THE LAW
OF
SPORTS

JOHN C. WEISTART
Professor of Law
Duke University

CYM H. LOWELL
Member
Atlanta, Georgia Bar

THE BOBBS-MERRILL COMPANY, INC.
PUBLISHERS
INDIANAPOLIS • NEW YORK • CHARLOTTESVILLE, VIRGINIA

With our deepest affection and thanks, we
dedicate this volume
To
Ruth, Lisa, and Whitney Weistart
and
Nancy and Whitney Lowell

whose support and encouragement has been exceeded
only by their extraordinary patience

SUMMARY TABLE OF CONTENTS

TABLE OF CONTENTS

CHAPTER 2. PUBLIC REGULATION OF SPORTS ACTIVITIES

CHAPTER 3. LEGAL RELATIONSHIPS IN PROFESSIONAL SPORTS

CHAPTER 5. ANTITRUST ASPECTS OF SPORTS ACTIVITIES

PREFACE

When we first began planning for this book in 1972, we had in mind a volume that would be modest in length and limited in topical coverage. At that time, a project of such moderate proportions seemed quite appropriate: the legal aspects of sports activities were largely unexplored in the literature and case developments were limited in number. Even a casual perusal of the materials which follow, however, will suggest that the final product bears little resemblance to the original design.

What happened between 1972 and the present to produce these changes in the nature of the project? To find the answer, one need simply compare the state of sports-related legal issues in 1972 and those which are treated in this book. In 1972, the antitrust exemption for baseball had been confirmed, and it appeared that the reserve clause was invulnerable to legal attack. In the other professional sports, the traditional player restraints were intact and there was a popular belief that the devices were not subject to serious antitrust challenge. On another front, player unions, which had appeared off and on in the early years of baseball, reappeared in a somewhat halting fashion in all of the professional sports. Because the unions were at their initial stages of development, their impact on league operations as of 1972 had been slight and their future seemed uncertain. In the tax area, professional sports franchises were attractive tax shelters, and they had not been specifically challenged. When a franchise was sold, the new owners were often unabashed in allocating all but a minute portion of the sales price to assets which would produce high depreciation deductions (and a rapid recovery of the initial capital investment).

On the amateur side in 1972, there were some cases testing the rules of high school athletic associations on matters relating to eligibility, athlete conduct, and the right to participate. The trend of precedent, however, was highly deferential to the authority of the athletic organization. At the collegiate level, suits against the NCAA were a rarity, and the meager precedents did not yield a coherent theory of the legal status of the NCAA. Indeed, any suggestion that actions of the NCAA might be reviewable under the antitrust laws seemed truly fanciful.

This state of affairs stands in rather sharp contrast to the developments which are treated in the following pages. In each of the areas mentioned, and in many others, the last half decade has seen changes of the most fundamental sort. In the early stages of the preparation of this book, the rapid legal developments were a source of some frustration. In several areas, the products of early research had to be discarded, or relegated to background discussion, as new theories replaced traditional approaches. In the final analysis, though, the litigation explosions on the antitrust, tax, labor, and amateur regulation fronts were welcome developments. On a general level, the cases of the mid-'70s served to finally strip away the myth that sports activities were recreational in nature and, thus, not subject to close legal scrutiny. But there was another benefit of the litigation which more directly affected the writing of this book. The litigation of the '70s did much to firm up our initial perceptions of the legal framework to be applied to sports-related issues. Theses which formerly could only be put forward in a tentative fashion can now be stated with the greater certainty that comes from successful testing in the courts. We certainly know much more about the legal implications of player restraints, collective bargaining, player contract depreciation, and amateur regulations than we did just a few years ago. As a result, predictions about the course of future developments can be made with more confidence than could have been generated in 1972.

This is not to suggest, however, that there are no interesting sports issues left to be pursued. Indeed, the exploration has probably only just begun. In the process of defining the proper framework for analysis of sports-related controversies in the litigation of the '70s, the courts significantly increased the potential for litigation. Actions and activities which were formerly thought to be unreviewable are now perceived as being well within the realm of judicial scrutiny. Thus, we hope that one effect of this book will be to suggest the need for further clarification in a great number of areas. For example, despite the persistence of the issue, the courts have yet to settle the question of whether there is anything like a constitutionally protected right to participate in amateur athletics. At the professional level, the courts have not yet given proper consideration to the difficult antitrust questions which arise in connection with league decisions limiting the number or location of club franchises.

It is also pertinent to note that during the early stages of the preparation of this book, we were drawn into discussions, both between ourselves and with others, about whether there really was any such thing as "the law of sports." The hypothesis to be dealt with was one which suggested that rather than having any law which was unique to sports, what we really had was "the law," and while this applied to sports, it also applied equally to other activities and industries. Hence, it could be doubted whether there was anything special to be said about the application of legal doctrine to sports issues.

While the early debates on this point were interesting — and, indeed, aided our development of a structure for the book — it soon became clear that there were many areas in which sports-related problems required a specially focused anaylsis. On some matters, there are legal doctrines which apply in the sports area and nowhere else. This is the case, for example, with respect to such diverse matters as baseball's antitrust exemption and some of the tax rules to be applied to the recapture of depreciation on player contracts. The more common situation, however, is one in which the doctrine applied to a particular sports problem is not unique, but the factual setting is sufficiently peculiar that the results are not the same as would obtain in other contexts. In the area of amateur sports, for example, the proscription against sex discrimination is based on the same political and sociological notions which have led to statutes and court decisions outlawing sex discrimination in employment, housing, and public benefits. However, none of these areas raise the issues (and tensions) which are posed by the significant differences in the revenue-generating potentials of traditional men's and women's sports. On the professional side, perhaps the most vivid illustrations of the factual uniqueness of sports problems can be found in the antitrust area. Sections 1 and 2 of the Sherman Act do not contain different language to be applied in sports cases. In that sense, then, the law relevant to the sports industry is the same as will be applied to other areas of commerce. A glance at the cases, however, will suggest that there is a good deal of judicial reasoning in the sports areas which is not very conventional. On many issues, a professional sports league is perceived as a blatant cartel, and one which enforces rules which have no purpose other than preventing competition. Nonetheless, through the course of litigation in the last several years, increasing numbers of courts have concluded that such behavior does not necessarily run afoul of the antitrust laws.

It has also become clear that, in addition to the possibly unique application of legal doctrine, there are a great number of areas in which sports problems are of sufficient factual uniqueness to require a specialized analysis. Our initial conclusions in this regard have been confirmed by the discovery of several areas in which the courts have been misled by drawing inappropriate analogies between sports activities and other endeavors. These are explored in the pages which follow. While it is true that the analysis of sports-related problems can be advanced by reference to the results achieved in non-sports contexts, we have found that this is an analytical technique which must be used with some care. Accordingly, the reader will find numerous instances in this text in which a significant part of the analysis is devoted to evaluating various non-sports precedent in terms of its appropriateness in the sports area.

An additional point that we should make about the preparation of this book is that it addresses the legal issues that are raised by an industry with vast contours. The sports industry ranges from the playing fields of elementary schools to the cavernous stadiums in which professional football games are played; from the aristocratic stables in which pure-bred horses are trained to the urban gymnasiums in which aspiring boxers prepare for their bouts; from the negotiating tables at which collective bargaining is conducted between representatives of owners and players to the tax planning that precedes the negotiation of an individual contract between player and team; from the grace of an Olympic gymnast to the violence that is frequently found in football and hockey; from the acquisition of elaborate equipment to build strong bodies to the injection of drugs to enhance performance; from the often informal administration of amateur athletics at the local level to the very formal procedures of the United States Congress as it deliberates over legislation proposed to regulate some aspect of athletics; from the often simplistic legal issues posed by an injury in a game to the frequently intransigent technicality of a federal antitrust challenge to a rule of a professional league; and from the terms of a collegiate scholarship to the rules relating to pari-mutuel betting.

The vastness of this industry crystallized as we searched to identify the legal principles that would apply to the various relationships in the industry. In our effort to adequately state these principles, we also quickly learned that the "law of sports" was not confined to contract and antitrust law. Rather, it includes a wide variety of legal subject areas. To facilitate the project, we divided the various subject areas between us. In the final product which appears here, our separate efforts can be identified on a chapter by chapter basis. Professor Weistart was responsible for the materials in Chapter 3 (Legal Relationships in Professional Sports), Chapter 4 (Enforcement of Professional Sports Contracts) and Chapter 5 (Antitrust Aspects of Sports Activities). Mr. Lowell prepared the balance of the material, in particular Chapter 1 (Regulation of Amateur Athletics), Chapter 2 (Public Regulation of Sports Activities), Chapter 6 (Collective Bargaining and Professional Sports), Chapter 7 (Federal Income

Taxation of Sports Activities) and Chapter 8 (Liability for Injuries in Sports Activities).

Finally, we should note that the materials in this book reflect authorities that were published through July of 1978. While there have certainly been important developments in the interim, it was not feasible to include them in this volume. These developments will be reflected in periodic supplements.

The authors are indebted to a large number of friends and colleagues who have in one way or another helped in the preparation of this book. We thank them all equally and hope that they will understand that individual acknowledgement would not be possible (or fair to those who were not mentioned). But we would like to express our sincere gratitude to our friend Ken Pye, who provided us with much of the encouragement and opportunity to begin this project. We would also like to publicly thank each other. During the gestation period of this book, we have each learned from the other and, more importantly, developed a close friendship, the fruits of which we will hope to enjoy in the years to come.

In addition, we would like to give particular recognition to the efforts of June Hubbard who has worked on the book for the past five years. Ms. Hubbard's contribution was unique in the truest sense of that word. Among other things, she conceived and implemented a system for gathering sports law-related articles from the major newspapers in the United States and Canada. In addition, she provided invaluable research and technical assistance, ranging from preparing the manuscript to introducing much needed rationality to our citation system. Her fine efforts in the preparation of this material are greatly appreciated. On another point, it must be noted that her knowledge of and devotion to the sport of hockey are truly significant, in no small part because they are maintained in a setting in which most others believe a puck to be a mischievous fairy.

John C. Weistart
Cym H. Lowell

November 11, 1978

CHAPTER 1

Regulation of Amateur Athletics

§ 1.01. In General.

The nature of the legal relationship between athletes, coaches, schools and athletic associations has been a subject of increasing attention in the last several years. This attention has primarily been the result of a rather large volume of litigation in which athletes have sought to challenge the authority of schools and associations to regulate their athletic activities. It has to a lesser extent involved similar action by schools with respect to the associations of which they are members. Although the precise nature of all aspects of these relationships is by no means settled, the courts have begun to identify the principles that will be utilized to decide disputes when they arise in the future. And the purpose of this chapter will be to analyze the legal relationships in amateur athletics in terms of these emerging legal concepts.

The principles that find application to amateur athletics disputes are derived from both private and public law sources. The private law principles flow from the nature of the relationship between athletes and their schools (especially private schools) and between schools and athletic associations in which they are members. The essence of the principles is that when the relationships are formed it is agreed, explicitly or implicitly, that specified rules or procedures will be binding. When disputes then arise, the parties should have the freedom to solve

1

them in accordance with the agreed upon internal procedures, and courts should intervene in only exceptional cases. The public law principles, on the other hand, are derived from the constitutional provisions that are applicable to schools and organizations which are public in nature, as well as from the delegations of authority from state legislatures to public schools. Because of the public interest involved, there is less judicial deference to private decision-making. Historically, disputes in amateur athletics which reached the courts were decided almost solely on the basis of private law principles, with the result that the complainant prevailed on a quite infrequent basis. In more recent years, however, there has been a rather apparent shift away from the ipso facto application of the private principles. This is primarily the result of the fact that cases tend to be brought and decided on constitutional bases, which supercede private law in those cases where the challenged conduct is subject to constitutional strictures. Even where strict constitutional principles are not applicable, there is a developing judicial attitude that the private principles may no longer be appropriate for resolution of some types of disputes.[1]

Although summarization on this general subject is hazardous, there are at least two preliminary observations that can be made. The first is that courts are increasingly reviewing the grievances of athletes and schools on their merits and that much (but not all) of this review is undertaken on the basis of constitutional authority. The second is that the nature of the regulatory process in amateur athletics is undergoing significant change. The process has historically been characterized by almost complete private regulation, but that regulation is increasingly being subjected to public supervision from the courts and, to a lesser extent, from legislative bodies. Although these are very broad generalizations, they will be reflected in the discussion throughout this chapter.

In the materials that follow, attention will initially be focused upon the administrative structure of amateur athletics in an effort to establish a basis for discussion of the various relationships in that structure in the balance of the chapter.[2] The discussion will then focus upon the status of the amateur athlete. The most difficult aspect of this subject is to determine whether the relationship between an athlete who receives financial aid and the college or university which grants it is gratuitous or contractual. This is a question of significant importance, and the little authority that does exist poses several problems to both athletes and their institutions.[3] Consideration will also be given to the athlete's interests in athletic participation,[4] as well as to the nature of the relationship between the athlete and his or her coach,[5] and the extent to which the activities of the athlete may be regulated by schools and athletic associations.[6] The focus of attention will then shift to the organizations and institutions which are responsible for administering amateur athletics. This discussion will involve an analysis of the basic legal principles, both constitutional and nonconstitutional, that apply to their activities and the basic functions that such entities perform.[7] These functions include primarily the

1. *See* § 1.14.
2. *See* § 1.02.
3. *See* §§ 1.03-.09.
4. *See* §§ 1.10-.11.
5. *See* § 1.12.
6. *See* § 1.13.
7. *See* § 1.14.

adoption and promulgation of rules and regulations for the administration of athletic activities[8] and the conduct of enforcement activities to insure compliance with the regulatory provisions.[9] The final subject for discussion will be to identify the extent to which legislative bodies have undertaken to involve themselves in amateur athletics.[10]

It should be noted that in undertaking these several areas of inquiry all levels of amateur athletics will be treated alike, although each could theoretically be singled out for separate treatment. Thus, a separate discussion could be undertaken for primary school, high school, college or university, and the other levels of amateur athletics. Such an approach would be justified by, for example, the fairly apparent differences between grade school games and intercollegiate athletics, since the younger the athlete the more the need for guidance and regulatory control. Similar distinctions could doubtlessly be drawn between each of the levels of amateur athletics. In the hope of avoiding the duplication that such a process would require, the approach in this chapter will be to create a single discussion of the legal problems and issues in amateur athletic regulation. We will state and discuss the rules and theories that will apply to the various subject matters, but will not attempt to identify how each such proposition would differentially apply to the various levels of amateur athletics. That step can be better taken as individual cases arise.

§ 1.02. Administrative Structure of Amateur Athletics.

In analyzing amateur athletics, the first step is to consider its basic administrative structure. This is an important and necessary inquiry because it is the breakdown in the relationship between amateur athletes and their schools and the institutions that regulate competition which precipitates the majority of the legal issues considered in the balance of this chapter. Thus, the present discussion will focus on the identification of customary administrative arrangements. Subsequent sections will analyze the various legal problems that result from those arrangements. It should be noted at the outset, however, that this structural discussion will be general only, and will not attempt to provide exhaustive commentary on the administrative organization of amateur athletics. Not only is that a task that is well beyond the scope of this text, but it has also been ably accomplished by others.[11]

As a means of facilitating discussion, amateur athletics may be considered as being composed of two broad types of competition, each having its own peculiar administrative organizations. The first will be referred to as "restricted competition," which includes all athletic competition that is restricted to a specific class of amateur athletes, such as those who are participants in high school or collegiate programs. The second broad category will be referred to as "unrestricted competition," in which all eligible amateur athletes may compete,

8. *See* §§ 1.15-.27.

9. *See* § 1.28.

10. *See* § 1.29.

11. *See generally* G. HANFORD, AN INQUIRY INTO THE NEED FOR AND FEASIBILITY OF A NATIONAL STUDY OF INTERCOLLEGIATE ATHLETICS (1974); E. SHEA & E. WIEMAN, ADMINISTRATIVE POLICIES FOR INTERCOLLEGIATE ATHLETICS (1967); THE CARNEGIE FOUNDATION FOR THE ADVANCEMENT OF TEACHING, AMERICAN COLLEGE ATHLETICS (Bull. No. 29, 1929); Cross, *The College Athlete and the Institution,* 38 LAW & CONTEMP. PROB. 151 (1973); Koch, *A Troubled Cartel; The NCAA,* 38 LAW & CONTEMP. PROB. 135 (1973).

regardless of class, category or group. "Unrestricted competition" would include, for example, the Olympic Games, and other forms of national and international competition in which any qualified athlete is eligible. Although these broad categories are distinct, they are not mutually exclusive—that is, an athlete could be involved in both types of competition.

a. Restricted Competition. The most prevalent form of amateur activity involves restricted competition, which will in almost all cases be at the high school and college levels. The administrative structure which is utilized to regulate restricted competition is essentially the same at both levels. Each school will normally have an athletic department to supervise its own athletes and the athletic activities in which they compete. The school may also be a member of a local or regional conference or association of similarly situated schools. The basic purpose for the establishment of these conferences will usually be to facilitate such matters as the scheduling of competition, the establishment of rules and procedures for the determination of athlete eligibility, and the general administration and supervision of the membership's athletic activities. Thus, the conferences serve several functions. First they enable schools with essentially common characteristics and objectives to compete one against the other, with the intensity of such competition being facilitated by the organization of tournaments and championships. Second, conferences provide a forum in which each member may benefit from the judgment, experience and expertise of other members in the joint analysis and solution of common problems.

The primary function of the conference in almost all cases, however, will be to serve as a legislative, judicial and executive body for the activities within its ambit of authority. In this sense, the conference or association will simply be a means of accomplishing the practical business of administering the various relationships involved in restricted competition. With respect to this particular function, it is well to note that "there are both moral and competitive reasons for the existence of self-imposed legislation in intercollegiate athletics: to keep people honest and to even out competition." [12] The administrative function will be performed through a more or less formal structure, which will facilitate and police the competitive activities of each member school in accordance with a constitution, bylaws and detailed rules and regulations setting forth policies and procedures for the conference. Each member will be bound to conduct its own affairs in compliance with these various provisions to the extent that they are lawful and enforceable.[13] To insure that the members do comply with these requirements, the conference or association will also engage in enforcement activities through which it can determine whether impermissible conduct has occurred, and, if it has, whether sanctions should be imposed upon the wrongdoing party.[14]

Although the conference arrangement is by far the most common form of organization for schools at both the high school and college level, there are also a large number of schools which are independent, in the sense that they are not as such members of a regional or local conference. Such schools conduct their athletic programs in accordance with their own self-imposed requirements,

---

12. G. HANFORD, *supra* note 11, at 89.
13. *See* § 1.15.
14. *See* § 1.28.

except to the extent that a statewide or national conference may impose additional requirements.

In addition to local or regional conferences, it is customary for schools to be members of statewide or national conferences, depending upon whether the school is, respectively, at the high school or college level. Such conferences serve, simply, as a central administrative body for all schools throughout the state or the country which are on the same educational and competitive level. They provide essentially the same functions as do the local or regional conferences, except that the administrative effort will involve a much broader spectrum of problems and activities. They are, in other words, additional administrative layers on the sports cake.

The administrative structure of restricted competition in amateur athletics is, therefore, relatively complex; and it is the complexity of structure, and the impact of the resulting regulatory efforts, which give rise to most of the problems that will be considered in this chapter.[15]

b. Unrestricted Competition. In addition to competition which is restricted to a specific group of athletes, amateur athletics also involves competition that is open to any athlete. This customarily includes international competition with athletes from other nations, and will include the Olympic Games, the Pan American Games, and all other events in which any amateur athlete is eligible to participate.

Consideration of the administrative structure which applies to this aspect of amateur athletics must begin with the United States Olympic Committee ("USOC"), which has under various names governed American participation in the Olympic Games since their revival in 1896, and which has operated under a federal charter since 1950.[16] The USOC is the sole organization recognized by the International Olympic Committee ("IOC") as the governing body for American participation in the Olympics. It is composed of more than 200 amateur organizations, but under IOC rules its voting control is lodged in the groups (national sports federations) which are recognized by international sports federations for the individual sports which compose the Olympics.[17]

The USOC, like the conferences and associations which regulate restricted competition, has a constitution and by-laws which govern its administrative functions. It does not as such, however, have a separate set of rules and regulations which must be observed by those involved in unrestricted competition. Rather, it normally requires that such persons conduct themselves in accordance with the rules and regulations of the IOC, or applicable international federation.

There have been several administrative problems in the unrestricted competition area, and these have related primarily to the public concern about the administrative activities of the USOC and the persistent jurisdictional squabbles that have raged for most of this century between the Amateur Athletic Union and the National Collegiate Athletic Association. Inasmuch as these several problems are noted in a subsequent section dealing with recent

---

15. The basic legal principles applicable to amateur athletic organizations are considered at § 1.14.
16. Act of September 15, 1950, ch. 975, 64 Stat. 902, *codified at* 36 U.S.C. §§ 371-83 (1970).
17. OLYMPIC RULES AND REGULATIONS, rule 24(b) (1972).

proposals to involve the federal government in amateur athletics,[18] they will not as such be discussed at this point.

c. Importance of the Administrative Structure. Even this brief review of administrative structure should suggest that the conduct of amateur athletics involves considerably more than the mere arrangement of games. The administration of amateur athletics is a difficult and complex undertaking, and the present structure is reflective of that complexity. The simple presence of a complex, and often overlapping, administrative framework is not as such of any particular significance. It is significant, rather, because of the consequences that it visits upon those who are subject to the regulatory effort, and it is these consequences which present the issues that will be discussed in this chapter.

§ 1.03. Status of the Amateur Athlete.

Having reviewed the basic administrative structure within which amateur athletics are conducted in this country, the next step is to analyze the status of the athletes who participate in athletic activities that are not formally professional—that is, where there is not an acknowledged play-for-pay system. This discussion could be conveniently short-circuited if there were a single, all-embracing concept that identified the status of athletes who compete in non-professional athletics. There is, for example, little real question about the "status" of professional athletes. One does not hear the question "what is a professional athlete" asked, and the reason is the general consensus that it is someone who performs for economic gain. All relevant issues relating to the professional athlete can be resolved in light of that "status." The situation for non-professional athletes, however, is much different. There is no single definition, and the question "what is an amateur athlete" is frequently asked. Probably the best answer that can be given is that it depends upon why the question is raised. As will be noted in the following section, all amateur organizations utilize the term "amateur" to define the class of athletes who are eligible for competition. It is universally used to distinguish sports participation of a vocational from an avocational nature, but the grounds of differentiation vary substantially. As used by these organizations, the term "amateur" has significance only for institutional purposes. Questions about the status of "amateur" athletes have also been raised in other situations. Thus, courts have examined the nature of the legal relationship between an athlete and an institution conferring financial aid, and in addition have inquired whether an athlete may be taxed on receipt of such aid or may qualify for workmen's compensation benefits. Each of these issues would be more easily resolved if there were a certain definition of "amateur," and the lack of such definition makes these questions more difficult. It also makes it difficult to draw clear conclusions from the cases that have been decided.

In order to survey the question of the status of the athletes who participate in amateur athletics, attention will be focused first upon the definition of "amateur" that is provided by the organizations which administer amateur athletics at both the international and domestic level. Attention will then be directed toward the case law that has been evolved by the courts as they have

18. *See* § 1.29.

decided cases which require the making of so-called status determinations with respect to the athletes who participate in amateur athletics.

§ 1.04. Organizational Definition.

The term "amateur" is utilized by all of the significant athletic regulatory bodies at both the international and domestic level, and the term is universally used as a means of drawing a line between those who do, and those who are deemed not to, receive pay for their play. The latter are "amateurs," and the former are not. Thus, the rules of the International Olympic Committee ("IOC"), which is responsible for the conduct of the quadrennial Olympic Games, define an eligible athlete as one who has "participated in sports as an avocation without having received any remuneration for his participation."[19] Although the eligible athlete may receive some types of assistance,[20] the rules specifically bar from "amateur" status "[i]ndividuals subsidized by . . . educational institutions . . . because of their athletic ability. . . ."[21]

The IOC definition of "amateur" has also been adopted by the United States Olympic Committee, which is responsible for the participation of the United States in the Olympic Games[22] and is largely followed in the definitions of domestic sports organizations. Thus, the Amateur Athletic Union ("AAU") defines an "amateur" as a person "who engages in sport solely for the pleasure and physical, mental or social benefits he derives therefrom and to whom sport is nothing more than avocation;"[23] and the National Collegiate Athletic Association ("NCAA") defines an "amateur" as "one who engages in a particular sport for the educational, physical, mental and social benefits he derives therefrom and to whom participation in that sport is an avocation."[24] With regard to the NCAA's "amateur" requirements, it should be noted that its financial assistance requirements may not be fully in keeping with the spirit of the IOC rules because they impose no bar to the award of an athletic scholarship solely on the basis of "athletic ability," as do the IOC rules. Indeed, the NCAA rules specifically provide that where a student's athletic ability is taken into account, the financial aid that is awarded shall not be for a period in excess of one academic year,[25] and the aid may be cancelled if the athlete renders himself ineligible[26] or withdraws from the sport for personal reasons.[27] Although these rules do not expressly so provide, they certainly lend themselves to the conclusion that financial aid to student-athletes is made only for the period in which they meet athletic requirements — a practice, which if present in fact,

---

19. OLYMPIC RULES AND REGULATIONS, rule 26(I) (1972).

20. These types of assistance are set forth in *id.* rule 26(III), and include such things as assistance for training, insurance coverage, scholarship and certain types of prizes.

21. *Id.* at 23. With regard to payments received from educational institutions, it should also be noted that receipt of a scholarship will not render an athlete ineligible so long as it is "dependent upon the fulfillment of scholastic obligations and not on athletic prowess." *Id.* rule 26(III)(3).

22. UNITED STATES OLYMPIC COMMITTEE CONST. art. II, § 5.

23. AMATEUR ATHLETIC UNION CODE art. 1, § 101.3(I) (1975).

24. CONSTITUTION OF THE NATIONAL COLLEGIATE ATHLETIC ASSOCIATION art. 3, § 1 (1977).

25. *Id.* art. 3, § 4(d).

26. With regard to "eligibility," it should be noted that an athlete may be ineligible if he or she simply quits playing. *See* Taylor v. Wake Forest University, 16 N.C. App. 117, 191 S.E.2d 379 (1972), which is considered in § 1.06.

27. CONSTITUTION OF THE NATIONAL COLLEGIATE ATHLETIC ASSOCIATION art. 3, § 4(c)(2) (1977).

would render the recipient ineligible for Olympic competition if the IOC definition were rigorously enforced, which is apparently open to question.[28]

The common denominator of each of the organizational definitions of "amateur" is that the athlete must pursue athletic activity as an "avocation," so that one whose participation constitutes a vocation will not be considered an amateur. One would have a vocation of performing in athletic activities, of course, if the *quid pro quo* for the play were some form of compensation. It should be emphasized that the organizational definitions are primarily important only to the extent that they define who is eligible for athletic competition. The definitions are certainly not binding upon courts which decide cases relating to amateur athletics. But the definitions, at least as suggested by the IOC, can be viewed as a normative statement that the term "amateurism" should only be applied to an athlete who performs for the sake of participation and not for compensation. If all non-professional athletes participated in this sense, then the questions to be considered in the following sections would probably not arise. Thus, questions would not be raised about whether the relationship between an athlete and an institution conferring financial aid is contractual or gratuitous, or whether an athlete may claim workmen's compensation benefits or will be subject to tax on the aid. These issues arise because the terms upon which some athletes participate deviate from that standard.

§ 1.05. Judicial Definitions.

Although the courts have not been, and are most unlikely to be, required to define the term "amateur," [29] opportunities have arisen, in context of lawsuits filed by athletes, which have required a determination of the status of the athlete seeking relief. For purposes of discussion, the decisions may be conveniently grouped into three categories: 1) scholarship cases; 2) workman's compensation cases; and 3) federal income tax cases.

In each of these categories of cases, the courts have been required to characterize the relationship between a student-athlete and the institution that provides him or her with financial support. The relationship could be viewed from either of two separate perspectives. It could be viewed, first of all, as a traditional academic relationship. The argument in favor of this view would be that athletics is a part of the general concept of education. Educational institutions are not monolithic and their programs include a wide variety of activities which contribute to the overall educational process. Indeed, the courts have in other contexts frequently concluded that athletics are a part of an institution's educational program.[30] In this sense, the student-athlete would be viewed as a member of an educational institution's student body who participates in athletic activities as part of the educational program and who receives financial aid to defray the cost of education. The fact that the aid given the athlete may be subject to the condition that he or she maintain athletic eligibility would not be seen to detract from its educational nature, since such conditions are frequently a part of the financial aid provided to students in other activities. The student-athlete would be perceived on the same basis as is, for example, a student who is required to maintain a given grade point average to

28. *See, e.g.,* S. REP. No. 93-850, 93d Cong., 2d Sess. 11-12 (1974).
29. The cases that have arisen are considered in § 1.17.
30. *See* § 1.11.

retain a financial award or a music or drama student who is given assistance with the expectation that he will engage in public performances as part of his educational program. It would also be argued that characterization of the relationship as academic would be consistent both with the fact that it exists in an academic environment between a student and the institution and with the conventional understanding of the parties to such relationships that they do not involve contractual or employment characteristics.

The relationship could, alternatively, be viewed as a contractual arrangement in which the athlete agrees to participate in athletics in exchange for the promise of the educational institution to provide financial support. The argument in favor of this view would essentially be that athletics is not a part of the educational process, but is, rather, in the nature of a business activity conducted by the institution. It would be argued that the financial aid given the athlete is in actuality compensation for services. Under this view, a condition requiring that the athlete maintain eligibility would be distinguished from similar conditions placed on grants to other students. A requirement that a student maintain a given grade average or participate in musical or dramatic activities would be seen as not contributing to the financial advantage of the institution, as compared to an athletic program that may in many schools make a significant financial contribution. It could, in addition, be noted that while public performances improve the skills which a music or art department seeks to "teach," the skills displayed in intercollegiate athletics bear a much less direct relationship to the educational functions of the institutions. It might also be suggested that the fact that the relationship occurs in an academic environment and is commonly believed to be non-contractual should be of little importance, since the law should be applied to the factual situation as it arises. If the relationship were so viewed, it would not be an academic relationship, as that term is commonly understood, and would subject the parties to all of the legal principles that attach to contractual or exchange transactions.

Although several cases have been decided in which issues about the status of amateur athletes were presented, it cannot be said that the courts' conclusions or reasoning provide a consistent view of the athlete-institution relationship. They do, however, suggest the serious problems that may be presented if the relationship cannot be characterized as academic.

§ 1.06. Scholarship Cases.

The legal relationship of the parties to a college or university award is a subject that has not received a great deal of attention, so that its precise nature is not as yet entirely clear.[30.1] The relationship could, as noted, be viewed as either academic or contractual. If it is viewed as academic, then the scholarship would constitute a gift from the institution, though it might be subject to conditions — for example, that the athlete maintain eligibility in accordance with specified rules and regulations — and the principal legal issue that it would raise would be whether the athlete could demonstrate that it constitutes an enforcible

---

30.1. *See generally* E. SHEA & E. WIEMAN, ADMINISTRATIVE POLICIES FOR INTERCOLLEGIATE ATHLETICS 129 (1967); CARNEGIE FOUNDATION FOR THE ADVANCEMENT OF TEACHING, AMERICAN COLLEGE ATHLETICS 253-59 (1929); Cross, *The College Athlete and the Institution,* 38 LAW & CONTEMP. PROB. 151, 166 (1973); Comment, *The Authority of a College Coach: A Legal Analysis,* 49 ORE. L. REV. 442, 447-48 (1970).

gift.[31] If the relationship is viewed as contractual, on the other hand, it will produce considerably more complex legal problems.

In the few cases that have interpreted financial aid awards, the courts have treated the awards in question as contractual arrangements, and found not only that the motivation for their conferral is often to induce the recipient to attend the conferring institution and be of assistance to its athletic program,[32] but also that there is inherent in the award a requirement that the athlete participate in that athletic program. Although the courts have analyzed the awards as constituting contractual arrangements, they have not considered the possibility that the awards could have been educational grants.

The most important of the cases dealing with financial aid awards, is *Taylor v. Wake Forest University,*[33] where a football scholarship had been awarded to a promising young athlete. The grant was for a period of four years and was conditioned only upon conformance to the rules of the Atlantic Coast Conference, the National Collegiate Athletic Association and Wake Forest University, all of which required the maintenance of eligibility. The University also had a policy of allowing the termination of financial aid if an athlete failed to attend practice sessions, though it was not put in writing until after the events in question. The athlete participated in the football program during his first year, but after achieving low grades decided not to participate further. The school then terminated the scholarship, and the express reason for termination was his failure to participate in football. When suit was subsequently brought to recover the expenses incurred by the athlete as a result of the termination, the court found that the scholarship was a contract, and that "in consideration of the scholarship award, [the athlete] agreed to maintain his athletic eligibility, and this meant both physically and scholastically." [34] When he then failed to maintain physical eligibility by not participating, the court concluded that the athlete "was not complying with his contractual obligations," [35] and could not, therefore, prevail.[36]

Although the result in *Taylor* — that the athlete was unable to recover the costs of his education — seems reasonable enough on its facts, the court's

31. If the relation were so viewed, the recipient's basic remedy for revocation of the scholarship would be on an estoppel basis. Thus, it would be argued that the donor had promised the scholarship to the recipient, which promise the donor would reasonably have expected to induce the recipient to enroll in the institution, which the recipient did in fact do in reliance upon the promise, and that as a result the promise would become binding upon the promisor-donor to avoid the injustice that revocation would cause. *See* RESTATEMENT OF CONTRACTS § 90 (1932); *see also* 1A A. CORBIN, CORBIN ON CONTRACTS §§ 193-209 (1963).

32. Buckton v. National Collegiate Athletic Ass'n, 366 F. Supp. 1152, 1158 (D. Mass. 1973) (actually involving constitutional issues).

33. 16 N.C. App. 117, 191 S.E.2d 379 (1972).

34. *Id.* 120-22, 191 S.E.2d at 382.

35. *Id.* 120-22, 191 S.E.2d at 382.

36. A similar approach was taken in Begley v. Corporation of Mercer Univ., 367 F. Supp. 908 (E.D. Tenn. 1973), where a scholarship had been awarded to a promising basketball player based upon a false assumption about the grading system of the player's high school. When it was subsequently learned that that assumption was incorrect and that the player's grades were actually too low, the court held that withdrawal of the scholarship was in order since the scholarship agreement required that all applicable rules and regulations be complied with, and one of those rules required a minimum level of achievement in high school. The propriety of withdrawal from the agreement was also indicated by the ordinary contract principle that where one party is unable to perform he cannot compel performance by the other party. *Id.* at 910.

opinion is troublesome because of the impact that its basic conclusion (that the athlete agreed to participate in consideration for the award) may have upon the legal status of the collegiate athlete. This conclusion is troublesome because if the ordinary financial aid award creates a contractual arrangement in which, as the court in *Taylor* concluded, the athlete undertakes to participate in consideration for the conferral of the award, then the recipient could well be found to be in violation of the "amateur" rules of the athletic administering organizations, which define "amateur" as a person who pursues sports activities as an avocation. If an award is granted in exchange for participation, the arrangement could be viewed as a vocational arrangement — that is, as compensation for personal services. And if the award is compensation for services, then the athlete might also be an "employee" of the institution for workmen's compensation purposes,[37] and the amount of the award may be taxable income for federal income tax purposes.[38] Although these results seem to be the logical implication of the *Taylor* opinion, they are, to say the very least, consequences which would not be commonly thought to flow from the award.

The court in *Taylor* did not consider the possibility that the award could have been construed as an educational grant with a condition that the student-athlete maintain eligibility in accordance with established rules and regulations of the school, conference, and national association.[39] This failure is regrettable since the court's conclusion could, as noted above and as will be considered in the following two sections, pose some rather severe collateral consequences to athletes and institutions if it were to be accepted as a more general proposition. If the award in *Taylor* had been characterized as an educational grant, the court could have reached the same ultimate conclusion — that recovery was denied — since the award could have been terminated for non-compliance with the condition.[40]

To the extent that the court did not consider the educational grant possibility, it should be less than authoritative as a precedent in future cases. When similar cases arise in the future, the argument of the institution will quite likely be that the award was an educational grant, not a contractual arrangement, and that the case should be decided on that basis. Again, this position will probably be taken because of the consequences that would follow if the relationship should be generally viewed as contractual.

With respect to the characterization of an award, it seems preferable that it be viewed as educational, and not contractual, at least where its language specifies only that the athlete must maintain eligibility under applicable rules and regulations. Such characterization would be consistent with the conventional understanding of both athletes and institutions.[41] There is no reason to believe that institutions assume a contractual relation to exist. Indeed, if such a relation did exist it would give the institution power to compel the athlete to perform the undertaking — for example, to preclude an athlete from leaving the

---

37. *See* § 1.07.
38. *See* § 1.08.
39. *See also* Begley v. Corporation of Mercer Univ., 367 F. Supp. 908 (E.D. Tenn. 1973).
40. *See, e.g.,* R. BROWN, THE LAW OF PERSONAL PROPERTY § 49 (2d ed. 1955).
41. *See* authorities cited note 30.1 *supra*.

institution. Such a situation would suggest a potential for coercion that is not present in other parts of the educational process.

A contractual characterization should be made only where the terms of an award cannot fairly be construed as anything other than a contractual arrangement, as was perhaps the case in *Taylor*. In this regard, it is important to note that even if the court in *Taylor* had considered the educational grant possibility, the language of the award under which the athlete agreed to maintain eligibility and abide by specified rules and regulations in consideration for its conferral, together with the institution's unwritten policy of terminating awards when athletes did not participate, may have precluded a conclusion that it was a gift. The distinction between gift and contract in such situations is a difficult line to draw in any case,[42] and where there is language in an award or an institutional policy indicating that the athlete specifically undertakes to perform in exchange for the amount in question, then it may not be possible to construe it as a non-contractual arrangement.

§ 1.07. Workmen's Compensation Cases.

The second group of cases in which the courts have had an opportunity to consider the status of the amateur athlete involves situations where athletes have sought workmen's compensation recovery for their injuries.[43] Workmen's compensation benefits in most jurisdictions are available only to "employees," so that a claimant must prove that he or she is an "employee," and not an independent contractor, or person of other status, who is excluded from coverage. Thus, the workmen's compensation cases are important to the extent that they indicate under what circumstances a collegiate athlete will be considered an "employee" of his or her institution.

Before reviewing the compensation cases, it is important to consider at least two preliminary matters. The first is to determine what an "employee" is for this purpose. Although there is normally a statutory definition in each jurisdiction, it can be said in general that a person's status will be determined in accordance with common law concepts and will depend upon an analysis of all the facts and circumstances of each particular case.[44] The second is whether the result in cases such as *Taylor v. Wake Forest University*[45] requires a finding that the athlete is an "employee" under the workmen's compensation laws. Where the award is an educational grant, it would not, but where there is a basis for a conclusion similar to that in *Taylor,* then the athlete will most likely be considered an "employee."

As a general proposition, a college or university athlete will not be considered an "employee" merely because he or she is the recipient of financial aid,[46] but where there is evidence that the performance of athletic services is the *quid pro*

---

42. R. BROWN, *supra* note 40, at § 49.

43. Workmen's compensation is a statutory scheme whereby an "employee" is able to recover for his or her employment-related injuries in an administrative proceeding, as opposed to seeking damages in a court of law. *See* § 8.12.

44. *See* 1A A. LARSON, THE LAW OF WORKMEN'S COMPENSATION § 43.10 (1972).

45. *See* § 1.06.

46. *See* Van Horn v. Industrial Accident Comm'n, 219 Cal. App. 2d 457, 33 Cal. Rptr. 169 (1963); State Comm'n Ins. Fund v. Industrial Comm'n, 135 Colo. 570, 314 P.2d 288 (1957).

quo for the aid [47] then the athlete may well be an "employee" for workmen's compensation purposes.[48] Inasmuch as employment status would be inimical to one's status as an amateur athlete — that is, if one were an "employee" in the sense of performing athletic services in return for financial aid, then he or she would almost certainly violate the institutional definitions of "amateur" [49] — and would require the institution to expend substantial resources for workmen's compensation insurance, it is important that attention be given to the cases that have evolved these general principles.

The first of the cases allowing recovery was *University of Denver v. Nemeth,*[50] where a football player had suffered a back injury during spring football practice. The player did not have a scholarship, but received a monthly payment from the university for cleaning litter from tennis courts, less an amount to cover meals, and paid no rent for his university accommodations since he cared for the building's furnace and sidewalks. The evidence established that the income, meals and lodging were all contingent upon his playing football and would be terminated if he dropped off the team. These facts, the court said, made it clear that the player had been hired by contract to perform work on campus and was required to play football as an incident to that work. He was, therefore, an "employee" entitled to a workmen's compensation recovery.[51] It is to be noted that *Nemeth* is an atypical case, since the athlete was not the recipient of the familiar type of athletic scholarship or grant-in-aid. He was, rather, given an income producing job, meals and lodging in exchange for performance on the football field. This was clearly a *quid pro quo* arrangement.

A similarly atypical situation was present in *Van Horn v. Industrial Accident Commission,*[52] involving an athlete who was killed in a plane crash while returning with the team from a regularly scheduled football game. The coach had offered to pay the athlete a specified amount per diem, which approximated the cost of tuition and books and an additional amount for rent, though neither payment was required to be used for tuition, books or rent. The amount paid per term was denominated an "athletic scholarship," though the funds were raised by a booster club. To be eligible to receive these payments, the player had to maintain a given grade average, be a member of an athletic team, and be recommended by the coach. These facts amply demonstrated, the court said, that the "scholarship" payments were received because of athletic prowess and participation, and that there was, therefore, a sufficient contract for hire to allow workmen's compensation recovery. In reaching this conclusion, however, the court was careful to limit its holding to the facts in question and specifically noted that not all athletes who receive athletic scholarships would be considered

47. That college or university athletes may be considered to be employed on a grand scale is suggested by Jones, *Playing the Payroll Game,* SPORTS ILLUSTRATED, April 23, 1973, at 20, which discusses the alleged use of federal "work-study" funds to support the University of Montana football program.

48. *See* Van Horn v. Industrial Accident Comm'n, 219 Cal. App. 2d 451, 33 Cal. Rptr. 169 (1963); University of Denver v. Nemeth, 127 Colo. 385, 257 P.2d 423 (1953). *See generally* 1 A. LARSON, THE LAW OF WORKMEN'S COMPENSATION § 22.21 (1972).

49. *See* § 1.04.

50. 127 Colo. 385, 257 P.2d 423 (1953).

51. *Id.* at 392, 257 P.2d at 430. After the initial award was paid in *Nemeth,* the player sought to gain an additional benefit. University of Denver v. Industrial Comm'n of Colorado, 138 Colo. 505, 335 P.2d 292 (1959).

52. 219 Cal. App. 2d 457, 33 Cal. Rptr. 169 (1963), *noted in* 11 U.C.L.A. L. REV. 645 (1964).

as "employees" of the donor institution. That status would be present only if the evidence of a particular case established the presence of a contract of employment.[53]

Nemeth and *Van Horn,* then, stand for the perfectly acceptable proposition that where there is a contractual relationship between an athlete and an institution, and the receipt of scholarship or other benefits is consideration for the performance of athletic services, then the athlete will be an "employee" for workmen's compensation purposes. Those cases clearly do not stand for the proposition that a truly "amateur" athlete — that is, one who participates in athletic activities as an avocation and who receives financial aid to defer educational expenses[54] — will be found to be an "employee." They seem to suggest that employee status will be present only where an award is given in consideration for performance and a contractual relationship is present. The lack of such an arrangement, then, should preclude the finding of an employment status. Thus, in *State Compensation Insurance Fund v. Industrial Commission ("Dennison"),*[55] a college football player had received a head injury on the opening play of a regularly scheduled football game, which led thereafter to his death. His widow brought a workmen's compensation proceeding, alleging that he had been the recipient of an athletic scholarship (in the form of tuition waiver) and had been hired by the college to manage a student lounge and do work on the college farm, though the college jobs were not related to his football performance. Although the court found that the athlete did indeed receive these benefits, it also found that they were not given in consideration for athletic participation,[56] which clearly distinguished the case from *Nemeth* where the taint of consideration was present.[57] Based on these facts, the court then found that there could be no workmen's compensation recovery, because the player was not under a contract of hire to play football and football was not a part of his other employment by the college.

The workmen's compensation cases, then, suggest that where there is a contractual relationship between the athlete and the institution, pursuant to which the athlete undertakes to participate in athletic activity in consideration for the payment of a scholarship or grant-in-aid, the athlete will be considered an "employee" for workmen's compensation purposes.[58] This conclusion poses

---

53. Specifically, the court noted that

> [i]t cannot be said as a matter of law that every student who receives an "athletic scholarship" and plays on the school athletic team is an employee of the school. To do so would thrust upon every student who so participates an employee status to which he has never consented and which would deprive him of the valuable right to sue for damages. Only where the evidence establishes a contract of employment is such inference reasonably to be drawn. *Id.* at 467, 33 Cal. Rptr. at 175.

54. *See* § 1.04.

55. 135 Colo. 570, 314 P.2d 288 (1957).

56. Thus, the court observed that

> none of the benefits he received could, in any way, be claimed as consideration to play football, and there is nothing in the evidence that is indicative of the fact that the contract of hire by the college was dependent upon his playing football, that such employment would have been changed had the deceased not engaged in the football activities. *Id.* at 572-73, 314 P.2d at 290.

57. 135 Colo. at 573-74, 314 P.2d at 290.

58. *See generally* Cross, *The College Athlete and the Institution,* 38 Law & Contemp. Prob. 151, 163-66 (1973); Hammond, *The Student Athlete and the Law,* 9 NASPA J. 302, 308-09 (1972); Randall,

little difficulty to the athlete who is indeed an "amateur," and who does not become a party to such a contractual relationship, but to athletes who are parties to documents such as the one construed in *Taylor,* the conclusion is simply further support for the implications of the *Taylor* case itself. And not only will such an athlete be in a contractual relationship with the institution and occupy the status of an employee for workmen's compensation purposes, but he or she may also fail to be an "amateur" for international athletic competition purposes.

§ 1.08.　Federal Income Tax Cases.

The final area in which the courts have had occasion to make determinations about the status of athletes who participate in amateur athletics has been in federal income tax cases. The most important federal income tax issue involving amateur athletes concerns the taxability of the stipend which the athlete receives in the form of a scholarship or grant-in-aid. Generally, the Internal Revenue Code provides that when a student receives a scholarship at an educational institution, the amount so received will not be includible within his or her gross income.[59] This exclusion will cover all services and accommodations provided,[60] as well as amounts received to cover expenses for travel and equipment, so long as they are incident to the scholarship and actually expended for that purpose by the recipient.[61] The exclusionary rule will not, however, apply to amounts received by a degree candidate which represent payments for the rendering of services in the nature of part-time employment as a condition to receipt of the award.[62] Thus, to qualify as non-taxable scholarships, awards must be in the nature of "relatively disinterested, 'no strings' educational grants, with no requirement of any substantial *quid pro quo* from the recipients." [63]

In light of these requirements of the Code, it would seem clear that if the factual circumstances of a given case indicated that the athlete received the scholarship in consideration for his or her athletic participation, then the award would not be within the exclusion provision because of the *quid pro quo*

Athletic Scholarships and Taxes: Or a Touchdown in Taxes, 7 GONZAGA L. REV. 297, 304 (1972); Steinbach, *Workmen's Compensation and the Scholarship Athlete,* 19 CLEV. ST. L. REV. 521 (1970).

59. INTERNAL REVENUE CODE OF 1954 § 117(a) (hereinafter referred to as "IRC").

60. IRC § 117(a)(1).

61. IRC § 117(a)(2).

62. IRC § 117(b)(1); Treas. Reg. §§ 1.117-2(a)(1), 1.117-4(c). Thus, graduate students are taxable on amounts paid to them for their teaching efforts, Rev. Rul. 68-146, 1968-1 Cum. Bull. 58; Edward A. Jamieson, 51 T.C. 635 (1969), as are medical interns and residents often taxable on their income received for services rendered. Rev. Rul. 73-89, 1973-1 Cum. Bull. 52; Rev. Rul. 68-520, 1968-2 Cum. Bull. 58; Rev. Rul. 57-386, 1957-2 Cum. Bull. 107; Aloysius J. Proskey, 51 T.C. 918 (1969); Parr v. United States, 469 F.2d 1156 (5th Cir. 1972); Hembree v. United States, 464 F.2d 1262 (4th Cir. 1972). *See also* Rev. Rul. 68-20, 1968-1 Cum. Bull. 55 (beauty contest winner taxable on scholarship when it required performance of services).

It is to be noted, however, that if such services are required of all scholarship or non-scholarship candidates for a particular degree, then the scholarship will remain non-taxable. Treas. Reg. § 1.117-2(a)(2). *See* Robert H. Steiman, 56 T.C. 1350 (1971).

63. Bingler v. Johnson, 394 U.S. 741, 751, 22 L. Ed. 2d 695, 89 S. Ct. 1439 (1969); Parr v. United States, 469 F.2d 1156, 1158 (5th Cir. 1972); Ussery v. United States, 296 F.2d 582, 586 (5th Cir. 1961); James B. Heidel, 56 T.C. 95 (1971).

It is to be noted that the *Bingler* definition of a "scholarship" is essentially the same as the requirement of the International Olympic Committee that an "amateur" must not receive financial aid from an educational institution as a result of athletic ability. *See* § 1.04.

arrangement, and would, therefore, be taxable. Certainly a factual finding similar to that which is implicit in *Taylor v. Wake Forest University* would seem to compel such a result.[64]

Although there are no cases which deal directly with the question of whether a college athlete who receives an athletic scholarship is entitled to the general exclusion, the issue has been considered in a recent public ruling by the Internal Revenue Service. In *Revenue Ruling 77-263*,[64.1] the Service was asked to rule on the taxability of awards given to students who expected to participate in athletics. The awards were governed by the rules of an intercollegiate conference, which required, *inter alia,* that the recipient be accepted by the university under its normal standards. In addition, the award could not be cancelled in the year of its award for non-participation. In view of these facts, the Service concluded (relying on the *Heidel* case discussed below) that the award was a non-taxable scholarship, reasoning that the recipient was not required to participate in order to receive the award:

> the university requires no particular activity of any of its scholarship recipients. Although students who receive athletic scholarships do so because of their special abilities in a particular sport and are expected to participate in the sport, the scholarship is not cancelled in the event the student cannot participate and the student is not required to engage in any other activities in lieu of participating in the sport.

In light of the Service's emphasis on the absence of a requirement that the recipient participate in athletics as a condition to the award (even if the non-participation is a result of "student's unilateral decision not to participate"), it is apparent that the presence of such a requirement would make the award taxable. With respect to the non-cancellation rules of the athletic association in question, it should be noted that they appear to have applied only to single-year awards, not to awards granted for the entire collegiate period (usually 4 years) of the athlete. The question raised by this situation is whether the Service would reach the same result if the grantor institution generally made one-year awards and renewed them for subsequent years only if the athlete in fact continued to participate — that is, non-participation would not result in termination of an existing award, but the award would not be renewed in the future. While *Revenue Ruling 77-263* did not focus on the question, it is possible that the awards of the institution would be subject to federal income taxation. If the institution followed such a procedure as to renewal of previously issued awards, the government could argue that there is no basis for an assertion that the institution required no athletic activity from the recipient. If such activity were required, the terms of the Ruling would not then be applicable.

The tax status of athletic grants-in-aid has also been considered in two cases in which athletes who received large professional bonuses upon completion of their collegiate eligibility sought tax relief under the income averaging rules.[65]

---

64. It also seems clear that the athlete could not succeed in making the argument that such services were required of all degree candidates, *see* note 62 *supra,* absent the showing that the services were part of a degree program.

64.1. 1977-2 Cum. Bull. 47.

65. The income averaging rules are contained in IRC §§ 1301-05, and provide, basically, that a

To qualify for these rules, a taxpayer must demonstrate, *inter alia,* that he has furnished more than one-half of his own support in each of the four years previous to the year in which income is sought to be averaged,[66] unless it can be shown, among other things, that more than one-half of the income sought to be averaged was attributable to work performed in two or more of the previous four years.[67] Thus, to qualify under either of these rules, an athlete would be required to show that an athletic scholarship constituted "support" or was attributable to "work" performed — that is, that the award was tendered in consideration for a reciprocal act or promise of the athlete (a *quid pro quo*).

The attempts to so qualify have failed. Thus, in *James B. Heidel,*[68] the taxpayer was a football player who had signed a professional contract after completing eligibility at the University of Mississippi. The player sought to utilize the income averaging rules to ameliorate the federal income tax liability produced by a large bonus. He maintained that the averaging rules were applicable because the athletic scholarship that he had received in college constituted "support" which he had furnished to himself, since he had been "required to play football for Ole Miss to continue to receive it." [69] In rejecting this argument, the court noted that it put the player on the horns of a dilemma, since if there was a *quid pro quo* for the scholarship it would not qualify for exclusion as a non-taxable scholarship; if, on the other hand, the award were indeed a scholarship, in the sense of being a "no-strings" educational grant, it could then not constitute "support" for income averaging purposes.[70] The court then concluded that it was more consistent with the intent of Congress to find that the value of the scholarship was not support "even leaving aside the implications *inherent* in treating the value of his scholarship as [having been] received by [the player] in return for playing college football." [71]

Having failed to establish the "support" requirement, the player then argued that he was within the exception to that requirement which requires a taxpayer to prove that the income in question is attributable to work performed during two or more earlier years. This argument was also rejected by the court's finding that the player had not carried his burden of proving that athletic performance in college was "work." [72] That participation in collegiate athletics is not ordinarily "work" for purposes of the income averaging provisions was made clear in *William L. Frost,*[73] where a star college baseball player signed a professional contract and sought to income average the bonus he received. In rejecting the player's contention that his collegiate experience was "work," the Tax Court stated that "work" for income averaging purposes means "gainful employment . . . which generates income." [74] The player did not meet this

---

taxpayer who has excessive income in the computation year may average it out over the preceding four years, the base period.

66. IRC § 1303(c)(1).
67. IRC § 1303(c)(2)(B).
68. 56 T.C. 95 (1971).
69. *Id.* at 104.
70. *Id.*
71. *Id.*
72. *Id.* at 105-06.
73. 61 T.C. 488 (1974).
74. *Id.* at 496.

requirement because he was not paid for his earlier efforts. The court did, however, gratuitously, but significantly, qualify its finding that the athlete had not been paid for his efforts by stating in a footnote that the player had received an athletic scholarship while in college and that

> these payments cannot be treated as payments (in the employment sense) for playing baseball. While it is true that an athletic scholarship is based on ability and the promise to participate in the specified sport, the purpose of the funds are to defray the educational costs of attending college and not for playing in the specified sport.[75]

Although neither *Heidel* nor *Frost* directly involved the taxability of the financial assistance given collegiate athletes, each will play an important part in making that determination when an appropriate case arises. Thus, in *Heidel* the court implicitly concluded that the award was an educational grant since it was not "support." It also noted that the implications of holding that athletic scholarships or grants-in-aid are given in return for a promise to participate in athletics are not to be lightly regarded. This admonition is well taken, since any such determination would, as already noted with regard to *Taylor v. Wake Forest University* and the workmen's compensation cases, indeed have potentially dire consequences. The admonition in *Heidel* was, however, only an admonition, since the court made no finding that would suggest the presence of a *quid pro quo* relationship between the scholarship there in question and the performance of football services by the athlete.

But such a finding was at least suggested by the same court a few years later in *Frost,* when it observed in the quoted footnote that an athletic scholarship is based on the "ability and the *promise* to participate." Although the court in *Frost* also stated that the athlete was not "paid for his effort" in collegiate athletics, it seems clear that it was referring to payment in the sense of general employment — that is, "work" for income averaging purposes. Thus, in the footnote the court observed that the payments were not made in the "employment sense" because they were intended to defray educational costs. The court in *Frost* did not, it should be emphasized, indicate whether the *quid pro quo* nature of the transaction would require taxation of the scholarship. Apparently it felt that such taxation would not be warranted, since it observed that the payments were not made in an "employment sense," but were, rather, intended to defray educational costs. That observation, however, is slightly off the point, since a "scholarship" for federal income tax purposes is a "no strings educational grant" which does not require any substantial *quid pro quo* from the recipient.[76] If the court meant to say that there was a *quid pro quo* for the award in *Frost,* as its statement that the athlete *promised* to participate would suggest, then the award might fail to meet the exclusionary test for a "scholarship." If such was the implicit conclusion in *Frost,* then other such athletic scholarships might be taxable to the extent that the trier of fact could discern a *quid pro quo* relationship between the award and athletic performance, as found in *Taylor v. Wake Forest University.*[77] Exclusion of the scholarship

75. *Id.* at 496 n. 6.

76. *See* notes 59-63 *supra.*

77. *See* Randall, *Athletic Scholarships and Taxes: Or a Touchdown in Taxes,* 7 GONZAGA L. REV. 297, 307 (1972).

To be sharply contrasted from the ordinary financial aid situation are the so-called "college

should be possible whenever such a finding cannot be made, as in *Revenue Ruling 77-263.*

§ 1.09. "Amateur" Status.

Having reviewed the limited case law which bears on the subject, it is important to return to the original question: What is the status of the athlete who participates in amateur athletics? As suggested earlier, the answer probably depends upon why the question is asked.[78] If the only issue is whether an athlete meets the requirements of an athletic organization, then attention can be focused upon whether he or she meets the organization's own definition. If, on the other hand, the issue arises outside of the organizational context and requires characterization of the relationship between an athlete and an institution, then the inquiry is much murkier. Such issues have, to date, involved essentially the same basic question: whether the athlete was compensated for athletic participation.[79] In response to this question, it would appear that an athlete who meets the normative requirements of organizational definitions of "amateur," at least that of the IOC, should not be found to have performed in consideration for compensation.

To the extent that the facts of a case depart from this standard, however, there is much less certain guidance. The courts have had ample opportunity to consider the relationship between the athlete and his or her institution in several different contexts. The most important of the cases has been *Taylor v. Wake Forest University,* where an athletic grant-in-aid was found to be a contract in which the athlete promised to participate in consideration of the conferral of the award. A similar observation could be found in *William L. Frost,* where the court remarked in a footnote that athletic scholarships are awarded on the basis of ability and the promise of participation. The conclusion in *Taylor* and the observation in *Frost* are troublesome. In each case, a court was concerned with a separate aspect of the collegiate athlete's status — in *Taylor* whether the athlete could recover his terminated scholarship, and in *Frost* whether income could be averaged for federal income tax purposes — but the language of each court has much wider ramifications. If a contractual relationship were indeed

scholarship plans," pursuant to which a player signs a contract to play for a professional team during the summer months, in return for which the club agrees to pay directly to the university a specified amount of his college expenses during the remainder of the year. Since these are amounts which are basically compensation for past, present or future employment services, Treas. Reg. § 1.117-4(c)(1), they will be includible within the recipient's gross income. Rev. Rul. 69-424, 1969-2 Cum. Bull. 15, *as modified* in Rev. Rul. 71-532, 1971-2 Cum. Bull. 356. *See also* Rev. Rul. 72-607, 1972-2 Cum. Bull. 82 (paid to college for engineering students by engineering companies).

78. *See* § 1.03.

79. With respect to the award of financial aid in collegiate athletics, it is worthwhile to note an observation by the court in Buckton v. National Collegiate Athletic Ass'n, 366 F. Supp. 1152 (D. Mass. 1973), that

the motivation behind [the] aid is . . . at least sometimes, an effort to induce a good athlete to attend a particular school in order to be of assistance to the athletic program. Even the most casual reader of our sports pages is aware that such inducements are an everyday fact of life in American amateur athletics. *Id.* at 1158.

See also, Jones, *Playing the Payroll Game,* SPORTS ILLUSTRATED, April 23, 1973, at 20 (discussing the alleged financing of the University of Montana football program with federal "work-study" funds).

present in *Taylor* and in *Frost,* then it might also be present with respect to other athletic scholarship or grant-in-aid arrangements. To the extent that such an arrangement is present, then the athlete may be entitled to workmen's compensation benefits (it will be recalled that even in *Dennison* the court couched its decision in terms of the lack of any *quid pro quo* arrangement); the amount of the financial aid may be subject to federal income taxation; and the athlete may not be an "amateur," as the term is defined by international rules and regulations.

The basic conclusion that may be drawn from the discussion of the cases that have considered the status of collegiate athletes is that financial aid arrangements should be structured with care to insure that they do not raise the specter of a contract, with the host of consequences that such status will visit upon the parties to the arrangements. So long as a given financial aid award is couched in terms of an educational grant, then the problems considered in the preceding discussion should not be present. To the extent that the terms of awards depart from this norm, it is to be anticipated that the status of the collegiate athlete receiving aid will slide away from the normative definition of "amateur." Where the dividing line is, or should be, between an educational grant and a contract is not, however, very clear. The result in any given case will inevitably be a function of the terms of the pertinent documents, the past practices of the institution and athletic association, and the presence or absence of non-financial reasons to explain why the action in question was taken.

§ 1.10. "Rights" of the Amateur Athlete.

In addition to determining an amateur athlete's status as an "amateur," it is also important to ascertain his or her "rights" with respect to participation in amateur athletics. Any given athlete may be subject to the direction of a coach, an athletic department, the administration of an educational institution, as well as the local, regional or national conferences in which the institution may be a member.[80] In the face of these many forms of administrative direction, it is important to determine what rights the athlete has in general, and the extent to which such rights will insulate the athlete from unnecessary and unreasonable forms of administrative action.

In identifying the rights of amateur athletes, attention will first be directed to the question of whether the athlete has a "right" to participate in amateur athletics.[81] The discussion will then consider the authority of coaches to direct the activities of the athlete,[82] as well as the extent to which the athlete may be protected from particular forms of administrative action.[83]

§ 1.11. The "Right" to Participate.

The first step in considering the rights of amateur athletes is to determine the status of the athlete's interest in his or her sport. When athletes have sought

80. *See* § 1.02.
81. *See* § 1.11.
82. *See* § 1.12.
83. *See* § 1.13.

judicial review of their grievances with those who direct their activities, the courts have struggled with the extent, if any, to which the "right" to participate is entitled to constitutional protection. If there is such a right in law, then the relationship between the athlete and the persons and organizations which administer his competitive activities may well be on a much different legal basis than it has traditionally been viewed.[84]

The question of whether there is such a "right" has most frequently arisen in situations in which an athlete has been the object of administrative sanction as the result of an alleged violation of a rule or regulation of a sports organization. Specifically, the question has been whether the athlete in a public insitution has a sufficiently important interest in athletic participation to require that before that interest can be adversely affected he or she must be given the procedural safeguards required by due process of law.[85] Although it is by no means certain what limits there are to the types of interests that will be accorded due process protection, it is clear that in order to be entitled to protection any given interest must involve liberty or rise to a "property" or "property-like" status.[86]

Amateur athletic participation will ordinarily arise in conjunction with the athlete's educational experience — that is, in all but a few circumstances, amateur athletics are conducted under the direct or indirect auspices of educational institutions. This fact has considerable significance. If the opportunity to participate in athletics is considered to constitute an integral and complementary part of the overall educational program of a school, whether at the elementary, secondary or collegiate level, then it may itself assume the stature of the student's interest in education. Few things are clearer in the law than that the student's interest in public "education" is subject to constitutional protection,[87] inasmuch as it is one of the most important interests in our society, is frequently deemed to be among the most important functions of government, and is regarded as the "principal instrument in awakening the child to cultural values, in preparing him for later professional training, and in helping him to adjust normally to his environment." [88] The relationship that does or should exist between athletics and education is, however, not clearly resolved. Those who include athletics within the generalized concept of "education" do so on the basis that the educational process is essentially a socializing function in our society, of which athletic participation is an important part. Thus, athletic participation is often credited with instilling in the athlete the aspiration for excellence; the

---

84. The traditional scope of review that has been applied to the actions of those persons or organizations who administer amateur athletics is considered at § 1.14.

85. The requirements of procedural due process of law are considered at § 1.28. As noted in §§ 1.12, 1.14, 1.15.1 and 1.28, constitutional protection is available only to athletes in public institutions.

86. Board of Regents of State College v. Roth, 408 U.S. 564, 33 L. Ed. 2d 548, 92 S. Ct. 2701 (1972). See also Goss v. Lopez, 419 U.S. 565, 39 L. Ed. 2d 465, 94 S. Ct. 1405 (1974). This issue is discussed more fully in § 1.28.

87. See, e.g., Dixon v. Alabama State Bd. of Educ., 294 F.2d 150 (5th Cir. 1961), cert. denied, 368 U.S. 930, 7 L. Ed. 2d 193, 82 S. Ct. 368 (1961).

88. Brown v. Board of Educ. of Topeka, 347 U.S. 483, 493, 98 L. Ed. 2d 873, 74 S. Ct. 686 (1954). "Education" is not, however, a "fundamental" right, in the sense of requiring strict judicial scrutiny. See San Antonio Independent School Dist. v. Rodriguez, 411 U.S. 1, 35-39, 36 L. Ed. 2d 16, 93 S. Ct. 1278 (1973).

life experience that is necessary for the building of character; and the internalization of the norms of teamwork, cooperation and motivation. Others, however, suggest that athletics is the antithesis of "education." At best, these persons would say, athletic participation is simple physical diversion, devoid of intellectual requirements. And at worst is anti-social to the extent that it is a simple manifestation of societal exploitation and an exposure of the young athlete to all of the immoral and unethical practices that are so often attributed, rightly or wrongly, to the athletic establishment.

Although these various positions have not been authoritatively resolved, several courts have reached the conclusion that athletic participation is indeed an integral part of the student's "education" and is, as such, entitled to the same protection as are other aspects of the educational experience.[89] Thus, it has been stated that "the right to attend school includes the right to participate in extra-curricular activities"[90] and that "[d]iscrimination in high school interscholastic athletics constitutes discrimination in education."[91] Participation in athletics is also an indispensable means for many secondary school students of modest resources to obtain a college education through athletic scholarships.[92] For these reasons, some courts have not had difficulty concluding that the athlete's interest in participation embodies a substantial element of educational opportunity and that when athletic eligibility is withdrawn the athlete is deprived of a part of his or her preparatory education.[93]

The interest in participation may also be analyzed as an economic interest. From this perspective, it is valuable to the athlete because of the potentially

---

89. Brenden v. Independent School Dist. 742, 477 F.2d 1292 (8th Cir. 1973); Moran v. School Dist. No. 7, Yellowstone County, 350 F. Supp. 1180 (D. Mont. 1972); Davis v. Meek, 344 F. Supp. 298 (N.D. Ohio 1972), *noted in* 22 BUFFALO L. REV. 634 (1973); Curtis v. National Collegiate Athletic Ass'n, Case No. C-71 2088 ACW (N.D. Cal. 1972); Kelley v. Metropolitan County Bd. of Educ. of Nashville, 293 F. Supp. 485 (M.D. Tenn. 1968); Cabrillo Community College Dist. of Santa Cruz County v. California Junior College Ass'n, 44 Cal. App. 3d 367, 118 Cal. Rptr. 708 (1975); Florida High School Activities Ass'n v. Bryant, 313 So.2d 57 (Fla. App. 1975); Thompson v. Barnes, 294 Minn. 528, 200 N.W.2d 921 (1972). Thus, in Tinker v. Des Moines Independent Community School Dist., 393 U.S. 503, 21 L. Ed. 2d 731, 89 S. Ct. 733 (1969), the court stated that "[a] student's rights . . . do not embrace merely the classroom hours. When he is in the cafeteria, *or on the playing field,* . . . ." *Id.* at 513 (emphasis added). Although *Tinker* was a First Amendment case, it is certainly indicative of the inclusiveness of the term "education."

90. Moran v. School District No. 7, Yellowstone County, *supra* note 89, at 1184.

91. Brenden v. Independent School Dist. 742, 477 F.2d 1292, 1298 (8th Cir. 1973); Gilpin v. Kansas State High School Activities Ass'n, Inc., 377 F. Supp. 1233 (D. Kan. 1973).

92. Regents of the University of Minnesota v. National Collegiate Athletic Ass'n, 560 F.2d 352 (8th Cir. 1977); Colorado Seminary v. National Collegiate Athletic Ass'n, 417 F. Supp. 885 (D. Colo. 1976); Wellsand v. Valparaiso Community Schools Corp., Cause No. 71 H 122(2) (N.D. Ind. 1971); Lee v. Florida High School Activities Ass'n, Inc., 291 So. 2d 636 (Fla. App. 1974).

93. Thus, in Davis v. Meek, 344 F. Supp. 298 (N.D. Ohio 1972), the court observed that

part of the function of educating children is to provide them with the basic knowledge and training necessary to become productive adult citizens. However much one may share Thomas Jefferson's scorn for games that are played with a ball, professional baseball is nowadays so important a commercial activity that questions are even raised as to whether or not in some of its manifestations it may come within the scope of the anti-trust laws. Hence it is difficult to refute the argument that a secondary school system that deprives a student of the opportunity to develop his full potential for entering the field of professional baseball is not functioning as it should. When this deprivation is not because the system is impoverished or limited in its educational offerings, but is because it desires to use the deprivation as a disciplinary measure in an attempt to attain objectives, however commendable, of doubtful legal validity, the problem becomes somewhat more sharply in focus. *Id.* at 301. *See also* Hoover v. Meiklejohn, 430 F. Supp. 164 (D. Colo. 1977).

large economic benefit that may be derived from participation in professional athletics. In this sense, the opportunity to participate is both a means of enabling the athlete to gain the requisite skill development for professional participation and to demonstrate those skills to the parties who "scout" talent for professional competition. The potential benefit of athletic participation is of such significance that in *Behagen v. Intercollegiate Conference of Faculty Representatives,*[94] the court took judicial notice of the fact that to many athletes "the chance to display their athletic prowess . . . is worth more in economic terms than the chance to get a college education." [95] Athletic participation may also be of economic importance to the extent that the athlete, through publicity and media exposure, becomes a public personality, thereby facilitating future employment.

The amateur athlete's interest in participation can, therefore, be viewed as having substantial value as a part of the educational process, and, in the case of those few athletes who are gifted with exceptional prowess, of potentially unlimited economic value in facilitating eventual participation in professional athletics. Notwithstanding the apparent substantiality of the interest, several courts have reached the conclusion that it is not within the range of interests protected by the Constitution. The leading case expressing this view is *Mitchell v. Louisiana High School Athletic Association,*[96] where the court, after noting that the Due Process Clause does not provide insulation from every injury at the hands of the state, concluded that "[t]he privilege of participating in interscholastic athletics must be deemed to fall . . . outside the protection of due process." [97] In reaching this conclusion, however, the court failed to undertake even the slightest analysis of the true significance and net worth of the interest as required by the standards for determining the interests that will be protected by due process of law.[98] Its conclusion rested, rather, on the simple assertion of non-protection.[99] Although protection was also denied in *Parish v. National*

---

94. 346 F. Supp. 602 (D. Minn. 1972).

95. *Id.* at 604. *See also* Buckton v. National Collegiate Athletic Ass'n, 366 F. Supp. 1152 (D. Mass. 1973); Kelley v. Metropolitan County Bd. of Educ. of Nashville, 293 F. Supp. 485, 494-95 (M.D. Tenn. 1968), *rev'd on other grounds,* 436 F.2d 856 (5th Cir. 1970). *See generally* Note, *Judicial Review of Disputes Between Athletes and the National Collegiate Athletic Association,* 24 STAN. L. REV. 903, 908-09 (1972). *But cf.* Samara v. National Collegiate Athletic Ass'n, 1973 Trade Cases ¶ 74,536 (E.D. Va.).

96. 430 F.2d 1155 (5th Cir. 1970).

97. *Id.* at 1158.

98. *See* note 86 *supra.*

99. Similarly, in Bucha v. Illinois High School Ass'n, 351 F. Supp. 69 (N.D. Ill. 1972), the court seemed quite surprised to be confronted by the suggestion that the interest in participation was protectible and, relying upon *Mitchell,* had little difficulty concluding that "[o]f course, it is clear that participation in interscholastic athletics is not a right guaranteed by the Constitution of the United States." *Id.* at 73 (emphasis added). As was true in *Mitchell,* the court in *Bucha* failed to even give passing consideration to the interests of the athlete that are embodied in the interest in participation. *See also* Hamilton v. Tennessee Secondary School Athletic Ass'n, 552 F.2d 681 (6th Cir. 1976); Albach v. Odle, 531 F.2d 983 (10th Cir. 1976); Walsh v. Louisiana High School Athletic Ass'n, 428 F. Supp. 1261 (E.D. La. 1977); Colorado Seminary v. National Collegiate Athletic Ass'n, 417 F. Supp. 885 (D. Colo. 1976); Dallam v. Cumberland Valley School Dist., 391 F. Supp. 358 (M.D. Pa. 1975); Stock v. Texas Catholic Interscholastic League, 364 F. Supp. 362 (N.D. Tex. 1973); Taylor v. Alabama High School Athletic Ass'n, 336 F. Supp. 54 (M.D. Ala. 1972); Paschal v. Perdue, 320 F. Supp. 1274 (S.D. Fla. 1970); Louisiana State Bd. of Educ. v. National Collegiate Athletic Ass'n, 273 So. 2d 912 (La. App. 1973); Marino v. Waters, 220 So. 2d 802 (La. App. 1969).

It has also been stated that the interest in participation is not protectible because it is not a vested interest, Sanders v. Louisiana High School Athletic Ass'n, 242 So. 2d 19 (La. App. 1970); Morrison

Collegiate Athletic Association,[100] the court at least recognized the need for some consideration of the nature of the interest but elected to follow the holding of *Mitchell.*[101]

The approach and result of *Mitchell* has, however, been rejected by other courts, which, after noting the significant educational and/or economic value of the interest in participation, have reached the conclusion that it is indeed of sufficient value to receive constitutional protection.[102] Probably the leading case expressing this view is *Behagen v. Intercollegiate Conference of Faculty Representatives,*[103] where the court reviewed the educational and economic significance of the interest, and concluded that the interest of a college athlete in participating in athletics is sufficiently substantial that it cannot be impaired without proceedings which comport with the minimum requirements of procedural due process of law.[104] Similar results have been reached by other courts.[105] While the court in *Behagen* suggested that "the direction in which this

---

v. Roberts, 183 Okla. 359, 82 P.2d 1023 (1938); Kissick v. Garland Independent School Dist., 330 S.W.2d 708 (Tex. Civ. App. 1959), that it is a mere privilege, Scott v. Kilpatrick, 286 Ala. 129, 237 So. 2d 652 (1970); Bruce v. South Carolina High School League, 258 S.C. 546, 189 S.E.2d 817 (1972); Tennessee Secondary School Athletic Ass'n v. Cox, 221 Tenn. 164, 425 S.W.2d 597 (1968), or that it is too speculative to be accorded the trappings of constitutional protection. Marino v. Waters, 220 So. 2d 802 (La. App. 1969).

100. 361 F. Supp. 1220 (W.D. La. 1973), *aff'd,* 506 F.2d 1028 (5th Cir. 1975).

101. The court justified its adherence to the *Mitchell* rule by noting that

> [o]ne of the plaintiffs (Parish [who was denominated as a superstar]) has an expectation, or — perhaps it is better to say — unless something happens, there is a substantial probability of his later attaining monetary rewards for his superior athletic abilities as a professional. But, as we later will develop, we do not visualize how, as a matter of law, restraint from participating in post-season games or championships, or in nationally televised games . . . will diminish his opportunity to gain monetary benefits of a significant order. As to the other plaintiffs' [who were not superstars] possibilities of professional employment, they are at least mere speculation. *Id.* at 1229.

On appeal, the athletes in *Parish* "wisely abandoned" the argument that the right to participate had constitutional significance, so that the Fifth Circuit was not required to reconsider its conclusion in *Mitchell,* 506 F.2d at 1034. The issue was specifically not decided in Regents of the University of Minnesota v. National Collegiate Athletic Ass'n, 560 F.2d 352 (8th Cir. 1977).

With regard to *Mitchell* and *Parish,* it is worth noting that the legal issues involved in each case did not require that the protectibility of the interest in participation be decided. Each case raised the primary issue of the permissibility under the Equal Protection Clause of a different form of eligibility rule, and the determination of that issue, unlike a procedural due process question, will not normally require, in the amateur athletics context, a finding as to the constitutional stature of the participation interest. The lack of necessity to squarely confront the issue, therefore, may well account for the summary consideration in *Mitchell,* and for the rejection of protection in *Parish. See* Chabert v. Louisiana High School Athletic Ass'n, 323 So.2d 774 (La. 1975).

102. *See* Behagen v. Intercollegiate Conference of Faculty Representatives, 346 F. Supp. 602, 604 (D. Minn. 1972).

103. *Id.* at 602.

104. *Id.* at 604.

105. In Brenden v. Independent School Dist. 742, 477 F.2d 1292 (8th Cir. 1973), for example, the court said "that at the very least, the plaintiffs' interest in participating in interscholastic sports is a substantial and cognizable one." *Id.* at 1299. Similarly, in Curtis v. National Collegiate Athletic Ass'n, Case No. C-71 2088 ACW (N.D. Calif. 1972), the court said that the interest in participation was "something very dear" to the athletes. *See also* Baltic Independent School Dist. No. 115 v. South Dakota High School Activities Ass'n, 362 F. Supp. 780 (D.S.D. 1973); Moran v. School District No. 7, Yellowstone County, 350 F. Supp. 1180 (D. Mont. 1972); Reed v. Nebraska School Activities Ass'n, 341 F. Supp. 258 (D. Nebr. 1972); Wellsand v. Valparaiso Community Schools Corp., Cause No. 71 H 122(H) (N.D. Ind. 1971); Kelley v. Metropolitan County Bd. of Educ. of Nashville, 293 F. Supp. 485 (M.D. Tenn. 1968), *rev'd on other grounds,* 436 F.2d 856 (1970); California State Univ., Hayward v. National Collegiate Athletic Ass'n, 47 Cal. App. 3d 533, 121 Cal. Rptr. 85 (1975); Sturrup v. Mahan,

area of the law is evolving" is to accord constitutional protection to the amateur athlete's interest in participation,[106] subsequent events have not fully supported this perceived movement of the law.[106.1] In this connection, it is important to note that the Supreme Court has recently indicated that it may be taking a very restrictive interpretation of the term "property," [106.2] and this may suggest that the views expressed in *Mitchell* will continue to receive substantial support from the lower courts.

There is some basis for the view that certain members of Congress have concluded that the interest in participation should be protected, though not on the basis of constitutional interpretation. In recent sessions, several bills have been introduced to affect reform in the administration of certain aspects of amateur athletics.[107] The implicit predicate of each of these measures is not only that the athlete has a right to participate, but that the right itself is of sufficient public importance that the Congress will intervene when it is adversely affected. In introducing a bill in the Senate, for example, a Senate sponsor stated that the proposed legislation would assure "that amateur athletes will be given sufficient rights to protect themselves from the arbitrary and capricious harassment that has unfortunately become an endemic part of the amateur sports scene." [108] Indeed, if the "right to participate" were not a thing of value, import and significance both to the athlete and to the nation as a whole, and if it were not worthy of protection from unreasonable interference, one might well ask why Congress would have any interest in considering legislation that would protect the athlete's freedom to participate.

§ 1.12. The Athlete-Coach Relationship.

Since the athlete is commonly understood to be subject to the supervision and direction of the coach, the first step in considering the athlete-coach relationship is to ascertain the parameters of the coach's authority.[109] A coach in a public institution is generally considered to have broad authority to control within reasonable and constitutional limits those aspects of the athlete's life which directly relate to his or her athletic performance.[110] This authority includes the power to establish and maintain health and training rules, to direct and conduct practice sessions, and to issue reasonable instructions during competition which

---

— Ind. —, 305 N.E.2d 877 (1974); Haas v. South Bend Community School Corp., 259 Ind. 515, 289 N.E.2d 495 (1972); Chabert v. Louisiana High School Athletic Ass'n, 323 So.2d 774 (La. 1975).

106. 346 F. Supp. at 604. *See generally* Cross, *The College Athlete and the Institution,* 38 LAW & CONTEMP. PROB. 151, 157 (1973); McGuire, *The NCAA—Institution Under Constitutional Siege,* 2 J. COLL. & UNIV. L. 175 (1974-75).

106.1. *See* notes 99-101 *supra.*

106.2. *See* § 1.28 at notes 530-531 and 535.1.

107. *See* § 1.29.

108. *See* 120 CONG. REC. S11975, 11977 (daily ed. July 9, 1974). *See also* S. REP. No. 93-850, 93rd Cong., 2d Sess. 17 (1974); 119 CONG. REC. S15670 (daily ed. August 3, 1973).

109. *See generally* Comment, *The Authority of a College Coach: A Legal Analysis,* 49 ORE. L. REV. 442 (1970). It should be noted that the principles discussed here, especially those of the First Amendment, are not restricted in application to the actions of a coach, but apply generally to any restriction imposed upon an athlete in a public institution. The principles are considered at this point because they arise most frequently in the relation between a coach and an athlete and illustrate the limits of a coach's authority.

110. Dunham v. Pulsifer, 312 F. Supp. 411 (D. Vt. 1970).

will be accepted and followed without question.[111] It would also include the power to impose sanctions for violation of such instructions.[112] The authority of the coach is not, however, all-inclusive, and does not include the right to regulate those aspects of athletes' lives which do not relate to athletic performance. Perhaps the best statement of the limits of the coach's authority is in *Dunham v. Pulsifer*,[113] where the court stated that "[a] coach may not demand obedience to a rule which does not in some way further other proper objectives of participation and performance." [114] A coach in a private institution will have much broader authority with respect to athletes under his or her direction, since constitutional requirements will not be applicable and reasonableness limitations may be subject to a much different construction.[115] Except as otherwise noted, the following discussion will specifically cover only public institutions.

It should be emphasized that there is no case law which deals specifically with the breadth of power that is possessed by the public school coach, though there have been several cases involving first amendment issues and they are discussed below. In order to suggest how a court would approach a specific exercise of authority, it may be helpful to consider a typical example. Assume that a coach in a public high school has adopted a rule which requires players to "hustle" at all times during practice. The coach then concluded that an athlete had failed to hustle and barred him from dressing for the next game. If the athlete then brought suit alleging that the suspension was illegal, the court's analysis would be along the following lines. If it is assumed that the court has jurisdiction over the case, its first inquiry would be whether the coach had authority to impose the hustle rule. His authority would include the power to adopt rules which relate to the athletic activity under his supervision, so long as the rules are reasonable and constitutional. In the assumed facts, the coach would be responsible for the training, discipline and performance of the school's team. Thus, the court would have to determine whether a rule requiring that athletes actively participate is directly related to those duties and, if so, whether the rule is reasonable in

---

111. Thus, Amos Alonzo Stagg is quoted as having described "the necessity for military obedience on a football field. A player must obey orders like a soldier where orders have been given, and, like a good soldier, act swiftly and surely on his own in an unforeseen contingency." CARNEGIE FOUNDATION FOR THE ADVANCEMENT OF TEACHING, AMERICAN COLLEGE ATHLETES 179 (1929).

112. *See* § 1.28.

113. 312 F. Supp. 411 (D. Vt. 1970) (length of hair rule held invalid).

114. *Id.* at 420. The court also noted that

> [i]t is bootstrap reasoning indeed to say that disobedience of any rule weakens the coach's authority or shows a lack of desire on the part of the competitor thus justifying obedience to any rule however arbitrary.
>
> If the rule is otherwise reasonable or, if in this case, it advances a compelling governmental interest vested in the school board, then it should be obeyed. But an otherwise arbitrary or unjustified regulatory classification cannot pull itself up by the bootstrap of its own existence.

Id. See also Clary v. Alexander County Bd. of Educ., 19 N.C. App. 637, 199 S.E.2d 738, 740 (1973) (an athlete must disregard a coach's order where "a reasonable man under similar circumstances would know that his compliance with such orders would result in injury"). It has also been observed that a coach's authority may sufficiently inhibit an athlete's volition as to preclude the normal assumption of the risk rule for participant injuries. *See* Martini v. Olymphant Borough School Dist., 83 Pa. D. & C. 206 (1952). The general assumption of the risk rule is considered at § 8.02.

115. *See* § 1.14, at note 168, and § 1.15.1.

application.[116] Existing authority in related areas would suggest an affirmative answer.[117] The second basic issue that a court would consider would relate to the process by which the athlete was suspended for one game. It would consider whether the coach's conclusion that the athlete had not hustled was justified, whether the athlete was entitled to notice and hearing prior to the imposition of the suspension, and whether the sanction (a one game suspension) was reasonably related to the offense committed.[117.1]

These factors should suggest that the precise inquiry that a court would make in this type of situation is actually fairly complex, but the purpose of the inquiry will be to resolve the very serious allegation of the athlete that he has been illegally deprived of his rights. Neither the allegation nor the resolution is simple. These elements of inquiry should not, however, be viewed as suggesting that the law imposes severe limitations on the authority of a coach to conduct the day-to-day instruction, supervision and discipline that is essential to the development of an athletic program. As will be indicated in subsequent portions of this chapter, the standards that would be used to resolve the inquiries require, in essence, only that the coach act in a fair and reasonable manner. Thus, the decision as to lack of hustle will be respected if it is based upon substantial evidence,[118] the required hearing procedures would probably be limited to the coach's advising the athlete of the finding and giving the athlete a chance to respond,[119] and the sanction would be upheld so long as it is reasonably related to the offense committed.[120] In other words, there is no clear and concise answer to the specific limits of a coach's authority, but it is possible to articulate how the outer limits of authority would be analyzed if a case challenging such authority were to arise.

Once the broad scope of authority of coaches has been established, it is next appropriate to consider how that authority affects the relationship between the amateur athlete and the coach. This effect is perhaps best illustrated by the cases which have considered the extent to which the coach may limit the rights of athletes to speak and conduct themselves. In light of the general principles already noted, one would anticipate that a coach would have the authority to limit such rights only in a reasonable and constitutional manner.[121] Thus, in order to be lawful, such limitations would have to be related to athletic performance and be consistent with the constitutional provisions which apply to the athlete's speech and conduct rights.

Constitutional requirements represent the most difficult aspect of cases in which a coach takes action which restricts the speech or conduct rights of athletes. The basic premise of these requirements is the simple phrase in the First Amendment that "Congress shall make no law . . . abridging the freedom of speech . . . ." [122] The shield of the First Amendment is not limited, however,

---

116. *See* § 1.15.

117. *See* § 1.16.

117.1. *See* § 1.28.

118. *See* § 1.28, at note 575.

119. *See* § 1.28, at notes 534-41, 546.

120. *See* § 1.28, at notes 576-81.

121. *See* notes 110, 111, 113-15 *supra.*

122. The First Amendment provides in full that

Congress shall make no law respecting an establishment of religion, or prohibiting the

to acts of Congress, inasmuch as interpretations of the Fourteenth Amendment have placed its requirements in full force upon the states and all of their instrumentalities,[123] though not upon the operations of privately operated schools.[124] What the First Amendment requires, in essence, is that absent constitutionally valid reasons, neither the state nor its instrumentalities may abridge the freedom of expression of its citizens,[125] including "pure speech" as well as so-called "symbolic" conduct.[126] Clearly, students do not shed their First Amendment rights at either the schoolhouse gate or the playing field entrance.[127]

The application of these principles to amateur athletics is illustrated by the following example. Assume that a college football player in a public school has decided that he wishes to protest some public event or policy by wearing a colored band around his arm during a game and by announcing the significance of the band publicly before the game. If the player's coach forbade him from undertaking such action, and suspended him from the team when he persisted, the issue would be whether the coach had abridged the constitutional rights of the athlete. This determination would be made by reference to the general case law that has dealt with the constitutional rights of students. The leading case in this area is *Tinker v. Des Moines Independent School District,*[128] in which several students had been suspended from school for wearing black armbands to protest American involvement in the Vietnam War, in contravention of a policy adopted by city school principals. In holding that the action of the school officials had abridged the First Amendment rights of the students, the Court noted that there was no evidence that the wearing of armbands would cause

free exercise thereof; or abridging the freedom of speech, or of the press; or the right of the people peaceably to assemble, and to petition the Government for a redress of grievances. U.S. CONST., amend. I.

123. *See, eg.,* West Virginia State Bd. of Educ. v. Barnette, 319 U.S. 624, 87 L. Ed. 1628, 63 S. Ct. 1178 (1943), where the Court observed that "[t]he Fourteenth Amendment, as now applied to the States, protects the citizen against the State itself and all of its creatures — Boards of Education not excepted." *Id.* at 637. *See also* Healy v. James, 408 U.S. 169, 171, 180, 33 L. Ed. 2d 366, 92 S. Ct. 2338 (1972). The application of the "state action" concept to sports organizations is considered at § 1.14.

124. *See* § 1.14, at note 168 and § 1.15.1.

125. The relation of governmental interest and First Amendment freedom was expressed in United States v. O'Brien, 391 U.S. 367, 20 L. Ed. 2d 672, 88 S. Ct. 1673 (1968), to be that

a governmental regulation is sufficiently justified if it is within the constitutional power of Government; if it furthers an important or substantial government interest; if the governmental interest is unrelated to the suppression of free expression; and if the incidental restriction on alleged First Amendment freedoms is no greater than is essential to the furtherance of that interest. *Id.* at 377.

See also Meyer v. Nebraska, 262 U.S. 390, 400, 67 L. Ed. 1042, 43 S. Ct. 625 (1923); Saunders v. Virginia Polytechnic Institute, 417 F.2d 1127, 1130-31 (4th Cir. 1969).

126. Brown v. Louisiana, 383 U.S. 131, 142, 15 L. Ed. 2d 637, 86 S. Ct. 719 (1966) (symbolic speech being the silent standing of blacks in a library to protest its segregationist policies); Russo v. Central School Dist. No. 1, 469 F.2d 623, 631 (2d Cir. 1972) (silent refusal to recite pledge of allegiance is protected expression); Ferrell v. Dallas Independent School Dist., 392 F.2d 697, 702 (5th Cir. 1968), *cert. denied,* 393 U.S. 856, 21 L. Ed. 2d 125, 89 S. Ct. 98 (1968) (length of hair is a form of expression).

127. Thus, in Tinker v. Des Moines Independent Common School Dist., 393 U.S. 503, 512, 21 L. Ed. 2d 731, 89 S. Ct. 733 (1969), the Court observed that "[a] student['s] rights . . . do not embrace merely classroom hours. When he is . . . on the playing field . . . he may express his opinions." *See also* Goss v. Lopez, 419 U.S. 565, 39 L. Ed. 2d 465, 94 S. Ct. 1405 (1975); Long v. Zapp, 476 F.2d 180 (4th Cir. 1973); Williams v. Eaton, 468 F.2d 1079, 1083 (10th Cir. 1972).

128. 393 U.S. 503, 21 L. Ed. 2d 731, 89 S. Ct. 733 (1969).

disruption and that no other constitutionally valid reason for the action had been offered.[129] Rather, the school authorities simply wished to avoid the controversy that such conduct might engender, and such a desire, the Court said, may not serve as a basis for the abridgement of First Amendment rights.[130] Such abridgement would be permissible only if the conduct in question "materially disrupts" the institutional process or "involves substantial disorder or invasion of the rights of others." [131]

In applying *Tinker* to the hypothetical facts, one would anticipate that the coach's action in suspending the player for wearing the armband would violate the athlete's First Amendment rights if the conduct did not involve a "material disruption" or did not provoke a "substantial disorder or invasion of the rights of others." [132] This was not, however, the result in the single case involving an amateur athlete which has to date presented the issue. In *Williams v. Eaton,*[133] the coach of the University of Wyoming football team had instituted a "coaching rule" against his players' participation in demonstrations or protests. A group of black athletes then informed the coach of their intent to wear black armbands to protest the alleged racially discriminatory policies of the Mormon Church and Brigham Young University, and the coach, with the later approval of the board of trustees, dismissed the players from the team for having violated this rule. The players then challenged the rule and the dismissal as being in violation of their civil rights, but the court held that their rights had not been violated. Although the court relied upon *Tinker* in reaching this conclusion,[134] it specifically stated that its holding was not based upon the presence of violence or disruption.[135] Rather, the court based its conclusion upon the finding that the action of the trustees "protected against invasion of the rights of others by avoiding a hostile expression to them by some members of the University

---

129. *Id.* at 511.
130. Specifically, the Court stated that

[i]n order for the State in the person of school officials to justify prohibition of a particular expression of opinion, it must be able to show that its action was caused by something more than a mere desire to avoid the discomfort and unpleasantness that always accompany an unpopular viewpoint. Certainly where there is no finding and no showing that engaging in the forbidden conduct would "materially and substantially interfere with the requirements of appropriate discipline in the operation of the school," the prohibition cannot be sustained. . . . *Id.* at 510.

See also Burnside v. Byars, 363 F.2d 744, 748-49 (5th Cir. 1966).
131. 393 U.S. at 513.
132. *See generally* Hammond, *The Student Athlete and the Law,* 9 NASPA J. 302, 302-05 (1972); Slusher, *Sport: A Philosophical Perspective,* 38 LAW & CONTEMP. PROB. 129, 133-34 (1973).
133. 468 F.2d 1079 (10th Cir. 1972). The case also had a substantial prior history, 310 F. Supp. 1342 (D. Wyo. 1970), *remanded,* 443 F.2d 422 (10th Cir. 1971), *on remand* 333 F. Supp. 107 (D. Wyo. 1971).
134. In addition to the freedom of expression issue in *Williams v. Eaton,* there was also an issue involving the establishment and free exercise of religion. Thus, the defendants had sought to defend their action, *inter alia,* on the ground that to permit the wearing of armbands would have violated the First Amendment's proscription of the establishment of religion and constituted an interference with the free exercise of religion. Although the district court had upheld the suspension of the players on the basis of this argument, 333 F. Supp. at 113-14, the court of appeals upheld the lower court's decision without deciding the religion question. 468 F.2d at 1084. The lower court's decision, in this regard, is criticized in Note, 19 KAN. L. REV. 316 (1971).
135. 468 F.2d at 1084. The district court had stated that the wearing of the armbands "might have tended to create disruption." 333 F. Supp. at 114.

team."[136] Presumably, the persons protected from "hostile expression" were those participating in, or witnessing, the football game, because the court noted that the limited circumstances with which it was concerned was the display of armbands "on the field and during the game." [137]

Although *Williams v. Eaton* does suggest that the First Amendment rights of amateur athletes may be subject to measurable abridgement by their coaches, the case appears to have been improperly decided. As noted, the basis for the court's decision was that barring the armband demonstration would avoid a "hostile expression" to others, which "hostile expression" would invade their rights. The natural desire to seek to avoid offending others is, however, not a constitutionally valid reason to regulate speech related activity. In *Tinker,* specifically relied upon in *Williams v. Eaton,* the Supreme Court stated that "the action of the school authorities [in suspending the students wearing armbands] appears to have been based upon an urgent wish to avoid the controversy which might result from the expression . . . .," [138] and that, the Court said, would not permit the denial of the freedom of expression.[139] The *Tinker* principles require a showing of potential disruption.[140] Since the court stated that such a showing could not be made in *Williams v. Eaton,* the dismissal of the athletes appears to have been constitutionally improper.[141]

Personal appearance and grooming is another area that a coach may seek to control. In *Long v. Zapp,*[142] for example, a football coach had decreed that all players must observe a "hair code," both during and after the season, under penalty of losing their letter for violation of the code. A player then let his hair grow after the football season, and the coach denied him his letter and an invitation to the annual athletic banquet. When the player brought suit, the court of appeals held, in a per curiam opinion, that the rule and its application were in violation of his First Amendment rights.[143] Although the court's opinion was limited to only the post-season application of the rule, it seems clear that such rules would be equally invalid during the season, absent the showing of some justifiable reason peculiar to athletes during the playing season but not present with regard to other students. In light of the fact that hair length does not in

136. 468 F.2d at 1084.
137. *Id.*
138. 393 U.S. at 510.
139. *Id.* at 514.
140. Perhaps the best way to evidence the showing that must be made is to compare the back-to-back decisions of Judge Gewin in Burnside v. Byars, 363 F.2d 744 (5th Cir. 1966), and Blackwell v. Issaquena County Bd. of Education, 363 F.2d 749 (5th Cir. 1966). In *Burnside* there was no showing of disruption, so that the wearing of "freedom buttons" could not be prohibited, but in *Blackwell,* where such a showing was made, prohibition was permissible. Similarly, in Karp v. Becken, 477 F.2d 171 (9th Cir. 1973), the court found sufficient disruption to infringe on speech-related activities when high school students threatened to disrupt an athletic award banquet and athletes threatened to disrupt the disrupters. *See also* Sword v. Fox, 446 F.2d 1091 (4th Cir. 1971), *cert. denied,* 404 U.S. 994, 30 L. Ed. 2d 547, 92 S. Ct. 534 (1971) (limiting right to demonstrate on campus is permissible).
141. *See* James v. Board of Educ. of Central Dist. No. 1, 461 F.2d 566 (2d Cir. 1972) (dismissal of teacher for wearing armband where no disruption violates the First Amendment), *on remand* 385 F. Supp. 209 (W.D.N.Y. 1974).
142. 476 F.2d 180 (4th Cir. 1973).
143. The court stated that

[a]wards, properly earned . . . cannot be used as instruments to enforce compliance with a "hair code," for the enforcement of which there is no compelling necessity. *Id.* at 181.

most sports affect the ability of an athlete to perform and that limitations on its length may serve no permissible objective of schools or school boards,[144] such a showing may be most difficult to make.[145]

With regard to the athlete-coach relationship, then, the public school coach has authority to exercise reasonable and constitutional control over the player's athletic activities. Where such control affects the player's rights of expression or conduct, the principles of *Tinker* will apply, and unless the coach, or other school authorities, can show that particular acts or expressions cause disruption, or otherwise materially and substantially interfere with appropriate discipline in the operation of the school or the athletic activity, then acts which abridge athletes' rights of expression will be held to be constitutionally impermissible.

§ 1.13. Freedom from Unreasonable Regulation.

The most significant aspect of the rights of the amateur athlete involves the extent to which athletic administering organizations may regulate the athlete's competitive activity. As suggested by the discussion of the athlete-coach relationship, such organizations will have substantial freedom to regulate athletic acitivity, but the emerging principles that the courts have developed in this area [146] will also insure that the athlete, at least in public schools, will have a zone of interests that may not be unreasonably impaired.[147] Thus, in analyzing different forms of regulation, it will be necessary to balance the respective interests of the athlete and the organizations which are responsible for regulating competitive activity. This may in many cases be a rather difficult and imprecise task, but it is possible to identify general principles to guide such determinations. As will be considered in the following discussion, it may be observed that rules and regulations which are sought to be imposed upon athletes will be enforceable so long as they are within the authority of the adopting organization, are adopted pursuant to a proper procedure, and are proper exercises of that authority.[148] If administrative action is taken with respect to an athlete, moreover, the action must be taken only in accordance with the requirements of procedural due process of law,[149] and any determinations made by an administrative organization will be subject to judicial review.[150] Each of these aspects of the relationship between the athlete and the athletic administering organizations will be considered in the following sections of this chapter.

---

144. Dunham v. Pulsifer, 312 F. Supp. 411 (D. Vt. 1970) (striking a hair rule on equal protection grounds).

145. Dostert v. Berthold Public School Dist. No. 54, 391 F. Supp. 876 (D.N.D. 1975); Jacobs v. Benedict, 35 Ohio Misc. 92, 301 N.E.2d 723 (Common Pleas 1973). In Zeller v. Donegal School Dist., 517 F.2d 600 (3d Cir. 1975), however, the court upheld such a rule, stating that the constitutionality of hair regulations does not present a substantial federal question and that the federal courts should defer to the judgment of school officials. See also Kelley v. Johnson, 425 U.S. 238, 47 L. Ed. 2d 784, 96 S. Ct. 1532 (1976) (upholding a grooming rule for police officers).

146. See § 1.15.

147. See §§ 1.15-28. The private school situation is considered at § 1.15.1.

148. See § 1.15.

149. See § 1.28.

150. See §§ 1.15, 1.28.

§ 1.14.   Amateur Athletic Organizations and Institutions.

Probably the most important aspect of the regulation of amateur athletics involves the relationships between athletes and their schools and the athletic organizations which perform the administrative and regulatory functions. Attention has already been devoted to the overall administrative structure formed by these organizations and institutions,[151] and this section focuses upon their legal status in performing administrative and regulatory functions in amateur athletics.

The question of the legal status of an organization will normally arise when it has taken action which affects the interests of a person who is subject to its regulatory control. It is an important inquiry because it will to a large extent determine the scope and nature of judicial review that may be available to the person whose interests have been affected. The status of an organization may involve both constitutional and nonconstitutional issues, and each will be considered separately.

    a. Constitutional Status. With respect to the constitutional status of an athletic organization or institution, the primary issue will be whether it is within the rubric of "state action" for purposes of the Fourteenth Amendment. The concept of "state action" defines the class of persons and organizations to which the requirements of the Equal Protection Clause of the Fourteenth Amendment are applicable.[152] Thus, Section 1 of the Fourteenth Amendment provides that "[n]o State shall make or enforce any law which shall . . . deny to any person . . . the equal protection of the laws." [153] As indicated by its explicit language, the "equal protection" requirement applies only to actions of the "State," and erects no shield against merely private conduct, regardless of whether it may be discriminatory and wrongful.[154] The term "State," however, has been interpreted to include all persons or organizations who are affected with "state action," and "state action" may be present because of the receipt of governmental assistance[155] or encouragement,[156] the performance of governmental functions,[157] or receipt of the imprimatur of governmental enforcement.[158] The gloss of state action, then, covers any person or organization associated with, or performing the functions of, duly constituted governmental entities.

---

    151. *See* § 1.02.

    152. It is also important for other purposes. *See* §§ 1.12, 1.28.

    153. U.S. CONST. amend. XIV. The equal protection requirements are specifically considered at § 1.15.

    154. Moose Lodge No. 107 v. Irvis, 40 U.S. 163, 32 L. Ed. 2d 627, 92 S. Ct. 1965 (1972); Shelley v. Kraemer, 334 U.S. 1, 92 L. Ed. 2d 1161, 68 S. Ct. 836 (1948). The status of private institutions is considered at notes 168-180 *infra. See also* § 1.15.1.

    155. Burton v. Wilmington Parking Autho., 365 U.S. 715, 6 L. Ed. 2d 45, 81 S. Ct. 856 (1961); Jacobson v. New York Racing Ass'n, Inc., 41 App. Div. 2d 87, 341 N.Y.S.2d 333 (1973), *modified on appeal* 33 N.Y.2d 144, 350 N.Y.S.2d 639 (1973) (receipt of parimutuel racing franchise); Garofano v. United States Trotting Ass'n, 78 Misc. 2d 33, 355 N.Y.S.2d 702 (1974) (private entity performing public function). *See* § 2.05.

    156. Reitman v. Mulkey, 387 U.S. 369, 18 L. Ed. 2d 830, 87 S. Ct. 1627 (1967).

    157. Food Employees Union v. Logan Valley Plaza, 391 U.S. 308, 20 L. Ed. 2d 603, 88 S. Ct. 1601 (1968); Terry v. Adams, 345 U.S. 461, 97 L. Ed. 2d 1152, 73 S. Ct. 809 (1953); Marsh v. Alabama, 326 U.S. 501, 90 L. Ed. 265, 66 S. Ct. 276 (1946).

    158. Shelley v. Kraemer, 334 U.S. 1, 92 L. Ed. 1161, 68 S. Ct. 836 (1948).

"State action" is certainly present with regard to the activities of public schools,[159] but private schools fall outside the category unless their activities meet one or more of the situations noted above.[160] Further, there is no longer any substantial question that the Equal Protection Clause applies to athletic associations which govern state-wide high school athletic programs.[161] Thus, in *Louisiana High School Athletic Association v. St. Augustine High School,*[162] the court observed that

> [t]here can be no substantial doubt that the conduct of LHSAA is state action in the constitutional sense. The evidence is more than adequate

159. *See, e.g.,* Dunham v. Pulsifer, 312 F. Supp. 411 (D. Vt. 1970).

160. *See* notes 168-180 *infra.*

161. Regents of University of Minnesota v. National Collegiate Athletic Ass'n, 560 F.2d 352 (8th Cir. 1977); Wright v. Arkansas Activities Ass'n, 501 F.2d 25 (8th Cir. 1974); Associated Students, Inc. v. National Collegiate Athletic Ass'n, 493 F.2d 1251 (9th Cir. 1974); Mitchell v. Louisiana High School Athletic Ass'n, 430 F.2d 1155 (5th Cir. 1970); Oklahoma High School Athletic Ass'n v. Bray, 321 F.2d 269 (10th Cir. 1963); Leffel v. Wisconsin Interscholastic Athletic Ass'n, 398 F. Supp. 749 (E.D. Wis. 1975); Dallam v. Cumberland Valley School Dist., 391 F. Supp. 358 (M.D. Pa. 1975); Buckton v. National Collegiate Athletic Ass'n, 366 F. Supp. 1152 (D. Mass. 1973); Howard Univ. v. National Collegiate Athletic Ass'n, 367 F. Supp. 926 (D.D.C. 1973), *aff'd,* 510 F.2d 213 (D.C. Cir. 1975); Parish v. National Collegiate Athletic Ass'n, 361 F. Supp. 1214 (W.D. La. 1973), *aff'd,* 506 F.2d 1028 (5th Cir. 1975); Samara v. National Collegiate Athletic Ass'n, 1973 Trade Cases ¶ 74,536 (E.D. Va.); Curtis v. National Collegiate Athletic Ass'n, Case No. C-71 2088 ACW (N.D. Calif. 1972); Bucha v. Illinois High School Ass'n, 351 F. Supp. 69 (N.D. Ill. 1972); Paschal v. Perdue, 320 F. Supp. 1274 (S.D. Fla. 1970); Cabrillo Community College Dist. of Santa Cruz County v. California Junior College Ass'n, 44 Cal. App. 3d 367, 118 Cal. Rptr. 708 (1975); Lee v. Florida High School Activities Ass'n, 291 So. 2d 636 (Fla. App. 1974); Haas v. South Bend Community School Corp., 259 Ind. 515, 289 N.E.2d 495 (1972); Josephine County School Dist. No. 7 v. Oregon Activities Ass'n, 15 Or. App. 185, 515 P.2d 431 (1973); School Dist. of City of Harrisburg v. Pennsylvania Interscholastic Athletic Ass'n, 453 Pa. 495, 309 A.2d 353 (1973). *But cf.* McDonald v. National Collegiate Athletic Ass'n, 370 F. Supp. 625 (C.D. Cal. 1974) (conclusion that NCAA not involve "state action," appears to be erroneous in light of other cases noted, and the *Associated Students* decision of the Ninth Circuit; see note 164 *infra*); Watkins v. Louisiana High School Athletic Ass'n, 301 So. 2d 695 (La. App. 1974); Sanders v. Louisiana High School Athletic Ass'n, 242 So. 2d 19 (La. App. 1970).

With respect to the "state action" issue, it should also be noted that the determination that a given organization is affected with state action will also establish the "color of law" requirement for 42 U.S.C. § 1983, which will provide an aggrieved athlete with a cause of action in federal court for most grievances with athletic organizations. *See, e.g.,* Mitchell v. Louisiana High School Athletic Ass'n, 430 F.2d 1155 (5th Cir. 1970); Taylor v. Alabama High School Athletic Ass'n, 336 F. Supp. 54 (M.D. Ala. 1972). The combining of the findings is a common procedure. *See, e.g.,* Monroe v. Pape, 365 U.S. 167, 171, 5 L. Ed. 2d 492, 81 S. Ct. 473 (1961); Moran v. School District No. 7, Yellowstone County, 350 F. Supp. 1180 (D. Mont. 1972). *See generally* McCormack, *Federalism and Section 1983: Limitations on Judicial Enforcement of Constitutional Protections, Part I,* 60 VA. L. REV. 1, 5-21 (1974).

In this consideration of equal protection requirements, it is also well to note that the availability of a constitutional remedy does not mean that the courts will countenance the assertion of frivolous cases. Thus, in Oklahoma High School Athletic Ass'n v. Bray, 321 F.2d 269 (10th Cir. 1963), the court dismissed a suit instituted by an aggrieved athlete as not being within the federal courts' cognizance, when it concluded that the "grievance with the Athletic Association lay only with the application of its . . . rule, the Board's refusal to grant an exception for hardship, and a general attack upon the amount of power delegated by the high schools to the Association. Such complaints are not within federal cognizance, are not subject to review in federal court, ..." *Id.* at 213. Although *Bray* fulminated against the frivolous use of § 1983 as a remedy to an aggrieved athlete, it also indicates the practical result that may be accomplished by filing the 1983 action. Thus, by filing the suit in the district court, the athlete in *Bray* was able to obtain an injunction which allowed him to play football for the then current season. *See also* Marino v. Waters, 220 So. 2d 802 (La. App. 1969). To the athlete who has been ruled ineligible, then, there may be considerable practical merit in the filing of suit challenging the validity of the action producing ineligibility and seeking a temporary injunction against its enforcement. *But cf.* Kupec v. Atlantic Coast Conf., 399 F. Supp. 1377 (M.D. N.C. 1975) (injunction denied).

162. 396 F.2d 224 (5th Cir. 1968).

to support the conclusion . . . that the Association amounts to an agency and instrumentality of the State of Louisiana. Membership of the Association is relevant — 85 per cent of the members are state public schools. The public school principals, who nominally are members, are state officers, state paid and state supervised, and together are the heads of all the white public high schools in Louisiana that participate in interscholastic athletics.

Funds for support of the Association came partly from membership dues, largely from gate receipts from games between members, the great majority of which are held in state-owned and state-supplied facilities. The paid staff of LHSAA is covered in part by the Louisiana Teachers Retirement Act and the staff members are legally defined as teachers.[163]

There is an apparent split of authority concerning the National Collegiate Athletic Association ("NCAA"), although the clear majority of cases have held it to be within the "state action" concept.[164] Thus, in *Buckton v. National Collegiate Athletic Association,*[165] the court, noting the *Louisiana High School Athletic Association* case, concluded that the NCAA was subject to constitutional requirements because it performed a "public function" and received substantial state support through its member institutions.[166] State action may also be present in some forms of non-school related sports activities.[167]

In considering the application of "state action" to athletic organizations, it is also important to consider the status of private educational institutions.[168] In

---

163. *Id.* at 227.

164. Regents of University of Minnesota v. National Collegiate Athletic Ass'n, 560 F.2d 352 (8th Cir. 1977); Rivas Tenorio v. Liga Atletica Interuniversitária, 554 F.2d 492 (1st Cir. 1977); Associated Students, Inc. v. National Collegiate Athletic Ass'n, 493 F.2d 1251 (9th Cir. 1974); Colorado Seminary v. National Collegiate Athletic Ass'n, 417 F. Supp. 885 (D. Colo. 1976); Jones v. National Collegiate Athletic Ass'n, 392 F. Supp. 295 (D. Mass. 1975); Buckton v. National Collegiate Athletic Ass'n, 366 F. Supp. 1152 (D. Mass. 1973); Parish v. National Collegiate Athletic Ass'n, 361 F. Supp. 1214 (W.D. La. 1973), *aff'd,* 506 F.2d 1028 (5th Cir. 1975); Samara v. National Collegiate Athletic Ass'n, 1973 Trade Cases ¶ 7,536 (E. D. Va.); Curtis v. National Collegiate Athletic Ass'n, Case No. C-71 2088 ACW (N.D. Cal. 1972).

165. 366 F. Supp. 1152 (D. Mass. 1973).

166. *Id.* at 1156. *But cf.* McDonald v. National Collegiate Athletic Ass'n, 370 F. Supp. 625 (C.D. Cal. 1974). The conclusion in *McDonald* was expressly rejected in Parish v. National Collegiate Athletic Ass'n, 506 F.2d 1028, 1032 (5th Cir. 1975) and in Howard Univ. v. National Collegiate Athletic Ass'n, 510 F.2d 213, 218-20 (D.C. Cir. 1975). *See* note 161 *supra.*

167. Such a situation is best illustrated by the status of Little League baseball. Although it has been thought that Little League activities are not so affected with state action as to be subject to constitutional requirements, Assmus v. Little League Baseball, Inc., 70 Misc. 2d 1038, 334 N.Y.S.2d 982 (1972), that conclusion may not always be correct. In 1964, Congress saw fit to establish and charter a federal corporation to be known as Little League Baseball, Incorporated. Pub. L. No. 88-378, 78 Stat. 325 (1964). The existence of a federal charter, as well as the presence of other factors, could require a finding of state action in some circumstances. *See* Fortin v. Darlington Little League, Inc., 514 F. 2d 344 (1st Cir. 1975); National Organization for Women v. Little League Baseball, Inc., 127 N.J. Super. 522, 318 A.2d 33 (1974); Paglia v. Staten Island Little League, Inc., 38 App. Div. 2d 575, 328 N.Y.S.2d 224 (1971) (failure of league to follow own procedures was unlawful). The presence of the federal charter need not, however, mean that the Little League is, for that reason alone, affected with state action. *See* King v. Little League Baseball, Inc., 505 F.2d 264, 267-68 (6th Cir. 1974). *See also* Greenya v. George Washington Univ., 512 F.2d 556 (D.C. Cir. 1975); Stearns v. Veterans of Foreign Wars, 394 F. Supp. 138 (D.D.C. 1975).

168. *See generally* O'Neil, *Private Universities and Public Law,* 19 BUFFALO L. REV. 155 (1970); Note, *State Action: Theories for Applying Constitutional Restrictions to Private Activities,* 74 COLUM. L. REV. 656 (1974). *See* § 1.15.1.

suggesting that constitutional duties should be placed upon private institutions, the argument has generally been that their non-athletic affairs are sufficiently affected with "state action" to make them, for constitutional purposes, indistinguishable from public institutions. It is argued that since the provision of educational services is a public function the provider must adhere to the constitutional duties of public bodies;[169] that sufficient "state action" is present where the private institution is the recipient of substantial state involvement, either in the form of financial aid, regulatory supervision, or the delegation of governmental powers;[170] or that the private institution bears the indicia of a public body.[171] Although it is true that "the amenability to constitutional commands of what was once widely assumed to be purely private activity is a fluid and developing concept," [172] private institutions need not, as a general matter, conform their actions to the explicit requirements of the Constitution.[173] Those requirements will most likely be applied only when state involvement in what would otherwise be private conduct becomes "so dominant as to afford basis for a contention that the state is merely utilizing private trustees to administer a state activity." [174]

---

169. Powe v. Miles, 407 F.2d 73 (2d Cir. 1968).

170. Greene v. Howard Univ., 271 F. Supp. 609 (D.D.C. 1967), *remanded* 412 F.2d 1128 (D.C. Cir. 1969).

171. Burton v. Wilmington Parking Auth., 365 U.S. 715, 722, 6 L. Ed. 2d 45, 81 S. Ct. 856 (1961).

172. Greene v. Howard Univ., 412 F.2d 1128, 1131-32 n. 2 (D.C. Cir. 1969).

173. Trustees of Dartmouth College v. Woodward, 17 U.S. (4 Wheat.) 518, 4 L. Ed. 629 (1819); Berrios v. Inter American Univ., 535 F.2d 1330 (1st Cir. 1976); Greenya v. George Washington Univ., 512 F.2d 556 (D.C. Cir. 1975); New York City Jaycees, Inc. v. United States Jaycees, Inc., 512 F.2d 856 (2d Cir. 1975); Wahba v. New York Univ., 492 F.2d 96 (2d Cir. 1974); Blackburn v. Fisk, 443 F.2d 121 (6th Cir. 1971); Magill v. Avonworth Baseball Conf., 364 F. Supp. 1212 (W.D. Pa. 1973) (private baseball league), *aff'd,* 516 F.2d 1328 (3d Cir. 1975); Brownley v. Gettysburg College, 338 F. Supp. 725 (M.D. Pa. 1972); Bright v. Isenbarger, 314 F. Supp. 1382 (N.D. Ind. 1970), *aff'd per curiam,* 445 F.2d 412 (7th Cir. 1972); Torres v. Puerto Rico Junior College, 298 F. Supp. 458 (D.P.R. 1969); Grossner v. Trustees of Columbia Univ., 287 F. Supp. 535 (S.D.N.Y. 1968); Greene v. Howard Univ., 271 F. Supp. 609 (D.D.C. 1967), *remanded,* 412 F.2d 1128 (D.C. Cir. 1969); Guillory v. Administrators of Tulane Univ., 212 F. Supp. 674 (E.D. La. 1962); Oefelein v. Monsignor Farrell High School, 77 Misc. 2d 417, 353 N.Y.S.2d 674 (1974). *But cf.* Belk v. Chancellor of Washington Univ., 336 F. Supp. 45 (E.D. Mo. 1970); Ryan v. Hofstra Univ., 67 Misc. 2d 651, 324 N.Y.S.2d 964 (1971).

174. Powe v. Miles, 407 F.2d 73, 81 (2d Cir. 1968). *See also* Jackson v. Metropolitan Edison Co., 419 U.S. 345, 39 L. Ed. 2d 466, 94 S. Ct. 1407 (1974); Moose Lodge No. 107 v. Irvis, 407 U.S. 163, 32 L. Ed. 2d 627, 92 S. Ct. 1965 (1972). These principles are also considered in a slightly different context in § 2.09.

The approach that the courts utilize in the private institution cases is well illustrated by *Powe v. Miles, supra,* where students had been suspended from Alfred University, a private institution, for violation of its demonstration and protest rules. Some of the students were enrolled in Alfred University as such, while others were enrolled in a state supported ceramics college which was a part of the university. The university was chartered pursuant to a special state statutory provision, and was subject to the regulatory powers of the state. For purposes of applying constitutional requirements, the court separated the university and the component college. With regard to the university, the court held that it was a private institution and that, as such, it was not bound by the constitutional standards applicable to public institutions. Judge Friendly stated that a private institution would be held to be public only if the specific act made the subject of complaint were a public, not a private, act. Since the act complained of — that is, the creation and invocation of demonstration and protest rules — was a private act, therefore, Alfred University could not be deemed a public institution. Thus, the facts that the state chartered the university, provided substantial financial support, enacted regulatory provisions which governed its activities, and maintained a public institution that was a part of its organization were not determinative because they were not the acts which were made the basis of complaint. The court also found that the football field upon which the protest had taken place was not a sufficiently public place as to cause the

Notwithstanding the general proposition that private institutions are not affected with state action for constitutional purposes, their athletic activities might be subject to a different rule. For purposes of this analysis, private institutions may be divided into three groups: 1) those which are not members of any athletic conference or association; 2) those which are members of an athletic conference of association composed entirely of private institutions; and 3) those which are members of athletic conferences or associations whose membership is composed of both public and private institutions. With regard to the first category, it seems clear that the athletic activities of those institutions do not constitute state action. There is nothing in the nature of athletic activity to require departure from the general rule. A similar result should be reached with respect to the second category, since a combination of private institutions would not create a different constitutional character for the common entity than that possessed by its component members, even if the private association adopts the rules and regulations of a state agency.[175]

Though there are two classes of private institutions which should not as such be affected by the principles of the Constitution, this fact will be of benefit to a relatively small number of schools because virtually all institutions are members of leagues or national regulatory associations such as the NCAA, the majority of whose members are public institutions. The more significant issue, therefore, is whether a private institution can lose its private action status by joining an athletic conference or association whose membership includes public institutions. It is now well established that such associations are themselves affected with state action, so that their own acts must adhere to constitutional requirements.[176] The act of joining such an association should not, however, cause a private institution to lose its private status for constitutional purposes. So long as it acts on its own initiative, utilizing its own rules and procedures, the private institution will apparently not be subjected to constitutional requirements. But if a private institution takes action as a result of the requirements or directives of a "public" athletic association of which it is a member, then the broadening of the state action concept suggests that it may then lose its private status as to such action.[177]

university to be deemed "public," because "it was open only to persons connected with the university or licensed by it to participate in or attend athletic contests or other events." 407 F.2d at 80.

The private status of the university was, therefore, upheld notwithstanding the presence of substantial state involvement. The *Powe v. Miles* court believed that such "privateness" would be disregarded only when the state involvement is "so dominant as to afford basis for a contention that the state is merely utilizing private trustees to administer a state activity." *Id.* at 81. This contention was then found to be present with regard to the ceramics college, since the state not only furnished its land, buildings and equipment, but also told the university what to do and how it should be done, *id.* at 83 — that is, the state made the university a private trustee to administer a state activity. *See also* Jackson v. Statler Foundation, 496 F.2d 623 (2d Cir. 1973) (suggesting that tax exemption alone may be a basis for a state action finding; though a strong dissent from a denial of rehearing en banc was filed by Judge Friendly, *id.* at 636-41); Braden v. University of Pittsburgh, 477 F.2d 1 (3rd Cir. 1973); Rackin v. University of Pennsylvania, 386 F. Supp. 992 (E.D. Pa. 1974); Isaacs v. Board of Trustees of Temple Univ., 385 F. Supp. 473 (E.D. Pa. 1974).

175. Stock v. Texas Catholic Interscholastic League, 364 F. Supp. 362 (N.D. Tex. 1973). Thus, in Howard Univ. v. National Collegiate Athletic Ass'n, 510 F.2d 213 (D.C. Cir. 1975), the court stated that "if the NCAA had no public members, its actions would be private for constitutional purposes." *Id.* at 220.

176. *See notes* 161-166, *supra.*

177. *See* Louisiana High School Athletic Ass'n v. St. Augustine High School, 396 F.2d 224, 228-29 (5th Cir. 1969); McDonald v. National Collegiate Athletic Ass'n, 370 F. Supp. 625 (C.D. Cal. 1974)

b. Nonconstitutional Status. In addition to the constitutional status of athletic organizations and institutions, it is also necessary to consider their status for nonconstitutional purposes. The following discussion will focus primarily upon the actions of athletic associations. In many situations, the action which is made the subject of judicial challenge will not raise constitutional issues, and its permissibility will largely be determined by the court's characterization of the relationship between the parties to the dispute. When disputes between athletes, schools and athletic associations have arisen, the courts have frequently analyzed them in terms of the so-called rules of "voluntary associations." [178] According to this body of law, an association, whether or not incorporated, consists of a group of persons or organizations who have combined to achieve a common objective or purpose. Because membership is purportedly voluntary, the rule has been that membership is a privilege which can be accorded or withheld at the will of the association, and not a right that can be judicially enforced. Thus, an association may adopt any rules, regulations or conditions as eligibility standards for membership so long as they are not in contravention of overriding legal standards.[179] If a membership application is rejected, moreover, the rejected party will be without legal remedy, unless it can show that its application properly meets the association's standards and the rejection was itself an arbitrary or illegal act.[180]

The basic organizational structure of the association will be established by a constitution or articles of association and by-laws which will define the rights and duties of both the association and its membership. To govern and police itself, the association may also adopt rules and regulations to cover all relevant aspects of its internal structure and the activities of its membership, even though the effect may be to limit the member's freedom of action. Once these rules and regulations have been adopted, the association will, according to this body of law, have the basic right to administer and interpret them without the intervention of the courts.[181] Moreover, when suits are brought seeking judicial interference in the actions of an association, the general rule has been that the decisions of its tribunals will be held to be conclusive, except when mistake,

---

(in an opinion that is questionable in several respects, see note 166 *supra* and § 1.28, the court stated that "[i]f NCAA action is state action, then the concurring action of its members—both public and private—is also state action." *Id.* at 632); Buckton v. National Collegiate Athletic Ass'n, 366 F. Supp. 1152, 1157 (D. Mass. 1973) (indirect suggestion that a private university—itself found to be affected by state action — might become "public" through membership in the NCAA). This issue was specifically not decided in Parish v. National Collegiate Athletic Ass'n, 506 F.2d 1028, 1032 n. 10 (5th Cir. 1975).

178. *See generally Developments in the Law — Judicial Control of Actions of Private Associations,* 76 HARV. L. REV. 983 (1963); Note, *Judicial Review of Disputes Between Athletes and the National Collegiate Athletic Association,* 24 STAN. L. REV. 903, 909-16 (1972).

179. Bruce v. South Carolina High School League, 258 S.C. 546, 189 S.E.2d 817 (1972). Thus, if a state statute requires that all high schools shall be eligible for membership in a high school athletic association, the association may not exclude parochial schools. South Dakota High School Interscholastic Activities Ass'n v. St. Mary's Inter-Parochial High School of Salem, 82 S.D. 84, 141 N.W.2d 477 (1966).

180. Louisiana High School Athletic Ass'n v. St. Augustine High School, 396 F.2d 224 (5th Cir. 1968) (membership of black high school required where it met the association's requirements). *See also* Tillman v. Wheaton-Haven Recreation Ass'n, Inc., 410 U.S. 431, 35 L. Ed. 2d 403, 93 S. Ct. 1090 (1973) (racially discriminatory rejection).

181. Art Gaines Baseball Camp, Inc. v. Houston, 500 S.W.2d 735 (Mo. App. 1973).

fraud, illegality, collusion or arbitrariness can be shown.[182] The extent of the court's review, in the absence of these factors, will be to determine whether the proceedings resulting in the court action were conducted in accordance with a valid rule or regulation of the association, in good faith and pursuant to the law of the land.[183] If these conditions are met, the association's action will, according to the traditional law of associations, be conclusive.[184]

In order to evaluate the law of associations, it is important to keep in mind that the courts have experienced considerable difficulty in dealing with challenges to the actions of such associations, and that difficulty is reflected in many of their opinions. When challenges to the actions of an association occur, a court is confronted with two distinct, but related, problems: whether a given case is suited for judicial resolution (or for intervening in the affairs of the association), and, if so, what criteria to use in deciding the merits of the dispute. In resolving these issues, a court must delicately balance competing policy considerations that involve a rather high level of abstraction and generality. Thus, it must consider the substantiality of the interests of the challenging party, the extent to which the challenged action may infringe upon those interests and the interests of similarly situated persons, the substantiality of the interests of the association, the degree of relationship between those interests and the action in question, the harm to the association if the challenged action is invalidated, the public interest in both the conduct of the challenger that may be limited by the action and the objectives of the association, whether the court can fashion meaningful standards to handle such disputes, whether it can provide meaningful relief, and whether intervention in the dispute would infringe upon any other articulated public policies.[185]

The evaluation and balancing of these factors is a difficult task and has not customarily been undertaken expressly in the decided cases. Rather, the cases have traditionally tended to blur the issues by the invocation of the principles of association law, which may provide a basis for decision but do little to illuminate the analytical process by which a court reached decision, especially if it in fact engaged in an unarticulated interest balancing process.

It is also necessary to keep in mind that the traditional principles in this area were designed to deal with social clubs, religious organizations and fraternal associations, whose affairs did not generally present a strong case for judicial intervention. The contemporary concept of "private association" is not, however,

---

182. Robinson v. Illinois High School Ass'n, 45 Ill. App. 2d 277, 195 N.E.2d 38 (1963); Anderson v. South Dakota High School Activities Ass'n, — S.D. —, 247 N.W.2d 481 (1976); Sanders v. Louisiana High School Athletic Ass'n, 242 So. 2d 19 (La. App. 1930); Brown v. Wells, 284 Minn. 468, 181 N.W.2d 708 (1970); State ex rel. National Junior College Athletic Ass'n v. Luten, 492 S.W.2d 404 (Mo. App. 1973); State ex rel. Ohio High School Athletic Ass'n v. Judges of Court of Common Pleas of Stark County, 173 Ohio St. 239, 181 N.E.2d 261 (1962); Oklahoma Secondary School Activities Ass'n v. Midget, 505 P.2d 175 (Okla. 1972); Bruce v. South Carolina High School League, 258 S.C. 546, 189 S.E.2d 817 (1972); Texas High School Gymnastics Coaches Ass'n v. Andrews, 532 S.W. 2d 142 (Tex. Civ. App. 1975).

183. Oklahoma Secondary School Activities Ass'n v. Midget, 505 P.2d 155 (Okla. 1972); Tennessee Secondary School Athletic Ass'n v. Cox, 221 Tenn. 164, 425 S.W.2d 597 (1968).

184. Sult v. Gilbert, 148 Fla. 31, 3 So. 2d 729 (1941).

185. The various factors that must be considered by a court in this respect are discussed in more depth in Chafee, *The Internal Affairs of Associations Not for Profit*, 43 HARV. L. REV. 993, 1020-29 (1930); *Developments in the Law — Judicial Control of Actions of Private Associations*, 76 HARV. L. REV. 983, 990-98, 1006-20 (1963).

limited to such bodies and encompasses a much broader range of institutions, including, for example, labor unions, professional associations and other types of institutions (such as athletic associations) whose actions may have a more significant effect upon the interests of their members and the requirements of broader public policy considerations.

In light of the very limited nature of judicial review reflected in the association principles, and the nature of the interests affected by many types of association action, the courts have in recent years shown a willingness to expressly undertake the balancing process suggested above to insure that the powers entrusted to associations are exercised in a manner that is consistent with the interests of their members and the more general requirements of felt public policies.[186] The effect of these decisions is to indicate that where substantial interests are affected by the action of an association, the courts will in many cases review that action on its merits and will fully articulate the balancing process that is necessary to determine whether judicial intervention is appropriate.

The basic issue raised by the voluntary association principles in the present context is whether they will be applied to disputes in amateur athletics. If they are, then a person who is aggrieved by the action of an athletic association will be most unlikely to find vindication, since a court would accord a very broad deference to the actions and determinations of the association. If, on the other hand, the rules are not applied or are not applied with full force, then a court would be far more likely to analyze the grievances presented on their merits. In determining whether and to what extent the principles are appropriately applied to amateur athletics, it is important to distinguish the two separate situations that will normally present the issue: disputes between an athletic association and a school that is one of its members, and disputes between an association and an athlete who is a student in a member-school, but who is not himself or herself a member.

The athletic association situation would seem to fit comfortably within the rubric of association law. An association would presumably be formed by its members for the purposes of achieving common goals and collectivizing their athletic relationships, and each institution would voluntarily become a member with the expectation that its interests would be thereby served. Upon becoming a member, moreover, each institution would agree to be bound by the actions and determinations of the association. In short, it could be suggested that the association would be the product of its members having joined together in order to regularize their relationships and achieve mutually desired objectives. One of the difficulties with this argument would be the premise that membership in such athletic associations is truly voluntary. As a practical matter,

---

186. *See, e.g.,* Marjorie Webster Junior College, Inc. v. Middle States Ass'n of Colleges & Secondary Schools, Inc., 432 F.2d 650 (D.C. Cir. 1969), *cert. denied,* 400 U.S. 965 (1970); Pinsker v. Pacific Coast Soc'y of Orthodontists, 12 Cal. 3d 541, 116 Cal. Rptr. 245, 526 P.2d 253 (1974); California State Univ., Hayward v. National Collegiate Athletic Ass'n, 47 Cal. App. 3d 533, 121 Cal. Rptr. 85 (1975); Jacobson v. New York Racing Ass'n, 33 N.Y.2d 144, 350 N.Y.S.2d 639, 305 N.E.2d 765 (1973); Falcone v. Middlesex County Medical Soc'y, 34 N.J. 582, 170 A.2d 791 (1961). *See also* Chafee, *The Internal Affairs of Associations Not for Profit,* 43 HARV. L. REV. 993, 1021-23 (1930); *see* note 177 *supra.* These principles are also considered with respect to professional sports in §§ 3.10(b), 3.15.

membership may be mandatory to enable a school to engage in athletics in a competitive manner. Membership may, for example, be required in order to compete for national recognition through association sponsored competition or championships, to attract top young athletes, or to share in the media revenues that are produced by the association's agreements with broadcasters. Thus, it has been observed that lack of membership in an association may make it "all but impossible to field a competitive team in any major sport . . . ." [187]

If an association's membership were viewed as being truly voluntary and a dispute arose between it and a member, one would anticipate that the association-type rules would have prima facie application, at least to the extent that they represent principles which retain current vitality. Thus, if an athletic association made a determination that affected the interests of one of its members, and the member brought suit challenging the action, the association principles would suggest that the court would limit its inquiry to determining whether the association's actions were infected by fraud, caprice, arbitrariness or illegality. Such a process is reflected in *Parsons College v. North Central Association of Colleges and Secondary Schools,*[188] where a college brought suit against an association to prevent it from terminating the school's membership, and thereby its accreditation, which would cause it substantial and irreparable harm. In analyzing the complaint of the college, the court began by noting that the association's actions were not affected with state action, so that the case did not present any federal constitutional issues. It then turned to private association principles, which indicated that

> the only law applicable to determine the propriety of the expulsion of a member from a private association is the law which he agreed to when he voluntarily chose to join the association, that is, the rules of the association itself.[189]

In light of these principles, the court rejected the relief sought by the college. The court did not undertake to balance the respective interests of the parties and did not elaborate on why the association principles were applicable to the relationship between them.

A significantly different approach to an essentially similar case was taken in *Marjorie Webster Junior College v. Middle States Association of Colleges & Secondary Schools, Inc.,*[190] where a college had sought accreditation from an association, but was rejected on the basis of the association's rule that it would not accredit a proprietary institution, such as the applicant college. When the college then brought suit against the association, the court assumed that the association's activities would constitute state action.[191] With respect to the extent of review that would be given, the court stated that

> [w]here membership in, or certification by, . . . an association is a virtual prerequisite to the practice of a given profession, courts have

187. Parish v. National Collegiate Athletic Ass'n, 361 F. Supp. 1214, 1222 (W.D. La. 1973), *aff'd,* 506 F.2d 1028 (5th Cir. 1975); Board of Regents, University of Oklahoma v. National Collegiate Athletic Ass'n, — Okla. —, 561 P.2d 499 (1977).
188. 271 F. Supp. 65 (N.D. Ill. 1967).
189. *Id.* at 70.
190. 432 F.2d 650 (D.C. Cir. 1969), *cert. denied,* 400 U.S. 965 (1970).
191. *Id.* at 658-59.

scrutinized the standards and procedures employed by the association notwithstanding their recognition of the fact that professional societies possess competence in evaluating the qualifications of an individual to engage in professional activities. The standards must be reasonable, applied with an even hand, and not in conflict with the public policy of the jurisdiction. Even where less than complete exclusion from practice is involved, deprivation of substantial economic or professional advantages will often be sufficient to warrant judicial action.[192]

With these principles in hand, the court analyzed the facts of the case before it, and, after observing that the college would not suffer a large degree of harm from the lack of accreditation, concluded that substantial deference should be accorded to the action of the association. The standard suggested in *Marjorie Webster* requires that where association action causes the loss of substantial economic or professional advantage a court will scrutinize that action to determine its reasonableness, which is a much different standard than that suggested in *Parsons College.* The difference may be attributable to the presence of state action in the former, or it may be attributable to the growing reluctance of the courts to dismiss complaints out of hand by reference to the vague association principles.[193]

As indicated above, the activities of an athletic association would appear to fit the classic mold to which the association principles were applicable, and to this extent it would not be unduly surprising to find courts applying the principles as was done in *Parsons College.*[194] There are, however, at least two elements present in the activities of most associations that may cause courts to at least follow the lead of *Marjorie Webster* and not apply the traditional principles of non-intervention on an ipso facto basis. The basic element is that membership in an athletic association may be a virtual prerequisite to successful athletic competition — *i.e.,* it is not truly voluntary.[195] In addition, some courts have held that the interests affected by association action are sufficiently substantial that they may be interfered with only after a proceeding in which procedural due process rights are accorded.[196]

In several of the more recent cases dealing with disputes between schools and athletic associations, there is a rather surprising lack of attention paid to the association principles. In some cases the issue of their application is not even considered by the court,[197] and in others they are applied in a manner that is quite similar to that suggested in *Marjorie Webster.* The fullest discussion of the later position is in *California State University, Hayward v. National Collegiate Athletic Association,*[198] in which the school had been suspended by

192. *Id.* at 655. *See also* Rockland Institute v. Association of Independent Colleges & Schools, 412 F. Supp. 1015 (C.D. Calif. 1976).

193. *See* note 186 *supra.*

194. *See* notes 203-204 *infra.*

195. *See* note 187 *supra.*

196. *See* §§ 1.11, 1.28. An additional element that may distinguish the cases is that state action was found to be present in *Marjorie Webster.* While this factor may be important, it seems clear that the court in *Marjorie Webster* was not basing its standard of review on constitutional principles.

197. *See* Howard Univ. v. National Collegiate Athletic Ass'n, 510 F.2d 213 (D.C. Cir. 1975); Cabrillo Community College Dist. of Santa Cruz County v. California Junior College Ass'n, 44 Cal. App. 3d 367, 118 Cal. Rptr. 708 (1975).

198. 47 Cal. App. 3d 533, 121 Cal. Rptr. 85 (1975). *See also* Chabert v. Louisiana High School Athletic Ass'n, 323 So.2d 774 (La. 1975); Board of Regents, University of Oklahoma v. National Collegiate Athletic Ass'n, — Okla. —, 561 P.2d 499 (1977).

.the NCAA for failure to dismiss two students who were apparently in violation of an NCAA rule, which the NCAA had interpreted inconsistently. The NCAA took the position that it was improper for the courts to intervene in the affairs of a private association in general, and specifically in this type of case where the party seeking intervention had no substantial interest. The court rejected both contentions. With respect to the insubstantiality of the interest, it referred to the rather large group of cases holding that the interest in participation is of sufficient weight to require constitutional protection[199] and observed that the interest of the school was substantial for a variety of reasons.[200] As to the general proposition that courts should not intervene, the court followed the lead of earlier cases which had suggested that courts would intervene where the association's action is in violation of its own rules, by-laws or constitution, or where it is otherwise in violation of the law of the land.[201]

The *California State* case is by no means a broad rejection of the association principles in the athletics context, but it does indicate that where substantial rights are involved, the courts may not apply those rules in such a manner as to obviate the need for judicial scrutiny of the grievances brought before them. This apparent trend is further supported by those cases in which the courts do not even refer to the association principles, though these cases tend to be decided on constitutional grounds, as well as by the cases which have analyzed the merits of various rules and regulations of athletic associations.[202] If substantial rights are not affected by associational action, then there is a much stronger case for the application of the traditional principles, as is suggested by *Marjorie Webster.* This might, for example, be the case if a member undertakes to challenge the adoption of rule approved by the requisite majority of members but disliked by the challenger.[202.1]

The second type of situation in which the application of the association principles may arise is in cases involving disputes between athletes and athletic associations. Although the courts have quite commonly applied the private association law to actions brought by amateur athletes,[203] they have never made it clear why these rules should be applicable to the relationship between athletes and those who regulate their athletic endeavors. The only reasonable basis would be that the associations, whether they be state high school athletic

---

199. *See* § 1.11.

200. 121 Cal. Rptr. at 90. These reasons included the opportunity to participate in post season championships, as well as damage to the school's athletic program that would result from the suspension.

201. 121 Cal. Rptr. at 91.

202. *See* §§ 1.15-.27. *See also* H. APPENZELLER, ATHLETICS AND THE LAW 131 (1975).

202.1. *See, e.g.,* Board of Regents, University of Oklahoma v. National Collegiate Athletic Ass'n, — Okla. —, 561 P.2d 499 (1977) (coaching staff limitation upheld against antitrust attack).

203. *See* Robinson v. Illinois High School Ass'n, 45 Ill. App. 2d 277, 195 N.E.2d 38 (1963); Watkins v. Louisiana High School Athletic Ass'n, 301 So. 2d 695 (La. App. 1974); Sanders v. Louisiana High School Athletic Ass'n, 242 So. 2d 19 (La. App. 1970); Brown v. Wells, 284 Minn. 468, 181 N.W.2d 708 (1970); State *ex rel.* National Junior College Athletic Ass'n v. Luten, 492 S.W.2d 404 (Mo. App. 1973); School Dist. of City of Harrisburg v. Pennsylvania Interscholastic Athletic Ass'n, 453 Pa. 495, 309 A.2d 353 (1973); State *ex rel.* Ohio High School Athletic Ass'n v. Judges of Court of Common Pleas of Stark County, 173 Ohio St. 239, 181 N.E. 261 (1962); Oklahoma Secondary Schools Ass'n v. Midget, 505 P.2d 175 (Okla. 1972); Bruce v. South Carolina High School League, 258 S.C. 546, 189 S.E.2d 817 (1972); Tennessee Secondary School Athletic Ass'n v. Cox, 221 Tenn. 164, 425 S.W.2d 597 (1968).

associations or collegiate conferences, are aggregations of schools which have voluntarily come together to regulate their athletic programs. Such reasoning might justify the application of the rules to the schools, which are the members of the association,[204] but it would provide a rather slender basis for application to the athletes themselves. The athletes will only rarely be members of the association, and in the ordinary case their only connection with it will be that they are students in a school which is a member. Thus, when application of the association principles to athletes is considered, there is the very substantial problem that they are not members and will have had no opportunity to exercise their volition (even if there could be any) about becoming a member.[205]

Even if the associational framework were applicable to athletes, the cases that have reviewed the activities of associations whose action deprives a person of substantial economic or professional advantage would seem to have prima facie application.[206] As has already been noted, the interest of athletes in athletic participation is a substantial interest, of both an educational and economic nature, and has frequently received protection for constitutional purposes.[207] Thus, it seems likely that even if the general associational framework were applicable, it might not prevent a court from scrutinizing the action in question.[208] It should in fairness, however, again be noted that there is a substantial body of precedent applying the association principles to athletes' grievances, though courts have seldom analyzed their application in terms of the problems suggested here.

Although there is not yet any clear answer as to when and under what circumstances the association-type principles will be applied to amateur athletics disputes, it can be said, as will be observed in much of the remainder of this chapter, that the courts regularly review the substantive and procedural propriety of the actions and determinations of athletic organizations and institutions. For example, eligibility rules that are adopted and procedures used in enforcement proceedings are reviewed on their merits pursuant to a standard of review that is much different than that which is suggested by the traditional association principles.[209] Whether these several decisions suggest that the voluntary association principles have been sapped of a great deal of their authority in the athletics context, that athletics disputes have been "constitutionalized," or that the rules serve only as convenient bases for

---

204. *See, e.g.,* School Dist. of City of Harrisburg v. Pennsylvania Interscholastic Athletic Ass'n, 453 Pa. 495, 309 A.2d 353 (1973).

205. *See* Chabert v. Louisiana High School Athletic Ass'n, 323 So.2d 774 (La. 1975).

206. *See* note 186 *supra.*

207. *See* §§ 1.11, 1.28.

208. Perhaps the best statement of this fact is contained in Reed v. Nebraska School Activities Ass'n, 341 F. Supp. 258 (D. Nebr. 1972), where the court said that the cases blindly invoking the rules of private associational law

> miss the mark in these respects: they assume that schools and activities associations may make any rule they choose to make, irrespective of whether there be any rational connection with a reasonable objective of the state; and they indicate and they assume that students have only "privileges" relating to sports activities. These assumptions may be proper as matters of state law, with which those state courts primarily were dealing, but as matters of federal constitutional law they are untenable in view of the declarations of the Supreme Court of the United States cited in this memorandum. *Id.* at 262.

See also Dumez v. Louisiana High School Athletic Ass'n, 334 So.2d 494 (La. App. 1976).

209. *See* § 1.15 (rule-making); § 1.28 (enforcement activity).

decisions upholding challenged action is unclear. It is apparent, however, that review is undertaken on a regular basis, that the principles utilized in such review often bear little similarity to the association rules, and that the courts invoke those rules on a much less frequent basis than has been true in the past.

§ 1.15. Rule-Making in Amateur Athletics.

⌈ The primary means by which the regulation of amateur athletics is accomplished is through the making and enforcing of rules and regulations (hereinafter "rules") by the organizations and institutions responsible for the conduct of athletic competition. This is one of the most important aspects of athletic regulation, since if it is properly performed it will advise participants of their rights and duties, foster the public's belief in the fair and honest administration of amateur athletics, and require the regulating bodies to think through the problems that exist in their sports in order to formulate appropriate rules.⌋

The inquiry in this section will be to determine how courts will review the rules that are adopted and promulgated by amateur athletic bodies.[210] The discussion will include the rule-making of public athletic associations and public schools, but will not include that of private schools, which is considered in the immediately following section. Athletic associations and public schools are discussed concurrently because the rule-making activities of each are essentially similar, as are the broad principles that will be utilized to determine whether a given rule will be enforced by a reviewing court.

In considering the rule-making actions of amateur athletic organizations and institutions, and the extent to which courts will review those actions, it is important to note at the outset that there is no clearly established standard that may be turned to for guidance. The question of the proper scope of review is one that has elicited a considerable amount of scholarly comment,[211] as well as numerous judicial expressions (which shall be considered in the sections that follow), but these have produced little consensus. In part this is due to the traditional invocation of principles such as those reflected in the law of associations,[212] in part to the deference that is properly accorded the decision-making of educational bodies,[213] and in part to the fact that many of the disputes that have reached the courts in recent years have involved constitutional issues.[214] The purpose of this section will be to suggest the

---

210. In almost all situations in which athletes or other parties challenge the validity of a rule or regulation, it will be through an injunction or declaratory judgment action, or a common law writ. These forms of action are noted in § 2.19 note 397.

211. N. EDWARDS, THE COURTS AND THE PUBLIC SCHOOLS 564-67 (Garber 3d ed. 1971); S. GOLDSTEIN, LAW AND PUBLIC EDUCATION (1974); E. REUTTER & R. HAMILTON, THE LAW OF PUBLIC EDUCATION 122-23 (1970); Van Alstyne, *Student Academic Freedom and the Rule-Making Powers of Public Universities: Some Constitutional Considerations,* 2 LAW IN TRANSITION Q. 1, 23 (1965); Wright, *The Constitution on Campus,* 22 VAND. L. REV. 1027, 1069 (1969); *Developments in the Law — Academic Freedom,* 81 HARV. L. REV. 1045, 1143-57 (1968); Note, *Judicial Review of Disputes Between Athletes and the National Collegiate Athletic Association,* 24 STAN. L. REV. 903 (1972).

212. *See* § 1.14.

213. *See* notes 215-216 *infra.*

214. *See* Goldstein, *The Scope and Sources of School Board Authority to Regulate Student Conduct and Status: A Nonconstitutional Analysis,* 117 U. PA. L. REV. 373, 376-77 (1969).

standards that appear to be applied by the courts in deciding challenges to the rules of athletic organizations.

As noted above, the courts have traditionally given broad deference to the actions of athletic associations,[215] and the same deference has been given to the actions of public schools. Although this deferrence has been limited in recent years by an increased judicial willingness to review such actions on their merits, the scope of a court's review continues to be quite limited. A court will not review a challenged rule to determine its wisdom or lack of wisdom.[216] These are issues which properly belong to the body who is vested with responsibility for making the rules, and the courts will not substitute their judgment for that of the appropriate entity. Rather, the scope of a court's review will be limited to determining whether the rule as adopted meets applicable legal standards. In order to make this determination, there are two levels of inquiry that may be appropriate in any given case. These include analysis of a challenged rule on nonconstitutional and constitutional bases, though the inquiries are not entirely distinct and may involve quite similar analysis.[217] Notwithstanding the similarity of the inquiries, the two should be separately considered, since both may not be involved in any given case—for example, when a court need not, or does not wish to, reach the constitutional issue.[218]

a. Nonconstitutional Inquiry. The nonconstitutional inquiry will focus upon whether the rule in question is a proper exercise of the rule-maker's authority. This will principally require consideration of two related factors: whether the rule is 1) within the authority of the rule-maker and 2) a reasonable exercise of that authority.[219] The authority of an organization to adopt rules will be dependent upon its own status. In most cases, the organizations will be either educational institutions or athletic conferences or associations, whose membership may include educational institutions. Establishment of the authority of such an organization is crucial, because if a particular rule is adopted and enforced without the requisite rule-making power, both the rule and the action taken pursuant to it will be void.[220] In most states, the authority to provide for the educational interests of the state is vested in the state legislature.[221] It is customary for the legislature to then delegate that authority

---

215. *See* § 1.14.

216. *See, e.g.,* Wood v. Strickland, 420 U.S. 308, 326, 95 S. Ct. 992, 43 L. Ed. 2d 214 (1975); Paschal v. Perdue, 320 F. Supp. 1274 (S.D. Fla. 1970); Louisiana State Bd. of Educ. v. National Collegiate Athletic Ass'n, 273 So. 2d 912 (La. App. 1973); Brown v. Wells, 288 Minn. 468, 181 N.W.2d 708 (1970), *noted in* 36 Mo. L. Rev. 400 (1971).

217. As will be observed in the following paragraphs of text, the nonconstitutional standards of review will involve essentially the same type of inquiry that will be required under the traditional permissive standard for fourteenth amendment purposes. The need for keeping the constitutional and nonconstitutional inquiries as distinct as possible is considered in Goldstein, *The Scope and Sources of School Board Authority to Regulate Student Conduct and Status: A Nonconstitutional Analysis,* 177 U. Pa. L. Rev. 373, 376-77 (1969).

218. *See, e.g.,* Cabrillo Community College Dist. of Santa Cruz County v. California Junior College Ass'n, 44 Cal. App. 3d 367, 188 Cal. Rptr. 708 (1975).

219. There may also be an issue with respect to whether the rule was adopted pursuant to the proper procedures, *see* Bunger v. Iowa High School Athletic Ass'n, 197 N.W.2d 555 (Iowa 1972), but the issue has seldom been raised in amateur athletics litigation.

220. Moran v. School Dist. No. 7, Yellowstone County, 350 F. Supp. 1180 (D. Mont. 1972).

221. *See, e.g.,* Iowa Const. art. IX, 1st, § 15 (1949); Mont. Const. art. XI, § 1 (1957).

to the school boards, or other supervisory authorities, of each school district.[222] This delegation will include the power to make rules for its own governance and that of the students in its charge, including regulation of extracurricular activities and participation in interscholastic athletics.[223]

Since athletic conferences and associations do most of the rule-making for amateur athletics, and such rules are considered binding on all their members, the more important question is whether any given conference or association has the power to perform this function. The answer depends on whether a school board can redelegate to an athletic association its delegated power to make rules for the governance of its students' activities. This is an issue that has received infrequent attention in the decided cases. This lack of attention may be explained by the conclusion that when schools join an athletic association they agree to abide by its rules and if those rules are unsatisfactory they may withdraw,[224] but that conclusion does little to answer the question of where the association gets its power and whether the conferral of such power is consistent with the educational statutes of the state. In some states this question has been answered by the legislative body through the enactment of statutory authority for school boards to join athletic associations.[225] Without such a provision, the validity of an association's rule-making activities is less clear since a delegated power requiring the exercise of judgment or discretion may not be further delegated unless there is a special power of substitution either express or necessarily implied from its original delegation. Thus, although a public body may properly authorize the performance of ministerial or administrative functions by others, it may not re-delegate matters of judgment or discretion.[226] The leading athletic association case considering this problem is *Bunger v. Iowa High School Athletic Association*,[227] where the state legislature had made no provision for re-delegation of rule-making power to an athletic association,[228] and the court held that the rules adopted by the association were invalid for lack of the requisite promulgating authority. In defense of its rules, the association had unsuccessfully contended that they were actually rules of each individual school board since each had agreed to abide by the rules when it joined the association,

---

222. *See e.g.,* IOWA CODE ANN. §§ 274.1, .7 (1972).

223. *See, e.g.,* MINN. STAT. ANN. §§ 123.17, .38 (1960). In Georgia, for example, the University of Georgia Athletic Ass'n is granted specific rule-making power. GA. CODE ANN. § 32-153 (1976).

224. *See* State *ex rel.* Indiana High School Athletic Ass'n v. *Lawrence Circuit Court,* 240 Ind. 114, 162 N.E.2d 250 (1959); Quimby v. School Dist. No. 21 of Pinal County, 10 Ariz. App. 69, 455 P.2d 1019 (1977).

225. *See e.g.,* KAN. STAT. ANN. § 72-130 (1972); MINN. STAT. ANN. § 129.121 (Supp. 1977); W. VA. CODE § 18-2-25 (1971). Such provisions have been upheld against attacks that they constitute impermissible delegations. Anderson v. South Dakota High School Activities Ass'n, — S.D. —, 247 N.W.2d 481 (1976).

226. Bunger v. Iowa High School Athletic Ass'n, 197 N.W.2d 555 (Iowa 1972). It should be noted that not all activities of an athletic association would be subject to the potential application of the delegation rule. Thus, even where the rule is found to be applicable, it would not preclude the delegation of authority to perform functions of an essentially ministerial nature — for example, arranging game schedules for members of the association.

227. 197 N.W.2d 555 (Iowa 1972).

228. Although there was a statutory provision allowing a school to join an association if the association met a number of specified requirements, this was held to not authorize a redelegation of rule-making power. *But cf.* South Dakota High School Interscholastic Activities Ass'n v. St. Mary's Inter-Parochial High School of Salem, 82 S.D. 84, 141 N.W.2d 477 (1968).

and by joining had adopted the rules as their own.[229] Although there are decisions which have reached a result contrary to that in *Bunger*,[230] and the delegation doctrine has itself been the subject of considerable criticism in recent years,[231] the court's conclusion may pose a sufficient barrier in states without explicit statutory provision to make the adoption of such a provision advisable. Similar issues may also arise with respect to the power of collegiate athletic associations, though the issues have not been presented in the reported decisions dealing with their rule-making power.

If the organization does have rule-making authority, it must still be determined whether a challenged rule is within the authority granted. As noted above, the authority of public schools, as well as that of athletic associations composed in whole or part of public schools, is derived, directly or indirectly, from the state, and the authority will include the power to adopt and promulgate rules to control the activities within their jurisdiction. As with all grants of power, this rule-making authority is subject to the inherent limitation that it may be used only for the purposes for which it is conferred, and its exercise must bear a proper relationship to those purposes.[232] Thus, when a court is asked to consider whether a given rule is a proper exercise of the authority of a public athletic organization, it must determine whether the rule is directly related to a subject matter that is a proper object of the organization, and,[233] if it is,

---

229. In rejecting this contention, the court observed that

> [w]e think this contention is inconsonant with the realities of the situation. The rules are actually association rules. A rule is initially adopted by majority vote of the association members. Bearing in mind that a school board cannot redelegate its rule-making power, how can we say that a school which votes against a proposed rule has itself promulgated that rule? Again, a school which joins IHSAA after a number of rules have been adopted has no choice as to the rules it will accept. It must take them all and abdicate its nondelegable responsibility to select the rules it wishes to have. Then what about a member school which becomes dissatisfied with a rule? It has no power to repeal the rule. To say the school can withdraw from the IHSAA is no answer. If it leaves IHSAA voluntarily, or involuntarily for violating the rule, its boys' interscholastic athletic program is at an end—except for playing Kalona. Its hands are tied. The power is actually in the association, not in each school board where the statute places it.
> What we have here, in fact, is an association which started out arranging inter-school games and tournaments and grew into an organization above individual schools, regulating all manner of affairs relating to athletes. The association did not usurp the regulatory functions of individual schools; the schools turned over those functions to the association. 197 N.W.2d 555, 561 (Iowa 1972).

Some of the issues raised by *Bunger* are considered in S. GOLDSTEIN, LAW & PUBLIC EDUCATION 742-45 (1974). *See also* Cabrillo Community College Dist. of Santa Cruz County v. California Junior College Ass'n, 44 Cal. App. 3d 367, 118 Cal. Rptr. 708 (1975) (holding that educational institutions can delegate to athletic associations only as much power as they themselves are given to delegate by the legislature).

230. *See* State *ex rel.* Ohio High School Athletic Ass'n v. Judges of the Court of Common Pleas of Stark County, 173 Ohio St. 239, 181 N.E.2d 261 (1962). In People v. Colorado High School Activities Ass'n, 141 Colo. 382, 349 P.2d 381 (1960), the court held that the legality of the contribution of public funds to a state high school athletic association was a proper subject of judicial inquiry.

231. *See* 1 K. DAVIS, ADMINISTRATIVE LAW TREATISE ch. 2 (1958); L. JAFFE, JUDICIAL CONTROL OF ADMINISTRATIVE ACTION 33-86 (1965). *See also* § 2.17.

232. *See, e.g.,* Sacher v. United States, 343 U.S. 1, 29, 96 L. Ed. 717, 72 S. Ct. 451 (1952) (Frankfurter, J., dissenting).

233. It should be noted that the question of whether a rule is directly related to a proper object of the organization is similar to the question of whether the rule-maker has authority to adopt rules, *see* notes 220-231, though it focuses more specifically upon a given rule.

whether the rule is reasonably drawn to achieve only the proper object.[234] Both inquiries involve primarily factual questions that will be answered by considering and balancing the facts and circumstances presented by a given case.[235] If either is answered negatively, the rule will not be enforced.[236]

In considering the application of these principles, it is important to reiterate that the court's review will be limited to insuring only that the rule in question is a proper exercise of the rule-maker's authority. It will not evaluate the wisdom or desirability of the rule as drafted, and will not substitute its judgment for that of the rule-maker, even if it would have adopted a different rule had the initial decision been its to make. With respect to many of the rules adopted by athletic organizations, the legal standard will normally be met so long as the rules relate to the conduct of athletic contests and other matters affecting on the field competition. Rules which define the type of competition to occur are within the legitimate purpose of the rule-maker to provide for the staging of athletic competition and would normally pose no problems in terms of the breadth of application. For example, rules which set forth the manner in which a game is to be played and the penalties that will be imposed for violation of these rules during the course of a game would be most unlikely candidates for judicial review. They do not result in the imposition of severe sanctions upon the party who violates them, at least in terms of a suspension of a team or, normally, an athlete, and they affect conduct only on the athletic field or floor (we are not here considering a 15-yard penalty in football or a technical foul in basketball to be penalties in a legal sense). As attention is focused upon rules which affect conduct or status that is not immediately related to athletic competition, and which may result in substantial penalties, then the rules will become progressively more subject to judicial scrutiny in terms of the standards suggested.

The application of these principles is illustrated by *Bunger*,[237] where the court considered the permissibility of a rule which precluded athletes from consuming, possessing, transporting, or being in a car containing alcoholic beverages at any

---

234. There are doubtlessly many other methods of phrasing the two aspects of this inquiry. Thus, it has been suggested that cases which deal with the validity of such rules involve two questions:

> The first is whether the school authorities have the power to adopt rules in this area. The second, assuming power, is whether the adopted rule and its accompanying sanction are reasonable.

S. GOLDSTEIN, LAW AND PUBLIC EDUCATION 230 (1974). *See also* N. EDWARDS, THE COURTS AND THE PUBLIC SCHOOLS 564-67 (Garber 3d ed. 1971); E. REUTTER & R. HAMILTON, THE LAW OF PUBLIC EDUCATION 122-23 (1970); Goldstein, *supra* note 214, at 387-89.

235. The types of interest balancing that will inevitably be a part of a court's decision-making process is suggested by the factors identified at § 1.14 note 185. *See generally Developments in the Law — Academic Freedom,* 81 HARV. L. REV. 1045, 1148-57 (1968); *Developments in the Law — Judicial Control of Actions of Private Associations,* 76 HARV. L. REV. 983, 1006-20 (1963).

236. Curtis v. National Collegiate Athletic Ass'n, Case No. C-71 2088 ACW (N.D. Cal. 1972); Bunger v. Iowa High School Athletic Ass'n, 197 N.W.2d 555 (Iowa 1972); Kinzer v. Directors of Independent School Dist. of Marion, 129 Iowa 441, 105 N.W. 686 (1906); Art Gaines Baseball Camp, Inc. v. Houston, 500 S.W.2d 735 (Mo. App. 1973).

In addition to the requirements noted in text, a given rule may also have to satisfy other legal principles in order to be enforcible. *See, e.g.,* Board of Regents of University of Oklahoma v. National Collegiate Athletic Ass'n, — Okla. —, 561 P.2d 499 (1977) (antitrust principles, discussed in § 5.12); College Athletic Placement Service, Inc. v. National Collegiate Athletic Ass'n, Civil Action 74-1144 (D.N.J. 1974) (antitrust principles).

237. 197 N.W.2d 555 (Iowa 1972).

time of the year, in or out of the playing season. During the summer months, the athlete in question had been in an automobile that contained beer, though he was in no way connected with it. In examining the authority for the rule, the court observed that a school could make a player ineligible if he drank beer during the playing season and could probably do so even if it occurred in the off-season or during summer vacation, since all of these acts would affect the school and its athletic program. In the case before it, however, the court found that the nexus between the rule and the conduct was simply too tenuous, since it took place "outside of football season, beyond the school year [and involved], no illegal or even improper use of beer." [238] Although the rule did not even pass the first inquiry, the court went on to consider its reasonableness, to furnish athletes, schools, athletic associations and other courts a standard by which to evaluate such rules. The rule was also found to exceed "the bounds of reason," since it was not confined to consumption, acquisition, disposition, possession or transportation, but included as well mere occupation of an auto containing beer. In reaching this conclusion, the court observed that "[w]e realize that the rule has been made broad in an effort to avoid problems of proving a connection between the student and the beer, but rules cannot be so extended as to sweep in the innocent in order to achieve invariable conviction of the guilty." [239]

b. Constitutional Inquiry. The second level of inquiry that may be appropriate when a rule of a public athletic organization is challenged involves its constitutionality. Although the constitutional inquiry may in many respects be similar to that already noted for nonconstitutional purposes, it may also involve several additional factors. When rules are subjected to constitutional challenge, the basic principles that will be applicable will involve equal protection and substantive due process of law.[240]

The first of these basic principles is the Equal Protection Clause of the Fourteenth Amendment. In pertinent part, Section I of the Fourteenth Amendment provides that "[n]o State shall make or enforce any law which shall . . . deny to any person . . . the equal protection of the laws." From these relatively simple and direct words has emerged a potent panoply of rules which circumscribe the actions of all persons and organizations within their ambit.[241] The Equal Protection Clause requires the courts to consider whether classifications brought into dispute constitute arbitrary and invidious discrimination.[242] In applying the Clause, the Supreme Court has consistently recognized that it does not deny the power to treat different classes of persons in different ways; rather, it denies only the power to differentiate among classes

---

238. *Id.* at 564.

239. *Id.* at 565.

240. Additional discussions of constitutional principles are in § 1.12 (first amendment principles) and § 1.28 (procedural due process). In considering the constitutional bases for challenge to athletic rules, it should be observed that attention here will be given to only principles of federal constitutional law and not to those that may flow from state constitutional provisions. In many situations, the principles will be quite similar since most state constitutions are patterned after comparable federal provisions.

241. The requirements of the Equal Protection Clause apply to only those persons or organizations who are affected with "state action," which is considered in § 1.14.

242. Loving v. Virginia, 388 U.S. 1, 18 L. Ed. 2d 1010, 87 S. Ct. 1817 (1967).

of persons when the purposes therefor are not constitutionally sufficient.[243] The sufficiency of the purposes behind any particular classification, moreover, is determined by applying the appropriate standard of review, which is itself determined by the type of interest affected by the classification in question.

Contemporary equal protection theory has adopted a "two-tier system," in which there are apparently two basic standards of review: the permissive and strict standards.[244] The traditional permissive standard, which will ordinarily be applied to test the validity of classifications, will uphold all classifications which are reasonably related to the purpose sought to be thereby achieved.[245] The courts will presume that the purposes sought to be achieved are proper, and the constitutionally required nexus will be present if the classification is reasonably related to the purpose.[246] Under the permissive standard of review, those who devise classifications have wide discretion to accomplish their purposes. This discretion will allow them to imprecisely draw their classifications. Thus, the classification may be permissible even though it is "under-inclusive"—that is, the burden created by the classification does not affect all persons similarly situated—if the purpose for the under-inclusion is to facilitate a step-at-a-time approach to the problem sought to be solved.[247] The classification may also be upheld though it is "over-inclusive"—that is, it sweeps within its ambit not only those who must be included to accomplish the purpose of the classification but also those who need not be included[248]—unless it is not reasonably related to the purpose for which it is drawn.[249] Even if a classification is fair and reasonable on its face, it may yet become constitutionally impermissible if its application or administration is uneven so as to result in illegal discrimination between persons similarly situated.[250]

The strict standard of review, on the other hand, requires that classifications within its purview be precise and substantively justified. This standard will apply whenever a questioned classification touches upon a "fundamental interest" [251] or is based upon "suspect criteria," [252] and its constitutional permissibility will

---

243. Reed v. Reed, 404 U.S. 71, 30 L. Ed. 2d 225, 92 S. Ct. 251 (1971).

244. It has been suggested that the Supreme Court has in recent years indicated the possibility that it may be evolving a new standard for equal protection analysis. *See* Gunther, *Foreword: In Search of Evolving Doctrine on a Changing Court: A Model for a Newer Equal Protection,* 86 HARV. L. REV. 1 (1972).

245. Royster Guano Co. v. Virginia, 253 U.S. 412, 64 L. Ed. 989, 40 S. Ct. 560 (1920).

246. Goesaert v. Cleary, 335 U.S. 464, 93 L. Ed. 163, 69 S. Ct. 198 (1948).

247. Williamson v. Lee Optical, 348 U.S. 483, 99 L. Ed. 563, 75 S. Ct. 461 (1955).

248. Hirabayashi v. United States, 320 U.S. 81, 87 L. Ed. 174, 63 S. Ct. 1375 (1943).

249. Associated Students v. National Collegiate Athletic Ass'n (Civil No. S-2754, E.D. Cal. 1973), *aff'd,* 493 F.2d 1251 (9th Cir. 1974); Curtis v. National Collegiate Athletic Ass'n, Civil No. C-21 2088 ACW (N.D. Cal. 1972).

250. Yick Wo v. Hopkins, 118 U.S. 356, 30 L. Ed. 220, 6 S. Ct. 1064 (1886). *See also* Haas v. South Bend Community School Corp., 259 Ind. 515, 289 N.E.2d 495 (1972).

251. The interests to date deemed "fundamental," have included voting, Reynolds v. Sims, 377 U.S. 533, 12 L. Ed. 2d 506, 84 S. Ct. 1362 (1964); criminal appeals, Griffin v. Illinois, 351 U.S. 12, 100 L. Ed. 891, 76 S. Ct. 585 (1956); marriage, Loving v. Virginia, 388 U.S. 1, 18 L. Ed. 2d 1010, 87 S. Ct. 1817 (1967); divorce, Boddie v. Connecticut, 401 U.S. 371, 28 L. Ed. 2d 113, 91 S. Ct. 780 (1971); and interstate travel, Shapiro v. Thompson, 394 U.S. 618, 22 L. Ed. 2d 600, 89 S. Ct. 1322 (1969).

252. "Suspect criteria" have included race, McLaughlin v. Florida, 379 U.S. 184, 13 L. Ed. 2d 222, 85 S. Ct. 283 (1964); alienage, Yick Wo v. Hopkins, 118 U.S. 356, 30 L. Ed. 220, 6 S. Ct. 1064 (1886) and Howard Univ. v. National Collegiate Athletic Ass'n, 367 F. Supp. 926 (D.D.C. 1973); wealth, McDonald v. Board of Election Comm'rs, 394 U.S. 802, 22 L. Ed. 2d 739, 89 S. Ct. 1404 (1969); Harper

be determined by whether it promotes a "compelling interest" of the organization drawing the classification.[253] A court confronted with such a classification will weigh the benefits sought by it to be achieved and the interests of the rule-maker against the harm to the personal interests affected. Although the weighing process may be a complex undertaking, it may cause a classification to be invalidated even though it is neither invidious nor unrelated to a legitimate public purpose.[254]

The primary question raised by the strict standard is whether the interest of amateur athletes in athletic participation is a "fundamental interest," entitled to the strict standard of review when classifications drawn by regulatory associations interfere with, or prevent, such participation. The courts have clearly indicated that the right to participate in amateur athletics is not "fundamental" and is not, therefore, entitled to the strict standard of review.[255] Even though the interest in participation will not itself qualify as a fundamental interest, that fact will not prevent a court from applying the strict standard if a challenged classification is based upon "suspect criteria"[256] or affects interests other than the simple right to participate which are fundamental.[257]

The second of the basic constitutional requirements is that of substantive due process of law. The principles are drawn from the Due Process Clauses of the Fifth and Fourteenth Amendments, and assure that no person shall be deprived of fundamental rights and liberties. Although the principle of substantive due process has within it strains of natural law philosophy [258] which has long been discredited by the Supreme Court,[259] it has not been utilized to strike down acts that are simply repugnant to the sensibilities of the Court. It has, rather, been used to strike down enactments which are overbroad in application, chill protected rights, or overlook alternative means of regulation which would be less restrictive of protected liberties.[260] Although the substantive due process theory is broad and often ambiguous, the Supreme Court has been careful to limit its impact to unnecessarily broad governmental regulation of a subject

v. Virginia Bd. of Elections, 383 U.S. 663, 16 L. Ed. 2d 169, 86 S. Ct. 1079 (1966); and possibly sex, Frontiero v. Richardson, 411 U.S. 677, 36 L. Ed. 2d 583, 93 S. Ct. 1764 (1973) (plurality).

253. Shapiro v. Thompson, 394 U.S. 618, 22 L. Ed. 2d 600, 89 S. Ct. 1322 (1969).

254. *See Developments in the Law—Equal Protection,* 82 HARV. L. REV. 1065, 1132 (1969).

255. Morris v. Michigan State Bd. of Educ., 472 F.2d 1207 (6th Cir. 1973); Mitchell v. Louisiana High School Athletic Ass'n, 430 F.2d 1155 (5th Cir. 1970); Colorado Seminary v. National Collegiate Athletic Ass'n, 417 F. Supp. 885 (D. Colo. 1976); Taylor v. Alabama High School Athletic Ass'n, 336 F. Supp. 54 (M.D. Ala. 1972); Scott v. Kilpatrick, 286 Ala. 129, 237 So. 2d 652 (1970); Sturrup v. Mahan, 261 Ind. 463, 305 N.E.2d 877 (1974); Sanders v. Louisiana High School Athletic Ass'n, 242 So. 2d 19 (La. App. 1970); Kissick v. Garland Independent School Dist., 330 S.W.2d 708 (Tex. Civ. App. 1959). *But cf.* Brenden v. Independent School Dist., 342 F. Supp. 1224 (D. Minn. 1972), *aff'd,* 477 F.2d 1292 (8th Cir. 1973) (court specifically said it was not deciding whether participation was a fundamental interest).

256. Such criteria have included sex (to an as yet unclear extent) and race, which are discussed, respectively, at §§ 1.22 and 1.24.

257. Such interests have included the right to marriage and interstate travel, which are discussed, respectively, at §§ 1.23 and 1.20.

258. The primary example of this philosophy is Lochner v. New York, 198 U.S. 45, 49 L. Ed. 937, 25 S. Ct. 539 (1905), where the Court held unconstitutional a state statute regulating the number of hours a baker could work.

259. *See, e.g.,* Olsen v. Nebraska *ex rel.* Western Reference & Bond Ass'n, 313 U.S. 236, 85 L. Ed. 1305, 61 S. Ct. 862 (1941); Nebbia v. New York, 291 U.S. 502, 78 L. Ed. 940, 54 S. Ct. 505 (1934).

260. Griswold v. Connecticut, 381 U.S. 479, 14 L. Ed. 2d 510, 85 S. Ct. 1678 (1965).

legitimately within the government's authority which thereby invades an area of protected activity.[261] In short, where governmental action seeks to regulate activities which involve personal liberty, the proper approach must be to require narrowly drawn regulatory provisions—that is, "precision must be the touchstone of legislation so affecting basic freedoms." [262]

Although the types of rules that have been adopted by amateur organizations cover most aspects of sport, and present a virtually endless list for discussion, subsequent sections will consider only those which have been made the subject of judicial scrutiny.

§ 1.15.1. Rule-Making by Private Institutions.

The principles developed in the preceding section related to the rule-making activities of public organizations and institutions. In light of the fact that private institutions also adopt and promulgate rules to regulate athletic competition, it is necessary to inquire whether, and to what extent, "privateness" should affect the doctrinal bases upon which courts will review their rule-making.

The essential distinction between public and private institutions relates to the extent of state involvement in their activities. Public institutions are creatures of the state, derive their authority, directly or indirectly, from the state legislative body,[263] and are bound by the requirements of the Constitution since their activities are affected with "state action." [264] Private institutions, on the other hand, derive their authority both from the instruments which bring them into existence and from the relationship with their members (primarily students),[265] and are not bound by the requirements of the Constitution since their activities are not affected with "state action."[266]

---

261. *See, e.g.,* Aptheker v. Secretary of State, 378 U.S. 500, 12 L. Ed. 2d 992, 84 S. Ct. 1659 (1964).

262. NAACP v. Button, 371 U.S. 415, 438, 9 L. Ed. 2d 405, 83 S. Ct. 328 (1963). *See also* Cleveland Bd. of Educ. v. LaFleur, 414 U.S. 632, 39 L. Ed. 2d 52, 94 S. Ct. 791 (1974); Roe v. Wade, 410 U.S. 113, 35 L. Ed. 2d 147, 93 S. Ct. 705 (1973).

Although the discussion of substantive due process of law might appear to be itself somewhat far afield from the law of sports, it has found application in the sports cases. The primary example of its invocation has been in Davis v. Meek, 344 F. Supp. 298 (N.D. Ohio 1972), *noted in* 22 BUFF. L. REV. 634 (1973), where a school board had adopted a rule which precluded married students from participating in extracurricular activities. *See* § 1.23.

When it was then challenged by a student who was thereby disabled from playing interscholastic baseball, the court struck the rule down as having placed an unendurable strain on the right to marital privacy. In reaching this result, the court relied upon *Griswold,* and its language clearly bears the stamp of substantive due process. Thus, the court stated that

> it seems clear that the effect of the enforcement of the rule . . . is to put what may be an unendurable strain upon the plaintiff's marriage. This Court feels that it cannot escape the obligation to protect from invasion by the power of the state that right to marital privacy that Griswold v. Connecticut, *supra,* holds to be protected by the Constitution. What greater invasion of marital privacy can there be than one which could totally destroy the marriage itself? 344 F. Supp. at 302.

263. *See* § 1.15.

264. *See* § 1.14.

265. *See* John B. Stetson University v. Hunt, 88 Fla. 510, 102 So. 637 (1925).

266. *See* § 1.14 notes 168-174. Although "private" institutions are not subject to constitutional requirements, it has been suggested that there is substantial question whether any educational institution can be truly considered private in the contemporary world, *see* Van Alstyne, *The Judicial Trend Towards Student Academic Freedom,* 20 U. FLA. L. REV. 290, 291-92 (1968), and that many private schools have, in any event, adopted procedures and policies that are at least consistent with the constitutional requirements applicable to public schools. *See* Wright, *The Constitution on the Campus,* 22 VAND. L. REV. 1027, 1035-36 (1969).

When a student in a private institution seeks judicial review of a grievance that he or she has with the institution, the first step will be to characterize the relationship between the student and the institution. The traditional view has been that the institution stands *in loco parentis* and has all of the authority to deal with a student that would have been possessed by the student's parents.[267] This view, which would give the institution a very broad range of authority, has been severely criticized on a number of grounds. For example, this characterization would not cover those students who are not minors; large impersonal institutions do not give the attention to each student that his or her parents would; and educational institutions utilize sanctions (expulsion) which would not be used by parents. As a result of these types of criticisms, the doctrine of *in loco parentis* has largely been repudiated.[268]

The most widely accepted characterization of the student-private institution relationship is to view it as "contractual." According to this view, the student and the institution enter a "contractual" relationship when the student enrolls in the institution.[269] The terms of the contract are said to be incorporated in the various publications, bulletins or catalogues of the school, and the act of registration is deemed to represent the student's voluntary assent to those terms.[270] If the student finds the terms to be distasteful, he or she may enroll elsewhere. Although this view has become quite popular with the courts, it is also subject to several criticisms. These would include the fact that the "terms" of the contract are seldom the result of bargaining by the putative parties, but are, rather, the result of a "take-it-or-leave-it" tender by the institution; the terms are frequently not brought within the conscious understanding of the student prior to enrollment; the institution will normally retain the right to change the "terms" by its unilateral act; and the relationship is seldom perceived by the parties as being contractual.[271] Notwithstanding these criticisms, the contractual model has also been viewed as a potential protector of student interests, since if rigorously applied it would accord the student certain rights that the courts have not often recognized. Thus, it has been suggested that any ambiguity in the terms of the contract should be construed against the institution since it is responsible for its drafting, and that terms may be voided which appear to be unconscionable.[272]

The application of the contractual model may be illustrated by considering *Carr v. St. John's University, New York,*[273] where a young man and woman had

---

267. *See, e.g.,* John B. Stetson Univ. v. Hunt, 88 Fla. 510, 102 So. 637 (1925); Gott v. Berea College, 156 Ky. 376, 161 S.W. 204 (1913).

268. *See* Van Alstyne, *The Judicial Trend Towards Academic Freedom,* 20 U. FLA. L. REV. 290, 291-92 (1968); *Developments in the Law — Academic Freedom,* 81 HARV. L. REV. 1045, 1144-45 (1968).

269. *See, e.g.,* Goldstein v. New York University, 76 App. Div. 80, 78 N.Y.S. 739 (1902); Samson v. Trustees of Columbia University, 101 Misc. 146, 167 N.Y.S. 202 (1917), *aff'd per curiam,* 181 App. Div. 936, 167 N.Y.S. 1125 (1917); Barker v. Trustees of Bryn Mawr College, 228 Pa. 121, 122 A. 220 (1923). It should be noted that the term "contractual" is used here in a much looser sense than was the case in § 1.06, where it was used to describe a traditional employment relationship.

270. *See, e.g.,* Carr v. St. John's University, New York, 17 App. Div. 2d 632, 231 N.Y.S.2d 410 (1962), *aff'd,* 12 N.Y.2d 802, 235 N.Y.S.2d 834, 187 N.E.2d 18 (1962).

271. *See* Van Alstyne, *The Student as University Resident,* 45 DENVER L.J. 582, 583-84 n.1 1968); *Developments in the Law — Academic Freedom,* 81 HARV. L. REV. 1045, 1146-47 (1968).

272. Van Alstyne, *supra* note 271, at 583-84 n. 1.

273. 17 App. Div. 2d 632, 231 N.Y.S.2d 410 (1962), *aff'd,* 12 N.Y.2d 802, 235 N.Y.S.2d 834, 187 N.E.2d 18 (1962).

enrolled in a private university operated by the Catholic church. At the time of their admission, the university bulletin provided that "[i]n conformity with the ideals of Christian education and conduct, the University reserves the right to dismiss a student at any time on whatever grounds the University judges advisable. Each student by his admission to the University recognizes this right." Shortly before their anticipated graduation, the students were married in a civil ceremony. When this fact became known to the university, the students were asked to justify their actions, and were subsequently dismissed. When the students then challenged the dismissal, the trial court concluded that the university's action was unreasonable because it was based upon a vague and indefinite rule.[274] This conclusion was reversed on appeal. The appellate court was of the opinion that when the students enrolled in the university a contractual relationship arose and an implied part of the contract was that they would not be guilty of misconduct. It observed that the students had understood that their actions would be viewed as misconduct by the university and concluded that

> [w]hen a university, in expelling a student, acts within its jurisdiction, not arbitrarily but in the exercise of an honest discretion, a court may not review the exercise of discretion [citations omitted]. Here, the discretion exercised by the University was of that character.[275]

The opinion in *Carr* is reflective of numerous other decisions dealing with the scope of review of grievances between students and private institutions.[276] While these several opinions do grant a very broad range of discretion to private institutions, the discretion is not without limit. Thus, it is said that the institution may not act arbitrarily, capriciously or in bad faith.[277] Some courts, however, have gone further and stated that when the student and the institution enter their contractual relationship the student agrees, expressly or impliedly, to be bound only by reasonable rules and regulations.[278] The use of the word

---

274. Carr v. St. John's University, New York, 34 Misc.2d 319, 231 N.Y.S.2d 403 (1962). Specifically, the court observed that

> There is also the implied understanding that the student will submit himself to reasonable rules and regulations for the breach of which, in a proper case, he may be expelled [citations omitted]. With respect to these rules and regulations the courts will not consider whether they are wise or expedient but whether they are a reasonable exercise of power and discretion of the college authorities. *Id.* at 408.

275. *Id.* at 414.

276. *See* Dehaan v. Brandeis University, 150 F. Supp. 626 (D. Mass. 1957); Booker v. Grand Rapids Medical College, 156 Mich. 95, 120 N.W. 589 (1909); People *ex rel.* O'Sullivan v. New York Law School, 68 Hunter 118, 22 N.Y.S. 663 (1892); Goldstein v. New York University, 76 App. Div. 80, 78 N.Y.S. 739 (1902); Samson v. Trustees of Columbia University, 101 Misc. 146, 167 N.Y.S. 202 (1917), *aff'd,* 181 App. Div. 936, 167 N.Y.S. 1125 (1917).

277. *See* Militana v. University of Miami, 236 So. 2d 162 (Fla. 1970), *cert. denied,* 401 U.S. 962 (1971); Edde v. Columbia University, 8 Misc.2d 795, 168 N.Y.S.2d 643 (1957), *aff'd,* 6 App. Div. 2d 780, 175 N.Y.S.2d 556 (1958), *app. dismissed,* 5 N.Y.2d 881, 182 N.Y.S.2d 829, 156 N.E.2d 458 (1959), *cert. denied,* 359 U.S. 956 (1959).

278. *See* John B. Stetson University v. Hunt, 88 Fla. 510, 102 So. 637 (1925); Kwiatkowski v. Ithaca College, 82 Misc.2d 43, 368 N.Y.S.2d 973 (1975); Miami Military Institute v. Leff, 129 Misc. 481, 220 N.Y.S. 799 (City Ct. 1926) ("there is one important provision upon which the entire law rests [when analyzing challenges to private institution rules], and that is that the rule or regulation must be reasonable"); Koblitz v. The Western Reserve University, 21 Ohio Cir. Ct. Rep. 144 (1901). *See generally Developments in the Law — Academic Freedom,* 81 HARV. L. REV. 1045, 1154-56 (1968).

It should also be noted that several proposals have been made recently that would subject private institution decision-making to a much stronger standard of review than is suggested by the cases

"reasonable" could, of course, impose a more searching scope of judicial review than is suggested by *Carr*.

Although these various views of the proper scope of review of private institution decision-making may not be entirely harmonious doctrinally, they may be reconciled for present purposes by suggesting that a private institution will have broad discretion in adopting and enforcing rules, and that when a court is asked to review such activities its scope of review will be quite narrow. It will not be concerned with the wisdom or lack of wisdom of the rules or whether it would have adopted them to accomplish the purpose sought to be achieved. Since the relationship between the student and the institution is one of volition — that is, the student will have decided to attend the private institution in preference to other alternatives for education — the central inquiry of the court will be to determine whether the rule in question was satisfactorily brought to the attention of the student.[279] So long as the student is properly notified of the rule, the volitional requirement of the relationship is satisfied, since if the student finds the rule offensive he or she may enroll elsewhere. If, on the other hand, the student is not notified of the existence of a questioned rule, or if what purports to be a rule is couched in such a manner as to not give fair notice of its supposed content, then the court must determine whether the rule is appropriate given the nature of the relationship. Whether the court's inquiry be couched in terms of determining "honest discretion" (as in *Carr*), arbitrariness or reasonableness, the analysis will be essentially the same. It will be seeking to determine whether the rule in question is one that relates to the recognized purposes of the institution and is one that could reasonably have been anticipated by the student.[280] Thus, the rule in *Carr* did not specifically preclude civil marriage ceremonies but the institution was a Catholic university and such a requirement could have been reasonably anticipated by (and, in fact, was known to) the students. On the other hand, where a military school specifies in published materials that students must attend churches in the local community, the adoption of a rule that students must attend a designated denominational church, even if in conflict with personal religious beliefs, could very well be viewed as an improper exercise of authority since it does not relate to a recognized purpose of the institution and might not have been foreseen by the student.[281]

considered herein. The thrust of these proposals is that students in such institutions have valuable property rights, and that these rights may be protected by an aggressive use of the principles of private association law. *See* Note, *Judicial Review of the University — Student Relationship: Expulsion and Governance*, 26 STAN. L. REV. 95, 102-17 (1973); Note, *Common Law Rights for Private University Students: Beyond the State Action Principle*, 84 YALE L.J. 120 (1974). These suggestions have not yet, however, been reflected in the case law.

279. Flint v. St. Augustine High School, 323 So.2d 229 (La. App. 1975); Baltimore University of Baltimore City v. Colton, 98 Md. 623, 57 A. 14 (1904); Miami Military Institute v. Leff, 129 Misc. 481, 220 N.Y.S. 799 (City Ct. 1926). *See also Developments in the Law — Academic Freedom*, 81 HARV. L. REV. 1045, 1154-56 (1968).

280. This inquiry could be framed in terms of the standards identified in § 1.15 for the review of rule-making by public organizations and institutions — that the rules of private institutions will be upheld so long as they are within the authority of the institution and constitute a proper exercise of authority — but the ultimate question would still be whether the student had clear notice of the rule at the time of enrollment.

281. Miami Military Institute v. Leff, 129 Misc. 481, 220 N.Y.S. 799 (City Ct. 1926).

When these principles are considered in terms of rule-making by private institutions, it is clear that the institutions will have broad authority to adopt rules which they deem appropriate. This authority would certainly include the vast majority of rules dealing with athletic participation and eligibility and would even include rules which do not as such relate to athletic competition if students had clear notice of their content. As an example, attention might be given to the rule that was involved in the *Bunger* case.[282] There the athletic association had adopted a rule that, in essence, precluded a student-athlete from even being present in a car containing beer in the off-season, and the court held that it was an improper exercise of rule-making authority. If the same rule had been adopted by a private institution, with the requisite advance notice, it seems clear that the rule would be upheld. The relationship between the student and the institution was volitional, and the terms of the relationship would be clear to both parties. If, on the other hand, the rule had not been formally adopted, or was vague in terms of content (as was the rule in *Carr*), then a court would be required to consider the relationship between the purposes of the institution and the rule, as well as whether a student could have anticipated such a rule. Should it find, for example, that the school has strong ties to a religion whose tenets frown on alcohol, then, as in *Carr,* it would probably uphold the rule; but if it finds that the school has never announced any purpose relating to alcohol and has not prohibited such conduct in the past, then the court would probably invalidate the rule, since it would be difficult to find that it was a part of the relationship of the parties.[283]

§ 1.16. Good Conduct.

In an effort to exercise control over the conduct of athletes, rules are often adopted to insure that amateur athletes conduct themselves in a manner that those who draft the rules deem appropriate. Although these rules vary widely in content, most essentially require that athletes maintain "good conduct" and specify that deviation from that norm will result in sanctions being applied to the errant athlete.[284] Inasmuch as the rules are general in content — that is, requiring that athletes engage in conduct that is "good" or which measures up to some other vaguely defined standard — they present a number of problems with respect to their legality and enforceability.

The propriety of a given rule depends upon whether it meets the nonconstitutional and constitutional standards.[285] With respect to the nonconstitutional standards, a good conduct rule would be authorized to the

---

282. *See* § 1.15 note 237.

283. *See* note 279 *supra.*

284. A typical example provides that

Any student whose habits and/or conduct, both in and out of school during the school year or during the summer months, are such as to make him unworthy to represent the ideals, principles and standards of his school and this Association shall be ineligible and it shall be the duty of the superintendent or his delegated principal to exclude him from interscholastic athletic participation until reinstated to eligibility by the local school administration. Bunger v. Iowa High School Athletic Ass'n, 197 N.W.2d 555, 557 (Iowa 1972).

285. *See* § 1.15.

extent that it could be proven to relate to a legitimate, athletics-related objective of the organization responsible for its promulgation. For example, a rule designed to insure that athletes conduct themselves in a manner befitting representatives of the organization while participating in athletics-related activities, would appear to be authorized. If, on the other hand, a rule seeks to regulate conduct that is not related to athletic activities, it would appear to be unauthorized.[286] Similarly, a rule would be a reasonable exercise of authority only if it affects persons whose conduct it is necessary to control — that is, athletes engaged in athletics-related conduct. If a rule also affects other persons, then it would be over-inclusive and, possibly, unreasonable.

The leading case applying these principles to a good conduct rule is *Bunger v. Iowa High School Athletic Association*,[287] where the association had adopted, as part of its good conduct provision a section known as the "beer rule," which essentially provided that an athlete would lose six weeks of eligibility if he possessed, consumed or transported alcoholic beverages or dangerous drugs. The same penalty would be imposed if the athlete were present in an autombile which contained any of those substances when stopped by law enforcement officers. The case arose when an athlete was stopped in a car which contained beer. Although the charges against him were dismissed, he was declared ineligible for the six week period. He then brought suit to enjoin enforcement of the rule. Utilizing the nonconstitutional standard, the court found that the rule was invalid and unenforceable. It found the rule to be unauthorized because the presence of an athlete in a car containing an alcoholic beverage out of season simply has no relation to the athletic program; and it found the rule to be unreasonable because it was over-inclusive and swept within its ambit the guilty and the non-guilty alike.[288] Good conduct rules have also been challenged when they were applied to participation in assaultive conduct,[289] and alleged lack of proper grooming.[290]

The constitutional requirements that a rule must meet will largely be dependent upon the specific nature of the rule and the facts and circumstances of the situation in which it is sought to be applied.[291] At least four separate constitutional problems may be identified. The first involves the Equal Protection Clause of the Fourteenth Amendment, which would be utilized to determine whether a classification created by a good conduct rule is constitutional. If such a rule separates otherwise similarly situated persons into different classifications without a reasonable basis, then it will be violative of

286. Bunger v. Iowa High School Athletic Ass'n, 197 N.W.2d 555 (Iowa 1972). Bunger is also discussed at § 1.15.

287. *Id.*

288. *See also* Thompson v. Barnes, 294 Minn. 528, 200 N.W.2d 921 (1972) (holding that temporary injunction not appropriate to enjoin rule precluding the possession or consumption of alcoholic beverages); O'Connor v. Board of Educ., 65 Misc. 2d 140, 316 N.Y.S.2d 799 (1970) (denial of athletic "letter" for violation of alcohol rule, which was held to be reasonable, invalidated when athlete not given fair hearing); Randol v. Newberg Public School Bd., 23 Ore. App. 425, 542 P.2d 938 (1975) (anti-smoking rule needs to be reasonable).

289. Hanger v. State Univ. of N.Y. at Binghamton, 39 App. Div. 2d 253, 333 N.Y.S.2d 571 (1972) (rules relating to maintenance of public order applied to temporarily suspend student following assaults in intramural basketball game).

290. Dunham v. Pulsifer, 312 F. Supp. 411 (D. Vt. 1970). *See* § 1.12.

291. Constitutional problems of good conduct rules not considered here are considered at § 2.05.

the equal protection requirements.[292] Such a result was reached in *Dunham v. Pulsifer,*[293] where a school board, pursuant to an athletic code which required, among other things, that males not have long hair,[294] had dismissed three members of the tennis team when their hair grew too long.[295] In holding that the rule was unconstitutional as being in violation of the Equal Protection Clause,[296] the court found that the code classified athletes apart from the remainder of the student body without any reasonable or compelling justification. Long hair had no effect upon the performance of athletes, created no dissension on the team, and served only to promote the unworthy goal of conformity and uniformity.

A second constitutional problem posed by good conduct rules is that the attempted regulation of what is believed to be conduct may constitute regulation of speech or speech-related conduct which is protected by the First Amendment. In that event, a completely different set of rules will determine the constitutional permissibility of the regulation.[297] Thirdly, good conduct rules may be subject to attack as being in violation of due process of law because of their vagueness or lack of specificity.[298] However, since any concept of proper conduct necessarily covers a wide variety of conditions and circumstances, it would be unrealistic to require that all possible types of misconduct be spelled out or defined with exactitude. Thus, the courts will give fair deference to rules adopted so long as they notify athletes of the conduct which they are expected to exemplify.[299]

Finally, a good conduct rule may also have difficulty if it has the effect of creating presumptions. For example, if a rule provided that participation in a given type of conduct would be presumed to be (or would have the effect of presuming) a violation of a good conduct standard, then the presumption would itself be unconstitutional unless it met the due process requirements. Those

---

292. *See* § 1.15.

293. 312 F. Supp. 411 (D. Vt. 1970).

294. The athletic code provided in full that

> In order to enhance *esprit de corps,* prevent adverse public reaction, prevent dissension on teams, and for the general welfare of teams and participants the following regulations governing dress and grooming for pupils participating in and traveling to and from interscholastic athletic activities are in effect:
>
> 1. Whenever eating and not traveling in team uniform, male athletes shall wear jacket and tie.
> 2. For males, hair must be cut tapered in the back and on sides of the head with no hair over the collar. Sideburns must be no lower than the earlobe and trimmed.
> 3. Males must be clean shaven and not wear beards and mustaches.
> 4. Females, when not traveling in team uniform, shall wear skirts (no slacks or shorts).
> 5. Cleanliness and neatness shall be maintained at all times.

295. The First Amendment consequences of limiting personal liberty by adopting a "hair" rule, are considered in § 1.13.

296. The general principles associated with the Equal Protection Clause are considered at § 1.15.

297. The regulation of speech and conduct is considered in § 1.12.

298. *See* Thornhill v. Alabama, 310 U.S. 88, 84 L. Ed. 1093, 60 S. Ct. 736 (1940); Soglin v. Kauffman, 295 F. Supp. 978 (W.D. Wis. 1968), *aff'd,* 418 F.2d 163 (7th Cir. 1969).

299. Kelley v. Metropolitan County Bd. of Educ. of Nashville, 293 F. Supp. 485, 496-97 (M.D. Tenn. 1968). *See also* Murray v. West Baton Rouge Parish School Bd., 472 F.2d 438 (5th Cir. 1973); Burnside v. Byars, 363 F.2d 744 (5th Cir. 1966); Alex v. Allen, 409 F. Supp. 379 (W.D. Pa. 1976); Wood v. Goodman, 581 F. Supp. 413 (D. Mass 1974) (teacher conduct). *See* § 2.05.

requirements are considered in a later chapter [300] and are noted here for their potential application to amateur athletics rules.[301]

§ 1.17. "Amateur" Standing.

Since participation in amateur athletics is, by theoretical definition, undertaken for reasons other than financial remuneration, rules have also been adopted which deny eligibility to those who receive any form of compensation for their athletic endeavors.[302] The objective of such rules is to insure that the amateur and non-professional status of individual athletes, as well as that of their teams and leagues, is not lost by the receipt of something that could be viewed as a payment for participation — that is, to insure that those who participate do so as an avocation and not as a vocation.

The enforceability of an amateur standing rule will, of course, be determined by the general standards noted above.[303] Such rules will normally be within the authority of the adopting institution, since a legitimate objective of any amateur organization will be to maintain the amateur status of the athletes subject to its control.[304] In order to be a reasonable exercise of that authority, however, the rules must affect only conduct which it is necessary to control.[305] Thus, a rule could reasonably forbid, or could reasonably be utilized to punish, the receipt of things that would affect the amateur standing of the recipient. If, on the other hand, an amateur standing rule forbade, or punished, the receipt of things that would not affect an athlete's "amateur" status, then it might to that extent be unreasonable.[306]

---

300. *See* § 2.07.

301. *See, e.g.,* Andrews v. Drew Municipal Separate School Dist., 371 F. Supp. 27 (N.D. Miss. 1973) *aff'd,* 507 F.2d 611 (5th Cir. 1975) (presumption that unwed parents were unfit for school employment held unconstitutional).

302. The term "amateur" is defined in § 1.04.

303. *See* § 1.15.

304. This conclusion seems appropriate enough in light of the fact that one of the most strongly established convictions in amateur athletics is the notion that those who participate do so for reasons other than financial compensation. The use of amateur standing rules is certainly consistent with the definitional requirements of international sports organizations, *see* § 1.04, and would appear to be a legitimate interest of domestic rule-makers. If athletes subject to their control were not "amateurs," in the sense that the term is used by international organizations, then such athletes would be ineligible for international competition, as would, perhaps, others who competed with or against those athletes. In addition, the receipt of compensation for participation would raise the other problems that were discussed in §§ 1.04-.09, though as those sections suggest the issue is present notwithstanding the amateur standing rules because of contemporary athletic grant-in-aid practices.

With respect to this discussion, it is perhaps important to note that the amateur requirements were originally adopted by collegiate organizations for the apparent purpose of preventing the results of contests from being skewed by the use of professionals or "ringers," especially when bookmakers were taking an active interest in the contests. Amateurism was seen as a positive virtue, and professionalism was not. *See* CARNEGIE FOUNDATION FOR THE ADVANCEMENT OF TEACHING, AMERICAN COLLEGE ATHLETICS 34-45 (1929). In light of the contemporary use of financial aid in collegiate athletics, one may question whether these purposes have been achieved by existing rules, *see* note 314 *infra,* and wonder whether the purposes could not be achieved much easier by a rule limiting eligibility to students in good standing.

305. Jones v. National Collegiate Athletic Ass'n, 392 F. Supp. 295 (D. Mass. 1975); Buckton v. National Collegiate Athletic Ass'n, 366 F. Supp. 1152 (D. Mass. 1973).

306. *But cf.* Morrison v. Roberts, 183 Okla. 359, 82 P.2d 1023 (1938) (rule violated by receipt of gold football award; though court did not attempt any consideration of the permissibility of the rule).

Although the amateur standing rules have not yet been the subject of extensive litigation, it appears that courts will uphold an organization's right to prohibit a pure play-for-pay arrangement. In *Jones v. National Collegiate Athletic Association*,[307] for example, a student was declared ineligible pursuant to an amateur standing rule because he had received compensation from Canadian "amateur" hockey teams for three years while in high school, and also for two years between high school and college. In upholding the rule and the action of the organization that had declared his ineligibility, the court noted that the athlete had received compensation for two years in which he had not been attending school, so that its receipt could not "be considered as coincidental to or in conjunction with his obtaining an education." [308] The court also rejected other theories put forth by the athlete,[309] and its language and approach indicates that in similar situations the rules will be upheld.[310]

An amateur standing rule may, however, be written or applied in such a manner as to raise other issues which will require that it be stricken. This is most likely to arise in situations where a rule, or its application, creates unreasonable classifications among otherwise similarly situated people. The leading case involving this type of situation is *Buckton v. National Collegiate Athletic Associations ("NCAA")*,[311] where two Canadian nationals had been declared ineligible to compete in interscholastic hockey due to their receipt of room, board, books and certain other expenses from teams on which they competed while prep players in Canada. The NCAA had adopted a rule which declared that participation in a specified Canadian Amateur Hockey Association league would violate "amateur" requirements, and it was in this league that the Canadians had competed. In holding that the rule deprived the athletes of their rights under the Equal Protection Clause,[312] the court found that the rule imposed disparate standards on students from the U.S. and those from Canada. It based this conclusion on the factual finding that prep competition in Canada was much different than in the U.S., and that to compete the young athletes were frequently required to join teams that were often a considerable distance from their homes, but received no more financial assistance than did their American counterparts.[313] The NCAA's rule, therefore, distinguished between the receipt

---

307. 392 F. Supp. 295 (D. Mass. 1975). *See also* Regents of University of Minnesota v. National Collegiate Athletic Ass'n, 560 F.2d 352 (8th Cir. 1977) (receipt of miscellaneous benefits); Colorado Seminary v. National Collegiate Athletic Ass'n, 417 F. Supp. 885 (D. Colo. 1976) (receipt of expenses from third parties).

308. *Id.* at 301.

309. Thus, the athlete argued that the rule constituted a form of wealth classification that violated Equal Protection standards, which the court rejected. 392 F. Supp. at 301-02. He also claimed that the rule constituted an unconstitutional irrebuttable presumption, but the court did not decide this question because of its view that the athlete could not benefit from the argument. The permissibility of irrebuttable presumptions is considered in § 2.07. Finally, the athlete raised an antitrust claim against the NCAA, which the court rejected. *See* § 5.12.

310. *See* Shelton v. National Collegiate Athletic Ass'n, 539 F.2d 1179 (9th Cir. 1976) (upholding a rule requiring loss of eligibility for signing professional contract, even if the contract is alleged to be invalid). *See also* Southern Methodist Univ. v. Smith, 515 S.W.2d 63 (Tex. Civ. App. 1974) (though not raising permissibility of rule).

311. 366 F. Supp. 1152 (D. Mass. 1973).

312. The equal protection requirements are considered in § 1.15.

313. Indeed, the evidence showed that the Canadians may actually have received less in Canada than they could have in the U.S., though if they had come to the U.S. the rule would not then have

of aid from one's school (in the case of U.S. athletes) and one's team (in the case of the Canadians). Such a distinction, the court said, violated the Canadians' equal protection rights. With regard to this distinction, it is important to note the court's comments that it would be

> naive to assume that because the source of aid happens to be a school, the motivation behind that aid is not, at least sometimes, an effort to induce a good athlete to attend a particular school in order to be of assistance to the athletic program. Even the most casual reader of our sports pages is aware that such inducements are an everyday fact of life in American amateur athletics. This fact of life underscores the frivolity, if not more, of holding student athletes responsible for the motives of their benefactors, whether they be American athletic directors or Canadian team managers.[314]

Although *Buckton* supports only the proposition that a rule which classifies recipients of aid by its source may be unenforceable, its language is broad enough to suggest that athletes who receive more than simple expenses should not be held responsible for the impermissible motives of their benefactors.[315] Such a view does not, however, appear to be the intent of the court, and its language should not be given that intent, because it is certainly not uncommon to impose sanctions on athletes for the derelictions of their coaches.[316]

§ 1.18. Participation in Non-Approved Events.

In order to control the competitive efforts of athletes, it is common for rules to be adopted which deny eligibility to athletes who participate in athletic events which are not sanctioned by the enacting organization. The objectives of such rules are to prevent the exploitation of athletes, to promote their overall development, and to equalize competitive opportunities.[317] Although sanctioning

been applicable. 366 F. Supp. at 1159. The situation in *Buckton* was specifically distinguished in *Jones.* 392 F. Supp. at 300-01.

314. 366 F. Supp. at 1158-59.

315. The receipt of such amounts could, of course, preclude the recipient from meeting the "amateur" definition. *See* § 1.04.

316. *See, e.g.,* Associated Students, Inc. of Calif. State Univ. v. National Collegiate Athletic Ass'n, 493 F.2d 1251 (9th Cir. 1974) (erroneous certification of eligibility); McDonald v. National Collegiate Athletic Ass'n, 370 F. Supp. 625 (C.D. Cal. 1974) (athletes suspended when coach used improper test scores).

317. The objectives of such rules have, specifically, been stated to be as follows:

> (1) Consistent with the desire of educators to provide students with a varied and comprehensive academic curriculum, one objective of the extracurricular program is to provide students with comprehensive and varied extracurricular experiences.
> (2) The schools hope, by the adoption of these rules, to protect students against pressures from their peers, their parents and community interests that would otherwise force them to specialize in limited activities.
> (3) The school program is designed to avoid professionalism or overemphasis of its extracurricular activities as compared to larger goals and responsibilities in life.
> (4) The schools fear that without the limitations imposed by these rules the public school athlete will be subject to exploitation by outside interests in the community who are motivated by economic profits that can be gained from sports programs.
> (5) The program has been designed to eliminate, to some extent, competitive advantages based solely on difference in economic resources.
> (6) The educators who develop the rules also want to give athletes an opportunity to develop skills in sports in which they can participate in later years.

Brown v. Wells, 288 Minn. 468, 181 N.W.2d 708 (1970), *noted in* 36 Mo. L. REV. 400 (1971). *See also* Art Gaines Baseball Camp, Inc. v. Houston, 500 S.W.2d 735 (Mo. App. 1973).

rules have been upheld on several occasions,[318] they must, in any case, meet the applicable standards.[319] A given rule will be authorized if it is directly related to a legitimate purpose of the enacting organization. The reasons cited in support of the rules are quite general,[320] and may not provide the "direct" relationship required to establish authority.[321] The essence of the cited reasons is that participation in events which are not sanctioned will in some manner subject athletes, or the more general athletic program, to undesirable consequences. In order for such reasons to provide a legitimate interest to which a sanctioning rule can be related, it must be demonstrated that such undesirable consequences are likely to exist in the future or have been present in the past.[322] If such a factual showing is made, then the rule would be within the rule-maker's authority. A rule must also be a reasonable exercise of authority in the sense that it affects only those whose conduct it is necessary to control. Thus, the organization must show that the rule is narrowly drawn and requires approval of only those events which require control in order to achieve the purposes of the rule. For example, if the purpose of a rule was to preclude the receipt of compensation for competing, then it would appear to be unreasonable to apply the rule to preclude competition in a local charity event. Finally, the rule must, of course, be constitutional.

The leading case dealing with such rules is *Brown v. Wells*,[323] where the state high school athletic association had adopted rules which denied hockey eligibility in its league to any student athlete who participated on an independent team, who participated in any hockey game, practice or activity in the "off-season," or who attended any hockey school, camp or clinic not sanctioned by the association. When these rules were challenged, the court upheld their validity by applying the ordinary principle of private association law that rules will be upheld unless they are arbitrary or capricious.[324] As is noted elsewhere in this chapter, such an approach may be out of step with contemporary concepts of judicial review,[325] which seem to suggest a different scope of review for the rule-making activities of amateur organizations.[326] When the conclusion of the court is viewed in terms of the standards identified above, it would appear that it is subject to substantial question. The rule would not appear to have been

---

318. Samara v. National Collegiate Athletic Ass'n, 1973 Trade Cases ¶ 74,536 (E.D. Va. 1973); Kinzer v. Directors of Independent School Dist. of Marion, 129 Iowa 441, 105 N.W. 686 (1906); Dumez v. Louisiana High School Athletic Ass'n, 334 So.2d 494 (La. App. 1976); Brown v. Wells, 288 Minn. 468, 181 N.W.2d 708 (1970); Fisher v. Rockland County P.S.A.L., 44 App. Div. 2d 552, 352 N.Y.S.2d 668 (1974); Art Gaines Baseball Camp, Inc. v. Houston, 500 S.W.2d 735 (Mo. App. 1973); Hawksley v. New Hampshire Interscholastic Athletic Ass'n, Inc., 111 N.H. 386, 285 A.2d 797 (1971); Assmus v. Little League Baseball, Inc., 70 Misc. 2d 1038, 334 N.Y.S.2d 982 (1972); Texas High School Gymnastics Ass'n v. Andrews, 532 S.W.2d 242 (Tex. Civ. App. 1975).

319. *See* § 1.15.

320. *See* note 317 *supra.*

321. *See* Bunger v. Iowa High School Athletic Ass'n, 197 N.W.2d 555 (Iowa 1972).

322. In Samara v. National Collegiate Athletic Ass'n, 1973 Trade Cases ¶ 74,536 (E.D. Va.), the court found that "there were in fact abuses in the past that gave rise to the need and desire for some regulation," but did not specify what those abuses were or why they justified the rule in question.

323. 288 Minn. 468, 181 N.W.2d 708 (1970), *noted in* 36 Mo. L. REV. 400 (1971).

324. *Id.* at 472-74, 181 N.W.2d at 711.

325. *See* § 1.14.

326. *See* § 1.15.

within the authority of the association, since the reason set forth in its support was that it would prevent schools from having to "prepare or train students for a career in professional athletics." [327] In the absence of a factual record indicating that this was a legitimate objective of the association and that the rule would aid in its achievement, it is difficult to see the required connection between the rule and a legitimate objective. In addition, the reason set forth disregards the fact that to many students the chance to develop and display athletic prowess may be of considerable value, both in terms of educational opportunity [328] and, for a few, enhancing the chances of a professional career.[329]

The sanction-type rules were also considered in *Samara v. National Collegiate Athletic Association*,[330] where the Amateur Athletic Union (AAU) was sponsoring a Russian-American track meet at Richmond, Virginia in 1973. Under the rules of the NCAA, athletes in member institutions would lose their eligibility if they participated in a meet that was not certified by the NCAA. When the AAU refused to apply for certification, several athletes brought suit to compel the NCAA to certify the meet. In dismissing their action,[331] and upholding the certification rule, the court stated that the general purposes of the NCAA were legitimate and that the rule was rationally related thereto.[332] Like the court in *Brown v. Wells,* the court in *Samara* neither evaluated the objectives of the rule nor determined whether it was narrowly drawn. The court did, however, indicate that its opinion was merely preliminary and that further inquiry was not foreclosed. Thus, it noted that the NCAA would have routinely granted certification had the AAU applied and that sanctions had not been applied to the athletes. If the certification were denied, or if sanctions were imposed, therefore, further review would apparently have been in order.

§ 1.19. Longevity.

In an effort to limit the period of eligibility, rules frequently restrict the period of time during which an athlete may compete. Such rules generally state that an athlete may remain eligible only during the period in which a person would customarily complete the particular level of education. For example, a rule relating to high school athletics will usually allow an athlete to remain eligible for a period of four years.[333] The objective of these rules is to prevent

---

327. 288 Minn. at 473, 181 N.W.2d at 711.

328. *See, e.g.,* Kelley v. Metropolitan County Bd. of Educ., 293 F. Supp. 485 (M.D. Tenn. 1968), *rev'd on other grounds,* 436 F.2d 856 (6th Cir. 1970).

329. Behagen v. Intercollegiate Conference of Faculty Representatives, 346 F. Supp. 602 (D. Minn. 1972). *But cf.* Samara v. National Collegiate Athletic Ass'n, 1973 Trade Cases ¶ 74,536 (E.D. Va.) (disregarding the theory of *Behagen). See* § 1.11.

330. 1973 Trade Cases ¶ 74,536 (E.D. Va. 1973).

331. The suit was brought in three separate causes of action: 1) interference with prospective advantage; 2) violation of the federal anti-trust laws; and 3) violation of constitutional rights. The present discussion refers to only the third, although all three were dismissed by the court.

332. Although the court also suggested a factual basis for this rule, *see* note 322 *supra,* it did not elaborate upon its suggestion.

333. A typical rule provides that

> A student must not have attended high school for eight semesters. (Attendance in school for twenty days shall be counted as a semester's attendance.)
> Beginning with the sixth grade, a student repeating any grade in school which he has

"red-shirting" — that is, to prevent the deliberate retention of promising athletes in order to have an experienced and veteran team.[334]

The longevity rules have generally been upheld. [335] In terms of a rule-maker's exercise of authority in adopting such rules,[336] longevity limits can generally be said to relate to an athletic organization's legitimate interest in insuring that educational goals are not subverted to the athletic policies.[337] They would also be a reasonable exercise of authority to the extent that they affect only those students whose extra-longevity in school is the result of athletic-related reasons.[338] However, if a longevity rule also affects a student whose excess longevity is not motivated by an athletic reason, it might be unreasonable as applied to that student, since its application would be over-inclusive. The legitimate purpose of the rule would be to prevent the excess longevity of students based solely upon athletic considerations, and its application to one who is in school in excess of the normal period for non-athletic reasons might be unreasonable because it would not be necessary to control that student's conduct.[339]

§ 1.20. Transfer of Residence.

The ability of an amateur athlete to participate is frequently subject to limitation when he or she changes places of residence. Such rules typically provide that an athlete who changes from one school to another without a bona fide change of residence, which generally refers to a change of residence by parents, shall be ineligible to participate for a given period of time, usually not more than one year.[340] The purpose of these rules is invariably stated to be the

passed shall lose his fourth year of eligibility in high school. Note: This does not apply to a student repeating a grade because of failure in that grade. Mitchell v. Louisiana High School Athletic Ass'n, 430 F.2d 1155, 11 (5th Cir. 1970).

334. Mitchell v. Louisiana High School Athletic Ass'n, 430 F.2d 1155 (5th Cir. 1970).

335. *Id.;* Howard Univ. v. National Collegiate Athletic Ass'n, 367 F. Supp. 926 (D.D.C. 1973), *aff'd,* 510 F.2d 213 (D.C. Cir. 1975); David v. Louisiana High School Athletic Ass'n, 244 So.2d 292 (La. App. 1971); Murtaugh v. Nyquist, 78 Misc. 2d 876, 358 N.Y.S.2d 595 (1974).

Rules have also been upheld which use age as a means of determining eligibility. Robinson v. Illinois High School Ass'n, 45 Ill. App. 2d 277, 195 N.E.2d 38 (1963), *cert. denied,* 379 U.S. 960, 13 L. Ed. 2d 555, 85 S. Ct. 647 (1965); State *ex rel.* West Virginia Secondary School Activities Comm'n, 152 W. Va. 533, 164 S.E.2d 775 (1968). *But cf.* Rivas Tenorio v. Liga Atletica Interuniversitaria, 554 F.2d 492 (1st Cir. 1977) (suggesting that age limitations applied only to aliens would be unconstitutional). These cases are, however, subject to the same comments that are noted in text. *See* note 339 *infra;* Florida High School Activities Ass'n v. Bryant, 313 So.2d 57 (Fla. App. 1975).

336. *See* § 1.15.

337. Mitchell v. Louisiana High School Athletic Ass'n, 430 F.2d 1155 (5th Cir. 1970).

338. Howard Univ. v. National Collegiate Athletic Ass'n, 367 F. Supp. 926 (D.D.C. 1973), *aff'd,* 510 F.2d 213 (D.C. Cir. 1975).

339. Thus, in Lee v. Florida High School Activities Ass'n, 291 So. 2d 636 (Fla. App. 1974), the court held that the application of a longevity rule to deprive an athlete of eligibility was arbitrary when the reason for the longer than normal longevity was the need of the athlete to drop out of school for a year to aid his family in overcoming a desperate financial situation. *See also* Florida High School Activities Ass'n v. Bryant, 313 So. 2d 57 (1975). *But cf.* David v. Louisiana High School Athletic Ass'n, 244 So. 2d 292 (La. App. 1971) (application of rule upheld even though athlete had to repeat a grade for reasons having nothing to do with athletic participation). This problem is avoided by the rule in note 333 *supra,* which excludes academic failure.

340. A typical rule provides, *inter alia,* as follows:

No pupil who enrolls in one high school and later transfers to, or enrolls in, another shall

prevention of recruitment activities designed to lure students from one school to another for athletic rather than academic reasons.[341]

Inasmuch as the prevention of recruiting and school-jumping may be justified as legitimate purposes of schools and athletic associations, the transfer of residence rules will in most cases be appropriate exercises of authority in a nonconstitutional sense.[342] If the rules limit permissible changes of residence to those of the athlete's parents, however, the rules might not be reasonable — that is, they may penalize more persons than those whose conduct it is necessary to control — because there may be any number of non-athletics motivated reasons for residence transfer other than those related to parents.[343] Notwithstanding this potential defect in the transfer rules, they have been upheld in the vast majority of cases.[344] Representative of these cases is *Marino v. Waters*,[345] where a star high school football player had transferred from a parochial school to a public school in the same district. The transfer was necessitated by the fact that the player had married and the parochial school prohibited attendance by married students. In order to comply with the state high school association rules, which allowed participation if the residence change was a bona fide change of residence by the parents, the player's parents then

---

be eligible to represent the latter school in any athletic contest with the following exceptions.
A student shall be considered as enrolled in a high school when he has enrolled and attended any class in that School.
. . . .
EXCEPTION III—A pupil whose parents make a bona fide move from one school district to another may transfer all his rights and privileges to his school district at the time the parents move. Marino v. Waters, 220 So. 2d 802 (La. App. 1969).

341. Sturrup v. Mahan, 261 Ind. 463, 305 N.E.2d 877 (1974); State *ex rel.* National Junior College Athletic Ass'n v. Luten, 492 S.W.2d 404 (Mo. App. 1973); Josephine County School Dist. No. 7 v. Oregon School Activities Ass'n, 15 Ore. App. 158, 515 P. 2d 431 (1973).

342. *See, e.g.,* Sturrup v. Mahan, 261 Ind. 463, 305 N.E.2d 877 (1974); State *ex rel.* National Junior College Athletic Ass'n v. Luten, 492 S.W.2d 404 (Mo. App. 1973); Bruce v. South Carolina High School League, 258 S.C. 546, 189 S.E.2d 817 (1972).

343. Thus, in Sturrup v. Mahan, 261 Ind. 463, 305 N.E.2d 877 (1974), the court stated that

the rules sweep too broadly, they create an over-inclusive class — those who move from one school to another for reasons wholly unrelated to athletics are grouped together with those who have been recruited or who have "jumped" for athletic reasons. In short, the purported objective of the transferee eligibility rules is to prevent the use of undue influence and school "jumping," but their practical effect is to severely limit the transferee eligibility in general. The rules as presently constituted penalize a student-athlete who wishes to transfer for academic or religious reasons or for any number of other legitimate reasons. *Id.* at 881.

344. Albach v. Odle, 531 F.2d 983 (10th Cir. 1976); Oklahoma High School Athletic Ass'n v. Bray, 321 F.2d 269 (10th Cir. 1963); Paschal v. Perdue, 320 F. Supp. 1274 (S.D. Fla. 1970); Scott v. Kilpatrick, 286 Ala. 129, 237 So. 2d 652 (1970); Quimby v. School Dist. No. 21 of Pinal County, 10 Ariz. App. 69, 455 P.2d 1019 (1969); State *ex rel.* Indiana High School Athletic Ass'n v. Lawrence Circuit Court, 240 Ind. 114, 162 N.E.2d 250 (1959); Chabert v. Louisiana High School Athletic Ass'n, 323 So. 2d 774 (La. App. 1975); Sanders v. Louisiana High School Athletic Ass'n, 242 So. 2d 19 (La. App. 1970); Marino v. Waters, 220 So. 2d 802 (La. App. 1969); State *ex rel.* National Junior College Athletic Ass'n v. Luten, 492 S.W.2d 404 (Mo. App. 1973); Josephine County School Dist. No. 7 v. Oregon School Activities Ass'n, 15 Ore. App. 185, 515 P.2d 431 (1973); Tennessee Secondary School Athletic Ass'n v. Cox, 221 Tenn. 164, 425 S.W.2d 597 (1968). *But cf.* Cabrillo Community College Dist. of Santa Cruz County v. California Junior College Ass'n, 44 Cal. App. 3d 367, 118 Cal. Rptr. 708 (1975) (invalidating transfer rule under state law provisions entitling every high school graduate to admission to junior colleges).

345. 220 So. 2d 802 (La. App. 1969).

moved into the athlete's new apartment. The state high school athletic association, however, concluded that there was no bona fide change of residence and declared the player ineligible under the rule. Although the court acknowledged that the application of the rule had an inequitable result, since the player really had no choice in making the transfer, it upheld the association's determination.[346]

As indicated in *Marino v. Waters,* the courts have generally upheld the transfer of residence rules. In the few cases in which the athlete in question did in fact transfer for the purpose of playing for a specific school,[347] the rules cause no inequity since they affect those whose conduct it is necessary to control. In many other cases, however, there is no evidence of improper motivation for the transfer, and in these cases enforcement of the rules causes considerable inequity to the athlete who has been required to make a school change for reasons that are beyond his or her control. Thus, the rules have been upheld in cases where the athlete was required to change schools due to inability to enroll at a previous school;[348] financial inability to continue attendance at private school;[349] parental move from out of state;[350] inability to attend a school that was closed due to racial strife;[351] closing of the prior school to effect integration;[352] and because of compulsion by a judge.[353] Again, one can question whether the transfer rules, in their common formulation, can be viewed as over-inclusive to the extent that they punish non-athletic motivated residence transfers.[354]

In addition to the inquiry into the authority of the enforcing entity, it must also be determined if the rules are constitutional, and there are several constitutional theories available to those against whom the transfer of residence rules are applied. The first is the Equal Protection Clause of the Fourteenth Amendment, which precludes the unequal treatment of persons similarly situated.[355] To invoke its protection, however, the rule sought to be challenged must create more than one classification either on its face or by its application. These rules will generally create separate classifications between those who move with their parents and those who do not.[356] The rules may also create other classifications as they are in fact applied. Under the permissive standard of constitutional review,[357] the transfer rules will be upheld, to the extent that they

---

346. The court's reasoning was that athletic participation was a privilege, and that it would not interfere in the affairs of a private association. The bases upon which these factors may be criticized are considered in §§ 1.11, 1.15.

347. *See, e.g.,* Josephine County School Dist. No. 7 v. Oregon School Activities Ass'n, 15 Or. App. 185, 515 P.2d 431 (1973).

348. Marino v. Waters, 220 So. 2d 802 (La. App. 1969). *See also* Chabert v. Louisiana High School Athletic Ass'n, 312 So.2d 343 (La. App. 1975) (no private school in public school district).

349. Tennessee Secondary School Athletic Ass'n v. Cox, 221 Tenn. 164, 425 S.W.2d 597 (1968).

350. State *ex rel.* Indiana High School Athletic Ass'n v. Lawrence Circuit Court, 240 Ind. 114, 162 N.E.2d 250 (1959).

351. Sanders v. Louisiana High School Athletic Ass'n, 242 So. 2d 19 (La. App. 1970).

352. Paschal v. Perdue, 320 F. Supp. 1274 (S.D. Fla. 1970).

353. Quimby v. School Dist. No. 21 of Pinal County, 10 Ariz. App. 69, 455 P.2d 1019 (1969).

354. *See* note 359 *infra* (for constitutional purposes).

355. *See* § 1.15.

356. Sturrup v. Mahan, 261 Ind. 463, 305 N.E.2d 877 (1974).

357. *See* § 1.15.

are properly related to a permissible objective of the rule-making party.[358] If a rule is over-inclusive and sweeps too broadly in its application, however, it may be unreasonable, and in violation of the Equal Protection Clause.[359] Such overbreadth is illustrated by *Sturrup v. Mahan*,[360] where a high school athlete moved from Florida to live with his brother in Indiana to avoid the "demoralizing and detrimental conditions" of his home and school environment in Florida. He was subsequently declared ineligible by the state high school athletic association under a residence transfer rule. In reviewing the application of the rule, the court noted that it was the result of the legitimate objective to forestall recruiting, but that it was unreasonable to the extent that it was written more broadly than necessary to accomplish that objective. Thus, it stated that the rule limits

> eligibility to those who move with their parents free of undue influence and to those whose move is necessitated by "unavoidable circumstances" free of undue influence. All other transferring student-athletes . . . are *automatically* denied the opportunity to participate in interscholastic athletics for the period of one year. The bylaws, in essence, create an irrebuttable conclusion of law that all other transferees have been the victims of unscrupulous practices. This is precisely where the rules sweep too broadly, they create an over-inclusive class — those who move from one school to another for reasons wholly unrelated to athletics are grouped together with those who have been recruited or who have "jumped" for athletic reasons. In short, the purported objective of the transferee eligibility rules is to prevent the use of undue influence and school "jumping" but their practical effect is to severely limit the transferee's eligibility in general. The rule as presently constituted penalizes a student-athlete who wishes to transfer for academic or religious reasons or for any number of other legitimate reasons. Surely, denying eligibility to such transferees in no way furthers [the association's] objectives.[361]

Sturrup v. Mahan was decided on constitutional grounds, but it is of interest that the court did not even note the several previous cases which had upheld the application of such rules in analogous situations under nonconstitutional state law.[362]

It may be argued that the transfer rules should be reviewed under the "strict" standard of review, which will require a compelling interest to support a classification which affects a "fundamental interest" or which is based upon "suspect criteria." [363] Since the operative element of these rules is the transfer of residence, the most likely source of a sufficiently protectible interest is in the right to freedom of travel, which has been denominated a "fundamental" interest entitled to the strict standard of review.[364] Although that interest originally applied to only interstate travel, it is now clear that "each citizen, adult

---

358. *See* note 342 *supra.*
359. *See* Sturrup v. Mahan, 261 Ind. 463, 305 N.E.2d 877 (1974).
360. 261 Ind. 463, 305 N.E.2d 877 (1974).
361. 305 N.E.2d at 881. *See also* Walsh v. Louisiana High School Athletic Ass'n, 428 F. Supp. 1261 (E.D. La. 1977) (rule held to be unconstitutional because of its exemption of four schools).
362. *See* notes 344-353 *supra.*
363. *See* § 1.15.
364. Shapiro v. Thompson, 394 U.S. 618, 22 L. Ed. 2d 600, 89 S. Ct. 1322 (1969).

or minor has a fundamental right to move freely from State to State and from city to city within the State." [365] Since the transfer of residence rules incumber the right to travel, by imposing what amounts to a residency requirement, it would be argued that a compelling interest must be shown to uphold the rule. In the only case to consider this question, the court held that the prevention of recruiting and school jumping did constitute a compelling interest,[366] but that statement was rejected without elaboration by the state's highest court on further review.[367] Whether the "strict" standard of review offers refuge from the rules, therefore, is yet to be authoritatively decided.

Even if a transfer of residence rule is supported by a compelling interest, it may also be attacked on the substantive due process theory [368] that it constitutes an overbroad means of attempting to protect a legitimate interest. The basis of this theory would be that a governmental purpose to control or prevent activities constitutionally subject to regulation may not be achieved by rules which sweep too broadly and invade protected rights.[369] Any such restrictions must, rather, be narrowly and precisely drawn to meet only the evil being attacked.[370] Thus, when the state seeks to regulate activities which are associated with the right to travel, its acts will be unlawful if they encumber the travel rights of those who are not within the class of persons affected by the evil which would be the legitimate subject of a narrowly drawn regulation.[371] In context of the transfer of residence rules, this theory would mean that if the rule is designed to prevent recruiting and school jumping, then it may not constitutionally affect those whose transfer of residence has nothing to do with those evils.[372]

§ 1.21. Grades.

Since amateur athletics are ordinarily conducted as a part of the educational activities of high schools and colleges, it is also common for there to be rules which limit eligibility to those who maintain a required grade average. Such a rule will ordinarily be a proper exercise of institutional authority, because it is normally both authorized and reasonable. It will be authorized because the fostering of scholastic, not athletic, achievement is the primary objective of the academic institution, and denying participation in extracurricular activities to those who are unable to render satisfactory academic performance is directly related to that objective. A rule will also be reasonable so long as its impact is felt only by those unable to maintain satisfactory academic standing.[373]

---

365. Dunn v. Blumstein, 405 U.S. 330, 31 L. Ed. 2d 274, 92 S. Ct. 995 (1972). *See also* Memorial Hosp. v. Maricopa County, 415 U.S. 250, 39 L. Ed. 2d 306, 94 S. Ct. 1076 (1974).
366. Sturrup v. Mahan, — Ind. App. —, 290 N.E.2d 69 (1972).
367. Sturrup v. Mahan, 261 Ind. 463, 305 N.E.2d 877 (1974).
368. *See* § 1.15.
369. NAACP v. Alabama, 357 U.S. 288, 307, 2 L. Ed. 2d 1488, 78 S. Ct. 1163 (1958).
370. NAACP v. Button, 371 U.S. 415, 438, 9 L. Ed. 2d 405, 83 S. Ct. 328 (1963).
371. Aptheker v. Secretary of State, 378 U.S. 500, 12 L. Ed. 2d 992, 84 S. Ct. 1659 (1964). Where the regulation is narrowly drawn, it will not be an unconstitutional infringement of the right to travel. Zemel v. Rusk, 381 U.S. 1, 14 L. Ed. 2d 179, 85 S. Ct. 1271 (1965).
372. *See, e.g.,* Sturrup v. Mahan, — Ind. App. —, 290 N.E.2d 64 (1972), *modified on appeal,* 261 Ind. 463, 305 N.E.2d 877 (1974).
373. Associated Students, Inc. v. National Collegiate Athletic Ass'n, 493 F.2d 1251 (9th Cir. 1974); Curtis v. National Collegiate Athletic Ass'n, Case No. C-71 2088 ACW (N.D. Cal. 1972).

Grade rules are also commonly used as a means of insuring that only academically qualified athletes are eligible for college competition. These rules pose a much different problem, since they do not relate to the maintenance of academic eligibility but to the achievement of some specified level of accomplishment at an earlier educational level. There may be a less direct connection between the interests of a college or collegiate association and an athlete's high school grades than there is to his or her college grades, especially if satisfactory work is in fact performed in college. When such rules are challenged, the rule-maker would be required to demonstrate a legitimate objective requiring that it exercise control on the basis of pre-admission grades, even for those athletes who make passing marks in college. The objectives of such rules are said to be to prevent the recruitment of persons having little chance of academic success and to encourage schools to maintain uniform minimum academic standards.

The permissibility of the lower level achievement rules is usually questioned when an athlete is declared ineligible after a finding that he or she was allowed to play without having achieved the requisite high school grades. In reviewing this type of rule, the courts have reached inconsistent results. In *Curtis v. National Collegiate Athletic Association*,[374] two athletes had been declared ineligible by the college athletic association although they were in good academic standing in their college. The athletes had originally been admitted to the school under a special program based upon factors of educational need and promise and not on high school class rank or scores on achievement tests. Since achievement test scores were not needed, the athletes did not take them. The association's rules, however, required that athletes could be eligible only if the combination of their high school grades or rank in class and score on a scholastic aptitude test "predicted" that they would achieve a "1.6" grade average (the equivalent of a D+ or C— in college). An official interpretation of that rule required that if an athlete received aid without qualifying under these requirements, he or she would be ineligible for intercollegiate competition. When the athletes brought an action to challenge the association's action, the court held that the grade "predicting" rule served as a means of distinguishing athletes, who were doing acceptable work but who had not "predicted" from those who were doing similar work and had "predicted," and that such a classification was unconstitutional as applied to the facts in question. Specifically, the court held that

> [a]s applied to these plaintiffs, the 1.600 rule of the NCAA, as interpreted, is unconstitutional insofar as the Rule makes a classification on the basis of the fact that 1) plaintiffs failed to predict a 1.600 grade point average prior to entrance to the University and 2) thereafter received financial aid based in part upon their athletic ability. The consequence of that classification is that plaintiffs are permanently ineligible to participate in intercollegiate athletics despite the fact that each of the plaintiffs is at present in good academic standing. The classification is neither necessary nor is it rationally related to any of

---

374. Case No. C-71 2088 ACW (N.D. Cal. 1972).

the objectives sought to be obtained by the NCAA in adopting the 1.600 Rule, or of any public policy or of any other policy of the NCAA.[375]

The grade prediction rule was held impermissible on the facts in *Curtis* because it was over-inclusive and rendered ineligible even those who were maintaining suitable grades in college. This approach has, however, been rejected by the majority of courts which have considered the issue. Thus, in *Associated Students, Inc. v. National Collegiate Athletic Association,*[376] the court, on facts essentially identical to those in *Curtis,* upheld the rule and its interpretation that had been stricken in *Curtis.* It began by noting that the purpose of the rule was to reduce exploitation of young athletes and to insure the academic standing of all student-athletes,[377] and concluded that the rule in question was reasonably related to these purposes, which were legitimate objectives of the NCAA. To uphold the rule on the reasoning of *Curtis,* the court said, would allow schools to recruit unqualified athletes and then, if they achieved satisfactory grades in their first year, utilize them in their athletic programs; and to allow such subterfuge would undermine the rule itself.

Associated Students, and the cases reaching similar conclusions,[378] state that the purpose of grade predicting rules is to insure recruitment of academically qualified students, and that the question of academic qualification must be made on the basis of high school marks, even though this produces an apparently inequitable result to the athlete who in fact makes satisfactory academic progress in college. Much of this inequity is minimized if the athlete who does not "predict" is allowed to sit out the first year of college, and if satisfactory work is accomplished during that period is then granted eligibility.[379]

§ 1.22. Sex.

Probably the most controversial of the rules in amateur athletics are those which classify persons who are eligible to participate on the basis of their sex.[380]

---

375. *Id.* at 8. *Curtis* is discussed at length in Note, *Judicial Review of Disputes Between Athletes and the National Collegiate Athletic Association,* 24 STAN. L. REV. 874 (1972).

376. 493 F.2d 1251 (9th Cir. 1974).

377. Specifically, the court stated that the purpose of the rule was

> to reduce the possibility of exploiting young athletes by recruiting those who would not be representative of an institution's student body and probably would be unable to meet the necessary academic requirements for a degree; and also to foster and preserve the concept of college athletics as a sport engaged in by athletes who were first and primarily college students, and to recognize the probability that any student who could not meet the requirements of the Rule should not engage in athletics during his freshman year, but should devote his full time to study. *Id.* at 1255.

378. McDonald v. National Collegiate Athletic Ass'n, 370 F. Supp. 625 (C.D. Cal. 1974); Howard Univ. v. National Collegiate Athletic Ass'n, 367 F. Supp. 926 (D.D.C. 1973), *aff'd,* 510 F.2d 213 (D.C. Cir. 1975); Parish v. National Collegiate Athletic Ass'n, 361 F. Supp. 1220 (W.D. La. 1973), *aff'd,* 506 F.2d 1028 (5th Cir. 1975).

379. This appears to be the present position of the NCAA. *See* Bylaws & Interpretations of the National Collegiate Athletic Association, art. 4, § 1 (j) (1977).

380. A typical rule provides that

> Boys and girls shall not be permitted to participate in interschool athletic games as united teams, nor shall boys' teams and girls' teams participate against each other in interschool athletic contests.

Haas v. South Bend Community School Corp., 289 N.E.2d 495 (Ind. 1972).

The sex rules normally exclude females from participating with or against males,[381] and have generally been justified by one or more of the following reasons:

1. Males consistently outperform females on the playing field.[382]
2. Males are physiologically superior to females.[383]
3. Separation of the sexes is necessary to prevent psychological injury to females.[384]
4. Separation of the sexes is necessary to the development of future, and preservation of present, female athletic programs.[385]
5. The cost of allowing females to compete with males would be prohibitive.[386]

With respect to the following discussion, it should be noted that no effort will be made to differentiate between the various levels of athletic competition in which females may be involved. As noted at the beginning of this chapter, see § 1.01, it would certainly be possible to distinguish the application of the rules considered in this section depending upon whether competition is at the primary, secondary or college and university level. It is our belief that not only would the principles discussed apply similarly at each level, but that separate consideration for each would unduly prolong the discussion and would of necessity be redundant. It should also be kept in mind that private institutions are not separately considered in this discussion. Since the principles involved are basically constitutional, they would not in any event apply to such institutions. See §§ 1.14, 1.15.1. Only the Title IX discussion would be applicable. See notes 463-479 infra.

An additional issue that may arise in the future concerns the dividing line between male and female. The issue was given prominence by tennis star Dr. Renee Richards. See, e.g., She'd Rather Switch — And Fight, SPORTS ILLUSTRATED, September 6, 1976, at 16.

381. See generally Gilbert and Williamson, Women in Sport, Part 1: Sport is Unfair to Women, SPORTS ILLUSTRATED, May 28, 1973 at 92-95; Stroud, Sex Discrimination in High School Athletics, 6 IND. L. REV. 661, 666-69 (1973); Note, Sex Discrimination in Intercollegiate Athletics, 61 IOWA L. REV. 420 (1975); Note, Sex Discrimination in High School Athletics, 57 MINN. L. REV. 339, 351-57 (1972); Comment, Sex Discrimination in Interscholastic High School Athletics, 25 SYRACUSE L. REV. 535 (1974); Note, The Case for Equality in Athletics, 22 CLEV. ST. L. REV. 570 (1973); Note, Equality in Athletics: The Cheerleader v. The Athlete, 19 S. D. L. REV. 428 (1974).

382. Bucha v. Illinois High School Ass'n, 351 F. Supp. 69 (N.D. Ill. 1972) (the court took judicial notice of this "fact").

383. Thus, in Brenden v. Independent School Dist., 342 F. Supp. 1224 (D. Minn. 1972), aff'd, 477 F.2d 1292 (8th Cir. 1973), the court observed that

> men are taller than women, stronger than women by reason of a greater muscle mass, have larger hearts than women and a deeper breathing capacity, enabling them to utilize oxygen more efficiently than women, run faster, based upon the construction of the pelvic area, which, when women reach puberty, widens, causing the femur to bend outward, rendering the female incapable of running as efficiently as a male. These physiological differences may, on the average, prevent the great majority of women from competing on an equal level with the great majority of males.

Id. at 1233. See also Fortin v. Darlington Little League, Inc., 376 F. Supp. 473 (D.R.I. 1974), rev'd, F.2d 344 (1st Cir. 1975); Ritacco v. Norwin School Dist., 361 F. Supp. 930 (W.D. Pa. 1973). The evidence of this contention is considered in Gilbert & Williamson, Women in Sports, Part 2: Are You Being Two Faced?, SPORTS ILLUSTRATED, June 4, 1973.

384. Bucha v. Illinois High School Ass'n, 351 F. Supp. 69 (N.D. Ill. 1972); Hollander v. Connecticut Interscholastic Athletic Conf., Inc., Cause No. 12497 (Super. Ct. Conn., New Haven County, 1971), noted in 1 WOMEN'S RIGHTS L. REP. No. 2 at 41 (Spring 1972), app. dismissed 164 Conn. 654, 295 A.2d 671 (1972); Gregoria v. Board of Educ. of Asbury Park, Cause No. A-1277-70 (N.J. Super. Ct. App. Div. 1971), noted in 1 WOMEN'S RIGHTS L. REP. No. 1 at 39 (1972).

385. Brenden v. Independent School Dist. 742, 477 F.2d 1292 (8th Cir. 1973); Haas v. South Bend Community School Corp., 289 N.E.2d 495 (Ind. 1972).

386. Haas v. South Bend Community School Corp., 289 N.E.2d 495 (Ind. 1972). This concern includes both the cost of coaching and training twice as many athletes, and the cost of duplicate facilities. With regard to facilities, one director of a state athletic association is reported to have justified sex separation because the "[g]irls haven't figured out yet how to use the urinals." Gilbert & Williamson, Women in Sports, Part I: Sport Is Unfair to Women, SPORTS ILLUSTRATED, May 28, 1973, at 95. See also Gregoria v. Board of Educ. of Asbury Park, Cause No. A-1277-70 (N.J. Super.

6. Separation of the sexes is necessary to achieve equitable competition.[387]

7. Separation of the sexes is a tradition in sports.[388]

Before considering the sex rules and their application, it is necessary to consider the status of sex-based classifications more broadly.

Classifications based on sex have in general been the subject of great concern in recent years, and developments in the area are proceeding at a rather rapid pace.[389] The courts traditionally showed little real concern with the use of sex as a means of classification, and, in the past, the Supreme Court has, for example, upheld sexual classifications which limited the hours women could work [390] and their ability to serve as bartenders.[391] It is said that the basis for this lack of concern was the long and unfortunate history of sex discrimination in this country, which has been rationalized by an attitude of romantic paternalism that has had the effect of placing females, rather than on a pedestal, in a cage.[392] This traditional deference has, however, recently been repudiated by the Court. The first step came in *Reed v. Reed,*[393] where the Court invalidated the use of sex as a statutory means to classify those who could be appointed as administrator of a decedent's estate. In reaching this conclusion, the Court noted that classifications must be "reasonable, not arbitrary, and must rest upon

---

Ct. App. Div. 1971), *noted in* 1 WOMEN'S RIGHTS L. REP. No. 1 at 39 (1972) (cost of hiring female trainer).

387. Brenden v. Independent School Dist. 742, 342 F. Supp. 1224 (D. Minn. 1972), *aff'd,* 477 F.2d 1292 (8th Cir. 1973).

388. Note, *Sex Discrimination in High School Athletics,* 57 MINN. L. REV. 339, 351-52 (1972). Perhaps the best summation of these reasons, and what their rejection would mean to females in general, is the following:

> The overemphasis on protecting girls from strain or injury, and underemphasis on developing skills and experiencing teamwork, fits neatly into the pattern of the second sex. Girls are the spectators and the cheerleaders. They organize the pep clubs, sell pompons, make cute, abbreviated costumes, strut a bit between halves and idolize the current football hero. This is perfect preparation for the adult role of women — to stand decoratively on the sidelines of history and cheer on the men who make the decisions. Women who have had the regular experience of performing before others, of learning to win and to lose, of cooperating in team efforts, will be far less fearful of running for office, better able to take public positions on issues in the face of public opposition. By working toward some balance in the realm of physical activity, we may indeed begin to achieve a more wholesome, democratic balance in all phases of our life. Gilbert & Williamson, *Women in Sports, Part 3: Programmed to Be Losers,* SPORTS ILLUSTRATED, June 11, 1973, at 73.

389. Sex rules are also considered with respect to state athletic commissions in § 2.10.

390. Muller v. Oregon, 208 U.S. 412, 28 S. Ct. 324, 52 L. Ed. 551 (1908).

391. Goesaert v. Cleary, 335 U.S. 464, 69 S. Ct. 198, 93 L. Ed. 163 (1948). *See generally* Ginsburg, *Gender and the Constitution,* 44 U. CIN. L. REV. 1, 2-8 (1975).

392. Frontiero v. Richardson, 411 U.S. 677, 684, 93 S. Ct. 1764, 36 L. Ed. 2d 583 (1973). Indeed, in his concurring opinion in Bradwell v. Illinois, 83 U.S. [16 Wall.] 130 (1873), Mr. Justice Bradley observed that

> Man is, or should be, woman's protector and defender. The natural and proper timidity and delicacy which belongs to the female sex evidently unfits it for many of the occupations of civil life. The constitution of the family organization, which is founded in the divine ordinance, as well as in the nature of things, indicates the domestic sphere as that which properly belongs to the domain and functions of womanhood. The harmony, not to say identity, to the family institution is repugnant to the ideas of a woman adopting a distinct and independent career from that of her husband. . . . The paramount destiny and mission of woman are to fulfill the noble and benign offices of wife and mother. This is the law of the Creator. *Id.* at 141.

393. 404 U.S. 71, 30 L. Ed. 2d 225, 92 S. Ct. 251 (1971).

some ground of difference having a fair and substantial relation to the object of the legislation, so that all persons similarly circumstanced shall be treated alike." [394] In light of this standard, it framed the question before it in terms of whether a difference in the sex of applicants bore the "rational relationship to a state objective" that was sought to be advanced by the classification. The only purpose put forth by the state was the desire to reduce the workload of probate courts. The Court held that while this interest had "some legitimacy," it did not justify the use of a sex-based classification.[395]

In *Reed v. Reed,* then, the Court appeared to have been requiring that sex-based classifications meet what is essentially the permissive standard of equal protection review, though it has been widely read to have actually applied a far more searching inquiry *sub rosa.*[396] A few years later, it expressly suggested the strict standard.[397] In *Frontiero v. Richardson,*[398] the plurality opinion of the Court made the use of sex as a means of classifying otherwise similarly situated persons a subject for the strict standard of review. In striking down a statutory scheme which differentiated between the spouses of male and female members of the armed services, the Court, after noting the history of sex discrimination in this country, stated that

> classifications based upon sex, like classifications based upon race, alienage, or national origin, are inherently suspect, and must therefore be subjected to strict judicial scrutiny.[399]

Although a majority of the Court has not adopted the position of the plurality in *Frontiero,* and though the specific standard by which sex classifications will be reviewed is by no means clear, the Court has continued to indicate that those who seek to use sex as a means of classifying otherwise similarly situated persons will have a heavy burden to carry.[400] Thus, it has stated that sex-based classifications will be held to be in violation of the Equal Protection Clause unless shown to rest upon a convincing factual basis going beyond "archaic and overbroad generalizations" about the differences between males and females.[401]

When a sex-based classification in amateur athletics is challenged, the court will determine its vitality for equal protection purposes by considering three separate criteria: 1) the character of the classification in question; 2) the

---

394. *Id.* at 76.
395. *Id.*
396. *See, e.g.,* Gunther, *The Supreme Court 1971 Term, Foreword: In Search of Evolving Doctrine on a Changing Court: A Model for a Newer Equal Protection,* 86 HARV. L. REV. 1 (1972); Note, *The Emerging Bifurcated Standard for Classifications Based on Sex,* 1975 DUKE L.J. 163, 177-78.
397. The standards of review are discussed in some detail at § 1.15.
398. 411 U.S. 677, 36 L. Ed. 583, 93 S. Ct. 1764 (1973).
399. *Id.* at 682. It must, however, be noted that only four members of the Court agreed to the "suspect criterion" portion of the decision.
400. *See* Turner v. Department of Employment, 423 U.S. 44, 96 S. Ct. 249, 46 L. Ed. 2d 181 (1975); Stanton v. Stanton, 421 U.S. 7, 95 S. Ct. 1373, 43 L. Ed. 2d 688 (1975); Weinberger v. Weisenfeld, 420 U.S. 636 (1975); Schlesinger v. Ballard, 419 U.S. 498, 95 S. Ct. 572, 42 L. Ed. 2d 610 (1975); Kahn v. Shevin, 416 U.S. 351, 94 S. Ct. 1734, 40 L. Ed. 2d 189 (1974). At least one state court decision had reached the conclusion that sex was a "suspect criterion" entitled to the strict standard of review before *Frontiero.* Sail'er Inn, Inc. v. Kirby, 5 Cal. 3d 1, 95 Cal. Rptr. 329, 485 P.2d 529 (1971).
401. Schlesinger v. Ballard, 419 U.S. 498, 508, 95 S. Ct. 572, 42 L. Ed. 2d 610 (1975). *See also* Gilpin v. Kansas State High School Activities Ass'n, 377 F. Supp. 1233, 1239 (D. Kansas 1974); Darrin v. Gould, 85 Wash. 2d 859, 540 P.2d 882 (1975).

individual interests affected by it; and 3) the interests asserted to support its use by the rule-maker.[402] The first inquiry will in most cases be rather clear, since the classification will seek to determine eligibility for a specified type of competition on the basis of sex, and its permissibility will be determined by the principles noted above. The interests affected by the sex classification will be the interests of females or males in participating in interscholastic athletics. As has been noted at length in an earlier discussion, some courts have taken the position that this interest is sufficiently substantial to be entitled to constitutional protection.[403] The interests of the entity responsible for the sex rule will generally be stated in terms of the need to protect females from physical or mental injury as a result of competition with or against males, to insure that female competition will be developed in an orderly manner by keeping it separate from the male program, or to insure that persons with similar qualifications compete only among themselves.[404] In support of these interests, the reasons identified at the beginning of this discussion will normally be cited.[405] The court will then evaluate the interests or purposes of the rule-maker under the applicable standard to determine whether there is a proper nexus between the rule and the proferred interests to justify the infringement of the complainant's interests.

The application of these principles in the amateur athletics context is indicated by *Brenden v. Independent School District 742,*[406] involving two female high school students who desired to participate in tennis and cross country skiing and running. Since their schools provided no female teams, they sought to qualify for a position on the male teams, but were precluded from doing so by a rule of the state athletic association that prohibited females from competing with or against males. In evaluating the merits of the females' claim that the rule violated their equal protection rights, the court began by noting that sex-based classifications were coming under increasing scrutiny from the courts, as well as legislative and executive bodies. It then found that the complainants' interest in athletic participation were "substantial and cognizable," since it constituted a part of their interest in education and was as valuable to them as it was to their male peers.[407] With respect to the purposes sought to be achieved by the rule, the athletic association had argued that it was necessary to insure that persons with similar qualifications competed among themselves, since, in the association's view, females could not equitably compete with males. The court then evaluated these purposes in terms of the principles of *Reed v. Reed,* as

---

402. Dunn v. Blumstein, 405 U.S. 330, 335, 92 S. Ct. 995, 31 L. Ed. 2d 274 (1972).

403. *See* §§ 1.11, 1.28.

404. *See, e.g.,* Brenden v. Independent School Dist. 742, 477 F.2d 1292 (8th Cir. 1973); Gilpin v. Kansas State High School Activities Ass'n, 377 F. Supp. 1233 (D. Kansas 1973); Haas v. South Bend Community School Corp., 280 N.E.2d 495 (Ind. 1972).

405. *See* notes 381-388 *supra.*

406. 477 F.2d 1303 (8th Cir. 1973).

407. *Id.* at 1297-99. Probably the best statement of this view has been that of Justice DeBruler in his concurring opinion in Haas v. South Bend Community School Corp., 289 N.E.2d 495 (Ind. 1972):

> Full and equal opportunity to participate in the curricular and extra-curricular educational activities of our public schools, with full and equal opportunity to receive the benefits flowing from such participation, is guaranteed to all public school students, be they male or female, by the equal protection clause of the Fourteenth Amendment. 289 N.E.2d at 502.

augmented by the particular sensitivity required in considering sex classifications, and concluded that the association had "failed to demonstrate that sex-based classifications fairly and substantially promote the purposes of the . . . rule." [408] In support of this conclusion, the court found that the complainants were capable of competing with males in the non-contact sports in question and that the evidence offered to establish that females could not so compete was quite subjective.[409] The court went further, however, and stated that even if it were shown that females could not compete with males in these sports generally, the rule would still not have been justified since *Reed v. Reed* "precludes a state from using assumptions about the nature of females as a class, to deny [them] an individualized determination of their qualifications for a benefit provided by the state." [410] In this part of its opinion, the court seems to be indicating that ultimately the only basis for the exclusion of females is their own respective ability (the same basis for the exclusion of males). In short, the court found that the rule as applied to these females violated equal protection requirements, and the court required that they be given an opportunity to qualify for the respective teams.

Brenden is reflective of the conclusion of other courts that have considered similar cases,[411] though contrary results have also been reached.[412] The thrust of cases such as *Brenden* is that the courts are sensitive to the possibility that sex rules are based largely upon stereotypes concerning the nature of females generally, and that the rules will be upheld only where a substantial and rational basis can be shown for the classification created. Although generalization from these cases is hazardous, it can be observed that a sex rule will probably not

---

408. 477 F.2d at 1300.

409. Aside from the subjectiveness of the testimony on this issue, the appellate court also noted that a study of male-female competition in New York had strongly recommended such competition after concluding that preliminary studies of such competition indicated that there were no medical reasons why females could not so compete. The only negative factor discovered in field observation was that it was not yet socially acceptable for a female to defeat a male. *See* REPORT ON EXPERIMENT: GIRLS ON INTERSCHOLASTIC ATHLETIC TEAMS (N.Y. Dept. of Educ. and Rec. 1972). 477 F.2d at 1300-01.

410. 477 F.2d at 1302. *See also* Darrin v. Gould, 85 Wash. 2d 859, 540 P.2d 882 (1975). The court also noted that the purpose of the rule was

> to insure that persons with similar qualifications will compete with each other. Yet, females, whatever their qualifications, have been barred from competition with males on the basis of an assumption about the qualifications of women as a class. The failure to provide the plaintiffs with an individualized determination of their own ability to qualify for positions on these teams is, under *Reed*, violative of the Equal Protection Clause.

Id. This language suggests the possibility that sex rules could be viewed as irrebuttable presumptions to the extent that individualized determinations are not provided. *See* § 2.07.

411. Bednar v. Nebraska School Activities Ass'n, 531 F.2d 922 (8th Cir. 1976); Morris v. Michigan State Bd. of Educ., 472 F.2d 1207 (6th Cir. 1973); Hoover v. Meiklejohn, 430 F. Supp. 164 (D. Colo. 1977)ˑ Gilpin v. Kansas State High School Activities Ass'n, 377 F. Supp. 1233 (D. Kansas 1973); Reed v. Nebraska School Activities Ass'n, 341 F. Supp. 258 (D. Neb. 1972); Haas v. South Bend Community School Corp., 280 N.E.2d 495 (Ind. 1972).

412. Ritacco v. Norwin School District, 361 F. Supp. 930 (W.D. Pa. 1973); Bucha v. Illinois High School Ass'n, 351 F. Supp. 69 (N.D. Ill. 1972); Hollander v. Connecticut Interscholastic Athletic Conf., Inc., Cause No. 12497 (Super. Ct. Conn., New Haven County, 1971), *app. dismissed,* 164 Conn. 654, 295 A.2d 671 (1972); Ruman v. Eskew, — Ind. App. —, 343 N.E.2d 806 (1976); Gregoria v. Board of Educ. of Asbury Park, Cause No. A-1277-70 (N.J. Super. Ct. App. Div. 1971). The *Hollander* and *Gregoria* cases were pre-*Reed* decisions, and *Ritacco* and *Bucha* each involved factual situations showing separate female teams in the sports in question. There is a basis in each, then, for the suggestion that they are not as such in conflict with the cases cited at note 411 *supra.*

be enforced where insufficient factual support is shown for the purposes offered to justify the rule, where there are no alternative female teams, and where the sport in question does not involve physical contact with males. Each of these factors will be noted below.

The emphasis in *Brenden* on the lack of factual support does not suggest that the courts have rejected the reasons offered to justify sex rules.[413] They have not.[414] The emphasis means only that if the rules are to be upheld on the bases commonly put forth, those bases must be proven to exist in fact. It bears emphasis, however, that even if such a factual predicate is shown, the court in *Brenden* seems to have been pointing toward a conclusion that ability may be the only ultimate basis for selection. Evidence of general physiological inferiority cannot, it said, be used as a basis for denying all females the chance to demonstrate that they can compete.[415] Although this view has not been widely embraced, it is evident in some other cases in this area.[416]

An additional aspect of the cases that must be considered involves the effect of separate female teams. The presence or absence of such teams has played an important part in most of the decided cases. In several of the cases holding that sex rules were unlawful as applied to the facts in question, the courts specifically indicated that there were no separate female teams in existence,[417] and in some the courts have suggested that their decision would be different if such teams in fact existed. Thus, in *Haas v. South Bend Community School Corp.*,[418] the court observed that there were no interscholastic athletic programs for female students, so that "the rule, in effect, prohibits females from participating in interscholastic athletics altogether. Although the difference in athletic ability is a justifiable reason for the separation of male and female athletic programs, the justification does not exist when only one athletic program is involved." [419] The clear implication of *Haas* is that where there are girls' athletic programs, the sexual classification rule would not have been found to be unlawful. This was, indeed, the result in *Bucha v. Illinois High School Association*,[420] where the court upheld such a rule, and noted that there was a statewide girls' program for the sports in question.

The presence of a separate female team raises several questions. The first is the extent to which such a team will provide support for the use of a sex rule. Where such teams are present, a rule-maker will be in a much better position

413. *See* notes 381-388 *supra.*

414. Indeed, the reasons have often been applauded, though not given force in the absence of the requisite factual proof. *See e.g.,* Gilpin v. Kansas State High School Activities Ass'n, 377 F. Supp. 1233, 1242-43 (D. Kansas 1973).

415. *See* note 410 *supra.*

416. *See* notes 450-462 *infra.*

417. Brenden v. Independent School Dist. 742, 477 F.2d 1292 (8th Cir. 1973); Gilpin v. Kansas State High School Activities Ass'n, 377 F. Supp. 1233 (D. Kan. 1973); Haas v. South Bend Community School Corp., 289 N.E.2d 495 (Ind. 1972).

418. 289 N.E.2d 495 (Ind. 1972).

419. *Id.* at 499, 501. *See also* Gilpin v. Kansas State High School Activities Ass'n, 377 F. Supp. 1233 (D. Kan. 1973).

420. 351 F. Supp. 69 (N.D. Ill. 1972), *noted* in 50 Chi.-Kent L. Rev. 169 (1973). *See also* Ritacco v. Norwin School Dist., 361 F. Supp. 930 (W.D. Pa. 1973); Seldin v. State Bd. of Educ. of N.J., Cause No. Civil 202-72 (D.N.J. 1972), noted in 1 Women's Rights L. Rep. No. 2 at 41 (1972) (suspended decision pending outcome of experimental program); Ruman v. Eskew, — Ind. App. —, 343 N.E.2d 806 (1976).

to justify the use of sex as a means of classification. It will then be able to demonstrate to the court that it provides athletic opportunity to both males and females through separate programs and will avoid the difficulty of arguing around the fact that females have no opportunity where there is only a male team. The only question will be whether there is a rational basis for separate competition. The rationale would inevitably be that because of the physiological and ability differences between males and females as a class, it is necessary to maintain separate teams if a program for the females is to be developed.[421] If the predicate — that there are such physiological and ability differences — can be proven, then it is possible that the rule would be upheld. Thus, in one of the cases holding a sex rule invalid in the absence of separate teams, it was noted that

> in light of the physiological differences between males and females, the Court agrees that separation of male and female interscholastic competition arguably *bears* a substantial relation to the advancement of that interest [developing a viable female program], *when* separate and substantially equivalent programs for males and females are in fact in existence.[422]

The presence of separate teams should not, however, foreclose inquiry. There would remain the question of whether the female teams provided competitive opportunity to the females that was substantially equivalent to that provided to males by the male teams.[423] The basic rationale of the cases which have stricken sex rules is that the effect of the rules is to deprive females of equivalent athletic opportunities.[424] Thus, if there were substantial differences between, for example, the financing, competition or coaching of male and female teams, it would seem clear that they would not provide equal opportunities to each sex and would not seem to meet the spirit of the courts' opinions. The difficult problem, of course, will be to determine what it is that constitutes substantial equivalency in the programs — a question that is not considered by the cases which have used the presence of separate teams to uphold sex rules.[425] An interpretation requiring absolute equality in terms of financial support, equipment, coaching, competitive opportunity and appropriate intangible factors such as prestige (to name only a few possible ingredients) would put a much different gloss on the matter than would, for example, an interpretation that the bare existence of separate teams is sufficient. Although there are few

---

421. It should also be noted that there is considerable support for the view that separate but equal teams are necessary to insure that there is an opportunity for female competition. It is feared that if there is a single team in each sport, females may be completely excluded from competition on an ability basis. *See* Fasteau, *Giving Women a Sporting Chance,* Ms. Magazine, July, 1973, at 58; *Hearings Before the House Subcomm. on Postsecondary Education of the House Comm. on Education and Labor,* 94th Cong., 1st Sess. 343 (1975).

422. Gilpin v. Kansas State High School Activities Ass'n, 377 F. Supp. 1233, 1242 (D. Kansas 1973) (emphasis supplied).

423. *See* Note, *Sex Discrimination and Equal Protection: Do We Need a Constitutional Amendment?,* 84 Harv. L. Rev. 1499, 1515-16 (1971).

424. *See* notes 411, 422 *supra.*

425. *See* cases in note 420 *supra. See* Hoover v. Meiklejohn, 430 F. Supp. 164 (D. Colo. 1977) (teams must be substantially equal, though differences could be justified on the basis of "neutral factors," such as student interest).

guideposts for the resolution of this question,[426] the Title IX Regulations may serve that purpose.[427]

Even if the male and female teams were in fact equal, it would also have to be determined whether the maintenance of "separate but equal" teams is sufficient for equal protection purposes. It could be argued that the use of such teams to justify sex rules, as was suggested in *Haas* and done in *Bucha,* is no more than a step towards the resurrection of the "separate but equal" theory of *Plessy v. Ferguson.*[428] Although *Plessy* involved racial separation by law on public transportation facilities, the "separate but equal" theory that it upheld was broadly rejected for all areas of education in *Brown v. Board of Education,*[429] where the Court concluded "that in the field of public education the doctrine of 'separate but equal' has no place. Separate educational facilities are inherently unequal." [430] The admonition in *Brown* against use of the "separate but equal" philosophy in education might include interscholastic athletics, as some courts have stated that athletic participation is a part of the educational process.[431]

Unlike situations involving racial discrimination, the constitutional viability of "separate but equal" in the area of sex discrimination is as yet unresolved. The issue was not raised in *Bucha,* though in another case the court approved the practice without really analyzing the question.[432] It has, however, been observed that "[a]nyone who would seek to support the rationality of the separatist principle served by such dual [athletic] systems would have a difficult burden indeed." [433] In other areas, the courts have occasionally rejected "separate but equal" to justify the use of sex-based classifications,[434] as have some,[435] but not other,[436] legislatures in dealing with sex discrimination in athletics, though recent federal regulations under Title IX have broadly approved its use.[437] Whether the "separate but equal" doctrine will be viable

426. *See* Sweatt v. Painter, 339 U.S. 629 (1950).

427. *See* notes 463-480 *infra.*

428. 163 U.S. 537 (1896).

429. 347 U.S. 483 (1954).

430. *Id.* at 495.

431. *See* § 1.11.

432. Thus, in Ritacco v. Norwin School Dist., 361 F. Supp. 930 (W.D. Pa. 1973), the court stated that " 'separate but equal' in the realm of sports competition, unlike that of racial discrimination, is justifiable and should be allowed to stand where there is a rational basis for the rule." *Id.* at 932. *See also* Ruman v. Eskew, — Ind. App. —, 343 N.E.2d 806 (1976).

433. Haas v. South Bend Community School Corp., 289 N.E.2d 495, 503 (Ind. 1972) (DeBruler, J., concurring). *See also* Commonwealth v. Pennsylvania Interscholastic Athletic Ass'n, 18 Pa. Commw. Ct. 45, 334 A.2d 839 (1975). *See generally* Stroud, *Sex Discrimination in High School Athletics,* 6 IND. L. REV. 661, 676-79 (1973); Comment, *Sex Discrimination in Interscholastic High School Athletics,* 25 SYRACUSE L. REV. 535, 556-58 (1974); Note, *Sex Discrimination in Intercollegiate Athletics,* 61 IOWA L. REV. 420, 448-52 (1975).

434. *See* NLRB v. Glass Bottle Blowers Ass'n Local 106, 520 F.2d 693 (6th Cir. 1975) (the maintenance of "separate but equal" locals of a labor union for male and female members held to be a union unfair labor practice); Kirstein v. Rector and Visitors of University of Virginia, 309 F. Supp. 184 (E.D. Va. 1970) (females must be admitted to the University of Virginia). *But cf.* Vorchheimer v. School Dist. of Philadelphia, 532 F.2d 880 (3d Cir. 1976) (upholding separate public high schools, though with a vigorous dissent), *aff'd by equally divided court,* 430 U.S. 703 (1977).

435. MICH. STAT. ANN. § 15.3379 (Supp. 1973).

436. CALIF. LEGISLATIVE SERVICE ch. 802 (1975) (specifying that provisions of act precluding sex discrimination in public school athletic programs would not require that males and females compete against each other).

437. *See* notes 463-479 *infra.*

in amateur athletics is, in other words, an open and debatable question. Even if it should eventually be concluded that separate but equal teams would suffice for constitutional purposes, there will remain other questions for which there is neither ready nor easy answer. The most important would be, as already noted, what "separate but equal" means in this context.[438] There will also be other problems, including whether females would be allowed to compete for a position on the male team, and, if so, whether the males would be allowed to compete for the female team.[439] If the females could but the males could not, there would then be the further question of whether such a benign policy could be justified.[440]

The final factor in the sex cases that requires consideration involves the distinction that many cases have drawn between contact and non-contact sports. Whether females should under any circumstances be allowed to compete in men's contact sports is a question that has been carefully avoided by most courts. Thus, in several of the non-contact decisions, the courts have expressly noted that a contact sport was not present,[441] and in at least one case it was conceded by the females' advocate that male-female classification was reasonable in contact sports.[442] The contact-non-contact distinction has also been noted by a statute which precludes sex discrimination rules in the former but not the latter,[443] and by a federal appellate decision which required that an injunction be rephrased by the district court to preclude discrimination in only non-contact sports.[444] Although these several factors might suggest that females may be barred from amateur athletics which involve contact, there is not as yet a clear answer to the issue.

As an element in sex classification cases, the contact issue would appear to raise only one basic issue: whether there is a rational basis for excluding females from sports involving physical contact with males. The reason that is generally said to support the exclusion is that females would face a greater likelihood of physical injury than would their male peers. As was observed to be true with respect to the reasons offered in support of sex rules in general, this reason would support a finding that there was a rational basis for the rule only if the factual assumption could be proven.[445] If such a showing could not be made, then there would be no reasonable basis for the imposition of the classification.[446]

438. *See* notes 424-427 *supra.*

439. *See, e.g.,* White v. Corpus Christi Little Misses Kickball Ass'n, 526 S.W.2d 766 (Tex. Civ. App. 1975) (denying male effort to compete on female team, though on basis of lack of state action).

440. These problems are commented upon in *Hearings Before the House Subcomm. on Postsecondary Education of the House Comm. on Education and Labor,* 94th Cong., 1st Sess. 343, 391, 526-28 (1975). There is some support for the exclusion of males from female institutions, *see, e.g.,* Williams v. McNair, 316 F. Supp. 134 (D. S.C. 1970), *aff'd,* 401 U.S. 951, 91 S. Ct. 976, 28 L. Ed. 2d 235 (1971), but it antedated even *Reed v. Reed.* Ameliorative sex classifications are considered in Note, *The Emerging Bifurcated Standard for Classifications Based on Sex,* 1975 DUKE L.J. 163.

It should be noted that there have been numerous proposals advanced about how male and female competition could be integrated in the best interests of all parties. These proposals are identified and evaluated in Comment, *Sex Discrimination in High School Interscholastic Athletics,* 25 SYRACUSE L. REV. 535, 556-66 (1974).

441. *See, e.g.,* Bucha v. Illinois High School Ass'n, 351 F. Supp. 69 (N.D. Ill. 1972); Haas v. South Bend Community School Corp., 289 N.E.2d 495 (Ind. 1972).

442. Haas v. South Bend Community School Corp., 289 N.E.2d 495 (Ind. 1972).

443. MICH. STAT. ANN. § 15.3379 (Supp. 1973).

444. Morris v. Michigan State Board of Education, 472 F.2d 1207 (6th Cir. 1973).

445. *See* notes 413-416 *supra.*

446. *See* Clinton v. Nagy, 411 F. Supp. 1396 (N.D. Ohio 1974).

Although this factual issue has been addressed by several courts, the results are not consistent. A practice of barring females from baseball participation was upheld in *Magill v. Avonworth Baseball Conference*,[447] where a young female athlete was precluded from competing in a summer baseball program, because of her sex. When suit was brought, the case was dismissed on the ground that the summer league was a private organization not within the "state action" concept for equal protection purposes.[448] The court, however, then went on to consider the merits of the challenge to the sexual exclusion. After noting the physical danger faced by little girls when they play baseball, it concluded that "sex is a rational distinction where a contact sport is involved." [449]

The result in *Magill* has not been followed by the courts that have been confronted with the issue since it was decided. In *National Organization for Women v. Little League Baseball, Inc.*,[450] the Little League had sought to bar females from participating in its baseball program for children aged 8 to 12. This policy was justified by the assertions that females are physiologically inferior and that the psychological balance of children required sexual segregation. These justifications were, however, rejected, when the court concluded that they were not supported by any evidence in the record. The evidence that was in the record, the court said, indicated that there was no reasonable basis upon which females could be excluded from playing baseball. Lacking such a basis, the sex policy was unlawful. Specifically, the court stated that the purpose of recent efforts to provide sexual equality as a legal reality have been designed "mainly to emancipate the female sex from stereotyped conceptions of its limitations embedded in our *mores* but discordant with current rational views as to the needs, capabilities and aspirations of the female, child or woman." [451] A similar view was expressed in *Darrin v. Gould*,[452] where two high school girls had been prohibited from playing on their school's football team by a sex rule of the state athletic association. This rule was said to be justified by the facts that most girls cannot compete with boys in football and the risk of injury for girls is greater than for boys. In holding that these reasons would not justify the rule, the court observed that

> [b]oys as well as girls run the risk of physical injury in contact football games. The risk of injury to 'the average boy' is not used as a reason

447. 364 F. Supp. 1212 (W.D. Pa. 1973), *vacated and remanded,* 497 F.2d 921 (3d Cir. 1974). *See also* Fortin v. Darlington Little League, Inc., 376 F. Supp. 473 (D.R.I. 1974), *rev'd,* 514 F.2d 344 (1st Cir. 1975).

448. *See* § 1.14.

449. 364 F. Supp. at 1217.

450. 127 N.J. Super. 522, 318 A.2d 33 (1974). It should be noted that the case arose under a public accommodations law, N.J. STAT. ANN. § 10:5-1 *et seq.* (Supp. 1974), which precludes denial of public accommodations on the basis of, *inter alia,* sex. Such statutory provisions are considered in § 2.22.

451. 318 A.2d at 38-39. In King v. Little League Baseball, Inc., 505 F.2d 264 (6th Cir. 1974), the court held that a complaint failed to state a cause of action since the plaintiff female was playing, but did not even mention the fact that baseball was a contact sport. It is to be noted that the federal charter of Little League Baseball, *see* § 1.14, has recently been amended to make it clear that its provisions apply to "young people" and not simply to "boys." Pub. L. No. 93-551, 88 Stat. 1744 (1974). *See* Rappaport v. Little League Baseball, Inc., 65 F.R.D. 545 (1975) (dismissing suit as moot after Little League adopted this policy). This amendment was said in Fortin v. Darlington Little League, Inc., 514 F.2d 344 (1st Cir. 1975), to imply "a finding by [the Little League] that girls are capable of playing Little League baseball without undue risk." *Id.* at 350. *See also* H.R. REP. No. 93-1409, 93rd Cong., 1st Sess. 2 (1974).

452. 85 Wash. 2d 859, 540 P.2d 882 (1975).

for denying boys the opportunity to play on the team in interscholastic competition. Moreover, the fact that some boys cannot meet the team requirements is not used as a basis of disqualifying those boys that do meet such requirements.[453]

The court then held that the rule could not be used to deprive the complainants of the right to participate as members of the football team. Although the case was specifically decided on the basis of the state Equal Rights Amendment (ERA), the court clearly suggested that it would have reached the same conclusion under the Fourteenth Amendment.[454]

The basic thrust of *National Organization for Women* and *Darrin v. Gould* is that where there is no proof that females are less able than males to compete in contact sports, they may not be excluded on the basis of assumptions concerning their physical ability. These views are consistent with those which have been expressed in other areas involving the use of sex-based classifications. For example, the cases that have arisen under Title VII of the Civil Rights Act of 1964,[455] have held, for purposes of the "bona fide occupational qualification" exception to the Act's prohibition against sex discrimination,[456] that females may not be precluded from performing certain tasks because of their presumed lack of physical stamina.[457] The same views have been expressed by the Supreme Court.[458]

453. *Id.* at 892. The court also found the suggestion that the rule was necessary to prevent disruption of the girls' program to be without any factual basis since the school had no contact football program for females, and because this fear had not stopped the association from allowing females to compete in non-contact sports.

454. *Id.* at 893. Such a step was taken in Clinton v. Nagy, 411 F. Supp. 1396 (N.D. Ohio 1974), in which a temporary restraining order was issued to allow a 12 year old female to participate in a football program. *See also* Hoover v. Meiklejohn, 430 F. Supp. 164 (D. Colo. 1977) (females allowed to participate in soccer); Carnes v. Tennessee Secondary School Athletic Ass'n, 415 F. Supp. 569 (E.D. Tenn. 1976) (baseball); Commonwealth v. Pennsylvania Interscholastic Athletic Ass'n, 18 Pa. Commw. Ct. 45, 334 A.2d 839 (1975), *noted in* 14 DUQUESNE L. REV. 101 (1975) (court invalidated a sex rule on the basis of the state ERA, and specifically included wrestling and football since "it is apparent that there can be no valid reason for excepting those sports from our order . . . .").

455. 42 U.S.C. § 2000e *et seq. See generally* Annot., 12 A.L.R. FED. 15 (1972).

456. *See* 42 U.S.C. § 2000e-2(e)(1). The "bona fide occupational qualification" exception provides that

> Notwithstanding any other provision of this subchapter, (1) It shall not be an unlawful employment practice for an employer to hire and employ employees, . . . on the basis of his [or her] . . . sex, ... where . . . sex . . . is a bona fide occupational qualification reasonably necessary to the normal operation of that particular business or enterprise . . . .

457. Thus, in Weeks v. Southern Bell Telephone Co., 408 F.2d 228 (5th Cir. 1969), the court observed that an employer seeking to defend such a rule

> would have us "assume," on the basis of a "stereotyped characterization" that few or no women can safely lift 30 pounds, while all men are treated as if they can. While one might accept, *arguendo,* that men are stronger on the average than women, it is not clear that

458. *See* notes 392-400 *supra.* In *Frontiero v. Richardson,* for example, the Court held that sex classifications are abhorrent because

> the sex characteristic frequently bears no relation to ability to perform or contribute to society. As a result statutory distinctions between the sexes often have the effect of invidiously relegating the entire class of females to inferior legal status without regard to actual capabilities of its individual members. 411 U.S. at 686-87.

See also Schlesinger v. Ballard, 419 U.S. 498, 95 S. Ct. 572, 42 L. Ed. 2d 610 (1975); Berkelman v. San Francisco Unified School Dist., 501 F.2d 1264 (9th Cir. 1974) (use of sexual stereotypes prohibited).

Darrin v. Gould also suggests the possibility of a broader principle that females may be excluded from athletic competition only on the basis of their own ability. The court expressed support for the proposition earlier suggested in *Brenden* that even if there was a basis for the conclusion that females as a class are less able than males, eligibility to compete in athletic events could be based only upon an individualized determination of ability to play, regardless of sex.[459] This proposition would appear to be consistent with the direction of employment discrimination cases involving women,[460] and would certainly be the result under the ERA. As noted in *Darrin v. Gould,* where the state constitution contained an ERA provision, discrimination on the basis of sex would be forbidden by that rule.[461] Although it is not yet clear whether ability will become the sole basis of classification, it would appear that the courts are certainly headed in that direction.

The use of ability as the criterion for selection is, in any event, the ultimate test whenever it is concluded that females must be given an opportunity to compete for a position on a team, since the Fourteenth Amendment requires only that females be given the same opportunity to qualify for competition as possessed by males, but does not require that they be utilized if their skills are inferior.[462] Even this proposition may, however, be subject to some question. If it were shown, for example, that females in an institution were given complete freedom to try out for male teams, but that few actually competed, there might then be a question as to whether the Equal Protection Clause would require that funds used for athletics purposes be allocated between males and females in such a manner as to provide equality of competitive opportunity.

any conclusions about relative lifting ability would follow. This is because it can be argued tenably that technique is as important as strength in determining lifting ability. Technique is hardly a function of sex. *Id.* at 235-36.

See also Griggs v. Duke Power Co., 401 U.S. 424 (1971); Pond v. Braniff Airways, Inc., 500 F.2d 161 (5th Cir. 1974); Rosenfeld v. Southern Pacific Co., 444 F.2d 1219 (9th Cir. 1971); Bowe v. Colgate Palmolive Co., 416 F.2d 711 (7th Cir. 1969); Nance v. Union Carbide Corp., 397 F. Supp. 436 (W.D.N.C. 1975); Kober v. Westinghouse Electric Corp., 325 F. Supp. 467 (N.E. Pa. 1971); Utility Workers Local 246 v. Southern California Edison Co., 320 F. Supp. 1262 (C.D. Calif. 1970). *See generally Developments in the Law — Employment Discrimination and Title VII of the Civil Rights Acts of 1964,* 84 HARV. L. REV. 1109 (1971); Annot., 12 A.L.R. FED. 15 (1972). Cases involving non-Title VII issues have reached a similar conclusion. *See* Smith v. City of East Cleveland, 363 F. Supp. 1131 (N.D. Ohio 1973); Hardy v. Stumpf, 37 Cal. App. 3d 958, 112 Cal Rptr. 739 (1974); Sontag v. Bronstein, 33 N.Y.2d 197, 351 N.Y.S.2d 389, 306 N.E.2d 405 (1973).

These cases are considered in the sex discrimination in athletics context in Brenden v. Independent School Dist. 742, 477 F.2d 1292, 1300-02 (8th Cir. 1973); Bucha v. Illinois High School Ass'n, 351 F. Supp. 69, 75 (N.D. Ill. 1972) (held to be inapplicable).

459. *See* notes 409-410 *supra.*

460. *See* notes 455-457 *supra.*

461. 540 P.2d at 893. *See also* Freund, *The Equal Rights Amendment Is Not the Way,* 6 HARV. CIV. LIB. — CIV. RTS. L. REV. 234, 238 (1971); Comment, *Sex Discrimination in High School Interscholastic Athletics,* 25 SYRACUSE L. REV. 535, 571 (1974).

462. Thus, in Commonwealth v. Pennsylvania Interscholastic Athletic Ass'n, 18 Pa. Commw. Ct. 45, 334 A.2d 839 (1975), the court observed that

[i]f any individual girl is too weak, injury-prone, or unskilled, she may, of course, be excluded from competition on that basis but she cannot be excluded solely because of her sex without regard to her relevant qualifications. *Id.* at 843.

The court then went on to indicate that its order would also cover the contact sports of football and wrestling. *See also* Fortin v. Darlington Little League, Inc., 514 F.2d 344 (1st Cir. 1975); Hoover v. Meiklejohn, 430 F. Supp. 164 (D. Colo. 1977).

In addition to the basic theory provided by the Equal Protection Clause, sexual classifications in amateur athletics may also be attacked through the provisions of Title IX of the Education Amendments of 1972,[463] which provide basically, that "[n]o person . . . shall, on the basis of sex, be excluded from participation in, be denied the benefits of, or be subjected to discrimination under any education program or activity receiving federal financial assistance. . . ."[464] Although it was originally unclear whether the provisions of Title IX applied to athletics, it was specifically made applicable to intercollegiate athletics in 1974.[465] The sanction for non-compliance with the non-discrimination requirements of Title IX is a loss of federal aid to the institution in question.[466] The statute does not as such provide an additional civil remedy for violations of its requirements — that is, a means for private persons to require conformity or seek damages for violations. While there is authority that might be utilized as a means for establishing such a remedy,[467] the courts have to date held that no such remedy exists.[467.1]

The language of the statutory provisions in Title IX is ambiguous and does not indicate what factors will be considered in determining when prohibited discrimination will be present in general or how it will be determined specifically with respect to athletic programs. This ambiguity was to be resolved by the promulgation of rules and regulations by the Department of Health, Education, and Welfare. These regulations have now been adopted,[468] and have been the center for a storm of controversy both as adopted and in their earlier drafts.[469] Inasmuch as females have not had a prominent part in many aspects of intercollegiate or interscholastic athletics in the past, one might have anticipated that the regulations would be rather detailed and precise in terms of defining what athletic departments must do in order to comply with the congressional mandate. Unfortunately, this has not been the case.

---

463. 20 U.S.C. § 1681-86 (Supp. III, 1973). For a detailed analysis of these requirements, see Cox, *Intercollegiate Athletics in the Wake of the HEW Regulations Under Title IX of the 1972 Education Amendments,* 46 GEO. WASH. L. REV. 34 (1977). *See generally* Buek & Orleans, *Sex Discrimination — A Bar to Democratic Education: Overview of Title IX of the Education Amendments of 1972,* 6 CONN. L. REV. 1 (1973); Koch, *Title IX and the NCAA,* 3 WEST. ST. L. REV. 250 (1976); Kuhn, *Title IX: Employment and Athletics are Outside HEW's Jurisdiction,* 65 GEORGETOWN L.J. 49 (1976); Comment, *Title IX's Promise of Equality of Opportunity in Athletics: Does It Cover the Bases?,* 64 KY. L. REV. 432 (1976); Comment, *HEW's Regulations Under Title IX of the Education Amendments of 1972: Ultra Vires Challenge,* 1976 B.Y.U. L. REV. 133; Note, *Sex Discrimination and Intercollegiate Athletics,* 61 IOWA L. REV. 420, 458-84 (1975).

464. 20 U.S.C. § 1681(a) (Supp. III, 1973).

465. Education Amendments of 1974, Pub. L. No. 93-380, § 844, 88 Stat. 484. Doubts as to coverage in the original enactment were reflected in the comments of Senator Bayh in the legislative history that "[w]e are not requiring that intercollegiate football be desegregated nor that the men's locker room be desegregated." 117 CONG. REC. 30407 (1971). Similar provisions have been adopted in some states, specifically dealing with sex discrimination in the athletic programs of publicly supported schools. *See, e.g.,* CALIF. LEGISLATIVE SERVICE ch. 789, 802, 838 (1975).

466. 20 U.S.C. § 1682 (Supp. III, 1973).

467. *See, e.g.,* Lau v. Nichols, 414 U.S. 563, 39 L. Ed. 2d 1, 94 S. Ct. 786 (1974). *See generally* Comment, *Title IX of the 1972 Education Amendments: Preventing Sex Discrimination in Public Schools,* 53 TEX. L. REV. 103, 120-21 (1974); AMERICAN CIVIL LIBERTIES UNION, SEX DISCRIMINATION IN ATHLETICS AND PHYSICAL EDUCATION, attach. 5, at 3-4 (1975).

467.1. *See* Cannon v. University of Chicago, 406 F. Supp. 1257 (N.D. Ill. 1976).

468. 40 FED. REG. 24,128 (June 4, 1975). As originally proposed, the Regulations appeared in 39 FED. REG. 22,232 (June 20, 1974).

469. These various controversies are explored in some depth in *Hearings, supra* note 440.

The regulations require that recipients of federal financial assistance (which is defined to include any public or private institution to which federal assistance is extended directly or indirectly and which receives or benefits from such assistance) [470] must conduct their athletic programs in such a manner that "[n]o person shall, on the basis of sex, be excluded from participation in . . . or otherwise be discriminated against in any interscholastic, intercollegiate, club or intramural athletics . . . ." [471] Although this basic requirement might be broad enough to impose the same requirements that the courts have imposed upon athletic programs through the Equal Protection Clause of the Fourteenth Amendment, the regulations do not go so far. They specifically provide that an institution may have separate teams for each sex where selection "is based upon competitive skill or the activity involved is a contact sport." [472] If separate teams are not maintained, and if athletic opportunities for the sex in question have previously been limited, then members of the sex for whom a team is not maintained must be allowed to try-out for the team *unless* it is a contact sport.[473] For these purposes, contact sports are defined to include boxing, wrestling, rugby, ice hockey, football, basketball and other sports involving bodily contact.[474] These provisions fall short of the view of some courts under the Equal Protection Clause that females may not be excluded from contact sports solely upon the basis of stereotypes concerning their physical ability and stamina as a class.[475]

To the extent that the regulations reach less far than do recent decisions on the subject, they could be said to fall short of the congressional purpose in enacting Title IX. As noted, the statutory provisions require that there shall be no discrimination on the "basis of sex." Presumably, Congress intended to preclude the same types of discrimination based upon stereotyped sexual classifications that the courts have banned under equal protection rubric. In defense of the breadth of the regulations, however, it must be kept in mind that Title IX poses a much more significant sanction than do remedies under the Equal Protection Clause. If Title IX requirements are violated, the institution may lose its federal financial assistance, while if equal protection requirements are not met, the result will in almost all cases be merely to allow a complaining person to participate or try-out for a given athletic team. The courts have not required the creation of new teams; they have only required that existing teams be open to all persons who are, absent sexual classifications, eligible. Thus, the

---

470. Reg. § 86.11.
471. Reg. § 86.41(a).
472. Reg. § 86.41(b).
473. Reg. § 86.41(b).
474. Reg. § 86.41(b).
475. Although these provisions of the Regulations could be read to state that an institution could preclude females from participating in contact sports by not maintaining a separate female team, since they could not try-out for the male team (a conclusion that seems to flow naturally enough from the language of Reg. § 86.41(b)), the interpretation that HEW has placed upon them is apparently to the contrary. Thus, in a memorandum which discusses the changes between the proposed and adopted provisions, it is said that

> an institution would be required to provide separate teams for men and women in situations where the provision of only one team would not 'accommodate the interests and abilities of members of both sexes.' This provision, of course, applies whether sports are contact or non-contact. 40 Fed. Reg. 24,134 (June 4, 1975).

Title IX regulations may appropriately seek to reach less far, but require more (in the sense of equal financial and program support) for the equality that it mandates.

The determination of whether equal opportunity has been provided by an institution, in those areas where it must be made available, will be determined by a list of several factors:

(i) Whether the selection of sports and levels of competition effectively accommodate the interests and abilities of members of both sexes;
(ii) The provision of equipment and supplies;
(iii) Scheduling of games and practice time;
(iv) Travel and per diem allowance;
(v) Opportunity to receive coaching and academic tutoring;
(vi) Assignment and compensation of coaches and tutors;
(vii) Provision of locker rooms, practice and competitive facilities;
(viii) Provisions of medical and training facilities and services;
(ix) Provisions of housing and dining facilities and services;
(x) Publicity.[476]

An additional factor will be the level of funding for the programs for each sex. Although the regulations specifically state that unequal aggregate expenditures for each sex or for male and female teams in the same sport will not constitute non-compliance, they do provide that the "failure to provide necessary funds" will be considered.[477] Absent some indication of what will constitute the provision of "necessary" funds, this last requirement is ambiguous. It is particularly troublesome because of the varying financing arrangements that are present in many educational institutions. At any given institution, financial support may include gate receipts, radio and television revenues, legislative appropriation, voluntary or mandatory student fee check-offs, and alumni contributions.

Without specific guidance on how these several factors will be considered to determine whether equal opportunity is present, those who are consulted for advice on how to comply with the letter and spirit of the regulations are left in a rather difficult position. The safest course, absent some indication to the contrary, would be to initiate a program to insure that all of the listed factors are provided on as close to an equal basis as possible by the date when compliance is mandatory.[478] With respect to funding, the provision of "necessary funds" would appear to be that level of funding which will provide equal opportunity in each of the listed factors. Although this would not necessarily require equal expenditures either on an absolute or team by team basis, it would certainly require the allocation of a substantial part of the athletic budget. It is unclear, however, what the budget level of an athletic department will be for purposes of the regulations. Given the various financing arrangements that are present in intercollegiate athletics, the budget capability for purposes of the

476. Reg. § 86.41(c). There is also a specific provision requiring proportional allocation of scholarships. Reg. § 86.37(c). This laundry list of items is intended to be illustrative only and not preemptive of other factors that HEW may wish to consider. *See* 40 Fed. Reg. 24,134.

477. Reg. § 86.41(c).

478. The Regulations specify that for secondary or postsecondary institutions compliance shall be "as expeditiously as possible but in no event later than three years from the effective date of this regulation." Reg. § 86.41(d). HEW has also taken the position, however, that it will seek earlier compliance "wherever possible." 40 Fed. Reg. 24,135.

regulations could be drawn in many different ways, but there is no guidance on how this will be accomplished. The most likely position will be that all funds, from whatever source, will be considered in determining whether the "necessary funds" have been provided.[479]

Although the specific requirements of Title IX are not yet clear, it is apparent that it will have potentially far reaching effect upon athletics in educational institutions. It is also likely to have a strong influence on the courts in cases which do not directly involve its provisions, in light of the strong public policy favoring sexual desegregation of sports that it reflects.[480] Whether it will have the destructive effect upon existing structures that has been widely proclaimed is a question that must wait the passage of time. The regulations that have been promulgated do indeed induce some concern over what exactly is required to meet their letter and spirit (a concern that may be allayed by ruling positions in the future), but they generally reflect the policy expressed in the statute itself that sexual classifications have no place in the athletic programs of educational institutions.

§ 1.23. Marriage.

Rules have frequently been adopted which exclude married persons from participating in interscholastic athletics.[481] The policy considerations which are cited in their support generally include the following:

1. Married students assume new and serious responsibilities. Participation in extracurricular activities tends to interfere with discharging these responsibilities.
2. A basic education program is even more essential for married students than for non-married students. Therefore, the married students' full attention should be given to the school program in order that he or she may achieve success.
3. Teenage marriages are on the increase. Marriage prior to the age set by law should be discouraged. Excluding married students from extracurricular activities may tend to discourage early marriages.
4. Married students need to spend time with their families in order that the marriage will have a better chance of being successful.
5. Married students are more likely to drop out of school. Hence, marriage should be discouraged among teenage students.

---

479. An amendment to delete from the revenues subject to Title IX those from so-called "revenue sports" (primarily football, basketball and ice hockey) was not adopted either in 1972 or 1974. *See* 40 Fed. Reg. 24,134.

480. *See, e.g.,* Brenden v. Independent School District 742, 477 F.2d 1292 (8th Cir. 1973). *See also* Comment, *Sex Discrimination in Interscholastic High School Athletics,* 25 SYRACUSE L. REV. 535, 567 (1974); Gilbert and Williamson, *Women in Sport: A Progress Report,* SPORTS ILLUSTRATED, July 29, 1974, at 27.

481. A typical rule will provide, simply, that "[m]arried pupils, either male or female, shall attend classes only and not be required to attend study hall. They may not participate in extracurricular activities." Moran v. School District No. 7, Yellowstone County, 350 F. Supp. 1180 (D. Mont. 1972). Regulation of married students is generally considered in Bolmeier, *Board of Education's Right to Regulate Married Students,* 1 J. FAMILY LAW 172 (1961); Goldstein, *The Scope and Sources of School Board Authority to Regulate Student Conduct and Status: A Nonconstitutional Analysis,* 117 U. PA. L. REV. 373 (1969); Knowles, *High School, Marriage, and the Fourteenth Amendment,* 11 J. FAMILY LAW 711 (1972); Comment, *Marriage vs. Education: A Constitutional Conflict,* 44 MISS. L.J. 248 (1973); Annot., 11 A.L.R.3d 996 (1967).

6. The personal relationships of married students are different from those of non-married students. Non-married students can be unduly influenced as a result of relationships with married students.

7. Married students may create school moral and disciplinary problems, particularly in the informal extracurricular activities where supervision is more difficult.[482]

8. If married students were present in locker rooms, the discussion would center around their sexual experiences. Hence, exclusion of married students will prevent locker room discussion of sex.[483]

The married student exclusion rules have generally been upheld,[484] though the courts have tended to rely upon the reasons noted above and the rubric of private association law,[485] rather than analyzing whether they are proper exercises of rule-making authority.[486] Unless it could be shown that the rules were directly related to a legitimate objective of the rule-making organization, they would not be authorized. Even if they were authorized it would also have to be shown that they were reasonable—that is, that they affected only those whose conduct it was necessary to control. Thus, if it were shown that the rules were necessary to insure that married students meet academic requirements, they would not be reasonable if, in addition to barring academically weak students, they also barred married students with a sound academic record. The rules must be narrowly drawn and may not be written so broadly as to snare those whose conduct need not be controlled.[487]

Notwithstanding the nonconstitutional inquiry, consideration of the marriage rules will focus primarily upon their constitutionality, which will involve at least two different principles. The first is the Equal Protection Clause of the

---

482. Board of Directors of Independent School Dist. of Waterloo v. Green, 259 Iowa 260, 147 N.W.2d 854 (1967). *See also* Moran v. School Dist. No. 7, Yellowstone County, 350 F. Supp. 1180 (D. Mont. 1972).

483. Wellsand v. Valparaiso Community Schools Corp., Cause No. 71 H 122(2) (N.D. Ind. 9/1/71); Romans v. Crenshaw, 354 F. Supp. 868 (S.D. Tex. 1971).

484. Board of Directors of Independent School Dist. of Waterloo v. Green, 259 Iowa 260, 147 N.W.2d 854 (1967); Estay v. LaFourche Parish School Bd., 230 So. 2d 443 (La. App. 1969); Cochrane v. Board of Educ. of Mesick Consol. School Dist., 360 Mich. 390, 103 N.W.2d 569 (1960); State *ex rel.* Baker v. Stevenson, 270 Ohio Op. 223, 189 N.E.2d 181 (1962); Kissick v. Garland Independent School Dist., 330 S.W.2d 708 (Tex. Civ. App. 1959); Starkey v. Board of Educ. of Davis County School Dist., 14 Utah 2d 227, 381 P.2d 718 (1963).

485. These rules are considered at § 1.14.

486. *See* § 1.15.

487. Thus, in Indiana High School Athletic Ass'n v. Raike, — Ind. App. —, 329 N.E.2d 66 (1975), *noted in* 52 N.D.L. Rev. 593 (1976), the court observed that a married student rule

is both over- and under-inclusive.
The classification is over-inclusive in that it includes some married students of good moral character who would not corrupt the morality of their fellow students or contribute to an unwholesome atmosphere.
It is under-inclusive in that it includes neither unmarried high school students who participate in athletics as team members, student managers or trainers, and yet may engage in premarital sex nor unmarried high school students who may be of a depraved nature, all of whom are as likely to be a corrupting influence as married high school students.
The classification simultaneously catches too many fish in the same net and allows others to escape. 329 N.E.2d at 77.

See generally Goldstein, *The Scope and Sources of School Board Authority to Regulate Student Conduct and Status: A Nonconstitutional Analysis,* 117 U. PA. L. REV. 373 (1969) (which uses married student rules as an example in analyzing several aspects of the rule-making function and its review by the courts).

Fourteenth Amendment,[488] which has been used by several courts to invalidate marriage rules.[489] In *Moran v. School District No. 7, Yellowstone County,* [490] for example, a school district had adopted a rule which precluded married students from participating in extracurricular activities and applied it to preclude a student, who had been lawfully married, from participating in high school athletics. In considering the permissibility of the rule under the Equal Protection Clause, the court noted that the school district would have a heavy burden in attempting to establish the predicate for its validity, that the ordinary reasons set forth for its adoption were unpersuasive, and that the rule was probably invalid. Although *Moran* did not as such declare the marital non-participation rule to be unconstitutional under the Equal Protection Clause,[491] other courts have made that decision.[492]

The second constitutional principle that militates against marital non-participation rules is that of substantive due process, which precludes the deprivation of fundamental rights and liberties.[493] Although the Bill of Rights does not as such specify a right to marry, the Supreme Court has recognized the right to marital privacy,[494] and this recognition might provide a basis for a substantive due process attack on marriage exclusion rules. The primary case applying this principle has been *Davis v. Meek,*[495] where a city board of education had adopted a rule that precluded married students, or males who contributed to pregnancy out of wedlock, from participating in extracurricular activities. The rule was then applied to prevent a star high school baseball player from competing, and he brought suit to stop enforcement of the rule. In granting that relief the court found that the rule was probably invalid, and observed that

> it seems clear that the effect of the enforcement of the rule which the defendants have promulgated under the color and authority of the state laws, is to put what may be an unendurable strain upon the plaintiff's marriage. This Court feels that it can not escape the obligation to protect from invasion by the power of the state that right to marital privacy . . . [which is] protected by the Constitution. What greater invasion of marital privacy can there be than one which could totally destroy the marriage itself?
> . . . .
> The defendants should not be faulted for trying, by the adoption of their rule, to discourage child marriages. Unfortunately, the laudable purposes of their rule fails to take into account the extremely limited deterrent value of punishment in areas where action is mainly governed

---

488. The parameters of the Equal Protection Clause are considered in detail at § 1.15.

489. *See* O'Neill v. Dent, 364 F. Supp. 565 (E.D.N.Y. 1973), Holt v. Shelton, 341 F. Supp. 821 (M.D. Tenn. 1972), *noted in* 22 BUFFALO L. REV. 634 (1973); 40 TENN. L. REV. 268 (1973).

490. 350 F. Supp. 1180 (D. Mont. 1972).

491. The reason for not declaring it invalid, was that the motion actually being considered asked only for a preliminary injunction, and resolution of that motion would not require a final decision; Indiana High School Athletic Ass'n v. Raike, — Ind. App. —, 329 N.E.2d 66 (1975).

492. Hollon v. Mathis Independent School Dist., 358 F. Supp. 1269 (S.D. Tex. 1973); Holt v. Shelton, 341 F. Supp. 821 (M.D. Tenn. 1972); Wellsand v. Valparaiso Community Schools Corp., Cause No. 71 H 122(2) (N.D. Ind. 9/1/71); Romans v. Crenshaw, 354 F. Supp. 868 (S.D. Tex. 1971).

493. *See* § 1.15.

494. Griswold v. Connecticut, 381 U.S. 479, 14 L. Ed. 2d 510, 85 S. Ct. 1678 (1965). *See also* Cleveland Bd. of Educ. v. La Fleur, 414 U.S. 632, 39 L. Ed. 2d 52, 94 S. Ct. 791 (1974); Roe v. Wade, 410 U.S. 113, 35 L. Ed. 2d 147, 93 S. Ct. 705 (1973).

495. 344 F. Supp. 298 (N.D. Ohio 1972), *noted in* 22 BUFFALO L. REV. 634 (1972).

by emotion. What the rule does, as distinguished from what it is intended to do, is to punish the one who has not been deterred at all even by the immediate prospect of the punishment, much less by the example it is supposed to offer.[496]

In light of these principles, the decisions upholding marriage-exclusion rules may no longer represent authoritative precedent.

§ 1.24. Race.

The most pernicious restrictions on who may participate in amateur athletics are those which have attempted to classify athletes according to their race. With regard to the maintenance of racially separate systems of education, of which interscholastic athletics are but a part,[497] there are few things in the law clearer than that such action is in violation of the Equal Protection Clause of the Fourteenth Amendment.[498] Racial classifications may be based only upon a compelling state interest, because classification by race is the most suspect of the "suspect criteria" which invokes the protection of the strict standard of review.[499]

The leading case dealing with racial classifications in sports is *Wesley v. City of Savannah,*[500] where a private golf association limited participation in an amateur golf tournament played for the city championship on a municipally owned course to its own membership, which was open to only white persons. Although the golf association was allegedly private, the court found that its activities were the product and remainder of a state-imposed system of racial segregation in the use of publicly owned recreational facilities and, thus, clearly sufficient for state action purposes.[501] In finding that the exclusion of blacks from the tournament violated the Equal Protection Clause, the court relied principally upon cases which have held that the exclusion of blacks from publicly owned recreational facilities is unlawful.[502] The court's opinion, however, was actually very narrow, inasmuch as it did not require that blacks be admitted to the association on the same basis as whites and did not hold that all of the association's tournaments on publicly owned courses be open to blacks. It held only that when a private association conducts an amateur tournament for the city championship on a public golf course, the tournament must be open to blacks and whites alike.[503]

A similar result was reached in *Louisiana High School Athletic Association v. St. Augustine High School,*[504] where the white state athletic association had

---

496. *Id.* at 302.

497. Kelley v. Metropolitan County Board of Educ. of Nashville, 293 F. Supp. 485 (M.D. Tenn. 1968). *See* § 1.11.

498. Brown v. Board of Educ. of Topeka, 347 U.S. 483, 98 L. Ed. 2d 873, 74 S. Ct. 686 (1954).

499. Loving v. Virginia, 388 U.S. 1, 18 L. Ed. 2d 1010, 87 S. Ct. 1817 (1967); McLaughlin v. Florida, 379 U.S. 184, 13 L. Ed. 2d 222, 85 S. Ct. 283 (1964).

500. 294 F. Supp. 698 (S.D. Ga. 1969).

501. The "state action," and other Equal Protection Clause requirements, are considered in detail at § 1.14.

502. These cases, and the theories underlying their result, are considered in detail at § 2.11; *see also* § 2.22.

503. 294 F. Supp. at 702.

504. 396 F.2d 224 (5th Cir. 1968).

arbitrarily refused to admit an all-black private high school to its membership, although the school had complied with all admission requirements. In affirming the district court's order requiring an immediate admission to membership, the court held that the vote denying membership was in fact arbitrary [505] and racially motivated, and that the association should be enjoined from engaging in any activity which discriminates against any school by reason of the race, creed or color of its students or faculty.[506]

Where racial classifications are found in state-related athletic activities, then, they will ordinarily be held to be in violation of the Equal Protection Clause of the Fourteenth Amendment. If such a classification results in separate athletic systems, moreover, the systems will be directed to merge.[507]

§ 1.25. Drugs.

In light of the increasing concern over the use of drugs in amateur athletics,[508] attention should also be given to the circumstances under which rules forbidding the use of drugs will be permissible.[509] The purpose of such rules would be to protect the health and well-being of the athletes subject to the rule and to prevent over-zealous persons from administering drugs to athletes in an effort to increase their athletic performance. In order for such a rule to be within an organization's authority, it would have to be proven that there was a factual basis for the purposes suggested. If it could be shown, for example, that there was a danger to athletes or that drugs were being used to artificially stimulate performance, then the purposes identified would be likely to support a legitimate objective to which the rules could be related. A rule would be reasonable so long as it affected only those persons whose conduct it is necessary to control. Thus, if a rule is narrowly drawn and affects those who are proven to have used or administered a drug which in fact detrimentally affects athletic competition, it will be reasonable. But if it affects persons whose conduct need not be the subject of control, because either they did not use or administer drugs or the drugs used cannot be proven to affect competitive activities, then it will not be reasonable.

A particular drug rule must also be constitutional. The primary basis upon which a drug rule might be constitutionally infirm is its use of presumptions—for example, a presumption that a coach or trainer is responsible for the presence of drugs in the blood of athletes under their direction or control. Such presumptions may be unconstitutional as a result of the limitations imposed by the due process clauses of the Fifth and Fourteenth Amendments upon the presuming of one fact from the proof of another fact. Although no such presumptions have yet been presented in situations involving amateur athletes,

---

505. The court defined "arbitrary" to mean "a vote to deny membership to an applicant which has met proper and reasonable membership requirements and standards as defined by the Association." *Id.* at 228.

506. *Id.* at 226.

507. Lee v. Macon County Bd. of Educ., 292 F. Supp. 363 (M.D. Ala. 1968).

508. *See Hearings Before the Senate Subcomm. to Investigate Juvenile Delinquency of the Senate Comm. on the Judiciary,* 93rd Cong., 1st Sess. (1973) (Proper and Improper Use of Drugs by Athletes).

509. *See* § 1.15.

there is a substantial body of law dealing with drug rule presumptions in the area of professional animal racing.[510]

The constitutional permissibility of a drug rule may also be raised by the inclusion of a provision requiring that athletes submit to blood or saliva testing. Such a testing procedure might be challenged under the Fourth Amendment's prohibition of unreasonable searches and seizures and the Fifth Amendment's privilege against self-incrimination, though the Supreme Court has indicated that such testing procedures are permissible, at least in criminal proceedings, so long as they constitute only minor personal intrusions and are conducted under proper medical supervision.[511]

§ 1.26. Spectator Disturbances.

An additional element of amateur athletic regulation involves the regrettably prevalent problems caused by spectator disturbances at athletic events. The athletic regulatory problems created by such disturbances deal primarily with whether a school's athletic team may be punished for the actions of its supporters. It will be noticed that this issue focuses upon rules which may be applied to schools or teams as opposed to athletes. Although the interests of a school or team are not quite identical to those of the athlete, the following discussion will utilize the same basic principles that have been identified with respect to rules relating to athletes. The authority of an athletic association to act with respect to such entities will in most cases be drawn from the same sources and invoke the same limitations as arise with respect to athletes.[512]

It is common for an athletic association to have a rule which provides that a team (or school) will be held responsible for the conduct of its own supporters, regardless of where the event may take place. Such a rule would be within a rule-maker's authority to the extent that it is shown to be directly related to a legitimate objective of the rule-maker, such as eliminating disturbances or turmoil at the events it sanctions. The rules will also be reasonable to the extent that they affect only those entities whose conduct it is necessary to control — that is, the team or school whose supporters are responsible for the disturbance.[513]

Even if a spectator disturbance rule is found to be authorized and a reasonable exercise of authority, it must also be constitutional. The primary constitutional issue that may be raised by a spectator disturbance rule is whether it contains sufficient standards of required conduct to meet due process requirements. The

---

510. *See* § 2.07.

511. Schmerber v. California, 384 U.S. 757, 16 L. Ed. 2d 908, 86 S. Ct. 1826 (1966). It should also be noted that drug questionnaires have been held to be unconstitutional invasions of the privacy of those questioned. Merriken v. Cressman, 364 F. Supp. 913 (E.D. Pa. 1973). *Merriken v. Cressman* also suggests the consent question that may be present in such cases. See § 2.07 n. 3.1.

512. *See, e.g.,* Kelley v. Metropolitan County Bd. of Educ. of Nashville, 293 F. Supp. 485 (M.D. Tenn. 1968).

513. School Dist. of City of Harrisburg v. Pennsylvania Interscholastic Athletic Ass'n, 453 Pa. 495, 309 A.2d 353 (1973); Watkins v. Louisiana High School Athletic Ass'n, 301 So. 2d 695 (La. App. 1974). In Taylor v. Alabama High School Athletic Ass'n, 336 F. Supp. 54 (M.D. Ala. 1972), a disturbance case was dismissed as a result of the court's conclusion that the right to participate was not protectible. The reasons why this aspect of *Taylor* may not be authoritative are considered at § 1.11.

necessity of such standards is suggested by *Kelley v. Metropolitan County Board of Education of Nashville*,[514] where spectators representing each of two teams in a post-season high school basketball tournament had created a substantial disturbance. At the end of the game, the cheering section of the victorious team rushed onto the playing area to congratulate their team, while the vanquished team's fans created confusion by improperly exiting the field. There was also evidence that fans from the losing team struck and verbally abused the referees and congregated in hallways and ramps and there engaged themselves in chanting and physical abuse of other fans. As a result of these acts, the losing team was subsequently suspended from all interscholastic competition for a period of one year by the school board. Although the board found that the school had failed to provide proper supervision, there were no rules which specified the conduct of spectators that the schools were required to enforce. In the absence of such pre-existing standards, the court concluded that the suspension was improper:

> [t]he imposition of penalties in the absence of prescribed standards of conduct is contrary to our basic sense of justice. The requirement that the official personnel of a public school shall have responsibility for the conduct of fans and spectators at an athletic contest itself carries a heavy burden and can be justified only on the basis of practical necessity. The burden is compounded when the penalty may entail the denial of athletic benefits to an entire group regardless of individual blamelessness. If group responsibility of such magnitude is to be upheld, no great inconvenience or burden is imposed upon a state agency by requiring it to specify the standards and rules to guide the actions of its subordinates and to delineate forms of punishment for the violation of such rules. Without some guiding standards the possibilities of arbitrary action are increased and individual interests are likely to suffer.[515]

If appropriate standards are provided, then the school will be advised of the conduct that will be required of its supporters and the punishment that will result from a failure to meet the conduct standards.

§ 1.27. Tournament Classifications.

In order to organize tournaments and other forms of championship competition, various teams or schools competing therein are often classified according to enrollment, geographic location or some other basis. So long as such classification efforts provide an equality of competitive opportunity between those being classified, they would not seem to be subject to attack. Where, however, the classification results in a disparity of competitive opportunity, it may be subject to challenge. The leading case dealing with an analogous situation is *Baltic Independent School District No. 115 v. South Dakota High School Activities Association*,[516] where two qualifying tournaments were held in South Dakota to determine which high school teams should participate in a national debating tournament. One tournament was sponsored by the same

---

514. 293 F. Supp. 485 (M.D. Tenn. 1968).
515. *Id.* at 493-94. The case also involved other procedural issues, which are considered in § 1.28.
516. 362 F. Supp. 780 (D.S.D. 1973).

organization which conducted the national tournament, while the other was conducted by a state high school organization which certified a winner to the national tournament. The state organization-sponsored tournament divided schools into two classes, "A" and "B", according to enrollment size, and only the winner of the "A" class had ever been certified for the national tournament. The effect of this classification was to give "A" schools two opportunities to qualify for the national tournament — by winning the qualifying tournament sponsored by the national organization or the one sponsored by the state organization — while the "B" schools had only one opportunity — through the qualifying tournament sponsored by the national organization. When the enrollment classification was challenged, the state organization argued that it was justified by the fact that it would achieve "fairer competition among classes [of schools] by enabling smaller schools to compete against schools of equal ability." [517] The court, however, held that the rule was in violation of the Equal Protection Clause,[518] since it denied "fair competition" by giving larger schools two chances to qualify and smaller schools only one chance. The court noted that the students in each size school had similar qualifications and ability and that participation in the national tournament could have an important bearing upon college debate scholarships. The court reserved judgment on whether enrollment based classifications would be unconstitutional in all circumstances.

In light of *Baltic Independent School District No. 115,* it seems clear that the classifications of schools for tournament purposes must be carefully reviewed to insure equality of competitive opportunity. Where such equality is not present, the classification may be unlawful.

§ 1.28. Enforcement Activities in Amateur Athletics.

The enforcement of rules and regulations adopted by amateur athletic organizations will consist of several activities, which may be described as investigatory, prosecutorial and adjudicatory. Thus, when it is believed that improper acts have taken place, the organization will investigate the surrounding circumstances, and, if there are grounds for believing that such acts have occurred, it will then conduct such proceedings as are necessary for it to determine whether its rules, regulations or other requirements have been violated. The enforcement power will generally be commensurate with the power permitting their adoption. Thus, although an organization's authority will normally be broad, it will not have unbridled discretion, and its enforcement activities must be conducted in a fair, reasonable and constitutional manner.

Probably the most important aspect of amateur enforcement activities is the validity of the procedures that are utilized by the organization, which will be determined by the requirements of procedural due process.[519] The Due Process Clause of the Fifth and Fourteenth Amendments specifies that no person shall be deprived of "life, liberty, or property without due process of law." Whether

517. *Id.* at 784.
518. *See* § 1.15.
519. The present discussion focuses only upon the procedural aspects of enforcement proceedings. The scope of review of rules and regulations is considered at § 1.15 (public institutions or organizations) and § 1.15.1 (private institutions and organizations).

the procedures to which the deprived person has been subjected meet the rudiments of fair play required by the Due Process Clause will be determined by judicial consideration of the circumstances and interests involved in each particular case.[520]

In order to trigger the due process requirements, two facts must be present. The first is an act undertaken by the "state," and the inclusiveness of that term will be measured by the same standard that applies to the "state action" concept of the Equal Protection Clause.[521] The second factor is the deprivation of a right or interest that is sufficiently important to require constitutional protection.[522] The delineation of protected from non-protected interests was at one time measured by an elusive doctrine that distinguished between "rights" and "privileges," and which held that only the former were constitutionally protectible.[523] While some amateur athletics cases have indeed followed this rule,[524] the demise of the "right-privilege" distinction suggests that they may no longer have precedential value.[525] Although the range of protected interests has not been defined with precision, it is clear that the courts will no longer employ fictions or labels, such as the "right-privilege" distinction, but will, rather, seek to determine whether a particular interest has a "property" or "property-like" status.[526] Such a status will be present if the complainant can demonstrate a "legitimate claim of entitlement" to the benefit sought to be protected, stemming from an independent source such as state law.[527] In *Goss v. Lopez*,[528] for example, students had been suspended from a public high school, and a sufficient property interest was found in the "legitimate claims of entitlement to a public education." [529]

---

520. *See* notes 534, 545, 547 *infra.*

521. *See* § 1.15.

522. Behagen v. Intercollegiate Conference of Faculty Representatives, 346 F. Supp. 602 (D. Minn. 1972).

523. *See, e.g.,* United States *ex rel.* Knauff v. Shaughnessy, 338 U.S. 537, 94 L. Ed. 317, 70 S. Ct. 309 (1950).

524. *See, e.g.,* State *ex rel.* Baker v. Stevenson, 27 Ohio Op. 2d 223, 189 N.E.2d 181 (Common Pleas 1962); Starkey v. Board of Educ. of Davis County, 14 Utah 2d 227, 381 P.2d 718 (1963).

525. Graham v. Richardson, 403 U.S. 365, 374, 29 L. Ed. 2d 534, 91 S. Ct. 1848 (1971); Reed v. Nebraska School Activities Ass'n, 341 F. Supp. 258 (D. Neb. 1972). *See generally* Van Alstyne, *The Demise of the Right-Privilege Distinction in Constitutional Law,* 81 HARV. L. REV. 1439 (1968).

526. Board of Regents of State College v. Roth, 408 U.S. 564, 33 L. Ed. 2d 548, 92 S. Ct. 2701 (1972); Brenden v. Independent School Dist. 742, 477 F.2d 1292 (8th Cir. 1973).

527. In defining the range of protected interests, the Supreme Court in *Roth* observed that the Fourteenth Amendment prevents a person from being deprived of life, liberty or property without due process of law, and stated that

> Certain attributes of "property" interests protected by procedural due process emerge from these decisions. To have a property interest in a benefit, a person clearly must have more than an abstract need or desire for it. He must have more than a unilateral expectation of it. He must, instead, have a legitimate claim of entitlement to it. It is a purpose of the ancient institution of property to protect those claims upon which people rely in their daily lives, reliance that must not be arbitrarily undermined. It is a purpose of the constitutional right to a hearing to provide an opportunity for a person to vindicate those claims.
>
> Property interests, of course, are not created by the Constitution. Rather they are created and their dimensions are defined by existing rules or understandings that stem from an independent source such as state law — rules or understandings that secure certain benefits and that support claims of entitlement to those benefits. 408 U.S. at 577.

See also Goss v. Lopez, 419 U.S. 565, 42 L. Ed. 2d 725, 95 S. Ct. 729 (1975).

528. 419 U.S. 565, 42 L. Ed. 2d 725, 95 S. Ct. 729 (1975).

529. *Id.* at 573.

With respect to amateur athletics, there is not yet a clear answer as to whether the interest of athletes (or institutions) in athletic participation will qualify as "property." As noted in the earlier discussion of this point, some courts have found a sufficient "entitlement" by viewing athletic participation as a part of the educational process (or as having economic significance). Many other courts, however, have concluded that the interest is not entitled to constitutional protection.[530] In this connection, it is important to observe that the Supreme Court appears to have recently adopted a rather restrictive view of the "entitlement" requirement,[531] and this may influence the lower courts to restrict the types of interests that will be accorded "property" status.

Constitutional protection will also be required if the action in question deprives an individual of "liberty." The liberty interest arises when "a person's good name, reputation, honor, or integrity is at stake because of what the government is doing to him. . . ." [532] Although this interest has not played a large part in the reported sports cases, suspensions or other administrative sanctions could certainly damage the athlete's standing and future opportunities in athletics.[533]

If it is determined that the interest in question is subject to due process protection, the next inquiry will be to determine what process is due. Before reviewing the types of procedures that may be required prior to the deprivation of constitutionally protected interests, it must be noted that the degree of procedural formality that will be required by the Due Process Clause is an area that is not clearly resolved. During the sixties and early-seventies, the courts (especially the lower federal courts) had tended to view due process expansively to require relatively elaborate procedures. In its most recent cases, however, the Supreme Court has indicated a more rigid view. In several cases, it has ruled that the procedures required for due process purposes may, where appropriate, be limited to those that are specified in the source of the interest in question.[533.1] In light of this perceptible shift in emphasis, it is difficult to articulate even the general standards that may be required to provide the requisite degree of procedural regularity. Accordingly, the following discussion will focus upon the basic principles that have been evolved by the courts over the past ten to fifteen years, though it should be kept in mind that the discussion may reflect more stringency than will actually be required in the future if the Court continues to relax the due process standards. We think that this type of presentation is appropriate because it reflects existing precedent, in the lower courts, and

---

530. *See* § 1.11.

531. *See, e.g.,* Bishop v. Wood, 426 U.S. 341, 96 S. Ct. 2074, 48 L. Ed. 2d 684 (1976).

532. Wisconsin v. Constantineau, 400 U.S. 433 (1973); *see also* Board of Regents of State College v. Roth, 408 U.S. 564, 572-73, 33 L. Ed. 2d 548, 92 S. Ct. 2701 (1972). The scope of the "liberty" interest has recently been restricted by the Court. Bishop v. Wood, 426 U.S. 341, 96 S. Ct. 2074, 48 L. Ed. 2d 684 (1976) (non-public reasons for discharge of police officer not affecting liberty interest); Paul v. Davis, 424 U.S. 693, 96 S. Ct. 1155, 47 L. Ed. 2d 405 (1976) (reputation alone does not imply "liberty" interest). *See also* Colorado Seminary v. National Collegiate Athletic Ass'n, 417 F. Supp. 885 (D. Colo. 1976).

533. *See* Goss v. Lopez, 419 U.S. 565, 95 S. Ct. 729, 42 L. Ed. 2d 725 (1975).

533.1. *See e.g.,* Dixon v. Love, 431 U.S. 105, 97 S. Ct. 1723, 52 L. Ed. 2d 172 (1977); Arnett v. Kennedy, 416 U.S. 134, 94 S. Ct. 1633, 40 L. Ed. 2d 15 (1974). *See generally* Van Alstyne, *Cracks in "The New Property": Adjudicative Due Process in the Administrative State,* 62 CORNELL L. REV. 445 (1977); Comment, *Democratic Due Process: Administrative Procedure After Bishop v. Wood,* 1977 DUKE L.J. 453.

because the unsettled nature of law in this area will require the passage of several years before clear precedent becomes available.

In order to determine the procedures that will be required by the Due Process Clause, the courts will balance the interests of the respective parties, including such factors as the importance of the jeopardized interest, the type of proceeding in which the interest is presented, the appropriateness of the procedure requested to prevent the arbitrary deprivation of a protected interest, and the costs of requiring such a procedure.[534] The seriousness of the sanction imposed may also be considered.[535]

Although the balancing process may demonstrate the necessity of specific procedures in particular circumstances, the basic requirement of procedural due process is that before any action may be taken, the affected person must be given a "fair hearing," which will include, in essence, notice and a hearing.[536] The degree of formality in the notice will depend upon the seriousness of the offense in question. When significant interests are at stake, the notice should recite the time and place of hearing, as well as a statement of the specific charges and the grounds which, if proven, would justify the imposition of a sanction, and should be given sufficiently in advance of the date of the hearing as to allow time for the preparation of a proper defense.[537] Although the nature

534. *See* Board of Regents of State College v. Roth, 408 U.S. 570, 33 L. Ed. 2d 548, 92 S. Ct. 2701 (1972); Joint Anti-Fascist Refugee Committee v. McGrath, 341 U.S. 121, 163, 95 L. Ed. 847, 71 S. Ct. 624 (1951) (Frankfurter, J., concurring).

535. *Compare* Kelley v. Metropolitan County Bd. of Educ. of Nashville, 293 F. Supp. 485 (M.D. Tenn. 1968) (strict procedural protection required for "drastic" sanction of suspension of school's entire athletic program) *with* School Dist. of the City of Harrisburg v. Pennsylvania Interscholastic Athletic Ass'n, 453 Pa. 495, 309 A.2d 353 (1973) (lesser procedures sufficient for probationary sanction). *See also* Goss v. Lopez, 419 U.S. 565, 576, 42 L. Ed. 2d 725, 95 S. Ct. 729 (1975) ("the length and severity of a deprivation, while a factor to weigh in determining the appropriate form of a hearing, 'is not decisive of the basic right' to a hearing of some kind"); Ingraham v. Wright, 525 F.2d 909, 918 n. 10 (5th Cir. 1976), *aff'd,* 430 U.S. 651 (1977).
The process that will be utilized by a court to determine the procedures required is illustrated by *Goss v. Lopez, supra,* in which students in a public high school had been suspended for a period of 10 days without any hearing. The Court first held that the nature of the students' interests required due process protection. With respect to the specific procedures that must be utilized for such short suspensions, the Court observed that due process would require at the very least that the students "be given *some* kind of notice and afforded *some* kind of hearing," but that the specific nature of the notice and hearing would depend upon an appropriate accommodation of the interests involved. *Id.* at 579 (emphasis in original). After noting the interests of the school in taking appropriate disciplinary measures and of the students in not being unfairly deprived of their ability to attend school, the Court held that in such short suspension situations a "student must be given oral or written notice of the charges against him, and, if he denies them, an explanation of the evidence the authorities have and an opportunity to present his side of the story." *Id.* at 581. *See generally* Kirp, *Proceduralism and Bureaucracy: Due Process in the School Setting,* 29 STAN. L. REV. 841 (1976). *But cf.* Ingraham v. Wright, 430 U.S. 651 (1977) (notice and hearing not required prior to imposition of corporal punishment).

536. Dixon v. Alabama State Bd. of Educ., 294 F.2d 150, 159 (5th Cir. 1961), *cert. denied,* 368 U.S. 930, 7 L. Ed. 2d 193, 82 S. Ct. 368 (1961).

537. Due process will also require that persons whose conduct is to be made subject to administrative regulation be warned in advance that sanctions will be applied to specified types of conduct. *See* discussion of *Kelley* in § 1.26. Thus, in Wright v. Arkansas Activities Ass'n, 501 F.2d 25 (8th Cir. 1974), the court held that a coach's due process rights had been violated when an association sought to punish him for beginning football practice before a specified date, without ever having warned him that such action might result in a specific sanction being applied to him. *See also* Regents of University of Minnesota v. National Collegiate Athletic Ass'n, 560 F.2d 352 (8th Cir. 1977) (no need for actual knowledge of violation at time of conduct).

of the hearing itself will depend upon the circumstances of each particular case,[538] it must enable the decision-maker to hear both sides of the situation, and should entail the rudiments of an adversary proceeding. Thus, in cases involving significant potential penalties, it may be necessary that the affected person be accorded the right to counsel, given a list of the charges that are to be presented, provided with a list of the names of, and facts to be elicited from, adverse witnesses, and be allowed to undertake reasonable discovery activities.[539] Once the hearing has been held, the findings and conclusions which are rendered may have to be presented in a written report that is available for inspection. In short, the person subjected to enforcement activities should have the opportunity to appear, be heard and make an intelligent and informed defense to the proferred charges.[540] With respect to these various procedural rights, it is important to emphasize again that not all of the rights will be required every time a sanction is imposed. For example, if an athlete failed to observe a coach's rule requiring "hustle" and was suspended for one game, the only procedural steps that would appear to be required would be that the coach advise the athlete of his finding and give the athlete an opportunity to respond.

538. Howard Univ. v. National Collegiate Athletic Ass'n, 367 F. Supp. 926 (D.D.C. 1973), *aff'd*, 510 F.2d 213 (D.C. Cir. 1975).

539. Esteban v. Central Missouri State College, 277 F. Supp. 649, 651-52 (W.D. Mo. 1967). In summarizing the procedural due process requirements, it has been stated that the essential elements of a fair procedure include (but may not be limited to) the following:

(1). Serious disciplinary action may not be taken in the absence of published rules that: (a) are not "so vague that men of common intelligence must necessarily guess at its meaning and differ as to its application;" and (b) do not depend upon the unqualified discretion of a particular administrator for their application.

(2). Where the rules are reasonably clear and their application does not depend upon uncontrolled discretion, a student still may not be seriously disciplined (as by suspension) unless: (a) the student charged with an infraction has been furnished with a written statement of the charge adequately in advance of a hearing to enable him to prepare his defense (for example, ten days); (b) the student thus charged "shall be permitted to inspect in advance of such hearing any affidavits or exhibits which the college intends to submit at the hearing"; (c) the student is "permitted to have counsel present . . . at the hearing to advise [him]"; (d) the student is "permitted to hear the evidence presented against him" or at least "the student should be given the names of witnesses against him and an oral or written report on the facts to which each witness testifies"; (e) the student "(not his attorney) may question at the hearing any witness who gives evidence against him"; (f) those who hear the case "shall determine the facts of each case solely on the evidence presented at the hearing. . . ."; (g) "the results and findings of the hearing should be presented in a report open to the student's inspection"; (h) "either side may, at its own expense, make a record of the events at the hearing."

Van Alstyne, *The Judicial Trend Toward Student Academic Freedom*, 20 U. FLA. L. REV. 290, 295-96 (1968). Additional aspects of procedural due process are considered at § 2.18.

540. Thus, in Behagen v. Intercollegiate Conference of Faculty Representatives, 346 F. Supp. 602 (D. Minn. 1972), the court stated that

[p]laintiffs should be given a written notice of the time and place of the hearing at least two days in advance. Accompanying such notice should be a specification of the charges against each, and the grounds which, if proven, would justify imposition of a penalty. The hearing should be such that the Directors of Athletics have an opportunity to hear both sides of the story. This does not require a full-dress judicial hearing, with the right to cross-examine witnesses. However, it should include the presentation of direct testimony in the form of statements by each of those directly involved relating their versions of the incident. Plaintiffs should be given a list of all witnesses who will appear, and should be allowed a written report specifying the Directors' findings of fact, and if there is to be any punishment the basis for such punishment. The proceedings should be recorded, and the tapes should be made available to plaintiffs in the event they wish to appeal . . . . If these minimal standards are followed in cases of this nature, it is this Court's opinion that the requirements of due process will have been met. *Id.* at 608.

There would be no need for a formal hearing and its various procedural trappings. In short, the procedural rights noted above would all apply only in situations where rather serious charges and potential penalties are involved.

The type of procedural steps that may be required in an amateur athletics enforcement situation, where a constitutionally protected interest is present, is illustrated by *Behagen v. Intercollegiate Conference of Faculty Representatives*,[541] in which two star college basketball players had been suspended after a brawl during a game between the University of Minnesota and Ohio State University, on January 25, 1972, in which several players and spectators were injured. Shortly after the fight committees from both the Big Ten conference and the University of Minnesota faculty undertook an investigation of the incident. The Commissioner of the Big Ten conducted his investigation by interviewing participants and other persons who were present, and viewing films of the game. He did not, however, provide the players who were suspended with an opportunity to appear and be heard in defense of charges made against them, although the conference procedures required such steps. The Commissioner then consulted with a committee from the University of Minnesota which had also investigated the incident. On January 28, it was agreed that the university would suspend the two players from further athletic competition for the remainder of the season, pending further investigation (which suspension was imposed on that date). On January 31, the conference concluded that the suspension should preclude participation in practice sessions. On February 1, the University of Minnesota appealed the conference's decision, but the decision was affirmed on that same date. The University committee then reopened its investigations on February 4, and on February 10 lifted its earlier suspension, concluding that it had contained "significant omissions regarding due process." On February 11, however, the Commissioner of the Big Ten suspended the players, which action he subsequently affirmed after a later reexamination, though he acted to convene an additional hearing before the Athletic Directors of all member-schools. At no time were the players given notice of any hearing, an opportunity to present their defense, or, indeed, notice that they were being investigated.

In evaluating the procedural permissibility of this action, the court considered only the procedures of the Big Ten. This was a two-step inquiry, inasmuch as there had been two suspensions: 1) the suspension from practice on January 31, and 2) the suspension on February 11. With regard to the first suspension, the court held that it violated the players' due process rights, because it involved a complete disregard of the conference's own procedures which would have given the players an opportunity to appear and be heard in their own defense.[542]

541. 346 F. Supp. 602 (D. Minn. 1972). *See also* Oklahoma High School Athletic Ass'n v. Bray, 321 F.2d 269 (10th Cir. 1963); Kelley v. Metropolitan County Bd. of Educ. of Nashville, 293 F. Supp. 485 (M.D. Tenn. 1968). *See generally* Note, *Judicial Review of Disputes Between Athletes and the National Collegiate Athletic Association*, 24 STAN. L. REV. 903 (1972).

542. *See also* United States *ex rel.* Accardi v. Shaughnessy, 347 U.S. 260, 98 L. Ed. 681, 74 S. Ct 499 (1954); Warren v. National Ass'n of Secondary School Principals, 375 F. Supp. 1043 (N.D. Tex. 1974); McDonald v. National Collegiate Athletic Ass'n, 370 F. Supp. 625 (C.D. Cal. 1974) (violation of due process for school to ignore its own procedures); Paglia v. Staten Island Little League, Inc., 38 App. Div. 2d 575, 328 N.Y.S.2d 224 (1971). *But cf.* Edwards v. Board of Regents of No. Western Mo. St. Univ., 397 F. Supp. 822 (W.D. Mo. 1975).

As to the second suspension, however, the court ruled that it was actually only a temporary suspension designed to preserve the status quo until a hearing before the Director of Athletics could be arranged. Such a suspension was, the court said, proper. It stated that it is consistent with the power of the commissioner to promote the general welfare of the conference that he have the authority to temporarily suspend players pending a properly assembled hearing. Such a suspension would violate due process only if it were imposed "arbitrarily and capriciously, and is in fact punitive." Since the second suspension was reasonable,[543] the court found it permissible so long as it continued no longer than would be reasonably necessary to convene the formal hearing — which it found would be not longer than 3 days from the date of its decision. Although the court's conclusion that the second suspension was proper seems somewhat incongruous in light of its decision as to the first suspension,[544] the impact of the incongruity is minimal in light of the fact that the second suspension would be dissolved unless a proper hearing were held within 72 hours.[545] Notwithstanding the court's sanction for short-term suspensions, the Supreme Court has recently indicated that such suspensions will normally require that the student in question be accorded minimal notice and hearing procedures, though even those steps will not be necessary where there is danger of disruption.[546]

543. In reaching the conclusion that the suspension in question was reasonable, the court observed that

> [i]t was reasonable for him [the Commissioner] to conclude that if the suspended players were permitted to participate in intercollegiate competition prior to a final determination of their case that other incidents might occur, regardless of model behavior on their parts or their best efforts to prevent them. The highly emotional aspects of the original altercation had been so fanned by needless post game comments of supposedly mature individuals and spectacular press coverage that the atmosphere surrounding the Minnesota basketball team was highly charged. 346 F. Supp. at 607.

544. The court justified the result by the fact that there was no need to conduct a hearing since it could assume that the earlier suspension would remain in force. In support of this result, it cited v. Metropolitan County Bd. of Educ., 293 F. Supp. 485 (M.D. Tenn. 1968), where the court had held a state high school athletic association's suspension of a school to be justified since the school had already been suspended by the local school board, though improperly, and it had told the principal that its hearing procedure was available if he wished a hearing, which he did not.

545. Short suspensions of students have frequently been upheld although not involving procedural due process safeguards, with the courts placing emphasis on the shortness of the suspension. Thus, in Fisher v. Rockland County P.S.A.L., 44 App. Div. 2d 552, 352 N.Y.S.2d 668 (1974), the court stated that "where the issue is interscholastic athletic eligibility, the exigencies of the sports schedule . . . permit a preliminary determination, and suspension, followed closely by an administrative conference. . . . *Id.* at 680. *See also* Murray v. West Baton Rouge Parish School Bd., 472 F.2d 438 (5th Cir. 1973); Greene v. Moore, 373 F. Supp. 1194 (N.D. Tex. 1974); Hanger v. State Univ. of N.Y. at Binghamton, 39 App. Div. 2d 253, 333 N.Y.S.2d 571 (1972) (suspension of student after fight in intramural basketball game).

546. With respect to such temporary suspensions, the Supreme Court has recently indicated that the due process safeguards may in fact be applicable. Thus, in Goss v. Lopez, 419 U.S. 565, 42 L. Ed. 2d 725, 95 S. Ct. 729 (1975), the Court held that before students could be suspended for 10 days or less they must be granted some form of notice and hearing. *Id.* at 581. It said that such notice and hearing could be held almost simultaneously with the conduct requiring suspension, but that the student be given an opportunity to explain his or her version of the facts and be advised of the accusations and their basis. The court also indicated that where the student's continued presence would pose a danger of disruption, notice and a hearing would not be necessary. *Id.* at 582-83. *Cf.* Sweet v. Childs, 518 F.2d 320 (5th Cir. 1975) (sufficient threat of disruption). Whether the factual situation in *Behagen* (see note 543 *supra*) would be within this exception is not yet clear. In any event, the temporary suspension cases must be viewed in light of *Goss v. Lopez*, which will require in most cases that some form of notice or hearing be given, even for short suspensions.

As indicated in *Behagen,* due process requirements are flexible, and will vary depending on the facts and circumstances which are present in any given case. Thus, in *Howard University v. National Collegiate Athletic Association,*[547] the court held that a university was not deprived of its rights by the failure of the investigating organization to disclose an investigation report or have witnesses present at a hearing, where the university did not contest the facts which underlay the alleged violation and had otherwise been given timely notice and a full and fair opportunity to defend itself. The court was careful, however, to note that "in some other context some type of confrontation with witnesses and/or access to investigative reports . . . might be required." [548]

Although the requirements of a full and fair hearing will depend on the facts and circumstances of each case, it is the specific elements that vary, not the applicability of the procedural due process concepts in general. The proposition that is applicable to enforcement proceedings in amateur athletics, in other words, comes down to this: 1) when a constitutionally protected interest is involved, 2) the rudiments of procedural due process must be applied when enforcement proceedings are instituted, and 3) the specific rudiments that will be required in any given case will depend upon its facts and circumstances. Due process formalities will not, however, be required if the interest in question is not entitled to protection,[549] and there is some question whether due process requirements will be applied in non-school related activities.[550]

With respect to procedural requirements in athletic controversies, it should be noted that the procedure followed by an athletic association to determine whether its rules and regulations have been violated may involve only the school which is its member, and not the athlete whose conduct may have precipitated the investigation. If a violation is found, the association may then impose a

---

547. 367 F. Supp. 926 (D.D.C. 1973), aff'd, 510 F.2d 213 (D.C. Cir. 1975).

548. *Id.* at 930-31. *See also,* O'Connor v. Board of Educ., 65 Misc. 2d 140, 316 N.Y.S.2d 799 (1970) (denial of athletic "letter" requires some due process safeguards). *But cf.* Southern Methodist Univ. v. Smith, 515 S.W.2d 63 (Tex. Civ. App. 1974) (in a questionable decision, the court held that a hearing was not required by a school which suspended an athlete where it would be futile since the NCAA had "unrestricted power" to make eligibility determinations).

549. The most apparent of these decisions is Taylor v. Alabama High School Athletic Ass'n, 336 F. Supp. 54 (M.D. Ala. 1972), where a school had been suspended from hosting or participating in invitational basketball tournaments for a period of one year following disruption of a tournament by its students. It appeared that the state high school athletic association had given notice to the principal of a hearing, but it did not specify the charges. It also appeared that the principal was not given a chance to present a defense at the hearing, and that the hearing conducted was in violation of the association's own rules. When these procedures were challenged, the court dismissed the action finding that the interest in participation was not constitutionally "protectible."

In light of *Kelley,* and of the discussion in § 1.11, *Taylor* certainly appears to be a questionable decision. *See also* Oklahoma Secondary School Activities Ass'n v. Midget, 505 P.2d 175 (Okla. 1972) (forfeiture of school's games because it used ineligible player upheld, although procedure in violation of association's own rules and regulations and not in accord with procedural due process, on the ground that principal had advised association of rule violation).

550. Where suspensions arise outside of public school oriented athletic associations, the procedural due process requirements may have no application, so that the propriety of the suspension may depend upon the rules and regulations of the entity in question. In Assmus v. Little League Baseball, Inc., 70 Misc. 2d 1038, 334 N.Y.S.2d 982 (1972), for example, the court held that due process requirements have no place in disputes arising in Little League athletic programs. But in Paglia v. Staten Island Little League, Inc., 38 App. Div. 2d 575, 328 N.Y.S.2d 224 (1971), the court overturned a suspension where the league had failed to follow its own procedures, which the court said was unlawful. *See* note 542, *supra.* Whether due process requirements should apply to organizations such as the Little League is considered in § 1.14 at note 167.

sanction upon the institution, and if the school does not take appropriate action with respect to the athlete additional sanctions may be imposed against it. Such a procedure raises the question of whether the athlete is entitled to procedural rights in the initial proceeding, even though he or she may not be a direct participant. The argument against granting the athlete such rights would emphasize that the institution, not the athlete, is involved in the association proceedings and that the institution need not take action against the athlete, though if it does not it may itself be sanctioned by the association. It would also be argued that the athlete may have no constitutionally protectible interest, so that there is no need for his or her participation. The athlete, on the other hand, would argue that he or she may have a protectible interest, at least in some circumstances, and that his or her rights are very much in question, since if a violation is found it is he or she who will feel the eventual punishment. Indeed, recent cases seem to confirm that the individual institution may have little real choice about complying with the association's decision, since failure may jeopardize its entire athletic program.[551]

The resolution of this issue is not yet clear. In *Parish v. National Collegiate Athletic Association,*[552] the NCAA applied sanctions to a college that had recruited athletes in violation of a grade-predicting rule,[553] and required that the college declare the athletes ineligible. The college, however, refused to impose this sanction on the athletes and brought suit against the NCAA. In connection with the question of the procedural rights of the athletes in the association-institution proceedings, the court noted that the college had not declared the athletes ineligible as it had been directed to do by the NCAA. This fact, the court said, obviated any need for answering the issue, since "the NCAA's responsibility for actions taken by the school in voluntary compliance with the association's mandate is not before us." [554]

The issue was given fuller consideration in *McDonald v. National Collegiate Athletic Association,*[555] which held that the athletes would have no procedural rights in the association-institution proceeding. It reached this conclusion by finding that the NCAA's action did not constitute "state action," so that it was not bound by the procedural due process requirements — a conclusion that rests upon a very weak base, since the court is alone in its conclusion that the NCAA's action does not constitute "state action." [556] It did, however, note that the athlete's interests would be significantly affected by the association hearing:

> [n]o one can deny that a declaration by the NCAA [or other such association] regarding an infraction of its rules, which declaration may affect the eligibility of a particular athlete to participate in intercollegiate sports, is a vital interest to the athlete. It affects his interscholastic athletic career and — depending upon his skills — can be of significant concern to his livelihood as a professional athlete.[557]

---

551. *See, e.g.,* Howard Univ. v. National Collegiate Athletic Ass'n, 510 F.2d 213 (D.C. Cir. 1975); Parish v. National Collegiate Athletic Ass'n, 506 F.2d 1028 (5th Cir. 1975).
552. 506 F.2d 1028 (5th Cir. 1975).
553. These rules are considered in § 1.21.
554. 506 F.2d at 1034 n. 16. *See also* Howard Univ. v. National Collegiate Athletic Ass'n, 510 F.2d 213 (D.C. Cir. 1975) (athlete failed to take advantage of procedures available to him).
555. 370 F. Supp. 625 (C.D. Cal. 1974).
556. *See* § 1.14 and notes 521-31 *supra.*
557. 370 F. Supp. at 631.

The court also concluded that before the school could declare the athletes ineligible, it must accord them procedural rights.[558]

Since the court in *McDonald* concluded that the athletes must receive procedural protection in the institution's decision-making process, it is possible that it would have reached the same result for the NCAA's proceedings if it had concluded (as have all other cases) that the NCAA's action is "state action." This resolution of the issue would resolve the inevitable dilemma that will be faced by institutions which have been directed to declare an athlete ineligible. Since the institution may have a contractual obligation to the association to take such action, and may be subjected to additional sanctions by the association if it does not, it will be under substantial pressure to do so. But the view expressed in *McDonald,* as well as the other authority considered in this section, may mean that the institution will have a constitutional duty to give the athlete procedural protections before doing so. If in this process it is determined that additional facts not presented in the association-institution proceeding require that the athlete not be punished, then the institutional decision-makers will be in a precarious position indeed. If they do not declare the athlete ineligible, the institution may face additional (contractual) sanctions from the association, but if it does make such a declaration, it might violate its constitutional duties to the athlete. In light of this potential dilemma, it has been suggested that the athletes should be given procedural rights in the initial proceeding.[559]

The presence of dual association and institutional hearing procedures may also raise the further question of whether the association can, consistent with constitutional requirements, compel the institution to declare an athlete ineligible *if* the institution's proceedings result in a finding that the athlete should not (or may not) be punished. This could theoretically pose a similar conflict between the contractual duty of the institution to follow the association's directive and its constitutional duty to the athlete. While the resolution of this issue is also not clear, it would appear that the institution's public constitutional duty would take precedence over its private contractual obligation if reasonable evidence is generated by its proceedings that there has been no violation. This was the result suggested by the court in *Regents of the University of Minnesota v. National Collegiate Athletic Association,*[560] where the institution had held hearings after being directed by the NCAA to declare the athletes in question ineligible. The hearings resulted in findings that the pertinent rules had been technically violated, but that there were mitigating circumstances that should preclude any penalty, and the university refused to follow the NCAA's directive. The court found that the institution could have followed the directive without violating its constitutional duties, since its hearings had provided sufficient evidence that the athletes had violated the rules (notwithstanding the mitigating factors). Accordingly, it was not required to

---

558. *Id.* at 631-32.

559. *See generally* Note, *Judicial Review of Disputes Between Athletes and the National Collegiate Athletic Association,* 24 STAN. L. REV. 903, 923-24 (1972) (concluding that the athlete should have procedural rights in the association-institution proceeding: "[i]t is the NCAA that has ruled that an athlete was not qualified to participate in athletics; and in making that determination, it is the NCAA that should be required to provide procedural protections to the penalized athlete").

560. 560 F.2d 352 (8th Cir. 1977).

decide the issue, which would have arisen if the institutional proceedings had demonstrated a satisfactory basis for a finding of no violation. The court did, however, assume, without deciding, that the constitutional duty would prevail in the event of conflict. The court also noted that its resolution of the matter left institutions with the "sometimes difficult task of declaring individuals ineligible when facts are found which reasonably reflect proscribed conduct and with not declaring them ineligible when such facts are not found." [561] While this situation may contain the potential for inevitable conflict, the court observed (somewhat circularly) that the association's authority was of the utmost importance to the achievement of its goals and that this authority could be overridden by constitutional requirements only where there is, in fact, no basis for a conclusion that a violation was present (the determination of which could pose the serious dilemma for the institution).

An additional aspect of enforcement activities that may raise interesting questions relates to the availability of pre-hearing judicial relief to compel the investigating organization to follow appropriate procedures. This is important because if improper preliminary procedures are utilized, a party will be likely to suffer irreparable damage which will not be easily remedied, even though an ultimate suspension or other penalty may eventually be overturned for lack of requisite procedural formality.[562] Accordingly, it is important to determine the extent to which a person may be able to compel the investigating organization to conform its procedures to applicable due process requirements or, if it has already adopted procedures that conform to those requirements, compel adherence to those procedures.

The only case which has actually involved this question is *Louisiana State Board of Education v. National Collegiate Athletic Association*,[563] where the NCAA was investigating allegedly improper recruiting practices by the University of Southwestern Louisiana ("U.S.L."). The official procedure of the NCAA at that time specified that a Committee on Infractions would conduct a preliminary investigation, and if it were determined that an official inquiry was necessary, one would be initiated by a notification letter fully informing the school of the allegations, and of its opportunity to respond to the charges. If the Committee wished officials of the school to appear, such appearance would be accomplished at a mutually convenient time and place. When the official inquiry was complete, the Committee was to make a report to the NCAA Council, with a copy to the school, and the school was to be afforded an opportunity to appear before the Council to challenge the Committee's findings and evidence. In the case at hand, the NCAA had been advised of alleged violations by U.S.L., but in a letter informing the school of its preliminary investigation on October 18, 1971, the Committee did not identify the suspected infractions. On November 2, 1972, the school was advised that an official inquiry was necessary, and the Committee specified the alleged violations in a 31 page, single-spaced letter. This letter also stated that the school was to respond to the charges by December 13, and directed its representatives to appear at a meeting on December 19.

561. *Id.* at 372.
562. The agony of such an investigation is well illustrated by Kennedy, *427: A Case in Point*, Sports Illustrated, June 10, 1974, at 87, June 17, 1974, at 24.
563. 273 So. 2d 912 (La. App. 1973).

Believing that there was insufficient time to prepare a response, the school requested an extension. Although the extension to respond was granted until March 3, 1973, the December 19 appearance was not continued. On January 3, 1973, the school received notice from the Committee that the committee's report was complete and would be submitted to the Council on January 9, 1973, at which time the school could make a presentation of its case. Believing that six days was an insufficient period within which to prepare its case, the school sought an extension, and, when this was not granted, brought suit to enjoin the NCAA proceedings.

At the trial court level, the proceedings were enjoined until August 15, 1973. The basis of this decision was that the NCAA had disregarded its own official procedures because the scheduled proceeding would not have afforded the school a hearing at a "mutually convenient" time and place or given it a reasonable opportunity to present its own case and defense. In addition, the NCAA had not advised the school of all charges against it prior to the January 3 report. The trial court decision, however, was reversed on appeal.

The Court of Appeals cited three reasons for its reversal. The first was that an injunction could have been properly issued only if irreparable injury were shown by the school. Such a showing was not made by the school, the court said, because it had shown only that an injury was purely speculative since no hearing had as yet taken place and no penalties had been imposed.[564] While there can be little question that the need for an irreparable injury showing is a necessary pre-condition to the issuance of an injunction, the court's approach is far too wooden. If an investigating organization were allowed to proceed in violation of its own procedures, which the court did not question would happen in the present case, the standing of a school in the athletic community could well suffer severe and irreparable damage, since it would not be able to adequately respond to charges for which the organization had built support over a substantial period. Its recruiting activities could be severely jeopardized, as could other aspects of its athletic program.[565]

The court's second reason for reversal was an invocation of the traditional principle of private association law that a court will not interfere in the internal

---

564. The court stated these factors as follows:

The injunction was improvidently granted because USL failed to show irreparable injury. USL's allegations of injury were at best purely speculative and conjectural inasmuch as no hearing had taken place and no penalties had been imposed. The allegations in respondent's petition illustrate the prematurity of the trial court's actions. USL alleged that if ". . . the hearing is held, and/or if any violations of NCAA regulations are determined by the Council and/or any penalties are assessed against the University, its personnel or student athletes, grievous and irreparable damage will be done to those persons and the Institution." This barest of allegations cannot be held sufficiently precise or compelling to sustain the harsh remedy of injunctive relief. There is no showing that if the hearing is held, USL will suffer injury, much less irreparable harm. It may very well be that USL will be completely exonerated of any wrong doing following a hearing by the NCAA. Until it is determined that a definite penalty will be imposed, the threatened irreparable harm is not imminent but is merely possible. If possibilities of irreparable harm were sufficient to serve as the bases for injunctive relief, courts could be called upon in the future to enjoin investigations by the NCAA of possible rule violations even before charges were made. The logical extension of USL's argument surely points in that direction. The sine qua non is infinite. It is for this reason that courts will only extend injunctive relief when irreparable injury is imminent. 273 So.2d at 915.

565. See, e.g., California State Univ., Hayward v. National Collegiate Athletic Ass'n, 47 Cal. App. 3d 533, 121 Cal. Rptr. 85 (1975).

affairs of a private association except where fraud, prejudice or caprice could be shown.[566] Though the general rule of association law has been stated in these terms, it is usually not applied where an association fails to follow its own procedures, since the courts have commonly intervened to insure that procedural rules are followed.[567] Where the association is subject to constitutional requirements, the failure to follow its own rules may also constitute a violation of due process of law.[568] The clearest statement of this latter view in the sports cases has been in *Behagen v. Intercollegiate Conference of Faculty Representatives,*[569] where the court stated that "[i]t is elemental that action beyond the scope of a body's own procedural regulations is a violation of due process of law." [570] Finally, the court sought to premise its opinion on the "fact" that state and federal courts have defined the right to participate in athletics as a privilege which is not protected by the due process safeguards.[571] There is a respectable body of law that stands for this proposition, but it has not been universally adopted.[572] In short, the Court of Appeals' decision in *Louisiana State Board of Education* is subject to serious criticism. The NCAA had failed to observe its own procedures, and the school may have been entitled to the injunction to insure that its rights were not unnecessarily prejudiced by the NCAA's wrongful action, as the trial court had originally held.

In considering the enforcement process, attention should also be given to the extent to which courts will review factual determinations made by an athletic organization. The review will in most cases be rather narrow, since if appropriate procedural practices have been followed (either as a result of the organization's rules or due process requirements, or both), those practices should have the effect of facilitating full development of the controlling facts in question.[573] Such a procedural process will also aid in preventing action from being taken on the basis of unwarranted or mistaken factual conclusions.[574] Where

---

566. *See* § 1.14.

567. The reasons and grounds for such action are considered in *Developments in the Law — Judicial Control of Actions of Private Associations,* 76 HARV. L. REV. 983, 1021-26 (1963). *See also* § 3.10(c).

568. *See* note 542 *supra.*

569. 346 F. Supp. 602 (D. Minn. 1972). *Behagen* is discussed in detail at notes 541-545 *supra.*

570. *Id.* at 606. This view was also reflected in the well written dissenting opinion of Judge Fruge in *Louisiana State Board of Education.* In rejecting the majority's opinion, he stated that

> [a]pplicant [NCAA] cites a series of cases in an attempt to show that actions taken by a voluntary association are subject to judicial interference only where there is fraud, oppression, or bad faith, or where the laws of society or the law of the land is illegal. In all of those cases, the plaintiffs were asking the courts to pass on the *merits* of the action taken by the various associations involved. In all of the enumerated cases, the actions had been taken by the associations involved in *complete accordance with the procedural rules of the associations;* the actions were taken only after fair notice and a fair opportunity to be heard . . . .
> I agree with applicant that the general rule in this state is that courts will not interfere with the internal affairs of an association so as to settle disputes between the members on questions of policy, discipline, or internal government. However, I note that the District Judge applied the well-settled exception to that general rule: courts *will* interfere if the association's rules are not fairly and honestly administered.

571. 273 So. 2d at 916.

572. *See* § 1.11.

573. *See, e.g.,* Goss v. Lopez, 419 U.S. 565, 579-80, 42 L. Ed. 2d 725, 95 S. Ct. 729 (1975).

574. *See generally* McCormack, *The Purpose of Due Process: Fair Hearing or a Vehicle for Judicial Review,* 52 TEXAS L. REV. 1257 (1974).

appropriate procedural steps have been followed, the scope of a court's review should be limited to determining whether, on the basis of the record as a whole, the factual findings are supported by substantial evidence.[575] If proper procedural practices have not been followed, then the case should be returned to the athletic organization with instructions to conduct a satisfactory hearing.

The final aspect of the enforcement process in amateur athletics that should be considered involves the sanctions that may be imposed upon a person who is found to have violated organizational rules. The rules will normally specify the penalty, or range of penalties, that may be imposed, and in amateur athletics these will in almost all situations involve suspensions that bar athletes or their schools or teams from competing for a specified period of time. Such suspensions may in some cases be quite severe. In the case of an athlete, a suspension may cause permanent loss of eligibility, and a school suspension may apply to its entire athletic program, not simply to the sport in which a violation occurred.[576] When a sanction is imposed, especially where it is severe, an inevitable question is whether the courts will review its imposition, and if so what will be the appropriate scope of review.

With respect to the availability of review, the applicable principles are the same as applied to the issues that have been considered in this chapter.[577] The scope of review, however, is a much more difficult question. The question has received very little attention in the decided cases, but the broad principles that would guide its resolution seem rather clear. Throughout this discussion, the basic proposition has been that such action must be reasonable, either in terms of the objectives sought to be accomplished or the facts and circumstances of an individual case.[578] In light of this, it would seem that a sanction would be upheld so long as it is reasonably related to the purposes of the rule violated and the severity of the offender's conduct.[579] In *Howard University v. National*

---

575. Esteban v. Central Missouri State College, 290 F. Supp. 622, 630-31 (W.D. Mo. 1968), *aff'd* 415 F.2d 1077 (8th Cir. 1969), *cert. denied,* 398 U.S. 965 (1970); Florida High School Activities Ass'n v. Bryant, 313 So. 2d 57 (Fla. App. 1975). A similar standard is applied for the review of such factual findings on a nonconstitutional basis, Goldstein, *The Scope and Sources of School Board Authority to Regulate Student Conduct and Status: A Nonconstitutional Analysis,* 117 U. PA. L. REV. 373, 429 (1969), and for private law purposes. *Developments in the Law — Judicial Control of Actions of Private Associations,* 76 HARV. L. REV. 983, 1036-37 (1963). The broader parameters of a substantial evidence standard are considered at § 2.19.

576. With respect to the imposition of sanctions upon an entire team or school, it should be observed that such "group" sanctions are not as such a constitutionally forbidden form of punishment, though they may call for particularly close adherence to procedural safeguards. *See* Kelley v. Metropolitan County Board of Education of Nashville, 293 F. Supp. 485, 495 (M.D. Tenn. 1968).

577. *See* §§ 1.14, 1.15.

578. *See* §§ 1.12, 1.15.

579. Although there is very little authority dealing with the scope of review of sanctions imposed in such proceedings, it is worthwhile noting that a similar situation has existed in the area of review of criminal sentences. *See* Kadish, *Legal Norm and Discretion in the Police and Sentencing Process,* 75 HARV. L. REV. 904, 916 (1962). In the criminal area, however, there has recently been strong sentiment for providing review of sentences, since in many criminal cases the only disputed issue is the sentence that should be imposed upon an admittedly guilty defendant, and in the absence of review the trial judge would have virtually unrestricted discretion. In order to provide appropriate review, one suggestion has been that the scope of review of criminal sentences would be as follows:

> The authority of the reviewing court with respect to the sentence should specifically extend to review of:
> (i) the propriety of the sentence, having regard to the nature of the offense, the

Collegiate Athletic Association,[580] for example, a rule was interpreted by the NCAA to require permanent ineligibility to an athlete whose academic standing had been improperly certified. With respect to this sanction, the court observed that "[a] penalty need not be the best that might have been provided, but only reasonably related to the rule's purpose." [581] The deference that will be accorded to those who impose sanctions is underscored by the fact that the court approved permanent denial of eligibility to athletes who may not personally have engaged in any improper conduct. A violation occurred because the academic standing of the athletes had been improperly certified by some third person, presumably in the athletic department of the school attended.

§ 1.29. Legislative Intervention in Amateur Athletics.

As was suggested in the introductory discussion to this chapter, the most fundamental aspect of the development of a law of amateur athletics has been the evolution from what was essentially a system of private administrative regulation to a system that increasingly involves public supervision of the acts of the private administrators.[582] This has been primarily a result of the willingness of the courts to review the merits of the grievances of those who are affected by amateur athletics administrators — a subject that has consumed much of this chapter. Although there has not, as yet, been a perceptible effort by legislative bodies to exercise supervision over the administration of amateur athletics, this is probably not so much a result of lack of concern, as it is a lack of strong incentive. Many of the conflicts that are commonly perceived to be present in amateur athletics administration have been resolved by judicial action. Legislative action would be anticipated, therefore, only where specific problems are either not resolved by the courts or are resolved in a manner that is not satisfactory to the legislative body.

In considering the possibility of legislative action that will affect amateur athletics, it is possible to identify two separate situations in which such action may arise. The first would involve legislation that is intended to remedy problems that are prevalent in our society generally, but which are also present in amateur athletics. In this type of situation, the legislative scheme would be developed to remedy the general problem and would not be specifically geared

---

character of the offender, and the protection of the public interest; and
(ii) the manner in which the sentence was imposed, including the sufficiency and accuracy of the information on which it was based.

AMERICAN BAR ASSOCIATION PROJECT ON STANDARDS FOR CRIMINAL JUSTICE, APPELLATE REVIEW OF SENTENCES § 3.2 (1968). These standards embrace a much broader scope of review than is suggested in the text, but it may reflect the types of inquiries that a court would feel appropriate to consider in reviewing a sanction in an athletics context. Certainly the concerns that underlie the need for review in the criminal situation are not significantly dissimilar from those in the athletics situation. *See* Colorado Seminary v. National Collegiate Athletic Ass'n, 417 F. Supp. 885 (D. Colo. 1976); Note, *Judicial Review of Disputes Between Athletes and the National Collegiate Athletic Association,* 24 STAN. L. REV. 903, 922-23 (1972).

580. 510 F.2d 213 (D.C. Cir. 1975). *See also* Associated Students, Inc. v. NCAA, 493 F.2d 1251, 1256 (9th Cir. 1974).

581. *Id.* at 221. It has also been suggested that sanctions should not be imposed without giving the offending party procedural rights. Note, *supra* note 579, at 922-23.

582. *See* § 1.01.

to the problem as it exists in athletics. The scheme could, as a result, have a rather severe impact upon relationships in the athletics community. The primary example of such legislation is Title IX of the Education Amendments of 1972, which prohibits discrimination on the basis of sex in federally funded educational programs.[583] The regulations that have been adopted to implement the Title IX requirements have met with significant controversy in the sports area, and this is partly the result of their failure to take account of the nature of athletic affairs in educational institutions. Indeed, some collegiate athletics administrators have suggested that the regulations could precipitate the demise of major college athletics as they are now known. Although the ultimate effect of the regulations is not yet clear, it is apparent that when Title IX was passed its impact upon athletics received little analysis.[584] Similar developments could occur in the future if statutory schemes of general application are imposed upon amateur athletics.[585]

The second type of situation in which legislative action could affect amateur athletics involves legislation that is specifically designed to resolve athletics problems. No such legislation has yet been enacted, but there have been proposals which suggest the extent to which some legislators may find intervention necessary. These proposals relate to the disputes that have existed between the organizations which are primarily responsible for international competition of American athletes. The proposals will be reviewed here as a means of illustrating the scope of legislative activity that is possible. Although the specific problems and proposals may be unique to the international area, the prospect of legislative intervention is of broader significance. It suggests that Congress is not committed to perpetuating vested interests in the athletics community where it is felt that the public interest is not being served. Moreover, these developments indicate a very real possibility that if legislation is forthcoming it might take the form of direct federal control of some aspects of amateur athletics. Once such control is established it would, of course, be a rather easy step to include all areas of amateur athletic activity within its purview.

The perceived need for legislative intervention in the administration of international competition reflects concern for several separate, but related, problems. The first relates primarily to the United States Olympic Committee ("USOC"), which has under various names governed American participation in the Olympic Games since their revival in 1896 and which has operated under a federal charter since 1950.[586] The USOC is the sole organization recognized by the International Olympic Committee ("IOC") as the governing body for American participation in the Olympics. The problems which have apparently been posed by the USOC relate chiefly to the allegation that the Amateur Athletic Union ("AAU") has been able to control the USOC and effectively

583. *See* § 1.22.

584. This seems especially clear in light of the fact that Title IX did not specifically apply to athletics when it was first enacted, though such coverage was provided by subsequent amendment. *See* § 1.22.

585. This could, for example, occur with respect to the Fair Labor Standards Act, 29 U.S.C. § 201 *et seq.* (1970), and the Occupational Safety and Health Act, 29 U.S.C. § 651 *et seq.* (1970). *See generally* H. Appenzeller, Athletics and the Law 145-60 (1975).

586. Act of September 15, 1950, ch. 975, 64 Stat. 902, *codified at* 36 U.S.C. § 371-83 (1970).

preclude any rival organization from gaining either control or a stronger voice in USOC affairs.[587]

After hearing testimony on the problems relating to the USOC, the Senate Committee on Commerce concluded that the USOC had failed to meet its obligations to its members, athletes and the American public because (1) neither the public nor the athletes have any voice in USOC activities; (2) some national sports federations have used the USOC to insulate their own position from challenge; and (3) groups which received international recognition in some sports at the turn of the century have retained their recognition notwithstanding the fact that they no longer have viable programs in some of those sports.[588] The cumulative effects of these factors, the Committee said, were that individuals administering sports organizations were often not directly responsive to the athlete and that the organizations themselves were not responsive to public criticism because "their source of authority and power lies in their recognition by private international organizations, which are beyond the influence of the American people and the Congress." [589]

A second, but closely related, problem has involved the feuding that has been prevalent in the administration of international amateur athletics. It is apparently a widespread belief in Congress that the various organizations that control amateur athletics have failed to perform their assigned tasks in a manner that meets the needs of either the athletes or their supporters. Indeed, it has been suggested that these organizations have demonstrated "an inordinate capacity to engage in petty disputes coupled with a fierce determination to perpetuate their own rule over amateur sports." [590] The focus of these comments is the struggle that has been waged for most of this century between the AAU and the National Collegiate Athletic Association ("NCAA") for primacy of control of amateur athletics in this country. Although this is certainly not the place for a detailed discussion of that struggle,[591] a few brief comments are in

---

587. S. REP. No. 93-850, 93rd Cong., 2d Sess. 9 (1974) (hereinafter referred to as S. REP. No. 93-850). Indeed, as a result of the alleged control of the AAU, and the nature of its entrenchment, the National Collegiate Athletic Association withdrew from the USOC on October 25, 1972. *Id.* at 8.

588. Specifically, the Committee found that

First, neither the public nor the athletes governed by USOC rules have a voice in the selection of the organizations which rule individual amateur sports and control American participation in the international Olympic Games. Private, international groups make such basic decisions, with no possibility of the athletes or the public having a role in the selection process.

Second, once selected, some national sports federations have used their position to insulate themselves and the USOC from challenges by groups which believe they can better perform the function of a national sports federation. The USOC rules cited above are part of that effort.

Third, groups which received charters half a century ago, when they were the dominant organization in particular sports, have continued to be the controlling national sports federations, even though other groups have developed larger and more comprehensive programs in these sports. The AAU, with its eight sports (and sparse programs in many of them), is the most prominent example of this problem. S. REP. 93-850 at 10-11.

589. *Id.* at 11.

590. *See Hearings Before the Senate Comm. on Commerce,* 93rd Cong., 1st Sess. 3 (1973) (statement of Senator James B. Pearson). *See also* 119 CONG. REC. S1249-98 (daily ed. June 29, 1973) (comments of Senator James B. Pearson).

591. *See generally* S. REP. 93-850 at 12-17; S. REP. No. 93-380, 93rd Cong., 1st Sess. 14-19 (1973); S. REP. No. 89-753, 89th Cong., 1st Sess. 3-4 (1965); 120 CONG. REC. S8779-86 (daily ed. May 21, 1974);

order. Since the founding of the AAU in 1888, and the predecessor of the NCAA in 1905, the two organizations have competed for control. In the early days, the struggle was over basketball. The AAU claimed that it had primary jurisdiction and enforced its rules on college teams which, in order to maintain schedules, were compelled to play against amateur, non-school clubs. Since some of the clubs were not under the control of the AAU, athletes who competed against them were suspended by the AAU. The struggle between the organizations has continued from that day to the present. Its effect has been to create confusion as to who has what authority over whom, with the ineluctible consequence of impeding athletic competition. In recent years, the struggle has surfaced most frequently in the form of refusal by one organization to sanction meets, generally of international character, sponsored or endorsed by the other.[592] In an effort to mediate the impasse between the two organizations, President Kennedy in 1962 requested General Douglas MacArthur to attempt resolution, but he was unsuccessful.[593] The Senate in 1965 then resolved that the Vice President of the United States be authorized to appoint an independent sports arbitration panel to produce a final and conclusive settlement between the AAU and the NCAA.[594] Although both organizations agreed at the outset to abide by the decision of the arbitrators, the NCAA repudiated the report when it was made public in February, 1968.[595] In light of this century-long struggle, and the failure of earlier efforts to mediate or otherwise resolve it, many members of Congress concluded that the only remedy was for the federal government to intervene.[596]

After holding lengthy hearings which evoked considerable testimony on all of these factors, the Senate Committee on Commerce concluded that "it is no longer advisable to permit elements of the present amateur sports structure of the United States to continue without substantial reform . . . [and] that needed change will not come about voluntarily, nor will further efforts on the part of Congress to seek voluntary change be successful." [597] It is as a result of this overall conclusion, then, that the Committee favorably reported and the Senate

A. FLATH, A HISTORY OF RELATIONS BETWEEN THE NATIONAL COLLEGIATE ATHLETIC ASSOCIATION AND THE AMATEUR ATHLETIC UNION OF THE UNITED STATES (1964); Note, *The Government of Amateur Athletics: The NCAA-AAU Dispute,* 41 S. CAL. L. REV. 464 (1968).

592. The refusal has, predictably, led to lawsuits seeking to compel sanctioning. *See* Samara v. National Collegiate Athletic Ass'n, 1973 Trade Cases ¶ 74,536 (E.D. Va. 1973).

593. The effort to mediate the dispute by General MacArthur is described in detail by Colonel Earl Blaik, his principal assistant in the effort, in *Hearings Before the Senate Comm. on Commerce,* 89th Cong., 1st Sess. 272-87 (1965).

594. S. RES. 147, 89th Cong., 1st Sess. (1965). *See* S. REP. No. 753, 89th Cong., 1st Sess. (1965); *Hearings, supra,* note 590, at 190-94.

595. S. REP. 93-850 at 16. The sports arbitration panel appointed by Vice President Humphrey was chaired by Theodore W. Kheel, the respected labor negotiator, who later observed that "[d]ealing with the Teamster problem is nothing when compared with working with the NCAA and AAU." *See Hearings, supra* note 590, at 149 (attributed to Mr. Kheel by Senator James B. Pearson). The NCAA apparently rejected the decision on the grounds that it awarded total sanctioning power to the AAU. 120 CONG. REC. S8783 (daily ed. May 21, 1974).

596. S. REP. 93-850 at 16. The other reasons that produced a belief that federal intervention was necessary included the need for centralized information about sports facilities and sports medicine, health and safety. *Id.* at 18.

597. S. REP. 93-380 at 7. *See also* Ford, *In Defense of the Competitive Urge,* SPORTS ILLUSTRATED, July 8, 1974, 16, 18 (opinion of the then Vice President of the United States describing the struggle between the AAU and the NCAA as a "petty conflict," and the need for restructuring the USOC).

passed, the Amateur Athletic Act of 1974.[598] It was not, however, enacted into law. While a more detailed analysis of the Act has been undertaken elsewhere,[599] it is appropriate for our purposes to at least identify its structure and suggest the impact that it would have had upon the amateur athletics community.

The legislative objectives of the Act were to (1) create a public mechanism to insure that the right to manage Olympic sports goes to the most representative and capable private organizations, (2) protect the rights of amateur athletes to compete without arbitrary controls, (3) provide for the coordination of all amateur sports groups, and (4) create a national sports development program to stimulate athletic activity. In order to achieve these objectives, the Act would have established the Amateur Sports Board as an independent agency of the federal government with the power to issue charters in each Olympic sport to the sports organization which most satisfactorily met the requirements of the Act and the regulations established by the Board. It would have protected the rights of amateur athletes by establishing a mandatory arbitration procedure, which would have given athletes, and other interested parties, the right to seek mandatory arbitration either before the Board or the American Arbitration Association. Coordination of sports groups would have been achieved by a sanctioning procedure, requiring an organization with a charter in one sport to sanction events in the sport sponsored by another organization. This would have precluded the types of jurisdictional disputes that have plagued international competition during at least the last decade. It would, finally, have provided a sports development program by the creation of a foundation which would have served as a clearinghouse for information and a conduit for development funds.

The Amateur Athletic Act of 1974 would have created a new, and independent, federal administrative agency to deal with the problems in international amateur competition. Its creation of a federal agency would have required that the procedures of the agency be undertaken in compliance with the requirements of federal administrative law. These requirements, of course, would have complicated the administrative process to a substantial degree, but they are part of the baggage that would accompany formal federal intervention in amateur athletics.[600] In this connection, it should be observed that the administrative structure that the Act would have created is essentially the same as the state athletic commissions which exist in almost every jurisdiction to govern professional sports which have in the past been unable to satisfactorily effect self- (that is, private) regulation.[601] The similarity between the Act and the state athletic commissions is significant because it provides vivid illustration of the extent to which public bodies will intervene in amateur athletics (or any other part of the athletic community) when private administrative action is unable to resolve issues in a manner that is deemed consistent with the public interest.[602]

---

598. S. 3500, 93rd Cong., 2d Sess. (1974), reported favorably by the Committee on Commerce, S. REP. No. 93-850, 93rd Cong., 2d Sess. (1974), and passed by a vote of 62-29. 120 CONG. REC. S12018 (daily ed. July 9, 1974).
599. *See* Lowell, *Federal Administrative Intervention in Amateur Athletics,* 43 GEO. WASH. L. REV. 729 (1975).
600. *Id.* at 748-64.
601. *See* § 2.02 *et seq.*
602. The issues raised by The Amateur Athletic Act of 1974 were analyzed in detail by the President's Commission on Olympic Sports during 1975 to 1977. *See* THE FINAL REPORT OF THE

The discussion of the Amateur Athletic Act is important because it provides a useful example of the type of legislative response that may be expected when unresolvable problems develop in the amateur sports community. Although it dealt only with international aspects of amateur competition by express provision, it seems certain that the legislative findings and conclusions that underlay its provisions portend potentially far reaching consequences to all other aspects of sports activity in this country. The clear message of its sponsors is that Congress will not allow the rights of either athletes or the public to be trammeled by those responsible for the administration of sports activities. Thus, the most important message of the Act is a warning to those who administer sports activities to keep their house in order, for if they do not, Congress (and, possibly, state legislative bodies) will intervene to insure that the interests of athletes in competitive opportunity, and of the public in the excellence of competition, are protected.

PRESIDENT'S COMMISSION ON OLYMPIC SPORTS 1975-1977 (1977). The recommendations of the Commission were introduced in Congress. *See, e.g.,* S. 2036, 95th Cong., 1st Sess. (1977).

CHAPTER 2

Public Regulation of Sports Activities

§ 2.01. In General.

The first step in our analysis of the law of sports has been to consider the legal principles defining the various relationships in amateur athletics.[1] Amateur athletics was the starting point because it is the area of sports which has been traditionally accorded the widest freedom to regulate itself. The self-regulation has, however, been significantly preempted by the intervention of public institutions (the courts and legislative bodies), and the result of this intervention has been the emergence of a developing body of judicial principles, and legislative judgments, defining the various relationships in the amateur athletic community. The reason for this development is the apparent perception of both courts and legislators that the interests of those who are involved in amateur athletics may, in some circumstances, require that acts which affect those interests be subjected to review by public bodies. Where, in other words, private regulation has failed, public regulation (either in the form of judicial or legislative action) has begun to take root.

The developments in amateur athletics are, of course, important in their own right, but they are also important as establishing a base from which to consider many other facets of the more general sports community, which have for a much longer period been the subject of public regulation. Thus, the title of this chapter is "Public Regulation of Sports Activities," and it includes the more or less formalized structures that have been legislatively created to deal with sports activities where self-regulation has failed. This title is, however, to some extent misleading since several of the remaining chapters in this treatise will also deal with specific types of regulatory schemes that affect sports activities. In

---

1. *See* ch. 1.

113

succeeding chapters, attention will be devoted to the application of the federal antitrust[2] and labor laws[3] to professional sports activities, as well as the impact of the federal income tax laws upon sports activities of all types.[4] Each of these chapters deals with public regulation, but the subjects considered in those chapters have been separated from the present discussion because each constitutes a sufficiently identifiable and distinct body of principles and precedent to warrant individual attention. Those chapters do, nonetheless, represent additional aspects of the public regulation of sports activities, and should be kept in mind as the materials in this chapter are considered.

This chapter continues the analysis initiated by the introductory chapter on amateur athletics, and considers how the public has imposed regulatory schemes on sports activities which are not undertaken for the sake of competition itself.[5] The discussion will focus primarily upon the activities of the state athletic commissions that have been created in almost all jurisdictions to regulate some sports. Attention will be specifically directed towards the policy judgments that have led to the creation of such commissions,[6] and the functions that the commissions perform. These functions include the issuance of licenses to all who participate, directly or indirectly, in the sport,[7] the adoption of rules and regulations,[8] and the enforcement proceedings that may be necessary to insure compliance with the rules and regulations.[9] It will also be important to consider the extent to which courts will review determinations made, and procedures utilized, by athletic commissions.[10]

The second broad area that this chapter will cover involves other aspects of public regulation which are not individually treated in subsequent chapters. These subjects include the regulation of gambling on sports events,[11] illegal sports activities,[12] and discrimination in the availability of athletic facilities.[13]

§ 2.02. Athletic Regulatory Commissions.

The most significant aspect of the public regulation of sports activities involves the statutory schemes in almost all states which establish athletic commissions to regulate specific sports.[14] The legislative purpose for the

---

2. *See* ch. 5.

3. *See* ch. 6.

4. *See* ch. 7.

5. *See generally* R. NOLL, GOVERNMENT AND THE SPORTS BUSINESS (1974).

6. *See* § 2.02.

7. *See* § 2.03.

8. *See* §§ 2.04-.17.

9. *See* § 2.18.

10. *See* § 2.19.

11. *See* § 2.20.

12. *See* § 2.21.

13. *See* § 2.22.

14. *See* notes 17-22 *infra*. The constitutionality of these provisions has frequently been upheld. *See, e.g.,* Western Turf Ass'n v. Greenberg, 204 U.S. 359, 51 L. Ed. 520, 27 S. Ct. 384 (1907); Grainger v. Douglas Park Jockey Club, 148 F. 513 (6th Cir. 1906); Louisiana Greyhound Club, Inc. v. Clancy, 167 La. 511, 119 So. 532 (1929), *aff'd,* 280 U.S. 525, 74 L. Ed. 593, 50 S. Ct. 87 (1929); Mullholland v. State Racing Comm'n, 295 Mass. 286, 3 N.E.2d 773 (1936); Heuchert v. State Harness Racing Comm'n, 403 Pa. 440, 170 A.2d 332 (1961). *See generally* J. HUMPHREYS, RACING LAW (1962) (two volume work which thoroughly discusses the legal aspects of racing); 9 E. MCQUILLEN, THE LAW OF MUNICIPAL CORPORATIONS § 26.152 (1964); Annot., 83 A.L.R. 696 (1933) (wrestling regulation).

establishment of athletic commissions is two-fold: the first is the desire to prevent, so far as possible, the abuses that may have been a part of the sport in the past; and the second is to promote and protect the public interest in the legitimate and sportsmanlike conduct of the sport.[15] The sports which have been made the subject of athletic commission control are, accordingly, those which are perceived to require state regulation, either as a result of their importance to the public or the failure of private regulation.[16] These sports have included horse and dog racing,[17] automobile racing,[18] jai-alai,[19] and boxing and wrestling.[20] Regulation has also been extended to certain aspects of other sports, such as ski-lift operation[21] and snowmobile ownership.[22] Although a

15. *See, e.g.,* Gilmour v. New York State Racing and Wagering Bd., 405 F. Supp. 458 (S.D.N.Y. 1975); Hubel v. West Virginia Racing Comm'n, 376 F. Supp. 1 (S.D. W. Va. 1974), *aff'd,* 513 F. 2d 240 (4th Cir. 1975); Fitzsimmons v. New York State Athletic Comm'n, 15 Misc. 2d 831, 146 N.Y.S. 117 (1914), *aff'd,* 162 App. Div. 904, 147 N.Y.S. 1111 (1914). The abuses sought to be overcome are well stated, in the case of boxing, in Tilelli v. Christenberry, 1 Misc. 2d 139, 120 N.Y.S.2d 697 (1953), as follows:

> The unsavory history of professional boxing in this State reveals why boxing matches and all who participate in them are by legislative policy and enactment made subject to the most inexorable and meticulous regulation, ... The Legislature was plainly apprehensive of the unwholesome influence exerted by gamblers, criminals and other disreputable persons who dominated professional boxing. Since it featured violence, the sport attracted full-blooded patrons who bet heavily on the outcome of the bouts. And since the moral stamina of pugilists, in that era at least, was often weaker than their physical stamina, many were not adverse to "fixing" fights at the behest of professional gamblers. Judging from newspaper comment in 1920, the public was revolted by the sordid spectacle presented by professional boxing. 1 Misc. 2d at 143, 120 N.Y.S.2d at 700.

See also George Foreman Assoc., Ltd. v. Foreman, 389 F. Supp. 1308 (N.D. Cal. 1974), *aff'd,* 517 F. 2d 354 (9th Cir. 1975); Wilson v. Sandstrom, 317 So.2d 732 (Fla. 1975), *cert. denied,* 423 U.S. 1053 (1976); Ali v. State Athletic Comm'n, 308 F. Supp. 11 (S.D.N.Y. 1969); Christensen v. Helfand, 208 Misc. 302, 143 N.Y.S.2d 285 (1955).

The legislative purposes are frequently stated in specific statutory provisions. *See, e.g.,* CAL. BUS. & PROF. CODE § 18804 (West Supp. 1977) (reciting that professional boxers as a group require aid in avoiding destitution, and then providing pension and disability insurance requirements); FLA. STAT. ANN. § 550.081(1) (1974); N.J. STAT. ANN. § 5:5-86 (1973).

16. Jacobson v. Maryland Racing Comm'n, 261 Md. 180, 274 A.2d 102 (1971). In considering state regulation of sports, it should be observed that proposals have been made for comparable regulation at the federal level for some aspects of amateur athletics. *See* § 1.29. Attention has also been given to the possibility of federal regulation in professional sports which are not now affected by the state athletic commissions. *See, e.g.,* Comment, *Discipline in Professional Sports,* 60 GEO. L.J. 771 (1972). When specific proposals have been made, however, they have not had much success. Thus, in a Report on Organized Baseball, a House Committee once observed that it "would be unwise in the extreme to saddle professional baseball with a new governmental bureau to control its destiny." H.R. REP. 2002, 82d Cong., 2d Sess. 231 (1952); *see also Hearings Before the Senate Antitrust Subcomm. of the Senate Comm. on the Judiciary,* 85th Cong., 1st Sess. 2657, 2671 (1957). The refusal to impose such regulatory control in the past is not, of course, a reliable precedent in the future.

17. *See, e.g.,* ARIZ. REV. STAT. ANN. §§ 5-101 *et seq.* (1974); FLA. STAT. ANN. §§ 550.01 *et seq.* (1974); ILL. ANN. STAT. tit. 8, § 37a *et seq.* (Smith-Hurd 1975); OHIO REV. CODE ANN. §§ 3769.01 *et seq.* (Page's 1971); W. VA. CODE §§ 19-23-1 *et seq.* (1977).

It should be noted that the authorization of horse racing will not, of itself, legalize dog racing. Hawthorne Kennel Club v. Swanson, 339 Ill. 220, 171 N.E. 140 (1930). Indeed, it is occasionally so provided by statute. *See, e.g.,* LA. REV. STAT. ANN. § 4:249 (1973).

18. N.J. STAT. ANN. §§ 5:7-8 *et seq.* (1973); VT. STAT. ANN. tit. 31, §§ 601 *et seq.* (1970).

19. FLA. STAT. ANN. § 551.01 (1974); R.I. GEN. LAWS §§ 41-7-1 *et seq.* (1977).

20. CAL. BUS. & PROF. CODE §§ 18600 *et seq.* (West 1970); MASS. GEN. LAWS ANN. ch. 147, §§ 32 *et seq.* (1972); NEV. REV. STAT. § 467.010 (1973); N.Y. UNCONSOL. LAWS §§ 8901 *et seq.* (McKinney 1974); PA. STAT. ANN. tit. 4, §§ 1 *et seq.* (Purdon's 1963); WASH. REV. CODE ANN. §§ 67.08.001 *et seq.* (1974).

21. MONT. REV. CODES §§ 69-6601 *et seq.* (Supp. 1974); VT. STAT. ANN. tit. 31, § 701 (1972). These provisions deal primarily with safety requirements. *See* § 8.02.

22. N.H. REV. STAT. ANN. §§ 269:B-1 *et seq.* (Supp. 1972); VT. STAT. ANN. tit. 31, §§ 801 *et seq.* (1970). These are primarily registration provisions.

sport may in general require regulation, some of its aspects may satisfy legislative objectives without the need of intervention by an agency of the state, and those aspects will, accordingly, be exempted from the commission's supervision.[23]

While the specific statutory schemes adopted to regulate sports activities vary substantially from state to state, and from sport to sport, their general design is sufficiently common to facilitate a general discussion. In order to provide a basis for analyzing the various functions of athletic commissions, this section will consider the basic structure and authority of the commissions, and subsequent sections will consider each of their basic functions.

In establishing an athletic commission, the legislature will customarily vest it with the primary jurisdictional power to direct, manage and control the sport which it is to regulate.[24] To accomplish these objectives, the commission will be expressly delegated certain powers. Thus, it is common for the commission to be granted power to promulgate and enforce rules and regulations, to issue licenses to those who wish to participate in the sport in any capacity, and to undertake appropriate administrative proceedings to insure that the various statutory directions, as well as its own rules and regulations, are observed by all persons subject to its jurisdiction. In addition to the express powers granted by the legislature, an athletic commission will also possess such other discretionary power as may be necessary and proper for it to achieve its regulatory objectives.[25] In short, an athletic commission will function as an administrative agency of the state and will be the statutory trustee of the express and implied powers with which it is vested.[26] As an agency of the state, moreover, the acts and determinations of an athletic commission will be subject to judicial review,[27] and its procedures must comport with the requirements of due process of law.[28]

The specific functions of an athletic commission may be broken into three

---

23. These exemptions are noted at § 2.03, n.2. It should be noted, however, that the exempt status of an organization may not be exploited by another group in an attempt to circumvent the regulatory requirements. *See* Inter-Continental Promotions, Inc. v. Miami Beach First Nat'l Bank, 441 F.2d 1356 (5th Cir. 1971), *cert. denied,* 404 U.S. 850, 30 L. Ed. 2d 89, 92 S. Ct. 85 (1971).

24. *See, e.g.,* ARIZ. REV. STAT. ANN. § 5-227 (1974); CAL. BUS. & PROF. CODE § 18670 (West 1973); FLA. STAT. ANN. § 550.02 (1974); N.J. STAT. ANN. § 5:2-5 (1973).

To insure exclusive control, it is also customarily provided that it shall be unlawful to engage in the sport other than pursuant to the statutory scheme. *See, e.g.,* ALA. CODE § 41-9-121 (1977); IND. STAT., BURNS' CODE ED. 35-31-2-1 (1975); ILL. ANN. STAT. tit. 8, § 37g (Smith-Hurd 1977). *See also* State *ex rel.* Esgar v. District Ct. of Ninth Jud. Dist. of Gallatin County, 56 Mont. 454, 185 P. 157 (1919).

25. Jones v. Kind, 61 So. 2d 188 (Fla. 1952). Thus, a commission will have the power to require surety bonds of licensees, even if there is no specific statutory provision therefor. McClare v. Massachusetts Bonding & Ins. Co., 266 N.Y. 371, 195 N.E. 15 (1935). *See* § 2.03.

If the legislature is fearful of disastrous results from its creation of an athletic commission, however, it may well place the commission in a straitjacket by giving it little discretion. If those results are not forthcoming, the legislature may then relent and grant the commission substantial discretionary powers. *See* Biscayne Kennel Club, Inc. v. Board of Bus. Reg., 239 So. 2d 53 (Fla. App. 1970) (describing such a shift).

26. West Flagler Amusement Co. v. State Racing Comm'n, 122 Fla. 222, 165 So. 64 (1935). Although federal antitrust suits have been brought against the athletic commissions, they have not been successful. *See* Karlinsky v. New York Racing Ass'n, 517 F.2d 1010 (2d Cir. 1975).

27. *See* § 2.19.

28. *See* § 2.18.

broad categories: [29] 1) the issuance of licenses to those involved in the sport; [30] 2) the adoption, amendment and promulgation of rules and regulations to govern the sport; [31] and 3) the conduct of enforcement activities to insure the achievement of the legislative objectives.[32] Each of these functions will be considered in detail in the sections that follow. In reviewing these functions it will be well to keep in mind that athletic commissions are administrative agencies of the state. Accordingly, their actions will be governed by the principles, both statutory and common law, that usually apply to administrative action.[33] Although no attempt will be made herein to set forth in detail the principles of administrative law,[34] specific principles will be considered when appropriate to the subject being discussed.

§ 2.03. Commission Issuance of Licenses.

Probably the most important function performed by athletic commissions is the issuance of licenses and permits to those who wish to take part in the sports events over which the commissions have jurisdiction. The applicable statutory provisions customarily require that all persons or organizations desiring to take part in the sport in question, whether as actual participants, referees, owners, trainers, event sponsors or promoters, or in any other capacity, must acquire a license from the appropriate athletic commission.[35] The provisions may, however, exempt certain categories of persons from the licensing requirements,[36] limit the number of licenses that may be issued,[37] or preclude certain classes of persons from obtaining licenses.[38] The purpose of requiring

29. *See generally* Hoffheimer, *Some Horse-Racing Tips for Lawyers,* 50 A.B.A.J. 250, 251 (1964).

30. *See* § 2.03.

31. *See* § 2.04.

32. *See* § 2.18.

33. As administrators of a state agency, for example, commission members may be held personally liable only for malicious, oppressive or willful conduct, but not for mere error in judgment or mistaken exercise of discretion. Keifer v. Smith, 103 Neb. 675, 173 N.W. 685 (1919) (not liable for issuing license to non-pure bred horse).

34. The subject of administrative law is, indeed, a field well covered by authoritative texts. *See* F. Cooper, State Administrative Law (1965); K. Davis, Administrative Law Treatise (1958); L. Jaffe, Judicial Control of Administrative Action (1965).

35. *See, e.g.,* Alaska Stat. § 05.10.010 (1973); Ariz. Rev. Stat. Ann. § 5-107.01 (1974); Ind. Code Ann. § 25-9-1-5 (Burns 1975); Ky. Rev. Stat. § 230.310 (1977); Nev. Rev. Stat. § 466.090 (1973); N.Y. Unconsol. Laws § 7915 (McKinney Supp. 1978), § 8907 (McKinney 1978).

Compliance with non-commission requirements will not suffice. State *ex rel.* Allen v. Rose, 123 Fla. 544, 167 So. 21 (1936) (A.K.C. registration no substitute for commission license).

36. *See, e.g.,* Cal. Bus. & Prof. Code §§ 18650-52 (West 1970) (exempt boxing matches under supervision of National Guard or Naval Militia, colleges or universities, and amateur organizations); Md. Ann. Code art. 56, § 127 (1972) (exempt matches under supervision of colleges or high school); Mich. Stat. Ann. § 18.966 (21) (1971) (exempt races conducted by county fair associations); Wash. Rev. Code Ann. § 67.08.015 (1974) (exempt matches sponsored by scholastic organizations). Such provisions have been held to be constitutional. Antlers Athletic Ass'n v. Hartung, 85 Colo. 125, 274 P. 831 (1928); National Drag Racing Enterprises, Inc. v. Kendall County, 54 Ill. 2d 83, 295 N.E.2d 712 (1972); Bridge City Athletic Club, Inc. v. Salberg, 234 App. Div. 309, 254 N.Y.S. 777 (1932).

37. The most common such provision is that which limits the number of race tracks within a given radius, *see, e.g.,* Fla. Stat. Ann. § 550.05(2) (1974), which has been upheld by the courts. Rodriguez v. Jones, 64 So. 2d 278 (Fla. 1953); State *ex rel.* Flagler County Kennel Club, Inc. v. Jones, 60 So. 2d 761 (Fla. 1952); Saratoga Harness Racing, Inc. v. New York State Quarter Horse Racing Comm'n, 74 Misc. 2d 1096, 347 N.Y.S.2d 613 (1972).

38. *See, e.g.,* Ariz. Rev. Stat. Ann. § 5-103.01 (1974) (excluding commission and other state employees). *See also* Murtha v. Monaghan, 1 App. Div. 2d 178, 148 N.Y.S.2d 615 (1956), *aff'd,* 2

the licensing of all persons or organizations involved in the sport is to enable the commission to maintain proper control over their activities in particular and to police the sport in general. Accordingly, the commission will be granted considerable discretion in its determination as to whether a license should be issued to any particular applicant[39] — that is, the issuance decision will, absent statutory provision to the contrary,[40] be discretionary and not merely ministerial.[41]

Although the types of licenses that may be issued by a commission vary considerably depending on the interest being licensed, the principles that apply to the issuance decision are essentially similar for all types of licenses. The basic question that a commission will consider is whether the public interest, and the best interests of the sport, will be served by issuing a license to any given applicant.[42] This consideration will require the evaluation of numerous factors,[43] and the commission may properly take into account all evidence from reliable and trustworthy sources that has a reasonable relation to the desirability of

N.Y.S.2d 819, 159 N.Y.S.2d 834, 140 N.E.2d 746 (1957), *cert. denied,* 355 U.S. 891, 2 L. Ed. 2d 190, 78 S. Ct. 264 (1957) (prohibition of public employees earning more than $5,000 from acquiring pari-mutuel clerk's license).

39. Medina v. Rudman, 545 F.2d 244 (1st Cir. 1977); Bay State Horse Racing & Breeding Ass'n v. State Racing Comm'n, 340 Mass. 776, 166 N.E.2d 711 (1960); North Hampton Racing & Breeding Ass'n v. Conway, 94 N.H. 156, 48 A.2d 472 (1946) (statutory "may" creates administrative discretion).

40. Brooke v. Moore, 60 Ariz. 551, 142 P.2d 211 (1943) ("may" issue means shall issue when statutory conditions are met); Arkansas State Racing Comm'n v. Southland Racing Corp., 226 Ark. 995, 295 S.W.2d 617 (1956) (same); State *ex rel.* Kinsella v. Florida State Racing Comm'n, 155 Fla. 387, 20 So. 2d 258 (1944) (statutory "shall" makes issuance mandatory upon compliance with requirements).

41. Ross v. State Racing Comm'n, 64 N.M. 478, 330 P.2d 701 (1958). The issuance may in some circumstances, however, become merely ministerial. Dubin v. Department of Business Regulation, 262 So. 2d 273 (Fla. App. 1972) (after license is once issued to horse trainer, renewal is ministerial); Charles Town Raceway, Inc. v. West Virginia Racing Comm'n, 143 W. Va. 257, 101 S.E.2d 60 (1957) (after local option approval has been obtained).

42. Palm Springs Turf Club v. California Horse Racing Bd., 155 Cal. App. 2d 242, 317 P.2d 713 (1957).

43. The New York racing statute, for example, provides as follows:

If the state racing commission shall find that the financial responsibility, experience, character and general fitness of the applicant are such that the participation of such person will be consistent with the public interest, convenience or necessity and with the best interests of racing generally in conformity with the purposes of this act, it shall thereupon grant a license. If the commission shall find that the applicant fails to meet any of said conditions, it shall not grant such license and it shall notify the applicant of the denial. The commission may refuse to issue or renew a license, or may suspend or revoke a license issued pursuant to this section, if it shall find that the applicant, or any person who is a partner, agent, employee or associate of the applicant, has been convicted of a crime in any jurisdiction, or is or has been associating or consorting with any person who has or persons who have been convicted of a crime or crimes in any jurisdiction or jurisdictions, or is consorting or associating with or has consorted or associated with bookmakers, touts, or persons of similar pursuits, or has himself engaged in similar pursuits, or is financially irresponsible, or has been guilty of or attempted any fraud or misrepresentation in connection with racing, breeding or otherwise, or has violated or attempted to violate any law with respect to racing in any jurisdiction or any rule, regulation or order of the commission, or shall have violated any rule of racing which shall have been approved or adopted by the commission, or has been guilty of or engaged in similar, related or like practices.

N.Y. UNCONSOL. LAWS § 7514(2) (McKinney 1961). *See also* ARIZ. REV. STAT. ANN. § 5-108(A)(1) (1974); LA. REV. STAT. ANN. § 4:151, 159 (1973); ORE. REV. STAT. § 462.075 (1974); W. VA. CODE § 19-23-8 (1977).

issuing a license to the applicant.[44] With regard to participants, these factors may include, for example, the applicant's personal conduct; [45] temperament, training or character; [46] physical condition; [47] and the completeness of the application.[48] Similarly, in considering the applications of persons or organizations wishing to promote sports events, the commission may wish to evaluate the applicant's financial condition [49] or past bookmaking activities; [50] the likely impact of issuance upon state revenue; [51] the prevailing community sentiment; [52] or the applicant's compliance with statutory requirements.[53] In making its determination, the commission may also require applicants to take examinations; [54] submit additional information that is reasonably related to the issuance decision; [55] comply with altered requirements for license applications, though a grandfather clause may exist to protect those already following the application process; [56] or meet reasonable conditions imposed upon the licenses

---

44. Fink v. Cole, 1 N.Y.2d 48, 133 N.E.2d 691 (1956). It should be noted that if, while an application is pending, the applicant challenges the propriety of a particular rule of the commission, it has been held that the commission should consider the application as if there were no such rule. It may not delay any decision until the suit is finally terminated. State ex rel. Beulah Park Jockey Club, Inc. v. Claypool, 53 Ohio L. Abs. 1, 84 N.E.2d 245 (1948).

45. In Christensen v. Helfand, 208 Misc. 302, 143 N.Y.S.2d 285 (1955), for example, the court stated that

> [t]he Commission has the power to inquire into the conduct of those who hold or apply for licenses. It must exercise its authority to prevent monopolistic combinations which seek to attain a strangle hold on the sport to the detriment of the boxers and the public which maintains it. It has the obligation to protect boxers and others in the profession, and the public from the unscrupulous and the venal, who from time to time infiltrate its ranks. The rules here involved are a part of the regulatory pattern designed to effectuate the governmental purpose. Id. at 303, 143 N.Y.S.2d at 286.

The requirement of "good conduct" is considered at § 2.05.

46. Zannelli v. DiSandro, 84 R.I. 76, 121 A. 2d 652 (1956).

47. Harris v. Commonwealth, State Athletic Comm'n, 10 Pa. Commw. Ct. 419, 310 A.2d 711 (1973); Fitzsimmons v. New York State Athletic Comm'n, 15 Misc. 831, 146 N.Y.S. 117 (1914), aff'd, 162 App. Div. 904, 147 N.Y.S. 1111 (1914); Zannelli v. DiSandro, 84 R.I. 76, 121 A.2d 652 (1956). It should be noted that both the Harris and Fitzsimmons cases provide a discussion of the power of a commission to bar a person from boxing to prevent further damage to an already damaged physical condition.

48. Greenhalgh v. McCanna, 90 R.I. 417, 158 A.2d 878 (1960).

49. State ex rel. Magnolia Park, Inc. v. Louisiana State Racing Comm'n, 231 La. 720, 92 So. 2d 699 (1956); Mount Clemens Harness Ass'n v. Michigan Racing Comm'n, 360 Mich. 467, 104 N.W.2d 363 (1960).

50. Wexler v. Ring, 125 So. 2d 883 (Fla. App. 1961).

51. North Hampton Racing & Breeding Ass'n v. Conway, 94 N.H. 156, 48 A.2d 472 (1946). See also South Haven Racing Ass'n v. Michigan Racing Comm'r, 42 Mich. App. 125, 201 N.W.2d 314 (1972) (to determine if additional time is needed for the sport to develop before issuing additional racing licenses).

52. Colorado Racing Comm'n v. Columbine Kennel Club, Inc., 141 Colo. 497, 348 P.2d 954 (1960) (dog racing); Rhode Island State Fair Ass'n v. Racing & Athletic Bd., 80 R.I. 486, 98 A.2d 821 (1953) (horse racing).

53. Young v. State Athletic Comm'n, 111 Cal. App. 33, 295 P. 61 (1931) (possess proper lease).

54. Vinas v. Gimma, 33 App. Div. 2d 538, 304 N.Y.S.2d 105 (1969).

55. In Simmons v. Hanton, 65 So. 2d 42 (Fla. 1953), the commission required applicants to submit fingerprints and a photograph with their application. In rejecting a challenge to this rule, the court stated that

> [s]oldiers and sailors, workers in government service, applicants to practice in some of the professions, babies in hospitals (footprinted), and countless thousands of employees in private industry are required to be thus identified. . . . Id. at 44.

56. See, e.g., Tweel v. West Virginia Racing Comm'n, 138 W. Va. 381, 76 S.E.2d 874 (1953) (local option election not applicable to existing trades). A "grandfather clause" will not as such violate the Equal Protection Clause, Vinas v. Gimma, 33 App. Div. 2d 538, 304 N.Y.S.2d 105 (1969).

that it in fact issues.[57] If the law changes while an application is pending, moreover, it has been held that the law as changed will govern the application.[58]

The discretionary nature of the issuance decision, and the extent to which the courts will review it, is well illustrated by *Man O'War Racing Association v. State Horse Racing Commission,*[59] where the commission had the duty of selecting four organizations from a large field of applicants to which it would issue licenses to conduct harness racing. When the decision was made, one of the disappointed applicants brought suit to contest the commission's action. In upholding the commission's decision, the court noted that the commission had a difficult task in making its selection and was required to balance many competing interests. It was because of this difficulty and the commission's expertise, the court said, that the state legislature had accorded it such broad and exclusive discretion. Accordingly, in order for a commission license-issuance decision to be overturned, the court concluded, there must be a clear abuse of its discretion, and even if the court "would have chosen different applicants, this [would] not cast doubt upon the determination made by the Commission [absent an abuse of discretion]." [60]

---

57. Bowers v. Calkins, 84 F. Supp. 272 (D.N.H. 1949) (condition requiring trainer to sign release and waiver to allow search of quarters for drugs); Sullivan County Harness Racing Ass'n v. Glasser, 30 N.Y.2d 269, 283 N.E.2d 603 (1972) (condition of harness racing license that racing not be conducted in conjunction with television broadcasts); Saratoga Harness Racing, Inc. v. New York State Quarter Horse Racing Comm'n, 42 App. Div. 2d 3, 344 N.Y.S.2d 95, aff'd, 33 N.Y.S.2d 666, 348 N.Y.S.2d 982, 303 N.E.2d 706 (1973) (different "buffer zone" requirements for some counties not unconstitutional); Lanchester v. Pennsylvania State Horse Racing Comm'n, 16 Pa. Commw. Ct. 85, 325 A.2d 648 (1947) (consent to search for prohibited articles). *But cf.* Ogden/Fairmount, Inc. v. Illinois Racing Bd., 30 Ill. App. 2d 707, 332 N.E.2d 610 (1975) (no power to impose condition as to prices).

Where the evidence presented in a license issuance proceeding indicates that there is a reasonable need for the imposition of conditions, the commission may be required to investigate the need and impose conditions where necessary. *See, e.g.,* Township of Cherry Hill v. New Jersey Racing Comm'n, 131 N.J. Super. 125, 328 A.2d 653 (1974), aff'd, 131 131 N.J. Super. 482, 330 A.2d 600 (1974).

It is frequently required that some types of licensees, especially promoters, post bonds. *See, e.g.,* ILL. ANN. STAT. tit. 8, § 373-10 (Smith-Hurd 1975); MD. ANN. CODE art. 56, § 113 (1972); N.J. STAT. ANN. § 5:2-9 (1973); TEX. STAT. ANN. § 8501-5 (Vernon's Supp. 1974). Such bonds will cover only the risks identified, State Athletic Comm'n of Calif. v. Massachusetts Bonding & Ins. Co., 46 Cal. App. 2d 839, 117 P.2d 80 (1941) (bond for one fight did not cover failure of promoter to stage a second fight), and when bond principals make payments, the surety will be entitled to credit therefor. State Athletic Comm'n of Calif. v. Massachusetts Bonding & Ins. Co., 46 Cal. 2d 823, 117 P.2d 75 (1941). If the surety accepts payment for the bond issued, moreover, it will then be estopped to deny its validity. McClare v. Massachusetts Bonding & Ins. Co., 266 N.Y. 371, 195 N.E. 15 (1935).

58. Selectmen of Topsfield v. State Racing Comm'n, 324 Mass. 309, 86 N.E.2d 65 (1949). Although licenses once issued are normally non-transferable, *see, e.g.,* FLA. STAT. ANN. § 550.21 (1974), transfer may properly be allowed in appropriate cases. Biscayne Kennel Club, Inc. v. Florida State Racing Comm'n, 165 So. 2d 762 (Fla. 1964). A statutory provision allowing transfer may, however, be unlawful if it is merely special legislation. West Flagler Kennel Club, Inc. v. Florida State Racing Comm'n, 153 So. 2d 5 (Fla. 1963).

59. 433 Pa. 432, 250 A.2d 172 (1969).

60. Specifically, the court stated that

[t]he importance of appreciating the number of technical and precise factors with which the Commission had to contend is only to emphasize what must be obvious. The Legislature vested this authority in the Commission because of the expertise and judgment required in making the important decision which corporations were to be granted licenses. Thus the Commission was required to exercise an administrative discretion which under the circumstances was exclusively committed to it under the statutory mandate of the Legislature. In our role as a reviewing court, we must enter upon the performance of our judicial function ever mindful of the deference we should show to the Commission's determinations. It is possible that if this Court had been called upon to carry out this important task, we might have chosen different applicants, perhaps because we might

A commission's discretion will not, however, be without limit, and the courts will review specific decisions to determine whether they exceed the permissible scope of discretion.[61] Thus, judicial intervention is appropriate where the denial of a license application is arbitrary or unreasonable.[62] A leading case expressing this proposition is *Ali v. State Athletic Commission*,[63] where the then former heavyweight champion of the world had been denied a boxing license because of his conviction for refusing to be inducted into the armed forces. Evidence in the commission's files indicated, however, that it had issued licenses to several hundred other applicants who had been convicted of crimes both before and after the denial of Ali's application. These facts were, the court observed, "overwhelming and undisputed proof of arbitrary, capricious, and unfounded discrimination [against Ali]," [64] which required a finding that the commission's denial "constituted an arbitrary and unreasonable departure from its practice in the case of other such applicants." [65] Its denial was, therefore, unlawful, and the commission was enjoined from denying Ali a license.[66] In short, a commission

have placed more emphasis on certain factors which the Commission did not consider especially important. *But even* if we would have chosen different applicants, this does not in any way cast doubt upon the determination made by the Commission. Because it was not this Court, but the Commission which has been charged with this responsibility. *Id.* at 450, 250 A.2d at 180-81 (emphasis in original).

See also Mount Clemens Harness Ass'n v. Michigan Racing Comm'r, 360 Mich. 467, 104 N.W.2d 363 (1960); Valley Forge Racing Ass'n v. State Horse Racing Comm'n, 449 Pa. 292, 297 A.2d 823 (1972). Judicial review of commission decisions is considered in detail at § 2.19.

61. Fink v. Cole, 1 N.Y.2d 48, 133 N.E.2d 691 (1956). *See* § 2.19.
62. Ali v. State Athletic Comm'n, 308 F. Supp. 11 (S.D.N.Y. 1969); Cloverleaf Kennel Club v. Racing Comm'n, 130 Colo. 505, 277 P.2d 226 (1954); State *ex rel.* Kinsella v. Florida Racing Comm'n, 155 Fla. 387, 20 So. 2d 258 (1944); Ross v. State Racing Comm'n, 64 N.M. 478, 330 P.2d 701 (1958).
63. 316 F. Supp. 1246 (S.D.N.Y. 1970).
64. *Id.* at 1252.
65. *Id.* at 1253.
66. In reaching this conclusion, the court stated the general rules as follows:

Although the state possesses broad powers to regulate boxing, however, it may not exercise those powers in such a way as to deny to an applicant the equal protection of the state's laws, which is guaranteed to him by the Fourteenth Amendment. A deliberate and arbitrary discrimination or inequality in the exercise of regulatory power, not based upon differences that are reasonably related to the lawful purposes of such regulation, violates the Fourteenth Amendment [citations omitted]. In determining whether there has been such an arbitrary denial of equal protection, the acts of the state's duly constituted Athletic Commission or similar agency are deemed to be those of the state itself [citations omitted]. In short, the exercise of state power by a state agency in the issuance or refusal of licenses to engage in a regulated activity should not represent the exercise of mere personal whim, caprice or prejudice on the part of such agency [citations omitted]. It should, and constitutionally must, have some rational basis. 316 F. Supp. at 1250.

Similar results have been reached in many other cases. *See* Arkansas State Racing Comm'n v. Southland Racing Corp., 226 Ark. 995, 295 S.W.2d 617 (1956) (failure to issue license to applicant who had met all statutory requirements and statute was mandatory); Cloverleaf Kennel Club v. Racing Comm'n, 130 Colo. 505, 277 P.2d 226 (1954) (commission decided that another track was not needed in the community); State *ex rel.* Kinsella v. Florida State Racing Comm'n, 155 Fla. 387, 20 So. 2d 258 (1944) (failure to issue license to applicant who had met all statutory requirements and statute was mandatory); Ross v. State Racing Comm'n, 64 N.M. 478, 330 P.2d 701 (1958) (rejection on grounds having no statutory basis; proof of financial success); People *ex rel.* Empire City Trotting Club v. State Racing Comm'n, 190 N.Y. 31, 82 N.E. 723 (1907) (rejection on grounds having no statutory basis; available racing dates already used up); Merritt v. Swope, 267 App. Div. 519, 46 N.Y.S.2d 944 (1944) (failure to follow statutory hearing procedures); Standard Athletic Club v. Cushing, 30 R.I. 208, 74 A. 719 (1909) (license granted with broader scope than allowed by statute: for one year and statute required license for each performance). *See also* Congregation Nachlas

may reject a license application only for good and reasonable cause.[67] With respect to license issuance, it should also be noted that it has been held that a commission may not delegate its statutory task to a private organization.[68]

Since the interest of the applicant in the license, should it be issued, has been frequently held to be of sufficient importance to warrant constitutional protection before it may be suspended or revoked,[69] the issue may also arise as to whether the issuance decision itself must be made in accordance with due process requirements.[70] This issue will arise only if an application is denied, since if the license is granted the applicant will have little concern over the absence of a hearing procedure.[71] The denial of a license application is similar in effect to the revocation of an existing license, and where the denial is based upon findings of fact it would appear that the considerations which require a hearing for revocation would also necessitate such procedures for denial of the initial application.[72] Although some courts have held that hearing procedures are not required in the absence of a specific statutory provision,[73] there is a substantial basis for the view that procedural safeguards are applicable, at least before an application may be denied. Support for this result can be found in *Goldsmith v. United States Board of Tax Appeals,*[74] involving an analogous situation. In *Goldsmith,* an accountant had applied to the Board to be enrolled on its list of attorneys, but was denied admission in an exercise of the Board's broad discretion to "deny admission, suspend or disbar any person." The application, however, was rejected in a process which gave the applicant no opportunity to be heard or answer charges against him. In holding that the applicant was entitled to notice and a hearing,[75] the Supreme Court stated that the broad discretion vested in the Board "must be construed to mean the exercise of a

Jacob Anshe Sfard of Jackson Heights v. Ball, 40 App. Div. 2d 769, 337 N.Y.S.2d 284 (1972) (applicant religious organization was created solely for the financial benefit of its leader).

Although actions have been brought to seek prohibition or revocation of the grant of a license to another applicant, those efforts have frequently been rejected. *See* State *ex rel.* Fronton Exhibition Co. v. Stein, 144 Fla. 387, 198 So. 82 (1940); State *ex rel.* Magnolia Park, Inc. v. Louisiana State Racing Comm'n, 231 La. 720, 92 So. 2d 699 (1956); Bay State Harness Racing & Breeding Ass'n v. State Racing Comm'n, 340 Mass. 776, 166 N.E.2d 711 (1960); Mullholland v. State Racing Comm'n, 295 Mass. 286, 3 N.E.2d 773 (1936); State *ex rel.* Masterson v. Ohio State Racing Comm'n, 164 Ohio St. 312, 130 N.E.2d 829 (1955); Keystone Racing Corp. v. State Harness Racing Comm'n, 405 Pa. 1, 173 A.2d 97 (1961). A person disappointed by the issuance of a license to another may, however, be able to appeal the decision. *See, e.g.,* Valley Forge Racing Ass'n v. Commonwealth, 449 Pa. 292, 297 A.2d 823 (1972); Valley Forge Racing Ass'n v. Commonwealth, 17 Pa. Commw. Ct. 271, 330 A.2d 570 (1975).

67. Kelly Downs v. Michigan Racing Comm'n, 60 Mich. App. 539, 231 N.W.2d 443 (1975); South Haven Racing Ass'n v. Michigan Racing Comm'n, 42 Mich. App. 125, 201 N.W.2d 314 (1972).

68. Fink v. Cole, 302 N.Y. 216, 97 N.E.2d 873 (1951); Murtha v. Monaghan, 7 Misc. 2d 568, 169 N.Y.S.2d 137 (1957), *aff'd,* 5 App. Div. 2d 695, 169 N.Y.S.2d 1010 (1957), *aff'd,* 4 N.Y.2d 897, 174 N.Y.S.2d 648 (1958). The issue was noted, but not decided, in Bailey v. McCann, 550 F.2d 1016 (5th Cir. 1977). It is not, however, uncommon for a commission to be authorized to adopt the rules and regulations of private organizations. *See, e.g.,* CAL. BUS. & PROF. § 19563 (West 1964); CONN. GEN. STAT. § 12-574 (1972); N.J. STAT. ANN. § 5:5-30 (1973). *See* § 2.17.

69. *See* § 2.18.

70. These requirements are discussed in general at § 1.28.

71. 1 F. COOPER, STATE ADMINISTRATIVE LAW 150 (1965).

72. *See* § 2.18. *See generally* 1 F. COOPER, STATE ADMINISTRATIVE LAW 149-51 (1965).

73. *See, e.g.,* Fink v. Cole, 1 N.Y.2d 48, 133 N.E.2d 691 (1956).

74. 270 U.S. 117, 70 L. Ed. 494, 46 S. Ct. 215 (1926).

75. The Court actually upheld the Board's action, because the applicant had failed to demand the safeguards.

discretion to be exercised after fair investigation, with such notice, hearing and opportunity to answer for the applicant as would constitute due process." [76] Thus, although a commission, or legislature, may require high standards of qualification before it will issue a license, its procedures may have to comport with procedural due process and the qualifications required should have a rational connection with the applicant's fitness for the license requested.[77] Fortunately, this particular issue is not open to debate in those jurisdictions in which the legislature has statutorily imposed procedural requirements upon commissions who refuse to issue licenses.[78] The procedural requirements have also been imposed upon refusals to renew licenses that have already been issued.[79]

An additional aspect of the licensing process in animal racing sports involves the annual issuance of racing dates to those who own or operate racing facilities. In most jurisdictions, there will be a finite number of racing dates available in a given geographical area for each year, and some of those dates may have significant competitive advantage over others. Thus, competition for the preferred dates may be intense among those entities licensed to conduct animal racing in the particular geographical area.

In making the racing date allocations, the commission is typically guided by a statutory provision which requires annual application for the dates and which spells out the conditions under, and the procedures pursuant to, which the dates will be awarded.[80] In exercising its discretionary authority,[81] the commission will normally take into consideration many factors. These may include the interests of the public in general, as well as specific factors relating to the resources, good will, financial responsibility and managerial skill of competing applicants.[82]

76. 270 U.S. at 123. See also Willner v. Committee on Character and Fitness, 373 U.S. 96, 10 L. Ed. 2d 224, 83 S. Ct. 1175 (1963).

77. Schware v. Board of Bar Examiners of the State of N.M., 353 U.S. 232, 239, 1 L. Ed. 2d 796, 77 S. Ct. 752 (1957). See also 1 K. DAVIS, ADMINISTRATIVE LAW TREATISE §§ 7.18-.19 (1958); Byse, Opportunity To Be Heard in License Issuance, 101 U. PA. L. REV. 57 (1952). But cf. Medina v. Rudman, 545 F.2d 244 (1st Cir. 1977) (no procedural rights for denial of authority to purchase stock in a corporate licensee).

78. See, e.g., ALASKA STAT. § 05.10.010 (1962); ARIZ. REV. STAT. ANN. § 5-108.01 (1974); IND. CODE ANN. § 25-9-1-12 (Burns 1975); ILL. ANN. STAT. tit. 8, § 37c-4 (Smith-Hurd 1977); N.J. STAT. ANN. § 5:5-52 (1973). See also Merritt v. Swope, 267 App. Div. 519, 46 N.Y.S.2d 944 (1944); Valley Forge Racing Ass'n, Inc. v. Commonwealth, 17 Pa. Commw. Ct. 271, 330 A.2d 570 (1975).

79. Dubin v. Department of Business Regulation, 262 So. 2d 273 (Fla. App. 1972).

80. See, e.g., ARIZ. REV. STAT. ANN. § 5-110 (1974); FLA. STAT. ANN. § 550.081 (1974); ILL. ANN. STAT. tit. 8, § 37b (Smith-Hurd 1977); N.Y. UNCONSOL. LAWS § 7909 (McKinney 1961).

81. Hialeah Race Course, Inc. v. Board of Business Regulation, 267 So. 2d 839 (Fla. App. 1972). If the applicable statute allows charity dates in addition to the regular number of dates to be issued, it has been held that the commission may, if the statute so provides, add these at either end of the statutory period. State ex rel. Gulfstream Park Racing Ass'n v. Florida State Racing Comm'n, 70 So. 2d 375 (Fla. 1953).

82. State ex rel. West Flagler Kennel Club v. Florida State Racing Comm'n, 74 So. 2d 691 (Fla. 1954); Bay State Harness Horse Racing & Breeding Ass'n v. State Racing Comm'n, 342 Mass. 694, 175 N.E.2d 244 (1961). See also Gulfstream Park Racing Ass'n v. Board of Business Reg., 318 So.2d 458 (Fla. App. 1975) (allocation to prevent financial failure at one track); Hialeah Race Course, Inc. v. Board of Business Regulation, 267 So. 2d 839 (Fla. App. 1972); Biscayne Kennel Club, Inc. v. Board of Business Regulation, 239 So. 2d 53 (Fla. App. 1970); Leach v. Inglis, 340 Mich. 202, 65 N.W.2d 746 (1954) (track too small and facilities insufficient). In State ex rel. Biscayne Kennel Club v. Board of Business Regulation, 276 So. 2d 823 (Fla. 1973), the court noted that "[u]nder ordinary circumstances, whatever is good for the tracks is usually good for the State." Id. at 829.

After considering these factors, the commission will then allocate the available dates in a manner that will best effectuate the objectives it seeks to accomplish. These objectives may require, for example, that the dates be allocated on an experimental basis in an effort to determine which of several licensees is best able to take advantage of the most favorable dates [83] or that particular licensees be allocated dates so as to facilitate the balancing of competition between horse and dog racing.[84] In allocating the dates, the commission may also have a duty to apportion the available dates among the applicants in an equitable manner.[85] This may require, for example, that the dates be assigned so as to afford substantially equal opportunity among all applicants for the beneficial enjoyment of their racing licenses.[86] It may also require that a licensee who has historically been the victim of a discriminatory allocation arrangement be given the choice dates as a means of affording "equal opportunity" and rectifying the historical abuses.[87] It should also be noted that if the licensees seeking the allocation reach an agreement as to how the dates should be allocated, it has been held that the agreement will not bind the commission and will be approved only if it is in the public interest.[88]

Notwithstanding its customarily wide discretion, a commission's freedom of allocation may in some situations be limited. Thus, where several tracks in a single county apply for racing dates that are not in conflict and the commission is required to allocate the dates requested, it may then have a simple ministerial duty to allocate those dates.[89] The commission will also be precluded from allocating dates in a manner that is unreasonable or in abuse of its discretion.[90]

Where there are several applicants for a finite number of racing dates, the athletic commission may be required to accord the applicants the procedural rights of notice and hearing,[91] so that each will have an opportunity to

83. West Flagler Associates, Ltd. v. Board of Business Regulation, 265 So. 2d 507 (Fla. 1972); West Flagler Associates, Ltd. v. Division of Pari-Mutuel Wagering, 251 So. 2d 856 (Fla. 1971).

84. Gleason v. Love, 14 Ore. App. 97, 511 P.2d 435 (1973).

85. Hialeah Race Course, Inc. v. Board of Business Regulation, 267 So. 2d 839 (Fla. App. 1972); West Flagler Amusement Co. v. State Racing Comm'n, 122 Fla. 227, 165 So. 64 (1935); Jefferson Downs, Inc. v. Louisiana State Racing Comm'n, 288 So. 2d 653 (La. App. 1974).

86. West Flagler Amusement Co. v. State Racing Comm'n, 122 Fla. 227, 165 So. 64 (1935). Thus, a statute which gives the best dates to the tracks that produce the most revenue has been held to be unlawful on constitutional grounds, inasmuch as it deprives other tracks of the opportunity of proving their ability to produce large revenue with good dates. Hialeah Race Course, Inc. v. Gulfstream Park Racing Ass'n, 245 So. 2d 625 (Fla. 1971). *See also* West Flagler Associates v. Board of Business Regulation, 262 So. 2d 23 (Fla. App. 1972) (abuse of discretion to always award best dates to same track).

87. Gulfstream Park Racing Ass'n v. Division of Pari-Mutuel Wagering, 253 So. 2d 429 (Fla. 1971); Hialeah Race Course, Inc. v. Board of Business Regulation, 267 So. 2d 839 (Fla. App. 1972) (applicant cannot request continuation of discriminatory favoritism by arguing that it has in the past allowed it to achieve a position of national prominence).

88. State *ex rel.* Biscayne Kennel Club v. Board of Business Regulation, 276 So. 2d 823 (Fla. 1973).

89. State *ex rel.* Biscayne Kennel Club v. Board of Business Regulation, 276 So. 2d 823 (Fla. 1973); West Flagler Associates v. Board of Business Regulation, 241 So. 2d 369 (Fla. 1970) (the court actually made the allocation originally requested); State *ex rel.* Broward County Kennel Club, Inc. v. Rose, 126 Fla. 288, 170 So. 710 (1936).

90. West Flagler Associates v. Board of Business Regulation, 262 So. 2d 23 (Fla. App. 1972); Jefferson Downs, Inc. v. Louisiana Racing Comm'n, 288 So. 2d 653 (La. App. 1974) (allocating dates in alphabetical order); Hazel Park Racing Ass'n v. Inglis, 343 Mich. 1, 71 N.W.2d 692 (1955); People *ex rel.* Empire City Trotting Club v. State Racing Comm'n, 190 N.Y. 31, 82 N.E. 723 (1907).

91. The safeguards of procedural due process are considered at §§ 1.28, 2.18.

demonstrate why available dates should be allocated in its favor.[92] Such a comparative hearing is a common requirement in administrative proceedings in which several persons seek mutually exclusive privileges or licenses and will allow the commission to effectively appraise the comparative merits of the applicants in light of the public interest.[93]

Once the racing dates are allocated, moreover, the commission may not have the power to alter them without according the licensees the procedural due process safeguards.[94] Thus, it has been held that a commission may not undertake to alter the dates allocated in a proceeding in which one or more of the affected licensees is not present.[95]

§ 2.04. Commission Rule-Making.

The primary means by which athletic commissions perform their statutory duties is through the making and enforcing of rules and regulations. As with all of the other basic functions of such commissions, the authority to make rules is the result of specific statutory authorization. These provisions customarily delegate broad rule-making power to the commission.[96] The New York statute provides, for example, that the commission "shall have power to adopt, amend and promulgate rules and regulations, not inconsistent with this act, to carry into effect its provisions." [97] The purpose of this delegation is, as suggested by the New York statute, to provide a means for implementing by executive action the legislative objectives and requirements as set forth in the athletic commission statute.

The most important issue with respect to rule-making by athletic commissions concerns the extent to which courts will review the rules adopted.[98] Although it is clear that review will be available in properly presented cases,[99] the scope

---

92. Bay State Harness Horse Racing & Breeding Ass'n v. State Racing Comm'n, 342 Mass. 694, 175 N.E.2d 244 (1961).

93. *See, e.g.,* Ashbacker Radio Corp. v. Federal Communications Comm'n, 326 U.S. 327, 90 L. Ed. 108, 66 S. Ct. 148 (1945); Federal Communications Comm'n v. National Broadcasting Co., 319 U.S. 239, 89 L. Ed. 1374, 63 S. Ct. 1035 (1943).

94. The safeguards of procedural due process are considered at §§ 1.28, 2.18.

95. State *ex rel.* Investment Corp. of So. Fla. v. Board of Business Regulation, 227 So. 2d 674 (Fla. 1969). *See also* West Flagler Associates v. Division of Pari-Mutuel Wagering, 251 So. 2d 856 (Fla. 1971).

96. Tilleli v. Christenberry, 1 Misc. 2d 139, 120 N.Y.S.2d 697 (1953.) The various issues involved in the delegation of power are considered in detail in 1 F. COOPER, STATE ADMINISTRATIVE LAW 31-94 (1965).

97. N.Y. UNCONSOLIDATED LAWS § 7908 (McKinney Supp. 1978). See also ALA. CODE § 36-19-20 (1977); ILL. STAT. ANN. tit. 8, § 37s.5 (Smith-Hurd 1977); MICH. STAT. ANN. § 18.966(6) (1971); OHIO REV. CODE ANN. § 3769.03 (Page 1974). The propriety of such delegation is considered in Southern California Jockey Club, Inc. v. California Horse Racing Bd., 36 Cal. 2d 167, 223 P.2d 1 (1950). The legislature may not, however, delegate such power to private corporations, Fink v. Cole, 302 N.Y. 216, 97 N.E.2d 873 (1951); Murtha v. Monaghan, 7 Misc. 2d 568, 169 N.Y.S.2d 137 (1957), *aff'd,* 5 App. Div. 695, 169 N.Y.S.2d 1010 (1957), *aff'd,* 4 N.Y.2d 897, 174 N.Y.S.2d 648 (1958), though it is common for the commissions to be specifically authorized to adopt the rules of private entities which exert nation-wide control over particular sports. *See, e.g.,* CAL. BUS. & PROF. CODE § 19563 (West 1960); CONN. GEN. STAT. ANN. §§ 12-574 (1972); N.J. STAT. ANN. § 5:5-30 (1973). Private entity rule-making is considered at § 2.17.

98. The scope of review in general is considered at § 2.19.

99. State *ex rel.* Mason v. Rose, 122 Fla. 413, 165 So. 347 (1936); Brennan v. Illinois Racing Bd., 42 Ill. 2d 352, 247 N.E.2d 881 (1969). *See* § 2.19.

of review that will be accorded is not so certain. The terms of the statutory delegation are, as indicated by the New York provision quoted above, quite broad, and the courts have generally interpreted the breadth of delegation as indicating that commissions are to be accorded considerable discretion in performing this function.[100] The accordance of discretion does not, however, mean that the courts will not scrutinize the rules which are adopted. Indeed, as will be indicated in the next several sections, the courts regularly review the substance of commission rules.

In determining the proper scope of review of rules adopted by administrative agencies, the courts have commonly distinguished between so-called interpretative and legislative rules.[101] Interpretative rules are those which are not adopted pursuant to a specific delegation of legislative authority, but which are issued for the purpose of interpreting statutory provisions, judicial decisions or other things believed to be in need of interpretation.[102] With regard to interpretative rules, the scope of review is quite extensive. When such rules are challenged, the issue will be whether they represent a correct interpretation, and since interpretative rules do not rest upon a legislative delegation it is said that a court may substitute its judgment for that of the agency.[103] Interpretative rules have apparently played a small role in athletic commission regulation, since commissions are customarily granted specific rule-making authority. There may, however, be situations in which a commission will adopt rules for the purpose of interpreting judicial opinions or statutory provisions for which it has no affirmative rule-making authority. In those situations, a court will uphold the interpretative rule only if it concludes that the rule represents a correct interpretation.

A legislative rule, on the other hand, is one that is adopted pursuant to a specific delegation of legislative power.[104] The scope of review of such rules is much narrower than it is for interpretative rules. The delegation of authority from the legislative body to the agency is generally viewed as committing questions of desirability and wisdom to administrative and not to judicial judgment. Accordingly, a court may not substitute its judgment for that of the agency as to the substantive content of a rule.[105] Its review will be limited to determining whether the rule is valid. Although the courts have certainly not agreed on the precise standards to be used in determining validity, they have

---

100. *See, e.g.,* Colella v. State Racing Comm'n, 360 Mass. 152, 274 N.E.2d 331 (1971).
101. *See* 1 F. COOPER, STATE ADMINISTRATIVE LAW 174-75 (1965); 1 K. DAVIS, ADMINISTRATIVE LAW TREATISE § 5.03 (1958).
102. Skidmore v. Swift & Co., 325 U.S. 134, 89 L. Ed. 2d 124, 65 S. Ct. 161 (1944).
103. 1 F. COOPER, STATE ADMINISTRATIVE LAW 265-66 (1965); 1 K. DAVIS, ADMINISTRATIVE LAW TREATISE § 5.05 (1958).
104. *See* 1 F. COOPER, STATE ADMINISTRATIVE LAW 175-76 (1965); 1 K. DAVIS, ADMINISTRATIVE LAW TREATISE § 5.03 (1958).
105. Thus, in American Telephone & Telegraph Co. v. United States, 299 U.S. 232, 81 L. Ed. 142, 57 S. Ct. 170 (1936), the Supreme Court stated that

> [t]his court is not at liberty to substitute its own discretion for that of the administrative officers who have kept within the bounds of their administrative powers. Id. at 236.

See also State *ex rel.* Mason v. Rose, 122 Fla. 413, 165 So. 347 (1936); Mahoney v. Byers, 187 Md. 81, 48 A.2d 600 (1946).

identified several maxims that have been used for that purpose.[106] The essence
of these several maxims is suggested by the view that "[a] legislative rule is
valid and is as binding on a court as a statute if it is (a) within the granted power,
(b) issued pursuant to the proper procedure, and (c) reasonable." [107] This view
is useful because it appropriately narrows the inquiry to the basic issues that
seem to underlie the courts' various pronouncements on the validity of
legislative rules, which is about all that can be expected of a general standard
in this area. Once the issues are so defined, it is then much easier to analyze
the factual details and policy implications of a given case.[108]

With respect to the quoted statement, it may be observed that the validity of
any given rule will be determined primarily by analysis of the first and third
requirements, since the second (propriety of the procedure used to issue the rule)
has played a very small role in the reported cases.[109] Thus, when a legislative
rule is challenged, a court will consider whether it relates to a subject matter
that is within the authority delegated to the commission,[110] and, if it is, whether

---

106. These maxims have been identified to state the following propositions:
   (a) A rule is invalid if it exceeds the authority conferred;
   (b) A rule is invalid if it conflicts with the governing statute;
   (c) Rules are void if they extend or modify the statute;
   (d) Rules having no reasonable relationship to statutory purpose are void;
   (e) Courts will set aside rules deemed to be unconstitutional or arbitrary or unreasonable.
1 F. COOPER, STATE ADMINISTRATIVE LAW 250-62 (1965).

These maxims have been reflected in decisions involving athletic commissions. *See, e.g.,* Salmore
v. Empire Racing Ass'n, 123 N.Y.S.2d 688 (Sup. Ct. 1953) (rule invalid if it is capricious, arbitrary,
discriminatory or an abuse of authority); Casarona v. Pace, 175 Misc. 269, 22 N.Y.S.2d 726 (1940)
(same); Grandview Raceway, Inc. v. Ohio State Racing Comm'n, 6 Ohio App. 2d 91, 216 N.E.2d 765
(1966) (rule invalid where exceed statute).

In his treatise on state administrative law, Professor Cooper also suggests the difficulties that
exist in attempting to identify any standards in this area:
> In a field so surcharged with delicate questions of policy, and the balancing of competing
> claims and divergent governmental theories, the law cannot live on logic. The approach
> must be realistically pragmatic. While the decisions are ordinarily couched in maxims that
> set forth general "tests" as to the validity of rules, yet these formal criteria often express
> the result of a judgment rather than describing the means by which that judgment was
> reached. In interpreting and evaluating the decisions, the circumstances under which the
> rule was issued — and as well the circumstances of the particular application of the rule
> in the case before the court — must be carefully appraised. The general "tests" announced
> by the courts cannot be taken as talismanic touchstones to decision of any particular case.
> *Id.* at 251.

As suggested in text, the standards there identified are intended to define the issues that must be
addressed with respect to the validity of a legislative rule and are certainly not suggested as
possessing a talismanic basis for decision.

107. 1 K. DAVIS, ADMINISTRATIVE LAW TREATISE § 5.03 at 299, § 5.05 at 314, and § 5.11 at 358
(1958).

108. *See* 1 F. COOPER, STATE ADMINISTRATIVE LAW 262-63 (1965).

109. *See, e.g.,* Colella v. State Racing Comm'n, 360 Mass. 152, 274 N.E.2d 331 (1971); State Racing
Comm'n v. Robertson, 111 Ohio App. 435, 172 N.E.2d 628 (1960) (presumption that rules were
regularly adopted and promulgated by the commission). Rules which are adopted will be applicable
to only those persons who have been fairly notified of their application. Moshier v. La Crosse County
Agrl. Soc'y, 90 Wis. 37, 62 N.W. 932 (1895) (fair notification not present, and owner of horses not
bound, even when notification of such application was contained in an advertisement).

110. *See* Department of Business Regulation v. Vandervoort, 273 So. 2d 66 (Fla. 1973); Chicago
Division of the Horsemen's Benevolent & Protective Ass'n v. Illinois Racing Board, 53 Ill. 2d 16,
289 N.E.2d 421 (1972); Hesseltine v. State Athletic Comm'n, 6 Ill. 2d 129, 126 N.E.2d 631 (1955);
Tassistro v. Louisiana State Racing Comm'n, 269 So. 2d 834 (La. App. 1972); Grandview Raceway,
Inc. v. Ohio State Racing Comm'n, 6 Ohio App. 2d 91, 216 N.E.2d 765 (1966); Ohio Thoroughbred
Racing Ass'n v. Ohio State Racing Comm'n, 114 Ohio App. 80, 180 N.E.2d 276 (1961).

the rule is reasonable.[111] A rule will be "reasonable" in this sense if it is drafted in such a manner as to achieve only the proper purpose of the delegated authority.[112]

The use of these two levels of inquiry is illustrated by *Brennan v. Illinois Racing Board,*[113] where the athletic commission had been concerned with the use of drugs to stimulate the performance of racing animals and had adopted a rule which imposed absolute responsibility upon a trainer for any drugs found in animals under his or her control. When this rule was challenged, the court held that the commission did have the power to prohibit the administration of such stimulants, but that the rule as drafted was not reasonable since by making all trainers absolute insurers the rule could be used to punish both those who were and those who were not guilty of administering drugs.[114] In other words, the rule was within the commission's authority but was not reasonable — it related to the delegated authority of the commission but was drafted too broadly.

In addition to what are identified as authority and reasonableness inquiries, a given rule must also meet applicable constitutional requirements.[115] Although

---

111. *See* Jones v. Kind, 61 So. 2d 188 (Fla. 1952); State *ex rel.* Paoli v. Baldwin, 159 Fla. 156, 31 So. 2d 627 (1947); Mahoney v. Byers, 187 Md. 81, 48 A.2d 600 (1946); Colella v. State Racing Comm'n, 360 Mass. 152, 274 N.E.2d 331 (1971); New York Standardbred Farm Owners, Inc. v. Agriculture & N.Y. State Horse Breeding Dev. Fund., 71 Misc. 2d 671, 336 N.Y.S.2d 825 (1972); Battles v. Ohio State Racing Comm'n, 12 Div. App. 2d 52, 230 N.E.2d 662 (1967).

The meaning of the term "reasonable" is not altogether clear. Professor Davis suggests that

> [t]he requirement of reasonableness stems both from the idea of constitutional due process and from the idea of statutory interpretation that legislative bodies are assumed to intend to avoid the delegation of power to act unreasonably. 1 K. DAVIS, ADMINISTRATIVE LAW TREATISE § 5.03, at 299 (1958).

This view does not define the term "reasonable" but, as will be developed in the succeeding sections, the term is generally used to express the idea that when a commission exercises rule-making power, over a subject that is within its authority, it may not adopt rules that affect persons whose conduct need not be regulated to achieve the purpose of the delegated authority.

112. It is to be noted that the analysis suggested here is roughly similar to that identified in chapter 1 with respect to rule-making by amateur athletic associations and institutions. See § 1.15. It is similar because the issues raised in both contexts (at least with respect to public rule-makers) relate to rule-making authority derived, directly or indirectly, from the appropriate legislative body. The major difference between the methods of analysis is that in chapter 1 more emphasis was placed upon the requirement that the rule-maker have authority to adopt a given rule, which would be satisfied if a rule was directly related to a legitimate objective of the rule-maker. In the present discussion, the authority issue is phrased more broadly, and requires only that a rule relate to a subject matter that is within the authority delegated to the athletic commission. The degree of relationship here is less than would be required in the amateur situation, and the reason is that the legislative delegation is usually much clearer with respect to athletic commissions than it is with respect to amateur athletic organizations, whose authority may be much more ambiguous in terms of both source and scope.

113. 42 Ill. 2d 352, 247 N.E.2d 881 (1969).

114. 247 N.E.2d at 884:

> No question is presented of the power to prohibit the administering of drugs or stimulants to horses, or to require reasonable measures to be taken for protection against such acts. But making the trainer an absolute insurer, at the peril of losing his license regardless of how innocent he may be, is arbitrary and unreasonable.

See also Harbour v. Colorado State Racing Comm'n, 32 Colo. App. 1, 505 P.2d 22 (1973); Colella v. State Racing Comm'n, 360 Mass. 152, 274 N.E.2d 331 (1971); *In re* Cline, 3 Ohio App. 2d 345, 210 N.E.2d 737 (1964); State Racing Comm'n v. Robertson, 111 Ohio App. 435, 172 N.E.2d 628 (1960) (rule within range of delegated authority, but unreasonable in scope); State *ex rel.* Morris v. West Virginia Racing Comm'n, 133 W. Va. 129, 55 S.E.2d 263 (1949).

115. Mones v. Austin, 318 F. Supp. 653 (S.D. Fla. 1970); Douglas Park Jockey Club v. Talbott, 173 Ky. 685, 191 S.W. 474 (1917). *See* § 1.15.

the constitutional and nonconstitutional analyses may theoretically overlap in some cases, it is important to keep them separate since it may not be appropriate or desirable to reach constitutional issues in some cases.

The types of rules that have been adopted by athletic commissions cover all aspects of the sports regulated and present a virtually endless list of potential subject matters for discussion, but the following sections will consider only those which have been made the subject of judicial scrutiny.

§ 2.05. Good Conduct and Character.

The primary purpose for the creation of state athletic commissions has been to establish or restore confidence in the honesty of competition through state regulation. Apparently, one of the basic factors which undermined such confidence was the presence of persons whose conduct or character was such as to raise a substantial question as to whether the sports events with which they were associated were being conducted in an entirely honest manner.[116] In order to insure public confidence to the greatest possible extent, athletic commissions have frequently adopted rules which require that licensees conduct themselves in a manner that is deemed appropriate by the commission.[117]

In considering the good conduct rules, it is first appropriate to consider the more general body of law dealing with the permissibility of good conduct and character requirements in professional licensing procedures. The Supreme Court has made it clear that a state has a substantial and constitutionally valid interest in determining whether an applicant for a professional license possesses the requisite character and fitness for that profession. Although the standards which it applies are inevitably vague and indefinite, the Court has indicated that the state's conduct requirements and findings must themselves be reasonably precise.[118] Thus, in *Konigsberg v. State Bar of California,*[119] an applicant for admission to the bar was denied certification because he had failed to establish "good moral character." In reviewing this determination, the Court observed that

> [t]he term "good moral character" has long been used as a qualification for membership in the Bar and has served a useful purpose in this respect. However, the term, by itself is unusually ambiguous. It can be defined in an almost unlimited number of ways for any definition

---

116. *See* § 2.02.

117. Such a rule may provide, for example, as follows:

If any licensed person uses improper language to the racing officials or threatens such officials, or if any person uses profane or indecent language, carries or exhibits a deadly weapon, or otherwise disturbs the peace of any race track enclosure, he may be ejected, fined, suspended or ruled off. Fischbach v. Ohio State Racing Comm'n, 76 Ohio L. Abs. 540, 147 N.E.2d 258 (1955).

The most common use of "character" rules is in statutory provisions setting forth grounds for the issuance or suspension of licenses. *See* §§ 2.03, 2.18.

118. Schware v. Board of Bar Examiners of State of N.M., 353 U.S. 232, 1 L. Ed. 2d 796, 77 S. Ct. 752 (1957); Konigsberg v. State Bar of California, 353 U.S. 252, 1 L. Ed. 2d 810, 77 S. Ct. 722 (1957). *See also* Arnett v. Kennedy, 416 U.S. 134, 40 L. Ed. 2d 15, 94 S. Ct. 1633 (1974); *In re* Griffiths, 413 U.S. 717, 37 L. Ed. 2d 190, 83 S. Ct. 2851 (1973); Law Students Research Council v. Wadmond, 401 U.S. 154, 27 L. Ed. 2d 749, 91 S. Ct. 720 (1971); Hoke v. Board of Medical Examiners of North Carolina, 395 F. Supp. 357 (W.D. N.C. 1975); Pennsylvania State Horse Racing Comm'n v. Dancer, 16 Pa. Commw. Ct. 525, 333 A.2d 196 (1975).

119. 353 U.S. 252, 1 L. Ed. 2d 810, 77 S. Ct. 722 (1957).

will necessarily reflect the attitudes, experiences, and prejudices of the definer. Such a vague qualification, which is easily adapted to fit personal views and predilections, can be a dangerous instrument for arbitrary and discriminatory denial of the right to practice law.[120]

In order to avoid arbitrary use of such standards, the Court indicated that the term "good moral conduct" must be defined. It was able to find a satisfactory definition in the decisions of the state supreme court.[121] The Court also required that there be evidence to support a conclusion that such good conduct had not been demonstrated by the applicant, and since such evidence was not present in the record of the instant case the denial of certification was held to be improper.[122] The *Konigsberg* case, then, suggests that the state may utilize good conduct requirements so long as there exists a reasonable definition of the types of conduct to which the standard may be applied.[123]

When good conduct rules are considered in the regulated sports context, it would appear that such rules would generally be within the authority of a commission. The basic purpose of state regulation of sports has been to eliminate factors which undermine public confidence and perhaps the most apparent factor has been the presence of certain types of undesirable individuals. The barring of such individuals from the sport would, therefore, appear to be within the rule-making authority of athletic commissions. In order to be enforceable, however, the rules must also be reasonable, and this will require that they affect only those persons whose conduct it is necessary to control.[124] Reasonableness, in this sense will mean that the standards of required conduct be defined and that such standards relate to the sport in question. The application of these principles is illustrated by *State Racing Commission v. Robertson*,[125] where a good conduct rule which provided that a license could be revoked for "improper practice . . . or for conduct detrimental to the best interests of racing" was found to be within the authority of the commission, but inapplicable to a jockey who had been charged with petit larceny. The court found it inapplicable because the words of the rule were too broad and indefinite and, as illustrated by the facts at hand, could be used to punish conduct that had no direct relationship to the conduct of horse racing.[126] The specific defects in the rule considered in *Robertson* were that the rule did not define the types of conduct required and the conduct in question (a petit larceny conviction) was not related to horse

120. *Id.* at 262-63.
121. Thus, it noted that the state court had defined "good moral character" in terms of "an absence of proven conduct or acts which have been historically considered as manifestations of 'moral turpitude.'" *Id.* at 263.
122. *Id.* at 273-74. *See also* Baird v. State Bar of Arizona, 401 U.S. 1, 27 L. Ed. 2d 639, 91 S. Ct. 702 (1971); Schware v. Board of Bar Examiners of State of N.M., 353 U.S. 232, 1 L. Ed. 2d 796, 77 S. Ct. 752 (1957).
123. Thus, in Pennsylvania State Athletic Comm'n v. Loughran, 9 Pa. D. & C.2d 427 (1956), the court held that the term "detrimental to the best interests of boxing" was not too vague. *See also* Arnett v. Kennedy, 416 U.S. 134, 161, 40 L. Ed. 2d 15, 94 S. Ct. 1633 (1974); Pennsylvania State Athletic Comm'n v. Graziano, 12 Pa. D. & C. 127, 70 Dauph. 257 (1957). *See* § 2.09 n. 17-18. *See generally* 2 F. COOPER, STATE ADMINISTRATIVE LAW 487-90 (1965).
124. State Racing Comm'n v. Robertson, 111 Ohio App. 435, 172 N.E.2d 628 (1960). *See* § 2.04.
125. 111 Ohio App. 435, 172 N.E.2d 628 (1960).
126. *Id.* at 632. *See also* Arkansas Racing Comm'n v. Emprise Corp., 497 S.W.2d 34 (1973) (rule which provided that corporate shareholders could be required to divest themselves of their interest because they were undesirable; *see* § 2.06).

racing. Where these defects are not present, the application of good conduct rules should be upheld.

Good conduct requirements have also been considered in a rather wide variety of circumstances and have been upheld where there was a record indicating indifferent and lackadaisical competition; [127] failure to participate in a scheduled event; [128] unauthorized entry into a horse stall; [129] the use of an electric prod by a jockey; [130] the failure of a manager to report the physical disabilities of a fighter; [131] a manager holding an improper financial interest in a boxer; [132] gambling activities; [133] a failure to disclose a criminal history on a license application; [134] and the giving of instructions to fighters and managers to lose a fight. [135] It has also been held that a good conduct rule could be utilized to bar a person with a record indicating a conviction for a felony or military offense. Thus, in *Ali v. State Athletic Commission*, [136] the court observed that

> [a]lthough conviction of a crime involving moral turpitude should have little or no effect upon a boxer's athletic skill or physical prowess in the ring, it could bear upon his proclivity to corruption or upon the general reputation of professional boxing as a sport. For these reasons the action of a state or its agency in barring convicted persons from certain types of employment affecting the public has been upheld as constitutional. [137]

The distinction between the type of crimes noted in *Ali* and the petit larceny conviction in *Robertson* would appear to be in terms of the connection that the crime itself bears to the sport being regulated, though in light of the language in *Ali* one might question the result in *Robertson*.

It should, finally, be noted that, as indicated by *Konigsberg* and *Robertson*, the primary issue which will be present in most cases involving conduct or

---

127. Beikrich v. New York State Racing & Wagering Bd., 48 App. Div. 2d 954, 369 N.Y.S.2d 36 (1975) (driving horse into path of oncoming animal); Application of Harner, 12 App. Div. 2d 987, 210 N.Y.S.2d 937 (1961); Mac Rae v. New York Racing & Wagering Bd., 48 App. Div. 2d 245, 368 N.Y.S.2d 313 (1975); Pennsylvania State Harness Racing Comm'n v. Dancer, 16 Pa. Commw. Ct. 525, 333 A.2d 196 (1975) (horse not in position at starting gate); Poisson v. State Harness Racing Comm'n, 5 Pa. Commw. Ct. 20, 287 A.2d 852 (1972) (driving rig not intending to win).

128. Ruane v. New York State Racing & Wagering Bd., 400 F. Supp. 819 (S.D.N.Y. 1975), *aff'd per curiam,* 532 F.2d 860 (2d Cir. 1976). *See also* Dougherty v. State Harness Racing Comm'n, 286 App. Div. 837, 142 N.Y.S.2d 421 (1955), *aff'd,* 309 N.Y. 992, 132 N.E.2d 898 (1956).

129. In re Cline, 3 Ohio App. 2d 345, 210 N.E.2d 737 (1964).

130. Arkansas Racing Comm'n v. Sayler, 249 Ark. 913, 462 S.W.2d 472 (1971); Durousseau v. Nebraska State Racing Comm'n, 194 Neb. 288, 231 N.W.2d 566 (1975); Dennehy v. American Horse Shows Ass'n, 82 Misc. 2d 846, 371 N.Y.S.2d 46 (1975).

131. Pennsylvania State Athletic Comm'n v. Loughran, 9 Pa. D. & C.2d 427 (1956).

132. Pennsylvania State Athletic Comm'n v. Moran, 6 Pa. D. & C.2d 611, 68 Dauph. 388 (1956). *See* § 2.14.

133. State Racing Comm'n v. Latonia Agrl. Ass'n, 136 Ky. 173, 123 S.W. 681 (1909).

134. Fineman v. New York State Harness Racing Comm'n, 33 App. Div. 2d 144, 306 N.Y.S.2d 271 (1970); Lombardo v. DiSandro, 8 R.I. 393, 103 A.2d 557 (1954).

135. Rudolph v. Athletic Comm'n of California, 177 Cal. App. 2d 1, 1 Cal. Rptr. 898 (1960). *See also* Pennsylvania State Racing Comm'n v. Di Santo, 29 Pa. Commw. Ct. 574, 372 A.2d 487 (1977) (instructing jockey not to win).

136. 316 F. Supp. 1246 (S.D.N.Y. 1970).

137. *Id.* at 1250 (rule actually held proper, but unconstitutional as applied; *see* § 2.03). *See also* Mules v. Maryland Racing Comm'n, 30 Md. App. 533, 353 A.2d 664 (1976) (conviction of veterinarian for offenses relating to controlled substances).

character is whether there is substantial evidence to support a finding that the rule was violated.[138] This matter is discussed at length in a later section.[139]

§ 2.06. Undesirable Shareholders.

Athletic commissions have also undertaken to control the types of persons who may be shareholders in corporate licensees. This is frequently the result of specific statutory direction that in determining whether to issue a license to a corporate applicant, the commission may refuse issuance if one or more of its shareholders has engaged in specified types of activities.[140] Statutory provisions have also been enacted which allow a commission to control who may become shareholders of a corporate licensee; [141] to revoke or suspend the license of a corporation with undesirable shareholders; [142] to refuse to license a corporation whose charter does not contain a provision requiring any shareholder to sell his or her shares upon the demand of the commission; [143] to regulate the transfer of shares in corporate licensees; [144] to preclude public officials or political party officers from owning shares in a corporate licensee; [145] and to require all corporate licensees to file lists setting forth the names and addresses of all

---

138. Fischbach v. Ohio State Racing Comm'n, 76 Ohio L. Abs. 540, 147 N.E.2d 258 (1955) (no evidence to support charge of creating a public disturbance); Bagley v. Pennsylvania State Horse Racing Comm'n, 15 Pa. Commw. Ct. 258, 326 A.2d 651 (1974) (no evidence that trainer had violated rule by entering a horse that was not in proper racing condition); Dancer v. Commonwealth Harness Racing Comm'n, 10 Pa. Commw. Ct. 642, 309 A.2d 614 (1973) (no evidence that harness driver had not maintained proper pace).

139. *See* § 2.19.

140. N.Y. UNCONSOL. LAWS § 8008 (5) (McKinney 1961), for example, provides as follows:

The commission may refuse to grant a license to an association or corporation if it shall determine that (a) any officer, director, member or stockholder of such association or corporation applying for a license, or of any association or corporation which owns stock in or shares in the profits or participates in the management, of the affairs of such applicant, or which leases to such applicant the track where it shall operate.
　(1) has been convicted of a crime involving moral turpitude;
　(2) has engaged in bookmaking or other forms of illegal gambling;
　(3) has been found guilty of any fraud or misrepresentation in connection with racing
　　or breeding;
　(4) has been guilty of any violation or attempt to violate any law, rule or regulation of
　　any racing jurisdiction for which suspension from racing might be imposed in such
　　jurisdiction;
　(5) has violated any rule, regulation or order of the commission; or
　(b) The experience, character or general fitness of any officer, director or stockholder of any of the aforesaid associations or corporations is such that the participation of such person in harness racing or related activities would be inconsistent with the public interest, convenience or necessity or with the best interests of racing generally; but if the commission determines that the interest of any stockholder referred to in this paragraph or in paragraph (a) of this subdivision is insufficient in the opinion of the commission to affect adversely the conduct of pari-mutuel harness racing by such association or corporation in accordance with the provisions of this article, the commission may disregard such interest in determining whether or not to grant a license to such association or corporation . . . .

See also CAL. BUS. & PROF. CODE § 18681.6 (West 1960); N.Y. UNCONSOL. LAWS § 8912 (McKinney 1974).

141. *See, e.g.,* N.J. STAT. ANN. § 5:5-34.1 (1973).

142. *See, e.g.,* ARK. STAT. ANN. § 84-2823.3 (b) (Supp. 1977).

143. *See, e.g.,* N.Y. UNCONSOL. LAWS § 8008(6) (McKinney 1961).

144. *See, e.g.,* ARIZ. REV. STAT. ANN. § 5-108.02(B) (1974) (may revoke license if sell more than 10% of shares); N.Y. UNCONSOL. LAWS § 8008(9) (McKinney 1961); PA. STAT. ANN. tit. 4, § 304 (Purdon's 1963) (must file reports when stock transferred).

145. *See. e.g.,* N.Y. UNCONSOL. LAWS § 8052(1) (McKinney Supp. 1978).

shareholders.[146] Inasmuch as the power to control the identity of shareholders is in derogation of the rights of those individuals to freely invest their moneys and energies, the statutory provisions will be strictly construed. Thus, where a commission is given only authority to revoke or suspend the license of a corporation with undesirable shareholders, it may not seek to eliminate some shareholders by a conditional revocation of the corporation's license.[147]

Where the commission is not granted specific statutory authority to control the shareholders in corporate licensees, its power to exercise such control will be limited by the extent of its general rule-making power.[148] Such rules would appear to be within the delegated authority to the extent that they seek to exclude from the sport persons whose character or conduct would be detrimental to public confidence in the sport, since the prevention of abuses and the protection of the public interest are the legislative objectives which athletic commissions are designed to accomplish.[149] The rules must also be reasonable, and this will mean that they may affect only those persons whose conduct it is necessary to control. Thus, if the rule is too broad in its coverage and affects persons whose conduct need not be controlled for achievement of the legislative objectives, it will then be unreasonable and unlawful.

The primary case dealing with attempts to control shareholders, in the absence of specific statutory authorization, is *Jones v. Kind,*[150] where the state racing commission had concluded that several of the shareholders of an applicant were "undesirable" and that their presence would be "hurtful to racing in this state." The commission then ordered those shareholders to dispose of their interests in the corporation. In holding that the commission's action was unlawful, the court stated that the descriptions of the shareholders in question as "undesirable" and "hurtful to racing in this state" were too vague and uncertain. The use of those descriptions as guidelines would, the court said, give the commission virtually unbridled and unlimited authority to determine who was desirable as a holder of stock in corporate licensees.[151] Although the court's

---

146. *See, e.g.,* N.Y. UNCONSOL. LAWS § 8051 (McKinney 1961).

147. Arkansas Racing Comm'n v. Emprise Corp., 254 Ark. 975, 497 S.W.2d 34 (1973). Similarly, where a statute allowed sanctions to be imposed only if officers, directors or employees of a corporate licensee had been convicted of a felony, a commission order suspending the license when a shareholder had been convicted was quashed. State *ex rel.* Volusia Jai-Alai, Inc. v. Board of Business Regulation, 304 So. 2d 473 (Fla. App. 1974).

148. *See* § 2.04.

149. *See* §§ 2.02, 2.05. *See generally* North Dakota Bd. of Pharmacy v. Snyder's Drugstores, Inc., 414 U.S. 156, 38 L.Ed. 2d 379, 94 S. Ct. 407 (1973).

150. 61 So. 2d 188 (Fla. 1952).

151. Specifically, the court stated that:

> There is no yardstick or limitation as to what would make, in the opinion of the members of the Commission, the stockholder "undesirable" and would cause him to be "regarded by all members of the Commission" as being undesirable and hurtful in this state and because of "public opposition" to the stockholder's connection with Florida racing.
> To many people who are opposed to pari-mutuel racing in Florida, all persons owning stock in a corporation conducting a race track may be "undesirable" and such people may be a part of the "public" which would constitute "public opposition" to the particular stockholder's connection with Florida racing and to all other persons owning stock in Florida racing. The words "undesirable" and "public opposition" are very elastic terms. To the owners of stock of a competing race track all stockholders of another race track may be undesirable and the owners of the stock or the competing corporation may be a part of the public which would be in opposition to stockholders owning stock in another corporation conducting racing. Many people in the state (a part of the public) are opposed

opinion is not entirely clear, it would appear that the specific defect in the commission's action was its failure to adopt a rule which specified the grounds upon which a person could be required to sever his or her relationship with a corporate licensee.[152] If such specification had been made, and if the grounds specified related to the conduct of the sport in question, then the commission's action would probably have been upheld, provided that there was also substantial evidence to support a finding that the complainant's conduct was covered by the specifications.[153] It has also been held that a commission could not arbitrarily compel minority shareholders to divest themselves of their shares;[154] or undertake an arbitrary and unbridled investigation into alleged interlocking stock ownership in corporate licensees.[155]

Although the statutory enactments and commission-adopted rules may be cast in broad and imprecise terms, their validity will be determined in the same manner as has already been considered with respect to good conduct and character rules.[156]

§ 2.07. Drugs.

The type of athletic commission rules which have most frequently been the subject of judicial scrutiny are those relating to the application of drugs to racing animals. The purpose of the drug control rules is to maintain the integrity and honesty of the sport by insuring that the outcome of races is not influenced by the use of stimulants or other drugs that will artificially increase the speed or performance of the animal in question.[157] In determining the validity of a particular drug rule, the first step will be to determine whether it is within the rule-making authority and is reasonable in scope.[158] In some cases, authority for such rules is specifically delegated,[159] but even where such specific authority is not present the power to regulate the administration of drugs would appear to be within the commission's general authority to maintain the integrity of the sport.[160] Whether the rules will be reasonable, however, will depend upon whether they affect only those persons whose conduct it is necessary to control and cover only drugs which in fact have a detrimental effect upon the racing

to race tracks, poolrooms, barrooms, cocktail lounges and many other things which may be distasteful to them, but which have been legalized and licensed to operate in this state. 61 So. 2d at 191.

152. To this extent the case is similar to *State Racing Commission v. Robertson,* discussed in § 2.05. Such specification would appear to be present, for example, in a rule that followed the New York provision cited at note 140 *supra.*

153. *See* §§ 2.05, 2.19.

154. Hazel Park Racing Ass'n v. Inglis, 336 Mich. 508, 58 N.W.2d 241 (1953).

155. Saratoga Harness Racing Ass'n v. Monaghan, 9 Misc. 2d 868, 169 N.Y.S.2d 520 (1958).

156. *See* § 2.05.

157. Hubel v. West Virginia Racing Comm'n, 513 F.2d 240 (4th Cir. 1975); Sandstrom v. California Horse Racing Bd., 31 Cal. 2d 401, 189 P.2d 17, 3 A.L.R.2d 90 (1948), *cert. denied,* 335 U.S. 814, 93 L. Ed. 369, 69 S. Ct. 31 (1948). The application of drugs to animals may also result in criminal conviction. *See, e.g.,* People v. Otash, 186 Cal. App. 2d 132, 8 Cal. Rptr. 878 (1960) (defendant convicted of conspiracy to administer drug to horse).

158. *See* § 2.04.

159. *See, e.g.,* N.Y. UNCONSOL. LAWS § 7908 (McKinney Supp. 1978).

160. *See, e.g.,* Sandstrom v. California Horse Racing Bd., 31 Cal. 2d 401, 189 P.2d 17 (1948), *cert. denied,* 335 U.S. 814, 93 L. Ed. 2d 369, 69 S. Ct. 31 (1948); Tassistro v. Louisiana State Racing Comm'n, 269 So. 2d 841 (La. App. 1972); Commonwealth v. Webb, 1 Pa. Commw. Ct. 151, 274 A.2d 261 (1971).

ability of the animal to which they are administered. Thus, where a rule made the owners of tracks the insurers of the drug-free condition of all horses racing on their track, it was found to be unreasonable and unlawful since it was too sweeping and encompassed persons whose conduct was not reasonably related to its purpose.[161] Similarly, it has been held that it is unreasonable to apply a drug rule in a situation where the drug discovered in the animal was not proven to have a direct effect on the animal's racing ability.[162]

The primary problem posed by the drug rules relates to their customary inclusion of a provision which specifies that if a drug is found in an animal, then the trainer, jockey or some other person shall be presumed to have had knowledge of, or to have been responsible for, its presence.[163] This presumption is variously stated in the rules to be "conclusive"[164] or "prima facie"[165] evidence, or that the trainer or other person is an "absolute insurer" of,[166] shall "be held responsible"[167] or shall have "strict accountability"[168] for the condition of the animal. The particular form in which the presumption is cast is not, however, crucial to its validity.[169] What is important is its operative effect. The constitutional issue posed by the inclusion of such a presumption is whether it would be consistent with the requirements of due process of law, which establish limitations on the propriety of making the proof of one fact (in this case a drug in the animal) evidence of the existence of the ultimate fact upon which guilt will be predicated.[170] The standard by which such presumptions will

---

161. Ohio Thoroughbred Racing Ass'n v. Ohio State Racing Comm'n, 114 Ohio App. 80, 180 N.E.2d 276 (1961).

162. *See* Battles v. Ohio State Racing Comm'n, 12 Ohio App. 2d 52, 230 N.E.2d 662 (1967).

163. An additional problem that may be present with respect to drug problems in regulated sports activities involves the validity of a consent that is often required of licensees for the commission to search any premises which the licensee occupies or controls. *See* § 2.03, at note 57. A consent to search and seizure will normally be upheld so long as it is given voluntarily and knowingly by the person in question. *See* AMERICAN LAW INSTITUTE, A MODEL CODE OF PRE-ARRAIGNMENT PROCEDURE 148-51, 532-38 (1975). Such a consent was specifically upheld in Lanchester v. Pennsylvania State Horse Racing Comm'n, 16 Pa. Commw. Ct. 85, 325 A.2d 648 (1974), where the court stated that

> [w]here an individual entering a traditionally regulated licensed field such as horse racing consents to a warrantless search of his person or premises directly related to or involved in that endeavor, his consent is held to constitute a waiver of his Fourth Amendment protections within the limits of valid regulation. *Id.* at 653.

Warrantless searches based upon statutory authorization have been approved by the Supreme Court with respect to licensed activities. *See, e.g.,* United States v. Biswell, 406 U.S. 311, 92 S. Ct. 1593, 32 L. Ed. 2d 87 (1972); Colonnade Catering Corp. v. United States, 397 U.S. 72, 90 S. Ct. 774, 25 L. Ed. 2d 60 (1970) (could not effect warrantless search with forcible entry).

164. Mahoney v. Byers, 187 Md. 81, 48 A.2d 600 (1946).

165. Tassistro v. Louisiana State Racing Comm'n, 269 So. 2d 834 (La. App. 1972).

166. Sandstrom v. California Horse Racing Bd., 31 Cal. 2d 401, 189 P.2d 17, 3 A.L.R.2d 90, *cert. denied,* 335 U.S. 814, 93 L. Ed. 369, 69 S. Ct. 31 (1948); State *ex rel* Paoli v. Baldwin, 159 Fla. 165, 31 So. 2d 627 (1947); Brennan v. Illinois Racing Bd., 42 Ill. 2d 352, 247 N.E.2d 881 (1969); Fogt v. Ohio State Racing Comm'n, 3 Ohio App. 2d 423, 210 N.E.2d 730 (1965).

167. State *ex rel.* Morris v. West Virginia Racing Comm'n, 133 W. Va. 179, 55 S.E.2d 263 (1949).

168. Jamison v. State Racing Comm'n, 84 N.M. 679, 507 P.2d 426 (1973).

169. *See* Christie & Pye, *Presumptions and Assumptions in the Criminal Law: Another View,* 1970 DUKE L.J. 919, 925 (1970).

170. Tot v. United States, 319 U.S. 463, 468, 87 L. Ed. 1519, 63 S. Ct. 1241 (1943); Manley v. Georgia, 279 U.S. 1, 6, 73 L. Ed. 575, 49 S. Ct. 215 (1929). *See generally* 1 WHARTON'S CRIMINAL EVIDENCE § 94 (13th ed. 1972).

be tested was stated by the Supreme Court in *Leary v. United States*[171] to be that a "presumption must be regarded as 'irrational' or 'arbitrary,' and hence unconstitutional, unless it can at least be said with substantial assurance that the presumed fact is more likely than not to flow from the proved fact on which it is made to depend." [172] Applying this standard to the facts before it, the Court in *Leary* struck down a statutory rule that one in possession of marijuana would be presumed to have knowledge of its illegal importation, since it could not be said with "substantial assurance that those who possessed marijuana would know it to have been illegally imported." [173] In short, the presumed fact of knowledge did not "more likely than not" flow from the proven fact of possession." [174]

In light of these principles, it would appear that presumptions in drug rules would be lawful only if the fact presumed (knowledge or responsibility) is more likely than not to flow from the proven fact (a drug in an animal subject to the defendant's control). Although this proposition would appear to be one that could be applied with relative ease, the courts have clearly split in several directions.[175] The numerical majority have reached the conclusion that such presumptions are lawful.[176] The leading case expressing this result is *Sandstrom v. California Horse Racing Board*,[177] where a rule made the trainer an "absolute insurer" of the condition of the horse, and when a drug was found in the horse in question, its trainer's license was suspended. In upholding the validity of the rule, the court concluded that its effect was to impose upon the trainer "strict liability" for the condition of the animal and as such required no proof of fault. Since the rule did not require proof of fault, the court said, it did not involve a presumption. The court then concluded that it was not "unreasonable, arbitrary or capricious

---

171. 395 U.S. 6, 23 L. Ed. 2d 57, 89 S. Ct. 1532 (1969).

172. *Id.* at 36. The Court in *Leary* relied upon its earlier formulation in Tot v. United States, 319 U.S. 463, 87 L. Ed. 1519, 63 S. Ct. 1241 (1943).

173. 395 U.S. at 53-54.

174. *Leary* was followed in Turner v. United States, 396 U.S. 398, 24 L. Ed. 2d 610, 90 S. Ct. 642 (1970). *See also* Cleveland Bd. of Educ. v. La Fleur, 414 U.S. 632, 39 L. Ed. 2d 52, 94 S. Ct. 791 (1974) (conclusive presumption that pregnant teachers are unfit after fifth month); Vlandis v. Kline, 412 U.S. 441, 37 L. Ed. 2d 63, 93 S. Ct. 2230 (1973) (irrebuttable presumption of non-residency); Stanley v. Illinois, 405 U.S. 645, 31 L. Ed. 2d 551, 92 S. Ct. 1208 (1972) (irrebuttable presumption that unmarried father is an unfit parent); Bell v. Burson, 402 U.S. 535, 29 L. Ed. 2d 90, 91 S. Ct. 1586 (1971) (conclusive presumption of fault from lack of automobile insurance). *Compare* Gainey v. United States, 380 U.S. 63, 13 L. Ed. 2d 658, 85 S. Ct. 754 (1965) *with* United States v. Romano, 382 U.S. 136, 15 L. Ed. 2d 210, 86 S. Ct. 279 (1965).

175. *See generally* Hoffmeier, *Some Horse-Racing Tips for Lawyers,* 50 A.B.A.J. 250, 251 (1964); Annot., 52 A.L.R.3d 206 (1973).

176. Sandstrom v. California Horse Racing Bd., 31 Cal. 2d 401, 189 P.2d 17, 3 A.L.R.2d 90, *cert. denied,* 335 U.S. 814, 93 L. Ed. 369, 69 S. Ct. 31 (1948); Taylor v. Wright, 84 Cal. App. 2d 521, 191 P.2d 73 (1948); Harbour v. Colorado State Racing Comm'n, 32 Colo. App. 1, 505 P.2d 22 (1973) (rule stated that presence of drug would be only "evidence" of responsibility); Tassistro v. Louisiana State Racing Comm'n, 269 So.2d 834 (La. App. 1972); Jamison v. State Racing Comm'n, 84 N.M. 679, 507 P.2d 426 (1973); Sanderson v. New Mexico State Racing Comm'n, 80 N.M. 200, 453 P.2d 370 (1969); Fogt v. Ohio State Racing Comm'n, 3 Ohio App. 2d 423, 210 N.E.2d 730 (1965); State *ex rel.* Spiker v. West Virginia Racing Comm'n, 135 W. Va. 512, 63 S.E.2d 831 (1951); State *ex rel.* Morris v. West Virginia Racing Comm'n, 133 W. Va. 179, 55 S.E.2d 263 (1949).

177. 31 Cal. 2d 401, 189 P.2d 17, 3 A.L.R.2d 90, *cert. denied,* 335 U.S. 814, 93 L. Ed. 369, 69 S. Ct. 31 (1948), *noted* in 22 S. Cal. L. Rev. 461 (1949).

to provide that the trainer guarantee the condition of a horse running in a race upon the results of which there is wagering." [178]

The result in *Sandstrom* is not, however, altogether persuasive for at least two reasons. The first is that the court sought to premise its decision as to the lawfulness of an administrative rule that had the effect of depriving a person of the right to engage in a professional activity without the necessity of proof of fault or improper conduct by analogy to "strict liability" concepts in tort law.[179] Although the strict liability concepts are an important development in tort law, they may not be a proper analogue for rules which deprive an individual of a professional license. The second reason that *Sandstrom* is not persuasive is its conclusion that the rule's requirement that the trainer be the "absolute insurer" of the condition of the horse in question did not involve a presumption. Regardless of what descriptive tag may be placed upon the rule considered in *Sandstrom,* it is clear that its effect was to make the fact of drug presence determinative of the trainer's responsibility therefor — that is, the presumed fact (responsibility) is made to flow *ipso facto* from the proven fact (a drug in the animal subject to the trainer's control). Even if the rule were not a presumption, its effect was to substitute the declaration of the rule-makers for the proof of facts, and such substitution is forbidden by the requirements of due process of law. Thus, the Supreme Court has stated that "[m]ere legislative fiat may not take the place of fact in the determination of issues involving life, liberty or property." [180] Inasmuch as the right of the trainer, or other party, to practice his or her licensed profession has been held to be a constitutionally protectible interest,[181] it would appear that rules such as that in *Sandstrom* may not be utilized to preempt a fact finding process, however they may be described.

Notwithstanding *Sandstrom,* several other courts have concluded that such presumptions are unlawful.[182] The leading case is *State ex rel. Paoli v. Baldwin,*[183] where a trainer's license had been suspended after a horse, for which he had been responsible, was found to have been drugged. The rule in question, like that in *Sandstrom,* provided that the trainer was the "absolute insurer" of the condition of the horses for which he was responsible. Unlike the court in *Sandstrom,* however, the court in *Baldwin* held the rule to be unlawful. It began by noting that the exercise of reasonable care by the trainer would be no defense under the rule. In the court's view, this fact indicated that "proof of the fact that a horse entered in a race has been administered a drug shall constitute irrebuttable evidence that the trainer violated [the rule]. This is the reason why

---

178. *Id.* at 412, 189 P.2d at 23. With respect to *Sandstrom,* it should also be noted that Justice Carter filed a very strong dissent. 31 Cal. 2d at 415-26, 189 P.2d at 25-31.

179. *See* 22 S. CAL. L. REV. 461, 464 (1949). Strict liability principles are considered at § 8.10.

180. Manley v. Georgia, 279 U.S. 1, 6, 73 L. Ed. 575, 49 S. Ct. 215 (1929).

181. *See* § 2.18.

182. State *ex rel.* Paoli v. Baldwin, 159 Fla. 165, 31 So.2d 267 (1947); Brennan v. Illinois Racing Bd., 42 Ill. 2d 352, 247 N.E.2d 881 (1969); Mahoney v. Byers, 187 Md. 81, 48 A.2d 600 (1946); Battles v. Ohio State Racing Comm'n, 12 Ohio App. 2d 52, 230 N.E.2d 662 (1967) (application of rule to specific drug held unreasonable, with the court distinguishing *Fogt v. Ohio State Racing Comm'n, noted at note 166, supra,* on the basis of the different drugs involved in each case). *See also* Samples v. Ohio State Racing Comm'n, 92 Ohio L. Abs. 481, 25 Ohio Op. 2d 265, 193 N.E.2d 552 (1963); Ohio Thoroughbred Racing Ass'n v. Ohio State Racing Comm'n, 114 Ohio App. 80, 180 N.E.2d 276 (1961).

183. 150 Fla. 165, 31 So. 2d 627 (1947).

[it] violates the due process clause of both our State and Federal Constitutions."[184] A similar result was reached in *Mahoney v. Byers*,[185] where the rule provided that the presence of drugs in a horse shall be "conclusive evidence" of knowledge or carelessness. The court held it to be unlawful since its effect was to create an irrebuttable presumption that prevented the proof of fact or demonstration of truth. In light of the requirements set forth by the Supreme Court in *United States v. Leary*,[186] it would appear that the results reached in *Baldwin* and *Mahoney v. Byers* are correct. As noted in discussing *Sandstrom*, a provision in a drug rule which makes a specific class of persons responsible for the presence of a drug in an animal does create a presumption however the rule be described, and to be permissible the presumed fact (knowledge or responsibility) must be more likely than not to flow from the proven fact (a drug in the animal under the control of the accused). Unless that nexus be shown, guilt may not be based upon presumption or fiat.

It should also be noted that after concluding that the presumption before it was unlawful, the court in *Mahoney v. Byers* suggested that if the goal to be achieved by drug rule presumptions is that of requiring the trainer, or other person, to provide for the continuous guarding of racing animals, then a rule should be adopted which imposes such a duty.[187] If such a rule were adopted, it would avoid the problem posed by the rules in *Sandstrom, Baldwin* and *Mahoney v. Byers*, since a violation could be found only if the trainer (or other person) were *proven* to have failed to meet the requirements of the rule.[188] The different process that would be required by such a rule is illustrated by *Commonwealth v. Webb*,[189] in which an athletic commission had adopted a rule requiring that all persons with responsibility for a horse "protect and guard the horse against the administration . . . of any drug. . . ." When a trainer was found to have violated the rule, he challenged the rule as constituting an irrebuttable presumption. In rejecting this argument, the court distinguished the rule in question from those in cases such as *Baldwin* and *Mahoney v. Byers*, since it contained no "absolute insurer" or "conclusive evidence" language. To the contrary, the rule required only that the trainer "protect and guard" his animals, and that a failure to meet that requirement could be found only by factual proof. Thus, the rule provided "ample opportunity for an embattled trainer to demonstrate his innocence, and likewise clearly provide that a penalty is not automatically imposed." [190] In light of the need for proof of violation, the court concluded that the rule contained no presumption. Since there was also substantial evidence in the record to support the commission's determination that the trainer had in fact violated the rule, his suspension was upheld.

---

184. *Id.* at 165, 31 So. 2d at 631.

185. 187 Md. 81, 48 A.2d 600 (1946).

186. *See* notes 171-74 *supra.*

187. 187 Md. at 88, 48 A.2d at 604.

188. Tassistro v. Louisiana State Racing Comm'n, 269 So.2d 834 (La. App. 1972); Maryland Racing Comm'n v. McGee, 212 Md. 69, 128 A.2d 419 (1957); Johnson v. Commonwealth State Horse Racing Comm'n, 5 Pa. Commw. Ct. 458, 290 A.2d 277 (1972); Conway v. State Horse Racing Comm'n, 2 Pa. Commw. Ct. 266, 276 A.2d 840 (1971); Commonwealth v. Webb, 1 Pa. Commw. Ct. 151, 274 A.2d 261 (1971).

189. 1 Pa. Commw. Ct. 151, 274 A. 2d 261 (1971).

190. *Id.* at 266. *See also* Edelberg v. Illinois Racing Bd., 540 F. 2d 279 (7th Cir. 1976) (rule allowed factual hearing as to whether animal was drugged).

Inasmuch as the presence of drugs in an animal is ascertained by the testing of saliva and/or urine samples by special laboratory processes, the finding that a drug was present in a particular animal may also raise issues concerning the testing process itself. The first will involve the certainty that the sample containing the drug was actually drawn from the animal in question. When the "chain of custody" issue has been raised, the courts have made it clear that the athletic commission will properly prove the "chain" by establishing regular procedures for the taking and analyzing of samples, that those procedures were in fact followed, and that there is reasonable certainty that the sample was taken from the suspected animal.[191] The second question that may arise is whether the person charged with having been responsible for the drug should have an opportunity to separately test the sample. Rules in some states specifically provide for this privilege,[192] and even absent such a provision it has been stated that "[f]airness and equity would dictate that [the person charged] ought to be provided with this additional device." [193]

§ 2.08. Minimum Fees.

In order to prevent disputes between licensed animal owners and athletes over compensation, athletic commissions have often adopted rules which set forth the minimum fees that must be paid for specified types of performances. The rules customarily specify that an athlete, in the absence of a special agreement to the contrary, must be paid a minimum fee for performing. The primary issue that has been raised by the minimum fee rules has been whether they are within a commission's authority absent specific statutory authorization. In order for a minimum fee rule to be upheld in these circumstances, it would appear that there would have to be a record indicating that the rule was necessary to the achievement of the general purposes of the commission. It has been suggested that the absence of a minimum fee requirement would produce disputes between owners and athletes over appropriate riding fees and that such disputes could interfere with the conduct of the sport. This argument would provide a basis for such a rule only if a factual showing could be made, for example, that the absence of minimum fees has produced disputes between owners and athletes or has otherwise interfered with the confidence of the public in the sport.

Although there are several cases that have considered the authority of commissions to adopt minimum fee rules, they do not provide much general guidance. In the one case that has found such authority to exist, the court noted that broad rule-making power had been delegated to the commission and then concluded that the minimum fee rule was within the power given.[194] It did not analyze the factors that would justify the authority, but simply concluded that the authority resulted from the general rule-making power. A similar approach

191. Tassistro v. Louisiana State Racing Comm'n, 269 So.2d 834 (La. App. 1972); Jamison v. State Racing Comm'n, 84 N.M. 679, 507 P.2d 426 (1973); Brown v. Waldman, 93 R.I. 489, 177 A.2d 179 (1962). If a person purposely changes samples taken from an animal in his custody, that act will itself violate the drug rules. *See* Norwood v. Pennsylvania Horse Racing Comm'n, 16 Pa. Commw. Ct. 219, 328 A.2d 198 (1974).

192. Tassistro v. Louisiana State Racing Comm'n, 269 So.2d 834 (La. App. 1972).

193. *Id.*

194. Colella v. State Racing Comm'n, 360 Mass. 152, 274 N.E.2d 331 (1971).

was used by another court to reach the opposite conclusion. In a short per curiam opinion, the court simply concluded that the power to establish minimum fees "is too broad . . . to be derived from the general statutes . . ." giving the commission rule-making power.[195]

While two of the three cases which have considered this question have held that authority does not exist,[196] it is difficult to generalize about the authority to adopt minimum fee rules. However, in the cases that have rejected such authority, it would appear that the commissions failed to persuade the courts of the factual basis establishing the necessity of such rules to the accomplishment of the commission's statutory purposes.[197] If such a showing can be made, then a minimum fee rule would appear to be within the authority generally granted to commissions.

If a minimum fee rule is found to be authorized, a question may also be raised as to whether it is reasonable. This objection would probably be framed in terms of reasonableness in the constitutional sense that the rule deprives an athlete of the right to fully negotiate a fee in violation of his or her equal protection or due process rights. In the only case to consider this question, the court found that such a rule did not abridge these rights since it established a minimum fee only in the absence of individually negotiated compensation arrangements.[198]

§ 2.09. Patron and Participant Exclusion.

One of the most frequently recurring questions in the regulated sports has involved the authority of an owner of a licensed sports facility to exclude persons from its premises. At common law, the owner of an athletic facility, unlike the owner of a public accommodation or a common carrier, had a right to exclude any person therefrom whom it did not desire to grant admission.[199] The leading

---

195. Department of Business Regulation v. Vandervoort, 273 So. 2d 66 (Fla. 1973). A similar result was reached in Chicago Div. of the Horsemen's Benevolent & Protective Ass'n v. Illinois Racing Bd., 53 Ill. 2d 16, 289 N.E.2d 421 (1972), though the court apparently relied upon a state statute precluding the commission from interfering in salary arrangements between a licensee and its employees, and a conclusion that the legislature intended to leave compensation questions to private resolution.

196. *See* notes 194-95 *supra.*

197. In Chicago Div. of the Horsemen's Benevolent & Protective Ass'n v. Illinois Racing Bd., 53 Ill. 2d 16, 289 N.E.2d 421 (1972), the court held that there was no authority for such a rule, but specifically noted that its decision was made "without considering the effect of the absence of any finding by the Board that the quality of horse racing in Illinois has suffered from or was threatened by a lack of competent jockeys . . . ." *Id.* at 432. Whether this comment means only that such a finding was not present, or that even if it were the commission would still lack authority is not clear. The presence of the evidence suggested in the text should, however, provide a basis for a conclusion that authority exists.

198. Colella v. State Racing Comm'n, 360 Mass. 152, 274 N.E.2d 331 (1971).

199. Griffin v. Southland Racing Corp., 236 Ark. 872, 370 S.W.2d 429 (1963); Jacobson v. New York Racing Ass'n, 33 N.Y.2d 144, 305 N.E.2d 765 (1973); Madden v. Queens County Jockey Club, Inc., 296 N.Y. 249, 72 N.E.2d 697 (1947), *cert. denied,* 332 U.S. 761, 92 L. Ed. 346, 68 S. Ct. 63 (1947); Kimball v. Windsor Raceway Holdings, 3 Ont. Rep. 307 (1972); Adrian Messenger Services & Enterprise, Ltd. v. Jockey Club, Inc., 2 Ont. Rep. 369 (1971). *See generally* Conard, *The Privilege of Forcibly Ejecting an Amusement Patron,* 90 U. PA. L. REV. 809 (1942); Turner & Kennedy, *Exclusion, Ejection, and Segregation of Theater Patrons,* 32 IOWA L. REV. 625 (1947); Annot., 1 A.L.R.2d 1165 (1965); Annot., 60 A.L.R. 1089 (1929); Annot., 30 A.L.R. 951 (1924).

case expressing this view was the English decision in *Wood v. Leadbitter,*[200] where a race track patron who had been forcibly ejected from a track brought suit against the owner for assault and false imprisonment. In rendering a decision upholding a verdict for the owner, the court stated that the owner of an amusement may for any reason order a ticket-holding patron to leave the premises, and if, after reasonable notice is given, the patron does not leave, the owner may effect removal by the use of reasonable force. The bases for this conclusion were that the ticket afforded the patron no interest in the property of the race track and that even if the ticket should be considered a license it would be revocable at the will of the owner.[201] The rule of *Wood v. Leadbitter* was implicitly adopted by the Supreme Court in *Marrone v. Washington Jockey Club of the District of Columbia,*[202] where a patron had been excluded from a race track on the grounds that he had earlier been involved in a conspiracy to drug a horse. In holding that the patron had no right to admittance, the Court stated that a ticket creates no "right in rem" and is "not a conveyance of an interest in the race track." [203] It then recited what it referred to as the commonly accepted rule that the owner may exclude any patron for any reason deemed by it to be sufficient. The results in *Wood v. Leadbitter* and *Marrone* have been followed by several courts in upholding the exclusion of patrons [204] and participants [205] from regulated athletic facilities.

Although the common law right of exclusion gives the owner of athletic facilities a considerable degree of authority, it may be subject to several limitations when it is considered in the regulated sports situation. The rules of

---

200. 13 M. & W. 836, 153 Eng. Rep. 351 (Exch. Ch. 1845). Liability for exclusion of spectators is considered at § 8.03.

201. The reasons for this result were described by Chief Justice Latham in Cowell v. Rosehill Racecourse Co., 56 C.L.R. 605 (Austl. 1937), as follows:

> The right to see a spectacle cannot, in the ordinary sense of legal language, be regarded as a proprietary interest. Fifty thousand people who pay to see a football match do not obtain fifty thousand interests in the football ground. A contrary view produces results which may be fairly described as remarkable. The Statute of Frauds would be applicable. A person who bought a reserved seat might be held to have what could be called "a term of hours" in the seat. *Id.* at 616.

The result in *Wood v. Leadbitter,* was rejected, but in no way overruled, by Hurst v. Picture Theatres, Ltd., [1915] 1 K.B. 1, where the court held that a ticket to an amusement was not arbitrarily revocable, and that a patron forcibly ejected upon the erroneous belief that an admission fee had not been paid could recover damages for assault and false imprisonment. The *Hurst* opinion was itself rejected in *Cowell v. Rosehill Racecourse Co., supra.*

202. 227 U.S. 633, 57 L. Ed. 679, 33 S. Ct. 401 (1913).

203. *Id.* at 636.

204. Watkins v. Oaklawn Jockey Club, 86 F. Supp. 1006 (W.D. Ark. 1949), aff'd, 183 F.2d 440 (5th Cir. 1950); Greenfield v. Maryland Jockey Club, 190 Md. 96, 57 A.2d 335 (1948); Neff v. Boomer, 149 Neb. 361, 31 N.W.2d 222 (1948); Tamelleo v. New Hampshire Jockey Club, Inc., 102 N.H. 547, 163 A.2d 10 (1960); Garifine v. Monmouth Park Jockey Club, 29 N.J. 47, 148 A.2d 1 (1959); Presti v. New York Racing Ass'n, 46 App. Div. 2d 387, 363 N.Y.S.2d 24 (1975); Vaintraub v. New York Racing Ass'n, 28 App. Div. 2d 660, 280 N.Y.S.2d 758 (1967); Gottlieb v. Sullivan County Harness Racing Ass'n, 25 App. Div. 2d 798, 269 N.Y.S.2d 314 (1960). *See generally* Wynne, *An Absolute Property 'Right' to Discriminate in New Hampshire? — Discussion of a Race Track Exclusion Case,* 3 N.H. B.J. 258 (1961). Where an excluded patron returns, moreover, he will be guilty of trespass. People v. Licata, 28 N.Y.2d 113, 268 N.E.2d 787, 320 N.Y.S.2d 53 (1971).

205. Martin v. Monmouth Jockey Club, 145 F. Supp. 439 (D. N.J. 1956), aff'd, 242 F.2d 344 (3d Cir. 1957) (jockey); Greenberg v. Hollywood Turf Club, 7 Cal. App. 3d 968, 86 Cal. Rptr. 885 (1970) (trainer).

state athletic commissions frequently contain provisions requiring licenses to exclude persons with certain characteristics from the use of their facilities.[206] Since these rules have the effect of *requiring* a license to exercise the power of exclusion, it is important to determine the validity of such an exclusion rule and the effect that it may have upon the common law power.

The exclusionary rules adopted by athletic commissions are in some states the result of specific statutory provision,[207] and even where such specific authority is absent, it would appear that the rules would be within a commission's more general rule-making authority. The basic purpose of athletic commissions is to police sports that have demonstrated the need for public regulation,[208] and in order to accomplish that purpose it may be necessary to exclude some persons whose conduct jeopardizes continued public confidence in the sport.[209] The reasonableness of an exclusionary rule would be determined by whether its operative effect is limited to persons whose exclusion is necessary to the accomplishment of a commission's purposes. If a rule (or similar statutory provision) affects persons who need not be excluded to accomplish those purposes, then it will to that extent be unreasonable.[210] In *Colorado Racing Commission v. Smaldone,*[211] for example, a provision allowing the commission to exclude any person who violated any federal or state law was found to be unreasonable on constitutional grounds because of its overbreadth.[212]

When the exclusion power is considered in terms of a commission rule, then, the authority is significantly narrower than it is under the common law view. A commission rule would authorize the exclusion of a person only when his or

---

206. A typical rule provides as follows:

> All persons guilty of any dishonest or corrupt practice, fraudulent act or other conduct detrimental to racing, committed while within or without any racing enclosure, shall be ruled off all racing enclosures under the jurisdiction of the California Horse Racing Board, and it shall be the duty of the stewards and those authorized by them to exclude from all places under their jurisdiction persons who commit such offenses or are so ruled off. Pacific Turf Club, Inc. v. Cohn, 104 Cal. App. 2d 321, 231 P.2d 527 (1951).

207. *See, e.g.,* CAL. PENAL CODE § 337.5 (West 1971); CAL. BUS. & PROF. CODE § 19572 (West 1962); MASS. GEN. LAWS ANN. ch. 128A, § 10A (West 1972); N.H. REV. STAT. ANN. § 284.39 (1966); OR. REV. STAT. § 462.080 (1971).

208. *See* § 2.02.

209. Martin v. Monmouth Jockey Club, 145 F. Supp. 439 (D. N.J. 1956), *aff'd,* 242 F.2d 344 (3d Cir. 1957); Flores v. Los Angeles Turf Club, Inc., 55 Cal. 2d 736, 361 P.2d 921, 13 Cal. Rptr. 201 (1961); Epstein v. California Horse Racing Bd., 222 Cal. App. 831, 35 Cal. Rptr. 642 (1964). *See* §§ 2.05, 2.06. Patrons and participants are said to submit to these rules by attending or participating in regulated sports. Grannan v. Westchester Racing Ass'n, 153 N.Y. 449, 47 N.E. 896 (1897).

210. Mones v. Austin, 318 F. Supp. 653 (S.D. Fla. 1970), which is discussed at notes 237-38 *infra.*

211. 492 P.2d 619 (Colo. 1972).

212. *Id.* at 620. *See also* Orloff v. Los Angeles Turf Club, 36 Cal. 2d 734, 227 P.2d 449 (1951) (rule could not enlarge instances in which owner could exercise common law power, and term "immoral" too vague); Pacific Turf Club, Inc. v. Cohn, 104 Cal. App. 2d 371, 231 P.2d 527 (1951). The specific statutory defect in *Orloff* was subsequently corrected, so that it does not preclude exclusion. Flores v. Los Angeles Turf Club, Inc., 55 Cal. 2d 736, 361 P.2d 921, 13 Cal. Rptr. 201 (1961).

It should also be noted that the exclusion of persons who have been found to have committed acts that are detrimental to the sport in question has been held to not constitute a form of double jeopardy. Mones v. Austin, 318 F. Supp. 653 (S.D. Fla. 1970); Epstein v. California Horse Racing Bd., 222 Cal. App. 831, 35 Cal. Rptr. 642 (1969). An exclusion requirement has also been held to not constitute a bill of attainder. Mones v. Austin, 318 F. Supp. 653 (S.D. Fla. 1970). A "bill of attainder" is a legislative act that inflicts punishment without judicial trial. Cummings v. Missouri, 71 U.S. (4 Wall.) 277, 18 L. Ed. 356 (1867).

her presence or conduct would be inconsistent with the accomplishment of the commission's purposes.[213] In light of this difference, the issue inevitably arises as to whether commission regulation will entirely preempt the owner's common law rights. Although there is authority suggesting that such regulation does not necessarily effect the authority provided by the common law rule,[214] the more recent cases appear to be moving in the other direction. The most significant of these cases is *Jacobson v. New York Racing Association,*[215] in which the New York Racing Association had denied stall space to a licensed owner after the owner's license had been suspended (though reinstated at the time of denial). This had the effect of essentially barring the owner from participating in racing activity in the state, since the Association owned all of the major thoroughbred tracks. In reviewing this action, the court noted that it had on several occasions recognized the common law right of exclusion that existed with respect to patrons at licensed facilities.[216] It did not, however, view those cases as providing any basis for the existence of authority to arbitrarily exclude licensed participants. If such a power existed, the court reasoned it would effectively deny the participant the right to exercise his profession, and there was no showing that such arbitrary authority was necessary to the protection of any of the Association's legitimate interests. Thus, it stated that "[i]n contrast to a racetrack proprietor's common-law right to exclude undesirable patrons, it would not seem necessary to the protection of his legitimate interests that the proprietor have absolute immunity from having to justify the exclusion of an owner and trainer whom the State has deemed fit to license." [217] Accordingly, the court concluded that the owner should have an opportunity to prove that his exclusion was arbitrary, though in so doing he would have a "heavy burden" to establish that his exclusion was "actuated by motives other than those relating to the best interests of racing generally." [218]

    Jacobson is a rather significant decision because it clearly holds that the common law right of exclusion may not be utilized to arbitrarily exclude a participant.[219] But the court did not hold that the common law rule was entirely

213. Rockwell v. Pennsylvania State Horse Racing Comm'n, 15 Pa. Commw. Ct. 348, 327 A.2d 211 (1974); Burrillville Racing Ass'n v. Garabedian, 113 R.I. 134, 318 A.2d 469 (1974).

214. In Tamelleo v. New Hamsphire Jockey Club, Inc., 102 N.H. 547, 163 A.2d 10 (1960), for example, the court stated that the regulatory provisions were declaratory of common law, though at the end of its opinion the court stated that the power could not be exercised in an arbitrary, capricious or unreasonable manner. This qualification hardly declares the common law view. It is, to the contrary, quite similar to the basic conclusion expressed in *Jacobson.*

215. 33 N.Y.2d 144, 305 N.E.2d 144, 350 N.Y.S.2d 639 (1973).

216. These cases were People v. Licata, 28 N.Y.2d 113, 268 N.E.2d 787, 320 N.Y.S.2d 53 (1971); Madden v. Queens County Jockey Club, 296 N.Y. 249, 72 N.E.2d 697 (1947), *cert. denied,* 332 U.S. 761, 92 L. Ed. 346, 68 S. Ct. 63 (1947).

217. 305 N.E.2d at 768.

218. *Id.* The court justified its requirement that exclusion could not be accomplished on an arbitrary basis even by a "private" person by reference to the cases that have applied similar limitations upon private associations whose actions may seriously effect the economic interests of their putative members. *See* §§ 1.14, 3.15. *See also* Greenberg v. Hollywood Turf Club, 7 Cal. App. 3d 968, 86 Cal. Rptr. 885 (1970). It is important to note that the court did not hold that a hearing must be held before a participant could be excluded. *See* notes 239-44 *infra.*

219. *See also* Greenberg v. Hollywood Turf Club, 7 Cal. App. 3d 968, 86 Cal. Rptr. 885 (1970) (could not arbitrarily exclude a trainer); Tamelleo v. New Hampshire Jockey Club, 102 N.H. 547, 163 A.2d 10 (1960); Rockwell v. Pennsylvania State Horse Racing Comm'n, 15 Pa. Commw. Ct. 348, 327 A.2d 211 (1974) (could not arbitrarily exclude patron); Burrillville Racing Ass'n v. Garabedian, 113 R.I. 134, 318 A.2d 469 (1974) (same).

preempted by the imposition of state regulation. It held only that a licensed participant could not be excluded on an arbitrary basis and, significantly, the court reaffirmed its view that the common law rule would apply to the exclusion of patrons.[220] Other courts have, however, taken this further step and held that specific statutory authorization for an athletic commission to direct owners to control admission would preempt the common law rule, so that even the exclusion of patrons could be accomplished only in accordance with the terms of the statute.[221] Although the scope of preemption may vary depending upon the jurisdiction considered, it is clear that the advent of commission regulation has substantially limited the scope of the common law power.

In addition to the restraints upon the common law power of exclusion that have resulted from commission regulation, additional limitations may be imposed by statutory and constitutional provisions that are not as such specifically related to the regulation of sports. For example, the right to exclude may be limited by statutory provisions which require that admittance be granted to those with proper tickets. Thus, in *Western Turf Association v. Greenberg,*[222] the Supreme Court held that a statute requiring admission of any ticketholder over the age of twenty-one, who was not inebriated, boisterous or of lewd or immoral character, would compel a race track owner to admit all such persons. In reaching this conclusion, the Court stated that the race track was a place of public entertainment and was "so far affected with a public interest that the state may, in the interest of good order and fair dealing, require [it] to perform its engagement to the public [to honor its tickets] . . . ." [223]

An additional statutory restriction on the power to exclude will result from the civil rights laws which preclude certain persons from discriminating on the basis of race, color, sex, religion or national origin. These enactments and their interpretations are considered in a subsequent section.[224]

The exclusionary power would also be limited by constitutional principles if the entity exercising the power is affected with "state action." The most likely basis for a state action finding would be the existence of a state issued license. However, the fact that an entity is licensed by an agency of the state will not of itself cause it to be affected with "state action" for equal protection purposes.[225] As noted in *Western Turf Association v. Greenberg,* athletic

220. 305 N.E.2d 768. *Jacobson* has not been interpreted to apply to non-licensed persons, who continue to be subject to the common law rule. Presti v. New York Racing Ass'n, 46 App. Div. 2d 387, 363 N.Y.S.2d 24 (1975). *But see* note 221 *infra.*

221. Rockwell v. Pennsylvania State Horse Racing Comm'n, 15 Pa. Commw. Ct. 348, 327 A.2d 211 (1974); Burrillville Racing Ass'n v. Garabedian, 113 R.I. 134, 318 A.2d 469 (1974). The basis of both decisions is the implied intention of the legislature to allow exclusion only upon reasonable bases, which is necessarily inconsistent with the common law rule. *See also* Narragansett Racing Ass'n v. Mazzaro, 116 R.I. 354, 357 A.2d 442 (1976).

222. 204 U.S. 359, 51 L. Ed. 520, 27 S. Ct. 384 (1970).

223. *Id.* at 364.

224. *See* § 2.22. *See also* Bonomo v. Lousisiana Downs, Inc., 337 So.2d 553 (La. App. 1976); Burrillville Racing Ass'n v. Garabedian, 113 R.I. 134, 318 A.2d 469 (1974).

225. Jackson v. Metropolitan Edison Co., 415 U.S. 912, 39 L. Ed. 2d 466, 94 S. Ct. 1407 (1974); Moose Lodge No. 107 v. Irvis, 407 U.S. 163, 32 L. Ed. 2d 627, 92 S. Ct. 1965 (1972); Watkins v. Oaklawn Jockey Club, 86 F. Supp. 1006 (W.D. Ark. 1949), *aff'd,* 183 F.2d 440 (15th Cir. 1950); Greenfield v. Maryland Jockey Club, 190 Md. 96, 57 A.2d 335 (1948); Tamelleo v. New Hampshire Jockey Club, Inc., 102 N.H. 547, 163 A.2d 10 (1960); Garifine v. Monmouth Park Jockey Club, 29 N.J. 47, 148 A.2d 1 (1959); Madden v. Queens County Jockey Club, Inc., 296 N.Y. 249, 72 N.E.2d 697, 1 A.L.R.2d 1160

facilities are indeed affected with sufficient "public interest" as to be subject to government regulation,[226] but recognition of a public interest in the activities of an otherwise private entity will not cause it to become an arm of the state.[227] The state may, however, become so far involved in the activities of an otherwise private entity that its activities become in essence those of the state itself, and when that point is reached it will be subject to the constitutional requirements placed upon the state.[228] Such involvement may occur, for example, when a franchise is granted to a basically public corporation which provides it with a monopoly in the franchised activity. Thus, in *Jacobson v. New York Racing Association*,[229] a non-profit racing corporation, which was required by statute to transfer its assets to a tax-exempt entity upon dissolution, had received a 25-year franchise to conduct pari-mutuel racing [230] at several race tracks in New York, which gave it a virtual monopoly over thoroughbred racing in the state. Although the Court of Appeals did not reach the question of whether this substantial state involvement constituted "state action," [231] the Appellate Division was persuaded that the pervasiveness of state involvement in, and the public nature of, the association's activities required the conclusion that it was affected with "state action" and could not, therefore, arbitrarily exclude an owner or trainer from its facilities.[232]

The Appellate Division, thus, reached two conclusions: that the activities of the racing association did constitute state action, and that it could not arbitrarily exclude licensed persons. The Court of Appeals, as has already been noted, agreed that exclusion could not be effected arbitrarily in the case of licensed persons, and disagreed only on the state action question, which it felt was unnecessary to its decision.[233] Given the similarity of the ultimate result—the ability to exclude participants only on a non-arbitrary basis—it is important to determine what effect a "state action" finding would have upon the exclusion

(1947), *cert. denied*, 332 U.S. 761, 92 L. Ed. 346, 68 S. Ct. 63 (1947); Vaintraub v. New York Racing Ass'n, 28 App. Div. 2d 660, 280 N.Y.S.2d 758 (1967).

"State action" and the Equal Protection Clause are considered at § 1.14.

226. *See* notes 222-23 *supra.* Thus, it is clear that the provisions of civil rights legislation apply to sports facilities. *See* § 2.22.

227. Madden v. Queens County Jockey Club, Inc., 296 N.Y. 249, 72 N.E.2d 697, 1 A.L.R.2d 1160 (1947), *cert. denied*, 332 U.S. 761, 92 L. Ed. 346, 68 S. Ct. 63 (1947); Grannan v. Westchester Racing Ass'n, 153 N.Y. 449, 47 N.E. 896 (1897). The "public interest" that justifies state regulation is not the same as the performance of a "public function" that may cause the activities of an otherwise private entity to be affected with state action. *See* § 1.14 note 157.

228. Burton v. Wilmington Parking Auth., 365 U.S. 715, 6 L. Ed. 2d 45, 81 S. Ct. 856 (1961). In making this determination, "the inquiry must be whether there is a sufficiently close nexus between the state and the challenged action of the regulated entity so that the action of the latter may be fairly treated as that of the state itself." Jackson v. Metropolitan Edison Co., 415 U.S. 912, 39 L. Ed. 2d 466, 94 S. Ct. 1407 (1974).

229. 33 N.Y.2d 144, 305 N.E.2d 765, 350 N.Y.S.2d 639 (1973).

230. "Pari-Mutuel" betting is considered in § 2.20.

231. 33 N.Y.2d at 150, 305 N.E.2d at 768.

232. 41 App. Div. 2d 87, 341 N.Y.S.2d 333 (1973). The Appellate Division's opinion was followed in Presti v. New York Racing Ass'n, 75 Misc. 2d 242, 347 N.Y.S.2d 314 (1973), *rev'd*, 46 App. Div. 2d 387, 363 N.Y.S.2d 24 (1975); Halpern v. Lomenzo, 81 Misc. 2d 467, 367 N.Y.S.2d 653 (1975), and cited with approval in Rockwell v. Pennsylvania State Horse Racing Comm'n, 15 Pa. Commw. Ct. 348, 327 A.2d 211 (1974). *See also* Gilmour v. New York State Racing & Wagering Bd., 405 F. Supp. 458 (S.D.N.Y. 1975).

233. *See* notes 215-23 *supra.*

power. It could have two possible consequences. First, if the excluding party is affected with state action, then the Equal Protection Clause of the Fourteenth Amendment would preclude it from excluding persons on unreasonable bases.[234] As noted above, the reason for exclusion is ordinarily that the person in question has a character or reputation that would make his or her presence at a facility detrimental to racing.[235] It seems unlikely that the exclusion of such persons, in light of the purpose of the state commission legislation, would be any more likely to offend constitutional standards than it would the non-constitutional reasonableness standard.[236] Thus, in *Mones v. Austin*,[237] the court held that a statute requiring the exclusion of any person who had been convicted of, or had been excluded from another race track for, bookmaking was constitutional, and that the legislative conclusion that bookmakers must be excluded from state-licensed racing activities was reasonable.[238] If the excluding entity were subject to constitutional requirements, it would also be precluded from exercising its power arbitrarily, but this same limitation was imposed by the Court of Appeals in *Jacobson* on non-constitutional grounds.

The second potential effect of a state action conclusion would be that the exclusion could only take place in accordance with the requirements of due process, which would require a hearing to determine whether there was in fact a reasonable basis for excluding the person in question.[239] If a person holding a license is excluded by direct action of an athletic commission, a hearing would almost certainly be required. The exclusion would then be accomplished by an agency of the state (the commission), the interest affected (the licensed right to practice a profession) would probably be entitled to constitutional protection,[240] and the result of commission-ordered exclusion would be similar in effect to the suspension of the license which would require a hearing.[241] If, on the other hand, a person is excluded by an otherwise private licensee of the commission—for example, a regulated racing facility—then a hearing could be required only if the entity were subject to constitutional requirements, or the applicable athletic commission statute were interpreted to require such a hearing.[242] Under the common law rule, no hearing would be required since the

---

234. *See* § 1.15.
235. *See* note 199 *supra*.
236. *See* note 209 *supra*.
237. 318 F. Supp. 653 (S.D. Fla. 1970).
238. *Id.* at 657. Specifically, the court stated that

[i]t is clear that the challenged statute bears a reasonable relationship to a legitimate state objective, that the classification established by the statute is neither arbitrary nor unreasonable, and, therefore, that the statute does not violate the equal protection clause of the Fourteenth Amendment. *Id.*

As to the legislative objectives, *see* notes 200-02 *supra*.
239. This was apparently the effect that the Appellate Division in *Jacobson* intended. 341 N.Y.S.2d at 337, 340. The court did not, however, specify the dimensions of due process that would be required. *Id. See* § 2.18.
240. *See* § 2.18.
241. *Id.*
242. *See* Rockwell v. Pennsylvania State Horse Racing Comm'n, 15 Pa. Commw. Ct. 348, 327 A.2d 211 (1974) (required by state administrative procedure law). *See also* Whetzler v. Krause, 411 F. Supp. 523 (E.D. Pa. 1976) (temporary suspension pending hearing); Greenberg v. Hollywood Turf Club, 7 Cal. App. 3d 968, 86 Cal. Rptr. 885 (1970).

owner could exclude a person on any grounds.[243] Even if the view of the Court of Appeals in *Jacobson* is followed to preclude arbitrary exclusion, there would not necessarily be a hearing requirement. The court held that the question of whether there was a non-arbitrary basis for exclusion would be determined in a civil suit against the excluding entity.[244]

§ 2.10. Sex Discrimination.

Athletic commissions have frequently promulgated rules which limit participation in the sports they regulate on the basis of sex. The validity of sex-based classifications is a subject that has attracted a great deal of attention and controversy in recent years, both in and out of the sports world. The validity of such classifications in amateur athletics has been considered in the previous chapter,[245] which should be consulted for a more general discussion of the issue than is presented here. The basic theme that was developed in the earlier consideration of sex classifications was that the courts, and legislative bodies, have taken a clearly skeptical view of the use of sex as a basis of classification. It is perhaps a result of this view that some state legislatures have specifically precluded discrimination on the basis of sex in regulated sports.[246]

In determining the validity of a commission rule which limits participation on the basis of sex, the first step will be to ascertain whether it is within a commission's rule-making authority. In the absence of a specific delegation, a commission would have authority to promulgate a sex rule only if the rule could be shown to be related to a proper purpose of the commission.[247] The difficulty that a commission may encounter in sustaining its authority to adopt a sex rule is illustrated by *Hesseltine v. State Athletic Commission*,[248] where a female had been denied a permit to wrestle on the basis of a rule which prohibited females from participating in wrestling exhibitions. The rule was invalidated because the commission lacked authority for its adoption. The court noted that the legislature had given the commission no express authority for the rule. Moreover, the court rejected the argument that such authority could be found in a provision allowing the adoption of rules to establish qualifications for those applying for an exhibitor's license, since the complainant was seeking only a competitor's license.[249] Although the court did not consider the possibility that authority could have been found in the general rule-making power of the commission, its opinion could be viewed as implicitly suggesting that a sex rule could not be justified on that basis.

If it could be found that a commission had authority to adopt a sex rule, the second, and perhaps more difficult question would be whether such a rule was reasonable. In the area of sex-based classifications, the reasonableness issue will normally be raised in terms of the requirements of the Equal Protection Clause

---

243. *See* Presti v. New York Racing Ass'n, 46 App. Div. 2d 387, 363 N.Y.S.2d 24 (1975).
244. *See* notes 217-18 *supra.*
245. *See* § 1.22.
246. *See, e.g.,* S.D. Comp. Laws § 42-7-18.1 (Supp. 1974).
247. *See* § 2.04.
248. 6 Ill. 2d 129, 126 N.E.2d 631 (1955).
249. 126 N.E.2d at 633.

of the Fourteenth Amendment. In considering the permissibility of similar rules in amateur athletics, it was observed that the courts have generally given little determinative weight to the use of presumptions about the presumed lack of physical ability of females as a class. Accordingly, it was suggested that sex rules would be upheld only where the rule-maker could demonstrate a reasonable factual basis for the reasons offered to justify the use of sex-based classifications.[250] Inasmuch as this view was premised upon constitutional requirements, the same standard would presumably be employed in regulated sports. Indeed, when a sex rule is adopted by an athletic commission, it will have the effect not only of precluding participation by the members of the excluded sex, but also of denying to those persons the right to earn a living. The approach that would be used to determine the validity of a sex rule is indicated by *New York State Division of Human Rights v. New York-Pennsylvania Professional Baseball League*,[251] in which a female had been denied employment as a baseball umpire because she failed to meet height and weight requirements and because it was alleged that females could not handle the duties of an umpire. The court held that the denial violated a state unfair employment practice law since the league had "not introduced evidence to support a factual basis for a belief that women are not qualified for the job of a professional baseball umpire." [252] In reaching this conclusion, the court placed heavy reliance upon the decisions arising under Title VII of the Civil Rights Act of 1964 which have required that before an employer can utilize the bona fide occupational qualification exception to justify discrimination on the basis of sex it must affirmatively prove that there is a factual basis for the belief that females could not safely perform the duties of the job in question.[253] Although the doctrinal base of the decision in *New York-Pennsylvania Professional Baseball League* is a state employment practices law, the court's approach is similar to that employed under the Fourteenth Amendment. It fully supports the view that sex-based classifications may be justified only if the rule-maker can demonstrate a factual basis for presuming that females cannot perform the tasks in question.[254]

It should be noted, however, that some courts have rendered opinions that are clearly not in line with the approach that is suggested here. The primary such

---

250. *See* § 1.22, at notes 389-412. *See generally* Johnston & Knapp, *Sex Discrimination by Law: A Study in Judicial Perspective,* 46 N.Y.U. L. REV. 675, 692-93 (1971).

251. 36 App. Div. 2d 364, 320 N.Y.S.2d 788 (1971), *aff'd,* 29 N.Y.2d 921, 279 N.E.2d 856, 329 N.Y.S.2d 920 (1972).

252. 320 N.Y.S.2d at 792.

253. These cases are discussed in § 1.22, at notes 455-57.

254. With respect to *New York-Pennsylvania Baseball League,* it must be observed that the court did not even refer to its earlier opinion in Calzadilla v. Dooley, 29 App. Div. 2d 152, 286 N.Y.S.2d 510 (1968), in which it had upheld a state athletic commission rule barring females from the sport of wrestling. The *Calzadilla* opinion is highly questionable because of the failure of the court to even consider the factual bases that would support the prohibition against female participation. Instead of making a factual inquiry, the court upheld the rule on the simple basis that the commission had authority to adopt it. Although this is one question that must be addressed, it begs the more difficult question of the reasonableness of the use of sex as a basis of classification. One could seek to distinguish the cases on the basis of the specific legal issue involved — in *New York-Pennsylvania Baseball League* the issue was employment discrimination and in *Calzadilla* it was the validity of a commission rule — but that difference would not explain the failure of the court in *Calzadilla* to even consider the existence of any factual basis to support the rule. *See also* Whitehead v. Krulewitch, 25 App. Div. 2d 956, 271 N.Y.S.2d 565 (1966) (dismissing petition of a female for a wrestler's license).

case is *State v. Hunter*,[255] where a female wrestler was charged with the "Crime of a Person of Female Sex Participating in Wrestling Competition and Exhibition," which, it was charged, was against the peace and dignity of the state of Oregon. The act of participating in a wrestling match by a female was criminal in nature, apparently, because the statute requiring licenses for wrestlers provided that "[n]o person other than a person of the male sex shall participate in or be licensed to participate in any wrestling competition or wrestling exhibition." In rejecting the athlete's challenge to this provision, the court stated that it was constitutional because the legislature could properly prevent the "ever-increasing feminine encroachment upon what for ages had been considered strictly as manly arts and privileges."[256] If the basis of the court's decision in *State v. Hunter* was, indeed, to prevent "feminine encroachment," it is almost certainly wrong. Whatever else may be said about the need to prevent "feminine encroachment," it can hardly be viewed as constituting a legitimate purpose of the state, absent a strong demonstration of a factual basis for the reason asserted.[257]

In short, when sex-based classifications are considered in the regulated sports context, they will present the same issues that have already been considered in more detail in the amateur athletics situation. Although the sex issue has not played as significant a role in regulated sports litigation as it has in amateur athletics, it is possible that the same types of issues will arise in the future. As females obtain more nearly equal opportunities at lower levels of competition, it seems likely that there will be greater pressure for their participation in regulated sports. When this occurs, the athletic commissions will be confronted with the same issues that have been present in amateur athletics. Thus, it will have to be decided whether females and males should be allowed to compete against one another, and, if so, whether this should be true in all sports. It will also have to be determined whether separate competition should be created for males and females. The resolution of these matters by an athletic commission could raise essentially the same legal issues that have arisen in amateur athletics. The principles developed in the amateur cases should apply as well to regulated sports. The only difference between the two areas is that the latter is subject to state regulation, and the ability to compete in the sports regulated

---

255. 208 Ore. 282, 300 P.2d 455 (1956).
256. *Id.* at 288, 300 P.2d at 458. Specifically the court stated that

> [i]t seems to us that its purpose, although somewhat selfish in nature, stands out in the statute like a sore thumb. Obviously it intended that there should be at least one island on the sea of life reserved for man that would be impregnable to the assault of woman. It had watched her emerge from long tresses and demure ways to bobbed hair and almost complete sophistication; from a creature needing and depending upon the protection and chivalry of man to one asserting complete independence. She had already invaded practically every activity formerly considered suitable and appropriate for men only. In the field of sports she had taken up, among other games, baseball, basketball, golf, bowling, hockey, long distance swimming, and racing, in all of which she had become more or less proficient, and in some had excelled. In the business and industrial fields as an employee or as an executive, in the professions, in politics, as well as in almost every other line of human endeavor, she had matched her wits and prowess with those of mere man, and, we are frank to concede, in many instances had outdone him. In these circumstances, is it any wonder that the legislative assembly took advantage of the police power of the state in its decision to halt this ever-increasing feminine encroachment upon what for ages had been considered strictly as manly arts and privileges?

257. *Id.*

will have a more immediate economic consequence for the females in question. As indicated by *New York-Pennsylvania Baseball League,* these differences should certainly not call for the application of any lesser standards.

§ 2.11. Race Discrimination.

Rules have also been adopted which attempt to preclude members of one race from competing with members of another race. Typically, these rules have been specifically drafted to prevent blacks and whites from competing.[258] Inasmuch as the constitutional impermissibility of racial discrimination is considered elsewhere, it will suffice to note that racial discrimination may be justified under the Equal Protection Clause only by the showing of a "compelling interest" of the classification drawing body.[259] Absent such a showing, racial discrimination in commission supervised athletics will be unconstitutional. Thus, in *Harvey v. Morgan,*[260] where a black boxer had applied for a permit to fight a white boxer, the court invalidated a statutory provision which purported to preclude any boxing or wrestling match between black and white participants, which the commission had relied upon to deny the boxers' permits. In defense of the provision, the athletic commission argued that racial separation was necessary to prevent riotous disturbances, but this was rejected by the court since there was evidence that blacks and whites were able to compete in other sports without unusual incident. In light of the constitutional proscription against racial discrimination, the statutory provision could not, the court said, be allowed to stand, so that the black boxer must, if otherwise qualified, be granted the requisite permit.[261]

§ 2.12. Qualification.

In order to provide the best possible competition in given sports, athletic commissions have also adopted rules which require varying forms of qualification. Whether such rules will be valid and enforcible will be determined by the principles already noted,[262] but since the rules are so varied in content and purpose it is not feasible to discuss all such rules here. It is possible, however, to mention the few cases that have been decided, which suggest how the courts have evaluated qualification rules that have been presented for decision. The leading case is *New York Standardbred Farm Owners, Inc. v. Agriculture and New York State Horse Breeding Development Fund,*[263] where

---

258. A Louisiana Athletic Commission rule, for example, provided as follows:

> There shall be no fistic combat match, boxing, sparring, or wrestling contest or exhibition between any person of the Caucasian or "white" race and one of the Negro or "black" race; and, further, it will not be allowed for them to appear on the same card. Dorsey v. State Athletic Comm'n, 168 F. Supp. 149, 150 (E.D. La. 1958), *aff'd per curiam,* 359 U.S. 533, 3 L. Ed. 2d 1028, 79 S. Ct. 1137 (1959).

259. *See* §§ 1.24, 2.22.

260. 272 S.W.2d 621 (Tex. Civ. App. 1954).

261. In reaching this conclusion, the court relied upon Brown v. Board of Educ. of Topeka, 347 U.S. 483, 98 L. Ed. 2d 873, 74 S. Ct. 686 (1954). *See also* Dorsey v. State Athletic Comm'n, 168 F. Supp. 149 (E.D. La. 1958), *aff'd per curiam,* 359 U.S. 533, 3 L. Ed. 2d 1288, 79 S. Ct. 1137 (1959) (boxing commission rule precluding black and white competition held unconstitutional).

262. *See* § 2.04.

263. 71 Misc. 2d 671, 336 N.Y.S.2d 825 (1972).

the sponsor of the "New York sire stakes" had adopted a point-qualification rule for the final races of the stakes, which required that a horse must have previously accumulated a sufficient number of points in races at smaller tracks. The rule had been adopted as a result of declining participation by the best horses at the smaller tracks. In upholding the validity of the rule, the court held first that the sponsor had the statutory power to adopt and promulgate the rule. It then went on to conclude that the rule was not arbitrary or capricious since it served the legitimate purpose of the sponsor to insure the entry of quality horses in each stakes race and to generate public interest therein. It has also been held that entrants may be required to be registered with a private organization,[264] and that a state office responsible for racing events had the authority to determine the qualifications of entrants in racing events.[265]

§ 2.13. Purses.

Both athletic commissions and state legislatures have from time to time issued rules, regulations or statutory provisions dealing with the purses awarded in given sports. The statutory provisions typically authorize the retention of purses where there is evidence of less than honest or good faith competition,[266] or establish minimum purses for different events.[267] Although the specific rules and regulations that have been adopted by athletic commissions are too diverse for discussion, it is appropriate to indicate how the courts have resolved cases involving purse rules.[268] The courts have held that purses may be withheld from the apparent winner of a race where it is subsequently determined that the horse had drugs in its urine[269] or where its owner had failed to pay the appropriate entry fee.[270] The courts have also upheld statutes establishing the sizes of purses in different size cities;[271] required that races be conducted under the name established by statute;[272] and allowed interest to be paid on improperly withheld purses.[273]

§ 2.14. Manager's or Agent's Contracts.

It has been felt that athletic commissions should exercise some degree of control over the contractual relationships between athletes and their managers,

264. State *ex rel.* Mason v. Rose, 122 Fla. 413, 165 So. 347 (1936) (American Kennel Club). Private entity rule-making is considered at § 2.17.

265. People *ex rel.* Empress Farms, Inc. v. Schneider, 1 Ill. App. 3d 147, 273 N.E.2d 61 (1971).

266. *See, e.g.,* Cal. Bus. & Prof. Code § 18747 (West 1962); Ind. Code Ann. § 25-9-1-18 (Burns 1975); N.H. Rev. Stat. Ann. § 285:23 (1966); Okla. Stat. Ann. tit. 3A, § 28 (1973).

267. *See, e.g.,* Pa. Stat. Ann. tit. 4, § 14 (Purdon 1963).

268. The validity of such rules or regulations would be determined in accordance with the principles set forth at § 2.04.

269. Edelberg v. Illinois Racing Bd., 540 F.2d 279 (7th Cir. 1976); Kentucky State Racing Comm'n v. Fuller, 481 S.W.2d 298 (Ky. 1972). Where the drug rule is held to be unlawful, however, the purse may then be due to the apparent winner notwithstanding the deficient urine test. *See* Wexler v. Maryland State Fair, 164 F.2d 477 (4th Cir. 1947). The drug rules are considered at § 2.07.

270. Baker v. Western Horsemen Co., 100 Ind. App. 595, 197 N.E. 697 (1935).

271. Douglas Park Jockey Club v. Talbott, 173 Ky. 685, 191 S.W. 474 (1917).

272. Schroeder v. Selkirk, 31 App. Div. 2d 47, 294 N.Y.S.2d 864 (1968).

273. People *ex rel.* Empress Farms, Inc. v. United States Trotting Ass'n, 13 Ill. App. 2d 327, 300 N.E.2d 18 (1973).

agents or other representatives, and many commissions have adopted rules for that purpose. Such rules normally require that persons wishing to represent athletes in athletic endeavors[274] subject to regulatory control be licensed by, and that their contracts with athletes be filed with, the commission.[275] In most circumstances, such rules would appear to be both within the commission's authority and reasonable.[276] They have frequently been held to be within the rule-making authority on the ground that one of the legitimate objectives of an athletic commission is to prevent the types of abuses that characterized the sports prior to commission-regulation, including the manipulation of athletes by unscrupulous managers, agents and other purported representatives.[277] The rules will also be reasonable so long as they affect only those whose conduct it is necessary to control. If, however, the rules purport to affect those whose conduct it is not necessary to control, then they will to that extent be unreasonable.[278]

These rules have most frequently been the subject of litigation when a boxing manager has sought to enforce a contract with a boxer. If the manager has not complied with the contract rules, either by not procuring the requisite license, by not filing a copy of the contract, or otherwise, the courts have clearly enunciated the general rule that the "manager" may not enforce a contract and his or her rights in a fighter will not be recognized.[279] Thus, in *Baksi v. Wallman*,[280] a professional boxer entered a contract with two managers, which was for a term of more than two years and called for the managers to receive more than $33^1/_3\%$ of the boxer's earnings. In addition to violating commission rules requiring that such contracts be filed and that the parties to it appear before the commission for approval, the contract also violated rules precluding contracts calling for a term of more than two years, compensation in excess of $33^1/_3\%$ and specifying more than one manager. When the boxer then brought suit to have the contract declared a nullity, the court held that, as a result of the infirmities noted, it was illegal and unenforceable *in toto*. Similar results

---

274. The rules will not normally apply to contracts whose subject matter is not directly related to the athletic performance. Wallman v. Wolfson, 184 Misc. 520, 53 N.Y.S.2d 586, *aff'd*, 269 App. Div. 689, 54 N.Y.S.2d 700, *app. denied*, 269 App. Div. 737, 54 N.Y.S.2d 702 (1945) (business manager).

275. *See, e.g.*, Wallman v. Wolfson, 184 Misc. 520, 53 N.Y.S.2d 586, *aff'd*, 269 App. Div. 689, 54 N.Y.2d 700, *appeal denied*, 269 App. Div. 737, 54 N.Y.S.2d 702 (1945). This requirement may also be imposed by statute. *See, e.g.*, OKLA. STAT. ANN. tit. 3A, § 21 (1973).

276. Casarona v. Pace, 175 Misc. 269, 22 N.Y.S.2d 726 (1940). *See* § 2.04.

277. Ali v. State Athletic Comm'n, 308 F. Supp. 11 (S.D.N.Y. 1969); Christensen v. Helfand, 208 Misc. 302, 143 N.Y.S.2d 285 (1955); Tilelli v. Christenberry, 1 Misc. 2d 139, 120 N.Y.S.2d 697 (1953); Fitzsimmons v. New York State Athletic Comm'n, 15 Misc. 831, 146 N.Y.S. 117, *aff'd*, 162 App. Div. 904, 147 N.Y.S. 1111 (1914); Norwood v. Pennsylvania Horse Racing Comm'n, 16 Pa. Commw. Ct. 259, 328 A.2d 198 (1974). *See* § 2.02.

278. Such "over-inclusiveness" might be present, for example, if a contract filing rule were sought to be applied to contracts with business managers, since their conduct might not be necessary to control for the achievement of the commission's regulatory objectives. *See* Wallman v. Wolfson, *supra* note 274. The definition of "manager" is in some states quite broad, and would include parties other than those who actually participate in matches. *See, e.g.*, Norwood v. Pennsylvania Horse Racing Comm'n, 16 Pa. Commw. Ct. 259, 328 A.2d 198 (1974) (term included a partnership that was to perform specified services in return for a portion of a fighter's revenues).

279. Baksi v. Wallman, 297 N.Y. 456, 74 N.E.2d 172 (1947); Casarona v. Pace, 175 Misc. 269, 22 N.Y.S.2d 726 (1940); Rosenfeld v. Jeffra, 165 Misc. 662, 1 N.Y.S.2d 388 (1937).

280. 297 N.Y. 456, 74 N.E.2d 172 (1947). *See also* Norwood v. Pennsylvania Horse Racing Comm'n, 16 Pa. Commw. Ct. 259, 328 A.2d 198 (1974).

have been reached when a duly licensed manager is suspended, even if the result is to deprive an otherwise blameless boxer of the opportunity to compete.[281] If, however, a manager has a valid license at the time his contract is breached by another party, it has been held that he need not be licensed at the time he seeks to assert his rights under the agreement.[282]

Rules requiring filing or approval of managerial contracts may or may not have an extra-territorial effect depending upon the choice of law rules that a court may apply. In *Zwirn v. Galento*,[283] for example, a contract had been executed in New York, pursuant to which the manager procured a fight for the boxer in New Jersey. When representatives of the manager brought suit to recover the percentage of earnings due him under the terms of the contract, the court held that the contract was enforceable even though the manager was not licensed in New York and the contract had not been filed with the appropriate athletic commission in New York. The court conceded that these failings would have caused the contract to be unenforceable in New York, but since the fight in question took place in New Jersey and there was no showing that such requirements existed in New Jersey, the New York requirements could not, the court said, be given extra-territorial power to vitiate a contract valid in the place of performance.[284] The conclusion in *Zwirn v. Galento* is premised upon the troublesome choice of law question as to what law will be applied to determine the validity of a contract, which is said to be "the most confused and uncertain area in conflicts law." [285] In *Zwirn v. Galento,* the court applied the law of the place of performance, but there are certainly many other possibilities.[286] An approach that is much different from *Zwirn* is suggested by *Foreman v. George Foreman Associates,*[287] where the court invalidated a contract under the California commission rules, even though it dealt with fights that would take place outside the state of California. The contract had specifically designated California law to be applicable to its construction, and the court upheld the designation.[288] It refused to apply a rule of validation, as the court in *Zwirn* had done, reasoning that "[t]he choice of law principles which favor validation of contracts function to protect the expectations of the parties. But the regulations governing boxing contracts exist to invalidate contracts *despite* the expectations of the parties by restricting the boxer's power to contract." [289] The court also indicated that it would invalidate the contract even if the boxer had intentionally designated California law knowing that it would cause invalidation. In addition, it suggested that to apply the law of some other state would pose the obvious difficulty of determining which law to apply, as well as the problem of whether

---

281. Christensen v. Helfand, 208 Misc. 302, 153 N.Y.S.2d 285 (1955).
282. Stephan v. World Wide Sports, Inc., 502 S.W.2d 264 (Mo. App. 1973).
283. 288 N.Y. 428, 43 N.E.2d 474 (1942).
284. Additional conflict of law theories that might be applicable in a given case or jurisdictions are considered in R. WEINTRAUB, COMMENTARY ON THE CONFLICT OF LAWS 263-95 (1971).
285. See Reese, *Power of Parties to Choose Law Governing Their Contract,* 1960 PROC. OF AMERICAN SOCIETY OF INT'L LAW 49-50. *See also* Yntema, *Contract and Conflict of Laws: 'Autonomy' in Choice of Law in the United States,* 1 N.Y.L.F. 46 (1955).
286. *See* note 284 *supra.*
287. 517 F.2d 354 (9th Cir. 1975).
288. *See* RESTATEMENT (SECOND) OF CONFLICT OF LAWS § 187 (1971).
289. 517 F.2d at 357.

such law would violate the public policy of the forum (California) — a concern that posed little difficulty on different facts in *Zwirn*. The choice of law problem in construing contracts governed by athletic commission rules is, as noted, quite difficult, and as indicated by *Zwirn* and *Foreman* the results and rationale of future cases may not be consistent. The cases do suggest, however, that those who draft commission-regulated contracts pay careful attention to the question of which forums' law will be applied to determine their validity.

In addition to commission rules relating to contractual relationships as such, it is also common for the legislative body to enact statutory provisions which forbid promoters of matches, or other persons, from having a financial interest in the athletes who compete therein.[290] A "financial interest," for this purpose, has been defined to mean "a money interest, a financial investment or derived gain, an expectation of money reward." [291]

§ 2.15. Decisions of Referees or Umpires.

In those sports where the determination of who should be the winner of a contest is made by the judgmental decision of a person or persons appointed for that purpose, it is not uncommon for an athletic commission to adopt rules to guide the rendering of those decisions. Inasmuch as any two people may, and probably will, disagree on the merits of the decisions rendered, it is inevitable that they will on occasion be challenged.[292] In most circumstances, such challenges will amount to little more than verbal protestations, since there will be no authoritative forum in which an aggrieved participant may seek review of the decision. When the sport in question is subject to the regulation of an athletic commission, however, those who feel that an improper decision has been rendered by a referee, umpire or other such person may be able to seek commission review of the decision.[293] When such review is sought, the general rule will be that, in the absence of bad faith or corruption, the decisions of judges, umpires or referees in athletic contests will be final, and will not be disturbed—that is, they will be presumptively correct.[294]

---

290. *See, e.g.,* ARIZ. REV. STAT. ANN. § 5-231 (1974); N.H. REV. STAT. ANN. § 285:25 (1966).

291. Pennsylvania State Athletic Comm'n v. Moran, 6 Pa. D. & C.2d 611, 68 Dauph. 388 (1956). *See also* Stephan v. World Wide Sports, Inc., 503 S.W.2d 264 (Mo. App. 1973).

292. The reason for such challenges was said, in Tilelli v. Christenberry, 1 Misc. 2d 139, 120 N.Y.S.2d 697 (1953), to be that

> [a]s in most money-making callings, a boxer's earning capacity is related to his reputation and his reputation is dependent upon his success. In the sports world the interested public follows the detailed records of individual athletes and teams with avidity. It flocks to watch the athletes with winning records; and the earnings of those athletes are related directly to the number of paying spectators they can attract. Spiritually, a professional boxer may emerge greater in defeat than in victory. Materially, however, his prestige and the purses he can command are lowered. Any action which affects his record so prejudicially of necessity impairs economic rights and interests sufficiently to give the petitioner legal standing to sue. *Id.* at 142, 120 N.Y.S.2d at 701.

293. Such review may also be available through appeal to a league commissioner in some professional sports. *See* § 4.19.

294. Wellington v. Monroe Trotting Park Co., 90 Me. 495, 38 A. 543 (1897); Finlay v. Eastern Racing Ass'n, 308 Mass. 20, 30 N.E.2d 859 (1941); Miller v. Lomenzo, 43 App. Div. 2d 997, 352 N.Y.S.2d 260 (1974); Tilelli v. Christenberry, 1 Misc. 2d 139, 120 N.Y.S.2d 697 (1953); State *ex rel.* Durando v. State Athletic Comm'n, 272 Wis. 191, 75 N.W.2d 451 (1956).

The basis for the rule has been described as being that

> [a]s in other professional competitive sports, such as tennis, baseball, football, basketball,

The leading case expressing this rule is *Tilelli v. Christenberry*,[295] where immediately after the two referees in a boxing match had rendered their decision, two members of the boxing commission who were in attendance called for the score cards and then altered one referee's decision, with the result that the boxer declared a winner by the referees became the loser. This action was justified by the commission on the basis of a rumor that a betting coup surrounded the boxer who became, by its action, the loser. When suit was then brought challenging the power of the commission to alter a referee's decision, the court held that the action in the case before it was improper and that the decision of the referee should not have been altered. It found that the commission had given no basis for its alteration of the decision, and that since "[t]he scoring of a prize fight is not a routine process, like the scoring of a tennis match," mere good faith or well-intentioned rationalization would not justify such unusual action.[296] Similar results have been reached when a disappointed boxer alleged that a referee failed to properly follow a rule for the counting-off of knockdowns;[297] a disappointed bettor challenged a decision of race track stewards in declaring a "false start;"[298] and a trotting driver challenged a commission decision to alter the finish positions.[299]

Notwithstanding the general rule that the decisions of umpires and referees will not be disturbed, it is clear that where a decision has involved corruption or bad faith, as opposed to an honest mistake or error in judgment which are a part of any decision involving the perceptiveness of human beings, a commission will have the power to undertake appropriate action to correct the decision.[300] Thus, in *Wellington v. Monroe Trotting Park Co.*,[301] a horse had won a race but before the winner was announced one of the three judges separately told each of the other two that he and the third judge had concluded that another horse had won the race. Since each of the other judges believed that a majority of the judges was in favor of the second horse, they acquiesced and the second horse was declared the winner. In overturning the decision, the court stated that

> hockey, boxing, and soccer, it has been found of great practical importance to have umpires, referees, timekeepers, and other officials in said sports, who are experienced, mentally alert, fair, and otherwise well-qualified to make immediate decisions, and whose decisions must be final and binding. In more than one sense, such officials are truly judges of the facts, since they are closer to the actual situation and characters involved, at the time, and as and when, and under the circumstances in which the events occurred. Surely their immediate reactions and decisions of the questions which arose during the conduct of the sport should receive greater credence and consideration than possibly the remote, subsequent, matter-of-fact observation by a court in litigation subsequently instigated by a disgruntled loser of a wager. Shapiro v. Queens County Jockey Club, 184 Misc. 295, 53 N.Y.S.2d 135 (1945).

But cf. O'Neil v. Pallot, 257 So. 2d 59 (Fla. App. 1972) (presumption of correctness does not apply to decisions of race track stewards); Williams v. Cabarrus, 1 N.C. 54 (1793) (decision of race track judges could be reviewed by a jury).

295. 1 Misc. 2d 139, 120 N.Y.S.2d 697 (1953).
296. *Id.* at 147, 120 N.Y.S.2d at 705.
297. State *ex rel.* Durando v. State Athletic Comm'n, 272 Wis. 191, 75 N.W.2d 451 (1956).
298. Shapiro v. Queens County Jockey Club, 184 Misc. 295, 53 N.Y.S.2d 135 (1945).
299. Miller v. Lomenzo, 43 App. Div. 2d 997, 352 N.Y.S.2d 260 (1974).
300. Tilelli v. Christenberry, 1 Misc. 2d 139, 120 N.Y.S.2d 697 (1953); Shapiro v. Queens County Jockey Club, 184 Misc. 295, 53 N.Y.S.2d 135 (1945). Thus, in State *ex rel.* Durando v. State Athletic Comm'n, 272 Wis. 191, 75 N.W.2d 451 (1956), the court indicated that a commission could adopt a rule giving it such power.
301. 90 Me. 495, 38 A. 543 (1897).

"[s]uch conduct was fraudulent, and the decision processed should not be permitted to . . ." stand.[302] The power to correct corrupt or fraudulent decisions is, indeed, a necessary means of insuring that the commission will be able to achieve the legislative objectives of inspiring public confidence in the honest and competent judging of athletic contests.[303]

§ 2.16. Championships.

Athletic commissions have also found it necessary to establish rules and regulations relating to championships in the sports subject to their regulation. These rules have normally involved the sport of boxing, and have been upheld to the extent that they require champions to defend their title[304] and preclude the holding of more than one championship title at a time.[305] The leading case in this area is *Robinson v. Krulewitch,*[306] where the New York State Athletic Commission had adopted a rule which required a boxer holding a championship title to defend it against a suitable contender within six months of winning the title. If such defense were not forthcoming, a contender could then challenge the champ, and if a fight were not then scheduled, the champ's license could be suspended. Although Sugar Ray Robinson had held the Middleweight title for more than six months, he had not defended its possession. Thus, when Carmen Basilio (whom Robinson had defeated for the title) issued a challenge that was not taken by Robinson, the Commission gave Robinson notice of its intention to vacate his title if a suitable fight were not scheduled by a specified date. When Robinson then brought suit to have this decision set aside, the court held that his action was premature because the commission had only served notice of its intention to vacate. Because of the importance of the issue, however, the court also reached the merits of the challenge to the rule itself. It held the rule to be lawful and enforceable because the existence of championship titles was integral to the sport of boxing, and the sport could be severely damaged if a champion could, once in possession of a title, simply sit back and refuse to fight.[307] Although the court in *Robinson v. Krulewitch* also suggested that a champion's interest in his or her title was not subject to due process protection,[308] that view may no longer be valid.[309]

---

302. *Id.* at 500, 38 A. at 545.
303. *See* § 2.02.
304. Robinson v. Krulewitch, 18 Misc. 2d 285, 187 N.Y.S.2d 937 (1959). *See also* Pender v. Krulewitch, 18 App. Div. 2d 975, 238 N.Y.S.2d 307 (1963).
305. Griffith v. Krulewitch, 51 Misc. 2d 352, 273 N.Y.S.2d 168 (1966).
306. 18 Misc. 2d 285, 187 N.Y.S.2d 937 (1959).
307. Thus, the court observed that

> just as the sport of baseball requires for its success the awarding of league championships as well as world's championships, so does the success of the sport of boxing require the awarding of world's championship titles for different weight classes and championships for subdivisions of the world, such as countries. The existence of championship titles may safely be said to be an integral and necessary part of the sport of boxing.
> . . . [w]ithout such a provision, a champion could refuse to fight in its defense and yet hold on to his title, thus destroying the incentive of others to improve their ability in the hope of winning a championship. *Id.* at 289, 187 N.Y.S.2d at 941-42.

308. *Id.* at 291, 187 N.Y.S.2d at 943-44.
309. *See* § 2.18.

§ 2.17. Private Entity Rule-Making.

In the sports that are subject to commission regulation, there are frequently private associations which seek to establish standards for the sport by the adoption of rules and regulations. The issue posed by such activity is whether an athletic commission may adopt the rules or regulations as its own, or otherwise defer to the authority of private associations.

With respect to legislative authority that is delegated to an administrative agency,[310] the traditional view has been that a delegated power requiring the exercise of judgment or discretion may not be re-delegated unless there is a special power of substitution either express or necessarily implied from the original delegation. In light of this principle, the courts have reached the conclusion that, as a general rule, an athletic commission may not delegate its authority to a private entity.[311] Similar views have been expressed with respect to direct delegation of authority from the legislature to a private entity. Thus, in *Fink v. Cole*,[312] the court held that the state legislature could not constitutionally delegate to private associations the licensing function for those involved in horse racing.[313] Such delegation was unconstitutional, the court said, because it was "such an abdication as to be patently an unconstitutional relinquishment of legislative power . . . ." [314] The court also noted that even had the power been delegated to a state agency, the delegation would be stricken if it did not contain proper guidance and standards.

The rule against delegation need not preclude an athletic commission from making use of some services provided by private entities, so long as the delegation of judgmental or discretionary power is not involved. The courts have, for example, upheld the requirement that animals competing in commission-sponsored sports be registered with a private entity.[315] In addition, the legislative bodies in some jurisdictions have enacted statutory provisions which specifically authorize the adoption of appropriate rules of private associations.[316] While such provisions would appear to facilitate adoption, the doctrine represented by *Fink v. Cole* could be a substantial impediment in the event of a court challenge to the adoption. Its rationale would suggest that a commission may have very limited authority to delegate its responsibilities to a private entity, which would almost certainly not include performance of the

310. *See* § 2.02.

311. People *ex rel.* Empress Farms, Inc. v. Schneider, 1 Ill. App. 3d 147, 273 N.E.2d 61 (1971) (could not delegate responsibility of determining the eligibility of a horse to race in the United States Trotting Association). *See generally* Liebmann, *Delegation to Private Parties in American Constitutional Law*, 50 IND. L.J. 650 (1975).

312. 302 N.Y. 216, 97 N.E.2d 873 (1951).

313. The licensing function of athletic commissions is considered at § 2.03.

314. 302 N.Y. at 225, 97 N.E.2d at 876. *See also* Murtha v. Monaghan, 7 Misc. 2d 568, 169 N.Y.S.2d 137 (1957), *aff'd,* 5 App. Div. 695, 169 N.Y.S.2d 1010, *aff'd,* 4 N.Y.2d 897, 174 N.Y.S.2d 648 (1938).

315. State *ex rel.* Mason v. Rose, 122 Fla. 413, 165 So. 347 (1936) (membership in American Kennel Club). *See also* Bailey v. McCann, 550 F.2d 1016 (5th Cir. 1977) (issue not reached). *But cf.* Halpern v. Lomenzo, 81 Misc. 2d 467, 367 N.Y.S.2d 653 (1975).
  Even if such private association rules should be applicable, it has been held that one will be bound by them only when he knows, or should know, that they are applicable. Moshier v. La Crosse County Agrl. Soc., 90 Wis. 37, 62 N.W. 932 (1895).

316. *See, e.g.,* CAL. BUS. & PROF. CODE § 19563 (West 1960); CONN. GEN. STAT. ANN. § 12-574 (1972); N.J. STAT. ANN. § 5:5-30 (1973).

functions for which it was created or powers which would be inconsistent with other acts of the state legislature.

The difficulty which may arise is illustrated by *Halpern v. Lomenzo,*[317] where the state racing commission had at an early date adopted the rules of a private entity as its own and promulgated them with little change. The regulations, as promulgated, granted to the race stewards (who included some persons appointed by private parties) the power to suspend those who were licensed by the commission. This procedure was invalidated on the basis of *Fink v. Cole,* since it involved the delegation of a part of the licensing power (the power to suspend a license). Similar results were reached with regard to regulations giving the stewards power to disqualify a person who could not prove that he was not "disqualified." The regulations also made specific delegations, including provisions requiring the registry of stable names and colors, the filing of all racing contracts and leasing agreements, and the payment of a filing fee to the private entity. They also gave the stewards power to disapprove any contract or arrangement that was potentially deceptive. The court invalidated the registry provisions on the ground that the legislature had adopted trade and assumed business name statutes, the effect of which would be nullified by the delegation in question.[318] The fee payment provision was stricken since it allowed the payment of public monies to a private entity.[319] The court also suggested that there were numerous other aspects of the relationship between the commission and the private entity that might be unlawful, but which were not then before it for decision.[320]

§ 2.18. Commission Enforcement Proceedings.

The third of the basic functions performed by an athletic commission involves the enforcement of its rules and specific statutory obligations.[321] The enforcement process will normally be comprised of several separate functions, which may be described as investigatory, prosecutorial and adjudicatory. When it is believed that improper acts may have taken place, the commission will investigate the surrounding circumstances, and, if there are grounds for believing that such acts have occurred, it will conduct such proceedings as are necessary for it to determine whether its rules, regulations or other requirements have been violated.[322] These functions will normally be facilitated by statutory provisions which provide the commission with the power to issue

---

317. 81 Misc. 2d 467, 367 N.Y.S.2d 653 (1975).

318. 367 N.Y.S.2d at 664.

319. *Id.* at 663.

320. These included, for example, a regulation giving the stewards power to impose a civil penalty, which was so lacking in standards as to pose constitutional problems, and power to supervise an apprentice system through which young jockeys must rise.

In considering the delegation rule, it is important to keep in mind that, notwithstanding cases such as *Fink v. Cole,* the rule has been the subject of rather strong criticism in recent years. *See* § 1.15 note 226.

321. *See* § 2.02.

322. The combination of functions will not, of itself, cause the person under scrutiny to be deprived of applicable due process rights. Withrow v. Larkin, 421 U.S. 35, 43 L. Ed. 2d 421, 95 S. Ct. 1456 (1975); Hoke v. Board of Medical Examiners of State of N.C., 395 F. Supp. 357 (W.D.N.C. 1975); Rudolph v. Athletic Comm'n of Calif., 177 Cal. App. 2d 1, 1 Cal. Rptr. 898 (1960).

subpoenas, administer oaths and examine witnesses.[323] Although a commission's investigatory authority will normally be broad, the grant of such authority will not give the commission unbridled discretion. Its enforcement activities must still be conducted in a reasonable manner—that is, the inquiry must be one the commission is authorized to make, it must be relevant, and it must be limited to the subject properly being investigated.[324] Thus, in *Saratoga Harness Racing Association v. Monaghan*,[325] a commission's action was held to be unreasonable when, in investigating alleged interlocking stock ownership, it requested documents pursuant to its subpoena power that included virtually every scrap of paper in the licensee's possession. It should also be noted that it has been held that a person subject to a commission's investigatory power may not divert or avoid the investigation by the fact that a license is expired,[326] or by surrendering an unexpired license.[327]

The focus of these several functions is to enable the commission to determine whether it should exercise its statutory power to revoke or suspend a license that it has previously issued,[328] or to impose other forms of sanction.[329] Sanctions may, for example, be imposed if a licensee is found to have violated a rule or regulation of the commission,[330] engaged in conduct that would be detrimental to the public interest or the best interests of the sport,[331] or acted

---

323. *See, e.g.,* ARIZ. REV. STAT. ANN. § 5-104(F) (1974); NEV. REV. STAT. § 466.080 (1973); N.Y. UNCONSOL. LAWS § 7912 (McKinney 1961), § 8010 (McKinney Supp. 1978).

324. *See* Oklahoma Press Publishing Co. v. Walling, 327 U.S. 186, 90 L. Ed. 614, 66 S. Ct. 494 (1946).

325. 9 Misc. 2d 868, 169 N.Y.S.2d 520 (1958). *See generally* 1 F. COOPER, STATE ADMINISTRATIVE LAW 299-313 (1965).

326. Application of D'Amato, 23 Misc. 2d 473, 198 N.Y.S.2d 119 (1960).

327. Wallman v. New York State Athletic Comm'n, 20 Misc. 2d 398, 194 N.Y.S.2d 213 (1959).

328. *See, e.g.,* ARIZ. REV. STAT. ANN. § 5-108.02 (1974); CAL. BUS. & PROF. CODE § 18681 (West 1960).

Revocation may normally occur only by the affirmative action of the commission. Florida State Racing Comm'n v. Bourquardez, 42 So. 2d 87 (Fla. 1949).

329. These normally include monetary fines. *See, e.g.,* ARIZ. REV. STAT. ANN. § 5-109.02(E) (1974); N.Y. UNCONSOL. LAWS § 8011 (McKinney 1961); ORE. REV. STAT. § 462.090 (1974).

330. Licenses will ordinarily be issued subject to the rules and regulations of the commission. *See, e.g.,* CAL. BUS. & PROF. CODE § 18682 (West 1960); OHIO REV. CODE ANN. § 3769.06 (Page 1971); Fitzsimmons v. New York Athletic Comm'n, 15 Misc. 2d 831, 146 N.Y.S. 117, *aff'd,* 162 App. Div. 904, 147 N.Y.S. 1111 (1914).

331. *See, e.g.,* DEL. CODE § 28-139 (1975); KY. REV. STAT. § 229.200 (1977); MASS. GEN. LAWS ANN. ch. 128A, § 5 (1974); N.J. STAT. ANN. § 5:5-33 (1973); N.Y. UNCONSOL. LAWS § 8010(2) (McKinney 1961); PA. STAT. ANN. tit. 4, § 12 (Purdon 1963). *See also* Pennsylvania State Athletic Comm'n v. Moran, 6 Pa. D. & C.2d 611, 68 Dauph. 388 (1956) (a manager's having a financial interest in a boxer was contrary to the best interests of boxing; *see* § 2.14).

Such provisions will not normally be unlawful as being too vague or uncertain. Thus, in Pennsylvania State Athletic Comm'n v. Loughran, 9 Pa. D. & C.2d 427 (1956), the court stated that

> We believe that the phrases "sham or collusive boxing match" and acts "detrimental to the interests of boxing" need no definition by our legislature. Where is there an individual, interested in boxing, who has not, at some time or other, attended a boxing bout or a wrestling bout, in which the actions of the contestants became so apparently indifferent or collusive, in which it appeared so clearly that they were not putting forth their very best efforts to win the contest, that the audience indulged in catcalls, verbal comments, stamping of feet, whistling and in various other manifestations of disapproval of the way the contest was being conducted? Any ten-year-old boy can quickly recognize such a spectacle. The public pays good money to see honestly conducted fights and expects each contestant to be in condition and to do his best. A veritable wave of protest has been sweeping over the whole United States against the way in which boxing generally has been conducted, and any person of ordinary intelligence knows that on many occasions the

in some other manner as to justify the conclusion that there is "just cause" for the sanction.[332] Although it is also provided in some jurisdictions that a license may be suspended or revoked for any cause deemed sufficient by the commission,[333] the commission's discretion will be limited by the rule that it may not act arbitrarily, capriciously or unreasonably.[334] When the commission does impose sanctions, moreover, they must be reasonable under the circumstances, and where they are not, appropriate relief will be granted.[335]

In performing these functions, it is common for athletic commissions to delegate portions of their supervisory power, or the power to investigate, determine and redress alleged rule violations, to subordinate bodies,[336] and this delegation will not deprive the delegating commission of its original powers.[337] Such delegation is, for example, customary in the case of horse racing, where stewards are appointed to supervise each authorized race in accordance with rules established for that purpose by the racing commission.[338]

Probably the most important issue raised by commission enforcement activity concerns the permissibility of the procedures that it utilizes, which will be determined by the applicable statutory provisions and by the requirements of procedural due process. It is increasingly common to find statutory provisions which require that before an athletic commission may take any action that will significantly affect the rights of a person subject to its jurisdiction, it must give that person notice of the proceedings and an opportunity to be heard.[339] This trend represents the apparent legislative conclusion that before the private rights of those involved in athletic endeavors may be affected, they should be

---

public has been hoodwinked and cheated out of their money. By this language we do not mean to judge this particular case, but we feel very strongly that the legislature knew exactly what it was saying when it put that language into the act and that no further definition is necessary. . . . *Id.* at 434-35.

See also Pennsylvania State Athletic Comm'n v. Graziano, 12 Pa. D. & C.2d 127, 70 Dauph. 257 (1957). Rules relating to good character or conduct are considered at § 2.05.

332. *See, e.g.,* Fineman v. New York State Harness Racing Comm'n, 33 App. Div. 2d 144, 306 N.Y.S.2d 271 (1970) (failure to disclose criminal charges on application); Lombardo v. Di Sandro, 81 R.I. 393, 103 A.2d 557 (1954) (same).

333. *See, e.g.,* DEL. CODE § 28-325 (1953).

334. Ali v. State Athletic Comm'n, 316 F. Supp. 1246 (S.D.N.Y. 1970). *See* § 2.03.

335. Arkansas Racing Comm'n v. Emprise Corp., 254 Ark. 975, 497 S.W.2d 34 (1973) (conditional revocation of license improper); Florida State Racing Comm'n v. Ponce De Leon Trotting Ass'n, 151 So. 2d 633 (Fla. 1963) (revocation improper where statute specifies willful conduct, and conduct in question was not willful); Tropical Park, Inc. v. Ratliff, 97 So. 2d 169 (Fla. 1957) (revocation of license too severe a penalty for conduct in question); De John v. New York State Athletic Comm'n, 12 App. Div. 2d 318, 210 N.Y.S.2d 706 (1961) (commission did not have power to bar boxing manager for life).

336. *See, e.g.,* CAL. BUS. & PROF. CODE § 19440 (West 1973); COLO. REV. STAT. ANN. § 12-60-104 (1974).

337. Colorado Racing Comm'n v. Conner, 30 Colo. App. 72, 490 P.2d 75 (1971).

338. *See, e.g.,* N.H. REV. STAT. ANN. § 284:20 (1972); N.Y. UNCONSOL. LAWS § 7914 (McKinney 1961). It has been held, however, that a steward may not impose fines on an ex parte basis without any hearing. Tappis v. New York State Racing & Wagering Bd., 46 App. Div. 2d 613, 359 N.Y.S.2d 780 (1974).

339. *See, e.g.,* ARIZ. REV. STAT. ANN. § 5-108.02(C) (1974); ARK. STAT. ANN. § 84-2745 (Supp. 1977); IND. CODE ANN. § 25-9-1-14 (Burns 1975); ILL. ANN. STAT. tit. 8, § 37c-4 (Smith-Hurd 1977); N.J. STAT. ANN. § 5:5-52 (1973); PA. STAT. ANN. tit. 4, § 318 (Purdon 1963). *See also* Pennsylvania Athletic Comm'n v. Bratton, 66 Dauph. 333 (1954), *rev'd on other grounds,* 177 Pa. Super. 598, 112 A.2d 422 (1955) (required by applicable administrative procedure act).

given an opportunity to present their case and have a fair hearing on the merits of the controversy.

Even if such procedural safeguards are not specifically required by statutory provision, they may be required by either of two other factors. The first may be based on a judicial construction of the phrase "just cause" in statutory provisions setting forth grounds for license revocation or suspension,[340] which may read the necessity of notice and hearing into "just cause." [341] The second and far more important basis for the imposition of procedural safeguards is the constitutional requirement of due process.[342] Due process safeguards will be applicable, of course, only if the interest of the affected person is constitutionally protectible.[343] The delineation of protected from non-protected interests was at one time measured by an elusive doctrine that distinguished between "rights" and "privileges," and which held that only the former were of such importance as to require constitutional protection.[344] Although some cases involving athletic commission licenses have indeed followed this rule,[345] the demise of the "right-privilege" distinction [346] indicates that those decisions may no longer

340. *See* note 332 *supra.*
341. Thus, in State *ex rel.* Orleans Athletic Club v. Louisiana State Boxing Comm'n, 163 La. 418, 112 So. 31 (1927), the court observed that

> since the only protection afforded an innocent holder of a license lies in the fairness, honesty, and efficiency of the members of the commission or public officials, and in the presumption that they will not act arbitrarily or capriciously in the performance of their official duties, it may well happen that, where an opportunity is given to a licensee to be heard on complaints or charges against him, he may make such defense or offer such explanation as will convince a conscientious and fair minded tribunal that said charges or complaints are unfounded or possess so little merit as not to require the imposition upon him of the extreme penalty of revocation of his license. *Id.* at 424, 112 So. at 33.

See also Carroll v. California Horse Racing Bd., 16 Cal. 2d 164, 105 P.2d 110 (1940); Narragansett Racing Ass'n v. Kiernan, 59 R.I. 79, 194 A. 49 (1937).
342. *See generally* 1 F. COOPER, STATE ADMINISTRATIVE LAW 273-93 (1965); § 1.28. In addition to the activities of the state athletic commissions, to whom the procedural due process requirements are clearly applicable (since they are state agencies), the requirements may also be applicable to the proceedings of other organizations involved in administering the sports which are subject to athletic commission regulation. Thus, in Garafano v. United States Trotting Ass'n, 78 Misc. 2d 33, 355 N.Y.S.2d 702 (1974), the court held that the U.S.T.A., a private organization which licenses member trotting drivers, trainers and racing officials, was required to conduct its enforcement activities in accordance with the procedural due process requirements. In reaching this conclusion, the court noted that its

> activities are so involved with the public interest and agential supervision of a spectator sport with dramatic and serious public impact, that its determinations must be characterized as sufficiently resembling "state" or "governmental" action. *Id.* at 38, 355 N.Y.S.2d at 708.

But see Bailey v. McCann, 550 F.2d 1016 (5th Cir. 1977). The extent to which procedural due process requirements are applicable to private institutions is considered in detail at § 1.14.
343. *See* § 1.28.
344. *See* § 1.28.
345. Arkansas Racing Comm'n v. Hot Springs Kennel Club, Inc., 232 Ark. 504, 339 S.W.2d 126 (1960); State *ex rel.* Mason v. Rose, 122 Fla. 413, 165 So. 347 (1936); North Hampton Racing & Breeding Ass'n v. Conway, 94 N.H. 156, 48 A.2d 472 (1946) (racing license is "a privilege such as the state may grant or withhold at its pleasure"); Sanderson v. New Mexico State Racing Comm'n, 80 N.M. 200, 453 P.2d 370 (1969); London Sporting Club, Inc. v. Helfand, 3 Misc. 2d 431, 152 N.Y.S.2d 819 (1956); Zannelli v. DiSandro, 84 R.I. 176, 121 A.2d 652 (1956).
346. Graham v. Richardson, 403 U.S. 365, 374, 29 L. Ed. 2d 534, 91 S. Ct. 1848 (1971). *See generally* Van Alstyne, *The Demise of the Right-Privilege Distinction in Constitutional Law,* 81 HARV. L. REV. 1439 (1968).

be valid to the extent that they deny constitutional protection.[347] In place of such artificial distinctions, the courts will attempt to separate protected from non-protected interests by analyzing whether they have a "property" or "property like" status. An interest will have such a status only if the affected person can demonstrate an entitlement to the benefit sought to be protected which flows from some independent source such as state law.[348] Although constitutional protection will also be available if the action in question interferes with a person's "liberty" interest, the Supreme Court has recently narrowed the scope of this interest for constitutional purposes.[349] It appears that the liberty interest has not played a large role in regulated sport litigation.

With regard to the action of state athletic commissions, the interest that will normally be affected is a commission-issued license which makes participation in the sport possible. The licensed interest will frequently provide the means by which the person licensed, if an individual, has chosen to earn his or her living. The Supreme Court has made it clear that before one's right to follow a profession can be interfered with, the person must be accorded the safeguards of procedural due process.[350] Since the interest represented by an athletic commission license is the right to pursue the profession of a boxer, jockey, trainer, owner, track operator or other related calling, the courts have generally held that it is an interest of sufficient magnitude[351] as to require the protection of procedural due process safeguards.[352]

Since the sanctions imposed in enforcement proceedings will not always involve lengthy suspensions or revocations of licenses,[353] it is appropriate to consider the extent to which due process rights will attach to the interests affected by lesser sanctions. The Supreme Court has recently indicated that entitlement to due process protection is determined by the nature of the interest affected and not by its weight. Thus, it has said that "as long as a property deprivation is not *de minimis,* its gravity is irrelevant to the question whether

---

347. With regard to the state cases adopting the "privilege" approach, it has been stated that

[t]he large body of state case law which relies upon the privilege concept to justify a denial of opportunity to be heard . . . is one of the most prominent areas of weakness in all judge-made administrative law. 1 K. DAVIS, ADMINISTRATIVE LAW TREATISE § 7.18 (1958).

348. Goss v. Lopez, 419 U.S. 565, 42 L. Ed. 2d 725, 95 S. Ct. 729 (1975); Board of Regents of State Colleges v. Roth, 408 U.S. 564, 33 L. Ed. 2d 548, 92 S. Ct. 2701 (1972).

349. *See* § 1.28, notes 532-33.

350. Willner v. Committee on Character & Fitness, 373 U.S. 96, 10 L. Ed. 2d 224, 83 S. Ct. 1175 (1963); Schware v. Board of Bar Examiners of State of N.M., 353 U.S. 232, 1 L. Ed. 2d 796, 77 S. Ct. 752 (1957); Goldsmith v. United States B.T.A., 270 U.S. 117, 70 L. Ed. 494, 46 S. Ct. 215 (1926).

351. State *ex rel.* Investment Corp. of South Florida v. Board of Business Regulation, 227 So. 2d 674 (Fla. 1969) (right to conduct dog racing is a "valuable property right"); Man O'War Racing Ass'n v. State Horse Racing Comm'n, 433 Pa. 432, 250 A.2d 172 (1969) (a "very valuable privilege").

352. *See, e.g.,* Hubel v. West Virginia Racing Comm'n, 376 F. Supp. 1 (S.D. W. Va. 1974), *aff'd,* 513 F. 2d 240 (4th Cir. 1975); State *ex rel.* Paoli v. Baldwin, 159 Fla. 165, 31 So. 2d 627 (1947); State Racing Comm'n v. McManus, 82 N.M. 108, 476 P.2d 767 (1970); Tappis v. New York State Racing & Wagering Bd., *supra* note 338; Garofano v. United States Trotting Ass'n, 78 Misc. 2d 33, 355 N.Y.S.2d 702 (1974); Presti v. New York Racing Ass'n, 75 Misc. 2d 242, 347 N.Y.S.2d 314 (1973). *See also* Suarez v. Administrador Del Deporte Hipico De Puerto Rico, 354 F. Supp. 320 (D.P.R. 1972) (a right that is "substantial and federal in nature").

In this connection, it should be noted that the Supreme Court has recently taken a restrictive view of the so-called "entitlement" doctrine, *see* § 1.28 at note 531, and this could mean that the extent of the protection for licensed interests may be subject to some question.

353. *See* note 329 *supra.*

account must be taken of the Due Process Clause." [354] This language would suggest that any sanction which involves a license suspension of even a very short period would normally require due process protection.[355] A more difficult issue is raised by the imposition of fines. It could be argued that a fine does not involve the type of punishment that would require procedural protection because it would not involve a direct loss of the ability to participate. In regulated sports, however, the existence of a fine may, depending upon the circumstances of its imposition, subject the licensee to further sanctions in the same or other states. This is particularly true if the fine is not promptly paid. Thus, the licensee may be subjected to a license suspension for non-payment.[356] Moreover, the good conduct and character rules of another commission may require that the licensee not be allowed to participate,[357] or the owner of a sports facility might conclude that such a person should be excluded from its facilities.[358] Although there is little authority on this particular issue, it would appear that due process protection may be required. Statutory provisions frequently require notice and hearing before the imposition of fines,[359] and in at least one case the court held that a commission's rules were unconstitutional "to the extent that they permit a fine . . . without affording a right to a prior hearing . . . ." [360]

In some cases, enforcement activities may affect a non-licensed person such as a spectator. Thus, a spectator may be excluded from a racing facility pursuant to an athletic commission rule.[361] The common law rule that a patron may be excluded on even arbitrary grounds would not give rise to procedural rights,[362] but a few courts have recently interpreted applicable statutory provisions to require that a spectator could be excluded only after notice and a hearing.[363]

If it is determined that the interest in question is subject to due process protection, the next inquiry will be to determine what process is due. As indicated in § 1.28, it must be noted that the degree of procedural formality that will be required by the Due Process Clause is an area that is not clearly resolved. In its most recent cases, the Supreme Court has indicated that it may be withdrawing from the expansiveness with which it had earlier viewed procedural requirements. Thus, in several cases it has ruled that the procedures required for due process purposes may, where appropriate, be limited to those that are specified in the source of the interest in question.[363.1] In light of this perceptible shift in emphasis, it is difficult to articulate even the general standards that may be required to provide the requisite degree of procedural regularity. Accordingly, the following discussion will focus upon the basic principles that

354. Goss v. Lopez, 419 U.S. 565, 576, 42 L. Ed. 2d 725, 95 S. Ct. 729 (1975).
355. *Id. But see* notes 379-87 *infra.*
356. Tappis v. New York State Racing & Wagering Bd., 46 App. Div. 2d 613, 359 N.Y.S.2d 780 (1974).
357. *See* § 2.05.
358. *See* § 2.09.
359. *See, e.g.,* N.Y. UNCONSOL. LAWS § 8022 (McKinney Supp. 1978).
360. Tappis v. New York State Racing & Wagering Bd., 46 App. Div. 2d 613, 359 N.Y.S.2d 780 (1974).
361. *See* § 2.09.
362. *See* § 2.09, at notes 199-205.
363. Rockwell v. Pennsylvania State Horse Racing Comm'n, 15 Pa. Commw. Ct. 348, 327 A.2d 211 (1974); Burrillville Racing Ass'n v. Garabedian, 113 R.I. 134, 318 A.2d 469 (1974).
363.1. *See* § 1.28 at note 533.

have been evolved by the courts over the past several years, though it should
be kept in mind that the discussion may reflect more stringency than will
actually be required in the future if the Court continues to relax the due process
standards. We think that this type of presentation is appropriate because it
reflects existing precedent, in the lower courts, and because the unsettled nature
of law in this area will require the passage of several years before clear
precedent becomes available.

In order to determine the procedures that will be required by the Due Process
Clause, the courts will balance the interests of the respective parties, including
such factors as the importance of the jeopardized interest, the type of proceeding
in which the interest is presented, the appropriateness of the procedure
requested to prevent the arbitrary deprivation of a protected interest, and the
costs of requiring such a procedure.[363.2] The seriousness of the sanction imposed
may also be considered.[364]

Although the balancing process may demonstrate the necessity of specific
procedures in particular circumstances, the basic requirement of procedural due
process is that before any action may be taken, the affected person must be
given a "fair hearing," which will include, in essence, notice and a hearing. The
degree of formality in the notice will depend upon the seriousness of the offense
in question. When significant interests are at stake the notice should recite the
time and place of hearing, as well as a statement of the specific charges and
the grounds which, if proven, would justify the rendition of a sanction,[365] and
should be given sufficiently in advance of the date of the hearing as to allow
the preparation of a proper defense.[366] Although the nature of the hearing will
depend upon the circumstances of the case, it must enable the decision-maker
to hear both sides of the situation, and should entail the rudiments of an
adversary proceeding.[367] Thus, in cases involving significant potential penalties,
the affected person may be entitled to counsel,[368] a list of the charges that are
to be presented, the names of, and the facts that will be elicited from adverse
witnesses and be allowed to undertake reasonable discovery activities.[369] Once
the hearing has been held, the findings and conclusions which are rendered

---

363.2. *See, e.g.,* Dixon v. Love, 431 U.S. 105, 97 S. Ct. 1723, 52 L. Ed. 2d 172 (1977).

364. *See* notes 353-60, *supra.*

365. Dubin v. Department of Business Regulation, 262 So. 2d 273 (Fla. App. 1972).

366. Brann v. Mahoney, 187 Md. 89, 48 A.2d 605 (1946); Narragansett Racing Ass'n v. Kiernan,
59 R.I. 79, 194 A. 49 (1937).

367. It has been held that procedural due process requirements will preclude a commission from
requiring that as a condition to a hearing a petitioner post a bond, which may be forfeited if the
petitioner is unsuccessful in the hearing. MacRae v. New York State Racing & Wagering Bd., 48
App. Div. 2d 745, 368 N.Y.S.2d 313 (1975).

368. In Merritt v. Swope, 267 App. Div. 519, 46 N.Y.S.2d 944 (1944), for example, the court held
that a fair hearing was not granted when the jockey's attorney was excluded during the hearing
of testimony. *See also* Amsley v. West Virginia Racing Comm'n, 378 F.2d 815 (4th Cir. 1967), *cert.
denied,* 397 U.S. 945, 25 L. Ed. 2d 127, 90 S. Ct. 963 (1970).

369. 1 F. COOPER, STATE ADMINISTRATIVE LAW 313-16 (1965). *See, e.g.,* Tappis v. New York State
Racing & Wagering Bd., 46 App. Div. 2d 613, 359 N.Y.S.2d 780 (1974) (entitled to cross-examination).
These requirements need not preclude a commission from undertaking investigative efforts in an
ex parte manner. Thus, in Norwood v. Pennsylvania State Horse Racing Comm'n, 16 Pa. Commw.
Ct. 219, 328 A.2d 198 (1974), the court held that an athletic commission could take statements from
potential witnesses without notice to the person being investigated and this would not violate due
process requirements "as long as [it] provides a fair opportunity for notice and cross-examination,
and makes no effort to conceal or suppress evidence favorable to that person." 328 A.2d at 202.

should be presented in a written report that is available for inspection.[370] In short, the affected person should have the opportunity to appear, be heard and make an intelligent and informed defense of the proferred charges.

In order for a hearing to be "fair," it must also be conducted in an impartial manner. Thus, when a chairman of an athletic commission made statements to the press before the affected person had been notified of the pending charges, and stated that the person would be suspended for a year regardless of what further evidence might be presented, a fair hearing was not provided.[371] Similarly, where there is evidence that the chairman of a commission is biased against the affected person, the hearing will not be deemed fair.[372]

The licensee will also be entitled to procedural due process protection after the issuance of the license—that is, the license may not, once issued, be altered by the arbitrary action of an athletic commission. Thus, a commission will violate the due process rights of a licensee by changing the racing dates that had originally been issued to it in a proceeding to which it was not a party.[373]

The type of procedure that will not meet the requirements of a fair hearing is illustrated by *Smith v. Commonwealth of Pennsylvania State Horse Racing Commission*,[374] where an owner-licensee had concluded that track conditions were so poor that it would be dangerous to race his horse. When he was unable to secure permission to withdraw the horse, he intentionally violated commission rules, including one requiring approval to "scratch" a horse. The stewards imposed a fine upon the owner, and the commission subsequently affirmed their findings and increased the fine. Upon review, the court found that the proceedings were defective in several respects. Prior to the commission hearing, the owner subpoenaed several commission staff members for depositions and sought the production of documents. The commission's counsel refused to comply with the discovery demands, asserting that there was no authority for such procedures. The court concluded that this was an erroneous conclusion, and that under applicable authority the owner was entitled to have discovery rights.[375] At the hearing, the trial examiner allowed the commission's counsel to introduce hearsay evidence over strenuous objection, precluded the owner's counsel from examining the owner on several relevant matters, and refused his proffer of other relevant evidence. The court noted that while such hearings are not bound by the rules of evidence, the conduct in this case raised serious questions as to its fairness and possible abuse of discretion by the hearing examiner.[376] The court was also disturbed by evidence that the commission's decision was issued less than 24 hours after the transcript was prepared. The court observed that it "taxes our imagination . . . to believe that the commission

---

370. Maywood Park Trotting Ass'n v. Illinois Harness Racing Comm'n, 15 Ill. 2d 559, 155 N.E.2d 626 (1959) (absence of findings makes basis of decision questionable); Bay State Harness Horse Racing & Breeding Ass'n v. State Racing Comm'n, 342 Mass. 694, 175 N.E.2d 244 (1961).

371. Brann v. Mahoney, 187 Md. 89, 48 A.2d 605 (1946).

372. Arkansas Racing Comm'n v. Emprise Corp., 254 Ark. 975, 497 S.W.2d 34 (1973); Franklin Fair Ass'n v. State Racing Comm'n, 347 Mass. 118, 196 N.E.2d 821 (1964).

373. State *ex rel.* Investment Corp. of South Florida v. Board of Business Regulation, 227 So. 2d 674 (Fla. 1969). *See* § 2.03.

374. 18 Pa. Commw. Ct. 1, 333 A.2d 788 (1975).

375. 333 A.2d at 804.

376. 333 A.2d at 806.

could have seriously considered . . . ." the lengthy transcript in such a short period of time, and that such serious consideration was essential to the requirements of a fair hearing.[377] Finally, the commission effectively precluded the licensee from filing a post-hearing brief, since he would have had to file it either before the transcript was completed (which would not have been meaningful) or before the issuance of the decision (which would not have been possible). This process also abridged the owner's procedural rights. In short, the procedure used by the commission precluded the owner from gathering and presenting evidence in his own defense, and its own deliberations suggested the lack of care necessary for a fair hearing, all of which indicated "shoddy conduct by the commission and its staff" and cast "serious doubt on the essential fairness of the hearings." [378]

Although a commission will generally be required to conduct its enforcement proceedings in accordance with due process of law, summary procedures may in some cases be permissible. The circumstances which will require such procedures will normally make instantaneous action essential to the achievement of the commission's objectives. Such circumstances were thought to be present, for example, in *Tilelli v. Christenberry*,[379] where members of an athletic commission were in attendance at a boxing match which was rumored to be fixed. When the decision of the referees was announced, the commissioners called for their score cards and, after review, concluded that one referee had failed to follow the proper standards in judging two rounds. Accordingly, the commissioners altered the referee's decision, and the outcome of the fight. The court held that the referee's decision could not be disturbed because there was no evidence of fraud,[380] but it did find that summary procedures such as had been used were appropriate. The court felt that if there had, indeed, been a betting coup which had interfered with the conduct or decision of the fight, the public interest would have required that proper action be taken instantaneously to ameliorate any effect on the outcome of the fight. To do otherwise, the court said, would be to disserve the legislative objective of maintaining the public confidence in the honesty of all aspects of the boxing match.[381]

---

377. 333 A.2d at 802.

378. 333 A.2d at 801, 806.

379. 1 Misc. 2d 139, 120 N.Y.S.2d 697 (1953). *See also* Hubel v. West Virginia Racing Comm'n, 376 F. Supp. 1 (S.D. W. Va. 1974).

380. The extent to which decisions of umpires and referees may be disturbed is considered in § 2.15.

381. Thus, the court observed that

> [g]iven the power in justifiable circumstances, and upon a finding of facts establishing the alleged fraud, the next question is whether it could be exercised in such summary fashion. According to the Chairman, the Commissioners were alerted to a closer scrutiny of this fight by "rumors of a betting coup." Now, a rumor in the boxing world comes close to being a reality—at least in its potentiality for shaking public confidence in the integrity of professional boxing. The sport has been given a bad name because too many of such rumors have been proven true in the past, and public relations have become a real consideration. Other administrative agencies may wait until a rumor dissipates from its own emptiness or achieves some factual dignity; but the Athletic Commisssion should and must act immediately to destroy or confirm the rumor. A dominant legislative purpose is to secure and maintain the spectator's confidence in the honesty of every aspect of the boxing match.
>
> . . . .
>
> What might be unseemly and dangerous haste by other administrators was justified,

Tilelli clearly sanctioned the use of summary procedures, but its conclusion might be questioned in terms of the Supreme Court's recent decisions in the area of suspensions from public schools. Thus, in *Goss v. Lopez*,[382] the Court held that a student must be accorded procedural rights before the imposition of even a very short suspension, though it did suggest that such procedures would not be required where immediate action was necessary to eliminate dangers to persons or property or prevent disruption of the academic process.[383] If such summary action is taken, it then specified that notice and hearing should follow the suspension "as soon as practicable." [384] This language would suggest that the summary procedures approved in *Tilelli* would be upheld today only if there was a clear need for immediate action and the suspension was only a step in a process that would provide notice and hearing shortly thereafter. These views are supported by the principal post-*Goss* decision involving regulated sports, in which the court held that suspension before the accordance of procedural rights may be appropriate. In *Hubel v. West Virginia Racing Commission*,[385] the court upheld a preliminary suspension of an owner's license without notice and hearing when drugs were found in one of his horses.[386] After noting the substantial interests that the state has in the regulation of horse racing,[387] the court stated that

> [s]hould the offense of "doping" a horse be committed, whether by intentional act of his handlers or negligence in protecting him from the depredations of outsiders, the offense is so serious and the consequences so severe that absolute protection to the horse and to the public is fully warranted until the matter can be formally resolved. The public is entitled to protection from the continuing danger that one who participates in drugging his horse will do so again, and that one who fails to protect his horse from drugging by others will repeat his negligence. We hold that these considerations justify the mandatory denial of a stay of any suspension for violation of the rules pending the notice and hearing that the due process clause requires.[388]

In light of *Hubel,* it would appear that the vitality of *Tilelli* has not been entirely drained by *Goss v. Lopez,* at least if the dangerousness or disruption requirements can be met and a satisfactory notice and hearing are provided as soon as practicable after the summary action has been taken.[389]

---

might even be required, in this case. First, as just stated, such rumors should be scotched as quickly as possible if unfounded; and prophylaxis should be applied as quickly as possible, if true. Second, it is of the essence of enjoyment of a sporting spectacle that the decision follow the event immediately. Sport followers, unlike lawyers, have no patience with reserved decisions.

The summary method in which the Commissioners acted, while it would be condemned in almost any other area of administrative jurisdiction, was appropriate here. 1 Misc. 2d at 145-46, 120 N.Y.S.2d at 702.

382. 419 U.S. 565, 42 L. Ed. 2d 725, 95 S. Ct. 729 (1975).
383. *Id.* at 582.
384. *Id.* at 582-83. *See also Dixon v. Love, supra* note 363.2 (post-suspension hearing for driver's license sufficient).
385. 513 F.2d 240 (4th Cir. 1975).
386. *See* § 2.07.
387. *See* § 2.07, at note 157.
388. 513 F.2d at 244.
389. *See also* Whetzler v. Krause, 411 F. Supp. 523 (E.D. Pa. 1976); Beikrich v. State Racing & Wagering Bd., — App. Div. 2d —, 369 N.Y.S.2d 36 (1975). The serious objections that could be raised

Notwithstanding the safeguards that will be required by procedural due process of law, the person affected by commission enforcement action may waive those safeguards by knowing and voluntary action. Thus, where a harness racing driver appeared in person before the commission, expressly indicated that he wanted to proceed without counsel, consented to the addition of additional charges to the original citation, and specifically waived any defects in the notice that had been given to him by the commission, he was then estopped from contesting the procedures utilized by the commission.[390]

With regard to commission enforcement proceedings, then, it may be concluded that the oft-recited proposition that commission-issued licenses are revocable at the will of the commission[391] is correct only to the extent that the will of the commission may not be arbitrarily imposed and that it is exercised in a manner that is consistent with procedural due process safeguards.

It should also be noted that determinations made by athletic commissions may on occasion result in the institution of a defamation action by the person or organization which is the object of the determination. The courts have made it clear, however, that in conducting hearings and in announcing decisions athletic commissions, and their members, will be protected by the privilege which attaches to the conduct of official proceedings.[392]

§ 2.19. Judicial Review of Commission Determinations.

When a person is aggrieved by some action of an athletic commission, the immediate question will be whether there is a means of having the action reviewed by the courts. In almost all cases, some form of judicial review will be available. Consideration of judicial review of commission actions will require discussion of two separate issues: how the person may proceed to seek judicial review of the action in question, and how the courts will conduct that review. With respect to the following discussion, it is important to note that there may be substantial variance among the specific principles applicable in the various jurisdictions. The limited purpose of this discussion is to identify the types of problems that will be present when a person seeks judicial review, and to indicate how they have been resolved by courts that have had an opportunity to consider them in the context of regulated sports.

The first issue will be how the person should proceed to achieve judicial review.[393] In every jurisdiction, there will normally be several methods by which the person may proceed. In many jurisdictions, the legislature has either

---

about a procedure that allowed sanctions to be imposed without any hearing are considered at § 3.10(c) (dealing with disciplinary action in non-regulated professional sports).

390. Fogt v. Ohio State Racing Comm'n, 3 Ohio App. 2d 423, 210 N.E.2d 730 (1965). *See also* Nation v. Oregon Racing Comm'n, 21 Or. App. 465, 536 P.2d 536 (1975) (failure to raise defects); Man O'War Racing Ass'n v. State Horse Racing Comm'n, 433 Pa. 432, 250 A.2d 172 (1969) (waive lack of formal hearing when not object).

391. *See, e.g.,* Fitzsimmons v. New York State Athletic Comm'n, 15 Misc. 2d 831, 146 N.Y.S. 117, *aff'd,* 162 App. Div. 904, 147 N.Y.S. 1111 (1914).

392. Porter v. Eyster, 294 F.2d 613 (4th Cir. 1961); Lloyds v. United Press Int'l, Inc., 63 Misc. 2d 421, 311 N.Y.S.2d 373 (1970). Defamation is discussed in detail at § 8.17.

393. *See generally* 2 F. COOPER, STATE ADMINISTRATIVE LAW 603-62 (1965); 3 K. DAVIS, ADMINISTRATIVE LAW TREATISE §§ 24.01 *et seq.* (1958); L. JAFFE, JUDICIAL CONTROL OF ADMINISTRATIVE ACTION (1965).

established a specific means of gaining review in the athletic commission statute itself,[394] or has made the state's administrative procedure act applicable to actions against the athletic commission.[395] If there are no statutory remedies available, review may be obtained through collateral attack of the action by way of injunction, declaratory judgment, or suit against commission members for damages.[396] Non-statutory review may also be available by use of the so-called common law writs.[397] As a condition to the institution of any form of court proceeding, the person seeking review may be required to exhaust all available administrative remedies.[398] Thus, if a hearing procedure is available, but is not requested, the plaintiff may be barred from instituting judicial proceedings.[399] Exhaustion of state judicial remedies may not, however, be a prerequisite to the institution of federal court proceedings.[400] A complainant's ability to have a grievance adjudicated may also be prevented by any of several other factors.

394. *See, e.g.,* CAL. BUS. & PROF. CODE § 18681 (West 1960); DEL. CODE § 28-325(b) (1975); IND. CODE ANN. § 25-9-1-14 (Burns 1971); ILL. ANN. STAT. § 37s.13 (Smith-Hurd 1977); MICH. STAT. ANN. § 18.966(8) (1975); N.J. STAT. ANN. § 5:5-60 (1973). *See also* Kentucky State Racing Comm'n v. Fuller, 481 S.W.2d 298 (Ky. App. 1972); Dancer v. Commonwealth, 10 Pa. Commw. Ct. 642, 309 A.2d 614 (1973).

395. *See, e.g.,* LA. REV. STAT. ANN. § 4:154 (1973). *See also* Bay State Harness Horse Racing & Breeding Ass'n v. State Racing Comm'n, 242 Mass. 694, 175 N.E.2d 244 (1961).

396. *See* 2 F. COOPER, STATE ADMINISTRATIVE LAW 631-44 (1965).

397. The general principles that are commonly said to apply to these methods of gaining review are easily stated, but such statements are prone to be quite misleading since the entire scheme of review in the state courts is so erratic, shifting and contradictory. Indeed, it is said that "[n]o branch of administrative law is more seriously in need of reform than the common law of the state courts concerning methods of judicial review," and "[a]n imaginary system cunningly planned for the evil purpose of thwarting justice and maximizing fruitless litigation would copy the major features of the extraordinary remedies." 3 K. DAVIS, ADMINISTRATIVE LAW TREATISE § 24.01, at 388-89 (1958).

Although this is not the place for a detailed analysis of the common law writs, *see* authorities in note 393 *supra,* it is necessary to at least identify them in their common formulation. The first is the writ of certiorari, which is said to be available for the review of judicial or quasi-judicial action but not for the review of non-judicial action. *See* West Flagler Amusement Co. v. State Racing Comm'n, 122 Fla. 222, 165 So. 64 (1935); North Shore Corp. v. Selectmen of Topsfield, 322 Mass. 413, 77 N.E.2d 774 (1948). The second, and most commonly used, writ is the writ of mandamus, which is usually said to be the proper remedy for controlling ministerial, but not discretionary, acts of public officers, and which is used to compel a public officer to perform a duty which the officer has refused to perform, which failure has violated a clearly established legal right. Brooke v. Moore, 60 Ariz. 551, 142 P.2d 211 (1943); West Flagler Associates v. Division of Pari-Mutuel Wagering, 251 So. 2d 856 (Fla. 1971); State *ex rel.* Investment Corp. of South Fla. v. Board of Business Regulation, 227 So. 2d 674 (Fla. 1969); State *ex rel.* Associated Outdoor Clubs, Inc. v. Lechner, 197 So. 2d 512 (Fla. 1967); State *ex rel.* Pensacola Greyhound Racing, Inc. v. Lechner, 195 So. 2d 206 (Fla. 1967); State *ex rel.* Tourist Attractions, Inc. v. Lechner, 191 So. 2d 555 (Fla. 1966); State *ex rel.* Volusia Jai-Alai, Inc. v. Ring, 122 So. 2d 4 (Fla. 1960); State *ex rel.* Pinellas Kennel Club, Inc. v. State Racing Comm'n, 116 Fla. 143, 156 So. 317 (1934); State *ex rel.* West Flagler Associates v. Board of Business Regulation, 238 So. 2d 677 (Fla. App. 1970); People *ex rel.* Empress Farms, Inc. v. Schneider, 1 Ill. App. 3d 147, 273 N.E.2d 61 (1971). The final common law writ would be the writ of prohibition, which is customarily available to prevent the exercise of judicial or quasi-judicial power in excess of the jurisdiction of the body in question. *See generally* 2 F. COOPER, STATE ADMINISTRATIVE LAW 659-62 (1965); 3 K. DAVIS, ADMINISTRATIVE LAW TREATISE § 24.04 (1958).

398. *See generally* 2 F. COOPER, STATE ADMINISTRATIVE LAW 572-85 (1965).

399. State Racing Comm'n v. McManus, 82 N.M. 108, 476 P.2d 767 (1970); Eldred v. Monaghan, 6 Misc. 2d 658, 164 N.Y.S.2d 202 (1957) (mere allegation that hearing procedure insufficient not sufficient grounds for refusing to follow that procedure).

400. Amsley v. West Virginia Racing Comm'n, 378 F.2d 815 (4th Cir. 1967), *cert. denied,* 397 U.S. 945, 25 L. Ed. 2d 127, 90 S. Ct. 963 (1970); Suarez v. Administrador Del Deporte Hipico De Puerto Rico, 354 F. Supp. 320 (D.P.R. 1972).

For example, review may be unavailable if the question presented is moot,[401] if the moving party is guilty of laches [402] or clearly not entitled to relief,[403] or if relief would in any event be meaningless.[404] Review may not be avoided by the mere fact that a sanction meted out by a commission has expired, since the presence of the sanction on the affected person's record may have a materially damaging effect upon the person's future in the sport.[405]

By whatever method judicial review is accomplished, the basic issue will involve the scope of review that will be applied to those determinations.[406] Consideration has already been given to the scope of review that will be accorded the rule-making function of athletic commissions,[407] and the present discussion will be limited to the question as it arises with respect to adjudicatory determinations.

Although the scope of review may be established by statutory provision,[408] or by the non-statutory collateral or common law forms of proceeding utilized to obtain judicial review,[409] it will in almost all cases be governed by the so-called substantial evidence rule.[410] This rule will cause the reviewing court to distinguish between the findings of fact and conclusions of law made by the commission.[411] The court will review conclusions of law on their merits, but will limit its review of findings of fact to determining whether they are supported by substantial evidence. The term "substantial evidence" may be defined as

---

401. State *ex rel.* West Flagler Associates v. Board of Business Regulation, 238 So. 2d 677 (Fla. App. 1970); Maywood Park Trotting Ass'n v. Illinois Racing Comm'n, 15 Ill. 2d 559, 155 N.E.2d 626 (1959); People *ex rel.* Mikel v. Illinois Racing Comm'n, 310 Ill. App. 68, 33 N.E.2d 893 (1941); National Jockey Club v. Illinois Racing Comm'n, 364 Ill. 630, 5 N.E.2d 224 (1936).

402. Wight v. New Jersey Racing Comm'n, 128 N.J.L. 517, 26 A.2d 709 (1942).

403. State *ex rel.* West Flagler Club, Inc. v. Florida State Racing Comm'n, 74 So. 2d 691 (Fla. 1954).

404. State *ex rel.* Dade County Kennel Club, Inc. v. Florida State Racing Comm'n, 116 Fla. 144, 156 So. 343 (1934) (charitable corporation could not be a licensee).

405. Pennsylvania State Athletic Comm'n v. Graziano, 12 Pa. D. & C.2d 127, 70 Dauph. 257 (1957) (even though suspension expired, suspended manager entitled to have blot on record removed when commission acted improperly); Brown v. Waldman, 93 R.I. 489, 177 A.2d 179 (1962).

406. The multitude of questions that may arise concerning the scope of judicial review in a given jurisdiction are considered in detail in 2 F. COOPER, STATE ADMINISTRATIVE LAW 603-779 (1965).

407. *See* § 2.04.

408. *See, e.g.,* Arkansas Racing Comm'n v. Emprise Corp., 254 Ark. 975, 497 S.W.2d 34 (1973); Dancer v. Commonwealth, 10 Pa. Commw. Ct. 642, 309 A.2d 614 (1973).

409. *See* notes 396-97 *supra.*

410. The criticisms that may be and are leveled against the "substantial evidence rule" are reviewed at 2 F. COOPER, STATE ADMINISTRATIVE LAW 724-37 (1965). Notwithstanding these deficiencies in the rule, it is set forth here as a general standard because it is utilized by the courts and because this is not the proper place to present a general evaluation of its usefulness or desirability.

In this vein, it is also well to point out what has been suggested as the somewhat "cynical rule-of-thumb" of attorneys practicing before administrative agencies:

> If the appellant can convince the appellate court that the administrative finding of facts is obviously wrong, and if the appellant can at the same time arouse in the court a zealous desire to correct the error, the court can always find means to do so, whatever labels must be applied. 2 F. COOPER, STATE ADMINISTRATIVE LAW 734 (1965).

411. Universal Camera Corp. v. NLRB, 340 U.S. 474, 490, 95 L. Ed. 456, 71 S. Ct. 456 (1951). It is worth noting that the differentiation is "often not an illuminating test and is never self-executing," Baumgartner v. United States, 322 U.S. 665, 671, 88 L. Ed. 1523, 64 S. Ct. 1240 (1944), because of the intrinsic difficulty in separating legal form from factual determinations. *See also* 2 F. COOPER, STATE ADMINISTRATIVE LAW 665-67 (1965).

"such relevant evidence as a reasonable mind might accept as adequate to support a conclusion." [412]

With regard to factual determinations, therefore, a court will accord athletic commissions, as expert bodies, a wide discretion in accomplishing their objectives, and will not substitute its judgment for that of the commission.[413] This judicial deferral is premised on the view that factual questions are peculiarly within the province of a commission's delegated authority. Accordingly, findings of administrative agencies on factual issues are, as a prima facie matter, viewed as being correct.[414] Thus, where a factual finding is supported by substantial evidence, it will not be disturbed even though the reviewing court might have reached a different conclusion had it made the original determination.[415] These principles are amply demonstrated by *Kentucky State Racing Commission v. Fuller,*[416] where the "winner" of the 1968 Kentucky Derby ("Dancer's Image") was deprived of the victor's purse by the steward's conclusion that there were drugs in the horse's urine.[417] This decision was upheld by the full athletic commission and was then appealed to the appropriate local trial court, which held that there was not substantial evidence to support the decision. In subsequent review of the trial court's decision, the court of appeals stated that the sole issue was whether the commission's factual conclusion was supported by substantial evidence. After noting the commission's broad authority and discretion, the court extensively reviewed the evidence presented to the stewards. Although there was some dispute as to the adequacy of the tests which were performed on the urine sample in question, it found that the stewards' decision had in fact been supported by substantial evidence. In reaching this conclusion, the court observed that the commission must be afforded great latitude in its evaluation of the evidence presented and the credibility of the witnesses heard; that it is the commission's, not the court's, duty to make the findings and conclusions of fact; and so long as there is substantial evidence in the record, those determinations should not be altered

---

412. Consolidated Edison Co. v. NLRB, 305 U.S. 197, 227, 83 L. Ed. 126, 59 S. Ct. 206 (1938). *See also* Consolo v. Federal Maritime Comm'n, 383 U.S. 607, 16 L. Ed. 2d 131, 86 S. Ct. 1018 (1966); Kentucky State Racing Comm'n v. Fuller, 481 S.W.2d 298 (Ky. App. 1972).

413. The best statement of this rule is in London Sporting Club, Inc. v. Helfand, 3 Misc. 3d 431, 152 N.Y.S.2d 819 (1956), where the court observed that:

> A great deal of latitude and discretion must be accorded a commission which is responsible to the people of the state for the maintenance of fair dealing, honesty, and clean sport in a field which has in the past been infected with undesirable elements. Its rules should be enforced by the courts unless shown to be clearly arbitrary. Its determinations, particularly when supported by evidence, should be upheld. *Id.* at 436, 152 N.Y.S.2d at 824.

See also Ruane v. New York State Racing & Wagering Bd., 400 F. Supp. 819 (S.D. N.Y. 1975); Mahoney v. Byers, 187 Md. 81, 48 A.2d 600 (1946); Fitzsimmons v. New York State Athletic Comm'n, 15 Misc. 2d 831, 146 N.Y.S. 117 (1914), *aff'd,* 62 App. Div. 904, 147 N.Y.S. 1111 (1914).

414. Maywood Park Trotting Ass'n v. Illinois Harness Racing Comm'n, 15 Ill. 2d 559, 115 N.E.2d 626 (1959); State *ex rel.* Durando v. State Athletic Comm'n, 272 Wis. 191, 75 N.W.2d 451 (1956) (commission determinations be accorded "great weight").

415. Vale v. Colorado Racing Comm'n, 510 P.2d 1382 (Colo. App. 1973); Wilkey v. Board of Bus. Reg., 314 So. 2d 17 (Fla. App. 1975); O'Neil v. Pallot, 257 So. 2d 59 (Fla. App. 1972); Miller v. Lomenzo, 43 App. Div. 2d 997, 352 N.Y.S.2d 260 (1974); Gleason v. Love, 14 Ore. App. 97, 511 P.2d 435 (1973); Pennsylvania State Athletic Comm'n v. Moran, 6 Pa. D. & C.2d 611, 68 Dauph. 388 (1956).

416. 481 S.W.2d 298 (Ky. App. 1972).

417. Drug rules are considered at § 2.07.

by subsequent court review, whether or not the court would reach the same conclusion if it were trying the case on a *de novo* basis.[418]

Notwithstanding the broad discretion accorded athletic commissions, the courts will overturn findings which are not supported by substantial evidence,[419] or which are so arbitrary or capricious as to constitute an abuse of discretion.[420] Thus, findings have been overturned when there was not substantial evidence in the record to support the conclusion that a jockey's petit larceny conviction was detrimental to the best interests of racing;[421] that an owner had created a public disturbance;[422] that a harness driver had failed to maintain a proper pace;[423] that a referee had failed to score a boxing match correctly;[424] or that a non-existent license could be suspended.[425] Sanctions have also been reduced when they were found to be too severe for the conduct in question.[425.1]

Although the courts will normally apply the substantial evidence rule in determining the appropriate scope of its review, they will retain the discretion, absent a statutory provision to the contrary, to specifically adopt a different scope of review in any particular case.[426]

§ 2.20. Public Regulation of Gambling on Sports Events.

Sports events have long been one of the most popular objects of gambling activity.[427] The football or basketball game which is ostensibly played for no

---

418. 481 S.W.2d at 308-09.

419. Carroll v. California Horse Racing Bd., 16 Cal. 2d 164, 105 P.2d 110 (1940); Rudolph v. Athletic Comm'n of Calif., 177 Cal. App. 2d 1, 1 Cal. Rptr. 898 (1960); State Racing Comm'n v. Robertson, 111 Ohio App. 435, 172 N.E.2d 628 (1960); Fischbach v. Ohio State Racing Comm'n, 76 Ohio L. Abs. 540, 147 N.E.2d 258 (1955); Smith v. Cole, 270 App. Div. 675, 62 N.Y.S.2d 226, *appeal granted,* 296 N.Y. 614, 68 N.E.2d 888 (1946); Narragansett Racing Ass'n v. Kiernan, 59 R.I. 79, 194 A. 49 (1937).

420. Vale v. Colorado Racing Comm'n, 510 P.2d 1382 (Colo. App. 1973) (suspension of non-existing license). Clearly within this category would be the failure of the commission to afford requisite procedural safeguards to the person affected by its action. *See* § 2.18.

421. State Racing Comm'n v. Robertson, 111 Ohio App. 435, 172 N.E.2d 628 (1960).

422. Fischbach v. Ohio State Racing Comm'n, 76 Ohio L. Abs. 540, 147 N.E.2d 258 (1955).

423. Dancer v. Commonwealth, 10 Pa. Commw. Ct. 642, 309 A.2d 614 (1973).

424. Tilelli v. Christenberry, 1 Misc. 2d 139, 120 N.Y.S.2d 697 (1953). The power of a commission or a court to disturb the decisions of umpires or referees is considered at § 2.15.

425. Vale v. Colorado Racing Comm'n, 510 P.2d 1382 (Colo. App. 1973).

425.1. *See, e.g.,* Pennsylvania State Horse Racing Comm'n v. DiSanto, 29 Pa. Commw. Ct. 574, 372 A.2d 487 (1977) (actions not so gross as to warrant multi-year suspension).

426. *See* 4 K. DAVIS ADMINISTRATIVE LAW TREATISE § 30.08 (1958). In determining whether it will adopt a different scope of review, Professor Davis suggests that the court will consider three factors:

    1) The comparative qualifications of the court and the administrative agency;

    2) The degree of legislative commitment of power to the agency; and

    3) The distinction between enunciating general principles and applying legal concepts to unique factual situations.

427. The term "gambling" itself has reference to the playing of a game of chance for stakes risked on an event, chance or contingency, Holberg v. Westchester Racing Ass'n, 184 Misc. 581, 53 N.Y.S.2d 490 (1945), and has been held to include, for example, a bet on a foot race between human beings, Jones v. Cavanaugh, 149 Mass. 124, 21 N.E. 306 (1889), on the physical ability of animals, Commonwealth v. Tilton, 8 Metc. (Mass.) 232 (1844) (cockfighting), and on a race between horses. McLain v. Huffman, 30 Ark. 428 (1875); Hawthorne Kennel Club v. Swanson, 257 Ill. App. 499, Transf. to 339 Ill. 220, 171 N.E. 140 (1930); Cheesum v. State, 8 Blackf. (Ind.) 332, 44 Am. Dec. 771 (1846); Ellis v. Beale, 18 Me. 337, 36 Am. Dec. 726 (1841); Kemp v. Hammond Hotels, 226 Mass. 409, 115 N.E. 572 (1917); Grace v. M'Elroy, 1 Allen (Mass.) 563 (1861); Wilkinson v. Tousley, 16 Minn. 299, 10 Am. Rep. 139 (1871); Shropshire v. Glascock & Garner, 4 Mo. 536, 31 Am. Dec. 189 (1837); Joseph v. Miller & Clouthier, 1 N.M. 621 (1876).

reason other than to promote interscholastic competition or provide spectator entertainment may also be the basis for substantial gambling activity.[428] Thus, there may be a significant relationship between sports and gambling activities, and the extent to which this relationship affects the conduct of sports events has been a subject of considerable concern for legislators at both the state and federal level. Although wagering on sports events was not a crime at common law,[429] it has been made unlawful in most states,[430] as well as by a series of federal statutory provisions.[431] In addition to enacting criminal legislation,

428. *See generally* L. MERCHANT, THE NATIONAL FOOTBALL LOTTERY (1973); Denison, *Big-Time Gambling — Menace to Pro Sports,* READER'S DIGEST (Aug., 1973).

429. *See, e.g.,* Grayson v. Whatley, 15 La. Ann. 525 (1860); Shropshire v. Glascock & Garner, 4 Mo. 536, 31 Am. Dec. 189 (1837); People *ex rel.* Weiner v. Barr, 131 Misc. 80, 225 N.Y.S. 346 (1927) (wager on boxing match); Misner v. Knapp, 13 Or. 135, 9 P. 65 (1885); All Texas Racing Ass'n v. State, 82 S.W.2d 151 (Tex. Civ. App. 1935), *aff'd,* State *ex rel.* Shook v. All Texas Racing Ass'n, 128 Tex. 384, 97 S.W.2d 669 (1936) (betting on dog races); McElroy v. Carmichael, 6 Tex. 454 (1851); Porter v. Day, 71 Wis. 296, 37 N.W. 259 (1888) (bet on horse race; citing cases). *But cf.* McLain v. Huffman, 30 Ark. 428 (1875); Nash v. Monheimer, 20 Ill. 215 (1858) (betting on horse race unlawful in Illinois); Hawthorne Kennel Club v. Swanson, 257 Ill. App. 499 (1930), Transf. to 339 Ill. 220, 171 N.E. 140 (general rule not followed in Illinois); Wilkinson v. Tousley, 16 Minn. 299, 10 Am. Rep. 139 (1871); Hoit v. Hodge, 6 N.H. 104, 25 Am. Dec. 451 (1833).

430. *See, e.g.,* CAL. PENAL CODE § 337.1 (West 1971); CONN. GEN. STAT. ANN. § 19-338 (1977); DEL. CODE § 28-165 (1975); KY. REV. STAT. § 436.500 (1975); MASS. ANN. LAWS ch. 128A, § 13 (1972); MICH. STAT. ANN. § 18.422(25) (1974); VA. CODE § 9-33 (1973). *See generally* Note, *Statutory Trends Toward Legalization of Gambling,* 34 IOWA L. REV. 647 (1949); Annot., 45 A.L.R. 998 (1926).

In light of the common law posture of betting or wagering on sports events, it is important to note that the general gambling laws are ordinarily intended to apply to the activities of persons involved in gambling as a profession or business, and are not designed to make the casual player, contestant or bettor who gambles for amusement or recreation criminally culpable. United States v. Tarter, 522 F.2d 520 (6th Cir. 1975) (applying federal law, *see* note 431 *infra*); People v. Solomon, 296 N.Y. 220, 72 N.E.2d 163 (1947); Watts v. Malatesta, 262 N.Y. 80, 186 N.E. 210 (1933); People v. Wilkerson, 73 Misc. 2d 895, 342 N.Y.S.2d 936 (1973).

431. The basic federal statute makes it unlawful for anyone to conduct a "gambling business," 18 U.S.C. § 1955, and is designed to include all syndicated gambling proscribed by state law. United States v. Harris, 460 F.2d 1041 (5th Cir. 1972); United States v. Schullo, 363 F. Supp. 246 (D. Minn. 1973); United States v. Kohne, 358 F. Supp. 1053 (W.D. Pa. 1973). The reference to gambling acts unlawful under state law has been upheld. *See, e.g.,* United States v. Smaldone, 458 F.2d 1333 (10th Cir. 1973). The type of gambling activity sought to be controlled is well illustrated by United States v. Sacco, 491 F.2d 995 (9th Cir. 1974), where the court upheld the constitutionality of the statute, and applied it to members of a gambling business involved with wagers on horse racing, football and basketball games. Those whose convictions were upheld included the proprietors of the business, the "splitters" (those who collect and pay-off bets), and the "layoff bettors" (those who share the risk with bookmakers who receive unbalanced bets on a given event). *See also* United States v. Schaefer, 510 F.2d 1307 (8th Cir. 1975).

Federal statutes also make it unlawful for anyone in the business of betting or wagering to knowingly use a facility of interstate commerce for the transmission of bets or wagers, or information which will be used to assist in the placement of bets or wagers on sporting events. 18 U.S.C. § 1084(a); Truchinski v. United States, 393 F.2d 627 (8th Cir.), *cert. denied,* 393 U.S. 831, 21 L. Ed. 2d 103, 89 S. Ct. 104 (1968) (stating elements of offense). *See also* ARK. STAT. ANN. § 411-2034 (1977); CAL. PENAL CODE § 337i (West 1971). The statute excludes from its coverage the transmission of information used in news reporting, Kelly v. Illinois Bell Tel. Co., 325 F.2d 148 (7th Cir. 1963) (an information sheet of racing results was within exception); *see also* ARK. STAT. ANN. § 41-2034 (1964), or which originates from, and/or concludes in, a state in which such betting or wagering is lawful. 18 U.S.C. § 1084 (b); *but cf.* Martin v. United States, 389 F.2d 895 (5th Cir.), *cert. denied,* 391 U.S. 919, 20 L. Ed. 2d 656, 88 S. Ct. 1808 (1968) (exception does not include information sent to a state where gambling is lawful from a state in which it is not). It also specifies that a public utility must, after reasonable notice, discontinue furnishing or maintaining any facility used by a customer for the transmission of betting or gambling information. 18 U.S.C. § 1084(d); Telephone News System, Inc. v. Illinois Bell Tel. Co., 220 F. Supp. 621 (N.D. Ill. 1963), *aff'd per curiam,* 376 U.S. 782, 12 L. Ed. 2d 83, 84 S. Ct. 1134 (1964). This provision does not affect the utility's

legislators have also utilized other means to affect specific control over the relationship between gambling and sports.[432]

The primary non-criminal method of control has been the use of public regulation concepts, which have already been noted in detail with respect to state athletic commissions.[433] These concepts have been most frequently manifested by legislation in some states which permits gambling on selected sports events, but requires that it be done in accordance with rules and regulations established by an agency of the state which is created for that purpose. The statutory provisions normally authorize the maintenance of pari-mutuel betting arrangements. The term "pari-mutuel" has reference to a form of betting in which all of the money wagered on a given event is placed in a single pool. When the outcome of the event is known, the pool, less a fixed percentage of the total deposits which is divided between the licensee who conducts the betting and the state (as a tax on the conduct of pari-mutuel betting),[434] is paid over to those

---

common law right to terminate service for illegal use. Delaware Sports Serv. v. Diamond State Tel. Co., 241 F. Supp. 847 (D. Del. 1965), *aff'd per curiam*, 355 F.2d 929 (3d Cir.), *cert. denied*, 385 U.S. 817, 17 L. Ed. 2d 55, 87 S. Ct. 38 (1966). There are also federal statutes which make it unlawful to transport gambling devices in interstate commerce, 18 U.S.C. § 1953, or to have connection with a gambling ship, 18 U.S.C. § 1082, which is defined as "a vessel used principally for the operation of one or more gambling establishments." 18 U.S.C. § 1081.

432. An additional means of controlling the relation between gambling and sports, has been statutory provisions which make it unlawful to offer or accept a bribe in a sports contest. The federal statute is 18 U.S.C. § 224(a), whose background was stated in H. REP. No. 1053, 88th Cong., 2d Sess., to be that

> During the past few years, we have witnessed a number of scandals in the sporting world in which attempts were made to influence sporting events by bribery. With the development of highly organized athletics, both professional and collegiate, gambling interests have become increasingly involved. Because of the heavy stakes, the temptation to fix games has become very great.
> Efforts have been made by dedicated men in collegiate and professional sports to preserve athletics from the influence of the gamblers and the underworld. States have passed laws providing criminal penalties for offering or accepting bribes in sporting contests. State law enforcement agencies have done much to uncover and prosecute violators of these statutes. However, it is felt that more must be done. Bribery of players or officials to influence the results of sporting contests is a challenge to an important aspect of American life — honestly competitive sports.

See also ALA. CODE § 13-7-36 (1977); ARK. STAT. ANN. § 41-903 (1977); CAL. PENAL CODE 337b (West 1971); CONN. GEN. STAT. §§ 12-568—12-578 (1973); DEL. CODE § 28-701 (1975); FLA. STAT. ANN. § 838.12 (Supp. 1973); GA. CODE ANN. § 26-2711 (1972); IND. CODE ANN. § 35-18-12-1 (Burns 1975); KY. REV. STAT. § 436.505 (1969); LA. REV. STAT. ANN. § 14:118-1 (1974); MD. ANN. CODE art. 27, § 24 (1975); N.H. REV. STAT. ANN. § 577.16 (1955); N.J. STAT. ANN. § 2A:93-10 (1969); WASH. REV. CODE ANN. § 67.04.010 (1974). It may also be provided that the mere payment of a bonus as an incentive to play better shall not be unlawful. *See e.g.*, WASH. REV. CODE ANN. § 67.04.070 (1974).

See United States *ex rel.* Sollazzo v. Esperdy, 187 F. Supp. 753 (S.D.N.Y. 1960), *aff'd*, 285 F.2d 341 (2d Cir.), *cert. denied*, 366 U.S. 905, 6 L. Ed. 2d 204, 81 S. Ct. 1049 (1961) (deportation for bribing amateur athletes); People v. Blanck, 188 Cal. App. 2d 808, 10 Cal. Rptr. 754 (1961) (must have corroborating evidence of bribe); People v. Phillips, 76 Cal. App. 2d 515, 173 P.2d 392 (1946) (bribe boxer to do less than best efforts). *See generally* Annot., 49 A.L.R.2d 1234 (1956).

433. *See* §§ 2.02 through 2.19.

434. *See, e.g.*, N.Y. UNCONSOL. LAWS § 7959 (McKinney Supp. 1978). It should also be noted that in order to facilitate this paying-off of the winning bettors, the amounts to be paid per ticket will often be rounded-off. This process may cause there to be a small amount left in the pool after all tickets have been paid, and this remainder has come to be called the "breaks." Because the "breaks" may, over a period of time, amount to a substantial amount of money, there will normally be a specific statutory provision dealing with their distribution. *See, e.g.*, ARIZ. REV. STAT. ANN. § 5-111.01 (1974); FLA. STAT. ANN. § 550.26 (1974). Absent such a provision, it has been held that the "breakage" may not be deducted from the pool. Delaware Steeplechase & Race Ass'n v. Wise,

persons who bet on the winner.[435] Thus, under the pari-mutuel system, every person who makes a bet becomes a bookmaker for every other bettor [436] — that is, the odds and returns are determined by the participants themselves according to the entrants they choose and the amount of their payments (bets) placed in the pool.[437]

Inasmuch as pari-mutuel betting would constitute an unlawful gambling pool[438] if it were not exempted from the anti-gambling laws,[439] it is common to find a statutory provision which authorizes it so long as conducted in accordance with the conditions set forth in the applicable statutory scheme.[440] Pari-mutuel

111 Del. 587, 27 A.2d 357 (1942). *See also* California Horse Racing Bd. v. Los Angeles Turf Club, Inc., 111 Cal. App. 2d 933, 245 P.2d 327 (1952) (not offset against "breakage" due state the amount of minus pools); Feeney v. Eastern Racing Ass'n, 303 Mass. 602, 22 N.E.2d 259 (1939) (definition of "breakage"); State v. Garden State Racing Ass'n, 136 N.J.L. 173, 54 A.2d 916 (1947) (payment to state is in the nature of a license fee); Saratoga Harness Racing Ass'n v. Agriculture and New York State Horse Breeding Dev. Fund, 22 N.Y.2d 119, 238 N.E.2d 730 (1968) (statutory direction as to payment of percentage of "breakage" constitutional).

435. Salmore v. Empire City Racing Ass'n, 123 N.Y.S.2d 688 (1953). In *Salmore,* the court made the following observation concerning the origins of the pari-mutuel system:

> Pari-mutuel betting originally known as "Paris-Mutuel" is generally believed to have been devised by one d'Ollier in France in about the middle of the 19th Century. It is said that the system of calculations was first devised in early 1908 by Col. Matt Winn and Judge Charles Franklin Price, an amateur mathematician of note in Louisville, Kentucky; that it was introduced to the public at The Kentucky Derby of that year, and was subsequently adopted by and still is employed at every race track in the United States and Canada holding pari-mutuel betting. *Id.* at 692.

See also Donovan v. Eastern Racing Ass'n, 324 Mass. 393, 86 N.E.2d 903 (1949). *See generally* 6A A. CORBIN, CONTRACTS § 1488 (1962).

436. Aliano v. Westchester Racing Ass'n, 265 App. Div. 225, 38 N.Y.S.2d 741 (1942).

437. Holberg v. Westchester Racing Ass'n, 184 Misc. 581, 53 N.Y.S.2d 490 (1945).

438. *See, e.g.,* CAL. PENAL CODE § 337a (Deering's Supp. 1975); CONN. GEN. STAT. § 12-515 (1973); IND. CODE ANN. § 35-1-104-8 (Burns 1975); MASS. GEN. LAWS ANN. ch. 271, § 17 (Supp. 1977). *See also* Reinmiller v. State, 93 Fla. 462, 111 So. 633 (1927); Pompano Horse Club v. State *ex rel.* Bryan, 93 Fla. 415, 111 So. 801, 52 A.L.R. 51 (1927); Swigart v. People, 154 Ill. 284, 40 N.E. 432 (1895); Commonwealth v. Simonds, 79 Ky. 618 (1881); State *ex rel.* Sorensen v. Ak-Sar-Ben Exposition Co., 118 Neb. 851, 226 N.W. 705 (1929); Barker v. Mosher, 60 N.H. 73 (1880); *In re* Opinion of Justices, 73 N.H. 625, 63 A. 505 (1906); State v. Lovell, 39 N.J.L. 458 (1877); State v. Feak, 60 Ohio App. 223, 20 N.E.2d 534 (1938); Hurt v. Oak Downs, Inc., 85 S.W.2d 294 (Tex. Civ. App. 1935). *But cf.* McCall v. State, 18 Ariz. 408, 161 P. 893 (1916) (operation of pari-mutuel pool not engaged in gambling); James v. State, 63 Md. 242 (1885) (pool-selling is not gambling).

439. *See* note 430 *supra.*

440. *See, e.g.,* ARIZ. REV. STAT. ANN. § 5-112(A) (1974); ARK. STAT. ANN. § 84-2748 (1977); CAL. BUS. & PROF. CODE §§ 19590 *et seq.* (West 1960); DEL. CODE § 28-361 (1975); FLA. STAT. ANN. § 550.16 (1974); IDAHO CODE § 54-2512 (Supp. 1977); ILL. ANN. STAT. tit. 8, § 37J (Smith-Hurd 1977); MAINE REV. STAT. ANN. tit. 8, §§ 274, 333 (Supp. 1974); MASS. GEN. ANN. ch. 128A, § 5 (Supp. 1977); MICH. STAT. ANN. § 18.966(12) (1974); NEV. REV. STAT. § 464.010 (1971); N.J. STAT. ANN. § 5:5-62 (1973); N.Y. UNCONSOL. LAWS § 7952 (McKinney Supp. 1978); OHIO REV. CODE ANN. § 3769.08 (Page Supp. 1977); PA. STAT. ANN. tit. 4, § 305 (Purdon 1963); R.I. GEN. LAWS § 41-4-1 (1970); WASH. REV. CODE ANN. § 67.16.060 (1974); W. VA. CODE § 19-23-9 (Supp. 1974).

These enabling provisions have been held to be constitutional. Rodgers v. Southland Racing Corp., 247 Ark. 115, 450 S.W.2d 3 (1970), *appeal dismissed,* 400 U.S. 809, 27 L. Ed. 2d 37, 91 S. Ct. 42 (1970); Longstreth v. Cook, 215 Ark. 72, 220 S.W.2d 433 (1949) (citing cases); People v. Sullivan, 60 Cal. App. 2d 539, 141 P.2d 230 (1943); Ginsberg v. Centennial Turf Club, Inc., 126 Colo. 471, 251 P.2d 926 (1952); People v. Monroe, 349 Ill. 270, 182 N.E. 439 (1932); State v. Saia, 212 La. 868, 33 So. 2d 665 (1947); Patton v. Fortuna Corp., 68 N.M. 40, 357 P.2d 1090 (1960) (only aggrieved persons may challenge); State v. Garden State Racing Ass'n, 136 N.J.L. 173, 54 A.2d 916 (1947); Mellman v. Metropolitan Jockey Club, Inc., 195 Misc. 121, 89 N.Y.S.2d 64 (1949) (statute authorizing manual computation of daily double tickets constitutional). *See generally* 27 CALIF. L. REV. 78 (1938); Annot., 85 A.L.R. 605 (1932).

The pari-mutuel provisions have also been held to not authorize unlawful lotteries or to violate the anti-lottery laws. Scott v. Dunaway, 228 Ark. 943, 311 S.W.2d 305 (1958); People v. Sullivan, 60

betting which is conducted in the absence of, or which is conducted outside of, such provisions will continue to be unlawful.[441] In considering pari-mutuel betting, it is significant to keep in mind that the purpose for its legalization is not legislative altruism, but is, rather, a means of effecting regulation and enabling the state to tap an additional source of revenue for the support of general governmental programs.[442] In light of the frequent assertion that animal racing could not survive economically without the funds made available through the pari-mutuel system,[443] it is said that without the enabling legislation making such gambling lawful it would be neither practical, lawful nor feasible to operate an animal racing and betting operation.[444]

The fact that the enabling legislation exempts pari-mutuel betting from otherwise applicable criminal laws has two immediate consequences. The first is that its conduct is a function of great public interest and importance, so that the state will be authorized to exercise greater control and utilize its police power in a more arbitrary manner than would be the case with enterprises over which the exercise of police power is not so essential for the public welfare.[445] The second consequence is that the scope of the pari-mutuel enactments will be strictly construed — that is, the activities made lawful will include only those specifically authorized by the legislature.[446] Thus, in *Northwest Greyhound Kennel Association v. State*,[447] a corporation formed to conduct dog racing challenged the constitutionality of the applicable pari-mutuel statute which applied only to horse racing, after it had been denied a license to operate a

---

Cal. App. 2d 539, 141 P.2d 230 (1943); People v. Monroe, 349 Ill. 270, 182 N.E. 439 (1932); Commonwealth v. Kentucky Jockey Club, 238 Ky. 739, 38 S.W.2d 987 (1931); Rohan v. Detroit Racing Ass'n, 314 Mich. 326, 22 N.W.2d 433 (1946); Panas v. Texas Breeders & Racing Ass'n, 80 S.W.2d 1020 (Tex. Civ. App. 1935); Utah State Fair Ass'n v. Green, 68 Utah 251, 249 P. 1016 (1926). *But cf.* State *ex rel.* Moore v. Bissing, 178 Kans. 111, 283 P.2d 418 (1955); State *ex rel.* Sorensen v. Ak-Sar-Ben Exposition Co., 118 Neb. 851, 226 N.W. 705 (1929) (pari-mutuel betting violates the lottery law in the absence of specific statutory authorization).

It has also been held that a statute which authorizes pari-mutuel betting on races will also authorize such betting on a multi-race basis. Donovan v. Eastern Racing Ass'n, 324 Mass. 393, 86 N.E.2d 903 (1949).

The socio-economic consequences of legalized gambling are reviewed in D. WEINSTEIN & L. DEITCH, THE IMPACT OF LEGALIZED GAMBLING (1974).

441. *See, e.g.,* ARIZ. REV. STAT. ANN. § 5-112(B) (1974); CAL. BUS. & PROF. CODE §§ 19593, 19595 (West 1960); IDAHO CODE § 54-2513 (Supp. 1977). *See also* State v. Del Bianco, 96 N.H. 436, 78 A.2d 519 (1951); *In re* Bromberger, 187 Misc. 593, 62 N.Y.S.2d 47 (1946); People v. Wilson, 4 N.Y.S.2d 592 (1938).

Enactment of a pari-mutuel law will not, moreover, affect the vitality of the ordinary anti-gambling laws. People v. Lightstone, 330 Mich. 672, 48 N.W.2d 146 (1951).

442. *See, e.g.,* N.Y. UNCONSOL. LAWS § 7952 (McKinney Supp. 1978); State v. Garden State Racing Ass'n, 136 N.J.L. 173, 54 A.2d 916 (1947); Saratoga Harness Racing Ass'n v. Agriculture and New York State Horse Breeding Dev. Fund, 22 N.Y.2d 119, 238 N.E.2d 730 (1968); Aliano v. Westchester Racing Ass'n, 265 App. Div. 225, 38 N.Y.S.2d 741 (1942).

443. Maine State Raceways v. La Fleur, 147 Me. 367, 87 A.2d 674 (1952); Jacobson v. Maryland Racing Comm'n, 261 Md. 180, 274 A.2d 102 (1971).

444. Northwest Greyhound Kennel Ass'n v. State, 8 Wash. App. 314, 506 P.2d 878 (1973).

445. Hialeah Race Course, Inc. v. Gulfstream Park Racing Ass'n, 37 So. 2d 692 (Fla. 1948), *appeal dismissed,* 336 U.S. 948, 93 L. Ed. 1104, 69 S. Ct. 882 (1949); State v. Garden State Racing Ass'n, 136 N.J.L. 173, 54 A.2d 916 (1947); Sullivan County Harness Racing Ass'n v. Schenectady Off-Track Betting Comm'n, 76 Misc. 2d 558, 351 N.Y.S.2d 56 (1973).

446. Maine State Raceways v. La Fleur, 147 Me. 367, 87 A.2d 674 (1952) (proper to allow pari-mutuel gambling in some but not other sports).

447. 8 Wash. App. 314, 506 P.2d 878 (1973).

pari-mutuel dog track. In upholding the statute, the court stated that in the area of social and economic evils, such as gambling, the legislature has broad discretion, and that if a court should hold the statute to be invalid because it did not include dog racing, "the judiciary would be determining what is primarily a political question in an area of almost complete legislative discretion and in an area vitally affecting public safety and morals."[448]

The pari-mutuel betting is often conducted by those who conduct the events upon which the bets are placed, provided that they have applied for and been granted a license by the appropriate athletic commission.[449] Since one of the primary purposes of the pari-mutuel system is to produce revenue for the state, the licensed party will act as an administrative agent of the state for collecting, holding and distributing the money wagered.[450] In performing these functions, the licensee will have statutory direction as to how to dispose of the moneys placed in the pari-mutuel pools.[451] In addition to issuing licenses, the supervising athletic commission will also be authorized to adopt rules and regulations to govern the conduct of pari-mutuel betting.[452] As with other types of athletic commission licenses,[453] the pari-mutuel license may be revoked if the licensee does not conduct its activities in accordance with the terms and conditions of the license, or the rules and regulations promulgated by the commission.[454] The commission may also be authorized to impose civil penalties and fines for violation of its rules and regulations.[455] In conducting such proceedings, moreover, the commission will generally be required to accord the licensee the safeguards of procedural due process of law, either by statutory mandate[456] or constitutional requirements.[457]

As a result of the success of pari-mutuel betting at race tracks, and the felt need to curb unlawful bookmaking and illegal wagering on racing events, pari-mutuel betting is now spreading to off-track locations.[458] The use of the

---

448. 506 P.2d at 882. *See also* Maine State Raceways v. La Fleur, 147 Me. 367, 87 A.2d 674 (1952).

449. *See, e.g.,* N.Y. UNCONSOL. LAWS § 7953 (McKinney 1961).

450. Holberg v. Westchester Racing Ass'n, 184 Misc. 581, 53 N.Y.S.2d 490 (1945).

451. *See, e.g.,* N.Y. UNCONSOL. LAWS § 7959 (McKinney Supp. 1978).

452. *See, e.g.,* ARIZ. REV. STAT. ANN. § 5-111 (1974); N.Y. UNCONSOL. LAWS § 7957 (McKinney 1961).

453. *See* §§ 2.03, 218.

454. N.Y. UNCONSOL. LAWS § 7968 (McKinney 1961).

455. *See, e.g.,* N.Y. UNCONSOL. LAWS § 7975 (McKinney 1961).

456. *See, e.g.,* N.Y. UNCONSOL. LAWS § 7969 (McKinney Supp. 1978).

457. *See* § 2.18.

458. *See generally* Samuels, *The Off-Track Betting Experiment in New York,* 17 How. L. REV. (1973); Samuels, *Legalization of Gambling on Sports Events,* 18 N.Y.L.F. 897 (1973).

The off-track betting normally differs from its on-track counterpart only to the extent that it is not conducted at the track where the races take place. In fact the off and on-track betting in a given region may be combined to form a common pool for the calculation of uniform odds and payouts for all tickets irrespective of whether the wager was placed on or off-track. *See, e.g.,* N.Y. UNCONSOL. LAWS § 8067(1) (McKinney Supp. 1978). Off-track operations may, however, involve bets on races not run in its region. *Id.* § 8067 (a)-(7). The difficulties that may be created by such procedures are suggested by Sullivan County Harness Racing Ass'n v. Schenectady Off-Track Betting Comm'n, 76 Misc. 2d 558, 351 N.Y.S.2d 56 (1973) (percentage that could be retained in interface). Off-track pari-mutuel betting is accomplished by a statutory scheme that is quite similar to those authorizing pari-mutuel betting at the tracks which have already been considered. The New York off-track betting system, for example, is carried out by the creation of a public benefit off-track betting corporation for each of several regions of the state. N.Y. UNCONSOL. LAWS § 8113

pari-mutuel system has also recently been expanded to include state-operated betting on professional football.[459]

One of the most important inquiries to be made with regard to pari-mutuel betting involves the relation between the person placing the bet and the organization which is authorized to accept it. As has already been noted, pari-mutuel betting involves the creation of a pool out of which winning bets are paid, so that the organization accepting the bets merely facilitates the creation of the pool and the generation of revenue for the state. Accordingly, the betting transaction is between the participants in the pari-mutuel pool, and the placing of the bet does not create a wagering contract or agreement between the bettor and the organization with whom it is placed.[460] Although a contract is not formed by the placing of a bet, the collection and distribution of the pari-mutuel pool must be conducted in accordance with the valid and properly adopted rules of the appropriate regulatory commission. Thus, when a person makes a decision to take part in a pari-mutuel betting system, he or she is presumed to know that the system has rules and that participation in the system requires that they abide by those rules.[461] Similarly, a licensee who acts as an agent in accepting bets will be required to collect, hold and distribute the pool in accordance with the same rules.

These principles are most commonly applied in cases where a disappointed bettor seeks to alter the rules pursuant to which his or her bet was placed. As a general rule, a disappointed bettor will be able to alter the rules that apply to bets placed only if it can be shown that the rules were improperly adopted or are not valid.[462] Thus, when a bettor seeks to have the method of calculating the odds on a race altered after the fact, the attempt will ordinarily be rejected.[463] The relation between the bettor and the organization which accepts his or her bets is illustrated by *Hochberg v. New York City Off-Track Betting Corp.,*[464] where a bettor had placed a bet in which he was required to pick in order the first four finishers in a horse race. At the time the bet in question was placed, there were only eight horses listed, but thereafter a ninth was listed, which, in fact, finished fourth. The bettor's first three choices were correct but

(McKinney Supp. 1978). *See also* Hochberg v. New York City Off-Track Betting Corp., 74 Misc. 2d 471, 343 N.Y.S.2d 651 (1973). The statutory scheme has been upheld against constitutional challenge. *See, e.g.,* Slisz v. Western Regional Off-Track Betting Corp., 382 F. Supp. 1231 (W.D.N.Y. 1974). Each such regional corporation is granted the power necessary to operate the off-track betting arrangement, N.Y. UNCONSOL. LAWS §§ 8114-20 (McKinney Supp. 1978), though in order to actually conduct the pari-mutuel operation they must submit a plan of operation for approval by the state racing and wagering board. The requirements of the plan are set forth in *id.* § 8065(1). The racing and wagering board is established by *id.* §§ 8161-66. If approval of a plan of operation is granted, it may be suspended if the betting is not conducted in accordance with the plan approved or the applicable rules or regulations of the racing and wagering board. *Id.* § 8066(1). The procedures that must be followed to affect such a suspension are set forth at *id.* § 8066(2).

459. This has occurred through a state-run lottery in Delaware, which is based upon the results of games played in the National Football League. The system has withstood an attrack by the League. National Football League v. Governor of the State of Delware, 435 F. Supp. 1372 (D. Del. 1977). *See generally* Looney, *Legalized Wagering? You Betcha!,* SPORTS ILLUSTRATED, September 6, 1976, at 22.

460. Hochberg v. New York City Off-Track Betting Corp., 74 Misc. 2d 471, 343 N.Y.S.2d 651 (1973).
461. Salmore v. Empire City Racing Ass'n, 123 N.Y.S.2d 688 (1953).
462. The permissibility of athletic commission-adopted rules is considered at § 2.04.
463. Salmore v. Empire City Racing Ass'n, 123 N.Y.S.2d 688 (1953) (odds on a dead heat).
464. 74 Misc. 2d 471, 343 N.Y.S.2d 651 (1973).

the fourth obviously was not. He then brought suit to have his bet declared a winner. In holding that the bettor had failed to state a claim upon which relief could be granted, the court observed that when he placed the bet, the bettor subjected himself to the rules and regulations of pari-mutuel racing and one of those rules was that the posting of betting information was solely for the convenience of the betting public, and that no liability could be incurred for the posting of inaccurate information. Thus, the court concluded that the organization accepting the bet was not a guarantor of the accuracy of the information posted, and that its only duty, if information was posted, would be to refrain from willfully posting inaccurate or erroneous information.[465] Similarly, it has been held that a bettor will be bound by a "false start" decision of the race track stewards.[466] It should also be noted that if pari-mutuel tickets are paid off in accordance with the order of an initially posted finish, a subsequent disqualification of the winner will generally not affect its payment.[467]

Inasmuch as pari-mutuel betting is physically accomplished by the bettor placing his or her wager and receiving a ticket in return, it is also necessary to consider the status of the ticket. Statutory provisions will ordinarily require that payment for winning tickets be tendered only upon the presentation of proper tickets[468] and all funds in the pool that remain unpaid on account of unredeemed tickets shall be paid over to the state.[469] A bettor may, then, obtain recovery from the pool only upon the presentation of a winning ticket,[470] and the licensee operating the pari-mutuel system has the right to pay on winning tickets immediately upon presentation without being subjected to liability by a third person making a claim upon one or more of the presented or unpresented tickets.[471] Thus, payment has been denied to a "winner" who destroyed his tickets by mistake, even though records showed that the amount unclaimed in the pool equaled the number of tickets allegedly destroyed;[472] claimed that his

---

465. *Id.* at 475-76, 343 N.Y.S.2d at 656. Specifically, the court stated that

bettors cannot expect and certainly do not have an absolute right or guarantee that they will win on any bet they place. Every wager is a gamble with often only a slight chance of winning. When a bettor places a wager on a horse or combination of horses which loses, he cannot demand a return of his money or be given a winning payoff because he failed to bet on horses other than those he actually did select. *Id.*

See also Greene v. New York City Off-Track Betting Corp., 76 Misc. 2d 935, 351 N.Y.S.2d 876 (1974) (relief denied to ticket-holder in superfecta when an entry was changed, which under O.T.B. rules voided the ticket, even though the order of pick eventually turned out to be a winner).

466. Shapiro v. Queens County Jockey Club, 184 Misc. 295, 53 N.Y.S.2d 135 (1945). The decisions of officials are considered at § 2.15.

467. Kentucky State Racing Comm'n v. Fuller, 481 S.W.2d 298 (Ky. App. 1972); Finlay v. Eastern Racing Ass'n, 308 Mass. 20, 30 N.E.2d 859 (1941) (excellent statement of reasons why this rule must prevail). *But cf.* Giordano v. Metropolitan Jockey Club, 176 Misc. 506, 29 N.Y.S.2d 939 (1941) (allowed bettor payment when his horse declared first after two disqualifications).

468. *See, e.g.,* N.Y. Unconsol. Laws § 7957 (McKinney 1961). *See generally* Annot., 165 A.L.R. 838 (1946).

469. *See, e.g.,* Fla. Stat. Ann. § 550.164 (1974).

470. Aliano v. Westchester Racing Ass'n, 265 App. Div. 225, 38 N.Y.S.2d 741 (1942).

471. Epps v. Yonkers Raceway, Inc., 21 App. Div. 2d 798, 250 N.Y.S.2d 751 (1964). The tickets might be compared to commercial paper that is payable to the bearer.

472. Carr v. State, 15 App. Div. 2d 709, 223 N.Y.S.2d 229, *motion for leave to appeal denied*, 11 N.Y.2d 645, 229 N.Y.S.2d 1025, 183 N.E.2d 329, *appeal dismissed*, 371 U.S. 14, 9 L. Ed. 2d 49, 83

tickets were stolen by someone who actually recovered the winning payments;[473] claimed that the teller punched out tickets showing the wrong number;[474] or intended to place a bet on a specific selection of horses but instead placed a bet on a different selection because the teller would not accept wagers on one of the original selections at the time the bet was placed.[475]

As has been considered at some length, the primary effect of statutes authorizing pari-mutuel betting is to legalize some forms of gambling on sports events. Since the type of gambling authorized is then lawful, activities associated therewith will also be made lawful. Thus, when contracts are made to facilitate pari-mutuel betting they will generally be lawful and enforceable.[476]

§ 2.21. Unlawful Sports Activities.

The nature of a particular sports activity or the conditions under which it is conducted may render it unlawful.[477] The principal factor that will cause a sports activity to be deemed unlawful is a finding that it is brutal, barbaric or otherwise objectionable.[478] Thus, it is common to find statutory provisions which make endurance contests,[479] cock-fights,[480] bull-fights[481] and automobile racing on the streets[482] unlawful.

a. Prize-Fighting. The treatment of such activities has received its fullest consideration with regard to the sport of mutual combat between human beings. The sport of mutual combat is doubtlessly one of the most ancient of sports still enjoying wide popularity. In its most familar form, this sport has involved the combat of two contestants by the use of their fists, which has been traditionally referred to as pugilism or prize-fighting. Until the final decade of the nineteenth century, these contests took the form of a bare knuckle fight to the finish under the so-called London Prize Ring Rules, which permitted the fighters to throw each other to the ground, jump on one another, and wear long spikes in each shoe. Each round lasted until one fighter fell or was knocked or thrown to the ground, and the contest was completed only when one of the fighters was unable to continue, either because of exhaustion or physical injury.[483] In the late nineteenth century, however, bare-knuckle fighting under the London Prize

S. Ct. 44 (1962); Aliano v. Westchester Racing Ass'n, 265 App. Div. 225, 38 N.Y.S.2d 741 (1942). *But cf.* Giordano v. Metropolitan Jockey Club, 176 Misc. 506, 29 N.Y.S.2d 939 (1941).

473. Mattson v. Hollywood Turf Club, 101 Cal. App. 2d 215, 225 P.2d 276 (1950); Epps v. Yonkers Raceway, Inc., 21 App. Div. 2d 798, 250 N.Y.S.2d 751 (1964).

474. Holberg v. Westchester Racing Ass'n, 184 App. Div. 581, 53 N.Y.S.2d 490 (1945).

475. Hochberg v. New York City Off-Track Betting Corp., 74 Misc. 2d 471, 343 N.Y.S.2d 651 (1973).

476. Monmouth Park Jockey Club v. Guth, 441 F.2d 1361 (3d Cir. 1971).

477. *See* § 2.02 (athletic commission-regulated sports); § 2.20 (relation of gambling laws to sports); § 2.22 (discrimination in the use of athletic facilities).

478. *See, e.g.,* C.E. America, Inc. v. Antinori, 210 So. 2d 443 (Fla. 1968).

479. *See, e.g.,* S.C. CODE § 47-1-50 (1977); VA. CODE § 61-8-19 (1977).

480. *See, e.g.,* TEX. PEN. CODE § 42.11 (Vernon's 1974); VA. CODE § 61-8-19 (1977).

481. *See, e.g.,* IOWA CODE ANN. § 726.7 (1957) (any type of animal fighting).

482. *See generally* 2 BLASHFIELD, AUTOMOBILE LAW & PRACTICE §§ 102.37-.39 (1965).

483. One of the better descriptions of such a fight is in Commonwealth v. McGovern, 116 Ky. 212, 75 S.W.261 (1903), where an injunction was granted against a scheduled prize-fight, and the court observed

> A fight between McGovern and Corbett would necessarily be one of the bloodiest of its kind, for the large money reward, and the more highly prized championship at stake, would furnish every incentive to fire the courage and enlist all the physical powers of the

Ring Rules was largely replaced by contests fought pursuant to the Marquis of Queensbury Rules, which essentially define and describe a boxing match as it is commonly known today.[484]

Although prize-fighting was apparently not as such an offense known to the common law of this country,[485] virtually all of the state legislatures have enacted statutes making prize-fighting a crime.[486] These statutes seldom define with any exactitude what acts constitute prize-fighting, and when indictments have been returned against alleged prize-fighters, or other participants, the courts have experienced considerable difficulty in working out an acceptable definition. This difficulty is illustrated by *Sullivan v. State,*[487] where an indictment was returned against John L. Sullivan, alleging that his match with Jake Kilrain on July 8, 1889, was an unlawful prize-fight. In holding the indictment defective, the court noted that the statute did not define prize-fighting, and in order to provide some guidance the court sought to distinguish acts that would be subject to the statute from that which was not:

> the evil sought to be protected against by the statute is the debasing and brutalizing practice of fighting in public place, or places to which the public or some part of it, is admitted as spectators. . . .
>
> . . . .
>
> . . . [T]he prize-fighting intended to be prohibited is that which is public in character and tends to disturb the peace and quiet of the community in which it occurs, and to debase not only the participants, but others, who are admitted as spectators. A private contest between individuals, whether amateurs, or professional fighters or boxers, though it be for a prize or wager, would not be in violation of the particular statute under consideration though the participants might be guilty of assault and battery, or of gaming.[488]

combatants. Blood would flow, and flesh be bruised and mangled, to the delight of the multitude of spectators present, whose applause would doubtless equal that of the Roman populace for the victorious gladiator, as, standing over his prostrate foe, he awaited the turn of the Emperor's thumb that he might know whether to slay or spare his victim. *Id.* at 264.

484. *See* Inter-Continental Promotions, Inc. v. MacDonald, 367 F.2d 293 (5th Cir. 1966), *cert. denied,* 393 U.S. 834, 21 L. Ed. 2d 104, 89 S. Ct. 105 (1968).

485. People v. Taylor, 96 Mich. 576, 56 N.W. 27 (1893); Sullivan v. State, 67 Miss. 346, 7 So. 275 (1890). Although it was not "as such" a crime, prize-fighting could be punished as a breach of the peace or as an assault and battery. Champer v. State, 14 Ohio St. 437 (1863). Mutual combat was apparently also not unlawful as a common law matter in England. Thus, it was held that a sparring match conducted in private and not for a money prize was lawful. Regina v. Young, 10 Cox's Crim. Cases 371 (Central Crim. Ct. 1866). Where the combat took place in public or involved a prize, however, it was held to be unlawful. The leading case expressing this view was Regina v. Coney, 8 Q.B.D. 534 (1882), in which the court held that prize-fighting was illegal. *See generally* 1 J. TURNER, RUSSELL ON CRIME 597-98 (1964). *Coney* has more recently been read to make illegal only fights conducted under the London Prize Ring Rules and not to affect those conducted as ordinary boxing matches under the Marquis of Queensbury Rules. Williams, *Consent and Public Policy,* 1962 CRIM. L. REV. 74, 80. This interpretation is consistent with that which has evolved in this country.

486. *See, e.g.,* FLA. STAT. ANN. § 21-1801 (1964); IOWA CODE ANN. § 727.1 (1950); KANSAS STAT. ANN. § 21-1801 (1964); MASS. GEN. LAWS ANN. ch. 265, § 9 (1968); TENN. CODE ANN. § 39-1201 (1975). *See also* London Sporting Club, Inc. v. Helfand, 3 Misc. 2d 431, 152 N.Y.S.2d 819 (1956).

487. 67 Miss. 346, 7 So. 275 (1890).

488. *Id.* at 352-531, 7 So. 275 at 276-77. Several other cases have also devoted considerable attention to the definition of prize-fighting. Inter-Continental Promotions, Inc. v. MacDonald, 367 F.2d 293 (5th Cir. 1966), *cert. denied,* 393 U.S. 834, 21 L. Ed. 2d 104, 89 S. Ct. 105 (1968); State v. Purtell, 56 Kans. 479, 43 P. 782 (1896); Commonwealth v. McGovern, 116 Ky. 212, 75 S.W. 261 (1903); People v. Taylor, 96 Mich. 576, 56 N.W. 27 (1893).

"Prize-fighting," then, was found to include only contests held in public, and did not cover private fights. Since this distinction could well make lawful the encounter between Sullivan and Kilrain, the court said, the indictment was insufficient to advise Sullivan of the nature and character of the alleged offense.[489]

The chief problem posed by the prize-fighting statutes is whether they prevent the staging of ordinary boxing or wrestling matches. The answer is often found in the prize-fighting statutes themselves, since several specifically except from their coverage matches conducted by specific organizations[490] or under the auspices of a state athletic commission.[491] Where the statute does not specifically except certain kinds of matches, some courts have rendered opinions with language broad enough to preclude any boxing or wrestling match conducted for financial gain.[492] Such decisions may, however, have little continuing authority since contemporary courts appear to interpret the prize-fighting statutes to bar only those matches which are debasing and brutalizing — such as bare knuckle fist fights, under the London Prize Ring Rules, which continue until one fighter is unable to continue — and not to make criminal the sports of boxing or wrestling. Perhaps the best statement of the view that prize-fighting statutes do not apply to the ordinary species of boxing or wrestling matches is in *Inter-Continental Promotions, Inc. v. MacDonald*,[493] where the promoter of the Cassius Clay-Sonny Liston heavyweight championship fight in December, 1964, had entered a contract to pay a corporation that owned both fighters a fixed sum for the live gate rights. When the actual gate receipts did not equal this amount, the promoter defaulted on the contract, and the corporation brought suit. In its defense, the promoter argued that the contract was unlawful since it was related to the promotion of a prize-fight, which was alleged to have been made criminal by the prize-fight statute. The court rejected this defense, and in so doing clearly differentiated between prize-fights, on the one hand, and boxing exhibitions on the other. To illustrate the point, the court noted two fights in which John L. Sullivan participated. The first was a clandestine bare knuckle fight lasting 75 rounds and two hours and sixteen minutes, under the London Prize Ring Rules; while the second was a gloved fight conducted under the Marquis of Queensbury

---

489. It should be noted that several courts have disagreed with the result in *Sullivan* that an indictment must state more than the mere statutory language. State v. Patten, 159 Ind. 248, 64 N.E. 850 (1902); Commonwealth v. Barrett, 108 Mass. (12 Browne) 302 (1871); Commonwealth v. Welsh, 73 Mass. (7 Gray) 324 (1856); People v. Taylor, 96 Mich. 576, 56 N.W. 27 (1893); Seville v. State, 49 Ohio St. 117, 30 N.E. 621 (1892).

490. *See. e.g.,* FLA. STAT. ANN. § 548.03 (1974). *See also* Fischer v. Cleveland, 42 Ohio App. 75, 181 N.E. 668 (1931) (matches approved by mayor).

491. *See, e.g.,* IDAHO CODE § 54-418 (1957); MASS. GEN. LAWS ANN. ch. 265, § 12 (1968); N.Y. CONSOL. LAWS §§ 8905, 8907 (McKinney 1974). *See also* City Island Athletic Club, Inc. v. Mulrooney, 141 Misc. 733, 253 N.Y.S. 768 (1931); Fitzsimmons v. New York State Athletic Comm'n, 15 Misc. 2d 831, 146 N.Y.S. 117, *aff'd,* 162 App. Div. 904, 147 N.Y.S. 1111 (1914). *See generally* Annot., 83 A.L.R. 696 (1933). The law relating to state athletic commissions is considered at §§ 2.02-.19.

If such a provision is present and not complied with, then the match will be unlawful. State *ex rel.* Esgar v. District Court of Ninth Judicial Dist. of Gallatin County, 56 Mont. 464, 185 P. 157 (1919); Tilelli v. Christenberry, 1 Misc. 2d 139, 120 N.Y.S.2d 697 (1953).

492. People v. Taylor, 96 Mich. 576, 56 N.W. 27 (1893); Seville v. State, 49 Ohio St. 117, 30 N.E. 621 (1892).

493. 367 F.2d 293 (5th Cir. 1966), *cert. denied,* 393 U.S. 834, 21 L. Ed. 2d 104, 89 S. Ct. 105 (1968).

Rules in a private facility known as the Olympic Club. The former, it said, was an unlawful prize-fight,[494] while the latter was in the nature of a mere boxing exhibition which was not unlawful.[495] The court then compared the Clay-Liston fight to the second Sullivan fight and concluded that it was not a prohibited prize-fight, so that the contract in question was not unlawful for that reason.[496] Although the court did engage in a lengthy analysis of relevant Florida statutes, its rationale supports the view that common boxing matches are not prize-fights and should not, therefore, be unlawful under prize-fighting statutes.[497]

The issue of the legality of prize-fights has generally been raised in criminal proceedings against participants,[498] promoters,[499] or other members of the prize-fighting "entourage." [500] It has also arisen in quo warranto actions to revoke the charter of corporations sponsoring or promoting the fights,[501] and

494. *But see* Sullivan v. State, 67 Miss. 346, 7 So. 275 (1890) (holding an indictment alleging violation of the prize-fighting statute to be improper on the same facts).

495. This view was supported by one decision of the Louisiana Supreme Court, State v. Olympic Club, 46 La. Ann. 935, 15 So. 190 (1894), though it was opposed by another. State v. Olympic Club, 47 La. Ann. 1095, 17 So. 599 (1895).

496. The contract in question was, however, declared to be unlawful on the basis of the Florida Prize-fight Statute because the fight was not conducted under the auspices of a qualified organization. Inter-Continental Promotions, Inc. v. Miami Beach First Nat'l Bank, 441 F.2d 1356 (5th Cir.), *cert. denied*, 404 U.S. 850, 30 L. Ed. 2d 89, 92 S. Ct. 85 (1971). Sports contracts have also been invalidated on unlawfulness grounds when they involved an unlawful horse race, Erickson v. North Dakota State Fair Ass'n of Fargo, 54 N.D. 830, 211 N.W. 597 (1926), or violated public policy by requiring another party to refrain from opposing, and indeed to advocate, the granting of a kennel license to another party. Colorado Racing Comm'n v. Columbine Kennel Club, Inc., 141 Colo. 497, 348 P.2d 954 (1960).

497. The distinction between prize-fights and ordinary boxing matches was also made in State v. Olympic Club, 47 La. Ann. 1095, 17 So. 599 (1895):

> There can be no reasonable objection to boxing as ordinarily understood. It is a manly, healthful, and vigorous training, and encouraged in some of our most respectable institutions.
> An interference with it by legislative power would be a great stretch of authority, bordering upon an infringement of personal liberty. And even boxing without gloves, for a display of skill, and for pastime, when there is no breach of the peace, and no intentional injury to the person, cannot be considered as embraced within the statute. But in a prize contest for a purse, with or without gloves, there is, despite the customary shaking of hands and the preliminary courtesies between the combatants, an intention to do an injury, and to break the public peace. The contest is directly within the spirit, if not exact definition, of an assault. In such a contest there cannot be an absence of intention to do an injury, for the purpose of the contest is to subdue an opponent by knocking him senseless, or so injuring him that he cannot, within a given time, continue the fight. *Id.* at 1097-98, 17 So. at 600.

See also State v. Purtell, 56 Kans. 479, 43 P. 782 (1896) ("Wrestling, fencing, boxing, and numberless other matches, in which the physical powers are employed by men in friendly contests with each other, are not punishable."); Parmentier v. McGinnis, 157 Wis. 596, 147 N.W. 1007 (1914). It is clear that the definitions of "prize-fighting" that are contained in the cases cited here (and in notes 488 and 492 *supra*) reflect little general agreement. These cases must, however, be considered in the context of their times (near the turn of the nineteenth century), see 367 F.2d at 298, and it would appear that the views expressed in *Inter-Continental Productions* represent a more contemporarily acceptable definition of the term.

498. *See, e.g.,* People v. Taylor, 96 Mich. 576, 56 N.W. 27 (1893); Sullivan v. State, 67 Miss. 346, 7 So. 275 (1890).

499. *See, e.g.,* Commonwealth v. McGovern, 116 Ky. 212, 75 S.W. 261 (1903) (injunction against holding of prize-fight); Sampson v. State, 180 Okla. Crim. 191, 194 P. 279 (1921).

500. *See, e.g.,* People *ex rel.* Weiner v. Barr, 131 Misc. 80, 225 N.Y.S. 346 (1927).

501. State v. Olympic Club, 46 La. Ann. 935, 15 So. 190 (1894); State v. Olympic Club, 47 La. Ann. 1095, 17 So. 599 (1895); State v. Business Men's Athletic Club, 178 Mo. App. 548, 163 S.W. 901 (1914).

as a defense to breach of contract[502] and libel actions.[503] Where a particular fight is an unlawful prize-fight, any agreement relating thereto will constitute a conspiracy to engage in a crime and will, as such, be unlawful and unenforceable.[504] In considering these several decisions, it should be kept in mind that most of the cases are several generations old, and the issues which they raise are primarily related to the legality of mutual combat. In light of the fact that boxing and wrestling have in most jurisdictions been subjected to regulation by state athletic commissions,[505] the contemporary legal issues raised by such activities will normally concern the validity of athletic commission action.[506] As suggested by *Inter-Continental Productions*, however, the legality issue has not entirely expired.[507]

An event may also be rendered unlawful by the conditions under which it is conducted. Thus, it is often unlawful to conduct certain kinds of games on Sunday.[508] Although it has been stated that a legislative body could prohibit the playing of baseball on Sunday,[509] the courts have refused to prohibit true sporting activity on Sunday in the absence of specific statutory provision to that effect.[510] Thus, in *Ex parte Neet*,[511] the court found that it was not unlawful in Missouri to play baseball on Sunday, since it is a game and not as such productive of the type of immorality to which the Sunday law was addressed.[512] The courts have also refused to enjoin the conduct of sports activities on Sunday on the ground that they are nuisances, unless the party complaining is able to show that the activity constitutes a public nuisance and that special damage has been suffered.[513]

b. Violence in Sports. The final aspect of legality that should be considered involves the extent to which a participant in a lawful sports event may be subject to criminal sanctions for his or her conduct. This issue would be raised, for example, by the act of a hockey or football player intentionally striking or kicking an opponent in clear violation of the rules of the sport. If the opponent is seriously injured, or killed, the criminal question that would be posed would

---

502. Magness v. Isgrig, 145 Ark. 232, 225 S.W. 332 (1920).

503. Inter-Continental Promotions, Inc. v. MacDonald, 367 F.2d 293 (5th Cir. 1966), *cert. denied,* 393 U.S. 834, 21 L. Ed. 2d 104, 89 S. Ct. 105 (1968).

504. Fitzsimmons v. New York State Athletic Comm'n, 15 Misc. 2d 831, 146 N.Y.S. 117, *aff'd,* 162 App. Div. 904, 147 N.Y.S. 1111 (1914); Seville v. State, 49 Ohio St. 117, 30 N.E. 621 (1892).

505. *See* § 2.02.

506. *See* §§ 2.03, 2.04, 2.18.

507. The legality would also be raised, for example, by activities that are not within the jurisdiction of an athletic commission.

508. *See, e.g.,* ALA. CODE § 41-9-122 (1977); COLO. REV. STAT. § 12-10-121 (1974); GA. CODE ANN. § 106-801 (1970); PA. STAT. ANN. tit. 4, § 82 (Purdon Supp. 1974). *See generally* Annot., 24 A.L.R.2d 813 (1952); Annot., 56 A.L.R. 813 (1928); Annot., 50 A.L.R. 1050 (1927); Annot., 4 A.L.R. 382 (1919).

Such laws are apparently based on the admonition in Exodus, 20:8-10, that the sabbath is to be kept a holy day, and that work shall not on that day be done.

509. *Ex parte* Roguemore, 60 Tex. Crim. 282, 131 S.W. 1101 (1910).

510. *Ex parte* Neet, 157 Mo. 527, 57 S.W. 1025 (1900); Orange Speedway, Inc. v. Clayton, 247 N.C. 528, 101 S.E.2d 406 (1958); *Ex parte* Roguemore, 60 Tex. Crim. 282, 131 S.W. 1101 (1910).

511. 157 Mo. 527, 57 S.W. 1025 (1900).

512. *Id.* at 536, 57 S.W. at 1027.

513. Warren Co. v. Dickson, 185 Ga. 481, 195 S.E. 568 (1938); McMillan v. Kuehnle, 78 N.J. Eq. 251, 78 A. 185 (1910); Commonwealth v. Smith, 266 Pa. 511, 109 A. 786 (1920). *See generally* Annot., 76 A.L.R.2d 874, 883-84 (1961). Nuisance liability is considered at § 8.16.

be whether the facts required the imposition of criminal sanctions.[514] The resolution of this question would involve a number of separate inquiries. It would first have to be determined whether the penal laws were intended to be applied to conduct in lawful sports events. If so, attention would then focus upon whether the elements of a particular crime—for example, assault, manslaughter or murder—were present. Finally, it would have to be determined whether the accused had a defense. The most important defense would be that the injured person had consented to the injury by voluntarily engaging in the sport. If the conduct had been provoked, it is possible that there could also be a self-defense argument. These are all difficult questions, and are not purely academic. Several criminal actions have been brought against athletes in recent years as the result of serious injuries suffered during athletic events.[515] These actions have produced a storm of protest from persons involved in sports, who argue that the imposition of criminal sanctions would destroy competition.[516] Although there are no clear answers to the questions identified above, there is precedent from other common law countries that may be consulted for general guidance.[517]

There can be little doubt at this point in time that the criminal laws apply to conduct in sports. There is nothing inherent in the nature of sport which should insulate it from penal sanctions of general applicability. Thus, if an athlete engages in conduct which could constitute assault, manslaughter or murder if performed in an alley, it will not have a different status simply because it is performed on an athletic field.[518] The more difficult question will be whether the athlete accused of committing such a crime can defend on the basis that the conduct was lawful on the facts of the case or that the injured person consented to the injury by engaging in the sport.

It is frequently said that the consent of a victim is not a defense for crimes which involve a wrong that affects the general public, since the public interest may not be frustrated by mere private license.[519] Consent is a defense, however, where it negatives an element of the offense. For example, an assault is generally said to be an unconsented-to touching. The consent which negates this offense may be found in connection with many bodily injuries sustained in properly conducted sports events. Thus, the *Model Penal Code* specifies as follows:

---

514. The civil liability aspects of the issue are considered at § 8.02.

515. The most celebrated action was brought by the state of Minnesota against hockey star David Forbes. After a complete trial, the jury was unable to reach a verdict and the prosecutor subsequently dropped the charges. N.Y. Times, August 12, 1975, at 24, col. 6. *See* notes 523-32 *infra. See also* New York Times, February 25, 1976, at 43, col. 5 (Dan Maloney of Detroit Red Wings in N.H.L. charged with assault in Toronto); Atlanta Constitution, July 1, 1976, at 7-D, col. 1 (Maloney acquitted by jury, but with a statement requesting an end to hockey violence).

516. *See generally* Reed, *Week of Disgrace on the Ice,* Sports Illustrated, April 26, 1976, at 22; Kennedy, *Wanted: An End to Mayhem,* Sports Illustrated, November 17, 1975, at 17; Kennedy, *A Nondecision Begs the Question,* Sports Illustrated, July 28, 1975, at 12; Cady, *Violence in Sports is a Growing Concern,* N.Y. Times, September 25, 1975, at 55, col. 1.

517. *See generally* Hallowell & Meshbesher, *Sports Violence and the Criminal Law,* Trial Magazine 27 (January, 1977); Comment, *The Consent Defense: Sports, Violence, and the Criminal Law,* 13 Am. Crim. L. Rev. 235 (1975).

518. Regina v. Bradshaw, 14 Cox's Crim. L. Cas. 83 (Leicester Spring Assizes 1878).

519. *See* W. Lafave & A. Scott, Handbook On Criminal Law 408 (1972); R. Perkins, Criminal Law 961-62 (2d ed. 1969).

When conduct is charged to constitute an offense because it causes or threatens bodily harm, consent to such conduct or to the infliction of such harm is a defense if:

    (a) the bodily harm consented to or threatened by the conduct consented to is not serious; or

    (b) the conduct and the harm are reasonably foreseeable hazards of joint participation in a lawful athletic contest or competitive sport . . . .[520]

The language of the *Model Penal Code* makes it clear that consent may be a defense to criminal charges arising out of conduct in a sports event.[521] It does not, however, do much to clarify the types of conduct that it would protect. The *Code* provides that the conduct and harm inflicted will be within the consent defense if they are "reasonably foreseeable hazards" of the sport.[522] The question, of course, is what are "reasonably foreseeable hazards." One possibility would be that such hazards would include only conduct sanctioned by the rules of the sport in question. But this view would have to be rejected as being too narrow, since it would exclude all conduct that technically violates a rule of the sport. For example, it would not cover intentional fouls in basketball that are committed for strategic purposes or conduct in a football game that violates a "roughing the kicker" rule but does not cause serious injury. Another possibility would be that the defense applies to the types of conduct that are customarily a part of a given sport. Thus, if fist or stick-fighting were found to be customary aspects of hockey competition, then they would be protected. The difficulty with this view is that it is too broad and would not put a limit on the injuries that could be inflicted. It is obviously one thing to say that stick-fights are customary in hockey so that the consent defense would apply to a routine fight in which a participant receives relatively minor injuries, but quite another to say that the defense would also cover an unprovoked, savage attack that causes death. A standard that looked only to custom in the sport would appear to cover the latter situation, since stick-fighting could be viewed as being customary in hockey.

It seems clear that there must be a limit on the nature of the conduct that will be protected. It has been frequently stated that the limitation on the consent defense must, in the final analysis, rest upon the general demands of public sentiment.[523] In the sports situation, this would suggest that one must articulate the point at which the public would no longer condone violence on a sports field. This is obviously less than a certain inquiry and there is very little authority that can be consulted for guidance. The most apparent touchstone would be the

---

520. MODEL PENAL CODE § 2.11(2) (1962). *See also* Williams, *Consent and Public Policy,* 1962 CRIM. L. REV. 74.

521. The consent that is suggested in § 2.11(2), as quoted in text, could be overcome if there was evidence that the injured athlete did not participate voluntarily. *See* MODEL PENAL CODE § 2.11(3) (d); R. PERKINS, CRIMINAL LAW 963 (2d ed. 1969). The primary basis upon which such a lack of voluntariness could be predicated would be a finding that the pressure of a coach or other persons forced an athlete to compete against his or her own will. Such facts have occasionally been suggested in civil damage cases. *See* § 8.02, note 28.

522. This is similar to the rule adopted in civil damage actions. *See* § 8.02.

523. *See* Hughes, *Criminal Law — Defense of Consent — Test to be Applied,* 33 CAN. B. REV. 88, 92 (1955).

provision of the *Model Penal Code* quoted above, in which it is said that the consent defense covers only bodily harm that is not "serious." However, this limitation is apparently not intended to apply to sports activities, since it is one of two disjunctive limitations on the defense and the second covers sports injuries. The apparent purpose for not placing a "seriousness" limitation on sports activities is that serious injuries are common occurrences in many sports even where no rules are violated. Although the "serious" rule may not apply to sports, it does reflect the policy that hazards which cause severe injury to an individual also injure the public and may not be sanctioned by mere private consent.

The nature of the limitation on the consent defense in sports may be most easily illuminated by considering two related illustrations. If in a football game a defensive player tackles a quarterback who is setting up to pass, few would suggest that there would be criminal culpability even if the quarterback was seriously injured with a concussion or broken bone. The object of a defensive lineman would be to tackle a quarterback as far behind the line of scrimmage as possible, and in the illustration this was accomplished with no more than reasonable force. But if the defenseman was not satisfied with simply tackling the quarterback and proceeded to beat him with fists or stomp him with feet, it then seems clear that criminal conduct may be present. The basic difference between the two situations is the nature of the defenseman's conduct. In the former, he is acting in a manner that is competitive and consistent with the objectives of the game, while in the latter his conduct can only be characterized as being either intentional or reckless. It is believed that this distinction suggests the outer limit of the consent defense in sports. It is certainly consistent with language used in the more recent English commonwealth decisions to define conduct that would result in criminal liability. These courts have spoken of "unprovoked savage attacks in which serious injury results," [524] and "malicious, unprovoked or overly violent attack[s]." [525]

Although it is hazardous to generalize in this area, in the absence of direct American authority, it is suggested that consent will be a defense to criminal charges arising from a sports injury so long as it is a reasonably foreseeable hazard of the sport and is not the result of intentional conduct having no reasonable relation to the sport.[526] This standard adopts the language of the *Model Penal Code* but adds a clause to limit its reach. It has not as such been adopted by any of the courts that have considered the issue to date, but it appears to reflect the underlying theories of the opinions that have been rendered.

---

524. Regina v. Green, 16 D.L.R.3d 137, 143 (Ontario Prov. Ct. 1970).

525. Regina v. Maki, 10 Crim. Rep. (n.s.) 268, 272 (1970).

526. This standard is similar to the views expressed by Glanville Williams, the noted English criminal law scholar:

> In . . . games [such as football], the consent by the players to the use of moderate force is clearly valid, and the players are even deemed to consent to an application of force that is in breach of the rules of the game, if it is the sort of thing that may be expected to happen during the game . . . A player may, however be convicted of battery or manslaughter if he does an act with intent to harm outside the bounds of the sport, or (in the case of manslaughter) if he is grossly negligent. Williams, *Consent and Public Policy*, 1962 CRIM. L. REV. 74, 81.

One of the earliest reported decisions is *Regina v. Bradshaw*,[527] in which an athlete was killed during a football (soccer) game. The decedent was "dribbling" the ball toward the opponent's goal and, as the accused approached, the decedent kicked it out of the former's reach. The accused charged, jumped in the air and struck the decedent in the stomach with his knee, rupturing the decedent's intestines. It was unclear, however, whether the accused's action took place before or after the decedent had kicked the ball. The decedent died the next day, and manslaughter charges were brought against the accused. In charging the jury, the court stated the parameters of an athlete's criminal responsibility for acts in a sports event as follows:

> If a man is playing according to the rules and practice of the game and not going beyond it, it may be reasonable to infer that he is not actuated by any malicious motive or intention, and that he is not acting in a manner which he knows will be likely to be productive of death or injury. But, independent of the rules, if the prisoner [the athlete causing injury] intended to cause serious hurt to the deceased, or if he knew that, in charging as he did, he might produce serious injury and was indifferent and reckless as to whether he would produce serious injury or not, then the act would be unlawful.[528]

After considering the case in light of this charge, the jury acquitted the accused of the manslaughter charges.

Although the charge in *Bradshaw* speaks of the intent of the accused athlete rather than the consent of the injured person, it is supportive of the standard suggested. It indicates that an athlete is criminally responsible for intentional and reckless acts. In terms of the consent defense, this view would mean that an athlete will not be deemed to have consented to intentional or reckless acts that are not reasonably related to the conduct of the sport in question.

In more recent cases, the courts have expressed views that are consistent with both the suggested standard and the jury charge in *Bradshaw*. The principal decisions have arisen from the prosecution of two National Hockey League players who were involved in a fight during a 1969 exhibition game in Canada between the Boston Bruins and the St. Louis Blues.[529] The facts of the cases indicate that Wayne Maki and Edward Green had pursued the puck behind the Boston net. A skirmish then developed in which Green struck Maki in the face with his glove. After a delayed penalty was called, the players came together again in front of the Boston net and engaged in a stick fight. Apparently Maki struck the first blow, but it was answered in kind. These events all took place in the space of approximately ten seconds. Criminal assault charges were subsequently brought against each player, and both were acquitted. In *Regina v. Green*,[530] the court based its acquittal upon the conclusion that Green's action

---

527. 14 Cox Crim. Cas. 83 (Leicester Spring Assizes 1878).

528. *Id.* at 84. A similar charge was given on closely comparable facts in Regina v. Moore, 14 Times L. Rep. 229 (Leicester Assizes 1898), but the jury found the accused to be guilty of manslaughter. *See also* Regina v. Young, 10 Cox Crim. Cas. 370 (Central Crim. Ct. 1866) (acquitted of manslaughter for a death in a lawful sparring match). *See generally* 1 C. TURNER, RUSSELL ON CRIME 459, 463, 597 (1964).

529. Regina v. Green, 16 D.L.R.3d 137 (Ontario Prov. Ct. 1970); Regina v. Maki, 10 Crim. Rep. (n. s.) 268 (1970).

530. 16 D.L.R.3d 137 (Ontario Provincial Court 1970).

was taken in self-defense and was reasonable under the circumstances.[531] Although the court did not specifically premise its opinion upon the consent of the other combatant to the injury, it did give attention to the issue and its language is supportive of the standard suggested:

> There is no doubt that the players who enter the hockey arena consent to a great number of assaults on their person, because the game of hockey as it is played in the National Hockey League . . . could not possibly be played at the speed at which it is played, and with the force and vigour with which it is played . . . unless there were a great number of what would in normal circumstances be called assaults . . . No hockey player enters on to the ice . . . without consenting to and without knowledge of the possibility that he is going to be hit in one of many ways once he is on that ice.[532]

Having made this broad statement of the hazards which must be consented to in a violent game such as hockey, the court then carefully noted that its comments were directed only to facts similar to those before it and that the consent would not be deemed to cover "unprovoked savage attacks in which serious injury results." [533]

Although there is certainly a difference of approach among the *Model Penal Code* and the decisions in *Bradshaw* and *Green,* they all seem to point in the same direction: An athlete will not be subject to criminal liability for acts that are reasonably foreseeable aspects of the sport and which are not the result of intentional or reckless conduct having no reasonable relation to the sport.

In considering criminal liability in sports events, it should also be noted that the criminal indictments that have been returned against athletes for competition-related injuries in recent years have resulted in several suggestions that sports leagues take action to forestall violence that results in injuries of such severity as to raise the specter of criminal indictment.[534] It has frequently been suggested that reform could be accomplished through the enforcement of specific rules precluding unnecessary violence.[535] If such rules were adopted and enforced, it is generally believed that criminal acts would be discouraged. In considering these proposals, it is well to keep in mind that such self-policing action will not preclude criminal actions from being instituted. Thus, it has been observed that "[n]o sports league, no matter how well organized or self policed

---

531. *Id.* at 142, 143. Self defense was also the basis for acquittal in Regina v. Maki, note 525 *supra.*

532. 16 D.L.R.3d at 140. Similarly, in *Regina v. Maki* the court observed that "all players when they step onto a playing field or ice surface assume certain risks and hazards of the sport and in most cases the defense of consent . . . would be applicable. But . . . there is a question of degree involved and no athlete should be presumed to accept malicious, unprovoked or overly violent attack." 10 Crim. Rep. (n.s.) at 272.

It bears repeating that the language in *Green* and *Maki* is almost undistinguishable from that which has been used by the courts in establishing an assumption of the risk rule for civil actions. *See* § 8.02.

The consent defense in sports is discussed in more detail in Williams, *Consent and the Criminal Law,* 1962 CRIM. L. REV. 74, 80-81; Comment, *The Consent Defense: Sports, Violence and the Criminal Law,* 13 AM. CRIM. L. REV. 235, 242-46 (1975) (in which the defense is criticized as being "a blunt instrument incapable of separating the abusive from the desirable aspects of the sport").

533. 16 D.L.R.3d at 143.

534. *See* note 519 *supra.*

535. *See, e.g.,* Kennedy, *Wanted: An End to Mayhem,* SPORTS ILLUSTRATED, November 17, 1975, at 21; Cady, *Violence in Sports is a Growing Concern,* N.Y. Times, September 25, 1975, at 59, col. 4.

it may be, should thereby render the players in that league immune from criminal prosecution." [536] The adoption and enforcement of such rules would, however, substantially reduce the likelihood of criminal prosecution.

§ 2.22. Regulation of Discrimination in the Use of Athletic Facilities.

The hand of public regulation is also found in requirements that athletic facilities be made available to all people on an equal basis. As a common law principle, the owner or operator of athletic facilities, unlike the owner or operator of an entity engaged in a "public calling" such as an innkeeper or common carrier, had the right to exclude therefrom any person for any reason.[537] Notwithstanding this common law right of exclusion, there is a substantial body of law evidencing the public interest in insuring that the ability to utilize athletic or recreational facilities is not limited to certain groups by the erection of discriminatory barriers by persons or organizations subject to legislative control or constitutional command. Attention has been given elsewhere in this chapter to the right of the owner or operator to exclude certain patrons or participants from sports events,[538] and that discussion will not be repeated in this section. Rather, consideration here will be directed toward the theories that may be invoked by those denied access to athletic facilities to overcome the rule allowing exclusion.

The basic theory by which one denied the use of athletic facilities may seek relief will be the Equal Protection Clause of the Fourteenth Amendment, which forbids any group or organization affected with "state action" from classifying, and thereby treating unequally, otherwise similarly situated persons.[539] The application of the Equal Protection Clause to discrimination in athletic and recreational facilities was made clear by two circuit court of appeals decisions in 1955, which were summarily affirmed without opinion by the Supreme Court. In *Dawson v. Mayor and City Council of Baltimore City,*[540] public authorities had enforced racial segregation in the use of public beaches and bathhouses. In declaring that such acts were in violation of the Equal Protection Clause, the court repudiated several earlier decisions which had upheld such segregation as a permissible exercise of the state's police power,[541] and stated that "racial segregation in recreational activities can no longer be sustained as a proper exercise of the police power of the state." [542] A similar result was reached in *Holmes v. Atlanta,*[543] where the city practiced a racially discriminatory policy with respect to its municipal golf courses. In holding that such policies were in contravention of the Equal Protection Clause, the court said that the city was

---

536. 10 Crim. Rep. (n.s.) at 272.

537. *See, e.g.,* Flores v. Los Angeles Turf Club, Inc., 55 Cal. 2d 736, 361 P.2d 921 (1961). *See generally* Note, *Public Access to Beaches: Common Law Doctrine and Constitutional Challenges,* 48 N.Y.U.L. REV. 369 (1973); Annot., 1 A.L.R.2d 1165 (1964).

538. *See* § 2.09.

539. The requirements of the Equal Protection Clause are considered in detail at § 1.14. The status of private institutions is also considered at §§ 1.14, 1.15.1.

540. 220 F.2d 386 (4th Cir. 1955), *aff'd,* 350 U.S. 877, 100 L. Ed. 774, 76 S. Ct. 133 (1955).

541. These cases were Boyer v. Garrett, 183 F.2d 582 (4th Cir. 1950) and Durkee v. Murphy, 181 Md. 259, 29 A.2d 253 (1942).

542. 220 F.2d at 387.

543. 223 F.2d 93 (5th Cir.), *aff'd,* 350 U.S. 879, 100 L. Ed. 776, 76 S. Ct. 141 (1955).

required to admit blacks to its golf courses on the same terms and conditions that are applicable to all other persons. These, and other,[544] decisions forbid discrimination in publicly owned and maintained athletic and recreational facilities.[545] Although most of the discrimination cases that have been decided involved racial discrimination, the equal protection theory would also apply to other forms of discrimination,[546] though the standards may be less strict for non-racial classifications.

As a means of evading their duty to make facilities available on a discrimination-free basis, some public authorities have apparently sought to divest the facilities of their public character. This has been attempted by a number of schemes, such as conveying the facilities to a "private" membership corporation,[547] leasing the facilities to non-public parties,[548] conveying them in fee subject to an option to repurchase,[549] and conveying to the transferee a fee simple subject to a condition subsequent.[550] The courts, however, have been alert to such subterfuges, and have had little difficulty in holding that the discriminatory practices of the transferees or lessees are no less in contravention of the teachings of the Equal Protection Clause. Notwithstanding these decisions, the public authorities retain the power to evade non-discrimination requirements by permanently closing or unconditionally selling the facilities.[551] This ability was considered by the Supreme Court in *Palmer v. Thompson,*[552] where it held that a city may close, and finally cease running, its public swimming pools rather than attempt to operate them on a desegregated basis and not be in violation of equal protection requirements. In reaching this conclusion, the Court specifically noted that there was no evidence that the city was any longer directly or indirectly involved in the funding or operation of the pools that were private in name only.[553] Although the Court also noted that the action of the city in turning over to the YMCA a pool it had previously leased was not in that case unlawful, it added the caveat that "[p]ossibly in a case where

544. Goodloe v. Davis, 514 F.2d 1274 (5th Cir. 1975); Scott v. Young, 421 F.2d 143 (4th Cir.), *cert. denied,* 398 U.S. 929, 26 L. Ed. 2d 91, 90 S. Ct. 1820 (1970); Greensboro v. Simkins, 246 F.2d 425 (4th Cir. 1957); Beal v. Holcombe, 193 F.2d 384 (5th Cir. 1951); Valle v. Stengel, 176 F.2d 697 (3d Cir. 1949); Sawyer v. Mobile, 208 F. Supp. 548 (S.D. Ala. 1961); Moorhead v. Ft. Lauderdale, 152 F. Supp. 131 (S.D. Fla.), *aff'd,* 248 F.2d 544 (5th Cir. 1957); Holley v. Portsmouth, 150 F. Supp. 6 (E.D. Va. 1957); Williams v. Kansas City, Mo., 104 F. Supp. 848 (W.D. Mo. 1952), *aff'd,* 205 F.2d 47 (8th Cir.), *cert. denied,* 346 U.S. 826, 98 L. Ed. 351, 74 S. Ct. 652 (1953).

545. *See* § 1.14. *See also* Golden v. Biscayne Bay Yacht Club, 530 F.2d 16 (5th Cir. 1976) (yacht club found to be private).

546. *See, e.g.,* Riegler v. Holiday Skating Rink, Inc., 48 Mich. App. 449, 210 N.W.2d 454 (1973) (suggesting that exclusion of long-haired males could be unlawful discrimination). *See* § 1.22 (sex discrimination in amateur athletics).

547. Castle Hill Beach Club, Inc. v. Arbury, 2 N.Y.2d 596, 162 N.Y.S.2d 1, 142 N.E.2d 186 (1957).

548. Wimbish v. Pinellas County, Fla., 342 F.2d 804 (5th Cir. 1965); Greensboro v. Simkins, 246 F.2d 425 (4th Cir. 1957).

549. Smith v. Young Men's Christian Ass'n, 316 F. Supp. 899 (M.D. Ala. 1970), *modified on appeal,* 462 F.2d 634 (5th Cir. 1972). *See also* Gilmore v. Montgomery, 417 U.S. 556, 41 L. Ed. 2d 304, 94 S. Ct. 2416 (1974).

550. Hampton v. Jacksonville, 304 F.2d 320 (5th Cir. 1962).

551. Hampton v. Jacksonville, *supra* note 550 (closing swimming pools); Montgomery v. Gilmore, 277 F.2d 364 (5th Cir. 1960) (closing city parks); Tonkins v. Greensboro, 276 F.2d 890 (4th Cir. 1960) (sale of swimming pool); Greensboro v. Simkins, 246 F.2d 425 (4th Cir. 1957).

552. 403 U.S. 217, 29 L. Ed. 2d 438, 91 S. Ct. 1940 (1971).

553. *Id.* at 222-26. A potential means of attacking even such "private" action in the case of racial discrimination is noted at the text subsequent to note 580 *infra.*

the city and the YMCA were both parties, a court could find that the city engaged in a subterfuge, and that liability could be fastened on it as an active participant in a conspiracy with the YMCA." [554] Not surprisingly, such cases have arisen.[555]

The second theory that has been utilized to invalidate racial discrimination in the use of athletic and recreational facilities is Title II of the Civil Rights Act of 1964.[556] Title II provides, broadly, that no person shall be denied the full and equal enjoyment of the facilities or privileges of a "place of public accommodation" on the basis of race, color, religion or national origin.[557] The term "public accommodation" is defined to include any covered establishment that serves the public if its operations affect interstate commerce[558] or its discrimination is supported by state action.[559] The types of establishment covered by the Act include those which provide lodging to transient guests,[560] sell food for consumption on the premises,[561] any sports arena, stadium or other place of exhibition or entertainment,[562] and any establishment either within a covered establishment or within which there is a covered establishment if it holds itself out as serving patrons of such a covered establishment.[563] In applying these provisions, moreover, the courts have afforded Title II a liberal construction to insure the carrying out of the purpose of Congress to eliminate the inconvenience, unfairness and humiliation of the prohibited types of discrimination.[564] The application of these requirements to recreational facilities is made quite clear by *Daniel v. Paul*,[565] where the owners of an establishment, which included swimming, boating and miniature golf facilities, denied admission to all non-white persons. The Court found that the recreational facility was a "public accommodation," subject to the provisions of Title II, for two separate reasons. The first was that there was a snack bar on the grounds which was itself a covered establishment, which would automatically bring the entire facility within the ambit of Title II.[566] The second was that it constituted a "place of exhibition or entertainment," even though its patrons participated in sports

554. *Id.* at 223-24.

555. Gilmore v. Montgomery, 417 U.S. 556, 41 L. Ed. 2d 304, 94 S. Ct. 2416 (1974); Smith v. Young Men's Christian Ass'n, 462 F.2d 634 (5th Cir. 1972); Wimbish v. Pinellas County, Fla., 342 F.2d 804 (5th Cir. 1965); Hampton v. Jacksonville, 304 F.2d 320 (5th Cir.), *cert. denied,* 371 U.S. 911, 9 L. Ed. 2d 170, 83 S. Ct. 256 (1962).

556. 42 U.S.C. §§ 2000a *et seq.* This approach would, of course, also include the statutory provisions adopted at the state level to deal with similar types of discrimination. *See, e.g.,* East Chop Tennis Club v. Massachusetts Comm'n Against Discrimination, 364 Mass. 444, 305 N.E.2d 507 (1973) (would not enjoin administrative proceedings to determine if unlawful discrimination were present).

557. 42 U.S.C. § 2000a(a).

558. "Commerce" is defined in 42 U.S.C. § 2000a(c).

559. "State action" is defined in 42 U.S.C. § 2000a(d). State action for purposes of the Equal Protection Clause is considered in detail at § 1.14.

560. 42 U.S.C. § 2000a(b) (1). *See* Heart of Atlanta Motel, Inc. v. United States, 379 U.S. 241, 13 L. Ed. 2d 258, 85 S. Ct. 348 (1964).

561. 42 U.S.C. § 2000a(b) (2). *See* Katzenbach v. McClung, 379 U.S. 294, 13 L. Ed. 2d 290, 85 S. Ct. 377 (1964).

562. 42 U.S.C. § 2000a(b) (3).

563. 42 U.S.C. § 2000a(b) (4).

564. Miller v. Amusement Enterprises, Inc., 394 F.2d 342 (5th Cir. 1968); United States v. Johnson Lake, Inc., 312 F. Supp. 1376 (S.D. Ala. 1970).

565. 395 U.S. 298, 23 L. Ed. 2d 318, 89 S. Ct. 1697 (1969).

566. *Id.* at 305. *See also* Fazzio Real Estate Co., Inc. v. Adams, 396 F.2d 146 (5th Cir. 1968); United States v. Johnson Lake, Inc., 312 F. Supp. 1376 (S.D. Ala. 1970); Evans v. Laurel Links, Inc., 261 F. Supp. 474 (E.D. Va. 1966).

activity and were not mere spectators.[567] Similar results have been reached when discrimination is practiced by those operating golf,[568] bowling,[569] swimming,[570] football [571] and general recreational facilities.[572] Unlawful discrimination may also be found where facially neutral rules or regulations have in practice a discriminatory effect.[573]

Title II of the Civil Rights Act of 1964, then, provides a potent means of insuring that athletic and recreational facilities are not operated in a discriminatory manner. As a result, it is not surprising that one of the more contested provisions of Title II is the exemption for private clubs or other establishments which are not open to the public.[574] To come within this provision, the establishment in question must not be a business operated for profit, and must have all of the attributes of self-government and member-ownership traditionally associated with private clubs. The simple identification of an establishment as a "private club" will not, for these purposes, suffice.[575] In determining whether a particular establishment is an exempt private club, a number of factors will be examined in light of Title II's clear purpose of protecting only the privacy of clubs whose membership is genuinely selective.[576] These factors will include the presence of limited membership, definite admission standards, regular meetings of the membership, and financing that comes from other than public sources.[577] The application of these limitations was clarified in *Sullivan v. Little Hunting Park, Inc.,*[578] where the Supreme Court held that a non-stock corporation which was organized to operate park and playground facilities was not a "private club" when "[t]here was no plan or purpose of exclusiveness. It is open to every white person within the geographic area, there being no selective element other than race." [579] Similarly, where an organization freely admits all whites to membership, with color of skin being the only criteria for admission, receives a substantial amount of its revenue from

567. 395 U.S. at 306-08. *See also* United States v. Slidell Youth Football Ass'n, 387 F. Supp. 474 (E.D. La. 1974); National Organization for Women v. Little League Baseball, Inc., 127 N.J. Super. 522, 318 A.2d 33 (1974) (playing field was a place of public accommodation under state statutory provision); Moose Lodge 145 v. Pennsylvania Human Relations Comm'n, 16 Pa. Commw. Ct. 433, 328 A.2d 180 (1974) (fraternal lodge bowling league a place of public accommodation under state law).

568. Wesley v. Savannah, 294 F. Supp. 698 (S.D. Ga. 1969); Evans v. Laurel Links, Inc., 261 F. Supp. 474 (E.D. Va. 1966).

569. Fazzio Real Estate Co., Inc. v. Adams, 396 F.2d 146 (5th Cir. 1968).

570. Tillman v. Wheaton-Haven Recreation Ass'n, Inc., 410 U.S. 431, 35 L. Ed. 2d 403, 93 S. Ct. 1090 (1973); Olzman v. Lake Hills Swim Club, Inc., 495 F.2d 1333 (2d Cir. 1974).

571. United States v. Slidell Youth Football Ass'n, 387 F. Supp. 474 (E.D. La. 1974).

572. Smith v. Young Men's Christian Ass'n of Montgomery, Inc., 462 F.2d 634 (5th Cir. 1972); Nesmith v. Young Men's Christian Ass'n of Raleigh, N.C., 397 F.2d 96 (4th Cir. 1968); United States v. Beach Associates, Inc., 286 F. Supp. 801 (D. Md. 1968).

573. Griggs v. Duke Power Co., 401 U.S. 424, 28 L. Ed. 2d 158, 91 S. Ct. 849 (1971); Yick Wo v. Hopkins, 118 U.S. 356, 30 L. Ed. 220, 6 S. Ct. 1064 (1886); United States v. Slidell Youth Football Ass'n, 387 F. Supp. 474 (E.D. La. 1974); Olzman v. Lake Hills Swim Club, Inc., 495 F.2d 1333 (2d Cir. 1974).

574. 42 U.S.C. § 2000a(e).

575. Daniel v. Paul, 395 U.S. 298, 301, 33 L. Ed. 2d 318, 89 S. Ct. 1697 (1969).

576. Nesmith v. Young Men's Christian Ass'n of Raleigh, N.C., 397 F.2d 96 (4th Cir. 1968).

577. *Id.*

578. 396 U.S. 229, 24 L. Ed. 2d 386, 90 S. Ct. 400 (1969).

579. *Id.* at 236. *See also* Tillman v. Wheaton-Haven Recreation Ass'n, 410 U.S. 431, 35 L. Ed. 2d 403, 93 S. Ct. 1090 (1973); Olzman v. Lake Hills Swim Club, Inc., 495 F.2d 1333 (2d Cir. 1974).

public sources, and is neither owned nor governed by its members, who never as such meet, it has frequently been held that it is not a private club and will not be exempted from the requirements of Title II.[580]

The final means by which racially discriminatory refusals to allow certain classes of persons to use athletic facilities may be redressed is through utilization of two additional statutory provisions, whose language may be traced to the Civil Rights Act of 1866.[581] The first is what is now referred to as "§ 1982," which provides that "[a]ll citizens . . . shall have the same right . . . as is enjoyed by white citizens . . . to inherit, purchase, lease, sell, hold, and convey real and personal property." [582] Its application to discrimination in athletic facility availability was considered in *Sullivan v. Little Hunting Park, Inc.*,[583] where the Supreme Court held that § 1982 would provide a remedy for racial discrimination in a community park and recreation facility which the party who had been discriminated against had a right to utilize by reason of a leasehold interest.[584] It has also been held that § 1982 would protect "the freedom of blacks to go and come as guests of a swim club member." [585] Probably the most important aspect of these cases is the extent to which they apply § 1982 to what is essentially private action. Thus, in *Sullivan* the Court stated that § 1982 "reaches beyond state action and operates upon the unofficial acts of private individuals. . . ." [586] The § 1982 remedy is, therefore, of particular importance since it provides a remedy for racial discrimination by private persons, who may not be subject to equal protection requirements.[587] Although it might be argued that the "private club" exception to the provisions of Title II of the Civil Rights Act of 1964 might yet protect such private action, that conclusion would appear to be inconsistent with the Supreme Court's approach in *Sullivan*. The Court has, however, specifically left the question open.[588]

The second statutory outgrowth of the Civil Rights Act of 1866 is what is now referred to as "§ 1981," which provides that "[a]ll persons . . . shall have the same right . . . to make and enforce contracts . . . and to the full and equal benefit

---

580. Smith v. Young Men's Christian Ass'n of Montgomery, Inc., 462 F.2d 634 (5th Cir. 1972); United States v. Slidell Youth Football Ass'n, 387 F. Supp. 474 (E.D. La. 1974); Bell v. Kenwood Golf & Country Club, Inc., 312 F. Supp. 753 (D. Md. 1970) ("private" country club); United States v. Young Men's Christian Ass'n of Columbia, 310 F. Supp. 79 (D.S.C. 1970). *See also* Anderson v. Pass Christian Isles Golf Club, Inc., 488 F.2d 855 (5th Cir. 1974). *But cf.* Application of New York Athletic Club of the City of New York, 56 Misc. 2d 565, 289 N.Y.S.2d 246 (1968) (upheld status as private club under similar New York statutory scheme).

581. Act of April 9, 1866, ch. 31, § 1, 14 Stat. 27.

582. 42 U.S.C. § 1982.

583. 396 U.S. 229, 24 L. Ed. 2d 386, 90 S. Ct. 400 (1969).

584. *Id.* at 236-38. The Court also held that damages may be available under § 1982. *Id.* at 238-40.

585. Olzman v. Lake Hills Swim Club, Inc., 495 F.2d 1333, 1339 (2d Cir. 1974).

586. 396 U.S. at 235. *See also* Runyon v. McCrary, 427 U.S. 160, 427 L. Ed. 2d 160, 96 S. Ct. 2586 (1976); Tillman v. Wheaton-Haven Recreation Ass'n, 410 U.S. 431, 35 L. Ed. 2d 403, 93 S. Ct. 1090 (1973). The "state action" concept for equal protection purposes is considered at note 539 *supra* and § 1.14.

587. *See* § 1.14.

588. Thus, in Tillman v. Wheaton-Haven Recreation Ass'n, 410 U.S. 431, 35 L. Ed. 2d 403, 93 S. Ct. 1090 (1973), the Court stated that "it is not necessary in this case to consider the issue of any implied limitation on the sweep of § 1982 when its application to a truly private club, within the meaning of § 2000a(e), is under consideration." *Id.* at 438-39. A similar issue exists under § 1981. *See* note 594 *infra*.

of all laws and proceedings . . . as is enjoyed by white citizens. . . ." [589] Inasmuch as § 1981 is derived from the same base as was § 1982,[590] it will be construed in a similar fashion.[591] Thus, § 1981 will be an appropriate remedy for discrimination which is based upon refusal to contract with certain persons on a racial basis.[592] This remedy has been used primarily in cases where the owner or operator of an athletic facility has refused to sell admission tickets to blacks.[593] It has also been utilized for refusals to grant membership in a YMCA branch.[594]

Where discrimination is encountered in the availability of athletic and recreational facilities, then, there are several remedies that may be utilized, depending upon the nature of the discrimination, to eliminate the discriminatory acts or policies.

An additional type of discrimination that may be present in the use of athletic facilities is competitive discrimination, pursuant to which some persons or groups may be precluded from using facilities on as favorable terms as are available to others. As has been discussed at length in this section, a party deprived of the use of athletic facilities may obtain a remedy if an actionable wrong can be proven. In the case of such competitive discrimination this may be a difficult burden to carry. Thus, in *D.D.B. Realty Corporation v. Merrill,*[595] the operator of a ski facility which was leased from the state had entered an agreement with a ski lodge association for its members to use the facilities at a lower than normal charge. When a ski lodge which was not a member of the association brought suit claiming that it had been unlawfully discriminated against, the court held that the plan was not discriminatory and noted that the complaining lodge was eligible to become a member of the association, and indeed had been a member in the past. A contrary result might be justified if membership in the association were not open to the complaining party and if the requisites of the theories considered heretofore could be established.

---

589. 42 U.S.C. § 1981.

590. *See* note 581 *supra.*

591. Scott v. Young, 421 F.2d 143 (4th Cir.), *cert. denied,* 398 U.S. 929, 26 L. Ed. 2d 91, 90 S. Ct. 1820 (1970). *See also* Olzman v. Lake Hills Swim Club, Inc., 495 F.2d 1333 (2d Cir. 1974).

592. Thus, § 1981 may have much broader applicability than to simply overturn racial discrimination in athletic and recreational facilities. It was sought to be utilized, for example, in Cooper v. Allen, 493 F.2d 765 (5th Cir. 1974), where a black golfer alleged that he had not been hired as a golf pro on a racially discriminatory basis. Although he lost the case, it does suggest additional areas in which § 1981 might provide a valuable remedy.

593. *See, e.g.,* Olzman v. Lake Hills Swim Club, Inc., 495 F.2d 1333 (2d Cir. 1974); Scott v. Young, 421 F.2d 143 (4th Cir.), *cert. denied,* 398 U.S. 929, 26 L. Ed. 2d 91, 90 S. Ct. 1820 (1970).

594. *See, e.g.,* Smith v. Young Men's Christian Ass'n, 316 F. Supp. 899 (M.D. Ala. 1970), *modified on appeal,* 462 F.2d 634 (5th Cir. 1972). *But see* Perkins v. New Orleans Athletic Club, 429 F. Supp. 661 (E.D. La. 1976) (§ 1981 did not apply where membership in private club was not widely offered to the public).

595. 232 F. Supp. 629 (D. Vt. 1964).

CHAPTER 3

Legal Relationships in Professional Sports

§ 3.01. Scope of Chapter.

Legal relationships in the professional sports industry have both private law and public law aspects. The public law in this area has its source in the various legislative enactments and administrative regulations which define the industry's responsibilities under the federal labor, antitrust, and tax laws. These matters are considered elsewhere in this treatise.[1] The present chapter is concerned with the private law of professional sports. In this connection, it will be seen that the law of contracts plays the predominant role in defining the rights and responsibilities of the various participants in the professional sports business. Virtually every important relationship in this area is covered by a private agreement in one form or another. The present discussion considers some of the legal questions which arise as the parties undertake to interpret and enforce these private arrangements.

The first topic to be considered concerns the interpretation of the employment contracts of professional athletes. The reader will note that the discussion which follows focuses on employment relationships in professional team sports. Most issues are discussed in terms of the relationship which exists between athletes and clubs in the major professional leagues. The contracts used in the team sports are similar in their basic structure and thus are more susceptible to a general analysis. The contracts which define the relationships in sports involving individual performances, such as boxing, tennis, and golf, often reflect greater variation in content, and these are not separately treated. It can be noted, however, that there are many similarities in the legal questions which arise in the two types of sports. The contracts in both team and individual sports often

---

1. *See* chs. 5 (antitrust), 6 (labor), 7 (tax).

include provisions dealing with such matters as the employer's right to assign the contract, the athlete's obligation to perform exclusively for the employer during the period of their relationship, and the respective rights of the parties to terminate the agreement. Thus, although the specific focus is on the standard player contracts in professional team sports, much of what is said can be transferred to other employment situations.

On another matter, it can be noted that while the problems addressed in the uniform player contracts used in the various leagues are basically the same, there are often differences in the solutions which are selected. This fact has influenced the analysis which is undertaken here. In the following sections, there are basically three different approaches which are used. Some matters, such as those involving the formation of contracts and the general rules of interpretation, are largely unaffected by the particular terms of the parties' agreement. The discussion of these points in the following materials focuses primarily on legal principles which have general applicability. There are other issues, such as those arising from the assignment of a player's contract, which require that the parties' agreement be read against the background of general contracts principles. On matters such as these, the emphasis in the following discussion is on the background concepts, for these are likely to have the most general application.

There is a third category of issues, including questions such as the employer's right to unilaterally renew the contract for an additional term, which depends entirely upon the particular language of the contract for resolution. Since there are few generalizations which can be made with respect to matters of this sort, the approach used in the following sections is to examine the language of particular contracts to illustrate how the problems are dealt with. The reader will note that in some instances reference is made to contract language which is no longer in current use. Where this is done, the purpose is either to indicate other approaches which might be taken or to provide background for issues which have appeared in litigation. This comparative approach, which is also indicated in footnote references to contracts from some now-defunct leagues, will hopefully be of use to those who are undertaking to draft new contract terms on these matters, as well as those who are seeking to interpret contracts used in other professional sports settings.

As the prior discussion suggests, the controversies which arise with respect to the employment of professional athletes cover a wide range of legal issues, and it may be worthwhile to give a more complete listing of the matters which will be considered here.

The most important issues which are discussed concern the extent of the athlete's obligation to the employer-club and the related question of the club's control over the player's job rights. Thus considerable attention is given to the club's right to terminate the contract so as to bring an end to the athlete's right to receive his salary.[2] It will be seen that the clubs retain broad powers in this regard, and the average player has relatively little job security. Some players enjoy the protection of no-cut contracts which are intended to limit the team's

_____

2. *See* §§ 3.07-3.08 *infra.*

right to terminate its obligations. These provisions warrant discussion because their terms are not always well-defined.[3]

The issue which has appeared most frequently in the decided cases concerns the club's responsibility to the athlete in the event he is injured.[4] This question is of critical importance in high-risk sports such as football. Predictably, the parties' contract will usually include one or more terms which are intended to define the employer's obligation first, to pay for expenses incurred in connection with the injury and second, to continue the player's salary for the period of disability. While the clubs generally accept some responsibility for these sums, their liability is usually limited by the terms of their agreements. Most controversies arise from the parties' varying interpretations of the limitations which are specified in their contract.

Another area of controversy in professional sports concerns the right of the club to demand performance from the athlete. The question usually arises in circumstances in which the parties differ on whether the athlete has the right to abandon his original contract and accept employment with another club. Some important aspects of this subject matter are treated in chapter 4, which deals generally with the enforcement of professional sports contracts. That chapter considers the legal issues which arise when the club seeks equitable enforcement of the athlete's promise to perform only for his existing employer.[5] The present discussion treats the remaining issues which arise when the athlete asserts his freedom to negotiate with other clubs. Attention is given to the player's right to terminate his contract.[6] In addition, the contractual aspects of option and reserve clauses are discussed.[7]

Another important feature of the player-club relationship is the club's power to subject the player to discipline in the form of a fine or suspension. The limits of this authority are defined in the typical player contract, although, as discussed below, this is not an area in which courts are likely to be wholly deferential to the parties' agreement.[8] Of similar importance is the club's right to assign players' contracts to other teams.[9] The athlete may be displeased that he is given very little to say in such a decision but, as will be seen, he typically has no legal bases upon which to object.

There are other private agreements in addition to those defining the athlete's employment status which play a significant role in the law of sports. The relationship between clubs within a league is basically contractual in nature.[10] The constitution and by-laws of the league, which are generally the product of the mutual agreement between league members, provide the terms by which most intra-league disputes are resolved. While the sections which follow consider the contractual nature of the relationship, the discussion is qualified by other principles from the law of private associations. There are limits on the power of the private association to take actions adverse to the basic economic

---

3. *See* § 3.09 *infra.*
4. *See* §§ 3.05-3.06 *infra.*
5. *See* §§ 4.02-4.14 *infra.*
6. *See* § 3.11 *infra.*
7. *See* § 3.12 *infra.*
8. *See* § 3.10 *infra.*
9. *See* §§ 3.13-3.14 *infra.*
10. *See* § 3.15 *infra.*

interests of one of its members. Thus, attention is given to the restraints which courts impose on the league's right to discipline its member clubs or otherwise affect their membership rights.[11]

Another contractual relationship treated in this section is that which exists between an athlete and his agent. The actions of many players' agents have been subjected to rather pointed criticism, including complaints about the general incompetence and lack of ethics of some agents.[12] While these have not always been translated into legal controversies, there are well-established principles from other areas of the law which serve to define the duties of such representatives. These and related legal principles affecting the emerging athletic management business are outlined below.[13]

§ 3.02. Interpretation of Standard Player Contracts: Problems in Contract Formation.

a. Introduction. In this section and those which follow, attention is given to some of the legal issues which arise in connection with the negotiation and interpretation of formal employment contracts between an athlete and his club. Initial consideration will be given to problems related to the formation of such player contracts. In subsequent sections, particular types of contract clauses will be examined.

It will quickly become apparent that there is much about the law of contracts in the sports area which is not unique. The legal principles which are applied here are the same as those used to interpret contracts in other contexts. Indeed, it is common for courts presented with controversies involving sports contracts to cite and rely upon precedent from general contracts cases.[14] While the law of sports necessarily draws upon legal doctrine from the body of general contracts law, it is nonetheless useful to separately examine selected issues pertaining to sports contracts. There is undeniably a factual uniqueness to many contracts questions in the sports area, and as with any legal analysis, the factual setting will dictate how general doctrine will be applied. In addition, the sports area often presents peculiar policy considerations in a particular case. Finally, on a few issues in the sports area, there is sufficient precedent from sports cases to support or refute interpretations which might otherwise be arguable under general contracts law doctrine. The following sections are written with the above points in mind. The emphasis will be on the special factual settings and the peculiar public and economic policies which seem to influence the contracts issues which arise in the sports area. These will be analyzed with particular reference to the case law developments relevant to sports law issues. Where such precedent is not available, more general authorities will be utilized.[15]

---

11. *See* § 3.16 *infra.*
12. *See* § 3.17 *infra.*
13. *See* §§ 3.18-3.19 *infra.*
14. *See, e.g.,* Hennigan v. Chargers Football Co., 431 F.2d 308 (5th Cir. 1970); Pasquel v. Owen, 186 F.2d 263 (8th Cir. 1950); Los Angeles Rams Football Club v. Cannon, 185 F. Supp. 717 (S.D. Cal. 1960).
15. Since the case citations in the following pages are generally limited to decisions arising from the sports area, the lawyer interested in more extensive case authority will want to consult traditional sources. *See generally* Restatement of Contracts (1932); Restatement (Second) of

b. Problems in Contract Formation: Offer and Acceptance. Some controversies involving sports contracts begin at the most basic level, often with the player contending that the elementary prerequisites for proper contract formation have not been met. That the conflict might dwell upon such basic issues is not surprising, for if the athlete is successful in his arguments, there is no contract, and he is free to contract with other eligible employers.[16] Thus, what appears to be a dispute over basic rules of contracts law may in reality be a dispute over which of two teams shall have the right to the athlete's services.

One might think that the contracting process in professional athletics was a simple one. The parties typically use a standard form contract, and it is normally assumed that except for matters of compensation and length of contract,[17] there is little room for negotiation.[18] The standard player's agreement is drafted by the team, and it is the team who usually seeks out the player. Thus, it might be assumed that, in terms of offer and acceptance, the team was the party making the offer and, when the player added his signature to the document, he was indicating his acceptance. Under that characterization, the player would lose the option to change his mind about entering into the contract when he signed.[19] Hence, it might appear that he could not thereafter abandon the contract and sign with another team without subjecting himself to liability. In fact, however, the player's signing of the contract may not signal the end of his freedom to sell his services to another team. It may be that the signed contract which the player returns to the team is only an offer,[20] and if it is not itself supported by consideration,[21] it may be withdrawn if that fact is communicated to the team before there has been an acceptance.[22] What determines whether the player's act of signing results in the formation of a binding contract or only authenticates a revocable offer? As with other issues in the area of contract formation, it will be the intent of the parties which dictates the legal characterization.[23] In most

CONTRACTS (Tent. Draft 1964); A. CORBIN, CORBIN ON CONTRACTS (1952) [hereinafter cited as CORBIN ON CONTRACTS]; J. MURRAY, MURRAY ON CONTRACTS (1974) [hereinafter cited as MURRAY ON CONTRACTS]; S. WILLISTON, A TREATISE ON THE LAW OF CONTRACTS (2d ed. 1957) [hereinafter cited as WILLISTON, CONTRACTS]; 17 AM. JUR. 2d Contracts (1964); 17, 17A C.J.S. Contracts (1963).

16. See, e.g., Los Angeles Rams Football Club v. Cannon, 185 F. Supp. 717 (S.D. Cal. 1960); American League Baseball Club of Chicago v. Chase, 86 Misc. 441, 149 N.Y.S. 6 (Sup. Ct. 1914); Metropolitan Exhibition Co. v. Ward, 9 N.Y.S. 779 (Sup. Ct. 1890).

17. Because of their greater bargaining power, superstars are sometimes able to secure variances in provisions of the standard player contract dealing with matters other than compensation and length of the contract. See, e.g., Munchak Corp. v. Cunningham, 457 F.2d 721 (4th Cir. 1972) (specially negotiated restrictions on the assignability of the contract).

18. See Matuszak v. Houston Oilers, Inc., 515 S.W.2d 725, 730 (Tex. Civ. App. 1974) (Tunks, J., dissenting). But see discussion at notes 26-29, § 3.04 infra.

19. This discussion assumes that the parties understand that there would be no binding contract until it had been reduced to writing. 1 CORBIN ON CONTRACTS § 30.

20. See generally 1 CORBIN ON CONTRACTS § 11; MURRAY ON CONTRACTS § 22.

21. See 1 CORBIN ON CONTRACTS §§ 42-44; MURRAY ON CONTRACTS § 36.

22. See, e.g., Detroit Football Co. v. Robinson, 186 F. Supp. 933, 934 (E.D. La.), aff'd, 283 F.2d 657 (5th Cir. 1960); Los Angeles Rams Football Club v. Cannon, 185 F. Supp. 717, 724 (S.D. Cal. 1960); RESTATEMENT OF CONTRACTS § 35 (1932); CORBIN ON CONTRACTS § 38; MURRAY ON CONTRACTS §§ 31, 35, 39.

23. Questions of interpretation arise not only where there is admittedly a contract, but also where the controversy is whether there is a contract. In determining this, interpretation must often be applied to words and other manifestations of intention as a preliminary to deciding whether an agreement amounts to a contract, or whether words or other

fact situations, the ultimate conclusion on this issue will depend upon whether the parties contemplated that further acts of execution remained to be performed. Thus, if the team had not yet signed the document, or if league approval were a precondition to the contract becoming binding, the player's act of signing would likely not have legal finality.[24]

Once the matter of identifying the offeror and offeree has been resolved, it is necessary to find that there has been a proper acceptance.[25] In many cases, there is a question of timing which underlies the dispute over the acceptance. That is, the player often seeks to show that his offer to play had been withdrawn before the team had entered its acceptance.[26] If that decision to withdraw the offer is communicated before the contract is accepted, then the player will be successful in his efforts to establish that he was free to sign with another team.[27] Acceptance is indicated by any manifestation which shows the parties' willingness to be bound by the precise terms of the offer.[28] Under this principle, there is no acceptance, and hence no contract, if the team seeks to accept a contract on terms different from those which the player understood as being operative.[29] Where the promisee's acceptance includes such a variance his communication is properly treated as a counter-offer, and it is then necessary to determine whether the counter-offer has been accepted by the original offeror.[30]

As the above analysis should suggest, the ultimate goal of the various legal rules governing contract formation is to insure that before a court proceeds to order enforcement, there is reliable evidence that the parties have, based on their outward manifestations, in fact reached an agreement.[31] Thus, enforcement should generally be reserved for those situations in which the acceptor has agreed to the same set of conditions which the offeror reasonably understood would provide the basis of the bargain.[32] But since the rules for offer and acceptance are concerned primarily with the reliability of the proof of the alleged agreement, it would seem to follow that the rules themselves should be interpreted in light of this goal and not in a wooden fashion which would deny a party the benefit of a contract where there is a common understanding even though it is imperfectly expressed.

Cases dealing with sports contracts reflect the increasing judicial sensitivity to this basic function of the rules governing offer and acceptance. In early cases,

---

manifestations of intention amount to an offer, an acceptance, a rejection, or revocation of an offer. RESTATEMENT OF CONTRACTS § 226, comment a at 305 (1932).

24. See 1 CORBIN ON CONTRACTS §§ 22-23; MURRAY ON CONTRACTS §§ 20, 22-24.

25. See generally MURRAY ON CONTRACTS § 44.

26. See, e.g., Detroit Football Co. v. Robinson, 186 F. Supp. 933 (E.D. La.), aff'd, 283 F.2d 657 (5th Cir. 1960).

27. RESTATEMENT OF CONTRACTS § 41 (1932); RESTATEMENT (SECOND) OF CONTRACTS § 41 (Tent. Draft No. 1, 1964); MURRAY ON CONTRACTS §§ 31, 35, 39.

28. See generally RESTATEMENT OF CONTRACTS §§ 20, 52 (1932); RESTATEMENT (SECOND) OF CONTRACTS §§ 20, 52 (Tent. Draft No. 1, 1964).

29. See Los Angeles Rams Football Club v. Cannon, 185 F. Supp. 717, 725 (S.D. Cal. 1960). See also 1 CORBIN ON CONTRACTS § 88; MURRAY ON CONTRACTS § 43.

30. See RESTATEMENT OF CONTRACTS § 38 (1932); RESTATEMENT (SECOND) OF CONTRACTS § 38 (Tent. Draft No. 1, 1964).

31. See 1 CORBIN ON CONTRACTS § 9.

32. See generally MURRAY ON CONTRACTS §§ 18-19.

enforcement was denied if the contract appeared to be no more than an agreement to agree [33] or if the parties had included terms which were so vague and indefinite as to suggest that neither side could have understood the substance of the bargain.[34] While the basic principle of those cases — that there must be reasonable evidence of agreement — would continue today, modern courts are generally more willing to supply terms and definitions which were not included in the parties' agreement.[35] Thus, when confronted with a term which is vague or indefinite on its face, the court will likely look to the customs and usage of the trade to supply a meaning.[36] Similarly, prior actions and expressions of the parties might be consulted.[37] In general, if the dealings between the parties otherwise indicated that they had manifested an intention to be bound, the court should make a strong effort to supply or define the terms of the agreement, subject to the limitation that no enforcement should be decreed where there is no certain basis upon which to fashion a remedy.[38]

Basic to the formation of a contract is an acceptance which is responsive to the offer. The potential for differing perceptions between the player and the team appears to be particularly acute where the matter in controversy is the duration of the contract,[39] although other matters have been the object of controversy.[40] Where the parties do have different views on the meaning of particular terms, the court must choose between two courses: either the court will deem the contract unenforceable because there never was any agreement [41] or the court will choose the interpretation given by one of the parties and proceed to enforce the now definite contract.[42] The decision as to which approach will be taken is usually made according to well-established principles. As previously stated, the normal rule is that the parties will be bound by a reasonable interpretation of their outward manifestations. Under this view a secret intention or private interpretation which does not comport with the parties' expressions and conduct cannot control.[43] Moreover, if a formal document

---

33. *See* Metropolitan Exhibition Co. v. Ewing, 42 F. 198, 204 (S.D.N.Y. 1890). *See generally* 1 CORBIN ON CONTRACTS § 29.

34. *See* Metropolitan Exhibition Co. v. Ward, 9 N.Y.S. 779, 782, 784 (Sup. Ct. 1890); Philadelphia Ball Club, Ltd. v. Hallman, 8 Pa. County Ct. 57, 62 (1890). *See also* Metropolitan Exhibition Co. v. Ewing, 42 F. 198 (S.D.N.Y. 1890).

35. *See* 1 CORBIN ON CONTRACTS §§ 29, 95-100.
The Uniform Commercial Code provides perhaps the most fully developed system for interpreting contracts which have few terms. *See* U.C.C. §§ 2-204, 2-305 to 2-310. While these provisions of the U.C.C. apply only to contracts for the sale of goods and thus are not technically applicable to employment contracts, it can be noted that the modern trend toward liberality of interpretation is found in other areas as well, including the area of contracts of employment. *See, e.g.,* Borg-Warner Corp. v. Anchor Coupling Co., 16 Ill. 2d 234, 156 N.E.2d 513 (1958).

36. *See, e.g.,* Egan v. Winnipeg Baseball Club, Ltd., 96 Minn. 345, 104 N.W. 947 (1905); Johnson v. Green Bay Packers, Inc., 272 Wis. 149, 74 N.W.2d 784 (1956). *Compare* Metropolitan Exhibition Co. v. Ewing, 42 F. 198, 202 (S.D.N.Y. 1890).

37. *See* Tollefson v. Green Bay Packers, 256 Wis. 318, 41 N.W.2d 201 (1950).

38. *Cf.* Soar v. National Football League Players' Ass'n, 550 F.2d 1287 (1st Cir. 1977).

39. *See, e.g.,* Los Angeles Rams Football Club v. Cannon, 185 F. Supp. 717 (S.D. Cal. 1960); Sample v. Gotham Football Club, Inc., 59 F.R.D. 160 (S.D.N.Y. 1973).

40. *See* Washington Capitols Basketball Club, Inc. v. Barry, 419 F.2d 472, 479 (9th Cir.), *aff'g* 304 F. Supp. 1193 (N.D. Cal. 1969) (alleged promise that franchise would not be moved).

41. *See* Los Angeles Rams Football Club v. Cannon, 185 F. Supp. 717 (S.D. Cal. 1960).

42. *See* Houston Oilers, Inc. v. Neely, 361 F.2d 36 (10th Cir. 1966); *cf.* Sample v. Gotham Football Club, Inc., 57 F.R.D. 160 (S.D.N.Y. 1973).

43. *See* RESTATEMENT OF CONTRACTS § 20 (1932); RESTATEMENT (SECOND) OF CONTRACTS § 20

executed by the parties is sufficient to constitute a contract, one party will not be allowed to introduce evidence of oral agreements for the purpose of showing that he had a different understanding of terms which have a plain meaning.[44] By application of these principles, courts are able to avoid many potential disputes about whether an agreement does in fact exist.

The sports area does, however, include one case, *Los Angeles Rams Football Club v. Cannon,*[45] in which the court gave great weight to the subjective understanding of the parties, particularly the athlete, in concluding that no binding contract had been formed. Following negotiations with the Rams' General Manager, Billy Cannon, a senior at Louisiana State University, signed three sets of NFL standard player contracts covering the 1960, 1961, and 1962 seasons. Shortly thereafter, however, Cannon signed another contract with the Houston Oilers of the then-rival American Football League and notified the Rams that he did not regard himself bound by his earlier negotiations with them. When the Rams sued to enjoin Cannon from playing with any other team, the central issue in the case was whether a binding contract had ever been formed between the parties. The court concluded that with respect to the last two seasons, 1961 and 1962, Cannon's signing only amounted to an offer, which he could revoke. The documents covering these seasons had never been approved by the league commissioner, an act which, as discussed in the next subsection, the court found was a necessary prerequisite to a binding contract. The document covering the 1960 season had, however, been signed by the commissioner. But when this writing was separately considered, it too was found to be insufficient to bind Cannon. In the court's view, this document lacked the most rudimentary characteristic of a contract for there had been no meeting of the minds between the parties on the fundamental point of the duration of the parties' agreement. While the athlete thought he was agreeing to a single three-year contract, the club, by using three one-year contracts and securing commissioner approval for only the first year, had structured the transaction so as to obligate it only on a year-to-year basis. Since there was no mutual understanding between the parties on the precise nature of their agreement, the court concluded that there was no contract and, thus, no basis to sustain the club's request that Cannon comply with the terms which obligated him to play exclusively for the Rams. The court's analysis, while giving greater weight to the player's peculiar perception of the transaction than is normally afforded,[46] is fully supportable on the facts. Two matters of evidence were of critical importance in the particular setting: on the one hand, the team's representative had done much to implant the erroneous characterization in the athlete's mind, and on the other, the player was not represented by counsel and did not possess sufficient personal sophistication to give a proper interpretation to the contract

(Tent. Draft No. 1, 1964). *Cf.* Houston Oilers, Inc. v. Neely, 361 F.2d 36 (10th Cir. 1966); Sample v. Gotham Football Club, Inc., 57 F.R.D. 160 (S.D.N.Y. 1973).

44. *See* RESTATEMENT OF CONTRACTS § 230, and comment *a* (1932); *cf.* Washington Capitols Basketball Club, Inc. v. Barry, 419 F.2d 472, 479 (9th Cir.), *aff'g* 304 F. Supp. 1193 (N.D. Cal. 1969). *See also* § 3.16 *infra.*

45. 185 F. Supp. 717 (S.D. Cal. 1960).

46. *Compare* Sample v. Gotham Football Club, Inc., 57 F.R.D. 160 (S.D.N.Y. 1973).

he signed.[47] Hence, in a real sense, it was the manifestations of the team's agent which produced the situation in which the parties shared different perceptions of what was being exchanged. When *Cannon* is viewed in this perspective, its importance is restricted to that increasingly limited class of cases in which a relatively naive athlete attempts to negotiate his own contract with a team which does not take care to insure that the terms are clearly understood.[48] Either adequate third party counseling for the athlete or more temperate practices by the team's negotiator would easily avoid the result reached here and lead to application of the more traditional rules for identifying whether an enforceable contract exists.

As previously indicated, it is often necessary to determine whether particular acts by one side or the other amount to an acceptance of the contract. A question which has received some attention in the courts is whether the athlete's acceptance of a bonus or other emolument evidences his intent to be bound to the proffered terms. The prevailing view appears to be that the legal significance of a bonus depends upon the intent with which it is received by the athlete. If the athlete thinks that he is not entitled to the money until some later time,[49] or receives it at a time when the contract has not been formalized,[50] the mere fact of receipt of the bonus will not be sufficient to indicate a binding agreement.[51]

c. The Role of Commissioner Approval. A question which has received the specific attention of the courts concerns the role of the league commissioner in the contracting process between players and their clubs. Most professional sports contracts provide for some mechanism whereby the commissioner is required to review and approve each individual contract signed between a team and a player. The purpose of this review procedure is to insure that no individual team negotiates terms which were not in the best interest of the league as a whole. The larger group interest which is protected has never been carefully articulated, but it seems to include both an interest in insuring equalized competition on the playing field and a more basic economic interest in preserving equal treatment of players on matters other than salary. For example, the league may have an interest in insuring that no player is offered improper bonuses for incidents of outstanding play. Similarly, the teams may reach a collective judgment that it is preferable that all players shall be subjected to the same rules for discipline so that punishments may be meted out uniformly and even-handedly. The league commissioner is usually designated as the party to insure that interests such as these are not ignored in the player employment contracts entered into by the individual clubs.[52]

---

47. 185 F. Supp. at 724-26.

48. *See also* Community Sports, Inc. v. Denver Ringsby Rockets, Inc., 429 Pa. 565, 240 A.2d 832, 837 (1968).

49. *See* Los Angeles Rams Football Club v. Cannon, 185 F. Supp. 717 (S.D. Cal. 1960).

50. *See* Detroit Football Co. v. Robinson, 186 F. Supp. 933 (E.D. La.), *aff'd,* 283 F.2d 657 (5th Cir. 1960).

51. *See* § 3.11 *infra.*

52. *See, e.g.,* Constitution and By-Laws for the National Football League § 15.4 (1972): "the Commissioner shall have the power to disapprove any contract between a player and a club executed in violation of or contrary to the Constitution and By-Laws of the League, or if either contracting party is or has been guilty of conduct detrimental to the League or to professional football."

Whether the requirement of commissioner approval is a pre-condition to the formation of a binding contract depends upon the language of the particular contract and the intention of the parties. Earlier versions of the NFL standard player contract provided:

> This agreement shall become valid and binding upon each party hereto only when, as and if it shall be approved by the Commissioner.[53]

The typical case in which this language was drawn into question was one in which an athlete had signed a standard player contract with one club and then, before that agreement was approved by the league commissioner, had repudiated his signing and entered into a contract with another team, usually in a rival league. When the club which originally signed the athlete sued to enjoin him from performing for the other team, the issue arose as to whether the original, unapproved agreement was binding. The plaintiff club usually argued that the contract was binding on the club and athlete when each had agreed to its terms and that commissioner approval was merely a pre-condition to the enforceability of the agreement. Under this view, the athlete is bound to the contract upon signing, but the commencement of his obligation to perform was delayed until the agreement had been approved.[54] While this characterization meant that a disapproval by the commissioner would have released the athlete from further obligations to the club, this point was seldom raised because the club was usually careful to secure the necessary approval before commencing litigation. The defendant athlete would urge a much different characterization of the disputed clause and suggest that approval by the commissioner was a pre-condition to the contract becoming binding at all. Under this view, the signed, but unapproved, standard player contract was a mere offer, which under normal contract rules could be effectively withdrawn if the decision to withdraw were communicated to the club before the steps for acceptance — that is, approval by the commissioner — had occurred.[55] Upon a proper withdrawal of the offer, the player would be free to contract with another team.

The courts had little difficulty agreeing that under the language quoted above, an unapproved standard player contract was not binding on the player and could be withdrawn.[56] It would have been permissible for the parties to have relegated commissioner approval to the status of a condition to performance, which would have virtually precluded the player's escape from the contract. But in the courts' view, the parties had not done that in language which was employed. In commenting on the then-standard form clause, the court in *Los Angeles Rams Football Club v. Cannon* [57] concluded:

---

53. This contract provision is quoted in Detroit Football Co. v. Robinson, 186 F. Supp. 933, 935 (E.D. La.), aff'd, 283 F.2d 657 (5th Cir. 1960); Los Angeles Rams Football Club v. Cannon, 185 F. Supp. 717, 721 (S.D. Cal. 1960).

54. *See* RESTATEMENT OF CONTRACTS § 250 (1932); RESTATEMENT (SECOND) OF CONTRACTS § 250 (Tent. Draft No. 7, 1973); 3A CORBIN ON CONTRACTS § 649. *Cf.* RESTATEMENT OF CONTRACTS § 262, *example* 2 (1932).

55. *See generally* RESTATEMENT OF CONTRACTS § 41 (1932); RESTATEMENT (SECOND) OF CONTRACTS § 41 (Tent. Draft No. 1, 1964); 1 CORBIN ON CONTRACTS §§ 38-39.

56. Los Angeles Rams Football Club v. Cannon, 185 F. Supp. 717 (S.D. Cal. 1960); Detroit Football Co. v. Robinson, 186 F. Supp. 933 (E.D. La.), aff'd, 283 F.2d 657 (5th Cir. 1960).

57. 185 F. Supp. 717, 722 (S.D. Cal. 1960).

This clause is too definite to be ignored. It jumps out at you. The words employed are too strong to permit of ambiguity. Their selection was obviously made with great care so that there would be no dispute about their meaning, and this court attaches to them the only meaning it can — that is, that the agreement shall only become valid and binding if, as and when approved by the Commissioner.

The decisions on this issue have had an effect upon industry practice. The leagues generally continue to endorse the notion that commissioner approval is a desirable feature in their collective business venture. However, the contracts have been redrafted to make clear that the athlete loses his right to contract with other teams at the point at which he and his employer sign the contract, and not at the later point at which it is approved by the appropriate league official.[58] Another change which can be noted is that approval often no longer requires an affirmative act by the commissioner. Unlike the earlier form which contemplated that the appropriate league official would actually consider and approve each contract, some present contracts provide, in effect, that approval will be automatic, and the contract will be fully effective, unless specific negative action is taken.[59]

§ 3.03.   Status of Agreements Collateral to the Standard Player Contract.

Before the legal relationship between an athlete and his club can be defined, it is necessary to determine the precise content of their contract. While the parties usually will have signed a standard player contract which provides most of the terms governing their relationship, questions will arise about the extent to which those standard provisions can be modified or supplemented by terms taken from other sources. In the sports area, disputes are likely to arise with respect to two types of collateral provisions: those which appear in league rules and by-laws and those which allegedly are the product of an oral agreement reached during the negotiations which preceded the signing of the printed form contract. In each case, legal precedents are available to define the extent to which these collateral terms will be recognized as part of the athlete's contract.

The by-laws which govern the teams within a league, as well as the rules of competition and decorum which the teams have devised, may obviously have a significant impact on a player's relationship with his employer if they are deemed to be part of his contract. The league rules may affect virtually every aspect of the individual's employment relationship, including such matters as the athlete's eligibility to play in the league,[60] the playing rules which govern his

---

58. Illustrative of the current contract is ¶ 17 of the Standard Player Contract, National Football League (1975):

> This contract shall be valid and binding upon the parties hereto immediately upon its execution. A copy of such contract shall be filed by the Club with the Commissioner within ten (10) days of the execution. The Commissioner shall have the right to terminate this contract by his disapproval thereof within ten (10) days after the filing thereof in his office . . . .

See also Uniform Player Contract, (Veteran — Single Season), National Basketball Association ¶ 14 (1976).

59. *See* Standard Player Contract, National Football League ¶ 17 (1975), quoted in note 58 *supra*. *See also* note 52 *supra*.

60. Constitution and By-Laws for the National Football League, art. XII (Eligibility of Players) (1972).

on-the-field conduct,[61] the terms and conditions under which the contract can be assigned,[62] and such minutia as the player's entitlement to complimentary game tickets.[63] Where the major professional sports are involved, there is little basis to suggest that league rules and by-laws are not part of the player's contract with the team. Indeed, most of the major team contracts include a general clause which recites that the league constitution and by-laws are incorporated.[64] In addition to these general provisions for incorporation, the contracts also typically make specific reference to league rules where matters such as player discipline and player "waivers" are involved.[65]

This process of general and specific incorporation of provisions which are not themselves subject to negotiation between the immediate parties has encountered relatively little judicial resistance. Courts not only read league provisions into the player's contracts, but also often do so without any expression of doubt as to the correctness of this approach.[66] These precedents suggest that there is little basis upon which to raise a wholesale objection to the incorporation technique. And to the extent that there is judicial resistance to applying such collateral provisions, the cases suggest no problem for which careful draftmanship does not provide a solution. One court's view of the outer limits of incorporation is as follows:

> If the rules of such associations are to be incorporated in private contracts between individuals they should at least be identified in some manner and referred to therein. Persons are not bound by rules and regulations except by their consent.[67]

At one time it might have been possible to raise the policy objection that the player should not be bound by rules which were not subject to his negotiation and which could be amended without his consent. That argument was given little, if any, credence in former times, a result which is not surprising in light of the fact that courts were generally willing to allow particular matters to be committed to the discretion of one of the contracting parties or an outsider.[68] The objection is even less persuasive today, for it is not in fact true that the league's rules are beyond the players' influence. To the contrary, any matter which can reasonably be characterized as a term or condition of the players' employment is a proper subject for negotiation by the players' collective

---

61. *Id.* at art. XI (Playing Rules).

62. *Id.* at art. XVI (Assignment of Player Contracts).

63. *Id.* at § 19.15 (Tickets for Players).

64. The Club and the Player, severally and mutually promise and agree to be legally bound by the Constitution and By-Laws of the League and by all the terms and provisions thereof, a copy of which shall be open and available for inspection by the Club, its Directors and Officers, and the Player, at the main office of the League and at the main office of the Club. Standard Player's Contract, National Hockey League ¶ 18 (1974).

65. *See, e.g.,* Uniform Player Contract (Veteran — Single Season) National Basketball Association, ¶¶ 15, 16, 20(f) (1976).

66. *See, e.g.,* Boston Professional Hockey Ass'n, Inc. v. Cheevers, 348 F. Supp. 261, 266 (D. Mass.), *remanded,* 472 F.2d 127 (1st Cir. 1972); Nassau Sports v. Peters, 352 F. Supp. 870, 878 (E.D.N.Y. 1972); American League Baseball Club of Chicago v. Chase, 86 Misc. 441, 149 N.Y.S. 6, 7-9 (Sup. Ct. 1914); Community Sports, Inc. v. Denver Ringsby Rockets, Inc., 429 Pa. 565, 240 A.2d 832, 836 (1968).

67. Middendorf v. Schreiber, 150 Mo. App. 530, 131 S.W. 122, 123 (1910).

68. *See generally* 1 A. CORBIN, CORBIN ON CONTRACTS §§ 16, 150 (1951) [hereinafter cited as CORBIN ON CONTRACTS]; 3 *id.* at §§ 644-47, 651.

bargaining representative.[69] As the various players' associations have become aware of their bargaining rights, they have directed their attention to an increasing number of matters which may have formerly been regarded as within the leagues' sole prerogative.[70]

An entirely different legal analysis is necessary when the issue is whether the player's contract will be deemed to include terms other than those which appear on the face of the written standard form agreement and related documents. In general, the law disfavors attempts by one party to establish that the content of the contract is different from that which appears in the written memorial. This policy is embodied in the parol evidence rule. As a tenet of substantive law, the rule requires two preconditions: the parties must have integrated all or part of their agreement into a written memorandum, and they must have intended that writing to be a final expression of the terms of their agreement. If these conditions are present, then the parties' contract is that contained in the written document, and other utterances, agreements, and promises made prior to or contemporaneous with the writing are not to be consulted for purposes of adding to or modifying the written terms.[71] This rule is the doctrinal embodiment of the notion that when the parties so intend, their final written expression of the terms in their agreement will be preferred over other expressions made in the course of negotiation. While the correctness of this principle cannot be doubted, a review of the literature and cases will suggest that there are many situations in which resort to parol evidence is not precluded. For example, extrinsic evidence may be used to determine the factual question of whether a particular writing was intended as a final written expression between the parties.[72] In addition, parol evidence may be consulted when there is an ambiguity in the language which the parties have used in their writing. Hence, a prior or contemporaneous expression can be consulted if the party seeking to introduce it can first establish that a particular term of the contract does not have a singular, apparent meaning.[73] In this context, the parol evidence is considered for the purpose of explaining or defining the term and not for the purpose of adding to or modifying the integrated expression. Further, even where the parties appear to have executed a formal, integrated memorandum, parol evidence is still admissible to establish that the parties had agreed that the contract would not become effective and binding until some prior condition was met.[74] Finally, the parol evidence rule is concerned only with prior and

---

69. *See* §§ 6.05-.08 *infra.*

70. *See, e.g.,* National Football League Players Ass'n v. NLRB, 503 F.2d 12 (8th Cir. 1974); National League Management Council, 1973 CCH N.L.R.B. ¶ 25,406.

71. *See generally* RESTATEMENT OF CONTRACTS §§ 228-31, 237-40(1), 242 (1932); RESTATEMENT (SECOND) OF CONTRACTS §§ 235-42 (Tent. Draft Nos. 5 & 6, 1971); 3 CORBIN ON CONTRACTS §§ 573-96; C. MCCORMICK, HANDBOOK ON THE LAW OF EVIDENCE ch. 24 (2d ed. 1954); J. MURRAY, MURRAY ON CONTRACTS §§ 103-08 (1974) [hereinafter cited as MURRAY ON CONTRACTS]; 4 S. WILLISTON, A TREATISE ON THE LAW OF CONTRACTS §§ 631-39 (3d ed. 1961) [hereinafter cited as WILLISTON, CONTRACTS].

72. *See, e.g.,* Mitchell v. Lath, 247 N.Y. 377, 160 N.E. 646 (1928); RESTATEMENT OF CONTRACTS §§ 229, 240(1) (1932); RESTATEMENT (SECOND) OF CONTRACTS §§ 236, 242 (Tent. Draft Nos. 5 & 6, 1971); 3 CORBIN ON CONTRACTS § 582; 4 WILLISTON, CONTRACTS §§ 633, 638-39.

73. *See, e.g.,* Martindell v. Lakeshore Nat'l Bank, 15 Ill. 2d 272, 154 N.E.2d 683 (1958); 3 CORBIN ON CONTRACTS § 579.

74. *See, e.g.,* Hicks v. Bush, 10 N.Y.2d 488, 180 N.E.2d 425 (1962); RESTATEMENT (SECOND) OF CONTRACTS § 243 (Tent. Draft No. 6, 1971); 3 CORBIN ON CONTRACTS § 589. *Cf.* Los Angeles Rams Football Club v. Cannon, 185 F. Supp. 717, 726 (S.D. Cal. 1960).

contemporaneous expression; it does not operate to preclude evidence that the parties subsequently modified their written agreement by parol evidence.[75] It should be noted, however, that the effectiveness of many such subsequent modifications will be precluded by another rule, that which requires that any additional agreement be accompanied by new consideration.[76]

It should be made clear that even when the offer of extrinsic evidence is not foreclosed by the parol evidence rule, there is no guarantee that the evidence will be received and weighed. There are many rules of interpretation which will operate to exclude evidence extrinsic to the parties' writings.[77] While matters of contract interpretation are subject to a wide range of discretion in the judge to whom the case is presented, both the "rules" of interpretation and the more formal parol evidence rule reflect a judicial inclination to accept the parties' written expression as the most reliable expression of the parties' understanding.

Since these standards expressing the law's preference for the integrated contract are applied throughout the law of contracts, it is not surprising to find that the results of particular sports cases have been determined by their application. Controversies in the sports area arise in part because of the "pie-in-the-sky" negotiating techniques which are frequently employed. Having had their expectations inflated by the praise and promise of the team's representative, the athletes are often disappointed to discover that there is a significant difference between verbalized promises and written contracts. The team does much to insure its protection under the parol evidence rule by including a clause in the contract which recites that the written contract is accepted by both parties as the final and complete agreement between them.[78] Such an integration clause is not conclusive evidence that the parties did not intend to be bound by other collateral agreements which may have been made.[79] But when the player's consent to this clause is considered in connection with other factors including the fact that it is customary in professional sports to deal on the basis of uniform written contracts and not oral understandings, the player will have a difficult time establishing that the contract was not intended as a final expression.

The athlete will encounter the greatest difficulty when he is attempting to modify the express terms of the contract. Thus, once the written document is signed and accepted, the player will usually not be able to secure enforcement of verbal assurances by a team representative that certain parts of the standard player contract will not be operative.[80] Similarly, the player will not be able to

---

75. *See generally* Wagner v. Graziano Constr. Co., 390 Pa. 445, 136 A.2d 82 (1957); 3 CORBIN ON CONTRACTS § 577; RESTATEMENT OF CONTRACTS §§ 238-39 (1932); RESTATEMENT (SECOND) OF CONTRACTS §§ 240-41 (Tent. Draft No. 6, 1971); MURRAY ON CONTRACTS § 108.

76. *See, e.g.,* Community Sports, Inc. v. Denver Ringsby Rockets, Inc., 429 Pa. 565, 240 A.2d 832, 836 n.5 (1968). *See generally* RESTATEMENT OF CONTRACTS §§ 76(a), 84 (1932); RESTATEMENT (SECOND) OF CONTRACTS §§ 76A, 84, 89D (Tent. Draft Nos. 1 & 2, 1964); Corbin, *Does a Pre-Existing Contract Defeat Consideration?,* 27 YALE L.J. 362 (1917).

77. *See generally* 3 CORBIN ON CONTRACTS §§ 539-40; MURRAY ON CONTRACTS §§ 109-110.

78. *See, e.g.,* Uniform Player Contract (Veteran — Single Season) National Basketball Association, ¶ 23 (1976): "This contract contains the entire agreement between the parties and there are no oral or written inducements, promises or agreements except as contained herein."

79. *See, e.g.,* RESTATEMENT (SECOND) OF CONTRACTS § 236, comment *b,* § 242, comment *e* (Tent. Draft Nos. 5 & 6, 1971).

80. *See* Johnson v. Green Bay Packers, Inc., 272 Wis. 149, 74 N.W.2d 784, 788 (1956).

use collateral oral agreements to modify or nullify the plain meaning of provisions found in the standard contract. For example, the standard contracts grant to a club a virtually unlimited right to assign the player's contract to another team. This sort of clause will usually operate to preclude the player from introducing evidence of oral representations from the team owners that neither the player nor the franchise would be moved.[81] In this context, the parol evidence is not offered for the purpose of defining or amplifying ambiguous terms, but rather to contradict the written document, precisely the sort of case which the parol evidence rule was intended to avoid.

Whether parol evidence will be consulted will often depend upon whether the contract is clear on its face, and in this regard courts are careful to avoid bootstrap uses of parol evidence, in which one party tries to introduce evidence which would render ambiguous, terms which are otherwise clear. Thus, a court with a proper view of the rules in this area will not allow a player to introduce extrinsic evidence to show that when he signed three separate one-year contracts for successive seasons, he really thought he was entering into one three-year agreement. Where the independent nature of the separate contracts is clear on the face of the documents, the player will be bound by that expression "even though it may not accord with the subjective intent of the parties."[82]

Before the rules excluding parol evidence can be applied, a determination must be made as to precisely what writings will be included in the final integration. The basis of the integration, of course, is the standard form contract. And, as indicated above, the final written memorial also typically includes the league's by-laws and rules, which usually become incorporated by specific reference in the standard player contract.[83] Finally, other terms in the integrated document may be added by the parties themselves. These may include both formal additions, such as no-cut clauses, or informal insertions made during earlier negotiations.[84] The degree of informality which will be acceptable is not subject to a precise test, but it is clear that courts are willing to enforce terms written in long-hand and those added on the back of a contract even when most other terms of substance are printed on the other side.[85] When terms are added by such informal notation, it is often true that they either contradict other terms or include phrases the meaning of which is not self-evident. In these cases, an ambiguity is created, and it is appropriate for the court to look beyond the contract to determine the meaning of the contract.[86]

§ 3.04. General Rules of Interpretation.

Commentators and other authorities have devoted a good deal of attention to identifying and defining the standards of interpretation which should be applied

---

81. *See* Washington Capitols Basketball Club, Inc. v. Barry, 419 F.2d 472, 479 (9th Cir.), *aff'g* 304 F. Supp. 1193 (N.D. Cal. 1969).

82. *See* Sample v. Gotham Football Club, Inc., 59 F.R.D. 160, 165 (S.D.N.Y. 1973).

83. *See* text at notes 60-70 *supra.*

84. *See* Johnson v. Green Bay Packers, Inc., 272 Wis. 149, 74 N.W.2d 784, 788-90 (1956). *See also* 3 CORBIN ON CONTRACTS § 548.

85. *See* Community Sports, Inc. v. Denver Ringsby Rockets, Inc., 429 Pa. 565, 240 A.2d 832 (1968).

86. *See* Johnson v. Green Bay Packers, Inc., 272 Wis. 149, 74 N.W.2d 784, 788-90 (1956). *See generally* MURRAY ON CONTRACTS § 122.

to give meaning to the agreement between two parties.[87] The analysis provided by these sources has general application throughout the law of contracts and, thus, applies equally to controversies which arise under sports contracts. Indeed, at least on the matter of the general rules of contract interpretation, the sports law area has not produced any special variations. However, the factual settings in the sports area are in many respects distinctive, if not unique, and these are worth noting. Hence, the discussion which follows, while based on generally accepted rules of interpretation, focuses upon those problems of interpretation which seem to recur in connection with sports contracts.

The basic question which is repeatedly presented concerns the circumstances which will justify a court in resorting to extrinsic aids and sources in interpreting the contract. Under the generally accepted view, the court is empowered to look beyond the contract in order to interpret it only if there is an ambiguity in the terms which are used. Such ambiguity is present, for example, where the parties have included a term not found in common usage.[88] But where the words which the parties used have a plain and readily understandable meaning, the court is normally to give effect to the intention of the parties as it is expressed in the words which were used.[89] Thus, it will be of no avail to a party to allege that he subjectively entertains a different understanding of the contract than that which appears on the face of the document.[90] A party is free, however, to show that the parties intended to attribute a special or uncommon meaning to an otherwise common term.[91] But this requires a showing that both sides subscribed to the uncommon meaning,[92] and apart from that special situation, courts in the sports area follow the guide of courts generally in giving to the words the meaning normally associated with them.[93] Thus, the rule emerges that a necessary first step in directing the court's attention to extrinsic aids to interpretation is to show that the words used in the contract are either ambiguous on their face or intended to connote an uncommon meaning. It will be noted that when a court looks beyond the face of the written contract and receives external evidence to aid its interpretation, it is not acting inconsistently with the parol evidence rule. The parol evidence, in this context, is consulted not for the purpose of adding to or modifying the written contract, but rather for the purpose of explaining its contents.[94]

As has already been suggested, the sports industry is one which depends heavily upon the use of pre-printed, standard form contracts to record the agreements between the various parties, particularly between teams and

---

87. *See* RESTATEMENT OF CONTRACTS §§ 226-36, 245-49 (1932); RESTATEMENT (SECOND) OF CONTRACTS §§ 226-36, 245-49 (Tent. Draft No. 5, 1970); 3 A. CORBIN, CORBIN ON CONTRACTS §§ 532-60 (1951) [hereinafter cited as CORBIN ON CONTRACTS]; J. MURRAY, MURRAY ON CONTRACTS §§ 109-23 (1974) [hereinafter cited as MURRAY ON CONTRACTS].

88. *See, e.g.,* Johnson v. Green Bay Packers, Inc., 272 Wis. 149, 74 N.W.2d 784 (1956).

89. *See* Hennigan v. Chargers Football Co., 431 F.2d 308, 314-15 (5th Cir. 1970); Sample v. Gotham Football Club, Inc., 59 F.R.D. 160, 164 (S.D.N.Y. 1973). *See also* MURRAY ON CONTRACTS §§ 109-10.

90. *See* Sample v. Gotham Football Club, Inc., 59 F.R.D. 160, 164-65 (S.D.N.Y. 1973).

91. *See* 3 CORBIN ON CONTRACTS § 542; MURRAY ON CONTRACTS § 109.

92. *See generally* MURRAY ON CONTRACTS § 109.

93. *See, e.g.,* Hennigan v. Chargers Football Co., 431 F.2d 308, 315 (5th Cir. 1970); *cf.* Keith v. Kellerman, 169 F. 196, 200 (S.D.N.Y. 1909).

94. *See* 3 CORBIN ON CONTRACTS §§ 576, 579; MURRAY ON CONTRACTS § 108.

players. Special problems of interpretation arise from the use of such form agreements. One court has characterized them as contracts of adhesion, a description which is intended to underscore the fact that the contract is typically presented to the player on a take-it-or-leave-it basis.[95] This absence of opportunity for bargaining will affect how the terms of the standard form are regarded by the court. While one might expect that the teams would take care to insure that there were no major inconsistencies or ambiguities in their agreements, that is not always the case. When a court is called upon to ascertain the meaning of an uncertain term, it may give recognition to the fact that it was the team which selected the terminology and which had the opportunity to avoid the uncertainty. Hence, a well-established rule of construction is that the terms of a contract will be construed against the party who drafted it.[96] Application of this principle requires that where a term is capable of two constructions, one favorable to a team and the other contrary to its interests, the latter construction is to be preferred.[97]

This rule has often been applied in the sports area.[98] But it should be noted that the cases on this matter were decided some time ago, and the doctrine in this area has not taken full account of modern developments. It is now generally true that the terms of the standard form player's contract are not as immune from player negotiation as they were in former times.[99] This fact should cause courts to rethink the question of whether the contracts are wholly one-sided, as once assumed. For example, in sports in which there are competing leagues, it is often true that star players entering the weaker league can secure variances in the standard agreement.[100] This is true even though league by-laws state that all contracts must be uniform. Of more general importance is the recent movement toward collective bargaining in professional sports. The players' union will usually include within its list of bargainable issues the terms of the uniform player agreement.[101] Thus, while the player may be unable to secure modifications in his individual negotiations, he may nonetheless seek changes through his collective bargaining representative. To the extent that there is labor-management bargaining about the player's agreement, the characterization of the contract as one of adhesion will have to be tempered. But each case will require an *ad hoc* assessment by the court, for the extent of actual,

95. *See* Lemat Corp. v. Barry, 275 Cal. App. 2d 671, 80 Cal. Rptr. 240, 245 (1969).
96. *See* O'Connor v. St. Louis American League Baseball Co., 193 Mo. App. 167, 181 S.W. 1167, 1174 (1916); Johnson v. Green Bay Packers, Inc., 272 Wis. 149, 74 N.W.2d 784, 791 (1956).
97. *See also* MURRAY ON CONTRACTS § 119.
98. *See* cases cited note 96 *supra*.
99. *But see* Matuszak v. Houston Oilers, Inc., 515 S.W.2d 725, 729 (Tex. Civ. App. 1974) (Tunks, J., dissenting).
100. *See, e.g.,* Munchak Corp. v. Cunningham, 457 F.2d 721, 725-26 (4th Cir. 1972).
101. *See, e.g.,* Basic Agreement Between the American League of Professional Baseball Clubs and the National League of Professional Baseball Clubs and the Major League Baseball Players Association, art. III (1973):

> The form of the Uniform Player's Contract between a Club and a Player is attached hereto as Schedule A which is incorporated herein by reference and made a part hereof. During the term of this Agreement, no other form of Uniform Player's Contract will be utilized. Should the provisions of any Contract between any individual Player and any of the Clubs be inconsistent with the terms of this Agreement, the provisions of this Agreement shall govern. Nothing herein shall limit the right of any Club and Player to enter into special covenants in the space provided in a manner not inconsistent with the provisions of this Agreement.

and even potential bargaining, will vary depending upon the sport, the strength of the union, and the particular clause involved.[102]

Another problem created by the use of standard form contracts relates to the weight to be afforded to modifying terms which conflict with the original language. In cases in which there has been individualized bargaining, it will often be true that new terms are written or typed directly onto the preprinted form. When the parties are not careful to conform the original terms of the contract to these new provisions, questions of interpretation will arise. To the extent that there is a conflict between the preprinted terms and those which are typed or written later, greatest weight will be given to the latter.[103] This same rule is applied even though the new terms are not directly integrated into the document, but rather are added more informally, as by handwriting on the back of the contract.[104] The principle which is followed here is wholly defensible, as it is intended to recognize the common sense notion that new terms added during the negotiations are more likely to be reflective of the parties' intent than those which were printed on a form even before negotiations were begun.

The terms of a contract must be interpreted in light of the commercial setting in which the contract is negotiated. That commercial setting may produce specialized definitions or otherwise unambiguous terms. A well-established rule of contract construction allows a court to consult these usages of the trade in order to give to the parties' contract the meaning which they were likely to have intended.[105] But before a trade usage can be read into a contract, the usage "must be proved to be known to the parties or be so general and well-established that knowledge and adoption of it may be presumed and it must be certain and uniform." [106] There are many terms and usages in professional sports which either are or should be known to persons who work in the industry. Courts have been responsive to this fact and have undertaken to admit such extrinsic evidence in a variety of circumstances. Thus, trade usages have applied to determine what was meant by a team's agreement not to "release" a player,[107] a club's specification that the player's contract was a "season contract," [108] and a player's agreement that the club had a "right to reserve" him for another season.[109]

The appropriateness of interpreting terms in light of their commercial meanings cannot be disputed as a general proposition. To the extent that legal issues continue to arise, it will likely be over the question of whether resorting to trade usages is appropriate in very particularized fact situations. In this connection it can be noted that courts may be hesitant to incorporate such usages

102. *See* Robertson v. National Basketball Ass'n, 389 F. Supp. 867 (S.D.N.Y. 1975); Kapp v. National Football League, 390 F. Supp. 73 (N.D. Cal. 1974).

103. *See* Egan v. Winnipeg Baseball Club, Ltd., 96 Minn. 345, 104 N.W. 947 (1905); Johnson v. Green Bay Packers, Inc., 272 Wis. 149, 74 N.W.2d 784, 785 (1956); Tollefson v. Green Bay Packers, Inc., 256 Wis. 318, 41 N.W.2d 201, 203 (1950). *See generally* 3 CORBIN ON CONTRACTS § 548; MURRAY ON CONTRACTS § 122.

104. *See, e.g.,* Johnson v. Green Bay Packers, Inc., 272 Wis. 149, 74 N.W.2d 784, 785 (1956).

105. *See generally* 3 CORBIN ON CONTRACTS §§ 555-57.

106. Baltimore Baseball Club & Exhibition Co. v. Pickett, 78 Md. 375, 28 A. 279, 280 (1894). *See also* MURRAY ON CONTRACTS § 121.

107. Egan v. Winnipeg Baseball Club, Ltd., 96 Minn. 345, 104 N.W. 947 (1905).

108. Johnson v. Green Bay Packers, Inc., 272 Wis. 149, 74 N.W.2d 784, 789 (1956).

109. Metropolitan Exhibition Co. v. Ewing, 42 F. 198, 200-02 (S.D.N.Y. 1890).

where the term could fairly be regarded as inconsistent with the parties' agreement.[110] Moreover, one can find older cases which suggest that resort to a trade usage as an aid to interpretation is appropriate only where it appears that a term would otherwise be "indefinite and equivocal." [111] But the modern, and better reasoned view recognizes that words need not be ambiguous on their face before reference to trade usages is appropriate.[112] The ultimate goal of contract interpretation is to enforce the agreement which the parties intended to make. Hence, if it can fairly be said that the parties contracted in light of a special meaning, that meaning ought to control even if the term has a different definition in ordinary usage.[113]

There are a variety of extrinsic aids in addition to trade usages which may be consulted by a court when it interprets the language of the parties' contract. While examples from sports law cases do not cover all of the possible external sources, they do illustrate the extent to which courts will look to the particular setting of the agreement to give it meaning. For example, the court in *Tollefson v. Green Bay Packers* [114] used extrinsic evidence to resolve an ambiguity in the salary term in the contract before it. One pre-printed term of the agreement specified that Tollefson's salary was to be $300 for each regularly scheduled game, while another provision gave the team the right to terminate the contract on forty-eight hours notice. During the negotiations of the contract, the club's manager had, in handwriting, added the words "minimum 3600 for season." Tollefson was cut from the team early in the season and was paid only $900 for the games he actually played. The athlete sued for the balance of the $3,600, alleging that he understood that he would receive the designated minimum salary even if he failed to exhibit sufficient skill to make the team. The club responded by arguing that the inserted language meant that Tollefson was assured of the minimum salary if he played the entire season. In concluding that the clause required payment of the player's salary even after he had been cut, the court considered, among other things, the background negotiations which led up to the contract.[115] Those negotiations revealed that the player had an offer to play for another team. Thus, in the court's view, it was not unreasonable to conclude that the parties intended the minimum salary term to provide the player with increased security so as to make this contract more attractive than that which might be offered by another team.[116]

There are other aspects of the relationship between an athlete and club which may be equally instructive in interpreting their agreement. Thus, it may be appropriate to consult other contracts which the parties have entered into concerning the same subject matter.[117] Moreover, where the breach in the parties' relationship occurs after the player's contract has been partially

---

110. *See* Baltimore Baseball Club & Exhibition Co. v. Pickett, 78 Md. 375, 28 A. 279, 280 (1894).
111. Metropolitan Exhibition Co. v. Ewing, 42 F. 198, 202 (S.D.N.Y. 1890). *See also* Dixon, Irmaos & Cia, Ltd. v. Chase Nat'l Bank, 144 F.2d 759 (2d Cir. 1944); Inman Mfg. Co. v. American Cereal Co., 133 Iowa 71, 110 N.W. 287 (1907).
112. *See* 3 CORBIN ON CONTRACTS § 555.
113. *See* MURRAY ON CONTRACTS §§ 109, 121.
114. 256 Wis. 318, 41 N.W.2d 201 (1950).
115. *See also* 3 CORBIN ON CONTRACTS §§ 536-37, 543; MURRAY ON CONTRACTS § 114.
116. 41 N.W.2d at 205. *See generally* 3 CORBIN ON CONTRACTS § 543.
117. *See, e.g.,* Metropolitan Exhibition Co. v. Ewing, 42 F. 198, 202 (S.D.N.Y. 1890).

performed, it is appropriate for the court to look at how the parties actually functioned under the contract.[118] In many cases the parties will have acted in a manner which clarifies the meaning of a particular term or clause which would have otherwise been ambiguous. Again, it should be emphasized that this resort to evidence apart from the face of the contract is quite appropriate since the context in which an agreement is negotiated and performed will be highly suggestive of what the parties understood their respective obligations to be.

There are rules of interpretation other than those mentioned above which will on occasion prove to be useful in determining the meaning of the player's agreement. As with the other rules, these embody principles which are generally applied throughout the law of contracts, and where the sports cases provide inadequate precedent for a particular point, it is appropriate to consult general contracts authorities.[119] One rule which has been particularly influential in the sports area is that which provides that contracts should, whenever possible, be construed so as to avoid rendering them illegal. It was this rule which led the court in *Central New York Basketball, Inc. v. Barnett*[120] to conclude that the option clause in the standard NBA contract ought to be interpreted to give the team a one-year option rather than an option of perpetual length, a characterization which would have rendered it unenforceable as an improper restraint on trade. Other courts have recognized that contract terms should be construed to avoid conflict with other laws and policies which would destroy the validity of the contracts.[121] Many of the other rules of interpretation have produced much less spectacular results in the sports area. Included in this category are rules such as those which admonish that specific terms in a contract are to govern more general statements in the same agreement[122] and that where two clauses of a contract appear to be in irreconcilable conflict, the clause first appearing in the contract will be given controlling weight.[123]

§ 3.05. Interpretation of Provisions Pertaining to Injuries and Physical Condition — The Basic Rights of the Parties.

One of the primary concerns of the professional athlete is the possibility that he might sustain an injury which prematurely ends his playing career. This risk is present in all sports, and in some, such as football, the risk is so high that it is almost a certainty that the player will be injured at least to the point of temporary incapacity sometime in his playing career. From an economic standpoint, the consequences of an injury can be quite severe, as the athlete's earning potential is reduced from that of a highly paid player to that of a poorly-trained, unspecialized male, who in many cases does not even have a

---

118. *See, e.g.,* Pasquel v. Owen, 186 F.2d 263, 268 (8th Cir. 1950); O'Connor v. St. Louis American League Baseball Co., 193 Mo. App. 167, 181 S.W. 1167, 1175 (1916).
119. *See generally* RESTATEMENT OF CONTRACTS §§ 235-36; 3 CORBIN ON CONTRACTS §§ 545-52; MURRAY ON CONTRACTS §§ 109-23.
120. 19 Ohio Op.2d 130, 181 N.E.2d 506 (1961).
121. *See, e.g.,* Nassau Sports v. Peters, 352 F. Supp. 870 (E.D.N.Y. 1972).
122. *See* Johnson v. Green Bay Packers, Inc., 272 Wis. 149, 74 N.W.2d 784 (1956). *See generally* 3 CORBIN ON CONTRACTS § 547.
123. *See* O'Connor v. St. Louis American League Baseball Co., 193 Mo. App. 167, 181 S.W. 1167, 1174 (1916). *See also* MURRAY ON CONTRACTS § 122.

college degree despite four years attendance at such an institution. In addition, the injured athlete faces the prospect of continued medical expenses, which may put strains on his meager non-sports earnings. In light of the potentially dramatic effects of an injury, it is not surprising that professional sports contracts include provisions detailing the respective obligations of players and team. This section will treat the contractual aspects of these injury questions. Other facets of the injury problem, including the player's potential recovery in tort [124] and under statutory workmen's compensation schemes [125] are discussed in subsequent sections.

The present discussion will indicate the respective rights and duties of the club and athlete under the terms of the most common standard player contracts. The footnotes include references to the actual language used in particular contracts to illustrate the points discussed in the text.[126] While not all of the major standard player contracts are cited in each instance, it can be noted that there is a good deal of similarity in the treatment of the injury question in the contracts used in the major professional leagues. Hence, the analysis presented here is generally applicable throughout the professional sports industry. Of course, the resolution of specific controversies which arise in practice may turn on the exact language used in the relevant contract. Thus, this analysis will not eliminate the need for careful attention to the particular terms of the applicable agreement.

The common law rule appears to be that in a contract for personal services, the employee's continuing physical capacity to render his performance is a condition precedent to the employer's obligation to pay the designated salary.[127] A disabling physical injury to the employee will permit the employer to treat his obligations under the contract as having ended. A somewhat expanded version of this same notion is found in most professional sports contracts and provides the starting point for our analysis. Under these contracts, the player typically represents that he is free from debilitating injuries. In addition, he

---

124. *See* §§ 8.06-.11 *infra.*

125. *See* § 8.13 *infra.*

126. Abbreviated forms of citation are used to identify the various contracts. The formal citations, and the shortened forms used here, are as follows: Uniform Player Contract, American Basketball Association (1973) [hereinafter cited as ABA Contract]; Uniform Player's Contract, American League of Professional Baseball Clubs (1973) (same as National League Uniform Contract) [hereinafter cited as Baseball Contract]; Uniform Player Contract (Veteran — Single Season), National Basketball Association (1976) (substantially the same as the National Basketball Association's (1) Rookie — Single Season and (2) Rookie or Veteran — Two or More Seasons Uniform Player Contracts (1976)) [hereinafter cited as NBA Contract]; Standard Player Contract, National Football League (1975) [hereinafter cited as NFL Contract]; Standard Players Contract, National Hockey League (1974) [hereinafter cited as NHL Contract]; Player's Contract, World Football League (1974) [hereinafter cited as WFL Contract]; Uniform Player's Contract, World Hockey Association (1973) [hereinafter cited as WHA Contract].

It will be noted that the NFL contract referred to above is that which was used in the 1975 season. In the 1977 collective bargaining agreement, the players and owners agreed that the standard form contract "will be revised to conform to the terms of this Agreement." Collective Bargaining Agreement Between the NFL Management Council and the NFL Players Ass'n, art. XII, § 1 (1977). A new contract form, apparently drafted by management, was put into use in 1977. At the time of this writing, the form had not been approved by the players' association and there is some question as to whether all of the terms would be found acceptable, particularly those relating to injuries. Where the new version of the contract is cited in the following discussion, it is identified as NFL Contract (1977).

127. *See, e.g.,* Hennigan v. Chargers Football Co., 431 F.2d 308, 317 (5th Cir. 1970); Strader v. Collins, 280 App. Div. 582, 585-86, 116 N.Y.S.2d 318, 322 (1952).

makes a general warranty that he is in good physical condition, which presumably means that his general overall state of physical well-being is such that he can endure the rigors of professional sports training and competition.[128] Often there is also a representation that the player will maintain himself in good physical condition throughout the season.[129] Under the normal rules of contract interpretation, these clauses would most probably be read as rendering the player's continuing physical condition a precondition to the team's duty to perform.[130] However, the clubs do not depend upon the application of such common law concepts, for the contracts themselves typically specify the consequences of a breach of these warranties by the player. Typically, the club is empowered to either suspend the player or terminate his contract.[131] In some contracts these are alternative remedies.[132] The former remedy, in one respect, is more coercive, since the suspended player is apparently still bound to the team, and thus is not free to negotiate with other teams, even though his income is temporarily interrupted.[133]

While the club does demand that the player maintain a good physical condition, it does not shift the risk of injuries completely to the player. With respect to certain types of injuries the team specifically accepts responsibility under the terms of the contract. There are basically two questions which are addressed by contract provisions pertaining to injuries: (1) what types of injuries is the team responsible for under the contract? and (2) what is the extent of its responsibility? It will be seen that the team typically accepts responsibility only for injuries arising from performance under the contract and then only for a portion of the loss incurred in connection with those injuries.

In answering the first question about the types of injuries for which the team accepts responsibility, it is useful to classify injuries by their relationship to the playing season and the athlete's performance under the contract. The injury provisions in a typical standard form player contract include language which is intended to exclude certain types of injuries from the scope of the team's responsibility. The critical language is an amplification of the player's basic warranty of physical fitness and usually gives the team the right to terminate or suspend the athlete if he fails to pass the physical examination administered at the commencement of the season.[134] The initial examination serves as a

128. Illustrative of this type of warranty is the NBA provision: "The Player agrees (a) to report at the time and place fixed by the Club in good physical condition; [and] (b) to keep himself throughout the entire season in good physical condition. . . ." NBA Contract ¶ 5.

129. *See id.*

130. *See* authorities cited at note 127 *supra.*

131. For example, one provision of the NBA Contract gives the team the remedy which would be available at common law:

> The Club may terminate this contract . . . if the Player shall . . .
> (1) . . . fail, refuse or neglect . . . to keep himself in first class physical condition. . . . *Id.*
> ¶ 20(b)(1).

Another clause in the contract provides that if the athlete is not in good physical condition at the start of the season or if his condition deteriorates thereafter, the club has the right to suspend the player and withhold his salary for the period of suspension. *Id.* at ¶ 6(a).

132. *See* NBA Contract, *supra* note 131. Under the NHL contract, the club appears to be given only the power to suspend the player. *Compare* NHL Contract ¶ 5 *with id.* ¶ 13.

133. *See* § 3.07 *infra.*

134. Illustrative of this type of provision is paragraph 5 of the NHL Contract:

> If the Player, in the sole judgment of the Club's physician, is disabled or is not in good physical condition at the commencement of the season or at any subsequent time during

screening device which enables the team to avoid responsibility for certain types of injuries. For example, the team may invoke the contract to preclude the player who has incurred an off-season injury from receiving his salary. A more important effect of such clause is not spelled out, but nonetheless arises by implication. Player contracts often cover only one season. A player who sustained a disabling injury while playing for the team in a prior season will not be able to pass the physical exam and, thus, the club may avoid responsibility for these injuries as well.[135]

But just as the contract enables the club to avoid liability for some injuries and physical defects, the contract also gives express recognition to the club's responsibility for other physical impairments. Typically, the club accepts liability for injuries to the player sustained in his performance under the contract. Various phrases are used to identify the types of injuries for which compensation will be provided. Under some contracts, the athlete must be injured while playing for the club,[136] while in others the covered class of injuries is potentially broadened by language which covers all performances under the contract.[137] With one possible exception, the contracts generally avoid phrasing which makes the team contractually liable for all injuries arising in the "course and scope" of the athlete's employment.[138]

Although the precise contours of some of these phrases will be in doubt until tested in a court or arbitration proceeding, some conclusions can be reached concerning their scope. It is clear, for example, that the team's responsibility extends to injuries sustained in the course of regular season competition. Also apparently covered would be those injuries sustained in practice sessions during the regular season. And, while the language of some contracts leaves some room

---

the season (unless such condition is the direct result of playing hockey for the Club) . . . it is mutually agreed that the Club shall have the right to suspend the Player for such period of disability or unfitness, and no compensation shall be paid for that period under the contract.

Very similar language is found in the NBA Contract ¶ 6(a), WFL Contract ¶ 7.1, WHA Contract ¶ 5.1, and ABA Contract ¶ 4(a).

135. *See* Hennigan v. Chargers Football Co., 431 F.2d 308 (5th Cir. 1970); Sample v. Gotham Football Club, Inc., 59 F.R.D. 160 (S.D.N.Y. 1973).

136. Under the NHL Contract, for example, the team accepts responsibility for "Player's injuries resulting directly from his playing for the Club . . . ." *Id.* ¶ 5.

137. Under the NFL Contract, the club accepts responsibility "if Player is injured in the performance of his services under this contract." NFL Contract ¶ 8 (1977). The suggestion that this language is potentially more inclusive is premised on the notion that the "services" required under the contract include more than merely playing for the club. The term "services" arguably includes any action taken by the player on behalf of the club, including travel with the team and participation in publicity events. *Cf.* Matuszak v. Houston Oilers, Inc., 515 S.W.2d 725 (Tex. Civ. App. 1974); World Football League v. Dallas Cowboys Football Club, Inc., 513 S.W.2d 102, 105 (Tex. Civ. App. 1974).

138. The most confusing of the phrases describing the scope of the club's liability is found in the NBA Contract. The contract, interestingly, has two different clauses obligating the team to continue the salary of an injured player. In one provision, the team's responsibility is said to arise if "the Player's injuries resulted directly from playing for the Club . . . ." NBA Contract ¶ 6(b). But in a subsequent clause dealing with the club's liability under a terminated contract, it is provided that the club will be liable for salary if the contract is terminated as a result of an injury "sustained in the course and within the scope of his employment hereunder . . . ." NBA Contract ¶ 20(c). As is well illustrated in the area of workmen's compensation law, the "course and scope" of one's employment may encompass much more than his performance of the particular task for which he was primarily employed. *See* 1 A. LARSON, THE LAW OF WORKMEN'S COMPENSATION §§ 27.00-.40 (1972).

for doubt, whatever liability the club has assumed would seem to extend to injuries sustained in pre-season training camps and exhibition games. Indeed, some of the litigated cases have involved pre-season injuries, and the team's liability for such impairments has generally been either assumed by the court or posited by the parties.[139] By the same token some injuries occurring during the season are excluded, more specifically those arising from activities unrelated to the contract. While this can reasonably be implied from the contract language in most cases, it is expressly recognized in contract-related documents in some sports.[140]

Once the types of injuries for which the club assumes liability have been identified, it is necessary to determine the extent of its liability. In general, the standard form contracts indicate in fairly precise terms the sorts of losses for which the club agrees to provide compensation. These are primarily of two types: (1) expenses for medical treatment and hospitalization and (2) loss of salary due to the injury. A typical provision covering medical expenses will obligate the team to pay the cost of hospitalization and hospital-related services as well as doctor's bills.[141] Often the club will retain the right to select the hospital and doctors to be utilized.[142] The time limit on the club's responsibility is not uniform among the various sports. In some cases, the team will pay medical expenses only for a stated number of weeks or months.[143] In others, the only apparent limitation is the length of the contract itself.[144] The printed terms of the contract do not give a complete picture of the protection which the player enjoys for it will often be true that the club or the player maintains a medical insurance policy which will cover injuries sustained on the playing field.[145] Such a policy may well provide the player with protection in the event of long-term or catastrophic disability not fully covered under the compensation provisions of the contract.

The typical salary-continuation clause provides that if the player is disabled as a result of an injury sustained while performing under the contract, his salary will be paid, at the normal contract rate, for the remainder of the season in which

---

139. *See* Sample v. Gotham Football Club, Inc., 59 F.R.D. 160 (S.D. N.Y. 1973); Schultz v. Los Angeles Dons, 107 Cal. App. 2d 718, 238 P.2d 73 (1951); Tillman v. New Orleans Saints Football Club, 265 So. 2d 284 (La. App. 1972); Houston Oilers, Inc. v. Floyd, 518 S.W.2d 836 (Tex. Civ. App. 1975).

140. For example, the collective bargaining agreement between the NFL clubs and the NFL Players Association establishes a procedure for resolving disputes concerning injuries. The agreement sets forth certain defenses which the club may raise. One of these is "[t]hat the player's injury arose solely from a non-football related cause subsequent to the physical examination. . . ." Collective Bargaining Agreement Between the NFL Management Council and the NFL Players Association, art. IX, § 3(d) (1977).

141. *See, e.g.,* NHL Contract ¶ 5:

> . . . the Club will pay the Player's reasonable hospitalization until discharged from the hospital, and his medical expenses and doctor's bills, provided that the hospital and doctor are selected by the Club and provided further that the Club's obligation to pay such expenses shall terminate at a period not more than six months after the injury.

142. *See* NHL Contract ¶ 5, *supra* note 141.

143. *See, e.g., id.* (six months).

144. *See, e.g.,* NFL Contract ¶ 14.

145. *See, e.g.,* Collective Bargaining Agreement Between the NFL Management Council and the NFL Players Association, art. VI, § 4 (1970):

> [T]he Member Clubs agree that all players and their families shall be covered during the four years beginning April 1, 1970, by a group major medical policy with benefits equal to those in effect during the 1969 season.

the injury occurs.[146] It is also specified in most contracts that the club's liability will be reduced by any award which the player receives under a governmental workmen's compensation scheme.[147] The duration of the player's rights under a salary continuation clause is not always clear. For example, a player who has signed a multi-year contract may assert that his salary should be continued through all the years remaining under the contract while the club may contend that it is obligated to pay only the salary due for the remainder of the particular season in which the injury occurred. In analyzing the problems presented in this situation, a number of points can be made. As an initial matter, it is necessary to distinguish contracts which include "no-cut" provisions. These raise special problems of interpretation, and discussion of them is undertaken in a subsequent section.[148] Another matter to consider, of course, is the language of the particular contract involved, for many contracts now are fairly specific in stipulating that the team's duty to continue the player's salary is only for the remainder of the year in which the injury occurs.[149]

There is a limited body of case law which bears on this question. In *Sample v. Gotham Football Club, Inc.,*[150] the issue was whether a player who had signed three one-year contracts was entitled to his salary for the third year following a disabling injury in the course of the second season. In *Hennigan v. Chargers Football Company,*[151] a similar suit for compensation was filed by a player who was injured in the last year of a three-year contract. The specific dispute concerned whether the athlete was entitled to be paid for the option year when his option was exercised after he had been injured. In both cases, the player was denied compensation for any period beyond the season in which the injury occurred. While each case has some facts which give rise to arguments wholly peculiar to the particular situation, a common issue which underlies them is whether the year for which compensation is sought can be said to be governed by the same contract under which the player was injured. Each court read the

---

146. *See, e.g.,* NBA Contract ¶ 6(b): "If in the judgment of the Club's physician, the Player's injuries resulted directly from playing for the Club and render him unfit to play skilled basketball, then, so long as such unfitness continues, but in no event beyond the term of one year . . ., the Club shall pay to the Player the compensation prescribed in . . . this contract." *See also* NHL Contract ¶ 5; ABA Contract ¶ 4(b)(1); WHA Contract ¶ 5.3; WFL Contract ¶ 7.3.

In some leagues, the collective bargaining agreement between the players and owners broadens the club's liability for injury-related payments. For example, the 1977 NFL collective bargaining agreement provides for an "injury protection benefit" under which a player may receive monetary payments in the season following that in which he is injured. This benefit is in addition to the player's right to receive his salary for the season in which the injury is sustained. The amount of the benefit is the greater of $37,500 or 50% of the player's salary for the season following the injury. The benefit is available if (a) the player is unable to play in the last game of the season of injury or undergoes club authorized surgery, and (b) the player undergoes any rehabilitation treatment ordered by the club, and (c) the player is cut in the next season because he cannot pass the pre-season physical examination in the following year due to the prior year's injury. *See* Collective Bargaining Agreement Between the NFL Management Council and NFL Players Ass'n, art. X (1977).

147. *See, e.g.,* NBA Contract ¶ 6(b). *See also* Houston Oilers, Inc. v. Floyd, 518 S.W.2d 836, 837 (Tex. Civ. App. 1975).

148. *See* § 3.09 *infra.*

149. Thus, the team's obligation under the NBA contract will not extend "beyond the term of one year" (NBA Contract ¶ 6(b)), under the NHL contract, "beyond the end of the current season" (NHL Contract ¶ 5) and under the ABA contract, "beyond the playing season during which such injury occurred" (ABA Contract ¶ 4(b)(1)).

150. 59 F.R.D. 160 (S.D.N.Y. 1973).

151. 431 F.2d 308 (5th Cir. 1970).

team's obligation for salary to continue no longer than the term of the contract pursuant to which the player was rendering his services at the time of his injury. Support for such a construction is found in the applicable contracts which in each case provided that the player was to be paid "in the event that [he] is injured in the performance of his services *under this contract.*" [152] Thus, in *Sample* the court found that each of the one-year agreements was intended to operate as a separate contract, and not as part of an integrated three-year contract.[153] In the same vein, the contract which resulted from the Chargers exercise of its option rights was regarded as a contract distinct from the one under which Hennigan was injured.[154]

The result in *Sample* is fully defensible once one accepts the court's premise that the parties did not manifest an intention to have a single three-year agreement. It would then seem to follow that the purpose of the contracts covering future years was only to peg the player's salary for those periods and not to relieve the player from annually establishing his physical fitness as a condition precedent to the club's obligation to perform.[155]

The *Hennigan* holding has less appeal on the surface, for the option which the Chargers had was an option to renew Hennigan's contract "on the same terms as are provided by [the original] contract." [156] One of the terms of the original contract was that which obligated the club to pay the player's salary in the event he was injured "in the performance of services under this contract." [157] Hence, it could be reasonably argued that one of the terms which continued upon exercise of the option was the obligation to pay the injured player's salary. It was only over a strong dissent that the court dismissed this contention.[158] While the majority opinion strains its analysis in finding a fine distinction between an "extension" and a "renewal" of the contract, it does eventually explain the ultimate result of the case with a rationale which is persuasive in its pragmatism. In the court's view, the player's suggested reading of the option clause would put the team to a decision which was so fraught with risk as not likely to have been intended when the contract was drafted. If the team's obligation to pay the injured player's salary continued into the option year, the team would be

---

152. *See* NFL Contract ¶ 14 cited 431 F.2d at 311, and 59 F.R.D. at 162-63.

153. 59 F.R.D. at 165-66.

154. 431 F.2d at 315-18.

155. There is some evidence that clubs are now more careful in characterizing the nature of the arrangement when they sign a player for more than one year:

> Clubs now are specifying when they announce signings for more than one season that the player has been given "a series of one-year contracts" instead of the former "multi-year contract."
>
> ... The players' union had argued that if a player was sidelined permanently by an injury in the first year of a "multi-year contract" that he be paid for the rest of the contract. The clubs specify that a player must pass a physical before every season of the "one-year contracts." Washington Post, May 16, 1976, at D6, col. 4.

The Uniform Player Contract (Rookie or Veteran — Two or More Seasons), National Basketball Association ¶ 6(b) (1976) expressly provides that the Club's obligation to pay the player following his injury shall not continue "after the Player has received his full salary for the season in which the injury was sustained. . . ."

156. *See id.* at 311.

157. *Id. See also* note 137 *supra*.

158. *See* 431 F.2d at 318 (Clark, J., dissenting).

faced with the prospect of having to choose to retain the player or lose him to another team, not knowing whether the player's physical condition was such that he would be able to play.[159] If the club exercised the option and had guessed wrong about the player's condition, the cost of this error would have been the amount of the player's salary. The court apparently felt that the contract terms were intended to provide the club something in the nature of a right of first refusal, rather than the extremely high risk choice which the plaintiff proposed in *Hennigan.*

Apart from the limitation on the duration of the club's obligation, there are other respects in which the contract language serves to limit the club's exposure to liability. It is clear from the terms of the contracts that the team does not obligate itself to provide compensation for all of the losses which a player might sustain. For example, the player has no contractual right to reimbursement for long-term medical expenses, such as those incurred after the expiration of the period designated in the contract and not otherwise covered by medical insurance. Thus, if two years after he has been cut by the team the athlete discovers that he needs extensive knee surgery, he cannot look for reimbursement under the contract. This is true even though the injury which necessitates the operation was sustained during the contract period. Other losses are similarly not within the team's contractual obligation. One important loss impliedly excluded under the contract is that resulting from the injury itself, including loss of physical capacity, diminution of future earning capacity, pain and suffering, and so on. Does the athlete have any legal avenue apart from the contract through which to secure compensation for these losses? The lawyer representing the athlete will want to explore at least two legal alternatives, one based on a tort theory and the other on the player's rights under the applicable workmen's compensation system. Subsequent portions of this book consider both the workmen's compensation question [160] and the potential for tort actions against the team,[161] those who manufacture protective equipment,[162] and others connected with professional sports operations.[163] For the present section, it is sufficient to note that any attempted tort litigation against the team may have to deal with a contractual provision releasing the club from liability beyond that specified in the agreement.[164] The legal effect of such releases must be tested against the general principles which define the extent to which a party can contract out of liability for his tortious conduct.[165]

---

159. *See id.* at 317.

160. *See* §§ 8.12-.15 *infra.*

161. *See* § 8.02 *infra.*

162. *See* §§ 8.09-.11 *infra.*

163. *See* §§ 8.02, 8.06-.07 *infra.*

164. Illustrative of these provisions is that found in the NBA contract. In the paragraph which states the club's liability for medical expenses and salary in the event of a contract-related injury, it is provided that "the Player hereby releases the Club from any and every other obligation or liability arising out of any such injuries." NBA Contract ¶ 6(b). *See also* NHL Contract ¶ 5; WHA Contract ¶ 5.3.

165. *See* § 8.04 *infra.*

§ 3.06. Determination of Club's Responsibility for Injuries.

a. Conditions Precedent to the Club's Liability. Under most professional sports contracts, the team's obligation to compensate the athlete for medical expenses and salary arises only if two preconditions are met. Typically the contract requires the player to establish that the injury arose in the course of his performance under the contract and, further, that notice of the injury was given within a time period specified in the agreement. Each of these requirements presents distinct problems of interpretation.

The issue of whether the injury arose during the player's performance under the contract is essentially a question of causation: was the cause of the injury one which can be related directly to the athlete's participation in practice or competition under the current contract, or was the injury a result of some action or condition which arose prior to the contract or in the course of an off-the-field activity? In many cases, this determination will be a difficult one, for injuries often have no single cause, or at least no single cause which is readily identifiable. Often a disability is the result of the combined effects of a single blow and a subsequent long-term deterioration of physical condition. Similarly, the disabling characteristic of a particular injury may not appear immediately, but only after the athlete has resumed playing for a period of time. This period may be weeks or months in length and extend beyond the contract term.

While the issue in these cases is difficult, it involves the sort of determination which legal institutions are perfectly well prepared to make. Indeed, courts and arbitrators are constantly asked to sift through complex fact situations to decide whether a particular action was or was not the cause of a given injury.[166] There is no reason to expect that they will be any less expert at making a similar determination in the present context.

A case which illustrates the type of analysis which may be undertaken is *Schultz v. Los Angeles Dons, Inc.*[167] In that case, the athlete sued to recover the balance of his salary under his contract, alleging that he had been discharged without pay following a disabling injury sustained in pre-season practice. The basic question was whether the cause of the disability was attributable to the four days of practice in which the athlete engaged or some condition which pre-dated the current contract. The court's decision, which affirms a lower court finding that the team was liable, is important for two reasons. First, it serves to underscore the critical importance of the pre-season physical examination in these controversies over causation. Second, the court's analysis comes very close to announcing a rule *of res ipsa loquitur* on this matter of causation.

Schultz, the athlete involved, had suffered a debilitating back injury in a prior season. When he reported for the current season with the Dons, who apparently had full knowledge of this condition, he was examined by two different physicians selected by the team. Both physicians reported that he was in excellent condition and did not have any symptoms suggesting a continuation of the prior back problem. But then after only four days of pre-season practice, he developed pain and numbness in his legs. The club cut him from the roster,

---

166. *See generally* W. PROSSER, HANDBOOK OF THE LAW OF TORTS §§ 41-45 (1971) [hereinafter cited as PROSSER, TORTS].
167. 107 Cal. App. 2d 718, 238 P.2d 73 (1951).

contending that he had breached his contractual promise to report in good physical condition.

In affirming that the team was liable, the court accepted the lower court's finding that the athlete had reported in good condition and without prior impairment. The apparent bases of this finding were the certifications made by the team-designated physicians. Thus, those examinations, whether accurate or not, made it very difficult for the club to argue that the prior injury was the cause of the disability. The continued effects of that earlier injury had been specifically discounted by the team's own agents. As the club had greater control than the player over the conducting of the exam, its implicit attack on the findings was understandably met with skepticism.

Once the court was able to find that the athlete was in good physical condition at the start of the training season, it seemed that, *ipso facto,* the subsequent disability occurred in the course of the athlete's performance under the contract. In the court's view:

> [T]he injury that caused respondent's disability must have been suffered after the execution of the contract. The only evidence offered or received of respondent's activities, after the contract date, whereby he could have been injured as found was that he had engaged in a strenuous conditioning program and during the four days of training, before his disability developed, had engaged in two scrimmages involving violent contacts with other players. Under such a state of the record the only finding that could reasonably have been made in that regard was that the injury causing respondent's disability was suffered during the performance of the required services.[168]

While this analysis does not present a true *res ipsa* situation,[169] it does suggest a method of analysis which effectively shifts to the team the burden of refuting the natural inference that the rigors of the athletic activities caused the injury. It can be emphasized again that the initial physician's certification effectively laid the groundwork for this inference as to causation. Had the findings of that examination been more equivocal, the court could not have dismissed other possible causes as readily as it did.[170]

---

168. *Id.* at 724-25, 238 P.2d at 76-77.

169. *See* Prosser, Torts §§ 39-40.

170. The situation considered in *Schultz* continues to be a major source of concern in the NFL. The problem arises with respect to a player who has suffered a serious injury in a prior season and then rejoins the team in the current season. If the player's contract is then terminated after a period of play in the current season, the question arises as to whether the team must pay the balance of the player's salary. In order to analyze this question, it is useful to distinguish between two different reasons which the club might give for its action. On the one hand, the club might contend that because of the lingering effects of the prior season's injury, the player was not physically fit at the time he entered training camp and thus breached his promise to report in good physical condition. The *Schultz* case suggests that once the player has passed the initial physical examination, a court or arbitrator should be reluctant to accept the team's characterization of the reason for the termination. This approach of giving controlling effect to a positive determination by the club's physician in the initial physical has been institutionalized in the collective bargaining agreement between the NFL owners and players. In the section dealing with injury grievances, it is provided that:

> If the player passes the physical examination of the club at the beginning of the pre-season training camp for the year in question, having made full and complete disclosure of his known physical and mental condition when questioned by the club physician during the physical examination, it will be presumed that such player was physically fit to play football on the date he reported.

The team has a legitimate interest in being informed of any injury sustained by its players in the course of a season or pre-season. Prompt notification will

Collective Bargaining Agreement Between the NFL Management Council and the NFL Players Ass'n, art. IX, § 2 (1977). In addition, the agreement lists a number of defenses which the club may raise to avoid liability. One of these is that the player did not pass the physical examination administered at the beginning of the pre-season training period. However, it is also stipulated that "This defense will not be available if the player participated in any team drills following his physical examination or in any pre-season or regular season game . . . ." *Id.* at art. IX, § 3(a). Thus, where the player actually joins the club in practices or games, the club cannot object that he did not enter the season in adequate physical condition.

When the player is eventually cut, however, there is a different justification which the team might put forth. Rather than asserting that the player lacked sufficient physical capacity, the club may assert that he was cut because he failed to exhibit sufficient skill compared to other players competing for positions on the club's roster. In these situations, the player will often assert that the reason for his decreased performance was that he had sustained a new injury in the current season. If the player is correct, he would be entitled to the balance of his salary. On the other hand, if the club is correct that the player simply was not able to perform up to the required standard — because of the lingering effects of the prior injury or otherwise — it would be free to cut the player without any further obligation on its part, just as it would be free to terminate any player who failed to exhibit sufficient skill. Thus, the basic question is one of causation — was there a new injury which affected the player's performance, or was the cause of the player's reduced skill the impairment resulting from an injury in the prior season?

The injury arbitration procedures used in the NFL have produced some decisions which bear on this question. (The injury arbitration procedure is described more fully in note 188 *infra*). For example, several arbitrators have adopted the view expressed in *In re* McCauley (Atlanta Falcons), Aug. 27, 1974 (Smith, Arbitrator):

> In a case like this — and there must be many in professional football — where a player enters a football season with a history of past injuries and yet is deemed not as yet physically incapacitated although possessing less physical capacity of certain kinds than he would have had but for the past injury or injuries, it seems to me that Article XI ought not to result, and was not intended to result, in salary liability for the year in which the player is terminated unless —
> (a) the pre-season physical evaluation was clearly wrong, and, in fact the player was even then physically incapacitated because of the prior injury or injuries, and his subsequent termination can properly be attributed to that incapacity and thus was in a sense chargeable to the Club's inadequate "physical," or
> (b) during the season there occurs a new football injury which . . . may reasonably be held to have contributed to the Club's decision to terminate the player, or
> (c) during the season there occurs through football participation a substantial aggravation of a prior injury, either associated with some specific incident (a blow, hit, or other traumatic event), or, contrary to prior expectations, simply as the result of the general physical stress of football practice and play, and this had the effect of reducing the player's physical capacity below the level anticipated at the time of his pre-season "physical", and such *reduction* in comparative capacity may reasonably be held to have contributed to the decision to terminate him.
> The rationale underlying this analysis, particularly with respect to the type (c) situation, is my belief that it is unreasonable to suppose the NFL clubs, or the NFLPA, or indeed the players, themselves, would deliberately have sought to produce a result where a history of prior football injuries would involve such risk to a club in connection with its decision whether or not to continue with the player for another contract year, or with its decision whether or not to trade for a player, that there would be a substantial reduction in the player's chances of continuing in professional football despite his desire to do so; or, to produce a result which would deprive a club, in effect, of the right to take into account, as a basis for terminating a contract with a player, without continuing salary liability, a non-disabling physical limitation which, at the outset, was known both to the player and to the club and despite which the player was willing to enter competition in an attempt to "make the team" and the clubs was willing to permit him to do so . . . .

Quoted in In re Williams (Washington Redskins), Mar. 15, 1977 at 25-26 (Stark, Arbitrator).

The view expressed here is similar to that suggested as a rationale for *Hennigan v. Chargers Football Company,* which is discussed in the text at notes 151-59, § 3.05 *supra.* As a matter of contract interpretation, it seems unlikely that the parties intended that if a club decided to give a previously injured player another chance to make the team, the club would automatically be

insure that the team can arrange for expert medical treatment immediately and thereby prevent any aggravation of the injury. Such timely action will serve a two-fold purpose as it enables the team to both protect its investment in the player and minimize its exposure to liability under the injury compensation provisions of the contract.[171] In order to protect its interests, the club often includes a contract provision which requires that the player give prompt notice of any injuries he sustains.[172] Some contracts expressly provide that such notification is a condition precedent to the club's liability for the injury,[173] while others do not.[174]

Where notice is a precondition to the team's duty to perform, legal disputes are likely to arise when the player either fails to give notice in the proper form or fails to give it within the time period specified. While the contract may be specific both as to the requirement of a writing and the matter of timeliness, the case law makes clear that the team will not always be allowed to insist upon precise compliance with the letter of the contract. With respect to each condition, the question to be asked is whether exact compliance was so essential to the operation of the agreement that the player can justly be held to have forfeited important rights when the form of his notice varied from that which was required.[175] In actual cases, this general question is translated into the specific doctrine of waiver, estoppel and excuse of conditions. Hence, when a contract required the player to give notice in writing and the player instead gave the team all the necessary information in non-written form, the court concluded that the team, by proceeding to act on the notice as given, had waived its right to insist upon written notice.[176] It was noted that the team was "as fully protected as if the required information had been given in writing" and a further written notice "would have been an idle act." [177] Where the player delays in giving notice, it may similarly be found that the time period specified in the contract has been waived.[178] This will often be the case where the team proceeds to act

---

responsible for his salary. Imposing such a heavy cost on the decision would likely discourage clubs from giving the player a second chance, and neither the interests of the club nor the interests of the player would be served by such a result. On the other hand, it would be going too far to suggest that a previously injured player who did earn the right to play waived his right to claim the benefit of the salary-continuation provision in his contract. Thus, if a new injury-occurrence can be shown, the contract rules on compensation should apply.

It will be noted that the issue considered here bears a close relationship to that which arose in *Tillman v. New Orleans Saints Football Club,* discussed at notes 182-84.

     171. *See* Schultz v. Los Angeles Dons, Inc., 107 Cal. App. 2d 718, 724, 238 P.2d 73, 76 (1951).

     172. Under the former NFL contract, for example, the team's obligation to pay medical expenses and continue the athlete's salary arose only "in the event the Player is injured . . . under this contract, and if Player gives written notice to the Club Physician of such injury within thirty-six (36) hours of its occurrence. . . ." NFL Contract ¶ 14 (1975). A more recent version of the NFL contract simply requires that the player must "promptly report" his injury. NFL Contract ¶ 9 (1977). (Shortened citation form used to refer to the various standard player contracts is explained in note 126, § 3.05, *supra.*

By contrast, the NHL contract omits any reference to a requirement that the club be notified of the player's injuries. *See* NHL Contract ¶ 5.

     173. *See id.*

     174. *See* NBA Contract ¶ 7. *See generally* 3A A. CORBIN, CORBIN ON CONTRACTS § 724, n. 63 (1951) [hereinafter cited as CORBIN ON CONTRACTS].

     175. *See generally* 3A CORBIN ON CONTRACTS §§ 722-23, 752, 759.

     176. *See* Schultz v. Los Angeles Dons, Inc., 107 Cal. App. 2d 718, 724, 238 P.2d 73, 76 (1951).

     177. *Id.* at 724, 238 P.2d at 76. *Cf.* Tillman v. New Orleans Saints Football Club, 265 So. 2d 284, 288-89 (La. App. 1972).

     178. *See generally* 3A CORBIN ON CONTRACTS § 722.

on the belated notice without raising an objection. But even where an immediate objection is raised, it is still necessary to find that time was of the essence under the contract.[179] Moreover, most courts will permit inquiry into the issue of whether the notice period under the contract is of reasonable duration.[180] In the case of sports contracts, resolution of this question would seem to require that a conclusion be reached about the likely consequences of any delay. Moreover, it would seemingly be relevant to inquire as to whether the rule was uniformly enforced, for if it was not, that fact would tend to undermine any argument by the club about the immediacy of its need for notice.

As the foregoing discussion suggests, a club will often not be able to avoid liability under the injury-compensation provisions of its contract merely because of the athlete's dereliction in giving formal notice of the injury. In many cases, the club will have sufficient notice of the injury simply because it occurred during a practice session or game observed by club personnel. Moreover, even where the injury or its effects are not immediately appreciated, the club may react in a manner which strongly suggests that it has waived its right to object to the intervening delay. Thus, the team's medical personnel may undertake to treat the injury and begin a program of rehabilitation to enable the athlete to return to the team. As suggested above, if this period of treatment proceeds without objection by the team, the basis will have been laid for a finding that the club had relinquished its right to insist upon immediate notice. This is not to suggest, however, that a contract provision requiring notice is to be ignored. As mentioned, the club has legitimate reason for insisting that it be informed of an injury as soon as possible after it occurs. Thus, in some cases, a failure to give notice of an injury within a reasonable time may preclude the athlete's claim for compensation. This would be true, for example, when it can be shown that the delay resulted in an aggravation of the injury which could have been prevented by more prompt medical attention.

b. Determination of Player Fitness. It is obvious that the question of the athlete's physical fitness is one of considerable importance in determining his rights under his contract. And it follows that of equal importance are the procedures and standards which are used to resolve any disputes as to fitness. Under the typical professional contract, there are three different times at which the question of the player's fitness to play may be drawn into sharp focus. First is the physical examination given the player when he reports to pre-season training camp. If the athlete fails this examination, he may usually be suspended without pay or his contract may be terminated.[181] The second critical determination will be at the point at which the player receives a serious injury while performing under the contract. Here a decision will have to be made whether the athlete is fit to continue. If he is found not to be, then he will continue to be a drain on the club's payroll without contributing to its revenue-producing ventures on the field. This is not to suggest that the player

---

179. *See generally id.* § 713.
180. *See generally id.* § 723.
181. *See, e.g.,* NBA Contract ¶¶ 6(a), 20(b)(1).
   There is very little non-technical literature on the actual practices followed by team physicians in evaluating the player's condition. General discussions of related issues can be found, however. *See* Ryan, *Medical Practices in Sports,* 38 LAW & CONTEMP. PROB. 99 (1973).

himself may not be displeased with a finding that he is disabled, for he may lose his playing position to a teammate who uses the period of the disability to sharpen his talents. Finally, once a player has been found to be disabled as a result of a contract-related injury, there will subsequently be another medical review to determine his fitness to return to play. This decision may have even greater consequences than those which immediately followed the injury.

A case which serves to underscore the importance of the decisions made as to the player's physical fitness is *Tillman v. New Orleans Saints Football Club*.[182] Tillman had injured his knee in a pre-season practice drill and later underwent an operation to repair the damage. After a period of recuperation, he was instructed to return to camp to begin an exercise program. Later the team physician declared that he was physically fit to return to full duty. Tillman's performance thereafter apparently did not measure up to the standards required to make the team, and he was cut from the squad. The consequence was that he lost his right to further salary for the season. Tillman disputed the physician's conclusion as to his fitness, and contended that since he was still suffering from an injury incurred in performance of the contract, he should have received the remainder of his salary under the salary-continuation clause. The court accepted the physician's finding of fitness, and thus rejected the player's contention. The case illustrates the point that once the player is disabled by an injury received in his performance under the contract, he is entitled to continue to receive his salary as long as the team physician declares him to be unfit to return to full playing duty, or until the expiration of the contract. After the period of rehabilitation, a critical decision is committed to the physician's discretion. If the player is still found not to be fit, then he can continue to draw his salary. But if the opposite conclusion is reached, the athlete must rejoin the team. The question then arises as to whether he still exhibits the minimum degree of skill necessary to make the team. If he does not, his contract may be cancelled and his salary terminated.[183]

This analysis suggests the important difference between an athlete's fitness and his skill under the existing professional sports contracts. Even where there is residual disability from the prior injury, the athlete may still be declared physically fit to resume play.[184] When the player returns to full duty, the lasting effects of the prior injury may have reduced his level of athletic finesse, so that he no longer exhibits the skill which he once had. And his new, reduced level of achievement may not be sufficient to warrant his retention by the team, with the ultimate consequence that his contract is terminated.

In light of the foregoing, it should be apparent that the procedures used to determine the athlete's fitness are of critical importance. There are some differences under the contracts in the various sports on the issue of who is empowered to make decisions as to the player's physical fitness. Each of the three decisions identified above could be committed to the sole discretion of a

---

182. 265 So. 2d 284 (La. App. 1972). *See also* Houston Oilers, Inc. v. Floyd, 518 S.W.2d 836 (Tex. Civ. App. 1975).

183. *See, e.g.,* NFL Contract ¶ 6 (1975); NFL Contract ¶ 11 (1977).

184. *See* Tillman v. New Orleans Saints Football Club, 265 So. 2d 284, 286 (La. App. 1972). *See also* Houston Oilers, Inc. v. Floyd, 518 S.W.2d 836 (Tex. Civ. App. 1975).

physician designated by the club.[185] Other contracts make distinctions between the three types of decisions. Under some agreements, the team physician is given sole discretion in evaluating the results of the pre-season physical examination, but while the team physician may make the initial determination of the player's fitness in other situations, procedures are established to provide independent review of a finding which is adverse to the athlete.[186] This is an area in which the emergence of collective bargaining has had a major impact on league practices. In several leagues, the players' associations have succeeded in bargaining for procedures which allow a player to have the club's fitness determination submitted to arbitration.[187] As might be expected, the types of arbitration procedures used and the standard of review to be applied vary from league to league.[188] It can be noted that controversies will most frequently arise in circumstances such as those in *Tillman* where a player alleges that he is not physically able to return to duty following a contract-related injury. The player may feel that if he were ordered to rejoin the team, he would subsequently be found to lack sufficient skill, and thus have his contract terminated.[189]

Apart from requiring that the athlete be physically able to perform the services required of him, the typical professional sports contract does not attempt to specify in detail the standard which will be applied to determine fitness.[190] But this is not to suggest that legal institutions will be presented with extensive arguments about whether the player was capable of continuing to

---

185. *See, e.g.,* NBA Contract ¶ 6 (1971). *See also* Standard Player's Contract, Canadian Football League ¶¶ 6, 21 (19—). The new NBA player contracts provide that disputes as to whether the player (1) is in sufficiently good physical condition to play skilled basketball, (2) was injured as a direct result of playing basketball, or (3) remains unfit to return to the active roster, shall be resolved in the manner provided by the collective bargaining agreement in existence between the league and the players association. NBA Contract ¶ 6(c).

186. *See, e.g.,* NHL Contract ¶ 5.

187. *See, e.g.,* Collective Bargaining Agreement Between the NFL Management Council and the NFL Players' Ass'n, art. IX (1977). *See also* note 185 *supra* (NBA).

188. Under the procedures outlined in the NFL collective bargaining agreement, a determination by the club physician that the player is unfit may, at the player's request, be reviewed by a neutral physician selected from a list approved by the players and owners. The decision of the neutral physician may then be appealed to an arbitrator selected from a previously approved pool of five arbitrators. The selection of the arbitrator for a particular case is made by the arbitrator who serves as chairman of the arbitration pool. It is agreed that the findings of the neutral physician will be conclusive with regard to the physical condition of the player. Thus, the arbitrator's decision will mainly focus on defenses raised by the club. The collective bargaining agreement sets forth a non-exclusive list of defenses which may be considered. These include assertions by the club that

 (a) the player did not pass the pre-season physical examination;
 (b) the player failed to make a complete disclosure of his physical and mental condition;
 (c) the player's injury occurred prior to the physical examination and the player executed a waiver of any claim based on that injury;
 (d) the player's injury arose from a non-football cause;
 (e) the player suffered no new football-related injury after the examination; or
 (f) the player suffered no aggravation of a prior injury after the examination which further reduced his capacity.

Id.

189. The NFL collective bargaining agreement recognizes that the situation mentioned in the text is a frequent source of controversy. An "injury grievance" is defined as "a claim or complaint that at the time . . . [the player's contract] was terminated by a club, the player was physically unable to perform the services required of him by that contract because of an injury incurred in the performance of his services under that contract." *Id.,* art. IX, § 1.

190. *See* NFL Contract ¶ 8 (1977); NBA Contract ¶ 6(a) (1976).

perform at a skilled level. It is often true that such review is foreclosed by other terms of the parties' agreement. In the standard form contracts used before the advent of collective bargaining by the players, it was often stipulated that the team physician would have sole discretion in the matter of determining fitness.[191] Under such a clause, the appropriate issue for review by a court or arbitrator would seem to be only whether there had been an abuse of discretion by the physician.[192] If the physician acted in good faith and had an acceptable level of skill and training, his or her judgment on the issue of fitness would appear to be binding. A subsequent section of this treatise includes a more complete discussion of the traditional approaches to this issue of the reviewability of discretionary decisions in the contracts context.[193]

It is understandable that the players might resist the notion that the physician employed by the club should play such a decisive role in the determination of their career opportunities. Thus, it is not surprising that the collective bargaining agreements entered into between the players and owners often include provisions which diminish the role played by the team physician. It is interesting to note, however, that even where reliance on the team physician's discretion has been abandoned in the new agreements, the parties often have not made the issue of the player's fitness one which is reviewable on the merits in an arbitration or judicial proceeding. Rather, the approach typically taken is to give controlling weight to the determination of a neutral physician.[194]

§ 3.07. Club's Right to Terminate Player Contracts.

If there is one aspect of the legal relationship between teams and players which most fans appreciate, it is that the clubs retain vast powers to terminate the contracts, and usually the careers, of the athletes they employ. The terminations occur for a variety of reasons. As noted in prior sections, a player's contract may be terminated under some circumstances where his performance has been impaired by injuries.[195] Moreover, even a physically fit athlete may have his contract prematurely ended because his performance in competition has been found inadequate. Most fans understand that the coach must retain broad prerogatives to make personnel changes in his search for the magic combination of talent, attitude, and leadership which will produce a winning team. Where the player has no trading value and only marginal skill or an undesirable attitude, he will often be cut from the team. Less frequent, but equally important, are the cases in which a player is terminated for reasons unrelated to his level of skill or physical fitness. Professional sports is a business which, like most, depends upon a perpetuation of its good will with its customers, the fans. Translated into sometimes unpopular terms, this requires that the *image* of the industry be maintained. That image is based primarily on the fans' belief in the integrity of the on-the-field competition. Anything which would suggest that the competition is less than genuine, such as gambling and point-shaving, is a major

191. *See* NFL Contract ¶ 6 (1975); NBA Contract ¶ 6 (1971).
192. *Cf.* 3A CORBIN ON CONTRACTS § 651.
193. *See* § 3.08 *infra*.
194. *See* note 188 *supra*.
195. *See* §§ 3.05-3.06 *supra*.

cause for concern to management. The quickest way to separate this sort of misconduct from the sport itself is to terminate the contracts of the individual athletes involved. Any termination, whatever the cause, must find some support in the terms of the written contract. This section explores some of the contractual aspects of the powers which a club exercises when it brings an end to its relationship with a player. The matter of terminations related to physical condition is subsumed in the prior discussion of the club's obligation to an injured player. That analysis is not repeated here, and the reader dealing with an injury-related termination will want to consider the prior sections in connection with the present discussion.

a. The Nature of the Employment Relationship. The starting point for defining the right of the team to terminate a player's contract is the proper characterization of the employment relationship which exists between the parties. The matter of classification is not without difficulty. Indeed the few litigated cases in this area contain often contradictory assertions about the nature of club-player contracts. In one recent case involving the NFL contract, for example, the court entertained the team's assertion that its right of termination is "unqualified" except for its obligation to continue the salary of an injured player.[196] On the other hand, in a case interpreting the same provision of the NFL contract, both the team and the court assumed that since the contract is one for employment for a fixed term, it can be terminated only for cause, the only dispute being over who has the burden of proof on this issue.[197] It is undeniable that the club's right of termination is quite broad. This is illustrated by the provisions of the NFL contract which give the team the right to terminate the contract where "in the sole judgment of the Club, Player's skill or performance has been unsatisfactory as compared with that of other players . . . ."[198] The contract may be terminated where these qualities are established to the satisfaction of the head coach or the team's physician. But even conceding the extreme breadth of the club's right to terminate, it is quite a different question whether that power is without limit.

Among the varieties of employment relationships which are recognized by the law, the least restrictive is one embodied in a contract "at will." Under such an arrangement either party is free to terminate at anytime, with or without cause, and presumably, without regard to the good faith or *bona fides* of the party ordering the termination.[199] While most workers in this country are employed

---

196. Sample v. Gotham Football Club, Inc., 59 F.R.D. 160, 162-63 (S.D.N.Y. 1973).

197. *See* Johnson v. Green Bay Packers, Inc., 272 Wis. 149, 160-61, 74 N.W.2d 784, 790 (1956).
The matter of characterizing the employment relationship is further complicated by the fact that earlier forms of professional sports contracts took a much different approach to the matter of termination by providing simply that the team could terminate the contract after a brief period following notice. *See, e.g.,* American League Baseball Club of Chicago v. Chase, 86 Misc. 441, 455, 149 N.Y.S. 6, 14 (Sup. Ct. 1914); Metropolitan Exhibition Co. v. Ward, 9 N.Y.S. 779, 782-84 (Sup. Ct. 1890). Under this sort of provision, the club had the right to release the player at any time with or without cause. *See* Tollefson v. Green Bay Packers, Inc., 256 Wis. 318, 321-23, 41 N.W.2d 201, 203 (1950).

198. NFL Contract ¶ 11 (1977). (The shortened citation used in earlier sections is adopted in the present discussion. *See* § 3.05, note 126 *supra*. — Eds.)

199. *See generally* 1 A. CORBIN, CORBIN ON CONTRACTS § 70 (1950) [hereinafter cited as CORBIN ON CONTRACTS].

under a "contract" of this sort, professional athletes cannot properly be said to work under this type of arrangement. An "at will" contract is unilateral in nature; that is, the employer promises to pay only in exchange for actual performance and the parties do not agree to be bound for a definite term.[200] The typical two party sports contract is bilateral, each side making definite promises and agreeing that the contract will run for a definite period, albeit subject to an early termination. Perhaps more persuasive in refuting the "at will" characterization is the fact that the parties themselves have included a provision which particularizes the grounds for termination. Even though those grounds are defined in most expansive terms, the parties have not agreed that the team's powers are without limitation.

The more correct view of the club's power of termination is that the team can only terminate the contract "for cause," but the notion of proper "cause" in these circumstances usually includes considerable deference to the desires and judgments of the team's agents. Again using the NFL contract as illustrative, it is clear that the team must identify one of the grounds specified there as the reason for termination. But if the reason given is that the player's work and conduct does not measure up favorably to that of others on the squad, the club is not obligated to bring forth detailed, objective performance evaluations to prove this point. And it most likely will be of little benefit to the player to show that others would strenuously disagree with the team's conclusion as to comparative performances. The reason is that the player's performance need be defective only in the sense that it is unsatisfactory "in the sole judgment of the Club." [201] A subsequent section of these materials considers in more detail the degree of discretion which the team would enjoy under this type of contractual provision.[202] As is suggested in that discussion, it will often be true that the only substantive limitation of the club's judgment is a requirement that it be made in good faith, meaning that the decision to terminate must be made honestly and without pretense. Even when such a broad right of termination is reserved to the club, it is inappropriate to characterize the arrangement as a contract at will. There are important limitations in both the employee's and employer's rights which are not found in situations in which the employment is truly at will. One obvious difference is that under the contracts discussed here, the employee-athlete has little, if any, discretion to bring the relationship to an end. Indeed, except in the limited situations considered elsewhere in this treatise,[203] the club may bind the player for the full term of the agreement, even if he has found the relationship wholly unsatisfactory.[204] With respect to the employer's options, it will be noted that despite the breadth of discretion which it retains, the club may still not terminate "at will" in the strict legal sense of that term. An employer with a right to terminate at will may do so for whatever reason,

---

200. *Id.* §§ 70, 647.

201. NFL Contract ¶ 11 (1977). *See generally* Comment, *Discipline in Professional Sports: The Need for Player Protection,* 60 GEO. L.J. 771, 780-81 (1972).

202. *See* § 3.08 *infra.*

203. *See* § 3.11 *infra.*

204. While the club may "bind" the player to the contract, that does not mean that it can compel the athlete to actually play for the team. Rather, if the athlete refuses to perform, the relief normally available to the club is an injunction prohibiting the athlete from playing for any other team. *See* § 4.02 *infra.*

subject only to special statutes prohibiting discrimination on the basis of race, sex, age and so on. Since the reason for the termination is generally irrelevant, there is no basis for judicial review of the grounds of the decision. By contrast, there are potential litigable issues where the contract requires that the employer's discretion be exercised in good faith. Thus, there are at least two important factual questions which the athlete may take to court: (1) was the employer's stated reason for termination in fact the real motivation for its action? and (2) even if it was, did the contract sanction a termination on that basis? A case for judicial relief would be stated, for example, if the player could show that while the club purported to cut him because of an unsatisfactory performance on the playing field, the action was in fact taken because some agent of the club found the athlete's friends objectionable on purely personal grounds. The use of such a subterfuge would seem to establish the absence of good faith.[205] Moreover, if the club has not reserved the right to consider the athlete's off-the-field activities in determining whether his actions are satisfactory, a termination because of the player's objectionable associations should not be sustained even if the club were candid in specifying the reason for its action.

It should be emphasized that in some cases, the limits on the club's discretion to terminate may be even more substantial than those mentioned above. Only by examining the actual language of the contract can one determine whether the team's decision will be judged by this sort of subjective standard, or whether the team must show that the performance was defective in an objective sense.[206] Whichever standard is applied, it can be accepted that the club's power of termination is not without limitation, despite occasional suggestions to the contrary.[207]

b. The Consequences of Termination. The consequences which flow from a termination depend, not surprisingly, upon whether it is proper or not. If the club exercises its power of termination in accordance with the provisions of the contract, then its legal relationship with the player is brought to an end, with all of the consequences which are implicit in such an event. Thus, the club has no further obligation to employ the player and, if the termination is other than for injuries sustained in the player's performance of his duties under the contract,[208] the team has no further obligation to pay the player,[209] except, of

205. *See generally* § 3.08 *infra.*
206. *See id.*
207. *See* Sample v. Gotham Football Club, Inc., 59 F.R.D. 160, 163 (S.D.N.Y. 1973). *See generally* Comment, *Discipline in Professional Sports: The Need for Player Protection, supra* note 201, at 780-81.
208. *See generally* §§ 3.05-.06 *supra.*
209. *See, e.g.,* Tillman v. New Orleans Saints Football Club, 265 So. 2d 284 (La. App. 1972). *See also* Comment, *Discipline in Professional Sports: The Need for Player Protection, supra* note 201, at 780-81. This analysis assumes that the player does not have a no-cut contract. It should be noted that some leagues have adopted what are in effect no-cut provisions of limited duration as a part of the standard player contract. In the NBA, for example, the players union successfully bargained for a clause which stipulates that if a player is cut for a lack of skill between December 16 and April 30, the club will be obligated to pay the balance of the player's salary. NBA Contract ¶ 20(b)(2), *quoted in* note 224 *infra. See also* National Basketball Players Ass'n Agreement, art. 1, § 2(k) (1976). By its literal terms, the clause still permits the club to terminate the player's contract during the designated period and only requires the club to pay the athlete's salary for the remainder of the

course, for salary or expenses which were earned or incurred prior to the termination.[210] By the same token, a proper termination ends all claims which the team may have to the player's services, and the player is free to market whatever skill he has remaining with other teams, including those who might compete with his original employer.[211] In most cases, of course, a team will not knowingly terminate the contract of a player who still has marketable skill, but rather will seek to sell his contract to another team in the same league. Even when that approach is not taken, the player is not allowed to slip away unnoticed, for league rules usually provide for a waiver system whereby a player must be offered to other teams for a stated waiver price.[212] Where such a waiver system is construed to be for the benefit of the player, strict compliance with its provisions is a necessary prerequisite to a valid termination.[213] But when all of these conditions are satisfied, the termination operates to free both the team and the player from any further obligation.

The team's premature, or otherwise improper, termination of the contract amounts to a breach of contract, and the player is entitled to damages in accordance with the normal rules for calculating damages under a contract of employment.[214] One aspect of the doctrine which operates in this area should be emphasized. Absent a breach, a player is entitled to receive his salary only if he has met certain conditions in the contract. He must, for example, establish that he was a member of the squad, that he possessed the requisite degree of skill, that he had committed no offenses for which discipline was appropriate. But if his contract is improperly terminated early in the season, can the player recover for the balance of the season even though he was not actually on the squad and even though he did not actually establish his playing ability? The basic legal issue raised by this question concerns the circumstances in which the law will excuse the player's nonperformance of conditions precedent to his right to receive his salary.[215] Some cases will present difficult questions of interpretation, as where there is a dispute about which party "caused" the

---

season. In legal effect, however, the clause operates like a traditional no-cut clause. While under such a clause, the club agrees not to cut the player from its roster, it appears that it may do so if it is prepared to pay the player's salary for the balance of the season. See § 3.09 *infra.*

210. *See, e.g.,* NBA Contract ¶ 20(d)-(e), providing for (1) payment of board, lodging, and expenses if contract terminated during training camp and (2) pro rata share of salary if contract is terminated for a reason other than a contract-related injury.

211. The famous "Catfish" Hunter episode illustrates the increased marketability which a player can enjoy when his contract is terminated. When his contract with the Oakland A's baseball club was terminated, Hunter's services were put up for bid by other clubs and he eventually signed with the New York Yankees for a total compensation estimated to be in the range of $3 million. *See* N.Y. Times, Jan. 1, 1975, at 1, col. 5; *id.,* Jan. 3, 1975, at 21, col. 2; *id.,* Jan. 4, 1975, at 19, col. 6; *id.,* Jan. 5, 1975, § 5, at 1, col. 1. But that case is atypical in that the contract was terminated by the player, and not the team, and the termination occurred through inadvertence as the team miscalculated the consequences of its acts. *See also* American & National Leagues of Professional Baseball Clubs v. Major League Baseball Players Ass'n, 59 Cal. App. 3d 493, 130 Cal. Rptr. 626 (1976).

212. *See, e.g.,* CONSTITUTION AND BY-LAWS FOR THE NATIONAL FOOTBALL LEAGUE art. 18 (1972).

213. *See* Baseball Players' Fraternity, Inc. v. Boston American League Club, 166 App. Div. 484, 492, 151 N.Y.S. 557, 563 (1915), *aff'd,* 221 N.Y. 704, 117 N.E. 1061 (1917).

214. *See, e.g.,* Pasquel v. Owen, 186 F.2d 263 (8th Cir. 1950); Schultz v. Los Angeles Dons, Inc., 107 Cal. App. 2d 718, 238 P.2d 73 (1951); Egan v. Winnipeg Baseball Club, Ltd., 96 Minn. 345, 105 N.W. 947 (1905).

215. *See generally* RESTATEMENT OF CONTRACTS §§ 274, 306; 3A CORBIN ON CONTRACTS §§ 653-60A, 752-71; J. MURRAY, MURRAY ON CONTRACTS §§ 186-96 (1974).

termination or where there is a question about the player's continued ability to perform. But most situations can be resolved under the general rule that where the team has "discharged [the player] without good cause and prevented him from performing, no further performance or offer to perform by [the player is] required." [216] Thus, while the athlete normally has to participate in team activities before he can draw his salary, actual performance is not a legal prerequisite where his participation is prevented by the action of the club. The breach by the team serves to excuse the player's further active participation.

Most standard form player contracts give the team the right to affect the player's employment status with some action short of a termination of his contract. Typical of these other rights is the authority given to a club to suspend a player. Thus, it may be provided that the player is subject to suspension if he fails to maintain himself in good physical condition [217] or if he fails to observe club rules pertaining to the conduct of its athletes.[218] Although the typical contract does not elaborate upon the effect of a suspension, some preliminary conclusions can be reached about how the consequences of a suspension differ from those which attend a termination.[219]

The critical difference between a suspension and a termination is the extent to which the team can continue to claim the exclusive right to the player's services. As indicated above, when a team terminates a player's contract, the rights of each party to the contract come to an end: the player loses his right to receive his salary and the team correspondingly loses its right to demand that the player perform for it and no one else. But when a player is suspended he finds himself in the worst possible position with respect to his right to receive his salary and the club's right to claim his services. On the one hand, he loses his right to be paid under the contract for the period of suspension, but on the other hand, he is still bound by the other terms of the agreement. This means that his promise to render his services for no other team continues to be fully effective, and although denied his source of income, the player may not market his services elsewhere. Thus, where a player is suspended by a team for improper or disruptive conduct or because he is not in good physical shape, it is of no avail to him that another team with a less impressive array of talent would regard him as a satisfactory addition. Assuming that the suspension is meted out in accordance with the terms of the contract, and for no greater duration than the contract itself, the contracting team has the right under the agreement to temporarily preclude the player from realizing any economic return from his special athletic skills. Because of this important effect of a suspension, it is fully appropriate that the exercise of this power be subjected to close scrutiny by legal institutions.[220]

c. **The Grounds for Termination.** The contracts used in the major professional team sports specify a variety of grounds upon which the club may

216. Schultz v. Los Angeles Dons, Inc., 107 Cal. App. 2d 718, 722, 238 P.2d 73, 75 (1951).
217. *See, e.g.,* NBA Contract (Veteran — Single Season) ¶ 6(a).
218. *Id.* ¶ 4.
219. A question exists as to whether there are not limits on the club's power to enforce a promise by an athlete to subject himself to a broad power of suspension and discipline. *See* § 3.10 *infra.*
220. *See* § 3.10 *infra.* The antitrust implications of player suspensions are explored in § 5.09 *infra.*

exercise its right to terminate its relationships with the athlete. There is virtually no case law interpreting these clauses except those pertaining to the termination of an injured player. This paucity of litigation is readily explainable: terminations for disciplinary reasons are rare; [221] and an otherwise healthy player who is not picked up by another club following his termination by the original employer will not likely be able to show that he possesses a degree of skill which should have been satisfactory to the contracting team. In light of the wide range of discretion which the club possesses to determine fitness and skill,[222] those giving legal advice to a player who has been terminated may well decide that there is little hope of impugning the legality of the team's decision, except perhaps in those cases in which the player has received an injury in his performance of service under the contract.[223]

A review of the grounds for termination specified in the common standard contracts reveals the broad scope of the club's powers. There are four bases for termination which are recognized in many of the contracts. It is usually provided that the club may end the contract if the athlete (1) is not physically fit, (2) fails to exhibit sufficient skill and ability in the particular sport, (3) fails to observe club and league rules, including disciplinary rules, or (4) otherwise materially breaches the contract.[224] The determination of whether the athlete is in proper

---

221. *But see* Molinas v. National Basketball Ass'n, 190 F. Supp. 241 (S.D.N.Y. 1961); Molinas v. Podoloff, 133 N.Y.S.2d 743 (S. Ct. 1954). *See generally* Comment, *Discipline in Professional Sports: The Need for Player Protection, supra* note 201.

222. *See* § 3.08 *infra.*

223. *See,* e.g., Hennigan v. Chargers Football Co., 431 F.2d 308 (5th Cir. 1970); Schultz v. Los Angeles Dons, Inc., 107 Cal. App. 2d 718, 238 P.2d 73 (1951); Tillman v. New Orleans Saints Football Club, 265 So. 2d 284 (La. App. 1972); Houston Oilers, Inc. v. Floyd, 518 S.W.2d 836 (Tex. Civ. App. 1975); Tollefson v. Green Bay Packers, Inc., 256 Wis. 318, 41 N.W.2d 201 (1950).

224. In contrast to provisions relating to injuries, see § 3.05 *supra,* the termination clauses used in the major professional leagues reflect some diversity in the extent to which the club's powers are explicitly set forth. This is in part due to the fact that the club's powers of termination are not always set forth in a single clause of the standard player contract. And even when a specific termination clause is included, it is often supplemented by terms found in other sections of the contract. The NBA contract is among the more specific, although as will be seen even its provisions require some interpretation. The basic termination clause in the NBA contract provides that the club may terminate the contract if the player should:

> (1) at any time, fail, refuse or neglect to conform his personal conduct to standards of good citizenship, good moral character and good sportsmanship, to keep himself in first class physical condition or to obey the Club's training rules; or
> (2) at any time, fail, in the sole opinion of the Club's management, to exhibit sufficient skill or competitive ability to qualify to continue as a member of the Club's team (provided, however, that if this contract is terminated by the Club, in accordance with the provisions of this subparagraph, during the period from December 16 through April 30 of any season, the Player shall be entitled to receive his full salary for said season; or
> (3) at any time fail, refuse or neglect to render his services hereunder or in any other manner materially breach this contract.

NBA Contract ¶ 20(b).

Under the NBA contract there is a separate section dealing with training and conduct rules. Under paragraph 4, the club is given broad power to "establish reasonable rules for the government of its players." That paragraph specifies fines and suspension as authorized sanctions, and termination is not specifically mentioned as a possible sanction. The failure to mention a right of termination in cases of discipline might give rise to an argument that the only sanctions are those specified. *See* 3 CORBIN ON CONTRACTS § 552. However, the alternative of termination would seem to be authorized by the portion of the termination clause requiring good citizenship and good moral conduct. The broad nature of those classifications would seem to indicate that the club intends to reserve to itself virtually unlimited authority to determine the type of conduct which may result in a termination.

physical condition or has the requisite degree of skill may be committed to the discretion of an agent of the club, usually a coach or team designated physician.[225] One difference which can be noted among the various standard player contracts is the degree to which they give express recognition to the club's right to terminate if the player fails to exhibit good moral character. Some contracts specifically require moral conduct and good citizenship as a fifth prerequisite to the athlete's continued rights under the agreement.[226] In others, the concern for the morality of the player's action appears to be treated under provisions empowering the club to enforce disciplinary rules.[227]

Many of these grounds for termination are treated in other sections of this chapter. The club's right to terminate for a lack of physical fitness, which is often related to a player's failure to exhibit sufficient skill, is discussed in the immediately preceding section.[228] The club's power to discipline a player for

While there may be a legally imposed limit of the club's right in that regard, *see* §§ 3.10, 5.09 *infra,* the club will likely be given particular discretion to punish such conduct where it has been proscribed in a previously announced rule. Thus, the rules of conduct might be viewed as providing, at least in part, the parties' definition of what amounts to conduct which may lead to a termination of the contract. *Cf.* Molinas v. National Basketball Ass'n, 190 F. Supp. 241 (S.D.N.Y. 1961); Molinas v. Podoloff, 133 N.Y.S.2d 743 (S. Ct. 1954).

In the version of the standard player contract used in the NFL prior to 1977, the club's basic right to termination is set forth in ¶ 6, which provided as follows:

> The Player represents and warrants that he is and will continue to be sufficiently highly skilled in all types of football team play, to play professional football of the caliber required by the League and by the Club, and that he is and will continue to be in excellent physical condition, and agrees to perform his services hereunder to the complete satisfaction of the Club and its Head Coach. Player shall undergo a complete physical examination by the Club physician at the start of each training session during the term hereof. If Player fails to establish his excellent physical condition to the satisfaction of the Club physician by the physical examination, or (after having so established his excellent physical condition), if, in the opinion of the Head Coach, Player does not maintain himself in such excellent physical condition or fails at any time during the football seasons included in the terms of this contract to demonstrate sufficient skill and capacity to play professional football of the caliber required by the League, or by the Club, or if in the opinion of the Head Coach the Player's work or conduct in the performance of this contract is unsatisfactory as compared with the work and conduct of other members of the Club's squad of players, the Club shall have the right to terminate this contract.

The listing of possible grounds for termination in this paragraph cover those which are normally asserted, but it is clear that the listing is not exclusive. Noticeably absent from this specification are express provisions dealing with the matters of player discipline and decorum. These are covered elsewhere in the contract. Thus, paragraph 11 specifically empowers the Commissioner of the NFL to cancel the contract of any player who engages in point-shaving, betting or "any conduct detrimental to the welfare of the League or of professional football." A similar array of broad powers in disciplinary matters is granted under paragraph 4. The player agrees to abide by "the Constitution and By-Laws, Rules and Regulations of the League, of the Club, and the decisions of the Commissioner of the League . . ." If the athlete fails to comply with these, "the Club shall have the right to terminate this contract as provided in Paragraph 6 hereof" or to take other action authorized in the applicable documents. NFL Contract ¶ 4 (1975).

The NFL standard form contract was redrafted in 1977. *See* note 126, § 3.05 *supra.* Under the new version, there are separate paragraphs dealing with the club's right to terminate a player for a lack of fitness [NFL Contract ¶ 8 (1977)]; unsatisfactory skill or performance [*id.* ¶ 11]; and disciplinable conduct [*id.,* ¶ 15]. The club still retains the right to terminate a player if his performance is unsatisfactory "in the sole judgment of [the] Club." ¶ 11. Also, the player must establish his fitness "to the satisfaction of the Club physician." The club's determination under these provisions are now subject to arbitration. *See* note 246, § 3.08 *infra.*

225. *See* NBA Contract ¶ 20(b), *supra* note 224. *See generally* Comment, *Discipline in Professional Sports: The Need for Player Protection, supra* note 201 at 781.

226. *See* NBA Contract ¶ 20(b), *supra* note 224. *See also* Baseball Contract ¶ 7(b)(1).

227. *Compare* NFL Contract ¶¶ 4, 6, 11 (1975).

228. *See* §§ 3.05-.06 *supra.*

improper conduct is considered below.[229] Finally, the issue of the scope of the club's discretionary powers, which affect grounds for termination, is treated separately in a subsequent section.[230]

One matter which remains to be considered is the legal effect of a clause which gives the club the right to terminate if the player should materially breach the contract. In light of the other clauses dealing with the conduct, character, physical fitness, and skill of the player, one might wonder what sorts of activities are intended to be covered by this section. The answer is found in the other provisions of the contract. In addition to these promises to conduct himself properly, to maintain his physical condition, and to possess sufficient skill, the player usually accepts a variety of other obligations under the contract. Thus, typically the player not only makes an affirmative promise to render his services for the team, but also promises to participate in promotional activities on behalf of the club and league,[231] to refrain from tampering with other players under contract,[232] to report promptly to an assigned team,[233] and, in some contracts, to avoid doing anything which is detrimental to the best interests of the club or league.[234] A "material breach" clause is intended to give the team an alternative to seeking damages or an injunction in situations in which the player fails to live up to these other promises.[235]

Such a clause, however, does not give the club an unqualified right to terminate for any dereliction by the player with respect to the non-playing aspects of his performance. Rather, the right of termination exists only for those breaches which are material. Hence the player's failure to carry out the contract in minor respects will not in itself justify a team's refusal to pay the stipulated salary. There are numerous precedents available from the general body of contracts law which will aid a court or arbitrator in making the necessary distinction.[236] The definition of a material breach is largely functional: it is a "non-performance of duty that is so material and important as to justify the injured party in regarding the whole transaction as at an end." [237] Thus, the breach has to be such that the player's non-performance deprives the team of some substantial advantage which it anticipated under the contract. In making this evaluation, particular emphasis is placed upon the consequences to the team when the player's performance is not precisely as called for. Thus, there

229. *See* § 3.10 *infra.*

230. *See* § 3.08 *infra.*

231. *See, e.g.,* NBA Contract ¶ 18.

232. *See, e.g., id.* ¶ 19.

233. *See, e.g., id.* ¶ 12.

234. *See e.g., id.* ¶ 5.

235. It must be recognized that the club would seldom exercise its right of termination in these circumstances against a star athlete. The contract of such a player may be quite valuable, and the club would be hesitant to totally relinquish its rights to the player's services, as would happen in the event of a termination. Rather, the club would likely pursue other remedies, including seeking an injunction against a continued infraction. *See* Matuszak v. Houston Oilers, Inc., 515 S.W.2d 725 (Tex. Civ. App. 1974). *Cf.* World Football League v. Dallas Cowboys Football Club, Inc., 513 S.W.2d 102 (Tex. Civ. App. 1974). However, a material breach by a marginal player is not likely to be treated as cautiously.

236. The notion that a contract may be terminated by a party injured by a material breach has long been recognized in the law of contracts, and the language used in the standard player contracts is merely a restatement of rights which otherwise exist. *See* authorities cited, note 238, *infra.*

237. 4 CORBIN ON CONTRACTS § 946.

obviously is a material breach when the athlete refuses to participate in a scheduled competition. Moreover, the athlete's total refusal to engage in any publicity activities will likely be found to be of the same quality. But a failure to show up for one picture-taking session probably does not lead to such a disadvantage as to justify a termination. A similar weighing of the resulting injury will be applied to the infinite variety of other situations which might arise.[238]

One other aspect of the club's right of termination deserves attention. A few contracts specifically provide that the death of the player will automatically terminate the agreement,[239] although most are silent on this point. The absence of a specific provision on this matter will usually have no significant consequence. Even in the absence of a specific agreement, the generally accepted rule is that where a contract involves a personal relationship, the death of one of the parties will automatically terminate each side's obligation.[240] The termination which is effected is complete and neither side has a further duty of performance.[241] This result would seem to be a further manifestation of the principle that the player's preparedness to perform is a precondition to the club's obligation to pay his salary.[242] Anything which impairs his ability to carry out his duties under the contract provides an excuse for the team to withhold its performance, unless the team has otherwise accepted responsibility for the debilitating condition.

Another consideration which may operate to limit the team's power of termination is the inclusion of a "no-cut" clause in the contract. Such a clause operates to nullify some provisions of the standard form contract which specify grounds for termination. The operation of these no-cut clauses is considered more fully in § 3.09 *infra*.

§ 3.08. The Role of Discretion in the Club's Power to Terminate a Player's Contract.

The standard form player contracts used in the major professional leagues grant to the clubs and their agents varying degrees of discretion in determining whether the contract will be terminated. In some, it is made clear that the question of whether the athlete exhibits sufficient ability is committed to the sole discretion of the head coach or manager.[243] Similarly the coach or manager

---

238. *See, e.g.,* Zancanaro v. Cross, 85 Ariz. 394, 339 P.2d 746 (1959); Walker & Co. v. Harrison, 347 Mich. 630, 81 N.W.2d 352 (1957); Rozay v. Hegeman Steel Prod., Inc., 37 Misc. 2d 10, 234 N.Y.S.2d 647 (Sup. Ct. 1962); Wm. G. Tannhaeuser Co. v. Holiday House, Inc., 1 WIS. 2d 370, 83 N.W.2d 880 (1957); RESTATEMENT OF CONTRACTS §§ 313, 317 (1932).

239. WHA Contract ¶ 7.6; NFL Contract ¶ 12 (1977).

240. *See, e.g.,* Berg v. Erickson, 234 F. 817 (8th Cir. 1916); Dumont v. Heighton, 14 Ariz. 25, 123 P. 306 (1912); Campbell v. Faxon, 73 Kan. 675, 86 P. 760 (1906); Clifton v. Clark, 83 Miss. 446, 36 So. 251 (1903); RESTATEMENT OF CONTRACTS § 459 (1932). *See generally* 17 AM. JUR.2D, *Contracts* § 487 (1964).

241. *See* RESTATEMENT OF CONTRACTS § 459, comment *a* (1932).

242. *See* discussion at note 127, § 3.05 *supra.*

243. *See, e.g.,* NBA Contract ¶ 20(b)(2), quoted in note 224, § 3.07 *supra.* (The citation form for references to standard player contracts is explained in note 126, § 3.05 *supra.* — Eds.) *See generally* Comment, *Discipline in Professional Sports: The Need for Player Protection,* 60 GEO. L.J. 771, 780-81 (1972).

The NBA contract lists the several different grounds for termination, but the club's "personal

may be expressly given discretion to determine whether the player's general conduct under the contract is satisfactory.[244] In the event that the athlete's performance is found lacking in either respect, his contract may be terminated.[245] Another variety of discretion is that given to the team physican to determine whether the player is physically fit to play.[246] Again, the physician's

satisfaction", is specifically mentioned as the determinative criteria with respect to only one of these. *See* NBA Contract ¶ 20(b), quoted in note 224, § 3.07 *supra.* This selective use of an express condition of personal satisfaction raises the obvious question of whether a difference in substance was intended. Aspects of this question are considered below.

244. Such a term requiring general conduct satisfactory to the head coach was found in the former NFL contract. *See* NFL Contract ¶ 6 (1975), quoted in note 224, § 3.07 *supra.* The new version leaves the determination of whether the player's skill and performance is satisfactory to the "sole judgment" of the club. The contract also provides that it may be terminated if the player's personal conduct is "reasonably judged by [the] Club to adversely affect or reflect on [the] Club . . . ." NFL Contract ¶ 11 (1977). For the effect of the arbitration provision of the league's collective bargaining agreement on these clauses, see note 246 *infra.*

245. *See generally* § 3.07 *supra.*

246. *See, e.g.,* NBA Contract ¶ 6:

> (a) If the Player, in the judgment of the Club's physician, is not in good physical condition at the date of his first scheduled game for the Club, or if, during the season, he fails to remain in good physical condition (unless such condition results directly from an injury sustained by the Player as a direct result of participating in any basketball practice or game played for the Club during such season), so as to render the Player, in the judgment of the Club's physician, unfit to play skilled basketball, the Club shall have the right to suspend such Player until such time as, in the judgment of the Club's physician, the Player is in sufficiently good physical condition to play skilled basketball . . . .
> (b) . . . If, in the judgment of the Club's physician, the Player's injuries resulted directly from playing for the Club and render him unfit to play skilled basketball, then, so long as such unfitness continues, but in no event beyond the term of one year referred to in paragraph 1 of this contract, the Club shall pay to the Player the compensation prescribed in paragraph 2 of this contract. . . .
> (c) Disputes arising under this paragraph (6) as to (i) whether the Player was in sufficiently good physical condition to play skilled basketball, as to (ii) whether the Player was injured as a direct result of participating in any basketball practice or game played for the Club, as to (iii) whether such injury rendered the Player unfit to play skilled basketball, . . . shall be resolved in the manner provided by the Agreement currently in effect between the National Basketball Association and National Basketball Players Association.

See also, § 3.06 *supra.* It should be noted that in several of the major leagues, the discretion given to the team physician to determine a player's fitness is modified in some situations by collective bargaining provisions pertaining to arbitration. For example, under the NFL player contract, the player must establish his "excellent physical condition to the satisfaction of the Club physician . . . ." NFL Contract ¶ 8 (1977). The terms of the contract are, however, subject to the collective bargaining agreement negotiated by the owners and the players' association. That document includes an injury arbitration procedure which permits a player who asserts he has been terminated in an injured condition to submit to an examination by a neutral physician. The matter may then be taken to arbitration, and in these proceedings the findings of the neutral physician are conclusive on the matter of the player's physical condition at the time of the examination. Thus, the initial determination of the team physician is supplanted and arbitration focuses on various defenses which the club may raise. This system is described in note 188, § 3.06 *supra.*

This type of review is undertaken only where the player's fitness is impaired by an injury. Other determinations of non-fitness — for example, where the player is overweight — are subject to the general arbitration provisions of the NFL collective bargaining agreement, which do not include special directives modifying the operation of the standard form contract. In those proceedings not involving injuries, the arbitrator would undertake to apply the terms of the player contract, including that which commits the fitness determination to the discretion of the team physician. Thus, it will be necessary to determine what standard of review will be applied. It is this issue which is addressed in the text of this section. In the same vein, it should be noted that the determination of whether the player possesses sufficient skill might also be arbitrated under a general arbitration provision. In the NFL, the relevant contract language commits this decision to the sole judgment of the club, see NFL Contract ¶ 11 (1977), and the principles discussed here concerning the breadth of review utilized in court proceedings may be relevant.

decision will have important consequences for the player's right to continue as a member of the team.[247]

A question immediately arises as to whether there are any effective legal limits on the manner in which these judgments are made. The athlete may well be concerned that a coach's or physician's loyalty to the team will influence his decision. Moreover, even apart from the possibility of bias, there may be cases in which the examination which precedes an adverse decision is conducted in a manner less thorough or less professional than the athlete would like.[248] On the other hand, the team can properly assert that it must be given considerable freedom in making personnel decisions. Such decisions are a fundamental part of the day-to-day operation of the team, and the efficiency of the club's operation could be substantially impeded if review were readily available in a court or arbitration proceeding.

The present section examines the extent to which legal institutions will defer to an exercise of discretion under the standard player contracts. The basic legal question which arises is whether the person making the decision must act in an objective, reasonable manner, or whether it is enough to show that without regard to objective standards, the decision was made with candor and in good faith.[249] It will be noted that the potential for disagreement in this area is not limited to those cases in which the contract expressly states that the team or its agent will have sole discretion to determine a matter which leads to a termination of the athlete's contract. Even in the absence of such an express term, the team will assert that its decision as to the athlete's fitness or skill is necessarily discretionary. Since the nature of the decision is the same whether or not the contract recognizes that fact, it might be argued that the team which omits a specific reference to the discretionary nature of its judgments ought not be less free from judicial intervention than the club which has exercised more careful draftsmanship. Moreover, a similar issue may be raised within a single contract, for it is not uncommon to find that the parties have expressly stated that certain decisions will be in the sole discretion of an agent of the team, while

---

247. *See generally* §§ 3.05-.06 *supra.*

248. This sort of complaint appears to have played a role in the athlete's successful suit for his salary in Houston Oilers, Inc. v. Floyd, 518 S.W.2d 836 (Tex. Civ. App. 1975). The player had been injured and placed on the disabled list. He was later ordered back to duty and promptly cut from the team, allegedly because of his failure to exhibit sufficient skill. The player then sued, contending that he was still suffering the effects of the contract-related injury when he was returned to the active list. *(See generally* § 3.06 *supra).* In that connection, the court considered the circumstances under which Floyd's fitness had been determined. The court observed:

> The evidence does not establish whether the club doctor was of the opinion that Floyd was physically able to perform services under the contract. The record shows only that Floyd was advised by the club trainer that he had been placed on the active player list. Floyd testified that the only reason given him by the club trainer for being reactivated was "that he had no choice other than to put me back on, because it was from higher up to reactivate me." It further appears from the evidence and the trial court's finding, against which no attack has been made, that Floyd's services were terminated less than seventy-two hours after he was restored to the active player roster. The evidence does not show that he was given the period of time specified in the contract to have an examination made by a physician of his own choice, even if he had decided to take that course of action. 518 S.W.2d at 839.

249. *See generally* Comment, *Discipline in Professional Sports: The Need for Player Protection, supra* note 243, at 781.

other decisions which are equally judgmental in nature are not so qualified.[250] While the selective use of language authorizing an exercise of discretion might suggest otherwise, the club would argue that it should be the nature of the decision, and not the exact phrasing used, which should determine the standard of review.[251]

It is not uncommon for two parties to agree that one of them will have discretion to determine an important aspect of their contractual relationship. There is a considerable body of precedent from the general law of contracts which defines the willingness of courts to scrutinize such an exercise of discretion.[252] A review of that precedent will suggest the type of analysis to be followed in the sports area. Courts have made clear that it is entirely appropriate for one party to agree to render a performance which the other side need not accept unless it meets his personal satisfaction. In determining whether an expression of dissatisfaction is legally effective, courts will apply either an objective or a subjective test, depending upon the nature of the promised performance. Under the objective standard, the party who disapproved the performance must show that his disapproval was reasonable and proper under the circumstances.[253] In its purest form, the objective test incorporates a reasonable man standard: the expression of dissatisfaction will be sustained if a hypothetical reasonable man would have been dissatisfied with that which was tendered.[254] This test, as applied in the sports area, would require a showing that the team's insistence upon a higher level of performance or physical fitness was not unreasonable given the extent to which these qualities were possessed by other players. The subjective test, on the other hand, affords a much wider range of discretion to the party who deems himself dissatisfied. Under this standard, the courts only require a showing that the party acted in good faith in making his judgment.[255] It is not required that the decision reached be one which most others would have made in the particular circumstances, nor need it be the one which a reasonable, prudent man would have made. But the suggestion of dissatisfaction must be made honestly, with candor, and without pretense.[256]

---

250. *See* NBA Contract ¶ 20(b), note 224, § 3.07 *supra.*

251. *Compare* Comment, *Discipline in Professional Sports: The Need for Player Protection, supra* note 243, at 781.

252. *See* generally 3A A. CORBIN, CORBIN ON CONTRACTS §§ 644-46 (1960) [hereinafter cited as CORBIN ON CONTRACTS].

253. The leading cases which discuss the various standards to be employed in reviewing one party's expression of dissatisfaction with the performance tendered by the other side are as follows: Ward v. Flex-O-Tube Co., 194 F.2d 500 (6th Cir. 1952); Shepherd v. Union Central Life Ins. Co., 74 F.2d 180 (5th Cir. 1934); Patterson v. Alabama Vermiculite Corp., 149 F.Supp. 548 (W.D.S.C. 1957); Kadner v. Shields, 20 Cal. App. 3d 251, 97 Cal. Rptr. 742 (Ct. App. 1971); Mattei v. Hopper, 51 Cal. 2d 119, 330 P.2d 625 (1958); Leighton v. Leighton, 10 Mich. App. 424, 159 N.W.2d 750 (1968); Isbell v. Anderson Carriage Co., 170 Mich. 304, 136 N.W. 457 (1912); Wood Mach. Co. v. Smith, 50 Mich. 565, 15 N.W. 906 (1883); Coker v. Wesco Materials Corp., 368 S.W.2d 883 (Tex. Civ. App. 1963).

254. *See* 3A CORBIN ON CONTRACTS § 646.

255. *See* Comment, *Discipline in Professional Sports: The Need for Player Protection, supra* note 243, at 781, n.50.

256. In addition to the cases cited in note 253 *supra, see* American Music Stores v. Kussel, 232 F. 306 (6th Cir. 1916); Zaleski v. Clark, 44 Conn. 218 (1976); Hawkins v. Graham, 149 Mass. 284, 21 N.E. 312 (1889); Brown v. Foster, 113 Mass. 136, 18 Am. R. 463 (1873); Gibson v. Cranage, 39 Mich. 49 (1818); Gutner v. Success Magazine Corp., 136 Misc. 257, 242 N.Y.S. 679 (Sup. Ct. 1928); Jenkins Towel Service, Inc. v. Tidewater Oil Co., 422 Pa. 601, 223 A.2d 84 (1966). *See generally* 3A CORBIN ON CONTRACTS § 646.

Over the course of time, the courts have also developed guidelines which can be employed to determine which of the two tests is to be applied in a particular case. In general, it can be said that whether the objective or subjective standard of review is selected will be determined by the nature of the performance which is in question. The more routine and mechanical the performance, the more likely the objective test will be chosen to test the party's expressed dissatisfaction. When the performance is one with respect to which tastes and preferences are likely to vary, the courts are inclined to conclude that the parties intended to sanction such personal choices under the contract. As expressed by one court, the cases involving contracts requiring a satisfactory performance

> have been divided into two primary categories and have been accorded different treatment on that basis. First, in those contracts where the condition calls for satisfaction as to commerical value or quality, operative fitness, or mechanical utility, dissatisfaction cannot be claimed arbitrarily, unreasonably, or capriciously . . . and the standard of a reasonable person is used in determining whether satisfaction has been received. . . . [T]he second line of authorities [deal] with . . . clauses . . . involving fancy, taste, or judgment. Where the question is one of judgment, the promisor's determination that he is not satisfied, when made in good faith, has been held to be a defense to an action on the contract.[257]

Other courts have similarly observed that the closeness of judicial scrutiny of a particular expression of dissatisfaction will depend upon whether the contracted-for performance is one which is generally regarded as mechanical or otherwise subject to independent evaluation.[258]

While the distinction between these two types of contracts is often made on an *ad hoc* basis, it is possible to categorize particular types of contracts according to the subject matter involved. In this regard, it is relevant to ask whether personal service contracts, such as those involved in professional sports, are more likely to be grouped in one category or the other. As one might suspect, when a contract provides that the continuation of an employment relationship depends upon the employer's satisfaction with the employee's performance, the contract will often be judged to be one of those requiring only honest or good faith dissatisfaction, rather than reasonable dissatisfaction. An employment contract often involves a personal relationship and whether the employer is satisfied with the employee's performance depends not only upon the results achieved, but also upon both the particular style of work and personality of the employee. The suitability of a particular person's personality or technique may be subject to widely varying judgments depending upon the preferences of the observer. Thus, to the extent that the employer's obligation depends upon his being "satisfied" with the employee's performance, most courts apply the subjective, good faith test. Indeed, where the contract includes an express term deferring to the employer's satisfaction and judgment, the courts are most receptive to the notion that the employer should have wide-range

---

257. Mattei v. Hopper, 51 Cal.2d 119, 123-24, 330 P.2d 625, 626-27 (1958).
258. *See* Shepherd v. Union Central Life Ins. Co., 74 F.2d 180 (5th Cir. 1934) and cases cited in note 253 *supra*.

discretion to declare himself dissatisfied.[259] Even where the employer's personal satisfaction is not an express term of the contract, it would seemingly be appropriate to look at the nature of the relationship which was created to see if it was one which likely rested on trust and confidence and similar subtleties. These qualities will be important in many employment relationships and where they are, the employer's discretion to terminate the contract ought to be relatively unfettered by judicial inquiry. Hence, application of the subjective standard is appropriate.

The only doctrinal uncertainty in these conclusions about the role of discretion in employment contracts stems from a line of cases holding that "where, in a given contract, it is doubtful whether the promise is intended to be conditional on the promisor's dissatisfaction or on the sufficiency of the performance to satisfy a reasonable man, the latter interpretation is adopted." [260] The basic thrust of this principle is sound, for it accepts that one will not be held to have given up the more substantial protection afforded by the requirement of objectivity unless there is a reliable indication that such a relinquishment was within the parties' contemplation.[261] But the intent and understanding which can properly be attributed to a party is not discerned solely from the expressed terms of the contract. Hence, the applicability of the subjective test should not depend only upon the presence or absence of an expressed term conditioning the employer's performance on his personal satisfaction with the proffered performance. While the omission of such a term is a fact to be weighed, it must be considered along with all other facts, including the personal nature of the particular employment relationship.

When the above principles are applied to sports contracts, some conclusions can be reached. Perhaps the least difficult case is presented by those contract clauses in which the particular ground for termination is specifically left to the judgment of satisfaction of the club or its coach. The existing precedents would suggest that the subjective standard should be applied to review an expression of dissatisfaction by the team,[262] and this result seems to be confirmed by the nature of the relationship. With respect to a contract term in which there is no mention of the extent of discretion assumed by the team, the conclusion is less certain. Here again, it is appropriate for the court or arbitrator to look at the type of relationship created by the contract and determine whether it is such that each side was likely to have understood that the employer retained

---

259. *See* Tow v. Miners Memorial Hosp. Ass'n, Inc., 305 F.2d 73 (5th Cir. 1962); Shepherd v. Union Central Life Ins. Co., 74 F.2d 180 (5th Cir. 1934); American Music Stores v. Kussel, 232 F. 306 (6th Cir. 1916); Hazen v. Cobb, 46 Fla. 151, 117 So. 853 (1928); Tyler v. Ames, 6 Lans. 280 (1872); Gutner v. Success Magazine Corp., 136 Misc. 257, 242 N.Y.S. 679 (S. Ct. 1928); Diamond v. Mendelsohn, 156 App. Div. 636, 141 N.Y.S. 775 (1913); Jenkins Towel Service, Inc. v. Tidewater Oil Co., 422 Pa. 601, 223 A.2d 84 (1966).

260. Johnson v. School Dist. No. 12, 210 Ore. 585, 312 P.2d 591 (1957). *See also* Stevens v. G. L. Rugo & Sons, Inc., 209 F.2d 135 (1st Cir. 1953); Kadner v. Shields, 20 Cal. App. 3d 251, 97 Cal. Rptr. 742 (Ct. App. 1971); Fulcher v. Nelson, 273 N.C. 221, 159 S.E.2d 519 (1968); Gould v. McCormick, 75 Wash. 61, 134 P. 676 (1913).

261. Some sports contracts are drafted in a manner which gives rise to uncertainty as to the parties' intent with respect to the extent of discretion available to the club. *See* note 243 *supra.*

262. *See* cases cited note 259 *supra. See also* Comment, *Discipline in Professional Sports: The Need for Player Protection,* 60 GEO. L. J. 771, 781 (1972).

wide-ranging discretion to invoke the particular ground for termination. If so, application of the subjective standard is again appropriate.[263]

An important factor in each case will be the reason for the termination. Where the player is cut for an alleged lack of skill or deficient attitude (which may be a component of skill), a court may decide not to require any more than candor and good faith by the team. Indeed, a persuasive argument can be made that the employment relationship in professional sports is one which presumes that the club and coach retain extensive discretion to make personnel changes, including those which result in a termination of player contracts. Because of the collective nature of the effort which is involved in a team sport, the suitability of a player depends not only upon his level of skill, but also upon his attitude toward the game and his relationship with his teammates. At times the coach may be looking for more "leadership"; at other times, he may feel that the concentration of the team is impaired because there are too many "leaders." Or the coach may change his strategy as to the type of player needed in a particular position. Often these changes in strategy are not purely objective and would not win the general approval of outside observers. Nonetheless, the subtle nature of the coach's decisions underscores the fact that the relationship between coach and player, and thus, between the team and player, is one which depends upon the coach's satisfaction in a most personal, subjective sense.[264] Since this fact is generally appreciated by all who enter the profession, it is not unreasonable to interpret their contracts in light of it.

---

263. See Shepherd v. Union Central Life Ins. Co., 74 F.2d 180 (5th Cir. 1934).

264. One of the few judicial inquiries into the personal aspects of team play was undertaken by the district court in Cincinnati Bengals, Inc. v. Bergey, 453 F. Supp. 129 (S.D. Ohio 1974), aff'd, Civil No. 74-1570 (6th Cir., Aug. 27, 1974). While the case involved a legal question different from that considered here, its findings are nonetheless relevant. The court undertook to examine the nature of interpersonal relationships in football. In that connection it quoted with approval the following testimony by Coach Paul Brown of the Bengals:

> Q. In the course of your experience as a football coach, have you reached any general conclusions concerning the major factors which influence the success and performance of football teams?
> A. Well, I've got a pretty firm opinion of what I think makes it go. To begin with a football team, when you get a franchise, you get a certificate that you hang on the wall, and really it's a lot more than that, and a heap of jerseys and pants and shoes and athletic supporters in the corner of a locker room. It comes down to nothing, really, but people. It's the getting of people, putting them together and getting them into the spirit and paying the price towards a common objective of trying to win a football game, is the name of the game, really.
> When I first go to camp with the football players, . . . I give them a talk [on] . . . all aspects of what I think make for a successful operation.
> [I] try to point out to them if they're ever a bad character or boozer or chaser or what not, we're that much farther away from winning what we're trying to win.
> . . . I'm really interested in getting their best efforts.
> And I tell them that this isn't for moral reasons. It's because we have the right in our agreements with them to receive their best. And I'm in the process of trying to prepare them physically and mentally to arrive at that point. More football players fail mentally and quicker from that standpoint than they do from the physical. District Court Opinion, at 135.

The court also accepted the testimony of one player that on a football team "there is a delicate balance — a fine honing — necessary to success." The court concluded that "In short, football is a scientific, sophisticated sport, and a delicate sort of mechanism." Id. at 135. While the court stated that football was "probably unique," its evaluation seems to have been directed more to the difficulty encountered in that sport because of the large number of players involved and not to the subjective nature of the coach's discretion.

The Bergey case is considered in more detail in § 4.14 infra.

The case for relatively unfettered team discretion is somewhat less persuasive where the alleged basis for the termination is, in the language of some contracts, the player's failure "to conform . . . to standards of good citizenship, good moral character and good sportsmanship. . . ." [265] In contrast to his athletic ability, the player's general morals and citizenship are farther removed from the essential purpose of the contract. Presumably, good morals and good citizenship are not indispensable components of successful athletic endeavors.[266] Nonetheless, a different point of analysis suggests that at least as far as the law of contracts is concerned,[267] the team should be afforded broad prerogatives in determining whether it is satisfied with the player's non-athletic conduct. The basis of this conclusion is that with respect to the qualities here involved, there are not readily-discernible objective criteria against which the player's actions can be judged. An assessment of one's moral standing or citizenship is necessarily subjective, and a termination decision premised on these grounds is most appropriately judged on that basis, although disciplinary sanctions short of termination may be evaluated more critically.[268]

The not-so-subtle implication of the prior discussion is that the athlete who seeks to contest his termination will encounter significant difficulty in establishing that the team exceeded the broad bounds of discretion which are afforded under the typical standard player contract. Indeed, the absence of any significant amount of sports-related case law on these matters may be explained by the fact that those who counsel athletes regard litigation in this area as futile. For most terminations, this assessment is probably correct. Despite the stories in the popular press about the arbitrariness of club owners, a club is not likely to terminate a player who still has a valuable contribution to make to the team. Such a decision would be contrary to the economic self-interest of the club, for, as explained above, the termination would end all rights which the club had in the player, including the right to trade or sell his contract.[269] Thus, it is difficult to imagine that there will be many cases of outright termination which are made on a wholly capricious basis. The athlete most likely to be terminated is one possessing talents which are only marginal compared to those of substitutes which might be readily found. And where such a player is released, it will be difficult to argue that the club could not have in good faith found his

---

265. NBA Contract ¶ 20(b)(1), quoted in note 224, § 3.07 *supra. See also* Baseball Contract ¶ 7(b)(1).

266. *But see* note 264 *supra.*

267. A decision to terminate a player for bad conduct which also has the effect of precluding him from playing for other teams may have antitrust implications. *See* § 5.09 *infra. See generally* Blalock v. Ladies Professional Golf Ass'n, 359 F. Supp. 1260 (N.D. Ga. 1973); Molinas v. National Basketball Ass'n, 190 F. Supp. 241 (S.D.N.Y. 1961); Comment, *Discipline in Professional Sports: The Need for Player Protection, supra* note 262, at 779-80.

268. It is important that a distinction be made between termination of a player's contract and other forms of discipline such as a fine or suspension. Assuming that there is no improper blacklisting of the player by other teams, see note 267 *supra,* the athlete whose contract is terminated will have an opportunity to seek employment with another club which finds his non-athletic conduct less offensive. *See generally* § 3.07 *supra.* But where the club employs other forms of discipline, such as a suspension the club attempts to both deny the athlete his salary and preclude him from seeking other employment. *See id.* In such a case, there is a greater restraint on the athlete's right to earn his livelihood, and courts are likely to be more concerned about the reasonableness of the club's action. The matter of player discipline is considered more fully below. *See* § 3.10 *infra.*

269. *See* text accompanying notes 211-14, § 3.07 *supra.*

performance to be less than satisfactory. The club would satisfy its legal obligation even if the basis of the termination were only a desire to fill the roster position with a younger or less well-known player who offered at least the potential for a more substantial contribution to the team. The mere fact that the terminated athlete was doing an adequate job would not provide a basis for judicial relief, for in many sports, there are a wealth of potential players who not only meet that standard but also have unproven potential in terms of skill, attitude, and the other qualities valued by professional teams.

However, one should not conclude that a club's exercise of discretion will never be subject to judicial review. Despite its rather amorphous content, the requirement of good faith will serve as an important limitation in some situations. What will be required, however, are rather extreme facts which suggest a substantial element of deception or vindictiveness on the part of the employer. While it would be difficult to anticipate the wide variety of fact situations which might arise, some examples can be suggested. As indicated in an earlier discussion,[270] the requisite candor would not be present if the club stated that the athlete was terminated for a lack of skill when the real basis for the decision was that a club official had petty objections to the character of the individual's friends. Likewise a termination based on false and malicious reports of off-the-field misconduct would raise a serious issue of the club's good faith. Finally, it would seem that the club could not ignore objective facts which plainly refuted the articulated basis for the termination. Thus, a running back could not be terminated because he was "too slow" if unbiased records showed that he consistently outperformed his competition. The athlete who has been terminated may find little solace in these examples for they hardly represent typical cases. This result is not surprising, however, for the clear import of the precedents developed in other areas is that the good faith standard is not to be used to test routine judgments made in the operation of a business enterprise.

A form of discretion which deserves special attention is that which is granted to the team's physician to determine the athlete's fitness for continued competition.[271] What is the legal standard of review where this decision is left to the "sole judgment" of the physician? [272] Does such a definition of the range of permissible discretion mean that the physician's decision is final subject only to the player's right to show that it was made dishonestly or in bad faith? Or is the physician obligated to exercise his judgment to reflect generally accepted medical practices? The latter standards would, of course, provide a basis of review which was essentially objective in nature. As with other similar provisions, the physician's discretion clause should be interpreted with a view to the purpose intended to be achieved. Where the issue of physical fitness is made a matter of the physician's sole discretion, the team is likely to have

---

270. *See* text accompanying notes 202-206, § 3.07 *supra.*

271. It is important to emphasize again that the discretion allocated to the team physician under the standard form player contract may be modified by the terms of a grievance procedure found in a collective bargaining agreement. This issue is discussed in note 246 *supra.* For a non-technical discussion of medical practices in the sports industry, *see* Ryan, *Medical Practices in Sports,* 38 LAW & CONTEMP. PROB. 99 (1973).

272. *See* NBA Contract ¶ 6 (1976); NHL Contract ¶ 5 (pre-season physical examination). *See generally* § 3.06 *supra.*

intended that its decision to take particular action would not be overruled by a court or arbitrator simply because the player is able to find others in the medical profession who disagree with the original judgment. Moreover, the team may seek this degree of finality even if there are a significant number of physicians who would disagree with the assessment made. On the other hand, the player properly views the team's medical adviser as a member of a profession and does not expect that the adviser will use procedures which would be disapproved by the profession. The seeming conflict in the team's interests and the player's expectations may be more apparent than real. As with the other decisions which are committed to a person's discretion, the basic standard against which the physician's judgment will be tested should be that embodied in the requirement of good faith. Thus, honesty and candor will be required, and any attempted subterfuge will provide a reason for judicial intervention.[273] By the same token, it will not be enough to show that others in the profession disagree with the judgment.[274] But even a subjective good faith standard would seemingly require that one who held himself an expert in a particular field possess the minimal skills demanded by that profession, including minimal familiarity with the generally-accepted procedures. Such a requirement may be viewed as an aspect of the good faith standard as applied in this specialized context. Thus, a physician who was not aware of important procedures for a particular injury or who otherwise ignored elementary techniques could not be said to have acted in good faith.[275] To proceed to treat a patient without such basic familiarity with the subject matter would appear to be the antithesis of candor and forthrightness.[276]

§ 3.09. No-Cut Contracts.

a. The Various Types of Job Security Clauses. It should be clear from the earlier discussion of the club's power of termination that many professional athletes enjoy relatively little job security.[277] Under the typical standard form contract, he gets paid only if he is a member of the team, and the coach and team physician have broad-ranging powers to determine who will be chosen and kept for those few positions.[278] An off-duty injury or the recurrence of an injury from a prior season,[279] as well as the team's acquisition of fresh new talent, may abruptly put an end to the player's right to further compensation. It is not surprising that individual athletes have sought to negotiate for greater job protection, which can be secured only by modification of the standard form player contract.[280]

---

273. The present inquiry bears some similarity to that which is made under commercial contracts which commit important matters to the discretion of an architect or other professional. *See* 3A Corbin on Contracts § 651.

274. *Cf. id.* § 651, at 118, n.22.

275. *Cf.* Tillman v. New Orleans Saints Football Club, 265 So. 2d 284 (La. App. 1972).

276. While the general level of medical practice in professional sports appears to be adequate, there are some cases in which the procedures followed are less than professional. *See* Houston Oilers, Inc. v. Floyd, 518 S.W.2d 836, 839 (Tex. Civ. App. 1975). *See also* Ryan, *Medical Practices in Sports, supra* note 271, at 111.

277. *See generally* § 3.07 *supra.*

278. *See generally* § 3.08 *supra.*

279. *See generally* § 3.05 *supra.*

280. *See, e.g.,* Comment, *Discipline in Professional Sports: The Need for Player Protection,* 60

Newspaper reports concerning the contracts signed by superstars tend to convey the impression that contract clauses which provide job security are rather uniform. Typically the specially-negotiated arrangement is referred to as a "no-cut contract." Through repeated use of this label, fans may be led to believe that such an agreement defines the player's protection in precise, well-understood terms. The reality of the sports world is quite different. For example, Billy Cunningham signed a contract with the Philadelphia 76'ers which contained all of the standard terms, provided for a salary of $225,000, and at the end recited simply:

> Anything hereinto the contrary not withstanding Club and Player agree that this shall be deemed a 'no-cut' contract and Player shall not be traded to any other Club without Player's consent.[281]

Under what conditions could the team interrupt the salary of a player with this type of contract? What if the player's ability were diminished because of the lingering effects of an off-season injury? What if he developed a bad attitude and refused to play to the best of his ability? And would he still receive his salary if he committed a disciplinary offense which would have otherwise led to his suspension from the team?

The contracts signed by other athletes present equally challenging cases for contract interpretation. For example, Lew Hudson signed a professional basketball contract which recited simply:

> This is a guaranteed no-cut contract for the 1966-67 season and the compensation referred to above shall be payable to the Player in any event.[282]

If the hypothetical situations suggested above are tested against this language, are the results the same as under the Cunningham contract? At least on the surface, it would appear that the use of the words guaranteeing the player's salary "in any event" are intended to do more than simply protect the player from being dropped from the team because he fails to exhibit the requisite level of ability.[283]

The above examples of job security clauses are of relatively recent vintage. If one examines the devices used in earlier contracts, even greater diversity appears. Thus, there are contracts (1) in which the team agreed not to release

---

GEO. L.J. 771, 781, n.51 (1972). It should be noted that players associations in some leagues have successfully negotiated for provisions in their collective bargaining agreements which provide the equivalent of partial season no-cut contracts for all players in the league. This is true in the NBA, for example, where it is now provided that if a player is cut for a lack of skill during the last part of the season (December 16 to April 30), his club is obligated to pay his salary for the balance of the season. See NBA Contract ¶ 20(b), quoted in note 224, § 3.07 supra. See also note 209, § 3.07 supra. While the contract clause technically allows the club to "cut" the player, the operation of the clause is similar to the more traditional versions of no-cut clauses. As is discussed below, a club which promises not to "cut" a player presumably still has the right to remove him from its roster if it continues to pay the athlete's salary. See text at notes 318-24 infra.

281. Cunningham's contract is part of the documents filed in connection with the case of Munchak Corp. v. Cunningham, 457 F.2d 721 (4th Cir. 1972). The portion of the contract quoted in the text is found in the Appendix of the Appellant, at A-95, filed in the United States Circuit Court of Appeals for the Fourth Circuit, Docket No. 71-1984.

282. Minnesota Muskies, Inc. v. Hudson, 294 F. Supp. 979, 981 (M.D.N.C. 1969).

283. See discussion at notes 310-17 infra.

the athlete; [284] (2) in which the club owner inserted a handwritten "minimum salary" term in the compensation clause; [285] and (3) in which a team official added a salary minimum and wrote the phrase "season contract" on the reverse side of the document.[286] Each of these forms would require separate analysis to determine precisely what sort of protection was intended to be afforded to the athlete.

In lieu of these cryptic references to no-cut and minimum salary rights, it would seem much more advisable if the parties made an effort to spell out precisely the protection which the player was to receive. That has been done in the better-drafted contracts. Indeed, there is a standard form no-cut provision which has been used in numerous football players' contracts as an amendment to the clause in the standard player contract which spells out the grounds upon which the club can terminate the contract.[287] This no-cut clause is as follows:

> Notwithstanding the foregoing, the Club, so long as the Player fulfills his representation and warranty that he has and will continue to have excellent physical condition and fulfills his agreement that he will perform services hereunder as directed by the Club and its Head Coach (except to the extent the Player is excused from such performance pursuant to Paragraph 15 hereof [relating to injuries received in the course of performance under the contract. — Eds.]), agrees that it will, not prior to the first day of May following the close of the football season beginning in the calendar year 19—, terminate this contract because of the Player's lack of skill or capacity to play professional football of the caliber required by the League and by the Club or because the Player's work or conduct in the performance of this contract is unsatisfactory as compared with the work and conduct of other members of the Club's squad of players.[288]

b. Interpretation of No-Cut and Salary Guarantee Clauses. Despite the differences which exist between the various types of job security clauses, general conclusions can be reached about the types of protection which such provisions afford. As a method of analyzing the clauses, it is convenient to first hypothesize different types of defects in the player's performance which might arise in the contractual relationship and then attempt to determine, to the extent possible, whether the athlete will continue to receive his salary despite the occurrence of the various difficulties. Thus, it can be noted that under the typical standard form player contract, there are a variety of conditions which might arise to cut off any right which the player otherwise had to his salary. With appropriate action by the team, the player may lose his right to compensation in any of the following situations:

(1) the athlete exhibits insufficient athletic skill; [289]

---

284. *See* Egan v. Winnipeg Baseball Club, Ltd., 96 Minn. 345, 104 N.W. 947 (1905).
285. *See* Tollefson v. Green Bay Packers, Inc., 256 Wis. 318, 41 N.W.2d 201 (1950).
286. *See* Johnson v. Green Bay Packers, Inc., 272 Wis. 149, 74 N.W.2d 784 (1956).
287. The no-cut amendment set out in the text was generally used in connection with the pre-1977 version of the NFL standard form contract. In that earlier version of the contract, the club's basic right to terminate a player for a lack of fitness or skill was set out in paragraph 6 of the uniform contract. *See* NFL Contract ¶ 6 (1975). The text of paragraph 6 is set forth in note 224, § 3.07 *supra*.
288. NFL, No-Cut Clause, Addendum to Standard Player Contract, quoted in Henningan v. Chargers Football Co., 431 F.2d 308, 310 (5th Cir. 1970).
289. *See, e.g.,* Tillman v. New Orleans Saints Football Club, 265 So. 2d 284 (La. App. 1972). *But*

(2) he develops a serious attitude problem and plays to less than his full ability; [290]
(3) he plays poorly because he is not in good physical condition due to poor eating habits or insufficient exercise;
(4) he is unable to perform because of an off-season or off-duty injury or one incurred in a prior playing season; [291]
(5) he has committed a disciplinary offense which subjects him to possible suspension from the team; [292]
(6) the athlete dies before the expiration of his contract.

Once these cases are posed, the question arises as to which of these events and conditions is eliminated as a potential ground for salary termination under a no-cut or salary guarantee contract. To simplify the analysis of this question, we can choose three types of clauses against which to test these cases. The three which are chosen are (i) the undefined no-cut clause, of the type found in the Cunningham contract; (ii) the more detailed clause illustrated by the standard form football addendum and (iii) a salary guarantee clause of the sort used in the Hudson contract.

At the outset, it should be emphasized that trade usages and trade customs in the particular sport will be of considerable importance in giving meaning to the terms "no-cut" and "salary guarantee." The terms have been used in professional sports for many years, and the occasions for application and interpretation of the various forms have been numerous. As long as these trade usages meet minimum legal conditions, which are discussed elsewhere in this treatise,[293] they can be used as aids in interpreting the contract. Because no-cut provisions and salary guarantee provisions are generally not well-defined and usually are not explained, or even mentioned, in the by-laws of the league, resort to evidence of the actual applications of the terms may be a particularly helpful interpretive device, as is evidenced in the decided cases.[294]

1. *The Undefined No-Cut Clause.*

While trade usages may produce some variations in interpretation from league to league, and even perhaps from team to team, there are nonetheless some general conclusions which can be reached about the operation of the clauses. For example, consider the undefined no-cut clause in the Cunningham contract, which, in essence, simply states: "This is a no-cut contract." [295] Here the words "no-cut" are highly suggestive of the intended meaning, for the notion of "cutting" a player from the team has a rather definite meaning in most sports. If a player is "cut" from the squad, that means that for reasons of skill, he is eliminated from the team's roster of active players. Thus, the action in cutting

---

see Johnson v. Green Bay Packers, Inc., 272 Wis. 149, 74 N.W.2d 784 (1956); Tollefson v. Green Bay Packers, Inc., 256 Wis. 318, 41 N.W.2d 201 (1950).

290. *Cf.* Pasquel v. Owen, 186 F.2d 263 (8th Cir. 1950).

291. *See, e.g.,* Hennigan v. Chargers Football Co., 431 F.2d 308 (5th Cir. 1970); Sample v. Gotham Football Club, Inc., 59 F.R.D. 160 (S.D.N.Y. 1973). *See also* Tillman v. New Orleans Saints Football Club, 265 So.2d 284 (La. App. 1972).

292. *Cf.* Molinas v. National Basketball Ass'n, 190 F. Supp. 241 (S.D.N.Y. 1961); Molinas v. Podoloff, 133 N.Y.S.2d 743 (Sup. Ct. 1954). *See generally* Comment, *Discipline in Professional Sports: The Need for Player Protection,* 60 Geo. L.J. 771 (1972).

293. *See* § 3.04 *supra.*

294. *See, e.g.,* Johnson v. Green Bay Packers, Inc., 272 Wis. 149, 158-60, 74 N.W.2d 784, 789 (1956).

295. *See* text accompanying note 281 *supra.*

the player reflects the coach's decision that when his talents were matched against those of the team's other personnel, they were found to be inadequate to warrant the club in continuing to carry the athlete on its squad, the size of which is regulated by league rules.[296] When the player is "cut," of course, his salary ordinarily terminates. Hence, a contract which declares that it is a no-cut agreement is presumably to insure that the salary will not be affected by an adverse decision about his athletic ability. Under this construction, the no-cut clause would operate to protect the player if he exhibited a level of ability less than originally anticipated by the club, or less than that of subsequently acquired players.

But the question arises as to whether an undefined no-cut clause also protects the salary rights of the player whose performance is impaired either because he has not maintained himself in good physical condition or because he suffers from injuries not related to his performance under the contract.[297] These are the conditions suggested in cases (3) and (4) above. The prior analysis suggests that the player is protected from being cut for a lack of skill. A good argument can be made that these situations also come within that principle. Thus, it would be contended that it is impossible to make a distinction between impaired physical condition and a lack of skill. It may be that a player exhibits inadequate athletic skill because his body is not well-conditioned or because he suffers the lingering effects of an injury. Yet, while it is true that there is often a direct relationship between the two qualities, they can, in fact, be viewed separately.[298] The quality of *athletic skill* can be said to be that degree of aptitude possessed by a player who has properly conditioned his body and who achieved the best recovery possible from any prior injuries. Hence, in the normal situation, a player who is hampered by a former injury will be cut for a lack of skill if he can anticipate no improvement in his condition.[299] But if he is terminated while still recovering from the injury, the cause of his termination would be physical — and not skill — related.[300] This distinction is also reflected in the standard form player contracts, where defects of skill and physical conditions are listed as separate grounds for termination.[301] Thus, the initial finding that a player with an undefined no-cut contract is protected from being cut for insufficient

---

296. *See, e.g.,* Constitution and By-Laws for the National Football League, art. XVII (Player Limits and Eligibility). *See also id.* § 17.3: "After the final reduction in the player limit to forty (40) Active Players and for the balance of that season, no club shall have more than forty-seven (47) players under contract . . . unless the player or players in excess of 47 is or are placed on the Reserve List . . . ."

297. If the player is incapacitated by an injury sustained while rendering his performance under the contract, the agreement, even if it does not contain a no-cut provision, will usually provide for the continuation of his salary. *See* §§ 3.05-3.06 *supra.*

298. *See also* discussion at note 184, § 3.06 *supra.*

299. *See, e.g.,* Tillman v. New Orleans Saints Football Club, 265 So.2d 284 (La. App. 1972).

300. Houston Oilers, Inc. v. Floyd, 518 S.W.2d 836 (Tex. Civ. App. 1975).

301. For example, ¶ 6 of the pre-1977 version of the National Football League contract, which defines the team's right of termination, gives the team a right to terminate either if the player "does not maintain himself in such excellent physical condition" or "fails to demonstrate sufficient skill and capacity to play professional football . . . ." NFL Contract ¶ 6 (1975), quoted in note 224, § 3.07 *supra.* (The abbreviated citation form for references to standard player contracts is explained in note 126, § 3.05 *supra*). A similar distinction is made in the termination clause used by the NBA, in which a lack of "sufficient skill and competitive ability" and the player's failure to "keep himself in first class physical condition" are treated in separate subsections. NBA Contract ¶¶ 20(b)(1)-(b)(2).

skill may also identify the dividing line between protected and unprotected defects in the player's performance. Absent a special agreement, such a no-cut clause will not likely be read to entitle the player to his salary regardless of defects in his physical condition. Viewed in this light the no-cut clause has the effect of relieving the player from the anxiety and risks which would be present if he had to constantly establish that his physical abilities were superior to those of other players seeking a position on the team roster. But the athlete is not relieved of the burden of maintaining his physical condition. He must keep himself in shape and avoid non-playing injuries.

It can be noted that this distinction between the type of protection afforded has a rational basis. At the time a club commits itself to the greater burden of a no-cut clause, it will usually have some basis upon which to evaluate the player's innate ability and, thus, usually will be able to make a reasoned judgment about the level of skill he will exhibit in the future. But the team has little basis upon which to predict the player's future physical condition and, hence, this characteristic represents a much greater risk to the team. Moreover, physical condition is something over which the player has some control, and by leaving that risk on the player, the team provides an incentive for him to do everything possible to maintain his condition.

The other cases hypothesized above require a somewhat different analysis. Situation (5) raises the question of whether the player with a no-cut contract is immunized from disciplinary action which would affect his salary, including both fines and suspension. The likely answer is that absent some strong indication to the contrary, the club probably did not intend to restrict the authority of its coaches to compel conforming behavior from the player.[302] By the same token, it is most unlikely that the team intended to relinquish its right to enforce rules designed to preserve the integrity of the sport. The morale problems created by an uneven disciplinary policy are potentially devastating, and it is unlikely that the team would invite such difficulty.

The matter of the player's death should present little problem. If the team does not become a guarantor of the athlete's physical condition, then surely it does not intend that the inclusion of a no-cut provision will alter the right which it otherwise has to terminate the player's salary in the event of his demise.[303]

---

302. The power of the club and league to discipline players is thought to be necessary to preserve the fans' belief in the integrity of the sport, and thus, to insure the fans' continued economic support of the industry. A variety of activities may be seen by the clubs as threatening fan support:

> Strong internal controls have ... been found necessary to protect professional sports from the greatest threat to athletic competition — organized gambling — which could completely destroy competition by tampering with or "fixing" the natural outcome of a game or event. To deal with this threat, most sports have imposed severe penalties on anyone who obviously puts forth less than his best efforts, who bets on any athletic contest, or who associates with reputed gamblers. Finally, to promote public relations and maintain spectator support, professional sports organizations have enacted broad regulations requiring all individuals with a nexus to the sport to refrain from any "conduct detrimental to the best interests" of their sport, regardless of the effect of their conduct on the level of competition.

Comment, *Discipline in Professional Sports: The Need for Player Protection,* 60 GEO. L.J. 771, 773-74 (1972).

See also Cady, The Rentzel Case, N.Y. Times, Aug. 5, 1973, § 5, at 1, col. 1; Anderson, In Defense of Discipline, *id.,* Aug. 5, 1973, § 5, at 2, col. 3.

303. *See* § 3.07 *supra. See generally* RESTATEMENT OF CONTRACTS § 459 (1932); 17 AM. JUR. 2d, *Contracts* § 487 (1964).

The final situation to be treated involves the athlete whose performance deteriorates because of attitude or emotional problems. A good case can be made for the view that the team ought to have the right to suspend the player's salary in these situations. In many respects, this problem is like that involving deteriorated physical condition. The cause of the problem is often one which is within the control of the athlete, and unless it has clearly and unequivocally been bargained away, the team should have the right to create an incentive for the player to deal with his problem. Moreover, it can probably be said that the team did not intend that the no-cut clause would operate to entitle it to anything less than the athlete's best efforts. But whatever the appeal of these arguments, the practicalities of the situation will most likely lead to the opposite result. Poor performance attributable solely to the athlete's attitude is difficult, if not impossible, to prove. One might go even further and suggest that attitude is indeed a part of skill.[304] Thus, a clause which was intended to protect a player from changing evaluations of his level of ability might be said to be directly applicable to this type of situation. In any event, the team that attempted to draw the fine line between skill and attitude would most likely find itself a party to a legal proceeding.

2. *The Football No-Cut Clause.*

Many of the questions which arise in connection with an undefined no-cut clause are avoided under a clause such as that commonly used in football contracts. Of particular significance is the language in the clause which is intended to make clear that inadequate physical condition continues as a grounds for termination. By the terms of the contract, the player must "continue to have excellent physical condition," although he is assured that he will not be terminated for a lack of skill or capacity.[305] Application of these principles to the cases identified above would suggest that the athlete's salary would continue in case (1), but a termination or interruption would be appropriate in cases (3) and (4). Since it is clear that physical condition continues to be a prerequisite to the player's entitlement to his salary, it would also follow that the club would have no continuing salary obligation in the event of the player's death, the situation presented by case (6) above. With respect to case (2), no different resolution of the problem of the interrelationship of attitude and skill is suggested by the language in the football clause. Indeed, the language which protects the player from comparative evaluation of his work and conduct serves to reinforce the conclusion that the player's salary will continue in the event his play is adversely affected by an attitude or emotional problem.

The matter of the suspension of a player's contract rights for disciplinary reasons requires some further analysis. Under the language of the no-cut clauses used in football contracts, the player is assured that he will not be terminated because his "work or conduct in the performance of this contract is

---

304. Coaches and others have recognized the inseparable relationship between mental attitude and skill. Coach Paul Brown of the Cincinnati Bengals has testified: "More football players fail mentally[,] and quicker from that standpoint[,] than do from the physical." *Cincinnati Bengals, Inc. v. Bergey*, 453 F. Supp. 129, 135 (S.D. Ohio 1974), *aff'd,* Civil No. 74-1570 (6th Cir., Aug. 27, 1974). Brown's testimony is considered more fully in note 264, § 3.08 *supra.*

305. The relevant language is set out in full in the text at note 288, *supra.*

unsatisfactory as compared with the work and conduct of other members of the Club's squad of players." [306] This language might be read to mean that the club is relinquishing the right to deem the player's *conduct* to be unsatisfactory. To the extent that these actions would otherwise be subject to disciplinary sanction, the club would have given up its right to demand conforming conduct. That would be a rather startling result.[307] Not only would the management and training of the team be made much more difficult, but, as suggested above, a lack of even-handedness in the disciplinary process would create severe morale problems. And if other clauses of the football contract are examined, it will be seen that discipline is treated in a separate provision of the agreement.[308] Since these disciplinary rights are covered elsewhere in the contract, they would seem to be unaffected by a no-cut clause which is inserted as an amendment to a different provision.[309] Moreover, simply as a matter of interpretation, it can be said that discipline falls outside the coverage of the termination clause and its no-cut amendment. When a player is disciplined, it is not because his conduct is unsatisfactory on a comparative basis, but rather because it is unsatisfactory in an absolute sense, given the prohibitions of the disciplinary rule. Thus, it would appear that the club's disciplinary powers are unaffected by its acquiescence to a no-cut clause.

3. *The Salary Guarantee.*

Unless it is precisely defined in the contract itself, a salary guarantee clause raises the most difficult problems of interpretation. Typical of this sort of provision would be the one used in the Lew Hudson contract.[310] That clause provided simply that the stipulated compensation "shall be payable to the Player in any event." [311] It appears from the situations in which these clauses are used that the player has negotiated for greater protection than would be afforded by a no-cut clause. Yet, it seems unlikely that the parties intended that the player should have an absolute, unconditional right to receive his salary. For example, should the player move to another team or retire before even playing a game, it is doubtful that the team understood that it would, nonetheless, be obligated to pay the full amount of his salary.

If the salary guarantee is, in fact, used as a device to give rights beyond those available under a no-cut clause, the conditions to which the protection is most logically extended are those relating to physical condition. And the most reasonable reading of an undefined salary guarantee clause is that it is intended to relieve the player of concerns about potential physical disabilities, as well as from the risk that his level of athletic ability might be found unacceptable. What types of physical disabilities are covered by the salary guarantee? Since the purpose of the guarantee clause is to afford the player greater protection than he would achieve under the terms of the basic standard player agreement, the injuries covered are presumably injuries other than those incurred in the course

---

306. *See id.*
307. *See* note 302 *supra.*
308. *See* NFL Contract ¶¶ 4, 11 (1975), discussed in note 224, § 3.07 *supra.*
309. The wording of the football no-cut clause indicates clearly that it is intended to operate as an amendment to ¶ 6 of the pre-1977 NFL Contract. *See* note 287 *supra.*
310. *See generally* Minnesota Muskies, Inc. v. Hudson, 294 F. Supp. 979 (M.D.N.C. 1969).
311. *See* text at note 282 *supra.*

of performance under the contract.[312] The custom of the trade is to lump all non-playing injuries into one category,[313] and presumably it is this broad group of physical deficiencies which are affected by the guarantee clause. Thus, the player with such a clause can be expected to be paid even when his performance is impaired by an off-season, off-duty, or pre-contract condition.

But what can the team expect in terms of performance by the player? Here the basic problem is to define the conditions which must be satisfied before the player is entitled to his guaranteed salary. As previously mentioned, it would be unreasonable to find that the club's obligation to pay was absolute. Surely, the parties expect that the player will perform some services on behalf of the team. A traditional contract analysis would suggest the limits of the player's right to receive his salary.[314] The player's basic duty is that which exists in any such arrangement; at a minimum, the club can expect that the athlete will make a good faith effort to perform the services called for under the contract. That means that the player must constantly be ready and willing to perform,[315] and he can do nothing which will impair the likelihood that he will be available when the time for performance arrives.[316] Thus, he will not be paid if he accepts other contractual commitments which interfere with the duty he owes the team. But of equal importance is the fact that the player must be willing to perform. Should the player decide to retire or otherwise abandon his playing effort, the team would have no obligation to pay him. By the same token, a less-than enthusiastic effort on the playing field, if deliberately staged, would give the team grounds for withholding salary, although the problems of proof in this connection would weigh heavily against any adverse decision by the club.

Finally, it must be asked whether a salary guarantee clause immunizes the athlete from disciplinary actions which might reduce or suspend his salary. For the reasons already outlined in connection with the other no-cut clauses,[317] it is doubtful that the parties intended that a player with a guaranteed salary should be treated any differently in disciplinary matters than the athlete who operates under the unmodified standard player agreement. The matter of player discipline is of such importance to the basic function of the team that it is reasonable to assume that the team would not relinquish its control in the absence of an express recognition of that fact in the contract documents.

c. Release of an Athlete Under a No-Cut Contract. Does a no-cut clause operate to assure an athlete a place on the team's roster, or does it simply mean that the team will have to continue to pay the player's salary if he is, in fact,

---

312. Under most standard player contracts, the club agrees to continue the player's salary if he is injured while performing under the contract. *See* §§ 3.05-3.06 *supra. See generally* Schultz v. Los Angeles Dons, Inc., 107 Cal. App. 2d 718, 238 P.2d 73 (Ct. App. 1951); Houston Oilers, Inc. v. Floyd, 581 S.W.2d 836 (Tex. Civ. App. 1973).

313. *See* § 3.05 *supra.*

314. The matter of the rights and obligations of parties to an employment relationship is discussed in 3A CORBIN ON CONTRACTS §§ 674-84. Corbin's treatment is necessarily general and does not take account of specially negotiated terms such as a salary guarantee clause. The discussion is, nonetheless, useful to set the general framework in which these problems will be resolved.

315. But as suggested above, he need not also be "able" to perform. While the player's availablility and attitude are his responsibility, the team presumably accepts the risks of physical incapacity.

316. *Cf.* 3A CORBIN ON CONTRACTS §§ 677-78.

317. *See* discussion at note 302 *supra.*

cut from the squad? Although there are no reported cases on this question, the latter interpretation is surely the correct one. This result is suggested by a number of different points of analysis. In order to put the problem in proper perspective, it should be kept in mind that the club has a strong incentive not to drop a no-cut athlete from its roster and most likely would do so only in the most dire circumstances. The club has a substantial investment in such a player, and presumably will make reasonable efforts to develop the player into a productive member of the team, either as a regular or as a reserve.[318] Thus, the athlete who is dropped in these circumstances is not likely to be one who has a stellar future ahead of him.[319]

It can be noted that under the no-cut provision used in football, the basic undertaking accepted by the club is a promise that it "will not . . . terminate [the] contract because of the Player's lack of skill or capacity." [320] If the club continues to pay the player's salary, which is usually the basic performance for which the player bargained, it is arguable that the contract has not been "terminated," even if the athlete is not allowed to remain on the active roster. This interpretation should prevail in most cases.

Some arguments can be made that the player has interest in a roster position distinct from his interest in salary. But when exposed to the practicalities of the professional sports world, these contentions lose much of their validity. For example, it might be argued that an athlete has an interest in remaining on the team's active squad because of the exposure and training value of such a position. Surely advertisers looking for athletes to endorse their products are not likely to be impressed by a player who spends most of his time watching the game from the end of the bench, as usually will be the case with an athlete who has to insist upon his right to a roster position. And while it is probably true that even the player at the bottom of the roster learns something from practice sessions and his occasional minutes of regular season play, the team should have no obligation to continue to try to train the player when it is apparent that its reasonable efforts are for naught. Since the club will presumably do what it can to recoup its investment in a player with a no-cut contract, it is difficult to imagine a situation in which there is any great likelihood that such a player would show substantial improvement by being retained on the active list beyond the point at which the club would otherwise decide to drop him. The better view is that by agreeing to a no-cut clause, the club intends to

318. There are some notable exceptions, however. Jim McDaniels, who received a $1.8 million, 18-year, no-cut contract from the Seattle SuperSonics, did not perform to the club's expectations and was eventually dropped from the team. He continued to draw his salary, however, which was to be paid over a period of 18 years. *See* Florence, *McDaniels, One of the Idle Rich, Says He Doesn't Like It,* Los Angeles Times, Jan. 31, 1974, pt. III, at 1, col. 5.

319. The athlete who is dropped from the roster of one team will often find that a large no-cut contract inhibits his ability to obtain a position with another team. On the one hand, other teams are likely to be unwilling to buy up his contract because it would obligate a new employer to a financial commitment which is not usually justified by the level of the player's talent. On the other hand, even if the player were willing to renegotiate the contract, the original employer is likely to insist that it receive substantial compensation for assigning its rights. Even though these rights may have little value to the present employer, the club may attempt to use the occasion of the assignment to attempt to recoup the substantial investment which it has in the unproductive player. *See* Florence, *Id.* (SuperSonics want $500,000 for rights to McDaniels).

320. *See* text at note 288 *supra.*

satisfy the player's interest in job-security, but does not intend to relinquish its right to attempt to field a competitive team. Both interests are satisfied under the suggested interpretation. Job-security is afforded by the assurance of salary continuation even if the athlete's skills are found to be wanting, and the club's continued control of the competitiveness of its team is assured if it has no absolute obligation to carry a particular player. While the club may be willing to accept the salary consequences of an erroneous evaluation of the playing potential of an athlete, it is not likely to have intended a result which could potentially impair its ability to attract spectators, whose dollars are basic to its continued existence.

One commentator has suggested that instead of simply bargaining for a no-cut clause, the athlete ought also insist that a no-release provision be added.[321] Such a clause would explicitly provide that the player had to be maintained on the club's active roster for the duration of his contract. It is not clear, however, that a clause of this sort has much value. One must ask what the consequences would be if a club violated a no-release clause. Presumably specific performance of the provision would not be ordered for reasons of public policy.[322] Rather, the athlete's only recourse would be compensation in money damages for the injury he suffered, and in the vast majority of cases, the only damages to be awarded would be the balance of the stipulated salary. While the player might try to argue that there were other losses flowing from his removal from the roster, he bears a significant burden in avoiding the club's rebuttal that either there is no injury [323] or any damages are wholly speculative.[324] The athlete would be better advised to expend his bargaining efforts on more substantive provisions.

§ 3.10. Contractual Aspects of Player Discipline.

a. Background. One of the most frequently disputed aspects of the relationships which underlie professional sports is the power claimed by the clubs and the league commissioners to discipline athletes.[325] The provisions for discipline may be invoked to discourage a wide variety of activities, including

---

321. *See* S. GALLNER, PRO SPORTS: THE CONTRACT GAME 90 (1974).

322. Courts generally do not award specific performance in personal service contracts, in part because of a public policy against using judicial powers to compel individuals to take actions against their will. In addition, there is a concern for the difficulty of administering an order with which compliance depends upon the good faith of the party restrained. *See* § 4.02 *infra.*

323. As suggested above, the club would often be able to argue that the athlete was not likely to receive outside income from endorsements and the like. In addition, there will often be no loss resulting from the club's failure to give the athlete additional training.

324. *See generally* 5 CORBIN ON CONTRACTS § 1022.

325. *See generally* Molinas v. National Basketball Ass'n, 190 F. Supp. 241 (S.D.N.Y. 1961); Molinas v. Podoloff, 133 N.Y.S.2d 743 (Sup. Ct. 1954); American League Baseball Club of New York v. Johnson, 109 Misc. 138, 179 N.Y.S. 498 (1919), *aff'd,* 190 App. Div. 932, 179 N.Y.S. 898 (1920); Alyluia, *Professional Sports Contracts and the Players' Association,* 5 MANITOBA L.J. 359, 386-70 (1973); Comment, *Discipline in Professional Sports: The Need for Player Protection,* 60 GEO. L.J. 771 (1972); Cady, *The Rentzel Case,* N.Y. Times, Aug. 5, 1973, § 5, at 1, col. 1; *Interview: Pete Rozelle,* Playboy, Oct. 1973, at 65.

Earlier chapters in this treatise consider aspects of sports-related discipline arising in other contexts. Legal questions which arise in regard to the disciplining of amateur athletes are considered in Chapter 1. Issues which arise from discipline in publicly regulated sports activities are considered in Chapter 2. While the legal doctrine which is applied in these other areas draws heavily on principles of constitutional law, the reader may find it useful to consult that earlier discussion to note how the problems of discretion and procedure are dealt with in those somewhat different contexts.

gambling,[326] criticizing umpires and referees,[327] associating with "undesirables," [328] and failing to observe the rules of competition.[329] This vast power of discipline must find its basis in the consent of the player. Thus, it is not surprising that the standard form player contract provides the necessary link between the player and the disciplinary authority of the team and the league.

This is not to suggest, however, that one will find an exhaustive listing of disciplinable offenses in the standard player contracts. Although there are exceptions, most contracts serve only the limited purpose of securing the player's agreement to abide by rules which the team or league may devise. Typically the standard player contract recites that the club may establish rules governing player conduct and exacts the player's express promise to abide by those rules.[330] The agreement also will usually indicate the types of sanctions

---

326. *See* Molinas v. National Basketball Ass'n, 190 F. Supp. 241 (S.D.N.Y. 1961); Molinas v. Podoloff, 133 N.Y.S.2d 743 (Sup. Ct. 1954); N.Y. Times, Apr. 2, 1970, at 48, col. 1 (baseball player Denny McLain suspended for gambling activities); *id.,* Mar. 17, 1974, at 41, col. 1 (football players Paul Hornung and Alex Karras suspended); *id.,* July 14, 1960, at 27, col. 3 (football players Merle Haper and Frank Filchock suspended).

327. *See* N.Y. Times, Mar. 19, 1975, at 63, col. 2; *id.,* Mar. 30, 1975, § 5, at 5, col. 1; *id.,* Apr. 1, 1975, at 43, col. 2.

328. *See* N.Y. Times, Apr. 2, 1970, at 48, col. 1 (baseball player Denny McLain suspended for associating with gamblers). *Cf.* N.Y. Times, July 20, 1969, § 5, at 1, col. 1 (NFL commissioner suggests that football players, including Joe Namath, avoid frequenting establishments suspected of housing gambling activities).

329. *Cf.* Blalock v. Ladies Professional Golf Ass'n, 359 F. Supp. 1260 (N.D. Ga. 1973).

330. The source of the club's disciplinary power in the NHL contract is paragraph 4 of the Standard Player's Contract:

> The club may from time to time during the continuance of this contract establish rules governing the conduct and conditioning of the Player, and such rules shall form part of this contract as fully as if herein written. For violation of any such rules or for any impairing the thorough and faithful discharge of the duties incumbent upon the Player, the Club may impose a reasonable fine upon the Player and deduct the amount thereof from any money due or to become due to the Player. The Club may also suspend the Player for violation of any such rules. When the Player is fined or suspended, he shall be given notice in writing stating the amount of the fine and/or the duration of the suspension and the reason therefor.

NHL Contract ¶ 4 (the abbreviated citation form used to refer to standard player contracts is explained in note 126, § 3.05 *supra*).

The primary disciplinary provision of the pre-1977 NFL contract is in ¶ 4:

> The Player agrees at all times to comply with and be bound by: the Constitution and By-Laws, Rules and Regulations of the League, of the Club and the decisions of the Commissioner of the League (hereinafter called "Commissioner"), which shall be final, conclusive and unappealable. The enumerated Constitution, By-Laws, Rules and Regulations are intended to include the present Constitution, By-Laws, Rules and Regulations as well as all amendments thereto, all of which are by reference incorporated herein. If the Player fails to comply with said Constitution, By-Laws, Rules and Regulations, the Club shall have the right to terminate this contract as provided in Paragraph 6 hereof or to take such other action as may be specified in said Constitution, By-Laws, Rules and Regulations, subject, however, to the right to a hearing by the Commissioner. All matters in dispute between the Player and the Club shall be referred to the Commissioner and his decision shall be accepted as final, complete, conclusive, binding and unappealable, by the Player and by the Club. The Player, if involved or affected in any manner whatsoever by a decision of the Commissioner, whether the decision results from a dispute between the Player and the Club or otherwise, hereby releases and discharges the Commissioner, the League, each Club in the League, each Director, Officer, Stockholder, Owner or Partner of any Club in the League, each employee, agent, official or representative of the League or of any Club in the League,

which may be imposed. Fines and suspensions are typically specified,[331] but contracts vary somewhat in the extent to which termination of the contract is expressly recognized as an available sanction.[332] Some contracts specify the

> jointly and severally, individually and in their official capacities, of and from any and all claims, demands, damages, suits, actions and causes of action whatsoever, in law or in equity, arising out of or in connection with any decision of the Commissioner, except to the extent of awards made by the Commissioner to the Player. The Player hereby acknowledges that he has read the present said Constitution, By-Laws, Rules and Regulations, and that he understands their meaning. *Id.*

The NFL disciplinary system underwent a significant change with the new collective bargaining agreement which was approved in 1977. The agreement prompted a change in the standard player contract. In the version of the new contract used at the time of this writing (*see* note 126, § 3.05 *supra*), two provisions are relevant:

> 14. Rules. Player will comply with and be bound by all reasonable Club rules and regulations in effect during the term of this contract which are not inconsistent with the provisions of this contract or of any collective bargaining agreement in existence during the term of this contract. Player's attention is also called to the fact that the League functions with certain rules and procedures expressive of its operation as a joint venture among its member clubs and that these rules and practices may affect Player's relationship to the League and its member clubs independently of the provisions of this contract.

> 15. Integrity of Game. Player recognizes the detriment to the League and professional football that would result from impairment of public confidence in the honest and orderly conduct of NFL games or the integrity and good character of NFL players. Player therefore acknowledges his awareness that if he accepts a bribe or agrees to throw or fix an NFL game; fails to promptly report a bribe offer or an attempt to throw or fix an NFL game; bets on an NFL game; knowingly associates with gamblers or gambling activity; uses or provides other players with stimulants or other drugs for the purpose of attempting to enhance on-field performance; or is guilty of any other form of conduct reasonably judged by the League Commissioner to be detrimental to the League or professional football, the Commissioner will have the right, but only after giving the Player the opportunity for a hearing at which he may be represented by counsel of his choice, to fine Player in a reasonable amount; to suspend Player for a period certain or indefinitely; and/or to terminate this contract.

NFL Contract ¶¶ 14, 15 (1977).

The NFL collective bargaining agreement also includes several important provisions. The players were successful in their efforts to make club discipline a matter for agreement between the union and the owners. Thus, it was agreed that "The NFLPA and the Management Council will agree upon and publish a maximum discipline schedule to be utilized beginning with the 1977 season; such a schedule will include maximum discipline for offenses or categories of offenses." Collective Bargaining Agreement Between the NFL Management Council and the NFL Players Ass'n, art. VI, § 1 (1977). Once this "maximum discipline schedule" is agreed upon, the individual clubs are required to publish a complete list of the sanctions which can be imposed for designated offenses, and the sanctions must be within the maximum limits agreed upon. Significantly, it is also agreed that matters of club discipline are subject to the non-injury grievance procedure under the collective bargaining agreement. *Id.,* art. VI, § 4.

The above provisions only pertain to club discipline, and the collective bargaining agreement recognizes the independent disciplinary authority of the Commissioner in matters pertaining to "conduct on the playing field" and "conduct detrimental to the integrity of, or public confidence in, the game of professional football ...." *Id.,* art. VIII, § 1. The collective bargaining agreement specifies the procedures which the commissioner must follow and provides for a hearing before the commissioner.

331. *See, e.g.,* NHL Contract ¶ 4, *supra* note 330; NFL Contract ¶ 4 (1975), *supra* note 330; WHA Contract ¶¶ 4, 10.2.1. *See generally* Kapp v. B.C. Lions Football Club, (1967) 61. W.W.R. 31.

332. *See, e.g.,* NFL Contract ¶ 4 (1975), *supra* note 330.

The NBA contract is somewhat unclear on this point. While the provision which empowers the club to make disciplinary rules specifies fines and suspensions as remedies, (NBA Contract ¶ 4) the termination clause of the contract states that the club may terminate if the player fails "to conform his personal conduct to standards of good citizenship, good moral character, and good sportsmanship." *Id.* ¶ 20(b)(1). Arguably the latter clause is broad enough to include some types of conduct which would otherwise be subject to a disciplinary rule. See discussion in note 224, § 3.07 *supra*.

procedural rights which the player will be afforded. The player is usually entitled to notice of the action taken [333] and there is frequently a provision for review of club-imposed discipline by the league commissioner.[334] In some cases, a right to a hearing is provided.[335]

Most agreements recognize that the league commissioner has independent disciplinary authority.[336] A typical standard player contract recites that the athlete agrees to be bound by league rules and regulations and that the league commissioner has authority to enforce these.[337] As with club-imposed discipline, the substance of the rules is often not stated in the contract.[338] Prohibitions on gambling are an exception,[339] and many agreements specifically empower the commissioner to impose severe penalties when the player is found to have engaged in gambling or gambling-related activities.[340]

b. Limitations on the Club's Disciplinary Power. An inquiry into the legal basis of the disciplinary power in professional sports suggests that this is another area in which the legal questions are in many respects unique. Moreover,

---

333. *See, e.g.,* NHL Contract ¶ 4, *supra* note 330; NBA Contract ¶ 4; WHA Contract ¶ 4.

334. *See, e.g.,* WHA Contract ¶ 4 ("In the event the Player believes the fine or suspension to be unreasonable, he may, within forty-eight (48) hours of notice of the fine or suspension, request the League President to rule on its reasonableness, and the President's decision shall be binding on Player and Club.")

In other contracts, the right of appeal would presumably arise under contract terms which empower the league commissioner to decide all disputes between an athlete and his club arising from the contract. *See, e.g.,* NHL Contract ¶ 18.

335. *See, e.g.,* NFL Contract ¶ 4 (1975), *supra* note 330. *See also* Molinas v. Podoloff, 133 N.Y.S.2d 743 (Sup. Ct. 1954).

336. *But see* American League Baseball Club of New York v. Johnson, 109 Misc. 138, 179 N.Y.S. 498 (1919), *aff'd,* 190 App. Div. 932, 179 N.Y.S. 898 (1920).

337. *See, e.g.,* NFL Contract ¶ 4 (1975), *supra* note 330.

Under the NHL contract, the legal basis for the league president's authority over a player is found in a provision in which the club and the player agree to be "legally bound by the Constitution and By-Laws of the League...." NHL Contract ¶ 18. The player then agrees separately that the league-imposed fines may be deducted from his salary (*id.* ¶ 18) and that the club may "put into effect" any suspension ordered by the league (*id.* ¶ 14).

338. The NBA contract is somewhat unique in that appended to the agreement is an excerpt from the league constitution which details the commissioner's fining authority and lists certain offenses. A clause of the NBA contract specifically incorporates this provision into the player contract. NBA Contract ¶ 15. Although the incorporated provision is broad enough to authorize league-imposed sanctions for gambling-related activities and for tampering with other parties already under contract, the standard player contract also includes provisions dealing with these matters and empowering the commissioner to take appropriate action. *See id.* ¶¶ 16, 19.

339. *See, e.g.,* NFL Contract ¶ 11 (1975):

> Player acknowledges the right and power of the Commissioner (a) to fine and suspend, (b) to fine and suspend for life or indefinitely, and/or (c) to cancel the contract of, any player who accepts a bribe or who agrees to throw or fix a game or who, having knowledge of the same, fails to report an offered bribe or an attempt to throw or fix a game or who bets on a game, or who is guilty of any conduct detrimental to the welfare of the League or of professional football. The Player, if involved or affected in any manner whatsoever by a decision of the Commissioner in any of the aforesaid cases, hereby releases and discharges the Commissioner, the League, each Club in the League, each Director, Officer, Stockholder, Owner, Partner, employee, agent, official or representative of any Club in the League, jointly and severally, individually and in their official capacities, of and from any and all claims, demands, damages, suits, actions and causes of action whatsoever, in law or in equity, arising out of or in connection with any such decision of the Commissioner.

See also NFL Contract ¶ 15 (1977), quoted in note 330, *supra.*

340. *See* Molinas v. Podoloff, 133 N.Y.S.2d 743 (Sup. Ct. 1954).

as with many other issues in the law of sports, there is no substantial body of case precedent dealing specifically with sports-related discipline. As a consequence, the analysis for the issues presented has to be made primarily by drawing analogies to other areas of the law. But even at this stage there may be disputes about the appropriate legal framework in which these questions should be analyzed. For example, one commentator has argued that the law of private associations ought to be applied.[341] Under this view, the status of the athlete would be regarded as similar to that of a member of an association, and the rights with respect to disciplinary actions would be determined under the precedents which define the right of a private group to expel or otherwise sanction its members for improper conduct.[342] The appeal of this analogy rests in the fact that courts have increasingly been willing to intervene into the affairs of such associations where the actions of the group have a significant effect upon important economic interests of the member who is disciplined.[343]

There are a number of problems with this approach however. As an initial matter, it can be noted that athletes are not, in fact, members of an association with their employers.[344] While there is no small difficulty in defining exactly what types of groups constitute associations,[345] it should be clear that the club owners and their athlete-employees do not have the singular community of interests which typifies most associations.[346] Indeed, the owner's interest in operating a profitable business and the player's interest in job security would seem to suggest that there is a basic antagonism. In light of that fact, it would seem more appropriate to place sports-related discipline problems into a legal context which was to a greater extent shaped by the adversary nature of the relationship involved.[347]

A further defect which can be noted in the association analogy is the fact that it fails to fully take account of the opportunity for bargaining between those

---

341. *See* Comment, *Discipline in Professional Sports: The Need for Player Protection, supra* note 325, at 782-86.

342. *See generally* Chafee, *The Internal Affairs of Associations Not for Profit,* 43 HARV. L. REV. 993 (1930); Comment, *Developments in the Law — Judicial Control of Actions of Private Associations,* 76 HARV. L. REV. 983 (1963).

343. *See, e.g.,* Pinsker v. Pacific Coast Soc'y of Orthodontists, 12 Cal. 3d 541, 526 P.2d 253, 116 Cal. Rptr. 245 (1974); McCune v. Wilson, 237 So. 2d 169 (Fla. Sup. Ct. 1970); Falcone v. Middlesex County Medical Soc'y, 34 N.J. 582, 170 A.2d 791 (1961).

344. *Compare* Comment, *Discipline in Professional Sports: The Need for Player Protection,* 60 GEO. L.J. 771, 782-83 (1972).

345. *Id.* at 782. *Cf.* Scott v. Lee, 24 Cal. Rptr. 824 (Dist. Ct. App. 1962).

346. The author of the comment recognizes that singularness of purpose is a common characteristic of "associations," but the writer goes on to conclude that professional athletes have such singular affinity with their clubs. *See* Comment, *Discipline in Professional Sports: The Need for Player Protection, supra* note 344, at 782. It is true that employees, in one sense, share a common purpose with their employers, for both have an interest in the success of the enterprise. But this common goal is usually not the only one which is sought by each of the parties. Thus, the employment relationship is more truly multidimensional than, say, an Elks Club or other similar organization.

347. The recent cases in which courts have intervened into the affairs of an association have typically involved groups which serve an important public purpose, such as medical societies. *See, e.g.,* Pinsker v. Pacific Coast Society of Orthodontists, 12 Cal. 3d 541, 526 P.2d 253, 116 Cal. Rptr. 245 (1974); Falcone v. Middlesex County Medical Soc'y, 34 N.J. 582, 170 A.2d 791 (1961). The associations involved typically controlled the extent to which important services were available to the public. It would not seem that a "group" which operated only to provide entertainment events, such as sports leagues, would present as urgent a case for judicial intervention under these principles.

enforcing discipline rules and those subjected to them. It is true that the members of an association may amend the rules which govern the group's affairs,[348] and this does allow for the possibility that individual interests will be considered. But associations quickly develop bureaucratic characteristics,[349] and the prospect of dynamic membership participation is usually more theoretical than real.[350] While the disciplinary process in the sports industry has historically been presented to the players on a take-it-or-leave-it basis, that is changing in some important respects. The advent of players' unions increases the likelihood of player-input into the disciplinary process.[351] The players' interests in this regard receive substantial support from the federal law which requires that the employer-clubs must bargain about all matters affecting "wages, hours, and other terms and conditions of employment." [352] Although the ultimate impact of representative bargaining has yet to be determined, there are indications that the players' unions have achieved some success in invoking their right to influence the disciplinary procedures in professional sports.[353]

What this suggests is that the matter of discipline in professional sports should be regarded as a matter of employer-employee relations, which, of course, is what it is. When framed in those terms, it will be seen that the system of discipline in the sports industry has two aspects: one arising from the controls imposed by the federal labor laws and the other based in common law precedents applicable to employment contracts. The federal labor law issues are considered elsewhere in this treatise.[354] The present discussion will be limited to a consideration of the issues which arise under the private law of contracts.

The starting point for analysis is the legal doctrine which has developed in connection with the use of disciplinary measures in other employment contexts. While that doctrine does suggest some useful points of analysis which can be applied in the sports area, two factors limiting the applicability of the precedents from other businesses can be noted. First, it must be accepted that the sports industry is probably atypical in the extent to which it depends upon fines and suspensions to control the behavior of its employees. While other businesses utilize such penalties in some situations, the power asserted is seldom as pervasive as that which is assumed to exist in the sports area. Secondly, even

---

348. Under the classic formulations, a member is said to be bound to the disciplinary rules of his association because he has consented to them, as evidenced by the fact that he accepted membership in the group. Moreover, the consent is thought to be effective in part because of the individual's opportunity to change the rules if he desires. *See generally* Chafee, *The Internal Affairs of Associations Not for Profit, supra* note 342.

349. *See* Comment, *Developments in the Law — Judicial Control of Actions of Private Associations, supra* note 342, at 989. *See generally* Blumer, *Collective Behavior,* in Principles of Sociology 167, 203 (2d rev. ed. 1951).

350. This phenomenon has received particular attention in connection with the internal government of labor unions. *See* Lipset, *The Political Process in Trade Unions: A Theoretical Statement,* in Labor and Trade Unionism: An Interdisciplinary Reader 216 (W. Galeson & S. M. Lipset eds. 1966).

351. *See generally* ch. 6, *infra;* Krasnow & Levy, *Unionization and Professional Sports,* 51 Geo. L.J. 749 (1963); Lowell, *Collective Bargaining and the Professional Team Sport Industry,* 38 Law & Contemp. Prob. 3 (1973).

352. National Labor Relations Act, § 8(d), 29 U.S.C. § 158(D) (1974).

353. The recent revisions of the NFL disciplinary system which resulted from the 1977 collective bargaining agreement between the owners and the players are discussed in note 330, *supra.*

354. *See* §§ 6.05-6.08 *infra.*

though there is some precedent available outside the sports area, it can hardly be said that the matter of the employer's disciplinary powers is well-defined at common law. In total, the body of precedent is rather meager, and the cases by no means follow consistent trends. Most courts seem to concede that the employer enjoys some right to use forfeiture and penalties to control his employees' conduct, but the precise scope of that power is not firmly settled.[355] With those qualifications in mind, we can undertake to outline the common law considerations which bear upon the exercise of disciplinary power by a club or a league.

A threshold question can be raised concerning the proper characterization of an employer fine. In many non-sports cases, it can be said that a fine, or more often a forfeiture of salary, is used by the employer as compensation for some injury which was sustained by the employer's business as the result of misconduct by the employee. Thus, the employer may attempt to make deductions for money missing from a cash drawer within the control of the employee,[356] or for losses sustained by the employer's property as a result of the employee's negligence.[357] In these cases, the forfeiture may be viewed as a method whereby the employer recovers damages for the injury which he has incurred. But even non-sports cases recognize that a forfeiture may operate where the employee's violation of an employer rule produces no readily quantifiable damage to the employer.[358] However, the allowance of recovery in these situations might be explained on a contract damage theory. Under this view, the fine or forfeiture would be regarded as a form of liquidated damages for some injury to the employer's interest. Although it does not appear that the forfeiture cases are decided under that theory, the rules which have been devised to determine the validity of an employer-imposed fine are strikingly similar to those used to adjudge the enforceability of a liquidated damage clause.[359] Thus, there must be a showing that the employee consented to the forfeiture provision, a requirement designed to insure that the matter becomes a part of the contract.[360] Moreover, the enforceability of the disciplinary provision is limited by a notion of reasonableness: only reasonable rules may be enforced, and the amount of any forfeiture must not be disproportionate to the harm which was likely to result to the employer.[361]

It can appropriately be asked whether a system for fining in professional sports should be regarded as a mechanism for liquidating damages. Despite the

---

355. *See generally* 53 AM. JUR. 2d *Master and Servant* § 85 (1970); 56 C.J.S., *Master and Servant* §§ 103-06, 114 (1948).

356. Gutierrez v. Hachar's Dept. Store, 484 S.W.2d 433 (Tex. Civ. App. 1972).

357. *See, e.g.,* Maratta v. Chas. H. Heer Dry Goods Co., 190 Mo. App. 420, 177 S.W. 718 (1915); Eaton v. Wooly, 28 Wis. 628 (1871).

358. Several early cases support this principle. *See, e.g.,* Preston v. American Linen Co., 119 Mass. 400 (1876); Noon v. Salisbury Mills, 85 Mass. (3 Allen) 340 (1962); Birdsall v. Twenty-Third St. Ry., 8 Daly 419 (N.Y.C.P. 1879); Matthews v. Industrial Lumber Co., 91 S.C. 568, 75 S.E. 170 (1911).

359. *See* RESTATEMENT OF CONTRACTS § 339 (1932).

360. *See, e.g.,* Borden v. Day, 197 Okla. 110, 168 P.2d 646 (1946); Matthews v. Industrial Lumber Co., 91 S.C. 568, 75 S.E. 170 (1911).

361. *See, e.g.,* Ressig v. Waldorf-Astoria Hotel Co., 185 App. Div. 4, 172 N.Y.S. 616 (Sup. Ct. 1918), *aff'd,* 229 N.Y. 553, 129 N.E. 912 (1920); Godt v. Henigson, 135 N.Y.S. 666 (Sup. Ct. 1912); Schrimpf v. Tennessee Mfg. Co., 86 Tenn. 219, 6 S.W. 262 (1887). *See generally* 56 C.J.S., *Master and Servant* §§ 103-06 (1948). *Compare* RESTATEMENT OF CONTRACTS § 339 (1932); Uniform Commercial Code § 2-718.

temptation to accept that analogy, the answer which must ultimately be reached is that it strains contract doctrine too much to say that fines are imposed primarily for the purpose of compensating the club or league for damages resulting from player misconduct. It is clear that the amount of a fine in the sports area is often determined, not on the basis of the "injury" sustained, but rather on the basis of the amount necessary to provide both a sufficient degree of "punishment" to the offender and deter others from similar misconduct. In pure contract theory, such a justification provides an insufficient basis upon which to enforce a provision for contractually-agreed upon damages.[362] It can be accepted, however, that many of the policies which underlie the limitations on the enforceability of liquidated damage clauses are also applicable to employer fines. As suggested, the meager case law pertaining to industrial fines indicates that courts in fact express similar concerns in each area.

From this background, a number of useful principles emerge on the nature of judicial review in discipline situations. It must be pointed out, however, that this discussion presumes a situation in which a court reviews the merits of a disciplinary action. In some sports leagues, such direct review is not available for many types of discipline because the parties have agreed to resort to arbitration as the means of resolving disputes.[362.1] But even in these situations, the analysis suggested here may be useful, for it is likely to be urged that the arbitrator should apply the same standard of review which a court would use. With that caveat, it can be noted that the traditional assumption has been that the matters of fining and discipline are not simply left to the agreement between the parties. While the parties will be given considerable freedom in defining that which amounts to misconduct and in deciding what sanctions will be imposed, the task of the court is not simply to enforce what the parties agreed upon, whether a fine and/or suspension is involved. The court will make an independent review to determine the fairness and reasonableness of the agreement which is reached.[363] The courts have never clearly articulated why it is that they are unwilling to simply enforce the disciplinary procedures which the parties have explicitly agreed upon. Nonetheless, the policies which prompt the judiciary to police this aspect of the agreement are probably the same as those pursued in analogous areas. For example, it can be said that the judiciary has a concern for its institutional reputation, and thus courts refuse to aid parties in enforcing penalty clauses which are supported by no compelling commercial necessity.[364] Closely related to that concern is a well-founded skepticism that the employment relationship is not one in which the parties have historically enjoyed real equality of bargaining. The contracts which are agreed to in the employment area are often negotiated in a setting in which the employer

---

362. *See* RESTATEMENT OF CONTRACTS § 339, comment *a* at 552 (1932).

362.1. For example, since the 1977 collective bargaining agreement, the NFL utilizes an internal grievance procedure to review player complaints about club-imposed discipline. *See* note 330 *supra.* The nature of arbitration as a dispute-settlement mechanism is discussed in §§ 4.15-4.20 *infra.*

363. *Compare* Gutierrez v. Hachar's Dept. Store, 484 S.W.2d 433 (Tex. Civ. App. 1972); Leemon v. Grand Crossing Tack Co., 187 Ill. App. 247 (1914).

364. *See generally* Brighton, *Liquidated Damages,* 25 COLUM. L. REV. 277 (1925); McCormick, *Liquidated Damages,* 17 VA. L. REV. 103 (1930).

has greater sophistication and, in general, a better understanding of the implications of particular terms of the agreement. Moreover, employment in some industries has traditionally been offered on a take-it-or-leave-it basis, and courts are properly hesitant to treat the resulting "agreements" in the same way as other commercial contracts.

The relative bargaining strength of the parties may be somewhat less of a concern in the sports area than in the settings in which the first industrial disciplinary cases were decided. While the early history of contract negotiation in the sports area was often characterized by the same one-sidedness found in other employment situations,[365] we have recently seen significant advances in the quality of individual and collective representation of athletes.[366] But this is not to suggest that the factors which caused concern have been completely eliminated. Rather, it is still true in many sports that employers treat discipline as a non-negotiable demand. Moreover, even with a well-functioning collective bargaining system, there is no assurance that the specialized interests of subgroups of employees will be protected. And in the final analysis, of course, the sort of bargaining which is likely to take place will never be sufficient to completely allay the further concern that legal institutions not use their good offices to enforce penalties for which there is no business justification. An increase in the effectiveness of the player's negotiating strength should entitle the parties' agreed-upon disciplinary scheme to greater deference from the judiciary. But it is unlikely that the systems of discipline in the sports area will ever develop to a point where they are regarded as unreviewable. Courts have never been totally uncritical of the agreements which they are asked to enforce. They continue to exhibit a healthy degree of skepticism with respect to other types of stipulated remedies, and there is little reason to expect a different result in the present context.[367]

This emphasis on the negotiations which take place between the parties serves to underscore another basic requirement which operates in this area: before an employer can take any steps to enforce a disciplinary system against his employees, he must show that the rudiments of contract have been met with respect to the disciplinary rules. Specifically, there must be showing that the employee has given his actual or implied consent to the arrangement.[368] The rules need not be an explicit part of the contract, and may be taken from some collateral source.[369]

---

365. *See, e.g.,* Los Angeles Rams Football Club v. Cannon, 185 F. Supp. 717 (S.D. Cal. 1960); American League Baseball Club of Chicago v. Chase, 86 Misc. 441, 149 N.Y.S. 6 (Sup. Ct. 1914). *See generally* § 4.13 *infra.*

366. *See generally* ch. 6, *infra;* Krasnow & Levy, *Unionization and Professional Sports, supra* note 351; Lowell, *Collective Bargaining and the Professional Team Sport Industry, supra* note 351; §§ 3.17-3.19 *infra.*

367. *See* 5A A. CORBIN, CORBIN ON CONTRACTS § 1057 (1960) [hereinafter cited as CORBIN ON CONTRACTS.] See generally Brighton, *Liquidated Damages, supra* note 364; Loyd, *Penalties and Forfeitures,* 29 HARV. L. REV. 117 (1915); McCormick, *Liquidated Damages, supra,* note 364.

368. *See* 56 C.J.S., *Master and Servant* §§ 102-03 (1948). *See generally* Preston v. American Linen Co., 119 Mass. 400 (1876); Hunt v. Otis Co., 45 Mass. (4 Met.) 464 (1842); Borden v. Day, 197 Okla. 110, 168 P.2d 646 (1946); Pottsville Iron & Steel Co. v. Good, 116 Pa. 385, 9 A. 497 (1887); Matthews v. Industrial Lumber Co., 91 S.C. 568, 75 S.E. 170 (1911).

369. *See, e.g.,* Preston v. American Linen Co., 119 Mass. 400 (1876) (rule printed on pay envelope); Pottsville Iron & Steel Co. v. Good, 116 Pa. 385, 9 A. 497 (1887) (rule printed on time card). This notion is important in the sports area, for many of the rules and regulations which are

This matter of consent raises interesting questions in the sports area because the parties typically agree to grant a wide range of discretion to league officials to define offenses and prescribe the punishment which will be imposed. In some cases, the precise punishment which will be imposed for a particular offense will not be known in advance; in other cases, particular offenses will not be defined until after the contract has been entered into. It might thus be asked whether there has been an effective consent by the player in these cases. Obviously there has not been actual consent to rules or sanctions which are subsequently devised. Nonetheless, a sufficient acquiescence by the employee can probably be found in most cases, for the proper characterization of the arrangement is that the employee has consented to granting another person discretion to administer, and in large measure to define, the disciplinary system.[370] The discretion which is granted in such cases is not without limitation, for it must be exercised in good faith [371] and without a vindictive motive.[372] Where the controversy involves a newly prescribed offense, it is presumably relevant in defining good faith in this context to ask whether the rule was totally unexpected and unforeseeable in light of the operation of the system in the past. Similarly, there will be a good deal of overlap with notions of reasonableness mentioned above.

The above analysis should suggest the general contours of the inquiry which will be made when a player attacks a disciplinary action. The court's focus will be on the effectiveness of the player's consent to the rule and the reasonableness of the proscription. The former will require an investigation of the extent to which the player had an opportunity, usually through his players' association, to affect the rule. Because of the varying intensity of the bargaining which takes place in the various professional sports, a detailed examination of the facts of the particular situation will be necessary.[373] Where effective consent is found, the disciplinary action will likely be upheld. Even if the opportunity for direct player input is lacking, the rule may still be sustained. As indicated above, a court is likely to uphold an employer's action if it is taken in furtherance of a legitimate interest,[374] assuming that there is a basis upon which to find that the player appreciated that his conduct would not be approved.

---

enforced are not found in the body of the standard player contract, although the agreement usually contains some reference to these collateral provisions. *See generally* § 3.03 *supra.*

370. *Cf.* Chicago City Ry. v. Blanchard, 35 Ill. App. 481 (1889); Sloan v. Hayden, 110 Mass. 141 (1872).

371. *See* Sloan v. Hayden, 110 Mass. 141 (1872); Adams-Smith v. Hayward, 52 Neb. 79, 71 N.W. 949 (1897); RESTATEMENT (SECOND) OF CONTRACTS § 231 (Tent. Draft No. 5, 1970).

372. *Cf.* Lowe v. Feldman, 11 Misc. 2d 8, 168 N.Y.S.2d 674, *aff'd,* 6 App. Div. 684, 174 N.Y.S.2d 949 (1957); 3A CORBIN ON CONTRACTS §§ 644-47.

One commentator has identified instances in which the club's disciplinary powers appear to have been exercised with improper motives. *See* Alyluia, *Professional Sports, Contracts and the Players' Association,* 5 MANITOBA L.J. 359, 368-70 (1973).

373. For example, in 1974 the NFL Players Association based their strike on a demand for negotiation of the so-called "freedom issues," many of which dealt with matters of discipline. Other player unions have been less vocal on these matters. *See* N.Y. Times, July 1, 1974, at 37, col. 1; *id.,* July 4, 1974, at 11, col. 1; *id.,* July 13, 1974, at 15, col. 2; *id.,* July 21, 1974, § 5, at 5, col. 1; *id.,* Aug. 19, 1974, at 19, col. 4. The NFL players and owners eventually approved a collective bargaining agreement in 1977, and this agreement included important modifications of the former disciplinary system. *See* note 330 *supra.*

374. *See generally* Comment, *Discipline in Professional Sports: The Need for Player Protection,* 60 GEO. L.J. 771, 773-74, 786 (1972).

c. Enforcement of Contract Provisions Affording Procedural Protection.
As previously noted, the standard player contracts provide varying degrees of
procedural protection to the athlete who is alleged to have violated a disciplinary
rule.[375] The procedural rights in the contract are often amplified in related
documents such as the constitution and by-laws of the league.[376] These
provisions are the product of private agreement and are enforceable under the
normal rules of contract law.[377] In the event of a breach, money damages would
not likely provide adequate compensation for the failure of the club or league
to provide the agreed-upon safeguards,[378] and thus the player should be entitled
to specific performance of the provisions.[379]

While the player's resort to equitable relief in these circumstances is fully
supported by general precedents, the decision in *Molinas v. Podoloff*[380] suggests
an important limitation. Although the holding of the case is subject to serious
criticism, a review of the court's analysis provides the occasion for an inquiry
into more general concerns about the player's entitlement to the procedural
protections provided in his contract. Jack Molinas, an NBA player, had signed
a statement during a police investigation in which he admitted that he had placed
bets on several games in which he played. NBA officials were summoned, and
later in the evening on which the confession was made, the league commissioner,
Podoloff, informed the player that he was indefinitely suspended from the
league. Molinas brought suit seeking to enjoin the suspension since he had not
been given notice and an opportunity for a hearing as required by the league
constitution.[381]

The court found it unnecessary to decide whether the face-to-face meeting
between Molinas and Podoloff satisfied the hearing requirement in the league
rule. Rather, the court applied the unclean hands doctrine and found that
Molinas was not entitled to equitable relief. The actions of the athlete which
prompted the court to find him an unworthy suitor were the gambling activities
themselves. In the court's view, the plaintiff was "morally dishonest," [382] and
his request for equitable relief was "an affront to the conscience of the
chancellor." [383]

---

375. *See* text at notes 333-35 *supra.*

Chapters 1 and 2 of this treatise discuss the procedural aspects of other types of sports-related
discipline. Section 1.28 considers this question as it arises in the context of amateur athletes. Section
2.18 reviews the statutory rules and case law precedents which have developed in the area of
publicly-regulated sports. In those sections, the reader will also find a discussion of the various
principles of constitutional law which apply to discipline procedures where the enforcing authority
is of a more public nature than those which are involved in professional sports.

376. *See* text at notes 337-39 *supra.*

377. *See generally* § 3.03 *supra.*

378. *See generally* 5A CORBIN ON CONTRACTS § 1142; H. McCLINTOCK, HANDBOOK OF THE
PRINCIPLES OF EQUITY § 60 (1936); RESTATEMENT OF CONTRACTS § 361 (1932).

379. *See generally* 5A CORBIN ON CONTRACTS §§ 1136-39, 1142; RESTATEMENT OF CONTRACTS
§§ 358-59 (1932).

380. 133 N.Y.S.2d 743 (Sup. Ct. 1954).

381 *See also* Molinas v. National Basketball Ass'n 190 F.Supp. 241 (S.D.N.Y. 1961).

382. 133 N.Y.S.2d at 747.

383. *Id.* The court expressed strong views about the adverse effects of an athlete's participation
in gambling activities:

When the breath of scandal hits one sport, it casts suspicion on all other sports. It does
irreparable injury to the great majority of the players, destroys the confidence of the

This aspect of the court's analysis has an interesting *Catch 22* quality to it: the plaintiff who seeks enforcement of disciplinary procedures is denied relief because he has engaged in disciplinable conduct. Surely such a rationale must be rejected if the agreed-upon protections are to have meaning. The court does, however, emphasize that Molinas admitted his offense in "open court." [384] While that fact might be relevant for other purposes, it would not seem to add meaningful support to a denial of relief under the doctrine of unclean hands. Presumably the plaintiff's candor and cooperativeness ought not be the basis upon which his entitlement to an agreed-upon remedy is denied. Indeed, the court's approach has the effect of preferring the plaintiff who obstructs a legitimate inquiry by the league.

The fact of Molinas' admission of misconduct might be used as a basis upon which to argue that no hearing should be ordered because its outcome would be preordained. While the court suggests this as a further reason for its decision,[385] two responses are appropriate. First, the supposed futility of the hearing has little to do with the unclean hands doctrine and ought not be used to buoy up the otherwise dubious conclusion that an athlete who fails to follow league rules is personally unworthy of equitable relief. Secondly, and more to the point of the case, the fact that misconduct has been admitted should not destroy the athlete's right to a hearing. The suggestion that the hearing would be meaningless in these circumstances assumes that the only purpose of such a proceeding is to determine whether the improprieties actually occurred.[386] But further analysis should suggest that the hearing serves other purposes as well.[387] For example, it gives the accused an opportunity to present evidence which might mitigate the apparent seriousness of his offense. Thus, by participating in the proceeding in which his future is determined, the player may be able to influence either the characterization of the offense or the severity of the sanction.[388] In addition, the hearing serves to facilitate subsequent review of the disciplinary action, whether by a court or an arbitrator.[389] Such a proceeding provides an opportunity for the accumulation of all relevant evidence. Moreover, through their participation, the parties are likely to sharpen

---

public in athletic competition, and lets down the morale of our youth. When the standards of fair play, good sportsmanship, and honesty are abandoned, sporting events become the property of gamblers and racketeers. *Id.* at 746.

384. *Id.* at 747. The court also stated:

This plaintiff wagered, and admitted it, ... If there was the slightest suggestion that the statement was involuntary or untrue, or a single suggestion offered to question it, if there was a triable issue, this court would have relegated the defendant to his contractual obligations and ordered a hearing. However, the testimony of the plaintiff before the court that the statement was free, voluntary and true eliminates any question as to the plaintiff's admissions. *Id.*

385. *Id.* In the court's view, to order a hearing "would be a mere futile gesture."

386. *Compare* Jacques v. International Longshoremen's Ass'n, 246 F. Supp. 857, 866 (E.D. La. 1965).

387. *See generally* McCormick, *The Purpose of Due Process: Fair Hearing or Vehicle for Judicial Review?*, 52 Texas L. Rev. 1257 (1974); Tribe, *Structural Due Process*, 10 Harv. Civil Rights-Civil Liberties L. Rev. 269 (1975); Comment, *Specifying the Procedures Required by Due Process: Towards Limits on the Use of Interest Balancing*, 88 Harv. L. Rev. 1510 (1975).

388. *Compare* Tribe, *Structural Due Process, supra* note 387, at 303-14.

389. *See* McCormick, *The Purpose of Due Process: Fair Hearing or Vehicle for Judicial Review?, supra* note 387, at 1258-59; Comment, *Specifying the Procedures Required by Due Process: Towards Limits on the Use of Interest Balancing, supra* note 387, at 1539-40.

their arguments, as dubious contentions are dropped and more basic contentions are solidified. Thus, the judge or arbitrator who is called upon to test the validity of the outcome may be presented issues which are more precisely defined.[390]

There is one respect in which the athlete's admission of misconduct would be highly relevant. It may be probative evidence on the question of whether he had waived his right to a hearing. A party is free to relinquish his right to insist upon precise performance of the contract,[391] and where such a waiver of rights occurs, the other side's non-performance of a promise cannot provide the basis for a breach of contract action.[392] But in the present situation, a "confession," standing alone, would seemingly not be a sufficient waiver. Basic to an effective waiver is a voluntary relinquishment of the rights in question.[393] Before a conclusion could be reached on that question, it would presumably be necessary to examine the other indicia of voluntariness. Thus, it would be relevant to ask such basic questions as whether the player knew that he was otherwise entitled to a hearing, whether he appreciated the potential severity of the punishment, whether he had an opportunity to consult with third parties, and whether he was subjected to any undue threats or pressures.

In short, the *Molinas* court seems to have been misled by its conclusion about the despicable nature of the player's actions. If promises of procedural safeguards are to be meaningful, the misconduct alone cannot be asserted as the reason for refusing the athlete's request for relief. A hearing will not have to be afforded in every case, but before non-performance of that part of the contract is approved, the court should find an excuse more substantial than the supposed unworthiness of the disciplined player.

d. Other Aspects of Player Discipline. Other questions involving the team's or league's power of discipline involve legal issues which are not strictly contractual in nature. A resolution of these issues will require the application of principles discussed in other portions of this treatise. For example, there may be important antitrust implications where the discipline takes a form which excludes the athlete from opportunities to earn his livelihood.[394] Also, as players'

---

390. The Supreme Court's decision in Goss v. Lopez, 419 U.S. 565 (1975), requiring that a student suspended from school be afforded rudimentary due process, may be read by some to detract from the analysis in the text, for the Court seems to imply that the requisite fairness is present as long as there is a face-to-face confrontation with the disciplining authorities in which the accused is given an opportunity to characterize his actions. Seemingly a confession would be such a characterization and would eliminate the need for further inquiry. But the theory of the case is distinguishable from that which would prevail in the present context for the court only dealt with "short suspensions" and specifically indicated that more elaborate protection might be necessary where the consequences of the discipline were more severe. In the case of an athlete faced with a possible indefinite suspension from a league, the interest at stake is quite substantial. Since due process in other contexts seems to be defined on a sliding scale reflecting the potential severity of the outcome of the proceeding, the athlete whose livelihood is threatened could seemingly demand that the requirement of a hearing not be treated lightly. *See generally* Friendly, *"Some Kind of Hearing,"* 123 U. PA. L. REV. 1267 (1975); Comment, *Procedural Due Process After* Goss v. Lopez, 1976 DUKE L. J. 409.

391. *See generally* 3A CORBIN ON CONTRACTS §§ 752-53, J. MURRAY, MURRAY ON CONTRACTS §§ 189, 193 (1974).

392. *See, e.g.,* Harris v. American Motorist Ins. Co., 240 Miss. 262, 126 So. 2d 870 (1961); Fain v. Texas-Hanover Oil Co., 354 S.W.2d 949 (Tex. Civ. App. 1962).

393. *See, e.g.,* Clark v. West, 193 N.Y. 349, 86 N.E. 1 (1908); 3A CORBIN ON CONTRACTS § 752.

394. *See* § 5.09 *infra. See also* Blalock v. Ladies Professional Golf Ass'n, 359 F. Supp. 1260

associations assume a more predominant role in the representation of athletes, the matter of discipline becomes increasingly enmeshed with the principles of federal labor law.[395] Many of the issues which will arise under the labor law will not differ from those which would appear under a traditional contract analysis. A critical question will involve the issue of whether the player has given his consent to be bound by particular disciplinary rules. Here again a proper resolution of the matter will depend upon an interpretation of the parties' agreement and an analysis of the breadth of the discretion which is granted to the team or league to define and punish misconduct.[396]

§ 3.11. The Player's Basic Rights Under the Contract: Compensation, Bonuses and the Right to Terminate.

a. The Athlete's Right to Compensation. While a standard player's contract typically specifies a definite salary to be paid to the athlete, the player's right to receive that salary will usually be qualified by other terms in the agreement. It is a truly rare case in which the athlete's right to the specified salary is unconditional. The presence of a "no-cut" clause will reduce the number of circumstances in which the player's contract may be ended before the expiration of its terms. But, as is indicated in the more complete discussion of these clauses which appears above,[397] even under a "no-cut" contract, there will be numerous contingencies which might arise to limit the player's right to salary. The present discussion will deal only with the more typical standard player contract which includes no special salary continuation clauses.

With respect to such contracts, there is little that needs to be said about the player's right to compensation apart from the prior discussion of the team's right to terminate his contract [398] and impose disciplinary measures which may reduce his salary.[399] The contract is usually for a specified term of one or more years [400] and states the annual salary which the player is to receive.[401] The player is thus entitled to receive his salary for the stated period *unless* the team takes some action, consistent with the contract,[402] to terminate its relationship or otherwise reduce its obligation for salary, as in the case of a player who is fined or

---

(N.D. Ga. 1973); Morris, *In the Wake of the Flood,* 38 LAW & CONTEMP. PROB. 85, 91-92 (1973). *Cf.* Silver v. New York Stock Exch., 373 U.S. 341 (1963).

395. *See* §§ 6.05-6.08 *infra.*

396. *See* National Football League Players Ass'n v. NLRB, 503 F.2d 12 (8th Cir. 1974).

397. *See generally* § 3.09 *supra.*

398. *See generally* § 3.07 *supra.*

399. *See generally* § 3.10 *supra.*

400. In some cases, there may be an initial dispute about the duration of the team's obligation. This particularly arises where the player has signed a series of one-year contracts. *See, e.g.,* Sample v. Gotham Football Club, Inc., 59 F.R.D. 160 (S.D.N.Y. 1973).

401. Although the typical contract states an annual salary, it is sometimes true that the player is paid on a per game basis. This is particularly true of minor and semi-professional leagues. *See, e.g.,* Connecticut Professional Sports Corp. v. Heyman, 276 F. Supp. 618 (S.D.N.Y. 1967). This type of arrangement would require an analysis somewhat different from that suggested in the text. As is noted, under an annual salary term, the player's right to compensation continues until the contract is terminated. Where salary is paid on a per game basis, however, the player will be entitled to his salary only if games are actually scheduled and he participates in them. The team has no obligation to pay if it chooses not to schedule games or otherwise eliminates the opportunity for the player's performance. No formal termination is necessary.

402. The "contract" under which the club's termination power is exercised may include terms other than those found in the formal document. Thus, the right of termination may arise by trade custom, which may become a part of the agreement. *See* Baltimore Baseball Club & Exhibition Co. v. Pickett, 78 Md. 375, 28 A. 279 (1894). *See also* §§ 3.03, 3.04 *supra.*

suspended without pay.[403] Thus, in a particular case, an inquiry into the athlete's right to be paid will usually focus on the issue of whether the club has taken proper measures to limit its obligation.

Perhaps the most frequently litigated factual pattern is one in which the player brings suit against a team which has terminated his contract and stopped his salary before the expiration of the term of the agreement.[404] The player typically alleges that the termination was not in accordance with the terms of the contract [405] and does not provide an excuse for the team's failure to continue to pay him.[406] Often the termination occurs while the player alleges he is injured.[407] If it is shown that the injury occurred in the course of the athlete's performance for the team,[408] the team usually has no right to interrupt payment of the stipulated salary.[409] If it attempts such a termination, the player is entitled to a judgment in the amount of his loss resulting from the breach.[410]

Thus, it is appropriate for the player to demand damages where the termination is based upon grounds which do not in fact exist [411] or upon grounds which are not recognized by the contract [412] or where the termination was not in accordance with league procedures.[413] Further, there is authority for the view that the player is entitled to recover when his salary is withheld for improper reasons, even though there may have been other grounds upon which the team could have properly ended its salary obligation.[414] And while the athlete's actual participation in team activities is normally a precondition to his right to receive his salary,[415] such participation is excused when the team has terminated the

---

403. *Cf.* Molinas v. Podoloff, 133 N.Y.S.2d 743 (Sup. Ct. 1954).

404. *See, e.g.,* Hennigan v. Chargers Football Co., 431 F.2d 308 (5th Cir. 1970); Sample v. Gotham Football Club, Inc., 59 F.R.D. 160 (S.D.N.Y. 1973); Hurley v. Great Falls Baseball Ass'n, 59 Mont. 21, 195 P. 559 (1921).

405. The terms which govern a termination may include league rules. Thus, a club's failure to comply with a league waiver system may invalidate its attempted waiver. Baseball Player's Fraternity, Inc. v. Boston American League Club, 166 App. Div. 484, 151 N.Y.S. 557 (1915), *aff'd,* 117 N.E. 1061 (1917).

406. *See, e.g.,* Pasquel v. Owen, 186 F.2d 263 (8th Cir. 1950); Schultz v. Los Angeles Dons, Inc., 107 Cal. App. 2d 718, 238 P.2d 73 (1951); Griffin v. Brooklyn Ball Club, 68 App. Div. 566, 73 N.Y.S. 864 (1902), *aff'd,* 174 N.Y. 535, 66 N.E. 1109 (1903); Houston Oilers, Inc. v. Floyd, 518 S.W.2d 836 (Tex. Civ. App. 1975); Johnson v. Green Bay Packers, Inc., 272 Wis. 149, 74 N.W.2d 784 (1956); Tollefson v. Green Bay Packers, Inc., 256 Wis. 318, 41 N.W.2d 201 (1950). *See also* O'Connor v. St. Louis American League Baseball Co., 193 Mo. App. 167, 181 S.W. 1167 (1916); Middendorf v. Schreiber, 150 Mo. App. 530, 131 S.W. 122 (1910).

407. *See, e.g.,* Hennigan v. Chargers Football Co., 431 F.2d 308 (5th Cir. 1970); Sample v. Gotham Football Club, Inc., 59 F.R.D. 160 (S.D.N.Y. 1973); Schultz v. Los Angeles Dons, Inc., 107 Cal. App. 2d 718, 238 P.2d 73 (1951); Houston Oilers, Inc. v. Floyd, 518 S.W.2d 836 (Tex. Civ. App. 1975).

408. *See* Schultz v. Los Angeles Dons, Inc., 107 Cal. App. 2d 718, 238 P.2d 73 (1951).

409. *See generally* § 3.05 *supra.*

410. *See, e.g.,* Schultz v. Los Angeles Dons, Inc., 107 Cal. App. 2d 718, 238 P.2d 73 (1951); Houston Oilers, Inc. v. Floyd, 518 S.W.2d 836 (Tex. Civ. App. 1975). *But see* Tillman v. New Orleans Saints Football Club, 265 So.2d 284 (La. App. 1972).

411. *See* Baltimore Baseball Club & Exhibition Co. v. Pickett, 78 Md. 375, 28 A. 279 (1894); Houston Oilers, Inc. v. Floyd, 518 S.W.2d 836 (Tex. Civ. App. 1975).

412. *See* Johnson v. Green Bay Packers, Inc., 272 Wis. 149, 74 N.W.2d 784 (1956); Tollefson v. Green Bay Packers, Inc., 256 Wis. 318, 41 N.W.2d 201 (1950). *Cf.* Egan v. Winnipeg Baseball Club, Ltd., 96 Minn. 345, 104 N.W. 947 (1905).

413. *See* Baseball Player's Fraternity, Inc. v. Boston American League Club, 166 App. Div. 484, 151 N.Y.S. 557 (1915), *aff'd,* 221 N.Y. 704, 117 N.E. 1061 (1917).

414. *See* Griffin v. Brooklyn Ball Club, 68 App. Div. 566, 576-77, 73 N.Y.S. 864, 871 (1902), *aff'd,* 174 N.Y. 535, 66 N.E. 1109 (1903).

415. *See* Egan v. Winnipeg Baseball Club, Ltd., 96 Minn. 345, 104 N.W. 947 (1905); Baseball Players' Fraternity, Inc. v. Boston American League Club, 166 App. Div. 484, 151 N.Y.S. 557 (1915),

contract [416] and thereby indicated its unwillingness to receive the athlete's services.[417]

A similar analysis would follow where the team had taken action short of termination of the contract, as where the team sought to suspend the player for a period or to reduce his salary by the amount of a disciplinary fine.[418] In either case, the rule to be applied is one which recognizes that the player is entitled to be paid the full amount of his salary unless any attempted salary reduction conforms to the terms of the agreement.[419]

In the event a player's contract is terminated prematurely for improper reasons, the amount which the athlete will recover may not be the full amount of the unpaid balance of his salary. Any claim for damages is subject to the requirement that the player attempt to mitigate the loss sustained.[420] Under this principle, the athlete who is wrongfully discharged will recover

> the amount he would have earned under the contract to the end of the term, less any amount received by him for services rendered to others or which he might have received by the exercise of due diligence in seeking employment after the date of his discharge and to the end of the term.[421]

Thus, the athlete must make a reasonable effort to secure other employment, and if he fails to make such effort, his recovery will be reduced by the amount of compensation he would have received elsewhere.[422] Of course, if the player is injured, he may be unable to work and thus need not attempt to reemploy himself.[423] But where the player is healthy and otherwise highly skilled he must accept positions which are available, including those offered by other teams.[424]

aff'd, 221 N.Y. 704, 117 N.E. 1061 (1917). See generally 3A A. Corbin, Corbin on Contracts §§ 657, 675-76 (1960) [hereinafter cited as Corbin on Contracts].

416. The termination must be complete before the player's performance is excused. Thus, where the athlete is hired as a player-manager at a single salary and is subsequently relieved of his duties as manager, he must continue as a player to be entitled to the salary promised. See Pasquel v. Owen, 186 F.2d 263 (8th Cir. 1950).

417. See, e.g., Schultz v. Los Angeles Dons, Inc., 107 Cal. App. 2d 718, 722, 238 P.2d 73, 75 (1951); Griffin v. Brooklyn Ball Club, 68 App. Div. 566, 575,73 N.Y.S. 864, 871 (1902), aff'd, 174 N.Y. 535, 66 N.E. 1109 (1903).

418. A few of the major standard player contracts expressly recognize that the club may deduct the amount of a disciplinary fine from the club player's salary. See, e.g., NHL Contract ¶ 4: "... the Club may impose a reasonable fine upon the Player and deduct the amount thereof from any money due or to become due to the Player." (The major standard player contracts are referred to by an abbreviated citation form explained in note 126, § 3.05 supra).

419. In the event of an improper suspension, it is proper for the player to sue to recover his salary for the period of his suspension. But, of course, he bears the burden of showing that the suspension was improper. See Molinas v. Podoloff, 133 N.Y.S.2d 743 (Sup. Ct. 1954).

420. See generally 5 Corbin on Contracts § 1095; D. Dobbs, Handbook on Remedies § 12.25 (1973); Annot., 91 A.L.R.2d 682 (1963).

421. Hurley v. Great Falls Baseball Ass'n, 59 Mont. 21, 195 P. 559, 561 (1921). See also McAleer v. McNally Pittsburg Mfg. Co., 329 F.2d 273 (3d Cir. 1964); Ridenour v. Kuker, 185 Neb. 321, 175 N.W.2d 287 (1970).

422. See, e.g., Runkle v. Fuess, 226 Ark. 447, 290 S.W.2d 433 (1956); Byrne v. Independent School Dist., 139 Iowa 618, 117 N.W. 983 (1908); Spurck v. Civil Service Bd., 231 Minn. 183, 42 N.W.2d 720 (1950). See also Griffin v. Brooklyn Ball Club, 68 App. Div. 566, 73 N.Y.S. 864 (1902), aff'd, 174 N.Y. 535, 66 N.E. 1109 (1903).

423. Compare Schultz v. Los Angeles Dons, Inc., 107 Cal. App. 2d 718, 238 P.2d 73 (1951).

424. See Pasquel v. Owen, 186 F.2d 263, 273 (8th Cir. 1950). See also Griffin v. Brooklyn Ball Club, 68 App. Div. 566, 73 N.Y.S. 864 (1902), aff'd, 174 N.Y. 535, 66 N.E. 1109 (1903).

b. The Legal Status of Bonus Payments. One of the benefits which a player might receive from his relationship with a professional sports team is a bonus which is ostensibly intended to reward the player for signing a contract with the team. While there has been relatively little legal controversy about the various forms of compensation which an athlete might receive,[425] the "bonus of signing" is an exception. The basic question which arises concerns the proper legal characterization of such payments and the conditions which govern the player's entitlement to the money.

The bonuses do not fit nicely into any of the traditional legal classifications. On the one hand, they are different from the ordinary salary because it is usually assumed that the athlete may retain the bonus money even if he is later cut by the team. Furthermore, it is the event of the signing of the contract, and not any actual athletic efforts, which prompt the bonus, further suggesting the inappropriateness of classifying the bonus as salary. On the other hand, it is clear that the team is paying for more than the athlete's act of signing the contract, and the team would not expect that the athlete could keep the bonus if he jumped to another league or retired immediately upon signing. Thus, the teams seem to offer bonuses with some expectation of a return performance.[426]

The uncertainty about the nature of the "bonus for signing" is reflected in the litigation which has occurred in this area. The bonus has been variously characterized by litigants and courts as a gift,[427] as "irregular compensation . . . to encourage . . . performance," [428] as an advance salary,[429] as payment for a binding option,[430] and as a means of apportioning income for tax purposes.[431]

Several of these characterizations can be refuted. The bonus is clearly not a gift, for some return performance is expected by the team.[432] Nor can the bonus usually be said to be the consideration which supports the player's granting of an option to the team. Usually the parties do not negotiate with an intent to enter this sort of arrangement.[433] And while the bonus is clearly a form of compensation, it is accompanied by conditions and assumptions which are different from those which accompany the ordinary salary term in the contract. For example, a player who is dropped from the team because he possesses

---

425. *But see* Pasquel v. Owen, 186 F.2d 263 (8th Cir. 1950); Hurley v. Great Falls Baseball Ass'n, 59 Mont. 21, 195 P. 559 (1921).

426. The parties are, of course, free to agree upon their own characterization of the bonus. Thus, they may agree that the bonus will be paid upon the signing of the contract and may be retained by the athlete whether he plays for the club or not. Such a commitment was apparently made when ABA star, George McGinnis, received a $500,000 bonus for signing with the New York Knicks of the NBA. It was subsequently determined that another NBA team had the draft rights to McGinnis and he was not permitted to play for New York. The owners of the New York team conceded that McGinnis could keep the money. *See* N.Y. Times, June 6, 1975, at 30, col. 1. McGinnis eventually signed with the other NBA team, the Philadelphia 76'ers, and it was reported that Philadelphia had assumed the Knicks' responsibility for the $500,000. *See* N.Y. Times, July 11, 1975, at 21, col. 4.

427. Pasquel v. Owen, 186 F.2d 263, 271 (8th Cir. 1950) (reference to instruction in the lower court).

428. *Id., citing* Willkie v. Commissioner, 127 F. 2d 953, 956 (6th Cir. 1942).

429. Detroit Football Co. v. Robinson, 186 F. Supp. 933, 935 (E.D. La.), *aff'd,* 283 F.2d 657 (5th Cir. 1960).

430. Detroit Football Co. v. Robinson, 186 F. Supp. 933, 935 (E.D. La.), *aff'd,* 283 F.2d 657 (5th Cir. 1960); Los Angeles Rams Football Club v. Cannon, 185 F. Supp. 717, 726 (S.D. Cal. 1960).

431. Los Angeles Rams Football Club v. Cannon, 185 F. Supp. 717, 725 (S.D. Cal. 1960). A discussion of the tax aspects of bonus payments can be found in §§ 7.05-.08 *infra*.

432. *See* Pasquel v. Owen, 186 F.2d 263, 271 (8th Cir. 1950).

433. *See* Detroit Football Co. v. Robinson, 186 F. Supp. 933, 935 (E.D. La.), *aff'd,* 283 F.2d 657 (5th Cir. 1960); Los Angeles Rams Football Club v. Cannon, 185 F. Supp. 717, 726 (S.D. Cal. 1960).

insufficient skill is not entitled to further salary payments,[434] but normally he need not return any portion of the bonus, even if he is cut before the team has engaged in any contests.

The most appropriate characterization of the bonus is that it is compensation paid to the athlete upon the event of his signing the contract and can be retained by him as long as he is ready and willing to perform the contract for its initial term.[435] Thus, it can be said that the bonus is a form of conditional payment, and the critical inquiry concerns identification of the conditions which must be met to continue the athlete's entitlement to the compensation. One contingency is that there must be a binding contract between the parties.[436] Moreover, it is usually understood that the athlete must show up for training camp.[437] But the performance expected of the athlete probably extends much further, although the issue has never been fully developed in litigation. Presumably the athlete must make a good faith effort to participate in the team's activities and, whether or not he is given a top position on the team's roster, the player must exhibit a continuing willingness to play for the team. The interesting case, which has not yet appeared in the reported decisions, would involve the player who received a large bonus, gave his best efforts for part of the season, and then went into permanent or temporary retirement. Would the athlete have to return all or any portion of his bonus? It might seem inequitable to allow the player to keep his entire bonus. To allow him to do so would impliedly assume that the bonus was given without any expectation of services, which is clearly not the case.[438] On the other hand, the team has gained some benefit from the player's participation. This analysis would suggest that it would not be inappropriate to attempt an apportionment of the bonus. Where the facts do not compel a different distribution, it might be appropriate to apply the criteria for apportionment used to define the player's entitlement to salary, which typically allocates salary on the basis of the proportion of the playing season which has been completed at the time of the player's departure.[439]

In an effort to avoid the risk of an unfavorable judicial characterization of a bonus payment, some leagues have adopted a standard form addendum to the uniform players contract which seeks to spell out the terms upon which the bonus is paid. A typical clause is that used in some football contracts:

> The Club hereby agrees to pay the Player a bonus of $_____, which bonus is separate and distinct from the sum set forth in paragraph 3 of the above-mentioned contract, and the Player acknowledges receipt of such amount.
> Notwithstanding the foregoing, if the Player fails to report to and remain at training camp at the times and places prescribed by the Club,

---

434. See generally §§ 3.06-.07 supra.

435. Under this characterization, the club, in effect is paying the player to give it the exclusive opportunity to put him through training to see if he can make the team. This is particularly important in sports in which there are competing leagues. The bonus serves to induce the player to sign with one league rather than the other. While it may turn out that the player is not able to meet the level of professional competition, the club which signs him has an obvious interest in being able to make the initial determination of that question.

436. Detroit Football Co. v. Robinson, 186 F. Supp. 933, 935 (E.D. La.), aff'd, 283 F.2d 657 (5th Cir. 1960).

437. Los Angeles Rams Football Club v. Cannon, 185 F. Supp. 717, 725, 727 (S.D. Cal. 1960).

438. See Pasquel v. Owen, 186 F.2d 263, 271 (8th Cir. 1950).

439. See, e.g., NBA Contract ¶¶ 20(d)-(e).

or fails to render the services required under the contract, or fails to perform such contract for any reason other than termination of such contract by the Club under paragraph 6 thereof or assignment of such contract by the Club under paragraph 9 thereof, the Player shall forthwith repay to the Club in full the amount of such bonus.[440]

It will be noted that under a provision of this sort, the situation involving a player who retires early is treated in a manner different from that suggested above. By the express terms of this clause a player would not be entitled to a proportionate part of the payment, but rather would have to return it in full.

There may be other situations involving a premature termination of the contract which give rise to similar issues concerning the athlete's right to retain bonus payments. The prior discussion, as well as the contract language quoted above, deals with cases in which the player has abandoned the contract even though the club has satisfied all of its obligations under the agreement. What principles will be applied to define the athlete's right to keep bonus money where he terminates the contract because the club has defaulted on its obligations? That question was addressed in *Alabama Football, Inc. v. Stabler.*[441] In April 1974, Stabler, then under contract with the Oakland Raiders of the NFL, signed a contract to play for the defendant club in the recently formed World Football League. This new contract called for Stabler to begin playing for the defendant in 1976, after he had fulfilled his commitment to the Raiders. Stabler was to receive a bonus of $100,000 in 1974 for signing the new agreement and yearly compensation thereafter totaling $775,000. Although the club paid Stabler $50,000 upon signing, it soon became clear that the franchise was encountering significant financial difficulty. Stabler later received an additional $20,000 of the 1974 payment, but the club eventually defaulted on a $30,000 note which represented the balance. Stabler sued, seeking to rescind the agreement.

The club argued that rescission was inappropriate because Stabler had not offered to restore the money which he had received under the contract. The court recognized that there was support for the club's argument. However, in the court's view, the "rule must be applied to comport with general equitable principles." [442] The court concluded that the athlete was entitled to keep the $70,000 bonus money he had received. The court did agree, however, that in order to "[balance] the equities between the parties," the club should be relieved of any further obligation on the unpaid $30,000 note.[443]

The court apparently perceived that there were two factors which supported Stabler's right to keep the portion of the bonus which had been paid to him. On the one hand was Stabler's opportunity cost in having signed the contract in question. The court noted that "he was prohibited from negotiating a contract with any other team so long as he was under contract with Alabama Football, Inc." [444] The other element weighing in favor of the athlete in the balancing

---

440. This form was originally drafted for use in the American Football League prior to its merger with the NFL.

441. 294 Ala. 551, 319 So. 2d 678 (1975).

442. *Id.* at 681.

443. *Id.*

444. *Id.* The element of foregone opportunities will be present in most contracts involving professional team sports. These are typically exclusive service contracts, so that the player necessarily forecloses the opportunity to play elsewhere by committing himself to a particular team. *See* §§ 4.02-.04 *infra.*

process was the fact that the club "had received benefits under the contract which Stabler was entitled to be paid for." [445] Since Stabler had never actually played for the defendant-club, the benefits were necessarily intangible in nature. In the court's view, the primary benefit consisted of the publicity value to the club of its having signed Stabler. The court noted that the club "exploited his notoriety as a successful quarterback with the Oakland Raiders to sell tickets to ballgames played in 1974; [and] he appeared at press conferences to publicize Alabama Football, Inc. and the World Football League." [446]

The court's allocation of the bonus money raises a number of interesting issues. Initially, there is a question as to the legal theory under which the court decided the case. As the court notes, it is generally accepted that when a party seeks to rescind a contract, he is obligated to return any part performance which he has received, a principle which might seem to apply to the bonus payments made to Stabler.[447] While the court chose not to apply this doctrine, its reason for declining to do so is not entirely clear. The court rather cryptically observed that "contracts involving professional athletes are somewhat unique," [448] but does not elaborate on the factors which contribute to the perceived uniqueness or the reasons why these should alter the rule which is usually applied. However, there may be a doctrinal framework which would clarify to some extent the court's treatment of the bonus question. Much of the court's language is similar to that which would have been used had the plaintiff's complaint formally requested an award in restitution for the services which the plaintiff had rendered.[449] Thus, Stabler's action might be viewed as encompassing a claim that the $70,000 actually paid represented an amount which would compensate Stabler for the publicity which he gave to the team.

If there is a weakness in the approach which the court took, it lies in the fact that the court greatly oversimplified the issue before it. By regarding the dispute as a matter to be resolved under its equitable discretion, the court was able to ignore important principles from the doctrine of restitution which would have required a more rigorous analysis.[450] Moreover, even if one were inclined

---

It should also be noted that the court's statement that Stabler was prohibited from "negotiating" with another team is probably not accurate. As is discussed in detail elsewhere, the defendant club would only have authority to prevent Stabler from performing for another club during the term of his agreement. He would, however, presumably be free to negotiate, and sign, an agreement to play following the expiration of his contract with the defendant. See §§ 4.12, 4.14 infra.

445. 294 Ala. at 553-54, 319 So. 2d at 681.

446. Id.

447. 5 CORBIN ON CONTRACTS §§ 1109, 1112, 1114.

448. 294 Ala. at 553-54, 319 So. 2d at 681.

449. The statement of fact in the court's opinion does not indicate that the plaintiff made such a claim. The substance of Stabler's complaint was summarized as follows:

> Stabler filed a complaint on December 4, 1974, seeking a declaratory judgment and other relief, contending that the defendant had breached its contract with Stabler by failing to pay the balance due in 1974 under the contract between the parties; that the terms of the contract prohibited him from negotiating a contract with any other professional football club; and that irreparable damage would result to him if the contract was not held to be null and void. Id. at 552, 319 So. 2d at 679.

450. The remedy of restitution was once thought to be equitable in nature, and some courts required that the plaintiff establish that he was "equitably" entitled to relief. But this characterization does not mean that the rules developed for granting relief should be abandoned in favor of a less precise analysis. See 5 CORBIN ON CONTRACTS § 1103 (entitled "Is Restitution an 'Equitable' Remedy? Effect of the Amalgamation of Equity and Common Law").

to agree that the plaintiff's plea was essentially equitable in nature, there are matters which warrant greater attention than the court gives. Particularly troublesome is the court's uncritical acceptance of the sum of $70,000 as appropriate compensation for the publicity which Stabler provided. If the action had been treated as one in restitution, it would have been necessary to find that this was "the reasonable value of the past performance rendered ... to the defendant." [451] Moreover, this determination is to be "uncontrolled by the contract price or rate or by any other term of the express contract." [452]

Yet on the face of the opinion, the only apparent reason for "awarding" $70,000 is that this was the amount actually paid to the athlete while the contract was in effect. The difficulty with this result is that the athlete's entitlement turns on such matters as the club's financial condition and its good faith in meeting its contractual obligations, rather than the more relevant, though admittedly less certain, criteria of the approximate value of the services rendered. The merit of the court's approach is further impaired if one considers that the schedule of payments agreed to in the contract was most likely dictated by considerations which bear little relationship to the particular legal question which was before the court. At least as far as the initial years of Stabler's contract were concerned, it is doubtful that the parties understood that the payments were being made for an equivalent exchange of services. Rather, the timing of payments was more likely the product of considerations such as the tax consequences to the player,[453] the club's anticipated revenues once it could field a full contingent of NFL veterans, and so on.

It must be accepted that a valuation problem of the sort raised in *Stabler* admits of no easy solution.[454] There are no ready guidelines for valuing the notoriety of a star player, much less his value to a new enterprise of questionable durability. But the weakness of the *Stabler* opinion is the apparent absence of any effort at all to relate the allocation of the disputed bonus payment to the injury which was supposedly being compensated. A number of factual questions might have been considered, such as the level of ticket sales before and after the publicity efforts; the comparative experience of other WFL franchises which had signed NFL veterans; the economic value, if any, of the athlete's opportunity cost; and so on. Because factors such as these seem not to have been considered in any detail, the precedential value of the *Stabler* case must necessarily be limited. While some courts in the future may also choose the rough justice of leaving the parties where they find them, others are likely to be mindful of the admonition of the venerable Professor Corbin that "care must be taken not to

---

451. *Id.* at § 1112. Corbin also observes that

By giving a judgment for restitution of value received by the defendant, the court is trying to put the plaintiff in a position as good as that occupied by him before the contract was made, at least so far as that result will be brought about by requiring the defendant to pay the reasonable value of what he may have received from the plaintiff by way of past performance. *Id.*

452. *Id.*

453. The facts of the *Stabler* case indicate that, as would be expected, the parties did give some attention to the tax consequences of their transaction. Stabler received $50,000, which was one-half of the 1974 payment, at the time the contract was signed. Payment of the balance was delayed, in part, because Stabler was interested in determining whether there was some method by which he might defer that income and "avoid taxes on monies due in 1974." When no suitable plan could be devised, Stabler demanded the balance of the 1974 payment. 294 Ala. at 552-53, 319 So. 2d at 680.

454. *See* 5 CORBIN ON CONTRACTS § 1112.

make the recovery so great that it operates as a penalty instead of compensation"[455] — or, one might add, so that it operates as a windfall for the club.

c. The Player's Right to Terminate the Contract. Most legal disputes involving the termination of a professional athlete's contract are likely to arise when it is the team which seeks to bring the contractual relationship to an end. Relatively rare are cases such as the *Stabler* decision, discussed above, in which the athlete is able to terminate his contract. As might be imagined the reason for the infrequency of this type of case is the fact that the player has relatively few grounds upon which he can terminate, and if the player is a star performer, the team will attempt to do everything it can to avoid providing a basis for termination.[456] Yet, that is not to suggest that a player, even one in a financially stable league, will not have an incentive to test his right to terminate the contract. Such an incentive will exist, for example, where the athlete has signed for a modest salary but later revealed that he possesses superstar talent. Another team might be willing to pay a salary commensurate with the player's ability, but only if the athlete can disengage himself from his present commitment. A complete "disengagement" before the expiration of the natural term of the contract would be possible only if proper grounds for termination existed.[457]

Uniform player contracts vary in the extent to which they recognize the player's right to terminate. Some include no termination clause.[458] Where such a clause does exist, it will typically specify the grounds for termination.[459] Thus,

---

455. *Id.* In Corbin's view, "it must be remembered that the defendant is a wrongdoer. Doubts and difficulties in the determination of this question of value should be resolved against the defendant." However, as mentioned in the text, Corbin urges caution so that the award not operate as a penalty.

It is not clear that the *Stabler* decision is any more defensible even if it is assumed that all "doubts . . . [were] resolved against the defendant." The point in doubt is Stabler's publicity value. Without a more precise analysis, there is little basis to peg that value at $70,000 rather than $100,000, or even a much larger or smaller sum.

456. The notion of a termination of the contract by the player is to be distinguished from the case in which the contract ends because the term of the contract has expired. Here, the concept of a *termination* is used to imply that the player has attempted to bring the contract to an end before he has rendered the full performance for which he was potentially accountable. This is to be contrasted with the case in which the athlete "plays out his option" and is released from further contractual duties only because he has done everything which was called for under the contract.

457. A classic case in this area is that involving the celebrated "Catfish" Hunter. Hunter's original employer, the Oakland Athletics, failed to pay Hunter the entire compensation which was due him and Hunter exercised his right under ¶ 7(a) of the Uniform Player's Contract of the American League of Professional Baseball Clubs to terminate the contract in the event the club defaulted in its obligation to pay his salary. *See* American and National Leagues of Professional Baseball Clubs v. Major League Baseball Players Ass'n, 59 Cal. App. 3d 493, 130 Cal. Rptr. 626 (1976). This termination enabled Hunter to negotiate a multi-million dollar contract and thereby increase his salary several fold. *See* N.Y. Times, Jan. 1, 1975, at 1, col. 5; *id.,* Jan. 3, 1975, at 21, col. 2; *id.,* Jan. 4, 1975, at 19, col. 6; *id.,* Jan. 5, 1975, § 5, at 1, col. 1.

458. *See, e.g.,* NFL Contract; WHA Contract.

459. *See, e.g.,* NBA Contract ¶ 20(a):

In the event of an alleged default by the Club in the payments to the Player provided for by this contract, or in the event of an alleged failure by the Club to perform any other material obligation agreed to be performed by the Club hereunder, the Player shall notify both the Club and the Association in writing of the facts constituting such alleged default or alleged failure. If neither the Club nor the Association shall cause such alleged default or alleged failure to be remedied within five (5) days after receipt of such written notice, the National Basketball Players Association shall, on behalf of the Player, have the right

the player may be given the right to terminate the contract if the club fails to pay his salary.[460] In addition, it may be recognized that the athlete may terminate for any other material breach by the club.[461] While the breach may thus relate to any aspect of the obligations imposed on the team by the contract, most material breaches will relate to the team's obligation to pay the athlete's salary.[462] Other breaches might include such things as the team's failure to reimburse the athlete for travel or medical expenses, but with respect to these items, there will often be a question as to whether the breach is material.

A player termination clause may also specify the procedures to be followed in the event of the club's default. Often the player must notify the club[463] and, in some cases, the league[464] and afford each an opportunity to render the promised performance. Although the league may be mentioned, the clause usually does not include a promise by the league to correct defaults by the club but gives the league the option to do so. Such a right might be exercised by the league, for example, were it desired to prevent the player from joining a rival league.

A question might arise concerning the rights of a player who has signed a contract which does not contain a clause specifically recognizing his right to terminate. Perhaps ironically, the player with that sort of agreement will often have somewhat greater rights than a player who has signed a contract with provisions such as those described above. As with many contract provisions purporting to grant affirmative protection to the player, the real intent of an express termination clause is often to qualify the rights which the athlete would otherwise enjoy at common law.

As far as the grounds for player termination are concerned, the athlete whose contract is silent on this point will often be in basically the same position as a player covered by an express provision. Under the common law principles, a party has the right to cancel a contractual relationship if there has been a total or material breach by the other side.[465] If the breach is only minor, then it amounts to a partial breach and does not excuse further performance by the injured party. While the partial breach is, nonetheless, a default under the

---

to request that the dispute concerning such alleged default or alleged failure be referred immediately to the Impartial Arbitrator in accordance with Article XV, Section 2(g), of the Agreement currently in effect between the National Basketball Association and National Basketball Players Association. If, as a result of such arbitration, an award issues in favor of the Player, and if neither the Club nor the Association complies with such award within ten (10) days after the service thereof, the Player shall have the right, by a further written notice to the Club and the Association, to terminate this contract.

See also NHL Contract ¶ 12; Baseball Contract ¶ 7(a).

460. *See, e.g.,* NBA Contract ¶ 20(a), *supra* note 459.

461. *Id.* Under the NHL contract, the player may terminate not only if he is not paid but also if the club "shall fail to perform any other obligation agreed to be performed by the club hereunder." NHL Contract ¶ 12. However, the player must give notice of the default and allow the club to correct it.

462. *See, e.g.,* Alabama Football, Inc. v. Stabler, 294 Ala. 551, 319 So. 2d 678 (1975).

463. *See, e.g.,* NHL Contract ¶ 12; Baseball Contract ¶ 7(a).

464. *See* NBA Contract ¶ 20(a), *supra* note 459.

465. This assumes that the promises which were exchanged by the parties were dependent promises, which would be true in the sorts of situations under discussion here. If the parties exchanged independent promises, then one side would have to perform despite the failure of the other side to deliver the promised performance. *See* 4 CORBIN ON CONTRACTS § 946.

contract, the remedy of the injured party is limited to an action for damages, and he may not use the breach as an occasion to bring the contract to an end.[466] The common law notion of a total or material breach is likely to be applied in the same fashion as the criteria specified in provisions such as those mentioned above. A default with respect to the payment of the player's salary will generally be the most frequent sort of material breach. Non-payment of an installment of the promised salary will be a material breach if there are other circumstances which indicate that the employer either cannot or does not intend to meet its salary obligation.[467] Most of the club's other obligations also involve the payment of money, usually under a promise to reimburse the player for traveling expenses, but because of the small amounts involved and the secondary nature of this type of obligation, the player will have a difficult time showing that the breach is material.[468]

The distinction between a total and partial breach is well-illustrated by the case of *Pasquel v. Owen.*[469] Jorge Pasquel, promoter of the Mexican Baseball League which operated briefly in the late 1940's as a challenge to the American and National Leagues,[470] hired Arnold Owen to serve the dual role of player-manager for one of his clubs. After about five weeks, Pasquel became dissatisfied with Owen's performance as manager and relieved him of his duties. Owen continued to play for the team, but then eventually became disenchanted and returned to the United States. In litigation which resulted, it became

---

466. *See* 4 CORBIN ON CONTRACTS §§ 943-46; J. MURRAY, MURRAY ON CONTRACTS §§ 166-72 (1974); RESTATEMENT OF CONTRACTS § 317 (1932).

467. The notion that one party's prospective inability to perform the contract may sustain the other party's demand for rescission has been recognized as a general principle of contracts law. *See* 4 CORBIN ON CONTRACTS § 958 at 850. It has also been specifically applied in at least one sports case. In *Alabama Football, Inc. v. Stabler,* the athlete, Stabler, sought a declaratory judgment rescinding his contract with the defendant on the grounds that the club had failed to pay a portion of his bonus payment after he had agreed to several extensions. Although the court's opinion is not clear on this point, the club apparently took the position that failure to pay the last $30,000 of the $100,000 was not a material breach since this represents only a small part of the amount to be paid over the life of the contract, which called for total payments of $875,000. Since the team's obligation to pay $775,000 did not arise until the future, there had been no actual breach as to this sum, and apparently in the view of the club, the failure to pay the $30,000 then due was not a material breach in light of its total obligation. In assessing the materiality of the breach, the court looked not only to the present default but also to the overall financial position of the club. The court concluded:

> The evidence adduced below relating to the financial condition of appellant is uncontroverted. It overwhelmingly supports a conclusion that it was unable to perform the contract with Stabler.

294 Ala. at 554-55, 319 So. 2d at 682.

The court identified the following rule of law as applicable to the case before it:

> The inability of a party to perform a contract after it is made is, as a rule, grounds for rescinding it. The fact that substantial performance by one party is impossible or that a party is unable to perform a material part of the contract is a ground for rescission.

Id. quoting 17 AM. JUR. 2D, *Contracts* § 506.

468. This assumes that there are not other circumstances indicating that the employer is insolvent or has otherwise repudiated the contract. *Id.*

469. 186 F.2d 263 (8th Cir. 1950).

470. *See also* American League Baseball Club of New York, Inc. v. Pasquel, 187 Misc. 230, 63 N.Y.S.2d 537 (Sup. Ct. 1946); Davis, *Self-Regulation in Baseball, 1909-71,* in GOVERNMENT AND THE SPORTS BUSINESS 349, 359-60 (R. Noll, ed. 1974).

important to determine whether Owen had the right to treat the contract as ended. He asserted that he could properly terminate the agreement as a result of Pasquel's breach in removing him from the position of manager. The contract did not contain a termination clause. In analyzing this issue, the court first stated the applicable common law rule:

> ... A breach of the contract by one party may, of course, be of such character as to warrant the other party in abandoning it, but to permit an abandonment the failure of performance by the other party must go to the substance of the contract and where there is no distinct refusal by the party in default to be bound by the contract in the future, his conduct must be such clearly to indicate that he does not intend to be bound by its terms. A breach committed by one of the parties may be a breach which the parties have not on a reasonable construction of the contract regarded as vital to its existence, in which event the breach does not discharge the other party or warrant his abandoning it.[471]

The court applied these principles to find that the athlete had no right to terminate the contract under the particular facts. The court reasoned that

> The contract here is specific in the matter of compensation. ... [I]t is not specific as to the obligations of the parties with reference to the defendant's duties. The parties apparently by their subsequent action indicated that the mere designation of the defendant as player-manager was not a vital provision. So far as the plaintiff was concerned there was at most only a partial breach of the contract as he at no time failed to pay the full consideration agreed upon ... .[472]

Thus, in the court's view, the essence of the parties bargain was the salary term. As long as that provision was complied with, a change in the nature of the player's assigned duties did not amount to a material breach.[473]

To the extent that there are differences between the operation of a contract with no termination clause and one with an express provision, they are likely to arise with respect to the procedures which the player must follow in effectuating a cancellation of the contract. At common law, the party who has been subjected to a material breach by the other side has an immediate right to bring the contract to an end.[474] He need not request that the other side correct the default, nor need he seek a substitute performance from a third party, such as the league. When a club inserts a player termination clause in its standard player contracts, it is typically seeking to temper the player's right to immediately declare an end to the relationship. Thus, as mentioned, the contract may call for notice and mandate a minimum period of delay to enable the party in default or its guarantor to rectify the breach. Contract provisions of this sort are permissible, and indeed are probably desirable to the extent that they insure against a termination caused by one party's inadvertence or mistake.

---

471. 186 F.2d at 269.
472. *Id.*
473. *But see* Mair v. Southern Minnesota Broadcasting Co., 226 Minn. 137, 32 N.W.2d 177, 4 A.L.R.2d 273 (1948); Marks v. Cowdin, 226 N.Y. 138, 123 N.E. 139 (1919); Collier v. Sunday Referee Pub. Co., 4 All E.R. 234 (1940).
474. *See* 4 CORBIN ON CONTRACTS § 946. *See also* RESTATEMENT OF CONTRACTS § 313 (1932). *But see* Alabama Football, Inc. v. Stabler, 294 Ala. 551, 319 So. 2d 678 (1975).

§ 3.12. Contractual Aspects of Option and Reserve Clauses.

One of the most controversial provisions of the standard player contracts used in some professional sports has been the clause which gives the team the right to unilaterally renew the player's contract at the end of its original term.[475] A clause which entitles the club to a one-year renewal is commonly referred to as an option clause, while provisions, such as those found in baseball, which give a team perpetual rights to the player's services are categorized as reserve clauses.[476] Whatever its form, the right to bind the athlete for a further term would presumably be exercised in cases in which the player did not voluntarily agree to extend the term of an existing arrangement.[477] Thus the right of unilateral renewal can be used by the team to secure the services of a player who would prefer to play elsewhere. Option and reserve clauses have long been resented by athletes, for they operate to significantly reduce the player's

---

475. *See generally* Flood v. Kuhn, 407 U.S. 258, 32 L. Ed. 2d 728, 92 S. Ct. 2099 (1972); Boston Professional Hockey Ass'n v. Cheevers, 472 F.2d 127 (1st Cir.), *remanding* 348 F. Supp. (D. Mass. 1972); Hennigan v. Chargers Football Co., 431 F.2d 308 (5th Cir. 1970); Robertson v. National Basketball Ass'n, 389 F. Supp. 867 (S.D.N.Y. 1975); Kapp v. National Football League, 390 F. Supp. 73 (N.D. Cal. 1974); Philadelphia World Hockey Club, Inc. v. Philadelphia Hockey Club, Inc., 351 F. Supp. 462 (E.D. Pa. 1972); Nassau Sports v. Hampson, 355 F. Supp. 733 (D. Minn. 1972); Nassau Sports v. Peters, 352 F. Supp. 870 (E.D.N.Y. 1972); Metropolitan Exhibition Co. v. Ewing, 42 F. 198 (S.D.N.Y. 1890); Metropolitan Exhibition Co. v. Ward, 9 N.Y. 779 (Sup. Ct. 1890); Central New York Basketball, Inc. v. Barnett, 19 Ohio Op. 2d 130, 181 N.E.2d 506 (1961); Philadelphia Ball Club, Ltd. v. Hallman, 8 Pa. County Ct. 57 (1890); Reeves v. Huffman, [1951] 3 W.W.R. (n.s.) 176 (K.B.); Philadelphia Eagles v. Armstrong, [1951] 3 W.W.R. (n.s.) 637 (K.B.); Canes, *The Social Benefits of Restrictions on Team Quality* in GOVERNMENT AND THE SPORTS BUSINESS 81 (R. Noll, ed. 1974); Noll, *Alternatives in Sports Policy* in *id.* 411; Rivkin, *Sports Leagues and the Antitrust Laws* in *id.* 387; Alyluia, *Professional Sports Contracts and the Players' Association,* 5 MAN. L.J. 359, 363-66, 380-81 (1973); Gilbert, *Some Old Problems in a Modern Guise: Enforcement of Negative Covenants,* 4 CAL. L. REV. 114 (1915); Rottenberg, *The Baseball Players' Labor Market,* 64 J. POL. ECON. 242 (1956); Comment, *Antitrust and Professional Sport: Does Anyone Play by the Rules of the Game?,* 22 CATHOLIC U.L.REV. 403 (1973); Comment, *Injunctions in Professional Athletes' Contracts — An Overused Remedy,* 43 CONN. B.J. 538 (1969); Comment, *Contractual Rights and Duties of the Professional Athlete — Playing the Game in a Bidding War,* 77 DICK. L. REV. 352 (1972); Comment, *The Super Bowl and the Sherman Act: Professional Team Sports and the Antitrust Laws,* 81 HARV. L. REV. 418 (1967); Comment, *Player Control Mechanisms in Professional Team Sports,* 34 U. PITT. L. REV. 645 (1973); Note, *Reserve Clauses in Athletic Contracts,* 2 RUTGERS-CAMDEN L.J. 302 (1970).

476. *See* Flood v. Kuhn, 407 U.S. 258, 259 n.1 (1972). *See generally* Comment, *Player Control Mechanisms in Professional Team Sports, supra* note 475; Note, *Reserve Clauses in Athletic Contracts, supra* note 475.

477. Typical of the option clauses which were the focus of litigation in this area is the following provision from the old NBA contract:

> On or before September 1 next following the last playing season covered by this contract and renewals and extensions thereof, the Club may tender to the Player a contract for the next succeeding season by mailing the same to the Player at his address shown below, or if none is shown then at his address last known to the Club. If the Player fails, neglects, or omits to sign and return such contract to the Club so that the Club receives it on or before October 1st next succeeding, then this contract shall be deemed renewed and extended for the period of one year, upon the same terms and conditions in all respects as are provided herein, except that the compensation payable to the Player shall be the sum provided in the contract tendered to the Player pursuant to the provisions hereof, which compensation shall in no event be less than 75% of the compensation payable to the Player for the last playing season covered by this contract and renewals and extensions thereof. Uniform Player Contract, National Basketball Association ¶ 22 (1971).

The NBA contract was subsequently amended to provide that the player's salary in the option year would be 100% of his salary under the original contract. *See* Robertson v. National Basketball Ass'n, 389 F. Supp. 867, 874, n.7 (S.D.N.Y. 1975). The new NBA contracts eliminate the option clause except in the contracts of first year players.

economic return. On the one hand, the player's attractiveness to another team, even one in another league, is limited to the extent that the original contracting club has an enforceable claim to the player's services.[478] He may thus be forced to pass up lucrative contract offers from other sources. By the same token, the player's bargaining position with respect to his own club is reduced. Since he cannot make an effective threat that he will leave the club to play for another, he must bargain without the advantage of the employee's ultimate weapon.[479]

The NFL uses provisions similar to those of the NBA. *See* NFL Contract ¶ 17 (1977). (The citation form for standard player contracts is explained in note 126, § 3.05 *supra*). Under the collective bargaining agreement reached between the NFL owners and the players in 1977, certain veteran players need not sign contracts which include option clauses. Those so exempted are players who have received four or more years of credited service under the league's pension plan. Such veterans may, however, agree to an option clause, but they must be separately compensated for its inclusion. Rookies are required to consent to an option clause, and the contracts of veterans with less than four years of service "may include an option year." The collective bargaining agreement also specifies that if the club exercises its rights under an option clause, it must pay the player, in the option year, no less than 100% of his original salary. *See* Collective Bargaining Agreement Between the NFL Management Council and the NFL Players Ass'n, art. XIV (1977).

The NHL formerly had a provision which used language similar to that used in the NBA, but which was interpreted to operate as a perpetual reserve system. *See* Philadelphia World Hockey Club, Inc. v. Philadelphia Hockey Club, Inc., 351 F. Supp. 462 (E.D. Pa. 1972). As a result of litigation attacking the system on antitrust grounds, the NHL in 1973 made a radical revision in its player retention system. The new arrangement has several unique features. A player in the NHL can readily secure free agent status and become eligible to negotiate with other teams. Basically, the arrangement provides for a number of options available to the club and player. In the final year of the original contract, the club may give the player the option of accepting a one-season termination contract or immediately claiming free agent status. If the club does not give the player that choice, it may renegotiate the original contract. If (1) the player takes no unilateral action and (2) if the parties cannot agree on a new contract, then the existing contract is, in effect, extended for one season with salary to be determined by neutral arbitration. But the new system contains one feature that is particularly worthy of note. The player is given a unilateral right to renew the contract for one season at the previous year's salary. Thereafter, he is a free agent. *See* NHL Contract ¶ 17. The new standard players contract, at least on its face, does not include a term allowing the club to terminate a player for insufficient skill. Also important to the operation of the system is an amendment to the League By-Laws providing for "Equalization Payments." As indicated in the league documents:

> The purpose of the equalization payment shall be to compensate a player's previous Member Club fairly for loss of the right, to his services when the player becomes a free agent and the right to his services is acquired by another Member Club or a club owned or controlled by another Member Club. NHL By-Laws § 9A(7).

The payment obligation may be satisfied by the acquiring club's assignment of another player's contract, transferring draft choices or paying cash.

The new arrangement for free agent status applies to all players in the NHL except amateurs and certain rookies.

The NHL system for player equalization payments is somewhat similar to that which operated in the NFL under the so-called Rozelle Rule. That arrangement was the focus of antitrust attacks. It is alleged that the requirement that a club acquiring a free agent compensate the original employer unlawfully restrains the player's right to market his services since potential employers within the league are discouraged from hiring him. This matter is considered more fully in the chapter of this book dealing with antitrust. *See* § 5.07 *infra. See also* Robertson v. National Basketball Ass'n, 389 F. Supp. 867 (S.D.N.Y. 1975); Kapp v. National Football League, 390 F. Supp. 73 (N.D. Cal. 1974). *See generally* Morris, *In the Wake of the Flood*, 38 LAW & CONTEMP. PROB. 85 (1973); Comment, *Player Control Mechanisms in Professional Team Sports, supra* note 475; Note, *Reserve Clauses in Athletic Contracts, supra* note 475.

478. The player's mobility within a league with an option system is affected not only by the terms of the clause in his contract, but also by league rules requiring that a club who hires a free agent compensate the athlete's previous employer for its loss. *See* note 477 *supra*. The present discussion does not treat this aspect of player retention systems, but rather is limited to an interpretation of the language included in the player's contract.

479. *See generally* Canes, *The Social Benefits of Restrictions on Team Quality, supra* note 475; Rottenberg, *The Baseball Players' Labor Market, supra* note 475.

As might be imagined, players have not accepted these methods of player restraints impassively. To the extent that their objections have been expressed in legal actions, they most commonly appear in litigation seeking to subject the restraints to judicial scrutiny under the antitrust laws.[480] The interpretations which have emerged from these controversies are treated in another chapter dealing with the antitrust aspects of professional sports.[481] But the athletes have not limited their legal objections to those which arise under the antitrust laws. There are potential problems of contracts law involved as well, and it is this facet of the common systems of player restraints which is examined here.

a. Duration of the Team's Right to Continue the Player's Contract. For a long period of time, there was considerable uncertainty in many leagues as to whether the league's contract renewal clause gave the club the right to renew in perpetuity or only for one additional year. This question received attention in a number of cases. However, those precedents are now largely of historical interest as far as the major professional leagues are concerned. In the antitrust actions brought in the mid-1970's the courts made clear that a clause giving a perpetual right of renewal could not be sustained.[482] This and other antitrust setbacks prompted more serious bargaining between the club owners and the players, and the consequence of these negotiations has been that contract renewal clauses have either been eliminated or rewritten to specifically provide for a single year renewal.[483]

While the question of the duration of the club's right to renew has thus been settled in the major leagues, it may be useful to mention some of the older precedents. These will serve to help explain how the present system evolved. In addition, there may be other less well-known leagues in which the process of interpreting the renewal clause may be aided by reference to the prior developments involving the major league contracts.

Under a clause giving the club a right of renewal for an additional term, the question frequently arose as to whether a club which has once exercised its right under the option clause has the further right to bind the player to an additional term following the expiration of the option year. The most frequently used types of clauses provided that the contract will be renewed "upon the same terms and conditions" as provided in the original agreement.[484] Thus, it might be argued that one of the terms of the original agreement is the option clause itself, and if that clause became part of the contract governing the option year, then presumably the team would have the right of a further renewal. This process could presumably continue indefinitely and, in effect, give the team a perpetual right to the player's services. Such a power in the team would not only raise serious antitrust problems [485] but might also be subject to the common law

---

480. *See, e.g.,* Flood v. Kuhn, 407 U.S. 258 (1972); Robertson v. National Basketball Ass'n, 389 F. Supp. 867 (S.D.N.Y. 1975); Kapp v. National Football League, 390 F. Supp. 73 (N.D. Cal. 1974); Philadelphia World Hockey Club, Inc. v. Philadelphia Hockey Club, Inc., 351 F. Supp. 462 (E.D. Pa. 1972).

481. *See* §§ 5.03-5.07 *infra.*

482. *See* Robertson v. National Basketball Ass'n, 389 F. Supp. 867 (S.D.N.Y. 1975); Kapp v. National Football League, 390 F. Supp. 73 (N.D. Cal. 1974).

483. *See* note 477 *supra.*

484. *See* NBA Contract, *supra* note 477. *See also* NBA Contract (Rookie-Single Season) ¶ 22 (1976); NFL Contract ¶ 10; ABA Contract ¶ 15.

485. *See* §§ 5.03-.07 *infra.*

objection that it is contrary to public policy.[486] On the other hand, depending on the language which the parties used and other indicia of their intent, it might be possible to interpret the option clause as giving the team the right to renew the player's contract only once. Under this view, the player would be free to sell his services to other teams after having fulfilled his obligations in the option year.[487]

The question of which of the above interpretations was most properly applied to the various systems of player restraints received a good deal of attention by the courts. The courts' responses were not uniform. In evaluating these cases, one must allow for variations which might be mandated by differences in the language which the parties use. Even so, the divergence of interpretations is significant.

The perpetual nature of the baseball reserve system was condemned in some of the early baseball cases.[488] A later review, limited to selected issues, dismissed many of the earlier objections.[489] More recently, however, a private arbitrator interpreted the standard form baseball contract as providing only a one-year option.[490] The first tests for the basketball option system resulted in decisions which construed the contract clauses as giving the team only a single, as opposed to a perpetual, right to renew.[491] Interestingly, this result was reached not because of the particular language of the contract or because of reliable evidence of the specific intent of the parties. Rather, in the primary decision on this point, the court applied the well-founded rule that a contract ought to be interpreted to preserve its validity. Since a contrary interpretation would raise serious antitrust problems, it seemed preferable to read the contract language more narrowly, and thereby insure the enforceability of the agreement.[492]

While some commentators regarded this decision as conclusive on the proper construction of the basketball clause,[493] subsequent courts were less certain. Indeed, in a preliminary decision in *Robertson v. National Basketball Association*,[494] an antitrust proceeding, the court expressed the view that it was by no means clear that the basketball clause created a single one-year option, rather than a perpetual claim, as the club alleged.[495] Moreover, the suggestion that an option clause ought to be interpreted to preserve the validity of the

---

486. *See, e.g.,* American League Baseball Club of Chicago v. Chase, 86 Misc. 441, 149 N.Y.S. 6 (Sup. Ct. 1914). *See also* § 4.13 *infra.*

487. *See* note 478 *supra.*

488. *See, e.g.,* American League Baseball Club of Chicago v. Chase, 86 Misc. 441, 149 N.Y.S. 6 (Sup. Ct. 1914).

489. *See* Flood v. Kuhn, 316 F. Supp. 271 (S.D.N.Y. 1970), *aff'd,* 443 F.2d 264 (2d Cir. 1971), *aff'd,* 407 U.S. 258, (1972). While the Supreme Court reviewed the antitrust aspects of the case, the lower court considered other issues, including the question of whether the reserve system created a condition of involuntary servitude violative of the Thirteenth Amendment. Ultimately, the reserve system was held to be immune from antitrust attack.

490. *See* § 5.02 *infra.*

491. *See, e.g.,* Lemat Corp. v. Barry, 275 Cal. App. 2d 671, 80 Cal. Rptr. 240 (1969); Central New York Basketball, Inc. v. Barnett, 19 Ohio Op. 2d 130, 181 N.E.2d 506 (1961).

492. *See* Central New York Basketball, Inc. v. Barnett, 19 Ohio Op. 2d 130, 132-33, 181 N.E.2d 506, 509 (1961).

493. *See, e.g.,* Comment, *Antitrust and Professional Sport: Does Anyone Play by the Rules of the Game?, supra* note 475, at 414; Comment, *Injunctions in Professional Athletes' Contracts — An Overused Remedy, supra* note 475, at 548.

494. 389 F. Supp. 867 (S.D.N.Y. 1975).

495. *Id.* at 890-91.

contract was not regarded as controlling when a similar question arose in connection with the player restraint system in hockey. In *Philadelphia World Hockey Club, Inc. v. Philadelphia Hockey Club, Inc.,*[496] the leading case subjecting the operation of the NHL to scrutiny under the antitrust laws, the court concluded that the NHL option clause created a perpetual obligation in the player.[497] This result was reached even though the language of the hockey option clause was quite similar to the basketball option provision which was given a more restrictive reading.[498] Once the hockey provision was characterized as creating perpetual rights, the court was then compelled to consider the antitrust implications of its finding. The consequence was that the system of player restraint was found to be impermissibly broad and in violation of federal proscriptions.[499]

If the question of the duration or rights created by a renewal clause should arise again, as in the case of a yet-unlitigated minor league contract, there are a number of considerations which the parties may wish to bring to the court's attention. For example, it is highly relevant to determine how the clause has actually been applied in practice.[500] Thus, the litigants should seek to identify specific instances in which the league or club officials have made interpretations affecting particular players, even if those cases never proceeded to litigation. In addition, despite the quaintness of the notion, the principle that a contract should be interpreted to avoid its illegality seems to be sound.[501] Unless there is convincing evidence to the contrary, it seems appropriate to presume that the parties did not purposely intend to render their agreement a nullity. Finally, it can be suggested that the meaning of a contract term need not be static. While the parties may have drafted the agreement with one interpretation in mind, their understanding of its meaning may change over time. Thus, changes in the league's operation, such as the advent of collective bargaining, may alter prior assumptions about the effect of language used in former agreements.[502] In the same vein, there may be situations in which a court can find that developments in other parts of the industry, such as adverse antitrust interpretations of another league's contracts, have altered the way in which parties not otherwise directly affected view their contractual relationships.

---

496. 351 F. Supp. 462, 480-81, 505-09 (E.D. Pa. 1972).

497. *See also* Nassau Sports v. Peters, 352 F. Supp. 870, 878-79 (E.D.N.Y. 1972); Nassau Sports v. Hampson, 355 F. Supp. 733 (D. Minn. 1972); Alyluia, *Professional Sports Contracts and the Players' Association, supra* note 475, at 363-64.

498. *Compare* Philadelphia World Hockey Club, Inc. v. Philadelphia Hockey Club, Inc., 351 F. Supp. 462, 475-76 (E.D. Pa. 1972) *with* Central New York Basketball, Inc. v. Barnett, 19 Ohio Op. 2d 130, 132-33, 181 N.E.2d 506, 509 (1961).

499. Philadelphia World Hockey Club, Inc. v. Philadelphia Hockey Club, Inc., 351 F. Supp. 462, 505-09 (E.D. Pa. 1972). *See generally* Alyluia, *Professional Sports Contracts and the Players' Association, supra* note 475.

500. *See generally* § 3.04 *supra.*

501. *See* text at notes 491-92 *supra.*

502. This approach seems to have been taken by Peter Seitz in interpreting the renewal clause in the professional baseball contract. The language of the clause left some uncertainty as to its precise meaning. However, it had historically been interpreted as providing for a perpetual right of renewal, and, indeed, it was this feature which prompted the litigation in *Flood v. Kuhn.* Nonetheless, Arbitrator Seitz stated that the recently-formed players union had never agreed to this interpretation and thus doubted whether it should control his reading of the clause. *See* National & American Leagues of Professional Baseball Clubs v. Major League Baseball Players Ass'n (John

b. The Manner of Exercising the Option. Under the typical option clause, including those which have emerged in the recent collective bargaining agreements, the team can secure a right to the player's services for the option year without the express consent of the player. The unilateral nature of the option rights is usually given explicit recognition. Thus, it may be provided that the club will tender a contract to the player and if the athlete fails or refuses to sign it, he is nonetheless bound.[503] The terms to which he is bound are usually the terms of the original contract, although salary is sometimes subject to adjustment.[504] Thus the player is often given the right to enter a new contract or have his old one extended.

Judicial interpretation of the option provisions has affirmed that the option can be exercised upon mere tender or notice by the club, and no separate acceptance or consent by the player is necessary.[505] Thus, if the club takes the proper action, the player is bound, and the fact that he fails to open the letter [506] or otherwise fails to acknowledge its terms [507] does not affect the existence of an obligation on his part. In many situations, the player will be well advised not to sign the tendered contract. Unless the original contract provides otherwise, the player's acceptance of the tendered contract may indicate his acceptance of a totally new contract, which itself contains an option clause exercisable by the club for still another year. Thus, by the player's signing of the proffered contract, the club avoids having to exercise its option, for the relationship which exists is one reached by mutual agreement, not by virtue of the club's unilateral right to claim an additional year of the player's services. If the player wants to "play out his option," he will usually have to indicate that choice by refusing to accept any new contract tendered by the team.[508]

The club will usually seek to renegotiate its contract with the athlete rather than abruptly exercise its option. In the process of renegotiation the team may tender a contract which includes terms which are different from those which would govern the option year. The question may arise as to whether these

A. Messersmith & David A. McNally), Grievance Nos. 75-27 & 75-28, Decision No. 29 (Dec. 23, 1975, Opinion of Impartial Chairman Peter Seitz).

503. *See, e.g.,* NBA Contract, ¶ 22, *supra* note 477. *Compare* NBA Contract (Rookie — Single Season) ¶ 22 (1976).

504. *See, e.g.,* NFL Contract ¶ 10 (1975) (not less than 90% of the compensation payable under the contract). *See also* note 477 *supra.*

505. *See* Lemat Corp. v. Barry, 274 Cal. App. 2d 671, 80 Cal. Rptr. 240 (1969); Central New York Basketball, Inc. v. Barnett, 19 Ohio Op. 2d 130, 181 N.E.2d 506 (1961); Dallas Cowboys Football Club, Inc. v. Harris, 348 S.W.2d 37 (Tex. Civ. App. 1961).

506. *See* Central New York Basketball, Inc. v. Barnett, 19 Ohio Op. 2d 130, 134-35, 181 N.E.2d 506, 511 (1961).

507. *See* Lemat Corp. v. Barry, 275 Cal. App. 2d 671, 674, 80 Cal. Rptr. 240, 242 (1960).

508. Central New York Basketball, Inc. v. Barnett, 19 Ohio Op. 2d 130, 181 N.E.2d 506 (1961), presents a situation which fits somewhere in between the mutual agreement of the team and player to a new contract and the team's unilateral exercise of its right to further services. In that case, the team based its case upon the fact that it had exercised its option to renew the contract, *id.* at 130-31, 181 N.E.2d at 507, but apparently contended that the player had agreed to a particular salary for the further year, a contention which the court upheld. *See id.* at 134-35, 181 N.E.2d at 511. Another possible construction of the facts which the court did not treat fully is that the player had in fact agreed to a new, separate contract, rather than merely to the salary to be paid in the option. The difference between the two interpretations, of course, may be of critical importance, for it would seem that if the parties agreed to a new contract, the club would still have an unexercised option. *See also* Reeves v. Huffman, (1951) 3 W.W.R. (n.s.) 176 (K.B.); Philadelphia **Eagles,** Inc. v. Armstrong, (1951) 3 W.W.R. (n.s.) 637 (K.B.).

actions by the club affect the validity of an attempted exercise of the team's option, particularly one which is prior to the offer of a new contract. The argument which would be made is that the club had waived its option rights by proceeding to consider a different arrangement.[509] Unless a case presents other facts suggesting a waiver, the team should not be penalized for attempting to secure a new contract with the athlete.[510] The realities of the situation are that the club would not lightly give up its rights to the player, and it can be assumed that the club intended to act to preserve its interest. The offer of a new or alternate contract can best be viewed as an attempt by the club to foster a good relationship with the player and provide him increased economic incentives to stimulate his performance. The team may truly prefer to avoid having to assert the rights afforded by the option, but this interest in preserving a congenial relationship is not mutually exclusive with the team's paramount interest in maximizing its investment.

c. The Terms Governing the Option Year. It is generally true that the terms which will define the parties' relationship in the option year will be the same terms as governed the original contract. This is often expressly recognized in the option clause itself, which may include language providing that a renewal is upon the same terms and conditions as provided in the original document.[511] But there are exceptions to this general incorporation, some of which arise by virtue of the express language of the contracts, others of which are supplied by judicial interpretation.

Player contracts sometimes provide that the athlete's salary for the option year may be different from that provided in the original contract. A typical provision stipulates that the player's salary may be set by the club, but in no event will be less than a stated percentage of the original salary.[512] It formerly was common for the contracts to specify that the player's salary in the renewal year was less than 100% of the original salary. While a clause of this sort clearly afforded the team the opportunity to adversely affect the player's economic status in the option year, it was often true that the original salary was not reduced at all, and indeed was actually increased.[513] Why would a team reserve the right to reduce the athlete's salary in the option-year? The historical explanation for the differential was that the "extra" salary provided during the

---

509. *Compare* 2A A. CORBIN, CORBIN ON CONTRACTS §§ 742-53, 755 (1951). *See also* Philadelphia Eagles, Inc. v. Armstrong, (1951) 3 W.W.R. (n.s.) 637 (K.B.).
510. *See* Dallas Cowboys Football Club, Inc. v. Harris, 348 S.W.2d 37, 46 (Tex. Civ. App. 1961):
    Certainly after one party has exercised his option under an existing contract, it is not illegal or improper for the parties to enter upon negotiations looking to the possibility of the execution of a new, separate and different contract, not entered into as a part of the original option agreement.
See also Central New York Basketball, Inc. v. Barnett, 19 Ohio Op. 2d 130, 134-35, 181 N.E. 2d 506, 511 (1961). *But see* Reeves v. Huffman, (1951) 3 W.W.R. (n.s.) 176 (K.B.).
511. *See, e.g.,* NBA Contract (Rookie — Single Season) ¶ 22 (1976).
512. The NBA formerly had a minimum option yearly salary of 75% of the original compensation, but this was recently changed to guarantee that the salary would not be changed. *See* note 477 *supra.*
513. *See* Lemat Corp. v. Barry, 275 Cal. App. 2d 671, 80 Cal. Rptr. 240 (1969); Central New York Basketball, Inc. v. Barnett, 19 Ohio Op. 2d 130, 181 N.E.2d 506 (1961). The club may decline to exercise its right to reduce the player's salary in order to induce the player not to exercise his ultimate weapon, which is to retire from professional sports altogether, or to encourage him to continue his performance at a high level.

original term was intended to compensate the player for two different things — his performance on the athletic field *and* his granting of option rights to the team. Once the contract was extended into the option-year, the need for the team to pay for the option had ended, and hence the compensation could appropriately be reduced to reflect the reduced value of the team's contract rights. Despite the superficial attractiveness of this characterization, it is unnecessary as a legal matter. There is no need for the team to offer extra consideration for the option. Whatever consideration supports the player's obligation to perform during the original term will also support the option.[514] The more likely explanation for the salary reduction clause is that it was the product of the team's superior bargaining position and was included for the primary purpose of providing a further potential disability to the player who is thinking about playing out his option.

The other limitations which serve to define the content of the option year contract are generally less certain than that which defines the player's salary rights. By way of background, it can be noted that courts used the occasion of the early baseball cases to make clear that a team has enforceable rights in the option year only if the terms which govern that extended term are clear and explicit.[515] If the applicable terms are not clear, and if they cannot be ascertained by the application of the normal rules of construction,[516] then there is no contract and the player is free to market his services elsewhere.[517] Most standard players contracts in the major professional sports avoid that problem by leaving none of the option-year provisions to the parties' future agreement.

The court's decision in *Hennigan v. Chargers Football Company*[518] has general significance in this area, for the opinion can be viewed as disproving the notion that the option contract incorporates all but the salary term of the original agreement. Hennigan was injured during the original period of his contract. The contract contained a provision under which the team was obligated to pay Hennigan's entire salary "in the event that Player is injured in the performance of his services under this contract."[519] The issue presented was whether Hennigan's right to compensation under this language continued into the option year when the defendant club subsequently exercised its option rights. This construction would seem to be supported by the contract language which seeks to treat the option year contract as merely incorporating and extending the terms of the original agreement. Hence a "right" which a player had under the original contract — in this case a right to compensation — would presumably be continued into the option-year. The court's conclusion was to the contrary, however. In its view, when the club exercised its renewal option, "a new contract was established," and it did not have the effect of carrying over obligations arising from the original agreement which were subject to expiration at the end

---

514. *See* Central New York Basketball, Inc. v. Barnett, 19 Ohio Op. 2d 130, 135-36, 181 N.E.2d 506, 512 (1961). *See generally* Gilbert, *Some Old Problems in a Modern Guise: Enforcement of Negative Covenants*, 4 CAL L. REV. 114, 118 (1915).

515. *See, e.g.,* Metropolitan Exhibition Co. v. Ewing, 42 F. 198 (S.D.N.Y. 1890); Metropolitan Exhibition Co. v. Ward, 9 N.Y.S. 779 (Sup. Ct. 1890); Philadelphia Ball Club, Ltd. v. Hallman, 8 Pa. County Ct. 57 (1890).

516. *See generally* §§ 3.03-.04 *supra.*

517. *See, e.g.,* Metropolitan Exhibition Co. v. Ward, 9 N.Y.S. 779 (Sup. Ct. 1890).

518. 431 F.2d 308 (5th Cir. 1970).

519. *Id.* at 311. *See generally* §§ 3.05-.06 *supra.*

of that contract.[520] Given the *Hennigan* precedent, the player cannot assume that any entitlement, whether it be compensation for injury or reimbursement in another form, will continue into the option year. Rather, the contract must be examined to determine if the benefit is expressly or impliedly limited to the terms of the original agreement.

Perhaps the most important teaching of *Hennigan* is that the option clause will be given a practical construction in light of the general unwillingness of the clubs to accept any great risk upon exercise of the option.[521] The court's view seems to be that the teams ought to be regarded as intending to preserve all rights which they have to a player's services, while carefully controlling their obligation to pay for anything other than services actually received. Thus, it can be assumed that the team which exercises its option on a player intends to start the relationship afresh as far as its duty to pay the player is concerned. The court's analysis presents what is probably an accurate characterization of the intention which underlies the club-drafted professional athlete's contract.[522]

§ 3.13. Assignment of Player Contracts — The Basis of the Club's Right to Assign.

A club's ability to trade players is an important, and perhaps an indispensable, part of the operation of a professional sports team. Often such trades are made for the purpose of improving the team's competitive position within the league. Thus, a weakness on the pitching staff might be cured by trading away a player in another position where the club has extra talent. While the team might like to have the public believe that all trades are of this sort, it should be recognized that a trade may be made for purely financial reasons, as where the team seeks to reduce the extent of its obligation to pay player salaries or where the team seeks to capitalize on the "profit" which it can claim under the draft and reserve system.[523] Each of these situations will necessarily involve the assignment of some player contracts. In other cases, the assignment of player contracts may occur on a wholesale basis, as where an existing franchise is sold to new owners and the contracts of all players are transferred as part of the sale.[524]

Whatever the reason for the assignment, it may give rise to a variety of objections by the player. He may be displeased with the prospect of having to move his family and abandon social ties.[525] Or he may have cultivated local business interests which would suffer if he left.[526] Even where the player's tenure in the assignor's city has not resulted in substantial business or social involvement, he may well object to the climate or playing conditions in the

---

520. 431 F.2d at 315.

521. *Id.* at 317.

522. The *Hennigan* case is discussed further in § 3.05 *supra*.

523. Because of the restrictions imposed on player mobility by the draft and reserve systems, a player will often be paid less than his fair market value. A team may desire to capture a portion of that differential by selling the player's contract to another team. *See generally* Rottenberg, *The Baseball Players' Labor Market*, 64 J. POL. ECON. 242 (1956).

524. *See, e.g.,* Minnesota Muskies, Inc. v. Hudson, 294 F. Supp. 979 (M.D.N.C. 1969).

525. *See, e.g.,* Flood v. Kuhn, 309 F. Supp. 793, 799 (S.D.N.Y. 1970). This case was eventually affirmed on a different point. 407 U.S. 258, 32 L. Ed. 2d 728, 92 S. Ct. 2099 (1972).

526. *See, e.g.,* Flood v. Kuhn, 309 F. Supp. 793, 799-800 (S.D.N.Y. 1970); Washington Capitols Basketball Club, Inc. v. Barry, 304 F. Supp. 1193, 1202 (N.D. Cal.), *aff'd,* 419 F.2d 472 (9th Cir. 1969).

assignee's city, or he may be skeptical of the ability of the assignee-owners to meet the financial commitments of his contract. What are the player's rights to object to an assignment of his contract? Does he have any assurance that the trade will not work to his economic or social detriment? These are questions which arise with some frequency in the day-to-day world of professional sports, and even with the dearth of reported cases in this area, rather certain answers are available for many of the issues.

In an industry in which assignment of contracts has such important consequences, it is not surprising that the contracts which define internal relationships have been drafted to anticipate many of the objections which might be raised. The typical standard player contract includes a term in which the athlete agrees that the club will have the right to assign the contract.[527] Often there is a further promise that the player will fully perform for the assignee team.[528] In addition, there may be a provision specifying the time limits within which the player must report to the new team [529] and the obligations of the respective parties with respect to moving and travel expenses.[530] But the relevant agreement concerning the club's right to assign is not limited to the standard player contract alone. The constitution and by-laws of the league, which may be incorporated into the individual player contracts by specific reference, often also contain provisions pertaining to assignments. These typically deal with procedural matters, such as the necessity for obtaining commissioner approval and for using league forms,[531] as well as with matters of substance, such as the respective salary obligations of the two teams and the impropriety of conditional trades.[532] The collective bargaining agreement between the players' association and club owners may also be relevant. Increasingly these agreements provide limitations on the club's rights. In some sports, for example, the contracts of veteran players cannot be assigned without their consent.[533] But with respect to most players, a club will be free to engage in player trades with little, if any, basis for legal objection by the athlete.

---

527. *See, e.g.,* NFL Contract ¶ 9 (1975):

> It is mutually agreed that the Club shall have the right to sell, exchange, assign or transfer this contract and the Player's services hereunder to any other Club in the League. Player agrees to accept such assignment and to report promptly to the assignee Club and faithfully to perform and carry out this contract with the assignee Club as if it had been entered into by the Player with assignee Club instead of with this Club.

(The abbreviated citation form for standard player contracts is explained in note 126, § 3.05 *supra.*) In 1977, the NFL began using a new contract which included the following assignment clause:

> 18. Assignment. Unless this contract specifically provides otherwise, Club may assign this contract and Player's services under this contract to any successor to Club's franchise or to any other Club in the League. Player will report to the assignee promptly upon being informed of the assignment of his contract and will faithfully perform his services under this contract. The assignee club will pay Player's necessary traveling expenses in reporting to it and will faithfully perform this contract with Player.

NFL Contract ¶ 18 (1977).

528. *See id.*

529. *See* NBA Contract ¶ 12.

530. *Id.* ¶ 11 ("... all reasonable expenses incurred by the Player in moving himself and his family ... shall be paid by the assignee club").

531. *See* CONSTITUTION AND BY-LAWS FOR THE NATIONAL FOOTBALL LEAGUE §§ 16.1, 16.8 (1972).

532. *Id.* §§ 16.3, 16.7. *But see* Macon Baseball Ass'n v. Pennington, 166 S.E. 35 (Ga. Ct. App. 1932).

533. *See, e.g.,* Basic Agreement Between the American League of Professional Baseball Clubs and the National League of Professional Baseball Clubs and Major League Baseball Players Association, Art. XIV, ¶ (A) (1973):

a. The Common Law Background. In analyzing the legal effect of a team's transfer of a player's contract, it is helpful to determine what is meant by an "assignment of the contract." In legal effect, the transaction is not a singular act, but rather has two separate aspects, each of which has different legal consequences. To the extent that there is an *assignment,* it is only an assignment of the club's *rights* under the contract.[534] The basic right which the club enjoys is a right to receive the player's performance. So one question is whether the team can transfer this "right" to performance to another club. A different question is presented when the original owner attempts to have another club assume its obligation to pay the player. Here the question is not whether some rights or benefits may be assigned, but rather whether a duty may be *delegated.*[535] Separate sets of rules govern these questions of assignment of rights and delegation of duties. We look first at the matter of assignment of rights.

The basic common law rule which governs an assignment of contract rights is one which favors assignability, and the general rule presumes that the person entitled to a right under a contract can assign that right to another.[536] But there are important exceptions to this rule, including one which has a direct bearing on personal service contracts of the sort involved in professional sports. These fall under an exception which disallows assignment of rights if

> the substitution of a right of the assignee for the right of the assignor would vary materially the duty of the obligor, or increase materially the burden or risk imposed upon him by his contract, or impair materially his chance of obtaining return performance.[537]

There is little question but that the transfer of a professional athlete's contract from one team to another will materially vary his duties and burdens. Indeed, such a transfer usually means that the athlete must move his home, a burden which was not part of the original contract.[538] In addition, the typical contract allocates certain decisions to the discretion of the original owners, a relationship which is highly personal.[539] After the assignment, the discretion resides in different individuals, none of whom the player has selected. Finally, the player will be asked to play in a different competitive situation, with different teammates, a different manager, and a different climate, all of which might affect his performance.[540] Because these sorts of changes are present to one

---

(1) The contract of a Player with ten or more years of Major League service, the last five of which have been with one Club, shall not be assignable to another Major League Club without the Player's written consent.
(2) The contract of a Player with five or more years of Major League service . . . shall not be assigned otherwise than to another Major League Club, without the Player's written consent.

534. *See generally* 4 A. CORBIN, CORBIN ON CONTRACTS §§ 856, 861 (1951) [hereinafter cited as CORBIN ON CONTRACTS].
535. *See generally* 4 CORBIN ON CONTRACTS §§ 865-66.
536. *See generally* RESTATEMENT OF CONTRACTS § 150 (1932); 6 C.J.S. *Assignments* § 24 (1937); 6 AM. JUR. 2d *Assignments* § 9 (1963); Crane Ice Cream Co. v. Terminal Freezing & Heating Co., 147 Md. 588, 128 A. 280 (1925).
537. RESTATEMENT OF CONTRACTS § 150 (1932). *See also* RESTATEMENT (SECOND) OF CONTRACTS §§ 149(1), 163 (Tent. Draft No. 3, 1967).
538. *See generally* 4 CORBIN ON CONTRACTS § 867-68.
539. *See* § 3.08 *supra.*
540. *See* 4 CORBIN ON CONTRACTS § 868.

degree or another any time a personal service contract is transferred, the exception to assignability identified above has resulted in a generally-recognized principle that absent special facts, rights under personal service contracts are not assignable.[541] Obviously, it would not be acceptable to the professional sports industry to function with a rule which precluded assignability, and it is not surprising that the clubs have undertaken to provide the "special facts" which will avoid this restriction. This is accomplished by securing the player's prior consent to the assignment in a contract provision such as those outlined above.[542] This contract language has the effect of bringing professional sports contracts within the doctrine which recognizes that "if . . . the obligor manifests assent to the future assignment of a right, . . . the power of assignment exists . . . despite any subsequent objection." [543] A question which remains, and which is examined below, is whether this contractual consent removes from the player the right to object no matter what new duties or new risks may result from the assignment.

When we move from the matter of an assignment of the team's rights under the contract to issues relating to the team's delegation of its duties, we find that the common law rules suggest an analysis similar to that given in the preceding paragraph. In general, the law does not disapprove the delegation of legal duties,[544] although it is generally true that a delegation cannot relieve the original obligor of legal liability should the duty not be performed properly.[545] But as in the case of an assignment, there are limitations on a party's right to delegate his duty. Most important for the present discussion is the notion that an attempted delegation will be disapproved if performance by the delegate (i.e., assignee team) "would vary materially from performance by the person named in the contract." [546] Such a material variation would normally exist where the contract contemplated duties which required the personal skill or judgment of the promisor.[547] Do the duties assumed by a club under a standard player contract involve matters of this sort? Under one view, the team's obligation is only a duty to pay the player's compensation, and the accepted view at common law is that a contractual duty to pay money can be discharged by anyone and thus is delegable.[548] Further analysis should suggest, however, that the team's obligations include much more than a mere duty to pay money. As already noted, the contracts allocate to the team a great deal of discretion to determine the athlete's fitness and qualifications for participating in the team's games.[549] The team literally has the discretion to determine whether or not the player will be

---

541. *See, e.g.,* Rochester Ry. v. Rochester, 205 U.S. 236, 51 L. Ed. 784, 27 S. Ct. 469 (1907); Munchak Corp. v. Cunningham, 457 F.2d 721, 725 (4th Cir. 1972); Sisco v. Empiregas, Inc., 286 Ala. 72, 237 So. 2d 463 (1970); 6 C.J.S. *Assignments* § 26 (1937).

542. *See* discussion at notes 527-30 *supra.*

543. RESTATEMENT OF CONTRACTS § 162(1) (1932). *See also* RESTATEMENT (SECOND) OF CONTRACTS § 152 (Tent. Draft No. 3, 1967).

544. *See generally* RESTATEMENT OF CONTRACTS § 160 (1932); 4 CORBIN ON CONTRACTS §§ 865-69; J. MURRAY, MURRAY ON CONTRACTS § 302 (1974).

545. *See generally* 4 CORBIN ON CONTRACTS § 866. *See also* discussion at notes 567-79 *infra.*

546. RESTATEMENT OF CONTRACTS § 160(3)(a) (1932). *See also* RESTATEMENT (SECOND) OF CONTRACTS §§ 150, 151 (Tent. Draft No. 3, 1967).

547. *See, e.g.,* Taylor v. Palmer, 31 Cal. 240 (1866); Carson v. Lewis, 77 Neb. 446, 109 N.W. 735 (1900); Deaton v. Lawson, 40 Wash. 486, 82 P. 879 (1905).

548. *See, e.g.,* Cannister Co. v. National Can Corp., 71 F. Supp. 45 (D. Del. 1947).

549. *See* § 3.08 *supra.*

entitled to receive his compensation. On this basis alone, it would seem that the club's duties under the contract are non-delegable unless additional facts were present. But, as in the case of the assignment of contract rights, the law permits a delegation where there is an express consent by the promisee,[550] and the teams have presumably intended to provide that consent in the standard form agreements discussed above.[551] While the language most typically used secures the player's acquiescence to an "assignment of the contract" and does not specifically exact a consent to a delegation of the team's duties, the phrase "assignment of the contract" is probably intended to cover both aspects of the transaction. Should any doubts remain, industry practice will provide convincing evidence that this result was intended.[552]

While the basic common law rules governing assignment and delegation can be simply stated, they have been the source of some confusion when they are applied to contracts in which the assignor is a corporation. Since many employers in the sports area do business in this form, some effort should be made to insure that the potential for confusion be minimized as much as possible. Why should it make any difference whether the employer operates as a corporation, rather than in some form of personal proprietorship? The argument would be as follows. The reason for not allowing assignment of employment contracts involving skill or judgment is that the original contractual relationship can be said to be based upon very subjective feelings of trust and confidence between the parties. Such a relationship requires the assent of each party. This being so, it is felt that one party should not be allowed to use the device of an assignment to introduce an outsider into the relationship, absent consent by the other side. It can be argued that this rationale does not apply where the person providing the service has contracted with a corporation. A corporation has no personality, exhibits no characteristics of trust and confidence, and therefore, can hardly be said to have entered into a "personal" relationship. Thus, an assignment of a personal contract from one corporation to another could not be objected to since no "personal" relationship ever existed. Similarly, it might be contended that one who contracts with a corporation knows that it can only act through delegates and thus has given his implied consent to the corporation's delegation of its duties.[553] A corollary to this view is that one who has contracted with a corporation cannot object when the corporation changes hands and is acquired by new owners.[554] Since the contract was with the corporation, and not with the shareholders, it is alleged, there can be no complaint.[555]

Despite the superficial logic of this argument, it must be rejected, at least to the extent that it seeks to present a general rule that a personalized relationship can never be developed with a corporation. The primary difficulty with the argument is that it fails to differentiate between types of corporations and

550. See RESTATEMENT OF CONTRACTS § 162(1) (1932). See also RESTATEMENT (SECOND) OF CONTRACTS § 155 (Tent. Draft No. 3, 1967).

551. See discussion at notes 527-30 supra.

552. Cf. Washington Capitols Basketball Club, Inc. v. Barry, 419 F.2d 472, 479 (9th Cir. 1969).

553. See generally L. SIMPSON, HANDBOOK ON THE LAW OF CONTRACTS § 276 (2d ed. 1965); 4 CORBIN ON CONTRACTS § 865.

554. See generally id.

555. See, e.g., Munchak Corp. v. Cunningham, 457 F.2d 721, 725 (4th Cir. 1972).

between the varieties of relationships which might arise in the corporate world. In particular, the argument ignores the fact that many closely-held corporate ventures very much retain the personality of the primary shareholders. It seems fatuous to suggest, for example, that one who contracts with a corporation which has one predominant shareholder, who is also the primary executive officer of the firm and its main source of business acumen, does not enter into a personal relationship. To accept that it is the presence of a corporate structure alone which changes the legal rules is surely to elevate form over substance.[556]

Arguments along these lines do not often appear in the sports law area, for resort to this "corporate-promisee exception" is unnecessary since another exception — the fact of the employee's consent — is also available. It will appear, however, in those cases in which a superstar has bargained for a contract which preserves his right to object to a transfer of his contract. *Munchak Corporation v. Cunningham* [557] was such a case. The court was called upon to decide whether a contract provision which prohibited assignment of the contract to another "club" without the player's consent also preserved to the player a right to object to a change in the identity of the shareholders. The court concluded that the player had no right to object in these circumstances. While this is a result which may have been defensible on other grounds not directly pertinent to the present discussion,[558] the court's rationale is seriously flawed. The court observes that "to us it is inconceivable that the rendition of services by a professional basketball player to a professional basketball club could be affected by the personalities of successive corporate owners." [559] If the court means to say that the rules and the object of the game are the same, no matter who owns the team, it is probably correct. But surely that is not the only relevant inquiry. Indeed, the history of professional sports would suggest that the personality of the owner may have a substantial effect on the demands which are placed on the player and may be a primary factor in defining the goodwill which exists between the player and his "corporate" employer.[560] And apart from these important personal factors, it is hopefully clear that the solvency of the franchise, and hence the value of the player's contract, is very much related to the financial position of the club's owners. Indeed, it is well-known that in

---

556. The venerable Professor Corbin would seemingly accept these views on the unsoundness of making the legal rule turn solely on the business form of the promisor. 4 CORBIN ON CONTRACTS § 865, at 450. *But see id.* at § 867, n.52 (Supp. 1971), where Corbin's revisers make the analytical error which Corbin earlier noted.

557. 457 F.2d 721 (4th Cir. 1972), *rev'g* 331 F. Supp. 872 (M.D.N.C. 1971).

558. A more appropriate analysis would have been to interpret the word "club" in the contract to mean "a different team or franchise," and not to include changes in the original team's ownership. This would have required a finding that Cunningham was most concerned that he not be moved to another franchise in a different location, and that he did not specifically bargain for a right to object to movements and changes in the original franchise. While the court recites no evidence on this matter of the parties' intent, the court apparently assumed that the above characterization was correct. Indeed, the result which the court announced presumed that Cunningham was primarily concerned about being traded to another team. 457 F.2d at 725-26.

559. *Id.* at 725.

560. Charles O. Finley, owner of a major league baseball club, is a prime example of a corporate employer whose flamboyant personality has affected the careers of large numbers of professional athletes in often controversial ways. *See, e.g.,* N.Y. Times, Jun. 19, 1971, at 21, col. 4; *id.,* Oct. 17, 1972, at 49, col. 3; *id.,* Oct. 18, 1972, at 31, col. 1; *id.,* Oct. 23, 1972, at 44, col. 2; *id.,* Nov. 2, 1972, at 60, col. 1; *id.,* Oct. 17, 1973, at 37, col. 1; *id.,* Oct. 18, 1973, at 59, col. 1; *id.,* Oct. 25, 1973 at 61,

marginal leagues, even though a franchise is organized in a corporate form, the corporate entity itself may operate near insolvency and the real sustaining force of the business is the principal shareholder's willingness to continue to commit personal funds. This is not to suggest, however, that the rule of law ought to assume that all contractual relationships in sports are highly personal and that the corporate-promisee doctrine ought to be abandoned wholesale. Rather, the more reasonable approach would be to avoid forcing all cases into one general rule, as the *Cunningham* rationale does, and instead approach each case on an *ad hoc* basis which would permit the introduction of evidence which tended to prove or disprove that a personal relationship was intended.[561]

One other matter deserves mention in this treatment of the common law background for assignment of professional sports contracts. The prior discussion has focused on that portion of common law doctrine which would disallow assignments and delegations which materially altered the relationship contemplated in the original contract. There is another "exception" to the rules favoring assignment and delegation which has received some attention in the sports law area, and that is the rule which would disallow a transfer of contract rights or duties if such a transfer were contrary to public policy.[562] The potential objection to the assignment of a player's contract would be stated in these terms: when such assignments are considered in the context of the draft system, which removes from the player the right to choose his initial employer, and the reserve or option system, which limits the player's freedom to subsequently seek employment elsewhere, it would appear that the industry has created a system which is akin to involuntary servitude.[563] To the extent that this public policy question has been addressed, players have generally found the courts unreceptive. The precedents rejecting this argument include a very early case in which the objection was squarely presented to the court [564] and a more recent decision in which the court noted in passing that the assignment provisions of the player's contract therein involved were not contrary to public policy.[565] Perhaps more influential, however, are the lower court decisions in *Flood v. Kuhn*,[566] in which the courts concluded that the restraint of the employee's right to choose his employer was not objectionable on these grounds as long as the

---

col. 7; *id.,* Oct. 29, 1973, at 49, col. 1; *id.,* Nov. 1, 1973, at 55, col 5; *id.,* Nov. 17, at 43, col. 3.

561. *See* 4 CORBIN ON CONTRACTS § 865, at 450:

> Under many circumstances the courts will "pierce the corporate veil" and see the human beings that are operating behind it. One who makes a bilateral contract with a corporation may not even see the "veil"; he is dealing with the officers who wear it, and it may be reasonable for him to require them to continue to do so and to perform in person some substantial part of the performance promised by the "corporation" acting through them.

562. *See* RESTATEMENT OF CONTRACTS §§ 151(b), 160(3)(b) (1932). *See also* RESTATEMENT (SECOND) OF CONTRACTS § 149(2)(b) (Tent. Draft No. 3, 1967). *See generally* Hall v. Carl G. Ek & Son Constr. Co., 17 App. Div. 2d 558, 562-63, 236 N.Y.S. 2d 555, 560, *aff'd,* 13 N.Y.2d 825, 192 N.E.2d 227 (1963).

563. *See generally* Schneiderman, *Professional Sports: Involuntary Servitude and the Popular Will,* 7 GONZAGA L. REV. 63 (1971).

564. *See* Augusta Baseball Ass'n v. Thomasville Baseball Club, 147 Ga. 201, 93 S.E. 208 (1917).

565. Washington Capitols Basketball Club, Inc. v. Barry, 304 F. Supp. 1193, 1198 (N.D. Cal.), *aff'd,* 419 F.2d 472 (9th Cir. 1969).

566. Flood v. Kuhn, 316 F. Supp. 271, 281-82 (S.D.N.Y. 1970), *aff'd,* 443 F.2d 264, 268 (2d Cir. 1971), *aff'd on other grounds,* 407 U.S. 258, 32 L. Ed. 2d 728, 92 S. Ct. 2099 (1972).

employee had the opportunity to abandon the particular trade and earn his livelihood in some other pursuit.

b. The Liability of the Original Contracting Team Following an Assignment. Another question which needs to be considered is whether the original team remains liable to pay the player's compensation should the assignee team fail to do so. This question has importance not only for the practical purpose of identifying the various avenues of recourse available to the player, but also for defining more clearly the degree of risk which an athlete assumes when he is traded to another team. The general rule is that a delegation of a duty, here from one club to another, does not extinguish the original obligor's liability to pay for the services called for under the contract.[567] Hence, the intended recipient of the duty will retain all rights which he had against the original obligor,[568] and may in addition secure rights against the assignee.[569] As is true of most general rules, this one is subject to modifications if other facts are present. In this regard, customs and usages of the trade may be highly relevant. In addition, it is relevant to consider the particular contract provisions used to secure the player's consent to the assignment.[570] Normally, a consent by one party that the other's duties may be delegated does not of itself release the original obligor from liability, *unless* an agreement for release may be inferred from the circumstances.[571]

If such a substitution of obligors is to be found in the typical standard player contracts, it would often require that special significance be attached to particular phrases in the agreements. Although there are exceptions,[572] the contracts usually do not explicitly state that the player accepts the assignee's obligation as a substitute for the promises made by the original team. Thus, it is necessary to interpret clauses such as those which recite that the player agrees "to accept the assignment and to . . . carry out this contract with the assignee Club as if it had been entered into by the Player with assignee Club instead of with this Club." [573] But under language such as this, it is doubtful that the player will be deemed to have relinquished his rights against the original employer. An unstrained reading of this language would suggest that it is in

---

567. *See* Griffin v. Brooklyn Ball Club, 68 App. Div. 566, 73 N.Y.S. 864 (1902), *aff'd,* 174 N.Y. 535, 66 N.E. 1109 (1903). *See also* Baseball Players' Fraternity, Inc. v. Boston American League Baseball Club, 166 App. Div. 484, 151 N.Y.S. 557 (1915), *aff'd,* 221 N.Y. 704, 117 N.E. 1061 (1917).

568. *See* Community Sports, Inc. v. Denver Ringsby Rockets, 429 Pa. 565, 240 A.2d 832, 836 (1968).

569. *See* RESTATEMENT OF CONTRACTS § 160, comment *b* (1932). *See also* George v. Kansas City American Ass'n Baseball Co., 219 S.W. 134 (Mo. Ct. App. 1920); RESTATEMENT (SECOND) OF CONTRACTS § 164 (Tent. Draft No. 3, 1967).

570. *Compare* Griffin v. Brooklyn Ball Club, 68 App. Div. 566, 73 N.Y.S. 864 (1902), *aff'd,* 174 N.Y. 535, 66 N.E. 1109 (1903).

571. *See, e.g.,* Hall v. Arnett, 31 S.W.2d 506 (Tex. Civ. App. 1929).

572. The baseball contract is one of the few which expressly recognizes that the assignee will accept the original employer's obligations:

> Upon and after such assignment, all rights and obligations of the assignor Club hereunder shall become the rights and obligations of the assignee Club; provided, however, that
> (1) the assignee Club shall be liable to the Player for payments accruing only from the date of assignment and shall not be liable . . . for payments accrued prior to that date. . . . Baseball Contract ¶ 6(d).

573. NFL Contract ¶ 9 (1975), *supra* note 527.

fact silent on the question of how the obligor's duty is to be treated, and is probably intended only to bind the player with respect to his own performance.[574] Hence, if a prior consent to the substitution of the assignee as sole obligor on the contract is to be found, the court or arbitrator will usually have to look beyond the language of the particular contract. In some cases, it may well be found that such a complete substitution is a well-known, generally accepted custom of the particular league, but here the original obligor bears a heavy burden of showing that the player should have been aware of this unwritten rule.[575]

In many cases it will be unnecessary to search for trade customs or special nuances in the contract language, for there is a third avenue through which a court or arbitrator might find that the original team's obligation to compensate the player under the contract had been extinguished and the assignee's undertaking substituted in its place. If the proper combination of facts is present, it will be possible to find that the player, by words or action, has acquiesced or ratified the club's attempted substitution.[576] There appears to be some difference of opinion as to exactly what facts will show the requisite acquiescence. Can such post-assignment consent be inferred from the fact that the player accepts his position with the assignee team and begins to perform as the employee of the latter? Both the original and the revised *Restatement* would seem to answer that question in the negative. Under this view, a substitution — or novation — requires more than a mere showing that the player accepted performance from the team to whom the original duty had been delegated. Such an acceptance of performance is determinative only if the original obligor first "manifests an intention not to perform" the duties imposed by the contract.[577] Yet, this insistence upon a seemingly separate, discernible manifestation of the original obligor's intent not to perform is not fully mirrored in the cases which have considered this question, and authority can be found which would, in effect, allow a court to infer such a manifestation where the employee willingly embraced the new employment relationship.[578] Regardless of whether the case law is in full harmony with the *Restatement*, it is obviously relevant to focus on the length of the period of the player's acceptance of the substituted performance.[579] Even without an explicit renunciation of its obligation by the original team, the athlete's continuing acquiescence in the assignee's payment of his compensation will be strongly suggestive of his ratification of the substitution of obligors.

---

574. *See generally* 4 CORBIN ON CONTRACTS §§ 865-66, 870.

575. *See generally* § 3.04 *supra*.

576. *See* Baseball Players' Fraternity, Inc. v. Boston American League Baseball Club, 166 App. Div. 484, 495, 151 N.Y.S. 557, 565 (1915) (dissenting opinion). *See also* Hofman v. Chicago Legaue Ball Club, 195 Ill. App. 249 (1915).

577. RESTATEMENT OF CONTRACTS § 165(1) (1932). *See also* RESTATEMENT (SECOND) OF CONTRACTS § 161 (Tent. Draft No. 3, 1967).

578. *See* Sisco v. Empiregas, Inc., 286 Ala. 72, 237 So. 2d 463 (1970). *But see* Mitchell-Huntley Cotton Co. v. Waldrep, 377 F. Supp. 1215 (N.D. Ala. 1974); *see generally* 4 CORBIN ON CONTRACTS §§ 866-67, especially discussion at pp. 456-68.

579. *See* Griffin v. Brooklyn Ball Club, 68 App. Div. 556, 572-73, 73 N.Y.S. 864, 869 (1902), *aff'd*, 174 N.Y 535, 66 N.E. 1109 (1903). *Compare* Hofman v. Chicago League Ball Club, 195 Ill. App. 249 (1915).

§ 3.14. Limitations on the Right to Assign a Player's Contract.

The discussion in the prior sections establishes that while normally rights under contracts for personal service cannot be assigned, that proscription can be avoided if the prior consent of the employee is secured. In the major sports, a provision for such prior consent is an integral part of the standard form contracts used.[580] But the question remains as to whether there are any legal limitations upon a team's right of assignment.[581] In short, does the player's grant of consent in a standard form clause remove from him all right to object to a transfer of his contract, no matter how adverse the resulting change in his employment conditions?

While the question of assignment of sports contracts has not been exhaustively litigated, there has been implicit judicial approval of the general notion of the importance of the team's right to transfer its players' contracts.[582] Such a right of assignment is preserved to the team to enable management to make adjustments in player personnel in order to "fine tune" the team's balance in terms of skill, temperament, and style of play. A prudent exercise of managerial judgment in this regard will mean that occasionally players with high degrees of skill will be traded in order to achieve a better balance among other qualities. Moreover, the team may properly demand the right to transfer player contracts for purely financial reasons unrelated to the team's playing activities. Thus, the team may sell players to generate cash or preferred draft positions [583] or, as is frequently the case in new leagues, there may be a wholesale assignment of player contracts when an entire franchise is transferred from an original location which proved to be unprofitable.[584] A transfer for any of these reasons is a part of the reality of professional sports. As noted by one court, it is unrealistic for a professional ball player to argue

> that he takes no risk of being traded or sold or . . . that the franchise might not be transferred or . . . that the embryonic club for which he was playing incurred no risk of becoming a financial failure.[585]

Because these risks are recognized in the operation of the sports industry, the athlete will not be heard to object that he bargained for immunity from these practices unless his contract is explicit.

a. Potential Objections by the Player. There are some specific types of objections which can be anticipated when a club transfers a contract. In general, these can be identified as player objections either (1) to the disruption of established social and business ties in the assignor's city or (2) to the conditions of employment which will exist when the assignee takes over the contract.[586] Thus, the player might object that his transfer to a distant locale will bring

---

580. *See* discussion at notes 527-30, § 3.13 *supra*.

581. *See generally* 4 A. CORBIN, CORBIN ON CONTRACTS § 870 (1951) [hereinafter cited as CORBIN ON CONTRACTS].

582. *See generally* Washington Capitols Basketball Club, Inc. v. Barry, 419 F.2d 472, 479 (9th Cir.), *aff'g*, 304 F. Supp. 1193 (N.D. Cal. 1969); Augusta Baseball Ass'n v. Thomasville Baseball Club, 147 Ga. 201, 93 S.E. 208 (1917).

583. *See* note 523, § 3.13 *supra*.

584. *See, e.g.,* Minnesota Muskies, Inc. v. Hudson, 294 F. Supp. 979 (M.D.N.C. 1969).

585. Washington Capitols Basketball Club, Inc. v. Barry, 419 F.2d 472, 479 (9th Cir. 1969).

586. These sorts of objections of course assume that the threshold requirements for an effective assignment have been met. Specifically, the assignment must strictly comply with the provisions

substantial injury to business interests which he has nurtured in the original club's city. The complaint may be that the business requires either his constant personal attention or the favorable publicity and name-identification which goes with his status as a local sports figure.[587] But arguments of this sort are not likely to be persuasive. Given the well-known custom of frequent trades and franchise shifts, it may be said that as between the player and the team, the player more appropriately bears the risk of economic losses which accompany contract assignments of this sort.[588] When a player enters into a business venture, he must surely foresee some possibility that his tenure in a given city will not be indefinite. As expressed by one court:

> Every famous athlete may suffer some damage to his local business and personal interests or other inconvenience when the assignment of his contract requires him to relocate in another city; but nothing is more commonplace in the history of organized professional sports in America than such moves, through trades and otherwise.[589]

It might be added that it is not totally inequitable to allocate to the player the risk that his contract might be traded. The player has the means available to protect himself: he can either choose business ventures which do not depend upon a local identification or he can negotiate a contract which affords him the right to object to an assignment of his contract, as many athletes have done.[590]

When the player's objection is directed to the conditions of his new employment, the analysis must necessarily start from the basis mentioned above. It is true that the player will be subjected to new personal relationships which he did not specifically contemplate at the time of his contract. Moreover, he will be asked to play under different conditions, some of which may affect

of the original contract governing the transferability of the player. *See* Baseball Players' Fraternity, Inc. v. Boston American League Baseball Club, 166 App. Div. 484, 492, 151 N.Y.S. 557, 562-63 (1915), *aff'd,* 221 N.Y. 704, 117 N.E. 1061 (1917); Griffin v. Brooklyn Ball Club, 68 App. Div. 566, 570, 73 N.Y.S. 864, 867 (1902), *aff'd,* 174 N.Y. 535, 66 N.E. 1109 (1903). In addition, the assignee club must agree to accept all of the terms and obligations of the original contract. *See* Griffin v. Brooklyn Ball Club, 68 App. Div. 566, 572-73, 73 N.Y.S. 864, 869 (1902), *aff'd,* 174 N.Y. 535, 66 N.E. 1109 (1903).

587. *See, e.g.,* Flood v. Kuhn, 309 F. Supp. 793, 799 (S.D.N.Y. 1970). This case was eventually affirmed on a different point in 407 U.S. 258, 32 L. Ed. 2d 728, 92 S. Ct. 2099 (1972).

588. The athlete who seeks to resist an assignment on the basis of his business or family connections may seek injunctive relief. The court in Flood v. Kuhn, 309 F. Supp. 793 (S.D.N.Y. 1970), considered the question of whether a player could show irreparable harm in this connection, which must be established before injunctive relief will be granted. In denying the request for an injunction, the court observed:

> Plaintiff will suffer undoubted loss of social and communal ties to St. Louis which he has developed during his twelve years as a ball player there. Additionally, his outside business interests in St. Louis may well suffer. These interests are both substantial, although the latter may be subject to monetary compensation and there appears no reason to expect that plaintiff could not develop similar social and business interests elsewhere. *Id.* at 800.

Flood's position was substantially weakened by the fact that he not only contested the assignment, but sought to become a free agent as well. In this regard, the court noted that

> the relief ultimately sought by plaintiff would not and could not compel the St. Louis Club to retain his services. He seeks to become a "free agent" which might or might not result in his remaining in St. Louis. Were he to contract to play for any club except St. Louis, these losses [to business and social interests] would be the same he would suffer playing for [the assignee]. *Id.*

589. Washington Capitols Basketball Club, Inc. v. Barry, 304 F. Supp. 1193, 1202 (N.D. Cal.), *aff'd,* 419 F.2d 472 (9th Cir. 1969).

590. *See, e.g.,* Munchak Corp. v. Cunningham, 457 F.2d 721 (4th Cir. 1972).

his own level of performance. But even though real changes in working conditions can be anticipated, that fact alone should not provide a basis for objection, again largely because the possibility of such changes was clearly foreseeable at the time the player gave his consent to the transferability of his contract.

The case of *Washington Capitols Basketball Club, Inc. v. Barry*[591] provides useful insights into the degree to which courts will allocate to players the risks which attend changes in the employer's identity. Rick Barry, the player in that case, had a basis for objection to the transfer of his contract which was more substantial than that which could be raised by most players. Under Barry's contract with an Oakland team, he was to receive a portion of the team's gate receipts.[592] That provided Barry with the basis for the argument, not normally available in such graphic terms, that his contract was uniquely tied to Oakland and, in his view, could not be assigned to another team which had a smaller arena, a different degree of fan interest in the sport, and so on. In effect, Barry was arguing that a transfer of his contract would not only change the conditions under which he worked, but would also alter the compensation to which he was entitled. It is generally true that a consent to assignment does not give the assignee the right to alter the terms of the contract,[593] particularly not the amount of compensation the employee is to receive.[594] Without rejecting this general principle, the court in *Barry* denied relief to the player, choosing instead to view the matter of an alteration in compensation as essentially a question of fact. Hence, the court found that while the assignee's stadium was indeed considerably smaller, the average attendance in Oakland was so small as to be readily accommodated in the assignee's facility.[595] Implicit in the court's approach was a refusal to analyze the player's objection in terms of his expectations at the time he signed the contract.[596] Such an analysis would have supported an argument by the player that the assignment had the effect of substantially reducing his *potential* compensation, if not his shortrun return. The court's unwillingness to make this pristine distinction can be explained in large measure by its premise that professional sports contracts must be construed in light of the established custom of frequent transfers of both franchises and player contracts.[597]

But even accepting the general willingness of courts to enforce contract assignments which operate to the disadvantage of a player, a question must still remain as to whether the assignor team can be totally unconcerned about the conditions which confront the player when he joins the assignee's franchise.

---

591. 304 F. Supp. 1193 (N.D. Cal.), *aff'd*, 419 F.2d 472 (9th Cir. 1969).

592. *See* 304 F. Supp. at 1198.

593. *See generally* RESTATEMENT OF CONTRACTS § 162 (1932). *See also* RESTATEMENT (SECOND) OF CONTRACTS § 155 (Tent. Draft No. 3, 1967). *Compare* Community Sports, Inc. v. Denver Ringsby Rockets, 429 Pa. 565, 240 A.2d 832, 836 (1968).

594. *See, e.g.,* George v. Kansas City American Ass'n Baseball Co., 219 S.W. 134 (Mo. Ct. App. 1920); Baseball Players' Fraternity, Inc. v. Boston American League Baseball Club, 166 App. Div. 484, 492, 151 N.Y.S. 557, 562-63 (1915), *aff'd*, 221 N.Y. 704, 117 N.E. 1061 (1917); Griffin v. Brooklyn Ball Club, 68 App. Div. 566, 73 N.Y.S. 864 (1902), *aff'd*, 174 N.Y. 535, 66 N.E. 1109 (1903).

595. *See* 304 F. Supp. at 1198.

596. *Compare* 3 CORBIN ON CONTRACTS §§ 538, 545.

597. *See* text at note 589 *supra. See also* Flood v. Kuhn, 309 F. Supp. 793, 799-800 (S.D.N.Y. 1970).

Among the potential objections which could be raised by the player, the one deserving closest scrutiny would be a contention that the financial position of the assignee franchise is so precarious that there is substantial reason to doubt whether the assignee will be able to pay the player's compensation.[598] As with most legal issues in this unexplored area of sports law, there is no simple answer to the issue which is raised. There are, however, general principles which can be put forth which will at least narrow the area of debate. The starting point for analysis would be the general proposition that a definition of the scope of the player's consent to assignment of his contract must necessarily begin with the specific language used in the contract. It is accepted that even where there is consent, the power of assignment must be exercised "in accordance with the terms of the manifested assent." [599] While the scope of the club's right of assignment is very broadly defined in the typical standard player contract, the contract language must always be construed in light of what the parties knew and understood at the time the contract was entered into.[600] On this point, it must certainly be true that a knowledgeable athlete, or a naive athlete with a knowledgeable agent, ought to be aware that there are differences, sometimes dramatic differences, between the financial stability of various franchises. Thus, it can be said that the athlete, by consenting to a subsequent assignment, assumed some risks with respect to differences in the financial position of various teams.[601]

But this inquiry into intent and expectations provides only the starting point for analysis. There are other matters which also have to be considered and which, in particular cases, will be decisive. In the hypothetical case, the player's primary objection is a perceived insecurity in the financial arrangements which he had negotiated with the original team. Such an argument assumes that the player's only security for his promised compensation is the assignee's pocketbook. In fact, in many situations there will be other persons legally obligated to meet the player's salary. Where such back-up obligors can be identified, the potency of this objection to an assignment evaporates. Thus, in some leagues, the requisite security for the player's right to compensation can be found in contractual provisions which obligate the league to pay the player's salary in the event of a default by the club.[602] Under such a provision, the player is given an assurance that his right to compensation does not depend upon the financial well-being of

---

598. *See generally* Fenn v. Pickwick Corp., 117 Cal. App. 236, 4 P.2d 215 (1931); Brassel v. Troxel, 68 Ill. App. 131 (1896); Pardee v. Konady, 100 N.Y. 121, 2 N.E. 885 (1885); 4 CORBIN ON CONTRACTS § 869.

599. RESTATEMENT OF CONTRACTS § 162 (1932). *See also* RESTATEMENT (SECOND) OF CONTRACTS § 155 (Tent. Draft No. 3 1967).

600. *See* 3 CORBIN ON CONTRACTS §§ 538, 545.

601. *See* Washington Capitols Basketball Club, Inc. v. Barry, 419 F.2d 472, 479 (9th Cir. 1969). *See also* text at 585 *supra.*

602. Such provisions are found in player contracts used in the World Football League and the World Hockey Association. In the WFL, the league's obligation was expressed in these terms:

> After the Effective Date, if Club defaults in any salary payment admittedly due to Player, and fails to make such payment within forty-eight (48) hours after written demand to Club, with a copy to League office, then payment of the amount in default will be mailed by certified or registered mail to Player by the League within seventy-two (72) hours after the receipt by the League of written notice that Club has failed to respond to Player's demand. WFL Contract ¶ 3.4.

the particular club which holds his contract. Another consideration which may be equally persuasive in removing the player's objection to the assignee's financial position is whether the assignor team continues to be obligated for the player's compensation even after the contract is assigned. As noted above, the general rule is that an assignment (or more correctly, a delegation) does not extinguish the assignor's obligation of performance,[603] but such a complete substitution of obligations can be found where the player has either expressly consented to such a result or implicitly indicated his acquiescence by entering into the service of the new employer.[604] The point which can be made is that where such a continuing obligation is found, an otherwise troublesome objection to assignment of a player's contract has been removed.

b. The General Obligation of Good Faith. As the above analysis suggests, the inquiry into limitations on the team's right of assignment does not reveal major restrictions on the club's prerogatives. But the question remains as to whether there is a generalized standard under which courts and arbitrators might make at least a cursory review of the validity of particular assignments. In fact, such a standard can be found, although it will necessarily respect the team's wide-ranging discretion to make judgments about player personnel. That limitation is embodied in the notion of good faith. It is now accepted that every right arising under a contract imposes an obligation of good faith.[605] That concept is variously defined according to an objective standard (commercial reasonableness) or a subjective standard (honesty and candor) depending on the setting in which it is invoked.[606] But in the present context the subjective sense of good faith provides the appropriate test. It is clear from the language of the player's contracts and the customs of the trade that the teams have reserved to themselves broad discretion in determining when and whether to assign a player's contract.[607] This would suggest that the team did not intend that its decision to assign a contract should be scrutinized by a court or arbitrator to determine whether a reasonable man would have made the same decision.[608] Rather what can be said to have been assumed by the parties is that each would act with good will toward the other. In the present context that suggests that

It should be noted that the degree of security provided by this clause is greatly influenced by the provisions of the contract which give a team the right to terminate the contract. Except in cases of no-cut contracts a team can avoid liability for salary by a prior termination of the contract. Moreover, the WFL may be a case in point on the practical limits of the security which the player enjoys under this sort of provision. The league subsequently went into bankruptcy, and while provision was made to pay most of the league debts, not all liabilities were covered. One provision of the bankruptcy plan provided that "all executory contracts of any description including all player's 'future' contracts, are hereby rejected." Raleigh (N.C.) News & Observer, June 1, 1975, pt. II, at 4, col. 1.

603. RESTATEMENT OF CONTRACTS § 160(4) (1932). *See also* Hofman v. Chicago League Ball Club, 195 Ill. App. 249 (1915).

604. This question is considered more fully at notes 567-79, § 3.13 *supra.*

605. *See* RESTATEMENT (SECOND) OF CONTRACTS § 231 (Tent. Draft No. 5, 1970). *Cf.* UNIFORM COMMERCIAL CODE § 1-203.

606. *See generally* § 3.08 *supra.*

607. *Cf.* Doyle v. Gordon, 158 N.Y.S.2d 248 (Sup. Ct. 1954); Peden Iron & Steel Co. v. Jenkins, 203 S.W. 180 (Tex. Civ. App. 1911).

608. A case which is instructive in the present context, although not strictly on point, is Mattei v. Hopper, 51 Cal. 2d 119, 330 P.2d 625 (1958). This case concerns a contract wherein a buyer of real property was bound to perform only on condition that he acquire a sufficient number of "satisfactory" leases. The seller claimed that as the buyer was given an ostensibly unlimited

the team may not make a trade of a player where the motivating cause was personal animosity against the athlete, such as a desire to make him suffer for past criticism of the management. Such might be the case where a player is assigned to a team which the assignor knew would be highly disagreeable and where there was no other justification for the transfer.[609] Similarly, an assignment undertaken as retribution against one involved in union activities would seemingly fail to meet the good faith test and provide a basis for objection in this context, as well as under the federal labor laws.[610]

It must be accepted, however, that given the range of discretion necessarily allocated to the teams, it will be a rare case in which the player is able to prove the requisite sort of improper motivation. Any allegation of impropriety will carry with it a difficult burden of proof, which the player must bear. If the court can find any plausible explanation for a trade which is founded in the team's personnel needs or financial condition, the player's level of performance, or even in management's dissatisfaction with the player's attitude or adjustment, then the team ought to prevail absent clear and compelling proof that a different motivation existed.

c. **Bargained-for Limitations on the Team's Right of Assignment.** Another type of limitation on the team's right of assignment is that which takes the form of an agreed-upon modification of the assignment clause of the standard player's contract. A typical provision would be one which gave the team authority to assign the player's contract only if the athlete approved the terms and conditions of the transaction. In this situation, the right to object may be given to certain

---

discretion to accept or reject any potential lessee, the contract lacked mutuality of obligation and ought not to be enforced. This court held that the buyer's judgment as to satisfaction could not be made capriciously but was restricted by the requirement of good faith. The obligations imposed by the contract were, therefore, fully mutual, and the contract was enforceable. Although the central issue of the case is different from that considered in the text, the analysis developed by the court is readily transferable to the issue presented here, and is the appropriate one for distinguishing between the applicability of a subjective or objective standard of good faith.

When a contract contains " . . . a condition calling for satisfaction as to commercial value, operative fitness, or mechanical ability . . ." the question of whether satisfaction has been received is judged by the standard of the reasonable man. *Id.* at 123, 330 P.2d at 626-27. This is roughly equivalent to the objective good faith test of commercial reasonableness and would apply when the elements of judgment are primarily quantitative. When a contract contains a satisfaction clause calling for an evaluation " . . . involving fancy, taste or judgment . . ." the determination of dissatisfaction, so long as it is made in good faith, would be sufficient. *Id.* at 123, 330 P.2d at 627. Like the subjective standard mentioned in the text, the emphasis here is on the genuineness of the promisor's decision. Obviously, a club's decision on the assignment of any given player's contract will ultimately depend on the preference and judgment of those making the decision. The good faith validity of a coach's claim of poor relations with a player could not, for instance, be judged by the same standards used where one claims dissatisfaction with the "operative fitness" of a recently purchased machine. In the former situation, the club's actions deserve a more lenient standard of review and subjective good faith and a sense of honesty or candor should be the criterion. *See also* Uniform Commercial Code § 1-201(19) (Supp. 1975).

609. Other definitions of *good faith* can be found in Wright v. Mattison, 59 U.S. 50, 14 L. Ed. 280 (1855) and Doyle v. Gordon, 158 N.Y.S.2d 248 (Sup. Ct. 1954).

According to one account, assignments of player contracts in hockey are sometimes utilized as a form of punishment. Such an action would raise a serious question as to whether the good faith limitation discussed above had been satisfied. *See* Alyluia, *Professional Sports Contracts and the Players' Association,* 5 Manitoba L.J. 359 (1973).

610. *See generally* Lowell, *Collective Bargaining and the Professional Team Sport Industry,* 38 Law & Contemp. Prob. 3, 4 n.8 (1973). *See also* § 6.03 *infra.*

classes of players, such as veterans.[611] The limitation on the team's prerogatives may also result from individual negotiations between player and club. But such a concession will usually only be made to superstars, who because of their superior bargaining position, are able to exact variances from the standard form contract which would not be conceded to players of lesser stature.[612]

The basic question which arises concerns the extent to which the negotiated clause is intended to reduce rights which the team would have under the standard assignment clause or at common law. Since the resolution of a controversy will depend upon the precise language used by the parties, it is difficult to generalize about the effect of these provisions. Nonetheless, there is one case, *Munchak Corporation v. Cunningham*,[613] which should be noted. In that case, it was held that a contract provision which prohibited assignment of the team's right to another "club" did not protect the player from a change in the ownership of the corporation which held the original franchise. As suggested above, the court may well have reached the right result, but for the wrong reason.[614] The basic inquiry which should be made on these facts is whether the intent of the parties was to give the player a right to object to any change in the operation or ownership of the original franchise, or whether the parties' intent was the more limited one of giving the player power to decline to participate in a disagreeable trade. Since the latter situation is more commonly the object of athletes' complaints and since existing owners are less likely to make concessions on matters of corporate ownership, there is some basis for the suggestion that the protection which the player had bargained for did not encompass a right to object to the composition of the team's ownership. The court in *Cunningham* chose, however, to explain the result in broad terms. The court implies, for example, that a player would have no reason to object to any change in corporate ownership. That is a difficult position to sustain in the real world of professional sports, and the better view is one which ascribes a less venturesome purpose to the changes agreed to by the parties.[615]

§ 3.15. The Legal Status of Professional Sports Leagues — The Nature of the Relationship Between Clubs Within a League.

Most litigation in the professional sports area involves controversies which arise between players and their clubs. But there is another relationship — that between the various clubs within a league — which is probably equally important in terms of the economic success of the sports industry.[616] Yet, the problems which arise in the course of the league's operation have only rarely surfaced in reported decisions. Thus, there is very little law on the particular

611. Such a provision is found in baseball, where players with ten or more years of major league service, the last five of which are with a single club, must give written consent to any assignment of their contract. *See* note 533, § 3.13 *supra.*

612. *See, e.g.,* Munchak Corp. v. Cunningham, 457 F.2d 721, 725 (4th Cir. 1972).

613. *Id. rev'g* 331 F. Supp. 872 (M.D.N.C. 1971).

614. *See* discussion at notes 557-61, § 3.13 *supra.*

615. *See id.*

616. The economic principles which prompt the formation of sports leagues are considered in Quirk & El Hodiri, *The Economic Theory of a Professional Sports League* in GOVERNMENT AND THE SPORTS BUSINESS 33 (R. Noll ed. 1974); Rottenberg, *The Baseball Players' Labor Market,* 64 J. POL. ECON. 242 (1956).

issues which arise in the sports context. Because of that limitation, the following discussion seeks only to suggest the general framework in which intraleague controversies will be resolved. The limited body of sports precedent does not mean that disputes between clubs will have to be resolved in a vacuum, however. Indeed, with respect to some issues, considerable guidance will be provided by precedent from analogous areas. In general, leagues are treated as a form of private association, and most legal questions which arise can be answered by application of precedents from the law of associations. As the present discussion will consider only selected issues which have particular importance in the sports area, a serious research effort in this area will necessitate the consideration of other sources.[617]

a. The League Constitution and Bylaws: The Contract Between the Clubs. The characterization which is given to the relationship between clubs within a league depends in part upon the purpose for which the question is asked. In the antitrust context, for example, it has been held that the various clubs within a league constitute an economic entity somewhat in the nature of a joint venture.[618] Thus, it is said the individual clubs "are not competitors in an economic sense," but rather "are acting together as one single business enterprise." [619] But for the purpose of analyzing most private law issues, it can be said that the basic relationship between clubs within a league is one of contract. The contract which defines the respective powers of the league and its component clubs is found in the league constitution and by-laws.[620] Through these documents the clubs give up some of the autonomy which they would otherwise enjoy. The relinquished power is typically transferred either to an official of the league, such as the commissioner,[621] or to some subunit within the league, such as a board of governors. But just as the constitution and by-laws are a source of power for the league, they are also a source of limitation, and it is generally accepted that the league or its commissioner or directors have

---

617. *See generally,* Chafee, *The Internal Affairs of Associations Not for Profit,* 43 HARV. L. REV. 993 (1930); Comment, *Development in the Law: Judicial Control of Actions of Private Associations,* 76 HARV. L. REV. 983 (1963); 6 AM. JUR. 2D *Associations and Clubs* (1963); 7 C.J.S. *Associations* (1939).

618. *See generally* Rivkin, *Sports Leagues and the Federal Antitrust Laws* in GOVERNMENT AND THE SPORTS BUSINESS 387, 402-407 (R. Noll ed. 1974); Comment, *The Super Bowl and the Sherman Act: Professional Team Sports and the Antitrust Laws,* 81 HARV. L. REV. 418, 426-430 (1967).

619. San Francisco Seals, Ltd. v. National Hockey League, 379 F. Supp. 966, 969 (C.D. Cal. 1974). *See also* Levin v. National Basketball Ass'n, 385 F. Supp. 149, 152 (S.D.N.Y. 1974).

620. *See, e.g.,* Atlanta National League Baseball Club, Inc. v. Kuhn, 432 F. Supp. 1213 (N.D. Ga. 1977); Charles O. Finley & Co. v. Khun, Docket No. 76-C-2358 (N.D. Ill., Mar. 17, 1977) (findings and judgment order); Professional Sports, Ltd. v. Virginia Squires Basketball Club, 373 F. Supp. 946, 950 (W.D. Tex. 1974); Riko Enterprises, Inc. v. Seattle SuperSonics Corp., 357 F. Supp. 521, 524 (S.D.N.Y. 1973); Boston Baseball Ass'n v. Brooklyn Baseball Club, 37 Misc. 521, 524-25; 75 N.Y.S. 1076, 1078 (Sup. Ct. 1902); Bradley v. Wilson, 138 Va. 605, 612, 123 S.E. 273, 275 (1924). A similar contractual analysis is applied to define the relationship between the major and minor leagues in baseball. *See* Portland Baseball Club v. Kuhn, 368 F. Supp. 1004, 1006 (D. Ore. 1971), *aff'd,* 491 F.2d 1101 (9th Cir. 1974). *Cf.* Macon Baseball Ass'n v. Pennington, 45 Ga. App. 611, 166 S.E. 35 (1932).

621. A much debated issue is whether the league commissioner acts merely as the agent of the member clubs or whether he in fact has an autonomous function. *See* § 4.19 *infra. See also* Davis, *Self-Regulation in Baseball, 1909-71* in GOVERNMENT AND THE SPORTS BUSINESS 349, 377-82 (R. Noll. ed. 1974); Comment, *Discipline in Professional Sports: The Need for Player Protection,* 60 GEO. L.J. 771, 772-79 (1972).

no authority to take actions which are not either authorized in or reasonably implied from the terms of the relevant documents.[622] To the extent that they take actions beyond those explicitly or implicitly authorized, their decisions have no validity and will not be enforced by the courts.[623]

While this sort of contract analysis represents the approach most typically taken to intraleague controversies, the courts have indicated that other principles may be applied in appropriate circumstances. For example, it is often held that membership in an association such as a league gives rise to property interests which are entitled to protection.[624] This characterization may be particularly apt in the sports context since the league serves a basic business function, and actions of the league may have a direct impact upon a member's access to certain "property" in the form of economic rewards.[625] In other contexts, it is useful to view the club's interest in its membership as a relational interest protected by tort concepts.[626] However, even where the property or relational aspects of a club's membership are emphasized, the "contract" which defines the club's rights and the league's powers will necessarily have to be consulted,[627] and it can be expected that the relevant documents, the constitution and by-laws, will serve as the focus for most controversies.

It is not suggested that courts will blindly apply the parties' agreed-upon rules. Obviously some of those rules may be offensive to the most basic notions of justice, and it can be expected that in this area, courts will be loath to enforce unconscionable terms, just as they are in other contexts.[628] Thus, it is often said that while the internal rules of a private association will be entitled to great respect, the organization's rules and procedures must not offend principles of natural justice.[629] Consistent with this basic concern that associations not become a law unto themselves, courts will also insist that associational rules not require actions which are contrary to established laws or public policy.[630] These general principles from the law of private associations have been applied in

---

622. *See, e.g.,* Professional Sports Ltd. v. Virginia Squires Basketball Club, 373 F. Supp. 946 (W.D. Tex. 1974).

623. *See, e.g.,* Atlanta National League Baseball Club, Inc. v. Kuhn, 432 F. Supp. 1213 (N.D. Ga. 1977); American League Baseball Club of New York v. Johnson, 109 Misc. 138, 179 N.Y.S. 498 (Sup. Ct. 1919), *aff'd,* 190 App. Div. 932, 179 N.Y.S. 898 (1920). *See generally* 6 AM. JUR. 2D *Associations and Clubs* § 11 (1963). *Cf.* Macon Baseball Ass'n v. Pennington, 45 Ga. App. 611, 166 S.E. 35 (1932).

624. *See, e.g.,* Metropolitan Base Ball Ass'n v. Simmons, 1 Pa. County Ct. 134, 138, 17 Phila. 419, 420 (1885); Chafee, *The Internal Affairs of Associations Not for Profit, supra* note 617, at 999-1001; Comment, *Development in the Law: Judicial Control of Actions of Private Associations, supra* note 617, at 983, 998.

625. *See* American League Baseball Club of New York v. Johnson, 109 Misc. 138, 140, 179 N.Y.S. 498, 500 (1919), *aff'd,* 190 App. Div. 932, 179 N.Y.S. 898 (1920); Metropolitan Base Ball Ass'n v. Simmons, 1 Pa. County Ct. 134, 138, 17 Phila. 419, 420 (1885).

626. *See* Comment, *Development in the Law: Judicial Control of Actions of Private Associations, supra* note 617, at 1005.

627. *See, e.g.,* Metropolitan Base Ball Ass'n v. Simmons, 1 Pa. County Ct. 134, 17 Phila. 419 (1885).

628. *See* § 4.18 *infra.*

629. *See, e.g.,* Cason v. Glass Bottle Blowers Ass'n, 37 Cal. 2d 134, 231 P.2d 6 (1951); Yeomans v. Union League Club, 225 Ill. App. 234 (1922); Crawford v. Newman, 13 Misc. 2d 198, 175 N.Y.S.2d 903 (Sup. Ct. 1958), *aff'd,* 10 N.Y.2d 865, 179 N.E.2d 505 (1961). *See generally,* Chafee, *The Internal Affairs of Associations Not for Profit, supra* note 617, at 1014.

630. *See, e.g.,* Mitchell v. International Ass'n of Machinists, 196 Cal. App. 2d 796, 16 Cal. Rptr. 813 (Dist. Ct. App. 1961); Schneider v. Plumbers Local Union No. 60, 116 La. 270, 40 So. 700 (1905); Spayd v. Ringing Rock Lodge No. 665, 270 Pa. 67, 113 A. 70 (1921). *See generally* 6 AM. JUR. 2D *Associations and Clubs* § 37 (1963); 7 C.J.S. *Associations* § 25(e) (1939).

sports cases, usually for the purpose of correcting deficiencies in the league's procedural rules.[631]

These judicially-defined limitations on the powers of leagues will be invoked only to prevent the most extreme sorts of abuses, and with respect to most aspects of their relationship, the clubs will be left free to structure the constitution and by-laws as they see fit. As has been suggested, this freedom of contract extends to both the substantive rules under which the league will operate, as well as the procedures to be followed in the enforcement of those rules. Once the agreement is formed, subsequent actions by the league or its agents must be consistent with the agreed-upon provisions. Most litigation in this area will concern the issue of whether particular league decisions were within the authority which had been granted.[632]

The arrangement between the parties need not be static, however, and may be changed from time to time, either by formal amendment of the documents which represent the club's contract or by the adoption of new administrative rules.[633] Amendments must be made in accordance with the procedures which have previously been agreed upon.[634] By the same token, powers originally granted to one group within the association's structure can usually be delegated to others within the entity. But the authority of the delegating group is not unlimited, and in the sports area, at least, the courts have indicated some reluctance to approve these informal redistributions of power, particularly where the action involved has an adverse effect on a fundamental interest of a league member.[635] Nonetheless, because of the flexibility which is afforded to the clubs to amend and redefine their governing rules, the determination of whether a particular decision was authorized may require an assessment of a

---

631. *See, e.g.,* Riko Enterprises, Inc. v. Seattle SuperSonics Corp., 357 F. Supp. 521, 526 (S.D.N.Y. 1973). State *ex. rel.* Rowland v. Seattle Baseball Ass'n, 61 Wash. 79, 111 P. 1055 (1910).

632. *See, e.g.,* Professional Sports, Ltd. v. Virginia Squires Basketball Club, 373 F. Supp. 946 (W.D. Tex. 1974); Riko Enterprises, Inc. v. Seattle SuperSonics Corp., 357 F. Supp. 521 (S.D.N.Y. 1973); American League Baseball Club of New York v. Johnson, 109 Misc. 138, 179 N.Y.S. 498 (Sup. Ct. 1919), *aff'd,* 190 App. Div. 932, 179 N.Y.S. 898 (1920).

One recent celebrated case involved Baseball Commissioner Bowie Kuhn's decision to disapprove an attempt by owner Charlie Finley to sell and trade three of the star players from his championship Oakland A's team. When the matter was subsequently litigated before Judge McGarr in the federal District Court for the Northern District of Illinois, the court declined to overturn Kuhn's actions. In his opinion, Judge McGarr offered the following perspective on the case:

> The fact that this case has commanded a great deal of attention in the vociferous world of baseball fans, and has provoked wide-spread and not always unemotional discussion, tends to obscure the relative simplicity of the legal issues involved. The case is not a Finley-Kuhn popularity contest — though many fans so view it. Neither is it an appellate judicial review of the wisdom of Bowie Kuhn's actions. The question before the court is not whether Bowie Kuhn was wise to do what he did, but rather whether he had the authority.

Charles O. Finley & Co. v. Kuhn, Docket No. 76-C-2358, Judgment Order at 1 (N.D. Ill., Mar. 17, 1977).

633. *See* Bradley v. Wilson, 138 Va. 605, 123 S.E. 273 (1924).

634. *See* Ace Bus Transp. Co. v. South Hudson County Boulevard Bus Owners' Ass'n, 118 N.J. Eq. 31, 177 A. 360 (Ch.) *aff'd,* 119 N.J. Eq. 37, 180 A. 835 (Ct. Err. & App. 1935); Hillery v. Pedic Soc'y, 189 App. Div. 766, 179 N.Y.S. 62 (1919). *See generally* 7 C.J.S. *Associations* § 7(c) (1939).

635. *See, e.g.,* Riko Enterprises, Inc. v. Seattle SuperSonics Corp., 357 F. Supp. 521, 524-26 (S.D.N.Y. 1973). In Riko, the court questioned the validity of an attempt by the league directors to refer a matter within their jurisdiction to the league commissioner, but the court ultimately found alternative grounds for disapproving the commissioner's action.

variety of formal and informal actions by the parties who share authority within the entity.[636]

Even when the various components of the "contract" of the league members is identified, there will be disputes about its interpretation. The courts are available to resolve these controversies if they cannot be settled internally. In construing provisions of the league constitution and by-laws, courts generally employ the same interpretative aids used in other contexts,[637] although there is some authority for the view that the judiciary should defer to the interpretation made by the appropriate league officials.[638] This process of judicial interpretation has been utilized in a variety of circumstances in the sports area. Thus, courts have been called upon to review league constitutions and by-laws to determine who, as between the individual club and the league president, has authority to discipline individual players; [639] to interpret the league's authority to block player trades; [640] to ascertain whether league officials were properly elected; [641] to determine which body within the league is empowered to discipline member teams; [642] to define the procedural rules to be followed in internal proceedings,[643] and to determine the propriety of an attempted league reorganization.[644]

---

636. *See* American League Baseball Club of New York v. Johnson, 109 Misc. 138, 179 N.Y.S. 498 (Sup. Ct. 1919), *aff'd,* 190 App. Div. 932, 179 N.Y.S. 898 (1920). In *Johnson,* the court was confronted with the argument that although the league constitution did not specifically authorize the league president to take the action in question, he in fact had done so on many previous occasions without objection by the member clubs. The court rejected the argument that this amounted to an implicit authorization:

> Although courts have placed great weight on the construction which parties have put upon contracts existing between them, such considerations must never violate the fundamental concepts of justice. If the original act was unauthorized, repetition does not invest the act with authority. If the construction did not convey power to the president, he cannot prescriptively acquire power by continual usurpation. If the opposite were true he would in effect effectuate an amendment of the constitution by usurpation. 190 App. Div. at 149-51, 179 N.Y.S. at 505.

A somewhat different approach is reflected in Charles O. Finley & Co. v. Kuhn, Docket No. 76-C-2358 (N.D. Ill., Mar. 17, 1977). There the question was whether a clause in the league constitution which empowered the commissioner to punish conduct which was "detrimental to the best interests of the national game of baseball" authorized the commissioner to disapprove a sale and trade transaction which would substantially reduce the talent on a former championship team. The court eventually concluded that the requisite authority was present. In its finding of facts, it made an extensive review of prior instances in which the commissioner had utilized the above-quoted clause to intervene in player trades. Thus, the interpretation of the disputed clause was substantially aided by reference to the league's prior practices.

637. *See, e.g.,* Metropolitan Baseball Ass'n v. Simmons, 1 Pa. County Ct. 134, 17 Phila. 419 (1885). *See also* Comment, *Judicial Control of Actions of Private Associations, supra* note 617, at 1025. *See generally* § 3.04 *supra.*

638. *Cf.* Bonacum v. Harrington, 65 Neb. 831, 91 N.W. 886 (1902). *See generally* Comment, *Development in the Law: Judicial Control of Actions of Private Associations, supra* note 617, at 1025-26.

639. *See* American League Baseball Club of New York v. Johnson, 109 Misc. 138, 179 N.Y.S. 498 (Sup. Ct. 1919), *aff'd,* 190 App. Div. 932, 179 N.Y.S. 898 (1920).

640. *See* Charles O. Finley & Co. v. Kuhn, Docket No. 76-C-2358 (N.D. Ill., Mar. 17, 1977); Professional Sports, Ltd. v. Virginia Squires Basketball Club, 373 F. Supp. 946 (W.D. Tex. 1974); Milwaukee American Ass'n v. Landis, 49 F.2d 298 (N.D. Ill. 1931).

641. *See* Boston Baseball Ass'n v. Brooklyn Baseball Club, 37 Misc. 521, 75 N.Y.S. 1076 (Sup. Ct. 1902).

642. *See* Riko Enterprises, Inc. v. Seattle SuperSonics Corp., 357 F. Supp. 521 (S.D.N.Y. 1973). *See also* Atlanta National League Baseball Club, Inc. v. Kuhn, 432 F. Supp. 1213 (N.D. Ga. 1977).

643. *See* Professional Sports, Ltd. v. Virginia Squires Basketball Club, 373 F. Supp. 946 (W.D. Tex. 1974); State *ex rel.* Rowland v. Seattle Baseball Ass'n, 61 Wash. 79, 111 P. 1055 (1910).

644. *See* Metropolitan Base Ball Ass'n v. Simmons, 1 Pa. County Ct. 134, 17 Phila. 419 (1885).

The powers of the league are derivative. Hence, they are necessarily limited and subject to whatever constraints the member clubs have specified. The individual clubs, which have their own identity for most business purposes, will typically retain some prerogatives. Two clubs may, for example, enter into transactions which are not subject to league control.[645] Controversies which arise from such dealings will be resolved according to traditional legal principles and not under league-designated procedures. Similarly a club will usually retain significant control over its relationships with its players, and to the extent that such authority has not been vested in the league, the individual clubs must be free to make personnel decisions free of league intervention.[646]

b. The Role of the Commissioner in League Governance. A major difference between professional sports leagues and other private associations is the extent to which the powers of the organization reside in a single individual. The league commissioner is typically given vast powers to approve player contracts; [647] to resolve disputes, both between clubs and between a club and its players; [648] to mete out discipline to players, clubs, and club owners; [649] and to make rules governing the administration of league affairs.[650] In light of the predominant role which the commissioner plays, it is not surprising that his actions generate most of the litigation in this area. One important aspect of the commissioner's function — his role as the final authority in resolving club and player disputes — is considered in another section of this treatise dealing with arbitration.[651] Many facets of the Commissioner's power have not been thoroughly tested in litigation, but the precedents which are available are sufficient to suggest the general restraints which operate on his exercise of authority.

The controversies which arise in this area suggest that two aspects of the commissioner's operation of his office are particularly subject to dispute. One recurring theme in the cases is the definite tendency of the commissioners to usurp powers which were either granted to other bodies within the league [652] or reserved to the member clubs.[653] This result is probably the natural consequence of the fact that the commissioner is more deeply involved in the day-to-day operation of the league than any other person. His primary concern is the smooth functioning of the organization and competition-related

---

645. *See* Professional Sports, Ltd. v. Virginia Squires Basketball Club, 373 F. Supp. 946 (W.D. Tex. 1974).

646. *See, e.g.,* American League Baseball Club of New York v. Johnson, 109 Misc. 138, 179 N.Y.S. 498 (Sup. Ct. 1919), *aff'd,* 190 App. Div. 932, 179 N.Y.S. 898 (1920).
The matter of the respective roles of the club and league in matters of player discipline is considered in section 3.10 *supra.*

647. *See, e.g.,* Charles O. Finley & Co. v. Kuhn, Docket No. 76-C-2358 (N.D. Ill., Mar. 17, 1977); Detroit Football Co. v. Robinson, 186 F. Supp. 933 (E.D. La.), *aff'd,* 283 F.2d 657 (5th Cir. 1960); Los Angeles Rams Football Club v. Cannon, 185 F. Supp. 717 (S.D.Cal. 1960). *See generally* § 3.02 *supra.*

648. *See, e.g.,* Riko Enterprises, Inc. v. Seattle SuperSonics Corp. 357 F. Supp. 521 (S.D.N.Y. 1973); Johnson v. Green Bay Packers, Inc. 272 Wis. 149, 74 N.W.2d 784 (1956). *See generally* § 4.19 *supra.*

649. *See, e.g.,* Atlanta National League Baseball Club, Inc. v. Kuhn, 432 F. Supp. 1213 (N.D. Ga. 1977); Molinas v. Podoloff, 133 N.Y.S.2d 743 (Sup. Ct. 1954). *See generally* § 3.10 *supra.*

650. *See, e.g.,* National Football League Player's Ass'n v. NLRB, 503 F.2d 12 (8th Cir. 1974).

651. *See* § 4.19 *infra.*

652. *See, e.g.,* Riko Enterprises, Inc. v. Seattle SuperSonics Corp., 357 F. Supp. 521 (S.D.N.Y. 1973).

653. *See, e.g.,* American League Baseball Club of New York v. Johnson, 109 Misc. 138, 179 N.Y.S. 498 (Sup. Ct. 1919), *aff'd,* 190 App. Div. 932, 179 N.Y.S. 898 (1920).

activities.[654] Thus, when a problem arises, it might appear quite reasonable for him to attempt to resolve it. It may be only later that the party who is adversely affected investigates the technical limits of his authority.

The other area of dispute which suggests a systemic problem involves the propensity of the commissioner to handle matters with less formality than is required by the documents which grant his authority. As in situations in which the commissioner assumes powers granted to others, the courts do not hesitate to correct these failures to follow prescribed procedures. Thus, where the applicable rules call for notice and hearing, it has been held that these are not satisfied by "informal discussions in the rooms and hallways of hotels." [655] Similarly, where there is confusion about the facts surrounding a particular controversy, it will be expected that the commissioner will make some effort to ascertain what those facts are before he acts.[656]

The judicial treatment of these issues serves to suggest the general principles which will be applied to judge the commissioner's actions. As is true with respect to the league itself, the commissioner has only those powers which are granted by the constituent members. To the extent that a particular subject matter has been reserved to the discretion of an individual club or some other group within the league, the commissioner is powerless to deal with it. The notion of the limited nature of the commissioner's authority applies to both his substantive powers [657] and the procedural aspects of his decision-making.[658] While he may be granted authority to promulgate regulations to govern a particular activity, he cannot use such a grant to extend the reach of his substantive authority.[659] However, it is likewise true that he does not lose his jurisdiction over a particular controversy merely because he originally treated it in an unauthorized fashion. He may correct his error if, in reasserting authority over the dispute, he follows the procedures spelled out in the by-laws which define his prerogatives.[660]

As the above discussion indicates, the definition of the commissioner's authority is critical to the determination of the balance of power within the various sports leagues. In many areas, the clubs have authorized the commissioner to take actions which are detrimental to the individual club's interests. When such actions are taken, it can be expected that the club will react. Its initial response will likely be to question whether the action actually was within the powers which have been delegated. Where there is a serious failure by the commissioner to respect the limitations on his office, the clubs will find the courts available as a forum for review of the controversy.

---

654. *See generally* Davis, *Self-Regulation in Baseball, 1909-71, supra* note 621, at 377-82; *Arbitration in Professional Athletics* in ARBITRATION OF INTEREST DISPUTES—PROCEEDINGS OF THE TWENTY-SIXTH ANNUAL MEETING OF THE NATIONAL ACADEMY OF ARBITRATORS 108 (1973).

655. Professional Sports, Ltd. v. Virginia Squires Basketball Club, 373 F. Supp. 946, 951 (W.D. Tex. 1974).

656. *See* American League Baseball Club of New York v. Johnson, 109 Misc. 138, 179 N.Y.S. 498, 506 (Sup. Ct. 1919) (dictum), 190 App. Div. 932, 179 N.Y.S. 898 (1920). *See also* National Football League Players Ass'n v. N.L.R.B., 503 F.2d 12 (8th Cir. 1974).

657. *See, e.g.,* American League Baseball Club of New York v. Johnson, 109 Misc. 138, 179 N.Y.S. 498 (Sup. Ct. 1919), *aff'd,* 190 App. Div. 932, 179 N.Y.S. 898 (1920).

658. *See* Riko Enterprises, Inc. v. Seattle SuperSonics Corp., 357 F. Supp. 521 (S.D.N.Y. 1973); *cf.* National Football League Players Ass'n v. N.L.R.B., 503 F.2d 12 (8th Cir. 1974).

659. *See* Professional Sports, Ltd. v. Virginia Squires Basketball Club, 373 F. Supp. 946, 952-53 (W.D. Tex. 1974).

660. *See id.* at 952.

§ 3.16. Membership Rights.

In general, the most frequently litigated controversies involving private associations concern the power of the organization to affect membership rights.[661] Considerable judicial attention has been given to the question of the right of associations to deny membership to applicants and to expel or otherwise discipline existing members. Despite the general frequency of suits involving these questions, professional sports leagues have been largely immune from this type of litigation.[662] The dearth of reported cases should not, however, suggest that the matter of membership control is not an important factor in the sports industry. Disciplinary actions are not uncommon,[663] and the formation of new leagues and clubs, as well as the normal changes in team ownership of existing teams, insure that the question of access to a league will continue to arise with some frequency.[664]

a. Admission to Membership. A decision by a sports league to deny membership to a party seeking to acquire a team franchise raises questions not only under the common law of private associations but under the federal antitrust laws as well.[665] While the relevant antitrust principles are considered in greater detail in another section of this treatise,[666] the present analysis of league admission decisions requires that attention be given to both the antitrust concerns and those which arise under the law of private associations.

A review of the general law applied to the admissions practices of associations suggests that a denial of membership by a sports league falls somewhere in between the two lines of cases which have emerged in this area. The judicial policy identified in the early cases and still applied in most situations is one of non-intervention into the admissions practices of private associations.[667] The premise of this view is that the members of a private group ought not be forced to associate with someone whom they find unacceptable. Moreover, where exclusion, rather than expulsion, is involved, the party affected does not yet have

---

661. See generally Chafee, The Internal Affairs of Associations Not for Profit, 43 HARV. L. REV. 993 (1930); Comment, Development in the Law: Judicial Control of Actions of Private Associations, 76 HARV. L. REV. 983 (1963).

662. But see Atlanta National League Baseball Club, Inc. v. Kuhn, 432 F. Supp. 1213 (N.D. Ga. 1977); Levin v. National Basketball Ass'n, 385 F. Supp. 149 (S.D.N.Y. 1974); Riko Enterprises v. Seattle SuperSonics Corp., 357 F. Supp. 521 (S.D.N.Y. 1973); Bradley v. Wilson, 138 Va. 605, 123 S.E. 273 (1924); State ex rel. Rowland v. Seattle Baseball Ass'n, 61 Wash. 79, 111 P. 1055 (1910).

663. See, e.g., Atlanta National League Baseball Club, Inc. v. Kuhn, 432 F. Supp. 1213 (N.D. Ga. 1977); Riko Enterprises v. Seattle SuperSonics Corp., 357 F. Supp. 521 (S.D.N.Y. 1973).

In 1975, the New York Knicks were reportedly fined $400,000 by NBA Commissioner Larry O'Brien for violating the draft rights of the Philadelphia NBA club by signing basketball player George McGinnis. See Putnam, Score a Basket for Brotherly Love, SPORTS ILLUSTRATED, June 23, 1975, at 22; N.Y. Times, June 6, 1975, at 29, col. 1.

664. See, e.g., N.Y. Times, Feb. 10, 1966, at 45, col. 2 (controversy over the manner of selecting site and owner for new NHL team).

665. See, e.g., Levin v. National Basketball Ass'n, 385 F. Supp. 149 (S.D.N.Y. 1974). See generally Comment, The Super Bowl and the Sherman Act: Professional Team Sports and the Antitrust Laws, 81 HARV. L. REV. 418, 426-30 (1967).

666. See § 5.11 infra.

667. See, e.g., Trautwein v. Harbourt, 40 N.J. Super. 247, 123 A.2d 30 (App. Div. 1956); Simmons v. Berry, 210 App. Div. 90, 205 N.Y.S. 442 (1924); Schroeder v. Meridian Improvement Club, 36 Wash. 2d 925, 221 P.2d 544 (1950); 6 AM. JUR. 2D Associations and Clubs § 18 (1963); 7 C.J.S. Associations § 23 (1939).

contract or property rights in the organization.[668] Thus, it is felt that his request for relief lacks a doctrinal basis. The results reached under these principles would appear to be sound where the purpose of the association is to serve the social needs of its members or to provide a mechanism for the collective expression of political or religious beliefs.[669] But there are other associations, such as medical societies, in which ideological and social goals are clearly secondary. These organizations may exercise considerable control over an individual's access to a trade or other trade-related economic advantages. Thus, there is a second line of cases which reflect a less tolerant view of the group's right to control its admissions practices where important economic interests are at stake.[670] Most of the cases in which courts have intervened involve medical groups.[671] In these situations the courts are obviously concerned both about the individual's economic opportunities and the public's access to the important services which are offered.[672]

For the present discussion, the basic issue is whether a sports league is entitled to the immunity from judicial scrutiny which most associations enjoy or whether the economic position of the league is such as to give rise to the same concerns which have prompted judicial review in the second group of cases.[673] Clearly leagues operate with goals which are primarily economic in nature, and social and ideological compatibility may not be necessary for the group's success. Also, it would appear that an unfavorable admissions decision may have a significant adverse effect on the applicant's access to economic opportunities.[674] Finally, it will be argued that like a medical society, the league often occupies a monopolistic position with respect to access to the particular sport.[675] These considerations might appear sufficient to support the conclusion that sports leagues lack many of the characteristics which underlie the judicial policy of non-intervention with respect to social, political, and religious associations.

There are, however, other factors which suggest that the courts have little role to play in regulating the admissions practices of sports leagues. It can be conceded that a league has few of the characteristics of a fraternal or social organization, and it is proper that the precedents which have developed with respect to such groups not be applied blindly. But it must be recognized that cases dealing with medical societies and real estate licensing boards also do not provide appropriate analogies. The gravamen of complaints directed against

---

668. *See, e.g.,* Hurwitz v. Directors Guild of America, Inc., 364 F.2d 67 (2d Cir. 1966); McKane v. Adams, 123 N.Y. 609, 25 N.E. 1057 (1890).

669. *See generally* Comment, *Development in the Law: Judicial Control of Actions of Private Associations, supra* note 661, at 1010-18.

670. *See generally id.* at 1037-55.

671. *See, e.g.,* Hawkins v. North Carolina Dental Soc'y, 355 F.2d 718 (4th Cir. 1966); Falcone v. Middlesex County Medical Soc'y, 62 N.J. Super. 184, 162 A.2d 324 (1960), *aff'd,* 34 N.J. 582, 170 A.2d 791 (1961).

672. *See, e.g.,* Pinsker v. Pacific Coast Soc'y of Orthodontists, 12 Cal. 3d 541, 550-52, 526 P.2d 253, 260-61, 116 Cal. Rptr. 245 (1974).

673. *Cf.* Comment, *Discipline in Professional Sports: The Need for Player Protection,* 60 GEO. L.J. 771, 782-86 (1972).

674. *See generally* Comment, *The Super Bowl and the Sherman Act: Professional Team Sports and the Antitrust Laws, supra* note 665, at 426-30.

675. *Compare* Falcone v. Middlesex County Medical Soc'y, 62 N.J. Super. 184, 162 A.2d 324 (1960), *aff'd,* 34 N.J. 582, 170 A.2d 791 (1961).

such organizations is that their admissions practices limit the economic opportunities of potential competitors. Thus, the basic concern is that the device of eligibility criteria might be used for anticompetitive purposes.[676] The admission practices of sports leagues present a different concern. An analysis of the relationship between clubs within a league suggests that the various league members do not compete with one another in an economic sense. Rather, a league is more like a partnership.[677] While each club initially contributes its own capital, the various participants to a large extent share in the joint profits of the venture. This participation in profits is achieved through various arrangements, such as the pooling of television receipts and the division of gate receipts between home and visiting clubs. Thus, a decision on access to membership is basically a decision as to whether particular individuals (or their business entities) will be allowed to participate in the partnership venture. Since the various members pool their efforts and do not engage in economic competition with one another, an adverse decision on membership in the usual case has no appreciable impact on the level of competition which will take place.[678] Again, this consequence appears to be much different from that which occurs when a medical society or similar organization restricts its membership. In those situations, the person seeking access can, if admitted, affect the amount of competition which occurs. The shift in precedent toward greater scrutiny of such groups' control can be seen as an effort to preserve the desirable consequences which flow from increased inter-firm rivalry, a concern which is not present in the sports context.[679]

The foregoing is intended to indicate that the basic issue which arises with respect to league admissions practices is whether present legal doctrine requires those who operate a joint business venture to have an obligation to apply non-arbitrary criteria in deciding who will be allowed to participate in the enterprise.[680] As is explained more fully in section 5.11 of a subsequent chapter on antitrust issues, the answer appears to be *no*. Once the concern for an adverse effect on competition is set aside, there is literally no case law which suggests that a group of investors is limited in its discretion to decide who will be given access to its mutual venture. The law of partnerships does not impose a reasonable access rule, and other bodies of precedents, including the law of private associations,[681] similarly do not yield precedents which would provide a basis for review where no element of restricted competition is at stake.

b. Discipline of Members. Up to this point, the discussion has considered league action which denies outsiders access to membership. When the focus is shifted to the power of the league to expel or otherwise discipline a member, there is less uncertainty concerning the availability of judicial review. Not only would the group's control of business opportunities continue as a basis for

---

676. *See* Pinsker v. Pacific Coast Soc'y of Orthodontists, 12 Cal. 3d 541, 526 P.2d 253, 116 Cal. Rptr. 245 (1974).

677. This analogy between a sports league and a partnership is developed more fully in § 5.11.

678. *See* Levin v. National Basketball Ass'n, 385 F. Supp. 149 (S.D.N.Y. 1974).

679. It can be suggested that a goal of increasing competition in the product market should focus on the competition which occurs between leagues since within a single league, the clubs do not compete with one another in the production of output. *See* § 5.11 *infra*.

680. *See* Pinsker v. Pacific Coast Soc'y of Orthodontists, 12 Cal. 3d 541, 557-59, 526 P.2d 253, 265-66, 116 Cal. Rptr. 245, 257-58 (1974).

681. *See* text at notes 667-72 *supra*.

judicial concern, but also the disciplined member will often be able to assert that it has definite economic interests which are entitled to protection.[682] In contrast to the disappointed applicant, the club which is subject to discipline most likely will have already made important financial commitments in connection with its franchise, and the success of its venture may be impaired even where the disciplinary action involves a penalty less drastic than a termination of membership.[683] Discipline in the form of a disqualification from a championship or an action affecting its players may produce substantial financial loss.[684]

Because of the impact which a disciplinary action might have on the club's economic position, antitrust considerations are highly relevant in defining the league's powers. These are outlined in subsequent sections,[685] but, as might be expected, many of the same concerns are reflected in the cases decided under common law principles. Because of the greater likelihood that a vested interest will be affected, courts have generally been more receptive to complaints about improper discipline than to those involving exclusionary practices.[686] Under the early disciplinary cases, however, the scope of judicial review was somewhat limited, as the courts professed a policy of affording wide discretion to the internal government of the association. Thus, while the court would intervene to the extent of determining whether the stated offense came within one of the group's disciplinary rules [687] and insuring that the internal proceeding was conducted in accordance with the procedures specified in the association's constitution and by-laws,[688] it was generally said that a court would not attempt to assess the wisdom or reasonableness of the rules defining disciplinable conduct.[689] But as was true with respect to admissions practices, courts gradually began to question the desirability of affording such limited review where the disciplinary action was taken by an organization which had essentially an economic, as opposed to a social or ideological, function.[690] Although the

---

682. *See, e.g.,* Metropolitan Base Ball Ass'n v. Simmons, 1 Pa. County Ct. 134, 138, 17 Phila. 419, 420 (1885). *See also* Atlanta National League Baseball Club, Inc. v. Kuhn, 432 F. Supp. 1213 (N.D. Ga. 1977).

683. *See id.* at 135.

684. *See* American League Baseball Club of New York v. Johnson, 109 Misc. 138, 140, 179 N.Y.S. 498, 499-500 (Sup. Ct. 1919): "Suspension of a player ... not only interferes with his individual contract, but may also interfere with the reputation and collective ability of the club. Inasmuch as the leading clubs of the leagues and their players are entitled at the end of the season to certain rights and privileges, which are unquestionably to be desired property rights, this interference with an individual player would confuse and possibly destroy the rights of the respective clubs and their players. . . ."

685. *See* §§ 5.09-5.11 *infra.*

686. *See, e.g.,* Hurwitz v. Directors Guild of America, 364 F.2d 67 (2d Cir. 1966); Falcone v. Middlesex County Medical Soc'y, 62 N.J. Super. 184, 162 A.2d 324 (1960), *aff'd,* 34 N.J. 582, 170 A.2d 791 (1961).

687. *See, e.g.,* Sweetman v. Barrows, 263 Mass. 349, 161 N.E. 272 (1928); Commonwealth *ex rel.* Burt v. Union League, 135 Pa. 301, 19 A. 1030 (1890); 6 AM. JUR. 2D *Associations and Clubs* § 33 (1963); 7 C.J.S. *Associations* § 25 (1939).

688. *See generally* Comment, *Development in the Law: Judicial Control of Actions of Private Associations, supra* note 661, at 1021-22; 7 C.J.S. *Associations* § 25(d) (1939).

689. *See, e.g.,* Efler v. Marine Eng'rs Local 12, 179 La. 383, 154 So. 2d 32 (1934); Commonwealth *ex. rel.* Burt v. Union League, 135 Pa. 301, 19 A. 1030 (1890).

There were, of course, exceptions as represented by Metropolitan Base Ball Ass'n v. Simmons, 1 Pa. County Ct. 134, 17 Phila. 419 (1885), upholding the right of an expelled club to notice and the opportunity to be heard before the final disciplinary action is taken.

690. *See, e.g.,* Mitchell v. International Ass'n of Machinists, 196 Cal. App. 2d 796, 16 Cal. Rptr. 813 (Dist. Ct. App. 1961); Bernstein v. Alameda-Contra Costa Medical Ass'n, 139 Cal. App. 2d 241, 293 P.2d 862 (Dist. Ct. App. 1956); Bernson Cooperative Creamery Ass'n v. First Dist. Ass'n, 284 Minn. 335, 170 N.W.2d 425 (1969); 6 AM. JUR. 2D *Associations and Clubs* § 33 (1963).

evolution of a more exacting standard of review for organizations of this sort is far from complete, the unmistakable trend is one in which the deference normally paid to the association's own rules and procedures gives way to a concern that the court not aid in an unreasonable deprivation of the member's property or economic advantage. Thus, it is increasingly held that the rules of such an association must be justified in light of the purposes for which the group was formed, and its disciplinary proceedings must meet minimum standards of due process.[691]

In light of a club's financial interest in its membership, there should be little dispute that a sports league will be included in the category of associations whose disciplinary actions are subjected to this more exacting level of judicial scrutiny.[692] The implications for the sports industry can be briefly stated. Rules defining disciplinable conduct will be evaluated in light of the purpose and essential needs of the league.[693] To the extent that the league can show that

---

691. *See* cases cited note 690 *supra. See also* McCrerry Angus Farms v. American Angus Ass'n, 379 F. Supp. 1008, 1018 (S.D. Ill. 1974); Normali v. Cleveland Ass'n of Life Underwriters, 39 Ohio App. 2d 24, 315 N.E.2d 482 (1974); Metropolitan Base Ball Ass'n v. Simmons, 1 Pa. County Ct. 134, 140, 17 Phila. 419, 422 (1885); *cf.* Pinsker v. Pacific Coast Soc'y of Orthodontists, 12 Cal. 3d 541, 526 P.2d 253, 116 Cal. Rptr. 245 (1974).

692. *See* Metropolitan Base Ball Ass'n v. Simmons, 1 Pa. County Ct. 134, 17 Phila. 419 (1885).

693. *See* Comment, *Judicial Control of Actions of Private Associations, supra* note 661, at 1010-18; *cf.* Pinsker v. Pacific Coast Soc'y of Orthodontists, 12 Cal. 3d 541, 557-59, 526 P.2d 253, 265-66 (1974).

The issue of the scope of judicial review of league disciplinary actions was considered in Atlanta National League Baseball Club, Inc. v. Kuhn, 432 F. Supp. 1213 (N.D. Ga. 1977). Baseball Commissioner Bowie Kuhn had suspended Atlanta Braves' owner Ted Turner for one year after finding that Turner had improperly "tampered with" a player under contract to another club. The actual punishment took the form of an order prohibiting Turner from exercising any powers in connection with the management of his baseball club. In addition, the commissioner ordered that Atlanta must give up its first round draft selection in a subsequent free agent draft. In the litigation which ensued, the court upheld the suspension of Turner but reinstated the club's draft rights, finding that the applicable league documents did not authorize this sort of sanction.

It is not entirely clear what standard of review the court used in upholding Turner's suspension. The case is perhaps not a good vehicle for testing the principles considered in the text, for there appeared to be little debate that the league had an interest in insuring that one club did not improperly interfere with the contract relationship that another club had with its players. Thus, the question of whether the commissioner's actions were within the scope of the league's legitimate interests was not specifically addressed.

The court's opinion does include a statement which suggests the standard of review which it applied. Thus, the court stated:

> In any event, the court must hold in check a close scrutiny of the reasons given for the Commissioner's decision to discipline Turner. The Commissioner has general authority, without rules or directives, to punish both clubs and/or personnel for any act or conduct which, in his judgment, is "not in the best interests of baseball" within the meaning of the Major League Agreement. What conduct is "not in the best interests of baseball" is, of course, a question which addresses itself to the Commissioner, not this court. He has made his finding that Turner's conduct was of this character. The court knows of no authority which prevented him from making it, and cannot say his decision was either arbitrary or wrong. There is no evidence that the Commissioner's decision was the result of bias or ill will, although, during the same period one other tampering violation was dealt with much less severely. The court therefore concludes, with some misgivings, that under this provision, the Commissioner did have authority to punish plaintiffs.

Id. at 1222. While this statement by the court seems to indicate a high degree of deference to the discretion of the commissioner, that conclusion is not necessarily inconsistent with the standard suggested in the text. In cases in which the particular regulation was found to bear a reasonable relationship to the purposes of the league, it would seem appropriate for the courts to generally respect the judgment of the league officials in matters of fact finding and the like. It can also be noted that the court's statement does imply that the matter of procedural fairness is an appropriate concern.

a legitimate interest is being furthered by its action, its exercise of control will be sustained.[694] Thus, the leagues will be given authority to insure that member clubs fulfill their financial obligations to the league; [695] comply with reasonable rules and regulations of the league, such as those requiring respect for the draft rights of other clubs; [696] refrain from conduct which would undermine the integrity of the sport; and generally, avoid taking actions which substantially undermine the league's orderly pursuit of its economic goals. On the other hand, to the extent that a reasonable relationship between the league's disciplinary action and its primary business functions is lacking, a basis for judicial intervention will exist. Of equal importance will be the judicial concern for the procedural fairness of the proceedings in which league discipline is meted out. Indeed, if there is any particular theme that emerges from the few reported decisions involving league actions, it is that in the absence of evidence of waiver,[697] clubs are to be apprised of charges against them and afforded an opportunity to participate in any proceedings which result.[698] This is not to suggest that courts are inclined to burden the leagues with the expense and inconvenience of elaborate proceedings. Rather, the decisions are largely directed toward placing a check upon the tendency of the league, or more often the commissioner, to take informal, wholly unilateral actions.[699]

Although the general move toward greater review of association actions is of relatively recent origin, it is based on principles which are by no means of startling proportions. The basic lesson for the leagues is that they must avoid using the associational relationship as the occasion to achieve conformity on matters which are irrelevant to the business.[700] When the league's view of its purposes is appropriately narrowed to those proportions, the league can proceed with a vigorous administration of its affairs. Since sound management practice would seem to dictate the same result any time diverse interests are joined in a business venture, it is doubtful that any radical adjustments will be necessary in the league which is already well-run.

---

694. *Compare* Comment, *Discipline in Professional Sports: The Need for Player Protection, supra* note 673, at 786 (suggesting that a similar analysis should be applied to test the propriety of player discipline).

695. *See* Metropolitan Base Ball Ass'n v. Simmons, 1 Pa. County Ct. 134, 139, 17 Phila. 419, 421 (1885); Bradley v. Wilson, 138 Va. 605, 123 S.E. 273 (1924).

696. *Cf.* Riko Enterprises, Inc. v. Seattle SuperSonics Corp., 357 F. Supp. 521 (S.D.N.Y. 1973) (discipline overturned on procedural grounds).

697. One context in which the waiver question arises is discussed in section 4.19 *infra. See also* State *ex rel.* Rowland v. Seattle Baseball Ass'n, 61 Wash. 79, 111 P. 1055 (1910).

698. *See* Riko Enterprises, Inc. v. Seattle SuperSonics Corp., 357 F. Supp. 521 (S.D.N.Y. 1973); American League Baseball Club of New York v. Johnson, 109 Misc. 138, 179 N.Y.S. 498 (Sup. Ct. 1919) (dictum); Metropolitan Base Ball Ass'n v. Simmons, 1 Pa. County Ct. 134, 17 Phila. 419 (1885); State *ex rel.* Rowland v. Seattle Baseball Ass'n, 61 Wash. 79, 111 P. 1055 (1910); *cf.* Professional Sports, Ltd. v. Virginia Squires Basketball Club, 373 F. Supp. 946 (W.D. Tex. 1974).

699. This is not to suggest that the parties might not empower the commissioner to take unilateral action in some cases. Indeed, notions of freedom of contract would seemingly give the parties wide latitude in specifying the degree of formality which must accompany the commissioner's decision-making. *See generally* § 4.18 *infra.*

700. *See generally* Comment, *Development in the Law: Judicial Control of Actions of Private Associations, supra* note 661, at 1010-18.

§ 3.17. Athletes and Their Agents — Background.

The relationship between an athlete and his agent is often as important as that which the player has with his club. The agent's influence may affect virtually every aspect of the player's career. At a preliminary level, the agent who negotiates the athlete's contract will determine whether he is properly paid for his athletic performances. But this is only one way in which the agent may influence whether the athlete realizes the full value of his talents. Thus, the agent who also serves as manager will determine whether the athlete properly exploits his publicity value from endorsements, appearances, publishing, and the like.[701] Even if he has secured the full financial rewards of the athlete's talents, the agent-manager's advice with respect to investments and tax planning has a significant impact on the extent to which the player is able to achieve lifetime security from the economic gains of his brief playing career. Without sound advice in his early years, the athlete may find that an otherwise substantial income is consumed by taxes [702] or lost in risky business ventures.

The direct financial ramifications of the athlete's relationship with his agent are not the only concern, for it is increasingly apparent that the agent's actions may also have an impact on his client's athletic performance. The athlete's mental condition, and his on-the-field performance, can be greatly influenced by his personal financial position. Any number of problems may arise. The athlete may see that other, less talented players receive more attractive salaries. Similarly he may feel exploited when he eventually develops superstar talents but finds himself obligated under a relatively low-paying long-term contract. Or he may become preoccupied, sometimes with the encouragement of a predatory agent, by offers from a rival league. Finally, he may experience the severe mental pressure which accompanies serious reversals in his business investments. A preoccupation with concerns such as these can be truly self-defeating as they adversely affect the athlete's performance and thus further limit the potential financial rewards of his playing career.[703]

The suggestion that agents have not always performed in the best interests of the athlete, or indeed of the sport generally, is by no means hypothetical. Perhaps no aspect of professional sports has been subjected to as much vilifying criticism. Despite the presence in the industry of several highly reputable managers,[704] the best efforts of these professionals are often overshadowed by

---

701. Successful management of the athlete's endorsements includes not only making placements in the advertising field but also controlling the nature of the endorsements so as to not limit future opportunities. For example, some young golfers have been criticized for associating themselves with less than prestigious products early in their careers and thereby limiting their opportunities for more lucrative endorsements when they achieve superstar status. *See* Kennedy, *On His Mark and Go-Go-Going,* SPORTS ILLUSTRATED, May 12, 1975, at 82.

702. Subsequent portions of this treatise consider the basic tax-planning principles which the athlete should follow. *See* Ch. 7, *infra.*

703. The discussion in the text focuses on the problems which are encountered when the athlete believes he is underpaid. Some authors have suggested that agents play a role in fostering a much different attitudinal problem. It is suggested that players whose agents have exploited interleague competition to secure lucrative contracts often develop nonchalant attitudes toward their sport with the consequence that the general level of competition suffers. *See* S. FISCHLER, SLASHING! 84-95 (1974).

704. *See, e.g.,* Oates, *What Kind of Lineup Has Doris Day and Henry Aaron?,* Los Angeles Times, Feb. 6, 1974, Pt. III, at 1, col. 2; Golenbach, *Now Calling Signals, The Lawyer-Agent,* JURISDOCTOR, Oct. 1971, at 49; Kennedy, *On His Mark and Go-Go-Going, supra* note 701.

the presence of a large number of less scrupulous operators. These are often individuals who lack training and experience in the skills which are important to proper management of an athlete's affairs, such as contract negotiation and tax and financial planning. In the view of their critics, the greatest talent of the worst of the agents is an ability to exploit naive college athletes. The general criticisms of this group of player-agents have ranged from allegations of basic incompetency to charges of blatantly unethical conduct.[705] Specific complaints are directed to the willingness of some agents to sign college players to management contracts in knowing violation of NCAA rules [706] and to secure these commitments by substantial cash payments to the athlete. The agent's efforts are often directed to the large number of college stars from impoverished backgrounds and thus are seen as exploitive.[707] Not all of the improper inducements are financial. A particularly distasteful ploy involves the agent's misrepresenting to a club that he has been retained by an athlete and then using any resulting salary offers to lure the athlete into a management contract.[708]

Even if the agent is eventually retained by the athlete, there is no reason to believe that his ethics will improve. Often the agent's lack of ethics and general

---

705. For a highly critical view of the role of player-agents in the sport of hockey, see S. FISCHLER, SLASHING! 84-95 (1974). Some of Fischler's criticisms seem to have been borne out by subsequent developments. One of the more sordid player-agent cases in recent years involves Richard Sorkin, an agent who represented several professional hockey players and a few professional basketball players. Sorkin pleaded guilty to seven counts of grand larceny after having been accused of misappropriating money which he had received from his clients. The total amount lost by his clients has not been established, but has been estimated to be about $1.2 million. The details of Sorkin's improprieties are reported in Montgomery, *The Spectacular Rise and Ignoble Fall of Richard Sorkin, Pros' Agent,* N.Y. Times, Oct. 9, 1977, § 5, at 1, col. 1. Sorkin later testified before a New York state legislative committee considering the question of whether sports agents should be licensed or otherwise brought within governmental control. In his testimony, Sorkin reported on a number of the questionable practices in which he engaged. He indicated, for example, that the owner of a hockey team paid him $20,000 to give the owner's team the "first crack" at negotiating with a player whom Sorkin represented. In addition, Sorkin admitted that he had signed several collegiate athletes to representational contracts while they were still competing in college sports, action which violates a specific NCAA proscription. Also Sorkin indicated that a junior hockey league in Canada had offered him and another party the exclusive right to represent players from the league in exchange for a percentage of the agency fees which would be generated. *See id.,* Feb. 2, 1978, at 57, col. 4.

The deficiencies of some agents have not gone unnoticed by the players' unions. Ed Garvey, executive director of the National Football League Players' Association, has suggested that players' unions in the various sports should compile lists of reputable agents and make these available to their members. Garvey has also indicated that he may register a formal complaint with the American Bar Association about the unethical conduct of some lawyer-agents representing NFL players. Globe & Mail (Toronto), Feb. 6, 1976, at 32, col. 1.

706. *See* Adams, *Pro Basketball War: Ugly Mess, Shrewd Agents,* Louisville Courier-Journal & Times, Aug. 8, 1971, reprinted in *Hearings on S.2373 Before the Subcomm. on Antitrust and Monopoly of the Senate Comm. on the Judiciary,* 92d Cong., 1st Sess., pt. 1, at 424-27 (1971).

707. Sam Gilbert, a Los Angeles businessman who has represented many UCLA basketball players has stated:

> I dislike super agents. They prey in unsuspecting black athletes with ghetto backgrounds. Agents like that ought to be paid an hourly fee, not on percentage. After all, no one is worth 10 percent of a player's earnings.

Quoted in Adams, *Agents Due Thinner Cuts, More Slices of Pro Basketball Pie After Merger,* The Louisville Courier-Journal & Times, Aug. 11, 1971, reprinted in *Hearings, supra* note 706, at 435. *See also* S. GALLNER, PRO SPORTS: THE CONTRACT GAME 52 (1974); Axthelm, *Marvin Barnes and the Work Ethic,* NEWSWEEK, Dec. 2, 1974, at 61; Golenbach, *Now Calling Signals, The Lawyer-Agent, supra* note 704, at 49.

708. *See* Adams, *Pro Basketball War: Ugly Mess, Shrewd Agents, supra* note 706, at 425.

incompetence will be reflected in the player contract which he negotiates on behalf of his client. A recurring criticism is that agents too frequently negotiate for terms which will insure that they are paid immediately. Thus, their fees may consume a large part of the player's bonus and initial salary payment and leave the player in a difficult financial position.[709] Moreover, whether from a lack of knowledge about the sport or an unabating concern for his own immediate financial gains, the agent may give inadequate attention to the athlete's suitability for a particular team. Unless the parties consider such things as the athlete's particular strength and weakness, the team's long-term personnel needs, and the quality of training and direction which will be provided, the result may be an abbreviated professional career for the client.[710] Even apart from those problems, the agent's lack of expertise may produce a contract in which promised long term benefits are illusory [711] or are otherwise unsound for their failure to consider tax ramifications.

The agent's inadequacies are also likely to be reflected in his post-contract services. Many agents are accused of providing no useful money-management services even though they have received fees which are equal to or greater than those charged by reputable firms which offer substantial investment and tax counseling in connection with the athlete's contract. In the better sports management firms, these matters are either handled by specialists within the firm [712] or by experts retained on a case-by-case basis.[713] The athlete usually has such an imperfect understanding of the business world that he is easily misled by the unscrupulous agent's representation of the range of his services.[714]

Some of the strongest criticism is reserved for the role of the misdirected agent in disrupting existing contractual relationships. Thus, an agent may seek

---

709. Many of these elements were involved in the suit by player Kenny Burrow of the Atlanta Falcons against his manager, Probus Management, Inc., and Norman Young, one of its officers. The district judge made several findings, one of which was that "the advice and counsel given by the Defendant Young ... to accept all of the bonus in one lump sum was advice not for the best interest of the Plaintiff but given for the purpose of acquiring immediate funds for the benefit of the Defendant which created additional tax liability in the amount of approximately twelve hundred dollars." Burrow v. Probus Management, Inc., Civil No. 16840, at 6 (N.D. Ga., Aug. 9, 1973) (unpublished order).

710. Mike Storen, former president of the ABA Kentucky Colonels has stated: "Agents can't appraise a boy's basketball talent or his future.... Does the agent ever really ask himself or the player 'Can the boy make it?' Look at Don May.... Did he go to the right team? He played hardly at all. But his agent sent him where the money was." Adams, *Agents Due Thinner Cuts, More Slices of Basketball Pie After Merger, supra* note 707, at 434.

711. *See* S. GALLNER, PRO SPORTS: THE CONTRACT GAME 104 (1974) (discussion of the Dolgoff Plan for deferring an athlete's compensation).

712. *See* Kennedy, *On His Mark and Go-Go-Going, supra* note 701, at 82.

713. *See* Golenbach, *Now Calling Signals, The Lawyer-Agent, supra* note 704, at 50.

714. In *Burrow v. Probus Management, Inc.,* the court noted that the agent had represented that he "would prepare all of [plaintiff's] income tax returns to his best advantage, would receive and manage his funds coming from income as a professional football player, would render tax advice and establish tax shelters for Plaintiff's benefit, would invest his funds in second mortgages and other investments and would pay interest on held funds of twelve percent per annum and would pay from his funds all of his bills and other living expenses, maintaining for him a good credit reputation and relationship with the public." The court found, however, that the defendant failed to pay bills submitted by the player's creditors, prepared false tax returns, failed to pay other creditors and failed to account for an additional $30,000. The court found that the agent had grossly misrepresented its services and awarded the player $60,000 in punitive damages, in addition to $30,000 in actual damages and $5,000 for attorney's fees. Civil No. 16840, at 3-7 (N.D. Ga., Aug. 9, 1973) (unpublished order).

to induce a player to abandon his existing contract and jump to another league.[715] Even when that opportunity is not available, the agent may convince the player that his existing contract is inadequate and seek to renegotiate it.[716] Even where there is no legal basis for demanding that the terms be changed, the agent may use ploys such as adverse publicity or a feigned retirement to encourage the club to increase the athlete's compensation.[717] Such tactics undermine the stability of sports contracts and, it is felt, erode fan support.[718] It is true that there may be legal remedies available to the club which is subjected to actions such as contract jumping,[719] but these often offer little solace. The resulting litigation may be protracted and, in any case, is likely to generate adverse publicity which distracts the public's attention from the club's primary venture. Even if the team prevails in the litigation, it may only regain a disgruntled player whose lack of loyalty has caused a further incremental erosion of fan interest. In short, it is clear that many athletes have not received the type of counseling which is conducive to a healthy respect for the role of the contract in professional sports.[720]

There is, however, reason for optimism about the future role of player agents. The business of sports management began on a major scale no more than two decades ago. The problems described above may simply be manifestations of the uncertainty of its formative years. There are signs that the number of athletes retaining reputable firms is increasing and the truly unscrupulous and incompetent operators are playing a less significant role. It can be hoped that this trend will continue as word of the performance of the established firms spreads further through the intercollegiate ranks. Yet, an uncertain factor for the future is the extent to which there will continue to be inter-team competition for the athlete's services. In the past, such competition has served to intensify the problems discussed here.[721] Even though the prospects for new, competing

---

715. *See* S. GALLNER, PRO SPORTS: THE CONTRACT GAME 70 (1974).

716. *See* Axthelm, *Marvin Barnes and the Work Ethic, supra* note 707, at 61.

717. The formation of a rival league may present the occasion for the athlete to demand that his contract be renegotiated. The sudden appearance of several new teams usually means that there are not enough experienced players to fill the clubs' needs. A particular player may use that fact as a leverage to increase his compensation. *See* S. FISCHLER, SLASHING! 89-90 (1974).

718. *See* Axthelm, *Marvin Barnes and the Work Ethic, supra* note 707, at 61.

719. *See generally* §§ 4.02-.03 *infra.*

720. Judge J. Skelly Wright, then a federal district court judge in Louisiana, expressed strong views on the matter of contract jumping when he was asked to adjudicate conflicting claims to football player Johnny Robinson: "This case is but another round in the sordid fight for football players, a fight which begins before these athletes enter college and follows them through their professional careers. . . . It is a fight which so conditions the minds and hearts of these athletes that one day they can agree to play football for a stated amount for one group, only to repudiate that agreement the following day or whenever a better offer comes along. So it was with Johnny Robinson." Detroit Football Club v. Robinson, 186 F. Supp. 933 (E.D. La.), *aff'd,* 283 F.2d 657 (5th Cir. 1960). At least on the reported facts, Robinson's actions were not induced by his personal agent, but by the competing clubs themselves. The case serves to illustrate that the clubs are not always the hapless victims of the problems discussed in the text. In fact, there is some evidence that the clubs have utilized their own agents to exploit untutored athletes. *See* Adams, *Pro Basketball War: Ugly Mess, Shrewd Agents, supra* note 707, at 426; Golenbach, *Now Calling Signals, The Lawyer-Agent, supra* note 704, at 49.

721. *See* Houston Oilers, Inc. v. Neely, 361 F.2d 36 (10th Cir. 1966); Detroit Football Club v. Robinson, 186 F. Supp. 933 (E.D. La.), *aff'd,* 283 F.2d 657 (5th Cir. 1960). *See generally* Adams, *Pro Basketball War: Ugly Mess, Shrewd Agents, supra* note 706, at 424-27.

leagues have entered a somewhat uncertain stage,[722] developments in the antitrust area seem to foreshadow increased competition of a different sort. Perhaps the market mechanism will eventually operate to eliminate the problems previously experienced and the actors who generated them. In such a situation, the reliable firms in the sports management field will be able to reveal, with fewer distractions, the positive contributions which they can make to the full realization of an athlete's potential as a professional.

In light of the intensity of the criticism directed at some segments of the sports management business, one might expect to find extensive litigation on the numerous legal issues which must necessarily arise. Such is not the case, however. Even when the class of relevant precedent is broadened to include the representation of entertainers generally, the body of reported decisions is quite small.[723] This is not to suggest that there are not substantial legal precedents to guide the attorney seeking to counsel a client in this area. Controversies which arise will raise basically questions of agency and contract, and case law from those general areas will provide the precedent for resolving sports-related controversies. The discussion in the sections which follow does not attempt to outline all of the questions which might be presented. Rather, along the lines of prior discussions, attention will be given only to a selected group of issues which seem to have particular ramifications for agency arrangements in the sports industry.

§ 3.18. Exclusive Agency Arrangements.

a. The Agent's Right to Compensation. The management contracts entered into in the sports industry typically provide that the agent is to serve as the "exclusive representative" of the athlete.[724] The exclusive nature of these arrangements has important consequences both for its effect upon the agent's right to receive compensation and for its definition of the quality of representation to which the athlete is entitled.[725] Questions about the agent's right to his commission are particularly apt to arise in two types of situations.

---

722. *The Sports Boom Is Going Bust . . .*, FORBES, Feb. 15, 1974, at 24. *See also* § 5.11 *infra.*

723. *See, e.g.*, Campas v. Olson, 241 F.2d 661 (9th Cir. 1957); George Foreman Associates Ltd. v. Foreman, 389 F. Supp. 1308 (N.D. Cal. 1974), *aff'd,* 517 F.2d 354 (9th Cir. 1975); Burrow v. Probus Management, Inc., Civil No. 16840 (N.D. Ga., Aug. 9, 1973) (unpublished order); Russell-Stewart Inc. v. Birkett, 24 Misc. 2d 528, 201 N.Y.S.2d 687 (Sup. Ct. 1960); Trammel v. Morgan, 158 N.E.2d 541 (Ohio App. 1957); and cases cited in Annot., 175 A.L.R. 617 (1948).

724. Examples of the standard contract forms used by some sports management firms can be found in S. GALLNER, PRO SPORTS: THE CONTRACT GAME 174-76 (1974). A typical provision recites: "You authorize us and we agree to serve as your exclusive personal representatives and business advisor [sic]." *Id.* at 174. The exclusive nature of the relationship is further confirmed by the compensation term which entitles the agent to 7-½% "of the gross consideration . . . from your professional employment contract or contracts entered into during the term of this agreement." It will be noted that the right to compensation is not specifically made dependent upon the agent's having negotiated the contract.

Samples of management contracts used in the movie industry are set forth in Annot., 175 A.L.R. 617, 636 (1948).

725. The accepted black letter rule is that an agency relationship will not be deemed exclusive unless the express terms of the contract so provided. *See* RESTATEMENT (SECOND) OF AGENCY § 449, comment *b* (1958). Under a non-exclusive arrangement, the agent receives his commission only if he completes the requested performance. The owner is free, however, to either do the specified act himself or appoint another agent to perform it. If there is a prior performance by either of these parties, the non-exclusive agent cannot complain that he was denied the opportunity to earn his

It may be, for example, that the athlete begins the negotiation of his player contract by working through his agent, but later rejects the agent's efforts and proceeds to deal directly with the club.[726] Or the athlete, perhaps as the result of outside inducement, may seek to end his affiliation with one agent and utilize the services of another.[727] In either case, if the contract is consummated without the assistance of an agent who has been offered an exclusive right to represent the athlete, it must be determined whether that agent is entitled to the commission he would have received had his services been accepted.[728]

As a preliminary matter it can be noted that many agents choose not to press the question of their right to compensation in these situations. It is by no means clear that such a response reflects the agent's assessments of his legal entitlements. A more likely explanation is that in the competitive atmosphere which pervades the sports management business, the agents are concerned about the potential adverse effects of the publicity which would attend the agent's resort to litigation or other aggressive collection tactics. Whatever the reason, the effect of the agent's acceptance of his client's decision to change his affiliation suggests that the assertion of legal rights will likely be reserved for cases in which the probability of damages is certain.

Case law from analogous situations suggests that merely because the parties describe the agency relationship as an exclusive one does not necessarily mean the agent is given the sole right to perform the specified act. In real estate brokerage contracts, for example, a distinction is often made between an "exclusive agency" arrangement and an "exclusive right to sell" the designated property.[729] In the former situation, the broker is assured that he is the only agent which will be selected, but he remains subject to competition from the principal.[730] In the latter case, the seller not only grants the agent authority to sell the property but also promises to personally refrain from doing so himself.[731] In the event that action is taken in contravention of either of these arrangements, the agent is entitled to damages, which, as discussed below, may or may not equal the amount of the promised commission.[732]

These principles provide the basic rules for analyzing cases in the sports area.

---

commission. *See, e.g.,* Potts v. Thompson, 61 N.J. Super. 424, 161 A.2d 284 (App. Div. 1960); Annot., 126 A.L.R. 1233 (1940). It would seem, however, that the customs of the particular trade would control over these general rules, and if it were generally understood that all agency relationships were exclusive, the mere appointment of the agent would imply an exclusivity in the relationship. Of course, there is often a substantial question as to whether a practice is so common as to elevate itself to the status of a trade custom. *See generally* UNIFORM COMMERCIAL CODE § 1-205; 3 A. CORBIN, CORBIN ON CONTRACTS §§ 555-56 (1960) [hereinafter cited as CORBIN ON CONTRACTS]; W. SEAVEY, HANDBOOK OF THE LAW OF AGENCY § 171 (1964) [hereinafter cited as SEAVEY, AGENCY].

726. An occasional complaint by agents is that club representatives will sometimes induce the player to shun the agent's assistance and deal directly with them in finalizing the arrangement. *See* Golenbach, *Now Calling Signals, The Lawyer-Agent,* JURISDOCTOR, Oct. 1971 at 49.

727. *See, e.g.,* Axthelm, *Marvin Barnes and the Work Ethic,* NEWSWEEK, Dec. 2, 1974, at 61.

728. *See generally* SEAVEY, AGENCY § 171, ¶ F.

729. *See generally* SEAVEY, AGENCY § 171; RESTATEMENT (SECOND) OF AGENCY § 449 (1958); Annot., 64 A.L.R. 395 (1930); Annot. 12 A.L.R.2d 1360 (1950).

730. *See, e.g.,* Wood v. Hutchinson Coal Co., 176 F.2d 682 (4th Cir. 1949); Welch v. Herbert, 78 Cal. App. 2d 392, 178 P.2d 25 (Dist. Ct. App. 1947).

731. *See, e.g.,* Louis Schlesinger Co. v. Rice, 4 N.J. 169, 72 A.2d 197 (1950); Bell v. Dimmerling, 149 Ohio St. 165, 78 N.E.2d 49 (1948).

732. *See, e.g.,* Meyers v. Nolan, 18 Cal. App. 2d 319, 63 P.2d 1216 (Dist. Ct. App. 1936); RESTATEMENT (SECOND) OF AGENCY § 449, comment *d* at 363 (1958).

In the absence of other facts, the athlete's promise to a sports management firm that it will be his exclusive representative would not preclude the player from entering into direct negotiations with the team. Under such a term, the principal remains free to forego representation and handle the transaction directly. On the other hand, the athlete would be liable if he repudiated the original agency relationship and selected another manager to represent him. These rules will not always be applied in this literal form, however.[733] Other considerations, including customs of the trade, the particular language of the contract, and other indicia of the parties' intent must be considered.[734] For example, in many management contracts it will be important to look at the term defining the agent's entitlement to compensation. Often the agent's commission will be based on the athlete's income from all contracts consummated during the term of the agency.[735] Such a provision might be read to mean that the commission is payable whether or not the agent handles the contract.[736] Relatedly, the sports management business has been in existence long enough that trade customs have undoubtedly developed. These may be consulted if the party seeking to take advantage of them first establishes that the other party either was or should have been aware that they would control interpretation of their contract.[737]

The player's breach of an exclusive agency contract does not necessarily entitle the agent to his commission. Technically, the agent is only entitled to damages for breach of contract.[738] These may be the same as the promised commission where the contract expressly so provides. Such a term will be enforceable if it otherwise satisfies the rules normally applied to liquidated damages.[739] In the absence of an agreement of this sort, the agent is entitled to the usual measure of damages. Thus, he will receive the value of the promised performance reduced by any expenses which he saved by his performance having been prevented.[740] In the sports context, this means that awards may be reduced by the amounts which would have been spent negotiating the contract, securing outside tax advice, and so on.[741] But there is a further element which must be considered: the agent is entitled to his commission only if he can show that had he been permitted to continue performance, he would have been able to consummate the contract or contracts upon which his claim for a commission is based.[742] There is usually no difficulty in making the necessary showing where the agent claims a commission for the contract negotiated with the club, since the court will often have definite proof as to whether the contract was eventually consummated.[743] More troublesome, however, will be the agent's claims for commission resulting from contracts for endorsements and the like.

733. See generally 3 AM. JUR. 2D Agency § 259 (1962).

734. See RESTATEMENT (SECOND) OF AGENCY § 449, comments b, c (1958).

735. See S. GALLNER, PRO SPORTS: THE CONTRACT GAME 174, 176 (1974). See also note 724 supra.

736. See also Annot., 175 A.L.R. 617, 636-37 (1948).

737. See generally 3 CORBIN ON CONTRACTS §§ 555-57; § 3.04 supra.

738. See generally 5 CORBIN ON CONTRACTS § 1025; RESTATEMENT (SECOND) OF AGENCY § 449, comment d (1958).

739. See generally 5 CORBIN ON CONTRACTS §§ 1054, 1057-63.

740. See generally 5 CORBIN ON CONTRACTS §§ 992, 997-98, 1038-39.

741. See generally 5 CORBIN ON CONTRACTS § 1038. But see Arnold v. Ray Charles Enterprises, Inc., 264 N.C. 92, 141 S.E.2d 14 (1965) (award not reduced by expenses).

742. Cf. Wisconsin Liquor Co. v. Park & Tilford Distillers Corp., 267 F.2d 928 (7th Cir. 1959); John B. Robeson Assoc. v. Gardens of Faith, Inc., 226 Md. 215, 172 A.2d 529 (1961).

743. See SEAVEY, AGENCY § 171.

The athlete may allege that the agent would not have been able to arrange the particular contracts which were eventually secured by other means. Or the agent may contend that he could have secured additional placements had his authority not been improperly revoked.[744] In each situation, the court must inquire as to the probability that the claimed commission would have been earned.[745]

It can be noted that in other related situations, there is an increasing tendency by courts to accept less certainty in the agent's proof of damages.[746] The apparent basis for a relaxation of the agent's burden is a desire to prevent the principal from benefiting from his wrongful termination.[747] But even in a jurisdiction which follows this more liberal rule, the agent will presumably still be required to show that there was a real possibility that the commission would have been earned. If a particular promotional venture was wholly speculative, the athlete should be able to claim the protection of the rule which disallows damages when the extent of the injury cannot be ascertained.[748]

b. The Duties of the Agent. The preceding discussion should serve to underscore the fact that the sports agent gains a considerable advantage from a contract which entitles him to serve as the exclusive representative of an athlete. As might be imagined, however, there are important legal duties which go with such status. The athlete has effectively limited his right to seek assistance from other sources and, thus, the realization of his economic potential as a professional athlete may be wholly dependent upon the efforts made by the party designated as agent.

What quality of representation can the athlete expect? This question can best be answered in terms of the general standards against which the agent's actions will be tested. Typically, the sports agent will perform a variety of different services which fall roughly into the categories of contract negotiation, investment advice, and promotional services.[749] It will be noted that the agent's performance of the first two tasks can be related to external standards. If the agent does an adequate job, the athlete's compensation under his playing contract will bear a reasonable relationship to that received by others with comparable skill. With respect to investments, the athlete ought to be able to expect a reasonable rate of return on his investment, subject, of course, to the normal risks which attend particular types of investments.[750] At the first level, the quality of the agent's representation in these matters will be judged against the level of skill possessed by others engaged in similar activities.[751] The sports

744. *See generally* 3 AM. JUR. 2D *Agency* § 260 (1962).

745. *See* 5 CORBIN ON CONTRACTS § 1025; RESTATEMENT (SECOND) OF AGENCY § 449, comment *d* (1958).

746. *See, e.g.,* Meyers v. Nolan, 18 Cal. App. 2d 319, 63 P.2d 1216 (Dist. Ct. App. 1936); John B. Robeson Assoc. v. Gardens of Faith, Inc., 226 Md. 215, 172 A.2d 529 (1961); Fister v. Henschel, 7 Mich. App. 590, 152 N.W.2d 555 (1967).

747. *See* 5 CORBIN ON CONTRACTS § 1020.

748. *See generally* 5 CORBIN ON CONTRACTS §§ 1020-22; 3 AM. JUR. 2D *Agency* § 260 (1962).

749. A typical management contract provides that the agent agrees to "1. Negotiate your employment contract or contracts as a professional athlete. 2. Advise you regarding financial investments and business opportunities. 3. Review tax saving possibilities. 4. Publicize and promote your name and abilities to benefit your reputation and possible draft position. 5. Seek profitable offers for your endorsements and service in Radio, T.V., Advertising, Merchandising, and other commercial fields." S. GALLNER, PRO SPORTS: THE CONTRACT GAME 174 (1974).

750. *See generally* SEAVEY, AGENCY § 27.

751. *See, e.g.,* Fleetwood Motors, Inc. v. John F. James & Sons, Inc., 38 Misc. 2d 499, 237 N.Y.S.2d 668 (Sup. Ct. 1963); RESTATEMENT (SECOND) OF AGENCY § 379 (1958); SEAVEY, AGENCY § 140; 3 AM. JUR. 2D *Agency* § 202 (1962).

agent who holds himself out as capable of negotiating sophisticated sports contracts or handling complicated investment plans must perform those tasks with the same expertise which is generally possessed by others in the trade.[752] This does not mean that the agent must always get the best possible contract, or that he must never make an investment which fails. It does mean, however, that he must adequately inform himself of the customs and practices of the trade and act in accordance with these.[753]

The agent's authority to handle the athlete's investments imposes additional duties beyond the general duty of care. The responsibility of the agent is similar to those of the trustee under a traditional trust arrangement.[754] Thus, the agent has a duty not to hold funds in unproductive accounts.[755] Moreover, he must invest only in such securities and business ventures "as would be obtained by a prudent investor for his own account, having in view both safety and income, in light of the principal's means and purposes." [756] Finally, he must monitor the investments and make appropriate adjustments when there are changes in the security of a particular venture.[757]

The agent's duties with respect to securing contracts for endorsements, personal appearances, and the like involve somewhat different responsibilities than those discussed above. In negotiating any contractual offers actually received, the agent, of course, must use the same degree of care previously identified. A separate question arises, however, as to the agent's duty to promote the athlete's services among potential sponsors. Whether the athlete eventually secures any publicity contracts will depend upon a great many factors not the least of which are the amount of time the agent devotes to the particular client, the agent's familiarity with the advertising industry, and his skill in developing a public image for the player. The legal standard which is used to judge the agent's performance requires, at a minimum, that the agent possess skill which is commensurate with his representation of his abilities.[758] But in addition he has an affirmative obligation to seek out placements for the athlete, for it is normally held that a grant of an exclusive agency imposes a duty on the agent to use his best efforts to secure the promised result.[759] Such a duty is implied from the fact that the principal is wholly dependent upon the agent by virtue of the exclusive nature of the authority granted.[760] In practical terms this means

---

752. See generally McCurin v. Kohlmeyer & Co., 347 F. Supp. 573 (E.D. La. 1972), aff'd, 477 F.2d 113 (5th Cir. 1973); United States Liability Ins. Co. v. Hardinger-Hayes, Inc., 1 Cal. 3d 586, 463 P.2d 770, 83 Cal. Rptr. 418 (1970); Highway Ins. Underwriters v. Lufkin-Beaumont Motor Coaches, Inc., 215 S.W.2d 904 (Tex. Civ. App. 1948).

753. See RESTATEMENT (SECOND) OF AGENCY § 379, comment c (1958).

754. See SEAVEY, AGENCY § 27.

755. See RESTATEMENT (SECOND) OF AGENCY § 425, comment e (1958).

756. Id. § 425, comment b at 291; cf. 3 A. SCOTT, THE LAW OF TRUSTS §§ 227.1-.3 (2d ed. 1956); see also Blondeau v. Sommer, 99 S.W.2d 668 (Tex. Civ. App. 1936); City Nat'l Bank v. Morgan, 258 S.W. 572 (Tex. Civ. App. 1924).

757. See RESTATEMENT (SECOND) OF AGENCY § 425, comment c (1958).

758. See id. § 379. See also Hardt v. Brink, 192 F. Supp. 879 (W.D. Wash. 1961); United States Liability Ins. Co. v. Hardinger-Hayes, Inc., 1 Cal. 3d 586, 463 P.2d 770, 83 Cal. Rptr. 418 (1970).

759. See, e.g., Heckard v. Park, 164 Kan. 216, 188 P.2d 926 (1948); Wood v. Lucy, Lady Duff-Gordon, 222 N.Y. 88, 118 N.E. 214 (1917); Tauchner v. Burnett, 32 Misc. 2d 839, 223 N.Y.S.2d 800 (Sup. Ct. 1961); cf. UNIFORM COMMERCIAL CODE § 2-306(2). See generally 3 CORBIN ON CONTRACTS § 567.

760. See Wood v. Lucy, Lady Duff-Gordon, 222 N.Y. 88, 118 N.E. 214 (1917) (Cardozo, J.).

that the athlete has no guarantee that the agent will ever secure one of these collateral contracts for his benefit. Nor is the agent required to expend time and effort beyond that which is justified by the athlete's level of achievement and reputation.[761] Yet, the agent cannot completely ignore his client. He must be able to show that he gave some attention to the matter of securing placements for the athlete.[762] And if his efforts are ever disputed, he presumably will be required to provide an explanation as to why he did not have greater success.[763]

It should be apparent from the preceding discussion that the athlete's dissatisfaction with his agent's work will not always be translatable into a legal cause of action. There are necessarily differences in the level of knowledge and skill possessed by the multitude of persons working in the sports management field. While the athlete will often be justified in thinking that he could have secured better services elsewhere, as a legal matter he can usually demand no more than a competent effort from the agent with whom he has contracted. This is not to suggest that the agent's duties are insubstantial. Indeed, even under the minimum legal standard, the agent who purports to offer a wide range of management services must be prepared to supply expertise in a number of complex areas. Whether the particular issue involves the quality of the agent's tax advice or his portfolio management, the athlete can insist that that which was promised is delivered. If it is not, he will not find the courts unreceptive to his claims.[764]

§ 3.19. Other Aspects of the Athlete-Agent Relationship.

a. Conflicts of Interest. Critics of the sports management business assert that players' agents are often insensitive to the potential conflicts which may arise between their own interests and those of the athlete. For example, it is alleged that significant problems are presented when an agent or his firm represents several different athletes. If two or more athletes are seeking contracts with the same team, there may be a tendency on the part of the agent to compromise one client's demands in order to secure a more favorable contract for another.[765] A similar problem may arise in connection with endorsements and other collateral arrangements. A manufacturer seeking to associate its products with well-known athletes may inquire about the terms upon which the services of various clients might be available. The agent is then put in a position of having to choose between several equally well-suited candidates. The athlete who is "screened out" by his agent might well have preferred that someone else represent him so that his interests could be more vigorously argued. Criticism is also directed to the manner in which agents negotiate their client's playing contracts. Questions are raised as to whether there is not a potential conflict

---

761. *Cf.* HML Corp. v. General Foods Corp., 365 F.2d 77 (3d Cir. 1966).

762. *See* Friedlander v. Stanley Products Inc., 24 Cal. App. 2d 677, 76 P.2d 145 (Dist. Ct. App. 1938).

763. *See* HML Corp. v. General Foods Corp., 365 F.2d 77 (3d Cir. 1966).

764. Burrow v. Probus Management, Inc., Civil No. 16840 (N.D. Ga., August 9, 1973), involved apparent misrepresentation by an agent of the extent of financial management which would be provided to his athlete-client. Because of the fraudulent nature of the promises which the agent made, the athlete not only recovered his actual losses but was also awarded $60,000 in punitive damages. The case is discussed in notes 709 and 714, § 3.17 *supra.*

765. *See* S. GALLNER, PRO SPORTS: THE CONTRACT GAME 68 (1974).

between the client's interest in having his income deferred as much as possible and the agent's interest in having the athlete receive sufficient cash to pay the agent's commission.[766] A similar conflict presumably could arise in connection with the agent's selection of investments.

There can be little dispute that the agent has a legal duty to avoid conflicts of interest in his representation of his athlete-clients.[767] However, when the principles which define that duty are applied to situations such as those identified above, many of the supposed conflicts will be found not to violate accepted legal standards. In this regard, the matter of multiple representation of athletes presents a somewhat different problem than the agent's efforts to protect his fee.

It should be apparent that a rule which prohibited an agent from representing athletes with potentially competing interests would have the effect of limiting the athlete's access to experienced counsel. The athlete may well feel that the desirability of having an agent with wide experience, which may include familiarity with the financial position and negotiating tactics of the club which will employ him, outweighs the potential disadvantages of utilizing a representative who must simultaneously accommodate the interests of other clients. At a minimum, there can be little debate that the athlete ought to be able to choose such a relationship if he desires. The relevant legal rules confirm this assessment. It is generally agreed that an agent is under a duty not to undertake to represent persons whose interests are in conflict.[768] But this proscription is not absolute and will be varied if there is express or implied acquiescence by the parties involved.[769] The usual way in which such approval is secured is through the agent's disclosure of his other relationships.[770] While a formal disclosure of the potential competing interest is the preferred mode,[771] the client's approval may be implied if joint representation is customary in the particular trade.[772]

The requisite degree of disclosure will generally be found in connection with the operation of the major firms and individuals who provide representation to athletes. The fact that they may represent several players with one club is usually well-known and is presumably accepted by new clients. To the extent

---

766. *See* Burrow v. Probus Management, Inc., Civil No. 16840 (N.D. Ga., Aug. 9, 1973) (unpublished order). This aspect of the *Burrow* cases is discussed in note 709, § 3.17 *supra*.

767. *See generally* RESTATEMENT (SECOND) OF AGENCY §§ 387, 394 (1958); W. SEAVEY, HANDBOOK OF THE LAW OF AGENCY §§ 147-54 (1964) [hereinafter cited as SEAVEY, AGENCY]; 3 AM. JUR. 2D, *Agency* §§ 220-25, 233-42 (1962).

768. *See, e.g.,* Merskey v. Multiple Listing Bureau, Inc., 73 Wash. 2d 225, 437 P.2d 897 (1968); Bockmuhl v. Jordan, 270 Wis. 14, 70 N.W.2d 26 (1955). *See generally* RESTATEMENT (SECOND) OF AGENCY § 394 (1958).

769. *See, e.g.,* McConnell v. Cowan, 44 Cal. 2d 805, 807, 285 P.2d 261, 265 (1955); Bell v. Strauch, 40 Tenn. App. 384, 292 S.W.2d 59 (1955).

770. *See* Bell v. Strauch, 40 Tenn. App. 384, 292 S.W.2d 59 (1955); Merskey v. Multiple Listing Bureau, Inc., 73 Wash. 2d 225, 437 P.2d 897 (1968); RESTATEMENT (SECOND) OF AGENCY §§ 392, 394, comment *b* (1958); SEAVEY, AGENCY § 150; 2 AM. JUR. 2D, *Agency* § 234 (1962).

771. Some of the standard form contracts used in the movie industry specifically recognize that the agent may represent other clients with competing interests. *See* Annot., 175 A.L.R. 617, 637 (1948). *Compare* S. GALLNER, PRO SPORTS: THE CONTRACT GAME 174-76 (1974).

772. *See* RESTATEMENT (SECOND) OF AGENCY § 394, comment *b* at 219 (1958). *Compare* 3 AM. JUR 2D § 235 (1962).

that there is an area for concern, it may be in connection with individuals, such as coaches, teachers, and lawyers, who undertake player representation as an incidental venture. In these situations, the agent would be well advised to make an express disclosure of any relationship which may present conflicts. But in the case of both the established firm and the more informal operator, mere disclosure of competing interests does not leave the agent with unlimited discretion to prefer one client over another. The player agent still has a duty to treat each client's interest fairly.[773] This requires that proper attention be given to the needs of each client and that the representative act impartially in accommodating their respective interests.[774] A preference of one client over another must be made for justifiable reasons. To the extent that the agent carries out his duties with disregard for his basic obligation to each client, the athlete may pursue the legal remedies which are available.[775]

With respect to conflicts other than those generated by an agent's representation of multiple clients, the standard against which the representative's action will be judged is the fundamental duty of loyalty which every agent owes to his principal. The agent is a fiduciary with respect to matters within the scope of his agency,[776] and he must take no actions which are detrimental to the economic or social interests of the principal.[777] The agent is particularly forbidden from entering into competition with his client[778] or from otherwise taking actions which have the effect of preferring his interests over those of the party which he has been hired to represent.[779] The strictness of these principles can be modified by agreement, however.[780] Thus, the parties may undertake, by formal contract, tacit agreement, or trade custom, to define the agent's obligation in particular circumstances. The client may consent to the arrangements designed to protect the self-interest of the agent and may even approve having the agent act as an adverse party.[781]

Many of the disputes which will arise in the sports area will raise the question of whether the client had effectively consented to actions taken by the agent on his own behalf. That issue is presented, for example, where the agent structures the compensation term of the athlete's employment contract so as to insure that cash is available to pay his commission. Even though the client

---

773. *See* RESTATEMENT (SECOND) OF AGENCY § 392, comment *a*. *But see id.* at § 394, comment *b:* "It is much easier to find that an agent is privileged to act for a competitor than to find that an agent is privileged to act for an adverse party, since acting for a competitor has merely a tendency to reduce the allegiance of the agent and not, as where the agent is acting for an adverse party, to cause him to give improper advice or to take improper action." *See also* SEAVEY, AGENCY § 150.

774. *Compare* SEAVEY, AGENCY § 149.

775. *See generally* RESTATEMENT (SECOND) OF AGENCY §§ 387, 399 (1958).

776. *See generally* SEAVEY, AGENCY §§ 140, 147.

777. *See, e.g.,* Nye v. Lovelace, 288 F.2d 599 (5th Cir. 1956); Baskin v. Dain, 4 Conn. Cir. 702, 239 A.2d 549 (1967); Cox v. Bryant, 347 S.W.2d 861 (Mo. 1961); Kribbs v. Jackson, 387 Pa. 611, 129 A.2d 490 (1957). *See generally* RESTATEMENT (SECOND) OF AGENCY § 387 (1958).

778. *See generally* SEAVEY, AGENCY §§ 149-51; 3 AM. JUR. 2D, *Agency* § 222 (1962); RESTATEMENT (SECOND) OF AGENCY § 393 (1958).

779. *See, e.g.,* Batson v. Strehlow, 68 Cal. 2d 662, 441 P.2d 101, 68 Cal. Rptr. 589 (1968); Blakely v. Bradley, 281 S.W.2d 835 (Mo. 1955); Ledirk Amusement Co. v. Shechner, 125 N.J. Eq. 209, 37 A.2d 823 (Ct. Err. & App. 1944).

780. *See generally* RESTATEMENT (SECOND) OF AGENCY §§ 387, 389-92 (1958).

781. *See, e.g.,* Phillips Petroleum Co. v. Peterson, 218 F.2d 926 (10th Cir. 1954); Moore v. DeGuire, 125 F.2d 486 (2d Cir. 1942); Fisher v. Lasey, 78 Cal. App. 2d 121, 177 P.2d 334 (Dist. Ct. App. 1947); Bell v. Strauch, 40 Tenn. App. 384, 292 S.W.2d 59 (1955).

might receive more favorable tax treatment under a different arrangement,[782] the parties are presumably free to agree between themselves how the athlete's obligations to the agent will be satisfied. A provision for a substantial initial payment may be seen as simply a method of providing security for the agent's claim.[783] If the athlete raises a complaint, it will usually be because he did not appreciate the consequences of the compensation arrangement, particularly where he finds himself short of cash despite a seemingly lucrative contract. The reputable agent, of course, will both explain the implications of the particular compensation arrangement and insure that the athlete has a cash flow adequate to meet living expenses. But even where these actions are not taken, the athlete will have a difficult time showing that he had not agreed to meet his obligation to his agent out of the initial payments under the contract.[784]

Situations suggesting outright deception or secretive double dealing by the agent will cause less difficulty. Clearly the agent's duty of loyalty to the athlete is breached in these circumstances, and remedies will be available for the injury which is caused. Despite the general dearth of reported precedent in this area, there are strong indications that the courts have little patience with those who take unconscionable advantage of unsuspecting athletes.[785]

b. The Duration of the Agency Contract. It should be apparent at this point in the discussion that the relationship between an athlete and his agent is one of contract. As with other such relationships the parties are given considerable freedom to specify the terms which govern their particular arrangement, including the term which specifies the duration of the contract.[786] Thus the parties may expressly provide that the agency relationship will continue for a stated period of years. In the absence of a specific provision of this sort, the general rule is that the agency relationship will continue for a reasonable period of time.[787] In the sports area, however, additional factors will be weighed to determine the duration of the contract which does not specify its own termination date. The precise scope of the agent's authority will have to be considered.[788] More particularly it must be determined whether the agent has been appointed for the limited purpose of negotiating the athlete's contract with his club or whether his authorization is broader and includes such additional duties as handling of the athlete's investments and securing endorsement and appearance contracts. If the agent is only to represent the athlete in a single contract negotiation with the club, then the agent's contract rights will terminate upon the completion of the particular performance.[789] On the other

782. *See generally* ch. 7 *infra.*
783. *Compare* Seavey, Agency § 176 (agent's lien).
784. *See* Seavey, Agency § 169.
785. *See* Burrow v. Probus Management, Inc., Civil No. 16840 (N.D. Ga., Aug. 9, 1973) (unpublished order) ($60,000 punitive damages awarded for gross misrepresentation by player's agents of extent and quality of services to be provided).
786. *See generally* Seavey, Agency § 170.
787. *See* Restatement (Second) of Agency § 105 (1958). *See also* Seavey, Agency § 170, ¶¶ A, C.
788. *Compare* Jack's Cookie Co. v. Brooks, 227 F.2d 935 (4th Cir. 1955); Glassell v. Prentiss, 175 Cal. App. 2d 599, 346 P.2d 895 (Dist. Ct. App. 1959); Cummings v. Kelling Nut Co., 368 Pa. 448, 84 A.2d 323 (1951).
789. *See, e.g.,* Robinson v. Merrill, Lynch, Pierce, Fenner & Smith, Inc., 337 F. Supp. 107, 111 (N.D. Ala. 1971), *aff'd,* 453 F.2d 417 (5th Cir. 1972); Holland v. Parry Navigation Co., 7 F.R.D. 471 (E.D. Pa. 1947); Restatement (Second) of Agency § 106 (1958).

hand, where the relationship is one which contemplates more extensive management services, the relationship, in the absence of agreement to the contrary, will be said to continue for a period which is reasonable in light of the objectives which are sought to be accomplished, the formality of the arrangement, and similar considerations.[790]

It should be noted that the issue of the duration of the agent's contract is different from the question of the athlete's right to terminate the agent's authority.[791] The player may at any time revoke previously granted authority, and thereafter the agent has no right to act on behalf of the athlete.[792] This power to strip the agent of his authority is unaffected by a term in the contract which specifies that the arrangement is an exclusive one or otherwise guarantees its continuance for a definite term.[793] The effect of such a clause, of course, is to give the agent an action in damages for the athlete's breach of the contract. In the event the agency is revoked before the end of the term, the agent will still be entitled to compensation for the injury he suffers when his further performance under the contract is prevented.[794] He may not, however, bind the athlete to contracts with third persons once his agency is effectively revoked.[795]

The question sometimes arises as to whether there are not limitations on the extent to which an agent can bind the athlete to a long term management contract. If his initial bargaining position is relatively weak, the young, unproven athlete may agree to terms in such an arrangement which are quite unfavorable when he later achieves superstar status.[796] Although the question is seldom litigated, it is clear that the parties' freedom to specify the duration of their contract is not unlimited. The limitations which do exist are manifestations of a public policy prohibiting excessive restraints on an individual's freedom to market his services.[797] This policy is sometimes expressed in statutes controlling particular types of management contracts. Thus, legislative regulations covering the sport of boxing commonly provide that contracts between the athlete and his manager may not exceed a stated period.[798] A more general

---

790. *See* RESTATEMENT (SECOND) OF AGENCY § 105, comment *b* (1958). *See also* cases cited note 788 *supra.*

791. *See generally* SEAVEY, AGENCY §§ 46, 170.

792. *See, e.g.,* Kravetz v. United Artists Corp., 143 N.Y.S.2d 539, 550 (Sup. Ct. 1955), *aff'd,* 2 N.Y.2d 880, 141 N.E.2d 623 (1957); Wilson Sullivan Co. v. International Paper Makers Realty Corp., 307 N.Y. 20, 25, 118 N.E.2d 573, 574 (1954).

793. *See, e.g.,* N.L.R.B. v. Marcus Trucking Co., 286 F.2d 583 (2d Cir. 1961); Shumaker v. Hazen, 372 P.2d 873 (Okla. 1962); Spence v. Northern Virginia Doctors Hosp. Corp., 202 Va. 478, 117 S.E.2d 657 (1961).

794. *See generally* SEAVEY, AGENCY §§ 171, 172; RESTATEMENT (SECOND) OF AGENCY § 118 (1958).

795. It can be noted, however, that a termination of the agent's authority may not become effective as to third parties until they have received notice of that fact. *See, e.g.,* Fischer Co. v. Morrison, 137 Conn. 399, 78 A.2d 242 (1951); Trane Co. v. Williams, 143 So. 2d 119 (La. App. 1962); Bernhagen v. Marathon Fin. Co., 212 Wis. 495, 250 N.W. 410 (1933). *See generally* SEAVEY, AGENCY §§ 51-53.

796. *Cf.* George Foreman Assoc. Ltd. v. Foreman, 389 F. Supp. 1308 (N.D. Cal.), *aff'd,* 517 F.2d 354 (9th Cir. 1975).

797. A similar question arises in connection with the negative covenants found in contracts between an athlete and his club, or an athlete and his promoter. *See generally* § 4.05 *infra.*

798. *See, e.g., id.;* Baksi v. Wallman, 271 App. Div. 422, 65 N.Y.S.2d 894 (1946), *aff'd,* 297 N.Y. 456, 74 N.E.2d 172 (1947). Other aspects of the public regulation of certain sports contracts are discussed in more detail in § 2.14, *supra.*

application of the policy is reflected in cases disapproving overly broad exclusive agency relationships as restraints on trade.

Even if the contract does not explicitly so state, an agreement that the agent will have the exclusive right to represent an athlete for a stated period will usually be construed to include an implied covenant of non-competition for the term of the contract.[799] This aspect of the contract will be subjected to the same general principles which apply to other restraints on competition, and a court may properly inquire as to whether the scope of the agent's claim is not so broad as to offend public policy.[800] However, the type of restraint under consideration here typically endures only for the term of the agreement employing the agent and thus is not scrutinized as vigorously as a covenant which seeks to bind a party after he has terminated his relationship with another.[801] The important difference is that the promisor — the athlete in the present situation — is not foreclosed from all access to the relevant market, but still has his agent to promote his interests.[802] Thus, whatever the outside limit on the duration of this type of agency contract, it presumably will be longer than that tolerated with respect to a naked promise not to compete.[803] Other factors to be considered in assessing the reasonableness of the period covered by the contract include such things as the amount of effort which the agent has expended in developing the athlete's placements, particularly in regard to advertising activities; financial commitments which are made in connection with the agent's representation; and the general equality of the parties' bargaining positions at the time the contract was made.[804]

---

799. *See generally* § 4.04 *infra.*

800. *See, e.g.,* Greer v. Lifsey, 128 Ga. App. 785, 197 S.E.2d 846 (1973); Heckard v. Park, 164 Kan. 216, 188 P.2d 926 (1948). *See generally* 6A A. CORBIN, CORBIN ON CONTRACTS §§ 1404, 1411-13 (1962); § 4.05 *infra.*

801. *See* 6A A. CORBIN, CORBIN ON CONTRACTS § 1411 (1962).

802. *See generally* § 3.18 *supra.*

803. *But see* Greer v. Lifsey, 128 Ga. App. 785, 197 S.E.2d 846 (1973) (disapproving a five-year exclusive management contract).

804. *See, e.g.,* Heckard v. Park, 164 Kan. 216, 188 P.2d 926 (1948). There are a number of cases in which management contracts of five years duration in the movie industry have been enforced, although generally without specific discussion of the reasonableness of their length. *See* Annot., 175 A.L.R. 617 (1948).

CHAPTER 4

Enforcement of Professional Sports Contracts

§ 4.01. The Coverage of This Chapter.

The present chapter considers some of the legal issues which arise in connection with the enforcement of professional sports contracts. The initial sections give attention to the doctrine which defines the club's right to judicial relief when an athlete breaches his employment contract. Such a breach usually occurs when the player repudiates his existing contract and accepts employment with another club. As will be seen, traditional legal remedies, particularly the remedy of money damages, are generally not available in these situations. Rather, the club will seek equitable relief in the form of an injunction enforcing the athlete's promise to perform exclusively for the plaintiff club for the period covered by the contract.[1]

The availability of equitable enforcement in the event of the player's abandonment of his contract is by no means a foregone conclusion. An injunction has historically been regarded as an extraordinary form of relief and is generally said to be available only when the plaintiff establishes that other types of remedies would not provide adequate compensation for the injury sustained. Moreover, a court of equity retains wide discretion in the exercise of its enforcement powers and the plaintiff must make a particular showing that it is entitled to the special protection of equity.

The specialized nature of equitable remedies gives rise to a number of issues which are of particular importance in the sports context. These are considered below. Attention is given to the requirement that the contract which is the basis of the plaintiff's suit be one which the court of equity could in good conscience enforce.[2] Relatedly, it is necessary to consider cases which have denied equitable

1. See § 4.02 infra.
2. See § 4.13 infra.

relief because the plaintiff itself has engaged in inequitable conduct and thus brought itself within the doctrine of unclean hands.[3] The terms of the athlete's employment contract also come under scrutiny in connection with the doctrine which would deny the enforceability of contracts which lack mutuality. While this doctrine was once a major impediment to the club's efforts to secure equitable relief, it now has much less significance. One section of the discussion which follows considers the origins of the requirement of mutuality and its role in present-day proceedings for equitable relief.[4]

Attention is also given to the nature of the injury which the club sustains when a player jumps to another team. In order to establish that the remedies at law would be inadequate, many courts require that the defendant-athlete possess unique skills, a requirement which is usually satisfied where a professional athlete is involved.[5] This subtopic also presents the occasion for a more careful examination of situations in which a remedy in the form of money damages might be fashioned.[6] Finally, a portion of the following discussion focuses on the sometimes troublesome principle that an employee is subject to injunction only if he engages in "unfair" competition with his original employer.[7]

A team's efforts to protect its contract rights will occasionally draw it into litigation with other clubs which attempt to hire away its athletes. Thus, it is necessary to consider the legal doctrine which creates a cause of action for tortious interference with contract. The appearance of new leagues in several sports in the 1960's and 1970's added to the legal precedent in this area, and it will be seen that considerable progress has been made in defining the legal bounds which must be observed as teams compete for another's players.[8]

There are many controversies which arise in connection with sports contracts which do not involve the unique problems raised when a player jumps to another club. Indeed, as the discussion in chapter 3 suggests, there will be numerous occasions for disputes between an athlete and his club as to whether the respective obligations under the contract have been met. Often the issues will concern whether the club acted properly in terminating the player's contract or in otherwise taking some adverse action, such as the imposition of disciplinary sanctions. It is increasingly true that the parties to professional sports contracts have agreed to forego traditional forms of litigation to resolve disputes of this sort and have instead obligated themselves to submit their private controversies to arbitration. Such agreements to arbitrate are common not only in contracts between players and clubs but also in the agreements which define the relationship between clubs within a league.

Although the device of arbitration in commercial settings is by no means of recent origin, developments both in the sports area and on a more general level suggest that this is a subject which deserves particular attention in the present treatise. The following discussion attempts to present a general review of the most important legal questions which are likely to arise.[9] Among the topics

---

3. *See* § 4.12 *infra.*
4. *See* § 4.11 *infra.*
5. *See* § 4.07 *infra.*
6. *See* § 4.09 *infra.*
7. *See* § 4.10 *infra.*
8. *See* § 4.14 *infra.*
9. *See* §§ 4.15-4.20 *infra.*

considered is the rather basic issue of whether controversies are to be resolved under federal or state law, an issue about which there has recently been some confusion.[10] Also considered is the scope of the arbitrator's authority and the respective roles of courts and arbitrators in producing a final resolution of the substantive and procedural controversies which arise under an agreement to arbitrate.[11]

Some of the arbitration agreements in professional sports designate the league commissioner as the party to serve as arbitrator. The commissioner's role in this regard has been the subject of much controversy. Because the commissioner is usually hired and paid by club owners, doubts have been raised about the commissioner's ability to remain impartial in disputes between clubs and players. The specific objections which have been raised, and the legal principles which will guide their resolution, are discussed below.[12]

The final sections of this chapter consider the basic question of the judicial forums which are available for the resolution of legal complaints against an athlete or a club.[13] The discussion which is presented has general application in the sports area. It is relevant not only for traditional breach of contract actions, but also in connection with a club's requests for equitable relief as well as proceedings for judicial review of arbitration controversies. The jurisdictional issues which arise in the sports context warrant special attention because of the unique aspects of the sports industry. The activities of clubs usually involve contacts with several states, any of which might be the plaintiff's preferred forum in a particular case.[14] By the same token, athletes are distinctively mobile and often establish relationships which would support jurisdiction in more than one forum.[15] The determination of a defendant's vulnerability to suit in a particular court requires application of rather general constitutional principles. The task which is undertaken here is to define more precisely the manner in which these concepts will be applied in the sports context.

§ 4.02. Judicial Enforcement of Player Contracts: The Nature of the Remedy.

By virtue of the contracts entered into with its individual players, a professional sports team obtains rights to its players' services which may have significant economic value. When an athlete breaches his contract, by jumping to another club or otherwise, his original employer will predictably turn to the courts for assistance in securing the economic advantage to which it believes it is entitled. While the normal rule is that one who breaches a contract must either provide the promised performance or provide its equivalent value in money, the professional sports team will find that the peculiar characteristics of its contracts limit its access to these traditional contract remedies. In lieu of direct enforcement of the athlete's promise to play, the club will normally be forced to seek a specialized form of equitable relief which limits the player's right to perform for others.

---

10. *See* § 4.15 *infra.*
11. *See* §§ 4.15, 4.18, 4.20 *infra.*
12. *See* § 4.19 *infra.*
13. *See* §§ 4.21-4.22 *infra.*
14. *See* § 4.21 *infra.*
15. *See* § 4.22 *infra.*

The uniqueness of the contract remedies in the sports context can be seen by a comparison with the type of relief normally afforded for the breach of a more typical commercial contract, such as one involving a sale of goods. The basic goal of contract remedies in the commercial context is to give the injured party the benefit of the bargain. Thus, the usual forms of judicial relief are designed to place the injured party in roughly the same economic position it would have enjoyed had the contract been fully performed. In contracts for the sale of goods the desired result can be achieved by an award of money damages. A disappointed buyer in such an arrangement will usually complain that the breaching seller had promised to deliver goods at a price which was less than the price at which equivalent goods are now available from other sources. The "advantage" which the buyer gained from this contract can be secured by a judicial order directing the seller to pay the buyer the difference between the market value of the promised performance and the amount which the buyer would have had to pay under the original contract.[16] The theory of such an award is that it gives to the buyer the true economic value of the performance which the seller promised to render, and the buyer is assured that he can go into the marketplace, secure a fully equivalent substitute performance, and pay no more than he would have under the original agreement. In some cases, of course, the goods involved are unique, so that the market offers no adequate substitute. Since money damages will not provide adequate compensation for the injury which has been caused, the law provides for extraordinary forms of relief in this situation. Consistent with the goal of giving the injured party the benefit of its contract, the injured party is entitled to an order compelling the defendant to perform exactly as he had promised, which, in the case of unique goods, will direct him to deliver the specific items covered by the contract.[17]

The remedial options available to a sports team seeking to enforce a player contract stand in rather sharp contrast to these traditional forms of relief. The team, of course, has as keen an interest in realizing the benefit of its bargain as any disappointed plaintiff. The primary benefit of its contract is the right to utilize the player's talents in connection with its efforts to field a competitive team which will attract public attention and thus generate revenues from ticket sales, concession receipts and television contracts. When the team goes to court to enforce its right to the player's performance, it will usually find that the normal remedy of money damages is unavailable. The services of star players are unique, and money damages would not enable the team to "buy" an equivalent performance from someone else, since, by definition, no exact equivalent is available.[18] Moreover, the amount of damages which flows from the athlete's breach is not susceptible to quantification. Because so many individuals and such diverse external factors influence the financial success of

---

16. *See* Uniform Commercial Code § 2-713.

17. *See* Uniform Commercial Code § 2-716.

18. Various courts have recognized the unique type of injury which is caused by a player's defection from an established team. *See* Philadelphia Ball Club v. Lajoie, 202 Pa. 210, 217, 51 A. 973, 974 (1902) ("The defendant is an expert baseball player in any position; . . . he has a great reputation as a second baseman; . . . his place would be hard to fill with as good a player; . . . his withdrawal from the team would weaken it, as would the withdrawal of any good player, and would probably make a difference in the size of the audiences attending the game."); Long Island American Ass'n Football Club, Inc. v. Manrodt, 23 N.Y.S.2d 858, 860 (Sup. Ct. 1940) ("Once the team is organized and the Football season begins, it may be extremely difficult to find adequate replacements for players about whom plays have been planned.")

a team, the effect of the loss of any one player, even the best player, is thought to be wholly speculative.[19]

Because the promised performance is legally irreplaceable, it might appear that the policies which compel specific performance in other contexts would warrant a similar response where a sports team is the disappointed plaintiff. However, the basic difference between a promise to render services rather than deliver inanimate goods precludes an extension of the traditional rule. As recognized in the *Restatement of Contracts*

> A promise to tender personal services . . . will not be specifically enforced by an affirmative decree.[20]

This principle has repeatedly been recognized, and reaffirmed, in litigation involving entertainers, generally, and athletes, in particular.[21]

Various reasons are put forth in support of this result. At one level, there is concern for the pragmatic problems of determining whether the athlete's performance was in compliance with the decree. In addition, there is an overriding concern that the power of the courts not be used to compel the performance of personal acts against the will of the performer.[22] With respect to the former, there is concern that even if the court were to order the athlete to perform, the matter would not end there. If, in subsequent appearances, the athlete did not perform up to what the club perceived as his capacity, the court might be called upon to adjudge that the athlete was not in compliance with the prior decree, the normal remedy for which would be a finding that the athlete was in contempt and therefore subject to further judicial penalties.[23] This prospect raises a variety of administrative problems for the court. It would be difficult, if not impossible, to ascertain whether the athlete's less-than-satisfactory performance represented a refusal to abide by the judicial decree or whether it was, in fact, the result of totally unrelated physical or emotional problems. The factors which influence the athlete's performance on a given day are truly innumerable and, in most cases, not subject to precise identification. Closely related to this concern is the prospect that the issue could arise repeatedly. Even if the court could make a judgment about the sincerity of a particular performance, that would not necessarily end the inquiry, as the team could theoretically call for a judicial evaluation any time the player performed poorly.[24] Thus, in order to avoid involving themselves in the constant supervision of the parties' further contractual relationships, the courts have

---

19. *See generally* RESTATEMENT OF CONTRACTS § 361 (1932). The difficulty of measuring the damages caused by a player's breach of his contract is considered more fully below. *See* §§ 4.07-4.09 *infra.*

20. RESTATEMENT OF CONTRACTS § 379 (1932).

21. *See, e.g.,* Allegheny Base-Ball Club v. Bennett, 14 F. 257, 260 (W.D. Pa. 1882); American League Baseball Club v. Chase, 86 Misc. 441, 443, 149 N.Y.S. 6, 8 (Sup. Ct. 1914); Metropolitan Exhibition Co. v. Ward, 9 N.Y.S. 779, 780 (Sup. Ct. 1890); Harrisburg Base-Ball Club v. Athletic Ass'n, 8 Pa. County Ct. 337, 338 (1890); Ford v. Jermon, 6 Phil. Rep. 6, 7 (1865).

22. *See* RESTATEMENT OF CONTRACTS § 379, comment *d* (1932). A thorough discussion of the various policies supporting the courts' refusal to grant affirmative relief can be found in STEVENS, *Involuntary Servitude by Injunction,* 6 CORNELL L.Q. 235, 239-47 (1921).

23. D. DOBBS, HANDBOOK ON THE LAW OF REMEDIES §§ 2.8-2.9 (1973).

24. These problems of shaping an effective decree were specifically addressed in one of the earliest cases of this sort in the entertainment law area. In explaining why it would not order an actress to fulfill her promise to perform for the plaintiff, the court in Ford v. Jermon, 6 Phil. Rep. 6, 7 (1865), observed that "[i]n order to render such a decree effectual, it would be necessary to

determined that the player's promise to perform is not one for breach of which a specific remedy is available.[25]

The second consideration, while less pragmatic in nature, has been found equally compelling. Courts have generally agreed that it would be repugnant to our system of jurisprudence to compel an individual to continue in the personal service of another against his will. To decree specific performance in this situation carries overtones of involuntary servitude, a type of relationship which at the time the earliest cases were decided, had been recently made the object of a specific prohibition in the Thirteenth Amendment of the United States Constitution.[26] While a court would have no reservations about awarding damages where appropriate, it is a much different matter to require an individual to accept a particular type of employment, since a basic premise of our governmental system is that the individual retains a wide range of prerogatives in choosing those with whom he will be intimately associated. The noteworthy feature of the courts' acceptance of this proposition is that it is often given recognition even though the individual has seemingly acted voluntarily in binding himself by contract to the plaintiff.[27] Despite this element of volition and despite the allegiance which is otherwise given to the principle of integrity of contractual promises, courts have seen the principles of personal freedom as occupying a clearly more predominant role.[28]

The plaintiff-team thus finds itself in a much different position than most parties who have been injured by a breach of contract. While an injured plaintiff is normally assured that he will receive either the promised performance or its market value equivalent, the club seeking to enforce a player contract usually has neither of these remedies. Indeed, the primary right which such a contract creates — the right to the player's service — is a right only to the extent that the promisor-athlete chooses to comply with the agreement; it is not a right for which there is a specific, compensating remedy. But this is not to suggest that the club does not have the benefit of judicial assistance in its efforts to secure the economic advantage for which it bargained. Judicial remedies are available, but they are of a different sort than those which normally obtain in breach of contract situations.

---

appoint a master whose duty should be to frequent the theatre and decide whether the mistakes or incongruities by which the part might be disfigured, were in contempt of the order of the court or unintentional." Interestingly, the court also saw this as a reason for denying any enforcement of the actress' negative covenant not to perform for others during the term of her contract. *Id.* at 7.

25. *See* Harrisburg Base-Ball Club v. Athletic Ass'n, 8 Pa. County Ct. 337 (1890); Philadelphia Ball Club, Ltd. v. Hallman, 8 Pa. County Ct. 57 (1890).

26. The tension between judicially enforced personal service and the thirteenth amendment has been recognized by the Supreme Court in other contexts. *See* Bouley v. Alabama, 219 U.S. 219 (1911); United States v. Reynolds, 235 U.S. 133 (1914). From these cases one commentator has gleaned the principle that "a contract of service from which the law permits no release except by the performance of the service produces a condition of involuntary servitude." STEVENS, *Involuntary Servitude by Injunction, supra* note 22, at 247.

27. *See, e.g.,* American Base Ball & Athletic Exhibition Co. v. Harper, 54 CENT. L.J. 449 (Cir. Ct. St. Louis 1902).

28. *See, e.g.,* Madison Square Garden Corp. v. Braddock, 19 F. Supp. 392, 393 (D.N.J. 1937). One court, considering the same issue in a somewhat different context, dismissed the alleged voluntariness of the association created by the contract, by finding that the fundamental right of personal liberty was not one which could be "bartered away by contract or consent," and that, thus, any contractual provision which seemed to have that effect was void as contrary to law. American Base Ball & Athletic Exhibition Co. v. Harper, 54 CENT. L.J. 449, 451 (Cir. Ct. St. Louis 1902).

The typical player's contract includes two different promises which are relevant to this discussion of remedies. One is the player's promise to perform for the team which, as mentioned, is the primary benefit which the team hopes to secure. But the club typically also exacts a promise that the athlete will not perform for any other club during the term of the contract.[29] Because of the speculative nature of the losses which would result from a breach, money damages would again not be an appropriate means of securing the benefit of this covenant. On the other hand, specific enforcement of this negative promise does not require the court to compel any specific action by the player and thus, does not seem to involve the same element of compulsion and administration which has prompted courts to refuse to order performance of the player's affirmative promise to play for the team. In light of the limitations of the availability of other forms of judicial assistance, it is not surprising that specific enforcement of this negative covenant has evolved as the club's primary remedy under its player contracts. And even though the available judicial relief extends only to this secondary promise not to perform for others, as might be expected, the legal distinction between that covenant and the athlete's promise to actually perform for the team loses its significance in practice. While the athlete could fully comply with the negative decree by merely sitting out for the duration of his contract and refusing to rejoin the club, the economic consequences of such a decision are usually sufficiently adverse that he will be prompted to rejoin the club when his negative covenant is specifically enforced.[30] Thus, while the club does not have the same assurances as other contracting parties that the benefit of its bargain can be secured in the courts, it is the beneficiary of independent economic forces which are likely to produce the same result.

It is important to note that the availability of specific enforcement of the player's negative covenant has not always been wholeheartedly accepted by the courts. The origin of the remedy is relatively recent by common law standards, and the court's acceptance of the propriety of the remedy evolved only gradually. Indeed, the rather unique remedy of the negative injunction originated in 1852 in the English case, *Lumley v. Wagner*.[31] In that case, the famous opera singer, Johanna Wagner, had entered into a contract with the plaintiff, Benjamin Lumley, to deliver certain specified operatic performances in a theatre which the plaintiff had rented. By specific agreement, Wagner agreed that she would not "use her talents at any other theatre, nor in any concert or reunion, public

---

29. *See* § 4.04 *infra.*

30. In most cases, the athlete would suffer significant financial detriment if he chose not to rejoin the team since his non-athletic endeavors are not likely to generate a salary comparable to that which he earns as an athlete. *See* Scoville, *Labor Relations in Sports* in GOVERNMENT AND THE SPORTS BUSINESS 188-89, 194-95 (R. Noll ed. 1974). Apart from financial considerations, the athlete who is subjected to a negative injunction may choose to rejoin his team to avoid other negative consequences of sitting out. Among these are the risks that (1) a period of inactivity will adversely affect his playing skills, (2) that the salability of his sports talents will be reduced if he removes himself from the limelight for a long period and (3) that a period of inactivity will reduce his attractiveness to advertisers who might otherwise pay him to endorse their products.

While the reaction of most athletes is to resume performance under their original contracts, there have been notable exceptions. A recent example is the basketball star, Rick Barry, who chose to temporarily withdraw from the sport when he was enjoined from jumping to a rival league. *See* Washington Capitols Basketball Club, Inc. v. Barry, 304 F. Supp. 1193 (N.D. Cal.), *aff'd,* 419 F.2d 472 (9th Cir. 1969); Lemat Corp. v. Barry, 275 Cal. App. 2d 671, 80 Cal. Rptr. 240 (1969).

31. 1 De G.M. & G. 604, 42 Eng. Rep. 687 (1852).

or private, without the written authorization of Mr. Lumley." [32] During the term of this agreement, Wagner entered into a contract to perform for another theatre manager, and Lumley brought suit in equity seeking to restrain Wagner from performing under her new arrangement.

The court, speaking through Lord St. Leonards, examined at length the various precedents on the question of equitable enforcement. By a process of distinguishing several analogous cases and declaring others to be wrongly decided, the judge reached the conclusion that Lumley was entitled to the restraining order requested. As perceived by Lord St. Leonards, the basic principle at hand was the integrity of one person's contractual commitment to perform services for another. Having thus framed the issue, he had little difficulty in finding the proper resolution: the stability of the contractual relationship should be insured, even though it is accepted that the breaching party would not be affirmatively compelled to give her services. In the judge's view

> Wherever this court has not proper jurisdiction to [affirmatively] enforce specific performance, it operates to bind men's consciences, as far as they can be bound, to a true and literal performance of their agreements. . . . The exercise of this jurisdiction has, I believe, had a wholesome tendency towards the maintenance of that good faith which exists in this country to a much greater degree perhaps than in any other. . . . [33]

Wagner pressed the objection that it seemed inconsistent to use the negative restraining order to bind her to the contract when the court clearly lacked power to order her to fulfill her commitment to work for Lumley. The court agreed that the "injunction may . . . tend to the fulfillment of her engagement" with Lumley, but the jurist specifically disclaimed the notion that he was "doing indirectly what I cannot do directly." [34]

The integration of *Lumley v. Wagner* into American law came about rather slowly. A Pennsylvania court in 1865, in one of the earliest decisions interpreting *Lumley,* regarded the case as anomalous and thought it not clearly consistent with earlier precedent.[35] The *Lumley* doctrine gained major support when, in 1874, it was accepted by the courts of New York, which have otherwise played a predominant role in shaping the principles governing the entertainment law field.[36] Doubts still lingered for some time in other jurisdictions,[37] as some

---

32. *Id.* at 606, 42 Eng. Rep. at 688.

33. *Id.* at 619, 42 Eng. Rep. at 693.

34. *Id.* at 620, 42 Eng. Rep. at 693. Whatever the court's hopes that its decree against Wagner might encourage her "to the fulfillment of her engagement," Lumley apparently never got the benefit of Wagner's further services and instead was left to pursue his damage remedies against the party who induced the breach of contract. *See* Lumley v. Gye, 2 El. & Bl. 216, 118 Eng. Rep. 749 (1853).

35. Ford v. Jermon, 6 Phil. Rep. 6 (1865). In commenting on *Lumley,* the court stated that "the fact that amidst the multitude of quarrels that have . . . disturbed the stage, there has been but one instance of such interference, may be thought to indicate that it should be regarded as a warning rather than followed as precedent." *Id.* at 7.

36. *See* Daly v. Smith, 38 N.Y. Super. Ct. Rep. 158 (1874).

37. The uncertain reception given *Lumley v. Wagner* is reflected in three Pennsylvania cases decided within four months of one another in 1890. The first, Philadelphia Ball Club, Ltd. v. Hallman, 8 Pa. County Ct. 57, 59 (1890), announced that "the decision in *Lumley v. Wagner* has . . . been generally followed both in England and in this country." Three months later this pronouncement by the *Hallman* court was regarded as presenting a well-settled rule in American Ass'n Base Ball Club of Kansas City v. Pickett, 8 Pa. County Ct. 232 (1890). But then one month later another

judges found that the court's analysis in *Lumley v. Wagner* "instead of . . . being, as some judges have thought, clear, logical, and convincing, . . . is to a considerable extent inconsistent and contradictory."[38] The reservation which was expressed went to the heart of the policy question which underlies this area. Courts felt that a request for enforcement of a negative covenant was in fact a request that the athlete be ordered to continue in the employ of the original contracting team. It was recognized that the athlete would most likely return to the plaintiff-employer if enjoined from performing elsewhere. Since the courts clearly had no authority to specifically compel the player's compliance with his affirmative promise to perform for the team, it was doubted that they were authorized to achieve that same result by merely casting their order in the negative.[39] Such a variation in the form of the order was seen as an insubstantial change and the offensive element, a judicially-coerced involuntary association, remained.[40] These doubts lingered into the early part of the Twentieth Century,[41] but thereafter quickly subsided.[42] In light of the increasing casualness with which some athletes approached their contractual commitments, the *Lumley* court's concern for the integrity of private contracts seems fully justified.[43] Since the *Lumley* remedy was the most practical and least offensive of the alternatives available, it has been accepted as the method for securing to the plaintiff club some of the advantages which it had sought to secure through its private agreements.[44]

Modern courts now routinely enforce negative covenants in professional sports contracts and typically do so without citation to either *Lumley* or the controversy which it generated.[45] But a review of the cases, particularly the

Pennsylvania court specifically rejected the *Hallman* view. The court in Harrisburg Base-Ball Club v. Athletic Ass'n, 8 Pa. County Ct. 337 (1890) reviewed a series of post-*Lumley* decisions which were highly critical of the result reached and concluded that *Lumley* "instead of settling the law, has really unsettled it." *Id.* at 341.

See also American Base Ball & Athletic Exhibition Co. v. Harper, 54 Cent. L.J. 449 (Cir. Ct. St. Louis 1902); STEVENS, *Involuntary Servitude by Injunction,* 6 CORNELL L.Q. 235 (1921).

38. Harrisburg Base-Ball Club v. Athletic Ass'n, 8 Pa. County Ct. 337, 341 (1890).

39. *See* Ford v. Jermon, 6 Phil. Rep. 6, 7 (1865). *See also* Madison Square Garden Corp. v. Braddock 19 F. Supp. 392, 394 (D.N.J.), *aff'd,* 90 F.2d 924 (3d Cir. 1937).

40. *See* Harrisburg Base-Ball Club v. Athletic Ass'n, 8 Pa. County Ct. 337 (1890); *cf.* Allegheny Base Ball Club v. Bennett, 14 F. 257 (Cir. Ct. Pa. 1882). *See generally* STEVENS, *Involuntary Servitude by Injunction, supra* note 37.

41. *See* American Base Ball & Athletic Exhibition Co. v. Harper, 54 CENT. L.J. 449 (Cir. Ct. St. Louis 1902); STEVENS, *Involuntary Servitude by Injunction, supra* note 37.

42. *See, e.g.,* Cincinnati Exhibition Co. v. Marsans, 216 F. 269 (E.D. Mo. 1914); Philadelphia Ball Club, Ltd. v. Lajoie, 202 Pa. 210, 51 A. 973 (1902).

43. *See* Philadelphia Ball Club, Ltd. v. Lajoie, 202 Pa. 210, 51 A. 973 (1902); *cf.* Weeghman v. Killefer, 215 F. 168 (W.D. Mich.), *aff'd,* 215 F. 289 (6th Cir. 1914).

44. *See generally* RESTATEMENT OF CONTRACTS §§ 379-80 (1932).

One of the last decisions to question the wisdom of the rule of *Lumley v. Wagner* was Madison Square Garden Corp. v. Braddock, 19 F. Supp. 392 (D.N.J.), *aff'd,* 90 F.2d 924 (3d Cir. 1937). There the court was asked to enjoin the boxer, James J. Braddock, from fighting Joe Louis until he had fulfilled his commitment to another promoter. While denying the injunction on grounds other than the inappropriateness of the *Lumley* decision, the judge added, in dicta, that his reading of the parties' briefs and the scholarly commentary mentioned above led him "to the conclusion that the last word has not yet been said upon the extent to which *Lumley v. Wagner* would be or actually is, followed in this country . . . ." *Id.* at 394. In the court's view, "there may be a question as to whether a federal court of equity could enjoin the violation of a negative covenant relating to unique personal services, where its very apparent object is an attempt to enforce the performance of such service under an affirmative covenant . . . ." *Id.*

45. *See* Central New York Basketball, Inc. v. Barnett, 19 Ohio Op. 2d 130, 181 N.E.2d 506 (1961); Dallas Cowboys Football Club, Inc. v. Harris, 348 S.W.2d 37 (Tex. Civ. App. 1961).

most recent ones, indicates that a team is by no means assured that its request for relief will be granted.[46] What this suggests is that the courts are still sensitive to the coercive effects of their negative orders and perceive the necessity for controlling the clubs' access to this remedy. The mechanisms for judicial control have become more sophisticated, however. No longer is the issue framed in the gross terms of whether negative enforcement is, or is not, a wise practice. Rather, courts now invoke their discretionary powers to make a determination of whether enforcement should be allowed in the particular case. Enforcement has been denied, for example, where the player's contract was too harsh,[47] where a restraining order would seriously inhibit the player's opportunity to realize the fair value of his services,[48] and where the plaintiff-team has otherwise secured unduly restrictive control over the player's mobility.[49] The results of this more flexible approach are much more palatable than those which obtained when courts felt that their only option was to accept or deny the validity of *Lumley v. Wagner.* Now there is some assurance that the club may acquire contract rights for which there is an effective remedy. But by the same token, there is a real opportunity to control the coercive effects of the remedy which is provided. Integrity of contract is preserved, but only if the agreement is one which is worthy of such respect.

§ 4.03. The Context in Which the Enforcement Questions Arise.

Subsequent sections focus on the various legal issues which arise when a club seeks an injunction to enforce an athlete's promise to perform exclusively for it. Before examining those specific questions, it should be noted that, as with most legal controversies, the disputes in this area gain much of their significance from the factual context in which they arise. The cases which provide virtually all of the relevant precedent for this aspect of sports law involve the same factual pattern. The basic ingredient is the presence of a recently formed league which seeks to attract players away from well-established teams. In order to gain a place in the fan's eye (and pocketbook), the teams in the new league must attract talent which makes a respectable showing on the playing field.[50] Thus

---

46. *Compare* Boston Professional Hockey Ass'n, Inc. v. Cheevers, 348 F. Supp. 261 (D. Mass.), *remanded,* 472 F.2d 127 (1st Cir. 1972); Nassau Sports v. Hampson, 355 F. Supp. 733 (D. Minn. 1972) (injunction denied); Minnesota Muskies, Inc. v. Hudson, 294 F. Supp. 979 (M.D.N.C. 1969) *with* Nassau Sports v. Peters, 352 F. Supp. 870 (E.D.N.Y. 1972); Matuszak v. Houston Oilers, Inc., 515 S.W.2d 725 (Tex. Civ. App. 1974) (injunction granted).

47. *See* Connecticut Professional Sports Corp. v. Heyman, 276 F. Supp. 618 (S.D.N.Y. 1967).

48. *See* Nassau Sports v. Hampson, 355 F. Supp. 733 (D. Minn. 1972).

49. *See* Nassau Sports v. Peters, 352 F. Supp. 870 (E.D.N.Y. 1972).

50. The need for this sort of instant respectability has been expressly recognized in several cases. For example, in an unpublished opinion in *Cincinnati Bengals, Inc. v. Bergey,* the court observed that

> Faced with the stiff competition for the sports dollar by the NFL, as well as other professional sports organizations, the WFL seeks to insure its future by signing established NFL players to give the new league "credibility" in the eyes of the public. The signing of professional players is also necessary to overcome the doubts of college players as to the future of the league. There was testimony that these doubts are very real, since players recognize that if they sign with the WFL and that league folds, they may face difficulty in attempting to sign with the NFL. . . . [One witness] stated that the signing of name players to future contracts is "essential" to the WFL's success, since the league's financial future is dependent in great part on the earliest possible public acceptance of the WFL as a marketer of "major league" professional football.

453 F. Supp. 129, 138 (S.D. Ohio), *aff'd,* Civil No. 74-1570 (6th Cir., Aug. 27, 1974). *See also* Philadelphia World Hockey Club, Inc. v. Philadelphia Hockey Club, Inc., 351 F. Supp. 462, 515 (E.D. Pa. 1972).

a special effort must be made to sign both the best players emerging from the amateur ranks and star performers from an established league. In each case, the immediate results are the same: a bidding war ensues in which the athlete may be confronted with alternative offers which make it worth his while to ignore previous commitments. The college athlete may have second-thoughts about the contract he previously signed and seek to market his services elsewhere.[51] Similarly, the established player may be hired away by a salary which pales his existing compensation.[52] Because of his knowledge of the uncertain, often abbreviated, duration of professional careers, the athlete may feel justified in assessing his new contractual opportunities for their practical, rather than legal, significance. When that occurs, the occasion arises for the first contracting team to seek a judicial determination of the availability of equitable relief under the terms of its contract.

The often unsavory contexts in which the legal questions arise have not gone unnoticed in many courts. Where the facts of the particular case are highly suggestive of team and player misconduct, judges have been explicit in voicing their view that the recreational aspects of the parties' endeavors should not cloud the fact that the enterprises are commercial in nature and depend upon contractual commitments for their success. An early expression of this impatience with player practices is found in cases involving the player wars between the Federal and National baseball leagues. William Killefer had repudiated his existing contract with the Philadelphia club, signed with Chicago in the new Federal League, and then, using the bargaining power gained by the new league's interest in his services, renegotiated a more attractive arrangement with the Philadelphia club, a fact pattern which has recurred with notable frequency.[53] The Chicago club eventually lost its suit to enjoin Killefer from playing for Philadelphia. Despite the victory for Killefer, his use of inter-league competition to enhance his financial position prompted the court to observe:

> This record shows that the defendant, Killefer, is a baseball player of unique, exceptional and extraordinary skill and expertness. Unfortunately, the record also shows that he is a person upon whose pledged word little or no reliance can be placed, and who, for gain to himself, neither scruples nor hesitates to disregard and violate his express engagements and agreements. . . . Viewed from the standpoint of common honesty and integrity, his position in this litigation is not an enviable one.[54]

A half-century later when a rival football league was formed, the basic elements of the controversies brought before the courts had not changed. In

---

51. *See, e.g.,* Houston Oilers, Inc. v. Neely, 361 F.2d 36 (10th Cir. 1966); Detroit Football Co. v. Robinson, 186 F. Supp. 933 (E.D. La.), *aff'd,* 283 F.2d 657 (5th Cir. 1960); Los Angeles Rams Football Club v. Cannon, 185 F. Supp. 717 (S.D. Cal. 1960).

52. *See, e.g.,* Boston Professional Hockey Ass'n, Inc. v. Cheevers, 348 F. Supp. 261 (D. Mass.), *remanded,* 472 F.2d 127 (1st Cir. 1972); Nassau Sports v. Peters, 352 F. Supp. 870 (E.D.N.Y. 1972).

53. *See also* Munchak Corp. v. Cunningham, 331 F. Supp. 872 (M.D.N.C. 1971), *rev'd,* 457 F.2d 721 (4th Cir. 1972); Minnesota Muskies, Inc. v. Hudson, 294 F. Supp. 979 (M.D.N.C. 1969).

54. Weeghman v. Killefer, 215 F. 168, 169 (W.D. Mich. 1914), *aff'd,* 215 F. 289 (6th Cir. 1914). (The spelling of the parties' names is different in the two opinions. Based on A. DANZIG & J. REICHLER, THE HISTORY OF BASEBALL: ITS GREAT PLAYERS, TEAMS AND MANAGERS (1959) the correct spelling of the parties' names is *Killefer* and *Weeghman* and is. therefore, used throughout this treatise).

1960, Judge J. Skelly Wright, then sitting on the Louisiana federal district court, was presented with the competing claims of the NFL Detroit Lions and the AFL Dallas Texans to the services of Johnny Robinson. As Wright viewed the case before him, it was

> . . . but another round in the sordid fight for football players, a fight which begins before these athletes enter college and follows them through their careers. It is a fight characterized by deception, double dealing, campus jumping, secret alumni subsidization, semi-professionalism and professionalism. It is a fight which has produced as part of its harvest this current rash of contract jumping suits. It is a fight which so conditions the minds and hearts of these athletes that one day they can agree to play football for a stated amount for one group, only to repudiate that agreement the following day or whenever a better offer comes along. So it was with Johnny Robinson.[55]

Although Robinson, or more precisely his AFL employer, was unable to undo the consequences of Robinson's signing with the Lions, Judge Wright was prompted to invoke the admonition delivered by the judge who had heard a similar case arising from the AFL-NFL raids:

> . . . in four or five, six or eight years, some day your passes are going to wobble in the air, you are not going to find that receiver. If you keep playing around here, with these professionals, and others, and jumping your contracts — you are all right this time, . . . but someday your abilities will be such that [your club] won't even send a twice disbarred attorney from Dogpatch to help you. They sent some dandy ones this time . . .[56]

Despite the negative overtones of these particular remarks, the courts have shown considerable tolerance of the sharp dealing which sometimes accompanies inter-league competition for the players.[57] This is in large measure due to the presence of an important countervailing consideration which must be weighed before a decision is entered on the plaintiff's request for an injunction. New leagues typically attempt to assert themselves into a sport which is dominated by a well-established, financially stable competitor, and courts are frequently quite willing to extend to the new entrant the benefits of the strong public policy which favors the development of economic competition between business enterprises.[58] Some courts will invoke this policy even to the extent of overlooking the fact that the new competitor has rather abruptly hired away new talent.[59] For most courts, the desirability of competition serves as a

55. Detroit Football Co. v. Robinson, 186 F. Supp. 933, 934 (E.D. La.), aff'd, 283 F.2d 657 (5th Cir. 1960).

56. 186 F. Supp. at 935-36, *quoting from* Chicago Cardinals Football Club, Inc. v. Etcheverry, (D.N. Mex., June 26, 1956) (unreported).

57. Indeed, both Killefer and Robinson were able to offer their services to the employers they had finally chosen. Weeghman v. Killefer, 215 F. 289 (6th Cir.), aff'g 215 F. 168 (W.D.Mich. 1914); Detroit Football Co. v. Robinson, 283 F.2d 657 (5th Cir.), aff'g 186 F.Supp. 933 (E.D.La. 1960).

58. *See, e.g.,* Cincinnati Bengals, Inc. v. Bergey, 453 F. Supp. 129, 138 (S.D. Ohio) ("[T]he court must conclude that if the injunction is granted there will be harm to the public interest in fostering free competition in the market place for the sports dollar."), aff'd, Civil No. 74-1570 (6th Cir., Aug. 27, 1974); Nassau Sports v. Hampson, 355 F. Supp. 733 (D. Minn. 1972); Philadelphia World Hockey Club, Inc. v. Philadelphia Hockey Club, Inc., 351 F. Supp. 462, 514-16 (E.D. Pa. 1972).

59. *See* Nassau Sports v. Hampson, 355 F. Supp. 733 (D. Minn. 1972).

justification for allowing rival employers to negotiate with the players of another team as long as any resulting agreements respect the rights of the original employer.[60]

There are at least two different interests which are promoted by encouragement of inter-league competition. On the one hand, there is the interest of the sports fan, who will presumably benefit as each league seeks to make its product more attractive so as to secure a larger share of the fans' sports dollar.[61] On the other hand, there is the interest of the professional athlete whose salary will be determined by the extent of demand for his services.[62] The significance of inter-league competition for this latter group is more susceptible to documentation. The evidence is strong that the formation of new leagues does prompt a general increase in players' salaries. The same evidence also suggests that competition-generated salaries more accurately reflect the player's competitive value. The experience of Billy Cunningham, a star basketball player, is a case in point. Originally employed by the Philadelphia 76'ers for a yearly salary of $55,000, he was able to secure a contract with the Carolina Cougars in the rival ABA for an average yearly compensation, including bonus, of $150,000. The competition for his services did not end there, for his defection had the predicted effect on his original Philadelphia employers. They sought to induce him to return to their team with a salary offer valued in excess of $225,000.[63] More general studies of both the escalating effects of inter-league competition, and the dampening effects of any subsequent inter-league merger, confirm that these trends are not of isolated significance.

As the foregoing will suggest, the court which is asked to enforce a player's negative covenant will seldom be able to ignore the broader implications of the issues which arise. If the case is well-developed, it will soon become clear that the issue before the court is not simply whether the athlete will play for one team or the other, but rather the extent to which a competing league will be allowed to intrude into the existing relationship between an established team and its players.[64] The court will often find that there is no easy choice between the desirability of competition, on the one hand, and the integrity of the

60. *See* Cincinnati Bengals, Inc. v. Bergey, 453 F. Supp. 129 (S.D. Ohio), *aff'd,* Civil No. 74-1570 (6th Cir., Aug. 27, 1974); Munchak Corp. v. Cunningham, 457 F.2d 721 (4th Cir. 1972). The *Bergey* case is discussed in § 4.14 *infra.*

61. *See* Philadelphia World Hockey Club, Inc. v. Philadelphia Hockey Club, Inc., 351 F. Supp. 462, 496 (E.D. Pa. 1972).

62. In *Boston Professional Hockey Ass'n, Inc. v. Cheevers,* the court undertook to balance the relative hardship between the plaintiff club and the defendant players who were seeking to join a new league. In the court's view, it appeared that "the balance of hardship from injunctive relief herein would clearly run in favor of the defendant hockey players, who have a limited number of high-earning years before them, having in mind their respective ages and the rigors of playing professional hockey with the always-present possibility of career curtailment caused by physical injury." 348 F. Supp. 261, 270 (D. Mass. 1972). *See also* Philadelphia World Hockey Club, Inc. v. Philadelphia Hockey Club, Inc., 351 F. Supp. 462, 496 (E.D. Pa. 1972).

63. Munchak Corp. v. Cunningham, 331 F. Supp. 872 (M.D.N.C. 1971), *rev'd,* 457 F.2d 721 (4th Cir. 1972).

64. Scoville, *Labor Relations in Sports* in GOVERNMENT AND THE SPORTS BUSINESS 185 (R. Noll ed. 1974). Scoville's data, gathered from the major sports of basketball, football, and hockey indicates that substantial increases in player salaries are more closely tied to periods of inter-league competition than other factors thought to effect wages such as the popularity or prosperity of the sport. Further, the effects of inter-league competition are shown to reach beyond those players who have proven themselves in the established leagues to players moving from minor leagues and intercollegiate sports. *Id.* at 198-200.

contracts, on the other. While the factual settings of the decided cases may be similar, the results are not. Thus, the particular facts of each case will have to be examined to determine which of the competing policies is to be favored.

§ 4.04. The Source of the Club's Exclusive Right to the Athlete's Services.

A club's right to enjoin the athlete from performing for another team has its basis in the contract which exists between the parties. The purpose of this section is to identify more precisely the extent to which the written contract will affect the employer's access to injunctive relief. The analysis will show that those who draft the standard form professional sports contracts generally leave little doubt as to the employer's intention to retain an exclusive claim to the athlete's services.

a. Relevant Contract Terms. It can safely be said that every standard form contract used in major professional sports enterprises includes one or more clauses intended to give the employer, whether a team or promoter, an exclusive right to the services of the athlete for the duration of the contract. While some earlier forms of player contracts did not include such a clause,[65] their inclusion in the agreement which the player signs avoids a potential legal controversy.

In the typical standard form player contract used by the major sports leagues, the team's claim of an exclusive right to the player's services can be related to not one, but three clauses in the contract. First, there is a clause which includes the player's basic promise — a promise to play for the team. This provision is usually worded to express the player's promise to play *only* for the designated team.[66] A second clause limits the player's right to engage in other athletic activities and is intended to minimize the player's exposure to injury. A typical provision limits the player's participation in sports, amateur and professional, other than his primary sport, and gives to the club the right to control all of the athlete's activities in the sport covered by the contract.[67] Thus, a basketball player may covenant not to participate in *any* unauthorized basketball activity.

---

65. *See* American Ass'n Base Ball Club of Kansas City v. Pickett, 8 Pa. County Ct. 232 (1890).

66. *See, e.g.,* NFL Contract, ¶ 2 (1975): "The Player agrees that during the term of this contract he will play football and engage in activities related to football only for the Club and as directed by the Club. . . ." *See also* note 68 *infra.* (Shortened citation form used to refer to standard player contracts is explained in note 126, § 3.05 supra).

67. *See, e.g.,* NFL Contract, ¶ 5 (1975):

> The Player promises and agrees that during the term of this contract he will not play football or engage in activities related to football for any other person, firm, corporation or institution, or on his own behalf, except with the prior written consent of the Club and the Commissioner, and that he will not, during the term of this contract, without the prior consent of the Club, engage in any other sport. . . . The Player likewise promises and agrees that during the term of this contract, he will not participate in any other outside football game not sponsored by the League unless such game is first approved by the League. . . .

The NFL contract was rewritten in 1977. *See* note 126, § 3.05 *supra.* There is now a new version of the provision quoted above. *See* note 68 *infra.*

In player contracts in some other sports, the athlete's covenant against participating in other sports is not worded as broadly as that found in the NFL contract. In the Uniform Player Contract of the National Basketball Association, for example, the covenant seems to be directed almost singularly to protecting the team's interest in the physical condition of the player and, thus, may not in itself support an action by the club to enjoin the player from accepting employment elsewhere. Further support for this interpretation is found in the fact that the NBA covenant, unlike the NFL

As expressed, this would preclude playing for another professional team. Finally, a third clause in the typical standard player contract addresses directly the question of the remedies available to the contracting club in the event the player accepts employment with another team.[68] The clause is intended to establish that the basic prerequisites for judicial relief are present. There is usually a recital that the player's services are unique so that their loss is not compensable in money. In addition, the clause specifically provides that the club is entitled to seek an injunction against the player should he undertake to play for any other team. In essence, this term of the contract purports to set up the foundation for a legal action and then identifies the specific instance in which the team may exercise its enforcement right.

The last of the three named clauses would likely provide a sufficient basis for judicial relief and is often the only clause cited in judicial opinions.[69] However, some courts also include references to the other clauses in identifying the source of the plaintiff club's claim of an exclusive right.[70]

version, includes its own provision for remedies. The enumerated remedies are fine and suspension, suggesting that the parties have agreed to rely solely on internal, rather than judicial, enforcement. The NBA provision is as follows:

> The Player and the Club acknowledge and agree that the Player's participation in other sports may impair or destroy his ability and skill as a basketball player. The Player and the Club recognize and agree that the Player's participation in basketball out of season may result in injury to him. Accordingly, the Player agrees that he will not engage in professional boxing or wrestling, or in motorcycling, auto racing, sky-diving or hang-gliding; and that, except with the written consent of the Club, he will not engage in any game or exhibition of basketball, football, baseball, hockey, lacrosse, or other athletic sport, under penalty of such fine and suspension as may be imposed by the Club and/or the Commissioner of the Association . . . .

NBA Contract, ¶ 17 (1976).

68. *See, e.g.,* NFL Contract, ¶ 8 (1975):

> The Player hereby represents that he has special, exceptional and unique knowledge, skill and ability as a football player, the loss of which cannot be estimated with any certainty and cannot be fairly or adequately compensated by damages and therefore agrees that the Club shall have the right, in addition to any other rights which the Club may possess, to enjoin him by appropriate injunction proceedings against playing football or any other professional sport, without the consent of the Club, or engaging in activities related to football for any person, firm, corporation, institution, or on his own behalf, and against any other breach of this contract.

When the NFL contract was rewritten in 1977, the covenant of exclusive service was rephrased and combined with another provision dealing with the player's outside activities. The new clause is as follows:

> 3. Other Activities. Without prior written consent of Club, Player will not play football or engage in activities related to football otherwise than for Club or engage in any activity other than football which may involve a significant risk of personal injury. Player represents that he has special, exceptional and unique knowledge, skill, ability, and experience as a football player, the loss of which cannot be estimated with any certainty and cannot be fairly or adequately compensated by damages. Player therefore agrees that Club will have the right, in addition to any other right which Club may possess, to enjoin Player by appropriate proceedings from playing football or engaging in football-related activities other than for Club or from engaging in any activity other than football which may involve a significant risk of personal injury.

NFL Contract ¶ 3 (1977).

Similar provisions concerning the employer's right to the exclusive service of the athlete are found in non-team sports. *See e.g., Madison Square Garden Corp. v. Carnera,* 52 F.2d 47, 48 (2d Cir. 1931); *Machen v. Johansson,* 174 F. Supp. 522, 526 n.4 (S.D.N.Y. 1959).

69. *See, e.g., Minnesota Muskies, Inc. v. Hudson,* 294 F. Supp. 979, 982 (M.D.N.C. 1969); *Connecticut Professional Sports Corp. v. Heyman,* 276 F. Supp. 618, 619 n.3 (S.D.N.Y. 1967).

70. *See, e.g., Central New York Basketball, Inc. v. Barnett,* 19 Ohio Op. 2d 130, 131-33, 181 N.E.2d 506, 508-09 (1961); *Dallas Cowboys Football Club, Inc. v. Harris,* 348 S.W.2d 37, 41-42 (Tex. Civ. App. 1961).

b. Enforcement in the Absence of an Express Covenant. In the past, courts have been presented with sports and entertainment contracts which did not include a specific promise by the performer that his employer would have the exclusive right to his services. Hence, the question arose whether such an express covenant was a necessary precondition to the employer's obtaining injunctive relief when the performer accepted employment with a third party during the term of the contract. The judicial response was somewhat equivocal in the early English entertainment law cases. In *Lumley v. Wagner,*[71] the case which laid the foundation for negative enforcement of entertainers' contracts, Lord St. Leonards thought that an employer had a right to enjoin his employee from working for another without regard to whether the performer had expressly covenanted not to do so. In the judge's view, such a covenant could be implied from the nature of the agreement: "I am of the opinion that if [Johanna Wagner] had attempted, *even in the absence of any negative stipulation,* to perform at another theatre, she would have broken the spirit and true meaning of the contract as much as she would now do with reference to the contract into which she has actually entered [which did include an express negative covenant]." [72] Although this pronouncement was only dicta in *Lumley,* it was subsequently accepted as controlling in one case [73] and then, some eighteen years later, repudiated in another.[74] However, the court's concern in this latter case seems to have been with the *Lumley* holding itself, for the court expressed strong objection to the notion that a court could do indirectly (force compliance with the affirmative covenants) what it could not do directly, a criticism which lingered for sometime after *Lumley.*[75]

The American courts experienced less uncertainty in upholding the employer's right to an injunction even in the absence of an express covenant. Support for this view can be found in early law review articles [76] and in cases involving entertainers generally [77] and athletes in particular.[78] For example, in one of the early baseball cases, the defendant attempted to distinguish a post-*Lumley* case arguing that the particular precedent did not apply "where the contract of service does not contain a negative clause...." [79] The court found that contention "wholly untenable." In its view, "Every express promise to do an act embraces within its scope an implied promise not to do anything which will prevent the promissor from doing the act he has engaged to do." [80]

---

71. 1 De G.M. & G. 604, 42 Eng. Rep. 687 (1852).
72. 1 De G.M. & G. at 618, 42 Eng. Rep. at 693.
73. Montague v. Flockton, [1873] L.R. 16 Eq. 189.
74. Whitwood Chemical Co. v. Hardman, [1891] 2 Ch. 416.
75. *Id.* at 427. *See generally* Gilbert, *Some Old Problems in a Modern Guise: Enforcement of Negative Covenants,* 4 CAL. L. REV. 114, 117 (1916); Tannenbaum, *Enforcement of Personal Service Contracts in the Entertainment Industry,* 42 CAL. L. REV. 18, 19 (1954).
76. *See* Gilbert, *Some Old Problems in a Modern Guise: Enforcement of Negative Covenants, supra* note 75, at 117; Schofield, *The Word "Not" as a Test of Equity Jurisdiction to Enjoin a Breach of Contract,* 2 ILL. L. REV. 217 (1907).
77. *See* Harry Rogers Theatrical Enterprises, Inc. v. Comstock, 225 App. Div. 34, 36, 232 N.Y.S. 1, 4 (1928).
78. American Ass'n Base Ball Club of Kansas City v. Pickett, 8 Pa. County Ct. 232 (1890).
79. *Id.*
80. *Id.*

This view has been generally accepted in other cases and endorsed by the *Restatement of Contracts.*[81] But as the *Restatement* makes clear, the question of whether a covenant of exclusive services is properly implied depends ultimately on the language which the parties used and other manifestations of their intent.[82] Basic to the plaintiff's cause of action is a finding that the performer's arrangement with his employer was intended to be an exclusive one. While that would almost always be the inference to be drawn where the athlete agreed to a definite-term contract involving a team sport, it might be less clear in connection with more individualized athletic endeavors, such as golf, tennis or boxing. In those cases, the particular language of the contract would have to be scrutinized to determine whether the performer who had committed himself to perform in one or more events also intended to exclude his appearance in other contests during the same period.

Also relevant to a determination of the parties' intent is their agreement with respect to the remedies to be available in the event of a breach. This principle is well-illustrated by the case of *Madison Square Garden Corporation v. Braddock.*[83] Braddock, a boxer, had entered into one agreement with the promoters in which he covenanted that he would not engage in competing performances for a stated term. This agreement was later superseded by another which differed in two respects: it did not include a promise of exclusive service and the parties had added a provision for liquidated damages. When litigation arose, the employer argued that the court ought to find that the parties intended that the original negative covenant would carry over to the second agreement. This contention had some merit since the boxer presumably would understand that the promoter had an interest in controlling the boxer's exposure in order to heighten public interest in the planned championship event. The court, however, found that the subsequent agreement evidenced a different intention. In the court's view, the parties' agreement with respect to liquidated damages impliedly negated the possibility of equitable relief[84] since the parties apparently intended that any breach could be compensated by money damages. While the inclusion of a liquidated damages clause will not always preclude equitable relief,[85] the court's interpretation is not unreasonable on the particular facts in *Braddock*. The parties had not only omitted one remedy from their agreement, but had also included a term which may well have been regarded as a substitute. In the absence of some other explanation for why the form of the original agreement was not continued, it seems reasonable to assume that changes in the terms of the contract were intended to effectuate changes in the substance of the agreement. To do otherwise gives the plaintiff considerable freedom to ignore the explicit terms of the contract and choose a remedy which better suits his needs.

---

81. RESTATEMENT OF CONTRACTS § 380, comment *a* (1932). The view that a negative obligation ought to be generally implied was not adopted in this country without opposition. *See* Carlson v. Koerner, 226 Ill. 15, 80 N.E. 562 (1907).

82. RESTATEMENT OF CONTRACTS § 380 (1932).

83. 19 F. Supp. 392 (D.N.J.), *aff'd*, 90 F.2d 924 (3d Cir. 1937). *See also* Note, *Specific Performance — Injunctions to Enforce Negative Covenants in Contracts for Personal Services,* 36 MICH. L. REV. 865 (1938).

84. Madison Square Garden Corp. v. Braddock, 90 F.2d 924, 927 (3d Cir.), *aff'g* 19 F. Supp. 392 (D.N.J. 1937).

85. *See* RESTATEMENT OF CONTRACTS § 378 (1932).

§ 4.05. Express Covenants and the Requirement of Reasonableness.

While courts now appear willing to enforce an express or implied covenant limiting the athlete's right to play for others during the term of the contract, the employer does not have unlimited prerogatives in attempting to control the player's activities in the event of breach. The restrictions imposed by the negative covenant must satisfy a test of reasonableness,[86] and the courts will monitor the parties' agreement to protect the athlete from overreaching by the employer.

While the requirement of reasonableness might be used to test other aspects of the typical covenant,[87] the question most frequently raised in the past has been whether the restrictions on the athlete's mobility are of reasonable duration. Analysis of this question is facilitated if a distinction is made between situations involving major team sports and those involving individual athletic performances, such as boxing and tennis. Cases of the latter sort reveal several instances in which courts have expressed concern about the reasonableness of the time period covered by the agreed-upon covenant.[88] By contrast, a review of cases construing the contracts used in major team sports reveals that the reasonableness of the duration of the covenant is less likely to be drawn into question.[89] This difference can be explained by an examination of the peculiar features of the contractual arrangements made in the two situations.

In the typical professional team sport contract, the team's right to limit the player's employment with another club will exist only for that period during which the team has a contractual right to make an affirmative claim to the player's services. Hence, the duration of the covenant of exclusive services is determined by the term of the particular contract, and as long as the plaintiff team's contractual rights are of a reasonable duration, the issue of the reasonableness of its claims under the negative covenant is not likely to be litigated.

In order to determine the duration of a contract, one must consider the effect of option and reserve clauses, provisions which give the team the right to renew the contract for an additional period.[90] It is also important to distinguish between

---

86. See generally Stevens, Involuntary Servitude by Injunction, 6 CORNELL L.Q. 235, 263-65 (1921).

87. Whether the covenant of exclusive service is of proper scope in terms of geography or in terms of the interest the employer seeks to protect is closely related to the issue, subsequently discussed, of whether the team must show that the player who breaches his contract is undertaking to play for an employer who is in economic competition with the plaintiff. See § 4.10 infra. If the new employer will not compete in the plaintiff's market — because a different sport or distant geographical area is involved — then it would seem that enforcement of the exclusive covenant would not be proper. At this point, it can be noted that some courts in entertainment and sports law cases have exhibited a willingness to closely scrutinize the geographical reach of a performer's covenant of exclusive service. Machen v. Johansson, 174 F. Supp. 522, 530 (S.D.N.Y. 1959); Greer v. Lifsey, 197 S.E.2d 846 (Ga. Ct. App. 1973).

88. See Machen v. Johansson, 174 F. Supp. 522 (S.D.N.Y. 1959); Madison Square Garden Corp. v. Braddock, 19 F. Supp. 392 (D.N.J.), aff'd, 90 F.2d 924 (3d Cir. 1937); Arena Athletic Club v. McPartland, 41 App. Div. 352, 58 N.Y.S. 477 (1899).

89. See Lemat Corp. v. Barry, 275 Cal. App. 2d 671, 675-78, 80 Cal. Rptr. 240, 243-44 (1969); Central New York Basketball, Inc. v. Barnett, 19 Ohio Op. 2d 130, 181 N.E.2d 506 (1961).

90. Typical of the option clauses involved in many of the prior cases is the following provision from a former version of the National Basketball Association contract:

> On or before September 1st . . . next following the last playing season covered by this contract, the Club may tender to the player a contract for the term of that season by mailing the same to the Player. . . . If prior to November 1 next succeeding said September 1, the Player and the Club have not agreed upon the terms of such contract, then on or

the intra-league and inter-league effects of those restraints, for the extent of
the club's rights in those two situations may vary. The injunction proceedings
in which the reasonableness of the duration of the contract is questioned will
likely involve a situation in which a player seeks to move from one league to
another. A particular option clause may have a different operation where the
athlete seeks to move between teams within the same league. In some sports,
league rules require that the acquiring team compensate the original employer
for the loss of the athlete who has played out his option. A separate body of case
law addresses the question of whether the option is effectively perpetual in these
situations.[91] Because such an indemnity rule only affects intra-league player
movements, it is not usually an element in the typical injunction proceeding
involving an athlete who is seeking employment in a different league.

Collective bargaining and a variety of antitrust litigation have produced rather
substantial changes in the option and reserve systems that formerly were in
effect. A detailed discussion of these developments is taken up later.[92] For the
present, it is sufficient to note that the trend is clearly toward a relaxation of
the extent to which clubs have the right to unilaterally renew an athlete's
contract.[93] These developments will have the effect of rendering it even less
likely that the duration of the player's contract will be found to be unreasonable.
In some sports, for example, the option clause will be removed entirely and
replaced with a clause which gives the player's original club the right to match
any salary offered by the other team.[94] As long as there is a real opportunity
for bargaining and the term of the contract is not clearly excessive, there will
be little basis for questioning the reasonableness of the length of such an
agreement.

Despite these developments, there is still good reason to discuss the law which
has developed in this area. There are indications that even in the major sports,
clubs will continue the right to unilaterally renew the contract in some
situations.[95] Moreover, there are a variety of other sports leagues which have

before 10 days after said November 1, the Club shall have the right by written notice to
the Player . . . to renew this contract for the period of one year on the same terms, except
that the amount of compensation payable to the Player shall be such as the Club shall
fix in said notice; provided, however, that said amount shall be an amount payable at a
rate not less than 75% of the rate stipulated for the preceding year.

NBA Contract ¶ 22(a), *quoted in* Central New York Basketball, Inc. v. Barnett, 19 Ohio Op. 2d
130, 132-33, 181 N.E.2d 506, 509 (1961). Many of the later versions of the standard player
contracts make clear that the contract is renewable for only a single additional season. *See, e.g.,*
NFL Contract, ¶ 10 (1975): ". . . after such renewal, this contract shall not include a further option
to the Club to renew this contract."

91. *See, e.g.,* Mackey v. National Football League, 543 F.2d 606 (8th Cir. 1976), *modifying* 407
F. Supp. 1000 (D. Minn. 1975); Robertson v. National Basketball Ass'n, 389 F. Supp. 867 (S.D.N.Y.
1975); Kapp v. National Football League, 390 F. Supp. 73 (N.D. Cal. 1974). While these cases support
the view that an indemnity rule violates the antitrust laws, it should be noted that such a system
was included in the 1976 collective bargaining agreement between the owners and players in the
National Hockey League. *See* N.Y. Times, Oct. 7, 1975, at 1, col. 8.

92. *See* §§ 5.03-.07 *infra.*

93. Some of the early 1976 developments in this area are summarized in Washington Post, Mar.
7, 1976, at D. 4, col. 1. *See also* § 5.03 *infra.*

94. The 1976 collective bargaining agreement in the NBA contains such a provision. *See id.*

95. For example, the 1976 NHL collective bargaining agreement gives the club and player the
option to agree to a contract which gives the club the unilateral right to renew. *See id.;* N.Y. Times,
Oct. 7, 1975, at 1, col. 8.

not been directly affected by the developments mentioned above.[96] Thus, it may be useful to consider some of the principles which bear on the issue of reasonableness.

Whether the reasonableness of this duration of the contract is seriously subject to question will, as an initial matter, depend upon the interpretation of the clause which gives the club a unilateral right to renew. While a true reserve clause is generally thought to give a team a right to renew the player's contract as often as it wishes, the effect of an option clause may be less certain. Some contracts specify that the option to renew can be exercised only once.[97] But others, particularly the standard player contracts which were the subject of earlier litigation, are less definite and merely specify that the club may renew the contract for an additional period.[98] The basic issue raised by such a general right of renewal is whether the option clause gives the team a right to renew for only one year or whether the right of renewal is perpetual. The analysis which suggests the latter view is this: when the team exercises its option to renew for an additional season, the new contract contains basically the same terms and conditions as the original agreement.[99] One of those terms is, of course, the option clause itself. Hence, the team might assert that the contract governing the option year includes a right of renewal, so that the team can renew for a second option year. Under this view, the continually incorporated option would give the team the right to bind the player in each successive year until he retires.

An interesting aspect of the history of sports law is that similar language in various standard player contracts has led to divergent interpretations and practices. In *Central New York Basketball, Inc. v. Barnett,*[100] the argument was made that the standard NBA contract and its option clause provided for perpetual service and was, therefore, void as against public policy. This argument was rejected. The court applied the well-known rule of contract interpretation that a contract ought to be construed whenever possible so as to avoid rendering it illegal or void. Hence, the court concluded that the right of renewal was for only one year and thus the contract did not provide for perpetual service.[101] This view was subsequently accepted by other courts.[102] A similar interpretation was assumed to be appropriate for the renewal clause used in some standard football contracts.[103]

The option clause used in hockey came under attack in a series of antitrust cases involving player movements between the established NHL and the recently formed WHA. The court which eventually produced the most authoritative ruling in this controversy had little difficulty in concluding that

---

96. It has been reported, for example, the World Team Tennis League functions under a reserve system similar to that traditionally used in baseball. *See* N.Y. Times, May 19, 1976, at 33, col. 3.

97. *See* note 90 *supra.*

98. *See* note 90 *supra.*

99. *See* note 90 *supra.*

100. 19 Ohio Op. 2d 130, 181 N.E.2d 506 (1961).

101. *Id.* at 132-34, 181 N.E.2d at 509-10.

102. *See* Lemat Corp. v. Barry, 275 Cal. App. 2d 671, 80 Cal. Rptr. 240 (1969); *cf.* Munchak Corp. v. Cunningham, 457 F.2d 721 (4th Cir. 1972).

103. *See* Carlson, *The Business of Professional Sports: A Reexamination in Progress,* 18 N.Y.L. FORUM 915, 920-21 (1972-73); Morris, *In the Wake of the Flood,* 38 LAW & CONTEMP. PROB. 85, 87-88 (1973).

hockey contracts in effect created a continuous reserve system and not simply a one year option, even though the language of the clause was similar to that used in the NBA contract.[104] The legal difficulties which flow from this interpretation were subsequently avoided when the NHL and the players' union agreed to a non-mandatory option clause providing for a one year renewal.[105]

The prior discussion should suggest why there have been no recent injunction cases questioning the reasonableness of the duration of a contract which contained an option clause. The reason is that there is little basis upon which to argue that the length of the covenant is unreasonable. While the concept of reasonableness has not been precisely defined in this context, it seems clearly to include a limitation of two or three years.[106] Further, the offensiveness of even this time period is substantially mitigated by the fact that the sports employer is offering employment to the athlete for each of the years that the covenant will operate. Hence, the athlete is not necessarily denied his means of livelihood. In this respect, the non-competition clauses in athletic contracts are distinguishable from situations in which a former employee promises not to compete with his original employer for several years *after* he has left the employ of the latter.[107] In most sports, the athlete can structure his affairs so that he earns his salary while playing out his option. In light of both the relatively short duration of the covenant of exclusive service and the fact that the athlete does not have to forego practicing his profession in order to satisfy his covenant, it is proper that there has never been substantial doubt about the reasonableness of the term of the negative covenant in the one-year option situation.

For most of its history, the reserve clause in baseball was thought to grant a club a perpetual right to the player's services. However, the validity of that assumption was refuted in late 1975 when an arbitrator, Peter M. Seitz, interpreted the language of the standard form contract as giving the clubs the right to unilaterally renew for only one year, an interpretation which was not overturned in subsequent judicial proceedings.[108] The owners and the players union subsequently approved a collective bargaining agreement which restructured the league's player reservation system. Under the new arrangement, the contract of an entering player is subject to the club's right of renewal for a period of six years. Thereafter, he may become a free agent and participate in a reentry draft. Once a player becomes a free agent, he may not become a free agent again for a period of five years. Other details of the new system are discussed in a subsequent section.[109]

Even prior to these developments, one would have thought that the common law requirement of reasonableness would have been invoked to question the

104. Philadelphia World Hockey Club, Inc. v. Philadelphia Hockey Club, Inc., 351 F. Supp. 462, 480-81, 505 (E.D. Pa. 1972).
105. *See* note 95 *supra.*
106. *Compare* Grober v. Strick, 77 F.2d 762 (3d Cir. 1935); Carter v. Alling, 43 F. 202 (C.C. Ill. 1890); Granger v. Craven, 159 Minn. 296, 199 N.W. 10 (1924).
107. *See, e.g.,* American Hot Rod Ass'n v. Carrier, 500 F.2d 1269 (4th Cir. 1974); Grober v. Strick, 77 F.2d 762 (3d Cir. 1935); Granger v. Craven, 159 Minn. 296, 199 N.W. 10 (1924).
108. *See* Arbitration of Messersmith, Grievance No. 75-27, Decision No. 29 (1975); Kansas City Royals Baseball Corp. v. Major League Baseball Players Ass'n, 409 F. Supp. 233 (W.D. Mo.), *aff'd,* 532 F.2d 615 (8th Cir. 1976).
109. *See* § 5.03 *infra.*

enforceability of the club's presumed right of perpetual renewal. Yet, a review of the cases indicates that the question has seldom been raised, and particularly not in recent years. There are several reasons for this. The most readily apparent is that, at least since the effective merger of the two baseball leagues, the factual setting in which the issue would otherwise be litigated has not arisen. As mentioned, the context in which the common law principles are usually applied is one in which a player jumps his contract to accept employment in another league. However, except for brief periods when the Federal and Mexican leagues foundered, there has been no inter-league competition for baseball players.[110]

Despite the absence of recent litigation on the question, there are several precedents which are worthy of note. On the one hand, a series of cases decided in an earlier period reveals that clubs experienced a remarkable lack of success in enforcing their players' promises of exclusive service.[111] The cases which denied enforcement were decided on a variety of grounds, but some courts gave attention to the issue of whether the contracts provided for perpetual service. While this issue was seldom considered precisely in terms of whether the promise of exclusive service was of unreasonable duration from the standpoint of equity, the language of the opinions supports such a conclusion. The reserve system was variously condemned as a system of "quasi peonage . . . contrary to the spirit of American institutions"[112] and as exhibiting a "want of fairness"[113] because of the team's right to bind the player for the duration of his professional career.[114] It is by no means certain, however, that a modern court presented with a request for equitable enforcement of a perpetual renewal clause would endorse these objections.[115] At least one potential public policy objection was implicitly decided in the club's favor in the lower court decision in *Flood v. Kuhn,*[116] the most recent antitrust case in this area. Curt Flood, in addition to attacking the reserve system as a restraint on trade, also objected that the arrangement violated the prohibition against involuntary servitude embodied in the Thirteenth Amendment. In both the trial court[117] and the court of appeals[118] this argument was rejected.[119] While the courts recognized that

110. Davis, *Self-Regulation in Baseball, 1909-71* in GOVERNMENT AND THE SPORTS BUSINESS 349, 368-72 (R. Noll ed. 1974).

111. In several cases, the club's request for judicial relief was denied. *See* Weeghman v. Killefer, 215 F. 289 (6th Cir. 1914); Brooklyn Baseball Club v. McGuire, 116 F. 782 (E.D. Pa. 1902); Metropolitan Exhibition Co. v. Ewing, 42 F. 198 (S.D.N.Y. 1890); Allegheny Base-Ball Club v. Bennett, 14 F. 257 (W.D. Pa. 1882); Cincinnati Exhibition Co. v. Johnson, 190 Ill. App. 630 (1914); Baltimore Baseball Club & Exhibition Co. v. Pickett, 78 Md. 375, 28 A. 279 (1894); American League Baseball Club of Chicago v. Chase, 86 Misc. 441, 149 N.Y.S. 6 (Sup. Ct. 1914); Metropolitan Exhibition Co. v. Ward, 9 N.Y.S. 779 (Sup. Ct. 1890); Columbus Baseball Club v. Reiley, 11 Ohio Dec. 272, 25 Wkly. Law Bul. 385 (1891); Philadelphia Ball Club, Ltd. v. Hallman, 8 Pa. County Ct. 57 (1890); Harrisburg Base-Ball Club v. Athletic Ass'n, 8 Pa. County Ct. 337 (1890).

112. American League Baseball Club of Chicago v. Chase, 86 Misc. 441, 465, 149 N.Y.S. 6, 19 (Sup. Ct. 1914).

113. Metropolitan Exhibition Co. v. Ward, 9 N.Y.S. 779, 783 (Sup. Ct. 1890).

114. *Compare* J. Schaeffer, Inc. v. Hoppen, 127 Fla. 703, 173 So. 900 (1937); Mandeville v. Harman, 42 N.J. Eq. 185, 7 A. 37 (1886); Interstate Tea Co. v. Alt, 271 N.Y. 76, 2 N.E.2d 51 (Ct. App. 1936). *See also* Annot., 41 A.L.R.2d 1.

115. *Cf.* Flood v. Kuhn, 407 U.S. 258 (1972); Toolson v. New York Yankees, 346 U.S. 356 (1953); Federal Baseball Club v. National League, 259 U.S. 200 (1922).

116. 316 F. Supp. 271 (S.D.N.Y. 1970), *aff'd,* 443 F.2d 264 (2d Cir. 1971), *aff'd,* 407 U.S. 258 (1972).

117. *Id.*

118. 443 F.2d 264 (2d Cir. 1971).

119. *See also* Augusta Baseball Ass'n v. Thomasville Baseball Club, 147 Ga. 201, 93 S.E. 208 (1917).

a real restraint on freedom existed, it was observed that for purposes of the narrow question issued by the Thirteenth Amendment, the player remained free to disassociate himself from the team and pursue other non-baseball endeavors. This analysis of the Thirteenth Amendment issue does not completely answer the objection which might be raised in an equitable proceeding, for there the courts will be more mindful of the public interest in permitting the individual to follow the profession for which he is specially trained.[120] Yet, the *Flood* decisions do serve to temper somewhat the objections of the earlier decisions which chose to characterize the arrangement as one akin to slavery.[121] A final implication of *Flood* which may be troubling to a common law court is its suggestion that state antitrust laws cannot be used to attack baseball's perpetual reserve system.[122] The premise of this view is that regulation of this aspect of the industry has been left to Congress. If a state court cannot declare the system to be unreasonable under its antitrust laws, it would seem somewhat anomalous if it were to achieve the same result under its inherent equity powers. Thus, while a court's common law equity powers have traditionally been regarded as distinctive, it is now less clear that a court could ignore the pointed precedents developed in these other areas.

While the above analysis should suggest that the question of the reasonableness of the duration of the athlete's covenant of exclusive service has limited viability in connection with the major team sports, the issue of the reasonableness is by no means dormant in the sports law area. As suggested above, it has appeared on several occasions in connection with athletes' contracts in non-team sports.

A typical factual pattern is presented in boxing. A boxer who is either the reigning champion or a prime contender for the championship enters into a contract with a promoter to appear in a fight which is to determine the championship in a particular weight class. Normally, the parties will stipulate the date by which the fight will be held. In order to preserve the fighter's publicity value and to insure that the fighter is not injured, the promoter secures a covenant from the fighter that he will not appear in other matches. The legal controversy arises when the boxer disregards this promise and agrees to a fight for another promoter. In the ensuing litigation, the original promoter will argue that the covenant precludes the boxer from participating in another match until he has fulfilled his original commitment. Under this construction, the negative covenant could potentially continue for an indeterminable period of time. Where this type of argument has been made, relief has uniformly been denied.[123] One court has analyzed the issue in these terms:

> Since it appears that the negative covenant here involved fails to fix any definite limitations as to the length of time of its existence and might therefore forever deprive Braddock of his right to make a living

---

120. *Compare* Greer v. Lifsey, 197 S.E.2d 846, 847 (Ga. Ct. App. 1973); Menter Co. v. Brock, 147 Minn. 407, 180 N.W. 553 (1920); Sternberg v. O'Brien, 48 N.J. Eq. 370, 22 A. 348 (1891).

121. *See* American League Baseball Club of Chicago v. Chase, 86 Misc. 441, 465, 149 N.Y.S. 6, 19 (Sup. Ct. 1914).

122. *See* 407 U.S. 258, 284-85. This aspect of the *Flood* case is considered in more detail in § 4.13 *infra*.

123. *See* Machen v. Johansson, 174 F. Supp. 522 (S.D.N.Y. 1959); Madison Square Garden Corp. v. Braddock, 19 F. Supp. 392 (D.N.J.), *aff'd on other grounds,* 90 F.2d 924 (3d Cir. 1937); *cf.* Arena Athletic Club v. McPartland, 41 App. Div. 352, 58 N.Y.S. 477 (1899).

in the occupation he has chosen, I am of the opinion that the covenant places an unreasonable restraint upon his liberty.[124]

Other courts have based their denial of relief on similar grounds of public policy.[125] It can be noted that these decisions serve to reaffirm that employers in the sports area do not have unlimited prerogatives in coercing athletes into fulfillment of their contracts. When the bounds of reasonableness are surpassed, the courts are prepared to invoke independent grounds of public policy to free the athlete from the imprudent bargain which he made.

The cases in this area also provide guidance on an important subsidiary issue. When the court denies relief in the circumstances described above, its primary concern is that the athlete not be held to a contract which unduly restricts his right to pursue his profession. But the oppressive feature in this situation is not the fact that the athlete may lose his right to perform for others, but rather that the restraint may endure for an unreasonably long period of time. Since the gravamen is the time period involved and not the fact of restraint as such, the question logically follows as to whether a court faced with a covenant of indeterminable length should not proceed to enforce it, but limit its operation to a reasonable period. This approach would remove the feature which would otherwise render enforcement offensive to valid public policies. Such a construction would seem to gain support from the well-known rule of contract interpretation that where the contract is subject to varying interpretations, the court should choose an interpretation which does not destroy the validity of the contract.[126] Moreover, an argument can be made that without such a redefinition of the employer's rights, the plaintiff may be left without an effective remedy, since affirmative injunctive relief is not available as a matter of public policy and damages may be deemed too speculative.[127] Hence, if the plaintiff is to have any remedy at all, it must be in the form of negative enforcement.

This question has not been squarely confronted in the sports law area, and thus a definitive answer cannot be given. The limited precedents available reveal a general reluctance on the part of courts to save the plaintiff's cause of action by implying a reasonable time limit. Once it is found that the team or promoter has tried to secure an unreasonable restraint on the athlete, the court typically indicates little enthusiasm for reforming the parties' agreement. In some cases, the courts do not state the reasons for their refusal to imply a reasonable limitation.[128] In others, the refusal is based on the well-worn axiom that a court will not rewrite the contract for the parties.[129] Whatever the reason, the results in these cases suggest that the general public policy in favor of the free marketability of personal services will take precedence over any inclination

---

124. Madison Square Garden Corp. v. Braddock, 19 F. Supp. 392, 394 (D.N.J.), *aff'd on other grounds,* 90 F.2d 924 (3d Cir. 1937).

125. Machen v. Johansson, 174 F. Supp. 522, 529-30 (S.D.N.Y. 1959); Arena Athletic Club v. McPartland, 41 App. Div. 352, 58 N.Y.S. 477 (1899).

126. *See* Central New York Basketball, Inc. v. Barnett, 19 Ohio Op. 2d 130, 181 N.E.2d 506 (1961). *See generally* 3 A. CORBIN, CORBIN ON CONTRACTS § 546 (2d ed. 1960).

127. *See* § 4.02 *supra.*

128. Madison Square Garden Corp. v. Braddock, 19 F. Supp. 392 (D.N.J.), *aff'd,* 90 F.2d 924 (3d Cir. 1937).

129. *See* Machen v. Johansson, 174 F. Supp. 522, 529, n. 6 (S.D.N.Y. 1959); Arena Athletic Club v. McPartland, 41 App. Div. 352, 58 N.Y.S. 477 (1899).

which a court might have to provide relief to a team or promoter who has been injured by an athlete's contract breach.[130]

§ 4.06. Validity of the Contract as a Prerequisite to Injunctive Relief.

Before a club can secure equitable enforcement, it must show that a valid contract exists between it and the defendant athlete. The basis of the enforcement action would be the athlete's promise to perform his services exclusively for the plaintiff. This promise is part of the alleged contract forming the basis of the suit. If for some reason no binding agreement were found to exist between the parties, then neither the exclusive covenant nor any other provision of the alleged contract will be entitled to judicial enforcement.

Despite the obviousness of these conclusions, the question of the validity of the player's contract has played an important role in the cases which have been decided to date. As the athlete typically has a substantial interest in resisting the plaintiff's efforts to secure an injunction, he is apt to assert whatever defenses he has, including the defense that the contract is invalid. It has been through such attacks that a substantial body of sports contracts law has developed.

The basic contracts law issues, which courts have been called upon to decide in the context of injunctive proceedings, cover a wide range. For example, some cases have raised the question of whether the fundamental prerequisites of a valid offer and proper acceptance are present. In at least two cases, injunctive relief has been denied because it was found that an offer of a contract to play professional football had not been properly accepted before it was rescinded.[131] Equally basic issues such as whether the statute of frauds has been satisfied have commanded the attention of courts.[132]

The athlete must do more than indicate his general willingness to perform for the team. Rather, courts are insistent that before injunctive relief will issue, whatever "agreement" exists between player and team must constitute a contract. Thus, it is not enough that the parties have entered into "an agreement to agree." In this sort of arrangement, the parties typically agree to later enter into a contract, with such important terms as salary and length of service left to subsequent negotiations. If there is no further agreement, enforcement is likely to be denied.[133] In a similar vein, courts have used the plaintiff's request for injunctive relief as the occasion to review the definiteness of the terms of the contract. If basic terms, such as salary, are not definitely stated, then the injunction will be denied.[134] While the extent of each party's obligations must

130. At least one sports case, Nassau Sports v. Peters, 352 F. Supp. 870 (E.D.N.Y. 1972), offers some support for reading in a "reasonable" limitation. This is a suggested remedy even when the covenant actually contains terms which are unreasonable. The suggestion, however, is made in dicta and is recognized as a minority view. *Id.* at 877.

131. *See* Detroit Football Co. v. Robinson, 283 F.2d 657 (5th Cir. 1960); Los Angeles Rams Football Club v. Cannon, 185 F. Supp. 717 (S.D. Cal. 1960).

132. *See* Houston Oilers, Inc. v. Neely, 361 F.2d 36, 42-3 (10th Cir. 1966).

133. *See* Metropolitan Exhibition Co. v. Ewing, 42 F. 198, 204-05 (S.D.N.Y. 1890); Allegheny Base-Ball Club v. Bennett, 14 F. 257 (W.D. Pa. 1882); Arena Athletic Club v. McPartland, 41 App. Div. 352, 353, 58 N.Y.S. 477, 478 (1899); Philadelphia Ball Club, Ltd. v. Hallman, 8 Pa. County Ct. 57, 62 (1890).

134. *See* Weeghman v. Killefer, 215 F. 168, 170 (W.D. Mich. 1914); Arena Athletic Club v. McPartland, 41 App. Div. 352, 353, 58 N.Y.S. 477, 478 (1899).

be precisely stated before equitable enforcement will be granted, courts will consult other sources to supply a term where such an incorporation of terms is reasonable in light of the parties' likely understanding. Thus, a term which is obvious, such as a promoter's obligation to employ a boxer who has agreed to fight with a particular opponent, will be implied even if such an undertaking is not explicitly set forth in the contract.[135] Similarly courts will give the terms of the contract the meanings commonly attributed to them in the trade.[136]

It should be emphasized that a plaintiff's request for injunctive relief provides the context in which any objection to the legal validity of the contract can be raised. While the above examples illustrate objections based on traditional contract notions, more far-reaching objections may also be considered. The court is empowered to find that the asserted contract lacks validity because it offends either general public policy or some specific legislative control. Thus, the player may use the injunction proceeding as the occasion upon which to question the validity of the contract under the antitrust laws.[137] As reflected in the decided cases, these antitrust objections have been most recently based on the federal antitrust laws,[138] although at least one earlier court considered a similar objection based on common law principles.[139] In each instance cited in the notes, the courts found reason to seriously question whether the reserve clauses in the contracts in question would withstand antitrust attack.

The basic lesson to be learned from these cases should be clear: the team's entitlement to injunctive relief presupposes that the plaintiff has used care to insure the enforceability of the contract which forms the basis of its action. While some issues with respect to the enforceability — such as possible public policy objections — are not subject to a clear *a priori* determination, others clearly are. Thus, clubs are encouraged to give particular attention to such matters as the validity of the acceptance, the definiteness of the agreement and the applicable interpretative tools which will define the language used.

§ 4.07. Requirement That the Athlete Possess Unique Skills: Inadequacy of Money Damages.

The club which seeks to enjoin an athlete from playing for another team contrary to the terms of a negative covenant bears the burden of showing that the athlete is "a person of exceptional and unique knowledge, skill and ability in performing the service called for in the contract."[140] The rule is of uncertain

---

135. *See* Madison Square Garden Corp. v. Carnera, 52 F.2d 47, 49 (2d Cir. 1931).

136. *See* Metropolitan Exhibition Co. v. Ewing, 42 F. 198, 202 (S.D.N.Y. 1890).

137. The defense that the contract is illegal or unconscionable is considered more fully below. See § 4.13 *infra*.

138. *See, e.g.,* Boston Professional Hockey Ass'n, Inc. v. Cheevers, 348 F. Supp. 261, 265 (D. Mass.), *remanded,* 472 F.2d 127 (1st Cir. 1972); Nassau Sports v. Hampson, 355 F. Supp. 733 (D. Minn. 1972).

139. *See* American League Baseball Club of Chicago v. Chase, 86 Misc. 441, 460-61, 149 N.Y.S. 6, 17 (Sup. Ct. 1914).

140. Dallas Cowboys Football Club, Inc. v. Harris, 348 S.W.2d 37, 42 (Tex. Civ. App. 1961). *See also* Washington Capitols Basketball Club, Inc. v. Barry, 419 F.2d 472 (9th Cir.), *aff'g* 304 F. Supp. 1193, 1197 (N.D. Cal. 1969); Boston Professional Hockey Ass'n, Inc. v. Cheevers, 348 F. Supp. 261, 263 (D. Mass. remanded on other grounds, 472 F.2d 127 (1st Cir. 1972); Nassau Sports v. Peters, 352 F. Supp. 870, 876 (E.D.N.Y. 1972); Winnipeg Rugby Football Club v. Freeman, 140 F. Supp. 365, 366 (N.D. Ohio 1955); Brooklyn Baseball Club v. McGuire, 116 F. 782, 783 (E.D. Pa. 1902); Safro v. Lakofsky, 238 N.W. 641 (Minn. 1931); American Base Ball & Exhibition Co. v. Harper, 54 CENT. L.J.

origin. It was not an element of *Lumley v. Wagner*,[141] nor of subsequent English cases. Its most likely source is an early treatise writer.[142] In any event, it has unquestionably become a part of the jurisprudence of the enforcement of personal service contracts, although courts vary in the extent to which they insist upon precise compliance with it.

a. Reason for the Rule. Courts often do not articulate the reason for the requirement that the athlete possess unique skills. However, the rule appears to be a specialized application of the more general principle that equity will not act unless the plaintiff can show that his remedies at law are inadequate.[143] In its essence, the requirement of uniqueness seeks to preserve to equitable enforcement the status of a special or extraordinary remedy. If the injury which the plaintiff receives can be fully compensated by the usual legal remedy of money damages, then there is no need for the application of the special powers of equity, and equitable enforcement will be denied.

A finding that the athlete has unique skills establishes that it is unlikely that the club could secure a replacement who would perform in precisely the same manner as the player who has defected. If a wholly comparable substitute were available, the club would presumably be able to maintain its team's performance at the levels achieved before the defendant breached his contract. In such a case, the club might suffer some economic loss, either because it had to pay the substitute more than the defendant received or because it incurred special costs in locating the substitute, but these losses could be compensated by money damages and there would be no need for a court of equity to intervene. Where the defendant's skills are unique, however, an exact equivalent performance, by definition, cannot be secured elsewhere and, thus, the injury caused by his departure is thought not to be susceptible to valuation in monetary terms.[144]

449, 450 (Cir. Ct. St. Louis 1902); Long Island American Ass'n Football Club, Inc. v. Manrodt, 23 N.Y.S.2d 858, 860 (Sup. Ct. 1940); Central New York Basketball, Inc. v. Barnett, 19 Ohio Op. 2d 130, 137, 181 N.E.2d 506, 514 (1961); Columbus Base Ball Club v. Reiley, 11 Ohio Dec. 272, 275 (1891); Philadelphia Ball Club, Ltd. v. Lajoie, 202 Pa. 210, 51 A. 973 (1902); *cf.* Frederick Bros. Artists Corp. v. Yates, 61 N.Y.S.2d 478, 482 (Sup. Ct.), *rev'd,* 271 App. Div. 69, 62 N.Y.S.2d 714 (1946); Harry Rogers Theatrical Enterprises, Inc. v. Comstock, 225 App. Div. 34, 36, 232 N.Y.S. 1, 3 (1928); Harry Hastings Attractions v. Howard, 119 Misc. 326, 328, 196 N.Y.S. 228 (Sup. Ct. 1922); Dockstader v. Reed, 121 App. Div. 846, 106 N.Y.S. 795 (1907).

    See generally Brennan, *Injunction Against Professional Athletes Breaching Their Contracts,* 34 BROOKLYN L. REV. 61, 65-67 (1967); Gilbert, *Some Old Problems in a Modern Guise: Enforcement of Negative Covenants,* 4 CAL. L. REV. 114, 116 (1915); Tannenbaum, *Enforcement of Personal Service Contracts in the Entertainment Industry,* 42 CAL. L. REV. 18, 21 (1954); Comment, *Negative Specific Performance of Personal Contracts,* 2 BAYLOR L. REV. 189, 200 (1950); Comment, *Injunctions in Professional Athletes' Contracts — An Overused Remedy,* 43 CONN. B.J. 538, 544-46 (1969); Note, *Reserve Clauses in Athletic Contracts,* 2 RUTGERS-CAMDEN L.J. 302, 318 (1970).

    141. De G.M. & G. 604, 42 Eng. Rep. 687 (1852).

    142. *See* Gilbert, *Some Old Problems in a Modern Guise: Enforcement of Negative Covenants, supra* note 140, at 116 n. 8, where it is suggested that the requirement of uniqueness had its source in Pomeroy's A TREATISE ON SPECIFIC PERFORMANCE CONTRACTS (2d ed. 1897).

    143. *See* 1 J. POMEROY, A TREATISE ON EQUITY JURISPRUDENCE §§ 216-22 (5th ed. 1941); 27 AM. JUR. 2d *Equity* §§ 86-101 (1966); Note, *Developments in the Law — Injunctions,* 78 HARV. L. REV. 993, 1002-03 (1965).

    144. The analysis suggested in the text represents the apparent rationale of those courts which required a showing of the uniqueness of the athlete's skills as a part of the plaintiff-club's cause of action. An argument might be made, however, that the uniqueness requirement is unnecessary and indeed, misperceives the nature of the plaintiff's cause of action. The suit by the club is one to enforce the athlete's negative covenant. Thus, the promise for which the plaintiff seeks a remedy is the athlete's promise not to play for another employer. Under this view of the case, the only

It can be noted that many courts give little or no attention to the requirement of uniqueness.[145] This seeming de-emphasis of the rule can probably be explained as the consequence of two developments. First, there is an increasing willingness on the part of courts to accept that any athlete selected to perform with a professional team probably has a level of skill sufficient to satisfy the requirement.[146] This assumption is particularly appropriate in light of the fact that most cases involve athletes who have established themselves as star performers. Indeed, if the defecting player is only a marginal success in the professional ranks, his employer-club is less likely to endure the expense of litigation to secure his return. The second consideration which may prompt a court to give less attention to the element of uniqueness is of a more general nature. There is increasing evidence that courts generally are not rigidly insisting that the plaintiff in a proceeding in equity establish that his legal remedies are inadequate. Indeed, it is often enough for the plaintiff to argue either that equitable relief has historically been available in the particular type of case or that damages, even if available, would not be as complete or satisfactory a remedy as injunctive relief. As early as 1932, the *Restatement of Contracts* recognized a trend toward "greater liberality in granting decrees of specific performance." [147] Developments in this direction have apparently

relevant inquiry is whether money damages would provide adequate compensation for the injury occasioned by the athlete's failure to render this performance. And it would be argued that there is no "performance" which could be purchased in the marketplace which would provide a substitute for what the athlete had promised. The promised activity, or more properly, abstention, is so inescapably unique as to be incapable of performance by anyone other than the promisor. This would seemingly be true whatever the level of the athlete's skills.

While no cases can be found which adopt this rationale, the *Restatement of Contracts* offers some support. Under § 361 of the *Restatement,* damages may be deemed inadequate, and hence specific enforcement ordered, if it is difficult to obtain a substantial equivalent performance. The drafters of the *Restatement* go on to observe that "[a] substantial equivalent [performance] is *never* available in the case of a negative contract, for example, a contract not to compete." § 361, comment *g* (emphasis added).

The correctness of this view is not beyond doubt, however. It would seem that the relative level of the athlete's skill may in fact be quite relevant. Assume that there is a case involving an athlete of sufficiently marginal quality that there are a number of uncommitted players available who could fill the minor role which he plays on the team. While a rival team might hire away such a performer, it could presumably have employed any number of others to fill the available position. Likewise, the original employer could readily find a substitute. An action for equitable enforcement by the original employer should fail, not because money damages would be adequate, but rather because it has suffered no loss as a result of the breach of the negative covenant. The purpose of such a provision is to protect the original employer from the injury to his competitive position which results when an employee goes to work for another team. In light of the readily-available supply of similar players in our case, it cannot be said that the rival club has gained any substantial competitive advantage by selecting this athlete rather than another.

If this analysis is correct, then under this alternative view of the plaintiff's case, it would still be necessary to show that the defendant was someone who could not be readily replaced. As is discussed later in the text, the existing case law defines *uniqueness* in terms of the ease of replacement. Since the alternative rationale discussed here would require this same sort of inquiry, it is by no means clear that the decided cases have reached the wrong result, even if the theory upon which they proceed might be disputed.

145. *See, e.g.,* Munchak Corp. v. Cunningham, 457 F.2d 721 (4th Cir. 1972); Nassau Sports v. Peters, 352 F. Supp. 870 (E.D.N.Y. 1972).

146. "It would seem that mere engagement as a basketball player in the NBA or ABA, carries with it recognition of his excellence and extra-ordinary abilities." Central New York Basketball, Inc. v. Barnett, 19 Ohio Op. 2d 130, 137, 181 N.E.2d 506, 514 (1961). *See also* Brennan, *Injunctions Against Professional Athletes Breaching Their Contracts, supra* note 140, at 65-67; Note, *Reserve Clauses in Athletic Contracts, supra* note 140, at 318.

147. Restatement of Contracts § 358, comment *d* (1932).

continued, for the author of a recent treatise on remedies concluded the issue of the adequacy of legal remedies "is of diminished importance today [and] [t]here are many cases in which the equity court proceeds without any discussion of adequacy." [148] There is little to suggest that the sports cases are not to be included in this trend.

b. Criteria by Which Uniqueness Is Determined. The above analysis is not intended to suggest that the requirement of uniqueness does not still play a role in the equitable proceedings to enforce an athlete's promise to play exclusively for his original employer. Many courts continue to inquire into the level of the defendant-athlete's skills. Thus, it is appropriate to review the precedents which establish the criteria by which the determination of uniqueness is made.

In 1902, the court, in *Philadelphia Ball Club, Ltd. v. Lajoie,*[149] made clear that the appropriate inquiry was not whether the athlete was irreplaceable in the sense that no other player existed who had skills as highly refined as the defendant's. Suggesting that the phrase "irreparable damage" was an unfortunate and misleading standard, the court concluded that the appropriate inquiry was whether replacement of the defendant on the playing field would involve a degree of difficulty which could not be readily translated into a money damage award.[150] Under this approach, the essential question is whether the player is readily replaceable in the existing labor market. Such a test would seem to impose only a minimal burden on the plaintiff-club. Human skills, particularly those of a star athlete, are seldom precisely duplicated. Moreover, there is even less likelihood of finding a good substitute for a player who is already a member of the plaintiff's team. Since a "team effort" requires that each member adjust to the level of skill and manner of performance of each of his teammates, it would seem that the plaintiff-club could always show that the introduction of another player would necessitate an indeterminable period of adjustment, during which the team might suffer financial losses of equally indeterminable proportions.[151] Most courts accept that a player, particularly an established member of a team, need not be of superstar quality to be deemed to have unique skills, and it is enough if there is informed opinion that the player is "average or above average." [152] Finally, as is recognized in the decided cases, the determination of substitutability requires that courts consider not only the difficulty of duplicating the defendant's skills and manner of performance, but also the difficulty of finding another player after the season has begun or after the point when all other players have been allocated to their respective clubs.[153] Thus, in light of the many variables involved, it will likely be a rare case where a court can make an *a priori* determination that adequate replacements are available.

---

148. D. DOBBS, HANDBOOK ON THE LAW OF REMEDIES 61 (1973).

149. 202 Pa. 210, 51 A. 973 (1902).

150. 202 Pa. at 216, 51 A. at 973-74. *See also* Dallas Cowboys Football Club, Inc. v. Harris, 348 S.W.2d 37, 44 (Tex. Civ. App. 1961); Frederick Bros. Artists Corp. v. Yates, 61 N.Y.S.2d 478, 482 (Sup. Ct.), *rev'd,* 271 App. Div. 69, 62 N.Y.S.2d 714 (1946).

151. *See* Philadelphia Ball Club, Ltd. v. Lajoie, 202 Pa. 210, 217, 51 A. 973, 974 (1902); Long Island American Ass'n Football Club, Inc. v. Manrodt, 23 N.Y.S.2d 858, 860 (Sup. Ct. 1940).

152. Dallas Cowboys Football Club, Inc. v. Harris, 348 S.W.2d 37, 45 (Tex. Civ. App. 1961).

153. Long Island American Ass'n Football Club, Inc. v. Manrodt, 23 N.Y.S.2d 858, 860 (Sup. Ct. 1940).

Other precedents in this area confirm that a club will normally have little difficulty in meeting its burden on the question of uniqueness. As previously mentioned, there are cases which adopt what is basically a *per se* rule. As succinctly stated by the court in *Central New York Basketball, Inc. v. Barnett,* [154] "Professional players in the major baseball, football, and basketball leagues have unusual talents and skills or they would not be so employed." Other courts have similarly endorsed the notion that the recruitment and signing of a professional athlete is itself evidence of his unique ability. [155]

Cases can be found in which courts have either implied or specifically found that an athlete did not have unique skills. But few of these are of recent vintage, and most were decided under criteria which have been impliedly rejected by modern courts as unduly restrictive. [156] In other cases, the factual setting does not mirror that typically found in current professional sports litigation. [157]

c. **Evidence of the Athlete's Unique Skill.** The history of litigation in this area suggests that courts occasionally will find it necessary to delve into the factual basis of a club's assertion of the player's uniqueness. Where such an inquiry is made, a wide variety of evidence may be found to be relevant. Testimony may be received from witnesses who have closely observed the athlete's performance, including other players [158] and those who manage the affairs of the team. [159] The weight to be afforded such evidence depends upon the interest which the witness has in the outcome of the litigation. Thus, uncomplimentary testimony from individuals associated with the athlete's new employer may be regarded as self-serving since the interests of the club are furthered if the athlete is found not to have unique skills. [160] On the other hand, where persons associated with the plaintiff-club disparage the athlete's ability, the testimony would support a finding of non-uniqueness. [161] Apart from such personal opinion testimony, consideration is also given to the relative level of the athlete's salary and to the amount of salary increases which he has received. [162]

---

154. 19 Ohio Op. 2d 130, 139-40, 181 N.E.2d 506, 517 (1961).

155. *See* Nassau Sports v. Peters, 352 F. Supp. 870, 876 (E.D.N.Y. 1972); Washington Capitols Basketball Club, Inc. v. Barry, 304 F. Supp. 1193, 1197 (N.D. Cal.), *aff'd,* 419 F.2d 472 (9th Cir. 1969). *See also* Brennan, *Injunction Against Professional Athletes Breaching Their Contracts,* 34 BROOKLYN L. REV. 61, 69 (1967); Note, *Reserve Clauses in Athletic Contracts,* 2 RUTGERS-CAMDEN L.J. 302, 318 (1970).

156. *See* American Base Ball & Athletic Exhibition Co. v. Harper, 54 CENT. L.J. 449, 450 (Cir. Ct. St. Louis 1902); Columbus Base Ball Club v. Reiley, 11 Ohio Dec. 272, 275 (1891); Brooklyn Baseball Club v. McGuire, 116 F. 782, 783 (E.D. Pa. 1902).

157. Safro v. Lakofsky, 238 N.W. 641 (Minn. 1931). *See also* Frederick Bros. Artists Corp. v. Yates, 271 App. Div. 69, 62 N.Y.S.2d 714, *rev'g* 61 N.Y.S.2d 478 (Sup. Ct. 1946); Dockstader v. Reed, 121 App. Div. 846, 852, 106 N.Y.S. 795, 797 (1907).

158. *See, e.g.,* American Base Ball & Athletic Exhibition Co. v. Harper, 54 Cent. L.J. 449, 450 (Cir. Ct. St. Louis 1902); Central New York Basketball, Inc. v. Barnett, 19 Ohio Op. 2d 130, 136, 181 N.E.2d 506, 513 (1961).

159. *See, e.g.,* Central New York Basketball, Inc. v. Barnett, 19 Ohio Op. 2d 130, 136, 181 N.E.2d 506, 513 (1961); Dallas Cowboys Football Club, Inc. v. Harris, 348 S.W.2d 37, 43 (Tex. Civ. App. 1961).

160. *See* Boston Professional Hockey Ass'n, Inc. v. Cheevers, 348 F. Supp. 261, 263 (D. Mass.), *remanded,* 472 F.2d 127 (1st Cir. 1972); Central New York Basketball, Inc. v. Barnett, 19 Ohio Op. 2d 130, 136, 181 N.E.2d 506, 513 (1961); Winnipeg Rugby Football Club v. Freeman, 140 F. Supp. 365, 366 (N.D. Ohio 1955).

161. *See* Matuszak v. Houston Oilers, Inc., 515 S.W.2d 725 (Tex. Civ. App. 1974).

162. *See* Philadelphia Ball Club, Ltd. v. Lajoie, 202 Pa. 210, 217, 51 A. 973, 974 (1902); Central New York Basketball, Inc. v. Barnett, 19 Ohio Op. 2d 130, 137, 181 N.E.2d 506, 514 (1961); *cf.* Dockstader v. Reed, 121 App. Div. 846, 106 N.Y.S. 795, 797 (1907).

The question also arises whether representations in the athlete's contract concerning the uniqueness of his skills ought to be viewed as controlling. Those who draft standard form player contracts typically include boilerplate warranties by the athlete that he has "special, exceptional and unique knowledge, skill and ability . . . the loss of which cannot be fairly or adequately compensated by damages." [163] With one possible exception,[164] such clauses have been given virtually no weight by the courts.[165] While the club might try to argue that it relied on the representation of uniqueness and, thus, the player should be estopped from contradicting it, it can be noted that the parties do not have power to confer jurisdiction upon a court of equity, and the court is under a duty to satisfy itself that the conditions for the exercise of its equity power in fact exist.[166] Moreover, since the warranty of uniqueness is typically not the subject of real bargaining between the player and team, any suggestion that the team relied on the boilerplate must be discounted.

§ 4.08. Related Requirements of Irreparable Harm to the Plaintiff Club.

One of the universal principles of equitable enforcement is that the particular remedy of injunctive relief will be granted only upon the plaintiff's showing that it is threatened with irreparable harm.[167] The question of irreparable harm may arise either in connection with the plaintiff's request for a temporary restraining order or at the stage where permanent relief is sought. While the requirement is often used in each context without special qualification, it appears to be more stringently applied where temporary relief is requested.[168]

What is meant by the concept of irreparable harm? As generally applied in injunction cases in the sports area, the term seems to embody the same meaning as the requirement that the plaintiff not have an adequate remedy at law. Hence, the plaintiff is often able to establish a threat of irreparable harm if it can show that a player's departure would cause injuries which could not be compensated by money damages. This equation of irreparable harm with inadequate damage remedies was specifically endorsed by the district court in *Washington Capitols Basketball Club, Inc. v. Barry:*

> Irreparable harm is that which cannot be compensated by the award
> of money damages; it is injury which is certain and great. . . . Such

In cases involving entertainers, courts have considered evidence from seemingly disinterested third parties, including other employers in the industry and newspaper commentators. *See* Harry Rogers Theatrical Enterprises, Inc. v. Comstock, 225 App. Div. 34, 37, 232 N.Y.S. 1, 3 (1928); Harry Hastings Attractions v. Howard, 119 Misc. 326, 330, 196 N.Y.S. 228, 231 (Sup. Ct. 1922).

163. NFL Contract ¶ 8 (1975). *See also* Baseball Contract ¶ 4(a) (1973); NHL Contract ¶ 6 (1974).

164. *Cf.* Frederick Bros. Artists Corp. v. Yates, 61 N.Y.S.2d 478, 481 (Sup. Ct.), *rev'd,* 271 App. Div. 69, 62 N.Y.S.2d 714 (1946).

165. *See* Dallas Cowboys Football Club, Inc. v. Harris, 348 S.W.2d 37, 43 (Tex. Civ. App. 1961); Dockstader v. Reed, 121 App. Div. 846, 106 N.Y.S. 795 (1907). *See also* Frederick Bros. Artists Corp. v. Yates, 271 App. Div. 69, 62 N.Y.S.2d 714, *rev'g* 61 N.Y.S.2d 478 (Sup. Ct. 1946); Harry Hastings Attractions v. Howard, 119 Misc. 326, 196 N.Y.S. 228, 230-31 (Sup. Ct. 1922); Tannenbaum, *Enforcement of Personal Service Contracts in the Entertainment Industry,* 42 CAL. L. REV. 18, 22-23 (1954).

166. *See* Dockstader v. Reed, 121 App. Div. 846, 106 N.Y.S. 795 (1907).

167. *See* D. DOBBS, HANDBOOK ON THE LAW OF REMEDIES 108 (1973); Note, *Developments in the Law — Injunctions,* 78 HARV. L. REV. 993, 1056-57 (1965).

168. *See* D. DOBBS, HANDBOOK ON THE LAW OF REMEDIES 108 (1973); Note, *Developments in the Law — Injunctions, supra* note 167, at 1056.

injury exists when an athlete's team is denied the service of an irreplaceable athlete.[169]

Under this view, the team can establish irreparable harm by simply showing that the athlete possesses unique or exceptional skills.[170] The *Barry* perception of irreparable harm is not new, for the same notion was embraced a half-century earlier in *Philadelphia Ball Club, Ltd. v. Lajoie,*[171] where the court looked at precedent defining the term "irreparable harm" and concluded, "We are . . . within the term whenever it is shown that no certain pecuniary standard exists for the measurement of the damages." [172] Thus, irreparable harm may be found not only where it would be extremely difficult to value the player's services, but also where it would be difficult to secure substitute performance during the current playing season.[173] However, the harm complained of must be harm resulting from wrongful activity. The requisite type of injury is not present if the plaintiff club is harmed only in the sense of being subjected to legitimate economic competition for its players.[174]

One development which must be noted is found in the district court opinion in *Boston Professional Hockey Association, Inc. v. Cheevers.*[175] There the court concluded that on the record before it, the plaintiff club had not established that it would experience irreparable harm as a result of the signing of two of its star players by a rival league. The court apparently applied the same test used in earlier cases, for it perceived that the essential issue was whether damages would compensate the plaintiff for the injury incurred by the loss of its players. But the court's analysis of this question differs markedly from that employed by other courts. In earlier cases, the courts made inquiry into the issue of irreparable harm only to the extent of determining whether the player had unique skill. If the requisite high level of skill was found, then the court assumed that money damages would not be adequate and hence that irreparable harm was present.[176] The *Cheevers* court did not adopt this shorthand analysis and instead made a detailed inquiry into the impact which the loss of the player would have on the plaintiff's general economic position. The court's examination revealed that the club's revenues had recently increased at a most favorable rate and that, in general, its market position seemed to be quite secure. Even though the skills of the two players involved would probably meet the traditional test of uniqueness, the court refused to find irreparable harm. The court concluded the financial consequences for the plaintiff team were at best "unknown" and that "on the present record, it cannot be proven that the Bruins will suffer any financial loss whatsoever in their operating revenues, ticket sales, television income, etc., due to the absence of these two players from their team." [177] The

---

169. 304 F. Supp. 1193, 1197 (N.D. Cal.), *aff'd* 419 F.2d 472 (9th Cir. 1969).

170. *See also* Nassau Sports v. Hampson, 355 F. Supp. 733 (D. Minn. 1972).

171. 202 Pa. 210, 51 A. 973 (1902).

172. *Id.* at 216, 51 A. at 974.

173. *See* Long Island American Ass'n Football Club, Inc. v. Manrodt, 23 N.Y.S.2d 858, 860 (Sup. Ct. 1940).

174. Cincinnati Bengals, Inc. v. Bergey, 453 F. Supp. 129 (S.D. Ohio), *aff'd,* Civil No. 74-1570 (6th Cir., Aug. 27, 1974). This case is discussed more fully below. *See* § 4.14 *infra.*

175. 348 F. Supp. 261 (D. Mass.), *remanded on other grounds,* 472 F.2d 127 (1st Cir. 1972).

176. *See* Washington Capitols Basketball Club, Inc. v. Barry, 304 F. Supp. 1193, 1197-98 (N.D. Cal.), *aff'd,* 419 F.2d 472 (9th Cir. 1969); Philadelphia Ball Club Ltd. v. Lajoie, 202 Pa. 210, 216, 51 A. 973 (1902).

177. 348 F. Supp. at 269.

court added that the club had "a complete and adequate remedy at law, consisting of a suit for money damages for breach of contract. . . ." [178]

The burden placed on a plaintiff club by the *Cheevers* analysis is substantial. It would usually be quite difficult for a team to project the extent of financial loss which would be caused by the departure of one or more of its players. Since such losses would most likely occur gradually over one or more seasons and since the hearing on a request for an injunction is usually held before the season starts, it is not clear what type of evidence the *Cheevers* court would expect the club to introduce. The fact that the financial consequences to the plaintiff team are "unknown," as the court recognized, would seem to be a factor which should favor the plaintiff's position, and not undermine it, as the court suggests. Also noteworthy is the court's refusal to accept the formerly almost unquestioned notion that money damages do not provide an adequate remedy for the loss of a unique player. The court offers no explanation as to why it is inappropriate to presume that the injury in this situation is not readily translatable into monetary terms.

On each point — the insistence on a specific showing of loss and the finding of an adequate legal remedy — the *Cheevers* court departs from prior trends. It can be doubted whether *Cheevers* foreshadows a permanent departure in this regard. A subsequent appellate review of the district court decision did not endorse its new approach, and while the case was remanded on other grounds, the appellate court seems to have doubted the correctness of the lower court's analysis of the irreparable harm question.[179] Moreover, a later case which endorsed the *Cheevers* court's analysis on another point chose to treat the question of irreparable harm under the traditional standard.[180] Other subsequent cases have similarly indicated no inclination to adopt the *Cheevers* approach.[181]

§ 4.09. Other Aspects of the Adequacy of Remedies at Law.

The prior discussion should make clear that the question of the adequacy of the plaintiff's money damage remedies is seldom expressly considered in suits to enforce an athlete's negative covenant. Typically, the issue is implicitly addressed only as courts inquire into the uniqueness of the defendant-athlete's skills. As a consequence, there is very little authority exploring the issue of whether money damages would ever be an appropriate remedy in this setting. Nonetheless, there are situations in which a club might want to assess the likelihood of its success in securing a money judgment rather than injunctive

---

178. *Id.*

179. 472 F.2d 127 (1st Cir. 1972). The First Circuit remanded the case for further consideration of three questions pertaining to the interpretation of the standard player contract. The court added

> We do not intend, by these questions, to intimate any views as to the likelihood of plaintiff's ultimate success. We are, however, of the view that the plaintiff, both because damages other than monetary are at stake and because of the impossibility of demonstrating the extent of the monetary damages, has made a sufficient demonstration that it would probably suffer irreparable damages.

Id. at 128.

180. *See* Nassau Sports v. Hampson, 355 F. Supp. 733 (D. Minn. 1972).

181. *See, e.g.,* Matuszak v. Houston Oilers, Inc., 515 S.W.2d 725 (Tex. Civ. App. 1974).

relief. The question may arise as a part of the club's general evaluation of its litigation options in the event of breach. Or there may be circumstances in which the club is not really interested in having the athlete return, but would like to recoup losses through litigation. Or it may be that the money damage alternative is suggested by a court which has refused to grant injunctive relief. As noted in the prior section, such a situation was presented by the district court's decision in *Boston Professional Hockey Association, Inc. v. Cheevers.*[182] In denying the club's request for injunctive relief against two players who had joined the rival WHA, the court concluded that "there is available to the [plaintiff] a complete and adequate remedy at law, consisting of a suit for money damages for breach of contract." [183] While the court's finding on the adequacy of damages makes the decision somewhat aberrational in terms of the general trend of recent cases, there have been other cases in which courts have concluded that an injured team could be adequately compensated in money for the loss of a player.[184]

If the team should sue for damages, it will likely ask for compensation for the athlete's breach of his affirmative promise to play for the club.[185] In such litigation, a question will immediately arise concerning the valuation of the club's loss.[186] The measures of damage which might be employed can be briefly outlined. The method of valuation likely to be given first consideration is that which compensated the team for expenses incurred in securing a substitute performer.[187] The direct "damages" here would be of two sorts: a salary differential — the difference between the salary paid the former player and the salary paid his substitute — and the expenses incurred in locating and negotiating with the replacement. In addition, the team would seemingly be entitled to consequential damages which would compensate it for all other damages directly and foreseeably related to the athlete's breach.[188] These might include such things as loss of revenues due to the departure of a star player, loss of tournament and championship opportunities, and so on.

There are obvious problems with attempting to peg damages to the cost of obtaining substitute performance. It can be anticipated that there will be lengthy debates about whether a player secured as a replacement has skills which are greater or less than those of the defendant, whether his temperament makes a more or less constructive contribution to the team, and whether his future potential approximates that of the defendant. It should not be surprising that

---

182. *See* Boston Professional Hockey Ass'n, Inc. v. Cheevers, 348 F. Supp. 261 (D. Mass.), remanded on other grounds, 472 F.2d 127 (1st Cir. 1972).

183. 348 F. Supp. at 269. The *Cheevers* analysis on this and a related point is criticized in § 4.08 *supra*.

184. *See* Connecticut Professional Sports Corp. v. Heyman, 276 F. Supp. 618, 621 (S.D.N.Y. 1967); Brooklyn Baseball Club v. McGuire, 116 F. 782, 783 (E.D. Pa. 1902); Columbus Base Ball Club v. Reiley, 11 Ohio Dec. 272, 275 (1891). *See also* Linseman v. World Hockey Ass'n, 439 F. Supp. 1315, 1323 (D. Conn. 1977).

185. While the club cannot secure equitable enforcement of the affirmative promise to play, the policies which dictate against that result do not seem to apply where the plaintiff seeks only money damages and not actual enforcement. *See* § 4.02 *supra*.

186. *See generally* D. DOBBS, HANDBOOK ON THE LAW OF REMEDIES 931 (1973); Annot., 61 A.L.R.2d 1013 (1958); 22 AM. JUR. 2d *Damages* § 74 (1965). 11 S. WILLISTON, WILLISTON ON CONTRACTS § 1362A (3d ed. 1968).

187. *See* 5 A. CORBIN, CORBIN ON CONTRACTS § 1096 (1964). *See also* Allegheny Base-Ball Club v. Bennett, 14 F. 257 (W.D. Pa. 1882).

188. *See generally* 5 A. CORBIN, CORBIN ON CONTRACTS, § 1096.

these difficulties would be encountered: it is precisely because of this difficulty of valuation that the legal remedy is thought to be inadequate and the equitable remedy better suited to the sports area. Yet, to the extent that courts direct the parties to the law side of the courts, these questions will continue to appear.

Another possible method of assessing the club's damages is that which considers the loss caused to the team's overall financial picture by the player's departure. The components of this method are basically the same as those which would identify the club's damages in the prior discussion. The only difference may be one of emphasis: in some cases, the team may choose not to establish the cost of substitute performance and instead identify the loss to the franchise in terms of reduced gate and concession receipts, reduced broadcast revenues, and the like. This approach again invites lengthy debates about whether particular losses are attributable to the player's departure or to other causes. While there is an indication that at least some courts are willing to make their damage assessments in terms which do not require precise calculation,[189] there is only the most rudimentary case authority on this matter, and it must be accepted that the law has not yet answered the very difficult question about the degree of precision which will be required in the plaintiff's offer of proof.

A third valuation approach is available which avoids many of the difficulties found in the formula set forth above. Under this theory, the "damage" which is caused to the plaintiff team is the difference between the salary which the plaintiff had agreed to pay and that which the player was to be paid by his new employer.[190] In many situations these amounts are readily determinable.[191] While this approach thereby reduces substantially the range of controversy, it should be emphasized that this method has been approved in only a few cases involving employment contracts, none of which involved athletes.[192] Nonetheless, this approach has much to recommend it. Evidence of the salary received by the athlete from his new employer is at least some evidence of the player's market value. When this amount is compared to the player's "contract price" with the original employer, the resulting sum is roughly a market price-contract price differential, which is the measure generally employed to determine damages for breach of contract. Further, this method of valuation identifies the extent to which the player has been unjustly enriched by selling his services in disregard of the rights of his original employer. The amounts

---

189. The appellate court opinion in Lemat Corp. v. Barry, 275 Cal. App. 2d 671, 80 Cal. Rptr. 240, 245 (1969), indicates that the trial court undertook to calculate the damages to the plaintiff franchise resulting from their star player's departure. The trial court's damage formula was based on the growth in revenues which the plaintiff team could have anticipated had Barry not left. This growth rate was assumed to be the average rate of growth experienced by all league teams. The appellate court neither reviewed the damage calculation nor endorsed the method used. Rather, the appellate court affirmed the issuance of an injunction and then observed that any finding in the court below on damages was surplusage, for a plaintiff is not entitled to both damages and equitable relief. 275 Cal. App. 2d at 680, 80 Cal. Rptr. at 245.

190. See D. DOBBS, HANDBOOK ON THE LAW OF REMEDIES 932 (1973); Annot., 61 A.L.R.2d 1013, § 5 (1958).

191. See, e.g., Boston Professional Hockey Ass'n, Inc. v. Cheevers, 348 F. Supp. 261, 264 (D. Mass. 1972); Munchak Corp. v. Cunningham, 331 F. Supp. 872, 875 (M.D.N.C. 1971). It may be necessary to prorate, or otherwise allocate, a bonus in order to identify salary figures which are subject to comparison.

192. See Roth v. Speck, 126 A.2d 153 (D.C. Mun. App. 1956); Triangle Waist Co. v. Todd, 223 N.Y. 27, 119 N.E. 85 (1918). See also Annot., 61 A.L.R.2d 1013, 1015-16 (1958).

received as a result of such improper enrichment might properly be viewed as belonging to the plaintiff team.[193]

§ 4.10. Unfair Competition as an Element of Plaintiff's Case.

In proceedings seeking enforcement of an athlete's negative covenant, a proper assessment of the nature of the plaintiff's cause of action would seemingly require that injunctive relief be granted only where the defendant-athlete had accepted employment with another club which was an economic competitor of the original employer. This element is seldom discussed in reported cases. The reason, of course, is that in the typical case, the player jumps to a club operating a team in the same sport but in a rival league. Even if the new team is located in a distant city, the requisite competition will be present for the relevant markets for most sports are considered to be nationwide and are not restricted to individual franchise areas. There are indications, however, that athletes are increasingly being attracted to teams outside of the domestic markets, particularly as other countries develop professional teams in the traditional American sports.[194] When an established player makes such a move to a foreign team, a court may be required to determine whether there has been an injury to the original employer's competitive position. While the subsequent discussion focuses on the movement of athletes between geographical markets, it can be noted that the legal issue discussed here might arise in other contexts, as, for example, where an athlete "retires" from active play and accepts a sports-related position with another club or other employer. In assessing its legal right to object to such a move, the original employer will have to consider not only whether acceptance of the new position contravenes the terms of the athlete's negative covenant, but also whether there has been a diminution of the competitive advantage which its contract was intended to secure.[195]

The requirement of an injury to the plaintiff's competitive position arises from the peculiar characteristics of the cause of action which supports the club's request for equitable enforcement. As previously noted, the contractual basis of the team's suit for injunctive relief is the athlete's promise not to play for another employer. When an athlete abandons his contract and accepts employment with another club, it is not enough for the plaintiff to show that there has been a breach of the covenant; it must also establish that it has

---

193. It should be noted that this attempt to find a rational damage standard may be of as much, if not more, interest to the player who wants to resist injunctive enforcement than to the team which is considering a suit for damages. A player who wishes to avoid an injunction may argue that in fact there is an adequate remedy at law, perhaps for damages according to the third formula. Obviously the player should be concerned that he may win the battle, but lose the war, as would be true if he won the injunction suit, but then in a second suit, had to pay damages according to this formula. Even with this risk, the theory may be worth the effort either because success in the injunction suit renders the team more willing to settle or because the player sees advantages other than salary in spending his option year in the new league city.

194. *See, e.g.,* N.Y. Times, July 4, 1975, at 11, col. 2 (former Manhattan College basketball player B. Campion signs contract with Italian professional team); *id.,* Aug. 30, 1974, at 41, col. 6 (former Utah State University basketball player B. Lauriski signs contract with Italian professional team); *id.,* May 19, 1974, § 5, at 2, col. 5 (baseball player J. Pepitone plays with Japanese team); *id.,* Feb. 3, 1973, at 26, col. 2 (Baltimore Orioles announce sale of D. Buford's contract to Japanese team); *id.,* March 12, 1972, § 5, at 8, col. 1 (comment on U.S. basketball players competing in France.)

195. *Cf.* Matuszak v. Houston Oilers, Inc., 515 S.W.2d 725, 729 (Tex. Civ. App. 1974).

suffered harm as a result. Yet, such harm occurs only if the player's defection changes the relative competitive positions of his new and old employers. If the new employer operates a business which has no immediate impact upon the success or failure of the plaintiff's enterprise, the necessary effect is not present and the plaintiff will be unable to establish an injury cognizable in a court of law.

It is true that the plaintiff may have been injured as a result of the loss of the player's services. However, harm of that sort can be related only to the athlete's failure to live up to his affirmative promise to perform for the plaintiff. By virtue of strong public policies, including a concern that an individual not be compelled to perform personal acts against his will, breach of such a covenant cannot provide the basis for equitable enforcement.[196] In short, the two types of injuries which the plaintiff club may suffer — one caused by the athlete's failure to deliver his services and the other by his acceptance of employment elsewhere — are to be treated as legally distinct, and an injury resulting from the athlete's breach of one of his two basic covenants cannot support an action based on the other.

Although the majority of sports-related injunction cases have been decided without any attention being given to the requirement of a loss of competitive advantage, numerous authorities can be found which support this limitation on the plaintiff's access to injunctive relief. One of the earliest expressions of the doctrine in the sports-entertainment law area is found in *Harrisburg Base-Ball Club v. Athletic Association,*[197] which was decided in 1890. In denying the plaintiff's request for an injunction, the court observed:

> The injury complained of here is distinctly stated in the bill to be the loss of receipts to the club by the absence of a player of such exceptional skill as the defendant.... There is no distinct allegation, anywhere in the bill, that complainant will be injured by the [athlete's] playing ... for the [new employer], except as such playing involves his loss as a player to complainant. Therefore, an injunction restraining [the athlete] from playing for the [new employer] would not, in any degree, lessen the injury and damage to the complainant, unless it should have the effect of compelling him to play for plaintiff. This it would not, and could not, do directly, and it is conceded by the counsel for the plaintiff that the court could not compel him, by its decree, to do this directly, and therefore ... ought not to attempt to do it indirectly.[198]

Modern courts are not likely to insist that the threat to competition be pleaded or proved in detail, and the requirement will usually be put in issue only if it is raised by the defendant. Nonetheless, there is evidence from other sources that the basic notion developed in *Harrisburg* continues to have validity, albeit on terms somewhat less stringent than those suggested by the court in that case. Subsequent cases have, with varying degrees of explicitness, recognized the presence of a competitive threat as an important prerequisite to the grant of injunctive relief.[199] Similarly, the *Restatement of Contracts* endorses the view that no injunction should issue in the absence of an injury to the plaintiff's

---

196. *See* § 4.02 *supra. See also* RESTATEMENT OF CONTRACTS § 380, comment *g* (1932).
197. 8 Pa. County Ct. 337 (1890).
198. *Id.* at 341-42.
199. *See* Frederick Bros. Artists Corp. v. Yates, 61 N.Y.S.2d 478, 480 (Sup. Ct.), *rev'd on other grounds,* 271 App. Div. 69, 62 N.Y.S.2d 714 (1946); *cf.* Metropolitan Exhibition Co. v. Ward, 9 N.Y.S. 779, 780 (Sup. Ct. 1890).

competitive position.[200] Still further support can be found in law review commentary. Legal scholars very early raised the objection that courts were not giving sufficient attention to the importance of the element of unfair competition.[201] Interestingly, one of the more recent commentaries reaches the same conclusion, with an equal degree of consternation over the failure of courts to show concern for the coercive effects of an injunctive order.[202]

As these authorities suggest, the determinative inquiry in this area is whether the athlete's new employer is in economic competition with his old one. If the athlete accepts a playing position with another team located in the same city or same metropolitan area as the former employer, there should be no question but that the requisite degree of competition is present. But assume that a player jumps from a team in New York City to a California franchise in a rival league. Would the original employer be able to establish that it suffered injury as a result of the player's accepting employment with a club in a distant city? Resolution of the question depends upon how the market for the product known as professional sports is defined. If teams compete only on a local or regional basis, then the plaintiff would have difficulty making the requisite showing. But if major professional sports operate in a market area which is nationwide, then the element of unfair competition would be present if the player defected to any other team in this country, regardless of its geographic location. This question of the relevant product market for professional sports has been raised in cases determining the propriety of various league practices under the antitrust laws. The presently prevailing view is that for questions relating to interclub and interleague competition, the major professional sports leagues should be regarded as operating in a national, rather than a local or regional, market.[203] Despite the difference in the context in which that determination has been made, it should be deemed persuasive for the present inquiry. The factors which are considered in defining the sports market for antitrust purposes would also be relevant in determining whether the hiring of a player by a club in one domestic league infringed upon the competitive advantage of the player's former employer in another league. Thus, in each situation, particular weight would be given to the distinctly national character of the leagues, the team's interest in securing national broadcast contracts, and in general, the highly integrated

---

200. *See* RESTATEMENT OF CONTRACTS § 380, comment *g* (1932). The RESTATEMENT also uses an example which seems to accept the result and rationale suggested above: "*A* contracts to work for *B* as a garage mechanic for one year and not to work in that capacity for anyone else during the year. *A* has such exceptional skills that his services are unique. In breach of his contract, *A* quits *B*'s service and goes to work for an employer whose business *is not* in competition with that of *B* .... [S]ince the breach of the negative promise does not in itself cause injury, *B* cannot get an injunction preventing *A* from working for this new employer. An injunction will not granted merely for the purpose of indirectly compelling *A* to continue in *B*'s service." *See also* 11 S. WILLISTON, WILLISTON ON CONTRACTS § 1450 (3d ed. 1968).

201. *See* Stevens, *Involuntary Servitude by Injunction,* 6 CORNELL L. Q. 235, 266-67 (1921). *See generally* Pound, *The Progress of the Law,* 33 HARV. L. REV. 420, 440 (1920).

202. *See* Comment, *Injunctions in Professional Athletes' Contracts — An Overused Remedy,* 43 CONN. B.J. 538, 552-54 (1969); *cf.* Note, *Negative Specific Performance of Personal Performance Contracts,* 2 BAYLOR L. REV. 189, 199-201 (1950). *See also* D. DOBBS, HANDBOOK ON THE LAW OF REMEDIES 935 (1973); Tannenbaum, *Enforcement of Personal Service Contracts in the Entertainment Industry,* 42 CAL. L. REV. 18, 20-21 (1954).

203. *See* American Football League v. National Football League, 205 F. Supp. 60 (D. Md. 1962), aff'd, 323 F.2d 124 (4th Cir. 1963). *See also* Rivkin, *Sports Leagues and the Federal Antitrust Laws* in GOVERNMENT AND THE SPORTS BUSINESS 387 (R. Noll ed. 1974).

relationship which exists between league clubs which are otherwise widely dispersed geographically.[204]

A somewhat different analysis is necessary where the athlete moves from a team in the United States to one in Canada. Can the Canadian team be deemed to be in competition with the American club? The answer, of course, will depend on the sport. In hockey, for example, the relevant market should be defined to include both the United States and Canada [205] and hence the requisite degree of interteam economic competition is presumably present in that sport. Football presents a slightly different case, for the football enterprises of the two countries in many respects operate independent of one another. But a final resolution of this matter would require a closer analysis of other market factors, particularly the extent to which games from one country are broadcast into the other, a factor which has had varying significance in recent years. Other sports would require a similar particularized analysis, but presumably there are some in which the other country's leagues are of such different scope that they cannot be regarded as economic competitors.

Where teams from foreign countries other than Canada are involved, there is much less reason for equivocation. In most instances, the foreign club — for example, a European basketball team — would seem to operate in a distinct economic market so that the defection of an American player to such an enterprise would not represent a serious economic threat to a former American employer.[206] In cases in which this is true, the domestic employer would not be entitled to the assistance of a court of equity in securing the player's compliance with his negative covenant.[207] This would appear to be the correct analysis at

---

204. *See* American Football League v. National Football League, 205 F. Supp. 60 (D. Md. 1962), *aff'd*, 323 F.2d 124 (4th Cir. 1963).

205. *See* San Francisco Seals, Ltd. v. National Hockey League, 379 F. Supp. 966 (C.D. Cal. 1974).

206. A small but growing number of players in basketball and baseball are opting to play in Europe and Japan where viable professional baseball and basketball leagues exist. *See, e.g.,* Raleigh (N.C.) News and Observer, Aug. 7, 1974, at 18, col. 1 (ABA player Randy Denton signs contract to play in European basketball league) and sources cited note 194, *supra.*

In many situations, particularly in baseball, the contracts of established American players are "sold" to foreign teams. *See* N.Y. Times, Feb. 3, 1973, at 26, col. 2 (Baltimore Orioles announce sale of D. Buford's contract to Japanese team); *id.,* Jan. 16, 1972, § 5, at 4, col. 8 (San Francisco Giants announce first international player transaction in major league baseball history). Where such an assignment is effected, the legal question discussed in this section will, of course, not arise since the assignor will have no further claim to the player's services. Since it is by no means clear that an American club could enjoin a player from moving to a team in another country, a question might arise as to why the foreign team makes a formal purchase of the domestic club's contract rights. There are a number of considerations suggesting the wisdom of such an arrangement. In light of the dearth of cases on the issue of the domestic employer's entitlement to an injunction in these situations, the foreign team may well conclude that the player's success in litigation is by no means certain. The lack of precedent on the question of whether the foreign baseball teams are actually in competition with the American clubs adds to this uncertainty. Hence, the foreign team may decide that it is worth the cost of securing an assignment to insure that the athlete will be available on a specific date. Moreover, such an arrangement, if it is part of a more general agreement, protects the foreign team from competition for its players.

207. The present standard form players' contracts used in the major sports do not specifically provide that a player's promise not to play for another club covers employment with teams outside the United States. Nonetheless, the language used is sufficiently broad to support an argument that nothing in the contract limits its operation to employment with other domestic teams. *See* NBA Contract (Veteran—Single Season), ¶¶ 5, 9 (1976); NFL Contract ¶ 5 (1975). But even if the contract clause is construed to cover these situations, that will not insure the success of a suit in equity by the original employer. As previously stated, the requirement of unfair competition is based on the necessity of the club's establishing that it was injured by the athlete's actions, and thus arises independent of the particular terms of the negative covenant.

least until recent proposals for expanding domestic leagues into Asia, Latin America and other foreign markets become a reality.[208]

§ 4.11. Requirement of Mutuality.

Perhaps no element of the plaintiff's cause of action has generated as much uncertainty as that which is embodied in the notion that equity will not enforce a sports contract which lacks mutuality.[209] In the early 1900's, a lack of mutuality was the reason most frequently given by courts for denying equitable enforcement of sports contracts.[210] The significant number of cases decided under the mutuality doctrine during that period might suggest that the requirement of mutuality had become an inalterable part of the law in this area.

---

208. *See, e.g.,* N.Y. Times, April 6, 1974, at 22, col. 1 (comments on proposed World Baseball Association); *id.,* Oct. 4, 1973, at 61, col. 3 (World Football League plans to establish franchises in Europe and Japan).

209. There is an extensive body of precedent and commentary pertaining to the mutuality question. The following listing indicates the most important authorities. These are classified according to whether they deal with the mutuality problem generally or more specifically in the context of sports.

Sports Authorities: Weeghman v. Killefer, 215 F. 289 (6th Cir. 1914); Brooklyn Baseball Club v. McGuire, 116 F. 782 (E.D. Pa. 1902); Nassau Sports v. Peters, 352 F. Supp. 870, 876 (E.D.N.Y. 1972); Connecticut Professional Sports Corp. v. Heyman, 276 F. Supp. 618 (S.D.N.Y. 1967); Madison Square Garden Corp. v. Braddock, 19 F. Supp. 392 (D.N.J.), *aff'd,* 90 F.2d 924 (3d Cir. 1937); Cincinnati Exhibition Co. v. Johnson, 190 Ill. App. 630 (1914); American Base Ball & Athletic Exhibition Co. v. Harper, 54 Cent. L.J. 449 (Cir. Ct. St. Louis 1902); Long Island American Ass'n Football Club, Inc. v. Manrodt, 23 N.Y.S.2d 858 (Sup. Ct. 1940); Metropolitan Exhibition Co. v. Ward, 9 N.Y.S. 779 (Sup. Ct. 1890); American League Baseball Club of Chicago v. Chase, 86 Misc. 441, 149 N.Y.S. 6 (Sup. Ct. 1914); Central New York Basketball, Inc. v. Barnett, 88 Ohio L. Abs. 40, 19 Ohio Op. 2d 130, 181 N.E.2d 506, 512 (1961); Philadelphia Ball Club, Ltd. v. Lajoie, 202 Pa. 210, 51 A. 973 (1902); Harrisburg Base-Ball Club v. Athletic Ass'n, 8 Pa. County Ct. 337 (1890); Philadelphia Ball Club, Ltd. v. Hallman, 8 Pa. County Ct. 57 (1890); Gilbert, *Some Old Problems in a Modern Guise: Enforcement of Negative Covenants,* 4 CAL. L. REV. 114 (1915-16); Robinson, *Equity: Specific Performances of Service Contracts,* 2 RUTGERS-CAMDEN L.J. 302, 314-15 (1970); Comment, *Injunctions in Professional Athletes' Contracts — An Overused Remedy,* 43 CONN. B.J. 538 (1969); Note, *Enforcement Problems of Personal Services Contracts in Professional Athletics,* 6 TULSA L.J. 40 (1969).

General Authorities: Lee v. Chicago League Ball Club, 169 Ill. App. 525 (1912); Frederick Bros. Artists Corp. v. Yates, 61 N.Y.S.2d 478 (Sup. Ct.), rev'd, 271 App. Div. 69, 62 N.Y.S.2d 714 (1946). *See also* Rutland Marble Co. v. Ripley, 77 U.S. (10 Wall.) 339, 19 L. Ed. 955 (1870); Norris v. Fox, 45 F. 406 (N.D. Mo. 1891); Gould v. Stelter, 14 Ill. 2d 376, 152 N.E.2d 869 (1958); Ulrey v. Keith, 237 Ill. 284, 86 N.E. 696 (1908); Epstein v. Gluckin, 223 N.Y. 490, 135 N.E. 861 (1922); RESTATEMENT OF CONTRACTS § 372 (1932); D. DOBBS, HANDBOOK ON THE LAW OF REMEDIES 49-52 (1973); E. FRY, A TREATISE ON THE SPECIFIC PERFORMANCE OF CONTRACTS §§ 460-76 (6th ed. 1921); H. MCCLINTOCK, HANDBOOK OF THE PRINCIPLES OF EQUITY §§ 68, 181-87 (2d ed. 1948); Ames, *Mutuality in Specific Performance,* 3 COLUM. L. REV. 1 (1903); Cook, *The Present Status of the "Lack of Mutuality" Rule,* 36 YALE L.J. 897 (1927); Durfee, *Mutuality in Specific Performance,* 20 MICH. L. REV. 289 (1922); Lewis, *The Present Status of the Defense of Want of Mutuality in Specific Performance,* 21 AM. L. REG. 591 (1903); Stevens, *Involuntary Servitude by Injunction,* 6 CORNELL L. REV. 235, 268-69 (1921); Stone, *The Mutuality Rule in New York,* 16 COLUM. L. REV. 443 (1916); Note, *Mutuality of Remedy in California Under Civil Code Section 3386,* 19 HASTINGS L.J. 1430 (1968); Note, *Equity — Specific Performance — Mutuality of Remedy,* 32 WEST VA. L.Q. 352 (1926).

210. *See* Brooklyn Baseball Club v. McGuire, 116 F. 782 (E.D. Pa. 1902); Cincinnati Exhibition Co. v. Johnson, 190 Ill. App. 630 (1914); American Base Ball & Athletic Exhibition Co. v. Harper, 54 CENT. L.J. 449 (Cir. Ct. St. Louis 1902); American League Baseball Co. of Chicago v. Chase, 86 Misc. 441, 149 N.Y.S. 6 (Sup. Ct. 1914); Metropolitan Exhibition Co. v. Ward, 9 N.Y.S. 779 (Sup. Ct. 1890); Harrisburg Base-Ball Club v. Athletic Ass'n, 8 Pa. County Ct. 337 (1890); Philadelphia Ball Club, Ltd. v. Hallman, 8 Pa. County Ct. 57 (1890). *But see* Philadelphia Ball Club, Ltd. v. Lajoie, 202 Pa. 210, 51 A. 973 (1902).

Yet, a reading of recent cases reveals that the element of mutuality is now largely ignored. It is seldom mentioned in the modern cases, but when it is, the court's treatment often fails to respond to the policy concerns upon which the earlier precedents were based.[211] While it can be safely said that the mutuality requirement in its strictest and most traditional form has been abandoned,[212] some remnants of the doctrine continue to be applied to decide sports cases.[213]

One reason for the confusion generated by the mutuality requirement is that courts have used the mutuality notion to express at least three different concepts. Courts which purported to be applying the same legal doctrine were in fact looking for different elements in the cases before them, a development which has predictably produced a most uneven, and in some cases, contradictory line of precedent. The differing views which were taken of the mutuality requirement did not appear in a precise and distinctive form, usually because a particular court was often unaware of the degree to which its formulation deviated from the views which had been taken in prior cases. But if one looks at what appears to have been the primary concern of these decisions, three different uses of the mutuality notion can be discerned. Some courts applied the mutuality concept to require mutuality of obligation in a fundamental contract sense.[214] Used in this manner, the insistence on mutuality is simply another way of requiring an exchange of consideration. Since such an exchange is a prerequisite to the formation of any bilateral contract, this type of mutuality serves no function which is peculiar to equity. But the second meaning of mutuality does convey a notion unique to proceedings for specific relief. Most courts used the concept to require mutuality of remedy, although there was considerable uncertainty as to just how mutuality was to be defined in this context.[215] While these courts generally had the proper view of the then-viable mutuality doctrine, a few courts gave mutuality a third meaning which was even more clearly equitable in nature: a contract was deemed to lack mutuality if its terms allocated grossly uneven rights and privileges between the two parties. This view of mutuality was given expression in an early case,[216] and to the extent

---

211. *See* Nassau Sports v. Peters, 352 F. Supp. 870, 874 (E.D.N.Y. 1972); Central New York Basketball, Inc. v. Barnett, 19 Ohio Op. 2d 130, 135-36, 181 N.E.2d 506, 512 (1961). Both of these cases seem to view the doctrine of mutuality as requiring only mutuality of obligation in an elementary contract sense. As used in the early cases, however, the doctrine was applied to require mutuality of a remedy, a substantially different concept. *See* text at notes 232-36 *infra*.

212. *See* RESTATEMENT OF CONTRACTS § 372 (1932).

213. *See* Connecticut Professional Sports Corp. v. Heyman, 276 F. Supp. 618 (S.D.N.Y. 1967).

214. *See* Nassau Sports v. Peters, 352 F. Supp. 870, 876 (E.D.N.Y. 1972); American League Baseball Club of Chicago v. Chase, 86 Misc. 441, 456, 149 N.Y.S. 6, 14 (Sup. Ct. 1914); Central New York Basketball, Inc. v. Barnett, 19 Ohio Op. 2d 130, 135-36, 181 N.E.2d 506, 512 (1961). *Compare* Keith v. Kellerman, 169 F. 196, 200 (S.D.N.Y. 1909). *See also* Note, 54 CENT. L.J. 451, 452-53 (1902).

215. *See* Madison Square Garden Corp. v. Braddock, 90 F. 2d 924, 927 (3d Cir. 1937); Weeghman v. Killefer, 215 F. 168 (W.D. Mich.), *aff'd,* 215 F. 289 (6th Cir. 1914); Brooklyn Baseball Club v. McGuire, 116 F. 782 (E.D. Pa. 1902); Cincinnati Exhibition Co. v. Johnson, 190 Ill. App. 630 (1914); American Base Ball & Athletic Exhibition Co. v. Harper, 54 CENT. L.J. 449 (Cir. Ct. St. Louis 1902); Metropolitan Exhibition Co. v. Ward, 9 N.Y.S. 779 (Sup. Ct. 1890); Harrisburg Base-Ball Club v. Athletic Ass'n, 8 Pa. County Ct. 337 (1890); Philadelphia Ball Club, Ltd. v. Hallman, 8 Pa. County Ct. 57 (1890). *But see* Long Island American Ass'n Football Club, Inc. v. Manrodt, 23 N.Y.S.2d 858 (Sup. Ct. 1940); Philadelphia Ball Club, Ltd. v. Lajoie, 202 Pa. 210, 51 A. 973 (1902). *Compare* Lee v. Chicago League Ball Club, 169 Ill. App. 525, 530 (1912); Frederick Bros. Artists Corp. v. Yates, 61 N.Y.S.2d 478, 483 (Sup. Ct. 1946).

216. Philadelphia Ball Club, Ltd. v. Hallman, 8 Pa. County Ct. 57, 63 (1890).

that the modern cases continue to give any credence to the mutuality notion, it is used in this sense to require that the contract sued upon meets the test of fundamental fairness.[217]

With respect to each of these mutuality theories, the courts' attention was frequently focused on one facet of the parties' contractual relationship. The provisions in question were those which permitted the team to terminate the contract within its discretion and with little advanced notice while at the same time reserving to the team the right to bind the player to a lengthy commitment, one which in some cases was seen as being perpetual.[218] These provisions could be identified as lacking mutuality no matter which of the three different theories was used. Thus, it could be said that since the team had not incurred any substantial obligation to the player, there was no mutuality of obligation, no exchange of consideration, and hence, no valid contract.[219] Similarly, if the second meaning of mutuality were applied, it could be said that there was no mutuality of remedy. While the contract purported to give the team the right to enforce its terms against the athlete, perhaps for an indefinite period, the athlete had no similar assurance of a prospective remedy against the team, since the team could avoid any such enforcement action by merely exercising its right of termination.[220] Finally, the power of termination seemed to underscore a lack of mutuality in an equitable sense. While the player was burdened with heavy commitments under the contract, including the loss of considerable freedom to market his services, the team's obligation appeared to be minimal. By a simple exercise of the power of termination, the team could avoid any obligation to further compensate the player.[221]

It should be noted that a far-reaching power to terminate continues as a part of many of the present-day player contracts.[222] Since questions will continue to arise concerning the effect of this right of termination upon the team's

---

217. *See* Connecticut Professional Sports Corp. v. Heyman, 276 F. Supp. 618 (S.D.N.Y. 1967); D. DOBBS, HANDBOOK ON THE LAW OF REMEDIES 51, n. 24 (1973).

218. *See, e.g.,* American League Baseball Club of Chicago v. Chase, 86 Misc. 441, 455, 149 N.Y.S. 6, 12 (Sup. Ct. 1914); Metropolitan Exhibition Co. v. Ward, 9 N.Y.S. 779, 783 (Sup. Ct. 1890).

219. *See* American League Baseball Club of Chicago v. Chase, 86 Misc. 441, 456, 149 N.Y.S. 6, 14 (Sup. Ct. 1914); Gilbert, *Some Old Problems in a Modern Guise: Enforcement of Negative Covenants, supra* note 209, at 121-24.

220. *See* American Base Ball & Athletic Exhibition Co. v. Harper, 54 CENT. L.J. 449, 450 (Cir. Ct. St. Louis 1902); Harrisburg Base-Ball Club v. Athletic Ass'n, 8 Pa. County Ct. 337, 342-43 (1890). *See also* American League Baseball Club of Chicago v. Chase, 86 Misc. 441, 456, 149 N.Y.S. 6, 14 (Sup. Ct. 1914).

221. *See* Philadelphia Ball Club Ltd., v. Hallman, 8 Pa. County Ct. 57, 62 (1890).

222. For example, the Standard Player Contract of the National Football League provides in ¶ 6 that

> [i]f, in the opinion of the Head Coach, Player does not maintain himself in . . . excellent physical condition or fails at any time during the football seasons included in the terms of this contract to demonstrate sufficient skill and capacity to play professional football of the caliber required by the League, . . . or by the Club, or if in the opinion of the Head Coach the Player's work or conduct is unsatisfactory as compared with the work and conduct of other members of the Club's squad of players, the Club shall have the right to terminate this contract.

The contract also gives the team a right of termination if the player is involved in gambling or point-shaving activities. *Id.* at ¶ 11. Finally, ¶ 7 spells out the team's obligation for salary in the event of termination. The team is obligated to pay the athlete any outstanding balance for traveling expenses, plus a pro-rata share of his salary, based on the percentage of the club's games which are completed prior to termination.

enforcement effort, it is appropriate to undertake a more detailed review of the mutuality requirement. What will be seen is that the mutuality concept in its strictest form no longer presents the impediment to enforcement which was evidenced in the early sports cases. Some aspects of the doctrine continue to have validity, however, and an inquiry into mutuality will still be made by some courts as a part of their more general inquiry into the relative equities of the parties involved in the litigation.

a. The Concern for Mutuality of Obligation. The notion of "mutuality" has long been used in the law of contracts, although in recent times it has been subjected to resounding criticism. In its most frequently employed sense, the inquiry into "mutuality" involves a determination of whether one of the rudimentary elements of contract formation has been met. The rule is often stated that "In a bilateral agreement both promises must be binding or neither is binding." [223] If a lack of mutuality in this sense is found, then it is said that no contract is formed; and hence no enforcement action is available. Most legal scholars reject the mutuality rule in this formulation, largely because there are numerous situations in which a contract may be enforced against one party but, for any one of a number of policy reasons, may not be enforceable against the other party.[224] While the mutuality of obligation notion is generally maligned, there is one area in which its validity is recognized. This is the area in which one of two promises in an alleged bilateral contract is found to be illusory. For example, if *A* promises to work for *B* for a definite term and if *B* is given discretion as to whether or not to pay *A* for the work performed, there is usually no enforceable contract, and some courts would explain the result on the basis of a lack of mutuality.[225] While many scholars would denounce the use of the term *mutuality* in these circumstances, most would agree that no contract had been formed absent other facts. The preferable characterization, however, is that there is no enforceable contract because there was no exchange of consideration. *B*'s promise is illusory and in effect is no promise at all.

Some of this same flavor of the mutuality concept appears in the sports law area. One of the earliest uses of this sense of mutuality was in *American League Baseball Club of Chicago v. Chase*.[226] The court looked at the duration of the respective promises of the parties and noted that while the player promised to play for the team for a potentially indefinite period, the team had the right to terminate its obligation at any time upon ten days' notice. The court was led to the conclusion that "the negative covenant, under such circumstances, is without a consideration to support it, and is unenforceable by injunction." [227] In the court's view there was both a lack of mutuality of obligation as well as an absence of mutual remedies. The "promise" which the team had given could so easily be avoided that the court thought that it was no promise at all. Thus, the

---

223. J. MURRAY, MURRAY ON CONTRACTS 191 (1974).

224. *See, e.g.,* Atwell v. Jenkins, 163 Mass. 362, 40 N.E. 179 (1895) (insanity of one party to the contract, not a defense available to the other); Kelley v. Riley, 106 Mass. 339 (1871) (plaintiff could sue on a marriage contract while defendant, already a married man, could not); Lewis v. Bannister, 82 Mass. (16 Gray) 500 (1860) (party who entered contract under duress may enforce contract if he wishes); Holt v. Ward, [1732] 93 Eng. Rep. 954, 2 Strange 954 (infant may sue upon a contract where other party is a person of age).

225. *See* J. MURRAY, MURRAY ON CONTRACTS 192, n.58 (1974).

226. 86 Misc. 441, 149 N.Y.S. 6 (Sup. Ct. 1914).

227. *Id.* at 452, 149 N.Y.S. at 14.

court found that the supposed agreement lacked the element of exchange which is necessary to the establishment of a binding contractual relationship.

While there are other early authorities which lend support to the rationale of the *Chase* decision,[228] the case is now largely of only historical interest, for there is a respectable body of authority which finds a sufficient exchange of consideration where the sport employer's right to terminate is limited by a requirement of notice. Thus, even if the team can terminate upon only three days' notice, mutuality can be found.[229] The basis of this view is that the team has agreed to render a performance and as long as there is some obligation, even if it be for a brief period, the requisite exchange between the parties is present and the court will not inquire into the sufficiency of the consideration.[230] A finding of sufficient mutuality of obligation in these circumstances is unquestionably correct. It is not merely the obligation of "notice" which gives substance to the employer's undertaking. Rather, the real "consideration" for the player's promise is the other affirmative obligations which the team assumes, most particularly a promise to pay a salary. These bind the team in a very substantial way and will continue to do so until the team takes specific action to negate them. The employer has a real obligation which surely satisfies the minimum requirements of consideration.[231]

b. Mutuality of Remedy. The matter of mutuality of obligation discussed above has played only a minor role in sports litigation. Indeed, a reasonable hypothesis can be put forth that the courts which denied enforceability because of an absence of mutual obligation either were pursuing archaic doctrine, or more likely, confused this form of mutuality with the more substantial objection that there was a lack of mutuality of remedy. As previously mentioned, this latter variety of mutuality has received much more attention in the sports cases and in general, raises legal objections which are less easily subjected to certain analysis. While there has been a great deal of discussion about mutuality of remedy, a review of the authorities suggests that the doctrine of mutuality of remedy did not represent a singular concept. This divergence of meaning can be seen in the language used by various courts. For example, some courts took a literal view of the requirement of mutual remedies. Representative of this approach is the statement that: "To entitle a party to a decree for specific performance, the contract must be mutual. Both parties must, by the agreement, have a right to compel specific performance." [232] Under this view, remedies were "mutual" only if each party had access to precisely the same form of judicial relief. Thus, if the plaintiff was seeking an injunction or other type of specific enforcement, the court, before it could enter a decree, had to find that the

---

228. See cases cited Note, 54 CENT. L.J. 451 (1902).

229. *See* Long Island American Ass'n Football Club, Inc. v. Manrodt, 23 N.Y.S. 2d 858, 860 (Sup. Ct. 1940); "Mutuality of obligation [is] not lacking, for the provision for notice makes the contract binding at least until notice is given."

230. *See also* Frederick Bros. Artists Corp. v. Yates, 61 N.Y.S.2d 478, 483 (Sup. Ct.), *rev'd on other grounds,* 271 App. Div. 69, 62 N.Y.S.2d 714 (1946); Gilbert. *Some Old Problems in a Modern Guise: Enforcement of Negative Covenants, supra* note 209, at 123. *Cf.* Central New York Basketball, Inc. v. Barnett, 19 Ohio Op. 2d 130, 135-36, 181 N.E.2d 506, 512 (1961).

231. *See generally* Gilbert, *Some Old Problems in a Modern Guise: Enforcement of Negative Covenants, supra* note 209, at 121-25.

232. Harrisburg Base-Ball Club v. Athletic Ass'n, 8 Pa. County Ct. 337, 342-43 (1890).

defendant would have been entitled to such relief had he been the injured party.[233] In sports contracts, such identity of remedies was missing, of course, because the employer typically had the option of terminating the contract, and thus avoiding any specific enforcement order.

Other formulations of the mutuality of remedies rule did not speak in terms of a precise identity of remedies, but rather asked only whether the party seeking equity enforcement had entered into an undertaking to which he could be bound by judicial action. As stated in an early treatise, and adopted by a court in one of the early baseball cases, the rule was that:

> A contract, to be specifically enforced by the court must be mutual; that is to say, such that it might at the time it was entered into have been enforced by either of the parties against the other of them. Whenever, therefore, whether from personal incapacity, the nature of the contract, or any other cause, the contract is incapable of being enforced against one party, that party is equally incapable of enforcing it against the other.[234]

Because the rule in this form apparently did not require a finding that specific performance would have been available against the plaintiff, it generally represented a less substantial obstacle to equitable relief, as there were often damage remedies available when specific performance was not. But in the sports area, even this more liberal view of the mutuality rule was an impediment, again because of the employer's right to terminate the contract. Since the employer had the right to terminate with little advance notice, the contract between the parties was one at least potentially "incapable of being enforced against the [plaintiff]" and hence not subject to equitable enforcement.[235] There might be some dispute as to whether the terminable contract is "incapable of enforcement" in the same sense as a contract entered into with one lacking mental competency. The rule denying specific enforcement seems much better suited to the latter situation where it can reasonably be said that the contractual relationship ceased to exist even before the breach occurred and without any direct action of the parties. But this distinction between degrees of susceptibility to enforcement was not accepted and indeed was implicitly rejected in a leading case from the United States Supreme Court.[236]

Each formulation of the mutuality requirement was almost immediately subjected to an ever-growing list of exceptions. In some cases, efforts were made to reject previous formulations altogether and replace them with newly

---

233. *See also* Madison Square Garden Corp. v. Braddock, 90 F.2d 924, 927 (3d Cir. 1937); Cincinnati Exhibition Co. v. Johnson, 190 Ill. App. 630, 632 (1914); Lee v. Chicago League Ball Club, 169 Ill. App. 525, 530 (1912).

234. E. FRY, A TREATISE ON THE SPECIFIC PERFORMANCE OF CONTRACTS § 286 *quoted in* Metropolitan Exhibition Co. v. Ward, 9 N.Y.S. 779, 783-84 (Sup. Ct. 1890).

235. *See* Weeghman v. Killefer, 215 F. 168 (W.D. Mich.), *aff'd*, 215 F. 289 (6th Cir. 1914); Metropolitan Exhibition Co. v. Ward, 9 N.Y.S. 779, 783-84 (Sup. Ct. 1890); American Base Ball & Athletic Exhibition Co. v. Harper, 54 CENT. L.J. 449, 450(Cir. Ct. St. Louis 1902).

The case which was most influential in precluding access to courts of equity for enforcement of terminable contracts was Rutland Marble Co. v. Ripley, 77 U.S. (10 Wall.) 339 (1870). In that case, specific enforcement was denied even though the notice-termination provision was considerably longer than those found in sports contracts. In *Ripley*, the plaintiff had the right to terminate the contract only upon giving one year's notice.

236. *See* Rutland Marble Co. v. Ripley, 77 U.S. (10 Wall.) 339 (1870).

refined versions.[237] Through this process of redefinition it became increasingly clear that the rule often produced highly questionable results and typically was inhibiting rather than helpful.

What is the present state of the law with respect to the requirement of mutuality of remedy? It can probably be concluded that this version of the mutuality requirement, at least in its most stringent forms, is now largely of historical interest. While, as explained below, mutuality in some forms still appears in a few jurisdictions, the mutuality problems which impeded early enforcement efforts have largely faded from American jurisprudence. The role of mutuality of remedy as an impediment to the enforceability of sports contracts was effectively refuted in the now famous case of *Philadelphia Ball Club, Ltd. v. Lajoie,*[238] decided in 1902. The case is important for present day litigation because the court examined a fairly representative sports contract, which included a liberal right of termination provision, and found that the contract did not manifest a lack of mutuality of remedy. The court was careful to state its rationale in terms which were responsive to the major arguments which had been made against the enforceability of sports contracts. On the matter of the right of termination, the court said

> Each party has the possibility of enforcing all the rights stipulated for in the agreement. It is true that the terms make it possible for the plaintiff to put an end to the contract in a space of time much less than the period during which the defendant has agreed to supply his personal services; but mere difference in the rights stipulated for does not destroy mutuality of remedy.[239]

The court also addressed itself to the notion that equity should not enforce a contract against a defendant who could not have secured such enforcement against the plaintiff:

> We cannot agree that mutuality of remedy requires that each party should have precisely the same remedy, either in form, effect, or extent. In a fair and reasonable contract, it ought to be sufficient that each party has the possibility of compelling performance of the promises which were mutually agreed upon.[240]

---

237. At various times, leading legal scholars participated in the efforts to find an acceptable statement of the mutuality requirement. A major contribution was made by Dean Ames, who renounced the rule which held that a plaintiff could secure specific relief only if he himself could have been the object of such a decree. In place of that rule, Ames proposed a meticulously structured statement of law:

> ... Equity will not compel specific performance by defendant, if, after performance, the common law remedy of damages would be his sole security for the performance of the plaintiff's side of the contract.

Ames, *Mutuality of Specific Performance, supra* note 209, at 2-3. While this redefinition may have introduced some glimmer of certainty into the mutuality muddle, it offered little encouragement to sports employers who sought negative injunctions, for even under this formulation, enforcement would seem to be inappropriate. Since an injunction against breach by the employer was not available, the player's only security for his performance would be an action in damages. Hence, Ames' conditions for denying enforcement would seemingly be present. *See also* H. MCCLINTOCK, HANDBOOK OF THE PRINCIPLES OF EQUITY § 66 (2d ed. 1948).

238. 202 Pa. 210, 51 A. 973 (1902).

239. *Id.* at 219, 51 A. at 975.

240. *Id.* at 220, 51 A. at 975.

Finally, the court interjected a bit of common sense into the mutuality cases. It said, in effect, that all of the talk about whether the defendant had remedies against the plaintiff was really somewhat beside the point. Not only was that lawsuit not before the court, but also the factual context of the cases indicated no immediate threat of the plaintiff-team's non-performance of its part of the bargain.[241]

Lajoie has clearly had a profound effect on the abolition of the mutuality impediment. Despite an initial reception which was at best mixed,[242] and in one case, disdainful,[243] the case has generally been followed. The court's holding and rationale have also received nearly universal approval from the commentators who have considered the problem.[244]

By 1932, when the first *Restatement of Contracts* was published, the most influential courts and scholars had concluded that the requirement of mutuality of remedy should be abandoned. The conclusion of the *Restatement* was emphatic:

> The fact that the remedy of specific enforcement is not available to one party is not a sufficient reason for refusing it to the other party.[245]

Today, most authorities agree that mutuality, at least as it was known in the early part of the century, is neither viable nor worth reviving.[246]

Many of the policy reasons which supposedly supported the imposition of the mutuality requirement have been rejected or specifically accommodated in the rules governing sports injunctions. Although the various formulations of the rule were not always consistent, the courts which invoked them can reasonably be said to have shared a common concern. There seemed to be basic agreement that a court should be hesitant to compel the defendant's compliance with the contract unless the defendant is reasonably assured of receiving a return performance from the plaintiff who is seeking the injunction. While mutuality as a formalistic requirement has been generally abandoned, this concern for the defendant's rights has not. For example, some courts are properly concerned that if the athlete is to be cut off from other potential employers by virtue of the injunction, his right to the club's performance must be secured. This "security" is now achieved by the issuance of a conditional injunction, one which is conditioned upon the club's continued compliance with its contractual commitments.[247] With careful attention from the player's attorney, the order of

---

241. *Id.* at 221, 51 A. at 976.

242. *See* Weeghmam v. Killefer, 215 F. 168 (W.D. Mich.), *aff'd*, 215 F. 289 (6th Cir. 1914); Brooklyn Baseball Club v. McGuire, 116 F. 782 (E.D. Pa. 1902); Cincinnati Exhibition Co. v. Johnson, 190 Ill. App. 630 (1914); American League Baseball Club of Chicago v. Chase, 86 Misc. 441, 149 N.Y.S. 6 (Sup. Ct. 1914).

243. American Base Ball & Athletic Exhibition Co. v. Harper, 54 CENT. L.J. 449 (Cir. Ct. St. Louis 1902).

244. *See* Gilbert, *Some Old Problems in a Modern Guise: Enforcement of Negative Covenants, supra* note 209, at 135-36; Comment, *Contractual Rights and Duties of the Professional Athlete — Playing the Game in a Bidding War,* 77 DICK. L. REV. 352 (1972-73); Note, *Enforcement Problems of Personal Services Contracts in Professional Athletics, supra* note 209, at 48.

245. RESTATEMENT OF CONTRACTS § 372 (1932).

246. *See* D. DOBBS, HANDBOOK ON THE LAW OF REMEDIES 49-51 (1973); Comment, *Injunctions in Professional Athletes' Contracts — An Overused Remedy, supra* note 209, at 547; Comment, *Contractual Rights and Duties of the Professional Athlete — Playing the Game in a Bidding War, supra* note 244, at 365-66.

247. *See* Long Island American Ass'n Football Club, Inc. v. Manrodt, 23 N.Y.S. 2d 858, 860-61 (Sup. Ct. 1940).

injunction can be so worded as to make the restraint terminate automatically upon the team's failure to comply with any term of the contract, particularly that relating to salary.

The *Restatement* also accepts the notion that the defendant is entitled to some assurance that his compliance with the contract, pursuant to the injunction, will not be without compensation. In the *Restatement* view, specific relief should be denied if the court is not satisfied that the plaintiff's performance will be forthcoming.[248] Under this standard, it is appropriate for the court to assess the economic incentives which the plaintiff has for rendering return performance, and if there are doubts in this regard, to make an appropriate adjustment in the form of the order.[249] Presumably it is proper for the court to assess the financial stability of the plaintiff team and determine whether it is likely that the team will be able to pay the defendant's salary should he perform under the contract.[250]

c. Mutuality of the Parties' Equities. While some recent cases have considered, and summarily rejected, objections raising the mutuality question,[251] *Connecticut Professional Sports Corporation v. Heyman*[252] is the most recent case in which a lack of "mutuality" is the primary reason for denying relief. There may be a question as to the extent to which the *Heyman* case can be viewed as providing authority for the continuing validity of the older mutuality notions. The decision is somewhat aberrational since it ignores *Lajoie* and its progeny and attaches itself to no line of modern precedent. Some have suggested that *Heyman* represents the continuation of a unique "New York rule" which still requires mutuality as a prerequisite to equitable enforcement.[253] But the better view of the case is that it does not revive the strict mutuality notion, in New York or elsewhere, but rather represents an entirely different concern.

After a successful collegiate basketball career at Duke University and a less distinguished record in the NBA, Heyman signed a contract to play for the Hartford Capitols in the Eastern Professional Basketball League. The contract included an option clause which gave the club a unilateral right to renew it for one year. Shortly after the American Basketball Association was formed, Heyman signed a contract with the New Jersey Americans of that league. The present litigation resulted when the Hartford club sued to enjoin Heyman from playing for any other team while he was still under contract to it.

The basic difficulty with the contract in *Heyman* was that it gave the plaintiff an extraordinary range of control over Heyman's opportunity to earn a salary,

---

248. RESTATEMENT OF CONTRACTS § 373 (1932).

249. *Id.* at comment *b.*

250. The *Lajoie* court early recognized the need for flexibility in structuring the injunction. Philadelphia Ball Club, Ltd. v. Lajoie, 202 Pa. 210, 222, 51 A. 973, 976 (1902). The court emphasized that the granting of an injunction was a truly discretionary matter. The court implied that one thing to be taken into account was the attitude of the plaintiff, suggesting that an attitude of vindictiveness or inclination to not give the return performance presented a reason for dissolving or refusing to issue the order. If the discretionary nature of injunctive relief is fully recognized, then other considerations, such as financial position, which undermines the likelihood that defendant would receive a return performance ought to be taken into account.

251. *See* Nassau Sports v. Peters, 352 F. Supp. 870, 876 (E.D.N.Y. 1972); Central New York Basketball, Inc. v. Barnett, 19 Ohio Op. 2d 130, 135-36, 181 N.E.2d 506, 512 (1961).

252. 276 F. Supp. 618 (S.D.N.Y 1967).

253. *See, e.g.,* Comment, *Injunctions in Professional Athletes' Contracts — An Overused Remedy, supra* note 209, at 547.

while removing from the athlete the right to market his talents with another team which might pay a salary greater than the meager one offered by the club. Heyman was to be paid on a per game basis, rather than for the entire season as is usually the case. Thus, if Heyman did not play, even if he were sidelined as a result of a basketball-related injury, he would not receive his $175 per night. In addition, the team retained control over the number of games to be played per season, and while the contract bound Heyman exclusively to the plaintiff for one year, the team had an unlimited right to terminate.

The court mentions mutuality and identifies the team's power of termination as "the primary reason for denying relief." [254] But apart from these elements and a citation to *American League Baseball Club of Chicago v. Chase,*[255] the court's analysis bears very little relationship to that used in cases which insisted upon mutuality of remedy. It is clear that the court was not concerned about the remedies available to the respective parties. Rather, the point of concern is the inequity of the contract. The court says, for example, that the terms of the contract are "too harsh and one-sided" to permit enforcement.[256] Similarly, the court notes that the contract could be used to "prevent defendant from earning a living wage from his basketball court activities." [257]

It is the court's use of the term "mutuality," and not the result which the court reaches, which is unfortunate. While other courts have also found it convenient to refer to the "fairness and mutuality" of the contract as a singular concept,[258] the potential for confusion with the now dormant mutuality of remedy is substantial. If the confusing mutuality language in *Heyman* is ignored, it can be said the court pursued a course amply supported by precedent. It appears that the court simply refused to enforce a harsh bargain and thus exercised a judicial power which courts of equity have long assumed was in their province.[259] While the court talks of mutuality, the case properly viewed, harbors none of the skeletons from the closets of the early baseball cases.

Thus, when the ultimate question is posed — is mutuality still a prerequisite to equitable enforcement of sports contract — the answer has to be a qualified "no." Certainly there is no reason to believe that cases such as *Chase* will continue to affect the jurisprudence in this area. And the fact that the parties do not have precisely the same remedies will no longer be relevant. But mutuality remains in at least two senses. First, as illustrated by *Heyman,* the term may continue to be applied — or more correctly, misapplied — to identify a different type of restriction on equitable relief, the requirement of basic fairness in the contractual bargain. Second, to the extent that the original insistence upon mutuality embodied a concern that the defendant be assured of receiving return performance, it can be expected that courts will continue to exercise their discretion to grant equitable relief only when the plaintiff's performance under the contract is reasonably certain and then only with an order which is conditioned upon that result.[260] Yet, in this pursuit of equity for

254. 276 F. Supp. at 621.
255. 86 Misc. 441, 149 N.Y.S. 6 (Sup. Ct. 1914). Discussed in text accompanying notes 226-27 *supra.*
256. 267 F. Supp. at 620.
257. *Id.* at 621.
258. *See* Metropolitan Exhibition Co. v. Ward, 9 N.Y.S. 779, 781, 783 (Sup. Ct. 1890); Philadelphia Ball Club, Ltd. v. Hallman, 8 Pa. County Ct. 57, 63 (1890).
259. *See* RESTATEMENT OF CONTRACTS § 367 (1932).
260. *See id.* § 373.

the defendant, courts need not resort to the old rhetoric of mutuality. Indeed, in light of the confusion which the term has caused, it is best that more neutral labels be chosen.

§ 4.12. Unclean Hands Defense.

a. **The Rule and Its Application.** It is a fundamental principle of equity that "he who comes into equity must have clean hands." [261] Because of the questionable practices occasionally used by those engaged in the recruitment of athletes, it is not surprising that this doctrine has played an important role in the sports area.[262] It is only in recent decisions, however, that firm principles emerge to guide the sports employer in avoiding the potentially harsh consequences of the doctrine.

The contours of the doctrine are aptly stated in *Weeghman v. Killefer,*[263] an early baseball case:

> Equity imperatively demands of suitors in its courts fair dealing and righteous conduct with reference to the matters concerning which they seek relief. He who has acted in bad faith, resorted to trickery and deception, or been guilty of fraud, injustice, or unfairness will appeal in vain to a court of conscience, even though in his wrong doing he may have kept himself strictly within the law .... Under this maxim any willful act in regard to the matter in litigation, which would be condemned and pronounced wrongful by honest and fairminded men, will be sufficient to make the hands of the applicant unclean.[264]

Other courts have confirmed that conduct which will deny equitable relief to the plaintiff need not be "illegal." That is, the misconduct need not amount to a criminal offense nor is it necessary that it violate any private legal duty so as to give rise to a legal claim.[265] It is sufficient that some of the plaintiff's actions were deceptive or otherwise lacking in the candor which would be presumed of an honest business operation. Another equally well-established corollary recognizes that the doctrine is not one of comparative fault. "[I]f plaintiff's hands are not clean, equity must deny him relief no matter how improper

---

261. *See generally* Precision Instrument Mfg. Co. v. Automotive Maintenance Mach. Co., 324 U.S. 806, 89 L. Ed. 1381, 65 S. Ct. 993 (1945); Triangle Film Corp. v. Artcraft Pictures Corp., 250 F. 981 (6th Cir. 1918); D. DOBBS, HANDBOOK ON THE LAW OF REMEDIES, 45-47 (1973); H. MCCLINTOCK, HANDBOOK OF THE PRINCIPLES OF EQUITY § 26, at 59 (2d ed. 1948); 2 J. POMEROY, A TREATISE ON EQUITY JURISPRUDENCE §§ 397-98 (5th ed. 1941).

262. *See* New York Football Giants, Inc. v. Los Angeles Chargers Football Club, Inc., 291 F.2d 471, 473-74 (5th Cir. 1961); Munchak Corp. v. Cunningham, 331 F.Supp. 872 (M.D.N.C. 1971), *rev'd,* 457 F.2d 721 (4th Cir. 1972); Washington Capitols Basketball Club, Inc. v. Barry, 304 F.Supp. 1193 (N.D.Cal.), *aff'd,* 419 F.2d 472 (9th Cir. 1969); Minnesota Muskies, Inc. v. Hudson, 294 F.Supp. 979 (M.D.N.C. 1969); Weeghman v. Killefer, 215 F. 168 (W.D.Mich.), *aff'd,* 215 F. 289 (6th Cir. 1914); Comment, *Injunctions in Professional Athletes' Contracts — An Overused Remedy,* 43 CONN. B.J. 538, 549 (1969); Comment, *Contractual Rights and Duties of the Professional Athlete — Playing the Game in a Bidding War,* 77 DICK. L. REV. 352, 372-79 (1973).

263. Weeghman v. Killefer, 215 F. 168 (W.D. Mich.), *aff'd,* 215 F. 289 (6th Cir. 1914). (For an explanation of the spelling of the parties' names see note 54, § 4.03 *supra.*)

264. 215 F. at 171.

265. *See* Precision Instrument Mfg. Co. v. Automotive Maintenance Mach. Co., 324 U.S. 806, 814-15 (1944); New York Football Giants, Inc. v. Los Angeles Chargers Football Club, Inc., 291 F.2d 471 (5th Cir. 1961). *See generally* 2 J. POMEROY, A TREATISE ON EQUITY JURISPRUDENCE § 404 (5th ed. 1941).

defendant's conduct may have been." [266] Access to the special powers of the court of equity is granted only upon a showing that the court will not be aiding a dishonest party if it were to issue the decree requested. Hence, before plaintiff is entitled to equity relief, it must appear that quite apart from the defendant's fitness, the plaintiff is one who in good conscience can be the beneficiary of a discretionary order from the court.

There are basically two situations in which the clean hands doctrine has been applied in the sports area. The most common situation involves an athlete under contract with a team who "jumps" from that team to another and then returns to his original employer, usually because the original employer has substantially increased the salary it is willing to pay. When the second employer sues to gain enforcement of its negative covenant, the athlete may allege that the employer's hands are unclean because it interfered with the original employment relationship.[267] The other situation which has received attention is one in which it is alleged that the plaintiff engaged in some deception of third parties in the initial hiring of the athlete. These cases usually involve a second interested employer, who will gladly employ the athlete if the plaintiff is denied relief, but unlike the contract jumping cases, the questioned activities often affect a third party other than another employer. Such a situation arises when a club secretively signs a contract with a college athlete in violation of an NCAA rule.[268]

b. Interference with Existing Contractual Relationships. One of the first cases dealing with the clean hands doctrine in the context of contract jumping is *Weeghman v. Killefer,*[269] a case arising out of the player raids which followed the formation of the Federal Baseball League in the early part of the century. The Chicago club in the Federal League offered Killefer a contract with a higher salary after Killefer had agreed to play for the Philadelphia National League club for the period covered by the contract. While this was a fairly blatant interference by the Chicago club with an existing relationship, the club had a substantial defense for its actions: under then existing precedents the player had no enforceable obligation to his original employer because their contract lacked mutuality of remedy.[270] When Killefer decided to stay with the Philadelphia club, the Chicago team sought an injunction. While the court in *Killefer* had to concede that the original contract with Philadelphia was probably not enforceable, it nonetheless concluded that the plaintiff had tainted his hands — and lost his right to equitable relief — by interfering with the relationship which did exist. In the court's view, Killefer "was under a moral, if not a legal," obligation to play for Philadelphia, and the plaintiff's actions of interference not

---

266. Washington Capitols Basketball Club, Inc. v. Barry, 304 F. Supp. 1193, 1199 (N.D. Cal.), *aff'd,* 419 F.2d 472 (9th Cir. 1969). *See also* Precision Instrument Mfg. Co. v. Automotive Maintenance Mach. Co., 324 U.S. 806, 814 (1944); Minnesota Muskies, Inc. v. Hudson, 294 F. Supp. 979, 990 (M.D.N.C. 1969).

267. *See* Munchak Corp. v. Cunningham, 331 F. Supp. 872 (M.D.N.C. 1971), *rev'd,* 457 F.2d 721 (4th Cir. 1972); Washington Capitols Basketball Club, Inc. v. Barry, 304 F. Supp. 1193 (N.D. Cal.), *aff'd,* 419 F.2d 472 (9th Cir. 1969); Minnesota Muskies, Inc. v. Hudson, 294 F. Supp. 979 (M.D.N.C. 1969); Weeghman v. Killefer, 215 F. 168 (W.D. Mich.), *aff'd,* 215 F. 289 (6th Cir. 1914).

268. *See* Houston Oilers, Inc. v. Neely, 361 F.2d 36 (10th Cir. 1966); New York Football Giants, Inc. v. Los Angeles Chargers Football Club, Inc., 291 F.2d 471 (5th Cir. 1961).

269. 215 F. 168 (W.D. Mich.), *aff'd,* 215 F. 289 (6th Cir. 1914).

270. *See* § 4.11 *supra.*

only were knowingly in contravention of that duty, but also were motivated solely by a desire for personal profit.[271]

The basic principle of *Killefer* remains unchallenged: the person who entices an employee to abandon an existing commitment to another employer cannot stand to complain in equity when the employee decides not to honor the improperly secured contract. Yet, cases subsequent to *Killefer* have considerably narrowed the range of activities which will be deemed to taint the hands of the person who hires another's employee. This decision to give outsiders increasing freedom to bargain for the services of an athlete or other employee is firmly based in the strong public policy favoring open competition in the marketplace. Unless competition for the player's skills is protected, indeed promoted, the athlete will likely be forced to accept a salary and other contract terms which do not reflect the fair value of his services. Moreover, the presence of competition in the long run substantially enhances the athlete's bargaining power and thus indirectly serves as a check on overly harsh contract terms. Not only is such a result desirable in itself, but it should also reinforce the willingness of courts to otherwise give the parties great latitude in structuring the terms which will govern their affairs. Of course, there must be some limitations on the extent to which a competitor can intrude into the existing employment relationship, and these are considered below. But the basic choice in favor of increased competition in the sports labor market would appear to reflect a proper concern for the interests of the player, the competing teams, and the public in general.[272]

The correctness of the policy decisions made in this area was succinctly assessed by the venerable Judge Learned Hand in a related context:

> Nobody has ever thought, so far as we can find, that in the absence of some monopolistic purpose everyone has not the right to offer better terms to another's employee, so long as the latter is free to leave. The result of the contrary would be intolerable, both to such employers as could use the employee more effectively and to such employees as might receive added pay. It would put an end to any kind of competition.[273]

Once the general policy favoring inter-employer competition is identified, it can be applied to a number of specific situations which appear in the sports context. For example, one issue which arises is whether the prospective employer can begin contract negotiations with the player while he is still under contract. The athlete's existing employer would like to insist that the player not begin negotiations with another employer until he has played out his option or otherwise properly terminated his relationship with the original club. But as a practical matter, such a restriction would greatly enhance the monopoly position of the original employer. The athlete would often be unwilling to sever his existing relationship, and thus lose whatever goodwill he had with his club, without some relatively firm assurance that another employment opportunity was available on more attractive terms. That assurance could only come if other

---

271. 215 F. at 172-73.

272. Similar policy questions arise when the original employer sues the new club for tortious interference with contract. The elements of this action are considered in another section. *See* § 4.14 *infra*.

273. Triangle Film Corp. v. Artcraft Pictures Corp., 250 F. 981, 982 (6th Cir. 1918).

prospective employers were permitted to make legally binding offers to the player while he was still under contract. This result is confirmed in the cases decided in this area.[274]

Even if it is accepted that a competing employer may negotiate for the athlete's future services, a question remains as to the point in time at which the new employment relationship may begin. The original employer can properly demand that its contract rights to the player's services be respected. This is achieved if the new agreement is structured so that the player is not obligated to begin performing under the new arrangement until after he has fulfilled his obligation under his existing contract. When this condition is met and the negotiations are otherwise proper, existing precedent supports the conclusion that the actions of the new employer involve "neither illegality nor unclean hands." [275]

Under these precedents, it is necessary to identify the point at which a player's commitment to his original employer terminates in order to determine whether the new employer has shown proper deference to the rights of the existing employer. Where the new contract specifies a starting date which is subsequent to the time that the player's option-year with his former team would end, the arrangement would appear to avoid the unclean hands defense.[276] By contrast, it would seemingly be improper for a new employer to sign a player to begin performance during the option-year of his original contract, and this would be true even if the team had not yet exercised its option.[277] Option rights are so commonly exercised in professional sports that it would be unreasonable for the new employer to contend that it entertained honest doubts about whether the original employer would claim the player's services for the final year.[278] A more difficult question is presented when the contract is one which contains a "reserve" rather than an "option" clause. Under the former, the original team may be able to claim the player's services for more than a year and, in fact, may have a perpetual claim. Except in baseball,[279] such reserve systems are of doubtful validity under the antitrust laws.[280] Where a reserve system is in effect, a question which confronts the new employer when it selects the commencement date of the new contract is whether it should assume that the reserve system is invalid *in toto,* so that the player can switch teams at the end of his regular contract year. Another possibility is that the original team will deny that the system is a reserve system and choose to characterize it as a more permissible

274. *See* Munchak Corp. v. Cunningham, 457 F.2d 721, 724 (4th Cir. 1972), *rev'g,* 331 F. Supp. 872 (M.D.N.C. 1971); Washington Capitols Basketball Club, Inc. v. Barry, 304 F. Supp. 1193 (N.D. Cal.), *aff'g,* 304 F. Supp. 1193 (N.D. Cal. 1969).

275. Munchak Corp. v. Cunningham, 457 F.2d 721, 724 (4th Cir. 1972), *rev'g,* 331 F. Supp. 972 (M.D.N.C. 1971). *See also* Washington Capitols Basketball Club, Inc. v. Barry, 419 F.2d 472 (9th Cir.), *aff'g,* 304 F. Supp. 1193 (N.D. Cal.1969).

276. *See* Munchak Corp. v. Cunningham, 457 F.2d 721 (4th Cir. 1972).

277. *See* Minnesota Muskies, Inc. v. Hudson, 294 F. Supp. 979 (M.D.N.C. 1969).

278. *See id.* at 983.

279. *See* Flood v. Kuhn, 407 U.S. 258 (1972). The 1973 baseball contract has, however, been interpreted as providing only a one-year option right. National and American Leagues of Professional Baseball Clubs v. Major League Baseball Players Ass'n (John A. Messersmith and David A. McNally), Grievance Nos. 75-27 & 75-28, Decision No. 29 (Dec. 23, 1975, Opinion of Impartial Chairman Peter Seitz). The *Seitz* decision was affirmed on judicial review. Kansas City Royals Baseball Corp. v. Major League Players Ass'n, 409 F. Supp. 233 (W.D. Mo.), *aff'd,* 532 F.2d 615 (8th Cir. 1976).

280. *See* Philadelphia World Hockey Club, Inc. v. Philadelphia Hockey Club, Inc., 351 F. Supp. 462 (E.D. Pa. 1972).

option clause.[281] While a pure reserve system in a sport other than baseball probably would not withstand judicial scrutiny, athletes have not generally been successful in their efforts to use the injunction proceeding as the forum in which to raise that question.[282] The better course for the new employer would be to treat the reserve system as only giving the team a one-year option, inform the original team of this construction, and structure the new contract on the presumed validity of this assumption.

While recent cases have served to add sensible refinements to the unclean hands doctrine in the sports area, there has yet to be a satisfactory resolution of the question of whether the new employer may properly offer financial or other economic inducements to the player while he is still under contract to the original club. Typical situations are those in which the new employer pays a bonus to the player upon the signing of the new agreement or otherwise agrees to make payments to the player during the option-year of his original contract. While an earlier case clearly held these financial inducements soiled the hands of the new employer,[283] a subsequent review of the same issue in *Munchak Corporation v. Cunningham* [284] produced an implied rejection of the notion that such payments were a reason for denying equitable relief. Under the particular arrangement involved in that case, the court found that there was an "incentive" for Cunningham to play during the option-year because he might make 25% more by playing than by sitting out. The court dismissed the fact that Cunningham would receive $80,000 from his new employer for not playing in the option period by pointing out that "Cunningham already had this right [to sit out] since he could not be required to render personal services against his will." [285] Somewhat surprisingly, the court fails to consider other intangibles which might reduce the attractiveness of a $20,000 "incentive" to play for an athlete already assured of a salary of $80,000. For example, some consideration should be given to the fact that the athlete considerably reduces his exposure to injury by sitting out. In addition, he has more time available to pursue other business interests, which might well produce a return greater than $20,000. And while there is probably a natural incentive for the athlete to continue to perform to keep his name in the limelight, there are some notable cases in which an athlete who "sat out" a year did not appreciably diminish his attractiveness at the gate.[286]

281. *See* Central New York Basketball, Inc. v. Barnett, 19 Ohio Op. 2d 130, 132-34, 181 N.E.2d 506, 509-10, (1961), where the court indicates that in doubtful cases such a construction will be favored because it will preserve the validity of the contract.

282. *See* Nassau Sports v. Peters, 352 F. Supp. 870, 878 (E.D.N.Y. 1972); Minnesota Muskies, Inc. v. Hudson, 294 F. Supp. 979, 989-90 (M.D.N.C. 1969); Central New York Basketball, Inc. v. Barnett, 19 Ohio Op. 2d 130, 139-40, 181 N.E.2d 506, 517 (1961); Matuszak v. Houston Oilers, Inc., 515 S.W.2d 725 (Tex. Civ. App. 1974); Dallas Cowboys Football Club, Inc. v. Harris, 348 S.W.2d 37, 47 (Tex. Civ. App. 1961). *But see* Boston Professional Hockey Ass'n, Inc. v. Cheevers, 348 F. Supp. 261, 267 (D. Mass.), *remanded,* 472 F.2d 127 (1st Cir. 1972); Nassau Sports v. Hampson, 355 F. Supp. 733 (D. Minn. 1972).

283. *See* Minnesota Muskies, Inc. v. Hudson, 294 F. Supp. 979 (M.D.N.C. 1969): "Notwithstanding its recognition of [the player's] obligation [to his original employer], the Muskies agreed to pay Hudson to sit out the 1967-68 season even if the Court should decree that the St. Louis contract was enforceable. This alone is sufficient for a court of equity to refuse relief." *Id.* at 990.

284. 457 F.2d 721 (4th Cir. 1972), *rev'g* 331 F. Supp. 872 (M.D.N.C. 1971).

285. 457 F.2d at 724. *Compare* Washington Capitols Basketball Club, Inc. v. Barry, 419 F.2d 472, 477 (9th Cir.), *aff'g* 304 F. Supp. 1193 (N.D. Cal. 1969).

286. Rick Barry may be the primary example. *See* Washington Capitols Basketball Club, Inc. v. Barry, 304 F. Supp. 1193 (N.D. Cal.), *aff'd,* 419 F.2d 472 (4th Cir. 1969); Lemat Corp. v. Barry, 275 Cal. App. 2d 671, 80 Cal. Rptr. 240 (1969).

In short, the matter of the propriety of payments of this sort deserves more careful consideration than that given by the *Cunningham* court. It is by no means clear that approval of such payments necessarily follows from the policies which favor allowing rival teams to compete for the athlete's future services. For the reasons previously given, competition among sports employers should be encouraged. But presumably a court should also be concerned that it allow no greater intrusion into the existing employment relationship than is necessary to achieve the desired competition. The court should look skeptically upon an outsider's attempt to gain any present advantage from its rights in the athlete's future service. Particular problems arise from payments intended to influence the athlete's decision concerning his option year. While it is undeniable that athletes have the "right" to sit out the option year, it is quite a different matter to conclude that the new employer may provide compensation if the "right" is exercised. Hopefully, it is obvious that a decision to sit out is more likely to be made when the athlete receives outside payments than when he does not.[287] Thus, while the original employer has no assurance that the athlete will play in the option year, the club will surely feel more comfortable with the odds which favor such a decision when the player's sole source of income is at stake. The implication of the *Cunningham* analysis that the original employer may have actually benefited by the particular form of payment used there ignores the more basic concern of whether the payments are compatible with the employer's rights under the existing contract.

This is not to suggest that courts should automatically condemn any type of payment from the future employer. While there are some forms of incentive payments that should not be tolerated,[288] a payment of the sort involved in *Cunningham* is less clearly susceptible to an absolute rule. What can be suggested is that courts should make an inquiry somewhat different from that made in *Cunningham*. Specifically, an attempt should be made to ascertain first, the reason for the outside compensation and second, its actual effect on the player's behavior. If no improper motive is found and if it appears that the athlete's performance will be unaffected, little harm would seem to flow from judicial approval of the payment. But if the new employer is seeking to achieve a present advantage from his contract, or if, as a result of the payment, the

287. *Cf.* Truax v. Raich, 239 U.S. 33, 60 L. Ed. 131, 36 S. Ct. 7 (1915); American League Baseball Club of New York v. Pasquel, 197 Misc. 230, 63 N.Y.S.2d 537 (Sup. Ct. 1946).

288. For example, the new employer should not be permitted to promise rewards which would influence the athlete's performance on the field while he is still in the service of the original club. Bonuses for scoring a certain number of points or gaining a specified number of yards would represent an infringement upon the existing employer's right to define the athlete's role as a member of the team, including the right to design plays which might limit the athlete's scoring and performance opportunities. This sort of intrusion should be strictly proscribed, even though the future employer has an interest in seeing that the athlete's status as a star performer is maintained while he is playing out his existing contract. Precedent from other areas would seem to provide sufficient support for the view that an employer can insist that his employees remain free from the influence of payments provided by outsiders. *See* Texana Oil & Ref. Co. v. Belchic, 150 La. 88, 90 So. 522 (1922); Commercial Club v. Davis, 136 Mo. App. 583, 118 S.W. 668 (1909); Barber v. Martin, 67 Neb. 445, 93 N.W. 722 (1903). *Cf.* Paramount Mfg. Co. v. Mohan, 196 Cal. App. 2d 372, 16 Cal. Rptr. 417 (Dist. Ct. App. 1961); Connelly v. Special Road & Bridge Dist. No. 5, 99 Fla. 456, 126 So. 794 (1930); RESTATEMENT (SECOND) OF AGENCY § 387 (1958).

player is likely to act adversely to the interest of his present employer, a court ought to disapprove the arrangement. It is true that reliable evidence of the player's reaction in the future may be hard to find. Yet, the inquiry is worth the effort, for it will often yield the sort of evidence which traditionally influences the exercise of judicial discretion in equity proceedings.[289]

c. Improprieties in Contract Negotiations. As suggested, the relevance of the unclean hands defense is not limited to cases in which a new employer's attempt to "hire away" an athlete is drawn into question. The defense may also be used to test the propriety of the team's conduct during original contract negotiations. Any fraud, dishonesty, or extreme lack of candor which can be attributed to the team is a proper subject for review by a court of equity when the team comes before it for injunctive relief. This inquiry should have the same contours as those undertaken in non-sports cases. The evaluation of the alleged misconduct is committed to the discretion of the court, and the court is empowered to deny relief even if the activities do not involve illegality in either a criminal law or private law sense.[290]

The secret signing cases illustrate the differing results which may be reached when judicial discretion is exercised in this area. The NCAA maintains a well-known rule which disqualifies athletes from collegiate competition if they are already under a professional contract. A team anxious to bring a college star into the fold as early as possible may sign a player during his last intercollegiate season but agree not to disclose that fact so as to avoid NCAA sanction. When the player later wants to abandon the contract he may try to use the fact of the knowing violation of the NCAA rule as a reason why the team is not entitled to equitable relief. The courts which have considered this question have reached divergent results on essentially identical facts. In *Houston Oilers v. Neely* [291] the fact of the secret signing was viewed as insufficient reason for denying equitable relief. While the court found the alleged conduct to be "regrettable" and not something it would condone, it felt that "it must be conceded that there is no legal impediment to contracting for the services of athletes at any time." [292] By contrast, the court in *New York Giants, Inc. v. Los Angeles Chargers Football Club, Inc.* [293] refused injunctive relief, characterizing the action as

---

289. *See, e.g.,* Cincinnati Bengals, Inc. v. Bergey, 453 F. Supp. 129 (S.D. Ohio), *aff'd,* Civil No. 74-1570 (6th Cir. Aug. 27, 1974). In *Bergey,* the District Court undertook to make findings about the effect of Bergey's signing with a new league upon his performance under his existing contract with the Bengals. Although the *actual* effect of the signing could not be judged until sometime in the future, the court made inquiry into such things as the extent of Bergey's dedication and his relationship with his teammates. While scientific certainty on matters of this sort cannot be attained, it is clear that District Judge Porter felt that the evidence was sufficiently reliable to be considered in connection with the question of whether the Bengals had suffered irreparable harm as a result of Bergey's signing. *See* District Court opinion, at 14-15. The *Bergey* case is considered more fully below. *See* § 4.14 *infra.*

290. *See, e.g.,* Precision Instrument Mfg. Co. v. Automotive Maintenance Mach. Co., 324 U.S. 806 (1944); New York Football Giants, Inc. v. Los Angeles Chargers Football Club, Inc., 291 F.2d 471, 473-75 (5th Cir. 1961); Weeghman v. Killefer, 215 F. 168 (W.D. Mich.), *aff'd,* 215 F. 289 (6th Cir. 1914); 4 J. POMEROY, A TREATISE ON EQUITY JURISPRUDENCE §§ 397-98. *But see* Houston Oilers, Inc. v. Neely, 361 F.2d 36, 40-42 (10th Cir. 1966).

291. 361 F.2d 36 (10th Cir. 1966).

292. *Id.* at 41.

293. 291 F.2d 471 (5th Cir. 1961).

intended "to deceive others who had a very material and important interest in the subject matter." [294] The difference between the two approaches appears to be the degree of deceitfulness which each court requires. The *Neely* court seemed to insist that the plaintiff's conduct rise to the level of illegality. On the other hand, the *Giants* court looked to the improper motives and deceptive actions of the club. When judged by precedent from other areas, the *Giants* approach is the more logical interpretation of the unclean hands doctrine. [295] It might also be noted that the mere fact that the rule which is broken is private in nature should not lessen the impropriety of the plaintiff's actions, for it is a rule upon which members of the general public have placed some reliance and, perhaps more importantly, with which the professional teams have at least outwardly agreed to abide. A more interesting question is whether a court of equity should feel free to evaluate the fairness and reasonableness of a rule such as that dealing with professionalization in college sports. It would not seem unreasonable to suggest that the injunction proceeding, which does not involve the NCAA, is not the proper forum for an attack upon such a provision. Moreover, it would seem that the deceptive quality of the plaintiff's conduct should be judged more by the actor's candor than by the propriety of the rule itself.

d. The Effect of an Assignment Upon the Unclean Hands Defense. The party seeking enforcement of the player's contract may not be the one which engaged in the alleged misconduct, but rather a club which secured a right to the player's future services by assignment from the supposed wrongdoer. This is particularly apt to occur where the disappointed new employer is a member of a recently-formed league. As the new league seeks to assert itself as a competitive challenger, it is common to find a large number of franchise shifts. If these are accompanied by changes in ownership, there will be typically an assignment of existing player contracts.

In determining the rights of the assignee, a distinction must be made between the defects which inhere in the contract and those which arise from the manner in which it is negotiated. If the new contract calls for performance by the player before the expiration of his commitment with the original employer, then it would seem that neither the club which negotiated it nor its assignee should be permitted to enforce. [296] In this case, the assignee has in effect adopted the contract as his own and will not be able to disassociate himself from the offending term. A more difficult question arises when a contract with otherwise proper terms is secured by improper means. Should the innocent assignee of a player's contract be precluded from equitable relief because of indiscretions of this assignor? The question might be analyzed in terms of basic contracts concepts: an assignee can get no greater rights than his assignor, and a limitation upon the enforceability of the original owner's rights must pass with the contract. [297] It might also be suggested that this conclusion is necessary to

---

294. *Id.* at 474.

295. *See* Comment, *Contractual Rights and Duties of the Professional Athlete — Playing the Game in a Bidding War, supra* note 262 at 372-79. *See also* RESTATEMENT OF CONTRACTS § 577 (1932).

296. *See* Minnesota Muskies, Inc. v. Hudson, 294 F. Supp. 979, 990 (M.D.N.C. 1969).

297. *See id.*

insure that the wrongdoer does not profit by his improper actions. The better view, however, is that such a result misconceives the nature of the clean hands defense. The basic issue is whether the defense is one which attaches to the contract or operates only against the particular plaintiff. A review of the historical origins of the defense suggests that it was thought to be personal in nature and no bar to enforcement by other suitors. The basis of the doctrine is that equity will not use its special powers to aid a wrongdoer.[298] While the equity order is highly discretionary, this concern would seemingly not apply where the party before the court had not in any way participated in the improper activities. While there is a divergence of views among the sports cases which have considered the point, the interpretation suggested above was specifically approved in *Washington Capitols Basketball Club, Inc. v. Barry*[299] where the district court accepted the view of Judge Learned Hand that

> conduct to be relevant must touch and taint the plaintiff personally . . . .
> The doctrine is . . . derived from the unwillingness of a court . . . of conscience to give its peculiar relief to a suitor who . . . has so conducted himself as to shock the moral sensibilities of the judge. It has nothing to do with the rights and liabilities of the parties . . . .[300]

In response to the point that the wrongdoer ought not be allowed to profit by selling his improperly-secured contract to a third party, it can be observed that there is still the possibility of a suit for tortious interference with contract by the injured party against the wrongdoer. If the wrongdoer's conduct violates the legal standard, the improperly gained advantages may be retaken from him, but the proceeding should be one more appropriate for that purpose.

§ 4.13. Illegality or Unconscionability as a Defense.

A plaintiff's request for equitable enforcement of a negative covenant may be used by the defendant as the occasion to attack the legality and fairness of the contract. In strict legal terms, the defenses of illegality and unfairness proceed from different doctrinal premises. The former is a defense which would render the contract unenforceable for all purposes [301] while the latter is most common to equity proceedings and is generally more discretionary in its application.[302] In the sports cases decided to date, differences in the nature of these doctrines have not played a major role. Whether the concern which is expressed is one of illegality or of unfairness, the object of the defendant's assertion is often the same — the system for player retention employed in the particular sport. At the heart of such a system is the reserve clause or option clause which is typically a part of a standard player contract. While each type of clause raises questions of the sort considered here, the reserve clause, which is the more restrictive of the two, has generated the most litigation in this area. Objections to player retention systems are usually expressed in one of three

---

298. *See generally* D. DOBBS, HANDBOOK ON THE LAW OF REMEDIES 45-47 (1973); H. MCCLINTOCK, HANDBOOK OF THE PRINCIPLES OF EQUITY § 26 (2d ed. 1948).

299. 304 F. Supp. 1193 (N.D. Cal.), *aff'd,* 419 F.2d 472 (9th Cir. 1969).

300. 304 F. Supp. 1193, 1199 (N.D. Cal. 1969), *quoting* Art Metal Works v. Abraham & Straus, 70 F.2d 641, 646 (2d Cir. 1934).

301. *See* RESTATEMENT OF CONTRACTS §§ 512-610, especially § 598 (1932).

302. *See id.* § 367; D. DOBBS, HANDBOOK ON THE LAW OF REMEDIES 47-49 (1973); H. MCCLINTOCK, HANDBOOK OF THE PRINCIPLES OF EQUITY § 71 (2d ed. 1948).

forms: it may be contended (a) that the relevant contract terms provide for perpetual and involuntary servitude in contravention of the Thirteenth Amendment [303] or (b) that the contract provisions, when contrasted with the owner's right to terminate the contract with little or no notice, are so harsh and unfair as to warrant a denial of enforcement [304] or (c) that the system for player retention operates as a restraint on trade and is thus illegal under a statutory or common law proscription.[305]

It should be pointed out that the questions considered here may have limited significance in the future at least in the major team sports. In the relatively short period of 1973 to 1976, there have been major developments in baseball, football, basketball, and hockey which have significantly reduced the power which clubs formerly enjoyed under traditional option and reserve clauses. These are discussed in detail in subsequent sections.[306] For the present discussion, it is sufficient to note that as a result of litigation and collective bargaining, the major leagues are experimenting with a variety of player retention devices.[307] In some leagues, the traditional option clause and reserve clauses have been eliminated entirely.[308] In others, the club's right to unilaterally renew an athlete's contract has been made the subject of individual negotiations between player and club.[309] Baseball has even relinquished its once sacred claim to a perpetual right to its players' services.[310]

The import of these developments should be clear. As the extent of the club's power to restrain an athlete's mobility is drawn more narrowly, and as the particular terms of the restraint system increasingly become the product of collective or individual bargaining, litigants will find courts less willing to entertain objections to the fairness or legality of the contract. Nonetheless, the prior cases which bear on this issue represent an important part of the existing body of sports law. Thus, they warrant attention in the present discussion of the enforcement of sports contracts.

An early case endorsed the notion that enforcement of a negative covenant, which is part of virtually every player contract, would constitute an

---

303. *See* American Base Ball & Athletic Exhibition Co. v. Harper, 54 CENT. L.J. 449, 454 (Cir. Ct. St. Louis 1902). *See also* Flood v. Kuhn, 316 F. Supp. 271, 281-82 (S.D.N.Y. 1970), *aff'd,* 443 F.2d 264 (2d Cir. 1971), *aff'd on other grounds,* 407 U.S. 258, 32 L. Ed. 2d 728, 92 S. Ct. 2099 (1972). *See generally* Schneiderman, *Professional Sports: Involuntary Servitude and the Popular Will,* 7 GONZAGA L. REV. 63 (1971); Comment, *Injunctions in Professional Athletes' Contracts — An Overused Remedy,* 43 CONN. B.J. 538, 550-52 (1969).

304. *See* Metropolitan Exhibition Co. v. Ward, 9 N.Y.S. 779, 783 (Sup. Ct. 1890). *See generally* Gilbert, *Some Old Problems in a Modern Guise: Enforcement of Negative Covenants,* 4 CAL. L. REV. 114, 132-38 (1915). *See also* § 4.05 *supra.*

305. *See e.g.,* Boston Professional Hockey Ass'n Inc. v. Cheevers, 348 F. Supp. 261, 267 (D. Mass.), *remanded,* 472 F.2d 127 (1st Cir. 1972); American League Baseball Club of Chicago v. Chase, 86 Misc. 441, 466-67, 149 N.Y.S. 6, 20 (Sup. Ct. 1914). *See generally* Note, *Reserve Clauses in Athletic Contracts,* 2 RUTGERS-CAMDEN L.J. 302 (1970).

306. *See* §§ 5.03-.07 *infra.*

307. For a summary of the developments in the major sports, *see* § 5.03 *infra.*

308. Under the 1976 collective bargaining agreement between the NBA players and owners, the traditional option clause will be eliminated entirely for veteran players. It is to be replaced by a system under which the original employer has the right to match any salary which the player may have negotiated with another team. *See also* NBA Contract (Veteran-Single Season), National Basketball Ass'n (1976).

309. The 1976 NHL collective bargaining agreement gives the club and players the option to agree to a contract which includes a clause giving the club a unilateral right to renew. *See id.,* N.Y. Times, Oct. 7, 1975, at 1, col. 8.

310. *See* note 100 § 4.05 *supra.*

infringement upon the athlete's constitutionally guaranteed right to "life and liberty." [311] However, the notion was not given much credence in later cases and was rather authoritatively laid to rest in the lower court decisions dismissing Curt Flood's attack upon the baseball reserve clause.[312] It must be conceded that a reserve system such as that formerly found in baseball operated to place a player under the pervasive control of one employer. The player was not free to market his athletic skills with other employers in the same league, and he could be forced to spend his entire career with one employer even though he might have strong preferences to the contrary. But before it can be said that these complaints rise to constitutional dimensions, it must be found that the player had "no way to avoid continued service." [313] And, of course, in the sports industry, even with the most restrictive variety of reserve system, the player has a way to avoid further service — he can leave the sport altogether and choose from a variety of alternative vocations.[314]

When the reserve system is attacked for its lack of fairness, the appeal is to the equitable sensitivities of the court, which has discretion to deny enforcement because of the harshness of a contract.[315] Early cases [316] and text writers [317] characterized the baseball reserve system in these terms, emphasizing the fact that while the player's obligations might be perpetual, the team usually retained for itself a liberal right of termination. Other cases took a more charitable view of the allocation of rights under the contract and failed to find the degree of harshness which would justify a denial of enforcement. Under this view, the relatively greater degree of control residing in the owner could be justified by "the peculiar nature and circumstances of the business." [318]

In many of the more recent cases the harshness objection either was not raised or was not seriously argued. This is understandable because most of this litigation has involved football and basketball, sports in which the method for player retention was the much less restrictive option system.[319] In addition, it was sometimes the case that the player had employment opportunities in competing leagues; thus, he might have been able to bargain for a salary sufficient to compensate him for the rights which he relinquished when he consented to the option arrangement. This is not to suggest that courts of equity will no longer evaluate the fairness of player contracts. Indeed, as recently as 1974 a court had serious doubts about the basic fairness of the NFL standard

---

311. American Base Ball & Athletic Exhibition Co. v. Harper, 54 CENT. L.J. 449, 451 (Cir. Ct. St. Louis 1902). *See also* Note, *id.* at 454.

312. Flood v. Kuhn, 316 F. Supp. 271, 280-82 (S.D.N.Y 1970), *aff'd*, 443 F.2d 264, 268 (2d Cir. 1971), aff'd on other grounds, 407 U.S. 258 (1972).

313. Flood v. Kuhn, 316 F. Supp. 271, 281 (S.D.N.Y. 1970), *quoting* United States v. Shackney, 333 F.2d 475, 486 (2d Cir. 1964).

314. *See* Flood v. Kuhn, 316 F. Supp. 271, at 280-82 (S.D.N.Y. 1970), *aff'd,* 442 F.2d 264, 268 *aff'd on other grounds,* 407 U.S. 258 (1972). *See generally* Schneiderman, *Professional Sports: Involuntary Servitude and the Popular Will, supra* note 303.

315. *See generally* H. McCLINTOCK, HANDBOOK OF THE PRINCIPLES OF EQUITY § 71 (2d ed. 1948).

316. *See, e.g.,* Metropolitan Exhibition Co. v. Ward, 9 N.Y.S. 779, 783 (Sup. Ct. 1890).

317. *See e.g.,* Gilbert, *Some Old Problems in a Modern Guise: Enforcement of Negative Covenants, supra* note 304, at 136-38.

318. *See* Philadelphia Ball Club Ltd. v. Lajoie, 202 Pa. 210, 221, 51 A. 973, 975 (1902).

319. *See, e.g.,* Washington Capitols Basketball Club, Inc. v. Barry, 304 F. Supp. 1193, 1197 (N.D. Cal.), *aff'd,* 419 F.2d 472 (9th Cir. 1969); Central New York Basketball, Inc. v. Barnett, 19 Ohio Op. 2d 130, 132-34, 181 N.E.2d 506, 509-10, (1961); Dallas Cowboys Football Club, Inc. v. Harris, 348 S.W.2d 37 (Tex. Civ. App. 1961).

player contract. The majority in *Matuszak v. Houston Oilers, Inc.*[320] found the NFL agreement to be "incredibly one-sided," a criticism which it directed to the contract generally and not just to the option system. The majority concluded, however, that the issue of fairness need not be resolved at a hearing on a preliminary injunction, as it could be raised in a full hearing on the merits. A dissenting judge was less deferential and would have dissolved the preliminary injunction without hearing further evidence. In his view,

> The evidence shows that many of the terms of the standard contract tendered [to Matuszak] were not negotiable. He was given only the option of accepting them or not playing professional football in the United States. Standing in such a position of overwhelmingly superior bargaining power, the Oilers compelled Matuszak to sign a contract which is grossly unfair to him. A court should not lend its equitable powers to the enforcement of a contract so termed and so procured.[321]

Thus, although option clauses may receive less specific attention than in the past, *Matuszak* and other recent cases [322] confirm the continuing acceptance of the general notion that the player contracts must not incorporate a bargain which is too strongly weighted in favor of the club.

The equitable defense which has received perhaps the most attention is that which suggests that the player retention provisions of the particular contract are illegal as a restraint on trade. The basis for this characterization, of course, is that such provisions, particularly true reserve clauses, substantially curtail the player's ability to generate competition for his services among the potential sports employers.[323] A detailed analysis of the antitrust aspects of the reserve and option clauses is undertaken in a later chapter of this text.[324] For the present discussion, however, it may be useful to indicate the reception which these antitrust objections have received in injunction proceedings. One of the leading early baseball cases, *American League Baseball Club of Chicago v. Chase*,[325] found this objection persuasive and characterized the baseball reserve system as one of "quasi-peonage." In a later period, it became clear that courts were much less willing to use the relatively simple injunction proceeding as the forum in which to dictate basic reforms for the professional sports industry. Thus, antitrust objections were summarily rejected.[326] In addition, courts indicated a willingness to construe the contract so as to temper the source of the antitrust concern.[327] In other cases, there was a strong suggestion that the antitrust attack ought to be carried on in a different proceeding, one in which the alleged illegality was the primary focus of the court's attention.[328] However, this

---

320. 515 S.W.2d 725, 729 (Tex. Civ. App. 1974).
321. *Id.* at 730 (Tunks, J., dissenting).
322. *See* Connecticut Professional Sports Corp. v. Heyman, 276 F. Supp. 618 (S.D.N.Y. 1967). *Cf.* Nassau Sports v. Hampson, 355 F. Supp. 733 (D. Minn. 1972).
323. *See generally* Note, *Reserve Clauses in Athletic Contracts, supra* note 305.
324. *See* ch. 5 *infra.*
325. 86 Misc. 441, 465, 149 N.Y.S. 6, 20 (Sup. Ct. 1914).
326. *See* Washington Capitols Basketball Club, Inc. v. Barry, 419 F.2d 472, 478 (9th Cir. 1969); Dallas Cowboys Football Club, Inc. v. Harris, 348 S.W.2d 37, 47 (Tex. Civ. App. 1961).
327. *See* Central New York Basketball, Inc. v. Barnett, 19 Ohio Op. 2d 130, 181 N.E.2d 506 (1961).
328. *See* Nassau Sports v. Peters, 352 F. Supp. 870, 878-81 (E.D.N.Y. 1972); *cf.* Minnesota Muskies Inc. v. Hudson, 294 F. Supp 979, 990 (M.D.N.C. 1969).

attitude of neutrality toward the reserve system on the part of courts of equity has not been universal. Indeed, litigation involving player raids by the World Hockey Association confirmed that some courts perceive the request for an injunction and the resulting antitrust complaint as very much interrelated, particularly as the resolution of each question may have a direct and substantial bearing on whether a fledgling new league will survive.[329] However, even in the hockey cases not all courts departed from the prior trend of avoiding antitrust complaints,[330] and thus it is by no means certain that the cases represent a new direction.

The hesitancy of the courts of equity to decide the antitrust claims may be quite defensible. The issues raised in an antitrust attack are usually quite complex, and an adequate resolution of them often requires that extensive factual evidence and expert testimony be received. By contrast, a proceeding on request for a preliminary restraining order is intended to be a truncated affair in which an immediate decision is rendered on limited findings of fact. Even a less-hurried hearing on a motion for a permanent injunction is usually not used for the purpose of making detailed inquiries into the basic operation of an entire industry. Moreover, there are several available alternative proceedings specifically designed to resolve antitrust complaints. The rules for access to these are generally so liberal that the judge in the injunction proceeding who directs the litigants to one of them can be confident that the defendant's objections will be entertained.[331]

Most cases limiting the role of antitrust defenses in injunction proceedings have arisen at the federal level. There is an additional reason why a state court should not entertain an assault on option and reserve clauses based on state antitrust laws. The lower court decisions in *Flood v. Kuhn* found that a state's right to regulate player retention practices in baseball had been preempted by the federal antitrust laws.[332] In the view of the Second Circuit,

> ... it is apparent that each league extends over many states, and that, if state regulations were permissible, the internal structure of the leagues would require compliance with the strictest state antitrust standard ... On the other hand, we do not find that a state's interest in antitrust regulation, when compared with its interest in health and safety regulation, is of particular urgency. Hence, as the burden on interstate commerce outweighs the states' interest in regulating

329. *See* Boston Professional Hockey Ass'n, Inc. v. Cheevers, 348 F. Supp. 261, 267 (D. Mass.), *remanded,* 472 F.2d 127 (1st Cir. 1972); Nassau Sports v. Hampson, 355 F. Supp. 733 (D. Minn. 1972).

330. *See* Nassau Sports v. Peters, 352 F. Supp. 870 (E.D.N.Y. 1972). The new hockey league's antitrust complaints were finally vindicated, but in a different proceeding and one in which the potential antitrust violations were the particular matter in controversy. *See* Philadelphia World Hockey Club, Inc. v. Philadelphia Hockey Club, Inc., 351 F. Supp. 462 (E.D. Pa. 1972).

331. Some courts have been quite candid in their reluctance to litigate complicated antitrust claims when they are raised by way of defense in a simple contract action. Even the U.S. Supreme Court has observed that "As a defense to an action based on contract, the plea of illegality based on violation of the Sherman Act has not met with much favor in this Court." Kelly v. Kosuga, 358 U.S. 516, 518, 3 L. Ed. 2d 475, 79 S. Ct. 429 (1959). There are several reasons given for this resistance to the introduction of antitrust issues in an action seeking enforcement of the contract. Among other things, it is felt that the antitrust claims may unduly complicate and prolong the contract litigation. Moreover, other forms of relief are available, and these are generally sufficient to achieve the goals of the antitrust laws. *See* Dickstein v. duPont, 443 F.2d 783 (1st Cir. 1971).

332. 316 F. Supp. 271, 278-80 (S.D.N.Y. 1970), *aff'd,* 443 F.2d 264, 267-68 (2d Cir. 1971), *aff'd on other grounds,* 407 U.S. 258, 284-85, 32 L. Ed. 2d 728, 92 S. Ct. 2099 (1972).

baseball's reserve system, the Commerce Clause precludes the application here of state antitrust law.[333]

When the Supreme Court reviewed the *Flood* case, it found that these points "adequately dispose of the state law claims." [334]

Flood involved a frontal attack on the reserve clause under the antitrust laws and thus arose in a much different procedural context than that in which a club's request for an injuction is considered. It might be argued that the *Flood* analysis does not apply to a state injunction proceeding, since the court in such a case would only deny relief to the plaintiff team and could not directly order a club or league to alter its basic practices. Thus, the impact of an adverse ruling on state antitrust grounds would not have precisely the same effects which were identified as a source of concern by the Second Circuit. Yet, it must be accepted that the club's access to injunctive relief is a critical part of a league's player retention system, for if that remedy is denied, the club may be left without any effective recourse against the player.[335] Hence, the spectre of divergent and conflicting state law rules and the concomitant infringement upon the interstate activities of sports leagues foreseen by the Second Circuit is not dispelled by the more limited nature of injunction proceedings. The initial state court interpretations of the *Flood* holding adopt this latter view.[336]

An interesting question which has not yet been subjected to close judicial analysis is whether the *Flood* rationale can be applied to preclude a defendant from attacking the standard player contract, not on formal state law antitrust grounds, but for its lack of fairness. It has always been assumed that the discretionary nature of equitable relief empowers the court to review a contract on that basis. But as suggested above, the type of objections which are reviewed under the guise of an inquiry into the fairness of the provisions of a standard player contract, particularly a reserve clause, are often indistinguishable from those which would be raised by a more direct antitrust attack.[337] A general finding by a state court that the standard player contract in football, for example, was unfair and thus unenforceable in equity would seem to have the same adverse effect on a league's interstate operation as a similar ruling based on local antitrust laws.[338] While a state court might properly decide that the concept of *fairness* should be defined by reference to federal antitrust doctrine, that proposition is more easily stated than put into practice, for the substance of federal antitrust law is not susceptible to easy application in particular fact situations. The most that can be said is that *Flood* seems to require that inquiries at the state level be made with some sensitivity to developments under relevant federal doctrine.

---

333. 443 F.2d at 268.
334. 407 U.S. at 285.
335. *See* § 4.02 *supra.*
336. *See* Matuszak v. Houston Oilers, Inc., 515 S.W.2d 725, 728-29 (Tex. Civ. App. 1974).
337. In Matuszak v. Houston Oilers, Inc., *id.,* the dissenting judge found the terms of the NFL Standard Player Contract to be oppressive on the grounds that they were foisted upon the player by the club without an opportunity for negotiation. In the judge's view, the club was able to do this because "as a result of the combination and agreement between the twenty-six teams in the National Football League, Matuszak could deal with and play for only the Houston Oilers." *Id.* at 730. Although the court purported to base these objections on the grounds that a court of equity ought not enforce a contract which is grossly unfair, it can be noted that a more formal antitrust attack would be expressed in much the same terms. *See, e.g.,* Robertson v. National Basketball Ass'n, 389 F. Supp. 867 (S.D.N.Y. 1975); Kapp v. National Football League, 390 F. Supp. 73 (N.D. Cal. 1974).
338. *See* Flood v. Kuhn, 407 U.S. 258, 284-85, 32 L. Ed. 2d 728, 92 S. Ct. 2099 (1972).

§ 4.14. Tort Aspects of Contract-Jumping: New Employer's Interference with the Existing Contractual Relationship.

a. Introduction. When a player "jumps" his contract and signs with another club, the original team will predictably be concerned about the legal actions which are available to protect its interests. One concern will be its rights to get the player back. The various legal principles which define the club's right in this regard are treated in the preceding sections. But the club may also desire to pursue its remedies against the third party who induced the player to leave. The nature of that action will be in tort, more specifically the tort of interference with contractual relationships.[339] The litigation between the club and the alleged tortious intruder may take a number of different forms. For example, the club may join the player and the offending club in a single action seeking injunctive relief against both.[340] The action against the athlete would seek to enforce his promise to play exclusively for the plaintiff, while the action against the other club would seek to enjoin further tortious interference. Or where the controversy is part of a systematic effort by a new league to sign up players from established clubs, the plaintiff may seek an injunction either against particular players to prevent their leaving or against the new league itself to prevent further attempts to entice away the plaintiff's players already under contract.[341] Finally, in some circumstances, the injured club may sue the alleged intermeddler and seek money damages rather than an injunction.[342]

The basic legal issue involved in these actions bears a close relationship to a matter previously discussed. A player who has once "jumped" his contract often has second thoughts about the wisdom of his action and later returns to his original employer. The club which had hired him away may then seek a judicial order enjoining the player from violating his promise not to play for any other team. This litigation, in which the new employer is the plaintiff, often gives rise

---

339. *See generally* 45 AM. JUR. 2d, *Interference* § 39 (1969); 86 C.J.S., *Torts* §§ 42-44 (1954); D. DOBBS, HANDBOOK ON THE LAW OF REMEDIES § 6.4 (1973); W. PROSSER, HANDBOOK ON THE LAW OF TORTS § 129 (1971) [hereinafter cited as PROSSER, TORTS]; RESTATEMENT OF TORTS § 766 (1939); RESTATEMENT OF (SECOND) (c. & s.c.) TORTS § 766 (Tent. Draft No. 14, 1969); Carpenter, *Interference with Contract Relations,* 41 HARV. L. REV. 728 (1928); Sayre, *Inducing Breach of Contract,* 36 HARV. L. REV. 663 (1923). The seminal case in this area is Lumley v. Gye, 2 El. & Bl. 216, 118 Eng. Rep. 749 (1853) which is an outgrowth of the controversy presented in Lumley v. Wagner, 1 D. G. M. & G. 604, 50 Eng. Rep. 466 (1852) which is discussed in an earlier section. *See* § 4.02 *supra.*

340. *See, e.g.,* Winnipeg Rugby Football Club v. Freeman, 140 F. Supp. 365 (N.D. Ohio 1955); Long Island American Ass'n Football Club, Inc. v. Manrodt, 23 N.Y.S.2d 858 (Sup. Ct. 1940).

341. The formation of the World Football League in 1973 prompted some National Football League teams to seek to enjoin the new league from soliciting the services of players already under contract. One of these cases, *World Football League v. Dallas Cowboys Football Club, Inc.* is reported at 513 S.W.2d 102 (Tex. Civ. App. 1974). Another important case is *Cincinnati Bengals, Inc. v. Bergey.* The lengthy opinion in that case, written by Judge Porter was recently published. *See* 453 F. Supp. 129 (S.D. Ohio 1974). After initially issuing a 10-day temporary restraining order, Judge Porter heard considerable evidence on the effects of the World Football League signings, and eventually entered an order denying the Bengals' motion for a preliminary injunction against both Bergey and the World Football League. Judge Porter's decision was affirmed on appeal. The per curiam opinion by the Sixth Circuit Court of Appeals is unpublished. *See* Civil No. 74-1570 (6th Cir., Aug. 27, 1974).

The appearance of the Mexican Baseball League in the mid-1940's produced another case involving a request for injunctive relief against player raids by the new league. Here the established league was more successful in its efforts to restrain the intrusion into its affairs. *See* American League Baseball Club of New York, Inc. v. Pasquel, 187 Misc. 230, 63 N.Y.S.2d 537 (Sup. Ct. 1946).

342. *Cf.* Munchak Corp. v. Riko Enterprises, Inc., 368 F. Supp. 1366 (M.D.N.C. 1973).

to the player's assertion that the new employer is not entitled to equitable relief because it comes before the court with unclean hands as a result of its having interfered with the player's pre-existing contractual obligation.[343] This defense raises many of the same questions which are involved in a direct action based in tort. Thus, it will be necessary to determine such matters as whether the new contract conflicted with the player's pre-existing obligation, whether the new employer used improper inducements and whether there was any justification for the new employer's action. Many of these overlapping questions are treated in an earlier section,[344] and the prior discussion will not be reiterated here. It is suggested, therefore, that the prior treatment be reviewed in connection with the present topic.

b. Elements of the Tort. The employer-club which brings an action in tort for meddling by another club must establish that:

(a) there was an existing relationship between it and the athlete who was hired away;

(b) the defendant club or league interfered with that relationship in a manner which denied to the original employer benefits to which it was otherwise entitled;

(c) the new employer acted in knowing and intentional disregard of the existing relationship; and

(d) the original employer was damaged by the interference.

Some statements of the elements of the tort suggest that it is necessary to find that the original contract must have been fully enforceable and that the interference must have amounted to a breach of that contract.[345] Other sources suggest that malice in the sense of ill-will is an element.[346] The listing set out above draws the contours of the tort in less absolute terms, and, it is thought, more accurately reflects the development of the case law in this area. For example, while the nature of the relationship protected by this cause of action is one of contract, it is not always necessary that there be an enforceable contract between the parties.[347] Moreover, the requisite degree of interference can be found even if there is no actual breach of the protected contract.[348] Finally, it is clear that the earlier requirement of a malicious interference has been substantially tempered, and while there is still some diversity of viewpoints on the precise degree of intention which is required, many courts require only

---

343. *See, e.g.,* Munchak Corp. v. Cunningham, 331 F. Supp. 872 (M.D.N.C. 1971), *rev'd,* 457 F.2d 721 (4th Cir. 1972); Washington Capitols Basketball Club, Inc. v. Barry, 304 F. Supp. 1193 (N.D. Cal.), *aff'd,* 419 F.2d 472 (9th Cir. 1969).

344. *See* § 4.12 *supra.*

345. *See, e.g.,* 45 Am. Jur. 2d, *Interference* § 39 (1969) where the essential elements are described as: "(1) the contract; (2) the wrongdoer's knowledge thereof; (3) his intentional procurement of its breach; (4) the absence of justification; and (5) damages resulting therefrom."

346. *See, e.g.,* Lumley v. Gye, 2 El. & Bl. 216, 118 Eng. Rep. 749 (1853).

347. *See, e.g.,* American League Baseball Club of New York, Inc. v. Pasquel, 187 Misc. 230, 63 N.Y.S.2d 537 (Sup. Ct. 1946); Prosser, Torts § 129 at 932-33.

348. *See, e.g.,* Prosser, Torts § 129, at 936. *See also* Cincinnati Bengals, Inc. v. Bergey, 453 F. Supp. 129, 146 (S.D. Ohio), ("[P]rocurement of the breach or, at least, substantial interference with its performance is an essential element of the tort."), *aff'd,* Civil No. 74-1570 (6th Cir., Aug. 27, 1974).

that the new employer appreciated that it was acting in disregard of another's rights.[349]

While any of the four elements listed may be determinative in a case involving a sports contract, it is not necessary to give attention to each of the considerations in the present treatise. Rather, the emphasis here will be upon those elements which will likely require special analysis in the sports context, and other sources should be consulted if a more general treatment is desired.[350]

c. Requirement of Improper Interference. In the sports area, the issue which is most frequently contested is whether the commitments which the new employer has exacted from the athlete represent an improper infringement upon the rights of the original employer. The tort arises only when the interference is found to be "improper," a term which represents the court's conclusion that the third party's actions have surpassed the level of intrusion which must be tolerated in order to preserve a healthy level of economic competition for the player's service. It is clear that some degree of infringement must be accepted by the existing employer. As is discussed below, the original employer will not be allowed to prevent his employee-athletes from entering into contracts to be performed in the future.[351] Moreover, there is precedent which suggests that the athlete can accept financial rewards from the outsider during his tenure under the original contract.[352] While in each of these cases the third party's actions represent an intrusion upon the original employer's control of the athlete's loyalty, that consequence is thought to be necessary in order to avoid excessive restrictions on the player's right to market his services. On the other hand, the courts are not insensitive to the obligations created by the original contract and are willing to provide relief where the new employer fails to show proper respect for the player's previous commitments.

The cases which cause the least difficulty are those in which the third party contracts for the player's services with performance to begin at a time when the athlete is still under contract to the original employer. The creation of this type of blatant conflict in the player's contractual duties is not tolerated by the courts and subjects the tortious stranger to appropriate judicial sanction.[353] But definite limits on the original employer's right to be free from competition are identified in other situations. Particularly important here are the cases in which the player, while under contract with his original employer, obligates himself to play for another team upon the expiration of his existing contract. The cases decided under the tortious interference doctrines seem to accept the basic distinction made in connection with the defense of unclean hands.[354] The critical

---

349. See generally PROSSER, TORTS § 129, at 927-29, 938-42.

350. See generally sources cited note 339 supra.

351. See, e.g., Cincinnati Bengals, Inc. v. Bergey, 453 F. Supp. 129 (S.D. Ohio), aff'd, Civil No. 74-1570 (6th Cir., Aug. 27, 1974); World Football League v. Dallas Cowboys Football Club, Inc., 513 S.W.2d 102 (Tex. Civ. App. 1974). See also Munchak Corp. v. Cunningham, 457 F.2d 721 (4th Cir. 1972); Washington Capitols Basketball Club, Inc. v. Barry, 419 F.2d 472 (9th Cir. 1969).

352. See. e.g., Munchak Corp. v. Cunningham, 457 F.2d 721 (4th Cir. 1972). See also § 4.12 supra.

353. See, e.g., Winnipeg Rugby Football Club v. Freeman, 140 F. Supp. 365 (N.D. Ohio 1955); Long Island American Ass'n Football Club, Inc. v. Manrodt, 23 N.Y.S.2d 858 (Sup. Ct. 1940).

354. Compare Munchak Corp. v. Cunningham, 457 F.2d 721 (4th Cir. 1972); Washington Capitols Basketball Club, Inc. v. Barry, 419 F.2d 472 (9th Cir.), aff'g 304 F. Supp. 1193 (N.D. Cal. 1969).

question concerns the point at which the player is obligated to perform under his contract with the new employer.[355] If the athlete's new obligations begin only after his existing commitment has been fulfilled, there is no improper intrusion on the first employer's rights.[356] Contrary to an earlier view,[357] it is of no consequence that the player carries on the negotiations and actually signs the contract while he is still under contract with the original club.

The cases which originally approved the player's freedom to contract with respect to his future services did not consider all of the arguments which the original employer might make concerning the disruptive effect of allowing an athlete to become contractually involved with another team. But the limits of the doctrine were subjected to more precise definition in the cases which arose when the newly-formed World Football League signed players from the National Football League.[358] One of the arguments made by the plaintiff in *Cincinnati Bengals, Inc. v. Bergey*[359] was that the player's signing with the WFL would potentially impair his ability to perform for the Bengals. Particular emphasis was given to the fact that Bergey's WFL contract included a term which accelerated his obligation to perform, and hence his right to receive the substantially higher WFL salary, in the event he was given an early release from the Bengals. As characterized by the court of appeals, the Bengals' argument was that the acceleration provision "will tempt Bergey to 'dog it' or otherwise perform in such a manner as to cause the Bengals to grant him an early release." [360] The appellate court rejected this argument, but did so largely on the basis of findings made by the district court that Bergey was personally committed to fulfilling his original contract. While this approach would seemingly require a court to make an explicit inquiry into the player's personality and sense of commitment, other courts seem less willing to require particularized findings on the question of whether the player's incentives will be impaired. The plaintiff in *World Football League, Inc. v. Dallas Cowboys Football Club, Inc.*[361] made a similar argument that players signing contracts for their future services "will not use their best efforts for the team." The court responded that "[T]hese facts, even if true, do not present grounds for equitable relief." [362] While the court did not present a specific rebuttal to the club's contention, its general view appears to be that any such concerns are outweighed by the desirability of protecting the player's freedom to contract.

Since the argument about impaired incentives could be made in any case, it must be met with skepticism lest it provide the basis for effectively binding the player to his original team for the remainder of his career. The case in which

---

355. *See* § 4.12 *supra.*
356. *See* Cincinnati Bengals, Inc. v. Bergey, 453 F. Supp. 129 (S.D. Ohio), *aff'd,* Civil No. 74-1570 (6th Cir., Aug. 27, 1974); World Football League v. Dallas Cowboys Football Club, Inc. 513 S.W.2d 102 (Tex. Civ. App. 1974). The courts in both *Bergey* and *Dallas Cowboys* give specific approval to the *Barry* and *Cunningham* decisions. *See* Cincinnati Bengals, Inc. v. Bergey, 453 F. Supp. 129 (S.D. Ohio), *aff'd,* Civil No. 74-1570 at 5-6 (6th Cir., Aug. 27, 1974); World Football League v. Dallas Cowboys Football Club, Inc., 513 S.W.2d 102, 105 (Tex. Civ. App. 1974).
357. *See* Munchak Corp. v. Cunningham, 331 F. Supp. 862 (M.D.N.C. 1971), *rev'd,* 457 F.2d 721 (4th Cir. 1972); Minnesota Muskies, Inc. v. Hudson, 294 F. Supp. 979 (M.D.N.C. 1969).
358. *See* note 341 *supra.*
359. 453 F. Supp. 129 (S.D. Ohio), *aff'd,* Civil No. 74-1570 (6th Cir. Aug. 27, 1974).
360. Civil No. 74-1570, at 4 (6th Cir., Aug. 2, 1974).
361. 513 S.W.2d 102, 105 (Tex. Civ. App. 1974).
362. *Id.*

a star athlete makes a calculated effort to reduce his performance below an acceptable level will be extremely rare and should not influence the formulation of the general rule in this area. The athlete has little incentive to purposely degrade his endeavor, for in the process, he would not only leave himself open to considerable interpersonal conflict with others on the team, but also he may ruin his standing with the fans and, hence, destroy the prime ingredient of his ability to command a premium salary. The *Dallas Cowboys* decision is clearly directed to the typical case in which this does not happen and is sound in the result it reaches. Should a case actually arise involving a deliberate attempt by the athlete to force his early release from his original contract, it can be dealt with separately. But the mobility of the vast majority of athletes ought not be impaired by a concern which is truly hypothetical in nature.

Another argument made in both the *Bergey* and *Dallas Cowboys* cases was that a player's signing would have a divisive effect on the rest of the team. The apparent premise of this argument is the notion that a high degree of cohesiveness is a necessary ingredient of a successful football team, and achievement of that bond requires that each player be perceived by his teammates as devoted to the group's ultimate goal. After a player has signed with another team, it would be argued, his loyalty would be questioned and distance would develop between him and the others.[363] This contention was rejected in both cases, in *Bergey* on the basis of a specific finding that Bergey continued to enjoy a good relationship with his teammates [364] and in *Dallas Cowboys* on the general grounds that even if true, the contention would not support the relief requested.[365]

It would seem that the club's concern for the effects of a signing upon others is even less meritorious than its concerns for the direct impact on the player's own performance. The player and his new employer cannot be held responsible for the reaction which others have to the signing. Those reactions may or may not be rational and may be based on a variety of feelings, including professional jealousy. The defendants have no control over these, short of refraining from dealing with each other, a response which would unduly restrict the player's right to realize the maximum value of his services. As to this argument, it can rightly be held that no particularized inquiry is necessary, and a general rejection of the sort found in *Dallas Cowboys* is fully warranted.

---

363. One of the unique aspects of Judge Porter's opinion in the *Bergey* case was the inquiry made into the nature of professional football. The opinion contains two lengthy excerpts from the testimony at trial which serve to describe the intangible aspects of building a successful football team. Coach Paul Brown, when asked what factors influence the success of a football team, responded: "It comes down to nothing, really, but people." Others elaborated on the need for emotional cohesiveness among the team members. Football was distinguished from other sports in the degree to which the individual had to mold himself into the team in order to produce a successful product. Judge Porter made an explicit finding on these points: "From all this the Court can and does find that football is probably unique in that, to a greater degree than other professional sports, it is a team sport. Also it takes time and money to develop the players and 'units' so they will be cohesive. In short, football is a scientific, sophisticated sport, and a delicate sort of mechanism." 453 F. Supp. 129, 134-36 (S.D. Ohio 1974). As is noted later in the text, these findings did not prompt Judge Porter to accept the Bengals arguments about the disruptive effects of Bergey's signing. The court made a specific inquiry into Bergey's relationship with his teammates and found no evidence that a significant gulf had developed. *Id.* at 137.

364. *Id.* at 137.

365. 513 S.W.2d at 105.

The relief which was sought in both *Bergey* and *Dallas Cowboys* included a request for an injunction prohibiting the new league from signing any other players presently under contract to the plaintiff teams. The district court in *Bergey* made an interesting finding in connection with this request for a blanket order. The club argued that it would suffer disproportionate harm if the new league were to sign a number of its starting players. The district court found that "it is likely that there would be an adverse effect on the Bengals as a team if 'several' members of the team were to sign contracts with the WFL. . . ." [366] In the court's view, a massive exodus of Bengals' players would substantially undermine the efforts which the club had put forth to develop cohesive units within the team. The court added, however, that "this finding is not tantamount to a conclusion that the Bengals will be 'irreparably harmed' in the legal sense by a denial of injunctive relief." [367]

The court's precise conclusion on this matter is not entirely clear. It is possible to construe the court's statements to mean only that the club failed to show the degree of harm necessary to warrant injunctive relief. The question would remain as to whether there was nonetheless a legal wrong for which some other sort of remedy might be appropriate. It is unlikely, however, that the court intended to endorse such an alternative cause of action. On first thought, one might have doubts whether a rival ought to be able to hire away such a large number of employees as to render it unlikely that the employer could sustain its business until appropriate replacements were secured. But further analysis would suggest that the employer has a number of tools available to prevent this result. It can, for example, outbid its rival for the future services of its employees,[368] or by advance planning, it can stagger the employment contracts of key employees to insure that all do not depart at once. Moreover, it would seem that a particular athlete's right to earn a better salary ought not depend upon whether he is the first or seventh player to enter into negotiations with another club. Thus, absent unusual circumstances, it can be doubted that the threat of multiple signings should entitle the employer to any greater protection than he receives in any case in which a highly-valued employee is hired away.

Once the courts made clear that a rival team had the right to contract with a player even before he was freed from his commitments to the original employer, the question necessarily arose as to the extent to which the new employer could capitalize on the player's publicity value. The signing of a star performer adds prestige to a new league, and the fact of the signing could be used not only to attract other players but also to sell season tickets, television rights, and franchises. The player's actual participation in such promotional efforts would, of course, enhance them greatly. On the other hand, the existing employer might properly be concerned that such activity would divert the athlete's attention from his primary duties as a member of the employer's team. Moreover, the original employer might well feel that since it was paying the

---

366. 453 F. Supp. at 134-35.

367. *Id.*

368. In another portion of the opinion, the district court in *Bergey* reasoned that the team could avoid the adverse effects of a single player's signing with another team by outbidding its rival. While this might involve significant expense, it was felt that there is no real "harm" involved, for the expense would not be the result of any legal wrong. *Id.* at 148. A similar analysis might apply to cases in which several players were signed.

player's salary, it should have an exclusive right to exploit the athlete's publicity value.

An interesting question might be raised as to whether a contract for the existing services of an athlete also entitles the club to claim an exclusive right to the player's promotional value to the sport. For most professional sports that question need not be answered in the abstract, for many of the major leagues utilize standard contract forms which grant the club an exclusive right to not only the player's services on the field but also his other activities related to the sport. Typical in this regard is the NFL contract, under which "the Player agrees that during the term of this contract he will play football *and engage in activities related to football* only for the Club. . . ." [369] The protection which this type of provision affords the employer-club has not been precisely determined, but some guidance is provided by the court's opinion in the *Dallas Cowboys* case. There the court found that no improper interference with the existing contractual relationship resulted from "the publicity necessarily attendant upon the signing of contracts with well-known players." [370] However, the court seemed to draw the line at publicity relating to the signing itself: "We should not be understood, however, as holding that other promotional and publicity activities for the benefit of future employers would not be subject to restraint as 'activities relating to football,' which the players are bound by their present contracts to reserve for the Club." [371] Under the distinction which the court seems to make, the press conferences which normally attend a new league's signing of a star athlete would seemingly be permissible. Conversely, the athlete could presumably be restrained from making personal efforts to attract other players or to promote season tickets or other franchises. The player's value in instilling fan or investor confidence in a rival enterprise would seem to be precisely the sort of "other activity" which the original employer intended to secure for itself. There will, however, be activities which fall somewhere in between the two types mentioned above. For example, the promoters of the new league might seek to use the athlete's picture or endorsement in connection with their own publicity efforts. While the league should be given some liberty to publicize an indisputable fact — that it has a right to the player's future services — particular promotional activities will have to be judged against the basic test of the degree to which they represent a diminution of the rights which the original employer has under its contract. Until the original contract expires, it is clear that the primary rights reside in the party entitled to the player's present services.

One further type of potential interference by the new employer deserves mention. Often the contract with the new employer will provide payments to be made to the player even before he begins performance under the agreement. These might include a bonus paid upon the signing of the contract or amounts to be paid to the athlete during the option year. The question might be raised as to whether the player's receipt of such financial rewards would not affect the manner in which he performed his duties under his existing contract. Even granting the athlete's right to contract for the sale of his future services, it does not necessarily follow that such a payment should be approved, particularly

369. NFL Contract ¶ 2 (1975).
370. 513 S.W.2d at 105.
371. *Id.*

where it is intended to influence the athlete's behavior under his existing contract.[372] While there are decided cases which involve this issue, the matter has not been subjected to detailed analysis by the courts, and it can be expected that the occasion for further consideration will be presented in the future.

An implied approval of bonuses-for-signing can be found in the *Bergey* case. There, Bergey was to receive a bonus of $125,000 for signing with the WFL, with $40,000 payable upon the actual execution of the contract.[373] The district court did not separately discuss this payment as a potential interference with Bergey's NFL contract, but the relevant issue seems to be subsumed in the discussion of whether Bergey's WFL contract would adversely affect his performance for the Bengals. The district court's conclusion about Bergey's high degree of dedication was presumably made in light of the financial rewards available from the WFL and thus can be read as not disapproving such payments.[374]

A somewhat different question is raised when the payment involved is not a signing bonus as such but rather a payment to be made in the event the player decides to sit out his option year. Such payments may take a variety of forms,[375] but whatever the device used, the basic question presented is whether a competing employer ought to be permitted to pay money where the known effect, if not specific purpose, will be to influence the employee's conduct under an existing contract. The limited case authority on this point suggests a judicial tolerance of this type of arrangement.[376] This precedent is discussed more fully in an earlier section.[377] For the present discussion it is sufficient to note that approval of payments of this sort is not necessarily compelled by the desire to permit competition for the player's services, and a future court would be justified in placing severe limitations on such arrangements if there were evidence that the payment would have a substantial effect upon the player's performance.

d. The Intent Requirement. While the tort of interference with contract is generally held to require an intentional intrusion into an existing relationship, there is considerable diversity in the case law on the question of whether a desire to injure or deceive the plaintiff is an element of the cause of action. The intentional quality of the tort is often expressed as a requirement that legal malice must be found. In the early cases, this was construed to mean that the intermeddler must possess ill-will toward the plaintiff.[378] But Professor Prosser reports that the term *malice* has since "undergone a gradual process of vitiation, until it now has all shades of meaning from active malevolence, through an intent to profit at the expense of the plaintiff, to a mere intent with knowledge of his interests, to do an act which will have the effect of interfering with

---

372. *See* § 4.12 *supra.*
373. *See* 453 F. Supp. 129, 133 (S.D. Ohio 1974).
374. *Id.* at 136.
375. Indeed, an alleged bonus-for-signing may in reality be intended as an inducement to the player to remove himself from active competition. Where such subterfuge is found, the court ought to evaluate the payment with the greater skepticism suggested in the discussion in section 4.12 *supra.* Presumably the intent with which the payment was made would be of primary importance in categorizing the reward.
376. *See, e.g.,* Munchak Corp. v. Cunningham, 457 F.2d 721 (4th Cir. 1972).
377. *See* § 4.12 *supra.*
378. *See, e.g.,* Lumley v. Gye, 2 El. & Bl. 216, 118 Eng. Rep. 749 (1853).

them." [379] Discussion of the implications of these various meanings is beyond the scope of the present treatise. What can be noted is that the modern trend is toward defining the malice element to require only that the third party acted in knowing disregard of the plaintiff's rights under an existing contract, without further qualification as to the acceptability of the stranger's motive. Indeed, once it is decided that the degree of interference exceeded the level which attends normal business competition, most modern courts will require no more than that the defendant was aware of the plaintiff's prior contract rights.[380] But as the discussion below indicates, not all courts have moved this far from a requirement of malevolence, and it will be necessary to research the decisions in the particular jurisdiction to determine its position on this matter.

The cases in the sports area have given some attention to the requirement of intent. There are cases in which the new employer asserted that it did not know that the player was already under contract when it signed him. While such a state of ignorance would normally preclude a finding that the interference was intentional,[381] the evidence necessary to sustain the defense often has been found lacking in the sports cases.[382] Indeed, the more common fact situation is one in which a new league or team specifically seeks to recruit the proven talent of an existing club. In such circumstances, the competing club cannot seriously assert that it was unaware of the potential infringement.

On the surface at least, the sports cases also reflect some differences in the degree of malevolence they require before liability will be found. In some cases involving the actual pirating of a player during the term of his existing contract, injunctions have been issued without a specific finding of deception or similar impropriety on the part of the defendant teams.[383] But dicta in the cases arising from the recruiting efforts of the WFL suggest that the use of "deceitful means" is an element of the tort.[384] For example, the district court judge in *Bergey*, in discussing a series of cases cited by the plaintiffs, observed that each of the proffered decisions involved the use of secretive or otherwise improper recruiting techniques by a rival employer.[385] After concluding that these cases did not require the issuance of an injunction on the facts before it, the court observed:

> There is no evidence whatsoever that the WFL has utilized such deceitful means. In other words, there is no evidence of legal malice. There is no evidence from which the Court can conclude that the WFL

---

379. PROSSER, TORTS § 129, at 928. Prosser's analysis includes citations to a number of cases which are said to illustrate the different interpretations given to the term.

380. *See id.* at 941-42. *See also* Winnipeg Rugby Football Club v. Freeman, 140 F. Supp. 365 (N.D. Ohio 1955); Long Island American Ass'n Football Club, Inc. v. Manrodt, 23 N.Y.S.2d 858 (Sup. Ct. 1940).

381. *See* Augustine v. Trucco, 124 Cal. App. 2d 229, 268 P.2d 780 (1954); Twitchell v. Nelson, 126 Minn. 423, 148 N.W. 451 (1914); Thomason v. Sparkman, 55 S.W.2d 871 (Tex. Civ. App. 1933).

382. *See* Winnipeg Rugby Football Club v. Freeman, 140 F. Supp. 365 (N.D. Ohio 1955); Long Island American Ass'n Football Club, Inc. v. Manrodt, 23 N.Y.S.2d 858 (Sup. Ct. 1940).

383. *See* authorities cited in note 382 *supra.*

384. *See* Cincinnati Bengals, Inc. v. Bergey, 453 F. Supp. 129, 146-47 (S.D. Ohio), *aff'd,* Civil No. 74-1570 (6th Cir., Aug. 27, 1974).

385. The court considered Wear-Ever Aluminum, Inc. v. Towncraft Indus., Inc., 75 N.J. Super. 135, 182 A.2d 387 (1962); Architectural Mfg. Co. v. Airatec, Inc., 119 Ga. App. 245, 166 S.E.2d 744 (1969); and Haggerty v. Burkey Mills, Inc., 211 F. Supp. 835 (E.D.N.Y. 1962).

has singled out the Cincinnati Bengals as a target of destruction the accomplishment of which is through improper interference with the contracts between the Bengals and its players, nor that the WFL seeks to destroy the National Football League by its actions in signing NFL players to contracts for future services.[386]

This statement might be read to mean that, in the court's view, deceit was an element of the plaintiff's case. If that were true, it might then be argued that a rival employer who acted openly and directly would not be subject to liability even if he secured the athlete's commitment to play during the term of his existing contract. But surely the *Bergey* court did not intend to suggest such a result, for the court elsewhere recognizes the sanctity of the athlete's original contract. Moreover, the cases which enjoin actual pirating of players without inquiry into the new employer's motives would seem to reach the correct result.[387]

It is possible to read the cases as presenting no real conflict in their differing emphasis on the propriety of the rival's recruiting techniques. It might be said that the hiring away of a player during the term of his existing contract will be deemed tortious if it appears that the defendant knew of the player's prior contract and acted in disregard of it. But even when the rival is careful to delay the beginning of the athlete's performance until the expiration of the original contract, egregious misconduct in the recruiting of the player may warrant judicial intervention. Since this matter is only treated in dicta in the existing case law, it is not possible to present an authoritative assessment of the type of deception which will fall into this category. But as suggested by the district court's statement in *Bergey* and the case precedent to which it responds, the sort of recruiting techniques which will be condemned must presumably have the essential characteristics of improper actions which might otherwise provide an independent basis for relief. Thus, while a court might not insist that the means employed meet all of the technical requirements necessary to support a cause of action based on fraud, deceit, or related torts, it may require a showing that the same basic public policies have been offended.[388] Such a standard would serve to underscore the fact that that which is to be disapproved is not business competition as such, but rather competition which is unfair because it is carried out by means which directly injure the plaintiff or otherwise induce him to rely, to his detriment, on an assumed state of facts.

e. The Justification for the Defendant's Action. In its classic formulation, the tort of intentional interference with contract is said to require an inquiry into the justification for the defendant's actions.[389] This element is not entirely distinct from the requirements of improper interference and improper intent, for the conclusions reached with respect to those considerations will often predetermine the court's assessment of whether there was justification for the defendant's action. But separately categorizing the issue of justification does

---

386. 453 F. Supp. at 146-47.

387. *See* note 380 *supra.*

388. *See, e.g.,* Hitchman Coal & Coke Co. v. Mitchell, 245 U.S. 229, 251-52, 62 L. Ed. 260, 38 S. Ct. 65 (1917); Truax v. Raich, 239 U.S. 33, 38, 60 L. Ed. 131, 36 S. Ct. 7 (1915); Chipley v. Atkinson, 23 Fla. 206, 1 So. 934 (1887); Walker v. Cronin, 107 Mass. 555 (1871).

389. *See generally* Freed v. Manchester Service, Inc., 165 Cal. App. 2d 186, 331 P.2d 689 (Dist. Ct. App. 1958); 45 AM. JUR. 2d *Interference* § 39 (1969); RESTATEMENT OF TORTS § 766 (1939).

serve to make clear that a determination of the defendant's liability requires more than a literal application of mechanical rules. Rather, as applied to commercial contracts, the tort requires a balancing of the competing policies of the plaintiff's right to stability in his relationships with his employees and the defendant's right to compete with the plaintiff for the services of those same parties. These concerns are embodied in the element of justification, which, in general terms, requires an inquiry into whether the interests which the defendant is pursuing are entitled to greater deference than those which the plaintiff seeks to protect.[390]

There are several cases which reflect the courts' efforts to undertake this sort of balancing with respect to the particular interests which are at stake in the professional sports industry, although the courts seldom characterize their inquiry as one involving the element of justification. For example, there appears to be agreement on the point that a highly-talented athlete ought to be free to enter the marketplace and seek the buyer who values his services most highly, subject, of course, to his fulfillment of his existing obligations. The competition which a rival league creates for the player's services is generally regarded as a positive force which should be encouraged.[391] Thus, the courts are willing to protect the right of the new league to correspond with the athletes on an established club.[392] Moreover, it is recognized that a club holding a player's existing contract cannot justifiably complain that as a result of another league's intermeddling, it may have to pay more to continue its relationship with its players beyond the term of their existing contracts.[393]

It is also recognized that a significant barrier to the formation of new leagues would be presented if the established clubs were permitted to insulate their players from competing offers for their future services. Consistent with the general public policy favoring economic competition between business entities, courts are willing to recognize the role which they can play in minimizing the difficulty which new entrants encounter in establishing a market position.[394] The desired result is achieved through case decisions which more clearly define the rights which established teams enjoy under their pre-existing contracts with their players. While a club will be permitted to insist upon full performance for the agreed-upon term, it will not be allowed to extend the reach of its claim so as to secure a preferential position with respect to future contracts.

To the extent that the major sports continue to be dominated by a single league, a new entrant should find a receptive judicial climate for its efforts to

---

390. *See* PROSSER, TORTS § 129, at 942-46.

391. *See also* § 4.12 *supra.*

392. *See, e.g.,* World Football League v. Dallas Cowboys Football Club, Inc., 513 S.W.2d 102 (Tex. Civ. App. 1974).

393. *See* Cincinnati Bengals, Inc. v. Bergey, 453 F. Supp. 129, 142 (S.D. Ohio 1974): "It is not the players' present services for which the clubs will have to pay more, for these are protected by contracts which can presumably be enforced in the usual manner. . . . It is only when the NFL chooses, (and such decision is likely) to join the competition for the later services of its players that it will incur these higher costs. In our best judgment, such higher costs will be attributable to competition and not unfair competition." *See also* World Football League v. Dallas Cowboys Football Club, Inc., 513 S.W.2d 102, 105 (Tex. Civ. App. 1974).

394. *See* Cincinnati Bengals, Inc. v. Bergey, 453 F. Supp. 129, 137-38 (S.D. Ohio), *aff'd,* Civil No. 74-1570 (6th Cir., Aug. 27, 1974). *See also* Nassau Sports v. Hampson, 355 F. Supp. 733 (D. Minn. 1972); Boston Professional Hockey Ass'n, Inc. v. Cheevers, 348 F. Supp. 261 (D.Mass.), *remanded,* 472 F.2d 127 (1st Cir. 1972).

sign established players. While this may or may not continue to be the case, existing precedent does yield the rather durable principle that the tort of interference with contract gains much of its meaning from the context in which the particular problem arises. Although the various elements of the tort identify the general considerations which will be important, the open-ended nature of many of these, especially the factor of justification, allows for a wide range of judicial discretion in assessing the role of competition in the particular setting. Thus, it should be apparent that the determination of the justification for the defendant's actions involves an *ad hoc* assessment, and the court must look at such things as the precise terms of the athlete's existing contract, the level of competition in the relevant market, and the particular consequences of the defendant's action for all of the parties involved.

§ 4.15. Arbitration in Professional Sports: The Legal Framework.

a. Nature of Arbitration. Previous sections of this chapter have been devoted to detailing the rights and obligations of the parties to a sports contract. Once it is determined that a party has certain rights, the question arises as to how he secures enforcement of those rights. In the traditional contract setting, of course, enforcement of the agreement is secured through primary resort to the judicial process, and a breach of contract may necessitate the commencement of a formal law suit. But under the regime which presently prevails in professional sports, it is contemplated that most contract disputes will never get into court; rather, the parties often agree that all disputes which arise will be submitted to arbitration. Where it is applicable, arbitration will be the exclusive remedy, and the player or club which agrees to arbitrate a dispute loses the right to have the claim adjudicated in the courts, a consequence which is not always understood by the athletes and their attorneys.[395]

An agreement to arbitrate is basically a contract between the parties in which they promise to resolve disputes by non-judicial means.[396] As with other contracts, the parties are afforded considerable freedom to define the terms of their agreement. They are free to designate the particular person to be arbitrator or to agree upon a method for selecting arbitrators as they are needed. There is no requirement that arbitrators be legally trained or that they otherwise resemble judges. Indeed, in the past, the standard form contracts used in professional sports often stipulated that the league commissioner would serve as arbitrator,[397] an arrangement which met with considerable objection from the players.[398] The parties can also agree to the procedures which will apply to their

---

395. *See, e.g.,* Davis v. Pro Basketball, Inc., 381 F. Supp. 1 (S.D.N.Y. 1974).

396. *See generally* M. DOMKE, THE LAW AND PRACTICE OF COMMERCIAL ARBITRATION § 1.01 (1968) [hereinafter cited as DOMKE, COMMERCIAL ARBITRATION]; R. GORMAN, BASIC TEXT ON LABOR LAW 540-48 (1976) [hereinafter cited as GORMAN, LABOR LAW]; St. Antoine, *Judicial Review of Labor Arbitration Awards: A Second Look at Enterprise Wheel and its Progeny,* 75 MICH. L. REV. 1137, 1139-40 (1977).

397. The role of the commissioner as arbitrator is discussed in § 4.19 *infra*.

398. *See generally Arbitration in Professional Athletics* in ARBITRATION OF INTEREST DISPUTES — PROCEEDINGS OF THE TWENTY-SIXTH ANNUAL MEETING OF THE NATIONAL ACADEMY OF ARBITRATORS 108 (1973) [hereinafter cited as ACADEMY PROCEEDINGS].

arbitration proceeding,[399] and since the issue is essentially one of freedom of contract, there is no general requirement that the stipulated procedures be as protective as those which would be obtained in a court of law.[400] Further, the parties may agree as to exactly which of their disputes will be subject to arbitration.[401] To the extent that some controversies fall outside the scope of the arbitration agreement, the parties still have available the traditional forms of legal remedies.[402] While a system of arbitration is intended as a substitute for traditional forms of litigation, the courts continue to play a limited role in overseeing the arrangement. The primary function of the courts in this regard is not to resolve the parties' dispute, but rather to enforce the parties' "contract" with respect to the method of dispute-resolution which will be observed.[403] Thus, except for the insuring of a minimum of fairness in the actual arbitration proceedings,[404] the court will be primarily concerned with such things as compelling a reluctant party to participate in the arbitration,[405] providing enforcement of the arbitrator's award,[406] and insuring that the arbitration proceeding is actually conducted in accordance with the procedures which the parties had agreed to in their arbitration "contract."[407]

The differences between arbitration and the traditional forms of judicial relief are fundamental. As Justice Black has observed:

> For the individual, whether his case is settled by a professional arbitrator or tried by a jury can make a crucial difference. Arbitration differs from judicial proceedings in many ways: arbitration carries no right to a jury trial as guaranteed by the Seventh Amendment; arbitrators need not be instructed in the law; they are not bound by rules of evidence; they need not give reasons for their awards; witnesses need not be sworn; the record of proceedings need not be complete; and judicial review, it has been held, is extremely limited.[408]

Why do parties operating in the sphere of professional sports choose arbitration? The reasons are much the same as those which are influential in other commercial settings.[409] In general, it can be said that arbitration may be

---

399. See generally DOMKE, COMMERCIAL ARBITRATION ch. 24.

400. There is a residual concern that the proceeding meet the minimum standards of due process, a matter which is discussed in a later section. See § 4.18 infra. See also Prima Paint Corp. v. Flood & Conklin Mfg. Co., 388 U.S. 395, 407, 18 L. Ed. 2d 1270, 87 S. Ct. 1801 (1967) (Black, J. dissenting); Professional Sports, Ltd. v. Virginia Squires Basketball Club, 373 F. Supp. 946, 951 (W.D. Tex. 1974); Riko Enterprises, Inc. v. Seattle Supersonics Corp., 357 F. Supp. 521, 526 (S.D.N.Y. 1973).

401. See DOMKE, COMMERCIAL ARBITRATION § 12.01.

402. See, e.g., Johnson v. Green Bay Packers, Inc., 272 Wis. 149, 74 N.W.2d 784 (1956).

403. See DOMKE, COMMERCIAL ARBITRATION ch. 17, Introduction; St. Antoine, Judicial Review of Labor Arbitration Awards: A Second Look at Enterprise Wheel and Its Progeny, supra note 396. See generally 6A A. CORBIN, CORBIN ON CONTRACTS §§ 1432-34 (1962) [hereinafter cited as CORBIN ON CONTRACTS].

404. See § 4.18 infra.

405. See generally DOMKE, COMMERCIAL ARBITRATION Pt. VI (Statutory Enforcement of Arbitration Agreements); O. FAIRWEATHER, PRACTICE AND PROCEDURE IN LABOR ARBITRATION 18-28 (1973) [hereinafter cited as FAIRWEATHER, LABOR ARBITRATION].

406. See generally DOMKE, COMMERCIAL ARBITRATION Pt. XII; FAIRWEATHER, LABOR ARBITRATION 352-73.

407. See generally DOMKE, COMMERCIAL ARBITRATION Pt. XI; GORMAN, LABOR LAW 584-603.

408. Republic Steel Corp. v. Maddox, 379 U.S. 650, 664 (1965) (Black, J., dissenting).

409. See generally D. DOBBS, HANDBOOK ON THE LAW OF REMEDIES § 12.27, at 936 (1973) [hereinafter cited as DOBBS, REMEDIES]; F. O'NEAL, CLOSE CORPORATIONS § 9.11 (1958); Wolaver, The Historical Background of Commercial Arbitration, 83 U. PA. L. REV. 132 (1934).

selected because the parties want to take advantage of the differences between arbitration and judicial proceedings. As Justice Black suggests, arbitration proceedings are usually conducted much more informally than judicial proceedings. There is usually less energy devoted to procedural niceties, and typically fewer people are involved. Thus, a resolution secured through arbitration is usually less costly than that available from the courts. And for the reasons just identified, an arbitration is usually less time-consuming, a result which has the two-fold advantage of saving costs and removing the factor of delay as a settlement tool.[410] There are other advantages of arbitration which are particularly attractive to those who participate in professional sports. Arbitration proceedings tend to be much more private than the traditional judicial proceeding.[411] This is particularly valuable to an industry which, on the one hand, is very conscious of its public image [412] and, on the other hand, is subjected to the constant probings of the news media. By resort to the secrecy of the arbitration proceeding, many disputes are resolved with only the barest of information being circulated publicly.[413] Finally, those involved in sports, like those involved in other commercial ventures, recognize that there is some advantage to be obtained from being able to participate in the selection of the person who will hear the case. In a court of law, a party has almost no opportunity to determine which judge will hear his case. In arbitration, the parties theoretically can contract with respect to the arbitrator's qualifications and the manner of his selection. This system serves to assure a party that he will be treated fairly,[414] and more importantly gives the parties an opportunity to avoid the situation in which their case is decided by someone totally unfamiliar with the nature of the industry and its particular requirements.[415] Through

410. *See* Prima Paint Corp. v. Flood & Conklin Mfg. Co., 388 U.S. 395, 415 (1967) (Black, J., dissenting).

411. *See* DOBBS, REMEDIES § 12.27, at 936.

412. *See, e.g.,* ACADEMY PROCEEDINGS 133-34 (remarks of Theodore W. Kheel, Labor Counsel to the NFL Management Council); Comment, *Discipline in Professional Sports: The Need for Player Protection,* 60 GEO. L.J. 771, 772-75 (1972).

413. For example, under the system for arbitration of players' salaries in baseball, it is explicitly provided that "there shall be no opinion and no release of the arbitration award by the arbitrator except to the Club, the Player, the Players Association, and the Player Relations Committee." *See* Basic Agreement Between the American League of Professional Baseball Clubs and the National League of Professional Baseball Clubs and Major League Baseball Players Ass'n, art. V(E)(5) (1976) [hereinafter cited as Baseball Collective Bargaining Agreement]. The baseball salary arbitration provisions are discussed more fully in a later section. *See* note 531, § 4.18 *infra.*

414. In many sports, the players formerly would contend that although they were bound to arbitration, they had virtually no opportunity to participate in the selection of the arbitrator. This complaint was raised particularly with respect to those systems in which the league commissioner was designated as arbitrator. Because of the commissioner's relationship to the club owners, and because he often had made the rules which he enforced, the athletes questioned his neutrality. *See* ACADEMY PROCEEDINGS 124-27 (remarks of Edward Garvey, Executive Director, National Football League Players Association). Because of player objections, the system of commissioner arbitration is in the process of being reformed. *Id.* at 108-10 (remarks of Richard Moss, Counsel, Major League Baseball Players Association).

But other aspects of sports arbitration bear out the principle that there is an advantage to be obtained from the use of an experienced arbitrator. For example, an important ingredient of the salary arbitrations in baseball is the vast amount of statistical information which can be introduced concerning the player's performance. *See* Seitz, *Footnotes to Baseball Salary Arbitration,* 29 ARB. J. 98 (1974). The arbitrator must have some understanding of the game to make proper use of this information, and the process of decision-making is certainly made more efficient if the arbitrator has participated in precisely the same form of hearing on prior occasions.

415. *See* Prima Paint Corp. v. Flood & Conklin Mfg. Co., 388 U.S. 395, 415 (1967) (Black, J., dissenting); DOBBS, REMEDIES § 12.27 at 935-36; Mentschikoff, *Commercial Arbitration,* 61 COLUM. L. REV. 846 (1961).

repeated use of the same arbitrators the parties eliminate the need to educate the decision-maker and can thus further streamline the proceedings.

Arbitration is used in several different forms in the professional sports industry. It is increasingly used as the primary means of resolving disputes between an individual player and the team which employs him. The provision which requires a player to arbitrate claims arising from his individual contract may be found in the contract,[416] or may be included in the collective bargaining agreement negotiated between the players' association and the club owners.[417] However, the use of arbitration is not limited to individual complaints. Most collective bargaining agreements also provide that arbitration will be the final step of the procedures used to resolve disputes between the players' association and the owners.[418] The accommodation of both individual and collective complaints is necessary because professional sports is one of the few industries in which unionized employees also separately negotiate individual contracts.[419] Finally, arbitration is often chosen as the exclusive method of dispute resolution in controversies which arise between the various clubs in a league. The league constitution and bylaws form a contract which binds the various clubs together, and a common feature of these agreements is that disputes between the clubs will be submitted to an arbitrator, who is often the commissioner.[420]

Not only is the device of arbitration widely used, but in addition there is an increasing trend toward the development of specialized forms of arbitration. This is particularly true with respect to controversies which arise under a player's employment contract. For example, in the NFL, disputes involving the right of an injured player to receive compensation are treated by a procedure different from that which governs all other disputes.[421] Moreover, while the NFL uses a single grievance arbitration procedure for most other matters, the commissioner is designated as the final decision-making authority for

---

416. *See* NFL Player Contract ¶ 20 (1977):

> 20. Disputes. Any disputes between Player and Club involving interpretation or application of any provision of this contract will be submitted to final and binding arbitration in accordance with the procedure called for in any collective bargaining agreement in existence at the time the event giving rise to any such dispute occurs. If no collective bargaining agreement is in existence at such time, the dispute will be submitted within a reasonable time to the League Commissioner for final and binding arbitration by him, except as provided otherwise in Paragraph 13 of this contract.

Paragraph 13 provides a grievance procedure to be used to deal with complaints for compensation by injured players. *See* §§ 3.05-.06 *supra*. (The origins of the 1977 NFL player contract are explained in note 126, § 3.05 *supra*. That note also indicates the abbreviated citation form used for other standard player contracts. — Ed.)

417. *See* Davis v. Pro Basketball, Inc., 381 F. Supp. 1 (S.D.N.Y. 1974). *See also* Baseball Collective Bargaining Agreement art. X (Grievance Procedure).

418. *See* Baseball Collective Bargaining Agreement art. X. A "grievance" under the basic agreement is defined as "a complaint which involves the interpretation of, or compliance with, the provisions of any agreement between the Association and the Clubs or any of them, or any agreement between a Player and a Club...."

419. *See generally* Lowell, *Collective Bargaining and the Professional Team Sport Industry,* 38 LAW & CONTEMP. PROB. 3, 25-28 (1973).

420. *See, e.g.,* Professional Sports, Ltd. v. Virginia Squires Basketball Club, 373 F. Supp. 946 (W.D. Tex. 1974); Riko Enterprises, Enterprises, Inc. v. Seattle SuperSonics Corp., 357 F. Supp. 521 (S.D.N.Y. 1973). The relationship of clubs within a league is discussed more fully in another section. *See* § 3.15 *supra.*

421. *Compare* Collective Bargaining Agreement Between the NFL Management Council and the NFL Players Association art. VII (Non-Injury Grievance Procedure) *with id.* art. XI (Injury Grievance Procedure) (1977) [hereinafter cited as NFL Collective Bargaining Agreement].

league-imposed discipline.[422] In baseball, there are three different procedures applying, respectively, to disputes about the amount of the player's salary, interpretation of the benefit plan, and all other controversies.[423] The movement away from a single arbitration procedure seems to be prompted by the increased bargaining power which the players have been able to wield. In general, the players and owner have agreed to reduce the former dependence upon the commissioner as the sole adjudicator of claims. And as the parties begin to construct new systems, they increasingly realize that there is sometimes a necessity to tailor the arbitration procedures to the particular subject matter in controversy, as is illustrated by the baseball salary negotiations.[424]

b. Law Applicable to Arbitration. While it is true that arbitration is largely a creature of the parties' agreement, it is important to identify the body of law which will be applied to questions relating to the enforceability and interpretation of the arbitration clause. In classifying the arbitration systems which exist in professional sports, a distinction must be made between those which arise from a collective bargaining agreement and those which have their source in other types of agreements. Much of the literature on arbitration assumes that "labor arbitration" — that is, arbitration to resolve disputes covered by a collective bargaining agreement — is an animal different from "commercial arbitration," the species of arbitration used to resolve other business disputes. It is true that there are some important differences in these two types of arbitration. For one thing, the Supreme Court has given much more attention to the role of arbitration in labor-related disputes than in other types of relationships.[424.1] In addition, the Court has made clear that arbitration in the labor context is to be regarded as closely entwined with federal labor policy.[424.2] A basic tenet of that policy is that management and unionized employees should be encouraged to settle their disputes in a peaceful manner so as to minimize the potentiality of strikes, lockouts, and similar coercive actions which would disrupt commerce. The preference for peaceful resolutions of industrial disputes has prompted the Court to adopt a position that both affirms the general enforceability of labor-related arbitration clauses and minimizes the role which courts are to play in reviewing the decisions made by arbitrators.[424.3] The Supreme Court's directives in this area have led to the development of an extensive body of precedent in the lower courts, and these decisions have contributed to the view of labor arbitration as a discreet subject matter.

---

422. *See id.,* art. VII.

423. *See* Baseball Collective Bargaining Agreement arts. V, X. *See also* ACADEMY PROCEEDINGS, 119 (remarks of John Goherin, Player Relations Committee, Major Leagues of Professional Baseball Clubs). The classification of the various types of grievances can be further subdivided, for Article X of the collective bargaining agreement, which generally applies to controversies other than salaries or benefits, takes a further distinction as to controversies arising from actions taken against a player "involving the preservation of the integrity of, or the maintenance of public confidence in the game of baseball." With respect to these matters, authority for adjudication is given to the commissioner, rather than the tripartite panel utilized in other disputes.

424. *See generally* Seitz, *Footnotes to Baseball Salary Arbitration, supra* note 414.

424.1. The hallmarks of the Court's extensive involvement in the area of labor arbitration are its decisions in the *Lincoln Mills* case and the *Steelworkers Trilogy* in 1960. These decisions and their progeny are discussed in GORMAN, LABOR LAW 540-74, 584-603; P. HAYS, LABOR ARBITRATION: A DISSENTING VIEW (1966); T. KHEEL, LABOR LAW (18E BUSINESS ORGANIZATIONS 1974) §§ 24, 26-27.

424.2. *See, e.g.,* Textile Workers Union v. Lincoln Mills, 353 U.S. 448 (1957).

424.3. *See* authorities cited in note 424.1 *supra*.

By contrast, the development of the law of commercial arbitration has generally been more uneven. While there have been Supreme Court decisions in the area of commercial arbitration, and while the Court has generally accepted that arbitration is a wholly proper mode of settling commercial conflicts, its endorsement of commercial arbitration has not been imbued with the same overriding concern for strong public policy found in the labor area. Until very recently, there was a substantial question as to whether state or federal law was to be predominant on such basic questions as the enforceability of commercial arbitration agreements. Congress adopted the Federal Arbitration Act [424.4] in 1925, but for many years, it seemed to have been assumed that the provisions of the Act would give way to contrary state law. Since some states continued to follow the common law view that arbitration agreements were unenforceable, there often was considerable doubt as to whether an agreement to arbitrate was enforceable at all. As is explained more fully below, there is now reason to believe that the federal law of commercial arbitration — primarily that developed under the FAA — will have preemptive effect over conflicting state laws.[424.5] Hence, the question of the enforceability of commercial arbitration is considerably less lively than it once was. But the fact remains that the "law" on commercial arbitration has not had the benefit of the extensive Supreme Court and lower court precedent which has allowed the area of labor arbitration to mature into a set of well-tested principles.

For many who practice in the respective areas of commercial and labor arbitration, it would be heresy to suggest that the two mechanisms for dispute resolution operate under the same basic legal principles. We do not choose to put forth a contrary proposition in this brief review of arbitration in professional sports. Moreover, proper deference for the attitudes reflected in the existing literature should prompt the prudent practitioner to concentrate his research in the case law which has emanated from the particular species of arbitration with which he is working. But even with that cautionary advice, it can be suggested that there is much about commercial and labor arbitration which does not differ. For example, on the question of whether an agreement to arbitrate is enforceable, the ultimate conclusion is the same for both types of arbitration: agreements to arbitrate are not only enforceable but are entitled to great deference by the courts. More importantly, there is much about the rationale for this result which is common to both areas. It is perceived that if both parties have agreed as a matter of contract to forego the normal sort of judicial review, with its attendant costs and delay, that agreement ought to be respected. In particular, one party ought not be allowed to renounce its commitment to the arbitration devices merely because of a subsequent change in his perception of the advantage which he will attain in a particular case. Beyond this initial question of enforceability, other common threads appear. Thus, as to both types of arbitration, it is accepted that if the system of private dispute resolution is to function properly, the courts must play a very limited role in reviewing the merits of the arbitrator's decision. Otherwise, arbitration will simply become another step in the traditional, costly litigation process, rather than a means for avoiding it. But by the same token, there has to be some limit to the extent of

---

424.4. 9 U.S.C. §§ 1-14 (1970).
424.5. This issue is discussed more fully in the text accompanying notes 426-56 *infra*.

judicial deference. In extreme cases, where there is a basis to conclude that the arbitrator was biased or was influenced by fraudulent activity, it would appear that the parties did not get what they bargained for when they agreed to arbitrate. Thus, whether commercial or labor arbitration is involved, the courts should not — and will not — proceed to enforce an award which arises from a tainted proceeding.

Again, it would be too much to suggest that precedents on commercial and labor arbitration are wholly interchangeable. It is not inappropriate, however, to recognize that the legal principles applicable to each are woven from a great number of common threads. The issues on which the law truly differs between commercial and labor arbitration are likely to be limited in number.

As has been suggested, the dividing line between "commercial" and "labor" arbitration turns upon the nature of the agreement which is the source of the obligation to arbitrate. If the obligation arises from a labor contract, most typically a collective bargaining agreement, it is properly analyzed under the body of federal labor arbitration law which the Supreme Court has devised. If the arbitration clause is not the product of union-management negotiations, it will be treated under the rubric of commercial arbitration, the species which is addressed in the FAA. In the major professional team sports, most questions concerning the athlete's employment contract, including such issues as the player's right to compensation, the club's responsibility for injuries, and the amount of job security enjoyed by the player, have been folded into the collective bargaining agreement provision for arbitration [424.6] and thus are to be treated as issues of labor arbitration law. On the other hand, the mechanisms for resolving internal league disputes between clubs on non-player matters are typically spelled out in the league by-laws. To the extent that the mechanism chosen can be regarded as involving arbitration, the relevant legal principles are those applicable to commercial arbitration.

It must be recognized, however, that the distinction between labor and commercial arbitration in professional team sports does not absolutely parallel the distinction between player versus club and club versus club disputes. For example, prior to the recent emergence of forceful collective bargaining by player unions, the typical standard player contract empowered the league commissioner to resolve disputes concerning a player's right under his contract.[424.7] Several courts chose to treat this arrangement as one calling for arbitration and applied the principles from the law applicable to other commercial agreements. While the labor contracts in effect in the major leagues will now generally require that the analytical framework of labor arbitration be applied, it is still possible that some player contract-related disputes will involve non-labor arbitration. This will be true, of course, for athletes not covered by an existing collective bargaining agreement. Thus, athletes participating in less prominent leagues may be subject to the general body of commercial arbitration law. Moreover, arbitration clauses in many non-league sports (golf, boxing, and so on) may be similarly treated. Finally, it must be recognized that even in the major leagues, the law of commercial arbitration may

424.6. *See* text accompanying notes 421-23 *supra*.
424.7. *See* § 4.19 *infra*.

still be relevant for player-related disputes. This situation arises because an arbitration clause in a labor agreement expires with the agreement itself.[424.8] The term of an individual athlete's employment contract may extend for a longer period, and it is thus possible that an individual contract dispute may arise at a time when there is no labor arbitration clause in effect. In this situation, it is necessary to determine whether there is a duty to arbitrate arising from another source. At least one league has anticipated this possibility and has provided for an alternative dispute settlement mechanism.[424.9]

c. The Enforceability of Agreements to Arbitrate.

1. *Commercial Arbitration.*

When a party consents to an arbitration clause, he has agreed to forego the traditional device of court litigation to secure an adjudication of controversies which fall within the scope of the agreement to arbitrate. For the greater part of our common law history, there were substantial doubts as to whether private parties had it within their power to so oust the courts from their jurisdiction over traditional contract disputes. Some of these reservations have lingered on into the present period. We begin by looking at this question of enforceability in the context of arbitration clauses which arise from a source other than a collective bargaining agreement.

The question of the enforceability of commercial arbitration agreements takes on particular significance because of widely differing state law rules on the matter. At early common law, courts were generally hostile toward agreements to arbitrate. As previously mentioned, the courts often objected that private parties had no power to preclude a court from hearing a controversy which was otherwise within its jurisdiction.[425] Some of these earlier doubts are still reflected in state statutes which severely restrict the enforceability of agreements to arbitrate.[426] More modern statutes, particularly those in

---

424.8. *See generally* GORMAN, LABOR LAW 563-65. *But see* Nolde Bros. v. Bakery Workers, 430 U.S. 243 (1977).

424.9. *See* note 416 *supra.*

425. *See generally* Kulukundis Shipping Co. v. Amtorg Trading Corp., 126 F.2d 978 (2d Cir. 1942); W.H. Blodgett Co. v. Bebe Co., 190 Cal. 665, 214 P. 38 (1923); Levy v. American Auto. Ins. Co., 31 Ill. App. 2d 157, 175 N.E.2d 607 (1961); United Ass'n of Journeymen & Apprentices of Plumbing, Local 525 v. Stine, 76 Nev. 189, 351 P.2d 965 (1960); 6A CORBIN ON CONTRACTS § 1433; DOBBS, REMEDIES § 12.27; Wolaver, *The Historical Background of Commercial Arbitration, supra* note 409. Although the common law courts often insisted that private parties could not "oust the court of jurisdiction," the precise objection has never been clear. *See* DOBBS, REMEDIES 926; 6A CORBIN ON CONTRACTS §§ 1431-33. It must be accepted that two parties have power to enter into a binding out-of-court settlement of a claim and that the effect of such a settlement is to preclude either side from seeking an adjudication of the original controversy. An agreement to arbitrate can be viewed as simply providing a more elaborate method of extra-judicial settlement. It is true that the arbitration agreement differs in that it may apply to claims which do not exist at the time the method of settlement is agreed upon. But this factor should be a source of concern only to the extent that the claim which does eventually arise is not one which the disappointed party could reasonably have anticipated at the time of the agreement to arbitrate. With respect to future claims which are reasonably foreseeable, the agreement to arbitrate seems to share the characteristics of a present release of a claim. And even as to unforeseen claims, the modern view should surely be that the parties are free to use the device of contract to allocate risks, even when those risks are not well-defined. The relevant limitation should be one of interpretation: is it likely that the parties intended and understood that the particular dispute would come within the terms of their agreement to arbitration?

426. *See generally* 6A CORBIN ON CONTRACTS § 1441.

industrial states and the Federal Arbitration Act at the national level, have abandoned the older hostility to arbitration and now are generally supportive of this method of private dispute settlement.[427] With the wide divergence in treatment between these various statutes, it is obviously important to determine which of the various legal rules will apply agreements to arbitrate to the sports area.

The potential sources of law applicable to non-labor arbitration agreements can be divided into three rough categories: (1) the Federal Arbitration Act,[428] which specifically sanctions the enforceability of arbitration agreements and which spells out the standard for judicial enforcement and review of arbitrational proceedings; [429] (2) state statutes which are also clearly supportive of arbitration agreements; in general, these are either based on the Uniform Arbitration Act [430] or are original enactments which accept the premise that agreements are entitled to judicial enforcement; and (3) state statutes under which the enforceability of agreements to arbitrate is either expressly or impliedly limited to controversies existing at the time the contract is made.[431] As is apparent from these classifications, there may well be a different result in a case depending upon the body of law which is applied to the transaction. The contrast between the doctrine represented in the first and third categories is obvious, and an agreement to arbitrate which was given full judicial sanction under the federal statute might be deemed a nullity in some of the courts which applied the rules identified in the third group. But there may also be important differences between the FAA and the state laws which are otherwise receptive to arbitration proceedings. One critical point of departure concerns the question of whether an arbitration agreement will be enforceable if it is contained in a contract the making of which has been induced by fraud.[432] As was made clear in *Erving v. Virginia Squires Basketball Club,*[433] the arbitration clause is treated as severable from the remainder of the contract under the FAA, and an allegation of fraud in the inducement of the contract does not eliminate the need for arbitration of the matter of fraud. By contrast, it is often much less clear

---

427. *See generally* DOMKE, COMMERCIAL ARBITRATION §§ 4.01-4.03.

428. 9 U.S.C. §§ 1-14 (1970).

429. *See generally* DOMKE, COMMERCIAL ARBITRATION § 4.03.

430. The Uniform Arbitration Act has provided the basis for the following state statutes: ALASKA STAT. § 09.43.010 (1973); ARIZ. REV. STAT. ANN. § 12-1501 (Cum. Supp. 1975); ARK. STAT. ANN. § 34-511 (Cum. Supp. 1973); FLA. STAT. ANN. § 682.01 (Cum. Supp. 1975); ILL. ANN. STAT. ch. 10, § 101 (1966); IND. STAT., BURNS' CODE ED. § 34-4-2-22 (1973); ME. REV. STAT. ANN. tit. 14, § 5927 (Cum. Supp. 1974); MD. ANN. CODE, Courts & Judicial Proceedings § 3-201 (1974); MASS. GEN. LAWS ch. 251, § 1-19 (Cum. Supp. 1974); MINN. STAT. ANN. § 572.08 (1969); NEV. REV. STAT. § 38.105 (1973); N.M. STAT. ANN. § 22-3-9 (1973); PA. STAT. ANN. tit. 1, § 5 (Cum. Supp. 1974-75); WYO. STAT. ANN. § 1-1048.1 (Cum. Supp. 1973).

431. *See* ALA. CODE ANN. tit. 7, § 829 (1960); DEL. CODE ANN. tit. 10, § 5701 (1975); GA. CODE ANN. § 7-101 (1973); IDAHO CODE ANN. § 7-901 (1948); IOWA CODE ANN. § 679.1 (1950); KAN. STAT. ANN. § 5-201 (1964); KY. REV. STAT. § 417.01 (1969); MISS. CODE ANN. § 11-15-1 (1972); MONT. REV. CODE ANN. § 93-201-1 (1970); N.D. CENT. CODE ANN. § 32-29-01 (1960); S.C. CODE ANN. § 10-1901 (1962); TENN. CODE ANN. § 23-501 (1955); UTAH CODE ANN. § 78-31-1 (1953); VA. CODE ANN. § 8-503 (1957); W. VA. CODE ANN. § 55-10-1 (1966). *See generally* DOBBS, REMEDIES § 12.27, at 937-38.

432. *See generally* 6A CORBIN ON CONTRACTS § 1444; DOMKE, COMMERCIAL ARBITRATION §§ 8.01-8.04.

433. 349 F. Supp. 716 (E.D.N.Y.), *aff'd,* 468 F.2d 1064 (2d Cir. 1972). The *Erving* court was following the Supreme Court mandate of Prima Paint Corp. v. Flood & Conklin Mfg. Co., 388 U.S. 395 (1967), which established the principle that a federal court is to determine the validity of an arbitration clause separately from the validity or invalidity of the main contract. 388 U.S. at 403-04.

whether a state court would reach the same result,[434] and some states would accept the argument that the presence of fraud renders the whole contract a nullity, including the agreement to arbitrate.[435] Under this view, the injured party could proceed directly with his judicial remedies.

The question of which law should control in particular settings has been the subject of considerable controversy in the last several years. While there are still a number of issues which have yet to be settled, it is clear that the FAA, adopted more than a half-century ago, has taken on new meanings and is assuming the predominant role in the most important controversies in the area of commercial arbitration. The present treatise will not be used as the forum in which to debate all of the procedural and constitutional questions which arise. But the general adoption of arbitration procedures in professional sports justifies a summary of the present state of the law.

In analyzing the FAA, there are two different questions of a jurisdictional nature which must be asked. The first is whether the contract which contains the arbitration clause in question comes within the terms of the Act. At the next level is the issue of whether the Act is the controlling law in the particular judicial forum in which the controversy is being reviewed. Each of these questions deserves attention in the context of professional sports contracts.

By its own terms, the FAA applies only to arbitration provisions in "a contract evidencing a transaction involving commerce" and in maritime agreements.[436] Thus, if the contract pertains to a transaction which is wholly *intra*state in nature, the relevant body of law will be found in state sources.[437] Do professional sports contracts evidence "transactions involving commerce," so as to come within the statute? Despite some arguments to the contrary, the answer would appear to be affirmative as to all of the varieties of contracts found in professional sports. Some judges would try to limit the FAA to contracts between merchants relating to the movement of goods between states,[438] and there is an older precedent, based on the Supreme Court's misdirection in *Federal Base Ball Club v. National League*[439] to the effect that contracts in the entertainment industry do not involve interstate commerce, even though they obviously contemplate the movement of players and performers between the several states.[440] But when the question of the application of the FAA to professional sports was directly confronted in *Erving v. Virginia Squires Basketball Club*,[441] the court had little difficulty finding both that the Act extended to contracts of employment and that professional sports contracts involved interstate commerce.[442] Other courts have similarly assumed that

---

434. *See* Prima Paint Corp. v. Flood & Conklin Mfg. Co., 388 U.S. 395, 400 n.3 (1967); Robert Lawrence Co. v. Devonshire Fabrics, Inc., 271 F.2d 402, 412 (2d Cir. 1959); Comment, *Federal Arbitration Act and Application of the "Separability Doctrine" in Federal Courts,* 1968 DUKE L.J. 588, 597 n.49.

435. *See generally* DOMKE, COMMERCIAL ARBITRATION §§ 8.03-8.04.

436. Federal Arbitration Act 9 U.S.C. § 2 (1970).

437. Bernhardt v. Polygraphic Co., 350 U.S. 198, 100 L. Ed. 199, 76 S. Ct. 273 (1956).

438. *See* Prima Paint Corp. v. Flood & Conklin Mfg. Co., 388 U.S. 395, 409 (1967) (Black, J., dissenting); Comment, *Federal Arbitration Act and Application of the "Separability Doctrine" in Federal Courts, supra* note 434, at 600 n.57.

439. 259 U.S. 200, 66 L. Ed. 898, 42 S. Ct. 465 (1922).

440. *See* Conley v. San Carlo Opera Co., 163 F.2d 310 (2d Cir. 1947).

441. 349 F. Supp. 716 (E.D.N.Y.), *aff'd,* 468 F.2d 1064 (2d Cir. 1972).

442. 349 F. Supp. at 719, *aff'd,* 468 F.2d at 1068-69. *See also* Dickstein v. duPont, 443 F.2d 783 (1st Cir. 1971).

sports contracts are within the scope of the statute.[443] Thus, except to the extent that some courts may be misled by contrary suggestions in the legislative history of the Act [444] or by now out-dated precedents, the general coverage of the FAA should not be in doubt as far as non-labor arbitration is concerned.

Once it is established that arbitration agreements in the sports industry meet the statutory requirements, it becomes necessary to determine the weight to be afforded the Act in courts at both the state and federal level. To the extent that federal courts are called upon to decide complaints seeking enforcement of professional sports contracts, the court's jurisdiction will likely be based on diversity of citizenship. Does the FAA control in that sort of proceeding? This issue has caused considerable difficulty for the courts. One view which prevailed for a period was that *Erie R.R. v. Tompkins* [445] and its progeny required that state law be preferred in diversity actions.[446] The difficulty with this view was that it would effectively emasculate the FAA, for virtually all federal court proceedings involving arbitration questions are based on diversity of citizenship.[447] Since it was unlikely that Congress intended its enactment to have such an insignificant role, it was necessary for the Supreme Court to give further consideration to the relationship between the statute and state law. This was done in *Prima Paint Corporation v. Flood & Conklin Manufacturing Company*,[448] in which the Court announced that the FAA was to be regarded as providing for federal substantive rights which were to be given controlling effect in federal diversity litigation.[449] The critical point of the *Prima Paint* decision is its holding that the FAA represents an exercise by Congress of its commerce power and is not simply based on Congress' Article III power to prescribe procedures to be followed in federal courts.[450] This clarification of the

There is a considerable body of Supreme Court precedent correcting the erroneous assumption of *Federal Baseball* that sports and entertainment activities did not involve commerce. *See* Flood v. Kuhn, 407 U.S. 258, 32 L. Ed. 2d 728, 92 S. Ct. 2099 (1972); Radovich v. National Football League, 352 U.S. 445, 1 L. Ed. 2d 456, 77 S. Ct. 390 (1957); United States v. International Boxing Club of New York, Inc., 348 U.S. 236, 99 L. Ed. 290, 75 S. Ct. 259 (1955); United States v. Shubert, 348 U.S. 222, 99 L. Ed. 279, 75 S. Ct. 277 (1955).

443. *See, e.g.,* Riko Enterprises, Inc. v. Seattle SuperSonics Corp., 357 F. Supp. 521 (S.D.N.Y. 1973).

444. Justice Black, in his dissent in *Prima Paint,* took the position that the Act applies only to the interstate transfer of goods between merchants and based this conclusion on selected aspects of the legislative history of the measure. *See* 388 U.S. at 409-10 nn.2-3 (Black, J., dissenting). Others have found the legislative history to support the broader scope of the Act suggested in the text above. *See* Comment, *Federal Arbitration Act and Application of the "Separability Doctrine" in Federal Courts, supra* note 434, at 600 n.57.

445. 304 U.S. 64, 82 L. Ed. 1188, 58 S. Ct. 817 (1938).

446. *See* Bernhardt v. Polygraphic Co., 350 U.S. 198, 202-04 (1956); Note, *The Consequences of a Broad Arbitration Clause Under the Federal Arbitration Act,* 52 B. U. L. REV. 571, 582-86 (1972); Comment, *Federal Arbitration Act and Application of the "Separability Doctrine" in Federal Courts, supra,* note 434, at 595-97.

447. *See* Robert Lawrence Co. v. Devonshire Fabrics, Inc., 271 F.2d 402, 404 (2d Cir. 1959).

448. 388 U.S. 395 (1967).

449. *See also* Robert Lawrence Co. v. Devonshire Fabrics, Inc., 271 F.2d 402 (2d Cir. 1959); Comment, *Federal Arbitration Act and Application of the "Separability Doctrine" in Federal Courts, supra* note 434. Note, *The Consequences of a Broad Arbitration Clause Under the Federal Arbitration Act, supra* note 446;

The *Robert Lawrence* case, which presaged the result in *Prima Paint,* is noted in 60 COLUM. L. REV. 227 (1960); 45 CORNELL L. Q. 795 (1960); 9 DE PAUL L. REV. 291 (1960); 73 HARV. L. REV. 1382 (1960); 7 SYRACUSE L. REV. 358 (1960); 34 TULANE L. REV. 831 (1960); 46 VA. L. REV. 340 (1960); 69 YALE L.J. 847 (1960).

450. *See* Prima Paint Corp. v. Flood & Conklin Mfg. Co., 388 U.S. 395, 404-05 (1967).

bases of the Act elevates it to the status of substantive federal law. Under this characterization, the statute not only creates a federal law to control certain transactions, but also removes the statute from the reach of the constitutional limitations found in *Erie R.R. v. Tompkins* and its progeny.[451] Under the mandate of *Prima Paint,* it is now impermissible for a federal court to apply state arbitration rules when the FAA would dictate a contrary result.[452]

Also to be resolved is the question of the weight to be afforded the FAA in state court proceedings where the transaction involved was one involving interstate commerce. While the Supreme Court made clear in *Prima Paint* that the statute created important federal rights, it was silent on the question of whether the doctrine of federal preemption required state courts to follow the federal rule rather than one based on state law. Predictably, however, the question has arisen in cases subsequent to *Prima Paint.* A few courts have held that state rules are not preempted and may still be freely applied in state court proceedings even though the contract in question is one which would otherwise come within the statute.[453] However, the majority of cases have held to the contrary, and there now appears to be an emerging consensus that with respect to transactions covered by the federal statute, the law to be applied should be the same whether the proceeding is brought in state or federal court.[454] The latter would appear to be the better reasoned interpretation. While the Supreme Court's failure to comment on the question is troublesome, a finding of federal preemption insures equal treatment of similar interstate transactions and thus avoids a serious constitutional question. This and other considerations have been identified as reasons for insuring federal-state uniformity in the treatment of arbitration clauses. As was well-articulated by Judge Fuld of the New York Court of Appeals, a failure to apply the FAA in state court proceedings would:

> (1) permit, indeed encourage, forum shopping; (2) prevent and undermine the need for nationwide uniformity in the interpretation and application of arbitration clauses in foreign and interstate transactions; and (3) permit individuals to circumvent the national law relating to arbitration agreements. . . .[455]

The recent affirmance of the predominance of the FAA has important implications for all non-labor arbitration agreements, including those found in the professional sports industry. There was a period in which the enforceability of these agreements to arbitrate was doubtful, particularly to the extent that a disappointed party could take the controversy to a state court. *Prima Paint* and subsequent lower court decisions would suggest that this era has passed.

---

451. *See* Comment, *Federal Arbitration Act and Application of the "Separability Doctrine" in Federal Courts, supra* note 434, at 594.

452. *See, e.g.,* Collins Radio Co. v. Ex-Cell-O Corp., 467 F.2d 995 (8th Cir. 1972); Aberthaw Constr. Co. v. Centre County Hosp., 366 F. Supp. 513 (M.D. Pa. 1973).

453. *See, e.g.,* Lesser Towers, Inc. v. Roscoe-Ajax Constr. Co., 271 Cal. App. 2d 675, 75 Cal. Rptr. 100 (1969); Pullman, Inc. v. Phoenix Steel Corp., 304 A.2d 334 (Del. Sup. Ct. 1973).

454. *See* West Point-Pepperell, Inc. v. Multi-Line Indus., Inc., 231 Ga. 329, 201 S.E.2d 452 (1973); A/S J. Ludwig Mowinckels Rederi v. Dow Chemical Co., 25 N.Y.2d 576, 255 N.E.2d 774, 307 N.Y.S.2d 660 (1970); AAA Con. Auto. Transp., Inc. v. Newman, 77 Misc. 2d 1069, 356 N.Y.S.2d 171 (Sup. Ct. 1974); Mamlin v. Susan Thomas, Inc., 490 S.W.2d 634 (Tex. Civ. App. 1973); REA Express v. Missouri Pacific R.R., 447 S.W.2d 721 (Tex. Civ. App. 1969); Pinkis v. Network Cinema Corp., 9 Wash. App. 337, 512 P.2d 751 (1973).

455. A/S J. Ludwig Mowinckels Rederi v. Dow Chemical Co., 25 N.Y.2d 576, 580, 255 N.E.2d 774, 776, 307 N.Y.S.2d 660, 662 (1970).

The FAA appears to be the primary statute to be applied, and the party seeking to compel arbitration will have available the explicit federal policy that the agreements to arbitrate will be specifically enforceable.[456] Moreover, the effect of *Prima Paint* will be to insure that precedents will develop in a more uniform pattern as the courts increasingly undertake to apply a single statute rather than the variety of state statutes which were given effect in the past.

This is not to suggest that the substantial body of state law has become totally irrelevant. Indeed, the specific mandate of *Prima Paint* would seem to be that only *conflicting* state law rules must give way to interpretations under the FAA. To the extent that state law fills gaps left in the federal statute, it will still be consulted.[457] Moreover, there are procedural aspects of the federal statute which may not be fully applicable to state court proceedings.[458] While some problems of accommodation between state and federal law remain, the basic point of the preeminence of arbitration procedures over traditional judicial remedies appears to be settled in the professional sports industry.

2. *Labor Arbitration.*

When the basic federal labor statute, the Wagner Act, was adopted in 1935, its primary concern was with insuring that workers had the right to organize and engage in collective activity to secure their desired goals. Relatively little attention was given to the legal treatment which would be afforded to promises made in a collective bargaining agreement once one had been negotiated. In the years immediately following the adoption of the Wagner Act, it was assumed that a labor agreement was like any other contract and thus subject to interpretation and enforcement by state courts. This view created difficulty when a union or employer sought to enforce an arbitration clause. In addition to confronting procedural questions about whether a union could sue or be sued as an entity, requests to enforce an agreement to arbitrate also often encountered the state law rules mentioned above which either disapproved executory arbitration agreements altogether or severely restricted the scope of issues which could be decided by the arbitrator. Thus, for a period, it appeared that labor arbitration would be subjected to the same uncertain future which was confronted in the commercial context.

Two subsequent developments in the labor law field changed this picture dramatically, and there is now no serious question about the enforceability of labor arbitration agreements. The first significant development occurred in 1947 when Congress adopted section 301 of the Taft-Hartley Act. The section gives the federal courts original jurisdiction to hear "suits for violation of contracts between an employer and a labor organization." [458.1] The federal forum is made available for this species of breach of contract action without regard to the amount in controversy or the diversity of the parties. The section did not, however, address the issue of whether state or federal law was to be applied in section 301 proceedings and thus there was some uncertainty as to whether

---

456. *See* 9 U.S.C. § 2 (1970).

457. *See, e.g.,* Riko Enterprises, Inc. v. Seattle SuperSonics Corp., 357 F. Supp. 521, 526 (S.D.N.Y. 1973).

458. *See* Comment, *Federal Arbitration Act and Application of the "Separability Doctrine" in Federal Courts, supra* note 434, at 611-13; Comment, *Scope of the United States Arbitration Act in Commercial Arbitration: Problems in Federalism,* 58 Nw. U.L. Rev. 468, 492-93 (1963).

458.1. 29 U.S.C. § 185(a) (1974). *See generally* Gorman, Labor Law 540-48; T. Kheel, Labor Law (18E Business Organizations 1974) § 27.

arbitration clauses would be found enforceable when the court was confronted with unsympathetic state law. This issue was disposed of in a second critical development — the Supreme Court's decision in *Textile Workers Union v. Lincoln Mills*.[458.2] The case involved a section 301 proceeding in which the plaintiff union sought an injunction to force the employer to abide by its earlier agreement to use arbitration to settle disputes which arose under the collective bargaining agreement. The Court read section 301 as authorizing the federal courts to "fashion a body of federal law" to govern the enforcement of labor contracts.[458.3] The predominance of federal interpretation over varying state substantive law rules was thought to be necessary in order to effectuate Congress' purpose of fostering industrial peace. Congress had encouraged the parties to engage in collective bargaining as a means of reducing strife, and that goal seemed best achieved by a policy which favored the enforceability of the agreement which was reached. To insure that this policy was uniformly applied, the Court concluded that federal interpretations, fashioned from the national labor laws, must control. The Court found the arbitration agreement before it to be enforceable, and *Lincoln Mills* has given rise to a now well-recognized rule of federal substantive law that compliance with similar agreements in other labor contracts will be mandated even when contrary to state statutory or common law rules.

Subsequent refinements of the *Lincoln Mills* decision have touched on several important matters. It is now clear that the decision was not intended to make the federal courts the exclusive forum in which labor arbitration clauses may be enforced. State courts retain their jurisdiction to consider requests for enforcement, but local contract law is not to be applied in such proceedings if it conflicts with federal interpretation based on national labor policy.[458.4] Thus, on the narrow issues of enforceability, the results ought not be different whether the proceeding is brought at the state level or in a federal forum. On another matter, it is now accepted that an individual employee may sue under section 301 to enforce his employer's agreement to arbitrate, assuming that the union has not reserved to itself the exclusive right to secure compliance with the grievance-arbitration machinery.[458.5]

d. Securing Compliance with the Agreement to Arbitrate.

1. *Commercial Arbitration.*

The fact that a player or club has originally agreed to arbitrate claims which arise under a contract does not insure that the party will not change its mind at a later point. Thus, it is necessary to deal with the question of how one secures compliance with the agreement to arbitrate.[459] The cases which arise in this regard differ depending upon whether the party who fails to submit himself voluntarily to arbitration is the one asserting a claim or the person against whom the claim is made. Hence, it may be that the injured party ignores the requirement of arbitration and proceeds to initiate an original proceeding in

---

458.2. 353 U.S. 448 (1957).

458.3. *Id.* at 451.

458.4. *See* Charles Dowd Box Co. v. Courtney, 368 U.S. 502 (1962); Teamsters Local 174 v. Lucas Flour Co., 369 U.S. 95 (1962).

458.5. *See* Smith v. Evening News Ass'n, 371 U.S. 195 (1962). *See generally* T. KHEEL, LABOR LAW (18E BUSINESS ORGANIZATIONS 1974) § 26.03[3].

459. *See generally* DOMKE, COMMERCIAL ARBITRATION §§ 17.01-17.04, 18.01-18.06.

court. Here the question of compliance with the agreement arises when the defendant asserts that the court lacks authority to hear the controversy and requests that the plaintiff be ordered to proceed with arbitration.[460] On the other hand, it may be that the party seeking recovery is ready and willing to proceed with arbitration but the alleged breacher refuses to participate in the proceedings. The injured party typically does not have the means available to coerce the participation of his reluctant opponent, and it is necessary that he look to the courts for assistance. Where commercial arbitration is involved, the FAA can be consulted to provide the general guidelines for securing compliance.

The federal statute provides remedies for each of these situations. In the first case, where the injured party has initiated litigation contrary to his agreement to arbitrate, Section 3 of the FAA provides that the court shall "stay the trial of the action until such arbitration has been had in accordance with the terms of the agreement." [461] The problem of the reluctant breacher is addressed in section 4 which provides for specific performance of the agreement to arbitrate.[462] The section also outlines the procedures to be followed in such a proceeding, including the procedures for determining whether an agreement to arbitrate had in fact been made.

A problem with these sections is that they are written in terms which suggest that they were intended to apply only in federal court proceedings. Yet, under the cases which have followed *Prima Paint,* the statute has been held to create substantive federal rights which must be observed by state courts.[463] Thus the question arises as to the procedures which will be available when action is taken in state court to secure compliance with the athlete's or club's promise to arbitrate.[464] Will state procedures control? What if the state has no procedures for securing compliance with the arbitration agreement? While it would not appear that Sections 3 and 4 of the FAA could be held to be directly applicable in state court, the Supreme Court has also made clear in another context that "the assertion of Federal rights, when plainly and reasonably made, is not to be defeated under the name of local practice." [465] Final resolution of the problem will have to await further case law developments. It can be noted, however, that litigants in state courts should not be treated substantially better or less well than they would have been in federal court. Without some assurance of basic parity between the two proceedings, at least as far as the outcome of the cases is concerned, the specter of forum-shopping again presents itself.[466]

It should be made clear that although the FAA provides important federal rights, it does not insure that an aggrieved party will have access to federal courts for the vindication of those rights. The statute itself does not grant jurisdiction to federal courts to hear claims otherwise coming within its terms, and it will be necessary for the litigant to show that the court has subject matter

460. *See, e.g.,* Davis v. Pro Basketball, Inc., 381 F. Supp. 1 (S.D.N.Y. 1974); Erving v. Virginia Squires Basketball Club, 349 F. Supp. 716 (E.D.N.Y.), *aff'd,* 468 F.2d 1064 (2d Cir. 1972).
461. 9 U.S.C. § 3 (1970).
462. *Id.* § 4.
463. *See* cases cited note 454 *supra.*
464. *See generally* Comment, *Federal Arbitration Act and Application of the "Separability Doctrine" in Federal Courts, supra* note 434, at 612-14; Comment, *Scope of the United States Arbitration Act in Commercial Arbitration: Problems in Federalism, supra* note 458, at 492-93.
465. Brown v. Western R.R., 388 U.S. 294, 299, 94 L. Ed. 2d 100, 70 S. Ct. 105 (1949).
466. *Cf.* A/S J. Ludwig Mowinckels Rederi v. Dow Chemical Co., 25 N.Y.2d 576, 580, 255 N.E.2d 774, 776, 307 N.Y.S.2d 660, 662 (1970).

jurisdiction under the traditional criteria.[467] In sports cases, the most frequently asserted basis of jurisdiction will be the diversity of the citizenship of the parties.[468] The requirement of independent jurisdiction may pose a problem where an athlete is suing his club over a matter covered by a non-labor arbitration clause. If the plaintiff-player lives in the jurisdiction where the team is located, recourse to federal court may be foreclosed, and it will be necessary for the moving party to take his FAA rights to state court.

2. *Labor Arbitration.*

Where the agreement to arbitrate arises from a collective bargaining relationship, the party seeking to compel arbitration has basically the same remedies available as in the case of commercial arbitration. However, the governing legal principles emanated from a different body of law where labor arbitration is involved. As already indicated, precedents developed under section 301 of the Taft-Hartley Act will control affirmative actions to secure compliance with the agreement to arbitrate. Section 301 gives the federal courts jurisdiction to hear such requests, and if the plaintiff establishes a controversy which comes within an enforceable arbitration clause, the court may enter an order requiring that the defendant submit to arbitration.[468.1] While the Norris-LaGuardia Act limits the use of injunctions in certain labor controversies, it has been held not to diminish the courts' power to compel arbitration.[468.2] A request for specific performance of the agreement to arbitrate might also be brought in state court, but in such a proceeding the court could not reach results which were inconsistent with section 301 principles.[468.3]

As in the case of a commercial arbitration, the request for compliance with the duty to arbitrate may be raised defensively. Where the plaintiff brings an action seeking traditional relief for breach of some other term of the contract, the defendant may raise the point that the matter is subject to arbitration and demand a stay of the proceedings. Again, if the defendant can establish that a valid arbitration clause is in effect and that the particular controversy comes within it, the court must stay the plaintiff's effort to secure a traditional adjudication of the asserted claim.[468.4]

§ 4.16.   Controversies Subject to Arbitration.

a. Interpretation of the arbitration clause. It is often important to determine whether a particular controversy which arises between two parties will be subject to arbitration. In both commercial and labor arbitration, the obligation to arbitrate arises from the contract which exists between the parties, and they are free to define the scope of the arbitration

---

467. *See* Robert Lawrence Co. v. Devonshire Fabrics, Inc., 271 F.2d 402, 408 (2d Cir. 1959); Sturges & Murphy, *Some Confusing Matters Relating to Arbitration Under the United States Arbitration Act,* 17 LAW & CONTEMP. PROB. 580, 586 and n.13 (1952).

468. The matter of jurisdiction in sports controversies is considered more fully in other sections. See §§ 4.21-4.23 *infra.*

468.1. *See generally* FAIRWEATHER, LABOR ARBITRATION 1-45; GORMAN, LABOR LAW 540-51; Aksen, *The Law of Labor Arbitration* in ARBITRATING LABOR CASES 28 (N. Levin, ed., 1974).

468.2. *See* Textile Workers Union v. Lincoln Mills, 353 U.S. 488 (1957).

468.3. *See* authorities cited in note 458.4 *supra.*

468.4. Aksen, *The Law of Labor Arbitration, supra* note 468.1, at 34. *See also* text accompanying note 461 *supra.*

clause. They may draft it to cover all controversies which arise, or they may bargain to limit its scope to particular types of disputes. To the extent that the agreed-upon arbitration clause does not extend to a particular claim, the injured party is free to pursue traditional judicial remedies.[469]

In determining the extent of a player's or club's obligation, it is necessary to consult the relevant contract and examine the actual language used. As is true with most other types of contract clauses, it is often necessary to subject the terms of the agreement to the process of interpretation in order to determine whether a particular dispute comes within the agreement to arbitrate. For example, in *Johnson v. Green Bay Packers*,[470] the court was presented with a player's contract which provided that "all matters in dispute between the Player and the Club shall be referred to the Commissioner and his decision shall be final, complete, conclusive, binding and unappealable by the Player and Club." The club asserted that this language should operate to preclude the court from hearing a case based on the player's claim that his contract was wrongfully terminated. The court rejected this argument, noting that the quoted sentence was included in a paragraph dealing with the player's obligation to observe club and league rules. Applying accepted rules of contract interpretation,[471] the court concluded that the agreement to be bound by the commissioner's decision drew its essence from the surrounding language and was thus limited to cases involving rule infractions.

As in any situation involving contract interpretation, the court can assume wide discretion in construing the agreement.[472] In many situations, there will be no precise evidence of the parties' intent, and the court will be required to choose among alternative constructions. A good deal of attention has been given to the question of whether, in cases of doubt, there ought to be a presumption in favor of arbitration. This is a point upon which one can discern a subtle difference between the treatment afforded commercial and labor arbitration agreements. The Supreme Court has made clear that there is a presumption of arbitrability which is to apply to controversies affected by a collective bargaining agreement. The Court has indicated that a matter is to be excluded from arbitration only if there is firm evidence that the parties specifically intended it to be non-arbitrable. In the Court's words,

> An order to arbitrate the particular grievance should not be denied unless it may be said with positive assurance that the arbitration clause is not susceptible of an interpretation that covers the asserted dispute. Doubts should be resolved in favor of coverage.[472.1]

This directive has generally been given an expansive reading in the lower courts.[472.2] In some cases, the presumption of arbitrability has been found to take precedence over other devices traditionally used to interpret a contract.

---

469. *See generally* M. DOMKE, THE LAW AND PRACTICE OF COMMERCIAL ARBITRATION §§ 12.01-12.02, 13.01-13.10 (1968) [hereinafter cited as DOMKE, COMMERCIAL ARBITRATION].

470. 272 Wis. 149, 161, 74 N.W.2d 784, 790 (1956).

471. *See generally* § 3.04 *supra*.

472. *See generally* DOMKE, COMMERCIAL ARBITRATION §§ 12.01-12.02.

472.1. United Steelworkers v. Warrior & Gulf Navigation Co., 363 U.S. 574, 582 (1960). *See generally* R. GORMAN, BASIC TEXT ON LABOR LAW 551-63 (1976) [hereinafter cited as GORMAN, LABOR LAW]; T. KHEEL, LABOR LAW (18E BUSINESS ORGANIZATIONS 1974) § 27.01[3]; Aksen, *History and Development* in ARBITRATING LABOR CASES 18-22 (N. Levin, ed. 1974).

472.2. The presumption in favor of arbitrability has had a significant impact in at least one sports case. The occasion was the well-known McNally-Messersmith arbitration, in which Arbitrator Peter

Thus, at least one circuit court of appeals ordered arbitration and specifically refused to consider evidence of the parties' bargaining history to show that the particular matter was not intended to be arbitrable.[472.3]

By contrast, the field of commercial arbitration operated for a long period under a rule which encompassed the opposite presumption. Many older cases contain language which suggests that a matter will not be subject to arbitration unless it is plainly within the scope of the parties' commercial arbitration clause.[472.4] This negative presumption appears to be fast eroding, however. Now that courts are generally less jealous in guarding their jurisdiction from usurpation by arbitrators, one finds many interpretations which liberally construe the coverage of non-labor agreements to arbitrate. Indeed it is increasingly accepted that the FAA is a manifestation of a federal policy favoring arbitration and that doubts as to the scope of the parties' arbitration clause should be resolved in favor of its coverage.[473]

The arbitration clauses found in professional sports typically have a broad reach. Although the drafters of the standard player contracts have generally included most common types of controversies within the respective arbitration provisions, some differences exist. Variations can be noted in the manner in which the contracts identify the *source* of the claims that are subject to arbitration. For example, some contracts specify that arbitration must be used to resolve all disputes arising from *any* agreement between the club and player.[474] This would presumably include claims under the standard player

Seitz found that the two baseball players became free agents after playing for one year under contracts which their clubs had unilaterally renewed. The clubs contended that their right to renew was perpetual and could be exercised for repeated one year terms. Seitz, however, construed the contract to provide for only a single one-year right of renewal. In subsequent judicial proceedings, the club owners sought to have the arbitration award set aside. The primary basis of their attack was a contention that the baseball reserve system was not subject to arbitration. While the collective bargaining agreement entered into with the players' union included a broad arbitration clause, the owners contended that the reserve system had been excepted. Much of their argument was based on Article XV of the collective bargaining agreement which stated both that "this Agreement does not deal with the reserve system" and that "during the term of this agreement, . . . there shall be no obligation to negotiate with respect to the reserve system." The owners contended, in effect, that since the collective bargaining agreement was not intended to cover the reserve clause, the arbitration clause contained in the labor agreement would not reach it. This contention was rejected by the Eighth Circuit in its subsequent review. Kansas City Royals Baseball Corp. v. Major League Baseball Players Ass'n, 532 F.2d 615 (8th Cir. 1976). The premise of the court's analysis was the Supreme Court's directive that doubts are to be resolved in favor of the coverage of an arbitration clause. The court reviewed the background of Article XV and found the evidence to be insufficient to establish a clear intent to remove the reserve clause from arbitration.

Judge Gibson, writing a concurring opinion, was quite explicit in identifying the presumption as the reason for the court's upholding the Seitz award. In Judge Gibson's view, "the preponderance of the evidence as to the purpose of Article XV . . . favors the Club Owners . . . . However, the Club Owners' evidence does not appear sufficient to satisfy the enhanced standard of proof [required by the relevant Supreme Court decisions] . . . . It thus appears to me that the Club Owners are stuck with the 'presumption of arbitrability' . . . ." *Id.* at 633-34.

472.3. A. S. Abell Co. v. Typographical Union, 338 F.2d 190 (4th Cir. 1964). *See generally* GORMAN, LABOR LAW 561-63.

472.4. *Compare* United Steelworkers v. Warrior & Gulf Navigation Co., 363 U.S. 574 (1960).

473. *See, e.g.,* Metro Indus. Painting v. Terminal Constr. Co., 287 F.2d 382 (2d Cir.), *cert. denied,* 368 U.S. 817, 7 L. Ed. 2d 24, 825 S. Ct. 31 (1961); Stockwell v. Reynolds & Co., 252 F. Supp. 215 (S.D.N.Y. 1965).

474. For example, the general arbitration clause in baseball applies to complaints which involve "the interpretation of or compliance with the provisions of any agreement between the Association and the clubs or any of them, or any agreement between a player and a club" with exceptions made for claims relating to benefits. *See* Baseball Collective Bargaining Agreement art. X(A), *supra* note 413, § 4.15.

contract, the collective bargaining agreement and any collateral contracts. In other agreements, the class of arbitrable controversies is specifically limited to those which arise under the standard player contract and the collective bargaining agreement.[475] In some arbitration clauses formerly used,[476] the range of arbitrable matters included tort claims.[477]

In the NBA, the scope of arbitration is defined to include disputes arising from the player contract and the collective bargaining agreement between the club owners' and the players' association. The uniform player contract is identified by its formal title, which gives rise to the question whether the obligation to arbitrate extends to other agreements between a player and a club which supplement or modify the player contract. There may be some specialized contractual arrangements between a player and club which deal with subjects totally distinct from those covered in the standard agreement, as when a superstar agrees to promote some unrelated business of the owner. If this type of separate arrangement does not have its own arbitration clause, then the normal judicial remedies would seem to be available, but such cases would be rare. The more typical sorts of modifying or supplementary agreements deal with matters such as compensation and termination which are also treated in the uniform contract. These types of arrangements, even though not strictly "uniform," should nonetheless be treated as part of the basic agreement between player and club, and thus subject to arbitration. This interpretation is supported by the court's decision in *Davis v. Pro Basketball, Inc.*[478] There the club and player entered into what they termed a "Modification of Agreement" which specified the grounds upon which the club could terminate the player's contract if a known knee injury adversely affected his performance. The player argued that this was not part of the uniform player contract, and thus was not subject to the arbitration clause. The court rejected this contention and concluded that "The two documents are to be read together, as one contract, and that contract is a Uniform Player Contract." [479]

b. Club's Right to Enjoin Player's Breach of Contract. While the collective bargaining agreements in most sports seek to channel all contract-related controversies into arbitration, there is an important exception which is recognized in most agreements. The agreements often recite that the club retains the right to resort directly to the courts to secure an injunction to enforce the athlete's promise to perform exclusively for the club during the term of the contract.[480] It is intended that the club will be able to continue to utilize the traditional judicial channels to prevent the player from jumping to another club.[481] Because of the expedited procedures available for preliminary injunctions, this is probably one situation in which arbitration represents no

---

475. *See* Collective Bargaining Agreement Between the National Basketball Ass'n and the National Basketball Players Ass'n, art. XV (1976).

476. *See* ABA Contract ¶ 13.

477. For a general discussion of the arbitrability of tort claims see DOMKE, COMMERCIAL ARBITRATION § 13.08.

478. 381 F. Supp. 1 (S.D.N.Y. 1974).

479. *Id.* at 4.

480. *See* NBA Collective Bargaining Agreement, *supra* note 475, art. XV, § 1.

481. *See generally* §§ 4.02, 4.04 *supra.*

substantial time-savings. And since the injured club would otherwise most likely have to look to the courts to secure compliance with an arbitration award in these situations,[482] the selection of this subject matter as one for direct judicial enforcement seems appropriate.

As is suggested in the previous discussion of the covenant of exclusive services,[483] there may be numerous factual issues which need to be resolved in connection with the club's request for relief in these situations, and thus, a question arises as to whether these matters are to be determined by the court or by the arbitrator. If the latter were to be the decision-maker, then presumably the proceeding for the injunction would have to be interrupted while the matter was sent to arbitration.

The request for an injunction could raise a wide variety of factual issues. For purposes of this analysis, the potential questions of fact can be divided into two categories. In one group are those which bear on the issue of whether the plaintiff has a contractual right to enjoin the defendant. The other questions pertain to the availability of the particular remedy of equitable enforcement. With respect to the former category, it can be noted that the plaintiff's request for an injunction affords the defendant the opportunity to make an attack upon the validity of the alleged contract.[484] Here the defendant can raise a number of questions which might normally be referrable to arbitration, including such things as whether there was fraud in the inducement of the contract, whether the pre-conditions of the player's performance have been fulfilled, and so on.[485] But even when there is a valid contract empowering the club to seek the particular remedy, a court may grant relief only if certain prerequisites are available, and these may require findings of fact. Included in this category are such matters as the uniqueness of the athlete's skill [486] and the existence of a threat to competition.[487]

A number of diverse arguments can be made with respect to the treatment of these questions. On the one hand, it can be noted that if the defendant has unlimited freedom to argue contractual defenses in court, then the operation of the arbitration system will be undermined on questions which are potentially of critical importance. And it seems incongruous that the athlete ought to be able to use the occasion of his own breach to get a judicial hearing on a matter which he would otherwise have had to take to arbitration. Further, questions such as those relating to the uniqueness of the player's skill involve judgments which are best made by someone with a high level of familiarity with the particular sport, a quality more likely to be found in the arbitrator. On the other hand, courts have traditionally been unwilling to issue preliminary injunctions without examining the contract and making an assessment of whether the plaintiff has an enforceable right. Moreover, courts have not generally been

---

482. Presumably many players who jump to another team in disregard of an existing contract would not voluntarily comply with an arbitrator's decree and the club would have to enforce the award in a judicial proceeding. *See generally* DOMKE, COMMERCIAL ARBITRATION §§ 37.01-37.03. Thus the matter is likely to get before a court in any case. By preserving the right of direct resort to equitable enforcement, the club may shorten the process somewhat.

483. *See* §§ 4.02-4.13 *supra.*

484. *See generally* 5A A. CORBIN, CORBIN ON CONTRACTS § 1140 (1964) [hereinafter cited as CORBIN ON CONTRACTS].

485. *See* § 4.06 *supra.*

486. *See* § 4.07 *supra.*

487. *See* § 4.10 *supra.*

hesitant to determine for themselves whether the prerequisites for judicial relief are present.[488]

This matter of meshing the player's agreement to arbitrate with the procedures for issuing injunctions has received little attention in the courts, largely because the extensive use of arbitration is of relatively recent origin.[489] And while a final accommodation must await further judicial developments, the broad contours of a solution can be suggested on the basis of the parties' likely intentions. Particular emphasis must be given to the fact that the parties have designated the injunction proceeding as an *exception* to an otherwise pervasive duty to arbitrate. That would seem to evidence an understanding that some matters were to be freed from the usual restraints of arbitration. Those matters which fit most logically into this exception are questions which relate directly to the availability of the judicial remedy, including the matters of unique skill, injury to competition, and so on. And while a reasonable argument can be made that the parties have no power to compel arbitration of questions going to the court's jurisdiction,[490] that contention need not be considered if the parties' intent is that the injunction against the athlete's performing for another team is to be available upon the same conditions as have been applied historically. As to questions which concern the respective performances under the contract, it is likely that the parties intended to rely primarily on arbitration to determine matters of this sort. It will be necessary for the court to satisfy itself that a contract does in fact exist, for otherwise there would be no basis for an injunction. But with respect to disputes about whether the team has properly performed its duty under the contract, it would be appropriate for the court to defer to the arbitrator. That need not mean that the injunction will be delayed. Where these questions arise, the court should proceed to issue the injunction, assuming the remedy is otherwise available, and require the parties to arbitrate any pure contract claims which the player may have.[491] The continuance of the injunction in this situation should be conditional upon the arbitrator's finding

---

488. *See, e.g.,* Dallas Cowboys Football Club, Inc. v. Harris, 348 S.W.2d 37, 43 (Tex. Civ. App. 1961); Dockstader v. Reed, 121 App. Div. 846, 106 N.Y.S. 795 (Sup. Ct. 1907); Tannenbaum, *Enforcement of Personal Service Contracts in the Entertainment Industry,* 42 CAL. L. REV. 18, 22-33 (1954).

489. The appellate court opinion in Erving v. Virginia Squires Basketball Club, 468 F.2d 1064 (2d Cir. 1972), contains a cryptic reference to the club's right to secure judicial enforcement of the covenant of exclusive service. The player apparently argued that there was a lack of mutuality of remedy because only the club was empowered to secure injunctive relief. *See generally* § 4.11 *supra.* The court dismissed this argument and then added: "The provision relative to 'obtaining an injunction or other equitable relief' is merely declaratory of existing legal rights." *Id.* at 1067. The court appears to have confused two different types of injunctions — one which would be used to restrain the player from performing for another team and one which would be used to enforce the agreement to arbitrate. In many cases these would have the same practical effect upon the player who sought to market his services elsewhere. Nonetheless, each involves somewhat different questions of fact. Moreover, the fact that the team's right to seek an injunction is removed from the broad reach of the general arbitration clause would seem to suggest that the parties intended to treat the matters differently.

490. An injunction is a discretionary remedy which historically was issued only when the conscience of the equity court was moved to agree that judicial intervention was necessary to avoid an injustice. *Compare* Molinas v. Podoloff, 133 N.Y.S.2d 743 (Sup. Ct. 1954). Presumably the parties would have no power to dictate how the court's conscience would be affected on matters which went to the basic issue of whether the court ought to act. Indeed the notion of "discretion" suggests that flexibility is to be retained in the judicial decision-making process.

491. *See* § 4.15 (subsection c) *supra.*

that the athlete's claims were not such as would excuse his performance under the contract.[492] This approach has the virtue of allowing for consistent enforcement of the agreement to arbitrate. By requiring the parties to take pure contract questions to arbitration, the court can insure that the manner in which particular contract disputes are resolved does not differ merely because the player had chosen to abandon the agreement.

c. Arbitrator's Role in Defining Arbitrability.

1. *Commercial Arbitration*

Judicial interpretation has provided further definition of the proper division of authority between courts and arbitrators in commercial arbitration controversies.[493] As the above analysis should suggest, there is often an issue as to whether a particular dispute is within the subjects which the parties have agreed to arbitrate. The issue arises as to whether the courts or the arbitrator will decide this question. The near universal response is that the question of arbitrability will normally be decided by the court, and the arbitrator does not have authority to define his own jurisdiction unless the parties have specifically empowered him to do so.[494]

Another group of cases which involve a determination of the respective powers of the court and arbitrator are those in which one party claims that the entire contract is voidable because it was induced by fraud or because of similar defects surrounding its execution.[495] The party raising such a claim would argue that resort to arbitration should not be necessary for this type of complaint because the enforceability of the arbitration clause depends upon the validity of the contract which contains it. Just as the arbitrator cannot define his own jurisdiction, it would be argued, he cannot determine the validity of a provision which creates his authority. As previously noted,[496] this was a question which produced divergent views in the courts. However, the matter now seems to be well-settled in judicial proceedings to which the Federal Arbitration Act will be applied. Under the doctrine of separability, an attack upon the general validity of the contract must be taken to arbitration.[497] The contract provision containing the parties' agreement to arbitrate will be regarded as severable from the rest

---

492. This division of responsibility between court and arbitrator would not produce results radically different from that which would be obtained if the arbitration clause made no exception for the enforcement of the covenant of exclusive services. Even under a general arbitration clause the team could often enjoin the player from jumping to another team until all disputes under the original contract had been determined by arbitration. *See* Erving v. Virginia Squires Basketball Club, 349 F. Supp. 716, 719-20 (E.D.N.Y.), *aff'd*, 468 F.2d 1064 (2d Cir. 1972). While the result might be the same without the exception for injunctions, there may be important differences in the types of issues which are presented, and the forums in which these are to be resolved. *See also* note 489 *supra*.

493. *See generally* DOMKE, COMMERCIAL ARBITRATION §§ 12.01-12.02; 6A CORBIN ON CONTRACTS § 1444A.

494. *See, e.g.*, International Union of Operating Eng'rs v. Flair Builders, Inc., 406 U.S. 487, 32 L. Ed. 2d 248, 92 S. Ct. 1710 (1972); Drake Bakeries, Inc. v. American Bakery & Confectionery Workers Int'l, 370 U.S. 254, 8 L. Ed. 2d 474, 82 S. Ct. 1346 (1962); Mutual Benefit Health & Accident Ass'n v. United Cas. Co., 142 F.2d 390, 393-94 (1st Cir. 1944); D. DOBBS, HANDBOOK ON THE LAW OF REMEDIES § 12.27, at 943 (1973).

495. *See generally* 6A CORBIN ON CONTRACTS § 1444; DOMKE, COMMERCIAL ARBITRATION §§ 8.01-8.04.

496. *See* discussion at notes 432-435, § 4.15 *supra*.

497. *See* Prima Paint Corp. v. Flood & Conklin Mfg. Co., 388 U.S. 395, 400, 18 L. Ed. 2d 1270, 87 S. Ct. 1801 (1967). *See also* Robert Lawrence Co. v. Devonshire Fabrics, Inc., 271 F.2d 402, 410 (2d Cir. 1959).

of the contract. Thus, the duty to arbitrate will be excused only if it is shown that the arbitration clause itself was induced by fraud.[498]

2. *Labor Arbitration*

Predictably, the same issues concerning the division of authority between courts and arbitrators appear in the labor arbitration context. At the threshold level, the question arises as to whether the court or the arbitrator is to decide whether a particular controversy comes within the parties' arbitration clause. This is another labor arbitration issue which has received attention by the Supreme Court. The Court has indicated that it is a judicial function to determine whether a particular subject matter is covered by an agreement to arbitrate.[499] While this general result is the same as that which operates in the area of commercial arbitration, there are some nuances of the issue that have been more fully explored in the labor area. For example, in defining the scope of the arbitration clause, the court in a labor case must be mindful of the strong presumption in favor of arbitration. In addition, the Supreme Court has cautioned that courts in labor cases are to decide only whether there is an arbitrable *subject matter* and not whether the underlying controversy has merit. Thus, even if the court believes that the party requesting arbitration will clearly lose on the merits, the matter must still be sent to arbitration if it is a subject coming within the parties' clause.[500] This principle has been carried to the point of suggesting that arbitration is necessary even if a complained of breach of the underlying contract is obviously frivolous and brought in bad faith, assuming again that the general subject matter is an arbitrable one.[501] Finally, the Supreme Court has recognized that it is within the power of the parties to agree that the arbitrator will decide questions of the coverage of the arbitration clause.[502] Thus, while the issue of subject matter arbitrability is normally decided by the court, the parties may provide otherwise and give the arbitrator the exclusive power to define his jurisdiction.

Related to the question discussed in the preceding paragraph is the issue of the respective roles of courts and arbitrators in determining whether agreed-upon prerequisites to arbitrability have been satisfied. For example, it is common for the parties to stipulate that a matter must be submitted to arbitration within a stated period. Such a provision serves as a private statute of limitations and may operate to remove a claim from the jurisdiction of the arbitrator and preclude the injured party from securing relief in any form.[502.1] Despite the jurisdictional flavor of questions of this sort, they are left to the

---

498. This distinction between fraud in the inducement of the contract generally and fraud in the execution of the arbitration clause in particular is based on the language of Section 4 of the Federal Arbitration Act. This section directs the court to order the matter submitted to arbitration "upon being satisfied that the making of the agreement for arbitration . . . is not in issue . . . . If the making of the arbitration agreement . . . be in issue, the court shall proceed summarily to the trial thereof." 9 U.S.C. § 4 (1970). *See generally* Comment, *Federal Arbitration Act and Application of the "Separability Doctrine" in Federal Courts,* 1968 DUKE L.J. 588. This distinction, and the arbitrator's authority to decide claims relating to fraud in the inducement of the contract, has been specifically recognized as applicable to professional sports contracts. *See* Erving v. Virginia Squires Basketball Club, 349 F. Supp. 716 (E.D.N.Y.), *aff'd,* 468 F.2d 1064 (2d Cir. 1972).

499. *See* United Steelworkers v. American Mfg. Co., 363 U.S. 564 (1960). *See generally* O. FAIRWEATHER, PRACTICE AND PROCEDURE IN LABOR ARBITRATION 23-26 (1973).

500. *See* United Steelworkers v. American Mfg. Co., 363 U.S. 564 (1960).

501. *See* GORMAN, LABOR LAW 554.

502. United Steelworkers v. Warrior & Gulf Navigation Co., 363 U.S. 574 (1960).

502.1. *See generally* DOMKE, COMMERCIAL ARBITRATION §§ 15.01-.02.

arbitrator's decision. In *Davis v. Pro Basketball, Inc.*,[502.2] where the issue of timeliness was specifically raised, the court yielded to the arbitrator, noting that "once a court has determined that a dispute must be submitted to arbitration, any 'procedural' questions which arise out of the dispute must be decided by the arbitrators." [502.3] The court did suggest, however, that there would be some cases in which it would be so clear that a party had lost its right to arbitrate that a judge could refuse to order arbitration.[502.4] This interpretation reflects a policy of saving the other side the expense of arbitration when it was clear that the matter should not be heard. Where arbitration is precluded by the injured party's failure to take timely action, the court has no power to hear the substance of the claim.

A final issue which deserves mention concerns the division of authority between courts and arbitrators with respect to a party's allegation that the underlying contract was induced by fraudulent representations. As already noted, in the area of commercial arbitration, such issues are to be decided by the arbitrator. Interestingly, this appears to be one issue for which less deference is given to labor arbitrators than their counterparts in commercial cases. There are labor precedents which suggest that a claim of fraud in the inducement of the contract is to be decided by the court.[502.5] The apparent rationale for this result would be the same as that used by those state courts which follow a similar rule: the arbitrator's authority arises from the contract, and if the contract is invalid, then his claim of authority is also invalid.[502.6] It is not clear that this rule of labor arbitration is invulnerable, however. Not only is it out of step with the most recent pronouncements of federal policy under the FAA, but in addition, it seems to ignore the reality of labor relations in which the parties typically choose to commit most, if not all, aspects of their relationship to the province of the arbitrator.

§ 4.17. Matters Not Subject to Arbitration.

A party which has a claim under its contract will sometimes wish to avoid arbitration. Thus, it may be useful to catalog the situations in which the presence of an arbitration clause will not preclude direct access to the courts. Broadly defined, there are three situations in which the traditional judicial remedies may be pursued. The first situation is that suggested by the prior discussion: arbitration is mandatory only if the particular type of controversy is covered by the terms of the parties' arbitration agreement.[503] Thus, in some cases, the injured party may find that the applicable arbitration clause can be construed as not extending to the claim which he asserts. The second situation is one in which the breaching party is deemed to have waived its right to insist upon arbitration. The final group of cases not subject to arbitration is that in which the court can identify some strong public policy which requires direct judicial enforcement of the claim. Cases in this group typically involve the assertion of

---

502.2. 381 F. Supp. 1 (S.D.N.Y. 1974).

502.3. *Id.* at 4, *citing* John Wiley & Sons v. Livingston, 376 U.S. 543, 557-58 (1964).

502.4. 381 F. Supp. at 4.

502.5. *See* Garment Workers v. Ashland Indus., 488 F.2d 641 (5th Cir.), *cert. denied,* 419 U.S. 840 (1974).

502.6. *See* GORMAN, LABOR LAW 563-64.

503. *See generally* § 4.16 *supra.*

rights embodied in statutes designed for the protection of important individual or public rights. The "exceptions" to arbitration presented by the second and third categories of cases are discussed here.

a. Waiver of the Right to Arbitration. The notion that a party may have waived his right to have a matter decided by an arbitrator rather than a court appears most frequently in the context of commercial (non-labor) disputes. As the footnote material will suggest, the following discussion of the waiver issue is drawn from cases involving commercial arbitration. The right to arbitration in this context arises from contract, and like other contract rights, it is subject to waiver when a party who might otherwise demand arbitration fails to insist upon compliance with the arbitration agreement.[504] The waiver argument is often made in situations in which the injured party initiates a lawsuit based on a claim which is covered by an arbitration clause. The defendant may proceed to respond to the complaint in traditional fashion by filing an answer, participating in discovery and perhaps even going to trial, all the time failing to take action which shows that he is insisting on arbitration. Then at some point before the judicial proceeding is brought to a conclusion, the defendant asserts his arbitration rights and seeks a stay of the court proceedings. The plaintiff will insist that the defendant, by participating in the litigation, has acted inconsistently with any contention that the matter should be resolved outside the judicial process. Thus, by virtue of the defendant's delay in requesting a stay pending arbitration, the plaintiff will allege, the defendant has waived any rights which he had under the arbitration clause. It is clear that a waiver will be found in some of these situations.[505] The basic issue which is raised concerns the extent to which the defendant can participate in the court proceeding before he is deemed to have relinquished his right to insist on compliance with the arbitration provision.

An examination of the cases suggests that various courts look at different factors in determining whether there has been an effective waiver. Some courts appear to be concerned primarily with the length of any delay which has preceded the assertion of the right to arbitrate.[506] Other courts emphasize the extent to which the judicial proceedings have progressed and are more inclined to find a waiver if the case has been developed to an advanced stage.[507] Courts have also attempted to identify general rules of thumb. Thus, it has been suggested that the earliest point at which a waiver might be found is when there has been a responsive pleading on the merits, which will usually be the defendant's answer.[508] But these general guidelines are not always followed. For example, while some courts hold that a defendant preserves his right to arbitration if he asserts it in his answer,[509] other courts have found a waiver

504. *See generally* M. DOMKE, THE LAW AND PRACTICE OF COMMERCIAL ARBITRATION § 19.01 (1968) [hereinafter cited as DOMKE, COMMERCIAL ARBITRATION]; Annot., 161 A.L.R. 1426 (1946).

505. *See, e.g.,* Demsey & Assoc. v. S.S. Sea Star, 461 F.2d 1009, 1017-19 (2d Cir. 1972); Almacenes Fernandez, S.A. v. Golodetz, 148 F.2d 625, 627 (2d Cir. 1945); Sulphur Export Corp. v. Carribean Clipper Lines, Inc., 277 F. Supp. 632, 634 (E.D. La. 1968).

506. *See* Erving v. Virginia Squires Basketball Club, 349 F. Supp. 716, 719 (E.D.N.Y.), *aff'd,* 468 F.2d 1064 (2d Cir. 1972). *See generally* Annot., 25 A.L.R. 3d 1171 (1969).

507. *See, e.g.,* Demsey & Assoc. v. S.S. Sea Star, 461 F.2d 1009, 1017-19 (2d Cir. 1972); Sulphur Export Corp. v. Carribean Clipper Lines, Inc., 277 F. Supp. 632, 634 (E.D. La. 1968); United Nations Children's Fund v. S/S Nordstern, 251 F. Supp. 833, 840 (S.D.N.Y. 1965).

508. *See* Chatham Shipping Co. v. Fertex S.S. Co., 352 F.2d 291, 293 (2d Cir. 1965).

509. *See, e.g.,* Michael v. S.S. Thanasis, 311 F. Supp. 170, 181 (N.D. Cal. 1970).

even though the defendant had raised the question of arbitration in an affirmative defense.[510]

Although the courts appear to be emphasizing somewhat different points in deciding whether the right to arbitration has been waived, most of the cases share a common concern — whether the other side has been prejudiced by the moving party's delay in requesting arbitration.[511] Under this approach the elapse of as much as eighteen months between the initiation of the suit and the request for a stay will not be deemed excessive if there is no evidence of appreciable injury resulting from the delay.[512] What exactly must be the "prejudice" which results from the failure to make a timely assertion of one's right to arbitration? The primary ingredient is expense to the other party, which will take the form of expenditures made in preparing for and participating in the trial of the matter.[513] But the court will presumably also consider other types of prejudice, including a significant change in the parties' positions. The concern for possible prejudice can be translated into rough guidelines as to which steps in the judicial proceeding — answer, discovery, motions, trial — are likely to suggest that the requisite degree of detriment has been incurred. Thus, if the request for arbitration is not made until after a trial on the merits, a waiver is likely to be found.[514] On the other hand, the filing of an answer will usually not preclude a later request for a stay.[515] Cases which fall in between these extremes will require a particularized evaluation.[516] These principles defining the operation of the waiver doctrine have been developed in the general case law in this area, and as might be expected, cases involving professional sports contracts have applied them without modification.[517]

One final point is worthy of mention. While the prior analysis has dealt primarily with situations in which waiver may be implied, it is also possible that the party has expressly agreed to waive its right to arbitration.[518] The courts seem to insist upon rather explicit evidence of such a waiver, especially in an industry such as professional sports where arbitration is the primary means of dispute resolution.[519] Thus, a party who bargains for a waiver would be well-advised to secure an express written statement from the other side that its arbitration rights are being relinquished.

---

510. *See* Demsey & Assoc. v. S.S. Sea Star, 461 F.2d 1009, 1017 (2d Cir. 1972).

511. *See, e.g.,* Corcich v. Rederi A/B Nordic, 389 F.2d 692, 696 (2d Cir. 1968) ("It is not 'consistency,' but presence or absence of prejudice which is determinative of the issue"). *See also* Michael v. S.S. Thanasis, 311 F. Supp. 170 (N.D. Cal. 1970); Commercial Metals Co. v. International Union Marine Corp., 294 F. Supp. 570, 573 (S.D.N.Y. 1968).

512. *See* Hilti, Inc. v. Oldach, 392 F.2d 368 (1st Cir. 1968).

513. *See* Demsey & Assoc. v. S.S. Sea Star, 461 F.2d 1009, 1018 (2d Cir. 1972).

514. *See, e.g.,* Demsey & Assoc. v. S.S. Sea Star, 461 F.2d 1009, 1017-19 (2d Cir. 1972); Sulphur Export Corp. v. Carribean Clipper Lines, Inc., 277 F. Supp. 632, 634 (E.D. La. 1968).

515. *See, e.g.,* Erving v. Virginia Squires Basketball Club, 349 F. Supp. 716, 719 (E.D.N.Y.), *aff'd,* 468 F.2d 1064 (2d Cir. 1972). *See generally* DOMKE, COMMERCIAL ARBITRATION § 19.01.

516. *See, e.g.,* Almacenes Fernandez, S.A. v. Golodetz, 148 F.2d 625, 627 (2d Cir. 1945); United Nations Children's Fund v. S/S Nordstern, 251 F. Supp. 833, 840 (S.D.N.Y. 1965).

517. *See* Erving v. Virginia Squires Basketball Club, 349 F. Supp. 716, 719 (E.D.N.Y.), *aff'd,* 468 F.2d 1064 (2d Cir. 1972).

518. At least one court has refused to accept a voluntary waiver and expressed its preference to have particular controversies resolved by an expert arbitrator. *See* Germany v. River Terminal Ry., 477 F.2d 546, 548 (6th Cir. 1973).

519. *See* Davis v. Pro Basketball, Inc., 381 F. Supp. 1 (S.D.N.Y. 1974).

b. Public Policy Limitations on the Exclusivity of the Arbitration Remedy.

The legal rights which an athlete or club enjoys will not be limited to those which are based on its contract. There are numerous rights which emanate from other sources and the question which arises is whether the party's agreement that arbitration will be his exclusive remedy precludes his direct access to the courts for vindication of these other rights. It should be apparent that the starting point for analysis of this issue is the arbitration agreement itself. Close scrutiny of that contract should indicate whether, as an initial matter, the parties intended to utilize arbitration for claims arising apart from the contract. In many cases, it will be found that arbitration governs only contract-related claims and the injured party, whether player or club, may pursue traditional judicial remedies where other types of relief are sought.

Yet, there will be cases in which the subject matter which forms the basis of a collateral right is also covered in the contract itself. This is particularly true with respect to certain rights created by federal legislative enactment. There are two claims of this sort — those arising under federal antitrust laws and those involving the federally-guaranteed right of equal employment opportunity — which warrant particular attention in the present context. While a number of other federal statutory rights might also be relevant, the analysis of these two will suggest the sort of inquiry which is usually made to determine whether a party is bound by his promise to use arbitration as his exclusive remedy.[520]

In the present era, it should be clear that the federal antitrust laws provide an important outlet for complaints about those aspects of professional sports contracts which limit the parties' rights to market their services or products as they would otherwise wish. Antitrust objections are raised not only by players who resist league-mandated restraints on their freedom to contract,[521] but also by clubs which seek greater freedom in the selection of a site for their franchise.[522] But the complaints which are raised are always intimately related to the contracts which define the plaintiff's relationship with others in the industry. And typically those contracts include arbitration clauses covering all claims which arise under the agreement.[523] Is the athlete's or the club's right to secure relief under the federal antitrust laws limited by a prior agreement to arbitrate? While this question has not received a great deal of attention in the sports cases, a convincing answer is found in other cases examining the reach of a commercial arbitration agreement. The near universal response is that a prior agreement to arbitrate does not restrict a party's right to seek direct adjudication of his antitrust complaints.[524] At least two different reasons are

---

520. For a discussion of other situations in which the exclusivity of the arbitration remedy may be denied on public policy grounds see DOMKE, COMMERCIAL ARBITRATION § 19.02.

521. *See* Flood v. Kuhn, 316 F. Supp. 271 (S.D.N.Y. 1970), *aff'd,* 443 F.2d 264 (2d Cir. 1971), *aff'd,* 407 U.S. 258, 32 L. Ed. 2d 728, 92 S. Ct. 2099 (1972); Kapp v. National Football League, 390 F. Supp. 73 (N.D. Cal. 1974).

522. *See* San Francisco Seals, Ltd. v. National Hockey League, 379 F. Supp. 966 (C.D. Cal. 1974).

523. *See* § 4.16 *supra.*

524. *See* Cobb v. Lewis, 488 F.2d 41 (5th Cir. 1974); Power Replacements, Inc. v. Air Preheater Co., 426 F.2d 980 (9th Cir. 1970); American Safety Equip. Corp. v. J. P. Maguire & Co., 391 F.2d 821 (2d Cir. 1968); *Cf.* Helfenbein v. International Indus., Inc., 438 F.2d 1068 (8th Cir. 1971).

The discussion in the text assumes that the plaintiff has a colorable antitrust claim which can be raised. It should be kept in mind, however, that many potential objections which a player might raise will be found to have been immunized from antitrust attack under the so-called labor exemption. If the subject matter is one which has been subjected to good faith, arm's-length collective

suggested in support of this result. The rationale which has a more general application is that which suggests that the antitrust laws are intended to protect not only the interests of the private litigant, but also those of the public in general. Thus, courts ought to hesitate to find that vindication of the public interest is precluded by a private arbitration agreement entered into without reference to the particular claim involved.[525] The other reason suggested by the courts is the notion that the courts are better able to deal with the peculiar complexities of antitrust than are arbitrators.[526] While an arbitrator may have special expertise in the customs of the business, he is not likely to have the requisite experience with respect to the broader economic implications of a particular industry practice.

Once the question of the independence of antitrust claims is established, it is necessary to determine how far the above policies will be extended. For example, it might be asked whether there is a collateral estoppel effect when a party actually takes a potential antitrust claim to arbitration and after losing at that level, petitions a court for an original adjudication of his complaint. Some courts have held that the subsequent lawsuit is not controlled by the findings made in the prior arbitration.[527] On the other hand, it has been recognized that a party may take actions which amount to either an express or implied waiver of his right to pursue an independent action.[528] This might occur where a party agreed to arbitrate a potential antitrust claim after it had arisen.[529] Since a party otherwise has some freedom to settle his private antitrust claims despite the larger public interest in these matters, he should retain a right to arrange for other sorts of settlements.

Where the player's alleged independent right arises not from the antitrust law but from the federal statute which mandates equal employment opportunity, the same basic conclusions are reached concerning the availability of direct judicial relief. Such a case might arise for example, where a black athlete alleges that the club, or some of its agents, were improperly influenced by racial considerations in establishing his salary.[530]

The Supreme Court has addressed the question of the relationship between the private cause of action provided in Title VII of the Civil Rights Act [531] and a prior agreement to arbitrate complaints based on discriminatory hiring practices. The Court's decision in *Alexander v. Gardner-Denver Company* [532] makes clear that the federal right has origins independent of any private commitment made by an employer, and the employee may seek an original adjudication of his claim in court.[533] This result obtains even if the employee has

bargaining between the players' union and the owners, a union member who is disadvantaged by any resulting agreement will ordinarily not be able to attack the offending term on antitrust grounds. The rationale and scope of the labor exemption are discussed more fully in §§ 5.04-.06 *infra*.

525. *See* American Safety Equip. Corp. v. J. P. Maguire & Co., 391 F.2d 821, 826 (2d Cir. 1968).
526. *See id.* at 827.
527. *See* Overseas Motor, Inc. v. Import Motors Ltd., 375 F. Supp. 499 (E.D. Mich. 1974).
528. *See* Cobb v. Lewis, 488 F.2d 41, 49 (5th Cir. 1974).
529. *See id.*
530. *Cf.* Scully, *Economic Discrimination in Professional Sports,* 38 LAW & CONTEMP. PROB. 67 (1973).
531. 42 U.S.C. § 2000e-2 (1964).
532. 415 U.S. 36, 39 L. Ed. 2d 147, 94 S. Ct. 1011 (1974).
533. 415 U.S. at 54.

previously received an unfavorable decision in an arbitration on the same issue.[534]

The results in these two areas would suggest that a general agreement to arbitrate will not displace important statutory rights. Since these rights are often created to protect interests which are frequently subverted in the negotiation of general provisions of a contract, a strong impetus exists for a court to decline to find an *a priori* waiver. Some types of statutory rights may not fit into the pattern of those discussed above, and a different result may be called for in those situations. But the party who seeks to subject legislatively protected rights to the broad reach of a private arbitration agreement bears a heavy burden in showing that the effectiveness of the legislative program would not be undermined.

§ 4.18. Procedural Aspects of Arbitration.

Courts of law, with considerable assistance from legislatures, go to great lengths to spell out the procedures which will govern the proceedings which are brought before them. Through case decision, judicial rule-making, and legislative enactment, efforts are made to define the type of hearing to be held, the kinds of evidence which will be admissible, the persons entitled to participate in the hearings, the types of motions which will be entertained, the burden which each side bears in supporting his case and a wide variety of other matters. When a party takes his claim to arbitration, he will likely encounter a much different situation. Seldom will he find procedural rules as detailed as those which obtain in a court of law, and generally the arbitration will be conducted much more informally than a traditional lawsuit.[535] There is no requirement that the parties utilize the same procedures which would be used in a court of law, and in fact the arbitrator may employ methods which would be unacceptable in a judicial proceeding.[536] Unless he has specified otherwise, a party who consents to arbitration must accept that the proceeding will be less highly structured and more loosely conducted than those conducted in traditional forums. Indeed, two of the primary reasons for selecting arbitration are to minimize costs and secure a speedy resolution of the controversies.[537] The informality of arbitration operates to promote these goals, as the arbitrator can insure both that the hearing is not bogged down by procedural technicalities and that his decision will be issued with a minimum of delay.[538]

There is no single set of procedural rules to be applied in arbitration. As with other aspects of the arbitration relationship, the question of procedures is a matter of contract between the parties, and they are afforded considerable freedom to make the arbitration proceeding as structured, or as informal, as they think best meets the needs of their particular situation. The arbitration

---

534. *See id.*

535. *See, e.g.,* Compania Panemena Maritima San Gerassimo, S.A. v. J.E. Hurley Lumber Co., 244 F.2d 286 (2d Cir. 1957); American Almond Prods. Co. v. Consolidated Pecan Sales Co., 144 F.2d 448 (2d Cir. 1944); Annot., 154 A.L.R. 1205 (1945).

536. *See generally* Walden v. Teamsters Local 71, 468 F.2d 196 (4th Cir. 1972); Alonso v. Kaiser Aluminum & Chem. Corp., 345 F. Supp. 1356 (S.D. W. Va. 1971); D. DOBBS, HANDBOOK ON THE LAW OF REMEDIES § 12.27, at 942 (1973).

537. *See* § 4.15 *supra.*

538. *See* Sobel v. Hertz & Warner Co., 469 F.2d 1211 (2d Cir. 1972).

agreements in the sports industry reflect the diversity which might be expected when the matter of procedure is left to the parties' agreement. In some agreements, the parties defer completely to the arbitrator and empower him to specify the procedures which will govern.[539] In other situations, particularly those in which the arbitration agreement is the product of collective bargaining, the applicable procedures are set forth in great detail. Thus, the parties often include rules concerning each side's right to representation, the type of evidence which may be introduced, the manner of receiving testimony, the availability of cross-examination, the necessity of a written decision and numerous other matters.[540] In specialized situations, the parties may even agree to limit the range of the arbitrator's discretion.[541]

While most disputes over procedure will be resolved on the basis of the parties' contract, there are also independent legal principles which bear on such controversies. A court will scrutinize the procedural aspects of the arbitration not only to insure that the contract is complied with but also to satisfy itself that fundamental fairness has been afforded in the procedures followed by the arbitrator. The present case law suggests that there is some confusion on the general content of this requirement of fairness. Many courts which articulate this concern go on to suggest that procedures used in arbitration must afford due process to the participants. Illustrative of this approach is *Professional Sports Ltd. v. Virginia Squires Basketball Club*,[542] in which the court struck down an attempt by the ABA commissioner to block a player trade, partly on the basis that the commissioner had taken action without holding a hearing on the matter. There was some doubt as to whether the applicable contract — the league bylaws — required that the parties be afforded an opportunity to be heard. In resolving the doubts about the meaning of the contract, the court indicated that it would be guided by principles of constitutional dimension. In the court's view,

> [S]ince proceedings of this nature could have the effect of depriving a party of some property right, these terms should be construed to require at least the minimum essentials of "due process." [543]

539. *See* NFL Contract ¶ 20 (1977) (Commissioner's arbitration), note 416, § 4.15 *supra*.

540. *See* Basic Agreement Between the American League of Professional Baseball Clubs and the National League of Professional Baseball Clubs and Major League Baseball Players Association, Appendix A (Rules of Procedures) (1977) [hereinafter cited as Baseball Collective Bargaining Agreement]. *See also* discussion at note 423, § 4.15 *supra*.

541. Perhaps the most interesting example of an agreement on procedural matters is found in the arbitration system used in baseball to determine the player's salary in the event he and the club cannot agree. *See* Baseball Collective Bargaining Agreement art. V(D). The parties go to great lengths to limit the discretion which the arbitrator will exercise. The arbitration agreement spells out the criteria which the arbitrator is to employ. Thus, in setting the salary, the arbitrator is to consider "... Player's contribution to this Club, ... the length and consistency of his career contributions, the record of the Player's past compensation, comparative baseball salaries ..., the existence of any physical or mental defects on the part of the Player, and the recent performance record of the Club ..." *Id.* Also, the agreement specifies that certain types of evidence are to be kept from the arbitrator: "The following items ... shall be excluded: (a) the financial position of the Player and the Club, (b) Press comments, testimonials or similar material ..., (c) offers made by either Player or Club prior to arbitration, (d) the cost to the parties of their representatives, attorneys, etc., (e) salaries in other sports or occupations." *Id.* And most significantly, the agreement strictly limits the arbitrator's choices in making his salary award. The club and player are to each submit a salary which it thinks is appropriate, and the arbitrator may only select one figure or the other. *See generally* Seitz, *Footnotes to Baseball Arbitration,* 29 ARB. J. (n.s.) 98 (1974).

542. 373 F. Supp. 946 (W.D. Tex. 1974).

543. *Id.* at 951.

The court relied heavily on cases defining the constitutional right of due process in concluding that the commissioner's actions were defective because there had been no notice of a hearing, no specification of charges, and no opportunity for the parties to present witnesses or other evidence.[544] The court strongly suggests, without actually so stating, that an arbitration proceeding which did not embody these procedures would not be entitled to judicial enforcement.[545]

But one must surely raise a question as to the legal doctrine which justifies the application of the constitutional requirement of due process to arbitration proceedings. The court in *Professional Sports Ltd.* seems to assume that a hearing before an arbitrator must be evaluated in the same terms as a judicial or administrative hearing.[546] If that were true, then presumably the parties would not be free to agree to arbitration procedures which did not provide for a hearing and other due process protections. It can be suggested, however, that the court's emphasis on traditional due process notions is misplaced. The court properly expresses a concern for the fairness of the arbitration proceedings, but analyzes the question of fairness in the wrong doctrinal framework. It is clear that had the losing party not agreed to arbitration, he could have pursued an action in a traditional judicial forum and there would have been entitled to a variety of constitutional protections, including the right to due process of law [547] and, in some cases, a right to have the matter tried by a jury.[548] But it is also clear that a party may waive these constitutional protections if he so desires.[549] The proper question to be asked is not whether the arbitration afforded due process, but rather whether the disappointed party had made an effective waiver of the constitutional protections which would otherwise obtain. Under this view, it is inappropriate to insist that all arbitration proceedings provide the protection of notice, hearing, and a full opportunity to present evidence.[550] Rather, the critical question which the court should ask is whether the waiver of important procedural rights was constitutionally sufficient, that is, whether it was knowingly and willingly made.[551]

---

544. *Id.*

545. *Compare* Molinas v. Podoloff, 133 N.Y.S.2d 743 (Sup. Ct. 1954).

546. In defining the nature of the hearing which must be afforded, the court relies on cases in which the requirement of a hearing is of constitutional dimensions. For example, the court cites Fuentes v. Shevin, 407 U.S. 67, 32 L. Ed. 2d 556, 92 S. Ct. 1983 (1972), a case clearly based on the impropriety of the *government* assisting in a deprivation of property without a hearing. While those precedents would generally seem to be inapposite, it is relevant to note that even where governmental instrumentalities are involved, the Supreme Court has not always required that fact-finding be accompanied by a full hearing, with a right of cross-examination and so on. Rather, the content of due process in these state-action cases depends upon the severity of the sanction, the need for immediate action, and so on. *See* Goss v. Lopez, 419 U.S. 565 (1975).

547. *See* U.S. CONST. amends. V, XIV.

548. *See* U.S. CONST. amend. VII.

549. *See, e.g.,* D.H. Overmeyer Co. v. Frick, 405 U.S. 174, 187, 31 L. Ed. 2d 124, 92, S. Ct. 775 (1972) (waiver of the due process protections of the fifth and fourteenth amendments); Rogers v. United States, 141 U.S. 548, 554, 35 L. Ed. 853, 12 S. Ct. 91 (1891); Wilson v. Corning Glass Works, 195 F.2d 825 (9th Cir. 1952) (waiver of seventh amendment right to trial by jury).

550. *Compare* DOMKE, COMMERCIAL ARBITRATION *Introduction* to ch. 24.

551. *See* Prima Paint Corp. v. Flood & Conklin Mfg. Co., 388 U.S. 395, 412-14, 18 L. Ed. 2d 1270, 87 S. Ct. 1801 (1967) (Black, J., dissenting). *See also* Comment, *Federal Arbitration Act and Application of the "Separability Doctrine" in Federal Courts,* 1968 DUKE L.J. 588, 606.

In making its evaluation, a court may properly compare the procedures which were actually used with those which would obtain under the Constitution.[552] The more fundamental the procedural rights which were allegedly waived, the more skeptical a court should be. Thus, in some cases, it might be doubted that the party understood that his entitlement to the particular protected right had been waived by his mere consent to arbitration. Moreover, the court can properly examine the form of the contract and the circumstances surrounding its negotiation.[553] These matters may be a particular concern with respect to some types of sports agreements, for the arbitration clauses used in professional sports are often part of standard form contracts not subject to particularized negotiation by the parties affected.[554]

It would be inaccurate to suggest that courts do, or should, evaluate the fairness of the arbitration proceedings only in terms of the effectiveness of the waiver of rights.[555] Rather, what the prior analysis seeks to establish is that despite the obvious temptation, it is inappropriate for a court to strictly apply traditional due process requirements to arbitration procedures, the approach which seems to be suggested by the opinion in *Professional Sports Ltd.* While an inquiry into the effectiveness of the contractual waiver provides a more useful framework for analysis, there are other considerations which may influence the court's evaluation. Indeed, an examination of the cases indicates that in some situations, courts will judge the fairness of arbitration proceedings in more general terms than would be required under a technical application of the rules pertaining to waiver.[556] The authority for the continued resort to this type of generalized inquiry can be found in at least two different sources. Initially, there is the general public policy that a court ought not lend its good offices to enforce a bargain which is lacking in fundamental fairness.[557] At stake is the integrity of the judiciary as an institution, and the basic concern is that the respect which the court now commands in the community might be lost if the court were to blindly enforce any arbitration award presented to it without regard to the harshness of the procedures under which it was obtained.

Further support for a judicial inquiry into the fairness of the arbitration proceeding emanates from the federal arbitration statute which will be applicable to many proceedings involving professional sports contracts. The Supreme Court has found that the FAA is not neutral on the issue of the quality of the arbitration proceedings which come within its reach. In a case involving an allegation that the arbitrator was not impartial, the Court examined the statutory language and concluded that Congress intended "to provide not

552. But such a comparison will not always be easy to make because the content of constitutional due process varies depending on the particular circumstances, including the gravity of the action involved. *See* note 546 *supra*.

553. *See generally* DOMKE, COMMERCIAL ARBITRATION § 5.04.

554. *Cf.* Matuszak v. Houston Oilers, Inc., 515 S.W.2d 725, 729 (Tex. Civ. App. 1974).

555. *But see* Prima Paint Corp. v. Flood & Conklin Mfg. Co., 388 U.S. 395, 412-14 (1967) (Black, J., dissenting).

556. *See, e.g.,* Riko Enterprises, Inc. v. Seattle SuperSonics Corp., 357 F. Supp. 521, 526 (S.D.N.Y. 1973).

557. *Id.:* "the papers and testimony before this court show that Commissioner Kennedy conducted no hearing and did not allow Seattle to submit any evidence to rebut the charges . . . . No court, state or federal, should fix its imprimatur to any such 'awards.'"

merely for *any* arbitration but for an impartial one." [558] Thus, when a court makes inquiry into the manner in which the arbitration was conducted, it will be furthering the congressional intent to insure that arbitration not be an instrument of abuse.

It should be apparent that there are common denominators to the inquiry into waiver and the concerns for institutional integrity and congressional design. The outcome of an evaluation on any of these grounds should be greatly influenced by the degree to which it appears that the party attacking the arbitration had knowingly accepted the procedures which were used. In the case in which there is evidence of actual consent to a truncated proceeding which lacked the usual provisions for a comprehensive hearing, the court should be inclined to enforce the award if it does not appear to be wholly arbitrary.[559] If the party has received what he bargained for, and as long as the result has some rational support, the integrity of the court is not tarnished by enforcement and the congressional design is not frustrated. But in an industry which depends upon standard form contracts, it is unlikely that the requisite consent to provisions for abrupt arbitration will always be found.[560] As long as the industry utilizes uniform agreements, which it probably must as a practical matter, there will be considerable pressure to provide for an arbitration procedure sufficiently fair to remove all bases for objection. This would most likely require proceedings which afforded adequate notice and a hearing. If those protections were waived in the course of meaningful collective bargaining by the players' association, then a court may well be willing to enforce an award entered in an abbreviated proceeding.[561] But the effectiveness of player bargaining has not reached all those who participate in the sports industry.[562] On a more general level, it can be noted that the cases which have been decided in the sports area to date clearly suggest that the courts have little enthusiasm for endorsing the procedures which are used in many segments of the industry.[563]

§ 4.19. Commissioner's Role as Arbitrator.

For the greater part of its history, the sports industry has operated under a form of government which allocates significant authority to a single person, the league commissioner. For a long period, the commissioner's powers included the authority to serve as final arbitrator of complaints by both players and clubs.

---

558. *See* Commonwealth Coatings Corp. v. Continental Cas. Co., 393 U.S. 144, 147, 21 L. Ed. 2d 301, 89 S. Ct. 337 (1968). Although the issue in the present context is procedural fairness generally and not specifically potential partiality, it is not likely that a legislative body concerned about the latter would be indifferent about the former.

559. *Compare* Thaler v. Alberman, 135 N.Y.S.2d 532, 534 (Sup. Ct. 1954).

560. *See generally* Goldberg, *A Supreme Court Judge Looks at Arbitration,* 20 ARB. J. 13, 16 (1965). *See also* Stone, *A Paradox in the Theory of Commercial Arbitration,* 21 ARB. J. 156 (1966).

561. *See* Goldberg, *A Supreme Court Judge Looks at Arbitration, supra* note 560, at 16.

562. *See* Kapp v. National Football League, 390 F. Supp. 73 (N.D. Cal. 1974); Philadelphia World Hockey Club Inc. v. Philadelphia Hockey Club, Inc., 351 F. Supp. 462, 481-86 (E.D. Pa. 1972).

563. *See* Professional Sports, Ltd. v. Virginia Squires Basketball Club, 373 F. Supp. 946 (W.D. Tex. 1974); Riko Enterprises, Inc. v. Seattle SuperSonics Corp., 357 F. Supp. 521 (S.D.N.Y. 1973). *See also* National Football League Player's Ass'n v. NLRB, 503 F.2d 12, 15 (8th Cir. 1974) (NLRB refused to defer to arbitration by commissioner where it would involve the commissioner reviewing his own action); Kapp v. National Football League, 390 F. Supp. 73, 82 (N.D. Cal. 1974) (court finds commissioner's "unilateral ... arbitration" to be "patently unreasonable" when used to enforce employee restraints).

The degree of reliance upon the commissioner's decision-making varied from sport to sport,[564] but until recently, the common pattern was to utilize the commissioner as the final authority in matters of player discipline, player compensation disputes, performance disputes, as well as interclub controversies such as those when a player moves or is traded from one team to another.[565] For all the faith which was placed in the various league commissioners, their decisions received a less than wholly enthusiastic reception in the courts. Thus, courts found that in particular cases, the commissioner had acted without authority,[566] used procedures which lacked fundamental fairness,[567] and personally lacked the impartiality which would command the deference of courts and administrative agencies.[568] Not all judicial decisions have been disapproving, of course,[569] and the leagues held on to their traditional form of government in spite of the occasional defeats.[570]

564. For a discussion which highlights the contrasts between the role of the commissioner in the major baseball and football leagues see *Arbitration in Professional Athletics* in ARBITRATION OF INTEREST DISPUTES — PROCEEDINGS OF THE TWENTY-SIXTH ANNUAL MEETING OF THE NATIONAL ACADEMY OF ARBITRATORS 108-37 (1973) [hereinafter cited as ACADEMY PROCEEDINGS].

565. *See, e.g.,* Professional Sports, Ltd. v. Virginia Squires Basketball Club, 373 F. Supp. 946 (W.D. Tex. 1974); Erving v. Virginia Squires Basketball Club, 349 F. Supp. 716 (E.D.N.Y.), *aff'd,* 468 F.2d 1064 (2d Cir. 1972).

566. *See* Professional Sports, Ltd. v. Virginia Squires Basketball Club, 373 F. Supp. 946, 952 (W.D. Tex. 1974).

567. *See* Professional Sports, Ltd. v. Virginia Squires Basketball Club, 373 F. Supp. 946, 951 (W.D. Tex. 1974); Riko Enterprises, Inc. v. Seattle SuperSonics Corp., 357 F. Supp. 521, 526 (S.D.N.Y. 1973).

568. *See* National Football League Players' Ass'n v. NLRB, 503 F.2d 12, 15 (8th Cir. 1974). *See also* Kapp v. National Football League, 390 F. Supp. 73, 82 (N.D. Cal. 1974); Erving v. Virginia Squires Basketball Club, 349 F. Supp. 716 (E.D.N.Y.), *aff'd,* 468 F.2d 1064 (2d Cir. 1972).

569. *See, e.g.,* Atlanta Nat'l League Baseball Club, Inc. v. Kuhn, 432 F. Supp. 1213 (N.D. Ga. 1977); Charles O. Finley & Co. v. Kuhn, Docket No. 76-C-2358 (N.D. Ill., Mar. 17, 1977); Milwaukee American Ass'n v. Landis, 49 F.2d 298 (N.D. Ill. 1931).

570. This discussion assumes that decision-making by the commissioner with respect to inter-club and player-club disputes will be regarded as an "arbitration." The correctness of that conclusion is not free from doubt, however. Often the documents which establish the commissioner's authority to decide particular matters indicate that his decision will be final, binding and conclusive. These decisions are sometimes made without a prior hearing. Such a dispute resolution procedure bears little resemblance to the typical sort of arbitration, which involves an adversary type hearing. Thus, a question might arise as to whether the commissioner's decisions will always be regarded as the equivalent of arbitration. Resolution of this issue will serve to define generally the body of law which will apply to review commissioner decisions. Hence, it will be determined whether the actions will be reviewed under an arbitration statute or under the more general common law standard applied in situations in which two contracting parties defer to the discretion of another. *See* discussion at §§ 3.06, 3.08 *supra.*

One court has already expressed doubts about whether particular actions of the commissioner constituted an arbitration under the Federal Arbitration Act. In Riko Enterprises, Inc. v. Seattle SuperSonics Corp., 357 F. Supp. 521 (S.D.N.Y. 1973), the court considered the operation of paragraph 24(K) of the NBA constitution and by-laws which provided that certain decisions by the league commissioner would be "final, binding and conclusive." A club which had received a favorable decision from the commissioner sought to enforce the "award" under the FAA. In a footnote, the court noted:

> The Court has serious doubts whether ¶ 24(K) and the NBA constitution constitute "A written provision in . . . a contract evidencing a transaction involving commerce to settle by arbitration a controversy thereafter arising out of such contract or transaction . . . ." [citation to FAA § 2.] The provisions of ¶ 24(K) read more like an agreement that the actions of the commissioner shall be considered as having *been* by arbitration rather than an agreement *to* arbitrate the issues.

357 F. Supp. at 524 n.2 (emphasis in the original).

The court went on to treat the commissioner's action as an arbitration, and ultimately found it deficient because of the absence of an opportunity for a hearing. *See id.*

A somewhat related issue concerning the definition of *arbitration* is considered in 6A A. CORBIN, CORBIN ON CONTRACTS § 1442 (1951) (arbitration compared with appraisal and valuation).

Changes in the commissioner's role were eventually forthcoming, but only with the indirect involvement of the courts. It was, rather, the institution of collective bargaining which produced the most substantial modifications in the traditional approach. In recent years, players' associations in most of the major leagues have been able to substantially diminish the commissioner's role in matters relating to player contracts. That area of the league official's former power has, with a few exceptions, now been replaced by dispute-resolution systems which rely upon independent arbitrators.[571]

It may be useful to examine the controversy which surrounded the former role of the commissioner in player disputes. Such a review, of course, helps to explain why the players' associations bargained so vociferously for a different arrangement. But the dispute which surrounded this feature of league governance is not only of historical interest. In most leagues, the commissioner retains authority over certain types of player-related matters, particularly those relating to discipline.[572] In addition, the commissioner may retain residual powers which become important upon the expiration of any applicable collective bargaining agreement. Finally, the new systems of arbitration attained through player collective bargaining have not affected all segments of the sports industry. Practices in less well-known leagues continue to follow the old pattern, and while the discussion here will focus on the past controversies in the major professional leagues, it should be kept in mind that the issue of the commissioner's role may raise itself again in other enterprises.

While the commissioner's role in mediating interclub disputes has not always been free from controversy,[573] objections were most frequently raised with respect to the commissioner's authority over player personnel. The complaints were particularly vociferous in leagues in which the commissioner was empowered to resolve disputes arising under the standard player contract and to administer the league system for discipline. Thus, the commissioner often had authority to determine the player's right to receive his salary, to control his exercise of personal freedoms,[574] and, indeed, to expel the player from the industry altogether.[575] What precisely were the objections which the players raised? The basic complaint was that given the commissioner's relationship to the team owners and the nature of the administrative tasks which are performed by his office, it was impossible for him to exercise his powers in an impartial manner. It was noted, for example, that the commissioner was generally dependent upon the owners.[576] They usually determined and paid his salary; had

---

571. *See generally* § 5.03 *infra.*

572. *See generally* text at notes 421-24, § 4.15 *supra.*

573. *See, e.g.,* Professional Sports, Ltd. v. Virginia Squires Basketball Club, 373 F. Supp. 946 (W.D. Tex. 1974); Riko Enterprises, Inc. v. Seattle SuperSonics Corp., 357 F. Supp. 521 (S.D.N.Y. 1973).

574. *See, e.g.,* N.Y. Times, July 25, 1973, at 51, col. 6; *id.,* July 28, 1973, at 18, col. 4; *id,* July 31, 1973, at 43, col. 3; *id.,* Aug. 4, 1973, at 15, col. 2 (articles concerning NFL Commissioner Rozelle's one year suspension of Lance Rentzel following the latter's conviction for possession of marijuana and indecent exposure). *See generally* § 3.10 *supra.*

575. *See, e.g.,* Molinas v. National Basketball Association, 190 F. Supp. 241 (S.D.N.Y. 1961); Molinas v. Podoloff, 133 N.Y.S.2d 743 (Sup. Ct. 1954). *See generally* ACADEMY PROCEEDINGS 122-24 (remarks of Edward Garvey, Executive Director, National Football League Players Association).

576. *See generally* Davis, *Self-Regulation in Baseball, 1909-71* in GOVERNMENT AND THE SPORTS BUSINESS 349, 377-82 (R. Noll, ed. 1974).

authority to modify the documents which defined his powers; and they retained the right to fire him. With this degree of control, it was alleged, the commissioner was not likely to render decisions which were contrary to the owners' basic interests.[577]

In addition to this concern for the owners' influence over the commissioner's loyalties, the players objected that the commissioner was so involved in matters which came before him for arbitration that it was unrealistic to expect that he could treat them with disinterest. For example, in addition to his role as arbitrator, the commissioner was often given power to promulgate rules concerning such things as player conduct and personnel procedures.[578] He might later be called to arbitrate a case in which the meaning of the rule, or his authority to promulgate it, was called into question. The players complained that he could hardly be expected to be objective when his own actions were under review.[579] In other situations the commissioner was empowered to decide player complaints about disciplinary actions which he himself had taken.[580] As in the case of rule-making, the commissioner ended up reviewing his own action.[581]

The club owners raised a number of points in defense of the extensive powers given to the commissioner. It was asserted, for example, that even though the commissioner was selected and paid by the owners, it was in their best interests to insure that he acted impartially.[582] The basic concern was for the integrity of the particular sport, and it was contended that if the commissioner were to act in a truly arbitrary manner, the public would lose confidence in the enterprise and fail to support it.[583] Thus, considerable care went into the selection of the commissioner, and in the words of one owner, "We pay him to be impartial." [584] While someone who was more independent could protect the integrity of the game,[585] it was felt that there was also a need for centralized control in the administration of the league. This insured that rules were uniformly applied and that all personnel were treated equally with respect to both the administration of their contracts and their vulnerability to discipline. Ultimately this uniformity would tend to preserve the equality of competition which is thought to be the primary ingredient of the financial success of professional sports.[586] This interest in centralized control also was said to explain why the commissioner was given authority to both formulate rules and interpret them.

Some case law has been developed on these questions of the commissioner's role as arbitrator, but the precedent is meager and there are still many fundamental questions which have yet to be explored in litigation. The case law which does exist, while indicating some skepticism about the commissioner's

---

577. *See generally* ACADEMY PROCEEDINGS 109-13, 123 (remarks of Richard Moss, Counsel, Major League Baseball Players Association and Edward Garvey, Executive Director, NFLPA).

578. *See, e.g.,* CONSTITUTION AND BY-LAWS FOR THE NATIONAL FOOTBALL LEAGUE § 8.5 (1972): "The Commissioner shall interpret and from time to time establish policy and procedure in respect to the provisions of the Constitution and By-Laws and any enforcement thereof."

579. *See* ACADEMY PROCEEDINGS 123 (remarks of Edward Garvey, Executive Director, NFLPA).

580. *See id.* at 125.

581. *See also* National Football League Players Ass'n v. NLRB, 503 F.2d 12 (8th Cir. 1974).

582. *But see* Davis, *Self-Regulation in Baseball, 1909-71, supra* note 576, at 380-81.

583. *See also* Molinas v. Podoloff, 133 N.Y.S.2d 743 (Sup. Ct. 1954).

584. ACADEMY PROCEEDINGS 123.

585. *See generally* Comment, *Discipline in Professional Sports: The Need for Player Protection,* 60 GEO. L.J. 771, 794-97 (1972).

586. *See* ACADEMY PROCEEDINGS 133-37 (remarks of Theodore Kheel, Labor Counsel to the Management Council of the National Football League).

role, is insufficient to permit an accurate assessment of future trends.[587] But with that caveat, the general contours of the legal issues in this area can be outlined.

An analysis of the commissioner's role will suggest that the commissioner's relationship to the owners presents a different legal issue than is suggested by the fact that he performs the dual functions of administrator and arbitrator. With respect to the former, the basic question would be whether the owners' control over the commissioner's salary, position, and powers results in the sort of partiality which will invalidate an arbitrator's actions. There is no doubt that a finding of partiality will permit a court to vacate an arbitrator's award. This was true at common law [588] and is true under the FAA, which specifically identifies "evident partiality" as a grounds for denying the enforceability of an award.[589] But the meaning of partiality in this context is somewhat tempered by the realities of commercial arbitration.[590] Unlike judges, arbitrators are not expected to remain aloof from the transactions which give rise to the disputes which are presented to them. Indeed, arbitrators are often specifically chosen for their experience and expertise in the particular field, and these qualities often exist because the arbitrator works in the relevant industry.[591] Thus, it is clear from the cases that neither the arbitrator's friendship with one of the parties [592] nor his prior or subsequent business dealings [593] will necessarily provide a basis for disqualification.[594] Moreover, while it is clear that the arbitrator has an obligation to disclose any relationship he has with one of the parties,[595] the courts are inclined to find that a party has waived the right to object if he agrees to the arbitration with knowledge of the arbitrator's relationship with the other party.[596]

When the relationship between league owners and the commissioner is tested against these principles, it is far from certain that a proper basis for legal objection existed.[597] The wide publicity which has been given to this relationship

---

587. Various proposals for increased government intervention into the operation of sports leagues would have the effect of considerably reducing the role of the commissioner. *See, e.g.,* Davis, *Self-Regulation in Baseball, 1909-71, supra* note 576, at 382-86; Comment, *Discipline in Professional Sports: The Need for Player Protection, supra* note 585, at 794-97.

588. *See generally* M. DOMKE, THE LAW AND PRACTICE OF COMMERCIAL ARBITRATION §§ 21.02-21.03 (1968) [hereinafter cited as DOMKE, COMMERCIAL ARBITRATION]; Annot., 65 A.L.R.2d 755, 759-61 (1959).

589. 9 U.S.C. § 10 (1970).

590. *See generally* Comment, *Bias, Fraud, Misconduct and Partiality of the Arbitrator,* 22 ARB. J. 161 (1967); Comment, *Judicial Review of Arbitration: The Role of Public Policy,* 58 NW. U.L. REV. 545 (1963); Comment, *Commercial Arbitration Under the Federal Act: Expanding the Scope of Judicial Review,* 35 U. PITT. L. REV. 799 (1974).

591. *See* Commonwealth Coating Corp. v. Continental Cas. Co., 393 U.S. 144, 150, 21 L. Ed. 2d 301, 89 S. Ct. 337 (1968) (White, J., concurring).

592. *See* Kentucky River Mills v. Jackson, 206 F.2d 111 (6th Cir. 1953).

593. *See, e.g.,* Sanko S.S. Co. v. Cook Indus., Inc., 495 F.2d 1260 (2d Cir. 1973); Cook Indus., Inc. v. C. Itoh & Co., 449 F.2d 106 (2d Cir. 1971); Ilios Shipping & Trading Corp. v. American Anthracite & Bituminous Coal Corp., 148 F. Supp. 698 (S.D.N.Y.), *aff'd,* 245 F.2d 873 (2d Cir. 1957).

594. *See generally* DOMKE, COMMERCIAL ARBITRATION § 21.02.

595. *See* Commonwealth Coatings Corp. v. Continental Cas. Co., 393 U.S. 144 (1968).

596. *See, e.g.,* Sanko S.S. Co. v. Cook Indus., Inc., 495 F.2d 1260, 1264-65 (2d Cir. 1973); Garfield & Co. v. Weist, 432 F.2d 849, 854 (2d Cir. 1970). *See generally* DOMKE, COMMERCIAL ARBITRATION § 21.04.

597. *But see* Kapp v. National Football League, 390 F. Supp. 73, 82 (N.D. Cal. 1974), quoted in note 608 *infra.*

would seem to provide the necessary disclosure. Moreover, it would seem that there is nothing inherently improper about a system in which only one party pays the arbitrator's salary, if the decisions reached are otherwise just.[598] Despite the player's resistance to this notion, it would seem that the fairness of the arbitrator may be judged on a basis other than the source of his compensation. Finally, while the owners do have control over the commissioner's powers and tenure, consideration must be given to the provisions of the league by-laws which protect the commissioner from removal by a small number of owners.[599] Thus, particularly on matters which affect only a single club, the commissioner may be insulated from vindictiveness on the part of a club owner.

This is not to suggest that the players were not rightly concerned that a system of commissioner-arbitrator is less desirable than other alternatives. Indeed, there are many difficulties which arise from this system.[600] But reliance on the commissioner is not so obviously inappropriate as to support a generalized legal objection. Thus, in looking for an outlet for their objections, it is appropriate that the players have relied on means other than those traditionally used to nullify an arbitrator's actions through the judicial process.[601]

The matter of the overlap between the commissioner's role as administrator and arbitrator requires a different analysis. It can be noted that this duality did not affect all of the commissioner's actions as arbitrator and was a concern primarily in those cases in which the commissioner undertook to review a rule or action which he previously directed. There are two important policies which came into conflict in these cases. On the one hand, there is the policy which favors giving the parties considerable freedom to devise a system of arbitration suitable to their needs.[602] In a particular industry, there may well be situations which are best handled through reliance on a single administrator. With respect to the matters of player discipline in professional sports, for example, an argument can be made that the concern for public confidence demands that the league be capable of taking firm and swift actions [603] and that this is best achieved by empowering a single person to administer the discipline system. On the other hand, legislative and judicial approval of the use of arbitration as a

---

598. *See generally* DOMKE, COMMERCIAL ARBITRATION § 42.01.

599. Under the National Football League Constitution, for instance, modification of Commissioner Rozelle's contract requires the affirmative vote of 2/3 of the league members, as well as approval by 12 of the 15 clubs which were members of the league in 1966. *See* CONSTITUTION AND BY-LAWS FOR THE NATIONAL FOOTBALL LEAGUE §§ 8.1 (b) & (c) (1972).

600. *See* ACADEMY PROCEEDINGS 108-16 (remarks of Richard Moss, Counsel, Major League Baseball Players' Association). *See also* Davis, *Self-Regulation in Baseball, 1909-71, supra* note 576, at 377-82.

601. The baseball players' association has recently received the owners' agreement to use neutral arbitration for many types of disputes. *See* discussion at notes 417-18, 422, § 4.15 *supra;* and at notes 539-41, § 4.18 *supra. See also* note 609 *infra.*

It should be noted that there are systems of government in other sports areas in which the rule-making and enforcement functions are performed by the same person or persons. This is true, for example, with respect to publicly-regulated sports supervised by an athletic commission or similar body. The powers of such groups are discussed in § 2.27 *supra.* Critics of the similar multiplicity of roles played by the league commissioner will point out that public athletic commissions have a much different legal status. They are typically agents of the state, and thus their actions must meet constitutional standards. The league commissioner, on the other hand, is typically not imbued with such state-action and the bases for judicial review of his actions are much more limited.

602. *See* DOMKE, COMMERCIAL ARBITRATION §§ 21.01-21.02.

603. *Compare* Molinas v. Podoloff, 133 N.Y.S.2d 743 (Sup. Ct. 1954).

substitute for traditional forms of adjudication seems to assume that at least some type of review will be made of an injured party's grievance.[604] If the only review afforded is that undertaken by the party who created the conflict, then surely the screening function normally attributed to arbitration is subverted.[605]

The latter policy favoring meaningful review of the commissioner's action has already found some expression in the reported decisions. In one case, the NFL commissioner had adopted a rule prohibiting players from leaving the bench to join a fight in progress on the field.[606] The players' association alleged that this was a unilateral change in employment conditions and should have been subjected to negotiation between the parties. Before reaching the merits of the complaint, the administrative law judge, and later the NLRB, had to decide whether the complaint should not have first been submitted to the parties' agreed-upon arbitrator, the commissioner. While deferral to arbitration is the Board's normal policy, both the administrative law judge and the Board declined to do so in this case. The reason was that the commissioner was not a disinterested party and the policies which underlie the deferral rule would not be satisfied "where the arbitrator was determining the merits of his own conduct." [607]

The issue in this case was not one which involved the enforceability of the arbitrator's award, but rather concerned the scope of a federal labor policy. Nonetheless, the implication is clear that the absence of effective review sets commissioner-dominated proceedings apart from the more typical arbitration.[608] Before a court will give credence to the other policy identified above — that favoring the parties' own definition of their dispute-resolution devices — it will need some evidence that in fact there was effective consent to the system of unilateral arbitration before the commissioner. That consent is likely to be found only where it is shown that such a system was approved in a vigorous collective bargaining session.[609]

---

604. *See* note 570 *supra.*

605. *Cf.* Professional Sports, Ltd. v. Virginia Squires Basketball Club, 373 F. Supp. 946 (W.D. Tex. 1974).

606. *See* National Football League Players Ass'n v. NLRB, 503 F.2d 12 (8th Cir. 1974).

607. *Id.* at 15.

608. *See* also Kapp v. National Football League, 390 F. Supp. 73, 82 (N.D. Cal. 1974).

   [T]he so-called "one-man rule" . . . , vesting the final decision in the NFL Commissioner, is also patently unreasonable (particularly where considered in light of principles of *impartial* arbitration embodied in the Federal Arbitration Act . . . and underlying the decision of the Supreme Court in Commonwealth Corp. v. Casualty Co. . . .) insofar as that unilateral kind of arbitration is used to interpret or enforce other NFL rules involving restrictions on the rights of players or clubs to free employment choice.

609. The 1973 agreement between the baseball clubs and the Players' Association seems to satisfy the consent requirement suggested in the text. The agreement generally introduces a major reform of the old commissioner-arbitrator system by providing for arbitration before a more traditional tripartite panel, consisting of one arbitrator selected by the club, one by the players and the third designated by the other two arbitrators. Interestingly, however, there is one important exception which retains for the commissioner a role he formerly played. The Basic Agreement provides a special category of grievances for disciplinary actions taken by the commissioner "involving the preservation of the integrity of, or the maintenance of public confidence in, the game of baseball." For actions of this sort, review is afforded, but it is in the form of a hearing before the commissioner. *See* Baseball Collective Bargaining Agreement art. X(A)(1)(b). It is also provided that collective negotiations on this matter can be reopened in any year. This type of system, which reflects the product of considerable negotiation between players and clubs, is entitled to considerable deference in the courts. The objection raised in National Football League Players Ass'n v. NLRB, 503 F.2d 12 (8th Cir. 1974), discussed *supra* at notes 606-07, would seem to be less compelling when applied in the context of the collective agreement in baseball.

§ 4.20. Grounds for Vacating an Arbitrator's Award.

Perhaps the most important question in the law of arbitration concerns the grounds upon which a court will vacate an award entered by an arbitrator. The answer to this question identifies the extent to which arbitration will truly be an alternative to traditional court adjudication of contract claims. In considering this topic, we again take the approach of treating separately the standards applied to commercial and labor arbitration. As with several other issues we have considered, the present topic is one for which it is difficult to make bright line distinctions between the principles applied to the two types of arbitration. Indeed, as will be seen, the courts often do not hesitate to take standards derived under the FAA and apply them in labor cases. We begin by considering the issue of judical review of arbitrator's awards in the commercial setting.

a. Commercial Arbitration. The geneal trend of judicial policy concerning the reviewability of arbitral awards is readily apparent. An examination of the case law clearly establishes that courts exercise great restraint in reviewing arbitration awards and will set them aside only in extreme cases.[610] This trend was established at early common law and continues today.[611] As the Supreme Court noted in an early arbitration case:

> Arbitrators are judges chosen by the parties to decide matters submitted to them, finally and without appeal. As a mode of settling disputes, it should receive every encouragement from courts of equity. If the award is within the submission, and contains the honest decision of the arbitrators, after a full and fair hearing of the parties, a court of equity will not set it aside for error either in law or fact.[612]

This general policy of judicial deference is supported by at least two different considerations. On the one hand, it is felt that a party who has freely bargained away his right to judicial remedies [613] — and presumably received something of value in return — ought not be allowed to abandon his bargain.[614] The mere fact that a party is disappointed in the outcome of the choice he has made does not warrant a disregard to the basic contractual nature of arbitration.[615] In addition, a policy of judicial restraint is necessary if the desirability of arbitration as a mechanism for dispute resolution is to be maintained. Parties choose arbitration in part because they want the greater efficiency and cost-savings

---

610. *See generally* D. DOBBS, HANDBOOK ON THE LAW OF REMEDIES § 12.27 at 941-43 (1973); Glick, *Bias, Fraud, Misconduct and Partiality of the Arbitrator,* 22 ARB. J. (n.s.) 161 (1967); Jolet, *Judicial Review of Arbitration: The Judicial Attitude,* 45 CORNELL L.Q. 519 (1960); Comment, *When May An Arbitrator's Award Be Vacated,* 7 DEPAUL L. REV. 236 (1958); Comment, *Judicial Review of Arbitration: The Role of Public Policy,* 58 NW. U.L. REV. 545 (1963).

611. Before the present policy of non-intervention by the courts could become fully effective, it was necessary for courts to overcome their earlier reluctance to accept the general enforceability of agreements to arbitrate. *See* M. DOMKE, THE LAW AND PRACTICE OF COMMERCIAL ARBITRATION §§ 34.01-34.02 (1968) [hereinafter cited as DOMKE, COMMERCIAL ARBITRATION]; 6A A. CORBIN, CORBIN ON CONTRACTS §§ 1433, 1439 (1962) [hereinafter cited as CORBIN ON CONTRACTS].

612. Burchell v. Marsh, 58 U.S. (17 How.) 344, 349, 15 L. Ed. 96 (1854).

613. There may be an initial issue as to whether the party acted freely when he consented to the arbitration provision. If the arbitration agreement is boilerplate in a non-negotiable, standard form contract, courts may either be reluctant to require a party to arbitrate or may scrutinize the arbitration more closely than they otherwise would. *See* DOMKE, COMMERCIAL ARBITRATION § 5.04; Goldberg, *A Supreme Court Justice Looks at Arbitration,* 20 ARB. J. 13, 16 (1965).

614. *See* 6A CORBIN ON CONTRACTS § 1432, at 385-87, § 1433, at 395.

615. *See, e. g.,* Gramling v. Food Mach. & Chem. Corp., 151 F. Supp. 853, 856 (W.D.S.C. 1957).

which result from a less formal hearing.[616] If judicial review were readily available these advantages would be lost as arbitration would become simply a preliminary step to litigation.[617] Consistent with the present judicial and legislative policies favoring the enforceability of arbitration agreements, the limited availability of judicial review insures that the incentives to resort to private dispute settlement are retained.[618]

The Federal Arbitration Act specifies certain circumstances in which an award may be vacated. Under section 10 of the statute, an arbitrator's decision may be reversed:

(a) Where the award was procured by corruption, fraud or undue means.

(b) Where there was evident partiality or corruption in the arbitrators or either of them.

(c) Where the arbitrators were guilty of misconduct in refusing to postpone the hearing, or in refusing to hear evidence pertinent and material to the controversy; or any other misbehavior by which the rights of any party have been prejudiced.

(d) Where the arbitrators exceeded their powers, or so imperfectly executed them that a mutual, final, and definite award upon the subject matter submitted was not made.[619]

This portion of the statute is by no means a model of clarity. Some of the terms chosen — such as "fraud" — have no single, readily identifiable meaning in the arbitration context.[620] While that characteristic of the statute has necessitated considerable judicial interpretation, the statutory classifications leave no doubt that it is not the function of the courts to determine whether the arbitrator's decision was "correct." The nature of judicial review is not a hearing *de novo,* but rather an inquiry into any allegations of impropriety or lack of authority in the arbitrator's determination.[621] Thus, even though the arbitrator's decision is based upon a misinterpretation of the law or upon erroneous findings of fact, it will be enforced if there is no other evidence that it was improperly entered.[622]

Courts have not felt compelled to treat the various statutory classifications as each presenting a precisely defined rule with respect to their power to vacate awards.[623] Largely because of the looseness of the criteria specified in the

---

616. See discussion at notes 410-15, § 4.15 *supra.*

617. *See, e.g.,* Shahmoon Indus., Inc. v. Steelworkers Local 5216, 263 F. Supp. 10, 14 (D.N.J. 1966). *See also* Burchell v. Marsh, 58 U.S. (17 How.) 344, 249 (1854); "A contrary course . . . would make an award the commencement, not the end, of litigation."

618. *See generally* DOMKE, COMMERCIAL ARBITRATION, *Introduction* ch. 34.

619. 9 U.S.C. § 10 (1970).

620. *See, e.g.,* Comment, *Commercial Arbitration Under the Federal Act: Expanding the Scope of Judicial Review,* 35 U. PITT. L. REV. 799, 806-08 (1974).

621. *See, e.g.,* Wilko v. Swan, 346 U.S. 427, 98 L. Ed. 168, 74 S. Ct. 182 (1953); Aerojet-Gen. Corp. v. American Arbitration Ass'n, 478 F.2d 248 (9th Cir. 1973); Timken Co. v. Steelworkers Local 1123, 482 F.2d 1017 (6th Cir. 1973); San Martine Compania Navegacion, S.A. v. Saguenay Terminals, Ltd., 293 F.2d 796 (9th Cir. 1961).

622. *See, e.g.,* Wilko v. Swan, 346 U.S. 427 (1953); Office of Supply, Gov't of the Republic of Korea v. New York Navigation Co., 469 F.2d 377 (2d Cir. 1972); Raytheon Co. v. Rheem Mfg. Co., 322 F. 2d 173 (9th Cir. 1963); Fukaya Trading Co., S.A. v. Eastern Marine Corp., 322 F. Supp. 278 (E.D. La. 1971).

623. *See* Comment, *Commercial Arbitration under Federal Act: Expanding the Scope of Judicial Review, supra* note 620, at 805-09.

statute, the courts have chosen to regard section 10 as an effort by Congress to identify only its general concerns about the integrity of the arbitration process. Under this approach, judges have assumed considerable discretion in molding the rough classifications of section 10 into workable rules. Although other grounds for vacating awards are occasionally used, there are basically three types of objections which are asserted by parties seeking to overturn the arbitrator's decision. Thus, it may be contended that the award should not be sustained because (a) the arbitrator exceeded his authority, (b) he was biased or partial, or (c) his deliberations failed to meet rudimentary requirements for meaningful review of the controversy before him.

The first two of these grounds for vacation are treated elsewhere in this chapter. As previously mentioned, an arbitrator is a creature of contract and has no greater authority than that which is granted to him by the parties' contract.[624] Thus, the arbitrator cannot decide an issue which is not within the parties' definition of the scope of the arbitration clause.[625] Similarly, the arbitrator must follow the parties' specifications on procedural matters, including such things as the nature of the hearing, the types of evidence to be considered and so on.[626] Where the arbitrator acts in disregard of the authority given him, his actions are a nullity.[627] If the unauthorized actions can be separated from other actions within the arbitrator's power, the latter are entitled to judicial enforcement.[628]

The issue of the arbitrator's partiality is considered in an earlier section in connection with the commissioner's role as arbitrator.[629] That discussion includes an outline of the relevant principles which emerge from the general case law under the federal act. The basic point to be made is that there is strong policy in favor of assuring each party an untainted review of his case,[630] but the concept of partiality in this context must take account of the realities of commercial arbitration, which often utilize arbitrators who have substantial involvement in the particular industry.[631] Thus, the fact of a prior or existing relationship with one of the parties does not produce automatic disqualification, but does give rise to an obligation in the arbitration to make known the extent of the involvement.[632]

It is with respect to the third category of objections listed above that the courts have had the greatest difficulty in expressing the standard of review to be applied. In one line of cases, it is said that an arbitrator's award will be

624. See § 4.16 supra.

625. See DOMKE, COMMERCIAL ARBITRATION §§ 12.01-12.02.

626. See Professional Sports, Ltd. v. Virginia Squires Basketball Club, 373 F. Supp. 946 (W.D. Tex. 1974).

627. See, e.g., Orion Shipping & Trading Co. v. Eastern States Petroleum Corp. of Panama, S.A., 312 F.2d 299 (2d Cir. 1963); Nuest v. Westinghouse Air Brake Co., 313 F. Supp. 1228 (S.D. Ill. 1970); States Marine Corp. v. Power S.S., Ltd., 127 F. Supp. 943 (S.D.N.Y. 1954).

628. Compare United Steelworkers v. Enterprise Wheel & Car Corp., 269 F.2d 327 (4th Cir. 1959), rev'd on other grounds, 363 U.S. 593 (1960).

629. See § 4.19 supra.

630. See Commonwealth Coatings Corp. v. Continental Cas. Co., 393 U.S. 144, 147, 21 L. Ed. 2d 301, 89 S. Ct. 337 (1968).

631. See generally DOMKE, COMMERCIAL ARBITRATION §§ 21.01-21.02; Glick, Bias, Fraud, Misconduct and Partiality of the Arbitrator, supra note 610.

632. See, e.g., Sanko S.S. Co. v. Cook Indus., Inc., 495 F.2d 1260 (2d Cir. 1973); Cook Indus., Inc. v. Itoh & Co., 449 F.2d 106 (2d Cir. 1971).

overturned if it is made with "manifest disregard for the law." [633] Other cases express the standard in terms of whether the arbitrator's decision is rationally related to the parties' substantive contract and their commercial relationship.[634] On its surface, at least, these two concepts would seem to deal with different considerations: the former asks whether there was a manifest disregard of legal principles, while the latter requires allegiance to the spirit and intention of the agreement. But the two are often treated together,[635] and analysis of the concepts would suggest that they share a unifying theme. Each concept is used by the courts as a means of expressing the concern that despite the great freedom afforded the arbitrator, each side is entitled to a consideration of his case which has at least the most elementary characteristics of a disinterested review. When a party consents to the arbitration remedy, he surely does not intend to empower the arbitrator to act totally irrationally, but rather is likely to have assumed that arbitration would truly be a *review* of the merits of his case.[636] If the arbitrator ignores the essence of the parties' contract, the parties have not received the type of evaluation which is embodied in the concept of "arbitration."[637]

Although there are rarely cases in which an arbitrator's award is actually overturned on these grounds, courts have undertaken to elaborate on the concepts. Thus it is said that a manifest disregard of the law "must be something beyond and different from a mere error in the law or failure on the part of the arbitrators to understand or apply the law." [638] Often the parties choose arbitration, not because they desire an interpretation that strictly adheres to prevailing legal principles, but rather because they want a disinterested, knowledgeable reading of their contract.[639] The fact that the arbitrator reaches a non-legalistic decision, or one different from that which a court might render, is not grounds for reversal by a court.[640] By the same token, if the award is lacking in "fundamental rationality," it will be overturned.[641] But "if the

---

633. *See* Wilko v. Swan, 346 U.S. 427 (1953); San Martine Compania Navegacion, S.A. v. Saguenay Terminals, Ltd., 293 F.2d 796 (9th Cir. 1961).

634. *See, e.g.,* Swift Indus., Inc. v. Botany Inc., 466 F.2d 1125 (3d Cir. 1972). *Compare* United Steelworkers v. Enterprise Wheel & Car Corp., 363 U.S. 593 (1960).

635. *See, e.g.,* Swift Indus., Inc. v. Botany Indus., Inc., 466 F.2d 1125, 1129-31 (3d Cir. 1972); San Martine Compania Navegacion, S.A. v. Saguenay Terminals, Ltd., 293 F.2d 796 (9th Cir. 1961); Comment, *Commercial Arbitration Under the Federal Act: Expanding the Scope of Judicial Review, supra* note 620, at 810-12.

636. The common law notions of the reviewability of arbitration awards embodied these same principles. Thus, it was said that when a party sought

> To impeach it [an award] on the ground that the arbitrators had reached a wrong conclusion, it was incumbent on plaintiff to show clearly that this conclusion was so at variance with any conclusion which could legitimately be drawn from the facts and evidence before them as to imply bad faith or a failure to exercise an honest judgment on their part.

Larson v. Nygaard, 148 Minn. 104, 108, 180 N.W. 1002, 1003 (1921).

637. One facet of the problem of defining exactly what is meant by the concept of arbitration is considered in note 570, § 4.19 *supra*.

638. San Martine Compania Navegacion, S.A. v. Saguenay Terminals, Ltd., 293 F.2d 796, 801 (9th Cir. 1961).

639. *See* St. Antoine, *Judicial Review of Labor Arbitration Awards: A Second Look at* Enterprise Wheel *and Its Progeny,* 75 MICH. L. REV. 1137, 1139-42 (1977) (discussion relevant to commercial arbitration).

640. *See, e.g.,* Sapp v. Barenfield, 34 Cal. 2d 515, 212 P.2d 233 (1949); D. DOBBS, HANDBOOK ON THE LAW OF REMEDIES 942 (1973).

641. Swift Indus., Inc. v. Botany Indus., Inc., 466 F.2d 1125, 1130 (3d Cir. 1972).

interpretation can in any rational way be derived from the agreement," it must be sustained.[642] An award will be found to be rational if it can fairly be said to be based on the terms of the parties' agreement, as interpreted in light of any prior practices or understandings.

It is clear that these concepts will not afford a basis for relief if the arbitrator has minimum familiarity with the industry and handles the case with some care. Only in the event of total inadvertence or gross incompetence will relief be available.[643] In professional sports the arbitrators are normally selected with some deliberation because each side understands the importance of what is at stake. While there are many arbitrators who are unfamiliar with the sports industry, and its special customs and usages, both sides are aware of this fact and carefully scrutinize their selection of arbitrators. It will be an extremely rare case in which a sports arbitration is decided by an arbitrator who is totally unprepared to handle it.[644]

b. Labor Arbitration. One area in which there has been a discernible coalescing of principles from the respective spheres of commercial and labor arbitration involves the matter of judicial review of arbitral awards. On some aspects of the reviewability issue, the application of common principles is quite explicit. Although a few court decisions continue to resist the notion, there is respectable authority for the view that a court may overturn a labor arbitrator's decision where there are "procedural" irregularities of the sort identified in section 10 of the FAA.[644.1] Thus, if there is proof that the arbitrator was biased, the award will not be enforced. This principle is applied in cases in which the arbitrator has a relationship with one of the parties that might influence the objectivity of his decision-making.[644.2] By the same token, consistent with section 10(c) of the FAA, a labor arbitration award may be overturned if a party's case is seriously prejudiced by the arbitrator's refusal to hear important evidence. To bring itself within this principle, the complaining party must make a compelling case. Normally the arbitrator will be given extreme leeway in

---

642. Ludwig Honold Mfg. Co. v. Fletcher, 405 F.2d 1123, 1128 (3d Cir. 1969).

There is some question as to which part of section 10 of the Federal Arbitration Act supports the application of the concepts of manifest disregard and fundamental rationality. It has variously been said to derive from subsection (d) which permits vacation where arbitrators have exceeded their authority, see Amicizia Societa Navegazione v. Chilean Nitrate & Iodine Sales Corp., 274 F.2d 805, 808 (2d Cir. 1960); subsection (a) which permits the rejection of awards secured by undue means, see San Martine Compania Navegacion, S.A. v. Saguenay Terminals, Ltd., 293 F.2d 796, 801 (9th Cir. 1961); and from subsection (b) which condemns partiality. See id.

643. Perhaps the best example of a case in which the application of these principles led to a reversal is Swift Indus., Inc. v. Botany Indus., Inc., 466 F.2d 1125 (3d Cir. 1972), where the arbitrator ordered one party to post a cash bond in the amount of $6 million. Since the party's maximum liability would not exceed $1.5 million, the court found the arbitrator's order to lack fundamental rationality and, therefore, ordered it set aside.

644. Cf. Professional Sports, Ltd. v. Virginia Squires Basketball Club, 373 F. Supp. 946 (W.D. Tex. 1974).

644.1. Pietro Scalzitti Co. v. Operating Engineers, 351 F.2d 576 (7th Cir. 1965); R. GORMAN, BASIC TEXT ON LABOR LAW 599-600 (1976) [hereinafter cited as GORMAN, LABOR LAW]; O. FAIRWEATHER, PRACTICE AND PROCEDURE IN LABOR ARBITRATION 3-7, 74-78 (1973); Aksen, Some Legal and Practical Problems of Labor Arbitration in ARBITRATING LABOR CASES 163 (N. LEVIN, ed., 1974).

644.2. Holodnak v. Avco Corp., 381 F. Supp. 191 (D. Conn. 1974), modified, 514 F.2d 285 (2d Cir. 1975); Buski v. Eastern Auto. Forwarding Co., 396 F.2d 32 (3d Cir. 1968); cf. Colony Liquor Distributors, Inc. v. Teamsters, 34 App. Div. 2d 1060, 312 N.Y.S.2d 403 (1970).

controlling the introduction and use of evidence. It is only when a party can show that the exclusion or disregard of evidence destroyed the fairness of the proceeding that a court will entertain an objection based on these grounds.[644.3]

As in commercial arbitration, the most important question confronted in labor arbitration concerns when, if ever, a court may reverse an arbitrator's decision, not because of bias or other "procedural" impropriety, but rather because it is thought to be substantively infirm. With respect to commercial agreements, we saw that in general, courts will intervene only if the arbitrator's award is found to be an irrational interpretation of the parties' agreement. The Supreme Court has addressed this matter of substantive reviewability in the labor context, and while it employs somewhat different terminology, the view put forth suggests a similarly limited opportunity for judicial intervention. The Court stated that

> [A]n arbitrator is confined to interpretation and application of the collective bargaining agreement; he does not sit to dispense his own brand of industrial justice. He may of course look for guidance from many sources, yet his award is legitimate only so long as it draws its essence from the collective bargaining agreement. When the arbitrator's words manifest an infidelity to this obligation, courts have no choice but to refuse enforcement of the award.[644.4]

In another case, the court made clear that the arbitrator is not limited to merely interpreting the words of the contract, but may also properly consult "the industrial common law," including practices both in the industry and in the particular company.[644.5] As is true with respect to commercial arbitration, it is not a sufficient objection that the arbitrator chooses not to follow a substantive "law," whether statutory or otherwise, which might control the controversy if it were tried in court. Again, the role of the arbitrator is primarily that of a contract reader, and his main task is to provide an interpretation of the parties' agreement.[644.6] The fact that a court, or another arbitrator, would have read the contract differently is not a basis for objection.

When is a court likely to find that the arbitrator's award does not "draw its essence from the collective bargaining agreement?" As might be imagined, this is a determination which is greatly influenced by the peculiar orientation of the court to which the issue is presented. The decided cases reflect noticeable variations in the extent to which the courts are willing to allow the arbitrator's interpretation to stray from the language of the parties' contract. While this state of affairs makes generalizations very risky, it is possible to identify certain trends in the manner in which various types of cases are treated. At one extreme are those cases in which the arbitrator enters an award that directly contradicts a specific term of the parties' contract. Unless some alternative explanation can be found outside the contract — such as in common law of the shop — the award will be treated as one that does not have the requisite fidelity to the parties' agreement. Thus, where a contract expressly granted the employer the right to discharge striking employees, the court was prepared to overturn an

---

644.3. *See* Textile Workers v. American Thread Co., 291 F.2d 894 (4th Cir. 1961); Harvey Aluminum v. United Steelworkers, 263 F. Supp. 488 (C.D. Cal. 1967). *See generally* O. FAIRWEATHER, PRACTICE AND PROCEDURE IN LABOR ARBITRATION 209-40 (1973).

644.4. United Steelworkers v. Enterprise Wheel & Car Corp., 363 U.S. 593, 596-97 (1960). *See generally* T. KHEEL, LABOR LAW (18E BUSINESS ORGANIZATIONS 1974) § 24.05[2].

644.5. United Steelworkers v. Warrior & Gulf Navigation Co., 363 U.S. 574 (1960).

644.6. *See generally* St. Antoine, *Judicial Review of Labor Arbitration Awards: A Second Look at Enterprise Wheel and its Progeny,* 75 MICH. L. REV. 1137 (1977).

arbitrator's decision which sought to compromise the grievances of discharged employees by ordering their reinstatement without back pay.[644.7]

At the other extreme are cases in which the contract specifically gives the arbitrator discretion to decide a matter. For example, the agreement may provide that, within a specified range, the arbitrator is to choose the punishment to be imposed for a particular disciplinable offense. In this type of situation, the arbitrator's decision is effectively unreviewable on substantive grounds. If review is to be had, it will occur only upon a showing of procedural impropriety, such as bias, fraud, or the like.

Another significant class of cases involves those in which the arbitrator is asked to decide a matter that comes within his general arbitral powers but which is not clearly controlled by a specific provision of the contract. It may be that the contract is silent on the particular point, or that a relevant term is vague on a critical matter.[644.8] Or it may be that the arbitrator finds a term to be unspecific when viewed in the light of external evidence.[644.9] In these situations, the prevailing tendency is for the courts to accept the arbitrator's decision. Here the rationale behind the general policy of judicial deference plays a significant role: the arbitrator was chosen by the parties to be their contract reader; they bargained for his interpretation of the contract as a substitute for the traditional court adjudication, and this aspect of their bargain ought to be respected.

The cases most likely to be heavily contested are those in which the arbitrator interprets a term of the contract in a manner that seems to conflict with the spirit of the agreement or industrial common law. A review of the cases involving awards with this characteristic reveals a decided tendency on the part of the courts to accept the arbitrator's decision.[644.10] While this trend might seem surprising at first blush, it can be defended in most situations. The explanation lies in the nature of the objection which is raised. For a court to say that an award contravenes the "spirit" of the agreement largely begs the question, for the "spirit" of the contract can be discerned only by a process of interpretation. But, of course, it is the arbitrator, and not the court, who has been designated to decipher the contract's meaning.[644.11] Thus, for the court to make the determination of what is or is not consistent with the "spirit" of the undertaking is to involve the court in the very process which was to be left to the sole province of the arbitrator.

While this analysis will suggest that the court must usually stay its hand, there appears to be an outside limit to the arbitrator's prerogatives in the type of case described. It is not, however, a limit which will offer much encouragement to a disappointed party. Before a court will intervene, it must find that the award is not merely dubious or even erroneous,[644.12] but rather that

644.7. Amanda Bent Bolt Co. v. Automobile Workers, 451 F.2d 1277 (6th Cir. 1971); Falls Stamping & Welding Co. v. Automobile Workers, 416 F. Supp. 574 (N.D. Ohio 1976). See also Torrington v. Metal Prods. Workers, 362 F.2d 677 (2d Cir. 1966).

644.8. Musicians v. Philadelphia Orchestra Ass'n, 252 F. Supp. 787 (E.D. Pa. 1966).

644.9. See, e.g., H.K. Porter Co. v. Steel Prod. Workers, 333 F.2d 596 (3d Cir. 1964).

644.10. See, e.g., Kansas City Royals Baseball Corp. v. Major League Baseball Players Ass'n, 532 F.2d 615 (8th Cir. 1976); San Francisco-Oakland Newspaper Guild v. Tribune Publishing Co., 407 F.2d 1327 (9th Cir. 1969); Machinists v. Campbell Soup Co., 406 F.2d 1223 (7th Cir. 1969); Safeway Stores v. Bakery Workers, 390 F.2d 79 (5th Cir. 1958).

644.11. See generally GORMAN, LABOR LAW 584-93.

644.12. See, e.g., Safeway Stores v. Bakery Workers, 390 F.2d 79 (5th Cir. 1968); Trailways of New England., Inc. v. Motor Coach Employees, 353 F.2d 180 (1st Cir. 1965). See generally T. KHEEL, LABOR LAW (18E BUSINESS ORGANIZATION 1974) § 24.05[2] n.24.1.

it totally lacks rationality. If the award has no modicum of plausability in light of the parties' agreement, then judicial intervention may be appropriate. But short of that extreme situation, the court should respect the work of the appointed contract reader.[644.13]

There are various decisions which test the limits of the irrationality test. The case perhaps most frequently debated for its application of this standard is *Safeway Stores v. Bakery Workers.*[644.14] There the employer unilaterally changed the day of the week on which pay checks were issued. To effectuate the change, the company had to make a one-time issuance of checks covering only two work days. The union filed a grievance under a contract provision which guaranteed forty hours of work per week. The employees had in fact received pay for all work performed and had not missed any work days. Nevertheless, the arbitrator found the employees were entitled to pay checks which provided a full week's compensation. He ordered the company to pay each employee for three additional days even though no work had been performed. In subsequent proceedings, the Fifth Circuit refused to overturn the award. The court admonished that the judiciary should resist "the temptation to 'reason out' a la judges the arbiter's award to see if it passes muster." [644.15] In the court's view, the award before it had to be upheld because it was clear that the arbitrator had drawn on the collective bargaining agreement as the source of his interpretation. In additon, the award represented "a passably plausible" interpretation of the wage-guarantee provision.[644.16] Although recognized as controversial, the result in *Safeway Stores* is generally discussed approvingly by commentators.

§ 4.21. Jurisdiction Questions in Sports Litigation: Suits Against Clubs.

Litigation between a player and club may take several different forms. The club may sue to enforce the player's negative covenant.[645] Where the athlete is the injured party, the lawsuit may be a traditional breach of contract action, often with the player seeking damages based on the club's alleged improper termination of his contract.[646] Even where arbitration has been chosen as the primary means for resolving contract disputes, the potential for court litigation is present. A legal action may be necessary either to secure the other party's compliance with his agreement to arbitrate or to enforce the arbitrator's award once it is entered.[647] In any type of litigation between an athlete and his club, an immediate question arises as to where the suit may be brought. The plaintiff can achieve a binding adjudication of the controversy only in a court which has jurisdiction, more specifically, *in personam* jurisdiction, over the defendant player or club.[648]

644.13. *See generally* St. Antoine, *Judicial Review of Labor Arbitration Awards: A Second Look at* Enterprise Wheel *and Its Progeny, supra* note 644.6.

644.14. 390 F.2d 79 (5th Cir. 1968).

644.15. *Id.*at 84.

644.16. *Id.*

645. *See* § 4.02 *supra.*

646. *See* § 3.11 *supra.*

647. *See* §§ 4.15, 4.20 *supra.*

648. *See generally* Pennoyer v. Neff, 95 U.S. 714, 24 L. Ed. 565 (1877); RESTATEMENT (SECOND) OF CONFLICT OF LAWS 100-01 (1971); CONGRESSIONAL RESEARCH SERVICE, LIBRARY OF CONGRESS, THE CONSTITUTION OF THE UNITED STATES OF AMERICA 799-801 (1973); 49 C.J.S. *Judgments* § 19(b).

The potential problems which may arise are reflected in several recent cases in which courts found it necessary to give extended treatment to jurisdictional questions, typically in the context where a plaintiff sought to sue a team in a forum far removed from the state with which the club is identified.[649] Many difficulties in the application of the traditional jurisdictional rules stem from the manner in which teams conduct their business. On the one hand, most teams seek a strong local identification. In an effort to generate a following of local fans, the team will expend efforts to emphasize that it is part of the local scene — it will choose a name which includes the label of a particular city; its nickname will often capture a piece of local culture; it will do extensive local advertising and identify itself as the home team; and, of course, it will usually maintain its business office in the particular locale. But viewed in its broader perspective, the club's operation is inherently interstate in nature. The club sustains itself only by entering into competition with teams in a variety of distant cities,[650] a competition which requires considerable interstate movement. If it is truly a major league team, it will also participate in network contracts which send broadcasts of its games across the country.[651] Finally, its search for new talent will by no means be localized, as most teams maintain an extensive interstate scouting and recruiting system,[652] to say nothing of the teams which operate subsidiary enterprises, such as farm teams, in various locales.

Among the many jurisdictions where teams have contacts, which provide appropriate forums in which to adjudicate controversies between a team and a player? The following discussion attempts to provide some guidance on that question.

The issues considered here are generally framed in terms of whether a state court can exercise *in personam* jurisdiction over various participants in the sports industry. The discussion generally assumes that the plaintiff has selected a state forum in which to litigate his claim. It can be noted, however, that the analysis suggested here will be directly applicable to an action brought in a

---

649. *See* Munchak Corp. v. Riko Enterprises, Inc., 368 F. Supp. 1366 (M.D.N.C. 1973); Erving v. Virginia Squires Basketball Club, 349 F. Supp. 709 (E.D.N.Y. 1972); Martin v. Detriot Lions, Inc., 32 Cal. App. 3d 472, 108 Cal. Rptr. 23 (1973); *cf.* Rodwell v. Pro Football Inc., 45 Mich. App. 408, 206 N.W.2d 773 (1973). *See also* Eckles v. Sharman, 548 F.2d 905 (10th Cir. 1977), *rev'g on other grounds sub nom.*, Mountain States Sports, Inc. v. Sharman, 353 F. Supp. 613 (D. Utah 1972). For cases dealing with the question of jurisdiction over a league, *see* Drysdale v. Florida Team Tennis, Inc., 410 F. Supp. 843 (W.D. Pa. 1976); Florida Team Tennis, Inc. v. World Team Tennis, Inc., 401 F. Supp. 117 (W.D. Pa. 1975).

650. *See, e.g.,* Erving v. Virginia Squires Basketball Club, 349 F. Supp. 709, 713 (E.D.N.Y. 1972).

651. *See, e.g.,* id. at 713. *See generally* Horowitz, *Sports Broadcasting* in GOVERNMENT AND THE SPORTS BUSINESS 275 (R. Noll. ed. 1974); Hockberg, *Second and Goal to Go: The Legislative Attack in the 92nd Congress on Sports Broadcasting Practices,* 18 N.Y.U.L. FORUM 841 (1973).

652. *See, e.g.,* Munchak Corp. v. Riko Enterprises, Inc., 368 F. Supp. 1366, 1369 (M.D.N.C. 1973); Erving v. Virginia Squires Basketball Club, 359 F. Supp. 709, 712-13 (E.D.N.Y. 1972); Martin v. Detroit Lions, Inc., 32 Cal. App. 3d 472, 475, 108 Cal. Rptr. 23, 24 (1973). *See also* Eckles v. Sharman, 548 F.2d 905 (10th Cir. 1977).

There are also two other sports cases, Hawkins v. National Basketball Ass'n, 288 F. Supp. 614 (W. D. Pa. 1968), and American Football League v. National Football League, 27 F.R.D. 264, 266-67 (D. Md. 1961), which deal with venue questions, but which are instructive here. *See* United States v. Scophony Corp., 333 U.S. 795, 807, 92 L. Ed. 1091, 68 S. Ct. 855 (1948) which suggests that the same tests are used to venue and service of process. *See also* Carter v. American Bus Lines, Inc., 169 F. Supp. 460 (D. Neb. 1959); Neris Carbon & Oil Corp. v. Transcontinental Oil Co., 156 F. Supp. 790 (S.D.N.Y. 1957); Satterfield v. Lehigh Valley R.R., 128 F. Supp. 669 (S.D.N.Y. 1955).

federal court.[653] The power of any court, whether state or federal, to subject a person to its processes is limited by the requirement of fundamental due process.[654] The discussion in this and the subsequent section has its primary focus on the due process issue. Thus, although the issues are generally analyzed with reference to state proceedings, the conclusions reached are equally applicable in federal court.

The interrelationship between the federal and state jurisdictional rules has other aspects in addition to the common constitutional basis. An issue entirely distinct from the constitutional question is whether the state law, as reflected in the local jurisdictional statute, or federal law is to be applied to determine the extent of *in personam* jurisdiction available to a federal court in an action based on diversity of citizenship.[655] Subject to some qualifications which are beyond the scope of this treatise,[656] it is generally true that in diversity cases the federal court is empowered to exercise authority only over such persons as would have been amenable to suit in a state court in the state in which the federal tribunal is sitting.[657]

a. **Standards Defining In Personam Jurisdiction.** The inquiry into whether a defendant is subject to the jurisdiction of a particular state involves consideration of both state statutory law and federal constitutional law. As succinctly stated in a jurisdictional controversy involving the former Carolina

---

653. *See generally* 4 C. WRIGHT & A. MILLER, FEDERAL PRACTICE AND PROCEDURE (CIVIL) § 1069 (1968) [hereinafter cited as WRIGHT & MILLER, FEDERAL PRACTICE].

654. *See* International Shoe Co. v. Washington, 326 U.S. 310, 90 L. Ed. 95, 66 S. Ct. 154 (1945); 4 WRIGHT & MILLER, FEDERAL PRACTICE § 1064, at 205-06.

655. *See generally* Comment, *Federal Jurisdiction Over Foreign Corporations and the Erie Doctrine,* 64 COLUM. L. REV. 685 (1964); Comment, *Personal Jurisdiction over Foreign Corporations in Diversity Actions: A Tiltyard for the Knights of Erie,* 31 U. CHI. L. REV. 752 (1964); Comment, *Choice of Law in the Federal Courts: Use of State or Federal Law to Determine Foreign Corporation's Amenability to Suit,* 1964 DUKE L.J. 351; Note, *Diversity of Jurisdiction of the Federal Courts Over Foreign Corporations,* 49 IOWA L. REV. 1224 (1964); Note, *Corporate Amenability to Process in the Federal Courts: State and Federal Standards,* 48 MINN. L. REV. 1131 (1964).

656. For example, in certain types of multiple-party litigation, federal service of process may be made on persons found within 100 miles of the place in which the action is commenced even if the party is outside the jurisdiction of the state. *See* FEDERAL RULES OF CIVIL PROCEDURE, Rule 4(f). A question arises as to whether federal or state law should govern the foreign party's amenability to process in these cases. An argument can be made that only federal standards should apply in this situation. *See, e.g.,* 4 WRIGHT & MILLER, FEDERAL PRACTICE § 1075, at 314; Kaplan, *Amendments of the Federal Rules of Civil Procedure, 1961-1963,* 77 HARV. L. REV. 601, 633 (1964). *See also* Sevits v. McKiernan-Terry Corp., 270 F. Supp. 887 (S.D.N.Y. 1967). Several courts have indicated, however, that the amenability question is to be resolved under state law. *See, e.g.,* Coleman v. American Export Isbrandtsen Lines, Inc., 405 F.2d 250 (2d Cir. 1968); McGonigle v. Penn-Central Transp. Co., 49 F.R.D. 58 (D. Md. 1969); Pierce v. Globemaster Baltimore, Inc., 49 F.R.D. 63 (D. Md. 1969); Karlsen v. Hanff, 278 F. Supp. 864 (S.D.N.Y. 1967).

657. *See, e.g.,* Caesar's World, Inc. v. Spencer Foods, Inc., 498 F.2d 1176 (8th Cir. 1974); Burchett v. Bardahl Oil Co., 470 F.2d 793 (10th Cir. 1972); Fontanetta v. American Bd. of Internal Medicine, 421 F.2d 355 (2d Cir. 1970); Wilshire Oil Co. v. Riffe, 409 F.2d 1277 (10th Cir. 1969); Pujal v. United States Life Ins. Co., 396 F.2d 430 (1st Cir. 1968); Atwood Hatcheries v. Heisdorf & Nelson Farms, 357 F.2d 847 (5th Cir. 1966); Mechanical Contractors Ass'n of America, Inc. v. Mechanical Contractors Ass'n of Northern California, 342 F.2d 393 (9th Cir. 1965); Arrowsmith v. United Press International, 320 F.2d 219 (2d Cir. 1963); Westcott-Alexander, Inc. v. Dailey, 264 F.2d 853 (4th Cir. 1959); Partin v. Michaels Art Bronze Co., 202 F.2d 541 (3d Cir. 1953).

Where a federal suit is based not on diversity of citizenship but on federal question grounds, courts have generally held that the defendant's amenability to suit is determined by application of a federal standard, which is thought to empower the federal courts to claim the entire range of jurisdiction available under the due process clause. *See, e.g.,* Lone Star Package Car Co. v. Baltimore & Ohio R.R., 212 F.2d 147, 148-54 (5th Cir. 1954); First Flight Co. v. National Carloading Corp., 209 F.Supp. 730, 735 (E.D.Tenn. 1962); Goldberg v. Mutual Readers League, 195 F.Supp. 778, 781 (E.D.Pa. 1961).

Cougars of the ABA and the defendant Philadelphia 76er's of the NBA, the following analysis is applied:

> When in personam jurisdiction is contested . . . the court must undertake a two-part inquiry. First, it must be determined if the applicable state law would allow the exercise of in personam jurisdiction over the party in question; second, assuming the answer of the first inquiry to be yes, the court must determine if the exercise of jurisdiction as authorized by state law comports with due process concepts embodied in the Fourteenth Amendment of the United States Constitution.[658]

The determination of whether the state has claimed the right to assert jurisdiction in a particular case depends upon the particular language of the relevant state statute and any cases decided under it. While there are important exceptions, the trend of modern statutes is to afford courts of the particular state as broad a scope of jurisdiction as is constitutionally permissible.[659] Where this approach has been taken, one of the two steps is satisfied and the critical inquiry is whether an exercise of jurisdiction would comport with the limitations imposed by the constitutional concern that the defendant be afforded due process. The analysis which follows focuses on the constitutional question, although the cases which are considered of necessity must deal with the threshold issue of the reach of the relevant state statute.

For the greater part of the judicial history of this country, the accepted view was that the only basis of a state court's jurisdiction over a non-resident defendant was a finding that the defendant carried on sufficient activity in the state to indicate that he was present there. Such a finding was necessary to satisfy the constitutional mandate that a defendant not be subjected to judicial procedures unless he was afforded due process.[660] The determination of "presence" required a more complex analysis when it was applied to a business enterprise such as a corporation. Since such an entity lacked a capacity for actual physical presence, it was necessary to look at other indicia of presence. Hence, it became necessary to determine such things as the amount of business which the non-resident conducted in the state, the amount of goods sent into the state,

---

658. Munchak Corp. v. Riko Enterprises, Inc., 368 F. Supp. 1366, 1368 (M.D.N.C. 1973). *See generally* Bowman v. Curt G. Joa, Inc., 361 F.2d 706 (4th Cir. 1966); Pulson v. American Rolling Mill Co., 170 F.2d 193, 194 (1st Cir. 1948); Johnston v. Time Inc., 321 F. Supp. 837 (M.D.N.C. 1970); RESTATEMENT (SECOND) OF CONFLICT OF LAWS § 102 (1971); Annot., 23 A.L.R. 3d 551, 561-62 (1969); Annot., 27 A.L.R. 3d 397, 406-07 (1969).

659. *See, e.g.,* Curtis Publishing Co. v. Golino, 383 F.2d 586, n.4 (5th Cir. 1967); Munchak Corp. v. Riko Enterprises, Inc., 368 F. Supp. 1366 (M.D.N.C. 1973); CAL. CIV. PRO. CODE § 410.10 (West Supp. 1970): ("A court of this state may exercise jurisdiction on any basis not inconsistent with the Constitution of this state or of the United States"); R.I. GEN. LAWS ANN. § 9-5-83 (1969) (authorizes the state's courts to exercise judicial jurisdiction where there are "the necessary minimum contacts . . . in every case not contrary to the provisions of the Constitution or laws of the United States"); *cf.* Hanson v. Denckla, 357 U.S. 235, 250, 2 L.Ed. 2d 1283, 78 S. Ct. 1228 (1958); McGee v. International Life Ins. Co., 355 U.S. 220, 222, 2 L.Ed. 2d 223, 78 S. Ct. 199 (1957). *See generally* Annot., 23 A.L.R.3d 551 (1969); Annot., 27 A.L.R.3d 397 (1969).

660. *See generally* Pennoyer v. Neff, 95 U.S. 714 (1877); Kurland, *The Supreme Court, the Due Process Clause and the In Personam Jurisdiction of State Courts,* 25 U. CHI. L. REV. 569, 570-86 (1958); Comment, *Long-Arm and Quasi in Rem Jurisdiction and the Fundamental Test of Fairness,* 69 MICH. L. REV. 300, 303-07 (1970); Note, *Developments in the Law: State-Court Jurisdiction,* 73 HARV. L. REV. 909, 919-23 (1960).

the frequency of visits by the defendant's agents and so on.[661] The process of assessing the availability of jurisdiction became largely a matter of counting up the number and extent of intrusions made by the foreign defendant into the state.[662] That approach underwent a radical redefinition in the Supreme Court's decision in the now well-known case of *International Shoe Company v. Washington.*[663] The Court rejected the "presence" test as ignoring the basic concept embodied in the due process clause of the U. S. Constitution. As viewed by the Court, that clause guaranteed that the defendant would be fairly treated and not be called upon to subject himself to suit in a forum in which he was a virtual stranger. The Court did not suggest that the standard to be applied was necessarily more stringent than the old "presence" test. Rather, the Court said that the proper standard was one which was more sensitive to the issue of whether the defendant should be expected to defend in a state where he is not physically located. In the Court's view,

> due process requires only that in order to subject a defendant to a judgment in personam . . . he [must] have certain minimum contacts with [the forum] that the maintenance of the suit does not offend "traditional notion of fair play and substantial justice."[664]

The sort of contacts with the forum state which are necessary are those which "make it reasonable in the context of our federal system of government to require the [defendant] to defend the particular suit which is brought there."[665]

The Court's opinion suggests that in determining whether it is "reasonable" to require the defendant to appear in a particular case, particular attention will be given to the nature and quality of the defendant's contacts with the forum state. But the Court also made clear that there are interests other than the defendant's which must be weighed.[666] In particular, consideration must be given to both the plaintiff's interest in not having to litigate the controversy in another forum and the interest which the state might have in seeing the matter litigitated in its courts.[667]

Although not explicitly mandated in the Supreme Court's decision in *International Shoe,* it is clear that the extent, quality, and number of contacts which are necessary to support *in personam* jurisdiction may vary from case to case depending upon the relationship between the plaintiff's cause of action and the defendant's association with the state. It is now accepted that a court must find that the defendant has more significant contacts with the forum state when the plaintiff's cause of action does not arise from those contacts than when the plaintiff's complaint is directly related to the non-resident's in-state activities.[668]

---

661. *See, e.g.,* People's Tobacco Co. v. American Tobacco Co., 246 U.S. 79, 62 L.Ed. 587, 38 S. Ct. 233 (1918); International Harvester Co. v. Kentucky, 234 U.S. 579, 58 L.Ed. 1479, 34 S. Ct. 944 (1914); Green v. Chicago B. & Q. Ry., 205 U.S. 530, 51 L.Ed. 916, 27 S. Ct. 595 (1907); Hutchinson v. Chase & Gilbert, 45 F.2d 139 (2d Cir. 1930).

662. *See* note, *Developments in the Law: State-Court Jurisdiction, supra,* note 660, at 922-33; Annot., 146 A.L.R. 948 (1943). *See generally* THE CORPORATION TRUST CO., WHAT CONSTITUTES DOING BUSINESS (1939).

663. 326 U.S. 310, 90 L.Ed. 95, 66 S. Ct. 154 (1945).

664. *Id.* at 316.

665. *Id.* at 317.

666. *Id.* at 319. *See also* note, *Developments in the Law: State-Court Jurisdiction, supra* note 660, at 924.

667. *See* note, *Developments in the Law: State-Court Jurisdiction, supra* note 660, at 924.

668. *See generally* Fisher Governor Co. v. Superior Court, 53 Cal. 2d 222, 225, 347 P.2d 1, 3, 1 Cal. Rptr. 1, 3 (1959); Long v. Mishicot Modern Dairy, Inc., 252 Cal. App. 2d 425, 60 Cal. Rptr. 432

Since the state is likely to have less interest in unrelated causes of action than in those directly arising from the defendant's association with it, the former case requires a greater showing that the quality of the defendant's presence is such as to make it reasonable that it be required to appear in a foreign jurisdiction.[669] Thus, as one deals with sports litigation it is important to ask as an initial matter whether the plaintiff's complaint is directly related to or arises from the defendant's in-state activities. If not, and if the plaintiff is asserting that the defendant ought to be amenable to the general jurisdiction of the court, then the plaintiff will have to introduce evidence about the totality of the defendant's contacts with the forum state to establish that he was generally "doing business" there. In most instances, the discussion which follows with respect to sports litigation deals primarily with the availability of this general jurisdiction, rather than with jurisdiction arising out of a controversy directly related to the defendant's activities. This approach is in part dictated by the cases which have been reported in the sports area, for it appears that the most frequently litigated case is one in which the court is asked to determine the defendant's general amenability to jurisdiction.[670]

b. Foreign State Contacts of Professional Sports Clubs: Receipt of Revenues. Among the cases treating jurisdiction questions in sports litigation, the most frequently raised issue concerns the out-of-state forums in which a team, as opposed to an individual player, is subject to suit.[671] While the question of foreign-state jurisdiction has been raised where one team is sued by another, it appears with greater frequency in litigation by athletes attempting to recover for an alleged breach of contract by the team.[672] Some of the factors which prompt the player to pursue the litigation in the foreign jurisdiction are the same as those found in other nonsports litigation: typically the player has relocated to the foreign state and finds it more convenient to pursue his claim in the more accessible courts of his home area. Other considerations affecting the plaintiff's choice of forum may be unique to sports litigation. If the player's departure from

---

(1967); RESTATEMENT (SECOND) OF CONFLICT OF LAWS § 85, Reporter's Note (Tent. Draft No. 3, 1956); 2 J. MOORE, FEDERAL PRACTICE ¶ 4.25[5], 1173 (2d ed. 1967); Currie, *The Growth of the Long-Arm: Eight Years of Extended Jurisdiction in Illinois,* 1963 U. ILL. L. FORUM 533, 585 (1963). *See* Carrington & Martin, *Substantive Interests and the Jurisdiction of State Courts,* 66 MICH. L. REV. 227, 233 (1967); Gorfinkel & Lavine, *Long-Arm Jurisdiction in California Under New Section 410.10 of the Code of Civil Procedure,* 21 HASTINGS L.J. 1163, 1180-81 (1970); Reese & Galston, *Doing an Act or Causing Consequences as Bases of Judicial Jurisdiction,* 44 IOWA L. REV. 249, 264 (1959); von Mehren & Trautman, *Jurisdiction to Adjudicate: A Suggested Analysis,* 79 HARV. L. REV. 1121, 1142-44 (1966); Note, *Developments in the Law: State-Court Jurisdiction, supra* note 660, at 930-32; *cf.* L.D. Reeder Contractors v. Higgins Indus., 265 F.2d 768 (9th Cir. 1959); Peters v. Robin Airlines, 281 App. Div. 903, 120 N.Y.S.2d 1 (1953); Hunter v. Calvaresi, 45 Misc. 2d 96, 256 N.Y.S.2d 356 (Sup. Ct. 1964); Trinity Steel Co. v. Modern Gas Sales & Serv., 392 S.W.2d 861 (Tex. Ct. App. 1965); Tyree Constr. Co. v. Dulien Steel Prods. Inc., 62 Wash. 2d 98, 381 P.2d 245 (1963).

669. *See* Fisher Governor Co. v. Superior Court, 53 Cal. 2d 222, 1 Cal. Rptr. 1, 347 P.2d 1 (1959); *cf.* Note, *Developments in the Law: State-Court Jurisdiction, supra* note 660, at 930-32.

670. *See, e.g.,* Munchak Corp. v. Riko Enterprises, Inc., 368 F. Supp. 1366 (M.D.N.C. 1973); Erving v. Virginia Squires Basketball Club, 349 F. Supp. 709 (E.D.N.Y. 1972); Martin v. Detroit Lions, Inc., 32 Cal. App. 3d 472, 108 Cal. Rptr. 23 (1973).

671. *See, e.g.,* Munchak Corp. v. Riko Enterprises, Inc., 368 F. Supp. 1366 (M.D.N.C. 1973); Erving v. Virginia Squires Basketball Club, 349 F. Supp. 709 (E.D.N.Y. 1972); Martin v. Detroit Lions, Inc., 32 Cal. App. 3d 472, 108 Cal. Rptr. 23 (1973); *cf.* Rodwell v. Pro Football, Inc., 45 Mich. App. 408, 206 N.W.2d 773 (1973).

672. *See* Martin v. Detroit Lions, Inc., 32 Cal. App. 3d 472, 108 Cal. Rptr. 23 (1973); *cf.* Erving v. Virginia Squires Basketball Club, 349 F. Supp. 709 (E.D.N.Y. 1972).

the team's home area was well-publicized and occurred under less than pleasant circumstances, the player may be concerned about the possibility of prejudice resulting from unfavorable, and perhaps exaggerated, publicity. The defendant club will often resist being subjected to litigation in a foreign state, perhaps with the same concerns for convenience and advantage in mind. In its efforts to establish the inappropriateness of the selected forum, the club typically emphasizes the numerically small number of occasions upon which the team is present in the foreign state. The defendant's arguments here may be particularly forceful where the plaintiff attempts to argue that the team is "doing business" in the state because it plays some of its games there. If a limited-schedule sport, such as football, is involved, the team is likely to play in a league-opponent's city only once a year or, as is often true, only every other year. Hence, the contention is made that the contacts do not satisfy the statutory or constitutional minimum.[673] But the matter of playing league games in a foreign state is only the most obvious contact which might come into question. Consideration must also be given to the team's recruiting and contract negotiation activities,[674] its broadcast arrangements,[675] and in general, its revenue-raising activities in the foreign state.[676] The relative significance of these various activities is considered in this and the following subsections.

In controversies involving a particular state court's jurisdiction of a professional sports club, there is likely to be a debate over the relevance of the fact that the foreign club's activities within the state do or do not generate gate receipts or other revenue. The premise of an inquiry of this sort seems to be that the extent of revenue-generating activity should be of considerable importance in evaluating the quality of the club's contracts. The revenue will usually arise from the regular-season games with another league team located within the forum state,[677] although it may arise from other sources such as the playing of exhibition games.[678]

In cases not involving sports contracts the *absence* of significant revenues from forum state activities has occasionally been identified as a reason for finding that the defendant's contacts are not sufficient to satisfy constitutional requirements.[679] The framing of the constitutional issue in these terms can be criticized as giving undue weight to the quantitative aspects of the defendant's activities and directing attention away from an inquiry into the nature, substance and continuity of the forum state contacts, the inquiry which seems

673. *See* Erving v. Virginia Squires Basketball Club, 349 F. Supp. 709, 713 (E.D.N.Y. 1972); Hawkins v. National Basketball Ass'n, 288 F. Supp. 614 (W.D. Pa. 1968); American Football League v. National Football League, 27 F.R.D. 264, 268 (D. Md. 1961).
674. *See* Munchak Corp. v. Riko Enterprises, Inc., 368 F. Supp. 1366, 1369 (M.D.N.C. 1973); Martin v. Detroit Lions, Inc., 32 Cal. App. 3d 472, 108 Cal. Rptr. 23 (1973); Rodwell v. Pro Football, Inc., 45 Mich. App. 408, 206 N.W.2d 773 (1973).
675. *See* Munchak Corp. v. Riko Enterprises, Inc., 368 F. Supp. 1366, 1369 (M.D.N.C. 1973). *See also* Eckles v. Sharman, 548 F.2d 905 (10th Cir. 1977).
676. *See* Erving v. Virginia Squires Basketball Club, 349 F. Supp. 709, 713 (E.D.N.Y. 1972); *cf.* Hawkins v. National Basketball Ass'n, 288 F. Supp. 614, 618 (W.D. Pa. 1968); American Football League v. National Football League, 27 F.R.D. 264, 267 (D. Md. 1961).
677. *Cf.* American Football League v. National Football League, 27 F.R.D. 264, 267 (D. Md. 1961).
678. *See* Eckles v. Sharman, 548 F.2d 905 (10th Cir. 1977). *Cf.* Hawkins v. National Basketball Ass'n, 288 F. Supp. 614, 617 (W.D. Pa. 1968).
679. *See* Buckley v. New York Times Co., 338 F.2d 470 (5th Cir. 1964); Dooly v. Payne, 326 F.2d 941, 946 (5th Cir. 1964); *cf.* Insull v. New York World-Telegram Corp., 273 F.2d 166 (7th Cir. 1959), *cert. denied,* 362 U.S. 942, 4 L. Ed. 770, 80 S. Ct. 807 (1960).

to be dictated by the *International Shoe* tests.[680] There will be cases in which the defendant will be able to show that its in-state activities are financially insignificant in terms of its total business operation, but in which the particular contacts in the state, when viewed in themselves, are of such significance that it is not unfair to make the defendant defend in the particular forum. Such a case would be suggested where, for example, the defendant's contacts are continuous and pre-arranged and where the smallness of the revenue generated is explained more by the relative absence of population in the forum state as compared to other marketing areas in which the defendant operates.[681]

The matter of forum state revenues requires special scrutiny in sports litigation. This is particularly so with respect to teams operating under a league agreement which allocates gate receipts only to the home team. This matter was raised in *Erving v. Virginia Squires Basketball Club*.[682] In resisting Erving's efforts to subject it to New York jurisdiction, the Virginia-based team emphasized that when it played games in New York against the Nets of the American Basketball Association, it did not earn any revenue from that activity since the "home team" was entitled to all gate receipts from regular season league competition. In concluding that an exercise of jurisdiction was proper, the court both rejected the premise of the Squires' argument and found other factors sufficient to establish the Squires' amenability to suit. In the court's view, the essential business nature of the team's contacts was undiminished by the arrangement which the related teams had made for the distribution of revenues.

This result seems to be the correct one. The argument put forth by the defendant is unpersuasive even on the question of whether the Squires' New York activities resulted in any economic advantage. While it is true that the games played in the foreign jurisdiction do not produce an immediate financial return, it is nonetheless clear that a substantial economic gain is related to that activity. In particular, by virtue of its agreement with other league teams, the visiting club gains the right to play the home team on its own court and, most importantly, to retain all of the gate receipts. It would seem inappropriate then to conclude that the activity carried on in the foreign jurisdiction does not result in any economic advantage to the visiting team.

The other situation which must be anticipated is the case in which it is established that the foreign club does in fact receive revenues from activities within the state, whether from gate receipts or other sources.[683] In this type of case, there will be some authority which might prompt a court to make a quantitative evaluation of the extent of those receipts in light of the team's total income. But again, the principles of the *International Shoe* case, properly viewed, do not contemplate that this sort of comparison should be determinative. Rather,

---

680. *See* International Shoe Co. v. Washington, 326 U.S. 310, 319, 90 L.Ed. 95, 66 S. Ct. 154 (1945).
681. *Compare* Curtis Publishing Co. v. Golino, 383 F.2d 586 (5th Cir. 1967).
682. 349 F. Supp. 709 (E.D.N.Y. 1972).
683. *See, e.g.,* Martin v. Detroit Lions, Inc., 32 Cal. App. 3d 472, 108 Cal. Rptr. 23 (1973); *cf.* Hawkins v. National Basketball Ass'n, 288 F. Supp. 614, 617-18 (W.D. Pa. 1968); American Football League v. National Football League, 27 F.R.D. 264, 267 (D. Md. 1961).

the court's attention should be directed to other issues relating to the purposefulness and durability of the defendant's contacts.[684]

While this is the more logical approach, it should be pointed out that some opinions which seem to analyze the issue in quantitative terms may in fact be taking account of the qualitative factors which should be controlling. An inquiry into whether the defendant's activities are economically substantial may be a shorthand method of evaluating the quality of those contacts. For example, if it can be shown that the defendant earns an appreciable portion of its income from activities in the forum state, that fact is suggestive of the type of substantial relationship with the local jurisdiction which will establish that the defendant is generally doing business there. This approach was reflected in the opinion of the California Court of Appeals when it was asked to determine whether Larry Martin's claim against the Detriot Lions could properly be adjudicated in the California courts.[685] In finding that the Lions were amenable to suit in California, the court identified a number of factors which established a substantial connection between the out-of-state team and the State of California. Among the facts which received particular attention was the fact that the team "derives a substantial part of its income from paying customers who attend professional football games,"[686] that the Lions "regularly" play California teams [687] and that "when the Detroit Lions play in California [the team] receives a portion of the California gate receipts." [688]

The court did not make a detailed inquiry into the portion of the total revenue of the team which was derived from California activity. Nor did it attempt to gauge the number of games played in the foreign state against any sort of constitutional "minimum contacts." Because of this rather singular emphasis upon revenue receipts, without a more specific investigation into the nature of the Lions' contacts, the opinion might be regarded by some as contributing to the view that the fact of the receipt of revenue by itself should be determinative of the jurisdictional question. Properly viewed, however, the court's approach should be seen as one in which the fact of forum state income is used to suggest both the extent of the Lions' activity in the foreign state as well as its importance. Under this view, the emphasis on the revenue-generating character of the Lions' California activity is intended as a response to any argument that the Lions' contacts with California were casual or insubstantial.[689] The opinion may have benefited by a greater elaboration of the court's reasoning on the point of the substantiality of the defendant's contact. Yet, the language used cannot be seriously misleading, if one keeps in mind that revenue-receipt has relevance not so much for its own quantitative aspects, but because it is suggestive of the enduring and purposeful nature of the foreign team's relationship with the state.

---

684. *See* Hanson v. Denckla, 357 U.S. 235, 253 (1958); Tauza v. Susquehanna Coal Co., 220 N.Y. 259, 267, 115 N.E. 915, 917 (1917); *cf.* Beja v. Jahangiri, 453 F.2d 959, 962-63 (2d Cir. 1972). *See also* Putnam v. Triangle Publications, 245 N.C. 432, 96 S.E.2d 445 (1957); Perkins v. Benquet Consol. Mining Co., 342 U.S. 437, 96 L. Ed. 485, 72 S. Ct. 413 (1952); von Mehren & Trautman, *Jurisdiction to Adjudicate: A Suggested Analysis, supra* note 668.

685. Martin v. Detroit Lions, Inc., 32 Cal. App. 3d 472, 108 Cal. Rptr. 23 (1973).

686. *Id.* at 475, 108 Cal. Rptr. at 24.

687. *Id.* at 475, 108 Cal. Rptr. at 24.

688. *Id.* at 475, 108 Cal. Rptr. at 24.

689. *See also* American Football League v. National Football League, 27 F.R.D. 264, 267 (D. Md. 1961). *But see* Eckles v. Sharman, 548 F.2d 905 (10th Cir. 1977).

c. Number of Games Played in the Forum State. If a court is to avoid a mechanical application of the revenue receipts test, it should focus on other aspects of the foreign team's activities in the forum state. Another factor which has received attention by the courts is the extent to which the team appears in the forum state to participate in contests with another league team.[690] Most professional team sports involve the scheduling of a limited number of games with other league teams. In some sports, such as football, the total number of games played annually is small. Even in the most heavily scheduled sports, such as baseball, it will barely exceed 160. When the fact of home-and-away scheduling is added, the result is that a particular team may appear in a foreign jurisdiction on only a few occasions in a given year.[691] The limiting aspect of these scheduling systems is seen most dramatically in professional football, where some teams may appear in a particular foreign state only once a year or every other year.[692] These facts can be woven into an argument on behalf of the club that it is not subject to the jurisdiction of the courts of the foreign state, at least not on causes of action which are unrelated to events which occur while it is playing there.[693] Thus, if a former player seeks to sue a football team for a breach of contract in a state where the club has only played two games in the preceding four years, the team will object that its contacts with the forum state are insubstantial and that it is not "doing business" there. If one looks at the team's performance in the forum state only in isolation and as a limited number of entries into the jurisdiction, it might seem reasonable to regard the club's contacts as quite minimal. Thus, where a football team plays only one game a year, or a basketball team only six games a year, in a particular state, there might be an appearance of casualness or intermittence of contact such that it could be said to be "unfair" to subject the club to the state's jurisdiction on causes of action not directly arising from the forum state activities.

On the surface, this argument has some appeal. Accepted principles in the area of jurisdiction recognize that a manufacturer or other seller of products does not subject himself to the jurisdiction of the forum state on unrelated causes of action if the seller has shipped goods into the state on only a few occasions.[694] A further analysis, however, should suggest that there are difficulties with this characterization. The appropriate response, supported by the few cases decided in this area, is to reject the above argument by a refutation of the premise that the club is to be analogized to the typical seller of a commodity or service.[695]

---

690. *See* Erving v. Virginia Squires Basketball Club, 349 F. Supp. 709 (E.D.N.Y. 1972); *cf.* Hawkins v. National Basketball Ass'n, 288 F. Supp. 614, 617 (W.D. Pa. 1968); American Football League v. National Football League, 27 F.R.D. 264, 268 (D. Md. 1961).

691. *See* Erving v. Virginia Squires Basketball Club, 349 F. Supp. 709 (E.D.N.Y. 1972); American Football League v. National Football League, 27 F.R.D. 264, 268 (D. Md. 1961).

692. *See* American Football League v. National Football League, 27 F.R.D. 264, 268 (D. Md. 1961); *cf.* Rodwell v. Pro Football, Inc., 45 Mich. App. 408, 412, 206 N.W.2d 773, 776 (1973).

693. On causes of action unrelated to a defendant's contacts with the forum state, the contacts must be more substantial to sustain jurisdiction than if the cause of action arose out of such contacts. *See* authorities cited note 668 *supra*.

694. *See, e.g.,* Dooly v. Payne, 326 F.2d 941, 946 (5th Cir. 1964); Fisher Governor Co. v. Superior Court, 53 Cal. 2d 222, 1 Cal. Rptr. 1, 347 P.2d 1 (1959); *cf. Ex parte* Emerson, 270 Ala. 697, 701, 121 So. 2d 914, 917 (1960).

695. *See* Hawkins v. National Basketball Ass'n, 288 F. Supp. 614, 619 (W.D. Pa. 1968):

> . . . the corporate members of this professional athletic venture are not to be governed by rules evolved with reference to manufacturing or selling, nor by "atomizing" or "pulverizing" their activities in minute parts or events in disregard of the actual unity and continuity of their whole course of conduct.

See also Erving v. Virginia Squires Basketball Club, 349 F. Supp. 709 (E.D.N.Y. 1972).

The typical seller conducts his activities from a single base of operations which often supports a major part of his enterprise in terms of production, warehouse facilities, and personnel. Moreover, the merchandiser typically is involved in such a volume of business that if only a few intermittent sales are made in a particular state, his involvement there can truly be characterized as casual as far as unrelated causes of action are concerned. The professional sports club, on the other hand, functions in a much different framework. Professional sports gains its popularity in large part because of the national character of the league. A particular team generates the interest of home town fans because it is able to attract into its area another team which represents another region of the country and which has acquired a reputation based on its performance elsewhere. Fan interest in a local team is heightened by the outcome in other matches on this national circuit: the fans will follow not only the outcome of foreign contests involving their team, but also the outcome of a contest between two foreign teams which will affect overall league standings. In order to maintain the national appeal of the enterprise and to exploit intersectional rivalries, the leagues must maintain a scheduling system which insures that each team makes repeated appearances on the national circuit.[696] The development of a home base for a club is not necessarily dictated by the sort of production efficiency which leads a manufacturer or seller to centralize its base of operation. Rather the club chooses a particular locale both to give it geographical identification and also to give it an advantage in at least one consumer market. In a real sense, the "production" activities of the team are not centralized, but carried on a broad national scope.[697]

The courts have used a number of concepts to identify the situations in which an entity's activities in a state subject it to the jurisdiction of that state or unrelated causes of actions. If the defendant's activities are "continuous and systematic," and not "casual" or "single or isolated items of activities," [698] then a strong showing can be made that an exercise of jurisdiction is appropriate. While this is the standard which defines when jurisdiction can be constitutionally exercised,[699] it is also frequently used to define the limits of a state jurisdictional statute which authorizes suits against an individual "doing business" in a particular state.[700] As a constitutional matter, an exercise of jurisdiction must

696. See Erving v. Virginia Squires Basketball Club, 349 F. Supp. 709, 713 (E.D.N.Y. 1972); Hawkins v. National Basketball Ass'n, 288 F. Supp. 614, 620-21 (W.D. Pa. 1968). The effort to generate national interest in contests is also of critical importance if the league hopes to attract broadcasting contracts with the major television networks.

697. Compare San Francisco Seals, Ltd. v. National Hockey League, 379 F. Supp. 966 (C.D. Cal. 1974).

698. See Traveler's Health Ass'n v. Virginia, 339 U.S. 643, 648 (1950); International Shoe Co. v. Washington, 326 U.S. 310, 320 (1945); International Harvester v. Kentucky, 234 U.S. 579, 585 (1914); Buckley v. New York Times Co., 338 F.2d 470 (5th Cir. 1964); Curtis Publishing Co. v. Cassel, 302 F.2d 132, 136 (10th Cir. 1962); Erving v. Virginia Squires Basketball Club, 349 F. Supp. 709, 714 (E.D.N.Y. 1972); Lumbermen's Mut. Cas. Co. v. Borden Co., 265 F. Supp. 99, 102 (S.D.N.Y. 1967); Kesler v. Schetky Equip. Corp., 200 F. Supp. 678, 680 (N.D. Cal. 1961); Boyd v. Warren Paint & Color Co., 254 Ala. 687, 49 So. 2d 559 (1950); Ackert v. Ausman, 29 Misc. 2d 962, 966, 218 N.Y.S.2d 822, 826 (Sup. Ct. 1961); Meyers v. Mooney Aircraft, Inc., 429 Pa. 177, 185, 240 A.2d 505, 510 (1967); von Mehren & Trautman, Jurisdiction to Adjudicate: A Suggested Analysis, supra note 668, at 1143-44; cf. Tauza v. Susquehanna Coal Co., 220 N.Y. 259, 267, 115 N.E. 915, 917 (1917).

699. See International Shoe Co. v. Washington, 326 U.S. 310, 318 (1945); cf. Peters v. Robin Airlines, 281 App. Div. 903, 120 N.Y.S. 2d 1 (1953).

700. See Ex parte Emerson, 270 Ala. 697, 121 So. 2d 914 (1960); Meyers v. Mooney Aircraft, Inc., 429 Pa. 177, 185, 240 A.2d 505, 510 (1967); cf. Seilon, Inc. v. Brema S.P.A., 271 F. Supp. 516 (N.D. Ohio 1967).

also satisfy the Supreme Court admonition that "it is essential in each case that there be some act by which the defendant purposefully avails itself of the privilege of conducting activities within the forum state, thus invoking the benefits and protection of its laws."[701]

Even though limited in number, the professional team's activities in other league states seem to meet these criteria.

a. *Continuous.* It is inappropriate to view the club's contacts simply in terms of a given number of games in a particular year. Rather, a broader view of league scheduling should be taken. As long as the league maintains a franchise in a particular state, it can be assumed that every other league team will make periodic appearances in that state for the purpose of engaging in competition. Although the number of appearances may be small even over a five or six year period, the effect of league scheduling is to insure that the contacts will be repeated, consistent with the cycle of home-and-away games necessary to insure an equalization of competition within the league.

b. *Purposeful.* The content of a league schedule is not determined haphazardly, and particular contests are not the product of immediate negotiation between the two competitors. Rather, the schedule is dictated in advance by the need to maintain the national character of the game and to insure that each would-be champion has proven its worth against all other competition.[702] In this sense, a team's appearance in a foreign state is a highly predictable and well-planned result which is inherent in the concept of a "league."

c. *Substantial.* The substantiality of the club's contacts should be defined in light of the club's and league's basic economic function. While the foreign-state activity might be viewed as merely involving the playing of a few games of a couple hours' duration, that is the sort of activity which forms the heart of the team's business function. Thus, the games are not incidental to some other venture by the defendant, but represent its reason for existence.[703] Moreover, the club's foreign state activity is never limited to the contest itself. As has been recognized by the courts, each visit to the forum state requires the movement of personnel in addition to the players and involves business contacts in the form of contracts for meals, lodging and transportation.[704] Thus, in both the game itself and in the preparations for the team's appearance, the club, in the language of *International Shoe,* "enjoys the benefits and protection of the laws of that state."[705]

Another refinement of the Supreme Court's jurisdictional standards seems to have particular application in the sports area. In cases not involving sports controversies, courts have recognized that there is a distinction between commericial operations which have an inherently national scope, as do professional sports leagues, and firms which are largely localized but which carry on interstate activities.[706] While each type of firm may be subject to foreign state jurisdiction, the essential character of the former makes it less likely to be casual or isolated.[707]

---

701. Hanson v. Denckla, 357 U.S. 235, 253 (1958).

702. *See* Erving v. Virginia Squires Basketball Club, 349 F. Supp. 709, 713 (E.D.N.Y. 1972); Hawkins v. National Basketball Ass'n, 288 F. Supp. 614, 620 (W.D. Pa. 1968); American Football League v. National Football League, 27 F.R.D. 264, 268 (D. Md. 1961).

703. *See* Erving v. Virginia Squires Basketball Club, 349 F. Supp. 709, 713 (E.D.N.Y. 1972).

704. *See id.* at 713-14; Hawkins v. National Basketball Ass'n, 288 F. Supp. 614, 617 (W.D. Pa. 1968).

705. 326 U.S. at 319.

706. *See* Curtis Publishing Co. v. Golino, 383 F.2d 586, 590-92 (5th Cir. 1967); *cf.* Erlanger Mills v. Cohoes Fibre Mills, 239 F.2d 502, 507 (4th Cir. 1956).

707. *See, e.g.,* Curtis Publishing Co. v. Golino, 383 F.2d 586, 590-92 (5th Cir. 1967).

As suggested above, a professional sports club by its nature is a part of the venture which is national in scope. Its interstate activities are an inherent part of its structure and cannot be regarded as random or fortuitous ventures.

That the essential criteria for the exercise of jurisdiction over foreign teams are present in professional sports league competition was confirmed in *Erving v. Virginia Squires Basketball Club*.[708] The court adopted the analysis of the judge in *Hawkins v. National Basketball Association,*[709] who was asked to determine the appropriateness of a foreign forum for federal antitrust venue purposes. Thus, the conclusion endorsed in *Erving* was that

> The only business a corporation-owned professional athletic league team could engage in profitably is to systematically play games with other member teams according to Association schedules and play exhibition games in metropolitan cities. . . . To say that these corporations transacted no business of any substantial character in this district would be to disregard the practical non-technical business standards applicable to professional athletic teams.[710]

Will the playing of league games in the forum state be sufficient, in itself, to subject a foreign team to the state's jurisdiction? The jurisdictional question has not been raised in these narrowest terms in any of the cases litigated to date. It probably never will, since as discussed below, it is likely that the team will have other contacts with the forum state. These other contacts may take the form of the employment of scouts or other agents in the state, as in *Martin v. Detroit Lions, Inc.,*[711] or the presence of league offices, as in *Erving v. Virginia Squires Basketball Club.*[712] But even were these other elements not established, a strong case can still be made for the exercise of general jurisdiction. Even when they appear in isolation, the contacts provided by competition continued to have their characteristics of being continuous, purposeful, and substantial. If attention is focused on the national character of the league undertaking, the assumption of jurisdiction would seem to be consistent with the notion of fairness which is inherent in the jurisdictional prescription of the constitutional and expansive state statutes.

d. Recruiting Activities. The operation of the typical sports team will give rise to interstate contacts in addition to those generated by league competition. The other types of contacts which most frequently appear will include those generated by player recruiting efforts,[713] the maintenance of training camps, the scheduling of exhibition games [714] and the transmission of radio and

---

708. 349 F. Supp. 709 (E.D.N.Y. 1972).
709. 288 F. Supp. 614 (W.D. Pa. 1968).
710. 394 F. Supp. at 714, *quoting* 288 F. Supp. at 619.
711. 32 Cal. App. 3d 472, 108 Cal. Rptr. 23 (1973).
712. 349 F. Supp. 709 (E.D.N.Y. 1972).
713. *See* Martin v. Detroit Lions, Inc., 32 Cal. App. 3d 472, 108 Cal. Rptr. 23 (1973); Rodwell v. Pro Football, Inc., 45 Mich. App. 408, 415, 206 N.W.2d 773, 775 (1973); *cf.* Eckles v. Sharman, 548 F.2d 905 (10th Cir. 1977); Munchak Corp. v. Riko Enterprises, Inc., 368 F. Supp. 1366, 1369 (M.D.N.C. 1973).
714. *Cf.* Hawkins v. National Basketball Ass'n, 288 F. Supp. 614, 617 (W.D. Pa. 1968).

television broadcasts into the state.[715] Although there is only limited judicial commentary on the weight to be afforded such foreign state activities, there is some indication that courts are hesitant to posit jurisdiction on the basis of these peripheral activities alone.[716] On the other hand, where the foreign team is shown to have appeared in games with home forum teams, the presence of other activities is often identified as additional reason to support the exercise of jurisdiction over a foreign team.[717] As with most of the prior discussion, this distinction is particularly evident where the plaintiff is seeking general jurisdiction over the defendant and is not alleging specifically that his complaint arises out of the defendant's activity in the forum state. For purposes of analyzing the jurisdiction question, it is useful to separately discuss the relevance of recruiting activity and broadcast transmissions. Our initial inquiry will be into the former.

A case which illustrates the judicial tendency to accept the cumulative effect of scouting activities is *Martin v. Detroit Lions, Inc.*[718] where the court, in addition to noting that the defendant played a regular schedule of games in California, also emphasized that the Lions employed a professional scout to recruit talent in California, that the scout lived there, and that he engaged in recruiting activities.

A case illustrating the other situation, where non-playing activities alone were examined, involved litigation by a North Carolina professional basketball team against a Pennsylvania club which had no regularly scheduled appearances in North Carolina.[719] Thus, the plaintiff team, in attempting to establish the jurisdiction of the North Carolina federal court, was forced to base its case on the efficiency of the defendant's non-playing contacts, in particular its recruiting activities and the fact that broadcasts of its games were carried into the state. The court found on the particular facts of the case that the requirements of the North Carolina jurisdiction statute had been met, but the court went on to investigate whether an exercise of jurisdiction would meet constitutional requirements. On this point, the court concluded that due process concerns articulated in *International Shoe* made it constitutionally impermissible for the court to subject the out-of-state club to its general jurisdiction.

With respect to the defendant's scouting activity, the court noted that agents of the team "frequently" entered the state for such purposes.[720] The court did not further analyze those contacts according to a quantitative standard and, instead, chose to emphasize their qualitative aspects. And here it found a basis for dismissing the importance of those contacts for jurisdictional purposes. The court emphasized the passive nature of the in-state activity by observing that the scouts entered the state "only" for the purpose of "evaluating the talents of local basketball players...."[721] The court noted that scouts had no

---

715. *See* Munchak Corp. v. Riko Enterprises, Inc., 368 F. Supp. 1366, 1369 (M.D.N.C. 1973); Hawkins v. National Basketball Ass'n, 288 F. Supp. 614, 617 (W.D. Pa. 1968); American Football League v. National Football League, 27 F.R.D. 264, 267 (D. Md. 1961). *But see* Eckles v. Sharman, 548 F.2d 905 (10th Cir. 1977).

716. *See* Munchak Corp. v. Riko Enterprises, Inc., 368 F. Supp. 1366 (M.D.N.C. 1973).

717. *See* Martin v. Detroit Lions, Inc., 32 Cal. App. 3d 472, 108 Cal. Rptr. 23 (1973).

718. *Id.*

719. Munchak Corp. v. Riko Enterprises, Inc., 368 F. Supp. 1366 (M.D.N.C. 1973).

720. *Id.* at 1374.

721. *Id.*

authority to negotiate contracts: "These scouts are without authority to recruit or even negotiate with local college players and, in fact, are prevented from doing so by the National Basketball Association by-laws." [722]

The court's approach correctly perceived that *International Shoe* mandates that the basic inquiry should be directed to the substantiality of the scouting contacts, rather than merely their number. Thus, it seems correct to make an inquiry into the nature of the duties pursued by the scout. But is it relevant to emphasize that the scout is merely observing and evaluating and not engaging in any contract negotiation, even of the most preliminary sort? A careful analysis of the Supreme Court's directives should suggest that these types of distinctions are well-founded. Among the factors which the Court identified as relevant to the determination of fairness is the interest which the forum state has in the litigation [723] and thus in the defendant's activity which preceded the lawsuit. It would seem that the state would have a heightened interest in assuming some control over the defendant's activity where that activity involved more than mere entries into the state for "observation" purposes. Where the activity is of such a passive nature, the involvement of state regulations and state substantive law is minimal, unless the particular litigation should involve some conduct arising directly from such a visit. But where the scout has broader powers, including the power to make representations about the player's opportunities with his team and to make preliminary contract overtures, then there is the beginning of a legal relationship, and a further inquiry is necessary. As a general rule, the standard for judging jurisdictional contacts seems to identify the foreign defendant's establishment of a durable relationship as the minimum which will satisfy constitutional prerequisites.[724] The state's interest here is related to the fact that it can properly assume a role in protecting its citizens in their contractual relationships.[725] In the sports area, this concern seems to be particularly justified because of the near-monopoly power of some teams and because of some evidence of overreaching by teams in their negotiation of player contracts in the past.[726]

Yet, even this analysis is not sufficient to lead to a general rule on when scouting activities will provide a jurisdictional basis. As has been repeatedly stated, the trial court must make an inquiry into the totality of the facts.[727] Thus,

722. *Id.* at 1369.

723. *See* text accompanying notes 666-67, *supra*.

724. *See, e.g.,* Travelers Health Ass'n v. Virginia, 339 U.S. 643, 648 (1950) ("continuing obligations"); Greco v. Bucciconi Eng'r Co., 246 F. Supp. 261 (W.D. Pa. 1965); Tauza v. Susquehanna Coal Co., 220 N.Y. 259, 267, 115 N.E. 915, 917 (1917); Ackert v. Ausman, 29 Misc. 2d 962, 966, 218 N.Y.S.2d 822, 826 (Sup. Ct. 1961); *cf.* International Shoe Co. v. Washington, 326 U.S. 310, 317, (1945); Lumbermens' Mut. Cas. Co. v. Borden Co., 265 F.Supp. 99, 102 (S.D.N.Y. 1967); Kesler v. Schetky Equip. Corp., 200 F. Supp. 678, 680 (N.D. Cal. 1961).

725. *See, e.g.,* McGee v. International Life Ins. Co., 355 U.S. 220 (1957); Travelers Health Ass'n v. Virginia, 339 U.S. 643 (1950); Compania de Astral, S.A. v. Boston Metals Co., 205 Md. 237, 107 A.2d 357 (1954), *cert. denied*, 348 U.S. 943 (1955). *See generally* Gorfinkel & Lavine, *Long-Arm Jurisdiction in California Under New § 410.10 of the Code of Civil Procedure,* 21 HASTINGS L. REV. 909, 926-28 (1960); Annot., 23 A.L.R.3d 551 (1969).

726. *See generally* Connecticut Professional Sports Corp. v. Heyman, 276 F. Supp. 618 (S.D.N.Y. 1967); Los Angeles Rams Football Club v. Cannon, 185 F. Supp. 717 (S.D. Cal. 1960).

727. *See* Agrashell, Inc. v. Bernard Sirotta Co., 229 F. Supp. 98, 102 (E.D.N.Y. 1964); Ackert v. Ausman, 29 Misc. 2d 962, 966, 218 N.Y.S. 2d 822 (Sup. Ct. 1961); *cf.* Perkins v. Benquet Consol. Mining Co., 342 U.S. 437, 445 (1952).

in addition to looking at the nature of the relationship between the scouting organization and the forum state, a court should direct its attention to the scope and continuity of the team's recruiting efforts.[728]

There are particular situations in which the conduct of scouting activities will be especially important. One situation is the case in which the defendant team carries on some other significant activities in the state, such as appearing in exhibition or regularly scheduled games. Here, even if the other activities are not sufficient in themselves to support the court's exercise of general jurisdiction, the scouting activities should be regarded as relevant for their cumulative impact in establishing the likelihood that the defendant should have anticipated that it might be called upon to defend in the foreign forum.[729] Another situation worthy of note involves different considerations. While the prior analysis was concerned with the jurisdiction question in suits based on causes of action unrelated to the defendant's forum state activities, it can be noted that most controversies between plaintiff players and defendant teams involve questions of contract.[730] In this context, the team's scouting activity can often be viewed as part of the contracting process. Thus, if the direct relationship between the initial scouting of a player and his subsequent signing with a team can be shown, a foundation is laid for suggesting that an eventual contract dispute "arose out of" the defendant's in-state activities. A reading of existing non-sports cases would suggest that this relationship between scouting and subsequent contracting is *only* a foundation and that jurisdiction would be sustained only if the actual negotiation of the contract itself involved significant contacts with the forum state.[731]

728. For nonsports cases holding that the constitutional prerequisites for coming within the general jurisdiction of the court were not met when the defendants' contacts with the forum were too insubstantial, see Wilcox v. Pennsylvania R.R., 269 F. Supp. 326 (S.D.N.Y. 1967); Fisher Governor Co. v. Superior Court, 53 Cal. 2d 222, 1 Cal. Rptr. 1, 347 P.2d 1 (1959); Hunter v. Calvaresi, 45 Misc. 2d 96, 256 N.Y.S.2d 356 (Sup. Ct. 1964); Peters v. Robin Airlines, 281 App. Div. 903, 120 N.Y.S.2d 1 (1953).

For nonsports cases holding that contract negotiations alone are not enough on which to base general jurisdiction, see National Television Sales, Inc. v. Philadelphia Television Broadcasting Co., 284 F. Supp. 68 (N.D. Ill. 1968); Verner v. Morgan Towing & Transp. Co., 258 F. Supp. 169 (S.D.N.Y. 1966); Amco Transworld, Inc. v. M/V Bambi, 257 F. Supp. 215 (S.D. Tex. 1966); Pan American Consulting Co. v. Corbu Indus., S.A., 219 Md. 478, 150 A.2d 250 (1959); cf. Lone Star Motor Import, Inc. v. Citroen Cars Corp., 288 F.2d 69 (5th Cir. 1961); contra, Liquid Carriers Corp. v. American Marine Corp., 375 F.2d 951 (2d Cir. 1967).

729. For nonsports cases holding that jurisdiction should be sustained when defendant's activities in the forum established that it should have anticipated the likelihood of being called upon to defend in that forum, see Gray v. American Radiator & Std. Sanitary Corp., 22 Ill. 2d 432, 176 N.E.2d 761 (1961); Coulter v. Sears, Roebuck & Co., 426 F.2d 1315 (5th Cir. 1970). *See generally* Comment, *Long-Arm and Quasi In Rem Jurisdiction and the Fundamental Test of Fairness,* 69 MICH. L. REV. 300, 312-14 (1970).

730. *See, e.g.,* Munchak Corp. v. Cunningham, 457 F.2d 721 (4th Cir. 1972); Washington Capitols Basketball Club v. Barry, 419 F.2d 472 (9th Cir. 1969); Houston Oilers, Inc. v. Neely, 361 F.2d 36 (10th Cir.), *cert. denied,* 385 U.S. 840 (1966); Nassau Sports v. Peters, 352 F. Supp. 870 (E.D.N.Y. 1972); Erving v. Virginia Squires Basketball Club, 349 F. Supp. 709 (E.D.N.Y. 1967); Connecticut Professional Sports Corp. v. Heyman, 276 F. Supp. 618 (S.D.N.Y. 1967); Los Angeles Rams Football Club v. Cannon, 185 F. Supp. 717 (S.D. Cal. 1960); Martin v. Detroit Lions, Inc., 32 Cal. App. 3d 472, 108 Cal. Rptr. 23 (1973); American League Baseball Club of Chicago v. Chase, 86 Misc. 441, 149 N.Y.S. 6 (Sup. Ct. 1914); Central New York Basketball, Inc. v. Barnett, 19 Ohio Op. 2d 130, 181 N.E.2d 506 (1961); Dallas Cowboys Football Club v. Harris, 348 S.W.2d 37 (Tex. Civ. App. 1961); *cf., e.g.,* Munchak Corp. v. Riko Enterprises, Inc., 368 F. Supp. 1366 (M.D.N.C. 1973).

731. *See, e.g.,* Liquid Carriers Corp. v. American Marine Corp., 375 F.2d 951 (2d Cir. 1967); National Gas Appliance Corp. v. AB Electrolux, 270 F.2d 472 (7th Cir. 1959); Temco, Inc. v. General Screw Prods., Inc., 261 F. Supp. 793 (M.D. Tenn. 1966); Aucoin v. Hanson, 207 So. 2d 834 (La. Ct.

e. Sports Broadcasts into Foreign Jurisdictions. Under present precedents, there is no basis upon which to suggest that a professional club is "doing business" in a state merely because that state receives league-sponsored broadcasts of the team's activities. Further, the fact that the club may derive some revenue from those broadcasts does not compel a different result. This view has been specifically sustained in one case [732] and finds some support in the non-sports cases interpreting *International Shoe*.[733] To the extent that such broadcasts may be viewed as relevant jurisdictional facts, their importance would seem to be limited to situations in which either (1) the broadcasts were club, rather than league, sponsored and negotiated or (2) as in the case of scouting activitites, the fact of the broadcast could be coupled with other types of contacts which *in toto* were sufficient to show a general, continuing, and purposeful interaction between the team and the forum state.[734]

One case in which the jurisdictional implication of sports broadcasting was considered was *Munchak Corporation v. Riko Enterprises, Inc.*,[735] a case discussed above. There the court rejected the suggestion that a Pennsylvania ball club was subject to North Carolina jurisdiction because of its scouting and broadcast activities in the state. The broadcast arrangement was between a national network and the league to which the Pennsylvania team belonged. The court noted that "the defendant is not a party to this contract, except perhaps as a third party beneficiary, nor has the defendant contracted with any North Carolina television station in this regard."[736] In rejecting the importance of this broadcast arrangement for jurisdictional purposes, the court emphasized two points: (1) any benefit to the defendant from the leagued-negotiated arrangement was indirect and (2) the role which the forum state played in total broadcast arrangement was relatively insignificant.

The court's analysis takes the proper perspective in analyzing league-sponsored broadcasting in light of *International Shoe*. Under the principles of that case, the mere receipt of some benefit from in-state activity is not enough to support jurisdiction.[737] Consistent with the Supreme Court's subsequent emphasis upon finding a purposefulness in the defendant's contact,[738] it seems most appropriate to consider the extent to which the in-state activity was directed and arranged by the defendant. The further removed the defendant club is from a position of directing its contacts with a particular state, the less importance should be attached to the fact that some benefit is derived

---

App. 1968); Longines-Wittnauer Watch Co. v. Barnes & Reinecke, 15 N.Y.2d 443, 261 N.Y.S.2d 8, 209 N.E.2d 68, 24 A.L.R.3d 508, *cert. denied,* 382 U.S. 905 (1965); *cf., e.g.,* Lone Star Motor Import, Inc. v. Citroen Cars Corp., 280 F.2d 69 (5th Cir. 1961). *See generally* Annot. 23 A.L.R.3d 551 (1969).

732. Munchak Corp. v. Riko Enterprises, Inc., 368 F. Supp. 1366 (M.D.N.C. 1973). *See also* Eckles v. Sharman, 548 F.2d 905 (10th Cir. 1977).

733. *See* Taylor v. Portland Paramount Corp., 383 F.2d 634 (9th Cir. 1967); *cf.* Gearhart v. WSAZ, 150 F. Supp. 98, 102 (E.D. Ky. 1957); Hoffman v. Carter, 117 N.J.L. 205, 187 A. 576 (1936), *aff'd,* 118 N.J.L. 379, 192 A. 825 (1937); *contra* WSAZ v. Lyons, 254 F.2d 242 (6th Cir. 1958); Wanamaker v. Lewis, 153 F. Supp. 195 (D. Md. 1957).

734. For the importance of a general, continuing and purposeful interaction, see cases cited note 698 *supra. See also* Eckles v. Sharman, 548 F.2d 905 (10th Cir. 1977).

735. 368 F. Supp. 1366 (M.D.N.C. 1973).

736. *Id.* at 1369.

737. *Cf.* Hanson v. Denckla, 357 U.S. 235 (1968).

738. *Id.* at 253.

from in-state performance. The same conclusion is reached when one examines the question of whether the club could have reasonably expected that the league broadcast arrangement would subject it to the jurisdiction of all states in which the broadcasts were received.[739] Because of the indirectness of the contacts and because the club plays a limited role in either the contract negotiation or the actual transmission of the events, it can hardly be said that the club understood that it was taking advantage of the benefits and privileges of the receiving state so that some day it might be called upon to defend in its courts activities totally unrelated to the broadcast.

As is true with scouting activities, a finding that broadcast transmission in itself provided constitutionally sufficient contacts would produce a foregone conclusion on the question of foreign state jurisdiction for major portions of the sports industry. The major baseball, football and basketball leagues have participated in network telecasts at various times.[740] Since these are received in every state, there would be literally no jurisdiction in which a team could claim immunity. While nothing in *International Shoe* forecloses the possibility of such a broad exposure to foreign litigation, the sports industry does not seem to provide an appropriate candidate for this treatment. Rather, a close analysis of the factors regarded as significant in *International Shoe* and its progeny would support the view that courts should find jurisdiction only after examination of the activities of the particular defendant and only when those activities establish a conscious effort on the part of the defendant to direct his business into the particular state.[741]

As the above analysis should suggest, the fact of sports broadcasts is more important in the jurisdictional equation when they emanate from the club's own broadcast network, as opposed to a league-negotiated arrangement. While the individual club can be viewed as a passive beneficiary in the latter case, in the former, any contracts which the club makes with foreign stations is not only purposeful, but also is likely to be continuous and substantial.[742] And unlike the situation with respect to league-controlled broadcast arrangements, the projection of the team activities into a particular state are likely to be specifically and selectively arranged, so that it is more reasonable to find that the promoter either did or should have formed specific expectations about the possibility of its being called upon to defend litigation in the foreign state. In an evaluation of this situation, the broadcast should be seen as directly related to the team's primary business activity: the marketing of an entertainment product. Whether a club-sponsored broadcast will be sufficient to support jurisdiction on unrelated causes of action will depend upon the facts of the particular case — the nature

739. For an explanation of the reasonable expectations test, see Comment, *Long-Arm and Quasi In Rem Jurisdiction and the Fundamental Test of Fairness, supra* note 729, at 312-14. *See also* Gray v. American Standard Radiator & Sanitary Corp., 22 Ill. 2d 432, 176 N.E.2d 761 (1961).

740. For a discussion of the economic importance to clubs of both national and local broadcasting arrangements see Horowitz, *Sports Broadcasting* in GOVERNMENT AND THE SPORTS BUSINESS 275, 286-298 (R. Noll.ed. 1974). *See also* Noll., *The U.S. Team Sports Industry: An Introduction* in *id.* at 1, 10-28.

741. *See, e.g.,* Hanson v. Denckla, 357 U.S. 235, 253 (1958).

742. *Compare* Wanamaker v. Lewis, 153 F. Supp. 195 (D. Md. 1957) *and* Gearhart v. WSAZ, 150 F. Supp. 98, 102 (E.D. Ky. 1957) *with* Taylor v. Portland Paramount Corp., 383 F.2d 634 (9th Cir. 1967) *and* Hoffman v. Carter, 117 N.J.L. 205, 187 A. 576 (1936), *aff'd,* 118 N.J.L. 379, 192 A. 825 (1937).

of the broadcast contract, the frequency of the broadcasts, the extent to which team representatives entered the forum state and, as always, the nature of the contacts which the team might have had. But assuming that a pervasive club-sponsored broadcast arrangement can be found, a more likely case for the exercise of foreign state jurisdiction can be said to exist.

§ 4.22. Jurisdiction over Players.

a. Importance of Proper Forum Selection. A club or other plaintiff which seeks to bring suit against a professional athlete will want to evaluate a variety of tactical considerations in selecting the forum in which to pursue the litigation. Many of these considerations will be the same one's which influence a party's selection in any type of litigation. Thus, attention will be given to the convenience of the forum, the availability of helpful local precedents, the possibility of local bias and so on. There is one concern which must be given particular attention. This relates to the long-unsettled issue of whether equitable decrees will be enforced by foreign courts under the full-faith-and-credit clause. When a club sues a player, the remedy sought will often be some form of equitable relief, most typically a negative injunction seeking to prohibit the player from playing for any other team.[743] Indeed, clubs consciously structure their agreements to posit the appropriateness of this type of relief rather than the legal remedy of monetary damages.[744] Assume that the team secures such a negative injunction in State X but the player has moved to distant State Y (probably to join his new team) with no intention of returning to State X. The normal procedure in an action at law would be for the plaintiff to prove his judgment from State X in the courts of State Y. The judicial machinery of State Y would then be invoked to aid the plaintiff in securing compliance with his decree. The deference which sister states pay to the original judgment is a matter of constitutional dimension, for Article IV, Section 1 of the United States Constitution provides:

> Full faith and credit shall be given in each State to the public acts, records, and judicial proceedings of every other state. And the Congress may by general laws prescribe the manner in which such acts, records, and proceedings shall be proved, and the effect thereof.[745]

Is a team holding a negative injunction entitled to this same assistance in securing compliance? Not necessarily, for there is a definite split of authority on the question of whether an equitable decree of the sort posited here comes within the constitutional mandate. A significant number of state courts refuse to enforce such equitable decrees,[746] and the Supreme Court has chosen not to make a definitive ruling on the issue. Even the otherwise progressive *Restatement (Second) of Conflict of Laws* has declined to take a position on this

---

743. *See generally* § 4.02 *supra.*

744. For examples of sports contracts which provide for a negative injunction, see Nassau Sports v. Peters, 352 F. Supp. 870, n. 17 (E.D.N.Y. 1972); Central New York Basketball, Inc. v. Barnett, 19 Ohio Op. 2d 130, 132-33, 181 N.E.2d 506, 509 (1961); Dallas Cowboys Football Club, Inc. v. Harris, 348 S.W.2d 37, 42 (Tex. Civ. App. 1961). *See also* § 4.04 *supra.*

745. *See generally* CONGRESSIONAL RESEARCH SERVICE, LIBRARY OF CONGRESS, THE CONSTITUTION OF THE UNITED STATES OF AMERICA 793-829 (1973).

746. *See* Philadelphia Baseball Club Ltd. v. Lajoie, 13 Ohio Dec. 504 (1902); Buswell v. Buswell, 377 Pa. 487, 105 A.2d 608 (1954). *But see* Rich v. Con-Stan Indus. Inc., 449 S.W.2d 323 (Tex. Civ. App. 1969); Allee v. Van Cleave, 263 S.W.2d 276 (Tex. Civ. App. 1953).

matter.[747] The view that these equitable decrees are not entitled to full faith and credit has been specifically endorsed in the professional sports context.[748] Various justifications are proposed in support of this result. One is that such decrees often endure for long periods of time, and changes in the circumstances surrounding the case may require that the decree be modified from time to time. Opponents of foreign state enforcement suggest that it would be awkward for a sister state to make these adjustments in a case which was not originally heard by it. Another objection is that because of the continuous enforcement effort required, an onerous burden might be placed on the sister state in a matter with which it had relatively little involvement.[749] While these objections have been criticized by commentators,[750] they continue to be regarded as persuasive by a number of courts.

If the club secures a decree in a jurisdiction in which the athlete is not directly subject to the court's powers, it may find that it is effectively precluded from enforcing the order. If the foreign state which has power over the person of the athlete is unwilling to accept the original decree, the club's only choice will be to initiate a new lawsuit.[751] The delay and added expense of such a maneuver can be avoided by the exercise of care in its initial selection of a forum. Thus, in planning for litigation against a player who has jumped to another team, the plaintiff club may well find it necessary to give consideration to forums other than that which would be most convenient for it. And in pursuing the alternative, the team must of necessity determine which of these other forums can constitutionally assert jurisdiction over the person of the player.

b. Player's Residence as an Appropriate Forum. The traditional forum for suing a natural person is his domicile — the place in which he has chosen to locate his social and political activities with an intent to remain indefinitely.[752] While there is no question that a player could be sued in the state of his domicile, the unique factual aspects of relationships in professional sports prompt the question as to whether other forums might not be equally appropriate. Thus, it might be asked whether the athlete may be sued in a state where he is a temporary resident.

Professional athletes are likely to come within the rather small segment of our society which maintains more than one residence. While many players choose to take up permanent residency, or domicile, in the state in which their team is located, many do not, either because they view their tenure with the team as of limited duration or because they feel that with a short playing season and constant road trips, there is no compelling reason to permanently relocate in an area or climate which they find disagreeable. But even when their association with the team's location is not permanent, the players are likely to take some steps which establish residency — the rental of living accommodations, the maintenance of a mailing address and so on.[753] This dislocation between domicile

---

747. RESTATEMENT (SECOND) OF CONFLICTS OF LAWS § 102, comment c (1971).

748. See Philadelphia Baseball Club, Ltd. v. Lajoie, 13 Ohio Dec. 504 (1902).

749. See generally RESTATEMENT (SECOND) OF CONFLICT OF LAWS § 102, comment c (1971); Reese, Full Faith and Credit to Foreign Equity Decrees, 42 IOWA L. REV. 183, 189 (1957).

750. See generally Reese, Full Faith and Credit to Foreign Equity Decrees, supra note 749.

751. See Philadelphia Baseball Club, Ltd. v. Lajoie, 13 Ohio Dec. 504 (1902).

752. See Milliken v. Meyer, 311 U.S. 457 (1940). See generally Reese & Green, That Elusive Word, "Residence", 6 VAND. L. REV. 561, 562-63 (1953); Note, Developments in the Law: State-Court Jurisdiction, 73 HARV. L. REV. 909, 941-43 (1960).

753. For a definition of residence see 77 C.J.S. Residence (1952).

and residence is likely to become of particular importance for jurisdictional purposes in the litigation which results when the player has jumped from one team to another. The former team would likely be pursuing its equitable remedies to secure compliance with the abandoned contract. If the team has reason to believe that the player will not choose to appear voluntarily in the forum in which the case is tried, the team will have to weigh the advantages and disadvantages of litigating in those places where the athlete is physically present.

The presently prevailing view is that domicile is not necessarily the only appropriate jurisdictional basis and that in many cases residency alone will subject the defendant to the jurisdiction of a local court.[754] As is true with respect to other potentially relevant jurisdictional facts, the basic question to be asked is whether the defendant's association with the forum state is such as to make an exercise of jurisdiction reasonable.[755] What are the limitations on the availability of this alternate jurisdiction? Again, the availability of jurisdiction in a particular case will depend upon the reasonableness of subjecting the defendant to the court's power.[756] Such reasonableness is determined by considering (1) the length of time the player spends in the particular state, (2) the types of activities he undertakes there and (3) the nature of the living arrangements which he makes.[757]

At least one of these — the nature of the individual's forum state activities — becomes especially important in the context of sports litigation. The inquiry into reasonableness is basically an inquiry into the significance and permanence of the player's in-state activities.[758] When the place of residency is also the place where the player's team is located, the requisite association would seem to be present, even if the residency is non-permanent.[759] The player is not a casual visitor to the state, nor are his contacts only incidentally related to his main enterprise. In fact, the type of residency under consideration here represents a substantial connection between the player and the local forum. The residence is truly a business home and represents the location from which the player conducts his professional activities. Because of this substantial economic connection, it can reasonably be said that the defendant has purposefully taken advantage of the benefits and privileges afforded by the forum state. It would seem, therefore, that local courts should be satisfied that the elements of constitutional fairness would not be offended by an exercise of jurisdiction. And because residency in this context shares several of the important characteristics

---

754. *See* Myrick v. Superior Court, 256 P.2d 348 (Cal. Dist. Ct.), *aff'd*, 41 Cal. 2d 519 (1953); State *ex rel.* Merritt v. Heffernan, 142 Fla. 496, 195 So. 145 (1940); Camden Safe-Deposit & Trust Co. v. Barbour, 66 N.J.L. 103, 48 A. 1008 (1901); Rawstone v. Maguire, 265 N.Y. 204, 192 N.E. 294 (1934); RESTATEMENT (SECOND) OF CONFLICT OF LAWS § 30 (1971); EHRENZWEIG, CONFLICT OF LAWS 95 (1962); GOODRICH, CONFLICT OF LAWS 119 (4th ed. 1963).

755. *See* International Shoe Co. v. Washington, 326 U.S. 310, 317 (1945). *See generally* Note, *Developments in the Law: State-Court Jurisdiction, supra* note 752, at 941-43.

756. Allen v. Superior Court, 41 Cal. 2d 306, 259 P.2d 905 (1953). *See also* cases cited note 754 *supra.*

757. *See* RESTATEMENT (SECOND) OF CONFLICT OF LAWS § 30, comment *a* (1971).

758. *See* text accompanying notes 698-700, § 4.21 *supra.*

759. For the significance of partial performance of a contract within the forum to the establishment of jurisdiction see Atwood Hatcheries v. Heisdorf & Nelson Farms, 357 F.2d 847 (5th Cir. 1966); Lone Star Motor Import, Inc. v. Citroen Cars Corp., 288 F.2d 69 (5th Cir. 1961); Aucoin v. Hanson, 207 So. 2d 834 (La. Ct. App. 1968). *See generally* Annot. 23 A.L.R.3d 551 (1969).

found in a more permanent domicile, it is not unreasonable to find that the scope of jurisdiction afforded is similar in each case. Thus, the fact that the cause of action in question might not be directly related to the player's present forum state activities — as where the player is being sued by a former team — should not provide a basis for the court's declining to exercise jurisdiction.

c. Place of Contracting. It is often said that a defendant who enters into the negotiation and consummation of a contract in a particular state thereby subjects himself to the jurisdiction of the courts of that state in any matter relating to the enforcement of the contract.[760] The basis of this rule is two-fold: first the defendant has voluntarily sought to take advantage of benefits and privileges afforded by the forum state (the right to engage in commercial activity); second and relatedly, the state has an interest in all activities, particularly those of a commercial nature, which occur within its borders.[761] These principles have a number of potential applications in the sports area, but the present discussion will deal with one particular facet of the problem. Our focus will be on the case in which the player's contract is at least partially negotiated in a state with which the player has no other permanent contacts. A number of different fact situations from the sports industry could be used to illustrate this problem, but one which arises with some frequency in team sports involves the case in which a college athlete who is attending an out-of-state school is heavily recruited by a professional team, which also has its permanent association in another jurisdiction. Often there will be extended negotiation over contract terms in the state where the athlete is temporarily in college, and it may be that the contract is eventually signed in the college state, although most teams attempt to avoid this situation. Our case presents an interesting test for the principles identified above. Even if the place of contracting is clearly identified as the state where the college is located, neither party has a durable association with that state [762] and, except perhaps for the initial bonus payments, often no part of the contract will be performed in the state. While the plaintiff would seldom have an incentive to sue the player in a forum which had both limited interest in the litigation and limited power over the player, such litigation might arise where (1) the plaintiff was seeking to take advantage of favorable local precedent or (2) important witnesses, such as the player's agent, were present in the forum or (3) a favorable local jury might be found because of tension in the athlete's prior relationship with the community. Despite the significance normally assigned to the place of contracting,[763] a

760. *See* McGee v. International Life Ins. Co., 355 U.S. 220 (1957); Travelers Health Ass'n v. Virginia, 339 U.S. 643 (1950); Clinic Masters, Inc. v. McCollar, 269 F. Supp. 395 (D. Colo. 1967); Compania de Astral, S.A. v. Boston Metals Co., 205 Md. 237, 107 A.2d 357 (1954), *cert. denied,* 348 U.S. 943, 99 L.Ed. 738, 75 S. Ct. 65 (1955); Anderson, Clayton & Co. v. Atlas Concrete Pipe, Inc., 41 Mich. App. 58, 199 N.W.2d 531 (1972). *See generally* Annot. 23 A.L.R. 3d 551 (1969); Comment, *The Isolated Contact as a Basis of Jurisdiction Over Non-Residents,* 22 U. CHI. L. REV. 674 (1955).

761. *See* McGee v. International Life Ins. Co., 355 U.S. 220, 223, (1957); Travelers Health Ass'n v. Virginia, 339 U.S. 643, 648 (1950). *See generally* Note, *Developments in the Law: State-Court Jurisdictions, supra* note 752, at 924.

762. *Compare* Tauza v. Susquehanna Coal Co., 220 N.Y. 259, 267, 115 N.E. 915, 917 (1917).

763. *See, e.g.,* National Television Sales, Inc. v. Philadelphia Television Broadcasting Co., 284 F. Supp. 68 (N.D. Ill. 1968); Clinic Masters, Inc. v. McCollar, 269 F. Supp. 395 (D. Colo. 1967); Pan American Consulting Co. v. Corbu Indus., S.A., 219 Md. 478, 150 A.2d 250 (1959); Compania de Astral, S.A. v. Boston Metals Co., 205 Md. 237, 107 A.2d 357 (1954), *cert. denied,* 348 U.S. 943 (1955); Park Beverage Co. v. Goebel Brewing Co., 197 Md. 369, 79 A.2d 157 (1951); Wirth v. Prenyl, 29 App. Div. 2d 373, 288 N.Y.S.2d 377 (Sup. Ct. 1968). *See generally* Annot. 23 A.L.R.3d 551 (1969).

close analysis of the situation outlined above should suggest that an exercise of jurisdiction would be inappropriate in light of the concern for fairness expressed by the Supreme Court. First, an examination of the precedents in this area reveals that in cases in which the fact of contracting is identified as supporting an exercise of jurisdiction, it is almost always true that plaintiff is a resident of the forum state.[764] Thus the relevant jurisdictional facts in these cases include more than the mere act of contracting; they present situations in which the defendant has chosen to enter into a relationship with a citizen of the forum state and has reason to know that the association with both the citizen and the state will be somewhat durable. By contrast, in our hypothetical case, the plaintiff — usually the team — can establish no such continuing connection between itself, the contract, and the state where the college is located. Secondly, it is clear that the courts which base jurisdiction on the fact that a contractual relationship arose in their boundaries also insist that a substantial part of the relationship be completed in the state.[765] Thus, merely carrying on a portion of the negotiation or even actually signing the document will not be sufficient if it is clear that the real locus of the relationship is elsewhere.[766] This distinction should indicate that courts are not inclined to accept jurisdiction where the involvement of the forum state has been qualitatively insubstantial. Courts have shown a strong tendency in these single-act jurisdictional cases to look closely at the extent of the state's interest. If neither the defendant nor the plaintiff can claim any continuing association with the state and if the professional contract is intended to be performed in other jurisdictions, there is a substantial likelihood that an exercise of jurisdiction would be deemed to be inappropriate. Courts seem inclined to the view that any doubts as to the fairness of an exercise of jurisdiction should be resolved in favor of the defendant if the plaintiff is unable to articulate a strong state interest in continuing to police a contract which has left its boundaries.[767]

---

764. *See, e.g.,* Atwood Hatcheries v. Heisdorf & Nelson Farms, 357 F.2d 847 (5th Cir. 1966); Aucoin v. Hanson, 207 So. 2d 834 (La. Ct. App. 1968); Anderson, Clayton & Co. v. Atlas Concrete Pipe, Inc., 41 Mich. App. 58, 199 N.W.2d 531 (1972); *cf.* Lone Star Motor Imports, Inc. v. Citroen Cars Corp., 288 F.2d 69 (5th Cir. 1961); Clinic Masters, Inc. v. McCollar, 269 F. Supp. 395 (D. Colo. 1967); Compania de Astral, S.A. v. Boston Metals Co., 205 Md. 237, 107 A.2d 357 (1954), *cert. denied,* 348 U.S. 943 (1955).

765. *See, e.g.,* Atwood Hatcheries v. Heisdorf & Nelson Farms, 357 F.2d 847 (5th Cir. 1966); Lone Star Motor Imports, Inc. v. Citroen Cars Corp., 288 F.2d 69 (5th Cir. 1961); Henry R. Jahn & Son, Inc. v. Superior Court, 49 Cal. 2d 855, 323 P.2d 437 (1958); *cf.* Clinic Masters, Inc. v. McCollar, 269 F. Supp. 395 (D. Colo. 1967); Aucoin v. Hanson, 207 So. 2d 834 (La. Ct. App. 1968). *See generally* Annot. 23 A.L.R.3d 551 (1969).

766. *See* National Television Sales, Inc. v. Philadelphia Television Broadcasting Co., 284 F. Supp. 68 (N.D. Ill. 1968); Baughman v. Hein, 44 Ill. App. 2d 373, 194 N.E.2d 664 (1963); Wirth v. Prenyl, 29 App. Div. 2d 373, 288 N.Y.S.2d 377 (Sup. Ct. 1968).

767. *See* Curtis Publishing Co. v. Birdsong, 360 F.2d 344 (5th Cir. 1966).

CHAPTER 5

Antitrust Aspects of Sports Activities

§ 5.01. Scope of Chapter.

The relationship between professional sports and the antitrust laws is a curious one. If the reader will tolerate a mild overstatement, it can be said that substantive antitrust rules had relatively little impact upon the first several decades of development in professional sports. And, for the future, it is quite possible that the antitrust laws will be of only limited significance, especially in the team sports. Yet, there can be no doubt that the Sherman Act has been the single most influential factor in forcing a fundamental restructuring of the basic relationships in professional athletics. What is the explanation for this seeming paradox? There are several considerations which must be taken into account.

The impotence of the antitrust laws in the past is in large measure attributable to the Supreme Court's decisions declaring baseball to be exempt from the antitrust laws.[1] This grant of immunity meant, of course, that baseball was allowed to develop institutional mechanisms which may not have been tolerated in other industries. While the exemption cases only involved baseball, and while the doctrinal basis of the initial grant of immunity was highly debatable,[2] the Court's treatment of baseball served to characterize the antitrust status of the entire sports industry for the first several decades of this century. During that period, the baseball leagues were the only professional sports ventures of economic significance, and even when professional teams appeared in other sports, they adopted the governmental forms, competition arrangements, and basic employment terms used in baseball. It was not until the late 1950's that the Supreme Court made clear that other sports would not enjoy the same exempt status as baseball.[3] But even with this decision, there was no flood of litigation in the antitrust courts. While the 1960's saw a few cases in which antitrust issues were raised, none of these seems to have posed a serious threat to the basic structure of the non-exempt leagues.[4]

---

1. *See* § 5.02 *infra.*
2. *Id.*
3. *See* International Boxing Club v. United States, 358 U.S. 242 (1959); Radovich v. National Football League, 352 U.S. 445 (1957).
4. *See, e.g.,* American Football League v. National Football League, 205 F. Supp. 60 (D. Md. 1962).

As even a casual reader of the sports pages knows, the era of actual and, later, effective immunity for football, basketball and hockey came to an abrupt end in the early 1970's. Each of the professional leagues involved in these sports became embroiled in antitrust litigation contesting some of the most basic attributes of the existing institutional structure, particularly the contractual devices which were used to control the movement of players among league clubs.[5] Most of the material in the present chapter is based on those developments. It will be seen that the intervention of the antitrust courts has prompted the leagues to reformulate the internal player control rules and to accept the basic notion that some inter-club competition for players' services must be tolerated. The fundamental nature of the reforms prompted by the antitrust litigation is separately documented.[6]

In light of the recent shift toward greater resort to the antitrust courts, the suggestion that substantive antitrust review will play a diminished role in the future might seem strange. Yet, the cases from the early 1970's themselves provide the basis for this view. Those decisions have laid the groundwork for application of another exemption which may remove many significant issues from the purview of the antitrust laws. The exemption in question is that which is afforded to employment-related agreements arrived at through collective bargaining.[7] If the players unions and clubs undertake to settle player-related issues at the bargaining table, and if agreement results from good faith bargaining, the labor exemption will likely operate to preclude the courts from undertaking a substantive review of the terms agreed upon.

This is not to suggest that we will return full circle to the earlier era when sports related matters never came before the antitrust courts. The labor exemption is a selective form of immunity, and there are numerous issues which do not come within its coverage. Player-related rules not approved in collective bargaining, league decisions with respect to franchise location, and other rules pertaining to league governance are examples of issues which will remain lively despite the labor exemption. Moreover, there is no assurance that the present patterns of collective bargaining will endure in all leagues, and it is conceivable that substantive antitrust review may again become a potent control device in some segments of the industry.

The following sections of this chapter explore the two antitrust exemptions mentioned above and examine the cases which provide the transition between the two periods of immunity. The discussion in turn prompts a consideration of some related issues which have not yet been fully developed in litigation.

The baseball exemption is considered first.[8] Interesting questions arise concerning the precise doctrinal basis for giving baseball a special status. In addition, it is noted that there is some uncertainty as to exactly which aspects of the sport come under the immunity umbrella. This is a question which has received only limited attention in the cases and which thus invites further debate about the reason for the exemption.

---

5. See, e.g., Mackey v. National Football League, 543 F.2d 606 (8th Cir. 1976); Robertson v. National Basketball Ass'n, 389 F. Supp. 867 (S.D.N.Y. 1975); Philadelphia World Hockey Club, Inc. v. Philadelphia Hockey Club, Inc., 351 F. Supp. 462 (E.D. Pa. 1972).

6. See § 5.03 infra.

7. See §§ 5.04-.06 infra.

8. See § 5.02 infra.

The next several sections deal with the issues which are suggested by the cases challenging the player restraints. In considering the labor exemption, we explore both the Supreme Court precedents which defined the exemption and the lower court decisions which considered its applicability in the sports context.[9] One section specifically examines the operation of the exemption in situations in which restrictions on the athlete's mobility have been approved in collective bargaining.[10] The player restraint cases also provide the basis for a discussion of the substantive antitrust issues raised by the leagues' attempts to control competition for player services. An effort is made to trace the development of the case law dealing with these matters and to explain why the courts have differed in their resolution of the issues which are presented.[11] This discussion of the cases provides the background for a consideration of how a league might modify its practices to avoid the antitrust controversy, a discussion which assumes that the practices have not otherwise been immunized through collective bargaining.

A point which is unmistakeable in the player restraint cases is that courts are not prepared to give the leagues complete freedom to control the level of competition in the sports labor market. This general concern for the role of the leagues in restricting the players' economic opportunities leads to the discussion of other issues which have received little attention in the cases. One section of the following materials examines how the antitrust laws might be applied to evaluate a variety of league rules, ranging from those which define the rules of competition to those which limit a club's acquisition of new players.[12] Separate consideration is given to the issue of whether the antitrust laws can be used to control the power of leagues and clubs to discipline players.[13] Such actions may lead to a player's exclusion from the sport, or some other severe economic consequence, and the concerns here are not wholly different from those which have appeared in other antitrust contexts.

In the last several sections of the chapter our focus moves away from the player-related issues in professional team sports to three topics involving different aspects of the sports industry. A section dealing with the exclusionary practices of sports associations discusses the antitrust restraints which must be observed by groups which undertake to sanction or sponsor commerical sports activities, such as professional golf and racing associations.[14] The antitrust concern arises because the eligibility and disciplinary decisions of these groups can have a significant effect upon the economic interests of the persons affected. A second section deals with the antitrust status of the organizations, particularly the NCAA, which regulate amateur sports.[15] As might be expected, there is a threshold issue as to whether the antitrust laws were intended to be applied to the activities of educational institutions. This issue is discussed, as is the equally important question of the standard of review to be applied to evaluate those aspects of NCAA regulation which are subject to antitrust scrutiny. A third topic which is considered concerns the antitrust implications of franchising decisions

9. *See* §§ 5.04-.06 *infra.*
10. *See* § 5.05 *infra.*
11. *See* § 5.06 *infra.*
12. *See* § 5.08 *infra.*
13. *See* § 5.09 *infra.*
14. *See* § 5.10 *infra.*
15. *See* § 5.12 *infra.*

by the major sports leagues.[16] It is clear that when a league undertakes to establish a new franchise or move an existing one, there are a number of parties who may be adversely affected by the action. Since the existing franchise-holders make the decisions as to how the franchises will be allocated, a question arises as to whether this is not an improper attempt to control the development of the market in the particular league. The discussion below considers this and related questions in light of the policies of the antitrust laws and the limited body of case law which has developed.

§ 5.02. Baseball's Antitrust Exemption.

As the previous chapters should indicate, there is a good deal of uncertainty in the law of sports. The industry is unique in many respects, and most issues have not received extensive attention in the courts. There is one issue which, on the surface at least, seems to stand as an exception. As a result of repeated affirmances by the Supreme Court, it is clear that the sport of baseball enjoys immunity from the antitrust laws.[17] Thus, while the antitrust status of player

---

16. *See* § 5.11 *infra.*

17. There is an extensive body of material relevant to baseball's antitrust exemption. In the list which follows the sources are classified under three categories: (1) case decisions; (2) legal publications; and (3) congressional materials. The listing includes major cases involving other entertainment activities in which the scope of the baseball exemption is discussed.

(1) Case Decisions.

Flood v. Kuhn, 407 U.S. 258 (1972), *aff'g* 443 F.2d 264 (2d Cir. 1971), *aff'g* 316 F. Supp. 271 (S.D.N.Y. 1970); Radovich v. National Football League, 352 U.S. 445 (1957); United States v. International Boxing Club, 348 U.S. 236 (1955); United States v. Shubert, 348 U.S. 222 (1955); Toolson v. New York Yankees, Inc., 346 U.S. 356 (1953), *aff'g per curiam,* 200 F.2d 198 (9th Cir. 1952), *aff'g per curiam,* 101 F. Supp. 93 (S.D. Cal. 1951); Kowalski v. Chandler, 346 U.S. 356, *aff'g per curiam,* 202 F.2d 413 (6th Cir. 1953); Corbett v. Chandler, 346 U.S. 356, *aff'g per curiam,* 202 F.2d 428 (6th Cir. 1953); Federal Baseball Club of Baltimore, Inc. v. National League of Professional Baseball Clubs, 259 U.S. 200 (1922), *aff'g* 269 F. 681 (D.C. Cir. 1920); Portland Baseball Club, Inc. v. Kuhn, 491 F.2d 1101, *aff'g* 368 F.Supp. 1004 (D. Ore. 1974); Amateur Softball Ass'n v. United States, 467 F.2d 312 (10th Cir. 1972); Salerno v. American League of Professional Baseball Clubs, 429 F.2d 1003 (2d Cir. 1970), *cert. denied,* 400 U.S. 1001 (1971); Portland Baseball Club, Inc. v. Baltimore Baseball Club, Inc., 282 F.2d 680 (9th Cir. 1960); Gardella v. Chandler, 172 F.2d 402 (2d Cir. 1949), *rev'g* 79 F. Supp. 260 (S.D.N.Y. 1948), *subsequent proceedings,* 1949 Trade Cas. ¶ 62,412 (S.D.N.Y.), *aff'd,* 174 F.2d 919 (2d Cir. 1949); Martin v. National League, 174 F.2d 917 (2d Cir. 1949), *aff'g* Martin v. Chandler, 1949 Trade Cas. ¶ 62, 397 (S.D.N.Y.); Niemiec v. Seattle Rainier Baseball Club, Inc., 67 F. Supp. 705 (W.D. Wash. 1946); American League Baseball Club of Chicago v. Chase, 86 Misc. 441, 149 N.Y.S. 6 (1914); Wisconsin v. Milwaukee Braves, Inc., 31 Wis. 2d 699, 144 N.W.2d 1, *cert. denied,* 385 U.S. 990 (1966).

(2) Legal Publications.

J. VON KALINOWSKI, ANTITRUST LAW AND TRADE REGULATION (16F BUSINESS ORGANIZATIONS 1971) §§ 50.01-.04 [hereinafter cited as VON KALINOWSKI]; Rivkin, *Sports Leagues and the Antitrust Laws* GOVERNMENT AND THE SPORTS BUSINESS 387 (R. Noll ed. 1974); Allison, *Professional Sports and the Antitrust Law: Status of the Reserve System,* 25 BAYLOR L. REV. 1 (1973); Eckler, *Baseball — Sport or Commerce?,* 17 U. CHI. L. REV. 56 (1949); Gromley, *Baseball and the Antitrust Laws,* 34 NEB. L. REV. 597 (1955); Johnson, *The Law of Sport: The Unique Performer's Contract and the Antitrust Laws,* 2 ANTITRUST BULL. 251 (1957); Keefe, *The Flood Case at Ebbtide,* 59 A.B.A.J. 91 (1973); Keith, *Developments in the Application of Antitrust Laws to Professional Sports,* 10 HASTINGS L.J. 119 (1958); Martin, *The Aftermath of Flood v. Kuhn: Professional Baseball's Exemption from Antitrust Regulation,* 3 WES. ST. U. L. REV. 262 (1976); Morris, *In the Wake of the Flood,* 38 LAW & CONTEMP. PROB. 85 (1973); Neville, *Baseball and the Antitrust Laws,* 16 FORD. L. REV. 208 (1947); Pierce, *Organized Professional Team Sports and the Antitrust Laws,* 43 CORNELL

restraints and league operating rules present lively issues in other sports, baseball has been given a special status which moots this controversy as far as that sport is concerned.

The extensive judicial treatment, however, has not completely settled all issues, and the certainty which otherwise exists begins to evaporate as one attempts to define the reach of the exemption. As mentioned, it seems clear that baseball's reserve system partakes of the immunity, and most issues relating to the structure of the leagues similarly appear to have been removed from

L. REV. 566 (1958); Topkis, *Monopoly in Professional Sports,* 58 YALE L.J. 691 (1949); Comment, *The Modern Trend in Antitrust and Professional Sports,* 22 ALBANY L. REV. 272 (1958); Comment, *Baseball's Antitrust Exemption: The Limits of Stare Decisis,* 12 B.C. IND. & COMM. L. REV. 737 (1971); Comment, *Boxing Exhibitions and Theatrical Productions Under the Sherman Antitrust Act,* 35 B.U.L. REV. 447 (1955); Comment, *Antitrust and Professional Sport: Does Anyone Play by the Rules of the Game?,* 22 CATH. U.L. REV. 403 (1973); Comment, *Effect of Gardella on the Treble Damages Suit,* 44 ILL. L. REV. 493 (1949); Comment, *Sherman Act — Amenability of Organized Baseball,* 34 IOWA L. REV. 545 (1949); Comment, *The Balance of Power in Professional Sports,* 22 MAINE L. REV. 459 (1970); Comment, *Reserve Clauses in Athletic Contracts,* 2 RUTGERS-CAMDEN L.J. 302 (1970); Comment, *Baseball and the Commerce Clause,* 20 TENN. L. REV. 770 (1949); Comment, *Player Control Mechanisms in Professional Sports,* 34 U. PITT. L. REV. 645 (1973); Comment, *Organized Baseball and Law,* 46 YALE L.J. 1386 (1937); Comment, *Monopsony in Manpower: Organized Baseball Meets the Antitrust Laws,* 62 YALE L.J. 576 (1953); Note, *Applicability of State Law to Baseball,* 8 B.C. IND. & COMM. L. REV. 341 (1967); Note, *Baseball Players and the Antitrust Laws,* 33 COLUM. L. REV. 242 (1953); Note, *Professional Football Held Within Purview of Sherman Act,* 57 COLUM. L. REV. 725 (1957); Note, *Monopolies—Professional Football,* 62 DICK. L. REV. 96 (1957); Note, *Commerce and Supremacy Clauses Exempt Professional Baseball from State Antitrust Statute,* 35 FORD. L. REV. 350 (1966); Note, *Sherman Act Application to Professional Boxing,* 23 GEO. WASH. L. REV. 606 (1955); Note, *Sale of Radio and Television Broadcast Rights Makes Modern Organized Baseball Interstate Commerce in the Constitutional Sense,* 37 GEO. L.J. 609 (1949); Note, *Professional Baseball May Constitute Interstate Commerce Within Antitrust Laws,* 62 HARV. L. REV. 1240 (1949); Note, *The Super Bowl and the Sherman Act: Professional Team Sports and the Antitrust Laws,* 81 HARV. L. REV. 418 (1967); Note, *Boxing as Trade or Commerce Within the Sherman Act,* 1 How. L.J. 281 (1955); Note, *Flood in the Land of Antitrust: Another Look at Professional Athletics, the Antitrust Laws and the Labor Law Exemptions,* 7 IND. L. REV. 541 (1974); Note, *Is Organized Baseball Interstate Commerce?,* 47 MICH. L. REV. 1214 (1949); Note, *Application of Sherman Act to Major League Baseball,* 33 MINN. L. REV. 428 (1949); Note, *Baseball and Interstate Commerce,* 25 MISS. L.J. 270 (1954); Note, *Boxing and Interstate Commerce,* 26 MISS. L.J. 271 (1955); Note, *Baseball and the Commerce Clause Pursuant to the Sherman Antitrust Act,* 28 NEB. L. REV. 616 (1949); Note, *Antitrust Law — Non-Applicability to Baseball,* 29 N.Y.U.L. REV. 213 (1954); Note, *Sherman Anti-Trust Act — Professional Sports,* 36 N.C.L. REV. 315 (1958); Note, *Baseball and the Antitrust Laws — A Game or a Conspiracy,* 24 NOTRE DAME LAW. 372 (1949); Note, *Curt Flood at Bat Against Baseball's Reserve Clause,* 8 SAN DIEGO L. REV. 92 (1971); Note, *Interstate Commerce — Professional Football,* 11 SW. L. J. 516 (1957); Note, *Live Presentation of Local Exhibitions as Constituting Trade or Commerce Within the Sherman Act,* 9 SW. L.J. 516 (1957); Note, *Live Presentation of Local Exhibitions as Constituting Trade or Commerce Within the Sherman Act,* 9 SW. L.J. 369 (1955); Note, *Promotion of Professional Boxing Contests Constitutes "Commerce" Within the Scope of the Sherman Act,* 29 TEMP. L.Q. 103 (1955); Note, *Use of the Doctrine of Legislative Silence in Implying Adoption of Judicial Interpretation — Toolson v. New York Yankees, Inc.,* 32 TEXAS L. REV. 890 (1954); Note, *Multistate Promotion of Professional Championship Boxing Contests,* 29 TUL. L. REV. 793 (1955); Note, *The Monopoly in Baseball,* 18 U. CINN. L. REV. 203 (1949); Note, *Monopoly — Baseball,* 22 U. KAN. CITY L. REV. 173 (1954); Note, *Professional Football Immune from Sherman Act as a Team Sport Not Constituting Interstate Commerce,* 105 U. PA. L. REV. 110 (1956); Note, *Baseball — An Exception to the Antitrust Laws,* 18 U. PITT. L. REV. 131 (1956); Note, *Baseball and the Law — Yesterday and Today,* 32 VA. L. REV. 1164 (1946); Note, *Baseball's Immunity from State Antitrust Law,* 13 WAYNE L. REV. 417 (1967); Note, *Baseball's Exemption and the Reserve System: Reappraisal of an Anachronism,* 12 WM. & MARY L. REV. 859 (1971).

(3) Congressional Materials.

S. REP. No. 462, 89th Cong., 1st Sess. (1965); *Hearings on S. 950 before the Subcomm. on Antitrust and Monopoly of the Senate Comm. on the Judiciary,* 89th Cong., 1st Sess. (1965); S. REP. No. 1303, 88th Cong., 2d Sess. (1964); *Hearings on S. 2391 before the Subcomm. on Antitrust and Monopoly of the Senate Comm. on the Judiciary,* 88th Cong., 2d Sess. (1964); *Hearings on S. 3483 before the*

judicial scrutiny.[18] But the status of other types of club and league activities, such as contracts for stadiums, transportation and so on, is far from settled.[19]

The following discussion begins with a review of the important cases which produced the exemption and attempts to identify the shift which has occurred in the Court's rationale for the immunity. The implications of the exemption for other sports is also considered, as is the question of baseball's status under state antitrust laws. A final subsection returns to the perplexing matter of the scope of baseball's immunity and proposes general guidelines which might be applied to identify the types of activities which remain subject to judicial scrutiny.

a. The Baseball Cases. While the issue of baseball's status under the antitrust laws had earlier been considered by other courts,[20] the Supreme Court first addressed the question in 1922 in *Federal Baseball Club of Baltimore, Inc. v. National League of Professional Baseball Clubs.*[21] The case arose when the only remaining team in the Federal League sued the National and American Leagues for treble damages in a private antitrust action. The complaint alleged that the defendants destroyed the Federal League by buying up some of its teams and otherwise inducing others to leave.[22] The Supreme Court found it unnecessary to consider the merits of the case, for the Court concluded that the defendants' activities did not involve interstate commerce and thus did not fall within the reach of the antitrust laws.[23] The Court's opinion suggests that there were two factors supporting this conclusion. The "business" involved was the giving of exhibitions of baseball, which in the Court's view, were "purely state affairs." [24] The Court recognized that the exhibitions required that "the Leagues must induce free persons to cross state lines," [25] but it held that under then-prevailing judicial standards,[26] "the transport is a mere incident, not the essential thing." [27] In addition to finding that the activity lacked the essential interstate character, the Court also concluded that it was not "commerce." In the Court's view, "personal effort, not related to production, is not a subject of commerce." [28]

Subcomm. on Antitrust and Monopoly of the Senate Comm. on the Judiciary, 86th Cong., 2d Sess. (1960); *Hearings on S. 616 and S. 886 before the Subcomm. on Antitrust and Monopoly of the Senate Comm. on the Judiciary,* 86th Cong., 1st Sess. (1959); *Hearings on H.R. 10378 and S. 4070 before the Subcomm. on Antitrust and Monopoly of the Senate Comm. on the Judiciary,* 85th Cong., 2d Sess. (1958); *Hearings on H.R. 5307 before the Antitrust Subcomm. of the House Comm. on the Judiciary,* 85th Cong., 1st Sess. (1957); H.R. REP. No. 2002, 82nd Cong., 2d Sess. (1952); *Hearings before Subcomm. on Study of Monopoly Power of the House Comm. on the Judiciary,* 82nd Cong., 1st Sess. (1951).

18. *See* text at notes 148-50 *infra.*
19. *See* text at notes 151-52 *infra.*
20. *See, e.g.,* American League Baseball Club of Chicago v. Chase, 86 Misc. 441, 149 N.Y.S. 6 (Sup. Ct. 1914). *See also* Comment, *Monopsony in Manpower: Organized Baseball Meets the Antitrust Laws,* 62 YALE L.J. 576-77 (1953).
21. 259 U.S. 200 (1922), *aff'g* 269 F. 681 (D.C. Cir. 1920), *noted in* 34 HARV. L. REV. 554 (1921).
22. *See* 259 U.S. at 207. The plaintiff's complaint was directed to an agreement which had been reached between the established leagues and all other members of the Federal League. The agreement effectively ended the new league, and the plaintiff, the only party not to accept it, alleged that it was damaged by the elimination of its opponents.
23. *See* Sherman Antitrust Act §§ 1, 2, 26 Stat. 209, 15 U.S.C. §§ 1, 2 (1970).
24. 259 U.S. at 208.
25. *Id.* at 209.
26. *Id.*
27. *See* Hooper v. California, 155 U.S. 648 (1895).
28. 259 U.S. at 209. Some have mistakenly read *Federal Baseball* as holding that baseball was not a business, but rather in the nature of a recreational activity, and exempt from the antitrust laws for that reason. That was clearly not the Court's holding, for it specifically recognized the

Both of these grounds were substantially undermined in the next thirty years. In that period the Court significantly expanded its definition of interstate commerce. By the same token, changes within the baseball industry itself greatly increased the magnitude of its multi-state involvement. By virtue of expansion of the industry and the increased broadcasting and recruiting activities, the business of baseball had become so embroiled in interstate commerce that it likely would have satisfied even the early standards for Sherman Act coverage articulated in the contemporaries of *Federal Baseball*.[29] In addition, Supreme Court decisions in the 1930's and 1940's had virtually overruled the specific precedents on which *Federal Baseball* was based. The threshold for finding an effect on interstate commerce had been dramatically reduced,[30] and the classification of "commerce" for the purposes of the Sherman Act had been extended to include personal services.[31]

Legal authorities began to espouse the view that *Federal Baseball* would no longer protect the sport from antitrust attack.[32] Lower courts began to question the general precedential value of the decision,[33] and finally in *Gardella v. Chandler*[34] the Second Circuit announced that it was prepared to find that the case no longer controlled in the baseball industry. Gardella, who had been under contract with the New York Giants of the National League, had jumped to the recently formed Mexican League. Alleging that he had thereby violated his obligation under the reserve system, the American and National Leagues ordered that Gardella be barred from playing in either major league for a period of years.[35] When the player then sued on antitrust grounds, the district court dismissed the complaint relying on *Federal Baseball*.[36] On appeal, however, two of the three judges on the Second Circuit panel found that *Federal Baseball* should not preclude further proceedings. Since this majority included the eminent jurists, Learned Hand and Jerome N. Frank, the case seemed to support the predictions of others that the demise of baseball's antitrust immunity was near.

However, the circuit court's opinion in *Gardella* could hardly be read as a wholesale repudiation of *Federal Baseball*. For his part, Judge Hand merely held

commercial nature of the venture involved. Rather, the Court found there was no *commerce* involved, under the narrow meaning which it had previously given that term. *Id.*

29. As early as 1923, Justice Holmes, in his opinion in Hart v. Keith Vaudeville Exchange, 262 U.S. 271, clarified the position he had taken in authoring the opinion in *Federal Baseball*. With respect to the matter of an enterprise's interstate activities, he noted that what "in general is incidental in some instances may rise to a magnitude that requires it to be considered independently." 262 U.S. at 274. *See also* Neville, *Baseball and the Antitrust Laws,* 16 FORD. L. REV. 208, 215 (1947).

30. *See, e.g.,* Apex Hosiery Co. v. Leader, 310 U.S. 469, 511 (1940); NLRB v. Jones & Laughlin Steel Corp., 301 U.S. 1 (1937).

31. *See, e.g.,* United States v. National Ass'n of Real Estate Boards, 339 U.S. 485 (1950); American Medical Ass'n v. United States, 317 U.S. 519 (1943). *See also* Comment, *Monopsony in Manpower: Organized Baseball Meets the Antitrust Laws, supra* note 20, at 611.

32. *Id.* at 612; Neville, *Baseball and the Antitrust Laws, supra* note 29, at 208; Topkis, *Monopoly in Professional Sports,* 58 YALE L.J. 691 (1949).

33. *See* Ring v. Spira, 142 F.2d 647 (2d Cir. 1945) (theatrical productions).

34. 172 F.2d 917 (2d Cir. 1949), *rev'g,* 79 F. Supp. 260 (S.D.N.Y. 1948), *noted in* 18 U. CINN. L. REV. 203 (1949); 34 IOWA L. REV. 545 (1949); 33 MINN. L. REV. 428 (1949); 37 GEO. L. REV. 618 (1949); 62 HARV. L. REV. 1240 (1949); 28 NEB. L. REV. 616 (1949); 47 MICH. L. REV. 1214 (1949); 20 TENN. L. REV. 770 (1949); 44 ILL. L. REV. 493 (1949). *See also* Gardella v. Chandler, 174 F.2d 919 (2d Cir.), *aff'g* 1949 Trade Cas. ¶ 62,412 (S.D.N.Y. 1949).

35. 172 F.2d at 403.

36. 79 F. Supp. 26 (S.D.N.Y. 1948).

that *Gardella* should be remanded to the district court for a specific determination of whether the industry's recently expanded interstate activities — particularly those involving broadcasting — were of such significance to the industry that the interstate aspects of the sport could no longer be characterized as incidental, as they had been in *Federal Baseball*.[37] Judge Frank, who also voted to remand, was willing to go further and concluded that sufficient interstate involvement had been established to distinguish the case from *Federal Baseball*.[38] Whatever hope there was that Justices Hand and Frank's opinions would force a reconsideration by the Supreme Court was lost when the *Gardella* case was later settled out of court.[39]

There is some basis to doubt, even as early as *Gardella*, whether *Federal Baseball* would stand or fall solely on the continued validity of the Supreme Court's analysis of the interstate commerce question. It is true that the Supreme Court's articulated basis for finding antitrust immunity in 1922 was the absence of interstate commerce. But even in the early period, an undercurrent of the exemption question was that the immunity ought to be extended on the pure policy grounds of the special needs of a sport which had captured the nation's interest. The perceived danger of judicial meddling in the National Pastime was a major part of the argument which the defendants presented to the Court in *Federal Baseball*.[40] It may have been that the Court was reluctant to let the fact that baseball games necessitated the crossing of state lines stifle the industry itself, particularly when the nature of the venture, in the view of some, was so obviously different from the sorts of commercial activity to which the antitrust laws were primarily directed.[41]

Since the articulated basis of *Federal Baseball* appeared to be losing its vitality, lower court challenges to the baseball exemption continued. The controversy eventually again found its way to the Supreme Court in 1953. The occasion for the Court's further consideration was *Toolson v. New York Yankees*,[42] a consolidation of cases in which players sought to renew the antitrust challenge to the baseball reserve system.[43] The players' complaints had been dismissed in the lower courts on the basis of *Federal Baseball*.[44] The Supreme Court affirmed the dismissal by a 7-2 vote. In a *per curiam* opinion, the Court stated:

> Without reexamination of the underlying issues, the judgments below are affirmed on the authority of *Federal Baseball* so far as that

37. 172 F.2d at 408.

38. *Id.* at 409-10.

39. *See* Martin, *The Aftermath of Flood v. Kuhn: Professional Baseball's Exemption from Antitrust Regulation*, 3 WES. ST. U. L. REV. 262, 265 n.15 (1976).

40. *See* Comment, *Monopsony in Manpower: Organized Baseball Meets the Antitrust Laws, supra* note 20, at 612-13. The emotional tenor of the argument is instructive. The case was argued on the eve of the opening of the playing season. Senator Pepper, arguing for the defendants, suggested that the very existence of the sport depended on the exemption. The case was argued to a bench headed by Chief Justice Taft who had been approached by organized baseball in 1918 to be its first commissioner.

41. *See* Judge Chase's opinion in *Gardella*, 172 F.2d at 403.

42. 346 U.S. 356 (1953).

43. The cases considered with *Toolson* were Kowalski v. Chandler, 202 F.2d 413 (6th Cir. 1953); Corbett v. Chandler, 202 F.2d 428 (6th Cir. 1953). The lower court decisions in *Toolson* are found at 200 F.2d 198 (9th Cir. 1952), *aff'g per curiam*, 101 F. Supp. 93 (S.D. Cal. 1951).

44. See cases cited in note 43 *supra*.

decision holds that Congress had no intention of including the business of baseball within the scope of the antitrust laws.[45]

The Court premised its decision on the fact that Congress had considered the baseball exemption and had not seen fit to abolish it. The Court took this fact as an indication that Congress did not intend that baseball should be subjected to antitrust regulation. Moreover, the Court observed that "the business has thus been left for thirty years to develop on the understanding that it was not subject to existing antitrust legislation." [46] In the Court's view, "if there are evils in this field which now warrant application to it of the antitrust laws it should be by legislation." [47]

Justice Burton added a somewhat curious dissent. The majority made no pretense of continuing the early conclusion of *Federal Baseball* that the sport did not involve the requisite interstate commerce. However, Justice Burton stated that the majority, "in effect, announced that organized baseball, in 1953, still is not engaged in interstate trade or commerce." [48] He then proceeded to devote the bulk of his opinion to documenting the sport's ever-expanding interstate involvement. He responded only briefly to the majority's primary finding of tacit congressional approval of the notion that baseball should not be subject to antitrust regulation. On this point, he merely observed that Congress "had enacted no express exemption . . . ." [49] Without more, Justice Burton's point was not wholly convincing, for the Court had previously carved out other exemptions without specific statutory direction.[50]

After *Toolson,* the Supreme Court's position seemed clear and, predictably, lower courts found little reason to question it.[51] Whatever encouragement *Gardella* had given for courts to test the premises of *Federal Baseball* had effectively been quieted by the refusal of the *Toolson* majority to rely on the interstate commerce rationale. While the decision was accepted by lower courts, it was not always vigorously defended. In *Salerno v. American League of Professional Baseball Clubs,*[52] Judge Friendly indicated that he would

> . . . freely acknowledge . . . that *Federal Baseball* was not one of Mr. Holmes' happiest days [and] that the rationale of *Toolson* is extremely dubious.[53]

---

45. 346 U.S. at 357.
46. *Id.*
47. *Id.*
48. *Id.*
49. *Id.* at 364.
50. *See, e.g.,* Parker v. Brown, 317 U.S. 341 (1943) (activities of state governments); United States v. Rock Royal Co-Op Ass'n, 307 U.S. 533, *rehearing denied,* 308 U.S. 631 (1939) (activities of federal government). *See also* FTC v. Raladam Co., 283 U.S. 643, *motion to modify judgment denied,* 284 U.S. 572 (1931) (medical profession). The judicially created exemptions are discussed generally in 16F VON KALINOWSKI § 44.03.
51. *See, e.g.,* Salerno v. American League of Professional Baseball Clubs, 429 F.2d 1003 (2d Cir. 1970), *cert. denied,* 400 U.S. 1001 (1971); Portland Baseball Club, Inc. v. Baltimore Baseball Club, 282 F.2d 686 (9th Cir. 1960). While *Toolson* introduced some certainty into the matter of baseball's antitrust status, it did little to settle the question of whether other sports enjoyed a similar immunity. As is discussed below, the treatment to be afforded other sports was later considered by the Supreme Court, and the Court made clear that the special exemption would be limited to the sport of baseball. *See* text at notes 82-98 *infra.*
52. 429 F.2d 1003 (2d Cir. 1970), *cert. denied,* 400 U.S. 1001 (1971).
53. 429 F.2d at 1005.

And while he had no doubt as to his obligation to continue to apply what was clearly the prevailing rule, he added that he and the judges for whom he spoke would not "fall out of our chairs with surprise at news that *Federal Baseball* and *Toolson* had been overruled . . . ."[54]

Toolson was an obvious invitation to those displeased with the exemption to take their case to Congress. One might have thought that the Court's effort to clearly demarcate this alternative strategy would have relieved the Court from further pressures to change the rule on its own. That was not the case, however, and in 1972, in *Flood v. Kuhn*[55] the Court considered the exemption for a third time, and ultimately reaffirmed its continuing vitality. It is interesting to note why this further reaffirmance of the exemption was necessary. Several different considerations can be identified. While the rationale of the grant of immunity to baseball had been found unconvincing by many observers, it seemed even less defensible when the Supreme Court subsequently made clear that the exemption would not extend to other sports and similar entertainment activities.[56] In the eyes of many observers, this distinction, which is discussed more fully below, was not based on a meaningful difference in the affected enterprises.[57] Moreover, baseball's ever increasing involvement in interstate activity continued to be seen as destroying the foundation upon which the exemption was based.[58] Finally, the baseball players, who bore the brunt of the sport's immunity in the form of the reserve system, were beginning to unionize, and a major focal point of their discontent was the pervasive controls which the clubs had over their employment opportunities.[59] This organizational effort not only heightened the level of discussion about the antitrust issue but also permitted the accumulation of the resources necessary to sustain the controversy.[60]

The focus of the antitrust complaint in *Flood v. Kuhn* was on the baseball reserve system. The petitioner, Curt Flood, objected that he was given no opportunity to approve, or avoid, an inter-team trade which would have required that he move from St. Louis to Philadelphia.[61] The case involved extensive

---

54. *Id.*

55. 407 U.S. 258 (1972), *aff'g* 443 F.2d 264 (2d Cir. 1971), *aff'g* 316 F. Supp. 271 (S.D.N.Y. 1970). Other aspects of the district court proceedings in Flood are reported at 312 F. Supp. 404 (S.D.N.Y. 1970) and 309 F. Supp. 793 (S.D.N.Y. 1970).

56. *See, e.g.,* Radovich v. National Football League, 352 U.S. 445 (1957); United States v. International Boxing Club, Inc., 348 U.S. 236 (1955); United States v. Shubert, 348 U.S. 222 (1955).

57. *See* text at notes 82-98 *infra. See also* Comment, *Baseball's Antitrust Exemption: The Limits of Stare Decisis,* 12 B.C. IND. & COMM. L. REV. 737 (1971); Note, *Baseball's Exemption and the Reserve System: Reappraisal of an Anachronism,* 12 WM. & MARY L. REV. 859 (1971).

58. *See* Note, *Baseball's Exemption and the Reserve System: Reappraisal of an Anachronism, supra* note 57, at 859; *cf.* Comment, *The Super Bowl and the Sherman Act: Professional Team Sports and the Antitrust Laws,* 81 HARV. L. REV. 418 & n.4 (1967).

59. *See generally* Scoville, *Labor Relations in Sports* in GOVERNMENT AND THE SPORTS BUSINESS 185, 204-211, 214-16 (R. Noll ed. 1974); Comment, *Flood in the Land of Antitrust: Another Look at Professional Athletics, the Antitrust Laws, and the Labor Law Exemption,* 17 IND. L. REV. 541 (1974).

60. The baseball players' union has played an active role in the effort to modify the traditional reserve system. Interestingly, its most important victory was achieved, not through traditional litigation, but through arbitration, where the uniform player contract was interpreted as giving the clubs a right to unilaterally renew a player's contract for only one year. *See* § 5.03 *infra.*

61. The *Flood* case is commented on in 16F VON KALINOWSKI §§ 50.01-.04; Rivkin, *Sports Leagues and the Antitrust Laws* in GOVERNMENT AND THE SPORTS BUSINESS 387 (R. Noll ed. 1974); Allison, *Professional Sports and the Antitrust Law: Status of the Reserve System,* 25 BAYLOR L. REV. 1 (1973); Keefe, *The Flood Case at Ebbtide,* 59 A.B.A.J. 91 (1973); Martin, *The Aftermath of Flood v. Kuhn: Professional Baseball's Exemption from Antitrust Regulation, supra* note 39; Morris, *In*

proceedings in the lower courts, but in each instance in which the antitrust issue was addressed, it was concluded that *Federal Baseball* and *Toolson* precluded a review of the merits of Flood's contentions.[62] When the case reached the Supreme Court, a 5-3 majority concluded that nothing in the facts of the case or collateral developments required a disavowal of the industry's special exemption.

The majority opinion, authored by Justice Blackmun, did attempt to settle some concerns generated by the prior cases. The Court premised its analysis with an explicit statement recognizing that professional baseball was a business and that it was involved in interstate commerce.[63] By thus dismissing the interstate commerce issue, the Court made clear that the exemption rested on grounds other than those upon which *Federal Baseball* was based. Moreover, the majority indicated that it appreciated the seeming anomaly of granting antitrust immunity to baseball while denying a similar status to other professional sports.[64] While the baseball exemption was thus an aberration, in the Court's view "the aberration is an established one." [65] And because the Court had affirmed the special immunity for baseball on at least five occasions in the past,[66] the exemption seemed to rest on a principle which was "fully entitled to the benefit of *stare decisis.*" [67] This result was accepted with express recognition that "other sports operating interstate . . . are not so exempt." [68]

Some may criticize *Flood* for adhering too rigidly to the principle of *stare decisis.* It has been emphasized that there is a danger that the principle will be applied mechanically and thus serve to perpetuate outmoded judicial policies.[69] The preferred approach is one which accepts previous decisions as controlling only when an examination of the underlying issues both confirms their initial soundness and establishes that nothing has occurred since the intervening period to require a different result.[70] It might be suggested that the *Flood* majority failed to follow this course when it sustained the exemption despite its recognition that the rationale of the original grant of immunity in *Federal Baseball* had been substantially eroded in light of the indisputable interstate character of the modern baseball industry. However, other portions of the *Flood* decision make clear that the Court did in fact make the sort of reassessment necessary for the proper application of *stare decisis.* But the rationale which the

the *Wake of the Flood,* 38 LAW & CONTEMP. PROB. 85 (1973); Comment, *Baseball's Antitrust Exemption: The Limits of Stare Decisis, supra* note 57; Comment, *Antitrust and Professional Sport: Does Anyone Play by the Rules of the Game?,* 22 CATH. U. L. REV. 403 (1973); Comment, *Flood in the Land of Antitrust: Another Look at Professional Athletics, the Antitrust Laws, and the Labor Exemption, supra* note 59; Note, *Baseball's Exemption and the Reserve System: Reappraisal of an Anachronism, supra* note 57.

62. *See* 443 F.2d 264 (2d Cir. 1971), *aff'g* 316 F. Supp. 258 (S.D.N.Y. 1970). *See also* 309 F. Supp. 793 (S.D.N.Y. 1970).

63. 407 U.S. at 282.

64. *Id.* at 282-83.

65. *Id.* at 282.

66. These included *Federal Baseball* and *Toolson,* as well as Radovich v. National Football League, 352 U.S. 445 (1957); United States v. International Boxing Club, 348 U.S. 236 (1955); United States v. Shubert, 348 U.S. 222 (1955). The latter cases, in which the Court refused to extend the baseball exemption to other sports and entertainment activities, are discussed at notes 82-98 *infra.*

67. 407 U.S. at 282.

68. *Id.* at 282-83.

69. *See* Helvering v. Hallock, 309 U.S. 106, 119 (1940) (Frankfurter, J.).

70. *See* Comment, *Baseball's Antitrust Exemption: The Limits of Stare Decisis, supra* note 57, at 744.

Court apparently thought warranted critical examination was that used in the more recent *Toolson* decision, not the less defensible premises of *Federal Baseball.* As has been indicated, the *per curiam* opinion in *Toolson* carefully avoided the interstate commerce question and introduced a different basis for continuation of the exemption. Specifically, the *Toolson* Court found that Congress' failure to enact legislative proposals to bring baseball under the antitrust umbrella indicated an intention to approve the industry's exemption. When the issue was reexamined in *Flood,* the Court found little basis upon which to repudiate this rationale. There had been further proposals for congressional abolition of the exemption in the period since *Toolson,* but none of these had been adopted, and the industry had been allowed to develop another two decades free of antitrust controls.[71] Further, this development had occurred even though Congress was fully aware that in *Toolson,* the Court had expressed an intention to remove itself from a policy-making role on the matter and had stated that if a change were to be made, "it should be by legislation." [72] In the intervening period, Congress had neither eliminated the exemption nor disclaimed that the initiative to do so rested with it. Thus, nothing had occurred which suggested that the *Toolson* approach ought to be abandoned.

The *Flood* majority took care to make clear that it was not simply Congress' failure to act which the Court found persuasive. The majority emphasized that specific proposals had been considered by Congress, but all had been rejected. In the Court's view, this involved more than "mere congressional silence and passivity." [73] Rather, through its "positive inaction," Congress had "clearly evinced a desire not to disapprove" the Court's earlier grant of immunity.[74] Thus, the Court perceived that by upholding baseball's exemption, it not only was showing proper respect for its own precedents but also was carrying out a legislative design which had been repeatedly reaffirmed.

Not surprisingly, the Court's treatment of the exemption question has generated considerable commentary in the legal literature.[75] Particular criticism has been directed to the *Toolson* notion that the baseball industry's entitlement to an exemption is enhanced by the fact that it has been allowed to develop free of antitrust scrutiny. One commentator rejects the idea that the industry has developed a reliance interest which is entitled to protection, for it would require that one accept that the Court "contracts" with affected parties when it defines legal principles.[76] It can be noted that the Court has on other occasions reversed precedents which had fostered the development of particular industries.[77] There is little evidence that these have had the disastrous effects which the Court seems to assume would be visited upon the sport of baseball.

---

71. *See* 407 U.S. at 281-83.
72. *See* Toolson v. New York Yankees, Inc., 346 U.S. 356, 357 (1953).
73. 407 U.S. at 283.
74. *Id.* at 283-84.
75. *See* sources cited note 61 *supra.*
76. *See* Note, *Baseball's Exemption and the Reserve System: Reappraisal of an Anachronism, supra* note 57, at 866.
77. *See, e.g.,* United States v. Southeastern Underwriters Ass'n, 322 U.S. 533 (1944). *See also id.* at 578 (Stone, J., dissenting); Neville, *Baseball and the Antitrust Laws,* 16 FORD. L. REV. 208, 226 (1947).

It is also predictable that many have been unpersuaded by the efforts of the *Toolson* and *Flood* Courts to fashion a purposeful intent from congressional inaction on the exemption question.[78] Justice Douglas added support to this skepticism in his dissent in *Flood* by his observation that as creator of the exemption, the Court should correct its "own mistakes." [79] Other commentators are more critical and emphasize that while Congress has refused to overturn the exemption, it has also refused to exact legislation which would have specifically sanctioned it.[80] Some carry this idea further and suggest that the Congress has the primary responsibility for defining who will be affected by the antitrust laws and the Court should not recognize exemptions in the absence of a specific statutory authorization.[81] While such criticisms may indicate that the Court's approach to the exemption question has not been wholly convincing, there are few who suggest that the Court could be persuaded to reverse its position. Indeed, when the *Flood* case is reduced to its essential principles, one finds that it is basically a four-square reaffirmation of *Toolson.* While the case does elaborate on some principles which appear only opaquely in the brief *per curiam* in *Toolson,* the more complete statement of the Court's position only serves to make unmistakable that it has chosen to remove itself from the process which will determine whether and how long the baseball exemption will continue.

b. Sports Other Than Baseball. As previously mentioned, the Court has been fully prepared to subject other sports and entertainment activities to the full force of the antitrust laws even while recognizing that these ventures are functionally indistinguishable from baseball. The process of limiting the reach of the baseball exemption began very soon after the *Federal Baseball* decision in 1922. In *Hart v. Keith Vaudeville,*[82] decided the next year, Justice Holmes

78. *See, e.g.,* Comment, *Baseball's Antitrust Exemption: The Limits of Stare Decisis, supra* note 57, at 741-42.

The Court's actions in other cases make clear that it does not always feel bound by congressional inaction. *See, e.g.,* James v. United States, 366 U.S. 213 (1961); Giroud v. United States, 328 U.S. 61 (1946); Helvering v. Hallock, 309 U.S. 106 (1940). Before *Flood,* at least one lower court expressed the view that the Supreme Court might be prepared to change its view of the importance of congressional inaction. Judge Friendly noted in *Salerno v. American League* that

> Boys Mkts., Inc. v. Retail Clerks' Local 770, 398 U.S. 235 (1970), . . . overruling Sinclair Refining Co. v. Atkinson, 370 U.S. 195 (1962), despite Congress' failure to act on invitations to do so, may presage a change from the attitude with respect to such inaction that was expressed in *Toolson* . . . . 429 F.2d at 1005.

Judge Friendly misjudged the Court's reaction. It is clear that the majority in *Flood* did not regard the *Boys Market* case as controlling. The apparent basis for this was the majority's perception that Congress' refusal to eliminate the baseball exemption involved more than "mere . . . silence." *See* 407 U.S. at 283.

79. 407 U.S. at 286. Justice Marshall made a similar point and noted that the Court's isolation of baseball might have ruined the players' chances to get Congress to take action in their behalf. *Id.* at 292.

80. *See* Comment, *Baseball's Antitrust Exemption: The Limits of Stare Decisis, supra* note 57, at 741-42; Note, *Baseball's Exemption and the Reserve System: Reappraisal of an Anachronism, supra* note 57, at 867. *See also* 407 U.S. at 287 (Douglas, J., dissenting); Comment, *Monopsony in Manpower: Organized Sports Meets the Antitrust Laws,* 62 YALE L.J. 576, 613 (1953).

81. *See* Allison, *Professional Sports and the Antitrust Law: Status of the Reserve System, supra* note 61, at 14, 23. *See also* Note, *Baseball's Exemption and the Reserve System: Reappraisal of an Anachronism, supra* note 57, at 867.

82. 262 U.S. 271 (1923).

refused to dismiss an antitrust action against certain vaudeville promoters and strongly implied that *Federal Baseball* did not settle the interstate commerce issue for all activities involving public performances. In dicta, Holmes indicated that an interstate aspect of a business which is "in general incidental, in some instances may rise to a magnitude that requires it to be considered independently." [83]

The major decisions specifically addressing the issue of the reach of the exemption in the entertainment and sports industries came some thirty years later. Two years after it had reaffirmed baseball's immunity in *Toolson v. New York Yankees, Inc.*, the Court considered *United States v. Shubert*[84] and *United States v. International Boxing Club, Inc.*[85] *Shubert* was a civil antitrust action in which the government sought to force the defendant theatrical producers to divorce the booking and production aspects of their business. In addressing the defendants' claim that they were not subject to the antitrust laws, the Court relied on *Hart* and found that the government's complaint had stated a cause of action with respect to the issue of an impact on interstate commerce. In the Court's view, the transportation of actors and equipment across state lines was more than incidental to the business and was enough to establish trade or commerce within the meaning of the Sherman Act.[86] The Court rejected the argument that *Federal Baseball* immunized all public exhibitions, observing that *Toolson* did "not necessarily reaffirm all that was said in *Federal Baseball.*"[87] The Court made clear that Toolson had embraced *Federal Baseball* only in the sense of continuing its general holding that Congress did not intend baseball to be covered by the Sherman Act. The Court stressed that the two prior baseball decisions had created a special exemption, not a general standard for immunizing all exhibitions.

The Court's opinion in the companion *International Boxing* case served to emphasize further that *Toolson* was to be limited to the unique factual setting of the baseball industry. In a 7-2 decision, the Court reversed a district court order dismissing the government's civil antitrust action against three promoters of professional boxing matches. With respect to the defendants' assertion of antitrust immunity, the majority stated emphatically that the case before it had none of the elements which had been found controlling in *Toolson*. Thus, there was no firm judicial pronouncement immunizing the boxing industry from antitrust scrutiny, and in the Court's view, *Hart* should have put the defendants on notice that no general exemption had been created for businesses involving public exhibitions.[88]

International Boxing should have made clear that the Court was committed to limiting *Federal Baseball* and *Toolson* to the baseball industry. No other sport or entertainment venture would be able to establish the critical elements of an early judicial grant of immunity and repeated refusals by Congress to remove

83. 262 U.S. at 274. On remand, the trial court dismissed the case at the close of the evidence. The Second Circuit affirmed, stating that the plaintiff's evidence failed to establish that the interstate transportation involved was more than incidental to the business of staging the performance. 12 F.2d 341 (2d Cir.), *cert. denied,* 273 U.S. 703 (1926).

84. 348 U.S. 222 (1955).

85. 348 U.S. 236 (1955).

86. 348 U.S. at 225-29.

87. *Id.* at 230.

88. 348 U.S. at 242.

the protection. Nonetheless, to settle some suggestions that *International Boxing* applied only to non-team sports,[89] in 1957 the Court found it necessary to hear the case of *Radovich v. National Football League.*[90] Radovich had played in the NFL and then jumped to a rival league. When he later sought to accept a position in a minor league affiliated with the NFL, he found that he had been blacklisted, allegedly for failing to fulfill his obligations to his previous NFL team. Radovich brought an action asserting that the NFL and its affiliate had violated sections 1 and 2 of the Sherman Act. The district court had dismissed the complaint and the Ninth Circuit affirmed this dismissal on the grounds that the *Federal Baseball - Toolson* exemptions extended to the defendants and that the complaint otherwise failed to state a cause of action.[91] The Supreme Court reversed on both points and held that Radovich was entitled to a trial on the merits of his antitrust claims. The Court quoted the language which it had used in *Shubert* and *International Boxing* to indicate the special nature of the *Federal Baseball* and *Toolson* cases. The Court then stated:

> It seems that this language would have made it clear that the Court intended to isolate these cases by limiting them to baseball, but since *Toolson* and *Federal Baseball* are still cited as controlling authority in the antitrust actions involving other fields of business, we now specifically limit the rule there established to the facts there involved, *i.e.,* the business of organized professional baseball. As long as the Congress continues to acquiesce, we should adhere to — but not extend — the interpretation of the Act made in those cases.[92]

As has already been discussed, the Court continued to give controlling effect to this congressional acquiescence when it reaffirmed the baseball exemption twelve years later in *Flood v. Kuhn.* While *Flood* directly involved only the narrow issue of the baseball exemption, the Court there reiterated in dicta that "Other professional sports operating interstate . . . are not so exempt." [93]

The Court's unequivocal statement in *Radovich* that it would "not extend" the reach of *Federal Baseball* and *Toolson* had the desired effect of clarifying the issue in the lower courts. Since *Radovich,* the courts have applied the Sherman Act to several other sports. Those deemed subject to the antitrust laws include basketball,[94] hockey,[95] golf,[96] and bowling.[97] In addition, it is clear that other types of sports and entertainment will not be allowed to share baseball's special status.[98]

---

89. *See* Radovich v. National Football League, 231 F.2d 620, 623 (9th Cir. 1956), *rev'd,* 352 U.S. 445 (1957).

90. 352 U.S. 445 (1957).

91. 231 F.2d 620 (9th Cir. 1956).

92. 352 U.S. at 451.

93. 407 U.S. at 282-83.

94. *See* Haywood v. National Basketball Ass'n, 401 U.S. 1204 (1971); Robertson v. National Basketball Ass'n, 389 F. Supp. 867 (S.D.N.Y. 1975).

95. *See, e.g.,* Philadelphia World Hockey Club, Inc. v. Philadelphia Hockey Club, Inc., 351 F. Supp. 462 (E.D. Pa. 1972); Peto v. Madison Square Garden Corp., 1958 Trade Cas. ¶ 69, 106 (S.D.N.Y.).

96. *See* Deesen v. Professional Golfers Ass'n, 358 F.2d 165 (9th Cir. 1966); Blalock v. Ladies Professional Golf Ass'n, 359 F. Supp. 1260 (N.D. Ga. 1973).

97. *See* Washington State Bowling Proprietors Ass'n v. Pacific Lanes, Inc., 356 F.2d 371 (9th Cir. 1966).

98. *See, e.g.,* Bridge Corp. of America v. American Contract Bridge League, Inc., 428 F.2d 1365 (9th Cir. 1970); National Wrestling Alliance v. Myers, 325 F.2d 768 (8th Cir. 1963); Heldman v. United States Lawn Tennis Ass'n, 354 F. Supp. 1241 (S.D.N.Y. 1973); STP Corp. v. United States Auto Club, Inc., 286 F. Supp. 146 (S.D. Ind. 1968); United States v. United States Trotting Ass'n, 1960 Trade Cas. ¶ 69,761 (S.D. Ohio).

c. State Antitrust Laws. The Curt Flood litigation provided the occasion for the federal courts to consider whether baseball, despite its federal immunity, might be subject to regulation under state laws. The plaintiffs in that case raised the point that if *Federal Baseball* was correct that the sport was purely a state affair and did not involve interstate commerce, then surely its operation was a proper subject for state regulation.[99] The three federal courts which reviewed the case considered this argument, but ultimately each decided against the plaintiffs and concluded that the states were precluded from antitrust regulation.

Judge Cooper, who heard the *Flood* case in the district court, noted that after *Toolson,* it could no longer be said that the baseball exemption was premised on the absence of interstate involvement.[100] Rather, the basis of immunity was a congressional intention not to subject the sport to antitrust regulation.[101] In Judge Cooper's view, the more relevant inquiry was whether the notion of federal supremacy precluded the application of state laws. He observed initially that the logic of the Supreme Court's decision in *Toolson* seemed to require that states stay their regulatory efforts:

> We believe it unlikely that the Supreme Court would have held, as it did, that baseball's reliance interests precluded overruling *Federal Baseball* and that "Congress had no intention of including the business of baseball within the scope of the federal antitrust laws," if it considered baseball vulnerable to state regulation.[102]

Judge Cooper did not confine his rationale to the apparent intent of the Court and Congress.[103] He also found that the "nationwide character of organized baseball combined with the necessary interdependence of the teams" required that the sport be subject to uniform regulation.[104] In the Court's view, such uniformity would be lost if states were permitted to apply their "various and diverse . . . laws." [105]

When the case reached the Second Circuit, Judge Cooper's conclusion was affirmed.[106] The appellate court observed that the issue of the proper accommodation of federal and state antitrust laws had not previoulsy been defined by the Supreme Court. Citing *Southern Pacific Company v. Arizona,*[107] the court thought it appropriate to resolve the issue before it under a balancing test which weighed the states' interest in regulating the matter against the burden which potentially diverse interpretations would place on the interstate aspects of the sport.[108] Applying this test, the court concluded that the question

99. *See* 309 F. Supp. 793, 806 (S.D.N.Y. 1970).
100. *See* 316 F. Supp. 271, 278-79 (S.D.N.Y. 1970).
101. *Id.* at 279.
102. *Id.*
103. The dual nature of Judge Cooper's analysis has been overlooked by some courts. *See, e.g.,* Robertson v. National Basketball Ass'n, 389 F. Supp. 867, 880 (S.D.N.Y. 1975).
104. 316 F. Supp. at 279-80. It will be noted that the doctrinal classification of this reasoning is somewhat different than that which would be applicable under the view that Congress intended to preserve this field to its sole regulation. While the latter is an argument for federal preemption, the former is based on the authority reserved to Congress under the Commerce Clause.
105. *Id.* at 280.
106. 443 F.2d 264 (2d Cir. 1971).
107. 325 U.S. 761, 774-75 (1945). *See also* Note, *The Commerce Clause and State Antitrust Regulation,* 61 COLUM. L. REV. 1469 (1961).
108. 443 F.2d at 267-68.

of baseball's antitrust status required a uniform resolution which could be provided only by federal law:

> On the one hand, it is apparent that each league extends over many states, and that, if state regulation were permissible, the internal structure of the leagues would require compliance with the strictest state antitrust standard. . . . On the other hand, we do not find that a state's interest in antitrust regulation, when compared with its interest in health and safety regulation, is of particular urgency. Hence, as the burden on interstate commerce outweighs the states' interest in regulating baseball's reserve system, the Commerce Clause precludes the application here of state antitrust law.[109]

The issue of state antitrust regulation was dealt with in a single paragraph when the *Flood* case reached the Supreme Court. The Court quoted Judge Cooper's statement about the need for uniform regulation and the Second Circuit's conclusion that the potential burden on interstate commerce outweighed the states' interest in regulation. It concluded that "these statements adequately dispose of the state law claims." [110]

While the *Flood* litigation specifically dealt only with state regulation of baseball's reserve system, there is authority extending federal supremacy to other aspects of the industry as well. In *Wisconsin v. Milwaukee Braves, Inc.,*[111] a case which predated *Flood,* the Supreme Court of Wisconsin refused to entertain the plaintiff's complaint alleging various state antitrust law violations by the National League in connection with the movement of the club franchise from Milwaukee to Atlanta. The majority opinion was premised on two somewhat different theories. Some members reasoned that the sport of baseball involved substantial interstate activities; that Congress had evidenced an intention to allow the sport to develop free of antitrust regulation; and that state regulation through local antitrust laws would conflict with the congressional design.[112] Others joining the majority apparently were less certain that any firm congressional policy could be discerned. They concluded, however, the interdependent nature of the league's operation required uniform regulation and since the activities involved substantial interstate commerce, any regulation was properly reserved for Congress.[113] The ultimate conclusion of *Milwaukee Braves* that states were prohibited from applying their antitrust controls, was discussed with approval by the district court in *Flood,*[114] but the case was not specifically endorsed in either the court of appeals or the Supreme Court.[115]

While the brevity of the Supreme Court's treatment of the state law issue in *Flood* leaves somewhat ambiguous the theory upon which its finding of federal supremacy rests,[116] the language used can be read as endorsing the notion that the limitation is premised primarily on the need for uniformity and the lack of

---

109. *Id.* at 268.
110. 407 U.S. at 285.
111. 31 Wis. 2d 699, 144 N.W.2d 1, *cert. denied,* 385 U.S. 990 (1966).
112. *See* 31 Wis. 2d at 730, 144 N.W.2d at 17.
113. *See* 31 Wis. 2d at 731, 144 N.W.2d at 18.
114. *See* 316 F. Supp. at 279-80.
115. The Supreme Court cited the *Milwaukee Braves* case, but did not use the citation to support any particular principle of law. *See* 407 U.S. at 284 n.21.
116. Other courts have found the Supreme Court's rationale to be unclear. *See, e.g.,* Robertson v. National Basketball Ass'n, 389 F. Supp. 867, 880 (S.D.N.Y. 1975).

a substantial local interest in regulation.[117] One advantage of this approach to the issue is that it does not necessarily require a finding of a firm congressional intent to reserve particular matters to federal control. This difference would seem to be important in cases such as *Milwaukee Braves* where matters other than the reserve system are challenged under state law. Whatever legislative intent can be found arises mainly from Congress' decision not to adopt particular controls. Since Congress has not considered legislation affecting all of the aspects of the industry which might arise in litigation,[118] a state law exemption which required evidence of a specific intent could encounter difficulty. The details of congressional deliberations become less important when the focus is on the need for uniform regulation of an interstate business. Under this approach, a court can more properly focus on the potential for actual disruption in the operation of the industry which would result from local control.[119] When this latter element is emphasized, it would appear that the decision in *Milwaukee Braves* to extend federal supremacy to issues raised by franchise shifts can be sustained. Local efforts to control the movement of teams could substantially inhibit the league's operation. For example, the league has an interest in insuring that its clubs operate in markets sufficiently lucrative to permit the clubs to pay and retain quality players. In addition, the league is properly concerned that its clubs maintain sufficient geographical diversity to continue to attract national broadcasting contracts. While there may be a need for regulation of the league's prerogatives in this regard, the controls should be uniform and not variable according to the intensity of local feeling on the matter.

Milwaukee Braves also presents an interesting case for evaluating the extent of the local interest in regulating the particular activity. On the one hand, it would appear that a state would have a greater interest in preventing the loss of a sports franchise than in controlling restrictions such as those involved in *Flood* which limit player mobility. While a state has some interest in protecting those within its borders from oppressive employment contracts, this is not an interest which is unique to any particular locale and presumably it could be raised in a national forum which established a uniform regulation. Moreover, those who bear the burden of restrictive contractual provisions often have only a limited identification with the state and may not even qualify as citizens. By contrast, the location of franchises, particularly the loss of one, may directly affect substantial state interests.[120] The franchise may have both a direct

117. In quoting from the lower court opinions, the Court seems to have emphasized the need for uniform regulation and the burdensome nature of state control. These concerns are closer to those which underlie the Commerce Clause than those which support a pure preemption theory. *See* note 104 *supra*. While these are the points which the Court seems to have stressed, an ambiguity arises from the fact that the court referred to its prior decisions in sustaining the lower court dismissals of the state law claims. Its prior cases had made much of the matter of congressional intent, which is an important element in a preemption theory. Despite this reference, the Court's specific endorsement of the lower court's "statements" about the need for uniformity would suggest that the Court was not limiting itself to a theory which required specific congressional action.

118. A partial listing of relevant legislative materials is set forth in note 17 *supra*.

119. *See* notes 104 and 117 *supra*.

120. *See generally* Okner, *Subsidies of Stadiums and Arenas* in GOVERNMENT AND THE SPORTS BUSINESS 325 (R. Noll ed. 1974); Quirk, *An Economic Analysis of Team Movements in Professional Sports*, 38 LAW & CONTEMP. PROB. 42 (1973).

connection with the local government, in the form of stadium leases, financing commitments and the like, and a significant effect on the local economy.[121] And since the degree of governmental and private involvement is likely to vary from case to case, effective regulation will be difficult to achieve at the national level.[122]

While these considerations weigh in favor of permitting local controls, they are properly found insufficient to overcome the preference for federal control. Two points deserve particular emphasis. On the one hand, it will be noted that the fact that a business has a significant effect on local commerce is usually not a sufficient reason to overcome the policies favoring federal supremacy. Indeed, any major industry will have such an effect. But if its operation is basically national in character, limitations on local regulation may be necessary to avoid undesirable burdens on interstate commerce. Moreover, the fact of a significant local economic interest may well be a reason for limiting the application of local antitrust policies. There is a greater likelihood of state action which discriminates in favor of its own financial interests and ignores the interests of other states.[123] In order to avoid situations in which such local self-interest is permitted to inhibit the development of the business,[124] it seems appropriate that disputes be resolved in a national forum which takes account of the competing interests of other areas. Thus, although the question raised in *Milwaukee Braves* is in several respects a closer one than that considered in *Flood,* this extension of the supremacy doctrine appears to be proper.

The exclusivity of federal control is not limited to the sport of baseball if one accepts that the courts' primary concern is the need for uniform regulation of a highly interdependent interstate business. Other sports leagues have the same basic structure and would seem to be similarly immune from state antitrust laws. While the *Flood* decision involved a finding of a congressional intent to afford baseball a unique status, that factor seems not to have been a controlling element in the Supreme Court's approval of the limitation on state regulation. As previously noted, the Court specifically approved Judge Cooper's statement about the need for a singular legal standard and accepted the Second Circuit's determination that state regulation would unduly burden interstate

---

121. *See* Comment, *The Super Bowl and the Sherman Act: Professional Team Sports and the Antitrust Laws,* 81 HARV. L. REV. 418, n. 4 (1967).

122. That the state or municipality might be inclined to sue is established by the fact that a number of such suits have already been lodged in baseball and other sports. Among the most notable are those involving the actual or threatened shifts of (1) the Milwaukee baseball franchise, Wisconsin v. Milwaukee Braves, Inc., 31 Wis. 2d 669, 144 N.W.2d 1, *cert. denied,* 385 U.S. 990 (1966); (2) the Seattle baseball franchise, N.Y. Times, Feb. 18, 1976, at 36, col. 5; Washington Post, Feb. 14, 1976, at D5, col. 3; N.Y. Times, Feb. 10, 1976, at 48, col. 3; Globe & Mail (Toronto), Dec. 12, 1975, at 32, col. 5; (3) the San Francisco franchise, Washington Post, Feb. 12, 1976, at C1, col. 7; N.Y. Times, Feb. 10, 1976, at 48, col. 3; Gazette (Montreal), Jan. 14, 1976, at 26, col. 2; Washington Post, Jan. 13, 1976, at D1, col. 7; and (4) the Buffalo basketball franchise, N.Y. Times, June 29, 1976, at 38, col. 3; *id.* June 19, 1976, at 16, col. 6; *id.* June 16, at 29, col. 1.

123. In the district court proceeding in *Flood,* Judge Cooper intimated that because of the greater likelihood of local discrimination, the argument for prohibiting state antitrust regulation of franchise moves might be even stronger than that which could be made with respect to reserve clause questions. *See* 316 F. Supp. at 279.

124. *See* Wisconsin v. Milwaukee Braves, Inc., 31 Wis. 2d 699, 144 N.W.2d 1, *cert. denied,* 385 U.S. 990 (1966). There the court stated:

> There may well be thought to be a national interest in a wider distribution of available franchises throughout the country, but it may be doubted that a state will be objective in deciding whether that is an appropriate consideration, nor [sic] what the answer should be in a given case. *Id.* at 731, 144 N.W.2d at 18.

commerce.[125] Under this approach, it is the national character of the enterprise, and not the particular content of the federal regulation, which requires that the states stay their hand.[126]

At least two courts have accepted this interpretation. In *Matuszak v. Houston Oilers, Inc.,*[127] the plaintiff attempted to establish that the NFL standard player contract violated the Texas antitrust laws. The Court of Civil Appeals of Texas refused to consider this claim, relying on the Second Circuit's conclusion in *Flood* that "the burden on interstate commerce outweighs the states' interests . . . ." [128] A similar conclusion was reached by the federal district court in *Robertson v. National Basketball Association* [129] with respect to the plaintiffs' complaint that certain league practices violated the antitrust laws of New York. Judge Carter read *Flood* as calling for the uniform regulation of the sport of baseball, and observed that "baseball and basketball are in the same business." [130]

d. The Scope of Baseball's Antitrust Exemption. Despite the considerable attention which baseball's federal antitrust exemption has received in the courts and in legal publications, very little effort has been made to define the types of industry practices which enjoy immunity. While *Flood* should make clear that baseball's reserve system is not subject to antitrust attack, there are many other aspects of the business which might be the subject of litigation. Antitrust issues might arise in connection with the movement of franchises, the denial of franchises to interested investors or their cities, league or club control of stadiums, and intrusions by established clubs on newly formed leagues. In addition, leagues and clubs enter into a variety of contracts which could give rise to allegations of antitrust violations. These include agreements with non-player employees, television and radio contracts, contracts with respect to concessions, and an almost endless variety of agreements affecting the staging of exhibitions and the transporting and housing of athletes. Which of these partake of the antitrust immunity found in the Supreme Court's decision? There is no short answer. But it seems unlikely that either the Court or Congress intended that every activity connected with baseball, no matter how tangential, enjoys the protection of the immunity umbrella.

A review of the Supreme Court's decisions provides little in terms of a definition of the scope of the exemption. The language used in *Toolson* suggests only that immunity extends to "the business of baseball." The Court there stated that it was affirming *Federal Baseball* "as far as that decision determines that Congress had no intention of including the business of baseball within the scope of the federal antitrust laws." [131] This phrasing rather strongly implies that the exemption extends to matters other than the rules relating to the allocation and retention of players. This interpretation is also supported in other statements used by the Court to explain the reasons for baseball's special status. In various opinions, the Court has expressed the concern that after the *Federal Baseball* decision, the business of baseball had been allowed to develop on the assumption

125. *See* text at notes 110, 117 *supra.*
126. *See* note 117 *supra.*
127. 515 S.W.2d 725 (Tex. Civ. App. 1974).
128. 515 S.W.2d at 728-29, *quoting* 443 F.2d at 268.
129. 389 F. Supp. 867 (S.D.N.Y. 1975).
130. 389 F. Supp. at 881.
131. 346 U.S. at 357.

that it enjoyed antitrust immunity and that a later decision to overturn the exemption would retroactively undermine this reliance interest. For example, in explaining the *Toolson* decision in his opinion in *Radovich,* Justice Clark noted that "vast efforts had gone into the development and organization of baseball since [*Federal Baseball*] and enormous capital had been invested in reliance on its permanence." [132] Presumably these investments were made on the assumption that the basic structure and operation of the leagues, and not just the reserve system, would remain undisturbed by the antitrust laws. Finally, the facts of *Federal Baseball* itself would suggest that the exemption extends to matters such as league structure and the acquisition of franchises. It will be recalled that the complaint in that case arose from the efforts of the established league to take over, and in some cases eliminate, franchises in the rival Federal League.[133] Although the cases which later affirmed *Federal Baseball's* grant of immunity involved complaints directed to the player restraints, those decisions contain no hint that the Court intended to limit its extension of the exemption only to the player controls.

The few lower court decisions involving other baseball-related controversies provide little guidance on the issue of the scope of the exemptions, although they seem to confirm that it extends to matters other than player relations. In most of the cases, there is no specific discussion of possible limitations on the sport's immunity, and the exemption is either applied summarily or wholly ignored. *Salerno v. American League of Professional Baseball Clubs* [134] involved a suit brought by an umpire who alleged that the defendant had discharged him because of his union activities. The plaintiff contended that his exclusion from the league involved various antitrust violations. Judge Friendly, writing for the Second Circuit, thought it doubtful that the plaintiff had stated a cause of action even if the antitrust laws applied, but found it unnecessary to answer this question because of the baseball exemption. Judge Friendly assumed that the exemption covered the league's relationship with its umpire-employees and his opinion does not indicate that the court had any reservation about whether immunity should be so extended.[135] The exemption question was treated even more summarily in *Portland Baseball Club, Inc. v. Kuhn.*[136] The plaintiff minor league club held territorial rights the value of which was lessened when the major leagues established two new teams on the West Coast. As a result of an arbitration proceeding, the plaintiff was compensated for the diminution of its rights. Apparently not satisfied with the award, the plaintiff sued, contesting the arbitration and alleging certain antitrust violations. The Ninth Circuit upheld the district court's dismissal of both counts of the complaint. Its treatment of the antitrust claim consisted of a one sentence statement that dismissal was proper, followed by a citation to *Flood v. Kuhn.*[137]

Other aspects of the internal structure of the baseball leagues were involved in *Wisconsin v. Milwaukee Braves, Inc.*[138] In that case, the State of Wisconsin

132. 352 U.S. at 450.
133. *See* text at notes 22-23 *supra.*
134. 429 F.2d 1003 (2d Cir. 1970).
135. *See* 429 F.2d at 1005.
136. 491 F.2d 1101 (9th Cir.), *aff'g* 368 F. Supp. 1004 (D. Ore. 1974).
137. *See* 491 F.2d at 1103. The district court's treatment of this issue was similarly brief. *See* 368 F. Supp. at 1007.
138. 31 Wis. 2d 699, 144 N.W.2d 1, *cert. denied,* 385 U.S. 990 (1966).

contested the movement of the Milwaukee baseball franchise to Atlanta. The suit was based on state antitrust law, and the court ultimately held that the complaint must be dismissed because the matter was within the exclusive regulatory authority of Congress.[139] In the course of its opinion, the court commented on the scope of the federally created baseball exemption:

> The type of [league] decision involved in this case, in essence, whether to admit a new member in order to replace an existing member which desired to move to a new area, appears to be so much an incident of league operation as to fall within the exemption.[140]

A similar result was reached in *Charles O. Finley & Company v. Kuhn*,[141] where one of the issues involved the applicability of the antitrust laws to limit the commissioner's authority to disapprove a trade between two league clubs. In granting defendant's motion to dismiss that portion of the complaint alleging an antitrust violation, the court noted that the Supreme Court precedents "do not . . . restrict the exemption of baseball only to the extent of the reserve clause system." [142] Another case which is worthy of noting largely for the court's apparent assumption that the exemption was not applicable to the particular facts is *Twin City Sportservice Inc. v. Finley* [143] which involved allegations by the defendant club owner that the plaintiff's long-term concession contract violated the antitrust laws. Neither the district court nor the court of appeals opinion mentions the exemption issue. The fact that the courts proceeded to consider the merits of the antitrust claims may suggest that they saw no serious immunity issue.

While these cases are suggestive in their holdings, they provide little in terms of presenting a standard which might be used to define the limits of the exemption. As already suggested, the major Supreme Court cases also have not addressed this question directly. Despite this lack of specific guidelines, there are aspects of the history of the exemption which may lay at least a general foundation for the formulation of limitations. In particular, the spirit of the Supreme Court decisions on the one hand and the exceptional nature of the immunity on the other would suggest that courts ought to be prepared to confine the exemption to the essential aspects of the league's sports function. The Supreme Court has not been hesitant to label the exemption an "aberration," [144] and it has made clear that other sports may not partake of it. Indeed, in *Radovich* the Court was emphatic that it would "adhere to — but not extend" the interpretation made in *Federal Baseball* and *Toolson*.[145] In light of the Court's

---

139. *See* text at notes 111-15 *supra*.
140. 31 Wis. 2d at 725, 144 N.W.2d at 15.
141. Cause No. 76 C 2368 (N.D. Ill. Sept. 7, 1976).
142. *Id.* at 7. The entirety of the court's analysis on this point was as follows:

> Defendant Kuhn also moves to dismiss Count II of the complaint herein for failure to state a claim upon which relief can be granted. Count II of the complaint seeks to establish a violation of the Sherman Anti-Trust Act. Baseball, the anomaly of antitrust law, is not subject to the provisions of that Act. Federal Baseball Club of Baltimore v. National League, . . .; Toolson v. New York Yankees, Inc., . . .; Flood v. Kuhn, ... The above cases apparently do not, as plaintiff urges, restrict the exemption of baseball only to the extent of the reserve clause system. *See* Portland Baseball Club, Inc. v. Kuhn, . . .; Salerno v. American League of Professional Baseball Clubs, . . . Accordingly, Count II of the complaint must be and is hereby dismissed. *Id.*

143. 512 F.2d 1264 (9th Cir. 1975), *rev'g* 365 F. Supp. 235 (N.D. Cal. 1972).
144. Flood v. Kuhn, 407 U.S. 258, 282 (1972).
145. 352 U.S. 445, 451 (1957).

effort to limit the "damage" which is done by the exemption, it can be plausibly argued the court had no intention of extending it further than is necessary to preserve the essence of the baseball enterprise.[146] On a more general level it can be noted that the exemption stands as a rather extraordinary exception in a pervasive legislative scheme of antitrust regulation. Proper deference to the larger federal policy of promoting free commerce would suggest that this exception ought to be confined wherever reasonable limitations can be drawn.[147] Absent a more specific statement of legislative intent, it cannot be assumed that Congress intended to wholly abandon its general preference for antitrust controls.

The exemption would seem to fulfill its purpose if it were applied to immunize only those contracts or arrangements directly related to the staging of sports competition for public consumption.[148] Clearly the relationship between teams and players is part of this. Moreover, the protective umbrella can logically be extended to non-playing personnel who are involved in the game, as was done in *Salerno*.[149] It should also be clear that the matter of league structure is also a critical part of the sport's operation. Thus, questions pertaining to the number of franchises, their location, and requirements for ownership would seem to be free from antitrust scrutiny.[150]

The limitation intended by the proposed standard becomes clearer when it is applied to contracts which are more tangential to the actual "sports" aspects of the enterprise. These might include contracts for the transportation of players, the supplying of uniforms, and the like. It is true that the "business of baseball" could not operate without these. For that reason, some might try to argue that the Court's repeated use of that phrase is intended to encompass any activity which is necessary to the operation of the enterprise.[151] But to

---

146. In *Wisconsin v. Milwaukee Braves, Inc.* the Supreme Court of Wisconsin has indicated that it feels that the exemption is limited to the essential aspects of the sport:

> We venture to guess that this exemption does not cover every type of business activity to which a baseball club or league might be a party and does not protect clubs or leagues from application of the federal acts to activities which are not incidental to the maintenance of league structure, but it does seem clear that the exemption at least covers the agreements and rules which provide for the structure of the organization and the decisions which are necessary steps in maintaining it. 31 Wis. 2d 699, 725, 144 N.W.2d 1, 15 (1966).

147. Support for this reasoning can be found in other Supreme Court cases not involving athletics. The Court has repeatedly taken the position in order to preserve the general objective of the antitrust laws to promote free competition and open markets, "immunity from antitrust laws 'is not lightly implied.'" United States v. First City Nat'l Bank, 386 U.S. 361, 368 (1967), *quoting* California v. Federal Power Comm'n, 369 U.S. 482, 485 (1962). *See also* Woods Exploration & Producing Co. v. Aluminum Co. of America, 438 F.2d 1286, 1302 (5th Cir. 1971). Thus, the Court is generally inclined to construe exemptions narrowly except where there is clear congressional guidance to the contrary. *See generally* 16F VON KALINOWSKI § 44.01[3].

148. *See* note 146 *supra*.

149. *See* text at notes 134-35 *supra*.

150. Several cases add support to the notion that the exemption extends to matters of league structure. *See* Federal Baseball Club of Baltimore, Inc. v. National League of Professional Baseball Clubs, 259 U.S. 200 (1922); Wisconsin v. Milwaukee Braves, Inc., 31 Wis. 2d 669, 144 N.W.2d 1, *cert. denied*, 385 U.S. 990 (1966); Portland Baseball Club, Inc. v. Kuhn, 368 F. Supp. 1004 (D. Ore. 1971); *aff'd*, 491 F.2d 1001 (9th Cir. 1974); Portland Baseball Club, Inc. v. Baltimore Baseball Club, Inc., 282 F.2d 680 (9th Cir. 1960).

151. *But see* Wisconsin v. Milwaukee Braves, Inc., 31 Wis. 2d 699, 725, 144 N.W.2d 1, 15, *cert. denied*, 385 U.S. 990 (1966).

accept this argument, one must believe that there is virtually no limit on the exemption since any contract which yields supplies or helps produce revenue is, in one sense, essential. However, as suggested above, the Court's efforts to confine the exemption and the otherwise pervasive reach of federal antitrust policy strongly suggests that limitations are properly imposed. Contracts of the sort mentioned can be distinguished from matters relating to league structure because they do not partake of any of the unique aspects of the exhibitions themselves. In these agreements, the league or club is simply another customer of the seller or provider. Unlike the player entering the sport or the owner buying a franchise, the contractor has little reason to believe that special restraints on his activities are necessary to get realistic, interesting athletic competition before the public.[152]

The courts will necessarily have to assume the burden of identifying the particular baseball activities which will enjoy immunity under the proposed standard.[153] The present dearth of authority makes any case involving peripheral activities a prime candidate for lengthy litigation. When that litigation does come, the courts involved will have to deal with a body of law which chooses to make a distinction among various segments of the sports industry which is not wholly rational. The basic question to be confronted concerns the lengths to which the distinction can be carried. As suggested above, it is believed that the courts will find that at some point a further extension of baseball's special immunity becomes indefensible in light of the general federal policy against anticompetitive restraints.

§ 5.03. The Player Restraints: An Overview.

The subject of controversy in most of the recent antitrust litigation in the sports area has been the various mechanisms which leagues employ to limit the movement of players between teams.[154] The following several sections deal with

---

152. It is also difficult to conceive that an owner would have invested in a baseball club expecting that he enjoyed complete immunity from antitrust regulation. To the extent there is a reliance interest, it is most logically defined in terms of the investors' expectation that the unique character of the sport would require special rules for the control of players and the maintenance of league structure. *See* text at notes 131-32 *supra.* Other activities of the sort discussed in the text are rather routine aspects of the operation of the business and presumably would be so viewed by the investor.

153. It will be noted that the problem of defining the scope of an exemption in the face of a general federal policy in favor of antitrust controls is one which the courts regularly confront. *See generally* 16F VON KALINOWSKI §§ 44.01-.04. The rules of interpretation applied by courts in other areas, including the concern that exemptions be narrowly construed, would seem to be fully applicable in the baseball context.

154. *See, e.g.,* Mackey v. National Football League, 543 F.2d 606 (8th Cir. 1976), *modifying* 407 F. Supp. 1000 (D. Minn. 1975) (Rozelle Rule); Bryant v. National Football League, Docket No. CV 75-2543 (C.D. Cal. July 30, 1975) (*tro granted*), *order dissolved, id.,* (C.D. Cal. Aug. 7, 1975) (Rozelle Rule); Robertson v. National Basketball Ass'n, 389 F. Supp. 867 (S.D.N.Y. 1975) (draft, reserve clause, uniform player contract); Kapp v. National Football League, 390 F. Supp. 73 (N.D. Cal. 1974) (Rozelle Rule, tampering rule); Philadelphia World Hockey Club, Inc. v. Philadelphia Hockey Club, Inc., 351 F. Supp. 462 (E.D. Pa. 1972) (reserve clause).

The player restraint mechanisms have also received extensive attention in secondary sources. *See, e.g.,* Canes, *The Social Benefits of Team Quality,* in GOVERNMENT AND THE SPORTS BUSINESS 81 (R. Noll ed. 1974); Noll, *The U.S. Team Sports Industry: An Introduction,* in *id.* 3-7; Rivkin, *Sports Leagues and the Federal Antitrust Laws,* in *id.* 387; H. DEMMERT, THE ECONOMICS OF PROFESSIONAL TEAM SPORTS 20-23, 32-39 (1973) [hereinafter cited as DEMMERT]; Morris, *In the Wake of the Flood,* 38 LAW & CONTEMP. PROB. 85, 87-88 (1973); Rottenberg, *The Baseball Players' Labor Market,* 64 J. POL. ECON. 242 (1956); Sobel, *The Emancipation of Professional Athletes,* 3 WESTERN ST. U. L. REV. 185 (1976); Topkis, *Monopoly in Professional Sports,* 58 YALE L.J. 691 (1949); Comment,

issues which arise when these restraints are subjected to scrutiny under the antitrust laws. As background for that discussion, it may be useful to briefly describe the various systems of player restraints. As will be seen, the primary impediments to the free movements of players between teams are (a) reserve or option clauses, (b) the draft system, and (c) rules which prohibit clubs from "tampering" with the players of another club. This preliminary inquiry will also provide the occasion for a look at some of the modifications in the traditional restraints which have been prompted by the recent litigation.

a. Reserve and Option Clauses. Typically an athlete will sign a contract to play for a club for a specified number of years. The contract will expressly state the obligations of the respective parties for the agreed-upon period. Among the terms of the standard form contract typically used is a provision which gives the club the unilateral right to renew the contract for a period beyond that to which the parties have expressly agreed.[155] The clauses used in some leagues provided that in the event the club exercised its right of renewal, the athlete's salary would be some percentage, usually 75 or 90 percent, of that provided for in the original agreement.[156] Apart from such a provision for salary reduction, the renewal clause typically states that the contract will be renewed on the same terms and conditions as governed the original contract.[157] The employer-club will exercise its right of renewal only if the athlete does not consent to sign another original contract with the team. Since a new contract would also include a clause providing for renewal by the club, a new agreement by the athlete may simply delay the issue of the club's unilateral right to renew.[158]

A critical question concerns the number of times the club may exercise its right of renewal. In this connection prior sections of this book have

---

Antitrust and Professional Sport: Does Anyone Play by the Rules of the Game?, 22 CATH. U.L. REV. 403 (1973); Comment, *The Super Bowl and the Sherman Act: Professional Team Sports and the Antitrust Laws*, 81 HARV. L. REV. 418 (1967); Comment, *The Balance of Power in Professional Sports*, 22 MAINE L. REV. 459 (1970); Comment, *Player Control Mechanisms in Professional Team Sports*, 34 U. PITT. L. REV. 645 (1973); Comment, *Monopsony in Manpower: Organized Baseball Meets the Antitrust Laws*, 62 YALE L.J. 576 (1953); Note, *Baseball Players and Antitrust Laws*, 53 COLUM. L. REV. 242 (1953).

155. *See, e.g.*, Baseball Contract § 10(a):

> 10. (a) On or before January 15 (or if a Sunday, then the next preceding business day) of the year next following the last playing season covered by this contract, the Club may tender to the Player a contract for the term of that year by mailing the same to the Player at his address following his signature hereto, or if none be given, then at his last address of record with the Club. If prior to the March 1 next succeeding said January 15, the Player and the Club have not agreed upon the terms of such contract, then on or before 10 days after said March 1, the Club shall have the right by written notice to the Player at said address to renew this contract for the period of one year on the same terms, except that the amount payable to the Player shall be such as the Club shall fix in said notice; provided, however, that said amount, if fixed by a Major League Club, shall be an amount payable at a rate not less than 80% of the rate stipulated for the preceding year.
>
> (b) The Club's right to renew this contract, as provided in sub-paragraph (a) of this paragraph 10, and the promise of the Player not to play otherwise than with the Club have been taken into consideration in determining the amount payable under paragraph 2 hereof.

The operation of option and reserve clauses is discussed more fully at §§ 3.12, 4.13 *supra*.

156. *See* note 155 *supra*.

157. *See* note 155 *supra*. *See also* § 3.12 *supra*.

158. In some cases it is unclear whether the right which a club asserts to the athlete's services is based on a newly executed agreement or upon a renewal of the original agreement. *See, e.g.*, Central New York Basketball, Inc. v. Barnett, 19 Ohio Op. 2d 130, 181 N.E.2d 506 (1961).

differentiated between "reserve" and "option" clauses,[159] although some writers use one term or the other to describe all types of renewal clauses.[160] Under the terminology used here, a reserve clause is one which gives the club a perpetual right to renew the player's contract. Thus, at the end of the mutually-agreed upon term of the contract, the club may have unilaterally renewed the contract for an additional year. If at the end of the renewal period, the parties still have not executed a second contract, the club, operating in a league with a reserve system could, at least theoretically, renew the original agreement for a second time.[161] Such reserve systems have historically been found primarily in baseball and hockey,[162] although there are other sports in which the club's right of renewal has at times been alleged to be perpetual.[163]

Under a pure option clause, the club has the right to renew the contract for only one additional year. Some contracts include express language to this effect,[164] while in other cases a one-year renewal limitation has been implied by courts interpreting the contract language.[165]

In those leagues which use an option, as opposed to a reserve clause, the athlete who "played out his option" and became a "free agent" could theoretically sell his services to any other club in the league. This free mobility was seldom realized, however. Typically, the option system was coupled with an interleague rule informally known as a "Rozelle Rule," which required that any club signing a free agent must compensate the original employer.[166] As the name suggests, the prototype for such a rule was developed in the NFL in which the league bylaws provided that if the original employer and acquiring club could not reach an agreement on the type and amount of the compensation to be paid, then the determination would be made by the league commissioner.[167] When the

---

159. *See* §§ 3.12, 4.12-.14 *supra.*

160. *See, e.g.,* DEMMERT 20-23.

161. Often it will not be clear from the face of the contract whether the right to reserve is perpetual or simply for one year. *See, e.g.,* Central New York Basketball, Inc. v. Barnett, 19 Ohio Op. 2d 130, 181 N.E.2d 506 (1961). Indeed, it was precisely this question of the meaning of the contract language which was at the heart of the controversy in the landmark baseball arbitration cases involving Andy Messersmith and Dave McNally. The case is discussed more fully in the text accompanying notes 247-54, *infra.*

162. *See* § 3.2 *supra.*

163. The renewal clause used in basketball has been given differing interpretations by the courts. In two earlier state court proceedings, the clause was specifically found not to create a perpetual option. *See, e.g.,* Lemat Corp. v. Barry, 275 Cal. App. 2d 671, 80 Cal. Rptr. 240 (1969); Central New York Basketball, Inc. v. Barnett, 19 Ohio Op. 2d 130, 181 N.E.2d 180 (1961). However, when the status of the renewal right was formally drawn into question in federal antitrust proceedings initiated by a group of NBA players, the correctness of this interpretation was disputed and the players contended that the club's right of renewal was in fact perpetual. *See* Robertson v. National Basketball Ass'n, 389 F. Supp. 867, 891 (S.D.N.Y. 1975). The players supported their interpretation by pointing to the fact that an indemnity requirement discouraged players from testing the operation of the clause.

164. The NFL contract expressly states that the club may renew the contract only for an additional one-year term. The clause is quoted in note 501, § 3.12 *supra.*

165. Lemat v. Barry, 275 Cal. App. 2d 671, 80 Cal. Rptr. 240 (1969); Central New York Basketball, Inc. v. Barnett, 19 Ohio Op. 2d 130, 181 N.E.2d 506 (1961). *But see* note 163 *supra.*

166. Additional information about the nature of the compensation rule can be found in the reported cases which have considered its antitrust implications. *See* Mackey v. National Football League, 407 F. Supp. 1000 (D. Minn. 1975), *modified,* 543 F.2d 606 (8th Cir. 1976); Robertson v. National Basketball Ass'n, 389 F. Supp. 867 (S.D.N.Y. 1975); Kapp v. National Football League, 390 F. Supp. 73 (N.D. Cal. 1974).

167. The text of the NFL's Rozelle Rule is as follows:

> Any player, whose contract with a League club has expired, shall thereupon become a free agent and shall no longer be considered a member of the team of that club following

commissioner intervened, the compensation to be paid by the club signing the free agent could consist of either the transfer of future draft rights or the assignment of the new employer's contract rights in other players.[168] In effect, the indemnification settlement is a forced trade, for the acquiring club must exchange valuable property rights in order to acquire the services of the supposed free agent.[169] The players have contended, and some courts have agreed,[170] that the requirement of compensation operates as a real restraint on player mobility. The prospect of having to relinquish important draft or player rights, or pay cash in a mutual settlement, effectively lessens the willingness of other teams to deal with the free agent and increases the likelihood that the free agent will choose to stay with his original employer.[171]

> the expiration date of such contract. Whenever a player, becoming a free agent in such manner, thereafter signs a contract with a different club in the League, then, unless mutually satisfactory arrangements have been concluded between the two League clubs, the Commissioner may name and then award to the former club one or more players, from the Active, Reserve, or Selection List (including future selection choices) of the acquiring club as the Commissioner in his sole discretion deems fair and equitable; any such decision by the Commissioner shall be final and conclusive. CONSTITUTION AND BY-LAWS FOR THE NATIONAL FOOTBALL LEAGUE, art. 12.1(H).

168. The four instances in which Commissioner Rozelle has intervened to establish the compensation for a free agent are described in Mackey v. National Football League, 407 F. Supp. 1000, 1004 (D. Minn. 1975).

169. It is not entirely clear what loss or injury suffered by the original employer is intended to be compensated under an indemnification provision such as the Rozelle Rule. It will be noted that the NFL rule is silent on this point and states only that the compensation, if not mutually agreed upon, shall be that which the commissioner deems to be "fair and equitable." *See* note 167 *supra*. Judge Larson's opinion in Mackey v. National Football League, 407 F. Supp. 1000 (D. Minn. 1975), might be read to suggest that the amount of compensation to be paid may take account of at least two considerations: (1) the desire of the team to recoup its "investment" in the player, which might consist of recruiting and training expenses and (2) the need to maintain competitive balance within the league. *Id.* at 1008. It should be clear that these are very different elements. If only the former were a concern, the indemnity award might be relatively modest, particularly if the athlete had played for a sufficient number of years to permit the club to recoup a portion of its investment. On the other hand, if the award is to be affected by the need to maintain the relative player strength of the original club, then it would be appropriate for the club to demand that it be given a player of equal quality or a high draft choice. The few instances in which the NFL commissioner has determined the compensation to be paid suggests that he perceives that his awards should focus on the need to preserve the competitive position of the original club. *See id.* at 1004.

The indemnity system adopted in the National Hockey League after its reserve clause was struck down in Philadelphia World Hockey Club, Inc. v. Philadelphia Hockey Club, Inc., 351 F. Supp. 462 (E.D. Pa. 1972), is more specific in defining the compensation which the original employer could expect. In 1973, the League's By-laws were amended to add section 9A dealing with free agents and equalization payments. Paragraph 7 of that section states:

> The purpose of the equalization payment shall be to compensate a player's previous Member Club for *loss of the right to his services* when that player becomes a free agent and the right to his services is acquired by another Member Club or a Club owned or controlled by another Member Club. (Emphasis added.)

Under this language, it would appear that the original club could demand that it receive contracts or draft rights which give it playing talent equivalent to that which it lost.

170. *See, e.g.,* Mackey v. National Football League, 407 F. Supp. 1000, 1006 (D. Minn. 1975), modified, 543 F.2d 606 (8th Cir. 1976).

171. Several economists agree that this is the effect of the Rozelle Rule. *See, e.g.,* DEMMERT at 38; Noll, *The U.S. Team Sports Industry: An Introduction* in GOVERNMENT AND THE SPORTS BUSINESS 1, 3-4 (R. Noll ed. 1974).

b. The Draft System. All of the leagues involved in major team sports utilize a draft system to allocate new players among existing teams.[172] In most cases, the players eligible for the draft are those who have not previously signed a professional contract and thus are usually athletes who are rising from the amateur ranks. The ostensible purpose of the draft is to equalize playing talent among the clubs within the league and the selection process is structured to enable the least successful clubs to secure the best of the new talent coming into the league. Thus, selections from the draft pool are made in the reverse order of the club's standing in league competition.

Once a club drafted a player, its right to contract with him was exclusive. The duration of this right varied among leagues. In a few leagues, it lasted only until the next draft was held.[173] If the athlete and the club could not come to terms, the player was returned to the draft pool and was eligible for selection by another club. In most leagues, however, the right to negotiate with the player was perpetual. In these situations, the drafting club continued to enjoy exclusive rights in the athlete even though no contract was ever entered into with him. Even if the athlete spent several years in another league or in some other endeavor, he had to reckon with the drafting club before he entered its league.[174]

While the draft thus identified the club which could initially contract with the athlete, in practice it had a much more lasting importance. If the athlete agreed to play for the drafting club, he would almost certainly sign a standard player contract which included a reserve or option clause. As explained above, such a clause gave the club a claim to the player which continued even after the stated-term of the contract has expired.

The complaint raised against the draft is that it operates to limit an athlete's bargaining power. Because the draft gives a club a "right to contract" which is exclusive in a particular league, there is effectively only one buyer for the player's services.[175] While other clubs might be interested in hiring him, they could do so only if they were willing to pay the drafting club whatever amount it demanded as compensation for relinquishing its rights. Thus, the advantage which the player might gain by using competing offers to bargain up his price is effectively eliminated.[176] There is little evidence suggesting the league's

172. Further commentary on the operation of the player draft can be found in the sources cited in note 166 *supra,* most of which deal generally with the player restraint mechanisms.

173. This is true in baseball. *See* BASEBALL BLUE BOOK 517-22 (1971).

174. One of the celebrated instances which illustrates the perpetual nature of a club's draft rights involved basketball player George McGinnis. McGinnis was drafted by the Philadelphia 76'ers in 1973 while he was still playing in the rival ABA. Two years later, McGinnis indicated a desire to join the NBA and eventually signed a lucrative contract with the New York Knicks of that league. Philadelphia objected that the New York club had no right to deal with McGinnis. When the controversy was eventually decided by Larry O'Brien, the league commissioner, he left no doubt that the validity of Philadelphia's unused draft rights continued. He not only revoked McGinnis' contract with New York but also decreed that New York would lose its first round selection in the next player draft and ordered the Knicks to reimburse Philadelphia for all expenses it had incurred in the matter. *See* N.Y. Times, June 6, 1975, at 23, col. 2. *See also* Putnam, *Score a Basket for Brotherly Love,* SPORTS ILLUSTRATED, June 23, 1975, at 22; N.Y. Times, May 31, 1975, at 1, col. 1; *id.,* June 7, 1975, at 17, col. 6. McGinnis eventually signed a multi-year contract with Philadelphia. *Id.,* July 11, 1975, at 21, col. 4.

175. *See, e.g.,* Robertson v. National Basketball Ass'n, 389 F.Supp. 867, 891-92 (S.D.N.Y. 1975); DEMMERT at 22-23: Comment, *The Super Bowl and the Sherman Act: Professional Team Sports and the Antitrust Laws,* 81 HARV. L. REV. 418, 422-25 (1967).

176. "The player's position is such that he is forced to bargain with a potentially discriminatory monopsonist." DEMMERT, at 22.

dispute that this is the effect of the draft system. Rather, the league's response is usually that the reduction in bargaining power must be accepted as an unavoidable consequence of the league's efforts to maintain competitive balance among teams and insure the stability of the various franchises.[177] This debate and similar justifications offered for reserve and option clauses are at the heart of the litigation considered in the following sections.

   c. The Prohibition on Tampering. The notion that a club had exclusive "rights" in a player was significantly reinforced by other league rules which limited the right of other clubs to compete for the athlete's services. Most league bylaws prohibit a club from "tampering" with players on other teams.[178] Under the typical provision it is improper for the outsider to "negotiate with or make an offer to" a player whose rights are held by another club.[179] Although some bylaws are silent on the point, it is generally assumed that such discussions may be held if the prospective employer first secures the permission of the club with which the player is connected.[180] The sanction for failing to respect another club's rights may be quite severe. Some leagues provide that mere tampering may be punished by the loss of a draft choice, and if the offense is intentional, with an additional fine, a portion of which will be paid to the offended club.[181]

   One might wonder why a rule against tampering was necessary in light of the other rules which defined the property right which an employer had in a player. Even if clubs were given free rein to negotiate with those under contract to another team, the reserve clause, or Rozelle Rule, would presumably insure that the competing club could not gain the employee's services until it had paid

---

   177. Some commentators have suggested that the available evidence indicates that the draft, and relatedly the reserve clause, have been ineffectual in equalizing the competitive strength of teams within a particular league. *See, e.g.,* Demmert 32-39; Canes *The Social Benefits of Restrictions on Team Quality* in Government and the Sports Business 81 (R. Noll ed. 1974).

   178. *See, e.g.,* Kapp v. National Football League, 390 F. Supp. 73 (N.D. Cal. 1974); Noll, *The U.S. Team Sports Industry: An Introduction* in Government and the Sports Business 4-5 (R. Noll ed. 1974); Rottenberg, *The Baseball Players' Labor Market,* 64 J. Pol. Econ. 242, 245 (1956).

   179. The quoted language is taken from the NFL By-Laws, the complete version of which is as follows:

> If a member Club or any officer, shareholder, director, partner, employee, agent or representative thereof, or any person holding an interest in said Club shall tamper, negotiate with, or make an offer to a player on the Active, Reserve or Selection List of another member Club, then unless the offending Club shall clearly prove to the Commissioner that such action was unintentional, the offending Club, in addition to being subject to all other penalties provided in the Constitution and By-Laws, shall lose its selection choice in the next succeeding Selection Meeting in the same round in which the affected player was originally chosen. If such affected player was never selected in any Selection Meeting, the Commissioner shall determine the round in which the offending Club shall lose its selection choice. Additionally, if the Commissioner decides such offense was intentional, the Commissioner shall have the power to fine the offending Club and may award the offended Club 50% of the amount of the fine imposed by the Commissioner. In all such cases the offended Club must first certify to the Commissioner that such an offense has been committed. Constitution and By-Laws of the National Football League, art. 9.2 (1972).

   180. The tampering rule used in baseball allows such negotiations only if the club holding rights in the player "shall have, in writing, expressly authorized such negotiations or dealings prior to their commencement." The rule is quoted in Flood v. Kuhn, 407 U.S. 258, 259 n.1 (1972). The authority of the baseball commissioner to impose sanctions in tampering situations is considered in Atlanta National League Baseball Club, Inc. v. Kuhn, 432 F. Supp. 1213 (N.D. Ga. 1977).

   181. *See* note 179 *supra.*

the existing employer for a release of its claim.[182] But it will be noted that the tampering rules typically go beyond simply requiring that the existing employer must agree to a release and purport to prohibit even preliminary negotiations between the player and the outside club. In the league's view, one justification for so restricting the athlete's opportunity for bargaining is that the limitation is necessary to preserve the image of the game as involving honest athletic competition.[183] If an athlete were known to be negotiating with another team, perhaps one which was trying to preserve a first place standing, there might be some risk that his play against that club would not be as aggressive as it otherwise would. And even if the athlete had not actually withheld his best performance, there is a risk that fans would perceive the situation in this light. Thus, a sub-par performance by the athlete might be thought to have been prompted by the player's interest in improving the position of his potential employer. If such perceptions ever became widespread, it is likely that the fans' loyalty and financial support would decline.[184]

There can be little doubt that a rule against tampering would be likely to further erode the player's bargaining position under the traditional rules. Not only did it discourage the athlete from affirmatively testing the market for his skills but also it insured that the existing employer would play a significant role in any negotiations which took place. Thus, in some cases, the employer might effectively cut off competing offers by refusing to give others access to its players. In other situations, the employer could easily dampen the enthusiasm of other clubs by making known that it would demand substantial compensation for release of its claim. Whether the concern for preserving the appearance of honest competition provides a sufficient justification for this effect is, predictably, a matter about which there is some disagreement.[185] Legal developments in the sports area have generally focused on the other restraints, and it remains to be seen what effect reforms in the area of the draft and player retention rules will have on the prohibition on tampering.

---

182. Presumably one club could not in any case ignore the draft or contract rights of another club. If the player did sign a contract with a new club, the original employer, at a minimum, would be entitled to damages. More importantly, even without a tampering rule, the offended club would be able to enjoin the player from actually performing for another club particularly if the athlete had previously signed a contract containing a covenant of exclusive services. *See* §§ 4.02-.03 *supra.* The league might have an interest in seeing that these situations never arise, even if it were likely that the original employer would prevail in any subsequent litigation. But the league's interest in this regard could be protected by a rule drawn much more narrowly than the tampering rules presently used. Since the existing rules prohibit even preliminary negotiations, their purpose must be one other than simply forestalling potential litigation, a point which is pursued in the text.

183. *See* Noll, *The U.S. Team Sports Industry: An Introduction* in GOVERNMENT AND THE SPORTS BUSINESS 4-5 (R. Noll ed. 1974).

184. It will be noted that this concern for dual loyalties is similar to the argument which the NFL made when it sought to enjoin the WFL from negotiating with its players, even after the WFL made clear that any contracts which were signed would specify that performance was to begin only after the athletes had fulfilled all obligations to their original employers. The NFL found that the courts generally gave little credence to its concerns. See §§ 4.12, 4.14 *supra.*

185. In the *Kapp* case, Judge Sweigert concluded that "the tampering rule . . . and the Standard Player Contract rule . . . are . . . patently unreasonable insofar as they are used to enforce other NFL rules . . . ." Kapp v. National Football League, 390 F. Supp. 73, 82 (N.D. Cal. 1974). It should be noted that one commentator who otherwise favors elimination of most player restraints concedes that the problem of a player developing split loyalties may be a valid concern and proposes that negotiations by outsiders be prohibited during the playing season. *See* DEMMERT 92. *See also* note 184 *supra.*

d. Recent Developments. The preceding describes the player restraint mechanisms as they existed prior to 1972. In subsequent years, a series of antitrust cases and the continuing maturation of collective bargaining produced some substantial changes in these traditional forms. These are summarized below. Because the evolution of new forms of restraints is continuing, it is impossible to accurately predict the types of systems which will eventually prevail in professional sports. If any general theme emerges from the most recent developments, it is that there may well be greater diversity among the restraints used in the various leagues than has been true in the past. As will be evident from the following discussion, there are already indications that player groups differ rather markedly in their willingness to accept the owners' contention that the uninhibited movement of players between clubs would destroy the economic viability of professional team sports.

Basketball. Perhaps the most radical revision of the traditional restraint mechanisms is that reflected in the 1976 collective bargaining agreement between the owners and the players' union in the NBA. The impetus for the changes was a preliminary ruling by Judge Carter in *Robertson v. National Basketball Association.*[186] The suit was initially brought in 1970 to enjoin the then proposed NBA-ABA merger, and an injunction against the merger was issued. The suit continued, however, on another count of the plaintiff-player's complaint which asserted that the NBA draft system, option clause, and indemnity rule violated the antitrust laws. In response to a variety of pretrial motions, Judge Carter issued a preliminary decision on February 14, 1975, which provided little encouragement for the owners' efforts to justify the rules in question. In rather dramatic fashion, Judge Carter pointedly indicated his doubts about the owners' claims that the restraints did not violate the antitrust laws and, alternatively, that the practices were exempt from antitrust scrutiny because they were the product of collective bargaining between the parties. With respect to the first contention, Judge Carter stated:

> The player draft and perpetual reserve system are readily susceptible to condemnation as group boycotts based on the NBA's concerted refusal to deal with the players save through these unfair restrictive practices. . . .[187]

He was equally skeptical about the claimed labor exemption:

> I must confess that it is difficult for me to conceive of any theory or set of circumstances pursuant to which the college draft, blacklisting, boycotts, and refusals to deal could be saved from Sherman Act condemnation, even if defendants were able to prove at trial their highly dubious contention that these restraints were adopted at the behest of the Players Association.[188]

Shortly after this decision, which was not a final ruling on the merits of the plaintiff's complaint, the parties resumed collective bargaining and in February, 1976, announced that they had reached agreement on new rules to supplant the league's existing player restraints.[189] The measures adopted represent the most

186. 389 F. Supp. 867 (S.D.N.Y. 1975). *See also* 1975 Trade Cas. ¶ 60,448 (S.D.N.Y.).
187. 389 F. Supp. at 893.
188. *Id.* at 895.
189. *See* Collective Bargaining Agreement Between the National Basketball Association and the

extensive revision of the traditional rules to date. Under the new system, a club will no longer have a right to renew a player's contract unilaterally, as it formerly had under the league's option clause. At the end of the stated term of the contract, the player will become a free agent and may negotiate with any team. The replacement for the unilateral right of renewal is a provision which, in effect, gives the employer-club a right of first refusal on the athlete's subsequent contracts. If the player receives a more attractive offer from another team, his original club is given a chance to match that offer, and if it does, the player must agree to continue in its employ on the new terms.[190] Thus, while the athlete is not completely free to choose his own team, he is assured that his salary can be determined by competitive bidding if he so desires. The collective bargaining agreement also provides that beginning in 1980, the league's counterpart to the Rozelle Rule indemnity system will be eliminated and the club which signs a free agent will no longer be required to compensate the original employer.[191]

The draft system will continue to be used to allocate new talent among existing teams. There is, however, an important change in the nature of the rights which a club acquires through the draft. Rather than acquiring a perpetual right to the athlete's initial professional contract, the club is allowed one year in which to sign the player. If the parties cannot agree to a contract within that period, the athlete goes back into the draft pool and he is eligible to be drafted by any club.[192]

Needless to say, the new rules have not been completely satisfactory to all owners. In commenting on the performance of the owners' bargaining committee in the negotiations, one management source stated, "I think they gave away the store." [193] The virtue of the settlement is its potential for ending the controversy which has attracted attention away from the league's athletic endeavors. Also, it serves to settle the major points of controversy in the *Robertson* litigation, a suit which consumed a tremendous amount of energy and money.[194]

Football. The NFL had little success in its efforts to gain judicial approval of its traditional draft, option, and player compensation rules. A preliminary ruling in *Kapp v. National Football League* [195] gave the first indication that it would not fare well in the courtroom. Kapp alleged that he had been improperly boycotted by the league because he had refused to sign a standard player contract. He further alleged that he had been damaged by the operation of certain league rules, including those providing for the player draft, the option

---

National Basketball Players Association (1976); N.Y. Times, Feb. 3, 1976, at 25, col. 6; *id.* Feb. 8, 1976, § 5, at 1, col. 1; Washington Post, Feb. 4, 1976, at D1, col. 7; *id.,* Mar. 7, 1976, at D4, col. 1.

   190. *See* N.Y. Times, Feb. 3, 1976, at 25, col. 6.

   191. *See* Washington Post, Feb. 4, 1976, at D1, col. 7.

   192. If the player does not sign after the second draft, he becomes a free agent and may sign with any club. *Id.*

   193. Washington Post, Mar. 7, 1976, at D4, col. 1 (source not identified).

   194. Some months prior to the settlement, the commissioner of the NBA indicated that the league's annual legal fees for the *Robertson* suit were "in the seven-figure-plus category." Winnipeg Free Press, Dec. 2, 1975, at 64, col. 7.

   195. 390 F. Supp. 73 (N.D. Cal. 1974).

clause, the Rozelle Rule, and the prohibition on tampering. The basic conclusion reached by Judge Sweigert in his preliminary ruling was that

> [I]n the present case, league enforcement of most of the challenged %H: rules is so patently unreasonable that there is no genuine issue for trial.[196]

While the league lost on this important question of the legality of its restraints, it was ultimately victorious in its attack upon the merits of Kapp's particular complaint. When the case was submitted to the jury, it remained to be determined whether Kapp had been injured by the illegal action and if so, to what extent. The jury ultimately agreed with the league that Kapp had not actually been injured and thus was entitled to no recovery.[197] The precise basis of the jury's conclusion is uncertain, but it appears that the result may be uniquely tied to the facts of the *Kapp* case and thus not necessarily a forecast of what might happen in other situations. Several facts weighed against the plaintiff's claim that he was injured. Kapp had originally assented to a memorandum outlining a $600,000 agreement and indicated that he would sign a standard player contract. Although he subsequently refused to execute a standard contract embodying these terms, it was argued that his earlier actions indicated his acceptance of the restrictive claims.[198] In addition, the defendant league presented evidence indicating that Kapp was not among the outstanding quarterbacks in the league, proof which may have supported the defendant's contention that the $600,000 salary adequately compensated Kapp.[199]

A second legal test of the Rozelle Rule occurred in August, 1975. Ron Jessie, an athlete of considerable talent, played out his option with the Detroit Lions

---

196. *Id.* at 82. In April, 1975, Judge Sweigert issued a supplementary order:

> As indicated in pre-trial conference on March 5, 1975, I have in mind the possibility that a reviewing court might hold that, although the application of "the rule of reason" (rather than the "*per se* rule") is proper, the issue of reasonableness should be tried as an issue of fact (rather than concluded as a matter of law) . . . . I do not want this case to come back on any such procedural, technical ground. . . . Accordingly, (and was much as we must have [sic] set a trial anyhow on the other remaining issues — the "option rule," the contract and the damage issues), I am going to allow the parties to take the few additional trial days that might be necessary to also introduce evidence on the issue of reasonableness.

> To accomplish this, I will modify my previous order by vacating it insofar as it concludes the issue of reasonableness as a matter of law, reserving, however, power to make such post trial rulings, including reinstatement of my previous ruling, as the record may then require. *Id.,* Docket No. C 72-537, April 11, 1975 (Order re Motions and Interim Pre-Trial Order).

However, Judge Sweigert later rescinded this modification of his original order. *See* N.Y. Times, Feb. 14, 1976, at 15, col. 7.

197. *See* N.Y. Times, Apr. 4, 1976, § 5, at 1, col. 1. The *Kapp* trial received extensive coverage in the press. *See, e.g., id.,* Mar. 2, 1976, at 28, col. 1 (discussion of defense strategy); *id.,* Mar. 4, 1976, at 37, col. 1, (opening arguments); *id.,* Mar. 5, 1976, at 25, col. 5 (Kapp testimony); Washington Post, Mar. 6, 1976, at D3, col. 1, (Kapp testimony); *id.,* Mar. 7, 1976, at C3, col. 8 (Kapp testimony); N.Y. Times, § 5, at 5, col. 3 (background on attorneys involved in trial); Washington Post, Mar. 24, 1976, at F3, col. 4 (Rozelle testimony); *id.,* Mar. 25, 1976, at D4, col. 1 (George Blanda testifies that nine of thirteen named NFL quarterbacks were better than Kapp); N.Y. Times, Mar. 25, 1976, at 50, col. 6 (coverage of final testimony); *id.,* Mar. 31, 1976, at 43, col. 5 (Judge Sweigert's instructions to the jury).

198. *See* N.Y. Times, Apr. 4, 1976, § 5, at 1, col. 1.

199. *Id. See also* Washington Post, Mar. 25, 1976 at D4, col. 1 (Kapp's skills evaluated by George Blanda).

and, upon becoming a free agent, signed a new contract with the Los Angeles Rams. When the Lions and Rams were unable to agree upon the compensation to be paid Detroit for the loss of Jessie, Commissioner Rozelle decreed that the Rams must give up running back Cullen Bryant.[200] Bryant then brought suit attacking the Rozelle Rule and seeking to enjoin enforcement of Rozelle's order that he report to Detroit. Judge Warren J. Ferguson of the U.S. District Court in Los Angeles issued a preliminary injunction against the league[201] stating that in his opinion, "the Rozelle Rule in conjunction with the standard player contract and the option clause violates Section 1 of the Sherman Antitrust Act." [202] The judge made clear, however, that his ruling was only preliminary and indicated that when a full hearing was held, the league would be able to introduce evidence to show that the broad powers granted to Commissioner Rozelle were "necessary for the effective management of the league." [203] Further litigation on the merits of the league's restraints was avoided, however, when Rozelle withdrew his order directing Bryant to move and instead required the Rams to compensate the Lions by giving them future draft choices.[204]

The *Bryant* case was somewhat unique. Among the few occasions when the league commissioner has had to intervene to determine compensation, this was the first time he had ordered the club signing a free agent to give up a veteran player, rather than draft choices or a recently-signed rookie.[205] While the case did not come to a final, authoritative legal conclusion, Judge Ferguson's decision may provide a good indication of how courts will respond when they are called upon to make a rough evaluation of the relative equities of the league and a player who has been transferred. The informal reports of the case indicate that Judge Ferguson was concerned that a player who had entered a private contract with a club and had worked hard to gain a starting position could be compelled to abandon his employer and move his household to a distant city by the simple fiat of the league commissioner's decree.[206] There was no indication that Rozelle had taken the steps which might be expected to precede a decision which had such a personal impact on the athlete. For example, it is not clear whether the commissioner considered the availability of other players who would have found the move less objectionable. Nor did it appear that Bryant himself was given

200. *See* Los Angeles Times, July 26, 1975, Pt. III, at 1, col. 1; *id.,* July 27, 1975, Pt. III, at 1, col. 1.

201. Bryant v. National Football League, Docket No. CV 75-2543 (C.D. Cal. July 30, 1975).

202. Los Angeles Times, July 31, 1975, Pt. III, at 1, col. 5.

203. *Id.:* "The economic power of the NFL as demonstrated by this case truly is awesome. That might be the way it has to be if there is going to be an NFL. The awesome control of the commissioner may be necessary for the effective management of the league. A trial might well show that. But the rule of reason cannot merely be wiped aside by such necessities."

204. *See* Los Angeles Times, Aug. 2, 1975, Pt. III, at 1, col. 1. *See also id.,* Aug. 5, 1975, Pt. III, at 1, col. 5.

After Rozelle changed his decision, Judge Ferguson accepted a stipulation dissolving the temporary restraining order. Bryant v. National Football League, Docket No. CV 75-2543 (C.D. Cal. Aug. 7, 1975) (Stipulation for Dissolution of Temporary Restraining Order and Vacation of Order to Show Cause re Preliminary Injunction).

205. The compensation ordered by Commissioner Rozelle in the four other cases where he was called on to make that determination is described in Mackey v. National Football League, 407 F. Supp. 1000, 1004 (D. Minn. 1975), *modified,* 543 F.2d 606 (8th Cir. 1976).

206. *See* Los Angeles Times, July 31, 1975, Pt. III, at 1, col. 5. Judge Ferguson added: "Football owes more to Mr. Bryant than is seen in this case. . . . Cullen Bryant is entitled to better treatment than fiat."

an opportunity to object. A third case involving an antitrust attack upon the NFL player restrictions is *Mackey v. National Football League.*[207] The plaintiffs were sixteen present and former NFL players who asserted that the league's Rozelle Rule amounted to an illegal restraint under the antitrust laws. The plaintiffs alleged that they were injured as a result of enforcement of the rule and thus sought money damages and injunctive relief. Apparently deciding that the status of the Rozelle Rule should be finally settled, the league used the *Mackey* case as the occasion for presenting its most exhaustive defense of the indemnity system. The proceedings in the case entailed fifty-five days of trial, involved over sixty witnesses and 400 exhibits and resulted in a trial transcript in excess of 11,000 pages.[208]

Despite this effort, the district court proceedings proved to be a major defeat for the league. On December 29, 1975, Judge Earl Larson issued a lengthy opinion which rejected virtually every contention which the league had made in defense of its rule. The court found that

> Under the Rozelle Rule each individual player is denied the right to sell his services in a free and open market.... As a result, the salaries paid by each club are lower than if competitive bidding were allowed to prevail.[209]

In responding to the justifications which the league had asserted for the rule, Judge Larson found, first, that the quality of play in the NFL would not decrease if the rule were eliminated[210] and second, that neither the Rozelle Rule nor "the other restrictive devices" had had a significant effect upon the competitive balance among the teams within the league.[211] The court further concluded that the labor exemption had not immunized the rule from antitrust attack. In the court's view the Rozelle Rule had "never been the subject of serious, intensive, arm's length collective bargaining." [212] The court entered an order enjoining further enforcement of the rule and indicated the matter of money damages would be determined in the subsequent proceedings.

The league appealed Judge Larson's decision, and the case provided the first occasion for appellate court review of the NFL restraints.[213] The Court of Appeals for the Eighth Circuit agreed that the Rozelle Rule violated the antitrust laws and that the league had failed to establish that the practices were immunized under the labor exemption. While the league thus failed to secure a reversal, the appellate court's opinion is carefully written in terms apparently

---

207. 407 F. Supp. 1000 (D. Minn. 1975).
208. *Id.* at 1002.
209. *Id.* at 1007.
210. *Id.* at 1008. Judge Larson added: "Even assuming the quality of play would decrease, that fact does not justify the Rules's anticompetitive nature." *Id.*
211. *Id.* Judge Larson also stated that even assuming that the player restrictions have served to maintain competitive balance, "other *legal* means are available to pursue this goal (*e.g.,* the Competition Committee, multiple year contracts and special incentives)." *Id.* (Emphasis added.)

The conclusion that the player restrictions have been relatively ineffective in equalizing playing strengths is shared by a number of economists who have studied the problem. *See, e.g.,* DEMMERT 31-39; Canes, *The Social Benefits of Restrictions on Team Quality* in GOVERNMENT AND THE SPORTS BUSINESS 81 (R. Noll ed. 1974).
212. 407 F. Supp. at 1010.
213. Mackey v. National Football League, 543 F.2d 606 (8th Cir. 1976).

intended to temper the harshness of Judge Larson's treatment of the issues. The lower court had found that the Rozelle Rule was a *per se* violation of the antitrust laws,[214] a classification which is usually reserved for the most pernicious forms of anti-competitive behavior.[215] The Eighth Circuit rejected this conclusion, finding instead that the unique economics of a sports league required that a more extensive inquiry be made into the reasonableness of the practices.[216] As an alternative grounds for its decision, the lower court had made this rule of reason analysis and concluded that the Rozelle Rule could not be sustained on this basis either. The appellate court agreed and held that the record established that the Rozelle Rule imposed a greater restraint than could be justified by the special needs of the league's venture.[217] But even in affirming the ultimate finding of illegality, the reviewing court gave some credence to the league's basic arguments about the need for competitive balance among the various clubs within the league. The court recognized that the NFL has "a strong and unique interest" in maintaining that balance.[218] Moreover, the court noted that its disposition of the instant case did not "mean that every restraint on competition for players' services would necessarily violate the antitrust laws." [219] It also observed that "the protection of mutual interests of both the players and the clubs" might require that reasonable restrictions be imposed.[220] In sum, then, while Judge Larson's opinion had raised doubts as to whether player restraints could ever be justified, the appellate court took some pains to dispel this notion.

The court also used its opinion to suggest that the question of the proper accommodation of the players' interest in mobility and the clubs' interest in competitive balance was a matter which should be resolved at the bargaining table. In the court's view, the parties themselves were better able than the courts to produce a satisfactory resolution of the issue.[221] The court had earlier indicated that an agreement arrived at after serious, good-faith bargaining would be immune from antitrust scrutiny. While it had not found such bargaining on the record in the present case,[222] its suggestion that the parties now return to the bargaining table carried the clear implication that a serious effort to resolve these matters would end the difficulties which the league had been experiencing in court.

During the same period that the *Mackey* case was being tried and appealed, the NFL found itself embroiled in another case, *Smith v. Pro-Football,*

---

214. 407 F. Supp. at 1007.

215. *See* Northern Pacific Ry. v. United States, 356 U.S. 1, 5 (1958).

216. 543 F.2d at 620. The court noted that the NFL assumes some of the characteristics of a joint venture; each member club is dependent on the survival and success of the other clubs. Moreover, the Eighth Circuit concluded that, in most instances, courts when faced with a unique or novel business situation have eschewed a *per se* approach in favor of the rule of reason analysis. *Id.* at 619.

217. *Id.* at 621-22.

218. *Id.* at 621. The court, nevertheless, agreed with Judge Larson's finding that the Rozelle Rule was more restrictive than necessary. *Id.*

219. *Id.* at 623.

220. *Id.*

221. *Id. citing* Kansas City Royals v. Major League Baseball Players, 532 F.2d 615, 632 (8th Cir. 1976).

222. 543 F.2d at 615-16.

Inc.,[223] which sought to invalidate its draft system. Plaintiff, James McCoy (Yazoo) Smith, a first-round pick in the 1968 draft, had signed a one year contract with the Washington Redskins. Smith was expected to become one of football's premier defensive backs, but his career was prematurely ended when he suffered a neck injury in the final game of the 1968 season. In his complaint, which was filed against both the club and the league, Smith alleged that the draft system operated to prevent him from negotiating a contract reflecting the free market or true value of his services.[224] Such a contract, he asserted, would have contained adequate guarantees against the loss of earnings in the event of injury.[225] In defense of its practice, the league argued that the NFL draft was outside the scope of the antitrust laws by virtue of the labor law exemption.[226] Alternatively, defendants contended that the draft was a reasonable restraint within the permissible limits of the antitrust laws.[227] The trial court's decision in *Smith* came down while the appeal in *Mackey* was pending. The result, reflected in an opinion authored by Judge Bryant, followed the pattern of the earlier decisions. Judge Bryant rejected the league's claimed labor exemption, and on the merits of the antitrust claim concluded, first, that the draft was *per se* illegal and alternatively, that it also was invalid under the rule of reason. On the labor exemption issue, the court noted that plaintiff had signed his contract with the Redskins prior to the time when the league and the players' association reached their initial collective bargaining agreement, and this critical factual ingredient of the immunity grant was missing.[228] In his review of the substance of the draft system, Judge Bryant labeled the draft "a group boycott in its classic and most pernicious form" and deemed it a naked restraint of trade "with no purpose except stifling of competition." [229] The court emphasized that "The current system is absolutely the most restrictive one imaginable . . . . [and that] significantly less restrictive alternatives are available . . . ." [230] Having ruled against both of defendants' defenses, the court compared Smith's contract to that received by a veteran free agent signed by the Redskins and computed Smith's actual damages to be $92,200. Accordingly, judgment was entered for treble damages, totaling $276,000, plus costs and attorneys' fees.

These decisions and their general disapproval of the traditional forms of player restraints prompted renewed collective bargaining efforts between the NFL players and owners. Finally in March of 1977, a new agreement was

---

223. 420 F. Supp. 738 (D.D.C. 1976).
224. *Id.* at 741.
225. *Id.*
226. *Id.* at 742-43. The labor exemption is discussed more fully in § 5.04, *infra.*
227. *Id.* at 745.
228. *Id.* at 742-43. The court further noted that the players' association did not become the exclusive bargaining agent for the players until two months after the 1968 draft. The restraints of the draft and its related rules were, therefore, imposed upon plaintiff before the labor exemption could, under any view of the law, be deemed operative. *Id.* at 742.
229. *Id.* at 744-45.
230. *Id.* at 746. Judge Bryant gave examples of two less restrictive alternatives to the present draft which he felt might be within the rule of reason. The first alternative would reduce the current draft from seventeen "rounds" to just two. This plan would still distribute the top player talent among the franchises, but would permit competition for the services of other players. The second suggestion would permit a player to be drafted by more than one team, but would restrict the number of players any one team could sign. *Id.* at 747. The latter alternative is similar to the new free agent draft system in baseball. *See* text accompanying notes 289-91, *infra.*

reached which modified the player control devices. Under the new arrangement, annual amateur player drafts will still be held.[231] However, the draft will involve only twelve rounds of selections, and players not picked by a club in one of these rounds will presumably be free to negotiate with any team. In addition, a drafted player who chooses to sit out his initial year qualifies for the next year's draft and may be selected by a different club. If the player sits out through two drafts, he becomes a free agent.

A rookie player must sign a contract which includes a one-year option clause. However, for veteran players with more than four years of service, the club cannot insist upon such a renewal clause, but one may be included if the veteran is separately compensated for it. It is recognized in the bargaining agreement that every player becomes a free agent when his original contract expires. However, his status as a free agent is encumbered by two rights which his original employer may retain. First, the employer may claim a right of first refusal on any offer which the player receives from another club. In addition, if the free agent eventually signs with another club, the original employer may be entitled to compensation. In order to acquire the right of first refusal and the right to compensation, the original employer must make an offer to the player which includes a minimum salary determined under a formula contained in the collective bargaining agreement. Compensation is awarded in the form of draft choices, and the quality of the draft choice received depends upon the salary which the original employer offered to the free agent. Thus, for example, if the original employer offered the player $125,000 in salary and chose not to exercise its right of first refusal when the player received a better contract from another club, the new employer is obligated to give the former employer both its first and second round choices in the next draft.

Hockey. In several respects, the recent history of the player restraints in the NHL has followed the pattern which has developed in other leagues. The club owners' asserted justification for the rules were largely rejected in a major antitrust proceeding. As a result, the parties intensified their efforts to settle the matter through collective bargaining and eventually agreed to a major reformation of the restraints. There is, however, a major difference in the results achieved in the hockey negotiations. While some other players' unions have been unequivocal in their opposition to a player compensation system such as the Rozelle Rule, the hockey players were willing to give their conditional assent to such a device.

The major case involving hockey, *Philadelphia World Hockey Club, Inc. v. Philadelphia Hockey Club, Inc.,*[232] differs from the cases discussed above in that it involved an interleague dispute, rather than an affirmative action by individual players against their own league.[233] The primary plaintiff, the then-recently

231. This provision and others which are discussed in the text can be found in Collective Bargaining Agreement Between the NFL Management Council and the NFL Players Association (1977).

232. 351 F. Supp. 462 (E.D. Pa. 1972).

233. The case was actually the consolidation of several actions precipitated by the WHA's attempts to sign veteran players. *See* In re Professional Hockey Antitrust Litigation, 352 F. Supp. 1405 (Jud. Panel on Multidistrict Litig. 1973). In addition to the action by the WHA against the NHL, the consolidated litigation included actions by NHL clubs to enforce the reserve clause against individual players.

formed World Hockey Association, brought an action against the established NHL alleging first, that the latter's reserve clause amounted to an improper restraint of trade and second, that the NHL, through its reserve clause, affiliation agreements and control of the supply of hockey players, had monopolized the market for hockey players in violation of the antitrust laws.[234] The event which prompted subsequent reforms in league practices was Judge Higginbottom's decision on November 8, 1972. While the court had doubts as to whether the plaintiff had made a sufficient showing in the preliminary proceedings to sustain the first count of the complaint,[235] it found that the initial evidence on the second point warranted the issuance of a preliminary injunction against continued enforcement of the reserve clause by the NHL.[236] Thus, while Judge Higginbottom left open the possibility that some type of player restraint might be essential to the successful functioning of a sports league,[237] he was persuaded that due to the dominant market position of the NHL, the league ought not be allowed to enforce the clause to the detriment of the emerging WHA. The order prohibiting the continued use of the reserve clause was broadly worded and did not differentiate between intra- and interleague uses of the device.[238]

After this preliminary defeat, the NHL entered into a settlement agreement with most of the WHA teams. Under the new arrangement, the perpetual reserve clause was replaced with an option device and a modified draft system.[239] Having thus settled with the competing league, the NHL owners

---

234. *See* 351 F. Supp. at 503-05.

235. *Id.* at 503:

> In arguments and briefs before this Court, the WHA has vigorously taken the position that the practices of the NHL constitute *per se* antitrust violations within the meaning of § 1 of the Sherman Act. . . . The WHA's legal analysis of § 1 could never be categorized as one which is without merit. However, I find that because of the nature of the hockey sports industry, and the relative paucity of litigation on this type of reserve clause that I should refrain from making a ruling at this preliminary stage as to the § 1 Sherman Act issues. . . . On the basis of the present record . . . , I have some doubts on the WHA's probability of ultimate success.

236. *Id.*:

> While I have doubts as to whether the WHA will ultimately succeed on the § 1 grounds, and though I would deny a preliminary injunction if the only claim rested on § 1, I have *no* such doubts as to whether § 2 requires preliminary injunctive relief. (Emphasis in the original.)

237. *See id.* at 503-05.

238. *See id.* at 519:

> [I]t is hereby ordered that the National Hockey League, its member clubs and teams, . . . are preliminarily enjoined from further prosecuting, commencing, or threatening to commence any legal proceeding pursuant to and/or to enforce the so-called "reserve clause" (presently Paragraph 17) of the National Hockey League Standard Player's Contract, against any player, coach or other person whose contract, but for the reserve clause, expired on or before November 8, 1972.

239. *See* In re Professional Hockey Antitrust Litigation (Multidistrict Litigation), M.D.L. No. 119 (E.D. Pa. Feb. 19, 1974) (Consent Decree). The Consent Decree dealt with a number of other matters as well. For example, the parties agreed that the WHA would be free to contract with NHL-affiliated minor leagues, that a series of WHA-NHL exhibition games would be held, and the WHA would have freer access to arenas and playing dates. The Consent Decree did not settle the claims of two of the WHA clubs and the litigation continued. However, the plaintiffs later encountered procedural difficulties and their action was dismissed. *In re* Professional Hockey Antitrust Litigation, 63 F.R.D. 641 (E.D. Pa. 1974), *rev'd,* 531 F.2d 1188, *rev'd sub nom.* National Hockey League v. Metropolitan Hockey Club, Inc., 427 U.S. 639, 96 S. Ct. 2778, 49 L. Ed. 2d 747 (1976).

turned their attention to securing an agreement from the NHL players' union on the matter of mobility restraints. After more than a year of bargaining, the parties came to terms and accepted an arrangement which modified the former restraints in several important respects.[240] In lieu of a mandatory reserve or option clause, it was agreed that the question of whether the club would have a unilateral right of renewal should be left to negotiations between the club and player.[241] Thus, the athlete could insist on a contract which included no renewal clause, or he could agree to give the club an option to renew the agreement for one or more years. In any event, the player would become a free agent upon fulfilling his obligations under the contract.

Perhaps the most significant feature of the collective bargaining agreement is its acceptance of a rule requiring that a club which signs a free agent compensate the athlete's former employer.[242] This indemnity system differs from the former Rozelle Rule in one important respect: the determination of what will be proper compensation is to be made, not by the league commissioner, but by an independent arbitrator agreed upon by the parties.[243]

Why would the NHL players be willing to accept such an indemnity system when athletes in the NFL were resisting it so strongly? A critical difference in the two situations is the existence of a second major league in hockey. Apparently it was felt that the presence of the WHA insured that there would be competition for players' services. Bidding between the two leagues would tend to raise players' salaries to a level more closely approximating their market value.[244] Indeed, the NHL players' consent to the indemnity arrangement was conditioned upon the continued rivalry between the two leagues. The owners stipulated that in the event the two leagues merged, the players' union may reopen negotiations on both the indemnification system and the free-agent rules.[245]

Baseball. It will be noted that for purposes of the discussion which follows in the next several sections, the player restrictions found in baseball do not stand on the same footing as those employed in football, basketball, and hockey. As previously discussed,[246] the baseball industry is exempt from the antitrust laws and thus its player retention systems cannot be attacked as impermissible restraints on trade. However, the other sports do not enjoy a similar blanket exemption, thus necessitating the detailed discussion in the remainder of this chapter. But while baseball does not come within the scope of the subsequent discussion, a review of the developments which have affected its reserve system will serve to round out this preliminary discussion.

---

240. *See generally* N.Y. Times, Oct. 7, 1975, at 1, col. 8; Gazette (Montreal), Oct. 7, 1975, at 16, col. 6; Winnipeg Free Press, Oct. 7, 1975, at 47, col. 1; Sporting News, Oct. 18, 1975, at 67, col. 1; *id.,* Oct. 25, 1975, at 16, col. 1 (editorial).

241. *See* N.Y. Times, Oct. 7, 1975, at 1, col. 8.

242. *Id. See also* Washington Post, Mar. 7, 1976, at D4, col. 1.

243. *See* N.Y. Times, Oct. 7, 1975, at 1, col. 8.

244. Alan Eagleson, executive director of the NHL Players Association, stated that "The only reason that we're making this deal, other than for financial considerations, is the fact that there is competition for talent from the World Hockey Association. . . . There is no way this agreement could have been written in without a WHA dealing for the same player in the NHL." Winnipeg Free Press, Oct. 7, 1975, at 47, col. 1.

245. *See id.*

246. *See* § 5.02 *supra.*

In many respects, the developments in baseball present an interesting contrast to the pattern of the reforms which have occurred in other leagues. As the prior discussion suggests, the impetus for change in the player restraint mechanism outside of baseball has typically come from the courts. In case after case, the courts have expressed their rather pointed disapproval of the justifications which the other leagues have offered for their player controls. The players' initial success in using the antitrust laws and the prospect of further expensive litigation have prompted the club owners to assume a more conciliatory stance in labor negotiations directed at producing new, less restrictive rules to govern intraleague movements by players. In baseball, however, the players' union has not been able to use the threat of antitrust litigation to overcome the owners' intransigence. Nonetheless, they have had some considerable success in their efforts to change what has historically been a perpetual reserve system. The players' major victory occurred in an arbitration proceeding which was initiated to secure an interpretation of the renewal clause in the standard player contract. The cases considered by the arbitrator involved players Andy Messersmith and Dave McNally. Both had completed the period of performance called for under the express terms of their contracts. Messersmith then played an additional year without signing a new contract, a tactic which forced his club, the Los Angeles Dodgers, to exercise its right to renew the agreement. McNally's case was similar except that he retired in the middle of his option year. The players' union, on behalf of the players, asserted that at the end of the option year Messersmith and McNally became free agents.[247] At the heart of the controversy was the interpretation of the language of paragraph 10(a) of the Uniform Players Contract which provided, in pertinent part, that if the parties could not agree upon the terms of a new contract, "the Club shall have the right . . . to renew this contract for the period of one year on the same terms. . . ." [248] The players' association argued that this language gave the clubs the right to extend the agreement for one year but that the contractual relationship of the parties ended upon the expiration of that term. The owners argued, however, that when the club renewed the contract, it renewed all terms including the term which gave the club a right to renew it. Thus, in the owners' view the club's right to renewal was perpetual.[249] Peter Seitz, the arbitrator who decided the case,[250] agreed with the players' association and ruled that Messersmith and McNally were free agents.[251] Seitz emphasized that his decision was not intended to reflect his

---

247. *See* National and American Leagues of Professional Baseball Clubs v. Major League Baseball Players Ass'n, (John A. Messersmith and David A. McNally), Grievance Nos. 75-27 & 75-28, Decision No. 29 at 1-2 (Dec. 23, 1975, Opinion of Impartial Chairman Peter Seitz) [hereinafter cited as Messersmith-McNally Arbitration].

248. The full text of the renewal clause is quoted in note 155 *supra*.

249. Similar questions about the interpretation of the renewal clause have arisen in other sports. These are considered more fully in § 3.12 *supra*.

250. The case was heard by a three-person arbitration panel which also included representatives selected separately by the leagues and the players' association. Seitz cast the deciding vote and wrote the arbitration opinion. He prefaced his opinion with the disclaimer that "The statements and views expressed in this Opinion are those of the Chairman and are not necessarily subscribed to by either of the other two members of the Panel." Messersmith-McNally Arbitration at 2.

251. *The Merits*: The grievances of Messersmith and McNally are sustained. There is no contractual bond between these players and the Los Angeles and Montreal clubs, respectively. Absent such a contract, their clubs had no right or power, under the Basic

belief as to the merits or demerits of a reserve system, but was merely an interpretation of the language of the parties' agreement.[252] While the parties could have expressly provided for a perpetual right of renewal, the language they employed suggested, in Seitz' view, a more limited right. This narrower interpretation, in the absence of a clear statement to the contrary, was felt to be particularly appropriate in light of the personal nature of the employment relationship in question.[253]

Since the issue before Seitz was purely one of contract interpretation, one might ask why the arbitrator did not give greater weight to the fact that it has

Agreement, the Uniform Player Contract or the Major League Rules to reserve their services for their exclusive use for any period beyond the "renewal year" in the contracts which these players had heretofore signed with their clubs. *Id.* at 62-63.

Seitz went on to order the leagues to inform their members that the Major League Rules did not prohibit clubs from negotiating with either player.

An interesting insight to the case was revealed by Seitz to columnist Jerome Holtzman. Seitz stated that he would have postponed his decision if the owners had expressed a desire to negotiate with the players on the reserve system. However, according to Seitz, the owners rejected his suggestion that negotiations proceed and instead demanded that he issue a decision, thus "forcing" Seitz to decide against them. *See* Holtzman, *Owners Wouldn't Bargain, Demanded Decision — Seitz,* Los Angeles Times, Mar. 3, 1976, Part III, at 7, col. 1.

252. Before stating some of the reasons for [the conclusion that the position of the Players Association has merit] I believe it to be appropriate and salutory to state how I approach this issue.

It would be a mistake to read this Opinion as a statement of the views of the writer either for or against *a* reserve system, or for that matter, the Reserve System presently in force. It is not my function to do so! The Arbitration Panel on which I sit has authority and power only to rule on grievances which involve the interpretation of, or compliance with the provisions of 'any agreement' between the Players Association and the Clubs or between a Player and a Club . . . .

It deserves emphasis that this decision strikes no blow emancipating players from claimed serfdom or involuntary servitude such as was alleged in the *Flood* case. It does not condemn the Reserve System presently in force on constitutional or moral grounds. It does not counsel or require that the System be changed to suit the predilections or preferences of an arbitrator acting as a Philosopher-King intent upon imposing his own personal brand of industrial justice on the parties. It does no more than seek to interpret and apply provisions that are in the agreements of the parties. To go beyond this would be an act of quasi-judicial arrogance! *Id.* at 36-37.

253. The point the leagues present must be based upon the implication or assumption, that if the renewed contract is "on the same terms" as the contract for the preceding year . . . the right to additional renewals must have been an integral part of the renewed contract, I find great difficulties, in so implying or assuming, in respect of a contract providing for the rendition of personal services in which one would expect a more explicit expression of intention. *Id.* at 43.

Seitz also noted that his interpretation was supported by the conclusions reached by courts interpreting the option clause in basketball. *See* Lemat Corp. v. Barry, 275 Cal.App. 2d 671, 80 Cal. Rptr. 240 (1969); Central New York Basketball, Inc. v. Barnett, 19 Ohio Op.2d 130, 181 N.E.2d 506 (1961).

Seitz also had to deal with the leagues' contention that a club's right to reserve a player was also insured by Rule 4-A(a) of the Major League Rules. That rule provides for the establishment of a "Reserve List" for each club consisting of the names of players, not to exceed 40, "whom the club desires to reserve for the ensuing season." Upon proper submission of the list, the rule provides that "thereafter no player on any list shall be eligible to play for or negotiate with any other club until his contract has been assigned or he has been released. . . ." Since the Major League Rules are explicitly made a part of each player's contract, the leagues argued that the grievants, both of whom had been "reserved by their respective clubs," were bound by the prohibition on negotiating with other clubs. After an extended analysis, Seitz rejected this contention and read the rule as rendering a player ineligible for negotiations with others only so long as he was under contract with the reserving club. In Seitz' view, it was incompatible with notions of freedom of contract to construe an agreement to bind an individual beyond the terms of the contract he had signed.

historically been assumed that baseball's right to renew was perpetual in nature.[254] It is generally accepted that particular terms of a contract are to be interpreted consistent with the customs and usages which the parties have developed under it.[255] Indeed, the early baseball injunction cases,[256] the more recent *Flood v. Kuhn*,[257] and most writers who have commented on the practices of the industry[258] have assumed that the reserve system was perpetual in nature. A federal district court, which was asked to review Seitz' action, issued a decision which suggests one explanation for the perceived irrelevancy of the prior interpretations. In that proceeding for review, which was captioned *Kansas City Royals Baseball Corporation v. Major League Players Association*,[259] the owners sought to have the court consider certain evidence which supported their contention that since as early as 1879, the industry had operated on the assumption that reserve rights were perpetual. This included materials drawn from the 1903 Peace Compact between the American and National Leagues, the record developed in the *Flood* litigation, and various congressional hearings.[260] While this evidence was offered by the owners to support their contention that Seitz did not have authority to consider the reserve clause, a separate issue considered below, the court's treatment of the proffered materials is instructive on the larger question of the soundness of Seitz' interpretation of the contract language. The court rejected most of the owners' proposals for findings incorporating the historical materials. As to the materials which predated the development of a collective bargaining relationship in baseball, the court concluded that

> The history of how club owners may have run their business in the 19th century and that portion of the 20th century before they entered into a collective bargaining agreement with a recognized labor organization representing its employees simply is not relevant or material to the determination of the legal questions presented in this case.[261]

Other evidence was offered to support the owners' argument from the period in which the players were unionized. But this too was found to be unpersuasive by the court. In Judge Oliver's view, the totality of the evidence presented to the arbitration panel and offered to the court indicated that "the words 'Reserve System' . . . were never the subject of any agreed meaning as understood by the parties to the collective bargaining agreement." [262] What the court seemed

---

254. Seitz recited some of the history of the reserve clause, see *id.* at 10-14, but in his discussion of the merits of the case made no particular effort to explain the relevancy of that background for the issue before him. The analysis which he uses suggests that the present controversy was one to be resolved on the basis of the agreements, statements, and other evidence arising from the collective bargaining relationship which produced the arbitration system in which he was operating.

255. *See generally* A. CORBIN, CORBIN ON CONTRACTS §§ 544-45, 556-58 (1951).

256. These cases are discussed in § 4.13 *supra. See also* Gilbert, *Some Old Problems in a Modern Guise: Enforcement of Negative Covenants,* 4 CAL. L. REV. 114 (1916).

257. Flood v. Kuhn, 316 F. Supp. 271 (S.D.N.Y. 1970), *aff'd,* 443 F.2d 264 (2d Cir. 1971), *aff'd,* 407 U.S. 258 (1972).

258. *See, e.g.,* DEMMERT 20-21; Noll, *The U.S. Team Sports Industry: An Introduction* in GOVERNMENT AND THE SPORTS BUSINESS 3 (R. Noll ed. 1974); Rottenberg, *The Baseball Players' Labor Market,* 64 J. POL. ECON. 242, 245-46, 252 (1956).

259. 409 F. Supp. 233 (W.D. Mo.), *aff'd,* 532 F.2d 615 (8th Cir. 1976).

260. *See id.* at 243-46.

261. *Id.* at 243.

262. *Id.* at 246.

to be saying was that as far as the current labor contract was concerned, the parties had never reached an understanding as to what the critical words meant. It may have been true that the owners created the reserve system in the 1800's intending it to give rise to perpetual rights and they may have continued to adhere to that interpretation in initial dealings with the union, but in the court's view, there was no convincing evidence that the union had ever conceded that the owners' interpretation should control the administration of the contract in the contemporary setting.[263] Thus it was not necessary for the players to dispute the historical record on the early meaning of the reserve system, for that evidence was beside the point. More important was the failure of prior collective bargaining sessions to produce a common understanding on the import of the language used.

On appeal, the owners repeated their arguments that the reserve system enabled a club to perpetually control a player and that this interpretation had been historically accepted by the players' association. The Eighth Circuit rejected these contentions, however, and affirmed the award granted by Judge Oliver.[264] The court concluded that although there was evidence on record establishing that the reserve clause operated as a perpetual control, the record also disclosed that various players' association representatives had interpreted the clause as allowing a player to become a free agent by playing for one year under a renewed contract.[265] Equally important support for the court's conclusion rested upon the fact that the collective bargaining agreement contained no express provision interpreting the contract language.[266]

Once the meaning of the contract language was shown to be uncertain, other well-established principles of law required that the court not consider whether Seitz had chosen the best or most correct interpretation of the disputed language. As is discussed in more detail in other sections, courts are normally without authority to determine whether an arbitrator's interpretation of a contract is correct.[267] Although this principle is followed in other types of arbitration, it is applied with particular strictness in labor arbitrations.[268] It is assumed that by agreeing to a system of binding arbitration the parties

---

263. The arbitrator was presented with another argument which used the apparent lack of agreement between the parties to bolster the owners' position. The leagues argued, that because there had been no agreement on the reserve system, this was a matter which was reserved to the prerogatives of management and thus not affected by the collective bargaining agreement at all. Seitz did not give detailed attention to this argument, although it was recognized in his opinion. One major difficulty with this view is that the fact refuted any notion that the players' association voluntarily agreed that the entire matter of defining and applying the reserve system was to be left up to management. Indeed, the association strenuously opposed every effort by the owners to interpret or otherwise assume control over the system.

264. Kansas City Royals Baseball Corp. v. Major League Baseball Players' Ass'n, 532 F.2d 615 (8th Cir. 1976).

265. 532 F.2d at 631. The court noted that Marvin Miller, Executive Director of the Players' Association, had expressed this view prior to the start of the 1971 season, and again during the negotiations preceding the execution of the 1973-75 collective bargaining agreement. *Id.* at 626-27.

266. *Id.* at 631.

267. *See* § 4.20 *supra.*

268. *See, e.g.,* United Steelworkers v. American Mfg. Co., 363 U.S. 564 (1960); United Steelworkers v. Enterprise Wheel & Car Co., 363 U.S. 593 (1960).

specifically bargained for a private, extrajudicial interpretation.[269] Moreover, strong policies engrained in the federal labor laws make arbitration the favored mechanisms for dispute-resolution. Proper respect for that system of informed, private decision-making requires that courts not make themselves available as alternative forums for review. Thus, as long as it appears that the arbitrator's decision "draws its essence from the collective bargaining agreement," [270] the arbitration award will be treated as final. Predictably, this was the ultimate conclusion reached in the *Kansas City Royals* case on the Seitz interpretation.[271]

The Messersmith-McNally arbitration involved another issue which should be noted. The club owners contended that Seitz had no jurisdiction to pass on the players association claim because the issues involving the reserve system were outside the parties' broad arbitration agreement. The primary basis for this contention was a provision of the collective bargaining agreement which stated that "this Agreement does not deal with the reserve system." [272] Since the agreement establishing a system of arbitration was part of the same document, the owners contended that the reserve system was removed from the class of arbitrable disputes. In addition, the fact that the parties had been unable to agree upon any modification of the reserve system even though the issue arose on several occasions suggests that they intended their "agreement" at the bargaining table to leave the restraints unaffected.[273] The owners' attempt to deny Seitz jurisdiction in the matter proved unsuccessful both before the arbitrator and in the subsequent judicial proceedings. Several factors supported this result. As an initial matter, the evidence of an intent to omit reserve system questions from the labor contract was equivocal. Despite the language suggesting that the reserve clause was not covered, the agreement specifically incorporated the Uniform Player Contract, one provision of which was the reserve clause in question.[274] Moreover, in the past, some reserve clause

---

269. *Compare* § 4.20 *supra. See also* United Steelworkers v. Enterprise Wheel & Car Co., 363 U.S. 593, 599 (1960):

> The question of interpretation of the collective bargaining agreement is a question for the arbitrator. It is the arbitrator's construction which was bargained for; and so far as the arbitrator's decision concerns construction of the contract, the courts have no business overruling him because their interpretation of the contract is different from his.

270. *Id.* at 597.
271. *See* 532 F.2d at 621.
272. Basic Agreement Between the American League of Professional Baseball Clubs and the National League of Professional Baseball Clubs and Major League Baseball Players Association, art. XV (1973). Article XV provides in full that:

> Except as adjusted or modified hereby, this Agreement does not deal with the reserve system. The Parties have differing views as to the legality and as to the merits of such system as presently constituted. This Agreement shall in no way prejudice the position or legal rights of the Parties or of any Player regarding the reserve system.
> During the term of this agreement neither of the Parties will resort to any form of concerted action with respect to the issue of the reserve system, and there shall be no obligation to negotiate with respect to the reserve system.

273. *See also* note 263 *supra.*
274. Seitz found this inconsistency particularly troublesome:

> Stated in the form of a question, the quandary and dilemma faced by the writer is this: What does it mean when the Basic Agreement professes not to "deal with the reserve system" if the Players Contract incorporated into and made a part of the Basic Agreement actually contains provisions which are components of that system? Messersmith-McNally Arbitration at 19.

questions, notably that involved in the Catfish Hunter case, had been submitted to arbitration without objection by the owners.[275] In addition, while the parties had used express language to remove some matters from the broad arbitration clause, the reserve clause was not mentioned, and the language elsewhere in the contract which stated that it did not "deal with" the player restraints was somewhat equivocal by contrast.[276] The conclusion that the parties had indicated no singular intent on the matter of arbitrability was critical to the outcome of the case. This finding invited the application of the fundamental principle of labor law that unless the evidence is clearly to the contrary, it will be assumed that the parties intended their system of arbitration to govern a dispute which arises between them.[277] The bases of this presumption are similar to those which support the nonreviewability of arbitrators' decisions: due to the complexity of any employment setting, it is understandable that the parties may not have thought of every situation in defining the coverage of their arbitration agreement; private dispute resolution is more likely to produce industrial peace; and courts, with their lack of expertise in labor matters, are less well-suited to resolve conflicts between labor and management.[278] When the issue of Seitz' jurisdiction was presented to the courts for judicial review, predictably it was these principles which provided the foundation for the affirmance of the appropriateness of the arbitration forum.[279]

After the Seitz decision, the owners and players' representatives returned to the bargaining table. As expected, a key objective was to reach an accord with respect to the future of the reserve clause. While no agreement was reached

---

Seitz examined the background of the parties' negotiations and eventually concluded that the statement that the Basic Agreement did not deal with the reserve system was not intended to remove it from the purview of the arbitration clause, but rather had a much more limited purpose. Seitz accepted the players' contention that the language was sought by the Players Association in an attempt to protect it from the legal liability which might result if it were found to be a co-conspirator in a scheme to restrain player mobility. Thus, the Association was, in Seitz' view, attempting to protect itself from a suit by an individual player and not agreeing to completely remove the reserve system from the purview of the collective bargaining relationship.

275. *See id.* at 27 n.1.

For background on the Hunter case, see N.Y. Times, Dec. 16, 1974 at 51, col. 5; *id.*, Jan. 4, 1975, at 19, col. 6. Charles Finley, the owner of the Oakland A's, who lost Hunter's services when the club failed to pay a portion of his salary, continued to seek review of the arbitrator's decision in court, but without success. *See* American and National Leagues of Professional Baseball Clubs v. Major League Baseball Players Ass'n, 130 Cal. Rptr. 626 (1976).

276. The Basic Agreement suggests that the parties used some care in defining which grievances they intended to exempt from the arbitration procedure which involved an outside arbitrator. Thus, the term "grievance" was broadly defined to include any dispute between the Players Association and the clubs or between a player and a club, but specifically did not include disputes concerning certain benefit plans, those arising from discipline by the commissioner, or those relating to the league's right to compel public appearances by players. *See* Basic Agreement, *supra* note 272, at art. X(A).

277. "An order to arbitrate the particular grievance should not be denied unless it may be said with positive assurance that the arbitration clause is not susceptible of an interpretation that covers the asserted dispute. Doubts should be resolved in favor of coverage." United Steelworkers v. Warrior & Gulf Navigation Co., 363 U.S. 574, 582-83 (1960).

See also, Aaron, *Arbitration in the Federal Courts: Aftermath of the Trilogy,* 9 U.C.L.A. L. REV. 360 (1962); Meltzer, *The Supreme Court, Arbitrability, and Collective Bargaining,* 28 U. CHI. L. REV. 464 (1961); Wellington, *Judicial Review of the Promise to Arbitrate,* 37 N.Y.U. L. REV. 471 (1962); *Symposium-Arbitration and the Courts,* 58 NW. U. L. REV. 466 (1963).

278. *See* authorities cited note 277 *supra.*

279. 409 F. Supp. at 246-49, *aff'd,* 532 F.2d at 629-30.

in the initial sessions, each side offered proposals which represented positions less stringent than those which they had taken in the course of the arbitration. The players were willing to agree that a club could reserve a player for a period as long as six years if other concessions were made.[280] In addition, the players seemed prepared to accept that some sort of indemnification system could be utilized.[281] The owners demanded a right to reserve for a longer period and wanted to limit both the number of teams which could bid for a free agent and the number of such players which could be acquired by any one team, proposals presumably reflecting the clubs' concern that competitive balance within the league be maintained.[282] An agreement was finally reached on the eve of the 1976 All-Star Game.[283] It was eventually ratified by both the players[284] and owners.[285] The new four-year contract includes the right of an unsigned player to become a free agent at the end of the 1976 season and of a signed player to become a free agent after playing out the renewal year in his current contract.[286] Moreover, any player who has spent six years in the major leagues may become a free agent by notifying his club after the season that he wants to be a free agent.[287] A player with five years of major league service has the right to demand a trade and the power to veto up to six teams as potential assignees of his contract. If he is not traded by the spring of the following season, he becomes a free agent.[288] The most interesting feature of the new contract is the draft system devised to allocate negotiating rights to free agents. Under the draft procedures, each ball club, choosing in inverse order of their finish in the standings, will be able to select negotiating rights to one free agent in each round of the draft. More than one club can "draft" a player under this system, but no player can be selected by more than twelve teams.[289] In order to avoid a situation in which all the best talent is *signed* by the franchise with the largest checkbook, a limit is imposed on the number of free agents a club may actually acquire. A team may sign only one player if the free-agent pool consists of less than fifteen ballplayers; two if there are between fifteen and thirty-eight, three if there are between thirty-nine and sixty-two, and so forth.[290] A club may exceed these limits where it has lost players because they became free agents. In that case, the club is allowed a selection for each player it loses. Once a player signs

---

280. *See* Washington Post, Mar. 4, 1976, at G7, col. 1; N.Y. Times, Feb. 28, 1976, at 17, col. 5; *id.* Mar. 4, 1976, at 37, col. 1; *id.* Mar. 17, 1976, at 27, col. 3.

281. *See* sources cited note 280 *supra.*

282. *See* N.Y. Times. Mar. 16, 1976, at 41, col. 5; *id.* Mar. 17, 1976, at 27, col. 3; Washington Post, Mar. 21, 1976, at D3, col. 1.

283. *See* N.Y. Times, July 13, 1976, at 1, col. 1; Washington Post, July 13, 1976, at D1, col. 5.

284. *See* N.Y. Times, Aug. 3, 1976, at 25, col. 7.

285. *See* Washington Post, July 20, 1976, at D1, col. 6.

286. *See* Basic Agreement Between the American League of Professional Baseball Clubs and the National League of Professional Baseball Clubs and Major League Baseball Players Association art. XVII (1976). *See also* N.Y. Times, July 25, 1976, § 5, at 8, col. 4.

287. *See id.*

288. *See id.*

289. *See id.* The player's former team retains negotiating rights to the athlete, thus giving him an effective choice of thirteen teams. If the player fails to agree to terms with either his former team or any of the twelve teams granted negotiating rights, four teams, chosen by lots from among all teams expressing an interest in the ballplayer (including teams not among the original dozen) will be granted new negotiating rights.

290. *See id.*

with a new club, he must remain with the club a minimum of five years, unless traded or sold.[291] The club is prohibited from selling him to another franchise until after the June 15th following his signing. The club may trade the player, but only if the player agrees to the trade. The new contract brings to an end more than a year of difficult negotiations,[292] which largely focused on the reserve system. The agreement reached will bring peace to baseball for at least four years, but it is unlikely to be the last chapter in sports longest running controversy.

§ 5.04. Labor Exemption: Background.

a. Introduction. An analysis of the antitrust status of player restraints logically begins with a review of the federal law doctrine under which certain agreements reached in the course of collective bargaining between employers and workers' unions are removed from scrutiny under the antitrust laws.[293]

---

291. *See* Washington Post, July 20, 1976, at D1, col. 6.

292. *See id.*; N.Y. Times, July 13, 1976, at 1, col. 1.

293. The reader interested in doing further research into the labor exemption will find that there are a significant number of sources which may be consulted. The following list is divided between general authorities and those which have particular relevance for the sports area.

General Authorities:

Connell Constr. Co. v. Plumbers & Steamfitters Local 100, 421 U.S. 616 (1975); American Fed'n of Musicians v. Carroll, 391 U.S. 99 (1968); UMW v. Pennington, 381 U.S. 657 (1965); Meat Cutters Local 189 v. Jewel Tea Co., 381 U.S. 676 (1965); Allen Bradley Co. v. Electrical Workers Local 3, 325 U.S. 797 (1945); United States v. Hutcheson, 312 U.S. 219 (1941); Apex Hosiery Co. v. Leader, 310 U.S. 469 (1940); Duplex Printing Press Co. v. Deering, 254 U.S. 443 (1921); C. Morris, Developing Labor Law 807-16 (1971); T. Kheel, Labor Law (18 Business Organizations 1971) §§ 4.01-.06 [hereinafter cited as Kheel]; St. Antoine, *Collective Bargaining and the Antitrust Laws* in Indus. Rel. Research Ass'n Proceedings: 19th Annual Meeting 66 (1966); Williams, *Labor and the Antitrust Laws* in Labor Law Developments: Proceedings 12th Annual Institute on Labor Law 5 (1966); Bernhardt, *The Allen Bradley Doctrine: An Accomodation of Conflicting Policies*, 110 U. Pa. L. Rev. 1094 (1962); Cox, *Labor and the Antitrust Laws: Pennington and Jewel Tea*, 46 B. U. L. Rev. 317 (1966); Cox, *Labor and the Antitrust Laws — A Preliminary Analysis*, 104 U. Pa. L. Rev. 252 (1955); DiCola, *Labor Antitrust: Pennington, Jewel Tea and Subsequent Meandering*, 33 U. Pitt. L. Rev. 705 (1972); Feller & Anker, *Analysis of Impact of Supreme Court's Antitrust Holdings*, 59 LRRM 103 (1965); Meltzer, *Labor Unions, Collective Bargaining and the Antitrust Laws*, 32 U. Chi. L. Rev. 659 (1965); Summers, *Labor Law in the Supreme Court: 1964 Term*, 75 Yale L.J. 59 (1965); Winter, *Collective Bargaining and Competition: The Application of Antitrust Standards to Union Activities*, 73 Yale L.J. 14 (1963); Comment, *Labor's Antitrust Exemption*, 55 Calif. L. Rev. 254 (1967); Comment, *Labor's Antitrust Exemption After Pennington and Jewel Tea*, 66 Colum. L. Rev. 742 (1966); Comment, *Labor Law and Antitrust: "So Deceptive and Opaque Are the Elements of These Problems,"* 1966 Duke L.J. 191; Comment, *Labor Immunities and the Public Interest*, 44 Tul. L. Rev. 297 (1970); Comment, *Union-Employer Agreements and the Antitrust Laws: The Pennington and Jewel Tea Cases*, 114 U. Pa. L. Rev. 901 (1966); Note, *Antitrust and Labor-Union Liability Under the Sherman Act*, 19 Sw. L.J. 613 (1965); Note, *Labor-Antitrust: Collective Bargaining and the Competitive Economy*, 20 Stan. L. Rev. 684 (1968).

Sports Authorities:

Flood v. Kuhn, 407 U.S. 258, 293-06 (1972) (Marshall, J., dissenting); Mackey v. National Football League, 543 F.2d 606 (8th Cir. 1976), *modifying* 407 F. Supp. 1000 (D. Minn. 1975); Robertson v. National Basketball Ass'n, 389 F. Supp. 867 (S.D.N.Y. 1975); Kapp v. National Football League, 390 F. Supp. 73 (N.D. Cal. 1974); Philadelphia World Hockey Club, Inc. v. Philadelphia Hockey Club, Inc., 351 F. Supp. 462 (E.D. Pa. 1972); Boston Professional Hockey Ass'n v. Cheevers, 348 F. Supp. 261 (D. Mass.), *remanded,* 472 F.2d 127 (1st Cir. 1972); Jacobs & Winter, *Antitrust Principles and Collective Bargaining by Athletes: Of Superstars in Peonage*, 81 Yale L.J. 1 (1971); Comment, *Antitrust and Professional Sport; Does Anyone Play by the Rules of the Game?* 22 Cath. L. Rev.

Where this labor exemption is available, the immunity from antitrust attack is complete, and it is not necessary to make further inquiry into the economic justification for the restraints or the extent to which the complaining party was injured by them. The next three sections of this chapter examine the nature of the labor exemption and the considerations which will determine its application to the professional sports industry. Subsequent sections then consider the substantive antitrust issues which arise in cases in which the labor exemption is not available.

That the so-called labor exemption may be relevant in antitrust controversies in professional sports is beyond dispute. However, the precise role which it will play in particular controversies is much less certain. The reasons for this uncertainty are of rather formidable proportions. On the one hand, the exemption doctrine itself is not well-defined. While the United States Supreme Court has considered the exemption on several occasions,[294] its decisions do not provide an unambiguous statement of the proper accommodation of the federal labor and antitrust laws.[295] Application of the labor exemption requires that basic public policy choices be made in defining the lengths to which organized labor can go in seeking to protect the interests of the employees it represents. While the federal labor laws provide some guidance on these matters, there are no precise congressional guidelines to direct the courts' interpretations, and the courts have assumed considerable discretion in defining the reach of the exemption in particular cases.[296] The basic choices which must be made are of the sort which are greatly influenced by the decision-maker's political philosophy and economic orientation. Thus, changes in the personnel of the Supreme Court and differences among lower court judges have resulted in considerable unevenness in the development and application of the exemption in the general labor field.

The unsettling effect of that doctrinal uncertainty is intensified in the sports area because of the peculiar nature of labor-management relations in that industry. Collective bargaining between leagues and their respective players' associations is of relatively recent origin.[297] Many issues which were drawn into controversy under the antitrust laws had not been subject to extensive negotiations between the parties. In many cases, the practices in question antedated by many years the development of representative bargaining.[298] None of the Supreme Court precedents dealt specifically with this type of situation,

---

403 (1973); Comment, *Flood in the Land of Antitrust: Another Look at Professional Athletics, the Antitrust Laws and the Labor Exemption,* 7 IND. L. REV. 541 (1974).

294. *See* Supreme Court cases cited note 293 *supra.*

295. Some of the uncertainties which remain in this area despite the Court's decisions are noted in KHEEL § 4.06 [3].

296. The Court has recently recognized that the labor exemption, as applied in many modern cases is a non-statutory, but proper, accommodation between the congressional policy favoring collective bargaining and the congressional policy favoring free competition. Connell Constr. Co. v. Plumbers & Steamfitters Local 100, 421 U.S. 616 (1975).

297. *See generally* Krasnow & Levy, *Unionization and Professional Sports,* 51 GEO. L.J. 749 (1963); Lowell, *Collective Bargaining and the Professional Team Sport Industry,* 38 LAW & CONTEMP. PROB. 3 (1974).

298. *See, e.g.,* Philadelphia World Hockey Club, Inc. v. Philadelphia Hockey Club, Inc., 351 F. Supp. 462, 498-99 (E.D. Pa. 1972).

and the significance of this lack of bargaining history has been a major issue in the cases.[299]

The situation presented in the professional sports cases is unusual in another respect. In other industries, the availability of the labor exemption is usually tested in a suit brought by an employer or third party which is adversely affected by a union-proposed restriction included in a collective bargaining agreement.[300] The union typically seeks to avoid liability by asserting the labor exemption as a defense. In the cases decided in the sports area, however, the plaintiff was usually a member of the union or the union itself. In that setting, the party raising the claim of immunity was typically the employer, and the defense was raised, not for the purpose of seeking immunity for a union-imposed restriction, but rather to immunize an employer-devised restraint which may or may not have been agreed to by the union.[301] In the general labor cases, including those which have produced the Supreme Court precedents, the critical question was whether the labor exemption would protect an exercise of union power, while in the sports area the employer defendant often sought to use the exemption against the apparent interests of the employee group. Thus, here again, the important Supreme Court cases did not provide clear guidance,[302] and the process of interpreting those somewhat nebulous precedents was complicated further.

The different posture in which the labor exemption controversy has been presented in sports litigation provides the occasion for a reexamination of the philosophical basis of the grant of immunity. Indeed, the sports cases raise an issue seldom confronted in prior decisions. What precisely is the labor exemption intended to protect? Is its purpose to protect an entity — the union — or is it intended to protect a process — the process of collective bargaining?[303] The historical origins of the exemption would point strongly to the former view, for the exemption was initially devised to protect the then infant labor movement from the powers of unsympathetic courts.[304] More specifically, the earlier forms of the exemption were intended to immunize certain types of union organizing tactics, particularly strikes and boycotts.[305] Little in the early history of the exemption suggests that it was intended as a device which might be used to aid employers in overriding important employee interests.

---

299. *See* § 5.06 *infra.*

300. *See, e.g.* Connell Constr. Co. v. Plumbers & Steamfitters Local 100, 421 U.S. 616 (1975); UMW v. Pennington, 381 U.S. 657 (1965); Meat Cutters Local 189 v. Jewel Tea Co., 381 U.S. 676 (1965).

301. This distinction was found to be of critical importance in the court's refusal to apply the labor exemption in Robertson v. National Basketball Ass'n, 389 F. Supp. 867, 884-86 (S.D.N.Y. 1975). *See also* § 5.06 *infra.*

302. Mr. Justice Marshall, dissenting in *Flood v. Kuhn,* recognized that no prior decisions of the Court had involved a case where the employer sought to immunize a practice which worked to the detriment of labor. 407 U.S. 258, 294 (1972).

303. *See generally* Clune v. Publishers' Ass'n, 214 F. Supp. 520 (S.D.N.Y.), *aff'd per curiam,* 314 F.2d 343 (2d Cir. 1963).

304. *See generally* UMW v. Pennington, 381 U.S. 657, 700-13 (1965) (Goldberg, J., dissenting in part); Allen Bradley Co. v. Electrical Workers Local 3, 325 U.S. 797, at 801-08 (1945).

305. *See generally* United States v. Hutcheson, 312 U.S. 219 (1941); Apex Hosiery Co. v. Leader, 310 U.S. 469 (1940). The legislative history of the earlier forms of the labor exemption is considered in E. BERMAN, LABOR AND THE SHERMAN ACT 3-54, 99-117 (1930) [hereinafter cited as BERMAN]; F. FRANKFURTER & E. GREENE, THE LABOR INJUNCTION 134-63 (1930) [hereinafter cited as FRANKFURTER & GREENE].

But later developments suggest that the labor exemption has assumed a broader function as the labor movement has matured. Just as the primary focus of union activity has shifted from the organization of workers to negotiation of agreements to protect their interests, the nature of the controversy in the labor exemption cases has shifted from disputes about particular union tactics to disputes arising from union-imposed trade restrictions.[306] While the exemption is still frequently used to protect union demands from attacks by employers and outsiders, it is increasingly apparent that the immunity doctrine is applied to protect the collective bargaining process from judicial intervention.[307] This result seems consistent with the strong policy of the federal labor law which, on the one hand, compels unions and employers to bargain about the basic terms and conditions of employment, but which, on the other hand, leaves the parties free to define the content of their agreement.[308] If this principle of freedom of contract is to be respected, then the occasions for judicial intervention must be minimized. Once it is perceived that the labor exemption serves to protect the institution of collective bargaining, and not simply union participation in that process, it would seem to follow that the employer may in some cases invoke the immunity doctrine to resist antitrust attacks by disgruntled employees.[309] This, of course, is what the employers have sought to do in the sports area.[310] But existing precedents provide only limited guidance in defining the extent to which management is protected. Because of the unmistakable pro-union bias of the original immunity grant, it is by no means clear that employers enjoy the same range of protection under the labor exemption as has traditionally been afforded union demands.[311] Thus, it is necessary to review the important cases from the general labor field in order to determine their applicability to the rather unique circumstances which arise in the sports context.

b. Supreme Court Precedents. The Sherman Act, enacted in 1890 and still a primary weapon in the antitrust arsenal, in general language condemns "every contract and combination in restraint of trade." While the language of the statute and the circumstances surrounding its adoption might suggest that it was intended only to regulate businesses in their dealings with other commercial enterprises,[312] the original version of the act contains no language specifically

---

306. *Compare* cases cited note 304 *supra with* Connell Constr. Co. v. Plumbers & Steamfitters Local 100, 421 U.S. 616 (1975) *and* Meat Cutters Local 189 v. Jewel Tea Co., 381 U.S. 676 (1965).

307. *See generally* UMW v. Pennington, 381 U.S. 657, 698-735 (1965) (Goldberg, J., dissenting in part).

308. For an excellent discussion of the basic federal policy with respect to collective bargaining see H. WELLINGTON, LABOR & THE LEGAL PROCESS, 49-90 (1968) [hereinafter cited as WELLINGTON].

309. *See* § 5.05 *infra.*

310. For example, in *Robertson v. National Basketball Ass'n,* the league attempted to argue that any matter which was a mandatory subject of a bargaining agreement between an employer and a union was exempt as long as the matter had no substantial effect upon persons outside of the bargaining unit. The court rejected this argument. 389 F. Supp. 867, 886-89 (S.D.N.Y. 1975). This aspect of the *Robertson* case is considered more fully below. *See* § 5.06 *infra.*

311. *See generally* Flood v. Kuhn, 407 U.S. 258, 288-96 (1972) (Marshall, J., dissenting).

312. The pertinent section of the Sherman Act provides:

> Every contract, combination in the form of trust or otherwise, or conspiracy, in restraint of trade or commerce among the several States, or with foreign nations, is declared to be illegal. . . .

exempting the activities of labor unions.[313] Some courts adopted the view that the Act applied to all types of combinations, including those between laborers, which interrupted the free flow of commercial activity.[314] Such an interpretation had potentially devastating consequences for the infant labor movement, for unions, by their very nature, were combinations of individuals which sought to restrain an employer's freedom to deal with his employees. Moreover, the most obvious forms of union collective action — strikes and boycotts — had the undeniable effect of restraining the movement of the employers' goods.[315]

When the effects of the early Sherman Act labor cases became apparent, unions sought relief from Congress.[316] After several years of agitation by labor groups, Congress passed legislation which seemed to provide a significant exemption for labor movement activities.[317] Section 6 of the Clayton Act, adopted in 1914, proclaimed that labor unions were not combinations in restraint of trade and that "nothing contained in the antitrust laws shall be construed . . . to forbid or restrain individual members of such organizations from lawfully carrying out the legitimate objects thereof." [318] Section 20 of the same act limited the power of courts to issue injunctions to restrain certain enumerated types of union organizational activities.[319]

---

313. The Supreme Court has indicated that the dominant purpose of the Sherman Act was the regulation of the commercial activities of business. *See* Allen Bradley Co. v. Electrical Workers Local 3, 325 U.S. 797, 803-06 (1945); *cf.* Apex Hosiery Co. v. Leader, 310 U.S. 469, 489-501 (1940). The legislative history tends to support this conclusion. 51 Cong. Rec. 13663 (1914) (remarks of Senator Ashurst); see 21 Cong, Rec. 2455-57 (1890) (remarks of Senator Sherman).

314. *See* Waterhouse v. Comer, 55 F. 149 (C.C.S.D. Ga. 1893); United States v. Workingmen's Amalgamated Council, 54 F. 994 (E.D. La. 1893). *See also* Berman 58-70.

315. *See, e.g.,* Gompers v. Bucks Stove & Range Co., 221 U.S. 418 (1911); Loewe v. Lawlor, 208 U.S. 275 (1908). *See generally* Berman 90-110; Kheel, §§ 4.01-.06.

316. Labor's objection to the treatment which it had received from the courts had two aspects to it. On the first level there was a concern for the substantive law being applied, which in general was based on federal or common law antitrust principles. But in addition, there was a concern for the remedial device — the injunction — which was typically applied to prevent union collective activity. Thus, when the unions appealed to Congress, they presented a request which, in effect, sought to limit the reach of the antitrust laws and also curtail the use of injunctions to control union activities. *See generally* Frankfurter & Greene 139-43. *See also* Allen Bradley Co. v. Electrical Workers Local 3, 325 U.S. 797 (1945).

317. For a general discussion of the legislative history of these congressional actions see Kheel §§ 4.03-.04.

318. Section 6 of the Clayton Act provides in full:
> The labor of a human being is not a commodity or article of commerce. Nothing contained in the antitrust laws shall be construed to forbid the existence and operation of labor, agricultural, or horticultural organizations, instituted for the purposes of mutual help, and not having capital stock or conducted for profit, or to forbid or restrain individual members of such organizations from lawfully carrying out the legitimate objects thereof; nor shall such organizations, or the members thereof, be held or construed to be illegal combinations or conspiracies in restraint of trade, under the antitrust laws. 15 U.S.C. § 17 (1970).

319. . . . [N]o restraining order or injunction shall be granted by any court of the United States, or a judge or the judges thereof, in any case between an employer and employees, or between employers and employees, or between employees, or between persons employed and persons seeking employment, involving, or growing out of, a dispute concerning terms or conditions of employment, unless necessary to prevent irreparable injury to property, or to a property right, of the party making the application, for which injury there is no adequate remedy at law, and such property or property right must be described with particularity in the application, which must be in writing and sworn to by the applicant or by his agent or attorney.

> And no such restraining order or injunction shall prohibit any person or persons, whether singly or in concert, from terminating any relation of employment, or from ceasing to perform any work or labor, or from recommending, advising, or persuading others by peaceful means so to do; or from attending at any place where any such person

Labor's belief that these provisions totally freed them from the rigors of the Sherman Act was soon proven to be unfounded, for the Supreme Court chose to give a very limiting interpretation to the statute and left many union activities vulnerable to antitrust attack.[320] Further congressional action was necessary, and the desired clarification came in the form of the Norris-LaGuardia Act which expanded the classifications of protected-union activities and further restricted the use of injunctions in labor controversies.[321] While most of the provisions of the Norris-LaGuardia Act were designed to protect union organizational activities,[322] specific recognition was given to the public importance of encouraging "concerted activity for the purpose of collective bargaining. . . ." [323] As interpreted by the courts in cases involving complaints against unions on antitrust grounds, the Norris-LaGuardia Act is not viewed as a tightly drawn specification of the types of permissible union activity. Rather the statute is seen as a general congressional reassertion of a general public policy, first stated in the Clayton Act, but later dismembered by the Supreme Court, favoring collective activity by employees.[324]

The Clayton Act and the Norris-LaGuardia Act continue to provide the most specifically identifiable statutory sources of the labor exemption. But it is clear that those statutes provide only limited guidance in answering many of the complex issues which arise in the context of contemporary labor-management negotiations. The statutes responded to the issues which were most pressing at the time they were enacted and thus are drafted so as to provide antitrust immunity for certain types of union tactics, including strikes, boycotts and other group actions. The statutes do not provide a standard which can be used to test the *substance* of labor-management agreements under the antitrust laws or to determine when those laws should be applied. The task of providing such standards has been assumed by the courts.[325]

The courts' deliberations in this regard are influenced not only by the policies embodied in the early exemption statutes, but also by the expression of

---

or persons may lawfully be, for the purpose of peacefully obtaining or communicating information, or from peacefully persuading any person to work or to abstain from working; or from ceasing to patronize or to employ any party to such dispute, or from recommending, advising, or persuading others by peaceful and lawful means so to do; or from paying or giving to, or withholding from, any person engaged in such dispute, any strike benefits or other moneys or things of value; or from peaceably assembling in a lawful manner, and for lawful purposes; or from doing any act or thing which might lawfully be done in the absence of such dispute by any party thereto; nor shall any of the acts specified in this paragraph be considered or held to be violations of any law of the United States. 29 U.S.C. § 52 (1970).

320. In Duplex Printing Press Co. v. Deering, 254 U.S. 443 (1921), the Court read the Clayton Act as exempting only those union activities which were directed against the employees' immediate employers. Union efforts to boycott the employer's products in the hands of other dealers and other secondary activities were said to be still subject to the Sherman Act proscription on trade restraints. Thus, the statutes were applied in a manner significantly limiting the types of economic power which a union could exercise in its effort to promote employee interests. *See generally* UMW v. Pennington, 381 U.S. 676, 701-04 (1965) (Goldberg, J., dissenting in part); Allen Bradley Co. v. Electrical Workers Local 3, 325 U.S. 797, 805-06 (1945).

321. 47 Stat. 70 (1932), as *amended* 29 U.S.C. §§ 101-15 (1970). For a discussion of the legislative history and purposes of the Norris-LaGuardia Act, see KHEEL §§ 4.01-.06. *See also* Brissenden, *The Labor Injunction,* 48 POL. SCI. Q. 413 (1933).

322. *See, e.g.,* Norris-LaGuardia Act § 4, 29 U.S.C. § 104 (1970).

323. 29 U.S.C. § 102 (1970).

324. *See generally* United States v. Hutcheson, 312 U.S. 219, 234-36 (1941).

325. *See, e.g.,* Connell Constr. Co. v. Plumbers & Steamfitters Local 100, 421 U.S. 616, 622 (1975).

legislative purpose found in the original National Labor Relations Act and its subsequent amendments.[326] These latter enactments, which constitute the nation's basic labor laws, were clearly designed to promote and protect the institution of collective bargaining among labor and management groups.[327] Congress did not undertake to specify the relationship between the NLRA and the antitrust laws. Yet, the courts have recognized that the antitrust laws could not be applied with full force to labor-management agreements if the policies embodied in NLRA were to be achieved.[328] Thus, it has been necessary for courts to accommodate the conflicting policies embodied in the two sets of laws.

It is appropriate at this point to review the leading Supreme Court precedents. This review must be prefaced with a caveat, however. As mentioned in the introduction, all of the important cases have arisen in fact situations in which the defendants have sought antitrust immunity for activities or agreements initiated or enthusiastically endorsed by the unions involved. Thus, the decisions are concerned primarily with the protection of union efforts.[329] In the sports context, however, it is usually the employer who argues for the applicability of antitrust exemption and often in circumstances which suggest that a finding in favor of antitrust immunity would be contrary to the articulated interests of at least some members of the employee group. Despite the different posture in which the question arises, the prior Supreme Court precedents provide the broad framework in which the issues in the sports area will be resolved.[330]

While there are several early cases which produced relevant precedent,[331] the Supreme Court's decision, in 1941, in *United States v. Hutcheson*[332] has had a most significant impact on the development of the principles which govern contemporary labor controversies. On its facts, *Hutcheson* dealt only with the propriety of certain tactics which a union used to bring pressure to bear on an employer and did not specifically consider the more troublesome questions of the types of union-employer agreements which were immune from the normal application of the antitrust laws. More specifically, two unions became embroiled in a dispute over which of the two groups had jurisdiction over construction work

---

326. *See* UMW v. Pennington, 381 U.S. 657, 711-12 (1965) (Goldberg, J., dissenting in part); Winter, *Collective Bargaining and Competition: The Application of Antitrust Standards to Union Activities,* 73 YALE L.J. 14, 17-30 (1963).

327. *See generally* WELLINGTON 45-90.

328. *See, e.g.,* Connell Constr. Co. v. Plumbers & Steamfitters Local 100, 421 U.S. 616, 622 (1975):
The non-statutory exemption has its source in the strong labor policy favoring the association of employees to eliminate competition over wages and working conditions. Union success in organizing workers and standardizing wages ultimately will affect price competition among employers, but the goals of federal labor law never could be achieved if this effect on business competition were held a violation of the antitrust laws.

329. *See* notes 300-11 *supra.*

330. It can be noted that in the few sports cases decided on this question, the courts have relied heavily on the basic precedents discussed here. *See, e.g.,* Robertson v. National Basketball Ass'n, 389 F. Supp. 867 (S.D.N.Y. 1975); Philadelphia World Hockey Club, Inc. v. Philadelphia Hockey Club, Inc. 351 F. Supp. 462 (E.D. Pa. 1972). However, courts have generally recognized that the existing Supreme Court precedents raise a substantially different issue to the extent that they deal with union-supported arrangements. Flood v. Kuhn, 407 U.S. 258, 293-96 (1972) (Marshall, J., dissenting); Kapp v. National Football League, 390 F. Supp. 73 (N.D. Cal. 1974).

331. For a more detailed discussion of the early cases affecting the development of labor exemption see BERMAN 99-179; Meltzer, *Labor Unions, Collective Bargaining and the Antitrust Laws,* 32 U. CHI. L. REV. 659, 661-68 (1965).

332. 312 U.S. 219 (1941), *noted in* 41 COLUM. L. REV. 532 (1941) *and* 54 HARV. L. REV. 887 (1941) *and* 89 U. PA. L. REV. 827 (1941) *and* 27 VA. L. REV. 895 (1941).

to be performed at a St. Louis brewery. When the work was awarded to the other union, the carpenters union, in apparent disregard of an agreement to arbitrate such controversies, called a strike against the immediate employer, the brewery, as well as against a construction company and a tenant on adjacent brewery property. The carpenters also employed other types of secondary pressure, including a request to union members and friends that they refrain from buying the brewery's products. Officials of the union were charged with engaging in a criminal conspiracy to violate the Sherman Act prohibition on combinations in restraint of trade.

The Supreme Court found that the union's activities were immune from the antitrust laws. The narrowest holding of the case was that the Norris-LaGuardia Act, although expressly only prohibiting the use of *injunctions* against a union's actions taken in furtherance of the group's employment-related goals, operated to immunize unions from antitrust criminal liability as well.[333] But the effect of the Court's decision was to confirm that the various labor and antitrust statutes were to be read as expressing a congressional intention to generally exempt legitimate union activities from the restraints applicable to other combinations having an adverse effect on competition.[334] Indeed, the Court appeared to present a test for gauging the scope of the exemption which defined the extent of immunity in very broad terms. In the Court's view, union actions were not subject to judicial interference "so long as [the] union acts in its self-interest and does not combine with non-labor groups."[335]

This pronouncement has served to underscore the fact that any inquiry into the availability of the exemption must give attention to the question of whether the union's participation in a particular scheme is motivated primarily by a desire to improve or preserve working conditions.[336] While subsequent cases make clear that self-interest is not the only ingredient in the exemption formula,[337] the emphasis in *Hutcheson* on this element serves to identify the congressional design as one in which the exemption operated as a device to protect collective action in the labor movement.[338] The general significance of the Court's disapproval of union actions undertaken in combination with "non-labor groups" is less certain.[339] Since *Hutcheson* involved a situation in which the union had acted unilaterally, the Court did not have to respond to either the general question of the sorts of groups which would be regarded as "non-labor" groups or the more specific issue of whether agreements with employers were outside the scope of protection which the Court had defined.

---

333. 312 U.S. at 235-36.

334. *See* Meltzer, *Labor Unions, Collective Bargaining and the Antitrust Laws, supra* note 331, at 668-70.

335. 312 U.S. at 232.

336. This aspect of the *Hutcheson* standard continues to be given considerable weight by the courts. *See, e.g.,* Intercontinental Container Transp. Corp. v. New York Shipping Ass'n, 426 F.2d 884 (2d Cir. 1970).

337. *See, e.g.,* Allen Bradley Co. v. Electrical Workers Local 3, 325 U.S. 797 (1945).

338. In a subsequent decision, the Supreme Court has indicated that the scope of legitimate union self-interest extends only to concerns for the elimination of competition over wages and working conditions and does not encompass efforts by the union to curtail competition based upon the efficiency of the employer. *See* Connell Constr. Co. v. Plumbers & Steamfitters Local 100, 421 U.S. 616, 623 (1975).

339. *See* KHEEL § 4.06 [2].

Some of these questions were subsequently addressed by the Court four years later in *Allen Bradley Company v. Electrical Workers Local 3*,[340] one of the first cases under modern labor statutes to find that particular union activity fell outside the protective veil of the labor exemption. The electrical workers were charged with conspiring with manufacturers of electrical supplies and contractors who installed these products to control the market for electrical equipment in New York City. The union initially secured closed shop and hot cargo agreements with local manufacturers and contractors. The manufacturers were obligated to sell their products in the local area only to contractors employing union members. By the same token, contractors were obligated to buy goods only from the unionized manufacturers. As the arrangement matured, there was increasing interaction by the three groups on an industry-wide basis. Understandings developed on a variety of matters including price and market controls. The three groups also joined together to effectively boycott non-participating contractors and manufacturers and to limit sales of goods manufactured by firms outside of the New York area.[341] The evidence before the Court clearly established that price and product competition had been effectively eliminated.[342] The court of appeals had refused to find that the union's participation in the plan was subject to antitrust attack. The appellate court reviewed the prior precedents and laid particular emphasis on the language in *Hutcheson* which seemed to protect union actions taken in furtherance of the members' self-interest.[343] Since these arrangements had the effect of both increasing employment opportunities for union members and enabling the workers to secure more favorable working conditions, the appellate court had found them to be exempt from the normal antitrust proscriptions.

The Supreme Court, in an opinion written by Justice Black, reversed, concluding that the mere pursuit of union self-interest was not enough to immunize market-wide controls of the type involved in the case before it.[344] In Justice Black's view, the element which carried these agreements beyond the scope of the labor exemption was the fact that the restraints were not simply the result of an agreement between a union and an immediate employer of its members. Rather, the participants in the arrangement included "non-labor" groups, more specifically those who supplied goods to or purchased products from the immediate employer.[345] Equally important in the Court's characterization of the case was the fact that the arrangement went well beyond the union's interest in bargaining for better wages and conditions for a specific employee-employer relationship.[346] While the Court reaffirmed that matters such as wages, length of work hours, and so on were properly objects of the union's concern, the vice of the present arrangement was that it not only sought to affect these conditions in the labor market, but also was intended to control

---

340. 325 U.S. 797 (1945), *noted in* 19 S. CAL. L. REV. 256 (1946).
341. Meltzer, *Labor Unions, Collective Bargaining and the Antitrust Laws, supra* note 331, at 670-71.
342. 325 U.S. at 798-801.
343. *See* 145 F.2d 215, 224 (4th Cir. 1944).
344. 325 U.S. at 808-11.
345. *Id.* at 809.
346. *Compare* Connell Constr. Co. v. Plumbers & Steamfitters Local 100, 421 U.S. 616 (1975).

important aspects of the product market in the local area. While an agreement upon the price at which labor was sold would necessarily affect the price at which the employer eventually sold his goods,[347] it seemed to be quite a different matter to say that the federal intent had been to authorize unions to participate directly in agreements to set product prices on an industry-wide basis. In the Court's view,

> . . . Congress never intended that unions could, consistently with the Sherman Act, aid non-labor groups to create business monopolies and to control the marketing of goods and services.[348]

To underscore the point that agreements between a union and the immediate employer of its members are to be treated differently from agreements reached with others with a less direct interest in the particular employment relationship, Justice Black addressed himself to the situation in which a union exacts an agreement from an employer under which the employer promises to buy goods only from firms employing union members. In Justice Black's view, "we may assume that such an agreement standing alone would not have violated the Sherman Act," even though it may have an effect on the level of competition in the particular trade.[349] But Black pointed out that the participants in the agreements in the present case were not limited to those concerned with the immediate employment relationship in a particular business entity. Rather, the *Allen Bradley* agreements involved

> a far larger program in which contractors and manufacturers united with one another to monopolize all the business in New York City, to bar all other businessmen from that area, and to charge the public prices above a competitive level.[350]

As the foregoing discussion suggests, the agreements which were under scrutiny in *Allen Bradley* were not simply collective bargaining agreements between a union and an employer but included parties who seemingly had neither an interest in nor control over the immediate employment relationship.[351] The element which seemed to be condemned in this arrangement was the union's participation in a scheme which involved outsiders. The question which *Allen Bradley* did not answer was the extent to which an agreement confined to the immediate employment relationship and involving only the union and the interested employer might be found to fall outside the labor exemption.[352] Such an agreement would normally be the product of traditional collective bargaining and presumably would deal with matters reflecting important employee interests. Since it was this sort of collective union action which the federal labor laws were intended to protect, a much stronger case can be made for the

---

347. This distinction between the direct and indirect effects of union activity upon the price which the employer charges for his goods is recognized in other opinions by the Court. *See, e.g.* UMW v. Pennington, 381 U.S. 657, 663-65 (1965).

348. 325 U.S. at 808.

349. *Id.* at 809.

350. *Id.*

351. Similar agreements have been subjected to antitrust scrutiny in various cases decided subsequent to *Allen Bradley. See, e.g.,* Las Vegas Merchant Plumbers Ass'n v. United States, 210 F.2d 732 (9th Cir. 1954).

352. *See generally* §§ 5.05-.06 *infra.*

application of the labor exemption in this setting. Thus, the issue of the precise limits of the exemption in the antitrust context promised to be a most difficult one.

The Supreme Court addressed this question in two cases, *United Mine Workers v. Pennington*[353] and *Meat Cutters Local 189 v. Jewel Tea Co.,*[354] decided the same day in 1965. *Pennington* serves to make clear that the mere inclusion of a matter in a collective bargaining agreement does not automatically immunize it from antitrust attack.[355] The allegations in that case were as follows. The union and a multi-employer bargaining unit which included several large coal companies entered into an agreement the apparent purpose of which was to deal with the problem of overproduction of coal in the coal industry. The union abandoned its resistance to mechanization in exchange for higher wages and other benefits. In order to insure that the large operators were not disadvantaged by the higher wages to which they had agreed, the unions promised to demand the same wage scale from smaller operators in subsequent contract negotiations. In addition, the union and the employer group agreed upon other steps to limit the production and marketing of non-union coal, a step which also served to protect the large operators from price competition from firms not bound to the new, higher wage scale.

The Supreme Court, speaking through Justice White, concluded that these alleged agreements went beyond the limits of the labor antitrust exemption. The Court's analysis made clear that the ultimate objective of the union's agreement was proper. The subject matter of the alleged agreement was wages, a matter which was clearly in the self-interest of the union members. The Court conceded that the goal of attaining and maintaining a higher wage scale for its members was a proper union objective and that the national labor laws were designed to protect union collective activity which sought to secure such important job-related benefits.[356] But the defect in the alleged scheme was the means which the union employed to achieve its objective. Specifically, it was the attempt by the union and the employer group to affect the costs and markets of operators who were not parties to the agreement which exposed the arrangement to antitrust attack. In Justice White's view,

> [T]here is nothing in the labor policy indicating that the union and the employers in one bargaining unit are free to bargain about the wages, hours, and working conditions of other bargaining units or to attempt to settle these matters for the entire industry.[357]

Justice White specifically noted that no antitrust violation would be found where a union reached a wage settlement in one unit and then sought to impose similar wage rates on other employers with which it bargained.[358] Thus, the critical element alleged in *Pennington* was the presence of a union-employer

---

353. 381 U.S. 657 (1965), *noted in* 7 B.C. IND. & COM. L. REV. 158 (1965) *and* 18 VAND. L. REV. 2027 (1965).

354. 381 U.S. 676 (1965), *noted in* 7 B.C. IND. & COM. L. REV. 158 (1965) *and* 18 VAND. L. REV. 2027 (1965).

355. 381 U.S. 657, 662-64.

356. 381 U.S. at 664.

357. *Id.* at 666.

358. *Id.* at 664.

"conspiracy" to control the conditions outside the area of their immediate bargaining concerns.[359]

In condemning the type of arrangement which was alleged to have existed between the U.M.W. and the large operators, the Court was clearly concerned about its effects on the product market, that is, the market in which coal was bought and sold.[360] But the Court's analysis suggests that there is a fine line between permissible and impermissible product market effects. The conspiracy alleged in *Pennington* was viewed as having an obvious anti-competitive effect. If the conspiracy were successful, wage-related production costs would be equalized and the potential for price competition would be lessened. In the process, marginal operators who could not pay the higher scale would be eliminated and the pool of potential competitors reduced. However, unilateral action by the union in seeking uniform wage scales throughout the industry would also have these effects to the extent that the union was successful in imposing its demands in its various bargaining units. The Court appeared to be prepared to accept this consequence.[361] The distinction which the Court seems to make is between a union agreement which deals with immediate employment-related concerns such as wages in the particular bargaining unit and one which is directed at matters less directly related to the terms and conditions under which the members of the particular unit are employed. While the former may necessarily have an impact beyond the immediate relationship of the parties, that consequence is unavoidable.[362] Agreements specifically directed at controlling conditions either in other units or in the product market itself seem to be unnecessary to the achievement of legitimate union goals, and protection of these is not necessary to effectuate the purposes of federal labor protection.[363]

359. Unilaterally, and without agreement with any employer group to do so, a union may adopt a uniform wage policy and seek vigorously to implement it even though it may suspect that some employers cannot effectively compete if they are required to pay the wage scale demanded by the union. The union need not gear its wage demands to wages which the weakest units in the industry can afford to pay. Such union conduct is not alone sufficient evidence to maintain a union-employer conspiracy charge under the Sherman Act. *There must be additional direct or indirect evidence of the conspiracy.* There was, of course, other evidence in this case, but we indicate no opinion as to its sufficiency. *Id.* at 665, n.2 (emphasis added).

360. *See generally* Meltzer, *Labor Unions, Collective Bargaining and the Antitrust Laws, supra* note 331, at 702-09.

361. We think it beyond question that a union may conclude a wage agreement with the multi-employer bargaining unit without violating the antitrust laws and that it may as a matter of its own policy, and not by agreement with all or part of the employers of that unit, seek the same wages from other employers, 381 U.S. at 664.

362. It is accepted, for example, that intra-unit agreements as to wages may have a direct and concrete effect upon the product market, particularly where a multi-employer unit is involved. UMW v. Pennington, 381 U.S. 657, 664 (1965). *See also* American Fed'n of Musicians v. Carroll, 391 U.S. 99 (1968); Teamsters Local 24 v. Oliver, 358 U.S. 283 (1959).

363. The *Pennington* court indicated that it would be impermissible for the union to attempt to control directly the prices at which the employer sold his goods, even though such a demand might be made for the purpose of increasing the employer's income and, thus, its ability to pay higher wages. As Justice White observed,

In such a case, the restraint, on the product market is direct and immediate, is of the type characteristically deemed unreasonable under the Sherman Act and the union gets from the promise nothing more concrete than a hope for better wages to come. 381 U.S. at 663.

In addition to underscoring the Court's concern for product market effects, this analysis affirms that the mere fact that an agreement is in the self-interest of the union does not itself justify a grant of immunity.

The distinction between agreements embodying matters of immediate union-employer concerns and those in which the parties attempt to control matters beyond the employment relationship also appears in the Court's analysis in *Jewel Tea*.[364] In that case, the butchers' union sought to impose certain marketing hours restrictions on retail stores in the Chicago area. Several employers agreed to continue a rule which restricted meat counter operating hours to the period from 9:00 a.m. to 6:00 p.m., six days a week and which provided that no customer would be served at any other time. Jewel, which desired to operate an expanded self-service meat counter, sought to bargain for modification of the rule for its stores, but the union refused to vary the provision. Under the threat of a strike, Jewel finally consented to the clause. Subsequently, however, it filed suit attacking the arrangement on antitrust grounds.

Jewel Tea is a particularly important precedent because, as the case is treated by the Court,[365] it involves no evidence of conspiracy between the union and outsiders. As the case was presented to the Court, the issue was the relatively straight forward question of the extent to which matters of direct collective bargaining are subject to scrutiny under the antitrust laws. The Court in *Jewel Tea* gave a carefully drawn response which eschewed any simple, absolute rule on this question.

The Court concluded that the portion of the rule which restricted the hours during which butchers had to work was not subject to review under the Sherman Act. The Court noted initially that this touched a matter — hours of work — which was a mandatory subject of bargaining.[366] In addition, it was a matter in which the concern of the union was "immediate and direct." [367] Although there was necessarily an effect on competition — small grocery stores which did not have self-service meat counters were protected from night hours competition by chain stores which did[368] — that effect, in the Court's view, was tolerable because of the important employee interest involved.[369]

Thus, the Supreme Court suggested that the applicability of the antitrust laws to the results of collective bargaining was to be determined by a balancing test.[370] It is wholly proper that attention be given to the effect of a particular provision upon business competition. But the degree of restraint must be weighed against the type of employee interest at stake. The subject matter must relate to wages, hours, and other terms and conditions of employment. And even for matters within these classifications, an inquiry must be made into the

---

364. 381 U.S. 676 (1965).

365. Interestingly, the Supreme Court's treatment of the case ignores a finding by the trial court that the union had agreed not to enter into a contract with any other employer on terms more favorable than those provided in the agreement in question. *See also* Meltzer, *Labor Unions, Collective Bargaining and the Antitrust Laws, supra* note 331, at 725 n.228.

366. 381 U.S. 676, 690.

367. [A]lthough the effect of competition is apparent and real, perhaps more so than in the case of the wage agreement, the concern of union members is immediate and direct weighing the respective interests involved, we think the national labor policy expressed in the National Labor Relations Act places beyond the reach of the Sherman Act union-employer agreements on when, as well as how long, employees must work. *Id.* at 691.

368. *See generally* Meltzer, *Labor Unions, Collective Bargaining and the Antitrust Laws, supra* note 331, at 691-96.

369. 381 U.S. at 691.

370. *Id. See also* note 367 *supra*.

immediacy and directness of the employee interest which is involved. Where the dispute relates to an issue such as whether employees will have to work nights or weekends, the employee interest is quite substantial and will outweigh the other concern about the effect on competition.[371]

The Court's opinion also includes some suggestions about how this analysis will apply to other types of collective bargaining provisions. Reiterating a point made in dicta in *Pennington,* the Court intimates strongly that the cloak of antitrust immunity would not extend to a union demand that the employer sell its products at prices set by collective bargaining.[372] Here the suggestion is that such an arrangement would have a substantial adverse effect upon competition and would not deal with a matter of immediate concern to the employee group. While prices and profits may affect employee wages, the union's concern for wages can be accommodated by an agreement — one which more specifically focuses on wage rates as such — which does not have the undesirable anticompetitive consequences.

The Court applied the same type of analysis to the second facet of the rule in *Jewel Tea* which sought to prevent stores from selling meat from self-service counters outside the designated operating hours period. The effect on competition was conceded and the primary question was whether this restriction promoted a substantial union interest. The employer argued that it did not since after-hours sales did not require that a butcher be in attendance and thus could not be supported by the employees' interest in not having to work inconvenient hours. The Court indicated that the employer's antitrust attack on the after-hours sales restriction "would have considerable merit" if it were indeed true that such evening and Sunday self-service sales could be made without increasing the butcher's work load or working hours.[373] In that case, the restraint on competition would "stand alone, unmitigated and unjustified by the vital interests of the union butchers." [374] However, the union argued that night operations would be impossible without an increase in butchers' work hours or load. Thus, it was necessary for the Court to make a factual inquiry into the conflicting views on the extent to which fundamental employee interests would be affected. The Court examined that question and upheld the trial court's finding in the union's favor on this point.[375] Having thus decided that one part of the balancing test was heavily weighed in the favor of legitimate employee concerns, the Court found that the concern for the anticompetitive effects of the rule had been outweighed and it could thus be sustained.[376]

---

371. *See generally* Meltzer, *Labor Unions, Collective Bargaining and the Antitrust Laws, supra* note 331, at 724-26.

372. Jewel, for example, need not have bargained about or agreed to a schedule of prices at which its meat would be sold and the unions could not legally have insisted that it do so. But if the unions had made such a demand, Jewel had agreed and the United States or an injured party had challenged the agreement under the antitrust laws, we seriously doubt that either the unions or Jewel could claim immunity by reason of the labor exemption, whatever the substantive questions of the violation might be. 381 U.S. at 689.

373. *Id.* at 692.

374. *Id.*

375. *Id.* at 694.

376. *See generally* Meltzer, *Labor Unions, Collective Bargaining and the Antitrust Laws, supra* note 331, at 691-93, 726-27.

Another case which should be noted is *Connell Construction Company v. Plumbers & Steamfitters Local 100*,[377] decided by the Supreme Court in 1975. In that case, the union represented employees in the plumbing and mechanical trades in Dallas. These workers were employed by firms which served as subcontractors on construction projects in the Dallas area. The dispute arose when the union sought to secure commitments from several general contractors that they would choose only those subcontractors which were parties to collective bargaining agreements with the union. The union disclaimed any interest in representing the employees of general contractors and limited its demands to the restriction which would insure more employment opportunities for union members. As a result of strikes and other pressures, the plaintiff-general contractor gave in to the union demand but then initiated litigation to upset the arrangement on antitrust grounds.

The situation which was presented to the Court, involving an attempt by the union to extend its influence beyond the immediate bargaining unit, is not one which is likely to be important in the sports context.[378] The decision is relevant for the present inquiry, however, because of the views which the Court expresses on the range of legitimate union interests which will be entitled to deference under the antitrust laws.

The Court concluded that the particular agreement in *Connell* was not protected by the labor exemption. Without designating it as such, the Court seems to have employed the same type of balancing test employed in *Jewel Tea*.[379] On the one hand, the Court found a direct and substantial restraint on competition in the business market. The effect of the union-imposed agreement would be to restrict the opportunity of non-union subcontractors to bid on jobs and secure work. Thus, firms which might offer important price or quality competition were restrained in their efforts to market their services.[380] On the other hand, the Court found that the union-proposed restraint went well beyond the union's legitimate concern for wages and other conditions of employment. The Court recognized that federal "labor policy requires tolerance for the lessened business competition" which results when unions attempt to standardize wages and employment conditions.[381] But the agreement in the instant case was not drawn so as to protect only the union's interest in those matters. In the Court's view,

> The agreements with Connell and other general contractors indiscriminately excluded non-union subcontractors from a portion of the market, even if their competitive advantages were not derived from substandard wages and working conditions but rather from more efficient operating methods. Curtailment of competition based on efficiency is neither a goal of federal labor policy nor a necessary effect of the elimination of competition among workers.[382]

This portion of the opinion can be read as suggesting that the area of union self-interest which is clothed with antitrust immunity is to be rather tightly

377. 421 U.S. 616 (1975) *noted in* 61 A.B.A.J. 1276 (1975).
378. *See* note 384 *infra*.
379. *See* discussion at notes 370-71 *supra*.
380. 421 U.S. at 625.
381. *Id.*
382. *Id.*

drawn around the most basic sorts of employee concerns relating to wages, hours of employment and the like. On the facts of *Connell* the union could have asserted that it sought the agreement in question for the purpose of protecting an interest other than that of simply increasing its membership. Thus, a union may desire this type of restraint because it wishes to increase employment opportunities for its members. In an industry, such as the construction industry, where employment is often periodic, this would seem to be a matter of considerable employee concern. By insuring that unionized subcontractors will be selected by major general contractors, the union may be able to increase the regularity with which its members work. Like wages, this is a matter which directly affects the employees' total income. *Connell,* in effect, holds that such a goal would not be protected by antitrust immunity, at least not in circumstances in which the union seeks to achieve its goal through direct and substantial market restraints.

Many people will likely read *Connell* as heralding a new era in which a more conservative Supreme Court begins to tighten the antitrust reins on the labor-management horse. As suggested above, this interpretation of *Connell* is likely to be based on the seemingly narrow view which the Court takes of the range of protected employee interests. In another sense, however, *Connell* is quite consistent with the balancing approach earlier devised by the Court.[383] *Connell* was a case in which the union-proposed market restraint was obvious and pervasive: the union wanted to drive non-union firms from the market (or into its fold) and it wanted to do so by a most direct means. In a balancing test, such a bold restraint on competition could be sustained only by a showing that the union was seeking to protect the most fundamental of job-related concerns. But as suggested by the Court, such a strong countervailing consideration was lacking on these facts. The union did not appear to be acting for the purpose of protecting the union pay scale from the threat of low wage competition. Nor was there any showing that the non-union firms represented a threat with respect to other job-related concerns. Viewed in that light, *Connell* is not a startling case. The primary importance of the decision would seem to be in its teaching that a direct, unmitigated market restraint will be sustained only where it is necessary to protect the most fundamental of employee interests.[384]

---

383. The balancing test suggested in *Jewel Tea* is examined more closely in Meltzer, *Labor Unions, Collective Bargaining and the Antitrust Laws, supra* note 331, at 724-26.

384. One interesting facet of the *Connell* decision is the fact that the Court had available an alternative rationale for the result which received only passing attention in the opinion. The agreements in question were agreements reached between a union and another party which was not the immediate employer of the employees affected. Thus, the case appeared to present a situation in which the union sought to act with an outsider to lessen market competition for the purpose of benefitting employees represented by the union. This attempt to extend union power beyond the immediate setting seemed to be quite similar to the sorts of "conspiracies" which were condemned in *Allen Bradley* and *Pennington,* and those cases would seem to have presented a basis for a ready disposition of the case. The Court did note that the union had no direct representational interest in Connell's operation and mentioned that it was not deciding what the result would have been had the market restraint been included in a collective bargaining agreement. While the absence of any immediate employment concern seems to have necessarily played a role in the result reached, this aspect of the case played a decided secondary role in the Court's approach, for the Court placed its primary emphasis on the fact that the hoped-for market restraints went well beyond the union's interest in protecting wages and conditions of employment. It seems likely that the Court's insistence that labor-related market restraints be based on immediate wage and working conditions concerns

c. Conclusion. These Supreme Court cases, developed over four decades, serve to bring into somewhat sharper focus the general principles which will determine the extent of antitrust immunity enjoyed by employment related agreements. At the threshold, it appears that immunity will be available only for those agreements arrived at between labor and management. The involvement of outsiders — those not directly involved in the immediate employment relationship — extends the reach of the agreement and will be condemned if an effect on competition is found.

Similarly, there are limits on the extent to which the employer and the union can themselves seek to project the terms of their agreement on others. The scope of antitrust immunity will be limited to matters which affect the immediate employment relationship, more specifically the terms and conditions under which the bargaining unit employees work. As illustrated by *Pennington,* the parties lose their protection from the antitrust laws when they attempt to influence the conditions which prevail in other employment settings. Finally, even when an agreement upon the relationship between the employer and employee is involved in the bargaining, there are limits on the types of restrictions which will be immunized. The agreements which will be scrutinized are those which impose significant restraints in the business market in which the employer functions. Yet, these will be sustained if it is shown that they are premised upon the protection of vital employee interests, such as avoiding inconvenient hours of work. More bold attempts to affect the product market, as by union-negotiated prices, are presumably invalid.

For purposes of the sports industry, perhaps the most important principle to emerge from these cases is one which is largely unstated. The Supreme Court seems to have assumed that labor and management enjoy very broad freedom to impose restraints upon themselves. Limitations on the parties' prerogatives in dealing with one another are a natural result of the process of collective bargaining. The Court has indicated no inclination to overturn the results of that process where it is only the participants who are affected. The strong implication of the cases is that it is only where the efficient operation of business markets is substantially impaired that the question of possible antitrust scrutiny even arises. If this is the proper inference to be drawn from the Court's decisions, it has important implications for the player restraints in the sports industry. The objections raised to those restraints have been concerned primarily with their impact on the employee group, not upon the product which is consumed by fans. Thus, to determine the availability of the labor exemption in the sports context, it becomes critical to examine the process through which the restraints have been devised and to determine the extent to which it shares the characteristics of traditional collective bargaining. It is this issue which is reviewed in the next several sections.

will appear in subsequent decisions, even those in which the conspiratorial character of the agreement is less obvious.

§ 5.05. Availability of Labor Exemption Where Parties Agree to Player Restraints Following Meaningful Collective Bargaining.

a. Statement of the Problem. Until very recently, there was a substantial question as to whether a league's player restraints could properly be regarded as the product of an agreement between labor and management. The players often contended that restraints such as the draft and option systems were unilaterally imposed by the team owners without the effective acquiescence of the players or their unions.[385] The prior review of Supreme Court precedents suggests that the exemption was designed to protect union activity and to foster the institution of collective bargaining.[386] Thus, it is clear that the degree of union participation in a particular arrangement is highly relevant. To facilitate the analysis of the exemption issue in the sports setting, the following sections will attempt to show the importance of this concern for bargaining history by looking at the antitrust issues from two different perspectives. The first part of the discussion, which is covered in this section, will assume a situation in which particular matters have been subjected to good faith bargaining between the parties. Thus, this portion of the chapter will focus on the consequences of a direct application of the substantive principles of the exemption. The next section, § 5.06, will deal with situations in which there is some question about the extent to which particular alleged restraints have been specifically approved by the players' union. In this latter treatment, attention will be focused on the cases decided to date, in which there has been considerable debate about the amount of bargaining which has occurred over the traditional restraints.

There are a number of different league practices which might give rise to disputes about the applicability of the labor exemption. Those which have received the most attention are the restraints on player mobility, particularly the draft system, reserve and option systems, and indemnity rules such as the so-called Rozelle Rule.[387] Because of the prominence which these have played in recent cases and scholarly writings, they will receive the most attention here.[388] In later paragraphs, the principles which are developed with respect to

---

385. *See* Comment, *Antitrust and Professional Sports: Does Anyone Play by the Rules of the Game?*, 22 CATH. U. L. REV. 403, 407-408, 410-11, 415 (1973).

386. *See* Robertson v. National Basketball Ass'n, 389 F. Supp. 867, 884-86, 894-95, (S.D.N.Y. 1975). *See generally* Winter, *Collective Bargaining and Competition: The Application of Antitrust Standards to Union Activities*, 73 YALE L.J. 14 (1963); Jacobs & Winter, *Antitrust Principles and Collective Bargaining by Athletes: Of Superstars in Peonage*, 81 YALE L.J. 1 (1971).

387. The litigation to date is summarized in § 5.02 *supra*.

388. *See generally* Flood v. Kuhn, 316 F. Supp. 271 (S.D.N.Y. 1970), *aff'd*, 443 F.2d 127 (1st Cir. 1971), *aff'd*, 407 U.S. 258 (1972); Mackey v. National Football League, 543 F.2d 606 (8th Cir. 1976), *modifying* 407 F. Supp. 1000 (D. Minn. 1975); Robertson v. National Basketball Ass'n, 389 F. Supp. 867 (S.D.N.Y. 1975); Kapp v. National Football League, 390 F. Supp. 73 (N.D. Cal. 1974); Philadelphia World Hockey Club, Inc. v. Philadelphia Hockey Club, Inc., 351 F. Supp. 462 (E.D. Pa. 1972); Nassau Sports v. Hampson, 355 F. Supp. 733 (D. Minn. 1972); Boston Professional Hockey Ass'n, Inc. v. Cheevers, 348 F. Supp. 261 (D. Mass.), *remanded*, 472 F.2d 127 (1st Cir. 1971); Rivkin, *Sports Leagues and the Federal Antitrust Laws* in GOVERNMENT AND THE SPORTS BUSINESS 387 (R. Noll ed. 1974); Jacobs & Winter, *Antitrust Principles and Collective Bargaining by Athletes: Of Superstars in Peonage*, 81 YALE L.J. 1 (1971); Morris, *In the Wake of the Flood*, 38 LAW & CONTEMP. PROB. 85 (1973); Comment, *Antitrust and Professional Sports: Does Anyone Play by the Rules of the Game?*, 22 CATH. U. L. REV. 403 (1973); Comment, *The Super Bowl and the Sherman Act: Professional Team Sports and the Antitrust Laws*, 81 HARV. L. REV. 418 (1967); Comment, *Monopsony in Manpower: Organized Baseball Meets the Antitrust Laws*, 62 YALE L.J. 576 (1953); Comment, *Player Control*

these restraints will be considered briefly in connection with other industry practices.[389]

What are the implications of the labor exemption for employment relationships in professional sports where a healthy collective bargaining relationship exists? While there were earlier periods in which professional athletes attempted to unionize, the presence of players' unions protected by the federal labor laws is a relatively recent phenomenon.[390] The extent of union organization and the degree of player support for the union varies considerably among the various professional sports. Nonetheless, several of the players' associations are rapidly maturing and in most leagues, the collective bargaining relationship has progressed to the point that most disputes are settled through a process of collective bargaining.[391] Thus, it is useful to consider the case in which a players' union has entered into collective bargaining over the type of player restraint system which will operate in the particular league. In order to provide a framework for the present discussion, we can hypothesize a case in which the players' union agrees to a continuation of some version of the restraints which have been the focus of controversy in the past. Thus, it will be assumed that the union has agreed to an arrangement which includes a draft system for allocating new players to various teams, a limited option system to restrict the players' mobility, and a system for compensating a team which loses an established player who fulfills the terms of his option and signs with another club.[392] In order to dispel some potential collateral issues,[393] we will assume that the union's acceptance of this system of player restraints is preceded by robust bargaining between the parties. Thus it will be posited that the union did not meekly accept proposals put forth by management, but engaged in extended negotiations with the employer in which its own demands and proposals influenced the final agreement. If there has been true bargaining between the parties, the owner-employer will have secured the advantages of these arrangements only after making important concessions to the union. These concessions may take the form of increased base salaries, more substantial pension contributions, less restrictive work rules or a variety of other

---

Mechanisms in Professional Sports, 34 U. PITT. L. REV. 645 (1973); Note, *Flood in the Land of Antitrust: Another Look at Professional Athletics, the Antitrust Laws and the Labor Exemptions,* 7 IND. L. REV. 541 (1974); Note, *The Balance of Power in Professional Sports,* 22 MAINE L. REV. 459 (1970).

389. *See* text beginning at note 503 *infra.*

390. *See generally* Krasnow & Levy, *Unionization and Professional Sports,* 51 GEO. L.J. 749 (1963); Lowell, *Collective Bargaining and the Professional Team Sport Industry,* 38 LAW & CONTEMP. PROB. 85 (1973); Note, *Flood in the Land of Antitrust: Another Look at Professional Athletics, the Antitrust Laws and the Labor Exemptions,* 7 IND. L. REV. 541 (1974).

391. *See* § 5.03 *supra.*

392. It will be noted that the agreement reached in the NHL contains all of these elements, although with important modifications which remove some of the most objectionable features. Thus, the option clause is not mandatory, and an individual player may refuse to have it included in his contract. Moreover, the amount of compensation required under the indemnity system is determined by an independent arbitrator and not by the league commissioner. *See* § 5.03 *supra.*

The NBA Players Association has agreed to accept a system which includes a player draft and an indemnity device. However, the drafting club's right to negotiate with a player expires after a year, and if no contract is signed, the player may be drafted by other clubs. Also, the indemnity system expires in 1980. *See* § 5.03 *supra.*

393. *See* discussion at notes 609-10, at § 5.06 *infra.*

benefits.[394] And, on the basis of the player restraint agreements reached thus far in the sports industry, it can be assumed that the employer's concessions will include modifications in the severity of the player restraints themselves.[395] But even assuming some liberalization of the player control mechanisms, an individual athlete may find the modified restraints objectionable and seek to contest them on the grounds that they improperly restrain his ability to freely market his services among competing employers.[396] A suit of this sort will present the occasion for considering the applicability of the antitrust laws.

b. A Preliminary Concern: Would a Union's Acquiescence to Player Restraints Violate Its Duty of Fair Representation? Before we begin our review of the principles which will control the application of the labor exemption to union-accepted player restraints, it may be useful to consider two preliminary questions: why would a players' union ever agree to a contract which restricted its members' employment opportunities? Further, would such an agreement be consistent with the union's duty of fair representation?

On the first point, the argument might be made that while a union agreement on wages, pensions, and the like is usually in the best interests of its members, acceptance of restraints on player mobility seems to be clearly antithetical to the employees' interests. It would be argued that players presumably have an interest in being free to play wherever they desire. Not only is such freedom highly valued in its own right, but also the athletes would be able to gain higher individual salaries if they were able to bid one job offer against another. Because these "obvious" advantages would be partially sacrificed if the union agreed to player restraints, it would be contended, the union could not be said to be acting in the best interests of the employee group.

Despite such contentions, there are a number of considerations which may explain why a union would vote to accept a collective bargaining agreement which included player restraints. As an initial matter, it must be recognized that the player restraints will not affect all members of the union equally. Indeed, there are many athletes for whom the restrictions have little impact. Athletes who possess only marginal skills, and who are thus readily replaceable, have relatively few opportunities for moving between teams.[397] These players may

---

394. In the 1975 football negotiations, for example, it appeared that the matter of the Rozelle Rule provided the most substantial impediment to agreement. When the union requested that the employers make their "best offer," the management group responded with a proposal which included a slight modification of the Rozelle Rule and substantially more generous concessions in the areas of pensions and minimum salaries. *See* N.Y. Times, Aug. 31, 1975, § 5, at 11, col. 4.

395. *See* note 392 *supra*.

396. The possibility that the union might agree to player restraints which are objectionable to some of its members is by no means theoretical. Indeed, this may be another of the issues with respect to which the small group of superstars and the much larger group of average and marginal players have antagonistic interests. Restraints on player mobility have their most substantial effect upon players whose services are in high demand by other teams. Other players may feel that they suffer little real disadvantage as a result of the restraints and may be willing to make concessions on these matters in order to gain benefits, such as increased compensation, which they value more highly. Other aspects of this potential for disagreement between superstars and others are considered elsewhere in this treatise. *See* discussion at notes 397-403 *infra*.

397. It would appear that it is the superstars with highly marketable skills who bear most of the burden of the draft and option systems. With respect to more marginal players, there is a much greater supply of potential talent and the demand for such a player is not likely to be as great. For many such players, the primary concern is not the opportunity to move to other teams but rather

be willing to accept restraints in favor of other concessions, particularly higher minimum salaries and increased job security. Thus, while there are some employees who may be disadvantaged, an agreement incorporating such restraints may not be regarded as injurious by all players, as some might argue.[398] Where the employer's concessions are substantial, the number of players willing to accept the restraints may be large enough that their preferences control the union's definition of its self-interest.

The union's acceptance of player restraints will not necessarily involve a sharp division within the employee group, however. It may simply indicate that a consensus has been reached among the members that there is some validity to the owners' traditional argument that unrestrained movement of players will ultimately be detrimental to the league's operation. The thesis of this argument is that without some form of restriction, there is a potential that the one or two teams in the most lucrative markets will attract all of the good players. In such a situation, the prospect of lopsided games would likely erode fan interest and eventually undermine the financial stability of the league.[399] While several economists have concluded that devices such as the draft and a reserve clause are relatively ineffective in insuring that weak franchises will keep quality players,[400] the union may well decide that the propensity for concentration of talent would be even more pronounced if restraints were entirely removed. Moreover, the union may be willing to accept the economists' conclusion that player restraints operate to provide a subsidy to weak franchises at the expense of the players.[401] In particular leagues, the employee-group may conclude that

---

the necessity of avoiding being cut from the team. Because of the significantly more limited demand for their services, many non-superstars would not experience any dramatic increase in salary by the elimination of player restraints.

For a general discussion of the economics of player restraints, see Quirk & El Hodiri, *The Economic Theory of a Professional Sports League* in GOVERNMENT AND THE SPORTS BUSINESS 33 (R. Noll ed. 1974); Canes, *The Social Benefits of Restrictions on Team Quality* in *id.* at 81; Noll, *Alternatives in Sports Policy* in *id.* at 441; Rottenberg, *The Baseball Players' Labor Market,* 64 J. POL. ECON. 242 (1956).

398. During the 1975 NFL labor negotiations some union members, apparently satisfied with the other terms offered by the team owners, publicly urged their union to reconsider its refusal to compromise on the Rozelle Rule. *See* N.Y. Times, Sept. 13, 1975, at 18, col. 1.

399. This is the argument traditionally put forth by league officials in defense of the player restraints. *See, e.g.,* Noll, *The U.S. Team Sport Industry: An Introduction* in GOVERNMENT AND THE SPORTS BUSINESS 2-7 (R. Noll ed. 1974); Canes, *The Social Benefits of Restrictions on Team Quality* in *id.* at 81; Comment, *The Super Bowl and the Sherman Act: Professional Team Sports and the Antitrust Laws,* 81 HARV. L. REV. 418, 420-25 (1967).

400. *See, e.g.,* H. DEMMERT, THE ECONOMICS OF PROFESSIONAL TEAM SPORTS 31-39 (1973) [hereinafter cited as DEMMERT]; Canes, *The Social Benefits of Restrictions on Team Quality, supra,* note 399, at 83-91.

Demmert states, for example, that

If, as the owners claim, the purpose of the reserve clause and the free agent draft is to prevent one club, or a small set of clubs, from dominating a particular sport, we can only conclude that they have failed miserably. The fact that the players' contracts and future draft selections are marketable commodities assures the impotence of these institutions in significantly altering the competitive market, distribution of playing talent. *Id.* at 37.

401. *See* DEMMERT 38:

The reserve clause and the free agent draft insure the viability of the league not through their effect on the inter-club distribution of playing talent, but by lowering the cost curves of *all* clubs in the league sufficiently to insure the economic survival of even the perennial losers.

such a subsidization is necessary in order to insure the continued operation of clubs in smaller geographical markets.

A union which endorsed player restraints on these grounds could seemingly be said to be acting in its self-interest. The ultimate goal which is achieved is job-preservation, for it is fully plausible that the employees' acceptance of reduced mobility would contribute to the financial stability of the league. Thus, the union might well conclude that in the long range interest of insuring continued employment for the majority of its members, it will accept restraints upon the players' intra-league mobility.

The suggestion that a players' union might acquiesce to such devices is hardly fanciful. The evidence that player unions are generally so inclined is rather substantial, although the degree of restriction which would be accepted varies from league to league. As previously indicated, most unions have already entered into contracts which accept modifications of the draft, option and indemnity rules.[402] There are also public statements by union leaders which seem to concede that excessive competition for players may be detrimental to the long-run interests of the sport.[403]

While it may thus be true that some unions will accept less than complete freedom of employment for their members, the question remains whether this would be legally permissible under the federal labor laws. If this issue is pursued, it is likely to be at the insistence of a superstar who would benefit from greater mobility. The legal issue which will be presented is whether the union, having acquiesced in a system of player restraints, has satisfied its duty of fair representation.[404]

The source of the union's duty to represent each employee fairly is its status as exclusive bargaining agent for the employee group.[405] Accompanying the union's right to serve as the sole spokesman of employee interests is an

---

402. *See* note 392 *supra. See also* § 5.03 *supra.*

403. A rather classic case involves Marvin Miller, executive director of the baseball players association. Although baseball's separate antitrust exemption removes it from the general scope of this section on the labor exemption, Miller's positions are germane to the limited point discussed in the text. Under the contract which prevailed in 1976, players could become free agents by playing out their option as a result of Peter Seitz' decision in the Messersmith-McNally arbitration. *See* § 5.03 *supra.* However, Miller and the players association indicated that they were prepared to accept some form of player reservation system for future years, including one which might bind players as long as six years. *See* Washington Post, Mar. 4, 1976, at G7, col. 1; N.Y. Times, Feb. 28, 1976, at 17, col. 5. Indeed, as early as 1969, Miller made it clear that "The players and the Players Association never have proposed to abolish the reserve rules. Rather, we seek to make appropriate amendments which will enhance the players position but which will not do harm to the game." Letter from Marvin Miller to all Major League Players, December 26, 1969, quoted in National and American Leagues of Professional Baseball Clubs v. Major League Baseball Players Association (John A. Messersmith and David A. McNally), Grievance Nos. 75-27, 75-28, Decision No. 29 (December 23, 1975, Peter Seitz, Arbitrator).

404. *See generally* Steele v. Louisville & Nashville R.R., 323 U.S. 192 (1944); Ford Motor Co. v. Huffman, 345 U.S. 330 (1953); Humphrey v. Moore, 375 U.S. 335 (1964); Vaca v. Sipes, 386 U.S. 171 (1967); C. MORRIS, DEVELOPING LABOR LAW 726-56 (1971) [hereinafter cited as MORRIS]; WELLINGTON, LABOR AND THE LEGAL PROCESS 145-84 (1968) [hereinafter cited as WELLINGTON]; Aaron, *Some Aspects of the Union's Duty of Fair Representation,* 22 OHIO ST. L.J. 3 (1961); Cox, *The Duty of Fair Representation,* 2 VILL. L. REV. 151 (1957); Cox, *Rights Under a Labor Agreement,* 69 HARV. L. REV. 601 (1956); Savern, *The National Labor Relations Act and Racial Discrimination,* 62 COLUM. L. REV. 563 (1962); Wellington, *Union Democracy and Fair Representation: Federal Responsibility in a Federal System,* 67 YALE L.J. 1327 (1958).

405. *See* Steele v. Louisville & Nashville R.R., 323 U.S. 192 (1944).

obligation to pay proper deference to minority interests. An employee who can show that he has been improperly discriminated against may secure appropriate relief.[406] Most cases involving a breach of the duty of fair representation involve either racial discrimination or improper handling of individual employee grievances.[407] Little attention has been given to the issue of how the duty will be applied where the individual's complaint is that the union failed to properly represent his economic interests at the bargaining table.[408] But if the existing fair representation precedents serve as a guide, it is most unlikely that an athlete disappointed with his union's acceptance of player restraints will find much solace in this doctrine. Indeed, the general trend of the cases indicates that the union enjoys broad-ranging discretion in carrying out its task as collective bargaining representative.[409]

Under the present prevailing view, "a breach of the statutory duty of fair representation occurs only when a union's conduct toward a member of the collective bargaining unit is arbitrary, discriminatory, or in bad faith." [410] It is clear that the union may satisfy its duty even though the economic interests of some of its members are substantially undermined. Moreover, it is not enough for a member to show that the union's actions were unwise, or that other less disruptive alternative courses of action were available.[411] If relief is to be provided, there must be a showing that the union's conduct was not undertaken in an honest effort to fulfill its bargaining function.

The leading cases in this area make clear that the union may assume a considerable discretion in accommodating the various interests which it represents. In a number of situations, unions have been allowed to take actions which were clearly detrimental to particular employees. In *Humphrey v. Moore*,[412] the union represented the employees of two employers which, for economic reasons, were going to have to consolidate their operations. This move involved a reduction in the total work force, and the union was forced to decide which of its members would be put out of work. The union eventually concluded that lay-offs would be determined on the basis of seniority. This arrangement had a disproportionate impact on the employees of one of the firms because they had generally accumulated less working time. Nonetheless, the Supreme Court found no violation of the duty of fair representation. The thrust of the Court's analysis is that the administration of any collective bargaining relationship will raise numerous instances in which the interests of various employee groups will come into conflict, and the courts are generally not to make themselves available

---

406. One of the more controversial aspects of the duty of fair representation has been the question of the proper form of relief to be afforded in the event of a breach. *See generally* MORRIS 730-40, 747-55.

407. *See, e.g.,* Vaca v. Sipes, 386 U.S. 171 (1967); Steele v. Louisville & Nashville R.R., 323 U.S. 192 (1944); Independent Metal Workers Union (Hughes Tool Co.), 147 NLRB 1573 (1964).

408. One of the few discussions of this issue is found in WELLINGTON 155-63.

409. *See generally* WELLINGTON 145-63; MORRIS 741-47; Blumrosen, *The Worker and Three Phases of Unionism: Administrative and Judicial Control of the Worker-Union Relationship,* 61 MICH. L. REV. 1435 (1963); Lewis, *Fair Representation in Grievance Administration: Vaca v. Sipes,* 1967 SUP. CT. REV. 81.

410. Vaca v. Sipes, 386 U.S. 171, 190 (1967).

411. *See, e.g.,* Humphrey v. Moore, 375 U.S. 335 (1964).

412. 375 U.S. 335 (1964).

to assess whether the union reached a proper accommodation.[413] Before a court will intervene, the aggrieved member must show that he or she was the object of hostile or wholly arbitrary action by the union. Noticeably absent from the Court's analysis is any effort to evaluate other techniques which the union might have used to lessen the impact of the lay-offs. Also instructive are the cases which uphold a union's refusal to process a member's grievance even though the individual is able to make out a *prima facie* case that the grievance had merit.[414] Again, the courts' primary concern is not whether the union made a reasonable accommodation of the competing interests, but only whether the decision was made in good faith and not with an intent to disadvantage the member for personal reasons.[415]

In light of the apparent willingness of courts to tolerate the "injury" to the employees' interests in these cases, it is unlikely that a breach of the duty of fair representation would be found where the union agreed to a system of player restraints.[416] As explained above, there are a number of considerations which would support a finding that such a concession was wholly consistent with the union's interest in preserving the stability of the industry in which its members work.[417] Moreover, it must be accepted that compromises on important employee interests are inherent in collective bargaining. Thus, a union may give up a demand for higher wages for one group of employees in order to gain improvement in a vacation plan which will affect a greater number of its members.[418] Or the union may make concessions intended to improve the economic position of a financially-troubled employer. It may consent to a reduction in the work force or in salaries or in the length of the work week. Employees will be disadvantaged by these changes, and it may be that some groups bear a disproportionate burden. But it cannot be seriously questioned that the union may well act in good faith in making these judgments. There is little reason to expect that a different analysis will be applied where the union's concession relates to other terms and conditions of employment, such as those which will be involved in bargaining over player restraints.

c. The Antitrust Laws as a Separate Concern. The prior analysis deals only with the limited question of whether a union which agreed to player restraints would expose itself to liability under the principles defining its duty of fair representation. The status of such an agreement under the antitrust laws is a separate concern. The remainder of the discussion in this section addresses the question of whether the judicially-defined labor exemption will be applied to insulate the bargained-for restraints from an antitrust attack. For this discussion, we will continue the assumptions made above.[419] Thus, it will be

413. *See* 375 U.S. at 349-50.
414. *See* Vaca v. Sipes, 386 U.S. 171 (1967). *See generally* Feller, *Vaca v. Sipes One Year Later,* N.Y.U. 21ST ANN. CONF. ON LABOR 141 (1969); Lewis, *Fair Representation in Grievance Administration, supra* note 409, at 81.
415. *See* WELLINGTON 178-84.
416. *See generally* Jacobs & Winter, *Antitrust Principles and Collective Bargaining by Athletes: Of Superstars in Peonage,* 81 YALE L.J. 1, 18-21 (1971).
417. *See* discussion at notes 397-401 *supra.*
418. *Cf.* McGrail v. Detroit Federation of Teachers, 82 LRRM 2623 (Mich. Cir. Ct. 1973).
419. *See* text at notes 390-96 *supra.*

posited that the union and employer agreed to a restraint system only after vigorous bargaining and that the union exacted significant concessions before it gave its approval.

Because a number of different points will be involved, it may be useful to state at the outset the general conclusions which are reached in the following discussion. Several tangential issues are resolved in two subsections which immediately follow. Because of confusion in the language used in some of the sports-related exemption cases, it is necessary to make clear that to the extent an exemption is available, it operates to protect both the union and the employer from potential antitrust liability.[420] This result seems to be necessary if the exemption is to achieve its intended purpose of fostering the system of collective bargaining established under the federal labor laws.

Next it is necessary to consider the extent to which the major Supreme Court decisions dealing with the labor exemption provide guidance on the immunity question as it is presented in the sports industry. An analysis of the *Allen Bradley* and *Pennington* decisions suggests that these are of limited precedential value because the Court's primary concern in those cases is with union-employer agreements which attempt to directly influence the affairs of parties who are not part of the bargaining process.[421] The Court's decision in *Jewel Tea* is somewhat more useful. It serves to underscore the point that for purposes of applying the exemption, a primary concern will be whether the agreement has an anticompetitive effect in the business market in which the employer operates.[422] It is further concluded that the Court's approach in *Jewel Tea* adds some support for the notion that restraints which operate wholly within the bargaining unit — as do the player restraints under consideration here — are to be evaluated under principles found, not in the antitrust statutes, but rather in the federal labor laws.

When one looks at the relevant doctrine from the labor area, it is difficult to find any general principle which supports the use of the antitrust laws as a basis for judicial scrutiny of the terms of a collective bargaining agreement. Indeed, existing doctrine seems to point rather firmly to the opposite conclusion. A recurring theme of the labor law is that it is inappropriate for courts to involve themselves in determining whether the terms of a collective bargaining agreement are reasonable and fair.[423] Rather, that is thought to be a matter for the parties to decide for themselves. A particular concern is that opening avenues of substantive judicial review would undermine the finality of the collective bargaining process and thus potentially impair the parties' willingness to participate in it. Such a result would be detrimental to the overall goal of minimizing the disruption of commercial activity which is precipitated by labor-management disagreements.

The final segment of the following analysis is intended to suggest that the antitrust laws may be a particularly inappropriate vehicle for reviewing the terms of collective bargaining agreements. As the Supreme Court has

---

420. *See* text at notes 425-37 *infra.*
421. *See* discussion at notes 439-53 *infra.*
422. *See* text at notes 458-59 *infra.*
423. *See* text at notes 461-86 *infra.*

recognized, unions are anticompetitive by their very nature. Many terms common to labor contracts have the effect of limiting the ability of an individual employee to sell his services on the most favorable terms.[424] Uniform wage rates, seniority provisions, and hiring halls are examples. There seems to be little basis for leaving these immune while scrutinizing a union-accepted provision on player restraints. Rather, the conclusion which seems to be compelled is that the area of immunity extends to all matters properly in the purview of collective bargaining. Such a result is consistent with the general theme that collective bargaining is to proceed with a minimum of governmental oversight of its substantive aspects.

The foregoing will suggest the respective roles which seem to have been assigned to the antitrust laws. On the one hand, the antitrust statutes will come into play when the parties attempt to extend the influence of their collective bargaining relationship beyond the immediate concerns of their employment relationship. But where the effects are primarily internal, the relevant legal framework is provided by the labor laws. And at least as presently designed, labor doctrine projects a marked preference for minimum involvement by the courts in judging the reasonableness of the terms agreed upon.

d. May an Employer Claim the Benefit of the Labor Exemption? A most likely defendant in such a suit attacking a bargained-for player restraint system is the employer group which negotiated the restrictions. An initial question to be considered is whether employers can assert the antitrust exemption by way of defense. As is evident from the history of the labor exemption,[425] and as the Supreme Court has recognized several times,[426] the primary purpose of the labor exemption is to protect *union* organizing and bargaining activity. Indeed, the discussion in the major Supreme Court cases focuses on the propriety of particular union actions or union-imposed restrictions.[427] Since the historical emphasis has been on insulating unions from antitrust attacks, it might well be asked whether the employer may also partake of its protection.[428]

This issue has played an important role in some of the sports cases decided to date. For example, in *Robertson v. National Basketball Association*,[429] a group of employees brought suit alleging that the NBA player restraint mechanisms violated the antitrust laws. The team owners countered that the labor exemption removed these matters from the purview of the antitrust laws. In the court's view this defense could be readily dismissed:

A simple and concise answer to defendant's contention is that the

---

424. *See* text at notes 487-502 *infra.*

425. *See generally* UMW v. Pennington, 381 U.S. 657, 700-13 (1965) (Goldberg, J., dissenting in part); BERMAN, LABOR AND THE SHERMAN ACT (1930) [hereinafter cited as BERMAN].

426. *See, e.g.,* United States v. Hutcheson, 312 U.S. 219, 229-30 (1941); Allen Bradley Co. v. Electrical Workers Local 3, 325 U.S. 797 (1945).

427. *See, e.g.,* Connell Constr. Co. v. Plumbers & Steamfitters Local 100, 421 U.S. 616 (1975); American Fed'n Musicians v. Carroll, 391 U.S. 99 (1968); Meat Cutters Local 189 v. Jewel Tea Co., 381 U.S. 676 (1965); United States v. Hutcheson, 312 U.S. 219 (1941).

428. *See* Clune v. Publishers Ass'n, 214 F. Supp. 520 (S.D.N.Y.), *aff'd per curiam,* 314 F.2d 343 (2d Cir. 1963); T. KHEEL, LABOR LAW (18 BUSINESS ORGANIZATIONS (1971) § 4.01[4] [hereinafter cited as KHEEL].

429. 389 F. Supp. 867 (S.D.N.Y. 1975).

exemption extends only to labor union activities and not to activities of employers.[430]

Other cases have suggested a similar distinction.[431] However, as is discussed more fully in a subsequent section,[432] statements to this effect are subject to a very significant qualification suggested by the factual setting in which they are made. On the facts of *Robertson,* the court had reason to doubt whether the employer rule in question had ever been submitted to collective bargaining.[433] If it was being imposed by unilateral employer action, without specific union approval or acquiescence, then it would indeed appear that the action ought not be immunized from the antitrust laws simply because it affected the employment relationship.[434]

Further analysis should suggest, however, that the rather sharp distinction between employer and union activities noted above would not apply where the employer sought to enforce a rule which was the product of collective bargaining. The impact of the grant of immunity in fostering employee collective activity in general and collective bargaining in particular would surely be limited if only the union could invoke it as a defense in an antitrust action. If the employer were still fully vulnerable to suit, it would presumably be unwilling to acquiesce in union demands for work restrictions which had an anticompetitive effect.[435] In such a climate, where one of two participants would seek to minimize its exposure to liability, it can be doubted that there would be full and robust bargaining over employee demands. In short, as the *Robertson* court ultimately concedes,[436] a one-way grant of antitrust immunity would not achieve the labor policies which the Supreme Court has found to be embodied in the labor exemption. Thus, for the present discussion, it would appear that a finding that the various player restraints come within the antitrust exemption would preclude an antitrust attack whether it was directed against the union or the employer.[437]

---

430. *Id.* at 884-85.

431. *See* Mackey v. National Football League, 543 F.2d 606 (8th Cir. 1976), *modifying* 407 F. Supp. 1000, 1008 (D. Minn. 1975); Philadelphia World Hockey Club, Inc. v. Philadelphia Hockey Club, Inc., 351 F. Supp. 462, 498 (E.D. Pa. 1972). *See also* Cordova v. Bache & Co., 321 F. Supp. 600 (S.D.N.Y. 1970).

432. *See* § 5.06 *infra.*

433. 389 F. Supp. at 895.

434. *Cf.* Cordova v. Bache & Co., 321 F. Supp. 600 (S.D.N.Y. 1970). *But see* UMW v. Pennington, 381 U.S. 657, 700-13 (1965) (Goldberg, J., dissenting in part).

435. *See generally* UMW v. Pennington, 381 U.S. 657, 711-12 (1965) (Goldberg, J., dissenting in part); KHEEL § 4.01[4], at 4-15, n.43.

436. The *Robertson* court noted that there was a sharp division of opinion between the league and the union on whether the player restraints had ever been subject to arm's-length bargaining. The court observed that resolution of that conflict "may be the most critical issue" in the case: "Conceivably, if the restrictions were part of the union policy deemed by the Players' Association to be in the players' best interest, they could be exempt from the reach of the antitrust laws." 389 F. Supp. 867, 895 (S.D.N.Y. 1975.) Such immunity would necessarily extend to the employers who were the defendants in the instant case. This aspect of the case is discussed more fully in § 5.06 *infra.*

437. Although the matter has not received extensive attention by the Supreme Court, there has been implicit recognition that employers may partake of the immunity granted to unions where the matter in controversy is embodied in a collective bargaining agreement. For example, in Jewel Tea, 381 U.S. 676 (1965), the plaintiff store brought suit against both the union and the retailers who were observing the operating hours restriction. While the Court discussed the cases largely

e. The Relevance of Prior Supreme Court Decisions. As discussed in section 5.04, the question of the scope of the exemption has received more than passing attention by the Supreme Court. Indeed, it can be said that in its modern applications, the exemption was in fact devised by the Court. It is appropriate then that we look more closely at the Court's decisions to determine the extent to which they support or refute the extension of the labor exemption to collective bargaining agreements incorporating player restraints. What we will find is that the *Allen Bradley, Pennington,* and *Jewel Tea* cases are of varying relevance to the problem considered here. Despite the fact that some litigants and courts continue to cite *Allen Bradley* and *Pennington,*[438] it can be shown that the issue before the Court in those cases is fundamentally different from that presented in the sports area. *Jewel Tea* is somewhat more germane. While the Court in that case does not specifically address the issue pertinent here, its opinion does serve to narrow the range of debate and at least suggest the principles which should be applied to a controversy of the sort involved in the sports industry.

The limited applicability of much of the existing precedent on the antitrust exemption is underscored when one considers the question of whether an agreement between team owners and the players' association pertaining to player restraints will have the elements of an improper conspiracy which were found in *Allen Bradley* and *Pennington.* The arrangements in those cases took differing forms. In *Allen Bradley,* there was a series of complex agreements and understandings among a group which included not only the union and employers but also others who had no immediate interest in the employment relationship. In *Pennington,* the agreement was between parties who had a common interest in the employment of the union employees, but the purpose of the agreement was to impose restraints upon persons who did not have that community of interest. In each case, there was an attempt to extend the power of the union and the employer beyond the area of the immediate employment relationship.[439]

In assessing the relevance of these precedents in the sports context, it is useful to distinguish between a collective bargaining provision which imposes restraints on existing players and those, such as the draft system, which affect new entrants. Restraints of the former sort, which include the option clause and the indemnity rules, cause the least difficulty. It should be clear that these do not contain the element of an improper external effect which played a predominant role in *Allen Bradley* and *Pennington.* Rather an agreement encompassing such restraints is directed to the particular employment relationship in which the two bargaining parties have an immediate concern.

---

in terms of whether the union demand was exempt from antitrust attack, the result reached made clear that its affirmative finding of immunity also served to protect the defendant employees from potential liability. *See also* Intercontinental Container Transp. Corp. v. New York Shipping Ass'n, 426 F.2d 884 (2d Cir. 1970).

438. For example, in Kapp v. National Football League, 390 F. Supp. 73 (N.D. Cal. 1974) the plaintiff apparently contended that collective bargaining would not immunize the various agreements in question. In support of this argument the plaintiff cited *Allen Bradley* and *Pennington.* As will be suggested, those cases are clearly distinguishable from the situation presented in *Kapp* because the agreements in question sought to restrain the activities of parties outside the immediate bargaining unit. The *Kapp* court based its decision for the plaintiff on other grounds and did not examine the limited applicability of the cited precedent.

439. *See also* Connell Constr. Co. v. Plumbers & Steamfitters Local 100, 421 U.S. 616 (1975).

Moreover, the parties adversely affected — the players who might want to move to another league-team free of the restraints and clubs which might want to hire athletes without regard to the restraints — have actually participated in the arrangement and presumably have opportunities to influence the form which the restraints take.[440] They are thus in a different position than the non-local manufacturers in *Allen Bradley* and the small operators in *Pennington* who were subjected to anti-competitive pressure over which they had little control and which did not relate directly to their collective bargaining obligations with their employees.[441]

There is one aspect of post-employment mobility restraints which deserves particular mention. It might be contended by some that devices such as an option clause or compensation rule do in fact have some effects beyond the immediate employment relationship between a player and his club. More specifically, it would be argued, the restraints also affect the player's relationship with other clubs within the league which might desire to employ him in the future. Since the effects of the restraints extend beyond the immediate employee-employer relationship, it might be argued that the *Allen Bradley* and *Pennington* precedents are not wholly inapposite. Further analysis should suggest, however, that the effects in question are clearly different from those condemned in these two cases. Indeed, in the sports context, it can be suggested that they are not even *external* in that they are well within the realm of proper employee-employer concerns. The basic question, of course, is how the scope of legitimate employment concerns will be defined. The answer suggested in existing Supreme Court precedents is that the range of employment matters subject to immunity is to be defined by reference to the nature of the bargaining unit involved. Multi-employer units, such as those found in the sports area,[442] are not treated substantially different from single-employer units in the extent to which the parties' bargains on purely intra-unit matters are free from scrutiny under the antitrust laws.[443] Indeed, such a result would seem to be compelled if the national labor policy in favor of multi-employer bargaining is going to be given full expression.[444] It is true that agreements within a multi-employer unit will, by definition, have a greater restraining effect upon competition, but the

---

440. Jacobs & Winter, *Antitrust Principles and Collective Bargaining by Athletes: Of Superstars in Peonage,* 81 YALE L.J. 1, 8-9 (1971). *Cf.* J.I. Case v. NLRB, 321 U.S. 332, 335-37 (1944).

441. The Court in *Pennington* made clear that it was supporting the right of individual economic units to be free from restraints imposed by external agreements. This right of economic self-determination, in the Court's view, provided the reason why a union could not agree with one employer to take particular action against another employer. As expressed in the majority opinion, "It is just such restraints upon the freedom of economic units to act according to their own choice and discretion that run counter to antitrust policy." UMW v. Pennington, 381 U.S. 657, 668-69 (1965). This analysis also suggests a limitation on the reach of antitrust policy: that agreements which affect mainly the participants and have no significant effects upon outsiders are not within the type of restraints to which the antitrust laws are directed.

442. In the major professional team sports, the unit for bargaining purposes has been defined to include all league teams. The legal principles which control the definition of the appropriate bargaining unit are discussed elsewhere in this treatise. *See* § 6.04 *infra.*

443. *See* UMW v. Pennington, 381 U.S. 657, 664-65 (1965). *See id.,* 381 U.S. 657, 712-13 (1965) (Goldberg, J., dissenting in part).

444. The commitment to multi-employer bargaining has generally been afforded a high priority in national labor policy. *See generally* NLRB v. Truck Drivers' Local 449, 353 U.S. 87 (1957); MORRIS 236-45. *But see* Meltzer, *Labor Unions, Collective Bargaining and the Antitrust Laws,* 32 U. CHI. L. REV. 659, 709-14, 720 (1965).

Court appears to accept that consequence in order to preserve the institution of multi-firm bargaining.[445] Thus, it can be concluded that even though a collective bargaining agreement validating player restraints will affect the employee's relationship with parties other than his immediate employer, those effects are quite different from the external restraints which prompted the court to deny immunity in the *Allen Bradley* and *Pennington* situations. Although the restraints are one step removed from the immediate relationship, unlike the restraints involved in the cited cases, they are not wholly beyond the control of the parties affected. By virtue of the governing collective bargaining relationship, the players retain the opportunity to affect the form which the restraints take.

It is appropriate to add a caveat to this analysis. Some courts which have considered the labor exemption in the sports setting have intimated that there might be some forms of league-wide restrictions which would be deemed illegal.[446] While in none of these cases is a clear rationale presented,[447] there is a strong implication that the courts feel that some types of restraints which reach beyond the relationship of a single employee and his employer do indeed have an impermissible "external" effect. However, all of the cases which suggest this view involved only the traditional forms of employer-imposed restraints. These typically operated to remove all competition for a player's services and gave the employers unconscionable control of the operation of the rules. The cases condemning these arrangements may impose an outside limit on the lengths to which a multi-employee bargaining agreement can affect inter-employer relations. For the present discussion, however, it is not necessary to define those limits or to assess the correctness of the conclusion of a few courts that they exist. It is enough to note that the fact situations considered in those cases are fundamentally different from that being examined here. In none of those cases had there been any effective employee inputs into the restraint system. Moreover, the restraints involved the clubs' or leagues' near absolute control over their operation and provided no compensatory benefits for the players. Here we are assuming that collective bargaining is not merely a guise for legitimating what are really employer controls. Rather we have posited that there has been effective negotiation by the players and that the pervasiveness of the employers' control has been tempered in that process.[448]

A draft system or similar restraint applied to new players requires separate analysis under the internal-external effects dichotomy. It would be argued that a collective bargaining provision of this sort is an attempt to extend the combined union-management powers beyond the immediate relationship. Such rules, by definition, are applied to persons who were not part of the bargaining unit. Somewhat like the non-local manufacturers in *Allen Bradley,* amateur players

---

445. *See* Jacobs & Winter, *Antitrust Principles and Collective Bargaining by Athletes: Of Superstars in Peonage, supra* note 440, at 21-22.

446. The district court opinion in Mackey v. National Football League, 407 F. Supp. 1000, 1009 (D. Minn. 1975), presents the strongest suggestion to this effect, although other cases may add some support. *See* Robertson v. National Basketball Ass'n, 389 F. Supp. 867, 890 n.41 (S.D.N.Y. 1975); Kapp v. National Football League, 390 F. Supp. 73, 86 (N.D. Cal. 1974). Further discussion of this issue can be found in § 5.06 *infra*.

447. *See* text at notes 572-78, § 5.06 *infra*.

448. *See* text at notes 390-96 *supra*.

would find that their chances for competitive opportunities were limited by an agreement over which they had no control. The validity of these arguments will be determined in large measure by the manner in which the range of interests of the bargaining unit employees is defined. Other cases in the labor area provide an answer to this question. The existing precedents seem to accept that a union may properly seek to control outsiders' access to employment opportunities within the relevant bargaining unit. This principle is most fully developed with respect to the use of hiring halls to allocate employees among various employers.[449] The cases which hold that the union has a right to press demands concerning the operation of such halls seem to implicitly recognize that there is a direct and unavoidable relationship between the terms upon which new employees are hired and the conditions under which existing employees will work.[450] New entrants will compete for jobs and wages with existing employees, and, given the union's interest in eliminating competition of this sort which undermines job security, it is recognized that the union may properly extend its sphere of influence to affect those who have not yet had opportunities to participate in union decision-making.[451]

In the area of professional sports, the argument would be made that the same considerations which might prompt a union to accept restraints on the mobility of existing players — concern for imbalance in the on-the-field competitiveness of teams and the concomitant undermining of fan interest and support [452] — would also cause the union to seek restraints on the ability of new entrants to choose their own employers. There may be considerable debate about whether a union should adopt this posture, but that need not be determined for the present discussion. The question being considered is only whether bargained-for restraints on new entrants have an impermissible external effect. On that narrow question, the answer would appear to be that despite an undeniable effect upon persons not members of the bargaining unit, those externalities do not share the defects which existed in the *Allen Bradley* and *Pennington* situations. Rather, they are intimately related to matters which fall squarely within the goals which Congress has ascribed to the collective bargaining institution.[453]

An examination of the Court's approach in *Jewel Tea* is somewhat more useful in providing affirmative support for the application of the labor exemption to bargained-for player restraints. As an initial matter it will be noted that *Jewel Tea* and, indeed, the other cases, as well, implicitly draw a distinction between

---

449. *See generally* Teamsters Local 357 v. NLRB, 365 U.S. 667 (1961); MORRIS 712-715.

450. *See, e.g.*, NLRB v. Houston Chapter, Assoc. Gen. Contractors of America, Inc., 143 NLRB 409, *enforced*, 349 F.2d 449 (5th Cir. 1965), *cert. denied*, 382 U.S. 1026 (1966).

451. *See generally* MORRIS 409.

452. *See, e.g.*, Comment, *The Super Bowl and the Sherman Act: Professional Team Sports and the Antitrust Laws*, 81 HARV. L. REV. 418, 420-23 (1967); Comment, *Player Control Mechanisms in Professional Sports*, 34 U. PITT. L. REV. 645, 651-52 (1973). *See also* text at notes 399-401 *supra*.

453. "Some may argue that such an issue [the draft system] is not subject to resolution by collective bargaining. We submit that it is and that many precedents in the industrial context support this conclusion. The method by which new players enter has an enormous effect on those already in the unit and by the collective agreement which governs them." Jacobs & Winter, *Antitrust Principles and Collective Bargaining by Athletes: Of Superstars in Peonage, supra* note 440, at 16.

the product market and labor market effects of particular restraints.[454] Thus, in *Jewel Tea* the Court was primarily concerned about the potential adverse effects of the marketing hours restriction upon the level of business competition among various types of stores engaged in selling meat products.[455] The relevant inquiry was whether the Court ought to intervene to protect the right of a particular business entity to market its products on terms which were free of artificial restraints. The implicit assumption of this approach is that relatively free competition is desirable to protect the interests of those who are the ultimate consumers of that which is marketed in the particular industry. To the extent that either competitors or methods of competition are restrained, the product market will, of course, not be a free market and consumer interests in low prices and high quality are likely to be subverted.

A critical point to be made is that these same concerns are not likely to be involved in cases which arise in the sports area. In that context, the primary dispute will concern the effect of the union-management agreement in the *labor,* not the *product,* market.[456] Thus, the complaining party is likely to be an existing or potential employee and not a business entity or consumer which is allegedly injured by the restraint. Indeed, it will likely be suggested that the product market effects of devices such as player restraints are advantageous to most consumers.[457]

Does the *Jewel Tea* case offer any guidance on when the labor exemption will be applied in cases in which the sole complaint is that the collective bargaining agreement restrains competitive advantage of an affected employee? While the case is not direct authority on this question, the balancing test which it

---

454. A review of the cases in which the Supreme Court has considered the application of the antitrust laws in the labor area will confirm that the Court is primarily concerned with the external, or product market, effects of particular restraints. Thus, in *Allen Bradley* the vice of the union-management scheme was the fact that other manufacturers would not be able to sell their products in the affected areas. *See* § 5.04 *supra.* Similarly, in *Pennington* and *Connell* the agreements were not directed exclusively at some matter affecting only the immediate employment relationship but at the relative competitive position of outsiders. *See id.* A similar concern is at the heart of the *Jewel Tea* balancing test. The assumption in that case seems to be that absent a design or effect which seriously reduces competition among business competitors, the Court will leave labor and management free to reach agreements governing the internal employment policies of the affected employer or employers. *See id.*

455. It is noteworthy that most commentators who have considered the labor-antitrust problem have identified product market effects as the primary area of concern. There is very little writing dealing with the antitrust implications of the labor market effects of union activity, a fact which suggests that most writers assume that labor market restraints are generally immunized. *See, e.g.,* Winter, *Collective Bargaining and Competition: The Application of Antitrust Standards to Union Activities,* 73 YALE L.J. 14, 17-30 (1963); Meltzer, *Labor Unions, Collective Bargaining and the Antitrust Laws, supra* note 444, at 728-34.

456. *See generally* Jacobs & Winter, *Antitrust Principles and Collective Bargaining by Athletes: Of Superstars in Peonage, supra* note 440, at 26-27.

457. The clubs may suggest that restraints on player mobility will ultimately work to the benefit of the consumers, more specifically the fans, who buy the product which is produced. It would be contended that the rules operate to equalize the playing strengths among various league clubs and thus result in more "interesting" athletic events. It will likely also be contended that without the restraints, it might not be possible to offer the product at all. The premise of this view is that a league which is continually dominated by a few teams will not attract a significant fan following and thus will not generate sufficient revenues to support the sort of product which is presently offered. *See* text at notes 399-401 *supra. See generally* Comment, *The Super Bowl and the Sherman Act: Professional Team Sports and the Antitrust Laws, supra* note 452, at 420-23; Comment, *Player Control Mechanisms in Professional Sports, supra* note 452, at 651-52.

announces strongly suggests that the grant of antitrust immunity is quite broad in these situations. It will be recalled that the majority in *Jewel Tea* indicates that in determining the availability of the exemption, a court is to weigh the extent of the injury to *business* competition against the extent and immediacy of the union's interest in the particular restriction.[458] In the case we have posited, the first half of this formula is eliminated as a source of concern; there are no product market effects which are being disputed. It would seem to follow that the presence of any bona fide union interest would tip the balance in favor of applying the exemption. As was shown in a previous analysis, a players' union may well be found to have such an interest in a system of player restraints.[459] Thus, *Jewel Tea* at least gives rise to an implication that the limitations which it imposes on the labor exemption leave unaffected agreements which relate directly to the terms and conditions of employment and which include no attempt to influence persons outside the bargaining unit.

While it might be questioned whether *Jewel Tea* should be read as granting absolute immunity to internal agreements, the case is nonetheless useful in providing a focus for a further discussion of the labor exemption issue. What it suggests is that we need to set aside concerns for business competition and look specifically at restraints which a union-employer agreement imposes within the bargaining unit itself. The critical question which arises is this: What legal principles will be applied to define the aggrieved employee's right to secure judicial review of his complaint? As this question suggests, the issue which is at the heart of the controversy considered here is whether an individual union member has the right to object to a term which has been agreed to by the union which represents him. It should quickly become apparent that the essential question is one of defining the proper role of a labor union in an industrial organization, an issue to which existing labor laws are specifically directed.

f. The Relevant Labor Law Principles. As previously noted, the controversy generated by the player restraints will focus on their effects within the bargaining unit itself, and not upon their significance in the business market. An initial question which arises is whether limitations on competition for labor are within the class of restraints to which the Sherman Act is directed.[460] Particularly in light of the subsequent legislation specifically exempting union activity from its purview,[461] the Act seems not to have been intended as a device to regulate union-employer agreements, which mainly affect the internal personnel policies of the firm. While there are cases in which the Act has been applied to restraints upon labor market competition, these are generally of little relevance for the present discussion, for they involved attempts by groups of employers to unilaterally set industry-wide policies.[462] Since there was no

---

458. *See* text at notes 231-37, § 5.03 *supra.*

459. *See* text at notes 399-401 *supra.*

460. The Supreme Court has noted on several occasions that the primary thrust of the antitrust laws is directed to business, not labor, combinations. *See, e.g.,* Allen Bradley v. Electrical Workers Local 3, 325 U.S. 797, 801-02 (1945); Apex Hosiery Co. v. Leader, 310 U.S. 469, 492-93 (1940). *See also* UMW v. Pennington, 381 U.S. 657, 700-01 (1965) (Goldberg, J., dissenting in part).

461. For a discussion of the history and purposes of the exempting legislation, see KHEEL §§ 4.02-.05.

462. *See* Anderson v. Shipowner's Ass'n, 272 U.S. 359 (1926). *See also* Cordova v. Bache & Co., 321 F. Supp. 600 (S.D.N.Y. 1970).

effective union input, there was little basis upon which to claim that the matter fell within the purview of federal labor policies.[463] The sports cases which found antitrust violations in the traditional player restraints are similarly of limited utility because they involved restraints imposed unilaterally by employers.[464] Our case is much different in that the agreement being examined is presumed to be the product of the sort of employee collective action which the exempting statutes were specifically intended to protect.

This analysis should suggest principles which can be applied to define the proper accommodation of the various federal labor and antitrust policies. As long as the controversy concerns only the terms and conditions under which unionized employees work, it would seem to be essentially a labor matter to be resolved in the context of the labor laws. It is only when an agreed-upon restraint has a spill-over effect on business competition that the difficult problem of harmonizing antitrust and labor policies presents itself. While this division seems to be suggested by the antitrust statute and its amendments, it gains its most substantial support from the general design of the body of federal labor legislation.

A review of the pertinent labor policies confirms that Congress did not intend that an employee should be able to object to a term negotiated on his behalf on the grounds that it restrains his ability to sell his services. Three principles of labor law are of particular importance. One is the requirement that all matters concerning "wages, hours, and other terms and conditions of employment"[465] are subject to mandatory collective bargaining between the union and the employer or employer-group.[466] Each side has an obligation to bargain in good faith about all issues which come within these categories.[467] Thus, neither the employer nor the union is free to unilaterally impose rules on these matters,[468] and any rule falling within these categories must be subjected to a process which provides for inputs from the affected party. A second fundamental tenet of federal labor policy is that the prevailing principle in union-employer bargaining is one of freedom of contract.[469] Except for a few matters specifically regulated by congressional action, the parties are left free to define for themselves the precise terms which will govern this relationship. There is no requirement that the terms demanded or agreed upon meet any external standard of reasonableness or that they be consistent with some *a priori* concept of what is appropriate.[470] A third principle which emerges in the area of federal labor law is that the individual employee loses his freedom to make his own individual

---

463. *See* Meltzer, *Labor Unions, Collective Bargaining and the Antitrust Laws, supra* note 444, at 719-20.

464. These cases are discussed in § 5.06 *infra.*

465. The quoted language is taken from section 8(d) of the NLRA which attempts to define the parties' obligation to bargain. *See* 29 U.S.C. § 158(d) (1970).

466. The respective duties of the employer and union to bargain collectively are found in sections 8(a)(5) and 8(b)(3) of the statute. 29 U.S.C. 158(a)(5) & (b)(3). The duty to bargain is discussed more fully in a subsequent chapter. *See* §§ 6.06-.08 *infra.*

467. *See generally* MORRIS 271-347; 18C KHEEL §§ 16.01-.04.

468. *See, e.g.,* NLRB v. Katz, 369 U.S. 736 (1962); NLRB v. American Mfg. Co., 351 F.2d 74 (5th Cir. 1965).

469. *See generally* WELLINGTON 49-125 (1968); Jacobs & Winter, *Antitrust Principles and Collective Bargaining by Athletes: Of Superstars in Peonage, supra* note 440, at 10-13.

470. *See* WELLINGTON 56-59.

contract with the employer.[471] Thus, the desires of an individual worker are subject to the will of the majority of the union to which he belongs. He may desire higher wages in lieu of longer vacations or prefer other trade-offs in his employment contract. But his preferences must give way to the union's determination of the larger group interest. This principle, while necessarily subversive of individual freedom, is at the basis of the federal policy to encourage unionism.[472] As repeatedly recognized by the Supreme Court, the very purpose of the union movement is to reduce competition among employees concerning wages and conditions of employment.[473] The union derives its strength from collective action, and the effectiveness of its efforts can be insured only if it is given a monopoly in advocating its members' concerns.[474]

It should be clear that Congress intended that the foundation of national labor policy would be the institution of collective bargaining. The congressional endorsement of that process is neither half-hearted nor incidental. Rather, Congress set out with the specific purpose of giving the parties as much freedom as possible to structure a bargain which would fit their individual situation. It will be noted that there are other models which Congress could have chosen but which were apparently rejected in favor of the present system. For example, Congress could have provided that the terms of the parties' collective bargaining agreement would be respected, but only so long as they were reasonable or not unduly inflationary [475] or not inconsistent with good sound personnel practices. Or Congress might have used a model which said that a union could negotiate only for "minimum" terms and if an individual member could strike a better bargain, he was free to do so.[476] Or Congress could have imposed a requirement of binding arbitration to supply contract terms which could not be agreed upon at the bargaining table.[477] But the point which needs to be emphasized is that Congress chose none of these devices and, rather, designed a system which, as interpreted by the courts, accepted that bargaining should be free and open.[478]

The reasons for this critical choice in favor of unfettered bargaining are important for the present inquiry into the application of antitrust laws to purely internal arrangements between unions and employers. First, there was a realization that there are no absolute standards of what is a reasonable contract

---

471. *See, e.g.,* J.I. Case v. NLRB, 321 U.S. 332 (1944). The union may consent to individual bargaining, but the scope of such negotiations is subject to definition by the majority of workers. *See* § 6.07 *infra.*

472. *See* 18C KHEEL § 16.04[6]; MORRIS 304-07; Jacobs & Winter, *Antitrust Principles and Collective Bargaining by Athletes: Of Superstars in Peonage, supra* note 440, at 7-10.

473. *See, e.g.,* Connell Constr. Co. v. Plumbers & Steamfitters Local 100, 421 U.S. 616 (1975); UMW v. Pennington, 381 U.S. 657, 664 (1965).

474. *See, e.g.,* NLRB v. Allis Chalmers Mfg. Co., 388 U.S. 175, 180 (1967); D. BOK & J. DUNLOP, LABOR AND THE AMERICAN COMMUNITY 102-107 (1969) [hereinafter cited as BOK & DUNLOP].

475. *See generally* WELLINGTON 298-333.

476. *See generally* sources cited notes 471-72 *supra.*

477. Compulsory arbitration is often suggested as a technique which might be used to resolve labor disputes in the public sector, where, it is argued, the public interest demands that employees not have the same freedom to strike as they do in private industry. Proposals for compulsory arbitration have frequently been criticized on the grounds that, as in the private sector, it is clearly preferable that the parties be responsible for defining the bargain by which they are bound. *See* BOK & DUNLOP 235-59.

478. The freedom afforded the parties is not complete, for they are denied the right to decline to bargain. *See generally* WELLINGTON 49-90.

term.[479] Such an assessment must necessarily turn upon myriad factors, such as the type of industry involved, the work performed, and so on, which are simply not susceptible to standardization. Relatedly, it is thought that the courts are particularly inappropriate institutions for reviewing the substance of collective bargaining agreements.[480] A determination of what is an appropriate term would require not only great familiarity with the situation in the particular bargaining unit, but also some real sensitivity as to how competing interests should be accommodated. If courts were to undertake this task, there is substantial doubt as to whether they could hope to devise a solution which was as good as the one which the parties themselves would find satisfactory. Finally, and most importantly, the ultimate goal of any labor policy should be to insure industrial peace, to reduce strife and work stoppages which interfere with productivity. If the terms of collective bargaining were subjected to significant oversight by a judge or arbitrator, there is a stronger likelihood that one or both parties would not find the results as satisfactory as in the case in which the ultimate agreements required the consent of each.[481] Terms imposed from the outside are likely to generate resistance and thus increase the likelihood of disruption. However, where each side is given an unfettered right to consent or make counter-demands, there is greater reason to believe that each will abide by the final product.

These rather firm principles of labor policy are particularly instructive when the focus is shifted to the specific question of whether the terms of a collective bargaining agreement in the sports industry should be subject to scrutiny under the antitrust laws. The primary concerns are those identified above. As an initial matter, it must be recognized that if the antitrust laws were extended with full rigor to collective bargaining terms which affected only the immediate parties — the clubs and the players — the desired goal of giving finality to the parties' agreement would be undermined. The chief concern would be that if a party had an opportunity to secure judicial review of the substantive terms of the labor contract, it might be less willing to accept the bargained-for result. Thus, turmoil and agitation may continue after the negotiations have ended and the hoped-for industrial peace sacrificed in the process.

An equally important concern is that application of the antitrust laws will disrupt the process of bargaining itself. On the one hand, agreement between the parties would be more difficult to achieve.[482] Real or feigned concern for

479. *See, e.g.,* NLRB v. Insurance Agents Int'l Union, 361 U.S. 477, 488-90 (1952); Jacobs & Winter, *Antitrust Principles and Collective Bargaining by Athletes: Of Superstars in Peonage, supra* note 440, at 12-13. *See generally* BOK & DUNLOP 207-16.

480. *See* WELLINGTON 52-56; Jacobs & Winter, *Antitrust Principles and Collective Bargaining by Athletes: Of Superstars in Peonage, supra* note 440, at 10-13.

481. *See* UMW v. Pennington, 381 U.S. 657, 709-20 (1965) (Goldberg, J., dissenting in part).

482. Some support for the notion that the prospect of antitrust review may inhibit bargaining is found in the 1975 NFL labor contract negotiations. A major impediment to agreement was the position of the players' union that it could not consent to the Rozelle Rule because the rule was illegal. *See* N.Y. Times, Aug. 31, 1975, § 5, at 11, col. 4. The owners' position was that any illegality would be removed if the rule were approved in collective bargaining. The parties never reached agreement in those negotiations.

The NFL conflict is also instructive on another matter. The NFL owners have alleged that the pending of the appeal in the *Mackey* case prevented the players union from continuing to bargain about the player restraints. In testimony before a House subcommittee, Mr. Theodore Kheel, attorney for the NFL Management Council, analyzed the situation in these terms:

the possible antitrust implications of a proposal may be given as a reason why it will not be accepted.[483] In such a situation, the focus of the parties' negotiations may quickly shift from meaningful discussion about what is desired and what is economically feasible to an interminable debate about what the courts will think of the proposal. On the other hand, the possibility of subsequent antitrust review may inhibit each side's willingness to make trade-offs in the search for a settlement.[484] Under a system in which the parties' agreement is

> This is the reality. I put it to Mr. Garvey [Executive Director of the Players Association] in Chicago on August 25. I said, "I dare you to bargain collectively on the subject matter of the Rozelle Rule."
> I ask you to put it to him today when we get through. You will not get an unequivocal answer. Ask him, "Yes or no, will you bargain collectively on the subject matter of the Rozelle Rule?" You will not get a straight answer. Do you know why? Because that immediately would go into the court record, and it would destroy this suit. *Hearings Before the Subcomm. on Labor-Management Relations of the House Committee on Education and Labor,* 94th Cong., 1st Sess., 65 (1975) (testimony of Theodore Kheel).

It should be emphasized that it is by no means clear that further bargaining at this time would necessitate a reversal of *Mackey.* Among other things, the players would still be entitled to damages for the part enforcement of the rule.

483. "To tell the parties that they must bargain about a point but may be subject to antitrust penalties if they reach an agreement is to stultify the congressional scheme." UMW v. Pennington, 381 U.S. 657, 711-12 (1965) (Goldberg, J., dissenting in part).

484. The argument that antitrust review might undermine the institution of collective bargaining was adopted by the NFL Management Council in its efforts to secure a final agreement on the controversial Rozelle Rule. The owners' position on these matters is reflected in the following statement of Sargent Karch, Executive Director of the NFL Management Council, prepared for a congressional subcommittee investigating labor relations in the NFL.

The Union's Reliance on Multiple Forums
Anyone who knows anything about collective bargaining knows that it can work effectively only through a process of hard-nosed bargaining. Both sides know that they can be hurt by a failure to reach agreement — and the football experience shows this. But hard bargaining is never going to be productive when either of the parties uses alternative forums for pursuing its collective bargaining interests. In football, the player union attempts to deal with collective bargaining issues, simultaneously and alternatively, before Federal agencies and courts and in Congressional committees. So long as they are willing and able to resort to these forums, the incentive to agreement is nullified. The alternatives offer an excuse for not finally resolving the issues at the bargaining table. . . .
The direct result of the use of one of these forums, the Federal court in Minneapolis, was that the union's chief negotiator, Mr. Garvey, made himself unavailable for bargaining for the better part of five months during this spring and summer.

The Consistent Refusal of the Union to Accept the Results of Collective Bargaining
On August 3, 1970, negotiators of the 1970 Agreement shook hands, settled their differences, called off the player strike, and left to the lawyers the task of putting their understandings on paper. Mr. Garvey, a late appearing counsel for the Players Association, thereafter spent almost a year raising new issues and reopening old ones — before the Agreement could finally be executed.
The ink was hardly dry on this four-year Agreement before the union was supporting an NFL player in a challenge of the express terms of the 1970 Collective Bargaining Agreement (Joe Kapp).
Less than a year later, Mr. Garvey was in New York, pledging his cooperation at a meeting of NFL clubs. And one day after that, the union itself undertook sponsorship of an antitrust challenge of the Agreement in Minneapolis.

. . . .

The Constantly Shifting Positions of the Union
In 1970, the union viewed the rules for player transfer and retention as proper subjects for negotiation. However, by 1974 the union's position had changed. It demanded that *all* such rules be eliminated, and buttressed this new position with a 42-day strike. This was followed by an unsuccessful petition to the NLRB asserting that the clubs had failed to bargain in good faith on the rules. This was then followed by a pursuit of an antitrust case in Minneapolis in which the union claimed that the rules had never been, and could not be, the subject of collective bargaining.

final and enforceable, one side will likely be willing to make important concessions because he knows precisely what he will get in exchange. Thus, the clubs may be willing to give greater pension benefits than they would like because the union has indicated a willingness to give up its demand for total elimination of a particular restraint. If the union or one of its members could later go out and secure a court order enjoining the restraint which it had earlier accepted, the clubs would surely have doubts about the wisdom of their full, good faith participation in future negotiations.[485] It would appear to them that the concessions won at the bargaining table could be quickly lost in court. The ultimate consequence would be that agreement would be increasingly more difficult to achieve.

The point which should be emphasized is that finality in collective bargaining is not simply a desirable social policy which *ought to be* fostered; it is the specific policy which Congress has mandated in its design of the federal labor laws. Again, while Congress might have chosen to provide for greater judicial oversight of the substantive terms of collective bargaining, it chose not to. Among the alternatives available, the present system, with its emphasis on freedom of contract and governmental non-intervention, was selected as the one most likely to produce industrial stability in the long-run.[486]

> The union then injected into the negotiations the claim that the union and its members could become liable under the antitrust laws if they negotiated with respect to these rules, *i.e.,* that all the members could be liable to all other members of the union if an agreement were reached. This was put forward despite the *fact* that the union was challenging *its own Agreement* in two other proceedings.
>
> The Management Council sought to meet this nonsense with an agreement to hold the union and its members harmless against suits brought by themselves against themselves. The union then changed its position and asked the clubs to agree that the rules were not collective bargaining issues at all and that the parties should agree on "arbitration" of these rules by Federal courts. And these positions were urged in the face of the union's position in all pending antitrust cases that collective bargaining is an absolute irrelevancy to player antitrust claims.
>
> All of this "jockeying" by the union has come pretty close to putting the union into a morass from which it cannot extricate itself. Its leadership cannot negotiate a settlement of their own antitrust action because their position is that they cannot even collectively bargain on the subject. If so, there is no way to make such a settlement binding on players generally. Moreover, no antitrust court can ever resolve the collective bargaining issues between the parties, since no court can ever deal with the full range of collective issues. Basic changes in the rules by an antitrust court would inevitably require the clubs to take different positions on such matters as pensions, group insurance, pre-season, etc. Even the issue of the right of players to negotiate individually for their own salaries would then necessarily have to be reopened.
>
> These are just passing illustrations of how the union's constantly shifting positions have frustrated effective collective bargaining. Indeed, the union has spent some five years testifying in one fashion before the NLRB, in another fashion before the antitrust courts, in a third fashion before Congressional committees, and putting forth different versions of each in the union newspaper and in public statements.
>
> . . . .

(The prior statement is taken from Mr. Karch's prepared remarks. It appears in a form somewhat more extemporaneous in *Hearings Before the Subcomm. on Labor-Management Relations of the House Comm. on Education and Labor,* 94th Cong., 1st Sess., 51-55 (1975).)

485. *See generally* WELLINGTON 26-30, 49-63; Jacobs & Winter, *Antitrust Principles and Collective Bargaining by Athletes: Of Superstars in Peonage,* 81 YALE L.J. 1, 7-9 (1971).

486. *See, e.g.,* UMW v. Pennington, 381 U.S. 657, 664 (1965); Connell Constr. Co. v. Plumbers & Steamfitters Local 100, 421 U.S. 616, 622 (1975). *See generally* A. REES, THE ECONOMICS OF TRADE UNIONS 61-64 (1962).

g. Tolerance of Other Anti-Competitive Labor-Management Terms. The preceding analysis should suggest that Congress intended to adopt a general policy against governmental intervention into the collective bargaining process. There are other considerations which suggest that antitrust principles in particular should not be applicable to the agreements which were fully bargained for, which affect only the union members themselves, and which do not unduly restrain the product market. The reason, quite simply, is that unionization by its very nature is anti-competitive, and if employee collective actions are to be tolerated at all, the prospect of restrictions on the operation of the labor market must be accepted. The purpose of a union is, of course, to eliminate competition among individual workers for wages and other employment related terms.[487] This is achieved by the individual employees giving up their separate bargaining rights in favor of exclusive representation by the union.[488] While each employee possesses some quantum of bargaining power, it is thought to be more desirable to channel these individual strengths into the collective device of union representation. It is assumed that the threat of massive employee work stoppages will prove a more effective tool in securing concessions from management than if the employees acted individually in attempting to secure more favorable terms. In essence, the employees agree to refrain from competing among themselves and instead accept that they will rely upon the collective judgment of the employee group in setting hours and conditions of employment.[489] As the union bargains, the emphasis will be on achieving the greatest advantage for the greatest number of employees. Inevitably this will produce standardization of employment terms for particular classes of employees. Such arrangements will usually be better than those which most employees could achieve by individual negotiation. But some employees are likely to be less well off, for their superior bargaining power will have been used by the union to secure greater minimum benefits for others in the relevant group.

What this suggests is that union-bargaining will sometimes produce agreements which in effect operate as a real restraint upon an individual employee's ability to secure a better bargain for himself. Typical collective bargaining arrangements suggest myriad examples. Thus, an agreement that employees in a particular classification will all be paid the same wages may operate to the disadvantage — that is, have adverse anti-competitive effects — on a particular employee who, because of greater skill or greater efficiency, could command a higher wage if wages were established on the basis of individual productiveness.[490] In the same vein, a seniority system is often anti-competitive. A younger worker with superior skills may find his employment opportunities limited because the union has agreed to a system under which older employees will be favored in allocating job assignments, effectuating reductions in the work force and so on.[491] Finally, hiring hall

---

487. *See* WELLINGTON 129-31.
488. *See generally* BOK & DUNLOP 102-07, 210-14.
489. *See* WELLINGTON 130.
490. *See* Jacobs & Winter, *Antitrust Principles and Collective Bargaining by Athletes: Of Superstars in Peonage, supra* note 485, at 8-9.
491. *Id.* at 16-17, 19-20.

arrangements, in which one's access to work opportunities is determined on the basis of not only longevity in the trade but also one's willingness to abide by hiring hall rules, may operate to restrict job opportunities for younger, but better skilled, workers or those who would otherwise be hired by employers but for the hiring hall rules.[492]

Cases from the labor area leave little doubt but that the validity of things such as uniform wage scales, seniority lists, and hiring halls is accepted by courts.[493] Despite the obvious restraining effects of these devices upon the job opportunities of some employees, the question of their validity under the antitrust laws is seldom raised. The fact that they are accepted should be of considerable persuasive value in establishing that labor-management agreements enjoy a broad labor exemption.

The next question to be asked is whether differentiation is to be made between the type of restraints which a union has accepted. That is, is a uniform wage scale to be treated differently from a seniority system? Are provisions on player restraints to be treated differently from more traditional types of restraints? As an initial matter it can be noted again that the Supreme Court precedents in this area may imply that purely internal matters of immediate employee-employer interest are to be free from scrutiny under the antitrust laws. As previously discussed, all of the cases in which a union agreement was found not to be exempt involved situations in which the extra-unit product market effects were the source of the objections raised.[494] Moreover, the balancing test of *Jewel Tea* requires a weighing of the injury to business competition against the immediacy of the union's interest.[495] The first element is not present in the case considered here, and the implication arises that any legitimate union interest would bring the balancing process to rest in favor of applying the exemption.[496] Under this view, then, the limitations on the exemption developed by the Court leave unaffected agreements which both relate directly to the terms and conditions of employment and include no attempt to influence persons outside the bargaining unit.[497]

---

492. *See, e.g.,* Teamsters Local 357 v. NLRB, 365 U.S. 667 (1961). *See also* Connell Constr. Co. v. Plumbers & Steamfitters Local 100, 421 U.S. 616, 622-24 (1975).

493. *See, e.g.,* Connell Constr. Co. v. Plumbers & Steamfitters Local 100, 421 U.S. 616 (1975); UMW v. Pennington, 381 U.S. 657 (1965); Allen Bradley Co. v. Electrical Workers Local 3, 325 U.S. 797 (1945).

494. *See* § 5.03 *supra.*

495. Some have argued that if a particular employment term has no appreciable external effects and is otherwise a mandatory subject of bargaining, then it ought to be immune from antitrust attack, even if it has never actually been subjected to the bargaining process. This argument was rejected in Robertson v. National Basketball Ass'n, 389 F. Supp. 867, 886-87 (S.D.N.Y. 1975). It can be noted that the present discussion, while suggesting a somewhat similar test, assumes that the provision in question has been agreed to in collective bargaining.

496. *See, e.g.,* Note, *Antitrust and Labor Union Liability Under the Sherman Act,* 19 Sw. L.J. 613, 616 (1965):

> This leads to the apparent conclusion that any management-union controversy over activities concerning wages, hours, and other terms and conditions of employment are exempt from anti-trust attack; *a fortiori* all controversies concerning mandatory subjects of bargaining — absent an *Allen Bradley* combination — are exempt from the anti-trust laws.

497. *See id.* at 616, 620. *See also* UMW v. Pennington, 381 U.S. 657, 709-11 (1965) (Goldberg, J., dissenting in part).

It must be accepted that once we move away from situations in which the antitrust concern is directed at the extra-unit effect of a particular union-employer agreement, there is very little case law raising the antitrust question directly. But one likely explanation is the fact that where such external effects are not present, the matter is viewed as raising purely labor law questions, which are generally decided by the National Labor Relations Board and the courts without specific concern for the possible anti-competitive effects of a particular agreement or action. But the absence of direct precedent can only be suggestive and is never persuasive in itself. What may be determinative is that there are many very strong policy reasons why no substantial limitations ought to be placed on matters which have their most immediate effect within the bargaining unit itself. It seems unlikely that Congress intended such a result. The basis of this conclusion is found in the analysis suggested above as to why outside review of the substantive terms of collective bargaining is not permitted.[498]

Some of the cases considering the player restraints in the sports industry include language which would not read the Supreme Court's precedents this broadly.[499] While none of the decisions has presented a fully-developed conclusion in this regard, one can discern a veiled implication that some types of collective bargaining terms which affected the player's employment opportunities with employers other than his own would be impermissible even when the other employer was in the same bargaining unit.[500] However, this "implication" in the cases must be regarded largely as dicta because none of the decisions involved a situation having the elements which are being considered here. Thus, in each of the decisions the restraints had been the product of a unilateral employer conspiracy; they had not been subjected to good faith, arms-length bargaining; and they were decidedly one-sided, reflecting none of the modifications which are likely to be imposed when the players have an effective input into the bargaining process. These cases may establish an outside limit on the form which player restraints may take, but it can be doubted that the systems which will be devised when there is vigorous collective bargaining will approach that boundary.[501]

Some might try to argue against the enforceability of any agreement reached in a multi-employer unit which has the effect of inhibiting the movement of employees among the employer-firms involved in the bargaining. But the mere fact of a restraining effect would not seem to be a sufficient objection, at least not if the institution of multi-employer bargaining is to be preserved. It will be noted that a variety of collective bargaining terms which are now widely accepted in multi-employer units have such an effect. A unit-wide system of

498. *See* text at notes 461-86 *supra.*

499. The decisions which suggest that the labor examination might not immunize all intra-unit restraints are: Mackey v. National Football League, 543 F.2d 606 (8th Cir. 1976), *modifying* 407 F. Supp. 1000, 1009 (D. Minn. 1975); Robertson v. National Basketball Ass'n, 389, F. Supp. 867, 890 n. 41 (S.D.N.Y. 1975); Kapp v. National Football Legaue, 390 F. Supp. 73, 86 (N.D. Cal. 1974). These are discussed in § 5.06 *infra.*

500. *See* text at notes 572-78, § 5.06 *infra.*

501. As previously noted, in the leagues where there has been effective collective bargaining, the parties have agreed to player restraint systems considerably less onerous than those which have been disapproved in the prior cases. *See* § 5.03 *supra.*

uniform wage rates, for example, limits the extent to which employers will compete for a worker's services and thus inhibit employee mobility. Similarly, a multi-employer hiring hall, common in the construction industry, will often operate to deny an employee access to employers who would otherwise hire him if he did not have to first satisfy the rules limiting his eligibility for referral. The fact that these practices are tolerated weighs strongly against any argument that there are substantial limits on the authority of the union to bargain for inter-employer as well as intra-employer limits on an employee's opportunities for selling his services. If the individual could object to terms previously agreed upon by his representative, then the effectiveness of the union, and the function of collective bargaining, would be substantially undermined. Rather than serving as the final and exclusive spokesman for the entire employee group, the union would represent only a portion of a fragmented array of employee interests. Because of the lack of finality in a union's concessions at the bargaining table, the employer would less likely be willing to engage in serious negotiation. In short, the fact that particular union agreements operate as a restraint hardly justifies the repudiation of the preference for collective bargaining.[502]

h. Application of Labor Exemption to Other Collective Bargaining Terms. Restrictions on player mobility are not the only provisions of professional sports contracts which give rise to questions about the applicability of the labor exemption. Indeed, similar questions may be presented anytime the union and employer agree to terms which restrict the employment opportunities of a group of employee-athletes. Such restrictions might take any of a number of different forms. For example, some athletes might object to agreements with respect to squad size, such as an agreement reducing the number of players permitted on the active roster.[503] It is clear that a league-wide agreement on a matter of this sort would limit the employment opportunities of some athletes. If the teams were not subject to this limitation, clubs might hire more players and thus provide jobs for athletes who otherwise would be cut if the restriction were in effect.

Questions might also be raised about any attempt to control player salaries. Perhaps in exchange for the owners' agreement to raise minimum salaries, the union might agree to a limit on maximum salaries.[504] The potential objections are obvious. The burden of such an arrangement would be borne by the star performers who would complain that they were being denied the right to sell

---

502. See generally Jacobs & Winter, *Antitrust Principles and Collective Bargaining by Athletes: Of Superstars in Peonage, supra* note 485, at 10-13.

503. The matter of squad size has been a subject of controversy in the NFL, but the dispute is of a different sort than that suggested in the text. In 1975, the owners took action to reduce the size of the active squad and the union raised the objection that the matter must be submitted to collective bargaining. *See* Washington Post, June 28, 1975, at E1, col. 2; Los Angeles Times, June 29, 1975, Pt. III, at 7, col. 1. The situation suggested in the text would arise if the union eventually acquiesced in the reduced squad limitations.

504. The NFL owners have suggested that such limitations will be necessary if the players' union succeeds in its effort to eliminate the player restraints. *See* N.Y. Times, Oct. 3, 1975, at 25, col. 7. Negotiated salary schedules are quite common in the industrial context, and theoretically could be utilized in the sports industry as well.

their labor for its fair value.[505] Another category of restraint which is worth noting includes agreements which have the effect of limiting the player's ability to sell his services in another league. As evidenced by the history of the contracting process in professional sports, these might take a number of different forms, but most likely will include provisions under which the club can unilaterally renew its right to the player's services for an additional term.[506] Thus, if a player seeks to jump to another league, the club may have the right to insist upon further performance by the athlete and seek to enjoin the attempted defection.[507] Again, the player may allege that to the extent that these restraints are the product of joint action by the union and the owners, there is a conspiracy to restrain his ability to trade his services.[508]

The prior discussion should suggest the analysis which will be applied to determine whether the labor exemption operates to immunize these restraints. As an initial matter, it must be determined whether the agreement in question has the effect of imposing restraints beyond the immediate bargaining relationship. Of particular concern are restraints upon the product market [509] and those which affect labor policies of other employers in the industry, as in *Pennington*.[510] If the facts suggest a purposeful conspiracy to limit the competitiveness of persons and firms outside the unit, then presumably the exemption is not available, and antitrust liability may be found.[511] But even if no actual conspiracy is present, the availability of the labor exemption is by no means assured. If there is in fact a restraining effect upon the product market, the court will apply the balancing test suggested in *Jewel Tea*,[512] which requires that the impact of the agreement upon competition be weighed against the immediacy and directness of the employee interest involved.[513] The greater the external restraint, the more substantial must be the employee interest which is being furthered. In evaluating the importance of the employee's interest, differentiations will apparently be made on the basis of the extent to which the particular arrangement is directly tied to fundamental matters such as wage rates, work load, hours of work, and so on.[514] Agreements not involving critical aspects of the employment relationship will be scrutinized quite closely if there is an appreciable effect upon business competition.[515]

---

505. The potential for conflict between superstars and marginal players has been noted in other contexts in this treatise. *See* text at notes 397-401 *supra.*

506. *See generally* § 3.12 *supra.*

507. *See, e.g.,* Nassau Sports v. Peters, 352 F. Supp. 870 (E.D.N.Y. 1972); Connecticut Professional Sports Corp. v. Heyman, 276 F. Supp. 618 (S.D.N.Y. 1967); Lemat v. Barry, 275 Cal. App. 2d 671, 80 Cal. Rptr. 240 (1969); Central New York Basketball, Inc. v. Barnett, 19 Ohio Op.2d 130, 181 N.E.2d 506 (1961); Dallas Cowboys Football Club, Inc. v. Harris, 348 S.W.2d 37 (Tex. Civ. App. 1961).

508. *Cf.* Philadelphia World Hockey Club, Inc. v. Philadelphia Hockey Club, Inc., 351 F. Supp. 462 (E.D. Pa. 1972); Boston Professional Hockey Ass'n, Inc. v. Cheevers, 348 F. Supp. 261 (D. Mass.), *remanded,* 472 F.2d 127 (1st Cir. 1972).

509. *See* Connell Constr. Co. v. Plumbers & Steamfitters Local 100, 421 U.S. 616 (1975); Allen Bradley Co. v. Electrical Workers Local 3, 325 U.S. 797 (1945).

510. UMW v. Pennington, 381 U.S. 657 (1965).

511. *See* discussion at notes 201-37, § 5.03 *supra.*

512. *See* text at notes 231-32, § 5.03 *supra.*

513. *See generally* Meltzer, *Labor Unions, Collective Bargaining and the Antitrust Laws,* 32 U. CHI. L. REV. 659, 723-26 (1965).

514. *See* discussion at note 233, § 5.03 *supra.*

515. *Cf.* Connell Constr. Co. v. Plumbers & Steamfitters Local 100, 421 U.S. 616 (1975), discussed at notes 238-45, § 5.03 *supra.*

An agreement which limits the player's ability to jump to another league is illustrative of the type of provision which raises the concern for effects beyond the immediate bargaining relationship.[516] Devices such as renewal clauses and broad reserve clauses may well have a detrimental effect not only on the player's ability to sell his services but also upon the ability of a new league to establish itself as a viable competitor.[517] Because of the serious nature of the resulting restraint on competition, these devices can be sustained only upon a showing that a very substantial and direct employee interest was being protected. It is doubtful that such a justification could be found. The rationale which would likely be put forth — relating to the employer's need to have stable employment patterns — would not seem to be sufficient in light of the obvious anti-competitive effects upon outsiders.

Not all disputed provisions will have such substantial extra-unit effects, however. Where matters such as salary limitations and restrictions on squad size are involved, there will necessarily be some external effects, but these will not likely be the primary object of any resulting controversy. Rather the focus of the dispute will be on the adverse effect of these arrangements within the bargaining unit itself. Where the element of extra-unit restraint is removed, the analysis would closely follow that which was previously applied to agreements on player restraints. It can be briefly summarized. Present labor policy dictates that unions and employers be given considerable leeway to structure their bargain on terms which they find mutually satisfactory. Minimal governmental control over the substance of the parties' agreement is a desirable goal, and if this is to be achieved, review under the antitrust laws must be foreclosed. A different result is not required merely because it can be shown that the particular arrangement may limit the ability of some employees to secure better employment opportunities or higher wages. Such restrictions are not only tolerated, but also thought to be essential if the union is to achieve its ultimate goal of improving the economic position of the majority of its members. Thus, for most restraints, the inquiry into a possible antitrust violation is likely to end at the point at which it is determined that the complained of effects are wholly within the bargaining unit.

A question arises as to whether all agreements resulting from employer-union bargaining should be treated the same way. There is some basis for suggesting that the exemption extends to all mandatory subjects of bargaining, those affecting "wages, hours, and other terms and conditions of employment." [518] Some authorities suggest that the wholesale exemption of mandatory bargaining subjects is dictated by federal labor policy, which imposes an affirmative duty upon each party to bargain in good faith on such matters.[519]

---

516. See generally Philadelphia World Hockey Club, Inc. v. Philadelphia Hockey Club, Inc., 351 F. Supp. 462 (E.D. Pa. 1972); Jacobs & Winter, Antitrust Principles and Collective Bargaining by Athletes: Of Superstars in Peonage, 81 YALE L.J. 1, 27-28 (1971).

517. This concern for the restraining effects of a reserve clause upon the formation of new leagues was given controlling weight by the court in Philadelphia World Hockey Club, Inc. v. Philadelphia Hockey Club, Inc., 351 F.Supp. 462 (E.D. Pa. 1972).

518. 29 U.S.C. § 158(d) (1974). See generally NLRB v. Borg-Warner Corp., 356 U.S. 342 (1958); MORRIS 389-423.

519. In his dissenting opinion in Pennington and Jewel Tea, Justice Goldberg took a position which suggested that any mandatory subject of bargaining should be exempt even if there were extra-unit effects. See UMW v. Pennington, 381 U.S. 657, 709-11 (1965).

Since the parties must bargain, and since the government will not attempt to influence the substance of the ultimate agreement, it is said to follow that the parties must be given complete discretion, free from antitrust and other restraints, in defining the particular terms which will govern their relationship.[520] One potential implication of this rationale is that the labor exemption need not be applied to agreements concerning non-mandatory subjects.

Much of the debate on this matter is directed to situations in which the particular agreement definitely restrains business competition in the product market. Even where this is true, some would argue that the extra-unit effects must be tolerated if the matter is a mandatory subject of bargaining.[521] In the present context, however, it is assumed that the primary restraint is upon persons within the bargaining unit itself. This distinction should cause a court to conclude that whatever the scope of the exemption in situations where the product market effects are the primary concern, it should be drawn more broadly where the only effects are within the unit. Again, it can be emphasized that restraints on labor competition are an inherent part of unionization. Moreover, where only intra-unit restraints are involved, those affected have opportunities to influence the particular form of the regulation. Finally, the goal of achieving industrial peace would suggest that where the parties have agreed upon a matter, even when they bargained without compulsion of federal law, their agreement ought to be respected. In light of these considerations, there is a substantial basis for suggesting that courts should be less hesitant to apply the exemption to these agreements than in the case of an agreement which has a substantial impact upon outsiders. Whether the topic is a mandatory subject of bargaining ought not be the determinative element where the concern for extra-unit effects has been removed.

§ 5.06. The Importance of the History of the Parties' Collective Bargaining Relationship.

a. The Sports Cases. The prior analysis, which concludes that the labor exemption should be available to immunize union-employer agreements restraining player mobility, proceeds on the assumption that these matters have been subjected to serious negotiation by the parties and that a mutually satisfactory arrangement has resulted. The question which remains to be considered is whether the exemption will be available where the bargaining process has yielded more equivocal results.[522] This issue has been addressed in

---

520. *See id.;* Jacobs & Winter, *Antitrust Principles and Collective Bargaining by Athletes: Of Superstars in Peonage, supra* note 516, at 25-27; Note, *Antitrust and Labor-Union Liability Under the Sherman Act,* 19 Sw. L.J. 613 (1965).

521. *See* UMW v. Pennington, 381 U.S. 657, 698-735 (1965) (Goldberg, J., dissenting in part).

522. It should be noted that an important assumption of this discussion is that the player restraints were originally imposed prior to the formation of the players' union. Under this assumption the employer would continue the restraints until a modification was agreed upon through collective bargaining. These assumptions about the timing of the initial imposition of restraints in relation to the unionization of the league reflect the situation which exists in most of the present sports leagues. *See, e.g.,* Robertson v. National Basketball Ass'n, 389 F. Supp. 867, 894-95 (S.D.N.Y. 1975); Philadelphia World Hockey Club, Inc. v. Philadelphia Hockey Club, Inc., 351 F. Supp. 462 (E.D. Pa. 1972).

several sports cases involving antitrust challenges to various league restraints on player mobility.[523] The results of these cases point to a legal standard which requires a specific inquiry into the degree of bargaining which has actually taken place between the parties.[524] However, because of the rather unique posture in which the issue has been presented, the courts have been required to proceed from premises which are not always clearly demarked in prior cases.[525] The consequence is that despite the emergence of a seeming consensus on the necessity for actual bargaining, the precise limits of these few decisions are somewhat uncertain.[526] It may be worthwhile, therefore, to review these decisions for the purpose of defining the contours of this debate more precisely.

The lawsuits precipitated by the formation of the World Hockey Association as a rival to the well-established National Hockey League provided an important test of the applicability of the labor exemption. In *Philadelphia World Hockey Club, Inc. v. Philadelphia Hockey Club, Inc.*[527] the WHA sought to establish that the NHL had violated the antitrust laws by using its reserve clause, affiliation agreements, and other devices to control the supply of professional hockey players. The court, in a proceeding which combined motions for summary judgment with a request for a preliminary injunction, concluded that the NHL reserve clause [528] violated the antitrust laws, that the league had not established that the clause was within the scope of the labor exemption, and that a preliminary injunction should be issued to prevent the league from initiating and prosecuting further proceedings to enforce the reserve clause against individual players who sought to join the new league.[529]

The court made numerous findings of fact concerning the extent to which the reserve clause had been treated in collective bargaining between the NHL owners and the players' association. The court noted that the reserve clause was initially inserted in the contracts of hockey players several years before the

---

A somewhat different legal issue would be presented if the employer attempted to impose player restraints *after* the union had been formed. In that case, the employer might well run afoul of the doctrine which prevents it from making any changes in working conditions without first bargaining with the union. *See generally* C. MORRIS, DEVELOPING LABOR LAW 323-24, 340-43 (1971) [hereinafter cited as MORRIS].

523. *See, e.g.,* Robertson v. National Basketball Ass'n, 389 F. Supp. 867, 894-95 (S.D.N.Y. 1975); Kapp v. National Football League, 390 F. Supp. 73 (N.D. Cal. 1974); Boston Professional Hockey Ass'n v. Cheevers, 348 F. Supp. 261 (D. Mass.), *remanded,* 472 F.2d 127 (1st Cir. 1972); *cf.,* Flood v. Kuhn, 316 F. Supp. 271, 282-83 (S.D.N.Y. 1970), *aff'd,* 443 F.2d 264 (2d Cir. 1971), *aff'd,* 407 U.S. 258 (1972).

524. *See* discussion at notes 609-10 *infra.*

525. As previously noted, none of the major Supreme Court precedents in this area consider the exemption question in precisely the same terms as it is presented in the sports contexts. *See* § 5.04 *supra.*

526. *See* discussion at notes 580-95, 630-35 *infra.*

527. 351 F. Supp. 462 (E.D.Pa. 1972). *See also* Boston Professional Hockey Ass'n v. Cheevers, 348 F. Supp. 261 (D. Mass.), *remanded,* 472 F.2d 127 (1st Cir. 1972). Background on the issues considered in these cases can be found in Alyluia, *Professional Sports Contracts and the Players' Association,* 5 MAN. L.J. 359 (1973); Comment, *Flood in the Land of Antitrust: Another Look at Professional Athletics, the Antitrust Laws and the Labor Law Exemption,* 7 IND. L. REV. 541 (1974).

528. The reserve clause in question, found in every Standard Player's Contract in the NHL, obligated a player to enter into another contract for the next season if so requested by the club. The clause provided that the new contract would be on the same terms and conditions as the contract under which the reserve rights were exercised except that the salary for the renewal period was to be determined by mutual agreement. *See generally* § 5.03 *supra.*

529. 351 F. Supp. at 517-19.

players' association came into existence. Thus, in its origins, it was clearly the unilateral creation of management. The court also found that Paragraph 17 of the NHL Standard Player's Contract, which contained the reserve clause, had been "one of the subjects about which [sic] the clubs and the Players' Association have discussed since 1967," [530] the year when the Players' Association was first recognized. However, in the court's view, a distinction is to be made between the parties merely discussing a matter and their subjecting it to collective bargaining. The court noted that on three different occasions the parties had entered into specific agreements dealing with the question of how a player's salary was to be established when a club exercised its right to renew the player's contract. The parties originally agreed that salaries under an extended contract would be set by arbitration and subsequently made various modifications defining the form of arbitration to be used. This history of bargaining prompted the court to conclude that "the negotiations with respect to *arbitration* . . . have been bona fide good-faith collective bargaining negotiations relating to genuine issues of employer-employee relations." [531]

The court, however, chose to differentiate between bargaining about this one aspect of the mechanics of the reserve clause and bargaining about the larger question of whether there should be a reserve clause at all. On the latter point, the court made a finding of fact that while the reserve clause had been "discussed," the evidence did not establish that it was the subject of "any 'collective bargaining'." [532] Among the facts which apparently led the court to this conclusion were the following:

(1) Despite the owners' statements to the contrary, there was no evidence in the record which indicated that the players' group had received any trade-offs in exchange for an agreement to continue the clause.

(2) In an early bargaining session, the players had requested a change in the renewal arrangement. Although the matter was mentioned on other occasions and although a committee was formed to consider the matter, the evidence suggested that neither side had ever modified its position, and the clause itself had never been modified.

(3) One of the owners' representatives at the bargaining sessions testified that he was hesitant to state that either side had made what could be termed "proposals" with respect to the reserve clause. While "there was an examination of various avenues," apparently neither side got to the point of defining the changes which he would find acceptable. The owners' negotiator testified: "No one said 'This is our proposal. If you accept this, we would do this.' They never got to that stage." [533]

In defining the principles of law to be applied to the case, the court traced the evolution of the labor exemption from the Supreme Court's decision in *Hutcheson* to its more recent pronouncement in *Jewel Tea*. The court noted that those cases involved situations in which the union had played an active role in

---

530. *Id.* at 482.
531. *Id.* at 484.
532. *Id.* at 485.
533. *Id.*

the creation and enforcement of an alleged restraint. In the court's view, the present case was different in that the offensive clause had been unilaterally instituted by management and consistently opposed by the union. In addition, the court noted that the agreements involved in the *Hutcheson* line of cases had generally been subjected to extensive collective bargaining. Relying on the findings of fact which it had made, the court identified the absence of collective bargaining as a determinative element in its conclusion that the labor exemption was not available to the defendant NHL.[534] Indirectly, the court also identified the standard which should be applied to determine whether there has been sufficient bargaining to warrant an application of the exemption. In the court's view, a critical defect in the NHL's position was that it had not shown that the reserve clause had been subjected to "serious, intensive, arm's-length collective bargaining." [535]

While the court was persuaded that there had not been sufficient bargaining in the case before it, it went on to suggest an alternative rationale which did not depend upon the degree of collective bargaining which has occurred. It was noted that the complaining party in the instant case was an economic competitor of the defendant league. The reserve clause severely limited the new league in its efforts to attract established players and operated as a serious restraint on its ability to compete. Thus, even if there had been extensive collective bargaining, the clause in question had the central characteristics which led the Supreme Court to condemn the arrangements in *Allen Bradley* and *Pennington*.[536] The impact of the clause in question was not limited to the immediate concerns of the bargaining unit. Rather the restraint extended into the business market and had the effect of injuring third parties.[537] Thus, in the court's view, the NHL defendants failed to gain the protection of the labor exemption both because the necessary collective bargaining was absent and because the scope of the restraint was beyond that which would be sanctioned in any case.[538]

Another case dealing with the labor exemption in the sports area is *Robertson v. National Basketball Association*.[539] In that case, a group of professional basketball players alleged that various NBA practices, including the draft and reserve system, operated as restraints on trade in violation of the Sherman Act. The league asserted that several of the disputed practices were protected by the labor exemption and thus were not subject to scrutiny under the antitrust laws.

The court's response to this contention was somewhat unclear. Under a section of its opinion entitled *Labor Exemption from Antitrust Laws* the court seemed to present an emphatic rejection of the defendant's argument that the questioned practices were within the labor exemption. In the court's view, the exemption was only intended to protect actions taken by a union.[540] The court quoted several passages from Supreme Court opinions which emphasized that

---

534. *Id.*
535. *Id.* at 499.
536. *See generally* discussion at notes 340-63, § 5.04 *supra*.
537. *See generally* Jacobs & Winter, *Antitrust Principles and Collective Bargaining by Athletes: Of Superstars in Peonage,* 81 YALE L.J. 1, 27-28 (1971).
538. 351 F. Supp. at 499.
539. 389 F. Supp. 867 (S.D.N.Y. 1975).
540. 389 F. Supp. at 884-86.

the immunity was intended to protect the rights of employees to join together in pursuit of common goals. As the court interpreted the congressional design, the exemption was one-sided and did not protect *employer* activities. On this basis, the court concluded that "there is no operative labor exemption barring or protecting the defendants from being sued for antitrust violations." [541]

Despite the lack of equivocation in that conclusion, a subsequent portion of the court's lengthy opinion indicates that the matter of the labor exemption was far from settled. In later addressing the question of whether the players were entitled to summary judgment, the court concluded that such an order was not proper because of a sharp factual dispute as to whether the various restraints had been subjected to collective bargaining.[542] The court conceded that resolution of that factual question was critical to the plaintiffs' case:

> Conceivably if the restrictions were part of the union policy deemed by the Players' Association to be in the players' best interest, they could be exempt from the reach of the antitrust laws.[543]

The court also seemed to recognize that it might be necessary to distinguish between different degrees of bargaining in applying the exemption. In this regard, the court adopted the test proposed in *Philadelphia World Hockey* and stated that the appropriate inquiry was whether the disputed practices "were ever the 'subject of serious, intensive, arm's-length collective bargaining'." [544] While the court expressed skepticism about the likelihood that the evidence at trial would establish that the players' union actually agreed to the restraints,[545] it did recognize that entry of judgment was inappropriate until the question of the bargaining history had been resolved.[546]

---

541. *Id.* at 884.

542. The court stated:

> ... A barrier to taking definitive action on these issues at this time, however, is the sharp controversy between the plaintiffs and the NBA defendants as to whether the controversial restraints came into being in the context of arm's-length union-employer negotiations, or were imposed unilaterally by the NBA.
>
> There is a total divergence of views between plaintiffs and defendants in addressing themselves to this question. There is disagreement as to when the Players Association was recognized as the exclusive bargaining agent for the players; whether the reserve clause and the assignment of contract provisions were ever the subject of collective bargaining; whether the draft, assignment and trading provisions of the Uniform Contract, and the compensation plan are regulated by collective bargaining agreements entered into between the NBA and the players; whether the reserve clause, draft, assignment and trading provisions of the Uniform Contract, and the compensation plan have been unilaterally adopted by the NBA and imposed on the players. Whether the restraints were ever the subject of serious bargaining, or whether they were acquiesced in in return for other benefits, or whether they were boldly imposed by the NBA cannot be determined except at trial. 389 F.Supp. at 895.

543. *Id.*

544. *Id., quoting* Phildelphia World Hockey Club, Inc. v. Philadelphia Hockey Club, Inc., 351 F. Supp. 462, 499 (E.D. Pa. 1972). The court proposed to follow the course set in *Philadelphia World Hockey* and explore the parties' bargaining history when the matter came to trial. 389 F. Supp. at 895 n.50.

545. Judge Carter stated:

> I must confess that it is difficult for me to conceive of any theory or set of circumstances pursuant to which the college draft, blacklisting, boycotts and refusals to deal could be saved from Sherman Act condemnation, even if defendants were able to prove at trial their highly dubious contention that these restraints were adopted at the behest of the Players Association. *Id.* at 895.

546. *See* note 542 *supra.*

The court does not indicate how its original conclusion that "there is no operative labor exemption . . . protecting the defendants" is to be reconciled with its subsequent conclusion that the availability of the exemption turns upon the extent of bargaining which has taken place. A close reading of the opinion suggests that what the court meant to say was that *if* the restraints were imposed by purely unilateral employer action, the labor exemption would not be available. If that is the intended meaning, it finds support in other precedents. But to accept this reading of the opinion, one must overlook the court's seemingly unequivocal conclusion that there was no exemption protecting the defendants in this case. In order to reconcile the two portions of the court's analysis, it is necessary to emphasize that the court eventually concluded that it had insufficient factual evidence upon which to conclude that the employers' action here was unilateral.[547] To the extent that a general principle emerges from the case, it seems to be the same point made by the court in *Philadelphia World Hockey* : the labor exemption will be applied only to those practices which have been approved by the union.[548] The approval which is given must be more than passive acquiescence [549] and be the product of serious, good faith bargaining.

The applicability of the labor exemption in the sports area was also considered in *Kapp v. National Football League.*[550] Kapp brought suit alleging that various league practices including the draft system, the Rozelle Rule, and the use of mandatory standard form contracts operated as unconscionable restraints upon his ability to market his services among competing employers. The defendant league responded that the practices in question were immunized from antitrust attack by virtue of the labor exemption. Specifically the league argued that all of the disputed practices were provided for in the standard player contract, either expressly or by virtue of a clause incorporating the league by-laws,[551] and all of the matters in the standard contract were subject to collective bargaining.[552] Kapp had not signed such a contract for the season which preceded the lawsuit, but the league argued that he was required to do so by virtue of a collective bargaining provision which specifically required a signing. In short, the league's view was that all of the matters about which Kapp complained were matters subject to union-employer bargaining and thus should not be open to objection by an individual employee dissatisfied with the terms which had been put into effect.

The court refused to accept this labor exemption defense, but on grounds which are not completely satisfactory. The court thought that the restraints were not the product of collective bargaining.[553] But the court went on to

---

547. *See* note 542 *supra.*

548. The notion that union approval might provide immunity is implicit in the analysis which the court applies to conclude that the employer here could not claim the labor exemption. The language quoted by the court emphasizes that the exemption was intended for the protection of unions. *See* 389 F. Supp. at 884-86.

549. The language used by the court suggests that the players' association would have to make a conscious decision that restraints on player mobility were in the interests of its members. *See* text at note 543 *supra. See also* discussion at notes 397-419, § 5.05 *supra.*

550. 390 F. Supp. 73 (N.D. Cal. 1974).

551. *See id.* at 77. *See also* § 3.03 *supra.*

552. *See* 390 F. Supp. at 78-79.

553. *See id.* at 85-86.

suggest that even if the requisite collective bargaining had been present, the league would not prevail. In the court's view, the labor exemption could not be used to immunize direct restraints on an employee's right to seek employment:

> We are of the opinion that, however broad may be the exemption from antitrust laws of collective bargaining agreements dealing with wages, hours, and other conditions of employment, that exemption does not and should not go so far as to permit immunized combinations to enforce employer-employee agreements which, being unreasonable restrictions on an employee's right to freely seek and choose his employment, have been held illegal on grounds of *public policy* long before and entirely apart from the antitrust laws.[554]

This conclusion by the court raises a number of problems. The court seems to suggest that the labor exemption may immunize union-management agreements from scrutiny under the antitrust laws but leaves them vulnerable to attack under common law prohibitions on unreasonable restraints. As an initial matter, it can be observed that this analysis assumes that the common law rules represent different public policies than those which are embodied in the antitrust laws. At least on the matters here in question, that is not the case. The early common law decisions suggest that agreements which unduly restricted one's ability to compete were not to be tolerated because they contravened a strong public policy in favor of competitive markets.[555] The antitrust statutes which were eventually adopted can hardly be said to represent a radically different policy.[556] Indeed, they seem to be merely a codification of these same concerns.[557] The more correct view would seem to be that the labor exemption is to be broadly viewed as a doctrine which exempts certain types of agreements from *all* attacks which are premised upon the unreasonableness of the restraint imposed. While there are limits on the types of agreements which will be tolerated under the exemption,[558] they are likely to be demarcated, not on the basis of a distinction between antitrust and public policy principles, but rather on the basis of a careful assessment of federal labor and antitrust policies of the sort which the Supreme Court has already made.[559]

The *Kapp* court's rationale also suggests that whatever the reach of the labor exemption, the league practices in question are not immunized because they limit the "employee's right to freely seek and choose his employment." The court cites no authority for the distinction which it suggests. In light of the policies which underlie the exemption, it is by no means clear that agreements which restrain access to initial job opportunities are to be treated more severely than those which limit job opportunities once a position has been secured. It should be

---

554. *Id.* at 86 (emphasis in original).

555. *See generally* 6A A. Corbin, Corbin on Contracts §§ 1381, 1385-92 (1951).

556. *See generally* 6A A. Corbin, Corbin on Contracts §§ 1381, 1401-02 (1951). *See also* Anderson v. Shipowners Ass'n, 272 U.S. 359 (1926); American Medical Ass'n v. United States, 130 F.2d 233 (D.C. Cir. 1942), *aff'd,* 317 U.S. 519 (1943).

557. J. von Kalinowski, Antitrust Laws and Trade Regulations (16 Business Organizations 1971) §§ 1.01-.03.

558. Justice Marshall, in his dissent in *Flood v. Kuhn,* recognized, that none of the labor exemption cases decided by the Court had directly confronted the question of whether there are limits on the right of labor and management to agree to restraints which only affect the employees involved. 407 U.S. 258, 295-96 (1972) (Marshall, J., dissenting).

559. *See generally* § 5.05 *supra.*

apparent that it is not enough simply to ask whether one aspect of the employment relationship or another is involved. Rather, as explained more fully above, the proper inquiry seems to be whether the matter in question is one in which the union can claim a direct and immediate interest in light of its basic goal of improving the terms and conditions under which its members work.[560] It may well be that some aspects of the employment relationship fall outside this area of legitimate union concern,[561] but that determination cannot be made on the *a priori* basis that employees have the right to freely seek employment with whomever they desire. On that general question, there is adequate precedent from the labor law area which recognizes that a union has a substantial interest in how new employees are hired since that process may have a direct effect upon the security enjoyed by existing employees represented by the union.[562] Moreover, the cases accept that the union may agree to arrangements which in fact restrain the ability of some employees to freely choose their employers.[563] In these instances, again, the restraints are thought to be necessary to achieve some broader union policy.

In short, the basic difficulty with the *Kapp* analysis is that it gives too much credence to common law notions of proper employment practices. The subject area before the court is one in which general notions of reasonableness have given way to more complex policy choices embodied in the federal labor and antitrust laws.[564] A problem such as that presented in *Kapp* can no longer be viewed in terms of whether the restraint in question strikes a particular judge as reasonable. Rather, the issue to be confronted is whether judicial tolerance of the particular restraint is compelled by the policies underlying the congressional decision to control improper combinations on the one hand and to encourage employee collective activity on the other.

The antitrust status of the NFL player restraints, and the related labor exemption question, was again raised in *Mackey v. National Football League.* [565] The focus of that case, which was brought by a group of NFL players and veterans, was on the league's indemnity system, the so-called Rozelle Rule. The plaintiffs alleged that the rule was an improper restraint of trade and sought both an injunction against its further use and monetary damages for the injuries allegedly sustained in its prior enforcement. The case developed into a major test for the labor exemption question. Unlike the three prior sports cases in which the exemption question was decided in preliminary proceedings, the district court opinion in *Mackey* followed a full evidentiary trial on the antitrust issues. The proceedings, which were tried without a jury before Judge Earl Larson, required fifty-five days of trial and involved more than sixty witnesses and over four hundred exhibits. The resulting transcript was in excess of 11,000

---

560. The concern for the directness and immediacy of the employees' interest is suggested by the Court's analysis in *Jewel Tea. See* § 5.04 *supra. See generally* Meltzer, *Labor Unions, Collective Bargaining and the Antitrust Laws,* 32 U. Chi. L. Rev. 659, 724-26 (1965).

561. *See* note 558 *supra.*

562. *See* discussion at notes 449-51, § 5.05 *supra.*

563. *See, e.g.,* Teamsters Local 357 v. NLRB, 365 U.S. 667 (1961) (hiring hall). *See generally* Morris 132-34, 712-15.

564. *See generally* Jacobs & Winter, *Antitrust Principles and Collective Bargaining by Athletes: Of Superstars in Peonage,* 81 Yale L.J. 1, 17-18 (1971).

565. 407 F. Supp. 1000 (D. Minn. 1975), *modified,* 543 F.2d 606 (8th Cir. 1976).

pages. Despite the league's massive effort to defend its practices, the district court proceedings proved to be a resounding defeat. Judge Larson, in a decision issued on December 29, 1975, upheld the players on every major issue and enjoined the league from further enforcement of the rule, reserving until a later proceeding the issue of damages. On the merits of the plaintiffs' antitrust claim, Judge Larson held the Rozelle Rule to be a *per se* violation of the Sherman Act. He went on to find that even when evaluated under the less stringent rule of reason test, the rule could not be sustained.[566] And more importantly for our present purposes, Judge Larson concluded the league's claim of immunity under the labor exemption to be unfounded. The defendant-league appealed the decision, contesting Judge Larson's conclusions on both the merits of the plaintiffs' antitrust claims and on the labor exemption question. This appeal provided the first occasion for a federal court of appeals to consider the immunity issue in the sports context. The Eighth Circuit eventually affirmed Judge Larson's basic conclusions that the antitrust laws had been violated and that the labor exemption could not be claimed by the defendants.[567] The appellate court's opinion offered some encouragement to the league, however, for it rather pointedly suggested that the defendants could avoid further antitrust problems by entering into meaningful collective bargaining with the players' union on the matter of player restraints.

On the matter of the labor exemption, the Eighth Circuit perceived the facts before it as involving a question of the proper accommodation of competing federal labor and antitrust policies. The court identified what it thought to be the basis upon which the accommodation was to be made. In the court's view, the availability of the exemption was to be determined under a three prong test:

> First, the labor policy favoring collective bargaining may potentially be given pre-eminence over the antitrust laws when the restraint on trade primarily affects only the parties to the collective bargaining relationship. . . . Second, federal labor policy is implicated sufficiently to prevail only where the agreement sought to be exempted concerns a mandatory subject of collective bargaining. . . . Finally, the policy favoring collective bargaining is furthered to the degree necessary to override the antitrust laws only where the agreement sought to be exempted is the product of bona fide arm's-length bargaining.[568]

In applying these "tests" to the facts before it, the court had little difficulty with the first requirement. The restraints in question had no appreciable impact upon competing leagues or others outside of the bargaining unit and thus the court could conclude that the restrictions affected "only the parties to the agreements sought to be exempted." [569] The court also found that the Rozelle Rule was a mandatory subject of bargaining. While the rule technically only dealt with the obligation of compensation owed by one employer to another employer, it was also true that the Rule had a definite effect upon the athlete's mobility and his salary. Since these were matters clearly within the statutory classifications of "wages, hours and other terms and conditions of

---

566. 407 F. Supp. at 1001-08.
567. 543 F.2d 606 (8th Cir. 1976).
568. 543 F.2d at 614.
569. *Id.* at 615.

employment"[570] — which defined the mandatory subjects of bargaining — the court concluded that the second element of its test had been satisfied.[571]

In treating this issue, the appellate court also undertook to clarify a critical analytical error which had been made by Judge Larson in the lower court. Judge Larson concluded that

> The Rozelle Rule is a nonmandatory, illegal subject of bargaining. . . . The Rozelle Rule, being a *per se* violation of the antitrust laws and otherwise violative of the antitrust laws under the Rule of Reason standard, cannot, because of its illegality, constitute a mandatory subject of bargaining as that phrase is used in labor law.[572]

There are two difficulties with this assessment. The first is the holding that the Rozelle Rule is not a mandatory subject of bargaining. The basis of the appellate court's rejection of this conclusion has already been stated. The other difficulty arises from the suggestion that the Rule is also an illegal subject of bargaining.

In the labor context, the term "illegal subject of bargaining" is used to designate matters which are illegal in the sense that they are prohibited by statute or other legal rule.[573] Common examples include closed shop[574] and hot cargo[575] agreements which are prohibited by explicit language in the basic labor statute. Similarly, a proposal which required that either the union or employer practice racial discrimination, which is strictly forbidden under the Civil Rights Act, is an illegal subject of bargaining.[576] Since an agreement which included such a term would be "illegal," neither party can insist that the other side bargain about the matter.[577] A conclusion that the Rozelle Rule was an illegal subject of bargaining in this sense would have potentially far-reaching consequences not only for the NFL but the entire sports industry as well. It would mean, in effect, that a league could not even schedule such an indemnity system as a topic for negotiation. Moreover, if the players' union were to consent to such a term, even in exchange for the most substantial concessions, the term would be unenforceable. And, of course, if the Rozelle Rule cannot legally become part of the labor contract, it might be doubted whether any other type of significant player restraint could be adopted.

The appellate court was careful to point out that it rejected Judge Larson's characterization.[578] The basic flaw in the lower court's analysis is that it begs the essential question. As indicated in the passage quoted above, Judge Larson suggests that the Rozelle Rule is "illegal" because it violates the antitrust laws. From this premise he concludes that it cannot be the subject of a collective bargaining agreement. But that avoids the issue inherent in the labor exemption: will bargaining between an employer and a union remove the matter from the purview of the antitrust laws? Thus, the fact that the Rozelle Rule violates the

---

570. *See* National Labor Relations Act, § 8(d), 29 U.S.C. § 158(d) (1974).
571. 543 F.2d at 615-16.
572. 407 F. Supp. at 1009.
573. *See generally* MORRIS 435-39.
574. *See, e.g.,* Pinello v. United Mine Workers, 88 F. Supp. 935 (D.D.C. 1975).
575. *See, e.g.,* Amalgamated Lithographers Local 17, 130 NLRB 985 (1961).
576. *Cf.* NLRB v. News Syndicate Co., 365 U.S. 695 (1961).
577. *See* MORRIS 438.
578. 543 F.2d at 616.

antitrust laws in the absence of bargaining is not a reason for concluding that it cannot be bargained about. As is rather clearly set forth in the relevant Supreme Court precedents, it is the process of collective bargaining which legitimizes terms which would otherwise be prohibited as improper anticompetitive restraints.

Having satisfied itself that the Rozelle Rule had its primary effect upon the parties involved in the collective bargaining relationship and that the Rule was a mandatory subject of bargaining, the court turned its attention to the critical third prong of its test: had the rule been subjected to bona fide arm's-length bargaining? It was on this point that the league's claim of immunity failed, for the appellate court concluded that there was substantial evidence to support the lower court's finding that there had been "no bona fide arm's-length bargaining" over the Rozelle Rule.[579] Since the restraints in question were thus not the product of a joint union-management agreement, it could not be said that the policies in favor of collective bargaining would be promoted by a grant of immunity.

While the Eighth Circuit framed its analysis in terms of the sufficiency of the evidence supporting the lower court's findings, it seems clear that the reviewing court did not intend to endorse all that Judge Larson had said about the nature of the parties' collective bargaining relationship. The district court had strongly suggested that the relationship had been dominated by management and that the interests of the player had been consistently overridden. While there had been two collective bargaining agreements signed between the parties, one in 1968 and one in 1970, the court found that the union "achieved little in the way of substantive benefits" in the first agreement and that the league had treated the Rozelle Rule as non-negotiable in the second.[580] Somewhat gratuitously, Judge Larson also made findings about the strength of the union. In his view,

> The union, from its inception through the present day, has been too weak vis-à-vis the clubs to obtain elimination of or even a reasonable modification of the Rozelle Rule.[581]

In this connection, the lower court also concluded that the usual weapon of the economic strike had not been available to the union. The apparent bases for this conclusion were that a strike was not feasible because of the union's financial position and because of the "substantial adverse public pressure" which it would generate.[582] Judge Larson did not state what ultimate inference was to be drawn from these findings. It appears, however, that he intended to suggest that this was a situation in which the union was so weak that the formality of a collective bargaining relationship ought not affect the antitrust analysis which was applied to the practices in question. The court also seemed to be hinting that any evidence of the union's acquiescence in the continuation of the Rozelle Rule should be ignored because of the position of extreme weakness from which the group operated.[583]

---

579. *Id.* at 616.
580. 407 F. Supp. at 1009.
581. *Id.* at 1010.
582. *Id.*
583. Although Judge Larson specifically found that the NFLPA had never agreed to the Rozelle Rule in either the 1968 or 1970 agreement, he failed to deal directly with the fact that the Rule was

Interestingly this inquiry into the relative strength of the union was largely ignored by the appellate court. There was no attempt to characterize the effectiveness of the union or to ascertain the extent to which it had succeeded in securing concessions on behalf of its members. Rather, the appellate court merely observed that the Rozelle Rule had been incorporated into the parties' agreements and then addressed the issue of whether the term was the product of bona fide bargaining.[584] While the court did adopt the lower court's finding that there had been no bargaining over the restraint, it did not venture further into the matter of the parties' bargaining power.

The court's avoidance of this aspect of the lower court's decision is understandable. Since there had been no bargaining, it was not necessary to inquire further into the parties' relationship. In this case, the labor exemption question could be resolved on narrower grounds. But there are other reasons why the court might choose to ignore the veiled implication of Judge Larson's decisions that even if the union had agreed to the restraint in question, it might still be appropriate to evaluate the group's relative bargaining strength. In fact, an analysis of this question suggests that the preferable approach is to limit the labor exemption inquiry to the question asked by the court of appeals — was the restraint the product of bargaining? — and not attempt to judge the quality of the union's efforts, except perhaps in extreme cases in which the bargaining is truly a sham.

The basic point to be made is that a labor exemption which turns upon the relative strength of the union has the potential for seriously disrupting the process of collective bargaining. The courts should be hesitant to develop a new doctrine which potentially allows employers to escape the obligations imposed by a collective bargaining agreement negotiated on their behalf. Any major exception of this sort would leave the employer in a most difficult position: it would be legally obligated to bargain with the union but would have no assurance that the points agreed upon would be given effect. If the finality of the bargaining process is undermined, there is likely to be a corresponding erosion in the employer's willingness to engage in meaningful negotiations.[585]

A further difficulty with any rule which turns upon the relative strength of the union is that there are likely to be extended, and unresolvable, debates about the employees' responsibility for their lack of bargaining power. In concluding that the NFLPA had operated from a position of weakness, Judge Larson emphasized the group's heavy financial burden and his belief that "adverse public pressure" precluded the union from waging an effective strike.[586] The persuasiveness of these points is not self-evident, however. Some may argue, for example, that a court would surely want to consider the extent to which the union's debt position represented a conscious choice by the leadership to launch

technically a part of those agreements to the extent that it was incorporated by reference. *Compare* 543 F.2d at 612-13. Judge Larson's extended findings concerning the weaknesses of the union may have been an indirect attempt to respond to the argument that the fact of incorporation indicated some type of acquiescence by the union.

584. *See* 543 F.2d at 616.

585. The argument made in the text is basically an argument in favor of limited judicial intervention into the parties' collective bargaining relationship. The policies which support this position are considered more fully in § 5.06 *supra.*

586. 407 F. Supp. at 1010.

expensive organizational drives or litigation campaigns rather than concentrating on more modest goals. By the same token, it would be argued that the "adverse public pressure" may have been the result of the union's having selected the "wrong" issues over which to strike.[587] Some might contend that a sports union which selects temperate goals for its bargaining effort will encounter a favorable public reaction. Ultimately a court might decide that none of these avenues of inquiry should be pursued, for any attempt to answer these points puts the judiciary in a position of second guessing the organizational and bargaining strategy of the employee group. Those are not matters for which courts are likely to be able to provide accurate evaluations. Rather than subjecting employers to the risk that their collective bargaining agreements will be ignored, the courts may well conclude that they should not review the union's bargaining posture.

Again, the appellate court in *Mackey* was able to avoid this entire controversy because the case before it raised only the question of whether the rule in question had been subject to bargaining. The court found that there had been no exchange between the employers and the union for the latter's acquiescence.[588] The discussion in the preceding paragraphs should suggest that in those cases in which an exchange or trade-off is found, the court should be hesitant to inquire further. As suggested, it is probably desirable that the judiciary recognize a "sham" exception, under which the plaintiffs could establish that an apparent exchange lacked substance or was otherwise the product of joint employer-union collusion. But apart from those extreme cases, the courts would appear to have no role to play in determining whether the union received "enough" concessions in exchange for its agreement to a restraint. This type of inquiry would lead the judiciary into an area where there are considerably more issues than there are answers.

There is other evidence which suggests that the *Mackey* appeals court did not share Judge Larson's concern about the impotence of the players' union. The reviewing court concluded its opinion by urging the parties to return to the bargaining table to redefine the player restraint system. The pointed implication of the statements was that if the parties did this, and if there was a "mutual resolution," the antitrust problems which had previously plagued the league would disappear under the veil of the labor exemption.[589] This advice would most

---

587. *See* Los Angeles Times, June 3, 1974, Pt. III, at 1, col. 1; Wall Street Journal, July 2, 1974, at 36, col. 1.

588. The appellate court specifically considered an argument made by the defendant to the effect that there had in fact been an exchange between the players and owners on the matter of the Rozelle Rule. The defendants had contended that the players had agreed to the Rule as a *quid pro quo* for the owners' granting increased pension benefits and giving the players the right to negotiate salaries on an individual basis. The defendants' support for this argument came from the testimony of Alan Miller, who had represented the players in the early negotiations. Miller had testified that he recalled "telling somebody" that if the owners insisted upon the collective negotiation of salaries, he would demand bargaining over the Rozelle Rule. Miller indicated that this point was "not a major topic of discussion." In response to this testimony, the *Mackey* court said:

> We cannot agree that [it] is indicative of a *quid pro quo.* First, the colloquy related by Miller seems to have been a side discussion rather than a focal point of the negotiations. Second, at the time this interchange occurred, the clubs had already agreed to individual salary negotiations in a separate agreement. 543 F.2d at 616, n. 17.

589. *Id.* at 623.

likely not have been given if the court believed that the question of the union's bargaining strength presented a serious legal issue.

The court of appeals gives a defensible resolution to the ultimate question of whether the Rozelle Rule could be said to be the product of a collective bargaining relationship. Other aspects of its labor exemption analysis are less free from doubt, however. As already noted, the court suggested that the availability of the labor exemption was to be determined under a three-pronged test. The first two "prongs" required a restraint (a) which "primarily affects only the parties to the collective bargaining relationship" and (b) which would pertain to a matter which was a mandatory subject of bargaining.[590] There is some basis to question whether these aspects of the court's test accurately reflect the principles developed in the leading precedents in this area.

On the first point, for example, it can be suggested that the Supreme Court has not limited the exemption solely to agreements which affect only the immediate parties. Rather, *Jewel Tea* seems to suggest that where there are such extra-unit effects, the availability of antitrust immunity depends upon a balancing test which weighs the effect upon competition against the strength of the union's interest in the matter.[591] Indeed, the facts of *Jewel Tea* illustrate the Supreme Court's willingness to tolerate some third party effects. In that case the Court extended the exemption to a restriction on a store's operating hours even though there was a definite effect on an important group of third parties — the consumers who shopped at the store.[592] The criticism of the *Mackey* court's second criterion is less certain. The court requires that the agreement affect a matter which is a mandatory subject of bargaining and includes non-specific citations to *Jewel Tea* and *Pennington* to support its position.[593] However, a review of those cases and the other leading Supreme Court precedents suggests that there has never been a specific holding that agreements on non-mandatory subjects cannot partake of immunity afforded by the labor exemption.[594] It is true that the statutory definition of the mandatory subjects serves to identify matters to which Congress ascribed a high priority in its pursuit of the policy of encouraging collective bargaining. But it

---

590. *Id.* at 614.

591. Meat Cutters Local 189 v. Jewel Tea Co., 381 U.S. 676, 691 (1965). This aspect of the *Jewel Tea* case is discussed more fully in § 5.04 *supra*.

592. *See generally* Meltzer, *Labor Unions, Collective Bargaining and the Antitrust Laws,* 32 U. Chi. L. Rev. 659 (1965).

593. 543 F.2d at 614.

594. The apparent basis for the *Mackey* court's conclusion that the labor exemption extends only to mandatory subjects of bargaining is a passage in the *Jewel Tea* case in which Justice White uses the example of a union-employer agreement on retail prices to illustrate the type of agreement which would not be entitled to immunity under the labor exemption. In his treatment of this matter, Justice White emphasizes that the price at which the employer sells his goods, unlike the matter of wages, is not a mandatory subject of bargaining under the federal labor statutes. The *Mackey* court may have read this distinction to mean that only agreements on mandatory subjects come within the exemption. Other portions of Justice White's opinion can be read as refuting this interpretation, however. In a footnote, White observed that "The critical determinant is not the form of the agreement — e.g., prices or wages — but its relative impact on the product market and the interests of the union members." 381 U.S. 690 n.5. This statement suggests that if a particular agreement has little or no effect on the product market and if it touches upon a matter which the employees regard as in their own self-interest, then the exemption should be available even if the topic is not a mandatory subject.

would be wrong to suggest that Congress intended to show no deference to the parties' agreements on other matters as well. If an agreement on a permissive subject had no significant effects beyond the immediate bargaining unit and if the agreement was the product of bona fide collective bargaining, it would seem that the general policy in favor of the peaceful resolution of industrial disputes should not lead courts to stay their antitrust hand.[595] But again, the important point to be made is that this issue is less firmly settled than the *Mackey* court suggests.

Even if these criticisms of the court's analysis are valid, however, the result in *Mackey* remains unaffected. It will be noted that the basic objection is that the court defined the scope of the exemption too narrowly and that other situations should also partake of the immunity. Since the court found that the facts before it satisfied the first two requirements which it imposed, the case presumably would be decided the same way under a test which stated these elements in broader terms. Thus, it appears that any defects in the court's analysis on these points have significance largely for limiting the precedential value of the case. Other courts can properly follow *Mackey's* insistence on actual bargaining. They should, however, give further consideration to other conditions which must be met before immunity will be granted.

The National Football League had another occasion to argue its labor exemption defense in *Smith v. Pro-Football, Inc.,*[596] Judge Bryant's decision in this case was rendered while the appeal in *Mackey* was pending in the Eighth Circuit. However, Judge Bryant's standards for applying the labor exemption are similar to those which controlled the resolution of *Mackey* in the appellate court. The plaintiff in *Smith* was a college All-American and the first-round draft pick of the Washington Redskins in the 1968 player selection draft. Expected to become one of the league's premier defensive backs, Smith had his career prematurely terminated when he suffered a serious neck injury in the last game of his first season. In his complaint against the Redskins and the league, Smith argued that the draft system constituted a group boycott under the antitrust laws.[597] Had he not been forced to deal with only one club, and to sign the standard player contract, Smith alleged, he would have been able to negotiate a contract reflecting the free market value of his services and containing adequate guarantees against loss of earnings in the event of injury.[598] The court, following trial, ruled the annual player draft a group boycott and a *per se* violation of the antitrust laws.[599] Moreover, the labor exemption was held not to bar recovery by the plaintiff.[600]

---

595. The distinction between mandatory and permissive subjects may be useful where the particular agreement has a significant extra-unit effect. Whether a topic is a mandatory subject serves as some evidence of the strength of the union's interest in the matter, for the definition of the mandatory subjects identifies matters of a most fundamental nature in the employment relationship. Thus, if the matter is not at the core of employee concerns and if there are appreciable external effects, the balancing test formulated in *Jewel Tea* would suggest that the exemption ought to be available. The statement in the text, however, assumes a situation in which the extra-unit effects are minimal. Where this is true, the presence of any serious union interest ought to tip the balance in favor of the exemption. *See also* note 594 *supra.*

596. 420 F. Supp. 738 (D.D.C. 1976).

597. *Id.* at 740-41.

598. *Id.*

599. *Id.* at 745. For a full discussion of the antitrust issues in *Smith,* see § 5.07 *infra.*

600. 420 F. Supp. at 741.

The defendants, the Redskins and the league, had argued that the draft was exempt from review under the antitrust laws. The court rejected this contention, noting that the initial collective bargaining agreement between the league and the players' association was reached after the time Smith had signed his contract with the Redskins.[601] Additionally, the 1968 draft had occurred prior to the players' association even becoming the exclusive bargaining agent for the players and, thus, in the court's analysis, prior to the exemption "under any view of the law hav[ing] been considered operative." [602] Apparently, the court felt it too much to expect that the mere potentiality for bargaining in a relationship not yet established could provide the basis for the exemption. Despite this conclusive finding of inapplicability, the *Smith* court went on to discuss the conditions it would require before the exemption could be found. Although largely dicta, the court's analysis should offer encouragement to the leagues willing to engage in collective bargaining on the issue of player restraints. The court first noted that the draft could constitute a mandatory subject of bargaining.[603] Drawing an analogy to the acceptance of hiring halls and seniority rules as determinants of the structure of the labor market in a particular industry, the *Smith* court concluded that each feature of the draft could be considered a term or condition of employment.[604] The court went on to make clear that it would limit the exemption to cases in which the restraint was the result of serious, intensive, arm's-length bargaining,[605] an element required by other courts.[606]

Central to the court's belief that the labor exemption would be available to a bargained-for draft system is its finding that the restraint imposed operated on the labor, as opposed to the product, market. The court recognized that the major purpose of the antitrust law is to protect the functioning of a free product market, and the protection of employees is a lesser concern.[607] Alternatively, conditions of employment are the central concerns of the labor laws. Unions are encouraged to "arrive at bargains that they consider in their best interests with respect to wages, hours, and other terms and conditions of employment." [608] In order to provide the necessary encouragement for peaceful, collective settlements, the courts must assume a posture of limited involvement, and the exemption provides the doctrinal framework through which this is achieved.

---

601. *Id.* at 742. The court stated:

> [A] scheme advantageous to employers and otherwise in violation of the antitrust laws cannot under any circumstances come within the exemption unless and until it becomes part of a collective bargaining agreement negotiated by a union in its own self-interest. Defendants' argument that plaintiff was not entitled to the protection of the antitrust laws must therefore fail, since the plaintiff entered into his contract with the Redskins prior to the time when the league and the players association . . . reached their initial collective bargaining agreement. *Id.*

602. *Id.*
603. *Id.* at 743.
604. *Id. See also* Jacobs & Winter, *Antitrust Principles and Collective Bargaining by Athletes: Of Superstars In Peonage,* 81 YALE L.J. 1, 16 (1971).
605. 420 F. Supp. at 743.
606. *See, e.g.,* Mackey v. National Football League, 543 F.2d 606 (8th Cir. 1976); Philadelphia World Hockey Club, Inc. v. Philadelphia Hockey Club, Inc., 351 F. Supp. 462, 484 (E.D. Pa. 1972).
607. 420 F. Supp. at 744.
608. *Id.*

b. Commentary on the Cases. As the prior discussion should suggest, there is some disagreement among the courts in their perception of how the labor exemption ought to operate in the sports area. The greatest potential difficulty is caused by the somewhat veiled implication of the *Kapp* case that player restraints partake of an illegality which can never be neutralized, even if subjected to the most vigorous form of bargaining. For the reasons previously given, it is thought that this characterization misperceives the essential purpose of the labor exemption. It will be noted, however, that if one looks beyond this difficulty in the cases, it is possible to find rough consensus. It appears that the courts would be inclined to apply the labor exemption to player restraints which were the product of serious, good-faith collective bargaining.[609]

To the extent that a rationale has emerged for this requirement of actual bargaining, it seems to be that proof of such negotiation serves to establish that the union actually approved of the restraint.[610] As perceived by the courts, the labor exemption is intended largely to protect union activity, and it is not enough that a particular agreement is potentially subject to union approval through collective bargaining. Rather, it appears that it is only when there is definite proof of union participation in a particular practice that the exemption will be applied. Implicit in the courts' view is the notion that if immunity were applied as the leagues have urged, the labor exemption would quickly become a tool for the oppression of labor rather than a device for protecting employees' collective activity as it was originally perceived.

There is one important aspect of the cases which warrants re-emphasis. The decisions have produced a body of authority which weighs against an argument which had received a considerable amount of attention in the early rounds of litigation. It had been argued by some that for certain types of employment terms, the labor exemption was to be applied whether or not they had been subjected to bargaining.[611] While this view has been expressed in varying forms, its basic thesis is that matters ought to be exempt from the antitrust laws if (1) a collective bargaining relationship exists between the parties; (2) the subject matter is a mandatory subject of bargaining; and (3) agreement on the matter would have its primary effects within the bargaining unit involved in the negotiations.[612] With respect to player restraints, it is, of course, contended that

---

609. *See also* Boston Professional Hockey Ass'n v. Cheevers:

> ... I am aware of the Bruins' argument that the Standard Player's Contract is a collective bargaining agreement exempt from the operation of the antitrust laws. I find and note that this contention has no support in the evidence. There is no document contained in the thousands of pages of this record which establishes that the portion of Clause 17 of the Standard Player's Contract which is commonly known as the reserve clause ever was the subject matter of negotiations between the National Hockey League team owners and representatives of the players. 348 F. Supp. 261, 267 (D. Mass. 1972).

610. *See, e.g.,* Robertson v. National Basketball Ass'n, 389 F. Supp. 867, 895 (S.D.N.Y. 1975); Philadelphia World Hockey Club, Inc. v. Philadelphia Hockey Club, Inc., 351 F. Supp. 462, 484 (E.D. Pa. 1972).

611. *See, e.g.,* UMW v. Pennington, 381 U.S. 657, 710 (Goldberg, J., dissenting in part); Note, *Antitrust and Labor Union Liability Under the Sherman Act,* 19 Sw. L.J. 616 (1965). *See also* Robertson v. National Basketball Ass'n, 389 F. Supp. 867, 895, n. 50 (S.D.N.Y. 1975).

612. Jacobs and Winter's excellent article on the exemption problem, while not reducing the relevant tests to terms as specific as those suggested in this text, seems generally to accept the basic distinctions made here. A major thesis of their article is that a distinction must be made between the product market and labor market effects of union-management agreements and as to

they qualify as mandatory bargaining subjects.[613] Those who endorse this view of the labor exemption assume that the *potential* for collective bargaining provides a sufficient basis to support a grant of immunity, and they would not require that the disputed restraints actually have been agreed to at the bargaining table. Those who take this approach contend, in effect, that while employees may feel themselves disadvantaged by particular practices, that condition is only temporary, for the employees through their union have available a number of tools which can be utilized to produce a change in the offensive condition. It is argued that since the federal labor statutes have designated the collective bargaining process as the vehicle for resolving disagreements on mandatory subjects of bargaining and have not adopted *a priori* notions of what is reasonable or fair, it was intended that the parties should take their disputes to the bargaining table.[614]

Perhaps the most complete hearing on these contentions was provided in the *Robertson* case. There the league argued that the availability of the labor exemption was to be determined under a two-step inquiry. In the league's view,

> The test for applicability of the labor exemption . . . is twofold: (1) Are the challenged practices directed against non-parties to the relationship; if they are not, then (2) are they mandatory subjects of collective bargaining? If the answer to No. 1 is no, and to No. 2 yes, the practices are immune. . . . [615]

The league argued that the authority which established the relevance of these tests was the Supreme Court's decisions in *Pennington* and *Jewel Tea*.[616] However, neither of those cases dealt specifically with the type of situation presented in the sports area, for in each the primary complaint was directed to the product market effects of a particular restraint.[617] Thus, it was possible for the *Robertson* court to conclude that neither case provided any support for the standard suggested by the league.[618] Moreover, the court found the league's reliance on *Pennington* particularly inappropriate because the explicit language of the case directly refutes the league's premise that the exemption was co-extensive with the category of mandatory subjects of bargaining. In a passage specifically quoted in *Robertson*,[619] Justice White stated in *Jewel Tea* that the majority, for which he was writing, did not intend

> to say that an agreement resulting from union-employer negotiations is automatically exempt from Sherman Act scrutiny simply because the negotiations involve a compulsory subject of bargaining, regardless of the subject or form or content of the agreement . . . . [T]here are limits to what a union or an employer may offer or extract in the name of

the latter, existing precedents and policies seem to suggest that the parties are to be subjected to judicial or administrative supervision. *See generally* Jacobs & Winter, *Antitrust Principles and Collective Bargaining by Athletes: Of Superstars in Peonage,* 81 YALE L.J. 1, 7-13 (1971).

613. Several courts have agreed with this characterization. *See* Mackey v. National Football League, 543 F.2d 606 (8th Cir. 1976); Smith v. Pro-Football, Inc., 420 F. Supp. 738 (D.D.C. 1976). *But see* Robertson v. National Basketball Ass'n, 389 F. Supp. 867, 889-90 (S.D.N.Y. 1975).

614. *See* text at notes 475-81, § 5.05 *supra.*

615. 389 F. Supp. at 886.

616. *See id.* at 887.

617. *See* text at notes 438-45, § 5.05 *supra.*

618. *See* 389 F. Supp. at 887-89.

619. *Id.* at 888.

> wages, and *because they must bargain does not mean that the agreement reached may disregard other laws.*[620]

The basic difficulty with the argument on automatic exemption is that it sweeps too broadly.[621] Some of its premises are sound. Thus it is true that in the scheme of the federal labor laws, collective bargaining has been chosen as the primary forum for resolving disputes.[622] It can also be accepted that courts are not empowered to intervene to make a substantive review of the parties' terms.[623] Moreover, the Supreme Court, in its major labor exemption decisions, has indicated that it is the third-party, and not the intra-unit, effects of collective bargaining agreements which trigger antitrust scrutiny.[624] But it does not follow from these premises that the parties' bargaining history is irrelevant. Indeed, to extend immunity to situations in which there has been no bargaining over an employer practice which is otherwise clearly illegal is to turn labor exemption on its head and allow it to be used against employees, rather than for their protection. The general labor policies do indicate, however, that the fact that labor participates in the process which defines the player restraints becomes the critical determinant of the court's power to review the agreement reached. This is the theme which is developed more fully in section 5.05 *supra* where the status of bargained-for restraints is examined.

Another aspect of the prior sports cases which warrants attention concerns the impact which these decisions will have on future collective bargaining between the parties. For reasons that are developed at length in section 5.05, it would seem that there is nothing inherently illegal in the owners and the players' association bargaining over the issue of player restraints. And as recent negotiations confirm, it is perfectly conceivable that the players' union will consent to the continuation of some type of restraint system, albeit one which reflects the modifications which will necessarily come with full, rigorous bargaining.[625] Whatever the antitrust implications of such restraints in other settings, the fact that they are the product of collective bargaining would seem to clothe them with immunity. And presumably this immunity would be available even if there had been a prior judicial proceeding disapproving restraints imposed by the league's unilateral action.

In light of the possibility that restraints might subsequently be reintroduced as a permanent league practice, it might be asked what precisely is achieved by the rule disapproving unilateral employer action in imposing them initially. It

---

620. *Id. quoting* 381 U.S. at 664-65 (emphasis in *Robertson*).

621. It is clear that the cases other than *Robertson* have little sympathy for the notion that the exemption is automatically available. The proponents of this view would apply it to immunize player restraints even in the absence of any actual bargaining between the parties. As noted, the decisions to date are uniform in their insistence that no exemption will be available in the absence of "serious, intensive, arm's-length collective bargaining." Smith v. Pro-Football, Inc., 420 F. Supp. 738 (D.D.C. 1976); Robertson v. National Basketball Ass'n, 389 F. Supp. 867 (S.D.N.Y. 1975); Philadelphia World Hockey Club, Inc. v. Philadelphia Hockey Club, Inc., 351 F. Supp. 462 (E.D. Pa. 1972). Again, such meaningful bargaining is necessary to provide concrete evidence that the players have in fact found that the restraints further their own self-interest.

622. *See* text at notes 460-86, § 5.05 *supra.*

623. *See* text at notes 479-86, § 5.05 *supra.*

624. *See* text at notes 438-45, § 5.05 *supra.*

625. Developments in the area of collective bargaining are discussed in § 5.03 *supra. See also* text at notes 390-94, § 5.05 *supra.*

cannot be asserted that the rule is necessary to preserve the players' absolute right to freely market their services, for that result is by no means insured. It would appear that the law accepts that the employees are afforded a wide range of discretion to define for themselves the extent of mobility which they will enjoy. If the labor exemption decisions from the sports area are assessed in more pragmatic terms, then, it would appear that the policy at stake is not precisely one involving the preservation of open, competitive markets. Indeed, it might be said that in large measure, what the courts have decreed is that it is better that the employees, rather than the employer, have the advantage in any negotiations which will take place over these rules.

In the absence of an order mandating that the league's player restraints be abandoned, sports employers have had a tactical bargaining advantage as they approached the bargaining table at which the restrictions were put into issue. In virtually every league where the question has been raised, the restraints were already in effect at the time the players unionized.[626] Thus, when collective bargaining began, the union faced the formidable task of attempting to force the employer to change an existing practice. Clearly the employers had the advantage in these negotiations for if the parties could not agree, the restraints would continue. Thus, if a change were to be forthcoming, it would require some affirmative action by the employer. However, the relative bargaining positions of the parties is dramatically changed if there is a judicial order forcing the employer to give up its system of player restraints. The employer which subsequently seeks the reinstatement of these devices must bargain from a position of relative weakness. It may make proposals, offer concessions, and seek a compromise, but if no agreement is forthcoming, the players' apparent interests are protected, absent the employer taking other drastic steps.[627] Thus, the effect of the adverse antitrust decision is to produce an important shift in bargaining power from the employer to the union. While it is true that the employees may never agree to give up their new freedom, that result is by no means assured. Indeed, if the system of player restraints is as important to professional sports as some contend, it is quite likely that the restraints will reappear in modified form and competition for players' services will again be less than free and open.

A question which has to be confronted is whether the courts are justified in using their powers to effectuate this rather dramatic shift in bargaining power. Critics of the courts' decisions will point to the fact that in the labor area there

---

626. *See, e.g.,* Robertson v. National Basketball Ass'n, 389 F. Supp. 867, 895 (S.D.N.Y. 1975); Philadelphia World Hockey Club, Inc. v. Philadelphia Hockey Club, Inc., 351 F. Supp. 462, 498-99 (E.D. Pa. 1972). *See also* note 612 *supra.*

627. The discussion in the text must be qualified in one respect. Under the theory of impasse bargaining, the employer is able to unilaterally impose conditions proposed at the bargaining table if the negotiations on the matter reach an impasse. *See generally* MORRIS 330-31; Schatzki, *The Employer's Unilateral Act — A Per Se Violation — Sometimes,* 44 TEXAS L. REV. 470 (1966); Comment, *Impasse in Collective Bargaining,* 44 TEXAS L. REV. 769 (1966). The sports employer might thus be able to establish player restraints even without union approval, although this is subject to considerable uncertainty. *See* text at notes 632-35 *infra.* However, in the fact situation assumed in the text, the employer is still at a distinct disadvantage, for there are many practical reasons why an employer might not exercise his rights upon impasse. For example, the employer may want to avoid antagonizing the union, or it may conclude that unilateral imposition of such restraints would only generate costly litigation.

is no statutory provision or other expression of legislative purpose which indicates that Congress intended that the judiciary should play a role in adjusting the relative bargaining position of the parties if each has otherwise satisfied its obligation to bargain in good faith.[628] Moreover, it will be suggested, there is no body of precedent which holds that weak unions are to be protected or that other imbalances are to be corrected by the courts.[629] How then can judicial intervention in these cases be upheld?

It is believed that a justification can be found and that it is important to an understanding of the implications of the sports cases decided to date. At the first level, there is a rather straightforward rationale supporting the courts' intervention in the parties' collective bargaining relationship. The fact is that in each of the decided cases, the advantage which the leagues obtained from continuing the pre-existing player restraints was an "illegal" one. Evaluated on independent antitrust grounds, the courts found, the player controls were improper restraints on trade. Moreover, as the cases were perceived, there was no real meddling in a collective bargaining relationship because, as far as the rules in question were concerned, they had never become part of that relationship. The courts may well have concluded that the leagues could not have it both ways: they could not both claim that the restraints were immunized by bargaining and at the same time withhold those rules from the negotiating process. Once the guise of collective bargaining was removed and the restraints were viewed as solely the design of the employers, they could not be sustained.

Further support for the courts' approach can be found in the federal policy of encouraging collective bargaining. What will likely happen — and indeed what has already occurred in some cases — is that the issue of player controls will become a central topic for discussion at the bargaining table. It is not clear that this bargaining process would have worked as Congress had planned if the players had been left in a position of having to use up valuable bargaining power to overcome an advantage to which the employers had no legal claim.

It should be noted, however, that this explanation for the courts' intervention also implies a limitation. Once the employers' improper advantage has been neutralized and the parties proceed to bargaining, a new set of legal rules applies. As the cases seem to recognize, collective bargaining represents the threshold of antitrust immunity, and if an agreement is forged as a result of an earnest exchange of concessions, it is no longer appropriate for courts to interject themselves. Thus, while the cases discussed above address an important point, it is a point which has limited utility once the courts have accomplished the initial task of pointing the parties to the bargaining table.

c. Deference to Future Bargaining. The fact that the parties may subsequently submit the matter of player restraints to collective bargaining

---

628. *See* discussion at notes 460-86, § 5.05 *supra. See generally* Jacobs & Winter, *Antitrust Principles and Collective Bargaining by Athletes: Of Superstars in Peonage*, 81 YALE L.J. 1, 7-13 (1971).

629. *Cf.* NLRB v. American Nat'l Ins. Co., 343 U.S. 395, 404 (1952): ("The Board may not, either directly or indirectly, compel concessions or otherwise sit in judgment upon the substantive terms of collective bargaining agreements."); NLRB v. Insurance Agents' Int'l Union, 361 U.S. 477, 488-89 (1960); Terminal R.R. Ass'n v. Brotherhood of R.R. Trainmen, 318 U.S. 1 (1943). *See generally* WELLINGTON, LABOR AND THE LEGAL PROCESS 57-60 (1968).

should have an impact on the court which hears the initial antitrust proceeding in which the pre-existing, non-bargained-for restraints are contested. In particular, the court should consider the potential for bargaining when it undertakes to fashion a remedy. Thus, the grant of relief will appropriately be in a form which does not unduly prejudice the bargaining rights of either side.

There are a number of respects in which this concern for the future bargaining relationship will influence the choice of remedies. As an initial matter, it would seem improper for a court to enter an order which sought to permanently enjoin the league-wide player restraints. If the player restraint or other device may be immunized by collective bargaining, the court should take steps to insure that opportunities for bargaining are not inhibited. If the existing precedents are to be respected, it must be accepted that the anti-competitive effect of player controls is less of a concern than the process through which they were devised. Thus, the court's judgment should not seek to permanently suppress such devices, but only to insure that they do not reappear apart from the bargaining process. Under this view, the courts' primary objective in fashioning a remedy would be to provide relief from the prior effects of the improper restraints and to insure that the future relationship of the parties proceeds on a lawful basis. Such retroactive relief will most often take the form of damages. To the extent that prospective relief was provided, it should be framed in terms which recognize the possibility that the "unlawful" restraints might be revived through collective bargaining. Thus, a permanent injunction, if one were issued, ought to be carefully limited so as only to preclude any future attempts by the employer to reimpose the restraints in disregard of his bargaining obligation.[630]

In addition, the order issued by the court ought to be framed so as to avoid restricting any right which either the employer or the union enjoys under the laws pertaining to collective bargaining. The judgment should not place undue restrictions on the right of either party to propose subjects for negotiation in future bargaining sessions. And whatever protection is afforded to individual players by the order which is entered, it must be accepted that the players' union can assume considerable prerogatives in bargaining away rights which the individual athletes would otherwise have if they had not bound themselves to a collective representative.[631]

It can probably also be agreed that the court's order should not operate to limit the steps which either side can take to further its own interests in the bargaining process. The exact implication of this general notion is somewhat uncertain, however. Presumably it can be accepted that the usual threats of strikes, lockouts, or other economic coercion should not be inhibited by the order emanating from a prior antitrust proceeding. A somewhat more difficult question is whether each side retains the prerogatives which it would otherwise

630. It should be noted that even though the district court in *Mackey* suggested that the Rozelle Rule was an illegal subject of bargaining, its injunction order directed only that the defendants refrain "from continuing, attempting to continue, or otherwise enforcing the Rozelle Rule...." It thus included no express prohibition on further bargaining between the parties. *See* 407 F. Supp. at 1011. The circuit court in *Mackey* went further. It rejected the characterization of the Rozelle Rule as an illegal subject of bargaining and specifically urged the parties to resolve their differences at the bargaining table. 543 F.2d at 623.

631. *See generally* text at notes 487-502, § 5.05 *supra*.

enjoy in the event there is no agreement in the negotiations. Particularly important are the rights which arise when an impasse is reached in the bargaining.[632] In such a situation, the federal labor law would normally permit the employer to make unilateral changes in working conditions as long as the changes are consistent with the terms previously offered to the union.[633] These rules on impasse raise an interesting problem for the court deciding the antitrust issue before serious arm's-length bargaining has taken place. Unilateral employer action following an impasse would appear to have the characteristics which have prompted courts to refuse to apply the exemption in the sports cases decided to date: a restraint imposed in these circumstances, on the one hand, inhibits competition and on the other, is not clothed with union approval. Yet, while the absence of union acceptance might normally foreclose application of the exemption,[634] it is not clear that this result should obtain where the unilateral action follows an honest attempt to secure agreement through collective bargaining. Some of the existing cases suggest that the availability of the labor exemption will be determined by a variable standard which takes account of the extent of bargaining which has actually occurred.[635] Future impasse cases on this point will likely present situations which differ markedly in the degree to which the substance of the employer's unilateral action has been influenced by the give and take of prior bargaining. In some situations, a court might well conclude that the union has had a sufficient impact in shaping the content of the employer's offers and that the matter ought to be resolved free of intervention by the courts. In light of that possibility, it would seem inappropriate for a court sitting in an antitrust proceeding to announce a rule which predetermined the result in the subsequent impasse situation. By the same token, it would seem that the court ought not take any action which might limit the employer's prerogatives in dealing with an impasse. That would seem to be a matter more appropriately dealt with after the question arises.

§ 5.07. The Player Restraints: The Substantive Antitrust Issues.

Prior sections have considered whether the player restraints used in professional sports will be immunized from antitrust scrutiny by application of

---

632. *See generally* NLRB v. U.S. Sonics Corp., 312 F.2d 610 (1st Cir. 1963); Pacific Gamble Robinson Co. v. NLRB, 186 F.2d 106 (6th Cir. 1950); NLRB v. U.S. Cold Storage Corp., 203 F.2d 924 (5th Cir.), *cert. denied,* 346 U.S. 818 (1953); MORRIS 330-31; Schatzki, *The Employer's Unilateral Act — A Per Se Violation — Sometimes,* 44 TEXAS L. REV. 470 (1966); Comment, *Impasse in Collective Bargaining,* 44 TEXAS L. REV. 769 (1966).

633. *See, e.g.,* Central Metallic Casket Co., 91 NLRB 572 (1950).

634. The existing precedents suggest that the labor exemption was intended for the protection and benefit of unions and, thus, union acquiescence in any resulting restraint is a necessary prerequisite before immunity will be granted. *See, e.g.,* Robertson v. National Basketball Ass'n, 389 F. Supp. 867, 884-86 (S.D.N.Y. 1975). *See* discussion at notes 609-10 *supra.*

635. It is interesting to note, for example, that the *Robertson* court did not specifically require an actual agreement on the matter of player restraints in suggesting the conditions under which immunity would be granted. The court stated: "Conceivably, if the restrictions were part of the union's policy deemed by the Player Association to be in the players' best interest, they could be exempt from the reach of the antitrust laws. . . . The proper inquiry in respect of this controversy is whether the challenged restraints were ever the 'subject of serious, intensive arm's-length collective bargaining.'" 389 F. Supp. at 895. Presumably the union's active participation in bargaining would indicate that it had "deemed [the restrictions] . . . to be in the players best interest," even if it had not approved the particular form of restraint.

the labor exemption.[636] It is clear that unless the restraints are the product of collective bargaining, that exemption will not be available[637] and, except in baseball,[638] the antitrust laws will apply with full force. In the present section, we examine the principles which will be applied when the merits of an antitrust claim are considered. As will be seen, this is another area in which the unique nature of the sports industry raises important questions about the applicability of doctrine which has been developed in other business settings. Thus, it is necessary to deal not only with the uncertainties of the antitrust law itself, but also with the larger question of whether the sports industry should be expected to act like other commercial ventures.

There are several different issues which arise in the controversy concerning the antitrust status of the player restraints. At the first level, there is a question as to whether the traditional restraints (reserve clause, indemnity rule, player draft) amount to *per se* violations of the antitrust laws. If no *per se* violation is found, it then must be determined whether those restraints are acceptable under the rule of reason. And even if these questions are answered as far as the traditional restraints are concerned, it is relevant to ask how other types of control devices, particularly those which are less restrictive, will be viewed by the courts. Some answers to these questions are suggested in the developing body of case law dealing with the traditional player restraints.[639] It must be accepted that the cases are not entirely consistent with one another, and there are many points which are yet to be explored in litigation. However, a review of the cases should indicate that the range of controversy has at least been narrowed somewhat.

The present discussion begins with the question: are the traditional player restraints *per se* violations of the antitrust laws? This issue has received considerable attention in the cases, and it is possible to give a somewhat more extensive analysis to this matter than to other aspects of the player restraint controversy. The case law which has developed also sheds some light on the other two issues mentioned above. Thus, we are given some indication of how the restraints will fare under a reasonableness standard, and at least some of the cases suggest the general characteristics of the restraints which leagues should adopt if they want to avoid antitrust problems in the future. The discussion of the cases in connection with the *per se* issue provides the occasion to indicate their implications for the other questions as well.

As suggested, we will begin by looking at the antitrust status of the traditional player restraints. The devices which have received the most attention in the cases are the draft system, the reserve clause, and the indemnity arrangements. An earlier section discusses the actual operation of these in more detail.[640] For the present, it is sufficient to note that the common characteristic of the restraints which have been involved in litigation is that they operate as

---

636. See §§ 5.04-.06 *supra.*

637. See § 5.06 *supra.*

638. As previously discussed, there is little doubt that baseball's antitrust immunity extends to matters concerning club-player relations. See § 5.02 *supra.*

639. A general listing of cases and commentaries dealing with the player restraints can be found at note 154, § 5.03 *supra.*

640. See § 5.03 *supra.*

a pervasive restriction on the players' mobility. Thus, the draft systems which have been contested are those which give the drafting team a perpetual right to negotiate for the player's services.[641] Similarly, the disputed reserve clauses have operated to bind the athlete to his club until his contract is sold or traded.[642] Although structurally different, the indemnity arrangements have also operated to grant perpetual rights to the club which employed an athlete.[643] Under such a system, the player can move to another team only if his former employer's right to compensation has been satisfied. In the following discussion, these will be referred to as the traditional or pervasive player restraints.

    a. Background. The question of the status of player restraints under the antitrust laws requires that attention first be given to the basic issue of whether the controls are to be evaluated under the rule of reason or are to be characterized as *per se* violations of the Sherman Act. Others have undertaken the task of explaining the origins of these two approaches to applying the prohibitions against restraints on trade.[644] For the present, it is sufficient to note the differences between them. On its face, section 1 of the Sherman Act states that "every" contract or combination in restraint of trade is illegal.[645] Despite the breadth of this condemnation, the Supreme Court early concluded that the language was intended to prohibit only those restraints which were unreasonable.[646] The determination of reasonableness normally required an extensive judicial inquiry into the nature, purpose, and effect of the restraint. When the reasonableness of a restraint is fully investigated, that which needs to be considered includes "the facts peculiar to the business to which the restraint is applied; its condition before and after the restraint was imposed; the nature of the restraint and its effect, actual or probable." [647] Also to be analyzed are "the history of the restraint, the evil believed to exist, the reason for

---

    641. *See, e.g.,* Smith v. National Football League, 420 F. Supp. 738 (D.D.C. 1976); Robertson v. National Basketball Ass'n, 389 F. Supp. 867 (S.D.N.Y. 1975).

    642. *See, e.g.,* Philadelphia World Hockey Club, Inc. v. Philadelphia Hockey Club, Inc., 351 F. Supp. 462 (E.D. Pa. 1972).

    643. *See, e.g.,* Mackey v. National Football League, 407 F. Supp. 1000 (D. Minn. 1975), *modified,* 543 F.2d 606 (8th Cir. 1976).

    644. There are numerous legal commentaries dealing generally with the *per se* and rule of reason standards. The reader looking for a basic introduction might wish to consult E. GELLHORN, ANTITRUST LAW AND ECONOMICS IN A NUTSHELL chs. 5-6 (1976). The intricacies of the issues in this area are treated in a more exhaustive fashion in Bork, *The Rule of Reason and the Per Se Concept: Price Fixing and Market Division, Parts I & II,* 74 YALE L.J. 775 (1965); 75 *id.* 373 (1966). Other general authorities include the following: J. VON KALINOWSKI, ANTITRUST LAWS AND TRADE REGULATIONS (16 BUSINESS ORGANIZATIONS 1971) §§ 6.01-.02 [hereinafter cited as VON KALINOWSKI]; Barber, *Refusals to Deal Under the Federal Antitrust Law,* 103 U. PA. L. REV. 847 (1955); Handler, *Recent Developments in Antitrust Laws: 1958-59,* 59 COLUM. L. REV. 843 (1959); von Kalinowski, *The Per Se Doctrine — An Emerging Philosophy of Antitrust Law,* 11 U.C.L.A. L. REV. 569 (1964); Van Cise, *The Future of Per Se in Antitrust Law,* 50 VA. L. REV. 1165 (1964); Note, *Trade Association Exclusionary Practices: An Affirmative Role for the Rule of Reason,* 66 COLUM. L. REV. 1486 (1966).

    645. Every contract, combination in the form of trust of   otherwise, or conspiracy, in restraint of trade or commerce among the several States, or with foreign nations, is hereby declared to be illegal. . . . Sherman Antitrust Act § 1, 15 U.S.C. § 1 (1970).

    646. *See, e.g.,* Chicago Board of Trade v. United States, 246 U.S. 231 (1918); Standard Oil Co. v. United States, 221 U.S. 1 (1911). *See also* United States v. American Tobacco Co., 221 U.S. 106 (1911).

    647. Chicago Board of Trade v. United States, 246 U.S. 231, 238 (1918).

adopting the particular remedy [and] the purpose or end sought to be attained . . ." [648] It is obvious that a full exploration of all of these matters at trial is likely to involve a great expenditure of time and effort. This, in fact, happens and antitrust litigation is typically a laborious process requiring extensive pre-trial discovery and review of documents, extensive fact gathering, and lengthy trial presentations, including complicated testimony by expert witnesses.

The Supreme Court recognized the burden which such litigation placed upon the plaintiff seeking redress under the antitrust laws. In the Court's view, the extensive economic inquiry was often unnecessary because prior cases had established that the particular practice would ultimately be found to be unreasonable. The Court's response was to announce that some types of activities could be deemed *per se* unreasonable:

> [T]here are certain agreements or practices which because of their pernicious effect on competition and lack of any redeeming virtue are *conclusively presumed* to be unreasonable and therefore illegal without elaborate inquiry as to the precise harm they have caused or the business excuse for their use.[649]

While there is a debate among scholars as to the precise procedural impact of the *per se* rule,[650] it can be noted that the rule is often used in summary proceedings to grant relief to the plaintiff without requiring an exhaustive factual inquiry.[651]

As the Supreme Court has candidly admitted, this approach not only lightens the plaintiff's burden but also recognizes limitations in the judicial institution itself:

> The fact is that courts are of limited utility in examining difficult economic problems. Our inability to weigh, in any meaningful sense, destruction of competition in one sector of the economy against promotion of competition in another sector is one important reason we have formulated *per se* rules.[652]

There are a number of different practices which have been found to be *per se* illegal. Those most commonly cited include (1) price-fixing, as where competitors at the same level (*e.g.* retail or wholesale) reach agreements which have the effect of lessening price competition;[653] (2) divisions of markets

---

648. *Id.*

649. Northern Pacific Ry. v. United States, 356 U.S. 1, 5 (1958) (emphasis added).

650. Some have argued that a finding of a *per se* violation creates a presumption of illegality which in some cases may be overcome by a showing of justification. *See* Van Cise, *The Future of Per Se in Antitrust Law, supra* note 644, at 1173-74. *See also* Bork, *The Rule of Reason and the Per Se Concept: Price Fixing and Market Division, Parts I & II, supra* note 644.

651. *See, e.g.,* Silver v. New York Stock Exchange, 373 U.S. 341 (1963); White Motor Co. v. United States, 372 U.S. 253 (1963); Kapp v. National Football League, 390 F. Supp. 73 (N.D. Cal. 1974); Blalock v. Ladies Professional Golf Ass'n, 359 F. Supp. 1260 (N.D. Ga. 1973); Denver Rockets v. All-Pro Management, Inc., 325 F. Supp. 1049 (C.D. Cal. 1971).

652. United States v. Topco Associates, Inc., 405 U.S. 596, 609-10 (1972).

It should be noted that policies other than the avoidance of burdensome litigation are promoted by the *per se* approach. The rule also serves to clearly demarcate certain types of prohibited conduct and thus affords businesses guidelines for structuring their affairs to comply with the antitrust laws. *See* Bork, *The Rule of Reason and the Per Se Concept: Price Fixing and Market Division, Part I,* 74 YALE L.J. 775, 832, 840-41 (1965). The *per se* prohibition on price-fixing is an example of the Supreme Court's efforts to minimize the potential for misinterpretation of the breadth of the intended restriction. *See, e.g.,* United States v. Socony Vacuum Oil Co., 310 U.S. 150 (1940).

653. *See, e.g.,* United States v. National Ass'n of Real Estate Boards, 339 U.S. 485 (1950). The prohibition extends to vertical price-fixing as well as the sort of horizontal agreements mentioned

between competitors, as where sellers mutually agree not to invade each others' sales territories; [654] and (3) tying arrangements, in which the sale of one product is conditioned upon the buyer's agreement to purchase another product from the seller, as where the manufacturer of a computer requires buyers to purchase all of their software needs from it; [655] and (4) group boycotts, where commercial entities agree to refuse to deal with another entity for the purpose of improperly influencing the latter's business practices.[656]

In the antitrust cases involving attacks upon the player restraint systems, a good deal of attention has been given to the question of whether the various control devices are sufficiently similar to the arrangements identified above to warrant their being classified as *per se* unreasonable and thus violative of the Sherman Act. Various characterizations have been used. There has been some suggestion that devices such as a player draft and a reserve clause should be regarded as amounting to an illegal scheme for the horizontal division of the market for athletic talent.[657] The premise of this view is that competitors operating at the same commercial level — club owners seeking to buy new talent — have divided up the market for playing talent by agreeing to respect the exclusive right of each club to deal with particular players. It has also been contended that these restraints are analogous to a price-fixing scheme since the "buyers" of athletic talent in the particular league have agreed not to compete with one another, with the result that the "price" which athletes receive for their talent is reduced.[658] However, the contention which has received the most attention in the cases is that the league's enforcement of the player restraints amounts to an impermissible group boycott.[659] The theory of this argument is that the clubs within the league are all potential competitors for the purchase of the players' services, but through various league rules, they have agreed among themselves not to deal with players except upon the uniform terms embodied in the player restraints. This concerted refusal to deal is alleged to be anticompetitive in at least two respects. Not only are players precluded from negotiating contracts which do not include the restraints,[660] but also the terms uniformly imposed are designed to lessen competition among the various clubs.[661] Predictably, the leagues take the position that the use of the *per se*

---

in the text. *See, e.g.,* United States v. Socony Vacuum Oil Co., 310 U.S. 150 (1940); Dr. Miles Medical Co. v. John D. Park & Sons Co., 220 U.S. 373 (1911).

654. *See, e.g.,* United States v. Topco Assoc., Inc., 405 U.S. 596 (1972); Timken Roller Bearing Co. v. United States, 341 U.S. 593 (1951).

655. *See, e.g.,* Fortner Enterprises v. United States Steel Corp., 394 U.S. 495 (1969); Northern Pacific Ry. v. United States, 356 U.S. 1 (1958).

656. *See, e.g.,* Klor's, Inc. v. Broadway-Hale Stores, 359 U.S. 207 (1959); Fashion Originators' Guild of America v. FTC, 312 U.S. 457 (1941).

657. *See* Robertson v. National Basketball Ass'n, 389 F. Supp. 867, 893 (S.D.N.Y. 1975).

658. *See id.*

659. *See, e.g.,* Mackey v. National Football League, 407 F. Supp. 1000 (D. Minn. 1975), *modified,* 543 F.2d 606 (8th Cir. 1976); Robertson v. National Basketball Ass'n, 389 F. Supp. 867 (S.D.N.Y. 1975); Kapp v. National Football League, 390 F. Supp. 73 (N.D. Cal. 1974).

660. In many proceedings, particularly those dealing with league practices other than the reserve system, there is often a question as to the extent to which the league will permit athletes to vary the terms of the standard player contract. *See, e.g.,* Chuy v. Philadelphia Eagles, 407 F. Supp. 717 (E.D. Pa. 1976). The cases considering such devices as the draft, indemnity rules and option clauses give little indication that these devices are ever modified in individual negotiations.

661. In light of the leagues' justification for the player restraints — that they serve to limit the right of successful clubs to continually acquire the best talent — there seems little basis for

classification is inappropriate and the restraints ought to be tested under the rule of reason.

The premise of the leagues' argument is that the peculiar needs of the sports industry require that the individual club-firms be allowed to engage in certain types of collective action which might not be tolerated by other businesses. Since this claim that "sports is different" is central to the *per se* — rule of reason controversy, it warrants a further elaboration. It should be noted that the arguments put forth by the leagues are really intended to answer two different points. In asserting that their sports ventures are economically unique, the leagues, of course, hope to avoid the *per se* classification. But they also expect that when their case is submitted to detailed examination under the rule of reason, the special needs of the industry will compel a finding that restraints on mobility are reasonable. Thus, while the argument which follows has its most immediate impact on the threshold question of the standard of review to be applied, it also anticipates the criteria which will be selected and addresses the merits of the controversy.

There are several facets to the league's defense of its practices. Most commentators, including those otherwise unsympathetic to the player restraints, have recognized that the success of a league's sports venture depends upon the unpredictability of the outcome of on-the-field competition between clubs.[662] Fan interest, and hence club revenues from gate receipts and television and radio contracts seem to bear a direct relationship to the league's ability to stage a series of events in which either participant has a realistic chance of winning.[663] And, of course, the greater the unpredictability of the outcome of particular contests, the more interest there will be in pennant races or other championship competition. The goal of "evenness" in on-the-field competition is

---

arguing that the restraints do not lessen competition for players' services. *See* text at notes 664-65 *infra.*

662. *See, e.g.,* H. DEMMERT, THE ECONOMICS OF PROFESSIONAL TEAM SPORTS 10-11 (1973) [hereinafter cited as DEMMERT]; Rottenberg, *The Baseball Player's Labor Market,* 64 J. POL. ECON. 242 (1956); Comment, *The Super Bowl and the Sherman Act: Professional Team Sports and the Antitrust Laws,* 81 HARV. L. REV. 418, 421 (1967); Comment, *Player Control Mechanisms in Professional Team Sports,* 34 U. PITT. L. REV. 645, 651 (1973); Note, *The True Story of What Happens When the Big Kids Say, "It's my football, and you'll either play by my rules or you won't play at all,"* 55 NEB. L. REV. 335, 346-47 (1976). *See also* Noll, *Alternatives in Sports Policy* in GOVERNMENT AND THE SPORTS BUSINESS 411, 415-17 (R. Noll ed. 1974); Quirk & El Hodiri, *The Economic Theory of a Professional Sports League* in *id.,* 33, 34-37.

663. The impact of relative team strength on attendance is illustrated by the findings of an informal study made by Professor Henry Demmert. Using the 1971 baseball season as a sample, Demmert classified clubs as "Good" or "Poor" depending on their league standings. He then made random samplings of attendance to determine the effect of various match-ups. As indicated by the following chart, there were significantly different results depending upon the relative quality of the competitors.

Visiting Team	Home Team	Attendance
Good	Good	24,610
Good	Poor	11,349
Poor	Good	16,066
Poor	Poor	9,806

While this rough survey does not fully take account of differences in metropolitan areas, weather and the like, it does serve to confirm the likelihood of a real relationship between unpredictability and fan interest. DEMMERT 11.

promoted to the extent that the playing strength of the respective clubs is balanced. Problems arise, however, because of the significant differences among the member franchises which will affect their ability to attract players. There are several differences which are thought to be important. For example, the notion that "nothing succeeds like success" may have particular relevance for professional sports. It is argued that if given a choice, most highly skilled athletes would prefer to play for a winning team. For a number of reasons, not the least of which are pride and personal satisfaction, weak clubs would likely encounter difficulty in attracting talent and, it is contended, the result would be that the clubs at the top of the standings would continually reinforce their position. On another level, there are differences among clubs in terms of their relative wealth. Franchises located in the largest metropolitan areas are usually able to attract more fans and thus generate more revenue than clubs which operate in smaller cities.[664] Without some restraint on a club's ability to acquire playing talent, it is argued, the franchises operating in the largest metropolitan areas would soon purchase the best players and dominate on-the-field competition.[665] And if the elements of "wealth" and "success" become concentrated in a few clubs, it would be difficult for other clubs to acquire the talent necessary to mount a successful on-the-field challenge. It is predicted that in the end, the quality of the sport's product would suffer, perhaps to the point that the league could no longer operate profitably.

Much of the debate in the sports area deals with the issue of the methods which the league can and should use to achieve a balance in playing strength. The owners contend that the player restraints are necessary to insure that less lucrative and less successful franchises have an opportunity to hire and retain high caliber talent. Thus, it is argued that a player draft, in which the clubs with the worst won-lost records are given the first selections, insures that weaker teams can replenish their playing talent. Relatedly, it is felt that some device is needed to insure that a team's strength is not diluted by a subsequent movement of a player to another club. The reserve and indemnity systems are thought to achieve this result.

The assumptions made about the stabilizing effects of the player restraints are subject to some debate.[666] However, for the present discussion it is sufficient to note that the basic thrust of the aforementioned arguments is that it is inappropriate to treat professional sports under the same precedents which govern the more common forms of business ventures. In this connection, it is emphasized that clubs within a league differ from businesses which compete against one another in other industries. A business firm normally seeks to sell as much of its product as it can and is typically indifferent whether, in doing so, it drives its competition out of business. But, for the reasons given above,

---

664. *See, e.g.,* DEMMERT 55-76; Quirk & El Hodiri, *The Economic Theory of a Sports League, supra* note 662, at 33-37.

665. It can be accepted that some franchises located outside of the largest metropolitan areas will enjoy economic success. This may be due to factors such as the particular managerial skills of the owners and the lack of other entertainment alternatives. By the same token, location in a metropolitan area is not the only ingredient of economic success. *See* Quirk & El Hodiri, *The Economic Theory of a Sports League, supra* note 662, at 41-45.

666. *See* text at notes 787-801 *infra.*

a sports club is vitally concerned about the financial well-being of other members of the same league.[667] A club cannot compete too well in its efforts to accumulate the best talent if the continued success of the league is to be preserved. Since the usual assumption about the desirability of inter-firm competition does not apply to leagues, it is argued, the courts ought not apply principles, such as the *per se* rule, which are premised on that notion.

b. Supreme Court Decisions. The debate about whether the leagues' player controls come within the *per se* doctrine has necessarily drawn heavily upon Supreme Court precedents. However, a review of those decisions suggests that they offer some support to each of the positions put forth and do not clearly compel the application of either the *per se* classification or the rule of reason. The cases suggest that while the Court is generally inclined to treat as *per se* unreasonable joint efforts of competitors which affect the competitive position of outsiders, it is also prepared to recognize that there may be exceptional cases in which the peculiar nature of the private regulation requires that a more detailed inquiry be made.

Klor's, Inc. v. Broadway-Hale Stores [668] is frequently cited for the proposition that all group boycotts involve *per se* violations. Klor's alleged that the large Broadway-Hale chain had used its massive buying power to exact agreements from certain manufacturers and distributors of name-brand appliances not to sell their goods to Klor's or to sell them only on unfavorable terms. The defendants did not deny this allegation but moved for dismissal of the complaint on the grounds that there was no public injury. There were hundreds of other dealers in the area who sold the brands in question, and it was alleged that there had been no proof that the restraint in question had any effect on the price which the public paid or the quality it received.[669] The Supreme Court held that the district court had acted improperly in dismissing the complaint. Significant for the present discussion is the Court's unequivocal statement that

> Group boycotts, or concerted refusals by traders to deal with other traders, have long been held to be in the forbidden [*per se*] category.[670]

It would be contended that an agreement among league members not to contract with a player when another club held his draft rights or reserve rights amounts to a refusal "by traders to deal with other traders" and hence falls within "the forbidden category." The leagues would insist, however, that the agreement upon the restrictions was reached in pursuit of a legitimate goal, that is, the preservation of relative playing strengths. Language in another Supreme Court case seems pertinent in determining whether such a justification can avoid the *per se* rule. In *Fashion Originators' Guild of America v. FTC,*[671] the plaintiffs included manufacturers and designers of original dress designs who attempted to discourage other manufacturers from copying or pirating the unpatented

---

667. *See, e.g.,* United States v. National Football League, 116 F. Supp. 319, 323 (E.D. Pa. 1953); Rottenberg, *The Baseball Players' Labor Market, supra* note 662, at 254-55.

668. 359 U.S. 207 (1959).

669. *Id.* at 209-10.

670. *Id.* at 212. The Court added that such boycotts "have not been saved by allegations that they were reasonable in the specific circumstances ...."

671. 312 U.S. 457 (1941).

designs and selling them at lower prices. The device chosen to stop this practice was a secondary boycott in which the Guild members refused to sell to retailers who also handled the cheaper copies. The Guild argued that the pirating by other manufacturers was tortious under state law and that the resulting boycott was thus undertaken for a proper purpose.[672] The Court upheld the FTC's refusal to hear this evidence. In the Court's view,

> the reasonableness of the methods pursued by the combination to accomplish its unlawful object is no more material than would be the reasonableness of the prices fixed by unlawful combinations.[673]

The Court suggested that the Guild should have directly pursued its state law remedies and not undertaken its own method of extra-judicial enforcement. The vices which the Court identified in the Guild's arrangement were similar to those which would be attributed to player restraints: the arrangement "narrowed the outlets" through which the affected parties could trade; it subjected non-complying parties to a boycott, and it "[took] away the freedom of action" of members of the combination in operating their businesses.[674]

Klor's and *Fashion Originators' Guild* could be read as supporting the principle that any concerted refusal to deal among commercial entities is *per se* a violation of the Sherman Act, without regard to the purpose or intent of the boycott. Some commentators have so interpreted the cases.[675] However, further analysis should suggest that the status of such combinations is not so easily resolved. Despite the language in *Klor's* which rather explicitly proscribes all group boycotts, it seems clear that neither the Supreme Court nor the lower courts are prepared to condemn out of hand every arrangement which might be characterized as a refusal to deal. Evidence of this is found in the Supreme Court's opinion in *Silver v. New York Stock Exchange*.[676] In that case the defendant Exchange had ordered several of its members to disconnect direct telephone connections with Silver, a non-member broker-dealer. The consequence was that Silver's business suffered considerably. Silver sued, alleging violations of sections 1 and 2 of the Sherman Act. The district court held the defendant's action to be a *per se* violation.[677] The court of appeals reversed, finding the Exchange exempt from the Sherman Act because it was exercising power granted by the Securities Exchange Act.[678] The Supreme Court, in an opinion authored by Justice Goldberg, reversed this finding of the appellate court. Justice Goldberg reviewed the facts and noted the significant volume of business which the plaintiff had lost as a result of the Exchange's action. Finding

---

672. *Id.* at 467.
673. *Id.* at 468.
674. *Id.* at 465.
675. *See, e.g.,* Comment, *Antitrust and Professional Sports: Does Anyone Play by the Rules of the Game?,* 22 CATH. U. L. REV. 403, 408-11 (1973). *See also* Sobel, *The Emancipation of Professional Athletes,* 3 WES. ST. U. L. REV. 185, 214-15 (1976).
676. 373 U.S. 292 (1963). Among the cases specifically commenting on the implications of *Silver* for the sports area are Blalock v. Ladies Professional Golf Ass'n, 359 F. Supp. 1260 (N.D. Ga. 1973) and Denver Rockets v. All-Pro Management, Inc., 325 F. Supp. 1049 (C.D. Cal. 1971). *See also* Note, *Trade Association Exclusionary Practices: An Affirmative Role for the Rule of Reason,* 66 COLUM. L. REV. 1486 (1966).
677. 196 F. Supp. 209 (S.D.N.Y. 1961).
678. 302 F.2d 714 (2d Cir. 1962).

that group action was present, he cited *Klor's* for the principle that such concerted refusals to deal were treated as *per se* unreasonable.[679] This general conclusion was significantly qualified, however, by the Court's further statement that "absent any justification derived from the policy of another statute or otherwise," the Exchange's action would violate the antitrust laws.[680] The Court went on to hold that no such justification could be found in *Silver*, for while the Exchange had disciplinary power under the securities acts, in this case it should have given the non-member notice and an opportunity to be heard, protections which the Court apparently felt were required by the antitrust laws themselves.[681]

The case is important for several reasons. Its most immediate impact has been in providing lower courts with a standard by which to evaluate the internal regulatory actions of legitimate private associations. The courts have been willing to accept the right of certain types of private groups to establish eligibility and disciplinary rules, but have insisted that these be administered in a manner which is procedurally fair.[682] For our present inquiry, *Silver* is important for its recognition that the *per se* prohibition on group action is not as pervasive as *Klor's* might suggest. Clearly the Court seems prepared to apply the rule of reason when a concerted refusal to deal is justified "by the policy of another statute or otherwise." Some might read this language as carving out a very narrow exception for internal discipline mandated by legislative action,[683] but a strong case can be made for the view that the Court in *Silver* was implicitly recognizing that *Klor's* had spoken in too broad terms. Both before and after *Klor's*, lower courts refused to condemn all joint action which had an effect on competition.[684] Indeed, in defining the antitrust offense, it appears that the controlling element is not the fact that a group of traders acted together, but rather the purpose for which they acted and the degree of economic harm which resulted.[685] Any suggestion in *Fashion Originators' Guild* that the question of justification is wholly irrelevant seems to have been significantly qualified in *Silver*, a qualification which conforms the Court's statement of the law to what lower courts were, in fact, doing.

The purpose or object of some group action will be so obviously impermissible as to warrant a *per se* condemnation. For example, *Klor's* and *Fashion Originators' Guild* can be read as holding that an intent to destroy or coerce a competitor will not be tolerated. But the applicability of the classification

---

679. 373 U.S. at 348.

680. *Id.* at 348-49.

681. *Id.* at 361-63.

682. *See, e.g.,* Carver v. New York Stock Exchange, 371 F.2d 661 (2d Cir. 1967); Blalock v. Ladies Professional Golf Ass'n, 359 F. Supp. 1260 (N.D. Ga. 1973). *See generally* Note, *Trade Association Exclusionary Practices: An Affirmative Role for the Rule of Reason, supra* note 676.

683. *See* Blalock v. Ladies Professional Golf Ass'n, 359 F. Supp. 1260, 1266-67 (N.D. Ga. 1973).

684. *See, e.g.,* Bridge Corp. of America v. American Contract Bridge League, Inc., 428 F.2d 1365 (1970); Deesen v. Professional Golfers' Ass'n, 358 F.2d 165 (9th Cir. 1966); STP Corp. v. United States Auto Club, Inc., 286 F. Supp. 146 (S.D. Ind. 1968); Molinas v. National Basketball Ass'n, 190 F. Supp. 241 (S.D.N.Y. 1961); United States v. United States Trotting Ass'n, 1960 Trade Cas. ¶ 69,761 (S.D. Ohio).

685. *See* Barber, *Refusals to Deal Under the Federal Antitrust Laws,* 103 U. PA. L. REV. 847, 876-7 (1955). *See also* Bridge Corp. of America v. American Contract Bridge League, Inc., 428 F.2d 1365, 1370 (9th Cir. 1970).

becomes less certain where the group's action lacks the explicit, self-serving object found in those cases.[686] Particularly difficult are cases in which there is an undeniable lessening of competition but where the group can allege that special circumstances necessitate the restraints.

The player restraints in professional sports present this difficulty. Devices such as the draft system, reserve clause, and Rozelle Rule unquestionably have an effect upon competition among the clubs which buy the services of professional ball players. The clubs will contend, however, that the sports industry is one in which the retraints can be justified "by ... statute or otherwise." The justification, it will be alleged, is found in the peculiar economics of the industry which, in distinct contrast to other industries, require that no firm compete too well in its efforts to acquire the highest quality raw materials available. But this justification is troublesome. It seeks to protect group action undertaken with a specific intent to eliminate competition, and the only rationale offered is that the *competition itself* is undesirable. While the Court may not have answered other group boycott questions in *Klor's* and *Fashion Originators' Guild*, it did seem to indicate that such a direct and specific anti-competitive purpose was not to be tolerated. Thus, the perplexing question which arises is whether the Court ever contemplated, in *Silver* or its other decisions, that such an explicit attempt to eliminate inter-firm bidding could avoid a summary condemnation.

c. The Sports Cases. The question of whether the traditional player restraints should be treated as *per se* illegal has received attention in several different lower court decisions. In light of the uncertain implications of the Supreme Court precedents discussed above, it is not surprising that the sports cases have not produced a uniform answer. The developments on this issue have followed an interesting pattern. The earliest decisions found the courts skeptical of the restraints but unwilling to apply the *per se* concept because of the peculiar economics of the industry.[687] Then there appeared a series of decisions in which the courts spoke in more bold terms and seemed prepared to find the restrictions illegal under the summary standard.[688] But these decisions did not represent the sort of formidable authority which would finally settle the controversy. There were defects in the analysis which was applied as well as a decided tendency to engage in mere label-pinning by summarily categorizing the practices as naked restraints on trade. These decisions turned out not to be the final word. In the first case to reach the appellate level, the court rejected the use of the *per se* concept.[689] In large measure, this decision represented a return to the reasoning of the earliest cases. The unique relationship between the clubs within

---

686. *See generally* Note, *Trade Association Exclusionary Practices: An Affirmative Role for the Rule of Reason, supra* note 676.

687. *See, e.g.,* Flood v. Kuhn, 309 F. Supp. 793, 801 n.26 (S.D.N.Y.), *final decision,* 316 F. Supp. 271 (S.D.N.Y. 1970), *aff'd,* 443 F.2d 264 (2d Cir. 1971), *aff'd,* 407 U.S. 258 (1972); Philadelphia World Hockey Club, Inc. v. Philadelphia Hockey Club, Inc., 351 F. Supp. 462, 503-04 (E.D. Pa. 1972).

688. Mackey v. National Football League, 407 F. Supp. 1000 (D. Minn. 1975), *rev'd on this point,* 543 F.2d 606 (8th Cir. 1976); Robertson v. National Basketball Ass'n, 389 F. Supp. 867 (S.D.N.Y. 1975); Kapp v. National Football League, 390 F. Supp. 73 (N.D. Cal. 1974).

689. *See* Mackey v. National Football League, 543 F.2d 606 (8th Cir. 1976), *modifying* 407 F. Supp. 1000 (D. Minn. 1975).

a league was thought to require a more deliberate inquiry into the justification for the restrictions on player mobility.

But the cases decided on the *per se* question also indicate that this may not be the issue which is ultimately most important. In two of the cases, the courts did not rely solely on their finding of *per se* illegality and went on to evaluate the restraints under the alternative rule of reason standard. In each instance, the league rules were found to be illegal under this criteria as well.[690] It appears that this view may be the one which prevails with regard to the traditional restraints. Thus, even if the leagues are able to avoid the *per se* classification, their victory may offer little solace.

A review of the cases will indicate more clearly how the range of controversy on both the *per se* and rule of reason issues narrowed as the courts gave increasingly more careful attention to the leagues' practices. This review should also provide the background against which we can consider the important issues which remain. As will be seen, the prospect of future litigation on other types of player restraints requires that there be a clearer definition of the role of the *per se* concept in this area. Further, the existing precedents provide the main source of guidance in defining the types of future controls which will be acceptable under a rule of reason analysis.

1. *Early Cases.*

The question of whether baseball's reserve clause was *per se* illegal was considered by Judge Cooper in the district court proceedings in *Flood v. Kuhn.*[691] The precedential value of this aspect of the case is somewhat debatable, for, as has been noted above, both the lower courts and the Supreme Court ultimately decided that baseball's reserve system was not subject to review under the antitrust laws. Yet, in light of the fact that the district court proceedings in *Flood v. Kuhn* involved a thorough inquiry into the sport's practices, Judge Cooper's view should not be lightly dismissed. In an initial proceeding on plaintiff's request for a preliminary injunction, Judge Cooper noted that most concerted refusals to deal are treated as *per se* violations, but added that he was

> impressed by defendant's argument that the rule of reason should govern here . . . since it is generally conceded that some form of reserve system is essential to the very maintenance of the "joint venture" of organized professional baseball.[692]

In support of this view, the court cited *Silver* and *an earlier case, Chicago Board of Trade v. United States,*[693] in which the Court recognized that some types of industry self-regulation should be evaluated under the rule of reason. Judge Cooper added, however, that the existing reserve system appeared to impose excessive restraints and was likely to be found unreasonable if reviewed on the merits.[694] Later, after a trial which involved extensive testimony on the operation of the reserve system, Judge Cooper issued another opinion in which

---

690. *See* Mackey v. National Football League, 407 F. Supp. 1000 (D. Minn. 1975), *modified,* 543 F.2d 606 (8th Cir. 1976); Smith v. Pro-Football, Inc., 420 F. Supp. 738 (D.D.C. 1976).

691. 309 F. Supp. 793 (S.D.N.Y.) *final decision,* 316 F. Supp. 271 (S.D.N.Y. 1970), *aff'd,* 443 F.2d 264 (2d Cir. 1971), *aff'd,* 407 U.S. 258 (1972).

692. 309 F. Supp. at 801 n.26.

693. 246 U.S. 231 (1918).

694. 309 F. Supp. at 801 n.26.

he reiterated, again in dicta, that the reserve system could not be condemned out of hand:

> Clearly the preponderance of credible proof does not favor elimination of the reserve clause. With the sole exception of plaintiff [Curt Flood] himself, it shows that even plaintiff's witnesses do not contend that it is wholly undesirable; in fact they regard substantial portions meritorious.[695]

Judge Cooper added that the parties should resort to arbitration or negotiation to "extract such troublesome fault as may exist in the present system." [696] Thus, while baseball's player controls might have encountered difficulty under the rule of reason standard, Judge Cooper apparently thought it inappropriate to classify the restraints as *per se* unreasonable.

Another form of reserve clause, that employed by the National Hockey League, was considered in *Philadelphia World Hockey Club, Inc. v. Philadelphia Hockey Club, Inc.*[697] The primary plaintiff in the case, the rival World Hockey Association, raised two separate complaints against the NHL and its reserve system. Relying on section 2 of the Sherman Act, the WHA alleged that the established league had used devices such as the reserve clause and various affiliation agreements to secure for itself a monopoly position in the supplying of hockey exhibitions. In a separate count of its complaint, the WHA alleged that even apart from the monopoly position of the NHL, the league's reserve clause constituted an improper restraint on trade under section 1 of the Sherman Act, a claim similar to that which would be raised by a player attacking his league's restraint system. The district court eventually issued a preliminary injunction on the basis of the section 2 (monopolization) complaint.[698] However, the court declined to grant relief on the section 1 claim and its reasons are instructive for the present inquiry.[699]

The plaintiffs had alleged that the player restraints constituted a *per se* violation of section 1. The court found that the WHA had presented "a not insubstantial" case in support of its contention, but ultimately declined to treat the matter in the critical summary proceeding. The court indicated that it desired "a fuller record" before deciding the issue and did not explicitly disclaim the possibility that it might later find a *per se* violation.[700] However, some of the language used strongly suggests that it was inclined to pursue the more complete inquiry required by a rule of reason approach. One passage from the court's opinion indicated that it was prepared to give some credence to the arguments traditionally made in favor of player restraints. The court stated:

> For maximum customer receptivity and profit it is in the best interest of any club that its opponents not generally be viewed by the public as totally incompetent and utterly unable to compete effectively. For if the latter occurs, thousands of customers will not spend their dollars for tickets to view hundreds of games when the contest seems to

---

695. 316 F. Supp. at 276.
696. *Id.*
697. 351 F. Supp. 462 (E.D. Pa. 1972).
698. *See id.* at 517-19.
699. *Id.* at 503-04.
700. *Id.* at 504.

present no more of a challenge than an ant confronting an elephant. Thus, if it is not possible to keep the competitive challenge of all teams within some reasonable parameters, some type of intraleague reserve clause or system may be desirable and in fact necessary.[701]

The further proceedings on the section 1 issue were never held. However, the NHL responded to the section 2 injunction by reaching an accord with the WHA concerning interleague movement of players.[702]

2. *Kapp Case.*

The NFL player restraints received their first major test under the *per se*-rule of reason dichotomy in *Kapp v. National Football League.*[703] The court's opinion used language which supported the use of the rule of reason, but the ultimate result was not much different than that which would have resulted under the *per se* test. In many respects, the opinion is truly puzzling and it is not certain that it provides clear precedent for either side of the present controversy. The case involved allegations by an individual player, Joe Kapp, that various league practices amounted to a group boycott. Specifically he claimed that the draft system, tampering rule, option clause, Rozelle Rule, and standard player contract were imposed upon him and other players by the implicit threat of the league clubs that they would boycott any player who refused to be bound by them. Kapp alleged that he had been subjected to such a boycott because of his refusal to sign a standard player contract.

In addressing the question of the standard against which the player restraints were to be tested, Judge Sweigert concluded that

> in this particular field of sports league activities the purposes of the antitrust laws can be just as well served (if not better served) by the basic antitrust reasonableness test as by the absolute *per se* test sometimes applied by courts in other fields.[704]

The court offered several reasons for its preference for the rule of reason test. It noted other cases, specifically *Flood v. Kuhn* and *Philadelphia World Hockey,* in which the courts had found the *per se* test to be "inappropriate [for] . . . league sports activities."[705] Further, various federal congressional and executive department interpretations seemed to favor this view.[706] The court also observed, probably incorrectly, that applying the *per se* label would tend to preclude subsequent collective bargaining on these matters between clubs and players' unions.[707] A final reason put forth was less clearly stated. The court

---

701. *Id.*

702. The subsequent history of *Philadelphia World Hockey* is discussed in § 5.03 *supra.*

703. 390 F. Supp. 73 (N.D. Cal. 1974), *noted in* 55 NEB. L. REV. 335 (1976); 4 FORD. URBAN L.J. 581 (1976).

704. 390 F. Supp. at 82.

705. *Id.* at 81.

706. The court referred to legislation which exempted the AFL-NFL merger and certain sports broadcasting practices from the antitrust laws, as well as proposals for broader sports exemptions. The executive action referred to involved the Justice Department's acknowledgment that the special nature of league sports required restraints which would not be tolerated in other industries. *See* 390 F. Supp. at 79-80, nn.4-5.

707. As discussed above, Judge Sweigert's view of the labor exemption finds relatively little support in existing precedents. *See* § 5.06 *supra.* The fact that a practice might violate the antitrust laws if unilaterally imposed by a group of employers does not necessarily preclude the parties from bargaining about it or from claiming the benefits of the labor exemption if an agreement is subsequently reached after meaningful collective bargaining. *See generally* § 5.05 *supra.*

cited what it termed the "well-settled rule of contract law," that a restraint on an employee's right to pursue his trade was illegal "*if, but only if,* the restraint is unreasonable. . ." [708] The court then stated that "even though the reasonableness test would have been applicable to [an] individual player contract," an agreement among all employers to boycott an individual contract breacher "falls within the antitrust law *per se* prohibition of combinations not to deal." [709] The facts in *Kapp* involved such a multi-employer boycott. Yet, the court was hesitant to apply the *per se* classification. Because league sports were a "unique field," it was "arguable" that the test to be applied to league rules should be "the same test, i.e. reasonableness test, as would be applicable to the individual player-club contract." [710]

The *Kapp* court seems to have misunderstood the nature of the inquiry required by the *per se*-rule of reason issue. The opinion suggests that the common law requirement of "reasonable" employment restraints precludes use of the *per se* test. Such an analysis assumes that there is a distinction between the two standards. In fact, however, the *per se* classification is merely a subset under the reasonableness criteria. Thus, although all restraints are to be evaluated in terms of their reasonableness, there are some which will be found to be *per se* unreasonable without a detailed inquiry into their purpose or actual effects.[711] The *Kapp* court should not have created for itself the artificial dilemma of individual contracts versus league restrictions. Having reached the conclusion, without citation of authority, that league restraints were *per se* prohibited, the court seems to feel that it was manipulating legal doctrine when it gave credence to the view that the unique aspects of league sports "arguably" warranted a different treatment. Had the court correctly perceived that the reasonableness of a restraint was the touchstone in any situation, it may well have found the case against use of the *per se* classification much stronger and modified the remainder of its opinion accordingly.

The court's confusion as to the nature of the inquiry required continues into the critical portions of the opinion where the NFL restraints are evaluated. For the reasons just given, the court states that it is going to test the complained-of practices against its reasonableness standard and not apply "the absolute *per se* test." But having said that, Judge Sweigert then concluded that "league enforcement of most of the challenged rules is so patently unreasonable that there is no genuine issue for trial" [712] and entered an order granting summary judgment in favor of the plaintiff on all of the restraints in question, with the exception of the option clause.[713] Thus, although disclaiming the applicability of the *per se* classification, the court treats the issues precisely as they would

---

708. 390 F. Supp. at 81.

709. *Id.*

710. *Id.*

711. It should be apparent that even though the general common law standard for testing employment restraints is stated as a requirement of reasonableness, some types of restriction could still be found to be so unreasonable on their face as to not require a detailed examination. Thus, a covenant not to compete which bound a former employee for his lifetime and covered the entire world could readily be held to be so patently unreasonable as to violate the common law without any specific showing as to its economic impact.

712. 390 F. Supp. at 82.

713. *Id.* at 81-82.

have been treated under that standard. Again, the difficulty seems to arise from the court's failure to perceive that the *per se* label is used to identify cases in which the restraints involved are so destructive of competition that it is appropriate to treat the issue of their reasonableness in summary fashion and save the plaintiff the burden of a lengthy trial on this aspect of his case.

If one chooses to ignore what the court said and focuses upon what it did, *Kapp* would seem to provide support for the view that pervasive player restraints amount to *per se* violations. But even this view of the case must be qualified. The court dealt only with the particular restraints before it, and its condemnation of them was based primarily on the perception that they were perpetual in nature. When a case arises involving somewhat less drastic restraints, the precedential value of *Kapp* becomes much less clear. As previously noted, the court gave credence to the arguments as to why a *per se* approach is inappropriate in the area of league sports. The implication is that a trial on the factual issue of reasonableness is required. But in light of the court's refusal to make this inquiry on the facts before it, a subsequent court looking to *Kapp* as precedent will likely be somewhat perplexed as to where Judge Sweigert intended to draw the line identifying cases requiring a full trial. On this question — which is the crux of the *per se*-rule of reason debate — *Kapp* offers no general standard and, in large measure, simply confirms that there are compelling countervailing considerations which make a resolution difficult.

There is some indication that Judge Sweigert himself may have had some doubts about his treatment of the reasonableness issue. In a subsequent unreported order, the judge indicated that he thought it possible "that a reviewing court might hold that, although the application of the 'rule of reason' (rather than the '*per se* rule') is proper, the issue of reasonableness should be tried as an issue of fact (rather than concluded as a matter of law)." [714] Not wanting the case to come back on what he termed a "procedural, technical ground," he modified his earlier order to permit the introduction of evidence on the issue of reasonableness. [715] If this had been permitted to stand, it would, in effect, have reversed the substance of the earlier order. The plaintiff would have had to meet the evidence offered by the defendant and, presumably, the court would have made specific findings with respect to the justifications which the league put forth. However, prior to trial, there was a third order on the matter and Judge Sweigert reversed himself again, finally indicating that he would stand on his original determination that the restraints were so patently unreasonable as to leave no issue for trial. [716]

3. Robertson Case.

The question of the proper standard of review to be applied to player restraints was also considered in *Robertson v. National Basketball Association*. [717] In this proceeding, Robertson and several other NBA players initiated a class action

---

714. Kapp v. National Football League, Docket No. C-72-537, Order re Motion and Interim Pre-Trial Order 1 (N.D. Cal. April 11, 1975).

715. *Id.* at 20.

716. *See* N.Y. Times, Feb. 14, 1976, at 15, col. 7. As noted elsewhere, the case eventually went to trial and the jury decided in favor of the league on the question of damages. *See* § 5.03 *supra.*

717. 389 F. Supp. 867 (S.D.N.Y. 1975). *See also* 1975 Trade Cas. ¶ 60,448.

in which, among other complaints, they alleged that the NBA had used its draft, reserve clause, uniform contract, and related rules to monopolize the sport of professional basketball and restrain competition for the plaintiffs' service. Judge Carter addressed the question of the appropriate standard of review in an opinion issued in response to several pre-trial motions, none of which directly involved the *per se*-rule of reason issue. Although it was thus not intended to finally resolve the matter, the court's opinion offered little encouragement to the league. Judge Carter clearly indicated how he was inclined to view the restraints. He accepted that "some degree of economic cooperation which is inherently anti-competitive may well be essential for the survival of ostensibly competitive sports leagues." [718] However, in his view, this rationale did not require a wholesale exemption:

> Because survival necessitates some restraints ... does not mean that insulation from the reach of the antitrust laws must follow. Less drastic protective measures may be the solution.[719]

He then proceeded to review the league's practices, as they were characterized by the plaintiffs, in light of the Supreme Court's decisions defining the proper standard of review. He found several of the traditional *per se* classifications applicable to the NBA restraints:

> The player draft and perpetual reserve system are readily susceptible to condemnation as group boycotts based on the NBA's concerted refusal to deal with the players save through these uniform restrictive practices.... The two control mechanisms are also analogous to price-fixing devices condemned as *per se* violative of the Sherman Act, for the draft and a perpetual reserve system allow competing teams to eliminate competition in the hiring of players and invariably lower the cost of doing business.... In addition the player draft and a perpetual reserve system can be viewed as devices creating illegal horizontal territorial allocations and product market divisions.[720]

Judge Carter recognized, however, that at least two important factual questions remained to be resolved. One concerned the extent to which the restraints were the product of good faith collective bargaining between the parties, for such bargaining might remove the practices from scrutiny under the antitrust laws. In addition, the league had rather vigorously disputed the plaintiffs' claim that its contract renewal clause operated as a perpetual reserve system. Thus, the court thought it necessary to hold further proceedings to determine how the renewal system worked in practice.

Although Judge Carter indicated that he was withholding a conclusion on the legality of the reserve system, his initial remarks were rather explicit in expressing disapproval. His statements that a draft and perpetual reserve system were "readily susceptible to condemnation as group boycotts" and analogous to price-fixing and market division devices might have been read to mean that the league's restraints would be found to be *per se* illegal if the league failed in its efforts to have the two remaining factual questions resolved in its

718. 389 F. Supp. at 892.
719. *Id.*
720. *Id.* at 893 (citations omitted).

favor. Under this view, any subsequent proceedings would be limited to those two questions and would not involve the myriad other issues which would arise when a restraint is tested under the rule of reason. The plaintiffs apparently so interpreted the court's original opinion, for Judge Carter later found it necessary to issue another opinion clarifying the matters to be considered in pre-trial discovery.[721] He noted that in his earlier consideration of the case, he had before him only the defendants' request for summary judgment. The factual record was incomplete and hence no final determination of the status of the restraints could have been made. In his view, the matter still required a full-scale hearing:

> Accordingly, defendants are not barred from raising all possible defenses to plaintiffs' action, including one based on the economic necessity of retaining the challenged restraints.[722]

Judge Carter added, however, that the plaintiffs could move to strike the rule of reason defense after pre-trial discovery. The court would then make a final ruling on whether the league's claim of economic justification was barred by the *per se* doctrine or would be considered at trial.[723]

As a result of this subsequent "clarification," the court's view of the restraints under the *per se* rule is somewhat unclear. Judge Carter's earlier statements were most pointed in their condemnation of the restraints and did not even hint at the facts which the league might show to salvage them. Indeed, the analysis in the original opinion concluded with the remark that

> The life of these restrictions, therefore, appears to be all but over, although their formal interment must await further developments in this case.[724]

But according to his subsequent ruling, there was no issue which was intended to be removed from further scrutiny. If this were true, the "formal interment" of the restraints would not appear to have been a foregone conclusion.

The court's apparent change of position should lead to interesting speculation about the precedential value of the original opinion. Some will argue that the earlier view must be wholly discounted and that Judge Carter was conceding that, upon further reflection, he had overstated the case. Others will contend that much like Judge Sweigert in his short-lived second ruling, the court was simply giving the league every opportunity to present its case so as to avoid a reversal on appeal. Perhaps the most that can be said is that Judge Carter's initial reaction — admittedly based on a very limited record and made in light of a basic disagreement among the parties on the precise nature of the restraints involved — was one of extreme skepticism about the defendant's ability to muster facts to support pervasive restrictions on player mobility.

It probably never will be known whether the NBA would have been able to garner sufficient proof to avoid a finding of *per se* illegality. In subsequent

---

721. Parts of Judge Carter's subsequent opinion are reported at 1975 Trade Cas. ¶ 60,448 (S.D.N.Y.).
722. 1975 Trade Cas. ¶ 60,448 at 67,004.
723. *Id.*
724. 389 F. Supp. at 895.

collective bargaining, the league and its players' association reached an agreement which produced a substantial liberalization of the league's player controls.[725] The result was that the issues in the pending litigation were settled. While the factors which prompt substantial collective bargaining concessions by management are never clear, the extent of the compromise in this case casts substantial doubt on any argument that pervasive restraints were essential to the survival of the league. Presumably most club owners feel that the league can exist without such devices as perpetual draft rights, a league-administered indemnity system, and the like. Nevertheless, the fact that some restraints were continued serves to reaffirm the point, implicit in the cases, that the league's defense of economic necessity cannot be dismissed out of hand.

4. *Mackey Case.*

The controversy concerning the status of player restraints received perhaps its most complete airing in *Mackey v. National Football League.*[726] The suit, initiated by a group of former and present NFL players, focused on the league's controversial Rozelle Rule, which the plaintiffs alleged constituted an unreasonable restraint on trade under the Sherman Act. The case involved a lengthy trial before Judge Larson in the District Court of Minnesota. The proceedings required fifty-five days of trial and included over 400 exhibits and testimony from more than sixty witnesses. In contrast to the treatment afforded the issue in some of the earlier cases, Judge Larson chose not to resolve the *per se*-rule of reason controversy in advance of trial. Hence, most of the testimony in the 11,000 page transcript addressed the issue of the economic justification for the restraints and included a detailed inquiry into the structure of the NFL and the operation of its player controls.

When Judge Larson issued his decision at the end of the trial, it amounted to an emphatic rejection of the traditional justifications for player restraints. The NFL appealed the decision to the Court of Appeals for the Eighth Circuit. That court, speaking through Judge Lay, eventually affirmed the lower court on the ultimate conclusion that the Rozelle Rule was illegal under the antitrust laws.[727] However, the appellate court did not accept Judge Larson's analysis in its entirety and instead chose to view the league's position in somewhat more sympathetic terms. The differences in the analysis of the district and appellate courts may become important for defining the type of restraints which will be found acceptable in the future. For that reason, it is useful to review the treatment which each of these courts afforded the case. We begin with a review of the district court's opinion.

With respect to the operation of the Rozelle Rule, Judge Larson found that the requirement of compensating the players' former employer effectively deterred clubs from signing free agents.[728] It limited the number of clubs willing to sign an athlete who played out his option and, thus, limited the player's opportunity for bargaining with other clubs. Moreover, the court found a "free agent" was not truly free to bargain with other clubs; his former employer "still

---

725. The agreement is discussed in § 5.03 *supra.*

726. 407 F. Supp. 1000 (D. Min. 1975), *modified,* 543 F.2d 606 (8th Cir. 1976), *noted in* 4 FORD. URBAN L.J. 581 (1976).

727. 543 F.2d 606 (8th Cir. 1976).

728. 407 F. Supp. at 1006-07.

controlled his ability to participate in football, even though there was no longer any contractual obligation whatsoever." [729] Thus, the Rozelle Rule had an effect "substantially identical" to a lifetime reserve system. The rule denied the player the right to sell his services in a free and open market, depressed players' salaries, and restricted freedom of movement.[730]

In the section of the opinion entitled "Conclusions of Law," Judge Larson succinctly disposed of the issue which had proved troublesome in earlier cases:

> 5.1 The Rozelle Rule constitutes a *per se* violation of the antitrust laws.
>
> 5.1.1 The Rozelle Rule and its related practices constitute a concerted refusal to deal and a group boycott on the part of the defendants.
>
> 5.1.2 These are practices which the courts have held to be *per se* violations of the Sherman Act. *Fashion Originators' Guild v. FTC*, 312 U.S. 457, 61 S. Ct. 703, 85 L.Ed. 949 (1941); *Klor's, Inc. v. Broadway-Hale Stores, Inc.*, 359 U.S. 207, 79 S. Ct. 705, 3 L.Ed.2d 741 (1959); *United States v. General Motors Corp.*, 384 U.S. 127, 145-47, 86 S.Ct. 1321, 16 L.Ed.2d 415 (1966).
>
> 5.2 The Rozelle Rule is so clearly contrary to public policy that it is *per se* illegal under the Sherman Act. It is also an unreasonable restraint of trade at common law.[731]

The court then analyzed the Rule under the rule of reason standard and, as could be predicted in light of its prior statements, found it invalid under that test as well. Judge Larson found the practice to be unreasonable in three respects: (1) the Rule was unreasonably broad in that it affected all players, not merely those who were likely to upset the competitive balance of the league; (2) it was unreasonable in its failure to provide procedures to inform a free agent of pending negotiations for his services and to guard against an existing employer's unreasonable actions which might discourage trades; and (3) the Rule was further unreasonable in its duration in that it operated as a perpetual restriction on the players' mobility.[732]

One of the more controversial portions of the opinion is that which contains the court's findings with respect to the league's proffered justifications for the Rule. The league had argued that the Rule was necessary to protect the clubs' investments in their players; to insure player continuity, and hence the quality of competition; and to maintain competitive balance within the league. The league also contended that an abrupt elimination of the rule would disrupt the sport as players moved from club to club, a process which could lead to the financial demise of franchises unable to endure a bidding war. The court rejected all of these contentions, and while the court's responses are not all directed to the question of whether the *per se* standard should be used, they do suggest the reasons why the court was willing to treat the Rule summarily. It should also be noted, however, that the court's responses on this are largely conclusory. Since there is no indication of the quality of the evidence which the court relied

---

729. *Id.* at 1006.
730. *Id.* at 1007.
731. *Id.*
732. *Id.* at 1007-08.

on, one cannot be certain that other courts making the same factual inquiry would agree with Judge Larson's assessments.[733]

In response to the argument that player continuity was necessary so that clubs had time to mold players into a team, Judge Larson stated simply that "[t]he quality of play in the NFL will not decrease with the elimination of the Rozelle Rule. . . ." [734] He did provide the alternative rationale that even if the quality of competition did decrease, that concern would not justify continuation of the Rule. But the factual basis for his initial conclusion is not stated, nor is there an attempt to deal with the question of what the relative decrease in quality might be. Presumably, the alternative rationale is persuasive only if the extent of decrease in quality is determined to be something less than that which would render the league's operation unprofitable.

The effects upon the league's operation were considered in another portion of the court's conclusions, but these included no greater effort to assess the relative impact of the basic change in league practices which would result from the demise of the indemnity system. Judge Larson stated that elimination of the rule would not have a significant disruptive effect on the sport, reasoning that relatively few players will play out their options at one time. He also stated that his ruling would not "cause a decrease in the number of franchises" in the NFL.[735] Despite this rather explicit rejection of one of the league's traditional arguments, the court offered little in the way of factual evidence or economic analysis to support its conclusions. The same was true for the summary statement that the player restraints "have not had any material effect on competitive balance" in the NFL.[736] The court did not cite specific evidence on this point, nor did it explain the basis of its implicit prediction that competitive balance would not be materially altered in the future.

The court's assessment of the operation of the Rozelle Rule had potentially important implications for defining the types of modified restraints which would be found acceptable under the antitrust laws. It is possible to read the opinion as suggesting that the leagues would encounter difficulty even with substantially less restrictive devices. It will be recalled that Judge Larson condemned the Rozelle Rule because of its universal application, its perpetual duration, and its lack of procedural safeguards. Assume that the league introduced a modified form of the rule which "corrected" these defects. Could such a rule be sustained under Judge Larson's analysis? At its heart, the rule of reason standard requires that a court weigh the harm to competition against the defendant's justification for the regulation in question.[737] While a modified indemnity system would have less severe effects upon competition, it would still restrain mobility to some extent. The critical issue would be whether the defendants had available a justification which offset the anticompetitive impact.

Judge Larson's findings, if accepted at face value, would seem to undermine

---

733. On appeal, the league raised the objection that the court's findings were too conclusory, but to no avail. *See* 543 F.2d at 622, n.30.

734. 407 F. Supp. at 1008.

735. *Id.* The court added, however, that "changes in location of franchises or reorganization of existing franchises may occur." *Id.*

736. *Id.*

737. *See* text at notes 645-48 *supra.*

the most likely explanations which the league would offer. The court concluded that the Rozelle Rule has *no* material effect on competitive balance. It seems unlikely that a *less* restrictive system would have a more positive impact. Relatedly, Judge Larson suggests that a total elimination of the restraints upon veteran mobility would have little effect on the number of franchises in the league. In light of that statement, it is not certain that the league would be able to produce a credible explanation for the reintroduction of modified restraints, for, again, less onerous controls are not likely to have more disruptive consequences.[738]

While Judge Larson's opinion thus had troublesome implications for the league's effort to control player movement, the problems raised were largely eliminated in the subsequent appellate review.[739] The Eighth Circuit's opinion produced an interesting transformation of the lower court decision. The court of appeals affirmed on the critical point that the Rozelle Rule was illegal. Moreover, the reviewing court chose not to directly undercut most of the factual conclusions made by Judge Larson. Yet, by suggesting important qualifications on the lower court's analysis, Judge Lay was able to dispel the most unsettling features of the Larson decision. One of the qualifications added by the appellate court was quite explicit, while the other was much more subtle.

Judge Lay expressly rejected the lower court's holding that the Rozelle Rule was *per se* illegal.[740] In turning away from the trend of several then-recent cases, the court concluded that the "unusual circumstances" of the sports inquiry precluded summary condemnation of the league's practices.[741] It noted that the *per se* concepts had been developed in cases involving agreements between traditional business competitors. But the court did not think it appropriate "to mechanically apply" these precedents in the sports area.[742] The critical point of Judge Lay's analysis was his willingness to give credence to the league's argument concerning the uniqueness of its enterprise. The thrust of this contention is that the clubs within a league cannot be viewed as wholly distinct business competitors, for unlike other businesses, each club has an economic stake in the financial survival of the other clubs.[743] The *per se* cases proceeded from an entirely different premise — that individual business units should compete vigorously with one another. Confronted with an industry in which that premise is not valid, the court was inclined to make a more

---

738. In one respect, the analysis in the text somewhat oversimplifies the implication of Judge Larson's opinion. It may be that the court did not intend to suggest that all restraints would be ineffective to preserve competitive balance. Perhaps it had in mind that even a restraint as pervasive as the Rozelle Rule would be ineffective as long as the owners were able to unilaterally upset the balance by trades and purchases. But it seems unlikely that a system which both eliminated these features *and* placed restrictions on voluntary player movement would be sustained. Thus, for the restraint systems which are within the realm of arguable validity, the criticism in the text would seem justified.

739. 543 F.2d 606 (8th Cir. 1976).

740. 543 F.2d at 619-20.

741. *Id.* at 619.

742. *Id.*

743. "No one club is interested in driving another team out of business, since if the League fails, no one team can survive." *Id.* at 619, *citing* United States v. National Football League, 116 F. Supp. 319, 323 (E.D. Pa. 1953).

particularized inquiry into the special conditions which might justify a restraint.[744]

The second, more subtle qualification made in Judge Larson's analysis came in the reviewing court's application of the rule of reason. That court affirmed the conclusion that the Rozelle Rule was unreasonable. In most respects, the opinion approved the lower court's disposition of this issue. The court generally accepted Judge Larson's factual findings and, indeed, specifically rejected the league's argument that the district court's analysis was too conclusory.[745] Moreover, Judge Lay endorsed the three-pronged reasoning that the Rozelle Rule was unreasonable because it treated all players alike regardless of ability, operated as a perpetual restraint, and failed to afford procedural safeguards to the affected athletes. However, a critical difference in the reviewing court's approach appears in its treatment of the issue of the league's interest in maintaining competitive balance among the member clubs. As indicated above, Judge Larson found that the Rozelle Rule had no material effect on competitive balance and rejected the league's attempt to justify the Rule on this basis. While the appellate court specifically accepted Judge Larson's reasons for rejecting the league's other justification, it carefully avoided placing any reliance on this finding. Thus, the court expressly agreed with Judge Larson that a desire to recoup player development costs or to insure player continuity would not justify the Rozelle Rule. But with respect to the lower court's assertion that the indemnity system had been ineffectual, the appellate court stated only that it recognized that "the NFL has a strong and unique interest in maintaining competitive balance among its teams." [746] The fact that it avoided any mention of Judge Larson's finding in its own conclusion strongly suggests that it was uncomfortable with the district court's treatment of this issue.

Other passages of Judge Lay's opinion seem to confirm that the court found the concern for competitive balance to be an important one. The court took care to point out that its decision disapproving the Rozelle Rule was not intended as a wholesale condemnation of restrictive devices. In the course of concluding remarks which urged the parties to settle their differences at the bargaining table, the court stated:

> [O]ur disposition of the antitrust issue does not mean that every restraint on competition for players' services would necessarily violate the antitrust laws.[747]

And the court was even more positive in encouraging a modification of the existing rules:

> It may be that some reasonable restrictions relating to player transfers are necessary for the successful operation of the NFL. The protection

---

744. The court offered another ground for rejecting the application of the *per se* rule. One of the reasons for using the summary classification was to avoid a lengthy factual inquiry into the reasons for a restraint, the needs of the industry, and the effects of the restriction upon competition. But that justification was not persuasive here, for the detailed evidentiary inquiry had actually been made in the trial court. *See* 543 F.2d at 619. Thus, the posture of the litigation did not compel an application of the *per se* concept, and the rule of reason standard provided a better vehicle for dealing with the extensive evidence which had been generated in the court below.

745. *Id.* at 622 n.30.

746. *Id.* at 621.

747. *Id.* at 623.

of mutual interests of both the players and the clubs may indeed require this.[748]

In its review of Judge Larson's analysis, Judge Lay states that the district court also recognized that competitive balance was a proper concern to the league.[749] That suggestion belies the more fundamental difference in the two approaches. While Judge Larson might have accepted competitive balance as a desirable end to be pursued in the sports industry, there is little indication that he believed that restraints on players were a proper means to achieve this. As indicated above, his conclusion as to the ineffectiveness of the Rozelle Rule is hardly a brief in favor of milder restraints. Moreover, Judge Larson appeared prepared to force the league to look to Congress for special dispensation,[750] a view which seems to imply that the league's interest cannot be accommodated under present antitrust doctrine. The court of appeals is clearly more encouraging on the prospect of some type of restraint being sustained under existing law. The basic difference in the two opinions goes on to the questions of whether such restraints would contribute to competitive balance and even if they did, whether they would be tolerated under present antitrust doctrine. The appellate court laid the foundation for an affirmative answer to these questions.

5. *Smith Case.*

While the *Mackey* appeal was pending, the NFL found itself in court again, this time attempting to defend its draft system from antitrust attack. The occasion was the case of *Smith v. Pro-Football, Inc.*[751] which was tried before Judge Bryant in the District Court for the District of Columbia. Plaintiff Smith, a collegiate All-American, had been selected by the Washington Redskins in the first round of the 1968 draft. He had a one-year standard player contract with the defendant Pro-Football, Inc. which owned the club. While Smith was regarded as a superb professional prospect, his career was abruptly ended when he received a serious neck injury in the final game of the 1968 season. Smith's antitrust theory was that by granting the Redskins the exclusive right to negotiate with him, the draft system operated to restrict competition for his services. As a result of this restraint, Smith contended, he was not able to realize the true value of his services and, further, was unable to negotiate contract terms which would have afforded him greater security in the event of an injury.[752]

Smith named both his former club and the NFL as defendants. The case went to trial before Judge Bryant and a sizable body of evidence was considered.[753]

---

748. *Id.*

749. *Id.* at 621.

750. Judge Larson concluded his review of the substantive antitrust issue with the admonition that

> If the effects of this decision prove to be too damaging to professional football, assuming justification existed, Congress could possibly grant special treatment to the National Football League based upon its claimed special status. 407 F. Supp. at 1008.

751. 420 F. Supp. 738 (D.D.C. 1976).

752. Apart from the allegation of special damage due to his inability to negotiate for greater protection against injuries, Smith's allegations were similar to those which are generally raised against the draft. *See* § 5.03 *supra. Compare* Tepler v. Frick, 112 F. Supp. 245 (S.D.N.Y.), *aff'd,* 204 F.2d 506 (2d Cir. 1953).

753. There are numerous newspaper stories dealing with the particular testimony and other evidence which was received. *See, e.g.,* N.Y. Times, May 26, 1976, at 42, col. 1 (Ed Garvey, Exec.

A decision was issued on September 8, 1976, and the league again found itself on the losing side. Judge Bryant's approach was similar to that taken by the district court in *Mackey* in that he analyzed the league's practices under both the *per se* doctrine and the rule of reason. While he found a violation under each of these standards, Judge Bryant's analysis under the latter criteria was not total rejection of the NFL's position and his opinion, like the appellate decision in *Mackey*, can be read as inviting the league to attempt a less restrictive form for player allocation.

Judge Bryant's conclusion that the draft was *per se* illegal was stated with little elaboration. He noted that the draft operated to authorize only one league club to deal with the player and described this as a "group boycott in its classic and most pernicious form." [754] He also saw the restrictions as "naked restraints of trade" which had "no purpose except stifling competition." [755] With respect to the league's suggestion that it could not survive without some limit on competition for players, the court quoted language from a Supreme Court decision to the effect that illegal conspiracies cannot be saved by a supposed need to maintain profits or preserve a particular method of doing business.[756] In the court's view, the agreement embodied in the draft was a "direct, explicit and purposive" restraint on competition which was inconsistent with the free market model on which the antitrust laws are based.[757]

While the court's *per se* analysis reflected little sympathy for the league's position, its alternative evaluation of the draft under the rule of reason indicated a somewhat more tolerant attitude. The league's arguments in support of the reasonableness of the draft were basically those which are offered to support other types of restraints: in order to sustain fan interest, it is necessary that the results of games and divisional contests be unpredictable; thus, the viability of league sports requires that there be competitive balance between the respective clubs; balance could not be achieved if there were a free market for players' services because the more wealthy or more glamorous franchises would acquire the best talent; restraints on player mobility are therefore necessary.[758] The court indicated that it was not prepared to dismiss these contentions out of hand. Rather, it was "persuaded that in a free market for college players the wealthiest owners would indeed make an effort to buy up as much player talent as possible ...." [759] The court went on, however, to observe that there were

Dir. of NFLPA, testified that draft should be kept but modified); Washington Post, June 15, 1976, at D3, col. 1 (Tex Schramm, president and general manager of Dallas Cowboys, expressed need for draft to maintain competitive balance in NFL); *id.,* June 13, 1976, at D6, col. 6 (Alan Miller, player agent, stated draft creates more jobs, franchises and higher salaries in NFL); *id.,* June 10, 1976, at D3, col. 3 (Gerald Phipps, owner of Denver Broncos, declared elimination of draft would double scouting expenses resulting in lower player salaries); *id.,* June 8, 1976, at D3, col. 1 (Willie Davis, former All-Pro player with Green Bay Packers, testified in favor of draft); *id.,* June 3, 1976, at C1, col. 3, (Bart Starr, Green Bay Packer coach and former quarterback, favored draft in testimony; Edward B. Williams, prominent attorney and president of Washington Redskins, testified on benefits of draft); *id.,* May 27, 1976, at D1, col. 1 (Roy Jefferson, Jerry Smith, Briggs Owen, Washington Redskin players, revealed starting salaries with Redskins and offers made by AFL teams when they were drafted).

754. 420 F. Supp. at 744.
755. *Id.* at 745, *quoting* White Motor Co. v. United States, 372 U.S. 253, 263 (1963).
756. *Id. quoting* United States v. General Motors Corp., 384 U.S. 127, 146 (1966).
757. 420 F. Supp. at 745.
758. *See* text at notes 662-67 *supra* and notes 787-801 *infra.*
759. 420 F. Supp. at 746.

factors other than the glamor of the city and the club's on-the-field success which influenced a player's choice of a team. Thus, the evidence on this point was equivocal. And the league had failed to establish other factual points which would have aided its case. The court noted that evidence offered by the league showed an insignificant correlation between a club's opportunity to draft early and improvement in its athletic performance.[760] Moreover, the defendants had presented no evidence to establish that in the absence of restraints the best players would be attracted to a few glamor clubs.

While the court did not completely close the door on the argument concerning the need for competitive balance, it concluded that the contention need not be resolved in the present litigation. In the court's view, the version of the draft which the league had selected was "significantly more restrictive than necessary," [761] even assuming that there was a legitimate need for equalization of playing talent. The court gave examples of other, less restrictive alternatives, although it indicated in a footnote that it was not necessarily suggesting that these would be acceptable under a rule of reason.[762] The court observed that in any one year less than sixty of the incoming players were likely to "make the team" in the professional ranks. In the court's view, these prospects could be allocated in a draft which was limited to two rounds so that each club acquired negotiating rights to only two players. As it was, each club had seventeen selections, and thus the restriction on competition affected many players who did not represent a threat to competitive balance.[763] The court also noted that the league's desire to allocate talent among league clubs could be achieved by mechanisms which still allowed for some competitive bidding for players. While the league may have been concerned that one club not acquire too much of the incoming talent, it chose a rule which went much further. The traditional NFL draft operated not only to restrict the number of players a club could sign but also to force the athlete to sign with the club which drafted him. The court regarded these two restraints as not inseparable. By way of example, it observed that the league could have allowed each player to be drafted by a number of clubs, while permitting each club to sign only one player out of each round of the draft. Having satisfied itself that the league's goals could have been achieved by other means, the court disposed of the rule of reason issue:

> [I]n light of the near-certainty that less restrictive alternatives are available to meet the alleged player distribution needs of the league, the current system cannot be regarded as "reasonable" within the meaning of the antitrust laws.[764]

---

760. *Id.* In an effort to refute the claim that the draft preserved competitive balance, the court noted that in the prior three seasons 22 of 24 of the play-off slots had been claimed by only nine teams. It is somewhat surprising that more sophisticated evidence was not used. A period of three seasons is not necessarily predictive of long-range trends. Moreover, the seasons selected included those in which the WFL competed for football players, a factor which may make the sample unrepresentative. Nor do the cited statistics answer the question of whether particular contests during the season were balanced.

761. *Id.* at 746.

762. *Id.* at 747 n.6.

763. It will be recalled that a similar point was made in *Mackey* concerning the Rozelle Rule. *See* 543 F.2d at 622. *See also* 407 F. Supp. at 1007.

764. 420 F. Supp. at 747.

Judge Bryant seems to have selected the proper framework for applying the rule of reason analysis. He first examined the factual record to determine whether there was evidence to sustain the league's contention that the draft served to promote competitive balance among league teams. He then shifted the focus to specifically address the reasonableness issue: was the restraint reasonable in light of the concern which gave rise to it? On this point he concluded that the league's rules did not reflect the sort of temperate approach which the rule of reason required. Indeed, the league had painted with a very broad brush when it wrote its draft rules. It used the regulation as the occasion not only to allocate players who probably would have little effect on competitive balance but also to strip all the NFL players of important bargaining tools. The league should have been more sensitive to the effect which its rules would have on competition for playing talent. There are numerous other techniques which could have been chosen which would have lessened the impact of the rules on the players while continuing to control the number and quality of acquisitions made by the clubs.

One difficulty with Judge Bryant's opinion is that his rule of reason analysis somewhat undercuts the strictness of his treatment of the *per se* issue. While Judge Bryant leaves no doubt that he believes the traditional draft cannot be sustained under the rule of reason, his opinion can be read as outlining the steps which the league should take in reforming its draft system. There is a rather clear suggestion that if the league chooses a less restrictive version of the draft and develops a somewhat more persuasive factual record on the movement of playing talent, it is likely to receive a more favorable hearing in antitrust court.[765] The court's *per se* analysis, however, is presented in more absolute terms and does not indicate a similar escape mechanism. For example, the court stated that the essence of the draft was that the club owners had "agreed among themselves that the right to negotiate with each ... graduating college athlete will be allocated to one team and that no other team will deal with that person." [766] In the court's view, this was an "outright, undisguised refusal to deal" of the sort which "has long been condemned as *per se* violation ..." [767] The difficulty is that the less restrictive draft mechanisms which the court identifies in its rule of reason analysis would seem to share the same basic characteristics which the court condemns in its finding of *per se* violation. Thus, even where three clubs rather than one are allowed to bid for a player, there is still an agreement among the clubs to limit competition. And the same feature would be present even if the number of clubs allowed to draft a player were

---

765. As noted above, in putting forth examples of less restrictive draft rules, Judge Bryant was careful to indicate that he was not suggesting that these would "necessarily" be within the rule of reason. *See* text accompanying note 762 *supra*. However, it seems likely that Judge Bryant believed that some type of draft system would be utilized. For example, he gave some credence to the notion that wealthy clubs might have to be restrained if competitive balance were to be maintained. Moreover, if he thought it wholly improper for the league to attempt to allocate players, then his listing of less restrictive alternatives would represent a most unusual analysis. Rather than comparing degrees of restraint, he presumably would have cast his opinion in terms which suggested that no significant control of competition could be justified. He did not take that approach, however, and instead mapped out reasonable alternatives to the NFL's traditional player allocation procedures.

766. 420 F. Supp. at 744.

767. *Id.*

increased to ten or twelve. Under the classic principles of the *per se* doctrine which the court purports to apply, no restraint on competition will be tolerated, and a court would not be permitted to speculate as to when there was " enough" competition to remove the violation.

Judge Bryant's *per se* analysis also broadly condemns the purpose behind the draft. He states that its goal is to stifle competition and then applies the principle that a restraint on competition is fundamentally inconsistent with the free market concepts embodied in the antitrust laws. But even if the number of clubs which can negotiate with a player is increased from one to three, or to ten or twelve, the basic "purpose" of the draft rules will not have changed: they still will be specifically designed to control the amount of competition which occurs for players' services.

Again, the basic difficulty with Judge Bryant's *per se* analysis is that it is framed in the terms used in the classic group boycott cases.[768] Those cases typically arise from an economic setting which is capable of operating according to the free market model. Thus, it is understandable that courts use language suggesting that any agreement among traders to limit competition will be summarily condemned. But before this approach to the *per se* rule can be applied to agreements such as those embodied in the player restraints, it must be asked whether the free market provides the appropriate frame of reference.[769] Judge Bryant fails to deal with that question in his discussion of the *per se* issue. Moreover, the approach which he takes in his subsequent rule of reason analysis suggests that he is not convinced that free market notions are wholly applicable. Thus, the court's use of a traditional *per se* analysis, with its resolute condemnation of all joint action, is not wholly persuasive.

What this suggests is that if *per se* illegality is to be found, it must be premised on some basis other than that the antitrust law will never tolerate an agreement to control the amount of competition which takes place. That view proves too much where league sports are involved, for it precludes the use of even relatively mild restraints. We will shortly consider an alternative analysis for finding the traditional restraints to *per se* illegality which does not require that all player controls be abandoned.

d. Comments on the Issue of Per Se Illegality. In looking at the cases considering the antitrust status of the traditional player restraints, one must be struck by the extent to which the *per se* issue has prompted differing opinions. Judge Cooper in *Flood v. Kuhn* seems not to have had much difficulty in deciding that the rule of reason was the more appropriate standard for review. By contrast, portions of the district court decisions in *Mackey* and *Smith* suggest that those courts thought that the restraints presented classic cases for application of the *per se* notions. The appellate court in *Mackey* then changed the direction of authority again and held that the summary classifications should not be used. These differing reactions will surely invite divergent interpretations. Some may conclude, for example, that the fact of disagreement

---

768. The cases which gave rise to the *per se* doctrine are discussed in the text accompanying notes 668-90 *supra.*

769. *Compare* Mackey v. National Football League, 543 F.2d 606, 619 (8th Cir. 1976).

simply confirms that the issue is a close one and that courts are likely to differ as to its resolution depending on a variety of factors ranging from the judge's understanding of economics to the quality and extent of proof offered by the parties. Such an assessment is not particularly encouraging, and indeed is somewhat ironic since one of the subsidiary goals of the *per se* doctrine is to provide clear guidelines to enable business entities to bring their practices into conformance with the antitrust laws.[770]

There is, however, another view of the *per se* issue which offers a more definite resolution. One point which is sometimes ignored as courts wrestle with the *per se* doctrine in new areas is that the classification has an evolutionary characteristic to it.[771] Thus, it was not expected that courts would create *per se* violations out of whole cloth, but rather, as stated by the Supreme Court, "it is only after considerable experience with certain business relationships that courts classify them as *per se* violations." [772] The clear implication of this assessment is that courts should approach new problem areas with some hesitancy, and it is fully appropriate that courts gain "experience" with unusual types of restraints by making the more detailed inquiry required under the rule of reason.[773] Among the courts deciding the player restraint cases, only the *Mackey* appeals court gives express recognition to this principle.[774]

The pervasive restraints in professional sports seem particularly suitable to this type of cautionary approach to the *per se* rule. The arguments made by the leagues in support of their practices were of a sort which required a detailed examination. The basic contentions were that severe restrictions on player movement were necessary to the economic viability of the league and that sports ventures were unique in that competition among firms was not necessarily desirable. In essence, it was argued that the free market model which worked well in other contexts would be self-destructive in the sports industry.

Whatever one thinks of the merits of those arguments, it can be observed that the major Supreme Court precedents provide little guidance in dealing with them. For example, the *Klor's* decision can be distinguished, for that case involved a rather bold attempt by the defendant to eliminate a direct competitor, and the restraint thus had a singularly pernicious purpose. *Fashion Originators' Guild* had contained much of the same element, for the intent of the Guild's action was to bring about the demise of competing firms. While the Guild offered a justification — the prevention of pirating of its members' styles — that was, as the Court observed, an attempt to justify an otherwise unlawful object. The player restraints spring from league motives which are less easily dismissed. As propounded by the leagues, the ultimate objective is not to prey upon the innocent players, but to enable the industry to function. Because the restraints have such an undeniable effect on one form of competition, and thus serve the self-interest of the clubs, the courts are necessarily troubled by them.

---

770. *See* note 652 *supra.*

771. *See* Worthen Bank & Trust Co. v. National BankAmericard, Inc., 485 F.2d 119 (8th Cir. 1973), *cert. denied,* 415 U.S. 918 (1974).

772. United States v. Topco Assoc., Inc., 405 U.S. 596, 607 (1972).

773. *See* Van Cise, *The Future of Per Se in Antitrust Law,* 50 VA. L. REV. 1165, 1174-75 (1964).

774. *See* 543 F.2d at 619: "In similar circumstances, when faced with a unique or novel business situation, courts have eschewed a *per se* analysis in favor of an inquiry into the reasonableness of the restraint under the circumstances."

Nevertheless, the courts must recognize that the cases considering the common type of refusals to deal are of limited precedential value. In none of those cases could it have seriously been argued that the very existence of the industry depended upon the participants' ability to control competition.

The contention that pervasive restraints were necessary is not one which could be dismissed out of hand, and it was necessary that courts make some attempt to examine the factual basis of its premises.[775] The *per se* approach does not permit that sort of inquiry, however. In order to achieve the purposes ascribed to the *per se* rule — reducing the plaintiff's litigation burden and promoting bright-line demarcations of proscribed behavior [776] — it is necessary that the standard be absolute and inflexible. This approach works well in those areas where it can confidently be assumed that unfettered competition is a desirable goal. But in cases in which this premise is put in doubt, a less rigid standard is necessary.[777] The desired flexibility can be found in the rule of reason. This alternative test requires an inquiry into the conditions which give rise to the restraint [778] and thus permits the courts to make a knowledgeable assessment of the league's claim that its industry required extensive restraints.

If this analysis is accepted, it is possible to differentiate among the cases decided to date. More particularly, it can be concluded that the decisions to be preferred are those which rejected a summary *per se* approach. The issues being explored had a virgin quality to them. Proper concern for the uncertain consequences of the decision warranted caution on the part of the courts empowered to make it.

It should be noted that while this analysis can be used to evaluate the prior decisions, there is a question as to how it will affect future litigation. The thesis developed here is that the application of *per se* classifications is proper only when courts have had sufficient experience with particular practices to warrant a general conclusion that their anticompetitive effects are unjustifiable. In the player restraint cases decided to date, that experience with the unique structure of the sports industry has been lacking and thus the more deliberate inquiry under the rule of reason was required. It might be asked, however, whether resort to the *per se* concept is entirely foreclosed in the sports area. The prior litigation has produced considerable knowledge about the operation of sports leagues and the economic effects of their restrictive practices. And, it will be noted, there have been repeated findings — albeit with varying degrees of reliability — that the leagues have claimed a greater degree of control than their special needs will justify. Despite this "experience" with the restraints, will future courts be compelled to undertake anew the cumbersome inquiry into the leagues' justification? Or can the courts now say that the leagues have had their

---

775. A concern for the lack of information about the structure of a previously unexplored industry was the basis for the court's refusal to apply the *per se* standard in Worthen Bank & Trust Co. v. National BankAmericard, Inc., 485 F.2d 119 (8th Cir. 1973), *cert. denied,* 415 U.S. 918 (1974).

776. *See* note 652 *supra* and accompanying text.

777. Commentators have noted the danger that the concept of a *per se* violation may be applied too mechanically and have counseled that each case must be examined to determine whether it shares the basic characteristics of other situations in which the *per se* rule has been used. *See* Elman, *"Petrified Opinions" and Competitive Realities,* 66 COLUM. L. REV. 625 (1966).

778. *See* text at 646-48 *supra.*

day in court on the issue of justification and, having failed to sustain their position, summary findings of illegality are appropriate?

Perhaps the best answer to this question is that while the *per se* concept may have a role to play in the future, there will be only a narrow range of cases in which it will be applied. Before summary illegality could be found, it would be necessary for a court to determine that the experience gained in the other sports cases could be transferred to the situation before it. This will give rise to several subsidiary issues.

A critical point to be made is that the prior experience should have limited applicability in situations in which the restraints used are appreciably different from the pervasive restraints considered in the prior cases. None of the courts have said that all player restraints are *per se* illegal, and most have specifically stated that some type of restriction on movement may be necessary.[779] This would suggest that the courts will continue to look for controls which achieve a proper balance between the players' interests in competition for their services and the league's concern for the relative playing strengths of its member clubs. There are no clear *a priori* notions of the type of restraints which would achieve this result. Where the league can show that its new practices have significantly increased the amount of voluntary player movement between clubs, the prior cases will be factually distinguishable, and it will be necessary to undertake the difficult inquiry of whether the degree of mobility permitted achieves the desired balance between the conflicting interests of the parties.

Assume, however, that a case does arise which squarely raises the issue of whether the existing precedents can be translated into a *per se* rule. We can assume, for example, that the controversy concerns restraints used in a professional league which has not had its practices examined under the antitrust laws.[780] And we will posit, as we must, that the restraints in question have the same basic characteristics as those which were condemned in prior decisions. The central issue raised is whether the findings of unreasonableness made as to other leagues' practices are transferable in the form of a *per se* rule.

It is believed that a case can be made for allowing courts some liberty to generalize among the various sports. In the cases decided to date, there have been relatively few arguments that the restraints in a particular league are justified by special characteristics of the sport.[781] Indeed the contentions made

779. *See* Mackey v. National Football League, 543 F.2d 606, 621-22 (8th Cir. 1976); Robertson v. National Basketball Ass'n, 389 F. Supp. 867, 892 (S.D.N.Y. 1975); Kapp v. National Football League, 390 F. Supp. 73, 81-82 (N.D. Cal. 1974); Philadelphia World Hockey Club, Inc. v. Philadelphia Hockey Club, Inc., 351 F. Supp. 462, 503-04 (E.D. Pa. 1972); Flood v. Kuhn, 309 F. Supp. 793, 801 n. 26 (S.D.N.Y. 1970).

780. It should be noted that there are likely to be few cases which provide a serious test for the issue raised in the text. Most potential cases will be eliminated on other grounds. As suggested, cases involving modified restraints are not appropriate candidates. Moreover, situations in which the restraints are arrived at through collective bargaining will not raise the issue, for the labor exemption will operate to preclude substantive antitrust review. Finally, the litigation to date has covered most of the pre-collective bargaining restraints in the major leagues, and there are few examples of non-exempt pervasive restraints left to be litigated. Thus, the issue of whether the existing precedents can be translated into a *per se* rule may not prove to be a critical one.

781. The NFL apparently attempted to argue that football was somewhat unique because it was more of a "team" sport and more time and effort were required to mold the unit. Basketball is often cited as a contrast, because a single performer can have a more direct impact on the outcome of the contest. Yet it is not certain that the differences between football and hockey, for example,

by the leagues in the hockey, football, and basketball cases are virtually identical. While there are differences in the length of the leagues' prior experience under their restraints, this does not appear to impose a substantial limitation on the precedential value of the judicial assessment of the justifications put forth. Hence, in defining the body of relevant experiences, the court should not be wholly foreclosed from drawing upon the findings made with respect to another league's practices.

It is necessary, however, to allow for the possibility that the particular league has truly extraordinary needs. This can be accommodated under a modified *per se* approach. A factual inquiry would be permitted, but only for the limited purpose of allowing the league to establish that the special circumsitances of its situation required player controls more restrictive than those which would be tolerated in other sports. If the defendant failed in this proof, and again assuming that the restraints closely resembled those found to be unreasonable by other courts, it would seem proper for the court to apply the *per se* rule and relieve the plaintiff of the further burden of showing the precise effect of the practices in question.

e. Player Restraints Under the Rule of Reason. The debate about whether the *per se* standard should be applied to pervasive player restraints may be important mainly for defining the parties' litigation burden, for it is not clear that the traditional controls will ultimately fare any better under the rule of reason. Several different courts have indicated a clear disposition against giving the leagues the right to impose perpetual controls. The theme which emerges from the cases was perhaps best summarized by Judge Carter in the *Robertson* case. Adopting a point made in an earlier law review commentary,[782] Judge Carter observed that

> Because survival necessitates some restraint, however, does not mean that insulation from the reach of the antitrust laws must follow. Less drastic protective measures may be the solution.[783]

This assessment really involves two points. On the one hand, the antitrust laws will operate to limit the league's freedom in restricting competition for players. On the other, the antitrust laws may not require that the market for athletic talent be as free and open as those expected in other industries.[784] Other courts have endorsed these notions,[785] and several recent law review commentaries add further support.[786]

---

justify a legal distinction. Moreover, there is evidence that the courts are not prepared to give any weight to football's supposed need for continuity. *See* Mackey v. National Football League, 543 F.2d 606, 621 (8th Cir. 1976).

782. *See* Comment, *The Super Bowl and the Sherman Act: Professional Team Sports and the Antitrust Laws,* 81 Harv. L. Rev. 418, 424 (1967).

783. 389 F. Supp. at 892.

784. It should be added that Judge Carter's opinion in *Robertson* is not very clear in indicating the types of restraints which would be found acceptable. Some language used suggests that he would define the permissible type of controls in very narrow terms. *See id.* at 893. However, another portion of the opinion suggests that Judge Carter's strong disapproval is intended to be directed primarily to controls which are perpetual in nature. *See id.* at 896.

785. The district court opinions in *Flood* and *Kapp* indicate approval of the idea that some restraints must be tolerated. Judge Higginbottom in *Philadelphia World Hockey* seems similarly inclined, but ultimately withholds judgment. *See* discussion at notes 691-716 *supra.*

786. *See, e.g.,* Morris, *In the Wake of the Flood,* 38 Law & Contemp. Prob. 86, 87-90 (1973);

1. *The Case for Total Elimination of Player Restraints: A Critique.*

It thus seems appropriate that some effort be made to identify the types of restraints which might be acceptable under the antitrust laws. That inquiry is undertaken below.[787] Before considering that matter, however, it is necessary to deal with one line of argument which some would use to define the constraint of the antitrust laws in more absolute terms. There are those who maintain that the player restraints achieve none of the goals which the leagues ascribe to them. While various contentions are made, there is one point in particular which warrants comment here.

It will be recalled that the district court in *Mackey* arrived at the rather startling conclusion that

> the existence of the Rozelle Rule and the other restrictive devices on players have not had any material effect on competitive balance in the National Football League.[788]

This statement repudiates the primary argument which the leagues have put forth to justify limiting inter-club competition for players [789] and, if generally adopted, might well mean that no form of league-enforced restraint could be imposed. The district court in *Mackey* gave no indication of the factual basis for its conclusion, and thus there is no direct refutation which can be offered as far as the particular league is concerned. However, it can be noted that various economists have made similar observations about the general ineffectiveness of devices such as the draft and reserve systems in insuring competitive balance within the leagues.[790] It is argued that even with restraints, movement of players will continue in the form of the trading and selling of players' contracts.[791] Ultimately the tendency will be for particular players to be claimed by the clubs valuing their services most highly, which may not be the clubs which "need" the particular talent to remain competitive.[792] Implicit in these observations is a condemnation of the player controls. It is felt that their primary effect is to deny the player the right to claim the "true value" of his service. Rather, it is contended, the system allows the club selling the player's contract to receive the value representing the difference between the athlete's salary and his true worth.[793]

Comment, *The Super Bowl and the Sherman Act: Professional Team Sports and the Antitrust Laws,* *supra* note 782, at 424-26; Comment, *Player Control Mechanisms in Professional Team Sports,* 34 U. PITT. L. REV. 645, 667-70 (1973); Note, *The Legality of the Rozelle Rule and Related Practices in the National Football League,* 4 FORD. URBAN L.J. 582, 587-89 (1976); Note, *The True Story of What Happens When the Big Kids Say, "It's my football, and you'll either play by my rules or you won't play at all,"* 55 NEB. L. REV. 335, 346-55 (1976).

787. *See* text at notes 802-17 *infra.*

788. 407 F. Supp. at 1008.

789. *See* text at notes 662-67 *supra.*

790. *See* DEMMERT 31-39, 55-76; Quirk & El Hodiri, *The Economic Theory of a Professional Sports League* in GOVERNMENT AND THE SPORTS BUSINESS 33 (R. Noll ed. 1974); Canes, *The Social Benefits of Restrictions on Team Quality* in *id.* 81; Rottenberg, *The Baseball Players' Labor Market,* 64 J. POL. ECON. 242, 247-48 (1956).

791. *See, e.g.,* DEMMERT 36-39.

792. *See* Canes, *The Social Benefits of Team Quality, supra* note 790, at 83-84; Rottenberg, *The Baseball Players' Labor Market, supra* note 790, at 253-55.

793. *See, e.g.,* DEMMERT 38-39.

Again, if it were true that player controls had no effect on competitive balance in the league and only operated to increase the financial return of the clubs, it would be difficult for leagues to defend restraints even substantially less restrictive than those traditionally employed. It must be conceded that the argument outlined above has some validity. For example, it can be accepted that in one sense, the restraints operate as a subsidy from the players to the club.[794] If all restrictions were removed, many players would receive salaries more closely approximating their "open market" value, and the clubs would lose the economic rents which they now claim in trades. But it is a somewhat different question as to whether this "subsidy" is improper or unfair. A resolution of that question ultimately turns on other issues which are considerably more difficult to analyze. Thus, it would need to be determined whether a complete abolition of restraints would reduce the total number of sports franchises, and hence the number of employment opportunities for players; whether fan interest, and thus club revenues, would be reduced; and whether relative salary levels in weak and strong franchises would be skewed. In short, since some critics are willing to concede that the restraints do contribute to the viability of the present league structure, it would seem to be important to develop more precise information on the effects of their wholesale removal.[795]

The suggestion that the player controls have been ineffective in maintaining competitive balance among clubs is also subject to some debate. The basic difficulty is that there has never been a convincing analysis of the *relative* impact of the restraints. As evidence of the ineffectiveness of these devices, commentators frequently point out that most major leagues have endured periods in which one or two teams have consistently won the championship competition.[796] Other data, including comparisons between professional and

---

794. Some commentators would likely object to the statement that the restraints operate as a subsidy only "in one sense" and would contend that the fact of subsidization should not be qualified. However, a question can be raised as to whether the notion of a player-to-owner subsidy is not somewhat misleading in the present context. It might be contended that such a characterization is appropriate only if one assumes that the market for players could otherwise operate free of all restraints. But if some type of controls are necessary to the league's successful operation — a point which has never been clearly refuted — to characterize them as "subsidies" may not be entirely appropriate. That concept carries a somewhat normative connotation to laymen which may serve to confuse the debate. It might be more useful to address the question of whether the free market model should be imposed on league sports operations. Some of the difficulties with the existing studies on this point are mentioned in the text.

795. Professor Demmert offers the following analysis of the restraints:

> Why ... do these constraints on labor mobility continue to exist? The answer ... is quite straight forward. The reserve clause and the free agent draft insure the viability of the league not through their effect on the interclub distribution of playing talent, but by lowering the cost curves of *all* clubs in the league sufficiently to insure the economic survival of even the perennial losers. DEMMERT 38.

Professor Demmert also suggests that the removal of restraints on players may significantly affect the viability of some existing franchises and raises the useful point that any effort to introduce reforms into the players (input) market should also consider the need for adjustments in the market in which the product (games) is sold. *Id.* at 87-88.

796. Frequently cited examples are the dominance of the New York Yankees in baseball, the Canadian clubs in hockey, and the New York and Cleveland clubs in football. *See, e.g.,* DEMMERT 36; Rottenberg, *The Baseball Player's Labor Market, supra* note 790, at 247. *See also* Quirk & El Hodiri, *The Economic Theory of a Sports League, supra* note 790 at 45-58.

college sports, are also cited in support.[797] These studies are convincing to the extent that they establish that particular clubs have tended to maintain competitive superiority despite the restrictions on player movement. However, there has been little attention devoted to the question of the effect of the restraints on preserving the competitiveness of the more marginal franchises. While it can be accepted that the draft and reserve system have not prevented the establishment of sports dynasties, it has not been convincingly established that the relative quality of non-championship teams has not been enhanced. Moreover, there have been few factual studies of how particular franchises, especially those in less desirable markets, would be affected by a complete removal of the restrictions.[798] Since the success of the league depends upon its ability to stage interesting contests throughout its various franchises, the question of whether player restraints enhance competition below the championship level would seem to be of critical importance.

It is understandable that most courts have been reluctant to embrace the argument in favor of total abolition of player restraints. As suggested, its validity depends upon a wealth of factual information which has not yet been gathered or analyzed. But even if this data could be accumulated, it would be necessary to make predictions about the future behavior of players, clubs, and fans. And in the final analysis, it would require that a number of critical policy choices be made.

Some economists have assumed that restrictions on mobility are not in the players' best interest and that it is inappropriate for the players to provide this subsidy to the clubs. Yet it appears that a number of players, and most players' unions, have disagreed.[799] While there has been substantial opposition to the pervasive controls used in the past, player groups in several leagues have accepted less rigorous forms.[800] This reaction seems appropriate in light of the speculative nature of any prediction that an outright elimination of the restrictions would not have a serious adverse impact on league operations. A

---

797. See Canes, *The Social Benefits of Team Quality, supra* note 790, at 87-90.

798. Both Demmert and Noll concede that the player restraints operate to increase the financial viability of weaker franchises. They argue, however, that these results could also be attained by other devices, such as greater revenue sharing among clubs. *See* DEMMERT 38; Noll, *Alternatives in Sports Policy* in GOVERNMENT AND THE SPORTS BUSINESS 411, 416-17 (R. Noll ed. 1974).

799. Support for the continuation of some form of player restraints has come from a variety of sources. As previously noted, Judge Cooper stated in *Flood v. Kuhn,* that those proceedings established that

> The preponderance of credible proof does not favor elimination of the reserve clause. With the sole exception of plaintiff [Flood] himself, it shows that even plaintiff's witnesses do not contend that it is wholly undesirable; in fact they regard substantial portions meritorious. 316 F. Supp. 271, 276 (S.D.N.Y. 1970).

See also Mackey v. National Football League, 543 F.2d 606 (8th Cir. 1976). Several congressional studies have similarly concluded that some type of restraints may be necessary. *See, e.g.,* H.R. Rep. No. 2002, 82d Cong., 2d Sess. 229 (1952) (baseball). Various law review commentators have come to a similar conclusion. *See* authorities cited in note 786 *supra* and Comment, *Monopsony in Manpower: Organized Baseball Meets the Antitrust Laws,* 62 YALE L.J. 576, 630-39 (1953). The statements and proposals of several players' unions also indicate support for some types of restraints. *See* § 5.03 *supra.* Finally, at least one attorney representing professional athletes has expressed strong support for a system of modified restraints, specifically one which binds a player to a club for no more than five years. *See* B. WOOLF, BEHIND CLOSED DOORS 265-66 (1976).

800. *See* § 5.03 *supra.*

similar concern gives credence to the judicial statements suggesting that milder forms of restraints are likely to be acceptable. The courts have a limited capacity for weighing complex economic data,[801] and it seems likely that they will proceed cautiously before imposing results which will have a highly uncertain effect. The arguments in favor of striking a balance between player mobility and league stability have not yet been refuted to an extent which justifies their wholesale rejection by the courts. Particularly in light of the players' willingness to accept some form of restraint, the judiciary is likely to continue its search for a reasonable accommodation between the competing concerns.

2. *General Characteristics of Reasonable Restraints.*

The cases decided to date provide relatively little guidance in defining the type of restraints which would pass scrutiny under the antitrust laws. Several of the reported opinions considered only preliminary aspects of the antitrust question and the courts did not have before them the sort of factual record which would permit a definitive statement of the standards to be applied in evaluating the issue of reasonableness. Other courts had more complete information but addressed only the issues specifically before them. Thus, it is not possible to give a detailed specification of the control devices which might be approved. However, one can identify certain general themes in the cases, and while there is not always complete unanimity on these, they do serve to identify some of the boundaries which must be observed.

Perhaps the clearest point which emerges from the cases is the courts' unwillingness to tolerate restraints which are perpetual in nature. Several courts identified this as a primary defect in the practices which they examined.[802] It can be noted further that the perpetual obligations which were deemed objectionable were not only those found in a true reserve system, but also those created by equalizing indemnity arrangements such as the Rozelle Rule. This would suggest that at a minimum, an acceptable restraint system must include *some* opportunity for a player to seek competitive bids for his service free of any *substantial* obligation to his former club.

It might be asked whether the cases establish that all forms of so-called equalization payments are prohibited. It must be concluded that the cases do not speak in sufficiently specific terms to provide a definitive answer.[803] However, some forms of indemnity may be sufficiently mild to survive an

---

801. *Cf.* United States v. Topco Assoc., Inc., 405 U.S. 596, 607 (1972), quoted in the text at note 652 *supra. See also* Bork, *The Rule of Reason and the Per Se Concept: Price Fixing and Market Division,* 74 YALE L.J. 775, 838-47 (1965).

802. *See, e.g.,* Kapp v. National Football League, 390 F. Supp. 73, 82 (N.D. Cal. 1974) ("We conclude that such a rule imposing restraints virtually unlimited in time and extent, goes far beyond any possible need for fair protection of the interests of the club-employers or the purposes of the NFL ...."); Robertson v. National Basketball Ass'n, 389 F. Supp. 867, 896 (S.D.N.Y. 1975) ("While a *perpetual* reserve system would also appear to be a *per se* violation of the Act, whether such a system exists, and how it operates and comes into being are unclear.") (emphasis added). Judge Larson in his opinion in *Mackey* seems to emphasize that a primary defect in the Rozelle Rule is that it operates as "a perpetual restriction on a player following him throughout his career." 407 F. Supp. at 1007. The appellate court in *Mackey* endorsed this reasoning. *See* 543 F.2d at 622.

803. The court in Smith v. Pro-Football, Inc., 420 F. Supp. 738 (D.D.C. 1976), suggests examples of less restrictive draft systems, but the court disclaims any intention to imply that these would be found acceptable under the rule of reason. *See id.* at 747 n.6.

examination under a rule of reason standard. It seems unlikely that the courts would tolerate, even to the extent of hearing evidence of economic justifications, an arrangement which required a club acquiring a free agent to give up an existing player.[804] Such arrangements have the aura of infringements upon important personal freedoms, a fact which seems to have recently been recognized in some leagues.[805] Whether more innocuous forms of compensation, such as draft choices or cash would be found acceptable, might well depend upon the factual question of the extent to which the movement of players between clubs increased after the system was instituted. In some cases, it might be found that the restraining effect was sufficiently low as to be outweighed by other league interests.

In this same vein, it can be noted, that some of the courts appear to be uncomfortable with restrictions which are largely discretionary on the part of the league. This is indicated most clearly in the opinions which disapprove systems in which a single league official, such as the commissioner, has wide ranging discretion to affect the mobility of particular players.[806] The basic concern appears to be that the greater the range of discretion, the less certainty there is in the consequences of a player's decision to move. The apprehension of the players and future employers about the unknown results of a move tend to make these parties less willing to exercise prerogatives which are otherwise available.[807] This would suggest that the courts are likely to favor controls which operate with clearly defined standards and limitations. A clearer specification of the conditions involved would allow all affected parties, particularly the

---

804. Perhaps the most explicit evidence that such an arrangement would be disapproved is found in the unreported decision in Bryant v. National Football League, Docket No. 75-2543 (C.D. Cal. July 30, 1975) where the court issued a preliminary injunction against Commissioner Rozelle's attempt to require that Cullen Bryant move to Detroit as compensation for a player whom his employer, the Los Angeles Rams, had signed. The case is discussed more fully in § 5.03 *supra*. The use of existing players, as opposed to draft rights, as compensation highlights the most coercive effects of the indemnity system, and because the infringement on personal freedom is so apparent, it is likely that most courts will react adversely to this type of arrangement.

It should be noted, however, that the players have apparently not been unanimously opposed to player-for-player compensation. After *Philadelphia World Hockey,* the NHL instituted an indemnity system which sanctioned the assignment of player contracts as a form of compensation. The NHL players union subsequently approved the indemnity arrangement in collective bargaining. While newspaper accounts are not entirely clear on whether the player-for-player term was retained, it appears that it was. *See* N.Y.Times, Oct. 7, 1975, at 1, col. 8. It will be noted, however, that the situation in hockey is somewhat unique, for it is the one sport in which there are two competing leagues. Moreover, the NHL system includes other protections which temper its impact on player mobility. Equalization decisions are made by an independent arbitrator who is to hear evidence concerning the player's worth. Moreover, free agency status can be readily achieved in the league and thus a player dissatisfied with his involuntary transfer will usually be able to free himself from his new club after one or two years.

805. The 1976 collective bargaining agreement in baseball provides for a partial indemnity system, but provides that the compensation to be given by a club signing a free agent shall be a second round selection in the next player draft. *See* N.Y. Times, July 25, 1976, § 5, at 8, col. 2. *See also* § 5.03 *supra*.

806. *See* Kapp v. National Football League, 390 F. Supp. 73, 82 (N.D. Cal. 1974). *See also* Mackey v. National Football League, 407 F. Supp. 1000, 1006-07 (D. Minn. 1975), *modified,* 543 F.2d 606 (8th Cir. 1976), (concern for fact that compensation under Rozelle Rule is unknown in advance and finding that the Rule does not afford reasonable safeguards to players).

807. *See* Mackey v. National Football League, 407 F. Supp. 1000, 1006 (D. Minn. 1975): "The fact that unknown compensation would be awarded has acted as an effective deterrent to clubs signing free agents without reaching a prior agreement on compensation with that player's former club."

players, to take account of the constraints in negotiating their contracts and evaluating their employment choices.[808]

On another matter, it can be noted that several courts have indicated a receptivity to the leagues' concern that they be permitted to take steps to restrain the strongest franchises from accumulating too much talent.[809] The courts' approval of this notion provides the basis for an argument in support of league rules which attempt to skew the athlete's choice of a new employer in favor of competitively weaker clubs. This could be achieved either by such obvious devices as restricting the clubs who compete for draftees and free agents to a certain number with the worst won-lost records [810] or by more subtle incentives such as an authorization for more favorable contract terms if the player selected such a club. Such devices are specifically structured to preserve or retain competitive balance within the league and appear to come within the concern which the courts seem to regard as paramount.

The existing case law disapproves draft systems which give perpetual rights to the drafting club. One issue which has not been specifically addressed, however, is whether such a perpetual system would be illegal if a league changed its practices to give players significantly greater mobility after fulfilling their first contract. Some may argue that the burden of perpetual draft rights will become "reasonable" if the clubs relinquish their control of the movement of veteran players. Thus, it will be contended that even if the player is initially forced to sign with one club which he may dislike, he will be free to move to another club two or three years thereafter. This argument, however, tends to cut both ways, for if the club has no assurance that it can keep a player beyond a few years, its interest in signing him initially is presumably lessened. The consideration which may ultimately be found persuasive is that which underlies the courts' rejection of perpetual reserve and indemnity systems: the leagues' need to allocate players is outweighed by the concern that the player retain some prerogatives in selecting his employer. A rejection of perpetual draft rights, in favor of rights which endure for a year or so, would seem to introduce a desirable balance into the matter of employer selection. If a player found a particular club wholly unacceptable for reasons of its location, management practices, or the like, he would have the choice of not signing.[811] There would,

---

808. An interesting proposal suggested by one commentator would make the amount of compensation under the indemnity system subject to negotiation between player and club at the time of the initial contract. *See* Note, *The True Story of What Happens When the Big Kids Say, "It's my football, and you'll either play by my rules or you won't play at all,"* 55 NEB. L. REV. 335, 354 (1976). This would seem to be a risky proposition for both parties since they would be required to bargain without full knowledge of one critical fact: the player's value at the end of the contract. A player who did not live up to the club's expectations might find that he had negotiated a ransom which was too high in terms of his value to other teams. By the same token, a club may underestimate the value of the player so that the agreed-upon buy-out price in no sense provides compensation for its loss.

809. *See, e.g.,* Kapp v. National Football League, 390 F. Supp. 73, 81 (N.D. Cal. 1974); Philadelphia World Hockey Club, Inc. v. Philadelphia Hockey Club, Inc., 351 F. Supp. 462, 504 (E.D. Pa. 1972). *See also* Flood v. Kuhn, 316 F. Supp. 271, 275 (S.D.N.Y. 1970).

810. The new arrangement in baseball includes a provision increasing the player's bargaining power, but limiting to twelve the number of clubs with which he may negotiate. Moreover, there are restrictions on the number of free agents which a single club can sign. *See* N.Y. Times, July 25, 1976, § 5, at 8, col. 2. *See also* § 5.03 *supra.*

811. *See* Note, *The True Story of What Happens When the Big Kids Say, "It's my football, and you'll either play by my rules or you won't play at all,"* *supra* note 808, at 353-54.

however, be incentives for him to sign, for he would face the prospect of having to sit out a year. This should prompt most players to overcome mild objections, but those whose complaints were more substantial would be assured that they need not give up their careers in order to avoid an unpleasant relationship.

To conclude this discussion of player restraints, it is appropriate that some mention be made of a line of analysis which has caused difficulty for the courts in other contexts. There are some cases which seem to suggest that a restraint of trade will be deemed reasonable under a rule of reason inquiry only if it is the "least restrictive" device which could be used to accomplish the legitimate objective.[812] The courts following this approach, however, erroneously focus their inquiry on finding an alternative which would be less restrictive on competition, no matter to how small a degree, rather than focusing on whether the restraint actually was reasonable.[813] Application of the "least restrictive alternative" test to the sports area would place an undue burden on the leagues and owners. A player control device designed to achieve the otherwise legitimate purpose of competitive balance among the teams would be subject to attack by anyone sufficiently inventive to devise an alternative which was incrementally less restrictive.[814] Moreover, courts would be placed in the unenviable position of second guessing business judgments concerning the restraint as well as being forced to determine whether the alternative proposed will accomplish the required legitimate commercial goal.[815]

Although relevant to ascertaining the reasonableness of a player restraint, the existence of a less restrictive alternative is not determinative of the restraint's lawfulness.[816] As noted by Judge Adams in *American Motor Inns,*

---

812. *See* Copper Liquors, Inc. v. Adolph Coors Co., 506 F.2d 934, 945 (5th Cir. 1975); Siegel v. Chicken Delight, Inc., 448 F.2d 43, 51 (9th Cir. 1971), *cert. denied,* 405 U.S. 955 (1972). *See generally* Robinson, *Recent Antitrust Developments: 1975,* 76 COLUM. L. REV. 191, 231-33 (1976).

813. *Cf.* American Motor Inns, Inc. v. Holiday Inns, Inc., 521 F.2d 1230, 1249 (3d Cir. 1975).

814. *Cf. id.*

815. *Cf. id.* at 1249-50.

816. [T]he Supreme Court has never indicated that, regardless of the other circumstances present, the availability an alternative means of achieving the asserted business purpose renders the existing arrangement unlawful if that alternative would be less restrictive of competition no matter to how small a degree. American Motor Inns, Inc. v. Holiday Inns, Inc., 521 F.2d 1230, 1249 (3d Cir. 1975).

The less restrictive alternative approach is merely one facet of the rule of reason inquiry into whether the restraint imposed is "reasonably necessary" to accomplish the legitimate objective. *See* Robinson, *Recent Antitrust Developments: 1975, supra* note 812, at 232. In IBM v. United States, 298 U.S. 131 (1936), the Supreme Court proposed various alternatives to the tying clause used by defendants (lessees of IBM equipment forced to use IBM punch cards). The Court's use of such alternatives was only to illustrate the unreasonableness of the existing restraint, "whose substantial benefit to [IBM was] the elimination of business competition and the creation of monopoly, rather than the protection of its good will, ..." 298 U.S. at 140. In International Salt Co. v. United States, 332 U.S. 392 (1947), the Court again struck down a tying clause. Such tying agreements were deemed unreasonable *per se.* 332 U.S. at 396. Noting that other alternatives were available, the Court stated: "Rules for use of leased machinery must not be disguised restraints of free competition, though they may set reasonable standards which all suppliers must meet." 332 U.S. at 398.

The less restrictive approach has been used by other courts to test the reasonableness of the restraint imposed. The court in Smith v. Pro-Football, Inc., 420 F. Supp. 738 (D.D.C. 1976), expressly stated that the alternatives suggested were "meant to show that the present draft is not a reasonable system." *Id.* at 747 n. 6. The court never suggested that the NFL be permitted to use only the restraint with the least impact on competition.

The purpose of the less restrictive alternative approach is to strip away defendant's rationale for

Inc. v. Holiday Inns, Inc., the proper inquiry in a rule of reason case "is whether the restriction actually implemented is 'fairly necessary' in the circumstances of the particular case, or whether the restriction 'exceed[s] the outer limits of restraint reasonably necessary to protect the defendant'." [817] In the current setting, as long as the player restraints imposed are reasonable, and do not extend beyond the limits necessary to achieve the competitive balance required for the continued viability of the sport, they should be deemed lawful.

§ 5.08. Other Antitrust Issues: Playing Rules; Limitations on Roster Size; and Acquisition Deadlines.

The controversy concerning restrictions on player mobility has served to focus attention on the capacity of the league to create and define the market for professional athletic talent. The draft, reserve, and indemnity rules determine the extent to which there will be a demand for players and thus directly affect the economic rewards which an athlete realizes. It should quickly become apparent, however, that the restraints on mobility are not the only league practices which have an effect upon the demand for players' services. There are a wide variety of rules, ranging from those defining the conditions of competition to those governing player discipline, which may affect the economic rewards of particular athletes. The present section and the one which follows consider the antitrust status of several of these league practices. The present section separately considers playing rules, acquisition or trading deadlines, and restrictions on squad size. The next section treats the matter of league discipline. Also relevant is a third section, § 5.10, which considers generally the authority of sports organizations to define participant eligibility. As will be seen, the antitrust principles applied in these three sections are quite similar, and the reader may wish to consult the other materials for further background.

a. Rules of Competition. It is apparent that one necessary attribute of league sports competition is the development of uniform rules to govern on-the-field competition.[818] In order to make league standings, and the eventual designation of a champion, meaningful, it is necessary to insure that all clubs compete under conditions which are essentially the same. In deciding what the particular rules of competition will be, the league will usually pursue a variety of objectives. There is typically an effort to make the professional competition resemble that

---

the restraint imposed. If it is *obvious* that a lesser restraint will suffice, there can be no plausible justification for one more onerous. Thus, the defendant is unable to establish that his conduct was reasonable. *See* Robinson, *Recent Antitrust Developments; 1975, supra* note 812, at 232.

817. American Motor Inns, Inc. v. Holiday Inns, Inc., 521 F.2d 1230, 1248-49 (3d Cir. 1975), *quoting* Walt Disney Productions v. American Broadcasting-Paramount Theatres, 180 F. Supp. 113, 117 (S.D.N.Y. 1960). In *Holiday Inns,* a franchisee sued the motel chain for various violations of the antitrust laws, including a restriction on the franchisee's ownership of motor inns other than those of defendant. Holiday Inns contended that the restraint was necessary to protect its reservation referral system ("Holidex"). The district court found the restraint to be an unreasonable restraint under section 1 of the Sherman Act, noting, among other things, that "[t]he Holidex system can be protected adequately without a 'device' as restrictive of competition as the non-Holiday Inn clause." American Motor Inns, Inc. v. Holiday Inns, Inc., 365 F. Supp. 1073, 1093-94 (D.N.J. 1973).

818. *See generally* Comment, *Antitrust and Professional Sports: Does Anyone Play by the Rules of the Game?,* 22 CATH. U. L. REV. 403, 405-06 (1973); Comment, *The Super Bowl and the Sherman Act: Professional Team Sports and the Antitrust Laws,* 81 HARV. L. REV. 418, 419-20 (1967).

found at the amateur and recreational level. Adjustments may be made, however, in an effort to heighten fan interest. Thus, a baseball league may lower the pitcher's mound and introduce a designated hitter to stimulate each club's scoring potential. In the same vein, a football league may change the position of the goal posts and alter other rules to lessen the impact of relatively unexciting field goals.[819] In its constant effort to achieve a proper balance between offensive and defensive aspects of a game, the league's decision will reflect an interesting mixture of concerns, including concerns for fairness of the competition, the integrity of the game, the safety of the participants, and above all, the economic consequences, as reflected in the level of fan interest and support.[820]

It should be apparent that many rules will have an effect upon the demand for athletic talent, particularly the talent of players with specialized skills. Cases can be hypothesized in which the effect is very direct. For example, if a football league were to totally eliminate field goals and extra-point kicking, the demand for a rather distinct group of players would be virtually eliminated. In the same vein, it can be observed that the introduction of the designated hitter rule in baseball had the effect of lengthening the careers, and not incidentally, enhancing the economic rewards of a number of players who formerly would have been forced into retirement.[821] In other situations, the effects upon economic opportunities are much less dramatic. Lowering the pitcher's mound, moving the goal posts, and the like may marginally reduce the value of some performers and enhance the worth of others. And if the reader will permit the notion to be carried to its logical extreme, it can be observed that such seemingly innocuous rules as those defining the points awarded to particular plays and even those prescribing the permissible forms of defense may affect the opportunities of particular athletes to participate in the economic rewards of professional sports.

The cases involving player restraints indicate that the courts are very much concerned about at least some aspects of the leagues' control of the players' economic opportunities.[822] Can that concern logically be extended to such matters as the rules governing on-the-field competition? An analysis of this question will suggest that the leagues are not likely to encounter significant difficulty under the antitrust laws in this area. But as with many other legal questions in the sports industry, this is not an area where there are specific legal precedents and the analysis necessarily draws upon principles which have developed in other contexts. While this general antitrust doctrine can be applied to resolve most questions in favor of affording the leagues broad prerogatives, there are some lingering doubts, although these stem from cases which are largely hypothetical in nature.

---

819. *See* N.Y. Times, July 18, 1976, § 5, at 8, col. 4 (states the impact on points scored).

820. *See, e.g.,* N.Y. Times, June 19, 1976, at 16, col. 6 (NFL players ejected from the game must leave field; change in unnecessary roughness penalty); Washington Post, June 9, 1976, at D1, col. 1 (NHL stiffens penalties for fighting); N.Y. Times, Dec. 3, 1975, at 54, col. 1 (NFL sudden-death overtime rule increases fan interest).

821. *See* Los Angeles Times, Oct. 30, 1975, Pt. III, at 2, col. 2 (AL votes to keep designated hitter); *id.,* July 17, 1975, Pt. III, at 4, col. 3 (NL votes against use of designated hitter).

822. *See* § 5.07 *supra.*

There are a number of considerations which bear on the issue of the league's rule-making prerogatives. One rather fundamental point is that a sports league cannot be expected to operate according to the free market model on matters of this sort. If the venture is to succeed, it must be accepted that there will necessarily be joint action among the participating firms.[823] The nature of the product involved, league sports, requires that the on-the-field competition be conducted in a manner which allows for fair comparisons to be made between the different entity-clubs, and hence, the establishment of a meaningful league standing. The fact that there is "collusion" between the clubs is not in itself a basis for objection.[824]

Another point which should be indisputable is that the league's decision with respect to the rules of competition will have an unavoidable effect upon the demand for playing talent. Whether the issue is one of defining the number of participants allowed on the playing field at one time or the offensive and defensive maneuvers which will be permitted, the rule which is established will necessarily be an important ingredient in defining the number and types of players a club will need. It would seem to follow, then, that without more, the mere fact that a rule affected the playing opportunities of particular players would not provide the basis for legal objection. Some players are going to be affected by whatever rules are adopted and because that result is inevitable, it would seem inappropriate to use the sole fact of an adverse effect as a reason for applying the antitrust laws.

Whatever limitation exists on the leagues' prerogative to define the rules of competition is likely to find its origins in the cases dealing with the exclusionary practices of private commercial associations.[825] A particularly important case in this area is *Chicago Board of Trade v. United States*.[826] The Board of Trade, which operated an institutional market in farm commodities, instituted a rule which required that certain after-hours grain purchases be made at the price established by the last bid received during regular market hours. This arrangement had an obvious price-fixing flavor to it and prompted a suit by the government to enjoin its enforcement as a violation of the antitrust laws. The Supreme Court's decision reversing a district court order in favor of the government is important in the present inquiry for its suggestion as to the general principles which should govern private group action. The Court refused to characterize the Board's regulation as *per se* illegal and indicated that illegality could be found only after inquiry into the purposes and effects of the rule.[827] It stated specifically that not all regulations which affected competition were to be condemned. Rather, the appropriate inquiry is whether a particular rule suppresses competition, or merely regulates it so that other desirable ends are achieved.[828] On the facts before it, the Court seems to concede that there

---

823. *Cf.* H. DEMMERT, THE ECONOMICS OF PROFESSIONAL TEAM SPORTS 16-20 (1973).

824. *Compare* Timberlake, *Standardization and Simplification Under the Antitrust Laws,* 29 CORNELL L.Q. 301 (1944); Verleger, *Trade Association Participation in Standardization and Simplification Programs,* 27 A.B.A. ANTITRUST SECTION 129 (1956).

825. *See generally* Comment, *Trade Association Exclusionary Practices: An Affirmative Role for the Rule of Reason,* 66 COLUM. L. REV. 1486 (1966).

826. 246 U.S. 231 (1918).

827. *Id.* at 238.

828. *Id.* at 238: "[T]he legality of an agreement on regulations cannot be determined by so simple

was some restraint on competition, but ultimately found the regulation proper in that it produced a more orderly market for the commodities involved.

Thus, *Chicago Board of Trade* can be read as a recognition by the Court that there are certain types of institutional settings which will justify competitive restraints designed to promote other desirable economic goals. More recent cases confirm this general principle [829] and suggest that the critical question is whether a particular group can establish that it possesses the characteristics which justify joint action.[830] A sports league concerned about playing rules should be permitted to have its actions evaluated under this doctrine, for, as previously noted, the need for uniformity of regulation is essential to the success of the venture.[831]

Chicago Board of Trade and related cases do not create a wholesale exemption for joint ventures of this sort. Rather the group actions will still be subject to review under a rule of reason standard.[832] But even under this test, it seems likely that the courts will find that few playing rules raise serious antitrust issues.[833] While most will have some effect upon the competition for athletic talent, this result will almost always be justified by the purpose of the rule and the special needs of the industry. In most cases in which a rule is instituted or modified, the league will be able to show that the modification was undertaken for the purpose of improving the product being offered. Thus, changes will be introduced to make the game more interesting, to provide for the safety of the participants, or to achieve some related goal. These are worthy goals, and if it appears likely that they will be achieved by the particular changes made, that fact should be sufficient to justify the consequences which are felt in the labor market.

While the rule of reason standard normally permits a detailed inquiry into the facts surrounding the adoption of any particular rule, there are many reasons why a court should be reluctant to impose too exacting a burden of proof on the leagues. It will be noted that the rules with which we are concerned are essentially decisions by a business entity as to what type of product it should sell. Thus, the league rule-makers are often deciding whether more or less offense or defense is desirable, whether one type of play will heighten, or dampen, fan interest, and so on. These represent the most basic sorts of business judgments. Such decisions can seldom be made with perfect information, and undoubtedly the best possible alternatives will not always be selected. But courts will not normally be in any better position to weigh the relevant

---

a test as whether it restrains competition. Every agreement concerning trade, every regulation of trade, restrains. To bind, to restrain, is of their very essence. The true test of legality is whether the restraint imposed is such as merely regulates and perhaps thus promotes competition or whether it is such as may suppress or even destroy competition."

829. *See, e.g.,* Silver v. New York Stock Exchange, 373 U.S. 292 (1963); Radiant Burners, Inc. v. Peoples Gas Light & Coke Co., 364 U.S. 656 (1961); Cowen v. New York Stock Exchange, 256 F. Supp. 462 (N.D.N.Y. 1966), *aff'd,* 371 F.2d 651 (2d Cir. 1967).

830. *See* Comment, *Trade Association Exclusionary Practices: An Affirmative Role for the Rule of Reason, supra* note 825, at 1499-1502.

831. *See* text at note 823 *supra.*

832. *See* Chicago Board of Trade v. United States, 246 U.S. 231 (1918).

833. *See* Comment, *Antitrust and Professional Sports: Does Anyone Play by the Rules of The Game?, supra* note 818, at 405-06; Comment, *The Super Bowl and the Sherman Act: Professional Team Sports and the Antitrust Laws, supra* note 818, at 419-20.

considerations. As in most business settings, a rational evaluation of the effects of a particular decision upon the success of the venture requires a familiarity with the nature of the product and the nature of the market. The nuances of these qualities are not easily conveyed in a litigation setting. Moreover, it should be appreciated that the concern for the effects of a particular rule upon the demand for athletic talent is seldom clear-cut. As noted above, any rule change is likely to have some effect in the labor market, and while some players with particular talents may be disadvantaged, others will usually find their value enhanced.[834] Because of the directness of these interrelations between the rules and the demand for special skills, it is difficult to formulate any ordering of the relative equities of the persons affected. And, again, it is doubtful that courts have any special insights which would insure a more efficient balance between the competing concerns.

The limitations on the judicial capacity for meaningful review do not lead to the conclusion that the courts should never intervene. What they do suggest, though, is that the courts should be prepared to deal summarily with complaints which do not include a showing of exceptional circumstances. While courts are normally reluctant to use summary judgment proceedings against plaintiffs in antitrust proceedings,[835] the present area is one in which the courts should look critically at the allegations made before subjecting the leagues to the burden of a full-blown rule of reason hearing. Thus, the court can make a preliminary inquiry into such matters as whether the rule change represents a good-faith business judgment, whether the primary motive was enhancement of the sports product, and whether there is any evidence of a hostile motive on the part of the decision-makers. It would seem that the plaintiff should be required to make a threshold showing of inappropriateness under these norms before being allowed to lead the court into the uncertain process of a detailed review of the economic considerations relevant to the rule.

What type of case would raise a serious antitrust question? The fact is that there are few realistic examples. The pattern of recent rule changes involving such things as the designated hitters, field goal restrictions, and the like, seem well within the bounds of reasonableness. If a case for judicial scrutiny arises, it will likely involve some element of bad faith by the rule-makers. Thus, one can hypothesize a situation in which playing restrictions are imposed to coerce a particular group of players who are demanding substantial salary increases or who are involved in efforts to form a rival league. These are extreme cases, of course. But the fact that they are far removed from the sorts of decisions which have routinely been made in the past serves to underscore the basic conclusion reached above. The matter of playing rules is not likely to be a fruitful source of litigation for those who are adversely affected, and the plaintiff will bear a substantial burden for showing that the leagues have misused their power to define the playing skills which will be in demand. As long as the decisions

---

834. For example, a decision to move the goal posts ten yards from the playing field produces a disadvantage for field goal kickers and may lessen their value; but by the same token, the value of the other players who would participate in the alternative scoring maneuver is marginally enhanced.

835. *See, e.g.,* Poller v. Columbia Broadcasting System, Inc., 368 U.S. 464, 473 (1962); Chuy v. Philadelphia Eagles, 407 F. Supp. 717 (E.D. Pa. 1976).

are based on the usual concerns for improving the sports product, they are entitled to the deference of the courts.

b. Roster Limitations and Acquisition Deadlines. League rules limiting the number of players which a club has on its roster and prohibiting the acquisition of new players after a certain date are closely related, at least in their objectives, to rules governing on-the-field competition. The apparent purpose of such rules is to promote the equality of competition by controlling the clubs' access to playing talent during the playing season. If clubs could freely add players, early season games would lose their significance, and the race for the championship would lose much of its appeal. While these restrictions are to be evaluated according to the same principles which apply to the playing rules discussed above,[836] it is useful to consider them separately because they represent much more explicit restraints upon the players' ability to market their services. The argument will be made that a limitation on roster size has an effect upon the total demand for professional athletes in the particular sport. If the restrictions were removed, it will be contended, some teams, particularly those with greater financial resources would hire more players and thus provide employment opportunities which are presently being denied.[837] It will be contended that an acquisition or trading deadline also restricts competition for players. The argument here is somewhat more elaborate. If the rule operates to prohibit new acquisitions in midseason, a free agent or other player not under contract will be denied the opportunity to contract with a club which might have been willing to compensate him well for contributing to its efforts to prevail in a close league race.[838] It may also be contended that a trading deadline affects the opportunities of players already under contract. But for the artificial restraint, both the player and his employer might accept an assignment of the contract which provided a substantial return to the original club and an increased salary for the player.[839] The likelihood of such a transfer is enhanced if the athlete is a star performer for a club clearly out of the pennant race and the prospective employer is a championship contender which could use the player's services to cover a weakness in its team. In most leagues, such last minute trades are not permitted solely by virtue of an agreement among the employer-clubs.

Again, the validity of these restraints is to be determined under the rule of reason. Thus, it is appropriate to investigate the effects of the rules to determine whether the restrictions are reasonable in light of the purposes sought to be achieved. The few commentators who addressed the question have found the restrictions to be justified under the same principles which sustain the league's specification of uniform playing rules.[840] However, there is one case, *Bowman*

---

836. *See* text at notes 825-33 *supra.*

837. *Cf.* Canes, *The Social Benefits of Restrictions on Team Quality* in Government and the Sports Business 81, 103 (R. Noll ed. 1974).

838. *See* Bowman v. National Football League, 402 F. Supp. 754 (D. Minn. 1975).

839. There have been numerous cases in which a club has renegotiated a player's salary following an assignment of his contract. A colorful account of Ken Harrelson's successful efforts to more than double his salary in a trade is given in B. Woolf, Behind Closed Doors 62-76 (1976).

840. *See* Comment, *Antitrust and Professional Sports: Does Anyone Play by the Rules of the Game?, supra* note 818, at 405-06; Comment, *The Super Bowl and the Sherman Act: Professional Team Sports and the Antitrust Laws, supra* note 818, at 419-20.

v. National Football League,[841] which casts some doubt upon the certainty of that conclusion. The *Bowman* case is the only decision to date which touches upon these issues and it is likely that it will not be the final word. The opinion is written in such sweeping terms that the decision could have a much greater unsettling effect than the limited issue before the court should warrant. However, a close examination of the court's treatment indicates that some of its broader implications were probably unintentional. The fact situation presented was rather unique, and the significance of the case can be limited accordingly.

The plaintiffs in *Bowman* were former WFL players who were seeking employment in the NFL after their league had gone out of business. Their complaint focused on a resolution which the NFL owners had adopted to deal with the potential influx of WFL players. The measure, adopted in September of 1975 when the demise of the rival league seemed imminent, provided as follows:

> Resolved, for 1975 only, that any player who has been under a 1975 contract as a player or coach in another major professional football league may not sign with any NFL club for 1975. The foregoing provision shall not apply to players who are without any further contractual obligation within such league and whose club or league ceases to operate. In no event may any such player be signed for 1975 play after cessation of intraconference trading at 4 p.m. Eastern Time Tuesday, October 28.[842]

It will be noted that the prohibition was to be applicable only for the 1975 season and closely coincided with the deadline applied to intraleague acquisitions. The NFL clubs presumably would be permitted to sign WFL free agents to play in 1976 and thereafter.

The WFL formally ceased operations on about October 22,[843] although several teams had folded before that date and the ultimate cessation of the league could have been forecast earlier. The NFL resolution was subsequently modified to establish the signing deadline at October 24, four days earlier than originally stated.[844] It appears that the deadline was advanced, at least in part, due to the announcement of John Bassett, owner of the WFL Memphis franchise that he would sue the NFL if it attempted to sign players to whom he had a claim.[845] It had been reported that Bassett would keep his team intact and attempt to secure an NFL franchise. The *Bowman* suit was filed after the NFL deadline had passed, and the initial decision granting a preliminary injunction was issued in the first week in November, which again was after the signing deadline and after the last day for interconference trades.

The league resisted the preliminary injunction on several grounds. It was

841. 402 F. Supp. 754 (D. Minn. 1975). The *Bowman* decision is commented on in Sobel, *The Emancipation of Professional Athletes,* 3 WES. ST. U. L. REV. 185, 218-20 (1976).

842. 402 F. Supp. at 755.

843. *See* Sporting News, Nov. 11, 1975, at 6, col. 1; Los Angeles Times, Oct. 23, 1975, Pt. III, at 1, col. 5; Gazette (Montreal), Oct. 23, 1975, at 28, col. 6 (announcements of the demise of the WFL).

844. 402 F. Supp. at 755.

845. *See* Los Angeles Times, Oct. 25, 1975, Pt. III, at 1, col. 5 (NFL teams barred from signing WFL players after threatened suit by WFL franchise owner); Washington Post, Nov. 6, 1975, at B1, col. 6 (analysis of effect of *Bowman* decision).

emphasized that the signing deadline, which effectively precluded WFL players from entering the NFL, was imposed in an effort to avoid upsetting the competitive balance among the NFL clubs as they entered the critical period which would determine the league's divisional leaders.[846] Moreover, it was argued that the action was appropriate in light of the threat of a lawsuit if the league interfered with the rights of the WFL owners.[847] Finally, it was emphasized that various NFL clubs held rights to most of the WFL players, and it would be difficult, and potentially disruptive, to attempt to resolve competing claims in mid-season.[848]

Judge Dewitt chose not to respond to these contentions and instead issued an opinion which consisted of a *pro forma* recital of the grounds upon which the preliminary injunction was issued. The court stated that it was likely that the plaintiffs would prevail on the merits. Thus, the court stated that they could show that the NFL agreement amounted to a conspiracy to restrain competition for the plaintiffs' services and that "the conspiracy has as its object the deprivation of plaintiff's [sic] rights to freedom of contract." [849] To support its conclusion that this established a likely violation of the antitrust laws, the court cited, without elaboration, two classic group boycott cases, *Klor's Inc. v. Broadway-Hale Stores, Inc.*[850] and *Fashion Originators' Guild of America v. FTC,*[851] and two sports decisions which found antitrust violations in other situations.[852] The court did not cite, or deal with, the several cases and considerable body of commentary which suggests that *Klor's* and *Fashion Originators' Guild* should not be literally applied in the sports area.[853] The implication of the court's selection of cases is that the NFL's action amounted to a *per se* violation of the antitrust laws. As noted, many courts have been reluctant to apply that standard to cases of first impression in the sports context.[854] Further, the basis for its application in *Bowman* is particularly unclear in light of the fact that the alleged boycott was not perpetual, but only for the balance of the playing season which had been partially completed.[855]

Apart from the merits of the plaintiffs' complaint, it was also necessary for the court to find that the grounds for granting preliminary relief had been met.

---

846. 402 F. Supp. at 755.

847. *Id.*

848. *Id.* It will be noted that the injunction issued in *Bowman* did not attempt to interfere with any prior rights which NFL clubs held in the returning WFL players. Thus, many of the players apparently did not enjoy complete freedom to seek employment in the NFL.

849. *Id.* at 756.

850. 359 U.S. 207 (1959).

851. 312 U.S. 457 (1941).

852. The other cases cited were Blalock v. Ladies Professional Golf Ass'n, 359 F. Supp. 1260 (N.D. Ga. 1973) and Denver Rockets v. All-Pro Management Inc., 325 F. Supp. 1049 (C.D. Cal. 1971). The court also cited Haywood v. National Basketball Ass'n, 401 U.S. 1204 (1971), which involved a limited review of the *Denver Rockets* decision.

853. *See, e.g.,* Kapp v. National Football League, 390 F. Supp. 73 (N.D. Cal. 1974); Philadelphia World Hockey Club, Inc. v. Philadelphia Hockey Club, Inc., 351 F. Supp. 462, 503-04 (E.D. Pa. 1972); Flood v..Kuhn, 309 F. Supp. 793, 801 n.26 (S.D.N.Y. 1970); Rivkin, *Sports Leagues and the Federal Antitrust Laws* in Government and the Sports Business 387, 395-402 (R. Noll ed. 1974); Comment, *The Super Bowl and the Sherman Act: Professional Team Sports and the Antitrust Laws, supra* note 818, at 420-26.

854. Some of the reasons why the classic group boycott cases may not be fully applicable in the sports context are discussed in the text accompanying notes 774-78, § 5.07 *supra.*

855. *See* text at notes 862-64 *infra.*

On the question of whether the plaintiffs would suffer irreparable damage unless a summary order were entered, Judge Dewitt stated that the plaintiffs would suffer harm "not compensable in terms of damages and that the court's capacity to do justice will thereby be rendered futile." [856] It is not clear, however, why the plaintiffs could not be made whole by a subsequent award of money damages which compensated them for any salary which would have been lost by their inability to play out the season, assuming that a full hearing on the merits established the necessary antitrust violation. The court made reference to the "physical and professional detriment" which the plaintiffs would suffer if denied employment.[857] Perhaps the court felt that the plaintiffs' playing skills would deteriorate if they were not allowed to play the last games of the season. However, there were only six to ten games remaining (depending on whether a prospective employer-club qualified for the playoffs), and the plaintiffs presumably had available other alternatives for maintaining their condition until the signing moratorium passed. In light of these facts, it can be debated whether the plaintiffs' interest in employment for a half-season satisfied the usual standards for irreparable harm.[858]

It was also necessary for the court to find that public policy would support the issuance of the injunction. The court's brief treatment of this issue contains perhaps the most controversial statement of the opinion. Judge Dewitt found that

> Professional sports and the public are better served by open unfettered competition for playing positions.[859]

The reason why this conclusion should cause no small pause arises from the timing of the order which was entered. The time had passed during which the clubs were allowed to bolster their rosters with players secured in intraleague trades. Thus, the league had identified the point at which clubs had to make their final personnel selections before entering the last important phases of the competition for the league championship. This was done presumably in an effort to avoid last minute acquisitions by one club which would undermine the significance of the advancements that other clubs had made in prior contests. That the prohibition on such new additions was extended to players from outside the league, as well as those within the conference, would hardly seem to represent a basic inequity. The court's statement embracing the desirability of "open unfettered competition for playing positions" could be read as disapproving any restraint on a club's acquisition of new talent. Moreover, under this reading of the case, the finding that this competition was "in the public interest" repudiates the league judgment that fan interest in the championship

---

856. 402 F. Supp. at 756.

857. *Id.*

858. There are other problems of proof in establishing the plaintiffs' monetary injury, but none of these appear to be insurmountable. There is an issue as to what the plaintiffs' compensation would have been had they actually signed. Presumably, the court could look to the player's previous salary, his salary for 1976, and average salaries for players with similar skills. There is also a question as to whether the player would have been signed at all and a damage award would be appropriate only if this could be established. While this, again, is not a matter subject to certain proof, a reasonable determination could be made in most cases based on the player's level of skill, his ability to secure employment in 1976, and the needs of NFL teams in 1975.

859. 402 F. Supp. at 756.

race is likely to be heightened if the composition of a team is stabilized for the final critical period of the competition.

The league's rationale for its action was undermined somewhat by the fact that the rules restricting late-season acquisitions apparently did not apply to free agents. Thus, the plaintiffs were able to allege that the distinction made between former WFL players and free agents was irrational.[860] The court did not use this point in its summary analysis. It is not clear, however, that it adds any particular support to the result reached. While a league prohibition on all new acquisitions would make its rules more consistent, the allowance for free agents does not necessarily destroy the defendant's case for restricting the entry of players from other leagues. As a practical matter there are likely to be very few free agents who have either the skills or the conditioning to make an immediate contribution to a club. At a minimum, a factual investigation would be warranted to determine whether this exception had been utilized with any frequency. The WFL players would seem to represent a much more realistic threat to the league's efforts to stabilize rosters for the last part of the season. Indeed, they would seem to stand on much the same footing as the players which might be acquired in intraleague trades. They have presumably already been through the physical conditioning and practice which would make them adaptable to a new club after a brief period of training. Thus, while the league had apparently not drawn its lines with precision, the flaws which appeared did not seem entirely germane to the controversy before the court.

In the final analysis, there is a question as to how broadly the *Bowman* decision should be read. As indicated above, some might interpret the decision as holding that it is impermissible for the league to prevent clubs from acquiring new talent during the playing season. The court's finding that the plaintiffs could likely establish that they had been deprived of their right to freedom of contract, its uncritical citations to the classic *per se* boycott cases, and its pronouncement on the desirability of "open unfettered" competition all lend support to this view. But the case also is susceptible to a much narrower reading. All the court really needed to decide was that the league had operated improperly in effectively foreclosing all opportunities for the WFL players to enter the NFL in the 1975 season. Thus, it would seem important that by advancing the signing deadline, the league had subjected the WFL players to a rule which was substantially more restrictive than that applied to intraleague acquisitions. The only apparent justification was the threat of litigation by the WFL franchise owner. Since the new signings would be limited to players who had been freed from their WFL contracts,[861] that threat may not have justified the action which was taken. Under this view, *Bowman* would be read as holding that since other types of acquisitions were permitted, the league should have afforded some limited period in which the WFL players could have been signed.

It should be emphasized that whatever interpretation is applied to the case, the *Bowman* court's treatment of the league's interest in stabilizing club rosters

---

860. *See id.* at 755.

861. *See* Winnipeg Free Press, Nov. 26, 1975, at 69, col. 3 (Memphis Chancery Court judge rules that players Willie Spencer and Ed Marshall are bound to WFL contracts under which they are still being paid). *See also* Washington Post, Nov. 6, 1975, at B1, col. 6 (NFL clubs deny that Willie Spencer is available to be signed).

is not very satisfactory and should not control future inquiries into the issue. The court merely recited the league's concerns and issued its order without specific reference to these. Nor is there an effort to state the significance which was attached to such factors as the dubious threat of litigation from WFL owners, the discriminatory nature of the NFL's treatment of the rival league's players, or the number of regular season games which remained to be played. Thus, the court's rationale takes account of neither the general defense offered to support limitations on acquisitions or the peculiar features of the fact situation before it. The question of the league's right to control mid-season acquisition of talent is of sufficient importance to warrant a more thorough treatment.

When the occasion does arise for a further inquiry, there are a number of points which should be considered. In this regard, it is useful to treat acquisition deadlines as raising somewhat different problems than roster size limitations. Despite *Bowman's* suggestion to the contrary, the league should be given some freedom to control the timing of a club's efforts to acquire new talent. There appears to be nothing sinister in the judgment that the final stages of championship competition ought to be a test of a club's ability to mold a given roster of players into an effective playing unit. It seems likely that fan interest in the league race will be enhanced if there is some assurance that a club cannot quickly change its advantage by importing new talent. It should also be noted that the league controls on new acquisitions, while they do represent some restraint on the players' freedom to contract, do not partake of the features which have led courts to question the validity of the more pervasive restraints embodied in the draft, reserve clause, and indemnity systems.[862] The lessening of competition which results from those devices operates for a substantial period of time, and indeed in the case of the pervasive restraints which have been the focus of the litigation to date, the effects follow the player throughout his career.[863] A trading or acquisition deadline, on the other hand, affects competition for only a limited period, and the restraint which is imposed disappears when the playing season ends. Further, it can be noted that a deadline for acquisitions does not have the same self-serving economic impact which is found in traditional player restraints. Those restraints raise difficult questions, for while they may promote the desirable goal of equalizing playing strengths, they also conveniently serve the clubs' interest in reducing the price paid for players. There is usually a question as to which of these provides the primary motivation for the league's continuation of the practices.[864] It is much less clear that clubs gain any substantial improper economic advantage by limiting the period in which new players may be acquired. Rather, the rules seem more singularly directed to enhancing the product of the league's joint venture.

---

862. *See generally* § 5.07 *supra.*

863. A number of courts have identified the perpetual nature of the mobility restraints as a primary source of concern. This aspect of the cases is considered in the text accompanying notes 726-69, in § 5.07 *supra.*

864. Among the authorities considering the importance of the purpose of a restraint are Bridge Corp. of America v. American Contract Bridge League, 428 F.2d 1365 (9th Cir. 1970); United States v. United States Trotting Ass'n, 1960 Trade Cas. ¶ 69,761 (S.D. Ohio); and Barber, *Refusals to Deal Under the Federal Antitrust Laws,* 103 U. PA. L. REV. 847 (1955). *See also* text at notes 675-85, § 5.07 *supra.*

Unless compelling evidence of a different purpose or of a more substantial injury to competition can be shown, the league's use of roster-stabilizing rules would seem to be justified.

Restrictions on total squad size are not as easily dealt with as limitations on new acquisitions. It will be argued that their effect on competition is more durable, and that while the rules may serve a useful business purpose, they also tend to further the economic self-interest of the leagues which enforce them. Thus, the rules may limit the club's demand for players and although this may help to equalize competitive balance within the league, it may also conveniently reduce the amount which a club has to spend for players in order to field a suitable team. Since other rules which have been called into question involve a similar coalescing of ulterior justification and potentially impermissible economic self-interest, it might be contended that restrictions on squad size should similarly be subjected to close scrutiny under the antitrust laws.

However, further analysis should suggest that the leagues are justified in taking some action in an attempt to insure that each club operates under similar restrictions as far as its available pool of playing talent is concerned. In approaching this matter, it is useful to distinguish between the question of whether the league may properly impose a uniform squad-size limitation and the issue of what the numerical limitation should be. There are several considerations which support the leagues' traditional practices of requiring uniformity. As has already been noted in connection with the discussion of restraints on player mobility, the league seems to have a legitimate interest in attempting to secure some balance between the relative strengths of its member clubs.[865] Because of differences in the skills of individual players, a precise balance is difficult, if not, impossible to achieve. Nonetheless, there are steps which can be taken to remove some of the more obvious opportunities for dominance by a few clubs. One of these is a rule limiting the number of players which a club has available to it. Such a measure has the effect of placing clubs on a somewhat equal footing as they go into competition. Moreover, it will be noted that such a control is very much related to the concern that league competition not be dominated by the clubs located in the most lucrative markets. These clubs presumably have more resources available and thus, could afford to maintain a larger roster than those operating in more marginal franchises.[866] While, again, it is not possible to remove all disparities which might arise, it seems proper for the leagues to attempt to control the extent to which these are manifest in on-the-field competition.

As in the case of the playing rules discussed above, the league's use of uniform roster limitations can also be seen as part of its effort to define the type of sports competition which is offered. The leagues have said, in effect, that the product they sell will involve efforts by various clubs to make the most effective use of a stated number of players to fill an allotted number of playing positions. The limitation thus provides an additional element of strategy as club managers are

---

865. *See* text at notes 662-67, § 5.07 *supra.*

866. For the economist's view of the relationship between the size of a metropolitan area and the likely success of a franchise located therein, see Quirk & El Hodiri, *The Economic Theory of Professional Sports League* in GOVERNMENT AND THE SPORTS BUSINESS 33 (R. Noll ed. 1974).

forced to decide how the restricted number of roster positions will be filled by the various types of playing specialties which are available. Because all clubs operate under the same limitation, comparisons between respective performances are appropriate, and these can be readily translated into a meaningful league standing.

This analysis suggests that the requirement of uniformity can be sustained under the antitrust laws even though it is shown to affect competition for players. While on the surface player limits have the characteristics of a classic group boycott, the special needs of the league's joint venture should be sufficient to avoid a *per se* condemnation. Moreover, assuming that the league can bring forth factual evidence to substantiate the relationship between roster restrictions and competitive balance, the resort to uniform controls should also survive scrutiny under the rule of reason standard.[867] The thrust of the arguments suggested above is that the free market model cannot be applied with full force to a joint venture such as a sports league. The success of the enterprise requires that the league be able to stage exhibitions between units which are generally comparable, and thus mechanisms such as the roster restrictions are necessary to minimize the natural advantage which some clubs would otherwise enjoy.

The analysis is somewhat less certain when the focus shifts to the issue of whether the league has acted properly in selecting a particular numerical limit. On the one hand, there will be a concern that the economic self-interest of the member clubs will prompt the league to adopt limits which are more restrictive than those which are necessary to insure the viability of its enterprise. Once each club is assured of a critical core of players, the marginal impact of the remaining roster positions is probably slight, and the addition or deletion of these slots may not have an appreciable impact on the quality of competition. In deciding what the cut-off point will be, the clubs' discretion may be influenced more by their desire to maximize profits than by concerns for competitive balance and economic viability. Since only the latter considerations provide a justification for uniform roster limits, the objection might be raised that the league should lose its right to special treatment under the antitrust laws when it uses its rule-making prerogatives to achieve other goals.

Despite the theoretical appeal of these arguments, a determination of the antitrust status of a particular numerical limit must take account of several other factors. For example, it must be accepted that the most important issues in this area are not susceptible to precise factual analysis. Whether one numerical limit or another best serves the "legitimate" purposes of a restriction on roster size is not an issue which can be readily resolved. By the same token, the addition or deletion of a particular number of positions is likely to have *some* effect upon the quality of on-the-field competition, and whether this marginal impact is desirable or necessary is likely to be a point upon which there will be honest differences of opinion. These difficulties would seem to weigh in favor of giving the clubs a range of discretion in selecting the limit which they will

---

867. *See* Comment, *Antitrust and Professional Sports: Does Anyone Play by the Rules of the Game?*, 22 CATH. U. L. REV. 403, 405-06 (1973); Comment, *The Super Bowl and the Sherman Act: Professional Team Sports and the Antitrust Laws*, 81 HARV. L. REV. 418, 419-20 (1967).

observe. As in the case of playing rules, it is doubtful that the courts would bring any special insights to bear on the matters in controversy, and there is real risk that the relevant framework for decision-making cannot be duplicated in the litigation setting.

These concerns should suggest that while judicial intervention might be appropriate in some cases, such action would require rather convincing evidence that the league's choice of a roster restriction did not further the goals of maintaining competitive balance insuring economic viability. It is doubtful that the plaintiff will be able to meet this burden in the types of cases which are likely to arise in practice. If the court found that a change in the player limit was linked to a particular cause, such as financial difficulty among some clubs or a general decline in fan interest, it should be prepared to accept the resulting effect on competition. Likewise, where a league has operated with a particular limit for sometime, it will be difficult for a plaintiff to mount a successful challenge. If the league's venture has been successful, that fact should weigh heavily in the determination of whether its judgment about the proper roster size was reasonable. While the clubs might be financially able to carry more players, it would presumably be necessary to show that an increase would contribute to the quality of the product and not simply add to the expense of producing it. Apart from the situations noted, the range of cases giving rise to serious controversy is relatively narrow. While the prospective plaintiff may feel that he has identified such an exceptional case, he should appreciate that he bears a substantial burden in establishing that the league's action fell outside the broad range of discretion which it is likely to be afforded.

§ 5.09.   Player Discipline.

An earlier section of these materials considers some of the private law aspects of the disciplinary systems used by sports enterprises.[868] In the present section we turn our attention to a different question, the extent to which the antitrust laws operate to protect the athlete from unreasonable discipline. While much of the following discussion deals with this discipline issue as it arises in the context of league sports, the principles which emerge are equally applicable to other professional sports activities, such as golf and tennis, which involve individual, as opposed to team, competition. Although the disciplining authority in individual sports usually has a different structure than in a league setting,[869] the principles applicable to both types of activities have a common source.[870]

It should also be noted that the present topic involves issues which are closely related to those which arise when sports associations undertake to sanction particular events or determine the eligibility of participants. Litigation may result when the sanctioning group refuses to approve the use of a particular

---

868. *See* § 3.10 *supra.* Note 325 of that section includes a list of cases and materials which bear on the question of discipline. As the shortness of that list suggests, this is not a matter which has received extensive attention by either courts or commentators.

869. *Compare* Molinas v. National Basketball Ass'n, 190 F. Supp. 241 (S.D.N.Y. 1961) *with* Blalock v. Ladies Professional Golf Ass'n, 359 F. Supp. 1260 (N.D. Ga. 1973).

870. *See generally* Comment, *Trade Association Exclusionary Practices: An Affirmative Role for the Rule of Reason,* 66 COLUM. L. REV. 1486 (1966).

facility [871] or declines to permit an individual to participate in the competition.[872] While a consideration of the antitrust applications of such restrictions on eligibility is reserved for the next section, it should be clear that the present topic involves similar questions of the right of sports groups to control an individual's access to competitive opportunities.[873] The reader may thus wish to consider the materials in section 5.10 in connection with the present discussion. The reader may also wish to consult sections 5.04-.06, for the present discussion proceeds on the assumption that the disciplinary action in question has not been immunized from antitrust review under the labor exemption, which is discussed in the sections identified.

The discipline situations most likely to attract the attention of courts are those in which a league or sports association imposes the severe sanction of suspending a participant from competition. While such action might be taken for a variety of reasons, the few cases in this area suggest that allegations that the participant has cheated in competition or has bet on the outcome of his or her performance are particularly apt to prompt such drastic measures.[874] Such a suspension has many of the attributes of a group boycott.[875] When a league denies an athlete the right to continue playing, there is, in effect, a joint agreement among the member clubs that they will refuse to deal with the player for the period of the suspension. This joint action produces an injury, for the athlete is precluded from selling his or her services to the group and thus is denied an important means of livelihood. If this characterization were accepted without qualification, the legal result would seem clear, for concerted refusals to deal are usually treated as *per se* unreasonable under the antitrust laws.[876] But while that result might be clear, it would also be absurd. It would be a rather startling notion if the antitrust laws meant that a business operation such as a league could not protect itself against actions of participants which might seriously injure, if not destroy, the enterprise. The success of most professional sports activities depends upon the fans' belief that games and matches represent honest competition. Except perhaps in professional wrestling, the premise upon which the exhibitions are offered is that they represent a true test of the skills, conditioning, and coaching of the opposing sides. It seems unlikely that the interest of fans would continue at present levels if they had reason to believe that the outcome of the competition was controlled by factors other than the personal efforts of those participating and the pre-established rules of the game.[877]

---

871. *See* Washington State Bowling Proprietors Ass'n v. Pacific Lanes, Inc., 356 F.2d 271 (9th Cir. 1966).

872. *See* Deesen v. Professional Golfers' Ass'n, 358 F.2d 165 (9th Cir. 1966).

873. *See generally* Comment, *Trade Association Exclusionary Practices: An Affirmative Role for the Rule of Reason, supra* note 870.

874. *See, e.g.,* Blalock v. Ladies Professional Golf Ass'n, 359 F. Supp. 1260 (N.D. Ga. 1973); Molinas v. National Basketball Ass'n, 190 F. Supp. 241 (S.D.N.Y. 1961); United States v. United States Trotting Ass'n, 1960 Trade Cas. ¶ 69,761 (S.D. Ohio).

875. *Cf.* Silver v. New Stock Exchange, 373 U.S. 292 (1963).

876. *See, e.g.,* Klor's, Inc. v. Broadway-Hale Stores, Inc., 359 U.S. 207 (1959); Fashion Originators' Guild of America v. FTC, 312 U.S. 457 (1941). The group boycott cases are discussed in more detail at notes 668-86, § 5.07 *supra.*

877. The potential repercussions of player misconduct are illustrated rather starkly by the Black Sox scandal of 1919 in which eight players confessed that they had accepted bribes to throw the

While the Supreme Court seemed to indicate at one time that all group boycotts were *per se* illegal,[878] it subsequently recognized that its pronouncements to this effect could not be applied literally. Particularly relevant in this connection is the Court's decision in *Silver v. New York Stock Exchange.*[879] The case, which is discussed more fully in a prior section,[880] arose when the stock exchange attempted to prevent Silver, a non-member, from gaining access to exchange transactions by means of a private telephone connection with certain member firms. *Silver* involves a number of issues which are relevant to our discussion of discipline, but particularly pertinent for the immediate inquiry is the Court's suggestion that the summary condemnation of concerted refusals to deal under the antitrust statutes will not be applied where there is a "justification derived from the policy of another statute or otherwise." [881] Because the controversy in *Silver* focused on the question of whether another statute — the Securities Exchange Act — provided a justification for the defendant's refusal to deal with the plaintiff, the case offers little indication of the types of facts which might "otherwise" avoid summary condemnation under the *per se* doctrine. However, other courts, both before and after *Silver,* have had occasion to address the question of the right of private groups to engage in self-regulation. These courts have generally accepted that there are certain types of group actions which cannot be adequately dealt with under the *per se* doctrine, but rather require a more detailed inquiry into the reasonableness of the action taken.[882] Among the groups which are entitled to this more deliberate treatment are those engaged in activities of a nature which require self-policing of standards of conduct and methods of competition.[883]

Sports enterprises would appear to present clear examples of groups which need this authority for self-regulation. Not only are rules necessary for the successful staging of competition,[884] but in addition, the groups have an interest in insuring that their ventures remain free of illegal and fraudulent activities which might undermine fan support. Moreover, it will be noted that private

World Series. *See generally* E. ASINOF, EIGHT MEN OUT (1963). The event produced a considerable public outcry about the integrity of the game and threatened the existence of the league as three clubs threatened to withdraw and join another association. *See* Davis, *Self-Regulation in Baseball, 1909-71* in GOVERNMENT AND THE SPORTS BUSINESS 349, 376-77 (R. Noll ed. 1974).

878. *See* Klor's, Inc. v. Broadway-Hale Stores, Inc., 359 U.S. 292, 312 (1963). *See also* text accompanying notes 668-70, § 5.07 *supra.*

879. 373 U.S. 292 (1963).

880. *See* text accompanying notes 675-85, § 5.07 *supra.*

881. 373 U.S. at 348-49. *See generally* Comment, *Trade Association Exclusionary Practices: An Affirmative Role for the Rule of Reason, supra* note 870.

882. *See, e.g.,* Bridge Corp. of America v. American Contract Bridge League, Inc., 428 F.2d 1365 (9th Cir. 1970); Deesen v. Professional Golfers' Ass'n, 358 F.2d 165 (9th Cir. 1966); Denver Rockets v. All-Pro Management, Inc., 325 F. Supp. 1049 (C.D. Cal. 1971); STP Corp. v. United States Auto Club, 286 F. Supp. 146 (S.D. Ind. 1968); Molinas v. National Basketball Ass'n, 190 F. Supp. 241 (S.D.N.Y. 1966); United States v. United States Trotting Ass'n, 1960 Trade Cas. ¶ 69,761 (S.D. Ohio). *But see* note 901 *infra.*

883. *See* Comment, *Trade Association Exclusionary Practices: An Affirmative Role for the Rule of Reason, supra* note 870, at 1501-02.

884. The essence of "league competition" is the race for the league championship. In order for the designation of the champion to be meaningful, it is necessary that the teams compete according to the same rules so that comparison can be made. Thus, the league has an interest in defining the types of plays which will be permitted, the types of individual on-the-field conduct which will be proscribed, and so on.

regulation is necessary because traditional public legal remedies — those secured through the criminal process or through civil actions — are typically inadequate. Depending on the nature of the violation, such remedies either are not available or afford a form of relief which does not provide sufficient protection of the group's interest in preserving the integrity of the competition. For example, cheating under privately-defined rules does not normally involve a violation of the public criminal law, and there is no clear body of civil law doctrine which would provide a complete remedy.[885] Since such misconduct represents a clear threat to the success of the private venture, it seems appropriate that the group which controls it be given authority to take corrective action.

The recognition that sports authorities enjoy some discretion to regulate the conduct of participants suggests, then, that disciplinary actions will normally be reviewed under the rule of reason standard. The concept of *per se* illegality, however, will continue to play a limited role. The prerogatives which a league enjoys can properly be limited by the conditions which give rise to the need for self-regulation. If the league uses its powers to achieve ends which clearly cannot be justified by the need for preserving the integrity of the sport, the *per se* doctrine should be applied.[886] Similarly, the procedural aspects of an otherwise-proper disciplinary action may be so lacking in fairness and objectivity as to warrant a summary disapproval under the *per se* standard.[887] But these will be extreme cases, and most situations are likely to call for an inquiry under the rule of reason test. Since this standard requires only a showing of the reasonableness of the action taken, a league which acts responsibly in defining its disciplinable offenses and affords adequate procedural protections should find that the antitrust laws represent no substantial intrusion into its efforts at self-regulation.

a. Procedural Aspects of Discipline. There are two different elements of a league's disciplinary action which might be called into question under the antitrust laws. The first may be described as a concern for the substantive aspect of the discipline: was the punished conduct a matter over which the league could properly assume control, and was the league's sanction appropriate in light of the interest which it sought to protect? A second, and separate, concern is whether the league followed reasonable procedures in determining that a violation had occurred. The following discussion treats these two issues separately and begins with consideration of procedural concerns.

---

885. A number of theories might be proposed. Perhaps cheating could be viewed as a breach of an implied term of the player's contract, or it might be seen as such an infringement upon the economic advantage of the league as to warrant a court in exercising its equity powers. But money damages are likely to be an uneffective remedy. They are likely to be speculative, and, moreover, would do little to satisfy the concern for fan reaction. Some form of injunction might be devised which would achieve the same purpose as a suspension. But a basic problem is that there is no clearly defined body of law which would afford these rights. Moreover, judicial procedures would be considerably more cumbersome than internal enforcement, a fact which might well limit the effectiveness of the discipline.

886. Such would be the case, for example, where a league used its disciplinary powers for anti-competitive purposes, as where it blacklisted athletes who played in a rival league. *See* text at notes 906-11 *infra*.

887. *Cf.* Silver v. New York Stock Exchange, 373 U.S. 292 (1963).

One might wonder how the antitrust statutes could be interpreted to require procedural safeguards in private group disciplinary action. Those laws are primarily concerned with practices which improperly limit competition and, at least on the surface, seem to have little to say about procedural fairness. Since it is the fact of exclusion which limits competition for a participant's services, and not the procedures which precede such a decision, it might appear that the only relevant question was whether the conduct involved was properly punishable. Under this view, it would be argued that the antitrust laws authorize a court to look only at the propriety of the end achieved and not at the means by which it was attained.

This is not the approach which has been taken, however. In *Silver,* the Supreme Court made clear that the procedural aspects of private self-regulation were an appropriate matter for inquiry by the antitrust court. This concern for procedure is supported by a number of considerations. It is thought that the requirement of notice and a hearing will facilitate the administration of the antitrust laws.[888] Such procedures serve to define more precisely the factual basis for the group's actions as well as the defenses and contentions of the accused. Thus, a court called upon to review the matter in an antitrust proceeding will be in a better position to determine whether a basis exists for the discipline and whether the action is justified in light of the group's purposes. In addition, the requirement that a group use reasonable and deliberate procedures tends to discourage arbitrary action and thus serves to foster compliance with the substantive antitrust rules.[889] If the group is required to state and defend its reasons for imposing the discipline, it will constantly be reminded of the need to have defensible rules and to apply them only when the proper factual basis exists. A structural hearing will serve to expose weaknesses in the group's position and is likely to encourage adjustments — such as a reduction in the offense charged or the punishment imposed — which will bring its actions into antitrust compliance without the need for litigation.

Silver is particularly useful in defining the nature of the inquiry a court should make into the question of procedural fairness. In one portion of the opinion, the Court attempts to define the general type of procedures to be followed. The Court stated that before self-regulation by private groups could be justified, there must be "some method of telling a protesting nonmember why a rule is being invoked . . . and allowing him to reply in explanation of his position." [890] Thus, it would appear that the charges must be examined in a specific proceeding designed for that purpose and the accused must be given an opportunity to participate. While the Court did not elaborate on how the proceeding should be structured, its concern for informing the accused and allowing him to respond would reasonably imply that there should be some type of advanced notice, which would allow the accused time to formulate his response and gather any pertinent evidence. By the same token, the opportunity to offer an explanation presumably must be a meaningful one, which would mean that it must precede the determination of guilt.

888. *See id.* at 362-63.
889. *Id.* at 361-62.
890. *Id.* at 361.

The *Silver* decision also serves to continue a role for the *per se* doctrine in these matters. The Court observed that the decision of the stock exchange to terminate Silver's private line connection with member firms had been made unilaterally without a statement of charges or an opportunity for Silver to be heard. In these circumstances, the Court concluded, a finding of *per se* illegality was appropriate.[891] Thus, it appears that a disciplined participant may be entitled to a summary finding of illegality if he or she can establish that the method for determining guilt was inherently defective. In such a case the court need not make a detailed inquiry into the basis of the discipline, its justifications, or its effects. Before a defense on the merits will be heard, the group must initially establish that its action has the characteristics of reliability which come from a more deliberate proceeding in which the accused participated.[892]

While *Silver* seems to indicate that notice and a hearing — or a change to explain — are necessary before drastic action can be taken, there are numerous other questions which may arise concerning the formalities which must accompany the decision-making of the disciplinary authorities. Can the accused insist that he or she be represented by counsel? Even if a representative is allowed, may attorneys be excluded? Does the accused have a right to cross-examine witnesses? Must a transcript, stenographic or otherwise, be provided? Must the accused be given the right to participate in the selection of the members of the tribunal hearing the case? What rules of evidence will be followed? What standard of proof must be applied to the determination of guilt? Must guilt be shown beyond a reasonable doubt, or only by reasonable evidence?

The existing case law has not developed to the point where specific answers can be given to these questions. There are, however, several considerations which should provide guidance. Because of the nature of the question raised, there is a temptation to view the matter of procedural safeguards in constitutional terms and to look to cases which define procedural due process in the areas of criminal law and administrative enforcement actions. Earlier chapters of this book consider in more detail the standards which are evolving in those areas.[893] A comparison with these areas would not appear to be entirely inappropriate. The purposes of the requirement of a fair hearing are similar, particularly where private self-regulation and governmental administrative enforcement are compared. In each instance, procedural fairness is required, in part, to insure the integrity of the process, to facilitate subsequent judicial review, and to foster voluntary compliance with the legal mandate.[894] But by the same token, it would seem inappropriate to view private group self-regulation in purely constitutional terms. On some matters, the relevant constitutional provision specifies the protections to be afforded in greater detail than is found in the antitrust area, where the requirement for procedural safeguards is judge-made. In criminal law, for example, limitations on

---

891. *Id.* at 364.

892. *See generally* Comment, *Trade Association Exclusionary Practices: An Affirmative Role for the Rule of Reason, supra* note 870, at 1508-10.

893. *See* §§ 1.28, 2.18 *supra.*

894. *Cf.* McCormick, *The Purpose of Due Process: Fair Hearing as Vehicle for Judicial Review?,* 52 TEXAS L. REV. 1257 (1974).

evidence-gathering are specifically mandated and reflect the particular needs of the areas to which they apply. On a more general level, it should be noted that the nature of private group decision-making is quite different from that found in cases where governmental action is involved. For example, private groups normally do not have, and should not be expected to maintain, the elaborate permanent institutions for the investigation, prosecution, and review of violations which are found in the public sphere. Relatedly, the private groups do not have available the option of broad-based taxation to support these institutions, and it can be expected that economic considerations will impose more significant restraints.

Again, the point is not that notions of constitutional due process should be ignored, but only that their application must be tempered in light of the peculiar nature of the private decision-making which will be reviewed under the antitrust laws. The central question concerns which of the constitutional protections will be incorporated, and in what form. In resolving this question, there are two considerations which will deserve particular weight: the concern for the reliability of the decision and the significance of the consequences to the individual. There is a high degree of interrelationship between these factors, for the more severe the consequences of a decision, the greater the need for a carefully structured proceeding.[895] Where the accused faces a suspension or expulsion which seriously restricts the opportunity to earn a living, a high degree of deference to his or her interests will be required.

As is implied in the above analysis, the extent of protection afforded will vary from case to case. The severity of the consequences may be an important ingredient, and the range of relevant considerations will include such things as the complexity of the factual issues and the sophistication of the accused. Because of the *ad hoc* quality of the question, there is little value in attempting to anticipate all of the issues which might arise. A few examples, however, will serve to illustrate the type of balancing which should be undertaken. For example, does the accused have a right to be represented by an attorney? The answer would seem to depend upon a number of considerations. If the enforcing agency conducts its affairs through professional counsel and if the participant has no particular sophistication on the matter of how to present his defense, it would seem that the fairness of the proceeding could be insured only if there were a balance in the relative professionalism of the two sides. But if the disciplinary proceeding is handled by non-legally trained personnel, and otherwise has the attributes of impartiality, it would seem that a court should accept that some individuals could adequately represent themselves, particularly if the factual issues were not overly complex.[896] The primary concern would be whether the accused was seriously disadvantaged by the denial of counsel, and that would seem to be a matter upon which no *a priori* judgment could be made.

A question which has perhaps more significant implications concerns the rules of evidence and standard of proof which the tribunal must apply. On a general level, the private group should not be expected to conform to the strict standards

---

895. *Cf.* Goss v. Lopez, 419 U.S. 565 (1975).

896. *Cf.* Cornelio v. Carpenters Union, 243 F. Supp. 126 (E.D. Pa. 1965), *aff'd,* 358 F.2d 728 (3d Cir. 1966), *cert. denied,* 386 U.S. 975 (1967).

imposed in the criminal area. The tribunals which are used do not have the sophistication of a court of law; and to expect them to operate with the same care and precision as found in criminal proceedings would require a fundamental restructuring which is not warranted in light of the nature of the decision involved. A primary antitrust concern is for the reliability of the decisions which are made. This can be insured even if some hearsay evidence is presented, the traditional notions of privileged testimony are ignored, and the decision is made on the preponderance of the evidence. If the opportunities for bias are removed and if there is an orderly presentation of evidence bearing on a particular issue, there would seem to be no inherent reason why the tribunal's decision should be suspect. But, of course, this does not mean that a reviewing court should be unconcerned about the quality of proof. If the tribunal ignores opportunities to hear direct testimony, admits considerable irrelevant and prejudicial evidence, and fails to pursue important issues, the resulting decision is not likely to be one which generates confidence and may properly be rejected.

It would seem that reviewing courts should be particularly sensitive to the possibility for bias or prejudice in the decision-making process. There are several attributes of the disciplinary systems in sports which suggest that bias or prejudice may present a particular problem in this area. Often disciplinary decisions are made by a commissioner or similar official who is not totally removed from the internal politics of the league's venture. While, as discussed in another section, it seems inappropriate to conclude generally that league-appointed commissioners are inherently biased,[897] there may be cases in which the commissioner does not act with the objectivity which should be demanded.[898] On another level, there may be a temptation by sports authorities to use players caught in rule infractions as scapegoats. For example, if it develops that there are widespread rumors of gambling in a particular sport, there may be a tendency to "throw the book" at the first player to be caught. Such action will give the appearance to the public that the problem has been taken care of and serve as a pointed reminder to other participants who might be involved. Because of the need for swift, forceful action in these cases, there is a risk that the guilt of those who are caught will be determined summarily or that the degree of the offense will be overstated.

Courts have dealt with the risk of bias in other situations involving private discipline.[899] These cases suggest that courts should be alerted to the fact that a group's procedures may not provide mechanisms which guard against the possibility of prejudice. If there is evidence that the decision-maker has made up his mind before hand or that there have been improper attempts by club owners to influence the proceedings, it is fully appropriate that the results not be accepted. It would seem that because of their more disinterested perspective, the courts are particularly well-suited to provide a buffer against overzealous action by league authorities anxious to rid themselves of a brewing scandal.

897. *See* § 4.19 *supra.*

898. For an interesting debate between owners and players' representatives on the problems of a commissioner form of government, see *Arbitration in Professional Athletics* in ARBITRATION OF INTEREST DISPUTES — PROCEEDINGS OF THE TWENTY-SIXTH ANNUAL MEETING OF THE NATIONAL ACADEMY OF ARBITRATORS 108 (1973).

899. *See, e.g.,* Falcone v. Dantinne, 420 F.2d 1157 (3d Cir. 1969); Cefalo v. Moffett, 78 LRRM 2112 (D.D.C. 1971).

A somewhat different aspect of the concern for bias was treated in *Blalock v. Ladies Professional Golf Association*.[900] Jane Blalock was accused of cheating in an LPGA sponsored tournament and upon being found guilty, was suspended from tournament play for a year. She sued, alleging that the suspension constituted a group boycott. The district court accepted the plaintiff's characterization and found the defendant's action to be *per se* illegal. The court's opinion can be read as presenting the highly-debatable conclusion that *Silver* permits private self-regulation only when it is supported by specific statutory authorization.[901] But that aspect of the case aside, the court reaches a sensible result and suggests an independent rationale. The court was primarily concerned about the structure of the disciplinary organ in the LPGA. The committee which decided the disciplinary matter was composed of golfers who competed with Blalock on the LPGA circuit. Moreover, in the court's view, the group was given "completely unfettered, subjective" discretion in determining the appropriateness of exclusion as the sanction for the alleged offense.[902] While the court did not dwell on the question of how this discretion might be affected by bias, it was clearly concerned about the fact that the decision was made by players who stood to gain if Blalock were removed as a competitor. In the court's view, this situation had the essential characteristics of *Fashion Originators' Guild,* where one group attempted to regulate practices in the trade for the purpose of eliminating a potential source of competition.[903]

It should be noted that the court did not find that any of the players on the discipline committee was actually biased. Rather, the central objection was that

---

900. 359 F. Supp. 1260 (N.D. Ga. 1973).

901. The court noted that in *Silver,* the Supreme Court had said that self-regulation might be appropriate where justified by "another statute [other than the antitrust statutes] or otherwise." The *Blalock* court also recognized that other lower courts had indicated that the structure of certain industries might present cases in which the justification for self-regulation arose "otherwise" than from a statute. Judge Moye, however, chose to give a more limited reading to the Supreme Court's inclusion of the "or otherwise" language:

> The question posed in *Silver* was whether the existence of a statutory framework for self-government in the security [*sic*] industry repealed the antitrust laws to that extent. The Supreme Court stated that "This means that any repealer of the antitrust laws must be discerned as a matter of implication, and '[i]t is a cardinal principle of construction that repeals by implication are not favored' " . . . *A fortiorari,* a private, nonstatutory rule to govern a private association cannot repeal by implication a federal statute, the "law of the land." 359 F. Supp. at 1267.

The primary difficulty with the court's analysis is that it would lead to the logical conclusion that a sports association had no authority to discipline participants, even those engaging in conduct, such as bribery and cheating, which threatened its very existence. The court does temper its analysis somewhat by a seemingly approving reference to Molinas v. National Basketball Ass'n, 190 F. Supp. 241 (S.D.N.Y. 1961), in which a lifetime suspension was sustained under the antitrust laws. The court distinguishes the case on the grounds that the punishment was not imposed by the athlete's competitors, which suggests that the *per se* rule of *Blalock* is intended to be limited to those situations.

A more correct reading of *Silver* would still have allowed the *Blalock* court to apply the *per se* rule on the facts before it. The court could have recognized that private groups enjoy some discretion to impose discipline and that normally the exercises of this right will be treated under the rule of reason. But as *Silver* rather clearly indicates, *per se* illegality will be found if the group fails to afford procedural safeguards to the accused. Since Blalock's discipline was imposed by competitors who might gain from her exclusion from the sport, it can be questioned whether the proceeding had the requisite procedural fairness.

902. 359 F. Supp. at 1268.

903. *See id.* at 1267-68. *Fashion Originators' Guild* is discussed at notes 671-74, § 5.07 *supra.*

the disciplinary process had not been structured to guard against this possibility. This result seems consistent with the teachings of *Silver,* in which the Court did not inquire into the correctness or propriety of the group's decision, but rather into the fairness of the procedures under which it was made. Thus, it will not always be necessary for the plaintiff to directly attack the integrity of particular members of the disciplinary tribunal, a tactic which would likely lead to unwanted repercussions. Some cases will provide the occasion for a less personalized criticism of the imperfections in the structure of the disciplinary mechanism.

While *Blalock* dealt with a sport involving individualized competition, it may have interesting implications in the league sports context. One criticism which has been raised in the major team sports is that the league commissioner, who is usually hired and paid by the club owners, is given sole discretion to administer the disciplinary system.[904] One logical reform would involve a restructuring of the disciplinary tribunal to include representatives of the players. An obvious question arises as to whether *Blalock* would permit this type of arrangement, since it might be argued that the player representatives from opposing teams are competitors of those who would be disciplined and thus their decision-making might be guided by improper considerations. It might be asserted that the decision-makers would be tempted to eliminate the accused so as to decrease his team's chance of winning the championship and securing the resulting rewards. There are, however, some weaknesses in the use of *Blalock* in this setting. Because competitive success depends upon a team, as opposed to a purely individual effort, it is less clear that a player decision-maker would gain any significant advantage from the exclusion of a single participant. Moreover, since the players are salaried and generally receive game-by-game compensation only in championship contests, the economic rewards of an improper exclusion are more speculative and for that reason represent a less certain risk. Yet, where the accused is a star quarterback or leading scorer, his exclusion may yield an advantage to rival teams which is not wholly unlike that which was the source of the court's concern in *Blalock.*

While its applicability is somewhat debatable, the *Blalock* decision should have the desirable effect of prompting the parties to consider alternatives other than direct participation for increasing player inputs into the disciplinary system. One approach would be to give the players a voice in the selection of an independent party who would be given authority in disciplinary matters. A less venturesome alternative would permit the players to participate in redrafting the rules defining punishable conduct for the purpose of limiting the discretion which is afforded the administering authority. A consideration of other techniques which are available should serve to underscore the fact that direct player participation is not an indispensable element in a fair disciplinary system and indeed may not be a desirable feature.

---

904. *See Arbitration in Professional Athletics* in ARBITRATION OF INTEREST DISPUTES — PROCEEDINGS OF THE TWENTY-SIXTH ANNUAL MEETING OF THE NATIONAL ACADEMY OF ARBITRATORS 108 (1973). Criticism of other aspects of the commissioner role is considered in § 4.19 *supra.*

b. Substantive Aspects of Discipline. Once it is accepted that leagues have authority to maintain a system for internal discipline, a critical question arises as to how broadly it may extend its regulatory authority. Unless some legal control is introduced, there is a risk that the disciplinary power may be used to achieve improper economic goals or to require conformity with a standard of morality which reflects more the idiosyncrasies of a commissioner or a group of owners than the needs of the sport. While some have concluded that the antitrust laws are not a particularly useful vehicle for controlling abuses in this area,[905] a review of the relevant doctrine does suggest a standard which could serve as an effective control. The courts have had few occasions to consider how antitrust principles, with their basically commercial orientation, should be adjusted to deal with the concern for ethics and morality which will arise in the disciplinary context. But it would appear that the goal of a legal restraint upon the disciplinary power of a sports enterprise bears a close affinity to the basic policy of the antitrust laws. In each instance, there is a concern for protecting an individual from undue restraints upon his competitive opportunities. Thus, it is not surprising that principles which were developed in a purely economic setting can be adapted to answer questions which, to some extent, involve matters of ethics.

Some of the limits on a league's disciplinary prerogatives can be stated rather easily. For example, there should be little debate that a sports authority cannot use its disciplinary power solely for the purpose of enhancing its economic position or restricting the competitive opportunities of a player.[906] Thus, it would not be permissible for a league to impose sanctions on players who entered into negotiations for future employment with a rival league.[907] Equally suspect would be cases in which a league blacklisted a player who abandoned his or her contract to play in a competing league.[908] While the action might amount to a breach of an existing contract, there are independent legal actions through which the injured club can seek compensation,[909] and the additional sanction of perpetual disbarment from the original league would seem to serve no legitimate purpose.

In the examples given, the disciplinary action has the same aspect of coercive use of market power which has been condemned in other settings, and the mere fact that a sports venture is involved should not change the analysis. The cases from other areas also suggest that such actions will be treated as *per se*

905. *See* Comment, *Discipline in Professional Sports: The Need for Player Protection,* 60 GEO. L.J. 771, 779-80 (1972).

906. *See* Comment, *Trade Association Exclusionary Practices: An Affirmative Role for the Rule of Reason,* 66 COLUM. L. REV. 1486, 1502-04 (1966).

907. Other aspects of a club's right to limit its players' contacts with rival leagues are considered in § 4.14 *supra,* which deals generally with the question of tortious interference with contractual relationships. While issues considered in that section arise in a different legal context, it can be noted that many of the same policy questions are involved. The few cases decided to date suggest that the courts are not inclined to allow the legal doctrine dealing with tortious interference to be used by clubs to achieve anticompetitive ends.

908. *See* Comment, *The Super Bowl and the Sherman Act: Professional Team Sports and the Antitrust Laws,* 81 HARV. L. REV. 418, 425-26 (1967); Comment, *The Balance of Power in Professional Sports,* 22 MAINE L. REV. 459, 465-67 (1970); *cf.* Radovich v. National Football League, 352 U.S. 445 (1957); Gardella v. Chandler, 172 F.2d 402 (2d Cir. 1949).

909. *See* ch. 4 *supra.*

illegal [910] and thus the court need not entertain evidence which the league might offer in justification.[911] While the more detailed inquiry required by the rule of reason will be appropriate in most group discipline situations, the present cases involve actions so clearly directed to anti-competitive ends that they are appropriately treated as naked restraints of trade for which there is no justification.

The issues of necessity and justification require more attention when the focus is shifted from discipline undertaken for purely anti-competitive reasons to that which is imposed to preserve the integrity of on-the-field competition.[912] As previously noted, there can be little debate that the league has an interest in protecting its ventures against those who violate important playing rules, engage in gambling activities, or otherwise undermine the appearances that the league's contests involve honest athletic competition. The difficulty is that the league's concern for protecting its public image can easily be corrupted into rules which regulate player conduct having little connection with what occurs on the field. There is a real risk that the definition of proper conduct will be drawn so narrowly as to be an infringement upon the political, religious, or social prerogatives of the players. Moreover, the problem of achieving an appropriate balance between the corporate interest and that of the players is complicated in no small measure by the fact that non-conforming behavior tends to attract the interest of the sports news media. Private actions of employees which would go unnoticed in other industries may appear as lead stories on the sports pages. Such coverage tends to blur the line between the player's public and private affairs and may prompt league authorities to assume that most aspects of an individual's off-the-field conduct are appropriate subjects for concern.[913]

The developing body of law dealing with the regulatory powers of private groups suggests the general standard which should be applied to define the range of the league's authority in controlling player conduct. It will be recalled that the courts seem to be prepared to permit private group regulation where such internal control is justified by the structure of the industry or the nature of the activity undertaken.[914] While the latter concerns identify the reasons for granting private regulatory powers, they also serve as a limitation on the prerogatives which are assumed.[915] The group, in this case the league, should be permitted only that range of control which can be justified by the special needs of its peculiar venture. In determining whether a particular disciplinary action bears the necessary relationship to the concerns which support

910. *See, e.g.,* Klor's, Inc. v. Broadway-Hale Stores, Inc., 359 U.S. 207 (1959); Fashion Originators' Guild of America v. FTC, 312 U.S. 457 (1941).

911. The *per se* doctrine is examined in more detail in § 5.07 *supra.*

912. *See generally* Comment, *Trade Association Exclusionary Practices: An Affirmative Role for the Rule of Reason, supra* note 906, at 1493-97, 1504-10.

913. The relationship between sports and the news media is an interesting one, for there are few other private commercial activities which receive as much free "advertising." Indeed, the fact of extensive news coverage has been an important ingredient in the economic success of modern sports. *See generally* J. MICHENER, SPORTS IN AMERICA 285-336 (1976).

914. *See* text at notes 882-85 *supra.*

915. *See generally* Bridge Corp. of America v. American Contract Bridge League, Inc., 428 F.2d 1365 (9th Cir. 1970); Barber, *Refusals to Deal Under the Federal Antitrust Laws,* 103 U. PA. L. REV. 847 (1955); Comment, *Trade Association Exclusionary Practices: An Affirmative Role for the Rule of Reason, supra* note 906.

self-regulation, the rule of reason will be applied, except, of course, where the action so clearly reflects an anti-competitive motive as to call for treatment under the *per se* doctrine.[916] Thus, for most rules related to the integrity of league competition, the relevant inquiry is whether the action is reasonable in light of the goals sought to be achieved, on the one hand, and the effect upon the players' competitive opportunities on the other.[917] In making this determination, it is appropriate for the court to consider evidence on a wide range of matters, including the prior experiences of the league,[918] practices of leagues in other sports,[919] the deliberations which preceded the definition of the offense, informed testimony on fan and player reaction to similar conduct, the availablity of less restrictive controls,[920] and, not least of all, the severity of the impact upon those who are disciplined. It must also be accepted that many points which will be called into controversy will not admit of certain proof. There are no clear answers as to how personal freedoms are to be valued when balanced against corporate concern for fan reaction. But it can be noted that legal institutions have considerable experience in making similar judgments on matters of personal liberties, and many of the issues which will appear will not be wholly foreign to the judicial forum.

The role to be fulfilled by the general standard identified above becomes clearer when specific types of misconduct are considered. The matter of gambling by players has been a source of considerable concern for sports leagues.[921] Especially apt to attract disciplinary action are cases in which a

---

916. *See* authorities cited note 915 *supra; accord,* STP Corp. v. United States Auto Club, 286 F. Supp. 146 (S.D. Ind. 1968); Molinas v. National Basketball Ass'n, 190 F. Supp. 241 (S.D.N.Y. 1961); United States v. United States Trotting Ass'n, 1960 Trade Cas. ¶ 69,761 (S.D. Ohio).

917. *Cf.* Chicago Board of Trade v. United States, 246 U.S. 231 (1918).

It should be noted that the Supreme Court has declined to say whether the appropriate standard of review is one of *reasonableness.* In *Silver,* the Court noted that since it decided the case before it on procedural grounds:

> There is no need for us to define further whether the interposing of a substantive justification in an antitrust suit brought to challenge a particular enforcement of the rules on its merits is to be governed by a standard of arbitrariness, good faith, reasonableness, or some other measure. It will be time enough to deal with that problem if and when the occasion arises.

It appears, however, that most lower courts and commentators feel that a reasonableness standard is the appropriate one. *See, e.g.,* Bridge Corp. of America v. American Contract Bridge League, Inc., 428 F.2d 1365 (9th Cir. 1970); Molinas v. National Basketball Ass'n, 190 F. Supp. 241, (S.D.N.Y. 1961); United States v. United States Trotting Ass'n, 1960 Trade Cas. ¶ 69,761 (S.D. Ohio); Comment, *Trade Association Exclusionary Practices: An Affirmative Role for the Rule of Reason, supra* note 906. *But see* Cowen v. New York Stock Exchange, 256 F. Supp. 462 (N.D.N.Y. 1966), aff'd 371 F.2d 661 (2d Cir. 1967).

918. In sustaining the suspension of a player for gambling in Molinas v. National Basketball Ass'n, 190 F. Supp. 241, 244 (S.D.N.Y. 1961), the court emphasized the fact that the league had experienced difficulties as a result of persistent rumors concerning betting activities.

919. The experiences and practices of leagues may not always be a useful guide. For example, some leagues, particularly those in the sport of hockey, are apparently willing to tolerate more violence than would be accepted elsewhere. *See generally* Kennedy, *Wanted: An End to Mayhem,* Sports Illustrated, Nov. 17, 1975, at 17; Smith, *Good Unclean Fun for All,* N.Y. Times, Nov. 9, 1975, § 5, at 5, col. 6 (critical of NHL disciplinary measures); Washington Post, April 21, 1976, at E1, col. 4 (same); Winnipeg Free Press, Mar. 20, 1976, at 72, col. 1 (same).

920. There is a growing body of literature on the issue of whether the antitrust laws require that an entity utilize only the "least restrictive" means of control or whether a broader range of discretion is afforded. *See, e.g.,* Robinson, *Recent Antitrust Developments: 1975,* 76 COLUM. L. REV. 191 (1976).

921. *See generally* J. MICHENER, SPORTS IN AMERICA 406-13 (1976); Comment, *Discipline in*

player bets on the outcome of games in which he participates.[922] While the results in specific cases will be influenced by their particular facts, an application of the above test is likely to weigh in favor of sustaining the league's efforts to control such conduct. For example, it is readily apparent that gambling falls within the category of activities which justify regulation. The league has a strong interest in insuring that its contests are solely tests of athletic skill and are not influenced by the desire of some participants to have the team perform better or worse than the odds-makers have predicted.[923] Moreover, the player-betting cases typically involve few delicate questions of personal liberty. The act of betting is illegal in most states, and this fact is usually well-known to the players. Moreover, the athlete is hired specifically to contribute his talents to the club's, and hence the league's, effort, and it can reasonably be implied that he will do nothing which suggests that his on-the-field performance had any other purpose.

A case which suggests that the courts will be willing to sustain league discipline in these instances is *Molinas v. National Basketball Association.*[924] Molinas, a player for the NBA Fort Wayne Pistons, admitted that he had placed several bets on his team to win particular games. The league had a specific prohibition on gambling, and pursuant to those rules, the NBA commissioner declared that Molinas was suspended indefinitely. The player applied for reinstatement on several occasions over the next several years, but his request was denied each time. Molinas eventually sued, alleging that the league's suspension and the subsequent denials of reinstatement amounted to unreasonable restraints on trade under the antitrust laws. The court rejected this contention. Its treatment of the issue indicated a willingness to afford sports leagues considerable deference in their efforts to minimize the influences of gambling:

> A rule, and a corresponding contract clause, providing for the suspension of those who place wagers on games in which they are participating seems not only reasonable, but necessary for the survival of the league. Every league or association must have some

Professional Sports: The Need for Player Protection, 60 GEO. L.J. 771, 772-79 (1972); N.Y. Times, June 27, 1976, § 5, at 9, col. 6 (review of controversial survey made for Commission on the Review of the National Policy Toward Gambling); Washington Post, June 25, 1976, at D1, col. 2 (national gambling report); N.Y. Times, Dec. 10. 1975, at 35, col. 1 (Jets' Steve Tannen cleared of bookmaking involvement).

922. *See* Molinas v. National Basketball Ass'n, 190 F. Supp. 241 (S.D.N.Y. 1961); Molinas v. Podoloff, 133 N.Y.S.2d 743 (Sup. Ct. 1954). For an account of lifetime suspensions meted out against two hockey players accused of wagering on their clubs, see R. BEDDOES, S. FISCHLER, & I. GITLER, HOCKEY! THE STORY OF THE WORLD'S FASTEST SPORT 293-96 (1973).

923. There are a number of indications which suggest that the leagues regard gambling as a serious threat. One is the harsh penalties which are meted out to those suspected of gambling. *See* cases cited in note 922 *supra. See also* Comment, *Discipline in Professional Sports: The Need for Player Protection, supra* note 921, at nn.7, 30-31. On occasion, leagues have attempted to block efforts to legalize gambling. In 1976, the NFL was denied a temporary restraining order which would bar the State of Delaware from beginning operation of a pro football lottery. In denying the order U.S. District Judge Walter Stapleton stated "The court is unpersuaded by the current record that irreparable injury to plaintiff is likely to occur during this relevant period." Washington Post, Aug. 28, 1976, at E1, col. 5. Subsequent proceedings in the Delaware case also failed to provide any relief for the NFL. *See* National Football League v. Delaware, 435 F. Supp. 1372 (D. Del. 1977).

924. 190 F. Supp. 241 (S.D.N.Y. 1961). *See also* Molinas v. Podoloff, 133 N.Y.S.2d 743 (Sup. Ct. 1954).

reasonable governing rules, and these rules must necessarily include disciplinary provisions. Surely, every disciplinary rule which a league may invoke, although by its nature it may involve some sort of a restraint, does not run afoul of the antitrust laws. And a disciplinary rule invoked against gambling seems about as reasonable a rule as could be imagined.[925]

Not all gambling cases will admit of such an easy resolution. There are types of conduct other than betting which a league may attempt to punish, and where a player's involvement with the gambling establishment is more attenuated, the range of the league's prerogatives will be more limited. At this juncture, it may be useful to point out that the relevant antitrust doctrine serves not only to limit the types of conduct which can be punished, but also to limit the sanctions which can be imposed. Again, the basic standard is one of reasonableness,[926] and it is appropriate to ask whether the particular punishment can be justified in light of the league's interest in controlling the particular conduct.[927] While less serious gambling offenses might support some form of disciplinary action, they might not justify the most serious sanction of perpetual suspension.

The *Molinas* court specifically approved the NBA lifetime suspension of the plaintiff in that case, but that holding should be read in light of the facts which established that the athlete had directly and knowingly involved himself with the gambling process.[928] The case actually lends support to the notion that

---

925. 190 F. Supp. at 243-44. For a brief account of Molinas' later involvement in other types of gambling activities with sports and his other questionable dealings, see N.Y. Times, Aug. 6, 1975, at 18, col. 1.

926. As noted earlier, the question of the appropriate standard of review is not entirely free from debate, although the trend of authority supports the inquiry into reasonableness. *See* note 917 *supra.*

927. Although no sports cases can be found in which a court refused to approve a penalty as being too harsh in light of the infraction involved, the notion that the sanctions used must be reasonable can be implied from the general principle that the league's disciplinary power can be used only to achieve legitimate goals of self-regulation. The imposition of long term suspensions for relatively minor infractions would seem to involve the sort of coercive action which the antitrust laws are intended to guard against. *Cf.* Comment, *Trade Association Exclusionary Practices: An Affirmative Role for the Rule of Reason, supra* note 906, at 1506-07.

928. With respect to Molinas' objection to the length of his suspension, the court stated:

> The same factors justifying the suspension also serve to justify the subsequent refusal to reinstate. The league could reasonably conclude that in order to restore and maintain the confidence of the public vital to its existence, it was necessary to enforce its rules strictly, and to apply the most stringent sanctions. One can certainly understand the reluctance to permit an admitted gambler to return to the league, and again to participate in championship games, especially in light of the aura and stigma of gambling which has clouded the sports world in the past few years. Viewed in this context, it can be seen that the league was justified in determining that it was absolutely necessary to avoid even the slightest connection with gambling, gamblers, and those who had business with gamblers in the future. 190 F. Supp. at 244.

Perhaps the most debatable part of the court's analysis was its observation, offered in further justification of the permanent suspension, that "conduct reasonable in its inception certainly does not become unreasonable through the mere passage of time, especially when the same factors making the conduct reasonable in the first instance are present." While it may be reasonable to impose an indefinite suspension initially, a player may subsequently engage in activities which serve to establish his integrity and thus cleanse his public image. Thus, the athlete may play in another league, assume some position of public responsibility, or undertake to convincingly express his regret for his earlier misconduct. Where the player has been able to improve his reputation, it would seem inappropriate to justify a continuing suspension on the basis that the action was "reasonable in the first instance." It should be noted, however, that the *Molinas* court suggested that the plaintiff there had made no such showing. *Id.* Molinas' subsequent difficulties with the law and with gambling indicate that this may not have been the best case for testing the point made here. *See* N.Y. Times, Aug. 6, 1975, at 18, col. 1.

differentiated punishments are required, for the court selects as its frame of reference the question of whether the league's actions were reasonable.[929] Presumably, the requirement of reasonableness would require a different sanction in a case, for example, where the player's only offense was that he had secured information about the predicted point spread for particular games. There are few legitimate uses for such data, and the league would seem justified in taking steps to prevent the player's involvement even to this limited extent. But the conduct would hardly warrant the league's permanent termination of the player's career, particularly if its investigation failed to establish a more substantial connection between the player and the gambling elements. Some sort of fine or probation would seem to be sufficient to stop the conduct, deter others, and satisfy the public with the seriousness of the league's purposes.

A similar analysis would apply when the focus is shifted to other types of misconduct. Infractions which involve violations of the rules of competition are particularly appropriate subjects for a differentiated treatment. Some forms of cheating directly affect the integrity of the game. The use of unapproved equipment or improperly advancing the ball, when done with an intent to deceive, are destructive of the sports authority's effort to avoid fan disgust and cynicism and would warrant harsh treatment. Alternatively, other misconduct, including some which is intentional, may not warrant any greater penalties than those which are imposed in the context of the competition itself. For example, offensive holding in football and intentional fouls in basketball normally only require action by the game officials.[930] On matters of this sort, one must often look to the community ethics within the sport to determine how the varieties of "cheating" should be viewed. While an absolutist would find it difficult to rank order various forms of dishonesty, it seems clear that differentiations can be made. The factors to be considered include the degree of deception involved; the motive with which it is practiced, including the immediacy of any economic gain; the risk of physical injury to others; and the degree of community tolerance.

Fighting among players, although it does not involve the same type of dishonesty found in some other rule infractions, is often a source of concern for league officials.[931] There have been numerous instances in which fighting and other activity which threatens the safety of participants have resulted in players being suspended from competition, although the suspensions are usually for

---

929. For example, the court observed that

> . . . plaintiff must show much more than he has here in order to compel a conclusion that the defendant's conduct was in fact unreasonable. Thus, it is clear, that the refusal to reinstate the plaintiff does not rise to the stature of a violation of the antitrust laws. 190 F. Supp. at 244.

930. If particular types of rule violations become too disruptive, the league may find it necessary to add a penalty in addition to that which is imposed by game officials. Thus, when technical fouls became a problem in the NBA, the league imposed an additional automatic fine. This escalation of the penalty apparently had the desired effect, for the number of technicals decreased in subsequent years. *See* N.Y. Times, Sept. 7, 1975, at 31, col. 1.

931. Some might suggest that not all leagues share the same concern for violence in their sports. The NHL has been criticized for its failure to take more forceful action to stem the recent escalation of assaults and fighting which has occurred in that sport. *See* sources cited in note 919 *supra*. Most other leagues have taken strong positions against such conduct, utilizing sanctions ranging from fines to suspensions. *See* sources cited in note 932 *infra*. *Cf.* National Football League Players Ass'n v. NLRB, 503 F.2d 12 (8th Cir. 1974).

short periods of time.[932] There should be little doubt that the league can take action to control such conduct.[933] It has a legitimate concern not only for the physical well-being of its players but also for the problems which might result if a brawl developed to the point where fans joined in. Finally, major altercations among players disrupt the contests in which they occur and tend to attract attention away from the regular competition, a result which undermines the league's efforts to focus fan attention on the game itself. That the league may be justified in controlling such unauthorized combat does not mean that its action will not be reviewed. As with other types of misconduct, the punishment for fighting which is imposed must not be excessive. Moreover, the league

932. *See, e.g.,* Globe & Mail (Toronto), Dec. 5, 1975, at 33, col. 6 (hockey player Phil Roberto suspended pending league review of incident involving spearing opposing player in throat); Gazette (Montreal), Jan. 30, 1976, at 24, col. 5 (hockey player Dave Schultz given two game suspension for butting opposing player); Washington Post, Feb. 4, 1976, at D6, col. 5 (hockey player Dave Hutchinson suspended for eight games without pay for spearing at head of opposing player); Gazette (Montreal), April 23, 1976, at 21, col. 7 (baseball pitcher Lynn McGlothen suspended five days for throwing beanball). *See also* N.Y. Times, May 1, 1976, at 18, col. 6 (president of American League threatens fines and suspensions for players of two clubs who stated they would retaliate for an earlier fight); Minneapolis Tribune, Aug. 12, 1975, at 2B, col. 3 (NHL players-owners council request rule automatically suspending player who deliberately attempts to injure an opponent).

933. While there can be little question that the league has an interest in stemming fights and violence among players, some might question whether league control is necessary in light of the public remedies available through the criminal laws. It might be argued that the leagues should defer to the more neutral policies of the criminal authorities. However, a closer analysis should suggest that separate league enforcement is desirable. It can be noted, for example, that public prosecutors have generally been reluctant to prosecute for assaults arising out of athletic competition. There have been few prosecutions in the past, and, even though the level of public law enforcement has increased markedly in response to the recent rise in violence in hockey, there are still those who are strongly critical of this use of the criminal law. *See* Kennedy, *Wanted: An End to Mayhem,* Sports Illustrated, Nov. 17, 1975, at 17 (some public prosecutors demand more criminal enforcement; league officials question necessity); Globe & Mail (Toronto), Apr. 26, 1976, at 52, col. 6 (survey of 30 criminal actions taken in hockey-related violence at professional and amateur levels); Winnipeg Free Press, Apr. 21, 1976, at 69, col. 8 (Philadelphia district attorney terms prosecution of 3 Philadelphia players a "perversion of office" by Canadian officials); *id.,* Apr. 22, 1976, at 74, col. 2 (Ontario attorney-general responds to criticism of his prosecution of Philadelphia players). The practicability of a league's reliance solely on criminal enforcement is further diminished by the fact that convictions may be difficult to obtain. Not only is the legal standard unclear, but there also appears to be a propensity for juries, particularly those with avid fans, to accept the notion that violence and assaults are part of the game. *See,* Kennedy, *A Nondecision Begs the Question,* Sports Illustrated, July 28, 1975, at 12 (hung jury in *Forbes* case); Hockey News, Sept. 1, 1975, at 3, col. 1. (effect of *Forbes* case on future enforcement of NHL rules); N.Y. Times, July 19, 1975, at 17, col. 2 (*Forbes* case ends in mistrial); *id.,* Sept. 25, 1975, at 55, col. 1 (*Forbes* case first time athlete in U.S. tried in criminal court for actions occurring during athletic event). In the final analysis, there is a good argument to be made for the notion that league enforcement may in fact be preferable to that which would come through the criminal process. The league is in a better position to define specific standards of conduct, which will be more useful than the standard which would emerge from a case-by-case interpretation. Further, the range of conduct which the league might wish to control may well include some types of actions which are of a sufficiently minor nature as not to warrant public prosecution. Thus, a system of league control may in fact be more orderly than that which would be found on the public side. Further a league system is likely to be more evenhanded, since it relies upon central administration and thus avoids the variance which might be reflected in the enforcement practices of individual prosecutors. Finally, and not least of all, it appears that the league has interests at stake which are not likely to be fully accounted for in a public enforcement. Concern for preserving the athletic contest as the primary focus of the fans' attention, concern for the individual club's responsibility to pay the medical expenses of players, and concern for the cost of crowd control are matters which are not typically taken account of in public prosecutions. This is not to suggest, however, that there might not still be a place for the use of the public criminal law to control particular types of violence. Some of the legal issues which arise in that connection are considered in § 2.21 *supra.*

should be prepared to show that it has pursued an even-handed enforcement policy.

The concern for the public image of the sport may prompt the league to extend its disciplinary authority to the off-the-field conduct of its athletes. It is in this area that there may be a particularly lively debate about the range of control which the league may assume. On the one hand, a player may insist that he is hired primarily for his athletic prowess and as long as he maintains his physical condition and performs to the best of his ability in practice and competition, he has fulfilled his contractual obligation. What he does off-the-field, it will be contended, is his own business. On the other hand, league officials may contend that fan interest in sports personalities does not end at the stadium exit and, due in no small measure to the active sports press, the image of the sport will often be influenced by the athlete's off-hours activities. Moreover, it will be contended that the fans' perception of the athlete on-the-field cannot be disassociated from what he has done elsewhere.

In trying to weigh the two positions, we again find little guidance in the case law. There are no sports cases directly on point. Moreover, there appears to be no other industry which practices the type of control found here, so there are no useful analogies.[934] The cases which do talk about the political and social rights of employees usually involve an application of constitutional principles.[935] While some would like to find that a sports league involved "state action" and hence was bound by the Constitution,[936] that appears not to be the case. But even in the absence of firm authority, some conclusions can be reached about the types of outside player conduct the league can hope to control. Again the relevant standard is one of reasonableness.[937] As suggested, that concept is sufficiently flexible to permit the court to make judgments about the relative weight to be afforded the respective corporate and individual interests.

There are some types of activities in which concern for the league's public image seems clearly outweighed by the player's right of personal freedom. While there may have been an earlier time when owners and league officials could have imposed rigid rules of personal conduct, we are presently operating in an era in which the individual's private prerogatives are entitled to greater respect. There are some types of outside activities which will have to be accepted

---

934. There is very little literature dealing with employer disciplinary action generally and even less which considers the special concerns which surface in the sports area. Some of the common law principles applicable to employment related discipline are treated in 56 C.J.S., *Master and Servant* § 102-08. The contractual aspects of sports discipline are discussed in § 3.10 *supra.*

935. *See, e.g.,* Cafeteria & Restaurant Workers Union v. McElroy, 367 U.S. 886 (1961); DeGrazio v. Civil Service Comm'n, 31 Ill. 2d 482, 202 N.E.2d 522 (1964). *See generally* Van Alstyne, *The Demise of the Right — Privilege Distinction in Constitutional Law,* 81 HARV. L. REV. 1439 (1968).

936. *See* Comment, *Discipline in Professional Sports: The Need for Player Protection,* 60 GEO. L.J. 771, 791-92 (1972). *But see* Charles O. Finley & Co. v. Kuhn, Cause No. 76 C 2358 (N.D. Ill. Sept. 7, 1976). In his suit against Commissioner Kuhn, for disapproving the sales contracts of players Vida Blue, Rollie Fingers and Joe Rudi, Charles O. Finley alleged a deprivation of due process under the fourteenth amendment. Cause No. 76 C 2358 at 7. Finley argued that the "state action" necessary for such a claim consisted of the use by some of the baseball clubs of state-owned stadiums and the "baseball exemption" from the antitrust laws. *Id.* Judge McGarr summarily dismissed Finley's argument, noting that "[F]or an otherwise private party to be engaged in state action, there must exist a nexus between the state and the particular activity being challenged." *Id.* at 8 (citation omitted). No such "nexus" had been alleged, *id.;* nor is one likely to be found.

937. *See* note 917 *supra.*

even though they may not project the image which some leagues might wish. Thus, despite the somewhat peculiar identification of sports and conservative politics,[938] the fact that an athlete is vocal in his support of an unpopular political cause is not a proper matter for concern by sports authorities.[939] It can be accepted that some fans may not like what the athlete says and may even lose enthusiasm for the team, but under a "reasonableness" criteria, the athlete's interest should predominate. It would appear inappropriate for the league to suppose that it has a duty to insulate its fans from non-conforming behavior which they find unpleasant. The fans do not receive such protection in their other social contacts, and it is not clear why they should expect it in the narrow area of sports activities. Moreover, it will be observed that it is common in other segments of the entertainment industry for the performers to align themselves with diverse political viewpoints without the need for direct controls. A performer may diminish his box office attractiveness by such activities. It is quite another matter, however, whether he should be disciplined for the stands he takes. Finally, there is the fundamental concern for the player's personal freedom. Whatever other roles the athlete may fulfill, he still continues to be a citizen in a political system which grants him the prerogatives to choose his ideological identification.[940] It will require rather compelling circumstances to establish that those rights have been relinquished. In light of the limited nature of the contract between an athlete and his club, the relationship hardly seems to present such a case.

This same analysis would apply to other matters as well. The fact that the athlete chose an unconventional life-style and ignored traditional mores on matters of marriage, family, and the like, would appear to be beyond the range of the league's proper concerns. It is true that some aspects of the athlete's life-style (his diet, for example) might affect his ability to perform on the field. There is no serious question but that the employer can demand that the athlete maintain his physical condition, and the typical standard player contract outlines the club's prerogatives to deal with these situations.[941] But the determination of whether the athlete has the necessary physical capacity must be made according to objective criteria and does not provide the occasion for the persons in authority to impose their personal preferences as to the life-style to be followed.

A final area which deserves attention involves cases in which the athlete is involved in criminal activity off-the-field. Some cases should not present much difficulty. Traffic offenses, scuffles with the police, and the like should not be viewed as within the area of appropriate concern for sports officials, even though these usually receive coverage in the news media and thus may affect how some fans view the sport. If the players are to retain freedom in conducting their private lives, such minor brushes with the law are likely to occur. It would

---

938. *See* J. MICHENER, SPORTS IN AMERICA 375-86 (1976). *See also* P. HOCH, RIP OFF THE BIG GAME 70-99 (1972).

939. *Cf.* Ali v. State Athletic Comm'n, 308 F. Supp. 11 (S.D.N.Y. 1969).

940. *Cf.* Mitchell v. International Ass'n of Machinists, 196 Cal. App. 2d 796, 16 Cal. Rptr. 813 (1961) (importance of individual's rights outweighs union interest in controlling political behavior; decided on non-constitutional grounds).

941. *See generally* §§ 3.05-.06, 3.08 *supra*.

seem that the leagues should be prepared to tolerate these in order to give some breathing room for more important personal rights.

As one moves up the scale of seriousness of offenses, however, the analysis is less simple.[942] The cases which are likely to cause concern are those involving capital crimes such as murder and rape and lesser sexual crimes which are apt to meet with strong disapproval from the fans. Although the accused murderer may be fully capable of performing his athletic duties on the field, his presence may prove to be a disruptive force, either to the fans or to other players. For example, it is not unusual for fans to seek out a player on their team upon whom to vent their frustration when the club is losing, and the accused player may well become the object for this derision. Moreover, the normal probing of the news media is likely to create a heightened sense of controversy, and the situation could easily develop to the point that the focus of public attention is shifted from the club's playing efforts to the turmoil surrounding the particular athlete. Not only would this undermine the league's main goal, but it could easily have a demoralizing effect upon the performance of the clubs involved.

There is reason to question whether the anticipated disharmony is sufficient to justify a suspension, for this same reaction might occur if a player takes a truly aberrational political position. And as indicated above, the fact that some third parties might react adversely seems not to provide a sufficient justification for allowing the league to control the behavior. The central argument made in that context — that neither the fans nor the leagues can insist that they be insulated from unpleasantness — would seem to have some application here.

The question is a close one, but in the final analysis, it seems preferable that the leagues be given some prerogative to suspend, at least temporarily, the

---

942. A case which illustrates the difficulty in defining the league's prerogatives in this area is that involving football player, Lance Rentzel. Rentzel, a star performer as a wide receiver for the Dallas Cowboys, was suspended from the NFL following two convictions for indecent exposure and an arrest for drug possession. League Commissioner Rozelle suspended him under a rule which authorizes such action when a player engages in "conduct detrimental to the welfare of the League, or professional football . . . ." The NFL Players Association, through its Executive Director, Ed Garvey, publicly criticized the suspension and assisted in the filing of legal actions to enjoin the continuance of the suspension. The public debate raised the issues which are considered here. Club owners argued for the need for discipline among players and expressed concern for the distraction which might be caused by the presence of a controversial figure on the field. Garvey, on the other hand, saw the suspension as an attempt by the Commissioner to legislate the moral standard to be followed by players. Others viewed the matter as illustrating the difficulty of drawing a line between "life-style" and truly detrimental conduct. The resulting debate is summarized in Cady, *The Central Issue: How Much Authority Should the Sports Authorities Have?*, N.Y. Times, Aug. 5, 1973, § 5, at 1, col. 1. *See also id.,* Aug. 4, 1973, at 15, col. 2 (Federal Judge C. H. Carr denies order to temporarily restrain NFL Commissioner Rozelle from suspending Lance Rentzel of the Los Angeles Rams; suit had been filed by Rentzel and NFLPA on ground that suspension for conviction of possession of marijuana and indecent exposure was "arbitrary, capricious, and discriminatory"); *id.,* Aug. 7, 1973, at 41, col. 3 (Los Angeles Superior Court Judge D. A. Thomas issues order for NFL and Los Angeles Rams to show cause for suspension of Rentzel by August 22, 1973); *id.* Aug. 24, 1973, at 27, col. 2 (Los Angeles Superior Court Judge Thomas refuses Rentzell injunction to end his suspension for conduct detrimental to NFL). Rentzel's suspension was eventually lifted and he was again permitted to play in the NFL. *Id.,* May 16, 1974, at 56, col. 1 (Lance Rentzel considers return to football with WFL after indefinite suspension by NFL Commissioner Rozelle in 1973); *id.,* May 18, 1974, at 22, col. 5 (Lance Rentzel reinstated by NFL Commissioner Rozelle after suspension of almost one year).

For a discussion of the range of discretion enjoyed by the commissioner of baseball in disciplinary matters see Durso, *Kuhn Can "Punish" Those Who "Undermine" Baseball, id.,* Aug. 5, 1973, § 5, at 2, col. 5.

player accused of a serious crime. The arguments made for requiring tolerance of unpopular political beliefs are not wholly applicable here. It is possible to make an ordering of the relative importance of particular types of conduct and on that scale, the exercise of basic political freedoms must surely come before actions which result in serious criminal charges. It should be kept in mind that the basic inquiry is whether the league's act of suspending the player was reasonable. The league which temporarily suspends the accused felon would seem to satisfy that standard. Such a suspension might in fact be quite desirable. It would allow a period for explanation and clarification and avoid the situation in which incomplete details of the event unnecessarily flamed emotions.

But as this analysis implies, a permanent suspension, or a refusal to hire an ex-felon, would be difficult to justify. While the player might not be able to wholly disassociate himself from his past, it would be difficult to find the requisite reasonableness in a rule which did not recognize the possibility of rehabilitation.[943] Some fans might refuse to accept the player's efforts to make a new start, but, again, we are presumably not operating in an era in which players must project a socially neutral image.

c. Fines v. Suspension. Up to this point, we have been considering situations in which the punishment imposed for player misconduct was an expulsion or suspension from the league. It might be asked whether the league's power to fine is treated under the same legal principles.[944] Some might question whether punishment in the form of a fine has the characteristics necessary to make out an antitrust violation.[945] It can be noted that the potential group boycott, or

---

943. *Cf.* note 928 *supra.*

944. Most leagues have reserved to themselves broad powers to impose fines, and these powers are frequently used. For example, in the five-year period prior to 1976, NFL Commissioner Rozelle collected $53,000 in fines from players and approximately $245,000 from NFL clubs. Brief for Appellants NFL and Alvin Ray Rozelle at 46, Mackey v. National Football League, 543 F.2d 606 (8th Cir. 1976). Fines are often used as a lesser penalty to punish conduct of the sort discussed above in the text in connection with league-imposed suspensions. Thus fines may be imposed against players who engage in fights or other activities which threaten player safety. *See, e.g.,* N.Y. Times, April 22, 1976, at 43, col. 1 (ABA Commissioner DeBusschere fines 14 players a total of $2,200 as a result of fight during basketball game) Washington Post, May 16, 1976, at D11, col. 5 (league fines pitcher and manager for beanball incident). Monetary assessments are also used when players are unduly abusive of referees and umpires, see N.Y. Times, Aug. 21, 1975, at 47, col. 1 (Chicago baseball player Bill Madlock fined $200 for throwing helmet and for abusive language in confrontation with umpire), and for other conduct which disrupts the orderliness of the game. (*See id.,* Oct. 7, 1975, at 31, col. 1 (NBA increases amount of automatic fines for technicals)).

Fines are also used to control conduct where individual sports are involved. One of the more celebrated cases involved the $6,000 fine which was levied against tennis player, Ilie Nastase for public profanity and "not using his best efforts to win" following a disputed line call. When Nastase initially refused to pay the fine, which was equal to his second-place prize money, he was suspended from further play by the Men's International Professional Tennis Council. He eventually paid and secured his reinstatement. *See* N.Y. Times, Mar. 11, 1976 at 49, col. 1; *id.,* Mar. 16, 1976, at 44, col. 6; *id.,* Mar. 17, 1976, at 26, col. 3.

Earlier, the concern for player conduct had prompted the international tennis council to adopt a schedule of fines covering a wide range of behavior. For example, a player could be fined $1,000 for physically or verbally abusing the umpire, opponents, or spectators; $1,000 for walking off the court or failing to appear in final ceremonies; $50 for "unprofessional" dress; and $50 for throwing a racket. A player who accummulated $3,000 in fines in any twelve-month period was to receive an automatic twenty-one day suspension. *See* Winnipeg Free Press, Dec. 9, 1975, at 48, col. 1.

945. It should be noted at the outset that there is very little authority either generally or in the sports area which has specifically considered the right of private groups to use fines to achieve compliance with their rules. In the few instances in which fining systems in other industries have

concerted refusal to deal, is more obvious where a suspension, as opposed to a fine, is imposed. When a player is suspended from the league all league teams are told, in effect, that it is improper for them to contract with the athlete. There is clearly a refusal to deal, and by virtue of the league's power to insure compliance by member clubs, the action is concerted. There is more difficulty in fitting a monetary fine into this same analysis. One can legitimately ask whether there is really any boycott, for if the athlete is only fined, he presumably is still allowed to play and earn his salary. Moreover, there might be some dispute about whether the requisite concerted action is present. Other clubs may refuse to deal with the athlete, but this usually has nothing to do with the fine. The reason, rather, is the fact that the player is under contract to his club and thus not available for employment with other clubs.[946]

Yet, it would seem somewhat anomalous if fines resulted in a wholly different analysis under the antitrust laws. In some cases, a fine might be a much more severe penalty than a suspension. For example, a low-paid athlete might prefer to endure a very short suspension rather than pay a fine of several thousand dollars. Moreover, it seems clear that the leagues regard fines and suspensions as part of a singular disciplinary system. The league's ultimate purposes in imposing punishment are basically the same in each case, and the choice of one sanction rather than the other may merely reflect differences in the seriousness of the offense, the mental state of the offender, or the quality of the factual proof.[947]

A closer analysis should dispel the difficulties mentioned above. The requisite concerted action can be found if one focuses, not upon the effect of the sanction in a particular case, but rather upon the system through which it is imposed. Thus, the antitrust objection should be directed to the characteristics of the arrangement which give the leagues power to exact monetary penalties. The clubs have, in effect, jointly agreed that the league will be empowered to exercise control over the conduct of their employees. The officials who mete out discipline thus serve as the administrative organ through which the group achieves its goals in these matters. Moreover, it is clear that there is a "refusal to deal." Any player coming into the league is bound by the preordained system, and no club will deal with a participant except on the terms which prescribe the league's authority. Thus, while the clubs may not act together in the imposition and enforcement of a particular fine, they have joined together in structuring the system through which the punishment is imposed.[948]

It appears, then, that league fines are to be judged under the same standards which the antitrust laws impose upon suspensions. Fines may only be used to punish conduct which is within the range of the league's self-regulatory powers. Such penalties cannot be used as a device to protect the league from outside competition, nor may they be used to control behavior which does not affect

---

been reviewed, the focus has usually been on whether the group can properly impose discipline at all, and the issue of whether monetary penalties are entitled to greater, or lesser, deference has typically not been raised. *See, e.g.,* Mechanical Contractors Bid Depository v. Christiansen, 352 F.2d 817 (10th Cir. 1965). *See also* E. ROCKEFELLER, ANTITRUST QUESTIONS AND ANSWERS 49 (1974).

946. *See* §§ 4.02-.04 *supra.*

947. *See* note 944 *supra.*

948. This same analysis could be applied to define the antitrust offense when a suspension, rather than a fine, was involved. While the earlier discussion of suspensions focused upon the coercive nature of the individual suspension rather than the system under which the power was exercised, it can be noted that the requisite refusal to deal could be found at either level.

legitimate league interests.[949] Moreover, the amount of the fine must be reasonably related to the quality of the interest at stake, and the disciplinary authorities must be sensitive to the need for differentiated treatment for the various degrees of misconduct which might arise.[950] Finally, an accused player is entitled to procedural safeguards in the proceeding in which the fine is imposed.[951] For very large fines, this may require procedures as elaborate as those which accompany suspension. Where small fines are involved, less formality will be tolerated.

d. Discipline by Individual Clubs. Most sports leagues recognize the right of individual clubs to enforce their own disciplinary rules.[952] These usually pertain to matters which are of a more direct interest to the club and may include such things as curfews and training rules, as well as general rules concerning the players' obligations to follow orders given by the coaching staff.[953] The sanctions imposed may range from small fines to suspensions.

Are the disciplinary actions of a club subject to review under the antitrust laws? On the surface, there might be reason to question whether they involve the sort of joint action which will establish a concerted refusal to deal. That feature is present in league disciplinary action because the league derives its authority from the collective agreement of the member clubs. Yet, where a club takes action which affects only its own employees, it is less clear that the requisite conspiracy is present.

There are no cases which address the question of how discipline by individual clubs should be characterized for antitrust purposes. But there is another view of the club's authority which suggests that it should be subject to the same standard of review which is applied to league imposed discipline. Rather than focusing on the particular disciplinary action — which appears to involve only a single employer and its employee — it is useful to consider the source of the authority which is being exercised. In most leagues, a club's right to control a player's conduct arises from the contract which is entered into with the employee.[954] But that contract is not wholly the product of individual negotiation between the two parties. In most cases, the basic outline of the agreement is prescribed by the league and embodied in a uniform player's contract which all clubs must use. One of the uniform terms is that which exacts the player's agreement to abide by the rules which the club imposes. There may be differences among leagues in the extent to which such terms are subject to modification through the individual negotiations between the player and the club.[955] But where such variations are not allowed, it can be argued that the club's disciplinary authority is indeed the product of a concerted refusal to deal.

---

949. *See* text at notes 906-11 *supra.*
950. *See* text at notes 926-29 *supra.*
951. *See* text at notes 888-904 *supra.*
952. The contractual basis of the club's authority to discipline is considered in § 3.10.
953. *See, e.g.,* N.Y. Times, Aug. 18, 1975, at 25, col. 3 (WFL player Anthony Davis fined $500 for disrespectful remarks to assistant coach); Los Angeles Times, Aug. 31, 1975, Pt. III, at 2, col. 2 (baseball player Dock Ellis suspended thirty days for "insubordination"; reinstated, but still to pay "substantial" fine). *See also* § 3.10 *supra.*
954. *See* § 3.10 *supra.*
955. *Cf.* Chuy v. Philadelphia Eagles, 407 F. Supp. 717 (E.D. Pa. 1976).

The clubs have in effect agreed that they will not contract with a player except upon terms which reserve to them authority to control the player's conduct. And while a club might otherwise have sought to retain that right even without the joint agreement, a uniform provision for club discipline is partially intended to serve the interest of the league as a whole. The image of the league as sponsoring competition between teams of athletes who are serious, dedicated, and well-trained will be promoted if each club accepts resonsibility for controlling its own employees. Thus, the common agreement on the need for discipline by individual employers can be seen as a part of the larger design to insure the success of the joint venture.

If this theory is accepted, discipline by individual clubs would be treated under the same standards applied to league discipline. As the prior discussion suggests, the fact that these matters are reviewable under the antitrust laws does not mean that sports authorities cannot control player conduct. Such controls seem fully appropriate in some areas and should not prompt extensive litigation. What the antitrust laws do mean, however, is that both the leagues and clubs must act responsibly in defining and administering their disciplinary systems. Proper restraint in defining the range of the entity's legitimate interest and in structuring the disciplinary proceeding should provide adequate protection against unwanted litigation.

§ 5.10. Exclusionary Practices of Sports Associations.

The basic concern of the previous several sections was the right of professional sports leagues to control the economic opportunities of the athletes who participate in those ventures. It should be clear, however, that there are many other groups which enjoy broad powers to determine an individual's access to the rewards of commercial sports activities. The groups involved, and the types of competition which they affect, cover a wide range. Thus, the concern for the private group's control may arise when the Professional Golfers' Association declares a player ineligible for participation in one of its lucrative tournaments or when a horsemen's association refuses to license a particular horse for participation in its races. The present section examines some of the legal principles which operate to limit the discretion of such groups. Specifically, we will consider the extent to which the antitrust laws might be used as a basis for judicial review of the group's decisions.[956]

At the outset, it is important to emphasize the diverse sorts of activities which raise potential antitrust issues. First, there is a wide variety of rules which might be called into question. Most of the cases decided to date have involved what might be described generally as rules of eligibility. These include not only the rules which determine the initial eligibility of participants,[957] but also those which are applied to approve or disapprove the use of particular facilities or

---

956. Some of the groups considered here are involved in sports activities which are subject to direct public regulation through legislatively-created commissions. These statutory schemes may provide additional remedies for the types of exclusionary actions which are discussed here. The reader may wish to consult chapter 2 of this text for a further discussion of the types of sports activities subject to direct public regulation and the issues likely to be dealt with in such a statutory scheme.

957. *See, e.g.,* Deesen v. Professional Golfers Ass'n, 358 F.2d 165 (9th Cir. 1966); United States v. United States Trotting Ass'n, 1960 Trade Cas. ¶ 69,761 (S.D. Ohio).

equipment.[958] Moreover, the principles examined here would seem to be equally applicable to disciplinary rules.[959] Thus, whether the group is determining the individual's right to enter the competition as an initial matter or his or her right to continue despite allegations of misconduct, the basic concern is the same: what are the limits of the group's authority to control the individual's access to economic opportunities.[960]

The term *sports association* will be used to describe the types of groups likely to be involved in the enforcement of the rules examined here. It should be clear, however, that not all of these organizations are concerned with "athletics" in a traditional sense. The range of activities which may be involved covers not only those which primarily test human physical skills, such as golf,[961] tennis,[962] and bowling,[963] but also those which involve other elements as well, such as horse racing[964] and automobile racing.[965] The common characteristic of all of these ventures is that they involve elements of both economic and non-economic competition. The non-economic competition is that in which the relative skills of human participants or the capacity of animals or machines are tested. But the competition has a decided commercial aspect to it as well, for the contests result in the award of prize money or produce some other economic advantage. It is this latter feature which typically gives rise to legal controversy. As has been seen in prior sections, the basic policy of the federal antitrust laws is to prohibit improper restraints upon economic competition, and it is not surprising that those who are disappointed by a group's eligibility determination might invoke the antitrust laws to test the propriety of the action.

---

958. *See, e.g.,* Bridge Corp. of America v. American Contract Bridge League, Inc., 428 F.2d 1365 (9th Cir. 1970); Washington State Bowling Proprietors Ass'n v. Pacific Lanes, Inc., 356 F.2d 371 (9th Cir. 1966); STP Corp. v. United States Auto Club, Inc., 286 F. Supp. 146 (S.D. Ind. 1968).

959. *See, e.g.,* Blalock v. Ladies Professional Golf Ass'n, 359 F. Supp. 1260 (N.D. Ga. 1973); United States v. United States Trotting Ass'n, 1960 Trade Cas. ¶ 69,761 (S.D. Ohio).

960. Under common law principles dealing with the powers of private associations, there is authority for the view that a court should be more willing to intervene in the association's affairs when it acts to expel an existing member than when it merely refuses to admit an outsider. It is reasoned that in the former case, the membership has created a legal relationship which is entitled to protection. In the latter, of course, no relationship has been formed. *See, e.g.,* Hurwitz v. Directors Guild, 364 F.2d 67 (2d Cir. 1966). Along these same lines, it might be argued in the antitrust context that someone who is denied an existing opportunity to compete ought to be entitled to a more exacting judicial review than one who is merely denied a prospective advantage. However, there is little in the cases which supports a distinction; and whether exclusion or expulsion is involved, the basic inquiry appears to be whether the association's controls were reasonable. *Compare* Deesen v. Professional Golfers Ass'n, 358 F.2d 165 (9th Cir. 1966) *with* Blalock v. Ladies Professional Golf Ass'n, 359 F. Supp. 1260 (N.D. Ga. 1973). *See also* STP Corp. v. United States Auto Club, Inc., 286 F. Supp. 146 (S.D. Ind. 1968).

961. *See* Deesen v. Professional Golfers Ass'n, 358 F.2d 165 (9th Cir. 1966); Blalock v. Ladies Professional Golf Ass'n, 359 F. Supp. 1260 (N.D. Ga. 1973).

962. *See* Heldman v. United States Lawn Tennis Ass'n, 354 F. Supp. 1241 (S.D.N.Y. 1973).

963. *See* Washington State Bowling Proprietors Ass'n, Inc. v. Pacific Lanes, Inc., 356 F.2d 371 (9th Cir. 1966).

964. *See* United States v. United States Trotting Ass'n, 1960 Trade Cas. ¶ 69,761 (S.D. Ohio).

965. *See* STP Corp. v. United States Auto Club, Inc., 256 F. Supp. 146 (S.D. Ind. 1968).

Other cases dealing with the same general problem involve bridge tournaments, Bridge Corp. of America v. American Contract Bridge League, Inc., 428 F.2d 1365 (9th Cir. 1970), and professional wrestling, National Wrestling Alliance v. Myers, 325 F.2d 768 (8th Cir. 1963). It should also be noted that there are many kinds of non-sport activities involving the same types of legal issues which are considered here. *See, e.g.,* McCreery Angus Farms v. American Angus Ass'n, 379 F. Supp. 1008 (S.D. Ill. 1974); Comment, *Trade Association Exclusionary Practices: An Affirmative Role for the Rule of Reason,* 66 Colum. L. Rev. 1486 (1966).

The complaints which have been litigated in this area typically allege violations of both section 1 and section 2 of the Sherman Act.[966] These provisions involve somewhat different theories.[967] It will be recalled that section 1 is primarily concerned with agreements or combinations which restrain commerce.[968] Thus, the plaintiff who has been declared ineligible — perhaps because he was found not to have exhibited sufficient skill or because his equipment did not meet the association's specifications — may allege that in adopting the particular rule, the membership of the association had joined, or conspired, together in pursuit of a policy which had the effect of limiting the plaintiff's ability to compete for the prize money or other rewards which were available. The section 2 theory is somewhat different. That provision provides a basis for relief when it is established that a person or group has monopolized, or attempted to monopolize, any part of trade or commerce. Under section 2, the primary concern is with a structural condition, the defendant's ability to control or monopolize a particular market. In the present context, this theory is often made tenable by the fact that the particular sports association may be the only one which has authority to decide questions of eligibility for the activity involved.

The courts, however, generally have not undertaken to separate the section 1 and 2 complaints in their treatment of the cases. For example, the section 2 theory would usually require an inquiry into whether the defendant had the requisite monopoly power.[969] That entails the further determinations of what the relevant market is, an issue which could necessitate a lengthy inquiry into the other competitive opportunities available to the participant.[970] But relatively few cases treat such questions in any detail. Rather the tendency is for courts to go directly to the question of whether the restraint which the group imposed was improper.[971] This approach is understandable, although not always wholly defensible. Both section 1 and section 2 ultimately seek the same end, prohibiting practices which result in improper market control. Under section 2, it is not enough to simply show that an entity possesses monopoly power. It must also be established that the group used that power for the purpose of excluding or limiting competition, and in this connection it is usually relevant to inquire whether the group has "abused" its market position or simply engaged in legitimate business activity.[972] Thus, although the complaint may frame

---

966. *See, e.g.,* Bridge Corp. of America v. American Contract Bridge League, Inc., 428 F.2d 1365 (9th Cir. 1970); Deesen v. Professional Golfers Ass'n, 358 F.2d 165 (9th Cir. 1966); Washington State Bowling Proprietors Ass'n, Inc. v. Pacific Lanes, Inc., 356 F.2d 371 (9th Cir. 1966); STP Corp. v. United States Auto Club, Inc., 286 F. Supp. 146 (S.D. Ind. 1968).

967. The reader desiring a basic introduction to the theories of the two sections should consult E. GELLHORN, ANTITRUST LAW AND ECONOMICS IN A NUTSHELL 112-97 (1976) or A. NEALE, THE ANTITRUST LAWS OF THE U.S.A. 32-178 (2d ed. 1970).

968. *See* § 5.07 *supra.*

969. *See, e.g.,* United States v. Grinnell Corp., 384 U.S. 563, 570 (1966).

970. *See, e.g.,* United States v. E.I. du Pont de Nemours & Co., 351 U.S. 377 (1956); United States v. Grinnell Corp., 384 U.S. 563 (1966); United States v. Aluminum Co. of America, 148 F.2d 416 (2d Cir. 1945).

971. *See, e.g.,* Deesen v. Professional Golfers Ass'n, 358 F.2d 165 (9th Cir. 1966); Washington State Bowling Proprietors Ass'n, Inc. v. Pacific Lanes, Inc., 356 F.2d 371 (9th Cir. 1966).

972. *See, e.g.,* American Tobacco Co. v. United States, 328 U.S. 781 (1946); United States v. United Shoe Machinery Corp., 110 F. Supp. 295 (D. Mass. 1953), *aff'd per curiam,* 347 U.S. 521 (1954); United States v. Aluminum Co. of America, 148 F.2d 416 (2d Cir. 1945).

separate section 1 and section 2 issues, the court may feel that the central question is the propriety of the control and proceed to treat that issue. It should also be noted that in the majority of cases decided to date, the courts have rejected the plaintiffs' contentions of illegality and sustained the groups' actions.[973] The courts may have decided that since the ultimate question under both section 1 and section 2 — whether there was an improper restraint on competition — was to be decided in favor of the sports group, it was unnecessary to go through the complex analysis of relevant markets, relative market power, and the like. Even if a section 2 monopoly were established, that condition is only preliminary to the issue of whether there was an abuse.

For purposes of the following discussion, we have chosen to focus on the section 1 issues because these suggest the approach which is likely to have the most universal application. With respect to most sports associations, there is usually little difficulty in establishing that the requisite combination or agreement is present, for, as mentioned, the enforcing authority derives its power from some type of joint action among those involved in staging the contests involved. Thus, the issue which requires the greatest attention is whether the power derived from this combination was used improperly. It is thus appropriate that we now turn to the question of the standards which will be applied to determine the propriety of particular eligibility and disciplinary rules.

a. The Nature of the Antitrust Inquiry. It would be misleading to suggest that the cases decided to date are in complete agreement on the standard of review to be applied to rule-making by sports associations. Some courts have been highly critical of attempts by such groups to control competitive opportunities of outsiders, and at least one case might be read to suggest that all attempts to limit who can compete are *per se* unreasonable and that the justification which the group might offer need not be evaluated.[974] Other courts have been quite deferential to the groups' rule-making, and while none suggest that judicial review is wholly foreclosed, some appear willing to apply standards which would invalidate exclusionary practices only in extreme cases.[975] But if

---

973. *Cases in which relief has been denied:* Bridge Corp. of America v. American Contract Bridge League, Inc., 428 F.2d 1365 (9th Cir. 1970); Deesen v. Professional Golfers Ass'n, 358 F.2d 165 (9th Cir. 1966); National Wrestling Alliance v. Myers, 325 F.2d 768 (8th Cir. 1963); Abendroth v. Professional Golfers Ass'n, No. 75-2358 (N.D. Cal., Dec. 19, 1975); Heldman v. United States Lawn Tennis Ass'n, 354 F. Supp. 1241 (S.D.N.Y. 1973); STP Corp. v. United States Auto Club, Inc., 286 F. Supp. 146 (S.D. Ind. 1968); United States v. United States Trotting Ass'n, 1960 Trade Cas. ¶ 69,761 (S.D. Ohio). *See also* Molinas v. National Basketball Ass'n, 190 F. Supp. 241 (S.D.N.Y. 1961). *Cases in which the court has intervened:* Washington State Bowling Proprietors Ass'n, Inc. v. Pacific Lanes, Inc., 356 F.2d 371 (9th Cir. 1966); Blalock v. Ladies Professional Golf Ass'n, 359 F. Supp. 1260 (N.D. Ga. 1973). *See also* Denver Rockets v. All-Pro Management, Inc., 325 F. Supp. 1049 (C.D. Cal. 1971).

974. *See* Washington State Bowling Proprietors Ass'n, Inc. v. Pacific Lanes, Inc., 356 F.2d 371, 376 (9th Cir. 1966). The case is considered more fully in the text at notes 42-55 *infra.*

975. For example, in STP Corp. v. United States Auto Club, Inc., 286 F. Supp. 146 (S.D. Ind. 1968), the court used language which suggests that judicial intervention is appropriate only in the most extreme cases. At one point in its lengthy opinion, the court suggested that it was going to apply a standard similar to that used at common law to determine the reviewability of actions by private associations. Thus, it is stated that a court should interfere in the actions of a private governing body "only if it finds that the powers were exercised in an unlawful, arbitrary or malicious fashion and in such a manner as to affect the property rights of one who complains . . . ." *Id.* at 151. *See also* § 3.16 *supra* (law of private associations). Later when the court specifically addressed the antitrust issue, it was similarly deferential to the group's inherent authority. The particular

one looks beyond the aberrational holdings of a couple of the cases and the loose language found in others, it is possible to discern a trend which provides a highly useful framework for analysis. It must be accepted that the sports area has not yet generated enough cases to provide firm precedent on each point of this analytical model, but there is not a total lack of guidance on the gaps which remain. The general orientation of the existing sports precedents and the cases decided in other areas, including the major Supreme Court decisions dealing with commercial boycotts, are helpful in defining the basic principles which should be applied.

At this point, it may be useful to note that the analysis which is used to test the eligibility determinations of sports groups closely resembles that which has been applied to other issues discussed in prior sections of this treatise. Particularly pertinent here are the sections dealing with the authority of professional sports leagues to discipline players [976] and to establish rules for on-the-field competition, squad size limits, and the like.[977] In those areas, as here, it is accepted that the nature of the enterprise may require that the entity be given some prerogatives to regulate its own affairs, and in each instance, the pertinent issue for antitrust purposes is whether the entity has exercised its regulatory powers consistent with the conditions which justify self-regulation. Because of the similarity of the inquiry which is made, the reader may wish to consult the prior discussion of the rule-making prerogatives of leagues in team sports. Those materials will suggest that while the special needs of league sports may provide some justifications which are not available to other types of ventures, the basic framework for judicial review is the same as that outlined here.[978]

In general, the courts have had little difficulty accepting that private sports associations can, consistent with the antitrust laws, assume the prerogative to regulate the activities which come within their particular areas of interest.[979]

---

controversy concerned a rule change which substantially reduced the likelihood that the plaintiff's turbine cars would be able to compete effectively in the Indianapolis 500 race. In rejecting the plaintiff's complaint, the court said that it did not

> consider that the adoption [or] modification . . . from time to time by defendant of its rules for safety [or] competitive reasons . . . impose [sic] any obstruction or obstacle . . . [or] appreciably affect interstate . . . commerce . . . . 286 F. Supp. at 171.

In the final analysis, the court concluded that

> such rules . . . do not rise to dignity for measurement [nor] are they within the proscription of the antitrust laws. *Id.*

976. *See* § 5.09 *supra.*

977. *See* § 5.08 *supra.*

978. There are many matters which will be of common concern for both professional leagues and other sports associations. Both groups are likely to define the rules of competition, establish safety standards, and devise measures to prevent cheating and thus promote the integrity of the sport. On the other hand, leagues may have special interests not shared by some types of sports associations. For example, leagues are different from many other sports groups in that their members are also the employers of the participants. It is understandable that the league would involve itself more in employment related matters than, for example, would the United States Auto Club. *See* STP Corp. v. United States Auto Club, Inc., 286 F. Supp. 146 (S.D. Ind. 1968). Also, the nature of the league's enterprise will likely cause it to be more concerned about the relative balance among competing units. *See* § 5.07 *supra.* Here again, concerns which are essentially employment related — the conditions upon which trades can be made, the players' freedom of movement, and so on — are likely to receive more attention than in other sports settings.

979. *See, e.g.,* Bridge Corp. of America v. American Contract Bridge League, Inc., 428 F.2d 1365 (9th Cir. 1970); Deesen v. Professional Golfers Ass'n, 358 F.2d 165 (9th Cir. 1966); Heldman v. United States Lawn Tennis Ass'n, 354 F. Supp. 1241 (S.D.N.Y. 1973); STP Corp. v. United States Auto Club,

A critical issue concerns the types of matters over which they can properly assume control. The basic principle which seems to be applied in making this determination is that there are certain types of regulations which ultimately serve to promote economic opportunities and, hence, increase the amount of economic competition which occurs, and group enforcement of these is proper.[980] For example, regulations which standardize the rules for non-economic competition serve to give the sport an identity and thus promote spectator interest, with the result that the economic rewards available to participants and promoters are increased.[981] By the same token, standardization enables potential participants to determine the type of skills or equipment which will be needed to compete and permits them to concentrate on acquiring or perfecting these, thus avoiding what might otherwise be wasteful expenditures of time and money.[982] Other regulations which seek to preserve the integrity of the sport or to insure the safety of participants and spectators can similarly be viewed as ultimately enhancing the economic activity which takes place.

When the regulatory activities of sports associations are scrutinized under the antitrust laws, there are three general issues which may be pursued.[983] Initially it is appropriate for the court to examine the purpose of the rule in question.

Inc., 286 F. Supp. 146 (S.D. Ind. 1968); United States v. United States Trotting Ass'n, 1960 Trade Cas. ¶ 69,761 (S.D. Ohio). *See generally* Comment, *Trade Association Exclusionary Practices: An Affirmative Role for the Rule of Reason, supra* note 965.

980. The Supreme Court early indicated that in trade restraint cases:

... The true test of legality is whether the restraint imposed is such as merely regulates and perhaps thereby promotes competition or whether it is such as may suppress or even destroy competition. Chicago Bd. of Trade v. United States, 246 U.S. 231, 238 (1918).

The Court was addressing a situation involving marketing restrictions imposed by a commodities exchange. The same principles would seem to be applicable to sports associations which have as their essential function the development of an effective market for a particular product — sports competition.

981. For example, an automobile racing group might decide that it wanted to offer a form of competition which was limited to cars of a certain body size with piston driven engines. It would not seem unreasonable for the association to conclude that other types of vehicles — motorcycles, turbine or jet propelled autos, or those of a much larger or smaller size — would not be permitted. *Cf.* STP Corp. v. United States Auto Club, Inc., 286 F. Supp. 146 (S.D. Ind. 1968). What the group has done in effect is to define the "sport" which it will sanction. This serves to inform the fans as to what they can expect at the contests that are held and serves to define the areas in which participants can seek to secure a competitive advantage.

While there should be little question that competitors can agree among themselves as to what their sport will be, it should also be clear that this power can be used improperly. Thus, the sport might be defined in terms which permitted participants to use only certain facilities when the only purpose was to favor the economic interests of existing members of the association. *Cf.* Washington State Bowling Proprietors Ass'n v. Pacific Lanes, Inc., 356 F.2d 371 (9th Cir. 1966). The matter of distinguishing between proper and improper exercises of the group's authority is, of course, the primary concern addressed in subsequent portions of the text. For the present, it is enough to note that a case can be made for affording the association some prerogative to define the nature of its venture.

982. The arguments made in the text about the desirability of standardizing the elements of competition gain some support by analogy from the general body of antitrust law dealing with product standardization by commercial trade associations. It appears that rules designed for that purpose will be upheld if they can be shown to have a legitimate business justification. However, those intended only to protect the trade association members from unwanted economic competition clearly will not be tolerated. *See* J. VON KALINOWSKI, ANTITRUST LAWS AND TRADE REGULATION (16J BUSINESS ORGANIZATIONS 1973) § 75.03; Timberlake, *Standardization and Simplification Under the Antitrust Laws,* 29 CORNELL L.Q. 301 (1944); Verleger, *Trade Association Participation in Standardization and Simplification Programs,* 27 A.B.A. ANTITRUST SECTION 129 (1956); Wachtel, *Products, Standards and Certification Programs,* 13 ANTITRUST BULL. 1 (1968).

983. *See generally* Comment, *Trade Association Exclusionary Practices: An Affirmative Role for the Rule of Reason, supra* note 965, at 1504-05.

It must be determined whether the regulation was intended to further legitimate goals of the sort identified above or to achieve some other purpose not sanctioned by the antitrust laws. But even if the goal of the regulation is proper, a second inquiry is necessary, and that is whether the measure in question is a proper means of achieving the justifiable end. There are usually a variety of approaches which can be taken to attain the group's legitimate purposes, and the lesson of the antitrust laws in this area is that the governing authority must not choose an alternative which unduly impedes economic competition. A third inquiry shifts the focus away from the substance of the rules and considers the procedural aspects of the group's regulatory activity. Thus, there is a concern that those who are subjected to the group's disciplinary powers be afforded basic procedural protection. Similarly, other exclusionary decisions by the group, such as a determination that certain participants or equipment will not be eligible for competition, must be made in a procedural setting which insures their objectivity.

The three general antitrust issues identified above provide the outline for the discussion which follows. Each involves a number of collateral concerns which require separate analysis. Again, the existing case law provides specific answers to only a few of these questions and is valuable largely for suggesting the general framework in which these matters should be analyzed.

1. *Purpose of the Rule.*

In evaluating a particular regulation of a sports association, a threshold question will be whether the rule can be justified in light of the conditions which warrant self-regulation by the group. It is appropriate, therefore, that the purpose of the rule be examined.[984] There are some goals which are clearly impermissible and warrant summary treatment by the courts. Thus, a rule intended solely to protect the association or some of its members from competition by outsiders would not be tolerated. There are, however, few rules

---

984. United States v. United States Trotting Ass'n, 1960 Trade Cas. ¶ 69,671 (S.D. Ohio), was one of the first sports association cases to suggest that private regulations are to be evaluated in light of the purposes for which the group was formed. In that case, the government had filed a complaint generally attacking the rules of the association which approved particular tracks, registered horses and licensed drivers. The court eventually concluded that the rules in question should be sustained. It emphasized the legitimacy of the purposes involved and the reasonableness of the means used to attain these:

> The defendant contends that the main purposes of the U.S.T.A. are lawful and that restraints, if any, incidental to its activities are reasonable and reasonably related to the attainment of those purposes. Defendant alleges that the main purpose behind the organization of U.S.T.A. was to provide a voluntary association open to all persons and organizations interested in the betterment of harness racing; that this main general purpose was implemented by the adoption of U.S.T.A. By-Laws, Rules and Regulations which set forth the expressed main purposes of U.S.T.A., i.e. the registration and identification of horses, rules of racing "within the fence," and the preservation of the integrity of harness racing.
>
> Plaintiff has failed to establish that the main purpose of U.S.T.A. is an unlawful or hidden one different from its expressed purposes just mentioned. To determine whether the manner or means utilized by a defendant to attain its purposes are unlawful, the rule to be applied is whether the restraint imposed, if any, is such as "merely regulates and perhaps thereby promotes competition or whether it is such as may suppress or even destroy competition." *Chicago Board of Trade v. United States,* 246 U.S. 231, 238. The Court cannot find upon this record that the activities of U.S.T.A. in maintaining and enforcing its Rules and Regulations are unlawful as unreasonable and undue restraints upon competition in interstate commerce. Nor can the Court find that such activities are anything more than reasonable restraints that merely regulate and standardize harness racing, promote competition in harness racing, and generally enable U.S.T.A. to attain its main and not unlawful purposes as contended by defendant. *Id.* at 76,957.

See also Deesen v. Professional Golfers Ass'n, 358 F.2d 165, 170 (9th Cir. 1966).

which reveal such an improper purpose on their face, and it will often be necessary for the court to make an inquiry to determine the real intent behind a particular control. For example, an association may adopt a rule limiting the types of facilities in which its contests may be held.[985] There are some circumstances in which a restriction of this sort might be justified, as where the layout of the facility was such as to change the basic nature of the competition. But it is also possible that upon closer examination, a court might find that a rule ostensibly adopted to standardize the type of competition held, was really intended to protect the economic interests of some association members by insuring that only their facilities would be used.

The determination of the true purpose of a rule will often not be an easy matter, but there are various types of evidence which might be considered. With respect to sanctioning facilities, for example, it would be relevant to inquire whether under objective criteria the arena or track which had been disapproved differed substantially from those which previously had been sanctioned. By the same token, it would be appropriate to examine conversations and correspondence between the owners of approved facilities to determine whether these revealed an improper purpose.

One legal issue which is likely to arise is whether these cases should be treated under the *per se* or rule of reason standard.[986] If it can be established that a rule had an anticompetitive purpose, the measure ought to be condemned summarily as *per se* illegal. But, of course, the purpose of the rule may not be clear, which might suggest that a more detailed inquiry, such as that allowed under a rule of reason approach, should be made. The rule of reason approach, however, is not wholly appropriate, for that standard usually involves a consideration of matters which would be irrelevant if the improper purpose were shown. For example, the rule of reason permits an inquiry into the effect of the restraint in question, which may entail a detailed factual examination of the number of persons affected, the severity of the impact, and the probable consequences for future development of the industry.[987] These matters would be irrelevant if an anticompetitive purpose were established. It would seem more appropriate that courts develop a modified *per se* approach in cases in which the plaintiff alleged that a particular restraint had no purpose other than serving the economic self-interest of persons already protected by the association. In these instances, the court should hear evidence on the question of the intent behind the rule, but not require the plaintiff to present detailed proof on other matters such as the actual or potential effect on competition. Such evidence would be relevant if the plaintiff were attacking a rule for which there was some justification based on legitimate concerns of the association, for the relevant inquiry there is whether the group's interest is sufficiently strong to require that the resulting effect on competition be tolerated.[988] But if the rule is wholly

985. Such a rule was involved in Washington State Bowling Proprietors Ass'n v. Pacific Lanes, Inc., 356 F.2d 371 (9th Cir. 1966). As is discussed later in the text, there is some basis to suggest that the court's condemnation of the rule in that case reflected the fact that the rule served to further the economic self-interest of those who controlled the sanctioning group. *See* text at notes 41-54 *infra.*

986. The differences between these standards, and their role in antitrust litigation, is discussed in § 5.07 *supra.*

987. *See, e.g.,* Chicago Bd. of Trade v. United States, 246 U.S. 331 (1918).

988. There will often be disagreement as to whether the justification which the defendant puts forth is one which can be rejected as a factual matter or is one which has sufficient validity to require

lacking in legitimacy, any suppression of competition is sufficient to justify its rejection and detailed proof is not necessary. If the plaintiff chooses to limit his case to an allegation that the rule has an anticompetitive purpose, he should be entitled to a hearing which focuses on that limited issue.

Again, on the general question of whether a particular rule was adopted for a proper purpose, the analysis should focus on the conditions of the sport which give rise to self-regulation. Where an effect upon competition can be shown, only those rules which respond to these conditions should justify further scrutiny. The group's attempt to secure other goals will usually warrant summary disapproval. As suggested, a selfish purpose to protect the economic interest of some members will not be countenanced. In the same vein, a sanctioning association will not be permitted to assume control over the political or religious beliefs of those within its jurisdiction.[989] Some might argue that factors such as this affect the image of the sport and hence the degree of fan support. But as is explained more fully in connection with the discussion of the disciplinary authority of leagues, it is neither possible nor proper to wholly insulate sports from the various political and religious currents which influence the country.[990] While the sports authority has no duty to provide specific opportunities for public expression on these matters, it also has no right to demand political, social, or religious conformance. The thrust of its regulatory effort clearly should be directed to other matters.

The sports association rules which are likely to generate the most controversy are those which do not have a purely anticompetitive purpose, but which nonetheless impose significant restrictions on the economic opportunities of some individuals. In such instances, the focus of the debate will be whether the purpose of the rule is a justifiable one.[991] There will be some rules which can be sustained even though they are specifically designed to limit the number of persons who can compete for the prize-money offered in association-sponsored events. Thus, it would seem permissible for a golf association to adopt a rule limiting the field of competitors in its tournaments to a predetermined number.[992] Similarly, the sponsors of automobile races may decide that only a stated number of cars will be allowed to run. There may be differing justifications for such rules. In the case of the automobile race, the primary concern may be that too many cars would clog the track and limit the level of non-economic competition which took place or endanger the safety of the drivers. In the golf match, the limitation is likely to reflect the concern that only a certain number of golfers can play through a course in the time allotted.

---

the more extensive rule of reason inquiry. It seems proper that the trial court play an affirmative role in determining the characterization of the rule. Thus, even if a legitimate explanation for a rule could be plausibly put forth, the court should be prepared to reject this if the group is unable to come forth with evidence to suggest that its adoption of the rule was in fact influenced by such a concern. In some cases, the particular rule may present such an inefficient means of correcting a problem that the court should conclude that some purpose other than that suggested by the group lay behind its adoption. Again, Washington State Bowling Proprietors Ass'n v. Pacific Lanes, Inc., 356 F.2d 371 (9th Cir. 1966), may involve such a determination. *See* text at notes 41-54 *infra*.

989. *Cf.* Ali v. State Athletic Comm'n, 308 F. Supp. 11 (S.D.N.Y. 1969).

990. *See* § 5.09 *supra*.

991. *See* note 984 *supra*.

992. *See* Deesen v. Professional Golfers Ass'n, 358 F.2d 165 (9th Cir. 1966); Abendroth v. Professional Golfers Ass'n, No. 75-2358 (N.D. Cal.. Dec. 19, 1975).

In devising the rules by which a limited number of participant-positions are filled, the group may take account of other goals. Thus, it would seem proper that only the best of the potential entrants be deemed eligible for its contests.[993] By so restricting entry, the group will achieve the legitimate goal of heightening the level of non-economic competition which occurs. This will serve to stimulate fan interest and may promote a level of economic competition which would not otherwise be possible if a purely free-market approach were required. It should be noted that there is a separate concern as to whether the group has used a proper system for determining which competitors will fill the designated number of slots. That concern is addressed below where we focus not on the purpose of the rule, but on the means through which it is implemented.[994] On the general question addressed here, there should be little question that a group can exercise its powers to define the level of non-economic competition which will occur even when that means the economic opportunities of some participants are restricted.[995]

There are other types of eligibility rules which are of a much more questionable nature. For example, a group may have a rule which denies eligibility to anyone who participates in events not sanctioned by it.[996] Particular versions of this type of regulation may add qualifications to the basic prohibition. Thus, there may be a mechanism under which a person can re-qualify after he or she has participated in an unapproved contest,[997] or the group may provide that the only unapproved events which result in ineligibility are those which are scheduled in direct conflict with its own contests.[998]

The purpose of these rules is not altogether clear. On the surface they might appear to have a purely anticompetitive objective. But this is seldom an adequate explanation, for the groups which impose them are often involved only in sanctioning and regulating contests and do not participate directly in the resulting economic rewards.[999] It is more likely that the measures were originally devised as a means to bolster the authority of the group as the regulatory agency for the particular sport. Many sports associations come into existence as a response to the demands of participants, sponsors, and others for more centralized regulation of the sport.[1] Such a movement toward a common government might be prompted by wholly proper concerns, such as a desire to promote public interest in the sport or a specific concern for eliminating corrupt practices. In order to maximize the impact of the association, the members might agree to give it their complete support and not to undermine its authority by

---

993. Again, the PGA rules are examples of rules which have this further purpose. *See id.*

994. *See* text at notes 8-16 *infra.*

995. *See generally* Barber, *Refusals to Deal Under the Federal Antitrust Laws,* 103 U. PA. L. REV. 847 (1955).

996. *See, e.g.,* Washington State Bowling Proprietors Ass'n, Inc. v. Pacific Lanes, Inc., 356 F.2d 371 (9th Cir. 1966); Heldman v. United States Lawn Tennis Ass'n, 354 F. Supp. 1241 (S.D.N.Y. 1973); STP Corp. v. United States Auto Club, Inc., 286 F. Supp. 146 (S.D. Ind. 1968); United States v. United States Trotting Ass'n, 1960 Trade Cas. ¶ 69,761 (S.D. Ohio).

997. *See, e.g.,* Heldman v. United States Lawn Tennis Ass'n, 354 F. Supp. 1241, 1244-45 (S.D.N.Y. 1973).

998. *See, e.g.,* STP Corp. v. United States Auto Club, Inc., 286 F. Supp. 146, 154 (S.D. Ind. 1968).

999. *But see* Washington State Bowling Proprietors Ass'n, Inc. v. Pacific Lanes, Inc., 356 F.2d 371 (9th Cir. 1966).

1. *See, e.g.,* United States v. United States Trotting Ass'n, 1960 Trade Cas. ¶ 69,671 (S.D. Ohio).

participating in unregulated events. The problem, of course, is that a measure which originally served the laudable purpose of introducing order into an unregulated and disorganized sport could easily become a tool through which those with a vested interest in the venture protect themselves from outside competition. The rule against participation in unauthorized contests may operate so that all participants, or sponsors, or equipment manufacturers are locked-in to the association's events and thus are not available to those who might attempt to stage competing exhibitions.[2]

Association rules seldom raise this issue in such simple terms, however, and there are usually a range of subsidiary points which must be considered. For example, it is usually necessary to determine how difficult it would be for an outsider to have its events approved by the association. Obviously if such approval is secured, the legal problem may be avoided, for the participants would no longer be part of an "unauthorized" competition. If it appears that the group will be willing to sanction the event, and if there is no undue expense or obligation involved, the case for judicial intervention is substantially weakened.[3] Particularly where the remedy sought is discretionary, the court may not be persuaded that the facts compel the granting of relief. In other cases, it will be necessary to determine the precise extent to which the group controls competitive opportunities within the sport. If there is a considerable amount of unapproved competition which occurs, or if there are other sanctioning bodies operating in the sport, these facts may affect the likelihood of the plaintiff's recovery. Finally, a court considering a case in this area will want to give particular attention to the nature of the group enforcing the rule in question. In some sports, the sanctioning association may be found to have a neutral character;[4] in other cases, it may be dominated by persons who have a direct economic interest in limiting outside competition.[5] Where a rule serves the self-interest of those who enforce it, a court should have more difficulty accepting that it was intended only to help standardize and improve non-economic competition.

The range of considerations identified in the prior paragraph should suggest that there is no specific answer to the question of whether a rule which limits participation in unauthorized events is legally permissible. On the narrow issue of whether the purpose of such a rule is a proper one, it can be noted that there is nothing inherently evil about a rule which says that those who join a voluntary organization will do their best to support its efforts. But the question of the "purpose" of the rule will seldom be presented in such a pure form. Almost always the measure will take on special nuances in light of its historic origins, the economic interests of those who enforce it, and the economic power of the group involved. To enable the court to take account of such qualifications in particular rules, a rule of reason approach should be used.[6] As is developed in

2. *See, e.g.,* Heldman v. United States Lawn Tennis Ass'n, 354 F. Supp. 1241 (S.D.N.Y. 1973).
3. *See* Heldman v. United States Lawn Tennis Ass'n, 354 F. Supp. 1241, 1251 (S.D.N.Y. 1973), *cf.* Samara v. NCAA, 1973 Trade Cas. ¶ 74,536 (D.C. Va.).
4. *See* STP Corp. v. United States Auto Club, Inc., 286 F. Supp. 146, 153-54 (S.D. Ind. 1968).
5. *Cf.* Washington State Bowling Proprietors Ass'n, Inc. v. Pacific Lanes, Inc., 356 F.2d 371 (9th Cir. 1966).
6. *See* Heldman v. United States Lawn Tennis Ass'n, 354 F. Supp. 1241 (S.D.N.Y. 1973); United States v. United States Trotting Ass'n, 1960 Trade Cas. ¶ 69,761 (S.D. Ohio); *cf.* STP Corp. v. United States Auto Club, Inc., 286 F. Supp. 146 (S.D. Ind. 1968). *Contra* Washington State Bowling Proprietors Ass'n, Inc. v. Pacific Lanes, Inc., 356 F.2d 371 (9th Cir. 1966).

more detail in an earlier section, the rule of reason allows the parties to develop proof on a range of matters, including the history of the restraint, its actual and potential effects, and the peculiar condition of the industry in which it is imposed.[7]

2. *Is the Particular Control a Reasonable Means of Achieving an Otherwise Proper Goal?*

It is not enough simply to require that sports association rules be adopted for proper purposes. There must also be a concern for the manner in which those policies are implemented.[8] It should be clear that there are a variety of means which might be used to achieve a particular goal and, there may be differences among these in the extent to which they operate to restrain competition. For example, a private horse racing association may seek to prevent the drugging of horses to stimulate their performance. In implementing this policy, the group could, of course, choose a disciplinary system which punished only those persons actually shown to be involved in a drugging scheme. But because of the difficulties of finding direct proof of who administered the drugs, the association might adopt a rule which automatically punished the jockey, trainer, and owner of a horse found to have been drugged.[9] Or an automobile racing association might have a legitimate concern that its races only be held on tracks which are of a safe construction. To achieve this end, the group might establish a set of safety standards and approve any track which meets them. But what if the group chose another approach and approved only those tracks which had been constructed under the direct supervision of its architects? Obviously the means selected for implementing the safety rule could have an important impact on the number of tracks which could offer association-sanctioned races since tracks constructed before the start of the supervision program would automatically be eliminated.

The general antitrust principles which operate in this area suggest the legal standard to be applied to test the mechanisms chosen to implement the group's goals. Sports associations clearly enjoy some prerogative to devise rules which may affect the level of economic competition which occurs. But by the same token, there is an ever present concern that an individual's economic opportunities not be unnecessarily sacrificed. In other situations in which restraints on competition are reviewed on their merits, the basic test is the reasonableness of the restraint.[10] That standard also proves to be useful in the present context, and the central inquiry is whether the particular rule is a reasonable implementation of an otherwise proper goal.[11] This concern will have

7. *See* § 5.07 *supra.*

8. *See, e.g.,* United States v. United States Trotting Ass'n, 1960 Trade Cas. ¶ 69,761 (S.D. Ohio). *See also* note 984 supra.

9. Other legal issues arising from rules of this sort are considered in Chapter 2 *supra.*

10. *See generally* A. NEALE, THE ANTITRUST LAWS OF THE U.S.A. 20-29 (1970); Barber, *Refusals to Deal Under the Federal Antitrust Laws,* 103 U. PA. L. REV. 847 (1955); Coons, *Non-Commercial Purpose as a Sherman Act Defense,* 56 NW. U. L. REV. 705 (1962); Note, *A Return to the Rule of Reason in Group Boycott Cases?,* 42 U. COLO. L. REV. 467 (1971).

11. Union Circulation Co. v. FTC, 241 F.2d 652 (2d Cir. 1957), is the leading case from outside the sports area involving a regulatory measure which was broader than necessary to implement a legitimate policy. A group of magazine subscription agencies agreed not to hire a salesman who had left another firm in the prior year. The ostensible purpose of this arrangement was to discourage fraudulent practices. The court, however, found that the device used by the association had an impermissible effect on the labor market. Because the rule tended to

somewhat different meanings depending on the type of rule involved. If the controversy concerns the standards used to determine the safety of a race track, for example, the court may properly ask whether the "tests" used are reasonably calculated to differentiate among levels of safety. In this connection, it is obviously relevant to determine the extent to which some of those tracks excluded reflect construction techniques as good or better than those of tracks deemed qualified. Where the measure is one intended to prohibit or discourage particular conduct, such as drugging of racing animals, the issue will be whether the particular form of the rule is reasonably designed to identify those who either engaged in misconduct or had an opportunity to prevent it. If the rule requires the exclusion of a person who is in no sense culpable, the injured party can properly demand that a less restrictive approach be used. Again, the basic concern is that economic opportunities not be unnecessarily restricted.

The "reasonableness" standard necessarily implies that the group involved will be given some discretion to choose among the alternatives available for implementing a policy. It does not appear that the group is required to choose the very best technique or the one which the court might prefer.[12] If the particular mechanism is reasonably designed to achieve the desired goal, the group's choice of it should be respected.[13] There is a range of factors which a court might consider in making this determination. For example, it is proper to consider the extent to which competition is restrained in the particular case. Courts may also properly impose a more exacting standard upon a rule which bars an individual from participation for life than upon a measure which disqualifies him or her from a single tournament or event.[14] In the same vein, where eligibility criteria are involved, a court may properly attempt to ascertain the number of excluded participants or facilities which might, under a different test, be shown to be satisfactory. If it appears that there is a relatively small percentage of the total candidates who would fare better under a more complicated test — and if no long term disability attaches to the determination

discourage movement between firms and thus lessened competition, it was enjoined. It seems clear that even if the group's ultimate purpose were a legitimate one, the means selected to implement it were more restrictive than were necessary. It seems to have affected all salesmen who wished to change jobs, whether or not they had been involved in unethical conduct. Moreover, the group had selected a most coercive form of regulation — that related to job rights — and a court might well conclude that other less drastic steps might be sufficient to protect the group's legitimate interests. *See generally* Hoffman, *Association,* 13 ANTITRUST BULL. 595 (1968); Hummell, *Antitrust Problems of Industry Codes of Advertising, Standardization, and Seals of Approval,* 13 ANTITRUST BULL. 607 (1968).

12. *See* American Motor Inns, Inc. v. Holiday Inns, Inc., 521 F.2d 1230, 1248-49 (3d Cir. 1975); *cf.* Anderson v. American Automobile Ass'n, 454 F.2d 1240, 1246 (9th Cir. 1972). To demand adoption of that arrangement which imposed the least restriction on competition would place upon the group an objectionable burden. Its practices would be open to challenge by any lawyer with an imagination capable of conjuring up some lesser restrictive approach. Moreover, courts would be placed in the unenviable position of second-guessing business judgments as to what means would or would not achieve the legitimate goal. *See* American Motor Inns, Inc. v. Holiday Inns, Inc., 521 F.2d 1230, 1249-50 (3d Cir. 1975).

13. *See* Deesen v. Professional Golfers Ass'n, 358 F.2d 165 (9th Cir. 1966); STP Corp. v. United States Auto Club, Inc., 286 F. Supp. 146 (S.D. Ind. 1968); United States v. United States Trotting Ass'n, 1960 Trade Cas. ¶ 69,761 (S.D. Ohio). *Cf.* Heldman v. United States Lawn Tennis Ass'n, 354 F. Supp. 1241, 1253 (S.D.N.Y. 1973).

14. Where the candidate has an opportunity to qualify again at a later time, the court may be willing to accept less precision in the eligibility standards. *Cf.* Deesen v. Professional Golfers Ass'n, 358 F.2d 165 (9th Cir. 1966). *See also* Blalock v. Ladies Professional Golf Ass'n, 359 F. Supp. 1260, 1268 (N.D. Ga. 1973).

made — the court may well conclude that the existing practice comes within the bounds of reasonableness. Moreover, it would be appropriate for the court to consider the matter of expense and delay in judging the adequacy of qualifying rules. While a lengthy battery of tests might be a better indication of the safety of a facility than a visual inspection by a neutral expert, cost considerations may not warrant the more elaborate inquiry. It does not appear that the disappointed candidate is entitled to absolutely the best examination available, but only one which is reasonable in the circumstances of the particular case.

Again, the basic issue is whether the group's rule represents a reasonable implementation of a proper policy. In situations in which the group has acted in good faith and exhibited appropriate sensitivity to the fact that its actions will affect the economic opportunities of others, the decisions it reaches should be entitled to great weight.[15] There should be little debate that those involved in the day-to-day operation of the sport are better able to devise appropriate regulations than a court which views the industry from some distance.[16] Thus, where there are critical choices to be made among a range of alternative control devices, it seems appropriate that a court should be as much influenced by the orderliness and neutrality of the group's decision-making channels as by the precision of the mechanism finally selected. While the latter will always be a concern, it is not unthinkable that the degree of imperfections which will be tolerated should partially depend upon the extent to which there were opportunities for the group's decision to be influenced by the self-interest of some of its members. If the risks of such improper influences are eliminated and if the resulting restraint is not obviously excessive, it is fully appropriate that the "reasonableness" standard be applied in a manner which generally defers to the group's decision.

3. *The Procedural Concern.*

The cases decided in this area leave no doubt that the courts will be vitally concerned about the procedural aspects of a group's rule enforcement.[17] In one sense, this is simply another element of the question asked above as to whether

15. The court in STP Corp. v. United States Auto Club, Inc., 286 F. Supp. 146 (S.D. Ind. 1968), endorsed the notion that the decisions of the private regulatory group were entitled to great weight. Indeed, the court seems to have gone further and suggested a standard of review less exacting than the reasonableness standard used by most other courts. *See* note 975 *supra.* United States v. United States Trotting Ass'n, 1960 Trade Cas. ¶ 69,761 (S.D. Ohio), also indicates great deference to rule-making by the private association. There the court sustained a variety of different rules without apparently making a detailed inquiry into the purpose and effect of each measure.

16. The argument in favor of judicial deference to rule-making by entities with special expertise is a familiar one in administrative law. 4 K. DAVIS, ADMINISTRATIVE LAW TREATISE §§ 30.09-.14 (1958). The analogy to public administrative agencies seems particularly apt in those cases in which the sports association is not directly involved in the financial aspects of the competition. *See* STP Corp. v. United States Auto Club, 286 F. Supp. 146, 153-54 (S.D. Ind. 1968). Where the association exists only for the purpose of standardizing the competition and promoting its integrity, it fulfills a role not wholly different from that defined for many public regulatory agencies, and its solutions for avoiding particular problems can similarly be assumed to reflect its special understanding of the industry.

17. *See* Deesen v. Professional Golfers Ass'n, 358 F.2d 165 (9th Cir. 1966); Abendroth v. Professional Golfers Ass'n, No. 75-2358 (N.D. Cal. Dec. 19, 1975); Blalock v. Ladies Professional Golf Ass'n, 359 F. Supp. 1260 (N.D. Ga. 1973); *cf.* McCreery Angus Farms v. American Angus Ass'n, 379 F. Supp. 1008 (S.D. Ill. 1974); Denver Rockets v. All-Pro Management, Inc., 325 F. Supp. 1049 (C.D. Cal. 1971). *See generally* Comment, *Trade Association Exclusionary Practices: An Affirmative Role for the Rule of Reason,* 66 COLUM. L. REV. 1486, 1508-10 (1966).

the group had chosen a reasonable means for implementing an otherwise legitimate policy. For example, a participant who is disciplined for improper conduct may object to the lack of procedural safeguards in the disciplinary mechanism. Thus, while the plaintiff may concede that the group had pursued a proper goal (*i.e.,* it could legitimately punish the type of conduct alleged to have occurred), he or she might object that the policy was implemented in an unreasonable manner in that the procedures followed did not insure the reliability of the decision which was made. By the same token, a rule which resulted in the automatic suspension of the trainer of a horse which was drugged might be attacked as an unreasonable implementation of an otherwise valid policy against drugging. But at its heart, the plaintiff's objection would be directed to the lack of procedural fairness in a system which presumed guilt on the basis of a relationship and did not permit the accused to disprove the culpability.

Despite the affinity of the procedural issues and the matter of implementation discussed above, it is useful to consider the procedural concerns somewhat separately. In many situations procedural objections are directed more to the administrative, rather than the legislative, function of the sports association. Thus, some procedural questions involve no conscious choice of one enforcement option over another, but may simply indicate a lack of attention to formalities in the routine administration of the group's affairs. In any case, where the issue is framed in terms of procedural fairness, we are likely to find our experiences in other areas to be useful in suggesting the standards to be applied. Because the concern for the integrity of a decision-making process appears in a variety of contexts ranging from the criminal area to public administrative law, it is understandable that certain basic concepts are transferred to the present inquiry, even though the legal premise of the antitrust laws is otherwise distinctive.

As suggested, the concern for procedural fairness will often be raised when the sports association undertakes to exercise its disciplinary power. The Supreme Court made clear in *Silver v. New York Stock Exchange* [18] that the antitrust laws required that before a private, self-regulatory group could take action which had a significant effect upon the commercial interests of persons subject to its control, the group must provide basic safeguards to insure the integrity of the decision which was made. A prior section of these materials discusses the significance of *Silver* for disciplinary actions by sports leagues.[19] While sports associations often involve a somewhat different relationship than is found in the league setting, that fact does not seem to require a different interpretation of *Silver* where discipline is involved. Indeed, most courts and commentators assume that the requirement of procedural fairness has basically the same meaning in the two areas.[20] The prior discussion indicates the issues which will arise in the sports association context and suggests the analysis to be applied there. That discussion is not repeated here and the reader may wish to consult the prior section.

18. 373 U.S. 292 (1963).
19. *See* § 5.09 *supra.*
20. *See, e.g.,* Blalock v. Ladies Professional Golf Ass'n, 359 F. Supp. 1260 (N.D. Ga. 1973); Denver Rockets v. All-Pro Management, Inc., 325 F. Supp. 1049 (C.D. Cal. 1971); Comment, *Trade Association Exclusionary Practices: An Affirmative Role for the Rule of Reason, supra* note 17.

In addition to the matter of discipline, the concern for procedural fairness is also likely to arise when the association makes eligibility determinations. There are a variety of settings in which this issue may arise. It may be that an investor seeking approval of a new piece of equipment objects that the association did not give him a fair opportunity to establish its merit.[21] Or the objection may come from an athlete who is denied the opportunity to play in an association-sponsored contest.[22] Here again the thrust of the plaintiff's attack may be directed to a lack of fairness in the eligibility determining process.

The latter type of situation was involved in *Deesen v. Professional Golfers' Association*.[23] The case is profitably considered here not only because it illustrates the type of issues which will arise, but also because the court is willing to accept some debatable features of the defendant's eligibility rules. The reasons the court gave for its deferential attitude may be important for prospective plaintiffs who are contemplating similar litigation. Deesen, who had lost his eligibility to play in PGA tournaments, brought an action attacking the group's qualification procedures on antitrust grounds. Deesen perceived several different defects in the group's approach. First, the rules appeared to be discriminatory. Persons who were members of the PGA were permitted to enter without separate qualification, while non-members had to achieve the status of an "approved tournament player." Among other things, this required that the individual demonstrate an ability to "finish in the money." [24] To maintain his approved status, the golfer had to participate in a stated number of tournaments and continue to exhibit the requisite ability. In contrast, a PGA member did not have to demonstrate continuing ability to be eligible. Moreover, membership could be obtained merely by establishing that one was employed as a club professional for five years. This disparity was a particular source of concern to Deesen. He had qualified as a tournament player at one time, but later was deemed ineligible when injuries hampered his play. His concern was that a PGA member would not have been subjected to the same treatment even though the member's average tournament scores were lower than his.

A second objection raised by Deesen was addressed to the system under which non-members were approved for tournament play. The basic complaint was that there were no clearly defined objective criteria, and the determination of eligibility could easily be influenced by the personal biases of those who made the decisions. Under the association's rules, a local committee initially determined whether the player had the requisite ability, integrity, and financial backing for tournament play. Although the local group interviewed the applicant and participated in several rounds of golf with him, there were no predetermined minimum standards which were to be applied in the group's formulation of its recommendation. The local committee's actions were later reviewed at the regional and national level, but again there apparently was no prescribed standard of review.

---

21. *See* Bridge Corp. of America v. American Contract Bridge League, Inc., 428 F.2d 1365 (9th Cir. 1970).

22. *See, e.g.,* Deesen v. Professional Golfers Ass'n, 358 F.2d 165 (9th Cir. 1966). *Compare* Denver Rockets v. All-Pro Management, Inc., 325 F. Supp. 1049 (C.D. Cal. 1971).

23. 358 F.2d 165 (9th Cir. 1966).

24. *Id.* at 167.

While the court separately addressed each of the plaintiff's objections, its analysis suggests that it had some doubt as to whether Deesen was the proper plaintiff to attack the qualifying system. Although he made arguments about the extent to which the group's decisions might be influenced by personal biases, he made no convincing showing that such factors had influenced his case. Indeed, the facts tended to suggest that the potential abuses which Deesen discerned had not materialized in this instance. The record was clear that Deesen had in fact been approved by the PGA committee process at one time. And while he was subsequently declared ineligible, this was only after his tournament performances, as evidenced by his average scores, had deteriorated.[25] That he was encountering difficulties with his quality of play seemed to be confirmed when he turned in marginal performances in test rounds which the PGA arranged after the litigation had begun.[26] Perhaps instructive of the court's view of the case is its statement that

> The evidence does not establish that Deesen possessed such ability as %H
> a golfer that it is unreasonable to bar him from entering PGA
> tournaments.[27]

Thus, the court may well have decided that it did not have before it a plaintiff who could show that he was injured by any imprecision which might exist in the qualifying procedures. The court did not specifically identify this as the reason for its sustaining the PGA's practices. Instead, the court offered a more specific analysis of the points Deesen raised. It is likely, however, that the court's view of these arguments may have been tempered by its doubts about whether the plaintiff had been injured.

In answering the plaintiff's objection about the apparent arbitrariness of the automatic eligibility granted PGA members, the court found the history of the rules to be important. The PGA was formed to promote the interests of club professionals and held tournaments for that purpose. It soon became clear, however, that many other types of golfers had both an interest in participating and the requisite talent. Thus, the category of a non-member approved tournament player was established to allow these "outsiders" to participate in the PGA's events and share in the economic rewards.[28] While it was true that members did not have to establish a minimum level of skill, other rule changes lessened the impact of the member-non-member distinction. One such rule extended PGA membership to those who had participated in the group's tournaments for five years, without regard to whether they had ever been club professionals.[29] Thus, as a tournament player became established, he was relieved of the burden of constantly proving his eligibility.

But even with this move toward more general membership criteria, the plaintiff's complaint raised an issue which warranted examination. Surely a court should be hesitant to uphold such an obvious disparity in qualifying rules if it could be shown that it consistently produced arbitrary results. For example,

25. *Id.*
26. *Id.* at 168.
27. *Id.* At an earlier pre-trial conference, the parties agreed to have Deesen play a number of rounds with various professional golfers in San Francisco.
28. *Id.* at 170.
29. *Id.* at 167.

if PGA members with distinctly inferior skills regularly occupied a great number of tournament positions to the exclusion of highly qualified non-members, and if membership were not easily obtainable, it is difficult to accept that the restraint on the latter's competitive opportunities was a reasonable one. Such a system would seem to present a classic case of a group of "insiders" using their positions to protect themselves from outside competition. Why wasn't that analysis followed in *Deesen*? In one telling passage of the opinion, the court concluded that the member-non-member distinction "was not, *on this record,* shown to be for the purpose of suppressing or destroying competition, *nor did it have that effect.*" [30] This suggests that plaintiff may not have been able to prove that any significant disparity had in fact resulted. Thus, even though the rule's structure had the potential for producing significant favoritism of the insider-members, the alternative arrangement for non-member qualifying may have operated in such a fashion that the general level of tournament performance between the two groups was similar. But, of course, there is nothing to preclude a plaintiff in another case from coming forth with evidence to establish that the effect of a member-non-member distinction was to arbitrarily limit the professional opportunities of better-qualified candidates.

The state of the factual record was also important in the *Deesen* court's treatment of the plaintiff's complaint about the lack of standards in the PGA's procedure for identifying "approved tournament players." The court's position seems to have been that the plaintiff simply had failed to establish that the potential evils of such a discretionary system had in fact materialized in the instant case. Thus, the court found evidence that personal biases had not influenced prior decisions by the several committees and seemed to accept the lower court's conclusion that Deesen had failed to show that he personally had been the object of such prejudice. [31]

It is possible to read the court's treatment of this second issue too broadly. The case might be interpreted as requiring a showing of actual bias in the particular case before a plaintiff's attack upon the lack of procedural safeguards will be sustained. It can be doubted, though, whether *Deesen* intended to announce a general rule to this effect. In this connection, it is instructive to consider *Blalock v. Ladies Professional Golf Association.* [32] There the court reversed disciplinary action taken against the plaintiff on the grounds that the tribunal which heard the case was composed of persons who were her competitors. Since the competitors might gain by Blalock's exclusion, the court apparently thought that this arrangement involved a potential for abuse. [33] It is important to note, however, that the court did not require Blalock to show that the board's decision was actually influenced by improper considerations. The potential for bias seems to have been enough. While the holdings of *Blalock* and *Deesen* might appear to be at odds on this point, it is possible to harmonize them. One basis for distinguishing the cases was suggested by the *Blalock* court itself when it noted that the decision-making tribunal in *Deesen* was made up of non-competitors. [34] Since those involved would gain no particular advantage

30. *Id.* at 171.
31. *Id.* at 168-70.
32. 359 F. Supp. 1260 (N.D. Ga. 1973).
33. This aspect of the case is discussed more fully in § 5.09 *supra.*
34. *See* 359 F. Supp. at 1267-68.

from Deesen's exclusions, it seems appropriate that their decisions be treated more deferentially.

Another distinction between the cases can be found in the nature of the decision involved. In *Deesen*, there was less reason to be concerned that personal bias might enter in. The decision which was made — that the golfer lacked the requisite skill — was more susceptible to objective verification than that involved in *Blalock,* where the disciplinary board was asked to both resolve a factual dispute and select an appropriate punishment. While the committee in *Deesen* enjoyed a range of discretion, there were practical limitations on its ability to exclude a golfer who had the necessary ability. The player's prior scores and subsequent performances in non-sanctioned tournaments would give some indication of whether the group's decision had been free of improper influences.[35] While these do not provide a perfect test of the correctness of the decision, they may be sufficient to prompt a court to require a specific showing of bias before it will overturn a committee determination which otherwise appears to be proper.

An interesting sequel to *Deesen* was presented in *Abendroth v. Professional Golfers Association.*[36] The latter case arose almost ten years after *Deesen,* and in that period the PGA had changed its rules to introduce somewhat more rational selection criteria. The grounds for PGA membership had been further liberalized, and any golfer could qualify after a period of 32 months if certain performance requirements were met. In addition, the method for selecting non-member approved tournament players was changed to require a specified level of performance at an annual qualifying school. If the non-member who so qualified thereafter failed to maintain the requisite standard of performance in actual tournament play, he normally would have to return to the qualifying school. However, the rules provided that PGA officials could grant extensions of eligibility to some golfers and thus temporarily relieve them of the burden of requalifying when the level of their tournament play deteriorated. Abendroth had qualified in the 1974 qualifying school, but his performance in subsequent tournaments fell below that required for continued eligibility, allegedly due to a family crisis. He tried to requalify at the 1975 qualifying school, but failed to do so, and the defendants did not give him an extension on his eligibility.

Abendroth's complaint had some of the same characteristics found in Deesen's action. It was based solely on antitrust grounds and alleged, in sum, that the PGA rules operated to produce unreasonable restrictions on his opportunities to compete with other golfers. Abendroth argued that there were no standards to govern the granting of eligibility extensions and that this led to arbitrary results. His complaint in this regard was underscored by his assertion that his play on the PGA tour was superior to that of some golfers who were permitted to continue to participate.

Abendroth's request for a preliminary injunction was denied. The court was prepared to agree that the plaintiff would suffer irreparable harm if the injunction were denied. Further, the court indicated that the harm to Abendroth

---

35. Indeed, on the facts of *Deesen* itself, the objective fact of the plaintiff's scores tended to support the decision which was made by the PGA. Scores recorded both before and after the decision to remove his eligibility indicated a decline in Deesen's overall level of performance. *See* text at notes 25-27 *supra*.

36. No. 75-2358 (N.D. Cal., Dec. 19, 1975).

would be much greater than that suffered by the PGA if the injunction were issued. While the court thus found that two of three prerequisites for granting preliminary relief were present, it denied the request on the third element, finding that it was unlikely that the plaintiff would prevail on the merits of his claim. The court was particularly influenced by the *Deesen* decision. It observed that the PGA rules had been modified since that decision and added that

> The only significant change in those rules . . . has been that formerly non-members of the PGA were selected for tournament play without any fixed criteria by a "tournament committee," whereas now such selection is by competitive performance criteria at the Qualifying School and on the subsequent PGA Tours. Thus if selection by committee, as in *Deesen*, did not violate the Sherman Act, it is unlikely that plaintiff will prove that the present competitive selection criteria do violate the Act.[37]

With regard to the apparent lack of standards for granting eligibility extensions, the court gave weight to the affidavit of PGA officials which asserted that extensions had only been granted to players who had experienced physical disabilities.[38]

Abendroth seems to confirm the implication of *Deesen* that it will not be enough for the disappointed athlete to allege that he has sufficient ability to perform better than some of those who were allowed to compete. In most situations, the sports association will not be able to devise a qualification system which predicts perfectly the candidate's level of performance in subsequent competition. Indeed, if such predictions could be made with great accuracy, the later events would not be very interesting. The inexactness of the qualities being judged requires that courts utilize a more general standard for review and give greatest weight to the overall effects of the qualification process. Moreover, it will usually not be enough for the plaintiff to allege that some association officials retain discretion in applying the qualifying rules. *Abendroth* adds support to the notion that where good faith administrative decisions are involved, it is not an absolute prerequisite that they be made according to specifically defined, preannounced criteria.[39] As in *Deesen,* the court here appears to be concerned that the plaintiff be able to show more than a mere potential for abuse.

b. Other Approaches. It should be clear from the prior discussion that an antitrust court will normally review the regulatory activities of sports associations under a rule of reason test. Except in the rare case where the group acts in pursuit of purposes which clearly bear no relationship to its legitimate functions,[40] resort to the summary treatment of the *per se* rule will be avoided. As has been seen, most of the existing case law supports this approach.[41] There

---

37. *Id.* at 5.

38. *Id.* at 6.

39. A different result is likely to obtain if the plaintiff can show that the officials could exercise the discretion to their own economic advantage, as where they are fellow competitors. *See* Blalock v. Ladies Professional Golf Ass'n, 359 F. Supp. 1260 (N.D. Ga. 1973). *See also* § 5.09 *supra.*

40. *See* text at notes 984-90 *supra.*

41. *See, e.g.,* Bridge Corp. of America v. American Contract Bridge League, Inc., 428 F.2d 1365 (9th Cir. 1970); Deesen v. Professional Golfers Ass'n, 358 F.2d 165 (9th Cir. 1966); Abendroth v. Professional Golfers Ass'n, No. 75-2358 (N.D. Cal. Dec. 19, 1975); Heldman v. United States Lawn Tennis Ass'n, 354 F. Supp. 1241 (S.D.N.Y. 1973); STP Corp. v. United States Auto Club, Inc., 286

are, however, a few precedents which are less tolerant of the controls exercised by sports associations and which thus lend support to the view that the *per se* rule should be more freely applied. The leading case in this regard is *Washington State Bowling Proprietors Association, Inc. v. Pacific Lanes, Inc.*[42] Because the case can be read as disputing the analysis suggested above, it warrants a closer examination. It is believed that such a review will establish that the case is not a wholly convincing refutation of the principles emanating from the other precedents.

Under the rules of the Bowling Proprietors Association of America (BPAA), a bowler would lose his eligibility to compete in BPAA tournaments if he participated in an organized event at an establishment which was not a member of the association. An operator of a non-member bowling alley brought suit against state and local affiliates of the BPAA, alleging that the rule, and other practices of the defendant, limited its ability to attract patrons for league and tournament play.[43] The critical feature of the case for our purposes concerns the defendant's attempt to have the jury consider the justification which it offered for the rule. The group argued that the rule was designed to prevent cheating by insuring that all organized events were held under supervised conditions. The trial court had failed to give instruction which would have allowed the jury to review specifically the reasonableness of the rule.[44] The court of appeals affirmed the lower court's action.

The appellate court's opinion could be read broadly to suggest that evidence of justification should not be heard, a holding which, needless to say, would substantially undermine the authority of sports associations. The court recited the well-honed phrase that "group boycotts are *per se* violations of the Sherman Act." [45] On the issue of the proffered justification, the court cited *Fashion Originators' Guild* [46] and seemed to adopt its suggestion that where a group boycott is found, no justification can save it from condemnation under the Sherman Act,[47] and thus arguments and evidence offered in explanation of the practice need not be entertained.

F. Supp. 146 (S.D. Ind. 1968); United States v. United States Trotting Ass'n, 1960 Trade Cas. ¶ 69,671 (S.D. Ohio); Comment, *Trade Association Exclusionary Practices: An Affirmative Role for the Rule of Reason,* 66 COLUM. L. REV. 1486 (1966); *cf.* Denver Rockets v. All-Pro Management, Inc., 325 F. Supp. 1049 (C.D. Cal. 1971); Molinas v. National Basketball Ass'n, 190 F. Supp. 241 (S.D.N.Y. 1961).

42. 356 F.2d 371 (9th Cir. 1966).

43. The actual defendants in the suit were the state and local trade associations of bowling proprietors and a number of individual bowling establishments. The national association was originally named, but it was later dropped. It appears, however, that the eligibility rule in question was adopted by the national association and enforced by the affiliate organization. *Id.* at 374.

It should be noted that while the substantive antitrust analysis of the court of appeals focused on the eligibility rule, the plaintiff had alleged other illegal practices including joint efforts to discourage over-building of bowling establishments and a mutual price fixing scheme. *Id.*

44. The defendants sought instructions to the effect that operator-members of the association "had the right to place restrictions on their business which were designed to prevent cheating such as 'sandbagging' or other abuses, even though such restrictions might incidentally restrict commerce." *Id.* at 376. *Compare* United States v. United States Trotting Ass'n, 1960 Trade Cas. ¶ 69, 761 (S.D. Ohio).

45. 356 F.2d at 376, *citing* Klor's, Inc. v. Broadway-Hale Stores, Inc., 359 U.S. 207 (1959). *See* § 5.07 *supra.*

46. 312 U.S. 457 (1941).

47. This aspect of *Fashion Originators' Guild* is examined in § 5.07 *supra.*

If the court of appeals intended to speak in these broad terms, its holding is clearly out of step with the several other cases which support the view that private regulations by sports groups are to be sustained if they are reasonable.[48] And, of course, the determination of reasonableness will require that the court and jury specifically consider not only the proffered justification, but also proof of the effect of the regulation, the condition of the industry before and after its adoption, and so on.[49] In this same vein, it should be noted that the *Bowling Proprietors* decision fails to deal with the Supreme Court's suggestion in *Silver v. New York Stock Exchange*[50] that some types of private group self-regulation fall outside the *per se* classification. At a minimum, the court should have considered whether the nature of tournament bowling required that the defendants be given regulatory powers which would not be tolerated if undertaken by other commercial groups.[51]

It may not be necessary, however, to read the *Bowling Proprietors* decision in terms which raise these doubts about the completeness of the court's analysis. There is some basis to suggest, for example, that the real problem with the defendants' justification was purely an evidentiary one. The court may well have thought that there was so little evidence to support the defense that it should not be allowed to impede the resolution of the case. It will be noted that the court agreed with the trial judge's assessment that "the evidence in the case did not justify or support [the] proposed instructions."[52] Under this view, the *Bowling Proprietors* decision means no more than that the defendant must establish that the proffered justification has some basis in fact and is not simply being used to divert attention away from other, less appealing characterizations of the rule.

It may have been that the trial court had heard enough evidence to convince it that the real purpose of the rule in question was the purely anticompetitive one of enhancing the profits of the operators who controlled local bowling tournaments.[53] If such a purpose were established, there is little question that the court should summarily condemn the restraint and not entertain evidence

48. *See* authorities cited note 41 *supra*.

49. *See, e.g.,* Chicago Bd. of Trade v. United States, 246 U.S. 231 (1918). *See* § 5.07 *supra*.

50. 373 U.S. 292 (1963). Interestingly, the *Silver* case is neither discussed nor cited by the court of appeals.

51. Even if the court found that the defendants could establish some rules for tournament activities, it does not necessarily follow that the court would approve the limitation on eligibility considered here. Given the nature of the organization as a combination of economic competitors, its demand for the exclusive loyalty of its bowlers would seem to raise serious antitrust problems. *See* text at notes 996-99, 1-7 *supra*.

52. 356 F.2d at 376.

53. The court made a specific reference to evidence which would support the view that the rule was prompted by an anti-competitive purpose. Interestingly, however, the reference does not appear in the portion of the opinion dealing with the *per se* — rule of reason analysis, but in a later segment in which the court deals with the defendants' contention that there was not sufficient involvement in interstate commerce to justify application of the federal antitrust laws. Despite the placement, this portion of the court's analysis seems to present a rather firm conclusion that the defendants were engaged in a course of conduct to protect their own economic self-interest. The court stated:

> The record in this case is replete with testimony and documentary exhibits showing that the national proprietors' association (to which all of the local proprietors belonged) as well as the two local proprietors' associations . . . had each, at various times involved in this suit, discussed with others, and acted in an attempt to implement, programs to raise and stabilize prices, and to keep out new competitors. . . . Appellee alleged a national conspiracy to monopolize and restrain trade in the bowling industry, including Western Washington. We believe that this was a reasonable inference, which the jury was free to draw, that all of the various programs (eligibility rule, price fixing, over-building committees) were part of the same conspiracy to that end. *Id.* at 380.

of industry conditions and the like.[54] Earlier in this section we discussed the type of inquiry which should be made to identify situations in which anticompetitive motives were being masqueraded under a more neutral facade.[55] That discussion argues that the court should make a separate inquiry into the limited question of the true purpose of the rule, and if it finds an intent only to promote economic self-interest, it should not hesitate to summarily condemn the practice. The court's treatment of the justification defense in *Bowling Proprietors* might be viewed as involving this same approach, albeit in a form less deliberate than that recommended above. Under this interpretation, it would be suggested that the court made a truncated inquiry into the purpose of the rule and was unpersuaded by the defendant's characterization. Again, if the court felt that the rule was designed merely to promote the self-interest of the defendants, its decision to summarily condemn the regulation seems proper.

§ 5.11. Antitrust Aspects of the Ownership and Location of Sports League Franchises.

There should be little debate that a league's decisions concerning the ownership and location of its club-franchises have important economic consequences for a variety of interested parties. Indeed, the diversity of interests involved, and the fact that these interests are often antagonistic, will almost certainly insure that the league's franchising decisions will generate controversy. For example, a league's decision to expand the number of its franchises may prove to be a great boon to the cities which will receive the new clubs. At the same time, however, expansion may be potentially devastating to those who are seeking to promote a rival league, for the effect may be to claim the few remaining desirable franchise locations. Similar conflicts are likely to arise where the decision concerns the movement of an existing franchise. For the owners of the franchise, the move may represent the opportunity to remove themselves from a market which has been unprofitable. It may also provide the occasion for a sale of the franchise which permits the owners to withdraw from the sports business. There are likely to be many parties who will object to the move, however. The city from which the club is being moved may object to the adverse impact which the decision will have on the local economy. Moreover, there are likely to be private parties, such as suppliers and local broadcast interests, which may have objections based on their particular involvement in the team's operation.

To what extent do the antitrust laws provide a vehicle for the review of franchising decisions? As might be imagined, there is no simple answer to that question.[56] Several different antitrust principles come into play, and the

---

54. *See* Radiant Burners, Inc. v. Peoples Gas Light & Coke Co., 364 U.S. 656 (1961); Klor's, Inc. v. Broadway-Hale Stores Inc., 359 U.S. 207 (1959); Fashion Originators' Guild of America v. FTC, 312 U.S. 457 (1941). *See generally* J. VON KALINOWSKI, ANTITRUST LAWS AND TRADE REGULATION (16J BUSINESS ORGANIZATIONS 1973) §§ 75.01-.06.

55. *See* text at notes 985-88 *supra.*

56. The following is a list of cases and secondary materials which bear on the antitrust aspects of franchising decisions.

Sports Cases.

American Football League v. National Football League, 205 F. Supp. 60 (D. Md. 1962), *aff'd,* 323 F.2d 124 (4th Cir. 1963); Buffalo v. Atlanta Hawks Basketball, Inc., Civil No. 76-0261 (W.D.N.Y., June 15, 1976) (temporary restraining order granted); San Francisco Seals, Ltd. v. National Hockey

applicability of any one of these often depends upon the nature of the objection being raised. Moreover, even when the relevant antitrust doctrine is identified, there is often uncertainty as to whether the peculiar economics of league sports ventures require a deferential application of the traditional principles.

In order to isolate the various doctrinal problems which arise, it is useful to consider the objections which will be raised by particular plaintiffs. The following discussion considers four situations which differ in terms of the party raising the objection and the type of complaint involved. First, we will examine the antitrust principles which will be applied to resolve franchising disputes among owners within a single league. Here, the central issue is whether a league decision disapproving an owner's request to move his franchise to another city raises a claim under the antitrust laws.[57] Then we will shift our focus to consider the objections which might be raised by a competing league. In that situation, it is likely to be alleged that an established league has exercised its franchising power to achieve or perpetuate monopoly control of the particular sports market.[58] The third situation considered is one in which the party objecting is a municipality. The plaintiff city may be opposing the league's attempt to take away its franchise or may be seeking to have a club located in its area. Here, a critical question is whether the defendant league has an obligation to establish the reasonableness of its decisions concerning the number and location of

---

League, 379 F. Supp. 966 (C.D. Cal. 1974); Levin v. National Basketball Ass'n, 385 F. Supp. 149 (S.D.N.Y. 1974); San Diego v. National League of Professional Baseball Clubs, Civil No. 73-529 (S.D. Cal. filed Dec. 12, 1973) (antitrust action; later withdrawn); Philadelphia World Hockey Club, Inc. v. Philadelphia Hockey Club, Inc., 351 F. Supp. 462 (E.D. Pa. 1972); Washington Professional Basketball Corp. v. National Basketball Ass'n, 131 F. Supp. 596 (S.D.N.Y. 1955), *subsequent proceeding,* 147 F. Supp. 154 (S.D.N.Y. 1956); San Diego v. National League of Professional Baseball Clubs, Docket No. 343508 (Cal. Super. Ct., July 10, 1973) (preliminary injunction denied), *aff'd,* Docket No. 12741 (Cal. Ct. App., July 19, 1973); Wisconsin v. Milwaukee Braves, Inc., 1966 Trade Cas. ¶ 71,738 (Wis. Cir. Ct.), *rev'd,* 31 Wis. 2d 699, 144 N.W.2d 1 (1966).

Secondary Authorities.
    H. DEMMERT, THE ECONOMICS OF PROFESSIONAL TEAM SPORTS (1973); L. SOBEL, PROFESSIONAL SPORTS AND THE LAW 368-79, 381-410, 491-535 (1977); Noll, *Alternatives in Sports Policy* in GOVERNMENT AND THE SPORTS BUSINESS 411 (R. Noll ed. 1974); Noll, *The U.S. Teams Sports Industry: An Introduction* in *id.,* at 1; Okner, *Subsidies of Stadiums and Arenas,* in *id.,* at 325; Quirk & El Hodiri, *The Economic Theory of a Professional Sports League* in *id.,* at 33; Rivkin, *Sports Leagues and the Federal Antitrust Laws* in *id.,* at 387; Bork, *Ancillary Restraints and the Sherman Act,* 15 ABA ANTITRUST SECTION 211 (1959); Koppett, *Sports and the Law: An Overview,* 18 N.Y.L. FORUM 815 (1973); Morris, *In the Wake of the Flood,* 38 LAW & CONTEMP. PROB. 85 (1973); Neale, *The Peculiar Economics of Professional Sports,* 78 Q.J. ECON. 1 (1964); Quirk, *An Economic Analysis of Team Movements in Professional Sports,* 38 LAW & CONTEMP. PROB. 42 (1973); Comment, *The Super Bowl and the Sherman Act: Professional Team Sports and the Antitrust Laws,* 81 HARV. L. REV. 418 (1967); Cady, When Do Franchises Have the Right to Relocate?, N.Y. Times, Apr. 20, 1977, at 43, col. 3; American Enterprise Institute, Pro Sports: Should the Government Intervene?, AEI Forum (J. Daly, moderator, 1977).
    57. *See, e.g.,* San Francisco Seals, Ltd. v. National Hockey League, 379 F. Supp. 966 (C.D. Cal. 1974). *See also,* Quirk, *An Economic Analysis of Team Movements in Professional Sports,* 38 LAW & CONTEMP. PROB. 42 (1973).
    58. *See, e.g.,* American Football League v. National Football League, 205 F. Supp. 60 (D. Md. 1962), *aff'd,* 323 F.2d 124 (4th Cir. 1963); Philadelphia World Hockey Club, Inc. v. Philadelphia Hockey Club, Inc., 351 F. Supp. 462, 510-13 (E.D. Pa. 1972). This case was part of a consolidated multidistrict proceeding which dealt with a number of issues arising between the WHA and NHL. Other facets of that litigation are considered in *In re* Professional Hockey Antitrust Litigation, 352 F. Supp. 1405 (Jud. Panel on Multidistrict Litig., E.D. Pa. 1973), 63 F.R.D. 641 (E.D. Pa. 1974), *rev'd,* 531 F.2d 1188 (3d Cir. 1974), *rev'd sub nom.* National Hockey League v. Metropolitan Hockey Club, Inc., 427 U.S. 639, 49 L. Ed. 2d 747, 96 S. Ct. 2778 (1976).

franchises.[59] The fourth case to be examined involves changes in the ownership of existing franchises, and the central issue raised is whether the antitrust laws provide a basis for review when the league exercises its right to disapprove a proposed transfer of ownership.[60]

In considering the antitrust implications of a league's franchising decisions, it is useful to keep in mind some basic differences in the nature of the legal theories available under the Sherman Act. There are two sections of that statute which should be mentioned by way of background. Under section 1 of the Sherman Act, "every contract, combination . . ., or conspiracy" which restrains trade "is . . . declared to be illegal. . . ." [61] The proscription of section 2 is directed to a different situation. The latter section is concerned with monopolization and declares that "every person who shall monopolize, or attempt to monopolize, or combine or conspire . . . to monopolize" is subject to legal liability.[62] A violation of section 1 requires that there be action by more than one person.[63] The gravamen of the section 1 offense is an agreement or other joint action among businessmen which seeks to limit or destroy competition.[64] The drafters of the Sherman Act intended section 1 to reflect their basic policy decision that the nation's private economy should function according to a free market model. In this model, business entities are to operate as separate competing units. Their success or failure is to depend upon their own individual efforts, and not upon advantages which might be gained by joining with other entities to limit the opportunities of third party competitors.[65] But, again, the section only condemns joint action and does not seek to limit the methods of competition which are chosen by a single firm. In general, a firm acting on its own, without the voluntary involvement of others, could not violate section 1.[66]

The requirement of duality of action is not an indispensible element of the section 2 violation. That section addresses itself to a particular market condition (monopoly).[67] The section condemns both the misuse of monopoly power and actions undertaken to secure or perpetuate a monopoly.[68] While section 2 violations may arise from agreements among firms which further an entity's monopoly goals, a violation may also result from the actions of a single firm acting alone.[69] Particularly to be condemned are a firm's efforts to utilize its

---

59. *See, e.g.,* Wisconsin v. Milwaukee Braves, Inc., 1966 Trade Cas. ¶ 71,738 (Wis. Cir. Ct.), *rev'd,* 31 Wis. 2d 699, 144 N.W.2d 1 (1966).

60. *See, e.g.,* Levin v. National Basketball Ass'n, 385 F. Supp. 149 (S.D.N.Y. 1974).

61. 15 U.S.C. § 1 (1974).

62. 15 U.S.C. § 2 (1974).

63. *See, e.g.,* Poller v. Columbia Broadcasting Systems, Inc., 368 U.S. 464 (1962); Whitley v. Foremost Dairies, Inc., 151 F. Supp. 914 (W.D. Ark. 1957), *aff'd,* 254 F.2d 36 (8th Cir. 1958); Graham v. Hudgins, Thompson, Ball & Assoc., Inc., 319 F. Supp. 1335 (N.D. Okla. 1970); Beacon Fruit & Produce Co. v. H. Harris & Co., 152 F. Supp. 702 (D. Mass. 1957).

64. *See generally* E. GELLHORN, ANTITRUST LAW AND ECONOMICS IN A NUTSHELL 159-204 (1976) [hereinafter cited as GELLHORN]; J. VON KALINOWSKI, ANTITRUST LAWS AND TRADE REGULATION (16 BUSINESS ORGANIZATIONS 1971) §§ 6.01-.02 [hereinafter cited as VON KALINOWSKI].

65. *See, e.g.,* Northern Pacific Ry. v. United States, 356 U.S. 1, 4 (1958); Apex Hosiery Co. v. Leader, 310 U.S. 469, 497-500 (1940).

66. *See* cases cited in note 63 *supra.*

67. *See* GELLHORN 23.

68. *See* 16 VON KALINOWSKI § 8.02[4].

69. The statutory prohibition extends to *"every person* who shall monopolize. . . ." 15 U.S.C. § 2 (1974) (emphasis added).

dominant market position to improperly inhibit the development of competition.[70] In addition to proscribing such misuses of monopoly power, the section also declares illegal "attempts to monopolize," that is, actions through which a firm might seek to improperly attain market dominance.[71]

Although both section 1 and section 2 share a common concern for avoiding undesirable limitations on the competitiveness of the market place, a finding of illegality under the two sections requires that somewhat different questions be considered. As we have. seen in prior sections of this treatise, a threshold question in section 1 cases is whether a court should inquire into the reasonableness of a particular restraint.[72] Certain joint agreements are thought to have such a pernicious effect on competition that they are deemed *per se* illegal, and the court will not consider factors which the defendant might offer in justification.[73] The allocation of market territories among competitors is an example of a practice thought to be *per se* illegal.[74] In some situations, however,

70. *See, e.g.,* United States v. Aluminum Co. of America, 148 F.2d 416 (2d Cir. 1945); United States v. United Shoe Mach. Corp., 110 F. Supp. 295 (D. Mass. 1953), *aff'd per curiam,* 347 U.S. 521 (1954).

71. There are certain elements of the offense of an improper attempt to monopolize which distinguish it from actual monopolization. For example, there is a requirement that an improper *intent* be proven to establish an illegal attempt. Actual monopolization does not normally require such a showing. Moreover, the possession of monopoly power need not be shown to prove an improper attempt. *See generally* Continental Ore Co. v. Union Carbide & Carbon Corp., 370 U.S. 690 (1962); 16A VON KALINOWSKI § 9.01; Smith, *Attempt to Monopolize: Its Elements and Their Definition,* 27 GEO. WASH. L. REV. 227 (1959). An examination of existing precedent suggests, however, that demarcation between attempts and actual monopolization is not altogether clear. For example, the courts hold that the plaintiff in an attempt case must establish that there was a dangerous probability of an actual monopoly in the acts attributed to the defendant. While the plaintiff need not establish that the defendant actually held a dominant market position, plaintiff must be able to show that the alleged offender had sufficient power that it was likely that it could establish a monopoly if its practices were left unchecked. Since actual domination would establish one of the elements of pure (as opposed to attempted) monopolization, it is necessary to attribute some definite meaning to the "dangerous probability" notion if the attempt offense is to have a distinct status. But the courts have not developed useful standards for defining the degree of market power which will establish an attempt, while falling short of market domination. *See, e.g.,* Walker Distrib. Co. v. Lucky Lager Brewing Co., 323 F.2d 1 (9th Cir. 1963); Becker v. Safelite Glass Corp., 244 F. Supp. 625 (D. Kan. 1965); Centanni v. T. Smith & Sons, Inc., 216 F. Supp. 331 (E.D. La.), *aff'd,* 323 F.2d 363 (5th Cir. 1963). *See generally* GELLHORN 156-58; Hibner, *Attempts to Monopolize: A Concept in Search of Analysis,* 34 ABA ANTITRUST L.J. 165 (1967).

The substance of the attempt offense is further clouded by uncertainty as to what actions establish an improper attempt. The difficulty here is in distinguishing between mere aggressive business behavior and that which is likely to have undesirable consequences. The line between the two is often very fine, and the courts again have not always contributed to a clarification of the matter. *Compare* Greenville Publishing Co. v. Daily Reflector, Inc., 496 F.2d 391 (4th Cir. 1974) *and* Pacific Engineering & Prod. Co. v. Kerr-McGee Corp., 1974-1 Trade Cas. ¶ 75,054 (D. Utah) *with* Schine Chain Theaters, Inc., v. United States, 334 U.S. 110 (1948) *and* Telex Corp. v. IBM Corp., 510 F.2d 894 (10th Cir. 1975) *and* N.W. Controls, Inc. v. Outboard Marine Corp., 333 F. Supp. 493 (D. Del. 1971). 15 U.S.C. § 2 (1974).

In addition to actual monopolization and attempts to monopolize, section 2 states a third offense, involving conspiracies to monopolize. If one accepts that the relevant entity for our purposes is the league and not the individual clubs, the concern for section 2 conspiracies is likely to play a limited role in the cases we are considering. *See generally* American Tobacco Co. v. United States, 328 U.S. 781 (1946); 16A VON KALINOWSKI § 9.02.

72. *See* § 5.07 *supra.*

73. *See, e.g.,* Northern Pacific Ry. Co. v. United States, 356 U.S. 1 (1958); Fashion Originators' Guild v. FTC, 312 U.S. 457 (1941).

74. *See, e.g.,* United States v. Topco Assoc., Inc., 405 U.S. 596 (1972); United States v. Sealy, Inc., 388 U.S. 350 (1967).

the courts find that the conditions of the industry justify joint action and will undertake a more lengthy inquiry into the reasonableness of particular practices.[75] Even if a rule of reason approach is found to be appropriate, there is often a lengthy debate about what is reasonable. This frequently involves a very particularized examination of the history of the industry, the economic effects of the restraint in question, and the feasibility of less restrictive alternatives.[76]

The section 2 concern for monopolization focuses on somewhat different questions. One premise from which section 2 proceeds is that in the absence of a showing of actual or attempted market dominance, a single firm enjoys greater freedom to establish its methods of competition than would be afforded a collection of firms attempting to compete through joint agreement. Thus, while price-fixing among a group of firms is *per se* illegal,[77] a single firm may price its products as it wishes, again assuming that its pricing policies are not linked to improper efforts at monopolization.[78] Thus, the mere fact that a firm engaged in activities which would otherwise be proscribed in a proper section 1 case is not necessarily a reason for concern under section 2.

What is needed to raise a serious section 2 issue is some proof that the defendant firm is guilty of monopolization. When a firm is accused of such conduct, an initial point of controversy is often whether the firm possesses monopoly power.[79] Several subsidiary issues immediately appear: What degree of market power must be shown to establish a section 2 offense? How is market power to be measured? What is the relevant product market in the particular case? The relevant geographical area?[80] Even when those questions are answered is a way which brings the case within section 2, a second critical question arises and that is whether the defendant has misused its market position.[81] It is recognized that certain activities which affect competitors — the development of new technology, for example — may simply be the product of legitimate business judgment. Distinguishing "improper monopolization" from "permissible business practices" is a major hurdle in a successful section 2 action. If there is proof that the defendant had a specific intent to destroy or discourage competition, a finding of a misuse of monopoly power is relatively easy.[82] But such specific proof is often lacking, and as the case law has

---

75. *See, e.g.,* Silver v. New York Stock Exchange, 373 U.S. 292 (1963); Mackey v. National Football League, 543 F.2d 606 (8th Cir. 1976); United States v. United States Trotting Ass'n, 1960 Trade Cas. ¶ 69,761 (S.D. Ohio). *See also* Comment, *Trade Association Exclusionary Practices: An Affirmative Role for the Rule of Reason,* 66 COLUM. L. REV. 1486 (1966).

76. *See, e.g.,* Chicago Board of Trade v. United States, 246 U.S. 231 (1918); Mackey v. National Football League, 543 F.2d 606 (8th Cir. 1976).

77. *See, e.g.,* United States v. Arnold, Schwinn & Co., 388 U.S. 365 (1967); United States v. Socony-Vacuum Oil Co., 310 U.S. 150 (1940).

78. *See* GELLHORN 112-13. *See also* Telex Corp. v. IBM Corp., 510 F.2d 894 (10th Cir. 1975); Greenville Publishing Co. v. Daily Reflector, Inc., 496 F.2d 361 (4th Cir. 1974).

79. *See generally* 16 VON KALINOWSKI § 8.02.

80. *See, e.g.,* International Boxing Club v. United States, 358 U.S. 242 (1959); United States v. E.I. DuPont de Nemours & Co., 351 U.S. 377 (1956).

81. *See, e.g.,* United States v. Griffith, 334 U.S. 100 (1948); Telex Corp. v. IBM Corp., 510 F.2d 894 (10th Cir. 1975); American Football League v. National Football League, 205 F. Supp. 60 (D. Md. 1962), *aff'd,* 323 F.2d 124 (4th Cir. 1963).

82. *See, e.g.,* United States v. Crescent Amusement Co., 323 U.S. 173 (1944); Noerr Motor Freight, Inc. v. Eastern R.R. Presidents Conf., 155 F. Supp. 768, 813 (E.D. Pa. 1957), *aff'd,* 273 F.2d 218 (3d Cir. 1959), *rev'd on other grounds,* 365 U.S. 127 (1961).

developed, it is not always necessary. The courts are willing to find section 2 violations even when there is no direct evidence of improper motive. But the standard which is applied in these non-intent cases is somewhat elusive. The courts suggest that violations will be found when there is a combination of a dominant market position and actions which effectively exclude the development of competition.[83] Thus, while a vigorous program for developing new markets would normally be tolerated in most business settings, it might not be when undertaken by a firm which is thereby enabled to extend significant monopoly power.[84] In evaluating various methods of competition and their effects on competition, the courts appear to emphasize the importance of differences in the degree and not to insist upon real differences in kind. The relative market position of the firm and the relative aggressiveness of its behavior will normally be weighed carefully.[85]

As we undertake our consideration of league franchising decisions, we will see that the differences between the section 1 and section 2 violations become important in focusing the antitrust inquiry. The requirement of joint action under section 1 is a particular point of controversy. A question arises as to how the entity which we know as a "league" should be characterized for antitrust purposes.[86] If the member clubs are regarded as separate competing units, then actions which they take through the governing device of the league would appear to have the requisite jointness to satisfy the section 1 requirement of a combination.[87] On the other hand, the relevant competing unit might be found to be the league itself, so that franchising decisions could be seen as single-firm activities.[88] In that case, the element of an inter-firm conspiracy would be missing, and relief, if available at all under the antitrust laws, would have to come from section 2.

It is important to note, however, that the effect of the league-firm characterization is not to require a wholly different antitrust inquiry, but merely to sharpen the focus on the section 2 proscription. Even if the separate status of the member clubs were given controlling effect, section 2 issues would likely arise.[89] It would be alleged that the particular franchising decision represented an effort by the clubs to attain or perpetuate a monopoly in the particular sport. Thus, the matter of characterizing the nature of a league is important for determining whether both section 1 and section 2 are to be applied or whether

83. *See, e.g.,* United States v. Griffith, 334 U.S. 100 (1948); United States v. United Shoe Mach. Corp., 110 F. Supp. 295 (D. Mass. 1953), *aff'd per curiam,* 347 U.S. 521 (1954).

84. *See, e.g.,* United States v. Aluminum Co. of America, 148 F.2d 416 (2d Cir. 1945); Credit Bureau Reports, Inc. v. Retail Credit Co., 358 F. Supp. 780 (S.D. Tex. 1971), *aff'd,* 476 F.2d 989 (5th Cir. 1973). *See also* Philadelphia World Hockey Club, Inc. v. Philadelphia Hockey Club, Inc., 351 F. Supp. 462, 510-13 (E.D. Pa. 1972).

85. *Compare* United States v. Aluminum Co. of America, 148 F.2d 416 (2d Cir. 1945) *with* Telex Corp. v. IBM Corp., 510 F.2d 894 (10th Cir. 1975).

86. *See, e.g.,* San Francisco Seals, Ltd. v. National Hockey League, 379 F. Supp. 966 (C.D. Cal. 1974); Levin v. National Basketball Ass'n, 385 F. Supp. 149 (S.D.N.Y. 1974). *See also* Bork, *Ancillary Restraints and the Sherman Act,* 15 ABA ANTITRUST SECTION 211, 231-34 (1959); Morris, *In the Wake of the Flood,* 38 LAW & CONTEMP. PROB. 85, 90 (1973); Neale, *The Peculiar Economics of Professional Sports,* 78 Q.J. ECON. 1, 4-5 (1964).

87. *See, e.g.,* Wisconsin v. Milwaukee Braves, Inc., 1966 Trade Cas. ¶ 71,738 (Wis. Cir. Ct.), *rev'd,* 31 Wis. 2d 699, 144 N.W.2d 1 (1966).

88. *See* authorities cited in note 86 *supra.*

89. *See, e.g.,* San Francisco Seals, Ltd. v. National Hockey League, 379 F. Supp. 966 (C.D. Cal. 1974).

the latter section alone will provide the standard for review. Of course, merely deciding that monopolization, rather than conspiracy, is the primary area of concern does not answer the ultimate question of when league franchising activities might result in antitrust liability. It can be said, though, that the search for a resolution of that issue is moved forward when the proper frame of reference is identified.

There are other preliminary points of analysis which should be mentioned. It might be asked, for example, whether the same characterization of a league venture should apply in all situations.[90] Is it possible that the league would be regarded as a single firm in some of its relationships but that the separate identity of the clubs would control the antitrust analysis in other settings?[91] The four franchising situations to be discussed below involve league decisions which affect somewhat different aspects of the professional sports market. It may be necessary to determine whether the type of market activity affected is relevant in defining the respective applicability of section 1 and section 2 of the Sherman Act. On another matter, it should be noted that even where the league is viewed as a separate firm, there may be other aspects of a case which make application of section 1 appropriate. The requisite duality may be found, for example, when the league joins with outsiders — broadcasters, stadium owners and so on — in an arrangement which improperly restrains the development of competition.[92] Such combinations may involve some aspect of the league's franchising efforts and provide the occasion for an antitrust complaint. This should suggest that even if section 2 monopolization theories receive first attention where franchising questions are involved, section 1 issues can never be wholly dismissed.

One might expect that a question as fundamental as the proper characterization of a sports league would have been the focus of judicial concern in the few franchising cases which have arisen to date. Our consideration of the four situations outlined above will provide the opportunity for a review of the decided cases. What we will find, however, is that the courts have shown widely varying degrees of interest in the nature of a league's operation. In some cases, this issue is determinative of the result reached.[93] In others, it is completely ignored.[94] This divergence in approach, predictably produces differences in the results reached. The difficulty in developing a coherent view of the role of the antitrust laws in the area of franchising is further complicated by the fact that many issues have yet to be explored in litigation. Thus, it is necessary not only to choose between the lines of precedent presently available, but also to assess their impact on future areas of controversies. But even though this double uncertainty leaves the resolution of many matters in a tentative state, a closer examination of the issues presented does serve to significantly narrow the range of controversy. An effort toward such a narrowing is undertaken in the following pages.

90. *See, e.g.,* Levin v. National Basketball Ass'n, 385 F. Supp. 149, 152 n.6 (S.D.N.Y. 1974).

91. *See generally* Bork, *Ancillary Restraints and the Sherman Act, supra* note 86, at 231-34.

92. *See, e.g.,* Hecht v. Pro-Football, Inc., 444 F.2d 931 (D.C. Cir. 1971). *Cf.* Murdock v. Jacksonville, 361 F. Supp. 1083 (M.D. Fla. 1973).

93. *See* San Francisco Seals, Ltd. v. National Hockey League, 379 F. Supp. 966 (C.D. Cal. 1974); Levin v. National Basketball Ass'n, 385 F. Supp. 149 (S.D.N.Y. 1974).

94. *See* Wisconsin v. Milwaukee Braves, Inc., 1966 Trade Cas. ¶ 71,738 (Wis. Cir. Ct.), *rev'd,* 31 Wis. 2d 699, 144 N.W.2d 1 (1966).

a. Movement of Existing Franchises: The Requirement of League Approval. The rules in effect in most major sports leagues give the league considerable control over the movement of franchises.[95] The "franchise" which each owner holds entitles it to operate a team in a specified geographical area. Often this right is exclusive, meaning that no other owner will be allowed to operate a club in the same locale.[96] The areas in which franchises will be operated are designated by agreement among the member clubs. A request by an owner to move his franchise to a new area usually is voted upon by other members of the league.[97] Most leagues require a substantial majority vote — approval by either two-thirds or three-fourths of the existing clubs — before a move will be allowed.[98] The requirement of league approval may, of course, limit an owner's freedom to operate his business. The question which we examine in this segment is whether the league's exercise of control raises significant antitrust issues. Before we get to the technical aspects of that issue, however, it is useful to indicate some of the business considerations which come into play in this area.

One concern raised against the requirement of member-club approval is that it may be exercised in an arbitrary manner and that fans in cities otherwise suitable for the location of a professional sports franchise will be denied the opportunity to have a hometown club.[99] It might also be feared that an owner will be forced to operate an unprofitable (or relatively less profitable) franchise "against his will."[100] While these may be realistic concerns in some cases, it can be noted that there are other considerations which suggest that instances of league-disapproval of a proposed move are likely to be rare. Support for this conclusion can be found in the baseball industry. In the twenty-year period prior to 1972, there were eleven requests involving the movement of baseball franchises. Only two of these were denied, and in each of these cases, the franchises were eventually relocated when the plans were reformulated.[101] A factor which weighs strongly in favor of member clubs approving a move is the financial interdependence of the various teams within the league.[102] Because each club shares in the fortunes of other clubs — through the division of gate receipts, as one example — there is a strong incentive to allow an owner to pursue his most lucrative market. An owner will usually seek to relocate his

95. *See generally* Quirk, *An Economic Analysis of Team Movements in Professional Sports,* 38 LAW & CONTEMP. PROB. 42 (1973); Comment, *The Super Bowl and the Sherman Act: Professional Team Sports and the Antitrust Laws,* 81 HARV. L. REV. 418, 429-30 (1967).

96. *See, e.g.,* San Francisco Seals, Ltd. v. National Hockey League, 379 F. Supp. 966 (C.D. Cal. 1974).

97. *See* Noll, *The U.S. Team Sports Industry: An Introduction* in GOVERNMENT AND THE SPORTS BUSINESS 1, 8-9 (R. Noll ed. 1974).

98. *See. e.g.,* CONSTITUTION AND BY-LAWS FOR THE NATIONAL FOOTBALL LEAGUE § 4.3 (1972):

Any transfer of an existing franchise to a location within the home territory of any other club shall only be effective if approved by a unanimous vote; any other transfer shall only be effective if approved by the affirmative vote of not less than three-fourths or 20, whichever is greater, of the member clubs of the League.

99. *See* Quirk, *An Economic Analysis of Team Movements in Professional Sports, supra* note 95, at 63-66.

100. *See* Noll, *The U.S. Team Sports Industry: An Introduction, supra* note 97, at 412: "It does not make sense to force the owner of a business to continue to sustain financial losses operating in one location when he believes he could do much better elsewhere . . . ."

101. *See* Quirk, *An Economic Analysis of Team Movements in Professional Sports, supra* note 95, at 49-51.

102. The nature of this financial interdependence is discussed more fully at notes 137-44, *infra.*

franchise because his existing location has proved unprofitable. His determination that profitability will increase in another locale is likely to be endorsed by the other clubs.[103]

This does not mean that litigation will never arise over league efforts to control franchise moves. The existing precedent belies that conclusion.[104] The analysis does indicate, however, that when controversies do arise, there are likely to be unusual circumstances involved. Perhaps the move interferes with league expansion plans or presents peculiar logistic difficulties.[105] While there may be cases in which disapproval results from improper motives, the general context in which this species of franchising decision is made suggests that the concern for improper interference by the league is less substantial than might appear at first blush.

Assume that a situation arises in which the voting members of the league do disapprove a proposed franchise move. Can the antitrust laws be used by the disappointed owner to secure judicial scrutiny of the reasons for the action? There is a rather sharp disagreement on this issue in the limited case law and commentary that is available. Some authorities suggest that league decisions in this area are not subject to review under existing antitrust doctrine.[106] Others assume that judicial scrutiny is appropriate and, while the doctrinal bases for judicial intervention are somewhat unclear, these sources would apparently invalidate a league decision disapproving a move if it were found to be "unreasonable." [107] We examine the basis of these divergent interpretations in the following paragraphs. To facilitate the analysis, separate consideration is given to the issues arising under section 1 and section 2 of the Sherman Act.

1. *The Section 1 Issues.*

As previously noted, section 1 of the Sherman Act prohibits agreements and combinations which have the effect of restraining competition. Among the arrangements which are particularly suspect under section 1 are those in which a group of firms operating on the same economic level (*e.g.*, retailers of the same type of product) divide a particular market among themselves.[108] The relevant market may be a geographic one. A group of firms may reach an understanding that each participant will refrain from intruding into the territories claimed by the others. In the portion of the market allocated to it, a firm will be freed from

103. *See* Quirk, *An Economic Analysis of Team Movements in Professional Sports, supra* note 95, at 46-47.

104. *See* San Francisco Seals, Ltd. v. National Hockey League, 379 F. Supp. 966 (C.D. Cal. 1974).

105. For a discussion of situations in which proposed moves have been disapproved, see Quirk, *An Economic Analysis of Team Movements in Professional Sports, supra* note 95, at 49-53; Comment, *The Super Bowl and the Sherman Act: Professional Team Sports and the Antitrust Laws, supra* note 95, at 429, n.59.

106. *See, e.g.,* San Francisco Seals, Ltd. v. National Hockey League, 379 F. Supp. 966 (C.D. Cal. 1974); *Hearings on Professional Sports Before the House Select Comm. on Professional Sports,* 94th Cong., 2d Sess., pt. 1, at 296 (1976) (testimony of Joe Sims, Deputy Ass't Att'y Gen., Antitrust Div., Dept. of Justice) [hereinafter cited as *1976 Hearings*].

107. *See, e.g.,* L. SOBEL, PROFESSIONAL SPORTS AND THE LAW 500-05 (1977) [hereinafter cited as SOBEL]; Comment, *The Super Bowl and the Sherman Act: Professional Team Sports and the Antitrust Laws, supra* note 95, at 429-30. *See also* Quirk, *An Economic Analysis of Team Movements in Professional Sports, supra* note 95, at 65. Some would go further and suggest, with apparent seriousness, that all forms of territorial restraints in the sports industry are illegal and that a true free market ought to prevail. *See 1976 Hearings,* pt. 2, at 448-51 (testimony of Rep. John Seiberling).

108. *See* cases cited in note 74, *supra. See generally* 16 VON KALINOWSKI § 6.02[3][e].

competition by others who are parties to the arrangement. The undesirable effects of such an allocation of territorial rights are obvious. Without the restraint of competition, prices may be set at artificial levels and the incentive to provide efficient service to consumers will be reduced. In short, this form of horizontal territorial restraint is a corruption of the free market model upon which the Sherman Act is premised.

Those who seek to apply section 1 to franchise relocation decisions note that those decisions have many of the characteristics of the restraints described above.[109] In such situations, a group of firms — those which own the individual clubs — are attempting to limit the territory in which one of their number can operate. The club owners have, in effect, divided up the national market in the sport and in the instance of a denial of a request to relocate, forced the petitioning owner to operate in the territory originally allocated to him.

Is the denial of such a request illegal under section 1? There are some refinements of section 1 doctrine which must be considered. The position traditionally taken by courts in cases not involving sports leagues is that horizontal territorial restraints are *per se* illegal.[110] Under this view, the restraint is to be condemned without regard to whatever explanation might be offered to support it. The justification for this absolutist approach is that the anti-competitive effects of market division schemes are so patent and enduring that they ought not to be tolerated in any case.[111] Yet there is a basis to question whether the *per se* approach is properly applied to a sports league, assuming that section 1 is applicable at all. The Supreme Court has recognized that there are some situations in which joint action among firms may be justified by the nature of the economic activity in question.[112] Where this is true, interfirm agreements may be excepted from the normal *per se* prohibitions and tested instead under the rule of reason. The latter approach requires an inquiry into the reasonableness of the action taken. Here the court is to consider the special needs of the industry involved and determine whether the restraint is reasonably designed to achieve a legitimate purpose of the group which controls it.[113]

The argument can be made that franchising by sports leagues is the sort of activity which warrants application of the rule of reason. A sports league differs from other business combinations in that each member-firm has a keen interest in the financial success of the other participants.[114] The success of the venture

---

109. *See, e.g., 1976 Hearings*, pt. 2, at 448-51 (testimony of Rep. John Seiberling); Comment, *The Super Bowl and the Sherman Act: Professional Team Sports and the Antitrust Laws*, *supra* note 95, at 429. *Cf.* Wisconsin v. Milwaukee Braves, Inc., 1966 Trade Cas. ¶ 71,738 at 82,403-04, *rev'd*, 31 Wis. 2d 699, 144 N.W.2d 1 (1966).

110. *See* cases cited in note 74 *supra*. *See also* Timken Roller Bearing Co. v. United States, 341 U.S. 593 (1951). For a more complete discussion of the background of the *per se* rule and rule of reason, see §§ 5.07, 5.10, *supra*.

111. *See, e.g.,* Northern Pacific Ry. v. United States, 356 U.S. 1 (1958).

112. *See* authorities cited in note 75 *supra*. *See also* §§ 5.07, 5.10 *supra*.

113. *See* cases cited in note 76 *supra*. *See generally* Comment, *Trade Association Exclusionary Practices: An Affirmative Role for the Rule of Reason*, 66 COLUM. L. REV. 1486 (1966).

114. *See* United States v. National Football League, 116 F. Supp. 319 (E.D. Pa. 1953); Bork, *Ancillary Restraints and the Sherman Act*, 15 ABA ANTITRUST SECTION 211, 231-34 (1959); Koppett, *Sports and the Law: An Overview*, 18 N.Y.L. FORUM 815, 830 (1973); Neale, *The Peculiar Economics of Professional Sports*, 78 Q.J. ECON. 1, 2-6 (1964); Comment, *The Super Bowl and the Sherman Act: Professional Team Sports and the Antitrust Laws, supra* note 95, at 418-19; American Enterprise Institute, Pro Sports: Should the Government Intervene?, AEI Forum 22 (J. Daly, moderator, 1977) (remarks of Rep. Jack Kemp).

depends upon the clubs' ability to stage interesting athletic contests, that is, contests in which the clubs are sufficiently evenly matched that the result of a particular contest is not preordained.[115] The location of individual franchises is an important consideration in the pursuit of this goal of competitive balance.[116] Unprofitable franchises will not generate revenues sufficient to enable them to acquire high quality athletic talent with the consequence that the balance within the league will be disrupted.[117] Thus, it will be contended that club owners as a group have an interest in determining the territories in which franchises will be located.[118]

Under this characterization of the league's economic venture, section 1 would not be applied to invalidate every denial of a relocation request. Because most of the case law dealing with territorial restraints applies the *per se* rule, there is no firm precedent on what the precise standard of review should be in the sports context.[119] The uncertainty as to the meaning of section 1 is reflected in some of the law review commentary on franchise moves. One writer has concluded that a league might be allowed to prevent an owner from relocating in a city occupied by another club, but could not preclude a move into a new area.[120] There is some difficulty in relating this analysis to the general precedents which have developed under section 1. If a *per se* approach is not appropriate, then presumably the rule of reason should be applied. Under that criteria it would be difficult to sustain a general rule that a request to relocate a franchise in a virgin territory must always be permitted. Rather the validity of a denial of such a request should depend upon the reasonableness of the decision as determined by the particular facts of the case. "Reasonableness" in this context is usually defined by reference to the special needs of the industry which made application of the *per se* approach inappropriate in the first instance.[121] Thus, the league would be permitted to impose those restraints which legitimately furthered its interest in insuring the economic stability of the individual franchises. If the league could establish that a proposed relocation city clearly could not support a franchise, its denial of the petitioning owner's request would appear to be reasonable under the criteria generally applied in this area.[122] The fact that the new territory was not occupied by another club should not be controlling.

The rule of reason standard could be applied to other cases as well. It could be used to fetter out those situations in which the denial of a request was based

---

115. *See* DEMMERT 10-11, 15-18; Neale, *The Peculiar Economics of Professional Sports, supra* note 114, at 1-2.

116. *See generally* Quirk & El Hodiri, *The Economic Theory of a Professional Sports League* in GOVERNMENT AND THE SPORTS BUSINESS 33 (R. Noll ed. 1974).

117. *See id.* at 36-37.

118. The considerations mentioned in this paragraph seem not to have been taken into account by those who advocate the unrestricted entry and movement of franchises. *See 1976 Hearings* pt. 2, at 448-51 (testimony of Rep. John Seiberling).

119. *See* Bork, *Ancillary Restraints and the Sherman Act, supra* note 114, at 232-33.

120. Comment, *The Super Bowl and the Sherman Act: Professional Team Sports and the Antitrust Laws, supra* note 95, at 429.

121. *See, e.g.,* Chicago Board of Trade v. United States, 246 U.S. 231 (1918); Mackey v. National Football League, 543 F.2d 606 (8th Cir. 1976). *See generally* Comment, *Trade Association Exclusionary Practices: An Affirmative Role for the Rule of Reason, supra* note 113.

122. *See 1976 Hearings*, pt. 2, at 478-79 (testimony of Lionel S. Sobel). *Cf.* Noll 11, *Alternatives in Sports Policy* in GOVERNMENT AND THE SPORTS BUSINESS 411, 414-15 (R. Noll ed. 1974).

on improper personal motives. For example, it has been suggested that some relocation requests have been denied because the petitioning owner was unpopular with his fellow owners.[123] If it could be established that a denial was not based on objective business considerations, the league would presumably not be insulated from an antitrust attack. In a similar vein, the league would likely encounter difficulty when its decision was based on inaccurate or incomplete data, even if personal animosities played no role. The rule of reason approach appears to require that actions having adverse effects on important economic interests be the result of formal, deliberate decision-making.[124]

There is a basis to suggest that the above analysis may be largely irrelevant. The prior paragraphs have assumed that section 1 of the Sherman Act should be applied to franchise relocation decisions. That premise is hardly free from doubt and, indeed, was rejected in the one instance in which adverse action by a league was contested in court. The occasion for this judicial inquiry was *San Francisco Seals, Ltd. v. National Hockey League.*[125] While the litigation did not proceed beyond the initial decision of the California district court, the court's analysis presents a rather formidable obstacle to those who would seek to use the antitrust laws in this area. A review of the decision will confirm that there are serious weaknesses in the argument which suggests that league franchising practices should be viewed in the same light as traditional forms of horizontal territorial restraints.

San Francisco Seals arose when the plaintiff-owner attempted to move his NHL franchise from San Francisco to Vancouver, British Columbia. The club had encountered financial difficulty in the Bay area and the owner perceived that Vancouver, located in an area where hockey was a favored sport, had greater market potential for his venture. When the relocation proposal was submitted to the Board of Governors of the NHL, it was denied,[126] and the plaintiff brought suit. The complaint raised claims under both section 1 and section 2 of the Sherman Act. For the moment, we will consider only the section 1 issues.

For the *San Francisco Seals* court, the important issue under section 1 was the one which we considered briefly in the introductory paragraphs above: What is the relevant "firm" for section 1 purposes? Is the league a single entity? Or should the league be regarded as a collection of individual firms? The answer is critical, for if there is only one "firm" involved, there can be no agreement or combination, and hence no section 1 violation.

The court's conclusion was unequivocal:

> The plaintiffs and defendants [all members of the NHL] are acting together as one single business enterprise, competing against other similarly organized leagues.[127]

---

123. *See* Quirk, *An Economic Analysis of Team Movements in Professional Sports, supra* note 95, at 49-53; Comment, *The Super Bowl and the Sherman Act: Professional Team Sports and the Antitrust Laws,* 81 HARV. L. REV. 418, 429, n. 59 (1967).

124. *Cf.* Silver v. New York Stock Exchange, 373 U.S. 292 (1963); Denver Rockets v. All-Pro Management, Inc., 325 F. Supp. 1049 (C.D. Cal. 1971).

125. 379 F. Supp. 966 (C.D. Cal. 1974).

126. *Id.* at 968.

127. *Id.* at 969.

The court confirmed that the dispute before it thus lacked the features which would invoke application of section 1. In its view, the purpose of the Sherman Act was

> to prohibit some competitors from combining with other competitors to gain a competitive advantage ... by creating impermissible restraints on trade or commerce ...[128]

The particular plaintiffs and defendants in this case were not competitors "in the economic sense." [129]

The court arrived at its characterization of the league as a single venture by a two-step analysis. It first defined the product market in which the parties operated. It found that the relevant activity involved the production of professional hockey games before live audiences in the United States and Canada.[130] The court then examined the relationship of the parties within that two-nation market. And here it found that the plaintiff and defendants were actually engaged in a joint effort to promote and sell their common product. The court observed that the Seals were not seeking to compete with the defendants and indeed would "continue cooperating with the defendants in pursuit of [the league's] main purpose." [131] In the court's view, the ultimate goal of the venture was "to assure all members of the league the best financial return."[132]

The basic lesson of *San Francisco Seals* is that it is inappropriate to view a league's franchising activity in the same terms as the market division arrangements traditionally condemned under section 1. An agreement with respect to the location of a sports team is unlike an agreement by manufacturers of like products that they will not sell in one another's territories. In that case, the firms would be real economic competitors but for their agreement.[133] The more appropriate analogy for a sports league is that of a single firm attempting to exploit a national market.[134] The firm will have to decide where to locate its various branch offices in order to maximize its economic return. The enterprise will seek to avoid competition and duplication among its various branches as this will only frustrate its effort to secure the best return in the largest market. In order to effectuate these goals, control of marketing policy will be centralized and not allocated to the various divisions, which would tend to pursue individualistic goals.

There are various types of national partnerships which present interesting analogies to sports leagues. One could imagine a large accounting firm organized as a partnership in which each of the partners contributed his own capital and in which the individual's economic return was influenced by both the output of the local offices which each controlled and the overall success of the business.[135] Thus, there might be a general sharing in partnership receipts as

128. *Id.*
129. *Id.*
130. *Id. See also* Philadelphia World Hockey Club, Inc. v. Philadelphia Hockey Club, Inc., 351 F. Supp. 462, 502 (E.D. Pa. 1972).
131. 379 F. Supp. at 969.
132. *Id.*
133. *See* United States v. Sealy, Inc., 388 U.S. 350 (1967); Timken Roller Bearing Co. v. United States, 341 U.S. 593 (1951).
134. *See* authorities cited in note 86 *supra.*
135. *Cf.* Levin v. National Basketball Ass'n, 385 F. Supp. 149, 152 (S.D.N.Y. 1974) (suggesting that clubs are partners in the operation of a sports league). *See generally* Neale, *The Peculiar Economics of Professional Sports, supra* note 114, at 4-6.

well as a system for rewarding individual output. In such a venture, decisions as to the location of offices are still likely to be made centrally since these decisions will affect the partnership's ability to compete with other national firms. Imagine that the firm had decided to locate an office in Louisville. The partner who managed that branch might feel that the revenues generated by his office, as well as his standing in the firm, would rise if he could relocate the office in Cincinnati. The partnership might refuse to allow the move because it thought that the Louisville location was necessary to service important national clients. If the proposed relocation were disapproved, there would appear to be little basis to apply section 1. Since competition among the firm's various offices is neither an intended nor a desirable goal of the particular form of business organization, there appears to be no reason to apply a rule of law which was designed to solve different problems.[136] While the analogy between a sports league and a partnership is not a precise one, there is considerable similarity, and on the element which is most relevant here — mutual interest in cooperative, rather than competitive action — the comparison seems appropriate.

As already noted, the system of shared control in sports leagues may be an economic necessity. The financial success or failure of each franchise affects the fortunes of the other clubs.[137] The mutual concern for the financial stability of all franchises is manifested in a variety of practices found in existing leagues. Many of these take the form of arrangements for the sharing of revenues among member clubs. In most leagues, the clubs have agreed that receipts from national television contracts will be shared equally among the member clubs even though some clubs will likely make a disproportionate contribution to the production of the televised events.[138] Many leagues also have agreements providing for a sharing of gate receipts between a home and visiting club.[139] While the formulas for the division of such game revenues usually favor the home club, the percentage received by the visiting club is, in some cases, substantial.[140] The purpose of such rules, again, appears to offset the disadvantage which some clubs experience by being located in more marginal markets. Another common form of revenue sharing involves the distribution of franchise fees paid when a new club joins the league. In most leagues, these

---

136. Professor Bork applies a similar analysis to sports leagues:

> The members of a league cannot compete in the way that members of other industries can. It is neither in the interests of the members of the league nor of the public generally that the more efficient teams should drive out the less efficient. If one team goes out of business, all are endangered. This suggests that the concept of business competition may be irrelevant as applied to the relationship between members of a league. Functionally, the league appears to be a joint enterprise for the production of amusement spectacles. Bork, *Ancillary Restraints and the Sherman Act,* 15 ABA Antitrust Section 211, 233 (1959).

See also Neale, *The Peculiar Economics of Professional Sports,* 78 Q.J. Econ. 1, 2-6 (1964).

137. *See* authorities cited in note 114 *supra.*

138. *See* Demmert 11-15; Horowitz, *Sports Broadcasting* in Government and the Sports Business 275, 299-310 (R. Noll ed. 1974); Morris, *In the Wake of the Flood,* 38 Law & Contemp. Prob. 85, 92-96 (1973).

139. *See* Demmert 19-20; *1976 Hearings* pt. 2, at 167 (statement of Professor Gerald W. Scully); Morris, *In the Wake of the Flood, supra* note 138, at 94-95.

140. It has been reported that in baseball, the home/visitor division of gate-receipts is 85-15; in football, 60-40; and in basketball 100-0. *See 1976 Hearings* pt. 2, at 167 (statement of Professor Gerald W. Scully). *See also* Demmert, 19.

fees are divided equally among existing members.[141] The apparent assumption of this form of distribution is that all of the clubs contributed to the popularity of the sport which in turn made the additional franchise valuable.

The fact that the clubs engaged in the equalization efforts mentioned above seems to underscore the point that a league is, in essence, an entity which produces a common product.[142] Embodied in these rules is a recognition that a club cannot be compensated solely according to the extent of its contribution to the league's success in the particular year, for such an approach would likely accentuate differences among the clubs and detract from the group's ultimate goal of staging interesting athletic contests.[143] It is perceived to be in the best interests of all clubs, including those in the most lucrative markets, to insure that each franchise has sufficient revenues to sustain itself as a worthy opponent.[144] In order to be able to offer the fans contests in which the outcome is not certain in advance, even the strongest clubs will give up some of the revenues which might otherwise be attributable to their efforts.

Thus, the realities of the major sports leagues' operations would seem to lend support to the conclusion reached in *San Francisco Seals*. The primary goal of section 1 of the Sherman Act is to insure that true economic competitors maintain a healthy distance from one another. The section was not intended to condemn all cooperative efforts in the business world. If a particular group of entrepreneurs are joint investors in a common venture which could not be carried on by anyone of them alone, the cooperation which results hardly seems improper.[145] In these instances, it is proper that the "agreements" in question are viewed as essentially internal marketing decisions.

---

141. *See* Defendants' Trial Memorandum on the Rule of Reason at 24, Mackey v. National Football League, 407 F. Supp. 1000 (D. Minn. 1975), *modified*, 543 F.2d 606 (8th Cir. 1976).

The memorandum cited above lists fifteen aspects of the NFL's operation which illustrate the cooperative nature of the league's venture. Many of these are well-known — the sharing of TV revenues, the use of a single authority to administer discipline, and the like. Some are less obvious, however. For example, the memorandum states that

> [t]he National Football Conference of the League pools and divides equally among its members each team's annual travel costs and road game receipts. This affords the League greater flexibility in arranging scheduling and in effecting divisional alignments. *Id.*

Also worthy of note is the fact that

> [t]he clubs have a common disaster plan under which all clubs have agreed to assign player contracts to any club which loses a major portion of its squad through an accident. *Id.*

There are few other industries in which the participants would agree in advance to relinquish a portion of their specialized employees to help staff the work force of another firm which experienced a disaster. While firms in other industries might be able to hire away another's employees, in most industries cooperative advance planning for this type of situation would not be seen as an economic necessity for the mutual self-protection of the industry itself.

142. *See* note 136 *supra*.

143. *Cf.* Quirk & El Hodiri, *The Economic Theory of a Professional Sports League* in GOVERNMENT AND THE SPORTS BUSINESS 33, 36-37, 58 (R. Noll ed. 1974).

144. Many commentators who are otherwise highly critical of the business practices of sports leagues concede that revenue-sharing is necessary to offset national differences between the profit potential of various franchises. Indeed, some argue that Congress should intervene to require substantial revenue-sharing. *See 1976 Hearings* pt. 2, at 175-76 (statement of Professor Gerald W. Scully); Noll, *Alternatives in Sports Policy* in GOVERNMENT AND THE SPORTS BUSINESS 411, 414 (R. Noll ed. 1974).

145. *See* Bork, *Ancillary Restraints and the Sherman Act,* 15 ABA ANTITRUST SECTION 211, 231-34 (1959).

Before leaving this matter of the status of a sports league under section 1, there is a final point to be mentioned. A question may arise as to the relevance of the judicial decisions applying the antitrust laws to the traditional player restraints, particularly draft systems and reserve and option arrangements.[146] These cases can be read as supporting the view that the various clubs are separate business firms which should be expected to compete with one another. Since the traditional player restraints represented agreements among these potential competitors and since they had the effect of virtually eliminating inter-firm competition, they were generally struck down.[147]

Despite the superficial similarity of the issue of the proper characterization of a league venture, the player restraint cases cannot be regarded as controlling in the present context. These decisions considered a different market than that involved here, for attention was focused on the group decision which restrained competition among the league clubs in the acquisition of playing talent.[148] The courts generally found that the controls which had traditionally been imposed in this input market were not justified by the nature of the league's operation. In contrast, franchising controversies focus on league activities which affect the output market, that is, the market in which the sports product is sold.[149] The fact that courts determine that greater inter-firm competition is warranted in one market should not control the view which is taken of the other. The economic consequences of the restraints, their effects upon third parties, and the considerations which justify them are fundamentally different in the two cases.

2. *The Section 2 Issues.*

The owner whose relocation request is denied may seek to attack the league's decision under section 2 of the Sherman Act. The thrust of his complaint will be that through its franchising decisions, the league is attempting to secure or perpetuate a monopoly in the particular sport. The *San Francisco Seals* case involved this sort of complaint and the court's disposition of the issue will be important for cases which arise in the future.

In that case, the plaintiff's section 2 complaint included specific allegations of monopolistic behavior on the part of the league. The petitioning owner contended that the NHL had sought to discourage the development of a rival league.[150] The league, according to the plaintiff, had increased the number of its franchises and had located the new clubs in areas which might be attractive to a new league. It was alleged that the denial of the plaintiff's requested move was part of this effort to dominate the professional hockey market. Specifically, the plaintiff argued that the league forced it to remain in San Francisco in order to discourage the establishment of rival franchises in that locale.[151]

The contentions made concerning the defendants' motives would normally be sufficient to present a colorable claim under section 2.[152] However, the plaintiff

---

146. *See* Mackey v. National Football League, 543 F.2d 606 (8th Cir. 1976), *modifying* 407 F. Supp. 1000 (D. Minn. 1975); Smith v. Pro-Football, Inc., 420 F. Supp. 738 (D.D.C. 1976); Robertson v. National Basketball Ass'n, 389 F. Supp. 867 (S.D.N.Y. 1975), *subsequent proceeding,* 1975 Trade Cas. ¶ 60,448 (S.D.N.Y.); Kapp v. National Football League, 390 F. Supp. 73 (N.D. Cal. 1974).

147. These cases are discussed in detail in §§ 5.03-.07 *supra.*

148. *See* Levin v. National Basketball Ass'n, 385 F. Supp. 149, 152 n.6 (S.D.N.Y. 1974).

149. *See generally* DEMMERT 81-88.

150. 379 F. Supp. at 971.

151. *Id.*

152. *See generally* United States v. Aluminum Co. of America, 148 F.2d 416 (2d Cir. 1945); 16 VON KALINOWSKI § 8.02.

in *San Francisco Seals* was not able to withstand the league's motion for summary judgment. The reason was that the Seals' owner was found to lack standing to object to the alleged violation.[153]

Under the antitrust statutes, judicial relief is available to "any person who shall be injured in his business or property by reason of" an antitrust violation.[154] The courts have found two important limitations on standing in the statutory scheme. One appears on the face of the statute in the language quoted. The plaintiff must have been injured in his "business or property." [155] The second limitation arises not from a specific statutory directive, but from a judicial assessment of the scope of liability which the antitrust laws were intended to create. The courts will not grant standing to those who are only indirectly or remotely affected by a violation.[156] Most jurisdictions apply a "target area" test to identify the parties who may maintain an action. Thus, the courts will entertain a plaintiff's complaint only if it "was within the target area of the illegal practices . . . ." [157] Moreover, the plaintiff must establish that it "was not only hit, but was aimed at." [158] The thrust of the target area concept is to identify the area of commerce to which the alleged conspiracy was directed and to limit recovery to those which operate in that sphere.[159] Because few commercial activities occur in isolation, a particular practice may have effects upon other traders outside the area of competition directly subject to the restraint. But if these traders were not "aimed at" — that is, if the effect upon them is incidental and not the main object of the conspiracy — they will not be allowed to enforce the alleged antitrust violations.[160]

The application of these concepts required a rejection of the plaintiff's section 2 count in *San Francisco Seals*. It was clear that in the alleged monopolization scheme, the NHL did not aim at the Seals, but rather at rival leagues. Under the plaintiff's own characterization, the specific purpose of the complained of

153. 379 F. Supp. at 972.

154. Clayton Act § 4, 15 U.S.C. § 15 (1974).

155. *See generally* Martin v. Phillips Petroleum Co., 365 F.2d 629 (5th Cir.), *cert. denied,* 385 U.S. 991 (1966); Clapper v. Original Tractor Cab Co., 270 F.2d 616 (7th Cir. 1959), *cert. denied,* 361 U.S. 967 (1960); Waldron v. British Petroelum Co., 231 F. Supp. 72 (S.D.N.Y. 1964); Broadcasters, Inc. v. Morristown Broadcasting Corp., 185 F. Supp. 641 (D.N.J. 1960).

156. For cases in which affected parties were found not to have standing, see Bowen v. New York News, Inc., 522 F.2d 1242 (2d Cir. 1975) (competitor-newspaper dealers could not object to restrictions imposed on exclusive dealers in defendant's papers); Jeffrey v. Southwestern Bell, 518 F.2d 1129 (5th Cir. 1975) (telephone subscribers were not in the target area of an alleged attempt by manufacturer to monopolize telephone equipment field); *In re* Multidistrict Vehicle Air Pollution, 481 F.2d 122 (9th Cir. 1973) (governments and farmers could not object to alleged conspiracy to suppress development of air pollution control devices); Calderone Enterprises Corp. v. United Artist Theatre Circuit, Inc., 454 F.2d 1292 (2d Cir. 1971), *cert. denied,* 406 U.S. 930 (1972) (landlord of movie theatre could not object to alleged conspiracy to control distribution of films).

157. Karseal Corp. v. Richfield Oil Corp., 221 F.2d 358, 365 (9th Cir. 1955). It should be noted that the target area test has been rejected in some circuits as being unduly restrictive. *See* Malamud v. Sinclair Oil Corp., 521 F.2d 1142 (6th Cir. 1975). *Malamud* would favor a test which focused on the question of whether the interest asserted by the plaintiff was one the statute was intended to protect.

158. 221 F.2d at 365.

159. *See* Mulvey v. Samuel Goldwyn Prods., 433 F.2d 1073 (9th Cir. 1970), *cert. denied,* 402 U.S. 923 (1971). *See generally* 16L VON KALINOWSKI § 101.02.

160. The courts have noted that to say that the plaintiff must be "aimed at" does not mean that there must have been a specific intent to injure this particular plaintiff. Rather, it is enough that the plaintiff establish that he was within the area of commerce to which the alleged illegality was directed. *See* Twentieth Century Fox Film Corp. v. Goldwyn, 328 F.2d 190 (9th Cir. 1964).

practice was to frustrate the efforts of potential competitors.[161] As the court concluded, borrowing language from another case, "the plaintiff was not aimed at and it was not hit." [162]

The result reached in *San Francisco Seals* is sound. It is difficult to believe that the plaintiff wanted to eradicate all barriers which might have been erected to frustrate the formation of a rival league. As the court pointed out, the Seals' owner wished to continue to enjoy "the monopolistic protection" which the league could afford; he merely wanted to enjoy it in a different locale.[163] In applying standing rules, the courts should be concerned that they select plaintiffs whose interests are sufficiently antagonistic to those of the defendants to insure a full vindication of federal antitrust policies. Where the plaintiff is a member of the entity for whose benefit the restraint was devised, it is possible that important aspects of the improper practices will be contested with less than full vigor. Unless the plaintiff has the proper incentive to attack the improper activity at its core, the issues in the case may not be properly developed and the results reached may fall short of opening the particular market to further competition. This risk was present in *San Francisco Seals* where the plaintiff would have been satisfied with relief considerably less expansive than that which would have cured the alleged defects in the market for rival leagues. Moreover, because the particular plaintiff had been — and presumably hoped to continue to be — a participant in the monopoly,[164] it is not clear that he could be expected to produce evidence establishing the full extent of the monopoly. A careful detailing of all aspects of the monopoly might expose the plaintiff to liability to third parties.[165] The court had little reason to expect to receive a record revealing all the corrective measures which should be taken. In sum, it seems preferable to insist that the plaintiff who receives antitrust protection be one who has a sincere interest in eliminating the illegal conduct.

If one steps back from the particular arguments about standing and proper parties, the fallacy of the Seals' complaint becomes even clearer. The plaintiff would have had the court use the antitrust laws, not as a vehicle for preserving a free market, but rather as a device for settling internal disputes within a business cartel. The plaintiff's real complaint was that in undertaking to monopolize the hockey market, the plaintiff's cartel had not treated it fairly. It seems unlikely that Congress intended that the antitrust laws would be used to insure equity in the division of monopoly benefits. The public interest to be vindicated under the Sherman Act is that flowing from the establishment of conditions for open competition. One can doubt whether that interest would have been significantly advanced even if the situation prompting the Seals' litigation had been corrected.

The court's rationale in *San Francisco Seals* would seem to transcend the particular facts of that case and should be found persuasive in other situations

---

161. *See* 379 F. Supp. at 972.

162. *Id., quoting* Affiliated Music Enterprises, Inc. v. Sesac, Inc., 160 F. Supp. 865, 976 (S.D.N.Y. 1958), *aff'd,* 268 F.2d 13 (2d Cir.), *cert. denied,* 361 U.S. 831 (1959).

163. 379 F. Supp. at 972.

164. *See id.*

165. In any action brought by a rival league to contest a monopoly by the NHL, the plaintiff in *Seals* would become an appropriate defendant. *See, e.g.,* American Football League v. National Football League, 205 F. Supp. 60, 61 (D. Md. 1962), *aff'd,* 323 F.2d 124 (4th Cir. 1963).

in which a club attempts to raise a section 2 complaint against the monopoly effect of its league's franchise practices. In every case, any monopoly would be intended to injure parties outside of the league itself. While a particular owner might not be pleased with the role that he was assigned to play in the effectuation of the monopoly, his injury is not within the main thrust of the antitrust prohibitions. Given the club's limited incentive to insure the attainment of a market which was truly free, the antitrust actions that might be available are properly reserved for those to whom the monopoly was directed.

b. Exercises of Monopoly Power: The Injury to Rival Leagues. The basic conclusion reached in the prior discussion was that the antitrust laws will provide little basis for a club to object to its own league's franchising activities. One of the points made in that analysis was that a member club is not a proper party to object to a league's effort to dominate the market in its sport. In the present discussion, we turn our attention to situations in which the obstacles created by the standing issue are set aside, for here we will consider cases in which the plaintiff raising the antitrust objection is a rival league which seeks to compete with the established clubs.[166] Since such a competing league is the likely target of any improper market dominance, there should be little doubt as to its right to invoke the antitrust laws.

There is one clarification of the nature of our inquiry which should be made at the outset. While we have generally been concerned about the franchising activities of a sports league, the objections raised by a rival league are likely to be more inclusive. The basic complaint which would be raised is that the established clubs have dominated the market in the particular sport and thereby have restricted the plaintiff's ability to compete. In the typical case, the plaintiff will attack not only the defendant's franchising practices, but also its practices with respect to the acquisition and retention of players and its arrangements with the national television networks.[167] With respect to franchising, it may be alleged that the defendant's decisions as to the location of its clubs were designed to capture the best sports markets, with the result that the plaintiff-rival league was unable to compete effectively.[168] In a similar vein, the plaintiff may also try to show that the defendant's domination of player and television markets limited the opportunities for the establishment of a rival league.[169] Thus, our inquiry here cannot be limited solely to franchising questions. As will be seen, however, the issues which arise with respect to club location usually play the central role in the competing league's antitrust attack.

As implied in the above paragraphs, the antitrust complaints of a competing league will focus on section 2 of the Sherman Act, which is concerned with monopolistic behavior. The section 1 prohibition on collusive, anti-competitive agreements may have little role to play in this area. Not only is section 2 more

166. In the late 1960's and early 1970's there were several competing leagues which appeared to challenge the established clubs. None of these established itself as a long-term competitor. Some of the antitrust implications of this situation are discussed in *1976 Hearings* pt. 2, at 285-302 (testimony of Joe Sims, Deputy Ass't Att'y Gen., Antitrust Div., Dept. of Justice).

167. *See, e.g.,* Philadelphia World Hockey Club, Inc. v. Philadelphia Hockey Club, Inc., 351 F. Supp. 462 (E.D. Pa. 1972); American Football League v. National Football League, 205 F. Supp. 60 (D. Md. 1962), *aff'd,* 323 F.2d 124 (4th Cir. 1963).

168. Objections to the franchising practices of the dominant league were raised in both of the cases cited in note 167 *supra.*

169. In American Football League v. National Football League, 205 F. Supp. 60 (D. Md. 1962), *aff'd,* 323 F.2d 124 (4th Cir. 1963), the court found no substance in the plaintiff's objection about

specifically designed to deal with the objections whicn will be raised, but also it can reasonably be argued that a league's operation lacks the duality necessary to invoke section 1. Thus, a court may well agree that the section 1 analysis developed in *San Francisco Seals* should be applied in the instant case even though we have a different plaintiff.[170] This result seems appropriate since the competition that will be the focus of our inquiry occurs on the league, as opposed to the club, level.[171]

The section 2 proscription against monopolization is stated in general terms. The statute simply provides that it is illegal for any person to "monopolize . . . any part of trade . . . or commerce."[172] It has been left to the courts to give texture to this broad prohibition and to define more precisely the types of actions to be condemned. Many, and indeed, most factual situations can be dealt with under what will be identified here as the traditional tests. Under this standard, the section 2 violation requires that two elements be present. It must be found that the defendant possessed monopoly power and that it took actions amounting to a misuse of this power.[173] Each of these elements often requires a lengthy and sensitive inquiry by the court.[174] A finding of monopoly power requires a determination of the relevent product and geographical markets plus evidence indicating that the defendants held a dominant position in these spheres.[175] If that condition is found to be present, the court must evaluate the quality of the defendant's actions. A misuse of market power exists if the defendant "undertook some course of action the consequence of which was to exclude competition or prevent competition. . . ." [176] As previously noted, this general standard often must be further refined to take account of actions representing legitimate business practices.

The applicability of the traditional section 2 tests to sports franchising decisions is considered below. It should be noted, however, that the present situation in the sports industry is susceptible to a frame of reference which is somewhat different from that assumed by the traditional tests. Those tests are most frequently applied in cases in which the relevant market is capable of supporting several different firms. In these situations, the courts are properly concerned that potential competitors not be deterred and hence an emphasis on the exclusionary effects of the defendant's action is fully appropriate. Some markets, however, give rise to natural monopolies.[177] In situations where only

the defendant's control of the player market. However, in Philadelphia World Hockey Club, Inc. v. Philadelphia Hockey Club, Inc., 351 F. Supp. 462 (E.D. Pa. 1972) the defendant's domination of the supply of hockey players was a major reason for the plaintiff's success.

170. *See* text at notes 125-49 *supra.*

171. A basic theme which arises from the few cases in this area is that it is most appropriate to view rival leagues as competing in a national market, rather than in various local submarkets. *See* cases cited in note 167 *supra.*

172. Sherman Act § 2, 15 U.S.C. § 2 (1974). *See also* note 71 *supra.*

173. *See* cases cited notes 80-81 *supra.*

174. *See generally* VON KALINOWSKI § 8.02.

175. *See* cases cited note 80 *supra.*

176. *See* American Football League v. National Football League, 205 F. Supp. 60, 63 (D. Md. 1962), *aff'd,* 323 F.2d 124 (4th Cir. 1963). *See also* Philadelphia World Hockey Club, Inc. v. Philadelphia Hockey Club, Inc., 351 F. Supp. 462 (E.D. Pa. 1972).

177. *See, e.g.,* John Wright & Assoc., Inc. v. Ullrich, 328 F.2d 474 (8th Cir. 1964); Union Leader Corp. v. Newspapers of New England, Inc., 284 F.2d 582 (1st Cir. 1960), *cert. denied,* 365 U.S. 833 (1961); United States v. Harte-Hanks Newspapers, Inc., 170 F. Supp. 227 (N.D. Tex. 1959). *See generally* 16A VON KALINOWSKI § 9.03[1]; Neale, *The Peculiar Economics of Professional Sports,* 78 Q.J. ECON. 1, 45 (1964).

a single firm can survive, the fact that others are unable to enter is not in itself a reason for concern.

A reading of the cases does not suggest that the traditional tests are abandoned in natural monopoly situations.[178] Rather, what appears is a slight shift in emphasis, and to the extent that there are differences in the judicial treatment of natural monopolies, they are only differences in the degree of tolerance of a non-competitive market. The fact that a potential competitor is unable to establish itself or that an existing firm is driven out of business is not a substantial concern.[179] Nor is it a cause for concern that these results occurred because of aggressive competitive behavior by the surviving entity. Only one firm can survive, and it is appropriate that the determination of which entity that will be is left to the normal market forces.[180] The view developed in the cases is that the courts have only a limited role to play as firms struggle to see which will become the natural monopolist. The role prescribed is that of a referee who is indifferent as to who wins but who stands by to insure that the fight is a fair one.[181] The leading precedents dealing with natural monopolies suggest that section 2 violations arise to the extent that one of the firms resorts to unfair methods of competition to secure or to improve its position. Secret arrangements with third parties, improper monetary inducements to third parties, and predatory pricing are examples of methods of competition likely to be disapproved.[182]

The question needs to be raised as to whether the markets for each of the major professional league sports do not lend themselves to natural monopolies. This is an issue that has not been explored in the cases although it has important consequences for defining the type of competition to be expected to exist between leagues.[183] The arguments for treating the major sports leagues as

---

178. *See, e.g.,* Union Leader Corp. v. Newspapers of New England, Inc., 284 F.2d 582 (1st Cir. 1960), *cert. denied,* 365 U.S. 833 (1961); Gamco, Inc. v. Providence Fruit & Produce Bldg., Inc., 194 F.2d 484 (1st Cir.), *cert. denied,* 344 U.S. 817 (1952).

179. *Cf.* American Football League v. National Football League, 323 F.2d 124, 131 (4th Cir. 1963); Bailey's Bakery, Ltd. v. Continental Baking Co., 235 F. Supp. 705 (D. Hawaii 1964).

180. Union Leader Corp. v. Newspapers of New England, Inc., 284 F.2d 582 (1st Cir. 1960), *cert. denied,* 365 U.S. 833 (1961).

181. "When one has acquired a natural monopoly by means which are neither exclusionary, unfair, nor predatory, he is not disempowered to defend his position fairly." American Football League v. National Football League, 323 F.2d 124, 131 (4th Cir. 1963).

182. *See, e.g.,* Union Leader Corp. v. Newspapers of New England, Inc., 284 F.2d 582 (1st Cir. 1960), *cert. denied,* 365 U.S. 833 (1961); United States v. American Optical Co., 39 F.R.D. 580 (N.D. Cal. 1966). *See also* Greyhound Computer Corp. v. IBM Corp., 1972 Trade Cas. ¶ 74,205 (D. Ariz.).

183. The natural monopoly concept has appeared in two inter-league antitrust cases, but neither discussion made the point which we will consider here. In American Football League v. National Football League, 323 F.2d 124, 131 (4th Cir. 1963), the court suggested that some individual clubs may enjoy natural monopolies in their particular franchise locations because the cities in question could not support more than one club. The court did not go further and inquire into the applicability of the concept as far as a league's position in the national market was concerned. At the time of this case, the broader inquiry was inappropriate, for the established league — the NFL — occupied only a few of the available franchise locations.

The district court opinion in Philadelphia World Hockey Club, Inc. v. Philadelphia Hockey Club, Inc., 351 F. Supp. 462 (E.D. Pa. 1972), also included a reference to natural monopolies, but the point the court intended to make is far from clear. The court noted that there had been increasing interest in the sport of hockey in the United States and Canada and that the expansion of the NHL appeared to be an attempt to capture this new interest. The court then observed:

Of course, if even this burgeoning interest in hockey in North America could nonetheless support only one supplier, then this court would be bound to conclude that the NHL enjoys a "natural monopoly." *Id.* at 511.

natural, and therefore legal, monopolies are set forth following our review of the traditional section 2 tests.

1. *The Traditional Tests: Monopoly Power and Its Misuse.*

To focus our discussion of the traditional tests for a section 2 violation, it is useful to consider *American Football League v. National Football League.*[184] The case arose in the early 1960's, and as a result of subsequent developments in professional football, several important factual premises of the decision may no longer be valid. However, the general approach that the district and appellate courts took to the plaintiff's section 2 complaint still provides a useful guide for sifting out the critical section 2 issues.

The case arose shortly after the American Football League was formed as a rival to the established National Football League. The AFL alleged that the older league was guilty of, alternatively, actual monopolization, attempted monopolization, or a conspiracy to monopolize.[185] Central to the plaintiff's case was its contention that the defendant controlled the most desirable locations for professional football franchises and thus dominated the market in that sport.[186] As evidence, the AFL pointed out that not only was the NFL firmly entrenched in the largest metropolitan areas but in addition had undertaken a program for expansion capturing other attractive locales in which the AFL had planned to establish itself.

While some NFL owners had discussed expansion several years before the AFL was organized, the actual addition of new NFL cities coincided with the birth of the new league.[187] The AFL based much of its case on the fact that the NFL added franchises in Dallas and Minneapolis, two cities in which the AFL had a great deal of interest. The new league actually established a team in Dallas, and the appearance of the older league there added substantial competition.[188] The NFL's moving into the Minneapolis market was similarly a matter of great concern. The AFL had already begun negotiations with a group of Minneapolis investors but had to abandon its efforts after the NFL's decision to locate there.[189] The AFL argued that the older league already had a dominant position in the professional football market by virtue of its having previously locked in the largest metropolitan areas and that its move into the Minneapolis area was evidence of its capacity to beat out the AFL in the few desirable franchise locations which remained.[190] The plaintiff offered proof that the NFL

The court, however, did not choose to analyze this concept further. It offered no opinion on whether professional hockey could support more than one league and gave no indication of how its statement about natural monopolies affected its analysis. It may have been that the statement quoted above was merely added as an interesting sidelight.

A more complete discussion of the applicability of the natural monopoly concept to sports leagues can be found in Neale, *The Peculiar Economics of Professional Sports, supra* note 177.

184. 205 F. Supp. 60 (D. Md. 1962), aff'd, 323 F.2d 124 (4th Cir. 1963).

185. 205 F. Supp. at 62-63.

186. The activities of the NFL complained of by the plaintiffs included more than the older league's franchising practices. It was also alleged that the NFL had used its control of the players' market and its arrangements with television networks to perpetuate its monopoly. *Id. See also* text at notes 167-69 *supra.* It is clear from the courts' opinions, however, that the defendant's franchising activities were of most concern to the plaintiffs.

187. 205 F. Supp. at 67-73.

188. *Id.* at 69-70.

189. *Id.* at 71-73.

190. *See* 323 F.2d at 131.

was aware of its plans for franchising locations, and in fact, had contact with many of the investors whom it was hoping to attract.

(a) *Monopoly power.*

On the charge that the NFL had actually monopolized the professional football market, the district court framed the issues in terms of the traditional section 2 tests identified above. To prevail on this aspect of the complaint, the plaintiff would have to show, first, that the NFL possessed monopoly power and, second, that it had misused that power — *i.e.,* that its actions prevented or excluded competition by the new league.[191] As the case was perceived by the district court, the monopoly power question was dispositive of the issues before it. The Court of Appeals for the Fourth Circuit agreed that this was the critical issue and affirmed the lower court's determination that the facts did not establish that the NFL possessed monopoly power.[192]

In a typical section 2 case, the question of whether the defendant possesses monopoly power often requires a lengthy inquiry. While there is less than complete agreement on the specific criteria to be applied,[193] the general issues are not in dispute. As an initial matter, it is necessary to identify the relevant market in which the defendant's position will be judged. This requires that efforts be made to define the proper geographic area to be considered as well as the product or products involved.[194] Next, the court will attempt to assess the particular share of the market claimed by the defendant. Finally, the analysis is further refined to consider other factors that might influence the defendant's power to maintain its market position. Here the court will consider such things as the difficulty — or lack of difficulty — competitors would encounter in seeking to enter the market or expand their share of it; the defendant's capacity to increase its own share; and the latter's ability to unilaterally control the terms upon which transactions in the market are made.[195]

Several of these elements received extensive attention in *AFL v. NFL.* Interestingly, one question which apparently was not strongly debated concerns the nature of the product involved in the litigation. This issue normally requires a court to consider the availability of substitutes for the product offered by the defendant.[196] In the sports context, there might be some who would ask whether the relevant product market should include all forms of entertainment, or the more limited class of all varieties of professional sports, or the narrow category

---

191. *See* 205 F. Supp. at 63.

192. 323 F.2d 124 (4th Cir. 1963).

193. The courts appear to select from a variety of tests in determining whether the defendant possesses monopoly power. In some cases, the courts will look for indications that the defendant's prices, profits and so on are different from those which would exist in a competitive market. In other situations, an inquiry is made to determine whether the defendant has been responsive to changes in its competitor's mode of operation. A third, and more common test, looks largely at the size of the defendant's market share. Here the court ascertains the number of competitors in the market and the percentage of sales or purchases controlled by each one. *See* 16 VON KALINOWSKI § 7.01[1]; GELLHORN 115-17.

194. *See* cases cited note 80 *supra.*

195. *See generally* GELLHORN 117; Stocking, *Economic Tests of Monopoly and the Concept of the Relevant Market,* 2 ANTITRUST BULL. 479 (1957).

196. *See, e.g.,* United States v. E.I. DuPont de Nemours & Co., 351 U.S. 377 (1956); Beacon Fruit & Produce Co. v. H. Harris & Co., 152 F. Supp. 702 (D. Mass. 1957), *aff'd per curiam,* 206 F.2d 958 (1st Cir. 1958), *cert. denied,* 359 U.S. 984 (1959).

of professional sports offered by the particular defendant.[197] To sustain the argument that the product market includes more than a single sport, it would be necessary to show, first, that there are other sports and entertainment products competing for the fans' or investors' dollars and, second, that the degree of interchangeability is so high that there is no basis for differentiating sub-markets.[198]

While there is more to be said on this point than has been considered in the few cases to date, the disposition of this issue implicit in *AFL v. NFL* seems correct. There it seems to have been assumed that football should be treated differently from other sports. Since the court did not elaborate on the point, the precise basis for this determination is not clear. But the limited information available provides the basis for a finding that professional football operations have sufficiently distinctive characteristics to warrant the recognition of a separate sub-market. Factors such as the relative popularity of the sport, the general level of operating costs, and the sport's needs in terms of stadium size and climatic conditions serve to set it apart from other ventures. In the same vein, it seems that professional football generates a following of fans who are not indifferent as to whether their sports dollars are spent on football or some other form of entertainment. Application of these same criteria to other sports would seem to suggest that they should similarly be treated as involving distinct products, although, again, the ultimate conclusion would depend upon the specific facts to be developed.[199]

Among the other criteria for evaluating market power, the issue of the relevant geographical market proved to be very controversial in *AFL v. NFL.* The plaintiff sought to draw the market rather narrowly to include those cities in which the NFL was actually operating and the four or five other locales which had been seriously considered as NFL expansion cities.[200] It is clear that this contention was critical to the plaintiff's case. If the geographical market could be limited to that actually affected by the NFL's present and future operations, then there would seem to be little doubt that the older league's market position would be found to be a dominant one. In that event, the plaintiff would have passed the first major hurdle under the traditional section 2 tests and could concentrate on the question of whether the NFL's expansion program amounted to a "misuse" of the league's market position.

The plaintiff's characterization of the relevant geographic market was not accepted, however. The court of appeals, for example, recognized that the two professional football leagues competed in several different markets. The competition for gate-receipts might be highly localized, while competition for

---

197. Even if the relevant "product" were narrowed to the particular sport in question, it would be necessary to determine whether the market should be defined to include minor league, semi-professional, and amateur versions of the sport. In one case in which this issue was considered, the court held that the product of the major professional league was sufficiently distinct to warrant its characterization as a separate market. *See* Philadelphia World Hockey Club, Inc. v. Philadelphia Hockey Club, Inc., 351 F. Supp. 462 (E.D. Pa. 1972).

198. *See* 16 VON KALINOWSKI § 8.02[2][a]. For a discussion of the economic competition which exists among various types of sporting events, see Neale, *The Peculiar Economics of Professional Sports,* 78 Q.J. ECON. 1, 11 (1964).

199. For one of the few extended discussions of the product market question in the sports context, see Philadelphia World Hockey Club, Inc. v. Philadelphia Hockey Club, Inc., 351 F. Supp. 462, 500-02 (E.D. Pa. 1972). *See also* San Francisco Seals, Ltd. v. National Hockey League, 379 F. Supp. 966, 969 (C.D. Cal. 1974).

200. *See* 323 F.2d at 129.

players occurred in a broader geographic area. But the type of competition providing the focus of the AFL's complaint concerned the location of the franchises through which the athletic contests would be offered. For this level of competition, the court concluded that the relevant market was nationwide.[201] It observed that the defendant NFL had not limited itself to any one region of the country and in fact had attempted to achieve a wide geographical spread in its selection of franchise locations. In the court's view, the fact that there were only a limited number of locations that could successfully support a team did not diminish the fact that the market being exploited was larger in scope. Language used by the court suggests that it thought the case to be analogous to the chain store which selects a limited number of store locations but intends to influence the market covering an entire city or a wider metropolitan area.[202] From the perspective of a competitor, the relevant market may not be simply the store location or the immediate neighborhood, but rather the whole local retail marketing area.[203]

Having thus identified the relevant market, the court turned its attention to evaluating the position which the defendant held in that sphere. The district court's approach was to first identify the total number of potential franchise locations available nationwide and then to inquire as to the number controlled by the defendant.[204] Various views were presented on the first issue. There was some proof that a professional football franchise could operate in any metropolitan area with a population in excess of 500,000. There were fifty-two such areas in the United States. The district court found, however, that a more conservative estimate of potential franchise sites was appropriate. It concluded, and the appellate court agreed, that the number of potential franchise areas should be limited to the thirty-one metropolitan areas having a population in excess of 750,000.[205]

This determination proved fatal to the plaintiff's case. In 1959, before expansion, the NFL had franchises in only eleven of the thirty-one cities indentified. Moreover, their claim to two of those cities was not exclusive, for the AFL had been successful in locating rival teams in those locales. As the court of appeals observed, "twenty of the thirty-one potentially desirable sites were entirely open to [AFL]."[206] Thus, it could not be said that the NFL had dominated the market by the control of the retail outlets.

The plaintiff alternatively urged that the court consider the older league's *potential* for domination. Here the AFL noted the preference which potential investors and fans would have for new franchises from the established league and pointed to the NFL's capturing of the Minneapolis location as evidence that the defendant "could have taken several other cities away from [the AFL] had it undertaken to do so."[207] The court of appeals was unpersuaded by this view

201. *Id.* at 130, *aff'g* 205 F. Supp. at 65.
202. *See* 323 F.2d at 130.
203. Courts in other sports cases involving section 2 issues have concluded that the relevant geographical market is nationwide. *See* San Francisco Seals, Ltd. v. National Hockey League, 379 F. Supp. 966 (C.D. Cal. 1974); Philadelphia World Hockey Club, Inc. v. Philadelphia Hockey Club, Inc., 351 F. Supp. 462 (E.D. Pa. 1972).
204. *See* 205 F. Supp. at 76-77.
205. *Id.* at 76, *aff'd,* 323 F.2d at 130-31.
206. 323 F.2d at 131.
207. *Id.*

of the defendant's market power. It noted that the AFL had beaten out the NFL in a battle over a franchise location in another city (Houston) and that the NFL's expansion plans were limited to only four of the several cities remaining unclaimed.[208]

It is clear that the AFL lost its case because the court believed that the NFL had captured only a limited segment of a national market that appeared to be capable of supporting two different professional football leagues.[209] While the NFL was more established, and for that reason perhaps more desirable in the eyes of fans and investors, in the court's view it was not yet invulnerable to outside competition. The AFL's position was further weakened by the fact that it had been able to establish itself and, at least at the time of this litigation, faced a somewhat optimisitic future. It had arranged for a national television contract, had successfully signed star college players, and had received applications from a number of additional cities seeking franchises. All of these factors gave credence to the notion that the difficulties the AFL was experiencing were not due to any improper dominance by the NFL in the national football market.

The NFL was thus able to resist the antitrust challenge mounted in *AFL v. NFL* by establishing that it did not have monopoly power, the first prerequisite for a section 2 violation. But the situation in professional football has changed dramatically since the time of this case, and there is a substantial basis to question whether the results would be the same if the monopoly power issue were relitigated today. It may be useful to note some of the points which would be made in the present setting.

(1) At the time of the *AFL v. NFL* suit, the NFL operated teams in eleven of the thirty-one metropolitan areas thought to be capable of supporting a franchise. The league was also undertaking an expansion that would have added three additional cities. Subsequently the NFL absorbed several AFL clubs and further enlarged its expansion program. In recent years, it has operated twenty-eight teams in twenty-six metropolitan areas. Unless the number of potential franchise areas has increased beyond the thirty-one identified in the early 1960's, the NFL's present market penetration would seem to require a different conclusion than that reached in *AFL V. NFL.*[210]

(2) Has the number of potential franchise locations changed? This is a question which warrants re-examination. Such an inquiry would have to take account of several different factors: changes in population in metropolitan areas; increases in the cost of operating a franchise, including increased player costs due to the recent liberalization of player restraints; and increases in club revenue from sources other than home team gate-receipts (television contracts, away-game revenue-sharing, etc.).[211]

---

208. *Id.*
209. *See id. See also* 205 F. Supp. at 77.
210. The issue of whether the major professional leagues presently hold a monopoly position in their respective markets is discussed in *1976 Hearings,* pt. 2, at 285-302.
211. An interesting perspective on the question of whether the financial picture of professional sports leagues has changed in recent years is suggested by the contrast in the tone of two articles published in financial magazines. *Compare* The Sports Boom Is Going Bust, Forbes, Feb. 15, 1975, at 24 *with* Burck, Why Those WFL Owners Expect to Score Profits, Fortune, Sept., 1974, at 142. *See also* Block, So You Want to Own a Ball Club, Forbes, Apr. 1, 1977, at 37; Lorges, Pro Hockey's Financial Woes Not a Joking Matter, Washington Post, Mar. 8, 1977, at D1, col. 1; Rottenberg, Superstars in Wage Bracket with Top U.S. Company Executives, Globe & Mail (Toronto), Nov. 11,

(3) The AFL had been able to secure a broadcasting contract with a major television network. Are such opportunities available for a rival league in the present market? Since the *AFL v. NFL* litigation, the NFL has entered into agreements parceling out various parts of its television rights to the three major networks. In addition, the greater market penetration of the NFL may have resulted in such a superior product from a broadcasting standpoint that a rival league would have a difficult time selling its television rights even if a network was available.[212]

(4) It is likely that a court called upon to re-examine the question of the NFL's monopoly power would want to inquire into the arrangements which NFL clubs have made for the use of stadiums. During the brief tenure of the World Football League, one point of controversy between the two leagues was the fact that many NFL clubs held exclusive leases on the most desirable arenas.[213] Such arrangements, which have the effect of limiting the access of a rival league to many local markets, are relevant to the present inquiry, for they bear on the issue of the relative market position of the established league.

An authoritative resolution of the ultimate question of whether the NFL presently possesses "monopoly power" will have to await the development of a factual record which answers the issues posed above. But the limited data available suggest that *AFL v. NFL* may have been less-than-complete victory for the older league. The case has served to establish a framework for inquiry which may return to haunt the NFL if courts continue to apply the traditional section 2 tests to its operation. As previously mentioned, we examine below the question of whether another theory — that of natural monopoly — is not more appropriately applied in these cases.

While the prior discussion has looked at the monopoly power question from the perspective of the NFL, it should be clear that the general approach taken here would also be applicable to other leagues. The first problem is to define the relevant market, particularly as to the matter of its geographic scope. There are indications from other cases that courts are likely to conclude that the other major professional leagues will be found to operate in markets which are at least nationwide and in some sports include Canada.[214] It will also be necessary to decide how many potential franchise locations are available in that market and then to assess the market share claimed by the established league. Finally, it is appropriate to consider other factors — such as broadcast arrangements, stadium controls, player restrictions, financial resources, and natural barriers

1976, at S5, col. 1; Rottenberg, Irrationality of System Explains Athletes' Salaries, *id.,* Nov. 22, 1976, at S7, col. 4; Rottenberg, Superstar Salaries Seen a Key Factor in Pushing Prices Out of Fans' Reach, *id.,* Nov. 24, 1976, at S2, col. 3; Jacobson, Moneyball, Los Angeles Times, Jan. 24, 1976, Pt. Ill. at 1, col. 1.

212. *See generally* Horowitz, *Sports Broadcasting* in GOVERNMENT AND THE SPORTS BUSINESS 275 (R. Noll ed., 1974); N.Y. Times, Aug. 15, 1976, § 5, at 5, col. 2; *id.,* Aug. 30, 1976, at 29, col. 1 (NFL radio and TV rights cost broadcasters $81.5 million).

213. *See* Hecht v. Pro-Football, Inc., 444 F.2d 931 (D.C. Cir. 1971).

214. *See* San Francisco Seals, Ltd. v. National Hockey League, 379 F. Supp. 966 (C.D. Cal. 1974); Philadelphia World Hockey Club, Inc. v. Philadelphia Hockey Club, Inc., 351 F. Supp. 462 (E.D. Pa. 1972).

to entry — which are relevant to define the strength of the defendant league's market position.[215]

(b) *Misuse of market position.*

Because the *AFL v. NFL* section 2 issue was disposed of on the grounds that the defendant did not possess monopoly power, neither the district court nor the court of appeals found it necessary to address directly the question of what would amount to a misuse of its market position by an established sports league. However, the general factual setting of the case can be used as the occasion for a closer examination of the content of the second prong of the traditional section 2 tests. Of particular interest here is a somewhat off-hand statement made by the district court in *AFL v. NFL.* In a footnote at the end of its analysis of the complaint of actual monopolization by the NFL, the court stated that if the defendant had been found to have possessed monopoly power, "the awarding of the franchise to Dallas for operation in 1960, and the offer of the franchise to Minneapolis in November, 1959, might well have been such acts as would have imposed liability for monopolization." [216] Although this observation is clearly dicta, it suggests an issue likely to be of considerable importance in the future. Most sports leagues have increased the number of their franchises since the time of the *AFL v. NFL,* and it is now less clear that cases such as this would be decided on the grounds used in that decision.

With the *AFL v. NFL* dicta in mind, we can examine the doctrine which has been developed in other antitrust contexts to give meaning to the concept of a misuse of monopoly power. This second prong of the traditional section 2 tests is most easily understood if one accepts that there are gradations in the quality of proof which a plaintiff might offer on this point. In rare cases, the plaintiff may have evidence clearly establishing the necessary misuse of power. But many, and probably most cases, will be more difficult, and the task of the complainant will be to prove instances of the defendant's actions from which a court can infer section 2 abuses. We will examine three gradations in the legal standard applied in this area. These include (1) cases in which there is specific evidence that a defendant intended to achieve or perpetuate a monopoly and, in the process, to exclude or injure competitors; (2) cases in which proof of specific intent is lacking, but in which it can be shown that the defendant used illegal or unfair means against competitors to acquire or maintain its monopoly position; and (3) cases in which the monopoly is legally attained but is perpetuated by the defendant's overly aggressive behavior in solidifying its market position.[217]

---

215. The dominant league's control of the market for hockey players was a major factor in the conclusion that the NHL was guilty of monopolization in Philadelphia World Hockey Club, Inc. v. Philadelphia Hockey Club, Inc., 351 F. Supp. 462 (E.D. Pa. 1972).

216. *See* 205 F. Supp. at 77 n.17.

217. It should be noted that the categories which we suggest here do not necessarily represent sharp demarcations. Most section 2 cases are decided without regard to how the plaintiff's proof is to be categorized. Rather the courts frequently make an assessment of the evidence offered and determine whether it indicates that the defendant has engaged in conduct which had the anticompetitive characteristics of actions condemned in other cases. Often the court will find evidence which would fit into more than one of the categories we have designed. Thus, it may be that the defendant both used illegal means to achieve its monopoly and in addition was overly aggressive in its efforts to solidify its market position. The categories set out in the text are nonetheless useful. They not only serve to help categorize existing precedent, but also provide a useful guide for judging the strength of the plaintiff's case. Where there is proof of a specific

(i) *Specific intent to monopolize.* The first class of cases — those involving proof that the defendant took actions for the specific purpose of acquiring or perpetuating a monopoly — need not long detain us. Such proof of a specific anti-competitive motive is rarely available, and cases with this element seldom appear.[218] But the point can be made that if the plaintiff has access to correspondence, memoranda, or conversations in which a defendant discussed specific plans to control a market and to drive competitors out of business, the complaining party will be relieved of a substantial part of the burden which most antitrust litigants confront. Proof of the necessary intent, coupled with evidence that the defendant's expansion policy, pricing policy, or other business practices were undertaken in pursuit of this goal, will make the plaintiff's case. In the context of a suit involving rival sports leagues, the court would be most interested in the discussions in which the defendant owners expressed their reaction to the competitive threat presented by the new league.[219] It must be recognized, however, that given the astuteness of the antitrust counsel which most leagues use, it is likely that any such conversations will be carefully framed so that the sharpest anti-competitive edges are removed.[220]

While proof of an intent to monopolize may be available in some situations, it is not an indispensible element of the plaintiff's case under section 2. The courts have recognized that such evidence is often lacking and have accepted that the element of a misuse of market power may be established by other means.[221] It is appropriate for the court to focus on the particular actions taken by the defendant and to assess the effects which these have upon the market position of competitors. Where a defendant possessing monopoly power engages in conduct "the consequence of which was to exclude competition or prevent

anticompetitive intent coupled with monopoly power, the plaintiff's case is relatively clear. However, as we move up the scale to cases in which the defendant is only accused of overly-aggressive behavior, the question of whether there is a legal wrong is likely to be much more debatable. The ultimate conclusion in these cases is often highly judgmental, requiring a careful assessment of what is, and is not, proper business behavior.

218. Among the few cases suggesting the presence of specific, illegal intent are United States v. Crescent Amusement Co., 323 U.S. 173 (1944); United States v. Reading Co., 253 U.S. 26 (1920).

219. In the *Philadelphia World Hockey* case, the court considered a number of aspects of the defendant-NHL's activities in concluding that the established league was guilty of monopolization. In addition to the league's control of the player market and its overly-aggressive expansion practice, the court seemed to suggest that there was evidence indicating a more specific intent to monopolize. In this connection, the court gave particular emphasis to a 1965 statement by Clarence Campbell, then president of the league, that his organization was undertaking to expand to insure that the NHL was "the only major professional hockey league operating from coast to coast in the United States or Canada." *See* Philadelphia World Hockey Club, Inc. v. Philadelphia Hockey Club, Inc., 351 F. Supp. 462, 512 (E.D. Pa. 1972).

There could be a good deal of debate about how this statement should be interpreted. If it were made as part of a public relations campaign to promote new franchises, it could easily be taken as nothing more than puffing about the quality and efficiency of the league. In this light, the statement is much like that made by a car manufacturer when it announces that it has the largest, most convenient network of service locations. To give weight to such statements for antitrust purposes would suggest that corporate representatives should assume a reluctant, self-depreciating attitude in making public announcements of their company's expansion plans.

220. "Intelligent businessmen, aided by expert legal counsel, simply do not say, or put in writing, that they are going to drive a competitor out of business." Noerr Motor Freight, Inc. v. Eastern R.R. Presidents Conf., 155 F. Supp. 768, 813 (E.D. Pa. 1957), *aff'd,* 273 F.2d 218 (3d Cir. 1959), *rev'd on other grounds,* 365 U.S. 127 (1961).

221. *See, e.g.,* United States v. Griffith, 334 U.S. 100 (1948).

competition," [222] the courts may simply infer that an intent to monopolize was present. It will be presumed that the monopolist understands what the natural consequences of his actions will be.[223]

(ii) *Monopolies achieved through secondary illegality or unfair conduct.* The courts are particularly inclined to find section 2 violations when an actual or potential monopolist engages in activities which are themselves illegal or which are otherwise inherently destructive of competition.[224] The second category of cases identified above includes these situations. The illegality of the actions may arise from application of provisions of the antitrust laws other than section 2. The section 1 prohibition on illegal restraints on trade and the Clayton Act disapproval of anti-competitive mergers are frequently applied to establish that the defendant's monopoly position was improperly acquired or misused.[225]

To illustrate how this approach to a section 2 violation might be used in the sports context, reference can be made to the complaint filed in *Buffalo v. Atlanta Hawks Basketball, Inc.*[226] The case arose when it was announced that the NBA Buffalo Braves planned to leave Buffalo and relocate in North Hollywood, Florida.[227] The city of Buffalo, which owned the stadium leased by the Braves, sued, alleging that the defendants, which included all the members of the NBA, were guilty of a section 2 violation. The case was eventually settled when the Braves agreed to stay in Buffalo.[228]

The reader will want to keep in mind that the following portions of the complaint are presented here for the limited purpose of illustrating the manner in which other antitrust violations may be relevant to section 2. We do not directly address the question of whether the complaint had merit, although we later offer observations which bear on the points raised.[229] Also, as noted, the complainant in this case was a municipality, not a rival league. For our limited present purposes, that fact is not critical. Again, the complaint is quoted only to indicate the manner in which the issues might be framed.[230]

Pertinent portions of the *Buffalo* complaint are as follows:

> 21. The defendants herein ... are engaged in a joint venture [%12] commonly known as the "National Basketball Association" ("NBA").

---

222. American Football League v. National Football League, 205 F. Supp. 60 (D. Md. 1962), *aff'd,* 323 F.2d 124 (4th Cir. 1963). *See also* United States v. United Shoe Mach. Corp., 110 F. Supp. 295 (D. Mass. 1953), *aff'd per curiam,* 347 U.S. 521 (1954).

223. *See, e.g.,* United States v. Griffith, 334 U.S. 100, 107-08 (1948).

224. *See, e.g.,* United States v. Grinnell Corp., 384 U.S. 563 (1966); United States v. Griffith, 334 U.S. 100, 106 (1948); United States v. United Shoe Mach. Corp., 110 F. Supp. 295 (D. Mass 1953), *aff'd per curiam,* 347 U.S. 521 (1954).

225. *See* United States v. Grinnell Corp., 384 U.S. 563 (1966); Times-Picayune Publishing Co. v. United States, 345 U.S. 594 (1953); Lorain Journal Co. v. United States, 342 U.S. 143 (1951).

226. Civil No. 76-0261 (W.D.N.Y., filed June 15, 1976).

227. For background information on the case see Washington Post, Jan. 21, 1976, at D2, col. 3 (Buffalo Braves owner receives offer from Miami group); Globe & Mail (Toronto), Feb. 25, 1976, at 34, col. 1, (Toronto brewery interested in buying Buffalo Braves); N.Y. Times, June 15, 1976, at 47, col. 6 (Irving Cowan of Hollywood, Fla., owner of Diplomat Hotel, given option to purchase Buffalo Braves; NBA asked to approve shift to Fla.).

228. *See* Washington Post, July 7, 1976, at D3, col. 3 (City of Buffalo drops $10 million state suit; $48 million federal suit charging NBA with monopolistic practices in limbo).

229. Subsequent portions of these materials consider the objections which might be raised to a league's restrictions on player mobility (*see* text at notes 267-71 *infra*) and its prior practices with respect to mergers (*see* text at notes 300-02 *infra*).

230. The antitrust objections which might be raised by a municipality seeking to acquire or retain a sports franchise are treated in a subsequent part of this section. *See* text beginning at note 313, *infra*.

Since the inception of the NBA in 1946, defendants and their various predecessors in interest have presented professional basketball games and exhibitions throughout the United States. By reason of various practices set forth at paragraph 22, defendants have promoted and maintained a monopoly in the presentation of a type of professional basketball ... which has been recognized by the public at large as a form of sports entertainment which is separate and distinct from the entertainment offered by college, amateur, semi-professional, and other professional basketball teams, leagues or organizations.

22. Pursuant to various agreements, defendants ... have and continue to engage in a concerted effort to control, regulate and dictate the terms, conditions and locations in and at which major league professional basketball is played, to allocate and to divide the limited market consisting of the amateur basketball players with the potential to play major league professional basketball, and to perpetuate their monopoly by boycotts, blacklists, and concerted refusals to deal. The practices whereby these ends are effectuated include, but are not limited to:

(a) A draft procedure, whereby the negotiating rights to a college player are assigned to a specific defendant, thereby precluding such player from fully benefitting from competition for his services, and lowering the cost of said player's services to the defendants;

(b) A uniform contract, containing a reserve clause, which similarly limits the bargaining power of potential major league basketball players and enables the defendants to secure their services at an unreasonably low price;

(c) The enforcement of the aforesaid restrictions by boycotts of and refusals to deal with players who, though desirous of playing with another defendant on more advantageous terms or conditions, may not do so by reason of the aforesaid draft, reserve clause, or other anti-competitive arrangement. Upon information and belief, the defendants have enforced these practices by imposing penalties, including fines, upon each other;

(d) Negotiation of a merger with the American Basketball Association ("ABA"), a rival organization formed in 1967, which would further enhance the defendants' monopoly position in major league professional basketball; and

(e) The division of geographical markets amongst the defendants, whereby the presence of NBA basketball in each major advertising market is assured regardless of the lack of profitability of such location for the particular defendant.

23. By reason of the foregoing acts and other activities in which the defendants have engaged and continue to engage in concert, defendants ... , with the specific intent to achieve and to maintain their monopoly power, have achieved maintained a monopoly in the market for major league professional basketball, and precluded entry into that market by potential competitors such as, *inter alia,* the ABA, which has recently announced that its few surviving teams shall seek to merge into the NBA.

24. Defendants have combined and conspired to monopolize, have attempted to monopolize and have monopolized interstate commerce in major league professional basketball by engaging in the aforesaid predatory and anti-competitive conduct, in violation of Section 2 of the Sherman Act (15 U.S.C. Sec. 2). By reason of and in furtherance of such

violation by defendants, upon information and belief, plaintiff shall be injured in the manner hereinafter set forth.[231]

The theory of the quoted complaint is that most, if not all, of the cited restrictive practices are separate violations of the antitrust laws. Thus, the plaintiffs attempted to borrow upon the sports cases which had found the player restraints to be illegal restraints on trade under section 1.[232] In a similar vein, the reference to the ABA-NBA merger is intended to raise the possibility that the merger was illegal under the Clayton Act.[233] In the plaintiffs' view, defendants used these illegal devices to attain and perpetuate a monopoly position. The plaintiffs do not allege that they were directly injured by these secondary antitrust violations, but rather that these are evidence of the defendants' misuse of their market power and that the plaintiffs were injured by the monopoly conditions which resulted. The specific injury is the alleged exclusion of competition from which the plaintiffs would have benefitted.[234] Since the secondary antitrust violations are not "personal" to these particular plaintiffs, they could form the basis for a complaint by other parties as well, including a rival league which attempted to establish itself.

If a plaintiff can establish that activities such as those alleged in the *Buffalo* complaint are illegal and that they contributed substantially to the defendant's monopoly position, it will make out a colorable section 2 case under the traditional tests.[235] Whether the particular plaintiff has standing to raise the complaint or has been injured by the monopoly are, of course, separate questions which must be answered under other antitrust doctrine.

The general body of antitrust law suggests that a section 2 violation may be found even if the practices by which the monopoly is achieved are not actually illegal but only unfair. Such might be the case, for example, where the defendant undertakes to disparage a competitor's product, harass the competitor or those who deal with him, or engage in secretive activities not part of normal business practices.[236] The courts have not been entirely clear in defining the parameters of the actions which will be considered "unfair" in this context.[237] Nor have they clearly articulated the basis upon which "unfair" conduct is to be distinguished

231. Buffalo v. Atlanta Hawks, Inc., Civil No. 76-0261, Complaint at 5-8 (W.D.N.Y., filed June 15, 1976).

232. The player restraints used by the NBA were considered in Robertson v. National Basketball Ass'n, 389 F. Supp. 867 (S.D.N.Y. 1975), *subsequent proceeding,* 1975 Trade Cas. ¶ 60,448 (S.D.N.Y.). The court there expressed the view that the restraints were illegal, but did not actually decide the issue. This and other cases involving player restraints are discussed in §§ 5.03-.07 *supra.*

233. The *Robertson* case, 389 F. Supp. 867 (S.D.N.Y. 1975), *subsequent proceeding,* 1975 Trade Cas. ¶ 60,448 (S.D.N.Y.), first began as a proceeding by NBA players to contest the proposed merger between the NBA and the ABA. This merger also was the subject of congressional hearings. *Hearings on S. 2373 before the Subcomm. on Antitrust and Monopoly of the Senate Comm. on the Judiciary,* 92d Cong., 1st Sess. (1971).

234. The plaintiff in the *Buffalo* case apparently felt that if the professional basketball market had been more competitive so that a competing league could have operated, it would have been more likely that the city could find a suitable tenant for its arena. *See* text at note 377 *infra.*

235. *See* cases cited in notes 224-25 *supra. See generally* 16 VON KALINOWSKI § 8.02[4][a].

236. *See, e.g.,* L.G. Balfour Co. v. FTC, 442 F.2d 1 (7th Cir. 1971); Power Replacement Corp. v. Air Preheater Co., 356 F. Supp. 872 (E.D. Pa. 1973); Michigan Bar Review Center, Inc. v. Nexus Corp., 1971 Trade Cas. ¶ 73, 700 (E.D. Mich.). *See also* Packard Motor Car Co. v. Webster Motor Car Co., 243 F.2d 418 (D.C. Cir.), *cert. denied,* 355 U.S. 822 (1957).

237. *See* United States v. United Shoe Mach. Corp., 110 F. Supp. 295, 342 (D. Mass. 1953), *aff'd per curiam,* 347 U.S. 521 (1954).

from that found in the third class of cases considered below, those involving what might loosely be described as overly aggressive behavior. To the extent that a difference can be discerned, it lies in the quality of the behavior involved. Actions which are secretive, unethical, or predatory, as well as actions which are specifically directed to limiting competitors' opportunities,[238] are particularly apt to be categorized as "unfair" rather than merely over-aggressive.

(iii) *Activities which solidify the monopolist's market domination.* The most difficult applications of section 2 arise in cases in which there is no proof that the defendant either had a specific intent to monopolize or engaged in illegal or "unfair" activities to attain or perpetuate its monopoly position. Even when those elements are missing, the courts are prepared to find a section 2 violation if it can be established that a defendant with monopoly power pursued business practices (1) which had the effect of excluding or limiting competition and (2) which were not simply the result of the defendant's superior product or skill or some natural advantage.[239]

The case most frequently looked to for precedent in this area is *United States v. Aluminum Company of America.*[240] The defendant, Alcoa, was charged with monopolization of the market for domestic primary aluminum ingot. While Alcoa clearly controlled this market, there was no proof that it had engaged in practices which were "unfair" or illegal under other statutes or that it had a specific intent to drive out competition or otherwise monopolize. Nonetheless, the court concluded that Alcoa had violated section 2. Judge Learned Hand found that the defendant was not merely a passive recipient of its monopoly position, but rather showed a "persistent determination" to maintain its dominance in the domestic market.[241] As evidence of this, Hand pointed out that Alcoa had expanded its capacity more rapidly than market conditions justified.[242] It thus appeared that the firm consistently prepared itself to meet yet unrealized future demand and as a result discouraged the entry of new firms which might have otherwise been formed as the market for ingot expanded. Again, there was no proof that the defendant had any specific anti-competitive intent, but the effects of overly aggressive actions in maintaining its dominant position were, in Hand's view, as harmful as in cases where improper intent is proved.[243]

Courts in subsequent cases have used various characterizations to identify fact situations which involve the *Alcoa*-type violations. Thus, courts will look for evidence that the defendant's monopoly power was consciously attained or that its actions had the inevitable effect of solidifying legally-acquired monopoly power.[244] In the same vein, courts will ask whether the defendant's continued monopoly is simply the result of neutral factors such as superior skill, a superior

---

238. *See id.*
239. *See generally* 16-16A VON KALINOWSKI §§ 8.02[4][c], 9.03[1].
240. 148 F.2d 416 (2d Cir. 1945).
241. *Id.* at 430.
242. *Id.* at 431-32.
243. *Id.* at 432.
244. *See, e.g.,* Industrial Bldg. Materials, Inc. v. Interchemical Corp., 437 F.2d 1336 (9th Cir. 1970); Philadelphia World Hockey Club, Inc. v. Philadelphia Hockey Club, Inc., 351 F. Supp. 462, 510-13 (E.D. Pa. 1972); United States v. United Shoe Mach. Corp., 110 F. Supp. 295 (D. Mass. 1953), *aff'd per curiam,* 347 U.S. 521 (1954).

product, a legal license or a natural advantage.[245] Particular business decisions made by the defendant may be found not to be of a neutral character. For example, the defendant's decision to enter new markets, to lower prices, or to lease, rather than sell, its goods may be taken as evidence of a desire to perpetuate a dominant hold on the market.[246] Such non-neutral actions will often have the effect of discouraging entry and growth by competitors and will lead a court to conclude that section 2 has been violated. When a court finds that the defendant possesses monopoly power and that the operation of its business has deterred competition, it appears that the defendant's primary line of defense must be to establish that its market advantage was unavoidable given the inherent characteristics of its business and its products.

Unless read carefully, some precedents in this area might be interpreted to mean that large size alone establishes a section 2 violation.[247] If a firm holds an undisputed dominant position, possesses superior financial resources, and operates with an astute business sense, its mere presence in the market may discourage potential competitors from entering. Thus, in one sense, the continuation of the large size of the firm is an action which deters competition.[248] But where courts have confronted the question directly, they have generally been quick to disclaim any intention to find illegal monopolization on the basis of size alone.[249] Something more is needed to make out a case under section 2, and that additional ingredient is the pursuit of business policies which have the effect of injuring competition and for which there is no other neutral explanation.[250]

(iv) *Application in the sports industry.* The prior general discussion of the concept of misuse of monopoly power under section 2 may have important implications for the sports industry. The precise application of the doctrine will, of course, depend upon the proof of facts which will only be developed in the context of litigation. The motives for league expansion, the owners' attitudes toward rival leagues, and the nature of the sports market in particular cities are matters about which few firm facts are generally available.[251] While any analysis of the league's vulnerability under section 2 must be rather general, the parameters of future controversies in this area can be identified.

The section 2 doctrine discussed above is useful in explaining the venturesome footnote in *AFL v. NFL* quoted earlier. It will be recalled that the court said

---

245. *See, e.g.,* United States v. E.I. DuPont de Nemours & Co., 351 U.S. 377 (1956); Clark Marine Corp. v. Cargill, Inc., 226 F. Supp. 103 (E.D. La. 1964), *aff'd,* 345 F.2d 79 (5th Cir. 1965), *cert. denied,* 382 U.S. 1001 (1966); Greyhound Computer Corp. v. IBM Corp., 1972 Trade Cas. ¶ 74,205 (D. Ariz.).

246. *Compare* Industrial Bldg. Materials, Inc. v. Interchemical Corp., 437 F.2d 1336 (9th Cir. 1970) *and* United States v. United Shoe Mach. Corp., 110 F. Supp. 295 (D. Mass. 1953), *aff'd per curiam,* 347 U.S. 521 (1954) *with* United States v. E.I. DuPont de Nemours & Co., 351 U.S. 377 (1956) *and* Telex Corp. v. IBM Corp., 510 F.2d 894 (10th Cir. 1975).

247. *See, e.g.,* United States v. Grinnell Corp., 236 F. Supp. 244, 247-48 (D.R.I. 1964), *aff'd in part and remanded in part,* 384 U.S. 563 (1966).

248. *See* United States v. Swift & Co., 286 U.S. 106, 116 (1932) ("size carries with it an opportunity for abuse").

249. *See, e.g.,* United States v. United States Steel Corp., 251 U.S. 417 (1920). *See also* Telex Corp. v. IBM Corp., 510 F.2d 894 (10th Cir. 1975); Bailey's Bakery, Ltd. v. Continental Baking Co., 235 F. Supp. 705 (D. Hawaii 1964).

250. *See* cases cited in notes 244-46 *supra.*

251. *See* note 219 *supra.* An example of the detailed inquiry which may be made into how owners in an established league viewed the emergence of a rival can be found in American Football League v. National Football League, 205 F. Supp. 60, 65-75 (D. Md. 1962), *aff'd,* 323 F.2d 124 (4th Cir. 1963).

that *if* the NFL had been found to possess monopoly power, then the league's decision to locate expansion franchises in Dallas and Minneapolis "might well have" involved actual monopolization under section 2.[252] It is not entirely clear which branch of section 2 doctrine the court had in mind when it offered this assessment. Some may feel that the facts of the case should be treated under the *Alcoa* line of cases, in which the dominant party pursued business policies — here expansion into new markets — that had the effect of excluding competitors.[253] While the selection of the doctrinal framework is not critical to the ultimate conclusion reached, we would suggest that *AFL v. NFL* is more properly placed in the second category of cases identified above. In particular, it can be ventured that the older league's expansion into Dallas and Minneapolis, in the context in which it occurred, amounted to "unfair" conduct designed to further a monopoly. Again the choice of a pigeon-hole for the case is not of ultimate importance, but the suggested categorization can serve to clarify some of the nuances which appear in section 2 doctrine.

The *Alcoa* approach does not precisely fit the facts of *AFL v. NFL,* for there is a neutral explanation for the NFL's expansion into Dallas and Minneapolis. On an objective basis, those cities seemed to offer good possibilities for becoming viable football towns.[254] If the NFL were going to expand, it is logical that those locales would be among the first selected. Thus, unlike *Alcoa,* where the expansion of facilities was not wholly warranted by the neutral factor of market conditions, the location of NFL teams in Dallas and Minneapolis had an independent justification. The reason why the moves are a source of concern arises from other factors, and these relate more to the context in which the action was taken, rather than the specific action itself. There are several aspects of the NFL's decision which suggest that it was "unfair" to its competitor — the AFL. For example, the timing of the moves was especially disruptive. The AFL was in its formative stages and thus more vulnerable than it would have been at a later stage of its development. Moreover, the NFL's selection of new cities involved markets which the AFL was actively pursuing. The new league had already devoted considerable time investigating the two cities, talking with investors, and planning for franchises there.[255] When the NFL preempted these efforts, the AFL had to quickly make other arrangements for staffing its league and, accordingly, was set-back in its efforts to get underway.[256] Thus, while there was no proof that the NFL actually intended to frustrate the formation of the AFL, its first move toward expansion carried a strong implication to that effect.[257] At a minimum, the expression of concern by the district court in *AFL v. NFL* serves to underscore the fact that an established league must pay careful attention to the methods of competition it selects in its effort to retain preeminence.

252. 205 F. Supp. at 77 n.17.
253. *Compare* Philadelphia World Hockey Club, Inc. v. Philadelphia Hockey Club, Inc., 351 F. Supp. 462, 510-13 (E.D. Pa. 1972).
254. *See* 205 F. Supp. at 66-67.
255. *See id.* at 69-73.
256. *See id.* at 73-75.
257. *Cf.* Woods Exploration & Prod. Co. v. Aluminum Co. of America, 438 F.2d 1286 (5th Cir. 1971); Credit Bureau Reports, Inc. v. Retail Credit Co., 358 F. Supp. 780 (S.D. Tex. 1971), *aff'd,* 476 F.2d 989 (5th Cir. 1973); Michigan Bar Review Center, Inc. v. Nexus Corp., 1971 Trade Cas. ¶ 73,700 (E.D. Mich.).

If we turn our attention away from *AFL v. NFL* and look at the present situation in the professional sports industry, we see conditions suggesting somewhat different section 2 issues. As already mentioned, the recent history of professional football has seen a rather significant expansion in the degree of market penetration by the NFL. The league now has twenty-eight franchises located in twenty-six cities. Leagues in the other sports have similarly expanded to several new cities, and the number of potential franchise locations appears to have been reduced significantly. If a competing league were formed, could it raise a substantial antitrust objection to the expansion policies of the existing leagues? Again, because of limitations on available data — and because of the absence of an actual case — no firm conclusion can be ventured on this point. We can, however, identify some of the issues which should be pursued.

Alcoa suggests that it would be pertinent to ask whether the expansion policies of the potential-defendant league were undertaken in response to objective assessments of the various local markets.[258] If not, the recent, rapid expansion in several leagues might be viewed as evidence of a "persistent determination" on the part of the established league to maintain its preeminent position.[259] In this regard, it would be highly relevant to inquire into the details of the discussions and planning which preceded the league decision to expand.[260]

Precedents from other industries suggest that it is also relevant to inquire into the profitablility of the new operations. Such an inquiry is usually made to determine whether a firm's expansion into new markets was undertaken on normal business terms. If it is found that some aspects of the venture are operated for less than a normal rate of return, this is sometimes taken as evidence that the firm had engaged in cost-cutting or below-cost operations primarily for the purpose of preempting the particular market from competition and not for more neutral reasons.[261]

There is strong reason to believe that any such inquiry into the profitablility of new sports franchises will yield inconclusive results as far as a section 2 inquiry is concerned. Where new franchises are found to have marginal profitability, there is likely to be a vigorous debate about why this is so. In several leagues, the period of greatest expansion was followed by other events which so completely changed the financial picture of the sport that it would be difficult to reach a decision as to the economic motives at work. Among the post-expansion problems leagues faced were increases in player costs caused by liberalization of the player restraints, changes in federal laws removing some of the tax advantages of club ownership, and increases in operating costs due

---

258. It can be noted that one court suggested in 1968 that *Alcoa* was "the only case condemning internal expansion." *See* Hiland Dairy Co. v. Kroger Co., 402 F.2d 968, 976 (8th Cir. 1968). In addition, a highly knowledgeable commentator noted in 1976 that section 2 has not been widely applied with the full rigor that might be suggested by *Alcoa* and its progeny. *See* GELLHORN 156. However, those cases continue to have a considerable impact in particular situations, and there is at least one case suggesting their applicability to expansion by sports leagues. *See* Philadelphia World Hockey Club, Inc. v. Philadelphia Hockey Club, Inc., 351 F. Supp. 462, 510-13 (E.D. Pa. 1972).

259. *See* Philadelphia World Hockey Club, Inc. v. Philadelphia Hockey Club, Inc., 351 F. Supp. 462, 510-13 (E.D. Pa. 1972).

260. *See* note 251 *supra*.

261. *See, e.g.,* Greenville Publishing Co. v. Daily Reflector, Inc., 496 F.2d 391 (4th Cir. 1974); Credit Bureau Reports, Inc. v. Retail Credit Co., 358 F. Supp. 780 (S.D. Tex. 1971), *aff'd,* 476 F.2d 989 (5th Cir. 1973); Pacific Engineering & Prod. Co. v. Kerr-McKee Corp., 1974-1 Trade Cas. ¶ 75,054 (D. Utah).

to general economic inflation.[262] In addition, some leagues have had difficulty maintaining fan support and securing national television contracts.[263] In a particular case, these facts may so coalesce as to suggest that any attempt to analogize to *Alcoa* is misplaced. It may be found that there were such significant counter pressures to any attempt at overzealous market penetration that an antitrust violation, if it is to be found, must rest on other facts.

There is another general observation about league expansion policies that can be made. Any argument to the effect that a league has engaged in excessive market penetration must take account of the fact that the established leagues are often accused of doing just the opposite. Indeed, in the present period, this complaint is the one most frequently raised to the leagues' franchising practices. As a specific example, many politicians, and some citizens, decry the fact that professional baseball has refused to locate a franchise in Washington, D.C.[264] Some proponents of this view suggest that their lack of success in securing a franchise is evidence of the league's monopolistic powers.[265] On a more general level, there are commentators who accuse the leagues of impropriety in establishing excessive internal barriers to the granting of new franchises.[266] It is difficult to reconcile these criticisms with the view that excessive expansion has precluded the formation of new leagues. At a minimum, the complaints about the league's refusal to enter allegedly lucrative markets substantially undermines a contention that the same owners are purposely holding on to marginal franchises.

It will be recalled that the *Buffalo* complaint quoted above identified the defendant club's control of the player market as one point of evidence supporting the contention that the defendants had obtained their monopoly illegally. Even accepting that the traditional player controls were illegal under other antitrust principles,[267] it is by no means clear that this fact adds significant support to a contention by a rival league that the monopoly of the established clubs is illegal. The basic difficulty is that illegal control of the market for playing talent may do little to enhance the defendant's monopoly position as far as a *competing league* is concerned. It should be asked whether the player restraints made it

---

262. *See* authorities cited in note 211 *supra*.

263. *See* Lorges, Pro Hockey's Financial Woes Not a Joking Matter, Washington Post, Mar. 8, 1977, at D1, col. 1; Sporting News, Mar. 12, 1977, at 12, col. 1, (sharp attendance decline for NHL teams; failure to obtain network TV contract); *id.* Dec. 18, 1976, at 33, col. 1, (NHL attendance predicted to drop half-million for season); N.Y. Times, Nov. 16, 1976, at 50, col. 1, (only 5 NHL teams drawing capacity crowds); Sporting News, Jan. 26, 1974, at 6, col. 2 (ABA needs merger because of inability to attract top TV contract).

264. Representative B. F. Sisk has been a major critic of the failure of the professional baseball leagues to re-establish a club in the nation's capital. *See 1976 Hearings,* pt. 1, at 525-30; pt. 2, at 364-66, 469; Boswell, Panel Postpones Vote on Baseball Exemption, Washington Post, Dec. 11, 1976, at B1, col. 1; Sporting News, Jan. 1, 1977, at 13, col. 1 (Sisk and fellow Congressmen threaten baseball with antitrust legislation if major league team not put in Washington, D.C.); N.Y. Times, Dec. 2, 1971, at 61, col. 1 (U.S. Reprs. Sisk, Horton, Broyhill, and Price attend baseball owners meeting with petition to obtain franchise for D.C.; issue warning that franchise must be restored by 1973 or face possible federal antitrust legislation). *See also* American Enterprise Institute, Pro Sports: Should Government Intervene?, AEI Forum 9-10 (J. Daly, moderator, 1977) (remarks of Ed Garvey, Exec. Dir., NFLPA).

265. *See, e.g.,* American Enterprise Institute, Pro Sports: Should Government Intervene?, *supra* note 264, at 9-10 (remarks of Ed Garvey, Exec. Dir., NFLPA).

266. *See, e.g.,* Noll, *Alternatives in Sports Policy* in GOVERNMENT AND THE SPORTS BUSINESS 411, 412-15 (R. Noll ed. 1974).

267. *See generally* § 5.07 *supra*.

more difficult for the rival to establish itself. In many situations, the answer will be that the restraints had only intra-league effects and did not significantly limit the players' freedom to play for clubs in other leagues. For example, a draft system may operate to require the athlete to play for only one club in the league, but as these systems have historically operated, they have not limited the availability of players to competing leagues.[268] As to post-draft player restrictions, serious inter-league mobility problems arise only where the league uses a perpetual reserve clause such as that formerly used in hockey.[269] Where the league had only an option arrangement, as in football, a competing league could still have reasonable access to veteran players.[270] If such access is found, any illegality which might arise between the established league and its players would appear to be somewhat beside the point as far as a competing enterprise is concerned.[271]

The foregoing is intended to suggest a few of the problems that a competing league will confront in attempting to establish a section 2 violation on the part of present leagues. The preceding review is far from exhaustive, however. In addition to the points mentioned, the plaintiff can appropriately give attention not only to the specific facts concerning the defendant's franchising activities, but also evidence bearing on its arrangements with broadcasters, stadium owners, and advertisers. Whether such an inquiry will uncover major areas of vulnerability cannot be forecast, of course. In one respect, however, the plaintiffs should find themselves in a better position than the complaining parties in *AFL v. NFL*. The question of the defendant's monopoly power was the major hurdle in that litigation. As has already been suggested, under the present situation in most sports leagues, that issue might receive a different resolution than was given in the AFL's suit. In that event, the court should be open to taking a closer look at evidence suggesting that there had been a misuse of market power.

2. *The Natural Monopoly Theory.*

Section 2 is most frequently applied in fact situations in which the relevant market is capable of supporting several different competing firms. In this context, the statute has the clear purpose of insuring that the competitive conditions of the market are preserved, and it is fair to say that national policy favors having more, rather than fewer, competitors. However, it must be recognized that for some markets, the assumption that many different firms will, or should, operate is not entirely realistic. Indeed, there are situations in which the market naturally lends itself to monopoly conditions. In these instances, it is necessary to make some adjustments in our expectations about the type of competition which will occur.

The fact that a market tends toward natural monopoly does not mean that we abandon our goal of preserving the conditions for competition. That is, the firm which holds a natural monopoly is not allowed to run away with the cookie

---

268. *See* American Football League v. National Football League, 205 F. Supp. 60 (D. Md. 1962), *aff'd,* 323 F.2d 124 (4th Cir. 1963). *Cf.* Detroit Football Co. v. Robinson, 186 F. Supp. 933 (E.D. La.), *aff'd,* 283 F.2d 657 (5th Cir. 1960); Los Angeles Rams v. Cannon, 185 F. Supp. 717 (S.D. Cal. 1960).

269. *See* Philadelphia World Hockey Club, Inc. v. Philadelphia Hockey Club, Inc., 351 F. Supp. 462 (E.D. Pa. 1972).

270. *See* American Football League v. National Football League, 205 F. Supp. 60 (D. Md. 1962), *aff'd,* 323 F.2d 124 (4th Cir. 1963).

271. *See generally* § 4.03 *supra.*

jar. We can still expect that there may be competition among firms to determine who will control the market. Thus, it is appropriate to impose legal limitations to insure that no firm advances its position unfairly.[272] In short, the battle among the potential monopolists must be a fair one and neither side may resort to tactics which unduly restrict its opponent's right to establish superiority.

As has been suggested, there is an argument to be made that the markets in which the major sports leagues operate lend themselves to natural monopolies.[273] It is appropriate that we spend a few paragraphs indicating why this may be so and suggesting the implications which this has for antitrust policy in the sports area. We will see that even if we find that natural monopoly conditions exist in the sports industry, the legal results will not necessarily be dramatically different from those which obtain under the traditional section 2 test. Again, the major impact of the natural monopoly theory is that it may prompt courts to take a somewhat more restrained view of some of the competitive tactics used by sports leagues.

To begin, it may be useful to say a word about how the term *natural monopoly* is being used here. In the cases decided under section 2, that term, rightly or wrongly, has been applied to a variety of different situations. For example, some courts suggest that a manufacturer enjoys a natural monopoly with respect to his name brand products.[274] In a similar view, it is often said that one who holds a patent has a legal monopoly.[275] In other situations, the terms natural, or legal, monopoly may be used to describe the situation in which a firm has been able to apply its superior skill or industry to gain a monopoly position in a market which could otherwise support several firms.[276] None of these uses of the natural monopoly concept describes the type of situation which is the focus of our inquiry here. We will be concerned with monopolies which are *natural* in the sense that they are not created by legal license, as is true of the monopolies resulting from trademarks and patents. In addition, and more importantly, we want to raise the question as to whether the conditions of the sports market are not such that is it likely that only one major professional league will survive. If this is true, our situation is different from that involving an otherwise competitive market which has been captured by a single firm with unique skill or industry.

Courts have recognized that there may be markets of the sort with which we will be concerned. Although not wholly analogous to our case, the most convenient example of such a situation is the newspaper market in small towns.

---

272. *See, e.g.,* American Football League v. National Football League, 323 F.2d 124, 131 (4th Cir. 1963); Union Leader Corp. v. Newspapers of New England, Inc., 284 F.2d 582 (1st Cir. 1960), *cert. denied,* 365 U.S. 833 (1961).

273. *See* text at note 183 *supra.* Others have mentioned the natural monopoly concept in the context of league sports. *See* American Enterprise Institute, Pro Sports: Should Government Intervene?, AEI Forum 11-12 (J. Daly, moderator, 1977) (remarks of Rep. Jack Kemp). *See also* note 183 *supra.*

274. *See, e.g.,* Industrial Bldg. Materials, Inc. v. Interchemical Corp., 278 F. Supp. 938, 958 (C.D. Cal. 1967), *rev'd,* 437 F.2d 1336 (9th Cir. 1970), *quoting,* Schwing Motor Co. v. Hudson Sales Corp., 138 F. Supp. 899, 902 (D. Md.), *aff'd per curiam,* 239 F.2d 176 (4th Cir. 1956), *cert. denied,* 355 U.S. 823, 78 S. Ct. 30, 2 L. Ed. 2d 38 (1957).

275. *See, e.g.,* 16A VON KALINOWSKI, § 9.03[2].

276. *See, e.g.,* United States v. E.I. DuPont de Nemours & Co., 351 U.S. 377 (1956); United States v. Aluminum Co. of America, 148 F.2d 416 (2d Cir. 1945); Greyhound Computer Corp. v. IBM Corp., 1972 Trade Cas. ¶ 74,205 (D. Ariz.).

Because of the small potential readership and the relative high costs of production, it is accepted that some towns are capable of supporting only a single paper.[277] Thus, while there may be vigorous competition to determine which paper survives, it is wholly natural that one firm may eventually achieve a monopoly position.

Before beginning our investigation of the relevance of the natural monopoly theory for the sports industry, it may be useful to state more precisely the point we will seek to make. It is not clear that the data presently available yields an unequivocal conclusion that the markets for the major professional sports are capable of sustaining only one league. But there are facts available which will support a somewhat more guarded version of this same hypothesis. Specifically, it can be suggested that the conditions in the major sports markets are such that those markets will *tend to be* dominated by a single firm. Whether a situation might ever evolve in which two leagues achieve parity *and* resist merger is a point we will not attempt to refute here. Our purpose is the more limited one of indicating why the courts and the public ought to be prepared to accept the general tendency toward single league dominance in the various sports.

It should be noted that the proposition put forth here runs counter to views emanating from several authoritative sources. For example, one of the leading law review commentaries on the legal problems of the sports industry has suggested that judicial policies should be structured "to encourage the creation and success of new leagues." [278] The authors concluded that the presence of competing leagues might be the most efficient mechanism for rectifying some of the undesirable conditions that they perceived to exist with respect to limitations on player mobility and restrictions on franchise ownership.[279] Similar optimism about the prospects for inter-league competition was expressed by a representative of the Justice Department, Antitrust Division, in testimony before a special congressional committee investigating professional sports.[280] But if the thesis developed in the present discussion is correct, one might well conclude that it is too much to expect that competition among leagues will be the vehicle through which the operations of the dominant clubs are made more responsive to the perceived needs of players, fans and investors. It is likely that such competition will exist from time to time, but any expectation that the sports industry will experience the same level of competition found in most other segments of the economy may be unrealistic. The devotion of great judicial or governmental energies to this goal may thus be misplaced.

What evidence is there to suggest that sports markets will evolve to sustain the dominance of a single league? Perhaps the most persuasive data come from the historical record. Each of the four major professional sports has gone through periods in which a new league was formed to challenge the dominance

---

277. Union Leader Corp. v. Newspapers of New England, Inc., 284 F.2d 582 (lst Cir. 1960), *cert. denied,* 365 U.S. 833 (1961); United States v. Harte-Hanks Newspapers, Inc., 170 F. Supp. 227 (N.D. Tex. 1959).

278. Comment, *The Super Bowl and the Sherman Act: Professional Team Sports and the Antitrust Laws,* 81 HARV. L. REV. 418, 430 (1967).

279. *Id.* at 430-34.

280. *See 1976 Hearings,* pt. 2, at 292-95 (testimony of Joe Sims, Deputy Ass't Att'y Gen., Antitrust Div., Dept. of Justice).

of the established organization, and in none of these instances did the rival sustain itself as a viable, wholly distinct competitor for a long period of time.[281] The reasons for the demise of direct competition varied from case to case. In some situations, the rival league simply ran out of money;[282] in others, the two leagues merged or entered into other forms of agreement eliminating competition between them.[283] In each case, though, the ultimate result was the same, and the free market model for the production of professional sports was refuted.

One must be quick to point out that the elimination of competition was not always the product of purely natural forces. In some instances, the dominant leagues engaged in behavior which appeared to be of the sort subject to control under the antitrust laws.[284] But the frequency with which the notion of inter-league competition has proven itself to be a short-lived phenomenon strongly suggests that there are other, more neutral factors at work.

There are a number of explanations for why the sports markets have tended to favor single leagues. If one looks generally at the role of the major sports in American society, a rather definite hierarchical structure can be identified. Each sport is played at several different levels, beginning with sandlot games and ranging up through various stages of amateurism to the pinnacle of professional sports. In this system, fans come to expect that there will be a level at which the sport is played at its very best, and at which the best talent is gathered together in the best facilities to compete under the best conditions.[285]

281. See generally 1976 Hearings, pt. 2, at 292-98 (testimony of Joe Sims, Deputy Ass't Att'y Gen., Antitrust Div., Dept. of Justice); Hearings on S. 2373 before the Subcomm. on Antitrust and Monopoly of the Senate Comm. on the Judiciary, 92d Cong., 1st Sess. (1971) (ABA-NBA merger); S. REP. NO. 1654, 89th Cong., 2d Sess. (1966), 1966 U.S. Code & Admin. News 4378 (AFL-NFL merger); DEMMERT 18; Davis, Self-Regulation in Baseball, 1909-71 in GOVERNMENT AND THE SPORTS BUSINESS 349, 371-75 (R. Noll ed. 1974); Noll, The U.S. Team Sports Industry: An Introduction in id. 1, 13-29; Rivkin, Sports Leagues and the Federal Antitrust Laws, in id. 387, 404-09; Morris, In the Wake of the Flood, 38 LAW & CONTEMP. PROB. 85, 96-97 (1973); Neale, The Peculiar Economics of Professional Sports, 78 Q.J. ECON. 1, 5-8 (1964); Comment, The Super Bowl and the Sherman Act: Professional Team Sports and the Antitrust Laws, supra note 278 at 430-34; Hockey News, July, 1977, at 3, col. 1 (NHL plan for merger with six WHA teams); N.Y. Times, June 25, 1977, at 13, col. 1 (NHL plan for merger with six WHA teams).

282. See Sporting News, Nov. 8, 1975, at 6, col. 1 (cites amount of WFL debts and NFL resolution for eligibility of WFL players); N.Y. Times, Oct. 23, 1975, at 51, col. 1 (collapse of WFL due to financial problems); Los Angeles Times, Oct. 23, 1975, pt. III, at 1, col. 1 (WFL folds as result of debts and losses in excess of $30 million).

283. This was true in the case of the AFL-NFL and the ABA-NBA, and appears to be the likely future of the WHA-NHL.

284. For example, the circumstances under which the National League overcame the competitive threat of the Federal Baseball League seems to raise important antitrust questions. See generally H. REP. NO. 2002, Organized Baseball, 82d Cong., 2d Sess. 16-50 (1952); § 5.02 supra. However, the litigation which resulted from this controversy led to the first Supreme Court ruling exempting baseball from the coverage of the antitrust laws. See Federal Baseball Club v. National League of Professional Baseball Clubs, 259 U.S. 200 (1922), aff'g 269 F. 681 (D.C. Cir. 1921).

285. See J. MICHENER, SPORTS IN AMERICA 93-119, 277-83 (1976). Cf. International Boxing Club, Inc. v. United States, 358 U.S. 242, 250 (1959) (championship boxing, as opposed to other forms of professional boxing, found to constitute a "separate, identifiable market").

An objection may be raised that one can have several leagues and that these leagues are, or should be, competing firms. As one surveys the history and present state of the sporting trades one must admit the possibility, but one must also recognize that as a matter of observation there appears to be a strong tendency toward a single league, and this for one good reason: only a single league can produce the most useful of all (joint products), the World Champion. Neale, The Peculiar Economics of Professional Sports, supra note 281, at 6.

Professional sports attempts to provide this premier competition and devotes considerable energy to insuring that the fans' expectations are fulfilled. Two different leagues may vie to see which in fact has the best product, but it is likely that the fans will eventually decide that one or the other has reached the pinnacle.[286] When that happens, it can be expected that fan support will shift toward the preferred league and away from the contender.

Those who purchase the broadcast rights for sports events can be expected to follow the fans' preferences. The broadcasters will have the keenest interest in the games of the league perceived as offering the best sports competition.[287] As the fans' support shifts towards one league or the other, the broadcasters' bids for television rights are likely to follow. A second league may still have some television appeal, but it is likely to find that it receives lower royalty payments and that it has to compete with Saturday afternoon wildlife shows.

The worst thing that can happen to a rival league is to have its product branded as inferior to that of its competitors.[288] Once that label is attached — by sports commentators, fans or advertisers — the prevailing notion of the hierarchical nature of sports competition begins to take hold, and the league is likely to face a snow-balling process eventually relegating it to a position somewhere between the major and semi-professional leagues. Refuting this image, as well as overcoming it initially, can be very expensive. The costs of acquiring star players, attracting a respectable at-home attendance, and securing adequate news coverage requires resources that may not be available from the operation itself. Even if the league were to succeed in improving its stature, the effect will not be to insure long-term competition, but only to shift the burden of establishing credibility to the other league. The ultimate outcome is likely to be that which we have seen before — one league will predominate and the other will disappear or be absorbed.

Limitations on the availability of franchise locations also serve to bolster the dominance that single leagues seem to enjoy. The limitations are of two types: there are only a limited number of cities capable of supporting a professional team, and further, there is considerable variance in the relative attractiveness of these locales.[289] Typically, a new league appears on the scene after another league has firmly established itself. It is increasingly true that the older league has so penetrated the market that there are few viable cities left. Since a firm must have franchise locations in a minimum number of cities if it is to offer true "league" competition,[290] the new entrant may find that there simply are not a sufficient number of unclaimed cities available. But more importantly, even if there are, many of those cities are likely to be of marginal quality in terms of

286. *See* Comment, *The Super Bowl and the Sherman Act: Professional Team Sports and the Antitrust Laws, supra* note 278, at 432.

287. *See* International Boxing Club, Inc. v. United States, 358 U.S. 242, 250-51 (1959).

288. *See* Red, White and Who?, Sports Illustrated, Oct. 4, 1971, at 20-23; ABA Competition Will be Stimulating but the Quality Is Second Best, *id.,* Sept. 22, 1969, at 30-32; Super Flop I, N.Y. Times Magazine, Jan. 12, 1975, at 10-11 (WFL lack of support).

289. *See* American Football League v. National Football League, 205 F. Supp. 60 (D. Md. 1962), aff'd, 323 F.2d 124 (4th Cir. 1963); Philadelphia World Hockey Club, Inc. v. Philadelphia Hockey Club, Inc., 351 F. Supp. 462 (E.D. Pa. 1972). *See generally* Quirk & El Hodiri, *The Economic Theory of a Professional Sports League* in GOVERNMENT AND THE SPORTS BUSINESS 33 (R. Noll ed. 1974).

290. *See* American Football League v. National Football League, 205 F. Supp. 60, 62, 76 (D. Md. 1962), aff'd, 323 F.2d 124 (4th Cir. 1963).

their ability to support a club. The established league will almost always have placed teams in the largest metropolitan areas, and while the new organization could attempt to share those local markets, there are presently few large cities capable of supporting a second or third team.

A league's ability to locate in at least some of the four or five largest metropolitan areas may be critical to its existence. Because of the very active sports press in those locales, an organization which is not anchored there runs a serious risk of being characterized as a bush league operation. Moreover, a league needs to have some claim to the television viewing audiences in the largest cities if it is to be successful in securing a national network contract. Finally, it is becoming increasingly apparent that the success of a league depends upon a good deal of subsidization among the member clubs.[291] While there are few hard figures available to confirm this proposition, it is likely that clubs located in the largest metropolitan markets provide a larger share of the subsidy than those in more marginal locales.[292] Again, if the older league has already claimed the major rewards to be gained from the most lucrative markets, that factor may operate as a substantial deterrent to the formation of a rival organization.

Assuming that a case can be made that professional sports tend to be naturally monopolistic, it remains to be determined how that fact will affect our antitrust analysis. As already mentioned, the fact that a firm operates in a market with monopolistic tendencies does not mean that it is freed from antitrust controls.[293] The case law which has developed with respect to natural monopolies provides guidance on the type of constraints which will be imposed. Many of these are simply more particularized applications of the traditional section 2 tests.[294] For example, the courts will look closely at how a firm's market power was obtained. A firm may take full advantage of its monopoly power as long as that power was acquired "by means which are neither exclusionary, unfair, nor predatory." [295] Of particular concern is the matter of how two firms conduct themselves as they are battling to see which will end up with control of the market.[296] In these instances the courts accept that one of the combatants may be driven out of business. To reiterate a point made earlier, the role of the courts appears to be that of a referee indifferent as to which party will prevail but concerned that the fight be conducted fairly. The existing cases give an indication of the methods of competition that will be regarded as "unfair." While the doctrine in this area is not yet fully developed, it appears that "unfairness" in this context has many of the same characteristics attributed to that concept under the traditional section 2 tests discussed above.[297] Thus, practices merely indicating bold and aggressive competitive behavior will not be condemned. On the other hand, the firm seeking to establish itself as a monopolist must avoid actions that are secretive or that involve misrepresentations. Particularly suspect are attempts to align outsiders with one's cause by means of secret

291. See text at notes 137-45.

292. See generally Quirk & El Hodiri, The Economic Theory of a Professional Sports League, supra note 289.

293. See text at notes 178-82, supra.

294. Those tests are discussed in the text accompanying notes 184-250 supra.

295. American Football League v. National Football League, 323 F.2d 124, 131 (4th Cir. 1963).

296. See, e.g., Union Leader Corp. v. Newspapers of New England, Inc., 284 F.2d 582 (1st Cir. 1960), cert. denied, 365 U.S. 833 (1961).

297. See text at notes 224-38 supra.

rebates or to develop such alignments under circumstances which might mislead third-parties as to the reasons for the outsiders' involvement.[298] And, of course, it would be "unfair" for one of the competitors to resort to boycotts or restraints that were illegal under other antitrust laws.[299]

It bears repeating that if courts accept that sports leagues operate in natural monopoly conditions, the results of an antitrust inquiry would not necessarily be markedly different from those which would flow from an application of the traditional section 2 tests. What can be suggested, however, is that the court's view of whether the market is capable of sustaining several competing firms may influence the characterization given to some league actions. This is particularly true with respect to a league's prior history of absorbing rivals by merger.[300] In other industries, a plaintiff may seek to support its section 2 complaint by showing that the defendant eliminated potential competitors by buy-outs or mergers. In some circumstances, the courts accept this as evidence that the defendant acquired its monopoly position improperly or otherwise misused its market power.[301] Where sports leagues or other natural monopolies are involved, however, such a history of mergers must be approached with a great deal of caution. There may be an entirely neutral explanation for why the second league did not survive — in particular, the fact that the market is incapable of supporting long-term competition.[302] Again, a prior history of acquiring competitors has more troublesome implications in markets where multiple firm competition is a realistic goal. When that goal is not attainable, it is appropriate for courts to be less suspicious of activities leading to consolidation and cooperation.

The theory of a sports league as a natural monopoly may also have some implications for the view taken of league expansion policies. The issue here is perhaps most easily framed by a reference to a suggestion put forth — albeit somewhat tentatively — in the law review commentary referred to earlier. As noted, the authors of the comment suggest that judicial energies should be devoted to encouraging "the creation and success of new leagues." [303] In developing that suggestion, reference is made to the role which the *Alcoa* case might play in this area. The authors state that Judge Hand's opinion "may be read as holding that Alcoa's policy of expanding as fast as the market grew was illegal; Alcoa — as a monopoly — apparently had a duty to leave part of the demand unsupplied in order to encourage competitors." [304] The authors then suggest how this notion might be applied to the expansion practices of a sports

298. *See, e.g.,* Union Leader Corp. v. Newspapers of New England, Inc., 284 F.2d 582 (1st Cir. 1960), *cert. denied,* 365 U.S. 833 (1961). *See also* United States v. Harte-Hanks Newspapers, Inc., 170 F. Supp. 227 (N.D. Tex. 1959).

299. *See* text at notes 224-34 *supra.*

300. It will be recalled that the NBA's prior merger with the ABA was one of the points raised by the plaintiff in the *Buffalo* case. The plaintiff suggested that the merger was an action intended to establish or perpetuate the defendant's alleged monopoly. *See* text at notes 230-31 *supra.*

301. *See e.g.,* United States v. Grinnell Corp., 384 U.S. 563 (1966); Credit Bureau Reports, Inc. v. Retail Credit Co., 358 F. Supp. 780 (S.D. Tex. 1971), *aff'd,* 476 F.2d 989 (5th Cir. 1973).

302. *See* text at notes 281-92 *supra. See generally* Neale, *The Peculiar Economics of Professional Sports,* 78 Q.J. ECON. 1, 4-9 (1964).

303. Comment *The Super Bowl and the Sherman Act: Professional Team Sports and the Antitrust Laws,* 81 HARV. L. REV. 418, 430 (1967).

304. *Id.* at 431.

league. It is observed that "if this somewhat extreme interpretation of *Alcoa* were followed, an existing league would be required to refrain from expansion into new cities or from increasing TV coverage when such actions would preempt part of the market which the new league sought to enter." [305]

Our response is to concur in part and dissent in part. It would seem to make some difference whether the "new league" is actually in existence. If the case supposed is one of which the new venture is locked into head-to-head competition with an established league, then the facts would not be dissimilar to those addressed in the suggestive footnote in *AFL v. NFL*. We have already indicated the grounds upon which an antitrust violation might be found where an established league quickly expands to usurp new territories upon which a new entrant has specific designs.[306]

A different analysis may be called for where the issue arises in the context in which a section 2 plaintiff is complaining about past expansion practices undertaken when there was no rival league on the scene. There seems to be little basis for suggesting that a league must forego expansion in the expectation that a competitor might some day appear. This is not only unnatural, but also may work to the detriment of legitimate public interests.[307] The practical effect of a league's passing up expansion opportunities will be to deny certain citizens — those in potential expansion cities — the right to enjoy live athletic performances. In addition, a failure to expand may mean that the league's revenue opportunities are not fully exploited and that the quality of its product is thus less than it would have otherwise been. Finally, purposeful non-expansion may lead to reduced employment opportunities for professional athletes.[308]

What the proponents of this view may have expected, of course, is that another league would develop to offer increased spectator opportunities, player employment, and so on.[309] But there are a number of difficulties with that assumption, all of which stem from the fact that the market may be naturally monopolistic. Thus, even without further expansion by the dominant league, the remaining market may be so meager as to discourage new entrants. Or the conditions may be such that a new entrant does appear, but is so short-lived, that it leaves a trail of frustration and bankruptcy which sets back some of the cities' prospects of securing a sports team. In short, it is not clear than an *a priori* policy of requiring that the door be left open for a competitor is either realistic or desirable.[310] It seems preferable that courts be prepared to accept the expansion policies of the natural monopolies as long as they are free of any hint of a purpose to frustrate competition which is known or immediately anticipated.

---

305. *Id.*

306. *See* text at notes 252-57 *supra*.

307. *See* Bork, *Ancillary Restraints and the Sherman Act,* 15 ABA ANTITRUST SECTION 211, 233 (1959). *But see* Philadelphia World Hockey Club, Inc. v. Philadelphia Hockey Club, Inc., 351 F. Supp. 462, 510-13 (E.D. Pa. 1972).

308. *See generally* American Enterprise Institute, Pro Sports: Should Government Intervene?, AEI Forum 8-12, 18-21, 38-40 (J. Daly, moderator, 1977) (various commentators).

309. *See, e.g.,* Comment, *The Super Bowl and the Sherman Act: Professional Team Sports and the Antitrust Laws, supra* note 303, at 432-33.

310. *See generally* Neale, *The Peculiar Economics of Professional Sports, supra* note 302. *But see* Philadelphia World Hockey Club, Inc. v. Philadelphia Hockey Club, Inc., 351 F. Supp 462, 510-13 (E.D. Pa. 1972).

3. Concluding Comments on the Antitrust Complaints of Rival Leagues.

The prior discussion of the application of the antitrust laws to interleague rivalries can be concluded by a few observations which, hopefully, appear obvious in light of what has been said. The basic point to be made is that the range of lively issues in these cases is narrower than might first appear. A casual look at the history of inter-league rivalries in most sports may lead one to conclude that the dominant leagues have exercised too much power over their challengers. No rival has survived intact, and many have gone down with heavy losses for their investors. Moreover, the dominant leagues have usually gone on to expand their control of the market, thereby reducing the chances that they will be seriously challenged again. And at the bottom line, the market for sports franchises does not appear to be very competitive. Leagues locate franchises where they want to and seemingly refuse to authorize clubs for cities desiring them.

To many observers, this situation may appear to present a classic case of the monopoly power that the antitrust laws were presumably designed to rein in.[311] One of the conclusions to be drawn from the foregoing is that the first part of this observation is probably correct — sports leagues are monopolistic in the economic sense of that term. But whether they are subject to legal sanction is a different matter. It is necessary to separate several critical issues which must be answered before a conclusion can be reached on that ultimate conclusion.[312] As far as the interests of a rival league are concerned, the most important legal issues arise not from the fact that the dominant league possesses a monopoly but from subsidiary facts bearing on such questions as, how did the established league acquire its monopoly? How did it treat rivals when they appeared? What factors influenced its expansion policies? And has it taken unnecessary liberties with the tremendous power it possesses? In the prior discussion we have attempted to identify the doctrine which will be applied to expose a league's vulnerability on these points. There clearly are some circumstances in which a good section 2 claim can be made. But a plaintiff's success in this regard will

---

311. *Mr. Horton* [Congressman].

    [i]t seems to me that there is a broad general question as to whether or not [professional sports] really are subject to the antitrust laws.

    I realize that we say they are, but the possibility of creating a new league or the possibility of creating any competitive advantage to a new league or the possibility of establishing a new league is almost non-existent . . . .

    It seems to me as though they are just as monopolistic as baseball is.
    . . . .

Mr. Sims [Deputy Ass't Att'y Gen., Antitrust Div., Dept. of Justice].

    The fact that it is difficult, the fact that there are entry barriers into a particular industry, does not indicate that there will be for all time a monopoly.

    In addition, it certainly doesn't indicate that there is an illegal monopoly. To be guilty of monopolization under the antitrust laws, you not only have to maintain or create a monopoly but you have to do something to create or maintain that monopoly which is not an honest industrial practice.

Mr. Horton

    The point I am trying to make is regardless of how you slice the baloney, it is still baloney . . . . *1976 Hearings* pt. 2, at 292-94.

312. *See* note 311 *supra.*

require that it do more than raise general complaints about the strength of the defendant's market position.

c. Antitrust Complaints by Municipalities and Local Investors.

When a city loses a professional sports franchise, there are many local interests which may be adversely affected. In most sports, franchises have a significant effect upon the local economy.[313] The franchise itself will usually make significant expenditures for wages, concession supplies, and various supporting services. In addition, it will attract large numbers of people to the city who will spend money with local merchants. The city's economic interest may be even more direct, as in cases in which it gains revenues from income or entertainment taxes or from rentals on a municipally-owned stadium used by the local club.[314] When the franchise departs, the city is likely to find that its disappointment is shared by a variety of merchants and business people as well as by the local fans who formerly took great interest in the fortunes of "their" team. The present subsection considers whether this disappointment can be translated into substantial antitrust objections.

Over the years, there have been several instances in which a club's decision to leave a city has been contested in litigation sponsored by local interests.[315] However, these lawsuits generally provide little guidance in defining the application of the antitrust laws in this area. In some of the suits, the controversies focused on the clubs' obligations under unexpired long-term leases

---

313. *See, e.g.,* Wisconsin v. Milwaukee Braves, Inc., 1966 Trade Cas. ¶ 71,738 at 82,375-377 (Wis. Cir. Ct.), *rev'd,* 31 Wis. 2d 699, 144 N.W.2d 1 (1966) (detailed findings concerning the value of the defendant's franchise to the local economy). *See generally* Okner, *Subsidies of Stadiums and Arenas* in GOVERNMENT AND THE SPORTS BUSINESS 325, 327-30 (R. Noll. ed. 1974).

314. *See* Okner, *Subsidies of Stadiums and Arenas, supra* note 313; Scannell, Pros Bully Municipal Landlords, Washington Post, Apr. 24, 1977, at D4, col. 1. *See also* New York City v. New York Jets Football Club, Inc., 429 F. Supp. 987 (S.D.N.Y. 1977); Buffalo v. Atlanta Hawks Basketball, Inc., Civil No. 76-0261 (W.D.N.Y., June 15, 1976) (discussed at notes 226-34 *supra*); San Diego v. National League of Professional Baseball Clubs, Docket No. 343508 (Cal. Super. Ct., July 10, 1973) (preliminary injunction denied), *aff'd,* Docket No. 12741 (Cal. Ct. App., July 19, 1973) (discussed in L. SOBEL, PROFESSIONAL SPORTS AND THE LAW 513-33 (1977)).

Another unreported case in which a city sought to enforce its stadium leases against a departing club involved the city of San Francisco and the baseball Giants, who were threatening to move to Toronto. The city was able to secure an injunction against the proposed move. *See* Washington Post, Feb. 12, 1976, at C1, col. 7 (injunction issued; *id.,* Feb. 4, 1976, at D1, col. 3 (temporary stay issued.) *See generally* R. Smith, Have Baseball Club, Will Travel, N.Y. Times, Jan. 16, 1976, at 13, col. 2; L. Koppett, Drastic Changes Loom in Baseball, *id.,* Feb. 18, 1976, at 35, col. 1.

Another celebrated case involved the complaints raised by the city of Seattle when the old Seattle Pilots became the Milwaukee Brewers in 1970. The plaintiff's complaint involved several different issues. One point of contention centered on allegations that the city had relied upon promises made by the club about its permanency and had committed itself to financing stadium construction. The American League eventually awarded a new franchise to the city for the 1977 season. For background on the Seattle case, see N.Y. Times, Jan. 24, 1970, at 36, col. 8 (Seattle mayor seeks injunction to bar move); *id.,* Mar. 17, 1970, at 50, col. 1 (State of Washington and City of Seattle get restraining order to bar shift; federal antitrust suit filed against AL); *id.,* Sept. 25, 1975, at 57, col. 1 (American League discussion of franchise for Seattle) *id.,* Jan. 15, 1976, at 41, col. 6 (American League votes to add Seattle franchise); *id.,* Feb. 6, 1976, at 16, col. 5 (negotiations concerning franchise); *id.,* Feb. 10, 1976, at 48, col. 3 (Seattle trial recessed pending settlement talks); *id.,* Feb 14, 1976, at 16, col. 7 (Seattle agrees to settle suit). *See also* Washington v. American League of Professional Baseball Clubs, 460 F.2d 654 (9th Cir. 1972).

315. *See* authorities cited *id.*

involving a municipally-owned stadium.[316] Even where the plaintiff did raise antitrust objections, the resolution of these was often not definitive, for it frequently occurred that the parties were able to reach a settlement before the merits of the antitrust claims were considered. In one case, *Wisconsin v. Milwaukee Braves, Inc.,*[317] a lower state court did consider a complaint based on state antitrust law and held the plaintiff's objections to be valid. However, its decision, resting on several questionable doctrinal premises, was never implemented.[318] A reviewing court found that the state tribunal had no authority to consider the case, for the subject matter was one over which the federal courts had exclusive jurisdiction.[319] Thus, while the not infrequent occurrence of the litigation confirms that local interest may be inclined to contest the loss of a franchise, it remains to be seen whether the federal antitrust laws provide an appropriate vehicle for a review of their complaints.

The present discussion encompasses the claims which might be raised by several different plaintiffs. Where the event precipitating the lawsuit is the movement of a local franchise, the objecting parties may include the city, local investors, or businesses which provided supporting services. Our discussion will give particular attention to the complaints which might be raised by the first of these, the city itself. The few previous cases in this area suggest that this is the most likely plaintiff [320] and that the city will be inclined to raise most of the issues which are of interest to the other local parties affected. It is conceivable, of course, that the event which gives rise to the antitrust concern is not the loss of an existing franchise, but rather a league's refusal to locate a club in a city in which investors have applied for one. The principles which are discussed below should have equal application in this situation. The primary factual distinction to be made in such a case is that the league's action will frustrate anticipated commercial relationships rather than disrupt existing ones. Under the antitrust doctrine which will be called into question, this distinction is not likely to produce a difference in the legal result.

1. *The Applicability of Section 1.*

In considering the antitrust objections available to a city which has lost a sports franchise, an initial question to be confronted is whether section 1 of the Sherman Act provides an avenue for judicial scrutiny of the league's decision.[321]

---

316. The *Buffalo, San Diego,* and *San Francisco* cases were largely based on the legal objection arising from the clubs' lease arrangements.

317. 1966 Trade Cas. ¶ 71,738 (Wis. Cir. Ct.).

318. While the lower court in the *Braves* case upheld the plaintiff's antitrust complaint, the rationale of the case is not wholly convincing. For example, the court seems to have assumed that the various clubs which comprised the defendant league should be regarded as separate business entities. As will be suggested below, a reasonable argument can be made that the league should be regarded as a single firm for antitrust purposes. The court also suggests that a sports league is somewhat like a public utility and its contracts, therefore, are subject to review under a reasonableness standard. 1966 Trade Cas. ¶ 71,738 at 82,402-03. Our discussion below raises the question of whether this analogy is appropriate. The *Braves* court also granted relief in a form which would have warranted careful scrutiny on appeal, had the merits of the case been considered. The court enjoined the Braves from playing in Atlanta unless the defendant league established an expansion club in Milwaukee. As is explained below, such a remedy encourages the league to expand and claim an unused franchise location, and hence is somewhat inconsistent with the goal of the antitrust laws to foster the development of competition.

319. 31 Wis. 2d 699, 144 N.W.2d 1 (1966).

320. *See* authorities cited in note 314 *supra*

321. The nature of the section 1 prohibition is discussed at notes 61-76 *supra*.

In our earlier discussions of situations in which a member club or a competing organization objects to a league's franchising practices, we concluded that section 1 was not properly applied.[322] Is a similar conclusion called for in the present context where we have a different plaintiff? The answer appears to be "yes." The type of section 1 objection raised by a municipality would be quite similar to that which would be asserted by the other plaintiffs whose objections were previously discussed. In structuring a section 1 complaint, the city is likely to allege that the league vote denying the plaintiff its franchise was (1) an agreement among the member clubs which (2) amounted to an illegal refusal by the clubs to deal with the municipality. We have noted in a prior discussion that the first element — the presence of an agreement or conspiracy — is critical to a section 1 complaint.[323] Where league actions are involved, the question arises as to whether internal decision-making by member clubs establishes the necessary conspiracy. The resolution of this point requires a decision as to whether the relevant firm, for antitrust purposes, is an individual league club or the league itself. If it is the latter, then the section 1 action must fail, for the element of duality of action will be missing.

We have seen that the league has been regarded as a single firm incapable of conspiring with itself where antitrust complaints were raised by a member club.[324] It would appear that the rationale used in that situation would be equally applicable here. In the case referred to, *San Francisco Seals v. National Hockey League*,[325] the court noted that section 1 required a showing of an agreement between two independent business entities to restrain trade. The court held that as far as a league's franchising activities were concerned, the individual club-members were not economic competitors of one another, but rather were participants in the venture of a single firm — the league.[326]

While a municipality has interests different from those represented by the complaining party in *San Francisco Seals*, the basis of a city's section 1 complaint would appear to be the same as that considered in the Seals' litigation. The focus of the city's objection would be on the internal decision-making apparatus through which the league effectuates its plan for dividing up the national market for franchises in its sport. Since the structure and purpose of the disputed agreement process is the same as that reviewed in *Seals*, it would seem to follow that its antitrust treatment ought not be different. It will also be noted that while the plaintiffs are different, both the *Seals* litigation and the situation considered here involve disputes about the local effects of the clubs' collective franchise decisions. The basic objection is directed to the resulting restraints upon the development of local markets. These effects were apparently not sufficient to dissuade the *San Francisco Seals* court from its ultimate conclusion that league franchise decisions do not involve the type of conduct which section 1 was intended to proscribe, and a similar treatment would seem appropriate here.[327]

322. *See* text at notes 108-49, 170-71 *supra.*
323. *See* text at notes 61-64 *supra.*
324. *See* text at notes 125-32 *supra.*
325. 379 F. Supp. 966 (C.D. Cal. 1974).
326. *Id.* at 969. *See also* text at notes 125-32 *supra.*
327. The *Seals* decision, as well as the courts' decisions in American Football League v. National Football League, 205 F. Supp. 60 (D. Md. 1962), *aff'd*, 323 F.2d 124 (4th Cir. 1963), suggests that in evaluating league franchising decisions under the antitrust laws, a court should focus on the league's operation in the national, rather than local, market. In both cases, the courts resisted the plaintiffs' efforts to fragment the defendants' market.

Thus, under this analysis, a municipality's section 1 complaint should fail, at least if it relies upon the theory of an intra-league conspiracy.

2. *The Section 2 Issues.*

A different line of attack for the city contesting the loss of a sports franchise is available under section 2 of the Sherman Act. The objective of section 2 is to provide remedies to a party who is injured when a defendant misuses a dominant market position.[328] The city is likely to contend that the defendant league enjoys a monopoly in the particular sport and that its refusal to continue its local franchise represents an illegal attempt to control the market for professional sports exhibitions.

The discussion of the likely validity of a municipality's section 2 complaints is facilitated if we distinguish between two different issues which might be raised. The basis for differentiation involves the question of whether the defendant's monopoly was legally acquired. We will first consider situations in which the plaintiff's real complaint is not that the league's monopoly was attained by illegal or improper means, but rather that the league's decision to remove the disputed franchise was an improper exercise of monopoly power. Here the central issue is whether section 2 can be used as a vehicle for regulating the terms upon which a lawful monopolist deals with outsiders. The other situation to be addressed is that which is assumed away in the first category of cases. Specifically, we will consider whether a municipality is a proper party to litigate the issue of whether a league has used illegal or improper means to acquire its monopoly position.

(a) *A duty to deal fairly?*

We want to begin our consideration of the first group of cases by assuming that the plaintiff-city establishes that the league possesses monopoly power but cannot show that the defendant attained its dominant position illegally. Even when the issue of illegal acquisition is set aside, there is still a question as to how the city must frame its objection to the league's withdrawal or denial of a local franchise. What is the league's duty with respect to establishing local franchises? Must it locate a club in any city which wants one, without regard to profitability? Or is its obligation only to franchise those cities showing a reasonable probability that a club will operate with a profit? Or could it be that the league has no legal obligation to deal with any particular city? It can be suggested that the area for real debate falls somewhere between the second and third questions, and that a correct application of existing doctrine supports the latter view — that the antitrust laws do not limit the league's discretion on matters of franchise location.

The first question — whether the league has an obligation to permit complete freedom of entry of franchises — need not long detain us. While there are some who suggest that leagues should be forced to operate a free market for sports franchises,[329] this position has received little serious attention. Its primary defect is a failure to understand the basic nature of a league's operation.

---

328. *See generally* text at notes 172-250 *supra.*

329. *See 1976 Hearings,* pt. 2, at 448-51 (testimony of Rep. John F. Seiberling). On the matter of the baseball leagues' failure to locate a franchise in the nation's capital, Congressman Seiberling stated:

> Let free enterprise function. If this area [Washington, D.C.-Baltimore] cannot support two clubs, then that will be determined after they try and either succeed or don't succeed. Maybe they are right and maybe they are wrong. Let the people who want baseball and are willing to pay for the price of admission decide that question. *Id.* at 449.

It has become increasingly clear that the success of a league depends upon a good deal of cross-subsidization among clubs. This is necessary to insure that natural inequities in the economic potential of various franchise locations do not totally destroy competitive balance within the league. As is explained more fully elsewhere in this section, the subsidies may take many different forms, including the sharing of broadcast revenues, sharing of gate receipts, provisions for the mandatory allocation of players and the like.[330] A legal rule mandating unrestrained entry of new franchises without regard to their potential profitability would seemingly have one of two effects, neither of which is desirable from the perspective of investors, fans, nor the cities housing the clubs. If there were complete freedom of entry, leagues would either have to extend their subsidization to all new entrants, and face the risk that the shared-resources would be severely diluted, or eliminate the subsidy arrangements and require that each franchise stand on its own financial feet. In either case, it is likely that the degree of competitive imbalance within the league would be greatly increased, and the quality of the league's product would diminish, with a resultant loss of fan and investor enthusiasm.[331]

The fact is that *league* competition is different from that which involves barn-storming or other haphazard arrangements.[332] The league has an interest in insuring not only that there is a reliable basis for comparative evaluations of the quality of its clubs but also that the prospects of lopsided individual contests are minimized. To achieve these goals, it appears to be necessary that the league provide financial support to weaker franchises.[333] To make this system work, the leagues must also retain control over the number of the teams participating in their competition. While it might be possible to stage a professional team sports competition in which each club arranged its own schedule and depended solely on its own economic resourcefulness, such a scheme would involve a product different from that involved in league sports. As far as we know, nothing in the antitrust laws suggests that there is a national policy to eliminate the latter from the marketplace.

If it is accepted that a league has discretion to control franchise entry and movement, the central question arises as to whether the antitrust laws will be applied to limit the group's decision-making. One who was prepared to argue for limitations on the league's discretion would have to articulate the standard to be applied. Some commentators contend that a reasonableness standard is appropriate and argue that a league should be compelled to grant or continue a franchise if the persons pursuing it can establish that the local operation will generate a reasonable profit.[334] Under this view, the league's denial of a new franchise, or its decision to relocate an existing one, would be upheld only if it were supported by objective data establishing the unsuitability of the local market.[335] Presumably, the issue as to the sufficiency of the evidence would be

---

330. *See* text at notes 137-44 *supra.*

331. The consequences of reducing the leagues' control of the output market for the production of professional sports are discussed in DEMMERT 81-94.

332. *See* Koppett, *Sports and the Law: An Overview,* 18 N.Y.L. FORUM 815, 839 (1973).

333. These points are discussed in more detail in the text accompanying notes 114-18, 137-44 *supra.*

334. *See* Noll, *Alternatives in Sports Policy* in GOVERNMENT AND THE SPORTS BUSINESS 411, 414-15 (R. Noll ed. 1974); *1976 Hearings,* pt. 2, at 478-79 (testimony of Lionel S. Sobel, attorney).

335. For an example of an inquiry into whether a city could "reasonably" support a sports franchise, see the trial court's decision in Wisconsin v. Milwaukee Braves, Inc., 1966 Trade Cas. ¶ 71,738 (Wis. Cir. Ct.), *rev'd,* 31 Wis. 2d 699, 144 N.W.2d 1 (1966). The court undertook a detailed

decided in a judicial proceeding, the same as other issues of fact arising under antitrust claims.

While the implications of this approach have not generally been thoroughly analyzed by those who propose it, it would seem that the appropriate subjects for judicial review would include many issues other than the reasonableness of the league's initial negative decision. If that decision were found not to be reasonable, it would be necessary for the court to insure that the city's initial victory was not sabotaged in subsequent negotiations by the league or the new club.[336] Thus, the court would have to supervise the terms and conditions upon which the franchise was offered, the terms of the stadium lease, and all of the myriad subcontracts which are necessary to the operation of the franchise.

There are two rather basic difficulties with the argument that the league's franchise decisions are reviewable under a reasonableness standard: it is not supported by existing case law, and, moreover, the proposed standard of review imposes a duty which courts are ill-suited to perform. This assessment should serve to indicate the ultimate conclusion reached here. We do not find any legal or policy support for applying section 2 to limit the league's discretion in deciding where to locate its franchises, assuming, again, that the league enjoys a lawful monopoly. The reasonableness standard is not compelled by section 2 doctrine, and we can identify few policy reasons which suggest that its application will improve the operation of the professional sports market. That which follows is an elaboration of this conclusion.

Before considering the relevant case law, attention should be given to the problems caused by the burden which a "reasonableness" standard would impose on reviewing courts. It is believed that these are of sufficiently formidable dimensions to call into question the wisdom of proposals for significant judicial review. For example, as mentioned, a court would be required to find that the plaintiff-city could support a sports franchise and that the club would generate a reasonable profit. It is by no means clear, however, that the answers to these questions are capable of objective verification.[337] With respect to most cities, the determination involves several evaluations which are highly judgmental in nature. While the size of the population base is an important ingredient, it is clear that other factors may be of equal or greater importance. The enthusiasm of the local sports press, the degree of support from local businesses, climatic conditions, competition from other sports and non-sports entertainment, and the general level of fan interest and sophistication have to be considered.[338] One may doubt whether these factors can be quantified. There

examination of the Braves' operation in Milwaukee and concluded that the city was capable of sustaining a major league baseball franchise. One of the more interesting aspects of the court's inquiry arose when it was forced to choose between different methods for accounting for certain player-related costs. The court was able to form an optimistic conclusion about the team's financial prospects only by rejecting the accounting method used by the Braves and most other major league clubs. *See* 1966 Trade Cas. ¶ 71,738 at 82,382-85.

336. *Cf.* Note, *Refusals to Deal by Vertically Integrated Monopolies,* 87 HARV. L. REV. 1720, 1754 n.190 (1974).

337. *See* Comment, *The Super Bowl and the Sherman Act: Professional Team Sports and the Antitrust Laws,* 81 HARV. L. REV. 418, 427-28 (1967).

338. Various courts have recognized that factors other than population must be considered in evaluating a city's suitability for a sports franchise. *See, e.g.,* American Football League v. National Football League, 205 F. Supp. 60, 76-77 (D. Md. 1962); Wisconsin v. Milwaukee Braves, Inc., 1966 Trade Cas. ¶ 71,738 at 82,389-91 (Wis. Cir. Ct.).

are a number of cities with adequate population which have proven themselves to be marginal sports towns.[339] By the same token, there are small cities in which the high degree of fan support is somewhat mystifying.[340]

A court is also likely to encounter difficulty in dealing with the question of "reasonable profitability." [341] For one thing, the claim which a particular city raises will often not appear in isolation. There are likely to be other cities actually or potentially interested in a franchise. The league may be unable or, for financial reasons, unwilling to undertake a sizeable expansion program. Thus, before the court could make a realistic appraisal of one city's claim, it would have to make a comparative evaluation of the suitability of other locations.[342] If there is a limit on the amount of expansion a league can undertake in a given period, the court should be sensitive to the relative degree of risk confronting league-investors. When one takes account of the dubious reliability of the "objective" data likely to be available, any such wide-ranging comparative evaluation takes on a decided aura of mere sophistry.

Finally, it should be noted that courts are ill-equipped to make the sort of sophisticated inquiry that would be necessary. The decisions involved require a formidable mixture of fact-gathering, business acumen, and expert economic evaluation.[343] Moreover, the focus of the controversy may eventually shift from whether the franchise should be granted to the issue of what the terms and conditions of the club's various local contracts will be. Here the court will continue to pursue the elusive question of what is "reasonable" under the circumstances.[344] Even more troubling is the prospect that the court will become

339. *See* Block, So, You Want to Own a Ball Club, Forbes, Apr. 1, 1977, at 37 (comments on financial problems of Baltimore's baseball franchise).

340. The success of the NFL franchise in Green Bay, Wisconsin is often cited as an example of the unusual capacity which some small cities have to support a club. *See, e.g.,* Quirk & El Hodiri, *The Economic Theory of a Professional Sports League* in GOVERNMENT AND THE SPORTS BUSINESS 33, 44 (R. Noll ed. 1974).

341. *See* Comment, *The Super Bowl and the Sherman Act: Professional Team Sports and the Antitrust Laws, supra* note 337, at 427-28. *Cf.* Note, *Refusals to Deal by Vertically Integrated Monopolies, supra* note 336, at 1754-61.

342. *See* Comment, *The Super Bowl and the Sherman Act: Professional Team Sports and the Antitrust Laws, supra* note 337, at 427.

343. That a substantial amount of business judgment and economic evaluation is involved in these decisions is illustrated by the lower court's decision in Wisconsin v. Milwaukee Braves, Inc., 1966 Trade Cas. ¶ 71,738 at 82,377-400 (Wis. Cir. Ct.). *See also* note 318 *supra.*

344. As already noted, it would seem to be necessary for the court to supervise the price and other terms upon which the league offered the franchise. This would be necessary for a proper implementation of the court's initial decision that a franchise should be offered. *Cf.* Note, *Refusals to Deal by Vertically Integrated Monopolies, supra* note 336, at 1754-61. For the same reason, the court presumably would not permit the club owners to make unreasonable demands as far as their stadium rental, concessions, and related contracts were concerned, for again obstinate bargaining could undermine the court's initial determination of the city's entitlement to a franchise. There are numerous subsidiary problems with requiring a court to resolve disputes about what a "reasonable" contract would be. These difficulties become apparent if we consider the manner in which contract terms are normally arrived at in private negotiations.

· The process of negotiation is a dynamic one. Each side will propose the terms upon which it wishes to contract and if these are not identical, the process of trade-off and compromise will begin. One party may demand that something be provided at a low price, as in the case of a sports team owner who seeks a favorable rent on a municipal stadium. *See* Scannell, Pros Bully Municipal Landlords, Washington Post, Apr. 24, 1977, at D4, col. 1. The other side, the city, may not agree to this offer and insist on a higher figure. Or it may decide that it will accept a lower rent if it receives other concessions in exchange, such as an extraordinarily long lease or a provision requiring the club to bear the cost of some future contingency (*e.g.,* future maintenance costs). *See* Noll, *Alternatives*

the long-term administrator of the parties' agreement and repeatedly involve itself in questions of contract interpretation and enforcement.[345] If we could have confidence that judges would perform well in this administrative role, the proposed reasonableness standard might be palatable. But there is reason to doubt whether the courts were designed for this purpose or that they have been given the tools to perform the job.[346]

The inherent difficulties in requiring courts to make what are essentially business judgments may explain, in part, why there is no great body of case law supporting the notion that a lawful monopolist has a duty to act fairly.[347] Before

in Sports Policy, supra note 334, at 412. In this bargaining process, one important negotiating tool which each side has is the right to refuse to deal: if it does not like the terms offered it may simply withdraw from the arrangement. In the case of the club owner, this may mean that he will find another stadium or that he may look for a more hospitable city.

The proposal to require reasonable contract demands on the part of sports clubs and leagues requires a radical departure from the bargaining process described above. Specifically, it introduces a third party — the court — and directs that agency to decide what will be included in the parties' agreement. The court is likely to find that this is a very difficult task. Initially the court will confront the not insubstantial burden of deciding what a reasonable term would be on particular matters. Those urging this role on the courts may suggest that the judge should simply look to the marketplace and adopt whatever terms have been agreed to by other parties in a similar situation. This may be the going market price for sports franchises, for stadium rentals, for concession supplies, or whatever. The theoretical simplicity of this approach is deceiving. In the real world, there are likely to be few true market equivalents for terms which are most critical to the negotiations between a city (or local investor) and a club or league. The value of a stadium lease in New York is likely to be different from that in a city with only a marginal capacity to support a professional club.

Another difficulty with the use of a judicial intermediary is that the court is not likely to be able to account for the strength of the preferences of the various parties. But for the availability of court intervention, a city, for example, might be willing to make substantial concessions on the rent it charges for its stadium in order to have a club locate in its area. The city may perceive that the sports venture will attract visitors and increase its tax revenues, or it may feel that the presence of the team will solidify its "big-city" image and thus increase the attraction for major businesses seeking to relocate. *See* Okner, *Subsidies of Stadiums and Arenas* in GOVERNMENT AND THE SPORTS BUSINESS 325, 327-28 (R. Noll ed. 1974). Absent the opportunity for judicial control of the bargain, the city may have been willing to accept less than a reasonable rent of the leased space it provides.

It is not likely that a court will be able to develop an appreciation for the various preferences which will operate, much less attach a price tag to them. And if the court opts for a preference-neutral market value standard, assuming one exists, the results achieved will have a characteristic of unfairness that is difficult to defend. In the example above, the city would be able to both realize its preference — securing or continuing a sports franchise — and receive rental fees much higher than it would have otherwise accepted. Thus, the term which the court selects will in fact not be "reasonable" in the particular context of the parties' bargaining. Moreover, the impediments to finding the "right" term would appear to be insurmountable. Realistically, there would appear to be no way that a court could put itself in the parties' shoes in this type of situation where many of the benefits of the proposed bargain contract are wholly intangible.

345. The prospect of continual judicial supervision was one reason given by the Supreme Court for its refusal to accept a lower court order requiring movie distributors to allocate films on the basis of competitive bidding. *See* United States v. Paramount Pictures, Inc., 334 U.S. 131 (1948) (§ 1 case).

346. *See generally* Bork, *Ancillary Restraints and the Sherman Act,* 15 ABA ANTITRUST SECTION 211, 231-34 (1959); Note, *Refusals to Deal by Vertically Integrated Monopolies, supra* note 336, at 1754-61.

347. *See* Note, *Refusals to Deal by Vertically Integrated Monopolies, supra* note 336, at 1754-61. The authors of this note observe that "a duty to deal imposed on a monopolist has no precedent in the concerted refusal cases, where the typical decree merely compels the defendants to deal with competitors on a nondiscriminatory basis." *Id.* at 1754.

looking at particular precedents in this area, it is useful to examine the general legal framework in which the issue of the monopolist's duty of fairness arises. For many people, the notion of monopoly produces an automatic negative reaction and leads to an assumption that because monopolies are bad, they must be subject to legal control.[348] The existing doctrine suggests, however, that there is a major slip'twixt the cup and the lip in that analysis.

It is not true that monopolies have been declared inherently illegal.[349] A sizeable portion of a prior discussion has been devoted to the point that there are many types of monopolies which are perfectly lawful under section 2.[350] While various doctrines are applied to control how monopolies develop and perpetuate themselves, a careful review of these will indicate that the law's main concern goes to a different point than that which is in issue here. The antitrust laws *do* seek to prevent the acquisition of monopoly power by illegal and unfair means.[351] And as we have seen, even where a firm has acquired its monopoly power legally, the entity may not use unfair means to frustrate the efforts of others who would seek to enter the market.[352] But with respect to each of these types of controls, the focus is on the effect of the monopolist's activities upon competitors. The purpose of section 2 in these cases is to attempt to open up the marketplace to encourage the development of competition.[353]

The objection which we are assuming here is of a different sort. We have posited that there is no illegal monopoly, and our primary concern is whether our non-competitor plaintiff — a city — can complain that the monopolist refused to deal with it. The main body of section 2 doctrine has very little to do with this issue. The plaintiff's real complaint is not with the fact that a competitor may have been frustrated, but rather that it did not fare well in its own individual bargaining. At the bottom line, it has to be appreciated that even if the courts were to accede to the plaintiff's demand for their intervention, such action would not produce more competition in the sports market and indeed might even serve to lessen that prospect by compelling the league to capture a potential franchise location.

A search of the existing case law reveals no clear body of precedent establishing a general rule that a monopolist must always deal fairly.[354] One does find certain instances in which the courts have intervened to supervise the contractual relations of a monopoly firm. But those cases deal with very specialized situations which possess few of the characteristics found in the sports market.

The first line of cases is not technically a part of section 2 jurisprudence. These are cases in which courts, usually applying common law doctrine, declare a

---

348. *See* note 311 *supra.*

349. *See, e.g.,* United States v. E.I. DuPont de Nemours & Co., 351 U.S. 377 (1956); Standard Oil Co. v. United States, 221 U.S. 1 (1911); *Handler, Nineteenth Annual Review of Recent Antitrust Developments — 1966,* 21 Record (N.Y.C.B.A.) 539, 557 (1966).

350. *See* text accompanying notes 172-82, 216-50, 272-312 *supra.*

351. *See* text accompanying notes 216-50 *supra.*

352. *See* text accompanying notes 239-50 *supra.*

353. *See generally* Gellhorn 20-23, 112-13; 16 von Kalinowski § 3.02[4].

354. *Cf.* Note, *Refusals to Deal by Vertically Integrated Monopolies,* 87 Harv. L. Rev. 1720, 1754 (1974).

venture to be a public utility and thus subject to judicial control.[355] These decisions are considered here because, as evidenced by one sports case, some courts may be inclined to intermingle public utility doctrine with section 2 principles.[356] In addition, the cases are useful because they suggest the techniques employed by the legal institutions to regulate monopolists controlling vital public services, an approach which, it will be argued, has little relevance to the sports industry.

If an enterprise were found to be a public utility, the courts, at least in an earlier period, were prepared to intervene to impose restrictions on the manner in which it conducted its business. Even though the assets belonged to private investors, the courts would decree that the firm could not cease doing business as long as reasonable profitability could be projected.[357] Moreover, the terms upon which the firm contracted with other parties were subject to regulation. Specifically, the agreements were reviewed to insure that the terms were reasonable.[358] The rationale of these cases was that where private investors committed their assets to important public uses, there arose an obligation of continued fair and equitable dealing so that the public's interest in the venture was not frustrated.[359]

A critical point for our purposes is that not all firms offering services to the general public were declared to be public utilities. The firms subject to this type of regulation were often monopolists, but the services they offered had another distinguishing characteristic: they typically involved activities vital to the basic public welfare.[360] The degree of public interest had to be strong enough to justify a judicial conclusion that the public could demand the service as a matter of right. The firms typically subjected to control were those which operated private water, gas, and electric companies. While there are isolated cases arising in other contexts which have stretched the definition of a *public utility* to an extreme,[361] the main body of case law follows a more temperate approach emphasizing the need for a fundamental public interest in the services offered.

It would be difficult to argue that a local sports franchise has the characteristics of a *public utility* as that term has been historically applied. While the services it offers may be of economic importance, that fact alone has not traditionally provided a reason for judicial control. Any firm with a large payroll

---

355. *See generally* Arterburn, *The Origin and First Test of Public Callings,* 75 U. PA. L. REV. 411 (1926); Burdick, *The Origins of the Peculiar Duties of Public Service Companies,*11 COLUM. L. REV. 514 (1911); Keezer, *Some Questions Involved in Application of the "Public Interest" Doctrine,* 25 MICH. L. REV. 596 (1927); Robinson, *The Public Utility Concept in American Law,* 41 HARV. L. REV. 277 (1928); Wyman, *Public Callings and the Trust Problem,* 17 HARV. L. REV. 156 (1904); 64 AM. JUR. 2D, *Public Utilities* §§ 1, 9.

356. *See, e.g.,* Wisconsin v. Milwaukee Braves, Inc., 1966 Trade Cas. ¶ 71,738 at 82,402-03 (Wis. Cir. Ct.).

357. *See, e.g.,* Railroad Comm'n v. Eastern Texas R.R. Co., 264 U.S. 79 (1923); Burgess v. Brockton, 235 Mass. 95, 126 N.E. 456 (1920); Block v. Lincoln Telephone & Telegraph Co., 170 Neb. 531, 103 N.W.2d 312 (1960).

358. *See, e.g.,* Shepard v. Milwaukee Gas Light Co., 6 Wis. 526 (1858); Wyman, *Public Callings and the Trust Problem, supra* note 355, at 227-28. *Cf.* Munn v. Illinois, 94 U.S. 113 (1876).

359. *See, e.g.,* Burgess v. Brockton, 235 Mass. 95, 126 N.E. 456 (1920). *Cf.* Munn v. Illinois, 94 U.S. 113 (1876).

360. *See* cases cited in notes 357-58 *supra. See also* Pulitzer Publishing Co. v. FCC, 94 F.2d 249 (D.C. Cir. 1937); Ginsberg v. Denver, 164 Colo. 572, 436 P.2d 685 (1968).

361. *See* Golf View Realty Co. v. Sioux City, 222 Iowa 433, 269 N.W. 451 (1936); Capen v. Portland, 112 Ore. 14, 228 P. 105 (1924).

or significant sales may be important to the local economy. The element missing from a sports operation, and from most other significant local enterprises, is the presence of an activity affecting the basic public need for food, shelter, and sanitation.[362] Even if the concept of "public welfare" were expanded to include emotional well-being, it would require a quantum leap to find that privately-run forms of entertainment were of vital importance. In short, there is little law to support the application of public utility concepts to sports enterprises.

A consideration of the public utility concept is also useful for another reason. If we look at how the regulation of public utilities has evolved, we can find further evidence of why principles from that area of law have little relevance to questions relating to sports franchising.

In the modern context, the regulation of firms providing basic public necessities has continued. But the form of regulation has developed into a more formal system. Now, rather than relying on case-by-case judicial controls, we favor the establishment of permanent governmental regulatory agencies to control the terms upon which these "public utilities" deal with their customers.[363] This fact is of some importance for the present discussion, for the presence of permanent specialized institutions serves to overcome the problems inherent in trying to use the courts as the vehicle for setting reasonable contract terms. The regulatory commissions often have been given specific legislative directions as to where the regulated firms must operate and what their profit margins can be. In addition, the staffs of the agencies include experts whose job it is to make the investigation necessary to insure that the regulated firms operate properly. Finally, because of their permanance, the agencies are capable of undertaking the long-term supervision necessary to carry out the general goal of insuring that the firms act fairly. In sum, this system is workable only because there has been both an agreement in advance (through legislative enactment) as to what the relevant standard of conduct should be and the establishment of an on-going regulatory structure.

It is relevant for our purposes that such an extra-judicial system of regulation was found to be necessary. There is a rather strong implication here that the judicial process is unsuited for the type of regulation necessary where public control of a private firm is desired.[364] But perhaps the most important implication to be drawn from this discussion goes to a different point. It needs to be emphasized that legislatures have chosen to impose permanent regulatory structures only on certain types of businesses, in particular those firms involved in providing vital public services. Sports franchises, and indeed many other monopolies, have not been included. This would seem to suggest rather strongly that these other firms are not thought to be engaged in activities which require the extraordinary step of public control of their private dealings. The differentiations which have been made are entitled to respect and may suggest a further reason why the general body of precedent under section 2 reveals no

362. Cf. Ginsberg v. Denver, 164 Colo. 572, 436 P.2d 685 (1968) (sports stadium not a public utility); Madden v. Queens County Jockey Club, Inc., 175 Misc. 522, 23 N.Y.S.2d 106 (1940) (race track); Woollcott v. Schubert, 217 N.Y. 212, 111 N.E. 829 (1916) (theater).

363. See generally M. BERSTEIN, REGULATING BUSINESS BY INDEPENDENT COMMISSIONS (1955); J. RAPHAEL, GOVERNMENTAL REGULATION OF BUSINESS 47-80 (1966); A. WEBBER, PRINCIPLES OF PUBLIC UTILITY REGULATION (1941); W. WHERRY, PUBLIC UTILITIES AND THE LAW (1928).

364. Cf. Note, Refusals to Deal by Vertically Integrated Monopolies, supra note 354, at 1754-61.

strong desire by courts to supervise the affairs of monopolists offering non-essential services.

There is a second line of authority, with a more direct connection with section 2, which needs to be considered. We have said that in general, the doctrine developed under section 2 does not appear to require fair dealing by a monopolist. There is, however, an exception which warrants comment in the present analysis. Those who would urge that a court may compel a monopolist-league to grant a franchise to a deserving city are likely to point to the Supreme Court's decision in *Otter Tail Power Company v. United States* [365] as authority. Otter Tail Power Company was prosecuted by the federal government for allegedly engaging in activities to monopolize the sale of electric power in certain areas of the Midwest. Otter Tail was involved in the relevant market at two levels. It held exclusive franchises for the provision of retail electric power in several cities and towns in the upper Midwest. In addition, it controlled the subsystem of power lines through which electricity was transmitted from the main power lines to the various local markets. Its section 2 difficulties arose when several of the towns it served decided to establish their own municipally-owned retail power companies after Otter Tail's franchises had expired. Otter Tail was found to have engaged in various activities to frustrate the formation of these competitors in the local market. Particularly pertinent to our present inquiry is the finding that Otter Tail had refused to sell power from its sub-transmission lines to service the new municipally-owned companies being formed.[366] In a very close decision (4-3, with 2 abstentions) the Supreme Court agreed with the district court's conclusion that this refusal to sell power at wholesale violated section 2 of the Sherman Act. The Court approved the lower court's order enjoining Otter Tail from further refusals to sell power to existing and proposed municipal power systems.[367]

The *Otter Tail* decision might seem to provide authority for the proposition that a monopolist may violate the antitrust laws by refusing to deal with those who wish to contract for its product. It can be suggested, however, that the case does not support a general rule to that effect and indeed is fundamentally distinguishable from the situations that arise with respect to sports franchises. The first point to be made is that the antitrust theory of *Otter Tail* does not cover the type of complaint that would be raised by a city which had been denied a franchise. In *Otter Tail,* the section 2 violation arose because the defendant was using its dominant market position to foreclose competition. The company controlled the transmission of wholesale electric power and by refusing to sell to municipally-operated firms, it was able to preclude the formation of retail competitors and solidify its dominance of the retail market. The invocation of section 2 in these circumstances was called for because of the very direct injury to competition.[368] As has already been discussed, that element is missing when

---

365. 410 U.S. 366 (1973).

366. *Id.* at 377-78.

367. *Id.* at 374, 381-82.

368. Other cases dealing with vertically integrated monopolists similarly reflect a strong concern for the injury to competition which results when the monopolist refuses to deal with outsiders. *See, e.g., Lorain Journal Co. v. United States,* 342 U.S. 143 (1951); *Eastman Kodak Co. v. Southern Photo Materials Co.,* 273 U.S. 359 (1927); *United States v. Klearflax Linen Looms, Inc.,* 63 F. Supp. 32 (D. Minn. 1945).

a city complains that a league has refused to award it a franchise. The awarding of a franchise will not encourage the formation of a competitor to the league and, in fact, may have the opposite effect, for a potential franchise location for a rival league will be foreclosed.

Read in the proper light, *Otter Tail* serves to confirm that the main thrust of the national policy with respect to monopolies is to insure that they not operate in a fashion which deters inter-firm competition.[369] As we have seen, that policy is also applied to firms enjoying natural monopolies.[370] But here again, the ultimate objective is to insure that the formation of a competitor is not improperly precluded. Where a monopolist's practices have no negative effect on competition, it would appear that they fall outside the province of section 2. The objection which a city raises in a franchise-denial case has little to do with the overriding concern for opening up the marketplace, and it would require a major refashioning of the policies embodied in section 2 to use that statute to vindicate the city's perceived injury.[371]

A second basis for distinguishing *Otter Tail* arises from the specialized factual setting of the case. It will be recalled that we earlier contended that meaningful judicial review of city-league franchising disputes might not be possible because of the great practical difficulty involved in deciding what were fair and reasonable terms for the franchise contract and related agreements.[372] Having once decided that a franchise should be granted, a court would necessarily have to assume a role in supervising, if not actually setting, the terms of the various contractual arrangements which would arise. But one might ask, why was this not a problem in *Otter Tail*? Once the defendant company was ordered to sell power to municipalities, it would be necessary to decide a wide variety of issues pertaining to the terms and conditions upon which the sales were made. Surely these questions could be as difficult as those which would arise in the franchising context. There is, however, a critical difference in the two cases. Otter Tail was involved in an industry which was subject to direct regulation by a governmental administrative agency.[373] While the trial judge ordered Otter Tail to cease its refusals to deal, it could also add that sales were to be made "under terms and conditions which are filed with and subject to approval by the Federal Power Commission." [374] Judicial intervention into Otter Tail's business relations was thus feasible because there was a pre-existing regulatory entity possessing the expertise to review the disputes which might arise as the power contracts were being negotiated.[375] With respect to the sports industry, there is, of course, no

369. *See generally* Comment. *Refusals to Sell and Public Control of Competition,* 58 YALE L.J. 1121 (1949); Note, *Refusals to Deal by Vertically Integrated Monopolies, supra* note 354.

370. *See* text accompanying notes 293-99 *supra.*

371. It can be suggested that the lower court in Wisconsin v. Milwaukee Braves, Inc., 1966 Trade Cas. ¶ 71,738 (Wis. Cir. Ct.), failed to appreciate the distinction indicated in the text. Many of the antimonopoly cases relied upon by the court involved situations in which the courts intervened to protect actual or potential competitors. *See* 1966 Trade Cas. ¶ 71,738 at 82,402-05. *See also* note 318 *supra.*

372. *See* text accompanying notes 337-46 *supra.*

373. Many aspects of Otter Tail's operation were subject to regulation by the Federal Power Commission. The statutes defining the authority of the FPC in this area are cited in Note, *Refusals to Deal by Vertically Integrated Monopolies,* 87 HARV. L. REV. 1720, 1725 n.38 (1974).

374. *Quoted* in 410 U.S. at 375.

375. *See* Note, *Refusals to Deal by Vertically Integrated Monopolies, supra* note 373, at 1725, 1755.

comparable administrative agency. Because the difficulty of establishing reasonable terms for a franchise arrangement is very real, *Otter Tail* may be read as only a very limited invitation for courts to involve themselves in matters of this sort. At a minimum, the case provides little indication that the potential problems in the franchising area can be easily solved.

By way of a conclusion, it can be observed again that there is no persuasive case law support for the notion that a league with a lawful monopoly is subject to judicial scrutiny when it denies a city's request for a franchise.[376] While we have seen situations in which courts have undertaken to order monopolists to deal with outsiders, these have involved specialized fact situations which bear little similarity to those found in sports. The courts seem to appreciate that this type of judicial oversight is appropriate only where there is a compelling public interest at stake. In the public utility cases, that interest relates to the critical importance of the services provided. In *Otter Tail,* on the other hand, the public policy which is vindicated is the desirability of encouraging the growth of competition. Where a city is denied a sports franchise, neither of these interests come into play and we seem to be left to the general principle that the law does not otherwise dictate to a business firm how it must operate its affairs in its pursuit of maximum profitability.

(b) *League Monopolies Acquired by Illegal or Improper Means.*

The prior discussion has dealt with situations in which the only injury alleged by a plaintiff-city was that the league had refused to deal with it on reasonable terms. We now turn our attention to cases in which the plaintiff's complaint is based on a different theory — that the defendant league acquired its monopoly by illegal or improper means. Our main concerns here will be whether a city or a local investor has standing to raise this type of complaint and even if it does, what the appropriate remedy should be if a violation is found.

The theory of a complaint based on the illegality of the league's monopoly overcomes one of the difficulties we identified in our earlier discussion of "pure" refusals to deal. There we encountered the rather basic problem that the refusal to deal seemed to have very little effect upon competition among sports leagues. Since the main thrust of section 2 is to encourage competition in the relevant market, this defect appeared to be critical. Where the plaintiff city attacks the illegality of the defendant's monopoly, the complaint seems more in line with the purposes of section 2. The theory of the suit would be that (1) the defendant used improper means to attain or perpetuate its monopoly; (2) these actions discourage the formation of a rival league; and (3) had the particular sports market been more competitive, the plaintiff would have been able to secure a franchise, either from the rival league or from the defendant. In essence, it would be alleged that there had been an injury to competition and that the plaintiff was disadvantaged by it. The disadvantage, again, would flow from the fact that the deterrence of competition had both eliminated the rival league's demand for franchise locations and lessened the established league's interest in expansion.[377]

---

376. A similar view has been expressed by Mr. Joe Sims, Deputy Ass't Att'y Gen., Antitrust Div., Dept. of Justice: "[I]t is not clear to me . . . that the antitrust laws . . . would have any effect on the decision of the leagues to move teams from one city to another." *1976 Hearings,* pt. 2, at 296.

377. *See* Comment, *The Super Bowl and the Sherman Act: Professional Team Sports and the Antitrust Laws,* 81 HARV. L. REV. 418, 433 (1967): "[C]ontinued competition [among the AFL and

An obvious first step in the plaintiff's proof of its case is to show that the defendant had in fact improperly acquired or perpetuated its monopoly. In an earlier subpart of these materials, we discussed the type of showing which must be made to sustain such a charge.[378] That discussion also includes a sample complaint illustrating the allegations which might be put forth. The complaint is taken from the case of *Buffalo v. Atlanta Hawks, Inc.,*[379] which involved the city-plaintiff's objections to the threatened loss of its NBA franchise.[380] As the discussion in the earlier subpart indicates, there is likely to be a lively debate as to whether certain league practices — particularly those with respect to player controls, expansion and mergers — will be found to involve the sort of impropriety which will sustain a charge that the league's monopoly was illegally attained or perpetuated.[381] We will not repeat our earlier discussion, but the reader may want to refer to the prior material, for the issue of the propriety of the league's prior conduct often cannot be easily resolved.

For our present purposes, we need to first address the question of whether the city can maintain suit to vindicate the injuries resulting from a league's alleged illegal monopoly. The basic issue here is one of standing. In general, before a party can secure relief for the type of antitrust violations we are concerned with, he must establish that he has been (1) directly injured (2) in his "business or property" as a result of the unlawful activity.[382] In order to distinguish between direct injuries and those which are indirect, and hence not remediable under the antitrust laws, most courts utilize a "target area" test.[383] Under this approach, a plaintiff must show that "he is within that area of the economy which is endangered by a breakdown of competitive conditions in a particular industry." [384] Moreover, some courts will require that the plaintiff show that he "was not only hit, but was aimed at." [385] The basic notion is that the plaintiff must have operated in the area of commerce to which the antitrust violations were directed.[386] If the alleged injury is only remotely or incidentally related to the illegal practices, the plaintiff will be found to lack standing.

The second requirement — an injury to business or property — is satisfied if the violations have an adverse economic impact on a commercial venture operated by the plaintiff or have an adverse effect on some property right to which the plaintiff is entitled.[387] Loss of profits, loss of a prospective economic advantage, or an unwarranted increase in costs may show the requisite injury.

NFL] would have been more conducive to future expansion because the members of a stable, profitable league may be unwilling to tamper with success by expanding, except to the most attractive of cities."

378. *See* text accompanying notes 224-38 *supra.*

379. Buffalo v. Atlanta Hawks Basketball, Inc., Civil No. 76-0261 (W.D.N.Y., June 15, 1976).

380. The *Buffalo* complaint is quoted in the text at note 231 *supra.*

381. *See* text accompanying notes 251-71 *supra.*

382. *See* authorities cited in notes 154-56 *supra.*

383. *See* authorities cited in notes 156-57 *supra.*

384. Conference of Studio Unions v. Loew's, Inc., 193 F.2d 51, 55 (9th Cir. 1951), *cert. denied,* 342 U.S. 919 (1952).

385. Karseal Corp. v. Richfield Oil Corp., 221 F.2d 358, 363 (9th Cir. 1955).

386. *See generally* 16L VON KALINOWSKI § 101.02.

387. *See, e.g.,* Waldron v. British Petroleum Co., 231 F. Supp. 72 (S.D.N.Y. 1964); Gottesman v. General Motors Corp., 221 F. Supp. 488 (S.D.N.Y. 1963), *rev'd,* 414 F.2d 956 (2d Cir. 1969), *on remand,*

While the general parameters of the standing rules can be identified, the application of those rules in particular fact situations is often unclear. In part this is due to the fact that there is not complete agreement among the circuits as to how exacting the standing requirement should be. Some circuits seem to favor interpretations which require that plaintiff be a potential competitor in the sphere of commercial activity in question.[388] On the other hand, at least one circuit would allow suits to be brought by anyone who had an interest in the activity which the defendant sought to control.[389] Because of the unsettled state of the law on the standing requirement, there are few safe conclusions that can be reached about which local interests can properly maintain an antitrust suit in sports franchising disputes. The reader confronted with a problem in this area will be well-advised to pay careful attention to the law in his circuit. In the present discussion, we will only attempt to outline the questions which are likely to arise and offer a few tentative conclusions.

The city as landlord. In order to evaluate the standing issue as it applies to municipalities, it is necessary to differentiate between various types of cases. The strength of a city's claim will depend upon the nature of the interest which it attempts to assert. The first cases to be examined are those involving a plaintiff-city which owns and operates a stadium or arena. In these situations, the city will argue that it is engaged in a proprietary, or commercial, activity and that its business — the business of leasing a sports facility — has been damaged by the alleged monopolistic practices of the defendant. But for the complained of activities — it will be alleged — the city would have been able to find a suitable tenant for its limited-use stadium and secure a more favorable financial return.[390]

It is by no means clear, however, that the city's interest as landlord will be sufficient to satisfy the standing requirement for antitrust claims. Under the section 2 theory set out above, the purpose of the defendant-league's allegedly improper activities was to deter the formation of a competing league and thus solidify the defendant's dominant market position. It might be said, then, that the real target of the illegal practices was a competing league and not a city which might serve as host for a franchise.[391] There are indications in some circuits that this analysis would be followed and that the city-lessor would be found to be outside of the primary target area. Particularly relevant are a series of cases in which the plaintiffs were lessors of movie houses. The lessors alleged that the defendant movie distributors had artificially controlled the availability of quality movies and hence had reduced the plaintiffs' return under their

---

310 F. Supp. 1257 (S.D.N.Y. 1970), *aff'd,* 436 F.2d 1205 (2d Cir.), *cert. denied,* 403 U.S. 911 (1971); Broadcasters, Inc. v. Morristown Broadcasting Corp., 185 F. Supp. 641 (D.N.J. 1960).

388. *See, e.g.,* Harrison v. Paramount Pictures, 115 F. Supp. 312 (E.D. Pa. 1953), *aff'd,* 211 F.2d 405 (3d Cir. 1954); Cromar Co. v. Nuclear Materials & Equip. Corp., 1975-1 Trade Cas. ¶ 60,373 (M.D. Pa.). *See also* General Beverage Sales Co. v. East Side Winery, 396 F. Supp. 590 (E.D. Wis. 1975); Carnivale Bag Co. v. Slide-Rite Mfg. Corp., 395 F. Supp. 287 (S.D.N.Y. 1975) (suggesting "competitors only" limitation only appropriate for exclusionary practices cases and not price-fixing).

389. *See* Malamud v. Sinclair Oil Corp., 521 F.2d 1142 (6th Cir. 1975).

390. *See* text accompanying note 377 *supra. See also* note 234 *supra.*

391. *Cf.* San Francisco Seals, Ltd. v. National Hockey League, 379 F. Supp. 966, 972 (C.D. Cal. 1974): "In the instant case, the area of the economy endangered by the defendant's alleged conspiracy to monopolize is that in which rival pro hockey leagues compete. The target of 'the defendant's' alleged conspiracy is any rival hockey league which might try to take over part of the National Hockey League's market."

percentage-lease arrangements. In several cases, most notably those in the Second and Third Circuits, the plaintiffs were found not to have standing to litigate the alleged antitrust violations.[392] The courts concluded that the lessors were not themselves targets of the alleged market restraints and that something more than the foreseeability of the resulting injury had to be shown.[393] The result of these cases is reinforced by subsequent decisions implying that in situations involving illegal exclusionary practices (rather than price-fixing), standing will be limited primarily to those who are competitors of the defendants.[394]

There are other precedents, however, which would offer more encouragement for the city-lessor. Other courts considering percentage-lease situations have refused to follow the lead of the Second and Third Circuits.[395] In addition, as mentioned, at least one circuit has suggested that the relevant inquiry is whether the interest which the plaintiff seeks to assert is within the zone of interests the statute was intended to protect.[396] Under this latter approach, the city-lessor would seem to have a strong claim. The antitrust laws could be read to reflect an intention to protect the competitiveness of professional sports markets. Most sports require unique facilities for the staging of events, and the availability of stadiums and arenas would seem to be an important ingredient in the level of competition which occurs. Thus, the willingness of cities to finance stadiums, and the type of financial return they generate, would seem to bear a close relationship to the basic concern of the statute.[397]

Injury to the local economy. Where the city does not operate a sports facility, it may attempt to assert that it is suing to vindicate the general injury to the local economy which results when a league withdraws an existing franchise or refuses to grant a new one. There is no doubt that the presence of a major league sports franchise may have an important effect in stimulating local commerce.[398] Whether a city can use this fact to overcome the standing hurdle is another question, however.

It should be noted that there is an initial reason to doubt whether the city is the proper party to seek vindication of the alleged local injury. The suit would appear to be in the nature of a *parens patriae* action, for the government would be suing to protect the interest of its citizens, as opposed to its own proprietary interest. Such suits are normally brought by the state through its attorney general, rather than by a city.[399] As a municipality's power is derived from the

---

392. *See* Calderone Enterprises Corp. v. United Artists Theatre Circuit, Inc., 454 F.2d 1292 (2d Cir. 1971), *cert. denied,* 406 U.S. 930 (1972); Melrose Realty Co. v. Loew's, Inc., 234 F.2d 518 (3d Cir.), *cert. denied,* 352 U.S. 890 (1956); Harrison v. Paramount Pictures, Inc., 115 F. Supp. 312 (E.D. Pa. 1953), *aff'd,* 211 F.2d 405 (3d Cir. 1954).

393. *See, e.g.,* Calderone Enterprises Corp. v. United Artists Theatre Circuit, Inc., 454 F.2d 1292, 1295 (2d Cir. 1971), *cert. denied,* 406 U.S. 930 (1972).

394. *See* cases cited in note 388 *supra.*

395. *See, e.g.,* Congress Bldg. Corp. v. Loew's, Inc., 246 F.2d 587 (7th Cir. 1957); Steiner v. 20th Century-Fox Film Corp., 232 F.2d 190 (9th Cir. 1956).

396. See Malamud v. Sinclair Oil Corp., 521 F.2d 1142 (6th Cir. 1975).

397. *See also* Tugboat, Inc. v. Mobile Towing Co., 534 F.2d 1172 (5th Cir. 1976); Johnson v. Ready Mixed Concrete Co., 318 F. Supp. 930 (D. Neb. 1970).

398. *See* authorities cited in note 313 *supra.*

399. *See, e.g., In re* Multidistrict Vehicle Air Pollution, 481 F.2d 122, 131 (9th Cir. 1973). *See also* Hawaii v. Standard Oil Co., 405 U.S. 251 (1972); Georgia v. Pennsylvania R.R., 324 U.S. 439 (1945); Illinois v. Brunswick Corp., 1963 Trade Cas. ¶ 70, 726 (N.D. Ill. 1963). *Cf.* Wisconsin v. Milwaukee Braves, Inc., 1966 Trade Cas. ¶ 71,738 at 82,369, 82,374-75 (Wis. Cir. Ct.).

state, the city is not a sovereign in its own right. The power to litigate *parens patriae* is usually thought to inure to the governmental unit which has ultimate responsibility for its citizens' well-being.[400] Hence, if a claim were to be based on the government's non-proprietary interest in the franchising dispute, the state would seem to be the more appropriate litigant.[401]

But even if the litigation is correctly captioned, there are other standing hurdles to be overcome. The plaintiff must still establish that the injury complained of resulted directly from the alleged illegal conduct, and the concern for defining the relevant target area will reappear.[402] A state-plaintiff would likely encounter difficulty in those jurisdictions which grant standing only to those persons who are directly involved in the sphere of commerce which was allegedly restrained. A court might well conclude that the citizens of the relevant geographical area were not "aimed at" and that any injury which they suffered was only incidentally a result of the defendant's scheme.[403]

In addition, there is a question as to whether the plaintiff could show that there had been an injury to "business or property" as required by the antitrust standing rules. Some authorities suggest that an injury to a state's general economy is too non-specific and does not qualify under the "business or property" branch of the standing requirement.[404] The plaintiff might assert that some of the citizens it represents suffered definite business or property injuries. It would be alleged that this was true as to those firms which would have provided goods and services to the franchise if it had located in the disputed area. There is some uncertainty as to how such a claim would be treated. Under prior law, the presence of identifiable individual injuries often precluded the assertion of these in a *parens patriae* suit.[405] The courts reasoned that since the individuals involved could separately sue to test their claims, to allow the state to pursue them might lead to duplicitous litigation and multiple recoveries.[406] The law in this area was changed by the Antitrust Improvements Act of 1976, which allows the state attorney general to sue *parens patriae* "for injury sustained by [a resident] natural person to [his] property" by reason of antitrust violations.[407] It appears that the statute was intended to have its main impact on triple damages actions, and its application to the types of cases we are considering, which may involve requests for other types or remedies, has not been clearly defined.[408]

---

400. *See generally* 16L von Kalinowski § 101.11 n. 4; Malina & Bleachman, Parens Patriae *Suits for Treble Damages Under the Antitrust Laws,* 65 Nw. U. L. Rev. 193 (1970).

401. Where a city has sustained an injury to a proprietary, as opposed to non-proprietary, interest, it may maintain its own suit. *See* Chattanooga Foundry & Pipe Works v. Atlanta, 203 U.S. 390 (1906).

402. *See* text accompanying notes 383-89 *supra.*

403. *Cf.* Hawaii v. Standard Oil Co., 431 F.2d 1282, 1285 (9th Cir. 1970), *aff'd,* 405 U.S. 251 (1972); In re Multidistrict Air Pollution Litigation, 481 F.2d 122 (9th Cir. 1973).

404. *See, e.g.,* Hawaii v. Standard Oil Co., 431 F.2d 1282 (9th Cir. 1970), *aff'd,* 405 U.S. 251 (1972); In re Multidistrict Air Pollution Litigation, 481 F.2d 122 (9th Cir. 1973). *gf.* Cosentino v. Carver-Greenfield Corp., 1970 Trade Cas. ¶ 73,390 (D. Neb. 1969), *aff'd,* 433 F.2d 1274 (8th Cir. 1970). *But see* Georgia v. Pennsylvania R.R., 324 U.S. 439 (1945).

405. *See, e.g.,* Pfizer, Inc. v. Lord, 522 F.2d 612, 617 n.2 (8th Cir. 1975); California v. Frito-Lay, Inc., 474 F.2d 774, 775 (9th Cir.) *cert. denied,* 412 U.S. 908, 93 S. Ct. 2291 (1973). *See also* Hawaii v. Standard Oil Co., 405 U.S. 251 (1972).

406. *See* Hawaii v. Standard Oil Co., 405 U.S. 251 (1972).

407. 15 U.S.C. §§ 15, 15c(a) (Supp. 1977).

408. *See generally* Olliff, Parens Patriae *Antitrust Actions for Treble Damages,* 14 Harv. J. Legis. 328 (1977).

The proper remedy. The foregoing should suggest that there will often be a serious debate about whether a city (or state) has standing to question the legality of the defendant-league's monopoly. This is not the only issue which is likely to be heavily contested, however. Even if the plaintiff is found to have standing and even if it is able to establish that the league used illegal or improper means to acquire its monopoly, the court must confront the difficult matter of choosing an appropriate remedy. The plaintiff would likely ask for some type of injunctive relief which either precluded the league from moving an existing franchise or compelled it to award a new one.[409] It can be doubted, however, whether such a remedy would be justified in most of the cases which are likely to arise.

A major difficulty with any attempt to compel a league to franchise a city is that this type of remedy seems inconsistent with the nature of the antitrust violation alleged. The plaintiff's basic complaint is that the league took actions which render the particular sports market less competitive.[410] An order which "forces" a dominant league to locate in a city capable of supporting a team would hardly serve to foster competition for that market. Apart from the few largest metropolitan areas, there appear to be few cities in which more than one club in a given sport can operate profitably. Moreover, if the order has the effect of forcing the league to expand the total number of its franchises, this fact would operate as a further incremental deterrent to the formation of a rival enterprise.[411] A potential location for one of the rival's franchises would have been consumed, and thus the rival would find it now more difficult to establish itself in the minimum number of cities necessary for the operation of a credible "league." [412]

In light of the nature of the antitrust violation asserted, it would seem appropriate that the court direct its attention to devising remedies which increased, rather than deterred, the competitiveness of the particular market.[413] The court presumably would want to give attention to the practices of the defendant league which indicated that its monopoly power had been illegally acquired. If the improprieties were capable of being corrected, the most appropriate remedies would be those directed to this end. For example, the plaintiff might have established that the defendant attained its monopoly through the use of exclusionary agreements with advertisers or other third parties.[414] It would seem fully appropriate for the court to ban these practices and require the league to renegotiate its arrangements. Or if the plaintiff

409. The lower court in the *Milwaukee Braves* case issued an order enjoining the threatened move unless an expansion franchise was awarded to the city. *See* note 318 *supra*. Also, in its case against the member-clubs of the NBA, the City of Buffalo sought an injunction barring a transfer of the NBA Braves franchise. Buffalo v. Atlanta Hawks Basketball, Inc., Civil No. 76-0261 (W.D.N.Y., June 15, 1976). *See also* text accompanying notes 226-34 *supra*.

410. *See* text accompanying note 377 *supra*. *See also* text accompanying notes 232-34 *supra*.

411. *See* Comment, *The Super Bowl and the Sherman Act: Professional Team Sports and the Antitrust Laws,* 81 HARV. L. REV. 418, 431 (1967).

412. *See* text accompanying notes 289-92 *supra*.

413. *Cf.* Comment, *The Super Bowl and the Sherman Act: Professional Team Sports and the Antitrust Laws, supra* note 411, at 430.

414. *Cf.* Philadelphia World Hockey Club, Inc. v. Philadelphia Hockey Club, Inc., 351 F. Supp. 462 (E.D. Pa. 1972).

establishes that a proposed merger with a rival league amounts to an illegal acquisition of monopoly power, an order preventing the merger might be appropriate. But again, it does not necessarily follow that the plaintiff-city is also entitled to an order granting it a franchise. As previously explained, such an order may well do more harm than good in improving the competitiveness of the market for sports franchises.[415]

The city might seek money damages instead of injunctive relief. Such a claim has some plausability: the city would assert that it (or its citizens) had been damaged by the defendant's illegal practices and that like other antitrust plaintiffs, it is entitled to be compensated for the injury sustained. It can be expected that the defendant will resist any such claim on the basis that the extent of the plaintiff's damage is speculative. Here the strength of the plaintiff's case will depend on the particular interest which is asserted. If the plaintiff's only claim is for the injury sustained by local businesses, it is likely to encounter significant difficulty in making a reasonable quantification of the actual damage inflicted.[416] Several factors contribute to the uncertainty of this calculation. For example, it would be necessary to define the relevant period of the injury. This in turn would entail a determination of the likelihood that the franchise would have operated profitably. If the franchise had not succeeded, the club would have been moved or disbanded, and the resulting "damage" would not be attributable to the alleged antitrust violation.[417] The relative success of the hypothetical franchise would also have to be determined in order to gauge other aspects of the claim injury. The degree of commerce which a club generates is closely related to its success on the athletic field. A poor performer is likely to attract few fans, and hence generate a reduced volume of business for local suppliers of goods and services.

Where the city sues as landlord of a major league sports facility, the range of speculation is somewhat reduced. There is now a single business involved, and it presumably will have a past history of operation which provides a basis for the damage calculation.[418] Moreover, there are other cities which operate similar facilities, and while it is doubtful that these have had a uniform experience in terms of their profitability, the availability of some "comparables" should serve to narrow the range of speculation. It will be noted, however, that

---

415. If the court were inclined to force the league to locate in a particular city, it would seemingly have to make a comparative evaluation of the relative merits of the plaintiff-city and other cities which might be interested in hosting a club. *See* text accompanying notes 341-42 *supra.*

416. On the issue of when the amount of damage is established with sufficient certainty, see Bigelow v. RKO Radio Pictures, 327 U.S. 51 (1946); Story Parchment Co. v. Paterson Parchment Paper Co., 282 U.S. 555 (1931); Farmington Dowel Prods. Co. v. Forster Mfg. Co., 421 F.2d 61 (1st Cir. 1969), *supplemental order,* 421 F.2d 91 (1st Cir. 1970); Denver Petroleum Corp. v. Shell Oil Co., 306 F. Supp. 289, 309 (D. Colo. 1969); Bal Theatre Corp. v. Paramount Film Distrib. Corp., 206 F. Supp. 708 (N.D. Cal. 1962).

417. In several cases, the courts have refused to afford remedies because they found the particular injuries to be due to factors other than the antitrust violation. *See* Atlas Bldg. Prods. Co. v. Diamond Block & Gravel Co., 269 F.2d 950 (10th Cir. 1959), *cert. denied,* 363 U.S. 893 (1960); Scott Publishing Co. v. Columbia Basin Publishers, 180 F. Supp. 754 (D. Wash. 1959), *aff'd,* 293 F.2d 15 (9th Cir.), *cert. denied,* 368 U.S. 940 (1961); Noyes v. Parsons, 245 F. 689 (9th Cir. 1917).

418. *Cf.* Fontana Aviation, Inc. v. Beech Aircraft Corp., 430 F.2d 1080 (7th Cir. 1970), *cert. denied* 401 U.S. 973 (1971); Autowest, Inc. v. Peugeot, Inc., 434 F.2d 556 (2d Cir. 1970). *But see* Farmington Dowel Prods. Co. v. Forster Mfg. Co., 421 F.2d 61 (1st Cir. 1969), *supplemental order,* 421 F.2d 91 (1st Cir. 1970).

a determination of the plaintiff's lost revenues will involve some of the same difficulties mentioned above. Thus, it will be necessary for the court to determine how well the tenant-club would have performed on the athletic field and how long it would have remained in the city.

Courts have generally exhibited great ingenuity in fashioning damage remedies in antitrust proceedings. The problems of proof which we have identified here are not unique to the sports area; similar issues arise anytime the plaintiff alleges lost profits resulting from an antitrust violation. The courts have held that the plaintiff need not establish the amount of its damages with mathematical precision and have often been quite liberal in structuring damage remedies.[419] But for our purposes, the central question is whether the degree of uncertainty on the damage issue in the franchising cases is so great that even with their otherwise liberal orientation, the courts will decline to sanction this remedy. In deciding how much uncertainty they will tolerate, it seems appropriate that courts also consider the availability of other remedies which may more certainly promote the goals of the antitrust laws. Thus, where the contingencies in the franchising cases render the damage question truly imponderable, a court may conclude that it is preferable to issue an order directed at correcting the actions which gave the defendant-monopolist an unfair advantage. By tearing down the barriers created by improper restrictive or exclusionary agreements, the court may be able to lessen the monopolist's hold on the market and encourage more responsive market behavior.

Where a damage calculation can be made within the bounds of uncertainty tolerated by general antitrust precedents, an order awarding monetary recovery would seem appropriate. Among the situations we have considered, those in which the city sues as lessor of a sports facility seem to be the most promising in terms of presenting tolerable uncertainty on the matter of damages. It should be kept in mind, however, that the damage issue will arise only if it is first determined that the city has standing to contest the legality of the defendant's monopoly. As already discussed, in some circuits, it appears unlikely that a municipality will be able to satisfy this requirement.[420]

d. Ownership Approval Requirements. The final group of franchising cases which we want to consider are those in which a league refuses to approve an individual or group seeking to acquire a club. The leagues have various rules limiting the types of persons who may own franchises. Some of these, such as the prohibition on ownership by persons involved in gambling activities, are intended to protect the sport from undesirable influences.[421] Others, such as the prohibition on interlocking ownership among clubs, have the purpose of preserving the appearance that the clubs represent truly independent competing

---

419. *See generally* Bigelow v. RKO Radio Pictures, 327 U.S. 251 (1946); Agrashell, Inc. v. Hammons Prods. Co., 479 F.2d 269 (8th Cir.), *cert. denied,* 414 U.S. 1022 (1973); South-East Coal Co. v. Consolidation Coal Co., 434 F.2d 767 (6th Cir. 1970), *cert. denied,* 407 U.S. 983 (1971); Autowest, Inc. v. Peugeot, Inc., 434 F.2d 556 (2d Cir. 1970); Poster Exchange, Inc. v. National Screen Serv. Corp., 431 F.2d 334 (5th Cir. 1970), *cert. denied,* 401 U.S. 912 (1971).

420. *See* text accompanying notes 391-94 *supra.*

421. *See generally* Comment, *The Super Bowl and the Sherman Act: Professional Team Sports and the Antitrust Laws,* 81 Harv. L. Rev. 418, 428-29 (1967).

Similar limitations are found in sports, such as horse racing, which are subject to direct public regulation. These are discussed in § 2.06 *supra.*

units as far as their on-the-field performances are concerned.[422] In addition to rules controlling particular types of activities by club owners, most leagues have a general ownership-approval requirement. Thus, the league may provide that any transfer of ownership must be approved by a three-fourths vote of the existing clubs.[423]

The question which we will consider is whether the antitrust laws operate to limit the league's discretion in approving or disapproving prospective owners.[424] We will assume that the decisions in question pertain to franchises already in existence. Thus, we separate from the present discussion the question of whether prospective owners can force the league to expand the number of its franchises. The principles bearing on that issue are discussed in the prior subpart and are not repeated here. For the present, our main concern is with the right of the league to control who may own its franchises and what the form of ownership will be.

The central controversy in this area is brought into rather sharp focus by the decision in *Levin v. National Basketball Association.*[425] Levin and Lipton had purchased the Boston Celtics and applied to the NBA for a transfer of NBA membership from the Celtics' previous owners to the partnership which they proposed to form. The NBA Board of Governors considered the plaintiffs' application on two occasions, one of which involved a personal appearance by the plaintiffs. The application was overwhelmingly rejected both times.[426]

Levin and Lipton subsequently sued. The thrust of the plaintiffs' complaint was that they were entitled to have the basis of the rejection reviewed under the antitrust laws. While the court's opinion does not include a statement of the precise standard of review proposed by the plaintiffs, their contention apparently was that the other member clubs could limit the plaintiffs' entry into the league only if there were reasonable, objective grounds for doing so.[427] There was a sharp dispute on the issue of why the new owners were rejected.

---

422. *See, e.g.,* CONSTITUTION AND BY-LAWS FOR THE NATIONAL FOOTBALL LEAGUE § 9.1(B) (1972):

> No member, or stockholder, officer, director, partner, or employee thereof, and no officer or employee of the League, including a game official, shall:
> (1) Own or have any financial interest directly or indirectly, in any other member club of the League.
> (2) Directly or indirectly, loan money to or become surety or guarantor for any other member club, or any player, coach, or employee thereof, or holder of an interest therein.
> (3) Directly or indirectly loan money or offer any gift or reward or become surety or guarantor for any game official or other official or employee of the League.
> (4) Act as the contracting agent or representative for any player, or shareholder or be financially interested in the compensation of any player in the League . . . .

423. *See* Comment, *The Super Bowl and the Sherman Act: Professional Team Sports and the Antitrust Laws, supra* note 421, at 428 n.51. *See also* CONSTITUTION AND BY-LAWS FOR THE NATIONAL FOOTBALL LEAGUE §§ 3.3, 3.5 (1972) (new members and transferees must be approved by affirmative vote of "three-fourths or 20, whichever is greater, of the members of the League").

424. This question is also considered in Comment, *The Super Bowl and the Sherman Act: Professional Team Sports and the Antitrust Laws, supra* note 421 at 428-29. The authors conclude that

> The tenuousness of the alleged legitimate purposes, the availability of alternatives, the serious restrictive effects on entry, and the possibility of abuse all suggest that these restraints on sale are not sufficiently justified by the peculiarities of the industry to survive antitrust challenge. *Id.*

The reader will note that we reach the opposite conclusion in the discussion which follows.
425. 385 F. Supp. 149 (S.D.N.Y. 1974).
426. *Id.* at 150.
427. *Cf.* L. SOBEL, PROFESSIONAL SPORTS AND THE LAW 498-99 (1977).

The plaintiffs contended that they were disapproved only because of their friendship with Sam Schulman, an existing NBA owner, who apparently was regarded as a disruptive influence by his fellow owners.[428] The league did not deny that the relationship between the plaintiffs and Schulman influenced its decision, but suggested that there were objective grounds for disapproving it. The league contended, for example, that the plaintiffs had various business dealings with Schulman, including stock-ownership in Schulman's Seattle club, which created potential conflicts of interest and violated a league prohibition on interlocking club ownership.[429]

Judge Owen of the federal District Court for the Southern District of New York disposed of the plaintiffs' complaint in a procedural setting which is worthy of note. The defendants presented a motion requesting summary judgment in their favor. It is generally recognized that motions such as this which preclude a trial on the merits should be granted sparingly in antitrust litigation because of the uncertainties in substantive antitrust doctrine and because of the difficulty plaintiffs encounter in gathering firm evidence before trial.[430] Judge Owen recognized that courts were usually inclined to be highly deferential to a plaintiff's antitrust claims, but nonetheless concluded that the case before him was sufficiently devoid of merit to warrant the unusual step of summary dismissal in favor of the defendant-league. The court apparently felt that the unresolved factual issue as to the real reason for the league's disapproval of the plaintiffs' application was not critical to the case. Judge Owen suggested that even if the plaintiffs were correct in their characterization of the grounds for the rejection, their action would fail.[431] In the court's view, the plaintiffs had not established that the defendant-league's requirement of membership approval involved any transgression of antitrust policy.

Judge Owen's opinion does not include a lengthy analysis of the antitrust issue, and some of the court's statements as to the intended effect of the antitrust laws can be disputed.[432] But with some extrapolation, the rationale for the court's rejection of the plaintiffs' complaint can be readily discerned. To understand the court's analysis, it is useful to develop a more complete statement of the plaintiffs' theory of the case. Again, the plaintiffs apparently contended that the league could disapprove an application for the transfer of a membership only if it did so on objective, reasonable grounds. This arguement involves an assumption that a league is similar to a trade association in which the various members have authority to vote to exclude other participants. Cases from other industries suggest that a rule of reason approach will usually be invoked to evaluate the practices of industrial groups which exclude potential

---

428. 385 F. Supp. at 150-51.
429. *Id.* at 151.
430. *See, e.g.,* Poller v. Columbia Broadcasting System, Inc., 368 U.S. 464 (1962).
431. 385 F. Supp. at 152.
432. For example, the court states that "The law is well established that it is competition, and not individual competitors, that is protected by the antitrust laws." *Id.* It is not clear that this is a point worth debating or that it is necessary to the court's analysis. In any case, to the extent that the antitrust laws provide remedies (*e.g.,* money damages) which are based on the peculiar characteristics of the plaintiff, it would not seem unreasonable to suggest that those statutes do in fact afford substantial protection to individual competitors.

entrants.[433] Under this view, the organization must first show that its exercise of self-government controls was justified by the nature of its enterprise. Then it must appear that the particular controls which were used furthered a legitimate associational purpose and were not simply designed to discourage competition by those who sought membership.[434] A decision to exclude a potential entrant might lessen or destroy its ability to function in the relevant market and thus reduce the degree of interfirm competition which occurs. To insure that the group's control does not have such anti-competitive effects, the courts require that exclusionary decisions be made according to neutral criteria which further a legitimate end. In *Levin,* the plaintiffs apparently argued that the defendant-NBA's decision should be evaluated under these principles and that, therefore, their complaint could not be disposed of until the court had identified the real grounds for the rejection of their membership application and determined whether those grounds were reasonable.[435]

While Judge Owen did not set out the plaintiffs' contention in the detail suggested above, his analysis is responsive to the argument we have outlined. The court's opinion can be read as taking the position that the trade association cases were not relevant for the situation before it. As indicated, the reason for judicial intervention in those cases is to insure that the trade association does not use its exclusionary rules for anti-competitive purposes. In Judge Owen's view the facts of *Levin* did not present a similar basis for concern about the competitiveness of the sports franchise market, for "[h]ere the plaintiffs wanted to *join* with those unwilling to accept them, *not to compete with them,* but to be partners in the operation of a sports league for plaintiffs' profit."[436] The emphasis indicated by italics was supplied by the court and suggests that the court did not perceive the case as raising a fundamental concern for competition. The exclusion of Levin and Lipton would not deter a competitor because they had no intention to compete with the other owners. Rather, the plaintiffs had hoped to become co-participants in the defendants' venture and share in the profits which it generated. Since the reason for judicial intervention under the antitrust laws was missing, the court concluded that those laws did not apply and, accordingly, granted judgment for the defendants.

It should be clear that if *Levin* is correct, a league's application of its ownership approval requirements will be largely free from review under the antitrust laws. The import of that decision is that controversies resulting from these rules generally fall outside of the purview of the antitrust statutes, for they have little to do with the amount of competition which occurs with respect to the product known as "league sports." The only type of controversy that might be reviewable is one in which the plaintiff can allege that it was

---

433. *See, e.g.,* Hatley v. American Quarter Horse Ass'n, 552 F.2d 646 (5th Cir. 1977). *See generally* Comment, *Trade Association Exclusionary Practices: An Affirmative Role for the Rule of Reason,* 66 COLUM. L. REV. 1486 (1966).

434. *See* Comment, *Trade Association Exclusionary Practices: An Affirmative Role for the Rule of Reason, supra* note 433, at 1504-10. *See also* § 5.10 *supra.*

435. As previously noted, the precise theory of the plaintiffs' case in *Levin* is not apparent from the reported decision. There is at least one passage which might suggest that the plaintiffs argued that the ownership limitations should be deemed *per se* illegal. *See* 385 F. Supp. at 152 n.6. As indicated in the text accompanying notes 433-34 *supra,* a rule of reason, rather than a *per se,* approach would have been more appropriate had the court undertaken to evaluate the reason for the rejection of the plaintiffs' application for membership.

436. 385 F. Supp. at 152.

disapproved for anti-competitive reasons, as where a league rejects a former promoter of a rival league solely for the purpose of punishing him for his prior efforts.[437] But such a case will rarely arise, and in the vast majority of situations, the relevant question will be whether the *Levin* approach should be sustained.

There are several principles discussed in other parts of this section 5.11 which bear on the result reached in *Levin*. A review of these will suggest that Judge Owen's decision is consistent with the characterizations which have been given to a league's operation in other contexts. And since there appears to be little in the ownership approval situations calling for a different approach, it would appear that *Levin* states a rule which should be sustained in future cases.

In large measure, *Levin* simply involves a particularized application of a question raised in the introduction to this section. We suggested that in franchising controversies, it is often critical to decide what is the relevant "firm" or entity for antitrust purposes.[438] If the individual clubs are regarded as separate firms with distinct competitive interests, then a collective decision by such clubs has some of the earmarks of a group boycott or a concerted refusal to deal. Such decisions will be subject to control under either a *per se* or rule of reason approach. On the other hand, if the league is identified as the relevant firm for franchising purposes, the range of antitrust concerns is narrowed considerably. Because there is no duality of action, much of the doctrine dealing with illegal restraints of trade is inapplicable and the focus of any antitrust inquiry must be on those principles used to control the acquisition and misuse of monopoly power.[439]

In its essence, Judge Owen's opinion assumes that as far as ownership approval rules are concerned, the league should be regarded as a single entity. He perceives the league as a firm in which the various co-venturers do not compete with one another, but undertake a cooperative effort to produce a common product. That conclusion is similar to the finding made in *San Francisco Seals* and is also supported by a real-world appraisal of the nature of a league's operation. The factors to be considered in that appraisal are discussed elsewhere in these pages.[440] The basic point made is that there is a great deal of economic interdependence among the clubs comprising a league. They jointly produce a product which no one of them is capable of producing alone. In addition, the success of the overall venture depends upon the financial stability of each club.[441] The members must, therefore, refrain from direct, interfirm economic competition and, in fact, do utilize various cross-subsidy devices to compensate for the natural inequities arising from differences in the economic potential of various franchise locations.

Since a league's member-clubs do not compete with one another, it seems inappropriate to make them subject to legal principles designed to control the

---

437. Such a rejection would have some of the characteristics of a league's decision to blacklist a player who played in a rival league, although different markets are involved. The blacklisting problem is discussed in § 5.09 *supra*.

438. *See* text accompanying notes 86-88 *supra*. *See also* text accompanying notes 127-45 *supra*.

439. *See* text accompanying notes 61-85 *supra*.

440. *See* text accompanying notes 133-45 *supra*.

441. *See generally* United States v. National Football League, 116 F. Supp. 319 (E.D. Pa. 1953); Bork, *Ancillary Restraints and the Sherman Act,* 15 ABA ANTITRUST SECTION 211, 231-34 (1959); Neale, *The Peculiar Economics of Professional Sports,* 78 Q.J. ECON. 1 (1964).

behavior of firms which are fundamentally different. In its basic nature, a league-firm is not a conspiracy. To treat it as such is to force results which are unlikely to achieve any purpose intended by Congress.

This is not to say that a league's operation enjoys complete antitrust immunity. Rather, what it means is that we must select a different antitrust frame of reference for judging the league's conduct. Again, the discussion in the prior portions of this section suggest the principles to be applied. The thesis developed above is that a league should be regarded as a single entity which is an actual or potential monopoly and that the relevant doctrine is that which seeks to control the acquisition and misuse of monopoly power.[442]

Some of the monopoly-related concepts discussed above are useful in evaluating the *Levin* decision. It should be apparent that the question presented in *Levin* is similar to that which arises when a league refuses to grant a franchise to a petitioning city.[443] In each instance, the basic complaint is that the league-monopolist has refused to deal with an allegedly-worthy applicant. In our discussion of the city's right to demand a franchise, we investigated the question of whether a firm holding a lawful monopoly had an obligation to deal fairly with those who wanted to contract with it. We found that the law generally does not require that a monopolist act reasonably in its treatment of noncompetitors.[444] The lessons of that earlier discussion would seem to be applicable here. The prospective owner who has been rejected would like to enlist the aid of the court in forcing the monopolist to conform to a standard of reasonableness. There is, however, little reason to think that this type of plaintiff will, or should, fare better than the city which did not receive the desired franchise. In neither case would judicial intervention make a significant contribution to the amount of competition occurring in the output market of the sports industry.

The foregoing should suggest that the result in *Levin* seems correct under the applicable legal doctrine. There is another view of the case which adds further support to the conclusion reached. The reader will recall that in an earlier discussion of the singular nature of a league enterprise, an analogy was made to a national accounting firm.[445] We posited a situation in which the firm operated various regional offices staffed by partners whose compensation was determined in part by their own productivity and in part by the overall success of the firm. It was suggested that this form of organization was not dissimilar to that found in a sports-league and that in each instance it would be appropriate to view the operation as involving a single integrated entity.

The accounting firm analogy is useful in the present context as well. The plaintiffs in *Levin* may be viewed as businessmen who would like to invest in an attractive league venture. The same desire could be attributed to an unassociated accountant who wished to participate in our hypothetical national accounting firm. The question that arises is whether either type of entity has an obligation to justify its decision to admit or reject a potential partner. The

---

442. *See* text accompanying notes 170-271 *supra*.

443. The analogy is not an exact one, however. A city, at least one which owns a sports facility, might be viewed as a potential supplier, while an owner applying for membership can be regarded as a potential investor. The difference in the position of the two parties, however, does not appear to be critical for the antitrust analysis.

444. *See* text accompanying notes 329-76 *supra*.

445. *See* text accompanying note 135 *supra*.

answer appears to be that it does not. The ventures involved are private affairs and in general the law has not seen fit to force unwilling parties into an on-going relationship. There may be many reasons why those who have built up a business may not wish to allow an outsider to participate in it. Some of the reasons may involve considerations which are objectively verifiable, but some may not. It may be that because of the peculiar temperament of either the potential investors or those in control, the judgment is reached that the relationship would not be a fruitful one. But at the bottom line, there is an assumption that the opportunity to participate in a wholly-private undertaking is a mere privilege which does not rise to the status of a legal right.[446] Since only private assets and private efforts are involved in the venture, the question of who will benefit from it seems to be largely a private affair.

It is true that there are some limitations on a private firm's freedom to pursue certain goals. But all of these limitations are stated in the negative — the firm cannot refuse to contract on certain grounds. And each of the negative directives are addressed to very particular types of evils. None gives rise to a general right to invest where one wishes, and none imposes a general duty of reasonable behavior. Thus, in the area of employment contracts, the law proscribes certain types of racial and ethnic discrimination, but does not provide that where that element is absent, the employer must otherwise make reasonable choices. More germane to our present discussion are the proscriptions of the antitrust laws which are applied to private monopolies. The law seems to say that the monopolist may not refuse to deal where its purpose is to injure competition.[447] But the law does not go further and impose a general duty of reasonable behavior. It is only where the private decision-making transgresses into one of the narrow areas defined by a negative directive that the occasion for judicial rebuke arises. Apart from those cases, the assumption seems to be that a private party is free to deal with whomever he wishes and only on the terms which he chooses. Thus, if a firm, whether it be an accounting partnership or a sports-league, decides that it finds a proposed relationship unattractive, the posture of legal institutions appears to be one of indifference.

§ 5.12. The NCAA and the Antitrust Laws.

Several of the preceding sections have dealt with the antitrust problems of the groups which undertake the regulation of sports activities. We first considered some of the regulatory efforts of the leagues which govern professional team sports [448] and then examined the activities of other types of sports associations, particularly those which administer and sanction events in non-team sports.[449] In each case we saw that the antitrust laws provided some

---

446. It is true that the right-privilege distinction has been discredited in many areas of the law. However, each of these areas involves situations in which there is substantial government involvement. *See* Van Alstyne, *The Demise of the Right-Privilege Distinction in Constitutional Law,* 81 HARV. L. REV. 1439 (1968). *See also* Van Alstyne, *Cracks in "The New Property": Adjudicative Due Process in the Administrative State,* 62 CORNELL L. REV. 445 (1977). The basic point to be made here, however, is that the ventures in question are private in nature and do not partake of the changes which have occurred with respect to public sector activities.

447. *See* text accompanying notes 365-71 *supra.*

448. *See* §§ 5.02-.09.

449. *See* § 5.10.

check on the powers which were exercised. It might be asked whether the antitrust laws will also be applied to groups, particularly the NCAA, which undertake to regulate school-related amateur athletes. It will be noted that in many respects, the powers of the NCAA are similar to those exercised by the groups considered above. Thus, the NCAA exercises a sanctioning power under which it approves or disapproves particular events.[450] Moreover, the group promulgates and enforces rules which define the eligibility of athlete-participants and their schools. Other rules are intended to preserve the integrity of the sports involved and empower the NCAA to punish member schools which fail to comply with regulations covering a wide array of matters.[451] It should be clear that these regulatory powers can be exercised in a fashion which produces a substantial disadvantage for particular individuals and schools.

With respect to many of the NCAA's functions, however, the analogy to other sports associations is not complete. In the situations previously considered, the sports activities were typically commercial ventures conducted purely for profit. The sports activities subject to control by the NCAA are of a different sort.[452] While it would be fanciful to suggest that colleges are not concerned about the profitability of their ventures, it is clear that other, non-commercial goals play a central role in their sports programs. Indeed, many of the functions of the NCAA are specifically designed to insure that intercollegiate athletics do not become separate from the basic educational function of the member institutions. If these educational goals were always predominant, there would probably be little reason for a serious antitrust inquiry. Difficulties arise, however, because there is considerable variance in the strength of the academic policy which is reflected in the association's various rules. Where a rule promotes a purely educational goal, the analogy to professional sports associations is not persuasive. However, where the NCAA uses its powers to control the economic aspects of revenue producing sports, the distinction is less clear.[453]

There is no question as to the importance of the NCAA as a regulator of intercollegiate athletics. The NCAA is a voluntary non-profit association which listed 830-member institutions as of March 1, 1976.[454] Its membership increased 128% between 1950 and 1970.[455] It has been judicially noted that it is the "dominant" intercollegiate sports organization.[456] Its main counterpart, the National Association of Intercollegiate Athletics (NAIA), has a membership primarily of smaller schools.

Member schools rely on the NCAA to conduct college championships in seventeen sports, and participation in these contests is limited to eligible students attending member schools.[457] The NCAA also organizes and accepts

450. *Compare* § 5.10.

451. *Compare* § 5.09.

452. *But see* Koch, *A Troubled Cartel: The NCAA,* 38 LAW & CONTEMP. PROB. 135 (1973).

453. *See* Hennessey v. NCAA, No. CA 76-P-0799-W (N.D. Ala. Sept. 27, 1976), *aff'd per curiam,* 564 F.2d 1136 (5th Cir. 1977); Board of Regents, Univ. of Okla. v. NCAA, No. C.D. 76-871 (Dist. Ct. Okla. County, August 23, 1976).

454. 1976-77 MANUAL OF THE NCAA at 148.

455. Martin, *The NCAA and the Fourteenth Amendment,* 11 N.E. L. REV. 383, 389 (1976).

456. College Athletic Placement Service, Inc. v. NCAA, 1975 Trade Cas. ¶ 60,117 (D. N.J.), *aff'd,* No. 74-1904 (3d Cir. Nov. 25, 1974).

457. *See* BY-LAWS OF THE NCAA, art. 6, at 68.

the bids of television networks for broadcast rights to the association's games and controls the extent to which members can make their own broadcast arrangements.[458] The association's activities are financed by a portion of the broadcast receipts and by membership dues.[459] In addition to making rules to control the affairs of its members, the NCAA also performs administrative and judicial functions in enforcing these rules. Generally, the NCAA chooses to enforce its rules by suspensions and expulsions directed to member institutions.[460] Often the effect of these actions is to require the school to discipline athletes or coaches, who are not themselves members of the NCAA.[461]

In recent years the NCAA has increasingly involved itself in regulating the purely economic aspects of college athletics. The NCAA held an Economic Conference in the summer of 1975 and later acted on the proposals suggested there.[462] These efforts were primarily aimed at controlling the costs of the members' athletic programs. Perhaps the most controversial rules adopted were those limiting the size of coaching staffs in Division I football and basketball [463] and those limiting squad size in those same sports. The latter was eventually abandoned after much protest and litigation.[464] Despite these ventures into economic regulation, it can be noted that the NCAA directs most of its efforts toward educational goals relating to the improvement and standardization of programs for student athletes.[465] The overwhelming majority of NCAA

458. The NCAA football contract netted fifteen million dollars in 1974, while the 1976 contract was in excess of sixteen million dollars. Comment, *National Collegiate Athletic Association's Certification Requirement: A Section One Violation of the Sherman Antitrust Act,* 9 VAL. U.L. REV. 193, 197 (1974); *see also* BY-LAWS OF THE NCAA, Exec. Reg. §§ 15-18, at 107-08; Martin, *The NCAA and the Fourteenth Amendment, supra* note 455, at 390.

459. BY-LAWS OF THE NCAA §§ 1-3, at 70-71. The NCAA administrative budget in 1974 was $749,461. Martin, *The NCAA and the Fourteenth Amendment, supra* note 455, at 390.

460. 1976-77 MANUAL OF THE NCAA § 7, at 119; *see also* CONSTITUTION OF THE NCAA art. 4; BY-LAWS OF THE NCAA art. 4, § 6.

461. Chapter 1 of this treatise contains a more complete discussion of the constitutional and private law issues which arise as a result of NCAA enforcement actions.

462. The Second Special NCAA Convention was held Aug. 14-15, 1975, a third was held Jan. 14, 1976. The proposals were considered at the 70th Annual NCAA Convention, Jan. 15-17, 1976.

463. BY-LAWS OF THE NCAA, art. 12, at 94-95.

464. On September 8, 1975, the University of Alabama football coach, Bear Bryant, obtained a ruling in U.S. district court in Alabama that the 48 player limit on traveling squads was unfair but the Fifth Circuit Court of Appeals reversed Judge Sam Pointer and reinstated the rule. *See,* Los Angeles Times, Sept. 5, 1975, Pt. III, at 5, col. 1; Washington Post, Sept. 18, 1975, at E5, col. 1. Indiana basketball coach, Bobby Knight, filed a similar suit in Indiana state court. *See,* N.Y. Times, Dec. 12, 1975, at 51, col. 5.

The NCAA Convention voted to abandon these restrictions on Jan. 17, 1976 in St. Louis. *See,* N.Y. Times, Jan. 18, 1976, § 5, at 1, col. 7.

465. *See* CONSTITUTION OF THE NCAA, art. 2, § 1:

Section 1. Purposes. The purposes of this Association are:

(a) To initiate, stimulate and improve intercollegiate athletic programs by student-athletes and promote and develop educational leadership, physical fitness, sports participation as a recreational pursuit and athletic excellence.

(b) To uphold the principle of institutional control of, and responsibility by all intercollegiate sports in conformity with the Constitution and By-Laws of this Association.

(c) To encourage its members to adopt eligibility rules to comply with satisfactory standards of scholarship, sportsmanship and amateurism.

(d) To formulate, copyright and publish rules of play governing intercollegiate sports.

(e) To preserve intercollegiate athletic records.

(f) To supervise the conduct of, and to establish eligibility standards for regional and national athletic events under the auspices of this Association.

(g) To cooperate with other amateur athletic organizations in governing and promoting national and international athletic events.

regulations have a basis in this concern for the protection of amateurism in college athletics. Where this object is being pursued in its pure form, the NCAA is likely to find that the antitrust laws provide little basis for judicial intervention into its activities. The group's vulnerability under those laws is a much more serious concern, however, with respect to those rule-making activities which have a discernible economic purpose behind them.

An inquiry into the status of the NCAA under the antitrust laws suggests that there are two different issues which are likely to be subject to debate. One is the fundamental question of whether the group should be subject to antitrust regulation at all. The other concerns the extent to which the group should be able to rely upon its non-commercial, educational purposes to justify the anti-competitive effects of its regulations. This latter issue is usually framed in terms of a debate about whether the *per se* or rule of reason standard provides a more appropriate basis for review. There is only a limited body of direct precedent dealing with these issues of the applicability of the antitrust laws and the proper standard of review, and much of the analysis in this area must depend upon principles developed in other factual settings. But a review of the relevant doctrine suggests several respects in which the range of the debate on the NCAA's antitrust status can be narrowed.

a. Applicability of the Sherman Act. On the question of whether the NCAA is subject to the prohibitions of the Sherman Act, it can be noted that a threshold requirement for the application of that statute is that the activity in question must involve or affect interstate commerce.[466] The present scope of NCAA activity should be sufficient to establish the necessary interstate involvement. The object of the group's regulation — college-level sports — has many interstate aspects to it. Athletes are often recruited on a nation-wide basis; the teams themselves frequently move between states; and the games are often broadcast over a wide area. Moreover, the NCAA itself engages in many activities of a distinctive interstate character. As already stated, the NCAA controls the bidding for interstate television broadcasting for all collegiate events; it also has rights over program content, radio broadcast policy and the composition of advertising at NCAA contests.[467] In addition, the NCAA undertakes to schedule games and tournaments which necessitate the transportation of teams across state lines.[468] Similarly, the interstate sale of tickets for NCAA events supports a finding that interstate commerce is

(h) To legislate, through Bylaws or by resolution of a Convention upon any subject of general concern to the members in the administration of intercollegiate athletics.

(i) To study in general all phases of competitive intercollegiate athletics and establish standards whereby the colleges and universities of the United States can maintain their athletic activities on a high level.

466. Sherman Antitrust Act § 1, 26 Stat. 209 (1890) *as amended,* 15 USC § 1.

467. 1976-77 MANUAL OF THE NCAA, Exec. Regs. §§ 15-18, at 107-08. *See* Comment, *National Collegiate Athletic Association's Certification Requirement: A Section One Violation of the Sherman Antitrust Act, supra* note 458, at 197.

468. 1976-77 MANUAL OF THE NCAA, Exec. Regs. § 13, at 106. *Cf.* Washington State Bowling Proprietors Ass'n v. Pacific Lanes, Inc., 356 F.2d 371, 379 (9th Cir.), *cert. denied,* 384 U.S. 963 (1966); Blalock v. Ladies Professional Golf Ass'n, 359 F. Supp. 1260, 1263 (N.D. Ga. 1973); Yonker's Raceway v. Standardbred Owners Ass'n, 153 F. Supp. 552 (S.D.N.Y. 1957). *But see* STP Corp. v. United States Auto Club, 286 F. Supp. 146 (S.D. Ind. 1968).

effected.[469] These NCAA actions have, at best, a secondary effect on trade and could be viewed as incidental to the association's non-profit activity. However, this distinction has not been held to bar the application of the Sherman Act at this threshold stage. The NCAA cases to date either found or assumed that the necessary interstate involvement was present.[470]

On the general question of the applicability of the antitrust laws, there is another issue which is likely to receive the most attention. Traditionally the Sherman Act has only been applied to commercial enterprises rather than non-profit organizations such as the NCAA.[471] Some will contend that this exception for non-commercial ventures immunizes the group from antitrust controls. While that contention may have been supportable at one time, it is now apparent that courts are increasingly unwilling to assume that a non-profit association enjoys a wholesale exemption. Rather, the trend of the cases is to require that organizations engaged in substantial economic activities defend their regulations on their merits.[472] It is recognized, however, that the evaluation of the rules under the antitrust laws will be sensitive to the nature of the organization and the special needs of the activity it regulates.

It is well settled that there is nothing in the nature of a sports organization itself to merit an antitrust exemption.[473] Nor will the concern with amateur sports provide blanket protection.[474] However, the NCAA's educational purpose is often cited to distinguish it from other sports associations. It has been argued that a presumption against application of the Sherman Act was accorded educational organizations in *Marjorie Webster College v. Middle States Association*.[475] That case involved a refusal by the defendant association to grant accreditation to the plaintiff school because it was operated for a profit. The District of Columbia Circuit Court held that because the Sherman Act was "tailored to the business world," it should not limit the action of an educational association in a non-commercial sphere. The court stressed that a decision as to the applicability of the Sherman Act required a dual inquiry into the nature of the association and the nature of the action being challenged.[476] This examination convinced the court that the rule in question was an incidental restraint of trade which had no anti-competitive intent or purpose and as such did not warrant application of the Sherman Act.[477] The Middle States Association

---

469. Hennessey v. NCAA, No. CA 76-P-0799-W (N.D. Ala., Sept. 27, 1976) at 17-18. *Cf.* National Wrestling Alliance v. Myers, 325 F.2d 768, 770-71 (8th Cir. 1963).

470. Hennessey v. NCAA, No. CA 76-P-0799-W (N.D. Ala., Sept. 27, 1976) at 17-18; Jones v. NCAA, 392 F. Supp. 295 (D.Mass. 1975); College Athletic Placement Service Inc. v. NCAA, 1975 Trade Cas. ¶ 60,117 (D.N.J.); Samara v. NCAA, 1973 Trade Cas. ¶ 74,536 (E.D.Va.).

471. *See, e.g.,* Apex Hosiery Co. v. Leader, 310 U.S. 469 (1940); Marjorie Webster College v. Middle States Ass'n, 432 F.2d 650 (D.C. Cir. 1970).

472. Nawalarie, *Motives of Non-Profit Organizations and the Antitrust Laws,* 21 CLEV. ST. L. REV. 97, 113 (1972).

473. *See, e.g.,* Radovich v. National Football League, 352 U.S. 445 (1957). *See generally* § 5.07 *supra.*

474. Amateur Softball Ass'n of America v. United States, 467 F.2d 312 (10th Cir. 1972); Tondas v. Amateur Hockey Ass'n, 438 F. Supp. 310 (W.D.N.Y. 1977).

475. 432 F.2d 650 (D.C. Cir. 1970). This case has been severely criticized in Note, *College Accrediting Association's Refusal to Evaluate Proprietary College Held Not a Sherman Act Violation,* 84 HARV. L. REV. 1912 (1971).

476. 432 F.2d at 653.

477. *Id.*

successfully argued that the rule reflected the group's professional judgment about a matter uniquely within its field of expertise, and the court refused to usurp this non-economic decision-making power.

It should be clear that *Marjorie Webster* would offer a good deal of encouragement to the NCAA. That group would argue that it had a special expertise in dealing with the sometimes very difficult matter of defining the role of intercollegiate athletics in undergraduate education. It, too, would ask that courts not interfere with its professional judgments on how to accommodate the various important interests which are at stake. On another matter, it can be noted that Judge Bazelon also emphasized the facts that Middle States was purely a voluntary association, that Marjorie Webster had existed for twenty-three years without accreditation, and that a new association of proprietary schools could be formed.[478] The NCAA could argue that the presence of the NAIA and some independent athletic programs as well as the possibility of new associations forming should satisfy the court that the organization is purely voluntary.

While *Marjorie Webster* does offer some encouragement to groups such as the NCAA which are seeking antitrust immunity, there are reasons to doubt whether the case will ultimately support a significant exemption. It should be noted, for example, that the case itself approves only a limited grant of immunity. The court stated in dicta that no immunity was created for educational organizations as a class. It noted that other restrictions on eligibility for accreditation might be shown to have little other than a commercial motive and in those cases antitrust law would presumably be applicable.[479] This language suggests that NCAA regulations formulated solely as cost-cutting or cost-equalizing measures might not be protected under *Marjorie Webster*. Further support for the view that whatever exemption exists is necessarily limited can be gleaned from earlier Supreme Court decisions dealing with group sanctioning practices. For example, in a case where professional accreditation was denied solely for economic reasons, the Supreme Court looked to the effect on the regulated group, rather than the association making the rule, in its decision that the commercial aspects of the case come within the purview of the Sherman Act.[480] The clear implication of the case was that no group enjoys complete freedom from antitrust scrutiny and that exercises of power which have substantial adverse economic effects are particularly suspect.

Any attempt to use *Marjorie Webster* to immunize the regulatory activities of a group such as the NCAA must confront another, potentially more devastating argument, and that is that the case may not reflect the present state of the law on exemption questions. *Marjorie Webster* was decided at a time when there was still some support for the view that the Supreme Court would recognize a variety of judge-made exemptions from antitrust laws. More recently, however, the Court has undertaken to clarify its position on these matters, and its pronouncement indicates little enthusiasm for finding implied

---

478. *Id.* at 655-58.

479. 432 F.2d at 654-55. At note 21, the court observes that a rule limiting accreditation to schools who purchase textbooks from suppliers who give special discounts for association members would be commercial and subject to attack under the Sherman Act.

480. American Medical Ass'n v. United States, 317 U.S. 519 (1943) *aff'g*, 130 F.2d 233 (D.C. Cir. 1942). *See also* Friends of Animals v. American Veterinary Medical Ass'n, 310 F. Supp. 1016 (S.D.N.Y. 1970).

exemptions under the Sherman Act. *Goldfarb v. Virginia State Bar* [481] involved an attack upon a bar association's minimum fee schedule. The defendants attempted to have the Court confirm that learned professions did not involve trade or commerce under the Sherman Act and thus the regulatory activities of their governing groups were not subject to antitrust review. The Court, however, specifically disclaimed any intention to recognize a learned professions' exemption and found the minimum fee arrangement to violate section 1 of the Act. Perhaps more important than the specific holding in *Goldfarb* was its clear implication that the court was prepared to read the reach of the Sherman Act quite broadly and depend upon Congress to provide any special exemptions. The Court's analysis was particularly pointed in rejecting the bar association's claim of blanket immunity:

> Congress intended to strike as broadly as it could in § 1 of the Sherman Act, and to read into it so wide an exemption as that urged on us would be at odds with that purpose. [482]

While *Goldfarb* was clearly intended to present a new view of the role of the laws in regulating the activities of professional groups, there is some uncertainty as to how broadly the case should be read. It might be contended that *Goldfarb* was intended to presage the end of all judge-made exemptions, including the educational exemption applied in *Marjorie Webster.* It will be noted, however, that the facts of *Goldfarb* did not require that the Court go that far. The particular activity in question in *Goldfarb* was the defendant bar association's attempt to maintain a minimum fee schedule. Such a regulation has a distinctive commercial flavor to it and is arguably distinguishable from rules which deal with matters more purely non-economic, such as rules which seek to define the minimum course-load which college athletes must carry. Narrowly interpreted, *Goldfarb* may represent only a partial erosion of the *Marjorie Webster* exemption. While the Supreme Court seems prepared to find a reviewable commercial or economic effect more readily than the court in *Marjorie Webster,* it did not wholly repudiate the premises from which the D.C. Circuit had proceeded. [483]

Despite the uncertainty as to the precise meaning of *Goldfarb,* some definite conclusions can be reached. It seems clear, for example, that the NCAA does not enjoy blanket immunity from the antitrust laws. *Marjorie Webster* does not support such a wholesale exemption, and *Goldfarb* rather pointedly indicates that the antitrust laws will be rigorously applied to achieve the goal of unrestrained business activity. The cases also serve to identify the types of NCAA regulations which are particularly apt to be subjected to close judicial scrutiny. *Goldfarb* makes clear that the antitrust laws will be applied where the activity or relationship involved is of a business character. [484] Moreover, the Court's view of the concept of "business" in this context seems to be quite broad and may include all undertakings which have significant economic consequences.

481. 421 U.S. 773 (1975).

482. *Id.* at 787.

483. *See id.* at 787-88.

484. *Id.*: "Whatever else it may be, the examination of a land title is a service; the exchange of such a service for money is "commerce" in the most common usage of that word. It is no disparagement of the practice of law or a profession to acknowledge that it has this business aspect..."

The employment relationship between a coach and the university certainly has this characteristic.[485] There is also some argument to be made that the NCAA definitions of student eligibility — which have potentially significant economic consequences for both the student and the school recruiting him or her — also share this attribute. In the final analysis, it must be recognized that there are good reasons to draw the exemption narrowly in this area. One elementary but important point is that subjecting a broad range of practices to antitrust scrutiny does not imply their illegality. It can be expected that even if a substantive review is undertaken most NCAA regulations will be sustained. The group's educational purposes will usually be of sufficient weight to justify collateral economic impingements. Yet, it seems desirable that courts be permitted to insist that the regulatory body come up with such a justification. Such potential for review is likely to insure that regulations are drawn with more care and promulgated after greater deliberation. It is difficult to argue that these are not worthy goals. Moreover, it can be noted that the normal concern for the defendant's litigation burden may not be particularly strong in this area. If an exemption is recognized, it would likely extend only to those matters which did not have important economic consequences. But that issue — the economic implications of a particular restraint — is also a significant part of the factual inquiry which would be undertaken if the restraints were reviewed on the merits. Thus, since the court is likely to find itself enmeshed in the economic question, it will, in many cases, impose only a slightly greater burden if it proceeds to a substantive review. In short, since it may not be possible to devise a clearly demarked exemption in this area, and since there are collateral virtues to a review on the merits, the courts may properly decide to direct most of their efforts to defining the substantive rules to be applied to groups such as the NCAA.

b. Nature of the Antitrust Review. Once it is determined that an NCAA rule is subject to review under the antitrust laws, the issue arises as to whether the particular restraint is *per se* illegal or subject to review under the rule of reason standard, which would allow the court to consider the actual economic effect of the rule and the group's justification for it.[486] The *per se* concept is a particular concern because many NCAA controls are similar to those which are summarily condemned when undertaken in a more traditional business setting. For example, the group has an extensive set of rules dealing with the recruiting of athletes. Some might argue that these measures are purposely anticompetitive. They in effect limit certain methods of competition and permit the association to punish those who compete too well—for example, schools which engage in aggressive recruiting. The punishments operate to limit the economic opportunities of the offending schools and their students. Again, this regulatory system has some of the characteristics of a group boycott, which is deemed *per se* illegal in other contexts.[487] As a further illustration, some will contend that while price-fixing among competitors is perhaps the clearest type of *per se* violation,[488] the NCAA, nonetheless, controls the price at which college athletes

485. *See* Hennessey v. NCAA, No. CA 76-P-0799-W (N.D. Ala., Sept. 27, 1976), *aff'd per curiam,* 564 F.2d 1135 (5th Cir. 1977).

486. For further background material on the *per se* and rule of reason standards, *see* § 5.07 *supra.*

487. *See* United States v. Topco Assoc., Inc., 405 U.S. 596 (1972); Fashion Originators' Guild of America v. FTC, 312 U.S. 457 (1941).

488. *See, e.g.,* United States v. Socony Vacuum Oil Co., 310 U.S. 150 (1940); United States v. Trenton Potteries Co., 273 U.S. 397 (1927).

can sell their services. It will be argued that the group's rules concerning financial aid place a ceiling on the price which a school can pay for the services of its student-athletes.[489] Since such jointly imposed wage controls are not tolerated in other contexts, it will be argued that they should similarly be condemned where the NCAA is involved.

Despite the similarities between NCAA actions and classic *per se* violations, it is doubtful that the notion of summary illegality will play a significant role in litigation in this area. As a threshold matter, it can be noted that the *per se* concept was devised to achieve the goal of preserving economic competition between traditional business entities. It is not self-evident that legal concepts intended to regulate purely commercial relationships would provide appropriate controls in an educational setting, even though economic concerns may be involved.[490] In order to determine whether the more flexible rule of reason standard should be applied, it is important to ask the question which has been posed in other context in this text: is the particular activity (here educationally-related athletics) one which is appropriately subject to private regulation? [491] That is to say, will self-regulation achieve purposes and goals which are desirable and which can be assured by the normal operation of the free market? If one finds that self-regulation is necessary and desirable, then it would seem to follow that the decision-makers will be given broader powers to control the particular activity than would be tolerated in the typical commercial setting.[492] The inquiry into the limits of these regulatory powers requires a more flexible standard than that provided by the *per se* concept, and the rule of reason seems to provide the appropriate standard for review.

---

489. Allegations of this sort were made by Chris Kupec in his complaint against the Atlantic Coast Conference. The relevant portions of the complaint were as follows:

49

Upon information and belief, the member institutions of the Atlantic Coast Conference have met together on a frequent and recurring basis to set and prescribe regulations pertaining to the maximum amount of compensation to be paid to a student athlete of said member institutions, which compensation consists of scholarship aid, living expenses, room and board, and other prescribed fringe benefits.

50

The actions of the member institutions of the Atlantic Coast Conference in combining to set maximum compensation to be received by student-athletes participating in intercollegiate athletics, have in the past unreasonably restrained, do at the present unreasonably restrain, and will in the future continue unreasonably to restrain the commerce of intercollegiate football, as participated in by the Plaintiff, in violation of the Sherman Act, 15 U.S.C. § 1. As a result of said unlawful combination to fix compensation to be received by student-athletes, the Plaintiff has been damaged in amounts which are impossible to calculate. Kupec v. Atlantic Coast Conference, No. C-75-105-D (D.N.C., filed March 26, 1975) at 11.

The court denied Kupec's request for a preliminary injunction, which was based on this and several other grounds. *See* Kupec v. Atlantic Coast Conference, 399 F. Supp. 1377 (M.D.N.C. 1975).

490. *See generally* Barber, *Refusals to Deal Under the Federal Antitrust Law,* 103 U. Pa. L. Rev. 847 (1955); Note, *Trade Association Exclusionary Practices: An Affirmative Role for the Rule of Reason,* 66 Colum. L. Rev. 1486 (1966).

491. *Compare* §§ 5.09 *and* 5.10 *supra.*

492. *See, e.g.,* Bridge Corp. of America v. American Contract Bridge League, Inc., 428 F.2d 1365 (9th Cir. 1970); Deesen v. Professional Golfers Ass'n, 358 F.2d 165 (9th Cir. 1966); Molinas v. National Basketball Ass'n, 190 F. Supp. 241 (S.D.N.Y. 1961); United States v. United States Trotting Ass'n, 1960 Trade Cas. ¶ 69,761 (S.D. Ohio).

It should be clear that one will rarely find that group self-regulation is proper where traditional business competitors are involved. For example, when a group of businessmen agrees to cease dealing with a competitor who is engaging in price-cutting, no desirable goal is being promoted. Indeed, the ultimate object of the restraint is antithetical to goals of the antitrust laws. In these sorts of cases, it is appropriate for the courts to summarily condemn the restraint. But where a group such as the NCAA is involved, the situation is much different. The general goals of the NCAA are to preserve the amateur quality of the sports it regulates and, relatedly, to promote the development of educationally related sports. There is nothing inherently improper about these objectives and, indeed, it can probably be agreed that they should be encouraged.[493]

It can be observed that the movement toward group control in college athletics is a natural tendency, prompted in large measure by the fact that the activity (college sports) requires considerable interaction between institutions. While one might hypothesize a system of college sports in which each individual institution retained control over its own program, it seems unlikely that such an arrangement would endure for very long, absent some outside control. Schools would want to join together in conferences, and it is likely that the conferences would begin to develop regulations to make the athletic competition more uniform, to institutionalize the elements which define the common interests of the schools, and generally, to promote the particular group effort. Once schools become aware of the extent to which others in the nation shared these interests, it is natural that they would join together to establish a more general regulatory structure. One can speak with some confidence about the inevitability of these developments, for the present system of conferences and NCAA regulation serves as rather persuasive evidence of the tendencies which are at work.

Of course, it is not enough to establish that the movement toward self-regulation is inevitable,[494] and it must be separately established that these are common concerns which warrant group-control. The consideration which should ultimately prove persuasive is that schools have a legitimate interest in attempting to discourage excessive professionalism in school-related athletics. It seems wholly proper that efforts be made to preserve amateur sports as a separate genre on the American athletic scene. Moreover, since colleges and universities are in a unique position to provide sponsorship for athletic programs, the special brand of sport which is being promoted can further be defined as *school-related* amateur sports.[495] Without regulation, it is likely that this particular type of sports venture would have a difficult time achieving a distinct identity. Perhaps the greatest concern is that schools would find themselves subjected to pressures which would cause them to either curtail significant athletic opportunities or to contribute further to the demise of the separate system of amateur athletics.[496]

Critics of the NCAA will contend that the group's real goal, at least as far as the major college programs are concerned, is not to preserve amateurism but rather to control the costs the institutions incur in operating semi-professional

---

493. *See generally* Comment, *Trade Association Exclusionary Practices: An Affirmative Role for the Rule of Reason, supra* note 490, at 1488-97.

494. *Cf.* Koch, *A Troubled Cartel: The NCAA,* 38 LAW & CONTEMP. PROB. 135, 139-40 (1973).

495. *Cf.* Jones v. NCAA, 392 F. Supp. 295 (D. Mass. 1975).

496. *See generally* Cross, *The College Athlete and the Institution,* 38 LAW & CONTEMP. PROB. 151 (1973).

teams.[497] There is some validity to the criticism that the NCAA has been operating under an increasingly hazy notion of amateurism, but that fact does not detract from the basic conclusion reached here that the schools which comprise the NCAA have a legitimate interest in defining the characteristics of their unique brand of sports activity. Once that point is accepted we have gone a long way in determining which standard of antitrust review should normally be applied to judge the group's rules.

If it is permissible for the NCAA to adopt rules to promote particular goals, then as to any particular regulation it will be necessary to determine (1) whether it does in fact achieve its apparent objective, (2) whether that objective is within the scope of the group's proper concerns, and (3) whether the means chosen for implementation of the goal are reasonable in light of the resulting economic effects.[498] These questions usually cannot be answered without an extensive factual inquiry. Moreover, a proper resolution of the last concern requires a balancing of competing interests. The rule of reason standard specifically contemplates this type of extensive, deliberate inquiry.[499] On the other hand, the *per se* rule, with its emphasis upon firm rules and summary litigation is inappropriate. It assumes that the court can make an *a priori* judgment that no regulation should be tolerated. While such a decision can be made about many commercial restraints, the special characteristics of the activities which the NCAA regulates requires a more detailed inquiry to determine the extent to which these are important in the particular case.

This is not to say that the *per se* rule could never be applied to an NCAA regulation. That concept would seem to provide a proper mechanism of control where the group took action intended solely to protect itself or its members from outside economic competition.[500] Thus, if the NCAA intentionally undertook to eliminate or otherwise seriously restrain other associations interested in assuming a role in the governance of college athletics, a case would exist for a *per se* condemnation of these efforts in the absence of extenuating circumstances.[501] As has been seen in other areas, the fact that a group has power to regulate does not mean that its authority is unlimited. Where the group seeks to extend its influence merely to preserve itself, or to achieve clearly improper economic goals, the courts need not exhibit the degree of tolerance which the rule of reason presumes is appropriate.[502]

c. Rule of Reason Standard. Again, the prior analysis should suggest that most NCAA regulations will be evaluated under a rule of reason standard which allows judicial deference to be paid to the non-commercial goals of the rule being challenged. The elements of the rule of reason test have already been discussed

---

497. *See* Koch, *A Troubled Cartel: The NCAA, supra* note 494, at 139-40. *See also* K. DENLINGER & L. SHAPIRO, ATHLETES FOR SALE (1975); J. DURSO, THE SPORTS FACTORY (1975).

498. *Compare* § 5.10 *supra. See also* Comment, *Trade Association Exclusionary Practices: An Affirmative Role for the Rule of Reason, supra* note 490, at 1504-05.

499. The nature of the inquiry required by a rule of reason analysis is discussed in more detail in § 5.07 *supra.*

500. *Cf.* Comment, *National Collegiate Athletic Association's Certification Requirement: A Section One Violation of the Sherman Antitrust Act,* 9 VAL. U.L. REV. 193 (1974).

501. *Cf.* Washington State Bowling Proprietors Ass'n, Inc. v. Pacific Lanes, Inc., 356 F.2d 371 (9th Cir. 1966); Philadelphia World Hockey Club, Inc. v. Philadelphia Hockey Club, Inc., 351 F. Supp. 462 (E.D. Pa. 1972).

502. *See* § 5.10 *supra.*

in an earlier section of this treatise.[503] For the present it is sufficient to note that there is no presumption of unreasonableness under this analysis, and the plaintiff must show that the practice is improper. Specifically, it must be established that the rule restrains trade and that the restraint is unreasonable when evaluated in light of the justification which the defendants have established. In the present context, the professed justification will be related to the desirability of promoting and protecting a system of educationally-related amateur athletics. Alternative methods of reaching the association's goal will also be considered if they show that by comparison the rule is an unreasonable way to effectuate an otherwise acceptable goal.

In order to illustrate the kind of arguments that the NCAA could use to protect its educational regulations, a challenge against the rule forbidding special monetary gifts to student athletes will be considered.[504] The plaintiff would likely attempt to show that the rule is a restraint on trade, specifically that it interferes with the right of the athlete to realize the maximum economic return his or her talent could otherwise generate. The NCAA's defense of the rule would focus on the close relationship between the activity regulated and the group's central objectives. The rule in question here is designed to protect the amateur stature of its athletes, so that the educational goals of promoting leadership and fitness will not be overshadowed by commercial pursuits. The NCAA can argue that it has superior knowledge of the educational effects of unlimited economic inducements to student-athletes and cite abuses that took place before the rule was enacted. Courts traditionally afford considerable weight to this kind of expert judgment.[505] The NCAA can also argue that its rule is designed to foster, rather than restrain, fair competition by defining the essential characteristics of the athletic competition which will be held.[506]

In considering the strength of the group's justification, the court should be willing to receive evidence that there are less restrictive mechanisms which could be used to effect the association's goals.[507] Although the availability of a less restrictive method is usually strong evidence for the plaintiff where he can show his livelihood is endangered, it is unlikely that the plaintiff will be able to use this approach to mount a significant attack on the rule in question.[508] While the prohibition on monetary gifts is absolute, such an absolutist approach seems warranted in light of traditional notions of what constitutes amateurism.[509]

The balance struck under the rule of reason test will reflect the court's respect for the policies which the rule seeks to protect. If, as here, the rule is intimately related to the NCAA's purposes, it should be deemed acceptable. The anticompetitive effects of the rules are likely to be deemed incidental and reasonable restraints in otherwise legitimate regulatory activity. The standard used will be a variable one. The greater the adverse economic impact, the stronger must be the objectives which are being pursued.[510] But because the present rule touches upon a matter which is at the heart of the NCAA legitimate

503. *See* § 5.07 *supra.*
504. *See* CONSTITUTION OF THE NCAA, art. 3, § 1.
505. *See* text at notes 476-77 *supra. Compare* § 5.10 *supra.*
506. *Cf.* STP Corp. v. United States Auto Club, 286 F. Supp. 146 (S.D. Ind. 1968).
507. *See* § 5.07 *supra.*
508. *Cf.* Robinson, *Recent Antitrust Developments: 1975,* 76 COLUM. L. REV. 191, 231-33 (1976).
509. The amateurism concept is considered more fully in chapter 1 of this treatise.
510. *Compare* Comment, *Trade Association Exclusionary Practices: An Affirmative Role for the Rule of Reason,* 66 COLUM. L. REV. 1486, 1506-08 (1966).

concerns — the amateur status of the activities it regulates — a greater degree of restraint will be tolerated than would be true for other types of regulations.

d. Case Developments. The issue of the NCAA's status under the antitrust laws has received varying degrees of attention in the decided cases. The early decisions are probably best described as incomplete. Either because the facts of the case did not require it or because the issue was improperly framed, the courts in these decisions did not explore the most difficult questions which needed to be answered. Perhaps the most that can be said of the initial decisions is that they confirm that there are no simple answers to the questions which are generated by the NCAA's regulatory efforts. In a more recent case, however, the antitrust question was considered in more detail. The following paragraphs, which briefly review the case developments, should give some hint of the evolutionary nature of the judicial treatment of these matters.

(1.) Early cases.

One of the first cases to consider a contention that the NCAA constituted an illegal group boycott was *Samara v. NCAA*.[511] In that case, collegiate track runners who had competed in an Amateur Athletic Union Russian-American Track and Field Meet asked for an injunction against NCAA enforcement of a rule which denied eligibility to athletes who participated in events not sanctioned by the NCAA. However, at the time of the hearing in the case, the NCAA had not yet attempted to bar the plaintiffs from its events. The court conceded that the group boycott theory was plausible but found it unnecessary to examine it in detail for no boycott had taken place and no economic harm had been proved. The opinion suggests that where the injury could be shown to be less speculative an antitrust claim might prevail. The context of this statement implies that a showing that the particular college sport has significant commercial impact on the professional market is required.[512]

In 1974, a New Jersey district court, in *College Athletic Placement Service, Inc. v. National Collegiate Athletic Association*,[513] refused to restrain the application of an NCAA rule which denied eligibility to student athletes who had used a private scholarship placement service. Unlike the *Samara* decision, this case directly addressed the merits of the group boycott allegation. The plaintiff, who had previously been assured by the NCAA that his service would not jeopardize his clients' eligibility, charged a fee to help students proficient at less popular sports find athletic scholarships. Later, the NCAA amended its constitution to deny eligibility to students who used such a service.[514] The court found that no group boycott had taken place because there was no evidence of anticompetitive intent by the NCAA under the rationale of *Joseph E. Seagram & Sons, Inc. v. Hawaiian Oke & Liquors, Ltd.*[515] In that case treble damages

---

511. 1973 Trade Cas. ¶ 74,536 (E.D. Va.).
512. *Id.* at 94,384.
513. 1975 Trade Cas. ¶ 60,117 (D.N.J.), *aff'd,* No. 74-104 (3d Cir., Nov. 25, 1974).
514. *See* CONSTITUTION OF THE NCAA, art. 3, § 1(c) *as amended,* 1976.
515. 416 F.2d 71 (9th Cir. 1969), *cert. denied,* 396 U.S. 1062 (1970).

were denied a distributor who had been cut off by its liquor suppliers because there was no evidence of an anticompetitive purpose for the termination. However, the standard for a *per se* violation in franchising and distribution cases is an especially rigorous one because the supplier's legitimate business judgment must be overbalanced by some clear violation of the law. It is difficult to see how this precedent would apply to the NCAA.[516]

The court's analysis under the rule of reason is also questionable, however. In sustaining the NCAA's action, the opinion focuses on the fact that the NCAA was not competing in the plaintiff's market.[517] While the court did not employ the usual balancing test under the rule of reason, its opinion identifies competing interests which would have made this inquiry a difficult one. Early in the opinion, the plaintiff's service is characterized as an aid to needy students who would otherwise be unaware of scholarship opportunities.[518] Later, however, the court summarily defers to the NCAA's alleged purpose in seeking to protect the integrity of the college admissions procedure without explaining how the plaintiff's service actually threatened that process. This obvious tension between the court's recognition of the usefulness of the plaintiff's venture and its unexplained deferral to the NCAA's judgment raises a question about the completeness of the court's analysis. Other courts might be more concerned about the anticompetitive effect of the rule, especially in light of the absence of any evidence of abuse in the operation on the plaintiff's service.

In *Jones v. National Collegiate Athletic Association*,[519] a college student who had played "amateur" hockey for compensation was denied a waiver of the eligibility provision of Section 1(a)I of the NCAA constitution. The Massachusetts district court abruptly denied an injunction to the player stating that it was unlikely that the rule had a nexus to commercial activity of the NCAA.[520] The court refused to find a violation of the Sherman Act because the intent of the threatened boycott was to implement its non-commercial goal of amateurism rather than stifle competition.[521] This contention may preclude application of a *per se* standard of review but leaves unanswered the question of how the rule of reason might operate in a case such as this. The case does suggest that a rule clearly within the NCAA goal of amateurism would not be vulnerable to antitrust attack.[522]

516. *See* E. A. McQuade Tours, Inc. v. Consolidated Air Tour Manual Committee, 467 F.2d 178 (5th Cir. 1972), *cert. denied*, 409 U.S. 1109 (1973). *See also* Note, *National Collegiate Athletic Association's Certification Requirement: A Section One Violation of the Sherman Act, supra* note 500, at 206.

517. 1975 Trade Cas. at 65,267.

518. The service provided by plaintiffs enables student athletes to obtain scholarships, particularly those for the less popular sports, for which most colleges provide little publicity or recruitment, and of which they would normally be unaware through lack of information, resources, time or the ability to travel. The student athlete is thus presented with a wider choice of colleges to attend, allowing him to select the one which suits him best, scholastically as well as athletically.

A large number of those students aided by plaintiffs require financial assistance in order to attend college. Therefore, many prospective students would be unable to enter college if it were not for plaintiff's services. *Id.* at 65,265.

519. 392 F. Supp. 295 (D. Mass. 1975).

520. *Id.* at 303.

521. *Id.* at 304.

522. *But see* Board of Regents, Univ. of Okla. v. NCAA, No. C.D. 76-871 (Dist. Ct. Okla. County, Aug. 23, 1976). This recent state court case strains to condemn rules which regulate outside the traditional noncommercial scheme by analogy to the federal antitrust laws.

2. Subsequent Developments.

The leading case dealing with the NCAA's status under the antitrust laws if *Hennessey v. National Collegiate Athletic Association.*[523] The case was brought by two assistant coaches at the University of Alabama to contest a then-recent NCAA bylaw which limited the number of assistant coaches which a Division I school could employ in its football and basketball program. At the time the rule went into effect, the number of assistant coaches employed by the University of Alabama in these two sports was greater than the number allowed under the rule, and the two plaintiffs were terminated in order to bring the University into compliance with the association's directive. The resulting litigation raised a number of issues, but the most important for our present discussion was the contention that the staff-size limitation was an improper restraint upon the labor market for the employment of assistant coaches.

The rule in question was ultimately sustained by Judge Pointer of the Alabama federal district court. However, the court's assessment of the rule's validity was quite guarded, and the opinion suggests that a different result may have been mandated if there had been more definite proof that the rule would have a significant adverse impact on the plaintiff's employment opportunities. When the case was appealed, the Fifth Circuit affirmed *per curiam* and endorsed the analysis put forth by Judge Pointer.[524]

Applying an analytical framework similar to that discussed earlier in this section, Judge Pointer held that the staff-size limitation was more appropriately treated under the rule of reason standard rather than the more stringent *per se* rule. Moreover, in addressing the question of the reasonableness of the regulation, the court considered the various factors which have developed in other association-restraint cases and which were identified in our previous discussion of the NCAA limitation on monetary gifts to athletes. Thus, the court inquired whether the staff-size rule was related to a legitimate objective of the association. Judge Pointer concluded that it was, for, in his view, the NCAA was properly concerned about the financial advantages which major schools with lucrative sports programs had over other institutions which operated with a less substantial commitment to their athletic ventures. In addition, the NCAA was found to be properly concerned about the extent to which a member's pursuit of sports revenue might interfere with the group's goal of preserving the predominance of educational objectives in intercollegiate athletic programs. As perceived by the court, "the fundamental objective . . . [underlying the rule] was to preserve and foster competition in intercollegiate athletics — by curtailing, as it were, potentially monopolistic practices by the more powerful — and to reorient the programs into their traditional role as amateur sports operating as part of the educational process." [525]

Consistent with the approach taken in other antitrust contexts, Judge Pointer observed that the legitimacy of the group's objective in promulgating the rule was only one factor to be considered.[526] Also to be evaluated are such factors as the degree of adverse impact of a rule on the persons regulated and the availability of less restrictive regulatory schemes. It was the former issue —

---

523. 564 F.2d 1136 (5th Cir.), *aff'g* No. Ca. 76-P-0799-W (N.D. Ala., Sept. 27, 1976).
524. *Id.*
525. *Id.* at 1153.
526. *See* text accompanying notes 498-99 *supra.*

the actual economic effects of the rule — which caused Judge Pointer to introduce a note of caution in his analysis.

There are several economic concerns raised by the staff-size limitation. The immediate impact of the rule, of course, would be to eliminate a number of existing jobs. In addition, it might be asked whether the rule would not reduce the long-term demand for coaches and create an oversupply of qualified applicants for available positions. It would be contended that not only would jobs be more difficult to get, but also the heightened competition among applicants would likely reduce the salaries and other benefits which assistant coaches could command. Thus, the rule might be viewed as an agreement among employers (the members of the association) which had the effect of impeding the normal market forces which would otherwise determine the number of jobs available and the compensation to be paid. And, it would be contended, the degree of restraint on employment opportunities could be quite severe.

Judge Pointer's doubts about the correctness of these economic projections proved to be determinative in his decision to uphold the regulation. The court did not, however, totally dismiss the coaches' concerns. Rather, Judge Pointer felt that the precise impact of the new rule was uncertain. The NCAA contended that the rule might actually benefit assistant coaches by strengthening the athletic programs at schools presently less competitive and thus preserve jobs which might be lost if the few institutions with heavily endowed programs were allowed to continue their dominant positions. Judge Pointer did not endorse this hypothesis, but thought it desirable to allow the "opportunity to build up experience on which the issue could ultimately be judged." [527]

The court made clear that its decision to sustain the rule was not necessarily the final word in the matter and that it would be appropriate to have the question of the reasonableness of the rule relitigated at a future time. Particularly relevant would be more concrete data as to the long-term effects of the rule. In Judge Pointer's view, "if actual experience under the Bylaw should run counter to the NCAA's expectation (of an insignificant adverse impact), such evidence would be available to a court evaluating the reasonableness of the restraint in a subsequent case." [528]

It is possible to imagine "a subsequent case" in which the factual record before the court would lead it to find that the staff-size limitation violated the antitrust laws. The plaintiffs in such a case would want to show by empirical data that persons who formerly would have secured assistant coaching positions at Division I schools either could not find any coaching jobs or could only secure positions at a lower level in the school sports hierarchy. To the extent that the latter was established, it would also be necessary to document that positions in other schools, such as the small colleges and high schools, were significantly less advantageous in terms of providing the assistants with the opportunity to move into top-level coaching jobs in major programs. In addition, the plaintiffs would want to document the effect which the NCAA restriction had on the particular contract terms under which assistant coaches were employed. It would be relevant to inquire whether, with an appropriate discount for inflation,

---

527. 564 F.2d at 1154.
528. *Id.*

assistant coaches received lower salaries, reduced fringe benefits, increased duties and the like. Finally, it would be appropriate to gather data on whether the relative dominance of the schools with moneyed athletic programs had been lessened. Here information on pre- and post-1976 won-loss records, recruiting success and the similar indicia of "athletic power" would provide useful information. A point which seems to be implicit in *Hennessey* is that if these proofs reveal a substantial negative impact on the employment opportunities of assistant coaches and relatively little change in the distribution of "power" among Division I schools, then the staff-size limitation would be invalid. Again, it was primarily the lack of firm evidence on these matters which caused the court in *Hennessey* to tip the balance in favor of the NCAA's restriction.

It can also be suggested that Judge Pointer's decision contains a word of warning to the NCAA if it continues to formulate rules to respond to the concerns which member schools have about the increasing costs of their programs. While *Hennessey* endorses the general principle that cost-control is a legitimate objective for the NCAA, the opinion also indicates that the association must be careful that the burdens of its controls not rest too heavily on groups which have significant economic interests at stake. The failure in *Hennessey* was a failure of proof. For other forms of regulation, the adverse impact may not be as much in doubt and where this is true, the NCAA is likely to encounter a rending of the veil of deference which clothes its activities.

In devising its regulations, it seems appropriate that the NCAA give some attention to precisely who it is that bears the burden of a specific control. Particular concern ought to be given to the directness of the connection between the persons regulated and those who actively participate in the formulation of association policies. Efforts by trade associations to control the opportunities of non-members have always been particularly suspect in the antitrust laws.[529] Some NCAA rules share this attribute even though they are framed in terms of direct controls on the group's membership. For example, one difficulty with the staff-size rule considered in *Hennessey* is that it singled out one class of persons (assistant coaches) to bear the brunt of the association's general concern for costs. Although employed by member schools, assistant coaches do not participate directly in the association's legislative process. In addition, one suspects that within the hierachy of individual institutions and their athletic departments, this group is probably among the least powerful and least well-organized. There is reason to be suspicious when the form of cost-control chosen from among the various alternatives is one which has its main impact on those who exercise little or no control over its formulation.

The point to be made here needs to be stated with some care. It cannot be suggested that antitrust cases make bright line distinction between association rules which have their primary effect on members and those which mainly burden a sub-group. It is clear that some rules which directly affect the members themselves may be illegal.[530] What can be suggested, however, is that courts

---

529. *See, e.g.* Mackey v. National Football League, 407 F. Supp. 1000 (D. Minn. 1975), *modified,* 543 F.2d 606 (8th Cir. 1976); Washington State Bowling Proprietors Ass'n, Inc. v. Pacific Lanes, Inc., 356 F.2d 371 (9th Cir. 1966); Smith v. Pro-Football, Inc., 420 F. Supp. 738 (D.D.C. 1976). *Cf.* Silver v. New York Stock Exchange, 373 U.S. 341 (1963).

530. *See, e.g.,* Vandervelde v. Put and Call Brokers and Dealers Ass'n, 344 F. Supp. 118 (S.D.N.Y. 1972). *See generally* Note, *Trade Association Exclusionary Practices: An Affirmative Role for the Rule of Reason,* 66 COLUM. L. REV. 1486 (1966).

are likely to be somewhat more cautious when confronted with a situation in which those who formulate their organization's rules choose to encumber the economic opportunities of unrepresented affiliates rather than bear the direct impact themselves. Translated into a workable legal principle, this may mean that where a rule has such a particularized effect upon an identifiable subgroup, the court should give serious attention to the availability of less restrictive alternatives. If there are alternative forms of regulation which would clearly achieve the same goal with a more diffused impact, it may be appropriate for the court to compel a reconsideration of the regulatory scheme.[531]

On a related matter, the NCAA ought to be particularly cautious in devising regulations which impose economic restraints more direct than that considered in *Hennessey*. For example, it is believed that the association would confront a substantial antitrust challenge if it had gone a step further than in the staff-size bylaw and had adopted a rule which limited the salaries which an assistant coach could be paid. It is true that such a regulation would be consistent with the objectives of cost-control and cost-equalization approved in *Hennessey*. But there are other features of this type of restraint which raise serious questions about its validity. The principal point to be made is that such a rule is simply a not-so-subtle form of price-fixing. While courts have had difficulty deciding what other sort of trade group regulations will be sustained, they have typically indicated little hesitancy in striking down direct controls on prices.[532] Such devices represent the most pernicious type of restraint on the operation of the free market, and they have met with a judicial disapproval which is notable for its consistency. Although the NCAA faces a difficult task in trying to provide an answer to the problem of rising costs in college athletics, it is not likely that the courts will feel that the NCAA enjoys any special license to tinker with the prices which coaches or others receive for their employment services. The group will likely be told that it must choose other, less intrusive forms of regulation to achieve its goals.

531. *See* text accompanying note 508 *supra*.
532. *See, e.g.,* Phelps Dodge Refining Co. v. FTC, 139 F.2d 393 (2d Cir. 1943); Vandervelde v. Put and Call Brokers and Dealers Ass'n, 344 F. Supp. 118 (S.D.N.Y. 1972), and cases cited therein.

CHAPTER 6

Collective Bargaining and Professional Sports

§ 6.01. In General.

An important development in the law of sports has been the formation of a system of collective bargaining in professional sports. Although this is a rather new occurrence in the sports community, it is a common feature of our economic system for representatives of labor and management to bargain over the terms of employment. Indeed, when one considers the familiar assertion that professional athletes are little more than "peons" [1] or "slaves," [2] and the fact that professional athletics has increasingly assumed the trappings of ordinary business enterprise,[3] it is hardly surprising that unionization has been steadily creeping into sports arenas.[4] The "creep" has, in fact, reached the point that

1. American League Club of Chicago v. Chase, 86 Misc. 441, 465, 149 N.Y.S. 6, 19 (Sup. Ct. 1914); 117 CONG. REC. S15451 (1971) (Senator Sam J. Ervin); Krasnow & Levy, *Unionization and Professional Sports,* 51 GEO. L.J. 749, 755 n.20 (1963).

2. Gardella v. Chandler, 172 F.2d 402, 409 (2d Cir. 1949) (Frank, J., dissenting); *Hearings Before the Senate Antitrust Subcomm. of the Senate Comm. on the Judiciary,* 85th Cong., 1st Sess., pt. 2, 2653 (1957); Schneiderman, *Professional Sport: Involuntary Servitude and the Popular Will,* 7 GONZAGA L. REV. 63, 69 (1971); Note, *The Balance of Power in Professional Sports,* 22 MAINE L. REV. 459, 469 (1970). The relationship between players and their respective clubs has also been described as being "paternalistic," Shulman & Baum, *Collective Bargaining in Professional Athletics — The NFL Money Bowl,* 50 CHI. B. REC. 173, 175 (1969); *Hearings Before the Special House Subcomm. on Labor of the House Comm. on Education and Labor,* 92d Cong., 2d Sess. 22 (1972), with the owners viewing the players as "dumb jocks." Brown, *The Owners Can Be Tackled Too,* SPORTS ILLUSTRATED, March 22, 1971, at 20. In this regard, it is interesting that during the baseball strike in the spring of 1972, the spokesman for the players said that "[t]he real issue is the owners' attempt to punish the players for having the audacity not to settle, and for having the audacity not to crawl." Washington Post, April 4, 1972, § D, at 1, col. 3-4. *See* notes 32-39 *infra* and accompanying text.

3. *See* Pierce, *Organized Professional Sports and the Antitrust Laws,* 43 CORNELL L.Q. 566, 606 (1958) (a "unique type of business"). *See also* Seligman, *The Higher Economics of Baseball,* FORTUNE, April, 1957, at 135; Krasnow & Levy, *Unionization and Professional Sports,* 51 GEO. L.J. 749, 750-54 (1963); Note, *The Superbowl and the Sherman Act: Professional Team Sports and the Anti-Trust Laws,* 81 HARV. L. REV. 418 (1967); Note, *Monopsony Power in Manpower: Organized Baseball Meets the Antitrust Laws,* 62 YALE L.J. 576, 580 (1953). *See generally* H.R. REP. No. 2002, 82d Cong., 2d Sess. (1952); Rottenberg, *The Baseball Players' Labor Market,* 64 J. POL. ECON. 242 (1956).

4. *See generally* S. GALLNER, PRO SPORTS: THE CONTRACT GAME 160-67 (1974); L. SOBEL, PROFESSIONAL SPORTS AND THE LAW 267-331 (1977); Scoville, *Labor Relations in Sports* in GOVERNMENT AND THE SPORTS BUSINESS, 185 (R. Noll, ed. 1974); Krasnow & Levy, *Unionization and Professional Sports,* 51 GEO. L.J. 749 (1963); Lowell, *Collective Bargaining and the Professional Team Sport Industry,* 38 LAW & CONTEMP. PROB. 3 (1973); Miller, *Some Modest Proposals for Collective Bargaining in Professional Sports,* 48 L.A.B. BULL. 155 (1973); Shulman & Baum, *Collective Bargaining in Professional Athletics—The NFL Money Bowl,* 50 CHI. B. REC. 173 (1969).

recognized exclusive collective bargaining agents — in the form of players' associations — currently represent most team players in collective bargaining with team owners.[5]

The emergence of the players' unions has not been a precipitous event. They have been a periodic characteristic of professional sports since the early days of organized baseball.[6] But only recently has collective bargaining become an ongoing feature of the sports industry. The current relationships began during the 1960's with the formation of players' associations in each of the professional leagues.[7] By the end of the decade, the associations were recognized as the exclusive bargaining agents for the players, and collective bargaining agreements were entered. The seriousness of these efforts was underscored in 1969 when the National Labor Relations Board (NLRB) made it clear that it would accept jurisdiction over professional sports.[8]

The advent of the players' associations as viable collective bargaining representatives has ushered in a new era in the employment relations in professional sports. The terms and conditions under which athletes perform now may be determined in the give and take of the collective bargaining process, and the actions of both owners and players may be controlled by the principles of federal labor relations law. The development of an institutionalized collective bargaining process has not, however, been free of controversy and recrimination in most of the leagues. The use of economic sanctions has been a relatively frequent tactic by both owners and players, as has been the filing of unfair labor practice charges with the NLRB. Since collective bargaining promises to be one of the primary elements in the future of professional sports, it is important to review the types of problems that have been the basis of controversy in the past and the responses of owners and the players to them.

The scope of the National Football League Players Association is considered in *Hearings Before the Special House Subcomm. on Labor of the House Comm. on Education and Labor,* 92d Cong., 2d Sess. 11 (1972).

5. *See, e.g., Hearings, supra,* note 4, at 91; *See also* Wall Street Journal, Aug. 23, 1967, at 1, col. 1. It is noteworthy, however, that the players' associations have often not thought of themselves as a union, but rather as an "association." *See Hearings Before the House Subcomm. on Antitrust and Monopoly of the House Comm. on the Judiciary,* 89th Cong., 1st Sess. 104 (1964). Regardless of how a collective bargaining agent chooses to identify itself, it is a statutory "labor organization." *See* National Labor Relations Act § 2(5), 29 U.S.C. § 152(5) (1970) (hereinafter cited only as "NLRA," with no cross-cite to the United States Code), if it meets the prescribed definition.

6. It has, thus, been observed that "players have [periodically] organized unions which thrived for a fleeting moment, made their impact on . . . [sports] law, and then faded into history." H.R. REP. No. 2002, 82d Cong., 2d Sess. 172 (1952). An interesting discussion of the fate of one such union is contained in Seymour, *St. Louis and the Union Baseball War,* 51 Mo. HIST. REV. 257 (1956) (players' union forming own league in 1880's); *see also* Krasnow & Levy, *Unionization and Professional Sports,* 51 GEO. L.J. 749, 762-66 (1963) (describing a union effort in baseball in 1959); N.Y. Times, April 3, 1972, at 51, col. 5 (describing the labor strife in baseball at the end of the nineteenth century and comparing it to the thirteen-day baseball strike in 1972).

7. The Major League Players Association was formed in 1954; the National Football League Players Association in 1956, the American Football League Players Association in 1963, and the two were consolidated in 1970 after the leagues merged; the National Hockey League Players Association in 1967; the National Basketball Association Players Association in 1962, and the American Basketball Association Players Association in 1968. The procedures used to make the National Football League Players Association a viable collective bargaining participant are described by its then counsel in Shulman & Baum, *supra* note 2. See also Soar v. National Football League Players' Ass'n, 438 F. Supp. 337 (D.R.I. 1975), *aff'd,* 550 F.2d 1287 (1st Cir. 1977) (describing development of the NFLPA).

8. *See* § 6.02.

The first major controversies which arose in the modern era of collective bargaining in professional sports involved the same basic dispute, and evolved in a remarkably similar manner. A significant dispute occurred prior to the beginning of the training and exhibition season of the National Football League in 1968 when the owners and the players' association were attempting to negotiate a collective bargaining agreement. Apparently all issues had been settled except for the players' demand that the owners agree to a contribution formula to the pension system for years after 1970, which the owners stated could not be done because of uncertainty about predictions of future income.[9] When negotiations proved fruitless, the players authorized the players' association to call a strike [10] and were subsequently advised by the association to boycott training camps until there was an agreement.[11] The owners then barred the players from the training camps,[12] and within a few days an agreement was reached.[13] Throughout the controversy, the players alleged that the owners were trying to break the players' association, and the owners issued dire predictions about the effect of the short-lived impasse.[14] The 1968 dispute was the first major labor dispute in professional sports since the late nineteenth century,[15] and it served as an accurate barometer of the ensuing controversies. Its effect on professional sports was summarized quite well by columnist William Wallace:

> Pro football will be marked. The players, newly organized in a union structure, will have achieved their goals under duress of a strike. Precedent has been set and the players know forever that the next time they are to sign a contract with the owners . . . all they must do is carry their demands to the end, that being a strike.
> That is how it is done in the transit field and the newspaper business . . . . It is rather sad that we now may consider a football player in the same context as a subway motorman or a linotype operator. That takes away a little of the romance. Fran Tarkenton and Bart Starr are no longer heroes. They are mere working stiffs living up to a union contract. They play for the pension plan.[16]

A similar controversy arose prior to the 1969 baseball season, when agreement could not be reached on the percentage of receipts from the league's national television contract that was to be contributed to the players' pension plan. As in the 1968 football controversy, the players were advised to boycott training camps until an agreement was reached,[17] and although the owners opened their camps most players heeded the advice and stayed away.[18] An agreement was

9. N. Y. Times, July 6, 1968, at 15, col. 7.
10. N. Y. Times, July 4, 1968, at 26, col. 1.
11. N. Y. Times, July 6, 1968, at 15, col. 7.
12. N. Y. Times, July 11, 1968, at 47, col. 1.
13. N. Y. Times, July 15, at 38, col. 1. An agreement had already been reached in the American Football League without a strike. N. Y. Times, July 11, 1968, at 47, col. 2.
14. N. Y. Times, July 13, 1968, at 20, col. 5.
15. See note 6 supra.
16. N. Y. Times, July 8, 1968, at 50, col. 4. See generally Maule, Pro at the Conference Table, SPORTS ILLUSTRATED, October 14, 1968, at 87; Shrake, "Let's Get Back to Playing Football," SPORTS ILLUSTRATED, July 22, 1968, at 54; Shrake, Pro Football Faces a Delay of Game, SPORTS ILLUSTRATED, May 27, 1968.
17. N. Y. Times, February 7, 1969, at 41, col. 1.
18. N. Y. Times, February 15, 1969, at 34, col. 3.

soon reached when the commissioner of baseball intervened,[19] but not before the players stated that the delay was caused by the owners' efforts to test the resolve of the players,[20] and the owners suggested that they would play the exhibition and regular season, if necessary, with minor leaguers.[21]

Labor controversy revived in the National Football League in 1970. Initially, the bargaining dispute involved the amount that was to be paid the players for pre-season games and whether the commissioner was to be included in the collective bargaining process. When these issues were resolved, the level of contributions to the pension plan again became the focus of controversy.[22] An impasse in bargaining developed and the owners locked the veteran players out of training camps.[23] The owners again stated that the demands of the players were financially unrealistic [24] and indicated that they might be forced to cancel the entire football season.[25] In order to increase the pressure on the owners, the players attempted to persuade rookies to boycott the annual College All-Star Game in Chicago (but later agreed that it should be played).[26] When the owners opened training camps, the players declined to attend,[27] and eventually voted formally to strike.[28] After three days of strike, the dispute was settled when the commissioner of football mediated a round-the-clock bargaining session.[29] As in the previous disputes, accusations and counter-accusations were freely exchanged, and one player publicly stated that players or teams who did not go along with the association might be subject to a much higher incidence of serious injury once the season started.[30] The 17-day lockout and 3-day strike in 1970 mirrored the previous bargaining controversies in 1968 and 1969. Its effect on professional sports was again effectively reviewed by a sports columnist. Thus, Leonard Koppett wrote

> [a]fter about 72 hours, the official strike of the football players is over, without cancellation of preseason exhibition games, and once again American civilization has been saved from disaster. Unfortunately for the sports-loving public, however, this isn't really the end of the story, but only a little bit past the beginning. Labor turmoil in professional sports is here to stay, with whatever consequences one wishes to attribute to its belated arrival, and no fan will again be free of periodic exposure to such melodramatic negotiations.
>
> Melodrama, of course, is a built-in feature of traditional labor-management practices. That it comes late to sports, a generation

---

19. N. Y. Times, February 26, 1969, at 50, col. 1.

20. N. Y. Times, February 22, 1969, at 39, col. 1.

21. N. Y. Times, February 21, 1969, at 34, col. 3.

22. N. Y. Times, July 15, 1970, at 43, col. 1.

23. N. Y. Times, July 14, 1970, at 43, col. 1.

24. N. Y. Times, July 17, 1970, at 25, col. 1.

25. N. Y. Times, July 24, 1970, at 21, col. 1.

26. N. Y. Times, July 15, 1970, at 43, col. 1. The game was played because of respect for its tradition and the role that it had played in the early development of the National Football League. N. Y. Times, July 25, 1970, at 17, col. 5. It was reported that the decision of the Kansas City Chiefs (the winners of the previous Super Bowl) had caused a split in the unity of the players. N. Y. Times, July 26, 1970, § 5, at 1, col. 3. The labor dispute did, however, result in the cancellation of at least one other charity exhibition game in Jacksonville. N. Y. Times, August 1, 1970, at 17, col. 5.

27. N. Y. Times, July 30, 1970, at 27, cols. 3, 6.

28. N. Y. Times, July 31, 1970, at 22, col. 1.

29. N. Y. Times, August 4, 1970, at 24, col. 1.

30. Thus, a well known player stated that any team that did not go along "might find itself suffering an unusual number of injuries." N. Y. Times, July 31, 1970, at 22, col. 1.

or two after its arrival in most other business, only increases the shock felt by participants and spectators; it doesn't really change anything and the cherished illusion that the sports business is in some essential way "different" — in its business aspects — is once again shattered.[31]

The next round of confrontation took place prior to baseball's spring training in 1972. The primary issue again involved the pension plan, focusing on the question of how excess contributions were to be utilized. After an impasse developed, the players called a strike [32] and proclaimed that the owners' purpose was to punish the players by making them "eat dirt" and "bend down and kiss the shoes of the owners."[33] It was also alleged that the owners were attempting to coerce players to abandon the association and had terminated the employment of some players because of union activity.[34] As a result of these acts, the association indicated that it would file unfair labor practice charges. The tension of the strike also caused a division among the owners.[35] When the impasse continued, the National Conciliation and Mediation Service was called in, and President Nixon expressed his desire to see the strike resolved promptly.[36] When the pension issue was settled, the dispute then centered on whether the regular season games that had been missed would be played and whether the players would be paid for such make-up games.[37] After 13 days of strike, a settlement was reached, and it was decided that the cancelled games would not be played and the players would not be paid for the 9 regular season days that had elapsed. Although neither party claimed victory in the dispute, each side offered an appraisal of the events. The commissioner of baseball stated that the loser in the dispute was the game of baseball itself,[38] and the director of the players' association proclaimed that the strike had been necessary for the protection and vindication of the players' "human dignity." [39]

The baseball strike of 1972 represented a quantum increase in the level of public controversy over the disputes in 1968, 1969, and 1970. It lasted a total of 13 days, interrupted the regular baseball season, and again indicated that the effect of collective bargaining, at least for the short term, was to increase, not decrease, the level of labor strife.

---

31. N. Y. Times, August 4, 1970, at 24, col. 7. This column also included an excellent discussion of the tactics that could be expected to be used in labor disputes in professional sports. *See generally* Wright, *The Owners and the Players Fumble on in Philly,* SPORTS ILLUSTRATED, August 3, 1970, at 46.

32. N. Y. Times, April 1, 1972, at 1, col. 2.

33. N. Y. Times, April 4, 1972, at 49, col. 6.

34. N. Y. Times, April 8, 1972, at 19, col. 5.

35. N. Y. Times, April 6, 1972, at 57, col. 5. A dispute also developed between the American and National League. *See* N. Y. Times, April 12, 1972, at 51, col. 1.

36. N. Y. Times, April 9, 1972, § 5, at 3, col. 7, and April 10, 1972, at 49, col. 4.

37. N. Y. Times, April 12, 1972, at 51, col. 1.

38. N. Y. Times, April 14, 1972, at 29, col. 1. A similar conclusion was expressed during the strike by columnist Dave Anderson. N. Y. Times, April 2, 1972, § 5, at 3, col. 3.

39. Specifically, he said that

[t]he real issue [did not] have anything to do with money. The essential question was one of human dignity. . . . It had to do with the importance and necessity of players being treated as adult human beings with all the dignity that that should command.

All fans should be proud of the players whose activity they follow on the field because they demonstrated great courage against tremendous odds in standing together. They have made the owners understand that they must be treated as adult human beings and as equals. N. Y. Times, April 14, 1972, at 30, cols. 5-6.

See generally The Week That Wasn't, SPORTS ILLUSTRATED, April 17, 1972, at 70.

When the collective bargaining agreement in the National Football League expired in 1974, the stage was set for another round of economic struggle. In keeping with the evolving pattern, the dispute that followed was the most prolonged and vitriolic in professional sports bargaining. However, unlike the previous disputes, the heart of the 1974 controversy was the so-called "freedom" issues. These were contained in a list of 63 separate demands that were served upon the owners by the players' association in mid-March.[40] The association staked out its position at an early date by proclaiming its slogan to be "No Freedom, No Football."[41] This slogan was emblazoned on buttons, bumper-stickers, and T-shirts which were sold to raise funds for the union.[42] The union filed unfair labor practice charges at a very early date and predicted that a long strike would take place.[43] Rookies were requested not to report to training camp,[44] and when the first training camp opened in San Diego, the association set up picket lines in an effort to publicize its demands and persuade rookies to join the strike. However, the effort failed.[45] The owners responded by filing an array of unfair labor practice charges against the association,[46] and stopped contributions to the pension plan when the existing agreement expired. As the impasse continued, the players announced plans to picket the All-Star Game in Chicago. The rookies voted not to play in the game,[47] and it was cancelled by its sponsors for the first time in its 41 year history.[48] The owners also stated that if the impasse were not resolved shortly, they would play all scheduled games with rookies and free agents and that it might be necessary to cancel the entire season.[49] The players continued to picket the training camps, but not without cries of protest from the fans. At one training camp, the fans threatened counter-pickets, observing that strikes are "for people who haven't sense enough to take care of themselves."[50] Other picketing plans were cancelled because of irate fans, and an informal public poll conducted in Milwaukee showed that 89 percent of the respondents favored the owners in the dispute.[51]

The prolonged nature of the strike began to take a toll on the cohesion of the

40. N. Y. Times, March 16, 1974, at 21, col. 3.
41. N. Y. Times, July 1, 1974, at 37, col. 1. With respect to the freedom issues, columnist Dave Anderson observed that
> [n]early 200 years after the American revolutionaries declared their independence, American football players have discovered the ring of the word "freedom," as if it were an audible that took two centuries to penetrate. "No Freedom, No Football," is today's battle cry in the National Football League Players' Association strike. N. Y. Times, July 4, 1974, at 11, col. 1.
42. N. Y. Times, July 2, 1974, at 41, col. 6.
43. N. Y. Times, July 1, 1974, at 37, col. 1; id., July 2, 1974, at 41, col. 6.
44. Id.
45. N. Y. Times, July 4, 1974, at 11, col. 1.
46. N. Y. Times, July 4, 1974, at 12, col. 7.
47. N. Y. Times, July 7, 1974, § 5, at 6, col. 7. By striking the game, the association apparently hoped to preclude its being played by obtaining the assistance of union workers and television technicians.
48. N. Y. Times, July 11, 1974, at 21, col. 7.
49. N. Y. Times, July 12, 1974, at 25, col. 5.
50. N. Y. Times, July 13, 1974, at 15, col. 7. One owner also observed that this was the first strike in which "$100,000 players are driving Mark IV's and Cadillacs to the picket line." N. Y. Times, July 15, 1974, at 19, col. 3.
51. N. Y. Times, July 16, 1974, at 25, col. 3. The reasons given by the fans for favoring the owners' position were that the players should not expect to support themselves for the rest of their lives from playing football, there are rules and regulations for employees in all lines of work, and freedom demands were out of line because there is a need for discipline and authority to accomplish any task. Id.

union, and the players began reporting to training camps in increasing numbers, a fact that was duly reported (by name and team) in the press.[52] In an apparent effort to solidify its position, the association called for binding arbitration of the freedom issues and for round-the-clock negotiations, the tactic which had resolved the 1970 strike.[53] The call was not heeded, and the talks which were being conducted collapsed.[54] Thereafter, the situation deteriorated badly. The parties traded accusations of bad faith bargaining. Although exhibition games were played, attendance was substantially below that of previous years, which had disturbing consequences to the charitable sponsors of some games.[55] The fans generally showed little sympathy for either side, and it was reported that the favorable position enjoyed by the owners early in the strike was eroding.[56]

Finally, the players' association announced that it would call a 14-day moratorium on its activities and advise all players to report to training camp.[57] Shortly after the announcement, the owners were warned by leaders in the House of Representatives that if a "fair contract compromise" were not shortly forthcoming, an inquiry would be undertaken to re-evaluate the antitrust position of the National Football League.[58] When the 14-day period ended, the players rejected an offer of the owners, but decided to stay in camp rather than return to the picket lines, and the moratorium was indefinitely extended.[59] Although the season opened on schedule, a new collective bargaining agreement was not reached during 1974.

The football strike of 1974 lasted for 44 days. It was clearly a severe test of the strength of both players and owners, as well as the patience of the general public. The long, contentious dispute produced a considerable reservoir of ill-feeling on all sides. As had been predicted by a sportswriter's earlier comments, the strike produced "a residue of bitterness that (would) not soon evaporate."[60] Indeed, the 1974 impasse continued into subsequent seasons. When negotiations stalled in 1975, players on at least 4 of the 26 teams voted to strike during the exhibition season.[61] However, there was apparently little support for the strike and the season began on schedule when the players agreed to a no-strike pledge and the owners agreed to make a substantial contract offer.[62] Although an offer was made, it was overwhelmingly rejected by the players.[63] In the months that followed, unfair labor practice charges were filed

52. N. Y. Times, July 20, 1974, at 27, col. 8.
53. N. Y. Times, July 18, 1974, at 42, col. 6.
54. N. Y. Times, July 23, 1974, at 45, col. 4.
55. N. Y. Times, August 5, 1974, at 17, col. 1.
56. N. Y. Times, August 9, 1974, at 21, col. 5. There was also an incident at the annual Hall of Fame Game to be played at Canton, Ohio. The association had indicated that it would picket the game, and the United Auto Workers stated that they would join the picketing. N. Y. Times, July 25, 1974, at 40, col. 6. When the game was played (with rookies and free agents), there also appeared a group of retired players who were picketing against the players. N. Y. Times, July 28, 1974, § 5, at 1, col. 4. Picketing at one training camp also resulted in the picketers being arrested for failure to comply with a court order restraining their activity. N. Y. Times, July 26, 1974, at 20, col. 6.
57. N. Y. Times, August 12, 1974, at 31, col. 1.
58. N. Y. Times, August 14, 1974, at 19, col. 5.
59. N. Y. Times, August 28, 1974, at 21, col. 1.
60. N. Y. Times, July 25, 1974, at 29, col. 1.
61. N. Y. Times, September 15, 1975, at 1, col. 5. The teams were the New England Patriots, New York Giants, Washington Redskins, and, arguably, the Detroit Lions.
62. N. Y. Times, September 19, 1975, at 1, col. 5.
63. N. Y. Times, September 25, 1975, at 55, col. 1.

by the players with the NLRB, numerous hearings were convened in Congress to study the situation,[64] and the 1975 season passed without a labor contract in the NFL.

Early in 1976, there appeared a glimmer of hope that the labor situation in professional sports would stabilize when a broad based agreement was reached in the National Basketball Association. After a federal court had rendered an opinion which was quite favorable to the players' position on mobility restrictions,[65] the owners and players in early January settled the case and, apparently, the issues that had produced both litigation and labor controversy. The owners agreed to pay damages to the players,[66] but of even more significance was the owners' agreement to settle the contract grievances of the players. Thus, the owners agreed to eliminate the option clause and allow a player to become a free agent at the end of a one year contract (though rookies would be subject to a one year option if they signed an initial one year contract), limit a team's rights to players selected in the draft to one year, and to eliminate the compensation rule in 1980 in favor of a rule giving a team a first refusal option — *i.e.*, if a player wished to sign with another team, his existing team would have an option to meet the terms offered by other teams and retain the player.[67] The owners also voted to stop any consideration of merger with the ABA.[68] When the settlement was announced, it was widely viewed as indicating that the fundamental issues which created labor dispute in professional sports could be amicably resolved by the parties, rather than by judicial decree.[69]

The situation in football and baseball, however, provided less room for optimism. The football stalemate continued without resolution. The players filed additional unfair labor practice charges with the NLRB, alleging that the owners had refused to bargain in good faith.[70] The owners threatened to terminate the pension plan in the face of a players' threat to sue over the lack of contributions.[71] The bargaining situation was apparently affected significantly by a federal district court decision holding that many of the player restraint mechanisms violated the antitrust laws.[72]

The results of litigation also affected baseball. An arbitrator in October, 1975, had ruled that the reserve clause was limited to only a one-year term, allowing a player to become a free agent at the end of the one-year "renewal" period.[73] Subsequent bargaining produced proposals to modify the reserve rule, but when agreement could not be reached the owners locked the players out of spring

64. N. Y. Times, October 15, 1975, at 28, col. 3.

65. The case was Robertson v. National Basketball Ass'n, 389 F. Supp. 867 (S.D.N.Y. 1975). *See* § 5.03.

66. The owners agreed to pay the players three million dollars in damages and to defray attorneys' fees. Atlanta Constitution, January 4, 1976, at 1D, col. 1.

67. Atlanta Constitution, January 4, 1976, at 1D, col. 1.

68. N. Y. Times, February 4, 1976, at 23, col. 2.

69. N. Y. Times columnist Leonard Koppett, for example, observed that "the fact of reaching agreement is much more important than the details of this particular system. The N.B.A. has proved that it is possible to reconcile such details through bargaining. . . ." N. Y. Times, February 8, 1976, § 5, at 1, col. 1. *See also* Looney, *The Start of a Chain Reaction?*, SPORTS ILLUSTRATED, February 6, 1976, at 18.

70. Atlanta Constitution, January 10, 1976, at 1D.

71. Atlanta Constitution, March 2, 1976, at 1D, col. 2.

72. The decision was Mackey v. National Football League, 543 F.2d 606 (8th Cir. 1976), *modifying* 407 F. Supp. 1000 (D. Minn. 1975). *See* § 5.03.

73. *See* § 4.05.

training camps.[74] Proposals were made in the days that followed,[75] and each side issued dire warnings. The owners suggested that the regular season might have to be cancelled and the players adverted to the possibility of forming their own league.[76] As negotiations progressed, it appeared that one of the basic problems for the union was fear that if it agreed to a new contract which compromised the rights acquired by the arbitration decision it might be subject to suit by players who were thereby deprived of existing rights.[77] Although a "last and final offer" of the owners was not accepted by the players,[78] progress was apparently made in the contract negotiations and the commissioner ordered the training camps to open.[79] This ended the 17 day lockout, but without the execution of a collective bargaining agreement. Execution of the agreement did occur, however, a few months later.[79.1] Agreements were also reached in due course in the other sports without the public displays that had been seen in earlier negotiating periods.[79.2] An important aspect of each of these agreements was the elimination of the traditional player resistant mechanisms and the introduction of new types of controls.[79.3]

As the preceding discussion suggests, collective bargaining in the sports business is capable of producing the same level of disruption that has been common in other industries for the past forty years. The recent history also indicates that there are viable economic sanctions available to both sides at the professional sports bargaining table, which neither party is reluctant to utilize to improve its position.[80] Whether future disputes will continue to escalate as they did between 1968 and 1976, or will stabilize remains to be seen. As Leonard Koppett said in 1970, however, it may be that "[l]abor turmoil in professional sports is here to stay . . . and no fan will again be free of periodic exposure to . . . melodramatic negotiations" which may culminate in further interruptions of these several American pastimes. Hopefully, such turmoil is only symptomatic of the parties' adjustment to the framework of collective bargaining and will ultimately produce greater tranquility in the labor relations in professional sports. In light of the agreements reached in 1976 and 1977, there is room to hope that such tranquility is possible.

This discussion of the labor disputes that have taken place should serve to provide a framework for analysis of the legal issues which will inevitably arise

---

74. N. Y. Times, February 24, 1976, at 43, col. 6. Not all owners agreed with this process, and Bill Veeck of the White Sox viewed it as a violation of his rights as an owner. N. Y. Times, February 24, 1976, at 43, col. 6. He subsequently opened the White Sox training camp to non-roster players. N. Y. Times, February 27, 1976, at 37, col. 5.

75. N. Y. Times, February 28, 1976, at 17, col. 5.

76. Smith, *Golden Age of Press Agentry,* N. Y. Times, March 8, 1976, at 35, col. 1.

77. N. Y. Times, March 9, 1976, at 40, col. 7. The union believed that it could not deprive a player of his individual rights "by simply reaching an industry-wide formula." N. Y. Times, March 11, 1976, at 50, col. 6. Specifically, the issue was whether a collective bargaining agreement would have retroactive effect and apply to individual contracts that had been signed before its effective date.

78. N. Y. Times, March 17, 1976, at 27, col. 3.

79. N. Y. Times, March 18, 1976, at 53, col. 1.

79.1. *See* MAJOR LEAGUE BASEBALL BASIC AGREEMENT (1976).

79.2. *See* NATIONAL FOOTBALL LEAGUE COLLECTIVE BARGAINING AGREEMENT (1977). The process leading to this agreement is described in Marshall, *Finding Square One,* SPORTS ILLUSTRATED, March 7, 1977, at 63.

79.3. These changes are discussed in detail in § 5.03.

80. *But cf.* Mackey v. National Football League, 543 F.2d 606 (8th Cir. 1976), *modifying* 407 F. Supp. 1000 (D. Minn. 1975) (suggestion that the National Football League Players Association did not have equal bargaining power with the owners).

as the collective bargaining process in professional sports matures. In the remainder of this chapter, we will focus on some of those labor law problems. The basic conclusion to be drawn is that when the owners and players enter into formalized collective bargaining, they literally start a new ball game. In that game, their relationship and conduct are governed by a scheme of laws and decisional rules which are the product of nearly a half century of experience in other areas of commerce. These rules may cause unexpected changes to occur in professional sports, and they will put the owner-player relation upon a new foundation. The owners can no longer dismiss collective bargaining by invoking the shibboleth that it would bring the sport to an early grave, or that it would be prohibitively expensive, because any item relating to wages, hours or other terms or conditions of employment is a mandatory subject of bargaining about which the owners have a *duty* to bargain in good faith.[81] On the other hand, the players need no longer take any part of their "condition" as a "fact of life", for they have within their grasp the power to make the owners bargain about its continued existence.[82] There is, however, a concomitant to that new power. Once within the "friendly confines" of the labor law, individual players may be required to accept the terms and conditions negotiated by their bargaining agent, for they are all equally bound by its actions.[83] This basic labor policy of submitting the will of the minority to that of the majority may bear most heavily upon the so-called superstars should a situation arise in which they are no longer able to bargain individually for salary or other terms of employment.

Perhaps the most important aspect of the advent of collective bargaining is that all courts should in the future treat labor disputes in this industry the same as they do labor disputes in the steel industry — that is, they should leave the parties to their remedies under the labor laws, either before the NLRB or the courts themselves.[84] In short, though the professional sports industry may present collective bargaining problems in some rather unique, perhaps even *sui generis,* circumstances, they are, nonetheless, labor problems and should be treated as such.

Before addressing the substantive labor law problems that may arise in professional sports, it is important to emphasize that many of these issues will be intimately related to the antitrust issues that we reviewed in chapter 5 of this treatise. For example, when attention is given to the validity of a term in a collective bargaining agreement, it is likely that the labor law issues raised by the term will be addressed only after it is determined whether the labor antitrust exemption is applicable.[84.1] Accordingly, the reader may want to review the pertinent provisions of the antitrust chapter as part of a review of the labor law principles that we will present in this chapter.

---

81. *See* §§ 6.05, 6.06.

82. It is important to note that in Flood v. Kuhn, 407 U.S. 258, 32 L. Ed. 2d 728, 92 S. Ct. 2099 (1972), Mr. Justice Marshall observed, in his dissenting opinion, that the Court had rendered the collective efforts of ballplayers "impotent." *Id.* at 292. This is, with all due respect, a slightly overbroad conclusion. As will be developed herein, players' associations are no more or less "impotent" than is any other labor organization. *But cf.* note 80 *supra.*

83. *See* § 6.11.

84. *Hearings, supra* note 4, at 87. It has been noted, however, that any such remedy may be somewhat illusory. *See Hearings, supra* note 2, at pt. 2, 2654. Though that objection may have some appeal, it has never dampened the attitudes of courts considering labor disputes in other industries.

84.1. *See* §§ 5.04-06.

§ 6.02. Coverage of the National Labor Relations Act.

The first issue that must be addressed when considering the relationship between a particular industry and the labor laws is whether the coverage of the National Labor Relations Act (NLRA) is broad enough to include the industry in question. It has long been a familiar rule that because the NLRA is based upon the commerce clause of the Constitution, its coverage is coextensive with that clause's reach.[85] Thus, every industry that is in or affects interstate commerce is subject to the provisions of the NLRA.[86]

In order to conclude that the NLRA covers the professional sports industry, it need only be found that its activities are involved in interstate commerce. Though this may at one time have been an issue of merit, its further consideration lacks even academic interest in light of the Supreme Court's recent pronouncement that "[p]rofessional baseball is a business and it is engaged in interstate commerce."[87] A similar determination has been made with regard to football;[88] basketball;[89] boxing;[90] hockey;[91] and golf.[92] It is, therefore, clear that the NLRA's coverage does include professional sports.[93]

Even though the NLRA is applicable, the NLRB has the statutory power to decline jurisdiction where, in its opinion, the impact of a particular industry on interstate commerce is not so "sufficiently substantial to warrant the exercise of its jurisdiction . . . ."[94] Although the Board has exercised this discretion to exclude some aspects of the professional sports industry,[95] it seems clear that

85. NLRB v. Fainblatt, 306 U.S. 601, 607, 83 L. Ed. 1014, 59 S. Ct. 668 (1939); NLRB v. Jones & Laughlin Steel Corp., 301 U.S. 1, 81 L. Ed. 893, 57 S. Ct. 615 (1937); Pappas v. American Guild of Variety Artists, 125 F. Supp. 343, 344 (N.D. Ill. 1954).

86. NLRB v. Fainblatt, 306 U.S. 601, 607, 83 L. Ed. 1014, 59 S. Ct. 668 (1939).

87. Flood v. Kuhn, 407 U.S. 258, 282, 32 L. Ed. 2d 728, 92 S. Ct. 2099 (1972); *see also* American League of Professional Baseball Clubs, 180 N.L.R.B. 189 (1969); *Hearings Before the Senate Antitrust Subcomm. of the Senate Comm. on the Judiciary,* 85th Cong., 1st Sess., pt. 1, 47. The "commerce" issue in the antitrust context is reviewed in detail in § 5.02.

88. Radovich v. National Football League, 352 U.S. 445, 1 L. Ed. 2d 456, 77 S. Ct. 390 (1957); *see also* National Football League Players Ass'n v. NLRB, 503 F.2d 12 (8th Cir. 1974); Kapp v. National Football League, 390 F. Supp. 73 (N.D. Cal. 1974).

89. Haywood v. National Basketball Ass'n, 401 U.S. 1204, 28 L. Ed. 2d 206, 91 S. Ct. 672 (1971); Robertson v. National Basketball Ass'n, 389 F. Supp. 867 (S.D.N.Y. 1975); Denver Rockets v. All-Pro Management, Inc., 325 F. Supp. 1049 (C.D. Cal. 1971); Washington Professional Basketball Corp. v. National Basketball Ass'n, 147 F. Supp. 154 (S.D.N.Y. 1956).

90. United States v. International Boxing Club, 348 U.S. 236, 99 L. Ed. 290, 75 S. Ct. 259 (1955).

91. Nassau Sports v. Peters, 352 F. Supp. 870 (E.D.N.Y. 1972); Boston Professional Hockey Ass'n, Inc. v. Cheevers, 1972 Trade Cases ¶ 74,227 (D. Mass.); Philadelphia World Hockey Club, Inc. v. Philadelphia Hockey Club, Inc., 351 F. Supp. 462 (E.D. Pa. 1972); Peto v. Madison Square Garden Corp., 1958 Trade Cases ¶ 69,106 (S.D.N.Y.).

92. Deesen v. Professional Golfers' Ass'n, 358 F.2d 165 (9th Cir. 1966), *cert. denied,* 385 U.S. 846, 17 L. Ed. 2d 76, 87 S. Ct. 72 (1967); Blalock v. Ladies Professional Golf Ass'n, 359 F. Supp. 1260 (N.D. Ga. 1973).

93. National Football League Players Ass'n v. NLRB, 503 F.2d 12 (8th Cir. 1974); New York State Div. of Human Rights v. New York-Pennsylvania Professional Baseball League, 36 App. Div. 2d 364, 320 N.Y.S.2d 788, 799 (1971) (Cardamone, J., dissenting); *Hearings, supra,* note 87, at pt. 1, 47 ("we have to recognize that professional football now is under the National Labor Relations Act"). Although it may have at one time been believed that the antitrust exemption enjoyed by some professional sports (baseball — *see* § 5.02) exempted them all from NLRA coverage, this view has been rejected on numerous occasions and need no longer be grounds for argument. The theory and its rejection are considered in Hoffman, *Is the NLRB Going to Play the Ball Game?,* 20 LAB. L.J. 239, 242-43 (1969).

94. NLRA § 14(c)(1).

95. *See, e.g.,* Yonkers Raceway, Inc. 196 N.L.R.B. 373 (1972) (Board declined to assert jurisdiction over harness racing because it lacked sufficient impact on interstate commerce); Centennial Turf Club, Inc., 192 N.L.R.B. 698 (1971) (same).

it will not do so with regard to the organized team sports. Thus, in *American League of Professional Baseball Clubs,*[96] a case involving baseball umpires, the Board held that professional baseball is an industry in or affecting commerce and is subject to NLRA coverage and NLRB jurisdiction.[97] The Board observed that its policy of encouraging collective bargaining through protection of employee rights to self-organization and choice of representation would be best fulfilled by asserting its jurisdiction and subjecting any labor dispute to resolution under the NLRA.[98] The Board has also exercised its jurisdiction over professional football.[99] There should, therefore, be little remaining uncertainty as to the coverage of the NLRA and the jurisdiction of the Board with regard to the professional team sports. Not only is the coverage of the Act and the jurisdiction of the Board broad enough to cover the players themselves, but it will also include all other employees in the industry from bat boys to maintenance men.[100]

With regard to coverage, the question might also arise as to whether the players' associations are "labor organizations" within the meaning of the NLRA.[101] A labor organization is defined to include "any organization . . . which exists for the purpose, in whole or in part, of dealing with employers, concerning grievances, labor disputes, wages, rates of pay, hours of employment, or conditions of work."[102] Thus, any employee group which deals with employers about wages and other conditions of employment is a labor organization. In *American League,* the League had also argued that the umpires' organization there in dispute was not a labor organization since the umpires were allegedly "supervisors." The Board, however, held that the umpires were not supervisors and that the organization was a labor organization since it existed for the purpose of dealing with employers about wages and conditions of employment,[103] indicating that the players' associations would also meet the statutory test.

§ 6.03. Protected Rights of Employee-Athletes.

One of the essential benefits to be gained by professional athletes upon entering collective bargaining with their employer-owner will be the conferral upon them of the rights provided to employees by § 7 of the NLRA. These include "the right to self-organization, to form, join or assist labor organizations, to bargain collectively through representatives of their own choosing, and to engage in other concerted activities for the purpose of collective bargaining or other mutual aid and protection, and . . . to refrain from any or all such activities

---

96. 180 N.L.R.B. 189 (1969).

97. 180 N.L.R.B. at 192-93. *See also* 35th ANNUAL REPORT OF THE NATIONAL LABOR RELATIONS BOARD 22-26 (1970). It is to be noted, however, that member Jenkins was of the opinion that the Board should decline to assert its jurisdiction over professional baseball. 180 N.L.R.B. at 194.

98. 180 N.L.R.B. at 192-93. *See generally* Hoffman, *Is the NLRB Going to Play the Ball Game?,* 20 LAB. L.J. 239 (1969); Note, *The Balance of Power in Professional Sports,* 22 MAINE L. REV. 459, 478 (1970). '

99. National Football League Management Council, 203 N.L.R.B. No. 165 (1973).

100. 180 N.L.R.B. at 193.

101. N.L.R.B. v. Cabot Carbon Co., 360 U.S. 203, 3 L. Ed. 2d 1175, 79 S. Ct. 1015 (1959).

102. N.L.R.A. § 2(5).

103. 180 N.L.R.B. at 192-93; *see also* Krasnow & Levy, *Unionization and Professional Sports,* 51 GEO. L.J. 749, 772-74 (1963).

. . . ."[104] In order to protect these rights, § 8 of the NLRA makes it an unfair labor practice for either an employer or a union to interfere with an employee's § 7 rights. The specific provisions of § 8 are quite detailed and all have potential application to the labor relationships in professional sports. As a means of providing a basic discussion of employee rights, this section will suggest some of the specific problems that may arise in the sports context and indicate how they would be resolved under the substantive provisions of § 8. No attempt will be made to set forth a broad survey of the myriad issues that could arise with respect to the protected rights. Such a discussion would be beyond the scope of this treatise and has been done comprehensively by others.[105]

In virtually all of the labor controversies that have been experienced in professional sports, the players have alleged that owners engaged in various efforts to coerce them into withdrawing support from their union. For example, it has often been alleged that the owners have attempted to break the unions through direct coercion of players [106] and by undermining their confidence in the ability of union leaders.[107] If these charges could be proven, they might constitute a violation of the basic employer unfair labor practice provision. Section 8(a)(1) makes it an unfair labor practice for an employer to "interfere with, restrain, or coerce employees in the exercise of the rights guaranteed in Section 7."[108] Probably the most difficult aspect of § 8(a)(1) is the extent to which it requires the showing of an anti-union motive by the employer. The NLRB has followed the rule that motive is not a critical element of a violation,[109] but the Supreme Court has been much more equivocal.[110]

Although allegations of conduct that could violate § 8(a)(1) have been made frequently in the sports leagues, there has been little authoritative analysis of § 8(a)(1) issues. The existing authority does, however, provide an illustration of how such allegations will be reviewed. Thus, the NFL Players' Association filed charges with the NLRB in 1974 alleging that the owners had threatened players who would not participate in an all-star game and coerced other players by publicizing salary data. After reviewing the allegations, the Regional Director of the NLRB concluded that there was no evidence to support them and refused to issue a complaint against the owners.[111] Violations were, however, found by an Administrative Law Judge in *National Football League Management Council*

---

104. NLRA § 7.

105. *See generally* 18B T. KHEEL, LABOR LAW ch. 10 (1973); C. MORRIS, THE DEVELOPING LABOR LAW 63-149 (1971).

106. *See* § 6.01, at notes 14, 33-34; and note 112 *infra*. Coercion has also been reported by players threatening other players who do not go along with union positions. *See, e.g.,* N. Y. Times, July 31, 1970, at 22, col. 1.

107. *Hearings Before the House Subcomm. on Labor-Management Relations of the House Comm. on Education and Labor,* 94th Cong., 1st Sess. 25, 31 (1975).

108. NLRA § 8(a)(1). It is also an unfair labor practice for a union to interfere with its employees' § 7 rights. NLRA § 8(b)(1)(A).

109. *See, e.g.,* Cooper Thermometer Co., 154 N.L.R.B. 502 (1965).

110. *See* 18B T. KHEEL, LABOR LAW § 10.03[3] (1973); C. MORRIS, THE DEVELOPING LABOR LAW 66-68 (1971).

111. The letter of the Regional Director is reproduced in *Hearings, supra* note 107, at 89-90.

A § 8(a)(1) unfair labor practice might also be committed through communications with players of a coercive nature. In line with the employer free speech provision in § 8(c), the courts have generally taken the position that so long as the employer's comments go no further than to predict the economic consequences of given activity, they will not constitute coercive conduct, but if the comments go beyond mere prediction, and indicate that the employer will respond in some specified manner if the employees pursue a given path, then the comments may be coercive within the meaning of § 8(a)(1). *See generally* 18B T. KHEEL, LABOR LAW § 10.03 (1973).

(II),[111:1] which also involved charges arising out of the 1974 NFL strike. The judge found that § 8(a)(1) had been violated when a team (the Dallas Cowboys) gave a rookie a "Notice of Contract Termination" when he left training camp in support of the strike. While this was apparently a routine procedure whenever a player left a club, its use during a strike was found to be destructive of the employees' freedom to engage in protected concerted activity (even though the team apparently had no intention of actually placing the player on waivers). Similarly, a violation resulted from the demands of two teams (the Miami Dolphins and San Diego Chargers) that strikers repay their bonuses, since this also had the effect of inhibiting the exercise of protected rights. A separate violation occurred because the coach of another team (the Houston Oilers) had advised the player representative that any discussion of strike-related issues would result in a fine, suspension or other disciplinary action.[111.2]

One of the most frequently voiced complaints of the players is that owners interfere with union activity by trading, or otherwise eliminating, player representatives from the teams that they represent for collective bargaining purposes.[112] If these complaints could be proven as a factual matter, it seems likely that they would constitute a violation of § 8(a)(1). Such conduct could also violate § 8(a)(3), which makes it an unfair labor practice for an employer to "discriminate in regard to hire or tenure of employment or any term or condition of employment to encourage or discourage membership in any labor organization."[113] The underlying philosophy of § 8(a)(3) is to insure that the employment rights of an employee who participates in, or supports, union activity are not imperiled by the action of an employer.[114] When an employer's conduct is challenged under § 8(a)(3), it is not necessary that a specific antiunion motive be proven in every case since it may often be inferred from the circumstances or the nature of the conduct.[115] The factual nature of the inquiry in § 8(a)(3) cases is suggested by the response of an NLRB representative to charges that were filed by the NFL Players' Association in 1974 alleging that owners had discriminated against player representatives of the various teams. The union apparently alleged that a large number of representatives had been traded or cut during collective bargaining negotiations in 1974 and that there was a "pattern of union discrimination by management."[116] The owners, on the

---

111.1. Case No. 2-CA-13379 (June 30, 1976—*see* note 217.7 *infra*). The designation "II" after the name of the case is to distinguish the decision from an earlier case with the same name. *National Football League Management Council (I)*, 203 N.L.R.B. 958 (1973).

111.2. Other allegations were rejected. Thus, it was found that two teams (the Dallas Cowboys and St. Louis Cardinals) had not prevented the union from communicating with the players when the union had adequate and reasonable means of contacting the players. The team's photographing of strike activities was also found to have no necessary impact upon protected rights.

112. *See, e.g.,* N.Y. Times, July 20, 1974, at 25, col. 4; N. Y. Times, April 8, 1972, at 19, col. 5; *Hearings, supra* note 107, at 13, 27-31; *Hearings Before the Special House Subcomm. on Labor of the House Comm. on Education and Labor,* 92d Cong., 2d Sess. 19 (1972); Brown, *Owners Can be Tackled Too,* SPORTS ILLUSTRATED, March 22, 1971, at 19-20.

113. NLRA § 8(a)(3). It is also an unfair labor practice for an employer to discharge or otherwise discriminate against an employee for the filing of charges with the NLRB, § 8(a)(4), or for a union to cause an employer to discriminate against an employee in violation of § 8(a)(3). NLRA § 8(b)(2). It should be noted that a violation of § 8(a)(3), as well as the other employer unfair labor practice provisions of § 8(a), will also constitute a derivative violation of § 8(a)(1).

114. Radio Officers' Union v. NLRB, 347 U.S. 17, 40 (1954).

115. NLRB v. Great Dane Trailers, Inc., 388 U.S. 26, 18 L. Ed. 2d 1027, 87 S. Ct. 1792 (1967). *See generally* 18B T. KHEEL, LABOR LAW § 12.02[1] (1973).

116. *See Hearings, supra* note 107, at 13 (in which player representatives discussed these charges).

other hand, suggested that the facts actually showed that very few representatives were not with the same team both before and after the negotiations and that most of those who did not continue as representatives had resigned voluntarily.[117] When the charges were reviewed by an NLRB regional director, he concluded that "the evidence obtained in the investigation is insufficient to establish that [the owners] . . . engaged in a general pattern of cutting, trading or waiving certain players for discriminatory reasons."[118] He did, however, find that there was evidence to support the charges relating to four former representatives and those charges were to be subjected to further processing.[119] This was provided by an Administrative Law Judge, in *National Football League Management Council (II)*,[119.1] who found that one of the players had been traded as part of a package deal that did not reflect any discriminatory treatment. The remaining three players, however, had been the subject of improper discrimination, since they had not been given a "fair opportunity" to make the team following their strike activities.[119.2]

The potential for § 8(a)(3) violations is certainly not limited to the disposal of union representatives and may rise in any situation in which an owner takes action that could affect protected activity.[120] One such situation that will be discussed in a subsequent section of this chapter involves economic sanctions that owners might utilize during contract negotiations (lockouts and replacement of striking players).[121]

The final type of activity that has generated substantial complaint in the professional sports area involves the refusal of one side or the other to engage in good faith bargaining. Section 8(d) of the NLRA provides that "collective bargaining" requires both the employer and the representative of the employees to meet and bargain in good faith with respect to the terms and conditions of employment,[122] and the failure by either party to so meet is an unfair labor practice.[123] The specific principles that may arise under the duty to bargain are

---

117. *Id.* at 47.
118. *Id.* at 89 (letter from the Regional Director).
119. *Id.* at 90.
119.1. Case No. 2-CA-13379 (June 30, 1976 — *see* notes 111.1 *supra* and 217.7 *infra*).
119.2. The remedy for these players was that they be given immediate and full reinstatement to the roster without prejudice to their seniority or other rights, and that they be made whole for any loss of earnings suffered by reason of the discrimination. The rights of economic strikers to reinstatement are considered in § 6.09.
120. For example, discrimination might also arise from the threat of an owner to move a team's franchise from one city to another. *See, e.g.,* Textile Workers v. Darlington Mfg. Co., 380 U.S. 263, 13 L. Ed. 2d 827, 85 S. Ct. 994 (1965); Surprenant Mfg. Co. v. NLRB, 341 F.2d 756 (6th Cir. 1965). Professional athletes' concern over such movements is described in *Hearings Before Special House Subcomm., supra* note 112, at 71. An actual movement will be permissible if made in the good faith belief that it is necessary for economic or other valid business reasons. NLRB v. Rapid Bindery, 293 F.2d 170 (2d. Cir. 1961); Mt. Hope Finishing Co. v. NLRB, 211 F.2d 365 (4th Cir. 1954); Royal Plating & Polishing Co., Inc., 152 N.L.R.B. 619 (1965), *enforcement denied,* 350 F.2d 191 (3d Cir. 1965); Dove Flocking & Screening Co., 145 N.L.R.B. 682 (1963). An actual transfer may, however, be an unfair labor practice under § 8(a)(3) if motivated by a desire to hinder or prevent union activity. Darlington Mfg. Co. v. NLRB, 397 F.2d 760 (4th Cir. 1968); NLRB v. Southland Paint Co., 394 F.2d 717 (5th Cir. 1968); NLRB v. Lewis, 246 F.2d 886 (9th Cir. 1957).
121. *See* § 6.09.
122. The specific language of § 8(d) is that the parties must "meet at reasonable times and confer in good faith with respect to wages, hours, and other terms and conditions of employment . . . ."
123. NLRA §§ 8(a)(5) (employer) and 8(b)(3) (union).

considered in a subsequent section of this chapter, and they are mentioned here only as an additional illustration of the type of conduct that may generate controversy in sports bargaining.[124]

§ 6.04. The Appropriate Bargaining Unit.

The initial step in any analysis of collective bargaining under the NLRA is to determine the appropriate unit for bargaining purposes.[125] This determination is important for several reasons. It will define the basic bargaining relationship by establishing the group of employees who will be represented by an exclusive bargaining representative in negotiations with their employer.[126] The size of the unit will also define the power of both a given union and its individual members. If a group of employees with essentially common interests are fragmentized into several units, the power of each bargaining representative may be much less than would be true if all employees were included in a single unit. But in a unit that covers all such employees, each employee may have a much smaller impact upon bargaining objectives and methods than would be the case in a smaller unit. These several factors have made bargaining unit issues a frequent subject of dispute in industrial labor relations. Although such issues have not as of this writing presented many problems in professional sports, there are several issues that are quite likely to arise in the future. We will consider these issues after attention is given to the existing unit classifications in the sports leagues.

a. Existing Units. With respect to the initial determination of the size of a bargaining unit, the employer and union may agree upon the size of the unit to be represented. If they fail to do so, or if the agreed upon unit is challenged, the NLRB will make the determination.[127] In performing this function, the Board has been accorded wide discretion and will take a flexible approach, in which it will consider a number of factors. These have normally included the extent and type of union organization of employees, the bargaining history in the industry, the similarity in skills and interests of the employees, the organizational structure of the company, and the desires of the employees.[128]

The determination of appropriate bargaining units in professional sports has not required a decision from the NLRB, since the parties in the various leagues have been able to agree upon unit size. The preferential size of the bargaining unit has invariably been the sport itself (except where there are two leagues within a sport in which there has not been a merger). Thus, the present unit in football, basketball and baseball is the entire sport,[129] while in hockey it is the

---

124. *See* § 6.06. *See also* National Football League Players Ass'n v. NLRB, 503 F.2d 12 (8th Cir. 1974).

125. NLRA § 9(a).

126. NLRA § 9(b).

127. *See* C. MORRIS, THE DEVELOPING LABOR LAW 200 (1971).

128. These factors are individually discussed in 18C T. KHEEL, LABOR LAW § 14.02 (1974); C. MORRIS, THE DEVELOPING LABOR LAW 217-22 (1970).

129. National Football League Collective Bargaining Agreement 1 (1977); Major League Baseball Basic Agreement, art. II (1976). *See also Hearings Before the Special House Subcomm. on Labor of the House Comm. on Education and Labor,* 92d Cong., 2d Sess. 65 (1972).

league,[130] there having been as yet no merger in that sport.[131] Since there are any number of possibilities for the size of the bargaining unit in sports, it is interesting to consider why organization has been undertaken on a league-wide basis. Although there is no clear answer to the question, it would appear that it reflects the view that the league has traditionally been the dominant force in professional sports. It is the entity which makes uniform rules to regulate the highly interdependent activities of its component teams. A league-wide unit would also reflect the facts that players may move from one team to another within a league and that all players in a given league possess similar skills and perform under essentially identical working conditions. The agreement of the player unions to bargain on a league-wide basis may, then, have represented a belief that the power was at the league level. It may also have been necessary for the unions to acquire as much bargaining power as possible. When the players' associations were formed or reorganized for collective bargaining purposes in the 1960's, the players had little power as a group to bargain with the owners and if bargaining were undertaken on less than a league-wide basis it is entirely possible that the ranks of the players could not have been maintained with the unity necessary for effective collective bargaining.

b. Changing the Size of the Unit. The present size of the bargaining unit in each sport is, however, relatively unimportant, since one may take as given the present units in the industry. The more important issue relates to the circumstances under which the size of an existing unit might be changed. Before focusing on the specific issues that would be raised by an attempt to make such a change, it is necessary to consider two of the basic principles that may have particular importance to unit determinations in professional sports.

The first is that the inclusiveness of the bargaining unit is an issue that is a proper subject for discussion at the bargaining table and when raised is a permissive subject of bargaining — that is, it is one for which the other party does not have a duty to bargain and which may not be insisted upon by the proposing party to the point of impasse.[132] Once a bargaining unit determination has been made, therefore, it may be altered either by the Board or by the parties' mutual agreement.[133] Thus, although bargaining unit determinations seem already to have been made in the sports industry, that fact would not preclude the parties from adjusting the size of the unit to meet their own convenience. It should be noted, however, that such a change would be allowed only if it did not disrupt the bargaining process.[134] One situation that might be deemed to

---

130. *Hearings Before the Senate Subcomm. on Antitrust and Monopoly of the Senate Comm. on the Judiciary,* 92d Cong., 1st Sess., pts. 1 & 2, at pt. 1, 194 (1971); *Hearings, supra,* note 129, at 65.

131. The merger question in basketball (before the demise of the A.B.A.) is considered in some detail in two volumes of hearings. *See Hearings Before the Senate Subcomm. on Antitrust and Monopoly of the Senate Comm. on the Judiciary,* 92d Cong., 1st Sess., pts. 1 & 2 (1971).

132. NLRB v. Wooster Div. of Borg-Warner Corp., 356 U.S. 342, 348-49, 2 L. Ed. 2d 823, 78 S. Ct. 718 (1958). Thus, in Douds v. International Longshoremen's Ass'n, 241 F.2d 278 (2d Cir. 1957), where the union resorted to a strike when bargaining reached impasse over its demand for a broad extension of the bargaining unit, the court held it in violation of its duty to bargain pursuant to § 8(b)(3). It said that "[s]uch a demand interferes with the required bargaining 'with respect to rates of pay, wages, hours and conditions of employment' in a manner excluded by the Act." *Id.* at 283. *See also* AFL-CIO Joint Bargaining Committee, 184 N.L.R.B. No. 106 (1970); Steere Broadcasting Co., 158 N.L.R.B. 487, 507 (1966).

133. Lever Bros. Co., 96 N.L.R.B. 448 (1951).

134. Douds v. International Longshoremen's Ass'n, 241 F.2d 278 (2d Cir. 1957).

cause such disruption would be an agreement that left some employees unrepresented when they had been earlier included in the unit.[135] This might, for example, preclude an agreement to exclude rookies from a league-wide unit.

The second group of rules that should be noted are those that have evolved to govern multi-employer bargaining, which refers to the common practice of several employers in one industry bargaining with a single union. Multi-employer bargaining is presently used in professional sports — that is, the players' associations negotiate with the representative of all the owners in the league — and is common in the larger entertainment industry.[136] Bargaining on a multi-employer basis does not raise any serious problems in professional sports, but it does bring forth a number of labor law principles that may be important in considering the size of bargaining units in the future.

The history of multi-employer bargaining long antedates the Wagner Act,[137] and was, at least in its origins, designed as a technique of countervailing power, whereby small employers could join together to match the bargaining strength of the union which represented its employees [138] — that is, the multi-employer representative would become the bargaining agent for the group.[139] The rules which have grown up to govern this bargaining technique all revolve around the central principle that participation in the wider bargaining unit is entirely a consensual matter.[140] Thus, in determining the appropriateness of such a unit, as opposed to the presumptively appropriate single employer unit,[141] the Board requires a controlling history of collective bargaining on a multi-employer basis (which is thought to evidence consent),[142] or a joint agreement between the employers and the union that a multi-employer unit is appropriate.[143] Similarly, the settled criterion for determining the inclusion of any particular employer within such a unit is whether it unequivocally intends to be bound in collective bargaining by the group, rather than pursuing its own individual bargaining.[144] Thus, delegation of authority to a common bargaining agent will signify the requisite intent,[145] though mere adoption of a contract already negotiated need

135. *See, e.g.,* Steere Broadcasting Corp., 158 N.L.R.B. 487 (1966) (unfair labor practice for employer to insist upon inclusion of a group of employees and then insist upon their exclusion).

136. *See, e.g.,* Cavendish Record Mfg. Co., 124 N.L.R.B. 1161 (1959) (musicians); National Broadcasting Co., 104 N.L.R.B. 587 (1953) (free lance writers); American Broadcasting Co., 96 N.L.R.B. 815 (1951) (actors); Television Film Producers Ass'n, 93 N.L.R.B. 929 (1951) (actors).

137. NLRB v. Truck Drivers Local 449, 353 U.S. 87, 96, 1 L. Ed. 2d 676, 77 S. Ct. 643 (1957).

138. *See generally,* 18C T. KHEEL, LABOR LAW § 14.03 (1974); C. MORRIS, THE DEVELOPING LABOR LAW 237 (1970).

139. NLRB v. Strong, 393 U.S. 357, 21 L. Ed. 2d 546, 89 S. Ct. 541 (1969). It is worth noting, however, that the group agreement is not cast in stone. Thus, individual negotiations at the local level will not cause dissolution, or withdrawal from, the multi-employer unit. *See* The Kroger Co., 148 N.L.R.B. 569, 573 (1964). Similarly, retention by the employers of the right to approve or disapprove the agreement negotiated will not invalidate the wider unit. *See* Quality Limestone Prods. Co., 143 N.L.R.B. 587, 591 (1963).

140. Retail Associates, Inc., 120 N.L.R.B. 388, 393 (1958).

141. Cab Operating Corp., 153 N.L.R.B. 878, 879 (1965); John Breuner Co., 129 N.L.R.B. 394 (1960); Weaver Motors, 123 N.L.R.B. 209, 212-13 (1959).

142. York Transfer & Storage Co., 107 N.L.R.B. 139, 142 (1953).

143. Western Ass'n of Eng'rs, 101 N.L.R.B. 64 (1952); *see also* Calumet Contractors Ass'n, 121 N.L.R.B. 80, 81 n.1 (1958).

144. Electric Theatre, 156 N.L.R.B. 1351 (1966).

145. When members of an association jointly bargain, their by-laws should specify that collective bargaining agreements negotiated by the association bind all members, *see* Governale & Drew, Inc., 106 N.L.R.B. 1316, 1319-20 (1953), because if loose group action is followed, the Board may find the absence of the requisite intent. *See, e.g.,* Electric Theatre, 156 N.L.R.B. 1351 (1966).

not render the adopting firm a member of the multi-employer group.[146] The corollary to these consensual inclusion rules is that any employer, regardless of previous bargaining policy or practice,[147] may withdraw from the wider unit at an appropriate time.[148] To be effective, the withdrawal must be shown to have manifested an unequivocal and timely intention to withdraw on a permanent basis.[149] When an employer so withdraws, moreover, its motive for doing so is immaterial.[150] These same withdrawal rules also apply to the union members of the unit, who may withdraw all employees of one or more employer.[151]

The multi-employer rules indicate, therefore, that owners and a union may withdraw from a presently established unit whenever it is determined that they could negotiate more advantageously in individual employer bargaining. Although such action seems unlikely as a practical matter to take place, it is important to note that the authority for it does exist and might be used as a viable bargaining tool by either side.

Considered together, these rules suggest that the scope of the bargaining unit is a matter that is subject to the consensual agreement of owners and a union. This view of the unit may be an important element in future collective bargaining in professional sports. One situation which might make it significant would be a sport in which there were two leagues but where merger was not feasible — because, for example, Congress would not grant an antitrust exemption for the merger.[152] In this situation, the owners and players in the two leagues might seek to acquire the benefits of formal merger by utilizing the multi-employer bargaining unit device, without the necessity of obtaining an antitrust waiver from the Congress. The results of formal merger could be obtained to the extent that they involved matters that were appropriate for collective bargaining consideration — such as a common player draft, reservation or option system, or "anti-raiding" rules.[153]

---

146. National Elec. Contractors Ass'n, 131 N.L.R.B. 550, 551-52 (1961); *see also* Jewish Bakery Ass'n, 100 N.L.R.B. 1245, 1246 (1952).

147. Johnson Optical Co., 87 N.L.R.B. 539 (1949).

148. C. MORRIS, THE DEVELOPING LABOR LAW 243-45 (1971).

149. B. Brody Seating Co., 167 N.L.R.B. 830 (1967). This is generally accomplished by notice, and the proper notice rule requires that written notice of the intention to withdraw be given before the contractually set date for modification. Retail Associates, Inc., 120 N.L.R.B. 388 (1958); *but cf.* Imperial Outdoor Advertising, 192 N.L.R.B. No. 183 (1971) (oral notice sufficient). If not so given, the notice is not timely. Thus, in NLRB v. Strong, 393 U.S. 357, 21 L. Ed. 2d 546, 89 S. Ct. 541 (1969), the Supreme Court refused to allow withdrawal where the employer gave notice after the negotiated agreement became effective.

150. Evening News Ass'n, 154 N.L.R.B. 1494, 1495 (1956); Bearing Rim & Supply Co., 107 N.L.R.B. 101, 103 (1953).

151. Evening News Ass'n, 154 N.L.R.B. 1494, 1495 (1965).

152. This was the recent experience in professional basketball. S2373, 92d Cong., 1st Sess. (1971) (in favor of merger); S2616, 92d Cong., 1st Sess. (1971) (opposed to the merger); *Hearings Before the Special House Subcomm. on Labor of the House Comm. on Education and Labor,* 92d Cong., 2d Sess. 67 (1972); 117 CONG. REC. S15451 (1971) (Speech by Senator Sam J. Ervin). *See generally Hearings Before the Senate Subcomm. on Antitrust and Monopoly of the Senate Comm. on the Judiciary,* 92d Cong., 1st Sess., pts. 1 & 2 (1971).

153. *Senate Hearings, supra* note 152, at pt. 2, 856. *See* § 6.08.

Although there have been no formal proposals for such a "constructive" merger — at least none have been made public — representatives of the N.B.A. suggested the possibility of "absorbing" or "amalgamating" the stronger franchises of the A.B.A. *See* Anderson, *Power to the Players, Especially the A's,* N. Y. Times, February 5, 1976, at 19, col. 1; N. Y. Times, February 24, 1976, at 43, col. 6. This has subsequently taken place, and is quite close to a more explicit merger for "bargaining" purposes.

In order to accomplish these results, the owners and unions in the two leagues would need to agree to bargain on a joint basis. By agreeing to do so, the owners would be agreeing to bargain via the multi-employer device, while the players' associations would, by agreeing to bargain as one, be presenting themselves in a coalition bargaining posture.[154] So long as all parties agreed to the procedure, their action would appear to be permissible as a matter of labor law — which is simply to restate the familiar shibboleth that the right of both employees and employers "to choose whomever they wish to represent them in formal labor negotiations is fundamental to the statutory scheme." [155] The provisions agreed upon should be immune from antitrust attack, so long as the terms negotiated relate to wages, hours or working conditions, were the result of bona fide collective bargaining, where the union met its duty of fair representation and did not conspire with the employers.[156]

Though such a "constructive" merger procedure would seem to be technically possible under the NLRA, it would require that the parties consent to the bargaining arrangement. When such issues have arisen in the past, the players' associations have shown little interest in merger. This is apparently a consequence of a fear of losing the bargaining power that inevitably accrues to players as a result of two competing leagues.[157] Such intransigence might be overcome if the owners were to agree to a particular bargaining demand of the union in return for the joint bargaining. This might not be an especially appealing prospect for the owners, however, because under the multi-employer rules the players could opt out of the unit after getting a favored term. Withdrawal might itself be precluded by making any such acquiescence conditional upon maintenance of the multi-employer unit, or by the negotiation of a long-term contract, if that were possible. The resistance of a union to such bargaining procedures might also be overcome by the existence of economic necessity — for example, if it were clear that a league would become insolvent if the benefits of merger could not be acquired.

c. Establishing Different Units of Players. The principles developed above suggest the possibility of adopting a unit size for bargaining purposes that differs from an existing league-wide unit. For example, the natural unit in team sports would appear to be the team, since players are employed by a team rather than a league. Bargaining on a team by team basis would facilitate negotiation over issues that are important to a given team and its players. There are also other possible arrangements that would allow players with similar interests to bargain together. There might, for example, be bargaining among pitchers in baseball, quarterbacks in football, goalies in hockey, the "superstars" in a league or any other sub-group within the larger population of athletes with

154. Coalition bargaining refers, simply, to the presentment of a common front by several unions to a single employer, just the converse of multi-employer bargaining. Recent cases have left little question that in the absence of a clearly improper motivation, coalition bargaining is as permissible as is its multi-employer counterpart. See General Elec. Co., 173 N.L.R.B. 253 (1968), aff'd, 412 F.2d 512 (2d Cir. 1969); American Radiator & Standard Sanitary Corp., 155 N.L.R.B. 736 (1965); Standard Oil Co., 137 N.L.R.B. 690 (1962), enforced, 322 F.2d 40 (6th Cir. 1963).

155. General Elec. Co. v. NLRB, 412 F.2d 512, 516 (2d Cir. 1969).

156. See §§ 5.04-.06.

157. In the basketball merger situation before the demise of the A.B.A., for example, the players in the N.B.A. were adamantly opposed to the merger. See House Hearings, supra, note 152, at 65-72; Senate Hearings, supra note 130, at pt. 2, 227, 303.

identifiable characteristics that set them apart from the other players. If the members of one of these sub-groups had undertaken to form their own bargaining unit at the inception of the recent collective bargaining activities in the 1960's, it seems reasonably clear that their efforts may well have been successful, and the Board's determining tests would have allowed each of them. Thus, there would have been little or no bargaining history in any of the sports, the necessary skills of those in each sub-group would have been essentially identical, the organizational interest of all employers would have been the same with respect to each sub-group, and the members of each sub-group could have desired organization on such a basis.[158]

While we have league-wide units at the present time, there is no assurance that they will continue to be accepted by all parties, especially specific groups of players. Thus, if it is assumed that there are many sub-groups of players which have identifiable interests apart from those of the mass of other players, the appropriate inquiry is whether such a sub-group could form its own unit for purposes of collective bargaining and not be bound by the terms negotiated by the representative of the other players. This issue would be likely to arise if all members of one team or all players with common interests (all quarterbacks or superstars, for example) desired to form a separate unit. Since each of these possibilities raises slightly different issues, they will be discussed separately.

If all of the players on a single team decided that they would prefer to bargain separately with their employer (the team), there would be several methods of accomplishing this result. One approach would be to have the team withdraw from the multi-employer unit (the league). As noted above, a single employer may withdraw from the unit.[159] If the employer will not withdraw, it would also be possible to have the union withdraw with respect to the single team. The Board has made it clear in recent years that a union may withdraw from a multi-employer unit with respect to one or more employers while continuing to bargain on a group basis with the remaining employers.[160] The reason for this view is that the consensual nature of multi-employer bargaining requires that withdrawal be allowed and it would be unfair to give a union less than the same withdrawal rights that are accorded to employer members of the unit. It is also intended to give employees the opportunity to solve local problems through local bargaining.[161] The obvious difficulty with this approach is that it would require the union to agree to such withdrawal.

If the union will not agree to withdrawal, or if the players on one team do not wish to remain members of the union,[162] then the situation becomes more difficult. Since the union would be the recognized, exclusive bargaining agent of the players in the league, the members of one team would have no power to

158. At the present time, however, these factors would take on a different meaning. *See* notes 175-76 *infra.*

159. *See* notes 147-51 *supra.*

160. Pacific Coast Ass'n of Pulp & Paper Manufacturers, 163 N.L.R.B. 892 (1967). *See also* NLRB v. Hi-Way Billboards, Inc., 500 F.2d 181 (5th Cir. 1974); Belleville News Democrat, 185 N.L.R.B. 1000 (1970).

161. Hearst Consolidated Publications, Inc., 156 N.L.R.B. 210 (1965), *enforced sub. nom.* Publishers' Ass'n of New York City v. NLRB, 364 F.2d 293 (2d Cir. 1966), *cert. denied,* 385 U.S. 971 (1966).

162. During the football dispute in 1975, for example, the players on some teams apparently expressed interest in leaving the union. *See, e.g.,* Atlanta Constitution, September 16, 1975, at 1-D, col. 3 (reporting that at least one team had dropped out of the union).

simply decide not to be bound by the union's bargaining efforts.[163] In order to get out from under the union's exclusive authority, the players would have to dislodge the union as the bargaining agent. The most direct method of achieving this result would be to convince a majority of all players in the league to vote the union out.[164] If such a vote could not be mustered, the only remaining possibility would be for the sub-group of players to establish themselves as a separate bargaining unit from the existing league unit through the severance procedures. As will be indicated below, the employees of one employer (team) may have difficulty meeting the severance requirements.[165] Thus, the players on one team would be able to achieve separate bargaining with their employer only if the employer were willing to withdraw from the multi-employer unit, the union were willing to partially withdraw from the unit to the extent of the one team, or the union could be voted out as the bargaining representative for the entire league.

The second type of sub-group that might seek separate representation would be players with interests that are not common to the mass of players in the league, such as quarterbacks or superstars. In order for such a sub-group to acquire separate representation, it would have to establish that all such players constitute a separate bargaining unit and should be severed from the existing league-wide unit. The severance of a category of employees involves an attempt to fragmentize the bargaining unit, and the Board has consistently followed the rule that a petition for separate representation of a sub-group of employees in a multi-employer situation will be denied if it seeks severance with respect to only one employer.[166] In order to be successful, the severance must be coextensive with the existing multi-employer bargaining unit and the petition must meet the requirements of an ordinary severance procedure.[167] This would indicate that an effort to establish a separate bargaining unit for the players of a single team would not meet the criteria,[168] but that a unit to represent a more general sub-group of players (for example, quarterbacks or superstars) might be permissible since it would constitute a coextensive severance of all players in the sub-group from the larger unit (the league).

In order to succeed, however, the player sub-group would also have to meet the severance rules themselves. Severance is common in industrial labor relations and when the issue arises the extent to which employees have organized in the past may not be given controlling weight in determining whether a new group is appropriate[169] — though bargaining history is important.[170] Severance questions have arisen primarily when a craft seeks

---

163. See § 6.07.

164. Questions concerning the representational status of a union are considered in C. MORRIS, THE DEVELOPING LABOR LAW ch. 8 (1971).

165. See notes 169-76 *infra.*

166. See, e.g., William T. Kirley Lumber Co., 189 N.L.R.B. 130 (1971); Midas Muffler Clinics, Inc., 162 N.L.R.B. 775 (1967); Ward's Cove Packing Co., 160 N.L.R.B. 232 (1966); Thos. de la Rue, Inc., 151 N.L.R.B. 234 (1965).

167. A.B. Hirschfield Press, Inc., 140 N.L.R.B. 212 (1962); Grand Rapids Gen. Motors, 131 N.L.R.B. 439, 440 (1961); see also Jahn-Tyler Printing & Publishing Co., 112 N.L.R.B. 167 (1955); United Can & Glass Co., 105 N.L.R.B. 69, 71 (1953).

168. Such a separate bargaining unit could be established only in accordance with the principles considered at notes 169-76 *infra.*

169. NLRA § 9(c)(5).

170. International Ass'n of Tool Craftsmen v. Leedom, 276 F.2d 514 (D. C. Cir.), *cert. denied,* 364 U.S. 815, 5 L. Ed. 2d 46, 81 S. Ct. 45 (1960).

severance from a larger industrial union, and although the NLRB has followed a somewhat erratic path in the past,[171] it has recently stated the standards that it would follow in making craft severance decisions. In *Mallinckrodt Chemical Works,*[172] the Board said that it would consider the following factors in craft severance cases: 1) whether a tradition of separate representation exists; 2) the history of collective bargaining of the employees and plant involved; 3) whether the employees have established and maintained their separate identity; 4) the history and pattern of collective bargaining in the industry involved; 5) the degree of integration in the employers' production process; and 6) the qualifications of the union seeking to "carve-out" a separate unit.[173] In spite of this array of factors, it has been reported that the Board will be quite reluctant to permit severance, because by so doing it will be "sowing the seeds of labor relations instability" by undermining the bargaining position of the majority employee group.[174]

Severance was denied in the *Mallinckrodt* case and it is useful to note why this result was reached. In denying severance to the instrument mechanics, the Board noted that (1) they were an integral part of the employer's production process, (2) they did not constitute an identifiable group since their separate interests had been submerged in the broader community, (3) the industrial union had adequately represented them, and (4) "the interests served by maintenance of stability in the existing bargaining unit... outweigh the interests of affording . . . [a few employees] the opportunity to change their mode of representation." [175]

Applying these criteria in the present context would not portend a promising result for a sub-group of players. All of the players on any team will inevitably constitute an integral part of the employer's business (staging athletic competition). The frequency of movement between teams in the league and the existence of league-wide rules would also establish a substantial community of interest at the league level. In addition, there would be no tradition of separate representation — individual salary negotiations do not constitute separate representation — there is an established history of sport or league-wide bargaining, and the group would not have maintained a separate identity.[176]

171. At an early date, the Board had taken the stand that no craft severance would be allowed so long as the industrial union had had a successful history of bargaining for the craft unit and had adequately represented the craft's interests. American Can Co., 13 N.L.R.B. 1252 (1939). This stance was softened slightly in General Elec. Co., 58 N.L.R.B. 57 (1944), but it was the Taft-Hartley amendments that turned the tide. Taft-Hartley added § 9(b)(2), which provides that a prior Board determination shall not preclude the establishment of a craft unit. NLRA § 9(b)(2). The Board, however, still limited severance, and in National Tube Co., 76 N.L.R.B. 1199 (1948), it held that severance would be denied where the industry in question was highly integrated. The Board then decided that, in essence, a craft could seek severance whenever it chose. American Potash & Chem. Corp., 107 N.L.R.B. 1418 (1954). Finally, the Board adopted its present position in *Mallinckrodt,* which effectively limits *American Potash. See generally* 18C T. KHEEL, LABOR LAW § 14.03[1] (1974).

172. 162 N.L.R.B. 387 (1966). *See also* E. I. duPont de Nemours & Co., 162 N.L.R.B. 413 (1966); Holmberg, Inc., 162 N.L.R.B. 407 (1966).

173. 162 N.L.R.B. at 397.

174. *See* J. ABODEELY, THE APPROPRIATE BARGAINING UNIT 111 (1971).

175. 162 N.L.R.B. at 399.

176. There is, however, room for the contention that superstars in at least one sport have in fact maintained their separate identity and that the league-wide bargaining was based only upon a special agreement. It has, thus, been reported that when the National Football League Players Association was formed, the superstars conditioned their joining upon an agreement that the Association would bargain only for a minimum salary term, leaving them free to use their greater bargaining power

Even if a sub-group were to prevail on the severance criteria issue, difficult problems could arise in identifying who would be a member of the new sub-unit.[177] If the sub-group included, for example, super-stars,[178] there would be a serious problem in distinguishing a "superstar" from a "non-superstar". Such distinction could be made on the basis of years in the professional league, salary or on some other basis such as batting average, average point production, earned run average, pass completion percentage or any other statistical measure. Even if a jurisdictional boundary could be reached, there would remain the problem that from year to year some players would not meet the statistical measure because of having had a bad year, sickness or some other factor. This would then present the problem of a bargaining unit whose membership could be constantly changing, which is a situation the Board would be reluctant to sanction because of the jurisdictional uncertainty that it would create.

In light of the present league-wide bargaining, the Board's effective preclusion of establishing separate representation for a single team without employer or union consent, the problems posed by the severance requirements, and the factual problems that could arise, it seems unlikely that a sub-group of players could successfully establish their own bargaining unit. The players must, therefore, expect to seek satisfaction of their interests and grievances within the larger bargaining community.

d. Inclusion of the Commissioner. The final point that should be mentioned with respect to the appropriate scope of the bargaining unit in professional sports, involves the periodic efforts of players in different leagues to include their league commissioner within the bargaining unit as an employer.[179] The objective of such efforts would apparently be to make the disciplinary powers of the commissioner a subject of collective bargaining.[180] If the purpose of these efforts is to gain control over the disciplinary powers, it is not clear why the commissioner must be made a member of the bargaining unit. Disciplinary powers are clearly within the meaning of the terms and conditions of employment and would, therefore, be a mandatory subject of bargaining.[181]

If there are other reasons for attempting to include a commissioner, attention would be appropriately focused upon whether the commissioner was an "employer" under the NLRA. The term "employer" is defined in § 2(2) to include "any person acting as an agent of an employer, directly or indirectly." [182] In determining whether a person is acting as an agent of an employer, Congress

for their own benefit. *Hearings Before the Special Subcomm. on Labor of the House Comm. on Education and Labor,* 92d Cong., 2d Sess. 91 (1972). In light of this agreement, one seeking to splinter a superstar unit in the NFL could well have a basis for arguing a compliance with at least one of the *Mallinckrodt* standards.

177. These difficulties would not, of course, arise if the sub-group was seeking a "positional unit."

178. The superstars might want to form their own bargaining unit, for example, if their interests should for some reason be merged into those of the general group of players. Such a situation might, again for example, occur when the agent is directed to negotiate for a scheduled salary structure, as opposed to the present minimum salary term. *See* § 6.07.

179. *See* N. Y. Times, July 8, 1972, at 52, col. 6 (effort by NFL Players Association in 1970); *Hearings Before the Special House Subcomm. on Labor of the House Comm. on Education and Labor,* 92d Cong., 2d Sess. 76, 92 (1972) (effort by the NFL Players Association in 1968).

180. These powers are considered in detail at § 3.10.

181. *See* § 6.08.

182. NLRA § 2(2). The determination of when an agency relation is present is covered by NLRA § 2(13).

apparently intended that ordinary common law concepts of agency would be applied.[183] In order for an agency relationship to exist, it would have to be shown that the person in question acted on behalf, and was subject to the control, of the purported principal.[184] In the present context, this would require a factual showing that a commissioner acted on behalf of the owners in a league and that he was subject to their control. Although there is little clear authority on this issue, several courts have used language that would indicate a belief that the commissioners in question were indeed agents of the owners. In *National Football League Players Association v. NLRB*,[185] for example, the court held that the employers (the council of owners) had committed an unfair labor practice by unilaterally changing a condition of the players' employment by adopting a rule which imposed a fine upon players who left the bench during a fight.[186] The rule had been originally prepared by the commissioner, but he then sought to have it approved by resolution of the owners. This action, the court said, was actually the action of the employers (owners), and that if the commissioner were indeed the agent of both players and owners, as the owners contended, then "one must assume a serious breach of ethics by the Commissioner if he talked to only one of his principals". [187] This decision does not, of course, insure that a commissioner would be included in a bargaining unit as an "employer", but it does suggest that in some situations a commissioner may act on behalf of the owners.[188]

The agency relationship between owners and a commissioner could also be premised upon the theory that the commissioner participates in the collective bargaining process on behalf of the owners. In support of this theory, reference could be made to the numerous cases which have dealt with the question of when

---

183. H.R. REP. No. 510, 80th Cong., 1st Sess. 36 (1947).
184. RESTATEMENT (SECOND) OF AGENCY § 1(1) (1958).
185. 503 F.2d 12 (8th Cir. 1974).
186. The unfair labor practice portion of the decision is considered at §§ 6.03, 6.06.
187. 503 F.2d at 17.
188. In this regard, it is worth noting that in American League of Professional Baseball Clubs, 180 N.L.R.B. 189 (1969), the Board used language which does, in fact, indicate its finding of a relationship between the commissioner and owners in the American League of Baseball which approaches that of an agency, though the question then before it was whether the Board should decline jurisdiction over baseball because of the commissioner self-government system. This system, the Board said, would not induce it to decline jurisdiction because
> [t]he system appears to have been designed almost entirely by employers and owners, and *the final arbiter* of internal disputes *does not appear to be a neutral third party* freely chosen by both sides, but rather an individual appointed solely by the member club owners themselves. We do not believe that such a system is likely either to prevent labor disputes from arising in the future, or, having once arisen, to resolve them in a manner susceptible or conducive to voluntary compliance by all parties involved. Moreover, it is patently contrary to the letter and spirit of the Act for the Board to defer its undoubted jurisdiction to decide unfair labor practices to *a disputes settlement system established unilaterally by an employer or group of employers. Id.* at 191 (emphasis added).

The clear inference of the Board's language is that it did view the commissioner of baseball as standing in a position vis-a-vis the owners that was similar to that of an agent. It should also be noted that there have been frequent allegations that commissioners are subject to the direct control of owners, but not players, since it is normally the owners who control their appointment, salary and tenure. American League of Professional Baseball Clubs, 180 N.L.R.B. 189 (1969); Krasnow & Levy, *Unionization in Professional Sports,* 51 GEO. L. J. 749, 755 (1963); *Hearings, supra* note 179, at 15. It has, thus, been said that "the commissioner isn't going to bite the hand that feeds him, and the owners make him." *Hearings Before the Senate Antitrust Subcomm. of the Senate Comm. on the Judiciary,* 85th Cong., 1st Sess., pt. 1, 1216 (1957). In spite of these facts, Bert Bell, one-time commissioner of the NFL, once said that he owed greater allegiance to the players than he did to the owners. *See Hearings, supra* note 128, at pt. 3, 2503; *cf. id.* at 2633 (players' rebuttal).

an employers' association will be deemed to be an "employer" within the meaning of § 2(2) and, thus, an appropriate member of the bargaining unit. It should be noted that these cases have generally involved unfair labor practice charges rather than unit determination disputes, so that their authority may be somewhat limited. The case law suggests that if an employers' association negotiates collective bargaining contracts on the member employers' behalf, it is their agent and, therefore, an employer itself.[189] Where the agency relationship is less clear, however, a contrary result is reached. In *Metro-Goldwyn-Mayer Studios,*[190] for example, the Board found that a motion picture producers' association was not an "employer" where, although it negotiated on behalf of some employers, there was no evidence to indicate that it was authorized to control labor policies or to handle the employment problems of its members.[191] Although the *MGM* cases was decided prior to the Taft-Hartley amendments which added the specific agency language to § 2(2),[192] it is a clear indication that to come within the term "employer," the association must be participating in the collective bargaining process on behalf of the employers and that the extent and character of the association's participation must be clear to all parties.[193]

Whether a commissioner could be included as an employer in a bargaining unit under this theory would, thus, require evidence that he participated as an agent of the owners in the collective bargaining process. Although there have been reports that different commissioners have taken a mediatory role in resolving protracted labor disputes,[194] this would appear to be short of the showing that must be made for inclusion.

§ 6.05. The Collective Bargaining Process.

The central area of concern in collective bargaining and professional sports is, first, the rights and duties of each party in the collective bargaining process, and, second, the extent to which a negotiated agreement is subject to collateral attack by members of the bargaining unit or by third parties. The rights and duties which the NLRA provides to those engaged in the collective bargaining

---

189. *See, e.g.,* NLRB v. E.F. Shuck Constr. Co., 243 F.2d 519 (9th Cir. 1957); Employing Plasterer's Ass'n of Chicago v. Operational Plasterers and Cement Masons Int'l Ass'n of U.S. & Canada, 172 F. Supp. 337 (N.D. Ill. 1959); Jan Power, Inc., 173 N.L.R.B. 798 (1968); Teamsters Local 386, 145 N.L.R.B. 1475 (1964); Utah Plumbing & Heating Contractors Ass'n, 125 N.L.R.B. 256 (1959); Broward County Launderers & Cleaners Ass'n, Inc., 142 N.L.R.B. 379 (1963); Williams Coal Co., 11 N.L.R.B. 579 (1930).

190. 7 N.L.R.B. 662 (1938).

191. *Id.* at 695.

192. The original NLRA had provided that a person was an "employer" if it acted "in the interest of an employer," Act of July 5, 1935, ch. 372, § 2(2), 49 Stat. 450, whereas the present language uses the express agency language. NLRA § 2(2).

193. 7 N.L.R.B. at 695. *See also* NLRB v. E.F. Shuck Constr. Co., 243 F.2d 519, 521 (9th Cir. 1957); Strickeler Motors, 87 N.L.R.B. 1313 (1949).

194. Thus, it was reported during the 1972 baseball strike that Commissioner Kuhn was "getting into the thick of things." Washington Post, April 5, 1972, § D, at 1, col. 2. The 1970 football strike-lockout was also settled through the round-the-clock mediation of Commissioner Rozelle, N. Y. Times, August 4, 1970, at 24, col. 1, and the 1969 baseball mini-strike was resolved after Commissioner Kuhn's intervention got talks moving. Although these reports indicate that commissioners have aided in the resolution of labor disputes, they do not indicate participation in the collective bargaining process.

process may be succinctly stated, but their application to professional sports presents a number of issues which are both difficult to resolve as an abstract matter and as yet are undecided by the NLRB or the courts.[195]

In summary, the principle that will evolve from the following discussion is that when an agent is recognized as the bargaining agent for a unit of employees it becomes the exclusive bargaining representative of all members of the unit.[196] When bargaining is undertaken, all of the "terms and conditions of employment" are matters about which each party will have a duty to bargain in good faith.[197] Thus, one of the primary benefits of the collective bargaining process to the players is the ability to have their bargaining representative air and resolve all grievances about the "terms and conditions" of their employment at the bargaining table. If the bargaining produces an agreement and both sides have met their bargaining duties, it will be binding upon all members of the unit, whether or not individual members are satisfied with the terms that have been negotiated.[198] Thus, the agreement will not be subject to collateral attack by union members so long as the union has fairly represented the majority of those in the bargaining unit.[199] In addition, specific provisions of the agreement may not be set aside as being in violation of the antitrust laws so long as they relate to wages, hours and working conditions, and were negotiated by the labor representatives in furtherance of its own objectives.[200]

§ 6.06. The Duty to Bargain.

Once the parties enter collective bargaining, the NLRA imposes upon them the reciprocal duty to bargain in good faith. This duty is defined in § 8(d), which provides that "to bargain collectively" the parties must "meet at reasonable times and confer in good faith with respect to wages, hours, and other terms and conditions of employment...," [201] and the failure by either party to do so will be an unfair labor practice.[202] Although "good faith bargaining" is not a concept that can be defined with precision, it basically encompasses a willingness to enter into negotiations with an open and fair mind and with a sincere desire to find a basis of agreement.[203] This does not, however, mean that the parties are bound to reach agreement on the substantive terms in question; it means

---

195. The chief difficulty in analyzing the terms or clauses in present or future collective bargaining agreements in the professional sports area is that such provisions often have no counterpart in the industrial labor relations situations heretofore dealt with by the NLRB and the courts. When a clause in a sports agreement is considered, therefore, resort must be made by rough analogy to situations that have arisen in industrial labor relations, and the rules that have been fashioned to deal with those situations.

196. *See* § 6.07.

197. *See* §§ 6.06, 6.08.

198. *See* § 6.07.

199. *See* § 6.07.

200. *See* §§ 5.04-.06.

201. NLRA § 8(d). *See generally* Cox, *The Duty to Bargain in Good Faith,* 71 HARV. L. REV. 1401 (1958).

202. NLRA §§ 8(a) (5) (employer), 8(b) (3) (union). It is to be noted that the duty as such applies only to "mandatory" subjects of bargaining. *See* § 6.08.

203. NLRB v. Truitt Mfg. Co., 351 U.S. 149, 100 L.Ed. 1027, 76 S. Ct. 753 (1956); H.J. Heinz Co. v. NLRB, 311 U.S. 514, 85 L. Ed. 309, 61 S. Ct. 320 (1941); NLRB v. Montgomery Ward & Co., 133 F.2d 676 (9th Cir. 1943).

only that they must meet and confer in good faith. Thus, hard bargaining is not itself proof of bad faith,[204] and at some point each side is entitled to make a firm and final offer.[205] Similarly, there need be no inconsistency between good faith bargaining and the use of economic weapons, since good faith bargaining and the availability of economic pressure devices are part and parcel of the bargaining process.[206] Where bad faith bargaining has been found, it is usually the result of a pattern of conduct evidencing a lack of a good faith desire to find a mutual basis of agreement. Bad faith has been found, for example, where there was a refusal to negotiate about a mandatory subject of bargaining as defined in § 8(d);[207] an initial "take it or leave it" proposal;[208] a unilateral change in the conditions of employment that are under negotiation;[209] and an attempt to by-pass the union representative.[210] In general, the presence or absence of good faith in bargaining will be determined by analysis of the totality of the facts and circumstances of each case.[211]

The duty to bargain issue has arisen frequently in professional sports. It has periodically been alleged by both owners and players that the other party has failed to bargain in good faith.[212] In *National Football League Management Council (I),*[213] for example, the union (the players' association) had demanded that the employer (the Council) bargain, *inter alia,* over the issue of artificial turf installation.[214] The employer, however, refused to bargain, stating that the parties had an existing agreement and that it need not bargain during the agreement's term. When the union filed unfair labor practice charges alleging that the employer had refused to bargain, the Board dismissed the charges, finding that there was no evidence that the employer had not proceeded in good faith on the turf issue, since it had negotiated with the union and had taken no

---

204. Dierks Forests, Inc., 148 N.L.R.B. 923 (1964).

205. Philip Carey Mfg. Co., 140 N.L.R.B. 1103 (1963), *enforced in part,* 331 F.2d 720 (6th Cir.), *cert. denied,* 379 U.S. 888, 13 L. Ed. 2d 92, 85 S. Ct. 159 (1964).

206. NLRB v. Insurance Agents' Int'l Union, 361 U.S. 477, 4 L. Ed. 2d 454, 80 S. Ct. 419 (1960). The economic pressure devices are considered at § 6.09.

207. NLRB v. Katz, 369 U.S. 736, 8 L.Ed.2d 230, 82 S. Ct. 1107 (1962).

208. General Elec. Co., 150 N.L.R.B. 192 (1964), *enforced,* 418 F.2d 736 (2d Cir. 1969), *cert. denied,* 397 U.S. 965, 25 L.Ed.2d 257, 90 S. Ct. 995 (1970). This bargaining technique is frequently referred to as "boulwarism," after its apparent founder at General Electric, and it has been alleged that football owners have used the tactic in negotiations with the union. *See Hearings Before the House Subcomm. on Labor-Management Relations of the House Comm. on Education and Labor,* 94th Cong., 1st Sess. 9 (1975).

209. NLRB v. Katz, 369 U.S. 736, 8 L.Ed.2d 230, 82 S. Ct. 1107 (1962); National Football League Players Ass'n v. NLRB, 503 F.2d 12 (8th Cir. 1974) (unilateral change present where employers (owners) adopted a rule requiring a fine for any player who left the bench during a fight on the playing field).

210. J.I. Case v. NLRB, 321 U.S. 332, 88 L.Ed. 762, 64 S. Ct. 576 (1944). Negotiation by individual athletes and their team owner pursuant to "so called" minimum standards contracts is considered at § 6.07.

211. The factors that will be considered in making the determination are reviewed in detail in 18C T. KHEEL, LABOR LAW §§ 16.03-16.04 (1974); C. MORRIS, THE DEVELOPING LABOR LAW 277-309 (1971).

212. *See* § 6.01. *See also Hearings, supra* note 208, at 16, 51 (alleged refusal to bargain about NFL owners' reduction in squad size from 47 to 43 in 1975).

213. 203 N.L.R.B. 958 (1973).

214. An additional issue involved a fine rule that had been adopted by the employer, which the Board held need not be the subject of bargaining. This finding was reversed on appeal, and is discussed subsequently. *See* notes 216-17 *infra.* "Arbitrability" of grievances is considered at § 6.10.

action to change the status quo without consulting the union.[215] In short, the employer had not breached its duty to bargain. Such a conclusion will not, however, be present where the employer undertakes conduct which unilaterally changes the conditions of employment without bargaining or prior consultation with the employees' representative. Thus, in another aspect of the *National Football League Management Council (I)* case, the circuit court of appeals[216] held that the employers (owners) had committed an unfair labor practice by unilaterally adopting a rule which required that a player be fined if he left the bench during a fight on the field.[217] Similarly, a player's union was found to have violated its duty to bargain by the General Counsel's office when it apparently refused to bargain over mandatory subjects of bargaining (player restraint mechanisms) on the ground that they violated the antitrust laws.[217.1]

An additional aspect of the bargaining duty that may be important in some situations relates to the obligation of an employer to furnish information to the union upon the latter's request. This has been found to be an element of the employer's duty to bargain in good faith, on the ground that a union will be able to properly discharge its bargaining duties only if it possesses sufficient information concerning the pertinent issues.[217.2] Accordingly, the refusal of an employer to provide information has been viewed as a violation of its duty to bargain "as if he had failed to meet and confer with the union in good faith." [217.3]

In order to trigger this duty, a union must make a good faith request for the information to be furnished, which must be relevant — *i.e.,* directly related — to the dealings between the employer and the union in its representative capacity.[217.4] When such a request has been made, the employer is obligated to make the information available with reasonable promptness, and in a form that will be reasonably useful to the union.[217.5] While there is no clear delineation

---

215. A Regional Director of the NLRB also dismissed charges that the owners had refused to bargain in 1974. In reaching this conclusion, he stated that the allegations would be

> deemed to be unsupported by the evidence which discloses that the [owners] responded [to union] proposals, made concessions and counterproposals and demonstrated a desire to reach an agreement. In view of the foregoing, . . . there is insufficient evidence to show bad faith or surface bargaining on the part of the [owners] . . . . *Hearings, supra* note 208, at 90 (letter of the Regional Director).

See also National Football League Management Council (II), No. 2-CA-13379 (June 30, 1976 — *see* note 111.1 *supra* and 217.7 *infra*) (Council did not violate § 8(a)(5) when it adopted "punt coverage" and "overtime" rules, since the union declined an adequate opportunity to bargain about the proposals; but did fail to bargain in good faith when it unilaterally instituted a pre-season pay scale).

216. 503 F.2d 12 (8th Cir. 1974).

217. Specifically, the court concluded t.....

> [t]he Employers, by unilaterally promulgating and implementing a rule providing for an automatic fine to be levied against any player who leaves the bench area while a fight or altercation is in progress on the football field, have engaged in unfair labor practices within the meaning of Section 8(a) (5) and (1) of the Act. 503 F.2d at 17.

The NLRB subsequently ordered the fines to repaid, with interest, to the players who had been fined. National Football League Management Council, 216 N.L.R.B. No. 74 (1975).

217.1. National Basketball Players Ass'n, 1976-7 CCH NLRB DECISIONS ¶ 20,014 (January 26, 1976). *See* § 6.08.

217.2. *See* J. I. Case Co. v. NLRB, 253 F.2d 149 (7th Cir. 1958); NLRB v. Whitin Machine Works, 217 F.2d 593 (4th Cir. 1954). *See generally* NLRB v. Truitt Manufacturing Co., 351 U.S. 149, 100 L. Ed. 1027, 76 S. Ct. 753 (1955).

217.3. C. MORRIS, THE DEVELOPING LABOR LAW 310 (1971); *see* Curtiss-Wright Corp. v. NLRB, 347 F.2d 61 (3rd Cir. 1965).

217.4. *See* NLRB v. Acme Industrial Co., 385 U.S. 432, 17 L. Ed. 2d 495, 87 S. Ct. 565 (1967); Otis Elevator Co., 170 N.L.R.B. No. 59 (1968).

217.5. *See* Colonial Press, Inc., 204 N.L.R.B. 852 (1973).

of what kinds of information must be furnished, the duty clearly (presumptively) extends to data relating to the terms and conditions of employment.[217.6]

The duty to provide information has played a prominent role in another recent labor dispute in professional football that arose as a result of bargaining efforts prior to, and during, the players' strike in 1974. In *National Football League Management Council (II)*,[217.7] an Administrative Law Judge considered eight different information requests. An illustrative issue was the union's request for raw data (reports) relating to player injuries. The Council supplied summaries of the data on a confidential basis, but refused to provide the raw data on the grounds that the records were priviledged and were not necessary for collective bargaining purposes. The judge found that safety rules and playing conditions "are conditions of employment subject to collective bargaining," so that the records were relevant and should be supplied, unless there was a valid medical privilege or the provision of summary data was sufficient. Both defenses were rejected. There was no privilege since the reports did not reflect the name of the injured party, and the summaries did not constitute sufficient compliance because they represented only a small part of the data requested and were not made generally available to the union. Since there was no substantial basis for not providing the requested information, the Council was found to have failed to meet its bargaining duty under § 8(a)(5). Similar results were reached with respect to requests for the commissioner's employment contract (his powers were proper subjects of bargaining), the standard player contracts (to ascertain wage-level information), copies of stadium leases (to determine if the owners had control over the type of playing surface in each arena), names and addresses of team physicians (to review the quality of medical care), and players on the retired-reserve list (who were still employees). The Council was, however, found to have committed no violation with respect to other issues, with respect to which it was found that the information was either available to the union (fines) or not available to the Council (names of players whose insurance claims were denied).

§ 6.07. Exclusive Representation, Individual Bargaining and the Union's Duty of Fair Representation.

In considering collective bargaining duties, it is also necessary to consider the relationship between a union and the members of the bargaining unit that it represents. Historically, contract negotiations in professional sports have been conducted on an individual basis between a player and a team. Once a bargaining representative is recognized, however, it becomes the exclusive bargaining agent for all employees within the unit,[218] whether or not they are members of the union or agree with the terms and conditions that are negotiated in their behalf. Individual employees may bargain on their own only if so provided in

217.6. *See* Ellsworth Sheet Metal, Inc., 224 N.L.R.B. No. 199 (1976). *See generally* MORRIS, *supra* note 217.3, at 318-21.

217.7. Case No. 2-CA-13379 (June 30, 1976). The text of the opinion is set forth in H. REP. No. 94-1786, 94th Cong., 2d Sess. 465-521 (1977). The case was apparently not heard by the full NLRB due to a settlement agreement between the union and the Council that was a part of the collective bargaining agreement executed on March 1, 1977.

218. NLRA § 9(a); Davis v. Pro Basketball, Inc., 381 F. Supp. 1 (S.D.N.Y. 1974). Thus, the opinion expressed in Senate hearings that the majority of the ballplayers could not bind the remainder, *see Hearings Before the Senate Subcomm. on Antitrust and Monopoly of the Senate Comm. on the Judiciary,* 88th Cong., 2d Sess. 110-11 (1964), is clearly in error.

the collective bargaining agreement.[219] If individual bargaining is carried on despite the existence of a certified bargaining agent and in the absence of such a provision, moreover, the employer may commit an unfair labor practice for its action may be deemed a failure to bargain collectively with the representative of the majority of its employees.[220]

A corollary to the exclusive representation of the bargaining agent is that the agent must fairly represent all members of the bargaining unit. This duty is known in labor law as the duty of fair representation, and is designed to insure that the interests of all members of the unit are fairly represented in the collective bargaining process.[221] It was originally established by the Supreme Court in a series of opinions arising under the Railway Labor Act,[222] but has since been applied to the NLRA.[223] The first pronouncement of the doctrine came in *Steele v. Louisville & Nashville R.R.*,[224] which was based on a complaint that a union had engaged in racial discrimination against its black members, who constituted a minority of the total membership. The Court held that a labor organization must "represent all its members, the majority as well as the minority, and it is to act for and not against those whom it represents " [225] — that is, the representative must act "without hostile discrimination" amongst its members.[226] The Court, however, allowed room for the union to make provision for differing treatment of some members by stating that variations in the terms of the contract may be made so long as they are based on "relevant differences" among the employees, "such as differences in seniority, the type of work performed, [and] the competence and skill with which it is performed." [227]

Although *Steele* would suggest that a bargaining representative has a rather limited ability to make agreements that adversely affect some of its members — that is, only where there are "relevant differences" — the Court subsequently

---

219. NLRB v. Allis-Chalmers Mfg. Co., 388 U.S. 175, 180, 18 L.Ed.2d 1123, 87 S. Ct. 2001 (1967); Steele v. Louisville & Nashville R.R., 323 U.S. 192, 200, 89 L.Ed. 173, 65 S. Ct. 226 (1944); *But cf.* International Ass'n of Bridge, Structural and Ornamental Iron Workers, Local 494, 128 N.L.R.B. 1379 (1960), where the Board held a union to be in violation of §§ 8(b)(1) and 8(b)(2) when it excluded an employee who had succeeded in obtaining higher pay on his own.

220. NLRA § 8(a)(5). *See also* National Licorice Co. v. NLRB, 309 U.S. 350, 357-59, 84 L.Ed. 799, 60 S. Ct. 569 (1940); Steelworkers v. NLRB, 536 F.2d 550 (3rd Cir. 1976). Thus, in Dazey Corp., 106 N.L.R.B. 553 (1958), the Board held that such action could violate § 8(a)(5) for failing to bargain with the majority, as well as § 8(a)(1) for encouraging the minority to abandon the majority.

The exclusive representation theory is criticized, and alternative proposals are suggested, in Schatzki, *Majority Rule, Exclusive Representation, and the Interests of Individual Workers: Should Exclusivity be Abolished?,* 123 U. PA. L. REV. 897 (1975).

221. *See* Schatzki, *supra* note 220, at 903.

222. Now codified at 45 U.S.C. §§ 151-58.

223. Syres v. Oil Workers, Local 23, 350 U.S. 892, 100 L. Ed. 785, 76 S. Ct. 152 (1955); Ford Motor Co. v. Huffman, 345 U.S. 330, 97 L. Ed. 1048, 73 S. Ct. 681 (1953).

224. 323 U.S. 192, 89 L. Ed. 173, 65 S. Ct. 226 (1944).

225. *Id.* at 202. *See generally* 18A T. KHEEL, LABOR LAW § 19.06 (1973); 18E T. KHEEL, LABOR LAW §§ 28.01-28.04 (1974); C. MORRIS, THE DEVELOPING LABOR LAW 343-46 (1971); Lehmann, *The Union's Duty of Fair Representation—Steele and Its Successors,* 30 FED. B.J. 280 (1971); Rosen, *Fair Representation, Contract Breach, and Fiduciary Obligations: Union, Union Officials and the Worker in Collective Bargaining,* 15 HASTINGS L.J. 391 (1964); Summers, *Individual Rights in Collective Agreements and Arbitration,* 37 N.Y.U.L. REV. 362 (1962); Note, *Federal Protection of Individual Rights Under Labor Contracts,* 73 YALE L.J. 1215 (1964). The doctrine is also considered at § 5.05.

226. 323 U.S. 203. *See also* Vaca v. Sipes, 386 U.S. 171, 177, 17 L.Ed.2d 842, 87 S. Ct. 903 (1967). The duty applies as well to the administration of an agreement. Tunstall v. Brotherhood of Locomotive Firemen and Enginemen, 323 U.S. 210, 89 L.Ed. 187, 65 S. Ct. 235 (1944).

227. 323 U.S. at 203.

indicated that the standard by which a union's activity will be judged is much less stringent. In *Ford Motor Company v. Huffman,*[228] for example, the Court found no breach of the duty where a union had agreed to a contract amendment that adversely affected some of its members. In reaching this conclusion, the Court clearly suggested a rather broad range of discretion:

> Inevitably differences arise in the manner and degree to which the terms of any negotiated agreement affect individual employees and classes of employees. The mere existence of such differences does not make them invalid. The complete satisfaction of all who are represented is hardly to be expected. A wide range of reasonableness must be allowed a statutory bargaining representative in serving the unit it represents, subject always to complete good faith and honesty of purpose in the exercise of its discretion.[229]

In order for the duty of fair representation to be violated, the Court has thus required a showing that the union acted arbitrarily or in bad faith.[230] In light of these views, a bargaining representative in professional sports will have a rather broad range of discretion with which to reach collective bargaining agreements with the owners, even when the provisions agreed upon have substantial adverse consequences for some of its members.

Although the bargaining agent will be the exclusive representative for members of the unit, this need not preclude the members from negotiating with the employer for terms or conditions of employment that are more favorable than those in the collective agreement. It has indeed been common for collective bargaining agreements in professional sports to cover only the minimum terms and conditions of employment for those covered by the agreement and to specifically provide that individual athletes may negotiate individually for better terms.[231] Given this situation, it is appropriate to consider the rules which will apply to individual bargaining on terms in excess of the common minimum.

As a general matter, an employer will be considered to have violated its statutory duty to bargain if it deals directly with an employee, or any other agent who is not the certified representative,[232] because by so acting it will undermine the authority of the union and prevent effective collective bargaining, a major purpose of the NLRA.[233] A collective bargaining agreement may, however,

---

228. 345 U.S. 330, 97 L. Ed. 1048, 73 S. Ct. 681 (1953).

229. 345 U.S. at 338. *See also* Humphrey v. Moore, 375 U.S. 335, 349, 11 L. Ed. 2d 370, 84 S. Ct. 363 (1964).

230. Vaca v. Sipes, 386 U.S. 171, 193, 17 L. Ed. 2d 842, 87 S. Ct. 903 (1967). *See also* Hines v. Anchor Motor Freight, Inc., 424 U.S. 554, 47 L. Ed. 2d 231, 96 S. Ct. 1048 (1976).

231. National Football League Collective Bargaining Agreement, art. XII (1977); Major League Baseball Basic Agreement art. III (1976). *See* Shulman & Baum, *Collective Bargaining in Professional Athletics—The NFL Money Bowl,* 50 CHI. B. REC. 173, 174 (1969); Note, *Curt Flood at Bat Against Baseball's Reserve Clause,* 8 SAN DIEGO L. REV. 92, 94 n.12 (1971).

232. Peoples Motor Express, Inc. v. NLRB, 165 F.2d 903 (4th Cir. 1948); Mutual Industries, Inc., 159 N.L.R.B. 885 (1966), *enforced,* 387 F.2d 275 (3rd Cir. 1967).

233. J.I. Case Co. v. NLRB, 321 U.S. 332, 88 L. Ed. 762, 64 S. Ct. 576 (1944); NLRB v. Cooke & Jones, Inc., 339 F.2d 580 (1st Cir. 1964); NLRB v. Union Mfg. Co., 179 F.2d 511 (5th Cir. 1950). This rule applies equally to the modification of contracts. Adolph Coors Co., 150 N.L.R.B. 1604 (1965); Williams Coal Co., 11 N.L.R.B. 579 (1939). A union may, however, acquiesce in a practice of non-representative negotiation, and when the employer then bargains with those employees, it is not in violation of its § 8(a)(5) duty.

authorize individual employees, but not the union,[234] to negotiate for individual contracts whose terms exceed, but do not derogate from, those contained in the collective agreement.[235] When such a contract is negotiated, moreover, it is subsidiary to the collective agreement and may not waive any of its benefits.[236]

The clearest application of these rules was made by the Supreme Court in *J.I. Case Company v. NLRB*,[237] in which it observed that "where there is great variation in [the] capacity of employees, it is possible for the collective bargain to prescribe only minimum rates or maximum hours or expressly to leave certain areas open to individual bargaining." [238] Any such practice must, however, be looked upon "with suspicion," since the conferral of such advantage may be "disruptive of industrial peace" and be "at the long-range expense of the group as a whole." [239] Where such contracts are permissible, moreover, the Court said that they may not "subtract from the collective ones." [240]

J.I. Case, then, provides a narrow area within which an athlete may negotiate for terms in excess of a minimum standards contract—that is, where there is a great variation in the capacity of the members of the bargaining unit and where the individual contracts are not less advantageous than the collective bargain. Although there are no decisions in this area involving professional athletes, there is authority in the entertainment field.[241] In *Midland Broadcasting Company*,[242] the employer negotiated a collective bargaining agreement which included a provision providing for the negotiation of better terms than those contained in the "union contract." Relying upon this provision, the employer then negotiated "talent" contracts with its artists, which afforded the artist an opportunity to earn a bonus over the minimum rates of pay guaranteed by the union contracts, but which also placed restrictions on the artists' performance for anyone except the immediate employer.[243] These

---

234. UAW Local 180 v. J.I. Case Co., 250 Wis. 63, 26 N.W.2d 305 (1947). *See also* NLRB v. Darlington Veneer Co., 236 F.2d 85, 89 n.2 (4th Cir. 1956).

235. J.I. Case Co. v. NLRB, 321 U.S. 332, 339, 88 L. Ed. 762, 64 S. Ct. 576 (1944); United Brewery Workers Local Union 67 v. Duquesne Brewing Co., 354 F. Supp. 1033 (W.D. Pa. 1973).

Although the provisions of the collective agreement will normally be read into individual contracts, this rule may not apply in all circumstances and with respect to all agreements negotiated between union and employer. Thus, in Philadelphia World Hockey Club, Inc. v. Philadelphia Hockey Club, Inc., 351 F. Supp. 462 (E.D. Pa. 1972), the court stated that an agreement reached between a players' association and an owners' association would be binding on pre-existing player contracts only if the player specifically agreed to, or ratified, the agreement. *Id.* at 507-08. *See also* Kapp v. National Football League, 390 F. Supp. 73 (N.D. Cal. 1974) (not apply collective bargaining agreement retroactively).

236. J.I. Case Co. v. NLRB, 321 U.S. 332, 336, 88 L.Ed. 762, 64 S. Ct. 576 (1944).

237. 321 U.S. 332, 88 L.Ed 762, 64 S. Ct. 576 (1944).

238. 321 U.S. at 338.

239. *Id.* at 338-39.

240. *Id.* at 339.

241. *See generally* Burkey, *The Creative Artist's Problems,* in BROADCASTING AND BARGAINING 153 (A. Koenig ed. 1970); Tower, *Labor Relations in the Broadcasting Industry,* 23 LAW & CONTEMP. PROB. 62, 89-90 (1958).

242. 93 N.L.R.B. 455 (1951). *See also* Television Film Producers Ass'n, 93 N.L.R.B. 929, 930 (1951); Knopf v. Producers Guild of America, 40 Cal. App. 3d 233, 114 Cal. Rptr. 782 (1974).

243. It is not without significance that the restriction bears more than a passing resemblance to the reserve and option clauses that have generated so much controversy in professional sports. Inasmuch as the Board sanctioned this type of clause in *Midland Broadcasting,* one might argue that the reserve clause is also a proper term in a collective bargaining contract under the NLRA. *See* § 6.08. Such an argument would also indicate that the status of the clause under the antitrust laws is largely irrelevant. *See* Jacobs & Winter, *Antitrust Principles and Collective Bargaining by*

individual contracts were challenged as being violative of the employer's duty under § 8(a) (5) to bargain in good faith, because the performance restrictions were less favorable terms than those present in the union contract. The Board, however, found no such violation, and upheld the contracts saying that "[i]t is not sufficient . . . to show that a particular provision of the talent contract, taken by itself, is less favorable than a particular term of the union contract."[244]

What the Board seems to have held, therefore, is that in determining the permissiblity of an individual contract, it is the totality of the contract that must be considered, not particular terms. Thus, according to *Midland Broadcasting,* a less favorable term may be negotiated without an employer violation of § 8(a)(5) so long as the totality of the individual contract is not less favorable than the totality of the union contract. Although the "totality theory" is attractive, it is thought that its underpinnings are rather weak. In light of the language in *J.I. Case* that less favorable terms may not be negotiated in individual contracts,[245] the course of wisdom may be to assume that the standard against which any individual provisions will be tested is one which compares the individual and union contracts "term by term", not by the totality of terms. This will be especially true if the collective bargaining agreement specifies that only more favorable terms may be negotiated.[246] This view would pose little difficulty for individual provisions dealing with salary, or no-cut or no-trade clauses,[247] since they would be more, not less, favorable than the standard contract provisions and would not run afoul of either the *J.I. Case* or *Midland Broadcasting* rules. The situation would be much different, however, if a given clause in an individual contract were less favorable than a term of the collective bargaining agreement. The validity of such a clause would depend upon whether the *Midland Broadcasting* majority opinion were accepted. If it were not accepted, then the owner who negotiated the clause would apparently have committed an unfair labor practice by refusing to bargain in good faith with the exclusive representative of its employees.[248]

It is clear, then, that athletes with superior bargaining power need not suffer economic loss because of the advent of collective bargaining, and that the club owner need not risk a § 8(a)(5) unfair labor practice by negotiating a minimum standards contract with the players' association and an individual contract with the more talented players, so long as the proper negotiation procedure is

---

Athletes: Of Superstars in Peonage, 81 YALE L.J. 1, 17-18 (1972). The opinion in Mackey v. National Football League, 407 F. Supp. 1000 (D. Minn. 1975), *modified,* 543 F.2d 606 (8th Cir. 1976), does, however, suggest the need for caution in this area. *See* § 6.08.

244. 93 N.L.R.B. at 456. The Board observed that

> If we were to strike down the burdensome provisions and leave only the bonus provisions . . ., we would be making a new and different contract for the parties. That is not the function of this Board. *Id.*

Two members of the Board, however, dissented on this point. *Id.* at 460.

245. *See* notes 237-40.

246. The provisions in existing agreements are rather imprecise. The baseball agreement simply provides that the terms of individual contracts may not be "inconsistent" with the collective bargaining agreement, Major League Baseball Basic Agreement art. III (1976). *See also* National Football League Collective Bargaining Agreement art. XII (1977).

247. *See Hearings Before the Senate Antitrust Subcomm. of the Senate Comm. on the Judiciary,* 85th Cong., 1st Sess., pt. 3, 2650 (1957). Such clauses are discussed in detail at § 3.09.

248. The result of such inconsistency is not clear. The majority in *Midland Broadcasting* thought it would require the terms to be invalidated, 93 N.L.R.B. at 456, while the dissenters believed it would simply constitute an unfair labor practice. *Id.* at 461. The thrust of *J. I. Case* would appear to suggest that such conduct would constitute an unfair labor practice. 321 U.S. at 337-39.

followed.[249] The association should first negotiate a minimum standards contract which contains all terms and conditions of employment, and which, as in *Midland Broadcasting,* [250] also contains a specific provision allowing individual members of the bargaining unit to negotiate for more favorable terms than those contained in the collective agreement.[251] When the collective agreement is complete, the individual may then negotiate for the more favorable terms that are deemed a necessary *quid pro quo* for his or her services, assuming always that the collective agreement is part and parcel of whatever individual agreement may be reached with the employer.

In considering the right to bargain individually, it is also necessary to consider the fact that the players' association may itself be subject to the charge that such a negotiation procedure violates its duty of fair representation.[252] The basis of such a contention would be that by negotiating for a contract which set merely minimum standards, the association failed to fairly represent the vast majority of its members, since if the contract had included provisions that were applicable to all members without individual bargaining authority, the majority would have benefitted from the inclusion of superstars in the uniform agreement. It seems reasonably clear that if provisions are negotiated which apply across the board, with no provision for individual bargaining, the package would benefit average players at the expense of superstars.[253] Any such arrangement would be, of course, highly detrimental to the superstars. The issue, therefore, is whether the duty of fair representation permits the union to negotiate a minimum standards contract which makes provision for additional compensation to the more talented members of the bargaining unit.[254]

There does not, unfortunately, appear to be any decisional authority dealing with a situation comparable to that involved in the negotiations for minimum standards contracts and individual bargaining by superstars. In light of the language in *Steele v. Louisville & Nashville R.R.*[255] that a bargaining agent may bargain for a variance in the terms of a contract depending on the skill of the members involved,[256] there is little chance that a union would be held to have violated its fair representation duty by negotiating the minimum standards contract which puts those with superior skill in an advantageous position vis-à-vis their less talented peers, assuming the absence of a discriminatory motive and the presence of overall membership benefit.[257]

Although individual bargaining is the current norm in professional sports, it

249. *See* Jacobs & Winter, *supra* note 243, at 9-10.
250. The specific clause involved in *Midland Broadcasting* was as follows:

> The Company further agrees that nothing in this contract shall be deemed to prevent any staff artist from negotiating for or obtaining better terms than the minimum terms provided herein . . . 93 N.L.R.B. at 455, n.1.

251. The existing provisions in baseball and football are identified at note 246 *supra.*
252. *See* notes 221-27 *supra.*
253. *See* note 259 *infra.*
254. It is to be noted that in *Midland Broadcasting,* the Board did not raise this question. It did seem to indicate, however, that if such a complaint were processed through the grievance procedure, it might then be a proper subject for its scrutiny.
255. 323 U.S. 192, 89 L. Ed. 173, 65 S. Ct. 226 (1944).
256. 323 U.S. at 203. *See* notes 224-27 *supra.*
257. *See also* Ford Motor Co. v. Huffman, 345 U.S. 330, 97 L. Ed. 633, 73 S. Ct. 35 (1953); Thomson v. International Alliance of Theatrical Stage Employees, 232 Cal. App. 2d 446, 42 Cal. Rptr. 785 (1965).

is less than clear that it will continue indefinitely. One possibility, for example, would be that a players' union would agree to negotiate over player salaries. If it agreed to such a procedure, the resultant collective bargaining agreement would contain maximum salary figures for each classification of player, which would resemble the salary agreements negotiated in most other industries.[258] Such a contract would, in fact, appear to make economic sense to the non-star players, who, presumably, would benefit from such a "common denominator" approach.[259] Since they would constitute a majority of the bargaining unit, the non-stars could surely compel the bargaining representative to negotiate such a contract. If a maximum salary contract were negotiated, moreover, the superstars would have no basis for legal complaint.[260] That contract would be for the overall benefit of the bargaining unit as a whole, and the mere substitution of majority for minority advantage would certainly not constitute

---

258. Although this suggestion may seem somewhat remote as a realistic possibility, it does have factual support. Schedular salary systems—that is, the payment of X dollars for Y years of service as salary—have been used in baseball. See H.R. REP. No. 2002, 82d Cong., 2d Sess., 32, 159, 173 (1952). Such systems have also been used as a means of determining minimum salaries in professional football. See National Football League Collective Bargaining Agreement art. XXII, § 4 (1977); Hearings Before the Special House Subcomm. on Labor of the House Comm. on Education and Labor, 92d Cong., 2d Sess. 78 (1972). In addition, it has been reported that the owners in the National Football League have considered proposing such a system in the event the players are successful in overturning the rules and policies which preclude their free movement from team to team. The most forceful statement of the owners' position was made in congressional hearings by labor counsel Theodore W. Kheel. Thus, in commenting upon individual bargaining he stated that:

> We acquiesced. We acquiesced because that was what we knew the union wanted. We knew also that the union was under pressure from the superstars to insist on this. Nevertheless, I say to you, Mr. Chairman, that in furtherance of the purpose of the National Labor Relations Act, to encourage the practice and procedure of collective bargaining which you are interested in doing, I urge you to urge the union to assume the full responsibility of bargaining collectively on all salaries, to come to the collective bargaining table like the steelworkers, and auto workers, and all other unions, and bargain not only on the multiplicity of money matters they want to get to but on salaries as well. I say to you that that would be the most constructive step in furtherance of the principles of the National Labor Relations Act. Hearings Before the House Subcomm. on Labor-Management Relations of the House Comm. on Education and Labor, 94th Cong., 1st Sess. 59 (1975).

In this respect, it is worth noting that Bob Feller, one-time head of the Major League Players Association, once said that "I definitely do not think that collective bargaining could be put into baseball in salary talks. . . ." Hearings Before the Senate Antitrust Subcomm. of the Senate Comm. on the Judiciary, 85th Cong., 1st Sess., pt. 2, 1330 (1957).

259. It has been observed that

> there are players, stars and superstars, who unquestionably have far greater bargaining power individually . . . than they would have if the bargaining was conducted for them by an [collective bargaining] agent [representing all players, stars as well as non-stars]. House Hearings, supra note 257, at 75.

It would also seem to put the players association in a more advantageous bargaining position. Thus, it has been observed that the effect of the minimum salary term has been to sharply reduce

> the Union's role as bargaining agent and has resulted in greater emphasis by the Union on the matters remaining within the area of collective bargaining. It has forced the Clubs to consider simultaneously the cost impact of money matters in collective bargaining and the cost impact of individual demands. Id. at 91.

260. This view has been expressed as follows:

> If minimum salaries can be negotiated, so too can maximum salaries. But if maximum salaries are held to be illegal in baseball because they discriminate against the best players, then they should also be illegal in the steel industry because they discriminate against the best steel workers. It is elitist to view industrial workers as fungible and to treat them as though there are no differences in efficiency. Jacobs & Winter, supra note 243, at 21.

the "hostile discrimination," arbitrariness or bad faith that would be necessary for a fair representation challenge. In addition, the superstars would be barred from negotiating on their own, for if the employer bargained with them as individuals, whether or not they were members of the union, he would be committing an unfair labor practice under § 8(a)(5).[261] Once a bargaining representative is elected, it represents all members of the bargaining unit in negotiations with employers on wages and all other terms and conditions of employment, and all members must rely on internal union politics to secure their own advantage.[262] The superstars would, moreover, probably be unable to successfully invoke partial withdrawal or severance procedures to establish their own bargaining unit should the majority seek to submit the individual benefit of the stars to the overall good of all players,[263] and would be unlikely to prevail if an antitrust suit were brought seeking to invalidate the salary system.[264]

§ 6.08.   The Subject Matter of Collective Bargaining.

One of the most important aspects of the collective bargaining process in professional sports concerns the subjects that may be considered at the bargaining table and the extent to which each party will be required to bargain over them. With respect to subject matter, the NLRA defines the term "collective bargaining" to include "wages, hours, and other terms and conditions of employment," [265] and the bargaining representative's authority is similarly defined to include authority to bargain about "rates of pay, wages, hours of employment, or other conditions of employment." [266] In other words, the subject matter of collective bargaining in professional sports will include all matters that relate to the terms and conditions of the employment of athletes.

In defining the duty of each party to bargain, the subject matter has been broken into two basic categories: mandatory and permissive subjects of bargaining. "Mandatory" subjects are those within the phrase "wages, hours, and other terms and conditions of employment," while "permissive" include all other matters.[267] The parties must bargain in good faith about mandatory subjects, but may refuse to bargain about permissive subjects.[268] In addition, a party may insist that the other agree to proposals with respect to mandatory subjects even to the point of impasse. If agreement is not forthcoming, the party may then resort to economic pressure without risking a § 8 (a) (5) or § 8 (b) (3)

---

261. *See* notes 218-20.

262. It has been recently observed that the "existence of unions in professional sports thus negates any possibility of individual bargaining except as permitted by the collective bargain." Jacobs & Winter, *supra* note 243 at 9.

263. *See* § 6.04.

264. *See* §§ 5.04-.06.

265. NLRA § 8(d). *See also* Fibreboard Paper Prods. Corp. v. NLRB, 379 U.S. 203, 13 L. Ed. 2d 233, 85 S. Ct. 398 (1964).

266. NLRA § 9(a).

267. NLRB v. Wooster Div. of Borg-Warner Corp., 356 U.S. 342, 2 L. Ed. 2d 823, 78 S. Ct. 718 (1958). A third category of illegal subjects of bargaining is discussed at notes 315-24 *infra*.

268. In NLRB v. Wooster Div. of Borg-Warner Corp., 356 U.S. 342, 2 L. Ed. 2d 823, 78 S. Ct. 718 (1958), the Court stated that "[t]he duty [to bargain] is limited to [mandatory] subjects, and within that area neither party is legally obligated to yield .... As to other matters, however, each party is free to bargain or not to bargain, and to agree or not to agree." *Id.* at 349.

unfair labor practice charge.[269] With regard to permissive subjects, however, the parties may make bargaining proposals, but may not require the other side's acceptance as a condition to agreement on mandatory terms.[270]

The distinction between mandatory and permissive subjects may thus be crucial, because it will determine the extent to which one party may compel the other to bargain over any given proposal. The distinction rests primarily upon the Supreme Court's opinion in *NLRB v. Wooster Division of Borg Warner Corporation*[271] in which it adopted the basic definitions noted above.[272] Although the Court did not specifically indicate how a particular proposal would be analyzed to determine whether it was mandatory or permissive, the provisions in question provide some guidance. These included a "ballot" clause, which specified the procedure that was to be followed before a strike could be called, and a "recognition" clause, which dealt with the relations between the union and the employees. The Court held that neither of the clauses were mandatory subjects. The "ballot" clause failed because it related only to strike procedures and settled no term or condition of employment; and the "recognition" clause failed, since it did not deal with the employment relation at all and attempted to subvert the position of the recognized bargaining representative.[273] In *Borg-Warner,* then, the Court defined mandatory subjects of bargaining to include those matters that have a direct bearing upon "wages, hours, and other terms and conditions of employment."[274] In a subsequent opinion, the Court provided more general guidance by stating that "[i]n general terms, the [mandatory] limitation includes only issues that settle an aspect of the relationship between the employer and employees."[275] The inclusiveness of the mandatory label has also been broadly defined by both the NLRB and the courts to include an expansive array of aspects of the employment relationship.[276]

One of the most difficult issues concerning the subject matter of collective bargaining in professional sports is whether the various provisions which restrain the voluntary mobility of players constitute mandatory subjects of bargaining. These include the reserve and option rules which limit the ability of players to move from one team to another, the "Rozelle"-type rules which have a similar effect, and the draft systems which preclude a rookie from negotiating with a team other than the one which acquires the rookie's draft

269. NLRB v. Katz, 369 U.S. 736, 8 L. Ed. 2d 230, 82 S. Ct. 1107 (1962); NLRB v. American Nat'l Ins. Co., 343 U.S. 395, 96 L. Ed. 1027, 72 S. Ct. 824 (1952). The subjects included in the "mandatory" category are considered in 18D T. KHEEL, LABOR LAW chs. 19-20 (1974); C. MORRIS, THE DEVELOPING LABOR LAW 391-423 (1971). Economic sanctions are considered in § 6.09.

270. NLRB v. Wooster Div. of Borg-Warner Corp., 356 U.S. 342, 2 L. Ed. 2d 823, 78 S. Ct. 718 (1958). The subjects included in the "permissive" category are considered in 18D T. KHEEL, *supra* note 269, at § 21.01; MORRIS, *supra* note 269, at 424-35.

271. 356 U.S. 342, 2 L. Ed. 2d 823, 78 S. Ct. 718 (1958).

272. *See* note 267 *supra.*

273. 356 U.S. at 349-50.

274. *See* 18D T. KHEEL, LABOR LAW § 18.02[3] (1974).

275. Allied Chem. & Alkali Workers v. Pittsburgh Plate Glass Co., 404 U.S. 157, 178, 30 L. Ed. 2d 341, 92 S. Ct. 383 (1971).

276. Mandatory subjects include, for example, pensions, hiring practices, seniority, promotions, discharges, transfers, safety practices, workloads, union security (dues check-off is an illustration), grievance and arbitration procedures, and no-strike clauses. *See* 18D T. KHEEL, LABOR LAW ch. 20 (1974). The characterization of such provisions as mandatory or permissive could also effect the extent to which they could qualify for the labor antitrust exemption. *See* § 5.05.

rights.[277] The issue may be of central importance in future collective bargaining sessions, since these provisions tend to be viewed by owners as being essential to a sport's economic health and by the athletes as unreasonable restraints on the ability to freely market their services. If they are mandatory subjects, then either party may compel the other to bargain over their content and inclusion in a collective agreement and may utilize all of its economic weapons in the process. If they are permissive subjects, on the other hand, the ability to compel bargaining will be much less.[278]

In order for these provisions to constitute mandatory subjects, it would have to be concluded that they have a direct bearing upon the terms or conditions of employment of professional athletes. Although there are no clear analogues to these provisions in industrial labor relations, there is a large body of decisional authority dealing with different aspects of employment security—for example, hiring practices, seniority, promotion and transfer. With respect to proposals relating to employment security, the courts and the NLRB have made it rather clear that they will be considered as "terms or conditions of employment" so long as they relate to the terms upon which employment will be afforded or withdrawn.[279] The principal decision on the status of these provisions is *Fibreboard Paper Products Corporation v. NLRB*,[280] where the Supreme Court held that the contracting out of work previously performed by employees in a plant was a mandatory subject. The basis for the conclusion was that the subject matter of the dispute was "well within the literal meaning of the phrase 'terms and conditions of employment' " since contracting out would terminate the employment of the employees who had previously performed the work. The Court also observed that

> [t]he inclusion of contracting out within the statutory scope of collective bargaining . . . seems well designed to effectuate the purposes of the National Labor Relations Act. One of the primary purposes of the Act is to promote the peaceful settlement of industrial disputes by subjecting labor-management controversies to the mediatory influence of negotiation. The Act was framed with an awareness that refusals to confer and negotiate had been one of the most prolific causes of industrial strife.[281]

The language in *Fibreboard* suggests a rather expansive view of the inclusiveness of mandatory subjects. A similar view has been expressed with respect to so-called hiring hall proposals, which are quite similar to the mobility restraints.[282] A hiring hall agreement would require an employer to hire only persons referred to it by a union and a union to refer applicants on a non-discriminatory basis.[283] In the principal case on the status of such provisions, the NLRB held that hiring hall proposals are mandatory subjects of

---

277. These provisions are discussed in detail at § 3.12 (contractual aspects) and §§ 5.03, 5.07 (antitrust aspects).
278. *See* notes 267-270 *supra.*
279. *See* 18D T. KHEEL, LABOR LAW § 20.03 (1974).
280. 379 U.S. 203, 13 L. Ed. 2d 233, 85 S. Ct. 398 (1964).
281. 379 U.S. at 210-11. *See also* Meat Cutters Local 189 v. Jewel Tea Co., 381 U.S. 676, 691, 14 L. Ed. 2d 640, 85 S. Ct. 1596 (1965).
282. *See* notes 287-92, 332-33 *infra.*
283. Teamsters Local 357 v. NLRB, 365 U.S. 667, 6 L. Ed. 2d 11, 81 S. Ct. 835 (1961).

bargaining.[284] The Board found that such proposals were within the "terms or conditions of employment" because the standards used to determine priority of employment "of necessity regulate relations between the employer and employees." [285] It also observed that

> those employees who are working in the industry and who have a deep concern not only about the length of their present jobs, but also about the opportunities for continued employment elsewhere when they are laid off, are clearly and directly affected by the job priority standards established by the hiring hall.[286]

This language is highly suggestive of the proposition that any provision which directly affects the employment rights of employees will be considered a mandatory subject of bargaining.

Although the mobility restraints are certainly not *a fortiori* cases, they do seem to fit within the views expressed in the hiring hall cases and *Fibreboard.* [287] Like the hiring hall cases, the mobility restraints have the essential consequence of determining how employment relationships are to be formed and continued in professional sports. The analogy is especially close with respect to draft arrangements.[288] If the restraints were the subject of bargaining, any agreement would certainly "settle an aspect of the relationship between the employer and employees" [289] — that is, the extent to which an employee will be able to freely select an employer. Unlike the clauses in *Borg-Warner,* a collective bargaining provision dealing with one or more of these issues would relate to the terms and conditions upon which athletes would be employed in professional sports, and would not constitute a mere advisory provision or relate to the ability of the certified representative to bargain with the employer.[290] In light of the long standing friction that has existed between the owners and the players over these provisions,[291] their characterization as mandatory subjects would also be consistent with the quoted view of the Court in *Fibreboard* that labor disputes should be subjected to the "mediatory influence of negotiation." [292]

In light of these several factors, several courts have recently concluded that mobility restraints are mandatory subjects. In *Mackey v. National Football*

---

284. Houston Chapter Associated Gen. Contractors of America, Inc., 143 N.L.R.B. 409 (1963), *enforced,* 349 F.2d 449 (5th Cir. 1965), *cert. denied,* 382 U.S. 1026, 15 L. Ed. 2d 540, 86 S. Ct. 648 (1966).

285. 143 N.L.R.B. at 412.

286. *Id. See also* NLRB v. Tom Joyce Floors, Inc., 353 F.2d 768 (9th Cir. 1965). *See generally* 18D T. KHEEL, LABOR LAW § 20.05[3] (1974); C. MORRIS, THE DEVELOPING LABOR LAW 712-14 (1971).

287. Thus, in Jacobs & Winter, *Antitrust Principles and Collective Bargaining by Athletes: Of Superstars in Peonage,* 81 YALE L.J. 1 (1971), it is said that

> [w]e find it difficult to construct even a hypothetical argument that a contractual provision [the mobility restraints] so intimately connected with determining the team for which an athlete will play and what salary and other benefits he may extract through individual bargaining is not a term and condition of employment. *Id.* at 10-11.

See also Lowell, *Collective Bargaining and the Professional Team Sport Industry,* 38 LAW & CONTEMP. PROB. 3, 34 (1973).

288. *See* notes 296, 332-33 *infra.*

289. *See* note 275 *supra.*

290. *See* notes 273-74 *supra.*

291. *See* §§ 3.12, 5.03, 5.07.

292. *See* note 281 *supra.*

League,[293] a group of players challenged the "Rozelle-rule"—requiring that a team signing a free agent must compensate the team the player left, either on a voluntary or compulsory basis—under the federal antitrust laws.[294] With respect to the bargaining status of the provision, the court held that it was a mandatory subject of bargaining. The premise of this conclusion was that "the Rule operates to restrict a player's ability to move from one team to another and depresses salaries." [295] A similar conclusion has been reached with respect to the draft in professional football.[296]

Other courts have reached a contrary conclusion.[297] The primary case is *Robertson v. National Basketball Association*,[298] in which the court "tentatively" concluded that they were not mandatory subjects.[299] In reaching this conclusion, the court found that *Fibreboard* was inapposite since the Supreme Court had indicated that its language would not require all provisions that are of interest to bargaining parties be mandatory subjects.[300] It also suggested that the hiring hall cases were "wholly unpersuasive", though it did not indicate why they were unpersuasive.[301] Unfortunately, the opinion in *Robertson* is almost completely devoid of the type of analysis that would appear to be necessary to determine whether there is a direct relationship between mobility restraints and the conditions under which professional athletes are employed. Although not clearly articulated in this part of the court's opinion, it would appear that the essential basis for its conclusion is that the mobility restraints were unlawful under the antitrust laws. As will be indicated below, the legality of a provision under the antitrust laws should have little bearing upon its propriety as a subject of collective bargaining.[302] In short, the opinion in *Robertson* should not be viewed as dispositive of the question, since it lacks the analysis that the issue requires and appears to have been premised on a very shaky foundation (that the mobility restraints are not even proper subjects for collective bargaining).

The mandatory subject of bargaining question may also arise with respect to other issues. The process that will be utilized to analyze such issues when they do arise is illustrated by *National Football League Management Council (I)*,[303] where the players' association had sought to bargain over the issue of artificial turf. Although the employer (the Council) agreed to discuss the issue, it denied that it had an obligation to bargain during the term of the existing collective

---

293. 543 F.2d 606 (8th Cir. 1976), *modifying* 407 F. Supp. 1000 (D. Minn. 1975).

294. The antitrust aspects of the case are considered at § 5.07.

295. 543 F.2d 606 (8th Cir. 1976), *modifying* 407 F. Supp. 1000 (D. Minn. 1975).

296. Smith v. Pro-Football, Inc., 420 F. Supp. 738 (D.D.C. 1976). *See also* National Basketball Players Ass'n, 1976-77 CCH NLRB DECISIONS ¶ 20,014 (January 26, 1976) (General Counsel conclusion that the college draft, option clauses, and compensation rules in the NBA were mandatory subjects of bargaining).

297. Mackey v. National Football League, 407 F. Supp. 1000 (D. Minn. 1975), *modified,* 543 F.2d 606 (8th Cir. 1976); Robertson v. National Basketball Ass'n, 389 F. Supp. 867 (S.D.N.Y 1975). A similar doubt had been suggested by the district court in *Flood v. Kuhn,* 316 F. Supp. at 278.

298. 389 F. Supp. 867 (S.D.N.Y. 1975).

299. 389 F. Supp. at 889-90.

300. 389 F. Supp. at 890. The court disposed of *Teamsters Local 24 v. Oliver,* discussed at notes 333-38 *infra,* on the same basis.

301. *Id.*

302. *See* notes 320-24 *infra.*

303. 203 N.L.R.B 958 (1973), *remanded on other issue,* 503 F.2d 12 (8th Cir. 1974).

bargaining agreement. When the players' association then filed a § 8 (a) (5) unfair labor practice charge for refusal to bargain, the Board held that the issue was a mandatory subject of bargaining about which the employer had a duty to bargain.[304] In reaching this conclusion, the Board did not undertake to analyze the issue in terms of decisional authority, but simply agreed with the decision of the Administrative Law Judge, who did not view it as posing a particularly difficult matter. Thus, he stated that the union's request for bargaining over the issue was "predicated on its view that artificial surfaces are more conducive to injury, the relation to conditions of employment is close and immediate, not remote, or merely esthetical." [305] Another issue about which the parties must bargain is the disciplinary system that exists in all sports. In most of the leagues, the commissioner is vested with sole authority to handle disciplinary matters, and in some leagues is deemed to be the sole arbiter of other types of dispute.[306] The players have repeatedly expressed their opposition to this authority, and recent collective bargaining agreements have produced modifications of the traditional devices. Although there is no case law on point, the courts and the NLRB have repeatedly held that grievance and arbitration arrangements are mandatory subjects of bargaining.[307]

The final issue that should be considered with respect to the subject matter of collective bargaining concerns the extent to which one may challenge the substantive terms that are agreed upon by the bargaining parties. There will generally be little basis for challenge. One of the primary policies of the labor law is to maximize the freedom of collective contract between an employer and its employees.[308] The parties are generally free to define the terms and conditions that will govern their relationship. With the exception of so-called illegal subjects of bargaining (which are noted below), there is no requirement that the terms included in a collective bargaining agreement meet any external standard of reasonableness or appropriateness (assuming that the antitrust exemption will be applicable). The basic limitation upon this freedom is the statutory requirement that the parties meet and bargain in good faith about the terms and conditions of employment.[309] If these procedural requirements are satisfied, the substantive terms that are incorporated in a collective bargaining agreement are generally not subject to review in the courts.[310]

In order to focus more specifically upon the bases that might be available to challenge the substantive provisions of an agreement, it might be assumed that

---

304. 203 N.L.R.B at 959.

305. 203 N.L.R.B at 962. *See also* National Football League Management Council (II), Case No. 2-CA-13379 (June 30, 1976 — *see* notes 111.1 and 217.7 *supra*) (following *National Football League Management Council (I)*, and Administrative Law Judge ruled that rules relating to punt coverage and overtime were mandatory subjects of bargaining).

306. *See* § 4.19.

307. *See, e.g.,* United Elec., Radio & Mach. Workers v. NLRB, 409 F.2d 150, 156 (D.C. Cir. 1969); NLRB v. United Nuclear Corp., 381 F.2d 972, 977-78 (10th Cir. 1967); NLRB v. Century Cement Mfg. Co., 208 F.2d 84, 86 (2d Cir. 1953); Hughes Tool Co. v. NLRB, 147 F.2d 69, 73 (5th Cir. 1945); Bethlehem Steel Co., 136 N.L.R.B 1500 (1962), *petition for enforcement denied on other grounds sub nom.* Marine & Shipbuilding Workers v. NLRB, 320 F.2d 615 (3rd Cir. 1963), *cert. denied,* 375 U.S. 984, 11 L. Ed. 2d 472, 84 S. Ct. 516 (1964). *See generally* 18D T. KHEEL, LABOR LAW § 20.06[1] (1974); C. MORRIS, THE DEVELOPING LABOR LAW 404 (1971).

308. *See* H. WELLINGTON, LABOR AND THE LEGAL PROCESS 52 (1968); Jacobs & Winter, *supra* note 287, at 11-13.

309. *See* § 6.06.

310. *See e.g.,* NLRB v. American National Ins. Co., 343 U.S. 395, 404 (1952).

the parties in a professional sports league had agreed to include mobility restraint provisions in an agreement. If a person were dissatisfied with their inclusion, the only basis for challenge (assuming that bargaining duties have been met on both sides) would be to allege that the provisions (1) violate the antitrust laws or (2) constitute illegal subjects of bargaining.[311]

When antitrust suits are brought challenging a provision in professional sports, the initial issue will be whether it has been adopted as part of a bona fide collective bargaining agreement. If it has, then attention will focus upon whether the provision is protected by the exemption from the antitrust laws which applies to terms in collective bargaining agreements. The coverage of the labor exemption, and its application to professional sports, has already been analyzed in detail in the antitrust chapter and we will not repeat it here except to suggest that the exemption will be available only if the provision in question has been the subject of bargaining between the parties and included in a collective agreement.[312] If such a process has been followed, then it is possible that a provision which would be illegal under the antitrust laws may be immunized by inclusion in a labor agreement.[313] But if the provision has not been the subject of bargaining, then it will not be entitled to the exemption and would be subject to antitrust scrutiny on its merits.[314]

The second basis upon which a substantive provision could be attacked would be that it constitutes an illegal subject of bargaining. Illegal subjects may not be included in a collective bargaining agreement and the insistence of either side that they be included will constitute a failure to bargain in good faith.[315] Such subjects include those which would be unlawful or inconsistent with the basic policies of the NLRA and have been held to include, for example, a closed shop, a hot cargo clause, racial separation of employees, and discrimination against non-union members.[316] Illegal subjects have not, however, been held to include provisions that would be comparable to the mobility restraints in professional sports.

Although it would seem that there is little basis for the view that the mobility restraints would constitute illegal subjects, the district court in *Mackey v. National Football League*[317] came to that conclusion. The court's reasoning is less than clear, but it would appear that the premise of its conclusion was a finding that the mobility restraints violated the federal antitrust laws.[318] Since the provisions were illegal under those laws, the court apparently concluded that they must constitute illegal subjects of bargaining. This conclusion was

---

311. A third issue that might be presented by the inclusion of such provisions in a collective bargaining agreement would be whether the bargaining agent could make such an agreement and still meet its duty of fair representation. *See* § 6.07. In light of the discretion that is granted the bargaining agent by that duty, it would appear that such provisions could be agreed to without violating the duty so long as there were no evidence of hostile discrimination against some members of the bargaining unit. *See* Jacobs & Winter, *supra* note 287, at 18-21.

312. *See* §§ 5.05, 5.06.

313. *See note* 321 *infra*.

314. *See* § 5.06.

315. NLRB v. Wooster Div. of Borg-Warner Corp., 356 U.S. 342, 349-50, 2 L. Ed. 2d 823, 78 S. Ct. 718 (1958).

316. *See* 18D T. KHEEL, LABOR LAW § 21.02 (1974); C. MORRIS, THE DEVELOPING LABOR LAW 388, 435-37 (1971).

317. 407 F. Supp. 1000 (D. Minn. 1975), *modified,* 543 F.2d 606 (8th Cir. 1976).

318. This aspect of the case is discussed at § 5.07.

summarily rejected by the court of appeals,[319] and it is important to emphasize that the district court's conclusion does not necessarily follow from the finding of antitrust illegality. If the provisions in question had been the subject of bona fide collective bargaining and were included in a labor contract, they would appear to qualify for the labor exemption from the antitrust laws.[320] If the exemption were applicable, it would then protect the provisions from antitrust scrutiny. Thus, it is important to note that in the antitrust exemption context, the Supreme Court has repeatedly indicated that an act or agreement provision that *is* in violation of the antitrust laws standing alone may yet be *lawfully* included in a collective bargaining agreement if it meets the exemption requirements.[321] When the labor exemption is applicable, there would seem to be no basis for a finding that the provisions in question constitute illegal subjects of bargaining. The opinion in *Mackey* is not necessarily inconsistent with this view, since the court also found that there had been no collective bargaining on the mobility restraints that it was considering.[322] In such a situation, the labor exemption would not be applicable. But even if the exemption were not available to protect such provisions in the context of a specific case, that fact would not prevent the parties from bargaining about the provisions and including them in a future collective agreement that would qualify for the exemption.[323] Thus, it would appear that if the mobility restraints are made the subject of bargaining they need not constitute illegal subjects.[324]

In light of the preceding discussion, it seems reasonably clear that specific provisions will not be subjected to substantive review by the courts or the NLRB if they are bargained about in good faith and included in a collective agreement. Under such circumstances they would apparently qualify for the labor exemption from the antitrust laws and should not be viewed as illegal subjects of bargaining.

Since there is substantial disagreement in several professional sports over the mobility restraint provisions, it is also appropriate to inquire whether there is

---

319. 543 F.2d 606 (8th Cir. 1976).

320. *See* §§ 5.04-.06.

321. *See* American Fed'n of Musicians v. Carroll, 391 U.S. 99, 107-12, 20 L. Ed. 2d 460, 88 S. Ct. 1562 (1968); Meat Cutters Local 189 v. Jewel Tea Co., 381 U.S. 676, 692-97, 14 L. Ed. 2d 640, 85 S. Ct. 1596 (1965); Allen-Bradley Co. v. Electrical Workers Local 3, 325 U.S. 797, 800-01, 89 L. Ed. 1939, 65 S. Ct. 1533 (1945); United States v. American Fed'n of Musicians, 47 F. Supp. 304 (N.D. Ill. 1942), *aff'd per curiam,* 318 U.S. 741, 87 L. Ed. 1120, 63 S. Ct. 665 (1943). Such a view is, of course, essential to prevent the exemption from being consumed. Thus, to suggest that a provision could not be within the labor exemption if it were in violation of the antitrust laws is to simply seek destruction of the exemption. If a provision does not violate the antitrust laws, an exemption is pointless, as it would be if a provision that is violative were excluded from its protection for that reason alone.

322. 407 F. Supp. at 1000 (D. Minn. 1975), *modified,* 543 F.2d 606 (8th Cir. 1976).

323. Mackey v. National Football League, 543 F.2d 606 (8th Cir. 1976), *modifying* 407 F. Supp. 1000 (D. Minn. 1975). *See also* National Basketball Players Ass'n, 1976-77 CCH NLRB DECISIONS ¶ 20,014 (January 26, 1976) (General Counsel conclusion that the presence of antitrust litigation over player restraint mechanisms did not affect their status as mandatory subjects).

324. In testimony before a House committee, for example, Mr. Theodore W. Kheel, labor counsel to the NFL owners, observed that

> what might be viewed as an illegal restraint of trade, if imposed unilaterally by employers, is clearly subject to what I would call the collective-bargaining exemption to the antitrust laws and becomes, through collective bargaining, a legal restraint.

Hearings Before the House Subcomm. on Labor-Management Relations of the House Comm. on Education and Labor, 94th Cong., 1st Sess. 60 (1975).

any specific labor law authority dealing with similar provisions. As noted, one of the basic policies of the labor law is to accord broad freedom of contract to the bargaining parties, subject only to the very narrow exceptions considered above. The purpose of the present inquiry is to determine whether the courts or the NLRB have dealt with provisions like the mobility restraints which would substantiate the apparent conclusion that they are proper bargaining subjects. Although there is very little case law dealing with provisions that are comparable to the mobility restraints, the available authority does suggest that there is nothing impermissible about such provisions as a matter of federal labor law.[325] This authority will be considered by focusing separately on the different types of restraint mechanisms.

The reserve and option-type clauses have the effect of limiting the ability of a player to leave one team and seek employment with another. Such limitations are common elements of personal service contracts, and are routinely upheld against attack so long as they are reasonable in scope.[326] Unfortunately, there is very little labor authority that deals with this type of restriction. It was present in the contracts before the Board in *Midland Broadcasting Company*,[327] where the employer had inserted in individual "talent" contracts, executed pursuant to a collective bargaining agreement provision, a restraint on the entertainers' performing for any other party.[328] The Board, however, failed to even comment upon the provision, except to note that its purpose was "designed . . . to assure that the . . . [employer] would receive the exclusive benefit of its investment in the artist"[329] — the same basic purpose behind the reserve and option clauses. Though this lack of comment does not, to be sure, indicate that the Board placed its imprimatur upon such restraints, it does suggest that the Board did not perceive its role as policing the bargaining parties' freedom to contract on common law grounds.

A similar conclusion would seem appropriate with respect to the player drafts. The drafts serve the same type of restrictive purpose as do the other mobility restraints — that is, to equalize playing talent by restocking weak teams in order that competition will be stimulating and intense.[330] If a player draft were included in a collective bargaining agreement,[331] it might be asked whether rookies could object to the draft on the ground that it deprives them (as new entrants to the market) of the right to make a bargain with the team of their choice at a time when they are not a part of the collective bargaining unit that agreed to the draft. Although that objection has merit, there is ample labor law authority for such provisions. The most directly analogous authority would be the cases that have upheld the use of hiring halls. As indicated earlier, the Board

325. This conclusion is also supported by the cases which have found the mobility restraints to be mandatory subjects of bargaining. See note 293-96, *supra*.

326. *See* 6A A. CORBIN, CORBIN ON CONTRACTS § 1394 (1962). The permissibility of these provisions are considered in §§ 3.12 (contractual aspects), § 5.07 (antitrust aspects).

327. 93 NLRB 455 (1951).

328. *See* § 6.07. With respect to the employment restraints that have been utilized in the entertainment industry, it is worth noting that the period of exclusivity is normally related to the actual period covered by an individual employment contract. *See* Burkey, *The Creative Artist's Problems*, in BROADCASTING AND BARGAINING 153, 156 (A. Koenig ed. 1970).

329. 93 NLRB at 456.

330. *See* R. ANDREANO, NO JOY IN MUDVILLE 184 (1965).

331. If the draft were not included in a collective bargaining agreement, then it would have substantial antitrust problems. *See* §§ 5.03, 5.07.

and the courts have repeatedly held that hiring hall provisions are mandatory subjects of bargainings.[332] Like the hiring hall, the draft is simply one means of accomplishing the desired result of allocating employees at the least cost and effort. The hiring hall is distinguishable to the extent that in it the employee may or may not accept the job to which he is referred, whereas the player draft is a mandatory arrangement in which the player has no choice (except to not play in the league). The drafts might also be distinguished on the ground that they restrain the salary that is paid to players by precluding them from selling their services to the highest bidder, though the hiring hall would normally produce the same result through uniform salaries. The hiring hall is, nonetheless, sufficiently similar to the draft to suggest that owners and players in a professional league have the freedom to include a draft arrangement in a collective bargaining agreement.

Support for this conclusion may also be found in two opinions of the Supreme Court. Thus, in *Teamsters Local 24 v. Oliver,*[333] the Supreme Court stated that a collective bargaining agreement could regulate the terms upon which a motor carrier employer could contract for the services of a person who owned his own truck, even though the owner-operators may not have been a part of the bargaining process. Similarly, in *Fibreboard Paper Products Corporation v. NLRB,*[334] the Court found that the "contracting out" of work that had previously been performed by members of a union to an independent contractor was a mandatory subject of bargaining and required the employer to bargain over it.[335] The requirement to bargain over the "contracting out" of work in the bargaining unit also has the effect of regulating the entry of non-present third parties to the work. In both *Oliver* and *Fibreboard,* the basis of the Court's conclusions was that the contracting out arrangements would have a direct and intimate effect upon the terms and conditions of employment of the members of the bargaining unit, so that bargaining was essential to the interests of the union membership.[336] The player drafts are similar to the contracting out arrangements in the sense that they may affect persons who are not members of the bargaining unit at the time agreement is reached.[337] They also have a close relation to the terms and conditions of employment of all professional athletes — because there is only a limited fund of money out of which salaries may be paid, and the structure of the draft may have substantial impact upon other contractual provisions — and would seem to stand on the same base as the provisions in *Oliver* and *Fibreboard.* The only significant factual difference is that in the draft situation it is groups of employers who are competing for the scarce talents of athletes, while in the industrial contracting out cases it is groups of employees who are competing for the work sought by the employers

332. *See* notes 283-86 *supra.*
333. 358 U.S. 283, 3 L. Ed. 2d 312, 79 S. Ct. 297 (1959). *Oliver* was specifically followed in Smith v. Pro-Football, Inc., 420 F. Supp. 738 (D.D.C. 1976), holding that the draft in football is a mandatory subject of bargaining but in violation of the antitrust laws in the situation presented.
334. 379 U.S. 203, 13 L. Ed. 2d 233, 85 S. Ct. 398 (1964).
335. 379 U.S. at 210-11.
336. 379 U.S. at 210-14; 358 U.S. at 293-95.
337. Although the Supreme Court held in Allied Chem. & Alkali Workers v. Pittsburgh Plate Glass Co., 404 U.S. 157, 30 L. Ed. 2d 341, 92 S. Ct. 383 (1971), that the pension rights of retired workers were not mandatory subjects of bargaining because they were not members of the bargaining unit, the Court specifically limited its decision to employees who had ceased work with no expectation of ever being available for hire again in the future. *Id.* at 168.

to be contracted out.[338] In both situations it is the allocation of employment opportunities that is in question. Whether it is employers or employees who are competing for the opportunities should make little difference.[339]

§ 6.09. Strikes and Lockouts.

The most tangible public indication of active collective bargaining in professional sports involves the labor disputes that have frequently erupted between owners and players during the negotiation of new collective agreements. These disputes have often resulted in the use of economic sanctions by both sides, in the form of strikes by the players and lockouts by owners which bar players from reporting to training camps. They have also produced numerous unfair labor practice charges by both sides, as well as an active exchange of accusation and denunciation in the press. As indicated in the introductory section to this chapter, the intensity of the disputes has generally increased with each successive round. Thus, in 1968 there was a short lockout of football players from training camps; in 1969 a short training camp boycott in baseball occurred; in 1970 there was a 3-day strike and a 17-day lockout in football; in 1972 a 13-day strike in baseball eliminated a portion of the regular season; and a 44-day strike erupted in football in the summer of 1974. There is some evidence, however, that this trend may be abating. Thus, the football season commenced in 1975 without economic activity and agreements were entered in most of the major sports in 1976 and 1977, though there was a strike prior to the 1976 baseball season.[339.1]

It is undeniable that labor turmoil is now a periodic part of the professional sports business, just as it is in most other industries. It is also clear that the owners and players may not hesitate to utilize their economic sanctions when an impasse develops at the bargaining table. Although the use of these sanctions does little for the public relations of either side, their use is evidence of the maturation of collective bargaining in sports. Economic warfare is, in a sense, the essence of the collective bargaining process,[340] because that process is simply a means of requiring opposing parties to modify their positions. When this cannot be done peacefully, then the contest of economic weapons becomes the means by which controversies are won, lost or compromised.

The primary weapon of the players is the strike, which is defined as the act of employees refusing to work as a means of coercing their employer to accede to a demand that they have made and it has refused.[341] Though neither the Constitution nor the common law provide employees with an absolute right to

---

338. *See* Jacobs & Winter, *supra* note 287, at 15-16.

339. *See* Mountain Pac. Chapter, 119 NLRB 883, 896 (1958), *enforcement denied,* 270 F.2d 425 (9th Cir. 1959).

339.1. It might also be noted that a single team threatened to strike its owner in 1976, when the owner (Charles O. Finley) refused to play three players after the commissioner's refusal to approve their sale to another team. *See* Atlanta Constitution, June 28, 1976, at D-1, col. 4.

340. Thus, in NLRB v. Insurance Agents' Int'l Union, 361 U.S. 477, 4 L. Ed. 2d 454, 80 S. Ct. 419 (1960), the Court noted that "[t]he presence of economic weapons in reserve, and their actual exercise on occasion by the parties, is part and parcel of the system . . . ." *Id.* at 489.

341. Jeffery-De Witt Insulator Co. v. NLRB, 91 F.2d 134, 138 (4th Cir. 1937). *See also* The Point Reyes, 110 F.2d 608, 609-10 (5th Cir. 1940) (equating "strike" with the presence of an employee-employer relation in which the former have quit work).

strike,[342] federal statutory law makes it a potent weapon. Early statutes provided that the action of employees terminating their employment or ceasing to perform work shall not violate the law of the United States,[343] and in addition denied federal courts the power to issue temporary restraining orders or temporary or permanent injunctions against activities growing out of labor disputes.[344] The most important provisions, however, are those contained in the NLRA, which guarantee employees the right to engage in strikes and other forms of concerted activities,[345] and provide that the right to strike shall not be impeded or diminished by any of its provisions, except as may be therein specifically stated.[346] These provisions indicate that the right to strike is accorded considerable protection, and that when properly employed [347] it is an economic weapon which "implements and supports the principle of the collective bargaining system." [348]

The right to strike is not, however, without limitation. Even when on strike the union will be bound by its obligation to bargain in good faith [349] and will lose its protection when it consents to the inclusion of a "no-strike" clause in a collective bargaining agreement,[350] or when it engages in activity that involves either an unlawful objective [351] or the use of improper means.[352] In addition, the

---

342. *See* Dorchy v. Kansas, 272 U.S. 306, 311, 71 L. Ed. 248, 47 S. Ct. 86 (1926).

343. Clayton Act § 20, 29 U.S.C. § 52 (1970).

344. Norris-LaGuardia Act § 1, 29 U.S.C. § 101 (1970). Similar anti-injunction provisions have been enacted by several states. *See generally* C. MORRIS, THE DEVELOPING LABOR LAW 522 n.22 (1970).

345. NLRA § 7. Section 7 also gives employees the right to refrain from participating in any such activities.

346. NLRA § 13. NLRB v. Erie Resistor Corp., 373 U.S. 221, 233, 10 L. Ed. 2d 308, 83 S. Ct. 1139 (1963). The specific exceptions to this rule are contained in NLRA § 8(b)(4), which restricts the right to strike for 1) secondary purposes, 2) recognition of a union in some circumstances, and 3) jurisdictional and work assignment purposes. A further restriction is in NLRA § 8(d), which requires that a party seeking to modify or terminate an existing collective bargaining agreement must give 60 days notice to the other party and continue to work during the period.

347. A strike will be protected under the NLRA only if it arises in a "labor dispute," which is defined to include

> any controversy concerning terms, tenure or conditions of employment, or concerning the association or representation of persons in negotiating, fixing, maintaining, changing, or seeking to arrange terms or conditions of employment, regardless of whether the disputants stand in the proximate relation of employer and employee. NLRA § 2(9).

In determining whether a labor dispute is present, moreover, "[t]he wisdom or unwisdom of the men, their justification or lack of it . . . ." cannot be utilized as determinative factors. *See* NLRB v. Mackay Radio and Telegraph Co., 304 U.S. 333, 344, 82 L. Ed. 1381, 58 S. Ct. 904 (1938).

348. NLRB v. Erie Resistor Corp., 373 U.S. 221, 234, 10 L. Ed. 2d 308, 83 S. Ct. 1139 (1963).

349. NLRA § 8(b)(3). In NLRB v. Insurance Agents' Int'l Union, 361 U.S. 477, 495, 4 L. Ed. 2d 454, 80 S. Ct. 419 (1960), the Court noted that an ordinary economic strike would not be evidence of a failure to bargain in good faith, and that the reason "is not that it constitutes a protected activity but that . . . there is simply no inconsistency between the application of economic pressure and good-faith collective bargaining." *Id.*

350. Boys Markets, Inc. v. Retail Clerks Local 770, 398 U.S. 235, 26 L. Ed. 2d 199, 90 S. Ct. 1583 (1970) (federal courts may grant injunction to enforce no-strike clause); NLRB v. Sands Mfg. Co., 306 U.S. 332, 83 L. Ed. 682, 59 S. Ct. 508 (1939). This will not be true where the strike is to protest an employer's unfair labor practices unless the right to strike is waived. *See* Mastro Plastics Corp. v. NLRB, 350 U.S. 270, 100 L. Ed. 309, 76 S. Ct. 349 (1956). "No-strike" clauses have been included in several of the most recent collective bargaining agreements. *See* National Basketball Association Collective Bargaining Agreement art. XIV (1976); National Football League Collective Bargaining Agreement art. III, § 1 (1977).

351. Such objectives are noted at note 346 *supra.*

352. *See, e.g.,* NLRB v. Insurance Agents' Int'l Union, 361 U.S. 477, 4 L. Ed. 2d 454, 80 S. Ct. 419 (1960) ("sitdown" strike); UAW-AFL Local 232 v. Wisconsin Employment Relations Bd., 336 U.S.

employer may undertake to impose sanctions upon the strikers. Its ability to do so, however, will be limited by the fact that striking employees retain their protected status as "employees",[353] and may not be punished for striking against an employer's unfair labor practices. Thus, if an unfair labor practice strike occurs, the employees who have not participated in strike misconduct or been discharged for cause [354] are entitled to reinstatement [355] and to vote in all elections,[356] even if replacements have been hired. In an economic strike, however, the employer may hire replacements and need not reemploy the striking employees,[357] but, because the strike is still protected activity, the employer may not discriminate against a striker on account of his strike activity,[358] unless that activity itself constitutes misconduct.[359]

When professional athletes resort to the strike as a means of coercing their employer's acquiescence or capitulation to their demands, therefore, they will encounter a substantial body of law that will determine the scope and permissibility of their actions, and of their employer's response, as well as the sanctions that may be applied to each. Although there have been numerous strikes in professional sports,[360] there has not yet been much opportunity for the courts or the NLRB to evaluate the conduct of either party. The activity of the parties during the strikes does, however, provide some basis for applying several of the principles noted.

Each of the past strikes in professional sports appears to have been in support of the collective bargaining position of the players' association in question, and thus would have been economic in nature. Thus, the owners would have had the ability to replace the striking players with others who were not on strike — for example, rookies, minor leaguers or free agents — with no specific obligation to rehire the strikers when the strike was settled. During the strikes, the owners frequently stated that they would play regularly scheduled games with replacements.[361] In the baseball strike in 1972, however, the owners allowed nine

---

245, 93 L. Ed. 651, 69 S. Ct. 516 (1949) (intermittent work stoppage); NLRB v. Fansteel Metallurgical Corp., 306 U.S. 240, 83 L. Ed. 627, 59 S. Ct. 490 (1939) (seizure of employer's property). In determining whether particular activity will be protected, the basic test is simply whether it would justify an employer in discharging the participating employees. Elk Lumber Co., 91 NLRB 333 (1950).

353. NLRA § 2(3); *see* NLRB v. Fleetwood Trailer Co., 389 U.S. 375, 378, 19 L. Ed. 2d 614, 88 S. Ct. 543 (1967).

354. NLRA § 10(c).

355. NLRB v. Mackay Radio & Tel. Co., 304 U.S. 333, 345, 82 L. Ed. 1381, 58 S. Ct. 904 (1938).

356. Tampa Sand & Material Co., 137 NLRB 1549 (1962).

357. NLRB v. Mackay Radio & Tel. Co., 309 U.S. 333, 345-46, 82 L. Ed. 1381, 58 S. Ct. 904 (1938).

358. *See, e.g.,* NLRB v. Fleetwood Trailer Co., 389 U.S. 375, 380-81, 19 L. Ed. 2d 614, 88 S. Ct. 543 (1967) (if strikers are available for reinstatement, the employer cannot hire new employees absent a legitimate and substantial business justification); NLRB v. Great Dane Trailers, Inc., 388 U.S. 26, 34, 18 L. Ed. 2d 1027, 87 S. Ct. 1792 (1967) (employer cannot accord vacation benefits depending upon strike activity); NLRB v. Erie Resistor Corp., 373 U.S. 221, 232-37, 10 L. Ed. 2d 308, 83 S. Ct. 1139 (1963) (employer cannot grant "super-seniority" to those who did not remain on strike); NLRB v. Mackay Radio & Tel. Co., 304 U.S. 33, 346-47, 82 L. Ed. 1381, 58 S. Ct. 904 (1938) (unfair labor practice when employer fails to rehire those who were active in the strike.)

359. *See, e.g.,* NLRB v. Fansteel Metallurgical Corp., 306 U.S. 240, 252, 83 L. Ed. 627, 59 S. Ct. 490 (1939); Firestone Tire & Rubber Co. v. NLRB, 449 F.2d 511, 513 (5th Cir. 1971).

It is also to be noted that what began as an economic strike may become an unfair labor practice strike. *See* NLRB v. Waukesha Lime & Stone Co., 343 F.2d 504, 508 (7th Cir. 1965). *See generally* Stewart, *Conversion of Strikes: Economic to Unfair Labor Practice — I,* 45 VA. L. REV. 1332 (1949), *II,* 49 VA. L. REV. 1297 (1963).

360. *See* § 6.01.

361. *See* § 6.01.

regular season days to pass without using replacements to play the scheduled games. Although replacements and non-strikers were used to play exhibition games during the football strike in 1974, attendance at the games slumped badly from previous years, suggesting the limited utility of this particular option.

The results of the past strikes are thus inconclusive in terms of identifying the extent to which the parties will utilize the maximum leverage that is lawfully available to them. The owners certainly recognize their ability to replace strikers, though on the one occasion when it was done the fans did not turn out in large numbers to watch the games. Although the owners would also have the power to permanently replace economic strikers, this seems unlikely in professional sports where "name" players are concerned. With respect to marginal players, however, strike activity may have a real impact. After the 1974 football strike, for example, it was reported that marginal players were hurt by their participation in the strike, since their positions had in many cases been filled by rookies and free agents, and many were cut from their teams.[362] It was also reported that some player representatives had been cut as a result of their strike activity. While economic strikers do not, as noted above, have extensive rights, an Administrative Law Judge found in *National Football League Management Council (II)*,[362.1] that the rights of the representatives had been violated when they were not given a "fair opportunity" to make their respective teams.[362.2] In reaching this conclusion, the judge stated that

> This is not to say that a striker who is a union official must be accorded special privileges not accorded other strikers, or preferences not accorded nonstrikers. It is only to say that he is protected from discriminatory conditions of reinstatement.
>
> On termination of a strike, an economic striker is entitled to reinstatement to his former position unless he has been permanently replaced in the meantime.
>
> Here reinstatement to the status quo meant reinstating the veterans to their prior positions on the squad.

In contrast to the power of the the players to strike, the primary economic weapon available to the owners is the ability to "lockout" [363] — that is, the power to withhold employment — as a means of economically coercing acquiescence at the bargaining table.[364] Although this power was at one time relatively restricted,[365] it is now quite clear that it is a perfectly permissible means of

---

362. N. Y. Times, August 29, 1974, at 39, col. 1.
362.1. Case No. 2-CA-13379 (June 30, 1976 — see notes 110.1 and 217.7 *supra*).
362.2. *See* § 6.03.
363. In addition to the lockout, the employer may also permanently replace economic strikers, *see* notes 357-59 *supra* and accompanying text, terminate his entire business, *see* Textile Workers v. Darlington Mfg. Co., 380 U.S. 263, 13 L. Ed. 2d 827, 85 S. Ct. 994 (1965), or stockpile supplies and products to withstand a work stoppage. *See* American Ship Building Co. v. NLRB, 380 U.S. 300, 316, 13 L. Ed. 2d 855, 85 S. Ct. 955 (1965).
364. NLRB v. Truck Drivers Local 449, 353 U.S. 87, 92-93, 1 L. Ed. 2d 676, 77 S. Ct. 643 (1957); Betts Cadillac-Olds, Inc., 96 NLRB 268 (1951).
365. This relatively restricted permissibility was the result of the fact that the Board held lockouts to be presumptively unlawful, except in single-employer lockouts, *see* Betts Cadillac Olds, Inc., 96 NLRB 268 (1951) (to avert immobilization of autos brought in for repair); International Shoe Co., 93 NLRB 907 (1951) (to forestall "quickie" strikes); Duluth Bottling Ass'n, 48 NLRB 1335 (1943) (to avoid spoilage due to sudden work stoppage); Link-Belt Co., 26 NLRB 227 (1940) (to prevent sit-down strikes), and in multi-employer situations where a "whipsaw-strike" tactic was utilized by the union. *See* Buffalo Linen Supply Co., 109 NLRB 447 (1954), *rev'd sub. nom.* Truck Drivers Local 449 v. NLRB, 231 F.2d 110 (2d Cir. 1956), *rev'd,* 353 U.S. 87, 1 L. Ed. 2d 676, 77 S. Ct. 643 (1957).

economic coercion, so long as bargaining is pursued in good faith and the lockout is utilized only after the bargaining process has reached stalemate or impasse.

The extent to which the lockout may be permissibly employed is best illustrated by *American Ship Building Company v. NLRB*,[366] where an impasse had developed after good-faith bargaining. Fearing that the union would call a strike at the most profitable time of the year, and thus produce the greatest economic leverage, the employer locked out the employees until an agreement was reached some two months later. In upholding the employer's action, the Supreme Court observed that the use of a temporary layoff solely as a means of bringing economic pressure to bear upon the union following an impasse in prior good-faith bargaining would not be an unfair labor practice.[367] This practice would not, it said, interfere with the right to bargain collectively [368] or the right to strike,[369] and would not of itself be evidence of a discriminatory animus toward the union involved.[370] Although there was considerable objection on the Court to the majority's opinion,[371] *American Ship* does accord to employers a potent economic weapon with which to wage economic warfare. This was made even more clear by *NLRB v. Brown*,[372] a companion to *American Ship*, in which the Court upheld the temporary use of non-union personnel to replace union members locked-out by a multi-employer group after a union had struck one of its members.[373] It has also been indicated that a pre-impasse lockout may be justified if there is present a good faith bargaining effort.[374]

Use of the lockout is not, however, without limitation. In analyzing its use in particular circumstances, the primary inquiry will be the motivation of the

---

366. 380 U.S. 300, 13 L. Ed. 2d 855, 85 S. Ct. 955 (1965).

367. *Id.* at 308-18.

368. The right to bargain collectively, the Court observed, "does not entail any 'right' to insist on one's position free from economic disadvantage." *Id.* at 309.

369. In this regard, the Court observed that

> [i]t is true that recognition of the lockout deprives the union of exclusive control of the timing and duration of work stoppages calculated to influence the result of collective bargaining negotiations, but there is nothing in the statute which would imply that the right to strike "carries with it" the right exclusively to determine the timing and duration of all work stoppages. The right to strike as commonly understood is the right to cease work — nothing more. No doubt a union's bargaining power would be enhanced if it possessed not only the simple right to strike but also the power exclusively to determine when work stoppages should occur, but the Act's provisions are not indefinitely elastic, content-free forms to be shaped in whatever manner the Board might think best conforms to the proper balance of bargaining power.
>
> Thus, we cannot see that the employer's use of a lockout solely in support of a legitimate bargaining position is in any way inconsistent with the right to bargain collectively or with the right to strike. *Id.* at 310.

370. *See* NLRB v. Dalton Brick & Tile Corp., 301 F.2d 886 (5th Cir. 1962); American Brake Shoe Co. v. NLRB, 244 F.2d 489 (7th Cir. 1957).

371. In concurring opinions, one by Mr. Justice White, 380 U.S. at 318-27, and the other by Mr. Justice Goldberg, joined by Chief Justice Warren, *id.* at 327-42, it was, essentially, stated that the facts of *American Ship* justified the result, but that the Court should have not utilized such broad language to reach it, inasmuch as other cases would not be quite so clear.

372. 380 U.S. 278, 13 L. Ed. 2d 839, 85 S. Ct. 980 (1965).

373. *Id.* at 288-90. In reaching this opinion, however, the Court was careful, as it was not in *American Ship*, to tie its decision to the facts at hand. *Id.* at 287-88. *See generally* Oberer, *Lockouts and the Law: The Impact of* American Ship Building *and* Brown Food, 51 CORNELL L.Q. 193 (1966).

374. Darling & Co., 171 NLRB 801 (1968), *enforced sub nom.* Lane v. NLRB, 418 F.2d 1208 (D.C. Cir. 1969). *See also* Sargent-Welch Scientific Co., 208 N.L.R.B. 811 (1974); Hess Oil Virgin Is. Corp., 205 N.L.R.B. 23 (1973).

employer for its utilization.[375] When it is used defensively — that is, when it is used only to defend against actual or threatened union action — as it was in *American Ship* and *Brown*,[376] the lockout is clearly permissible under a motive inquiry. Where the lockout is used offensively, however, the motivation is more likely to be non-economic. Thus, although the lockout has been allowed as an offensive measure, it is not clear whether an employer may couple it with the use of non-union replacements.[377] The lockout will be unlawful if used by an employer who demonstrates a hostility to the principles of collective bargaining;[378] who has engaged in bad-faith bargaining;[379] who uses the lockout as a means to avoid bargaining,[380] to interfere with union organizational efforts,[381] to retaliate against striking employees,[382] or to punish those engaged in union activities;[383] or who has no substantial business interest to justify its action.[384] In short, when the lockout is inherently destructive of employee rights and does not support a legitimate and substantial economic objective of the employer, it will be unlawful.[385]

Just as the strike has been used frequently by the players in professional sports, so has the lockout been used by the owners. It was used briefly in the football dispute of 1968, and resulted in a 17-day lockout during the 1970 impasse.[386] As it has been used on these occasions, the lockout is clearly a lawful economic sanction of the owners, and could be used as a viable bargaining tactic

---

375. Thus, in *American Ship,* the Court observed that

> [p]roper analysis of the problem demands that the simple intention to support the employer's bargaining position as to compensation and the like be distinguished from a hostility to the process of collective bargaining which could suffice to render a lockout unlawful.

380 U.S. at 309. *See also* NLRB v. Great Dane Trailers, Inc., 388 U.S. 26, 32-34, 18 L. Ed. 2d 1027, 87 S. Ct. 1792 (1967); NLRB v. Brown, 380 U.S. 278, 289-92, 13 L. Ed. 2d 839, 85 S. Ct. 980 (1965); Inland Trucking Co. v. NLRB, 440 F.2d 562, 565 (7th Cir.), *cert. denied,* 404 U.S. 858, 30 L. Ed. 2d 100, 92 S. Ct. 106 (1971); Lane v. NLRB, 418 F.2d 1208, 1210-12 (D.C. Cir. 1969).

376. Thus, in *American Ship* the lockout was in response to a threatened, and feared, strike during the peak business season which would cripple the business, 380 U.S. at 303-04, and in *Brown* the union had already struck one member of the multi-employer group. *Id.* at 281. *See* Inland Trucking Co. v. NLRB, 440 F.2d 562, 564-65 (7th Cir.), *cert. denied,* 404 U.S. 858, 30 L. Ed. 2d 100, 92 S. Ct. 106 (1971).

377. *Compare* Inland Trucking Co. v. NLRB, 440 F.2d 562, 564-65 (7th Cir.), *cert. denied,* 404 U.S. 858, 30 L. Ed. 2d 100, 92 S. Ct. 106 (1971) (such action held to be *per se* impermissible) *with* Inter-Collegiate Press, Graphic Arts Div. v. NLRB, 486 F.2d 837 (8th Cir. 1973), *cert. denied,* 416 U.S. 938, 40 L. Ed. 2d 288, 94 S. Ct. 1939 (1974) (allowing such procedures); Johns Manville Products Corp., 223 NLRB No. 189 (1976). The issue had specifically not been decided in *American Ship.* 380 U.S. at 308 n.8. *See generally* 85 HARV. L. REV. 680 (1972); 50 TEX. L. REV. 552 (1972).

378. American Ship Building Co. v. NLRB, 380 U.S. 300, 309, 13 L. Ed. 2d 855, 85 S. Ct. 955 (1965).

379. NLRB v. Bagel Bakers Council of Greater New York, 434 F.2d 884, 888-89 (2d Cir. 1970), *cert. denied,* 402 U.S. 908, 28 L. Ed. 2d 648, 91 S. Ct. 1380 (1971).

380. *See, e.g.,* NLRB v. Tak Trak, Inc., 293 F.2d 270 (9th Cir.), *cert. denied,* 368 U.S. 938, 7 L. Ed. 2d 337, 82 S. Ct. 379 (1961). *See also* NLRB v. Truck Drivers Local 449, 353 U.S. 87, 93 n.18, 1 L. Ed. 2d 676, 77 S. Ct. 643 (1957).

381. *See, e.g.,* NLRB v. Somerset Classics, Inc., 193 F.2d 613 (2d Cir.), *cert. denied,* 344 U.S. 816, 97 L. Ed. 635, 73 S. Ct. 10 (1952); NLRB v. Long Lake Lumber Co., 138 F.2d 363 (9th Cir. 1943).

382. NLRB v. Golden State Bottling Co., 353 F.2d 667 (9th Cir. 1965).

383. *See, e.g.,* Sagiman Aggregates, Inc., 191 N.L.R.B. No. 104 (1971).

384. NLRB v. David Friedland Painting Co., Inc., 377 F.2d 983, 988-89 (3rd Cir. 1967); *see also* Newspaper Drivers & Handlers' Local 372 v. NLRB, 404 F.2d 1159 (6th Cir. 1968), *cert. denied,* 395 U.S. 923, 23 L. Ed. 2d 240, 89 S. Ct. 1775 (1969).

385. International Molders & Allied Workers Local 155 v. NLRB, 442 F.2d 742, 747 (D.C. Cir. 1971); Lane v. NLRB, 418 F.2d 1208, 1212 (D.C. Cir. 1969).

386. *See* § 6.01.

in the future, so long as the owners are careful to observe the limits that the courts have placed upon its use.

When economic sanctions are considered as bargaining tools in professional sports, there is ample authority to evaluate the permissibility of particular actions under the circumstances. Since there is nothing in the nature of professional sports that would justify exceptional rules, moreover, the ordinary strike-lockout rules of industrial labor relations will apply with full force to economic warfare in sporting disputes as will all the rest of the federal labor law.

§ 6.10. Grievances and Arbitration.

An additional element of the collective bargaining environment that has become a common part of the relations between owners and professional athletes is the grievance-arbitration procedure, which is commonly included in collective bargaining agreements. The arbitration provision will be adopted as a means of establishing an exclusive procedure for resolving the types of grievances specified in the contractual provision, and of achieving "peace" between the parties.[387] Such arbitrable grievances may typically include those concerning injuries, salaries, fines or othe.· sanctions, and the interpretation of the provisions of the standard player contract and relevant league documents.[388] The arbitration provision may also specify the procedure to be followed in seeking resolution of a grievance and provide that the decision will at some point become final.

Since the content and interpretation of arbitration agreements in professional sports is discussed in considerable detail in an earlier chapter,[389] our discussion here will focus primarily upon the labor and collective bargaining issues which arise. The principles discussed in the earlier chapter will be repeated only to the extent necessary to provide a proper perspective.

The basic point that should be made with respect to grievance provisions is that they are mandatory subjects of bargaining about which the parties have a duty to bargain in good faith.[390] Thus, the form and content of the arbitration agreement are subjects that should be resolved at the bargaining table to the mutual satisfaction of both parties. Since the arrangement is a subject of bargaining, moreover, the parties may generally establish whatever terms they desire in the agreement.

As a result of the fact that agreements to arbitrate will frequently not be self-executing, the first step for a party desiring arbitration will be to follow

387. United Steelworkers v. Warrior & Gulf Navigation Co., 363 U.S. 574, 4 L. Ed. 2d 1409, 80 S. Ct. 1347 (1960). This is, indeed the congressionally sanctioned procedure. See Labor Management Relations Act § 203(d), 29 U.S.C. § 173(d) (1970). See generally Gregory, Arbitration of Grievance Under Collective Labor Agreements, 1 GA. L. REV. 20 (1966).

388. See generally Arbitration in Professional Athletics, in PROCEEDINGS OF THE TWENTY-SIXTH ANNUAL MEETING, NATIONAL ACADEMY OF ARBITRATORS 108 (1974) (describing arbitration arrangements in football and baseball, and the experience that has been obtained in the process); Seitz, Footnotes to Baseball Salary Arbitration, 29 ARB. J. 98 (1974) (discussion by arbitrator in baseball salary arbitrations of 1974, which used the "high-low" procedure); Note, Arbitration of Grievance and Salary Disputes in Professional Baseball: Evolution of a System of Private Law, 60 CORNELL L. REV. 1049 (1975).

389. See §§ 4.15-4.20.

390. See § 6.08.

the agreement established procedures. If the other party is reluctant to arbitrate then action may be taken to enforce the agreement by judicial order.[391] Although courts originally followed the rule that arbitration agreements were not judicially enforceable,[392] the Supreme Court has made it clear that they are specifically enforceable, and that the courts are to fashion a substantive common law from the policy of the labor laws for the purpose of enforcing the agreements.[393] Arbitration agreements will also be enforced if contained in contracts other than collective bargaining agreements.[394]

When the courts are called upon to enforce arbitration agreements, their inquiry will be limited "to ascertaining whether the party seeking arbitration is making a claim which on its face is governed by the [arbitration] contract" and will not weigh the merits of the grievance in question.[395] Doubts as to the coverage of the arbitration clause will, moreover, be resolved in favor of coverage.[396] In *Kansas City Royals Baseball Corporation v. Major League Baseball Players Association,*[397] for example, an arbitration provision had empowered an arbitration panel to "interpret, apply or determine compliance with the provisions of agreements" between the owners and players in baseball. When a grievance was filed with respect to the reserve system, the panel held that it was within the scope of its jurisdiction. This conclusion was upheld in a subsequent challenge. The court noted that a broad arbitration provision could be deemed to exclude a given category of grievances only if there was an express exclusion or the terms of exclusion were ambiguous and there was a record which contained "forceful evidence" that the parties intended to exclude the grievance in question. Although it found that the agreement at hand was ambiguous on the exclusion issue, the court held that the reserve system grievance was within the arbitrators' jurisdiction because the record indicated that the parties did not intend to exclude reserve system grievances.[398]

The second basic issue involved in arbitration proceedings will be the extent to which a reluctant party may attempt to avoid arbitration by seeking to have the courts or the NLRB decide the dispute. This essentially involves a question of when the courts and the NLRB will defer to the arbitration agreement. As a general rule, deferral will be proper where the dispute in question is covered by the agreement. When a party to a collective bargaining agreement with an arbitration provision seeks to have an arbitrable dispute resolved in the courts,

---

391. *See* § 4.15; *see generally,* Rosen, *Arbitration in the Entertainment Industry—Selected Problems and Suggestions,* 7 J. BEVERLY HILLS BAR ASS'N 32, 36-37 (Nov.-Dec. 1973).

392. *See e.g.,* Red Cross Line v. Atlantic Fruit Co., 264 U.S. 109, 68 L. Ed. 582, 44 S. Ct. 274 (1924).

393. Textile Workers Union v. Lincoln Mills, 353 U.S. 448, 1 L. Ed. 2d 972, 77 S. Ct. 912 (1957). In reaching this conclusion, the court relied upon § 301(a) of the Labor Management Relations Act, 29 U.S.C. § 185(a) (1970). *See* § 4.15.

394. Erving v. Virginia Squires Basketball Club, 468 F.2d 1064 (2d Cir. 1972). *See* Federal Arbitration Act, 9 U.S.C. § 4.

395. United Steelworkers v. American Mfg. Co., 363 U.S. 564, 4 L. Ed. 2d 1403, 80 S. Ct. 1343 (1960).

396. United Steelworkers v. Warrior & Gulf Navigation Co., 363 U.S. 574, 4 L. Ed. 2d 1409, 80 S. Ct. 1347 (1960). *See also* Gateway Coal Co. v. UMW, 414 U.S. 368, 38 L. Ed. 2d 583, 94 S. Ct. 629 (1974).

397. 532 F.2d 615 (8th Cir. 1976).

398. 532 F.2d at 629-30.

therefore, the courts will properly defer to the arbitral procedures. The operation of this principle is illustrated by *Davis v. Pro Basketball, Inc.*[399] There, a basketball player sought to bring an action in a federal court against his team for breach of his player contract. The collective bargaining agreement then in force, however, specified that "[a]ny dispute involving the interpretation or application of . . . a Uniform Player Contract . . . shall be resolved in accordance with the Grievance and Arbitration Procedure . . . ." In light of this provision, the court concluded that the dispute must be submitted to arbitration under the procedures required by the collective bargaining agreement.[400] Similarly, in *Erving v. Virginia Squires Basketball Club*,[401] where a star professional basketball player had sought to have a federal district court set aside a player's contract that he had entered with the team, the court held that the arbitration clause in the contract required that the action be stayed pending the arbitration proceeding.[402]

While the complaining party may seek to avoid arbitration through resort to the NLRB, it, too, will normally defer to the arbitral process. Although the NLRB's power is specifically stated to be unaffected by any other means of adjustment that may have been agreed upon,[403] and it has been held that arbitral awards do not alter its jurisdiction,[404] the Board has made it clear that it will favor deferral to the arbitration process when the parties have so agreed. The primary statement of this policy came in *Collyer Insulated Wire*,[405] where an employer and a union had executed a collective bargaining agreement, but had

---

399. 381 F. Supp. 1 (S.D.N.Y. 1974).

400. 381 F. Supp. at 4. The court also rejected the players' contentions that the team had waived the arbitration procedures, and that the procedures did not apply if there was a modification of the Uniform Player Contract. *Id.*

401. 468 F.2d 1064 (2d Cir. 1972).

402. The action in *Erving* was based upon the Federal Arbitration Act, which provides that a federal court may stay any suit which involves issues which are referable to arbitration under a written agreement. 9 U.S.C. § 3. Although the Act applies to only arbitration provisions in contracts "evidencing a transaction involving commerce," *id.* § 2, it seems clear that professional sports are covered by that provision. Erving v. Virginia Squires Basketball Club, 468 F.2d 1064, 1068-69 (2d Cir. 1972). *See* § 4.15.

With respect to the Federal Arbitration Act, it should be noted that it is not yet clear whether it applies to collective bargaining agreements. Although the Supreme Court did not decide the issue in *Textile Workers v. Lincoln Mills,* 353 U.S. 448, 1 L. Ed. 2d 972, 77 S. Ct. 912 (1957), and Mr. Justice Frankfurter explicitly rejected its applicability, *id.* at 466, the lower courts have taken the position that it does apply and that there is nothing in it that requires different treatment for labor than for commercial agreements. *See, e.g.,* Electronics Corp. v. Elec. Workers, 492 F.2d 1255 (1st Cir. 1974); International Ass'n of Machinists v. General Elec. Co., 406 F.2d 1046 (2d Cir. 1969); Paramount Bag Mfg. Co., Inc. v. Rubberized Novelty & Plastic Fabric Workers, 353 F. Supp. 1131 (E.D.N.Y. 1973). *See generally* Burstein, *The United States Arbitration Act—A Reevaluation,* 3 VILL. L. REV. 125 (1958); Smith & Jones, *The Supreme Court and Labor Dispute Arbitration: The Emerging Federal Law,* 63 MICH. L. REV. 751, 801-02 (1965); Note, *Labor Arbitration: Appealing the Procedural Decisions of Arbitrators,* 59 MINN. L. REV. 109, 114-19 (1974).

403. NLRA § 10(a).

404. Carey v. Westinghouse Elec. Corp., 375 U.S. 261, 11 L. Ed 2d 320, 84 S. Ct. 401 (1964).

405. 192 N.L.R.B. 837 (1971). It should be noted that a strong dissent was filed by members Fanning and Jenkins. *See also* Joseph Schlitz Brewing Co., 175 N.L.R.B. No. 23 (1969); International Harvester Co., 138 N.L.R.B. 923 (1962). *See generally* 18E T. KHEEL, LABOR LAW ch. 25 (1974); Miller, *Deferral to Arbitration—Temperance or Abstinence,* 7 GA. L. REV. 595 (1973); Teple, *Deferral to Arbitration: Implications of NLRB Policy,* 29 ARB. J. 65 (1974).

not included a special wage increase that the employer desired for one category of employees. When subsequent negotiations failed to provide an agreement on the increase, the employer announced that it would unilaterally make an increase. The union then filed an unfair labor practice charge, and the employer contended that the dispute was covered by a broad arbitration provision in the collective bargaining agreement which was intended to provide the exclusive forum for resolving contract disputes. The Board agreed that deferral was proper in this type of case, stating that "disputes such as these can better be resolved by arbitrators with special skill and experience in deciding matters arising under established bargaining relationships . . . ."[406] In reaching this conclusion, it specifically noted that the parties had enjoyed a long and harmonious bargaining relationship, that the employer was willing to resort to arbitration under a clause that was "unquestionably broad enough to embrace [the] dispute," and that the dispute was eminently suited to arbitration since it involved the collective contract and its meaning.[407] The Board was careful to make clear, however, that it was not compelling the parties to arbitrate but was "merely giving full effect to their own voluntary agreements to submit all such disputes to arbitration, rather than permitting such agreements to be side-stepped and permitting the substitution of [Board] processes . . . ."[408] In subsequent decisions, the Board has substantially clarified the *Collyer* doctrine.[409] If the Board does defer, it will reassert its jurisdiction if one of the parties refuses to arbitrate.[410] Deferral is inappropriate, of course, if the issue before the Board is not covered by the arbitration agreement.[411]

The *Collyer* doctrine has not yet played an extensive role in the disputes that have arisen in professional sports, but its application in one case provides at least an illustration of scope of the doctrine and the circumstances in which the Board will not find deferral to be proper. In *National Football League Management Council (I)*,[412] the players' association had brought two unfair labor practices charges against the owners (the Council), who contended that the Board should exercise its deferral policy on the facts in dispute. The charges involved a rule which imposed fines upon players who left the bench during a fight on the field, which the union alleged was unilaterally imposed by the owners, and the installation of artificial turf as a playing surface, about which the union said the owners had not bargained in good faith. The collective bargaining agreement

---

406. 192 N.L.R.B. at 839.

407. 192 N.L.R.B. at 842.

408. 192 N.L.R.B. at 842. *See also* William E. Arnold Co. v. Carpenters, 417 U.S. 12, 40 L. Ed. 2d 620, 94 S. Ct. 2069 (1974).

Even though the Board may defer to arbitration, it does have power to resolve arbitrable disputes that are necessary to the adjudication of unfair labor practices. *See* NLRB v. Strong, 393 U.S. 357, 21 L. Ed. 2d 546, 89 S. Ct. 541 (1969); NLRB v. C & C Plywood Corp., 385 U.S. 421, 17 L. Ed. 2d 486, 87 S. Ct. 559 (1967).

409. *See* General American Transportation Corp., 228 N.L.R.B. No. 102 (1977); Roy Robinson, Inc., d/b/a Roy Robinson Chevrolet, 228 N.L.R.B. No. 103 (1977); 18E T. KHEEL, LABOR LAW § 25.02 (1974).

410. Medical Manors, Inc., d/b/a Community Convalescent Hosp., 203 N.L.R.B. No. 124 (1973) (employer engaged in "foot-dragging" by insisting upon unfounded preconditions to arbitration).

411. Adelson, Inc., 163 N.L.R.B. 365 (1967).

412. National Football League Players' Ass'n v. NLRB, 203 N.L.R.B. 958 (1973), *remanded on other issue,* 503 F.2d 12 (8th Cir. 1974).

provided a non-injury grievance procedure for all claims concerning the interpretation or application of the standard player contracts or league documents to the extent that their interpretation related to wages, hours and working conditions, or their application to an individual player. The procedure called for the submission of a written grievance to a team within 60 days of the occurrence of the action that gave rise to it. If the matter was not then settled within 10 days, it would be referred to the commissioner who would be the sole and final arbitrator. The Board concluded that *Collyer* deferral was not necessary on either issue. With respect to the bench fines, the Board observed that the commissioner "was an intimate participant in the events surrounding the dispute," and under such circumstances it "would be hard pressed to conclude that [he] is a disinterested party . . . ."[413] The Board did not reach the question of deferral on the artificial turf issue, for it found that the owners had not taken any action that would breach either their contractual or statutory duties.[414] However, the Administrative Law Judge had stated that deferral would not be proper because the agreement did not cover the grievance in question.[415]

In light of the fact that the commissioner in some sports may be granted authority to act as arbitrator of some disputes, the Board's conclusion that deferral would not be proper on the bench fine issue because the commissioner was not a disinterested arbitrator, poses substantial question as to whether deferral will be possible in many sports disputes. The Board apparently found the need for a "disinterested" arbitrator in the general policy requirements of the NLRA, but it is not clear why the arbitrator must be disinterested if he is agreed upon by both parties in bona fide collective bargaining.[416] There does not appear to be any such requirement in *Collyer,* where the Board concluded that "[w]hen the parties have contractually committed themselves to mutually agreeable procedures for resolving their disputes . . . we are of the view that those procedures should be afforded full opportunity to function."[417] It also observed that if the process chosen by the parties failed to function consistently with the NLRA, then its reserved jurisdiction would guarantee that statutory rights would not be sacrificed.[418] Given this generalized policy of deference to the agreed upon procedures for dispute resolution, the conclusion of the Board in *NFL Management Council (I)* seems inappropriate. Although disinterest of an arbitrator might be an appropriate basis for not deferring in situations where the other party was unaware of the bias at the time of agreement or designation, or where there has been no meaningful bargaining over the issue, it should have much less weight where the status and "interestedness" of the arbitrator in the type of grievance in question was known to all parties at the time the agreement was negotiated. This seems especially true in professional sports, where the powers of the commissioner have been a frequent topic of dispute between the

413. 203 N.L.R.B. at 959.

414. 203 N.L.R.B. at 960, n.5.

415. 203 N.L.R.B. at 966.

416. *See* §§ 4.19, 6.04. *See* Commonwealth Coatings Corp. v. Continental Casualty Co., 393 U.S. 145, 21 L. Ed. 2d 301, 89 S. Ct. 337 (1968) (arbitrators must disclose partiality).

417. 192 N.L.R.B. at 842-43.

418. 192 N.L.R.B. at 842.

players and the owners.[419] In short, it would appear that the policy goals that *Collyer* was designed to foster are frustrated when the Board refuses to defer to an arbitration arrangement, which was the result of bona fide collective bargaining, merely because the arbitrator who has been mutually designated is found to be not disinterested, and where that interest was not only known to the parties but also a subject of negotiation. Indeed, not deferring in such situations allows the agreed upon procedures to be "side-stepped and permitting the substitution of [Board] processes"—specifically what the Board said it was avoiding in *Collyer*.[420]

In applying the *Collyer* doctrine to professional sports, then, there will be several hurdles to overcome. The first will be establishing that there is a long and harmonious collective bargaining relationship between the parties, and that the employer has not demonstrated enmity toward employee or union rights under the NLRB. Although the period of the bargaining relation in professional sports covers less than a decade, the actual length of the relationship will not be determinative.[421] Similarly, the use of economic sanctions by either or both parties will not prevent deferral, unless they constitute a deliberate disregard of statutory obligations[422]—a situation that has not yet been found in professional sports. The second hurdle will be whether the grievance in question is covered by the applicable arbitration agreement. This should pose little difficulty where the agreement is worded broadly enough to cover all grievances, but as indicated by the administrative law judge's view in *NFL Management Council (I)*, the wording of an agreement may make it difficult to determine whether the grievance is covered.[423] The most difficult problem will be the necessity of establishing that deferral would serve the purposes of the NLRA. This will be especially important in situations like *NFL Management Council (I)*, where the arbitrator designated in the agreement is the commissioner, who may be involved in the factual dispute which he or she is supposed to arbitrate. In such situations, the Board may not defer because deferral to an interested arbitrator would not serve the policies of the Act. As indicated above, however, it is believed that the Board's view is too narrow, at least in situations where the interest of the commissioner was known to the

---

419. *See* §§ 4.19, 6.04.

With respect to the inclusion of the commissioner as an arbitrator in a collective bargaining agreement, it is of interest to note that although the players' association in football agreed to such inclusion, it has stridently taken the position that it is not a reasonable procedure. This approach, of course, prevailed in the *NFL Management Council (I)* case. Indeed, in a discussion of arbitration in professional sports, the executive director of the players' association identified it as "comical," and in detail described the difficulties that the procedure presented in practice. *See* PROCEEDINGS OF THE TWENTY-SIXTH ANNUAL MEETING, NATIONAL ACADEMY OF ARBITRATORS 126-28 (1974). He did, however, observe that the commissioner arbitration system had been the result of collective bargaining, in which the players had unsuccessfully attempted to obtain "impartial" arbitration. *Id.* at 122. The response of the labor counsel for the owners was, predictably enough, that the procedure should bind the parties since it was the result of collective bargaining, and could be changed at the next bargaining session. *Id.* at 135-36.

420. It should also be noted in this respect that the interest of an arbitrator has not been a ground for not enforcing commercial arbitration awards where all parties are duly notified of the interests that are present. *See* § 4.19.

421. *See, e.g.,* L.E.M. d/b/a Southwest Engraving Co., 198 N.L.R.B. No. 99 (1972); Coppus Eng'r Corp., 195 N.L.R.B. 595 (1972).

422. *See* 18E T. KHEEL, LABOR LAW § 25.02[1][c] (1974).

423. *See* note 415 *supra*.

parties at the time the procedure was agreed upon and where the agreement was the result of bona fide collective bargaining.

Apart from the question of the complaining parties' access to judicial or administrative review, the issue will also arise as to whether the use of economic pressure to support a grievance is consistent with an agreement to arbitrate. This issue would arise, for example, if a union instituted a strike over a particular dispute, rather than pursue the remedy provided by an arbitration agreement. In such a situation, a question would be whether an injunction could be granted to compel the striking union to cease its strike activity and proceed with arbitration. Since the Norris-LaGuardia Act generally precludes the issuance of injunctions in labor disputes,[424] the Supreme Court originally followed the rule that injunctions would not issue.[425] That position has, however, been overruled, in light of the fact that without the ability to enjoin such strikes the effectiveness of arbitration agreements would be greatly reduced.[426] In reaching this conclusion, the Court stated that "a no-strike obligation, express or implied [in the collective bargaining agreement], is the *quid pro quo* for an undertaking by the employer to submit grievance disputes to the process of arbitration."[427] Thus, if the dispute in question is arbitrable, the players may be enjoined if they strike, as may be the owners if they seek to institute a lockout.[428]

When arbitration is undertaken, the basic issue will be whether the grievance is "arbitrable"—that is, whether it is within the range of matters that were intended to be resolved through the grievance procedure. As a general matter, the question of arbitrability is one that will be decided by the courts,[429] though in doing so the courts will resolve doubtful disputes in favor of arbitrability because "[t]he processing of even frivolous claims may have therapeutic values of which those who are not a part of the [employment] environment may be quite unaware."[430] The parties may, however, specifically provide that arbitrability shall be determined by the arbitrator, and in that event the issue will be withdrawn from the courts.[431] The question of arbitrability may also be determined by the Board as an implicit part of its decision as to whether it shall defer to the arbitration of a given dispute. Once it is determined that the dispute is arbitrable, it will then be necessary to determine what procedure will be followed in the arbitration proceeding. In most cases, the procedures will be specified in the agreement. The most difficult aspect of the procedure issue is

424. Norris-LaGuardia Act § 4, 29 U.S.C. § 104 (1970).

425. Sinclair Ref. Co. v. Atkinson, 370 U.S. 195, 8 L. Ed. 2d 440, 82 S. Ct. 1328 (1962).

426. Boys Markets, Inc. v. Retail Clerks Local 770, 398 U.S. 235, 26 L. Ed. 2d 199, 90 S. Ct. 1583 (1970). *But see* Buffalo Forge Co. v. United Steelworkers, 428 U.S. 397, 49 L. Ed. 2d 1022, 96 S. Ct. 3141 (*Boys Market* does not apply to sympathy strike not directed at a dispute with employer).

427. 398 U.S. at 249 (emphasis in original). *See also* William E. Arnold Co. v. Carpenters, 417 U.S. 12, 140 L. Ed. 2d 620, 94 S. Ct. 2069 (1974) (state court may enjoin); Gateway Coal Co. v. UMW, 414 U.S. 368, 38 L. Ed. 2d 583, 94 S. Ct. 629 (1974) (no-strike obligation implied in agreement). In addition to an injunction, it is also possible that a damage action would be available. *See* 18E T. KHEEL, LABOR LAW § 27.03 (1974).

428. Strikes and lockouts are considered at § 6.09.

429. United Steelworkers v. Warrior & Gulf Navigation Co., 363 U.S. 574, 583 n.7, 4 L. Ed. 2d 1409, 80 S. Ct. 1347 (1960).

430. United Steelworkers v. American Mfg. Co., 363 U.S. 564, 569, 4 L.Ed. 2d 1403, 80 S. Ct. 1343 (1960).

431. *See, e.g.,* Metal Prods. Workers Local 1645 v. Torrington Co., 358 F.2d 103 (2d Cir. 1966).

the extent to which the courts may require that the procedures adopted by the parties meet more generalized legal requirements, such as procedural due process of law [432]—a question that we have considered in detail in the earlier discussion.[433]

Once an arbitration decision has been reached, a significant issue arises concerning the extent to which the Board and the courts will honor the decision. Although the Board's decision will clearly prevail in the event that it finds the arbitrator's conclusion to be incorrect,[434] the Board has indicated that it will honor such decisions so long as certain standards are met. Thus, an arbitral award will not be contravened by the Board where "[t]he proceedings appear to have been fair and regular, all parties agreed to be bound, and the decision . . . is not clearly repugnant to the purposes and policies of the Act."[435] Similarly, the Supreme Court has indicated that the courts will enforce an arbitrator's award so long as it is properly based on the arbitration agreement, even though the court might have reached a different result.[436] Awards may not be enforced, however, where the dispute is not covered by the agreement or where the arbitration was not properly convened or conducted. Thus, in *Professional Sports, Ltd. v. Virginia Squires Basketball Club Limited Partnership,*[437] the court held that a decision of the commissioner of the American Basketball Association was not enforceable, or binding, because it did not relate to a dispute covered by the agreement. The agreement had required final arbitration where there was a dispute over which party had contract rights to a player. In the case at hand, however, there was no dispute as to ownership (the parties had agreed to a sale of a contract), except to the extent that uncertainty was created by the commissioner's own action, so that the decision of the commissioner was not authorized by the agreement, and not, therefore, enforceable or binding in the federal courts.[438]

§ 6.11. Comment on Collective Bargaining in Professional Sports.

Collective bargaining is now a permanent part of professional sports in this country. Although it is as yet a young institution, having begun on a serious

---

432. *See, e.g.,* Board of Regents of State College v. Roth, 408 U.S. 564, 33 L. Ed. 2d 548, 92 S. Ct. 2701 (1972); Professional Sports, Ltd. v. Virginia Squires Basketball Club Ltd. Partnership, 373 F. Supp. 946 (W.D. Tex. 1974). These requirements are discussed in detail at §§ 1.28, 2.18.

433. *See* § 4.18.

434. Carey v. Westinghouse Elec. Corp., 375 U.S. 261, 11 L. Ed. 2d 320, 84 S. Ct. 401 (1964); NLRA § 10(a).

435. Spielberg Mfg. Co., 112 N.L.R.B. 1080 (1955). *See generally* 18E T. KHEEL, LABOR LAW § 25.01[2][b] (1974).

436. United Steelworkers v. Enterprise Wheel & Car Corp., 363 U.S. 593, 4 L. Ed. 2d 1424, 80 S. Ct. 1358 (1960); Portland Baseball Club, Inc. v. Kuhn, 368 F. Supp. 1004 (D. Ore. 1971), *aff'd,* 491 F.2d 1101 (9th Cir. 1974). *See also* Kansas City Royals Baseball Corp. v. Major League Baseball Players Ass'n, 532 F.2d 615 (8th Cir. 1976); Federal Arbitration Act, 9 U.S.C. § 9. Under the Federal Arbitration Act, a federal district court may vacate an arbitration award where it was procured by corruption, fraud or undue means, where the arbitrators were guilty of misconduct, or where the arbitrators exceeded their powers. 9 U.S.C. § 10.

The Supreme Court has recently indicated that the "finality" rule will not be applied in situations where a union's handling of a grievance violates its duty of fair representation. Hines v. Anchor Motor Freight, Inc., 424 U.S. 554 (1976). The duty of fair representation is considered at § 6.07.

437. 373 F. Supp. 946 (W.D. Tex. 1974).

438. Other aspects of the case are considered at § 4.18.

basis only in the late 1960's, collective bargaining has already had a substantial effect upon all involved in professional sports, and will continue to do so for the foreseeable future.

From a broad perspective, the bargaining process in sports functions in a manner that is customary in American labor relations.[439] The parties meet at the bargaining table to negotiate about the terms and conditions upon which employees of the industry shall be employed. Each side comes to the table with issues and positions that it will seek to impose upon the other and which it will be prepared to support by using economic sanctions (strikes and lockouts) if an impasse is reached in the negotiations. In addition to economic pressure, the period of contract negotiation is marked by the filing of unfair labor practice charges with the NLRB, and by the exchange of accusation, often of a distinctly vituperative nature, as to the motives and lack of good faith of the other party. After agreement is reached, the parties continue to have disputes over the provisions and their interpretations, and these disputes also result in the filing of charges and the melodramatic exchange of comment in the media.

Despite these similarities with labor relations in other industries, it is clear that professional sports is not just another industry. It is an entertainment business which commands the attention and admiration of a large segment of the population. Thus, when disputes erupt in sports bargaining, they produce a public response that is disproportionate to the economic significance of the industry. This may be a result of the status that has normally been accorded athletes in our society, or perhaps it is a function of the fact that many people enjoy spectator escapism and resent its being interrupted by labor disputes whose merits and implications may be imprecisely conveyed to the public. Whatever may be the reason for the public response, it is indicative of the public interest that many feel to be implicit in professional sports. This public interest is itself reflected in a general manner in the principles of the National Labor Relations Act, which apply to labor disputes in sports. It is also reflected in the more specific rounds of congressional hearings that are held on a nearly annual basis, in which different aspects of professional sports are analyzed to determine whether additional legislation is necessary to protect the public interest. The public nature of sports in general and labor disputes in particular is, or should be, important to those in professional sports because when it is felt that the public interest is not being served, then it can be assumed that appropriate legislation will be enacted to insure that it is served. For example, during the 44-day football strike in 1974 over the so-called "freedom issues," the chairman of a House committee advised the professional sports owners that if a fair contract compromise were not forthcoming in a short time, his committee would reevaluate the antitrust exemption that had earlier been given to the merger of the two football leagues.[440] This is, of course, the same process that occurs in the industries which have special significance to the nation's well-being.

---

439. It should be noted, however, that in Mackey v. National Football League, 407 F. Supp. 1000 (D. Minn. 1975), *modified,* 543 F.2d 606 (8th Cir. 1976), the court found that there had been no meaningful collective bargaining in professional football. If this conclusion were generally followed, then the statement in text would obviously require qualification.

440. *See* § 6.01, at note 58. *See also Hearings Before the House Subcomm. on Labor-Management Relations of the House Comm. on Education and Labor,* 94th Cong., 1st Sess. (1975) (oversight hearings on labor-management disputes in professional football).

Collective bargaining in professional sports has had its most direct effect upon the players and owners who are the participants in the bargaining process. The most apparent consequence of their entry into the collective bargaining arena is that the acts and policies of each are now judged in terms of their compliance with the requirements of the National Labor Relations Act. It is also beginning to have a more subtle effect. When the players' associations were formed in the mid-sixties, they had little bargaining power and in order to acquire it organized on a wide basis. The initial collective bargaining agreements changed few of the essential aspects of the employment situation and simply formalized many of the arrangements. As the process has continued, however, the ranks of the associations have closed, and they have acquired more solid bargaining power at the collective table. This increasing power has been reflected in changes in the terms and conditions of employment, and the beginning of a process in which the fundamental complaints of players are either being resolved or at least made the subject of bargaining.[441] This process is the grist of collective bargaining and indicates that the bargaining arrangement is functioning in the sports business.

Bargaining over these fundamental complaints has not, however, been conducted in a vacuum. It has been conducted concurrently with a spate of litigation in which athletes have used the antitrust laws to challenge the most basic rules of the leagues.[442] The plaintiff-athletes have invariably been members of the players' association, and in almost all cases the rules in question are otherwise mandatory subjects of bargaining. The concurrent processing of the same basic complaints both in collective bargaining and federal court litigation may have some significant consequences. The first involves the need to find a means of balancing the public interests reflected in voluntary collective bargaining agreements against the merits of the antitrust complaints which are filed with respect to the same basic issues. Although there is not as yet a definitive answer which strikes this balance, it appears that it will be done by an exemption from the antitrust laws for terms which have been the subject of bona fide collective bargaining, and the rigorous application of the antitrust laws in the absence of such bargaining.[443] If this view is taken by the courts, as seems fairly certain in one degree or another, then the parties will be precluded from challenging the results of collective bargaining in the courts but will, rather, be required to seek vindication of their grievances and objectives at the bargaining table.

The second effect of the concurrent existence of collective bargaining and rigorous antitrust litigation is to clearly define the legal status of the many aspects of professional sports which have for decades been ambiguous. If the courts uphold or invalidate the rules or procedures that are being challenged, then that action will have an inevitable effect upon the bargaining relationship of the parties. If it is decided that a given provision which the players find to be objectionable is in fact lawful under the antitrust laws or otherwise, then the players will have a difficult time winning concession at the bargaining table. If

441. This process is illustrated particularly well by the 1976 settlement in the National Basketball Association. *See* § 6.01, at notes 65-69.

442. *See* §§ 5.03, 5.07.

443. *See* §§ 5.04-.06.

it constitutes a mandatory subject of bargaining, the owners would be required to bargain about it, would not be required to reach an agreement and could use economic weapons in support of their bargaining position. If, on the other hand, it should be decided that the same provision is unlawful under the antitrust laws, but may be the subject of exemption if contained in a collective bargaining agreement, then the players will have acquired substantial new bargaining power; for if the owners wish to retain the provision in the structure of professional sports, then they must find a means of having it included in a collective bargaining agreement for exemption purposes. In short, as heretofore unanswered questions are answered by the courts, the relative bargaining position of each party may be significantly altered.

A third and related point is that the results of court litigation may have a pronounced effect upon the types of proposals presented at the collective bargaining table. If, for example, a traditional aspect of the structure of a sport (such as the draft system or option clause in football) is held to be illegal, the owners may, instead of seeking agreement for the term for antitrust exemption purposes, simply propose a new form for the collective bargaining agreement. Such a situation could drastically change the nature of the employment situation in professional athletics, and the interests of many players could be significantly changed.[444]

The potential for a dramatically changed employment situation perhaps brings the discussion full circle. Our discussion began with the players' associations being formed at a point when the players felt that they had common interests and were being abused as a class by their employers, but had little bargaining power. As the associations acquire more power, and as legal issues from related litigation are decided, it is not so clear that the players as a group will continue to have the same community of interests. As the bargaining situation matures, each group of players with similar interests may begin to view its interests as distinct from those of other players and seek to find a means of bargaining on their own. These players may find, however, that they have little success in this direction because of labor law principles that preclude such action and require that they seek vindication of their interests in the existing union (in which they may have little actual power). The collective bargaining process may require the individual to be subordinated to the collective good of his or her peers.

Perhaps the most important point that must be made about collective bargaining and professional sports is that it is an activity in which the public has a very real interest, and it is as a result of that interest that Congress enacted the National Labor Relations Act. The result of this legislative action and its judicial interpretation has been the creation of an extensive body of law which defines the relations between employers and employees in all industries, and establishes the rights and duties of all parties in the collective bargaining process. These principles were developed for regulating employment relations in general and have not been developed with sports in mind. Thus, when they are applied to labor disputes in the sports business, they may produce results that few foresaw when they entered the collective bargaining process, and would not have entered if they had known the results.

---

444. *See* §§ 6.04, 6.07.

CHAPTER 7

Federal Income Taxation of Sports Activities

INTRODUCTORY NOTE.

Before considering the federal income tax problems that may be involved in sports activities, it is important to specifically note that the following discussion is intended to be illustrative of the problems that may be present in the types of activities, and for the types of taxpayers, considered. Each subject will be treated in as much depth as is appropriate in a treatise of this nature, but the discussion is not intended to be a substitute for professional counsel. Rather, the following is only a general guide to the types of federal income taxation problems that may be present in specified types of sports activity.

As this book was going to press, Congress enacted the Revenue Act of 1978, which alters a few of the tax principles discussed in this chapter. Where provisions of the Act affect the discussion, an asterisk will be set in brackets — [*] — at the end of the pertinent footnotes. These changes will be reflected in the first supplement to the book.

§ 7.01. Taxation of Professional Athletes.

Many professional athletes are highly compensated for their competitive activities, and for the promotional utilization of their name, picture, or other personal attributes. The athlete is certainly not unique in this respect, but the peculiar situation in which many athletes find themselves in their high income producing years does pose some relatively unique tax problems. The high compensation will be the result of a physical prowess that is a depletable resource and will assure athletic achievement for only a short period of the athlete's life. For most highly compensated athletes, then, the federal income tax problems that they face are not so much those of determining tax liability for a given taxable year, as those of planning their affairs in such a manner as to maximize the life-long benefit from the short span during which their athletic skills will produce a high level of income.

In order to provide as useful a primer on the federal income tax problems of professional athletes as possible, given the nature of this book, the following discussion will focus on the basic principles and indicate how they relate to the professional athlete.

In very broad terms, the tax liability of all taxpayers, including professional athletes, is based upon the application of given tax rates to the net (taxable) income during a taxable year, which will normally be a twelve month period.[1] The first step in determining tax liability, therefore, is to ascertain the gross amount of all income of the taxpayer attributable to the taxable year in question. The inclusiveness of "gross income" will be considered in the immediately following section.[2] The second step is to subtract from this gross amount all deductions that are available to the taxpayer, a subject that will also be considered in a subsequent section.[3] When the second step has been completed, the taxpayer will then have a "taxable income" figure,[4] from which the tax liability will be determined by applying the tax rates which range, as a general rule for married individuals filing joint returns for taxable years after December 31, 1976, from a minimum of 14 percent for taxable income not over $3,200 to a marginal rate of 70 percent for taxable income in excess of $203,200.[5]

These rates are subject to a maximum marginal rate of 50 percent in the case of "personal service income." [6] The 50 percent ceiling will be beneficial to the individual whose taxable income is in excess of $40,200, and the married individual filing a joint return whose income is in excess of $55,200.[7] The 50 percent maximum tax applies to only "personal service income," which is defined to include earned income—"wages, salaries, or professional fees, and other amounts received as compensation for personal services actually rendered ...." [8]

In considering the rates that will be applied to taxable income, it is also important to note that if a professional athlete receives a disproportionately large amount of income in a given year, he or she may seek to reduce the amount of tax thereon by utilizing the so-called income averaging rules, which provide a means of levelling out unusual fluctuations in income from year to year.[9] In order to be eligible to utilize the income averaging rules, a taxpayer must be a citizen or resident of the United States throughout the computation year [10] and must have furnished more than one-half of his or her own support in each of the previous four years.[11] The support requirement will not apply if 1) the year

---

1. *See generally* J. CHOMMIE, FEDERAL INCOME TAXATION § 9 (2d ed. 1973).

2. *See* § 7.02.

3. *See* § 7.04.

4. "Taxable income" is defined in INT. REV. CODE of 1954, § 63(a). All references in this chapter to the Internal Revenue Code of 1954 shall be identified as "IRC" and the applicable section number.

5. IRC § 1(a).[*]

6. IRC § 1348(a). *See generally* Asimow, *Section 1348: The Death of Mickey Mouse?*, 58 CAL. L. REV. 801 (1970); Herskovitz, *Techniques Available to Shield the High Income of the "Superstar,"* 34 J. TAXATION 270 (1971); Reichler, *The Impact of the Maximum Tax on Earned Income on Compensation Planning,* 29 N.Y.U. FED. TAX INST. 1321 (1971).

7. Examples of how the calculation of the maximum tax is accomplished are set forth at Proposed Treas. Reg. § 1.1348-2(d)(4).[*]

8. IRC § 1348(b)(1) (for specific definition, § 1348(b)(1) cross-references to §§ 401(c)(2)(C) and 911(b) (which is quoted in text)). The term "personal service income" was added by the Tax Reform Act of 1976. Prior to this amendment (applicable to taxable years beginning after December 31, 1976), § 1348 applied to "earned income," which had a slightly less inclusive definition. One aspect of the expansion of the definition—to include "deferred compensation"—is considered in § 7.06.

9. IRC §§ 1301-05. The application of these rules requires consideration of a five-tax-year period, with the year in which the rules are to be applied being referred to as the "computation year," IRC § 1302(c)(2).

10. IRC § 1303(a). Non-resident aliens are specifically excluded. IRC § 1303(b).

11. IRC § 1303(c)(1); Treas. Reg. § 1.1303-1(c); James B. Heidel, 56 T.C. 95 (1971).

in which the averageable income is received occurs after the 25th birthday and during at least four taxable years after attaining age 20 the taxpayer was not a full-time student;[12] 2) more than one-half of the taxable income for the computation year was attributable to work performed during two or more of the base period years;[13] or 3) the taxpayer provided not more than 25% of the adjusted gross income reported on a joint return.[14] If the taxpayer is eligible, the income averaging rules may then be utilized if the taxpayer has "averageable income" in excess of $3,000 for the computation year.[15] It should also be noted that if a taxpayer elects to utilize the income averaging rules, then the maximum tax on personal service income[16] will be inapplicable for that taxable year.[17] This need not, however, be an unattractive feature of the averaging rules, since they will be equally applicable to earned as well as unearned income.[18] Thus, the income averaging rules could provide a taxpayer with a large amount of unearned income the benefit that would not be available from the maximum tax.

The income averaging rules will, then, be of substantial benefit to the athlete who has a disproportionate increase in taxable income in a particular year. In the ordinary case, the established athlete should have little difficulty establishing his or her eligibility for the rules. Difficulty will, however, arise when a rookie, or other athlete with less than four years of professional experience, seeks to take advantage of the rules. As has already been noted, an athlete will be ineligible if he or she is unable to meet the self-support rule,[19] and most new professional athletes will have spent their immediate pre-professional years as students in a college or university. Under such circumstances, it is unlikely that they would be able to demonstrate sufficient self-sufficiency.[20]

In addition to use of the income averaging rules as a means of reducing the tax bite on income after it has been received, there are also a variety of other methods by which the athlete can reduce or delay the tax on the relatively large amounts that may be derived from the years in which participation in professional athletics is possible.[21]

---

12. IRC § 1303(c)(2)(A). The term "student" is defined in IRC § 1303(d).

13. IRC § 1303(c)(2)(B). *See* William L. Frost, 61 T.C. 488 (1973) ("work" does not include participation in collegiate athletics).

14. IRC § 1303(c)(2)(C); Wilson v. United States, 322 F. Supp. 830 (D. Kan. 1971) (Miss America award not attributable to work in prior years); James B. Heidel, 56 T.C. 95 (1971) (professional football bonus not attributable to work in prior years). *See also* Rev. Rul. 75-40, 1975-1 CUM. BULL. 276.

15. IRC § 1301. The term "averageable income" is defined to mean the amount by which taxable income in the computation year exceeds 120 percent of the average base period income. IRC § 1302(a)(1); Treas. Reg. § 1.13021-1.

16. *See* notes 6-8 *supra*.

17. IRC § 1304(b)(5).

18. *See* Herskovitz, *Techniques Available to Shield the High Income of the "Superstar,"* 34 J. TAXATION 270, 273 (1971).

19. *See* note 11 *supra*.

20. *See* William L. Frost, 61 T.C. 488 (1973); James B. Heidel, 56 T.C. 95 (1971). These cases are considered at § 1.08. *See also* § 7.14.

21. *See* §§ 7.05-.13.

§ 7.02. The Athlete's Gross Income — Inclusiveness.

The first step in ascertaining the taxable income to which the rate structure will be applied, is to determine the gross income of the professional athlete. This determination requires consideration of both the inclusiveness of the concept of "gross income" for federal income tax purposes (discussed in this section), as well as the concepts utilized by the courts and the Internal Revenue Service (IRS) to prevent taxpayers from assigning that income to other persons in the hope of reducing overall tax liability (discussed in the following section).

The federal income tax includes within the concept of gross income all income from whatever source derived unless it is specifically excluded.[22] Although it has been observed that not every benefit received from a taxpayer's labor or investment will necessarily result in "income" and that there is no single and conclusive criterion with which to determine when the imposition of the income tax is appropriate,[23] it can be safely said that taxpayers must report as gross income most forms of money, property and services received during the taxable year.[24]

The primary source of income to most professional team sport athletes will be the compensation received for their services pursuant to an employment, or personal service, contract with a team. Constituting as it does compensation for personal services rendered, there can be little question that it must be included in the athlete's gross income in the taxable year during which it is actually or constructively[25] received. Similarly, income received in the form of bonuses for signing contracts[26] and tournament-prize money by athletes who compete individually will be included by the recipient in the year received. Income from endorsements or other uses of the name, likeness or reputation will also constitute an item to be included in gross income in the year of receipt.[27] The

---

22. IRC § 61(a). *See* Commissioner v. Glenshaw Glass Co., 348 U.S. 426, 430, 99 L.Ed. 483, 75 S. Ct. 483 (1955); Eisner v. Macomber, 252 U.S. 189, 207-08, 64 L.Ed. 521, 40 S. Ct. 189 (1920).

23. Treas. Reg. § 1.61-1(a). The power "to lay and collect taxes" is granted to Congress by the Sixteenth Amendment, which grants it the power "to lay and collect taxes on incomes, from whatever source derived, without apportionment among the several States, and without regard to any census or enumeration." U.S. CONST. amend. XVI. *See also* U.S. CONST. art. I, § 8. In enacting § 61(a), and its predecessors, moreover, Congress intended to use the full measure of its taxing power. *See* Helvering v. Clifford, 309 U.S. 331, 334, 84 L.Ed. 788, 60 S. Ct. 554 (1940).

24. Commissioner v. Wilcox, 327 U.S. 404, 407, 90 L.Ed. 752, 66 S. Ct. 546 (1946).

25. The reference to "constructively received" income has reference to situations in which moneys earned in one year are not actually received until later years as the result of a contractual, or other, arrangement, but because of the facts and circumstances of the particular case the entire amount is deemed to have been received in the year earned. *See* § 7.08.

26. Cecil R. Hundley, 48 T.C. 339, 344 (1967). *See also* James B. Heidel, 56 T.C. 95 (1971) (where the taxpayer argued that a bonus was attributable to "work" performed as a college football player, so as to qualify for the income averaging rules, which are considered at § 7.01); Richard A. Allen, 50 T.C. 329 (1968); Rev. Rul. 58-145, 1958-1 CUM. BULL. 360; Rev. Rul. 55-727, 1955-2 CUM. BULL. 25.

Merely because the bonuses must be included in the athlete's income, however, need not mean that they will always be "wages" for withholding tax purposes of the team. Thus, the IRS has ruled that bonuses paid to an athlete to sign an initial contract that are not contingent upon continued playing or employment are not "wages," so that withholding taxes need not be withheld; but where payments are made pursuant to a bonus requiring continued employment, then they are "wages" to which the withholding requirements apply. In either case, the bonus payments will be treated as ordinary income to the athlete-recipient. Rev. Rul. 58-145, 1958-1 CUM. BULL. 360.

27. This is the implicit holding in Paul V. Hornung, 47 T.C. 428 (1967), where the Tax Court held a prominent professional football player taxable on the rental value of an automobile provided to

treatment of the various types of deferred income arrangements that may be used by professional athletes to avoid the bunching of income—that is, to spread amounts earned in one year out over several years—are considered in §§ 7.07-7.10.

Professional athletes also customarily receive room and board while participating in pre-season training camps.[28] The Code contains a specific provision which excludes from gross income the value of meals and lodging provided employees in certain narrowly defined circumstances.[29] The value of meals is excluded if they are furnished on the business premises of the employer and for the employer's convenience.[30] The value of lodging provided will also be excluded if it meets the above tests, as well as the requirement that the employee be required to accept it as a condition of employment.[31] Under these requirements, it would appear that the value of meals and lodging provided by professional teams at training camps to the athletes who are, or who are seeking to become, members of the team will often not be includible in income. Thus, they are frequently furnished on the business premises of the employer (the training camp); furnished for the convenience of the employer, since they satisfy the business purpose of the employer to have its athletes confined to a supervised training regimen;[32] required as a condition of employment (if all athletes had to be lodged in the facilities provided during the training period); and furnished in kind.

In addition to the provision of meals and lodging during training periods, it is also common for professional teams to provide athletes with periodic payments of at least two separate types. The first involves simple per diem or subsistence payments that are made to the athletes during the training period.[33] The second involves meal allowances for periods when the athletes are required to travel away from the home city of their team.[34] So long as such payments are for the purpose of reimbursing subsistence and travel expenses of the athletes, they may not be required to be included in the athletes' gross income.[35] To the extent that the payments are for other purposes, however, they will be taxable.[36]

him for purposes of obtaining the intangible benefits of the player's "implied endorsement." *Id.* at 437-41.

The possibility of converting the ordinary income from such endorsement receipts into income taxed at capital gains rates, by trademarking the athlete's name, is considered in Herskovitz, *Techniques Available to Shield the High Income of the "Superstar,"* 34 J. TAXATION 270, 274 (1971). The basic theory of such an arrangement would be that after the athlete has obtained a trademark for his or her name, its subsequent sale would be entitled to capital gains treatment by the negative implication of IRC § 1253(a).

28. *See, e.g.,* National Football League Collective Bargaining Agreement art. XXI, § 2 (1977).

29. IRC § 119.

30. Treas. Reg. § 1.119-1(a).

31. Treas. Reg. § 1.119-1(b).

32. It should also be noted that the mere fact that all of the convenience is not on the side of the employer will not preclude exclusion. George I. Stone, 32 T.C. 1021 (1959).

33. *See, e.g.,* Major League Baseball Basic Collective Bargaining Agreement art. IV, § C (1976); National Football League Collective Bargaining Agreement art. XXI, §§ 3-5 (1977).

34. *See, e.g.,* Major League Baseball Basic Collective Bargaining Agreement art. VI, § B (1976); National Football League Collective Bargaining Agreement art. XXIII, § 1 (1977).

35. Rev. Rul. 77-351, 1971-40 I.R.B. 8; Rev. Rul. 74-433, 1974-2 CUM. BULL. 92; Treas. Reg. §§ 1.162-17, 1.274-5(e).

36. *See, e.g.,* Commissioner v. Kowalski, 434 U.S. 77 (1977) (cash meal allowances included when no accounting requirement and no limitation on how the money would be spent); Cockrell v.

The professional athlete may also receive reimbursement for moving expenses incurred when he or she is traded from one team to another.[37] This is, again, an area in which the Code provides explicit guidance. Thus, it provides that gross income shall include as compensation for services any amount received, directly or indirectly, as payment or reimbursement for the expenses of moving from one residence to another in connection with one's employment.[38] The taxpayer is also allowed a deduction for the moving expenses paid or incurred with respect to such a change of principal place of work.[39] Although there are limitations on the availability of the deduction,[40] it should have the effect in most cases of equalizing the income inclusion of the reimbursement received for the expenses, unless the amount of the reimbursement is more or less than the expenses actually incurred.[41]

The Code also contains rules concerning the taxation of prizes, awards and gifts. It requires, as a general matter, that all prizes and awards be included in gross income.[42] Exceptions are made, however, for non-taxable scholarships

---

Commissioner, 321 F.2d 504 (8th Cir. 1963); Higgins v. United States, 1973-1 U.S.T.C. ¶ 9275 (E.D. Cal. 1972); Darrell S. Courtney, 32 T.C. 334 (1959); Henry M. Lees, 12 T.C.M. 327 (1965); Justin T. Fong, 34 T.C.M. 230 (1975).

Although it might also be argued with respect to the in-season meal allowances that they fall within the exclusion for meals furnished by the employer, the argument would probably fail. The payments are, first of all, in the nature of reimbursement for the meals consumed while traveling, and the meal exclusion applies to only meals provided in kind. Treas. Reg. § 1.119-1(c)(2); S. REP. No. 1622, 83rd Cong., 2d Sess. 190 (1954); Commissioner v. Kowalski, 434 U.S. 77 (1977); Wilson v. United States, 412 F.2d 694 (1st Cir. 1969); Burl J. Ghastin, 60 T.C. 264 (1973); Henry M. Lees, 12 T.C.M. 327 (1965).

The athlete would also have difficulty meeting the other requirements of exclusion. Since the payments are made only when away from the home city, the employer business premises requirement could probably not be met. Similarly, the employer convenience requirement might not be met, since the requisite convenience could be present only if the meal provision satisfied a noncompensatory business purpose of the employer, other than providing additional compensation to its employees. Treas. Reg. § 1.119-1(a)(2). In light of the examples in the regulations, id. at § 1.119-1(d), it seems unlikely that such a purpose could be shown. The deductibility of such expenses, if they must be included in income, is considered at § 7.05.

37. See, e.g., Major League Baseball Basic Collective Bargaining Agreement art. VII; National Football League Collective Bargaining Agreement art. XXV (1977).

38. IRC § 82.

39. IRC § 217(a). See generally Allington, Moving Expenses and Reimbursements, 56 A.B.A.J. 495 (1970); Millett, Proposed Regulations on Moving Expenses: Planning Opportunities to Watch For, 36 J. TAXATION 176 (1972).

40. The limitations take several forms. The first limits the amount of deduction available for expenses incurred in searching for a new residence and occupying temporary quarters to $ 1,000, and for a qualified residence sale to $ 2,500, reduced by the above amounts, for married taxpayers filing a joint return. IRC § 217(b)(3)(A) (these amounts are increased to $1,500 and $3,000, respectively, for taxable years beginning after December 31, 1976). The second limitation provides that the deduction is allowed only if the taxpayer's new residence is at least 50 (35 in taxable years beginning after December 31, 1976) miles further from the former residence than was the former principal place of work (or former residence if no former place of work), id. § 217(c)(1), and that the taxpayer is a full-time employee during at least 39 weeks of the 12 months following arrival at the new residence (or 78 weeks out of the following 24 month period, of which not less than 39 weeks are during the first 12 month period). Id. § 217(c)(2).

41. If the reimbursement exceeds the actual moving expenses, then the amount of inclusion under § 82 will, of course, exceed the amount of deduction under § 217, so that the athlete will recognize the excess as income. If, on the other hand, the reimbursement is less than the actual moving expenses incurred, then the deduction under § 217 will exceed the inclusion under § 82, so that the athlete will get the benefit of deducting the excess expense.

42. IRC § 74(a). See generally Mansfield, Income from Prizes and Awards and Scholarships and Fellowship Grants, 19 N.Y.U. FED. TAX INST. 129 (1961).

or fellowships,[43] and for amounts received "primarily in recognition of religious, charitable, scientific, educational, artistic, literary, or civic achievement . . . .," if the recipient neither took action to enter the contest nor was required to render any future services as a condition to receiving the award.[44] In determining whether a particular award is within the quoted categories, the crucial test is the nature of the activity being rewarded. The exclusion will be granted to only those awards which recognize "genuinely meritorious achievements." [45] This, of course, reflects the types of achievement excepted and is consistent with the rule that the provisions of the Code are to be construed in their ordinary, everyday sense.[46]

The taxability of awards to athletes has been the subject of several court decisions. The first was in *Paul V. Hornung,*[47] where the taxpayer had received a new car for having been the outstanding player in the 1961 National Football League championship game. In support of his position that the award was not taxable, the taxpayer argued that it was for a civic achievement.[48] The court, however, rejected the argument and held the fair market value of the automobile to be taxable because professional football was not an educational, artistic, scientific or civic endeavor, and to hold otherwise, it said, would be to distort the commonly understood meaning of the word. Similarly, in *Wills v. Commissioner,*[49] the court held both an automobile and the "Hickok" belt (awarded to the taxpayer for having been the outstanding athlete of the year) taxable. Although the court found the taxpayer's argument that the belt was merely a valuable trophy to have an equitable appeal, it held that there was no basis in the Code for the argument and that the only criterion in considering the taxability of awards and gifts was the nature of the activity and not the form of the award.[50]

Under these rules, the receipt of a purely athletic award will ordinarily result in income inclusion. The amount to be included, however, is not clear. The IRS has taken the position that the amount subject to tax is the amount of money or the fair market value of goods or services received,[51] but some courts have been reluctant to require inclusion of the full fair market value of non-cash prizes.[52] It should also be noted that bills have been introduced in Congress to amend § 74(b) to include "athletic" awards, thereby making them non-taxable,

---

43. IRC § 74(a). The rules relating to scholarship and fellowship grants are contained in IRC § 117, and are discussed at some length in § 7.14.

44. IRC § 74(b).

45. Simmons v. United States, 308 F.2d 160, 163 (4th Cir. 1962). These achievements must, moreover, be apart from the employment relation. *See* Treas. Reg. § 1.74-1(b).

46. Malat v. Riddell, 383 U.S. 569, 571, 16 L.Ed. 2d 102, 86 S. Ct. 1030 (1966).

47. 47 T.C. 428 (1967).

48. In making this argument, the court said, the taxpayer had shifted into a "shotgun formation," but that he "should be caught behind the line of scrimmage on this particular offensive maneuver." 47 T.C. at 436.

49. 411 F.2d 537 (9th Cir. 1969).

50. 411 F.2d at 543. In both *Hornung* and *Wills,* the taxpayers also argued unsuccessfully that the awards were gifts, as is noted at notes 56-60 *supra.*

51. Treas. Reg. § 1.74-1(a)(2).

52. *See e.g.,* L.W. McCoy, 38 T.C. 841 (1962) (taxed only on amount that could be realized from sale of prize); Reginald Turner, 13 T.C.M. 462 (1962) (taxable value of airline tickets less than cost).

but the efforts have failed and serve only to provide further evidence of the apparent Congressional intent to tax such awards.[53]

The receipt of gifts raises similar problems. As a general rule, the Code provides that gifts are not includible in gross income.[54] To qualify as a gift, however, the transfer must be the product of a "detached and disinterested generosity" made "out of affection, respect, admiration, charity or like impulses," [55] and the mere fact that there is no moral or legal obligation to make the transfer will not of itself be sufficient for this purpose.[56] The application of these principles is illustrated, again, by *Paul V. Hornung,* where the taxpayer had been given an automobile by the manufacturer to drive during the football season, but was not required to perform any services in return therefor. After reviewing the above principles, the court concluded that the rental value of the automobile was not a gift, but was, rather, taxable income because the manufacturer had been motivated by primarily commercial motivations, not by a detached and disinterested generosity.[57] Where property is gratuitously transferred to a sports celebrity, therefore, it may be quite difficult to find a nontaxable gift. But if it can be shown that the gratuity was an instance of detached and disinterested generosity, it will not be taxable.[58]

Payments received as a result of injuries may present an additional source of income to professional athletes, though they will be excluded in many situations. Gross income generally does not include compensation for personal injuries or sickness if received under workmen's compensation acts[59] or health or accident insurance policies.[60] If the payments are received pursuant to health or sickness insurance maintained by an employer, the Code provides that such payments will be included in income to the extent that they are attributable to contributions of the employer that were not included in the taxpayer's income[61] or are paid by the employer.[62] This rule of inclusion is, however, applicable to very few payments, since it is subject to several broad exceptions. Payments may be excluded to the extent that they (1) reimburse the athlete for expenses incurred for medical care which have not been claimed as medical expense

53. These amendments are considered in Wills v. Commissioner, 411 F.2d 537, 542-43 (9th Cir. 1969).

54. IRC § 102(a).

55. Commissioner v. Duberstein, 363 U.S. 278, 285, 4 L.Ed. 2d 1218, 80 S. Ct. 1190 (1960); *see also* Commissioner v. LoBue, 351 U.S. 243, 100 L.Ed. 1142, 76 S. Ct. 800 (1956); Robertson v. United States, 343 U.S. 711 (1952); DeJong v. Commissioner, 309 F.2d 373, 379 (9th Cir. 1962). Although the Court in *Duberstein* did state the principles noted in text, its primary "learning" is that an appellate court should be reluctant to reevaluate the evidence presented to the trial court.

56. Old Colony Trust Co. v. Commissioner, 279 U.S. 716, 730, 73 L.Ed. 918, 49 S. Ct. 499 (1929).

57. 47 T.C. at 438-41.

58. Thus, in *Hornung* the court observed that the taxpayer had failed to prove the motivation of the donor, so that it was left to speculate on the reasons for the transfer. It then speculated that the company could have believed that the use of its automobiles by renowned football stars would be valuable implied endorsements of the autos, which speculation was supported by the fact that other players on the team had also been provided similar autos by the same manufacturer. 47 T.C. at 439-41. The court made it clear, therefore, that its decision left room for a recipient to receive a gift, but to establish that fact the athlete must undertake to prove the donor's motivation, which will be a difficult burden to carry.

59. IRC § 104(a)(1).

60. IRC § 104(a)(3).

61. Such employer payments would normally be excluded under IRC § 106.

62. IRC § 105(a).

deductions;[63] (2) constitute compensation for the loss of bodily members or functions and are not computed with respect to absence from work;[64] or (3) constitute qualified wage continuation arrangements.[65] If the athlete brings suit seeking compensation for injuries sustained, a recovery will generally be excluded from income.[66] For example, compensatory damages received from a suit for libel or slander or for injuries sustained because of improper medical care would probably not be taxable.[67] The recoveries in such actions will be excludable, however, only if they are compensatory in nature and relate to personal injuries. An award would be taxable to the extent that it represented punitive or exemplary damages.[68] It might also be taxable if the athlete is unable to prove that the award was in fact paid "on account of personal injuries."[69] Thus, if an athlete were cut from a team and brought suit seeking damages for the team's action, an eventual recovery would be excluded only if the athlete could show that it related to a personal injury (such as libel or slander). If the recovery was in fact paid to compensate the athlete for lost income due under a contract of employment, then the award would probably be taxable.[70] The requirement that the recovery be on account of personal injuries suggests the virtue of keeping the tax consequences of the recovery in mind while trying a suit or negotiating a settlement.[71]

The professional athlete may also receive income from other, less obvious sources. These might, for example, include the receipt of loans from the owner of a team or other interested party.[72] Although funds received in the form of

---

63. IRC § 105(b).

64. IRC § 105(c).

65. IRC § 105(d). There are several specific limitations on the exclusion of wage continuation plan receipts. *Id.*

66. IRC § 104(a)(2). *See, e.g.,* Dudley G. Seay, 58 T.C. 32 (1972); Theodate P. Riddle, 27 B.T.A. 1339 (1933). Amounts which are attributable to, and not in excess of, deductions for medical expenses in prior years will not be excluded. IRC § 104(a); Rev. Rul. 75-230, 1975-1 CUM. BULL. 93.

67. C. A. Hawkins, 6 B.T.A. 1023 (1927) (libel and slander); Rev. Rul. 58-418, 1958-2 CUM. BULL. 18 (same).

68. Commissioner v. Glenshaw Glass Co., 348 U.S. 426, 75 S. Ct. 473, 99 L. Ed. 483 (1955) (antitrust violation); Rev. Proc. 67-33, 1967-2 CUM. BULL. 659 (same).

69. Knuckles v. Commissioner, 349 F.2d 610 (10th Cir. 1965); Agar v. Commissioner, 290 F.2d 283 (2d Cir. 1961); W. C. Richards Co., Inc., 25 T.C.M. 884 (1966) (failure to prove arbitration award as personal injury). It should be noted, however, that a "personal injury" award may include payment of income lost due to the injury. *See* Fouts, *Payments Received in Settlement of Litigation and Claims,* 25 N.Y.U. FED. TAX INST. 555, 558, 562-63 (1967).

See generally Barnes, *Taxation of Tort Recoveries,* 48 L.A. BAR BULL. 258 (1973); Spaht, *Income Tax Effects on Personal Injury Recoveries,* 30 LA. L. REV. 72 (1970).

70. *See, e.g.,* Durkee v. Commissioner, 162 F.2d 184 (6th Cir. 1947); Anna Levens, 10 T.C.M. 1083 (1951).

71. Thus, in Dudley G. Seay, 58 T.C. 32 (1972), the taxpayer had filed a claim against a former employer alleging that his firing had been a breach of his employment contract, and that the circumstances and publicity of the firing had caused him serious personal injury. When the claim was settled, the settlement agreement specified that some $45,000 was for damages from the adverse publicity. The Tax Court then upheld the taxpayer's claim that the $45,000 was excludable under § 104(a)(2), since it was proven that this amount was paid "on account of personal injuries." The approach of the court in *Seay* is criticized in Comment, *Tax Treatment of Post-Termination Personal Injury Settlements,* 61 CAL. L. REV. 1237 (1973).

72. An additional example would be free tickets that are received by athletes. The IRS at one point suggested that they might not be taxable, though its suggestion related specifically to airline passes received by employees of airlines. Discussion Draft of Prop. Regs. § 1.61-16. However, these proposals have not been formally proposed.

a loan do not ordinarily constitute income for federal income tax purposes,[73] such an advance may be taxable if at the time it is made there is no obligation, express or implied, on the part of the recipient to repay the loan, or any restriction as to its disposition.[74] Thus, taxpayers are required to include in income all sums to which they have a claim of right with no restriction on disposition, even though a repayment obligation may be adjudged at a later time.[75] If the transaction is a bona fide loan with an obligation to repay a sum certain at a fixed point in time, however, it will not be includible within the athlete's gross income.

An athlete may also receive loans that are interest-free. An interest-free loan will be of benefit to the athlete because it will provide an opportunity to use the moneys loaned for personal or investment purposes without any obligation to pay interest thereon. It will also be difficult for the IRS to assert that such a benefit is includible within the athlete's gross income. Although the IRS may "impute" an interest payment—that is, attribute an interest payment where none is actually made—in a loan transaction between directly or indirectly related parties,[76] there is little authority for doing so when the parties stand at arm's length. Thus, the interest-free loan, so long as it is a bona fide loan transaction, should not result in taxable income.[77]

§ 7.03. Assignment of Income.

Because of the progressive nature of the federal income tax rate structure, taxpayers frequently attempt to avoid realizing income from their services by assigning a portion of it to a related third person. The purpose of such an assignment would be to reduce the overall tax liability by having the income spread among persons who are in lower marginal tax brackets than the taxpayer. Before considering the principles that will be utilized to determine the validity of such assignment procedures, it should be emphasized that the income splitting objective may in many cases be accomplished by carefully planning the transaction in advance, having in mind the tax and non-tax consequences of the various methods of accomplishing the objective. Since the specific methods that

---

73. United States v. Rosenthal, 470 F.2d 837 (2d Cir. 1972).

74. James v. United States, 366 U.S. 213, 6 L. Ed. 2d 246, 81 S. Ct. 1052 (1961).

75. North American Oil Consol. v. Burnet, 286 U.S. 417, 76 L. Ed. 1197, 52 S. Ct. 613 (1932).

76. IRC § 482; Liberty Loan Corp. v. United States, 498 F.2d 225 (8th Cir. 1974); Kerry Inv. Co. v. Commissioner, 58 T.C. 479 (1972). *See* § 7.12.

77. J. Simpson Dean, 35 T.C. 1083 (1961), *non. acq.* 1973-2 CUM. BULL. 4. *See generally* Herskovitz, *Techniques Available to Shield the High Income of the "Superstar,"* 34 J. TAXATION 270, 273 (1971) (which also suggests the possibility, and problems, of investing the proceeds in tax-exempt securities).

It should be noted that in Mason v. United States, 513 F.2d 25 (7th Cir. 1975), the court held that a charity received an economic benefit from a low interest rate on a purchase obligation to the taxpayer and allowed the taxpayer a charitable deduction for the amount of interest foregone. This case could be utilized by the government to support the argument that an interest-free loan confers an economic benefit on the recipient. *See* Duhl & Fine, *New Case Allowing Interest Deduction Calls for Reappraisal of No-Interest Loans,* 44 J. TAXATION 34 (1976).

The interest-free loan should not result in a gift tax to the lender. *See* Johnson v. United States, 254 F. Supp. 73 (N.D. Tex. 1966) (interest-free loan not a gift); Lester Crown, 67 T.C. 1043 (1977) (same). *See generally* C. LOWNDES, R. KRAMER & J. McCORD; FEDERAL ESTATE AND GIFT TAXES § 24.3 (3d ed. 1974); Frazier, *Interest-Free Loans Between Family Members: What Practitioners Can Expect After Crown?;* 48 J. TAXATION 28 (1978).

will be available for any given case will vary widely depending upon the specific facts and circumstances, the focus here will primarily be upon the basic principles of income assignment.

Such transactions will be successful only if they can avoid the so-called "assignment of income" doctrine, which provides that one who is entitled to receive income from personal services may not avoid personal tax liability by causing it to be paid to another through an anticipatory assignment.[78] The classic statement of the doctrine was in *Lucas v. Earl*,[79] where an attorney had entered an agreement with his wife to the effect that they would become joint tenants in the earnings of each other. The Court held the attorney taxable on all of his income, noting that he was the only party who had earned the salary and fees in question. In reaching this decision, Mr. Justice Holmes stated that the income tax laws will not give force to anticipatory arrangements "by which the fruits are attributed to a different tree from that on which they grew."[80] In other words, income is taxable to its owner, since the power to dispose of income is equivalent to its ownership and the exercise of that power to procure payment to another is the enjoyment and realization of the income.[81]

An athlete who desires that a portion of the income from his or her services be taxed to another must, then, carefully plan the transfer to insure that the assignment of income doctrine will not be invoked to nullify the transaction. If it is foreseen, for example, that a young athlete will receive a large bonus upon signing a professional contract and that it will be advantageous to have a portion of the bonus taxed to a parent or spouse, the transfer can be accomplished only if there is a legitimate basis for the other person receiving the income. One method of accomplishing this result is to establish that the recipient has performed valuable services for the athlete which have aided in the production of the bonus — such as training and coaching the athlete or conducting the negotiations which resulted in the bonus contract. Where such a showing can be made, the transfer may be effective for tax purposes.[82] If it cannot, then the assignment of income principles will be applied to defeat the attempted transfer

---

78. United States v. Basye, 410 U.S. 441, 35 L. Ed. 2d 412, 93 S. Ct. 1080 (1973); Harrison v. Shaffner, 312 U.S. 579, 85 L. Ed. 1055, 61 S. Ct. 759 (1941); Helvering v. Eubank, 311 U.S. 122, 85 L. Ed. 81, 61 S. Ct. 149 (1940); Helvering v. Horst, 311 U.S. 112, 85 L. Ed. 75, 61 S. Ct. 144 (1940); Lucas v. Earl, 281 U.S. 111, 74 L. Ed. 731, 50 S. Ct. 241 (1930); Rev. Rul. 58-127, 1958-1 CUM. BULL. 42. *See generally* Lyon & Eustice, *Assignment of Income: Fruit and Tree as Irrigated by the P.G. Lake Case,* 17 TAX L. REV. 295 (1962).

79. 281 U.S. 111, 74 L. Ed. 731, 50 S. Ct. 241 (1930).

80. 281 U.S. at 115. *See also* Helvering v. Horst, 311 U.S. 112, 85 L. Ed. 75, 61 S. Ct. 144 (1940).

81. Harrison v. Shaffner, 312 U.S. 579, 85 L. Ed. 1055, 61 S. Ct. 759 (1941) (assignment of income from a trust); Parmer v. Commissioner, 468 F.2d 705 (10th Cir. 1972) (assignment of crop shares); Paul A. Teschner, 38 T.C. 1003 (1962) (assignment of prize).

If the taxpayer desires to assign income from property, as opposed to income from services, this may be accomplished by transferring the entire income producing property. Helvering v. Eubank, 311 U.S. 122, 85 L. Ed. 81, 61 S. Ct. 149 (1940) (assignment of insurance renewal commissions); Blair v. Commissioner, 300 U.S. 5, 81 L. Ed. 465, 57 S. Ct. 330 (1937) (assignment of trust property); Fontaine Fox, 37 B.T.A. 271 (1938) (assignment of personal services contract).

82. In Cecil R. Hundley, Jr., 48 T.C. 339 (1967), for example, the Court upheld the transfer of a share of a large bonus to the athlete's father, who had served as coach, advisor and contract negotiator. In cases such as *Hundley*, the athlete will actually be required to include the whole amount in income, but will be entitled to a deduction for the payment to the parent or spouse for the services rendered. *See* § 7.04. The net result will be essentially the same as an assignment of income.

of earnings. Thus, in *Richard A. Allen*,[83] a young baseball player had signed a professional baseball contract that included a substantial initial bonus. A large portion of the bonus was paid to the player's mother, allegedly to compensate her for having caused him to have done the "right thing." Notwithstanding the formal diversion to the mother, the Tax Court held that the entire bonus was taxable to the player. This result was required, the court said, because he alone was the source of the income and "[r]egardless of the motives involved, the situation remains one of deflection of a portion of [the player's] bonus income to his mother, and he cannot escape the tax consequences thereof." [84]

Where a satisfactory basis cannot be established for the initial assignment to another person, more sophisticated arrangements will have to be undertaken to accomplish the desired result. One such procedure might call for the athlete to enter a personal service contract with his sports employer, and then sell the contract to another person at a discounted price. The courts have, however, been alert to the income shifting possibilities in such arrangements. Thus, in *Jones v. Page*,[85] a famous golfer had entered into a contract for the production of a series of movies showing his form and style. The contract called for him to receive $120,000, plus a 50 percent royalty on the net receipts of the movies. After the payment of a $20,000 advance, the golfer assigned the contract to his father for nominal consideration. The father then created trusts for the golfer's children, transferred his rights in the contracts to the trusts, and then renegotiated the original contract with the movie company. The golfer also executed a collateral agreement which guaranteed that he would perform the acts and duties for which his father had contracted. When payments were subsequently made to the father as trustee, the court held that the golfer was taxable on the income generated from the contract, stating that he had simply sought to use his father "as a conduit in an attempt to reduce or avoid taxes that would be otherwise assessable against compensation derived from his own personal services." [86] The plan sought to be utilized in *Jones v. Page* would be successful only if the sale price were its fair market value at the time of sale,[87] though in that event there may be little income shifting potential.

If a personal services contract is sold, it will also be necessary to determine how the proceeds will be taxed to the seller. This is an area that has received considerable attention,[88] and the principles that will apply in any given case are relatively clear. The basic principle will be that a right to compensation for services, even if secured by a contract, does not constitute a capital asset in the hands of the taxpayer who is to, or has already, performed the services.[89] Accordingly, when the right (or contract) is sold, the proceeds will be accorded

---

83. 50 T.C. 329 (1968), *aff'd per curiam*, 410 F.2d 398 (3rd Cir. 1968).

84. 50 T.C. at 477.

85. 102 F.2d 144 (5th Cir. 1939), *cert. denied*, 308 U.S. 562, 84 L. Ed. 472, 60 S. Ct. 43 (1939).

86. 102 F.2d at 145. *See also* Greer v. United States, 408 F.2d 631 (6th Cir. 1969) (assignment of "racing interests" in a race horse to the assignor's grandchildren held ineffective for federal income tax purposes).

87. *See, e.g.,* Est. of Stranahan v. Commissioner, 472 F.2d 867 (6th Cir. 1973).

88. *See* Lyon & Eustice, *Assignment of Income: Fruit and Tree as Irrigated by the P.G. Lake Case,* 17 TAX L. REV. 295, 393-96 (1962); Mintz, *Entertainers and the Capital Gains Tax,* 4 TAX L. REV. 275 (1949); Rosenbaum, *Entertainer's Corporations and Capital Gains,* 12 TAX L. REV. 33 (1956).

89. Hubert L. Luna, 42 T.C. 1067 (1964); Nat Holt, 35 T.C. 588 (1961), *aff'd,* 303 F.2d 687 (9th Cir. 1962). *See also* Roth v. Commissioner, 321 F.2d 607 (9th Cir. 1963); Ralph Bellamy, 43 T.C. 487 (1965).

ordinary income, not capital gain, treatment.[90] Capital gain treatment will be available only if there is a property element in the sale apart from the personal service element.[91] It should be noted, however, that even if there is an apparent capital element, the IRS will carefully scrutinize any transaction which appears to constitute a device for the avoidance of federal income taxes by disguising a sale of personal services as a sale of a capital asset.[92] In most cases, the question of whether the asset sold is the right to receive compensation income or a genuine capital interest will be a question of fact.[93]

An additional device for splitting the income of professional athletes would be through the establishment of a personal service corporation. This would be accomplished by organizing a corporation, having the athlete enter a contract with the corporation for his or her personal services, and then having the corporation enter a contract with the team or other entity seeking the services of the athlete. The income splitting objective could then be accomplished by having a portion of its shares issued to the person who the athlete desires to share in the service income. If properly organized, the personal service corporation might be an effective means of splitting income, and its advantages and disadvantages are discussed in detail later in this chapter.[94]

§ 7.04. Deductible Expenses of Professional Athletes.

After the "gross income" of the athlete-taxpayer has been determined,[95] the next part of the tax computation process is to ascertain the "taxable income." In the case of individual taxpayers, this is a two-step process. The first step requires that gross income be reduced by the deductions available for expenses of an essentially business or income-producing nature, which will result in a figure identified as "adjusted gross income." [96] The second step then requires that adjusted gross income be reduced by certain personal expense deductions allowed by the Code.[97] These will include excess itemized deductions (the amount of itemized deductions in excess of the zero bracket amount (a stated figure [98])) and the deductions for personal exemptions.[99] When these steps have been

---

90. *See* Commissioner v. P.G. Lake, Inc., 356 U.S. 260, 266-67, 2 L. Ed. 2d 743, 78 S. Ct. 691 (1958).

91. Commissioner v. Ferrer, 304 F.2d 125 (2d Cir. 1962) (sale of lease; allocation required); Julius H. (Groucho) Marx, 29 T.C. 88 (1957) (sale of partnership interest); Fred MacMurray, 21 T.C. 15 (1953) (sale of story); Jack Benny, 25 T.C. 197 (1955) (sale of stock). The IRS has acquiesced in these cases. 1958-2 CUM. BULL. 6.

92. Rev. Rul. 59-325, 1959-2 CUM. BULL. 185.

93. Thus, in Lyon and Eustice, *Assignment of Income: Fruit and Tree as Irrigated by the P.G. Lake Case,* 17 TAX L. REV. 295 (1962), it is noted that

[t]his question is essentially a factual one, and the *Benny* case is merely a striking illustration of the benefits which may flow to a taxpayer who is fortunate enough to be well represented by astute tax counsel throughout the transaction. *Id.* at 395, n. 398.

94. *See* §§ 7.11-7.13.

95. *See* §§ 7.02-7.03.

96. IRC § 62. The principal use of the "adjusted gross income" figure is as a base for the determination of the amount of other deductions. *See, e.g.,* IRC §§ 170(b) (charitable contributions); 213(a) (1), (b) (medical expenses).

97. IRC § 63(b).

98. IRC § 63(d) (presently, it is $3,200 for married taxpayers filing a joint return).

99. IRC § 63(b), 151.

completed, the resultant figure will be that of "taxable income," which serves as the base for the application of the tax rates.[100]

Although any athlete may, and probably will, have numerous possible deductions, the discussion in this section is limited to the types of deductions that seem to be peculiarly related to a taxpayer's status as a professional athlete. Thus, this section illustrates the types of deductions that may be available to professional athletes, but it is not, and it is not intended to be, a comprehensive guide for the determination of the precise tax liability of a particular taxpayer. Such a determination is a task for professional counsel, who will be able to ascertain the complete range of deductions, and other considerations, that will be necessary to properly determine federal income tax liability.

It is well to begin this survey by observing that unlike the term "gross income" which is liberally construed in favor of inclusiveness,[101] the determination of whether any given expense is deductible is a narrow inquiry and deductibility will result only if there is a specific statutory provision authorizing it.[102]

The principal basis for deductions by professional athletes as such is a provision in the Code which allows taxpayers to deduct from gross income all of the "ordinary and necessary" expenses paid or incurred during the taxable year in carrying on a trade or business.[103] A particular expense qualifies for deduction if the taxpayer can show that it was incurred in his or her trade or business,[104] and was not a mere personal expense; [105] that the expense could not have been capitalized; [106] and that it was "ordinary and necessary" to the trade or business.[107] Whether these conditions are met, moreover, will depend on the facts and circumstances of each particular case.[108]

Professional athletes are considered to be engaged in a trade or business and will be able to deduct all of the ordinary and necessary expenses incurred in connection with performance in athletic events. These include expenditures for the tools of the trade,[109] traveling,[110] professional association dues,[111]

---

100. *See generally* M. ROSE & J. PLATT, A FEDERAL INCOME TAXATION PRIMER 39-40 (1973).

101. *See* § 7.02.

102. *See generally* J. CHOMMIE, FEDERAL INCOME TAXATION § 44 (2d ed. 1973).

103. IRC § 162(a). The Code also allows the deduction of certain non-trade or business deductions in IRC § 212. These non-trade or business expenses include those for the production or collection of income, the management, conservation or maintenance of property held for income producing purposes, and for the determination, collection or refund of taxes. Treas. Reg. § 1.212-1(a).

104. Commissioner v. Heininger, 320 U.S. 467, 470, 88 L. Ed. 171, 64 S. Ct. 249 (1943). The "trade or business" requirement is considered with respect to sports investments in § 7.21.

105. Truman C. Tucker, 55 T.C. 783 (1971). Personal expenses are also denied deductibility by IRC § 262, which provides that "[e]xcept as otherwise expressly provided in this chapter, no deduction shall be allowed for personal, living or family expenses." Oppewal v. Commissioner, 468 F.2d 1000 (1st Cir. 1972).

106. Treas. Reg. § 1.162-1(a).

107. Treas. Reg. § 1.162-2. In Welch v. Helvering, 290 U.S. 111, 78 L. Ed. 212, 54 S. Ct. 8 (1933), Mr. Justice Cardozo made it clear that both the "ordinary" and "necessary" requirements must be satisfied. Thus, he concluded that "necessary" meant "appropriate and helpful," *id.* at 113, and that ordinary referred to the expenses that experience showed were "common and accepted" in the situation of the business in question. *Id.* at 114.

108. Commissioner v. Heininger, 320 U.S. 467, 475, 88 L. Ed. 171, 64 S. Ct. 249 (1943).

109. Rev. Rul. 70-476, 1970-2 CUM. BULL. 35; G.C.M. 7133, VIII-2 CUM. BULL. 85, declared obsolete in 1969-2 CUM. BULL. 307.

110. *See* notes 128-49 *infra*.

111. S. Charles Lee, 5 T.C.M. 240 (1946). Inasmuch as most professional athletes now belong to

entertainment,[112] professional services,[113] necessary gratuities,[114] and any and all other expenses that can be justified as being ordinary and necessary in the trade or business.[115]

There are several categories of expenses that should be of particular interest to professional athletes. The first involves fees paid to an agent to represent them in contract negotiations or other matters related to the business of athletic performance. As a general matter, a deduction is allowed for salaries or other compensation paid for personal services actually rendered to the taxpayer,[116] and the test of deductibility in the case of compensation payments is whether they are reasonable and are in fact payments purely for services.[117] Although a considerable body of law has developed to determine what constitutes reasonable compensation,[118] the basic principle is that compensation may not exceed what is reasonable under all of the circumstances.[119] The services of agents for professional athletes are often determined on a contingency basis, with the agent receiving a fixed percentage of the athlete's income. Although contingent compensation arrangements do invite special scrutiny, they are not treated, on a fundamental basis, any differently than are flat rate compensation schemes.[120] Thus, so long as the basis for the payments is a free bargain concluded before the services are rendered, and is not influenced by considerations other than securing services on fair and advantageous terms, payments actually made should be allowed as a deduction even though they turn out to be larger than would ordinarily be paid for such services.[121]

players' associations or unions, see ch. 6, it should also be noted that dues paid to a labor union are generally deductible. Marc P. Girard, 27 T.C.M. 357 (1968); Jeff Rubin, 13 T.C.M. 1094 (1954). Though deductible, the dues are non-business expenses and must be itemized.

112. Entertainment expenditures must, however, be incurred primarily for the benefit of the business of the taxpayer, and not for personal purposes. IRC § 274(a)(1)(A); George W. Randall, 56 T.C. 869 (1971); Robert L. Henry, 36 T.C. 879 (1961). In addition, IRC § 274(d) requires that any such expense be properly substantiated. John L. Ashby, 50 T.C. 289 (1968). The provisions of § 274 are, moreover, in addition to those of § 162. William F. Sanford, 50 T.C. 568 (1968), aff'd per curiam, 412 F.2d 201 (2d Cir.), cert. denied, 396 U.S. 841, 24 L. Ed. 2d 92, 90 S. Ct. 104 (1969).

113. Lou Levy, 30 T.C. 1315 (1958) (legal expenses); Olivia de Havilland Goodrich, 20 T.C. 323 (1953) (agent); Meldrum & Fewsmith, Inc., 20 T.C. 790 (1953); Kamen Soap Prods. Co., Inc., 15 T.C.M. 777 (1956).

114. Olivia de Havilland Goodrich, 20 T.C. 323, 331-32 (1953).

115. See generally Cohen, Taxation of Professional Athletes, 12 CLEV.-MAR. L. REV. 320 (1961).

116. IRC § 162 (a)(1).

117. Treas. Reg. § 1.162-7(a). Payments to a boxer's manager were disallowed in Ray S. Robinson, 44 T.C. 20 (1965), where the taxpayer failed to prove the purpose of the payment.

118. See generally J. CHOMMIE, FEDERAL INCOME TAXATION § 52 (2d ed. 1973) (citing appropriate commentaries).

119. Treas. Reg. § 1.162-7(b)(3). The Regulations go on to provide that

[i]t is, in general, just to assume that reasonable and true compensation is only such amount as would ordinarily be paid for like services by like enterprises under like circumstances. The circumstances to be taken into consideration are those existing at the date when the contract for services was made, not those existing at the date when the contract is questioned.

In addition to establishing that the compensation was reasonable, the taxpayer will also have to give satisfactory proof that the payments were actually made. Thus, in Robert S. Howard, 32 T.C. 1284 (1959), the Tax Court denied a deduction for "stakes to jockeys" because the taxpayer had made no showing as to what was actually paid over to the jockeys.

120. Treas. Reg. § 1.162-7(b)(2). See generally Note, Contingent Compensation Agreement Leads to Disallowance of Corporate Deduction for Salary to Nonshareholder Because of Lack of Free Bargain, 53 CAL. L. REV. 1544 (1965).

121. Treas. Reg. § 1.162-7(b)(2). See also Harold's Club v. Commissioner, 340 F.2d 861 (9th Cir.

These rules are well illustrated by two recent opinions involving the fees paid to the agents of professional baseball players. In *Cecil R. Hundley, Jr.,*[122] the taxpayer entered an oral agreement with his father, pursuant to which the father was to act as the taxpayer's coach, business agent, manager, publicity director and agent in negotiating a professional baseball contract. In return for these duties, the father was to receive 50 percent of any bonus received by the taxpayer for signing a baseball contract. Thereafter, the father performed all duties with great success and because of his "expert and shrewd" handling of contract and bonus negotiations the taxpayer received a contract and an extraordinarily large bonus.[123] On these facts, the Tax Court held the contingent compensation agreement to be reasonable in amount, though it noted that a father-son agreement should be carefully scrutinized, inasmuch as the father had performed substantial services and the agreement was reached at a time when it was uncertain whether any bonus would be received.[124] The amount paid to the father, therefore, was a deductible business expense in the taxpayer's trade or business of being a professional athlete.

The 50 percent figure held reasonable in *Hundley* is, of course, quite large.[125] It should be anticipated that where the agent does not supply clearly "expert and shrewd" services to the athlete, and it is clear at the time of agreement that a contract will be obtained, the size of the percentage fee that will be found to be reasonable in amount may be less than 50 percent. In *Richard A. Allen,*[126] for example, the Tax Court held that no compensation was reasonable when the purported agent performed none of the functions done by the father in *Hundley.*[127]

A second category of expenses that will be deductible by the professional athlete includes traveling expenses incurred by the athlete while away from home in the pursuit of his or her trade or business. The deduction includes amounts expended for meals, lodging and other expenses incident to travel, so long as they are not lavish or extravagant under the circumstances.[128] Before

---

1965); Austin v. United States, 28 F.2d 677, 678 (5th Cir. 1928); Roy Marilyn Stone Trust, 44 T.C. 349, 362 (1965); Olivia de Havilland Goodrich, 20 T.C. 323, 331 (1953); California Vegetable Concentrates, Inc., 10 T.C. 1158, 1165-66 (1948). The best example of these rules is probably *Olivia de Havilland Goodrich,* where the taxpayer had engaged her stepfather to act as her financial manager. Their original agreement provided that the father was to receive 25 percent of taxpayer's income, but this was reduced to 15 percent because of an IRS audit. When the 15 percent figure was thereafter challenged, the Tax Court upheld the arrangement, finding that it was the result of an arm's length agreement and reasonable in light of the services performed.

122. 48 T.C. 339 (1967). The IRS has acquiesced in *Hundley.* 1967-2 CUM. BULL. 2.

123. The bonus was $110,000, to be paid over a five-year period at the rate of $22,000 per year.

124. 48 T.C. at 345-47.

125. The mere size of the compensation is not, however, determinative of its reasonableness. William S. Gray & Co. v. United States, 35 F.2d 968 (Ct. Cl. 1925); Auburn & Associates v. United States, 336 F. Supp. 457 (W.D. Pa. 1971).

126. 50 T.C. 329 (1968), *aff'd per curiam,* 410 F.2d 398 (3rd Cir. 1969).

127. In *Allen,* the taxpayer's mother had claimed $40,000 of a $70,000 bonus in return for her doing whatever was best for her son and seeing that he did the "right thing." She possessed no financial knowledge, knew nothing about baseball, and had nothing to do with her son's development as a baseball player. There was, in addition, no agreement reflecting the duties to be performed and the amount of the contingent compensation to be received by the agent. 50 T.C. at 478 n.7. In other words, the agent in *Allen,* was at the opposite end of the spectrum from the agent in *Hundley.*

128. IRC § 162(a)(2); Treas. Reg. § 1.162-2(a). The items that may be claimed as traveling expenses are considered in J. MERTENS, LAW OF FEDERAL INCOME TAXATION § 25.92 (1972). Before a deduction may be claimed for meals, the taxpayer must "sleep or rest" while away from home.

a traveling expense deduction can be taken, however, the taxpayer must show that the expense was reasonable and necessary, that it was incurred while away from home in the pursuit of business,[129] and that it was not a mere commuting expense.[130] The most difficult of these three conditions is the "away from home" requirement.[131] The definition of "home" for these purposes involves no small amount of controversy. Thus, while the Internal Revenue Service,[132] the Tax Court,[133] and some circuit courts of appeal[134] have taken the position that "home" means the business location of the taxpayer, other circuit courts have concluded that "home" refers to the residence of the taxpayer.[135] Although the Supreme Court has considered the problem, its decision held merely that the "home" of military servicemen is their duty station, which would be their place of business. It refrained from applying the decision to all classes of taxpayers.[136]

Since the view of the Tax Court and the IRS is the more generally accepted position, the professional athlete should assume, except in those circuits where the court of appeals has adopted a contrary view, that "home" for this purpose will be the place of business — that is, the "club town" for team sport athletes.[137]

United States v. Correll, 389 U.S. 299, 19 L.Ed. 2d 537, 88 S. Ct. 445 (1967); I.T. 3395, 1940-2 Cum. Bull. 64. Whether a particular trip is primarily related to the taxpayer's trade or business will depend on the facts and circumstances of the particular case. Treas. Reg. § 1.162-2(b)(2). *See also* Commissioner v. Flowers, 326 U.S. 465, 470, 90 L. Ed. 203, 66 S. Ct. 250 (1946); Commissioner v. Heininger, 320 U.S. 467, 88 L. Ed. 171, 64 S. Ct. 249 (1943).

The taxability of amounts received to reimburse such expenses is considered at § 7.02.

129. Commissioner v. Flowers, 326 U.S. 465, 470, 90 L. Ed. 203, 66 S. Ct. 250 (1946); *see also* Peurifoy v. Commissioner, 358 U.S. 59, 60, 3 L. Ed. 2d 30, 79 S. Ct. 104 (1958).

130. Commissioner v. Flowers, 326 U.S. 465, 473-74, 90 L. Ed. 203, 66 S. Ct. 250 (1946); James A. Kistler, 40 T.C. 657, 663 (1963).

131. *See generally* Haddleton, *Traveling Expenses "Away From Home,"* 17 Tax L. Rev. 261 (1962); Note, *A House Is Not a Tax Home,* 49 Va. L. Rev. 125 (1963).

Before one can be away from "home," of course, he or she must have a home. Thus, where a taxpayer is unable to show a "home," the traveling expense deduction will be unavailable because he or she will then not be "away from home." Rosenspan v. United States, 438 F.2d 905, 912 (2d Cir. 1971).

The purpose of the "away from home" rule is to mitigate the burden on a taxpayer who must maintain two places of abode because of the exigencies of his or her trade or business. Ronald D. Kroll, 49 T.C. 392 (1968).

132. Rev. Rul. 75-432, 1975-2 Cum. Bull. 60; G.C.M. 23672, 1943 Cum. Bull. 66, 67.

133. Truman C. Tucker, 55 T.C. 783 (1971); Ronald D. Kroll, 49 T.C. 392 (1968); Clinton H. Mitchell, 42 T.C. 953 (1964). The starting point in this line of authority was Mort L. Bixler, 5 B.T.A. 1181 (1927).

134. Lewia v. Commissioner, 75-1 U.S.T.C. § 9145 (D.C. Cir. 1974); Jones v. Commissioner, 444 F.2d 508 (5th Cir. 1971); Jenkins v. Commissioner, 418 F.2d 1292 (8th Cir. 1969). All of the "home is place of business" cases have been criticized as not actually supporting the rule set forth, Rosenspan v. United States, 438 F.2d 905, 911 (2d Cir. 1971), and as placing too harsh a result on taxpayers. Peurifoy v. Commissioner, 358 U.S. 59, 62, 3 L. Ed. 2d 30, 79 S. Ct. 104 (1958) (Douglas, J., dissenting).

135. Six v. United States, 450 F.2d 66 (2d Cir. 1971); Rosenspan v. United States, 438 F.2d 905 (2d Cir. 1971), *cert. denied,* 404 U.S. 864, 30 L. Ed. 2d 108, 92 S. Ct. 54 (1971); Burns v. Gray, 287 F.2d 698 (6th Cir. 1961); Wallace v. Commissioner, 144 F.2d 407 (9th Cir. 1944).

136. Commissioner v. Stidger, 386 U.S. 287, 296, 18 L. Ed. 2d 53, 87 S. Ct. 1065 (1967). In *Stidger* the taxpayer was stationed in Japan and his wife and children maintained a residence in California, so that the place of business-residence distinction was crystallized for its decision that "home" meant duty station, though there was a strong dissent. *Id.* at 297-99 (Douglas, J., dissenting). The Court had faced a similar problem in Commissioner v. Flowers, 326 U.S. 465, 90 L. Ed. 203, 66 S. Ct. 250 (1946), but its decision there turned on the presence of a necessary relation of the expenses to a business.

137. Rev. Rul. 54-147, 1954-1 Cum. Bull. 51; Wills v. Commissioner, 411 F.2d 537 (9th Cir. 1969); Ronald C. Gardin, 64 T.C. 1079 (1975) (professional football player); *see also* Walter Schmidt v. Commissioner, 11 B.T.A. 1199 (1928). *Rev. Rul. 54-147* came to this conclusion by relying upon

Thus, a professional athlete may, generally, deduct only those traveling expenses incurred in connection with work-related travel while away from the club town. The trade or business requirement will, moreover, preclude the deduction of "commuting expenses" — that is expenses incurred in traveling between one's residence and place of business — inasmuch as they are considered to be non-deductible personal expenses.[138] It should also be noted that if an athlete's family travels with the athlete, their traveling expenses will generally not be deductible since such expenses are often viewed as non-deductible personal living expenses.[139]

The traveling expense rules will also be applicable to non-team sport athletes who are required to travel from place to place as the site of competition changes. In the case of professional golfers or tennis players, for example, the normal course of events is for them to travel from one part of the country to another as the situs of tournaments changes. In such cases, the athlete will be entitled to a deduction for the traveling expenses incurred while on temporary, but not indefinite or indeterminate, absences from his or her place of permanent residence.[140] The availability of the deduction in such cases is illustrated by *Pierce v. United States*,[141] where the taxpayer (a race track steward) maintained a residence in Hot Springs, Arkansas, but worked at various race tracks throughout the country during most of the year. His wife accompanied him while he was away from Arkansas and they always returned to Arkansas when not otherwise employed. The facts showed that the taxpayer had no future employment commitment when he completed his work at a given track and was able to arrange his schedule for the year only upon receiving requests for his services in January. On these facts, the court held that the taxpayer's tax "home" was in Arkansas, and that his employments at tracks away from Arkansas were "temporary" employments away from his tax home. He was, accordingly, entitled to travel expense deductions while traveling away from his tax home.[142] Similar results have been reached in numerous other cases involving comparable factual situations.[143] The IRS at one time issued an opinion

Commissioner v. Flowers, and *Wills* reached it by relying upon *Rev. Rul. 54-147* and the familiar rule that an appellate court must give great weight to the factual findings of the trial court. 411 F.2d at 540. Inasmuch as neither Rev. Rul 54-147 nor *Wills* analyzed the cases reaching the "home = residence" rule, there is room to argue the converse of their holdings, especially in light of the reasoning of Judge Friendly in Rosenspan v. United States, 438 F.2d 905, 908-12 (2d Cir. 1971).

138. Commissioner v. Flowers, 326 U.S. 465, 473-74, 90 L. Ed. 203, 66 S. Ct. 250 (1946); Treas. Reg. § 1.162-2(e).

139. Walter Schmidt v. Commissioner, 11 B.T.A. 1199, 1200 (1928). *But see* United States v. Disney, 413 F.2d 783 (9th Cir. 1969) (spouse's expenses deductible where she assisted in business activities).

140. Peurifoy v. Commissioner, 358 U.S. 59, 60, 3 L. Ed. 2d 30, 79 S. Ct. 104 (1958); Rev. Rul. 75-432, 1975-2 CUM. BULL. 55; Rev. Rul. 60-189, 1960-1 CUM. BULL. 60.

141. 271 F. Supp. 165 (W.D. Ark. 1967).

142. In reaching this conclusion, the court quoted from the dissenting opinion of Justice Douglas in *Peurifoy* (which did not reach the "home" issue), to the effect that the contention of the IRS that the taxpayer was not entitled to the deduction while away from Arkansas would mean
> that the taxpayer who is forced to travel from place to place to pursue his trade must carry his home on his back regardless of the fact that he maintains his family at an abode which meets all accepted definitions of "home." I do not believe that Congress intended such a harsh result when it provided a deduction for traveling expenses.

271 F. Supp. at 174 (358 U.S. at 62).

143. Burns v. Gray, 287 F.2d 698 (6th Cir. 1961) (race track starter); Alois J. Weidekamp, 29 T.C. 16 (1957) (pari-mutuel calculator); Lucien Boyer, 36 T.C.M. 1329 (1977) (professional ice skaters);

that a professional golfer would be entitled to a travel expense deduction when attending tournaments away from his home,[144] and, although that opinion has been declared obsolete by the IRS,[145] it would appear, in light of the line of authority of which the *Pierce* case is an example, to represent the proper result for most cases involving golfers, tennis players and other itinerant professional athletes.[146]

In light of the fact that many professional athletes maintain off-season businesses, consideration must also be given to the problems posed by the situation where a taxpayer has more than one business. In such cases, the taxpayer's "home" for purposes of the traveling expense deduction will be the location of the principal place of business,[147] and the taxpayer will be entitled to deduct traveling expenses incurred while away from the principal place of business.[148] When these rules are applied to professional athletes who have additional trades or businesses, the IRS has ruled that if the principal place of business of a team sport athlete is not in the club town, then the athlete will be entitled to deduct traveling expenses while in that city; but if the principal place of business is in the club town, then traveling expenses are deductible while away from that locale in pursuit of the trade or business, even though the permanent residence is located at the situs of the minor business post.[149]

There are also several other types of deductions that may be available to professional athletes. An athlete would be able to deduct expenses incurred for the purpose of maintaining the physical condition that is necessary for athletic competition.[150] Similarly, expenses for special coaching or instruction will be deductible to the extent that they are for the purpose of maintaining or

---

Daniel French, 29 T.C.M. 1473 (1970) (professional jockey); Curtis L. Ralston, 27 T.C.M. 1312 (1968) (exercise boy); Nat Glogowski, 26 T.C.M. 1202 (1967) (race track auditor); Judy L. Gooderham, 23 T.C.M. 938 (1964) (professional skater); Patricia A. Ruby Hall, 23 T.C.M. 930 (1964) (professional skater); Estate of Robert S. Shelley, 4 T.C.M. 668 (1945) (racing handicapper); Charles J. McLennan, 4 T.C.M. 672 (1945) (race track starter). *See also* Shaefer v. United States, 1976-1 U.S.T.C. ¶ 9277 (M.D. Fla. 1976) (auditor allowed deduction in two of three years). *But cf.* Dyer v. Bookwalter, 230 F. Supp. 521 (W.D. Mo. 1964) (exercise jockey).

144. G.C.M. 7133, VIII-2 CUM BULL. 85. In reaching this conclusion, the General Counsel stated that

> [a]ccordingly, a professional golf player traveling from his home to other places for the purpose of giving for compensation exhibitions of golf playing or of competing in professional golf tournaments for prizes or other consideration, is entitled to deduct his ordinary and necessary traveling expenses paid or incurred while away from home in pursuit of such business. *Id.* at 87.

145. 1969-2 CUM. BULL. 307.

146. *See* note 143 *supra.* See also 16 Federal Tax Coordinator ¶ L-4119 (1978).

147. In determining which is the principal place of business, the factors to be considered are the amount of time spent at, the amount of business transacted at, and the relative financial return of each place of business, with the latter factor being most important in the case of services performed as an employee. Rev. Rul. 54-147, 1954-1 CUM. BULL. 51, 52; Joseph H. Sherman, 16 T.C. 332, 337 (1951).

148. Rev. Rul. 55-109, 1955-1 CUM. BULL. 261, 262; Rev. Rul. 55-604, 1955-2 CUM. BULL. 49, 50; James A. Kistler, 40 T.C. 657, 663 (1963); William L. Heuer, Jr., 32 T.C. 947, 951 (1959), *aff'd per curiam,* 283 F.2d 865 (5th Cir. 1960); Joseph H. Sherman, 16 T.C. 332, 337 (1951).

149. Rev. Rul. 54-147, 1954-1 CUM. BULL. 51, 52-53.

150. *See* Reginald Denny, 33 B.T.A. 738 (1935) (motion picture actor); Charles Hutchinson, 13 B.T.A. 1187 (1928) (stunt actor). The IRS has not, however, acquiesced in the decisions on the training expense issue. XV-1 CUM. BULL. 7, 30; VIII-1 CUM. BULL. 22, 55.

improving athletic skills.[151] For example, a professional golfer would be able to deduct the expenses of instruction designed to improve his or her putting technique.[152] Such expenses would not be deductible, on the other hand, if their purpose was to qualify the athlete for a new trade or business,[153] such as that of a golf instructor.[154] An athlete may also be able to deduct expenses incurred for the purpose of seeking employment as a professional athlete,[155] so long as the athlete is at the time engaged in the trade or business of being a professional athlete.[156] A deduction may also be available for moving expenses incurred in certain situations. This deduction has already been noted with regard to the income inclusiveness of moving expense reimbursements [157] and will not be repeated here. Finally, a deduction may be available for expenses incurred for federal tax planning.[158] Thus, an athlete will be able to deduct fees paid for tax counselling, preparation of tax returns, or the handling of proceedings to determine the extent of tax liability.[159]

§ 7.05. Tax Planning Possibilities for Professional Athletes.

Since many professional athletes receive substantial income over a relatively short period of time, it is imperative in many cases that the athlete undertake a tax planning program for the purpose of maximizing the benefit from the high income-producing years. This will frequently require efforts to minimize the tax liability from income earned through athletic performance. Although the possibilities that exist for such planning are limited only by the knowledge and resourcefulness of the athlete's advisers, there are a number of different approaches that have over the years been common in tax planning for athletes and other highly compensated persons (such as entertainers). These approaches have customarily included the utilization of deferred compensation arrangements, tax sheltered investments, and the organization of a personal service corporation. Each of these broad approaches will be considered in the following discussion.

§ 7.06. Deferred Compensation Arrangements.

The most common type of tax planning that will be utilized by professional athletes involves so-called deferred compensation arrangements. These

---

151. *See* Reg. § 1.162-5(a); Coughlin v. Commissioner, 203 F.2d 307 (2d Cir. 1953). The athlete must, however, be engaged in the trade or business of being a professional athlete at the time the expenses are incurred. Johnson v. United States, 332 F. Supp. 906 (E.D. La. 1971).

152. *See, e.g.,* Elliott v. United States, 250 F. Supp. 322 (W.D. N.Y. 1966) (cost of lessons to improve skills as a concert harpist).

153. Reg. § 1.162-5(b)(3). The expenses would also be non-deductible if they were necessary to meet some minimum educational requirements. *Id.* § 1.162-5(b)(2).

154. *See, e.g.,* Samuel W. Marshall, Jr., 14 T.C.M. 955 (1955), *aff'd,* 240 F.2d 185 (5th Cir. 1957 (could not deduct expenses to qualify as a piano teacher).

155. *See* Rev. Rul. 75-120, 1975-1 CUM. BULL. 55; Leonard F. Cremora, 58 T.C. 219 (1972); David J. Primuth, 54 T.C. 374 (1970).

156. *See* Morton Frank, 20 T.C. 511 (1953).

157. *See* § 7.02.

158. Reg. § 1.212-1(a).

159. *See* Sidney Merians, 60 T.C. 187 (1973) (20 percent of attorney's fee deductible as estate planning advice attributable to tax planning); Rev. Rul. 72-545, 1972-2 CUM. BULL. 179. *See generally* Allington, *Deductibility of Estate Planning Fees,* 60 A.B.A.J. 482 (1974).

arrangements will have the overall purpose in most cases of deferring income from the years in which it is earned until future years, with the hope of deferring the incidence of taxation and achieving an overall reduction in the federal income tax liability that attaches to the amount in question. Thus, in order to be effective a deferred compensation arrangement must allow the athlete to earn income in early years, defer it until later years, and incur federal income tax liability only in the later years when the income is actually received and when applicable tax rates will possibly be lower. There are a number of different means by which these deferral objectives may be achieved — *e.g.*, pension plans, deferral by contract and deferral by the receipt of "restricted property" — and each will be separately discussed.

Before considering the different means of achieving deferral, however, several preliminary comments are in order. The first is to note again that although "deferred compensation" was originally excluded from the favorable provisions of the 50 percent maximum tax on personal service income, the Tax Reform Act of 1976 expanded the scope of the maximum tax to include such compensation.[160] This expansion eliminates one of the disadvantages of deferred compensation arrangements that existed before the effective date of the Act (taxable years beginning after December 31, 1976).[161] If the maximum tax is utilized, however, the taxpayer will be barred from using the income averaging rules.[162]

The second preliminary comment that should be made is that before a deferred compensation arrangement is undertaken, the athlete's financial future should be analyzed to determine whether deferral will actually be of economic benefit. Thus, it must be determined whether deferral will simply add additional ordinary income to the athlete's gross income in later years when he will have the same or a higher lever of income. If this is likely to be the case, deferral may not be advantageous since the athlete may not realize a reduction in the tax paid and may be economically poorer to the extent of the income that could have been earned in the interim years by the after-tax dollars. If, on the other hand, it is

---

160. *See* § 7.01. For purposes of determining tax liability in years to which pre-Tax Reform Act of 1976 law applies, the term "deferred compensation" was defined to include any payment for services pursuant to a plan, or method having the effect of a plan, which deferred the taxation of such payment to a taxable year later than that in which the services were rendered. The recipient need not have been an employee of the person making the payment for it to have been considered "deferred compensation." Notwithstanding this general exclusion, the term "deferred compensation" did not include any amount received before the end of the taxable year following the first taxable year of the taxpayer in which his or her right to receive the compensation was not subject to a condition that would result in a substantial risk of forfeiture. Thus, if an athlete entered an agreement to engage in an athletic contest in 1971, and compensation therefor was to be paid in equal amounts in 1971, 1972, 1973 and 1974, the payments in 1971 and 1972 would have been "earned income," while the payments received in 1973 and 1974 would not because they would have constituted "deferred compensation" — that is, they would have been received later than the end of the first taxable year (1972) following the year in which the athlete's right to receive the amounts was not subject to a substantial risk of forfeiture. *See* Proposed Treas. Reg. § 1.1348-3(b)(4)(ex. 16)(professional boxer) (published December 15, 1971).

161. In light of the possible exclusion of "deferred compensation" from the maximum tax, it was important in pre-Tax Reform Act of 1976 years to determine whether the advantage of deferral in a given case might not have been largely eliminated by the fact that the maximum tax may not have been applicable to the deferred income when it was actually received by the athlete. If it had not been available, the income averaging rules would have provided some relief. *See* § 7.01.

162. IRC § 1304(b)(5).

believed that the athlete's income will decrease in future years, deferral will be more attractive since it will be more likely to result in a reduced tax liability. Even in this case, however, the period of deferral should not be extended too far into the future, since loss of the use of the after-tax dollars in the deferral period may result in a net economic loss if the amount that could thereby be earned exceeds the amount of tax reduction.[163]

In addition to considering the financial future of the athlete, it is also important that the terms of a deferred compensation arrangement be analyzed to insure that its economic substance meets both the needs and expectations of the athlete. It is common to read accounts in the sports pages of the multi-million dollar contracts periodically received by gifted athletes for signing sports contracts, but the specific terms of the contract may suggest a much different situation than the stated figures would indicate. What is identified as a multi-million dollar contract may in fact be a combination of many different types of compensation that will provide benefits to the athlete for the remainder of his or her life.[164] Whether such an arrangement is consistent with the needs and expectations of any given athlete can only be determined by considering that athlete's own situation. For example, if an athlete is to receive a large bonus for signing a contract, it could make a great deal of difference whether it will be paid in a single lump sum payment, a series of equal installments over a five year period beginning immediately, a series of installments over a twenty year period beginning when the athlete reaches age forty, or in some other manner. Each of these methods of payment may be satisfactory for some athletes, but they may also be unsatisfactory for others. There are innumerable methods of arranging deferred compensation payments and it is essential that the tax and economic consequences of an agreement be consistent with the objectives of the athlete in question before it is executed.

The problems that may be posed by an arrangement that does not meet the apparent objectives of an athlete is suggested by the situation that arose after basketball star Spencer Haywood signed a six year contract to play for the Denver Rockets of the ABA with a contract reported to be worth 1.9 million dollars. Apparently the terms of the contract called for some $400,000 to be paid in salary over the six years,[165] with the remaining 1.5 million to be deferred under a plan which called for the team to invest in mutual fund shares during

---

163. *See* Gemmill, *Deferral of Compensation Frequently Results in Overall Economic Loss,* 19 J. TAXATION 276 (1963); Herskovitz, *Techniques Available to Shield the High Income of the "Superstar,"* 34 J. TAXATION 270 (1971). *See generally* Thomas, *Income Tax Planning for Unincorporated Professional Athletes and Entertainers,* in COUNSELING PROFESSIONAL ATHLETES AND ENTERTAINERS 351 (1972).

164. Probably the best recent example of this phenomenon involves the contract signed by Jim "Catfish" Hunter with the New York Yankees in January, 1975. Hunter, who was believed to be the best pitcher in baseball, had been declared a free agent by an arbitrator's ruling and his services were open for bidding. After a much publicized bidding period, Hunter signed a contract with the Yankees that was said to call for 3.75 million dollars in payments to Hunter. This amount was reported to include a $1,000,000 bonus for signing (apparently to be paid immediately), $1,000,000 in salary payable over a five year period at $200,000 per year, $100,000 in life insurance on Hunter's life, $500,000 in retirement payments ($50,000 per year for 10 years), $200,000 in attorney's fees, and $50,000 of life insurance on Hunter's children. N. Y. Times, January 2, 1975, at 52, col. 6.

165. This was to be payable at the rate of $47,000 for the first two years, and $75,000 for the remaining four years. Denver Rockets v. All-Pro Management, Inc., 325 F. Supp. 1049, 1052 (C.D. Calif. 1971).

a ten year period. The athlete would be allowed to withdraw income from the fund at the end of the ten year period if certain conditions were met.[166] The terms of this arrangement were apparently inconsistent with the understanding and objectives of the athlete, and he thereafter repudiated the contract and signed with a team in the rival league.[167]

A final preliminary comment is that the purpose of the following discussion is to provide a general guide to the principles that relate to the types of deferred income arrangements commonly utilized by professional athletes. Thus, it is imperative that the discussion be viewed as only an outline of the subject, and that whenever deferred compensation arrangements are contemplated an athlete obtain professional counsel for drafting contractual provisions, establishing deferral plans, analyzing economic reality, and for determining or planning tax consequences.

§ 7.07. Pension Plans.

The first type of deferred compensation arrangement that ought to be considered is a pension plan that may be created by, or for the benefit of, professional athletes.[168] Such plans are commonly the result of collective bargaining agreements in the team sports. A pension plan that is "qualified" under the Code [169] will provide several benefits. The basic benefits are that

---

166. This type of arrangement is known as the "Dolgoff Plan," in honor of the person who originally formulated it. In essence, the plan calls for a team to invest a specified sum each month in specified types of securities (such as those of mutual funds), which are held in a fund that is the exclusive property of the team. The team is also given the right to sell parts of the fund and to use the proceeds to reimburse it for any taxes incurred with respect to the fund, the premiums on insurance policies that are taken out on the athlete's life, or for other related payments. The plan will then provide that the athlete may receive a specified percentage (usually 10 percent) of the fund each year beginning a number of years after the term of the contract (often as long as 20 years) has expired, though such payment may be contingent upon the athlete's performance of additional consulting duties. Finally, the plan will provide that if the athlete's employment with the team is terminated he or she will have no further interest in the fund, and that the team will have no obligation to the athlete. *See* S. GALLNER, PRO SPORTS: THE CONTRACT GAME 202-03 (1974). In light of the vast freedom that a team has to terminate an athlete's employment, *see* §§ 3.07-.09, this type of plan gives the athlete an extraordinarily small amount of security. Thus, in Denver Rockets v. All-Pro Management, Inc., 325 F. Supp. 1049 (C.D. Calif. 1971), the court observed that the contract of Spencer Haywood, which is outlined in text, was "illusory and indefinite" in terms of its deferred compensation provisions, which were in the form of the Dolgoff Plan. *Id.* at 1053.

167. Denver Rockets v. All-Pro Management, Inc., 325 F. Supp, 1049 (C.D. Calif. 1971). The situation is discussed in S. GALLNER, PRO SPORTS: THE CONTRACT GAME 102-05, 171-73 (1974).

168. The provisions mentioned with regard to "qualified" pension plan arrangements might apply as well to other types of plans (including profit sharing plans), which will be used by, or be available to, few athletes. The plans are, however, noted with respect to personal service corporations. *See* § 7.13.

169. The requirements for "qualification" are set forth in IRC § 401(a). *See generally* 4A J. MERTENS, LAW OF FEDERAL INCOME TAXATION §§ 25B .05 - .16C (1972).

With regard to qualified pension plans, it should be noted that the Code also contains provisions designed to deal with plans that do not "qualify" under IRC § 401(a). Although such plans do not appear to be of widespread use in professional athletics, the principles should at least be noted. If the plan is not qualified, then IRC § 402(b) provides that contributions are to be included in the employee's income under the terms of § 83, which is considered at § 7.09. The result of the application of § 83 principles is that an employee will be subject to tax when the employee's interest (which will be the amount of the contribution) is no longer subject to a substantial risk of forfeiture. When income inclusion is required for the employee, the employer will be entitled to a corresponding deduction. IRC § 404(a)(5).

personal service income of the athlete may be deferred to later years to the extent of employer contributions or cost,[170] the employer's contribution or cost is deductible to it as a business expense,[171] and income received by the pension plan fund is exempt from federal taxation.[172]

The primary aspect of qualified pension plan arrangements that will be of interest to professional athletes, naturally, will be the extent to which they will be taxed on the proceeds. In most cases, the athlete will be entitled to receive a series of monthly payments upon reaching the age of retirement eligibility, or upon the happening of some other specified event such as total or performance-related disability. Such payments will be included in the athlete's income in accordance with the rules provided for the income inclusion of annuity payments.[173] These rules require that a taxpayer exclude from income an amount equal to that portion of the payment which is determined by the application of an "exclusion ratio." [174] The exclusion ratio is ascertained by dividing the taxpayer's investment in the annuity by its expected return (using mortality tables provided in the regulations),[175] and the amount of the payment to be excluded from income will equal the figure that is then produced by multiplying the payment by the percentage (the exclusion ratio).[176] If, as may often be the case in the professional team sports, the athlete does not personally make any contributions to the plan, then the whole of payments received would be included in income. In addition to receiving benefits as a series of monthly payments, the plan might also give the athlete the option of receiving the benefits in a lump-sum distribution, in which case the taxability of the payments would follow a different scheme. If the total benefits due are paid out within one year of death or other separation from service in a lump-sum payment, and in a taxable year beginning after December 31, 1973, then that portion of the payment which is attributable to pre-1974 service will be entitled to preferential capital gains treatment. A separate tax will be applied to that part of the taxable portion of the distribution which is attributable to post-1973 service.[177] The application of the separate tax for post-1973 service is, however, subject to a special ten-year forward averaging rule which will reduce the tax consequences of the bunching of income in the year of distribution.[178] If the athlete dies and his or her heirs are entitled to receive a payment from a qualified plan, the value

---

170. *See* notes 173-78 *infra.*

171. IRC § 404(a). There are, however, a number of limitations to deductibility, which are set forth in IRC § 404.

172. IRC § 501(a).

173. These rules are set forth in IRC § 72, and the regulations thereunder.

174. IRC §§ 72(b); 402(a); 403(a).

175. Treas. Reg. § 1.72-9.

176. These rules may be made more clear by way of a simple example. If it be assumed that a taxpayer invested $12,650 in the plan, that he was to receive payments of $100 per month, and that the expected return (total payments) would equal $16,000 (determined by use of the mortality tables), the exclusion ratio would be 79.1 (the result of dividing $12,650 by $16,000). If the taxpayer then received $1,200 in payments during the taxable year (twelve $100 payments), then he would exclude $949.20 (79.1% x $1200), and the remainder would be taxable income. Treas. Reg. §§ 1.724(a)(2).

177. IRC § 402(e). Since the capital gain portion would be subject to the tax preference rules of §§ 56-58, *see* § 7.10, this separation may not be as beneficial as it would appear. In order to eliminate this problem, the Tax Reform Act of 1976 amended § 402(e)(4)(B) to give the taxpayer an election to treat the entire distribution as ordinary income.

178. IRC § 402(e).[*]

of such payments may also be excludible from the athlete's estate if they are not paid in a lump sum.[179]

The second type of pension plan arrangement which should be considered is that which is available to the athlete who does not participate in a team or league established plan. This category will include primarily those professional athletes who do not participate in team sports. The Code allows the self-employed person to be treated as both an "employer" and an "employee" for pension plan purposes. Plans adopted for self-employed persons provide the same basic benefits noted above, but are subject to a number of restrictions that are not applicable to pension programs for the non self-employed.[180] The most important of these is that for taxable years beginning prior to January 1, 1974, the maximum deduction that could be claimed for pension plan contributions by a self-employed person was the lesser of 10 percent of earned income from the trade or business for which the plan was established or $2,500. In an attempt to equalize the position of self-employed persons and corporate employees, the Pension Reform Act of 1974 [181] made several changes with respect to pension arrangements for the self-employed. The basic change was the increase of the deduction ceiling for taxable years beginning after December 31, 1973, to the lesser of 15 percent of earned income or $7,500,[182] though a deduction of $750 (or 100 percent of earned income), is available without regard to the 15 percent and $7,500 limitations.[183] The Act also provides a means of translating the maximum contribution limits (the 15 percent or $7,500 limitation) into approximately equivalent limitations on benefits under defined benefit plans — that is, plans in which the employee (athlete) will receive a fixed benefit, as opposed to a defined contribution plan in which he or she receives upon retirement, or other separation from service, a benefit that is determinable by the performance of the trust fund into which the contributions are deposited.[184] The basic allowable benefit that could be accrued annually under a defined benefit plan would be the sum of the products of the self-employed person's earned income (but not in excess of $50,000) and the applicable percentage from a table provided by the Act.[185] Inasmuch as the maximum annual benefit that a self-employed person could receive under such a defined benefit plan would be limited only by the general limitation of the lesser of $75,000 (subject to a cost of living increase) or 100 percent of the participant's compensation for the three highest paid years in which he or she was a participant in the plan,[186] the effect of these provisions may be to encourage self-employed athletes to establish such plans at as early an age as possible to facilitate the achievement of the maximum benefit level. The provisions relating to self-employed persons are substantially more restrictive than those which apply to corporate

179. IRC §§ 2039(c), 2039(e).
180. These restrictions are contained in IRC § 401(d). *See generally* 4A J. MERTENS, LAW OF FEDERAL INCOME TAXATION §§ 25C.01-.27 (1972).
181. Pub. L. No. 93-406, 88 Stat. 829.
182. IRC §§ 404(e)(1), 401(d)(5).
183. IRC § 404(e)(4). This provision does not apply if the taxpayer's adjusted gross income exceeds $15,000. *Id.*
184. IRC § 401(j).
185. IRC § 401(j)(3)(A).
186. IRC § 415(b)(1).

employees, and this difference may provide an incentive for the athlete to form a personal service corporation.[187]

With respect to distributions from self-employed plans, the tax results are essentially the same as those noted for ordinary plans for corporate employees. Thus, installment payments would be subject to the annuity rules, and lump sum distributions would be subject to the capital gain-ordinary income rules depending upon whether the payment was attributable to service before or after December 31, 1973.[188]

The final type of pension arrangement to which attention should be given concerns another provision of the Pension Reform Act of 1974 which creates a new scheme called Individual Retirement Accounts.[189] Such accounts would be available to persons who are not active participants in a qualified plan,[190] and could be created by the individual, or by an employer or labor union.[191] If an account is created, the individual could contribute and deduct a maximum amount of the lesser of 15 percent of the compensation included in gross income for the taxable year or $1,500.[192] Withdrawals from the account could not be made without penalty [193] prior to age 59½, and the benefits must begin by age 70½. When withdrawals or distributions are made from the account, they would be taxed in full as ordinary income [194] and would not be subject to the special ten-year forward averaging rule applicable to lump sum payments under qualified plans,[195] though they would qualify for the general averaging rules in the Code.[196]

---

187. The discussion of the self-employed situation in the text is highly simplified, and does not attempt to even summarize the specific issues that must be considered in deciding whether to establish a plan. The basic rules relating to corporate plans are considered at § 7.13 *infra*. For discussions of the relative desirability of self-employed and corporate plans for professional persons, see Irish, *Impact of the New Pension Law on H.R. 10 and Subchapter S Retirement Plans,* 42 J. TAXATION 144 (1975); Kalish & Lewis, *Professional Corporations Revisited (After the Employees Retirement Income Security Act of 1974),* 28 TAX LAW. 471 (1975); Siegel, *The Utility of the Professional Corporation: A Rejoinder,* 29 TAX LAW. 265 (1976); Thies, *Keogh Plan v. Qualified Corporate Plan: An Analysis of the Respective Advantages,* 42 J. TAXATION 9 (1975); Zalutsky, *An Analysis of the Post-ERISA Advantages of Incorporation for the Professional,* 42 J. TAXATION 240 (1975). Although these articles deal specifically with the tax situation of doctors, lawyers and other "professionals," the underlying principles would appear to apply as well to a professional athlete.

188. *See* notes 177-78 *supra*.

189. IRC § 408. Requirements for establishment of the account are set forth in IRC §§ 408(a)(1)-(7). It should also be noted that once established, the funds in the account could be utilized to purchase an annuity or certain life insurance endowment contracts, or could be invested in qualified retirement bonds. IRC §§ 219, 408. The account would also be tax exempt. IRC § 408(e)(1). *See generally* Stevenson, *The New Individual Retirement Accounts: What They Are and How They Operate,* 42 J. TAXATION 91 (1975).

190. IRC § 219(b)(2). If both a husband and a wife have compensation income and are eligible, each may establish his or her own account. IRC § 219(c)(2). An account may also be established for a taxpayer and his or her spouse. IRC § 220.

191. IRC § 408(c), which also contains the requirements that the account, or trust, must satisfy.

192. IRC § 219(b)(1). Whether or not the deduction is allowable, the amount of the contribution made by an employer would be includible in the gross income of the employee. IRC § 219(a).

193. The penalty for premature withdrawal will be an additional tax of 10 percent. IRC § 408(f)(1).

194. IRC § 408(d)(1).

195. *See* note 178 *supra*.

196. IRC §§ 1301-05. The income averaging rules are discussed at § 7.01.

§ 7.08. Deferral by Contract.

A second type of deferred compensation arrangement would involve deferring the receipt of income by contractual agreement. A contract could be executed, for example, in which income from the performance in an athletic event or the signing of a contract would be paid to the athlete in equal sums in each of the subsequent five years. The advantage to be obtained by such an arrangement would be based on the proposition that income is, as a general matter, included in a taxpayer's gross income in the taxable year in which it is received, unless his or her accounting method would require inclusion in a different period.[197] Since most professional athletes will utilize a cash receipts and disbursements method of accounting,[198] items of income will normally be includible in gross income when received.[199] Thus, if the receipt of income actually earned in the present could be postponed into the future, there would result a *pro tanto* deferral of taxation.[200]

The viability of such arrangements, however, can be properly considered only in conjunction with the so-called "constructive receipt" doctrine, the purpose of which is to limit the availability of such income and tax deferral tactics. The doctrine provides, broadly, that although income is not actually reduced to a taxpayer's possession during the taxable year, it will be "constructively" received during the taxable year in which it is credited to his account, set apart, or otherwise made available so that he is able to draw upon it, unless the taxpayer's control of receipt is subject to substantial limitations or restrictions.[201] Thus, a taxpayer to whom income is available may not arbitrarily select the year in which to report it,[202] nor may this be done by private agreement.[203] Whether a particular attempt to defer compensation will be an appropriate occasion to invoke the constructive receipt doctrine, moreover, will depend upon the specific factual situation involved.[204] If the constructive receipt

---

197. IRC § 451(a).

198. The permissible methods of accounting under the IRC are set forth in IRC § 446(c), which allows the cash receipts and disbursements method, the accrual method, any other method permitted by the chapter, or any combination of those methods as permitted by the regulations. It is to be noted, however, that IRC § 446(b) enables the IRS to compute a taxpayer's income pursuant to a method that clearly reflects income if the taxpayer has not regularly used any method, or if the method used does not clearly reflect the income actually received.

199. The cash receipts and disbursements method is defined in Treas. Reg. § 1.446-1(c)(1)(i) as follows:

> Generally, under the cash receipts and disbursements method in the computation of taxable income, all items which constitute gross income (whether in the form of cash, property, or services) are to be included for the taxable year in which actually or constructively received. Expenditures are to be deducted for the taxable year in which actually made.

200. Commissioner v. Oates, 207 F.2d 711 (7th Cir. 1953); Rev. Rul. 77-420, 1977-2 CUM. BULL. 172, *amplifying* Rev. Rul. 69-650, 1969-2 CUM. BULL. 106.

201. Treas. Reg. § 1-451-2(a); Rev. Rul. 72-25, 1972-1 CUM. BULL. 127. The doctrine does not, for fairly obvious reasons, apply to taxpayers using the accrual method. Ray S. Robinson, 44 T.C. 20 (1965); Harbor Plywood Corp., 14 T.C. 158 (1950), *aff'd per curiam*, 187 F.2d 734 (9th Cir. 1951). See generally Metzer, *Constructive Receipt, Economic Benefit and Assignment of Income: A Case Study in Deferred Compensation*, 29 TAX L. REV. 525 (1974); Watts, *Some Problems of Constructive Receipt of Income*, 27 TAX LAW. 23 (1973); Zysman, *Constructive Receipt of Income*, 16 TAX LAW. 715 (1938).

202. The Hamilton Nat'l Bank of Chattanooga, as Admin. of Estate of S. Strang Nicklin, 29 B.T.A. 63 (1933).

203. James E. Lewis, 30 B.T.A. 318 (1934).

204. Rev. Rul. 60-31, 1960-1 CUM. BULL. 174, 180.

doctrine is applied, it could be economically disastrous, since the athlete would be taxed currently but might not have the cash to satisfy the tax liability.[205]

The application of the constructive receipt doctrine to the contractual arrangements of professional athletes has been considered on several occasions. The first of these was in an example in *Revenue Ruling 60-31*,[206] where a professional football player entered a two year standard player contract and, in addition to a specified salary, received a substantial bonus for signing the contract. Although he could have received the entire bonus amount at the time of signing, the player negotiated a provision whereby the team would pay the bonus to a bank as an escrow holder. The escrow agreement then provided that payments would be made to the player, together with interest, over a five-year period. The agreement contained several provisions apparently designed to limit the player's ability to draw upon the account prematurely — that the escrow account would bear the player's name, payments would be made only in accordance with the terms of the escrow, the agreement would be binding upon all successors and assigns, and upon the player's premature death the balance of the account would become a part of his estate.[207] Although the player had thus put the bonus effectively beyond his reach for a multi-year period, the IRS found that its total amount would be includible in his income in the year the contract was signed because at that point in time the club had unconditionally paid the bonus amount to the designate of the player.[208] To defer income by contractual provision, therefore, the athlete must enter an arrangement which does not make the income directly or indirectly available to the athlete or his designate.

A better procedure is suggested by *Ray S. Robinson*,[209] where the taxpayer had his contract for an ensuing title fight drafted so that his percentage of the gate, closed circuit television rights and other forms of income from the fight would be paid to him by the promoter in four installments, 40 percent immediately and the remaining 60 percent in equal installments over a three-year period.[210] The payment of these amounts was guaranteed by several

---

205. Kroll, *Deferred Compensation Arrangements* A-2, 20-4th TAX MANAGEMENT PORTFOLIOS (1972).

206. Rev. Rul. 60-31, 1960-1 CUM. BULL. 174 (ex. 4).

207. 1960-1 CUM. BULL. at 176-77.

208. 1960-1 CUM. BULL. at 179-80. In reaching this result, the IRS relied upon Rev. Rul. 55-727, 1957-2 CUM. BULL. 25, where it had held that a bonus paid to a baseball player for signing a contract was ordinary income, not capital gain, though no escrow-type arrangement for deferral was there present. It also relied upon E.T. Sproull, 16 T.C. 244 (1951), *aff'd per curiam,* 194 F.2d 541 (6th Cir. 1952), where a taxpayer's employer had paid a sum to a trust which was to pay it to the taxpayer over a two-year period, and the Tax Court had held the entire amount includible in the year paid to the trustee since it was at that time that it was paid out for the taxpayer's sole benefit.

The example in *Rev. Rul. 60-31* and *Sproull* also illustrate application of the economic benefit theory, which is closely related to the constructive receipt doctrine and requires current taxation when the taxpayer receives an economic benefit which is equivalent to cash. Gale R. Richardson, 64 T.C. 621 (1975). This theory finds its primary application in situations where a taxpayer receives an employer's funded obligation to make future deferred compensation payments. Its application is reviewed in detail in Kroll, *Deferred Compensation Arrangements* A-7 to A-9, 20-4th TAX MANAGEMENT PORTFOLIOS (1972).

The payments involved in the example in *Rev. Rul. 60-31* and *Sproull* might also be analyzed in terms of the assignment of income doctrine. *See* § 7.03.

209. 44 T.C. 20 (1965).

210. These provisions were contained in a separate contract, which was in addition to the standard contract required by the supervising boxing commission. 44 T.C. at 25.

persons who were third parties to the agreements. There was no provision for payment of these funds into a separate account, as in the *Revenue Ruling 60-31* example. The taxpayer was simply in the posture of a general creditor of the promoter, though payments were made to the taxpayer to settle various claims of creditors and the IRS. On these facts, the Tax Court stated that the question was *when,* not *whether,* the amounts were includible in the gross income of the taxpayer.[211] The question was answered by finding that the amounts were includible when paid, not in an aggregate amount as of the date of the first payment as had been contended by the IRS.[212] Constructive receipt was not appropriate, the court said, because once the contract was executed it defined the parties' rights and bound them equally.[213]

In *Ray S. Robinson,* therefore, the Tax Court clearly indicated that the constructive receipt doctrine can be avoided, but to do so the professional athlete must insure that the income deferral is done through a binding contractual agreement and that the income is not simply paid to a designate for later disbursement to the athlete. Thus, in *Revenue Ruling 60-31* the IRS stated that the constructive receipt doctrine would not apply to a bonus provision in a professional baseball player's contract which called for the bonus payment to be spread out over two years, inasmuch as the player was contractually barred from receiving the entire amount in the first year.[214] In short, the contractual deferral arrangement will avoid the constructive receipt doctrine only if it makes the athlete a general creditor of the other party to the agreement.[215]

Although it is generally said that the promise to pay must be no more than a simple promise to pay by the payor, it should be kept in mind that in *Ray S. Robinson* the athlete also received the guarantees of several persons who were not parties to the basic agreement, and the presence of these guarantees did not appear to have any effect on the Tax Court's conclusion that the deferral arrangement would be upheld.[216] With regard to deferral by contract, it should also be noted that the provisions of the Pension Reform Act of 1974 may be applicable to some types of deferred compensation arrangements, although at the time of this writing specific application is not yet clear.[217]

The final point to be made with respect to contractual deferral arrangements is that the IRS has recently indicated that it will no longer issue advance rulings on whether any given arrangement will be viewed favorably for federal income

---

211. 44 T.C. at 33.

212. The IRS had also contended that the taxpayer was engaged in a joint venture with the promoter, so that the entire amount would be included in the year earned. This argument was based upon another example in *Rev. Rul. 60-31,* 1960-1 CUM. BULL. 174 (ex. 5), where the IRS had stated that a joint venture was present on similar facts. Since this position was rejected in *Robinson,* and since the IRS acquiesced in the decision, 1970-34 I.R.B. 6, the example in *Rev. Rul. 60-31* was amended to coincide with *Robinson,* Rev. Rul. 70-435, 1970-2 CUM. BULL. 100, by changing the facts from a boxing match to a theatrical performance. Thus, the IRS still, apparently, favors the joint venture theory as a means of interdicting efforts to defer current income.

213. 44 T.C. at 37.

214. The facts stated were those in Rev. Rul. 55-727, 1955-2 CUM. BULL. 25.

215. A more secure position may be achieved by using IRC § 83. *See* § 7.09.

216. *See* Herskovitz, *Techniques Available to Shield the High Income of the "Superstar,"* 34 J. TAXATION 270 (1971).

217. *See* Kroll, *Deferred Compensation Arrangements,* at ERISA-1 to ERISA-7 (Special Supplement), 20-4th TAX MANAGEMENT PORTFOLIOS (1972).

tax purposes.[218] It has also suggested that it may take a much more aggressive position with respect to such arrangements. Thus, the IRS has issued proposed Regulations, which, if adopted, would have a significant impact on nonqualified deferred compensation plans offering the recipient-taxpayer an election to defer the receipt of compensation.

Under the proposed Regulations, a taxpayer (whether or not an employee) who individually chooses under a plan or arrangement (other than a "qualified plan") to have the payment of a portion of his or her current compensation deferred until a later year, will have the amount deferred treated as having been received in the earlier taxable year.[218.1] This result will occur even if the taxpayer's rights in the deferred amount become forfeitable by reason of the exercise of the option. For purposes of this proposal, "compensation" is defined to include, in addition to basic or regular compensation, supplemental payments such as bonuses.

The proposed Regulations do, however, contain a "grandfather" clause, which provides that the amendment will not apply to the amount of any payment which the taxpayer has chosen to defer under a plan or arrangement in existence on February 3, 1978, if the amount would have been payable, but for exercise of the option, prior to a date 30 days following the final adoption of the Regulations.

In announcing these proposals, the IRS identified certain of its previous rulings which would no longer be applied,[218.2] and stated that its acquiescence in two Tax Court decisions (including *Ray S. Robinson*) would be reconsidered,[218.3] if the new Regulations are adopted. In each of these rulings or decisions, the deferral was a result of the specific individual election or request of the receipient-taxpayer. The Service also identified other rulings (including two examples in *Revenue Ruling 60-31*) which would be reexamined to determine whether the deferral was at the individual option of the taxpayer who earned the compensation.[218.4] These rulings include situations in which the deferral was mandatory and not elective. Thus, it appears that the Service may attempt to permit deferral only when it is made at the insistence of the obligor, as opposed to deferral made at the request of the taxpayer.

The proposal raises a number of problems. For example, the apparent distinction between deferred compensation arrangements undertaken at the request of the taxpayer and those imposed by the obligor will be difficult to draw and will undoubtedly turn on subjective issues of intent and conduct, such as whether the obligor would have been willing to pay compensation currently and

---

218. *See* IR-1881 (Sept. 7, 1977). This altered its previous practice of issuing such rulings. Rev. Rul. 64-279, 1964-2 CUM. BULL. 121. *See generally,* Warner, *The IRS Freeze on Deferred Compensation Rulings — Prospects for the Future,* 78-1 THE COMPENSATION PLANNING J. 3 (1978).

218.1. Prop. Treas. Reg. § 1.61-16 (Jan. 31, 1978). Specifically, the Regulations provide,

> if under a plan or arrangement [other than a qualified plan] ... payment of an amount of a taxpayer's basic or regular compensation fixed by contract, statute, or otherwise (or supplements to such compensation, such as bonuses ...) is, at the taxpayer's individual option, deferred to a taxable year later than that in which such amount would have been payable but for his exercise of such option, the amount shall be treated as received by the taxpayer in such earlier taxable year.

218.2. These rulings were Rev. Rul. 71-149, 1971-2 CUM. BULL. 220; Rev. Rul. 69-650, 1969-2 CUM. BULL. 106; Rev. Rul. 68-86, 1968-1 CUM. BULL. 184; Rev. Rul. 67-449, 1967-2 CUM. BULL. 1973.

218.3. In addition to *Robinson,* the other case is James F. Oates, 18 T.C. 570 (1952).

218.4. In addition to Rev. Rel. 60-31, these included Rev. Rul. 72-24, 1972-1 CUM. BULL. 127; Rev. Rul. 69-99, 1969-1 CUM. BULL. 193.

the reasons for adoption of a deferral arrangement. In addition, the Service's position that it will henceforth be "immaterial" that the taxpayer's rights in the deferred amount become forfeitable by reason of the election to defer is not only inconsistent with its former position, but also with long-standing concepts of "constructive receipt" and other sections of the Code which deal with the effect of a substantial risk of forfeiture on the receipt of compensation for services.[218.5] Finally, it is far from clear that the Regulations would be enforced by a court, inasmuch as they would purport to overrule the results of several long-standing judicial interpretations. In light of the venerable tradition of deferral, the courts may very well conclude that the deferral privilege cannot be overturned by mere executive decision, but will, rather, require Congressional action.

At the time of this writing (August, 1978), it is not clear whether the IRS will adopt the proposal, or, if it does, how broadly the final language will reach. In any event, it is apparent that the proposed Regulations would, if adopted in substantially the same form as proposed, have a significant impact upon contractual deferral arrangements in professional sports. These Regulations also indicate that the IRS is, at the very least, considering a much more aggressive position in this area, and its action should be watched closely.[218.6]

§ 7.09.   Deferral by Receipt of "Substantially Non-Vested Property."

If the athlete wishes to take advantage of the benefits of deferring income, cannot partake of a qualified pension plan, and wants to be in a more secure position than he or she would be as a "general creditor" under a contractual deferral arrangement,[219] attention should be given to the use of so-called "substantially non-vested property." The term "substantially non-vested property" refers to property, other than money or an unfunded and unsecured promise to pay deferred compensation (such as a contractual deferral arrangement) which is transferred in connection with the performance of services.[220] The advantage offered by such property is that its value (determined by subtracting the amount paid for it from its fair market value, which is determined without regard to any restriction other than a restriction that will never lapse) is not required to be included in the recipient's income until the first time that the beneficial interest in it becomes substantially vested — i.e., transferable or no longer subject to a substantial risk of forfeiture.[221] The

---

218.5. *See* IRC § 83, discussed in § 7.09.

218.6. As this book went to press, the Revenue Act of 1978 was enacted and provided, in § 132, that the year of inclusion of payments under this type of deferred arrangement will be determined in accordance with the law as of February 1, 1978 — *i.e.,* as it stood before the proposed Regulations.

219. *See* § 7.08.

220. Treas. Reg. § 1.83-3(e). The final regulations were adopted on July 24, 1978. 43 Fed. Reg. 31911.

221. IRC § 83(a). This rule will not apply if the property is sold prior to the time it is transferable or no longer subject to a substantial risk of forfeiture. IRC § 83(a). When the recipient of the property is required to include its value in income, the transferor would be entitled to a deduction for the amount of inclusion to the recipient in the taxable year of the recipient's inclusion. IRC § 83(h).

See generally Baker, *Restricted Property — Section 83,* 262 TAX MANAGEMENT PORTFOLIOS (1972); Hindin, *Internal Revenue Code Section 83 Restricted Stock Plans,* 59 CORNELL L. REV. 298 (1974); Note, *Deferred Compensation Arrangements Under Section 83 of the Internal Revenue Code: Is Restricted Property Still a Viable Means of Compensation?,* 70 MICH. L. REV. 1202 (1972).

recipient may, however, elect to include the value of the property in income in the year of receipt, and the amount of inclusion would be the excess of its fair market value (determined as indicated above) at the time of transfer over the amount paid for it.[222] For purposes of these rules, a "substantial risk of forfeiture" is defined to occur when the recipient's rights to full enjoyment of the property are conditioned upon the performance, or the refraining from performance, of substantial services by any individual,[223] and the property will be "transferable" when the rights of the recipient are no longer subject to a substantial risk of forfeiture.[224]

The restricted property provisions, then, offer the professional athlete significant tax planning opportunities. Their primary usefulness to most athletes will be as a means of deferring the recognition of income and providing a security device.[225] Thus, the rules will allow an athlete to acquire possession of property at the time services are rendered while permitting the deferral of taxation until the point in time at which the substantial risk of forfeiture lapses. This result is to be contrasted to the contractual deferral arrangement, where the athlete would achieve deferral but would remain an unsecured general creditor of the employer.[226] In order to take advantage of these rules, the athlete will simply have the party for whom services are to be rendered take the amount which is to be deferred and purchase whatever type of property the athlete desires — for example, corporate stock or any other form of personal or real property.[227] The property would then be transferred to the athlete with a restriction that would qualify as a "substantial risk of forfeiture" — such as a provision requiring the athlete to return the property to the transferor in the event that the athlete terminates his or her services during a specified period.[228]

In drafting restricted property agreements, it is important to keep in mind that a risk of forfeiture can be written in several ways to state the same type of risk, but the language may place control of forfeiture in one or the other party. For example, if the risk is to be that an athlete perform for a team for a five year period, it will make a considerable difference whether forfeiture occurs if the athlete fails to remain a member of the team for five years or fails to make himself available to the team for five years. In the former situation, the team would control the risk since it could cut the athlete for many reasons

---

222. IRC § 83(b). It should be noted that if the property is subsequently forfeited, the recipient would generally be entitled to no deduction, IRC § 83(b), though the regulations would allow a loss, equal to the excess of the amount, if any, that the taxpayer actually paid for the property over the amount realized. Treas. Reg. § 1.83-2(a).

223. IRC § 83(c) (1); Treas. Reg. § 1.83-3(c). *See also* Estate of James M. Harrison, 62 T.C 524 (1974) (amount paid into trust upon resignation of decedent not included in year of payment because of the condition that the decedent not work for other groups). *But cf.* Gale R. Richardson, 64 T.C. 621 (1975).

224. IRC § 83(c)(2).

225. It should be noted that when included in income, the "substantially non-vested property" will qualify for the 50 percent maximum tax on personal service income. IRC § 1348(b)(1). *See* § 7.01.

226. *See* § 7.08.

227. Although § 83 deals primarily with the stock of an employer corporation which is transferred to corporate employees as compensation for services, it includes as well all forms of real and personal property other than money or an unfunded and unsecured promise to pay deferred compensation. Treas. Reg. § 1.83-3(e).

228. This will be a sufficient "substantial risk of forfeiture." Treas. Reg. § 1.83-3(c)(1).

which would give the athlete no basis for complaint[229] and preclude the restricted property from vesting. In the latter situation, however, the athlete would control the risk since he would determine whether to be available.

If the athlete desires to avoid a bunching of income in the taxable year when the restrictions lapse, it could be specified that the restrictions would lapse at a pro rata rate during the period of restriction, and that all restrictions would lapse if the transferor became insolvent or bankrupt. As a result of these provisions, the athlete would have possession of the property and would be required to include its value in income only as the restrictions serially lapse.[230]

The athlete could also use the restricted property rules to insure that appreciation in the value of the property would be taxed at capital gain rates. If an athlete were, for example, to sign a contract with a team and were to receive shares of stock in the team, he or she could elect to include the value of the stock in income in the year of receipt.[231] If the team then prospered, subsequent appreciation in the value of the stock would be taxed at capital gains rates when the restrictions lapse or the property is sold or exchanged, assuming that the stock would otherwise qualify as a capital asset.[232]

The restricted property rules will also be important in situations where an athlete is successful in negotiating for options to acquire shares of stock in the team. If a non-statutory stock option[233] is granted which has a readily ascertainable fair market value at the time of grant,[234] the person performing the services will realize compensation income in accordance with the general principles of § 83.[235] When the option is exercised there will be no additional compensation income, since the compensatory event occurred when the option was granted.[236] If an option is granted that does not have a readily ascertainable fair market value, it is excluded from § 83 altogether so that no income will be realized at the time of grant.[237] When this latter type of option is exercised, the § 83 rules would then come into play. Thus, if the stock received upon exercise was transferable and not subject to a substantial risk of forfeiture, then the athlete would be required to recognize income under § 83.[238] If the property received were non-transferable or subject to a substantial risk of forfeiture, then taxation would be postponed unless an election were made for immediate inclusion.[239]

---

229. *See* §§ 3.07-.09.

230. Treas. Reg. § 1.83-3(c)(4) (ex. 3).

231. *See* note 222 *supra.*

232. *See* Treas. Reg. § 1.83-2(a); Herskovitz, *Techniques Available to Shield the High Income of the "Superstar",* 34 J. TAXATION 270, 271 (1971).

233. The term "non-statutory" stock options refers to options that are not qualified under IRC §§ 422(b) or 424(b). *See* Baker, *Nonstatutory Stock Options,* 87-3rd TAX MANAGEMENT PORTFOLIOS (1974). Statutory stock options are considered in Baker, *Stock Options (Statutory) — Taxation,* 183-2nd TAX MANAGEMENT PORTFOLIOS (1970), though they were essentially eliminated on a prospective basis by § 603 of the Tax Reform Act of 1976.

234. An option will normally have a readily ascertainable fair market value only if it is traded on an established market, Treas. Reg. § 1.83-7(b)(1), unless the fair market value can be measured by some other reasonably accurate method. *Id.* § 1.83-7(b)(2).

235. Treas. Reg. § 1.83-7(a). *See* note 221 *supra.*

236. Baker, *Nonstatutory Stock Options* A-19, 87-3rd TAX MANAGEMENT PORTFOLIOS (1974).

237. IRC § 83(e)(4); Treas. Reg. § 1.83-7(a).

238. Treas. Reg. § 1.83-7(a).

239. *See* note 222 *supra.*

With regard to the use of stock options, attention should also be given to so-called "phantom stock

§ 7.10. Tax Sheltered Investments.

A second type of tax planning that might be considered by professional athletes involves the use of tax sheltered investments. The effectiveness of such investments was substantially limited by the Tax Reform Act of 1976. Since some athletes may be involved in "shelters" not affected by the Act, and not all "shelters" were eliminated by it, the following discussion will develop the general principles that apply to "shelters" and identify the changes made by the Act.

The term "tax shelter" is used to describe a wide variety of transactions, and the common element is an investment which allows the taxpayer to offset certain tax or accounting losses—that is, losses which are sustained for tax purposes but which do not represent actual economic losses—against income from the investment and, hopefully, from other sources.[240] To the extent that an investment actually produces these results, it will have the effect of "sheltering" (through the deductions) income from federal income tax liability. It should be emphasized, however, that the use of tax shelters will in most cases not avoid the bite of federal income taxation, but they will allow the taxpayer to defer its imposition. Accordingly, it has been observed that a successful tax shelter is simply a "means of moving income from high tax brackets to low tax brackets."[241]

The use of tax sheltered investments could, then, be quite beneficial to professional athletes whose athletic talents will produce high income during a relatively short period of time. Such investments could enable the athlete to earn income from investments without the imposition of current federal income tax and, perhaps more importantly, use the shelter benefit to offset income from athletic endeavors. As with most of the other subjects considered in this chapter, the desirability of specific tax shelter investments for any given athlete can be determined only after careful analysis of his or her situation.

There are a variety of investments that may produce tax shelter benefits, but they generally fall into three broad categories.[242] The first may be described as an investment that produces "capital gain conversion." This benefit could be achieved by investments which produce current deductions that the taxpayer can use to offset other ordinary income, with the intent of recouping the invested

---

plans". The purpose of such plans is to defer income, and the amount of income deferred is determined by the value or growth in the "phantom" stock account of the employee. The stock is described as "phantom" because there may actually be no shares in the employee's account. The account would be handled by an entry which would credit a certain number of shares in the employer's stock (or any other issue of stock) to the employee's account. The account would also be credited with dividends on the stock and any other additions of "phantom" stock value. The value of the "phantom" stock would be determined by its market value at the time it is credited to the employee's account. The balance of the account could then be paid out to the employee at some future date, depending upon the provisions of the governing agreement, and income would be recognized in the year in which the account, or the value which it reflects from the various entries plus appreciation in value, is received by the employee. See generally 2 F. O'NEAL, CLOSE CORPORATIONS, LAW AND PRACTICE § 8.11 (1971); Herskovitz, supra note 232, at 270-71.

240. Joint Committee on Internal Revenue Taxation, Overview of Tax Shelters: Prepared for the Use of the House Committee on Ways and Means, 94th Cong., 1st Sess. 4 (1975). See also Adams, Tax Shelter in Real Estate Investments, 1 UTAH B.J. 13 (1973).

241. Pennell, Analyzing a Tax Shelter for Its True Consequences—A Case Study in Detail, 1974 So. FED. TAX. INST. I-1.

242. Pennell, supra note 241, at I-1 to I-2.

funds and hopefully a profit in the future at preferential capital gains rates.[243] This type of shelter has principally involved investment in real estate. The taxpayer could, for example, invest the funds in a new residential apartment complex. The apartments would produce income from rentals, and against this income the taxpayer would be able to deduct depreciation, interest, real estate taxes and other expenses required to maintain and operate the apartments.[244] The major deduction would be for depreciation,[245] but it would be a non-cash expense in the sense that it would not require a cash disbursement.[246] If the deductions exceed the rental income, there would then be a net operating loss from the apartment business. Although this would be a loss for tax purposes, it is possible that it would not be an economic loss since the major deduction item would be depreciation which would not have required a cash expenditure. Thus, it is also possible that the investment could produce a positive cash flow, in the sense that the taxpayer could receive income from the apartments that would be sheltered by the net operating loss. The loss could also be used to offset (shelter) income from other sources (such as income from sports competition). Finally, when the investment property (the apartment building) is sold, the taxpayer could be entitled to claim capital gains treatment on the gain,[247] which would essentially enable the taxpayer to convert current ordinary income (which has been offset by previous deductions from the investment) into gain taxed at capital gain rates. The benefits to be obtained from capital gain conversion shelters are, however, available only in a limited number of situations.[248]

The second type of tax shelter investment involves the favorable deferral of ordinary income. This type of benefit would be obtained by investing in such a manner as to obtain current deductions which the taxpayer could offset against other ordinary income, with the intent of recouping the investment, and a profit, as ordinary income in future years that will be subject to more favorable rates. The most common method of accomplishing this type of benefit has been

---

243. The rates of taxation applicable to capital gains are preferential because the taxpayer is allowed to deduct one-half of net long-term capital gain in determining taxable income. IRC § 1202. For a taxpayer in the 70 percent tax bracket, this means that the effective rate applied to the net gain would be 35 percent. There is also an alternative method of calculating the capital gains tax under IRC § 1201(b), which in essence allows the taxpayer to calculate the tax on the gain by subjecting the first $25,000 of gain to a maximum tax of 25 percent with the remainder being taxed at one-half of the marginal rates that would otherwise be applicable to the income. The benefit of these rates has been reduced by the Tax Reform Act of 1976. See notes 271-75 *infra*.[*]

244. *See* IRC §§ 163(a) (interest), 164(a)(1) (real estate taxes), 162(a) and 212.

245. IRC § 167(a).

246. The amount of the depreciation deduction is determined by applying an appropriate method of calculating the rate of depreciation to the depreciable basis of the property. *Id.* §§ 167(b), (g). The depreciable basis is the cost or other basis of the property determined under § 1011, § 167(g), and this basis would include any liabilities that are incurred by the taxpayer to acquire the property. *See* notes 256-57 *infra*. This basis is reduced as depreciation deductions are utilized. IRC § 1016(a)(2).

247. *See* note 243 *supra*.

248. Capital gains conversion is principally limited by the depreciation recapture provisions that were enacted in 1969. IRC §§ 1245, 1250 (amended in 1976). Section 1245 is discussed at § 7.19, in connection with professional sports contracts.

Conversion would still be possible with respect to real property that is depreciated on a straight-line method, IRC § 1250(b)(1), and, to a limited extent, low income housing. Capital gain conversion may also be possible in other investments, including professional team sport franchises (*see* § 7.20).

Even where the recapture rules apply, they preclude capital gain conversion but do not affect the benefits to be derived from ordinary income deferral. *See* notes 252-54 *infra*.

through oil and gas drilling operations, where the cost of drilling is deductible against ordinary income.[249] The benefit of such investments has, however, been sharply reduced by the substantial restriction of the oil depletion allowance [250] and the provision of the Tax Reform Act of 1976 requiring recapture of the drilling expenses upon sale of the well.[251]

The final type of basic tax shelter investment involves the simple deferral of ordinary income. This benefit may be obtained by investing in an activity for which deductions can be claimed in one year even though income is not generated until a later year.[252] This causes a mismatch to occur with respect to the income and deductions attributable to the investment, with the accelerated deductions exceeding (sheltering) the income. The excess produces a net operating loss, which in turn may be used to offset (shelter) other income of the taxpayer. The net effect of the transaction is to defer tax liability on the sheltered income, and this has the effect of providing the taxpayer with an interest-free loan from the Treasury. To taxpayers in high tax brackets, the benefit from this loan can be substantial.[253] Although the taxes that are reduced in these early years will generally be shifted to later years, the taxpayer will have had the use of the unpaid taxes (the so-called interest-free loan) in the interim, and if his or her marginal tax rates are lower in the later years the actual tax liability may be reduced. In addition, the taxpayer may be able to avoid taxes even in the later years by investing in another sheltered investment.[254]

With respect to these deferral benefits, it is to be noted that they were in some cases substantially restricted by the Tax Reform Act of 1976. In essence, Congress sought to preclude the acceleration of deductions for several types of investment by requiring that certain expenses be capitalized and amortized over a specified period.[255] The effect of these provisions is to prevent the intentional mismatch of deductions and income in the covered investments.

The benefits to be derived from a tax shelter may be even greater to the extent that a taxpayer can utilize borrowed funds to make a large part (or all) of the shelter investment. These additional benefits are said to be the result of the taxpayer's having "leveraged" his or her own equity investment with borrowed funds. The leveraging is beneficial because for tax purposes borrowed funds are treated as if they were the taxpayer's own funds.[256] An illustration will make the benefits of leveraging more clear. If a taxpayer in the 70 percent tax bracket uses entirely his own assets to make an investment of $100,000, and it produces

---

249. IRC § 263(c); Reg. § 1.612-4.

250. For taxable years beginning after December 31, 1974 the benefits of percentage depletion will be available only for certain domestic gas wells, IRC § 613A(b)(1), and small producers of oil and gas. *Id.* § 613A(c)(1).

251. IRC § 1254 (applicable to taxable years beginning after December 31, 1975).

252. *See Overview of Tax Shelters, supra* note 240, at 5.

253. The amount of the "loan" or deferred tax liability increases as the tax bracket of the taxpayer increases. Thus, if taxpayer is entitled to a $1,000 deduction from a sheltered investment, it will provide a $200 benefit if he or she is in a 20 percent marginal bracket but a $700 benefit in a 70 percent bracket.

254. *See, e.g., Overview of Tax Shelters, supra* note 240, at 5.

255. This treatment is required for construction period expenses on real property improvements, IRC § 189, certain farming expenses, IRC §§ 464, 2780(b), 447, and prepaid interest. IRC § 461(g).

256. The classic case supporting this proposition is Crane v. Commissioner, 331 U.S. 1, 91 L. Ed. 1301, 67 S. Ct. 1047 (1947).

$20,000 of accelerated deductions in the first year, he will receive a benefit of $14,000 in the first year ($20,000 of deductions multiplied by the 70 percent marginal tax rate). In effect, the taxpayer is recovering $14,000 of the investment in the first year. If, on the other hand, the taxpayer uses $90,000 of borrowed money, then the first year benefit will still be $14,000, but the taxpayer's investment situation is much different. He will have invested only $10,000 of personal assets, and will receive $14,000 in tax benefits during the first year. Thus, the entire equity investment of $10,000 will be returned, and the taxpayer will get an additional tax (shelter) benefit of $4,000. By using borrowed funds, the taxpayer frees his own capital for other investments, and materially increases the rate of return on the equity that is invested. In addition, the equity funds that are invested will be recovered much more quickly (as illustrated by the above example), and the effect of this rapid recovery is that the Treasury will finance the investment through an additional form of interest-free loan.[257]

The benefits of leveraging may be increased if the taxpayer can obtain borrowed funds without personal liability (so called "non-recourse" loans), since he can then obtain tax shelter benefits with a minimum amount of legal risk—that is, liability to repay the loan out of personal assets. The benefits to be derived from non-recourse financing were sharply restricted by the Tax Reform Act of 1976. Its principal provision in this respect is new § 465, which limits the loss (excess of deductions over income) that may be deducted in the case of certain investments to the amount that the taxpayer has "at risk" in the activity.[258] These amounts include the amount of money and adjusted basis of property contributed, and liabilities to the extent that the taxpayer is personally liable or has pledged qualified property as security.[259] The provisions of § 465 apply to activities which involve films or video tapes, farming, leasing of personal property, and oil and gas exploration.[260] While § 465 applies to a limited range of activities, a much broader provision was added to preclude non-recourse liabilities from being used for loss deduction purposes by partners in a partnership.[261] The partnership provision does not, however, apply to real estate activities.[262] In short, the use of non-recourse liabilities will be limited in the future with the principal exception of real estate investments.

Even where borrowed funds are used, it should not be assumed that there is no tax risk. The principle that allows taxpayers to treat borrowed funds on a par with equity funds is a two-edged sword. Its other edge is that when a taxpayer is relieved of responsibility for borrowed funds—for example, through assumption by a third party—the relief is treated as a taxable payment of cash to the taxpayer, even in the case of non-recourse liabilities. This can be a very tangible risk. For example, if a taxpayer borrows $100,000 through a

---

257. This effect is discussed in *Overview of Tax Shelters, supra* note 240, at 6.

258. IRC § 465(a). Any unused loss may be carried forward to the year in which the taxpayer has additional amounts "at risk."[*]

259. IRC § 465(b). There are also other limitations on the source and terms of such borrowed funds. *See* IRC §§ 465(b)(3) and (c).

260. IRC § 465(c)(1).[*]

261. IRC § 704(d).[*]

262. *Id.*

non-recourse loan to invest in a tax shelter investment, the "shelter" turns out to be an economic disaster, and the taxpayer allows the lender to foreclose on the property securing the loan, then he will realize $100,000 of taxable income in the year of foreclosure. The $100,000 will, however, be "constructive" income in the sense that the taxpayer will actually receive no income in an economic sense, so that other funds will have to be found to discharge any resulting tax liability.

Although the discussion of tax sheltered investments presented here is a brief outline of an exceptionally complex subject, it should be sufficient to suggest the usefulness of such investments to professional athletes. Most athletes will be able to reap large income from their athletic ability for only a few years, and it is essential that this income be received and utilized with maximum advantage to the athlete. Since the large amounts of income will produce proportionately large tax liabilities, the athlete will be benefitted to the extent that the tax liabilities are reduced. One method of accomplishing this would be through investments that shelter the income in the year actually received. For example, if an athlete were to receive $250,000 for signing a contract, the substantial tax liability on the bonus could be avoided (deferred) if the athlete could invest in a manner that would provide a $250,000 deduction. If this could be arranged through 100 percent non-recourse financing, then the athlete would be in a rather attractive situation. The $250,000 would be received tax free (because of the sheltering deductions), and the athlete would have none of his or her own assets at risk in the investment. This is obviously only an illustration of the manner in which tax shelters could be utilized, but it does suggest the potential benefit.

It must also be emphasized that tax shelters are not a universal solvent for tax problems. Just as they may provide large benefits to some taxpayers, they may provide equally large problems to others. Thus, it is essential that the situation of any given athlete be analyzed in detail before he or she is advised to enter a tax shelter arrangement.[263] Attention must be given to his or her objectives. It will make a difference, for example, whether the athlete desires (or should desire) to obtain cash immediately, defer the realization of income or achieve a capital gains conversion. Attention must also be given to the extent to which the athlete is willing to undertake risks of a legal, tax or economic nature. Whether "legal" risk will be present depends on the nature of the organizational form that is utilized for the investment. If a corporation is used, the athlete will have legal risk only to the extent of the equity investment. If, on the other hand, it is a general partnership or sole proprietorship, the investor will have unlimited liability. If it is a limited partnership, and the athlete is a limited partner, the legal risk should, like the corporation, be limited to the investment.[264] Legal risk may also be present in either the corporation or the limited partnership if lenders require the athlete to assume personal liability on borrowed funds, as will often be the case. A "tax" risk will be present if the tax consequences of the investment are uncertain. This is true of many tax

---

263. The discussion in text is drawn from Pennell, *Analyzing a Tax Shelter for its True Consequences—A Case Study in Detail,* 1974 So. FED. TAX INST. I-1 to I-8 to I-11.

264. See § 7.16.

shelters, and because of their potential benefits they are prime targets for IRS audit. Thus, unless an IRS ruling can be obtained to insure favorable tax consequences, an investment may pose substantial tax risk to the investor. An economic risk will be present to the extent that there is a chance that the investment will be an economic loser, as opposed to a mere tax loser but economic winner. Experience in recent years suggests that many shelters do indeed raise this problem.

The final characteristic of the athlete that must be considered is his or her income structure. It is important to determine the amount of income that the athlete will realize during the period of the investment as well as the nature of that income. This is, of course, an uncertain inquiry to the extent that the size or nature of income in the future is not subject to reliable prediction. The purpose of the inquiry is to make a determination as to whether the athlete's income is such as to make a tax shelter sensible. The essential question will be whether the investor's income qualifies as "personal service" income for purposes of the 50 percent maximum tax.[265]

If an investor has only personal service income, it may not be worth sheltering, since the tax advantages may not outweigh the risk that will be required by the shelter. An example will help make this point clear. If a taxpayer has personal service income of $200,000 and files a joint return, the amount of tax thereupon will be $90,460.[266] If he receives a deduction from a tax shelter in the amount of $50,000 (assume an investment of $50,000 in the same year), the tax benefit will be a reduction in tax liability of $25,000. If the taxpayer recoups the investment in a later year, and if we assume the same income structure (all personal service income), then the best that the investor could hope to achieve would be payment of the $25,000 tax due in the earlier year, but deferred until the year of payment. Thus, the investor would have achieved an "IRS loan" through deferral. Unfortunately, the result to the investor may not even be this bright, since the return of the investment may be taxed as non-personal service income and not be subject to the protective ceiling of the 50 percent maximum tax. If this is the case, the taxpayer could have a substantially greater tax liability in the year of payment than would have existed in the original year of deduction.

Although one might assume that capital gains conversion could be beneficial to an investor with all personal service income, this may no longer be true because of the expansion of the tax preference rules by the Tax Reform Act of 1976.[267]

The above discussion suggests that there may be only limited advantages to be derived from sheltering personal service income, so that attention must be focused on the benefits of sheltering non-personal service income. For purposes of discussion, let us use the same taxpayer considered above, but assume that he has personal service income of $160,000, other income of $40,000 and taxable

---

265. IRC § 1348(a). The maximum tax is discussed at § 7.01.

266. This is the result of applying the rate structure in IRC § 1(a), as limited by the maximum tax of § 1348, which would impose a tax of $18,060 on the first $55,200 plus 50 percent of the taxable income in excess of $55,200 ($144,800) or $72,400, totalling $90,460.[*]

267. The tax preference rules are discussed at notes 271-75 *infra*.[*]

income of $200,000. The tax on the personal service income would be $70,460.[268] The $40,000 of other income would be subject to tax in the amount of $27,304.[269] If the tax shelter created a deduction of $50,000 (again, in the amount of the investment assumed), then the tax liability would be $65,460, which would produce a tax saving of $32,304.[270] Since a large portion of the income sheltered by the deduction is other income, the taxpayer will not lose even if the deduction is recouped in a later year as non-personal services income. If it is recouped in a manner that allows capital gain treatment, of course, there may be an additional benefit.

With regard to the athlete's characteristics, it is also essential to determine the effect of the minimum tax on preference items.[271] These items include, *inter alia,* accelerated depreciation on leased property, intangible drilling costs, excess itemized deductions, and one-half of net long-term capital gains.[272] Tax preference items in excess of the greater of $10,000 or one-half of the regular tax liability are taxed at a rate of 15 percent,[273] which is in addition to other taxes that are due.

The fact of the 15 percent tax is not, however, the only problem posed by the minimum tax. It will also have the effect of reducing the amount of income subject to the maximum tax. Thus, each dollar of preference income offsets personal service taxable income on a dollar for dollar basis.[274] Thus, the effect of tax preference items to an investor with personal service income is to subject the "tax-preferenced" dollars to a maximum of 70 percent taxation instead of 50 percent. In addition, the minimum tax may cause the effective rate of tax on capital gains to approach the 50 percent level if the taxpayer has substantial personal service income.[275]

The final inquiry that ought to be made concerning a prospective tax shelter investment, after it is understood what type of shelter the taxpayer is seeking

---

268. This calculation would be made in a similar manner as in note 266 *supra,* and the only difference would be that the 50 percent maximum rate would be applied to the $104,800 in excess of $55,200. Thus, the tax liability would be a function of the combination of $18,060 plus $52,400 (50 percent of $104,800).[*]

269. This figure is equal to the tax determined under the applicable § 1 rates without regard to the maximum tax over the tax computed with reference solely to the personal service income. IRC § 1348(a)(3). In effect, this process isolates the other income at the highest marginal bracket of the taxpayer, as if there had been no maximum tax. Specifically, the calculation would be as follows:

(a) Tax on $55,200 of earned income	14,060
(b) 50% of earned income in excess of $55,200 ($104,800)	52,400
(c) Tax computed under § 1 on taxable income ($200,000)	108,772
(d) Tax computed under § 1 on earned taxable income ($160,000)	81,468
(e) Item (c) less item (d)	27,304
(f) Tax (total of items (a), (b) and (e)	$97,764

See Proposed Treas. Reg. § 1.1348-2(d)(4)(illus. 1).[*]

270. This would be the result of the $50,000 having offset (sheltered) $40,000 of other income, which produces a tax savings of $27,304, *see* note 269 *supra,* and $10,000 of personal service income, which produces a savings of $5,000 (50 percent of $10,000).[*]

271. *See* IRC §§ 56-58.[*]

272. IRC § 57(a).

273. IRC § 56(a). These provisions are effective for taxable years beginning after December 31, 1975.

274. IRC § 1348(b)(2).

275. This will be the result of the maximum capital gains rate of 35 percent, plus the minimum tax on one-half of the net long-term gain, and the increase in ordinary tax rates that will result from the tax preference offset to personal service income.

and how it would affect his or her tax situation, is to analyze the investment itself. This inquiry starts from the simple premise that a tax shelter, whatever else it may be, is an investment, so that it is necessary to determine how much cash the investor must contribute, what rate of return it is likely (as opposed to what it is advertised) to produce, and what its likely economic results will be to the investor. If the shelter is being publicly promoted, it will also be necessary to analyze the promoter and the investment results that are predicted. Thus, one would have to ascertain, for example, who the promoter is, what kind of track record it has, and whether it has the ability to carry the investment through to a successful completion. One would also want to determine if the projections made by the promoter are realistic—for example, if it is to be a housing project, whether the occupancy rates, maintenance costs and ultimate selling price projections are realistic.

§ 7.11. Personal Service Corporations.

In addition to the deferred compensation arrangements and tax sheltered investments considered above, it has also been suggested that professional athletes may benefit from the use of a personal service corporation as a means of tax planning. The term "personal service corporation" refers to a corporation that is organized for the purpose of utilizing the individual's athletic, or other, abilities. In the ordinary situation, the athlete would form the corporation and become the sole or majority shareholder, depending upon the objectives of the athlete, and then enter into a contract with the corporation which would obligate the athlete to perform specified services. The corporation would then contract with the sports team or other person which desires to acquire the services of the athlete.

The personal service corporation would provide the athlete with several significant benefits.[276] These would include the deferral of income by the adoption of a corporate pension and profit-sharing plans and a corporate fiscal year, the ability to adopt corporate fringe benefit programs, and the various estate planning advantages offered by the corporate form of organization. Each of these benefits will be considered in the following discussion. Before undertaking that discussion, however, several preliminary observations should be made. The first is that although the usefulness of the personal service corporation has been reduced by the maximum tax on personal service income,[277]

---

276. *See generally* Herskovitz, *Techniques Available to Shield the High Income of the "Superstar,"* 34 J. TAXATION 270, 273-74 (1971); Kauder, *The Service Corporation as the Taxpayer's Alter Ego: Variations on the Borge Theme,* 28 N.Y.U. FED. TAX INST. 1109 (1970); Kopple, *Tax Planning for Professional Athletes and Entertainers,* in COUNSELING PROFESSIONAL ATHLETES AND ENTERTAINERS 327 (1972).

277. *See* Asimow, *Section 1348: The Death of Mickey Mouse?,* 58 CAL. L. REV. 801, 866-67 (1970). The maximum tax is considered in § 7.01. The reason why the maximum tax might limit the usefulness of the personal service corporation is that it would reduce the maximum tax on the personal service income of the athlete to 50 percent. Since the maximum permanent rate on the taxable income of corporations is 48 percent, IRC § 11, the benefit to be derived from incorporation would be lessened by the slight difference in marginal tax rules. The corporation will, however, continue to offer the other benefits of the corporate form, which will be considered in the following discussion.

With respect to the tax rates applicable to corporations, it should be noted that the Tax Reduction and Simplification Act of 1977 reduced the rates to a limited extent, and this reduction has been

and by the Pension Reform Act of 1974,[278] it may still be a viable planning concept for some athletes. The second is that notwithstanding these benefits, the personal service corporation will pose several distinct problems because of the theories that might be invoked to limit those benefits. Since these theories are so significant, they will be considered in the following discussion before attention is given to the benefits. As will be noted, the existence of these several bases for challenging the use of a personal service corporation may limit its usefulness as a tax planning device.

The basic point to be kept in mind with respect to personal service corporations is that the use of such corporations cannot be evaluated in a vacuum. As is the case with the other planning techniques discussed in this chapter, the value of this device can only be evaluated in the context of the particular facts and circumstances presented by an individual athlete's situation. The service corporation may provide substantial benefits to one athlete, while posing serious hazards to another. Accordingly, it is not feasible (or advisable) to generalize as to the benefits that can be derived from such corporations, except to point out the various advantages and disadvantages that seem to exist in connection with their utilization. Whether the balance of these factors will favor incorporation in any given case can be decided only after careful analysis by knowledgeable counsel. In the absence of such analysis, one should travel very cautiously in this area of tax planning, for, as will be noted below, the hazards may be significant.

With these preliminary comments in mind, we will identify the basic problems and benefits that may be posed by a personal service corporation in this and the following two sections.

§ 7.12. Problems Posed by the Corporation.

The IRS has traditionally been skeptical of the use of personal service corporations, and has attempted to utilize a number of theories to limit their benefits.[279] Although each of these theories is of sufficient importance to warrant separate consideration, they will not necessarily preclude effective utilization of such corporations. But they will require careful analysis to determine whether they outweigh the benefits to a particular athlete, as well as more precise planning and attention to form and detail.

a. Viability of the Corporation and Assignment of Income. The first basis upon which a personal service corporation may be subject to challenge is that it is not a viable corporation, and may, for that reason, be disregarded for federal income tax purposes. Although the IRS has set forth a specific list of requirements that a corporation must meet in order to be treated as a

---

extended through 1978. If this reduction is made permanent, it will increase the benefit potential of a personal service corporation.[*]

278. *See* §§ 7.07, 7.12.

279. *See generally* Hobbet, *The Corporate Entity: When Will It Be Recognized for Federal Tax Purposes?,* 30 J. TAXATION 74 (1969); Rosenbaum, *Entertainer's Corporations and Capital Gains,* 12 TAX L. REV. 33 (1956); Scheifly, *The Commissioner's Attacks upon Personal Service Corporations,* 19 TUL. TAX INST. 336 (1970).

corporation for tax purposes,[280] the corporate form may also be disregarded if it is not in substance and actuality, as opposed to mere form, a viable business corporation.[281] If the corporate form of a personal service entity is disregarded in a given case, the result will be that its income will be taxed directly to the athlete-shareholder when received by the corporation [282]—one of the things sought to be avoided by use of the corporation in the first place.

Since personal service corporations have been a favorite tax planning vehicle for a long time, and since their viability has been frequently considered, there are enough decisions to provide guidance in planning the affairs of such a corporation. Although the issue of disregarding the corporate form is not clearly resolved, it appears that one who derives his or her income chiefly from personal services may conduct business through a personal service corporation, and so long as the corporation is operated and maintained as a viable business entity having a meaningful business purpose its status as a separate entity will be respected for tax purposes. In the early cases, the courts recognized the tax status of a corporation that had been organized to exploit the services of its sole or primary shareholder.[283] In each of these cases, the corporation met the basic

---

280. Treas. Reg. § 301.7701-2. The requirements for "corporate" status include what are commonly understood to be the characteristics of a corporation. These include the presence of associates, an objective to carry on business, continuity of life, centralization of management, limited liability, and free transferability of the interests in the corporation held by the shareholders. Treas. Reg. § 301.7701-2(a)(1).

281. Higgins v. Smith, 308 U.S. 473, 477-78, 84 L. Ed. 406, 60 S. Ct. 355 (1940). *See also* Moline Properties, Inc. v. Commissioner, 319 U.S. 436, 439, 87 L. Ed. 1499, 63 S. Ct. 1132 (1943); Gregory v. Helvering, 293 U.S. 465, 469-70, 79 L. Ed. 596, 55 S. Ct. 266 (1935); National Investors Corp. v. Hoey, 144 F.2d 466, 468 (2d Cir. 1944); American Sav. Bank, 56 T.C. 828, 838 (1971); Jerome J. Roubik, 53 T.C. 365, 378-79 (1969). The premise of the corporate disregard theory is that in determining tax consequences substances and not form will prevail. The clearest exposition of this rule was in Court Holding Co. v. Commissioner, 324 U.S. 331, 89 L. Ed. 981, 65 S. Ct. 707 (1945), where the Supreme Court stated that

> [t]he incidence of taxation depends upon the substance of a transaction . . . the whole transaction must be viewed as a whole, and each step, from the commencement of negotiation to the consummation of the sale is relevant . . . . To permit the true nature of the transaction to be disguised by mere formalisms, which exist solely to alter tax liabilities, would seriously impair the effective administration of the tax policies of Congress. 324 U.S. at 334.

The amount of business activity that must be conducted is quite small. *See, e.g.,* Harrison Property Management Co., Inc. v. United States, 475 F.2d 623 (Ct. Cl. 1973), *cert. denied,* 414 U.S. 1130 (1974); Tomlinson v. Miles, 316 F.2d 710 (5th Cir. 1963); William B. Strong, 66 T.C. 12 (1976).

282. *See, e.g.,* Floyd Patterson, 25 T.C.M. 1230 (1966), which is considered at notes 285-89 *infra.*

283. The earliest and most venerable of the cases in this regard was Fontaine Fox, 38 B.T.A. 271 (1938), where a cartoonist had organized a corporation in 1924, in which he held 98 of the 100 issued shares. The board of directors authorized the corporation to execute a contract with the cartoonist whereby he assigned his copyrights to all cartoons theretofore published to the corporation and agreed to provide his exclusive services as an author and artist to the corporation, all in return for a stated monthly compensation. The corporation then entered a contract with a syndicator for the daily distribution of the cartoons. All funds received by the corporation were deposited in its own bank account and were reported in its tax returns in all applicable years. The cartoonist also executed, on his own, contracts for the manufacture and sale of toys using his cartoon characters in 1921, and for the motion picture rights and advertising and merchandising rights in 1926, all of which were assigned to the corporation in 1932. The record showed that the cartoonist conducted the affairs of the corporation as its president, was the only person authorized to draw checks on its account, and in 1925, without board of director authorization, negotiated a corporate loan with which to purchase land for a summer residence which included a studio for his own use. In 1932 and 1933, the corporation received $113,482.30 from the contracts executed by, or assigned to, it for varying uses of the caricatures created by the cartoonist. Of this amount it paid him only $30,000.

requirements of business function and purpose. In more recent cases, however, the courts have disregarded several corporations, though in each case it was clear that the corporation had not been treated by its organizers as either a viable separate entity or having a meaningful business purpose.[284]

The failure of a personal service corporation to muster the requisite "corporateness" is, perhaps, best illustrated by *Floyd Patterson*,[285] where the former heavyweight champion of the world organized Floyd Patterson Enterprises, Inc., in 1956, to handle all of his ancillary rights, such as movie, radio and television rights. At the time of its organization, Patterson received ten shares of its common stock and his manager received five shares, but the corporation received no payment for the shares.[286] Patterson then entered an exclusive personal services agreement with his manager, and pursuant to that agreement the manager executed contracts on Patterson's behalf for boxing matches. Although the corporation was intended to handle Patterson's ancillary rights, no such rights were assigned to it, and not until 1958, two years after its organization, did the corporation undertake to perform any business function. At that time, it entered a contract to sell ancillary rights to an upcoming championship fight to another corporation. All receipts from the fight were deposited in the corporation's bank account, and were disbursed to Patterson and his manager to pay fight-related expenses. The facts also demonstrated that funds changed hands between the corporation, Patterson and his manager without accounting; the accounting records were simple worksheets and miscellaneous folders; the corporation's records showed no director meetings subsequent to the organizational meeting, and only one shareholder's meeting; the corporation had no employees; and it shared a one-room office with Patterson, had its name on the office door and its own telephone number, though it owned none of the furniture. On these facts, the Tax Court had little difficulty concluding that the corporation would be disregarded for tax purposes since it was performing no business function.[287] As opposed to *Fontaine Fox* where the

---

Although the IRS then sought to disregard the corporation and treat its entire income as that of the taxpayer, the Board of Tax Appeals disagreed, stating that it did "not think the facts here warrant disregarding [the corporation] as a separate entity." *Id.* at 277. *See also* Commissioner v. Laughton, 113 F.2d 103 (9th Cir. 1940) (corporation formed by an actor); Pat O'Brien, 25 T.C. 376 (1955) (same).

284. *See* Johansson v. United States, 336 F.2d 809 (5th Cir. 1964); Richard Rubin, 51 T.C. 251 (1968); Floyd Patterson, 25 T.C.M. 1230 (1966).

285. 25 T.C.M. 1230 (1966).

286. This is in direct contrast to *Fox* and *Laughton,* see note 283 *supra,* where the shareholders paid a substantial sum for their shares. Thus, in *Fox* $94,000 worth of cash and market value securities were contributed in return for issued stock, 37 B.T.A. at 272, and in *Laughton* the figure was 6,000 English pounds and royalties due to be paid the taxpayer. 113 F.2d at 104.

287. 25 T.C.M. at 1234. Thus, the court noted that
> the corporation merely served as an instrument by which income and expenses could be arbitrarily allocated to serve the tax interests of petitioner [the boxer taxpayer] and D'Amato [his manager] and therefore should not be recognized for income tax purposes . . . . *Id.* at 1236.

In reaching this conclusion, the court specifically distinguished *Fox,* and contrasted *Laughton. Id.* at 1235-36.

A result similar to that in *Patterson* was reached, ironically enough, in the case of Ingemar Johansson, Floyd Patterson's frequent championship rival, who organized a Swedish corporation found by the district court to
> have no legitimate business purpose, but was a device which was used by Ingemar Johansson as a controlled depository and conduit by which he attempted to divert

taxpayer had put flesh on his corporation's bones,[288] the court found the corporation before it so transparent as to be more properly classified as a "wraith"—that is, as a ghost.[289]

Although *Patterson* does not by any means suggest that all personal service corporations will be disregarded for federal income tax purposes, it and other recent cases could be viewed as suggesting "a trend towards disregarding a corporate entity where it is organized and operated primarily to shelter personal service income of one or a few individual taxpayers."[290] The corporation should not, however, be disregarded in cases where it is operated and maintained as a viable entity with a meaningful business purpose. The mere fact that the corporation is in essence a one-person entity should not deprive it of corporate status for federal income tax purposes.[291] In other words, the personal service corporation should be disregarded only in cases, such as *Patterson,* where the requirements of business function and purpose are clearly not present.[292]

Even if the IRS does not seek to have the corporation disregarded for tax purposes, it may accomplish the same result by a slightly different attack. Instead of contending that the corporation is a sham, the IRS might contend that the transaction by which the income from the personal services of the athlete was paid to the corporation was a sham. Thus, instead of disregarding the

---

temporarily, his personal income, earned in the United States, so as to escape taxation thereon by the United States. Johansson v. United States, 336 F.2d 809, 813 (5th Cir. 1964). The efforts of Ingemar Johansson to avoid United States taxation provided the courts with a sound opportunity to consider a foreign personal service corporation, as well as many other issues. The avoidance efforts continued even after assessment. *See* United States v. Johansson, 447 F.2d 702 (5th Cir. 1971).

288. *See* note 283 *supra.*

289. "Wraith" is, thus, defined as "a ghost, specifically, the spectral figure of a person supposedly seen just before or after his death." WEBSTER'S NEW WORLD DICTIONARY 1686 (College ed. 1962).

290. Hobbet, *The Corporate Entity: When Will It Be Recognized for Federal Tax Purposes?,* 30 J. TAXATION 74, 77 (1969). This "trend" could prove troublesome for the personal service corporation to overcome inasmuch as taxpayers may

> be hard-pressed to prove that the corporations are really engaged in business or, perhaps, that they are really corporations at all. For, if they involve the services of only one man, who is also the sole shareholder of the corporation, a court might well look to the practicalities of the situation and say that the corporation cannot exist beyond the life of the shareholder without undergoing such a radical change that it would indeed be a different entity; that there can be no centralized management when there is only the activity of one professional person to manage, and that limited liability is a fiction because the shareholder is intimately involved in every activity of the corporation. *Id.*

291. *See* B. BITTKER & J. EUSTICE, FEDERAL INCOME TAXATION OF CORPORATIONS AND SHAREHOLDERS ¶ 2.07 (3rd. ed. 1971).

292. Although there are no fixed ingredients to insure corporate viability, the corporation must have real business functions. These might include the following: (a) negotiating and executing contracts for personal services, and obtaining income from personal appearances, endorsements or other uses of the athlete's name and likeness; (b) its records and books of account must be fully and completely maintained; (c) it should have the sole contractual right to all the services of the athlete to insure that he or she will be its employee, *see* Jerome J. Roubik, 53 T.C. 365 (1969) (doctors held not to be bona fide employees of their professional service corporation) and American Sav. Bank, 56 T.C. 828, 841-42 (1971); (d) all contracts executed by the athlete personally should be terminated and replaced by contracts executed by the corporation; (e) the athlete should pay for his or her stock in the corporation in money or money's worth; (f) the affairs of the athlete and the corporation must be kept entirely separate; and (g) the corporation should have offices, leased in its own name, employees, and all ordinary business expenses that it incurs must be paid for by the corporation. In short, the athlete's personal service corporation must simply be operated as is any viable, functioning business entity. Kopple, *Tax Planning for Professional Athletes and Entertainers,* in COUNSELING PROFESSIONAL ATHLETES AND ENTERTAINERS 336-37 (1972).

corporation as an entity, use of this theory would simply seek to ignore it to the extent of the personal service income of the athlete. There are two legal bases for this theory. The IRS could take the position that the income from the athlete's personal services was in substance the athlete's and should, accordingly, be included in his or her income. It could also be argued that by forming the corporation the athlete had simply sought to assign income from personal services to the corporation, and under the familiar assignment of income principles the income must be taxed to its earner, not its assignee.[293] With respect to this "transactional" theory, it should be noted that the IRS has successfully utilized it in cases where the corporation would have been vulnerable to the corporate disregard theory (as in *Patterson*). Thus, one might draw the same conclusion that has already been reached with respect to the viability of the corporation itself: so long as the corporation has a business function and purpose, it and its transactions should be respected for federal income tax purposes.

b. Reallocation of Income. If the personal service corporation is found to be a viable entity for federal income tax purposes, a second theory that the IRS might utilize to eliminate its benefits is to "reallocate" a portion of the income received by it as a result of the athlete's services to the athlete pursuant to the provisions of § 482 of the Code. Section 482 provides that where two or more organizations, trades, or businesses are owned or controlled, directly or indirectly, by the same interests, the IRS may "distribute, apportion, or allocate gross income, deductions, credits, or allowances" between or among such enterprises if necessary to prevent tax evasion or to clearly reflect the income of any such enterprise.[294] Instead of attempting to tax all of a corporation's income to its shareholder, as is done when the corporate entity is sought to be disregarded in cases such as *Floyd Patterson*,[295] the § 482 approach is to allocate a portion of its income to the shareholder who alone was responsible for its production.[296]

The premise of the § 482 argument would be that the furnishing of personal

---

293. The prime example of this approach is Richard Rubin, 51 T.C. 251 (1968), where a taxpayer controlled two corporations and arranged for one corporation to retain his personal services as a corporate manager and make payment therefor to the second corporation. In holding that the income from those services was taxable in full to the taxpayer, the Tax Court relied upon both of the theories noted in text. Thus, it concluded that in substance the taxpayer worked directly for the retaining corporation, and that the income should, accordingly, be included in his income under IRC § 61(a). The court also noted that the same result could be reached by application of the assignment of income principles (*see* § 7.04). Subsequent decisions involving the same facts are noted at note 301 *infra*. *See also* Commissioner v. Laughton, 113 F.2d 103 (9th Cir. 1940); Elvin W. Jones, 64 T.C. 1066 (1973); Rev. Rul. 77-336, 1977-2 CUM. BULL. 202. *See generally* Kauder, *The Service Corporation as the Taxpayer's Alter Ego: Variations on the Borge Theme,* 28 N.Y.U. FED. TAX INST. 1109, 1125-29 (1970).

294. IRC § 482; Commissioner v. First Security Bank of Utah, N.A., 405 U.S. 394, 31 L. Ed. 2d 318, 92 S. Ct. 1085 (1972). *See generally* B. BITTKER & J. EUSTICE, FEDERAL INCOME TAXATION OF CORPORATIONS AND SHAREHOLDERS ¶ 15.06 (1971); Jenks, *Treasury Regulations Under Section 482,* 23 TAX LAW. 279 (1970); Simon, *Section 482 Allocations,* 46 TAXES 254 (1968).

In addition to § 482, the IRS could also make reference to § 446(b), which gives it authority to require that a taxpayer utilize a method of accounting which clearly reflects income.

295. *See* notes 284-89 *supra*.

296. Borge v. Commissioner, 405 F.2d 673, 676 (2d Cir. 1968), *cert. denied,* 395 U.S. 933, 23 L. Ed. 2d 448, 89 S. Ct. 1994 (1969).

services by the athlete to the corporation was itself a trade or business, which theory has been given judicial sanction in some circumstances.[297] Thus, an athlete who performs services for a service corporation might be viewed as owning or controlling two "organizations, trades or businesses"—that is, the corporation and the "trade or business" of performing athletic services—and, if § 482 applies, the reallocation rules may be applied to defeat, or lessen, the tax advantages sought to be obtained by the use of the corporate form.

The leading case applying § 482 in this manner is *Borge v. Commissioner,*[298] where a well-known entertainer had formed a corporation for the purpose of avoiding limitations on the deductibility of losses from his poultry business. To provide the corporation with income, the taxpayer agreed to perform entertainment and promotional services for the corporation during a five-year period. In return for these services, the corporation was to pay him $50,000, approximately one-third of his net earnings from entertainment for the years in question. The corporation, however, provided no services or other aid or assistance to the taxpayer's entertainment business activities, and all parties contracting with the corporation for his services required his personal guarantee. In upholding the IRS's reallocation of a portion of the entertainment income received by the corporation to the taxpayer, the court noted the absence of any service provided by the corporation and emphasized that such a contract would not have been entered by an unrelated party. The transaction appeared, it said, to be an assignment of a portion of the taxpayer's income to the corporation.[299] It concluded that

> the income from Borge's two businesses has been distorted through Borge's having arranged for Danica [the corporation] to receive a large part of his entertainment income although Danica did nothing to earn that income, and the sole purpose of the arrangement was to permit Danica to offset losses from the poultry business with income from the entertainment business.[300]

It should be noted that a tax avoidance purpose is not a necessary element for the imposition of § 482,[301] so that reallocation is apparently permissible whenever the facts of a particular case indicate that it is necessary in order to clearly reflect the income of the businesses under an athlete's control.[302] In light

297. Borge v. Commissioner, 405 F.2d 673, 675-76 (2d Cir. 1968), cert. denied, 395 U.S. 933, 23 L. Ed. 2d 448, 89 S. Ct. 1994 (1969). *See also* Rubin v. Commissioner, 460 F.2d 1216, 1218 (2d Cir. 1972).
298. 405 F.2d 673 (2d Cir. 1968), *cert. denied,* 395 U.S. 933, 23 L. Ed. 2d 448, 89 S. Ct. 1994 (1969).
299. 405 F.2d at 676. The assignment of income principles are noted at § 7.04. The approach of the court is similar to that in *Jones v. Page,* discussed in § 7.04, at notes 286-87.
300. 405 F.2d at 677. *See also* Elvin W. Jones, 63 T.C. 1066 (1973).
301. Richard Rubin, 56 T.C. 1155, 1159 (1971), *aff'd,* 460 F.2d 1216 (2d Cir. 1972). In *Rubin,* § 482 was applied to allocate income to a taxpayer who had, as a 70 percent shareholder, formed a corporation to provide management services to a second corporation. These services were to be performed by the taxpayer, but there was no apparent tax avoidance purpose as in *Borge.*
The several decisions involving Richard Rubin provide an excellent analysis of the relation between § 482 and other theories that might be used to interdict the tax avoidance efforts of taxpayers. Thus, the Tax Court initially held the taxpayer taxable under a broad § 61 income-inclusiveness theory, 51 T.C. 251 (1968), *see* note 293 *supra,* but the Second Circuit thought it erred and should have considered § 482, 429 F.2d 650 (2d Cir. 1970), which it then applied, 56 T.C. 1155 (1971), to the approval of the Second Circuit, 460 F.2d 1216 (2d Cir. 1972).
302. Borge v. Commissioner, 405 F.2d 673, 677 (2d Cir. 1968), *cert. denied,* 395 U.S. 933, 23 L. Ed 2d 448, 89 S. Ct. 1994 (1969).

of the fact that § 482 is written in broad and comprehensive language, moreover, the courts will be slow to give it a narrow reading,[303] and will accord the IRS a broad discretion in invoking its application,[304] so that a reallocation may be difficult to overcome once made.

The imposition of § 482 might seem to conflict with the decisions sustaining the viability of personal service corporations for tax purposes,[305] since reallocation does in a very real sense disregard the corporate entity. But the courts have pushed the conflict aside. This conclusion has been reached on the basis of the fact that § 482 reallocates only a portion of the earned income, whereas the cases allowing complete disregard reallocate it all.[306] If such reasoning is upheld, the inevitable result may be that the IRS will normally utilize § 482, the application of which is less severe and, presumably, less difficult to support, instead of a complete corporate-disregard theory, whether or not the facts of a particular case might support the latter.[307]

Despite the apparent potency of the § 482 approach, its impact is diminished by several factors. The first is that it allows reallocation of only a portion of the income received by the corporation, and the portion allocated may often be a relatively small portion of the income actually earned. Thus, in *Borge* the corporation received an average of $166,465 from the taxpayer's entertainment services, but only $75,000 was reallocated to him, of which $50,000 was the amount specified in the personal services contract between the taxpayer and the corporation.[308] The second factor is that, if applied, § 482 will require the athlete to simply pay the tax on the reallocated income that would have been due in any event if the corporation had not been used. Since the incidence of the taxation will be delayed for several years, the athlete (or the corporation) will have been able to use the funds for other income generating purposes. When the reallocation is made, moreover, the corporation will be able to distribute an amount equal to that reallocated without the imposition of further taxation.[309] Though § 482 is a hazard, therefore, its impact may not be severe, and even if applied will not have made the use of the personal service corporation

---

303. Pauline W. Ach, 42 T.C. 114, 125 (1964), *aff'd,* 358 F.2d 342 (6th Cir.), *cert. denied,* 385 U.S. 899, 17 L. Ed. 2d 131, 87 S. Ct. 205 (1966).

304. Local Fin. Corp. v. Commissioner, 407 F.2d 629, 631-32 (7th Cir. 1969); Grenada Indus., Inc., 17 T.C. 231, 255 (1951) (prior law).

305. *See* notes 279-93 *supra.*

306. Borge v. Commissioner, 405 F.2d 673, 676 (2d Cir. 1968), *cert. denied,* 395 U.S. 933, 23 L. Ed. 2d 448, 89 S. Ct. 1994 (1969).

307. Thus, in *Borge* the court upheld application of § 482 although it found the corporation to have had no business function with regard to the entertainment activities, 405 F.2d at 676, 677, a finding which might have allowed disregard of the corporate form for income tax purposes. *See* National Investors Corp. v. Hoey, 144 F.2d 466, 468 (2d Cir. 1944). *But cf.* Advance Mach. Exch. v. Commissioner, 196 F.2d 1006, 1008 (2d Cir.), *cert. denied,* 344 U.S. 835, 97 L. Ed. 650, 73 S. Ct. 45 (1952), where the court observed that while the predecessor of § 482 permitted the Commissioner to reallocate income, it did not permit him to disregard valid tax entities altogether. *See also* Rubin v. Commissioner, 460 F.2d 1216 (2d Cir. 1972), which is discussed at note 301.

308. 405 F.2d at 677. The court viewed the amount so reallocated to be "entirely reasonable—indeed, generous . . . ." *See* Kauder, *The Service Corporation and the Taxpayer's Alter Ego: Variations on the Borge Theme,* 28 N.Y.U. FED. TAX INST. 1109, 1130-32 (1970).

309. Rev. Proc. 65-17, 1965-1 CUM. BULL. 833, as amplified by Rev. Proc. 65-31, 1965-2 CUM. BULL. 1024, and Amendment I, 1966-2 CUM. BULL. 1211. *See also* Rubin v. Commissioner, 429 F.2d 650, 653-54 n.7 (2d Cir. 1970).

necessarily disadvantageous. At worst, it will require the delayed payment of tax on a portion of the full income that would have ordinarily been taxable.

c. Personal Holding Company Status. The final theory that might be invoked by the IRS to deny an athlete the benefit of a personal service corporation is that it is a personal holding company. The personal holding company concept is of interest because in a series of provisions the Code imposes a special penalty tax on personal holding company income.[310] A personal holding company is defined to include any corporation that meets the prescribed income and stock-ownership tests. The income test requires that at least 60 percent of the adjusted ordinary gross income of the corporation for the taxable year in question be personal holding company income.[311] The stock ownership test, on the other hand, requires that more than one-half of the value of the corporation's outstanding stock be owned, directly or indirectly, by or for not more than five individuals at any time during the last half of the taxable year.[312] If these tests are met, the undistributed personal holding company income of the corporation is subject to a penalty tax of 70 percent.[313] In calculating the undistributed personal holding company income figure, however, the corporation may disregard all personal holding company income that it has distributed to its shareholders.[314]

The primary inquiry, therefore, is whether the personal service corporation established by an athlete would meet the two tests that are determinative of personal holding company income status. Inasmuch as it is unlikely that the corporation would be able to avoid the stock ownership test,[315] the primary inquiry will be whether it will also meet the income test. As noted, the income test requires that 60 percent of the adjusted ordinary gross income be personal holding company income.[316] Although it includes other forms of income, the primary ingredient of personal holding company income, as far as professional athletes are concerned, is income from personal service contracts.[317] Income from such contracts is personal holding company income if a person other than the corporation has the right to designate the individual who is to perform the

---

310. IRC §§ 541-47. *See generally* B. BITTKER & J. EUSTICE, FEDERAL INCOME TAXATION OF CORPORATIONS AND SHAREHOLDERS ¶¶ 8.20-8.25 (1971).

311. IRC § 542(a)(1). Personal holding company income is defined in IRC § 543(a). *See* Pacific Security Co., 59 T.C. 744 (1973).

312. IRC § 542(a)(2). The rules for determining stock ownership are contained in IRC § 544.

313. IRC § 541.

314. IRC §§ 545(a), 561. Other calculations and adjustments are set forth in the definition of undistributed personal holding company income in IRC § 545.

It is to be noted that even if a distribution is not made and the personal holding company tax is imposed, the Code makes allowance for a deficiency dividend procedure that will allow the corporation to retroactively reduce the tax liability. IRC § 547.

315. It will be almost certain to meet the shareholder test because it is unlikely that the stock would be held in a sufficiently public manner as to be more than 50 percent owned by five or fewer persons. Even if it were, it is likely that the persons owning the stock would be so situated as to run afoul of the constructive stock ownership rules. *See* IRC § 544.

316. IRC § 542(a)(1).

317. "Personal holding company income" includes, in addition to personal service contract income, income from dividends, interest, royalties and annuities, IRC § 543(a)(1), rents, IRC § 543(a)(2), mineral, oil and gas royalties, IRC § 543(a)(3), copyright royalties, IRC § 543(a)(4), produced film rents, IRC § 543(a)(5), amounts received as compensation for the use of corporate property by shareholders, IRC § 543(a)(6), and income from estates, trusts and beneficiaries, IRC § 543(a)(8).

services or if the performer is designated in the contract, provided that more than 25 percent of the value of the outstanding stock is owned, directly or indirectly, by the individual who is or will be designated to perform the contracted-for services.[318] If a designation is not made,[319] or if the services required are not unique,[320] then the income will not be personal holding company income. In light of the fact that any contract for professional sports services would almost certainly involve a designation of who would perform those services, it is likely that the income from the contract would be personal service company income.[321] Thus, in order to avoid imposition of the personal holding company tax, the corporation would have to derive at least 40 percent of its adjusted ordinary gross income from sources that would not taint it as personal holding company income.[322] If the corporation receives less than 40 percent of its income from these other sources, then it will almost certainly be subject to the penalty tax.

Although the personal service corporation of a professional athlete will, thus, be subject to the personal holding company tax in many cases, that fact need not deter the athlete from its use. As noted, in calculating "personal holding company income" the corporation will be entitled to a deduction for dividends paid during its taxable year.[323] If, therefore, the corporation distributes all of its taxable income prior to the end of its taxable year, it will not incur the personal holding company penalty tax.[324] The necessity for such a distribution may, however, seriously impair the viability of the corporation to the athlete.

---

318. IRC § 543(a)(7); Treas. Reg. § 1.543-1(b)(8); Kurt Frings Agency, Inc., 42 T.C. 472 (1964), *aff'd per curiam,* 351 F.2d 951 (9th Cir. 1965). If services are required by other persons in such personal service contracts, and they are important and essential, then only that portion of the amount received which is attributable to the 25 percent shareholder shall constitute personal service income. Treas. Reg. § 1.543-1(b)(8)(ii). The amounts attributable to a 25 percent shareholder are calculated according to a fraction set forth in Proposed Treas. Reg. § 1.543-10(c)(1) and (2), and if more than one contract is involved, the computations are to be made separately for each. Proposed Treas. Reg. § 1.543-10(c)(3).

319. S.O. Claggett, 44 T.C. 503 (1965); Rev. Rul. 59-172, 1959-1 CUM. BULL. 144.

320. Rev. Rul. 71-372, 1971-2 CUM. BULL. 241.

321. It should be noted in this respect that the IRS has recently ruled that a one-person professional corporation may normally avoid the designation problem. Rev. Rul. 75-67, 1975-1 CUM. BULL. 169. The theory of this ruling may be of assistance to planners of personal service corporations.

322. *See* Kauder, *The Service Corporation as the Taxpayer's Alter Ego: Variations on the Borge Theme,* 28 N.Y.U. FED. TAX INST. 1109, 1114-15 (1970).

323. *See* note 314 *supra.*

324. It is also to be noted that if the corporation's fiscal year is different than the taxable year (probably the calendar year) of the athlete-shareholder, there will be no interference with the deferral benefit of utilizing the personal service corporation. *See* § 7.13.

In addition to the personal holding company tax, the IRS might also invoke, depending upon the circumstances, one of several additional provisions of the Code. These would be most likely to include the accumulated earnings tax, which imposes a special tax on the unreasonable accumulation of earnings of a corporation, IRC §§ 531-37; and the collapsible corporation provisions, which would tax the disposition of the shares in a corporation at ordinary income rates in some situations. IRC § 341. Both of these additional provisions, and some other possibilities, are considered in Kauder, *The Service Corporation as the Taxpayer's Alter Ego: Variations on the Borge Theme,* 28 N.Y.U. FED. TAX INST. 1109 (1970).

§ 7.13. Benefits to the Athlete.

The benefits that a personal service corporation may provide to a professional athlete are several. The first would be the ability to defer income. Attention has already been given to the various types of deferred income arrangements that may be utilized by athletes outside of a corporate form of organization,[325] and the present discussion will focus on the additional arrangements that may be utilized through the corporate form. These basically will include the use of corporate pension and profit-sharing plans, though consideration will also be given to the other benefits that can be derived from such corporations.

a. Deferral Through Qualified Plan. The most important advantage to be derived from a personal service corporation will, in many cases, be the deferral benefits that can be derived through the adoption of pension and profit-sharing plans. Attention has already been given to the general effects of pension plans upon the taxable income of athletes who are employees of a team, or who establish self-employed plans on their own.[326] The present discussion will require a relatively detailed consideration of the benefits that may be derived from the corporate adoption of pension and profit-sharing plans. As noted in the earlier discussion, there are three basic benefits to be derived from the adoption of qualified plans: [327] 1) income that would otherwise be compensation income to the employees of the corporation may be deferred until distributions are received from the plan, 2) the employer's contributions to the plan are deductible in the year of contribution, and 3) income that is earned on the contributions by the trust into which they are paid is exempt from taxation in the year in which it is earned by the trust.

While the specific details of the consequences of these various types of qualified plans are rather complex (and will be discussed below), the essential point to be made is that such plans will provide a significant advantage to the athlete. They will enable the athlete to defer current taxation on a relatively large amount of his or her current compensation, and may provide a significant degree of flexibility in arranging distributions from the plan. This will be particularly true in the case of a profit-sharing plan, where the corporate contributions can be fixed by a percentage of the compensation paid to the employees covered by the plan (principally to the athlete) and distribution can be made prior to retirement age. These benefits will provide a means of spreading out the income earned by the athlete during the relatively short period of his or her playing career. In this sense, the corporate plans could be viewed as a method of establishing a forced savings plan (the income from which will be tax exempt), that will help to assure the long-term financial security of the athlete (assuming, of course, that the plan is properly administered).

As with all other aspects of the personal service corporation, a decision as to whether such arrangements will be advantageous to any given athlete can only be made after analyzing the facts and circumstances of his or her personal

---

325. *See* §§ 7.07-7.09.

326. *See* § 7.08. *See generally* Zalutsky, *An Analysis of the Post-ERISA Advantages of Incorporation for the Professional,* 42 J. TAXATION 240 (1975); *see* § 7.07, at note 187.

327. The requirements for "qualification" of a pension or profit-sharing plan are noted briefly in § 7.07, at note 169.

situation. This would require consideration of whether the athlete's income level would justify the expense of installing such an arrangement, and whether participation in such plans would be preferable to those that may be available through a team or collective bargaining agreement (if the athlete is in a team sport), or the type of plans that could be created by the athlete as a self-employed individual.[328] In addition, attention should be given to whether the athlete would prefer deferral to current consumption, and whether it would be feasible for the corporation to remain in existence for a reasonable period of time.[329] This will not be a simple task, and it is difficult to articulate any generalized advice that would be applicable to a wide spectrum of athletes.

There are three types of plans that will be attractive for adoption by most personal service corporations. The first two include the different types of pension plan arrangements: defined benefit and defined contribution plans. A defined benefit plan is a pension plan in which the employee is guaranteed a fixed retirement benefit, which will normally be determined in accordance with a specific formula.[330] A defined contribution plan, on the other hand, is one in which the employer is obligated to make contributions in a fixed amount, and in which the benefit to the employee will depend upon the performance of the trust into which the employer's contributions are paid. The third type of qualified plan that will be attractive for most personal service corporations is a profit-sharing plan, which is a defined contribution plan that is established and maintained by the employer to allow participating employees to share in its profits.[331] To facilitate discussion, the two pension plan arrangements will be considered apart from the profit-sharing arrangement.

With respect to the tax consequences of the pension plan arrangements, it has already been noted that two of the primary benefits of such plans are that they enable the employer to deduct contributions to a pension plan trust and the amount of the contribution will not be included in the participants' income in the year of contribution.[332] Thus, it is first of all necessary to ascertain the maximum benefits that may be obtained from a plan, and the maximum amount of contributions that may be deducted by the employer. The extent of benefit is dependent upon the type of plan that is utilized. In the case of a defined benefit plan, the maximum benefit that a participant could receive upon retirement, or other separation from service, would be the lesser of $75,000, which amount will

---

328. *See* § 7.07.

329. If there is not a likelihood that the plan will be an on-going arrangement (*i.e.,* if it can be terminated at will), there may be additional requirements in order to "qualify" the plan. *See* Treas. Reg. § 1.401-4(c). The IRS has, however, ruled that the "normal retirement" age in a defined benefit plan may be less than 65, though if it is less than 55 the amount of the benefit may be reduced. Rev. Rul. 78-120, 1978-14 I.R.B. 7; Rev. Rul. 71-147, 1971-1 CUM. BULL. 116.

It should also be noted that the IRS has ruled that a corporate plan will not fail to "qualify" merely because it is established by an employer operated for the purpose of selling the services, abilities, or talents of its only employee who is also its principal or sole shareholder.

Rev. Rul. 72-4, 1972-1 CUM. BULL. 105.

330. A "defined benefit" plan is specifically defined as any plan that is not a "defined contribution" plan. IRC §§ 414(j), 415(k).

331. Treas. Reg. § 1.401-1(b)(2)(ii).

332. *See* § 7.07.

be subject to a cost-of-living adjustment,[333] or 100 percent of the participant's income during the three highest paid years during which he or she was a participant in the plan.[334] With respect to defined contribution plans, on the other hand, there is no maximum benefit level as such, but there is a limitation on the amount of annual contribution by the employer. The amount of the limitation is the lesser of $25,000, also subject to a cost-of-living adjustment, or 25 percent of the participant's annual compensation.[335] If an individual is a participant in both a defined benefit and a defined contribution plan maintained by the same employer, then the determination of whether the limitations on benefits or contributions have been exceeded will be determined by applying the so-called rule of 1.4.[336] These limitations on benefits in defined benefit plans, contributions in defined contribution plans, and on combined plans, are required for the plans to "qualify" under the Code.[337]

In addition to these qualification requirements, there is also the question of how much an employer may deduct in each year for the contributions made to the plan. In most cases, the deductible amount will be the amount which is necessary to fund the pension plan. Thus, for taxable years after December 31, 1975,[338] the maximum allowable deduction will be either the level cost of funding past or present employee service credits or the normal cost of the plan plus an amount that would be required to amortize past service credits over a ten-year period.[339] The deduction limitations are, in other words, keyed to the amount that is required to fund the pension plan itself.

The final point to be made with respect to pension plans that might be established by a personal service corporation is that when the benefits of the plan are made available to the participant, he or she will be taxed in the same manner as earlier noted in the discussion of pension benefits which might be received from plans established by a professional team. Thus, if the proceeds are received in a series of periodic payments, they will be taxed to the recipient in accordance with the rules for the taxation of annuities; and if the proceeds are received in the form of a lump sum payment, then the payment will be allocated between that portion attributable to pre-1974 and post-1973 service, with the former being entitled to taxation at capital gains rates and the latter at the ordinary income rates applicable to single individuals.[340]

Although the tax consequences of profit-sharing plans are slightly different from those of pension plans, the provisions are essentially the same in terms of structure. The plan itself must have a pre-determined formula for allocating the contributions of the employer among the participants, and for the eventual

---

333. IRC § 415(d). *See generally* Wilf, *Limitations on Benefits and Contributions for Corporate Employees Under New Pension Law,* 41 J. TAXATION 280 (1974).

334. IRC § 415(b)(1).

335. IRC § 415(c)(1).

336. IRC § 415(e). The "rule of 1.4" is actually a formula that is derived from fractional calculations for both defined benefit and defined contribution plans. *Id.* §§ 415(e)(2), (3). The sum of the fractions must not exceed 1.4, and if they do, then one of the plans will be disqualified.

337. "Qualification" of the plan is, as has been noted on several occasions, a complex subject that is not as such considered in this discussion. *See* note 332 *supra.*

338. For taxable years after December 31, 1975, in the case of plans which were in existence on January 1, 1974, the maximum deduction limits are as set forth in the Pension Reform Act of 1974.

339. IRC § 404(a)(1)(A).

340. *See* § 7.07, notes 177-78.

distribution of the accumulated contributions.[341] Inasmuch as the profit-sharing plan will be a defined contribution plan, the maximum contribution will be the $25,000 or 25 percent of compensation limitation already noted.[342] Unlike other types of defined contribution plans, however, the profit-sharing plan has a specific limit on the amounts that may be deducted by the employer. Thus, the maximum amount that may be deducted is an amount equal to 15 percent of the compensation of all participants during the taxable year in which the contribution is made.[343] This limitation may cause the employer to adopt a second type of defined contribution plan, or establish a non-profit-sharing plan, in order to take maximum advantage of the contribution allowances.[344] If the employer has both a pension and profit-sharing plan, moreover, the maximum deductible contribution in any given taxable year will be the greater of 25 percent of the compensation of the participants in the plans, or the amount of contributions necessary to meet the minimum funding standard.[345] With respect to the tax consequences of distributions from the profit-sharing trust, the applicable principles would be the same as those already noted for pension plan distributions.[346]

In considering profit-sharing plans, it is also appropriate to make two other observations. The first is that distributions from the profit-sharing trust may be made prior to retirement or total disability. Thus, distribution is possible "after a fixed number of years, the attainment of a stated age, or upon the prior occurrence of some [other] event . . . ."[347] This may be an important consideration in evaluating such plans for professional athletes, since their playing careers will almost certainly end well before normal retirement age. The second point is that since the contributions that must be made by the employer under the plan hinge upon the profitability of the enterprise, contributions can be limited to profitable years, unlike a pension plan in which the obligation to contribute is fixed without regard to profitability.

b. Deferral Through Corporate Fiscal Year. Deferral can also be accomplished by the adoption of a corporate fiscal year,[348] which will defer income to the extent that it delays taxable receipt from one year to the next. Although the adoption of the fiscal year will not result in lower taxation, unless the rates are decreased in the second year, it may enable the athlete to have use of the moneys (taxable "receipt" of which is deferred) for a year without having to pay tax during that period.

---

341. Treas. Reg. § 1.401-1(b)(1)(ii).

342. *See* note 335 *supra.*

343. IRC § 404(a)(3)(A). If less than 15 percent is contributed in any given taxable year, then the employer may carry to succeeding taxable years the unused portion of the 15 percent. The maximum deduction in such succeeding years is limited, however, to 15 percent of the compensation of all participating employees in the succeeding years, and the amount deductible for the succeeding year and the carryover from the earlier year may not exceed 25 percent. *Id.*

344. *See* Wilf, *Limitations on Benefits and Contributions for Corporate Employees Under New Pension Law,* 41 J. TAXATION 280, 282 (1974).

345. IRC § 404(a)(7). The "minimum funding standard" is set forth in IRC § 412.

346. *See* note 339 *supra.*

347. Treas. Reg. § 1.401-1(b)(1)(ii). The "other events" would include illness, disability, retirement, death or severance of employment. *Id.*

348. The term "fiscal year" is defined in IRC § 441(e).

The benefits of the corporate fiscal year may be best illustrated by an example, which would assume an athlete, who is a married, calendar-year taxpayer filing a joint return, with a professional contract paying him $150,000 per year, $12,500 per month, for his personal services. The athlete forms a corporation on February 1 of 1978, with a fiscal year ending January 31, and is thereafter employed by the corporation which furnishes his services to the team. The athlete receives compensation from the corporation in the amount of $75,000 per year ($6,250 per month) with a $75,000 bonus paid in January, 1979, representing the same $150,000 earned prior to incorporation. As a result of these facts, the tax consequences to the corporation and the athlete would be as follows: 1) the corporation would be required to pay no federal income tax because it would have no taxable income for its fiscal year ending January 31, 1979; [349] and 2) the athlete would have gross income of $81,250 in calendar year 1978 ($12,500 salary from team in January, plus $6,250 per month from corporation for February through December, 1978), and assuming (for illustration) that taxable income were also $81,250, the federal income tax would be $31,085 (based on a joint return, using the maximum tax on personal service income), which would be due and payable by April 15, 1979.[350] Had incorporation not taken place, the athlete's taxable income would have been $150,000, on which the federal income tax liability would have been $65,460. Use of the corporate fiscal year, therefore, results in deferral of the $75,000 bonus paid in January, 1979, which was earned in 1978 ($68,750), with the consequence that, except for income tax withheld from the bonus, tax will not be due until April 15, 1980.[351] Thus, by deferring until 1979 the $68,750 of income earned in 1978, the athlete has improved his cash position (through having the tax-free use of cash that would otherwise be paid to the IRS in the form of taxes) by the amount of tax ($34,375) that would have been paid in April 1979, but will, as a result of deferral, be paid in April 1980.[352]

c. Other Benefits. A personal service corporation may also provide the athlete with several advantageous fringe benefits. Thus, the corporation could adopt, without tax consequences to the athlete, a medical and health plan to reimburse

---

349. Although the corporation would have no taxable income, the IRS could seek to deny deduction for the salary on the basis that it was unreasonable in amount. *See* Charles McCandless Tile Serv. v. United States, 422 F.2d 1336 (Ct. Cl. 1970). *See* § 7.04. This will, however, be a difficult argument for the IRS to carry. *See* Klamath Medical Serv. Bureau v. Commissioner, 261 F.2d 842 (9th Cir. 1958), *cert. denied,* 359 U.S. 966, 3 L. Ed. 2d 834, 79 S. Ct. 877 (1959). If it did succeed, the corporation would then have taxable income to the extent of the disallowed deductions, and the athlete would have dividend income equal to the amount by which the disallowed deductions exceed the corporation's tax liability thereupon. The athlete could avoid the corporate tax by having the corporation make a subchapter S election, pursuant to IRC § 1372. The subchapter S election may not, however, be desirable for the athlete in this context because of its limitation on the deductibility of amounts contributed to a pension plan. IRC § 1379(b).

350. The amount of tax would, of course, be significantly altered by the deductions, exclusions, exemptions or credits that may be available to any given athlete for the taxable year in question. Deductible expenses of athletes are considered at § 7.04.[*]

351. The IRS could, of course, argue that the bonus was "constructively" received in 1973, but that seems unlikely to prevail unless the bonus were credited to the athlete's account and could be withdrawn at that time. *See* § 7.08.[*]

352. *See* Kopple, *Tax Planning for Professional Athletes and Entertainers,* in COUNSELING PROFESSIONAL ATHLETES AND ENTERTAINERS 331-32 (1972).[*]

the athlete and his or her family for all their medical expenses,[353] a disability income policy,[354] or group term life insurance.[355] If the athlete should die, moreover, the corporation could make a payment up to $5,000 to the beneficiaries of the estate of the athlete which would not be included in the recipient's gross income.[356] Whether these arrangements will be beneficial in a given situation may be problematic (depending upon whether such benefits are already provided by a team or union plan), but they should be given consideration when analyzing the benefits to be derived from a personal service corporation.

An additional benefit that could be derived from such a corporation would be theoretical estate planning flexibility. We use the word "theoretical" here to emphasize the fact that the advantages noted below are important, but it may be far from clear that they will provide significant present benefits to a young professional athlete (who may or may not be concerned with estate planning). As with all of the other factors relating to personal service corporations, the benefits to be noted below must be evaluated in terms of the facts and circumstances of each athlete's own situation (and personal objectives).

The corporate form of organization would enable the athlete-shareholder to take advantage of a lifetime gift program to transfer the value of assets owned by the corporation (the athlete's personal service contract and any other assets that have been transferred to, or acquired by, it) to the objects of the athlete's bounty.[356.1] This would be accomplished by a transfer of shares of stock, which would not result in a current gift tax if the value of the stock transferred to each donee were $3,000 per year or less,[356.2] or if the value of the transfer were within the limit of the unified credit and occurred more than three years prior to the date of the athlete's death.[356.3] An additional advantage could be derived, if the corporation established a qualified pension plan arrangement, from a provision of the Code which would exclude from the athlete's estate (in the event of his or her death) the value of payments to be received from the qualified plan.[356.4]

---

353. IRC § 105(b). The amount of such reimbursement may not, however, be unlimited. *See* Edward D. Smithback, 28 T.C.M. 709 (1969).

354. IRC §§ 105(d), 106.

355. IRC § 79. The insurance would be tax-free to the athlete-employee if the amount of premiums were less than $50,000 per taxable year and there were more than one employee.

356. IRC § 101(d).

356.1. *See generally* Hood & Logan, *Close Corporations in Estate Planning after the Tax Reform Act of 1976,* 2 J. CORP. LAW 207 (1977).

356.2. IRC § 2503(b).

356.3. IRC §§ 2010(a) (a phased-in tax credit, which will amount to $42,500 in 1980), 2035 (gifts within 3 years of death are included in the estate).

356.4. IRC § 2039(c) (if not paid in a lump sum). This benefit was also extended to non-corporate plans by the Tax Reform Act of 1976.

Prior to the 1976 Act, there was an additional benefit that could be derived through a personal service corporation. This involved the ability to avoid "income in respect of a decedent" problems if the athlete died at a time when there was earned income from personal services which had not yet been paid. This could pose a problem, since, as a general rule, when a person dies the property received by heirs or beneficiaries will be subject to federal estate taxation. IRC § 2033. Before the enactment of the 76 Act (noted above), such property would obtain a new (stepped-up) basis equal to its fair market value on the date of death (or alternate valuation date) in the receipient's hands. IRC § 1014(a). This rule did not, however, apply to "income in respect of a decedent," which was defined to include "amounts to which the decedent was entitled . . . but which were not properly includible in computing his [or her] taxable income for the taxable year ending with the date of his

§ 7.14. Taxation of College Athletes.

The primary tax problem of college or university athletes concerns the taxability of the amounts received by them in the form of athletic scholarships or grants-in-aid. As a general matter, the Code provides that when a student receives a scholarship or fellowship at an educational institution, the amount so received will not be includible within his or her gross income.[357] This exclusion will include all services and accommodations provided,[358] as well as amounts received to cover expenses for travel and equipment, so long as they are incident to the scholarship and actually expended for that purpose by the recipient.[359] The exclusionary rule will not, however, apply to amounts received by a degree candidate which represent payments for the rendering of employment-like services as a condition to receipt of the scholarship or fellowship.[360] Thus, in

[or her] death. . . ." Treas. Regs. § 1.691(a)-1(b). Such income would clearly include compensation for personal services of the decedent rendered during his or her lifetime. *See* Brown, *Income In Respect of a Decedent,* 55 Cornell L. Rev. 211, 216-23 (1970); Ferguson, *Income and Deductions in Respect of Decedents and Related Problems,* 25 Tax L. Rev. 5, 28-41 (1969). Although income in respect of a decedent under pre-76 law was subject to federal estate taxation, it did not receive a stepped-up basis at the date of death. IRC § 1014(c). Instead, the income was taxable to the estate or other person acquiring the right to it by reason of the decedent's death, IRC § 691(a), though such person would be entitled to a deduction for the estate taxes paid. IRC § 691(c).

Income in respect of a decedent was to be avoided if possible, therefore, because it would be taxed in full to the recipient and not be subject to the general rule allowing a step-up in basis upon the death of the decedent. The use of a personal service corporation was thought to be a means of avoiding these difficulties. If such a corporation were formed, and it entered a contract with a third party for the athlete's personal services, then it would possess a right to receive future income which would have been "income in respect of a decedent" had the decedent owned it at the time of death. The difficulties noted above were said to be avoided if the corporation distributed the right in a complete liquidation, because on liquidation the right would receive a new basis in the hands of the decedent's estate equal to its fair market value on the date of liquidation under IRC § 334(a) — *i.e.,* liquidation would be a taxable exchange, so that the assets received (including the income in respect of a decedent) would get a basis equal to their fair market value, though gain or loss would presumably not be realized since the basis of the stock would be its fair market value under § 1014 — and the estate would be entitled to amortize the basis as it received the income. *See* B. Bittker & J. Eustice, Federal Income Taxation of Corporations and Shareholders ¶ 11.05, at 11-14 (1971). If this procedure were followed, the income would then receive a tax-free step-up in basis in the hands of the shareholder-beneficiary, so long as the income were not taxed to the corporation and the estate realized no gain on the liquidation. *See generally* Brawerman & Kopple, *Income Tax Planning for Composers, Entertainers and Others Performing Personal Services,* 49 Taxes, 211, 221-24 (1971); Kopple, *Tax Planning for Professional Athletes and Entertainers,* in Counseling Professional Athletes and Entertainers 329, 341-45 (1972).

This use of a personal service corporation will be less beneficial in the case of decedents dying after December 31, 1976, since the Tax Reform Act of 1976 replaced the step-up in basis rule of § 1014 with a "carryover" basis provision in new § 1023. This will require that the basis of property received from a decedent be equal to its basis in the decedent's hands immediately before death, § 1023(a)(1), with certain adjustments. *See* IRC §§ 1023(c) (increase for estate and inheritance taxes paid), 1023(h) (so called "fresh-start" adjustment). As a result of this provision, there could be no artificial step-up in basis through liquidation.[*]

357. IRC § 117(a). The amount that may be excluded is limited to $300.00 per month by IRC § 117(b)(2)(B). Since, moreover, § 117 is controlling in all matters relating to scholarships and fellowships, any amount in excess of this amount will be taxable, notwithstanding the exclusion of gifts in IRC § 102 and certain prizes and awards in § 74(b). Treas. Reg. § 1.117-1(a).

358. IRC § 117(a)(1).

359. IRC § 117(a)(2).

360. IRC § 117(b)(1); Treas. Reg. §§ 1.117-2(a)(1), 1.117-4(c). Thus, graduate students are taxable on amounts paid to them for their teaching efforts, Rev. Rul. 68-146, 1968-1 Cum. Bull. 58; Edward A. Jamieson, 51 T.C. 635 (1969), as are medical interns and residents generally taxable on their income received for services rendered. Rev. Rul. 73-89, 1973-1 Cum. Bull. 52; Rev. Rul. 68-520,

order to qualify for non-taxability, awards must be in the nature of "relatively disinterested, 'no strings' educational grants, with no requirement of any substantial *quid pro quo* from the recipients."[361]

Although there are no cases which deal directly with the question of whether a college or university athlete who receives an athletic scholarship or grant-in-aid is entitled to the general exclusion, the issue has been considered in a recent public ruling issued by the IRS [361.1] and in a line of Tax Court cases dealing with the income averaging rules.[362] The issue has also been raised indirectly by the various judicial opinions which have dealt with the status of the athlete who participates in amateur athletics. Inasmuch as these authorities and their ramifications are considered in detail in an earlier chapter,[363] the discussion will not be repeated here. For present purposes, it will suffice to note that there is authority for the proposition that some collegiate scholarships and grants-in-aid may be awarded in such a manner as to facilitate the conclusion that they are awarded on a *quid pro quo* basis—that is, given in consideration of the athletic ability and promise to perform of the recipient. To the extent that such a finding could be made in any given case, the award could not qualify as a "no strings educational grant," and would, accordingly, be fully taxable to the recipient.[364]

§ 7.15. Taxation of Professional Teams.

One of the most controversial issues in the area of federal income taxation of sports activities involves the tax consequences of professional team ownership. A professional team is a business enterprise which is similar to other commercial undertakings except that its business involves sports instead of more traditional forms of commercial activity. Accordingly, the federal income tax principles that apply to the income of professional teams do not differ in general from those that are applicable to other business organizations. A differential exists only to the extent that the types of assets owned by professional teams may raise some relatively unique tax problems.

As will be noted in the following discussion, the tax treatment of some team assets to some team owners may make team ownership very attractive from a tax standpoint. This attractiveness may help to explain some of the common transactions in sports leagues. Thus, it is possible to view the turnover of existing franchises, expansion of existing leagues and the proliferation of new

---

1968-2 CUM. BULL. 58; Rev. Rul. 57-386, 1957-2 CUM. BULL. 107; Aloysius J. Proskey, 51 T.C. 918 (1969); Parr v. United States, 469 F.2d 1156 (5th Cir. 1972); Hembree v. United States, 464 F.2d 1262 (4th Cir. 1972). *See also* Rev. Rul. 68-20, 1968-1 CUM. BULL. 55 (beauty contest winner taxable on scholarship when it required performance of services).

It is to be noted, however, that if such services are required of all scholarship or non-scholarship candidates for a particular degree, then the scholarship will remain non-taxable. Treas. Reg. § 1.117-2(a)(2). *See* Robert H. Steiman, 56 T.C. 1350 (1971).

361. Bingler v. Johnson, 394 U.S. 741, 751, 22 L. Ed. 2d 695, 89 S. Ct. 1439 (1969); Parr v. United States, 469 F.2d 1156, 1158 (5th Cir. 1972); Ussery v. United States, 296 F.2d 582, 586 (5th Cir. 1961).

361.1. *See* Rev. Rul. 77-263, 1977-2 CUM. BULL. 47.

362. IRC §§ 1301-05. The income averaging rules, and the Tax Court cases are discussed in this chapter at § 7.01. They are also discussed in the amateur athletics chapter at § 1.06.

363. *See* §§ 1.05-1.09.

364. *See* Rev. Rul. 77-263, 1977-2 CUM. BULL. 47; Randall, *Athletic Scholarships and Taxes: Or a Touchdown in Taxes,* 7 GONZAGA L. REV. 297, 307 (1972).

leagues as being a partial result of the very favorable tax situation that exists for some owners (at least prior to the Tax Reform Act of 1976). The tax principles that relate to sports teams may also help to explain the economic realities of team ownership, which may be much different than would be suggested by simple perusal of a team's income statement at the end of its taxable year. These comments should not, however, be understood to suggest that all teams produce tax consequences that are relatively more attractive than other forms of investment. This is certainly not the case. The sports pages in recent years have reported many situations in which teams, and leagues, have produced substantial economic losses. Theoretical tax advantage is of little benefit in the face of genuine economic loss.

In the sections that follow, attention will be focused on the basic tax issues that appear to have special significance to sports teams.

§ 7.16. Forms of Organization.

The first step in considering the federal income tax consequences of professional team ownership is to survey the different organizational forms that may be utilized for a team. This inquiry is important because the tax consequences of team ownership may differ significantly depending upon the form of organization. As is true in any type of business enterprise, there are several forms available to facilitate professional team ownership and choice among them can only be made after thoroughly analyzing the needs and objectives of a potential team owner. The discussion that follows is intended to be only a thumbnail sketch of the basic attributes of each form.[365]

a. Subchapter C Corporation. The first form of organization that might be considered is a subchapter C corporation,[366] which is an ordinary business corporation. Its basic advantages are those that are inherent in the corporate form of organization: limited liability, centralized management, continuity of life and free transferability of interest. There are, in addition, other advantages, including the ability to borrow at rates that might be considered usurious if charged to individuals or unincorporated entities. The disadvantages which stem from the use of a subchapter C corporation, however, may be significant. As will be discussed subsequently,[367] many owners of professional sports teams desire to obtain so-called tax shelter benefits, and this objective will not be possible through the use of a subchapter C corporation, assuming that it is not a member of an affiliated group that is eligible to file a consolidated income tax return.[367.1] It is a separate entity for federal income tax purposes, and its use precludes the pass-through of benefits that is essential to the accomplishment of tax shelter objectives. Use of the corporate form also raises a wide range of limitations imposed by the Internal Revenue Code.[368] Primary among these are

365. *See generally* Braun & Pusey, *Taxation of Professional Sports Teams,* 7 TAX ADVISER 196, 204 (1976).

366. The "subchapter C" designation is used because the corporate tax rules are contained in §§ 301-395 of the Internal Revenue Code, which collectively comprise subchapter C of the Code.

367. *See* § 7.20.

367.1. The consolidated return provisions are set forth in IRC §§ 1501-05. The issues raised by the losses of an affiliated member are substantial, and are well beyond the scope of this treatise.

368. Though there are many disadvantages, there are also a few tax advantages. Probably the most important of these is that no gain or loss is recognized to either the transferor or the

the personal holding company,[369] collapsible corporation [370] and unreasonable accumulation of income rules.[371]

Thus, although the subchapter C corporation has many non-tax advantages, it will often be unsuited for use as a form of organization for professional sports teams if shelter objectives are desired (and consolidated return treatment is not available) because of tax disadvantages. If shelter objectives are not present (or consolidated return treatment is available), then the subchapter C corporation could be a very attractive vehicle.

b. Subchapter S Corporation. A second potential form of organization is the subchapter S corporation,[372] which, if qualified, may elect to have its income taxed directly to the shareholders without tax at the corporate level.[373] In addition, most tax benefits will pass through to shareholders with the same characterization that they would have had at the corporate level.[374] The subchapter S corporation, therefore, provides the ordinary corporate benefits of limited liability while allowing a favorable pass-through of financial results, all of which may make it an attractive vehicle for professional sports ownership.[375]

corporation if property is transferred to the corporation by one or more persons solely in exchange for stock or securities, and such persons immediately thereafter control eighty per cent of the corporation's voting stock. IRC §§ 351(a), 358(a), 362(a). This need not be a factor in choosing between the corporation and the partnership, however, since § 721 provides for non-recognition in the case of property contributed to a partnership.

369. The personal holding company provisions are considered at § 7.12, at notes 310-24.

370. Although the collapsible corporation rules in IRC § 341 are quite complex, their basic principle is that gain realized by a shareholder in a transaction that would normally produce capital gain will be considered gain from the sale of a non-capital asset if the corporation was formed with a view to effecting such sale before the corporation had realized a substantial part of the income to be derived from its activities. *See generally* B. Bittker & J. Eustice, Federal Income Taxation of Corporations and Shareholders ¶¶ 12.01-09 (3rd ed. 1971).

371. To prevent shareholders from allowing the corporation to accumulate all its income, which they may later "bail out" at capital gain rates, the Code provides that any corporation formed or availed of for the purpose of avoiding income tax to its shareholders by permitting earnings and profits to accumulate instead of being divided or distributed shall be subject to a special accumulated earnings tax. IRC § 532. The accumulation of earnings and profits "beyond the reasonable needs of the business is determinative of the purpose to avoid the income tax" to shareholders. *Id.* § 533(a). If the requisite tax avoidance purpose exists, the corporation is taxed at a rate of 27 and ½ per cent on its "accumulated taxable income" not in excess of 100,000 dollars, and 38 and ½ percent on its "accumulated taxable income" in excess of 100,000 dollars. *Id.* § 531. "Accumulated taxable income" is defined in § 535. *See generally* Bittker & Eustice, *supra* note 370 ¶ 8.09.

372. This designation arises from the special rules in §§ 1371-78 of the Internal Revenue Code, which collectively comprise subchapter S of the Code.

373. To be eligible for the election, the corporation must be a "small business corporation," as defined by IRC § 1371(a). Thus, to be eligible a corporation must not (1) be a member of an affiliated group, (2) have more than 10 (or, in some cases, 15) shareholders, (3) have a shareholder (other than an estate, a grantor or a voting trust) who is not an individual, (4) have a nonresident alien shareholder, or (5) have more than one class of stock. IRC § 1371(a). *See* Bittker & Eustice, *supra* note 370, ¶ 8.09.[*]

374. Thus, earnings and profits, whether or not they are distributed, IRC § 1373(a), and capital gains both retain their corporate character in the shareholder's hands. *Id.* § 1375(a)(1). It is to be noted, however, that gain on § 1231 property loses its special identity at the shareholder level, where it is reported as a simple long-term capital gain. *See* Bittker & Eustice, *supra* note 370, ¶ 6.06. Although net operating losses also pass through with the usual carryback and carryover of § 172, to the extent of the shareholder's adjusted basis in his stock and any indebtedness of the corporation to him, long-term capital losses do not. *Id.* ¶ 6.07.

375. In considering a subchapter S election, attention must also be given to the numerous circumstances in which the election may be terminated by voluntary or involuntary action. Thus,

As compared to the partnership, however, the subchapter S corporation may be relatively unattractive because of the difference in the ability to deduct net operating losses, which will be of substantial importance where the team is sought to be utilized as a tax shelter investment. In both the subchapter S corporation and the partnership, a shareholder or partner may deduct losses only to the extent of his basis.[376] In the case of the partnership, basis may include a pro rata share of partnership liabilities,[377] but in the subchapter S corporation only indebtedness of the corporation to the stockholder may be used to increase the basis.[378] This distinction may make the subchapter S corporation less attractive   a basic vehicle for team ownership.

   c. General Partnership. The primary attraction of the partnership as a form of organization stems from the significant tax advantages that it provides its partners. Under the partnership tax rules, each partner includes in income his or her distributive share of all items of income, gain, loss, deduction or credit.[379] The distributive share of each partner may, in turn, be fixed by the partnership agreement,[380] so long as the allocation has substantial economic effect.[381] This flexibility, of course, sharply differentiates the partnership from the subchapter S corporation, where each shareholder must report his pro rata share of the net income without any ability to specially allocate particular items.[382] In addition, use of the partnership form avoids the corporate tax hazards of the personal holding company and accumulated earnings rules, and the impact of the "collapsibility" rules is much less stringent.[383]

   Although these tax advantages may be attractive, the general partnership may not be suitable for team ownership for several reasons. First, the partnership itself lacks any real continuity, since death, withdrawal or bankruptcy will cause dissolution. Second, a partnership, like an individual, but unlike a corporation, is generally subject to applicable usury laws, and may thus be effectively precluded from borrowing the capital that may be necessary for a successful sports investment. The chief drawback, however, is that the general partnership form subjects its partners to unlimited liability for all debts and obligations of the partnership. Thus, the general partnership would not provide

---

the election may be terminated if new shareholders refuse to file a timely consent, IRC § 1372(e) (1), a revocation is filed with the unanimous consent of the shareholders, *id.* § 1372(e) (2), the corporation ceases to be a small business corporation, *id.* § 1372(e) (3), too much income is derived from foreign sources, *id.* § 1372(e) (4), or if 20 percent of the corporation's gross receipts constitutes "passive investment income," which is defined to include, for example, income from royalties, rents, dividends, interest, or the sale or exchange of securities. *Id.* § 1372(e) (5).

   376. IRC §§ 704(d), 1374(c) (2).

   377. *See* Treas. Reg. § 1.752-1(e).

   378. IRC § 1374(c) (2) (B).

   379. IRC §§ 701, 702.

   380. IRC § 704.

   381. IRC § 704(b)(2). *See* Stanley C. Orrisch, 55 T.C. 395 (1970), aff'd in unpublished opinion (9th Cir. 1973).

   382. The Code provides that each shareholder in a subchapter S corporation "shall include in his gross income . . ., the amount he would have received as a dividend, if on such last day there had been distributed pro rata . . . an amount equal to the corporation's undistributed taxable income. . . ." IRC § 1373(b). A similar rule is provided for net operating losses. *Id.* § 1374(c) (1). *See generally* BITTKER & EUSTICE, *supra* note 370 at ¶ 6.07.

   383. Section 751 of the Code defends against the use of a "collapsible" partnership. *See* A. WILLIS, PARTNERSHIP TAXATION §§ 20.17-.18 (1971).

the requisites of limited liability and (possibly) facilitation of borrowing, though it would provide a pass-through of tax benefits.

d. Limited Partnership. The limited partnership is the half-way house between the partnership and corporation, enjoying most of their advantages, while avoiding most of their drawbacks. This results from its basically two-class structure where limited partners have a status essentially resembling that of a corporate shareholder, while general partners retain the characteristics of a partner in a general partnership. The limited partnership resembles the general partnership to the extent that death of a general partner will ordinarily cause dissolution.[384] It tends to resemble a corporation in that the partnership agreement may provide for continuity if the business is continued by the remaining partners after an act of dissolution [385] and death of a limited partner has no effect upon the continuation of the business.[386] Despite this two-class structure, the limited partnership is taxed as a partnership, so that it retains the significant tax advantages of the partnership rules.[387]

The limited partnership will, thus, provide the limited partners with limited liability and will both provide the requisite pass-through of tax benefits and allow great flexibility in their allocation. For these reasons, and because of the drawbacks of the other forms, the limited partnership may be an attractive form of organization where no business consideration requires the utilization of a corporation.

e. Sole Proprietorship. The final form of organization that could be utilized for team ownership would be the sole proprietorship, in which an individual would be the sole owner of the team. There would be no entity interposed between the individual and the business. In a proprietorship, the income or loss of the business would be taxed to the proprietor in its entirety and the rate of taxation would be dependent upon his or her tax bracket and marital status. The principal advantages of the sole proprietorship are its simplicity and the fact that the owner has sole control over its operations. Its disadvantages, however, are significant. Like a partner in a general partnership or a general partner in a limited partnership, the sole proprietor is personally responsible for all liabilities of the business. The sole proprietor will also be precluded from putting together a group of persons to own the team, and will be limited in raising capital to his or her own credit standing.[388]

§ 7.17. Acquisition of Individual Player Contracts.

One of the central aspects of professional team ownership involves the tax consequences of the player contracts that provide the talent necessary to the fielding of a team. Players may be acquired from other teams, through

---

384. UNIFORM LIMITED PARTNERSHIP ACT § 20 (1969).

385. *Id.*

386. UNIFORM LIMITED PARTNERSHIP ACT § 21 (1969).

387. In order to be taxed as a partnership, the entity must meet the requirements of Treas. Reg. § 301.7701-3.

388. *See generally* W. PAINTER, CORPORATE AND TAX ASPECTS OF CLOSELY HELD CORPORATIONS § 1.1 (1970).

organized player drafts sponsored by the league of which it is a member, from arrangements with minor league teams which are obligated to make their players available, or by individual contact without utilizing formal acquisition procedures. Regardless of the method utilized, the team will incur potentially substantial acquisition costs (aside from salary costs) in securing new players, and the basic tax issue presented by those costs is how they will be treated for federal income tax purposes.

From a very early date, both the IRS and the federal courts held that such costs must in general be treated as an ordinary expense incurred in the trade or business of the team and be deducted on a current basis.[389] In more recent rulings, however, the IRS has retreated from the "expense" view, at least with respect to professional teams,[390] and ruled that the acquisition costs of player contracts must be capitalized and depreciated (amortized) over their useful lives.[391] The basis for the change of position was stated in *Revenue Ruling 67-379,*[392] to be that the reserve clause in a professional baseball contract[393] gives the team the exclusive right to the player's services during his baseball career, so that the contract (the asset representing that right) has a useful life which extends substantially beyond the taxable year in which the contract is acquired. Since the contract is of a potentially long duration, the IRS reasoned that its cost must be capitalized and depreciated (amortized) over its useful life in accordance with the depreciation provisions of the Code.[394] This reasoning was later utilized to reach a similar conclusion with respect to contracts acquired by professional football teams. Although the football contracts then in force did

---

389. Helvering v. Kansas City Am. Ass'n Baseball Co., 75 F.2d 600 (8th Cir. 1935); Commissioner v. Chicago Nat'l League Ball Club, 74 F.2d 1010 (7th Cir. 1935); Commissioner v. Pittsburgh Athletic Co., 72 F.2d 883 (3d Cir. 1934); Rev. Rul. 54-441, 1954-2 CUM. BULL. 101; I.T. 4078, 1952-1 CUM. BULL. 39; I.T. 2932, XIV-2 CUM. BULL. 61. *See generally,* 4A J. MERTENS, THE LAW OF FEDERAL INCOME TAXATION § 25.46 (rev. ed. 1972).

390. A similar rule would be followed with respect to minor league contracts. *See* Houston Baseball Ass'n, 24 B.T.A. 69 (1931). If the view that minor league teams ordinarily hold their contracts primarily for sale to major league teams, *see* Hollywood Baseball Ass'n v. Commissioner, 423 F.2d 494 (9th Cir.), *cert. denied,* 400 U.S. 848, 27 L. Ed. 2d 85, 91 S. Ct. 35 (1970) (which had a lengthy prior history in Hollywood Baseball Ass'n, 42 T.C. 234 (1964), *aff'd,* 352 F.2d 350 (9th Cir. 1965), *vacated and remanded,* 383 U.S. 824, 16 L. Ed. 2d 291, 86 S. Ct. 1221 (1966), *on remand* 49 T.C. 237), is followed, however, this rule would require additional consideration.

391. Rev. Rul. 71-137, 1971-1 CUM. BULL. 104; Rev. Rul. 67-380, 1967-2 CUM. BULL. 291; Rev. Rul. 67-379, 1967-2 CUM. BULL. 127. *See generally* Klinger, *Tax Aspects of Buying, Selling and Owning Professional Sports Teams,* 48 L.A.B. BULL. 162, 164-67 (1973); Note, *The Professional Sports Team as a Tax Shelter — A Case Study: The Utah Stars,* 1974 UTAH L. REV. 556, 560-61; Note, *Professional Sports Franchising and the IRS,* 14 WASHBURN L.J. 321 (1975); *Hearings Before the Senate Subcomm. on Antitrust and Monopoly of the Senate Comm. on the Judiciary,* 92d Cong., 1st Sess., pt. 1, 410-11 (1971). A similar rule had been followed, in the case of players who stayed with their teams for more than one year, in I.T. 2993, XV-2 CUM. BULL. 146, but it was revoked by I.T. 4078, 1952-1 CUM. BULL. 39. As is discussed at notes 404-13, it may still be possible to expense some acquisition costs.

The bases upon which this view may be questioned are identified in Holdmann, *Amortization of Intangibles—General Rules,* TAX MANAGEMENT PORTFOLIO 209, A-7, 8 (1969).

The depreciation rules are discussed at notes 416-30 *infra.*

392. 1967-2 CUM. BULL. 127. The conditions under which a team may change from expensing to capitalizing these costs are identified in Rev. Rul. 70-318, 1970-1 Cum. Bull. 113.

393. The "reserve" clause is a provision in the standard baseball contract which has the effect of binding a player to one team for his or her entire career. It is discussed in detail in § 4.05.

394. IRC § 167. The depreciation (amortization) principles that relate to player contracts are considered at notes 416-30 *infra.*

not contain a "reserve" clause, they did contain an "option" clause,[395] which the IRS concluded also gave the contract a useful life substantially longer than a single year.[396]

In light of the reliance of these rulings upon the reserve or option clauses in professional contracts, it is important to note that the demise of those clauses, either through judicial, legislative or collective bargaining action,[397] may have a material impact upon the tax status of the contracts. Thus, if the contracts have only a one-year duration, and the team does not have a right to the player's services for a period substantially in excess of one year, then it is possible that the costs of acquiring a contract would have to be expensed instead of capitalized. This was, of course, the position of both the courts and the IRS prior to the IRS's conclusion that the contracts had a longer useful life.[398] Current expense treatment of acquisition costs could, however, be even more beneficial to a team than capitalization.[399]

In those circumstances where capitalization is appropriate, the rulings noted above will allow the team to capitalize and amortize its "cost" of contract acquisition, and the term "cost" is defined to mean the amount paid or incurred to purchase the contract, as well as the bonuses paid to the player for signing the contract.[400] There are, thus, two categories of "cost" that must be considered in determining the amount that is to be capitalized as the basis in the contracts. The first occurs when a team purchases a contract from a third party (such as another team), and it is allowed to capitalize both the amount actually paid and the amount incurred to acquire the contracts. This means that if a team purchases contracts and incurs an obligation to make future payments, it will be allowed to capitalize the actual as well as the incurred payments.[401]

The second type of "cost" would arise when a team acquires a contract by direct negotiation with the player. The tax issues raised by such acquisitions are not clearly resolved and there is certainly room for disagreement over how the costs should be treated. Before considering these issues, it will be helpful to distinguish between the three basic types of payments that may be paid to the athlete by a team. The first involves a lump-sum payment that is made to induce the player to sign a contract with the team ("bonus payment"). The second would include contract-signing payments that are paid in increments over a period of

---

395. The "option" clause differs from the "reserve" clause to the extent that it purports to tie a player to the team for only the option period, which is normally one year. It is discussed in detail in § 4.05.

396. Rev. Rul. 71-137, 1971-1 CUM. BULL. 104. It should also be noted that the conclusion that such contracts have a useful life in excess of one year is crucial to the availability of depreciation, *see* notes 400-14 *infra*, inasmuch as that showing must be made to depreciate any type of contract. *See* 4 J. MERTENS, THE LAW OF FEDERAL INCOME TAXATION § 23.65 (rev. ed. 1972).

397. The contractual aspects of such clauses are considered at §§ 4.04, 4.05; the antitrust aspects are considered at §§ 5.03, 5.07; and the collective bargaining principles that apply to them are considered at § 6.08.

398. *See* note 389 *supra*. It is worthy of note that in Dallas Athletic Ass'n, 8 B.T.A. 1036 (1927), the Tax Court found the player's contracts to be of indefinite duration so as to not qualify for the exhausting deduction, though it was allowed in Houston Baseball Ass'n, 24 B.T.A. 69 (1931), where their useful life was stipulated to be 10 years.

399. *See* notes 404-05 *infra*.

400. Rev. Rul. 71-137, 1971-1 CUM. BULL. 105; Rev. Rul. 67-379, 1967-2 CUM. BULL. 127.

401. *See* Crane v. Commissioner, 331 U.S. 1 (1947).

time ("deferred bonus payment"). Finally, the team may be obligated by the contract to make annual salary payments to the athlete for services rendered during each period of the contract ("salary payments").

The position of the Service is, apparently, that a team may capitalize only the amounts *actually* paid to a player for signing a contract. Thus, the rulings state that the cost to be capitalized is the amount *"paid* to the players for signing." This language clearly suggests that a team may not capitalize deferred bonus payments. Inasmuch as large bonuses are frequently negotiated, this issue may be of substantial importance to some teams. At least one writer has reached the conclusion that such signing bonuses may be capitalized even if deferred. The premise of the conclusion is that the cost basis for assets generally includes deferred obligations (liabilities) and no different rule should be followed with respect to sports contracts.[402] If a bonus is viewed as an acquisition cost, as is suggested by the language of the published rulings, then this conclusion would appear to be supported by general basis principles.[403]

In considering the treatment of bonuses, attention should also be given to the possibility of deducting the deferred portion of the bonus currently as a compensation payment. This might be even more beneficial to the team than capitalizing the obligation for at least two reasons. Current deduction would allow the team to claim the entire amount as a deduction in the year the obligation is incurred (whether or not actually paid), whereas capitalization would require that the amount be recovered (depreciated or amortized) over the longer period of the asset's (the contract's) useful life.[404] In addition, if the obligation were treated as deductible compensation, then the team could possibly avoid depreciation recapture upon sale of the contract.[405]

As might be expected, the question of the deductibility of deferred bonus payments is far from being resolved. If the team is on the cash method of accounting, then it would be entitled to salary expense deductions only for the taxable year in which payments are actually made to the athlete.[406] An accrual basis team, on the other hand, would generally be able to deduct an unpaid expense in the taxable year in which all events occur to fix the liability for payment.[407] This principle has apparently been used by some teams as a basis for currently deducting deferred bonus obligations.[408] The current deduction of deferred compensation payments is, however, limited by at least two factors. The first is that an employer may deduct contributions to nonqualified deferred compensation plans only in the taxable year in which they are includible in the income of the recipient-employee,[409] which generally will be the year during

402. Klinger, *Professional Sports Teams: Tax Factors in Buying, Owning and Selling,* 39 J. TAXATION 277, 278, n.6 (1973). The basis for this view is *Crane, supra,* note 401.
403. *See* 3A J. MERTENS, LAW OF FEDERAL INCOME TAXATION § 21.11 (1968).
404. *See* notes 416-30 *infra.*
405. If there were no other acquisition costs, then the basis of the contract would be zero and there could be no depreciation. Since there would be no depreciation, there would also be no depreciation recapture under IRC § 1245. *See* Okner, *Taxation and Sports Enterprises,* in GOVERNMENT AND THE SPORTS BUSINESS 159, 171-72 (1974). "Recapture" is discussed in § 7.19.
406. Treas. Reg. § 1.461-1(a)(1).
407. Treas. Reg. § 1.461-1(a)(2).
408. Okner, *supra* note 405, at 170-71.
409. IRC § 404(a)(5).

which there is not a substantial risk of forfeiture.[410] Thus, the IRS has ruled that payments under deferred compensation arrangements will be deductible when they are actually paid to the recipient.[411] The second limitation would be the requirement in the Regulations that an expenditure which results in the creation of an asset having a useful life extending beyond the taxable year may not be deductible, or be deductible only in part, in the year in which it is incurred.[412] Both of these factors have been cited to support the view that deferred payments to athletes cannot be deducted currently.[413]

The tax treatment of deferred bonus payments is obviously unsettled. The government's position is apparently that such obligations may be neither capitalized (since it allows such treatment for only actual payments) nor currently deducted. This position seems anomalous. If the bonus is to be treated as an acquisition cost, as the Service now suggests, then it should be treated the same as any other such cost, which would presumably require capitalization of the incurred (deferred) amount. Indeed, the Regulations seem to require this result, since capitalization is specified when an expense results in the creation of an asset having a useful life extending beyond the taxable year. Actual payment in the taxable year is not a condition precedent to capitalization, since such treatment is required of accrual basis taxpayers.[414] If, on the other hand, the bonus is to be indirectly treated as a compensation payment in the sense that it may be deducted (or capitalized) only in the year in which it is actually paid, then it should not be referred to as a cost of the contract. Such bonus payments are, of course, treated as compensation income to their athlete-recipient.[415]

Once the contract has been acquired, the next inquiry will be the extent to which it may be depreciated—since the player contracts are actually intangible assets, the proper word is "amortized", but "depreciated" will be utilized since it is a more familiar term—over its useful life. The ability to depreciate the contract will enable the team to claim a tax deduction, essentially as an operating expense, for each contract it owns or controls in an amount equal to a reasonable allowance for its exhaustion, wear, tear and obsolescence.[416] The allowance is the amount which should be set aside in the taxable year, pursuant to a reasonably consistent plan, so that the aggregate of the amounts so set aside, plus the salvage value of the property, will at the end of its useful life equal its cost or other applicable basis.[417] The components necessary for the calculation of the annual allowance are the basis of the property, its useful life

410. IRC §§ 83, 402(b), 403(c).
411. Rev. Rul. 60-31, 1960-1 CUM. BULL. 174. The Tax Court has recently indicated that § 404(a)(5) will not be literally applied. Latrobe Steel Co., 62 T.C. 456 (1974). This case could provide a basis for current deduction. *See also* Lukens Steel Co. v. Commissioner, 442 F.2d 1131 (3d Cir. 1971); Note, *Deductibility of Deferred Compensation Plans under the "All Events" Test,* 30 Tax. Law. 780 (1977).
412. Treas. Reg. § 1.461-1(a)(2).
413. H. REP. No. 94-658, 94th Cong., 1st Sess. 79-80 (1975).
414. Treas. Reg. § 1.461-1(a)(2).
415. Rev. Rul. 55-727, 1955-2 CUM. BULL. 25. If the payments were not so treated, an athlete might seek to argue that a bonus constituted a purchase transaction and that he or she should be entitled to capital gains treatment on receipt of the bonus. It was apparently this theory that was intended to be shot down by *Rev. Rul. 55-727.*
416. IRC § 167(a). *See also* 4A J. MERTENS, THE LAW OF FEDERAL INCOME TAXATION § 25.46 (rev. ed. 1972).
417. Treas. Reg. § 1.167(a)-1(a).

and salvage value. The basis for this purpose is the adjusted basis of the property for determining the gain or loss from its sale or disposition,[418] which will ordinarily be its cost.[419] The useful life will be the period over which the property is reasonably expected to have value to the team.[420] The salvage value will be the amount which, at the time of acquisition, is estimated will be the realizable value of the property, by sale or other disposition, when it is no longer useful in the taxpayer's trade or business.[421] Although there are several methods of "accelerated depreciation" which enable a taxpayer to write-off its depreciable assets in short periods of time,[422] professional sports contracts are considered to be intangible property [423] so the only permissible method is the so-called straight-line method.[424] Under this method, the basis of the property less its salvage value is deductible in equal annual amounts during its estimated useful life [425]—which, in the case of professional sports contracts may be as little as three to five years.[426]

In applying these rules to professional teams, the only real problem is the determination of the basis of the contracts. As noted, the basis of property is generally its cost to its owner.[427] In determining its cost basis in sports contracts, a team may include only amounts paid or incurred upon their purchase and bonuses paid to players for signing,[428] but may not include working agreement development costs.[429] Thus, the owner's basis in its sports contracts will equal the amounts paid or incurred in their acquisition, less claimed and deducted depreciation, but will not include amounts paid to players in the form of simple salary.[430]

§ 7.18. Acquisition of a Team.

Significant tax issues are also raised by the acquisition of an entire team franchise in a single transaction. Such an acquisition may actually be accomplished by a variety of methods, each of which may produce significantly

---

418. IRC § 167(g).

419. IRC §§ 1011, 1012. *See* notes 400-15 *supra*.

420. Treas. Reg. § 1.167(a)-1(b), which includes a listing of the factors to be considered in making the period determination.

421. Treas. Reg. § 1.167(a)-1(c)(1).

422. IRC §§ 167(b)(2)-(4).

423. Rev. Rul. 71-137, 1971-1 CUM. BULL. 104; Rev. Rul. 67-379, 1967-2 CUM. BULL. 127. It is to be noted that intangible assets are properly the subject of depreciation only if it is known from experience or other factors that it will be of use for only a limited time. Treas. Reg. § 1.167(a)-3. Because the contracts are intangibles, they are not subject to the investment credit. Rev. Rul. 71-137, 1971-1 CUM. BULL. 104.

424. IRC § 167(c).

425. Treas. Reg. § 1.167(b)-1(a).

426. *See Hearings Before the Senate Subcomm. on Antitrust and Monopoly of the Senate Comm. on the Judiciary*, 92d Cong., 1st Sess., pt. 2, 534, 575, 617, 1035 (1972). *See also* Madison Square Garden Corp. v. Commissioner, 500 F.2d 611 (2d Cir. 1974) (use of 7-year useful life); Laird v. United States, 391 F. Supp. 656 (N.D. Ga. 1975), *aff'd,* 556 F.2d 1224 (5th Cir. 1977) (use of 5¼-year useful life approved).

427. IRC § 1012.

428. Rev. Rul. 71-137, 1971-1 CUM. BULL. 104; Rev. Rul. 67-379, 1967-2 CUM. BULL. 127. *See* notes 400-15 *supra*.

429. Rev. Rul. 67-379, 1967-2 CUM. BULL. 127.

430. The availability of the depreciation arrangement will have a material bearing upon the tax shelter potential in the team itself. *See* § 7.20.

different tax results to the new owner. The principal methods of acquisition would be through (a) the purchase of a new franchise from a league; (b) purchase of a franchise from an existing owner, either through purchase of the assets, shares of stock or partnership interests of the entity that owns those assets; (c) acquisition of a franchise in a non-taxable exchange or reorganization, either by acquiring the existing owner's assets or shares of stock; (d) gift from an existing owner; or (e) as a result of the operation of law (such as by descent or bequest from a deceased owner).

Regardless of the method of acquisition, the central issue that will concern the new owner will be the tax basis for the team and its component assets.[431] The basis of the team and its components is important because it will determine the amount of depreciation that may be claimed by the new owner,[432] as well as the amount of gain or loss that would be recognized upon eventual sale. The new owner will generally have two basic objectives. The first will be to acquire a basis that is as high as possible to facilitate maximum depreciation benefits, and the second will be to allocate as much of the basis as possible to depreciable, as opposed to non-depreciable, assets. Each of these objectives will be considered in this section.

Although we do not undertake a detailed analysis of the basis results of the several types of transactions that may be involved in team acquisitions,[433] it is appropriate to note that the basis figure may vary substantially depending upon the method of acquisition. In order to provide an illustration of this difference, the basis rules for each type of transaction will be summarized. These general principles are all subject to the provisions of § 1056, which will be noted below.

The most straightforward type of acquisition would be through purchase, either of a new franchise from a league or an existing team from its present owner. This would involve a simple asset purchase. The new owner's basis would be equal to its cost of acquisition,[434] and the basis would generally be allocated among the acquired assets in accordance with their relative fair market values.[435] If an existing team is owned by a corporation, the new owner could

---

431. The acquisition of a team will also raise significant tax issues to the person or entity from which it is acquired. *See* § 7.19. If a team is acquired in a purchase transaction, the seller (either of assets or stock) would be required to recognize gain or loss on the transaction, IRC §§ 61(a) (3), 1002, the amount of which would be determined by the difference between the adjusted basis of the property and the amount realized upon sale. IRC § 1001(a). The character of the gain or loss (ordinary or capital) in an asset transaction would be determined by the status of each asset under IRC §§ 1221, 1231, 1245. If stock in a corporation or interests in a partnership were sold, the character of the gain or loss would generally be capital (assuming a sufficient holding period). IRC §§ 1221 (definition of a capital asset), 741 (a partnership interest is generally a capital asset, subject to the provisions of § 751). If the existing owner wishes to avoid recognizing gain or loss, this could be accomplished by transferring the team in a like-kind exchange under IRC § 1031(a), a reorganization qualifying under IRC § 368(a) (1) if the owner is a corporation, a gift, or (in the case of an individual) through a transfer by death. *See* § 7.19.

432. *See* § 7.17.

433. A detailed analysis of basis consequences in these several types of transaction is provided in B. BITTKER & J. EUSTICE, FEDERAL INCOME TAXATION OF CORPORATIONS AND SHAREHOLDERS (3rd ed. 1971); 3A J. MERTENS, THE LAW OF FEDERAL INCOME TAXATION ch. 21 (1968); J. PENNELL & J. O'BYRNE, FEDERAL INCOME TAXATION OF PARTNERS & PARTNERSHIPS (1970); R. STEPHENS, G. MAXFIELD & S. LIND, FEDERAL ESTATE & GIFT TAXATION (1974); A. WILLIS, PARTNERSHIP TAXATION (1976).

434. IRC § 1012.

435. *See* 3A J. MERTENS, LAW OF FEDERAL INCOME TAXATION § 21.32, at 99 (1968); *see also* Treas. Reg. §§ 1.167(a)-5, 61-6(a) (apportion equitably).

also make the acquisition through a purchase of the corporation's stock, and the stock would be held at a cost basis. However, the assets of the corporation would continue to have their pre-acquisition basis, which could be much lower than the purchase price of the stock.[436] If a new owner is an individual or partnership and desires a higher basis for the assets—for example, to maximize depreciation—this could be accomplished by liquidating the corporation. The assets would then have a basis equal to their fair market value,[437] but the new owner would possibly have to recognize gain or loss on liquidation,[438] unless a special one month liquidation procedure were utilized.[439] If, on the other hand, the new owner is a corporation, then it could acquire a cost basis through a stock acquisition without much difficulty. This could be accomplished by adhering to the specific requirements of the Code, which would allow it to liquidate the acquired corporation, recognize no gain or loss on liquidation and receive the assets at a basis equal to the cost of the stock.[440] Such a procedure would require that the cost basis of the stock be allocated among the assets received in accordance with their relative net fair market values.[441] If the existing team is owned by a partnership, the new owner could buy the outstanding partnership interests and would receive a cost basis in those interests.[442] Although the

---

436. This lower figure could be the result of previous depreciation of the assets, or a significant appreciation in the value of the assets transferred. *See* note 438 *infra*.

437. IRC § 334(a).

438. IRC § 331(a)(1). A gain would not have to be recognized if the new owner had purchased the stock of the existing corporation for an amount that was equal to the fair market value of the latter's assets, since in that event the liquidation would result in the amount realized (the value of the assets distributed) being equal to the adjusted basis of the stock (which was purchased for the fair market value of the underlying assets).

439. IRC § 333. In order to meet the elective requirements for non-recognition in a liquidation under § 333, there would have to be a complete liquidation of the corporation pursuant to a plan within a one calendar month period. Treas. Reg. § 1.333-1(b)(1). If these requirements are met, then a qualified electing shareholder (defined by § 333(c)) would generally not recognize gain or loss on the liquidation. IRC § 333(a). Gain would, however, be recognized to the extent of the greater of the shareholder's ratable share of the corporation's earnings and profits or the sum of money and fair market value of stock and securities received. In the case of a non-corporate shareholder, the gain would be taxed as a dividend to the extent of the earnings and profits and the remainder, if any, as a capital gain. If the shareholder is a corporation, the entire gain would be treated as a capital gain. IRC §§ 333(e), (f).

If a liquidation qualifies under § 333, then the shareholder's basis for the assets received would be the same as the basis in the stock cancelled in the liquidation, decreased by the amount of money received and increased by the amount of gain recognized. IRC § 334(c).

440. The statutory requirements are set forth in IRC § 334(b)(2), which requires that the corporation acquire 80 percent of the stock of another corporation by purchase in a period of 12 months and then completely liquidate the acquired corporation pursuant to a plan adopted within 24 months after the stock ownership requirement is achieved. If these requirements are met, then the basis of the assets received in the liquidation will be the cost basis in the stock with respect to which the liquidation was made. *Id.* The liquidation will also not require the recognition of gain or loss. IRC § 332. This procedure could provide the new corporate owner with considerable flexibility in terms of the acquisition procedure. *See, e.g.,* Madison Square Garden Corp. v. Commissioner, 500 F.2d 611 (2d Cir. 1974) (acquisition by "purchase" included percentage increase caused by redemption of other shareholders).

If the requirements of § 334(b)(2) are not satisfied, then the new owner would receive a basis in the assets received through liquidation equal to that of the corporation being liquidated, IRC § 334(b)(1), if it met the stock ownership requirements of § 332. The inequities of this rule are reviewed in B. Bittker & J. Eustice, *supra* note 433, at 11-26 to 11-27, 11-35 to 11-36.

In such liquidation transactions, the corporation being liquidated would generally not recognize gain or loss. IRC § 336.

441. Treas. Reg. § 1.334-1(c)(4)(viii); B. Bittker & J. Eustice, *supra* note 433, at 11-38 to 11-39.

442. IRC § 742; Treas. Reg. § 1.742-1.

adjusted basis of the partnership assets would generally carry over,[443] the new owner would be entitled to an election to adjust the basis upwards to reflect the cost basis in the acquired partnership interests.[444]

In each of the transactions identified above, the new owner would acquire a team in a transaction that would require the recognition of gain or loss by the seller.[445] If the seller (transferor) does not wish to have such a recognition event, then there are other forms in which the transaction could be cast, though the purchaser (transferee) may not be able to acquire a cost basis in the team. One such transaction would involve a reorganization, which would require that the new owner be a corporation and acquire an existing team through one of several types of reorganization.[446] In a reorganization, the new owner's basis for the property acquired would be the same as it was in the hands of the transferor, plus any gain recognized by the transferor.[447] If the new team were acquired in a like-kind exchange,[448] the new owner's basis would be equal to the basis of the property transferred, with certain adjustments.[449] Finally, if the team were acquired in a gift transaction, the new owner's basis would be the same as it was in the hands of the transferor.[450] In each of these non-purchase acquisitions, the new owner would not receive a cost basis, which would limit the new owner's ability to depreciate the assets acquired. For this reason, such transactions may not be attractive to the new owner whose objectives require maximum benefit from depreciation or other factors that are tied to the basis of the acquired assets. If the new owner has other objectives, however, such transactions may be much more attractive. For example, if the existing team has incurred a substantial net operating loss, the new owner may desire to acquire the loss carry-forward to offset post-acquisition income.[451] In such

---

443. IRC § 743(a).

444. IRC § 743(b). The basis adjustment of § 743 would be available if an election were in effect under § 754, and would allow the partnership to increase the adjusted basis of its assets by the excess of the basis of the transferee partner (the new owner) in the partnership interest over his or her proportionate share of the adjusted basis of the partnership assets, or to decrease the adjusted basis in the converse situation. IRC § 743(b). If such an adjustment is made, then it must be allocated among the partnership assets in accordance with some rather complicated provisions of the regulations under § 755. Treas. Reg. § 1.755-1(a). *See generally* J. PENNELL & J. O'BYRNE, FEDERAL INCOME TAXATION OF PARTNERS AND PARTNERSHIPS 135-61 (1970); 2 A. WILLIS, PARTNERSHIP TAXATION ch. 28 (1976).

445. *See* note 431 *supra.*

446. The different types of "reorganization" are specified in IRC § 368(a)(1), and for purposes of acquiring a sports team will generally include a statutory merger (a type "A" reorganization), a stock for stock exchange (type "B"), or a stock for property exchange (a type "C").

447. IRC § 362(b). If the transaction fails to qualify as a "reorganization" under § 368(a)(1), then it would be treated as a purchase transaction and the basis to the purchaser (transferee) would be the cost basis under § 1012.

448. *See* § 7.19.

449. IRC § 1031(d). The adjustments would include a decrease in basis by the amount of money received by the taxpayer and an increase or decrease by the amount of gain or loss recognized in the transaction. *Id.*

450. IRC § 1015. If the team were acquired from a decedent, then the team would have a basis to the recipient equal to its adjusted basis in the hands of the decedent, though with several upward adjustments (including a "fresh start" basis), in the case of decedents dying after December 31, 1976. IRC §§ 1014(a), 1023.[*]

451. This was, for example, reported to be one of the objectives of a group which acquired control of the Chicago White Sox in 1975. Veeck, *Back Where I Belong,* SPORTS ILLUSTRATED, March 15, 1976, at 73, 77.

circumstances, the acquisition transaction will have to be planned with exceptional care to insure that the losses may be carried over.[452]

Although this discussion of the types of transaction that could be utilized to acquire a sports team is only a very general summary, it should be sufficient to suggest that there are numerous possibilities and the tax consequences of each may be quite dissimilar. A specific method of acquisition can be selected only by analyzing the objectives of both the buyer and seller and working out an arrangement that is as mutually beneficial as possible.

Once it is determined what the basis in the acquired team will be as a gross figure,[453] it will then be necessary to determine the basis at which the various assets will be held. The difficulties that will be faced in this regard may be illustrated by considering the situation of a team that is acquired in an asset purchase transaction in which the new owner receives in exchange for the purchase price several categories of assets. These will include the franchise (which may or may not include other "rights," such as an interest in a league broadcast contract), player contracts, and office and sports equipment with which to operate the team. Inasmuch as all of these assets will in most cases be acquired for a single purchase price, the primary tax issue is how the purchase price will be allocated among the assets for federal income tax purposes. The allocation issue is of particular importance because it may to a considerable extent determine the economic profitability of the team as an investment.[454]

The reason that the allocation issue may pose difficulty, and be subject to the careful scrutiny of the IRS, is that the player contracts will be depreciable assets in the hands of the acquiring team,[455] while the franchise (and rights in league broadcast contracts) will not be depreciable to the extent that they are viewed as having indeterminate useful lives.[456] Thus, the acquiring team will in almost all cases wish to allocate as high a percentage of the purchase price as possible to the depreciable player contracts, since it will naturally desire a high tax basis for the depreciable contracts and a low basis in the non-depreciable assets.

In reviewing transactions in which a group of assets have been acquired in a single transaction, the IRS has frequently sought to limit the ability of the purchaser to achieve a favorable allocation of the purchase price between depreciable and non-depreciable assets. The basic rule is that where tangible and intangible assets are acquired in a single transaction, the portion of the purchase price allocated to the intangible assets may not be made the subject of a depreciation deduction to the extent that they have an indeterminate useful

---

452. In order for such an acquisition to be effective for tax purposes, it would have to successfully negotiate a labyrinthian series of provisions in the Code, as well as judicial precedent. These hurdles would include IRC §§ 269, 381, 382 and 482, and, possibly, the Supreme Court's opinion in Libson Shops, Inc. v. Koehler, 353 U.S. 382 (1957). Analysis of these several factors is well beyond the scope of this treatise, and is comprehensively discussed in B. BITTKER & J. EUSTICE, *supra* note 433, at ch. 16.

453. *See* notes 432-50 *supra.*

454. *See* INQUIRY INTO PROFESSIONAL SPORTS, FINAL REPORT OF THE SELECT HOUSE COMM. ON PROFESSIONAL SPORTS, 94th Cong., 2d Sess. 92-107 (1977); Jones, *Amortization and Nonamortization of Intangibles in the Sports World,* 53 TAXES 777, 778-79 (1975) (which discusses the benefit of depreciation or amortization in detail).

455. *See* notes 431-50 *supra.*

456. Laird v. United States, 391 F. Supp. 656 (N.D. Ga. 1975) *aff'd,* 556 F.2d 1224 (5th Cir. 1977). *See also* Toledo TV Cable Co., 55 T.C. 1107 (1971); Rev. Rul. 66-140, 1966-1 CUM. BULL. 45.

life.[457] In addition, the IRS has frequently invoked the so-called "mass" or "indivisible" asset theory to preclude allocation in the first place. This theory may be applied if a group of assets are acquired in a single transaction, all or a large portion are intangible, and the mass of assets will not decrease in value by the passage of time (due to the addition of new components as old ones expire or are terminated). When these conditions are present, it is apparently the view of the Service that the entire asset (the "mass" of which is "indivisible") is non-depreciable since it has an indeterminate and unascertainable useful life.[458]

The government has not, however, been very successful in securing judicial approval of this theory. For example, in *Commissioner v. Seaboard Finance Company*,[459] the taxpayer had acquired several small loan businesses as part of an expansion program. In determining the value of each business, it rated and then placed a value on the loan contracts held by the businesses. The resulting figure was then offered as the purchase price, though in each case the taxpayer actually paid an amount in excess of the face amount of loans outstanding and the value of the fixed assets acquired. The taxpayer sought to allocate this "premium" to the loan contracts which were to be depreciated over a 3-5 year period, but the IRS determined that the "premium" had been paid for non-depreciable goodwill. When the matter was presented to the Tax Court, it held that the evidence would justify an allocation of 70 percent of the premium to the contracts and the remaining 30 percent was non-depreciable goodwill. In upholding this determination, the circuit court rejected the IRS' position that the premium did not have an ascertainable life. In the court's view, the evidence justified the conclusion that the contracts to which 70 percent of the premium was allocable did have a life that could be estimated with reasonable accuracy. It also rejected the "mass" or "indivisible" asset theory because the taxpayer "apparently made an honest attempt to value the premium paid, under the impression that a depreciation deduction would be allowed. Each contract was individually analyzed to determine its ultimate worth."[460] The rationale reflected in *Seaboard Finance* has been utilized by several other courts, with the result that a purchase price for a group of assets may be allocated between the depreciable and non-depreciable portions thereof in as accurate a manner as possible based upon its facts and circumstances, even though such allocation may not be accomplished with mathematical precision.[461] The portion allocated to the intangibles will be subject to a depreciation deduction so long as the asset can be shown to have a reasonably ascertainable future life,[462] and the "mass" or "indivisible" asset rule will be inapplicable if the taxpayer can carry the burden of establishing that the assets have such a useful life and an ascertainable value separate and distinct from goodwill.[463] The use of a

457. *See* § 7.17.
458. *See* Golden State Towel & Linen Serv., Ltd. v. United States, 373 F.2d 938 (Ct. Cl. 1967).
459. 367 F.2d 646 (9th Cir. 1966).
460. *Id.* at 652.
461. *See, e.g.,* Miami Valley Broadcasting Corp. v. United States, 499 F.2d 677 (Ct. Cl. 1974) (allocating in a manner different from that sought by each party). The courts have repeatedly held that the issues of amortizability and allocation are inherently factual matters. *See* Houston Chronicle Publishing Co. v. United States, 481 F.2d 1240 (5th Cir. 1973).
462. *See, e.g.,* Miami Valley Broadcasting Corp. v. United States, 499 F.2d 677 (Ct. Cl. 1974); Houston Chronicle Publishing Co. v. United States, 481 F.2d 1240 (5th Cir. 1973); Super Food Servs., Inc. v. United States, 416 F.2d 1236 (7th Cir. 1969).
463. *See, e.g.,* Richard S. Miller & Sons, Inc. v. United States, 537 F.2d 446 (Ct. Cl. 1976); Houston Chronicle Publishing Co. v. United States, 481 F.2d 1240 (5th Cir. 1973); Super Food Servs., Inc. v.

reasonable valuation and appraisal procedure, as in *Seaboard Finance,* will not necessarily be indispensable to the taxpayer's efforts to avoid the "mass" or "indivisible" asset rule,[464] but failure to follow such a procedure may be a convenient premise for the conclusion that the rule is applicable or that allocation and depreciation is not appropriate for some other reason.[465] In short, when a taxpayer acquires a group of assets consisting in whole or part of intangible assets, it should be certain to establish the reasonable value and useful life of each asset with the greatest accuracy possible under the circumstances.

As indicated above,[466] the acquisition of a professional sports team will involve the purchase of a group of assets, some of which will be depreciable and others non-depreciable. In light of the principles just reviewed, it would appear that the allocational objectives of the acquiring owner may be substantially achieved if the transaction is satisfactorily planned. The application of the allocation rules to professional team acquisition is illustrated by *Laird v. United States,*[467] involving a corporation organized to purchase the Atlanta Falcons as an expansion team in 1966. The total purchase price was $8,500,000, and the agreement of sale specified that the price of the player contracts to be acquired from existing teams in the league was $8,450,000 and the price of the franchise itself only $50,000. For tax purposes, the team allocated $7,722,914 of the purchase price (approximately 91 percent) to the player contracts.[468] It allocated

United States, 416 F.2d 1236 (7th Cir. 1969); Harry A. Kinney, 58 T.C. 1038 (1972); Manhattan Co. of Virginia, Inc., 50 T.C. 56 (1968).

When the burden is not carried, the rule will be applied. *See, e.g.,* Sunset Fuel Co. v. United States, 519 F.2d 781 (9th Cir. 1975); Tomlinson v. Commissioner, 507 F.2d 723 (9th Cir. 1975); Marsh & McLennan, Inc. v. Commissioner, 420 F.2d 667 (3rd Cir. 1969); Golden State Towel & Linen Serv., Ltd. v. United States, 373 F.2d 938 (Ct. Cl. 1967); Commissioner v. Indiana Broadcasting Corp., 350 F.2d 580 (7th Cir. 1965), *cert. denied,* 382 U.S. 1027 (1966); Westinghouse Broadcasting Co. v. Commissioner, 309 F.2d 279 (3d Cir. 1962), *cert. denied,* 372 U.S. 935, 9 L. Ed. 2d 766, 83 S. Ct. 881 (1963); Thrifticheck Serv. Corp. v. Commissioner, 287 F.2d 1 (2d Cir. 1961); Keith Misegades, 53 T.C. 477 (1969); Gulf Television Corp., 52 T.C. 1038 (1969). *See also* Rev. Rul. 74-456, 1974-2 CUM. BULL. 65.

See generally 4 J. MERTENS, LAW OF FEDERAL INCOME TAXATION § 23.67 (1973); Holdmann, *Amortization of Intangibles—General Rules,* TAX MANAGEMENT PORTFOLIO 209 (1969); Holdmann, *Amortization of Intangibles—Specific Industries and Types of Property,* TAX MANAGEMENT PORTFOLIO 218 (1969); Note, *Amortization of Intangibles: An Examination of the Tax Treatment of Purchased Goodwill,* 81 HARV. L. REV.. 859 (1968); *Depreciation of Mass Assets — Current Developments,* Tax Management Memorandum 73-20, at 3 (1973); *Amortization of Intangibles—Recent Developments Under the Mass Asset Rule,* Tax Management Memorandum 70-06, at 3 (1970); *Depreciation of Intangibles—The Indiana Broadcasting Case and Related Questions,* Tax Management Memorandum 65-25, at 2 (1965).

464. Thus, in Houston Chronicle Publishing Co. v. United States, 481 F.2d 1240 (5th Cir. 1973), the court specifically noted that the purchase price of the assets had been paid in a lump sum "none of which was allocated among the various items prior to the time of sale." *Id.* at 1243. Although the assets were appraised after the sale, this later process did not appear to be in any way dispositive of the court's conclusion, as it had been, for example, in *Seaboard Finance* and the cases cited in note 465 *infra. See also* KFOX, Inc. v. United States, 510 F.2d 1365 (Ct. Cl. 1975) (court upheld conclusion that there was no allocation by agreement, but upheld the allocation in fact made by the taxpayer); Richard S. Miller & Sons, Inc. v. United States, 537 F.2d 446 (Ct. Cl. 1976). *See* note 487 *infra.*

465. *See, e.g.,* Winn-Dixie Montgomery, Inc. v. United States, 444 F.2d 677 (5th Cir. 1971); Boe v. Commissioner, 307 F.2d 339 (9th Cir. 1962).

466. *See* notes 455-56 *supra.*

467. 391 F. Supp. 656 (N.D. Ga. 1975), *aff'd,* 556 F.2d 1224 (5th Cir. 1977), *noted in* 42 J. TAXATION 332 (1975). *See also* Kauffman v. United States, 77-2 U.S.T.C. ¶ 9664 (Ct. Cl. 1977) (government not estopped by acceptance of valuation in previous years).

468. The difference between the contract stipulation for the player contracts ($8,450,000) and the amount actually sought to be allocated ($7,722,914) was accounted for by deferred interest, which the parties agreed was deductible by the team.

only a nominal amount to the league franchise and nothing to the rights it acquired in league broadcast contracts. When these determinations were audited, the IRS sought to reduce the amount allocated to the player contracts substantially (to $1,050,000), and to allocate the difference to the non-depreciable league franchise. At trial, however, the government abandoned this position and argued instead that no value could be assigned to the player contracts.[469]

In analyzing the case, the district court began by noting that the franchise entitled the team to "substantial and valuable rights and benefits" which it reviewed in detail. The first element considered was the right to participate in league television broadcast revenues. The court found that the team could expect to receive a significant annual income from its share of the television broadcast contracts, which were found to have a present value of $4,277,043. This amount was determined by applying a 5 percent discount factor to the revenues that the team could expect to receive from the 1966-69 contract with CBS. Although the court thus found that the television rights had an ascertainable fair market value, it went on to conclude that they did not have a determinable useful life and could not be depreciated.[470] This treatment of the broadcast rights would appear to be subject to some question, since the court made the value determination by reference to the four year contract with CBS and then found that the rights had no determinable useful life. If the rights had no such useful life, then the use of the four year period for valuation purposes seems inconsistent. On the other hand, if the rights had a value equal only to the present value of the income that could be expected to be received over a four year period, then consistency would seem to require that they also have a useful life of four years. It is possible that the court considered other factors that would more clearly explain its conclusions, but they were not set forth in its opinion. This aspect of the opinion seems to raise more questions than it answers.[471] For example, it is not clear why the broadcast rights should be considered as a separate asset for tax purposes or why they should not be treated as part of the franchise acquired. It is also unclear why the court failed to consider the expenses that would be incurred by the Falcons in performing the services (*i.e.,* fielding a team) that would be necessary for it to earn a share of the television pool.[471.1] Hopefully, these issues will be clarified in the future.

---

469. *See* Weill, *Depreciation of Player Contracts—The Government is Ahead at the Half,* 53 TAXES 581, 582 (1975) (article by the trial attorney for the government in *Laird*).

470. 391 F. Supp. at 665.

471. *See* Blum, *Valuing Intangibles: What are the Choices for Valuing Professional Sports Teams,* 45 J. TAX. 286 (1976); Jones, *Amortization and Nonamortization of Intangibles in the Sports World,* 53 TAXES 777, 786 (1975); Braun & Pusey, *Taxation of Professional Sports Teams,* 7 TAX ADVISER 196, 200-02 (1976); Weill, *supra* note 469, at 585-86. The taxpayer in *Laird* specifically appealed this aspect of the court's decision, but the court of appeals provided no additional explanation, 556 F.2d 1224, 1235-37.

471.1. Thus, in Bradley, *Planning for Amortization of Intangibles,* 35 N.Y.U. FED. TAX INST. 445, 467 (1977), it is observed that

> [t]he method used by the District Court [in *Laird*] to value the right to share in the television contract is unpersuasive. In valuing the television rights, the Court considered it to be an assured income stream. It failed to take any account of the charge against that income — the obligation placed on the Falcons to field a professional football team, and the costs involved in that endeavor. A pro rata portion of that cost should be applied against the television income, thereby reducing the value of the contract right.

See also Blum, *Valuing Intangibles: What are the Choices for Valuing Professional Sports Teams,* 46 J. TAXATION 286 (1976).

After finding that the broadcast rights had a value of $4,277,043, the district court then substracted this amount from the figure allocated by the team to the player contracts ($7,772,914), and the difference was the amount that it determined was potentially available for allocation to the contracts ($3,445,871). In order to determine how much of this amount could be allocated to the contracts, the court was required to ascertain their reasonable value. It noted that the team had produced expert witnesses who testified that the value of the contracts was approximately what the team had originally allocated to them, but rejected these appraisals because they exceeded the amount available for allocation, and one had been based on an improper method of valuation.[472] The court gave more credence to a method used by the original coach of the Falcons which apparently focused upon the relative, prospective skills of each player, rather than using a standard figure for different classes of players (as had been used by the other experts). This method produced a figure of $3,035,000, which the court concluded was their total fair market value "allowable as depreciable intangible assets."[473] The remaining amount available for allocation ($410,871) was allocated to the non-depreciable franchise.

The *Laird* opinion is important for several reasons. From the perspective of team owners, it is important because of the court's rejection of the government's "indivisible asset" argument.[474] The court emphatically stated that it did "not accept the Government's contention that it is impossible to establish, except in an arbitrary manner, a reasonably accurate basis for depreciation of the veteran player contracts . . . ."[475] It is also significant to both the government and owners to the extent that it concluded that allocation of the purchase price to depreciable player contracts is proper,[476] and that the only real issue is the reasonable value of the contracts at the time of acquisition. This determination, in the court's view, involves less than exact measurement:

> [v]aluation is, under the best of circumstances, a difficult task because the fair market value of any asset may depend upon, or at least be influenced by, a large number of factors and variables which may be difficult both to identify and to evaluate. But when the asset to be valued is the employment contracts of a group of forty-two professional football players, the task of arriving at a reasonably accurate result is unusually arduous. The court must evaluate (as best it can) all of the evidence in the record and arrive at the most reasonable result possible under the circumstances, fully realizing that such a result may necessarily be imprecise.[477]

The considerations that induce owners to seek substantial allocations to player contracts and the inherent factual problems that are raised by such allocations

---

472. It was improper, the court said, because it was based in part upon a comparison of veteran players selected in the expansion draft with rookies in the college draft. 391 F. Supp. 666.

473. 391 F. Supp. at 667. It should be noted that the court of appeals agreed with the ultimate figure allocated to the player contracts, but suggested that the "subtraction-out" method used by the district court was improper. 556 F.2d at 1237.

474. *See* notes 457-66 *supra*.

475. 391 F. Supp. at 670.

476. This conclusion seems to rest upon solid ground, in light of the broad authority which upholds the allocation of purchase price between depreciable and non-depreciable assets in comparable, non-sports, contexts. *See* note 466 *supra*. *See also* KFOX, Inc. v. United States, 510 F.2d 1365 (Ct. Cl. 1975) (similar conclusion with respect to disc jockey contracts, which was reached by analogy to professional athletics contracts).

477. 391 F. Supp. at 670. *See* note 461 *supra*.

(as illustrated by *Laird*), caused Congress to amend the Code to provide more definitive rules in the Tax Reform Act of 1976.[478] With respect to basis allocation, the Act adds new section 1056 to the Code.[479] It provides that when a franchise to conduct any sports enterprise is sold or exchanged, and there is a transfer of a contract for the services of an athlete, the basis of the contract in the hands of the transferee may not exceed the sum of the adjusted basis of the contract in the hands of the transferor immediately before the transfer plus the gain, if any, recognized by the transferor on the transfer of the contract.[480] Section 1056(d) also adds a presumption that not more than 50 percent of the consideration for a sports franchise may be allocated to player contracts, unless it is established that a larger allocation is proper.[480.1] It is also provided that there is no presumption that an allocation of less than 50 percent is proper. These allocation limitations are not applicable to a like-kind exchange or to the transfer of property from a decedent.[481] Where the allocation provisions are applicable, there is also a requirement that the transferor furnish certain information to the Service, and the figures so furnished will be binding upon both the transferor and transferee.[482]

Although § 1056 provides more definitive rules with respect to the allocation of the purchase price of a franchise to player contracts, it does not eliminate the types of controversies that are so well illustrated by the *Laird* decision. It would not appear to apply at all to the creation of new leagues (there would presumably be no transfer of player contracts as a part of the franchise transfer), and its application to new franchises in an existing league is not clear. In most expansions, a new owner acquires a franchise and the right to draft players from the existing teams (or from the rookie draft). This arrangement would be within § 1056 only if the transfer of the player contracts were "in connection with" the sale or exchange of the franchise. The Service has ruled that a "sale or exchange" does take place upon transfer of players pursuant to an expansion draft,[483] and it will presumably include such transactions within § 1056 in the regulations. An additional issue that is not clear is whether § 1056 will preclude the Service from invoking the "mass" asset rule in the future. Since § 1056(d) specifically states that even an allocation of less than 50 percent will not be presumed to be correct, it would appear that the Service could continue to attempt to impose the rule.

Even where § 1056 is applicable, it will not end controversy. As noted above, it will limit the basis of a contract to its basis in the hands of the transferor plus

478. *See* S. REP. No. 94-938, 94th Cong., 2d Sess. 86-91 (1976); H. REP. No. 94-658, 94th Cong., 1st Sess. 115-118 (1975).

479. Section 1056 is applicable to transfers of player contracts in connection with a sale or exchange of a franchise after December 31, 1975.

480. IRC § 1056(a). A gain not recognized to a corporate transferor because of IRC § 337 will be treated as recognized for purposes of § 1056 to the extent that it is recognized by the corporation's shareholders. *Id.*

480.1. In the court of appeals' opinion in *Laird,* the court referred to the presumption in § 1056(d) as a benchmark in affirming the district court's allocation to the player contracts. 556 F.2d at 1241.

481. IRC § 1056(b). Like-kind exchanges are noted at § 7.19.

482. IRC § 1056(c).

483. Rev. Rul. 71-123, 1971-1 CUM. BULL. 101; *see* S. REP. No. 94-398, 94th Cong., 2d Sess. 90 (1976) (indicating that § 1056 will apply to the creation of new franchises).

any gain recognized by the transferor. This will allow the transferee to obtain a relatively high basis only if the transferor has a high basis (for example, because of recent acquisition or little depreciation) or is willing to recognize a substantial amount of gain. If the transferee is able to obtain a high basis in the contracts, it must then confront the 50 percent presumption of § 1056(d). This will require that it justify an allocation of more than 50 percent of the consideration to the contracts. An allocation of less than 50 percent will also continue to require justification.

These factors suggest that the valuation and allocation problems raised in *Laird* will not be buried by § 1056. Thus, the core issue of that case will continue: How much is "properly allocable" to player contracts in a franchise acquisition? Section 1056(a) indicates the gross amount that may be allocated (transferor's adjusted basis and gain), but § 1056(d) will allow an allocation of more than 50 percent of the total purchase price only if such amount is shown to be "properly allocable." Although there is no clear indication of how a team will be able to demonstrate that more than 50 percent is "properly allocable," it does seem reasonably clear that the team will have to establish a fair and reasonable basis for such an allocation. The pre-§ 1056 case law would indicate that a team will be well advised to individually analyze and appraise each of the assets that is to be acquired, including each of the player contracts, so that a specific portion of the purchase price, or basis, may be intelligently assigned to each asset and be justified under § 1056. This process will not necessarily preclude application of the § 1056(d) presumption or an effort by the IRS to apply the "mass" or "indivisible" asset rule, but it would certainly aid the team's likelihood of success.[484] In establishing the propriety of an allocation, it would also be helpful if the agreement which memorializes the terms of the acquisition could reflect the desired allocation on its face (though this would not be possible in an expansion situation when players are selected after the price is agreed upon).[485] Such an agreement would, however, require that the buyer and seller agree on the terms of the acquisition, and, as will be noted subsequently, they may have different allocational objectives.[486] Such agreement has not, in any event, been required by some courts which have refused to apply the indivisible asset rule.[487]

---

484. Thus, in Commissioner v. Seaboard Fin. Co., 367 F.2d 646 (9th Cir. 1966), the court stated that "the 'indivisible asset' rule is inapplicable where the purchase price was derived by appraising the value of each individual asset . . .," and in "our case a definite cost was assigned to each contract purchased . . . ." *Id.* at 652-53. *See also* Super Food Serv., Inc. v. United States, 416 F.2d 1236 (7th Cir. 1969); Boe v. Commissioner, 307 F.2d 339 (9th Cir. 1962) (rule applied where "[t]here was no valuation of any particular contract, no assignment of any part of the purchase price to any contract or group of contracts. There was simply bargaining between the parties as to what would be paid for the business as a whole").

485. The usefulness of such an agreement, and the extent to which the IRS would be bound by it, is considered in Klinger, *Tax Aspects of Buying, Selling and Owning Professional Sports Teams,* 48 L.A.B. BULL. 162, 167, 176 (1973).

486. *See* § 7.19.

487. *See* notes 464-65 *supra.*

With respect to an agreed-upon valuation in the sales contract, it should also be noted that the courts have not given dispositive weight to the failure to include such a provision as a result of the conflicting tax interests of the buyer and seller. In Winn-Dixie Montgomery, Inc. v. United States, 444 F.2d 677 (5th Cir. 1971), for example, the court noted that the purchase price was stated as a lump sum "so that neither side would be definitively precluded by the wording of the pact from urging its most advantageous tax position to the revenue officials," *id.* at 679, and then went on to conclude that allocation was not available on the facts of the case. In Harry A. Kinney, 58 T.C. 1038 (1972), on the other hand, the court noted that no allocation had been made by the parties

It may also not be required under § 1056(d), though the statement filed by the transferor under § 1056(c) will bind the transferee whether or not the latter agrees with the information contained therein.

With regard to the allocation of purchase price, then, it would appear that if the professional team undertakes a reasonable valuation and appraisal process, which is generally suggested by the *Laird* opinion, and if it can meet the requirements of § 1056(a), then it may achieve its allocational objectives. Even if such a process is followed, the IRS will, of course, have the authority to audit the transaction itself; and although a recent study has suggested that "the probability of resulting adjustment appears to be low,"[488] *Laird,* the favor with which the "mass" asset rule is apparently viewed by the government, and new § 1056 would appear to indicate that future efforts to interdict the allocational objectives of professional teams are likely.

§ 7.19. Sale or Exchange of Contracts and Teams.

Tax issues will also arise upon the sale, exchange or other transfer of player contracts or the team itself. The principles that determine the consequences of these issues are similar, and in some cases repetitive, of those already considered, but they may have slightly different planning considerations from the seller's point of view than from that of the buyer.[489]

The player contracts held by professional teams are what the Code refers to as § 1231 property—that is, depreciable property used in the trade or business.[490] Status as "1231 property" will require that the team aggregate its gains and losses [491] from the sale, exchange or involuntary conversion [492] of

---

because of an inability to agree upon the amount to be allocated (without indicating that the reason for such inability was divergent tax objectives), *id.* at 1043, and then went on to allow an allocation to be made. These cases can only be said to be indicative of a facts and circumstances resolution.

Although an agreement was present in *Laird,* it reflected only lump-sum figures and was between the league and the expansion team, as opposed to the buyer and seller of an existing team who would more clearly have inconsistent allocational objectives, as well as what would more normally be viewed as countervailing (arm's length) bargaining power.

488. Okner, *Taxation and Sports Enterprises,* in GOVERNMENT AND THE SPORTS BUSINESS 159, 166 (R. Noll, ed. 1974). This study also reports that the incidence of IRS adjustment is quite low. *Id.*

489. Attention in this section will be devoted to only two basic types of transactions: sales and like-kind exchanges. There are also other possibilities, including gift, death and reorganization transactions, but these are not specifically discussed because of the apparently small role that they actually play in sports transfers. *See* § 7.18, at note 431 (discussing the basic tax results of these types of transaction).

490. Rev. Rul. 71-137, 1971-1 CUM. BULL. 104 (football); Rev. Rul. 67-380, 1967-2 CUM. BULL. 291 (baseball). It is significant in this regard to note the requirements of § 1231. Thus, to qualify as § 1231 property, an asset must be subject to depreciation, be held for more than six months, and not be inventory or other property held primarily for sale to customers. IRC § 1231(b). The only one of these requirements that would pose any hurdle to professional sports contracts might be the requirement that the assets not be held primarily for sale to customers. Thus, in Hollywood Baseball Ass'n v. Commissioner, 423 F.2d 494 (9th Cir. 1970), *cert. denied,* 400 U.S. 848 (1970), the court held that professional baseball contracts in the hands of a minor league team were inventory held by the team for sale in the ordinary course of its business. In reaching this conclusion, the court placed principal reliance upon the fact that the team was obligated by contract to make its players available for sale, either by player draft or pursuant to a working agreement with a major league team. The rule of *Hollywood Baseball* would not, therefore, apply to major league professional teams, absent a showing that they were obligated to make all of their players available for sale. See note 514 *infra.*

491. The computation of gains or losses is made in accordance with the provisions of IRC § 1001.

492. The term "involuntary conversion" has reference to the conversion of property into money or to other property as a result of complete or partial destruction, theft, seizure, requisition or

§ 1231 assets, and if the gains exceed the losses, such gains or losses will be considered as long-term capital gains and losses; but if the gains do not exceed the losses, then the gains and losses will be treated as ordinary gains and losses.[493] A "sale" for these purposes will be considered to exist, unless otherwise excluded, at any time a contract changes hands in return for consideration and would, of course, include the transfer of a contract for a valuable consideration (such as cash or future draft choices) to another team. It would also include other customary transactions in the professional sports business. Thus, in *Revenue Ruling 71-123*,[494] a "sale" was said to exist when a team assigned three contracts to an expansion team, for which it received a share of the amount paid to the league by the expansion team for its franchise.

As a general rule, then, the sale or exchange of player contracts will produce capital gain or loss to the selling team, subject to the aggregation requirements of § 1231. However, an additional provision of the Code may cause a portion of the gain to be taxed at ordinary income rates instead of at the preferable capital gains rates. This involves the depreciation recapture rule of § 1245,[495] which will, to the extent that it is applicable, override § 1231. The recapture rule provides that, in the case of a sale or exchange of § 1245 property,[496] the amount by which the lower of the "recomputed basis" of the property, or the amount realized, exceeds its adjusted basis shall be treated as ordinary income—that is, as the gain from the sale or exchange of property which is neither a capital asset nor § 1231 property.[497] The effect of these provisions is to require the taxpayer to pay tax at ordinary income rates on the depreciation deductions previously taken (to the extent of the realized gain). This result is not, however, unfavorable. Although tax on the earlier deductions may eventually have to be paid, it will have been deferred for possibly several years, so that the taxpayer will have had tax-free use of the money in the interim.[498]

The Service has for several years taken the position that professional player contracts are § 1245 property.[499] As part of its effort to reduce the tax benefits of team ownership in the Tax Reform Act of 1976,[500] Congress expanded the application of § 1245 to player contracts that are sold or exchanged after December 31, 1975. The Act adds new § 1245(a)(4), which provides that if a team franchise is sold or exchanged and player contracts are transferred in connection therewith, the "recomputed basis" of the player contracts to the transferor will be equal to their adjusted basis increased by the greater of the previously unrecaptured depreciation on contracts acquired by the transferor at the time of acquisition of the franchise or the player contracts involved in the transfer.

---

condemnation. Treas. Reg. § 1.1231-1(e)(1). Although it has been observed that when a player is cut from a team an involuntary conversion results, *Hearings Before the Senate Subcomm. on Antitrust and Monopoly of the Senate Comm. on the Judiciary*, 92nd Cong., 1st Sess. pt. 1, 373 (1971), that conclusion seems hardly to be consistent with the requirements of the regulations.

493. IRC § 1231(a); Treas. Reg. § 1.1231-(b); Rev. Rul. 67-380, 1967-2 Cum. Bull. 291.

494. 1971-1 Cum. Bull. 104.

495. IRC § 1245.

496. The definition of "section 1245 property" is contained in IRC § 1245(a)(3).

497. IRC § 1245(a)(1). In the event of a "like-kind" exchange, the amount of gain to be taken into account will not exceed the amount of gain recognized ("boot") plus the fair market value of specific other property. IRC § 1245(b)(4). The "like-kind" exchange rules are considered at notes 515-26 *infra*.

498. The benefits of this type of deferral are suggested in § 7.10.

499. Rev. Rul. 71-137, 1971-1 Cum. Bull. 104; Rev. Rul. 67-380, 1967-2 Cum. Bull. 291.

500. *See* § 7.18, at notes 478-88.

The term "previously unrecaptured depreciation with respect to initial contracts" is defined to be the excess, if any, of the sum of depreciation deductions allowed or allowable on player contracts acquired by the transferor at the time of the acquisition of the franchise, plus any loss deductions with respect to such contracts, over the aggregate of the amounts treated as ordinary income by § 1245 with respect to prior dispositions of such player contracts acquired upon acquisition of the franchise.[501] A similar definition is provided for the previously unrecaptured depreciation on the contracts actually transferred.[502]

This amendment expands the potential reach of the recapture rules. In essence, it will require a team to recapture at least the amount of depreciation (amortization) claimed on the contracts acquired upon original acquisition of the franchise. In the absence of § 1245(a)(4), the recapture rules would only apply to the contracts actually transferred.[503] Although the Act was intended to provide definitive rules with respect to recapture, it does raise some question about its application. For example, it is not clear how it would apply when a new franchise is created in an existing league. In such situations, a few contracts are transferred by each team to the new franchise. If the creation of the new franchise constitutes a "sale or exchange" of a franchise,[504] then the § 1245(a)(4) rules would be applicable. It is not clear, however, how its provisions would be applied. Section 1245(a)(4) states that the recomputed basis is the greater of the unrecaptured depreciation on the contracts originally acquired or actually transferred. If only a few contracts were transferred, does the original contract rule apply or is the actual transfer rule alone applicable? If the former, is a share of the original unrecaptured depreciation allocated to the contracts transferred? These, and other, questions will hopefully be answered by the issuance of regulations.

Even if the depreciation recapture rules were not for some reason applicable, ordinary income might also be produced upon sale of player contracts by application of the so-called tax benefit doctrine. This doctrine provides that where amounts previously deducted from income (producing a tax benefit) are later recovered by the taxpayer, the amount recovered will be included in income for the taxable year of recovery.[505] Although application of the doctrine is less

---

501. IRC § 1245(a)(4)(B).[*]

502. IRC § 1245(a)(4)(C).[*]

503. Section 1245(a)(4) was designed to limit the advantage to a person who acquires a team franchise and holds it just long enough to reap maximum tax benefit, but it will impose a penalty upon owners who have held teams for a substantial period of time and who, presumably, have not engaged in the type of practices that are sought to be circumscribed. The penalties, moreover, are dissimilar from the tax principles that apply to the ownership of non-sports assets. See Jones, *Amortization and Nonamortization of Intangibles in the Sports World,* 53 TAXES 777, 788 (1975) (discussing the original House version of this provision).

The divergence of § 1245(a)(4) from the principles applied to the seller of other types of assets has met with some Congressional criticism. See INQUIRY INTO PROFESSIONAL SPORTS, FINAL REPORT OF THE HOUSE SELECT COMM. ON PROFESSIONAL SPORTS, 94th Cong., 2d Sess. 100 (1977).[*]

504. See § 7.18, at note 483.

505. See Nash v. United States, 398 U.S.1, 26 L. Ed. 2d 1, 90 S. Ct. 1550 (1969); Rev. Rul. 68-104, 1968-1 CUM. BULL. 361. The specific coverage of the doctrine has, however, been subject to some confusion. It has frequently been used to suggest that if a deduction provided no tax benefit in a previous year then recovery of the item in a subsequent year will be excluded from income. See, e.g., Alice Phelan Sullivan Corp. v. United States, 381 F.2d 399 (Ct. Cl. 1967); IRC § 111. See generally S. SURREY, W. WARREN, P. MCDANIEL & H. AULT, FEDERAL INCOME TAXATION 738-44 (vol. 1, 1972).

than clear, it could apply in situations where a team expenses (currently deducts) acquisition costs of player contracts and subsequently sells them at a gain.[506] The issue could also arise in a slightly different context if the option and reserve systems that exist as of this writing are eliminated in the future. It will be recalled that the premise of the Service's position that contract acquisition costs must be capitalized and depreciated is that the contracts have a useful life substantially in excess of one year.[507] If these player restraint mechanisms are modified to the extent that the contracts no longer have such a useful life, then acquisition costs would be deducted and not capitalized,[508] the contracts would apparently not be depreciable [509] and, if so, would not be § 1231 assets.[510]

In either situation, the recapture rules of § 1245 would not be applicable because no depreciation would be claimed on the contracts, and in order to achieve ordinary income treatment the Service could turn to the tax benefit rule. This would be consistent with its past treatment of player contracts.[511] The position that could be taken is reflected by *Revenue Ruling 68-102*,[512] in which a taxpayer was engaged in a diaper rental business and the diapers were expensed in the year of acquisition, since experience showed that they would have a useful life of less than one year. The short useful life precluded depreciation and status as § 1231 assets. The taxpayer then sold the rental business, and the IRS ruled that amounts attributable to the diapers that were transferred must be treated as ordinary income "since the proceeds from the sale of diapers represent a recovery of amounts previously deducted for Federal income tax purposes."[513] Neither of the situations suggested here has been currently pursued by the Service in team sport cases, but the theories are certainly available and should be kept in mind by teams when they expense acquisition costs or agree to arrangements that reduce the period over which they can control the mobility of athletes.[514]

---

506. *See* § 7.17, at notes 404-414.

507. *See* § 7.17, at notes 397-99.

508. *Id.*

509. *See, e.g.,* Rev. Rul. 68-104, 1968-1 CUM. BULL. 361.

510. IRC § 1231(b)(1).

511. Thus, in Rev. Rul. 54-441, 1954-2 CUM. BULL. 101, the Service ruled that when a group of player contracts is sold, the gain would be treated as ordinary income. Although the ruling was revoked by Rev. Rul. 67-379, 1967-2 CUM. BULL. 127, it is perhaps reflective of a theory that the Service could again utilize if the nature of player contracts undergoes substantial change.

512. 1968-1 CUM. BULL. 361.

513. Similar principles have been developed for the sale of expensed items under IRC § 337. Anders v. United States, 462 F.2d 1147 (Ct. Cl. 1972); Spitalny v. United States, 430 F.2d 195 (9th Cir. 1970); Commissioner v. Anders, 414 F.2d 1283 (10th Cir.), *cert. denied,* 396 U.S. 958 (1969); Estate of David B. Mutter, 63 T.C. 663 (1975). *See also* Rev. Rul. 72-396, 1972-2 CUM. BULL. 106 (liquidations under §§ 331, 333 and 346). *See generally* Okner, *Taxation and Sports Enterprises,* in GOVERNMENT AND THE SPORTS BUSINESS 159, 172 n. 29 (R. Noll, ed. 1974).

514. In addition to the theory noted in text, the IRS may also have other theories in the quiver to seek ordinary income treatment on the sale of player contracts if the terms of the contracts are materially changed from their present format. For example, if a player were allowed to gain free agent status in a short period of time, and if a mandatory compensation system (such as the so-called "Rozelle Rule") were adopted, then the IRS might argue that the contracts are held "primarily for sale to customers in the ordinary course of business" to exclude them from § 1231. IRC § 1231(b)(1)(B); International Shoe Machine Corp. v. United States, 491 F.2d 157 (1st Cir. 1974), *cert. denied,* 419 U.S. 834 (1974). Where such a finding could be made with respect to minor league baseball contracts, the Ninth Circuit has suggested that ordinary income treatment would be in order.

In considering the sale or exchange of player contracts, it is also important to note the "like-kind" exchange rules, which may provide a means for a team to avoid having to recognize gain on the transfer of its contracts. Inasmuch as the contracts are § 1231 property, they will qualify for the like-kind exchange rules of § 1031,[515] which provides that no gain or loss shall be recognized if property used in the trade or business or held for investment is exchanged solely for property of a like-kind.[516] If non-like-kind property is received in addition to the like-kind property, then the gain, if any, to the recipient must be recognized to the extent of the money or non-like-kind property (commonly referred to as "boot") received.[517] If the non-like-kind exchange results in a loss, the loss will not be recognized.[518] When gain is recognized under § 1031 because of the receipt of "boot," the gain will be included in the year-end § 1231 aggregate computation,[519] but if neither gain nor loss is recognized then there will be no additional figure to place in the § 1231 aggregate.[520] It is to be noted, however, that § 1031 specifically excludes from its provisions stock in trade or other inventory property held primarily for sale [521]—that is, property purchased and sold in the regular course of business.[522] Although it has been held that a minor league baseball team holds its contracts primarily for sale,[523] that would not be the case for ordinary major league professional teams, because they have no similar obligation to make their player contracts available for sale.[524] Thus, the exclusions should pose no hurdle for tax-free exchanges between major league professional teams. Since multi-player and multi-team exchanges have been negotiated, it is also important to note that multi-sided exchanges will not preclude a taxpayer from obtaining non-recognition treatment of its transaction.[525] Such exchanges will require only that more care be exercised in structuring the transaction, and in this area of the tax law, at least, form seems to prevail over substance.[526]

Hollywood Baseball Ass'n v. Commissioner, 423 F.2d 494 (9th Cir. 1970), *cert. denied,* 400 U.S. 848 (1970) (applying the doctrine of Corn Products Refining Co. v. Commissioner, 350 U.S. 46, 100 L. Ed. 29, 76 S. Ct. 20 (1950) to depreciable property used in the trade or business under § 1231).

515. Rev. Rul. 71-137, 1971-1 CUM. BULL. 104; Rev. Rul. 67-380, 1967-2 CUM. BULL. 291.

516. IRC § 1031(a). A "like-kind" exchange would, of course, include the trade of one player for another, and might include the exchange of a player for a future draft choice. *See* Okner, *Taxation and Sports Enterprise,* in GOVERNMENT AND THE SPORTS BUSINESS 159, 173 (R. Noll, ed. 1974).

517. IRC § 1031(b).

518. IRC § 1031(c).

519. IRC § 1231(a). *See* notes 491-93 *supra.*

520. Treas. Reg. § 1.1231-1(d)(4).

521. Regals Realty Co. v. Commissioner, 127 F.2d 931 (2d Cir. 1942).

522. Burkhard Inv. Co. v. United States, 100 F.2d 642 (9th Cir. 1938); Winter Holding Co., 31 B.T.A. 1185 (1935); Biscayne Trust Co., 18 B.T.A. 1015 (1930).

523. Hollywood Baseball Ass'n v. Commissioner, 423 F.2d 494 (9th Cir. 1970). *See* Note, *The Sale of Minor League Baseball Players During Liquidation—The Application of Corn Products to Depreciable Property,* 45 TEMPLE L.Q. 291 (1972).

524. Baltimore Baseball Club, Inc. v. United States, 481 F.2d 1283 (Ct. Cl. 1973). Such an obligation may be present in some circumstances. One example would be an expansion draft, in which all teams must make all players (except those on a special list) available to the expansion teams.

525. Coastal Terminals v. United States, 320 F.2d 333 (4th Cir. 1963); Alderson v. Commissioner, 317 F.2d 790 (9th Cir. 1963); W.D. Haden Co. v. Commissioner, 165 F.2d 588 (5th Cir. 1948); Leslie Q. Coupe, 52 T.C. 394 (1969); Mercantile Trust Co. of Baltimore, 32 B.T.A. 82 (1935), *aff'd,* 43 F.2d 39 (8th Cir. 1939).

526. Leslie Q. Coupe, 52 T.C. 394 (1969), (Simpson, J., concurring, and Raum, J., dissenting); *see also* Carlton v. United States, 385 F.2d 238 (5th Cir. 1967); Halpern v. United States, 286 F. Supp. 255 (N.D. Ga. 1968); John M. Rogers, 44 T.C. 126 (1965), *aff'd,* 377 F.2d 534 (9th Cir. 1967).

An additional factor that should be kept in mind when player contracts are sold is the potential application of the installment reporting rules of § 453. The purpose of these rules is to simply defer payment of the tax on gains until the proceeds of the sale have been received.[527]

If the owner of the team undertakes to sell the entire team, there will be additional factors to be considered. As was true with respect to the acquisition of a team,[528] when a team is sold the major problem will involve the allocation of the purchase price between the assets transferred. The objectives of the owner will normally be to maximize the economic gain while minimizing the federal income tax liability from the sale. These objectives will be achieved by allocating the purchase price to the assets that will produce the most in capital gains and the least in recapturable depreciation.[529] Since all of the broad categories of assets sold will normally be either capital or § 1231 assets—that is, the franchise,[530] player contracts[531] and office and sports equipment—the object will be to avoid recapture, which is a problem only with regard to the contracts and the equipment, and since the equipment will normally be a small item it will be excluded from consideration. The contracts will be subject to recapture if the seller has already claimed depreciation upon them,[532] and, as has been discussed at length, a "basis" for depreciation may be established only by the payment of bonuses or other contract acquisition costs.[533] If the contracts in the owner's hands are highly depreciated, it will seek to allocate the purchase price to the franchise or other capital assets not subject to depreciation. But if the contracts are not, for one reason or another, highly depreciated, then the owner may have no reason to prefer allocation to one asset over another, since essentially the same result will be produced from sale of any of the assets so long as they are all capital or § 1231 assets in the owner's hands. Thus, the selling owner may or may not share the desire of the buyer to allocate the

---

527. The rules provide in substance that sellers in qualifying installment sales—including regular and casual sellers of personal property—may report as income therefrom in any taxable year that proportion of the installment payments actually received in that year which the gross profit, realized or to be realized when payment is completed, bears to the total contract price, IRC § 453(a)(1); provided that in the taxable year of disposition there are no payments or that the payments actually made do not exceed 30 percent of the selling price. IRC § 453(b)(2)(A). Thus, under the installment method, the gross profit from a sale—that is, the selling price less the adjusted basis under § 1011—is prorated over the period in which installment payments are to be received, so that the amount reported as gross profit in any taxable year is the amount determined by applying the gross-profit percentage of the sale as a whole to the payments received in the taxable year. To be applicable, however, the transaction must involve an actual installment sale and not mere deferred payment. In Baltimore Baseball Club, Inc. v. United States, 481 F.2d 1283 (Ct. Cl. 1973), for example, installment reporting was denied when a professional baseball team sold six of its players to an expansion team, with the purchase price to be made in a single lump-sum payment in the first fiscal year of the seller after the date of the sale. This did not comply with the installment rules, the court said, because there must be more than one payment due to qualify as an installment sale. The seller was required, therefore, to recognize the entire gain in the year of sale.

528. See § 7.18.

529. See notes 495-98 supra.

530. With respect to the franchise itself, a brief comment is in order. Although franchises are not as a general rule treated as capital assets for federal income tax purposes, IRC § 1253(a), a specific exception to that rule exists for a "franchise to engage in professional football, basketball, baseball, or other professional sport," IRC § 1253(e), so that their purchase or sale will be subject to capital gain or loss treatment. Rev. Rul. 71-123, 1971-1 CUM. BULL. 227.

531. See notes 490-94 supra.

532. See notes 495-98 supra.

533. See § 7.17.

purchase price primarily to the depreciable player contracts. If their objectives are consistent, that fact will facilitate the preparation of an agreement memorializing the terms of sale which on its face allocates the purchase price between the various assets.[534] If their objectives are not consistent, then the buyer and seller will have more difficulty agreeing to an allocation.

In considering such allocations, it is also important to consider the effect of new § 1056. As noted earlier, § 1056(a) limits the basis of a new owner (transferee) in player contracts to the adjusted basis of, and gain, if any, recognized by, the seller (transferor).[535] In addition, the seller is required to provide a statement setting forth these figures to the Service, and the statement will bind both the buyer and seller.[536] Section 1056 will have the effect in many situations of forcing the buyer and seller to reach an agreement on the amount to be allocated to player contracts. In other words, the tax results are to some extent left to the frequently adverse self-interests of the buyer and seller. Since the seller is required to file the mutually binding statement, the inability of the parties to reach agreement may limit the benefits to be derived by the buyer from player contract depreciation. At the very least, the provisions of § 1056 will preclude the parties from taking completely inconsistent positions on the amount of the purchase price allocated to the player contracts.

§ 7.20. Professional Teams as Tax Shelters.

Consideration of the federal income taxation of professional teams would not be complete without a brief discussion of the extent to which a team may be used as a tax shelter by its owners. As was considered in more detail in an earlier discussion, the term "tax shelter" covers a rather wide variety of investments.[537] One form of tax shelter benefit would be created by an investment that produces ordinary tax deductions that exceed the actual economic expenditures that it requires. This excess could then be used to offset (shelter) other income of the investor. When the investment is eventually sold, moreover, the proceeds could be realized at capital gains rates, and, to the extent that the gain is not recaptured, the investor would have converted ordinary income (which has been offset by previous deductions from the investment) into gain taxed at capital gain rates. Even if capital gains treatment could not be achieved, in whole or part, the investor would, as a result of the deductions, have benefitted by the tax-free use of the dollars that would otherwise have been paid into the federal treasury in the earlier years.

The professional team is, in theory, at least, easily utilized as a tax shelter. As has been noted throughout this discussion, player contracts are depreciable assets and may be, and frequently are, depreciated over rather short periods of time (often in as little as 3 - 5 years).[538] Thus, when an investor purchases a team and a significant portion of the purchase price is allocated to player contracts, the depreciation from the contracts may thereafter exceed the actual

---

534. The benefits of such agreement, and the extent to which the IRS will be bound by it, are considered in Klinger, *Tax Aspects of Buying, Selling and Owning Professional Sports Teams,* 48 L.A.B. BULL. 162, 163, 167, 176 (1973).

535. *See* § 7.18, at notes 478-83.

536. IRC § 1056(c).

537. *See* § 7.10.

538. *See* § 7.17.

economic expenditures required to maintain the team, and the total of the deductions may exceed the gross income of the team. If this is the case, the team will have a net operating loss, and if it is organized as a partnership [539] or a subchapter S corporation,[540] the investor may utilize the loss to shelter other income.[541] When the period in which the depreciation of a newly acquired group of player contracts has expired, moreover, the owner may then have an economic incentive to dispose of the team.[542]

Although this brief discussion highly simplifies the many complex factors that are part and parcel of tax shelter investments,[543] it is sufficient to indicate how the professional team may be utilized as a shelter and thereby provide economic consequences to the team owners that are much more attractive than might be indicated by simple perusal of the team's net operating results for any given taxable year.[544] This is not to say, however, that all professional teams are operated as tax shelters, because they certainly are not. It simply suggests that the professional team may be utilized for that purpose under interpretations of the relevant provisions of the Internal Revenue Code, at least as they existed prior to the Tax Reform Act of 1976.[545]

The extent to which a professional team may serve as a tax shelter was limited by the Tax Reform Act of 1976, or at least that was the stated purpose of Congress.[546] As noted in earlier discussions, the Act makes two significant

539. *See* § 7.16, at notes 374-78. If the team is organized as a partnership, the partners will themselves be able to deduct the net operating loss of the partnership, at least to the extent that such deductions do not exceed each partner's basis in the partnership interest (which may include indebtedness of the partnership). IRC §§ 704(a), 704(d), 752(a); Treas. Reg. § 1.752-1(e).

540. *See* § 7.16, at notes 380-87. If the team is organized as a subchapter S corporation, it will have made an election to not be subject to the federal income tax, with the result that the tax consequences of corporate operations will be borne by its shareholders. Thus, the shareholders will be entitled to deduct the net operating losses of the corporation, IRC § 1374(a), subject to a limitation which will be determined by the adjusted basis of the corporate stock in their hands plus any indebtedness of the corporation to them. IRC § 1374(c)(2).

If loss experience is continuous, attention should be given to the "hobby loss" rules, which are considered in § 7.21. The application of the "hobby loss" rules to sports teams is considered in INQUIRY INTO PROFESSIONAL SPORTS, FINAL REPORT OF THE SELECT HOUSE COMM. ON PROFESSIONAL SPORTS, 94th Cong., 2d Sess. 104-05 (1977).

541. Even if the team is organized as an ordinary corporation, the loss created by the rapid depreciation of the player contracts may be carried forward or backward to offset profits in other taxable years that would otherwise be, or have been, subject to corporate income taxation. IRC § 172. If the corporation were a member of an affiliated group, the loss could then be utilized as part of a consolidated return to offset income of other members.

542. *See Hearings Before the Senate Subcomm. on Antitrust and Monopoly of the Senate Comm. on the Judiciary,* 92nd Cong., 1st Sess., pt. 1, at 381-82 (1971).

543. *See* § 7.10 (where the factors are considered in some detail).

544. *See generally,* Burck, *Why Those W.F.L. Owners Expect to Score Profits,* FORTUNE, September, 1974, at 142; Okner, *Taxation and Sports Enterprises,* in GOVERNMENT AND THE BUSINESS 159 (R. Noll, ed. 1974); *Hearings Before the Senate Subcomm. on Antitrust and Monopoly of the Senate Comm. on the Judiciary,* 92d Cong., 1st Sess., pt. 1, 410-13, pt. 2, 1001-07 (1971); Klinger, *Tax Aspects of Buying, Selling and Owning Professional Sports Teams,* 48 L.A.B. BULL. 162 (1973); 39 J. Taxation 276 (1973); Note, *The Professional Sports Team As A Tax Shelter — A Case Study: The Utah Stars,* 1974 UTAH L. REV. 556.

545. The most detailed analysis of the operating results of professional teams available at this time is in Okner, *Taxation of Sports Enterprises,* in GOVERNMENT AND THE SPORTS BUSINESS 159 (R. Noll, ed. 1974) (which also includes, at pages 176-83, an evaluation of investments in professional teams, and the effect of pre-Tax Reform Act of 1976 interpretation of the relevant provisions of the Code on the organization of professional sports).

546. S. Rep. No. 94-1358, 94th Cong., 2d Sess. 86-91 (1976) H. REP. No. 94-658, 9th Cong., 1st Sess. 27-28 (1975). A more far reaching amendment of the Code (adding a so-called "limitation on artificial losses" passed the House, H. 10612, 94th Cong., 1st Sess. § 101(a) (1975), but was dropped in the Senate in favor of the provisions noted in text.

alterations in the tax treatment of professional teams. Thus, it limits the amount of the initial purchase price of a team that may be allocated to player contracts,[547] and expands the impact of the depreciation recapture rules upon the sale of a franchise.[548] These provisions will limit the benefits to be derived from team ownership, but they will not necessarily preclude a sports franchise from providing some tax shelter benefits.[549] Although some such benefits may remain, the 1976 amendments, and the judicial developments in the tax treatment of franchises,[550] may suggest that the allegedly rapid turnover and escalating prices of sports franchises may be a trend with an uncertain future.

§ 7.21. Taxation of Sports Investments.

An additional area in which sports activities may present substantial federal income tax issues, involves what might be loosely described as sports investments. Although this description is a misnomer to the extent that it would include some of the material already considered—there is, of course, a sports "investment" in any professional team — the description is a fair label to the extent that it identifies investments that are not related to professional teams. The federal income tax aspects of sports investments are not dissimilar from other types of investment, but they do present several issues that may have peculiar relation to the sports nature of the venture. Attention will be focused on such issues in this section.

The basic issues which arise relate to the nature of the investments themselves and the types of persons who become investors. Thus, sports investments are often made by financially secure persons who are interested in sports and who wish to sponsor entries in sports events, which will most frequently involve the ownership of horses or racing vehicles, but may also involve the sponsorship of athletes engaged in non-team sports (such as golf, boxing or tennis). Since such investments normally require the expenditure of substantial sums for current operating expenses, often produce substantial losses, and may, at least in part, be made for reasons other than the desire to realize profits, the issue that will inevitably arise is the extent to which the expenses and losses will be deductible to the person making the investment. This will require analysis of several specific provisions of the Code, some of which are present to allow deduction, while at least one is intended to limit deduction. Each raises similar issues, but will be discussed separately in the materials that follow.

As a general proposition, the Code in § 162(a) allows a deduction for the ordinary and necessary expenses incurred in carrying on a trade or business.[551]

---

547. See § 7.18.

548. See § 7.19. There are also other aspects of the 76 Act that will affect the viability of a sports team as a tax shelter. For example, the application of the "at risk" rule to partnerships will limit the leveraging of investments through the use of non-recourse loans in a limited partnership. See § 7.10, at notes 258-62. See also Zaritsky, *The Taxing Business of Sports Franchises*, 1977 PRENTICE-HALL TAX IDEAS ¶ 17,014,3(4)(1977).[*]

549. See §§ 7.18, 7.19.

550. See § 7.18 (especially the discussion of the *Laird* case).

551. IRC § 162(a). The requirements of § 162 are also considered with respect to the deductions of professional athletes in § 7.05. Deduction may also be authorized by § 212, which allows expenses paid or incurred for the production or collection of income, among other things. *See* Treas. Reg. § 1.212-1; note 569 *infra*. The primary distinction between deductions under §§ 162 and 212 is that a deduction under the latter would not be allowed as an "above the line" deduction in arriving at adjusted gross income. Thus, one would want to structure the arrangement in a manner that would produce deduction under § 162 if at all possible — *i.e.*, so that there would be a trade or business.

The primary element of § 162 that will cause difficulty in the effort to deduct the expenses of carrying on a sports investment is the "trade or business" requirement. Whether a given investment constitutes a "trade or business" for this purpose has normally been determined by the presence or absence of a profit motive. This requirement is well illustrated by *Norman C. Demler,*[552] where the taxpayer had become seriously interested in auto racing. He was primarily engaged in the business of manufacturing cider and vinegar, renting searchlights and grain farming. In pursuit of his interest in auto racing, the taxpayer designed a racing car of his own, and then expended a considerable sum to have it constructed. After it was built, the "Demler Special" was entered only in the Indianapolis 500 each Memorial Day, and was stored at the taxpayer's residence in New York during the remainder of the year. The taxpayer himself performed much of the mechanical work on the racer, and spent an entire month in Indianapolis getting it ready for the big race. In order to limit his exposure to liability due to the dangerous nature of racing, the taxpayer organized a corporation to conduct the racing activities and it engaged in no other business. The corporation incurred substantial expenses and the IRS sought to deny deduction by alleging that they did not arise from a trade or business under § 162. In holding that the racing activities did indeed constitute a "trade or business," the Tax Court noted that the taxpayer was a professional in the racing sport, having devoted many years in developing his talents; that the taxpayer had himself designed the racer; that if the Indianapolis 500 had been won in any year there would have been a substantial profit; and that a profit was realized during one of the years in question. These facts demonstrated, the court concluded, that the taxpayer had a profit motive in his racing efforts and that the corporation was engaged in a trade or business, so that the expenses incurred in connection with racing activities were deductible under § 162.[553] Thus, where it can be shown that there is a profit motive associated with an investment, the courts may find that the activity in question is a trade or business and allow the expense deductions.[554] Where the profit motive is absent, however, the courts will find that the activity is a sport, hobby or recreational undertaking and disallow deduction.[555]

552. 25 T.C.M. 620 (1966).

553. Specifically the court stated that

[w]e see no need to delineate the exact point in the wide spectrum between contempt or indifference to profit, on the one hand, and the sole compulsion of profit, on the other, which divides a hobby from a "trade or business." Where the critical factor is a person's intent or motive, there is a twilight zone which defies precise definition. Attempts to evolve a computer-like standard under such circumstances tend to compound rather than to dispel the confusion. [citations omitted]. It is enough if the taxpayer is found to have had a profit motive to a degree sufficient to convince the trier of the facts that he was carrying on a "trade or business."

We hold that the Corporation was engaged in a trade or business and that the requirements of section 162 have, therefore, been met. 25 T.C.M. at 627.

554. Worrell v. United States, 254 F. Supp. 992 (S.D. Tex. 1966) (horse breeding); Theodore Sabelis, 37 T.C. 1058 (1962) (horse breeding); Margaret E. Amory, 22 B.T.A. 1398 (1931) (racing stables); James Coe, 33 T.C.M. 592 (1974); Rex B. Foster, 32 T.C.M. 42 (1973) (horse breeding); George Thacker, 28 T.C.M. 1433 (1969) (horse breeding); Lang Chevrolet Co., 26 T.C.M. 1055 (1967) (auto racing activities of auto dealership); Estate of Lillian Solomon, 26 T.C.M. 919 (1967) (horse breeding); Herbert C. Sanderson, 23 T.C.M. 1723 (1964) (horse breeding).

555. Abrams v. United States, 449 F.2d 662 (2d Cir. 1971) (horse breeding); Bessenyey v. Commissioner, 379 F.2d 252 (2d Cir. 1967), *cert. denied,* 389 U.S. 931, 19 L. Ed. 2d 283, 88 S. Ct. 293 (1967) (Hungarian horse breeding); Virgin v. United States, 1975-1 U.S.T.C. ¶ 9288 (S.D. Fla. 1974)

A similar inquiry is necessitated if an investor in a sports activity seeks to deduct a loss incurred in the activity. As a general rule, § 165 of the Code allows non-individual taxpayers a deduction for any "loss" sustained during the taxable year which is not compensated for by insurance or other payments.[556] In order to be deductible, the "loss" must be bona fide, actually sustained and be evidenced by a closed transaction—that is, an event that is fixed and which requires no additional steps to complete.[557] If the investor is an individual, the rules for loss deduction are, however, significantly different. Individual losses will be deductible only if incurred in a trade or business,[558] in a transaction that is entered for profit,[559] or as a result of a casualty.[560] The "trade or business" and "entered into for profit" requirements have been interpreted in a manner that is similar to the "trade or business" provision in § 162—that is, there must be a profit motive.[561] Thus, a loss deduction will be available to an individual, under those provisions, only if the activity in question was entered with a profit-motive[562] and will be denied where no such motive is present.[563]

The necessity of demonstrating a "profit motive" is also reflected by the requirements of the so-called hobby loss rule of § 183.[564] This provision codifies the "profit motive" requirement, but also provides several objective benchmarks that aid the taxpayer in establishing that motive. Specifically, § 183 provides as a general rule that no deduction shall be allowable to an individual or a

(boat racing); American Properties, Inc., 28 T.C. 1100 (1957), aff'd per curiam, 262 F.2d 150 (9th Cir. 1958) (motor boat racing); Harry C. Fisher, 29 B.T.A. 1041 (1934), aff'd, 74 F.2d 1014 (2d Cir. 1935) (horse breeding); Gloria B. Zimmerman, 35 T.C.M. 559 (1976) (motorcycle racing); Edward J. Drew, 31 T.C.M. 799 (1972) (horse breeding); Morris A. Stoltzfos, 29 T.C.M. 1610 (1970) (horse breeding); Edward M. Stout, 12 T.C.M. 52, aff'd per curiam, 210 F.2d 607 (6th Cir. 1954) (horse breeding). See generally J. HUMPHREYS, HORSEMAN'S TAX GUIDE 1-46 (1963); Note, Breeding Farms and Racing Stables—Hobby or Business?, 54 KY. L.J. 92 (1965).

556. IRC § 165(a).

557. Treas. Reg. § 1.165-1(a). If a loss deduction is allowed, the amount of the deduction will be the adjusted basis of the property in question under IRC § 1011. Id.

The discussion in text relates only to "ordinary losses." A taxpayer may also have a loss from the sale or exchange of a capital asset, IRC §§ 1211-12, or § 1231 assets. See § 7.20, notes 592-98 infra.

558. IRC § 165(c)(1).

559. IRC § 165(c)(2).

560. IRC § 165(c)(3). In order for there to be a "casualty," the event causing the loss must be a sudden, unexpected or unusual cause. Thus, where a race horse had to be destroyed because of pain caused by a bowed tendon, and other horses had to be destroyed because of disease, "casualty" loss treatment was denied because the cause which precipitated the horses' demise was not a "sudden, unexpected or unusual" event. Campbell v. Commissioner, 504 F.2d 1158 (6th Cir. 1974). See also Curvin S. Miller, 34 T.C.M. 37 (1975) (could not add personal time to basis for casualty loss purposes).

561. See notes 551-55 supra. See generally 5 J. MERTENS, THE LAW OF FEDERAL INCOME TAXATION § 28.74 (rev. ed. 1969).

562. See, e.g., Brodrick v. Derby, 236 F.2d 35 (10th Cir. 1956); Alden B. Starr, 28 T.C.M. 167 (1969); Leonard P. Sasso, 20 T.C.M. 1068 (1961); Louis Hall, 12 T.C.M. 564 (1953); James L. Byrne, 4 T.C.M. 1096 (1945).

563. See, e.g., Abrams v. United States, 449 F.2d 662 (2d Cir. 1971); Imbesi v. Commissioner, 361 F.2d 640 (3rd Cir. 1966); Wise v. Commissioner, 260 F.2d 354 (6th Cir. 1958); Waddell F. Smith, 10 T.C. 701 (1948); Glenn H. Morton, 30 T.C.M. 671 (1971); W. Jane Luce, 29 T.C.M. 894 (1970).

564. Section 183 was enacted in 1969 in an effort to resolve difficulties that arose with respect to its predecessor. Section 270 had been enacted in 1954, and denied a taxpayer the right to deduct more than $50,000 per year from other income if the trade or business in question produced losses in excess of that amount for each of the five consecutive years prior to the taxable year. The difficulties caused by § 270 were that if a taxpayer had more than one trade or business, each would have to be analyzed separately in applying the five-year test; the five-year period was easily broken; and a taxpayer would be allowed $50,000 of deductions regardless of the nature of the "trade or business."

shareholder in a subchapter S corporation with respect to any activity that is "not engaged in for profit."[565] The application of this general rule is limited to some extent by two additional provisions. The first is that deductions attributable to an activity not engaged in for profit will be allowed for those items which would be deductible under other provisions of the Code without regard to whether the activity was engaged in for profit,[566] and for those deductions which would be allowed if the activity were engaged in for profit and which are not in excess of the gross income of the activity (as reduced by the deductions noted in the first part of this sentence).[567] The second factor limiting the general rule is a presumption that an activity is "engaged in for profit" if its gross income for two or more taxable years in a period of the last five (or seven in the case of horse breeding, training, showing or racing) consecutive taxable years ending with the taxable year in question exceeds the deductions attributable thereto.[568] If the presumption is satisfied, then the burden will be upon the IRS to prove that the activity was not engaged in for profit.

The primary question with respect to § 183 is, of course, whether the activity in question is "engaged in for profit." For this purpose, § 183 largely codifies the case law under §§ 162 and 212 and defines the phrase "activity not engaged in for profit" to mean any activity which is not within the provisions of §§ 162 or 212,[569] unless it is covered by the presumption.[570] As already noted, these provisions allow a deduction only if a profit-making motive is present with respect to the activity in question.[571] The regulations under § 183 go on to specify that profit-motive will be determined by making reference to objective standards, taking into account the facts and circumstances of each particular

---

565. IRC § 183(a). *See generally* Flick & Schmidt, *Is Incorporating Horse or Cattle Operations the Answer to Avoid the Rules of Section 183?,* 39 J. TAXATION 90 (1973); Lee, *A Blend of Old Wines in a New Wineskin: Section 183 and Beyond,* 29 TAX L. REV. 347 (1974); Sharpe, *New "Hobby Loss" Rule is Tougher but "Engaged in for Profit" Dilemma Remains,* 32 J. TAXATION 289 (1970); Comment, *Section 183: Work Horse or Hobby Loss,* 20 CATHOLIC L. REV. 716 (1971).

The IRS has also ruled that § 183 applies to partnerships, though the statute directly mentions only individuals and subchapter S corporations. Rev. Rule. 78-22, 1978-1 CUM. BULL. —; 77-320, 1977-2 CUM. BULL. 78.

The definition of what constitutes an "activity" is set forth in Treas. Reg. § 1.183-1(d), and the problems that it may pose are considered in Diamond & Horne, *Hobby Losses; Miscellaneous Individual and Corporate Problems,* 23 TAX L. REV. 431 (1970). The "activity" concept was considered under the predecessor of § 183 in Joseph M. Collins, 34 T.C. 592 (1960), where the Tax Court held that a taxpayer who abandoned one National Football League franchise after another, forming new teams with each new franchise, was engaged in more than one "activity." *See generally* Lee, *A Blend of Old Wines in a New Wineskin: Section 183 and Beyond,* 29 TAX L. REV. 347, 365-80 (1974) (an exhaustive discussion of the "activity" problems).

566. IRC § 183(b)(1). Such expenses would include, for example, interest expenses under IRC § 163, casualty losses under IRC § 165(c)(3), and state taxes under IRC § 164(a).

567. IRC § 183(b)(2); Treas. Reg. 1.183-1(b)(2).

568. IRC § 183(d). If the taxpayer has not engaged in the activity for a sufficiently long period to allow this determination to be made, an election may be filed under IRC § 183(e), but such an election will require the taxpayer to waive the statute of limitations as to each of the taxable years that will be included in the determination period.

569. IRC § 183(c). Section 212 would allow an individual a deduction for the expenses of producing or collecting income or of managing, conserving or maintaining property held for the production of income. Like § 162, the deduction under § 212 will not be available for expenses incurred with respect to an activity which is not engaged in for profit. Treas. Reg. § 1.212-1(c).

570. *See* note 568 *supra.*

571. *See* notes 551-55 *supra.*

case.[572] Section 183, thus, raises issues that are similar to those that have evolved under §§ 162 and 212, in the sense that it attempts to preclude the deduction of expenses relating to "activities which are carried on primarily as a sport, hobby or for recreation."[573]

Although there is not yet sufficient case law under § 183 to provide authoritative guidance to its application in the sports investment area, it seems clear that the decisions under §§ 162 and 212 will be an important part of future cases under § 183. The issue of whether an activity is "not engaged in for profit" is specifically phrased in terms of qualification under §§ 162 and 212,[574] and the factors identified in the regulations are essentially distilled from the case law under those sections. For example, the factors considered by the court in *Norman C. Demler* are quite similar to those specified in the regulations. Notwithstanding the similarity of the basic issues raised by § 183 and §§ 162 and 212, it is important to emphasize that § 183 provides the taxpayer with benefits that may not have been available under the other sections. Thus, it allows the deduction of expenses, whether or not the activity is engaged in for profit, to the extent that they would otherwise be deductible or that the income from the activity is not in excess of such otherwise deductible expenses.[575] The presumption will also allow a taxpayer to deduct all expenses so long as a profit can be shown in 2 out of 5 (or 7) years. The regulations are also beneficial to the extent that they provide more specific guidance on the profit-motive issue than is discernible from much of the case law under §§ 162 and 212.

With respect to § 183 it should, finally, be noted that it applies to only individuals and subchapter S corporations,[576] and is inapplicable to the ordinary business corporation. This may be an important element in planning for investment in sports-related activities, inasmuch as an investor who could not meet the presumption requirements may find it beneficial to incorporate the activity and not make a subchapter S election.[577] If such a course is followed, there will still be other problems that must be confronted. The first is that the deductibility issue will then be resolved pursuant to the "trade or business"

---

572. Treas. Reg. § 1.183-2(a). In making this determination, the regulations identify several factors that will be considered. These include the manner in which the activity is carried on; the expertise of the taxpayer; the time and effort expended by the taxpayer; the expectation of appreciation in value of the assets used; the success of the taxpayer in the activity; the relation of profits to losses; the financial status of the taxpayer; and the elements of personal pleasure and recreation inherent in the activity. Treas. Reg. § 1.183-2(b).

573. Treas. Reg. § 1.183-2(a).

574. *See* notes 569-70 *supra.*

575. *See* Lee, *A Blend of Old Wines in a New Wineskin: Section 183 and Beyond,* 29 TAX L. REV. 347, 390-95 (1974); Sharpe, *New "Hobby Loss" Rule Is Tougher but "Engaged in for Profit" Dilemma Remains,* 32 J. TAXATION 289, 290 (1970).

576. Thus, IRC § 183(a) provides that it applies to "an activity engaged in by an individual or an electing small business corporation...." The term "electing small business corporation" has reference to the election in IRC § 1372(b) (the so-called "subchapter S" election), which allows a qualifying corporation to elect to not be subject to federal income taxation, and to have the tax liability fall upon its shareholders. *See* note 583 *infra.*

577. *See* Flick & Schmidt, *Is Incorporating Horse or Cattle Operations the Answer to Avoid the Rules of Section 183?,* 39 J. TAXATION 90, 91-92 (1973). If such a corporation is formed, it will also be necessary to insure that the losses generated may be effectively utilized.

Even where § 183 applies, the individual or subchapter S corporation may still deduct expenses to the extent that they are otherwise deductible or do not exceed income from the activity. *See* note 567 *supra.*

requirements of § 162, which have already been considered.[578] The second is that the investor may be confronted with the IRS challenge that the corporation is merely a sham,[579] or was organized solely for the purpose of securing the benefit of deductions which would not otherwise be available.[580] These additional problems will not, however, prevent utilization of the corporation; they will simply require careful planning.

When investments are made in the types of activities considered here, it will also be important to determine the nature of the assets acquired for tax purposes.[581] One such inquiry will be whether the assets are depreciable. Assets such as racing animals and vehicles will be subject to a depreciation deduction so long as they are used in a trade or business or held for the production of income.[582] In order to determine the amount of deduction, the taxpayer would have to establish the useful life of the assets[583] and their salvage value, and choose a method of depreciation.[584] Although it has been held that the owner of a race horse could claim a full year's depreciation if it was acquired in the last month of the taxable year on the ground that the horse would "age" a full year for racing eligibility purposes,[585] that conclusion appears to conflict with the position expressed in the regulations [586] and has been rejected in a more recent case.[587] Since racing animals and vehicles are tangible personal property, the taxpayer might also be entitled to claim bonus depreciation in the first year,[588] and vehicles would also qualify for a reduction in salvage value.[589] The

578. *See* notes 551-55 *supra.*

579. This was, for example, the successful position of the IRS in Borge v. Commissioner, 405 F.2d 673 (2d Cir. 1968), *cert. denied,* 395 U.S. 933, 23 L. Ed. 2d 448, 89 S. Ct. 1994 (1969), where the taxpayer had incorporated a poultry business with the hope of avoiding the limitations of the predecessor of § 183, which is noted at note 556 *supra.* The principles involved in the question of whether a corporation will be disregarded for federal income taxes purposes are discussed in detail in § 7.13.

580. Under IRC § 269, such a conclusion would have the result of allowing the IRS to disallow any such deductions.

581. The issues discussed here are considered more fully with respect to professional sports teams in §§ 7.17-.19.

582. IRC § 167(a). *See* § 7.17.

583. *See, e.g.,* Taylor S. Hardin, 32 T.C.M. 892 (1973), *aff'd per curiam,* 507 F.2d 903 (4th Cir.) (useful life of race horse was 3 years). If the taxpayer elects to utilize the class life ADR system, the useful life of horses used for breeding or work purposes is specified to be 10 years. Rev. Proc. 72-10, 1972-1 CUM. BULL. 121, 123. This period is consistent with taxpayer positions that have received judicial approval. *See, e.g.,* Jerald O. Finney, 27 T.C.M. 1510 (1968) (useful life of 10 years).

The courts have held that if there is a decrease in the value of a horse in a subsequent year the taxpayer must treat the reduction as a loss and not readjust the useful life or salvage value of the horse. Estate of Whitaker, 259 F.2d 379 (5th Cir. 1958) (bowed tendon); George W. Offutt, III, 22 T.C.M. 589 (1963), *aff'd on other grounds,* 336 F.2d 483 (4th Cir. 1964).

584. IRC § 167(b).

585. Reineman v. United States, 61-1 U.S.T.C. ¶ 9386 (N.D. Ill. 1961), *aff'd on other grounds,* 301 F.2d 267 (7th Cir. 1962).

586. Treas. Reg. § 1.167(a)-10(b).

587. Taylor S. Hardin, 32 T.C.M. (1973), *aff'd per curiam,* 507 F.2d 903 (4th Cir. 1973) (allowing only depreciation for the month during which the race horse was actually owned).

588. IRC § 179(a). The bonus depreciation in the first year is 20 percent of the cost of the property, subject to a maximum "cost" of $10,000 in the case of single taxpayers. IRC § 179(b).

589. IRC § 167(f). The salvage value under § 167(f) may be reduced by an amount equal to 10 percent of the depreciable basis (determined under § 167(g)) of the property. Livestock (including horses) is excluded from § 167(f). *See* Treas. Reg. § 1.167(f)-1(b)(1). The assets may also be able to qualify for the investment credit of § 39, although horses are excluded from coverage. IRC § 48(a)(6).

assets acquired through a sports investment may also involve a contract with a boxer, golfer or other athlete. In such situations, the contracts will be intangible assets and be subject to slightly different rules than those noted with respect to tangible personal property (horses and vehicles). The treatment of such contracts would be similar to the player contracts held by professional teams, a subject discussed in some detail in earlier portions of this chapter.[590] A contract would be depreciable to the extent that it has a limited useful life that can be estimated with reasonable accuracy.[591] If such a useful life is present, then acquisition costs would be capitalized and depreciated (amortized) over that period.

To the extent that the assets acquired are depreciable, they would also be likely to qualify for the benefits of § 1231 on sale or exchange.[592] With respect to racing horses, the Regulations specifically provide that a horse held for racing purposes is within the provision allowing § 1231 treatment for horses used for sporting purposes.[593] A horse will be held for "racing purposes" if it has raced at a public track,[594] or, if not so raced, it has been trained to so race but does not meet objective standards used by the taxpayer to determine suitability for racing.[595] Contracts with golfers, boxers or other athletes would also be likely to qualify for § 1231 if they are depreciable in the taxpayer's hands.[596] This is, again, similar to the treatment afforded player contracts held by professional teams.[597] It has been suggested that the sale of an undivided interest in such assets will be treated the same as would a sale of the entire asset.[598] When assets that qualify for § 1231 treatment are sold, it will also be necessary to consider the effect of the depreciation recapture rules of § 1245, which will require

---

590. See §§ 7.17-7.19.

591. Treas. Reg. § 1.167(a)-3. See also Birmingham News Co. v. Patterson, 224 F. Supp. 670 (N.D. Ala. 1963), aff'd per curiam, 345 F.2d 531 (5th Cir. 1965); Stewart Title Guaranty Co., 20 T.C. 630 (1953).

592. The requirements and benefits of § 1231 are discussed with respect to professional teams in § 7.19.

593. IRC § 1231(b)(3)(A). Prior to the addition of the "sporting purposes" language in the Tax Reform Act of 1969, the case law had reached a position essentially similar to that suggested in the regulations at notes 594-95. Thus, in several cases it was held that where horses had been trained for racing and breeding, but had been culled because of failure to meet the taxpayer's standards, the sale or exchange would be within § 1231. See McKinley Kirk, 47 T.C. 177 (1966); Anderson Fowler, 37 T.C. 1124 (1967); Beverly J. Hill, 26 T.C.M. 1287 (1967) (in claiming race); Neil S. McCarthy, 22 T.C.M. 129 (1963); H. Arnold Jackson, 11 T.C.M. 939 (1952). If there was no evidence of an intent to race or breed the horses, however, other cases held that they were held primarily for sale to customers in the ordinary course of business and would not qualify for § 1231. See Nowland v. Commissioner, 244 F.2d 450 (4th Cir. 1957); Robert B. Jewell, 25 T.C. 109 (1955) (suggesting the factual difficulty that may be presented when several horses are sold in the same year).

594. Treas. Reg. § 1.1231-2(c)(1)(i). See also Rev. Proc. 71-33, 1971-2 CUM. BULL. 572 (application of regulation to years before 1970).

595. Treas. Reg. § 1.1231-2(c)(1)(ii). A horse that has neither been raced nor trained to race will generally not qualify for § 1231 treatment, Id. § 1.1231-2(c)(1)(iii). But cf. Launce E. Gamble, 68 T.C. No. 69 (1977) (IRC § 1231(b)(3)(A) is not exclusive).

596. See, e.g., Estate of John F. Shea, 57 T.C. 15 (1971).

597. See § 7.19.

598. Harry F. Guggenheim, 46 T.C. 559 (1966) (sale of an undivided ownership interest in a racing and breeding horse produced § 1231 treatment for the taxpayer).

ordinary income treatment to the extent that the taxpayer has claimed post-1962 depreciation of the assets.[599]

A final matter to be considered concerns the syndication of sports investments. Although syndication is usually thought of as a means of bringing numerous investors together for the purpose of investing in real estate, oil and gas rights, cattle or other types of familiar investments, it is also a means that may be utilized to provide financial support for a sports investment. A syndicate might, for example, be organized to back a promising boxer, golfer or tennis player; to exploit a famed horse as a stud; to promote a group of race cars or horses; or to purchase a professional sports franchise.[600] Regardless of the object of the syndicate, the first step that must be taken will be to select a form of organization. The choice will itself be largely influenced by the objectives of those who are to be investors in, or promoters of, the syndicate. Thus, an objective to simply contribute money to, and be associated with, a worthwhile sports activity might suggest use of an organizational form that differs from that which would be used by investors who sought to maximize both profit and federal income tax benefits. When the objectives are known, it will then be possible to select a form of organization for the syndicate that will be most likely to achieve those objectives.

There are several forms of organization which may be considered by investors. These include an ordinary business corporation, a subchapter S corporation, a general partnership and a limited partnership.[601] Inasmuch as the form of organization that will be most appropriate for any given group, as well as the consequences that its adoption will pose, can be determined only after careful review of the objectives, facts and circumstances of any given group of investors or promoters, it is not possible, given the limited scope of this discussion, to present a detailed analysis of the factors bearing on the advantages and disadvantages that might flow from each form of organization. Suffice it to say that selection of a form of organization may be a difficult and sophisticated task that must take into account not only the objectives of the investors or promoters, but also the legal consequences of conducting the sports activity contemplated through the form chosen—not the least of which will be the federal income tax and securities regulation consequences.

---

599. *See* § 7.19.
600. *See* § 7.20.
601. These forms are briefly discussed with respect to professional sports teams in § 7.16.

CHAPTER 8

Liability for Injuries in Sports Activities

§ 8.01. In General.

The area of the law of sports which has received the most frequent judicial analysis, and which has produced a correspondingly large body of decisional authority, is the liability which may result from injuries sustained in sports activities. The issues that are raised by the liability cases are actually not very broad, and the question presented by any given case is quite likely to fall within a very narrow range of applicable legal principles. Although one might conclude from this fact that a discussion of injury liability could be easily, and succinctly, presented, that is unfortunately only a partially correct conclusion. The relevant principles may indeed be easily stated, but the principles have been invoked in such a voluminous body of case law that accurate presentation necessitates a more lengthy analysis. In order to present these principles and systematize the case law as clearly as possible, and with the least consumption of space, the following discussion will state the basic principles in the textual discussion and provide in the footnotes an extensive citation of the decided authorities.

§ 8.02. Liability for Injury to Participants.

The most direct type of liability resulting from sports activity is that which arises as a consequence of the injuries suffered by participants. Such injuries may be the result of the zeal of competitive activity at close quarters, but will more often be the product of other forces which are not an ordinary component of the sport. Regardless of the specific cause of injury, however, the basis upon which recovery will be sought by the injured participant will in most cases be the same. Thus, when a participant seeks to recover for his or her injuries, the most frequent allegation, and claim for relief, will be that the person from whom recovery is sought was "negligent." [1]

1. In addition to the discussion in this section, additional aspects of participant recovery are considered in subsequent sections. *See* § 8.05 (injury in school sponsored athletics); § 8.06 (liability of coaches); § 8.07 and § 8.08 (liability for medical treatment); §§ 8.09-8.11 (liability for defective equipment); § 8.12 (workmen's compensation).

Although this is certainly not the place for an exhaustive analysis of the law of negligence,[2] it is important, as a preliminary matter, to briefly review the basic principles that will be considered throughout much of this chapter. As a general proposition, "negligence" is conduct which falls below the standard established by law for the protection of others against unreasonable risks of harm.[3] In most cases, the standard against which any particular act or omission must be tested to determine whether it is negligent is the conduct expected of an ordinary, reasonable person under like circumstances.[4] In other words, negligence is either the failure to do something which would have been done by a reasonable person, guided by those considerations which ordinarily regulate the conduct of human affairs or doing something which the prudent and reasonable person would not do.[5] The law of negligence is, thus, concerned with risk, and the circumstances in which a person must act to ameliorate risk or be prepared to accept responsibility for the harm that it visits upon others. The question, of course, is when must a person recognize that a risk exists requiring action, or inaction, on his or her part. Again, the answer is that one must recognize that conduct involves a risk of injury to another if such would have been perceived by a reasonable person.[6] If a particular injury is unforeseeable or could not have been prevented by the exercise of reasonable caution, it may then be an unavoidable accident which will not be actionable.[7] The mere existence of risk, however, will not alone be the basis of negligence liability, since the law requires only that a person refrain from creating situations where there is an *unreasonable* risk of injuring others. There must, therefore, be an unreasonable risk that has not been eliminated.[8]

Even if a person has been "negligent," liability may be avoided in appropriate cases under either of two doctrines which bar recovery by the victim as a result of the latter's own conduct. The first of these doctrines provides that recovery will be denied if the injured party was engaged in "contributory negligence," which refers to conduct by the injured party which falls below the standard that

2. *See generally* RESTATEMENT (SECOND) OF TORTS ch. 12 (1965); 2 F. HARPER & F. JAMES, THE LAW OF TORTS ch. 16 (1956); W. PROSSER, THE LAW OF TORTS ch. 5 (4th ed. 1971).

3. RESTATEMENT (SECOND) OF TORTS § 282 (1965). Although it was once contended that these principles should not apply to the conduct of games, that contention has been rejected and it is clear that ordinary negligence principles apply to the determination of liability for the injuries that arise as a consequence of sporting activity. *See* Cleghorn v. Oldham, 43 L.T.R. (n.s.) 465, 467 (K.B. 1927).

4. RESTATEMENT (SECOND) OF TORTS § 283 (1965).

5. RESTATEMENT (SECOND) OF TORTS § 284 (1965); Blyth v. Birmingham Water Works Co., 11 Ex. 781, 784, 156 Eng. Rep. 1047, 1049 (1856). In addition to the standard of the reasonable person, standards may also be established by legislative enactment, or by rules of the game in question, so that violation of those standards may be the basis of a negligence finding. Hudson v. Craft, 33 Cal. 2d 654, 204 P.2d 1 (1949) (failure to have boxing promoter license); Duncan v. Monark Boat Co., 281 So. 2d 382 (Fla. App. 1973) (failure to have boat seating capacity tag); Nabozny v. Barnhill, 31 Ill. App. 3d 212, 334 N.E.2d 258 (1975). Similarly, where a baseball league has established rules to govern the conduct of games, those rules may be admissible as evidence of the standard of care of those participating in the game. Toone v. Adams, 262 N.C. 403, 137 S.E.2d 132 (1964) (rules for minor league baseball in case involving injury to an umpire). *But cf.* Barrett v. Phillips, 29 N.C. App. 220, 223 S.E.2d 918 (1976) (eligibility rule violation does not alone constitute negligence).

6. RESTATEMENT (SECOND) OF TORTS § 289 (1965).

7. Thus, in Curtis v. Portland Baseball Club, 130 Ore. 93, 279 P. 277 (1929), the court said it was an accident that a spectator had been injured by a foul ball that had curved around a protective screen, inasmuch as such an occurrence could not have been reasonably anticipated. *See also* Johnson v. Krueger, 36 Colo. App. 242, 539 P.2d 1296 (1975) (unforeseeable that stump in adjoining lot would result in injury to football player).

8. The presence of an unreasonable risk is considered with respect to spectator injuries in § 8.03.

is necessary for his or her own protection, and which is a legally contributing cause in bringing about the injury.[9] Contributory negligence is similar in all respects to ordinary negligence and thus requires proof of the same elements, except that ordinary negligence has reference to unreasonable risk to third parties, while contributory negligence involves an unreasonable risk created by the injured party himself. Contributory negligence may result from the victim's having intentionally or unreasonably exposed himself to the danger created by the other person's negligence, of which the injured party knew or had reason to know, or from any other conduct that falls below that required by the reasonable person standard.[10] When proven to be a substantial factor in bringing about injury, contributory negligence will in most cases bar recovery by the injured party.[11]

A second doctrine precluding recovery by an injured party is the so-called "assumption of the risk" doctrine, which finds significant application to sports injuries. This doctrine states that a party who voluntarily assumes a risk of harm arising from the conduct of another cannot recover if harm in fact results.[12] Assumption of risk may arise in any of four separate circumstances. The first is where one by express consent relieves another of an obligation to exercise care for his or her protection and agrees to take the chance of injury from a known or possible risk.[13] Perhaps the clearest example of such undertakings in the sports world is the common contractual agreement between a participant and a sports promoter, whereby the former assumes the risks incident to a particular sports activity.[14] The second is where one enters a relationship with another which involves a known risk. In these circumstances, the party is deemed to have impliedly relieved the other of responsibility for that risk.[15] The clearest example of this in sports is the case of the spectator who is injured by

---

9. *See generally,* 2 F. HARPER & F. JAMES, THE LAW OF TORTS §§ 22.1-.11 (1956); W. PROSSER, THE LAW OF TORTS § 65 (4th ed. 1971).

10. RESTATEMENT (SECOND) OF TORTS §§ 465-66 (1965).
Even if contributory negligence is shown to exist, an injured party may yet recover if he or she can come within the doctrine of last clear chance, which assumes that both parties were negligent, and that the negligence of each was a contributing cause to the accident, but that the defendant had the last clear chance to avoid injuring the plaintiff. If the defendant does not take advantage of this last clear chance, then the defense of contributory negligence will be cut off and liability will be found on the basis of the defendant's originally negligent action. *See generally* 2 F. HARPER & F. JAMES, THE LAW OF TORTS §§ 22.13-.14 (1956); W. PROSSER, THE LAW OF TORTS § 66 (4th ed. 1971). This doctrine would have its clearest applicability in the law of sports to the golf cases where a ball is errantly struck and there is sufficient time to warn a person who has negligently placed himself in a zone of danger. Wood v. Postelthwaite, 6 Wash. App. 885, 496 P.2d 988 (1972) (indicating that it may be difficult to find a case where the doctrine would apply).

11. The contributory negligence doctrine may cause hardship when the injured party's negligence is only slight while the actor's negligence is great. As a result, some states have adopted so-called comparative negligence statutes. These statutes commonly provide that recovery will be determined by the relative negligence of the parties. Thus, if the actor's conduct is found to be twice as negligent as that of the injured party, the latter will recover only two-thirds of his damages. *See generally* W. PROSSER, THE LAW OF TORTS § 66 (4th ed. 1971).

12. *See generally* RESTATEMENT (SECOND) OF TORTS § 496A (1965); 2 F. HARPER & F. JAMES, THE LAW OF TORTS §§ 21.4-.8 (1956); W. PROSSER, THE LAW OF TORTS § 68 (4th ed. 1971); Bohlen, *Voluntary Assumption of the Risk,* 20 HARV. L. REV. 14 (1906); James, *Assumption of Risk,* 61 YALE L.J. 141 (1952).

13. RESTATEMENT (SECOND) OF TORTS § 496B (1965).

14. *See* § 8.04.

15. RESTATEMENT (SECOND) OF TORTS § 496C (1965).

the conduct of the activity being observed.[16] The third occurs when one is explicitly aware of a risk caused by the potential negligence of another, and yet proceeds to encounter it voluntarily.[17] Such assumption is made, for example, by athletes when they participate in athletic contests.[18] Finally, one may proceed to encounter a risk that is so unreasonably great as to render the party guilty of contributory negligence, so that recovery is barred both by assumption of the risk and contributory negligence principles.[19]

In an ordinary case involving the assertion of negligence liability, therefore, the courts will undertake a two-step process in determining whether the plaintiff may obtain a recovery from the defendant: the court will consider, first, the duty owed by the defendant to the plaintiff to ameliorate unreasonable risks to the plaintiff, and second, the duty owed by the plaintiff to himself. If the first duty has been violated, then the plaintiff should recover, unless the plaintiff has violated the second and thereby precluded such recovery. Although this same process is utilized in cases involving injuries to participants in sports activities, those cases are perhaps best analyzed by directing initial attention to the legal position of the participant. For these purposes, the term "participant" includes all persons who, in one way or another, take part in the activity (including actual participants, coaches,[20] managers, and umpires or referees,[21] and would, as well, include bat boys, caddies, sideline yard-mark holders, scorekeepers or any other person involved in the contest, whether or not taking human form).[22]

From this point of reference, it may be stated as a general rule that voluntary, *sui juris* [23] participants in lawful sporting activity assume, as a matter of law, all of the ordinary and inherent risks in the sport, so long as the activity is played in good faith and the injury is not the result of an intentional or willful act.[24]

---

16. *See* § 8.03; RESTATEMENT (SECOND) OF TORTS § 496C, illustration 4 (1965).

17. RESTATEMENT (SECOND) OF TORTS § 496D (1965).

18. *See, e.g.,* Thomas v. Barlow, 5 N.J. Misc. 764, 138 A. 208 (1927), *noted in* 26 MICH. L. REV. 322 (1928). It is this subject, of course, that will consume much of the remainder of this section.

19. *See* Tite v. Omaha Coliseum Corp., 144 Neb. 22, 12 N.W.2d 90 (1943).

Though there are situations where both contributory negligence and assumption of the risk can be present, their differences must be kept in mind. Assumption of the risk, first of all, concerns itself with the subjective state of the person's mind, while contributory negligence operates upon an objective standard of the reasonable person, which is completely external to the party in any particular context. Morris v. Cleveland Hockey Club, 157 Ohio St. 225, 105 N.E.2d 419 (1952). A second difference is that assumption of the risk can bar recovery for reckless conduct and conduct which is subject to strict liability, in addition to ordinary negligence, whereas contributory negligence can be a bar only to simple negligence recovery. These factors are all considered in RESTATEMENT (SECOND) OF TORTS § 496A, comment *d* (1965).

20. McGee v. Board of Educ., of New York 16 App. Div. 2d 99, 226 N.Y.S.2d 329 (1962).

21. Davis v. Jones, 100 Ga. App. 546, 112 S.E.2d 3 (1959) (official timekeeper at wrestling match); Toone v. Adams, 262 N.C. 403, 137 S.E.2d 132 (1964) (umpire may recover for assault by irate fan). *See generally* Annot., 10 A.L.R.3d 446 (1966).

22. Thus, in Jolley v. Chicago Thoroughbred Enterprises, Inc., 275 F. Supp. 325 (N.D. Ill. 1967), the "participant" rules were discussed with regard to injuries suffered by a thoroughbred racing horse during a race at Arlington Park.

23. A "sui juris" person is one possessed of full legal capacity. If the participant is not so possessed — for example, if he or she is a minor — then the general rule will be applied on a much less strict basis, inasmuch as a minor would be less able to appreciate the risks of the sport. Diker v. City of St. Louis Park, 286 Minn. 461, 130 N.W.2d 113 (1964) (minor injured in hockey game apply general rule, but not as a matter of law).

24. This principle has been applied in the following cases:

Alpine Skiing. Wright v. Mt. Mansfield Lift, 96 F. Supp. 786 (D. Vt. 1951) (assume risk of striking uneven spot on slope); Houser v. Floyd, 220 Cal. App. 2d 778, 34 Cal. Rptr. 96 (1963) (unexplained fall from lift chair); McDaniel v. Dowell, 210 Cal. App. 2d 26, 26 Cal. Rptr. 140 (1962) (assume risk

The clearest statement of the general rule was made by Judge Cardozo in *Murphy v. Steeplechase Amusement Company, Inc.,*[25] where a vigorous young

of being hit by other skiers who have lost control of downhill flight); Math v. State, 37 Misc. 2d 1023, 237 N.Y.S.2d 478 (1962) (failure to heed instructions); Kaufman v. State, 11 Misc. 2d 56, 172 N.Y.S.2d 276 (Ct. Cl. 1958) (assume risk of striking uneven spot on slope); Vogel v. State, 204 Misc. 614, 124 N.Y.S.2d 563 (1953), *appeal dismissed,* 284 App. Div. 993, 136 N.Y.S.2d 376 (1954) (get ski poles caught in lift mechanism). *See generally* Lisman, *Ski Injury Liability,* 43 U. COLO. L. REV. 307 (1972); Wells, *Liability of Ski Area Operators,* 41 DENVER L.J. 1 (1964); Rosenblatt, *After the Fall,* 5 TRIAL 44 (No. 2, 1969); Annot., 24 A.L.R.3d 1447 (1969); Annot., 19 A.L.R.3d 184 (1968); Annot., 94 A.L.R.2d 1431 (1964). In order to limit the ability of skiers to recover for participation-related injuries, several state legislatures have recently passed broad "assumption of the risk" statutes. Thus, MAINE STAT. ANN. tit. 26, § 488 (Supp. 1978), provides that

> each skier or passenger shall be deemed to have assumed the risk of and legal responsibility for any injury to his person or property arising out of his participation in Alpine or downhill skiing or the use of any passenger tramways associated therewith.

See also N. H. REV. STAT. § 225-A:26 (Supp. 1975).

Balance Beam. Bush v. Norwalk, 122 Conn. 426, 189 A. 608 (1937) (negligent failure to clean slippery and oily floor).

Baseball. Chase v. Shasta Lake Union School Dist., 259 Cal. App. 2d 612, 66 Cal. Rptr. 517 (1968) (running into obstruction while chasing fly ball); Tavernier v. Maes, 242 Cal. App. 2d 532, 51 Cal. Rptr. 575 (1966) (improper slide to second base); Dudley v. William Penn College, 219 N.W.2d 484 (Iowa 1974) (hit by foul ball while sitting on bench); James v. Hillerich & Bradsby Co., 299 S.W.2d 92 (Ky. App. 1957) (splintering of baseball bat); Richmond v. Employers' Fire Ins. Co., 298 So. 2d 118 (La. App. 1974) (hit by bat that slipped out of fungo batter's hands); Praetorius v. Shell Oil Co., 207 So. 2d 872 (La. App. 1968) (cleat marks in batter's box); Lutterman v. Studer, 300 Minn. 507, 217 N.W.2d 756 (1974) (player hit by bat that slipped from another's hands, failed to keep proper lookout); Niemczyk v. Burleson, 538 S.W.2d 737 (Mo. App. 1976) (baserunner collided with shortstop in basepath); Luftig v. Steinhorn, 21 App. Div. 2d 760, 250 N.Y.S.2d 354 (1964) (trip while trying to catch fly ball); McGee v. Board of Educ. of New York, 16 App. Div. 2d 99, 226 N.Y.S.2d 329 (1962) (injury in bunting practice); Scala v, New York, 200 Misc. 475, 102 N.Y.S.2d 790 (1951) (tripping over curb surrounding playing area); Weitzen v. Camp Mooween, 163 Misc. 312, 295 N.Y.S. 640 (1937) (sliding into stone home plate).

Basketball. Kerby v. Elk Grove Union High School Dist., 1 Cal. App. 2d 246, 36 P.2d 431 (1934) (hit by thrown ball); Albers v. Independent School Dist. No. 302 of Lewis County, 94 Idaho 342, 487 P.2d 936 (1971) (colliding with other players); Nunez v. Isidore Newman High School, 306 So.2d 457 (La. App. 1975) (moisture on floor); Paine v. Young Men's Christian Ass'n, 91 N.H. 78, 13 A.2d 820 (1940) (falling over bleachers after having been unintentionally propelled by an opposing player); Thomas v. Barlow, 5 N.J. Misc. 764, 138 A. 208 (1927) (unintentional blow to jaw); Spiegel v. Jewish Community Center, 24 App. Div. 2d 926, 264 N.Y.S.2d 771 (1965) (tripped over rolling ball); Frazier v. Y.M.C.A. of Little Falls, 286 App. Div. 464, 144 N.Y.S.2d 448 (1955), *aff'd,* 1 N.Y.2d 904, 154 N.Y.S.2d 963, 136 N.E.2d 908 (1956) (colliding with other players); Kaufman v. New York, 30 Misc. 2d 285, 214 N.Y.S.2d 767 (1961) (colliding with other players); Maltz v. Board of Educ. of New York, 32 Misc. 2d 492, 114 N.Y.S.2d 856 (1952), *aff'd,* 282 App. Div. 888, 124 N.Y.S.2d 911 (1953) (brick wall under goal); Clary v. Alexander County Bd. of Educ., 26 N.C. 160, 212 S.E.2d 160 (1975) (colliding with glass panels). *See also* Berger v. Miller, 241 F. Supp. 282 (E.D. Pa. 1965).

Blanket Toss. Rook v. State, 254 App. Div. 67, 4 N.Y.S.2d 116 (1938).

Boat and Water Skiing. Harmon v. United States, 532 F.2d 669 (9th Cir. 1975) (rafters on river should have known of the danger of high water conditions); Isaacson v. Jones, 216 F.2d 599 (9th Cir. 1954) (being thrown off the gunwale of a boat when skier fails to pay attention to the customary sharp turns); King v. Testerman, 214 F. Supp. 335 (E.D. Tenn. 1963) (water skier is injured as a result of a collision caused by improperly crossing the wake of his tow boat); Dunion v. Kaiser, 124 F. Supp. 41 (E.D. Pa. 1954) (boat damaged by a collision during organized boat race); Christian Appalachian Project, Inc. v. Berry, 487 S.W.2d 951 (Ky. App. 1972) (failure to ask for life preserver); Alberti's Adm'rx v. Nash, 282 S.W.2d 853 (Ky. 1955) (renting a canoe without asking for a life preserver when he knew he could not swim); Hennington v. Curtis, 248 Miss. 435, 160 So.2d 193 (1964) (injured by others in party); Mintz v. State, 47 App. Div. 2d 570, 362 N.Y.S.2d 619 (1975) (injury caused by severe weather conditions); Reddick v. Lindquist, 484 S.W.2d 441 (Tex. Civ. App. 1972) (improperly crossing wake); Harrop v. Beckman, 15 Utah 2d 78, 387 P.2d 554 (1963); Polsky v. Levine, 73 Wis. 2d 547, 243 N.W.2d 503 (1976) (comparative negligence); Mazurkiewicz v. Pawinski, 32 Wis. 2d 211, 145 N.W.2d 186 (1966) (playing near a ski jump ramp). *See generally* Annot., 8 A.L.R.3d 675 (1966).

---

25. 250 N.Y. 479, 166 N.E. 173 (1929).

man had been injured when he voluntarily went upon an amusement device known as the "Flopper." [26] The object of the amusement was to provide

Bobsled. Kaiser v. State, 55 Misc. 2d 576, 285 N.Y.S.2d 874 (1967), *rev'd,* 30 App. Div. 2d 482, 294 N.Y.S.2d 410 (1968); Clark v. State, 195 Misc. 581, 89 N.Y.S.2d 132 (1949); Cunningham v. State, 32 N.Y.S.2d 275 (1942). *See generally* Annot., A.L.R.2d 1431 (1964).

Chinning Bar. Fein v. Board of Educ. of New York, 305 N.Y. 611, 111 N.E.2d 732 (1953).

Fishing. Kaplan v. Hammer, 161 F. Supp. 625 (E.D.N.Y. 1958) (no recovery for slip on wet deck of fishing cruiser); Toca v. Rojas, 152 La. 317, 93 So. 108 (1922) (no recovery for fish hook in eye when no evidence of negligence); Hawayek v. Simmons, 91 So. 2d 49, 61 A.L.R.2d 1264 (La. App. 1956) (did not assume risk of mother's negligence which resulted in a fish hook in the eye); Rabiner v. Rosenberg, 176 Misc. 885, 28 N.Y.S.2d 533 (1941) (fish hook in eye).

Football. The application of the general rule in the football cases is illustrated quite well by Vendrell v. School Dist. No. 26C, Malheur County, 233 Ore. 1, 376 P.2d 406 (1962), where a high school football player was rendered a permanent paraplegic as a result of a broken neck sustained when he tried to use his head as a battering ram to avoid onrushing tacklers. When the player then brought suit to recover for his injuries, the court denied recovery. After noting that he had received extensive training, practice and play under the competent instruction and supervision of his coaches, the court stated that the reasons for the general rule of participant nonrecovery in football were that

> [t]he playing of football is a body-contact sport. The game demands that the players come into physical contact with each other constantly, frequently with great force. The linemen charge the opposing line vigorously, shoulder to shoulder. The tackler faces the risk of leaping at the swiftly moving legs of the ball-carrier and the latter must be prepared to strike the ground violently. Body contacts, bruises, and clashes are inherent in the game. There is no other way to play it. No prospective player need be told that a participant in the game of football may sustain injury. That fact is self-evident. It draws to the game the manly; they accept the risk, blows, clashes and injuries without whimper.

233 Ore. at 15, 376 P.2d at 412-13. *See also* Cramer v. Hoffman, 390 F.2d 19 (2d Cir. 1968); Board of Educ. of Waycross v. Bates, 114 Ga. App. 343, 151 S.E.2d 524 (1966); Davis v. Allstate Ins. Co., 206 So. 2d 748 (La. App. 1968); Whipple v. Salvation Army, 261 Ore. 453, 495 P.2d 739 (1972).

Golf. In approaching the golf-injury cases, the first step must always be to keep the nature of the game in mind. It is common knowledge, of course, that golf is a game of exact precision requiring a perfect co-ordination of mind and body, and it does not require an intimate knowledge of geometry to know that the slightest deviation of the club during the swing will cause the golf ball to do many peculiar things. It is apt to slice, pull, hook or travel straight at an angle, with neither hook nor slice. No player, moreover, has ever achieved such perfection in his game that he does not occasionally cause the ball to travel such errant paths, and with ordinary players such results are common occurrences. Thus, to hold that a golfer is negligent merely because his ball does not travel in the straight line he intended, would be to impose "a greater duty of care than the Creator endowed him with facilities to carry out." Page v. Unterreiner, 106 S.W.2d 528, 533 (Mo. App. 1937); *see also* Strand v. Connor, 207 Cal. App. 2d 473, 24 Cal. Rptr. 584 (1962) (slice); Walsh v. Machlin, 128 Conn. 412, 23 A.2d 156 (1941) (assume risk of a very bad shot); Kelly v. Forester, 311 S.W.2d 547 (Ky. 1958) (failure to not make a hook shot around a tree); Katz v. Gow, 321 Mass. 666, 75 N.E.2d 438 (1947); Hornstein v. State, 46 Misc. 2d 486, 259 N.Y.S.2d 902 (1965), *aff'd,* 30 App. Div. 2d 1012, 294 N.Y.S.2d 320 (1968) (hook or slice); McWilliams v. Parham, 273 N.C. 592, 160 S.E.2d 692 (1968); Gardner v. Heldman, 82 Ohio App. 1, 80 N.E.2d 681 (1948); Benjamin v. Nernberg, 102 Pa. Super. 471, 157 A. 10 (1931); Tannehill v. Terry, 11 Utah 2d 368, 359 P.2d 911 (1961) (aware of club being swung); Andrew v. Stevenson, 13 Scots L.T.R. 581 (1905). Thus, one who participates in the game of golf, should know that hard balls are hit at high velocity in an area which may contain many people, Ratcliffe v. Whitehead, [1933] 3 W.W.R. 447, and that those balls may be spread at all angles from any spot on the course. One does not play golf in a vacuum, but plays, to the contrary, in a situation of predictable danger from errantly hit golf balls.

In light of these circumstances, it is certainly not surprising that the courts have followed the general rule noted in text. *See, e.g.,* Wegener v. Foster, 120 Cal. App. 260, 8 P.2d 154 (1932) (miniature golf course); Rindley v. Goldberg, 297 So. 2d 140 (Fla. App. 1974); Meisenhamer v. Pharr, 99 Ga. App. 163, 107 S.E.2d 875 (1959) (driving range); Rose v. Morris, 97 Ga. App. 764, 104 S.E.2d 485 (1958); Foust v. Kinley, 254 Iowa 690, 117 N.W.2d 843 (1962) (driving range); Fink v. Klein, 186 Kan. 12, 348 P.2d 620 (1960) (member of a tournament rules committee not keeping lookout when staking off hazards); Nesbitt v. Bethesda Country Club, Inc., 20 Md. App. 226, 314 A.2d 738 (1974)

---

26. The "Flopper" was a moving belt, upon which passengers stood or sat, that ran upward on an inclined plane between padded walls on either side.

enjoyment through the tumbling of bodies and the accompanying screams and laughter. When the young man entered the "Flopper," however, he was injured

(driving range); Salamuff v. Godfrey, 344 Mass. 750, 182 N.E.2d 482 (1962) (indoor driving range); Young v. Ross, 127 N.J. Laws 211, 21 A.2d 762 (1941) (miniature golf course); Fresk v. Stinson, 7 App. Div. 2d 1027, 184 N.Y.S.2d 717, *appeal denied,* 8 App. Div. 2d 838, 190 N.Y.S.2d 335 (1959); Wood v. Postelthwaite, 6 Wash. App. 885, 496 P.2d 988 (1972).

Similar rules have been held to apply to caddies. Jesters v. Taylor, 105 So. 2d 569 (Fla. 1958); Stober v. Embry, 243 Ky. 117, 47 S.W.2d 921 (1932); Pouliot v. Black, 341 Mass. 531, 170 N.E.2d 709 (1960) (caddy struck while shagging); Simpson v. Fiero, 237 App. Div. 62, 260 N.Y.S. 323 (1932), *aff'd,* 262 N.Y. 461, 188 N.E. 20 (1933); Berry v. Howe, 39 Wash. 2d 235, 235 P.2d 170 (1951) (where caddy went out ahead to watch the drives, but neglected to observe the ball that hit him in the eye).

Gym Horse. Sayers v. Ranger, 16 N.J. Super. 22, 83 A.2d 775 (1951) (assume risk of dangerous exercise); Kanofsky v. Brooklyn Jewish Center, 265 N.Y. 634, 193 N.E. 420 (1934) (assumption of obvious risks).

Gym Mat. Cambareri v. Board of Educ. of Albany, 246 App. Div. 127, 284 N.Y.S. 892 (1936), *aff'd,* 283 N.Y. 741, 28 N.E.2d 968 (1940).

Handball. Waxenberg v. Crystal Baths, 129 N.Y.S.2d 71 (Sup. Ct. 1954) (assume risk of uneven floor).

Hockey. Diker v. City of St. Louis Park, 268 Minn. 461, 130 N.W.2d 113 (1964).

Horse Pulling. Bolduc v. Crain, 104 N.H. 163, 181 A.2d 641 (1962).

Horseback Riding. Stephenson v. Misericordia College, 376 F. Supp. 1324 (M.D. Pa. 1974).

Horseshoe Pitching. Carrillo v. Kreckel, 43 App. Div. 2d 499, 352 N.Y.S.2d 730 (1974) (recovery denied to by-stander); Kane v. Basralian, 16 N.J. Super. 496, 85 A.2d 4 (1951) (recovery denied for child who ran in path of horseshoe).

Ice and Roller Skating. Mortiboys v. St. Michael's College, 478 F.2d 196 (2d Cir. 1973) (defective surface known); Lattanzi v. San Moritz Club, 202 Cal. App. 2d 546, 20 Cal. Rptr. 847 (1962) (ice shaving machine obvious to plaintiff); Johnson v. County Arena, Inc., 29 Md. App. 674, 349 A.2d 643 (1976) (struck by guard); Farinelli v. Laventure, 342 Mass. 157, 172 N.E.2d 825 (1961) (unintentional collisions); Reay v. Reorganization Inv. Co., 224 S.W.2d 580 (Mo. App. 1949) (unintentional collisions); Humbyrd v. Spurlock, 345 S.W.2d 499 (Mo. App. 1961); Cassady v. Billings, 135 Mont. 390, 340 P.2d 509 (1959) (pitted ice); McCullough v. Omaha Coliseum Corp., 144 Neb. 92, 12 N.W.2d 639 (1944) (ice shavings and ruts on ice); Frye v. Omaha & C.B. St. Ry., 106 Neb. 333, 183 N.W. 567, 22 A.L.R. 607 (1921) (equipment known to be defective); Shields v. Van Kelton Amusement Corp., 228 N.Y. 396, 127 N.E. 261 (1920) (ice melted); Shaver v. Rotterdam, 22 App. Div. 2d 834, 253 N.Y.S.2d 893 (1964) (sand on ice); Filler v. Stenvick, 79 N.D. 422, 56 N.W.2d 798 (1953) (cracks in ice); Amon v. Shemaka, 419 Pa. 314, 214 A.2d 238 (1965). *See generally* Annot., 24 A.L.R.3d 911 (1969).

Monkey Bar. Hillman v. Greater Miami Hebrew Academy, 72 So. 2d 668 (Fla. 1954) (no amount of supervision would have prevented accident); Hunt v. Board of Educ. of Schenectady, 43 App. Div. 2d 397, 352 N.Y.S.2d 237 (1974) (no supervision).

Mutual Combat. The one sport in which the courts have not adopted an assumption of the risk posture is in mutual combat. Thus, although the risks and dangers of such contests are apparent, the courts have developed two clearly divergent rules, one allowing and one denying recovery to the injured combatant. The majority rule states that those who engage in mutual combat are each civilly liable to the other for any physical injury inflicted during the fight and the fact that the parties voluntarily engaged in the combat will be no defense to an action brought by the injured combatant. Adams v. Waggoner, 33 Ind. 531 (1870); McCulloch v. Goodrich, 105 Kan. 1, 181 P. 556 (1919); McNeil v. Mullin, 70 Kan. 634, 79 P. 168 (1905); Grotton v. Glidden, 84 Me. 589, 24 A. 1008 (1892); Morris v. Miller, 83 Neb. 218, 119 N.W. 458 (1909); Stout v. Wren, 8 N.C. (1 Hawks) 420, 9 Am. Dec. 653 (1821); Bell v. Hansley, 48 N.C. (3 Jones) 131 (1821); Barholt v. Wright, 45 Ohio St. 177, 12 N.E. 185 (1887); Teeters v. Frost, 145 Okla. 273, 292 P. 356 (1930), *noted in* 79 U. PA. L. REV. 509 (1931); Colby v. McClendon, 85 Okla. 293, 206 P. 207 (1922); Willey v. Carpenter, 64 Vt. 212, 23 A. 630 (1892); Strawn v. Ingram, 118 W. Va. 603, 191 S.E. 401 (1937); Shay v. Thompson, 59 Wis. 540, 18 N.W. 473 (1884); Reid v. Mitchell, 22 Scots L.T.R. 748 (1885). *See generally* 1 T. COOLEY, TORTS § 92 (4th ed. 1932); Bohlen, *Consent as Affecting Civil Liability for Breaches of the Peace,* 24 COLUM. L. REV. 819 (1924). The apparent basis for the rule was the venerable English decision in Boulter v. Clark, *noted in* F. BULLER, TRIALS AT NISI PRIUS 16 (7th ed. 1817), where it was held that the voluntary consent given by one participant in a boxing contest to his opponent was no defense to an action for injuries thereby inflicted, inasmuch as the act of boxing was then unlawful. The decision in *Boulter v. Clark* was imported into the jurisprudence of this country at an early date, see Stout v. Wren, 8 N.C. (1 Hawks) 420, 9 Am. Dec. 693 (1821), although it is, and was, a clear departure from the principles that apply to participant injuries in almost all other contexts. As is noted in an earlier chapter, boxing and

when he was thrown from his feet and fractured a knee cap. In denying recovery, Judge Cardozo outlined the conditions upon which a participant may recover for injuries related to sporting activity:

> One who takes part in such a sport accepts the dangers that inhere in it so far as they are obvious and necessary, just as a fencer accepts the

wrestling are no longer unlawful so long as they are conducted under the auspices of the appropriate state athletic commission. *See* §§ 2.02, 2.03.

The minority rule, on the other hand, would deny recovery to a mutual combatant injured in the contest, on the ground that the act of each combatant may be an unlawful breach of the peace and the law should leave the parties where they are found, unless a showing can be made that the injury is the result of excessive force or malicious intent to do serious injury upon the part of the defendant. Smith v. Simon, 69 Mich. 481, 37 N.W. 548 (1888); Galbraith v. Fleming, 60 Mich. 403, 27 N.W. 581 (1886); Parmentier v. McGinnis, 157 Wis. 596, 147 N.W. 1007 (1914). Even where the mutual combat is not unlawful, many courts have denied civil recovery on the basis that the parties had engaged in a mere sporting contest, and the fact of death or serious injury is not itself evidence of negligence. McAdams v. Windham, 6 Ala. App. 577, 94 So. 742 (1922); Parmentier v. McGinnis, 157 Wis. 596, 147 N.W. 1007 (1914). The minority rule is in essence the same as the general rule considered in text, though it may be phrased a little differently. Thus, it essentially provides that one may not recover for injuries caused by the ordinary and inherent risks of the sport of mutual combat. For example, in Rosensweig v. State, 5 App. Div.2d 293, 171 N.Y.S.2d 912 (1958), *aff'd*, 5 N.Y.2d 404, 158 N.E.2d 229 (1959), the court held that recovery for injuries suffered by a professional boxer was barred by the fact that he had "assumed the risks known to be inherent in the fight." 171 N.Y.S.2d at 914.

Although the majority rule has long prevailed, its infirmity as a basis for deciding cases brought by injured fighters has become increasingly clear. It seems to be inconsistent with the general rule that a participant in an athletic contest assumes all of the ordinary and inherent risks of the sport in question. Boxing, wrestling and other forms of mutual combat do not present unique circumstances that should require a different rule. The majority rule may also be criticized on the basis that it prevents the courts from following two of the most prevalent principles in tort law: 1) that one who has consented to an invasion cannot recover for the injuries caused thereby, and 2) that one shall not profit from his own wrongdoing. Hart v. Geysel, 159 Wash. 632, 294 P. 570 (1930). Following this reasoning, the *Restatement (Second) of Torts* has repudiated the majority rule, and stated that though each boxer in a boxing match may be in breach of the peace, neither is civilly liable to the other because of their advance consent to (or assumption of) the risks of the contest. RESTATEMENT (SECOND) OF TORTS § 60, illustration *1* (1965). Similarly, in Hudson v. Craft, 33 Cal. App. 2d 654, 195 P.2d 857 (1948), *noted in* 23 So. CAL. L. REV. 135 (1949); 2 VAND. L. REV. 301 (1949), the court held that a young man who had been injured as a result of his participation in a boxing contest at a circus was not entitled to recovery for his injuries, because by engaging in the match with his eyes opened to the possibility of bodily injury, he had assumed the risk of, and assented to, any injuries in fact received. *See also* Stafford v. Catholic Youth Organization, 202 So. 2d 333 (La. App. 1967) (contributorily negligent to sit on edge of mat); Rosensweig v. State, *supra*. The views expressed in the *Restatement* and *Hudson v. Craft* would presumably not bar recovery for injuries caused by risks not inherent to the sport (which are not assumed or consented to by the participant). To this extent, the minority rule is consistent with the prevailing rules of athletic participant recovery, and courts should in the future apply its rationale to deny an injured combatant recovery for his combat-related injuries, at least so long as they are the result of the ordinary and inherent risks of the sport.

See generally, Bohlen, *Consent as Affecting Civil Liability for Breaches of the Peace,* 24 COLUM. L. REV. 819 (1924) (criticizing *Boulter v. Clark); *Chamberlain, *Legal and Moral Aspects of Prize-Fighting,* 19 CASE & COM. 169 (1912); Moore, *Civil or Criminal Liability for Injuries in Field Sports,* 19 CASE & COM. 163 (1912); Annot., 71 A.L.R. 189 (1931).

Parallel Bars. Rodrigues v. San Jose Unified School Dist., 157 Cal. App. 2d 842, 322 P.2d 70 (1958); Quigley v. School Dist. No. 45J3, 251 Ore. 452, 446 P.2d 177 (1968).

Polevalulting. Johnson v. Municipal Univ. of Omaha, 184 Neb. 512, 169 N.W.2d 286 (1969) (not assume risk of wooden box placed in such a way that descending pole vaulter fell upon it).

Pool. See generally Annot., 15 A.L.R.3d 1420 (1967).

Racing. Jolley v. Chicago Thoroughbred Enterprises, Inc., 275 F. Supp. 325 (N.D. Ill. 1967) (collision in thoroughbred racing); Gulf Stream Park Racing Ass'n, Inc. v. Miller, 119 So.2d 749, 87 A.L.R.2d 1174 (Fla. App. 1960) (horse's excitable nature known); Brokaw v. East St. Louis Jockey Club, 12 Ill. App. 2d 243, 139 N.E.2d 850 (1956) (jockey could have elected not to ride on allegedly defective surface); Gray v. Pflanz, 341 Ill. App. 527, 94 N.E.2d 693 (1950) (defective eyesight of

risk of a thrust by his antagonist or a spectator at a ballgame the chance
of contact with the ball. The antics of the clown are not the poses of
the cloistered cleric. The rough and boisterous joke, the horseplay of

horse); McLeod Store v. Vinson, 213 Ky. 667, 281 S.W. 799 (1926) (alleged irregularities in race
course); Pardue v. Charlotte Motor Speedway, 273 N.C. 314, 159 S.E.2d 857 (1968) (no liability for
failure to erect barriers that cannot be demolished by a racer traveling at 150 miles per hour); Franks
v. Smith, 251 Ore. 98, 444 P.2d 954 (1968) (collision in motorcycle race); Luckey v. Adams, 397 S.W.2d
519 (Tex. Civ. App. 1965) (mechanical failure in suit against owner of dragster, who was said to have
no duty to instruct experienced driver in how to drive); Walker v. Yellow Belly Drag Strip, 351 S.W.2d
353 (Tex. Civ. App. 1961) (alleged irregularities in race course). Recovery has also been denied when
the amount of damages was too speculative, Cain v. Vollmer, 19 Idaho 163, 112 P. 686 (1910)
(employer action for injury to jockey), and when the injury was caused by an intervening cause.
Denemark v. Arlington Park Jockey Club, Inc., 326 Ill. App. 256, 61 N.E.2d 285 (1945) (horse forced
off track by another horse, and then became entangled in wire).

Rodeo. Rosenberger v. Central Louisiana Dist. Livestock Show, Inc., 312 So. 2d 300 (La. 1975).

Rope Jumping. Wire v. Williams, 270 Minn. 390, 133 N.W.2d 840 (1965).

Skydiving. Freeman v. United States, 509 F.2d 626 (6th Cir. 1975) (recovery allowed where air
traffic controller misidentified plane, which caused release of divers over Lake Erie).

Snowmobiling. Ujifusa v. National Housewares, Inc., 24 Utah 2d 219, 469 P.2d 7 (1970) (recovery
allowed when injury caused by going over bump too fast); Rock v. Concrete Materials, Inc., 46 App.
Div. 2d 300, 362 N.Y.S.2d 258 (1975), *app. dismissed,* 36 N.Y.2d 770, 368 N.Y.S.2d 841 (1975).

Springboard. Grant v. Lake Oswego School Dist. No. 7, 15 Ore. App. 325, 515 P.2d 947 (1973).

Soccer. Moore v. Jones, 120 Ga. App. 521, 171 S.E.2d 390 (1969); Nabozny v. Barnhill, 31 Ill. App.2d
212, 334 N.E.2d 258 (1975) (injury caused by intentional contact in "penalty area"); Darrow v. West
Genesee School Dist., 41 App. Div. 2d 897, 342 N.Y.S.2d 611 (1973); Keesee v. Board of Educ. of
New York, 37 Misc. 2d 414, 235 N.Y.S.2d 300 (1962).

Still Rings. Armlin v. Board of Educ. of Middleburgh Central School Dist., 36 App. Div. 2d 877,
320 N.Y.S.2d 402 (1971) (negligent supervision); Lueck v. Janesville, 57 Wis. 2d 254, 204 N.W.2d 6
(1973).

Surfing. Grob v. State, 42 Misc. 2d 791, 249 N.Y.S.2d 184 (1964) (negligence for lifeguard on
surfboard to jump off board and allow it to injure others).

Swimming. Cleary v. Indiana Beach, Inc. 275 F.2d 543 (7th Cir.), *cert. denied,* 364 U.S. 825, 5 L.
Ed. 2d 53, 81 S. Ct. 62 (1960) (diving into water known to be too shallow); Des Isles v. Evans, 225
F.2d 235 (5th Cir. 1955) (injured when dive into another); Atkins v. Bisigier, 16 Cal. App. 3d 414, 94
Cal. Rptr. 49 (1971) (diving into water known to be too shallow); Fowler Real Estate Co., Inc. v.
Ranke, 181 Colo. 115, 507 P.2d 854 (1973) (goes swimming shortly after having eaten so much food
as to cause cramps, swims in the deep end of the pool after his father, because he is a poor swimmer,
had warned him against swimming in that part of the pool); Webb v. Thomas, 133 Colo. 458, 296
P.2d 1036 (1956) (diving into water known to be too shallow); Brody v. Westmoor Beach & Blade
Club, Inc., 524 P.2d 1087 (Colo. App. 1974) (sliding into water with which familiar); Lincoln v. Wilcox,
111 Ga. App. 365, 141 S.E.2d 765 (1965) (another swimmer diving on injured party); Mouton v.
Vanguard Ins. Co., 293 So. 2d 604 (La. App. 1974) (beer can on bottom of pool); Caruso v. Aetna
Ins. Co., 186 So. 2d 851 (La. App. 1966) (diving into water known to be too shallow); Beck v. Broad
Channel Bathing Park, 255 N.Y. 641, 175 N.E. 350 (1931) (slipping on diving ladder); Englehardt
v. Philipps, 136 Ohio St. 73, 23 N.E.2d 829 (1939) (slipping on diving tower); Toole v. Levitt, 492
S.W.2d 230 (Tenn. App. 1973) (dives into a pool which has been closed for the season because of a
defective filter, with the result that the level of the pool had dropped and algae, scum, cans, dead
animals and other objects floated on the surface); Knight v. Wandermere Co., 46 Wash. 2d 768, 284
P.2d 1106 (1955) (diving into water known to be too shallow).

Table Tennis. Hoffman v. Silbert, 24 App. Div. 2d 493, 261 N.Y.S.2d 494 (1965) (recovery denied
for running arm through glass door).

Tennis. Manassa v. New Hampshire Ins. Co., 332 So.2d 34 (Fla. App. 1976) (comparative
negligence); Morrow v. Smith, 22 Misc. 2d 564, 198 N.Y.S.2d 737 (1960) (recovery denied when ran
into wall); Lobsenz v. Rubinstein, 258 App. Div. 164, 15 N.Y.S.2d 848 (1939), *aff'd,* 283 N.Y. 600,
28 N.E.2d 22 (1940) (contributory negligence for plaintiff to play on damaged surface).

Toboggan. Van Der Veen v. United States, 349 F.2d 583 (9th Cir. 1965) (plaintiff thrown from
toboggan, but unable to show fault); Grummitt v. Sturgeon Bay Winter Sports Club, 354 F.2d 564
(7th Cir. 1965) (toboggan flew out of chute because of ice build-up); Dickson v. Bounds, 190 Ark.
86, 37 S.W.2d 456 (*res ipsa loquitur* applies when sled leaves groove); Moore v. Edmonds, 384 Ill.
535, 52 N.E.2d 216 (1943); Powers v. Huizing, 9 Mich. App. 437, 157 N.W.2d 432 (1968) (negligence
to allow run to become slushy); Goodwin v. Bean, 99 N.H. 382, 112 A.2d 51 (1955); Williams v.
Poughkeepsie, 266 App. Div. 874, 42 N.Y.S.2d 495 (1943); Broderson v. Rainier Nat'l Park Co., 187
Wash. 399, 60 P.2d 234 (1936); Meyer v. Val-Lo-Will Farms, Inc., 14 Wis. 2d 616, 111 N.W.2d 500
(1961). *See generally* Annot., 19 A.L.R.3d 184 (1968); Annot., 94 A.L.R.2d 1431 (1961).

the crowd, evokes its own guffaws, but they are not the pleasures of tranquility. The plaintiff was not seeking a retreat for meditation. Visitors were tumbling about the belt to the merriment of onlookers when he made his choice to join them. He took the chances of a like fate, with whatever damage to his body might ensue from such a fall. The timorous may stay at home.

A different case would be here if the dangers inherent in the sport were obscure or unobserved, or so serious as to justify the belief that precautions of some kind must have been taken to avert them. Nothing happened to the plaintiff except what common experience tells us may happen at any time as the consequence of a sudden fall. Many a skater or a horseman can rehearse a tale of equal woe. A different case there would also be if accidents had been so many as to show that the game in its inherent nature was too dangerous to be continued without change . . . . Some quota of accidents was to be looked for in so great a mass. One might as well say that a skating rink should be abandoned because skaters sometimes fall.[27]

Although these principles will preclude recovery by participants in many cases, they do not preclude the possibility that actionable negligence may be present in some situations. For example, the voluntariness of participation which is the basis for the general rule may in extreme situations be overcome by the pressures that are an implicit part of the competitive atmosphere.[28] More importantly, the general rule will be inapplicable where the injured participant can establish that the injuries were either the result of other than good faith competition or the product of risks which are not ordinary or inherent in the sport in question.[29] Such factors may be present in several circumstances. The first might involve the acts of other participants. An unreasonable risk of injury may be created by the lack of skill or improper conduct of other participants or by the manner in which a particular activity is conducted. Such risks would not be assumed by the participant to the extent that they did not constitute the ordinary and inherent risks of the sport.[30] For example, in *Bourque v. Duple-*

Trampoline. Ragni v. Lincoln-Devon Bounceland, Inc., 91 Ill. App. 2d 172, 234 N.E.2d 168 (1968) (no duty to warn experienced participants); Daniel v. S-Co. Corp., 255 Iowa 869, 124 N.W.2d 522 (1963) (assume risk of dangers where sign says ask if in need of instruction); Berg v. Merricks, 20 Md. 666, 318 A.2d 220 (1974) (injury caused by own improper execution); Kungle v. Austin, 380 S.W.2d 354 (Mo. 1964) (citing cases); Williams v. Lombardini, 38 Misc. 2d 146, 238 N.Y.S.2d 63 (1963) (assume risk); Chapman v. State, 6 Wash. App. 316, 492 P.2d 607 (1972). *See generally* Annot., 8 A.L.R.3d 1427 (1966).

Tumbling. Bellman v. San Francisco High School Dist., 11 Cal. 2d 576, 81 P.2d 894 (1938) (negligent failure to prevent medically unfit student from participating); Passafaro v. Board of Educ. of New York, 43 App. Div. 2d 918, 353 N.Y.S.2d 178 (1974) (no proof of negligence); Rodriguez v. Seattle School Dist. No. 1, 66 Wash. 2d 51, 401 P.2d 326 (1965) (negligent supervision); Walter v. Everett School Dist. No. 24, 195 Wash. 45, 79 P.2d 689 (1938).

See generally 2 F. HARPER & F. JAMES, THE LAW OF TORTS § 21.5, at 1181-82 (1956); W. PROSSER, THE LAW OF TORTS § 68, at 446 (4th ed. 1970); Annot., 7 A.L.R.2d 704 (1949); Annot., 98 A.L.R. 400 (1935).

27. 250 N.Y. at 482083, 166 N.E. at 174-75 (citations omitted).

28. Thus, in Martini v. Olymphant Borough School Dist., 83 Pa. D. & C. 206 (1952), the court observed that

> [i]t is also debatable whether or not the usual disciplinary authority of the coach, the presence of school spirit, the probable odium attached to refusal to play, both by his fellow-players and his schoolmates, might not have robbed him of volition under the circumstances.

83 Pa. D. & C. at 211.

29. Foley v. Union Free School Dist. No. 17, Town of Oyster Bay, 259 App. Div. 837, 19 N.Y.S.2d 198 (1940); Oberheim v. Pennsylvania Sports & Enterprises, 358 Pa. 62, 55 A.2d 766 (1947).

30. This principle has been applied in the following cases:

chin,[31] one Duplechin was on first base during a softball game when a teammate hit a ground ball. The ball was fielded by the shortstop, thrown to the second

Alpine Skiing. Ninio v. Hight, 385 F.2d 350 (10th Cir. 1967) (recover from skier who fails to observe the "rules of the road" on a ski slope).

Basketball. Alpert v. Finkelstein, 42 App. Div. 2d 515, 344 N.Y.S.2d 649 (1973) (another basketball player's throwing a ball across court at eye level); Falk v. Whitewater, 65 Wis. 83, 221 N.W.2d 915 (1974) (struck plaintiff with fist; complaint stated cause of action).

Boat and Water Skiing. Shahinian v. McCormick, 59 Cal. 2d 554, 30 Cal. Rptr. 521, 381 P.2d 377 (1963) (run over by own boat); Allman v. Bird, 186 Kan. 802, 353 P.2d 216 (1960) (sudden acceleration of tow boat); Carroll v. Aetna Casualty & Surety Co., 30 So. 2d 406 (La. App. 1974) (negligent operation of boat); Greathouse v. Wolff, 360 S.W.2d 297 (Mo. App. 1962) (sudden acceleration of tow boat); McDonald v. Hanneson, 263 Ore. 612, 503 P.2d 674 (1972) (water skier and his tow boat operator cause the tow rope to "snake" across a swimming float); Harrop v. Beckman, 15 Utah 2d 78, 387 P.2d 554 (1963) (struck by an on-coming boat while trying to retrieve his skis in the water); Nugen v. Hildebrand, 145 W. Va. 420, 114 S.E.2d 896 (1960) (water skier run over by another boat).

Football. Hackbart v. Cincinnati Bengals, Inc., 435 F. Supp. 352 (D. Colo. 1977) (assumed risk of violent act given nature of professional football).

Golf. Strand v. Connor, 207 Cal. App. 2d 473, 24 Cal. Rptr. 584 (1962) (drive ball off a green); Brady v. Kane, 111 So. 2d 472 (Fla. App. 1959) (practice swing in crowd); Carroll v. Askew, 119 Ga. App. 224, 166 S.E.2d 635 (1969) (practice swing in crowd); Allen v. Pinewood Country Club, Inc., 292 So. 2d 786 (La. App. 1974) (others in foursome not noticing movement); Nesbitt v. Bethesda Country Club, Inc., 20 Md. 2d 226, 314 A.2d 738 (1974) (practice swing in crowd); Schmidt v. Orton, 190 Neb. 257, 207 N.W.2d 390 (1973) (playing ball into group ahead); McWilliams v. Parham, 273 N.C. 592, 160 S.E.2d 692 (1968) (failure to observe the rules or customs of the game, which other golfers and caddies are entitled to assume will be observed); Everett v. Goodwin, 201 N.C. 734, 161 S.E. 316 (1931) (play into those in front on a constant basis); Patterson v. Weatherspoon, 17 N.C. App. 236, 193 S.E.2d 585 (1972) (not observing customs of game); Getz v. Freed, 377 Pa. 480, 105 A.2d 102 (1954) (plays a third ball while his companions are on the fairway looking for the first two duffed balls); Nepstad v. Randall, 82 S.D. 615, 152 N.W.2d 383 (1967) (not observing customs of game); Rasmussen v. Richards, 7 Wis. 2d 22, 95 N.W.2d 791 (1959) (failure to observe customs of game); Ratcliffe v. Whitehead, [1933] 3 W.W.R. 447 (playing ball into foursome ahead, even though the group played into had given its permission); Cleghorn v. Oldham, 43 L.T.R. 465 (K.B. 1927) (swing in crowd).

Perhaps the greatest controversy in the golf cases involves the duty to give a warning — which generally refers to the traditional and time-honored yell of "FORE." As a general rule, the golfer will not be required to give the warning unless there are other players in such a position of danger that injury is to be reasonably anticipated if they are not warned — that is, a warning need be given to only those in a predictable zone of danger. Boynton v. Ryan, 257 F.2d 70 (3rd Cir. 1958); Houston v. Escott, 85 F. Supp. 59 (D. Del. 1949); Strand v. Connor, 207 Cal. App. 2d 473, 24 Cal. Rptr. 584 (1962); Rose v. Morris, 97 Ga. App. 764, 104 S.E.2d 485 (1958); Stober v. Embry, 243 Ky. 117, 47 S.W.2d 921 (1932); Page v. Unterreiner, 130 S.W.2d 970 (Mo. App. 1939); Schmidt v. Orton, 190 Neb. 257, 207 N.W.2d 390 (1973); Toohey v. Webster, 97 N.J. Law 545, 117 A. 838 (1922); Povanda v. Powers, 152 Misc. 75, 272 N.Y.S. 619 (1934); Rogers v. Allis-Chalmers Mfg. Co., 153 Ohio St. 513, 92 N.E.2d 677 (1950); Alexander v. Wrenn, 158 Va. 486, 164 S.E. 715 (1932). *But cf.* Thomas v. Shaw, 217 Ga. 688, 124 S.E.2d 396 (1962) (holding that a warning should be given to one not in the predictable zone of danger — an adjoining fairway). Circumstances requiring a warning will be present, for example, when the other player is unknown to himself in the intended line of flight, Oakes v. Chapman, 158 Cal. App. 2d 78, 322 P.2d 241 (1958); Allen v. Pinewood Country Club, Inc., 292 So.2d 786 (La. App. 1974); Turel v. Milberg, 10 Misc. 2d 141, 169 N.Y.S.2d 955 (1957); Alexander v. Wrenn, 158 Va. 486, 164 S.E. 715 (1932); would not expect the duffer to hit three tee shots, Getz v. Freed, 377 Pa. 480, 105 A.2d 102 (1954); or where a greenskeeper is not aware of the approaching golfers. Robinson v. Meding, 52 Del. 578, 163 A.2d 272 (1960). Absent such circumstances — as when the injured golfer was in an adjoining fairway, Houston v. Escott, 85 F. Supp. 59 (D. Del. 1949); Rocchio v. Frers, 248 App. Div. 786, 290 N.Y.S. 432 (1936); Trauman v. New York, 208 Misc. 252, 143 N.Y.S. 2d 467 (1955) — the warning need not be given, and failure to give it will not of itself be evidence of negligence. Mazzuchelli v. Nissenbaum, 355 Mass. 788, 244 N.E.2d 729 (1969). Even if otherwise required, warnings will not be required where the injured party was aware that the ball was about to be hit, but did not take action to protect himself. Oakes v. Chapman, 158 Cal. App. 2d 78, 322 P.2d 241 (1958); Walsh v. Machlin, 128 Conn. 412, 23 A.2d 156 (1941); Rose v. Morris, 97 Ga. App. 764, 104 S.E.2d 485 (1958); Stober v. Embry, 243 Ky. 117, 47 S.W.2d 921 (1932); Jenks v. McGranaghan, 30 N.Y.2d 475, 334 N.Y.S.2d 641 (1972); Turel v. Milberg, 10 Misc. 2d 141, 169 N.Y.S.2d 955 (1957); Wood v. Postelthwaite, 6 Wash. App. 885, 496 P.2d 988 (1972).

---

31. 331 So. 2d 40 (La. App. 1976).

baseman (Bourque) and then to the first baseman for a double play. After his throw, Bourque stood five feet from second base toward the pitcher's mound. Although Duplechin was forced out by the throw, he continued to run toward Bourque, who was not in the basepath, at full speed. When he ran into Bourque, Duplechin delivered a blow under the former's chin with his arm, which caused a serious injury. Bourque then brought suit against Duplechin and the court found that he was entitled to recover for the injuries caused by Duplechin's blow. Although Duplechin alleged that Bourque had assumed the risk of the injury, the court found that such intentional misconduct was not a risk assumed by softball players:

> Bourque did not assume the risk of Duplechin going out of his way to run into him at full speed when Bourque was five feet away from the base. A participant in a game or sport assumes all of the risks incidental to that particular activity which are obvious and foreseeable. A participant does not assume the risk of injury from fellow players acting in an unexpected or unsportsmanlike way with a reckless lack of concern for others participating.[32]

A second situation in which recovery would be possible involves risks created by the negligent acts of third persons. Such risks have frequently been created by the conduct of coaches. Thus, the courts have imposed liability where an injury is caused by the athlete's having been required by his or her coach to compete while injured;[33] by the failure of the coach or team physician to render proper medical attention;[34] by the failure of the coach to provide proper equipment;[35] and by the negligent instruction of a coach.[36] Liability has also been imposed when an injury is the result of the negligence of a referee in not

---

Not requiring a warning except when an unreasonable risk would otherwise be posed is supported by the view that in order to properly address the ball, a golfer must cast his or her vision downward upon the ball and cannot be expected to break that concentration the moment before the swing to look up and see if someone has entered the zone of danger, even if he or she were to be clairvoyant enough to determine where, if the ball does not go straight, the zone might be located. To require otherwise would be to ignore the physical requirements of the game and would be productive of more, not less, injury, since it would require the golfer to take his or her eyes off the ball before the swing. It would however, require the golfer to look around before getting set for the shot. *See generally* Annot., 82 A.L.R.2d 1183 (1962); Annot., 138 A.L.R. 541 (1942).

Hunting. Shurley v. Hoskins, 271 So. 2d 439 (Miss. 1973) (hunter not assume risk of companion's negligence); West v. Williams, 245 So. 2d 591 (Miss. 1971) (landowner may not shoot hunter); White v. Levarn, 93 Vt. 218, 108 A. 564 (1918) (recovery for shooting by another hunter on Sunday); Edgar v. Brandvold, 9 Wash. App. 899, 515 P.2d 991 (1973). *See generally* Annot., 26 A.L.R.3d 561 (1969).

Racing. McKay v. Irvine, 10 F. 725 (N.D. Ill. 1882) (intentionally fouling another horse).

Snowmobiling. Carpenter v. Mattison, 300 Minn. 273, 219 N.W.2d 625 (1974) (speeding of other snowmobile); Olson v. Hansen, 299 Minn. 39, 216 N.W.2d 124 (1974) (reckless driving of a snowmobile).

Soccer. Nabozny v. Barnhill, 31 Ill. App. 3d 212, 334 N.E.2d 258 (1975), *noted in* 42 Mo. L. Rev. 347 (1976) (intentional contact in the "penalty area").

32. 331 So. 2d at 42. *See also* Agar v. Canning, 54 W.W.R. 302 (1965), *aff'd,* 55 W.W.R. 384 (1966) (not assume risk of retaliatory blow struck in anger).

33. Morris v. Union High School Dist. A, King County, 160 Wash. 121, 294 P. 998 (1931). *But cf.* Hale v. Davies, 86 Ga. App. 126, 70 S.E.2d 923 (1952) (assume such risk unless coach acts willfully or wantonly). Liability of coaches is considered at § 8.06.

34. Welch v. Dunsmuir, Joint Union High School Dist., 326 P.2d 633 (Cal. App. 1958); Mogabgab v. Orleans Parish School Bd., 239 So. 2d 456 (La. App. 1970). *But cf.* Duda v. Gaines, 12 N.J. Super. 326, 79 A.2d 695 (1951) (no liability where no immediate need to call medical assistance). Liability for medical treatment rendered for athletic injuries is considered at §§ 8.07, 8.08.

35. Martini v. Olymphant Borough School Dist., 83 Pa. D. & C. 206 (1952).

36. Stehn v. Bernarr MacFadden Foundation, Inc., 434 F.2d 811 (6th Cir. 1970).

detecting the use of an illegal wrestling hold,[37] or failing to properly supervise a game.[38]

The participant may also suffer injury as a result of abuse from spectators excited by the events on the playing field. The chief difficulty in such cases will be the determination of who should be responsible for the injuries inflicted. If the spectator who throws the bottle, vegetable or other missile is identifiable, there should be little difficulty in holding that person liable for the consequences of the proven acts. More difficult, however, are cases in which the plaintiff seeks to impose responsibility upon a participant who precipitated the spectator reaction that ultimately resulted in the injury. This difficulty is suggested by *Toone v. Adams,*[39] where an umpire at a minor league baseball game had made several calls that were adverse to the home team. After each call, the manager of the home team charged onto the field and engaged the umpire in a strident verbal exchange. During one of these confrontations, the manager stated that if another bad call were made he would behave in such a manner as to engender the partisan spectators' extreme hostility toward the umpire. During the ninth inning, there was another disputed call made against the home team, and, true to his word, the manager charged onto the field and behaved in a manner that engendered the spectators' hostility. After the game, the fans poured onto the field cursing and challenging the umpire to fight. Before he could get to the dressing room, the umpire was struck on the head by a spectator. He then brought suit against the manager, the home team, and the spectator who delivered the blow. In dismissing the claim against the manager and the home team, the court stated that the unsportsmanlike conduct of the manager was not contemporaneous with the assault, and the manager could not be held responsible for the acts of the spectators. To do so, the court said, would be "an intolerable burden upon managers" because they would then become responsible "for the actions of every emotionally unstable person who might arrive at the game spoiling for a fight and become enraged over an umpire's call which the manager had protested."[40] *Toone v. Adams* should not, however, be viewed to state that a manager or other participant would never be legally responsible for injuries incurred by another participant in such situations. For example, if a manager had reason to know that fans would shower an umpire with bottles, hot coins or other missiles if he strongly protested a call against the home team, proceeded to so protest, and the umpire was in fact injured by such missiles from the stands, then the manager may be responsible for the injuries.

The most important risk that will not be assumed by participants is that posed by the negligence of others who have a specific duty of care toward them. Primary in this group are the operators of the sports facilities in which the activities take place.[41] When actions are brought against operators for injuries

---

37. Carabba v. Anacortes School Dist. No. 103, 72 Wash. 2d 939, 435 P.2d 936 (1967) (the hold was a "full-nelson").

38. Rosensweig v. State, 208 Misc. 1065, 146 N.Y.S.2d 589 (1955), *rev'd on other grounds,* 5 N.Y.2d 404, 158 N.E.2d 229 (1959). *See also* Crohn v. Congregation B'nai Zion, 22 Ill. App. 2d 625, 317 N.E.2d 637 (1974) (failure to supervise summer day camp baseball game).

39. 262 N.C. 403, 137 S.E.2d 132 (1964).

40. 262 N.C. at 412, 137 S.E.2d at 139.

41. For purposes of simplicity, the term "operators" will be used in the discussion even though it would be more precise to use the phrase "owners or operators." The latter phrase would be more accurate since the facilities in, or on, which sports activities take place may be leased from their

suffered by participants, the legal issue will generally be whether they have met their duty to the participants utilizing their facilities. As business invitors, operators are subject to the same liability imposed on other possessors of land. They will be liable for conditions on their premises which cause physical harm to their invitees (the participants) if they know, or should reasonably have discovered, that the condition exists, that it poses an unreasonable risk of harm which the invitee-participants will not discover or protect themselves against,

owner by the operator. Thus, in many cases it may become necessary to consider how liability will be allocated when the facilities are subject to the ownership or control of more than one party. The allocation of liability between the owner and the operator for defective conditions will be determined in accordance with the rules relating to the lessor-lessee relationship, which will generally be present. As a general rule, the lessor of athletic facilities will not be liable to his lessee or others for physical harm caused by any dangerous condition, whether material or artificial, which existed when the lessee took possession. RESTATEMENT (SECOND) OF TORTS §§ 355-56 (1965). *See also* Pollan v. Dothan, 243 Ala. 99, 8 So.2d 813 (1942); Sam v. Theriot, 49 So.2d 484 (La. App. 1950); Smith v. Camden, 115 N.J. Law 503, 181 A. 160 (1935); Schimenti v. Nansen Properties, Inc., 20 App. Div. 2d 653, 246 N.Y.S.2d 273 (1964); Fort Worth v. Barlow, 313 S.W.2d 906 (Tex. Civ. App. 1958). *But cf.* Atlantic Rural Exposition, Inc. v. Fagan, 195 Va. 13, 77 S.E.2d 368 (1953) (lessor and lessee equally liable). There are, however, several exceptions to this general rule. The first is that if the lease covers the use of athletic facilities for only a very short period, the lessee is entitled to rely upon the apparent safety of the premises, and the facilities thereupon, and need not inspect them for non-apparent defects. When injuries then result because of dangerous or defective conditions, the lessor will bear potential liability. Witherspoon v. Haft, 157 Ohio St. 474, 106 N.E.2d 296 (1952); Greene v. Seattle Athletic Club, 60 Wash. 300, 111 P. 157 (1910) (one night); Novak v. Delavan, 31 Wis. 2d 200, 143 N.W.2d 6 (1966) (single game). A second exception states that the lessor will be liable if 1) the lessor, as such, has contracted by a covenant in the lease or otherwise to keep the land in repair; 2) the disrepair creates an unreasonable risk to persons upon the land which the performance of the lessor's agreement would have prevented; and 3) the lessor fails to exercise reasonable care to perform its obligations. RESTATEMENT (SECOND) OF TORTS § 357 (1965); Brown v. Cleveland Baseball Co., 158 Ohio St. 1, 106 N.E.2d 632 (1952). This exception will not apply where the lessor merely reserves the privilege to enter and make repairs. RESTATEMENT (SECOND) OF TORTS § 357, comment *b.1.* (1965). A third exception is that liability will result where the lessor conceals or fails to disclose a condition, whether natural or artificial, which involves unreasonable risk of physical harm to those upon the land if the lessee does not know, or have reason to know, of the condition, and the lessor knows, or has reason to know, that the lessee will not discover the condition or realize the risk. RESTATEMENT (SECOND) OF TORTS § 358 (1965); Tulsa Entertainment Co. v. Greenlees, 85 Okla. 113, 205 P. 179 (1922) (rotten bleachers and lessor did not want to expend money to fix). A fourth exception, which will have particular relevance to sports facilities, concerns the lease of land for purposes which involve the admission of the public, and the lessor will then be liable if it 1) knows, or by the exercise of reasonable care could discover, that a condition involves an unreasonable risk of harm; 2) has reason to expect that the lessee will admit the public before the land is put in a safe condition for their reception; and 3) fails to exercise reasonable care to discover or remedy the condition. RESTATEMENT (SECOND) OF TORTS § 359 (1965). *See also* Ward v. United States, 208 F. Supp. 118 (D. Colo. 1962); Larson v. Santa Clara Valley Water Conservation Dist., 218 Cal. App. 2d 515, 32 Cal. Rptr. 875 (1963); Fitchett v. Buchanan, 2 Wash. App. 2d 695, 472 P.2d 623 (1970).

The "public purpose" exception is well illustrated by the following example:

> *A* leases his baseball park to the *B* Baseball Club for the baseball season. The lease contains a covenant by the lessee to make necessary repairs. Two months after *B* takes possession the grandstand falls because of the bad condition of the woodwork supporting it, which a reasonable inspection would have disclosed to either *A* or *B* Baseball Club when possession was given to the *B* Club. *C,* a spectator in the grandstand, is hurt by the collapse of the stand. *A* is subject to liability to *C* if, in spite of the covenant, he had reason to believe that the repairs would be neglected. RESTATEMENT (SECOND) OF TORTS § 359, comment *i,* illustration 2 (1965).

See also id. illustration 7 (baseball stands); *id.* illustration 8 (swimming pool). This exception will not, however, be of any benefit to a participant in an athletic event, since it does not apply to a participant who was injured on parts of the premises not in any way thrown open to members of the public. Regan v. Seattle, 76 Wash. 2d 501, 458 P.2d 12 (1969). The lessor will also be liable for dangerous conditions on those parts of the land that are retained within its control. RESTATEMENT (SECOND)

and fail to exercise reasonable care for protection of the invitee.[42] Thus, operators have the duty to exercise reasonable care to protect participants from injury caused either by the condition of the premises and equipment located thereon or by the conduct of the other invitee-participants or third parties, provided that the injury could have been prevented by the exercise of reasonable care.[43] This duty will include the duty to maintain the premises in a reasonably safe condition and to supervise the conduct of those on the premises. The operator is not, however, the insurer of the participants' safety, and to recover for injuries sustained on its premises, a participant must prove both that specific acts or omissions amount to a breach of the operator's duty of care and that the breach was the proximate cause of the injury sustained.[44] The operator may also assume that all participants will obey the rules and customs of the game.[45] Thus, liability will occur only when the participants have met their duty to exercise reasonable care for their own protection and the owner or operator has defaulted on its own duty.[46]

OF TORTS §§ 360, 361 (1965). Finally, the lessor will be liable when in making repairs it makes the land more dangerous or gives it a deceptive appearance of safety. RESTATEMENT (SECOND) OF TORTS § 362 (1965); Regan v. Seattle, 76 Wash. 2d 501, 458 P.2d 12 (1969). Liability for defective seating facilities is considered at § 8.03.

42. RESTATEMENT (SECOND) OF TORTS § 343 (1965). *See also* Panoz v. Gulf & Bay Corp. of Sarasota, 208 So. 2d 297 (Fla. App. 1968); Taylor v. Hardee, 232 S.C. 338, 102 S.E.2d 218 (1958); Cappel v. Board of Educ., Union Free School Dist. No. 4, Northport, 40 App. Div. 848, 337 N.Y.S.2d 836 (1972); Juntila v. Everett School Dist. No. 24, 183 Wash. 357, 48 P.2d 613 (1935); Copeland v. Larson, 46 Wis. 2d 337, 174 N.W.2d 745 (1970). *See generally* Note, *Negligent Design of Sports Facilities,* 16 CLEV.-MAR. L. REV. 275 (1967).

The duty of the owner or operator of some types of sports facilities may be subject to a different standard of care as the result of specific statutory enactments. One such provision is designed to encourage the owners of land or water areas that could be used for recreational purposes to make them available to the public for recreational purposes. *See, e.g.,* GA. CODE ANN. § 105-403 (Supp. 1970); W. VA. CODE § 19-25-1 (1971). The encouragement is accomplished by limiting the liability of the owners who make their land or water areas so available. *See, e.g.,* GA. CODE ANN. § 105-406 (1968); Est. of Thomas v. Consumers Power Co., 58 Mich. App. 486, 228 N.W.2d 786 (1975). In order for the limited liability provisions to apply, however, the owner must actually make the facilities available for public use. Thus, if "keep out" signs are posted around the facilities, or if only a few individuals, as opposed to the public in general, are allowed to use the facilities, then the limited liability provision will not apply. *See, e.g.,* Georgia Power Co. v. McGruder, 229 Ga. 811, 194 S.E.2d 440 (1972) (boy drowned in lake posted with "keep out" signs); Herring v. Hauck, 118 Ga. App. 623, 165 S.E.2d 198 (1968) (not apply to neighbors in swimming pool); Boileau v. De Cecco, 125 N.J. Super. 263, 310 A.2d 497 (1973) (not apply to residential swimming pool); O'Connell v. Forest Hills Field Club, 119 N.J. Super. 317, 291 A.2d 386 (1972) (not apply to excavation on golf course). *See also* Krievics v. Ayars, 141 N.J. Super. 511, 358 A.2d 844 (1976).

43. Lincoln v. Wilcox, 111 Ga. App. 365, 141 S.E.2d 765 (1965).

44. Panoz v. Gulf & Bay Corp. of Sarasota, 208 So. 2d 297 (Fla. App. 1968); Smith v. Village of Pine River, 232 N.W.2d 241 (Minn. 1975); Everett v. Goodwin, 201 N.C. 734, 161 S.E. 316 (1931); Juntila v. Everett School Dist. No. 24, 183 Wash. 357, 48 P.2d 613 (1935).

45. *See, e.g.,* Petrich v. New Orleans City Park Improvement Ass'n, 188 So. 199 (La. App. 1939); Schlenger v. Weinberg, 107 N.J. Law 130, 150 A. 434 (1930); Everett v. Goodwin, 201 N.C. 734, 161 S.E. 316 (1931); Amon v. Shemaka, 419 Pa. 314, 214 A.2d 238 (1965).

46. Cases involving defects in premises and equipment include the following:

Alpine Skiing. Marietta v. Cliffs Ridge, Inc., 385 Mich. 364, 189 N.W.2d 208 (1971) (defective markers on slalom course); Seidl v. Trollhausen, Inc., 232 N.W.2d 236 (Minn. 1975) (hit by ski instructors on slopes); Elliott v. Taos Ski Valley, Inc., 83 N.M. 575, 494 P.2d 1392, *aff'd,* 83 N.M. 763, 497 P.2d 974 (1972) (injured skier allowed to walk too soon); Morse v. State, 262 App. Div. 324, 29 N.Y.S.2d 34, *appeal dismissed,* 287 N.Y. 666, 39 N.E.2d 288 (1941) (allowing sledding and skiing on same facilities at same time).

The owners and operators are held to a slightly higher standard of care when they undertake to operate ski lift apparatuses to get skiers to the top of the ski runs. As a result of the fact that when they transport the public for a fee, the owners or operators of skiing facilities become common

These principles are aptly illustrated by *Dawson v. Rhode Island Auditorium, Inc.,*[47] involving the Harlem Magicians basketball team. The players had

carriers, Fisher v. Mt. Mansfield Co., 283 F.2d 533 (2d Cir. 1960); McDaniel v. Dowell, 210 Cal. App. 2d 26, 26 Cal. Rptr. 140 (1962); Grauer v. State, 15 Misc. 2d 471, 181 N.Y.S.2d 994 (1959), they must exercise a duty of highest care under the circumstances to protect those being transported — that is, they must undertake every precaution and safeguard to protect their patrons. Fisher v. Mt. Mansfield Co., 283 F.2d 533 (2d Cir. 1960) (failure to help skier out of lift cage); Sabo v. Brechenridge Lands, Inc., 255 F. Supp. 602 (D. Colo. 1966) (failure to take action to aid skier dangling from lift); Winn v. Ski Club of the Ass'n of Fellows of Mayo Foundation, 207 F. Supp. 448 (D. Minn. 1962) (malfunction of safety device); Arapahoe Basin, Inc. v. Fischer, 28 Colo. App. 580, 475 P.2d 631 (1970) (failure to take action to aid skier dangling from lift); Summit County Dev. Corp. v. Bagnoli, 166 Colo. 27, 441 P.2d 658 (1968) (violate safety provisions for public contract); Ford v. Black Mountain Tramways, Inc., 110 N.H. 20, 259 A.2d 129 (1969); Albert v. State, 80 Misc. 2d 105, 362 N.Y.S.2d 341 (1975) (no negligence); Friedman v. State, 54 Misc. 2d 448, 282 N.Y.S.2d 858 (1967) (stranding skier aloft in lift); Math v. State, 37 Misc. 2d 1023, 237 N.Y.S.2d 478 (1962); Grauer v. State, 15 Misc. 2d 471, 181 N.Y.S.2d 994 (1959) (failure to advise patrons of safety instructions); Vogel v. State, 204 Misc. 614, 124 N.Y.S.2d 563, *appeal dismissed,* 284 App. Div. 993, 136 N.Y.S.2d 376 (1953) (violate statutory safety provisions); Marshall v. Brattleboro, 121 Vt. 417, 160 A.2d 762 (1960) (lift mechanism that caught skier's clothes). It should also be noted that some states have enacted legislation which provides that ski lift operators can be held negligent only if they fail to conform to administrative regulations, but such statutes will not apply to non-lift related accidents. Adie v. Temple Mountain Ski Area, 108 N.H. 480, 238 A.2d 738 (1968) (negligent instruction).

The courts have also refused to apply the doctrine of *res ipsa loquitur* to ski lift accidents. Houser v. Floyd, 220 Cal. App. 2d 778, 34 Cal. Rptr. 96 (1963); Jordan v. Loveland Skiing Corp., 503 P.2d 1034 (Colo. App. 1972).

Baseball. Forkash v. New York, 27 App. Div. 2d 831, 277 N.Y.S.2d 827 (1967) (glass in outfield); Schmerz v. Salon, 26 App. Div. 2d 691, 272 N.Y.S.2d 404 (1966), *aff'd,* 19 N.Y.S.2d 846, 280 N.Y.S.2d 409, 227 N.E.2d 322 (1967) (holes in base paths); Turano v. New York, 17 App. Div. 2d 191, 233 N.Y.S.2d 330 (1962) (defectively designed baseball field).

Basketball. Nunez v. Isidore Newman High School, 306 So. 2d 457 (La. App. 1975); Webber v. New York, 30 App. Div. 2d 831, 292 N.Y.S.2d 574 (1968) (remanded to receive evidence on defectively designed basketball court); Stevens v. Central School Dist. No. 1, 25 App. Div. 2d 871, 270 N.Y.S.2d 23 (1966) (failure to install impact-resistant glass in a door under the basket); Bauer v. Board of Educ. of New York, 285 App. Div. 1148, 140 N.Y.S.2d 167 (1955) (overcrowded condition of the gym in which the game is played); Dawson v. Rhode Island Auditorium, Inc., 104 R.I. 116, 725, 242 A.2d 407 (1968) (failure to prevent water puddles from accumulating on the court).

Boat and Water Skiing. Glenview Park Dist. v. Melhus, 540 F.2d 1321 (7th Cir. 1976) (canoe trip on high water river); Kaiser v. Traveler's Ins. Co., 359 F. Supp. 90 (E.D. La. 1973) (injury from striking a partially submerged and unmarked barge); Larson v. Santa Clara Valley Water Conservation Dist., 218 Cal. App. 2d 515, 32 Cal. Rptr. 875 (1963) (water level in lake too low); Sorenson v. Hutson, 175 Cal. App. 2d 817, 346 P.2d 785 (1959); Gainesville v. Pritchett, 129 Ga. App. 475, 199 S.E.2d 889 (1973) (collision with improperly located jump).

Bowling. Sykes v. Bensinger Recreation Corp., 117 F.2d 964 (7th Cir. 1941) (application of "safe place" statute); Murphy v. El Dorado Bowl, Inc., 2 Ariz. App. 341, 409 P.2d 57 (1965) (question of fact if negligence to construct walking lane next to bowling lane); Taylor v. Centennial Bowl, Inc., 65 Cal. 2d 114, 52 Cal. Rptr. 561, 416 P.2d 793 (1966) (negligent failure to protect patron from assault); Repka v. Rentalent, Inc., 477 P.2d 470 (Colo. App. 1970) (no evidence of negligence when patron struck by a drunken patron); Nance v. Ball, 134 So. 2d 35 (Fla. App. 1961) (negligent failure to restrain bowler with known propensity to assault other competitors); Georgia Bowling Enterprises, Inc. v. Robbins, 103 Ga. App. 286, 119 S.E.2d 52 (1961) (recovery for assault by employee on child patron); Meyer v. Whipple, 94 Idaho 260, 486 P.2d 271 (1971) (no evidence of negligence in fall on bowling lane); Kincaid v. Lagen, 71 Ill. App. 2d 307, 218 N.E.2d 856 (1966) (no evidence of negligence when one bowler hit in head by arc of another's practice swing); Guidani v. Cumerlato, 59 Ill. App. 2d 13, 207 N.E.2d 1 (1965) (negligent failure to remove wetness on floor that may cause bowler to slip in delivery); Burns v. Goldammer, 38 Ill. App. 2d 83, 186 N.E.2d 97 (1962) (negligent failure to remove gum from approach); True v. Larimore, 255 Iowa 451, 123 N.W.2d 5 (1963) (no evidence of negligence in fall while delivering ball); Nelson v. Midwest Mortgage Co., 426 S.W.2d 149 (Ky. App. 1968) (same); Spiers v. Lake Shore Enterprises, Inc., 210 So. 2d 901 (La. App. 1968) (same); Messina v. Massachusetts Bonding & Ins. Co., 171 So. 2d 705 (La. App. 1965) (owner not required to foresee that bowler would swing a ball in such a way as to hit a patron sitting at a snack bar); Marra v. Botta Corp., 356 Mass. 569, 254 N.E.2d 418 (1970) (question of fact whether owner responsible for

---

47. 104 R.I. 116, 242 A.2d 407 (1968).

assembled in a circle near the middle of the court to demonstrate their unusual dexterity and wizardry in the art of ball handling. At the completion of this

assault); McGillivray v. Eramian, 309 Mass. 430, 35 N.E.2d 209 (1941) (negligence to allow delivery lane to deteriorate to extent that bowler got splinter while delivering ball); Cronin v. Northland Bowling Lanes Co., 389 S.W.2d 863 (Mo. App. 1965) (no evidence that sticky substance on approach was known to owner); Houston v. Cannon Bowl, Inc., 433 Pa. 383, 278 A.2d 908 (1971) (no evidence of foreign substance on lane); Fagan v. Williamsport Lodge No. 145 of Loyal Order of Moose, 361 Pa. 446, 64 A.2d 805 (1949) (same); Belkin v. Playdium, Inc., 194 Misc. 950, 87 N.Y.S.2d 813 (1949) (no negligence by owner when bowler bowls in stocking feet); Preston v. Newburgh Y.M.C.A., 271 App. Div. 797, 65 N.Y.S.2d 254 (1946) (no negligence by owner when bowler put hand between balls on rack and return ball causes impact which crushes bowler's finger). *See generally* Koch, *Bowling Alley Tort Liability*, 16 CLEVE.-MAR. L. REV. 284 (1967); Annot., 141 A.L.R. 1315 (1942); Annot., 97 A.L.R.2d 1074 (1964).

Golf. Dashiell v. Keauhou-Kona Co., 487 F.2d 957 (9th Cir. 1973) (improper golf cart path markings); Steele v. Jekyll Island State Park Authority, 122 Ga. App. 159, 176 S.E.2d 514 (1970) (algae under sand at bottom of ditch); Richards v. Mohawk Country Club, 301 Ill. App. 403, 23 N.E.2d 207 (1939) (poorly lighted tent stakes and support ropes); Brooks v. Bass, 184 So. 222 (La. App. 1938) (allow golfers to play into workmen); Gresser v. Taylor, 276 Minn. 440, 150 N.W.2d 869 (1967) (failure to prevent auto from rolling onto course and injuring tournament player); Country Club of Jackson v. Turner, 192 Miss. 510, 4 So. 2d 718 (1941) (employing a vicious and dangerous person); Gifford v. Bogey Hills Golf & Country Club, 426 S.W.2d 98 (Mo. 1968) (failure to inspect and repair golf cart brakes); Jones v. New Mexico School of Mines, 75 N.M. 326, 404 P.2d 289 (1965) (ice on fairway); Lowe v. Gastonia, 211 N.C. 564, 191 S.E. 7 (1937) (defective bridge); Everett v. Goodwin, 201 N.C. 734, 161 S.E. 316 (1931) (failure to promulgate or enforce rules); Slotnick v. Cooley, 166 Tenn. 373, 61 S.W.2d 462 (1933) (employing a starter who allows one group to tee off before another group is out of range); Texaco Country Club v. Wade, 163 S.W.2d 219 (Tex. Civ. App. 1942) (defective electrical equipment). *See generally* Annot., 17 A.L.R.3d 1430 (1974) (defective golf carts). Liability for defective athletic equipment is considered at § 8.09, where many golf cart cases are discussed.

Liability has, however, been denied in a number of cases. United States v. Marshall, 391 F.2d 880 (5th Cir. 1968) (not negligent to rent golf cart to one who causes it to overturn); Gillespie v. Chevy Chase Golf Club, 187 Cal. App. 2d 52, 9 Cal. Rptr. 437 (1960) (not negligent to rent cart to man who would drink three beers on course); Campion v. Chicago Landscape Co., 295 Ill. App. 225, 14 N.E.2d 879 (1938); Pais v. Pontiac, 372 Mich. 582, 127 N.W.2d 386 (1964) (no negligence when golfer slipped on asphalt floor); Hutchins v. Southview Golf Club, 343 S.W.2d 323 (Mo. App. 1960) (*res ipsa* not apply to golf cart accident); Farfour v. Mimosa Golf Club, 240 N.C. 159, 81 S.E.2d 375 (1954) (hole containing water connections out of area of play not such a condition as to give rise to negligence liability). An owner or operator will also not be liable for the acts of independent contractors. Petrich v. New Orleans City Park Improvement Ass'n, 188 So. 199 (La. App. 1939) (golf professional), and, since they are not insurers of safety on their premises, will owe no duty to trespassing children who swim in water hazards. Mason v. Carroll, 289 Ala. 610, 269 So. 2d 879 (1972).

Ice and Roller Skating. Johnson v. County Arena, Inc., 29 Md. App. 674, 349 A.2d 643 (1976) (patron struck by guard); Farinelli v. Laventure, 342 Mass. 157, 172 N.E.2d 825 (1961) (patrons who do not observe rules); Ducas v. Prince, 336 Mass. 555, 146 N.E.2d 677 (1957) (broken laces on roller skates); Mackey v. Island Bob-Lo Co., 39 Mich. App. 64, 197 N.W.2d 151 (1972) (failure to remove water from roller rink); Humbyrd v. Spurlock, 345 S.W.2d 499 (Mo. App. 1961) (roller skate wheels locked); Schamel v. St. Louis Arena Corp., 324 S.W.2d 375 (Mo. App. 1959) (patrons who do not observe rules); Murphy v. Winter Garden & Ice Co., 280 S.W. 444 (Mo. App. 1926) (failure to prevent obvious misconduct of patrons); England v. State, 162 N.Y.S.2d 921 (Ct. Cl. 1957); Schmidt v. State, 100 N.Y.S.2d 504 (Ct. Cl. 1950) (defective surface); Filler v. Stenvick, 79 N.D. 422, 56 N.W.2d 798 (1953); Brown v. Tulsa Exposition & Fair Ass'n, 429 P.2d 767 (Okla. 1967) (defective surface on ice rink); Benoit v. Marvin, 120 Vt. 201, 138 A.2d 312 (1958) (water from leaking roof dripping on skating surface).

Racing. Hertz v. Graham, 292 F.2d 443 (2d Cir.), *cert. denied*, 368 U.S. 929, 7 L. Ed. 2d 192, 82 S. Ct. 366 (1961) (wild horse on race track); Shandy v. Sombrero Ranches, Inc., 525 P.3d 487 (Colo. App. 1974) (provision of flighty horse to beginning rider); McClain v. Lewiston Interstate Fair & Racing Ass'n, 17 Idaho 63, 104 P. 1015 (1909) (dog on horse racing course); Herendeen v. Hamilton, 317 Ill. App. 644, 47 N.E.2d 335 (1943) (improperly protected starting gate); North Manchester Tri-County Agricultural Ass'n v. Wilcox, 4 Ind. App. 141, 30 N.E. 202 (1892) (spectator on horse racing course); Fairmont Union Joint-Stock Agricultural Ass'n v. Downey, 146 Ind. 503, 45 N.E. 696 (1897) (horses going wrong direction); Nikolas v. Kirner, 247 Iowa 231, 73 N.W.2d 7 (1955) (wild horse on race track); Goodale v. Worcester Agricultural Soc'y, 102 Mass. 401 (1869) (horse and sulky on horse racing course); Hoyt v. Northern Maine Fair Ass'n, 121 Me. 461, 118 A. 290 (1922) (automobile on horse racing course); Maryland St. Fair & Ag. Soc., Inc. v. Lee, 29 Md. App. 374, 348 A.2d 44

demonstration, one player was to dash toward the basket, receive a softly thrown lead pass and then propel himself through the air and at the height of his leap "dunk" the ball through the hoop. When the player undertook this maneuver, however, he slipped on "something slick" and fell with a hard bang to the floor. The slick spot was actually a puddle of water which was the result of a defective roof known by the owner to be riddled with leaks. As a result of the fall, the player sustained, in addition to doubtlessly crushing ignominy, serious injuries which terminated his career as a professional athlete. The player brought suit against the owner of the arena, and the appellate court upheld a

---

(1975) (failure to maintain safe conditions); Lane v. Minnesota State Agricultural Soc'y, 62 Minn. 175, 64 N.W. 382 (1895) (wild horse on race track); Keaton v. Good, 350 S.W.2d 119 (Mo. 1961) (failure to maintain clear race course); Simmons v. Kansas City Jockey Club, 334 Mo. 99, 66 S.W.2d 119 (1933) (holes in fence around horse track); Hotels El Rancho v. Pray, 64 Nev. 591, 187 P.2d 568 (1947) (craters on horse track); Cole v. New York Racing Ass'n, 24 App. Div. 2d 933, 266 N.Y.S.2d 267 (1965), aff'd, 17 N.Y.2d 761, 217 N.E.2d 144 (1966) (raised concrete footing on guard rail); Killary v. Burlington-Lake Champlain Chamber of Commerce, Inc., 123 Vt. 256, 186 A.2d 170 (1962) (yachts on motor boat race course); Benedict v. Union Agricultural Soc'y, 74 Vt. 91, 52 A. 110 (1902) (horses on bicycle race course); Regan v. Seattle, 76 Wash. 2d 501, 458 P.2d 12 (1969) (water on race track).

Rodeo. Rosenberger v. Central Louisiana Dist. Livestock Show, Inc., 312 So.2d 300 (La. 1975) (failure to close gate).

Snowmobiling. Est. of Thomas v. Consumers Power Co., 58 Mich. App. 486, 228 N.W.2d 786 (1975) (no recovery when injury caused by improper lights on snowmobile); Isler v. Burman, 232 N.W.2d 818 (Minn. 1975) (insufficient inspection); Rock v. Concrete Materials, Inc., 46 App. Div. 2d 300, 362 N.Y.S.2d 258 (1975), *appeal dismissed,* 36 N.Y.2d 772, 368 N.Y.S.2d 841 (1975) (no recovery for existence of a condition that was not concealed and which was known to snowmobilers generally).

Swimming. Burgert v. Tietjens, 499 F.2d 1 (10th Cir. 1974) (murky water); Montes v. Betcher, 480 F.2d 1128 (8th Cir. 1973) (too shallow for diving); Boyce v. Pi Kappa Alpha Holding Corp., 476 F.2d 447 (5th Cir. 1973) (empty swimming pool); Keating v. Jones Development of Missouri, Inc., 398 F.2d 1011 (5th Cir. 1968) (lack of proper supervision); Adams v. United States, 239 F. Supp. 503 (E.D. Okla. 1965) (too shallow for rope swinging); Ide v. St. Cloud, 150 Fla. 806, 8 So. 2d 924 (1942) (deep hole off bathing beach); Pleasant v. Blue Mound Swim Club, 128 Ill. App. 2d 277, 262 N.E.2d 107 (1970) (presence of diving board implied representation that water sufficiently deep for diving); State v. Collier, — Ind. App. —, 331 N.E.2d 784 (1975) (lifeguard on surfboard in path of diver); Wong v. Waterloo Comm. School Dist., 232 N.W.2d 865 (Iowa 1975) (*res ipsa loquitur* not applicable to swimming pool death); Vukas v. Quivira, 166 Kan. 439, 201 P.2d 685 (1949) (too shallow for diving); Waddel's Adm'r v. Brashear, 257 Ky. 390, 78 S.W.2d 31 (1935) (too shallow for diving); Johnson v. Bauer, 292 Mass. 534, 198 N.E. 739 (1935); Bofysil v. State, 44 Mich. App. 118, 205 N.W.2d 222 (1972) (too shallow for diving); Perkins v. Byrnes, 364 Mo. 849, 269 S.W.2d 52, 48 A.L.R.2d 97 (1954) (high water and strong undercurrent in swimming area); McLaughlin v. Rova Farms, Inc., 56 N.J. 288, 266 A.2d 284 (1970) (too shallow for diving); Valls v. Paramus Bathing Beach, Inc., 46 N.J. Super. 353, 134 A.2d 743 (1957) (failure to prevent frolicking in pool); Levy v. Cascades Operating Corp., 289 N.Y. 714, 46 N.E.2d 343 (1942) (too shallow for sliding); Curcio v. New York, 275 N.Y. 20, 9 N.E.2d 760 (1937) (lack of proper supervision); Cummings v. Borough of Nazareth, 427 Pa. 14, 233 A.2d 874 (1967) (too shallow a pool a "dangerous instrumentality"); Childress v. Martens, 444 S.W.2d 362 (Tex. Civ. App. 1969) (iron pipe fell on swimmer); Fort Worth v. Barlow, 313 S.W.2d 906 (Tex. Civ. App. 1958) (too shallow for rope swinging); Grove v. D'Allessandro, 39 Wash. 2d 421, 235 P.2d 826 (1951) (too shallow for sliding); Gould v. Allstar Ins. Co., 59 Wis. 2d 355, 208 N.W.2d 388 (1973) (too shallow for diving, and "safe place" statute). Even if a warning is made by posting a sign, it will be effective as a bar to liability only if all participants had knowledge of its provisions and proceed with knowledge that the owner or operator has disclaimed any duty to protect them from the warned about danger. Blanchette v. Union St. Ry., 248 Mass. 407, 143 N.E. 310 (1924).

The owner or operator will also have a duty of having suitable persons in attendance, and necessary equipment on hand, so that swimmers who get in trouble may be properly rescued. Kopera v. Moschella, 400 F. Supp. 131 (S.D. Miss. 1975); Langheim v. Denison Fire Dep't. Swimming Pool Ass'n, 237 Iowa 386, 21 N.W.2d 295 (1946) (one lifeguard for 48 novice swimmers insufficient); Stillwell v. Louisville, 455 S.W.2d 56 (Ky. 1970); Williams v. Baton Rouge, 252 La. 770, 214 So. 2d 138 (1968) (negligence for lifeguard to refuse aid); Kreiner v. Yezdbick, 22 Mich. App. 581, 177 N.W.2d 629 (1970); Gluckauf v. Pine Lake Beach Club, Inc., 78 N.J. Super. 8, 187 A.2d 357 (1963); Harris v. Laquinta-Redbird Jt. Venture, 522 S.W.2d 232 (Tex. Civ. App. 1975). Liability may also

verdict in his favor,[48] finding that the owner had notice of the condition and had failed to exercise reasonable care to correct it.[49]

§ 8.03. Liability for Injury to Spectators.

There is always danger that sports activity will cause injury to spectators when errantly hit or thrown balls escape the field of play, when improperly driven race cars or horses leave the track, when wrestlers are thrown from the ring, or when over-eager tacklers pursue their game into the sidelines.[50] An injured spectator can be expected to seek recovery from the person who is responsible for those injuries. In these cases, the inquiry of the court will be similar to that which has already been considered with respect to injuries to participants.[51] Thus, although a court in a negligence case would normally analyze the duties and conduct of the defendant first, the spectator cases (like the participant cases) may be more easily analyzed by directing initial attention to the legal position of the spectator himself. From this point of reference, it should be noted first that most risks that attend athletic activities are normally readily apparent to any person of reasonable intelligence, even on the first visit to any given sport. In light of this apparent awareness of risk, the courts have evolved the general rule that spectators at sports activities assume, as a matter of law, all of the ordinary and inherent risks of the sport which they are observing.[52] This is frequently framed in terms of a "common knowledge"

result from rescue efforts. Brumm v. Goodall, 16 Ill. App. 2d 212, 147 N.E.2d 699 (1958) (allowing unidentified stranger to administer artificial respiration); Durham v. Commonwealth, 406 S.W.2d 858 (Ky. App. 1966) (hit swimmer's head while rescuing which caused death).

Simply because a swimmer is found dead in a swimming pool, however, raises no inference of negligence. Curcio v. New York, 275 N.Y. 20, 9 N.E.2d 760 (1937); Maher v. Madison Square Garden Corp., 242 N.Y. 506, 152 N.E. 403 (1926); Boldoc v. Coffin, 133 Vt. 167, 329 A.2d 655 (1974).

See generally, Annot., 48 A.L.R.2d 104 (1956).

48. The actual-holding of the case was that the player should have a new trial, since error had been committed during the first trial which had resulted in a jury verdict for the owner.

49. In reaching this conclusion, the court stated that the owner

owed a duty of care which required it to take such measures to provide a reasonably safe place for the purposes of the invitation extended to plaintiff, namely, the playing of basketball . . . . It seems to us, . . . that in order for defendant (the owner) to exculpate itself from a finding of negligence on its part, it had to show one of two things: first, that having become aware of the leaky roof, it had undertaken such action which would assure a reasonable auditorium owner that all the leaks in its building were corrected — in substance, to make certain that its building was watertight; or secondly, show, as an alternative to eliminating all the leaks, it had apprised plaintiff, before his scheduled performance on the court, of the actual conditions of the building and at the same time issued him a warning of the risk of harm which those conditions presented to anyone choosing to play basketball at defendant's auditorium.

104 R.I. at 129, 242 A.2d at 415. *Compare* Nunez v. Isidore Newman High School, 306 So.2d 457 (La. App. 1975) (no liability for moisture on floor when it was found not be be in unreasonably dangerous condition).

50. The danger to spectators at sports events has been well summarized, as follows:

A defect inherent in the nature of man is that perversity of spirit which attracts us to spectacles of danger in which our fellow men risk death for our amusement. Although the events in the coliseums of ancient Rome were somewhat different from those held in their modern counterparts, spectators were perhaps subject to similar risks for there must have been occasions when a lion escaped the arena to prowl among the patrons or a gladiator lost control of his weapon to the detriment of a front row observer. Capital Raceway Promotions, Inc. v. Smith, 22 Md. App. 224, 322 A.2d 238 (1974).

51. *See* § 8.02.

52. *See generally* Restatement (Second) of Torts § 496C, illustration 4 (1965); 2 F. Harper & F. James, The Law of Torts §§ 21.2, at 1169-70, 21.3, at 1183-84 (1956); Colapietro, *The*

rule—that is, that the risks posed to spectators at sports activities are such a matter of common knowledge that any person of reasonable intelligence could not help but realize their potentiality and must, for that reason, be deemed to have accepted or assumed the risk of injury therefrom as a matter of law.

Promoter's Liability for Sports Spectator Injuries, 46 CORNELL L.Q. 140 (1960); James, *Assumption of Risk,* 61 YALE L.J. 141, 148, 159-60, 161-62 (1952); Keeton, *Personal Injuries from Open and Obvious Conditions,* 100 U. PA. L. REV. 629, 640-41 (1952); Malone, *Contributory Negligence and the Landowner Cases,* 29 MINN. L. REV. 71, 75-80 (1945); Thomas, *Torts: Liability of Exhibitor to Spectators at Public Exhibitions: Assumption of the Risk,* 24 CALIF. L. REV. 429 (1936); Note, *Injuries to Spectators in the Course of Sporting Activities,* 25 MOD. L. REV. 738 (1962); Note, *Negligence — Landowners — Duty of Baseball Club to Protect Invitees from Injurious Acts of Third Parties,* 12 VAND. L. REV. 299 (1958).

The application of this principle to specfic sports is considered in the following cases:

Baseball. The application of the general rule in the baseball cases is best illustrated by Hudson v. Kansas City Baseball Club, 164 S.W.2d 318 (Mo. 1942), *noted in* 41 MICH. L. REV. 742 (1943), involving a sixty-four year old man who was a fee paying invitee at a baseball doubleheader. He requested the "best reserved seat" and was escorted to the grandstand, where there was no screen, though he alleged that he had stated a desire for a screened seat. Thereafter, he was struck and injured by a foul ball, and brought suit against the operator of the stadium. In affirming a judgment for the operator, the court reviewed in detail the cases relating to baseball spectator injuries and stated that

> [t]he plaintiff says he was 'subject to the ordinary impairments of eyesight' of a man sixty-four years of age, but he does not say his vision was so impaired that he could not see that which was plainly before him. By reason of his attending the game we do not suppose he would have us infer that his allegation means anything less than that his vision was that of the ordinary person of that age and that he could see the obvious.
>
> Because of the special circumstances of his intention, his past experience and his impression he says the defendant was therefore negligent in not screening a specified area of the grandstand; in selling seats without a definite classification and notice as to whether they were screened or not; in selling reserved seats of both classes of seats, screened and unscreened, and thereby creating a false impression that a reserved seat was protected and giving the plaintiff reason to believe a screened seat would be protected and in failing to notify him that the designated seat he purchased was unscreened.
>
> Assuming that all the plaintiff's allegations are true, yet there is nothing in them indicating that he was not fully aware of the obvious fact that he was sitting in an unscreened area of the grandstand and subject to the well known personal hazards of a ball game, especially that of being hit by a foul ball. Even though the defendant did not screen a given section of the grandstand, even though there may have been some confusion about the manner of the defendant's selling seats, etc., yet the plaintiff while watching the game 'which was then going on' (he does not say how long) must have seen that he was not sitting behind a wire screen. Despite his allegations of negligence we yet have a condition so open and obvious that it was apparent or would have been had he been looking. Because of these allegations he cannot be said to have lost his former knowledge of the facts of baseball, the hazards and perils usually incident to the game, as well as the position of the spectator. The most that can be said for the special circumstances of his past experience, his present intention and impression is that he knew he was sitting in an unscreened area where he might be struck by a foul ball, but simply forgot it or ignored the fact, neither of which is excused by his allegation. [citations omitted]. He, therefore, voluntarily elected to watch the game with full knowledge of the dangers incident to it and of the possibility of injury to himself and his petition does not contain averments of special circumstances which, if true, would entitle him to recover. 164 S.W.2d at 324-25.

See also Quinn v. Recreation Park, 3 Cal. 2d 725, 46 P.2d 144 (1935); Mann v. Nutrilite, Inc., 136 Cal. App. 2d 729, 289 P.2d 282 (1955); Brown v. San Francisco Ball Club, 99 Cal. App. 2d 484, 222 P.2d 19 (1950); Ratcliff v. San Diego Baseball Club of the Pacific Coast League, 27 Cal. App. 2d 733, 81 P.2d 625 (1938) (batting practice); Hunt v. Thomasville Baseball Co., 80 Ga. App. 572, 56 S.E.2d 828 (1949) (practice); Maytnier v. Rush, 80 Ill. App. 2d 336, 225 N.E.2d 83 (1967) (rule not apply to ball thrown from bullpen); Emhardt v. Perry Stadium, 113 Ind. App. 197, 46 N.E.2d 704 (1943); Benedetto v. Travelers Ins. Co., 172 So. 2d 354 (La. 1965); Lorino v. New Orleans Baseball & Amusement Co., 16 La. App. 95, 133 So. 408 (1931) (practice); Jones v. Alexandria Baseball Ass'n, 50 So. 2d 93 (La. App. 1951); Shaw v. Boston American League Baseball Co., 325 Mass. 419, 90 N.E.2d 840 (1950); Blakeley v. White Star Line, 154 Mich. 635, 118 N.W. 482 (1908); Aldes v. Saint Paul Ball Club, 251 Minn. 440, 88 N.W.2d 94 (1958); Christianson v. Hager, 242 Minn. 41, 64 N.W.2d 35 (1954)

Probably the most elaborate illustration of the rule was given by Lord Justice
Greer in the classic English decision in *Hall v. Brooklands Auto Racing*

(assault by another spectator); Brisson v. Minneapolis Baseball & Athletic Ass'n, 185 Minn. 507, 240
N.W. 903 (1932); Wells v. Minneapolis Baseball & Athletic Ass'n, 122 Minn. 327, 142 N.W. 706 (1913);
Anderson v. Kansas City Baseball Club, 231 S.W.2d 170 (Mo. 1950); Hudson v. Kansas City Baseball
Club, 164 S.W.2d 318 (Mo. 1942); Brummerhoff v. St. Louis National Baseball Club, 149 S.W.2d 382
(Mo. App. 1941) (practice); Grimes v. American League Baseball Co., 78 S.W.2d 520 (Mo. App. 1935);
Olds v. St. Louis National Baseball Club, 232 Mo. App. 897, 104 S.W.2d 746 (1937) and 119 S.W.2d
1000 (Mo. App. 1938); Edling v. Kansas City Baseball & Exhibition Co., 181 Mo. App. 327, 168 S.W.
908 (1914); Crane v. Kansas City Baseball & Exhibition Co., 168 Mo. App. 301, 153 S.W. 1076 (1913);
Berrum v. Powalisz, 73 Nev. 291, 317 P.2d 1090 (1957); Philpot v. Brooklyn National League Baseball
Club, 303 N.Y. 116, 100 N.E.2d 164 (1951) (hit by beer bottle); Kozera v. Hamburg, 40 App. Div. 2d
934, 337 N.Y.S.2d 761 (1972) (practice); Robert v. Deposit Central School District No. 1, 18 App. Div.
2d 947, 237 N.Y.S.2d 680 (1963); Baker v. Topping, 15 App. Div. 2d 193, 222 N.Y.S.2d 658 (1961);
Zeitz v. Cooperstown Baseball Centennial, 31 Misc.2d 142, 29 N.Y.S.2d 55 (1941) (batting practice);
Adonnino v. Village of Mount Morris, 171 Misc. 383, 12 N.Y.S.2d 658 (1939); Blackhall v. Albany
Baseball & Amusement Co., 157 Misc. 801, 285 N.Y.S. 695 (1936) (batting practice); Cates v.
Cincinnati Exhibition Co., 215 N.C. 64, 1 S.E.2d 131 (1939); Cincinnati Baseball Club v. Eno, 112 Ohio
St. 175, 147 N.E. 86 (1925) (common knowledge rule not apply during practice session); Stradtner
v. Cincinnati Reds, Inc., 39 Ohio App. 2d 199, 316 N.E.2d 924 (1972); Hummel v. Columbus Baseball
Club, 49 Ohio App. 321, 49 N.E.2d 773 (1943); Ivory v. Cincinnati Baseball Club Co., 62 Ohio App.
514, 24 N.E.2d 837 (1939); Lang v. Amateur Softball Ass'n of America, 520 P.2d 659 (Okla. 1974);
Hull v. Oklahoma City Baseball Co., 196 Okla. 40, 163 P.2d 982 (1945); Hunt v. Portland Baseball
Club, 207 Ore. 337, 296 P.2d 495 (1956), *noted in* 1 WILLAMETTE L. J. 405 (1960); Curtis v. Portland
Baseball Club, 130 Ore. 93, 279 P. 277 (1929); Iervolino v. Pittsburgh Athletic Co., 212 Pa. Super.
330, 243 A.2d 490 (1968); Schentzel v. Philadelphia National League Club, 173 Pa. Super. 179, 96
A.2d 181 (1953); Kallish v. American Baseball Club of Philadelphia, 138 Pa. Super. 602, 10 A.2d 831
(1940) (injury due to overcrowding of arena); McNiel v. Fort Worth Baseball Club, 268 S.W.2d 244
(Tex. Civ. App. 1954) (batting practice); Knebel v. Jones, 266 S.W.2d 470 (Tex. Civ. App. 1954);
Williams v. Houston Baseball Ass'n, 154 S.W.2d 874 (Tex. Civ. App. 1941); Hamilton v. Salt Lake
City, 120 Utah 647, 237 P.2d 841 (1951); Leek v. Tacoma Baseball Club, 38 Wash.2d 362, 229 P.2d
329 (1951); Kafavian v. Seattle Baseball Club Ass'n, 105 Wash. 215, 181 P. 679 (1919); Powless v.
Milwaukee County, 6 Wis. 2d 78, 94 N.W.2d 187 (1959); Lee v. National League Baseball Club of
Milwaukee, 4 Wis. 2d 168, 89 N.W.2d 811 (1958), *noted in* 18 MD. L. REV. 355 (1958); 32 TEMPLE L.Q.
127 (1958).

See generally Note, *Duty of Baseball Club to Spectator,* 24 MICH. L. REV. 76 (1925); Note, *Theaters
and Shows — Assumption of Risk — Spectators at a Baseball Game,* 17 MICH. L. REV. 594 (1919);
Note, *The Liability of Proprietor of a Baseball Park for Injuries to Spectators Struck by Batted or
Thrown Balls,* [1951] WASH. U.L.Q. 434; Annot., 16 A.L.R.2d 912 (1951); Annot., 142 A.L.R. 868
(1942).

Football. Colclough v. Orleans Parish School Bd., 166 So. 2d 647 (La. App. 1964); Ingerson v.
Shattuck School, 185 Minn. 16, 239 N.W. 667 (1931), *noted in* 30 MICH. L. REV. 1121 (1932); Cadieux
v. Board of Educ. of Schenectady, 25 App. Div. 2d 579, 266 N.Y.S.2d 895 (1966); Perry v. Seattle
School Dist. No. 1, 66 Wash. 2d 800, 405 P.2d 589 (1965). *See generally* Colapietro, *The Promoter's
Liability for Sports Spectator Injuries,* 46 CORNELL L.Q. 140, 155 (1960). A similar rule was stated
by the King's Bench in Hall v. Brooklands Auto Racing Club, [1933] 1 K.C. 205, 214-15, where football
was used as a "common case" of the spectator assumption of the risk rule. *See also* Weldy v. Oakland
High School Dist. of Alameda County, 19 Cal. App. 2d 429, 65 P.2d 851 (1937) (no recovery for
spectator hit by glass bottle at football game).

Golf. Thompson v. Sunset Country Club, 227 S.W.2d 523 (Mo. App. 1950) (tripped over rock in high
rough during tournament).

Hockey. See notes 55-56 *infra.*

Racing. Barrett v. Faltico, 117 F. Supp. 95 (E.D. Wash. 1953); Morton v. California Sports Car Club,
163 Cal. App. 2d 685, 329 P.2d 967 (1958); Jerrell v. Harrisburg Fair & Park Ass'n, 215 Ill. App. 273
(1919); Johnson v. City of New York, 186 N.Y. 139, 78 N.E. 715 (1906); Baldwin v. Locomobile Co.
of America, 143 App. Div. 599, 128 N.Y.S. 429, *aff'd,* 147 App.Div. 901, 131 N.Y.S. 1103 (1911); Blake
v. Fried, 173 Pa. Super. 27, 95 A.2d 360 (1953). *But cf.* Goade v. Elks, Lodge 789, 213 Cal. App. 2d
189, 28 Cal. Rptr. 669 (1963) (not apply rule as a matter of law). *See generally* 2 BLASHFIELD,
AUTOMOBILE LAW & PRACTICE § 102.38 (1965). *See also* James v. Columbia County Agricultural,
Horticultural & Mechanical Ass'n, 321 Pa. 465, 184 A. 447 (1936) (horse slipping on muddy track
is ordinary and inherent risk of horse racing).

In addition to injuries suffered by spectators at motor and horse races, injuries have also been
sustained by spectators at soap box derby events, which are races conducted by

Club.[53] *In holding that a spectator at a sports car race could not recover for injuries suffered when a car hurtled into the spectator area, he stated that*

> [a] spectator at Lord's or the Oval runs the risk of being hit by a cricket ball, or coming into collision with a fielder running hard to stop a ball from going over the boundary, and himself tumbling over the boundary in doing so. Spectators at football or hockey or polo matches run similar risks both from the ball and from collisions with the players or polo ponies. Spectators who pay for admission to golf courses to witness important matches, though they keep beyond the boundaries required by the stewards, run the risk of the players slicing or pulling balls which may hit them with considerable velocity and damage. Those who pay for admission or seats in stands at a flying meeting run a risk of the performing aeroplanes falling on their heads.[54]

Although most courts have applied the "common knowledge" rule, it has not found universal acceptance. This has been especially true where the risks of a given sport are found not to be a matter of common knowledge because it is a new activity in the locale in which the injury occurred. The difficulty in applying the "common knowledge" rule in such situations is best exemplified by the cases which have involved injuries suffered by spectators at hockey matches, where the primary cause of spectator injuries has been pucks propelled from the iced playing surface into the crowd surrounding the rink. With respect to such injuries, the courts have been unable to agree upon whether the "common knowledge" rule should apply to prevent recovery as a matter of law. The majority have concluded that the risks of watching a hockey match are not of such common knowledge as to hold that spectators assume, as a matter of law, the risks of injury therefrom.[55] Many other courts have, however, adopted

---

momentum-propelled, home-made vehicles driven by children. These races are ordinarily sponsored by local businessmen and are conducted over a specially marked-off portion of a sufficiently inclined public street, and usually have only the most rudimentary means of protecting spectators from out-of-control racers. Under these circumstances, the courts have not been able to construct a legal rule of general application, preferring, rather, to treat the cases as presenting issues of fact that are to be decided by the triers of fact. Watford v. Evening Star Newspaper Co., 211 F.2d 31 (D.C. Cir. 1954); Cummings v. General Motors Corp., 146 Conn. 443, 151 A.2d 884 (1959); Macon Telegraph Publishing Co. v. Graden, 79 Ga. App. 230, 53 S.E.2d 371 (1949); Murphy v. Jarvis Chevrolet Co., 310 Ill. App. 534, 34 N.E.2d 872 (1941); Bango v. Carteret Lions Club, 12 N.J. Super. 52, 79 A.2d 57 (1951); Schaaf v. Record Publishing Co. of Erie, 35 Erie Co. L.J. 53 (1949). *See generally* Annot., 72 A.L.R.2d 1137 (1960). Thus, in the soap box derby races the courts have not felt, as they have with spectator injuries in other sports, that the dangers involved are sufficiently a matter of common knowledge to justify the application of a rule barring recovery for all injuries that are the result of dangers which are an ordinary and obvious part of the sport in question. Soap box derbies are, however, phenomena that present the same dangers as do ordinary auto races — that is, of the racers leaving the race course and injuring spectators — and, as such, should be subject to the same legal rules. Macon Telegraph Publishing Co. v. Graden, 79 Ga. App. 230, 53 S.E.2d 371 (1949) (Felton, J., dissenting); Judd v. Scranton Republican, 32 Pa. D. & C. 712 (1938).

Wrestling and Boxing. Davis v. Jones, 100 Ga. App. 546, 112 S.E.2d 3 (1959) (wrestler diving out of ring); Klause v. Nebraska State Board of Agriculture, 150 Neb. 466, 35 N.W.2d 104 (1948); Pierce v. Murnick, 265 N.C. 707, 145 S.E.2d 11 (1965) (wrestler thrown out of ring); Whitfield v. Cox, 189 Va. 219, 52 S.E.2d 72 (1949). *But cf.* Silvia v. Woodhouse, 356 Mass. 119, 248 N.E.2d 260 (1969); Caldwell v. Maupin, 61 Ohio App. 161, 22 N.E.2d 454 (1939); Dusckiewicz v. Carter, 115 Vt. 122, 52 A.2d 788 (1947). *See also* Uhrich v. Minneapolis Boxing and Wrestling Club, 268 Minn. 328, 129 N.W.2d 288 (1964) (spectator causing own injury). *See generally* Annot., 14 A.L.R.3d 993 (1967).

    53. [1933] 1 K.B. 205, [1932] All E.R. 208. *See also* Murray v. Harringay Arena, Ltd., [1951] 2 K.B. 529, 534.

    54. [1933] 1 K.B. at 209, [1932] All E.R. at 210.

    55. Thus, in Thurman v. Ice Palace, 36 Cal. App. 2d 364, 97 P.2d 999 (1939), the court observed that the "common knowledge" rule applied in the baseball cases was inapplicable to hockey injuries

the "common knowledge" rule invoked with respect to other sports.[56] Inasmuch as the basis for the assumption of risk doctrine is the plaintiff's voluntary consent to accept risk and look out for himself, it is entirely appropriate to inquire whether those in the locality of the injury would be aware of the risks and dangers of watching hockey matches. Where that inquiry shows that the risks and dangers are commonly known, then it will be appropriate to apply the "common knowledge" rule, but where they are not so known, then it should not be applied. Since it is this analysis that courts following each position have applied, their results are not inconsistent; they represent, rather, different conclusions as to the general level of knowledge in the localities in question. When hockey is as much a matter of common knowledge as is baseball, then the courts will surely implement the general "common knowledge" rule.

While the general rule will, thus, preclude the spectator from recovering for many injuries suffered while attending a sports activity, it does not by any means always prevent recovery. The spectator will be deemed to have assumed only the ordinary and inherent risks of attending a sports activity and will not assume other risks.[57]

for the reason that the average person of ordinary intelligence in this country is familiar with the game of baseball and it is reasonable to presume that such person appreciates the risk of being hit by a pitched or batted ball without being specifically warned of the danger. Hence a spectator at this nationally-known game may ordinarily be held to assume such a risk. However, the average person does not have the same knowledge respecting ice hockey or the risk of being hit by a flying puck while observing such a game. The game of ice hockey is practically a new game so far as the state of California is concerned and has only been played at regular intervals in this state for approximately twelve years last past. 36 Cal.App.2d at 368, 97 P.2d at 1001.

See also Uline Ice, Inc. v. Neely, 255 F.2d 540 (D.C. Cir. 1958); Uline Ice, Inc. v. Sullivan, 187 F.2d 82 (D.C. Cir. 1950); Shurman v. Fresno Ice Rink, 91 Cal. App. 2d 469, 205 P.2d 77 (1949); Thurman v. Clune, 51 Cal.App.2d 505, 125 P.2d 59 (1942); Thurman v. Ice Palace, 36 Cal.App.2d 364, 97 P.2d 999 (1940); Lemoine v. Springfield Hockey Ass'n, 307 Mass. 102, 29 N.E.2d 716 (1940); Shanney v. Boston Madison Square Garden Corp., 296 Mass. 168, 5 N.E.2d 1 (1936); Tite v. Omaha Coliseum Corp., 144 Neb. 22, 12 N.W.2d 90 (1943); Aaser v. Charlotte, 265 N.C. 494, 144 S.E.2d 610 (1965); Morris v. Cleveland Hockey Club, 157 Ohio St. 225, 105 N.E.2d 419 (1952), *noted in* 26 TEMPLE L. REV. 206 (1952), and 22 U. CINN. L. REV. 118 (1953); James v. Rhode Island Auditorium, 60 R.I. 405, 199 A. 293 (1938).

56. As representing the courts which have adopted the "common knowledge" rule, Sutherland v. Onondaga Hockey Club, 245 App.Div. 137, 281 N.Y.S. 505 (1935), is probably the most explicit. In affirming a verdict adverse to a spectator who had been struck by a flying puck, the court stated that she

occupied precisely the same status as a spectator at a baseball game and that the same rules should be applied in each instance. There was no obligation on the part of the respondents to protect appellants against a danger incident to the entertainment which any reasonable spectator could foresee and of which she took the risk. The risk of being hit by a baseball or by a puck at a hockey game is a risk incidental to the entertainment and is assumed by the spectators. . . . . It is common knowledge that the puck may leave the ice when the players are shooting for a goal. 245 App.Div. at 319, 281 N.Y.S. at 508.

There was, however, a strong dissent in *Sutherland,* advocating a contrary result. *Id.* at 140-43, 281 N.Y.S. at 509-12. *See also* Murray v. Harringay Arena, Ltd., [1951] 2 K.B. 529, [1951] 2 All E.R. 320; Elliott v. Amphitheatre Ltd., [1943] 3 W.W.Rep. 225; Modec v. Eveleth, 224 Minn. 556, 29 N.W.2d 453 (1947), *noted in* 31 MARQ. L. REV. 298 (1948); Sutherland v. Onondoga Hockey Club, 245 App.Div. 137, 281 N.Y.S. 505 (1935), *noted in* 10 So. CAL. L. REV. 67 (1936); Hammel v. Madison Square Garden Corp., 156 Misc. 311, 279 N.Y.S. 815 (1935).

See generally Annot., 14 A.L.R.3d 1018 (1967); Annot., 149 A.L.R. 1174 (1944).

57. This principle is illustrated by the following cases:

Baseball. Bonetti v. Double Play Tavern, 126 Cal.App. 2d 848, 274 P.2d 751 (1954) (a ball thrown into the stands by a player frustrated over his having dropped a pop fly that lost his team a championship); Atlanta Baseball Co. v. Lawrence, 38 Ga. 497, 144 S.E. 351 (1928) (player charged into stands and assaulted spectator).

The most important risk that the spectator will not assume is the risk that the owner or operator of the arena in which the sports event is conducted will fail to meet its duty of care.[58] As business invitors, the operators of sports facilities will be liable for conditions on their premises which cause physical harm to invitee-spectators if they know, or should reasonably have discovered, that the condition exists, that it poses an unreasonable risk of harm which the invitee-spectators will not discover or protect themselves against, and fail to exercise reasonable care for their protection.[59] Thus, the operators have the duty

Basketball. McFatridge v. Harlem Globe Trotters, 69 N.M. 271, 365 P.2d 918, 89 A.L.R.2d 1154 (1961) (player hit spectator with basketball in attempt to perform trick shot with a basket on the side of the court).

58. Waiver and release of liability by spectators is considered at § 8.04.

59. RESTATEMENT (SECOND) OF TORTS § 343 (1965); Hartzell v. United States, 539 F.2d 65 (10th Cir. 1967). *See* § 8.02. As noted in § 8.02, at note 41, the term "operators" will be used to cover all invitors.

The duty of the operators of athletic facilities to protect invitee-spectators from defective conditions has received judical attention most frequently in cases involving seating facilities. In these circumstances, large groups of patrons are typically confined at close quarters, and some can be expected to move about in response to the excitement of the contest. The courts have held that the duty of reasonable care requires that the operators provide their invitees with reasonably safe places to sit and watch the contest, having due regard for the character of the exhibition being presented and the customary conduct of spectators — who, it has been observed, do not "comport themselves as would staid adults witnessing a religious drama." Wright v. Downing, 116 Utah 465, 211 P.2d 211 (1949). *See also* Schofield v. Wood, 170 Mass. 415, 49 N.E. 636 (1898); Lawson v. Clawson, 177 Md. 333, 9 A.2d 755 (1939); Parker v. Warren, 503 S.W.2d 938 (Tenn. App. 1973). *See generally* Annot., 21 A.L.R.2d 420 (1952); Annot., 14 A.L.R.3d 993, 1003-07 (1967). When invitee-spectators use seating facilities at sports events, moreover, they are entitled to rely upon their safe condition and are not expected to conduct their own inspection. Scott v. University of Michigan Athletic Ass'n, 152 Mich. 684, 116 N.W. 624 (1908); Miratsky v. Beseda, 139 Neb. 229, 297 N.W. 94 (1941).

Thus, an essential element of an operator's duty will be to make reasonably thorough inspections of the seating facilities from time to time to insure that they are safe for occupancy. Lawson v. Clawson, 177 Md. 333, 9 A.2d 755 (1939). If such inspections are not made on a timely basis, or are made in an improper manner, the owner or operator will be charged with the knowledge that would have been revealed therefrom, even if the defective condition is concealed. Logan v. Agricultural Soc'y of Lenawee County, 156 Mich. 537, 121 N.W. 485 (1909). A municipal inspection will not, however, necessarily preclude a finding of negligence, inasmuch as such inspections may be little more than mere formalities. Hardy v. Philadelphia National League Club, 99 Pa. Super. 326 (1929).

Applying these general rules, the courts have held operators liable for injuries suffered when the seating structure simply collapsed, Schweikert v. Palm Beach Speedway, 100 So.2d 804 (Fla. 1958); Lawson v. Clawson, 177 Md. 333, 9 A.2d 755 (1939); Brown v. Cleveland Baseball Co., 158 Ohio St. 1, 106 N.E.2d 632 (1952); Winterow v. Christensen, 68 Utah 546, 251 P. 360 (1926); Hayward v. Downing, 112 Utah 508, 189 P.2d 442 (1948); when a bench was unable to withstand the predictable displays of excitement by spectators, Welsh v. Jefferson County Agri. Soc'y, 121 Neb. 166, 236 N.W. 331 (1931); Gallin v. Polo Grounds Athletic Club, 126 Misc. 550, 214 N.Y.S. 182 (1926); when there was a hole in the pathway from the seats, Johnson v. Zemel, 109 N.J. Law 197, 160 A. 356 (1932); when seats were not attached to floor as required by public safety regulations, Camp v. Rex, Inc., 304 Mass. 484, 24 N.E.2d 4 (1939); when railings were unable to withstand spectators leaning upon them, Agricultural & Mechanical Ass'n of Washington County v. Gray, 118 Md. 600, 85 A. 291 (1912); Schofield v. Wood, 170 Mass. 415, 49 N.E. 636 (1898) (at polo match); when there were no braces, or other structures, to protect those sitting on the highest row of the bleachers, Jackson v. McFadden, 181 Miss. 1, 177 So. 755 (1937); Witherspoon v. Haft, 157 Ohio St. 474, 106 N.E.2d 296 (1952); Stroud v. Bridges, 275 S.W.2d 503 (Tex. Civ. App. 1955); Bent v. Jonet, 213 Wis. 635, 252 N.W. 290 (1934); when bolts were allowed to come loose, Board of Educ. of Richmond County v. Fredericks, 113 Ga. App. 199, 147 S.E.2d 789 (1966); *see also* Cachik v. United States, 161 F. Supp. 15 (S.D. Ill. 1958) (bleacher blew over due to insufficient anchor); when rotten planks were used in the construction of bleachers, Taylor v. Hardee, 232 S.C. 338, 102 S.E.2d 218 (1958); Tri-State Fair v. Rowton, 140 Tenn. 304, 204 S.W. 761 (1918); and when needed repairs were not undertaken. Sawaya v. Tucson High School Dist. No. 1 of Pima County, 78 Ariz. 389, 281 P.2d 105 (1955); Tulsa Entertainment Co. v. Greenlees, 85 Okla. 113, 205 P. 179 (1922); Bruss v. Milwaukee Sporting Goods Co., 34 Wis. 2d 688, 150 N.W.2d 337 (1967); *see also* Kasper v. Buffalo Bills of Western New York, 42 App. Div. 2d 87, 345 N.Y.S.2d 244 (1973) (discussing evidentiary problems in a bleacher case).

to maintain the premises in a reasonably safe condition and to supervise the conduct of those on the premises to prevent injury.[60] Therefore, a spectator

The collapse of bleachers would also appear to be an appropriate event for the application of the doctrine of *res ipsa loquitur,* which is an evidentiary principle that shifts the burden of proof from the plaintiff to the defendant. The elements of the doctrine are usually stated to be that the injury 1) was of a kind that does not ordinarily occur in the absence of someone's negligence; 2) was caused by an event or instrumentality within the exclusive control of the defendant; and 3) was not due to any voluntary action or contribution of the plaintiff. *See* 9 J. WIGMORE, EVIDENCE § 2509 (3rd ed. 1940). Where these elements have been present, several courts have applied the *res ipsa loquitur* rule to bleacher-fall cases. Thus, in Miratsky v. Beseda, 139 Neb. 229, 297 N.W. 94 (1941), the court stated that

> [i]n the ordinary course of things, such bleachers do not collapse if proper care is used in their construction and maintenance. The collapse of the bleachers affords reasonable evidence, in the absence of explanation by the defendant, that the accident arose from a want of care. 139 Neb. at 232, 297 N.W. at 95.

See also Parker v. Warren, 503 S.W.2d 938 (Tenn. App. 1973).

60. These principles have been applied in the following cases:

Baseball. The primary risk in the game of baseball that may, under some circumstances, be unreasonable, is the risk posed by errant balls, inasmuch as they "are thrown and batted with great force and swiftness . . . often go in the direction of the spectators." Blakely v. White Star Line, 154 Mich. 635, 118 N.W. 482 (1908); Wells v. Minneapolis Baseball and Athletic Ass'n, 122 Minn. 327, 142 N.W. 706 (1913); Crane v. Kansas City Baseball and Exhibition Co., 168 Mo. App. 301, 153 S.W. 1076 (1913); Cincinnati Baseball Club v. Eno, 112 Ohio St. 175, 147 N.E. 86 (1925). To protect their spectators against this risk, it has almost universally been stated that the owners or operators have a duty to provide some seats that are protected by screens from errant balls to those spectators who desire, and are willing to pay for, such protection. Hummel v. Columbus Baseball Club, 71 Ohio App. 321, 49 N.E.2d 773 (1943); Grimes v. American League Baseball Co., 78 S.W.2d 520 (Mo. App. 1935); Cates v. Cincinnati Exhibition Co., 215 N.C. 64, 1 S.E.2d 131 (1939). The requirement for providing some screens does not, however, require that overhead protection be provided as well, Cates v. Cincinnati Exhibition Co., 215 N.C. 64, 1 S.E.2d 131 (1939) (no roof needed over bleachers); Leek v. Tacoma Baseball Club, 38 Wash. 2d 362, 229 P.2d 329 (1951) (perpendicular backstop screen sufficient), or that provision of screens be made for all seats, since many spectators would desire seats unhindered by such an obstruction. Anderson v. Kansas City Baseball Club, 231 S.W.2d 170 (Mo. 1950); Cates v. Cincinnati Exhibition Co., 215 N.C. 64, 1 S.E.2d 131 (1939). The fact that a particular spectator sought, but could not get, a screened seat, because of the inordinately large crowd, will not itself be a sufficient basis of liability. Quinn v. Recreation Park, 3 Cal. 2d 725, 46 P.2d 144 (1935); Shaw v. Boston American League Baseball Co., 325 Mass. 419, 90 N.E. 2d 840 (1950); Schentzel v. Philadelphia National League Club, 173 Pa. Super. 179, 96 A.2d 181 (1953). It will be sufficient if the operator provides as many screened seats as will be required under ordinary circumstances. Cates v. Cincinnati Exhibition Co., 215 N.C. 64, 1 S.E.2d 131 (1939).

Cases allowing baseball spectators recovery have also included the following: Cincinnati Baseball Club Co. v. Hines, 264 F.2d 60 (6th Cir. 1959) (sticky substance in grandstand); Atlanta Baseball Co. v. Lawrence, 38 Ga. 497, 144 S.E. 351 (1928) (player charged into stands and assaulted spectator); Emhardt v. Perry Stadium, 113 Ind. App. 197, 46 N.E.2d 704 (1943) (hit by ball thrown by another spectator, which was apparently a common practice at this ball park); Dean v. Martz, 329 S.W.2d 371 (Ky. 1959) (ball through screen); Aldes v. Saint Paul Ball Club, 251 Minn. 440, 88 N.W.2d 94, 16 A.L.R.2d 904 (1958) (where an usher asked a spectator, out of friendship, to take a more dangerous seat); Olds v. St. Louis National Baseball Club, 119 S.W.2d 1000 (Mo. App. 1938) (the protective screen did not extend to an exit so that a spectator could enter, sit and leave without fear of being struck by errant balls, *but cf.* Baker v. Topping, 15 App. Div. 2d 193, 222 N.Y.S.2d 658 (1961) (no recovery for spectator hit while being shown to seat, with the court declaring *Olds* to be against the great weight of authority and to be in the minority rule)); Hughes v. St. Louis National League Baseball Club, 359 Mo. 993, 224 S.W.2d 989 (1949) (injury caused by skylarking boys hired to pick up cushions after a game); Grimes v. American League Baseball Co., 78 S.W.2d 520 (Mo. App. 1935) (temporary bleachers installed for a forthcoming World Series game which deflected a ball); Edling v. Kansas City Baseball & Exhibition Co., 181 Mo. App. 327, 168 S.W. 908 (1914) (defective screen allowing ball to pass through); Berrum v. Powalisz, 73 Nev. 291, 317 P.2d 1090 (1957) (holes in wire screen allowing passage of a part of a Little Leaguer's bat); Lee v. National League Baseball Club of Milwaukee, 4 Wis. 2d 168, 89 N.W.2d 811 (1958) (trampled in a scramble for a foul ball).

Football. Brown v. Cleveland Baseball Co., 158 Ohio St. 1, 106 N.E.2d 632 (1952) (bleacher collapse); Witherspoon v. Haft, 157 Ohio St. 474, 106 N.E.2d 296 (1952) (same); Kasper v. Buffalo Bills of Western New York, 42 App. Div. 2d 87, 345 N.Y.S.2d 244 (1973) (same).

using an athletic facility may assume that the operator has exercised reasonable care to make the facilities safe for the purposes of the invitation. This will include the original construction of the premises, as well as any subsequent

Golf. Rockwell v. Hillcrest Country Club, Inc., 25 Mich. App. 276, 181 N.W.2d 290 (1970) (spectator was injured when an over-crowded bridge collapsed, and the club failed to exercise reasonable care for the protection of the spectators); Buck v. Clauson's Inn at Coonamessett, Inc., 349 Mass. 612, 211 N.E.2d 349 (1965) (spectator fell in hole on golf course during tournament, but sued wrong party).

Hockey. Uline Ice, Inc. v. Sullivan, 187 F.2d 82 (D.C. Cir. 1950); Tite v. Omaha Coliseum Corp., 144 Neb. 22, 12 N.W.2d 90 (1943); Sutherland v. Onondaga Hockey Club, 245 App. Div. 137, 281 N.Y.S. 505 (1935); Rich v. Madison Square Garden Corp., 149 Misc. 123, 266 N.Y.S. 288, *aff'd,* 241 App. Div. 722, 270 N.Y.S. 915 (1933). *See also,* Shurman v. Fresno Ice Rink, 91 Cal. App. 2d 469, 205 P.2d 77 (1949) (warnings will not relieve owner or operator from liability, though they will be evidence of an attempt to comply with the reasonable care standard).

Racing. Liability in the racing cases has resulted from operation of a track with knowledge of the presence of defective conditions, Fitchett v. Buchanan, 2 Wash. App. 2d 965, 472 P.2d 623 (1970); the failure to provide barriers of sufficient strength to protect spectators from coming in dangerous proximity to out-of-control racers, Celli v. Sports Car Club of America, Inc., 29 Cal. App. 3d 511, 105 Cal. Rptr. 904 (1972); Goade v. Elks Lodge 789, 213 Cal. App. 2d 189, 28 Cal. Rptr. 669 (1963) (no protection); Barker v. Colorado Region — Sports Car Club of America, Inc., 35 Colo. App. 73, 532 P.2d 372 (1955); Capital Raceway Promotions, Inc. v. Smith, 22 Md. App. 224, 322 A.2d 238 (1974); Ellingson v. World Amusement Service Ass'n, 175 Minn. 563, 222 N.W. 335 (1928); Arnold v. State, 163 App. Div. 253, 148 N.Y.S. 479 (1914); Blake v. Fried, 173 Pa. Super. 27, 95 A.2d 360 (1953); Rogers v. Black Hills Speedway, Inc., — S.D. —, 217 N.W.2d 14 (1974); Shacklett v. Naylor, 358 S.W.2d 952 (Tex. Civ. App. 1962) (rotten crossties); Kuemmel v. Vradenburg, 239 S.W.2d 869 (Tex. Civ. App. 1951) (cable size too small); Regan v. Seattle, 76 Wash. 2d 501, 458 P.2d 12 (1969) (hay bales not sufficient in "go-cart" race); the failure to warn spectators about, or protect them against, the risk of parts flying into spectator areas, Khanoyan v. All American Sports Enterprises, Inc., 229 Cal. App. 2d 785, 40 Cal. Rptr. 596 (1964) (applying *res ipsa loquitur* doctrine in a case where a fan blade flew off in a destruction derby; very poor decision, inasmuch as this is an obvious situation where "common knowledge" rule should apply); Alden v. Norwood Arena, 332 Mass. 267, 124 N.E.2d 505 (1955); Williams v. Strickland, 251 N.C. 767, 112 S.E.2d 533 (1960); Atlantic Rural Exposition, Inc. v. Fagan, 195 Va. 13, 77 S.E.2d 368 (1953); Fitchett v. Buchanan, 2 Wash. App. 2d 965, 472 P.2d 623 (1970); Kaiser v. Cook, 67 Wis. 2d 460, 227 N.W.2d 50 (1975), the lack of sufficient seats to properly seat or protect all spectators, Ellingson v. World Amusement Service Ass'n, 175 Minn. 563, 222 N.W. 335 (1928); Virginia State Fair Ass'n v. Burton, 182 Va. 365, 28 S.E.2d 716 (1944), the negligent maintenance of competing racers, Zieman v. World Amusement Service Ass'n of South Dakota, 209 Iowa 1298, 228 N.W. 48 (1929) (steering wheel improperly anchored); or the failure to provide adequate policing of the racing area. Saari v. State, 203 Misc. 859, 119 N.Y.S.2d 507, *aff'd,* 282 App. Div. 526, 125 N.Y.S.2d 507 (1953). *See also* Harms v. Lee County Fair Ass'n, 209 Ill. App. 103 (1918) (motorcycle rider thrown over guardrail); Boetsch v. Rockland Jaycees, 288 A.2d 102 (Maine 1972) (snowmobile racing).

Similar rules are followed in the horse racing cases. Thus, recovery has been allowed where spectator injuries were caused by allowing spectators to enter an arena where wild horses were present, Nicholas v. Tri-State Fair & Sales Corp., 82 S.D. 450, 148 N.W.2d 183 (1967) (rodeo); by the assault of a steward, Cowan v. Eastern Racing Ass'n, 330 Mass. 135, 111 N.E.2d 752 (1953); by a gap in a fence surrounding the race course through which horses could pass, Windeter v. Rush County Fair Ass'n, 27 Ind. App. 92, 59 N.E. 209 (1901), *but cf.* Haberlin v. Peninsula Celebration Ass'n, 156 Cal. App. 2d 404, 319 P.2d 418 (1958) (not negligence as a matter of law); by the failure to construct seats around a corral, Tomlin v. Miller, 335 Ill. App. 267, 81 N.E.2d 760 (1948); by allowing a horse with vicious tendencies to compete, Talizin v. Oak Creek Riding Club, 176 Cal. App. 2d 429, 1 Cal. Rptr. 514 (1959), Redmond v. National Horse Show Ass'n of America, 78 Misc. 383, 138 N.Y.S. 364 (1912); and by failing to contain a raging brahma bull. Tom v. Days of 47, Inc., 16 Utah 2d 386, 401 P.2d 946 (1965). Although most spectator injuries at horse races are caused by horses jumping into the spectators, the owner or operator does not, as a matter of law, have a legal duty to construct fences of sufficient height as to make such jumps impossible, Clarke v. Monroe County Fair Ass'n, 203 Iowa 1107, 212 N.W. 163 (1927), and the ordinary three to four foot railing will ordinarily be sufficient to meet the duty of care. Hallyburton v. Burke County Fair Ass'n, 119 N.C. 526, 26 S.E. 114 (1896); James v. Columbia County Agricultural, Horticultural & Mechanical Ass'n, 321 Pa. 465, 184 A. 447 (1936).

Wrestling and Boxing. Caldwell v. Maupin, 61 Ohio App. 161, 22 N.E.2d 454 (1939) (wrestler thrown out of ropes); Camp v. Rex, Inc., 304 Mass. 484, 24 N.E.2d 4 (1939) (failure to comply with city regulations requiring seats to be fastened to floor); Lawson v. Clawson, 117 Md. 333, 9 A.2d

alterations, and will require that the premises be inspected to discover their actual condition, as well as any latent defects, and that all necessary repairs, safeguards or warnings will be made for the spectators' protection.[61]

The operator will not, however, be the insurer of the spectator's safety and to recover for injuries sustained on the premises, the spectator must prove both that specific acts or omissions amount to a breach of the duty of care and that the breach was a proximate cause of the injury sustained.[62] As has been noted

755 (1939) (collapsed bleachers); Klause v. Nebraska State Board of Agriculture, 150 Neb. 466, 35 N.W.2d 104 (1948) (referee trying to separate wrestlers carrying on their battle outside of the ring, it not being commonly known that one may be hurt by a referee); Johnson v. Zemel, 109 N.J.L. 197, 160 A. 356 (1932) (fell through hole in walkway); Gallin v. Polo Grounds Athletic Club, 126 Misc. 550, 214 N.Y.S. 182 (1926) (not sufficiently strong benches); Dively v. Penn-Pittsburgh Corp., 332 Pa. 65, 2 A.2d 831 (1938) (fell down unlighted stairs); Hayward v. Downing, 112 Utah 508, 189 P.2d 442 (1948) (platform collapsed). *See also* Stevenson v. Kansas City, 187 Kan. 705, 360 P.2d 1 (1961); Silvia v. Woodhouse, 356 Mass. 119, 248 N.E.2d 260 (1969).

Inasmuch as the wrestlers are often themselves the cause of spectator injuries, the question of who is responsible for their actions has also been a frequently litigated issue. This is important because one is ordinarily responsible for the acts of his employees but not his independent contractors. These categories are distinguished by the right of the principal to exercise control over the actions of the person in question. One "controls" an employee but not an independent contractor. Silvia v. Woodhouse, 356 Mass. 119, 248 N.E.2d 260 (1969); Langness v. Ketonen, 42 Wash. 2d 394, 255 P.2d 551 (1953) (in making the "control" determination, a local statute precluding such control as to pre-determine the outcome of a "fight" will not be dispositive). Boxers and wrestlers are ordinarily brought together in a given exhibition by a promoter who enters specific contracts with each contestant. In evaluating this relation, however, the courts have not used a singular classification, having concluded that the wrestler may be either an employee, Caldwell v. Maupin, 61 Ohio App. 161, 22 N.E.2d 454 (1939), or independent contractor, Silvia v. Woodhouse, 356 Mass. 119, 248 N.E.2d 260 (1969), of the promoter or matchmaker. In light of this split, perhaps all that can be said is that the requisite "control" may depend on local custom, Langness v. Ketonen, 42 Wash. 2d 394, 255 P.2d 551 (1953), though the contract may have effect on the result. The prudent promoter or matchmaker will, therefore, include in its contracts a specific reference to the fact that there is present only an independent contractor relation between it and the wrestler or boxer. Even if an employment relation should be present, the employer will not be liable for acts outside the scope of exhibition-related activities, such as intentional assaults by contestants upon spectators, it being assumed that·one does not employ a wrestler to assault spectators, Wiersma v. Long Beach, 41 Cal. App. 2d 8, 106 P.2d 45 (1940); Ramsey v. Kallio, 62 So. 2d 146 (La. App. 1952).

61. RESTATEMENT (SECOND) OF TORTS § 343, comment *b* (1965).

62. This principle is illustrated by the following cases denying spectator recovery:

Baseball. Townsley v. Cincinnati Gardens, Inc., 39 Ohio App. 2d 5, 314 N.E.2d 409 (1974) (spectator assaulted in washroom).

Hockey. McDonald v. Chicago Stadium Corp., 336 Ill. App. 353, 83 N.E.2d 616 (1949) (injured by a third party while waiting for usher to remove another patron from spectator's seat); Klish v. Alaskan Amusment Co., 153 Kan. 93, 109 P.2d 75 (1941) (recovery denied when a spectator was injured by the jostling of a large crowd); Aaser v. Charlotte, 265 N.C. 494, 144 S.E.2d 610 (1965) (injured by children playing in a corridor); Rich v. Madison Square Garden Corp., 149 Misc. 123, 266 N.Y.S. 288, aff'd, 241 App. Div. 722, 270 N.Y.S. 915 (1933) (injured by errantly swung hockey stick where such action was foreseeable).

Racing. Leslie v. Delaware Racing Ass'n, 275 F. Supp. 354 (D. Del. 1967) (patron assaulted and robbed of winning tickets at winner's window, *but cf.* Hartigan v. Eastern Racing Ass'n, 311 Mass. 368, 41 N.E.2d 28 (1942)); Barrett v. Faltico, 117 F. Supp. 95 (E.D. Wash. 1953) (being in dangerous spot where spectators not supposed to be); Colgrove v. Lompoc Model T Club, 51 Cal. App. 2d 18, 124 P.2d 128 (1942); Indianapolis Motor Speedway Co. v. Shoup, 88 Ind. App. 572, 165 N.E. 246 (1929) (trespasser); Kelley v. Sportsman's Speedway, 224 Miss. 632, 80 So. 2d 785 (1955) (in pits without permission); Arnold v. State, 163 App. Div. 253, 148 N.Y.S. 479 (1914); Lynn v. Wheeler, 260 N.C. 658, 133 S.E.2d 514 (1963) (wheel flew off and no evidence of negligence); Grahn v. Northwest Sport, 210 Ore. 249, 310 P.2d 306 (1957) (on racetrack at wrong time); Shula v. Warren, 395 Pa. 428, 150 A.2d 341 (1959) (in pits without permission); Mercurio v. Burrillville Racing Ass'n, 95 R.I. 417, 187 A.2d 665 (1963) (taking pictures in wrong place); Aughtrey v. Wiles, 106 S.C. 416, 91 S.E. 303 (1917) (trespasser); Endorf v. Johnson, 59 S.D. 549, 241 N.W. 519 (1932) (crossing track during race); Shacklett v. Naylor, 358 S.W.2d 952 (Tex. Civ. App. 1962); Corpus Christi Speedway v. Morton, 279 S.W.2d 903 (Tex. Civ. App. 1955) (hit by bottle thrown by other spectators). *See also* Gulf Stream

earlier, the operator will be obligated to take precautions to ameliorate only unreasonable risks.[63] A risk will be considered unreasonable when the probability of injury outweighs the burden of taking adequate precautions to prevent its occurrence.[64] The amount of caution required by the operator will increase, then, in proportion to the probability that its activities will cause serious injury to others.[65] One of the classic examples of determining when a risk becomes unreasonable, is the English decision of *Bolton v. Stone,*[66] where a member of a visiting cricket team drove a cricket ball out of the playing field and into an adjacent public roadway where it struck and severely injured a lady who stood in its path. Although the House of Lords found that such an occurrence was foreseeable, it having happened six times in twenty-eight years, it found the defendants blameless inasmuch as the risk was so small that a reasonable person would have been justified in disregarding it and taking no precautions to prevent its occurrence.[67] *Bolton v. Stone* thus involved a simple

---

Park Racing Ass'n v. Miller, 119 So. 2d 749 (Fla. App. 1960) (disregard of known tendencies of horse: stablehand who knew that maiden two year olds had nervous tendencies); Toole v. Erlanger Fair Ass'n, 207 Ky. 441, 269 S.W. 523 (1925) (spectator at horse race in improper position); Morrison v. Union Park Ass'n, 129 Maine 88, 149 A. 804 (1930) (horse racing); Hallyburton v. Burke County Fair Ass'n, 119 N.C. 526, 26 S.E. 114 (1896) (failure to obey admonition to move away from horse barrier).

Recovery has also been denied for injuries that have been suffered as a result of jostling by other spectators in the crowd. Porter v. California Jockey Club, 134 Cal. App. 2d 158, 285 P.2d 60 (1955); Carr v. Mile High Kennel Club, 125 Colo. 251, 242 P.2d 238 (1952); Waterman v. President & Fellows of Harvard College, 290 Mass. 535, 195 N.E. 717 (1935); Shtekla v. Topping, 23 App. Div. 2d 750, 258 N.Y.S.2d 982 (1965); Futterer v. Saratoga Ass'n for Improvement of Breed of Horses, 262 App. Div. 675, 31 N.Y.S.2d 108 (1941); Aaser v. Charlotte, 265 N.C. 494, 144 S.E.2d 610 (1965); Bacon v. Harris, 221 Ore. 553, 352 P.2d 472 (1960).

Wrestling and Boxing. Sample v. Eaton, 145 Cal. App. 2d 312, 302 P.2d 431 (1956) (thrown bottle presents jury question); Wiersma v. Long Beach, 41 Cal. App. 2d 8, 106 P.2d 45 (1940) (intentional participant assault: wrestler hit spectator over head with a chair); Reynolds v. Deep South Sports, Inc., 211 So. 2d 37 (Fla. App. 1968) (thrown bottle); Shayne v. Coliseum Building Corp., 270 Ill. App. 547 (1933) (surging crowd trying to avoid spectator gun fight pushed plaintiff off balcony); Stevenson v. Kansas City, 187 Kan. 705, 360 P.2d 1 (1961) (spectator assaulted while proceeding to ladies' room); Ramsey v. Kallio, 62 So. 2d 146 (La. App. 1952) (intentional participant assault: wrestler beat up husband and wife spectators); Camp v. Rex, Inc., 304 Mass. 484, 24 N.E.2d 4 (1939) (surging crowd around wrestlers fighting out of ring pushed plaintiff off chair); Pierce v. Murnick, 265 N.C. 707, 145 S.E.2d 11 (1965); C. & M. Promotions v. Ryland, 208 Va. 365, 158 S.E.2d 132 (1967) (injuries caused by local policeman when arresting a disorderly spectator); Whitfield v. Cox, 189 Va. 219, 52 S.E.2d 72 (1949) (thrown bottle).

For a discussion of liability for assaults on spectators, see Annot., 34 A.L.R.2d 373, 422 (1954); Annot., 29 A.L.R.2d 911 (1953).

63. *See* § 8.02.

64. United States v. Carroll Towing Co., 159 F.2d 169 (2d Cir. 1949). Judge Hand stated the proposition to be that

if the probability be called P; and the injury L; and the burden B; liability depends upon whether B is less than L multiplied by P; i.e., whether B is less than PL. 159 F.2d at 173.

In addition to the burden of taking precautions, the utility of the actor's conduct must also be considered. RESTATEMENT (SECOND) OF TORTS § 292 (1965).

65. 2 F. HARPER & F. JAMES, THE LAW OF TORTS § 16.9 (1956), where all of these factors are considered at length.

66. [1951] A.C. 850, [1951] 1 All E.R. 1078.

67. Thus, Lord Justice Radcliffe stated that

a reasonable man, taking account of the chances against an accident happening, would not have felt himself called upon either to abandon use of the ground for cricket or to increase the height of his surrounding fences. He would have done what the appellants did: in other words, he would have done nothing. [1951] A.C. at 869, [1951] All E.R. at 1087.

See also Hall v. Brooklands Auto Racing Club, [1930] 1 K.B. 205, 224 (risk that auto would plunge through a barrier and injure spectators remote).

finding that the burden of precaution outweighed the probability of loss, and that reasonable people do not act to prevent the occurrence of largely speculative injuries. In other words, the risk of a cricket ball striking a person beyond the playing field boundaries was not an unreasonable risk, and when that event occurred, it would not be the result of negligent conduct.[68] The principle expressed in *Bolton v. Stone* appears to be sound, although contemporary courts might take a less tolerant view of what constitutes a reasonable risk than did the House of Lords in that case.

These several principles are perhaps best illustrated, again, by the decision in *Hall v. Brooklands Auto Racing Club*,[69] where a collision had propelled a sports car over a four and a half foot fence and into a spectator area, killing and injuring many of the spectators. Apparently no auto had ever entered the spectator areas before and the iron railing had always provided satisfactory protection. When an injured spectator then brought suit for his injuries, the court's first step was to determine the duty owed by the operator of race courses to paying spectators, who attend a spectacle the nature of which "is known to all people of ordinary intelligence who go to see it." [70] This duty, it said, was to exercise reasonable care for the safety of the spectators. The requirements of reasonable care "would depend on the perils which might be reasonably expected to occur, and the extent to which the ordinary spectator might be expected to appreciate and take the risk of such perils." [71] The duty would not, however, require the operator to warrant the safety of the spectators. Applying these principles to the case at hand, the court ruled that the defendants had fulfilled their duty and that the plaintiff-spectator had assumed the risk of the accident. Thus, Lord Justice Greer stated that

> a man taking a ticket to see motor races would know quite well that no barrier would be provided which would be sufficient to protect him in the possible but highly improbable event of a car charging the barrier and getting through to the spectators. The risk of such an event would be so remote that he would quite understand that no provision would be made to prevent its happening, and that he would take the risk of any such accident.[72]

A second risk that will not be assumed by the spectator, and which is distinct from the liability of owners or operators, is the risk of unreasonable conduct by participants, which is not an ordinary or inherent risk of any sport. Thus, a spectator has recovered for injuries caused by a baseball player's having intentionally thrown a ball into the stands in frustration after he dropped a crucial fly ball.[73] In most cases involving spectator injuries from participant

---

68. *See also* Curtis v. Portland Baseball Club, 130 Ore. 93, 279 P. 277 (1929) (a reasonable man would not undertake to prevent a baseball from curving around a protective screen, it being a remarkable feat); Leek v. Tacoma Baseball Club, 38 Wash. 2d 362, 229 P.2d 329 (1951) (failure to provide overhead protection to fans behind home plate was not an unreasonable risk).

69. [1930] 1 K.B. 205, [1932] All E.R. 208, *noted in* 49 L.Q. REV. 156 (1933).

70. [1930] 1 K.B. at 214, [1932] All E.R. at 212.

71. [1930] 1 K.B. at 214, [1932] All E.R. at 213.

72. [1930] 1 K.B. at 224, [1932] All E.R. at 217.

73. Bonetti v. Double Play Tavern, 126 Cal. App. 2d 848, 274 P.2d 751 (1954) (liability imposed upon employer who sponsored the team upon which the participant played, on the basis of respondeat superior). See note 57 *supra*.

conduct, however, recovery will be barred, since the risk producing the injury will be an ordinary and inherent risk of the sport, which will be assumed by the spectator. Thus, spectators will be held as a matter of law to have assumed the risk of injury caused by good faith and non-negligent competition.[74]

The classic exposition of the liability of participants to spectators is the decision of the English Court of Appeal in *Wooldridge v. Sumner*,[75] where a professional photographer had been injured by a horse during the course of a championship race. On the infield side of the grass racecourse was a low cement ridge with cables, and about two feet inside of that was a row of tubs, filled with rhododendrons and other shrubs, with benches between some of the tubs. The photographer was standing behind one of the benches. The accident occurred when the horses, which were "heavy hunters," rounded a turn and galloped toward a stretch in front of the grandstand. A horse mis-named "Work of Art," was too close to the shrub-filled tubs, jumped two of them, knocked a third down, and then straightened its course and passed about four feet behind the benches. At the approach of the horse, the photographer, who was inexperienced with horses and was taking little interest in the race, took fright and stepped or fell into its path while trying to pull a lady friend off the bench. The impact caused the jockey to be thrown, but a sufficient recovery was made so that the horse won the race, becoming supreme champion of its class. The photographer then brought suit against the owner of the horse for the negligence of his jockey-agent, and the organizers of the race, who also owned the stadium. The trial court dismissed the suit against the organizers, but held the owner liable, finding that the jockey was negligent in causing the horse to take the turn too fast. The Court of Appeal, however, unanimously reversed.

The case presented, in the view of Lord Justice Sellers, the question of "whether liability should be placed on a competitor who is merely seeking to excel and to win, it being the very purpose on which he is engaged and the very endeavor which people have assembled to witness and applaud."[76] The standard to be applied in answering this question was best stated by Lord Justice Diplock to be that

> [a] person attending a game or competition takes the risk of any damage caused to him by any act of a participant done in the course of and for the purpose of the game or competition, notwithstanding that such act may involve an error of judgment or a lapse of skill, unless the participant's conduct is such as to evidence a *reckless disregard* of the spectator's safety.[77]

---

74. Wooldridge v. Sumner, [1962] 2 All E.R. 978. *See also* Douglas v. Converse, 248 Pa. 232, 93 A. 955 (1915); Davis v. Jones, 100 Ga. App. 546, 112 S.E.2d 3 (1959).

75. [1962] 2 All E.R. 978. Although *Wooldridge v. Sumner* dealt primarily with negligence of the jockey, and not the assumption of risk by the spectator, it is illustrative of the approach that a court would take in analyzing this type of spectator injury case.

76. [1962] 2 All E.R. at 981.

77. [1962] 2 All E.R. at 989-90 (emphasis added). Lord Justice Diplock also noted that

[a] reasonable spectator attending voluntarily to witness any game or competition knows, and presumably desires, that a reasonable participant will concentrate his attention on winning, and if the game or competition is a fast-moving one will have to exercise his judgment and attempt to exert his skill in what, in the analogous context of contributory negligence, is sometimes called 'the agony of the moment'. If the participant does so concentrate his attention and consequently does exercise his judgment and attempt to exert his skill in circumstances of this kind which are inherent in the game or competition in which he is taking part, the question whether any mistake he makes amounts to a breach

Applying this standard, Lord Justice Diplock then found that the jockey had misjudged the speed at which "Work of Art" could take the turn, and the centrifugal force of the horse caused it to come in contact with the line demarcated by the tubs of shrubs. This showed at most, he said, "an error or errors of judgment or a lapse of skill," which was "not enough to constitute a breach of the duty of reasonable care which a participant owes to a spectator." [78] The photographer had, furthermore, caused his own injury by, in a moment of panic, stepping and stumbling out of his place of safety on the bench.[79]

The final issue that should be considered in discussing liability for injuries suffered by spectators, involves the extent to which spectators may seek recovery when they are excluded from an athletic facility by its operator. When such an action is brought, the spectator will be unlikely to prevail. As a general rule, the operator of an athletic facility, unlike the owner of a public accommodation or a common carrier, has a common law right to exclude any person therefrom whom it does not desire to grant admission.[80] The leading case expressing this right is the English decision in *Wood v. Leadbitter,*[81] where a

of duty to take reasonable care must take account of those circumstances. [1962] 2 All E.R. at 989.

A similar standard was expressed by Lord Justice Sellers, who said that

provided the competition or game is being performed within the rules and the requirement of the sport and by a person of adequate skill and competence, the spectator does not expect his safety to be regarded by the participant. If the conduct is deliberately intended to injure someone whose presence is known, or is reckless and in disregard of all safety of others so that it is a departure from the standards which might reasonably be expected in anyone pursuing the competition or game, then the performer might well be held liable for any injury his act caused. [1962] 2 All E.R. at 983.

See also Barker v. Colorado Region — Sports Car Club of America, Inc., 35 Colo. App. 73, 532 P.2d 372 (1975) (participant liable for negligently responding to signal); Douglas v. Converse, 248 Pa. 232, 93 A. 955 (1915) (participants liable for *reckless* conduct).

78. [1962] 2 All E.R. at 991-92.

79. [1962] 2 All E.R. at 991. Lord Justice Diplock also stated that while the photographer's own ignorance of horseracing and his concomitant panic may be understandable and excusable, they would not aid his case, inasmuch as

a reasonable competitor would be entitled to assume that spectators actually in the arena would be paying attention to what was happening, would be knowledgeable about horses, and would take such steps for their own safety as any reasonbly attentive and knowledgeable spectator might be expected to take. [1962] 2 All E.R. at 991.

This "assumption of the risk" element was also noted by Lord Justice Danckwerts. [1962] All E.R. at 984.

A similar result was reached in Davis v. Jones, 100 Ga. App. 546, 112 S.E.2d 3 (1959), where a wrestler, trying to escape peril at the hands of an enraged opponent, dove through the rope and injured a timekeeper sitting at ringside. In denying the timekeeper's recovery, the court was of the opinion that the wrestlers' duty was to warn spectators in proximity to their match of any "unusual dangers" which they may anticipate, a category that did not include their acts in question.

Where it is determined that the participant is liable for an injury, it will then be appropriate to consider whether his or her employer can also be charged with liability for the act. This will include a simple determination of whether it was done within the scope of the participant's employment. M. J. Uline Co. v. Cashdan, 171 F.2d 132 (D.C. Cir. 1948). This question has often been considered in the wrestling cases. See note 60 *supra.*

80. Madden v. Queens County Jockey Club, 296 N.Y. 249, 72 N.E.2d 697 (1947), *cert. denied,* 332 U.S. 761, 92 L. Ed. 346, 68 S. Ct. 63 (1947). *See generally* Conard, *The Privilege of Forcibly Ejecting an Amusement Patron,* 90 U. PA. L. REV. 809 (1942); Turner & Kennedy, *Exclusion, Ejection, and Segregation of Theater Patrons,* 32 IOWA L. REV. 625 (1947); Annot., 1 A.L.R.2d 1165 (1948); Annot., 60 A.L.R. 1089 (1929); Annot., 30 A.L.R. 951 (1924).

81. 13 M. & W. 836, 153 Eng. Rep. 351 (Exch. 1845).

race track patron had been forcibly ejected from the track by its owner, and then brought suit for assault and false imprisonment. In rendering a decision upholding a verdict for the owner, the court stated that the owner of an amusement may for any reason order a ticket-holding patron to leave the premises, and if, after reasonable notice is given, the patron does not leave, the owner may effect removal by the use of reasonable force. The bases for this conclusion were that the ticket afforded the patron no interest in the property of the race track, and that even if the ticket were considered a license, it would be revocable at the will of the owner.[82] The rule of *Wood v. Leadbitter* was implicitly adopted by the Supreme Court in *Marrone v. Washington Jockey Club of the District of Columbia*,[83] where a patron had purchased a ticket and then been excluded from the race track on the grounds that he had earlier been involved in a conspiracy to drug a horse. In holding that the patron had no right to admittance, the Court stated that a ticket creates no "right *in rem*" [84] and is "not a conveyance of an interest in the race track." It then adopted what it referred to as the commonly accepted rule that the owner may exclude any patron for any reason deemed by it to be sufficient.

The results of *Wood v. Leadbitter* and *Marrone* have been followed in several spectator cases. Thus, in *Finney v. Seattle Baseball Club*,[85] a spectator at a baseball game had been ejected because of his acts in betting on games and making monetary payments to players. In holding that the excluded spectator could not recover damages from the owner of the facilities, the court stated that the proprietor of a baseball park is engaged in a private business, and although it is conducted for the entertainment of the public, the proprietor has the right to control admission and exclusion at its will in the absence of a statutory provision curbing that power.[86]

It seems quite clear, then, that a spectator ejected from a sports facility will, as a general rule, be unable to recover damages for the ejection. In considering this rule, however, it should be noted that it may be subject to several qualifications, which we discussed in an earlier analysis of the exclusion power in chapter 2.[87] Specifically, the ability to exclude may be limited by constitutional

---

82. The reasons for this result were described by Chief Justice Latham in Cowell v. Rosehill Racecourse Company, 56 Commonwealth L. Rep. 605 (Australia 1937), as follows:

> The right to see a spectacle cannot, in the ordinary sense of legal language, be regarded as a proprietary interest. Fifty thousand people who pay to see a football match do not obtain fifty thousand interests in the football ground. A contrary view produces results which may be fairly described as remarkable. The Statute of Frauds would be applicable. A person who bought a reserved seat might be held to have what would be called 'a term of hours' in the seat. 56 Commonwealth L. Rep. at 616.

The result in *Wood v. Leadbitter,* was rejected, but not overruled, by Hurst v. Picture Theatres, Ltd., [1915] 1 K.B. 1, where the court held that a ticket to an amusement was not arbitrarily revocable, and that a patron forcibly ejected upon the erroneous belief that an adminission fee had not been paid could recover damages for assault and false imprisonment. The *Hurst* opinion was itself rejected in *Cowell v. Rosehill Racecourse Company, supra.*

83. 227 U.S. 633, 57 L. Ed. 679, 33 S. Ct. 401 (1913).

84. 227 U.S. at 636 (emphasis in original).

85. 122 Wash. 276, 210 P. 679 (1922).

86. *See also* Toms v. Tiger Lanes, Inc., 313 So2d 852 (La. App. 1975); Mandel v. Brooklyn National League Baseball Club, 179 Misc. 27, 37 N.Y.S.2d 152 (1942); Levine v. Brooklyn National Baseball Club, 179 Misc. 22, 36 N.Y.S.2d 474 (1942). It has also been held that punitive damages may not be recovered for alleged false imprisonment of a spectator at a race track parking lot in an attempt to search for evidence of bookmaking. Alterauge v. Los Angeles Turf Club, 97 Cal. App. 2d 735, 218 P.2d 802 (1950).

87. These limitations are considered in §§ 2.09, 2.22.

requirements and statutory provisions requiring admission or forbidding discrimination on the basis of race, color, sex, religion or national origin.

§ 8.04. Waiver and Release of Liability.

In light of the extensive liabilities inherent in the conduct of any sporting enterprise, it is not surprising that those who sponsor sports events posing a substantial risk of injury to participants or spectators seek to acquire a release from any liability arising therefrom. Such releases will typically purport to release the promoter, or other party, from any and all liability resulting from any loss that may be sustained by the athlete during the event in question.[88]

These provisions are known in the law as exculpatory agreements, since their effect is to relieve the one party of all or a part of its responsibility to the other.[89] Exculpatory agreements are generally considered as matters of contract law since they are, at least in theory, consensual agreements, although their effect is to alter the ordinary negligence principles which would otherwise apply. Such agreements, therefore, create a tension between the fundamental tenet of contract law that all persons should have freedom to contract as they wish and the fundamental principle of negligence law that one should be held responsible for negligent acts which cause injury to others.[90] The difficulty created is that when the freedom of contract "expresses itself in a provision designed to absolve one of the parties from the consequences of his own negligence, there is danger that the standards of conduct which the law has developed for the protection of others may be diluted." [91] The tension has been resolved in favor of the general enforcibility of exculpatory agreements,[92] except where there is a

---

88. As evidencing the scope and nature of such releases, the following are a sample of those that have come before the courts:

> In consideration of the acceptance by A.C.R.A, Inc. [Auto Championship Racing Association, Inc.] of my license application and issuance of license, and in consideration of the foregoing, I do hereby release, remise and forever discharge A.C.R.A., Inc. the promoters presenting races or other events under A.C.R.A., Inc. sanction and the owners and lessees of premises in which A.C.R.A., Inc. sanctioned races or other events are presented . . . of and from all liability, claims, actions and possible cause of action, whatsoever that may accrue to me or to my heirs, . . . from every and any loss, damage and injury (including death) that may be sustained by my person and property while in, about, en route into and out of premises, where A.C.R.A., Inc. sanctioned races or other events are presented. *Quoted in* Morrow v. Auto Championship Racing Ass'n, 8 Ill. App.3d 682, 291 N.E.2d 30 (1972).

> Whereas, the undersigned wishes to compete in Auto Racing Events sanctioned by the New Bremen Speedway, Inc., and

> Whereas, the undersigned knows the perilous nature of his undertaking as it relates to loss of life and/or limb, therefore it is agreed as follows:

> That in consideration of being allowed to compete in auto racing events for prize money and other valuable consideration to be offered by the New Bremen Speedway, Inc., the undersigned hereby voluntarily assumes all risk of accident or damage to his person or property and hereby releases the New Bremen Speedway, Inc., and its promoters from every claim, liability or demand of any kind for or on account of any personal injury or damage of any kind sustained, whether caused by the negligence *of* the said New Bremen Speedway, Inc., and its promoters or otherwise. Seymour v. New Bremen Speedway, Inc., 31 Ohio App. 2d 141, 287 N.E.2d 111 (1971).

89. Note, *The Significance of Comparative Bargaining Power in the Law of Exculpation,* 37 COLUM. L. REV. 248, 248-49 (1937).

90. Morrow v. Auto Championship Racing Ass'n, 8 Ill. App. 3d 682, 291 N.E.2d 30 (1972).

91. O'Callaghan v. Waller & Beckwith Realty Co., 15 Ill. 2d 436, 155 N.E.2d 545 (1958).

92. RESTATEMENT OF CONTRACTS § 574 (1932); Winterstein v. Wilcom, 16 Md. App. 130, 293 A.2d 821 (1972). Such provisions have also received legislative approval. *See, e.g.,* TENN. CODE ANN. § 66-405 (1976) (approving the practice of participants releasing racing promoters).

strong public policy which would be frustrated or where the party obtaining the agreement is in a clearly dominant position to the party signing away his rights.[93] Some courts have indicated that this result will follow even though one party may claim not to have read or otherwise been aware of the release. This is consistent with the general rule of contract law that a party is bound by contracts which he has signed, unless there is evidence of fraud, misrepresentation or duress.[94] To be enforcible, however, the waiving party must have had an opportunity to know the terms of the release.[95] Thus, the waiver must be conspicuous,[96] result from free and open bargaining,[97] and its express terms must be applicable to the particular misconduct of the party whose potential liability is waived.[98] Moreover, exculpatory clauses will not be enforcible to insulate a party from liability for damage resulting from wanton, intentional or reckless misconduct.[99] Finally, some courts have allowed recovery for the negligence of the operator of sports facilities, notwithstanding the presence of a waiver purporting to bar any recovery, where the release does not apply to the negligence of the operator.[100] Since the clauses are subject to contract principles, moreover, they may be repudiated (disaffirmed) if the signer is a minor.[101]

When exculpatory clauses have been signed by participants in athletic activities, they have, as a general rule, been upheld, with the courts considering and applying the same principles noted above. The application of these rules to athletic participants is illustrated by *Garretson v. United States*,[102] where an entrant in an amateur ski-jumping contest had been asked to sign an entry blank which contained a broad release clause. When the skier subsequently brought suit for injuries suffered as a result of an unfortunate landing, the court upheld the release as a bar to recovery. In reaching this result, the court noted that the athlete had known what he was signing, the release was itself conspicuous on the entry form, and the operation of the release in the circumstances present was reasonable.[103]

---

93. RESTATEMENT OF CONTRACTS § 575 (1932). Thus, Professor Prosser has stated that

> it is generally held that a contract exempting an employer from all liability for negligence to his employees is void as against public policy. The same is true as to the efforts of public utilities . . . . A carrier who transports goods or passengers for hire, or a telegraph company transmitting a message, ...

W. PROSSER, THE LAW OF TORTS § 68, at 442-43 (4th ed. 1971). *See generally* Note, *The Significance of Comparative Bargaining Power in the Law of Exculpation,* 37 COLUM. L. REV. 248 (1937); Annot., 175 A.L.R. 8 (1948); Annot., 8 A.L.R.3d 1393 (1966); Annot., 97 A.L.R. 582 (1935).

94. Theroux v. Kedenburg Racing Ass'n, 50 Misc. 2d 97, 269 N.Y.S.2d 789 (1965); *see also* Lee v. Allied Sports Associates, Inc., 349 Mass. 544, 209 N.E.2d 329 (1965).

95. Moore v. Edmonds, 384 Ill. 535, 52 N.E.2d 216 (1943).

96. Baker v. Seattle, 79 Wash. 2d 198, 484 P.2d 405 (1971). *Cf.* UNIFORM COMMERCIAL CODE § 2-316 (1962).

97. Winterstein v. Wilcom, 16 Md. App. 130, 138-39, 293 A.2d 821, 824 (1972).

98. RESTATEMENT (SECOND) OF TORTS § 496B, comment *d* (1965); Phibbs v. Ray's Chevrolet Corp., 45 App. Div. 2d 897, 357 N.Y.S.2d 211 (1974) (where waiver used only word "automobile" it did not include motorcycles).

99. Winterstein v. Wilcom, 16 Md. App. 130, 293 A.2d 821 (1972); French v. Special Services, Inc., 107 Ohio App. 435, 159 N.E.2d 785 (1958); W. PROSSER, THE LAW OF TORTS § 68 (4th ed. 1971).

100. Kaiser v. State, 55 Misc. 2d 576, 285 N.Y.S.2d 874 (1967) (based on specific statutory provision).

101. Del Santo v. Bristol County Stadium, 273 F.2d 605, 607-08 (1st Cir. 1960).

102. 456 F.2d 1017 (9th Cir. 1972).

103. 456 F.2d at 1020-21. *See also* Hewitt v. Miller, 11 Wash. App. 72, 521 P.2d 244 (1974) (release by scuba diving student upheld).

Exculpatory agreements have been most frequently reviewed by courts in the area of automobile racing. As a general rule, when participants in such contests have signed the agreements, they have barred any recovery for injuries. Thus, in *Winterstein v. Wilcom*,[104] a drag race driver was severely injured when he lost control of his racer when it struck a large engine component on the track. Before the race, however, he had executed a broadly worded exculpatory clause which stated that he knew the risks and dangers involved in drag racing and had inspected the premises. The clause also provided that the signer would assume all risks of injury to his person and property and release the owners, promoters and sponsors from any liability.[105] In upholding the validity of the agreement, the court observed that there is ordinarily no public policy to prevent parties from contracting as they see fit. Thus, they are free to provide that one party will undertake the responsibility of looking out for himself.[106] Finding that there was nothing in the case before it to prevent application of the general rule of enforcibility, the court stated that

> [t]here was not the slightest disadvantage in bargaining power between the parties. Winterstein [the driver] was under no compulsion, economic or otherwise, to race his car. He obviously participated in the speed runs simply because he wanted to do so, perhaps to demonstrate the superiority of his car and probably with the hope of winning a prize. This put him in no bargaining disadvantage.[107]

Similar results have been reached in many other cases.[108]

---

104. 16 Md. App. 130, 293 A.2d 821 (1972).
105. The release provided as follows:

REQUEST AND RELEASE

I, the undersigned, hereby request permission to enter the premises of 75-80 DRAG-A-WAY, PIT AREA, STAGING AREA, and participate in auto timing and acceleration runs, tests, contests and exhibitions to be held this day. I have inspected the premises and I know the risks and dangers involved in the said activities, and that unanticipated and unexpected dangers may arise during such activities and I assume all risks of injury to my person and property that may be sustained in connection with the stated and associated activities, in and about the premises.

In consideration of the permission granted to me to enter the premises and participate in the stated activities, and in further consideration of the provisions of a insurance and medical plan, I do hereby, for myself, my heirs, administrators and assigns, release, remise and discharge the owners, operators, and sponsors of the said premises, of the activities, of the vehicles, and of the equipment therein, and their respective servants, agents, officers, and officials, and all other participants in the stated activities of and from all claims demands, actions, and causes of action of any sort, for injuries sustained by my person and/or property during my presence in said premises and participation in the stated activities due to negligence or any other fault.

I represent and certify that my true age is stated below, and if I am under the age of 21 years, I do represent and certify that I have the permission of my parents and/or guardians to participate in the stated activities, and that they have full knowledge thereof.

I certify that my attendance and participation in the stated activities is voluntary, and that I am not, in any way, the employee, servant, or agent of the owners, operators or sponsors of the premises and the activities therein.

I HAVE READ AND UNDERSTAND THE FOREGOING REQUEST AND RELEASE.
16 Md. App. at 131-32, 293 A.2d at 822.

106. 16 Md. App. at 135, 293 A.2d at 824.
107. 16 Md. App. at 138, 293 A.2d at 825.
108. Rutter v. Arlington Park Jockey Club, 510 F.2d 1065 (7th Cir. 1975) (fire in horse stable); Gore v. Tri-County Raceway, Inc., 407 F. Supp. 489 (M.D. Ala. 1974); Cash v. Street & Trail, Inc., 136 Ga. App. 462, 221 S.E.2d 640 (1975); Morrow v. Auto Championship Racing Ass'n, 8 Ill. App. 2d 682, 291 N.E.2d 30 (1972); Lee v. Allied Sports Associates, Inc., 349 Mass. 544, 209 N.E.2d 329

The general rule that exculpatory agreements will be enforcible may not apply, however, in states where the legislature has established a public policy requiring the application of a different rule. Thus, in *McCarthy v. National Association for Stock Car Auto Racing, Inc.,*[109] the driver was badly injured when his stock car burst into flames following the race. When he brought suit against the stadium owners, the supervising racing association, and the track inspector, the defendants set forth as their defense a release that had been signed by the driver. Although the court noted the many decisions upholding such clauses in racing situations, it held that such releases were not valid in New Jersey because the legislature had undertaken to regulate the activity involved and had enacted statutory provisions designed for the safety of both participants and spectators. To allow these requirements to be contracted away, the court said, would be to nullify "the salient protective features of the legislation." [110] This was especially clear in the case before it, inasmuch as the statute specifically required an inspection of all vehicles and such an inspection had not been made of the auto in question. A contrary decision would, indeed, allow the parties to contractually overrule the act of the legislature.

Exculpatory agreements also have been found in "membership health plan" facilities, where a gymnasium or health spa makes its facilities available only to those who purchase "membership contracts," which are ordinarily simple installment contracts for the use of the facilities. In *Ciofalo v. Vic Tanney Gyms, Inc.,*[111] for example, the plaintiff had agreed in her membership contract to assume full responsibility for any injuries which might befall her as a result of the defendant's negligence. The defendant sought to assert this provision when she sued for injuries resulting from a fall in a swimming facility. In sustaining the agreement, the court noted the general rule that such agreements are enforcible so long as they do not abridge a relationship upon which public policy engrafts special rules. The court found that on the facts before it there was no special legal relationship and no overriding public interest which would render ineffectual an agreement freely entered.[112] Other facts may, however, require a contrary result. Thus, exculpatory clauses may not be enforced where the

---

(1965); Gervasi v. Holland Raceway, Inc., 40 App. Div. 2d 574, 334 N.Y.S.2d 527 (1972) (mechanic); Solodar v. Watkins Glen Grand Prix Corp., 36 App. Div. 2d 552, 317 N.Y.S.2d 228 (1971); Theroux v. Kedenburg Racing Ass'n, 50 Misc. 2d 97, 269 N.Y.S.2d 789 (1965); Seymour v. New Bremen Speedway, Inc., 31 Ohio App. 2d 141, 287 N.E.2d 111 (1971); Hine v. Dayton Speedway Corp., 20 Ohio App. 2d 185, 252 N.E.2d 648 (1969); French v. Special Services, 107 Ohio App. 435, 159 N.E.2d 785 (1958); Corpus Christi Speedway v. Morton, 279 S.W.2d 903 (Tex. Civ. App. 1955). *But cf.* Del Santo v. Bristol County Stadium, 273 F.2d 605 (1st Cir. 1960) (release signed by minor not enforcible when disaffirmed by bringing suit within six months of reaching majority). *See generally* 2 BLASHFIELD, AUTOMOBILE LAW & PRACTICE § 102.38 (3rd ed. 1965).

  109. 48 N. J. 539, 226 A.2d 713 (1967).

  110. 48 N. J. at 543, 226 A.2d at 715. This legislation is N. J. STAT. ANN. §§ 5:7-7 — :7-18 (1973).

  111. 10 N.Y.2d 294, 177 N.E.2d 925 (1961).

  112. 10 N.Y.2d at 298, 177 N.E.2d at 927. Specifically, the court stated that

> Defendant, a private corporation, was under no obligation or legal duty to accept plaintiff as a 'member' or patron. Having consented to do so, it had the right to insist upon such terms as it deemed appropriate. Plaintiff, on the other hand, was not required to assent to unacceptable terms, or to give up a valuable legal right as a condition precedent to obtaining employment or being able to make use of the services rendered by a public carrier or utility. She voluntarily applied for membership in a private organization, and agreed to the terms upon which this membership was bestowed. She may not repudiate them now.

Id. See also Bers v. Chicago Health Clubs, Inc., 11 Ill. App. 3d 590, 297 N.E.2d 360 (1973); Empress Health & Beauty Spa, Inc. v. Turner, 503 S.W.2d 188 (Tenn. 1973).

member does not sign the writing in which it is contained [113] or where the language is not clear.[114]

Although the majority of the cases have also enforced exculpatory agreements against spectators at sports events,[115] the courts have demonstrated somewhat more reluctance to give them force. Perhaps the best evidence of this reluctance is *Celli v. Sports Car Club of America, Inc.,*[116] where three spectators had been injured when a sports car skidded into the pit area of the track. Although the injuries were caused by the failure of the promoter to provide adequate barriers to protect spectators against such occurrences,[117] the promoter sought to avoid liability on the basis of an exculpatory clause contained on the pit pass issued to the spectators. This clause provided that the spectator released "every claim, demand, action or right of action whatsoever kind or nature . . . from or arising out of any accident or other occurrence . . . ." In holding that the clause did not release the track owner or race promoter from liability for the injuries caused by their negligence, the court stated that the language of the pit pass must be construed against the owner and promoter since it was a product of their draftsmanship and sought to whittle the customer's ordinary rights. The basis of the court's decision, however, was that the waiver did not purport to waive or release claims for negligence, so such claims were not affected thereby. Although the clause did not specifically mention negligence, its use of broad, general language could be interpreted to have implicitly included negligence.[118] Thus, the court's ruling seems to have been predicated on its reluctance to enforce the clause, not on the absence of the additional word. Indeed, the court went on to state that even if the clause had expressly mentioned negligence, it questioned "whether public policy . . . would permit judicial enforcement of a provision printed in such small type and designed to permit a tortfeasor to shift the risk of injury to the victims even where the release is sufficient to encompass defendant's own negligence."[119]

---

113. Bernstein v. Seacliff Beach Club, Inc., 35 Misc. 2d 153, 228 N.Y.S.2d 567 (1962).

114. Hertzog v. Harrison Island Shores, Inc., 21 App. Div. 2d 859, 251 N.Y.S.2d 164 (1964).

115. Lee v. Allied Sports Associates, Inc., 349 Mass. 544, 209 N.E.2d 329 (1965) (spectator in pits); Kotary v. Spencer Speedway, Inc., 47 App. Div. 2d 127, 365 N.Y.S.2d 87 (1975); Church v. Seneca County Agricultural Society, 41 App. Div. 2d 787, 341 N.Y.S.2d 45 (1973) (spectator in infield); Hine v. Dayton Speedway Corp., 20 Ohio App. 2d 185, 252 N.E.2d 648 (1969) (owner in pits). A valid waiver need not bar recovery by others who have causes of action based on an injury to a spectator. *See, e.g.,* Barker v. Colorado Region-Sports Car Club of America, Inc., 35 Colo. App. 73, 532 P.2d 372 (1975) (loss of consortium by spouse); Kotary v. Spencer Speedway, Inc., 47 App. Div. 2d 127, 365 N.Y.S.2d 87 (1975) (father's medical expenses).

116. 29 Cal. App. 3d 511, 105 Cal. Rptr. 904 (1972).

117. The liability of operators of race tracks for failure to provide sufficient barriers is considered at § 8.03.

118. Thus, in Hine v. Dayton Speedway Corp., 20 Ohio App. 2d 185, 252 N.E.2d 648 (1969), the court stated that

> The release does not specifically refer to the word "negligence," but there can be no doubt that its exculpatory language is thorough and comprehensive. Specifically, the plaintiff released the defendants from *all* causes of action and from *all* liability for injuries.
>
> Contracts purporting to relieve one from the results of his failure to use ordinary care must be strictly construed, but it is not necessary to use the word "negligence" if the intent of the parties is expressed in clear and unequivocal terms. 252 N.E.2d at 651.

119. 29 Cal. App. 3d at 521, 105 Cal. Rptr. at 911.

§ 8.05. Liability for Injuries in Educational Programs.

Unquestionably the most common context in which sports activities take place is on the fields, and in the gyms, of public and private educational institutions. This is also the context in which a proportionately large number of sports-related injuries occur. Although the basic legal principles which govern the respective rights and liabilities of those involved in these predictable mishaps do not materially differ from those that apply in other contexts, the circumstances in which they will be applied present sufficiently distinct issues to require separate discussion.[120]

Before undertaking that inquiry, however, it will be useful to state several factors which bear upon the potential liability of those involved with education-related sports activities. The first is that schools are populated by young people who have a definite propensity for frolic and play. Thus, injuries in sports activities are probably inevitable even when those in charge exercise due care in controlling and directing the activities. A second consideration is that the wide variety of factual situations that may be present in school-related activities precludes the articulation of precise standards of legally required conduct. Instead, the particular facts of each case will have to be evaluated in terms of the broad, general rules that have evolved. Finally, although the vast majority of the cases that will be reviewed are the result of activities in grammar or high schools, the principles considered are of equal applicability to the activities conducted or sponsored by institutions of higher learning.[121]

When actions are brought to seek compensation for school-related sports injuries, the first step will always be to ascertain the legal status of the entity which has responsibility for the school or activity in question. This will involve two basic inquiries. The first will be to determine whether the institution is subject to suit. In many jurisdictions, the institution may be immunized from liability by the doctrines of sovereign or charitable immunity,[122] and where these doctrines are still viable, suit against that particular entity will be fruitless. If suit may be maintained against the institution, the second inquiry will be to ascertain the statutory requirements for the proper institution of such an action. Statutory provisions in particular jurisdictions may specify steps that must be taken before suit may be begun against an educational institution (such as presentation of claims to the institution within a specified period of time),[123] and

---

120. *See generally* K. ALEXANDER & E. SOLOMON, COLLEGE AND UNIVERSITY LAW ch. 10 (1972); A. GRIEVE, THE LEGAL ASPECTS OF ATHLETICS (1969); H. LEIBEE, LIABILITY FOR ACCIDENTS IN PHYSICAL EDUCATION ATHLETICS RECREATION (1952); J. MOHLER & E. BOLMEIER, LAW OF EXTRACURRICULAR ACTIVITIES IN SECONDARY SCHOOLS 119-160 (1968); Franklin, *Tort Liability of Schools*, U. ILL. L. F. 327 (1958); Mancke, *Liability of School Districts for the Negligent Acts of Their Employees*, 1 J. L. & EDUC. 109 (1972); Miller, *Personal Injury Litigation in School Cases*, 20 LAW & CONTEMP. PROB. 60 (1955); Seitz, *Legal Responsibility Under Tort Law of School Personnel and School Districts as Regards Negligent Conduct Toward Pupils*, 15 HASTINGS L. J. 495 (1964); Annot., 38 A.L.R. 3d 908 (1971) (private school liability for lack of supervision); Annot., 38 A.L.R. 3d 830 (1971) (public school liability for lack of supervision); Annot., 160 A.L.R. 7 (1946); Annot., 56 A.L.R. 164 (1928); Annot., 24 A.L.R. 1070 (1923); Annot., 21 A.L.R. 1328 (1922); Annot., 14 A.L.R. 1392 (1921); Annot., 9 A.L.R. 911 (1920).

121. *See, e.g.,* Wells v. Colorado College, 470 F.2d 158 (10th Cir. 1973).

122. The sovereign and charitable immunity that may apply to the tort liability of public and private educational institutions is considered in detail at § 8.18.

123. *See, e.g.,* N.Y. EDUC. LAW § 3813 (McKinney 1970). *But see* Hunter v. North Mason High School, 85 Wash. 810, 539 P.2d 845 (1975) (holding such a "non-claim" statute unconstitutional).

failure to comply therewith may well bar the action. Such procedural requirements will not be considered here because the rules vary greatly among jurisdictions and do not directly relate to the present inquiry.

With respect to the athletic activities conducted under their auspices, educational institutions have the duty to exercise reasonable care to prevent reasonably foreseeable risks [124] and, where such risks are foreseen, to take sufficient precautions to protect the students in their custody.[125] This general duty can be translated into several specific obligations. Thus, the institution may be required to establish,[126] and enforce,[127] rules for the maintenance of discipline in sports and recreational activities (though they need not cover every possibility presented by the boundless natural instincts of children for self-amusement); [128] provide adequate supervision for the sports or recreational activities held under their auspices and exercise due care in the selection of supervisors; [129] and provide suitable equipment and facilities for the conduct of sports and recreational activities.[130] Although these responsibilities have primary

124. Charonnat v. San Francisco Unified School District, 56 Cal. App. 2d 840, 133 P.2d 643 (1943); Underhill v. Alameda Elementary School Dist. of Alameda County, 133 Cal. App. 733, 24 P.2d 849 (1933); Cambareri v. Board of Educ. of Albany, 246 App. Div. 127, 284 N.Y.S. 892, 127 (1936), aff'd, 283 N.Y. 741, 28 N.E. 2d 968 (1940).

125. Carabba v. Anacortes School Dist. No. 103, 72 Wash.2d 939, 435 P.2d 936 (1967); Briscoe v. School Dist. No. 123, Grays Harbor County, 32 Wash.2d 353, 201 P.2d 697 (1949).

126. Selleck v. Board of Educ. of Central School Dist. No. 1, 276 App. Div. 263, 94 N.Y.S.2d 318 (1949); Garber v. Central School Dist. No. 1 of Sharon, 251 App. Div. 214, 295 N.Y.S. 850 (1937).

127. Tashjian v. North Colonie Central School District No. 5, 50 App. Div. 2d 691, 375 N.Y.S.2d 467 (1975); Germond v. Board of Educ. of Central School Dist. No. 1, 10 App. Div. 2d 139, 197 N.Y.S.2d 548 (1960).

128. Hoose v. Drumm, 281 N.Y. 54, 22 N.E.2d 233 (1939).

129. Brittan v. State, 200 Misc. 743, 103 N.Y.S.2d 485 (Ct. Cl. 1951) (providing non-qualified student as supervisor is an act of negligence). See also Hunt v. Board of Educ. of Schenectady, 43 App. Div. 2d 397, 352 N.Y.S.2d 237 (1974); Darrow v. West Genesee Central School Dist., 41 App. Div. 2d 897, 342 N.Y.S.2d 611 (1973); Garber v. Central School Dist. No. 1 of Sharon, 251 App. Div. 214, 295 N.Y.S. 850 (1937).

130. Freund v. Oakland Bd. of Educ., 28 Cal. App. 2d 246, 82 P.2d 197 (1938) (locker fell over on student); Bridge v. Board of Educ. of City of Los Angeles, 2 Cal. App. 2d 398, 38 P.2d 199 (1934) (protruding concrete box on playing field); Bush v. Norwalk, 122 Conn. 426, 189 A. 608 (1937) (failure to provide mat under balance beam or to prevent its slipping on a greasy floor); Fein v. Board of Educ. of New York, 305 N.Y. 611, 111 N.E.2d 732 (1953) (failure to supply mat beneath chinning bar); Bradley v. Board of Educ. of Oneonta, 243 App. Div. 651, 276 N.Y.S. 622 (1935), aff'd, 274 N.Y. 473, 8 N.E.2d 610 (1937) (no mats covering sharply projecting part of gym wall). But cf. Shelton v. Planet Ins. Co., 280 So. 2d 380 (La. App. 1973) (school officials owe teachers no duty to provide safe athletic facilities).

Liability for the provision of defective equipment is considered in §§ 8.09-8.11.

Educational institutions may also incur liability from the transportation of their students to and from athletic functions. Thus, liability has been imposed for the failure to provide a suitable vehicle and proper supervision, Beardsell v. Tilton School, 89 N.H. 459, 200 A. 783 (1938), and the negligence of a coach in directing that members of the tennis team be taken home after practice by another team member known to be reckless. Hanson v. Reedley Joint Union High School Dist., 43 Cal. App. 2d 643, 111 P.2d 415 (1941).

Several cases have involved situations in which school officials have authorized team members to be transported by private automobile. The results of the cases have not, however, been in complete harmony. In one, the court upheld liability against the driver, and held a guest statute, which provides that guests may recover from their host only for injuries that are the result of wanton or willful conduct, was inapplicable. Kitzel v. Atkeson, 173 Kans. 198, 245 P.2d 170 (1952). In another case, the court denied liability because of the guest statute. Fessenden v. Smith, 255 Iowa 170, 124 N.W.2d 554 (1963). In neither case was an educational institution made a party, a probable result of their sovereign immunity status. Where that immunity does not apply, the institution that authorizes its students to travel by private automobile to athletic activities should bear responsibility for injuries that result therefrom. In such circumstances, the driver may become, in effect, the agent of the institution, especially if his or her expenses are reimbursed. But cf. Fessenden v. Smith, 255 Iowa 170, 124 N.W.2d 554 (1963) (driver not agent of school where neither control nor compensation).

application to endeavors which are part of the curriculum of the institution, they apply as well to extra-curricular activities.[131]

Notwithstanding the doubtlessly correct statement that "[p]arents do not send their children to school to be returned to them maimed because of the absence of proper supervision or abandonment of supervision," [132] educational institutions are not insurers of their students' safety,[133] and will be held liable for injuries suffered by students only when the institution, or someone for whom it is legally responsible, fail to meet the prescribed duty of care. Thus, in *Underhill v. Alameda Elementary School District*,[134] the court stated that

> [baseball, basketball, volleyball and handball] contribute to the physical development of the pupils participating, and there is nothing inherently dangerous about any of them. They seldom result in injury to either the participants or spectators and are ordinarily played by school children of all ages without adult supervision. Nevertheless, it is also a matter of common knowledge that children participating in such games and in fact in any form of play may injure themselves and each other, and that no amount of precaution or supervision on the part of parents or others will avoid such injuries. The injuries which may result from the playing of said games are ordinarily of an inconsequential nature and are incurred without fault on the part of anyone. In such cases there is no liability and, of course, the fundamental rules governing liability remain the same, even though the particular injury may prove to be of a more serious nature. The law does not make school districts insurers of the safety of the pupils at play or elsewhere and no liability is imposed upon a district under the above-mentioned section, in the absence of negligence on the part of the district, its officers or employees.[135]

Liability will, therefore, be denied for injuries that no amount of precaution, except elimination of the activity itself, could have prevented.[136] Liability will also be denied where the injury is solely the result of the unpreventable acts

---

See generally Annot., 34 A.L.R.3d 1210 (1970) (liability of public schools for transportation accidents).

131. Albers v. Independent School Dist. No. 302 of Lewis County, 94 Ida. 342, 487 P.2d 936 (1971). These principles apply with equal force to public and private institutions. Stehn v. Bernarr MacFadden Foundations, Inc., 434 F.2d 811 (6th Cir. 1970); Martin v. Roman Catholic Archbishop of Los Angeles, 158 Cal. App. 2d 64, 322 P.2d 31 (1958); Stafford v. Catholic Youth Organization, 202 So. 2d 333 (La. App. 1967); Marques v. Riverside Military Academy, 87 Ga. App. 370, 73 S.E.2d 574 (1952); Hillman v. Greater Miami Hebrew Academy, 72 So. 2d 668 (Fla. 1954); Sheehan v. St. Peter's Catholic School, 291 Minn. 1, 188 N.W.2d 868 (1971).

132. Ohman v. Board of Educ., 300 N.Y. 306, 311, 90 N.E.2d 474, 476 (1949) (Conway, J., dissenting). *See also* Berg v. Merricks, 20 Md. App. 666, 318 A.2d 220 (1974).

133. Cambareri v. Board of Educ. of Albany, 246 App. Div. 127, 284 N.Y.S. 892 (1936), *aff'd*, 283 N.Y. 741, 28 N.E.2d 968 (1940); Read v. School Dist. No. 211 of Lewis County, 7 Wash. 2d 502, 110 P.2d 179 (1941).

134. 133 Cal. App. 733, 24 P.2d 849 (1933).

135. 133 Cal. App. at 735-36, 24 P.2d at 851.

136. Weldy v. Oakland High School Dist. of Alameda County, 19 Cal. App. 2d 429, 65 P.2d 851 (1937) (a rowdy spectator throwing a bottle at a football game); Kanofsky v. Brooklyn Jewish Center, 265 N.Y. 634, 193 N.E. 420 (1934) (a failure by an able student to complete a simple exercise); Passafaro v. Board of Educ. of New York, 43 App. Div. 2d 918, 353 N.Y.S.2d 178 (1974) (slip in stocking feet during tumbling exercise); Cambareri v. Board of Educ. of Albany, 246 App. Div. 127, 284 N.Y.S. 892 (1936), *aff'd*, 283 N.Y. 741, 28 N.E.2d 968 (1940) (slip on tumbling mat); Gordon v. Deer Park School Dist. No. 414, 71 Wash. 2d 119, 426 P.2d 824 (1967) (a baseball bat slipping from the hands of a teacher); Read v. School Dist. No. 211 of Lewis County, 7 Wash. 2d 502, 110 P.2d 179 (1941) (an injury which could be explained only by the presence of many children playing a game).

of fellow-students,[137] and where contributory negligence or assumption of the risk are present.[138]

Probably the most difficult issue present in this area, is the extent to which an educational institution can be held liable for the negligent acts of its employees if its own duties have been satisfactorily performed. The traditional and majority rule is that, absent statutory provision to the contrary, an educational institution is not liable for the negligent acts of its teachers or instructors if they were selected with due care and the institution has met each of the other duties noted above.[139] The courts have relied upon a number of different considerations to support this rule. Thus, courts have reasoned that the institution's statutory duty is fully discharged if its own duties are satisfactorily performed; [140] that they are not subject to negligence liability as a result of the sovereign or charitable immunity doctrine; [141] or that teachers or instructors are not ordinary employees so that the doctrine of respondeat superior, which makes a master responsible for its servant's negligent acts, is not applicable.[142]

The traditional, or majority, rule will not be applicable in states which have either expressly made educational institutions liable for the negligence of their teachers or instructors,[143] or where the state has simply waived its sovereign immunity.[144] The trend of states to increasingly fall into one or another of these

---

137. McCloy v. Huntington Park Union High School Dist. of Los Angeles County, 139 Cal. App. 237, 33 P.2d 882 (1934).

138. These principles are discussed in detail at § 8.02. See Wright v. San Bernardino High School, 121 Cal. App. 342, 263 P.2d 25 (1953) (contributorily negligent when run into flight of ball); Albers v. Independent School District No. 302 of Lewis County, 94 Ida. 342, 487 P.2d 936 (1971) (assume risk of injury in pick-up basketball game in school gym on weekend); Gaspard v. Grain Dealers Mutual Ins. Co., 131 So. 2d 831 (La. App. 1961) (assume risk in recess baseball game); Robert v. Deposit School Dist. No. 1 of Town of Sanford, 13 N.Y.2d 709, 191 N.E.2d 901 (1963) (student baseball game spectator assume risk of injury). Since the participants in educational programs will frequently be minors, a slightly different standard may be applied with respect to both contributory negligence and assumption of risk. See RESTATEMENT (SECOND) OF TORTS §§ 464, 496D (1965).

139. Perkins v. Trask, 95 Mont. 1, 23 P.2d 982 (1933); Sherwood v. Moxee School Dist. No. 90, 58 Wash. 2d 351, 363 P.2d 138 (1961); Read v. School Dist. No. 211, Lewis County, 7 Wash. 2d 502, 110 P.2d 179 (1941).

140. Graff v. Board of Educ. of New York, 258 App. Div. 813, 15 N.Y.S.2d 941 (1939) (duty satisfied by provision of competent teacher).

141. Sawaya v. Tucson High School Dist. No. 1 of Pima County, 78 Ariz. 389, 281 P.2d 105 (1955); Hibbs v. Independent School Dist. of Green Mountain, 218 Iowa 841, 251 N.W. 606 (1933); Whitfield v. East Baton Rouge Parish School Bd., 23 So.2d 708 (La. App. 1945); Richards v. School Dist. of City of Birmingham, 348 Mich. 490, 83 N.W.2d 643 (1957); Mokovich v. Independent School Dist. of Virginia, No. 222, 177 Minn. 446, 225 N.W. 292 (1929); Rhoades v. School Dist. No. 9, Roosevelt County, 115 Mont. 352, 142 P.2d 890 (1943); Anderson v. Board of Educ. of Fargo, 49 N.D. 181, 190 N.W. 807 (1922); Martini v. Olymphant Borough School Dist., 83 Pa. D. & C. 206 (1952). The doctrines of sovereign and charitable immunity are considered at § 8.18.

142. Graff v. Board of Educ. of New York, 258 App. Div. 813, 15 N.Y.S.2d 941 (1939); Katterschinsky v. Board of Educ. of N.Y., 215 App. Div. 695, 212 N.Y.S. 424 (1925).

143. A typical provision provides that

[a] public entity is liable for injury proximately caused by an act of omission of an employee of the public entity within the scope of his employment if the act or omission would, apart from this section, have given rise to a course of action against that employee or his personal representative.

CAL. GOVT. CODE ANN. § 815.2 (Deering's 1973). See Dailey v. Los Angeles Unified School Dist., 2 Cal. 3d 741, 87 Cal. Rptr. 376, 470 P.2d 360 (1970); Lee v. Board of Educ. of New York, 263 App. Div. 23, 31 N.Y.S.2d 113 (1941).

144. Rook v. State, 254 App. Div. 67, 4 N.Y.S.2d 116 (1938).

patterns is well evidenced by *Domino v. Mercurio,*[145] which arose in New York where schools had traditionally been immune from liability for the negligence of their teachers. When, however, the state waived sovereign immunity by statute, the court held that public schools and school boards were no longer protected by that doctrine, so that they became liable for the negligence of their teachers and instructors under the general rule of respondeat superior.

Where educational institutions are charged with responsibility for their employees' actions, their duty toward their students is somewhat altered. They still have the duty to exercise due care to protect the students from unreasonable risks and dangers, but this duty will not be fulfilled simply by the use of reasonable care in delegating its performance to others. Rather, it will be satisfied only if the person to whom the duty of protection and supervision is delegated fulfills it in a non-negligent manner.[146] In other words, if the teacher or instructor fails to properly perform the supervisory duty, then the employer-institution will be vicariously liable under the doctrine of respondeat superior for all resulting injuries.[147] In the absence of any such employee negligence, the institution will be liable only for breaches of its own duties.[148]

Since the athletic facilities owned or maintained by educational institutions will inevitably be used by non-students for non-school purposes, it is also necessary to consider the institutions' duties under such circumstances.[149] In

---

145. 17 A.D.2d 342, 234 N.Y.S.2d 1011 (1962), *aff'd,* 13 N.Y.2d 922, 193 N.E.2d 893 (1963).

146. Carabba v. Anacortes School Dist. No. 103, 72 Wash. 2d 939, 435 P.2d 936 (1968).

147. Buzzard v. East Lake School Dist. of Lake County, 34 Cal. App. 2d 316, 93 P.2d 233 (1939) (negligent teacher supervision); Brown v. Board of Educ. of New York, 37 App. Div. 2d 836, 326 N.Y.S.2d 9 (1971) (teacher failed to follow prescribed syllabus); Armlin v. Board of Educ. of Middleborough Central School Dist., 36 App. Div. 2d 877, 320 N.Y.S.2d 402 (1971) (teacher failed to follow prescribed syllabus); Domino v. Mercurio, 17 App. Div. 2d 342, 234 N.Y.S.2d 1011 (1962), *aff'd,* 13 N.Y.2d 922, 193 N.E.2d 893 (1963) (teacher failed to properly supervise a softball game, with the result that a player fell over spectators who had gotten too close); Rivera v. Board of Educ. of New York, 11 App. Div. 2d 7, 201 N.Y.S.2d 372 (1960) (teacher compelled students to use defective equipment); Lee v. Board of Education of New York, 263 App. Div. 23, 31 N.Y.S.2d 113 (1941) (teacher compelled children to play football in busy street); Rook v. State, 254 App. Div. 67, 4 N.Y.S.2d 116 (1938) (teacher compelled children to play with defective equipment); Keesee v. Board of Educ. of New York, 37 Misc. 2d 414, 235 N.Y.S.2d 300 (1962) (teacher failed to follow prescribed syllabus); Brooks v. Board of Educ. of New York, 29 Misc. 2d 19, 205 N.Y.S.2d 777 (1960), *aff'd,* 15 App. Div. 2d 495, 222 N.Y.S.2d 184 (1961) (teacher compelled children to compete in a dangerous sport where participants were unevenly matched); Bard v. Board of Educ. of New York, 140 N.Y.S.2d 850 (1955) (prospective physical education teacher was compelled to complete exercise and was injured due to defective equipment); Quigley v. School Dist. No. 45J3, 251 Ore. 452, 446 P.2d 177 (1968) (negligent supervision); Guerrieri v. Tyson, 147 Pa. Super. 239, 24 A.2d 468 (1942) (teacher provided negligent medical assistance; liability for medical treatment of athletic injuries is considered at § 8.07); Carabba v. Anacortes School Dist. No. 103, 72 Wash. 2d 939, 435 P.2d 936 (1968) (wrestling referee, employed by the school board, negligently supervised match causing serious injury when an illegal hold was utilized); Rodriguez v. Seattle School Dist. No. 1, 66 Wash. 2d 51, 401 P.2d 326 (1965) (negligent supervision); Briscoe v. School Dist. No. 123, Grays Harbor County, 32 Wash. 2d 353, 201 P.2d 697 (1949) (negligent supervision); Morris v. Union High School Dist. A., King County, 160 Wash. 121, 294 P. 998 (1931) (football coach required injured player to compete; liability of coaches is considered at § 8.06); Cirillo v. Milwaukee, 34 Wis. 2d 705, 150 N.W.2d 460 (1967) (negligent supervision). Liability has also been imposed for injuries that have occurred during a high school letterman's initiation ceremony. Sherwood v. Moxee School Dist. No. 90, 58 Wash. 2d 351, 363 P.2d 138 (1961) (death). *See also* Chappel v. Franklin Pierce School Dist., 71 Wash. 2d 17, 426 P.2d 471 (1967) (social club).

148. Ostrowski v. Board of Educ. of Coxsackie-Athens School Dist., 31 App. Div. 2d 571, 294 N.Y.S.2d 871 (1968).

149. *See generally* Annot., 37 A.L.R.3d 738 (1971); Annot., 37 A.L.R.3d 712 (1971).

general, the duty of educational institutions to non-students using their athletic facilities is to exercise reasonable care under the circumstances. Thus, the institutions must keep equipment and facilities in a safe and suitable condition so that those using them will not be subjected to unreasonable risks of physical harm. If dangerous conditions do exist and cannot be immediately corrected, then the school must warn the non-students of the conditions so that they may avoid the danger.[150] This duty to non-students was considered in *Kelly v. Board of Education of the City of New York*,[151] where a public school had made its gymnasium available for use by a community center to provide recreation to neighborhood youths in the evening. On the evening in question, the youths moved a springboard to the center of the floor, for the purpose of propelling themselves over a gymnastic "buck" which was placed in front of the springboard. The springboard was defective and the defects had existed for several weeks. One of the youths was injured when he attempted to use the device. On these facts, the court held the school district liable, stating that

> [t]he duty, therefore, rested upon the board of education to use reasonable care to keep the premises and appliances in a safe and suitable condition, so that invitees would not be unnecessarily and unreasonably exposed to danger. It was shown that this springboard had been out of repair for three or four weeks, and that such condition had been reported to the director. The duty of the [school] board was then to remove this defective apparatus, and not leave it in the gymnasium, or to take some means of notifying the invitees of its dangerous condition and prohibit its use.[152]

A similar result was reached where injury was the result of improper glass having been installed in a door directly under a basketball goal.[153] Educational institutions are not, however, the insurers of the safety of non-students using their facilities, and will not be responsible for injuries caused by their own contributorily negligent conduct or for which they assumed the risk.[154] In addition, if the institution simply makes its facilities available for use by non-students and assumes no responsibility for the conduct of the activities undertaken, it will have no duty to supervise those activities.[155] In short, the institution will owe no different duty to its non-student invitees than would any

150. Fitzsimmons v. State University of New York at Stonybrook, 42 App. Div. 2d 636, 345 N.Y.S.2d 171 (1973); Kelly v. Board of Education of New York, 191 App. Div. 251, 180 N.Y.S. 796 (1920); Leahey v. State, 46 N.Y.S.2d 310 (Ct. Cl. 1944).

151. 191 App. Div. 251, 180 N.Y.S. 796 (1920).

152. 191 App. Div. at 253, 180 N.Y.S. at 797.

153. Stevens v. Central School Dist. No. 1 of Town of Ramapo, 25 App. Div. 2d 871, 270 N.Y.S.2d 23 (1966), aff'd, 21 N.Y.2d 780, 288 N.Y.S.2d 475, 235 N.E.2d 448 (1968).

154. Chase v. Shasta Lake Union School Dist., 259 Cal. App. 2d 612, 66 Cal. Rptr. 517 (1968) (collision in adult evening softball game with an incinerator known to be close while chasing a fly ball); Iacona v. Board of Educ. of New York, 285 App. Div. 1168, 140 N.Y.S.2d 539 (1955) (participant in an informal boxing match simply dropping dead during the second round); Lutzker v. Board of Educ. of New York, 262 App. Div. 881, 28 N.Y.S.2d 496 (1941), aff'd, 287 N.Y. 822, 41 N.E.2d 97 (1942) (struck by a bat while watching a game); Hanna v. State, 46 Misc. 2d 9, 258 N.Y.S.2d 694 (1965); Maltz v. Board of Educ. of New York, 32 Misc. 2d 492, 114 N.Y.S.2d 856, aff'd, 282 App. Div. 888, 124 N.Y.S.2d 911 (1953) (a collision with a brick wall located dangerously close to a basketball goal when the non-student had played upon the court frequently); Scala v. New York, 200 Misc. 475, 102 N.Y.S.2d 790 (1951) (tripping over a curb that was obviously protruding while chasing a ball).

155. Orsini v. Guilderland Central School Dist. No. 2, 46 App. Div. 2d 700, 360 N.Y.S.2d 288 (1974); Bennett v. Board of Educ. of New York, 16 App. Div. 2d 651, 226 N.Y.S.2d 593 (1962), aff'd, 13 N.Y.2d 1104, 246 N.Y.S.2d 634, 196 N.E.2d 268 (1963); Glatstein v. New York, 6 App. Div. 2d 824, 176 N.Y.S.2d 234 (1955).

other landowner,[156] and will not be burdened with the duties that are ordinarily owed to its students, unless it agrees to supervise the activities.

Apart from the liability of the institution which has overall responsibility for a sports program, it is also necessary to consider the potential liability of the teachers or instructors who are directly in charge of those programs.[157] The primary duty owed by teachers to their students is the duty to supervise the activities in which the students participate.[158] A teacher involved in physical education activity has the duty to supervise in a sufficiently diligent manner to prevent the students from confronting unreasonable risks of injury.[159] Perhaps the best statement of this duty is that

> [a] teacher occupies a position in relation to his pupils comparable to that of a parent to children. He has the duty to instruct and warn pupils in his custody of any dangers which he knows or in the exercise of ordinary care ought to know are present in the gymnasium; and to instruct them in methods which will protect them from these dangers, whether the danger arises from equipment, devices, machines, or other causes. A failure to warn students of such danger or to instruct them in the means of avoiding such danger is negligence.[160]

The teacher's duty of supervision does not, however, render the teacher the insurer of the safety of the students under his or her supervision. Even if the duty is properly performed, accidents will inevitably occur, and it is clear that a teacher will not be responsible in many cases. In *Nestor v. City of New York,* [161] for example, a teacher was supervising a group of children, most of whom were trying to catch fly balls. While the teacher was 30 feet away distributing milk, one of the children tried to hit a descending ball with a bat, rather than catch it as the others were doing. In the process, the batter struck the head of another child who was trying to catch the same ball. The court held the teacher's supervision to be free of negligence, since the injury was an unforeseeable accident. The court's language is instructive:

> Even if the teacher had had the game under steady observation and the measure of his supervision had been constant, an assumption that he could have anticipated what ensued would be without justifiable warrant. The teacher would be required to be invested with a profound prescience to have foreseen that Michael would attempt, after batting the ball, to run to catch it and that Tony, would suddenly run towards the ball with bat in hand and, without warning, swing with his bat at the descending ball while Michael was endeavoring to snare it.
>
> To urge that the teacher should have anticipated each of the separate occurrences constituting the links in the chain of events hereinabove

---

156. Streickler v. New York, 13 N.Y.2d 716, 241 N.Y.S.2d 846, 191 N.E.2d 903 (1963).

157. The closely analogous question of the liability of coaches is considered in § 8.06.

158. Kerby v. Elk Grove Union High School Dist., 1 Cal. App. 2d 246, 36 P.2d 431 (1934).

See generally Proehl, *Tort Liability of Teachers,* 12 VAND. L. REV. 723 (1959); Seitz, *Legal Responsibility Under Tort Law of School Personnel and School Districts as Regards Negligent Conduct Toward Pupils,* 15 HASTINGS L.J. 495 (1964); Note, *Negligence Liability of Schoolteachers in California,* 15 HASTINGS L.J. 567 (1964); Annot., 32 A.L.R.2d 1163 (1953).

159. Pirkle v. Oakdale Union Grammar School Dist., 40 Cal. 2d 207, 253 P.2d 1 (1953); Albers v. Independent School District No. 302 of Lewis County, 94 Ida. 342, 487 P.2d 936 (1971); Luce v. Board of Educ. of Johnson City, 2 App. Div. 2d 502, 157 N.Y.S.2d 123 (1956); La Valley v. Stanford, 272 App. Div. 183, 70 N.Y.S.2d 460 (1947); Reynolds v. State, 207 Misc. 963, 141 N.Y.S.2d 615 (1955).

160. Lueck v. Janesville, 57 Wis. 2d 254, 204 N.W.2d 6 (1973).

161. 28 Misc. 2d 70, 211 N.Y.S.2d 975 (1961).

recited, or that a blast by the teacher on his whistle would have frozen the two boys into instant immobility and averted the accident which ensued, is indulgence in pure speculation. This reasoning is fortified by the fact that Anthony Occhuzzio said that he saw Michael at the last moment but that he could not check his swing. This was an accident that could occur equally in the presence or absence of the teacher.

In the context of all the foregoing, it would be without judicial sanction to conclude that the circumstances described were within the orbit of reasonable apprehension.[162]

The question involved in the duty of supervision, therefore, will be whether a reasonably prudent person in the position of the teacher should have had reason to believe that the situation presented the possibility of serious injury to anyone participating in the activity.[163] If such a basis for apprehension is present, then the supervising teacher will have the duty to undertake reasonable actions to prevent an injury from occurring. If such actions are not undertaken, then the teacher will be liable for the injuries caused thereby.[164] Even if a teacher

---

162. 28 Misc. at 71-72, 211 N.Y.S.2d at 977 (citations omitted). *See also* Reithardt v. Board of Educ. of Yuba County, 43 Cal. App. 2d 629, 111 P. 2d 440 (1941) (student horse-play prior to start of class); Brackman v. Adrian, 472 S.W.2d 735 (Tenn. 1971) (catcher injured by thrown bat); Benedetto v. Travelers Insurance Co., 172 So. 2d 354 (La. 1965) (plaintiff hit by bat that slipped from batter's hands during recess softball game); Segerman v. Jones, 256 Md. 109, 259 A.2d 794 (1969) (calisthenics); Wire v. Williams, 270 Minn. 390, 133 N.W.2d 840 (1965) (unavoidable accident in physical education class); Passafaro v. Board of Educ. of New York, 43 App. Div. 2d 918, 353 N.Y.S.2d 178 (1974) (tumbling); Kaufman v. New York, 30 Misc. 2d 285, 214 N.Y.S.2d 767 (1961); Gordon v. Deer Park School Dist. No. 414, 71 Wash. 2d 119, 426 P.2d 824 (1967) (bat slipped from teacher's hands).

163. Reynolds v. State, 207 Misc. 963, 141 N.Y.S.2d 615 (1955).

164. Dailey v. Los Angeles Unified School Dist., 2 Cal. 3d 741, 87 Cal. Rptr. 376, 470 P.2d 360 (1970) (leave students unsupervised); Pirkle v. Oakdale Union Grammar School Dist., 40 Cal. 2d 65, 253 P.2d 1 (1953) (failure to warn about dangers in touch football); Bellman v. San Francisco High School Dist., 11 Cal. 2d 576, 81 P.2d 894 (1938) (failure to take into consideration the athletic aptitude and physical and emotional strength of a student, as well as the nature of the activity, in determining the kind of instruction to be given individual students); Rodriguez v. San Jose Unified School Dist., 157 Cal. App. 2d 842, 322 P.2d 70 (1958) (failure to limit the number of students being supervised); Ogando v. Carquinez Grammar School Dist. of Contra Costa County, 24 Cal. App. 2d 567, 75 P.2d 641 (1938) (failure to follow rule to supervise playground); Wright v. San Bernardino High School, 121 Cal. App. 342, 263 P.2d 25 (1953) (failure to warn about dangers in handball); Sheehan v. St. Peter's Catholic School, 291 Minn. 1, 188 N.W.2d 868 (1971) (leave students unsupervised); Gardner v. State, 281 N.Y. 212, 22 N.E.2d 344 (1939) (failure to properly instruct about acrobatic stunt); Darrow v. West Genesee Central School Dist., 41 App. Div. 2d 897, 342 N.Y.S.2d 611 (1973) (failure to properly instruct about soccer); Armlin v. Board of Educ. of Middleborough Central School Dist., 36 App. Div. 2d 877, 320 N.Y.S.2d 402 (1971) (failure to follow rule to have students and equipment in view at all times); Domino v. Mercurio, 17 App. Div. 2d 342, 234 N.Y.S.2d 1011 (1962), *aff'd,* 13 N.Y.2d 922, 193 N.E.2d 893 (1963) (failure to keep spectators from congregating so closely to the playing field as to pose dangers to the students); Rivera v. Board of Educ. of New York, 11 App. Div. 2d 7, 201 N.Y.S.2d 372 (1960) (failure to provide safe equipment); La Valley v. Stanford, 272 App. Div. 183, 70 N.Y.S.2d 460 (1947) (failure to warn about dangers in boxing); Lee v. Board of Educ. of New York, 263 App. Div. 23, 31 N.Y.S.2d 113 (1941) (failure to refrain from "compelling a physical training class to engage in a game of football on Forty-Second Street, Manhattan, during a congested traffic hour"); Graff v. Board of Educ. of New York, 258 App. Div. 813, 15 N.Y.S.2d 941 (1939) (failure to warn about dangers in using a rubber ball); Rook v. State, 254 App. Div. 67, 4 N.Y.S.2d 116 (1938) (failure to provide safe equipment); Keesee v. Board of Educ. of New York, 37 Misc. 2d 414, 235 N.Y.S.2d 300 (1962) (failure to follow prescribed syllabus); Guerrieri v. Tyson, 147 Pa. Super. 239, 24 A.2d 468 (1942) (failure to refrain from rendering medical treatment not competent to provide; liability for medical treatment of athletic injuries is considered at § 8.07); Briscoe v. School Dist. No. 123, Grays Harbor County, 32 Wash. 2d 353, 201 P.2d 697 (1949) (failure to closely supervise a rough or dangerous activity to insure that it is properly conducted); Cirillo v. Milwaukee, 34 Wis. 2d 705, 150 N.W.2d 460 (1967) (leave students unsupervised).

is held liable for sports-related injuries, many states have enacted statutory provisions which will save the teacher harmless from personal liability.[165]

If, however, the teacher had no reason to believe that the situation presented the possibility of serious injury to anyone participating in the event, then, as suggested by *Nestor,* there will be no liability because the teacher's duty of supervision would not have required the undertaking of any special procedures.[166] Similarly, if the students are properly instructed in the rules and procedures of the activity, the teacher will, absent special circumstances, not be required to constantly observe every phase of the activity as it is being conducted.[167] There will also be no liability where the injured student is contributorily negligent or assumes the risk of the act which caused the injury.[168]

In light of the potential liabilities which confront institutions which conduct sports activities, it may well be asked whether the assets of the institution may be insulated from sports-related liabilities.[169] As a traditional proposition, the most effective means of conducting relatively high-risk activities without subjecting all of one's assets to the liabilities thereof is to form a separate corporation through which the activities will be conducted. The corporation provides asset-insulation because it is a legal entity separate and distinct from its shareholders. Thus, when injury recoveries are awarded the only assets available for their satisfaction are those of the corporation, and the shareholders are liable only for the limited amount of capital which they have exchanged for their shares of stock.

165. *See e.g.,* Conn. Gen. Stat. § 10-235 (1977); N.J. Stat. Ann. § 18A:60-4 (1968); N.Y. Education Law § 3023 (McKinney Supp. 1978). *See also* Kobylanski v. Chicago Bd. of Educ., 63 Ill. 165, 347 N.E.2d 705 (1976) (statute giving teachers *in loco parentis* authority, so that they will be liable only for wilful or wanton action). *But see* Baird v. Hosner, 46 Ohio St. 2d 273, 347 N.E.2d 273 (1976) (denying *in loco parentis* protection in the absence of statute).

166. Kerby v. Elk Grove Union High School Dist., 1 Cal. App. 2d 246, 36 P.2d 431 (1934) (teacher did not know of aneurism of student, so no duty to undertake special precautions); Stafford v. Catholic Youth Organization, 202 So. 2d 333 (La. App. 1967) (no liability where teacher simply wrestled with students). Thus, there would be no negligence, for example, where a teacher, who was well-acquainted with his students and had rendered proper instruction, paired-off a class of thirty students for wrestling exercises without exactly matching the size and weight of each pair. Reynolds v. State, 207 Misc. 963, 141 N.Y.S.2d 615 (1955). *See also* Pirkle v. Oakdale Union Grammar School Dist., 40 Cal.2d 207, 253 P.2d 1 (1953) (touch football selection); Underhill v. Alameda Elementary School Dist. of Alameda County, 133 Cal. App. 733, 24 P.2d 849 (1933) (baseball game). *But cf.* Brooks v. Board of Educ. of New York, 29 Misc. 2d 19, 205 N.Y.S.2d 777 (1960), *aff'd,* 15 App. Div. 2d 495, 222 N.Y.S.2d 184 (1961) (physical education teacher picked randomly for a dangerous game).

167. Lopez v. New York, 4 App. Div. 2d 48, 163 N.Y.S.2d 562 (1957), *aff'd,* 4 N.Y.2d 738, 171 N.Y.S.2d 860 (1958); Nestor v. New York, 28 Misc. 70, 211 N.Y.S.2d 975 (1961) (teacher distributing milk 30 feet from accident); Chapman v. State, 6 Wash. App. 316, 492 P.2d 607 (1972) (teacher 30-40 feet away supervising other students in physical education class); Lueck v. Janesville, 57 Wis. 2d 254, 204 N.W.2d 6 (1973); Fagan v. Summers, 498 P.2d 1227 (Wyo. 1972).

168. Cox v. Barnes, 469 S.W.2d 61 (Ky. 1971) (student contributorily negligent at school outing and drowned); Stafford v. Catholic Youth Organization, 202 So. 2d 333 (La. App. 1967) (assume risk of wrestling with teacher); Berg v. Merricks, 20 Md. App. 666, 318 A.2d 220 (1974) (improperly executed exercise); Sayers v. Ranger, 16 N.J. Super. 22, 83 A.2d 775 (1951) (assume risk when jumping over gymnastic horse with unconventional method known to be dangerous). The contributory negligence and assumption of the risk principles are considered at § 8.02.

169. This result may of course, be accomplished in most circumstances by the purchase of insurance. *See* A. Grieve, The Legal Aspects of Athletics 111-16 (1969).

If an educational institution is authorized to form such a corporation, the basic legal question that it will present is whether the corporation will be a viable legal entity. As a general rule, a corporation will be recognized as a separate entity. If the facts in any given case, however, indicate that the corporation is merely the alter ego of its organizers, and is not in fact operated as a separate entity, then it may be disregarded, with the result that there would then be no limited liability advantage to its shareholders.[170] A corporation formed to conduct athletic activities will normally be recognized as a viable entity so long as it has control of its own decision-making, and is independent of the educational institution that is responsible for its initial organization.[171] To the extent, however, that the corporation is subject to the control, either financial or administrative, of the institution, or is set up with the evidently dominant purpose of avoiding specific tort liability, the corporation's separate identity will be more likely to be disregarded.[172] The provision of financial support or other

170. *See generally* 1 W. FLETCHER, CYCLOPEDIA OF CORPORATIONS § 41-46 (1963); E. LATTY, SUBSIDIARIES AND AFFILIATED CORPORATIONS ch. 2 (1936); Dobbyn, *A Practical Approach to Consistency in Veil Piercing Cases,* 19 KANSAS L. REV. 185 (1971); Gillespie, *The Thin Corporate Line: The Loss of Limited Liability Protection,* 45 N.D.L. REV. 363 (1969).

171. Scott v. University of Michigan Athletic Ass'n, 152 Mich. 684, 116 N.W. 624 (1908) (unincorporated association which conducted university's intercollegiate sports activities was indicated to be viably separate where it was essentially independent of university control); Plattsburgh College Benevolent and Educ. Ass'n v. Board of Assessors of the Town of Peru, 43 Misc. 2d 741, 252 N.Y.S.2d 229 (1964) (separate identity upheld where corporation operated entirely independently of the college); Faculty-Student Ass'n of the New York State College for Teachers, Albany, Inc. v. City of Albany, 17 Misc. 2d 404, 191 N.Y.S.2d 120 (1959) (separate identity of corporation organized to conduct operation of dormitories, bookstores and other student services upheld where it was completely self-governing and independent of the university).

Although it does not involve an educational institution, perhaps the strongest case indicating that separate incorporation of an athletic program may be viable is Klinsky v. Hanson Van Winkle Munning Co., 38 N.J. Super. 439, 119 A.2d 166 (1955), where an employer had separately incorporated an athletic association to conduct all employee athletic events. Hoping to get to the deeper pocket of the employer, the plaintiff, who had been injured by a bat that slipped from the hands of a batter at a family outing, alleged that the corporation was a mere instrument of the employer to maintain good labor relations. The court rejected this argument, however, and upheld the legal status of the athletic corporation, since the employer did not have or exercise ultimate control of its activities. Although the court noted that the employer provided financial support for the athletic corporation, it did not believe this fact to be of sufficient significance to alter the result.

172. Thus, in Rubtchinsky v. State University of New York at Albany, 46 Misc. 2d 679, 260 N.Y.S.2d 256 (1965), suit was brought against a university for injuries suffered by a student in an athletic program sponsored by the Student Association, a separate unincorporated association in the university community. Although the university sought to defend on the ground that the Association was a separate and distinct entity, the court rejected the defense. It found that under the constitution of the Association, the president of the university had a final veto power, which the court believed to be

consonant with the effort to grant college students as much autonomy as possible in their extracurricular activities while still retaining final control in the hands of adult authority.

46 Misc. 2d at 681, 260 N.Y.S.2d at 259. A similar result was reached in Carabba v. Anacortes School Dist. No. 103, 72 Wash. 2d 939, 435 P.2d 936 (1968), where the court observed that

[t]he fact that the wrestling matches were nominally staged by the student-body associations of the schools can afford no shield against liability on the part of respondent school districts under the facts appearing in this record, e.g. the participation of the faculty in the governing and operating of the student associations, and the full veto power possessed by the schools over proposed actions of the student associations.

Id. at 957 n.8, 435 P.2d at 947 n.8. *See also* T. BLACKWELL, COLLEGE LAW 186 (1961); Westbrook v. University of Georgia Athletic Ass'n, 206 Ga. 667, 58 S.E.2d 428 (1950) (not a separate entity for business competition purposes); People *ex rel.* Regents of University of Michigan v. Pommerening, 250 Mich. 391, 230 N.W. 194 (1930) (viability of corporation organized to conduct intercollegiate

services will not be determinative of the result, but it goes without saying that the more direct the financial support the less likely it is that separate viability will be found.

In short, the separate incorporation of an entity to conduct educationally-related athletic programs is an expedient means to *minimize the likelihood* of institutional tort liability. It must be borne in mind, however, that persuasive arguments may be readily mustered to pierce that corporate status, and the institution will seriously jeopardize its effort by retaining financial or administrative control. The further removed the institution is from the corporation, the more likely the avoidance of liability.[173]

§ 8.06. Liability of Coaches.

Since coaches normally have the most direct control of the activities of athletes, it is not surprising that they are frequently named as defendants in suits brought by injured athletes. In these cases, the critical inquiry will be whether the coach has fulfilled the duty to exercise reasonable care for the protection of the athletes under his or her supervision, which duty will be satisfied by providing proper instruction in how to play the game and by showing due concern that the athletes are in proper physical condition. The coach is not, however, an insurer of the athletes' safety, and the duty of care will be satisfied if the coach takes all reasonable steps to minimize the possibility of their injury in games that involve an inevitable amount of physical contact.[174] Thus, a coach who has properly instructed the players will not be liable for injuries caused when a first baseman hits another participant with a wildly thrown ball [175] or when a slightly injured player is sent home without first receiving medical aid.[176]

A pertinent case in this area is in *Vendrell v. School District No. 26C, Malheur County,*[177] where a high school football player suffered a broken neck, and became a permanent paraplegic, when he charged head first into approaching tacklers. When the player brought suit alleging that several acts of his coach were negligent, the court absolved the coach, and the school district, of liability, holding that the duty of care had been fully satisfied. The court began its analysis by noting that all students on the football team had to be pronounced physically fit by a physician and once fitness was determined they were put through a training program that included calisthenics, classes on physical conditioning and training rules, and instruction in the fundamental skills of the game, including the technique of using protective equipment to absorb blows.

---

athletics not upheld where Board of Regents appointed its officers, and its control was to be in such officers as the governing body of the university should designate, since these facts indicated that it was but an operating agency of the Regents which was at all times under the Regents control); Wallace v. Weiss, 82 Misc. 2d 1053, 372 N.Y.S.2d 416 (1975) (power to exercise control).

173. These same principles have been considered with regard to separate incorporation of student publications to protect the university from libel liability. Abbott, *The Student Press: Some First Impressions,* 16 WAYNE L. REV. 1, 13 (1969); Note, *Tort Liability of a University for Libelous Material in Student Publications,* 71 MICH. L. REV. 1061, 1074-75 (1973).

174. McGee v. Board of Educ. of City of New York, 16 App. Div. 2d 99, 226 N.Y.S.2d 329 (1962).

175. McGee v. Board of Educ. of City of New York, 16 App. Div. 2d 99, 226 N.Y.S.2d 329 (1962).

176. Duda v. Gaines, 12 N.J. Super. 326, 79 A.2d 695 (1951). Liability for medical treatment of athletic injuries is considered at §§ 8.07 — 8.08.

177. 233 Ore. 1, 376 P.2d 406 (1962).

The coach had stressed these "fundamentals" as an essential aspect of successful play and self-protection. In short, the player had undergone extensive training and practice under competent supervision and instruction. In reaching its conclusion of non-liability, the court summarized the responsibility of an athletic coach by observing that

> [n]o one expects a football coach to extract from the game the body clashes that cause bruises, jolts and hard falls. To remove them would end the sport. *The coach's function is to minimize the possibility that the body contacts may result in something more than slight injury.* The extensive calisthenics, running and other forms of muscular exercise to which the ... coaches subjected the ... squad were intended to place the players in sound physical condition so that they could withstand the shocks, blows and other rough treatment with which they would meet in actual play.[178]

Where the coach does not conduct the activities, or the persons, under his or her direction in such a way as to minimize the possibility of injury, the coach will be liable for the injuries thereby caused. Thus, liability has been found where a coach requires a player to compete when he or she knows, or in the exercise of ordinary care should have known, that the player was already suffering from serious injuries to his back and spine;[179] directs that a severely injured player be carried from the field without awaiting the arrival of medical assistance;[180] allows a team to compete against an opponent whose players are grossly disproportionate in size and ability;[181] allows spectators to congregate so closely to the playing field as to pose dangers to the players;[182] fails to properly instruct his wrestlers in the uses of, and defenses to, certain holds that may pose dangers of physical injury;[183] or instructs one team member to drive others home after practice, although the driver is known to be a reckless driver of an unsafe jalopy.[184]

The coach's duty to his players also encompasses activities which are not, as such, part of the sports activity. In *De Gooyer v. Harkness*,[185] for example, a coach was in charge of a high school lettermen's society. During an initiation ceremony, which was under the coach's direction, it was decided that each initiate should be subjected to a slight electrical shock. When it was found that the customarily used electrical apparatus was not available, the group decided

---

178. 233 Ore. at 15, 376 P.2d at 413. *See also* Berg v. Merricks, 20 Md. App. 666, 318 A.2d 220 (1974) Lovitt v. Concord School Dist., 59 Mich. App. 415, 228 N.W.2d 479 (1975).

179. Morris v. Union High School Dist. A., King County, 160 Wash. 121, 294 P. 998 (1931). *But cf.* Hale v. Davies, 86 Ga. App. 126, 70 S.E.2d 923 (1952) (coach liable only if wanton or wilful act; very poor decision). The playing of injured athletes is discussed in H. Savage, American College Athletics 145 (Carnegie Fndn. 1929).

180. Welch v. Dunsmuir Joint Union School Dist., 326 P.2d 633 (Cal. App. 1958). *See also* Mogabgab v. Orleans Parish School Bd., 239 So. 2d 456 (La. App. 1970) (failure to summon medical assistance after football player collapsed from heat stroke while running windsprints). *But cf.* Duda v. Gaines, 12 N.J. Super. 326, 79 A.2d 695 (1951) (no liability where no real need to summon medical assistance).

181. This possibility was raised in Vendrell v. School District No. 26C, Malheur County, 226 Ore. 263, 360 P.2d 282 (1961).

182. Domino v. Mercurio, 17 App. Div. 2d 342, 234 N.Y.S.2d 1011 (1962), *aff'd,* 13 N.Y.2d 922, 193 N.E.2d 893 (1963).

183. Stehn v. Bernarr MacFadden Foundations, Inc., 434 F.2d 811 (6th Cir. 1970).

184. Hanson v. Reedley Joint Union High School Dist., 43 Cal. App. 2d 643, 111 P.2d 415 (1941).

185. 70 S.D. 26, 13 N.W.2d 815 (1944). *See also* Sherwood v. Moxee School Dist. No. 90, 58 Wash. 2d 351, 363 P.2d 138 (1961).

to attach a cord to an electric light socket, pass the current through a rheostat (a glass jar full of water) and then to the initiate. Even though this procedure caused severe shock to the first several initiates, it was not stopped, and on a subsequent use one of the initiates was electrocuted. Inasmuch as the coach was in full control of the initiation proceedings, the court imposed personal liability upon him for the death, finding that he had failed to take proper precautions to prevent such an unfortunate occurrence.

§ 8.07. Liability for Providing Medical Treatment for Athletic Injuries.

When an injury occurs in a sports activity, it will frequently require medical treatment. In order to consider the legal principles that apply to such treatment, it is important to focus on two related issues. The first concerns the responsibility of those who conduct sports activities to provide medical care to persons who are injured in such activities, and will be considered in this section. The second issue involves the legal responsibilities of doctors who provide medical treatment to athletes, which will be considered in the next section.

The persons and organizations in charge of sports activities will have a duty to secure or provide reasonable medical assistance to injured participants or spectators as soon as possible under the circumstances.[186] Whether the duty has been met in any given case will normally depend upon the quality of the treatment, and the speed with which it is rendered. When satisfactory medical assistance is provided within a reasonable period of time, the duty will have been fulfilled. Thus, liability would presumably not be found where a doctor in attendance at a sports event provided immediate, and reasonable, medical assistance to an injured participant. When such assistance is not immediately available, the duty of care will require that the injured party be transported to a place where it can be rendered as quickly as reasonably possible.[187] It will also require that the injured party be properly cared for until medical attention can be obtained. Thus, a football coach was held liable for serious injuries suffered by one of his players when, despite suspicions that the player had suffered a severe neck or back injury, he directed that the player be carried from the field by eight of his teammates without awaiting the arrival of a physician.[188] Liability will be denied, however, where the delay in summoning medical assistance does not cause or aggravate an injury.[189] Moreover, if the injuries do not reasonably appear to be serious, there may then be no need to summon medical assistance.[190] The circumstances of a particular injury may also indicate that transportation to a hospital is preferable to summoning a physician who would

---

186. "Reasonable medical assistance" will require the provision of reasonable facilities and equipment as well as persons with the necessary degree of skill and experience. Clark v. State, 276 App. Div. 10, 93 N.Y.S.2d 28 (1949), aff'd, 302 N.Y. 795, 99 N.E.2d 300 (1951).
    See generally Ryan, Medical Practices in Sports, 38 LAW & CONTEMP. PROBS. 99 (1973).
187. Clark v. State, 276 App. Div. 10, 93 N.Y.S.2d 28 (1949), aff'd, 302 N.Y. 795, 99 N.E.2d 300 (1951). See also Mogabgab v. Orleans Parish School Bd., 239 So. 2d 456 (La. App. 1970).
188. Welch v. Dunsmuir Joint Union High School Dist., 326 P.2d 633 (Cal. App. 1958) (inter-school football scrimmage). See also Durham v. Commonwealth, 406 S.W.2d 858 (Ky. App. 1966) (fatally injured a swimmer when he was improperly pulled from water).
189. Pirkle v. Oakdale Union Grammar School Dist., 40 Cal. 2d 207, 253 P.2d 1 (1953) (junior high school touch football); Clark v. State, 276 App. Div. 10, 93 N.Y.S.2d 28 (1949), aff'd, 302 N.Y. 795, 99 N.E.2d 300 (1951).
190. Duda v. Gaines, 12 N.J. Super. 326, 79 A.2d 695 (1951) (high school football tackling practice). See note 194 infra.

be ready and able to come to the scene of the injury.[191] If the person in charge of the activity is not possessed of medical training and undertakes, in the absence of an emergency, to render medical assistance, the acts may then be determined to be unnecessary or positively detrimental, in which event there may well be liability.[192] This will be especially clear if the injured person protests the proferred aid upon learning of the non-medical status of the person offering the assistance.[193] Those in charge of sports activities are not, however, the insurers of the medical safety of the participants, and if the nature or seriousness of an injury could not reasonably be expected to have been discovered by a layman, then there may be no basis for liability.[194]

The leading case applying these principles is *Clark v. State*,[195] where a bobsled competing in the North American Championship failed to negotiate a reverse curve and hurtled over an almost perpendicularly banked curve into a snow-covered and wooded mountainside. Upon impact, Clark, one of the participants, sustained several injuries, including fractures of his left leg, collapse of his left lung, profound shock, and numerous cuts and bruises. Immediately after the accident, state employees carried Clark by stretcher to the first of several trucks used to transport him to a hospital where, following X-rays, a cast was put on the leg. Between the time of the accident and admission to the hospital, a total of 43 minutes had elapsed. After the cast had been applied, however, normal circulation did not return to the injured leg. When gangrene set in, the leg had to be amputated. Clark then brought suit against the state, which was the owner of the bobsled run, but not the sponsor of the event. He alleged negligence in the state's failure to provide sufficiently prompt medical care after the accident had taken place.[196] Clark conceded that the original accident was not due to any improper act of the state. On these facts, the court held that Clark could not prevail for three separate reasons. The first was that there was a lack of proof that the state's actions had caused the complications suffered by Clark. The second was that Clark, a participant in the bobsled contest, had assumed the risk of not only his injuries,[197] but of the resultant complications as well.[198] Finally, the court found that the state had adequately

191. Sayers v. Ranger, 16 N.J. Super. 22, 83 A.2d 775 (1951) (physical education class injury).

192. Mogabgab v. Orleans Parish School Bd., 239 So. 2d 456 (La. App. 1970) (applying ill-advised treatment to football player who suffered heat stroke); Guerrieri v. Tyson, 147 Pa. Super. 239, 24 A.2d 468 (1942) (teacher held liable for rendering unnecessary medical aid).

193. Clayton v. New Dreamland Roller Skating Rink, 14 N.J. Super. 390, 82 A.2d 458 (1951).

194. Pirkle v. Oakdale Union Grammar School Dist., 40 Cal. 2d 207, 253 P.2d 1 (1953) (spleen and kidney problems discovered several hours after time of injury when blood passed in urine). *See also* Cramer v. Hoffman, 390 F.2d 19 (2d Cir. 1968).

195. 195 Misc. 581, 89 N.Y.S.2d 132 (Ct. Cl. 1949), *aff'd,* 276 App. Div. 10, 93 N.Y.S.2d 28 (1949), aff'd, 302 N.Y. 795, 99 N.E.2d 300 (1951).

196. More specifically, Clark alleged that "he suffered undue exposure to cold through an unreasonable delay in removing him from the snow, lack of sufficient covering, and transportation in unheated open vehicles; and that such exposure greatly aggravated his shock condition, caused the failure of circulation, the ensuing gangrene and the resulting amputation." 195 Misc. at 583-84, 89 N.Y.S.2d at 134.

197. The general rule that participants in sports activities assume the risk of the ordinary and inherent dangers of the game, is considered in detail at § 8.02.

198. Specifically, the court stated that

[a] person responsible for an injury must respond for all damages resulting directly from and as a natural consequence of the wrongful act according to common experience and in the usual course of events, whether the damages could or could not have been foreseen by him.' [citation omitted]. This applies to aggravation of injuries through an error in treatment by a physician. [citations omitted]. While we find no case so asserting, we believe

discharged its duties to Clark after the original accident, inasmuch as it had promptly produced stretchers, blankets and a doctor, and had caused him to be promptly transported to a hospital.[199]

§ 8.08. Liability of Doctors in Treating Athletic Injuries.

In considering the medical care that is provided for sports injuries, it is also important to analyze the legal responsibilities of the doctors who provide the care. Unfortunately, the specific nature of those responsibilities is less than clear. There have been very few reported decisions involving injuries which are allegedly the result of improper medical care of athletes and those which exist provide little real guidance in resolving the many issues that appear to be present in the practice of sports medicine. The lack of such authoritative precedent makes discussion of the issues less certain than would otherwise be the case, but it certainly does not preclude an effort to develop the issues in terms of more general authority. There is a large body of law dealing with the legal duties of physicians generally and the principles that have been developed in those cases should be equally applicable in the sports medicine context. In light of the lack of specific guidance in this area, the purpose of the following discussion is to identify the legal principles that would apparently be applied to cases when they do arise and to suggest some of the issues that seem to have particular importance in sports medicine.

a. General Considerations. The first step in considering the legal responsibility of the sports doctor is to identify the basic principles that would be utilized to determine liability in any given case. When it is alleged that a

> the converse is also true, namely that one who assumes the risk of injury assumes also the risk of consequential injuries or damages, whether or not he could have foreseen them. In this case severe shock, some exposure to cold, some delay in hospitalization, possible error in treatment, were natural consequences of the severe injury and the situation. We believe that failure of the circulation in the badly injured leg, and the resulting gangrene, while certainly uncommon results, were still direct and natural consequences of the injury, shock and other factors. [citation omitted]. They were included in the risk assumed, even though of course unforeseen.

195 Misc. at 589, 89 N.Y.S.2d at 139-40. The Appellate Division however, disagreed with this statement to the extent that it required a participant to assume the risk of negligence. Thus, it stated "it may well be that known dangers of exposure to cold and the possibilities of delay in hospitalization were inherent in the risk assumed. However, such assumption would not cover delay and exposure due to negligence on the part of the State, had such been established." 276 App. Div. at 13, 93 N.Y.S.2d at 31.

199. In reaching this conclusion, the court stated that

> [t]he claimant concedes that the State violated no duty so far as the original accident is concerned. This being so, the State's subsequent position is most closely analogous to that of the volunteer, who, in no way responsible for the original accident, injury or occurrence, assumes the care of an injured person. It is now well established that such a volunteer is charged with a duty of common or ordinary humanity to provide proper care and attention so that at least the injured party is made no worse. [citations omitted]. Unreasonable delay in securing medical attention for an injured person of whom one has taken charge can constitute a violation of this duty. [citations omitted].
>
> We do not find any breach of this duty by the State in the present case. It promptly produced stretchers and blankets, and under the supervision of a physician, Dr. Bergamini, placed claimant and his teammates thereon, covered them, removed them with reasonable expedition to a vehicle, and transported them to a hospital without undue delay. 195 Misc. at 590, 89 N.Y.S.2d at 140.

The court also noted that the state, as owner of the facility, had no duty to provide an ambulance and medical attendant on the scene, although the Association had done so in the past, since the Association, not the state, had assumed that responsibility in the past.

doctor has not treated a patient properly, the basis for the allegation will in almost all cases be that the doctor has been negligent.[200] The basic principles of negligence liability noted earlier will continue to be the touchstones of a doctor's liability, but they will be modified slightly to take account of the professional nature of the conduct in question (medical treatment). As noted, the basic premise of the standard of care for negligence liability is that of the reasonable person under like circumstances.[201] Thus, when a doctor's conduct is alleged to be negligent the standard by which the conduct is to be judged must take into account the skill and knowledge of the medical profession as a whole. The specific standard may vary from jurisdiction to jurisdiction, but it may be said as a general rule that the doctor must practice with the level of reasonable skill and knowledge that is common for members of the medical profession in good standing.[202]

There are several aspects of this standard that should be emphasized. The first is that it only requires a doctor to act reasonably, as measured by what doctors with reasonable skill and knowledge would do or not do in a similar situation. The doctor is not rendered an insurer of the success of all treatment and procedures and will not be held liable for honest mistakes of judgment where the proper treatment is open to reasonable doubt.[203] Liability will occur only when the doctor's conduct has been unreasonable in terms of the general skill and knowledge of the profession. The second is that the standard was traditionally limited by a "locality" gloss which required a doctor to act only in accordance with medical practices in the locality in which he or she practiced.[204] However, improvement in communications, facilities, training and availability of expert consultants and literature have led to an abandonment of the locality requirement as a fixed rule in many jurisdictions. The community in which a doctor practices continues to have general importance in those jurisdictions only as a factor to be considered in applying the standard of care.[205] The third point to be mentioned is that the components of reasonable skill and knowledge will normally be established by the testimony of expert witnesses who are familiar therewith.[206] If there is more than one school of thought on how a given injury or disease should be treated, then the doctor's conduct will be judged in light of the school that he or she follows, if its principles can be established and the school is recognized by at least a respectable part of the profession.[207] Finally, it should be noted that the standard of care is not altered by the fact that the doctor is acting gratuitously,[208] though good samaritan statutes have been

200. If a different basis of liability is alleged, it will probably be that the doctor has breached a contract or warranty. *See* W. Prosser, The Law of Torts 162 (4th ed. 1971).

201. *See* § 8.02.

202. *See* W. Prosser, The Law Of Torts 162 (4th ed. 1971); McCoid, *The Care Required of Medical Practitioners,* 12 Vand. L. Rev. 549, 558-69 (1959).

203. *Id.*

204. *See, e.g.,* Small v. Howard, 128 Mass. 131 (1880).

205. Speed v. State, 240 N.W.2d 901 (Iowa 1976); *see generally* D. Harney, Medical Malpractice § 3.3 (1973); A. Holder, Medical Malpractice Law 53-55 (1975); W. Prosser, The Law of Torts 164 (4th ed. 1971).

206. Such testimony will not be required, however, in those cases where the questions presented are within the common knowledge of laymen. *See, e.g.,* Corn v. French, 71 Nev. 280, 289 P.2d 173 (1955).

207. *See* D. Harney, Medical Malpractice § 3.2 (1973).

208. *See, e.g.,* Dubois v. Decker, 130 N.Y. 325, 29 N.E. 313 (1891).

enacted in some states that would limit liability to situations involving intentional misconduct or grossly negligent practice.[209]

When these principles are considered in the sports medicine context, they essentially state that when a doctor in general practice undertakes to treat a sports injury, he or she will have a duty to perform with the degree of reasonable skill and knowledge that would be utilized by members of the profession in good standing. Although this is, of course, a rather general standard, it does carry the essential message that a doctor's conduct will only be judged in terms of what is reasonable in the profession generally. These basic principles are illustrated by one of the very few decisions in which a doctor was found to be negligent in treating a sports injury. In *Welch v. Dunsmuir Joint Union High School District*,[210] a high school football quarterback was participating in an inter-school scrimmage and on a "quarterback sneak" play was tackled and thrown to the ground. After the play, he was unable to get to his feet. When the coach arrived at his side, the athlete was able to move his hands at the coach's direction. The athlete was then carried to the sidelines by teammates but with no supervision as to the manner of carriage. When he arrived at the sidelines, however, the athlete was unable to move either his hands or feet. Although there was a doctor in attendance at the scrimmage, the evidence was unclear whether he examined the injured player on the field or only on the sidelines. In any event, the boy was rendered a permanent quadriplegic by these events and brought suit against the school, coach and doctor. Testimony at trial indicated that the spinal cord was not severed at the time of injury, since the athlete could move his hands, so that the severance could only have occurred when he was carried from the field. The jury returned a verdict for the athlete against all defendants (including the doctor). With respect to the doctor's conduct, the court found that the evidence sustained the jury's verdict.[211] The apparent basis of the doctor's liability was his negligence in not treating the injury immediately and in allowing the injured athlete to be removed from the field via the hands of his teammates instead of by stretcher. In terms of the principles noted above, the court implicitly concluded that a doctor of reasonable skill and knowledge would have treated the athlete immediately to determine the nature of the injury and would have instructed that he be removed from the field in a manner that would not cause further injury.

If the doctor practices as a specialist in sports medicine, or a more generic specialty (such as orthopedics), then the standard of care will be slightly altered. Since the doctor would then hold himself out as being a special expert in the field of treating sports injuries (or some other type of injuries), the standard will be adjusted to take account of this self-proclaimed expertise. The specialist will be held to a standard of care that is measured in terms of the specialty itself rather than the standard of the medical profession in general. In other words, the sports practitioner would be required to perform with the degree of reasonable skill and knowledge that would be utilized by sports medicine experts.[212] In light of

209. *See* D. HARNEY, MEDICAL MALPRACTICE § 1.5 (1973).
210. 326 P.2d 633 (Cal. App. 1958).
211. *Id.* at 639.
212. *See, e.g.,* Lewis v. Read, 80 N.J. Super. 148, 193 A.2d 255 (1963); Belk v. Schweizer, 268 N.C. 50, 149 S.E.2d 565 (1966); Dinner v. Thorp, 54 Wash. 2d 90, 338 P.2d 137 (1950). *See generally* Annot., 21 A.L.R.3d 944 (1966).

this higher standard of care, it is possible that the conduct of a sports doctor treating a sports injury could be found to have been negligent even though the same conduct by a general practitioner might not have been negligent.

In considering the basic standards of care for sports doctors, it is also important to note that there may be other elements of an action for negligence that could be important in sports injury cases. One such element would be that a doctor will be held legally responsible for an injury only if some reasonable connection can be demonstrated between the conduct of the doctor and the injury that has been suffered. This is usually referred to as the need for establishing that an injury was proximately caused by the defendant's conduct. Although this is certainly not the place for a detailed analysis of legal causation,[213] several aspects of the problem may be considered. The basic issue in determining causation is to identify when a person's conduct will be a legal cause of an injury. The most appropriate response is that conduct will be the legal cause if it is a "substantial factor" in bringing the injury about.[214] This is an inherently factual issue and the burden of establishing the connection between the conduct and injury will be upon the injured person.[215] In many situations, the burden may not be difficult to carry. For example, if a football player dropped dead of heart failure and the day before he had been given a physical examination which failed to disclose an obvious defect, it is quite possible that the legal cause of the injury would be the failure of the doctor to discover the defective condition.[216] In some situations, however, it may be much more difficult to establish causation, especially where the conduct of more than one person could potentially have been a factor in the injury. Under the "substantial factor" standard, it is possible that the conduct of more than one person could be a legal cause.[217] In the situation of the football player with the weak heart, for example, if the player had told his coach that he had severe chest pains and the coach continued to require the boy to participate in the summer heat, it seems likely that the coach's conduct would also be a "substantial factor" in bringing the injury about. In order for the conduct of more than one person to be a legal cause, it must be shown that each was a substantial factor.[218]

In several of the sports medicine cases that have involved causation issues, the courts have held that the doctor's conduct, in the facts presented, was not a legal cause of the injury in question. Thus, in one case it was found that a doctor's conduct in taking and reading X-rays was not a legal cause of injury to a football player when it did not aggravate the injury,[219] and in another case

---

213. *See generally* W. Prosser, The Law of Torts 161 (4th ed. 1971).

214. *See generally id.* §§ 41-45.

215. *Id.* at 240. An additional standard of causation that has been widely utilized is the "but for" test, which would say that a person's conduct is not the legal cause of injury if the injury would have occurred without the conduct of the defendant. The principal difficulty with this test is that it does not deal with the situation in which more than one person's conduct contributed to an injury.

216. A doctor's examination duties are considered at notes 247-251 *infra.* It should be emphasized that "causation" is only one element of the negligence action and the plaintiff would still have to establish the other elements—for example, that the doctor had breached his or her duty of care to the athlete.

217. *See* W. Prosser, The Law of Torts 239-40 (4th ed. 1971).

218. *See, e.g.,* Fish v. Los Angeles Dodgers Baseball Club, 56 Cal. App. 3d 620, 128 Cal. Rptr 807 (1976); Welch v. Dunsmuir Joint Union High School District, 326 P.2d 633, 639 (Cal. App. 1958).

219. Cramer v. Hoffman, 390 F.2d 19 (2d Cir. 1968).

several doctors were exonerated by the court's finding that an athlete's injury was a result of competition and not their conduct.[220] These cases obviously do not indicate that a doctor's conduct will not constitute a legal cause of an injury when more than one person's conduct is involved, but they do suggest that causation is implicitly a factual matter and that it may be quite difficult in some situations to prove the necessary connection between a doctor and an injury incurred in athletic competition.

In order to illustrate the application of these general standards of conduct, it is appropriate to consider some of the issues that seem to have special relevance to doctors engaged in a sports practice.

b. Relationship of Doctor to Athlete. The first issue that might be considered relates to the nature of the relationship between a sports doctor and the athlete. If a doctor is consulted by an athlete, or an athlete's family, for the purpose of acquiring treatment for a sports injury, the doctor will be under no legal duty to accept the athlete as a patient.[221] If the athlete is accepted as a patient, there will then exist a doctor-patient relationship and the doctor will be obligated to treat the athlete in accordance with the standard of care noted above. These duties will not be affected by the fact that the doctor is acting gratuitously.[222]

Inasmuch as the reason for consulting the sports doctor will normally be to secure treatment for an injury that may require surgery, it is important to consider the extent to which the doctor must obtain consent for a specific type of treatment or surgical procedure. Under normal circumstances, it seems clear that a doctor must obtain the consent of an adult patient before medical care can be administered.[223] The situation with respect to minors is much less certain. Consent must still be obtained and the question will frequently arise whether a minor may give valid consent or whether it must be obtained from the minor's parents or guardian. The general rule has been that consent for treatment of minors must be obtained from the parents or guardian, since the minor is deemed to be incapable of giving valid consent.[224] This general rule is, however, subject to several exceptions which allow a minor to give valid consent when an emergency exists, the parent or guardian is inaccessible, or the child is near majority and able to give a knowingly informed consent.[225] The application of these exceptions is suggested by a recent case in which a seventeen year-old girl injured her finger at a hospital and her family doctor recommended minor surgery. The girl's mother was under sedation and her divorced father lived some 200 miles away. In holding that the girl's consent was lawful, the court

---

220. Rosensweig v. State, 5 App. Div. 2d 293, 171 N.Y.S.2d 912 (1958), *aff'd on another ground,* 5 N.Y.2d 404, 158 N.E.2d 228 (1959). The court reached this conclusion as follows:

> It is clear that the immediate proximate cause of the injury which resulted in death was the severe blow to the head which [the athlete] suffered in the final fight. [The representative of the athlete] has failed to establish that this blow alone, irrespective of previous condition, would not have produced the fatal result. 171 N.Y.S.2d at 914.

221. *See, e.g.,* Hurley v. Eddingfield, 156 Ind. 416, 59 N.E. 1058 (1901).
222. *See* note 208 *supra.*
223. *See, e.g.,* Schloendorff v. Society of New York Hosp., 211 N.Y. 125, 105 N.E. 92 (1914).
224. *See* D. HARNEY, MEDICAL MALPRACTICE § 2.1(B) (1973).
225. Bakker v. Welsh, 144 Mich. 632, 108 N.W. 94 (1906); Lacey v. Laird, 166 Ohio St. 12, 139 N.E.2d 25 (1956); Smith v. Seibly, 72 Wash. 2d 16, 431 P.2d 719 (1967). There are also statutes in some states specifying when a minor may give consent to medical procedures.

observed that she was intelligent and capable for her age.[226] A similar result should follow when an athlete is treated under comparable circumstances.

In addition to the question of who may give consent, it may also be important to consider the type and scope of the consent that is to be obtained. The consent should always be in writing if that is possible under the circumstances. This will insure that there is evidence of the fact of consent and the terms upon which it was given. The consent should be drafted so that its terms and scope are clear, and should provide the doctor with both the general and specific authority to perform the necessary procedures in a particular case.[227] The consent should not, however, be written in such broad and ambiguous language as to purportedly provide blanket authority to do whatever the doctor deems appropriate, since it may then be invalidated on the grounds that it in fact authorized nothing.[228] The need for specificity is underscored by the view that a court may strictly construe consents in favor of the patient in light of the facts that consent forms are in almost all cases drafted by representatives of the doctor or hospital and the patient will be required to "consent" as a condition precedent to treatment.

In order for a consent to be valid, it must also be shown that it is the product of the "informed" consent of the patient. The patient is said to be "informed" when the doctor has "imported some quantum of medical information, relevant to a proposed treatment which is sufficient to enable the patient to make an *intelligent choice* as to whether he should undergo such treatment." [229] This would typically include a reasonable disclosure of the alternative procedures that are available to treat a given injury or disease and the dangers of each, as well as an indication of their relative advantages and disadvantages to the patient. The requirements of "informed" consent have attracted a rather large amount of attention.[230] The vagaries of its interpretation will not be summarized here, except to note that the general standard by which disclosure and subsequent consent appear to be analyzed is what would good medical practice require under the circumstances.[231]

If consent cannot be obtained from a patient, it may be implied from the circumstances in which treatment is given. This has especially been true in emergency situations where it has in some cases been concluded that a doctor was privileged to act because of the assumption that the patient would have consented to treatment if he had been competent to do so.[232]

An additional aspect of the doctor-patient relationship that may have particular importance in the sports medicine context involves the disclosure by the doctor of information relating to the physical condition of the athlete. It is

---

226. Younts v. St. Francis Hospital & School of Nursing, Inc., 205 Kan. 292, 469 P.2d 330 (1970).

227. Sample forms are reproduced in D. HARNEY, MEDICAL MALPRACTICE 44-46 (1973).

228. Compare Danielson v. Roche, 109 Cal. App. 2d 832, 241 P.2d 1028 (1952) (upholding such general language) *with* Rogers v. Lumbermens Mutual Casualty Co., 119 So. 2d 649 (La. App. 1960) (invalidating such language).

229. D. HARNEY, MEDICAL MALPRACTICE 58 (1973) (emphasis in original).

230. *See, e.g.,* Markham, *Doctrine of Informed Consent—Fact or Fiction,* 10 FORUM 1073 (1975); Norton, *Contract Law as a Viable Alternative to Problems of Informed Consent,* 21 CATHOLIC U. L. REV. 122 (1975).

231. *See* Plant, *Informed Consent—A New Area of Malpractice Liability* in MEDICAL MALPRACTICE 29, 36 (Shapiro, Steingold & Needham eds. 1965).

232. *See, e.g.,* Dunham v. Wright, 423 F.2d 940 (3rd Cir. 1970); Kritzer v. Citron, 101 Cal. App. 2d 33, 224 P.2d 808 (1950).

apparently common for professional and college scouts (or team doctors) to contact a doctor who has treated an athlete to determine the condition of the athlete. When such contacts are made, the primary issue that the doctor will have to determine is whether he or she may make any disclosure or statement about the athlete's condition. This may in some cases be an exceptionally important issue. For example, if a star college football player had suffered a knee injury which was hopefully corrected by subsequent surgery, it seems almost certain that a professional team would seek some assurance of rehabilitation before signing the athlete to a substantial contract. It could, of course, have its own doctors test the athlete, but it may also seek the opinion of the attending surgeon. In this situation, the surgeon would be in a rather delicate position. Ethical and legal standards may preclude him from disclosing any information without the consent of the athlete, and a disclosure made with consent may subject him to potential liability if the team relies upon his statements which turn out, for one reason or another, to be inaccurate.

It is axiomatic that the doctor-patient relationship is a fiduciary relation,[233] in which the doctor will have a duty to maintain the confidence of disclosures made by the patient during the course of treatment. The purpose of the duty is to insure a free flow of information between patient and doctor, which will enable the doctor to learn all pertinent facts upon which a diagnosis may be based. The duty of confidentiality is indeed a part of the Hippocratic Oath, and is required by statutory provision in some states.[234] Although there was some doubt in early cases,[235] it now seems clear that a doctor may be held liable for the disclosure of confidential information relating to a patient. Thus, it has been held that "[t]he unauthorized revelation of medical secrets or *any* confidential communication given in the course of treatment, is tortious conduct which may be the basis for an action in damages." [236] In light of this potential liability for disclosure of medical information without consent from the patient, a sports doctor should give no information to a team which is interested in a patient-athlete without the specific written consent of the athlete.

If information is given in response to such an inquiry, it is also important to consider what is to be communicated. The doctor should normally restrict the disclosure to a statement of the nature of the injury and method of treatment. Such a disclosure is limited to the objective facts of the injury and leaves the team with the burden of determining the current fitness of the athlete. But if the doctor is asked to go further and state whether the athlete has fully recovered from the injury, then the doctor should exercise a high degree of caution. In such situations, the doctor would be asked to render his opinion on the physical condition of an athlete in circumstances where it is foreseeable that

233. *See, e.g.,* Hammonds v. Aetna Casualty & Surety Co., 237 F. Supp. 96 (N.D. Ohio 1965); Berkey v. Anderson, 1 Cal. App. 3d 790, 82 Cal. Rptr. 67 (1969).

234. The statutes are discussed in D. HARNEY, MEDICAL MALPRACTICE § 1.6(B) (1973), and generally provide that if a doctor violates the confidentiality of the relationship his or her license may be revoked.

235. *See, e.g.,* Nelson v. Nederland Life Ins. Co., 110 Iowa 600, 81 N.W. 807 (1900).

236. Hammonds v. Aetna Casualty & Surety Co., 243 F. Supp. 793, 802 (N.D. Ohio 1965). *See also* Simonsen v. Suenson, 104 Neb. 224, 177 N.W. 831 (1920); Alexander v. Knight, 197 Pa. Super. 79, 177 A.2d 142 (1962); Barry v. Moench, 8 Utah 2d 191, 331 P.2d 814 (1958). *See generally* Note, 28 OKLA. L. REV. 658 (1975).

the team will to some extent rely upon the opinion in determining whether to sign the athlete. The danger in rendering such opinions is that, for example, a professional team might then sign the athlete to a substantial contract and if the athlete turns out to be physically disabled because of the injury said to have been corrected, the team could theoretically seek damages from the doctor for the erroneous opinion. It would be alleged that the doctor was negligent in making the disclosure. When one person makes a statement of opinion to another with knowledge that the other will rely upon it, that person may be responsible for damages incurred because of the inaccurateness of the opinion even though it is rendered in good faith and gratuitously. The inaccuracy would constitute negligence if there was a failure to exercise reasonable care in determining the facts upon which it was based or an absence of the skill and knowledge required by standards of the profession in formulating the opinion.[237] Although the specific parameters of liability in this type of situation are less than clear, there is authority which suggests that persons may be liable for damages caused by the rendering of gratuitous opinions in the course of professional activities which fail to meet the standards noted above.[238] With such authority in mind, a doctor should be rather circumspect in giving gratuitous opinions about the condition of athletes who have been treated by the doctor.

c. Relationship of Doctor to School or Team. In many situations, a doctor treating sports injuries will be retained by the educational institution for whom the athlete is competing. (Although an athlete may compete directly for a team — for example, a professional team—the legal issues would be essentially the same as in the school situation and for purposes of simplicity only the latter will be specifically discussed herein.) When so engaged, the doctor will have a duty to the school to perform services in accordance with the express or implied requirements of the contract and may be responsible for damages caused by a failure to perform those requirements. This should pose little real problem in most cases since the duties of the doctor will be relatively clear—for example, to provide medical care for a school's athletic program—and the doctor will use his or her best efforts to perform those duties. Difficult issues may arise, however, if it is alleged that the doctor performed the services required but did so in a negligent manner.[239] When such allegations are made, it will be necessary to determine who may be held responsible for the alleged negligence. The initial candidate would be the doctor whose conduct is alleged to have been negligent. In order for the doctor to be legally responsible to the patient, it would be necessary to find that a doctor-patient relationship existed. As a means of avoiding such a relationship, it might be argued that the doctor's only responsibility was to the school who had contracted for his services and that no relationship existed between the patient-athlete and the doctor. Although the appropriate response to the argument is certainly not clear, there is authority which holds that a doctor-patient relationship exists between an employee and a doctor who is hired to examine the employees by an employer.[240] This authority

237. *See* W. PROSSER, THE LAW OF TORTS 704 (4th ed. 1971).
238. *See, e.g.,* Virginia Dare Stores v. Schuman, 175 Md. 287, 1 A.2d 897 (1938). There are several additional aspects of the negligent misrepresentation question, and they are all considered in W. PROSSER, THE LAW OF TORTS § 107 (4th ed. 1971).
239. *See* notes 216-228 *supra.*
240. *See* Hoffman v. Rogers, 22 Cal. App. 3d 655, 99 Cal. Rptr. 455 (1972); Dubois v. Decker, 130 N.Y. 325, 29 N.E. 313 (1891); Beadling v. Sirotta, 41 N.J. 555, 197 A.2d 857 (1964) (holding that the

would appear to generally support a conclusion that a doctor-patient relationship will exist when a doctor treats students pursuant to a contract with the athlete's school. If the relation does exist, then the doctor would be directly responsible to the athlete for negligent conduct. This was, for example, the result in *Welch v. Dunsmuir Joint Union High School District.*[241]

An additional candidate for liability would be the school who had undertaken to provide medical care. Such liability could be imposed on at least two theories. The first would be that the school has a duty to provide reasonable medical care to athletes who are injured in the course of school-related athletic programs, and that the duty would not be fulfilled by providing a doctor who in fact rendered negligent care. Although there is apparently no specific authority for this proposition, there are several cases holding that a school must provide reasonable medical care and which have imposed liability when deficient care was rendered by persons who were not doctors.[242] While these cases are not dispositive of the issue, they do suggest that the theory is viable.[243] A second approach would be to argue that the school is responsible for the conduct since the doctor was acting under the school's authority—that is, that the school is vicariously liable for the conduct of the doctor.[244] In order to ascertain whether such liability could be imposed, it would be necessary to determine the specific nature of the relationship between the doctor and the school. Such liability may be imposed on a school only if the doctor is acting as an employee as opposed to an independent contractor. The basis for distinction between these two categories is whether the school exerts control over the physical conduct of the doctor.[245] If such control exists, then the doctor will be an "employee" or "servant" and the school will be vicariously liable; but if it does not exist then, the doctor will be an "independent contractor" and the school will not be vicariously liable. In many situations, the school will contract with a doctor to provide medical care to one or more participants in its athletic program but will not retain a right to control the doctor's physical conduct in providing such care.[246]

---

doctor owed a duty of reasonable care to the employee whether or not a doctor-patient relationship existed). *But cf.* Lotspeich v. Chance Vought Aircraft, 369 S.W.2d 705 (Tex. Civ. App. 1963). *See generally* McCoid, *The Care Required of Medical Practitioners,* 12 VAND. L. REV. 549, 554 (1959).

241. *See* notes 210-211 *supra. See also* Fish v. Los Angeles Dodgers Baseball Club, 58 Cal. App. 3d 620, 128 Cal. Rptr. 807 (1976).

242. *See* § 8.07.

243. One might view Welch v. Dunsmuir Joint Union High School District, 326 P.2d 633 (Cal. App. 1958), to stand for this proposition, but the court merely upheld a jury verdict against a doctor and a school district. The school district was apparently responsible for the negligent acts of the coach (its employee), but not for the acts of the doctor since the court stated that there was no evidence that he was its employee.

244. *See generally* W. PROSSER, THE LAW OF TORTS §§ 69-71 (4th ed. 1971); Fahr, *Legal Liability for Athletic Injuries,* in D. MATTHEWS & R. THOMPSON, ATHLETIC INJURIES 219, 220-21 (1963). *See* § 8.05.

245. RESTATEMENT (SECOND) OF AGENCY § 2 (1958).

246. In Cramer v. Hoffman, 390 F.2d 19 (2d Cir. 1968), for example, the evidence showed that a university had no discretion to control how a doctor treated injuries to its student-athletes and the court held that he was an independent contractor whose negligence could not be imputed to the University. *See also* Fish v. Los Angeles Dodgers Baseball Club, 58 Cal. App. 3d 620, 128 Cal. Rptr. 807 (1976) (issue not considered); Rosensweig v. State, 5 N.Y.2d 404, 158 N.E.2d 229 (1959) (doctors who examined boxers pursuant to statutory requirements were not employees of the state and the state was not responsible for their conduct).

d. Examination of Athletes. One of the most frequent procedures that will be performed by the doctor who is retained to treat members of an athletic program will be to examine its participants. Such examinations are commonly required of all athletes who seek to participate in athletic activities to insure that they are physically able to stand the rigors of competition. The scope of examination may vary substantially depending upon the circumstances under which it is performed. It may constitute little more than a rapid perusal of all members of a junior football team or it may require a thorough analysis of the physical condition of a single athlete. In light of the differing circumstances in which physical examinations may occur, it is difficult to articulate a precise standard by which a doctor's conduct would be evaluated. A court would inevitably apply the same basic standard noted earlier, which would require that in conducting physical examinations a sports doctor must act with the skill and knowledge that would be utilized by other members of the profession acting in similar circumstances.[247] In applying this standard, a court would consider the purpose of the examination, nature of the conditions under which it was performed, procedures generally utilized by the profession in conducting such examinations, and the requirements of good medical practice in responding to the results of the examination.

The situation in which a doctor's liability will most likely arise is when an athlete has been seriously injured and alleges that the injury could have been prevented by a reasonable medical examination. For example, if a football player died as the result of a heart attack it might be alleged that a doctor who gave the player a physical exam before the season began was negligent since death was the result of a defect or injury that should have been discovered in the examination. The approach that a court would take in determining liability in this type of situation is suggested by *Rosensweig v. State*,[248] in which a boxer died shortly after being knocked out in a professional fight. The evidence showed that the boxer had suffered technical knockouts (TKO's) in two previous fights within a three week period. After the second fight, the boxer was examined by doctor #1 who found nothing wrong. Ten days later, the boxer sought permission for another fight but a sports commission representative required that he have an electroencephalogram (EEG) made before permission would be given. The boxer was then examined by doctor #2, the EEG showed a "normal record," and after doctor #3 examined him permission was granted. Before the fight, doctor #4 gave him an additional examination. Although this doctor thought that the boxer should not fight because of the two TKO's, he allowed the fight to proceed in light of the custom of boxing doctors to defer to the judgment of the doctor who examined a fighter after the most recent fight. Since doctor #1 had found nothing wrong with the fighter, doctor #4 certified him for the fight. As luck would have it, the boxer was knocked out and died shortly thereafter. An autopsy apparently showed that he had suffered brain injuries in the previous fights. Representatives of the boxer then filed suit and the trial

247. *See* notes 202-212 *supra. See also* Speed v. State, 240 N.W.2d 901 (Iowa 1976) (insufficient examination of member of basketball team). The examination may require that the doctor determine whether an athlete should be allowed to participate. *See* Colombo v. Sewanhaka Central High School Dist. No. 2., 87 Misc. 2d 48, 383 N.Y.S.2d 518 (1976) (court upheld a doctor's decision that an athlete who was deaf in one ear should not be allowed to participate in contact sports).

248. 208 Misc. 1065, 146 N.Y.S.2d 589 (1955).

court held that all of the doctors had been negligent for several reasons. The first was that a reasonable medical examination should have discovered the brain injury. The second was based upon its finding that good medical practice would require that a person who has received a severe beating to the head (as had this boxer) should be kept inactive for approximately two months to avoid the risk of further trauma. The failure of the doctors to follow this practice was also evidence of negligence.[249] Finally, the court found that the custom of boxing doctors to defer to the diagnosis of the doctor who examined a fighter after the last fight was no defense, since it required a doctor to disregard his or her own medical knowledge and experience.[250]

Although the court did not enunciate a clear doctrinal base for its conclusions, the essence of its reasoning would appear to be that good medical practice in this context required an examination that would discover an injury to the part of the boxer's anatomy which had suffered severe beatings (the head) and that the fighter be held out of further competition for a suitable period of recuperation. To this extent, the court's analysis is consistent with the general standard suggested above, since the court's findings are reflective of a failure of the doctors to perform with the skill and knowledge that is utilized by other members of the profession. The trial court decision was, however, reversed on appeal.[251] The appellate court obviously disagreed with the trial court's conclusion that there was negligence, but the doctrinal basis for disagreement is not clear. The court stated that a "standard examination" had revealed no injury, but gave no indication of what such a standard examination required or what facts indicated that such an examination had been given in the present case. It also noted that the boxer had signed a medical history that disclosed no brain injury, but surely this fact could have little relevance to the negligence of the doctors. It also found that there was no duty to hold the boxer out of competition since the state boxing commission had adopted no such rule. It did not suggest why a doctor would not have a duty to take such action if it was, as the trial court had concluded, required by the standards of good medical practice. Finally, the court stated that the actual cause of death was the blows received in the fatal bout. In short, the appellate court found no negligence but undertook almost no effort to indicate why it came to that conclusion. Its reasoning would appear to be that a doctor is required to give only a standard examination (which it did not define) and since such examinations had been given here (though it did not say why) there was no basis for a conclusion that the doctors had been negligent.

The *Rosensweig* case is important because it is one of the few cases to focus specifically upon the potential liabilities of a sports doctor in conducting physical examinations of athletes.[252] Although the reasoning of the courts is not as clear

249. 146 N.Y.S.2d at 596-97.

250. *Id.* at 597.

251. 5 App. Div. 2d 293, 171 N.Y.S.2d 912 (1958). The decision of the appellate court was affirmed on subsequent appeal to the state's highest court, 5 N.Y.2d 404, 158 N.E.2d 229 (1959), but the court limited its consideration to whether the state could be held liable for the acts of the doctors. It did not address the question of whether the doctors' conduct was negligent. *Rosensweig* is noted at 14 Syracuse L. Rev. 79 (1962).

252. *See also* Fish v. Los Angeles Dodgers Baseball Club, 56 Cal. App. 3d 620, 128 Cal. Rptr. 807 (1976) (involving duties in examination of child hit by foul ball, but case remanded for proper instructions).

as it could have been, the positions of the trial and appellate court suggest the parameters of how examination questions will be analyzed when they arise.

e. Prescription of Drugs. One of the most interesting issues involved in the medical treatment of athletic injuries is the extent to which liability may be imposed for injuries caused by the administration of drugs to athletes.[253] It has been reported that drugs are in some situations administered to athletes in an attempt to increase their performance or delay the need for corrective surgery.[254] Suits have also been filed by some athletes. The basic allegation of such suits would be that a doctor was negligent in prescribing drugs that could cause, or worsen an existing, injury, or that the athlete could not validly consent to such prescription absent a clear disclosure of the dangers that the drugs might pose.[255]

Although there has apparently not yet been a reported decision involving these issues in the sports medicine field, the principles that a court would apply in such cases seem reasonably clear. The doctor's duty in prescribing drugs is the same as has been considered throughout this section: to utilize the level of reasonable skill and knowledge that is common for members of the medical profession (or for doctors practicing a given specialty).[256] The principal issue that would arise under this duty in the drug situation would be whether good medical practice would allow prescription of the drug in question to a given athlete in the manner and dosage utilized.[257] For example, if a football player were suffering from an injured knee and a doctor prescribed a pain killer to allow the player to continue competition, it would have to be determined whether good medical practice would allow use of such a drug in the circumstances that existed at the time of prescription for the particular athlete. This would be a factual question that would be resolved on the basis of testimony from experts in sports medicine (or whatever specialty of internal medicine would deal with the type of injury in question). Attention would also have to be given to whether the athlete had made an informed consent to the administration of the drug. As noted earlier, a doctor must make a disclosure to the athlete of the dangers of the drug prescribed and the existence of any procedures that would be alternatives to its administration.[258] The necessity of such "informed" consent has been subsumed within the concept of good medical practice, and if it was not obtained prior to the prescription of a drug the failure might itself constitute negligence by the doctor.[259] Again, the resolution of this issue would be a factual

---

253. *See generally* R. GOODMAN & P. RHEINGOLD, DRUG LIABILITY: A LAWYERS HANDBOOK ch. 8 (1970).

254. *Hearings Before the Senate Subcomm. to Investigate Juvenile Delinquency of the Senate Comm. on the Judiciary,* 93rd Cong., 1st Sess. 9, 107, 124, 140-74 (1973) (Proper and Improper Use of Drugs by Athletes); *see also* H. SAVAGE, AMERICAN COLLEGE ATHLETICS 145 (Carnegie Fndn. 1929).

255. *See, e.g.,* N.Y. Times, September 14, 1976, at 50, col. 5 ($600,000 settlement of suit by former football star Dick Butkus, who made these allegations).

256. *See* notes 202-213 *supra.*

257. This issue has been considered in some non-sports drug cases. *See, e.g.,* Chrestman v. Kendall, 247 Ark. 802, 448 S.W.2d 22 (1969); Talcott v. Holl, 224 So. 2d 420 (Fla. App. 1969); Incollingo v. Ewing, 444 Pa. 263, 282 A.2d 206 (1971). *See generally* D. HARNEY, MEDICAL MALPRACTICE § 9.6 (1973).

258. *See* notes 229-231 *supra.*

259. Failure to make such disclosure has been found to constitute negligence in some non-sports cases. *See, e.g.,* Koury v. Follo, 272 N.C. 366, 158 S.E.2d 548 (1968); Sharpe v. Pugh, 270 N.C. 598, 155 S.E.2d 108 (1967). *But cf.* Challett v. Pirkey, 171 Colo. 271, 466 P.2d 466 (1970). *See generally* D. HARNEY, MEDICAL MALPRACTICE § 2.4(K) (1973).

determination that would be made on the basis of expert testimony as to what types of disclosure would be required by good medical practice.

§ 8.09. Liability for Defective Athletic Equipment — Negligence Liability.

When an athletic participant is injured as a result of defective equipment, there are several different theories that will be available through which recovery may be sought. In the ordinary case, each of the theories discussed in this and the following two sections may be employed simultaneously, but they are sufficiently distinct to warrant separate discussion.

The first theory that should be considered involves negligence liability. The suppliers of athletic equipment have a duty to exercise care for the protection of those who use their equipment or who may be endangered by its use. As a general rule, one who supplies a chattel for the use of another is liable for physical harm caused by the use of the chattel in the manner for which it was supplied if 1) it has reason to know that the chattel is dangerous for the use for which it is supplied; 2) it has no reason to believe that those who use the chattel will realize its dangerous condition; and 3) it fails to exercise reasonable care to inform them of the chattel's condition or of the facts which make it likely to be dangerous.[260]

a. Suppliers of Athletic Equipment Without Charge. This duty arises most commonly when those in charge of athletic activities provide equipment to the participants without charge. In this circumstance, the supplier's duty is, simply, to exercise reasonable care to supply equipment that is in a safe and suitable condition for the purposes for which it is provided.[261] The supplier of equipment is not, however, the insurer of the safety of those using its equipment, and will be held liable only for injuries that are proximately caused by its failure to meet its duty of care.[262] Similarly, the user of the equipment may be barred from recovering for defects in the equipment by his or her own contributory negligence or assumption of the risk.[263]

These principles were applied in *Vendrell v. School District No. 26C, Malheur County,*[264] where an injured high school football player brought an action alleging, *inter alia,* that the equipment that had been given to him was defective. The evidence showed that the player had selected the equipment from a table upon which it had been placed the day after he reported for practice, and that it consisted of the usual helmet, pads and uniform used in competitive football. Thereafter, the helmet originally selected developed a crack, and the player selected another from several that were available. He used the helmet although he knew that "it was just a bit loose," as were his shoulder pads, and that others were readily available. The court held that there had been no negligence in the provision of the equipment, and noted that the player

> conceded that he did not mention to the manager, the coaches, or any other school representative the fault that he found with his gear. He

---

260. RESTATEMENT (SECOND) OF TORTS § 388 (1965). *See also* Telak v. Maszczenski, 248 Md. 476, 237 A.2d 434 (1968).

261. Diker v. City of St. Louis Park, 268 Minn. 461, 130 N.W.2d 113 (1964), *noted in* 49 MINN. L. REV. 142 (1964).

262. Hillman v. Greater Miami Hebrew Academy, 72 So. 2d 668 (Fla. 1954) (monkey bars).

263. Hanna v. State, 46 Misc. 2d 9, 258 N.Y.S.2d 694 (1965) (failure to wear protective equipment around batting cage). These principles are discussed generally at §§ 8.02, 8.03.

264. 233 Ore. 1, 376 P.2d 406 (1962).

also conceded ... that he had the privilege of returning any of his equipment and of selecting a substitute. .... We have studied the evidence with care and have found no indication that the plaintiff's equipment, if it was not proper, had any bearing upon the happening of his injury.

If it was in any way unsuitable to the plaintiff's needs, he was intimately familar with that fact and voluntarily decided to proceed. This, we believe, is a proper case in which to employ the rule denoted by the phrase volenti non fit injuria [assumption of the risk].[265]

Similar results have been reached when the injuries complained of are the consequence of failing to wear the prescribed protective equipment.[266] Liability will result, however, when actually defective equipment is provided;[267] or where proper equipment is not supplied at all.[268]

b. Lessors of Athletic Equipment. The liability of suppliers of athletic equipment arises in a slightly different context when the equipment is rented or leased to the user by the supplier. The scope of liability does not, in general, differ from that of any other supplier.[269] The principles are, however, phrased to take specific account of the nature of the lease relationship. Thus, liability will be imposed where a lessor who leases a chattel for another to use, knowing or having reason to know that it is or is likely to be dangerous for the purpose for which it is to be used.[270] If a chattel is leased for an immediate use that is known to the lessor, then the lessor will have a duty to exercise reasonable care to make it safe for such use and to disclose its actual condition to those who may be expected to use it.[271] The beneficiaries of this duty are those persons who can be expected either to use the chattel or be endangered by its probable use, though liability will result only if the chattel is used in the manner for which it was leased. Inasmuch as a user who leases a chattel for immediate use cannot be expected to do more than cursorily examine the chattel, the lessor will be required to examine it for defects.[272] The lessor will also incur liability for its failure to properly repair the equipment it leases. Thus, liability has been imposed for injuries caused by the failure of the lessor to inspect and repair the

265. 233 Ore. at 14, 376 P.2d at 412.

266. Hanna v. State, 46 Misc. 2d 9, 258 N.Y.S.2d 694 (1965).

267. Rivera v. Board of Educ. of City of New York, 11 App. Div. 2d 7, 201 N.Y.S.2d 372 (1960); Rook v. State, 254 App. Div. 67, 4 N.Y.S.2d 116 (1938).

268. Diker v. City of St. Louis Park, 268 Minn. 461, 130 N.W.2d 113 (1964); Fein v. Board of Educ. of New York, 305 N. Y. 611, 111 N.E.2d 732 (1953).

269. RESTATEMENT (SECOND) OF TORTS § 388, comment c (1965).

270. RESTATEMENT (SECOND) OF TORTS § 407 (1965). It is worth noting that the older cases dealing with the rental of athletic equipment stated that since the rental was no more than a bailment for hire, the provider had the duty to use the highest degree of care to protect its customers, and was bound to know the condition of the equipment and the purpose for which it was to be used. The duty also required that the bailor deliver it in good and proper condition. Moore v. City of Ardmore, 188 Okla. 74, 106 P.2d 515 (1940). This duty was often expressed in terms of an implied warranty by the provider that its equipment is fit for the purpose for which it is reasonably known that it will be used. Alberti's Adm'rx v. Nash, 282 S.W.2d 853 (Ky. App. 1955).

271. RESTATEMENT (SECOND) OF TORTS § 408 (1965). See also Shandy v. Sombrero Ranches, Inc., 525 P.2d 487 (Colo. 1974) (provision of flighty horse to beginner); Chanaki v. Walker, 114 N.H. 660, 327 A.2d 610 (1974) (improper supervision of persons renting horses); Tarlowe v. Metropolitan Ski Slopes, Inc. 28 N.Y. 2d 410, 372 N.Y.S.2d 665, 271 N.E.2d 515 (1971) (skis and ski boots).

272. RESTATEMENT (SECOND) OF TORTS § 408, comment a (1965). See also Vignone v. Pierce & Norton Co., 130 Conn. 309, 33 A.2d 427 (1943).

brakes,[273] or other equipment,[274] on a golf cart and the laces or wheels of roller skates.[275]

The lessor does not, however, guarantee the safety of its lessees, and will be held liable only when there is evidence of its own negligent acts or omissions.[276] Thus, liability will not be imposed merely because an injury occurs.[277] The lessor will also not be held liable for injuries caused by the contributorily negligent acts of its lessees or for risks assumed by them.[278]

Some of these principles were considered in *Moore v. City of Ardmore*,[279] where a fisherman who had rented a boat drowned when the boat sank in a storm. In holding the lessor-defendant not liable, the court noted the duty of the lessor, but found that the sinking of the boat was not the result of any defect attributable to the defendant. It found that no reasonable person would venture upon a body of water in a boat without some apprehension of danger from the unusual and unfavorable acts of nature, and that the lessor of the boat could not "be held to impliedly warrant that his boat is so built and equipped that it will be preserved in all of the situations that arise from the use of it." [280] Similar results have been reached when the renter of a golf cart drove it into the rough and then overturned it down a hill;[281] a participant knowingly used defective equipment;[282] a boat was taken into choppy water;[283] and a golfer stood up and caused his golf cart to overturn.[284]

c. Manufacturers of Athletic Equipment. Liability for defective sports equipment may also arise with regard to the manufacturers of the equipment. Although the rule was once followed that only those who dealt directly with the manufacturer could recover for injuries caused by its products,[285] that rule has been generally repudiated,[286] and it is now clear that any user whom the manufacturer should expect to use the product may recover for injuries caused by acts or omissions of the manufacturer.[287]

---

273. Gifford v. Bogey Hills Golf & Country Club, 426 S.W.2d 98 (Mo. 1968).

274. Ft. Lauderdale Country Club, Inc. v. Winnemore, 189 So. 2d 222 (Fla. App. 1966).

275. Ducas v. Prince, 336 Mass. 555, 146 N.E.2d 677 (1957) (laces); Humbyrd v. Spurlock, 345 S.W.2d 499 (Mo. App. 1961) (wheels).

276. Gillespie v. Chevy Chase Golf Club, 187 Cal. App.2d 52, 9 Cal. Rptr. 437 (1960); Dixon v. Outboard Marine Corp., 481 P.2d 151 (Okla. 1971).

277. Clark v. Detroit & M. Ry., 197 Mich. 489, 163 N.W. 964 (1917).

278. Powell v. Alaska Marine Equipment, Inc., 453 P.2d 407 (Alaska 1969) (not paying attention to terrain when riding snowmobile); Miller v. Robinson, 241 Md. 335, 216 A.2d 743 (1966) (golf cart accident); Albert v. State, 80 Misc. 2d 105, 362 N.Y.S.2d 341 (1975) (ski gondola fall); Dixon v. Outboard Marine Corp., 481 P.2d 151 (Okla. 1971 (golf cart accident); Moore v. City of Ardmore, 188 Okla. 74, 106 P.2d 515 (1940).

279. 188 Okla. 74, 106 P.2d 515 (1940).

280. 188 Okla. at 77, 106 P.2d at 518. *See also* Mintz v. State, 47 App. Div. 2d 570, 362 N.Y.S.2d 619 (1975).

281. United States v. Marshall, 391 F.2d 880 (5th Cir. 1968); Annot., 17 A.L.R.3d 1430 (1968).

282. Frye v. Omaha & C. B. Ry., 106 Neb. 333, 183 N.W. 567 (1921).

283. Alberti's Adm'rx v. Nash, 282 S.W.2d 853 (Ky. App. 1955).

284. Dixon v. Outboard Marine Corp., 481 P.2d 151 (Okla. 1971).

285. Winterbottom v. Wright, 10 M. & W. 109, 52 Eng. Rep. 402 (1842).

286. The early and leading case was MacPherson v. Buick Motor Co., 217 N.Y. 382, 111 N.E. 1050 (1916).

287. Cova v. Harley-Davidson Motor Co., 26 Mich. App. 602, 182 N.W.2d 800 (1970); RESTATEMENT (SECOND) OF TORTS § 388, comment *a* (1965); W. PROSSER, THE LAW OF TORTS § 96 (4th ed. 1971). *See generally* Annot., 78 A.L.R.2d 738 (1961).

While manufacturers of chattels have the same general duties as other suppliers,[288] they are also subject to several other rules as well. For example, a manufacturer must exercise reasonable care in the manufacture of a product which it should know would involve an unreasonable risk of physical harm if not carefully made.[289] The manufacturer also has the duty to exercise reasonable care in the adoption of a safe design for its products and may be liable for injuries to foreseeable users caused by a design which makes the product dangerous for the uses for which it was manufactured.[290] In addition, the producer has a duty to test for [291] and warn against [292] any hidden dangers. Despite these several duties, the circumstances of a particular case may allow the manufacturer to avoid liability. Thus, it will not be responsible for injuries caused by uses other than those for which the product was intended, by the user's failure to follow properly given instructions, by subsequent changes in the product, by improper maintenance, or by the predictable deterioration of the product at the end of its useful life.[293] The duties discussed here will be applicable to one who holds itself out as the manufacturer, even though the product was actually produced by someone else.[294] Thus, a vendor who applies its name to a product manufactured by another will assume liability not only for its own negligence but also for that of the actual manufacturer.[295]

The liability of a manufacturer was raised in *Dudley Sports Company v. Schmitt*,[296] where a high school had purchased an automatic baseball pitching machine that bore the name of Dudley Sports Company, though it had actually been manufactured by another company. Although the machine posed a serious danger in that the metal throwing arm could be unintentionally released, the only warning was contained on a tag which stated that the operation of the pitching arm should be understood before uncrating the machine. No operating instructions were provided. When the machine was unpacked, it was stored in a room to which students had access. The next day a student sweeping in the room was seriously injured by the sudden descent of the pitching arm. When the student then brought suit, the court held that Dudley Sports Company had been negligent in its sale of the machine. A manufacturer's products "must not be traps for the unwary," the court said, and Dudley was negligent in failing to warn of the latent danger posed by the tendency of the machine to self-activate. In the court's view,

> [a]lthough a manufacturer may assume that the purchaser will properly use the product and avoid obvious dangers, such reliance is improper if the product contains latent dangers and no notice is given thereof. Because no specific operating instructions were sent to the High School and no warning was given as to the specific latent dangers

---

288. RESTATEMENT (SECOND) OF TORTS § 394 (1965). *See generally* 1 L. FRUMER & M. FRIEDMAN, PRODUCTS LIABILITY § 5 (1973).

289. RESTATEMENT (SECOND) OF TORTS § 395 (1965).

290. RESTATEMENT (SECOND) OF TORTS § 398 (1965). The general rules and defenses of negligence liability are considered at §§ 8.02, 8.03.

291. McCormick v. Lowe & Campbell Athletic Goods Co., 240 Mo. 708, 144 S.W.2d 866 (1940).

292. Dudley Sports Co. v. Schmitt, 151 Ind. App. 217, 29 Ind. Dec. 285, 279 N.E.2d 266 (1972).

293. W. PROSSER, THE LAW OF TORTS § 96 (4th ed. 1971).

294. RESTATEMENT (SECOND) OF TORTS § 400 (1965). *See also* Telak v. Maszczenski, 248 Md. 476, 237 A.2d 434 (1968).

295. Dudley Sports Co. v. Schmitt, 151 Ind. App. 217, 29 Ind. Dec. 285, 279 N.E.2d 266 (1972).

296. 151 Ind. App. 217, 29 Ind. Dec. 285, 279 N.E.2d 266 (1972).

of the machine, it was reasonably foreseeable that a high school student might be the victim of such negligence.[297]

The court also noted that the mere fact that a product meets or exceeds the requirements of the industry is not conclusive of its reasonable safety.[298] Similar results have been reached by the failure of a manufacturer to properly test vaulting poles that it sold to pole vaulters;[299] to make shatterproof the sunglasses it sold to baseball players;[300] to so design a boat and propeller as to prevent injury to a water skier;[301] and to affix a tag to a boat specifying its seating capacity.[302]

The mere fact that an injury occurs, or that equipment fails to function properly, will not of itself be the predicate for a negligence recovery, since the manufacturer is not the insurer of the safety of the users of its products.[303] The critical question, of course, is whether the requisite breach of duty has been shown. The difficulty which may be caused by that issue is suggested by *James v. Hillerich & Bradsby Company, Inc.*,[304] where a pitcher was struck by a piece of a baseball bat which had broken off when the batter swung. In denying the pitcher's recovery against the manufacturer, the court stated that

> [t]he ordinary risks of personal injury involved in a baseball or softball game, from the breaking of even a properly made bat, are such that a defective bat cannot be said to materially increase the risk or . . . to create an 'unreasonable' risk. It is common knowledge that bats frequently break, and we think it is immaterial that a properly made bat ordinarily will splinter with the grain while one made of defective wood may break across the grain. The risk of injury is not materially altered.[305]

Although *James v. Hillerich & Bradsby* may be subject to considerable question to the extent that it denies recovery for injuries caused by an admittedly defective product, it does illustrate the proposition that sports equipment manufacturers do not underwrite the safety of athletes using their equipment.[306]

In addition to liability for physical injury, the manufacturer may also incur liability for economic loss. Thus, in *Cova v. Harley Davidson Motor Company*,[307] where a purchaser of golf carts had brought suit seeking recovery for allegedly defective products which had caused economic loss, the court held that he could recover for the profits lost as a result of defects in the product.[308]

---

297. 279 N.E.2d at 275.
298. 279 N.E.2d at 276.
299. McCormick v. Lowe & Campbell Athletic Goods Co., 240 Mo. 708, 144 S.W.2d 866 (1940).
300. Filler v. Rayex Corp., 435 F.2d 336 (7th Cir. 1970).
301. Standard v. Meadors, 347 F. Supp. 908 (N.D. Ga. 1972) (actual holding only that complaint stated a cause of action); Marrillia v. Lyn Craft Boat Co., 271 So. 2d 204 (Fla. App. 1973) (negligent design of boat steering cable).
302. Duncan v. Monark Boat Co., 281 So. 2d 382 (Fla. App. 1973).
303. Olson v. Arctic Enterprises, Inc., 349 F. Supp. 761 (D. N.D. 1972) (snowmobile); Powell v. Alaska Marine Equipment, Inc., 453 P.2d 407 (Alaska 1969) (same); Becker v. Aquaslide 'in Dive Corp., 35 Ill. App. 2d 479, 341 N.E.2d 369 (1976) (injury caused by diving on floating chairs, not defects in pool); Llewellyn v. Lookout Saddle Co., 315 So. 2d 69 (La. App. 1975) (doctrine of *res ipsa loquitur* not apply).
304. 299 S.W.2d 92 (Ky. App. 1957).
305. 299 S.W.2d at 94.
306. *But cf.* § 8.10.
307. 26 Mich. App. 602, 182 N.W.2d 800 (1970).
308. 182 N.W.2d at 805.

§ 8.10. Liability for Defective Athletic Equipment — Strict Liability.

The suppliers of athletic equipment may also be held liable for defective products on the basis of the principles of strict liability. Under this doctrine, one who sells a product which is unreasonably dangerous because of a defective condition is subject to liability for the physical harm caused thereby to the ultimate user or customer, provided that the seller is in the business of selling such products and the product has not been substantially changed.[309] For purposes of this doctrine, a product will be defective if it is not reasonably fit for the ordinary purposes for which such products are sold and used.[310] The strict liability doctrine will apply even though the seller has exercised all possible care and the ultimate user or customer is not in a privity relationship with the seller.[311] The seller may avoid liability by giving proper instructions and warnings which, if followed, will make the product safe.[312] The seller may also reasonably assume that such directives will be read and followed.[313] Under the strict liability rule, there is no defense for contributory negligence to the extent that the negligence consists of the mere failure to discover the defect or guard against its existence, though the doctrine of assumption of the risk, as well as other forms of contributory negligence, will be fully applicable.[314]

The strict liability rule was applied in *Filler v. Rayex Corporation,*[315] where a manufacturer of sunglasses promoted them by stating that one could acquire

---

309. RESTATEMENT (SECOND) OF TORTS § 402A (1) (1965). The justification for the theory is

> that the seller, by marketing his product for use and consumption, has undertaken and assumed a special responsibility toward any member of the consuming public who may be injured by it; that the public has the right to and does expect, in the case of products which it needs and for which it is forced to rely upon the seller, that reputable sellers will stand behind their goods; that public policy demands that the burden of accidental injuries caused by products intended for consumption be placed upon those who market them, and be treated as a cost of production against which liability insurance can be obtained; and that the consumer of such products is entitled to the maximum of protection at the hands of someone, and the proper persons to afford it are those who market the products. *Id.* § 402A, comment *c.*

See also Byrns v. Riddell, Inc., 113 Ariz. 264, 550 P.2d 1065 (1976) (question as to whether football helmet had been altered by addition of a facemask); O. S. Stapley Co. v. Miller, 103 Ariz. 556, 447 P.2d 248 (1968) (not apply where boat substantially altered). The most prominent issue relating to the strict liability doctrine in recent years has involved injuries allegedly caused by defective football helmets. The issue has been sharpened by recent jury verdicts involving substantial awards to injured athletes. *See* DuPree, *Sports Equipment on Trial,* Washington Post, December 31, 1977, at D1, Col. 3; Keese, *Sporting Goods Officials Worrying Amid Prosperity,* N. Y. Times, January 29, 1978, § 5, at 8, Col. 1. *See also* Byrns v. Riddell, Inc., 113 Ariz. 264, 550 P.2d 1065 (1976).

310. Bailey v. Montgomery Ward & Co., 6 Ariz. App. 213, 431 P.2d 108 (1967); Hauter v. Zogarts, 14 Cal. 3d 104, 120 Cal. Rptr. 681 (1975); Santor v. A and M Karagheusian, Inc., 44 N. J. 52, 207 A.2d 305 (1965).

311. RESTATEMENT (SECOND) OF TORTS § 402A (2); Simpson v. Powered Products of Michigan, Inc., 24 Conn. Super. 409, 192 A.2d 555 (1963) (defective golf cart). *See generally* 1 L. FRUMER & M. FRIEDMAN, PRODUCTS LIABILITY § 16.A[4.] [c.] (1973).

312. The failure to give a warning about a known defect may also support the strict liability doctrine. *See* Nissen Trampoline Co. v. Terre Haute First National Bank, 332 N.E.2d 820 (Ind. App. 1975); Degen v. Bayman, — S.D. —, 241 N.W.2d 703 (1976).

313. RESTATEMENT (SECOND) OF TORTS § 402A, comment *j* (1965).

314. RESTATEMENT (SECOND) OF TORTS § 402A, comment *n* (1965); Colosimo v. May Dept. Store Co., 466 F.2d 1234 (3d Cir. 1972) (cause of accident improper jump into swimming pool); O. S. Stapley Co. v. Miller, 103 Ariz. 556, 447 P.2d 248 (1968); Genteman v. Saunders Archery Co.,   Ill. App. , 355 N.E.2d 647 (1976) (misuse of archery equipment); Kinka v. Harley-Davidson Motor Co., Inc., 36 Ill. App. 2d 752, 344 N.E.2d 655 (1976).

315. 435 F.2d 336 (7th Cir. 1970).

"Instant Eye Protection with Rayex Baseball SUNGLASSES Professional FLIP-SPECS." However, except for the flip-down feature and an elastic strap at the rear of the frame, the glasses resembled ordinary sunglasses. The thinness of the lenses was not readily apparent because of the thinness of the frames. Several pairs of the glasses were purchased by a high school baseball coach, and were used during a varsity baseball practice. The plaintiff was injured when a flyball he was attempting to catch tipped his glove and struck the right side of his sunglasses, shattering the right lens into sharp splinters which pierced his right eye, necessitating its eventual removal. These facts warranted the application of the strict liability, the court found, because "the thinness of the lenses made them unreasonably dangerous to users." [316]

The doctrine was also considered in *Bailey v. Montgomery Ward & Company*,[317] where a child was injured by a pogo stick a few hours after he began using it. In holding that the doctrine required recovery for the injured boy, the court stated that

> [w]e take judicial notice that a pogo stick is expected to be used in a rugged manner. The manufacturer must expect that a pogo stick will be subjected to harsh contact with pavement, dirt, and asphalt, and that it may on occasion be dropped or, the rider falling or tossed off, it may be thrown into a tree or a wall or knocked violently to the ground. We conclude that since the plaintiff was acquainted with the use of the pogo stick and had merely jumped on it "about six times" the jury may reasonably have inferred that the direct result of the pogo stick's flying apart and injuring the plaintiff was due to a defect in the design or manufacture of the stick.[318]

These words should apply with equal force to injuries caused by defective sports equipment which is not reasonably fit for the purposes for which it was sold.[319]

The strict liability doctrine will not apply to all equipment-related injuries, however, simply because it is applicable only where the equipment is so defective as to be unreasonably dangerous. For example, the doctrine has been held to be inapplicable to the design of a swimming pool.[320]

Several other questions warrant attention. The first is whether the strict liability doctrine applies to parties other than "sellers." Although the doctrine as formulated by the *Restatement of Torts* expressly applies to only those who *sell* defective products, several courts have extended its coverage to lessors of defective products.[321] This question is of considerable importance to the present inquiry since the rental or leasing of sports equipment is so common. It was considered in *Katz v. Slade*,[322] where the plaintiff suffered injuries as a result

316. 435 F.2d at 338. *See also* Blevins v. Cushman Motors, 551 S.W.2d 602 (Mo. 1977) (golf cart); Byrns v. Riddell, Inc., 113 Ariz. 264, 550 P.2d 1065 (1976) ("unreasonably dangerous" defect as to impact characteristics of football helmet).

317. 6 Ariz. App. 213, 431 P.2d 108 (1967).

318. 6 Ariz. App. at 218-19, 431 P.2d at 113-14.

319. Curtiss v. Young Men's Christian Ass'n of Lower Columbia Basin, 82 Wash. 2d 455, 511 P.2d 991 (1973) (parallel bars).

320. Colosimo v. May Dept. Store Co., 466 F.2d 1234 (3d Cir. 1972); Telak v. Maszczenski, 248 Md. 476, 237 A.2d 434 (1968); Vincer v. Esther Williams All-Aluminum Swimming Pool Co., 69 Wis. 2d 326, 230 N.W.2d 794 (1975). *See also* Parker v. Warren, 503 S.W.2d 938 (Tenn. 1973) (not apply to lumber used for bleachers where unclear what grade of lumber was purchased).

321. Price v. Shell Oil Co., 2 Cal. 3d 245, 85 Cal. Rptr. 178, 466 P.2d 722 (1970); McClaflin v. Bayshore Equipment Rental Co., 274 Cal. App. 2d 446, 79 Cal. Rptr. 337 (1969); Cintrone v. Hertz Truck Leasing, 45 N.J. 434, 212 A.2d 769 (1965).

322. 460 S.W.2d 608 (Mo. 1970).

of a defective golf cart which had been rented from a municipal golf course. In rejecting the application of the strict liability doctrine, the court distinguished the cases applying the doctrine in lease transactions from the case before it on the ground that those cases involved mass leasing by commercial entities for commercial purposes. Thus, it said that

> [i]n contrast this is a municipally operated, nonprofit, recreational and amusement facility — a golf course. Golf carts are supplied to those patrons who desire to use them, as a casual operation, a strictly incidental and collateral convenience. They are rented for use solely on the golf course, for short periods of time, for small fees. There is no indication that patrons are stimulated or induced to rent by widespread advertising. There is no element of forced reliance by the patron, or [sic] that there is anything to prevent the prospective user from inspecting or trying out the carts before hiring one. It may not in any realistic sense be said that this is an operation essentially commercial in character, or that this is a 'marketing' of these carts, or a mass leasing of them as a part of the over-all marketing enterprise, or a commercial distribution by a profit-making concern to a public forced to depend upon the representation of the city that the carts are suitable and safe for use. The transaction more closely resembles a license than a lease; the 'renter' is more like the patron who buys a ticket to ride on a merry-go-round than he who leases a Hertz Drive-Ur-Self automobile for a weekend or a week of travel on the public highways. Traditionally the law has imposed upon proprietors of places of public amusement the duty of exercising the degree of care reasonably commensurate with the character of the amusement or game presented or played within the place, but they have not been held to be insurers of the safety of invitees, and we see no reason to disturb this salutary rule. The rights of persons injured by golf carts in the circumstances of this case will be fully protected by affording them relief under the established rules of liability for negligence which have heretofore governed such transactions.[323]

The distinction drawn in *Katz v. Slade* may be subject to some question. It could be argued that the rental of golf carts, or other sports equipment, is no less a commercial enterprise than is the leasing of automobiles and should not result in the differential application of legal standards. Imposition of strict liability in such situations would seem to be consistent with the underlying bases of the doctrine that a person who makes products available for use by others represents that they are fit and safe for use, has both the expertise and opportunity to inspect and make repairs, and is better able to distribute losses caused by defects in the products. Authority for the proposition that the strict liability doctrine should apply to lessors as well as to sellers is provided by analogy to the cases which have applied the warranty provisions of the Uniform Commercial Code to the lessors of sports equipment, notwithstanding their express application to only "sellers." [324]

A second coverage problem posed by the strict liability doctrine concerns the extent to which a bystander may recover for injuries suffered as a result of another's use of an unreasonably dangerous product. Although liability to bystanders has been denied in the past,[325] some courts have recently indicated

---

323. 460 S.W.2d at 613 (citations omitted).
324. See § 8.11.
325. RESTATEMENT (SECOND) OF TORTS § 402A, comment *o* (1965).

that bystanders might be able to recover.[326] The only sports case that appears to have considered this point is *Katz v. Slade*,[327] where, as already noted, a golfer was injured as a result of a defect in a golf cart which made it unsafe for its intended use. Unfortunately, the court did not reach the question, though it did note its presence in the case. In light of the authority which grants strict liability recovery to bystanders, however, recovery may be available in an appropriate case.

§ 8.11. Liability for Defective Athletic Equipment — Warranty Liability.

Warranty liability provides a third potential basis of liability for manufacturers of defective athletic equipment.[328] This type of liability may involve several specific types of warranties. These either arise by express statement or are implied by law and are set forth in the Uniform Commercial Code (U.C.C.). A seller of goods creates an express warranty by any "affirmation of fact or promise," description of the goods, or sample or model which is made a basis of the bargain between seller and buyer.[329] Actual words of warranty or guarantee are not required, since any statement or representation concerning quality will suffice.[330] Implied warranties, on the other hand, arise not by the words or action of the parties, but by operation of law.[331] There are two implied warranties set forth in the U.C.C. The first is the implied warranty of merchantability, which is implied in every contract for the sale of goods.[332] To satisfy this warranty, the goods must be suitable for the ordinary purpose for which they are sold. The second is the implied warranty of fitness for a particular purpose. It arises when the seller has reason to know the particular purpose for which the goods are purchased and the seller knows that the buyer is relying upon the seller to select or furnish suitable goods.[333] The basic difference between express and implied warranties, then, is that the former rest upon the "dickered" aspects of the individual bargain, while the latter arise from the nature of the transaction and thus require no affirmative act of the parties.[334]

---

326. Sills v. Massey-Ferguson, Inc., 296 F. Supp. 776 (N.D. Ind. 1969); Moning v. Alfonio, 400 Mich. 425, 254 N.W.2d 759 (1977) (not a § 402A case); Piercefield v. Remington Arms Co., 375 Mich. 85, 133 N.W.2d 129 (1965) (not a § 402A case). *See generally* 1 L. FRUMER & M. FRIEDMAN, PRODUCTS LIABILITY, § 16.A [4.] [c.] (1973); Note, *Strict Products Liability and the Bystander,* 64 COLUM. L. REV. 916 (1964).

327. 460 S.W.2d 608 (Mo. 1970).

328. The concept of warranty liability is similar to the "strict liability" considered in § 8.10, which had its original basis in the breach of implied warranties. *See* RESTATEMENT (SECOND) OF TORTS § 402A, comments *b, m* (1965).

329. UNIFORM COMMERCIAL CODE § 2-313(1) (1962). Thus, in Rinkmasters v. City of Utica, 75 Misc. 2d 941, 348 N.Y.S. 2d 940 (1973), an express warranty arose from an illustration in a catalog depicting ice hockey equipment. *See also* Pacific Marine Schwabacher, Inc. v. Hydroswift Corp., 525 P.2d 615 (Utah 1974). *But cf.* Salk v. Alpine Ski Shop, Inc., 115 R.I. 309, 342 A.2d 622 (1975) (no evidence that newspaper advertisements created an express warranty).

330. UNIFORM COMMERCIAL CODE § 2-313(1) (1962). In considering express warranties, it should be noted that there are also several disclosure requirements that must be satisfied. *See* 15 U.S.C. §§ 2301-2312.

331. Hauter v. Zogarts, 14 Cal. 3d 104, 534 P.2d 377 (1975).

332. UNIFORM COMMERCIAL CODE § 2-314 (1962). *See* Pacific Marine Schwabacher, Inc. v. Hydroswift Corp., 525 P.2d 615 (Utah 1974).

333. UNIFORM COMMERCIAL CODE § 2-315 (1962).

334. UNIFORM COMMERCIAL CODE § 2-313, comment *I* (1962).

Express warranties, once made, may be excluded from the bargain only by conspicuous language known to the buyer; the implied warranty of merchantability may be excluded only by conspicuous language specifically mentioning merchantability; and the implied warranty of fitness for a particular purpose may be excluded by general language if it is conspicuous and in a writing.[335]

Perhaps the most important questions in the area of warranty liability involve the extent of coverage or protection provided by the warranties where they do exist. The first concerns the types of transactions that are covered. It is clear that the warranties apply to sales transactions, but the U.C.C.'s application is not limited merely to "sales." It applies, instead, "to transactions in goods," unless the context otherwise requires,[336] and the term "transactions" is broader than the term "sales."[337] This is suggested with respect to the warranty provisions by the comment to U.C.C. § 2-313 that

> [a]lthough this section [dealing with express warranties] is limited in its scope and direct purpose to warranties made by the seller to the buyer as part of a contract for sale, the warranty sections of this Article are not designed in any way to disturb those lines of case law growth which have recognized that warranties need not be confined either to sales contracts or to the direct parties to such a contract. They may arise in other appropriate circumstances, such as in the case of bailments for hire, whether such bailment is itself the main contract or is merely a supplying of containers under a contract for the sale of their contents . . . . Beyond that, the matter is left to the case law with the intention that the policies of this Act may offer useful guidance in dealing with further cases as they arise.[338]

The issue of the extent of coverage of the warranties in sports equipment cases will most often arise with respect to equipment rentals. In light of the comment to § 2-313 that the warranties may arise in the case of bailments for hire, it is possible that the warranty provisions would apply to lease or rental situations. Several courts have reached this conclusion.[339]

The application of these principles to sports equipment cases is well evidenced by two rented golf cart cases in which the courts reached directly opposite results. In *Bona v. Graefe*,[340] a golfer injured when the brakes on a rented golf cart failed to operate brought suit against the driver, the owner of the cart, the golf course (the lessee of the owner) and the manufacturer. Against the golf course and the manufacturer, the golfer alleged, *inter alia*, breach of the U.C.C.

---

335. UNIFORM COMMERCIAL CODE § 2-316 (1962).

336. UNIFORM COMMERCIAL CODE § 2-102 (1962). Lewis v. Big Powderhorn Mountain Ski Corp., 69 Mich. App. 437, 245 N.W.2d 81 (1976) (not apply to services, such as "a weekend of skiing").

337. R. DUESENBERG & L. KING, SALES & BULK TRANSFERS § 7.01[2], at 7-4 (1976).

338. UNIFORM COMMERCIAL CODE § 2-313, comment 2 (1962).

339. KLPR T.V., Inc. v. Visual Electronics Corp., 327 F. Supp. 315 (W.D. Ark. 1971), *modified on other grounds,* 465 F.2d 1382 (8th Cir. 1972); Sawyer v. Pioneer Leasing Corp., 244 Ark. 943, 428 S.W.2d 46 (1968); W. E. Johnson Equipment Co. v. United Airlines, Inc., 238 So. 2d 98 (Fla. 1970); Cintrone v. Hertz Truck Leasing & Rental Service, 45 N.J. 434, 212 A.2d 769 (1965); A-Leet Leasing Corp. v. Kingshead Corp., 150 N.J. Super. 384, 375 A.2d 1208 (1977); Hertz Commercial Leasing Corp. v. Transportation Credit Clearing House, 59 Misc. 2d 226, 298 N.Y.S.2d 392 (1969), *rev'd on other grounds,* 316 N.Y.S.2d 585 (1970); *see also* Farnsworth, *Implied Warranties of Quality in Non-Sales Cases,* 57 COLUM. L. REV. 653, 655 (1957); Murray, *Under the Spreading Analogy of Article 2 of the Uniform Commercial Code,* 39 FORDHAM L. REV. 447, 449 (1971).

340. 264 Md. 69, 285 A.2d 607 (1972).

warranty provisions. Thus, he sought to impose U.C.C. warranty liability in a rental transaction upon both the lessor and his lessor's lessor. In rejecting this theory, the court characterized as "anomalous" the authority holding, or recommending, that the warranty provisions apply to such transactions, and stated that "[f]or us to accept [this] contention would take us beyond the limits of judicial restraint and into the area of judicial legislation, a journey which we [refuse] to make . . . ." [341] The journey was, however, made in *Baker v. City of Seattle,*[342] where another golfer was injured as the result of defective brakes on his rented golf cart. Unlike *Bona v. Graefe,* the court did apply the warranty provisions of the U.C.C. to the transaction, and did so without really questioning their applicability. Specifically, the court applied the U.C.C.'s provisions dealing with the enforceability of a disclaimer of warranty liability to invalidate a disclaimer signed by the golfer. In light of the cases which have applied the U.C.C. warranty provisions to leases or bailments for hire, it would appear that *Baker,* and not *Bona v. Graefe,* may present the preferred resolution of this particular problem.

A second important question under the U.C.C. warranty provisions concerns the extent to which protection is afforded to those who are not buyers of the defective product and thus are not in privity with the seller. As a general matter, the courts in recent years have frequently acted to prevent parties from invoking the traditional "privity" rule as a defense for the defective products which they have put on the market.[343] The status of the privity rule in the warranty area is less than clear. The basic privity principle of the U.C.C. is expressed in § 2-318, which provides that warranties extend to certain members of the buyer's family and household.[344] This section provides a very narrow opening in the privity rule and could be viewed to require privity in all other situations. The comments to this and other sections are, however, more equivocal. Thus, the official comments to § 2-318 suggest that the section is not intended to "enlarge or restrict the developing case law . . . ." in other areas.[345] This language is similar to the comment under § 2-313, quoted above, which states that warranty provisions "need not be confined . . . to the direct parties to the contract." [346] The uncertainty caused by the text of § 2-318 and these comments has resulted in court decisions that are less than harmonious on the privity issue. It has also caused some states to adopt language which is alternative to that used in § 2-318 in an effort to eliminate as much uncertainty as possible.[347] Although the variant language of § 2-318 from jurisdiction to jurisdiction precludes the identification of a general rule, several courts have not required privity for purposes of the

---

341. 264 Md. at 74, 285 A.2d at 601.

342. 79 Wash. 2d 198, 484 P.2d 405 (1971).

343. Thus, in 1931 the New York Court of Appeals was able to say that "[t]he assault upon the citadel of privity is proceeding these days apace." Ultramares Corp. v. Touche, 255 N.Y. 170, 174 N.E. 441 (1931).

344. UNIFORM COMMERCIAL CODE § 2-318 (1962).

345. UNIFORM COMMERCIAL CODE § 2-318, comment 3 (1962).

346. *See* note 338 *supra.*

347. The case law and language variations are considered in 3 R. DUESENBERG & L. KING, SALES & BULK TRANSFERS §§ 7.05[3], [4] (1976).

warranty provisions.[348] In *Filler v. Rayex Corporation,*[349] for example, a user of baseball sunglasses was able to bring a warranty action against the manufacturer although he was not a buyer, since the court found that privity was not required. In reaching this conclusion, the court did not even refer to § 2-318.

Several of the warranty principles were considered in *Hauter v. Zogarts,*[350] in which a father had purchased a "Golfing Gizmo" to aid his son's swing. The carton containing the device stated that it was "Completely Safe Ball Will Not Hit Player." However, when the boy used it he suffered severe brain damage when the ball hit him in the head. In a subsequent suit by the boy, the court held that the manufacturer was liable on both express and implied warranty grounds. It found that the quoted words created an express warranty, which became a part of the bargain when the father read and relied upon it. The manufacturer also breached the implied warranty of merchantability, since the device failed to meet the promises on its label and was not fit for the ordinary purposes for which it was sold.[351] The court rejected the manufacturer's argument that its liability was limited by instructions which illustrated only "proper" golf shots. It noted that disclaimers would be effective only if they were clearly stated and would, in any event, be strictly construed against the seller. Since the manufacturer had not made a clear disclaimer, its argument could not prevail. Finally, the court held that the boy was not barred from recovering by the fact that he was not in privity with the manufacturer (the "Gizmo" had been purchased by his father). It found that privity was not required for express warranties in California, and although privity was apparently necessary for implied warranties the boy came within the exception for members of the purchaser's family.[352]

§ 8.12. Workmen's Compensation Liability.

When an athlete is injured, the principal means of securing recovery for the injuries will be through a lawsuit based upon common law principles of tort liability.[353] In some situations, however, an alternative path is available through the workmen's compensation statutes. These laws provide a scheme under which an employee may secure compensation for employment related injuries through a fund created for that purpose.[354] Although the development of the workmen's

---

348. Greeno v. Clark Equipment Co., 237 F. Supp. 427 (N.D. Ind. 1965); Schipper v. Levitt & Sons, Inc., 44 N.J. 70, 207 A.2d 314 (1965); Marrillia v. Lyn Craft Boat Co., 271 So. 2d 204 (Fla. App. 1973); Electronics Corp. of America v. Lear Jet Corp., 55 Misc. 2d 1066, 286 N.Y.S.2d 711 (1967); Fairfield Lease Corp. v. Commodore Cosmetique, Inc., 7 UCC Rep. Service 164 (N.Y. Civ. Ct. 1969); Kassab v. Central Soya, 432 Pa. 217, 246 A.2d 848 (1968). *See also* 1 L. FRUMER & M. FRIEDMAN, PRODUCTS LIABILITY § 16.A[4.] (1973); R. NORDSTROM, THE LAW OF SALES § 92, at 284 (1970) ("The Code ought not be quoted to require a need for privity of contract between the manufacturer and the person who is injured by a defect in the goods."). *But cf.* Salmon Rivers Sportsman Camps v. Cessna Aircraft Co., 97 Ida. 348, 544 P.2d 306 (1975) (privity required for economic loss under implied warranty); Sparling v. Podzielinski, 32 Misc. 2d 227, 223 N.Y.S.2d 10 (1962) (privity required in ski tow rope accident).

349. 435 F.2d 336 (7th Cir. 1970).

350. 14 Cal. 3d 104, 534 P.2d 377 (1975).

351. 534 P.2d 385-86.

352. 534 P.2d at 383 n.8.

353. *See* § 8.02.

354. The nature of workmen's compensation is considered in 1 A. LARSON, THE LAW OF WORKMEN'S COMPENSATION §§ 1.10-3.40 (1972).

compensation laws provides a fascinating study in the evolution of statutory remedies to fill gaps in common law coverage,[355] it is sufficient for present purposes to state that their general effect is to strike a socially-enforced bargain in the employment relationship. This bargain requires that employees give up their rights to pursue an uncertain, but full, recovery under common law theories in the courts, in return for a certain, but limited, award before the workmen's compensation agency.[356] The employer, on the other hand is forced to relinquish its common law defenses, in return for an assurance that the recoveries of employees will be limited.[357] The coverage of the workmen's compensation scheme, moreover, extends beyond ordinary commercial enterprise and includes all kinds of public and private, charitable and educational institutions.[358] In general, the workmen's compensation laws will be liberally construed to bring as many cases as possible within their protective coverage, a policy that is thought to be necessary to insure that the remedial purpose of the statutes are achieved.[359]

To be within the scheme of the workmen's compensation provisions, however, an injured party must prove that he or she is an "employee" and that the injury occurred in an activity which was within the course of employment.[360] Among those not covered are independent contractors and others who participate in relationships which do not involve employment. Determining whether a given person is an independent contractor requires that an "often blurred and shadowy" line be drawn, and on which side of the line a particular case may fall will depend upon an analysis of all its facts and circumstances.[361] The factors that are generally considered in making this determination include the right to control the manner in which the work is done, which is the primary factor, the method of payment, the right to discharge, the skill required in the work to be done, and who furnishes the tools, equipment or materials needed to accomplish

---

355. The need for workmen's compensation-type legislation was chiefly a by-product of the evolution of the "fellow servant," "contributory negligence," and "assumption of the risk doctrines," which left the injured employee remedyless unless it could be proven that the employer's conduct was itself the cause of injury. *See* Owens v. Union Pacific Railroad Co., 319 U.S. 715, 720-21, 87 L.Ed 1683, 63 S. Ct. 1271 (1943). The development of workmen's compensation statutes to fill this void is comprehensively considered in 1 A. LARSON, THE LAW OF WORKMEN'S COMPENSATION §§ 4.10-5.30 (1972).

356. Metropolitan Casualty Ins. Co. of New York v. Huhn, 165 Ga. 667, 142 S.E. 121 (1928).

357. Van Horn v. Industrial Accident Comm'n, 219 Cal. App. 2d 457, 33 Cal. Rptr. 169 (1963).

358. The workmen's compensation liability of colleges and universities for athletic injuries is considered at § 8.14.

359. Rodwell v. Pro Football, Inc., 45 Mich. App. 408, 206 N.W.2d 773 (1973); Gross v. Pellicane, 65 N.J. Super. 386, 167 A.2d 838 (1961).

360. An injury not having any particular connection to the employment relation is not generally "compensable." *See, e.g.,* Illinois Country Club, Inc. v. Industrial Comm'n, 387 Ill. 484, 56 N.E.2d 786 (1944) (golf caddy being struck by lightning not compensable); Colarullo's Case, 258 Mass. 521, 155 N.E. 425 (1927) (an injury to golf caddy caused by being struck by a car was a "street risk" and, therefore, not compensable since the risk was common to all persons).

361. Moore v. Clarke, 171 Md. 39, 187 A. 887 (1936). The "employee" question has been most frequently considered in sports cases with respect to boxers and wrestlers, *see* § 8.02, and golf caddies. With respect to caddies, they have frequently been considered as "employees" of the club at which they work. *See* Claremont Country Club v. Industrial Accident Comm'n, 174 Cal. 395, 163 P. 209 (1917); Indian Hill Club v. Industrial Comm'n, 309 Ill. 271, 140 N.E. 871 (1923); Bird v. Lake Hopatcong Country Club, 119 N.J. Law 415, 197 A. 282 (1938); Essex County Country Club v. Chapman, 113 N.J. Law 182, 173 A. 591 (1934); Boyd v. Philmont Country Club, 129 Pa. Super. 135, 195 A. 156 (1937). *But cf.* City of Miami v. Fulp, 60 So. 2d 18 (Fla. 1952) (caddy not "employee" for workmen's compensation purposes). A club that simply allows neighborhood youngsters to carry club members' bags, however, may not be an employer, *see* Rice Lake Golf Club v. Industrial

the work.[362] An injury will be considered to have occurred within the course of employment, on the other hand, when it takes place during the period of employment, at a place where the employee may reasonably be, and at a time when the employee is fulfilling assigned duties or engaging in activities incidental thereto.[363]

§ 8.13. Professional Athletics.

In considering the application of workmen's compensation schemes to professional athletics, there are two separate types of athletes to be considered: the athlete who is a member of a professional team, and the athlete who participates in a sport where competition is on an individual, not a team, basis.

It seems clear that an athlete who is a member of a professional athletic team will frequently be an "employee" for purposes of the workmen's compensation statutes, except in those jurisdictions where professional athletes are specifically excluded from coverage.[364] The leading case expressing this view is *Metropolitan Casualty Insurance Company of New York v. Huhn*,[365] where two minor league baseball players had been killed in an automobile accident while traveling to the location of their next game. In rejecting the contention that the players were not "employees" within the statutory scheme, the court stated that the workmen's compensation law did not apply solely to industrial accidents, but rather was broad enough to include within its coverage employees engaged in athletic business.[366]

Comm'n, 215 Wis. 284, 254 N.W. 530 (1934), and an unlawfully employed minor may not pursue a workmen's compensation recovery. Fritsch v. Pennsylvania Golf Club, 355 Pa. 384, 50 A.2d 207 (1947).

362. Clark v. Industrial Comm'n, 54 Ill. 2d 311, 297 N.E.2d 154 (1973).

363. *See, e.g.,* Trent v. Employers Liability Assurance Corp., 178 So. 2d 470 (La. App. 1965) (award for injuries suffered by a coach while traveling to a football game which he intended to scout); McManus' Case, 289 Mass. 65, 193 N.E. 732 (1935) (caddy not within scope of employment when playing golf himself); Bird v. Lake Hopatcong Country Club, 119 N.J. Law 415, 197 A. 282 (1938) (caddy climbing tree at direction of superior within scope of employment); Boyd v. Philmont Country Club, 129 Pa. Super. 135, 195 A. 156 (1937) (caddy looking for flowers at direction of lady golfer within scope of employment); Milwaukee v. Industrial Comm'n, 160 Wis. 238, 151 N.W. 247 (1915) (award for injuries suffered by a coach when struck on the head with a ball while coaching a basketball team). *See generally* 1 A. LARSON, THE LAW OF WORKMEN'S COMPENSATION § 14.00 (1972).

364. The Massachusetts statute, for example, excludes from the definition of "employee"

persons employed to participate in organized professional athletics, while so employed, if their contracts of hire provide for the payment of wages during the period of any disability resulting from such employment.

MASS. ANN. LAWS ch. 152, § 1(4) (1976). *See also* OKLA. STAT. ANN. tit. 40, § 234 (Supp. 1978) (professional athlete ineligible for unemployment insurance).

365. 165 Ga. 667, 142 S.E. 121 (1928).

366. Thus, the court stated that

[i]t is true the baseball player for whose death the claim is made was not engaged in a 'productive industry' at the time of the happening of the occurrence which resulted in his death; but he was engaged in a 'business operated for gain or profit.' Section 2(a) of the Compensation Act is in part as follows:
'Employers shall include any . . . individual, firm, association or corporation engaged in any business operated for gain or profit, except as hereinafter excepted.'
And section 2(b) in part is as follows:
'Employee shall include every person, including a minor, in the service of another under any contract of hire or apprenticeship, written or implied,' etc.
In this case the baseball player who was killed was a person 'in the service of another under any contract of hire,' and therefore was an 'employee' under section 2(b). The title of the act in part is as follows:

When workmen's compensation recovery is sought by professional team sport athletes, there will also be a question as to where the claim should be filed. This issue will arise as a result of the fact that many such athletes will live in state A, their team's home town will be in state B, and they will regularly play in many other states. Fortunately, the injured athlete will frequently have a choice of bringing the action in either the state of residence or the state in which the team is primarily located. Thus, In *Rodwell v. Pro Football, Inc.*,[367] a college football player had signed a professional contract at his home in Michigan with a team located in Washington, D.C., and was injured during tackling practice at the team's training camp in Pennsylvania. When the player then brought a workmen's compensation claim against the team in Michigan, the state of his residence, the court held that the team was subject to the Michigan workmen's compensation act even though the injury took place out of state and involved a contract which would be performed for the most part outside of Michigan. In reaching this conclusion, the court noted that the relevant statutory provision specifically applied to Michigan residents injured out of state while performing under contracts signed in Michigan. It also stated that had the action been a civil suit, the Michigan courts would have jurisdiction under the applicable personal jurisdiction ("long-arm") statute. In the court's view, the team's active recruitment of the player and the actual contract signing in Michigan, as well as that state's interest in protecting its residents, were sufficient bases for the jurisdictional finding.[368]

In addition to those athletes who are members of organized teams, there are also many others who perform on an individual basis for different promoters. When these athletes are injured, the central question will be whether they are "employees" of any of the persons or organizations who provide their income.

This issue has received its primary consideration in the cases that have involved injured jockeys. There are two methods used by owners and trainers to employ jockeys. The first is on a "contract rider" basis, where the jockey is bound to ride whatever horse the owner or trainer may designate. The second and most common relationship is what is referred to as "free-lance" riding, in which the jockey contracts on a race by race basis. Most "contract-riders" are allowed to undertake "free-lance work" when there is no "contract" work to be performed. Where the jockey is performing as a "contract" rider, there should

'An act to prevent industrial accidents; . . . to establish rates of compensation for personal injuries or death sustained by employees in the course of employment; to provide methods of insuring the payment of such compensation; to create an Industrial Commission for the administration of this act and to prescribe the powers of such commission, and for other purposes.'

If the title had read, 'An act to establish rates of compensation for injuries or death sustained by employees engaged in industrial pursuits or in industrial business,' there would have been more force in the objection raised to including the baseball player who was killed among those who are covered by the act. But the words in the caption, 'to prevent industrial accidents,' cover only in the most general way the purpose of the act, and other words following in the caption are broad enough to cover the case of employees engaged in other businesses. The deceased baseball player was an employee under the provisions of section 2(b) of the act. 165 Ga. at 677-78, 142 S.E. at 125-26.

See also Harrington v. New Orleans Saints Football Club, 311 So.2d 555 (La. App. 1975).

367. 45 Mich. App. 408, 206 N.W.2d 773 (1973).

368. *See also* Metropolitan Casualty Insurance Co. of New York v. Huhn, 165 Ga. 667, 142 S.E. 121 (1928) (Georgia proper forum for injury to member of Georgia team in South Carolina). Jurisdictional problems in professional sports litigation are considered at §§ 4.21-4.22.

be little question that he or she is an employee and entitled to compensation for the racing-related injuries.

With regard to "free-lance" jockeys, however, the courts have split in all directions when faced with the question of the application of the workmen's compensation laws. Although the clear majority of courts have held free-lance jockeys to be employees, a few have held them to be unprotected casual employees. The leading case expressing the majority view is *Gross v. Pellicane,*[369] where a jockey who was a contract rider for an owner agreed through his agent to serve as a free-lance jockey for another trainer for one race. The jockey's compensation was determined by the state racing commission and was to be paid by the owner to track officials who would in turn pay the jockey on a weekly basis, though no taxes or fees were withheld from these payments. Before the race in question, the trainer met the jockey in the paddock and gave him instructions as to the handling of the horse. These facts indicated, the court believed, that the jockey was an employee, and not an independent contractor, of the trainer. Thus, it said that

> [t]he evidence in the instant case clearly shows that the [jockey] was subject to the control of the trainer and was duty-bound by his contract to follow her instructions as to the manner in which the race should be run. The fact that the instructions given in the instant case may appear to be merely informative as to the speed and capabilities of the horse is of no consequence. It is the existence of the right of control and not the actual exercise of this right which is determinative. . . .
>
> The fact that the [jockey] would have to use his own judgment concerning unanticipated problems which arose during the race, and that he could not be discharged after the race had been commenced, does not belie the existence of the right to control and discharge, but is merely due to the practical exigencies of the industry in question. It is of no consequence that because of physical inability the trainer was unable to communicate his exercise of such authority to [the jockey].[370]

Similar results have been reached in several other cases.[371]

A second rule, followed apparently by only the courts of Maryland, is that a free-lance jockey is a "casual employee," [372] which is an employee who is only fortuitously connected with the employer and who is customarily excluded from workmen's compensation coverage.[373] This view is best stated in *Moore v. Clarke,*[374] where a free-lance jockey was killed during a race. Although the facts appeared to be identical to those in *Gross v. Pellicane,* the court concluded that

369. 65 N.J. Super. 386, 167 A.2d 838 (1961).

370. 65 N.J. Super. at 392, 167 A.2d at 841-42.

371. Isenberg v. California Employment Stabilization Comm'n, 30 Cal. 2d. 34, 180 P.2d 11 (1947); Drillon v. Industrial Accident Comm'n, 17 Cal. 2d 346, 110 P.2d 64 (1941); Biger v. Erwin, 108 N.J. Super. 293, 261 A.2d 151, *aff'd,* 57 N.J. 95, 270 A.2d 12 (1970); Rice v. Stoneham, 254 N.Y. 531, 173 N.E. 853 (1930); Pierce v. Bowen, 247 N.Y. 305, 160 N.E. 379 (1928). *See also* Nikolas v. Kirner, 247 Iowa 231, 73 N.W.2d 7 (1955) (free lance jockey was servant of owner for common law negligence purposes); Simmons v. Kansas City Jockey Club, 334 Mo. 99, 66 S.W.2d 119 (1933) (same). *But cf.* Rock v. Commissioner of Revenue, 83 N.M. 478, 493 P.2d 963 (1972) (jockey not "employee" for state gross receipts tax; court held the rationale of the workmen's compensation cases to be inapplicable). Free-lance jockeys are also considered "employees" for federal income tax purposes. Rev. Rul. 73-232, 1973-1 CUM. BULL. 541; Rev. Rul. 70-573, 1970-2 CUM. BULL. 221; McCormick v. United States, 531 F.2d 554 (Ct. Cl. 1976) (trainer employer of "hotwalker").

372. East v. Skelly, 207 Md. 537, 114 A.2d 822 (1955); Moore v. Clarke, 171 Md. 39, 187 A. 887 (1936).

373. *See generally* A. LARSON, THE LAW OF WORKMEN'S COMPENSATION § 51.00 (1972).

374. 171 Md. 39, 187 A. 887 (1936).

the jockey was a casual employee, and not an employee, and as such excluded from coverage. It stated that the employment extended over a short period and was an isolated event that was fortuitous and connected with no past or future employment.[375] It is worth noting that the view of the court in *Moore v. Clarke* was distinguished in *Gross v. Pellicane* on the basis of the presence of a different statutory definition of "casual employee." In the latter case, the court rejected the casual employee argument by noting that "[t]he employment of a jockey is an integral part of the business of racing horses, the occasion for which does not arise by chance or accident.[376]

A third position, apparently adopted only by the Illinois courts, is that a free-lance jockey is an independent contractor.[377] This view is best expressed by *Clark v. Industrial Commission*,[378] where a free-lance jockey had been injured when thrown by his mount. The evidence indicated that the jockey had ridden for the owner in question about twenty times during the year; had signed in as a self-employed jockey when admitted to the hospital; his winnings and bonuses were to be paid by the owner to track officials, who would then distribute them on a once per week basis without withholding for income, social security or unemployment compensation tax purposes; and just prior to the race the trainer and owner had met the jockey in the paddock and instructed him in how to handle the horse during the race. On these facts, the court held that the claim for compensation must be rejected since the jockey was an independent contractor and not an employee. In reaching its conclusion, the court viewed the above factors to indicate that the owners "did not possess that degree of control over the details of the [jockey's] riding of their horse . . . [as] would render him their employee during that race." [379] The facts in *Clark* were in all essential respects identical to those in *Gross v. Pellicane*, so that the opinions of the two courts are simply at odds. In this regard, it should be noted that in *Clark* the court dismissed *Gross v. Pellicane* and the other jockey cases by simply noting that they were all "distinguishable in one respect or another." [380] They are distinguishable, however, only to the extent that the results the respective courts reached are different. As has already been noted, the view expressed by *Gross v. Pellicane* is clearly the majority view, so that *Clark* represents a view apparently limited to Illinois.

The applicability of workmen's compensation statutes to athletes has also been considered, though only indirectly, with regard to professional club golfers. In *Ridge Country Club v. United States*,[381] an action had been brought by a country club to recover taxes for a resident professional paid under a federal unemployment act, which required employer contributions on behalf of all employees. The professional had been hired as an instructor and received a

375. 171 Md. at 50-51, 187 A. at 894.

376. 65 N.J. Super. at 394-95, 167 A.2d at 843. *See also* Biger v. Erwin, 108 N.J. Super. 293, 261 A.2d 151, *aff'd*, 57 N.J. 95, 270 A.2d 12 (1970).

377. Whalen v. Harrison, 51 F. Supp. 515 (N.D. Ill. 1943); Clark v. Industrial Comm'n, 54 Ill.2d 311, 297 N.E.2d 154 (1973). *See also* Laurel Sports Activities v. Unemployment Compensation Comm'n, 135 N.J.L. 234, 51 A.2d 233 (1947), *aff'd per curiam* 136 N.J.L. 637, 57 A.2d 387 (1948) (wrestlers, boxers, referees and timekeepers not employees of promoter).

378. 54 Ill. 2d 311, 297 N.E.2d 154 (1973).

379. 54 Ill. 2d 317-18, 297 N.E.2d at 156-57.

380. 54 Ill. 2d at 318, 297 N.E.2d at 157.

381. 135 F.2d 718 (7th Cir. 1943).

salary for performance of that function, but was also allowed to conduct a pro shop on the premises, the profits of which the club turned over to him. The court found that the pro was an employee in connection with his instruction responsibilities, but an independent contractor with respect to his income from the pro shop. This latter result was required, the court believed, because the club did not receive a percentage of the income derived from the shop, the risk of loss and benefit belonged entirely to the pro, and he alone could direct the manner in which he would execute his duties.[382]

The jockey and golf cases should also provide a sufficient basis of authority to enable the courts to make similar determinations with regard to other types of non-team sport professional athletes.[383]

§ 8.14. College and University Athletics.

Doubtlessly the most complex problem involved in the area of workmen's compensation liability for athletic injuries, is the extent to which college or university athletes may recover for their participation related injuries. Although it is clear that employees may often be injured in athletic endeavors that are considered to be a part of their employment,[384] and that college or university students may, under some circumstances, be "employees" of their school,[385] it is far from clear whether such circumstances include participation in athletic activities. Fortunately, there is a sufficient body of law to indicate when, and under what circumstances, an athlete will be an employee. As a general rule, it may be stated that a college or university athlete will not be considered an employee simply because he or she is the recipient of an athletic scholarship or grant-in-aid.[386] Where, however, the performance of athletic services is the *quid pro quo* for the scholarship or grant-in-aid award,[387] the athlete will be an employee for purposes of workmen's compensation coverage.[388]

Inasmuch as the workmen's compensation cases involving college or university athletes are considered in detail in an earlier chapter,[389] the discussion will not be repeated here. For present purposes, it will suffice to note that there is authority for the view that some collegiate scholarships and grants-in-aid are

---

382. 135 F.2d at 720-21.

383. *See, e.g.,* Gale v. Greater Washington Softball Umpires Ass'n, 19 Md. App. 481, 311 A.2d 817 (1973) (umpire was an independent contractor, and could not recover benefits for an assault by a player).

384. *See* § 8.15.

385. Thus, in Evanson v. University of Hawaii, 52 Hawaii 595, 483 P.2d 187 (1971), the court observed that the fulfillment of educational requirements does not destroy the possibility of the employee-employer relation, and that "a person may occupy the dual status of an employee and student." Id. at 599, 483 P.2d at 190. *Cf.* Davis v. University of Delaware, 240 A.2d 583, 585 (Del. 1968). *See also* Anaheim General Hospital v. Workmen's Compensation Appeals Board, 3 Cal. App. 3d 468, 83 Cal. Rptr. 495 (1970); Union Lumber Co. v. Industrial Accident Comm'n, 12 Cal. App. 2d 588, 55 P.2d 911 (1936); Gentili v. University of Idaho, 91 Ida. 116, 416 P.2d 507 (1966) (recovery denied); Judd v. Sanatorium Comm'n of Hennepin County, 227 Minn. 303, 35 N.W.2d 430 (1948).

386. *See* Van Horn v. Industrial Accident Comm'n, 219 Cal. App. 2d 457, 33 Cal. Rptr. 169 (1963); State Compensation Insurance Fund v. Industrial Comm'n, 135 Colo. 570, 314 P.2d 288 (1957).

387. *See* § 1.07.

388. *See* Van Horn v. Industrial Accident Comm'n, 219 Cal. App. 2d 457, 33 Cal. Rptr. 169 (1963); University of Denver v. Nemeth, 127 Colo. 385, 257 P.2d 423 (1953). *See generally* 1 A. LARSON, THE LAW OF WORKMEN'S COMPENSATION § 22.21 (1972); Cross, *The College Athlete and the Institution,* 38 LAW AND CONTEMP. PROB. 171, 163-66 (1973); Steinbach, *Workmen's Compensation and the Scholarship Athlete,* 19 CLEV. ST. L. REV. 521 (1970).

389. *See* § 1.07.

awarded in such a manner as to facilitate the conclusion that they are awarded
on a *quid pro quo* basis—that is, that the award is given in consideration of the
athletic ability and promise to perform of the recipient.[390] To the extent that such
a finding could be made in any given case, the athlete in question would then
be an employee for workmen's compensation purposes.[391]

§ 8.15. Employer Sponsored or Sanctioned Athletic Activities.

The final type of situation in which an athlete may be able to have recourse
to the workmen's compensation laws involves injuries sustained during athletic
activities sponsored or sanctioned by an employer. These activities may take
many forms, ranging from pick-up games during the work period to formally
sponsored athletic teams that engage in league competition. In all of these
situations, recovery will be possible so long as the injured athlete is an
"employee" and is able to prove that the athletic activity is within the course
of his or her employment. Whether the injured athlete is an "employee", will
be determined by applying the tests stated above,[392] and this determination will
pose little problem in the ordinary case.

The more difficult question is whether the athletic activity was within the
employment environment. As a general rule, it has been stated[393] that athletic
activities will be considered to be within the course of employment in the
following cases: 1) when they occur on the employer's premises during a period
that is a regular incident of employment;[394] 2) when the employer brings the
activity within the course of employment by expressly or impliedly requiring
participation;[395] and 3) when the employer derives substantial direct benefit
from the activity beyond the intangible benefit derived from the improvement
of employee health and morale.[396] If any one of these links is found in a
particular case, then the injury should be compensable. The course of
employment does not, however, include every injury suffered by an employee,
and where none of the above situations is present, the injury will not be
compensable. Thus, compensation has been denied when an employee is injured

---

390. *See* § 1.07.

391. *See* note 388 *supra*.

392. *See* § 8.12.

393. 1 A. LARSON, THE LAW OF WORKMEN'S COMPENSATION § 22.00 (1972). *See also* Comment,
Workmen's Compensation — Recreational Injuries, 24 TENN. L. REV. 870 (1957); Comment,
Workmen's Compensation Awards for Recreational Injuries, 23 U. CHI. L. REV. 328 (1956).

394. Nichols v. Workmen's Compensation Appeals Board, 269 Cal. App. 2d 598, 75 Cal. Rptr. 226
(1969) (softball during free period); Geary v. Anaconda Copper Mining Co., 120 Mont. 485, 188 P.2d
185 (1947) (noon hour handball); Tocci v. Tessler & Weiss, Inc., 28 N.J. 582, 147 A.2d 783 (1959) (noon
hour softball); DiPerri v. Boys Brotherhood Republic of New York, Inc., 31 N.Y.2d 215, 335 N.Y.S.2d
405, 286 N.E.2d 897 (1972) (basketball at nearby gym); Brown v. United Services For Air, Inc., 298
N.Y. 901, 84 N.E.2d 810 (1949) (noon hour volleyball); Dowen v. Saratoga Springs Comm'n, 267 App.
Div. 928, 46 N.Y.S.2d 822 (1944) (recreation period swimming); City of Oklahoma City v. Alvarado,
507 P.2d 535 (Okla. 1973) (recreation period volleyball); Henry v. Lit Bros., 193 Pa. Super. 543, 165
A.2d 406 (1960) (noon hour football); Salt Lake City v. Industrial Comm'n, 104 Utah 436, 140 P.2d
644 (1943) (recreation period handball).

395. Turner v. Willard, 154 F. Supp. 352 (S.D.N.Y. 1956) (bowling league); Boyd v. Florida
Mattress Factory, Inc., 128 So. 2d 881 (Fla. 1961) (fishing trip to entertain customers); Lybrand Ross
Bros. & Montgomery v. Industrial Comm'n, 36 Ill. 2d 410, 223 N.E.2d 150 (1967) (golf tournament);
Sargeant v. Tile Roofing Co., 18 App. Div. 2d 1037, 238 N.Y.S.2d 645 (1963) (softball at picnic).

396. U. S. Fiber Glass Industries v. Uland, 137 Ind. App. 278, 206 N.E.2d 385 (1965) (attend Notre
Dame-Oklahoma football game with customer).

in a recreational basketball game held at a gym maintained by the employer,[397] or away from the employer's premises;[398] during a strictly voluntary touch football game at the noon hour;[399] at a golf club maintained by an employer;[400] on the way to an evening bowling,[401] baseball,[402] or basketball game;[403] on a pheasant hunting trip not connected with the employer;[404] while watching a noon hour softball game;[405] and when engaging in noon hour games not shown to be part of the course of employment.[406]

The application of these principles is most aptly demonstrated by considering two decisions of the New York Court of Appeals. In *Wilson v. General Motors*,[407] an employee was injured while participating in a softball game sponsored by an employees' league at a General Motors aircraft engine plant. The evidence showed that the league had been organized by the employees without the encouragement of the management and the games were not played during working hours or on the employer's premises. The employees furnished their own transportation, and were subject to wage deduction if they missed working time. Although the employees procured their own equipment, the employer paid for it. It was also shown that the games were not advertised and received no local publicity. On these facts, the court held that the game was not within the course of the employees' employment, and the injuries were not, therefore, compensable. In reaching this conclusion, the court stated that

> [t]hese ball games, the record makes plain, were out-of-hours, off-the-premises, personal diversions of the men, and were not only optional with the employees but were exclusively for their own recreation and indulgence, without business advantage to the employer. The games were neither initiated nor sponsored by the employer, in no way connected with its affairs, and in no manner subject to its control. Even if the company had so desired, it could not have halted the ballplaying or changed the program in any way. In other words, totally lacking is any basis for an inference that it controlled the activity or sought to compel or induce any employee to participate in it. On the contrary, indication almost positive that the activity was separate and removed from the employment is found in the fact that the employer actually penalized employees who, as a result of playing or practicing, reported late for work. Neither the circumstance that

---

397. Clark v. Chrysler Corp., 276 Mich. 24, 267 N.W. 589 (1936).

398. Gordon v. United Aircraft Corp., 24 Conn. Super. 262, 189 A.2d 792 (1962); Davis v. Liberty Mutual Ins. Co., 214 Tenn. 287, 379 S.W.2d 777 (1964) (customer's gym).

399. Beiring v. Niagara Frontier Transit System, Inc., 23 App. Div. 2d 611, 256 N.Y.S.2d 365 (1965).

400. Nevada Industrial Comm'n v. Holt, 83 Nev. 497, 434 P.2d 423 (1967).

401. Tom Joyce 7-Up Co. v. Layman, 112 Ind. App. 369, 44 N.E.2d 998 (1942); Youngberg v. Donlin Co., 264 Minn. 421, 119 N.W.2d 746 (1963); Jablonski v. General Motors Acceptance Corp., 22 App. Div. 2d 724, 254 N.Y.S.2d 168 (1964).

402. Industrial Comm'n of Colo. v. Murphy, 102 Colo. 59, 76 P.2d 741 (1938); Pate v. Plymouth Manufacturing Co., 198 S.C. 159, 17 S.E.2d 146 (1941).

403. Auerbach Co. v. Industrial Comm'n, 113 Utah 347, 195 P.2d 245 (1948).

404. Aetna Casualty & Surety Co. v. Industrial Comm'n, 127 Colo. 225, 255 P.2d 961 (1953).

405. Luterman v. Ford Motor Co., 313 Mich. 487, 21 N.W.2d 825 (1946). *But cf.* Conklin v. Kansas City Public Service Co., 226 Mo. App. 309, 41 S.W.2d 608 (1931) (spectator-employee hit by bat at noon hour baseball game compensated); Kingsport Silk Mills v. Cox, 161 Tenn. 470, 33 S.W.2d 90 (1930) (spectator who fell on basketball floor at noon hour game compensated).

406. Theberge v. Public Service Electric & Gas Co., 25 N.J. Misc. 149, 51 A.2d 248 (1947) (baseball); Long v. Gorham Corp., 100 R.I. 711, 219 A.2d 214 (1966).

407. 298 N.Y. 468, 84 N.E.2d 781 (1949), *noted in* 34 CORNELL L. Q. 676 (1969).

management gave its permission to employees to take part in the sport, nor even that it cooperated in the program, can be said to spell out compulsion or constraint, and no evidence on that score is supplied by testimony that a foreman once remarked that a particular game might have been won had claimant been playing. And, as indicated, we look in vain for evidence of any business advantage or benefit accruing to the company from the employees' participation in the contests. Too tenuous and ephemeral is the possibility that such participation might perhaps indirectly benefit the employer by improving the workers' morale or health or by fostering employee good will.

Personal activities of employees, unrelated to the employment, remote from the place of work and its risk, not compelled or controlled by the employer, yielding it neither advantage nor benefit, are not within the compass of the Workmen's Compensation Law. Nor is it of any operative consequence that the employer acquiesced in, or contributed some financial aid to, such activities. The slight support thus given by the employer, without attendant advertising or consequent business advantage, should be accepted for what it really was, a gratuitous contribution to its employees' social and recreational life.[408]

Similar results have been reached in many other cases.[409]

Opposed to *Wilson* are those cases in which the employer does bring the sports activity within the course of employment. The leading case considering such employer action is *Tedesco v. General Electric Company,*[410] where an employee had been injured in a softball game conducted by an employees' organization which had been organized at the instigation of the owner. The evidence showed that the employer had a member on the organization's board of directors, provided a building for the organization rent free, and made up its deficits. The sports activities were advertised in the employer's plant newspapers and received substantial local publicity. Games were held on the employer's premises and the employer provided transportation for games played on outside fields. These facts justified, the court believed, a finding that the employer had brought the activities within the course of employment, so that the injuries complained of were compensable. In reaching this result, the court stated that

[t]here was, it seems to us, more than adequate basis for the board's conclusion that claimant's injury was incurred out of and in the course of his employment. All of the activities of GEAA, which are conducted on the employer's property, are obviously carried out with the sole purpose of providing an integrated plan of recreational activity in which the employer is dominant. However beneficial to the employees such plan may be, its primary motivation is undoubtedly the furtherance of

---

408. 298 N.Y. at 472-73, 84 N.E.2d at 784.

409. Lindsay v. Public Service Co. of Colo., 146 Colo. 579, 362 P.2d 407 (1961) (baseball league); Jewel Tea Co., Inc. v. Industrial Comm'n, 6 Ill. 2d 304, 128 N.E.2d 699 (1955) (softball league); McDonald v. St. Paul Fire & Marine Ins. Co., 288 Minn. 452, 183 N.W.2d 276 (1971) (intramural softball); McFarland v. St. Louis Car Co., 262 S.W.2d 344 (Mo. App. 1953) (softball league); Complitano v. Steel & Alloy Tank Co., 34 N.J. 300, 168 A.2d 809 (1961) (softball league); Leventhal v. Wright Aeronautical Corp., 25 N.J. Misc. 154, 51 A.2d 237 (1946); Porowski v. American Can Co., 15 N.J. Misc. 316, 191 A. 296 (1937) (softball league); Konrad v. Anheuser-Busch, Inc., 48 N.J. Super. 386, 137 A.2d 633 (1958) (softball league) (interdepartmental softball game); Padula v. Royal Plating & Polishing Co., 14 N.J. Super. 603, 82 A.2d 225 (1951) (softball league); Iacovino v. National Biscuit Co., 18 App. Div.2d 741, 235 N.Y.S.2d 511 (1962) (softball league); Miller v. Young, 25 Ohio Op. 2d 268, 193 N.E.2d 558 (1961) (softball league); Biggs v. Presto Lite Div. of Eltra Corp., 462 P.2d 641 (Okla. 1969) (baseball team); Slick v. Boyett, 160 Okla. 111, 16 P.2d 237 (1932) (baseball league, even though hired for that purpose).

410. 305 N.Y. 544, 114 N.E.2d 33 (1953).

employee relations and the building of an *esprit de corps* and good will which redound to the benefit of the employer. The inseparable connection with the employment and the complete and ultimate control not only possessed, but exercised, by the employer could hardly be better illustrated than by the complete cessation of association activities during the 1945 strike. The contrast between this and the Wilson case . . . is thus aptly epitomized in that fact alone. Moreover, the inapplicability of that case is also illustrated by the presence here, and the absence there, of the following factors, among others: (1) the activities were on the premises; (2) the financial support was substantial, not slight; (3) the control by the employer was dominant; (4) advertising and business advantage benefited the employer; (5) the employer could halt the program at any time.[411]

Similar results have been reached in many other cases involving essentially identical facts.[412] Compensation has also been awarded for injuries suffered in an employer sponsored college scholarship benefit basketball game;[413] a basketball game in which the employer said participation was a part of the employees' "duties";[414] a pheasant hunting expedition with the employer's customers;[415] a fishing trip to entertain the employer's customers; [416] on the ski slope of the employer;[417] and in an auto race while driving a car sponsored by the employer.[418]

§ 8.16. Nuisance Liability.

Because of the light, noise and sometimes errant missiles associated with many sports activities, it is appropriate to examine the principles which define nuisance liability.[419] The law of nuisance is divided into two basic parts. The first

411. 305 N.Y. at 550, 114 N.E.2d at 36. With regard to athletic teams sponsored by employees, it is worthy of note that the employer may be able to deduct the costs thereof for federal income tax purposes. Rev. Rul. 70-393, 1970-2 CUM. BULL. 34.

412. Stephenson v. Industrial Comm'n, 23 Ariz. App. 424, 533 P.2d 116 (1975) (lunchtime baseball); Federal Mutual Liability Ins. Co. v. Industrial Accident Comm'n of Calif., 90 Cal. App. 357, 265 P. 858 (1928); Hendren v. Industrial Comm'n, 19 Ill. 2d 44, 166 N.E.2d 76 (1960) (baseball); Le Bar v. Ewald Bros. Dairy, 217 Minn. 16, 13 N.W.2d 729 (1944); Mack Trucks, Inc. v. Miller, 23 Md. App. 271, 326 A.2d 186 (1974) (acquiescence in touch football at coffee-break); Esposito v. Western Electric Co., 30 App. Div. 2d 750, 291 N.Y.S.2d 378 (1968) (softball league); Rafti v. Merrill, Lynch, Pierce, Fenner & Smith, Inc., 20 App. Div. 2d 592, 245 N.Y.S.2d 223 (1963); Nahabedian v. Equitable Life Ins. Co., 16 App. Div. 2d 713, 226 N.Y.S.2d 881 (1962) (softball league); McCarty v. Dahlstrom Metallic Door Co., 12 App. Div. 2d 673, 207 N.Y.S.2d 713 (1960) (baseball league); Sorino v. Remington Rand, Inc., 1 App. Div. 2d 720, 147 N.Y.S.2d 34 (1955) (intra-plant softball); Tobias v. Stormco Co., Inc., 282 App. Div. 1087, 126 N.Y.S.2d 120 (1953) (baseball); Huber v. Eagle Stationery Corp., 254 App. Div. 788, 4 N.Y.S.2d 272 (1938) (baseball league); Holst v. New York Stock Exchange, 252 App. Div. 233, 299 N.Y.S. 255 (1937) (soccer); Columbia Gas of Ohio, Inc. v. Sommer, 44 Ohio App. 2d 69, 335 N.E.2d 743 (1974); Ott v. Industrial Comm'n, 83 Ohio App. 13, 82 N.E.2d 137 (1948).

413. Zuckerman v. Board of Educ., Central High School Dist. No. 3, 35 App. Div. 2d 757, 314 N.Y.S.2d 814 (1970).

414. City & County of Denver v. Lee, 168 Colo. 208, 450 P.2d 352 (1969). *See also* DiPerri v. Boys Recreation Republic of New York, Inc., 31 N.Y.2d 215, 335 N.Y.S.2d 405, 286 N.E.2d 897 (1972).

415. Continental Casualty Co. v. Industrial Comm'n, 26 Wis. 2d 470, 132 N.W.2d 584 (1965).

416. Boyd v. Florida Mattress Factory, Inc., 128 So. 2d 881 (Fla. 1961).

417. Dorsch v. Industrial Comm'n, 185 Colo. 219, 523 P.2d 458 (1974).

418. Truck Ins. Exchange v. Industrial Comm'n, 22 Ariz. App. 58, 524 P.2d 1331 (1974). *See also* St. Paul Insurance Co. v. Van Hook, 533 S.W.2d 472 (Tex. Civ. App. 1976) (boxing match to settle dispute).

419. Since nuisance is a field of tort liability, rather than a separate species of tortious conduct, it may be the result of intentional or negligent conduct, or conduct which falls within the concept of liability without fault. Nussbaum v. Lacopo, 27 N.Y.2d 311, 317 N.Y.S.2d 347, 265 N.E.2d 762 (1970). In the ordinary case, the nuisance will result from the knowing creation of a condition that

refers to "private nuisances," which involve interference with the use and enjoyment of privately owned land. A "public nuisance," on the other hand, includes interference with the rights of the general public.[420] Any person whose use or enjoyment of land is interfered with by a private nuisance may bring an action for damages or injunctive relief, where appropriate, against the party responsible therefor. Public nuisances, however, are ordinarily actionable only by the appropriate governmental authority, though private parties may bring such actions if they are able to prove that the public nuisance has caused them special damages [421] — that is, damage over and above that caused to the public at large.[422] Some courts have sought to establish a third class of nuisances that are actionable under all circumstances (so-called *per se* nuisances).[423] Whether concern is specifically directed at the requisites of recovery for public or private nuisance, the basic inquiry is the same — that is, whether the use of one person's land interferes with the rights of others.

As a general rule, every person has the right to exercise, without the interference of others, such exclusive dominion over his property as may best suit his private purposes. This does not, however, give a person the right to use property so as to occasion unreasonable damage or annoyance to neighboring landowners.[424] In determining whether any particular use creates an actionable nuisance, a court will ordinarily balance the utility of the landowner's conduct against the gravity of harm that it produces.[425] The "utility of the conduct" will be determined by considering its social value, suitability to the character of the locality in which it takes place, and the impracticality of preventing or avoiding invasion of the rights of others.[426] The "gravity of the harm," on the other hand, will be determined by considering the extent and character of the harm, the social value of the land use, the suitability of the land use to the character of the locality, and the burden that would be placed on the injured person to avoid the harm.[427] If the gravity of the harm outweighs the utility of the conduct, then the injured party will be able to seek nuisance recovery. The fact that the party whose activity creates the nuisance is a municipal corporation, which as a governmental entity might otherwise be protected by the doctrine of sovereign immunity,[428] need not preclude recovery, since several courts have taken the

may, or will, result in an interference with the rights of others. Certainly this is the case with respect to most nuisances that arise as by-products of sports activity. The creation of such conditions may, depending on the circumstances, be the product of intentional or negligent conduct, though the basis of liability will rarely be determinative of ultimate recovery.

420. *See generally* 1 F. Harper & F. James, The Law of Torts §§ 1.23-.30 (1965); W. Prosser, The Law of Torts § 88 (4th ed. 1971).

421. Saari v. State, 203 Misc. 859, 119 N.Y.S.2d 507, *aff'd,* 282 App. Div. 526, 125 N.Y.S.2d 507 (1953).

422. W. Prosser, The Law of Torts § 89 (4th ed. 1971).

423. Vickridge First & Second Addition Homeowners Ass'n, Inc. v. Catholic Diocese of Wichita, 212 Kans. 348, 510 P.2d 1296 (1973) (acknowledging *per se* approach, but finding that baseball and football fields did not come within that definition. *See also* Board of Educ. of Louisville v. Klein, 303 Ky. 234, 197 S.W.2d 427 (1946) (football not *per se* nuisance); Buddy v. State, 59 Mich. App. 598, 229 N.W.2d 865 (1975) (toboggan not nuisance *per se*); Riffey v. Rush, 51 N.D. 188, 199 N.W. 523 (1924) (baseball nor *per se* nuisance); Lieberman v. Township of Saddle River, 37 N.J. Super. 62, 116 A.2d 809 (1955) (same).

424. Gleason v. Hillcrest Golf Course, Inc., 148 Misc. 246, 265 N.Y.S. 886 (1933).

425. Lee v. Rolla Speedway, Inc., 494 S.W.2d 349 (Mo. 1973).

426. Restatement (Second) of Torts § 827 (1965).

427. Restatement (Second) of Torts § 828 (1965).

428. The doctrine of sovereign immunity is discussed at § 7.18.

position that the immunity will not protect municipalities from nuisance liability.[429] Recovery will not, however, be granted where the nuisance is merely anticipatory — that is, where it has not yet occurred — unless the injury is imminent and certain to occur.[430] Recovery may also be denied where the defendant does not have control of the activity which is the subject of complaint,[431] or where the activity has been licensed by the state.[432]

Since the law of nuisance is so often inextricably intertwined with the property rights of adjoining landowners, the courts have often experienced predictable difficulty in fashioning a remedy for land uses found to be nuisances. This is an especially difficult problem when the remedy sought is injunctive relief which would cause the offending party to cease engaging in a worthwhile use of the land. To resolve this difficulty, a court will generally utilize a balancing process similar to that noted above. Thus, it will balance the offending land use against the economic hardship that the injunction will cause, the good faith of the parties, and the social utility of the conduct in question. A good example of such balancing is provided by *Downey v. Jackson*,[433] where the court found that the erection of floodlights on an amateur baseball field was a nuisance to the extent that it created glare to adjoining homeowners. In reviewing a lower court order granting a permanent injunction of the night games, the court observed that the field was used for the purpose of building strong bodies in the youth of the community, rather than for commercial sports purposes, and that the glare could be eliminated by the erection of a suitable screen. Finding that a complete injunction would stop an activity having considerable public benefit, and that the nuisance could be eliminated by a less burdensome order, the court modified the injunction to enjoin the casting of glare upon the homeowner's property only to the extent that it could be done by the erection of a screen suitable to achieve that result.[434] In other words, the court struck a slightly different balance than had the lower court.

The issue of potential nuisance liability frequently arises when a person, who is neither a spectator nor participant, is injured when balls leave the field of play. Such cases involve injury to the person as opposed to property rights. Injuries have often been inflicted upon those near a golf course as a result of an errantly hit ball escaping the course. The leading case dealing with this problem is the English decision in *Castle v. St. Augustine's Links*,[435] where a man had lost an

---

429. Downey v. Jackson, 259 Ala. 189, 65 So. 2d 825 (1953). *See generally* W. PROSSER, THE LAW OF TORTS § 131, at 982-83 (4th ed. 1971). *But cf.* Buddy v. State, 59 Mich. App. 598, 229 N.W.2d 865 (1975).

430. Wuillamey v. Werblin, 364 F. Supp. 237 (D.N.J. 1973) (construction of sports complex); Vickridge First & Second Addition Homeowners Ass'n, Inc. v. Catholic Diocese of Wichita, 212 Kans. 348, 510 P.2d 1296 (1973) (baseball diamond and football field); Dudoussat v. Louisiana State Racing Comm'n, 133 So. 2d 155 (La. App. 1961) (race track); Mullholland v. State Racing Comm'n, 295 Mass. 286, 3 N.E.2d 773 (1936) (race track).

431. Miller v. Iles, 72 Ohio Abs. 30, 132 N.E.2d 648 (1955).

432. Township of Cherry Hill v. New Jersey Racing Comm'n, 131 N.J. Super. 125, 328 A.2d 653 (1974), *aff'd*, 131 N.J. Super. 482, 330 A.2d 600 (1974). Other actions to enjoin licensed racing activities have also failed. *See, e.g.,* Kiper v. State, 310 So. 2d 42 (Fla. App. 1975); Bamonte v. New York City Off-Track Betting Corp., 80 Misc. 2d 980, 364 N.Y.S.2d 777 (1975).

433. 259 Ala. 189, 65 So. 2d 825 (1953). *See generally* Annot., 62 A.L.R. 782 (1929).

434. 259 Ala. at 194, 65 So. 2d at 828. *See also* Sans v. Ramsey Golf & Country Club, Inc., 29 N.J. 438, 149 A.2d 599 (1959).

435. 38 Times L. Rep. 615 (1922).

eye as a result of a golf ball striking the windshield of a taxicab which he was driving. The accident had occurred as the taxicab passed along a public highway that ran parallel to the 13th tee of the golf course. The evidence showed that balls from the tee frequently landed on the highway and had struck vehicles on several occasions. These facts demonstrated, the King's Bench said, that the risk of balls being sliced onto the highway was a public danger, and was a foreseeable consequence of people driving from the tee. It held, therefore, that the tee and the hole were a public nuisance, and granted judgment for the injured passerby.[436] *Castle* has been followed by several American decisions, which have held that fairways that are so close to public roadways as to interfere with their free and unmolested use are nuisances, and persons injured thereby may recover for their injuries.[437] A similar result has been reached for injuries suffered by a passenger in a car struck by a golf ball while traveling on a private roadway that cut across a fairway on the golf course.[438] Liability for such conditions could be theoretically eliminated by the erection of suitable barriers that would preclude balls from escaping the field of play.[439]

Errant golf balls have also caused injury to persons whose residences abut the fairways of a golf course. When these injuries occur, the courts have often held that the injured party may not recover, since the risks and dangers of living close to a golf course are readily apparent to even the most casual of observers and will be deemed to have been assumed by the abutting homeowner.[440] Thus, in *Nussbaum v. Lacopo*,[441] recovery was denied to a homeowner who had been struck and injured by a golf ball from a fairway closely adjacent to his property. Despite the fact that the injured man's patio and the 13th fairway were separated by approximately 20 to 30 feet of rough and a barrier of 45 to 60 foot-tall trees, errant balls were a relatively frequent occurrence on his property (1 to 2 per week). In denying the homeowner recovery, the court distinguished the highway-user cases, such as *Castle,* and held that "one who deliberately decides to reside in the suburbs on very desirable lots adjoining golf clubs and thus receive the social benefits and other not inconsiderable advantages of country club surroundings must accept the occasional, concomitant annoyances." [442] Although the result in *Nussbaum* was doubtlessly correct, since the evidence showed a substantial natural barrier between the fairway and the home, it should not preclude recovery by one injured as a result of deficient layout of the course and its adjacent homes. Thus, in *Sans v. Ramsey Golf & Country Club, Inc.,*[443] a private nuisance was found when two tees were moved

436. 38 Times L. Rep. at 616.

437. Gleason v. Hillcrest Golf Course, 148 Misc. 246, 265 N.Y.S. 886 (1933); Townsley v. State, 164 N.Y.S.2d 840 (Ct. Cl. 1957).

438. Westborough Country Club v. Palmer, 204 F.2d 143 (8th Cir. 1953).

439. This principle is, for example, reflected in the cases involving similar injuries from baseballs. *See* notes 448-454 *infra.*

440. Nussbaum v. Lacopo, 27 N.Y.2d 311, 317 N.Y.S.2d 347, 265 N.E.2d 762 (1970); Patton v. Westwood Country Club Co., 18 Ohio App. 2d 137, 247 N.E.2d 761 (1969). *See generally* Annot., 68 A.L.R.2d 1331 (1959).

441. 27 N.Y.2d 311, 317 N.Y.S.2d 347, 265 N.E.2d 762 (1970).

442. 27 N.Y.S.2d at 316-17, 317 N.Y.S.2d at 351, 265 N.E.2d at 764. The court also held that the facts that precluded recovery against the club would also preclude recovery against the player who had hit the ball, who had been a trespasser on the course. *Id.* at 318, 317 N.Y.S.2d at 352-53, 265 N.E.2d at 766-67.

443. 29 N.J. 438, 149 A.2d 599 (1959). *See also* Mruskovic v. McMullen, 65 Montgomery County L. R. 257 (Pa. 1949) (driving of golf balls from driving range into trailer court was an enjoinable continuing trespass).

so close to an adjoining residence that the ordinary and comfortable life of its occupants was rendered virtually impossible.

Errantly hit golf balls may also cause injury to other golfers on the golf course,[444] and, in seeking recovery for their injuries, such golfers have sought to argue that the construction of a golf course in such a manner as to allow injury by other golfers constitutes an actionable nuisance. The argument has not, however, met with much success.[445] While the design of a golf course may in some cases be sufficiently defective as to justify relief, when the person seeking that relief is another golfer the cause of action will probably be negligence, not nuisance.

Similar injuries have occurred as a result of baseballs that are hit or thrown out of the arena of play. When such injuries occur, the courts have often concluded that the playing of baseball, even if close to a public roadway, does not of itself constitute a nuisance which would make the operator of the grounds an insurer of the safety of persons lawfully using the highway.[446] Inasmuch as the baseball cases involve essentially the same type of hazard as is presented in the golf cases — escaping balls — it is appropriate to inquire why the courts have frequently concluded that baseball parks located close to public highways are not nuisances while a contrary conclusion has been reached in the golf cases. The distinction would appear to involve the factual issue of the frequency with which balls leave the field of play.[447] Thus, where there is evidence that balls frequently escape a baseball field, the courts have required that the operator take reasonable precautions for the protection of the public. The types of reasonable precautions required will depend upon the facts and circumstances of each particular case, which will include the inherent nature of the game and its past history in the particular location.[448] Thus, the operator of the playing field will be liable for allowing a nuisance to persist on its property if it has knowledge that the sport has caused, or is likely to cause, more than infrequent injury to persons on adjoining highways or property and does not use reasonable care to obviate the danger.[449] Applying these principles, a nuisance will be present where ball games are played so closely to public roads that batted or thrown balls often drop on the road and strike passersby,[450] and sufficient precautions to protect them have not been undertaken.[451] A nuisance will not

444. The principles that govern recovery for such injuries are discussed at § 8.02.

445. Trauman v. City of New York, 208 Misc. 252, 143 N.Y.S.2d 467 (1955) (parallel fairways not nuisances).

446. Alexander v. Tebeau, 24 Ky. 1305, 71 S.W. 427 (1903); Harrington v. Border City Mfg. Co., 240 Mass. 170, 132 N.E. 721 (1921); Young v. New York, N. H. & H. R. Co., 136 App. Div. 730, 121 N.Y.S. 517 (1910). In this regard, it is appropriate to note Louisville Baseball Club v. Hill, 291 Ky. 333, 164 S.W.2d 398 (1942), wherein the court applied the doctrine of *res ipsa loquitur* to an injury caused to a passerby from a ball hit out of a baseball park. As is indicated by the general rules discussed in text, the *Louisville Baseball* decision seems to be subject to some question. Applying the *res ipsa loquitur* rule bypasses the factual inquiry that must be made.

447. *See* note 456 *infra*.

448. Salevan v. Wilmington Park, Inc., 45 Del. 290, 72 A.2d 239 (1950).

449. Lane v. City of Buffalo, 232 App. Div. 334, 250 N.Y.S. 579 (1931).

450. Jones v. Kane & Roach, Inc., 182 Misc. 37, 43 N.Y.S.2d 140 (1943) (industrial league baseball teams regularly played on irregular diamond close to roadway because regular diamond in muddy condition); Lamm v. City of Buffalo, 225 App. Div. 599, 233 N.Y.S. 516 (1929); Wills v. Wisconsin-Minnesota Light & Power Co., 187 Wis. 626, 205 N.W. 556 (1925) (commercial recreation park in too close proximity to roadway).

451. Salevan v. Wilmington Park, Inc., 45 Del. 290, 72 A.2d 239 (1950) (2-3 balls per game escape ball park); Honaman v. City of Philadelphia, 322 Pa. 535, 185 A. 750 (1936).

be present, however, where it is so unforeseeable that a ball could reach the roadway that reasonable persons would not take precautions against it; [452] where an injury is caused by two boys playing a simple game of catch near the roadway; [453] or where there is no evidence that a nuisance was present under the facts and circumstances of the case.[454]

These principles were considered in the English decision in *Bolton v. Stone*,[455] where a lady, who was standing outside of her house, was struck and injured by a cricket ball that had been hit out of a park across the highway. The evidence showed that balls being so propelled were an infrequent occurrence, having taken place five or six times in the 28 years prior to the injury in question. On these facts, the trial court held that a nuisance had not been established, and that no recovery should be allowed to the injured lady. The Court of Appeal reversed, holding that the cricket club had been negligent in not preventing such occurrences, though it agreed with the lower court's nuisance determination. The House of Lords restored the trial court's decision, and although it did not hear argument on the nuisance cause, its decision clearly evidenced its belief that none was present. Thus, in distinguishing *Castle v. St. Augustine's Links*, Lord Justice Porter observed that it had "rested upon a different set of circumstances in which a succession of players driving off alongside a road might be expected from time to time to slice their ball over or along the road and, therefore, the possibility of injury to those using the highway was much greater." [456] The lack of a nuisance, then, was predicated on the infrequency of occurrence, which made injury a legally unforeseeable consequence of the activity.

Nuisance liability has also arisen in connection with racing activities, which are commonly known to be dangerous and often result in the racing vehicles, or their parts, flying into the crowd of spectators. In light of the rules followed in the golf and baseball cases, it may be said that where the conduct of racing activities results in an unreasonable and foreseeable risk of injury to the person or property of those in proximity to the racing event, nuisance liability will be present.[457] Thus, an actionable nuisance has been held to be present when an automobile race was conducted over an unprotected portion of the public highways, even though the road had been specifically set aside for that purpose.[458] A similar result was reached when speed tests were conducted over unprotected portions of the public highways.[459] The liability which is imposed may also extend to the governmental body which authorizes the race or is responsible for its safety. Thus, in *Saari v. State*,[460] the state of New York had issued a racing permit to those who sponsored the Watkins Glen Grand Prix, which was conducted on public roadways specifically designated for that

452. Bolton v. Stone [1951] A.C. 850, [1951] 1 All E.R. 1078.
453. Lane v. City of Buffalo, 232 App. Div. 334, 250 N.Y.S. 579 (1931).
454. Dwyer v. Edison Electric Illuminating Co., 273 Mass. 234, 173 N.E. 594 (1930).
455. [1951] A.C. 850, [1951] 1 All E.R. 1078.
456. [1951] A.C. at 860, [1951] 1 All E.R. at 1082.
457. Lee v. Rolla Speedway, Inc., 494 S.W.2d 349 (Mo. 1973); Township of Bedminster v. Vargo Dragsway, Inc., 434 Pa. 100, 253 A.2d 659 (1969). *See generally* Annot., 41 A.L.R.3d 1273 (1972).
458. Saari v. State, 203 Misc. 859, 119 N.Y.S.2d 507, *aff'd,* 282 App. Div. 526, 125 N.Y.S.2d 507 (1953).
459. Johnson v. City of New York, 186 N.Y. 139, 78 N.E. 715 (1906) (remanded for the nuisance determination by the trier of fact).
460. 203 Misc. 859, 119 N.Y.S.2d 507, *aff'd,* 282 App. Div. 526, 125 N.Y.S.2d 507 (1953).

purpose. As a condition to the issuance of the permit, the state law required that the roadways be fully and efficiently patrolled. Inasmuch as such patrolling would ordinarily be the duty of the state police, the court held that the effect of the permit was to delegate to the permit-holder the duty of, but not the responsibility for, the patrol duty. When the race course was then improperly patrolled, with the result that an injury occurred to a person watching the race when a racer left the track, the court concluded that the state could be held liable for the nuisance created, both because of its act in licensing the race and its inadequate performance of the duty to patrol.[461] A similar result has been reached when a permit was unlawfully granted.[462]

In addition to nuisances that may be created by objects that spill out of the area of the contest, nuisances may also be created by the light or noise emanating therefrom. As a general rule, it may be said that activities which cause light, noise or other disturbance to adjoining landowners will be considered nuisances only if the injury thereby caused is of such a character as to materially diminish the value of the property and thus seriously interfere with the comfort and enjoyment of its owners.[463] Perhaps the best example of such nuisances, is *Downey v. Jackson,*[464] noted above, where a city had erected floodlights on a public baseball stadium utilized by a local federation of amateur baseball teams. The lights, however, created a glare to the adjoining landowners, who brought a nuisance action seeking to enjoin any further night games. Although the evidence showed that only 14 night games were played during the season in question, that all games were over by 10:30, and that the games were not accompanied by undue noise, rowdyism or disturbance, the court held the lighting to be a nuisance because of the annoyance it created to the adjoining homeowners.[465]

The various types of nuisance-producing activities considered to this point have involved actions for private injuries. Sports events have also resulted in public nuisance actions brought by a governmental body to stop an event that is thought to be damaging to the rights, health, morals or safety of the public as a whole. Activities subjected to such actions have included gambling,[466] prostitution,[467] nude dancing,[468] automobile speed races,[469] bullfights,[470]

---

461. 203 Misc. at 872, 119 N.Y.S.2d at 521.
462. Johnson v. City of New York, 186 N.Y. 139, 78 N.E. 715 (1906).
463. Baker v. Odom, 258 Ark. 826, 529 S.W.2d 138 (1975) (dirt motorcycle track). Slaird v. Klewers, 260 Md. 2, 271 A.2d 345 (1970) (private swimming pool); Gilbough v. West Side Amusement Co., 64 N.J. Eq. 27, 53 A. 289 (1902) (baseball).
464. 259 Ala. 189, 65 So. 2d 825 (1953).
465. 259 Ala. at 192-93, 65 So. 2d at 828.
466. People v. Lim, 18 Cal. 2d 872, 118 P.2d 472 (1941); Valdez v. State *ex rel.* Farrior, 194 So. 388 (Fla. 1940); Pompano Horse Club v. State *ex rel.* Bryan, 111 So. 801 (Fla. 1927); Respass v. Commonwealth, 131 Ky. 807, 115 S.W. 1131 (1909); State v. Sportsmen's Country Club, 214 Minn. 151, 7 N.W.2d 495 (1943).
467. State v. Ellis, 201 Ala. 295, 78 So. 71 (1918); State *ex rel.* Orr v. Kearns, 304 Mo. 685, 264 S.W. 775 (1924).
468. Weis v. Superior Court of San Diego County, 30 Cal. App. 730, 159 P. 464 (1916).
469. Johnson v. City of New York, 186 N.Y. 139, 78 N.E. 715 (1906); Saari v. State, 203 Misc. 859, 119 N.Y.S.2d 507, *aff'd,* 282 App. Div. 526, 125 N.Y.S.2d 507 (1953). *See generally* Annot., 166 A.L.R. 1264 (1947).
470. State ex rel. Attorney General v. Canty, 207 Mo. 439, 105 S.W. 1078 (1907). *See also* C. E. America, Inc. v. Antinori, 210 So. 2d 443 (Fla. 1968) ("such an exhibition shocks the sensibilities of any person possessed of human instinct.")

prize-fights,[471] and endurance contests.[472] The bases for injunctive relief in these cases are, perhaps, best stated in *Commonwealth v. McGovern*,[473] where the court enjoined a prize-fight and observed that

> [s]uch a meeting . . . would doubtless have attracted many of the better and law-abiding class of citizens, curious to see such a spectacle as a prize-fight; but for every such reputable citizen thus attending there would have been present a dozen gamblers, confidence men, bunco steerers, or pickpockets, gathered from all parts of the United States, men of idle, vicious, and criminal habits and practices, whose business is to prey upon the public in some form or other, and many of them would remain in the community after the combat to ply their nefarious callings. Such an assembly would easily be led into a riot, or other unlawful disturbance of the public peace. In addition to the evils suggested, there would be the contaminating effect of such a meeting upon the youth of the city and state, which might prove of incalculable injury to their morals and future welfare. Such a gathering, too, would demand increased vigilance in the protection of the property of the city and its inhabitants, be a menace to good order, and disturb the peaceful pursuits and happiness of citizens who would be unwilling to patronize such an enterprise.[474]

Although this reasoning expresses a laudable social objective — the suppression of evil — it is sufficiently broad as a legal standard as to sweep within its coverage any type of public gathering thought to be evil by those holding the reins of prosecutorial power. Rather than subjecting any sports event which attracts large crowds to a public nuisance action, a better approach might be to hold that only unlawful sports events constitute public nuisances as such; and that lawfully held events could be deemed public nuisances only if it could be proven that they no longer attracted an ordinary cross-section of society, but had been allowed to degenerate to a point that they served as mere rallying places for undesirable elements of society.[475]

§ 8.17. Defamation and Invasion of Privacy.

The world of sports is also affected by those principles of law which determine the right of an athlete, or other person, to seek recovery for defamatory statements. A statement will be considered to be defamatory if it causes damage to one's interest in a good name or reputation and is false. Thus, it is said that a defamatory statement is one that will "diminish the esteem, respect, goodwill or confidence in which the plaintiff is held, or . . . excite adverse, derogatory or unpleasant feelings or opinions against him." [476]

With the development of the printing press, the law of defamation split into two distinct causes of action, one for the written, and one for the spoken, statement. In the case of the former, the action was called "libel", and in the latter "slander". Since it was presumed that a written word, with its greater

---

471. Commonwealth v. McGovern, 116 Ky. 212, 75 S.W. 261 (1903).
472. Sportatorium, Inc. v. State, 104 S.W.2d 912 (Tex. Civ. App. 1937).
473. 116 Ky. 212, 75 S.W. 261 (1903).
474. 116 Ky. at 235-36, 75 S.W. at 266.
475. Alexander v. Tebeau, 24 Ky. 1305, 71 S.W. 427 (1903) ("drunkards, rowdies, bullies, and men of like kidney").
476. W. Prosser, The Law of Torts § 111, at 739 (4th ed. 1971).

permanency, could cause far more damage than one spoken, all forms of libel were presumed to be actionable without proof of special damage, whereas only certain types of slander were so considered. Libelous statements may be divided into two classifications: those that are libelous on their face, and those that are libelous only by the introduction of extrinsic facts which show a seemingly innocent statement to be, in fact, defamatory of a particular person. Slanderous statements, on the other hand, are generally not presumed to be actionable — that is, actual damage must be proved — unless the statements contain an imputation of crime, a loathsome disease, unchastity to women, or affect the defamed party's business, trade, profession or calling,[477] which latter category may include one's activities in the sporting world.[478] Although defamation actions usually involve a single party, an entire football team may be defamed, and the mere size of the group will be no bar to recovery.[479] To be actionable, moreover, the defamatory statement must be published — that is, it must be communicated to some third person or persons.[480]

Although a statement may be defamatory, the defamed party may not be able to obtain recovery. The first bar to recovery may be the rule that the truth of the statement will be a complete defense to either written or spoken defamation.[481] Recovery may also be barred by the fact that it is no more than "fair comment" about an athlete's performance,[482] or that it was published as an incident of an activity which is accorded privilege — that is, immunity from liability. The privilege may be absolute, as in the case of judicial or administrative proceedings,[483] or conditional, which will depend upon the seriousness of the defamatory statement, the type of interest involved, and the seriousness of the threatened harm.[484]

Although these various rules are of wide application, their importance has been, in recent times at least, largely subordinated to the inquiry of whether recovery is barred by the First Amendment protection of the freedom of speech and press. In order to prevent defamation judgments from muzzling the press through protective self-censorship, the Supreme Court has erected a stringent barrier to such recoveries in a series of opinions. The cornerstone of the constitutional barrier is *New York Times v. Sullivan,*[485] where the court held that a "public official" could not recover for a defamatory falsehood relating to his official conduct unless he could prove that the statements were made with

---

477. *See generally* 1 F. HARPER & F. JAMES, THE LAW OF TORTS § 5.9 (1956).

478. *See, e.g.,* Grayson v. Curtis Publishing Co., 71 Wash. 2d 999, 436 P.2d 756 (1967) (college coach).

479. Fawcett Publications, Inc. v. Morris, 377 P.2d 42 (Okla. 1962), *cert. denied,* 376 U.S. 513, 84 S. Ct. 964, 22 L. Ed. 2d 968 (1964) (allegation that entire University of Oklahoma football team used drugs).

480. 1 F. HARPER & F. JAMES, THE LAW OF TORTS § 5.15 (1956).

481. *Id.* at § 5.20.

482. Cohen v. Cowles Publishing Co., 42 Wash. 262, 273 P.2d 893 (1954) (comment on sports page that jockey did poor job of riding was "fair"). *See also* Moresi v. Teche Publishing Co., Inc., 298 So. 2d 901 (La. App. 1974) (newspaper report that water at beach was too polluted for water sports not defamatory); Iacco v. Bohannon, 70 Mich. App. 463, 245 N.W.2d 791 (1976) (coach could criticize suspended player).

483. *See, e.g.,* Porter v. Eyster, 294 F.2d 613 (4th Cir. 1961) (posting of notice on bulletin board stating that a veterinarian had been ruled-off premises was privileged); Lloyds v. United Press Int'l, 63 Misc. 2d 421, 311 N.Y.S.2d 373 (1970) (report of official proceedings of Florida State Racing Commission is absolutely privileged when investigating an alleged drugging of a race horse).

484. *See generally* W. PROSSER, THE LAW OF TORTS §§ 109-10 (4th ed. 1971).

485. 376 U.S. 254, 84 S. Ct. 710, 11 L. Ed. 2d 686 (1964).

"actual malice," [486] which would require publication with knowledge that they were false or with reckless disregard of whether or not they were false.[487] The "malice" rule of *New York Times* was then extended to include "public figures" [488] — defined to include those who command a substantial amount of independent public interest at the time of publication [489] — who, like public officials, would be able to recover for defamatory falsehoods only upon clear and convincing proof that the falsehood was "made with knowledge of its falsity or with reckless disregard for the truth." [490] The Court has more recently ruled that the terms "public official" and "public figure" do not include "private individuals" — that is, those who have "achieved no general fame or notoriety in the community." [491] In order for such a private individual to obtain recovery for actual damages in a defamation action, the Court requires that there be evidence of some "fault" on the part of the publisher-defendant, which requirement will be defined by the law of each state.[492] In order to recover for presumed or punitive damages, however, the private person must meet the same showing as that required for "public officials" and "public figures." [493] Inasmuch as sports figures will rarely be "private individuals," it seems clear that the "public figure" category will frequently be sufficient to cover them.[494]

The constitutional privilege of the First Amendment has found frequent application in the world of sports, and has been invoked in cases involving professional baseball players,[495] professional boxers,[496] golf,[497] a college athletic

---

486. The term "public official" was again considered by the court in Rosenblatt v. Baer, 383 U.S. 75, 15 L. Ed. 2d 597, 86 S. Ct. 669 (1966). *See also* Monitor Patriot Co. v. Roy, 401 U.S. 265, 28 L. Ed. 2d 35, 91 S. Ct. 621 (1971) (candidate for public office treated as public officeholder); Ocala Star-Banner Co. v. Damron, 401 U.S. 295, 91 S. Ct. 628, 28 L. Ed. 2d 57 (1971) (same).

The same "malice" standard has also been applied to the extent to which a state may pursue criminal defamation prosecutions—that is, one is free to comment about public figures so long as the statements do not amount to constitutional malice. Garrison v. Louisiana, 379 U.S. 64, 67, 85 S. Ct. 209, 13 L. Ed. 2d 125 (1964).

487. 376 U.S. at 279. Three of the justices concurred in the result, but believed that the First and Fourteenth Amendments precluded recovery by a public official without regard to the presence of malice. 376 U.S. at 293 (Black, J., concurring, joined by Douglas, J.); 376 U.S. at 298 (Goldberg, J., concurring, joined by Douglas, J.).

488. Curtis Publishing Co. v. Butts, 388 U.S. 130, 87 S. Ct. 1975, 18 L. Ed. 2d 1094 (1967).

489. 388 U.S. at 154.

490. Gertz v. Robert Welch, Inc., 418 U.S. 323, 334, 94 S. Ct. 2997, 41 L. Ed. 2d 789 (1974); Vandenburg v. Newsweek, Inc., 507 F.2d 1024 (5th Cir. 1975).

491. Gertz v. Robert Welch, Inc., 418 U.S. 323, 352, 94 S. Ct. 2997, 41 L. Ed. 2d 789 (1974). This conclusion received strong dissent from Justices White and Brennan, who preferred the rule announced in a plurality opinion in Rosenbloom v. Metromedia, 403 U.S. 29, 91 S. Ct. 1811, 29 L. Ed. 2d 296 (1971), where the Court held that

> [i]f a matter is a subject of public or general interest, it cannot suddenly become less so merely because a private individual is involved. The public's primary interest is in the event: the public focus is on the conduct of the participant and the content, effect, and significance of the conduct, not the participant's prior anonymity or notoriety. *Id.* at 43.

Rosenbloom was, however, overturned by *Gertz*.

492. Gertz v. Robert Welch, Inc., 418 U.S. 323, 347, 94 S. Ct. 2997, 41 L. Ed. 2d 789 (1974). *See also* Time, Inc. v. Firestone, 424 U.S. 448, 96 S. Ct. 958, 47 L. Ed. 2d 154 (1976).

493. Gertz v. Robert Welch, Inc., 418 U.S. 323, 348-50, 94 S. Ct. 2997, 41 L. Ed. 2d 789, (1974).

494. Vandenburg v. Newsweek, Inc., 507 F.2d 1024 (5th Cir. 1975); Time, Inc. v. Johnston, 448 F.2d 378 (4th Cir. 1971).

495. Cepeda v. Cowles Magazines and Broadcasting, Inc., 392 F.2d 417 (9th Cir. 1968), *cert. denied,* 393 U.S. 840, 89 S. Ct. 117, 21 L. Ed. 2d 110 (1968) (recovery denied); Spahn v. Julian Messner, Inc., 18 N.Y.2d 324, 274 N.Y.S.2d 877, 221 N.E.2d 543 (1966), *app. dismissed,* 393 U.S. 1046, 89 S. Ct. 676, 21 L. Ed. 2d 600 (1969) (privacy recovery allowed for purported biography).

496. Cohen v. Marx, 94 Cal. App. 2d 704, 211 P.2d 320 (1949) (privacy recovery denied); Dempsey v. Time, Inc., 43 Misc.2d 754, 252 N.Y.S.2d 186, *aff'd,* 254 N.Y.S.2d 80 (1964).

497. Sellers v. Time, Inc., 423 F.2d 887 (3rd Cir. 1970), *cert. denied,* 400 U.S. 830, 91 S. Ct. 61, 27 L. Ed. 2d 61 (1970).

director,[498] a college basketball coach,[499] a basketball scouting service,[500] and a popular resort hotel at a famous golf tournament.[501] These cases indicate that a sports personality or institution will be unable to obtain a defamation recovery for statements involving activities in the sports world,[502] unless the burden of proving actual malice is satisfied.[503] This rule of non-recovery will also preclude recovery for statements made about an athlete's professional activity long after he or she has left the active professional arena, inasmuch as mere passage of time will create no "rule of repose" so long as newsworthiness and public interest attach to the achievements of the past.[504]

The defamation cases in the sports area have evolved from many different contexts, and their resolution has made quite clear the type of case which the plaintiff must present to justify recovery. The prime case allowing recovery is *Curtis Publishing Company v. Butts,*[505] where the athletic director of the University of Georgia brought suit against a national, weekly magazine, alleging that he had been defamed by an article which reported that he participated in fixing a college football game. The evidence at trial indicated that the magazine, interested in cultivating a "sophisticated muckraker" image, had ignored even the most elementary precautions to insure publication of the truth and established that the allegations in the article were not supported by credible evidence. This, the Court said, was sufficient to establish the presence of "highly unreasonable conduct," which would constitute the requisite publication with reckless disregard for the truth to satisfy the constitutional malice standard.

Where such unreasonable conduct on the part of the publisher is not present, however, recovery will be denied. Thus, where a sports magazine quoted a coach as saying that his star player had destroyed an opponent both mentally and physically, it was held that so long as the publication accurately quoted another's statement about a matter of legitimate public interest the protection of the First Amendment would apply.[506] Recovery was similarly denied where a professional baseball star could not prove that statements questioning his competence and value as a team player were printed maliciously; [507] as it was when a major

---

498. Curtis Publishing Co. v. Butts, 388 U.S. 130, 87 S. Ct. 1975, 18 L. Ed. 2d 1094 (1967) (defamation recovery denied).

499. Grayson v. Curtis Publishing Co., 72 Wash. 2d 999, 436 P.2d 756 (1967) (defamation recovery denied), *noted in* 144 WASH. L. REV. 461 (1969). *See also* Basarich v. Rodeghero, 24 Ill. App. 2d 889, 321 N.E.2d 739 (1974) (high school coach a public figure).

500. Garfinkel v. Twenty-First Century Publishing Co., 30 App. Div. 2d 787, 291 N.Y.S.2d 735 (1968) (recovery denied for characterization of scouting report service as a "flesh peddler").

501. Bon Air Hotel, Inc. v. Time, Inc., 426 F.2d 858 (5th Cir. 1970) (defamation recovery denied to hotel in Augusta, Georgia, site of the Masters).

502. Statements relating to one's private life, however, may justify a cause of action based upon the right of privacy, which is discussed at notes 509-20 *infra.*

503. Championship Sports, Inc. v. Time, Inc., 71 Misc. 2d 887, 336 N.Y.S.2d 958 (1972). The public agony and acrimony that can surround a defamation suit involving prominent professional athletes and coaches is illustrated by the suit brought by a defensive backfield star (George Atkinson) against an opposing coach (Chuck Noll) resulting from the latter's statement that the former had committed criminal acts during a game between their respective teams. *See* Johnson, *A Walk on the Sordid Side,* SPORTS ILLUSTRATED, August 1, 1977, at 10.

504. Time, Inc. v. Johnston, 448 F.2d 378, 381 (4th Cir. 1971) (12 years); *see also* Cohen v. Marx, 94 Cal. App. 2d 704, 211 P.2d 320 (1949) (10 years). *But cf.* Dempsey v. Time, Inc., 43 Misc. 2d 754, 252 N.Y.S.2d 186, 254 N.Y.S.2d 80 (1964) (reaching back 45 years is too great a period of time).

505. 388 U.S. 130, 87 S. Ct. 1975, 18 L. Ed. 2d 1094 (1967). *See also* Carson v. Allied News Co., 529 F.2d 206 (7th Cir. 1976).

506. Time, Inc. v. Johnston, 448 F.2d 378 (4th Cir. 1971).

507. Cepeda v. Cowles Magazines & Broadcasting, Inc., 392 F.2d 417 (9th Cir. 1968), *cert. denied,* 393 U.S. 840, 89 S. Ct. 117, 21 L. Ed. 2d 110 (1968).

college basketball coach was unable to prove maliciousness in the publication of an article by a referee, which portrayed the coach as one who incited crowds to such a point of hysteria as to result in physical abuse of the referees.[508]

Closely related to the law of defamation are the principles that protect one's right of privacy. While the former seeks to provide compensation to persons whose reputation has been damaged by the public exposure of allegedly false matter, the right of privacy exists to compensate the mental distress caused by public exposure of correct, but private, facts concerning one's life.[509] Thus, the right of privacy may be defined, simply, as "the right to be left alone; to live one's life as one chooses, free from assault, intrusion or invasion except as they can be justified by the clear needs of community living under a government of law." [510]

When such actions are brought, however, the complainant will be met with the same constitutional privilege that has evolved in the law of defamation. This defense was first made applicable to privacy cases in *Time, Inc. v. Hill,*[511] where a national magazine had published a story concerning a play that was a partially fictionalized version of a family's experience of having been held hostage in their home by criminals. In remanding a damage award for the family, the Supreme Court held that the malice standard of *New York Times v. Sullivan* should apply to privacy actions against publishers. In the Court's view, the constitutional protections of freedom of speech and press would preclude privacy recovery "in the absence of proof that the defendant published the report with knowledge of its falsity or in reckless disregard of the truth."[512]

The law of privacy has similarly produced a sizeable number of claims by sports personalities. These cases indicate that recovery in a privacy action will be obtainable only where the published matter dealt with the athlete's private, as opposed to his public professional life, or where the publisher is not entitled to the constitutional privilege because of its malicious conduct. The primary obstacle in privacy cases will be the issue of whether the material published affects purely personal matters. When one enters the athletic arena in search of public adulation and acclaim, it is said that he or she relinquishes the right to privacy on all matters pertaining to professional activity and may not "at his will and whim draw himself like a snail into his shell" to pin liability on those who comment on publicity seeking acts.[513] One does not, moreover, gain immunity from public comment on his or her professional activities simply by retirement from the playing field, inasmuch, as is true in the law of defamation, the mere passage of time creates no "rule of repose."[514]

---

508. Grayson v. Curtis Publishing Co., 71 Wash. 2d 999, 436 P.2d 756 (1969).

509. Time, Inc. v. Hill, 385 U.S. 374, 413, 87 S. Ct. 534, 17 L. Ed. 2d 456 (1967) (Fortas, J., dissenting). *See also* T. COOLEY, THE LAW OF TORTS 29 (2d ed. 1888).

510. *See* Rosenbloom v. Metromedia, Inc., 403 U.S. 29, 48, 91 S. Ct. 1811, 29 L. Ed. 2d 296 (1971). *See generally* S. HOFSTADER & G. HOROWITZ, THE RIGHT OF PRIVACY (1964). There are, however, some states which have not yet recognized any such right. *See, e.g.,* Carson v. National Bank of Commerce Trust and Savings, 501 F.2d 1082 (8th Cir. 1974).

511. 385 U.S. 374, 87 S. Ct. 534, 17 L. Ed. 2d 456 (1967).

512. 385 U.S. at 388. *See also* Cantrell v. Forest City Publishing Co., 418 U.S. 909, 94 S. Ct. 3202, 41 L. Ed. 2d 1156 (1974).

513. Cohen v. Marx, 94 Cal. App. 2d 704, 211 P.2d 320 (1949); *see also* Time, Inc. v. Johnston, 448 F.2d 378 (4th Cir. 1971).

514. Time, Inc. v. Johnston, 448 F.2d 378 (4th Cir. 1971).

The only sports case in which a recovery for infringement of privacy has been allowed in *Spahn v. Julian Messner, Inc.,*[515] where a publisher had published a fictitious biography of Warren Spahn, the famed major league baseball pitcher. In upholding a verdict for Spahn, the court said that he was a public personality only in his professional career, in which he had no right of privacy, but that he retained the right to the privacy of his personal life. As the biography publicized aspects of his personal, private life, the court was of the opinion that the biography was "an unauthorized exploitation of his personality for purposes of trade . . . ," and presented, therefore, a sufficient predicate for a privacy recovery.[516]

The important question about *Spahn,* of course, is whether it represents good law in the light of *Time, Inc. v. Hill.* Although the *Spahn* court considered the impact of *New York Times v. Sullivan* on its decision, it found the case inapplicable since it dealt only with public officials, which Spahn was not. The Court in *Hill* suggested that this approach was incorrect to the extent that it would allow privacy recovery for "false reports of matters of public interest in the absence of proof that the defendant published the report with knowledge of its falsity or in reckless disregard of the truth."[517] It is of interest in this regard to note that the constitutional standard would apparently have been justified by the opinion of the trial court in *Spahn.*[518]

Where the malice finding cannot be made, relief for invasion of privacy will be unavailable where comment is limited to public facts. Thus, recovery has been denied where a retired boxer's reputation as a "canvasback" was made the subject of a Groucho Marx comedy routine,[519] and where a retired professional basketball player's physical and mental humiliation at the hands of a legendary opponent was portrayed.[520]

An additional aspect of the privacy theory is the protection against the appropriation of one's name or likeness for the benefit or advantage of another. Under this theory, one may recover when his or her name or likeness has been used without consent by another to advertise its products, add luster to its name, or for any of its other business purposes.[521] Except for the most blatant use of an athlete's name or likeness for such purposes, however, recovery will not be likely. In *Namath v. Sports Illustrated,*[522] for example, pictures of a famous professional quarterback were used by a sports magazine for the purpose of promoting subscriptions. The athlete complained that he derived "several"

---

515. 18 N.Y.2d 324, 274 N.Y.S.2d 877, 221 N.E.2d 543 (1966), *app. dismissed,* 393 U.S. 1046, 21 L. Ed. 2d 600, 89 S. Ct. 676 (1969).

516. 18 N.Y.2d at 330, 274 N.Y.S.2d at 881, 221 N.E.2d at 546. *See also* Virgil v. Time, Inc., 527 F.2d 1122 (9th Cir. 1975); Motschenbacher v. R. J. Reynolds Tobacco Co., 498 F.2d 821 (9th Cir. 1974).

517. 385 U.S. at 388.

518. Thus, the trial court observed that
[w]hile untrue statements do not necessarily transform a book into the category of fiction, the all-pervasive distortions, inaccuracies, invented dialogue, and the narration of happenings out of context, clearly indicate, at the very least, a careless disregard for the responsibility of the press and within the context of this action, an abuse of the public's limited privilege to inquire into an individual's life. 43 Misc. 2d 219, 230, 250 N.Y.S.2d 529, 541 (1964).

519. Cohen v. Marx, 94 Cal. App. 2d 704, 211 P.2d 320 (1949).

520. Time, Inc., v. Johnston, 448 F.2d 378 (4th Cir. 1971).

521. W. PROSSER, THE LAW OF TORTS § 112 (4th ed. 1971); Treece, *Commercial Exploitation of Names, Likeness, and Personal Histories,* 51 TEX. L. REV. 637 (1973).

522. 80 Misc. 2d 531, 363 N.Y.S.2d 276 (1975), *aff'd,* 48 App. Div. 2d 487, 371 N.Y.S.2d 10 (1975). *aff'd,* 39 N.Y.2d 897, ·352 N.E.2d 584 (1976).

hundred thousand dollars from commercial endorsements, and that the magazine's actions had violated his right of privacy. In rejecting this claim, the court noted that the athlete was newsworthy and that his picture had appeared in the magazine for many years in connection with cover and feature stories.[523] However, if a picture is used without the athlete's actual or implied consent, or in a manner in excess of the consent, then recovery may be possible.[524]

§ 8.18. Sovereign and Charitable Immunity.

In considering the liability principles that apply to sports activities, it is finally necessary to give attention to the traditional immunity of governmental and charitable institutions, since they are so often involved in the sports liability cases. Each of these immunities once provided their beneficiaries with a broad cloak of protection that often precluded tort liability. In recent years, however, the courts and legislatures have begun to make wholesale inroads into the doctrines, with the result that in many states both public and charitable institutions are accorded the same status as are most other tortfeasors—that is, they must compensate those who are injured by their wrongful acts. Although the following discussion will not by any means undertake an exhaustive analysis of the law in each jurisdiction,[525] we will consider the present state of each doctrine as a general matter and note the sports decisions that have turned on the sovereign or charitable immunity issue.

In its broadest formulation, the doctrine of sovereign immunity provides that a state shall not be subject to suit without its consent.[526] The immunity is variously said to rest upon several policy bases. These include the view that as a sovereign entity the state can do no wrong; that public agencies have limited funds and can expend them for only public purposes; that public bodies cannot be responsible for the torts of their employees; and that public bodies have no authority to commit torts. The immunity in its pure form will cloak the actions of all public bodies, including school districts, school boards or other authorities operating public schools, inasmuch as they are considered to be the agents or

---

523. 363 N.Y.S.2d at 279-80. Specifically, the court observed that
   [i]t is understandable that plaintiff [Namath] desires payment for the use of his name and likeness in advertisements for the sale of publications in which he has appeared as newsworthy just as he is paid for collateral endorsement of commercial products. This he cannot accomplish under existing law of our State or Nation. Athletic prowess is much admired and well paid in this country. It is commendable that freedom of speech and the press under the First Amendment transcends the right to privacy. This is so particularly when a [person] seeks remuneration for what is basically a property right—not a right to privacy.
363 N.Y.S.2d at 280. *See also* Cepeda v. Swift & Co., 415 F.2d 1205 (8th Cir. 1969); O'Brien v. Pabst Sales Co., 124 F.2d 167 (5th Cir. 1941); University of Notre Dame Du Lac v. Twentieth Century-Fox Film Corp., 15 N.Y.2d 940, 259 N.Y.S.2d 832, 207 N.E.2d 508 (1965); Gautier v. Pro-Football, Inc., 304 N.Y. 354, 107 N.E.2d 485 (1952).

524. Kimbrough v. Coca Cola/USA, 521 S.W.2d 719 (Tex. Civ. App. 1975).

525. *See generally* W. PROSSER, THE LAW OF TORTS § 131 (4th ed. 1971); Borchard, *Government Responsibility in Tort, A Proposed Statutory Reform,* 34 YALE L.J. 1 (1924); Davis, *Tort Liability of Governmental Units,* 40 MINN. L. REV. 751 (1956); Shumate, *Tort Claims Against State Governments,* 9 LAW & CONTEMP. PROBS. 242 (1942).

526. RESTATEMENT (SECOND) OF TORTS § 895B (Tentative Draft No. 19, 1972). *See generally* W. PROSSER, THE LAW OF TORTS § 131, at 975 (4th ed. 1971).

instrumentalities of the state itself.[527] Even where the doctrine is in full force, however, it will not cover all entities formed to govern the athletic activities of public institutions.[528]

Although the sovereign immunity doctrine once provided broad immunity to state agencies, consent to suit has been given by the legislatures in many jurisdictions to a greater or lesser extent. Where such consent has not been given, courts in several jurisdictions have responded to the mounting criticism of the doctrine and abrogated it by judicial action. Indeed, the extent of abrogation has proceeded sufficiently far to justify the conclusion that "the modern rule is that the state and its agencies are subject to liability in tort,"[529] though the liability may be subject to legislative restriction or common law exceptions in any given jurisdiction.[530] For example, in *Lowe v. Texas Tech University*,[531] a football player alleged that a knee injury had been caused by the failure of the university to provide proper equipment. The court noted that in Texas the doctrine of sovereign immunity was still viable, but that the state legislature had waived the immunity to some extent through a tort claims act. In holding that the athlete's suit was not barred by the immunity, the court construed the waiver to cover the alleged failure to provide satisfactory equipment.

In considering the sovereign immunity doctrine, it is important to distinguish between the state and municipal (local government) corporations. Municipal corporations have been regarded by the law as having a dual character, which

---

527. Thus, in Hall v. Columbus Board of Educ., 32 Ohio App. 2d 297, 290 N.E.2d 580 (1972), the court stated that
> [b]oards of education are public agencies of the state established for the sole purpose of administering the state system of public education, and in the performance of their authorized duties or functions they take on a public or governmental character.

290 N.E.2d at 583. *See also* Harris v. Tooele County School District, 471 F.2d (10th Cir. 1973); Bragg v. Board of Public Instruction, Duval County, 160 Fla. 590, 36 So. 2d 222 (1948); Boyer v. Iowa High School Athletic Ass'n, 256 Iowa 337, 127 N.W.2d 606 (1964); George v. University of Minnesota Athletic Ass'n, 107 Minn. 424, 120 N.W. 750 (1909); O'Dell v. School Dist. of Independence, 521 S.W.2d 403 (Mo. 1975), *cert. denied,* 423 U.S. 865 (1976); Barchers v. School Dist. of Kansas City, 501 S.W.2d 502 (Mo. App. 1973). *See generally* Annot., 33 A.L.R.3d 703 (1971).

528. In Coughlon v. Iowa High School Athletic Ass'n, 260 Iowa 702, 150 N.W.2d 660 (1967), for example, the court held that a state high school athletic association would not so qualify. The court distinguished its activities from those commonly associated with the sovereign by noting that
> [a]lthough [the association] be characterized as serving a beneficial purpose, we still take judicial notice of the fact that it engages to some extent at least, in activities of a general business nature. . . .
> And where as here unincorporated associations exercise the rights and powers of a legal entity, it should, to the extent reasonably possible, be held to assume corresponding duties and obligations. Anything else would be unjust and unreasonable.

529. *See* RESTATEMENT (SECOND) OF TORTS § 895B, comment *b* (Tentative Draft No. 19, 1972).
Thus, in Arnold v. State, 163 App. Div. 253, 148 N.Y.S. 479 (1914), the court observed that "[t]he history of legislation on the subject [of sovereign immunity] shows progressive growth . . . with continuous enlargement of power to determine claims against the state." 163 App. Div. at 262, 148 N.Y.S. at 484. *See also* Johnson v. Municipal University of Omaha, 184 Neb. 512, 169 N.W.2d 286 (1969); Cromley v. Loyalsock Township School Dist., 226 Pa. Super. 433, 310 A.2d 330 (1973). *But cf.* Cantwell v. University of Massachusetts, 551 F.2d 879 (1st Cir. 1977); Brown v. Wichita State Univ., 219 Kan. 2, 547 P.2d 1015 (1976) (although court had abrogated sovereign immunity, legislature could constitutionally reimpose it).

530. The common law exceptions that may be present in any given jurisdiction are considered in general at notes 532-550 *infra.*

531. 540 S.W.2d 297 (Tex. 1976).

has affected their liability for tortious acts. A municipal corporation is both a subdivision of the state, performing governmental and political functions, and a corporation with special and local interests which are similar to those of a private corporation, and which are not shared by the state itself. As a consequence of this dual character, the law has attempted to distinguish between the respective capacities. Thus, immunity is provided for the acts of the municipal corporation in its governmental or public capacity,[532] but not those undertaken in its corporate, private or proprietary capacity.[533] The distinction is, in theory at least, rather easily stated, since a governmental function can be defined as one which is necessary to the well being of the community.[534] Thus, it is generally concluded that public education, training for self-preservation and good citizenship, and safeguarding the public health are governmental functions, while the provision of mere amusement or entertainment is not.[535] Perhaps the best example of the governmental-proprietary function distinction is provided by the cases that have turned upon the status of the party utilizing a publicly owned stadium for the holding of athletic events. When the stadium is being used by a public school, the courts have usually found that the holding of athletic contests therein is a part of the educational function of the state, and as such are governmental functions to which the doctrine of sovereign immunity applies in full force, in the absence of statute or case law abrogating it.[536] Where,

532. The application of the sovereign immunity doctrine to municipal corporations in this country began with the decision in Mower v. Leicester, 9 Mass. 247 (1812), in which the court followed the earlier English decision in Russell v. Devon, 2 Term Rep. 667, 100 Eng. Rep. 359 (K. B. 1759). This reception of the doctrine, and the doctrine itself, are criticized in Borchard, *Government Responsibility in Tort*, 34 YALE L.J. 129, 129-138 (1924).

533. *See* RESTATEMENT (SECOND) OF TORTS § 895C (Tentative Draft No. 19, 1972). *See generally* W. PROSSER, THE LAW OF TORTS § 131 at 977-84 (4th ed. 1971); Fuller & Casner, *Municipal Tort Liability in Operation*, 54 HARV. L. REV. 437 (1941); Repko, *American Legal Commentary on the Doctrines of Municipal Tort Liability*, 9 LAW & CONTEMP. PROBS. 214 (1942).

A second distinction has been between ministerial and governmental functions, with the immunity attaching to only the latter. The basis of this distinction is that liability should be imposed for ministerial functions, which comprise the execution of already formulated policies, but not for governmental functions, which involve the formulation of policy itself, since to interfere with policy-making would jeopardize the quality and efficiency of government. Elgin v. District of Columbia, 337 F.2d 152 (D.C. Cir. 1964); Van Dyke v. City of Utica, 203 App. Div. 26, 196 N.Y.S. 277 (1922). This exception is well illustrated by the rule that school districts are immune from liability for torts committed by employees performing duties involving the exercise of judgment and discretion. *See* Hall v. Columbus Board of Education, 32 Ohio App. 2d 297, 290 N.E.2d 580 (1972). Thus, in Fustin v. Board of Education of Community Unit Dist. No. 2, 101 Ill. App.2d 113, 242 N.E.2d 308 (1968), a school district was held not liable to a basketball player who was struck in the face during a game because of the alleged negligence of its coach in allowing an aggressive player to compete, reasoning that the coach was a public decision-maker and should not have his discretionary decisions made the subject of liability.

Although these distinctions are noted here with respect to municipal bodies, they have also been applied in some cases to other public bodies.

534. In Hoffman v. Scranton School Dist., 67 Pa. D. & C. 301, 308 (1949), for example, the court stated that

[t]he only rational distinction between a governmental or a corporate and proprietary function, it seems to us, is the distinction of necessity, that is, a governmental function is one which is performed by some agency of government in pursuance of the duty of government to provide for the safety, health and welfare of its citizens. On the other hand, those functions are corporate or proprietary which are performed by such an agency for the convenience or comfort of the persons served by such an agency and which could as well be performed by private individuals if the agency chose not to perform them.

535. Downey v. Jackson, 259 Ala. 189, 65 So. 2d 825 (1953); Plaza v. City of San Mateo, 123 Cal. App. 2d 103, 266 P.2d 523 (1954); Plaza v. City of Utica, 203 App. Div. 26, 196 N.Y.S. 277 (1922).

536. Richards v. School Dist. of Birmingham, 348 Mich. 490, 83 N.W.2d 643 (1957); Holzworth v. State, 238 Wis. 63, 298 N.W. 163 (1941).

on the other hand, a public school leases its stadium for use by others, courts have concluded that it will be conducting a proprietary activity (leasing) and will, therefore, be liable for injuries sustained as a result of the negligent maintenance of the facility.[537]

In most cases, however, it is not so easy to draw the line, and there is no rule of thumb which can be applied with any certainty of result.[538] Although the charging of a fee has often been used as a convenient standard, it should only be one factor in reaching the proper result.[539] The difficulty in drawing clear distinctions is amply demonstrated by comparing those functions that have been held to be governmental with those which have been held to be proprietary. Thus, it has been held that governmental functions include the sponsorship of high school football games [540] and basketball tournaments,[541] as well as the ownership or operation of swimming facilities,[542] municipal arenas,[543] public playgrounds,[544] ski lifts,[545] and parks used to conduct amateur baseball.[546] Proprietary functions, on the other hand, have been held to include the sponsorship of high school football games,[547] as well as the ownership or operation of swimming facilities,[548] a municipal golf course,[549] and an automobile race at fairgrounds facilities.[550] This simple recitation of the functions that have been held to be either, or in some cases both, governmental or proprietary functions, serves as mute testimony to the fact that the distinction often produces results that are justifiable only to lawyers and bear little relation to the fundamental bases of tort liability.

The doctrine of sovereign immunity, both at the state and local level, has been the subject of widespread criticism, and at the present time is clearly on the decline in most jurisdictions.[551] Since it may, however, protect a governmental entity which is made a defendant in a sports injury suit, it will be imperative

---

537. Sawaya v. Tucson High School Dist. No. 1, 78 Ariz. 389, 281 P.2d 105 (1955). *But cf.* Smith v. Hefner, 235 N.C. 1, 68 S.E.2d 783 (1952) (temporary lease of baseball field a governmental act); Kellam v. School Bd. of City of Norfolk, 202 Va. 252, 117 S.E.2d 96 (1960) (leasing auditorium is governmental function).

538. Plaza v. City of San Mateo, 123 Cal. App. 2d 103, 266 P.2d 523 (1954).

539. Plaza v. City of San Mateo, 123 Cal. App. 2d 103, 266 P.2d 523 (1954); Thompson v. Board of Educ., City of Millville, 12 N.J. Super. 92, 79 A.2d 100 (1951); Rich v. City of Goldsboro, 282 N.C. 383, 192 S.E.2d 824 (1972).

540. Lovitt v. Concord School Dist., 59 Mich. App. 415, 228 N.W.2d 479 (1975); Vendrell v. School District No. 26C, Malheur County, 226 Ore. 263, 360 P.2d 282 (1961).

541. Boyer v. Iowa High School Athletic Ass'n, 256 Iowa 337, 127 N.W.2d 606 (1964).

542. Crone v. City of El Cajon, 133 Cal. App. 624, 24 P.2d 846 (1933); Macy v. Town of Chelan, 59 Wash. 2d 610, 369 P.2d 508 (1962). *See generally* Annot., 55 A.L.R.2d 1434 (1957).

543. Howard v. Village of Chisholm, 191 Minn. 245, 253 N.W. 766 (1934); Fetzer v. Minot Park Dist., 138 N.W.2d 601 (N.D. 1965). *See generally* Annot., 47 A.L.R.2d 544 (1956).

544. Lane v. City of Buffalo, 232 App. Div. 334, 250 N.Y.S. 579 (1931).

545. Marshall v. Town of Brattleboro, 121 Vt. 417, 160 A.2d 762 (1960).

546. Downey v. Jackson, 259 Ala. 189, 65 So. 2d 825 (1953).

547. Hoffman v. Scranton School Dist., 67 Pa. D. & C. 301 (1949).

548. Ide v. City of St. Cloud, 150 Fla. 806, 8 So. 2d 924 (1942) (described as a "local function" for which a city would assume the same degree of care as private persons).

549. Plaza v. City of San Mateo, 123 Cal. App. 2d 103, 266 P.2d 523 (1954); Lowe v. City of Gastonia, 211 N.C. 564, 191 S.E. 7 (1937).

550. Arnold v. State, 163 App. Div. 253, 148 N.Y.S. 479 (1914). *See also* Johnson v. City of New York, 186 N.Y. 139, 78 N.E. 715 (1906) (city resolution allowing use of public highways for speed racing held unlawful).

551. See note 529 *supra.*

for an attorney litigating in this area to ascertain the extent of protection that the doctrine provides in the jurisdiction in question.[552]

The doctrine of charitable immunity, where applicable, will provide a veil of insulation for charitable institutions that is similar to that provided public institutions by principles of sovereign immunity. The bases of this immunity are many, though the most prevalent is the so-called "trust fund theory" which assumes that the funds of charitable institutions are held in trust for charitable purposes and may not be diverted for other uses. A second theory has been that charities are immune from the doctrine of respondeat superior (that employers are liable for the acts of their employees), and are not, as a consequence, responsible for the injury-causing actions of their employees, since no profit is derived from their labor. The other bases that have been advanced can be conveniently subsumed within a "public policy" theory which, of course, would include the previously mentioned theories as well.[553]

Even where the immunity applies in full force, it is rife with exceptions and distinctions which sap much of its effect. One such distinction is that charities may be liable to strangers, but cannot be liable to their beneficiaries—that is to the recipients of their charity.[554] A second distinction has been drawn between employees and non-employees, with only the former being allowed to recover from the charity.[555] A third view has been that liability can result only from the acts of the charity itself, since it is immune from the usual rule of respondeat superior.[556] Finally, it has been held that charities may be held liable for activities which involve non-charitable undertakings,[557] for which an admission fee is charged,[558] or which constitute nuisances.[559]

The charitable immunity doctrine has, however, been the subject of substantial criticism, and has been rejected in a sufficient number of

---

552. A compilation indicating the status of the doctrine in every jurisdiction, as respects both state and local governmental entities, is provided in a special table in the RESTATEMENT (SECOND) OF TORTS 12-22 (Tentative Draft No. 19, 1972). *See also* Leflar & Kantrowitz, *Tort Liability of the States,* 29 N.Y.U.L. REV. 1363 (1954) (compilation as of 1954).

An additional aspect of the sovereign immunity doctrine that should be noted is that even where the immunity is in full force, the authorized purchase of liability insurance may be held to constitute an implied waiver of the immunity to the extent of the insurance coverage. *See* Longpre v. Joint School Dist. No. 2 Missoula & Mineral Counties, 151 Mont. 345, 443 P.2d 1 (1968); Johnson v. Municipal University of Omaha, 184 Neb. 512, 169 N.W.2d 286 (1969); Clary v. Alexander County Bd. of Educ., 286 N.C. 525, 212 S.E.2d 160 (1975); Supler v. School Dist. of North Franklin Twp., Washington County, 407 Pa. 657, 182 A.2d 535 (1962); Vendrell v. School Dist. No. 26C, Malheur County, 226 Ore. 263, 360 P.2d 282 (1961). *See generally* W. PROSSER, THE LAW OF TORTS § 131, at 484-85 (4th ed. 1971); Gibbons, *Liability Insurance and the Tort Immunity of State and Local government,* 1959 DUKE L.J. 588.

553. Each of these theories is considered in detail in President and Directors of Georgetown College v. Hughes, 130 F.2d 810, 822-25 (D.C. Cir. 1942). *See generally* W. PROSSER, TORTS § 133 (4th ed. 1971); Annot., 25 A.L.R.2d 29 (1952).

554. President & Directors of Georgetown College v. Hughes, 130 F.2d 810, 825-27 (D.C. Cir. 1942); Pomeroy v. Little League Baseball of Collingswood, 142 N.J. Super. 471, 362 A.2d 39 (1976).

555. Southern Methodist University v. Clayton, 142 Tex. 179, 176 S.W.2d 749 (1943).

556. Young Men's Christian Ass'n of Metropolitan Atlanta, Inc., 107 Ga. App. 417, 130 S.E.2d 242 (1963); Hamburger v. Cornell University, 240 N.Y. 328, 148 N.E. 539 (1925).

557. Morehouse College v. Russell, 109 Ga. App. 301, 136 S.E.2d 179 (1964).

558. Langheim v. Dension Fire Dept. Swimming Pool Ass'n., 237 Iowa 386, 21 N.W.2d 295 (1946).

559. Peden v. Furman University, 155 S.C. 1, 151 S.E. 907 (1930). See § 8.16.

jurisdictions, to justify the conclusion that one engaged in charitable activities is not for that reason immune from tort liability.[560]

Although there are, thus, quite a variety of means by which the protections of sovereign and charitable immunity have been abrogated, either fully or partially, they still remain substantial hurdles in the path to recovery in some states. When the sports activities of public or private bodies give rise to injury, therefore, the first step in seeking recovery will be to ascertain the status, if any, of the applicable immunity in the jurisdiction in question.

---

560. *See* RESTATEMENT (SECOND) OF TORTS § 895F (Tentative Draft No. 18, 1972). A compilation indicating the current status of the doctrine in each jurisdiction is set forth in *id.* at 64-69. *See generally* W. PROSSER, THE LAW OF TORTS § 133 (4th ed. 1971). *But see* Pomeroy v. Little League Baseball of Collingswood, 142 N.J. Super. 471, 362 A.2d 39 (1976).

TABLES OF CASES

Cases in italic type are discussed in the Text as indicated.

A

AAA Con. Auto Transp., Inc. v. Newman, § 4.15, n. 454
Aaser v. Charlotte, § 8.03, nn. 55, 62
AB Electrolux, National Gas Appliance Corp v., § 4.21, n. 731
Abendroth v. Professional Golfers' Ass'n, § 5.10, nn. 973, 992-93, 17, 36-38, 41
Aberthaw Constr. Co. v. Centre County Hosp., § 4.15, n. 452
A. B. Hirschfield Press, Inc., § 6.04, n. 167
Abraham & Straus, Art Metal Works v., § 4.12, n. 300
Abrams v. United States, § 7.21, nn. 555, 563
Accardi v. Shaughnessy, § 12.8, n. 542
Ace Bus Transp. Co. v. South Hudson County Blvd. Bus Owners' Ass'n, § 3.15, n. 634
Ach, Pauline W., § 7.12, n. 303
Ackert v. Ausman, § 4.21, nn. 698, 724, 727
Acme Indus. Co., NLRB v., § 6.06, n. 217.4
Adams, Fazzio Real Estate Co., Inc. v., § 2.22, nn. 566, 569
Adams, Luckey v., § 8.02, n. 24
Adams, McKane v., § 3.16, n. 668
Adams, Terry v., § 1.14, n. 157
Adams, Toone v., § 8.02, nn. 5, 21, 39-40
Adams v. United States, § 8.02, n. 46
Adams v. Waggoner, § 8.02, n. 24
Adams-Smith v. Hayward, § 3.10, n. 371
Adelson, Inc., § 6.10, n. 411
Adie v. Temple Mountain Ski Area, § 8.02, n. 46
Administrador, Suarez v., § 2.18, n. 352; § 2.18, n. 400
Administrators of Tulane Univ., Guillory v., § 1.14, n. 173
Adolph Coors Co., § 6.07, n. 233
Adolph Coors Co., Copper Liquors, Inc. v., § 5.07, n. 812
Adonnino v. Village of Mount Morris, § 8.03, n. 52
Adrian, Brackman v., § 8.05, n. 162
Adrian Messenger Servs. & Enterprises, Ltd. v. Jockey Club, Ltd., § 2.09, n. 199
Advance Mach. Exch. v. Commissioner, § 7.14, n. 307
Aerojet Gen. Corp. v. American Arbitration Ass'n, § 4.20, n. 621
Aetna Cas. & Sur. Co., Carroll v., § 8.02, n. 30
Aetna Cas. & Sur. Co., Hammonds v., § 8.08, nn. 233, 236
Aetna Cas. & Sur. Co. v. Industrial Comm'n, § 8.15, n. 404
Aetna Ins. Co., Caruso v., § 8.02, n. 24
Affiliated Music Enterprises, Inc. v. Sesac, Inc., § 5.11, n. 162
AFL-CIO Jt. Bargaining Comm., § 6.04, n. 132
Agar v. Canning, § 8.02, n. 32
Agar v. Commissioner, § 7.02, n. 69
Agrashell, Inc. v. Hammons Prods. Co., § 5.11, n. 419
Agricultural Soc'y, Logan v., § 8.03, n. 59
Agricultural & Mech. Ass'n v. Gray, § 8.03, n. 59
Agriculture & N.Y. State Horse Breeding Dev. Fund, New York Standardbred Farm Owners, Inc. v., § 2.04, n. 111; *§ 2.12,* n. 263
Agriculture & N.Y. State Horse Breeding Dev. Fund, Saratoga Harness Racing Ass'n, Inc. v., § 2.20, nn. 434, 442
Air Preheater Co., Power Replacements, Inc. v., § 4.17, n. 524; § 5.11, n. 236
Airatec, Inc., Architectural Mfg. Co. v., § 4.14, n. 385
Ak-Sar-Ben Exposition Co., Sorensen v., § 2.20, nn. 438, 440
Alabama, Bouley v., § 4.02, n. 26
Alabama, Marsh v., § 1.14, n. 157
Alabama, NAACP v., § 1.20, n. 369
Alabama, Thornhill v., § 1.16, n. 298

B

Benedetto v. Travelers Ins. Co., § 8.03, n. 52; § 8.05, n. 162
Benedict, Jacobs v., § 1.12, n. 145
Benedict v. Union Agri. Soc'y, § 8.02, n. 46
Benjamin v. Nernberg, § 8.02, n. 24
Bennett, Allegeheny Base-Ball Club v., § 4.02, nn. 21, 40; § 4.05, n. 111; § 4.06, n. 133; § 4.09, n. 187
Bennett v. Board of Educ., § 8.05, n. 155
Benny, Jack, § 7.03, n. 91
Benoit v. Marvin, § 8.02, n. 46
Benquet Consol. Mining Co., Perkins v., § 4.21, nn. 684, 727
Bensinger Recreation Corp., Sykes v., § 8.02, n. 46
Bent v. Jonet, § 8.03, n. 59
Berea College, Gott v., § 1.15.1, n. 267
Berg v. Erickson, § 3.07, n. 240
Berg v. Merricks, § 8.02, n. 24; § 8.05, nn. 132, 168, § 8.06, n. 178
Berger v. Miller, § 8.02, n. 24
Bergey, Cincinnati Bengals, Inc. v., § 3.08, n. 264; § 3.09, nn. 304-06; § 4.03, nn. 50, 58, 60; § 4.08, n. 174; § 4.12, n. 289; *§ 4.14,* nn. 341, 348, 351, 356, 359-60, 363-64, 366-68, 373-74, 384, 386, 393-94
Berkelman v. San Francisco Unified School Dist., § 1.22, n. 458
Berkey v. Anderson, § 8.08, n. 233
Bernard Sirotta Co., Agrashell, Inc. v., § 4.21, n. 727
Bernarr McFadden Foundation, Inc., Stehn v., § 8.02, n. 36; § 8.05, n. 131; § 8.06, n. 183
Bernhagen v. Marathon Fin. Co., § 3.19, n. 795
Bernhardt v. Polygraphic Co., § 4.15, nn. 437, 446
Bernson Coop. Creamery Ass'n v. First Dist. Ass'n, § 3.16, n. 690
Bernstein v. Alameda-Contra Costa Medical Ass'n, § 3.16, n. 690
Bernstein v. Seacliff Beach Club, Inc., § 8.04, n. 113
Berrios v. Inter American Univ., § 1.14, n. 173
Berrum v. Powalisz, § 8.03, nn. 52, 60
Berry, Christian Appalachian Project, Inc. v., § 8.02, n. 24
Berry v. Howe, § 8.02, n. 24
Berry, Simmons v., § 3.16, n. 667
Bers v. Chicago Health Clubs, Inc., § 8.04, n. 112
Berthold Public School Dist., Dostert v., § 1.12, n. 145
Beseda, Miratsky v., § 8.03, n. 59
Bessenyey v. Commissioner, § 7.21, n. 555
Betcher, Montes v., § 8.02, n. 46
Bethesda Country Club, Inc., Nesbitt v., § 8.02, nn. 24, 30
Bethlehem Steel Co., § 6.08, n. 307
Betts Cadillac Olds, Inc., § 6.09, nn. 364-65
Beulah Park Jockey Club, Inc. v. Claypool, § 2.03, n. 42
Big Powder Horn Mt. Ski Corp., Lewis v., § 8.11, n. 336
Bigelow v. RKO Radio Pictures, § 5.11, nn. 416, 418
Biger v. Erwin, § 8.13, nn. 371, 376
Biggs v. Presto Lite Div. of Eltra Corp., § 8.15, n. 409
Billings, Cassady v., § 8.02, n. 24
Bingler v. Johnson, § 1.08, n. 63; § 7.14, n. 361
Bird, Allman v., § 8.02, n. 30
Bird v. Lake Hopatcong Country Club, § 8.12, nn. 361, 363
Birdsall v. Twenty-Third St. Ry., § 3.10, n. 358
Birdsong, Curtis Publishing Co. v., § 4.22, n. 767
Birkett, Russell-Stewart, Inc. v., § 3.17, n. 723
Birmingham News Co. v. Patterson, § 7.21, n. 591
Birmingham Water Works Co., Blyth v., § 8.02, n. 5
Biscayne Bay Yacht Club, Golden v., § 2.22, n. 545
Biscayne Kennel Club, Inc. v. Board of Bus. Reg., § 2.02, n. 25; § 2.03, nn. 82, 88-89
Biscayne Kennel Club, Inc., Florida State Racing Comm'n v., § 2.03, n. 58
Biscayne Trust Co., § 7.19, n. 522
Bishop v. Wood, § 1.28, nn. 531-32
Bisigier, Atkins v., § 8.02, n. 24
Bissing, Moore v., § 2.20, n. 440
Biswell, United States v., § 2.07, n. 163
Bixler, Mort. L., § 7.04, n. 133

Broderson v. Rainier Nat'l Park Co., § 8.02, n. 24
Brody v. Westmoor Beach & Blade Club, Inc., § 8.02, n. 24
Brokaw v. East St. Louis Jockey Club, § 8.02, n. 24
Bromberger, *In re,* § 2.20, n. 441
Bronstein, Sontag v., § 1.22, n. 457
Brooke v. Moore, § 2.03, n. 40; § 2.19, n. 397
Brooklands Auto Racing Club, Hall v., § 8.03, nn. 52-54, 67, 69-72
Brooklyn Ball Club, Griffin v., § 3.11, nn. 406, 414, 417, 422, 424; § 3.13, nn. 567, 570, 579; § 3.14, nn. 586, 594
Brooklyn Baseball Club, Boston Baseball Ass'n v., § 3.15, nn. 620, 641
Brooklyn Baseball Club v. McGuire, § 4.05, n. 111; § 4.07, nn. 140, 156; § 4.09, n. 184; § 4.11, nn. 209-10, 215, 242
Brooklyn Jewish Center, Kanofsky v., § 8.02, n. 24; § 8.05, n. 136
Brooklyn Nat'l Baseball Club, Levine v., § 8.03, n. 86
Brooklyn Nat'l League Baseball Club, Mandel v., § 8.03, n. 86
Brooklyn Nat'l League Baseball Club, Philpot v., § 8.03, n. 52
Brooks v. Bass, § 8.02, n. 46
Brooks v. Board of Educ., § 8.05, nn. 147, 166
Brooks, Jack's Cookie Co. v., § 3.19, n. 788
Brotherhood of Locomotive Firemen & Engineers, Tunstall v., § 6.07, n. 226
Brotherhood of R.R. Trainmen, Terminal R.R. Ass'n v., § 5.06, n. 629
Broward County Kennel Club, Inc. v. Rose, § 2.03, n. 89
Broward County Launderers & Cleaners Ass'n, Inc., § 6.04, n. 189
Brown v. Board of Educ. (N.Y.), § 8.05, n. 147
Brown v. Board of Educ. (Topeka), § 1.11, n. 88; *§ 1.22,* nn. 429-30; § 1.24, n. 498; § 2.11, n. 261
Brown v. Cleveland Baseball Co., § 8.02, n. 41; § 8.03, nn. 59-60
Brown v. Foster, § 3.08, n. 256
Brown v. Louisiana, § 1.12, n. 126
Brown, NLRB v., § 6.09, nn. 372-73, 375-76
Brown, Parker v., § 5.02, n. 50
Brown v. San Francisco Ball Club, § 8.03, n. 52
Brown v. Tulsa Exposition & Fair Ass'n, § 8.02, n. 46
Brown v. United Servs. For Air, Inc., § 8.15, n. 394
Brown v. Waldman, § 2.07, n. 191; § 2.19, n. 405
Brown v. Wells, § 1.14, nn. 182, 203; § 1.15, n. 216; *§ 1.18,* nn. 317-18, 323-24, 327
Brown v. Western R.R., § 4.15, n. 465
Brown v. Wichita State Univ., § 8.18, n. 529
Brownley v. Gettysburg College, § 1.14, n. 173
Bruce v. South Carolina High School League, § 1.11, n. 99; § 1.14, nn. 179, 184, 203; § 1.20, n. 342
Brumm v. Goodall, § 8.02, n. 46
Brummerhoff v. St. Louis Nat'l Baseball Club, § 8.03, n. 52
Brunswick Corp., Illinois v., § 5.11, n. 399
Bruss v. Milwaukee Sporting Goods Co., § 8.03, n. 59
Bryan, Pompano Horse Club v., § 2.20, n. 438; § 8.16, n. 466
Bryant, Cox v., § 3.19, n. 777
Bryant, Florida High School Activities Ass'n v., § 1.11, n. 89; § 1.19, nn. 335, 339; § 1.28, n. 575
Bryant v. National Football League, § 5.03, nn. 154, 201, 204; § 5.07, n. 804
Bucciconi Eng'r Co., Greco v., § 4.21, n. 724
Bucha v. Illinois High School Ass'n, § 1.11, n. 99; § 1.14, n. 161; *§ 1.22,* nn. 382, 384, 412, 420, 441-42, 457
Buchanan, Fitchett v., § 8.02, n. 41; § 8.03, n. 60
Buck v. Clauson's Inn, § 8.03, n. 60
Buckley v. New York Times Co., § 4.21, nn. 679, 698
Bucks Stove & Range Co., Gompers v., § 5.04, n. 315
Buckton v. NCAA, § 1.06, n. 32; § 1.09, n. 79; § 1.11, n. 95; *§ 1.14,* nn. 161, 164, 177; *§ 1.17,* n 305, 311, 313-14
Buddy v. State, § 8.16, nn. 423, 429
Buffalo v. Atlanta Hawks Basketball, Inc., § 5.11, nn. 56, 231, 234, 300, 314, 316, 379-80, 409
Buffalo, Lamm v., § 8.16, n. 450
Buffalo, Lane v., § 8.16, nn. 449, 453; § 8.18, n. 544
Buffalo Bills, Kasper v., § 8.03, nn. 59-60
Buffalo Forge Co. v. United Steelworkers, § 6.10, n. 426
Buffalo Linen Supply Co., § 6.09, n. 365

C

E

F

K

O

V